BARRON'S NEW STUDENT'S CONCISE ENCYCLOPEDIA

Second Edition

Compiled by the Editors of
Barron's Educational Series, Inc.

BARRON'S

PICTURE CREDITS

Photographs appearing in this book came from the sources listed below.

ART

1-3 (left), Jensen/Art Resource, New York; 1-3 (right), SCALA/Art Resource, New York; 1-4, 1-5, Marburg/Art Resource, New York; 1-6, Martin/Art Resource, New York; 1-7 (both), Giraudon/Art Resource, New York; 1-8, Marburg/Art Resource, New York; 1-9, Giraudon/Art Resource, New York; 1-10 (left), Art Resource, New York; 1-10 (right), Martin/Art Resource, New York; 1-11 (left), Giraudon/Art Resource, New York; 1-11 (right), 1-14, 1-15, Marburg/Art Resource, New York; 1-16 (left), SEF/Art Resource, New York; 1-16 (right), Alinari/Art Resource, New York; 1-17, Marburg/Art Resource, New York; 1-18, Martin/Art Resource, New York; 1-19, 1-20 (left), Giraudon/Art Resource, New York; 1-20 (right), SEF/Art Resource, New York; 1-21, Alinari/Art Resource, New York; 1-22 (left), Marburg/Art Resource, New York; 1-22 (right), Giraudon/Art Resource, New York; 1-23 (left), Giraudon/Art Resource, New York; 1-23 (right), Alinari/Art Resource, New York; 1-24, SCALA/Art Resource, New York; 1-25, Marburg/Art Resource, New York; 1-27, Giraudon/Art Resource, New York; 1-31, Art Resource, New York; 1-32 (left), Giraudon/Art Resource, New York; 1-32 (right), Marburg/Art Resource, New York; 1-33, Alinari/Art Resource, New York; 1-34 (left), Art Resource, New York; 1-34 (right), Giraudon/Art Resource, New York; 1-35, Marburg/Art Resource, New York; 1-36, Giraudon/Art Resource, New York; 1-38 (left), Art Resource, New York; 1-38 (right), Marburg/Art Resource, New York; 1-39, 1-40 (left), Alinari/Art Resource, New York; 1-40 (right), Giraudon/Art Resource, New York; 1-41 (left), Art Resource; 1-41 (right), 1-42, Giraudon/Art Resource, New York.

EARTH AND SPACE SCIENCE

5-3, NASA; 5-14, U.S. Geological Survey; 5-24, 5-33, NASA.

GOVERNMENT

7-9, 7-23, The Bettmann Archive.

HISTORY—U.S.

10-5, 10-9 (both), The Bettmann Archive; 10-18, Picture Collection, The Branch Libraries, The New York Public Library; 10-19, The Bettmann Archive; 10-23, National Park Service; 10-25 (left), U.S. Department of Agriculture; 10-25 (right), U.S. Department of the Interior, National Park Service, Edison National Historic Site; 10-26, The Bettmann Archive; 10-33, The collections of Henry Ford Museum & Greenfield Village; 10-34, Picture Collection, The Branch Libraries, The New York Public Library; 10-36, 10-37, 10-39, The Bettmann Archive; 10-45, UPI/Bettmann Archive; 10-47, 10-48, The Bettmann Archive; 10-50, Picture Collection, The Branch Libraries, The New York Public Library; 10-50, The Bettmann Archive; 10-51, UPI/Bettmann Newsphoto; 10-53, courtesy of General Douglas MacArthur Memorial; 10-55, Official U.S. Navy Photograph; 10-60, 10-65, The Bettmann Archive; 10-73, Friends of the Governor's Mansion, Austin, Texas; 10-75, 10-76, The Bettmann Archive.

HISTORY—WORLD

11-3, 11-12, 11-13, 11-18, 11-21, 11-25, 11-26, 11-29, 11-36, 11-50, 11-52, The Bettmann Archive; 11-57, The Bettmann Archive/BBC Hulton; 11-69, 11-72, 11-75, 11-82, 11-83, 11-100, 11-113, 11-117, The Bettmann Archive; 11-118, UPI/Bettmann Newsphoto; 11-125, 11-129 (left), The Bettmann Archive/BBC Hulton; 11-129 (right), The Bettmann Archive; 11-134, UPI/Bettmann Newsphoto.

LITERATURE

15-8, 15-13, 15-20, 15-38, 15-49, 15-51, The Bettmann Archive.

MUSIC

17-3, 17-4, 17-12, 17-18, 17-19, 17-25, 17-32, 17-33, 17-36, The Bettmann Archive.

MYTHOLOGY

18-3, 18-5, 18-7, 18-10 (both), 18-12, 18-15 (both), The Bettmann Archive.

PHILOSOPHY

19-3, 19-7, 19-12, 19-14 (both), 19-20, 19-22, The Bettmann Archive.

PSYCHOLOGY

21-12, 21-20, The Bettmann Archive.

RELIGION

22-4 (both), Picture Collection, The Branch Libraries, The New York Public Library; 22-7, The Bettmann Archive/BBC Hulton; 22-12, The Bettmann Archive; 22-16, 22-21, Picture Collection, The Branch Libraries, The New York Public Library.

FOUR-COLOR BIOLOGY ILLUSTRATIONS

Reprinted by permission of D.C. Heath and Company from *Heath Biology*, ©1991.

All inquiries should be addressed to:
Barron's Educational Series, Inc.
250 Wireless Boulevard
Hauppauge, New York 11788

Library of Congress Catalog Card No. 93-1066
International Standard Book No. 0-8120-6329-5

Library of Congress Cataloging-in-Publication Data

Barron's new student's concise encyclopedia / compiled by the editors of Barron's Educational Series, Inc. — 2nd ed.
    p.   c.m.
    Rev. ed. of: Barron's student's concise encyclopedia.
    Includes index.
    Summary: A guide and reference book providing overviews of subjects covered in high school.
    ISBN 0-8120-6329-5
    1. Encyclopedias and dictionaries. [1. Encyclopedias and dictionaries.] I. Barron's Educational Series, Inc. II. Barron's student's concise encyclopedia.
AG6.B37   1993
031—dc20   93-1066
                                                         CIP
                                                         AC

Printed in the United States of America
3456   8800   987654321

ACKNOWLEDGMENTS

The publisher gratefully acknowledges the following sources:

"Approximate Energy Expenditure By a Healthy Adult Weighing About 150 Pounds," reprinted by permission of The ServiceMaster Company, copyright © 1988 The ServiceMaster Company L.P. Terms from the Dictionary and Index from *Bulfinch's Mythology* by Thomas Bulfinch. Copyright © 1970 by Harper & Row, Publishers, Inc. Reprinted by permission of HarperCollins Publishers. *Bulfinch Pocket Dictionary of Art Terms* edited by David Diamond. Copyright © 1992 by Little, Brown and Company (Inc.). By permission of Little, Brown and Company. *Concise Dictionary of World History*, by Bruce Wetterau, copyright © 1983 by Bruce Wetterau. Reprinted by permission of John Hawkins & Associates, Inc. "Congressional Leadership" and "How a Bill Becomes a Law," reprinted by permission of The National Association of Towns and Townships. *The Dictionary of Art and Artists* by Peter and Linda Murray. Copyright © 1978 Peter and Linda Murray, Thames & Hudson, Ltd. Food Pyramid courtesy of U.S. Department of Agriculture/U.S. Department of Health and Human Services. *Making the Most of Your Money* by Jane Bryant Quinn. Copyright © 1991 by Berrybrook Publishing, Inc. 1983 Metropolitan Height and Weight Tables, reprinted courtesy of Metropolitan Life Insurance Company. " Not-So-Fast Food Fare " reprinted with permission from the August 1992 issue, *Tufts Diet & Nutrition Letter*, 53 Park Place, New York, New York 10007. *The Penguin Dictionary of Music* by Arthur Jacobs (Penguin Books, 1958, 5th Edition, 1973), copyright © Arthur Jacobs, 1958, 1967, 1968, 1970, 1973, 1977, 1991. *The Penguin Dictionary of Psychology* by Arthur S. Reber (Viking/Penguin Books, 1985), copyright © Arthur S. Reber, 1985. "Recommended Dietary Allowances" tables reprinted with permission from *Recommended Dietary Allowances: 10th edition.* Copyright © 1989 by the National Academy of Sciences. Published by the National Academy Press, Washington, DC. U.S. Area Code and Time Zone Map, Copyright © NYNEX Information Resources Company, 1993. Printed by permission of NYNEX Information Resources Company.

The following Barron's books, from which text, illustrations, and charts have been used, are copyrighted by Barron's Educational Series, Inc. as follows:

The Alchemist by Ben Johnson. Copyright © 1965. *Algebra the Easy Way* by Douglas Downing. Copyright © 1989. *American History at a Glance* by Nelson A. Klose and David A. Midgley. Copyright © 1966. *Biology the Easy Way* by Gabrielle Edwards. Copyright © 1990. *Building an Effective Vocabulary* by Murray Bromberg and Cedric Gale. Copyright © 1979. *Business Statistics* by Douglas Downing and Jeffrey Clark. Copyright © 1992. *Calculus the Easy Way* by Douglas Downing. Copyright © 1988. *The Compact Homer: The Iliad* by Homer. Translated by Andrew Lang, Walter Leaf, and Ernest Myers. Copyright © 1971. *Dictionary of Business Terms* by Jack P. Friedman. Copyright © 1987. *Dictionary of Computer Terms* by Douglas Downing and Michael Covington. Copyright © 1992. *Dictionary of Finance and Investment Terms*, Second edition by John Downes and Jordan Elliot Goodman. Copyright © 1987. *Dictionary of Legal Terms* by Steven H. Gifis. Copyright © 1983. *Dictionary of Medical Terms* by Mikel Rothenberg and Charles F. Chapman. Copyright © 1989. *Dictionary of Math Terms* by Douglas Downing. Copyright © 1987. *Economics* by W.J. Wessels. Copyright © 1987. *Essentials of American Government*, Second revised edition, by Ernst B. Schulz. Copyright © 1975. *Essentials of Biology*, Revised edition by C. Leland Rodgers. Copyright © 1967, 1974. *Essentials of English*, Fourth edition, by Vincent F. Hooper, Cedric Gale, and Ronald C. Foote. Revised by Benjamin W. Griffith. Copyright © 1990. *Essentials of Physics*, Sixth edition by Herman Gewirtz. Copyright © 1974. *Global Studies* by Erwin Rosenfeld and Harriet Geller. Copyright © 1987. *How to Prepare for the Advanced Placement Examination: American History*, Third edition, by William Kellogg. Copyright © 1988. *How to Prepare for the Advanced Placement Examination: Biology*, Fourth edition, by Gabrielle Edwards and Marion Cimmino. Copyright © 1992. *How to Prepare for the College Board Achievement Test: American History/Social Studies*, Eighth edition, by David A. Midgley and Phillip Lefton. Copyright © 1990. *How to Prepare for the College Board Achievement Test: Biology*, Tenth edition, by Maurice Bleifeld. Copyright © 1991. *How to Prepare for the College Board Achievement Test: Chemistry*, Fourth edition, by Joseph Mascetta. Copyright © 1990. *How to Prepare for the Graduate Management Admission Test*, Ninth edition, by Stephen Hilbert and Eugene D. Jaffe. Copyright © 1991. *Medical Dictionary for the Nonprofessional* by Charles F. Chapman. Copyright © 1984. *Medieval Mystery Plays, Moralities, and Interludes*, edited by Vincent M. Hopper and Gerald B. Lahey. Copyright © 1962. *Physics the Easy Way* by Robert Lehrman. Copyright © 1990. *Pocket Guide to Correct Spelling* by Francis Griffith. Copyright © 1990. *Pocket Guide to Literature and Language Terms* by Benjamin Griffith. Copyright © 1985. *Regents Exams and Answers: Biology* by Gabrielle Edwards and Marion Cimmino. Copyright © 1992. *Regents Exams and Answers: Chemistry* by David Kiefer. Copyright © 1992. *Regents Exams and Answers: Earth Science* by David Berey. Copyright © 1992. *Regents Exams and Answers: Physics* by Herman Gewirtz. Copyright © 1992. *Student Success Secrets* by Eric Jensen. Copyright © 1989. *Study Tactics*, by William H. Armstrong and M. Willard Lampe II. (Also published as *Study Tips*, Second edition.) Copyright © 1983. *Trigonometry the Easy Way* by Douglas Downing. Copyright © 1990. *United States History*, Vols. I and II by Nelson Klose. Copyright © 1983. *Young Chef's Nutrition Guide and Cookbook* by Carolyn E. Moore, Mimi Kerr, and Robert Shulman. Copyright © 1990.

CONTRIBUTORS

MANAGING EDITOR: Grace Freedson
PROJECT EDITOR: Lorraine De Pietro
EDITORIAL STAFF: Donna Marie Domenichello, Denise Nolty, Sally Strauss

CONTRIBUTING AUTHORS, SECOND EDITION: Marcos Bisticas-Cocoves, Michael A. Covington, John Downes, Douglas Downing, Gabrielle Edwards, Don H. Fontenelle, Morris Gall, Patrick Grim, Ted Kalivoda, Lawrence Leff, Robert Lehrman, Tedd Levy, Janet Lowe, Norah Martin, Joseph Mascetta, Sonia-Ivette Roman, Mikel A. Rothenberg, William Streitwieser, William Wallis

CONTRIBUTING AUTHORS, FIRST EDITION: Stewart Benedict, Murray Bromberg, Dora Clark, Joanne Dolinar, Douglas Downing, Gabrielle Edwards, George Ehrenhaft, Morris Gall, Richard Goldone, Philip Lefton, Robert Lehrman, Tedd Levy, Judy Makover, Gloria Marotta, Joseph Mascetta, John McGeehan, Jackie Reading, Mark Rush, Lester Schlumpf, Sue Weinberg

TABLE OF CONTENTS

EXHIBITS

COLOR ILLUSTRATIONS

MAPS

MAP-READING BASICS

Maps are usually accompanied by information presented in a key or legend to help you in interpreting the map. The title, scale, and map projection are usually given. As you use the many maps provided in this book, it may be helpful to review the following information.

Scale: A scale shows the relationship between distances on a map and on the earth's surface. A scale can be represented in different ways. One way is by stating that a distance on a map equals a certain number of miles or kilometers. Another way a scale is expressed is by using a representative ratio, such as 1:100,000, meaning one unit on the map represents 100,000 units on the earth's surface. The final way the scale can be shown is by a line or bar marked off in units that represent a distance. The maps in this volume utilize this last method, providing you with the scale in both miles and kilometers.

Grids: These vertical and horizontal lines on a map are used to locate points on a map. The North and South Poles are connected by lines called *meridians* that extend halfway around the globe. It is accepted internationally that a line passing through Greenwich, England, is the point from which meridians will be counted. This is 0° or the *Prime Meridian*. Halfway around the globe is 180°. The angle between meridians is the degree of *longitude*.

The equator is halfway between the North and South Poles. A line around the globe at the equator is 0° *latitude*. The North Pole is 90° North and the South Pole is 90° South. *Parallel* lines to the equator create angles that are measured as degrees of latitude.

Map Projections: The earth is a sphere or a globe in space. When you project a map onto paper, you are flattening the globe, and inevitably there will be some areas that will be distorted. Many types of projections have been developed over the years, but most maps are one form or another of three basic types, all of which are based on geometric shapes. They are the *conic, cylindrical,* and *azimuthal* projections.

1. *Conic Projections* are based on projections of a globe onto a cone. When the cone's open end touches the globe and the lines from the point of contact are transferred, there will be an accurate map along that line of latitude. All Conic maps are most accurate in the middle latitudes. One variation is the Polyconic, which puts together many cones from different latitudes. It is suited for showing an area's surface features. The Lambert-Conformal Conic uses straight lines that converge at the poles for the meridians and concentric circles for parallels. It is very useful for air navigation. The Bonne is a modified Conical Equal Area projection with one standard parallel and all the meridians are curved except for the central meridian, which is straight. For example, see pages 24-26 and 24-27 (Conic), 22-22 and 24-23 (Polyconic), and 24-74 (Bonne).

2. *Cylindrical Projections* are projections of a globe onto a cylinder. If the lines from the point at which the cylinder touches the globe are transferred, there will be an accurate map along a line of latitude. However, all meridians will be parallel and will never meet at the poles. Land masses near the pole, such as Greenland, will appear larger than near the equator. Variations include the Mercator, in which all parallels and meridians are at right angles, and the Robinson, which bends parallels slightly but not enough to converge at the poles. They are all helpful for navigation. An example of the Mercator appears on page 24-51. The Robinson is used for this volume's endpaper map.

3. *Azimuthal Projections* are projections of a globe on a flat surface that touches the globe at a certain point. A variation is the Lambert Azimuthal Equal Area, which is good for map projections of large areas, such as hemispheres and continents. (See the map of Africa on pages 24-16 and 24-17.) The Azimuthal Equidistant depicts the shortest distance between points. The shortest distance between the central point and any other is a straight line, creating a great circle route, useful for measuring distances. This projection is used by airline pilots.

Types of Maps: Maps can be used to depict not only capitals, cities, rivers, etc., but also population density, vegetation, climates, topography, and other features. In this volume, we have provided vegetation regions for six continents. See the color maps in the World at a Glance section.

Introduction

Whether you're in high school, in college, or on the job, you need information, and you need it fast. You'll get it from this book—a treasury of practical knowledge for students, researchers, writers, or anyone with a need for concise, accurate information drawn from every major field of academic study. In these pages you'll find virtually everything you've learned in school but have probably forgotten. At a time when there is so much to know, you can't expect to remember it all. Therefore, BARRON'S NEW STUDENT'S CONCISE ENCYCLOPEDIA may be the next best thing to having a computer implanted in your brain. (See *"Artificial intelligence,"* p. 4-3.)

In these pages, information is laid out clearly and attractively, giving you immediate access to thousands of facts about literature and the arts, American and world history, geography, politics, business, economics, technology, religion, and more. No other desktop reference book offers as much—not only as an aid for getting your facts straight while writing papers, doing homework, or settling an argument, but as a place to browse, enrich your knowledge, and sharpen your understanding of the world.

Turn to any page at random. In a moment you're sure to find something you already know. But you'll also have your memory jogged by a long-forgotten fact or two. Read on, and you'll add new bits of important information to your store of knowledge. Perhaps your curiosity will be stimulated. You'll want to know more about metaphysics or DNA. Each page contains boundless possibilities for intellectual growth and discovery. A single entry—short, to the point, and definitive—can start a chain reaction.

At the same time, however, this volume has more practical uses. It can serve as a survival guide for young people living on their own—away from home and family. For instance, the Health and Medicine section offers everyday advice on nutrition, weight control, and meal planning. The Life Skills section helps students prepare for exams, write term papers, use the library, manage checking accounts, get a passport, use the metric system, and more.

There's no limit to this book's usefulness. Just imagine:

You're in the middle of writing a term paper. No time for a trip to the library. You need to know the facts about the Los Angeles riots. Turn to page 10-52.

In class today, your professor said that the west coast of South America is farther east than the east coast of the United States. Could that really be right? Check the encyclopedia's color maps.

It's noon, and you need to telephone a business associate in Australia. If you call now, will you wake him or catch him at tea time? Consult the table of the world's time zones on page 14-40.

What is a bitmap? Where is Uzbekistan? When did the Persian Gulf War start? What happened at Tiananmen Square? How high is the highest waterfall in the world? What is an Azimuthal Equidistant projection in mapmaking? What happened at Three Mile Island? When did Caligula rule? What is Zoroastrianism? You'll find the answers in this concise encyclopedia.

To be useful, a reference book must not only be clear, accurate, and up-to-date—its contents must be accessible. Each of the 24 sections in this book is clearly organized either alphabetically or by topical area. Thousands of vivid charts, exhibits, tables, diagrams, maps, and illustrations make vast amounts of information easily accessible. Numerous cross-references, both within sections and between sections, lead you to related information. A comprehensive index, keyed both to page numbers and exhibits, further aids your search for information.

Because this encyclopedia has been published in one handy volume, it omits far more than it includes. The editors have been selective. You won't find lengthy discussions of highly technical or arcane subjects (the workings of the stock market, for instance, or quantum physics). Instead, you'll find a brief summary—a glimpse into innumerable fascinating topics and ideas. Regard this volume as a directory to basic human knowledge. It has been written as a ready reference guide, not a complete compilation of all there is or ever was. Knowing that this book is meant to provide a quick fix on a fact, the reader in search of information should look here first. Although there's only so much that can be crammed into 1,250 pages, you won't often be disappointed.

ART

Abstract Art Art in which elements of form have been stressed in handling the subject matter—which may or may not be recognizable. Wassily Kandinsky is generally credited with having created the first purely abstract artwork in 1910.

Abstract Expressionism This school of art amounts to little more than automatic painting—i.e., allowing the subconscious to express itself by creating involuntary shapes and dribbles of paint. Supposedly it derives from the intricate mesh of paint that forms the surface of Monet's last pictures, as, half-blind, he struggled to find pictorial equivalents of his optical sensations. This school of art is believed by many to be the first wholly American art movement. Abstract Impressionism has been defined by de Kooning as "retaining the quiet uniform pattern of strokes that spread over the canvas without climax or emphasis . . . the Impressionist manner of looking at a scene but leaving out the scene."

Academy Originally, the garden near Athens where Plato taught. Art academies developed in reaction to medieval guilds and became schools for the practical and theoretical training of artists. Rigorous study of the human form and highly structured teaching based on classical standards characterized most academy instruction.

Action Painting Splashing and dribbling paint on canvas without involving thought or planning. The basic assumption is that the unconscious will take over and produce a work of art. The technique is claimed to go back to Leonardo da Vinci, who suggested using stains on walls as a starting point for designing. The essential difference is that Leonardo used the method solely as a means of stimulating the creative imagination, not as an end in itself. Action painting should not be confused with the intellectual type of Abstract Art in which thought is necessary, but its advocates claim that the beauty of the movements of the artist's wrist constitute its justification. The term was invented in this country to describe the forceful, unpremeditated work of Jackson Pollock.

Afro-American Art (Black Art) The commonality of this artistic movement lies not with any one particular style or technique, but rather with its themes of protest and search for the historic roots of African-Americans.

Air Brush An atomizer of compressed air used to apply a fine spray of paint or liquid. This technique can make paintings resemble photographs and is also used as a touch-up for photographic work.

American Scene Painting This term describes art movements popular between 1850 and 1950 when painters depicted typical and distinctly American landscape scenes and aspects of the daily life of their subject matter. The style of these paintings was realistic and literal.

Angelico, Fra (1400?–1455) Fra *Giovanni da Fiesole,* known as the Blessed Angelico, was a Dominican friar. He used his art for didactic rather than mystic purposes, and the style he evolved was correspondingly simple and direct; conservative, and yet based on a largeness of form. The convent of St. Marco was taken over by his religious order in 1436, and he decorated it with a series of about fifty frescoes, most of them in the cells of the friars and intended to aid contemplation. He was called to Rome to decorate a chapel in the Vatican. He died in Rome in 1455. The biggest collection of his works is in the Museo di St. Marco, Florence, his own monastery.

Armature A metal or wire framework constructed by the sculptor as a skeleton for clay or wax in the making of a piece of sculpture.

Art Deco A style of the 1920s and 1930s seen in architecture, applied arts, interior design, and graphic design, which combines some highly decorative elements of late Art Nouveau with streamlined geometric forms inspired by current industrial design.

Art Nouveau "New Art" that spread across Europe and America in the 1890s. This highly stylized type of decoration, found mainly in architecture and interior decoration, flourished in Belgium and Britain. Art Nouveau utilized flat patterns of writhing vegetable forms based on a naturalistic conception of plants rather than a formalized type of decoration. The influence of this art form is still with us, as is evidenced by cast-iron lilies and copper tendrils as well as furniture with heart-shaped holes in it. Art Nouveau reached its height of popularity between 1895 and 1905.

Art Therapy The practice of free-expression painting, modeling, etc., as a curative activity by individuals with mental disorders or by others for psychomedical reasons.

Ashcan School A group of 19th- and 20th-century American realist painters and illustrators whose interest in the sordid side of city life (especially in New York City) justifies the nickname.

Assemblage A modern, abstract movement in which sculpture and paintings are assembled using ready-made objects, fragments, bits of paper, etc. *See* **Collage.**

Atelier (Fr. studio) The atelier is a common feature of the Continental art world. It is a free studio that provides a nude model for fixed sessions, but without benefit of an instructor. The most famous atelier was opened around 1825 in Paris by a model called Suisse and was used by Delacroix, Courbet, Manet, Monet, Pissarro, Cezanne, and other Impressionists.

Attribution When a picture is signed or recorded in a document, there can be little doubt that it is by the painter to whom it is attributed. "Attribution," however, usually means assigning a picture to its painter on the basis of its likeness to works known to be the artist's. Such grounds can range from certainty to mere guesswork, depending on the number of certain works known to the person making the attribution, as well as the degree of his intimacy with them.

Audubon, John James (1785–1851) An American artist and naturalist who became deeply involved in the study of birds. His over 400 color engravings of different species (with accompanying text) comprise the four volumes of *Birds in America,* for which he is most famous. Although his illustrations have been criticized for being tightly and precisely rendered, he created an interesting double vision, combining the use of large form and minute detail. His sensitive approach tended to be

AUDUBON
Snowy Heron

one more of devotion to his subject than of a strict objectivity.

Automatism   Doodling. Shut your eyes and draw—the subconscious will do the rest; hence it was a favorite Surrealist technique.

Avant-garde   A term coined around 1910 to mean new and experimental concepts in the arts. It is used most frequently to describe works that are innovative and often highly unconventional.

B

Bacon, Francis (1910–1992)   Bacon was a self-taught painter who destroyed a large part of his output, so much so that virtually nothing of his early work has survived. Through his highly personal subject matter, which concentrates chiefly on dogs, carcasses, and evocations of men, including elderly tycoons, and Velazquez's *Innocent X,* caged in plate glass and screaming in a silent world of horror, dissolution, and fear, he expressed with energy and singleness of aim all the gradations of emotion from pity and disgust to horror, traumatic revulsion, and the unbalance of panic. His work, which can be interpreted as an attempt to evoke catharsis in the spectator, raises in its most acute form the problem of the relationship between art and pleasure.

Barbizon School   A mid-19th-century group of landscape painters, centered on the village of Barbizon in the Forest of Fountainbleau. Their aims were an exact and unprettified rendering of peasant life and scenery, painted on the spot; this last point identifying them as the precursors of Impressionism.

Baroque   The style is seen at its purest in the so-called High Baroque, which is virtually confined to Italy and to the period covered by the years around 1630–1680. The High Baroque, at its best and fullest, is a union of the arts of architecture, painting, and sculpture, acting on the emotions of the spectator; inviting him, for example, to participate in the agonies and ecstasies of the Saints. Its blend of illusionism, theatrics, light and color, and powerful movement is calculated to overwhelm the spectator by a direct emotional appeal. At the end of the century, some Roman artists developed the classical and intellectual aspects of the Baroque style, almost to the exclusion of its emotional side. Outside Italy, astute politicians were quick to see that the religious style could easily be made to serve the glorification of the monarch, but in this process a good deal of pomposity was superimposed on the original religious fervor. The style lasted longest in Catholic Germany and Austria, and had the least influence in Protestant countries.

Bas-relief   A sculpture existing in a shallow relief, so that it does not project too far out from the surface from which it rises.

Bauhaus   This is the most famous school of architecture, design, and craftsmanship of modern times and has had an inestimable influence on art school training all over the world. It was founded in 1919 at Weimar, in Germany, by Walter Gropius, the architect. It moved eventually to Berlin, where, in 1933, it was closed by the Nazis. Its great importance lay in the fact that its teachers included Klee and Kandinsky, and that it attempted to face the problem of machine production by advocating an integration between art and technology.

Beardsley, Aubrey (1872–1898)   Beardsley was an illustrator whose highly wrought, stylized black-and-white drawings express perfectly the Art Nouveau of which they were an ingredient.

BACON
Study for Velazquez Pope

Beaux Arts   An architectural style of the late 19th and early 20th centuries that supported neoclassical themes through symmetry and plentiful sculptured ornamentation.

Black Art   *See* **Afro-American Art**.

Blake, William (1757–1827)   An artist and poet who earned a meager living by working for publishers as an engraver, usually of other men's designs. However, between his bread-and-butter work he produced his own poems in books that he made and published himself, engraving the text and surrounding it with an illustration that he colored by hand. In this manner he issued the *Songs of Innocence* (1789) and *Songs of Experience* (1794). His greatest works are his twenty-one large watercolors illustrating the *Book of Job* and his illustrations to *Dante*. His early work was neoclassical, but as his verse and philosophy acquired a more visionary and truly mystic quality, he turned to forms and ideas evolved from medieval examples. He then abandoned logical arrangement in space, and developed a purely subjective use of color, light, and form to give substance to his visions. Whatever his sources, he always transmuted everything by the power of his imagination.

Blaue Reiter, Der (Ger. The Blue Rider)   Members of this Munich group of artists, formed in 1911, included Kandinsky and Klee. Their work is considered the most important modern art in Germany pre-World War I, stressing anti-naturalism, magic, and primitivism.

Bonnard, Pierre (1867–1947)   A French painter, influenced by Gauguin and by Japanese art, Bonnard eventually gave up his work in graphics because of his desire to work more fully with color. In his paintings of nudes, landscapes, and still lifes he displayed great softness and gentleness while using tones of deep intensity.

Bosch, Hieronymus (1450–1516?)   Perhaps the greatest master of fantasy who ever lived. His obsessive and haunted world is that of Gothic twilight fraught with deep levels of symbolism. Bosch's work is the best surviving expression of some aspects of the waning of the Middle Ages, although it is now largely incomprehensible. The Surrealists have claimed him as a sort of Freudian, but it is certain that his pictures had a very definite significance and were not free expressions of the unconscious mind. In recent years there has been an elaborate attempt to "explain" many of the pictures as altarpieces painted for a heretical cult that was addicted to orgiastic rites. Not only is there no evidence for this, but it also fails to explain why so many of Bosch's pictures belonged to people of unimpeachable orthodoxy.

Botticelli, Sandro (1445–1510)   The most individual if not the most influential painter in Florence at the end of the 15th century. The chronology of his work ranges between vigorous realism and languorous and antinaturalistic ecstasy. We know that he was neurotic, and that he was accused of pederasty (though this charge was made freely in 15th-century Florence; and usually without much evidence). His most celebrated mythological pictures have very involved allegorical and Christianizing meanings and were probably painted for a

BOSCH
Garden of Earthly Delights

member of the Medici family, then still ruling Florence. During the last twenty years of the 15th century he ran a large shop for the production of Madonnas of a gently devout kind, well suited to the piety of the age: these made him prosperous, although many of them were copied by other artists. By about 1500 his style was so obviously opposed to the new ideas of Leonardo da Vinci and Michelangelo that he suffered a decline in popularity and the last ten years of his life are a mystery.

Brancusi, Constantin (1876–1957)   A Rumanian sculptor whose most successful works are often simple, highly polished shapes. He settled in Paris in 1904 and was influenced by Rodin, but by 1907 was more concerned with abstract shape: He was the friend of Modigliani and induced him to turn to sculpture. Brancusi exhibited in New York (1913) and was involved in a notorious case in 1926–1928, when the U.S. Customs refused to admit a work of his as sculpture, claiming that it was turned metal and thus dutiable.

Braque, Georges (1882–1963)   Braque began as an apprentice in a decorator's business, and hence his superb technique. He was at the Ecole des Beaux-Arts in Paris, but preferred to work on his own. By 1906 he was in the Fauve circle, but by 1909 he knew Picasso well, and with him had started to work out the basis of a new approach to painting that developed into Cubism. By the outbreak of war in 1914 this close collaboration was at an end and his acknowledgment of realism led to his vigorous and splendid still life and figure compositions, with a perfection of balance and harmony between color and design, which he continued to develop for the rest of his life.

Brueghel (Breughel), **Peter I** (1525 or 1530–1569) Sometimes also called "Peasant Brueghel," he was the most important satirist in The Netherlands after Bosch, and one of the greatest landscape painters. The Alps, and to a lesser extent the scenery of Italy, made a tremendous impact on him, as may be seen from the development of his landscape style. However, the art of Italy seems to have made almost no impression on him. His drawings for engravers were very much in the manner of Bosch and dealt with the same subjects. In the last ten or twelve years of his life he produced genre scenes and religious subjects set in vast landscapes that are his finest works. The old nickname "Peasant Brueghel" is misleading if it is held to mean that he was himself a peasant: On the contrary, he was highly cultivated. His attitude is hard to define since it is not merely condescending but seems to show a real interest in village customs coupled with a satirical approach to drunkenness, gluttony, and other sins. His paintings are among the great landscape paintings of the age, both in their feeling for nature and the unity of man and his surroundings.

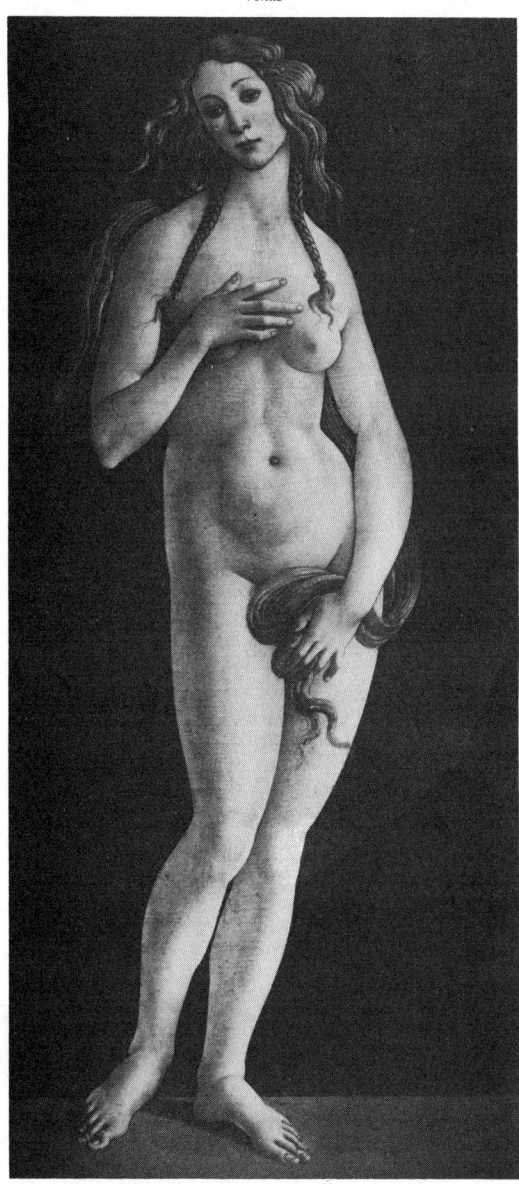

BOTTICELLI
Venus

Brush Drawing Drawing executed entirely with brush and usually in a wash. The favored technique of Oriental painting.

Brushwork With the development of the technique of oil painting, it soon became clear that the use of stiff bristle brushes charged with oil paint and applied to a grainy surface (i.e., canvas) could give a special texture. This quality was aesthetically pleasing in itself, independent of its function in representing form. A painter's brushwork is as personal as handwriting (and is occasionally referred to as such) and it is even harder to imitate. The encrustations of Rembrandt, the frenzied drama of van Gogh's brush, the thin film of Gainsborough, the gemlike luminosity of Vermeer's small dabs of paint—all these are possible in one and the same medium, so that brushwork is one of the painter's most powerful tools. In some cases it becomes the end rather than the means: In certain forms of Abstract Expressionism the word can perhaps hardly be legitimately applied to paint trickled rather than brushed onto the surface.

Buonarroti, Michelangelo *See* **Michelangelo Buonarroti.**

Byzantine Art Art of the Eastern (Greek) Empire called Byzantium. First seen in the 5th century, it lasted until the mid-15th century and the destruction of the Empire by the Turks. At times it exhibits strongly stylized or hieratic qualities owing to important oriental components. At other times classical realism from Greek art appeared in the style.

Cadmus, Paul (b. 1904) An American painter with a highly detailed, frequently photographic style whose graphic depiction of sex and horror often caused a reaction of shock. His recreation of daily life is negative and perverse, executed in a precise and highly technical style.

Caillebotte, Gustave (1848–1894) Born in Paris, he earned a law degree and inherited a large fortune from his father that enabled him to pursue the study of art at the Ecole des Beaux Arts in 1876. Caillebotte began as a solid realist artist but was captivated by the impressionists. He adapted the high keyed broken color technique of the impressionists, participated in several of their exhibitions and, by helping his artist friends financially, became known as the "patron of the impressionists."

Caldecott, Randolph (1846–1886) An English graphic artist whose abiding interest was in illustration. Caldecott's work appeared frequently in *Punch,* and he was the illustrator of many classic children's books. Today "Caldecott" is best known as the coveted award given annually for expertise in the world of children's book illustrations.

Calder, Alexander (1898–1976) An American sculptor, abstract painter, and illustrator of children's books. Calder was originally an engineer whose main invention, mobiles, can be regarded as a marriage between engineering and sculpture. His paintings were influenced by Miró.

Calligraphy Fine or elegant handwriting. When a drawing is described as calligraphic, it is linear, with flowing, rhythmic strokes and a distinctively personal quality.

Canaletto, (Giovanni) Antonio (1697–1768) A Venetian artist who went to Rome and acquired a special talent by teaching himself to paint city views. This skill became a lucrative occupation because of the popularity of travel in Europe; tourists wished to take home mementos of the cities they visited on the Grand Tour. When he returned to Venice his works were characterized by strong contrasts of light and shade that eventually served to make him famous. He had a strong sense of harmony, and his depiction of architecture is scrupulous, as if his buildings were painted with the use of a ruler and other geometric instruments.

Caravaggio, Michelangelo Merisi da (1573–1610) His earliest works were still life subjects and small dramatized self-portraits of a distinctly Northern and vaguely Venetian character, utilizing strong chiaroscuro and detailed execution. He then turned to religious subject matter, frequently creating controversial altar pieces. Basically, the objections to these works were on the grounds of indecorum—the dirty feet of the pilgrims, the peasant air of the Virgin, and the coarse types used to depict the Apostles. In one, the bloated figure of the dead Virgin was reputed to have been painted from a drowned prostitute fished out of the Tiber. These accusations were founded on Caravaggio's vivid realism, his use of contemporary costumes and settings, his rejection of idealization, and the simplicity of his approach. But all his rejected works found ready buyers among cardinals and noblemen, against whom no accusations of insincerity and sensationalism could be made. His reputation as a stormy petrel was probably added to by the numerous fracases with the police caused by his violent temper. His last works, painted in Malta and Sicily, are very dark and somewhat damaged, but their direct iconography, their inspired simplicity and poignancy embody a new intensity of dramatic feeling. His technical methods were revolutionary and brought him into endless controversy: He is recorded as painting directly onto the canvas from a model, instead of working from sketches. However, his methods and ideas were both admired and emulated by Rubens and Rembrandt.

Caricature First used in England in 1748, this word describes an ancient portrait technique that exaggerates characteristic physical features in order to stress traits of the subject's personality, for the sake of humor or satire.

Cartoon Nowadays this normally means a drawing with a humorous or satirical intention, but the original meaning is quite different. A cartoon was a full-size drawing for a painting, usually worked out in complete detail, ready for transfer to wall, canvas, or panel. The cartoon was rubbed on the back with chalk and the main lines were then gone over with a stylus, thus transferring them to the canvas or panel.

Cassatt, Mary (1845–1926) An American painter, printmaker, and pastelist, Cassatt was born in Pittsburgh, the daughter of a banker who offered her little encouragement with her painting. In 1868, after traveling widely in Europe, she settled in Paris to study and became interested in Courbet, Manet, and the Impressionists. In 1877 she met Degas, who invited her to exhibit with the Impressionists, which she did. Cassatt's paintings are frequently of mothers and children, but despite their subject matter, they are known to lack sentimentality. The color prints which she did in the 1890s are memorable for their discipline of line and subtlety of color.

CASSATT
Woman in Raspberry Costume

Casting In sculpture, the process of duplicating the original wax or clay model in metal, plaster of Paris, or other material by means of a mold.

Cellini, Benvenuto (1500–1571) Florentine sculptor, goldsmith, and amorist, Cellini is best known for his *Autobiography,* which gives a glimpse of the processes of artistic creation as well as insight into the troubled Italy of the years following 1527. Cellini's love life is also featured here in considerable detail, although not all of it is credible. As an artist, Cellini was first influenced by Raphael but later came very much under the shadow of Michelangelo. He was also a designer of coins and medals.

Cézanne, Paul (1839–1906) Probably the greatest painter of the last 100 years, Cézanne was born in Aix-en-Provence, the son of a wealthy banker and tradesman. In 1861, after abandoning the study of law, he went to Paris, where he met Pissarro, and from 1862 Cézanne devoted himself to painting. In

CÉZANNE
Self Portrait

the 1860s his ardent Southern temperament expressed itself in a series of more or less erotic and melodramatic pictures, which were not received with enthusiasm. While closely associated with Pissarro, Cézanne began to paint landscapes in an Impressionist technique. One of his pictures incurred the greatest public displeasure. It was the most extraordinary of all the erotic fantasies, the *Modern Olympia.* This painting represents a fat squatting female being disrobed by a black woman while a man (probably Cézanne himself) watches with interest. In the midst of the chaste Impressionist landscapes the effect must have been startling, particularly as these early pictures are painted with a palette knife. During the 1870s Cézanne digested the theories of color and light that the Impressionists were then developing. He gradually calmed his exuberant romantic temperament, and from about 1900 his genius was widely recognized. In the last years of his life he returned to some of his favorite early themes in which his lyricism and use of space and color became evident. Cézanne is thought to be the innovating source of the movements in 20th-century art.

Chagall, Marc (1887–1985) A Russian-Jewish painter who moved to Paris in 1910, Chagall had a highly imaginative style and painted more or less recognizable objects either in unusual juxtapositions or floating in space. His color was rich, and his subject matter often combined mystical elements with poetic evocations of Russian village life; although in later years he came increasingly to paint religious pictures. His fantasies greatly influenced the Surrealists.

Charcoal This medium is made from twigs of willow or vine, and used for drawing on paper and making preliminary drawings on walls or canvases as the first stage in a painting. In charcoal mistakes can easily be rubbed off and new renditions made.

Chardin, Jean-Baptiste-Siméon (1699–1779) The finest 18th-century French painter of still life, Chardin's works are modest in size and are restricted in their range of subjects. They are composed of the simplest elements—kitchen utensils, vegetables, game, baskets of fruit, fish, and similar materials—and are exceptional in their solid color and depth of tone.

Chasing A method of ornamenting metal surfaces by embossing, hollowing, or engraving with steel tools. Also, the finishing of bronze casts by removing small imperfections and smoothing rough spots.

Chiaroscuro (Ital. light-dark) As generally used, chiaroscuro means the balance of light and shadow in a picture, and the skill shown by the painter in

CHAGALL
The Green Violinist

the management of shadows. The word tends to be used mainly to describe painters like Rembrandt or Caravaggio, whose works are predominantly dark in tone. In contemporary life, the term is often used to describe efforts in interior design and trends in women's clothing.

Chirico, Giorgio de' (1888–1978) An Italian painter, founder of the quasi-Surrealist movement, who was preoccupied with mystery and the unknown as exemplified through dreams and the unconscious. His work, suffused with stark geometric forms and rigid architecture, is executed in solid blocks of color, with little attention to detail.

Classicism In the broadest artistic sense, art based on the study of classical models; art that emphasizes qualities considered to be characteristically Greek and Roman in style and spirit, i.e., reason, objectivity, discipline, restraint, order, harmony.

Cloisonné Enamel A technique of enameling in which the design is laid down in thin metal strips on a metal or porcelain ground, forming chambers (cloisons) to receive the vitreous enamel pastes.

Cole, Thomas (1801–1848) This first great American landscape painter, a member of the Hudson River School of painting, was born in England and worked as an engraver before emigrating to the United States in 1818. His initial efforts in landscape met with little success, but when he settled in New York in 1825, he began to be recognized. His works are often described as dramatically romantic—he could render a view accurately, yet still make that same view seem alive and spiritual as it acted out nature's drama.

Collage (from Fr. *coller,* to stick) A picture built up wholly or partly from pieces of paper, cloth, or any other material stuck onto canvas or other surface. This device was much used by the early Cubists, who would stick pieces of newspaper onto pictures painted in an otherwise normal way, and by the Dadaists. In his last years, Matisse used pieces of colored paper as a complete substitute for painting. *See* **Montage** for comparison.

Complementary Color A term meaning that each primary color—red, blue, yellow—has a complementary, formed by a mixture of the other two (thus green, mixing blue and yellow, is the complementary of red). It is part of Impressionist theory that every primary color has its complementary color in the shadow it casts. Thus, a yellow object will have violet in its shadow.

Composition The art of combining the elements of a picture or other work of art into a satisfactory visual whole: In art, the whole is very much more than the sum of its parts. A picture is well composed if its constituents—whether figures, objects, or shapes—form a harmony that pleases the eye. This is the sole aim of most abstract painting; however, in more traditional art, the task is made much more difficult by the need to piece forms in an ordered sequence without losing their effectiveness as a pattern.

Constable, John (1776–1837) With Turner, the major English landscape painter of the 19th century, Constable is highly recognized for his skill in composition and his brilliant use of chiaroscuro as a unifying factor. His work is characterized by the vivid,

CONSTABLE
The Hay Wain

dewy greens of water meadows and mills under fresh, windy skies. His art lay in the representation of nature modified by the tradition inherited from the Dutch landscape painters of the 17th century, and he was the last great painter in this tradition.

Constructivism Principally a Russian movement that utilized hanging and relief constructions, abstract in concept, and made of a variety of materials, including wire, glass, and sheet metal. The idea behind the movement was to "construct" in art. Constructivist ideas have had considerable influence on architecture and decoration, and their manifestations include abstract sculpture, employing nontraditional materials, or industrial methods in which welding is used.

Continuous Representation In many medieval pictures continuous representation conotes several successive incidents in the story shown as taking place in different parts of the same picture. For example, a picture of the martyrdom of a saint may show all his miracles dotted about in the background.

Copley, John Singleton (1738–1815) A Boston painter, almost completely self-taught, Copley evolved a distinguished and direct portrait style for his New England clientele. In 1774 he left America to visit Italy and much of Europe before settling in London. Although he profoundly altered his style to compete with other English painters, his portraits of children still retained their engaging vivacity.

Corot, Jean-Baptiste-Camille (1796–1875) Born in Paris, Corot's early training was with classical landscape painters. In 1825 he went to Italy, where he developed his sensitive treatment of light, form, and distance in terms of tone rather than by color and drawing. His muzzy treatment of landscape and trees in soft, gray-green tones became immensely popular. However, his very late portraits and figure studies are entirely free from this blurred and formless approach. He was a prolific painter, and examples of his work hang in almost every sizable museum in the world.

Correggio, Antonio (1489–1534) An Italian painter greatly influenced by Leonardo da Vinci, from whom he developed the very soft, voluptuous style characteristic of all his oil paintings. Correggio's art represented a great range of emotion—from the commonplace to the sublime. Though he worked during the High Renaissance, many characteristics of his work mark him as a forerunner of the Baroque art of the 17th and 18th centuries.

Coulisse (Fr., wing, as in a theater) Compositional elements—clumps of trees, groups of figures, buildings, etc.—arranged in tiers at the sides of a picture to direct the eye into the center picture space. Common in Baroque painting.

Courbet, Gustave (1819–1877) Teaching himself partly by copying in the Louvre, Courbet evolved a vigorous naturalism that he used in scenes from everyday life, portraits, nudes, still lifes, and landscapes. He was rabidly anticlerical, depicting drunken priests, and he further injured himself by meddling in politics and involving himself in the aftermath of the 1848 Revolution. Strongly anti-intellectual, Courbet rejected all idealization in art and rebelled against both classicism and romanticism for their literary and exotic subjects. He proclaimed that only realism was truly democratic and that the noblest subject for the artist was the worker and the peasant. His eventual flight from France in 1873 prevented him from knowing much of the work of the Impressionists. Courbet was a convivial Bohemian of inordinate vanity and one with an unendearingly caustic tongue. His technique was imperfect; his brushwork often as insensitive as his color, although in his best works this same brushwork can be extraordinarily rich. He is recognized for his use of chiaroscuro and his vivid unconventional approach, which is dramatically exciting. Many of his nudes range from the mildly to the highly erotic.

Crackle A network of fine cracks on the glaze of oriental and modern porcelain, produced by intentional crazing. Also, the surface of an oil painting when broken by a network of small cracks (craquelure).

Cubism A form of Modern Art, and the parent of all Abstract Art forms, Cubism grew out of the efforts of Picasso and Braque to replace the purely visual effects of the Impressionists with objects that had a more intellectual conception in form and color. Cubists deliberately gave up the representation of things as they appear in order to give several views of an object, expressing an idea rather than any one view of the subject. The first exhibition of Cubistic works was in 1907 in Paris.

Currier, Nathaniel (1813–1888) and **Ives, James Merritt** (1824–1895) American lithographers and printing partners who employed handcoloring on a mass-production system in which one person worked with each color. For some fifty years they published three new prints each week on every aspect of American life—the Wild West; Indian, sporting, and pioneering scenes; fires and other disasters; the Civil War, and temperance and political tracts—all of which reached into the farthest corners of the land and also had a considerable following abroad.

Dada (Fr. hobby-horse) An art form that began in 1915 (also an international movement in literature and drama) and flourished between Cubism and Surrealism; its purpose was to produce in its audience both hysteria and shock. Dada was deliberately antiart and antisense, intended to outrage and scandalize, and its most characteristic piece was the reproduction of the *Mona Lisa,* decorated with a mustache and bearing the obscene caption *Elle a chaud au cul.* Other manifestations included colored paper cut out at random and shuffled; ready-made objects, such as the "signed" bicycle wheel; bits of machinery with incongruous titles; and a lecture given by 38 lecturers in unison. Supposedly the name Dada was picked by sticking a pin down onto the page of an open dictionary.

Dali, Salvador (1904–1989) A Spanish painter, Dali was originally a Cubist but became one of the leading Surrealists until he abandoned Marxism and returned to the Catholic Church. Dali frequently used nightmares, visionary experiences, and mental aberrations for subject matter, all related with photographic exactness and great attention paid to every detail. He is also famous for paintings of great spiritual beauty. Dali the man was flamboyant, and not many claim to have really known this master of pose and disguise.

DALI
Premonition of the Civil War

Daumier, Honoré (1808–1879) A cartoonist and bitter political and social satirist, Daumier's watercolors and wash drawings of scenes from everyday life are untouched by any romantic feeling for picturesque poverty. His large oil paintings are loosely handled, with calligraphic brushwork and intense light and shadow. He delighted in painting the sordid side of great cities by exposing evil characters and carefully hidden secrets. In old age Daumier became blind and was eventually rescued from desperate poverty by Jean-Baptiste-Camille Corot.

DAUMIER
The People of Justice

DAVIES
Rapt at Rappaport's

David, Jacques-Louis (1748–1825)   During the French Revolution, David became dictator of the arts and designed huge propaganda pieces. He also painted memorial portraits of the martyrs of the Revolution. Later he met Napoleon and became an ardent Bonapartist, painting several laudatory works to aid Napoleon's public relations. After Waterloo, David fled to Switzerland and eventually retired to Brussels, where he died. Several contradictory strains combine in David's art—from the stern neo-classicism of his youth he moved, in the Napoleonic pictures, toward a Venetian use of color and light. Yet contemporary and later pictures of Classical subjects show a concentration on drawing and a rigid antiquarianism at variance with all that Venetian influence implies. His portraits are always supremely well designed and full of realism; however, his later Classical subjects betray a progressive sweetening of style, perhaps due to the stultifying influence of his self-imposed exile, cut off from the stimulating conflict of ideas resulting from the rise of Romanticism.

Davies, Arthur Brown (1862–1928)   An American artist, he studied in Europe where he was influenced by the dreamlike paintings of Giorgione. His paintings are distinguished by a poetic, fanciful symbolism based on figures moving gracefully within mysterious landscapes and wooden glens. He also executed mural decorations as well as tapestry designs for the Gobelin Factory. As a member of the Society of Independent Artists, Davies arranged the Armory Show of 1913.

Davis, Stuart (1894–1964)   An American abstract artist influenced by Léger, Davis frequently painted recognizable objects in "foreign," abstract settings. For one year his only subject matter was an egg beater, an electric fan, and a rubber glove.

Degas, Edgar (1834–1917)   Born in Paris of a wealthy family, Degas' early works—family portraits and some history pictures—suggest that he was to develop into an academic painter. However, his first pictures of dancers were painted about 1873, and from then on ballet girls, working girls, models dressing and bathing, and cabaret artists became his principal subject matter. He recorded the manners and movements of a society he observed almost as if it were another world. Technically, he was one of the greatest experimenters and innovators. In later life, he used pastel more than any other medium, and as his eyesight weakened his handling became broader and freer. There are also seventy-four pieces of sculpture—late works—including ballet dancers and figures in movement, originally executed in wax, but now generally cast in bronze.

de Kooning, Willem (b.1904)   A Dutch-born artist, de Kooning was a leader in the Abstract-Expressionist movement. In 1926, he settled in the United States permanently, and here his work took on the new dimensions of Symbolism and Surrealism. He was famous for his depictions of the female form in primitive and strident colors, distorted shapes, and tragic expressions.

Delacroix, Eugène (1798–1863)   The major painter of the Romantic movement in France, Delacroix had a great interest in English art and in animal painting. In 1832 he visited North Africa, and this opened to him a whole new field of subjects: scenes from Arab and Jewish life, animal subjects, and innumerable illustrations of Byron abound in his gigantic output after this. But the works he is happiest with are small, freely handled, colorful subjects—battles, hunts, animals in combat, and

DEGAS
Study of a Dancer

portraits of intimate friends, such as Chopin. He left no artistic succession, for the essence of Romanticism is its personal quality. He contributed greatly to the struggle of the nonconforming artist against entrenched classicism.

Donatello (1386?–1466) Not only the greatest Florentine sculptor before Michelangelo, Donatello was the most influential individual artist of the 15th century. Practically every later sculptor, including Michelangelo, was deeply indebted to him, and the heroic types he invented have colored our whole conception of 15th-century Florence. He created a new kind of humanity, slightly larger than life and exemplifying qualities that were highly prized in the early Renaissance. His later work is saturated in the spirit of antiquity which he understood more fully than any other 15th-century artist.

Doré, Gustave (1832–1883) A French painter and lithographer, Doré's powerful imagination made him recognized as a master of mystery, drama, and satire. His most famous illustrations appear in editions of Dante's *Inferno* and Cervantes' *Don Quixote*—works that provide a wealth of material for an artist who shaped visions and dreams.

Dragging The technique of applying paint over a previous, tacky layer in order to create the effect of broken color.

Drybrush A technique of drawing, watercolor, and also oil painting in which little color is put onto a brush and then skimmed over a surface. Color is left only on the raised points of that surface, which gives a soft, sketchy tone and effect.

Dubuffet, Jean (1901–1985) He was inspired by graffiti on walls ("the art of the ordinary man") and produced works that are made of junk—tar, sand, glass, and so on—which were scratched, colored, and manipulated into shapes resembling human beings, e.g., aggressively female women. He preferred amateur spontaneity to professional skill, and had a large collection of what he called *art brut* (raw art), much of it produced by psychotics.

Dufy, Raoul (1877–1953) Dufy worked in a sub-Impressionist manner until 1905, when he adopted simplified form and bright color. He designed textiles and ceramics and developed a gay, light-hearted, decorative style, eminently suited to his range of subjects—esplanades, racecourses, regattas, etc.

Dürer, Albrecht (1471–1528) The son of a goldsmith, Dürer began in the art world by producing woodcut book illustrations for a painter. Later he studied mathematics, geometry, Latin, and humanist literature and sought the company of scholars rather than that of fellow artisans. This departure in mode of life and thought was common enough in Italy, but it was unprecedented in Germany. Dürer's enormous work consists of woodcuts and engravings and paintings. He was the main channel through which Italian Renaissance forms and ideas were introduced into the North. His greatest influence was through his graphic work. He is one of the supreme masters of woodcut and copper engraving, and carried his technique and style all over Europe. All his works combine vivid imagery, technical refinement, expressiveness, and masterly draftsmanship.

DÜRER
His Mother

ART

Eakins, Thomas (1844–1916) An American painter, principally of portraits, Eakins went from Philadelphia to Paris in 1866, where he came under the influence of Manet's realism. He eventually became a successful teacher in Philadelphia where his quest for realism led him to attend medical classes to improve his knowledge of anatomy. However, in his later period of portrait painting, Eakins' scientific bent gave way to intense psychological study.

Early Christian Art Term referring to the early centuries of Christian art (3rd to 6th) when Christian subject matter was rendered in the prevailing styles of late Roman art.

Earth Art An umbrella term for related movements originating in the mid-1960s in which substances like dirt, rocks, snow, and grass are embraced as the artist's media.

Easel Picture Small- or moderate-size painting executed at an easel. Renaissance artists began painting easel pictures to meet the demand of collectors, and they were often displayed on easels. Also called cabinet picture.

Egg-and-Dart Classical decorative motif consisting of an alternation of oval forms with pointed, dart-like shapes.

Enamel Colorless, white, or colored glass fused by heat to a metal or porcelain base. Also, an object produced by the technique.

Engraving A generic title often used to cover all the methods of multiplying prints. The three main types of engraving may be classified as (1) Relief or cameo, (2) Intaglio, and (3) Lithography. (1) *Relief.* The main techniques are woodcut and wood-engraving. A plain block of wood, if covered with printing ink and pressed on a sheet of paper, would print as a black rectangle, but if channels were cut into the surface with a gouge these would not catch the ink and would print as white patches. The principle of a woodcut is, therefore, to leave the black lines or patches untouched. A single black line has to have the wood on each side of it cut away, and this is done with special knives and gouges. Woodcuts are done on blocks of soft wood and give hundreds, or even thousands, of impressions before wearing out. Color prints are produced by cutting a special block for each color as well as a key-block,

---

EXHIBIT 1.1
History of Architecture

Greek (750–720 B.C.) Temples and theaters constructed basically from marble were the main examples of buildings in this era. These were characterized by columns: Doric, a single molded top with no base; Ionic, a base with a scrolled top; and Corinthian, a base and an ornate top with bell-shaped leaves for ornamentation.

Roman (100 B.C.–370 A.D.) A style of many different types of buildings—amphitheaters, basilicas, aqueducts, baths, temples—constructed largely of stone, concrete, and brick, and featuring the development of the arch. Roman columns were either Tuscan—plain Doric-style, or Composite, which utilized Ionic scrollwork, with the addition of Corinthian leaves.

Byzantine (330–1450) The dome characterized this architectural period, and plaster was added to outside surfaces as a building medium. Interiors were brightly colored and ornate, using marble and mosaics for frescoes and decoration. The Byzantine era was greatly influenced by Eastern styles and Roman design.

Romanesque (Norman) (850–1250) Vaults and arches created from stone marked Romanesque architecture which was also characterized by the building of thick walls and massive pillars. Interior decoration was simple and severe, with primarily geometric design.

Gothic (1140–1560) High naves with flying buttresses (bridges of stone) and large windows sectioned into many small panes by stonework are features of this style of architecture. The Gothic era saw the development of pointed arches, elaborate carving, and curved windows and doors.

Renaissance (1420–1650) This "new" style was a revival and an adaptation of Greek and Roman architecture, featuring domes and rectangular columns that were frequently embedded in walls.

Baroque (1600–1770) An ornate style, often described as rococo, with elaborate carvings and decorations using gilt, plaster, and paint in flowing curves and designs.

Industrial Age (1800–1915) A period marked by the utilitarian construction of factories, apartment houses, stores, railroad stations, etc. Durability was stressed in the use of steel, iron, cement, and wrought iron; reinforced glass was also used to create domed ceilings.

Art Nouveau (1880–1920) An architectural style exemplified by long flowing lines and asymmetrical design. Interior motifs borrowed from natural forms such as flowers and leaves, waves and fire to create elaborate ornamentation.

Art Deco (1920–1940) Nonfunctional geometric design was characteristic of this architectural era, which was infuenced by Egyptian art. Materials such as plastic and glass were heavily relied on, as was steel in the construction of buildings.

Modern Architecture (1920–present day) The evolving new technology created new design needs and low, steel-constructed buildings with glass walls covering large areas were the vogue at the beginning of this era. Later, a reaction to such severe simplicity set in, and by the 1950s new decorative features and carving were once again in use, adding personality to buildings while managing to avoid a trend toward revivalism.

usually printed black, which carries the linear structure. (2) *Intaglio*. The intaglio techniques include all forms of engraving on metal, usually copper, and they are distinguished from other techniques by the method of printing. When the plate has been engraved, it is dabbed all over with a thin printing ink, which is then rubbed off, leaving the ink in the engraved furrows. A piece of paper is then dampened and laid on the plate, and both are rolled through a heavy press not unlike a mangle. The damp paper is forced into the engraved lines and so picks up the ink: when dry the engraved lines stand up in relief. (3) *Lithography*. The one major process that involves no cutting into the block or plate, and therefore no engraving in the proper sense, is lithography, usually executed on a thick slab of stone or zinc. The whole technique is based on the fact that water runs off a greasy surface. The design is drawn or painted on the stone with a greasy chalk, and then the stone is wetted. When the greasy ink is rolled on the stone it will not take on the wet parts, but it sticks on the parts that are already greasy, from which the water runs off. This process is used very widely for posters and other forms of commercial art. Its great advantage is that there is almost no limit to the number of prints it is possible to produce.

Environment Art   Not to be confused with earth art, in its broadest sense environment art refers to the work of artists who manipulate the man-made environment. Controlled spaces—whether sculpted or constructed of building materials or light beams or sound—are intended to be experienced with all the senses. Environment art has appeared sporadically in several 20th-century movements, including Dada, Surrealism, and Pop Art.

Epstein, Sir Jacob (1880–1959)   Born in New York, Epstein spent his life in England. In 1907 he was commissioned to carve 18 statues for the British Medical Association building. They were erected in 1908 and caused great scandal because people thought them indecent. After that, it became customary for any new imaginative work of his to be greeted with an uproar. His portraits in bronze have an over-life-size quality partly due to the handling. Reminiscent of Rodin, Epstein's works are generally admired by the public and receive great critical acclaim.

Ernst, Max (1891–1976)   Of German origin, a naturalized French artist, Ernst was a leading Surrealist and one of the founders of Dada. His works, sometimes referred to as "reveries," often had a mysterious quality and were sometimes peopled by strange animals moving through unusual and disturbing landscapes. Ernst was thought to be the most effective and moving when he endeavored to re-create the ideas and things with which he was obsessed.

Etching   A process in which an etching needle is used to draw the design into a wax ground applied over a metal plate. The plate is then subjected to a series of acid bitings, is inked, wiped, and then printed. Also, a print made by this process.

Expressionism   The contemporary search for expressiveness of style by means of exaggerations and distortions of line and color. Expressionism is a simplified style that carries great emotional impact, an art movement in which the artist's emotions become more important than a faithful rendering of the subject matter. For instance, van Gogh's use of a drastically simplified outline and very strong color, and Munch's hysterical art, which is one of the foundations of the movement. The tendency to sentimental hysteria and the clear derivation from African art are two of the factors that explain Hitler's denunciation of "Degenerate Art" (Expressionism) and also the esteem it now enjoys. Expressionism in Modern Art means the display of distortion and exaggeration.

 **Fauvism**   In the post-Impressionist Paris of 1905, the works of a number of painters (Matisse, Rouault, Dufy, etc.) were hung together in one room and a critic dubbed them *Les Fauves* (the wild beasts) because their pictures were full of distortions and flat patterns, and painted in violent colors that created a furor. They were not, until then—or even afterward—a particularly coherent group, but they stayed together temporarily mostly out of rebellion and because their brightly colored works could be hung in no other company. By 1908, the Fauves had fallen apart as a group and a number of members had seceded to Cubism. Fauvism is known as the first artistic revolution of the 20th century.

Fayum Portrait   Realistic portrait of a deceased person painted on a mummy case or on the linen shroud itself, in Fayum, a province of Egypt.

Federal Style   An American architectural style of about 1780 to 1820, which reflected English Georgian models, especially the influence of Robert Adam. Symmetrically designed facades, smooth surfaces, and restrained classical ornament typify buildings in that style.

Flying Buttress   A bridge of masonry that transmits the thrust of a vault or roof to an outer support.

Folk Art   The arts of peasant societies, both past and present. Characterized by naive subject matter and a vivacious style, folk art both perpetuates very ancient decorative traditions and draws selectively from art forms of sophisticated cultural traditions, e.g., the adaptation of 18th-century rococo motifs in European folk art. Paintings, sculpture, ceramics, metalwork, costume, needlework, implements, and tools all may be folk art.

Foreshortening   Perspective is used to create a three-dimensional effect. An arm pointing directly at the spectator so that little more than the hand can be seen is said to be strongly foreshortened.

Found Object (*Objet trouvé*)   In Surrealist theory, an object of any kind that is regarded by the artist as aesthetically significant—a shell found on a walk can be a work of art. If a little judicious touching up has been indulged in, the object is known technically as a "Found Object Composed."

Fouquet, Jehan (ca. 1420–1481)   The major French painter of the 15th century, Fouquet brought back from Italy theories of perspective then unknown to the French. He was famous for miniatures, court and religious paintings, and was a renowned illuminator of manuscripts. His eclecticism also earned him plaudits as a sculptor of tombs and the designer of stained-glass windows.

Foxing   A discoloration of paper in books, on prints, etc., due to dampness. Seen as brown spots.

FRAGONARD
The Love Letter

Fragonard, Jean-Honoré (1732–1806) The typical painter of gallant and sentimental subjects in the reign of Louis XV during the ascendancy of Mme. du Barry. Fragonard worked in a lighthearted and sometimes frankly erotic vein with great success. The French Revolution put an end to his patrons and to the demand for his kind of art; he died in Paris, almost totally forgotten.

Francesca, Piero della (de' Franceschi) (1410–1492) Long neglected, della Francesca is now probably the most popular painter of the 1400s. This is due to the mathematical perfection of his forms, which gives a timeless and serene air/to his works, increased by his pale and soft colors. His meditative mind gave a calm dignity to his work, enhanced by his masterful sense of order. His style has been described as both heroic and earthy at the same time.

Francis, Sam (b.1923) A San Francisco artist, he received an M.A. degree from the University of California at Berkeley and settled in Paris. His work has been exhibited in the major galleries and museums in New York since the 1950s. Influenced by Gorky and Rothko, his paintings are marked by cellular-like shapes and glowing colors. He utilizes spatter technique and runs of pigment and also renders expressive gestural forms against vast white space.

Fresco (Ital. fresh) Wall painting, in a medium like watercolor on plaster. Practiced in Italy from the 14th century and perfected in the 16th century, it is one of the most permanent forms of wall decoration known. The wall is first rough plastered and then the cartoon is traced. The cartoon is then painted with pigments mixed with plain water or lime water. Because the plaster is still damp, a chemical reaction takes place and the colors become integrated with the wall itself. The use of a detailed, full-size cartoon means that several assistants can work simultaneously on different parts of the wall, provided that all work is done from the top downward so that the splashes fall on the unpainted parts.

Frieze The middle section of the entablature . . . where relief sculpture was sometimes applied. Also, in interiors, the broad band between wall paneling and ceiling.

Fugitive Pigment Pigment that either fades with prolonged exposure to light, is susceptible to atmospheric pollution, or tends to darken when mixed with other substances.

Fuller, Richard Buckminster (1895–1983) American avant-garde architect, Fuller became famous for his geodesic domes (structures made from connected elements that are light and straight)—frameworks of steel ribs, covered in plastic, cardboard, metal, etc.

Funk Art A term coined in the 1960s to describe a class of art that emerged in the San Francisco Bay area. It was often witty, sometimes deliberately distasteful, with a diversity of styles ranging from comic-strip derivations to William Wiley's use of found objects. Funk artists looked to popular culture rather than traditional canons of fine art.

Futurism This word was used to mean any art more recent than 1900; the only important modern movement to be largely independent of Paris (for which reason it is not popular in France) dated from Italy in 1909 to its virtual demise in World War I. Futurists wished to represent machines or figures actually in motion, and their exhibitions caused scandal and riots all over Europe. Futurism was a reaction against static art, which was considered unsuited to the dynamism of the modern world. In Futurist language, it is not good enough to portray the picture of a man eating a sandwich—the artist must also express the feelings, ideas, and thoughts associated with the action.

G **Gainsborough, Thomas** (1727–1788) An English landscape painter, Gainsborough turned for a period of time to portraiture, executing full-length life-size figures, such as *The Blue Boy*. An artist who, in his scene paintings, depended more on composition than observation and was much in rivalry with Reynolds. Gainsborough is known as the most poetic illustrator of the English personality and was the official court painter of the 1780s.

Gargoyle A familiar grotesquerie in Gothic architecture: a bizarrely weird creature whose open mouth was functional in that it helped to serve as a gutter to direct and carry water from the walls.

Gaudí, Antonio (1852–1956) A Spanish architect, Gaudí was one of the major figures in the representation of Art Nouveau, although that was only one of his many styles. He explored both the Gothic and Avant-garde, and many of his works seem to be representations of the 1950s in style. Gaudí worked for forty years on the Church of the Sagrada Familia in Barcelona. This masterpiece of blended architecture was treated by him as a piece of sculpture. The porches contain their own worlds of animals and plants in a Baroque fantasy; the gables and pitched roofs of carved stone are created as imitation snow

GAUGUIN
Indian Ocean Maiden

from which emerge shapes that represent events in the life of Christ. He also designed apartment buildings in Barcelona without straight surfaces, so that they appear to move like waves in constant undulation.

Gauguin, Paul (1848–1903) A Parisian stockbroker, Gauguin was a Sunday painter who collected the works of the Impressionists and joined in their exhibitions. He eventually gave up his job, separated from his family, and went to live in Brittanny before leaving for Tahiti in 1891. The rest of his life was spent painting and living in the South Sea islands. His last years were spent in poverty, illness, and the continual struggle with authorities to champion native causes. His early works may be ranged with those of the Impressionists, but his rejection of Western civilization led to his departure for Tahiti, and to Naturalistic tradition—he depicted the simplicity of life among primitive and unspoiled peoples. Gauguin's influence has been enormous, because he is one of the main sources from which non-Naturalistic 20th-century art has emanated.

Genre This style of painting depicts scenes from everyday life without trying to idealize the subject matter.

Giacometti, Alberto (1901–1966) A Swiss artist who created imaginary, symbolic structures from rough blocks. In 1930, Giacometti joined the Surrealist movement and began to mold smaller and smaller pieces, until one bust of his was no bigger than a book of matches. Later he returned to more realistic figures (emaciated in form), built by working with plaster of Paris on an armature.

Gibson, Charles Dana (1867–1944) An American painter and illustrator, Gibson became involved in depicting and ridiculing New York society and turn-of-the-century social practices. He was most famous for the popular illustrations of his wife, who became the American symbol of manners and fashion (high neck, full sleeves, wasp waist), known still as the "Gibson girl."

Gilding The practice of applying a thin layer of gold leaf to the surface of an object, then burnishing it.

Giotto (1266–1337) A Florentine, Giotto is generally regarded as the founder of modern painting, since he broke away from the stereotyped forms of Byzantine art and tried to give his figures solidity and naturalism while imbuing passion and imagination into his scenes. His dramatic power can be felt in his frescoes, filled with the humanity St. Francis brought to the religious life of the 13th century that had a potent influence on the arts. In Giotto's art, people are revealed for the first time as human beings whose feelings express the deep emotions of Christianity.

Gisant A sculptured figure, memorializing the deceased, that lies on the lid of the deceased's tomb.

Glazing The process of applying a transparent layer of oil paint over a solid one so that the color of the first is profoundly modified. Thus, a transparent glaze of crimson over a solid blue will give effects of purple to mulberry color, depending on the thickness of the glaze or the intensity of pigment used. The use of glazes is now very rare, as it implies a deliberation and a craftsmanly approach to painting that is often thought inconsistent with inspiration. *See* **Scumbling**.

Gogh, Vincent van (1853–1890) The son of a Dutch pastor, van Gogh became a missionary in a coal-mining district in Belgium, where he shared the poverty and hardships of the miners. He did not begin to become an artist until he was living in great poverty after his dismissal from the mission in 1880. Then he joined his brother Theo in Paris and came immediately into contact with the works of the Impressionists, which Theo endeavored to sell in the gallery devoted to Modern Art that he directed. He met Toulouse-Lautrec, Pissarro, Degas, Seurat, and Gauguin, and in 1888 went to Arles, where he was later joined by Gauguin. In December 1888 he became mentally imbalanced, and from then until his death suffered intermittent attacks of manic depression. During the intervals he painted with a frenzy and passion in asylums or wherever he found himself living. In July 1890 he shot himself. His brother Theo, to whom most of his long and revealing letters were addressed, and who was his constant support, moral and financial, died six months later. Van Gogh's Dutch period is characterized by his use of dark color, heavy forms, and subject matter chiefly drawn from peasants and their work. He ignored Theo's advice to lighten his palette as the Impressionists were doing. Later he adopted the Impressionist technique and turned to flowers, views of Paris, and portraits and self-portraits that enabled him to experiment with new ideas. He painted many landscapes and portraits in heightened color and with a vivid expression of light and feeling. His paintings are vivid in color and with writhing, flamelike forms in the drawing, completely expressive of his tormented sensibility.

VAN GOGH
The Sunflowers

Gothic A term used to describe the medieval architectural style of Northern Europe from the early 12th century until the 16th. It is also used to describe the other arts of the same period, particularly when emphasizing their transcendental qualities distinct from Renaissance art. The cathedral was Gothic art's greatest contribution, with its elaborate architecture and grand stained-glass panels.

Gouache Opaque watercolor paint (known to many people as poster paint). With gouache, effects very similar to those in oil painting may be achieved with less trouble, so that it is a useful means of making studies for a large picture in oils, although it has the defect of drying much lighter in tone than it seems when wet.

Goya (y Lucientes), **Francisco de** (1746–1828) The official Spanish portrait painter, Goya also produced works that, he said, were "to make observations for which commissioned works generally have no room, and in which fantasy and invention have no limit." This fantasy was typified in a series of etchings that are savagely satirical attacks on manners and customs and on abuses in the Church. Goya was a rebel and a revolutionary, and what seems difficult to understand is how the Bourbons could continue to employ him, for his portraits of Charles IV and his family have been described as making them look like prosperous grocers, to appear brutish, moronic, and arrogant. In later years Goya began to practice the new art of Lithography and produced some bullfighting scenes as well as prints and etchings.

Graffiti Drawing and writing (sometimes just scratching with haste) on particularly nonaesthetic surfaces, such as trains, cars, school desks, and bathroom walls. Occasionally quite pleasing and color-ful, graffiti is infrequently raised to the level of an art form.

Graphic Arts The phrase refers to those arts involving writing, drawing, engraving, or any representation or decoration onto a flat surface.

Greco, El (Domenikos Theotocopoulos) (1541–1614) Known as "The Greek," his early works show his wide range of sources—Titian, Michelangelo, Raphael, Dürer—and, underlying all these, Goya's Byzantine heritage. It is not known why he went to Spain, but he is recorded in Toledo from 1577 until his death, where his ecstatic and passionate style became heightened with time, often increasing with successive repetitions of a subject, and so personal that his pupils and assistants did not even attempt to follow his example. Greco's use of color often eerie and strident, with sharp contrasts of blue, yellow, shrill green, and a livid mulberry pink, the elongated limbs and nervous tension of his fingers, the feeling that the draperies swathing them have a life of their own—all these suggest the intensity of the painter's mystical experience and the catharsis he found in his art.

Guild In the Middle Ages tradesmen formed themselves into Guilds for economic, religious, and social purposes, and often several different trades would unite in a single Guild; at Florence, for example, painters belonged to the doctors' and apothecaries' Guild. Much of our knowledge of early painting comes from Guild records, since all painters had to join unless they were in the personal

GRECO
The Annunciation

service of the ruling prince. Only a master could set up in business and take pupils. To become a master it was necessary to submit a masterpiece to the Guild as evidence of competence. The Guild officers also supervised the conditions of work and also the working materials. The tendency to uniformity of style and mentality led to painters like Leonardo and Michelangelo insisting on the freedom and originality of the artist and his status as a professional man. This new conception of the inspired being, instead of the honest tradesman, led to the decline of the Guilds and the rise of the Academies.

Halftone   In photoengraving, a process in which gradations of light are obtained by manipulating the density of minute dots on the printing surface.

Hals, Frans (1580–1666)   An artist who spent most of his life in The Netherlands, Hals had a great gift for portraiture, especially for catching the fleeting expression. He is best known for his portraits of the huge but lively groups of the companies of archers and musketeers raised during the wars against Spain. These groups solve the very difficult problem of composing a picture out of a number of figures, all of whom demanded the same prominence (since all the sitters subscribed to and bought the paintings), thus precluding the classical solution of subordinating the minor figures. The whole is perhaps a little like a school photograph, but the very informality caused his work to be a great influence on Manet and the Impressionists. In his single figures his dazzling skill sometimes runs away with him, and he never quite achieved the sympathy and insight of his greater contemporary Rembrandt. After the peace of 1648 the military

HALS
Mother with Child

companies were disbanded, but their place was taken, for artists, by the great group portraits commissioned by regents. Hals painted several of these, particularly in his last years when he was destitute and dependent on charity for himself and his wife. These paintings have greater feeling for character and greater humanity than many of his earlier groups, and they are also closer to Rembrandt in handling.

Happening   Happenings developed from a combination of assemblage and environment art, as artists sought to free art further from the constraints of the wall and the frame. Resembling performance, these events often involved sculpture, sound, time, motion, and living persons. While participants began with a plan, there was no rehearsal and no repeat performance.

Hard-edge Painting   A term used by critic Jules Langsner in 1959 in speaking of paintings executed in broad, flat areas of color delineated by precise, sharp edges.

Hartung, Hans (b.1904)   One of the leading representatives of Abstract Art whose works are a mesh of calligraphic brushstrokes, usually dark on a light ground. His paintings have no titles, but are distinguished by a style in which a sweep of paint or an ink stain is imposed on a highly colored surface. Hartung's later technique, dominated by a display of dark lines, gave his drawings the appearance of finely wrought engravings.

Hassam, Childe (1859–1935)   Born and trained in New England, Hassam was the foremost American impressionist painter. He first worked as an illustrator and watercolor artist. In Paris he adapted the impressionist principles of color division, spontaneity of brushstroke and atmospheric effects that distinguished his style. In New York he helped found the group called "The Ten"—made up of leading impressionist landscape painters such as Twachtman, Weir, and Metcalf. He exhibited at the Armory Show and was a member of the American Academy of Arts and Letters.

Hatching   Shading executed by closely spaced parallel lines; crosshatching is shading when another group of lines crosses the first at an angle.

Hepworth, Barbara (1903–1975)   A British abstract sculptor, Hepworth is a direct carver in wood and stone. In 1931, with Henry Moore, she began piercing holes in her sculpture and creating hollowed-out forms. In 1938, she began carving abstract forms in which large masses are set off by string or wire, giving the effect of a musical instrument.

History Painting   Dating from the Renaissance to the 19th century in fully developed academic theory, it was the noblest form of art, consisting of generalized representations of the passions and intellect as symbolized in Classical history or mythology or in themes taken from Christian subject matter.

Hockney, David (b.1937)   British painter and etcher, he studied at the Royal College of Art and became known for pictures in the Pop style idiom. His work conveys a strong sense of design, pattern, visual rhythm, and a light illusive imagery. In the 1960s he concentrated on such visual phenomena as moving water and reflective glass. His realistic portraits and domestic scenes reveal high-keyed color, flat acrylic textures, and an almost surrealistic aura.

ART

Hogarth, William (1697–1764) Beginning as a draftsman, Hogarth then began painting small groups and conversation pieces, and by 1729 he had begun to make a name. He said of himself, "I have endeavored to treat my subjects as a dramatic writer; my picture is my stage, and men and women my players, who by means of certain actions and gestures, are to exhibit a [pantomine]." The first of his moral subjects was the *Harlot's Progress*, showing the downfall of a country girl at the hands of the wicked Londoners (several of whom were recognizable). His fame is most firmly based on these "moral" engravings, which have to be read, detail by telling detail, rather than contemplated as works of art; nevertheless, all through his life he was capable of pieces of superb painting.

Holbein, Hans, the Younger (1497?–1543) Probably the most accomplished and penetratingly Realist portrait painter the North has produced. His early portraits show his gift for characterization, and his religious works show him as either grimly realist or decorative rather than devotional. His international reputation as a portraitist was established by 1532, and eventually he painted for Henry VIII, who also employed Holbein as a goldsmith's designer and sent him abroad to paint prospective brides. His later practice of painting from drawings, instead of from the sitter, was strengthened by the requirements of extensive court portraiture. His portraits—life-sized and in miniature—became more linear in style and more formal in treatment than his early works, partly through their emphasis on detail, partly because working only from drawings led him to be less sensitive in handling and perception.

Holograph Term used to describe a three-dimensional image created by a beam of laser light passing through a hologram wave interference photograph.

Homer, Winslow (1836–1910) With Eakins, one of the most influential of the late 19th-century American painters, he earned his living first as an illustrator—recording the Civil War—and this sense of actuality remained in all his works even after 1875, when he devoted himself to painting. In the 1880s and 1890s he revolutionized American painting by his Impressionist-like style in studies of the sea and shooting and fishing subjects appealing to

HOPPER
Eleven A.M.

the American male. He was also affected by the Japanese craze, which arrived in Europe in the 1860s and is visible in his work in the 1870s. Homer achieved fame in many different areas: as a naturalist, lithographer, and watercolorist.

Hopper, Edward (1882–1967) An American artist, he beautifully evoked the lonely moods of city life by depicting deserted buildings in glaring light, the lonely atmosphere of a predawn diner, and the daily worker captured in a state of *ennui*. His scenes are both bleak and surreal, and not infrequently he infuses his audience with a sense of despair.

Hudson River School A school of mid-19th-century American landscape painting, highly Romantic in feeling and glorifying the wonders of nature as visible in the American landscape. The Hudson River artists were highly realistic, and their work was encouraged by the vogue of having landscape paintings as parlor decorations.

Icon (*Ikon*, Gk. image) Originally meant a picture of Christ or a saint on a panel, as distinct from a wall painting. These icons were extremely limited in subject matter, and the actual forms and shapes were prescribed and maintained unchanged for centuries in the Greek Orthodox world: Thus, the earliest surviving examples may date from the 6th and 7th centuries but are virtually indistinguishable from those painted as late as the 17th century or even later. Iconology is the knowledge of the meanings to be attached to pictorial representations.

Ideal Art "Any work of Art that represents not a material object, but the mental conception of a material object, is in the primary sense of the word ideal; that is to say, it represents an idea, and not a thing" (Ruskin). According to Plato the only realities are ideas, and everything perceptible to the senses is merely an imperfect realization of the primary idea: Thus, the idea of a dog is the true dog, and all dogs in the visible gutter merely approximate to the idea of dogness. From this arises a perennial theory that the true function of art is to mirror those ideal forms that are the sole realities, approaching them by way of the physical phenomena that are their distorted images.

Illumination Describes an illustration, ornamental initial, or pattern painted on the vellum or parchment leaves of a manuscript as an adornment of the text.

Illusionism The use of techniques, such as perspective and foreshortening, to deceive the eye into taking that which is painted for that which is real. When such technical skill is lavished on things like a fly painted on a frame or a view through a nonexistent window, the French term *trompe-l'oeil* ("deceive the eye") is often used.

Imari A type of Japanese export porcelain made at Arita. Imari-ware combines red and gold over blue underglaze decoration.

Impasto An Italian word used to describe the thickness of the paint applied to a canvas. When the paint is so heavily applied that it stands up in lumps, the tracks of the brush, palette knife, or other tool become clearly evident.

Impressionism The derisive name given to the most important artistic phenomenon of the 19th century and the first of the modern movements. The name was derived from a picture by Monet, *Impression, Sunrise,* which represents the play of light on water, with the spectator looking straight into the rising sun. The true aim of Impressionism was to achieve ever greater naturalism, by exact analysis of tone and color and by trying to render the play of light on the surface of objects. This is a form of sensualism in which traditional ideas of composition and drawing were bound to suffer. The flickering touch, with the paint applied in small, brightly colored dabs, the lack of firm outline, and the generally high key undoubtedly alienated the public. The great decade of Impressionism was 1870–1880, but most of the major figures, such as Monet and Pissarro, continued to produce masterpieces in a more or less Impressionist style for many more years. Degas, Renoir, and Cézanne are only dubiously Impressionists and they very soon moved away from it. The main weakness of the movement was its lack of intellectual rigor; nevertheless, most painting of the last 90 years has been profoundly affected by it. The very nature of the movement was its emphasis on painting landscapes outdoors and catching the fleeting impression.

Industrial Design   The application of aesthetic principles to the design of machine-made articles, with a canon of standards quite independent of those for hand-made objects. Chiefly a phenomenon of the last hundred years, it was first espoused by members of the arts and crafts movement. Also called industrial art.

Ingres, Jean-Auguste-Dominique (1780–1867) Ingres became the main prop of a rigid classicism in opposition to the Romantic movement. His main works were portraits—which he professed to dislike, and in which he was influenced by early

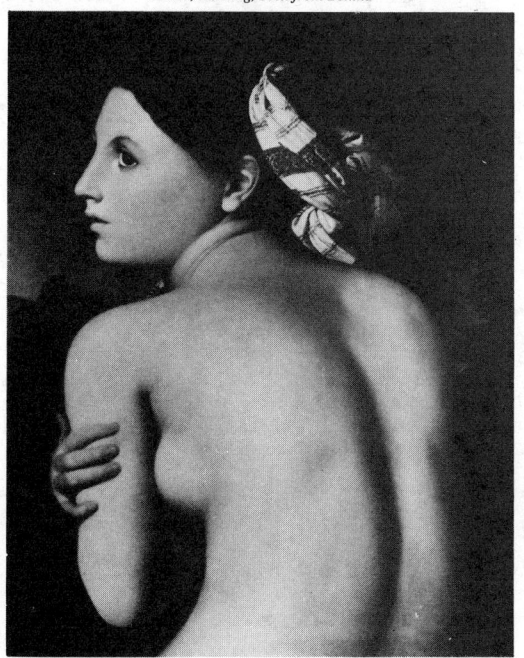

INGRES
Bather, Bustling, Seen from Behind

photographs—but he also painted subject pictures and poeticized Oriental scenes providing an excuse for voluptuous nudes. His style changed almost not at all, and to the end he pursued his piercingly exact vision, his sinuous line, and his supreme draftsmanship.

Inness, George (1825–1894)   A leading American landscape painter, Inness was influenced by Hudson River artists such as Cole and Durand. He portrayed vast panoramic scenes in sharp, clear detail. During the 1870s he was impressed by the Barbizon School and his canvases became more limited in scale with suggestive forms rendered in fluid brushstrokes reminiscent of Corot.

Isocephaly   A method of composing groups of figures in such a way that all are shown at the same height, regardless of posture or purpose. Characteristic of classical Greek art.

Itten, Johannes (1888–1967)   He founded an art school in Vienna before joining the faculty of the Bauhaus at Wiemar, Germany. A Swiss painter, he developed an accepted method of teaching art and when he left the Bauhaus in 1923, founded his own school in Berlin. Later he was director of an art school in Zurich, where he died. Influenced by the Cubists and the Blaue Reiter, he rendered recognizable and geometric forms within a compressed abstract design with bright colors and a surrealistic quality.

Ives, James Merritt   *See* **Currier, Nathaniel**.

J **Johns, Jasper** (b.1930)   A major Pop artist, Johns's paintings of cool blown-up images, such as *Flags* and *Targets,* adhere to the picture surface and are made like "art." A highly regarded and influential contemporary artist, he created an ambiguity between abstraction and representation as he explored the tension between a painting as a painted surface and as an object.

Jones, Inigo (1573–1652)   He introduced classical forms into England that provided the basis of the late Renaissance and Georgian styles of architecture. Born in England, he traveled across Europe but was impressed by Roman monuments and the buildings of Palladio in Venice. At the courts of James I and Charles I, he designed stage sets, became the king's surveyor, and designed buildings that embodied Palladian principles such as the Queen's House in Greenwich and the Royal Banqueting Hall in Whitehall, London. He also made designs for St. Paul's Church and Covent Garden.

Jugendstijl   The German term for the style known elsewhere as Art Nouveau. Named after the unofficial organ of the movement in Germany, the magazine *Jugend,* founded in 1896.

K **Kandinsky, Wassily** (1866–1944) Born in Moscow but trained in Munich, after abandoning a legal career, Kandinsky painted his first purely Abstract (non-realistic) work in 1910 and was therefore one of the founders of that genre. His work is characterized by a fury of lines and passionate color. Eventually he began to translate the intellectual aspects of his art into geometric form, heavily relying on shape, flat color, and rhythm to express his themes and subject matter. Both romantic and lyric, he produced some of the most original paintings in the Abstract movement.

Kent, Rockwell (1882–1971) American painter and illustrator whose works sometimes resemble the style of Homer, although Kent's brushwork tends to be more lyric and flowing. Kent greatly admired the art of Blake, but his own tones and forms tend to be both darker and stronger and his forms more geometric. He frequently employed woodcuts in his illustrative work.

Kinetic Art Art that moves, driven by atmospheric forces (e.g., Alexander Calder's mobiles) or by motors, magnets, etc. This sculpture in motion includes some of the most Avant-garde art since the 1960s.

Kirchner, Ernest Ludwig (1880–1928) German expressionist painter and graphic artist, he was one of the founders of Die Brucke in 1905. Influenced by German Medieval art, Dürer, van Gogh, Japanese prints, and tribal art, he painted brutalized forms within a distorted perspective with thickly applied brilliant colors. Some scenes attacked the depravity of life in Germany after World War I. He sought a subjective and symbolic value in art. He committed suicide one year after the Nazi purge of Modern Art.

KLEE
Senecio

Klee, Paul (1879–1940) A Swiss painter and etcher, whose art of free fantasy is perhaps the most poetic of modern times, defined in his own words as "taking a line for a walk." Klee seemed to "see" through his use of line—bold or delicate, curving under itself or waving—and color, usually in soft, pure tones. All of his works can be seen as a signature, bearing the mark of genius. There is a joy, an innocent and lighthearted spirit about Klee that is not often duplicated.

Kokoschka, Oskar (1886–1980) An Austrian painter who developed a highly imaginative Expres-

sionist style. In his portraits he explored the multi-faceted nature of his subjects, minutely examining the hands as well as the eyes and exploring the depths of emotion with a bold yet precise brush. His portraits, landscapes, and views, often seen almost in bird's-eye view, are vivid in color, and possess a restless energy of drawing; he also painted many allegories, inspired by legends or, more commonly, by ideological themes.

Kollwitz, Käthe (1867–1945) One of the most powerfully emotional German artists of this century, she married a doctor in 1891 and settled in Berlin, where she soon began to make etchings, woodcuts, and lithographs mainly of the mother and child theme and often with left-wing intentions. Most of her best works are tragic, and many of them are specifically pacifist—her son was killed in 1914 and her grandson in 1942. Her works are bold and forthright, displaying a combination of compassion and romanticism.

Kore In archaic Greek art, a statue of a standing, draped maiden; counterpart to the male *kouros*.

L **Lane, Fitz Hugh** (1804–1861) An American landscape artist, Lane re-created scenes of his native Gloucester, Massachusetts (oldest fishing port in the country), primarily in lithographs that he sold to the townspeople. He had a very precise and balanced style, and his signature can be seen in a very low and sweeping horizon above which clouds bank in a luminous sky.

Lay Figure A lifelike, jointed wooden figure, which can be used either to arrange drapery on or as a guide to a complicated pose.

Léger, Fernand (1881–1955) Léger's art quickly evolved from his early block-like figures into a form of Cubism, dependent on the shapes of machinery and their geometrical bases: cones, cylinders, cogged wheels, etc. These forms also influenced his massive, robotlike figures and increased the effect of his clear grays and strong, unbroken colors. Among his last works were the huge murals for the United Nations building in New York. Léger's paintings are beautiful examples of mechanical precision combined with dynamic areas and blocks of color.

LÉGER
Leisure Time

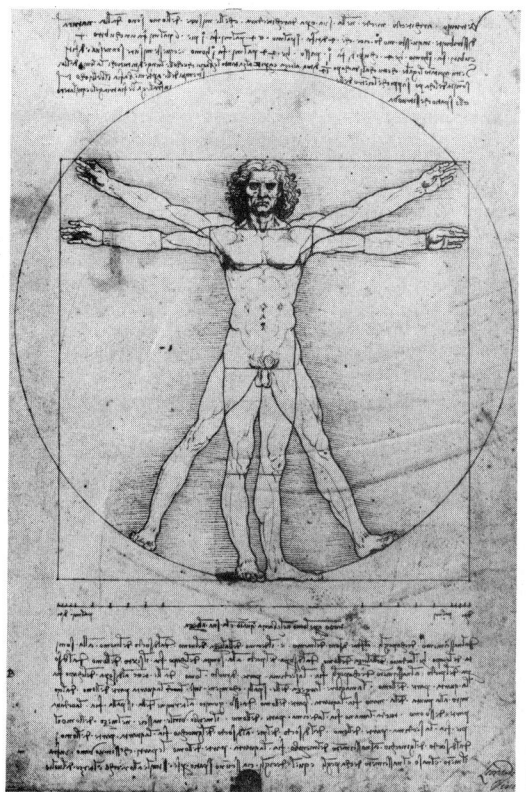

LEONARDO DA VINCI
Vitruvian Man

Leonardo da Vinci (1452–1519)   One of the greatest of the universal men produced by the Renaissance. Da Vinci's intellectual powers were such that he anticipated many later discoveries in anatomy, aeronautics, and several other fields, as well as being one of the greatest of Italian artists. His intellectual powers were so diffused over an enormous range of interests that he brought hardly any major enterprise to a conclusion: He almost discovered the circulation of blood, he invented the first armored fighting vehicle, projected several aircraft and helicopters, and anticipated the submarine; however, not one of these discoveries was completed. In the same way he left thousands of notes and drawings but only a handful of paintings, and fewer still completed ones. His earliest datable work is a landscape drawing (1473) that shows his interest in rock formation and the structure of the earth. One major work, the *Last Supper,* stresses the psychology of the disciples and the tension of the moment when Christ announces that one of them is about to betray him, a subtlety of interpretation quite foreign to the 15th century. The stories of Leonardo's slowness in working on this wall painting and his search for psychological expressiveness justify the claims made by a later generation. They regarded Leonardo as the originator of the idea of the artist as a contemplative and creative thinker, the equal of the philosopher, not a mere artisan who was paid to cover so many square yards of wall a day. Certainly

all the 16th-century ideas on the dignity of the artist can be traced back to the example set by him. His last years were spent mainly in scientific pursuits.

Lettrism   A phenomenon since the 1950s, lettrism is the juxtaposition of letters, words, signs, and pictographic symbols with visual effect as the primary concern and with meaning (if any) of secondary importance.

Lichtenstein, Roy (b.1923)   An artist of the 20th century, Lichtenstein began as an Abstract Expressionist, became involved in cartoonlike illustrations and new interpretations of the Old West paintings of Remington, and then began making art from industrial products, satirizing in his wake mass production and contemporary commercial art.

Light Sculpture   Sculpture in which light sources (fluorescent and neon bulbs, incandescent bulbs, laser beams, and sunlight) are the primary medium or source of visual interest.

Lipchitz, Jacques (1891–1973)   Born in Lithuania, Lipchitz's sculpture shows the influence of Cubism. However, by 1925 he had evolved a personal style of openwork sculpture. The small clay sculptures he began to model in 1941, after his arrival in the United States, became his stamp and genius. These consisted of points projected into space or solid masses rising from the earth.

Lippi, Fra Filippo (*ca.* 1406–1469)   An Italian painter, Lippi's frescoes are perhaps his major achievement and show the development of a dramatic style, with great interest in the problem of movement. In 1464, he was tried for fraud and his abduction of the nun Lucrezia. He later married her, after receiving dispensation from his friends and patrons the Medicis. In spite of his activities, his late works are infused with religious feeling and are far more lyrical than the earlier ones.

Lyrical Abstraction   This term . . . generally refers to the so-called third generation of abstract expressionism, which developed in the early 1970s and was characterized by more sensuous and subjective abstract interpretations than those of the second generation . . . Pop Art, Hard-edge Painting, and Minimal Art, for example.

M **Maculature**   The weak impression that results when a print is made without re-inking the plate.

Magic Realism   Related to Surrealism, this 20th-century art movement uses the unexpected combinations of objects to create disturbing images from everyday experiences.

Magritte, René (1898–1967)   Belgian born, one of the most important Surrealist painters, Magritte's dreamlike images combine a realistic technique with an "absurd" consciousness to convey the terror of an incomprehensible world. He used the juxtaposition of ordinary objects and the precision of his technique to create feelings of unrest in the viewer. The unusual titles of his paintings rarely describe the actual subject matter, but serve to add new dimensions to his work.

Maillol, Aristide (1861–1944)   Beginning as a tapestry maker, Maillol was a French sculptor whose works were devoted almost exclusively to the female nude. He returned to the ideals of Greek art of the 5th century B.C. in a reaction against Rodin's

MAILLOL
The Three Graces

them in newspaper criticisms: "Manet's gang." At the end of his life he was given the Legion of Honour and the vilification of his works abated. The tragedy of his life was that he was the perfect academic painter, unrecognized and rejected by the body whose dying traditions he alone could have revivified.

Mannerism   A term developed in the present century to describe the artistic manifestations, principally Italian, of the period around 1520–1600. The word *mannerism* was used by some to describe an art based on intellectual preconceptions rather than direct visual perceptions. Much of Mannerism consists of deliberately flouting the rules deduced from Classical Art and established during the Renaissance. The principal characteristics of a Mannerist work of art are an insistence, first on the human figure, which is set in strained poses, willfully distorted and elongated, and whose muscles are sometimes grossly overemphasized. The composition is usually forced and unclear, with the principal subject set in a corner or in the background. The color

MANET
The Fifer

fluid forms and dramatic content. By contrast, Maillol stressed the static and monumental qualities of the human figure, and throughout his work his style changed only slightly. He was successful in the rebirth of a classical idealism, and although his figures mark an end of a tradition, their power and life will always distinguish them.

Majolica   Commonly refers to the richly painted, enameled pottery produced in Italy.

Makemono   Far Eastern painting on a long horizontal scroll.

Manet, Edouard (1832–1883)   Although his well-to-do bourgeois father reluctantly allowed him to study art, Manet reacted very strongly against academic history painting and began his career as an artistic rebel. His brilliant technique was founded on painting directly from the model with intense immediacy and on a restricted palette in which black was extremely important. His early works include many Spanish subjects inspired by troupes of dancers visiting Paris. These works were frequently rejected and, if hung, were ill-received by critics. Eventually he adopted the Impressionist technique and palette, abandoning the use of black and his genius for analysis and synthesis, for a lighter, sweeter color and a freer handling. He also tended more to sentimental subjects, lacking the sober gravity of his earlier works. He always longed for official recognition and refused to take part in the Impressionist exhibitions, bitterly resenting being coupled with of a Mannerist picture is always vivid and often harsh, since it is intended to heighten the emotional effect rather than describe the forms. It is essentially an unquiet style, subjective and emotional. On the whole, Mannerism is a style best adapted to neurotic artists, all of whom produced major works, as well as such great masters as Michelangelo, Tintoretto, and El Greco. There were also many very dull painters who strained every nerve to be neurotically interesting but produced only frenziedly gesticulating and twisted figures.

Marquetry　　Detailed woodwork in which different colored woods and other materials are inlaid into furniture and other wooden surfaces to form patterns.

Matisse, Henri (1869–1954)　　The principal artist of the Fauve group, Matisse was strongly influenced by Impressionism. In 1910, he saw the exhibition of Near Eastern art at Munich and it is clear that this highly decorative and brilliantly colored art had a deep and lasting influence on him, particularly in his development of flat patterns with flowered backgrounds and in his use of brilliant and pure colors. In 1914 he went to Nice for the winter, to remain for most of the rest of his life on the Riviera, where he painted the still life subjects that are his main work.

Meissonier, Ernest (1815–1890)　　French painter and illustrator, he is best known for sentimental genre scenes based on the *Little Dutch Masters.* He also executed large military scenes, such as the battles of Napoleon. His style is marked by remarkable realism and scrupulous love of detail.

MATISSE
Jazz: Icarus

MICHELANGELO
David

Michelangelo Buonarroti (1475–1564)　　He carved the first of his major works, the *Pietà*, in 1496, showing that he had solved the problem presented by the representation of a full-grown man stretched out nearly horizontally on the lap of a woman, the whole contained in a pyramidal shape: This is the consummation of everything the sculptors of the 15th century had striven to attain. A cartoon, *Bathers,* with its exclusive stress on the nude human body as a sufficient vehicle for the expression of all emotions the painter can depict, had an enormous influence on the subsequent development of European art. This influence is more readily detectable in his most important work, the ceiling of the Sistine Chapel. Dissatisfied with the normal working methods and with the abilities of the assistants he had engaged, Michelangelo determined to execute the whole of this vast area virtually alone, working under appalling difficulties (amusingly described in one of his own sonnets), most of the time lying down and never able to get far enough away from the ceiling to be able to see what he was doing. From its completion, Michelangelo was universally regarded as the greatest living artist, although he was then only 37 and this was during the lifetimes of Leonardo and Raphael (who was even younger). From this moment, too, dates the idea of the artist as in some sense a superhuman being, set apart from ordinary men. At 75, Michelangelo became increasingly active as an architect, and all his late works were created solely for the glory of God.

Mies van der Rohe, Ludwig (1886–1969)   A German-born American architect and furniture designer, Mies van der Rohe was one of the masters of modern architecture. The impersonality of his designs created the formal purity of his constructions. Relying on the richness of his materials and severe projections, he designed the now classically famous steel-framed furniture and produced the "Barcelona chair." He was also a builder of skyscrapers and private homes.

Millais, Sir John Everett (1829–1896)   An infant prodigy, Millais developed into a fashionable and technically brilliant academic painter of portraits, costume history, and genre pieces. Because of his fidelity to nature as the basis of art, he was bitterly criticized by the Victorians, and especially incurred the wrath of Dickens.

Millefiori   A technique used to create decorative glass pieces by bundling and fusing together a group of glass rods, then slicing through the group transversely.

Millet, Jean-François (1814–1875)   The son of a peasant, Millet was trained under a local painter at Cherbourg and his earliest works are imitations of the pastorals of the 18th century and rather erotic nudes. Eventually, his choice of subject matter led to accusations of Socialism. In 1849 he began painting scenes of peasants and their labors and also some ordinary landscapes and marines, which show his unusually sentimental approach. His works are particularly well represented in America.

Miniature   A small painting, usually a portrait, executed in watercolor. The 16th-century type of miniature was normally painted on playing cards or on vellum, the material used by the medieval illuminator. This type of portrait, with its allegories and symbolism, is a direct descendant of manuscript illumination. In the 17th century, the portrait miniature became more closely allied to contemporary oil painting.

Minimal Art   In the contemporary movements, this art form is of a more neutral and impersonal quality than most. Minimalist artists reject emotional expression and stress the importance of color, composition, and precise execution. Restraint, understatement, and lack of personal involvement are the characteristics of this genre.

Miró, Joan (1893–1983)   A Surrealist painter of Spanish origin, Miró lived for some time in the United States. Of his work he wrote: "For me a form is never something abstract, it is always a sign of something. It is always a man, a bird, or something else. For me painting is never form for form's sake." Miró painted in the realm of the fantastic, the only area in which he was comfortable. In later years he created enormous works merely by allowing a single line to wander over a colored background. His whimsical world is peopled by oddly shaped filaments, amoebas, and tubes that achieve a life that reaches outside the canvas to make the viewer smile with pleasure.

Mobile   A kinetic sculpture invented in 1932 by Calder, consisting of a series of shapes cut from different materials. Mobiles hang at varying levels so that a gentle touch will cause the whole to revolve, giving an ever-changing sequence of planes, solids, and colors in three-dimensional movement.

Modern Art   In strict historical terminology, modern art began in the middle of the 19th century with the realism of Gustave Courbet. At that time, art began to free itself from the strict requirements of subject matter and developed increasingly toward preoccupation with form.

Modigliani, Amedeo (1884–1920)   The artist of elongated faces and necks who was referred to as *un peintre maudit* (the cursed painter). Born in Leghorn of a distinguished Italian-Jewish family, Modigliani spent the rest of his life in Paris, working at first in a manner influenced by Toulouse-Lautrec. Later his real style was based on African sculpture, Cézanne and Picasso, and, above all, his Italian heritage. He became known as the greatest Italian artist of the 20th century, not a French painter at all. Modigliani was handsome, amorous, and addicted to drink and drugs. He said of himself, "I am going to drink myself dead," and he did just that. Pity, tenderness, and a sense of melancholy pervade his most famous works of children and the poor.

Mondrian, Piet (1872–1944)   A Dutch abstract painter, Mondrian went to Paris in 1911 and abandoned his Realistic landscapes for Cubist ones. His form of Abstraction was a peculiarly rigorous one, which consisted principally of restricting forms to purely geometrical shapes, set at right angles and colored in the primary colors, with the addition of white, black, or gray. The only enlivening touch he permitted himself was in his titles—*Broadway Boogie Woogie,* for example.

MODIGLIANI
The Brown Haired Girl

Monet, Claude (1840–1944)   Monet was the leading member of the Impressionist group, and the one who for the longest time practiced the principles of absolute fidelity to the visual sensation, painting directly from the object and, if necessary, outdoors. Cézanne is said to have described him as "only an eye, but my God what an eye!" This description is certainly true in that his constant search for certain truths led at times to a neglect of form. From about 1890, Monet began to paint a series of pictures of one subject, representing it under various conditions and at different times of day. His most famous work of all, *Water Lilies,* was painted in the elaborate garden he had made for himself. It has recently been claimed that these shimmering pools of color, almost totally devoid of form, are the true starting point of Abstract Art. They were the logical outcome of Monet's lifelong devotion to the ultimate form of Naturalism, the truth of retinal sensation.

Montage   The sticking of one layer over another, especially when photographs of objects are applied to a photograph of an unusual or incongruous background. The technique was much used by the Cubists and is now much exploited by advertising agents. *Compare* **Collage**.

Moore, Henry (1898–1986)   Moore, an eminent British sculptor, always used his material to express natural forms in terms of stone or wood. His characteristic swelling and undulating shapes expressed his feelings about the close relationship existing between man and nature, what he termed "the organic" rather than the geometric.

Mosaic   One of the oldest and most durable forms of mural decoration, mosaic was in constant use from the earliest times up to about the 13th century, when it was largely superseded by other forms of painting that are cheaper and more adaptable to a realistic style. Recently, however, mosaic has been revived as a decorative art. The technique is simple but laborious. A drawing is executed on a wall, and a small area is covered with cement. Then small cubes (tesserae) are chipped from slabs of colored stone, marble, and glass, and stuck into the cement. Great care was taken in the best early mosaics to ensure that all the pieces were not perfectly flat and level, since an uneven surface catches the light and reflects it in different ways. Mosaics were used frequently for the decoration of Early Christian and Byzantine churches.

Moses, Anna Mary Robertson (Grandma) (1860–1961)   An American primitive painter who, at the age of eighty, began her public career. There is great pleasure to be found in her simple depictions of the life, seasons, landscapes, and people of New England. Moses created a world where imagination traveled far beyond nature, and her unique perception and sincerity are apparent in each brushstroke.

Motherwell, Robert (b.1915)   An American Abstract Expressionist painter who began by studying philosophy at Harvard. He has said: "Without ethical consciousness, a painter is only a decorator." Dating from the 1950s his works have exhibited wide, massive black shapes applied to a white background. He then extended this impact by using space invaded by symbols.

MUNCH
The Scream

Mound Builders   A civilization in the east-central United States that created art from A.D. 300 until the end of the 1800s. Some of the mounds built were in the form of different animals, others resembled pyramids with walkways to the top. All that now remains of these creations are the holes into which the framework was driven. A wealth of art, both utilitarian and ornamental, was discovered inside these mounds, created from wood, ceramics, copper, bone, shells, decorated leather, etc. Among the finest objects recovered were stone pipes, intricately detailed, carved into the shapes of human heads, animals, birds, and reptiles, with great attention paid to expression.

Mucha, Alphonse (1860–1939)   Czech Art Nouveau designer of jewelry and decorative arts, he studied in Munich, Vienna, and Paris. Mucha gained fame for his posters, illustrations, and murals for theaters and public buildings. He had opened a design studio with James McNeil Whistler and worked on jewelry for L.C. Tiffany.

Munch, Edvard (1863–1944)   A Norwegian painter whose childhood was filled with depression and tragedy, Munch was one of the forerunners of Expressionism. His subjects deal with basic themes of love and death, and his art, although powerful, is always neurotic and frequently hysterical, evoking empathetic feeling in the viewer. Munch wished to create his concept of the world through his work. He painted in long, flowing lines, choosing passionate and expressive colors.

Murillo, Bartolomé Esteban (1617–1682)   Born in Seville, where he passed the greater part of his life, Murillo started as a painter of the kind of pictures that are sold at fairs. The Spaniards mark his stylistic progression by his changes in the use of color. First, the rather hard Naturalism of the early beggar-boy pictures; then the early religious subjects, cool, detached, with only a little idealization; and then the devotional image, with idealized forms, a certain Baroque flutter to the draperies, a certain artificiality, but with warmth, charm, and quiet religious feeling. His late works all tend toward the softening and sweetening of style and color, to the sentimental emotionalism of a pious image. His later beggar-boy scenes also exploit this sentimental attitude, and he found a ready market for these glamorized, picturesque urchins in fancy-dress rags, exuding the charms of bohemianism and serving to negate poverty by robbing it of its power to inspire pity and horror. He had a large shop with many assistants, and his simple undemanding pictures enjoyed huge popularity, so much so that "Murillos" were painted until well into the 19th century, as a style in art, not primarily as forgeries.

Naive Art   Synonymous with the definition of Primitive Art—a term often used to refer to artists who worked subjectively and with no conscious concern for realism. Self taught, these artists invent and create according to personal psychological concepts unaffected by instruction and culture. Their paintings are marked by distortion of form and absence of geometric perspective.

Nast, Thomas (1840–1902)   An American illustrator and cartoonist, best known for his pictorial reporting and ultimate exposure of the Tweed Ring and Tammany Hall. He was responsible for creating the symbol of the donkey for the Democratic party.

Naturalism   The precise representation of an object—true to life in every detail and irrespective of subject matter or time period.

Neoclassism   *See* **Exhibit 1.2**, page 1-28.

Netsuke   Japanese belt toggle often made of ivory and carved in the form of an animal or animals.

Nocturne   A night piece. The term was first used by Whistler, who frequently gave his paintings musical titles, but the idea of painting landscapes as night scenes goes back to the 1600s.

Nolde, Emil Hansen (1867–1956)   A German painter who preferred solitude, Nolde's work has been described as rough and untamed. Most of his paintings were created in the barren northern region of Germany where he was born and where he could commune with his wild, exciting visions. He is characterized by distortion of form and vivid color, and his subject matter includes a frenzy of sunflowers, storm-ridden landscapes, and exotically portrayed scenes from the Bible.

Obelisk   A tall, four-sided free-standing pillar tapering to a pyramidal terminus.

Objet d'art (Fr.)   A work of art of small size, as a miniature painting, statuette, vase, or snuffbox.

Oiling Out   A process of rubbing a drying oil (such as linseed oil) over those colors in a painting that have lost their luster. Although brilliance is restored for a while, the ultimate effect is to darken them further.

Oil Painting   The "invention" of oil painting is traditionally credited to the Eycks. There are two principal ways of painting pictures in oil. One, known as "direct" painting, consists of putting on the paint and hoping it comes out right. If this fails, the proper cure is to take another canvas and start again. The second, more elaborate, technique is the one favored by the Old Masters. This involves a good deal of planning ahead. The canvas is first drawn on, then covered with one or more single-color layers of paint, and then color is added in built-up layers so that the underlying layers show through to give tone and shading. This technique, in the hands of a master craftsman, is capable of almost unlimited subtlety and variety, which is why oil painting has practically superceded all its rivals.

O'Keeffe, Georgia (1887–1987)   American painter who was greatly influenced by the New Mexican landscapes, the play of light on the bones and flowers of the desert. Many of her works are large, depicting a single object, and are open to varying interpretations.

Oldenburg, Claes (b.1929)   American sculptor, Oldenburg was one of the initiators of the Happening movement of the 1960s. He frequently created art by using such diverse elements as ice cubes and cars to portray a theme or idea. He opened his own store in New York City, aptly called "The Store," and there he sold food and other items reproduced in plaster, and so began the first glimmerings of Pop Art. Oldenburg abandoned "hard" sculpture for "soft" stuffed representations in vinyl, canvas, and other textured materials that often relied on the way they were placed, or fell, for interpretation.

Op Art (optical art)   Painting based on optical illusion, perception, and their physical and psychological effects. Also called retinal painting and perceptual abstraction.

Optical Mixing   The involuntary mixing of juxtaposed colors by the eye and brain. Thus, at a certain distance, juxtaposed dabs of red and yellow pigment produce the sensation of orange. The colors seen by optical mixing appear clearer and more brilliant than those obtained by mixing colors on a palette.

Ormulu   Gilded bronze mount used in decorating certain styles of furniture. Also, an article made or decorated with such mounts.

Orozco, José (1883–1949)   A Mexican painter, Orozco used an Expressionist style for his frequently huge decorations (often in fresco or in imitations of fresco, sometimes using modern building materials). Most of his works have strong political overtones, and many were commissioned by revolutionary governments.

Papiers Collés   Pictures created from cut and glued pieces of paper, cardboard, newsprint, playing cards, etc. This trompe l'oeil technique was first employed by cubist Georges Braque in 1909.

Passage   *See* **Exhibit 1.3**, page 1-30.

Pastiche   This is a piece of art that has been created in the style of a particular artist or movement but has not been faked, as in a deliberate forgery.

Patina   Originally, a green layer that formed on old bronze. Now extended to mean any type of mellowing with age.

Pellicle The skin that forms on the surface of drying oil paint.

Pentimento When a painter changes his or her mind in the course of a picture and alters, for example, the position of a leg, it sometimes happens that the old form will begin to show through in a ghostly way; this ghost is a pentimento. It is sometimes inferred that because there are pentimenti visible a painting must be an original—since it shows the artist changing his mind—and not a copy. The validity of this argument is open to doubt.

Perspective A quasimathematical system for the representation of three-dimensional objects in a two-dimensional surface. The basic assumption of all perspective systems is that parallel lines never meet, but that they appear to do so; and that, further, all parallel lines going in any one direction meet at a single point on the horizon known as a vanishing point. A system was further evolved that uses two vanishing points on the horizon, and more if necessary to obtain up-hill and down-dale effects. A further refinement is the use of measuring points, which allow the exact representation of objects to scale. All this can be learned by a moderately mathematically minded art student in a few hours; for this very reason, many artists are no longer interested in perspective and prefer either to renounce the representation of the third dimension altogether (as most abstract artists do), or create a spatial illusion of their own, stressing the independence of the world created by the artist from the laws that govern appearance in the physical world. *Aerial* perspective deals with the changes in tone and color values observable in objects receding from the spectator. Because of the density of the atmosphere, all tone contrasts are muted and all colors tend toward blue in proportion to their distance from the observer. Thus, mountains in the background are always bluish. The difference between the atmospheres of Northern Europe and the Mediterranean accounts for the greater interest in aerial perspective to be found in the North, particularly among the Impressionists.

Petard A piece of art that draws attention to itself through the unusual qualities of the colors used, subject matter, and composition.

Picasso, Pablo Ruiz y (1881–1973) As a boy Picasso showed exceptional talent and experimented with the styles of Munch, Toulouse-Lautrec, Renoir, Gauguin, and other Late Impressionists before settling on a passion for blue, which became the dominant color for his portrayal of the squalid tragedy of the Paris streets—the beggar, the harlot, the sick child, and the hungry. He questioned the whole basis of painting and was therefore unable to follow still further the Impressionist road. Picasso's *Les Demoiselles d' Avignon of* 1907 was begun in the vein of his harlequin series but ended as a semi-abstract composition in which the forms of the nudes are broken up into planes compressed into a shallow space. The influence of African sculptures also fitted in with his quest for expression in form and helped, by the bizarre nature of such forms, to release him from the tyranny of the representational tradition in art. In 1907 he met Braque and they found that they faced the same problems and were

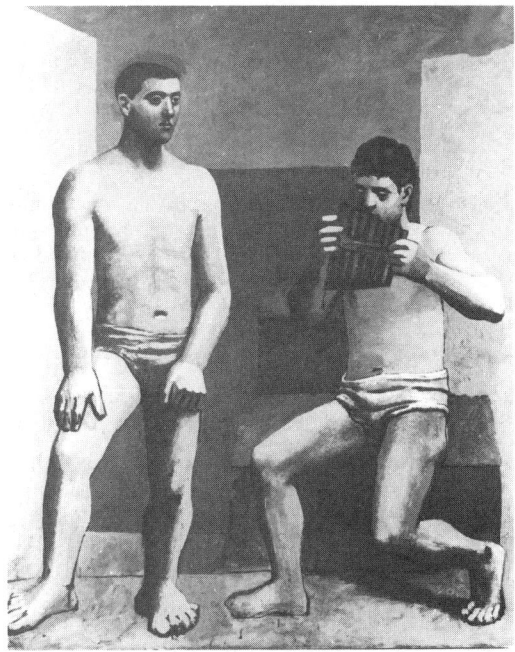

PICASSO
Pan Pipes

striving to solve them in the same way. Both rejected decorative arabesques and bright, sensuous color and were striving to devise a pictorial language without descending to the imitation of superficial appearances. Together they evolved what is now called Analytical Cubism. By 1912, color had begun to creep back among Picasso's grays, olive-greens, and drab browns, and actual objects—a piece of cane seating, a newspaper heading—were imported. Collage was the natural extension. Objects could be literally reconstituted with bits of wood, wire, paper, and string, their forms distorted by the artist into a flat composition whose inherent third dimension is only alluded to. In 1917 Picasso returned to a traditional vision, with parallel works in a glitteringly sophisticated idiom. Finally, contact with Classicism ushers in a series of paintings and drawings by him of monumental female nudes, at first almost motionless and then galvanized into terrifying movement that distorts them into frightening caricatures before dissolving them into convulsive and repellent distortions. In the 1930s he began the series of bullfighting subject that culminated in the imagery present in *Guernica,* a huge composition, prompted by the Spanish Civil War, which expresses in complicated symbolical language, comprehensible after careful study, the artist's abhorrence of the violence and beastliness of war. This dark mood persists in the dislocated forms and frightening imagery of his work during the Second World War. No man has changed more radically the nature of art. Like Giotto, Michelangelo, and Bernini, he stands at the beginning of a new epoch.

Pietà *See* **Exhibit 1.3**, page 1-31.

Pissarro, Camille (1831–1903) Born in St. Thomas in the West Indies, the son of a Creole mother and a father of Portuguese-Jewish descent, Pissarro worked as a clerk in his father's general store. Then, in 1852, he ran away to Venezuela with a Danish painter, after which his reluctant parents resigned themselves to his becoming an artist. In France he worked on landscapes painted entirely in the open, but he could sell almost nothing and he and his family lived in poverty. In 1870 he fled before the German invasion, where eventually news reached him that his house had been used as a butchery by the invaders, and his store of 200–300 pictures had become duckboards in the muddy garden. In 1872 he took part in the first Impressionist exhibition. From 1895 severe eye trouble forced him to give up working outdoors, and he painted many town views from the windows of Paris. His production was enormous and in all techniques—chiefly oil painting, but also pastel, gouache, drawing in all media, etching, and lithography.

Plaster Casting An intermediate stage in the production of a piece of sculpture, which is often the last process actually to be carried out *by* the sculptor. Once the model has been cast in plaster it can be regarded as a finished work, rather fragile in nature, or it can be executed in bronze, lead, or any other

---

EXHIBIT 1.2
Major Art Movements

Abstract Expressionism (1940s–1950s) American art movement stressing spontaneous, nonrepresentational creation. First truly American school of art, characterized primarily by Pollock, who dribbled and spattered paint on canvas to create subconscious reality.

Art Deco (1920s–1930s) Highly decorative art, utilizing streamlined geometric forms inspired by industrial design. Interior designs in glass, plastic, and chrome. Architecturally, New York's Chrysler Building is an example of this style.

Art Nouveau (1895–1905) Characterized by motifs of highly stylized flowing plants, curving lines, and fluent forms. Found in dress design, illustration, architecture, and interior design.

Ashcan School (ca.1908) American Realist painters who abandoned idealized subject matter for representations of the more sordid aspects of urban life.

Barbizon School (1830s–1860s) Landscape artists who rejected the classical and romantic to portray nature directly as they perceived it. Rousseau was the principal artist. The movement was a forerunner of Impressionism.

Baroque (1580–1720) Developed in Italy, a movement of grand theatrical effects and elaborate ornamentation. Palace of Versailles is an excellent example. Baroque's greatest achievement was the fusion of architecture, sculpture, and painting.

Beaux Arts (1890–1920) Primarily an architectural style using formal and classical techniques, derived from the inspiration of the great European academies.

Black (Afro-American) Art The various styles of black American artists, inspired by protest, the search for individual identity, and the desire to trace historical roots.

Classicism Art that emphasizes qualities characteristically Greek or Roman in both spirit and style. Noted for harmony, objectivity, and discipline.

Constructivism (1920 ff.) Creation of three-dimensional abstract art in Russia, using iron, plastic, etc. to express technological society. Mobiles of Calder are an excellent example.

Cubism (1907–1915) A modern art reaction to Impressionism, led by Picasso and Braque, that portrayed geometric forms in nature as a departure from representational art.

Dada (1915–1923) International anti-art movement reflecting the cynicism of the post-World War I era by producing such bizarre works as the Mona Lisa with a mustache. Dada represented the absurd and the nonsensical.

Expressionism Twentieth-century art in which the expression of the artist took precedence over rational and faithful rendering of subject matter. Stress on emotion and inner visions. The art of El Greco and van Gogh.

Fauvism The work of early 20th-century post-Impressionists characterized by strident color, distortions, and bold brushwork. Matisse and Roualt were leaders of the movement.

Futurism Italian artistic movement of 1910 that stressed motion and sought to glorify the age of the machine by painting and sculpting multiples of moving parts.

Impressionism Late 19th-century French school that stressed the depiction of light and color in nature at a given moment. Emphasis on visual impressions. Some chief Impressionists: Monet, Renoir, Degas, Pissarro.

Mannerism (1520–1590) School of art and architecture characterized by the exotic and confusing, also the distortion of the elongated human figure. El Greco was a major Mannerist.

Neoclassicism (1790–1830) A rejection of rococo and a return to classical style and motifs. An art form characterized by clarity, restraint, and balance.

Op Art (1960s) Nonobjective art based on optical illusions created by geometric forms whose colors the eye must blend at a distance.

Pop Art (1960s) Primarily an American movement derived from both popular culture and commerical art. Representational works culled from everyday life—soup cans, comics, etc. The art of Warhol, Lichtenstein, and Oldenberg, for example.

Rococo (1730–1780) European art of glorified asymmetrical ornamentation on paneling, porcelain, and jewelry to display a love of elegance and gaiety.

Surrealism (1924 ff.) An art form that sought to reveal the psychological reality behind appearances. Subject matter stressed dreams, fantasy, and the subconscious. The art of Magritte, Dali, and Miró.

metal. Any work of sculpture that is not a piece of direct carving in some hard substance is normally depicted in clay or wax. If a head has been modeled in wax it can be left at that; if in clay it will dry up and crumble to pieces unless it is either kept permanently damp or transformed into terra-cotta or plaster. Terra-cotta is really no more than baking the clay, in the same way as a common flower pot is produced. The result is the same in texture. A plaster cast is much more complicated, but also more durable, and more frequently used.

Plasticity   The quality of appearing three-dimensional. A painting is said to have great plasticity if it gives the impression that the figures are fully modeled and are capable of moving freely in the pictorial space. Plasticity is often obtained by emphasizing the tonal contrasts and by keeping the greater part of the picture in shadow.

Pointillism   An art form, developed by Seurat at the end of the 1880s, that created colors and forms from tiny dots of paint that would, when viewed from a distance, take the shape of people, objects, etc.

Pollock, Jackson (1912–1956)   The chief American exponent of Action painting, Pollock made studies for his apparently unpremeditated works, done on continuous lengths of canvas tacked to the floor and later cut up with selective care. He abandoned the use of brushes in 1947, pouring the paint straight onto the canvas, but later he began to employ brushes again. He said of his paintings: "I don't work from drawings or color sketches. My painting is direct . . . I want to express my feelings rather than illustrate them . . . When I am painting I have a general notion as to what I am about. I *can* control the flow of paint: There is no accident, just as there is no beginning and no end." He used metallic paints and ordinary commercial synthetic enamel and plastic paint, with results that are already unfortunate since these are not durable art mediums. Pollock was one of the most famous Abstract Expressionists, freeing the United States for the first time from European dominance in the world of art. "Dripping" was the form of calligraphy he chose. He often used sticks, trowels, and knives as painting tools. His works are considered masterpieces in which tenderness and violence alternate with each other.

Polyptych   Technically, a work of art comprising two or more panels. However, since the terms diptych (two panels) and triptych (three panels) are widely used, the work polyptych is usually used for a work of more than three panels, nearly always an altarpiece.

Pop Art   An Avant-garde movement that began in New York in the late 1950s that used the expressions of popular culture and commercial art to exemplify the "bare bones" of reality and expose the modern world of mass production and utility. "Pop" endeavored to raise the ordinary, fleeting experiences of daily life to an art form, using as its medium of exploration everything from comic strips to carnage. See the works of Warhol, Lichtenstein, and Oldenburg, for example.

Porcelain   Hard, dense, white, and translucent ceramic material invented in China between A.D. 600 and 900 and reinvented in Europe in 1708. Regarded as the most refined of all ceramic wares.

Poussin, Nicolas (1594–1665)   The greatest of the French Classical painters, who made many experiments in his early Roman years, one being a combination of Classical form and Venetian color raised to the most supreme beauty. He turned from religious to Classical subjects and mythologies, and then to compositions filled with figures grouped in dramatic poses. Later in his life he chose Classical themes of Roman moral victory and sacrifice, or dramatic Biblical themes in which the action turns on the psychological impact of the moment. His late works are essays in solid geometry, with facial expressions eliminated and immobile figures. By comparison with his early works they are frigid and cerebral, but they are the logical exposition of his theories: A picture must contain the maximum of moral content expressed in a composition that conveys its intellectual content; the pattern must be pleasing in itself, not conflict with the two-dimensional quality of the picture plane; the color must offer no sensuous charm to lessen the unity of vision. Nowhere is this severe attitude expressed with more finality than in his landscapes.

Priming   A layer of white (commonly white lead or zinc combined with linseed oil) applied over a sized canvas in preparation for painting.

Primitivism   In 20th-century art, this term largely refers to the charming and "naive" style of such painters as Rousseau, Wood, and Grandma Moses. It is a craftlike approach to painting, using solid colors on a flat background, frequently highly stylized. Great importance is given to minutia—the finite detail of people and things, the intricacies of a subject. Modern primitivists often came from unpretentious backgrounds in which art lay outside their cultures, so they were, therefore, "late bloomers"; however, the charm and joy inherent in their creations have earned them an important place in the world of art.

 **Quadratura**   Illusionistic painting on a ceiling or wall in which perspective and foreshortening of architectural members, figures, etc., give the impression that the interior is open and limitless.

Raphael (1483–1520)   The youngest of the three great creators of high Renaissance (including Leonardo and Michelangelo) and the most eclectic of great artists. In 1500 he was 17, Leonardo was 48, and Michelangelo 25—and yet in less than 10 years this provincial youth, who had not had their advantage in being born and brought up in Florence, was generally admitted to be their equal. In 1508 Raphael went to Rome, where he rapidly became the principal master employed in the Vatican, with the sole exception of Michelangelo, who was then painting the ceiling of the Sistine Chapel. At 26 Raphael was in the front rank, and there he remained for the rest of his short life. His style eventually became larger and simpler and showed how the conception of the Madonna had changed from the simple Naturalism of the 15th century to the superhuman being, which in the 16th century was thought more appropriate to the Mother of God—hence the figure floating in the clouds. Raphael was known for delicate treatment in the portrayal of his subject matter and also for the personification of his calm, serene mind. When he died at the age of 37, he occupied a unique social position, in terms of friendship with cardinals and princes, a position never before attained by an artist. The false rumor current at his death that the Pope had intended to make him a cardinal is the most eloquent proof of the change that had come over the status of the artist, a change wrought principally by Leonardo, Michelangelo, and Raphael.

Rauschenberg, Robert (b.1925) One of the forerunners of Pop Art, Rauschenberg relied heavily on the portrayal of violence, scenes of city life, and irony in his art. His challenge to modern civilization made him a transitional link between Abstract Expressionism and Pop imagery.

Ray, Man (1890–1976) A Renaissance man, being painter, designer, photographer, sculptor, and printmaker, Ray was one of the founders of the Dada movement. Rather than develop a personal style, he

---

EXHIBIT 1.3
Useful Art Terms

Brush Drawing Generally an Oriental technique of painting that relies on varieties of brushwork, usually executed over a wash of diluted watercolor.

Caricature The exaggeration of features in portrait work for the sake of humor, or to satirize.

Chasing Ornamentation on metal by embossing (carving or stamping a design) or engraving (cutting lines into wood, metal, etc.).

Coulisse Objects and figures arranged at the sides of a painting in order to focus the eye onto the central piece of the work.

Dragging A technique of applying paint lightly over a textured surface to gain the effect of both light and dark "broken" color.

Easel Picture During the Renaissance, a small painting meant to be displayed on an easel rather than hung. These popular works of art were also called cabinet pictures.

Egg-and-Dart Used in classical art, a decorative technique that alternated arrowlike shapes with oval forms.

Enamel Glass that has been heated to form a base of porcelain, which is then decorated with scenes or designs. Popular in the 15th and 16th centuries.

Etching A process in which a special needle is used to draw a design on a metal plate overlaid with wax. The plate is then treated with acid, inked, and finally used to print reproductions of the design.

Foxing A brown spotting that discolors prints, caused by dampness.

Fugitive Pigment Inferior pigments that tend to fade when exposed to sun, or disintegrate in a polluted atmosphere.

Gilding Gold leaf applied to surfaces and then burnished.

Gisant A figure that is recumbent on the stone lid of a tomb.

Gouache An opaque color medium in a water base.

Hard-edge Painting A painting executed in long and thick flat color areas, all of which have sharply defined edges.

Imari Japanese porcelain with a decorated blue underglass over which the colors of red and gold are laid.

Isocephaly Reflected in classical Greek art, this technique poses groups of figures all the same height, regardless of the action or purpose of each figure in the painting.

Kore A draped maiden in ancient Greek art; the young male is known as the kouros.

Lay Figure A wooden model of the human body that is jointed so that it can be posed and arranged in clothing; used by artists and sculptors.

Lettrism Letters, symbols, and words placed in artistic juxtaposition with concentration on form and color rather than meaning. An art form popular in the 1950s.

Light Sculptures A form of sculpture that utilizes light bulbs, the sun, and laser beams as the primary medium of expression.

Maculature A "thin" or partially obscured print made from a plate that needs re-inking.

Majolica The richly colorful pottery produced in Italy.

Makemono A painting, generally Oriental, on a long scroll.

Marquetry Refers to colored or varnished woods, ivory, or other materials that are inlaid flush with the surface of an object, especially furniture.

Millefiori A technique in glassmaking in which flowerlike sections appear from sticks of colored glass that have been cut on the transverse. Sometimes used for beads in jewelry-making; also embedded in shapes of clear glass to form paperweights.

Netsuke A small Japanese figure (predominantly animals) usually carved from ivory and used to decorate belts, purses, tobacco pouches, etc. Highly collectable, these miniature works of 16th-century art are said to have an "aura" about them the more they are handled.

Obelisk Primarily Egyptian, a pillar that tapers into the shape of a pyramid; used in monument decoration.

Oiling Out Process of rubbing oil into a painting to brighten up colors. Although a luster is restored for a while, the ultimate effect is to further darken the shades.

Optical Mixture The visual mixing of colors performed by the eye from a distance; i.e., dabs of blue and yellow paint combine to give the sensation of green.

Ormolu A gilded bronze used to decorate furniture.

Papiers Collés (Fr. pasted papers) Pictures made from bits of paper, tissue, cardboard, etc., that have been glued together in artistic color or form.

Passage A term in art used to mean many different things: a particular part of a painting; the transition from one shade to another; a special technique; or an area in a painting that has been painted over by someone other than the artist.

Pellicle The fine "skin" that forms when oil paints dry.

preferred "to paint as much as possible unlike other painters. Above all to paint unlike myself, so that each...work...shall be entirely different..." He experimented with airbrush work to produce paintings that would resemble photographs in an attempt "to create great confusion" between the worlds of art and photography. His Surrealist paintings are famous for grotesque juxtaposition of objects.

Realism   Signifies the search for the squalid and depressing as a means of life enhancement. It is, in

Pétard   An artwork produced to draw attention to itself through unusual composition, subject matter, etc.

Pietà   The name given to the depiction in painting or sculpture of the Virgin holding the body of the dead Christ.

Polyptych   A work of art involving two or more panels. However, most frequently referring to more than three panels, since diptych (two panels) and triptych (three panels) are more commonly used as designation.

Porcelain   Hard white ceramic material invented A.D. 800 in China and reinvented in 1710 in Europe. Porcelain is regarded as the finest ceramic.

Priming   The application of a coat of white paint (usually zinc or lead) to a sized canvas in order to prepare it for painting.

Psychedelic Art   Visionary works created by a person who seems to be under the influence of hallucinogenic drugs.

Quadratura   Painting on a ceiling or wall to create the illusion of limitless space.

Repoussé   Decorative art worked in metal with the design hammered into relief from the reverse side.

Representative Art   An art form that endeavors to show figures and objects exactly as they appear to the eye.

Retreating Color   Shades of green or blue used to suggest distance.

Squaring   The transferral of a small sketch to a larger space by dividing the sketch into numbered squares and copying the design in each square onto the larger surface.

Tactile Values   In art, giving an illusion of the tangible so that the viewer's senses react to temperature, motion, texture, etc.

Tinsel Painting   A painting on glass that has been backed by tinfoil; popular fad in the 19th century. Also called Oriental or crystal painting.

Tole   Objects made of tin and decorated with colorful designs.

Underpainting   The initial painting of a picture in one color to lay out the composition.

Vanitas   A still life art form developed in the 17th century to reflect the transience of life. Usually depictions of such objects as dead flowers, skulls, hourglasses, etc.

Veduta   A painting of a city or town that is lucid and faithful enough so that the location can be easily identified.

Woodcut   A print whose design has been cut into a block of wood so that the parts not cut away are reproduced.

RAPHAEL
Saint George and the Dragon

fact, the total repudiation of Ideal Art and should not be confused with Naturalism, which is no more than the pleasure in being able to make an accurate transcript of nature. Realistic Art was not for the squeamish, and it underwent different transformations according to the individual painter's nationality, school of art, and particular vision. The style is one of paying strict attention to scrupulous detail.

Relief   Sculpture that is not free-standing, and, in having a background, approximates painting. The design in this type of sculpture comes from its background, which is either deep (altoriliero) or shallow (bas-relief).

Rembrandt van Ryn (1606–1669)   A Dutch painter whose earliest works show great interest in light and represent scholars in lofty rooms, or are studies of old age. Eventually, Rembrandt moved to Amsterdam and set up as a portrait painter, attracting attention and prospering by producing highly finished likenesses. In 1634 he married a woman who brought him a considerable dowry as well as good connections that allowed him to live well beyond his means. In 1642, a group portrait, the *Night Watch,* was painted. It was one of several such commemorative groups of the volunteer militia enlisted to defend Amsterdam. Each man depicted in the group paid according to the prominence given to his portrait. After 1642 Rembrandt's business declined and bankruptcy followed. His son Titus "employed" him from 1660 onward, thus affording him some relief from creditors. During these years he turned to biblical subjects, creating a Protestant

REMBRANDT
Self Portrait with Sprouting Beard

iconography, landscapes, and studies of the Jews among whom he lived. He had been painting religious subjects from the start of his career, but the later works are deeper in emotional content and far less superficially dramatic. The same contrasts can be seen in his etchings. His portraits of the 1650s and 1660s include masterpieces of psychological penetration painted to please himself. A long series of self-portraits records every stage of his career, every moment of disillusion, with ever-deepening self-analysis. Rembrandt's influence has never died. His output was prodigious, and there are about 650 paintings by him (of which some 60 are self-portraits), as well as about 300 etchings and 1500–2000 drawings.

Remington, Frederic (1861–1909) American painter, illustrator, and sculptor of the Old West. Remington's work abounded in scenes of native America and the cowboy life and customs that he eventually turned into illustrations, famous for their direct appeal to the emotions. He did not attempt to document the West, but rather to popularize it by his vivid romantic portrayals.

Renaissance (Fr., or Ital. rebirth) Usually defined as the revival of art and letters under the influence of Classical models in the 14th–16th centuries. This age lent a new dignity to man and his works. The period from 1420–1500 is now generally called the Early Renaissance, and the term "High Renaissance" is reserved for the tiny span of time when a pure, Classical, balanced harmony was attained, and when artists of the first rank were in absolute control of their techniques, able to render anything they wanted with maximum fidelity to nature. It is this mastery of technique that, with the elimination of superfluous detail, is one of the distinguishing marks between Early and High Renaissance. A passion for Classical models is a distinguishing mark, so Renaissance style must also have the Classical qualities of serenity and harmony.

Renoir, Pierre-Auguste (1841–1919) One of the greatest painters affected by Impressionism. Renoir worked from the age of 13 in a china factory, and his early training as a painter on porcelain predisposed him toward the light palette of Impressionism. All his life he was conscious of the need to study art in museums and dissatisfied with the purely visual aspects of Impressionism. In 1868 he and Monet worked together on the Seine, and as a result of painting continually outdoors—and of Monet's influence—his color became lighter and higher in key and his handling freer, the whole canvas managed in patches of colored light and shadow without any definite drawing. His early works include portraits, landscapes, flowers, and groups of figures in settings of café, dance-hall, boats, or riverside landscapes; his late works are mostly nudes, or near nudes. The warmth and tenderness of pink and pearly flesh entranced him and gave him full scope for his favorite color schemes of pinks and reds. In 1906 he settled in the south of France, but he was already crippled with arthritis, which finally rendered him completely helpless, so that his last pictures were painted with brushes stuck between his twisted fingers. America is particularly rich in Renoirs, since they were bought there when the artist was still unappreciated in Europe.

Replica An exact copy of a picture, made by the painter of the original or at least under his supervision. It is often used to describe two or more paintings, exactly alike, when one is in doubt about which is the original.

RENOIR
On the Terrace

Repoussé   Ornamental metalwork in which the design is hammered into relief from the reverse side. Often incorrectly used to mean embossing.

Representational Art   In contrast with nonobjective and abstract art, representational art strives to depict figures and objects as they appear to the eye.

Retreating Color   A cool color, e.g., blue, which suggests distance, or at least does not appear to come to the fore.

Reynolds, Sir Joshua (1723–1792)   Historically the most important figure in British painting, Reynolds was born in Devon, where his father was headmaster of the Grammar School and a former Fellow of Balliol. This is worth mentioning because it shows that Reynolds was born and brought up in an educated family at a time when most English painters were hardly more than ill-educated tradesmen. Reynolds himself did more to raise the status of the artist in England through his learning and personal example than by his actual quality as an artist. The fundamental basis of his art was the deliberate use of allusion to the Old Masters. This appeal to the educated eye is the essence of his own style and the reason for the rise in public esteem for the visual arts that is so marked a feature of his age. Reynolds's practice as a portrait painter was profoundly influenced by the few weeks he spent in Venice in 1752. He was knighted in 1769 and the works of the years following show him at his most Classical and most learned. In 1781 he made a journey to Flanders and Holland and was profoundly influenced by the force and freedom of Rubens's handling; from then until his sight failed in 1789 his works are less consciously Classical and painted with greater warmth and feeling. The overwhelming majority of his vast output consists of portraits, which include almost every man and woman of note in the second half of the 18th century.

Robbia, Luca della (1400–1482)   Ranked as one of the great innovators at the beginning of the 15th century, he was one of the leading marble sculptors of the Early Renaissance and is considered the inventor of glazed terra-cotta, usually of white figures against a blue background. To some extent this discovery was the ruin of his art, for he was able to found a flourishing family business that later undertook some very large and highly colored commissions.

Rococo   Immediately after the death of Louis XIV of France in 1715 there was a reaction of relief against the excessive splendor and pomp of Versailles and the whole ceremonial "Sun King" way of life. One of the results was to transfer the center of French life back to Paris and to build new townhouses that were both smaller and much more comfortable than the Baroque palaces. Rococo—which comes from a French word *rocaille,* meaning rockwork—is basically a style of interior decoration, and consists principally of the use of curves, and the love of elegance. Porcelain, gold, and silversmiths' work portray these tendencies admirably. The characteristics of small curves, prettiness, and gaiety can also be found in painting and sculpture of the period. England did not take to Rococo, and in France it fell out of fashion in the 1740s. The countries in which Rococo produced numerous great works of art was Germany and Austria. There Rococo Art can be seen in scores of absurdly beautiful churches and statues, which are elegant, modish, and deeply moving.

Rodin, Auguste (1840–1917)   The most celebrated sculptor of the late 19th century, who achieved during his lifetime a fame that has done much to obscure his real qualities. He worked as a mason from about 1864, and supplemented his technical training by studying in museums, where he became interested in the works of Michelangelo. In 1875 he visited Italy, and soon after began working on his first independent free-standing figure. Its lifelike quality, accuracy of proportion and anatomy, and rendering of movement gave rise to the tale that it had been made from a cast taken from a live model. Most of his public commissions were unlucky: His original *Thinker* was not erected as he wished and was savaged by a vandal; his *Hugo* was produced in several versions to meet endless objections and was finally not put up as planned; his *Balzac* monument was refused by the commissioning committee and only erected much later. Rodin was the creator of a new form in sculpture—the fragment as a finished work, usually a head and trunk, but sometimes a pair of hands only—and he also employed a variant of Michelangelo's unfinished figures, giving to some parts a waxy delicacy of finish while leaving others buried in the hardly touched block. His great influence was through his expression of emotion and movement, his use of symbolism and distortion, and the amazing sensitiveness of his modeling. He was the product of Romanticism and a forerunner of Modern Art.

RODIN
The Kiss

ART

Romanticism   A current throughout the history of art laying stress on the importance of fantasy and the imagination as opposed to reason and order—a return to nature. See the works of Blake, Daumier, and Goya.

Rose Window   Very ornate circular window, primarily with religious themes, intricately worked in stained glass and particularly representative of Gothic architecture. One of the most famous examples is the rose window of Notre Dame cathedral in Paris.

Rossetti, Dante Gabriel (1828–1882)   Poet and painter, Rossetti's subjects were drawn mostly from Dante and from a medieval dream world also reflected in his verse. In 1850 he met Elizabeth Siddal, who had posed for Millais, and under his inspiration she developed into an artist of both poetic and neurotic intensity. His best work was produced during the years of their uneasy association. They married in 1860; in 1862 she died of an overdose of narcotics and he became virtually a recluse and eventually a chloral addict. Rossetti's works are characterized by a typically Victorian clutter of composition and a brooding pensiveness.

Rothko, Mark (1903–1970)   Rothko was born in Russia but in 1913 came to America, where he became influenced by Surrealism and so created a transparent aquatic world peopled by tentacled plants and animals. As he developed his own style he began painting abstract pictures that consist of horizontal bands of color with muzzy edges.

ROUAULT
Bitter Lemon

RUBENS
Portrait of Hélène Fourment

Rouault, Georges (1871–1958)   His early works were overworked oil paintings of biblical subjects with heavy dark contours enclosing areas of violent color; they express the painter's loathing of vice, hypocrisy, cruelty, and complacency. Eventually Rouault developed one of the purest forms of Expressionism. His themes were of religious subjects—chiefly of the Passion (Rouault was a devout Catholic)—landscapes of bleak and hostile country, and an occasional bouquet of flowers. He painted with hard, thick brushstrokes and dark outlines that were reminiscent of the early work he had done in stained glass. He used colors violently, and his figures were massive, larger than life.

Rousseau, Henri (1844–1910)   Called an amateur or "Sunday" painter, Rousseau achieved greatness with a direct, simple, and hauntingly naive vision. He painted unusually large and complicated pictures of elaborately fanciful, exotic subjects in a "primitive" technique with the use of strong color. He combined a certain peasant shrewdness and bland self-esteem with gullible simple-mindedness. Rousseau kept a school where he taught elocution, music, and painting, wrote two plays, got himself involved, although guiltlessly, in a trial for fraud, and finally died, it is said, as a result of a disappointment in love in his pursuit of a third wife.

Rubbing (Fr. *frottage*)   Technique of capturing designs and textural effects by placing paper over objects that have raised surfaces and rubbing the paper with graphite, wax crayon, etc.

Rubens, Sir Peter Paul (1577–1640)   After a lifetime appointment as court painter to the Spanish Governors of The Netherlands, Rubens settled in Antwerp, where he built himself an Italianate palace, married Isabella Brandt, and started on what was perhaps the most energetic and fruitful career in the history of art, one that made him the most important artist in Northern Europe and the greatest Northern exponent of the Baroque. He developed a dramatic style that was less passionate than his predecessors' so that numerous assistants could work under him to fulfill the multitude of commissions that poured in. Rubens carefully controlled the execution of his designs, and in most cases he did the final work on a picture himself. Without the methods he devised for the division of labor, his vast output over so many years could never have been achieved, much less maintained, at so high a standard. His practice was to make smallish sketches, very free in handling, usually on panels with a light streaky buff or gray ground, the loose drawing touched in with indications of color for his assistants to follow. He produced countless altarpieces, portraits, hunting scenes, landscapes, religious pictures, mythology scenes, tapestry designs, and book illustrations. After the death of his wife he married the sixteen-year-old Hélène Fourment, who became the theme and inspiration of his late mythologies and the subject of many portraits.

S **Sargent, John Singer** (1856–1925) A highly skilled American portrait painter who settled in London, Sargent painted high society in Edwardian and Georgian times, but is best known for his portraits and brilliant watercolors. He visited Spain, and the technical skill and simple color schemes of most of his portraits reflect Velazquez. His compositions were both unusual and skillful, and he often used light to obscure details and soften

SARGENT
Lady Hamilton

edges. Toward the end of his life he painted murals for the Boston Museum of Fine Arts and the Widener Library at Harvard.

Sarto, Andrea del (1486–1531) The best painter in 16th-century Florence, who had more feeling for tone and color than most of his contemporaries. He was the first Florentine to depart from the colored drawing approach in favor of composition by patches of colored light and shade. Del Sarto went to France in 1518–1519 at the invitation of François I and was well received, but he broke his contract in order to return to his wife, who, in the opinion of contemporaries, ruined him. He failed to live up to his great promise, but his works are of great importance in the evolution of Florentine painting.

Scaling The flaking-off of oil paint from the ground, caused by careless priming or mixing of pigment or varnish, rolling or folding the canvas, or moisture attacking the back.

Sculpture The art of creating forms in three dimensions or in Relief. Basically, there are two opposed conceptions of sculptural form: glyptic, which means carved, and consists essentially in removing waste material until the form is freed from the matter in which it was imprisoned (this neo-Platonic conception was Michelangelo's), and its opposite, in which form is created from nothing by building up in some plastic material. Carving and modeling are thus two separate and complementary aspects of sculpture, the present tendency being to exalt direct carving and the feel of the material at the expense of modeling, which involves using clay or wax as a preliminary material for translation into plaster, bronze, lead, or even stone.

Scumbling The opposite of Glazing, it consists of working an opaque layer of oil paint over another layer of a different color so that the lower layer is not entirely obliterated. The two processes of glazing and scumbling together demonstrate the range of effects, from transparency to opacity, possible in the oil medium, effects that ensured its universal adoption.

Serial Art (serial imagery) The repetition, with slight variations, of an image in the same work of art, whether a single canvas or related modules of a sculptured work.

Serigraphy Also known as silk screen printing, the basic principles are those of a stencil, in that it is a method by which paint is brushed over a screen so that the color penetrates those parts of the screen that have not previously been masked. By using successive masks on the same screen it is possible to produce prints in several colors and also to obtain color mixtures by printing one color over another—for instance, printing blue over yellow to make a green. The screen itself is made of fairly fine silk, and the masks are usually of paper; paint is brushed on and soaks through the silk in the parts that have not been masked. The process was originally developed for commercial purposes, since it is possible to use unskilled labor to make prints once the masks have been prepared. In recent years, however, first in America and later in Europe, the technique has been greatly developed as a method of making large numbers of artist-produced prints that can be sold at fairly low prices, although each print is, like a lithograph, an original work of art.

ART

Seurat, Georges (1859–1891)   Seurat evolved first a theory of painting (*See* **Pointillism**) in which the color of the light is broken down. For instance, bright yellow-green grass contains reflections from the sky and from other nearby objects. This objective was realized by the fine and delicate use of dots of paint on canvas to create color and form. He also evolved a formal type of composition based on the relation of objects within the picture space to one another and to the size and shape of the picture and on the balance of verticals and horizontals. The Impressionists stressed the flickering quality of light and figures caught in movement, but Seurat aimed at a static quality. His early death at 32, however, meant that his ideas were developed only by followers and imitators.

SEURAT
Study for the Kickup

Shahn, Ben (1898–1969)   This Russian-born American artist's use of photographic realism and some of the technical devices of advertising set him apart from most modern American painters; however, his art has always been a vehicle for ideas. The Sacco and Vanzetti case (when two immigrant anarchists were judicially murdered) led to the production of a series of biting comments in the form of drawings, which are only one example of Shahn using art as social commentary. He was much influenced by Rouault and Rivera, collaborating with the latter on the Radio City murals in 1933. Other murals are in the Bronx Post Office, New York, and the Social Security Building, Washington. He has also written on art. The people who live in his paintings are extremely stylized but not characterized. He is known for his use of bright colors, extreme detail, and the absence of perspective.

Sketch   A rough draft of a composition or part of a composition, made in order to satisfy the artist on certain points of scale, composition, lighting, etc. It is the trial run—or one of many—for the full-scale work, but must be carefully distinguished from a Study. A sketch by a landscape painter is usually a small and rapid note of the effect of light on a given scene, and is intended for future reference and reworking if necessary. The quality of some artists' sketches is, however, so high that what they would have considered their important works are now often undervalued: Rubens and Constable are examples.

Soft Sculpture   Sculpture made of pliable and sometimes impermanent materials, such as latex, vinyl, feathers, rope and string, hair, etc. Seen since the early 1960s, soft sculpture defies the tradition of hard and permanent material as the only suitable medium for sculpture.

Squaring   A way of transferring a small sketch to a larger surface by dividing both into the same number of squares, and then copying the design in each square of the smaller drawing onto the corresponding square of the larger surface.

Stained Glass   Designs or figures made from pieces of colored glass, held together by strips of lead, which form the outlines of the design. Apparently a Byzantine invention that soon became a distinctively Western and medieval art. Eventually this painstaking art died away, only to find its rebirth among 20th-century craftspeople in the form of hanging ornaments, mobiles, glass boxes, etc.

Still Life   Emerging as a subject in its own right in the 16th century, it appeared before that in religious pictures and portraits as part of the setting. When it became popular, still life was developed along various lines, the chief being a collection of objects chosen and arranged to remind the spectator of the transience and uncertainty of life (hourglasses, skulls, flickering candles, butterflies); in the symbolic type, the objects portrayed have a significance beyond their individual appearance (bread, wine, water in religious subject matter with references to the Trinity, etc.). Into this latter category come many still life subjects that at first sight appear no more than members of the third type—collections of objects arranged to display the painter's virtuosity. There are also large still life pieces of the "furniture picture" type—kitchen interiors, with quantities of raw and cooked food, flowers, guns, dogs, and cookmaids.

Study   A drawing or painting of a detail, such as a figure, a hand, or a piece of drapery, made for the purpose of study or for use in a larger composition. A study should never be confused with a Sketch, which is a rough draft of the whole, whereas a study may be very highly wrought but does not usually embrace more than a part of the composition.

Surrealism   This art movement claims a long artistic ancestry on a continuum with the art of Bosch and any other artist who has expressed the weird and fantastic. After the demise of Dada in 1922, André Breton gathered up the remnants of the group, took over the word *Surrealism* and defined it as "pure psychic Automatism, by which it is intended to express verbally, in writing, or in any other way, the true process of thought. It is the dictation of thought, free from the exercise of reason." The object was to free artists from the normal association of pictorial ideas and from all accepted means of expression so that they might create according to the irrational dictates of their subconscious mind and vision. Surrealism developed in two directions: pure fantasy, and the elaborate reconstruction of a dream world. The first produced such objects as a bottle dryer, a bicycle wheel, and a bird cage filled with sugar cubes and a thermometer—a random assortment of bric-a-brac. The second took the form of highly detailed likenesses of objects, straight or distorted, or three-dimensional abstractions, in a fantastic and unexpected juxtaposition, or in a setting of a hallucinatory kind: Chirico, Tanguy, Dali, Man Ray's photographs, and much of Picasso's painting and sculptures. Surrealism has been described as the feverish search for the unexpected: "Beautiful as the chance encounter of a sewing machine and an umbrella on an operating table." The movement has had as much currency in literature and drama as in the visual arts and has had a liberating influence. Its ideas of strange juxtapositions have been widely commercialized—particularly in sophisticated window dressing—and it survives in the world of art as a ghost of hauntingly incoherent incantations that speaks of and to the dark and unformed side of the mind—the little animal that lies trapped inside us all.

Symbolism   A movement that developed in 1885 among painters and poets in an attempt to refute a "picture" of the world as a faithful representation and depict it instead through the visionary eye of dreams and allusions.

Tactile Values   Texture. In painting, the illusion of tangibility—that which stimulates the imagination to sense in a physical way the plastic qualities of an object represented: its weight, mass, distance, texture, motion or stability, warmth or coolness.

Tanguy, Yves (1900–1955)   A French-born American Surrealist, Tanguy began life as a merchant seaman and took up painting after seeing a picture of Chirico's. Of all the Surrealists, it was Tanguy who was known best for his creation of a reality freed from the one known to the senses. His forms seem to grow as if from the floor of a dream and rise like smoke and ghosts up into the canvas, to re-form in steep cliffs and castles. Sometimes using imagery that seems to have arisen from the bottom of the sea, we watch as jellyfish and smoothly polished stones lift and float before our eyes.

Tchelitchew, Pavel (1908–1957)   An American artist of Russian origin, Tchelitchew often used such substances as sand and coffee grounds mixed into his paints to give texture and substance. He became increasingly involved in the metamorphosis within each of his paintings, as when a scene of winter transforms into a fierce tiger with a snake in its mouth, or in his famous *Hide and Seek*, in which at once a child and then a gnarled tree is present, repeatedly echoing into the center of the large canvas. In later years he did "interior landscapes"—figures whose skeletons or veins showed through their skin.

Tempera   This word really means any kind of binder that will serve to "temper" powder color and make it workable. For many years it was usual to paint most of a picture in tempera—which dries in minutes—and then to apply only the final touches in oil. In the last few years a small number of painters have returned to the pure tempera medium (the paints can now be bought ready mixed).

Terra-cotta   A hard, fired but unglazed clay ranging in color from pink to purple-red, but usually a brownish-red. Used since ancient times for sculpture and pottery, later for architectural decoration.

Throwing   This term is used in ceramics to describe the way a pot, a vase, etc., is "built up" on a spinning potter's wheel.

Tinsel Painting   A picture painted on glass and backed by crinkled tinfoil. A popular 19th-century parlor art.

Tintoretto, Jacopo (1518–1594)   In his early works, Tintoretto composed his figures across the picture in a frieze, with elegant elongated forms. He made his reputation with large and crowded compositions, brilliant color, and a concentration on one moment and incident. Later he evolved compositions based on violent movement. Tintoretto kept a huge workshop where his assistants worked extensively on altered variants of his original compositions. There are few mythologies in his work, for he had no Classical interest; neither does he show great range and inventiveness in portraits. After his death, painting in Venice dwindled significantly.

Titian (Tiziano Vecelli) (1487–1576)   The greatest Venetian painter and, in some senses, the founder of modern painting, Titian's *Assumption* laid the foundations of his fame. It is an enormous picture, in the "modern" style, and marks the beginning of the High Renaissance in Venice. Titian became a personal friend of the Emperor Charles V—an unheard-of honor for a painter of the 16th century, comparable only with Michelangelo's relationship with the Popes. After the abdication of Charles V in 1555, he continued to work for his successor, Philip II of Spain, who, however, employed him less as a portraitist than as a painter of poesie (Titian's own word for more or less erotic mythologies). During these years the old painter developed a very free style, almost anticipating Impressionism in its disregard for contours and its concentration on the rendering of form as patches of color. In the 1560s there were many criticisms of his failing powers, but, in fact, he was developing a sublime late style. He was said to have laid in his pictures with a mass of color that served as a groundwork for what he wanted to express: "With the same brush dipped in red, black, or yellow he worked up the light parts and in four strokes he could create a remarkably fine figure. Then he turned the picture to the wall and left it for months without looking at it, until he returned to it and stared critically at it, as if it were a mortal enemy. The final touches he softened, occasionally modulating the highest lights into the half-tones and local colors with his finger; sometimes he used his finger to dab a dark patch in a corner as an accent, or to heighten the surface with a bit of red like a drop of blood. He finished his figures like this and in the last stages he used his fingers more than his brush."

Tole Items of tinware painted with decorative designs.

Toulouse-Lautrec, Henri-Marie-Raymond de (1864–1901) Toulouse-Lautrec had the misfortune to break both his legs in childhood, as a result of which he was stunted in growth. In 1882 he began to study art seriously in Paris, and by 1885 had a studio in Montmartre where his first posters brought him immediate recognition. In 1898 his health began to suffer from drink, and he spent three months in a clinic recovering from an attack of delirium tremens. During his convalescence he worked on a series of drawings of the circus. After his recovery, he resumed his old life, but in 1901 he broke down completely and was taken to his mother's country house, where he died. His first teacher had encouraged him to paint animals, particularly horses; after he began studying in Paris he met van Gogh, and he was deeply influenced by the technique and subject matter of Degas, and by Japanese prints, the influence of which was pervasive in Impressionist circles. His subject matter was centered narrowly around the life he led: some portraits, many painted outdoors, scenes from dance-halls and cafés in Montmartre, such as the Moulin Rouge, figures of actresses, female clowns, circus artists seen backstage, and a great number of nudes, either *á la* Degas—washing, dressing—or seen sitting around in brothels, waiting for customers. He loathed posed models; these naked women just walking or sitting about provided him with models in movement and were under no restraint either in pose or behavior.

His technical range was very wide. He was a superb draftsman with a gift for conveying rapid movement and the whole atmosphere of a scene with a few strokes. Most of his paintings are in spirit-thinned oil paint on unprimed cardboard, using the neutral buff tone of the board as an element in design. He was not interested in light as were the Impressionists, only in form and movement. He subscribed to no theories, was a member of no artistic or aesthetic movement, and the works in which he records what he saw and understood contain no hint of comment—no pity, no sentiment, no blame, no innuendo.

Triptych Three panels, arranged or joined side to side by hinges. Usually the central panel is twice the width of the wings so that they can be folded over to protect it. A common form of triptych, as an object of private devotion, is to have a madonna as the center and one's patron saints on the wings: The backs of the wings, which become visible when the triptych is shut, usually bear the owner's coat of arms.

Trompe-l'œil (Fr., deceive the eye) · *See* **Illusionism**.

Turner, Joseph Mallord William (1775–1851) A precocious talent in 1792, Turner made the first of the sketching tours that were to take up so much of his time for the next half-century. At first he was exclusively a watercolorist, but eventually he worked in oils, and his paintings tend more and more to the pale brilliance he had already achieved in watercolor. He began to think in terms of colored light or, in Constable's phrase, "tinted steam." In 1828 his Venetian watercolors showed magical effects of light. The "cataclysmic" paintings of his later years show his involvement in the warring elements in nature.

TOULOUSE-LAUTREC
Jane Avril

TURNER
The Fighting Temeraire

Underpainting   The first painting of a picture, in monochrome, which lays out the general composition. Also called dead coloring and abbozzo.

Utrillo, Maurice (1883–1955)   The son of Suzanne Valadon (herself a talented painter who was encouraged by Renoir, Degas, and Toulouse-Lautrec, for whom she posed as a model), Utrillo developed early into an alcoholic and a drug addict, spent many years in clinics and sanatoriums, and his drinking bouts often ended in the police station. His mother made him learn to paint as a distraction and a form of therapy. His art shows nothing of this wild and melodramatic background. His paintings are almost all town views that are transformed from the everyday into poetry—narrow streets and lonely courtyards, and the houses of Montmartre whose walls and posters flake away into dust. They show a sensitive understanding of tone, are delicate and almost monochromatic in color (especially his milky whites, which cannot be analyzed), with precise drawing and a strange feeling for the atmosphere of a particular street or building.

Valadon, Suzanne (1867–1938) Valadon began drawing in 1883, the year Utrillo, her son, was born. Degas, for whom she modeled, was impressed with her artistic ability. Her landscapes and still lifes are famous for her use of color and composition, and her nudes (her favorite subject) are renowned for an intense and realistic style. Valadon outlined her figures with lines that recall the leading in stained glass.

Values   The gradations of tone from light to dark observable in any solid object under the play of light. Tone values are independent of color and are best perceived by half-closing the eyes so that color effects are diminished (a photograph is an example of pure tonal effect).

van Dyck, Sir Anthony (1599–1641)   In Genoa, van Dyck laid the foundation of his great career as a portrait painter and evolved the repertory of patterns from which he made such constant use during his years in England. In his finest portraits he was sensitive to his sitter's individuality, which he expressed with an unfailing sense of style that reflects something of his own introspective melancholy. In religious works, he leaned heavily on Rubens, Titian, and Correggio. He was famous for the "insights" he brought to his portraits and was thought inimicable in his re-creation of fabrics in paint, i.e., the heavy folds of white satin and the light blue of silk.

van Eyck, Jan (ca. 1390–1441) and **Hubert** Flemish painters, brothers. Although there is a great debate in the art world about whether Hubert existed, here they are referred to in the plural. For a long time the brothers were credited with the invention of oil painting, and although this is no longer a reasonable idea, it is clear that Jan perfected an oil medium and varnish that has enabled his brilliant color to survive almost unchanged. It is through the capacity to observe the minute that the van Eycks achieve a complete expression of the whole, and their technique is the perfect servant of realistic, unidealizing, and unemotional attitudes. Jan's ability and inventiveness make him easily the major

VAN DYCK
Portrait of Charles V

artist of the early Netherlands School, although few of the van Eycks are signed and still fewer documented. The van Eycks' originality is expressed in fantasy and illusion and with great attention to detail. Their subject matter was largely religious.

Vanishing Point   In perspective, the point, or points, on the horizon line at which receding parallel lines meet and seem to disappear.

Vanitas   A type of still life in which the objects depicted are reminders of the transience of temporal life. Developed in the 17th century, vanitas employed motifs such as the hourglass, skull, mirror, scales, dying or decaying plant life, and books.

Veduta   Representation of a town or city that is faithful enough to identify the location.

Velazquez, Diego Rodriguez de Silva (1599–1660)   His early paintings show his interest in the naturalistic representation of things seen in strong light. Velazquez was a slow worker with a deliberate technique and sober color used against a plain background for many of his portraits, so that the figure stands out as a silhouette. His court appointment gave him few opportunities for religious painting. His later work showed his preoccupation with the male nude and his fuller range of color. His brilliant use of color, panoramic landscape background, and heightened realism transcend any derivation. In the finest of his portraits, that of the little Infanta Margareta Teresa with her retinue of ladies and dwarfs, called *Las Meninas,* he reaches perhaps his highest point in the blending of realism with atmosphere and

ART

a deeply sensitive appreciation of character. During the 1630s and 1640s he painted a series of portraits of the court dwarfs, playmates of the royal children, for they interested him as character studies much as old age, wrinkles, and rags interested him in his imaginary portraits, and as did the aging face of the sick and gloomy King Philip, whom he painted all through his long reign, and who acknowledged the greatness of his painter by making him a Knight of the Order of Santiago in 1658.

Vellum   Fine grade of parchment made from the skins of calves or lambs. Used for manuscripts and bookbinding.

Vermeer, Jan (1632–1675)   The most calm and peaceful of all the Dutch masters, the recognition of his greatness has been long delayed. Very little is known of his life, and his pictures were completely forgotten until the mid-19th century. He died in 1675, leaving a widow and eleven children and an enormous debt to the baker, who held two pictures of his. Vermeer was obviously a very slow worker, for only about 40 pictures are generally accepted as his and most of them are quite small. They usually represent domestic interiors with one or two figures writing, doing housework, or playing musical instruments. The splendor of the color and the play of light, falling in little pearls of paint on everything in the picture, transform the everyday scenes into poetry, totally unlike the sober prose of the average Dutch master.

Vignette   An ornament of leaves and tendrils; the flourishes around a capital letter in a manuscript; a small decoration or embellishment found in beginning or ending sections of a book or manuscript; a small picture or illustration not enclosed by a definite border but shading off into the surrounding page.

VERMEER
The Lacemaker

VELAZQUEZ
Pope Innocent X

Vuillard, Édouard (1868–1940)   Fascinated with Japanese prints, the best of Vuillard's work reflects the influence of Oriental art. His scenes of family living show how well he could re-create the atmosphere of a clutter of objects and furniture in a snug, warmly lighted room. Paintings of his family, most particularly his mother, were frequent and of special delight to him.

Warhol, Andy (1928–1987)   An American Pop artist with a life-style both affluent and elegant, Warhol began by making paintings based on comic strips and advertisements. His early works showed the influence of Abstract Expressionism. One of the crucial qualities of Warhol's images is their extreme obviousness: Campbell Soup cans, portraits of Marilyn Monroe, dollar bills, and the reproduction of the *Mona Lisa*—all making a silent statement without being "transformed" into art. He began printing paintings to make art based on mass-produced imagery, rendered meaningless by constant repetition. The most striking effect of his paintings is his vivid and highly expressive use of color. Warhol died in 1987 as an indirect result of a routine gallbladder operation. He is most commonly quoted for writing, "Everyone is famous for fifteen minutes."

Wash   A thin, transparent layer of watercolor or ink, usually applied in broad areas.

Watercolor   The classical English method—and pure watercolor is almost an English monopoly—is to use the white paper as the highest lights and to apply transparent washes one over another to obtain gradations of color and tone.

Watteau, (Jean) Antoine (1684–1721)   A Flemish artist, Watteau began work as a hack painter of theatrical scenes. He had tuberculosis and at an early age showed symptoms of chronic restlessness that

WARHOL
Ten-foot Flowers

dominated the rest of his short life. Rubens was the main influence in the formation of his style. His pictures have a mood for a subject, a fleeting and melancholy sense of the transitoriness of all pleasure and all life. All Watteau's pictures were composed by taking the required number of figures from the big bound volumes in which he kept hundreds of his superb drawings. Studies of figures, heads, hands, and draperies were made in three-color crayon—black, red, and white for the highlights—and were then used when needed. Many hundreds of these still exist, usually in better condition than most of his paintings. Because the same drawing may have been used over and over again, all his pictures have a strong family likeness.

Watts, George Frederic (1817–1904)　At first he led the sheltered life of a tame genius and then began to paint large allegorical pictures while earning his living as a portraitist. His portraits of beauties and celebrities make a real attempt at more than a successful superficial likeness. In his series of famous men he strove to portray the whole man—character, personality, and appearance—and for this reason would only paint men he could like or admire. Watts, a true Victorian, was one of the last grand allegorical history painters, expressing idealized forms with a striving for sublime feeling that results in a divorce from reality, both physical and intellectual.

Whistler, James Abbott McNeill (1834–1903) Born in Lowell, Massachusetts, he attended West Point Military Academy. Failing there, he worked as a Navy cartographer, which taught him the technique of etching, before going to Paris to study painting in 1855. He lived as a dandy and had a deserved reputation as a biting wit, well able to keep up with his friend Oscar Wilde. After one particularly clever remark Wilde is supposed to have said admiringly, "I wish I had said that." Whistler replied, "You will, Oscar, you will!" Whistler's style, despite his early influence by French painting, shows a distinctly English bargain between

WATTEAU
The Storyteller

discipline and innovation. He became famous for his technique of placing a figure against a background that was virtually empty and colorless, as in the popular painting that has come to be known as *Whistler's Mother.*

Wood, Grant (1891–1942)　An American artist who spent his life in Iowa as a "regional" painter, he sought to put a finish to America's dependence on the European art world by expounding the experiences of "local"/"locale" life. Although he was first influenced by Impressionism, the majority of his work is in the primitive style. His renowned painting, *American Gothic,* is an example of this style that earned him world recognition.

Woodcut　Print made from a woodblock cut with the grain on which the parts not cut away form the design.

Wren, Sir Christopher (1632–1722)　An English architect, Wren's initial fame grew from his being a mathematician. Then the age of reconstruction that followed the Great Fire of London made it possible for Wren to undertake the complete and massive reconstruction of St. Paul's Cathedral and 51 parish churches. This work also gave him the opportunity for stylistic departure in his concepts of onion domes and galleries, etc., and occupied most of his time for 36 years. One of the most important aspects of Wren's creativity lay in the distinction he made between the beauty encapsulated in geometric form (absolute beauty) and the other beauty found in more usual, everyday shapes (relative beauty). He believed both to be equal in importance.

Wright, Frank Lloyd (1867–1959)　An innovative American architect, Wright used materials only in their natural, untouched state—stone, oven brick, nonvarnished woods. He frequently designed the furniture for the houses he built, using the Japanese motif of building directly into the walls. One of his most famous houses, *Falling Waters,* stands in Pennsylvania, a structure of cantilevered "decks" that hang suspended over a waterfall. A controversial work can be found in New York City's Guggenheim Museum, a huge spiral of stone in which museumgoers literally find themselves traveling around in circles to view an exhibition.

Wyeth, Andrew (b.1917)   An American painter, Wyeth won fame at the age of twelve for his polished illustrations in an edition of *Robin Hood.* His style is both precise and minute in detail, a Realist influenced by the exacting techniques of photography. Pennsylvania, Maine, the artist's family, and neighbors comprise most of his subject matter, and he is easily recognized by his dimly lit and deserted landscapes in tones of gray and brown, which convey feelings of both loneliness and solitude.

WHISTLER
Arrangement in Black and Grey: The Artist's Mother

BIOLOGY

Abiotic factors Physical and chemical conditions that affect the ability of a given species to live and reproduce in a particular place. Included in the abiotic factors are temperature, light, water, oxygen, pH (acid-base balance) of soil, type of substrate, and the availability of minerals. Certain kinds of plants and animals will flourish in a natural community if the conditions are present that permit their survival. Species interact to influence the survival of one another. One important principle of ecology is that no living organism is independent of other organisms or of the physical environment, if they share the same community.

Abscisic acid A growth-inhibiting plant hormone produced in the bud that helps to prepare the plant for winter by directing the leaf primordia to form scales and by inhibiting cell division in the vascular cambium.

Abscission layer A layer along which a leaf or fruit naturally separates from the stem.

Absorption The passage of dissolved materials through the cell membrane, into and out of the cell.

Acetylcholine A neurotransmitter secreted by motor neurons. When an impulse arrives at the knobs in the axon branches of a motor neuron, a neurotransmitter is released from the synaptic vesicles. Neurotransmitters are chemical substances that diffuse across the synaptic gap and initiate a second impulse when chemoreceptors on the dendrites are stimulated. Cholinergic cells secrete the neurotransmitter, acetylcholine. Adrenergic cells secrete the neurotransmitter, epinephrine.

Acid rain This is rainfall that can be as acid as vinegar. It is formed when gases of nitrogen oxide and sulfur dioxide are given off into the atmosphere as by-products of fuel combustion by automobiles, homes, factories, and power plants. As the fumes are carried into the air by wind currents, they combine with water vapor molecules and are transformed into microscopic drops of nitric acid and sulfuric acid. When it rains or snows, the precipitation returns the acids to earth, sometimes thousands of miles from their origin. Lakes and streams have become so acidified that the populations of trout, salmon, and other fish are being destroyed. There is also concern about the possible effects of acid rain on soil minerals and nitrogen-fixing bacteria.

Acquired characteristics Variations that cannot be passed from parent to offspring. These variations are not in the individual's gene pool. Lamarck (1809) advanced the hypothesis that acquired variations are transmitted to the offspring. According to him, structures that are in use are better developed and preserved, whereas unused organs eventually disappear. Characteristics thus acquired through use could be inherited, he thought, by the next generation. Facts do not seem to support his conclusions.

Acromegaly A condition of overgrowth of the bones in the hands, feet, and jaw brought on by an oversecretion of somatotropin by the pituitary gland.

Acrosome The forward tip of an animal sperm that contains the enzymes that help the sperm penetrate the egg. *See* **Sperm**.

ACTH (adrenocolticotropic hormone) Stimulates the cortex of the adrenal gland to produce a number of hormones, including cortisone. In severe cases of rheumatoid arthritis, it has brought about dramatic relief from disability and pain.

Actin One of the major proteins of muscle. The other muscle protein is myosin. Actin makes up the Z band of a sarcomere.

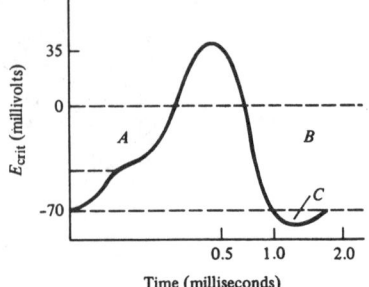

A Depolarization   B Repolarization   C Refractory period

Action potential

Action potential The graph of an action potential demonstrates the sequence of events involved in the transmission of a nerve impulse. A threshold value ($E_{crit.}$) must be attained before depolarization occurs. Once the threshold value is reached, an impulse is generated throughout the nerve fiber. A nerve cell will transmit the impulse either totally or not at all. There are no graded responses. This maximal firing condition is referred to as an "all or none response."

Activation energy The smallest amount of energy that must be available from an outside source that enables a chemical reaction to start.

Active site The specific place on the surface of an enzyme where a substrate attaches by weak chemical bonds and where catalysis occurs.

Active transport The movement of a substance across the cell membrane against a concentration gradient, that is, from a region of low concentration to a region of high concentration. Active transport involves the expenditure of energy.

Adaptation A trait that aids the survival of an individual or a species in a given environment. An adaptation may be a structural characteristic such as the hump of a camel, a behavioral characteristic such as the mating call of a bull frog, or a physiological characteristic controlling some inner workings of tissue cells. Adaptations permit the survival of species in environments that sometimes seem forbidding. For example, some bacteria are able to live in hot springs that have temperatures up to 80°C (175°F). They have adaptations that permit the carrying out of metabolic functions at extremely high temperatures.

Adaptive radiation The evolutionary division of a single species into several species adapted to divergent forms of life. For example: Darwin's finches.

Adenine A nitrogenous base contained in DNA.

ADH (antidiuretic hormone) Also called vasopressin. A hormone secreted by the hypothalamus that prevents the excretion of urine by stimulating the kidney nephrons to reabsorb water.

Adrenals Compound glands located at the top of the kidneys. They have an outer zone known as cortex and an inner one known as medulla. The cortex secretes a complex of substances appearing to be closely related chemically. Their combined action controls sodium, potassium, and chloride metabolism, which affects water balance, causes the change of glycogen to glucose, and influences sex. Deficiency results in a syndrome known as Addison's disease. The patient suffering from it experiences a general decline in muscular strength and sexual activity, a lowering of blood pressure, disturbance of digestion, and a bronzing of the skin. The best-known cortical secretion is cortisone, which has been used in treating arthritis and allergies. The medulla secretes a hormone called epinephrine (adrenaline), which is produced in accelerated quantities when one is stimulated by anger or fear. Apparently it is the only endocrine gland directly responding to nervous stimuli. The influence of epinephrine on the conversion of glycogen to glucose, stimulation of heart muscles, enrichment of blood supply to muscles, and acceleration of blood coagulation are without doubt useful to provide more and quick energy or to stop bleeding in times of stress or injury.

Afferent or sensory neurons Nerve cells that transport impulses from sense receptors to the central nervous system.

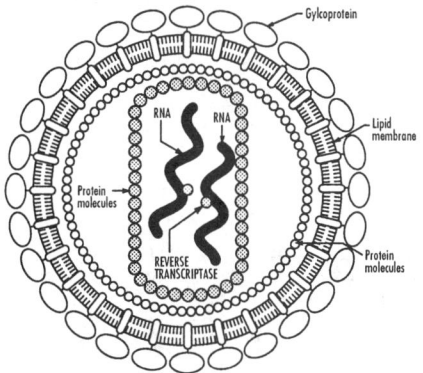

Diagram of AIDS virus

AIDS AIDS is a baffling disease that has recently attracted considerable attention. The name stands for "acquired immune deficiency syndrome." It refers to a severe breakdown in the body's immune system. A person with AIDS is vulnerable to a variety of infections and tumors that would normally be attacked by the body's white blood cells. As a result, the person becomes weak and dies. The cause of AIDS is a virus. It was identified in 1984 by Dr. Luc Montagnier of the Pasteur Institute in Paris, who called it LAV- I, and also named by Dr. Robert C. Gallo of the National Cancer Institute, HTLV-III. It is now known as HIV, or human immunodeficiency virus. It is believed that the AIDS virus kills a specialized type of white blood cell, called the helper T4 cell, which normally protects the body from infection by destroying foreign substances that enter it. The disease is believed to be passed through blood and semen, but not passed by casual contact, such as sneezing or using the same utensils. In the United States, certain groups of people have the greatest risk of getting the disease: male homosexuals, intra-

venous drug users who share contaminated needles, and babies born to infected mothers. Before 1987, recipients of contaminated blood transfusions contracted AIDS. In Central Africa where AIDS is prevalent the disease is also spread by heterosexual contact. Heterosexual transmission is also becoming more common in the United States. Considerable research is being conducted to develop a defense against the disease. In 1986, a drug, azidothymidine (AZT), was found to be effective against a form of pneumonia common among AIDS patients. It appears to interfere with reproduction of the virus inside the body cells. In the near future, it is hoped that research will produce a vaccine against the virus. *See also* the Health and Medicine section on page 8-17.

Air sac *See* **Alveolus (air sac)**.

Albinism An inherited trait requiring two recessive genes resulting in individuals without pigment.

Algae Simple photosynthetic organisms. Algae may be composed of a single cell, a filament of cells, or a flat plate of cells. Cell walls of algae are made of cellulose. Algae have some characteristics of animal cells. With the exception of the red algae, most algal cells have centrioles. During cell division, most algal cells form a cell furrow like those in animal cells.

Alimentary canal *See* **Digestive system**.

Allantois An embryonic membranous sac that stores the nitrogenous wastes of reptiles and birds up to the time of hatching. In mammals, it forms part of the placenta.

Alleles Two or more genes that have the same positions on homologous chromosomes. Alleles are separated from each other during meiosis and come together again at fertilization when homologous alleles are paired, one from the sperm cell and one from the egg cell. Two or more alleles determine a trait.

Allergy The sensitivity of some people to substances that are quite harmless to most other people. The cells of these sensitive people produce antibodies to ward off whatever substance affects them. The antibodies become attached to the tissue cells, rendering the person sensitized. Whenever that particular substance enters the body again, it reacts with the attached antibodies and damages the cells. These damaged cells prompt certain symptoms such as itching, sneezing, tearing eyes, red welts, large hives, fever, and a general feeling of not being well.

Allopatric speciation Speciation brought about when an ancestral population becomes separated by one or more geographical barriers that prevent dispersal. An example is Death Valley where each isolated spring has its own water temperature and salinity and each is a habitat for a different species of pupfish.

Alternation of generations The sea lettuce *Ulva* is a green algae that lives in saltwater. The life cycle of *Ulva* is described as alternation of generations because one generation of *Ulva* is produced sexually by gametes while the next generation is produced asexually by zoospores. The gametophyte generation is a haploid thallus from which small, flagellated gametes are released into the water. They pair off and fuse. Each fused pair of gametes forms a zygote that, after a short time, becomes a diploid thallus of a new generation of *Ulva*. The diploid thallus is the sporophyte generation. It produces haploid zoospores that develop and grow into a haploid thallus, which is now the gametophyte. Many other simple organisms also have an alternation of gametophyte and sporophyte generations.

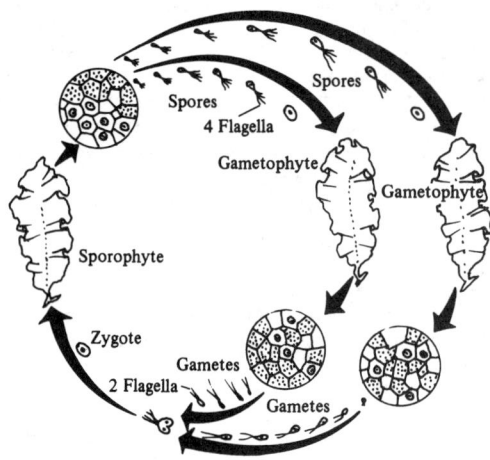

Alternation of generations in sea lettuce (*Ulva*)

Alveolus (air sac)   A minute air sac in the lungs through which oxygen enters the bloodstream and through which carbon dioxide and water are excreted from the bloodstream.

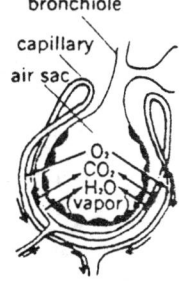

Gas exchange in the air sac (alveolus)

Alzheimer's disease   Progressive mental deterioration more often in older people. Recent research has revealed that nerve cells in parts of the brain are damaged by an accumulation of amyloid proteins.

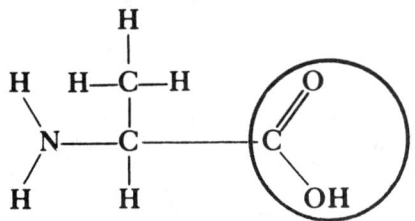

The structural formula of an amino acid
(The acid group of the molecule is circled.)

Amino acids   All proteins are built from small molecular units known as amino acids. The amino acid molecules link together in a particular way through peptide bonds. A dipeptide consists of two amino acids. A polypeptide contains many amino acid molecules. A protein is composed of one or more polypeptide chains.

Amniocentesis   The procedure of amniocentesis in which a small amount of amniotic fluid is removed from a pregnant woman and is used to study cells of the embryo. In this way certain chromosomal defects can be determined before birth.

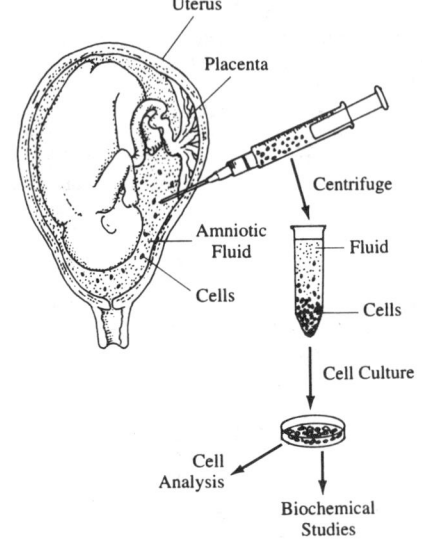

Amniocentesis is a safe method of determining if a newborn will be afflicted with a birth defect

Amnion   *See* **Embryonic membranes**.
Amniotic fluid   The fluid that surrounds the developing embryo in mammals, birds, and reptiles.

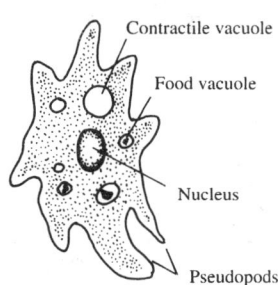

Amoeba *proteus*

Amoeba   The members of the phylum Sarcodina are described as being amoeboid. Amoeba *proteus* is the species most often studied. Species included in the Sarcodina move by means of pseudopods, flowing extensions of the flexible and amorphous body. The pseudopods also serve in food-catching. Most of the sarcodines live in fresh water. A contractile vacuole, an organelle designed to expel excess water from the protist cell body, plays an important role in maintaining water balance. Food is temporarily stored in a food vacuole where it is digested by the action of enzymes.

Amphibian   An amphibian must spend part of its life cycle in the water where its eggs are laid and fertilized. The eggs develop into a larval stage, or tadpole, that has fish-like characteristics. In tadpoles breathing is by means of gills, blood is pumped by a two-chambered heart, and swimming is by means of tail and body movements made possible by muscles in the body wall. Most amphibians undergo metamorphosis into a lung-breathing adult with a 3-chambered heart.

Anaerobic   Referring to a type of cellular respiration that occurs without oxygen such as fermentation. Referring also to certain species of bacteria, such as the *tetanus bacilli*, that live in an atmosphere devoid of oxygen.

Anaphase   A stage in mitosis in which the chromosomes are pulled apart. *See* **Mitosis**.

Angiosperms   Flowering plants that form seeds inside ovaries. Examples are apple, rose, and dandelion.

Animal kingdom   All animals belong to the kingdom Animalia, a grouping of 29 phyla. Twenty-eight of these phyla include animals called invertebrates because they do not have a vertebral column, or true backbone, the 29th phylum includes the vertebrates, animals with a vertebral column.

Annelid   The annelids are segmented worms that live in soil, fresh water, or the sea. Most of the annelids are free-living, although some of the marine forms burrow in tubes and some species (class Myzostoma) are parasites on echinoderms. The body of an annelid is divided into a series of similar segments and is said to be metamerically segmented. Most annelids have a closed circulatory system where the blood is contained in vessels. Enlarged muscular blood vessels function as hearts and pump the blood through the system of vessels. Annelids may be dioecious (have separate sexes) or hermaphroditic. Most annelid species go through a ciliated larval stage known as the trochophore larva. This is a larva of evolutionary importance because the same type appears in several phyla.

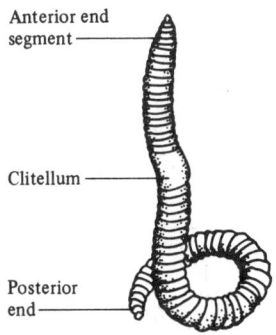

Earthworm

Annual   A plant in which the life cycle is completed in a single year or growing season, such as corn, tomato, and beans.

Anther   Pollen producing organ in the flower.

Antibiotic   An organic compound that is made and secreted by a living organism (commonly a mold) and is able to prevent the growth and reproduction of another species. Example: Penicillin is synthesized and secreted by the mold *Penicillium notatum*.

Antibodies   The body produces substances known as antibodies to fight disease-producing agents. Antibody production is a relatively slow process. FIrst of all, the body cells must recognize the invading agent as "foreign"—an antigen—and then produce an antibody that is exactly right to immobilize the protein invader. Finally, the blood cells must go into full scale production of this specific antibody. An antibody is specific against "a particle" type of germ. For example: diphtheria antibodies will not be effective against scarlet fever antigen.

Anticoagulant   A substance that prevents blood from clotting. Heparin is an anticoagulant.

Anticodon   A "triplet" of nucleotides in transfer RNA that is able to pair with a complementary triplet (a codon) in messenger RNA, thus arranging transfer RNA to the proper site on the messenger RNA.

Antigen   A foreign protein that stimulates the formation of antibodies by the immune system.

Antitoxin   An antibody that works against a specific toxin.

Anus   The body opening at the posterior end of the alimentary canal.

Aorta   A large artery that carries blood away from the heart. *See* diagram **Heart structure**.

Apical dominance   A process in which the terminal bud (top of the stem) in plants inhibits the growth of buds at the sides of the stem.

Appendix   A small protruding pouch without function positioned where the small intestine joins the large intestine. *See* **Digestive system**.

Arachnids   The class to which spiders belong. The body of the spider is divided into the cephalothorax and the abdomen. The cephalothorax has six pairs of jointed appendages. Spinnerets at the end of the abdomen are projections through which the spider spins webs. Most spiders breathe by book lungs. Other members of the class Arachnida are mites, ticks, scorpions, horseshoe crabs, and harvestmen.

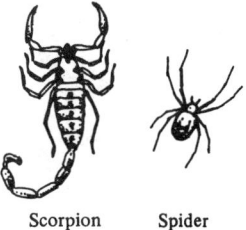

Scorpion   Spider

Arachnida

Archegonium   The multicellular, water-retaining structure, in which a single egg is produced and fertilized in the liverworts, mosses, and hornworts.

Archenteron   The cavity appearing in the early embryo during the gastrula stage that ultimately becomes the gut cavity.

Arteriole   A small artery.

Artery   A blood vessel that transports blood from the heart to the organs and tissues of the body.

Arthropods   The arthropod group is by far the largest group of animals with respect to the number

BIOLOGY

of species it contains. They share the common characteristics of having segmented bodies, jointed appendages, and exoskeletons.

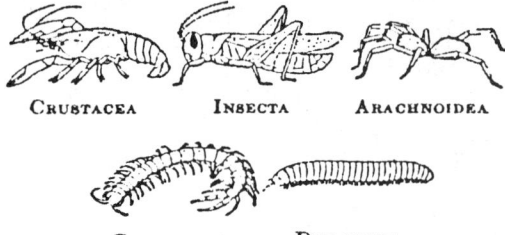

CRUSTACEA   INSECTA   ARACHNOIDEA

CHILOPODA   DIPLOPODA

Representative arthropods

Asexual reproduction   Involves only one parent. The parent may divide and become two new cells, thus obliterating the parent generation. Or the new individual may arise from a part of the parent cell; in such a case, the parent remains. Types of asexual reproduction are binary fission, sporulation budding, regeneration, and parthenogenesis.

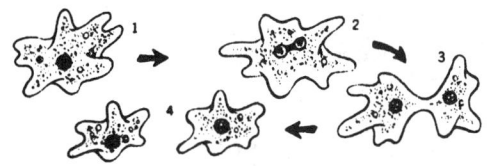

Fission in Amoebae

Assimilation   Involves the changing of certain nutrients into the protoplasm of cells.

Atoms   Elements are made of invisible building blocks called atoms. Each atom has a central nucleus surrounded by a definite number of moving negatively charged *electrons*.

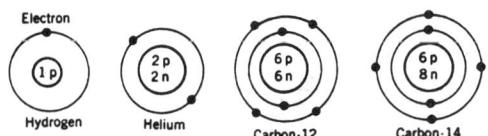

Electron

1p — Hydrogen

2p 2n — Helium

6p 6n — Carbon-12

6p 8n — Carbon-14

Atomic structure

ATP (Adenosine triphosphate)   The compound that stores energy produced during cellular respiration and releases this energy when needed for the cell's work. Energy produced during cellular respiration is passed on to adenosine diphosphate (ADP), which then becomes upgraded to ATP.

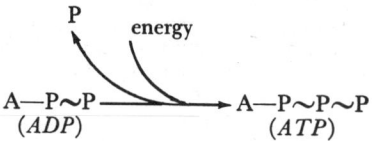

$$\text{A—P} \sim \text{P} \xrightarrow{\text{energy}} \text{A—P} \sim \text{P} \sim \text{P}$$
$$(ADP) \qquad\qquad (ATP)$$

Atrium   The chamber of the heart (also known as the auricle) that receives blood and passes it to the ventricle for pumping.

Autonomic nervous system   *See* **Nervous system, autonomic**.

Autosome   A chromosome that does not determine sex. Human cells have 22 pairs of autosomes.

Autotrophs   Organisms that are able to change inorganic materials into organic compounds. Among these are the photosynthetic bacteria and the green plants that use light energy to produce food. The chemosynthetic bacteria are capable of oxidizing the inorganic compounds of ammonia, nitrites, sulfur, or hydrogen gas into high-energy, organic compounds without the need of light energy.

Auxins   Plant hormones called auxins are produced by actively growing plant tissues like the growing tips of roots and branches, developing leaves, or flowers and fruits. They promote cell enlargement, which is one phase of growth (the other is cell division).

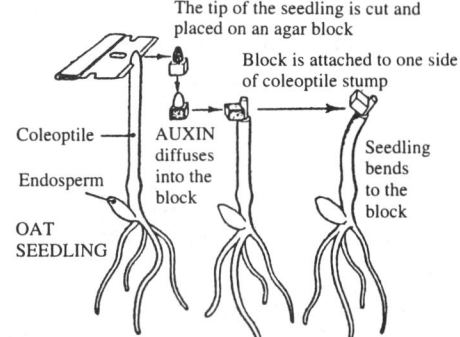

The tip of the seedling is cut and placed on an agar block

Block is attached to one side of coleoptile stump

Coleoptile

AUXIN diffuses into the block

Endosperm

Seedling bends to the block

OAT SEEDLING

Method of testing for effect of auxins

Axon   Extension of the neuron (nerve cell) that can carry impulses; is often the longest and least branched process of the cyton (cell body) and usually carries impulses away from the cell body of the neuron.

B cell   A white blood cell known as a lymphocyte produced in the bone marrow that works with T cell lymphocytes to destroy germs.

Back cross (test cross)   Plant and animal breeders mate an individual with a particular dominant trait to an individual that is recessive to determine if the dominant trait is pure or hybrid. As a result of this mating, if organisms appear that have the recessive trait, then the breeder knows that the parent individual is hybrid (heterozygous) for the dominant trait.

Bacteria   Bacteria are the smallest living organisms. They range in length from 0.2–7 micrometers; in diameter from 0.2–2 micrometers. As you recall, the unit used to measure bacteria is the micrometer and is equivalent to 1/1000 of a millimeter. The smallest cells known are the mycoplasmas, which have only one-half the DNA of other bacterial cells. The mycoplasmas are bacteria that live only as parasites on or in the bodies of plants and animals. Despite their small size bacteria are true cells: they provide their own genetic material (DNA and RNA) and the necessary cytoplasm for their own reproduction; they have multienzyme systems to control biochemical activities necessary for the life of the cell; and they build their own ATP molecules and use the stored energy to synthesize other organic compounds. Bacterial shapes include spheres (cocci), rods (bacilli), and spirals (spirilla). *See also* **Eubacteria—true bacteria**.

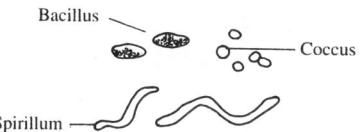

Bacteriophage A virus that infects a bacterial cell.

Biennial A plant for which the life cycle is two years. Vegetative growth occurs during the first year; flowering, the second. Beets and carrots are examples.

Bilateral symmetry Two sided, as demonstrated by animals that have an anterior (head end) and a posterior (tail end), a right and left side that are similar. For example: a human being shows bilateral symmetry, as does a horse. If sliced down the middle, each has two identical halves.

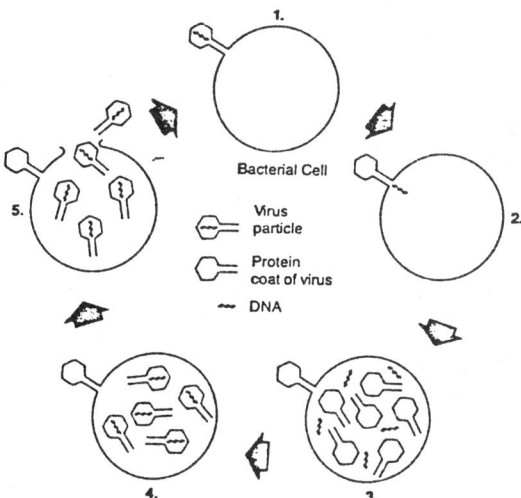

Replication of a bacteriophage inside of a bacterial cell

Binary fission A form of asexual reproduction in which a parent organism divides into two identical daughter cells. The nucleus goes through mitosis. The cytoplasm divides equally.

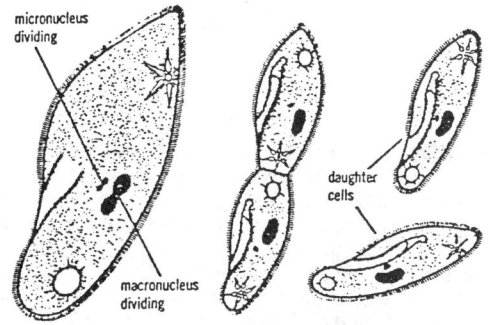

Binary fission in the paramecium

Binomial nomenclature The scientific naming of species by a double name. The first name in the binomial is the genus name. This system was developed by Carolus Linnaeus (1707–1788) and has become a worldwide standard for classifying and naming organisms.

The Genus Quercus

Scientific Name	Common Name
Quercus alba	white oak
Quercus coccinea	scarlet oak
Quercus montana	chestnut oak
Quercus rubra	red oak
Quercus suber	cork oak
Quercus virginiana	live oak

Biogenesis The doctrine that living things come only from other living things of like kind.

Biogeochemical cycles Certain compounds cycle through the abiotic portion and the biotic communities of ecosystems. These compounds contain elements that are necessary to the biochemical processes that are carried out in living cells. Among these elements are carbon, hydrogen, oxygen, and nitrogen. In elemental form, they are useless to cells and must be combined in chemical compounds. Let us trace the pathways of some of the vital compounds from the earth to living organisms to the atmosphere and back to earth. This cycle of events is best described by the term biogeochemical cycles. See figure.

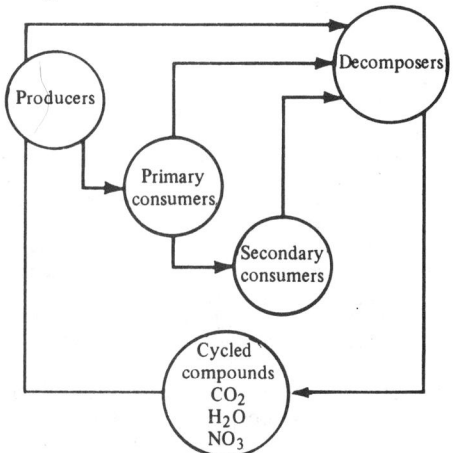

Biogeochemical cycle

Biology The study of living things; an extensive science including botany, zoology, bacteriology, genetics, physiology, anatomy, and many others.

Biome A climax community in a broad geographical area having one type of climate. Examples of biomes are the Taiga, coniferous forests of Canada; the Desert, regions where the annual rainfall is less than 6.5 centimeters; the Grasslands, annual rainfall is low and irregular; the Tropical Rain Forest, characterized by high temperatures and constant rainfall; and the Marine biome, the sea.

Biomes, world A climax community in a broad geographical area having one type of climate is known as a biome. The earth is divided into several biomes.

The Tundra. Vast stretches of treeless plains surrounding the Arctic Ocean where cold is the limiting factor. Plant life consists of lichens, mosses, grasses, and sedges. Animal life includes the musk ox, caribou, polar bears, wolves, foxes, and some marine mammals.

The Taiga. The coniferous forests of Canada and Russia where spruce and fir trees predominate. The kinds of mammals that live in this region are the black bear, the wolf, lynx, and squirrel.

The Deciduous Forest. These are forests of temperate regions, where broad-leaved trees that lose their leaves in the winter predominate. The types of animals that live in these forests are deer, fox, squirrel, skunk, woodchuck, and raccoon.

The Desert. Deserts form in regions where the annual rainfall is less than 6.5 centimeters and where evaporation of water is high. Creosote, sagebrush, and cacti are plants adapted for the desert. The animals include lizards, insects, kangaroo rats, and arachnids.

The Grasslands. These regions have low annual rainfall. Grasslands are located in regions that are sheltered from moisture-laden rainfall. The animals that predominate in temperate grasslands, called steppes or prairies, are bobcats, badgers, hawks, kit foxes, owls, and coyotes. Typical animals of tropical grasslands or savannas are zebras, giraffes, baboons, and gazelles.

The Tropical Rain Forest. The tropical rain forest is characterized by high temperatures and constant rainfall. This type of biome is found in Central and South America, in Southeast Asia, and in West Africa. The trees are tall and the vegetation is so thick that the forest floor is shaded from light. The animals of the rain forest include monkeys, lizards, snakes, and birds.

The Sea. Ocean waters cover almost three fourths of the earth's surface and support the greatest abundance and diversity of organisms in the world. Averaging 3.5–4.5 kilometers in depth, a marine biome constitutes the thickest layer of living things in the biosphere. The dominating physical factors determine the type of living organisms that compose its communities.

Biometrics The science that combines mathematics and statistics needed to deal with the facts and figures of biology. Biologists handle enormous numbers that must be organized and simplified so that they become useful in the analysis of data.

Biotic environment The part of the environment that is living and has some effect on other living organisms.

Bipedalism The ability to walk on two legs instead of four. Bipedalism has freed the forearms for doing work.

Birds Birds are terrestrial vertebrates with feathers. Feathers are the distinctive feature of birds: all birds have them and no other animals are so covered. The forelimb is modified into wings for flight, leaving the hindlimbs for walking (bipedal locomotion). Birds are built for flight; special adaptations in body structure effect lightness in weight, efficiency, and strength. Not only are the feathers light in weight

and easily moved and lifted by wind, but they also create warmth next to the body. Body heat warms the air that is in contact with the bird's body. Warm air becomes lighter and rises. Other adaptations for flight are the compact, but hollow, bones, numerous air sacs occupying all available body spaces, reduced rectum, loss of teeth, and feathers replacing a bony tail.

Bivalves Animals, such as clams, that have the body encased within two hinged shells. Lining the inner surfaces of the shells is a membranous mantle. The cavity inside of the shells is the mantle cavity.

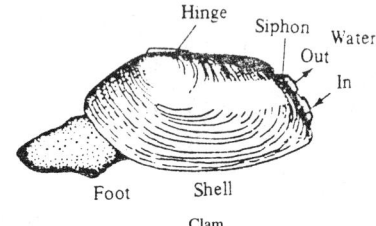

Clam

Blastula An early stage in animal embryology; a hollow ball of cells surrounding a central cavity. *See* **Cleavage**.

Blood A liquid tissue consisting of a liquid medium called plasma and three kinds of cells: red blood cells (erythrocytes), white blood cells (leucocytes), and platelets. There are about 25 trillion red blood cells in the human body. For each 600 red blood cells there is one white blood cell. Blood cells number in the billions. The red blood cells carry oxygen. The white blood cells function in immune reactions.

Blood clotting Platelets are the smallest blood particles. When a capillary is cut, the platelets collect at the site of the injury. There they break into smaller fragments and initiate the complicated chemical process of blood clotting in which more than 15 factors, including thromboplastin, calcium (Ca^{27}), and fibrinogen, are involved in the formation of a clot containing blood cells in a fibrin meshwork.

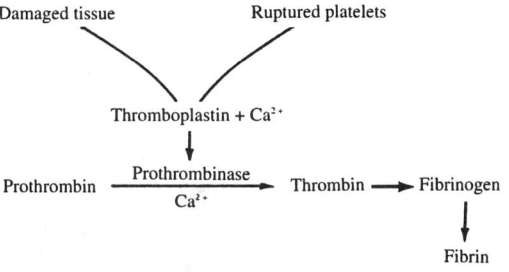

Some steps of the blood clotting process

Blood types The main types of blood are A, B, AB, and O. Transfusions of blood are possible only when the blood types are compatible. If the blood types are not compatible proteins in the plasma will recognize foreign antigens on red blood cells and respond by causing the cells to agglutinate, or clump, a condition that causes blockage in small blood vessels and often death. The following table summarizes the blood proteins involved in blood types.

Proteins of Blood Types

Blood Type	Cell Antigen	Plasma Antibody
A	A	b
B	B	a
AB	AB	none
O	none	a and b

Note: Type AB—universal recipient
Type O—universal donor

Bone   The living tissue that comprises the skeleton. Bone tissue is made of cells that are surrounded by hardened calcium phosphate.

Bowman's capsule   *See* **Nephron.**

Brain   The brain and the spinal cord compose the central nervous system. In the vertebrate body, the organs of the central nervous system are well protected by being wrapped in connective tissue and enclosed in bone. The brain, covered by the membranous meninges, rests in the skull cavity where it is enclosed by the cranium. The spinal cord, also covered by connective tissue, is circled by the vertebral column. The human brain is divided into many parts, each with special functions. Among the most important parts are the cerebrum, cerebellum, and medulla.

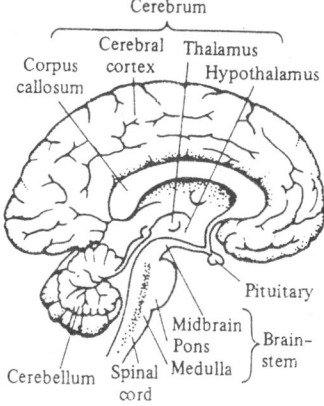

The human brain

Bronchi (Bronchus)   Two tubes made of cartilage rings that extend from the windpipe (trachea) into the lungs (*see* **Lungs**).

Bronchioles   Small tubes in the lungs that branch off from the bronchi. Each bronchiole ends in an air sac called the alveolus. *See* **Respiratory system.**

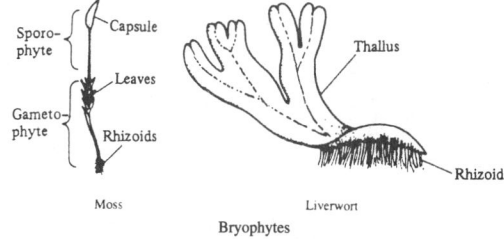

Bryophytes

Bryophytes   The bryophytes are the first green land plants. They are primitive, small, and inconspicuous. Although multicellular, the tissue differentiation is quite simple. Bryophyte species have no tissues that are specialized for water-carrying and no cambium specialized for growing new cells. Bryophyte species do not have true stems, leaves, or roots. Simple root-like structures called **rhizoids** anchor the plants to the ground and absorb moisture from the soil.

Budding   A form of asexual reproduction in which the parent cell body gives rise to a bud. The bud has the same number and kind of chromosomes as the parent cell, but has much less cytoplasm than the parent cell. The bud develops into a new individual. Example: yeast cells reproduce by budding.

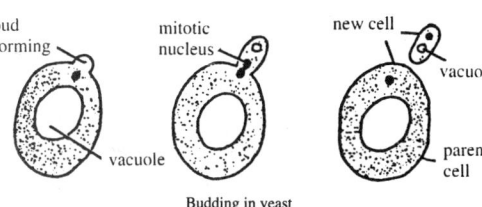

Budding in yeast

C

Calorie   The amount of heat required to raise the temperature of one gram of water by one degree Celsius (1°C). (A kilocalorie is the amount of heat needed to raise the temperature of one kilogram of water by 1°C.)

Calvin cycle   The second major stage of photosynthesis involves reductive carbon dioxide fixation. Because the cyclic reactions that function at this time do not require light as a source of energy, the term dark reaction has been used to designate this phase of photosynthesis. Calvin and his associates determined the path of carbon in the carbon dioxide by the use of ^{14}C. *See* **Photosynthesis.**

Cambium   *See* **Woody stems.**

Capillary   The smallest blood vessel.

Carbohydrates   Are characteristically composed of carbon, hydrogen, and oxygen in the proportion of CH_2O. The hydrogen and oxygen are in the same proportion in carbohydrates as in water.

Carboxyl group   *See* **Amino acids.**

Carcinogen   Any substance or radiation that causes cancer; asbestos, the herbicide dioxin, or radiation from radioactive materials, sunlight, or X rays are examples.

Carnivores   Flesh eaters such as snakes, frogs, hawks, and coyotes.

Carrier-facilitated diffusion   Transport of a substance across the plasma membrane by carrier molecules but without energy. This process cannot effect the net transport of a substance from a region of low concentration to a region of high concentration. This is a form of passive transport.

Carrying capacity   In ecology, the largest number of organisms of a given species that can be maintained indefinitely in a particular part of the environment.

Cartilage   A specialized type of dense connective tissue not as hard as bone, in which the cells are contained in a rubbery matrix that is smooth, firm, and flexible: occurs in joints, at the end of bones, and in the ears, nose, and windpipe.

Cell, animal

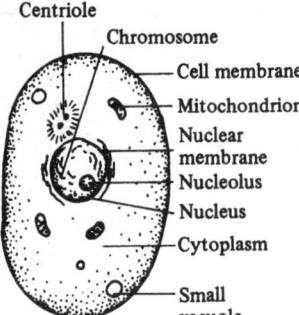

Typical animal cell

Cell, electron micrograph

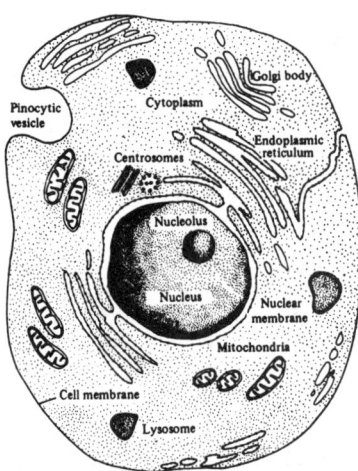

Electron micrograph of a cell

Cell, plant

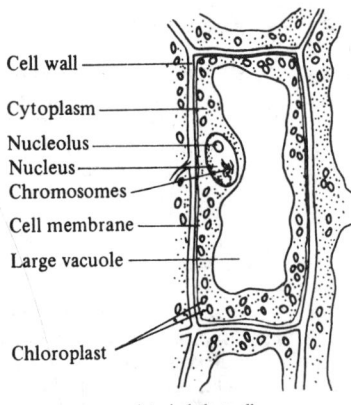

A typical plant cell

Catalyst   A chemical substance that speeds up a reaction without itself being used up in the overall course of the reaction. Enzymes are biological catalysts.

Cell   Each cell is a living unit. Whether living independently as a protist or confined in a tissue, a cell performs many metabolic functions to sustain life. Each cell is a biochemical factory using food molecules for energy, repair of tissues, growth, and ultimately, reproduction. On the chemical level, the cell carries out all of the life functions. Living organisms function the way they do because their cells have the properties of life. *See also* illustrations on pages 2-14 and 2-15.

Cell division   When a cell reaches a certain size it divides into two new cells, identical to each other and very similar to the original parent cell. The new cells are known as daughter cells. The events marking cell division differ in prokaryotes and eukaryotes. *See* **Mitosis**.

Cell membrane   The outer boundary of the cell, also called the *plasma membrane*, about 10 nanometers in width. The cell membrane controls the movement of substances into and out of the cell in a process known in general as *transport*. Highly selective as to the substances that cross its boundary, the cell membrane is said to be *semi-permeable*. Using the concept demonstrated by the *fluid mosaic model*, biologists explain how some molecules are able to penetrate the cell membrane while others cannot. According to this model, the core of the membrane is made up of *phospholipids*. Large circular proteins are set into the membrane; smaller proteins lie on the surface. The proteins and the phospholipids have special functions and form certain structural pathways that serve to admit or deny passage to specific molecules.

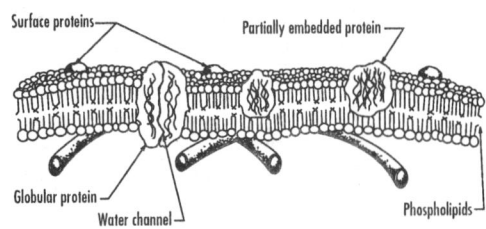

Fluid mosaic model of cell membrane

Cellulose   A straight chain polymer of glucose molecules secreted by plants and used as structural supporting material.

Cell wall   A relatively rigid structure composed of cellulose that encloses the cells of plants. The cell wall gives these cells their shape and limits their expansion in hypotonic media. *See* diagram **Cell, plant**.

Central nervous system   *See* **Brain**.

Centrioles   Paired structures that lie just outside of the nucleus of nearly all animal cells and some cells of lower plants. They are absent in cells of higher plants. Under the light microscope, the centrioles look like two insignificant granules, but the electron microscope demonstrates that they have a very intricate structure.

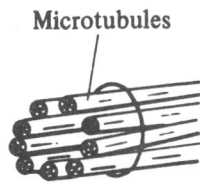

Microtubules

The fine structure of a centriole

Centromere   *See* **Chromatid** (diagram).

Cerebellum   *See* **Brain.**

Chemosynthesis   The production of high-energy organic compounds from inorganic raw materials without the aid of light energy by some bacteria that live on ammonia, nitrogen, and sulfur.

Chitin   Tough, nitrogen-containing polysaccharide that is present in the exoskeletons of insects and in the cell walls of most species of fungi.

Chlorophyll   *See* **Chloroplasts.**

Chloroplasts   A group of structures that has the general name *plastid*. Plastids are membrane-bound organelles found only in plant cells. Usually plastids are spherical bodies that float freely in the cytoplasm, holding pigment molecules or starch. Chloroplasts contain the green pigment chlorophyll, a substance that gives plants the green color. Chlorophyll is a special molecule that has the ability to trap light and to convert it to a form of energy that plants can use in carrying out the chemical steps of the food-making process known as photosynthesis. Each chloroplast is surrounded by a double membrane. Inside the chloroplast are numerous flattened membranous sacs called thylakoids (formerly called grana). The thylakoids are the structures that contain the chlorophyll and it is within these sacs that photosynthesis takes place. Stroma is the name given to the dense ground substance that cushions the thylakoids. Animal cells do not have chloroplasts and therefore cannot make their own food. The figure shows the fine structure of a chloroplast.

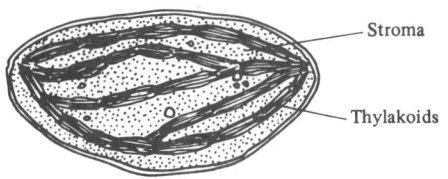

Stroma

Thylakoids

A chloroplast

Chordates   Set apart from lower animals by several distinguishing characteristics in addition to having a notochord. First, all chordate embryos have the three primary germ layers from which all specialized tissues and organs develop. Second, chordates are bilaterally symmetrical animals with anterior-posterior differentiation. Third, the body has a true coelom and a digestive tract that begins with a mouth and ends with an anus. Other characteristics that differentiate the chordates from other animals are the presence of pharyngeal gill slits and the dorsal hollow nerve cord.

Chromatography   A technique of separating substances, such as proteins in a complex liquid, by varying their rates of absorption on media such as filter paper or in a column of silicia gel.

Chromosomes   In the nucleus of the nondividing cell is a tangle of very fine threads that absorb stain quite readily. In the granular stage these threads are known as chromatin. The chromatin threads come together, shorten and thicken forming chromosomes that can be seen quite prominently in the dividing cell.

Chromosome Numbers of Some Common Species

Organism	Haploid No.	Diploid No.
mosquito	3	6
fruit fly	4	8
gall midge	20*	8*
evening primrose	7	14
onion	8	16
corn	10	20
grasshopper (female)	11	22
grasshopper (male)	10	21**
frog	13	26
sunflower	17	34
cat	23	38
human	23	46
plum	24	48
dog	39	78
sugar cane	40	80
goldfish	47	94

*   In the fertilized egg of the gall midge, 32 chromosomes become nonfunctional leaving 8 functional chromosomes.

**   The male grasshopper has only one sex chromosome.

Chromatid

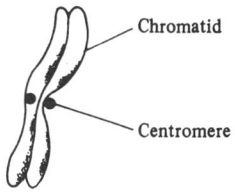

Chromatid

Centromere

Chromosome pair or chromatids hold together at centromere

Cilia   *See* **Flagella and cilia.**

Circulation   Distribution of blood pumped from the heart, through the arteries, arterioles, and capillaries to the body tissues. Blood is carried back to the heart by veins. *See* figure, page 2-12.

Circulatory system   The human circulatory system consists of the heart and the system of blood vessels that transport blood throughout the body. *See* **Heart.**

BIOLOGY

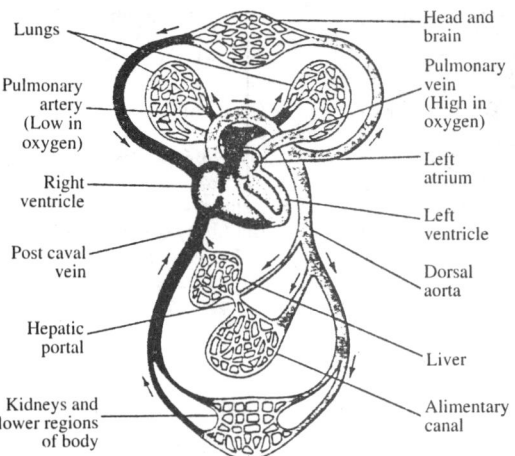

Lungs — Head and brain

Pulmonary artery (Low in oxygen) — Pulmonary vein (High in oxygen)

Right ventricle — Left atrium

Post caval vein — Left ventricle

Hepatic portal — Dorsal aorta

Kidneys and lower regions of body — Liver

— Alimentary canal

Cistron   The genetic unit of function, considered equivalent to a gene. Each cistron contains the genetic information for a single polypeptide chain.

Classification   The design of the classification system is a simple and practical one that easily lends itself to the addition of new names of organisms as they are discovered. Each group of organisms within the scheme is known as a taxon (plural, taxa). The classification groupings are as follows: kingdom, the largest and most inclusive group, followed by the phylum, class, order, family, genus, and species.

Cleavage   The fertilized egg goes through a series of cell divisions in which there is no growth in size of the zygote nor separation of the cells.

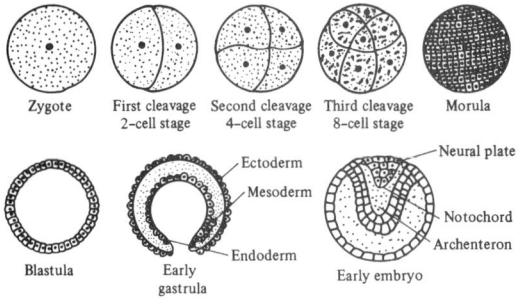

Zygote   First cleavage 2-cell stage   Second cleavage 4-cell stage   Third cleavage 8-cell stage   Morula

Blastula   Early gastrula   Early embryo

Ectoderm   Mesoderm   Endoderm   Neural plate   Notochord   Archenteron

Stages of cleavage

Climax community   A stable ecological community where one or two large trees predominate.

Clone   A population of cells (or whole organisms) that has descended from an original parent cell, which was stimulated to reproduce by asexual means.

Codominance   A form of inheritance in which neither of the allelic genes that determine a characteristic is dominant over the other. The result of this inheritance is a blend. When red-flowered primroses are crossed with white-flowered primroses, the offspring have pink flowers.

Codon   A "triplet" of three nucleotides in messenger RNA that directs the order of a particular amino acid in a protein molecule.

Coenzyme   An organic compound, not a protein, that supports the catalytic activity of an enzyme. Vitamins are coenzymes.

Coenocyte   A cell bounded by a single plasma membrane but containing many nuclei.

Cold-blooded animal   Poikilotherm. An animal whose body temperature changes with the external environment. Examples: fish, amphibians, reptiles.

Commensalism   *See* **Nutritional relationships**.

Community   All of the plant and animal populations living and interacting in a given environment are known as a community.

Compounds   Classified as organic or inorganic. Organic compounds are generally thought of as most compounds of carbon. Inorganic compounds are compounds made of other elements and a few carbon compounds similar to earthlike substances, like calcium carbonate ($CaCO_3$). Organic compounds are called organic because of the original belief that they came from living organisms. Today thousands of organic compounds not found in nature are being synthesized in laboratories. Both organic and inorganic compounds are necessary to life.

Conditioned behavior   A type of learned response in which a new response becomes associated with an original stimulus.

Conifers (cone bearers)   *See* **Gymnosperms**.

Conjugation   A form of sexual reproduction that is occasionally demonstrated by the ciliates. Two organisms will join together at the oral groove. The micronucleus of each will undergo meiosis, producing several cells. All but two of these in each organism disintegrate. One of these haploid micronuclei remains in each cell, while the other migrates into the other cell, fusing with the stationary gamete. The new nucleus—which is now diploid and contains a new genetic combination—goes through cell division producing a new macronucleus and a new micronucleus.

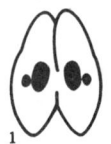 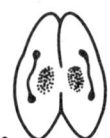 

1
Union by oral grooves.

2
Micronucleus of each undergoes meiosis; disintegration.

3
One micronucleus of each migrates to other cell.

4
Fusion with gamete; separation.

5
Fused nucleus undergoes division.

6
New organisms are formed.

Conjugation in paramecia

Consumers   Primary consumers—herbivores, or plant-eaters. Herbivores come in all sizes: crickets, leaf cutters, deer, and cattle. The carnivores, or flesh-eaters, such as snakes, frogs, hawks, and coyotes are secondary consumers because they feed on the herbivores. The tertiary consumers are those that feed on the smaller carnivores and herbivores as well. There are also scavengers in the ecosystem. Earthworms and ants feed on particles of dead

Human Respiratory System

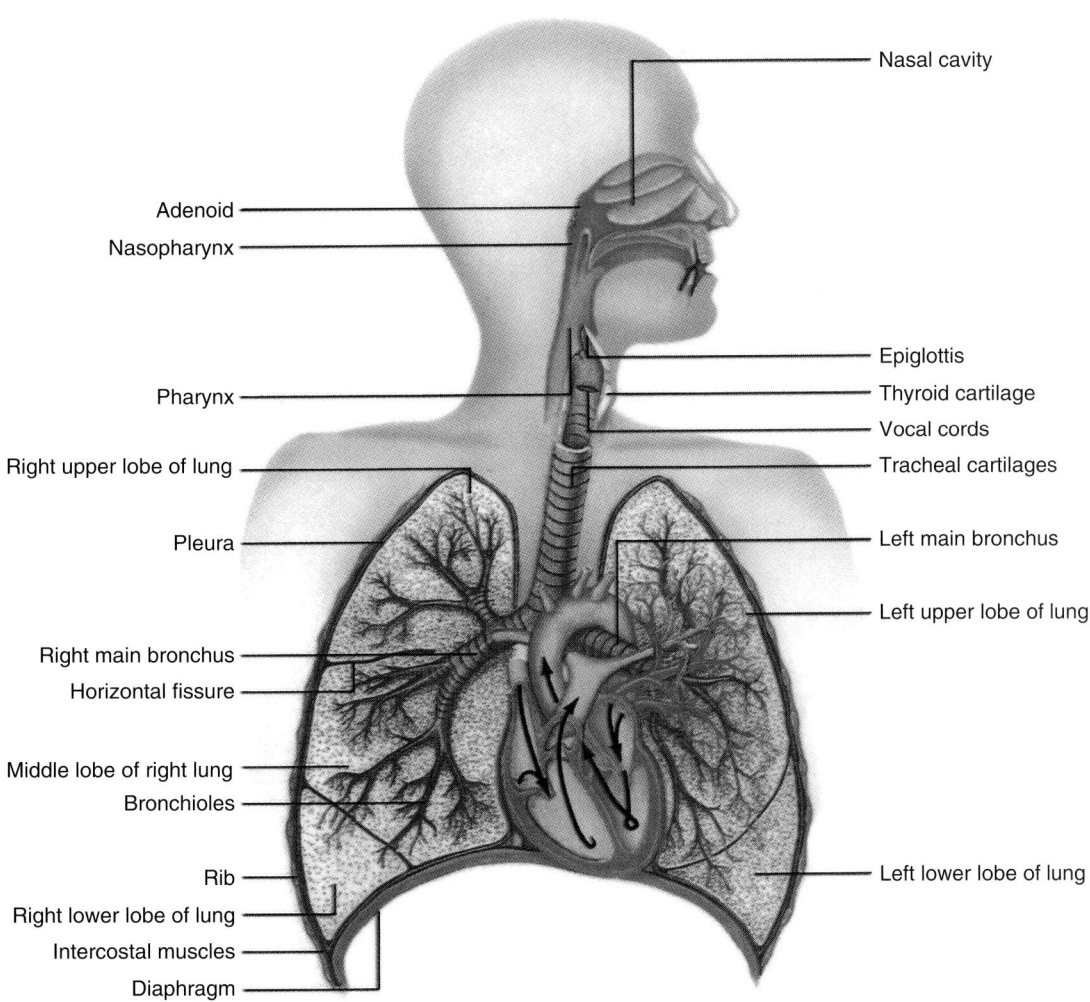

Nasal cavity

Adenoid

Nasopharynx

Epiglottis

Pharynx

Thyroid cartilage

Vocal cords

Right upper lobe of lung

Tracheal cartilages

Pleura

Left main bronchus

Left upper lobe of lung

Right main bronchus

Horizontal fissure

Middle lobe of right lung

Bronchioles

Rib

Left lower lobe of lung

Right lower lobe of lung

Intercostal muscles

Diaphragm

SOURCE: *Heath Biology*, ©1991. Reprinted by permission of D.C. Heath and Company.

Typical Animal Cell

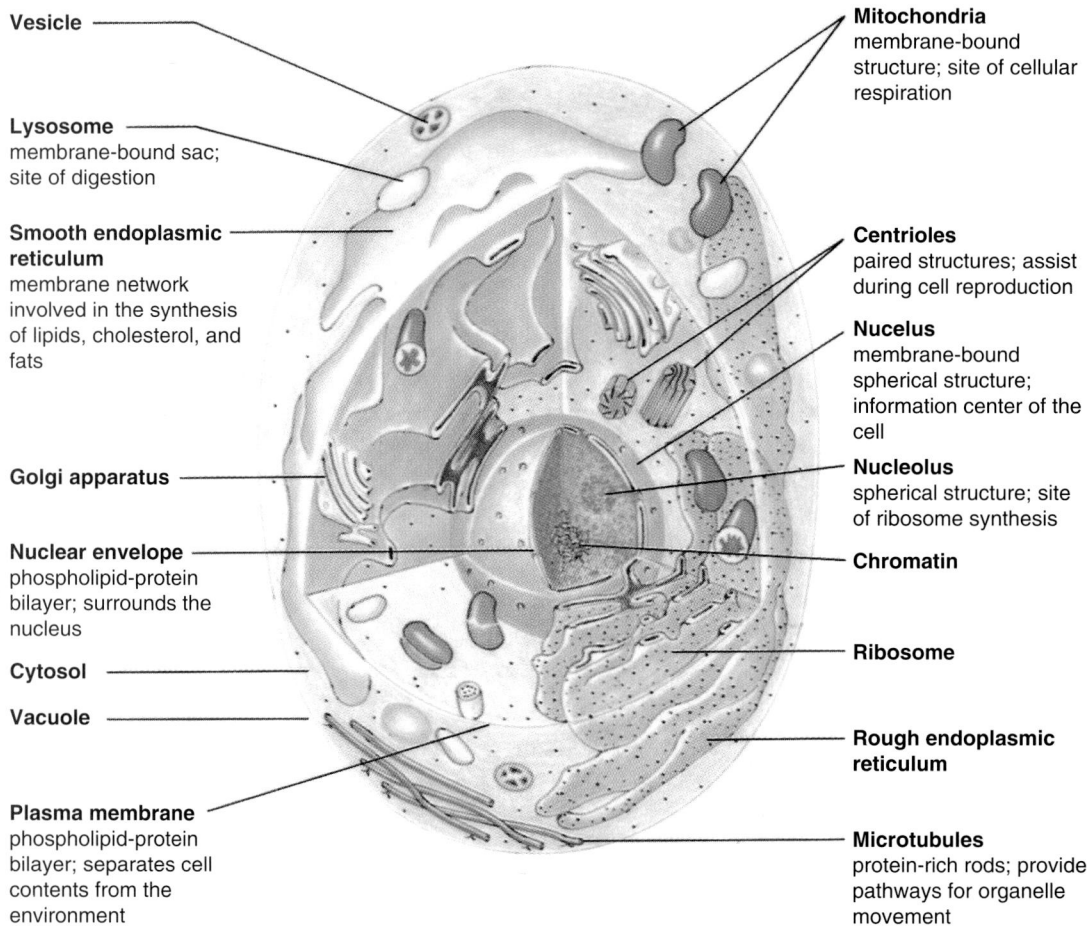

Vesicle

Lysosome
membrane-bound sac;
site of digestion

Smooth endoplasmic reticulum
membrane network
involved in the synthesis
of lipids, cholesterol, and
fats

Golgi apparatus

Nuclear envelope
phospholipid-protein
bilayer; surrounds the
nucleus

Cytosol

Vacuole

Plasma membrane
phospholipid-protein
bilayer; separates cell
contents from the
environment

Mitochondria
membrane-bound
structure; site of cellular
respiration

Centrioles
paired structures; assist
during cell reproduction

Nucelus
membrane-bound
spherical structure;
information center of the
cell

Nucleolus
spherical structure; site
of ribosome synthesis

Chromatin

Ribosome

Rough endoplasmic reticulum

Microtubules
protein-rich rods; provide
pathways for organelle
movement

SOURCE: *Heath Biology*, ©1991. Reprinted by permission of D.C. Heath and Company.

Typical Plant Cell

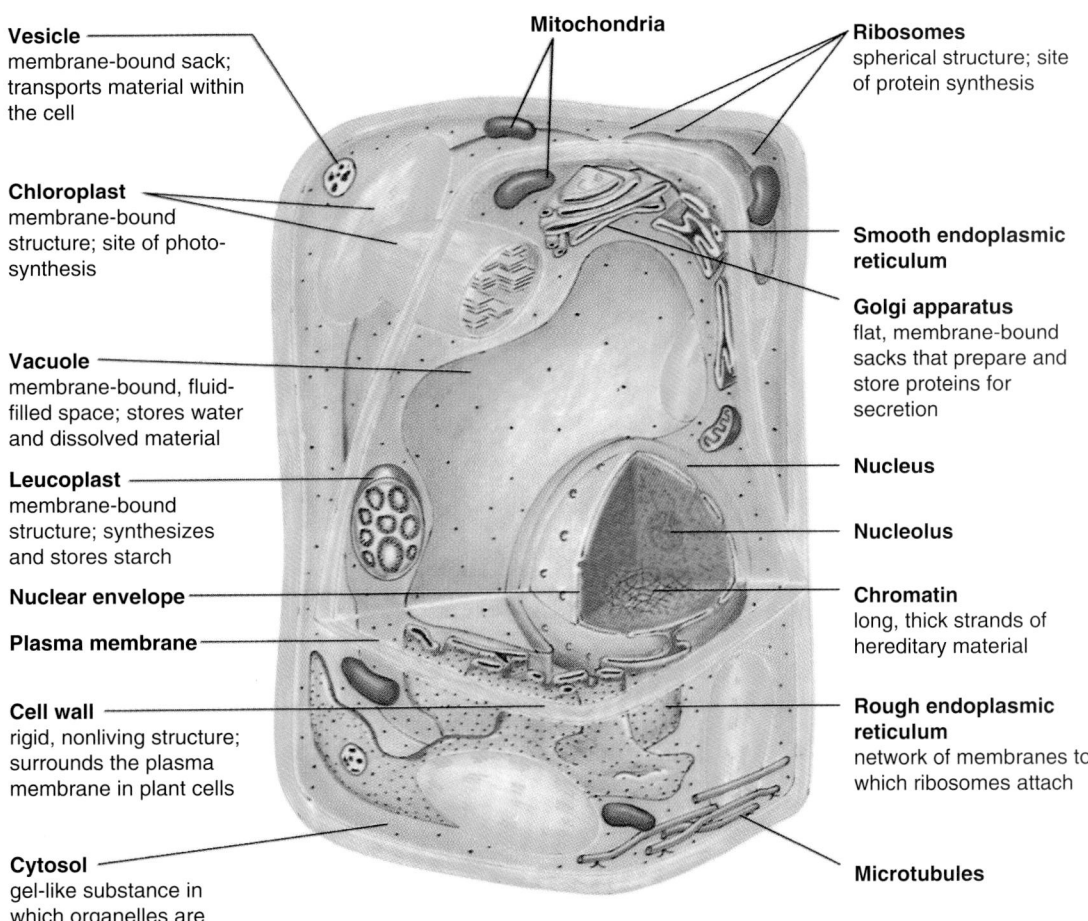

Vesicle
membrane-bound sack; transports material within the cell

Chloroplast
membrane-bound structure; site of photosynthesis

Vacuole
membrane-bound, fluid-filled space; stores water and dissolved material

Leucoplast
membrane-bound structure; synthesizes and stores starch

Nuclear envelope

Plasma membrane

Cell wall
rigid, nonliving structure; surrounds the plasma membrane in plant cells

Cytosol
gel-like substance in which organelles are suspended

Mitochondria

Ribosomes
spherical structure; site of protein synthesis

Smooth endoplasmic reticulum

Golgi apparatus
flat, membrane-bound sacks that prepare and store proteins for secretion

Nucleus

Nucleolus

Chromatin
long, thick strands of hereditary material

Rough endoplasmic reticulum
network of membranes to which ribosomes attach

Microtubules

SOURCE: *Heath Biology*, ©1991. Reprinted by permission of D.C. Heath and Company.

Evolutionary History of Life

3.5 Billion Years Ago	570 Million Years Ago

PRECAMBRIAN ERA	**PALEOZOIC ERA**

- First cells
- Simple, many-celled animals in ocean

- Simple ocean plants
- First fish
- Plants invade land

- First land animals (ancestors of spiders and insects)

SOURCE: *Heath Biology*, ©1991. Reprinted by permission of D.C. Heath and Company.

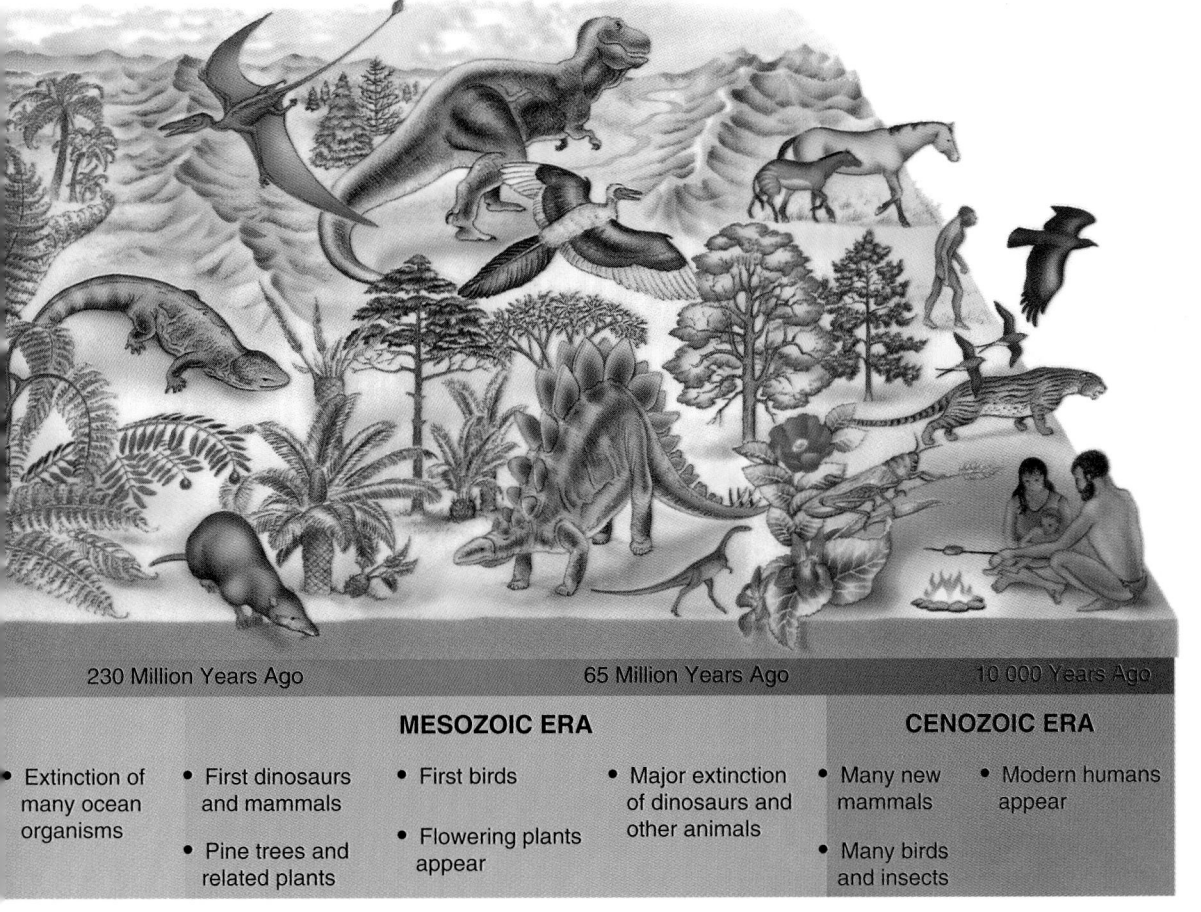

230 Million Years Ago		65 Million Years Ago		10 000 Years Ago
	MESOZOIC ERA			**CENOZOIC ERA**
• Extinction of many ocean organisms	• First dinosaurs and mammals • Pine trees and related plants	• First birds • Flowering plants appear	• Major extinction of dinosaurs and other animals	• Many new mammals • Many birds and insects	• Modern humans appear

Five Kingdoms of Living Things

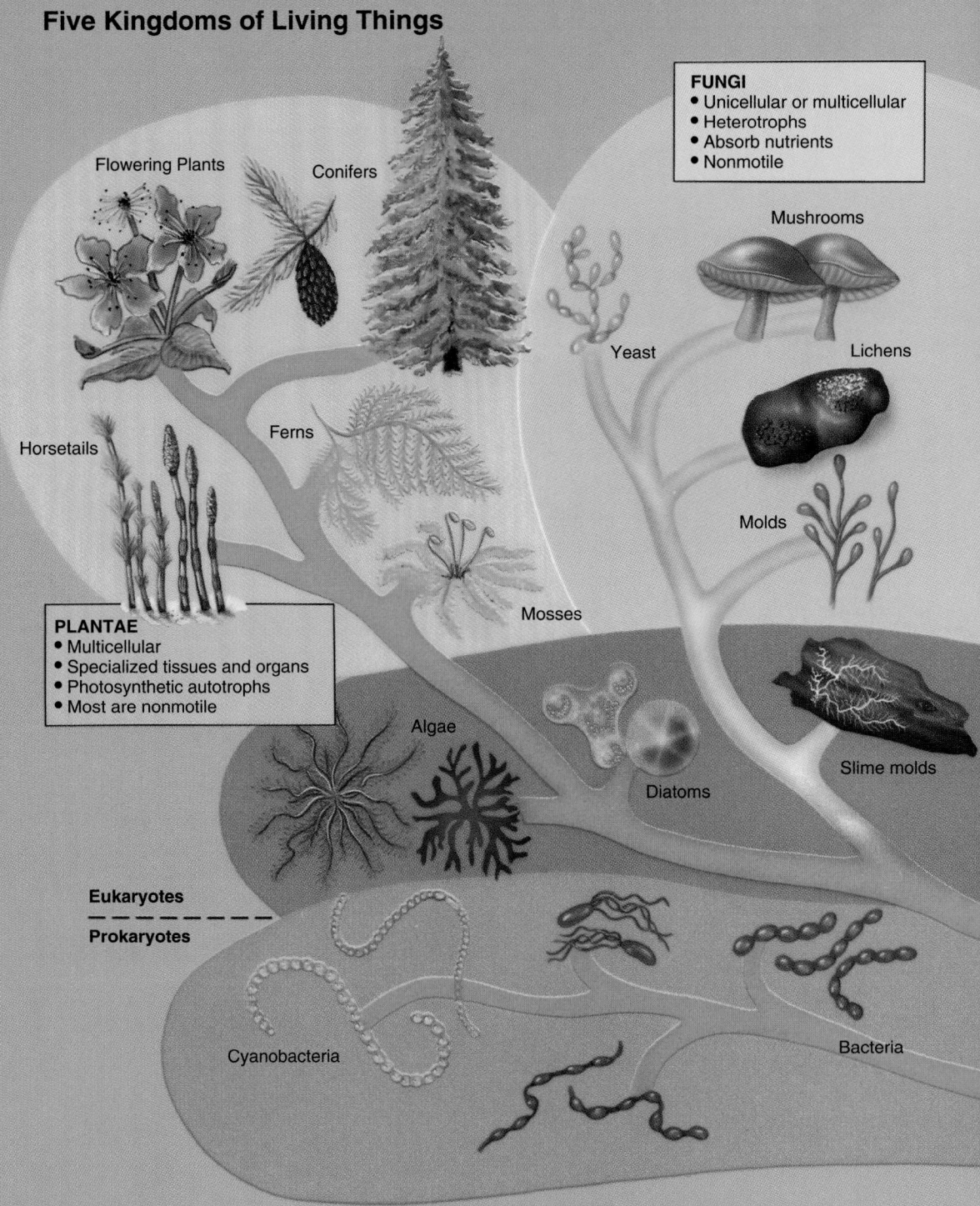

FUNGI
- Unicellular or multicellular
- Heterotrophs
- Absorb nutrients
- Nonmotile

Flowering Plants

Conifers

Mushrooms

Yeast

Lichens

Horsetails

Ferns

Molds

PLANTAE
- Multicellular
- Specialized tissues and organs
- Photosynthetic autotrophs
- Most are nonmotile

Mosses

Slime molds

Algae

Diatoms

Eukaryotes
— — — — — — — — —
Prokaryotes

Cyanobacteria

Bacteria

SOURCE: *Heath Biology*, ©1991. Reprinted by permission of D.C. Heath and Company.

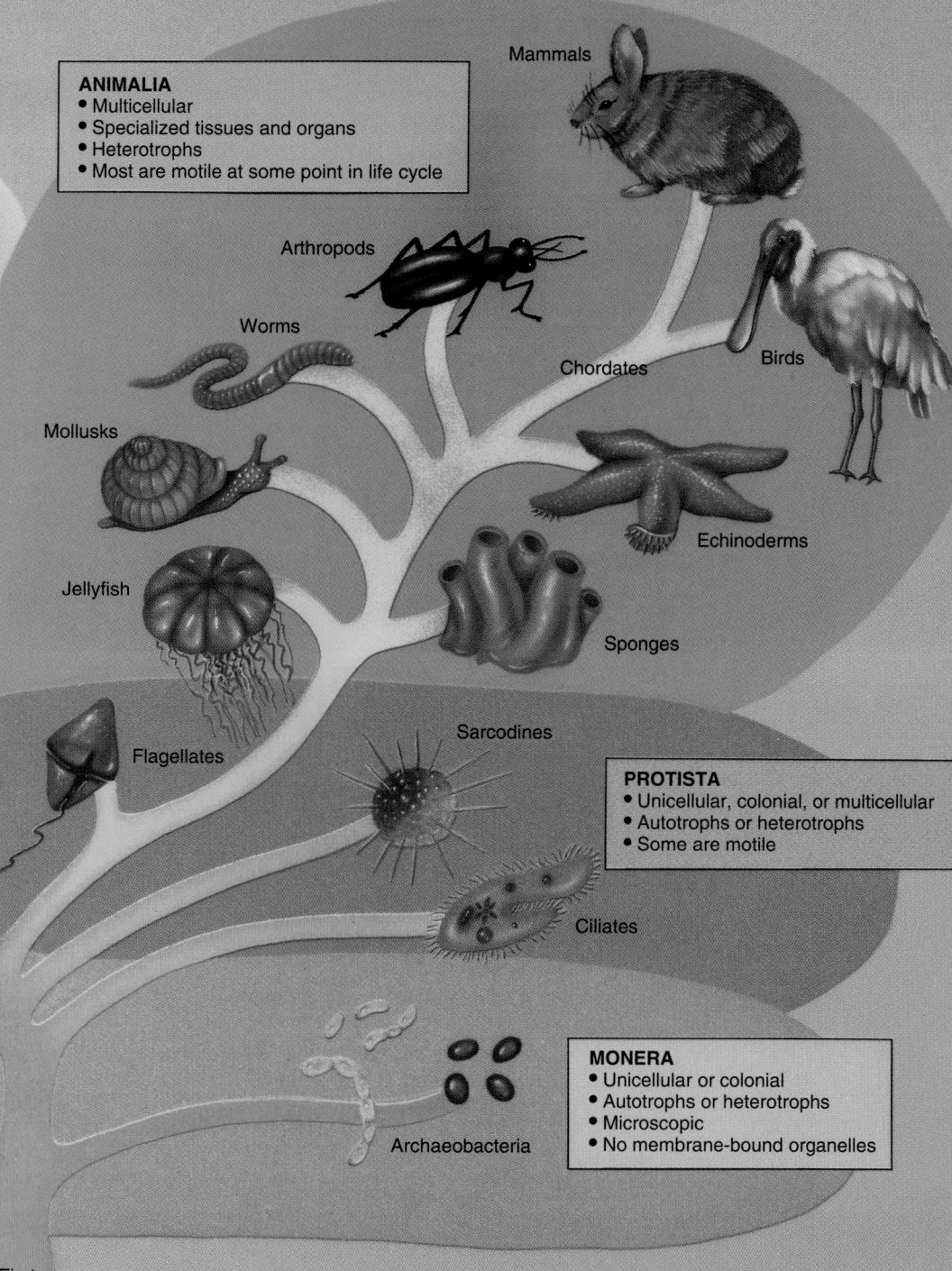

ANIMALIA
- Multicellular
- Specialized tissues and organs
- Heterotrophs
- Most are motile at some point in life cycle

Mammals

Arthropods

Worms

Chordates

Birds

Mollusks

Echinoderms

Jellyfish

Sponges

Flagellates

Sarcodines

PROTISTA
- Unicellular, colonial, or multicellular
- Autotrophs or heterotrophs
- Some are motile

Ciliates

MONERA
- Unicellular or colonial
- Autotrophs or heterotrophs
- Microscopic
- No membrane-bound organelles

Archaeobacteria

First cells

Human Muscle System

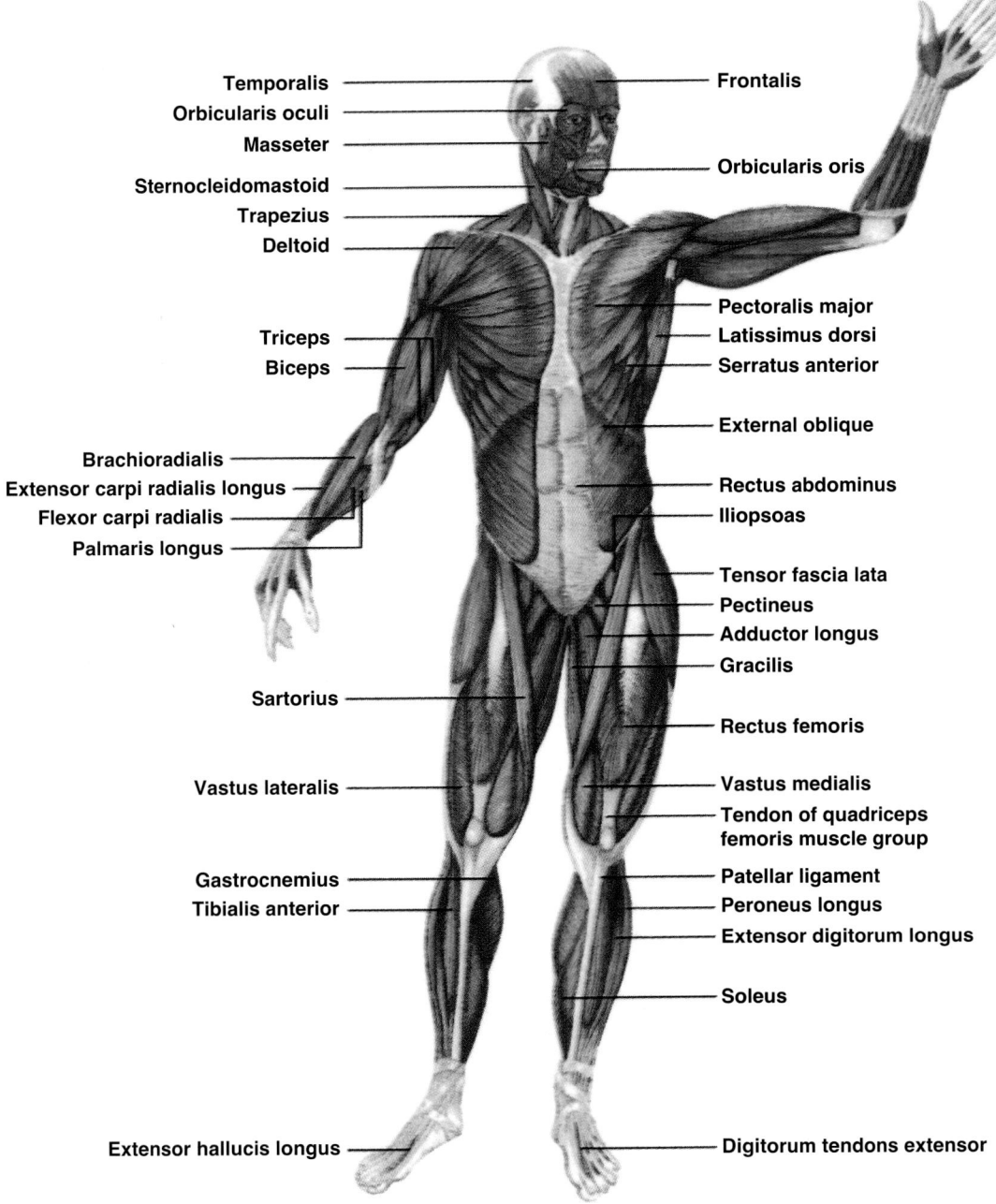

Temporalis — Frontalis

Orbicularis oculi

Masseter

Sternocleidomastoid — Orbicularis oris

Trapezius

Deltoid

Pectoralis major

Triceps — Latissimus dorsi

Biceps — Serratus anterior

External oblique

Brachioradialis

Extensor carpi radialis longus — Rectus abdominus

Flexor carpi radialis — Iliopsoas

Palmaris longus

Tensor fascia lata

Pectineus

Adductor longus

Gracilis

Sartorius

Rectus femoris

Vastus lateralis — Vastus medialis

Tendon of quadriceps femoris muscle group

Gastrocnemius — Patellar ligament

Tibialis anterior — Peroneus longus

Extensor digitorum longus

Soleus

Extensor hallucis longus — Digitorum tendons extensor

SOURCE: *Heath Biology*, ©1991. Reprinted by permission of D.C. Heath and Company.

organic matter that have decayed in the soil. Vultures eat the bodies of dead animals.

Contractile vacuole   *See* **Paramecium**.

Cotyledons   The first leaves of a plant; they are often strikingly different from later leaves. In some plants like the bean, they contain large quantities of stored food that get the embryo off to a good start until it can shift for itself. They are the two halves of the bean seed. Cotyledons usually persist for only a short while after germination.

Crossing over   Genes are linked on chromosomes and are inherited in a group on a particular chromosome. However, linkage groups are broken by *crossing over*, a phenomenon that may occur during meiosis when homologous chromosomes are intertwined during synapsis. It is at this time that chromosomes may exchange homologous parts and thus assort linkage groups.

Crustacea   Derived from the Latin crusta meaning crust, the name Crustacea describes the lobsters and their relatives aptly. The body is covered by a tough exoskeleton arranged in the form of arched plates that thin out at the joints to permit maximum movement. The lobster is representative of this class.

Cyclic AMP (cAMP; cyclic adenosine monophosphate)   A compound formed from ATP that regulates the effects of numerous hormones in animals (second messenger).

Cyclosis   The circulation of cytoplasm within cells. This is especially true in plant cells where there are large vacuoles. Protoplasm flows around the margins and in cytoplasmic strands that sometimes extend through the vacuoles. Protoplasm in adjacent cells may flow in opposite directions, or it may reverse directions in any particular cell. Light and temperature especially influence this action in plant cells, but the exact cause of movement is unknown. Circulation results in a thorough mixing of protoplasm and its contents. Cyclosis of protoplasm in palisade cells of leaves may prevent the overexposure of chloroplasts to light, since they remain in a position of maximum exposure only momentarily.

Cytochromes   Iron-containing red proteins; molecules of the electron-transfer machinery in photosynthesis and respiration.

Cytokinesis   The division of cytoplasm occurring during the last state (telophase) of mitosis.

Cyton   Nerve cell body. *See* **Nerve cell (neuron)**.

Cytoplasm   The ground substance of the cell that supports all of the cell's organelles. *See* **Cell**.

Cytosine   A nitrogen base that pairs with guanine in DNA and RNA.

D **Dark reaction**   The stage of photosynthesis in which carbon dioxide fixation occurs, resulting in the formation of sugar. See **Calvin cycle**.

Daughter cells   *See* **Cell division**.

Deciduous forest   The forests of the temperate regions are dominated by broad-leaved trees that lose their leaves in the winter. Examples of the kinds of trees that compose these hardwood forests are oak, hickory, chestnut, beech, maples, willows, cottonwood, and sycamore. The types of animals that inhabit these forests are deer, fox, squirrel, skunk, woodchuck, and raccoon.

Decomposers   Decomposers form an important part of ecosystems. Bacteria and fungi are organisms that break down dead organic matter and release from it organic compounds and minerals that are returned to the soil. Many of the materials returned to the soil are used by the producers in the process of food-making. Without the work of the decomposers the remains of dead plants and animals would pile up, not only occupying space needed by living organisms, but also keeping trapped within their dead bodies valuable minerals and compounds.

Dehydration synthesis   As the two molecules join, a molecule of water is produced during the process in addition to the double sugar. A synthesis of this type is known as dehydration synthesis.

$$C_6H_{12}O_6 + C_6H_{12}O_6 \rightarrow C_{12}H_{22}O_{11} + H_2O$$
glucose + glucose → maltose + water

Within living cells, carbohydrates, proteins, and fats are formed by dehydration synthesis.

Dendrite   *See* **Nerve cell (neuron)**.

Denitrifying bacteria   Soil bacteria that change nitrates back to atmospheric nitrogen. The cycle then repeats.

Deoxyribonucleic acid (DNA)   DNA molecules are the particular type of nucleic acid out of which genes are made. Genes are the bearers of hereditary traits from parent to offspring. *See also* **Replication**.

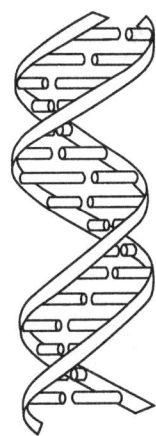

DNA: Double helix

Desert   Deserts form in regions where the annual rainfall is less than 6.5 centimeters, or where rain occurs unevenly during the year and the rate of evaporation is high. The temperature changes drastically from hot days to cold nights. Plants that survive in the desert have specific adaptations for low moisture and high temperature. Examples of desert plants are creosote, sagebrush, cacti, and cheat grass. Examples of desert animals are lizards, insects, kangaroo rats, and arachnids.

Diaphragm   The muscular structure that separates the chest cavity from the abdominal cavity in mammals; in a microscope, the part that regulates light entering the lens system.

Dicotyledon (dicot)   A type of angiosperm plant in which the embryo plant is contained between two seed leaves or cotyledons.

Differentiation   *See* **Embryo**.

Diffusion   The movement of molecules from an area of greater concentration to an area of lesser concentration. Diffusion is a type of passive transport.

Digestion   Begins in the mouth. Teeth grind the food while three pairs of *salivary glands* pour salivary juice (saliva) into the mouth. Saliva contains the enzyme salivary amylase (ptyalin), which begins the digestion of starch. The moistened, chewed food is swallowed and moves through the throat into the food tube, or esophagus. The esophagus has no digestive function but moves the food into the stomach by waves of muscle contractions called peristalsis. Chemical digestion is known as *hydrolysis*. Extracellular digestion takes place outside of cells. Intracellular digestion takes place inside of cells within cell vacuoles.

Digestive system   The human digestive system begins with a mouth and ends with an anus, and is often described as a "tube within a tube." Variously called the gut, alimentary canal, or the *gastrointestinal tract*, the digestive system extends from the lower part of the head region through the entire torso. Essentially, this system carries out five separate jobs that have to do with the processing and distribution of nutrients. First, it governs ingestion or food intake. Second, it transports food to organs for temporary storage. Third, it controls the mechanical breakdown of food and its chemical digestion. A fourth function is the absorption of nutrient molecules. Its final piece of work is the temporary storage and then elimination of waste products.

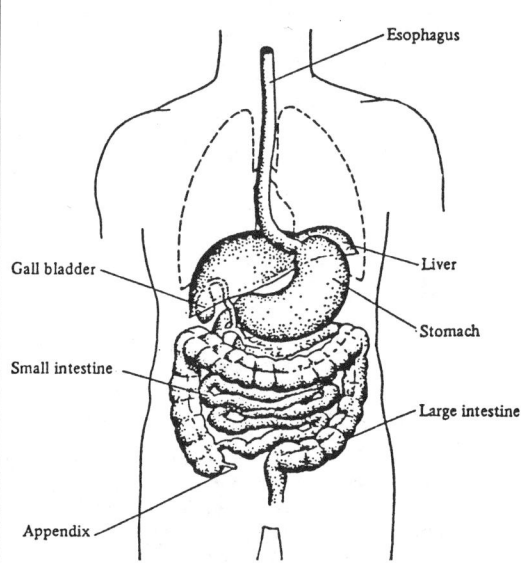

The human digestive system

Dihybrid   Mixed genes for two traits. *See* **Heredity, Mendelian**.

Dinoflagellates   Dinoflagellates are small protists and usually unicellular. Most of these organisms have two unequal flagella, one extending longitudinally from the posterior end of the cell, the other encircling the central part of the cell. Some dinoflagellates extend trichocysts like the paramecium; others have *nematocysts,* stinging cells common in

the coelenterates. Some species—*Noctiluca*, for example—are bioluminescent, giving off light like a firefly.

Diploid number   The full complement of chromosomes in somatic (body) cells designated by the symbol 2N; also known as the species number or chromosome number.

Disease   A disease is a disorder that prevents the body organs from working as they should. In general, diseases can be classified as being infectious or noninfectious. Infectious diseases are caused by organisms that invade the body and do harm to the cells, tissues, and organs. As a rule, there is disease specificity when a specific disease-producing organism causes a particular disease. Disease-producing organisms are said to be pathogens and are described as being pathogenic. Noninfectious diseases are caused by factors other than pathogenic organisms. Among the factors that are responsible for noninfectious diseases are genetic causes, malnutrition, exposure to radiation, emotional disturbances, organ failure, poisoning, endocrine malfunctioning, and immunological disorders. Whatever the cause, a disease works counter to the well being of the diseased organism.

Dominant trait   When organisms with contrasting traits are crossed, the trait that shows up in the F_1 generation is called the dominant trait. The trait that is hidden is called the recessive trait.

Double helix   *See* **Deoxyribonucleic acid (DNA)**.

Droplet infection   A common method of passing germs along. Disease germs are present in droplets ot water that escape from the nose and mouth when sneezing, coughing, and talking. If these infected droplets are inhaled or taken in by mouth, the germs then enter the body of another person.

E   **Ear and hearing**   The human ear is made up of three divisions: the outer ear, middle ear, and inner ear. The figure shows the structure of the ear. The outer ear catches sound waves and transports them to the eardrum, a membrane that stretches across the outer canal separating it from the middle ear. Sound waves cause the eardrum to vibrate. The middle ear contains three very small bones called the hammer, anvil, and stirrup. These are the smallest bones in the body. These bones accept the vibrations from the eardrum and transmit them to the oval window, one of two small membrane-covered openings

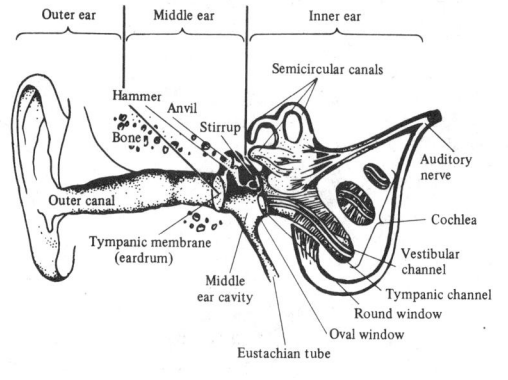

Structure of the human ear

between the middle ear and the inner ear. The inner ear, which is entirely encased in bone, has a fluid-filled structure called the cochlea, so named because it resembles a snail in shape. The cochlea has numerous canals that are lined with hair cells. The vibrations from the oval window are transmitted to the hair cells in the cochlea and thence on the auditory nerve, which conducts the vibrations to the brain. In the brain, signals are interpreted into sounds.

Echinoderms　Spiny-skinned invertebrates that include the starfish, brittle stars, sand dollars, sea urchins, and sea cucumbers. Although they do not look very much like vertebrate animals, the development of the echinoderm embryo strongly resembles that of the chordates in the early stages. The larval stage is free-swimming and shows bilateral symmetry.

Ecological niche　An important concept of ecology is that of the niche. An ecological niche is a feeding pattern exhibited by species that compose a community. A niche is a feeding way-of-life in relationship to other organisms.

Ecology　The science that studies the interrelationships between living species and their physical environment. The word "ecology" was coined in 1869 by the German zoologist Ernst Haeckel to emphasize the importance of the environment in which living things function. The environment includes living or biotic factors and nonliving factors referred to as abiotic factors.

Ecosystem　The living community and the non-living environment work together in a cooperative ecological system known as an ecosystem. An ecosystem has no size requirement or set boundaries. A forest, pond, and field are examples of ecosystems. So is an unused city lot, small aquarium, the lawn in front of a residential dwelling, or a crack in a sidewalk. All of these examples reflect areas where interaction is taking place between living organisms and the nonliving environment.

Ectoderm　*See* **Embryo**.

Effectors　The kind of responses that organisms can make is related to their own body equipment. The responding part is the effector. Most animal effectors are either muscles or glands. In considering responses one ordinarily thinks about rapid, visible muscular responses. Glandular responses are much more subtle.

Embryo　The stage in human or animal development following cleavage. During embryonic development the tissues and organs are being built. When the embryo takes human or animal form, it is known as a fetus. The process in which tissues are formed is known as differentiation.

Differentiation of the
Three Primary Germ Layers

Ectoderm	Endoderm	Mesoderm
skin	lining of lungs	muscles
nervous system	lining of digestive system	skeleton
sense organs	pancreas	heart
	liver	blood vessels
	respiratory system	blood
		ovaries, testes
		kidneys

Embryonic membranes　The embryo produces several membranes that do not form any part of the new baby but which are necessary to the development and well being of the embryo. One of these membranes is the amnion, a waterfilled sac that completely surrounds and protects the embryo. The water absorbs shocks and prevents friction that might damage the embryo. The implanted embryo is attached to the uterus by means of the umbilical cord, a structure that contains blood vessels that function in carrying nutrients and oxygen to the embryo and transporting wastes away from the embryo. The umbilical cord connects with the placenta, a vascularized organ made up of tissues of the mother and embryo. *See* **Allantois**.

Endocrine system　Made up of the pituitary gland, thyroid gland, parathyroid glands, the adrenal gland, the isles of Langerhans in the pancreas, the thymus gland, the pineal gland, and the gonads—testes in the male and ovaries in the female. Certain secretions of the stomach and small intestine are also hormones and thus part of the endocrine system. Through their secretions the endocrine glands regulate growth, rate of metabolism, response to stress, blood pressure, muscle contraction, digestion, immune responses, and the development and functioning of the reproductive system. Hormones exert their influence by becoming involved with the genetic machinery of cells and by affecting the metabolic activities of cells working through the cellular respiration pathways.

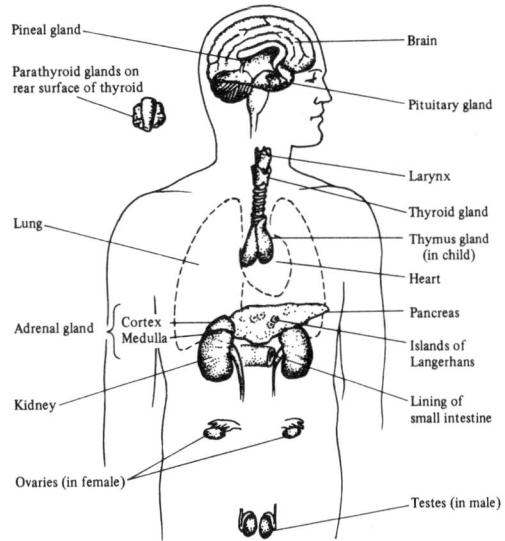

The location of the major endocrine glands: pineal, pituitary, thyroid, parathyroid, thymus, pancreas (part), lining of the small intestine, adrenal glands, and sex glands

Endoderm　*See* **Embryo**.

Endoplasmic reticulum　Spreading throughout the cytoplasm, extending from the cell membrane to the membranes of the nucleus is a network of membranes that form channels, tubes, and flattened sacs; this network is named the endoplasmic reticulum. One function of the endoplasmic reticulum is the movement of materials throughout the cytoplasm and to the plasma membrane. The endoplasmic reticulum has other important functions related to the synthesis of materials and their packaging and distribution to sites needed.

Enzyme-substrate complex   An enzyme affects the rate of reaction of the substrate molecule that fits the enzyme's activity site. In order for this to happen, a close physical association must take place between enzyme and substrate. This association is called the enzyme-substrate complex. *See* **Substrate**.

Enzymes (organic catalysts)   A catalyst is a molecule that controls the rate of a chemical reaction but is itself *not* used up in the process. Enzymes are proteins that control the rate of chemical reactions that take place in cells, tissues, and organs. Each chemical reaction that occurs in a living system requires the assistance of a specific enzyme (*enzyme specificity*).

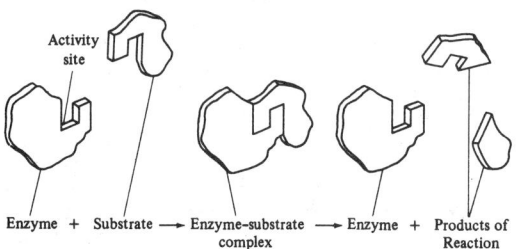

Enzyme + Substrate ⟶ Enzyme-substrate ⟶ Enzyme + Products of
                                   complex   Reaction

Enzyme-substrate complex

Epinephrine   The hormone secreted by the medulla of the adrenal gland; also called *adrenaline*. It is secreted as a result of stress and produces effects on the circulatory system and on glucose mobilization.

Epithelial tissue   *See* **Tissues**.

Estrus   The period of maximum sexual receptivity in the female mammal. Estrus is also the time of the release of eggs in the female.

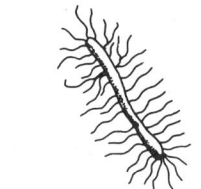

A flagellated bacterium

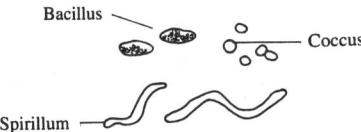

Bacillus

Coccus

Spirillum

Three shapes of bacteria

Eubacteria—true bacteria   This group, referred to as the true bacteria, represents a large number of species. All of these bacteria have thick and rigid cell walls. Some of the species are nonmotile (nonmoving), while others are motile, using flagella or a sling motion to move from place to place. Species belonging to the eubacteria are identified by their shapes. The rod-shaped bacteria are known as bacilli

(bacillus, sing.), the round bacteria as the cocci (coccus, sing.), and the spiral-shaped as spirillae (spirillum, sing.). Some species typically remain attached: diplococci occur in pairs, streptococci in chains, and staphylococci in clusters. *See also* **Bacteria**.

Eukaryotes   Organisms whose cells contain the genetic material (DNA) enclosed in a nucleus; includes all organisms above the level of bacteria and blue-green algae.

Evolution   Concerns the orderly changes that have shaped the earth and that have modified the living species that inhabit the earth. Evolution is a fusion of biological and physical sciences that have provided supporting data that confirm the fact that over periods of time major changes have occurred in the interior of the earth and on its surface, accompanied by modifications in climate. All of the changes in the earth are classified as nonbiological or inorganic evolution. Changes that have taken place in living organisms are known as biological or organic evolution.

Evolution, evidences of   Evidence that evolution—gradual change over a period of time—has occurred in living things is provided by many sciences and includes facts from the geologic record, the study of fossils, and evidence from cell studies, biochemistry, comparative anatomy, and comparative embryology. *See also* illustration on page 2-16.

Evolution, theories of   Since the eighteenth century several theories have been proposed to explain evolution. Among these are the use and disuse theory of Lamarck and the theory of natural selection formulated by Charles Darwin. Recent advances in genetics cell biology, and functional anatomy and biochemistry have led to the formulation of a modern theory of evolution based on Darwin's concept of natural selection.

Excretion   Removes waste products of cellular respiration from the body. The lungs, skin, and kidneys are excretory organs in humans that remove carbon dioxide, water, and urea from the blood and other body tissues. Guttation is the excretion of drops of water from plants during periods of high humidity.

Excretory system   In human beings, the lungs, skin, and urinary system work to expel the wastes produced in metabolic activities. The lungs excrete carbon dioxide and water. The skin expels water and salts from the sweat glands and a small amount of oil from the sebaceous glands. The urinary system handles the major work of excretion.

Exocrine glands   Glands, such as salivary and sweat glands, from which the secretions are discharged through ducts directly into an organ or onto the surface of the body.

Exoskeleton   A hard covering on the outside of the animal body. The exoskeleton of arthropods has the same functions of support as the bony internal skeleton of vertebrates.

Eye   The human eyeball measures about 2.5 centimeters in diameter. Most of the eyeball rests in the bony eyesocket of the skull. Only about one sixth of the eye is exposed. External structures associated with the eye are eyelids, lashes, and eyebrows. A transparent protective membrane, the cornea, covers the eye. Six small muscles attach the eye to the eyesocket. Secretions from tear glands help to keep the eye moist. The lens is a transparent body that focuses light on the light-sensitive retina where images are formed.

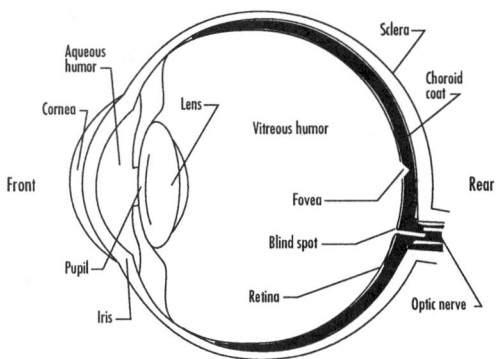

Structure of the human eye

![F]**Fats**   Organic compounds that supply cells with energy. Fats are usually insoluble in water. A fat results from the combination of one glycerol and three long-chain fatty acids joined through dehydration synthesis. Certain fats are essential to the structure and function of body cells, to the building of cell membranes, and to the synthesis of certain hormones. Fats also aid in the transport of fat-soluble vitamins. Foods rich in fats include butter, bacon, egg yolk, cream, and certain cheeses.

Fermentation   *See* **Anaerobic.**

Ferns   The fern plant used in flower bouquets is the sporophyte generation. The sporophyte generation produces asexual spores. The mature fern has true roots, leaves, and stem. Ferns growing in temperate climates have an underground stem called a rhizome that grows in a horizontal position. The rhizome not only stores food materials, but also gives rise to new fern plants that grow along its length. The stems of tropical species grow upright in a vertical position and serve as trunks of tree ferns.

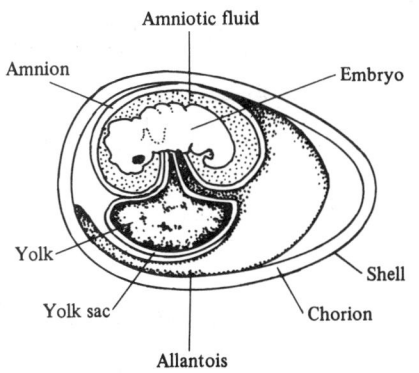

Development of the bird embryo

Fertilization, birds   Fertilization is accomplished during mating at which time the male and female place their cloacas close together. Sperm swim from the cloaca of the male into the female cloaca and up

into the oviduct. Fertilization takes place high up in the oviduct before the albumen and the other surrounding membranes are secreted by the oviduct cells. Most birds lay a clutch of less than six eggs. However, ducks may lay as many as 15 eggs at one time. *See* **Allantois.**

Fertilization, fish   Many sperm never reach the eggs and many fertilized eggs die before development. Hence there is an overproduction of gametes to ensure the survival of the species. In a few fish species fertilization is internal and parental care is given to the fertilized eggs. The stickleback male, for example, takes care of the fertilized eggs in nests and the male seahorse carries them around in a brood pouch.

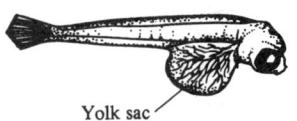

An immature fish

Fertilization, frogs   In frogs, fertilization is external. Sperm leave the testes through tubules called vasa efferentia that communicate with the kidney. The sperm cells then pass into the Wolffian duct that leads to the cloaca, a passageway that opens to the outside of the body. In the female, large egg masses are released into the body cavity from two ovaries, located at the anterior end of each kidney. Beating cilia sweep the eggs into coiled tubules known as oviducts where they are propelled to the cloaca and then out of the body. As the eggs pass through the oviducts they are coated with a thin layer of jelly-like material. At the time when the female is depositing eggs in the shallow waters of a pond or brook, the male deposits sperm over them. The sperm swim to the eggs and as each sperm reaches an egg, it digests its way through the jelly and into the egg, effecting fertilization. After fertilization the jelly coating on the eggs swells due to the absorption of large amounts of water. The swelling of the black jelly causes the eggs to adhere together and protects them from predation by fish and other animals. The fertilized egg, or zygote, undergoes cleavage, forming a tadpole.

Flagella and cilia   Fine threads of cytoplasm that extend from the surfaces of some cells. Both of these structures are involved in the locomotion of some protist species. Cilia are relatively short extensions but appear in great numbers, usually surrounding the body of the protist. Flagella are much longer than cilia and appear in fewer numbers. In addition to serving the locomotive needs of one-celled organisms, flagella and cilia help functions of other types of cells. Sperm cells of animals and plants are propelled through fluid media by the whip-like actions of their flagella. Tissue cells of the human windpipe are lined with cilia that wave back and forth catching dust particles and pushing them away from the lungs. The microstructure of the flagella and cilia resembles that of the centrioles.

Flatworms   The simplest of the flatworms demonstrate bilateral symmetry. This phylum represents a step up the evolutionary scale showing a recognizable head end and definite development of excretory, nervous, and reproductive systems. Most of the flatworms are hermaphrodites, as well as parasites. Some flatworms are serious parasites of humans and other animals. Among the flatworms are the planaria, flukes, and tapeworms.

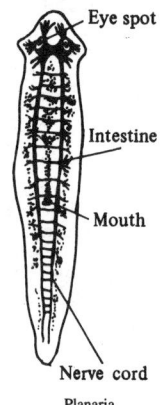

Planaria

Flower, parts of The reproductive structure of the angiosperm is the flower that encloses the male and female sex organs. The green leaflike sepals protect the flower when in the bud stage. Collectively, sepals are known as the calyx. Just inside of the calyx are colored petals. All of the petals in a flower are known as the corolla. The stamens are the male reproductive structures; pollen grains are produced in the anther. The pistil is in the center of the flower. The top portion of the pistil is the stigma. The style is the long stalk that leads to the rounded portion of the pistil called the ovary. Inside of the ovary are one or more ovules. The pistil and its many parts compose the female portion of the flower.

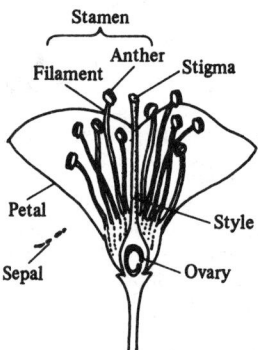

Parts of a flower

Flower, reproduction in Involves the maturation of the pollen grain during which three nuclei are produced. One is a pollen tube nucleus; the other two are sperm nuclei. As the sperm nuclei are traveling down the style, each ovule is going through a maturation process that results in the formation of a viable egg cell and a double nucleus. The sperm nuclei fertilize the egg cell and also the double nucleus.

The zygote goes through a series of changes that lead to seed formation.

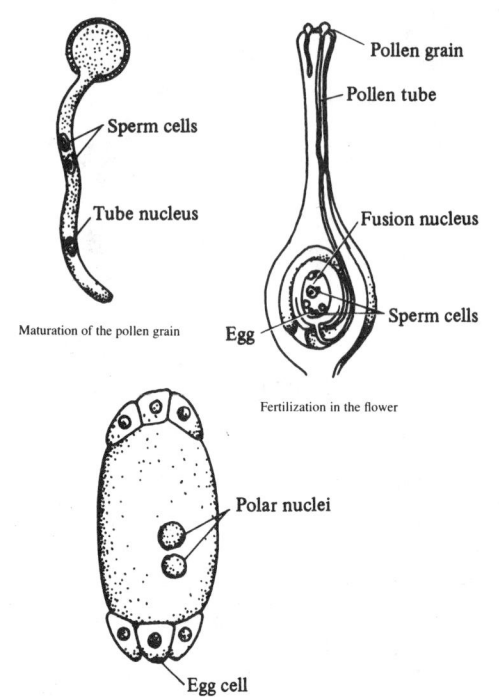

Maturation of the pollen grain   Fertilization in the flower

Maturation of ovule

Fluid Mosaic Model *See* **Cell membrane**.

Food chain The flow of energy through an ecosystem can be studied by way of food chains which show how energy is transferred from one organism to another through feeding patterns. An example of a food chain on a cultivated field might be as follows:
Lettuce → Rabbit → Snake → Hawk
The flow of energy in a food chain is in a straight line pattern. Most of the energy is concentrated in the level of the producer. At each succeeding level the energy is decreased. However, the feeding relationships among organisms in an ecosystem are not usually this simple, and, in actuality, are more complex, forming a food web.

Food pyramid Another way of illustrating energy flow in an ecosystem. The autotrophs at the base of the pyramid support all of the heterotrophs (consumers) that exist at each nutritional level and there is a decrease of available energy at each nutritional level.

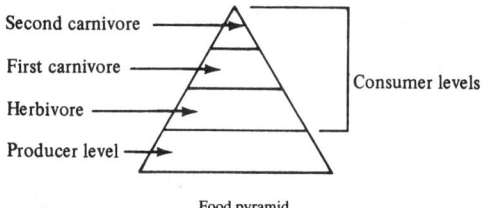

Food pyramid

Food web Shows that there are several alternative energy pathways in a food web. It is the alternative pathways that enable an ecosytem to keep its stability. One species does not eradicate another in the quest for food.

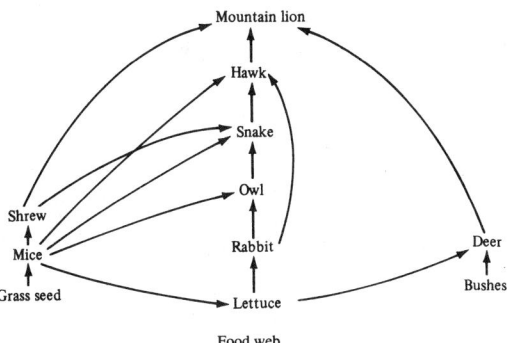

Food web

Fossils   The preserved remains of plants and animals, usually found in sedimentary rock. The age of fossils is estimated by the use of carbon dating, the ratio of radioactive carbon (carbon 14) to non-radioactive carbon (carbon 12). The fossil records contained in the layers of sedimentary rock provide reliable evidence of change in plant and animal species. The lower down the rock layer, the older the fossil. Top layers contain more recent fossil remains of more complex species.

Fruit   A ripened (mature) ovary bearing one or more seeds. A *simple fruit* develops from a single ovary; examples are tomatoes, plums, and pears. An *aggregate fruit* develops from a group of ovaries produced in a single flower; examples are raspberries and blackberries. A *multiple fruit* develops from the ovaries of a cluster of flowers that are carried on the same stalk; examples are pineapples, figs, and mulberries.

Fungi   Eukaryotic, multicellular, and multinucleate organisms. Yeasts are unicellular forms. The cells of fungi are different from those of other species because the boundaries separating the cells are either entirely missing or only partially formed. Thus fungi are primarily coenocytic organisms; this means that the cells have more than one nucleus in a single mass of cytoplasm. However, the characteristic that most distinguishes the fungi from other organisms is their mode of nutrition. Fungi are saprophytes, absorbing organic nutritive matter from decaying plant and animal bodies.

**Gametes**   Sex cells; male sex cells are called sperm and are produced in gonads called testes or spermaries. Female sex cells are the eggs or ova and are produced in female gonads called ovaries. All gametes have the haploid (monoploid) number of chromosomes.

Gametophyte   In alternation of generations, the gametophyte generation produces haploid gametes. Fusion of the haploid gametes forms a diploid zygote, which grows into a sporophyte (plant). The sporophyte produces haploid reproductive spores. Each spore grows into a multicellular haploid plant, the gametophyte. The cycle repeats.

Gamma globulin   A protein in the blood plasma from which antibodies are made. Antibodies, pro-

duced by the lymphocytes in the immune system, are molecules that inactivate or destroy antigens.

Ganglia (*ganglion*, sing.)   Functional groups of nerve cell bodies that lie outside of the brain and spinal cord, allowing parts of the nervous system to coordinate activities without involving the whole system.

Gastrula   A stage in embryonic development when the three primary tissue layers (ectoderm, mesoderm, and endoderm) develop and the primitive gut (archenteron) forms. *See* **Cleavage**.

Gene   Around 1911, Thomas Hunt Morgan introduced the tiny fruit fly *Drosophila melanogaster* as the new experimental organism for work in the field of heredity. The experimental work of Morgan resulted in the discovery of the chromosome as the means by which hereditary traits are transmitted from one generation to another. Morgan's chromosome theory of inheritance includes the concept that chromosomes are composed of discrete units called genes. Genes are the actual carriers of specific traits and move with the chromosomes in mitotic and meiotic cell divisions. Morgan further proposed that genes control the development of traits in each organism. When genes change, or mutate, the traits they control change. Morgan's work was based on the chromosome theory of inheritance, which began to take shape in 1902 from the work of Walter S. Sutton.

Genetic code   The DNA molecule carries coded instructions for controlling all functions of the cell. At the present time, scientists know most about the functions of the genetic code that controls protein synthesis. They have determined that triplet combinations of bases code for each of 20 amino acids. The coded sequence of amino acids determines the formation of different types of proteins. The code for proteins is present in messenger RNA molecules that are complementary to DNA molecules. For example: let us suppose that a portion of a DNA molecule carries a code such as AAC GGC AAA TTT. Its mRNA complement would be as follows: UUG CCG UUU AAA.

Genetics   The science of heredity.

Genome   The complete store of an organism's genetic material, which consists of genes on chromosomes.

Genotype   The genetic makeup of an individual. For a given trait an individual may have two like genes or two unlike genes. Genotype determines whether the dominant or recessive trait will show and whether or not the individual is dominant or recessive for the trait. Following is a chart showing the genotypes of human blood.

Blood Group Genotypes

Blood Type	Genotype
A	$I^A I^A$ or $I^A i$
B	$I^B I^B$ or $I^B i$
AB	$I^A I^B$
O	ii

Geotropism   Different parts of a plant may respond differently to the same stimulus. Thus the stem and leaves will grow upward, away from gravity; they show negative geotropism. On the other hand, the roots will grow downward, toward gravity; they show positive geotropism.

Germs   Organisms that invade the body of animals and plants and cause disease. Organisms that cause disease are bacteria, spirochetes, viruses, and parasitic worms.

Gibberellin   Plant growth substance isolated from the fungus *Gibberella fujikuroi* that has the following effects on plants:
1. It causes corn, wheat, and many other plants to grow very rapidly, showing an increase in height that is three to five times the normal in a short period of time.
2. It makes dwarf plants that by heredity should always be stunted, such as dwarf pea or dwarf corn, grow to the size of normal plants.
3. Seeds that are soaked overnight in it germinate ahead of time.
4. Biennial plants such as foxglove and carrot, that flower in the second year of their life cycle, burst into bloom in only one year.
5. Tomatoes and cucumbers develop from flowers that are not pollinated if the flower buds are sprayed with it.
6. Garden and house plants, such as geranium and petunias, bloom ahead of time, and have large flowers.

Glycogen   A multibranched glucose storage polysaccharide deposited in the liver and muscles of animals; also known as "animal starch."

Glycolysis   The anaerobic degradation of glucose into pyruvic acid; the initial stage of cellular respiration. *See* **Anaerobic**; **Respiration**.

Gonads   The sex organs of male (testes) and female (ovaries). Sex cells (gametes) are produced in the sex organs. Male sex cells are called sperm; female, ova (ovum, sing.)

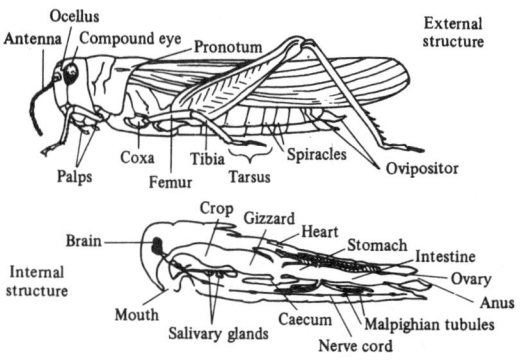

Parts of the grasshopper

Grasshopper   Belongs to a large group of organisms classified as *arthropods*. The name arthropod in literal translation means "jointed foot," a distinctive characteristic of this group, expressed traditionally as "jointed appendages." The arthropods are segmented animals protected by an exoskeleton made of protein and the flexible but tough carbohydrate chitin. The chitinous exoskeleton is fashioned in articulating plates held together by hinges covering both the body and the appendages, and attached to muscles that make possible quick and unencumbered movements.

Greenhouse effect   The amount of carbon dioxide in the atmosphere has been found to be increas-ing. Much of this is coming from the burning of fossil fuels (coal, oil, and natural gas) by factories, homes, and automobiles. Since trees use carbon dioxide in photosynthesis, the cutting down of the world's forests over the years is preventing some of this CO_2 from being absorbed. The actual effects of this increase are not fully known. Some scientists claim that carbon dioxide, like the glass of a greenhouse, allows visible sunlight to pass through to the earth. As the earth warms up, it gives off infrared rays. These are absorbed by the carbon dioxide in the atmosphere, instead of being given off into space. It is believed that this "greenhouse effect," as it is called, will cause the earth's atmosphere to eventually warm up. Some of the possible effects of such an increase in atmospheric temperature might be: spread of desert areas; reduction of food crop production; warmer climate; melting of polar ice, with the raising of sea levels and the consequent flooding of heavily populated areas along the coast.

Growth   Describes the increase of cell size and increase of cell numbers. The latter process occurs when cells divide in response to a sequence of events known as mitosis.

Guard cells   Cells in the epidermis of the leaf that regulate the opening and closing of the stomates. *See* **Leaf cross section**.

Gymnosperms   Gymnosperms are cone-bearers. They are woody plants, chiefly evergreens, with needle-like or scale-like leaves. Cone-bearing plants grow in many parts of the world including tropical climates. However, most species are found in the cooler parts of temperate regions. Examples of gymnosperm species are pines, spruces, firs, cedars, yews, California redwoods, bald cypresses, and Douglas firs. Most biologists think that the gymnosperms evolved directly from progymnosperms present during the Devonian period.

H **Haploid number**   The organism's sex cells, or gametes—eggs and sperm, contain half the species number of chromosomes. This number is called the haploid number and abbreviated N. Meiosis is the kind of nuclear division that leads to the formation of sperm and egg cells.

Hardy-Weinberg principle   A population includes all members of a species that live in a given location. Modern geneticists are concerned about the factors in populations that affect gene frequencies. All of the genes that can be inherited (heritable genes) in a population are known collectively as the gene pool. The Hardy-Weinberg principle uses an algebraic equation to compute the gene frequencies in human populations. The conditions set by the Hardy-Weinberg principle for determining the stability of a gene pool are as follows: large populations, random mating, no migration, and no mutation.

Heart   The human heart lies in the chest cavity behind the breastbone and slightly to the left. The heart is a bundle of cardiac muscles specialized for rhythmic contractions and relaxations known as heartbeat. The rate of average heartbeat is 72 times per minute. The inside of the heart is divided into four chambers. The two chambers at the top are the receiving chambers, or the atria. The lower chambers, the ventricles, are pumping chambers. Each atrium is separated from the ventricle below by a valve. The atrium and the ventricle on the right are separated from the left atrium and ventricle by a thick wall of muscle called the septum.

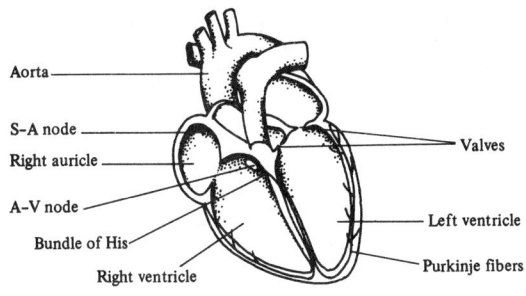

Aorta
S-A node
Right auricle
A-V node
Bundle of His
Right ventricle
Valves
Left ventricle
Purkinje fibers

Structure of the heart

Hemoglobin   An iron-protein complex in red blood cells that functions as an oxygen carrier.

Heredity, Mendelian   Gregor Mendel, an Austrian monk, began the first organized and mathematical study of how traits are inherited. Using the garden pea as the test organism, Mendel identified seven different traits that were easily recognizable in this self-pollinating plant. He called each of these traits *unit characters*. Mendel not only identified characteristics that seemed to be inherited, but for each unit character, he identified an opposite trait. For example: if the unit character was height, the opposite traits were short and tall. If the unit character was seed coat color, the opposite traits were yellow and green. Mendel formulated three major laws or principles of inheritance.

The Law of Dominance: If two organisms that exhibit contrasting traits are crossed, the trait that shows up in the first filial generation (F_1) is the dominant trait. For example: when a pure-bred tall pea plant is crossed with a short pea plant, all of the offspring will be tall. The offspring will not be pure tall, however, and are therefore known as hybrids. The factor for shortness is hidden. We say today that the phenotype of the F_1 plants is tall. A phenotype refers to the traits that we can see. The genotypes of genetic makeup of these plants is said to be hybrid or heterozygous, meaning mixed.

The Law of Segregation: When hybrids are crossed, the recessive trait segregates out at a ratio of three individuals with the dominant trait to one individual with the recessive trait. The 3:1 ratio is known as the phenotypic ratio, because it refers to the traits that can be seen and not those factors hidden in the germplasm. The hybrid cross is also known as the F_1 cross and the offspring produced by this cross are known as the second filial generation or F_2. In terms of modern knowledge, the F_2 generation also produces another type of ratio called the genotypic ratio which refers to gene makeup. The genotypic ratio is 1:2:1, translated into 1 homozygous dominant (pure) individual: 2 heterozygous (hybrid) individuals: 1 homozygous recessive. Only the homozygous recessive shows the recessive trait.

The Law of Independent Assortment: Mendel believed that each trait is inherited independently of others and remains unaltered throughout all genera-

tions. We now know that Mendel's "factors" are genes that are linked together on chromosomes and that if genes are on the same chromosome, they are inherited together.

Hermaphrodite   An animal that has both male and female reproductive organs and produces both eggs and sperm. Lifestyles such as burrowing (earthworms), living attached to objects (barnacles), or living within the body of another organism (tapeworms) make it difficult for such organisms to meet with a member of the opposite sex. Hermaphroditism solves the problem of reproduction. Most hermaphrodites mate with another member of the same species each donating sperm to fertilize the eggs of the other. *Sequential hermaphroditism* is a reproductive pattern exhibited in some reef fish that are able to change their sex from male to female or vice versa as conditions warrant.

Heterotroph   An organism that cannot synthesize its food from inorganic materials such as carbon dioxide and water. A heterotroph must obtain its nutrition by the intake of preformed organic molecules. All animals are heterotrophs.

Heterotroph-autotroph hypothesis   The first organisms on earth were probably heterotrophs utilizing the organic pool for nutrition. As time went on, the early heterotrophs must have faced a serious crisis because oxygen from photodissociation (atmospheric reactions) began to increase in concentration. This changed the atmosphere. Oxygen and hydrogen peroxide (H_2O_2) destroyed many heterotrophs. Eventually, photosynthetic organisms—autotrophs such as blue-green algae—evolved, increasing the oxygen content of the atmosphere and thereby threatening the continued existence of the heterotrophs. An ozone layer in the atmosphere developed from the high concentration of oxygen, which further diminished the organic compounds available to the beleaguered heterotrophs. Some heterotrophs developed pathways for utilizing oxygen in energy production (aerobic respiration). The carbohydrates produced by autotrophs and the oxygen of the atmosphere supplied the new heterotrophs with the nutritive materials necessary for survival (heterotroph-autotroph hypothesis). Thus the stage was set for the development of life on the scale that is known today.

Homeostasis   The term used to describe the stable internal environment of the cell and the organism as a whole. Homeostasis is a condition necessary for life. The internal chemical balance of the cell must be maintained at a steady state to promote innumerable biochemical activities that foster the production and use of energy. The concept of homeostasis was initially developed by the nineteenth century physiologist Claude Bernard.

Homologous structures   A comparative study of the bone structures and body systems of animals from the various phyla reveals a great deal of similarity. A comparative study of the skeletal systems of vertebrates shows that many of the bones are very much alike. Much of our evidence for evolution comes from a study of homologous structures. Homologous structures are bones that look alike and have the same evolutionary origin although they may be used for different purposes. The flipper of a whale, the arm of a human, and the wing of a bird are

EXHIBIT 2.1
Classification of *Homo Sapiens*

Category	Taxon	Characteristics
Kingdom	Animalia	Multicellular organism requiring preformed organic material for food, having a motile stage at some time in its life history
Phylum	Chordata	Animals having a notochord (embryonic skeletal rod), dorsal hollow nerve cord, gills in the pharynx at some time during the life cycle
Subphylum	Vertebrata	Backbone (vertebral column) enclosing the spinal cord, skull bones enclosing the brain
Class	Mammalia	Body having hair or fur at some time in the life; female nourishes young on milk; warmblooded; one bone in lower jaw
Order	Primates	Tree-living mammals and their descendants, usually with flattened fingers and nails, keen vision, poor sense of smell
Family	Hominidae	Bipedal locomotion, flat face, eyes forward, binocular and color vision, hands and feet specialized for different functions
Genus	*Homo	Long childhood, large brain, speech ability
Species	**Homo sapiens	Body hair reduced, high forehead, prominent chin

* *Homo* = Latin: man
** *sapiens*: wise

homologous structures having the same evolutionary origin and maintaining similarity of structure.

Hormones Secretions from the endocrine glands that regulate the activities of body organs. Examples: growth hormone regulates growth of the long bones; thyroxin regulates body metabolism; adrenaline controls the release of sugar from the liver. Hormones are secreted directly into the bloodstream, which then carries them to their target organs.

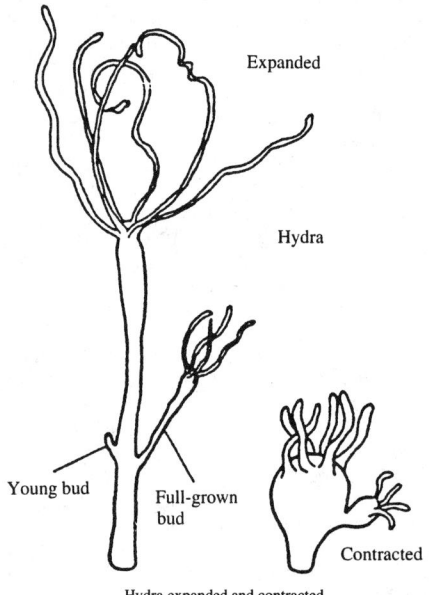

Hydra expanded and contracted

Hybrid An organism having mixed genes for a trait.

Hydra A freshwater coelenterate that is representative of a genus of the same name. Hydra is a polyp and has no medusa form in its life history. In length, each hydra is about 12 millimeters and has about eight tentacles that surround the mouth-anus. Hydras move about by somersaulting, end over end. The animal's locomotion is made possible by cells that have contractile fibers called myonemes. These epitheliomuscular cells have locomotor and sensory functions. Reproduction in hydra is sexual and asexual. A single organism produces both egg and sperm, which are discharged into the water where fertilization takes place. Asexual reproduction occurs by budding.

Hydrolysis *See* **Digestion**.

Hypothalamus The region of the brain that controls body temperature, osmoregulatory activities, maturity, thirst, hunger, and sex drive. The hypothalamus is also the region where the nervous and hormonal systems interact.

I **Immunity** Ability to resist the attack of a particular disease-producing organism. Immunity to one kind of disease germ does not automatically make a person immune to other types of disease germs. Active immunity is brought about by antibody production by a person's own body cells. Active immunity can be stimulated in either of two ways; by getting the disease and recovering from it or by being immunized against the disease. Immunization that produces active immunity involves the injection of weakened disease agents that stimulate antibody production but produce only mild symptoms or none at all. Active immunity is longlasting because the body cells continue to produce the antibodies. An injection of gamma globulins can give a person temporary immunity against certain specific diseases. This means that a person has borrowed antibodies in the blood and not those made by his (her) own cells. This kind of immunity is called passive immunity. It lasts only as long as the antibodies last; when they are used up, the immunity ceases.

Infectious diseases Caused by pathogens (germs). These pathogenic microorganisms include certain bacteria, protozoans, spirochetes, richettsias, mycoplasmas, and fungi. Parasitic worms and viruses also often produce disease in humans. Most infectious diseases are contagious—capable of being passed from one person to another by means of body contact or by droplet infection.

Ingestion The taking in or procuring of food. Digestion refers to the chemical changes that take place in the body by which nutrient molecules are converted to forms usable by cells.

Inheritance, intermediate Geneticists have discovered that in many cases a trait is not controlled by a single gene, but rather by the cooperative action of two or more genes. There are many instances in which Mendel's "law of dominance" does not hold true. A case in point is what was once called blending inheritance, or incomplete dominance. It is now known as codominance. When red-flowered evening primroses are crossed with white-flowered primroses, the hybrids are pink. Neither red nor white color is dominant and therefore the result is a blend. In sweet peas, the expression of red or white flowers is dependent upon two genes: a (C) gene for color and an (R) gene for enzyme. If C and R are inherited together, the flower color is red. If the dominant C is missing, the flower is white and if the dominant R is missing, the color is white. Therefore white flowers are the result of several different genotypes: ccrr, ccRR, CCrr, Ccrr.

Invertebrates Animals without backbones. About 90 percent of all animal species are invertebrates. Just like all members of the kingdom Animalia, invertebrates are multicellular. They are composed of cells that lack walls. Most invertebrates are capable of locomotion and have specialized cells with contractile proteins that facilitate movement. However, the adult forms of some lower invertebrate species are sessile, belonging to a group of filter feeders. These animals use cilia, flagella, tentacles, or gills to sweep smaller organisms from the currents of water that flow over or through their bodies into the digestive cavities. Some of the lower invertebrates reproduce vegetatively by budding. Other invertebrate species reproduce sexually, utilizing sperm and egg. Still other species reproduce asexually by parthenogenesis in which an unfertilized egg develops into a complete individual. Some invertebrates have marvelous powers of regeneration, the growing back of lost parts or the production of a new individual from an aggregate of cells or from a piece broken off from the parent organism. Examples of invertebrates are sponges, jelly fish, worms, clams, starfish, insects, crabs.

Involuntary muscle *See* **Muscle, smooth.**

Karyotype A technique of producing a photograph of matched chromosome pairs developed in 1956 by Joe Hin Tjio and Albert Levan.

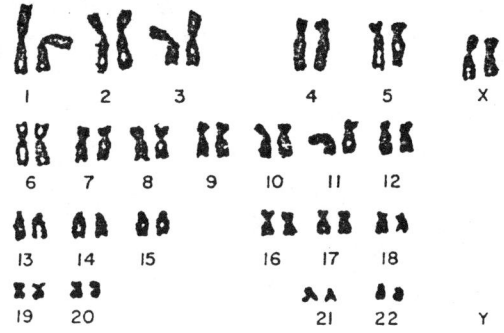

Karyotype of the Human Female

Kidneys Paired organs of the human urinary system located dorsally in the abdomen. The kidneys reabsorb water, sodium, glucose, and some proteins. Excess water and the protein waste, urea, pass into the collecting duct and are stored temporarily in the urinary bladder until released from the body. *See* **Urinary system.**

Kingdom system of classification, five The largest and most inclusive classification category is the kingdom. For many decades, living things were considered to be either plants or animals and thus were grouped into one of the two established king-

---

EXHIBIT 2.2
The Five Kingdom System

Kingdom	Characteristics
Monera	All monera are single-celled organisms. The monerans lack an organized nucleus, mitochondria, chloroplast, and other membrane-bound organelles. They have a circular chromosome. Examples are bacteria and blue-green algae.
Protista	Protists are one-celled organisms that have a membrane-bound nucleus. Within the nucleus are chromosomes that exhibit certain changes during the reproduction of the cell. Other cellular organelles are surrounded by membranes.
Fungi	Fungi are nonmotile, plant-like species that cannot make their own food. The fungi (fungus, singular) absorb their food from a living or nonliving organic source.
Plantae	The plant kingdom includes mosses, ferns, grasses, shrubs, flowering plants, and trees. Most plants make their own food by photosynthesis and contain chloroplasts.
Animalia	All members of the animal kingdom are multicellular. The cells have a discrete nucleus that contains chromosomes. Most animals can move and depend on organic materials for food.

doms. In 1969, the ecologist Robert Whittaker proposed an updated system of classification in which living things are grouped into one of five kingdoms, based on the extent of their complexity and the methods by which their nutritional needs are met. *See* **Exhibit 2.2** and illustration on page 2-18.

Krebs cycle　*See* **Respiration**.

Kwashiorkor　A serious protein deficiency disease is kwashiorkor. This disease, which threatens the lives of many children in Africa, causes misshapen heads, barrel chests, bloated stomachs, spindly legs and arms, decreased mental abilities, and poor vision.

Leaf　The most important function of green leaves is to carry out photosynthesis, the food-making process in which inorganic raw materials are changed into organic nutrients. A leaf consists of two parts: a stalk or petiole and the blade. The petiole attaches the blade to the stem. The blade is the place where photosynthesis takes place. Leaves vary greatly in shape.

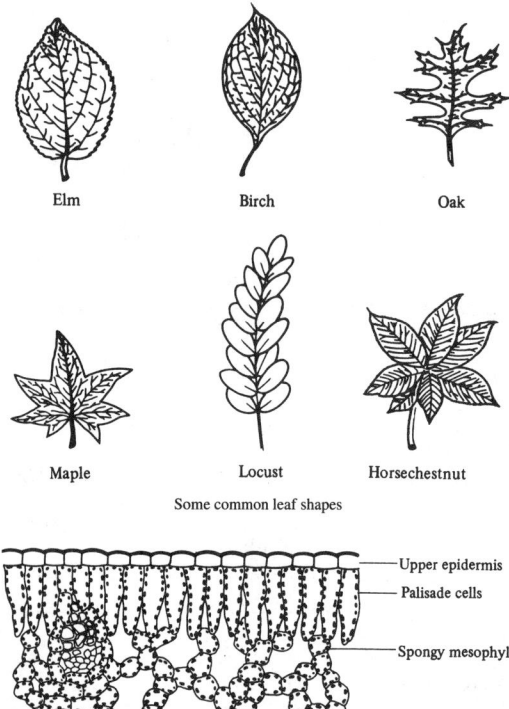

Elm　　　　Birch　　　　Oak

Maple　　　Locust　　　Horsechestnut

Some common leaf shapes

Upper epidermis
Palisade cells
Spongy mesophyll
Lower epidermis
Guard cell　Stomate

Leaf cross section

Leaf cross section　Study of a leaf cross section under the microscope reveals three types of tissue: upper and lower epidermis, mesophyll, and the vascular bundles. The mesophyll consists of palisade cells and spongy cells. The epidermis is a single layer of cells at the upper and lower surfaces of the leaf. The cells have thick walls made of cutin and lack chloroplasts. Their main function is to protect

the underlying or overlying tissues from drying, bacterial invasion, and mechanical injury. On the underside of the leaf, the lower epidermis has pores known as stomates, the size openings of which are regulated by a pair of guard cells. The stomates serve as passageways for oxygen and carbon dioxide.

Legionnaires' disease　An acute, pneumonia-like respiratory infection caused by an air-borne bacterium and associated with water in air conditioning towers. Symptoms are a feeling of malaise, chest pain, muscle aches, shortness of breath, and a dry cough. Other symptoms include a high fever, chills, abdominal pain, and sometimes abnormalities of the kidney and liver. If treated promptly with the antibiotic erythromycin, the infected person recovers. Without prompt treatment, the disease is fatal in 15 percent of cases.

Lichens　Lichens are pioneer organisms that can inhabit bare rock and other uninviting substrates. They live on the barks of trees and even on stone walls. A lichen is a combination of two organisms—an alga and a fungus—that live together in a mutualistic relationship. The alga carries on photosynthesis, while the fungus absorbs water and mineral matter for its partner. The fungus also anchors the lichen to the substrate.

Life functions　Living things are highly organized systems. They are self-regulating, self-reproducing, and capable of adapting to changes in the environment. To satisfy all of the conditions necessary for life, all living systems must be able to perform certain biochemical and biophysical activities which collectively are known as life functions. Nutrition is the sum total of those activities through which a living organism obtains nutrients (food molecules) from the environment. Life functions include nutrition as well as the processes of ingestion, digestion, and assimilation; respiration which encompasses breathing and cellular respiration; reproduction of cells; synthesis involving the biochemical processes of cells; regulation encompassing processes of control by hormones, enzymes, coenzymes, and utilized by the nervous system and the endocrine system; reproduction, both sexual and asexual.

Light reactions　*See* **Photosynthesis**.

Linked genes　Genes occurring on the same chromosome are inherited together. They are said to form linkage groups. Crossing over breaks linkage groups.

Lipids　The lipids are a group of organic compounds that include the fats and fat-like substances. A lipid molecule contains the elements carbon, hydrogen, and oxygen similar to a carbohydrate. Unlike the carbohydrates, however, in lipid molecules the ratio of hydrogen to oxygen is much greater than 2:1. Most lipids are made up of two basic units: alcohol (usually glycerol) and a class of compounds called fatty acids.

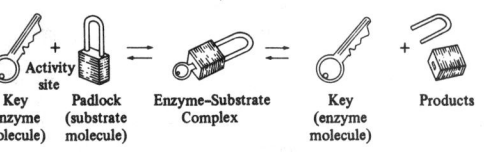

Key　　　Padlock　　Enzyme-Substrate　Key　　　Products
(enzyme　(substrate　　Complex　　　(enzyme
molecule)　molecule)　　　　　　　molecule)

Activity site

Lock and key analogy of an enzyme and its substrate

Lock and key　A simple analogy is used to explain the specificity of enzymes. Specificity refers to the characteristic of enzymes that permits a particular enzyme to form a complex with a specific substrate molecule only. The "lock and key" analogy explains enzyme specificity: the substrate is viewed as a padlock and the enzyme as the key able to unlock it. When unlocked (in the analogy) or acted upon by the key, the padlock comes completely apart. The key remains unchanged and ready to work again on another padlock of the same type.

Lungs   The human body has two lungs. Each of these is enclosed in a double membranous sac known as the pleural sac. Not only is this sac airtight, but it also contains a lubricating fluid. The pleural sac and the lubricating fluid prevent friction that might be caused by rubbing of the lungs against the chest wall.

Lyme disease   A flu-type disease transmitted from ticks to humans. The cause of the disease is a species of spiral bacteria injected in the human bloodstream through a bite by the infected deer tick, *Ixodes dammini*. Early treatment with antibiotics will prevent the development of arthritic symptoms. *See also* Health and Medicine section, page 8-42.

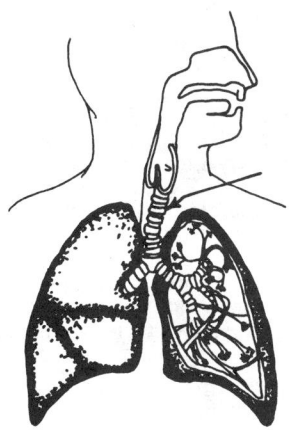

Lungs

Lymph   The body cells are bathed with tissue fluid called lymph. Lymph comes from the blood plasma, diffusing out of the capillaries into the tissue spaces in the body. Lymph differs from plasma in that it has 50 percent fewer proteins and does not contain red blood cells. Lymph has the important function of bringing nutrients and oxygen to cells and removing from them the waste products of respiration.

Lymphocytes   White blood cells that are produced in the lymph nodes and function in immune reactions of the blood.

M **Malpighian tubules**   These are long slender tubules, attached at one end to the digestive tract controlling excretion in insects and certain other arthropods. Nitrogen-containing wastes in the body fluid are changed into uric acid, which is then moved through the Malpighian tubule to the end of the digestive tract where it is ultimately excreted as dry crystals.

Mammals   The characteristics that set mammals apart from other animals and made them adaptable to a wide range of habitats are as follows:

1. Mammals have mammary glands (from which the name mammal) that supply the young with milk directly after birth.
2. At some time during the life cycle, all mammals have hair.
3. Mammals are warm-blooded. Constant body temperature is due, in part, to the four-chambered heart, a device that prevents the mixing of oxygenated and deoxygenated blood.
4. Most species of mammals have sweat glands that provide a secondary means of excreting water and salts.
5. Mammalian teeth have evolved into three different types: incisors for tearing, canines for biting, molars and premolars for grinding.
6. All but a few species have seven vertebrae in the neck. These neck bones are known as cervical vertabrae.
7. A muscular diaphragm separates the thoracic cavity (containing the lungs and the heart) from the abdominal cavity (housing part of the digestive system, the reproductive organs, and the excretory system).

For more information on the development of mammals, *see* illustration on page 2-16.

Marsupials   The marsupials are primitive mammals that do not have a placenta. The young are about 5 centimeters long at birth and are in an extremely immature condition. At birth they crawl into the mother's pouch or marsupium. The rounded mouth is attached to a nipple and the mother expresses milk down the throat of the helpless fetus. As development occurs, the young marsupial is then able to obtain milk by sucking. There are 29 living genera of marsuspials, 28 of which live in Australia. The opossum Didelphys is indigenous to North, South, and Central America and Caenolestes inhabits regions of Central America only. Besides the opossum, other marsupials are the kangaroo, koala, Tasmanian wolf, wombat, wallaby, and native cat.

Mastigophora   The Mastigophora are protozoa that have one or more flagella. Some species are free-living and inhabit fresh or salt water. Other Mastigophora species live in a symbiotic relationship with organisms of other species. For example, several species live in the intestines of termites, cockroaches, and woodroaches, where they digest cellulose for these insects. The genus Trypanosoma includes parasites that cause debilitating diseases in human beings. *Trypanosoma gambiense* is the zooflagellate that causes African sleeping sickness. Humans are infected with the trypanosome by the bite of an infected tsetse fly.

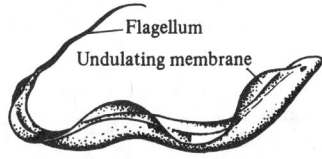

The causative organism of African sleeping sickness, *Trypanosoma gambiense*

Meiosis   Or reduction division, is cell division that occurs in the primary sex cells leading to the formation of viable egg and sperm cells. Meiosis reduces the number of chromosomes to one half in each gamete so that upon fertilization (the fusing of sperm and egg nuclei) the species chromosome number is kept constant.

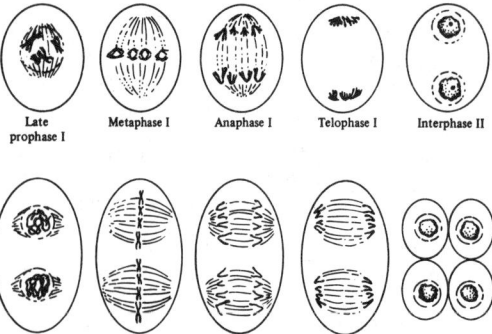

| Late prophase I | Metaphase I | Anaphase I | Telophase I | Interphase II |
| Prophase II | Metaphase II | Anaphase II | Telophase II | Four Haploid Cells |

Stages of meiosis

Menstruation　The process in which a nonfertilized egg is discharged from the body. The vascularized lining of the uterus, known as the endometrium, disintegrates in response to decreased levels of estrogen and progesterone in the blood. Menstrual bleeding lasts four to seven days in humans.

Messenger RNA　The mRNA, carrying a code for a specific protein, moves from the nucleus to the cytoplasm. The mRNA attaches itself to several ribosomes, each having its own ribosomal RNA. Specific transfer RNA (tRNA) molecules bring to the ribosomes their own kind of activated amino acids. Transfer RNA molecules that fit the active sites of mRNA's on the ribosomes temporarily attach to them. As a result, amino acids are lined up in the proper sequence. The RNA code is a triplet code with one triplet, or codon, made up of three base coding for a specific amino acid. *See also* **Protein synthesis.**

Metabolism　An inclusive term concerning all of the biochemical activities carried on by cells, tissues, organs, and systems necessary for the sustaining of life. Metabolic activities in which large molecules are built from smaller ones or in which nutrients are changed into protoplasm are called anabolic activities, or anabolism. Destructive metabolism in which large molecules are degraded for energy or changed into their smaller building blocks is called catabolic activity, or catabolism.

Metamorphosis　The change from tadpole to adult frog is known as metamorphosis, a process controlled by the thyroid gland. The adult amphibian loses the gills, lateral line senses, tail, unpaired fins, and muscles controlling them—the fish characteristics—and develops structures adapted for life on land. An adult amphibian breathes by means of lungs and has a three-chambered heart that is more efficient at pumping blood between the lungs, heart, and rest of the body. In most species the adult has limbs for movement, but no tail.

Change in body form takes place in some insects, such as from caterpillar to butterfly.

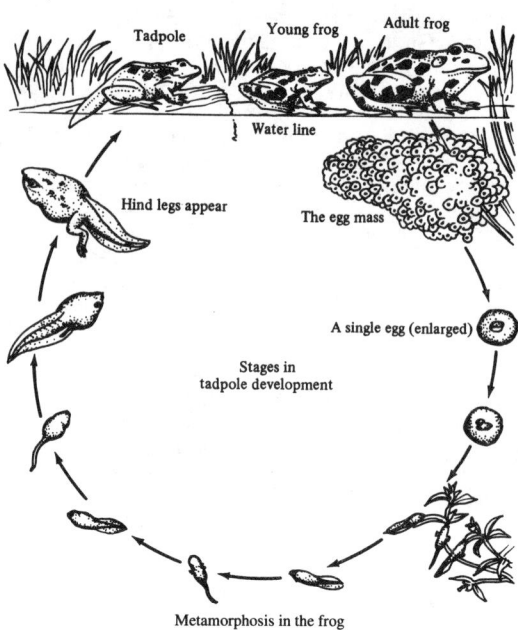

Metamorphosis in the frog

Microscope, electron　Magnification more than 200,000 times. Using electrons instead of light and magnets in place of lenses, the electron microscope has revolutionized the study of the cell. The scanning electron microscope has improved upon the resolution of fine detail made possible by electron microscopy. A fine probe directs and focuses electron beams over the material being studied, affording quick scanning and giving finer detail than is possible with the standard electron microscope.

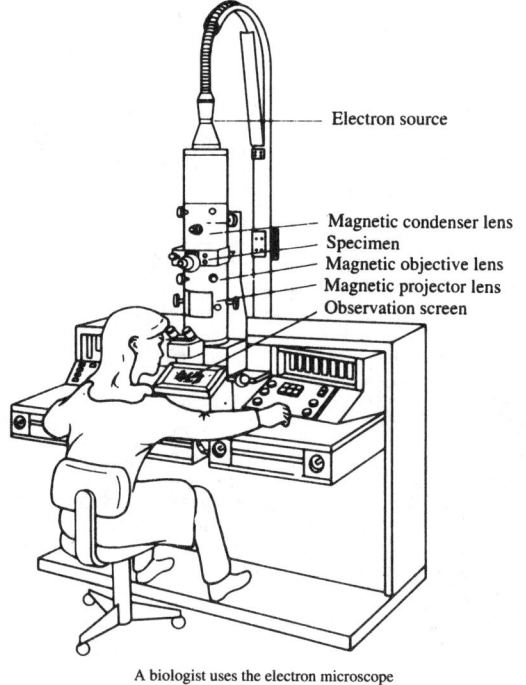

A biologist uses the electron microscope

Microscope, light The best light microscope is capable of magnifying objects 2,000 times. The phase contrast microscope makes transparent specimens visible, while the darkfield or the ultramicroscope gives vivid clarity to fragile and transparent organisms such as the spirochetes that cause syphilis. The ultraviolet microscope is used for photographing living bacteria and naturally fluorescent substances.

Mitochondrion A membranous cellular organelle. It consists of a smooth outer membrane and a folded inner membrane. The folds are called cristae. Like the cell membrane, the mitochondrion membrane is composed of proteins and phospholipids. The mitochondria are necessary for aerobic respiration to take place in cells.

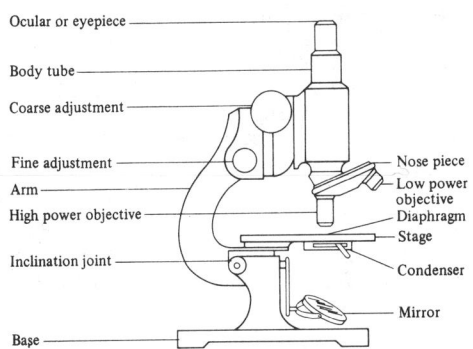

Parts of the compound (light) microscope

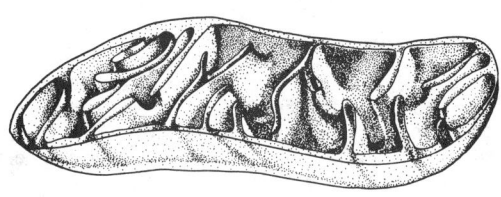

Mitochondrion

Mitosis Mitosis (also known as karyokinesis) concerns the cell nucleus and its chomosomes. Before the onset of mitosis, the cell is in a stage known as interphase. During interphase, the chromosomes are exceptionally long and very thin, appearing as fine granules through the light microscope. It is during this stage that DNA molecules in the nucleus replicate. The result of replication is that each chromosome now has an exact copy of itself. When interphase comes to an end, the cell has enough nuclear material for two cells. The orderly process that divides the chromosomes equally between the two daughter cells is known as mitosis. There are four stages of mitosis: prophase, metaphase, anaphase, and telophase. The significant events that mark each of these stages and interphase are shown below:

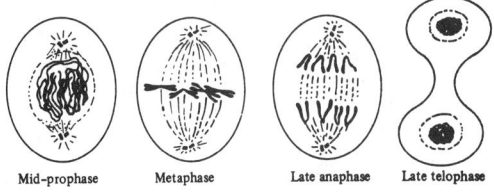

| Mid-prophase | Metaphase | Late anaphase | Late telophase |

Stages of mitosis

Mollusks Soft-bodied, nonsegmented, and usually enclosed within a calcium carbonate shell. They are most abundant in marine waters, although some species inhabit fresh water and others live on land. All mollusks have a mantle, a flattened piece of tissue that covers the body and that may secrete the calcareous shell. The body of the mollusk is described as being a head-foot, a muscular mass having different shapes and functions in the various classes. The mollusks include the chitons, snails, clams, scallops, squids, and octopuses. This is one of the largest animal phyla and includes about 1,000 species.

Monera The monerans are prokaryotic cells. They lack a nuclear membrane, mitochrondria, endoplasmic reticulum, Golgi apparatus, and lysosomes. The prokaryotes do not have any membrane-bound organelles in the cytoplasm. The monera are unicellular organisms usually invisible to the naked eye. Most monerans live as independent cells, although some may occur in filaments (chains of cells) or colonies of cells held together by a gelatinous coat. This kingdom includes bacteria, blue-green bacteria, also known as blue-green algae.

Monotremes The monotremes are primitive egg-laying mammals. The eggs, large and full of yolk, house the developing monotreme embryos. Examples of the monotremes are the "duckbill" or platypus (*Ornithorhynchus*) indigenous to Australia and Tasmania; the spiny anteater (*Echidna*), also an inhabitant of Australia; and a long snouted anteater (*Proechidna*) indigenous to New Guinea. Modified sweat glands of the anteater secrete a milk substitute that the young lick up from tufts of hair on the mother's belly.

Motor neuron *See* **Nerve cell (neuron).**

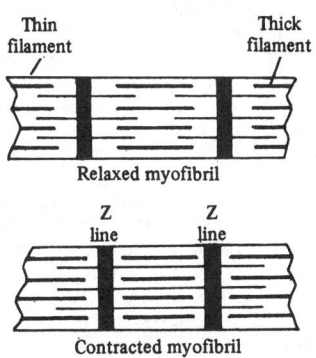

Sliding filament mechanism of muscle contraction

Muscle contraction Muscles contract due to a sliding filament mechanism. When the thick and thin filaments slide past each other, the Z lines of the sarcomeres are pulled closer together: in effect, contracting. Z lines form the boundary between sarcomeres. When the sarcomeres contract, the myofibrils contract, which causes the contraction of muscle fibers. Myofibrils are the basic units of muscle fibers. The figure illustrates the sliding filament mechanism of muscle contraction.

Muscular system   Muscles represent 40 percent of the total weight of the human body. Muscle tissue is characterized by contractility and electrical excitability, two distinctive properties that enable it to effect movement of the body and its parts. There are three types of muscle tissue: smooth, striated, and cardiac.

Muscle, cardiac   Cardiac muscle is present only in the heart, where the cells form long rows of fibers. Unlike other muscle tissue, cardiac muscle contracts independently of nerve supply since reflex activity and electrical stimuli are contained within the cardiac muscle cells themselves.

Muscle, smooth   Smooth muscle is present in the walls of the internal organs, including the digestive tract, reproductive organs, bladder, arteries, and veins. Because smooth muscle is contained in organs that do not respond to the will of a person, these muscles are called involuntary muscles.

Muscle, striated   Striated muscle is variously referred to as striped muscle, voluntary muscle, or skeletal muscle—terms describing its structure and function. Located in the legs, arms, back, and torso, striated muscles attach to and move the skeleton; since they are moved by the will of the person, they are often termed voluntary muscles. *See also* illustration on page 2-20.

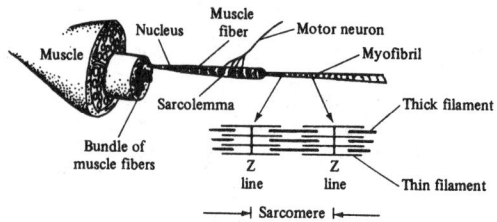

The fine structure of skeletal muscle

Mutations   Genes can change and changes in genes are known as mutations. Mutations are usually recessive and they are usually harmful. Mutations usually occur at random and spontaneously. However, mutations may be induced by radiation or by chemical contamination. There are several types of mutations. A loss of a piece of a chromosome is known as a deletion. The genes on the broken off piece of chromosome are lost. Sometimes a broken piece of chromosome sticks on to another chromosome, thus adding too many genes; this type of mutation is known as duplication. Sometimes a piece of chromosome becomes rearranged in the chromosome where it belongs, thus changing the sequence of the genes on that chromosome; this is known as an inversion, and it prevents gene for gene matching when chromosomes line up during meiosis. Point mutations are changes in individual genes.

Natural selection   Charles Darwin (1809–1882) was an English naturalist who together with his cousin, Alfred Russel Wallace (1823–1915), developed a theory of evolution that laid the groundwork for modern biological thinking. Darwin's theory of natural selection can be summed up thusly: large numbers of new plants and animals are produced by nature. Many of these do not survive because nature "weeds out" weak and feeble organisms by killing off those that cannot adapt to changing environmental conditions. Only the strongest and most efficient survive and produce progeny. Specific tenets of the Darwin-Wallace theory of evolution follow:

Overproduction: Every organism produces more gametes. If every gamete produced by a given species united in fertilization and developed into offspring, the world would become so overcrowded that there would be no room for successive generations. This does not happen because a balance is maintained in the reproduction of all species. Therefore natural populations remain fairly stable.

Competition: There is competition for life among organisms: competition for food, room, and space. Therefore there is a struggle for existence in which some organisms die and the more hardy survive.

Survival of the Fittest: Some organisms are better able to compete for survival than others. The differences that exist between organisms of the same species making one more fit to survive than another can be explained in terms of variations. Variations exist in every species and in every trait in members of the species. Therefore some organisms can compete more successfully for the available food or space in which to grow or can elude their enemies better. These variations are said to add survival value to an organism.

Nematodes   *See* **Worm-parasites**.

Nephridia   Coiled tubules that serve as excretory organs in the segmented worms. The nephridia filter out waste materials.

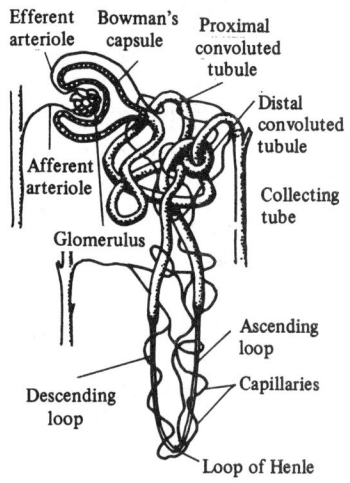

The nephron

Nephron   The unit of structure and function of the kidney is the nephron. There are about one million of these microscopic units in each kidney. They actively remove waste products from the blood and return water, glucose, sodium ions, and chloride ions to the blood. The nephron is made up of several structures. The first of these is a knot of capillaries called the glomerulus. The glomerulus fits into a second portion—the Bowman's capsule, a cup-shaped cellular structure that leads into the third part, the kidney tubule. There are four main parts of each kidney tubule: the proximal convoluted tubule, the loop of Henle, the distal convoluted tubule, and the collecting duct.

Nerve cell (neuron)   The basic unit of function of the nervous system is the *neuron*, or nerve cell. The parts of the nerve cell are the cyton, or cell body, the dendrites, and the axon. The dendrites receive signals from sense organs or from other nerve cells and transmit them to the cyton. The cell body passes signals to the axon, which then conducts the signals away from the dendrites and cell body. The axon terminating in

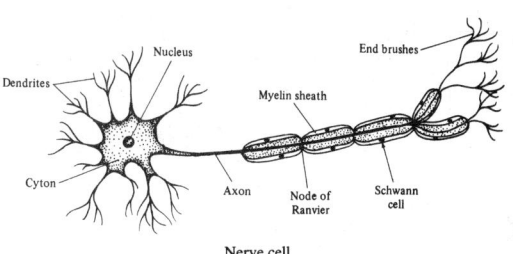

Nerve cell

end brushes (known also as terminal branches) is popularly called a nerve fiber. The nervous system has three types of neurons. Sensory or afferent neurons re-

---

EXHIBIT 2.3
The Autonomic Nervous System

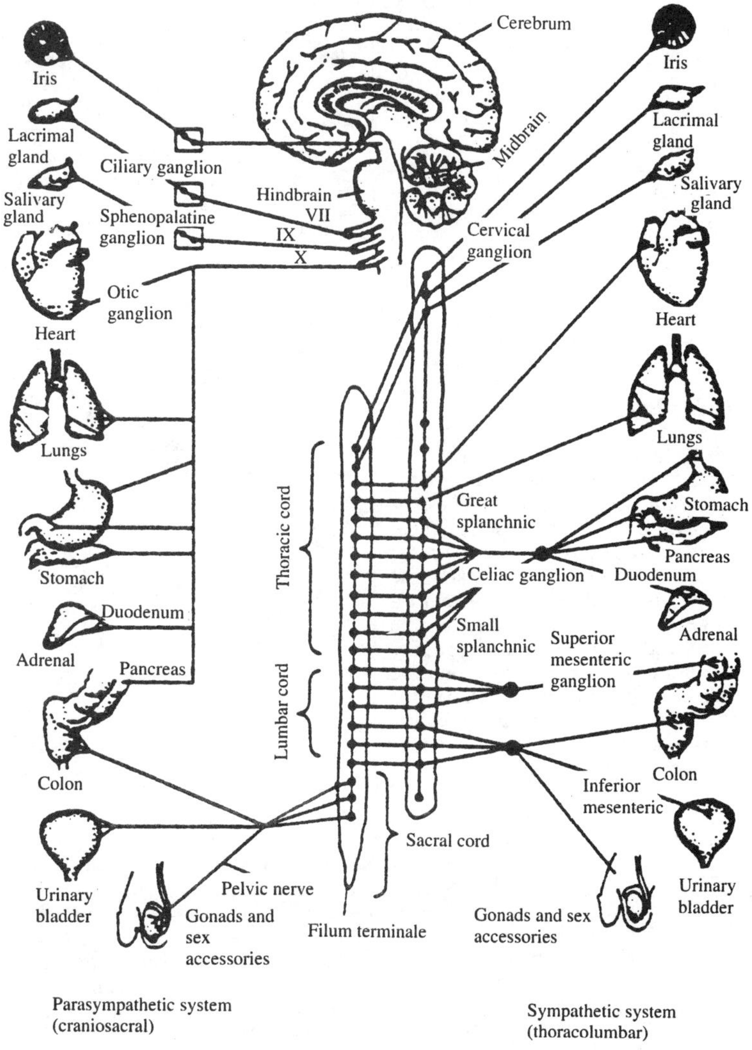

Cerebrum

Iris

Lacrimal gland

Ciliary ganglion

Salivary gland

Sphenopalatine ganglion

Otic ganglion

Heart

Lungs

Stomach

Duodenum

Adrenal

Pancreas

Colon

Urinary bladder

Pelvic nerve

Gonads and sex accessories

Filum terminale

Midbrain

Hindbrain

VII

IX

X

Cervical ganglion

Thoracic cord

Great splanchnic

Celiac ganglion

Small splanchnic

Superior mesenteric ganglion

Lumbar cord

Sacral cord

Inferior mesenteric

Iris

Lacrimal gland

Salivary gland

Heart

Lungs

Stomach

Pancreas

Duodenum

Adrenal

Colon

Urinary bladder

Gonads and sex accessories

Parasympathetic system (craniosacral)

Sympathetic system (thoracolumbar)

ceive impulses from the sense organs and transmit them to the brain or spinal cord. Associative or interneurons are located within the brain or spinal cord. These transmit signals from sensory neurons and pass them along to motor neurons. Motor or efferent neurons conduct signals away from the brain or spinal cord to muscles or glands, so-called effector organs.

Nerve impulse Communication in the nervous system is made possible by signals or impulses carried in a one-way direction along nerve cells. These impulses are electrical and chemical in nature. When a neuron is not carrying an impulse, it is at resting potential. When a nerve cell is stimulated to carry an impulse, its electrical charge changes and it has an action potential. Action potentials (nerve impulses) from any one nerve cell are always the same. All impulses are of the same size, there being no graded responses. This is known as the "all or none response," meaning that a nerve cell will transmit an impulse totally or not at all.

Nerve net The simple nervous system in Hydra consisting of pointed sensory cells scattered throughout the endoderm and ectoderm, specialized to receive impulses.

Nervous system, autonomic A network of nerves known as the autonomic nervous system controls the body's involuntary activities and the smooth muscles of the internal organs, glands, and heart muscle. It is composed of motor (efferent) neurons leaving the brain and spinal cord and also of peripheral efferent neurons. The autonomic nervous system is divided into the sympathetic system and the parasympathetic system. These subsystems are antagonists. When one set of nerves activates the smooth muscles of the body, the other set inhibits the action. For example: the parasympathetic nerves dilate the blood vessels and slow the heartbeat; the sympathetic nerves constrict the blood vessels and quicken heartbeat. *See* **Exhibit 2.3.**

Nervous system, human The human being has a complex nervous system that is composed of the principal functioning units of the central nervous system and the autonomic nervous system. The central nervous system is composed of the brain, spinal cord, and the nerves that radiate from the spinal cord. The brain is divided into three main parts: the forebrain, midbrain, and hindbrain. The forebrain controls all intelligent activities, voluntary muscle movements, speech, and interpretation of sensory data. The midbrain relays sensory information. The hindbrain controls all vital involuntary activities such as breathing, heartbeat, digestion, and the like. The central nervous system is the control center for all regulating activities in the body. *See* **Brain.**

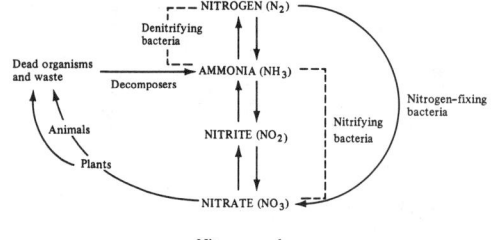

Nitrogen cycle

Nitrogen cycle The cycle of events through which nitrogen in the air becomes useful to plants and subsequently to heterotrophic organisms.

Nodules Bumps on the roots of leguminous plants (beans, clover, alfalfa) that house nitrifying bacteria. The nitrifying bacteria convert ammonia, released into the soil by breakdown of proteins to nitrites and then to nitrates.

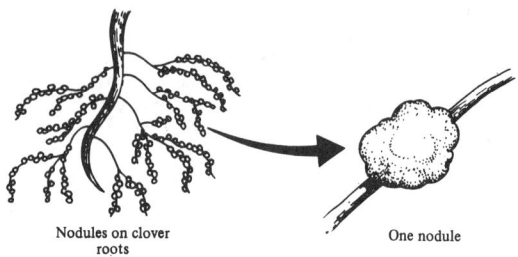

Nodules on clover roots   One nodule

Nodules

Nucleic acids DNA is an important part of the chromosome structure of all cells. DNA is a nucleic acid as is RNA. The unit of structure and function in the nucleic acid is called a nucleotide. A nucleotide is composed of a phosphate group, a five-carbon sugar, and a protein base. If the five-carbon sugar is ribose, the nucleic acid is ribonucleic acid (RNA). If the five-carbon sugar is deoxyribose, then the nucleic acid is deoxyribose nucleic acid (DNA). The protein bases in nucleic acids are ring compounds. Those bases with single rings are pyrimidines. Bases with double rings are purines. The pyrimidines in nucleic acid are thymine, cytosine, and uracil. The purines are adenine and guanine. The four bases that make up the DNA molecule are adenine (A), guanine (G), thymine (T), and cytosine (C). The four bases that make up the RNA molecule are adenine (A), guanine (G), cytosine (C), and uracil (U).

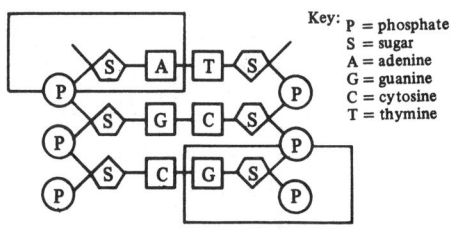

Key: P = phosphate
S = sugar
A = adenine
G = guanine
C = cytosine
T = thymine

Nucleotides are the units on which DNA molecules are built

Nutrition Is the totality of methods by which an organism satisfies the energy, fuel, and regulatory needs of its body cells. Those substances that contribute to the nutritional needs of cells are the nutrients. Animals take these nutrients into the body by the ingestion of food. Food, therefore, refers to edible materials that supply the body nutrients. Nutrients needed in large amounts are classified as macronutrients: carbohydrates, proteins, and fats. Micronutrients—vitamins and minerals—are needed in smaller amounts. Vitamins are organic compounds; minerals are inorganic. Malnutrition results from the improper intake of nutrients.

Nutritional relationships When two different species of organisms live together, the relationship is called symbiosis. If the relationship is of mutual benefit to both species, it is called mutualism. When one species benefits and the other does not but is not harmed by the association, the condition is known as commensalism. When one species lives at the expense of another, doing harm to its host, the relationship is parasitism. Disease-producing organisms are parasites.

Obligate aerobes Most species of the eubacteria are aerobic, using molecular oxygen in the process of breaking down carbohydrates to carbon dioxide and water. Obligate aerobes are those organisms that can live only in an environment that provides free or atmospheric oxygen. An example of an obligate aerobe is *Bacillus subtilis*.

Obligate anaerobes Some bacteria are obligate anaerobes and derive their energy by fermentation. These organisms cannot live in an environment of free oxygen. Many obligate anaerobes are disease producers; included in this group are *Clostridium tetani*, the causative organism of tetanus, and *Clostridium botulinum*, the bacterium that induces food poisoning. Still other bacteria are facultative anaerobes. These are basically aerobic bacteria, but they can live and grow in an environment that lacks free oxygen.

Oogenesis The maturation of the egg cell in which the primary oocyte (egg cell) goes through reduction division (meiosis). The outcome of these divisions is the production of one viable egg cell and two or more polar bodies.

Open circulatory system Characteristic of mollusks and the arthropods such as the grasshopper in which the blood is not confined in blood vessels and has contact with body tissues.

Organelles Organized structures that are parts of cells, such as ribosomes, nuclei, mitochondria, chloroplasts, cilia, contractile vacuoles, and endoplasmic reticulum.

Organs Are groups of tissues that work together to carry out a special function. Examples of organs are the heart, lungs, liver, and stomach.

Osmosis Is the diffusion of water through a membrane. Osmosis is a form of passive transport.

Ovary Is the female gonad where egg cells (ova) are produced. At times the ovary produces hormones and thus functions as an endocrine gland.

Oviparous Egg-laying, as in birds.

Ovoviviparous A condition in which eggs develop but are retained and hatched inside the mother's reproductive tract, as in cartilaginous fish (sharks) and a few snakes.

Ovulation The release of an egg cell (ovum) from a follicle in the ovary. Within the follicle a mass known as the *corpus luteum* forms in mammals and secretes the hormone *progesterone*. If the egg is not fertilized, the *corpus luteum* disintegrates and an egg is released from another follicle during the next menstrual cycle.

Ovules Immature seeds contained within the ovary of the flower.

Paramecium Representative of the ciliata. The cytoplasm in ciliates is differentiated into rigid outer ectoplasm and a more fluid inner endoplasm. A pellicle lies just inside of the cell membrane. Some species respond to adverse environmental stimuli by discharging elongated threads called trichocysts that serve as defense mechanisms or a means of anchoring the protist to floating pond material while feeding. Characteristic of the ciliata is the presence of two kinds of nuclei. The macronucleus controls metabolic activities, while the smaller micronucleus directs cell division. The figure shows the structure of the paramecium, a typical representative of the ciliata.

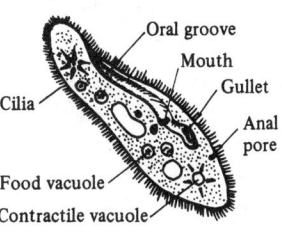

Paramecium

Parasites An organism that lives on or inside of the body of a plant or animal of another species and does harm to the host. Parasites offer physical discomfort to the host and tend to kill slowly, meanwhile having had time to reproduce themselves for several generations. Ectoparasites live on the host's body; body lice, dog fleas, ticks. Endoparasites live within the host's body and exhibit several adaptations for life in an intestine or in muscle or blood.

Parthenogenesis Although an egg will not develop unless it has been fertilized by sperm, some lower animals reproduce by parthenogenesis—in which eggs develop without sperm. This is true of aphids, or plant lice, water fleas, and others. In bees the drone, or male, develops from an unfertilized egg. Artificial parthenogenesis has been accomplished by scientists experimenting with the eggs of sea urchins and frogs. Jacques Loeb stimulated frog eggs to go through cleavage and eventually to form frogs without fertilization by sperms; he used various stimuli, such as pricking the membrane with a needle, and treatment with salt solutions or acids. Dr. Gregory Pincus was successful in producing "fatherless rabbits" by removing the ova from female rabbits, treating the ova with salt solutions and implanting them in other female rabbits. The baby rabbits that developed were females, and were subsequently mated to produce normal offspring.

Parturition The birth process is known as parturition. In humans the period of gestation (period of embryo development) is about 9 months or 40 weeks. At the end of that time, the uterus begins to contract in a process called labor to expel the baby. The onset of uterine contractions is probably caused by the release of oxytocin into the bloodstream by the posterior pituitary. The human newborn passes through the neck of the uterus (cervix) head first and then through the vagina to the outside.

Perennials Plants that live for many years, such as trees, shrubs, and grasses. Fire, disease, and mismanagement by humans causes the death of perennials.

pH The number of hydrogen ions in a solution is the basis of pH. The pH scale ranges from 0–14. A pH of 7 is neutral. Below the pH of 7, the number of H^+ ions increases and the solution becomes more acidic. The lower the pH number, the stronger the acid. A pH above 7 indicates that there are more OH^- ions than H^+ ions and the solution becomes more alkaline. Blood has a pH of 7.3. Special indicators are used to show the acidity or alkalinity of a solution.

Phagocytosis A process by which a cell first surrounds and engulfs a particle and then ingests it. Solid particles are ingested by cells through a process known as phagocytosis. White blood cells ingesting bacteria serve as an example of phagocytosis.

Phenotype The traits of an organism that can be seen.

Phloem Water-carrying (vascular) tissue in the plant leaf and stem specialized for conducting water with dissolved nutrient molecules downward to the root.

Photoperiodism The physiological response made by plants to changes in day length is known as photoperiodism. Some plants (short-day) flower only if they are exposed to light for less than a certain amount of time each day, other plants (long-day) must have a certain minimum length of photoperiod. Researchers explain the ability of plants to measure time by the action of phytochrome, a light absorbing pigment that is associated with the cell membrane and with some of the cell's internal membranes.

Light Reaction (Hill Reaction)

Light

Ch α_1

$2e^-$ Reducing substance

Photosystem I (700)

Z → FX Ferredoxin

Ch$^+$ α_1 4 ATP

Cyclic Phase   FP Flavoprotein

Plastocyanin PC

cyt b_6

cyt f

NAD$^+$ P → NADPH$_2$

Photo system II (680)

Light

Ch α_{11} 2e   Noncyclic Phase   cyt b_3

Q → Plastoquinone

Ch$^+$ α_{11} 4 ATP

Carrier Y

$2H_2O \rightarrow 2H^+ + 2OH^- \rightarrow \boxed{2e} + H_2O + \frac{1}{2}O + \boxed{2H^+}$

Photolysis

The pathways of photosynthesis involve many steps and many intermediate products and catalysts, including flavoprotein and cytochrome (cyt).

Photosynthesis Photosynthesis takes place inside of chloroplasts, structures within the cells of the leaf. Chloroplasts have fine structures within—

flattened membranous sacs named thylakoids. On the membranes of the thylakoids, chlorophyll and the accessory pigments are organized into functional groups known as photosystems. Each of these photosystems contains about 300 pigment molecules that are involved directly or indirectly in the process of photosynthesis. Photosynthesis involves four sets of biochemical events: photochemical reactions, electron transport, chemiosmosis, and carbon fixation. The photochemical reactions and electron transport activities take place on the membranes of the thylakoids. The oval membranes of a thylakoid surround a vacuole or reservoir in which hydrogen ions are stored until needed in the Calvin cycle, or carbon fixation. Each thylakoid rests in the stroma or ground substance of the chloroplast. The stroma is the place where carbon fixation occurs.

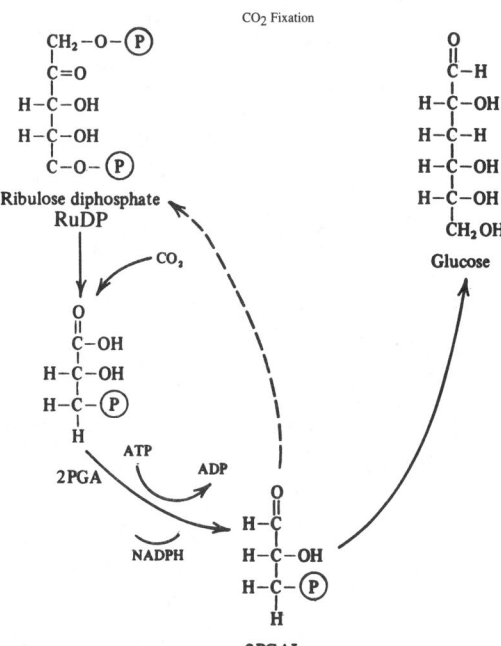

The Calvin cycle showing the complex steps leading from ribulose diphosphate (biphosphate) to glucose, a 6-carbon sugar.

Pinocytosis Cell drinking. The engulfing of molecules in solution through the cell membrane requiring the use of the cell's energy.

Plants, green Green plants are grouped in the kingdom Plantae. Members of the kingdom Plantae contain the green pigment chlorophyll. Not only does chlorophyll color plant leaves and some stems green, it, more importantly, traps light energy which is used in the process of photosynthesis. As an outcome of photosynthesis nutrient molecules are made, serving as food for both plants and animals. Most species of the kingdom Plantae are nonmotile, anchored to one place, and unable to move about, but a few of the lower plants are motile for at least part of the life cycle. However, the evolutionary trend exhibited in green plants is toward stationary organisms that carry out their life functions on land in locations where they remain for life. Lower plant species equipped to swim live in salt and fresh water. Higher plants are terrestrial (land-dwelling)

Pollination   The transfer of pollen from the anther to the stigma. Most flowers are insect- or wind-pollinated. Insect-pollinated flowers have petals and nectar that attract insects. The pollen tends to be sticky and clings more easily to insect bodies. Wind-pollinated flowers lack petals; or if present, they are relatively inconspicuous. They seldom produce nectar. Pollen is light and dry and sometimes has membranous appendages, all these characteristics making it easier to become wind-borne. Windblown pollen is produced in large quantities enhancing the chances for pollination.

Polymorphism   The honeybee exhibits a specialized social structure called polymorphism, a condition in which individuals of the same species are specialized for different functions. In a honeybee colony, three classes of individuals arise: fertile males called drones; fertile females, or queens; and sterile females, or workers. The workers have a special concave surface on the second pair of walking legs called a pollen basket used to carry pollen. The queen bee receives sperm from the drone once during her lifetime. The sperm are stored in a special organ called the spermatotheca in which they may live for years. Fertilized eggs give rise to females, most of which remain workers. A special female may be selected by the colony and fed a diet of "royal jelly" that causes her to grow larger than the others and become fertile. This fertile female will become a queen, and either take over the existing colony or start a colony of her own. Drones develop from unfertilized eggs by the process of parthenogenesis.

Population genetics   *See* **Hardy-Weinberg principle**.

Predation   This is the process of one species feeding upon another. The *predator* is the consumer that seeks out the *prey* to be consumed. Predators have special adaptations that enable them to hunt and catch their food supply: speed and agility, stingers, fangs, poisons, claws, and camouflage. Plant species have certain adaptations that protect them against predation such as thorns, microscopic spines, and the production of poisons such as nicotine, morphine, strychnine, mescaline, and aromatic compounds such as cinnamon and cloves. Animal defenses against predation include protective coloration, spines of the porcupine, the odor of the skunk, and the ability to hide through camouflage.

Proteins   Complex molecules built from amino acids. About 20 amino acids are essential to living systems. From these a large number of different kinds of proteins are formed. The great variety of protein molecules is possible because of the many ways in which amino acid molecules can be arranged. Changing the sequence of just one amino acid in a chain will change the protein molecule. Much of the work of the cell is concerned with the synthesizing of protein molecules. Some of these proteins such as hormones, enzymes, and hemoglo-

bin are used in complex biochemical activities. Other proteins contribute to the structure of cells such as those that make up the plasma membrane and other cellular membranes.

Protein synthesis   The code for proteins is present in messenger RNA molecules, which are complementary to DNA molecules. For example: let us suppose that a portion of a DNA molecule carries a code such as AAC GGC AAA TTT. Its mRNA complement would be as follows: UUG CCG UUU AAA. The mRNA, carrying this code, now moves from the nucleus to the cytoplasm. The mRNA attaches itself to several ribosomes, each having its own ribosomal RNA. Specific transfer RNA (tRNA) molecules bring to the ribosomes their own kind of activated amino acids. Transfer RNA (tRNA) molecules, each with a particular amino acid attached, attach temporarily to the codons on the mRNA and their amino acids are linked together in the correct sequence, one amino acid at a time. Note that the RNA code is a triplet code with one triplet, or codon, made up of three bases coding for a specific amino acid. *See also* **Messenger RNA**.

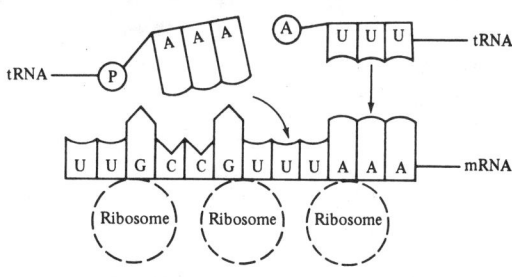

Protein synthesis

Protists   All of the species assigned to the kingdom Protista are eukaryotic, for example, Amoeba and Paramecia. Most protists carry out their lives within a single cell as free-living organisms. However, some protist species are organized into colonies where each cell carries out its own life functions and where, also, there may be some simple division of labor among the cells in the grouping. An impressive variety of species are classified as protists, and they probably descended from diverse evolutionary lines. The protists themselves represent evolutionary modification and are probably the ancestors of the modern fungi, plants, and animals.

Protozoa   Protozoa, meaning "first animals," are one-celled heterotrophs. Species of protozoa number in the thousands. They live in fresh water, salt water, dry sand, and moist soil. Some species live as parasites on or inside of the bodies of other organisms. Reproduction in the protozoans is usually described as being asexual by means of mitosis, but recent research has revealed that many protozoa augment asexual reproduction with a sexual cycle. Usually, the sexual cycle occurs during periods of adverse environmental conditions, and the cell arising from the fusion of gametes (zygote) can resist unfavorable conditions. The thick wall and the decreased metabolic rate of the cyst permits

BIOLOGY

survival during periods of cold, drought, or famine. The protozoa are divided into four phyla, based primarily on the methods of locomotion.

Punctuated equilibrium   There is a time frame for evolution. The concept of gradualism supports the idea that evolutionary change is slow, gradual, and continuous. The concept of punctuated equilibrium sets forth the idea that species have long periods of stability, lasting for four or five million years, and then change as the result of some geological or other environmental change.

Punnett square   A Punnett square is a diagrammatic device used to predict the genotypic and phenotypic ratios that will result when certain gametes fuse. Remember that as a result of meiosis each gamete has only one half the number of chromosomes that are in the somatic cells.

Problem: In fruit flies, long wing (L) is dominant over vestigial wing (l). What is the result of a cross between two flies that are heterozygous (Ll) for wing length?

Solution:

Parents: Male   ×   Female
            Ll Ll

Gametes: Ⓛ Ⓛ   Ⓛ Ⓛ

Punnett square

	L	l
L	LL	Ll
l	Ll	ll

F_2 LL = 1 homozygous dominant long winged fly
    Ll = 2 heterozygous dominant long winged flies
    ll = 1 homozygous recessive short winged fly

R   **Race** All humans belong to the species *Homo sapiens*. This means that the genetic material of all people is so similar that all humans can interbreed and produce fertile offspring. The human species is really a group of interbreeding populations. Populations that have adapted to certain environments become genetically different based on the frequency with which certain genes appear. Skin color, hair texture, body build, and facial bone structure are a few of the characteristics that identify human population groups known as races. Although we can make broad generalizations about the identifying characteristics of racial groups, not every member of each group fits these specifications. A set of physical characteristics can be drawn up that will fit individuals of several different races. Therefore, it is difficult for biologists and anthropologists to agree on the number of human races.

Radioactive dating   Scientists have determined that certain elements disintegrate by giving off radiations spontaneously and at a regular rate. Such elements are said to be radioactive. In the process of emitting radiations, the radioactive substance changes to something else. For example: uranium-238 changes to lead. The *half-life* of U-238, the rate at which one half of the uranium in a rock sample will change to lead, is 4.5 billion years. Uranium's rate of decay is not affected by any chemical or physical conditions. Therefore measuring the uranium-lead ratio in a sample of rock is a very reliable method for estimating the age of the rock. Dating of the oldest rocks found on earth indicates that they are about 3 billion years old. To allow time for the original formation of the rocks, geologists add another 2 billion years to this figure, thus arriving at the 4.5–5 billion-year estimate of the age of the earth.

Recessive trait   A characteristic that will appear if there are two like (recessive) genes for the trait. A trait that is masked by a dominant gene. For example: in sheep, white wool is dominant over black wool. A sheep with black wool must have two recessive genes for the trait.

Recombinant DNA   Recombinant DNA is DNA combined from two different organisms to produce characteristics not found in nature. The technique for doing this involves the use of a class of special enzymes called "restriction enzymes." These enzymes have the ability of splitting a DNA strand. The fragments of DNA have sticky ends, and when they touch a strip of DNA from another organism, they stick to it. In this way new genes can be introduced into an organism. Once done, the cell can synthesize the protein coded for by the newly acquired genes. Some proteins that have been produced in this way are interferon, insulin, and human growth hormone.

Red blood cells (Erythrocytes)   The human body contains about 25 trillion erythrocytes, each one lasting about 120 days. New red cells are produced by the bone marrow at the rate of one million per second. Erythrocytes contain hundreds of molecules of the iron-protein compound hemoglobin. In the lungs, oxygen binds loosely to hemoglobin forming the compound oxyhemoglobin. As erythrocytes pass body cells with low oxygen content, oxygen is released from hemoglobin and diffuses into tissue cells. Carbon dioxide combines with another portion of the hemoglobin molecule and is transported to the lungs where it is exhaled.

Reflex   If you accidentally touch a flame, your finger is automatically pulled back. A sensory neuron carries the impulse from the receptor, at the end of your finger, to the spinal cord, here an associative neuron receives it and sends it over a motor neuron to a muscle in your arm, which contracts, and pulls your finger away. There is no thought involved in the reaction. It is centered in the spinal cord. A moment later, you are aware of it, because impulses are sent up the spinal cord to the brain. Fortunately you do not have to think about such stimuli. The response is inborn and is a factor in your survival. Such a reflex protects you.

Regulation   Encompasses all processes that control and coordinate the many activities of a living thing. Chemical activities inside of cells are controlled by enzymes, coenzymes, vitamins, minerals, and hormones. The nervous and endocrine systems of higher animals integrate and coordinate body activities. Growth and development of plants is regulated by auxins and other growth-control substances. Gene activity is regulated by special molecules that turn the gene on and off.

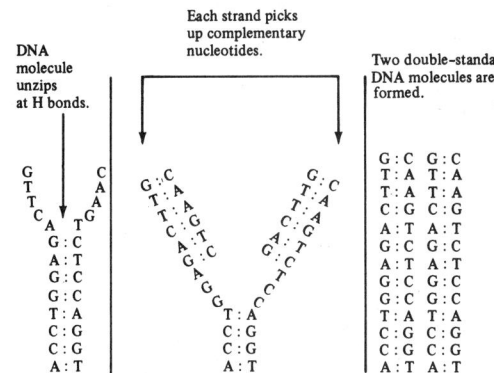

The replication of DNA

Replication   The process through which a DNA molecule makes an exact duplicate of itself.

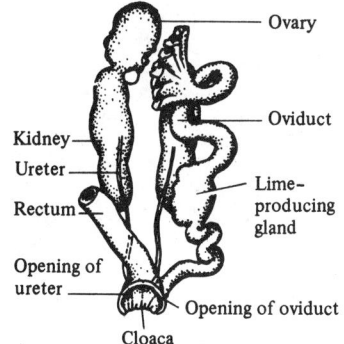

Reproductive system of the female bird

Reproduction   The process by which new individuals are produced by parent organisms. Basic to the understanding of reproduction is the concept that organisms produce the same kind of individuals as themselves. There are two major kinds of reproduction: asexual and sexual.

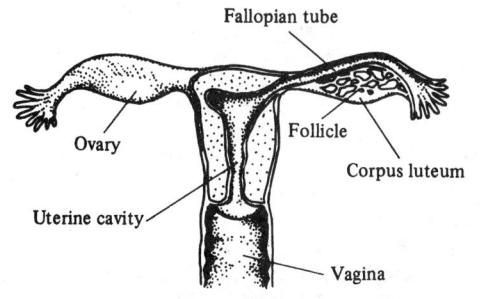

Female reproductive system

Reproductive system, female   The female reproductive system serves three important functions: the production of egg cells, the disintegration of nonfertilized egg cells, and the protection of the developing embryo. The reproductive system has spe-

cialized organs to carry out these functions. Two oval-shaped ovaries lie one on each side of the midline of the body in the lower region of the abdomen. On a monthly alternating basis each ovary produces a mature egg. Eggs are located in spaces in the ovary called follicles. As an egg matures, it bursts out of the ovarian follicle and is released into the appropriate branch of the fallopian tube, a tube that leads from the region of the ovary to the uterus. If the egg is fertilized, it becomes implanted in the uterus where it goes through a series of cell divisions known as cleavage.

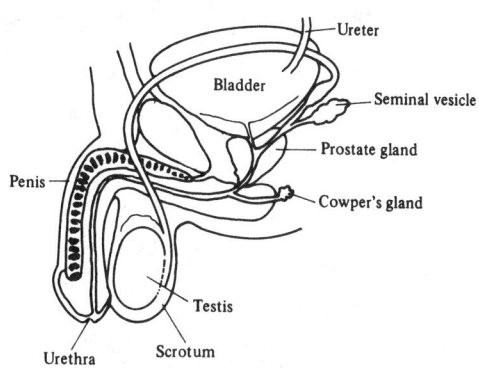

Male reproductive system

Reproductive system, male   In the male reproductive system some organs are located outside of the body and others are positioned internally. The scrotum contains the testes, glands that produce sperm, and the male hormone testosterone. Also positioned outside of the body is the penis, the organ that delivers the sperm into the body of the female. Each testis contains thousands of seminiferous tubules. Within these tubules, the sperm cells are manufactured. Each epididymis tubule functions as a storage place for sperm and also serves as a pathway that carries the sperm to a duct called a vas deferens. In its travels to the vas deferens, the sperm pass the seminal vesicles where they obtain nutrients. From the vas deferens, the sperm are conducted to the urethra, a single tube that extends from the bladder through the penis. Sperm cells leave the body through the penis. *See* **Sperm**.

Reptiles   Reptiles have a dry leathery skin covered with epidermal scales. A somewhat flattened skull contains a brain having a cerebrum much larger than that of the fish or amphibians. The eyes have secreting glands that keep the surface moist. Reptiles are air-breathers and have rather well-developed lungs. The heart is composed of two atria and a ventricle; in some species the ventricle is almost divided into two compartments, an evolutionary signpost pointing to the four-chambered heart. The body temperature of reptiles is not constant, changing with the external environment. In popular speech, such animals are called cold-blooded; in technical language, poikilotherms or ectothermic.

Respiration   Consists of breathing and cellular respiration. Breathing refers to the pumping of air into and out of the lungs of air-breathing animals

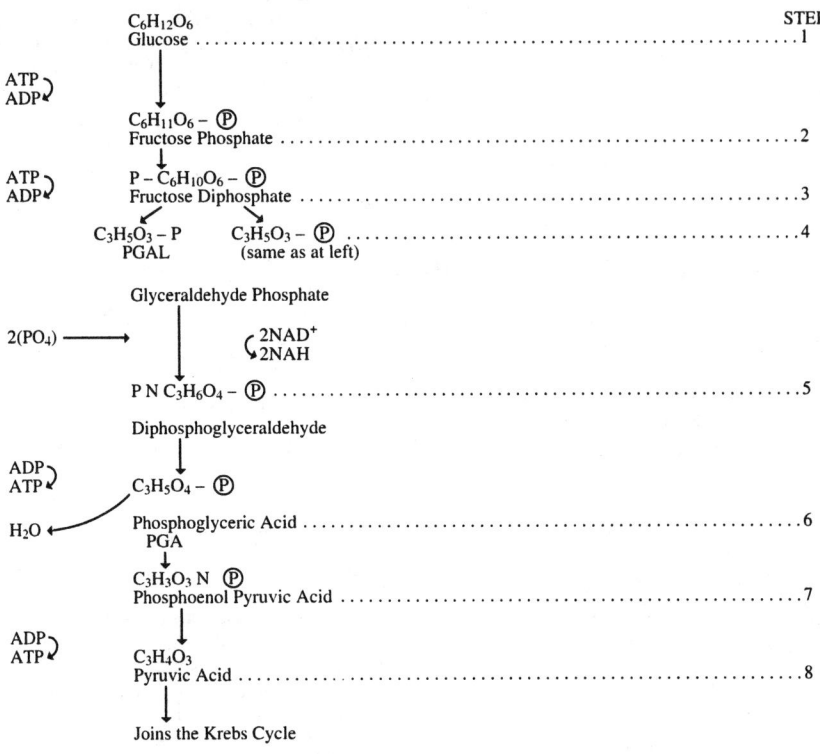

EXHIBIT 2.4
Anaerobic Respiration,
or Glycolysis

$C_6H_{12}O_6$
Glucose . . . . STEP 1

ATP
ADP

$C_6H_{11}O_6 - (P)$
Fructose Phosphate 2

ATP
ADP

$P - C_6H_{10}O_6 - (P)$
Fructose Diphosphate 3

$C_3H_5O_3 - P$ $C_3H_5O_3 - (P)$ 4
PGAL   (same as at left)

Glyceraldehyde Phosphate

$2(PO_4)$ ———→

$2NAD^+$
$2NAH$

$P N C_3H_6O_4 - (P)$ 5

Diphosphoglyceraldehyde

ADP
ATP

$C_3H_5O_4 - (P)$

H_2O ←

Phosphoglyceric Acid 6
PGA

$C_3H_3O_3 N (P)$
Phosphoenol Pyruvic Acid 7

ADP
ATP

$C_3H_4O_3$
Pyruvic Acid 8

Joins the Krebs Cycle

or the movement of water over the gills of fish. During breathing, oxygen diffuses into the air sacs in the lungs and carbon dioxide moves out of the lungs through the nose and mouth. Cellular respiration is a combination of biochemical processes that release energy from glucose and store it in ATP (adenosine triphosphate) molecules. *See* **Exbihits 2.4 and 2.5.**

Respiratory system The respiratory system includes the structures through which oxygen comes into the body to reach the bloodstream, and through which carbon dioxide and water vapor leave. Summary of route of air through respiratory system: (1) nostrils, (2) nasal cavity and sinuses, (3) pharynx, (4) larynx, (5) trachea, (6) bronchi, (7) bronchial tubes in the lungs, (8) air sacs (alveoli). *See* illustration on page 2-13.

Retrovirus A virus in which the genetic information is coded in ribonucleic acid (RNA) instead of in deoxyribonucleic acid (DNA). HIV, the virus of AIDS, is a retrovirus that produces *reverse transcriptase*, an enzyme that enables the retrovirus to replicate, and to make more of itself.

Ribonucleic acid (RNA) A nucleic acid consisting of a large number of nucleotides, each of which contains ribose sugar and four bases, including uracil, and a phosphate radical. *See also* **Protein synthesis.**

Ribose A sugar of chemical formula $C_5H_{10}O_5$: one of the building blocks of nucleic acid.

Ribosome A small organelle that is the site of protein synthesis.

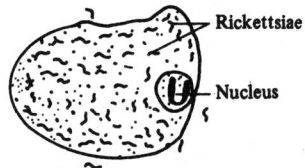

Rickettsiae in tissue cells

Rickettsiae The rickettsiae are very small Gram negative intracellular parasites. They were first described in 1909 by Harold Taylor Ricketts, who found them in the blood of patients suffering from Rocky Mountain spotted fever. The rickettsiae are nonmotile, nonspore forming, nonencapsulated organisms. In length, these organisms range from 0.3–1 micrometers. They live in the cells of ticks and mites and are transmitted to humans through insect bites. The rickettsiae are responsible for several febrile (fever-producing) diseases in humans, such as typhus fever, trench fever, and Q fever.

Roots Roots anchor plants to the soil and absorb water and dissolved minerals from the ground. The

EXHIBIT 2.5
Krebs Citric Acid Cycle

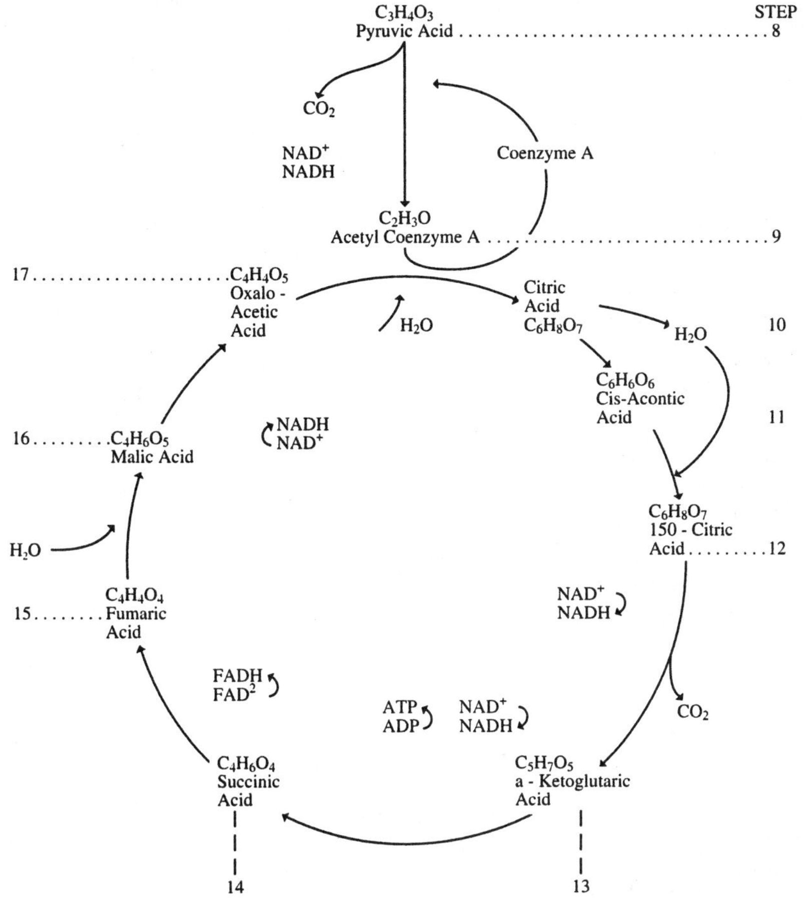

$C_3H_4O_3$
Pyruvic Acid . . . . STEP 8

CO_2

NAD^+
$NADH$

Coenzyme A

C_2H_3O
Acetyl Coenzyme A 9

17 . . . . $C_4H_4O_5$
Oxalo - Acetic Acid

H_2O

Citric Acid $C_6H_8O_7$

H_2O 10

$C_6H_6O_6$
Cis-Acontic Acid   11

16 . . . . $C_4H_6O_5$
Malic Acid

$NADH$
NAD^+

$C_6H_8O_7$
150 - Citric Acid 12

H_2O

15 . . . . $C_4H_4O_4$
Fumaric Acid

NAD^+
$NADH$

$FADH_2$
FAD^2

ATP NAD^+
ADP $NADH$

CO_2

$C_4H_6O_4$
Succinic Acid

$C_5H_7O_5$
a - Ketoglutaric Acid

14   13

---

absorbed materials enter the root by way of root hairs which are one-cell extensions of the epidermis. From the root hairs, dissolved materials pass through the cortex, endodermis, and pericycle into xylem cells. The xylem cells conduct the dissolved materials upward. The root cortex serves in the storage of food and water.

Root types

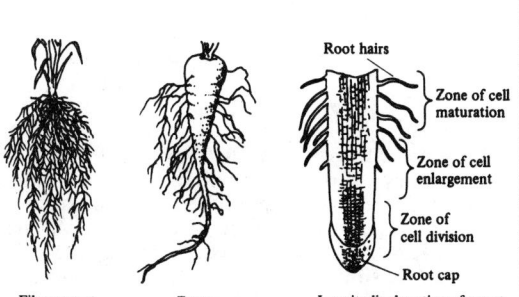

Fibrous root   Taproot   Longitudinal section of a root

Root hairs

Zone of cell maturation

Zone of cell enlargement

Zone of cell division

Root cap

Saprophytes (saprobes) These organisms obtain their food by absorbing nutrients from dead organic matter. Examples are some species of eubacteria and species of fungi. The fungus has specialized structures that secrete digestive enzymes into the food substrate on which they live, such as dead logs. The digestive enzymes liquefy the small portions of the log, releasing organic molecules that are absorbed by the fungus. Saphrophytic bacteria secrete digestive enzymes onto the food substrate for digestion. The released organic molecules then are absorbed by the bacteria.

Scientific method Scientific problem solving depends upon accuracy of observation and precision of method. Inherent in scientific thinking is orderliness of approach, which invites the forming of conclusions from hypotheses, theories, principles, generalizations, concepts, and laws. Scientific problem solving follows a pattern of behaviors that are collectively known as the scientific method.

Semi-permeable membrane The cell membrane controls the passage of materials into and out of the cell. It is often referred to as a living gatekeeper. The cell membrane is semi-permeable and highly selective: not every ion or molecule can cross its boundary. The movement of materials across the cell boundary and into or out of the cell is given the general term of transport. It is controlled by the globular proteins, phospholipids, and pores of the membrane and by the electrochemical nature of protoplasm, the living substance of the cell.

Sense organs The human body has five major senses—sight, hearing, taste, smell, and touch—that provide information about the external environment and transmit the stimuli to sensory nerves and ultimately to the brain for processing.

Sex determination In human beings, there are 22 pairs of autosomes, chromosomes that affect all characteristics not involved in sex determination. One pair of chromosomes determines the sex of an individual. In normal females, the sex chromosomes are designated as XX. In normal males, the sex chromosomes are XY. Certain disorders are sex-linked, usually passed from mother to son by a defective gene on the X chromosome; red-green color blindness is one such sex-linked trait that is found more frequently in males and hardly at all in females. Hemophilia is another sex-linked trait that affects males with greater frequency than females.

Sharks Cartilaginous fish in which the skeleton is made of cartilage instead of bone. The body of the shark is covered with placoid scales which arise from the ectoderm, also forming teeth in the jaws and on the roof of the mouth. Sharks have no swim bladder and the gill slits are uncovered. The fertilization is internal; the embryos are nourished from food from the egg.

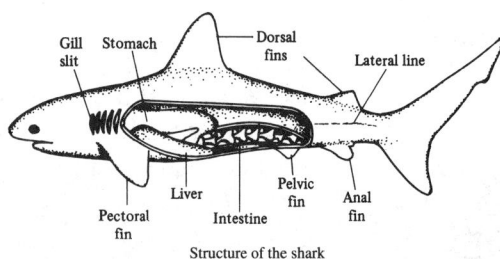

Structure of the shark

Sinoatrial node Each heartbeat is started by self activating electrical activity of the heart's pacemaker known as the sinoatrial node (S-A node), positioned in the wall of the right atrium. From the S-A node, the impulse spreads throughout the atrium to the antrioventricular node (A-V node), a specialized bundle of cardiac muscle located on the atrium near the ventricles. The impulse spreads from the A-V node to all parts of the ventricles causing simultaneous contractions in the ventricles.

Skeletal system The human skeleton, like that of all vertebrates, is a living endoskeleton that grows with the body. At birth, the human baby has a body that is made up of 270 bones. Due to the fusion of separate bones, the mature skeleton is composed of 206 bones. The human skeleton is a magnificent feat of engineering. The primary purpose of the skele-

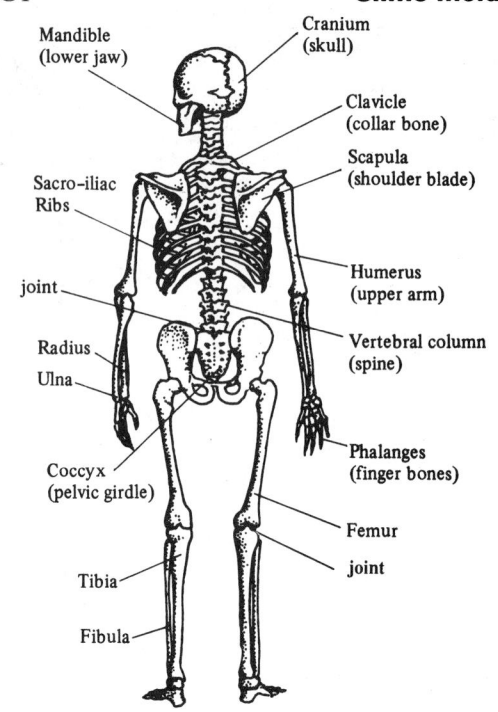

Some bones of the human body

ton is to carry the weight of the body and to support and protect the internal organs. The skeleton must be strong and able to absorb reasonable amounts of shock without fracturing. At the same time, the body framework must be flexible and light enough in weight to permit movement. Skeletal bones move in response to muscles that work like levers, allowing a variety of movements such as walking, running, hopping, sitting, bending, lifting, and stooping.

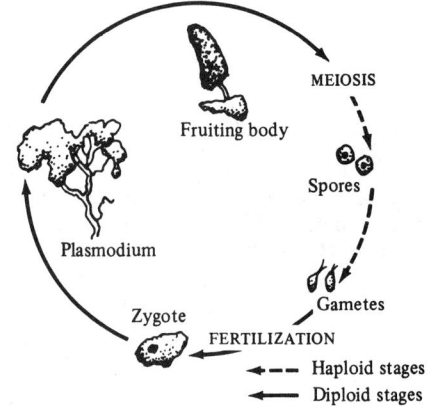

Life cycle of a true slime mold

Slime molds Slime molds live on the forest floor where they grow in damp soil, on or around rotting logs and on decaying vegetation. They appear to be shapeless globs of slime of varying colors: white, yellow, or red. The life cycle includes either an amoeboid slime mass called a plasmodium or a plant-like sporangia stage that is supported by stalks called fruiting bodies. A multicellular mass is called a plasmodium. A multinucleated mass is called a pseudoplasmodium. The diagram above shows stages in the life cycle of true slime mold.

Sodium-potassium pump   At times molecules are forced out of cells by exocytosis, a means by which they are carried to the cell surface by vacuoles or vesicles. The sodium-potassium pump is a means by which excess sodium ions are forcibly extruded from nerve cells while potassium ions are pulled into the cell.

The mule, an infertile hybrid

Species   The basic unit of classification is the species. A species is a group of similar organisms that can mate and produce fertile offspring. The red wolf, African elephant, red oak, house fly, hair cap moss—each belong to a separate and distinct species. For example, the red wolf belongs to the red wolf species in which the male mates with the female and produces fertile red wolf offspring. Upon maturity these red wolf offspring will reproduce just as their parents did. Species is a reproductive unit, not one defined by geography. Once brought together, a Mexican male Chihuahua can mate with a female Chihuahua born in France because they are species compatible. In rare instances, members of closely related species—horses and donkeys, for example—can mate and produce offspring. But the products of interspecies matings are not fertile and therefore cannot reproduce. When a male donkey mates with a female horse (mare), a mule is produced. The mule is an infertile hybrid. The mating of a male horse (stallion) and a female donkey results in a hinny, also an infertile hybrid.

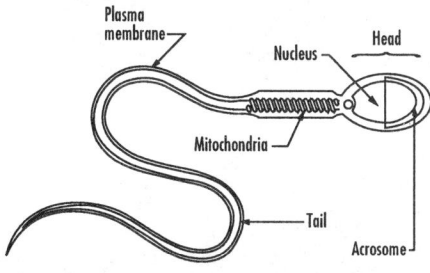

Diagram of a sperm cell

Sperm   The male gamete is structured for motility. It leaves the male reproductive system and is able to swim through the female reproductive system where it may fertilize (penetrate) an egg cell.

Sperm cells are haploid, having half the number of chromosomes of a fertilized egg.

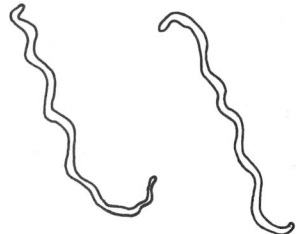

Spirochetes are highly motile but they lack polarity

Spirochetes   Most bacteria belonging to this group are anaerobic; many are disease producers. These bacteria are long, thin, and curved, moving with a wriggling, corkscrew-like motion, made possible by an axial filament. In some ways, the spirochetes resemble protozoa, but they are nonnucleated. They do not form spores or branches. They reproduce by transverse fission. The spirochete *Treponema pallidum* causes syphilis.

Spongy cells   *See* **Leaf cross section**.

Sporozoa   The Sporozoa are parasitic spore-formers. The adult forms are incapable of locomotion, although immature organisms may move by means of pseudopodia. Some species of sporozoa go through a complicated life cycle requiring different hosts during different life stages. For example, the species *Plasmodium vivax*—the agent that causes malaria—requires two hosts: the *Anopheles* mosquito and a human.

Starfish   The starfish is an excellent representative of the echinoderms. It has all of the distinguishing characteristics: pentaradial symmetry, spiny skin, tube feet controlled by a water vascular system, no head, excretory or respiratory system. Protruding from the wall of the coelom and extending out between the calcareous plates into the sea water, are the papulae, sac-like structures that function as respiratory and excretory organs. The mouth is located in the center of the disc on the underside of the body. The nervous system is composed of a nerve ring located in the disc from which a ventral and radial nerve branch into each arm. Starfish sexes are separate. Starfish have remarkable powers of regeneration. If an arms breaks off, the arm grows back. Should a piece of the central disc be attached to the amputated arm, a new individual will grow from the dismembered part. Starfish prey on oysters.

Stem   *See* **Woody stems**.

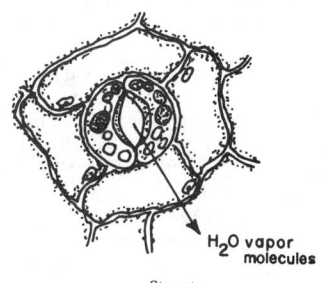

H_2O vapor molecules

Stomate

Stoma or stomate Small pore in the plant epidermis that permits gas exchange. Each stoma is bounded by a pair of guard cells whose osmotic status regulates the size of the opening.

Substrate The molecules on which an enzyme exerts catalytic action. The surface that supports any organism. *See* **Enzyme-substrate complex**.

Synthesis Involves those biochemical processes in cells by which small molecules are built into larger ones. As a result of synthesis, amino acids, the building blocks of proteins, are changed into enzymes, hormones, and protoplasm.

Tadpole *See* **Fertilization, frogs**.

Tapeworm The life cycle of the tapeworm includes two hosts. A mature proglottid contains a sac filled with hundreds of fertilized eggs. When the proglottid walls rupture, the ground becomes infected with fertilized eggs. If these eggs are ingested by a pig, the protective walls surrounding each egg are digested, releasing developing embryos of the tapeworm into the digestive system of the pig. These embryos bore into the pig's capillaries and are carried by the blood to the muscles where the scolex forms a cyst. The worm now remains encysted in the muscles (meat) of the pig. If the butchered pig (now called pork) is improperly cooked and eaten by a human, the encysted worm becomes activated. Its head begins to bud proglottids and the cycle of infection repeats.

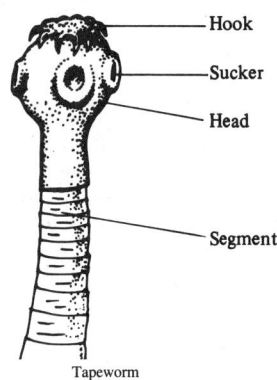

- Hook
- Sucker
- Head
- Segment

Tapeworm

Taste buds The taste buds, which receive stimuli for the four taste sensations of sweet, sour, bitter, and salty, are located in different parts of the tongue. The senses of taste are related to that of smell. When we have a bad head cold, or hold our nose, taste is affected.

Testes Male gonads that produce sperm, the male sex cells. Each gonad consists of tightly coiled *seminiferous tubules* where sperm production begins.

Thallophyta Most algae are not differentiated into roots, stems, and leaves. The simple body of the plant—either a single cell or a flat sheet of simple cells—is known as a thallus. Thallophytes do not have specialized tissues to carry water, anchor the plants, or to grow new cells. As a rule, the sex cells of the thallophytes are produced in rather simple sex organs that are not protected by a surrounding wall of cells. The zygotes of the thallophytes do not develop into embryos that are contained in a female reproductive organ. Most species of thallophytes live in fresh water, although there are a few saltwater forms. Some species live in damp soil or on the bark of trees.

Tissues Cells in the body of the multicellular organism are arranged in structural and functional groups called tissues. A tissue is a group of similar cells that work together to perform a particular function. Tissues that are grouped together and work for a common cause form organs. Groups of organs that contribute to a particular set of functions are called systems. The ability of cells to carry out special functions in addition to the usual work of cells exemplifies specialization. When different jobs are accomplished by the various tissues in an organ, we call this division of labor.

Transpiration Loss of water vapor through plant leaves is termed transpiration, a process that is responsible for the rise of sap in trees. Guttation is the loss of liquid water through the leaves of plants with short stems. Guttation is caused by the effect of root pressure on water flow and has hardly any physiological advantage to the plant.

Transport Involves the absorption of materials by living things, including the movement and distribution of materials within the body of the organism. There are several transport methods, including diffusion, active transport, and circulation. Diffusion is the flow of molecules from an area where these molecules are in great concentration to an area where there are fewer of them. Active transport is the movement of molecules powered by energy. Circulation is the movement of fluid and its dissolved materials throughout the body of an organism or within the cytoplasm of a single cell.

Turtles and tortoises The chelonians are the turtles and tortoises. The skeleton is modified to form a box-like covering, the upper curved portion of which is called the carapace, the lower part, the plastron. The head, tail, and legs are the only movable parts of the animal. The jaws are horny and toothless. Chelonians live on land, in freshwater, and in the sea. More turtles live on the American continent than anywhere else.

Turtle

Twins There are two types of twins: identical and fraternal. Identical twins result from the fertilization of one egg and have the same genetic makeup. They are of the same sex and are almost identical in appearance. They develop in a common chorionic sac and share a common placenta. However, the umbilical cords are separate. Fraternal twins develop from two separate fertilized eggs. They do not share a common genetic makeup and are no more alike than siblings born at separate times. The sexes may be different. Each fraternal twin has its own chorionic membrane and its own placenta.

Umbilical cord The implanted embryo is attached to the uterus by means of the umbilical cord, a structure that contains blood vessels that function in carrying nutrients and oxygen to the embryo and transporting waste away from it. The umbilical cord connects with the placenta, a vascularized organ made up of tissues of the mother and the embryo. The blood of the embryo that circulates in the capillaries of the placenta is separated from the blood of the mother by layers of cells thin enough to allow diffusion between the two circulatory systems. There is no mixing of the blood of the mother with the blood of the embryo. (The term fetus is used in mammalian embryos after the organs have formed.)

Urinary system The human urinary system is located dorsally in the abdomen. This system consists of two kidneys, tubes known as ureters extending from each kidney to a urinary bladder and a single urethra, a tube that leads out of the bladder.

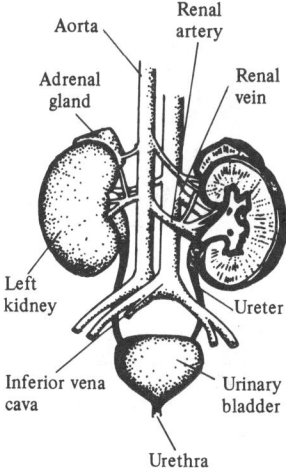

The urinary system

Uterus A muscular sac inside the body of the female mammal specialized for holding the developing young.

Vacuole A space in the cytoplasm enclosed by a membrane and filled with liquid. Some vacuoles are digestive vesicles; some are storage areas. Contractile vacuole is an organelle that pumps excess water out of freshwater protozoans such as the Paramecium.

Vascular plants The vascular plants are truly land-dwelling plants. They have developed adaptations that permit them to live on land independent of bodies of water. The word "vascular" means that these plants have a water-carrying system. Water is conducted upward from the roots by xylem tubules. Fluid compounds are conducted downward from the leaves to lower plant organs by the phloem tubules.

Vegetative propagation In some cases, flowering plants can reproduce more of their kind without the use of flowers, but from stems, leaves, or roots.

Since these are the vegetative parts of the plant normally used for nutrition, this method of reproduction is known as vegetative propagation. It is a form of asexual reproduction, since it involves only one parent.

Values of vegetative propagation:

1. The plants are of the same type as the parents. They do not vary, as might usually be the case in sexual reproduction, where the characteristics of two parents are inherited.
2. Plants are reproduced much more quickly and in larger numbers, than if they were grown from seeds.
3. Seedless fruits such as oranges and grapes can be maintained and propagated.

Venereal diseases (VD) Largely spread through sexual intercourse between people who are infected with the germs that cause the diseases. The infection of two such diseases, syphilis and gonorrhea, generally takes place through the mucous membranes of the reproductive organs or the mouth. A pregnant woman who has one of these diseases may give birth to a deformed or dead baby. Blindness may also affect the newborn. As a precaution, it is common practice in hospitals to treat the eyes of newborn babies with silver nitrate.

Vertebrates Animals that have a true backbone composed of segmented parts called vertebrae belong to the chordate subphylum Vertebrata. The vertebrae may be made of cartilage or bone: if made of the latter, cartilage cushions prevent the bones from rubbing together. The backbone is built around the notochord and usually obliterates it. Vertebrates vary in size from large to small, but all have a living endoskeleton usually made of bone. All vertebrate species have marked development of the head where a brain is enclosed in a cranium. Blood is pumped through a closed circulatory system by means of a ventral heart, having at least two chambers: an atrium and a ventricle. The hepatic portal system carries blood laden with food from the intestines to the liver before it reaches the body cells. Vertebrate red blood cells contain the iron-bearing pigment hemoglobin that is specialized to carry oxygen. Such a system of closed blood vessels prevents blood from entering the body cavity. Most vertebrates (except humans) have a post-anal tail that is a continuation of the vertebral column. Although there are never more than two sets of paired appendages, some adult vertebrates show only one such set or none at all, the appendages having been lost over evolutionary time. Evidence of lost appendages may be seen in embryonic forms or may be demonstrated by vestigial structures. The coccyx bone in humans is a remnant (vestigial structure) of a post-anal tail. Other characteristics of vertebrates include a mouth that is closed by a movable lower jaw and a thyroid gland derived from the ventral wall of the pharynx. In the invertebrate chordates, the endostyle is an evolutionary signpost pointing to the development of the thyroid gland.

Viruses Viruses are not living. They are not cells and they do not exhibit the characteristics of life as do cells. Viruses can reproduce only within living cells. The virus particle is known as a virion. It

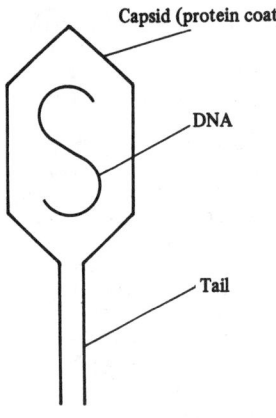

Capsid (protein coat)

DNA

Tail

Structure of a virus

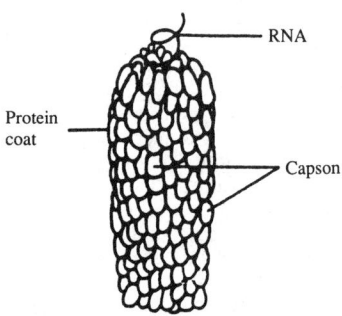

RNA

Protein coat

Capson

Tobacco mosaic virus

Water, conservation of   Water is rendered useless for drinking, bathing, irrigation, and as a habitat for fish when polluted by the chemical wastes from industry and by human sewage. Sewage treatment plants clean up sewage before it is dumped into waterways. Special treatment must be given to chemical wastes to detoxify them before disposal. Water is a renewable resource. However, people on the earth are using more water than ever before in industry, refrigeration, agriculture, and the like. Humans are dependent on rainfall to maintain an adequate water table (level of groundwater) and to replenish water stores in reservoirs. The wasting of water through careless use can have serious consequences for human life.

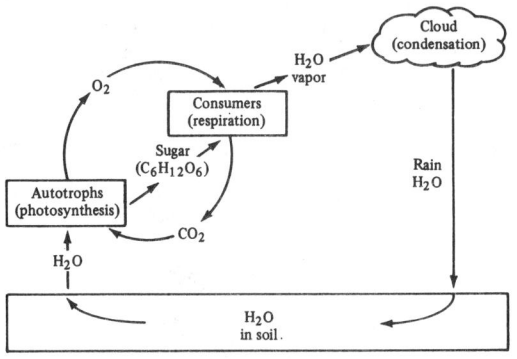

Water cycle

merely consists of a protein coat and a nucleic acid core. The protein coat, called a capsid, may be shaped like a rod, be polyhedral, or have a tail with extending fibers. In some viruses, including those that cause influenza, a cytoplasmic membrane surrounds the protein coat. This surrounding envelope may come from the plasma membrane of the host cell or may be synthesized by the host's cytoplasm. However, virologists have found that the envelope contains proteins that are virus-specific. Viral nucleic acid may be a single molecule consisting of as few as five genes or may have as many as several hundred. Viral nucleic acid may be single or it may be double-stranded; it may be circular or linear. Some viral nucleic acid is made of DNA (deoxyribonucleic acid); others have only an RNA (ribonucleic acid) core. Viruses never contain both DNA and RNA. *See* **Bacteriophage**.

Vitamins   Are organic compounds. They are classified as water soluble or fat soluble. In general, the water soluble vitamins are coenzymes necessary to the proper sequence of biochemical events that occur during cellular respiration. It is interesting to note that the primates (*Homo sapiens* included) and guinea pigs are the only vertebrate animals that cannot synthesize their own vitamin C from carbohydrates. Therefore, the daily requirements of ascorbic acid must be met through food intake. The functions of the fat soluble vitamins are not clearly understood. For detailed information on vitamins, *see* the Health and Medicine section, pages 8-2 to 8-7 and page 8-60.

Water cycle   There are three ways in which water vapor enters the atmosphere. Water evaporates from land surfaces and from the surfaces of all bodies of water. Water vapor enters the air as a waste product of respiration of animals and plants. For example: every time you exhale, water vapor is released into the air. Great amounts of water are lost from plants through the openings in the leaves; this water loss due to evaporation is called transpiration. Water vapor in the air is carried to high altitudes where it is cooled and forms clouds by condensation. Eventually, clouds fall to the earth in the form of precipitation: rain, snow, or sleet. Most of the precipitation returns to the oceans, lakes, or stream and less than 1 percent of it falls on land. Of the water that does fall on land, about 25 percent of it will evaporate from the various land surfaces before it can be absorbed by plants or used by animals. Water that does not evaporate enters the soil and becomes available to plant roots and soil organisms. Soil water that is not absorbed by plants seeps down into the ground until it reaches an impervious layer of rock. The water moves along this rock as groundwater until it reaches an outlet into a larger body of water such as a lake or an ocean. The water cycle repeats.

White blood cells (Leucocytes)   There are five types of white blood cells, functioning to protect the body against invading foreign proteins. The amoeboid-like neutrophils and monocytes behave as phagocytes, engulfing bacteria and other foreign proteins. Eosinophils detoxify histamine-like secretions. Lymphocytes participate in immune responses and basophils produce anticoagulants.

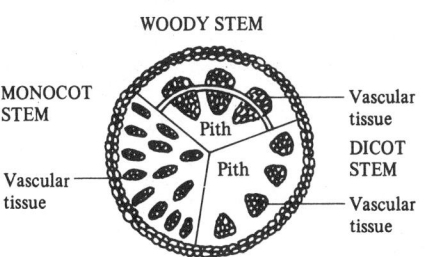

WOODY STEM

MONOCOT STEM

Vascular tissue

Pith

Pith

Vascular tissue

DICOT STEM

Vascular tissue

Comparison of monocot, herbaceous, and woody stems

Woody stems   Stems have three major functions. First, they conduct water upward from the roots to the leaves and conduct dissolved food materials downward from the leaves to the roots. Second, stems produce and support leaves and flowers. Third, they provide the mechanisms for the storage of food. Woody stems are composed of primary and secondary tissues. Primary tissues are those that develop from the meristems (embryonic tissue) of the buds on twigs during the first year of growth. After the first year, growth in the woody stem takes place in the secondary tissues. These are tissues that arise from the cambium.

Worm-Parasites and Diseases

Diseases Caused by Flatworms	Diseases Caused by Roundworms
Tapeworm Infection	Hookworm
Sheep Liver Fluke Infection	Trichinosis
Chinese Liver Fluke Infection	Ascaris Infection
	Pinworm Infection
	Filariasis

Xylem   Water-carrying (vascular) tissue in plants that conducts water from the roots upward.

Zoospores   Free-swimming cells with flagella that are produced by asexual cell division of the green algae *Chlamydomonas*. The zoospores mature, develop a large chloroplast, and become vegetative *Chlamydomonas* cells.

Zygote   Fertilized egg formed by the union of egg and sperm. The zygote has the 2N chromosome number. Following zygote formation, the cell goes into a series of divisions known as cleavage.

CHEMISTRY

Absolute temperature Temperature measured above absolute zero on the Kelvin scale. Celsius temperatures are converted to Kelvin or absolute temperatures by adding 273. *See* **Temperature scales.**

Acetaldehyde *See* **Aldehydes.**

Acetic acid The common name for ethanoic acid, CH_3COOH, a colorless liquid that is miscible in all proportions with water and in the aqueous solutions acts as a weak acid. Pure acetic acid is called glacial acetic acid, which freezes slightly below room temperatures. *See* **Organic Acids**, under **Organic chemistry**, for structure and preparation. *See* **Table J** in **Exhibit 3.13**, page 3-66, for relative strength in aqueous solution.

Acetone Or dimethyl ketone, or 2-propanone, CH_3COCH_3. The simplest of the organic chemicals called ketones. *See* **Ketones** for structure and preparation.

Acetylene First member of the alkyne series; common name for ethyne, C_2H_2. *See* **Alkyne series**, under **Organic chemistry**, for structure.

Acid anhydride The name given to a nonmetallic oxide that reacts with water to form an acid such as sulfuric acid or phosphoric acid. For this reason, these oxides are referred to as acid anhydrides. Some common examples are:

$CO_2 + H_2O \rightarrow H_2CO_3$ carbonic acid
$SO_3 + H_2O \rightarrow H_2SO_4$ sulfuric acid
$P_2O_5 + 3H_2O \rightarrow 2H_3PO_4$ phosphoric acid

In general then,

Nonmetallic oxides + $H_2O \rightarrow$ acids

Acids and bases (Since *acid-base theory* is interwoven, both acids and bases are covered here.)

Definitions and Properties
Acids: There are some characteristic properties by which an acid may be defined. The most important are as follows.

- Water solutions of acids conduct electricity. This conduction depends on their degree of ionization. A few acids ionize almost completely; others ionize only to a slight degree. Exhibit 3.1 indicates some common acids and their degrees of ionization.
- Acids react with metals that are more active than hydrogen ions to liberate hydrogen. (Some

acids are also strong oxidizing agents and do not release hydrogen. Somewhat concentrated nitric acid is such an acid.)

- Acids have the ability to change the color of indicators. Some common indicators are litmus and phenolphthalein. Litmus is a dyestuff obtained from a lichen plant. When litmus is added to an acidic solution, or paper impregnated with litmus is dipped into an acid, the neutral purple color changes to pink-red. Phenolphthalein is red in a basic solution and becomes colorless in a neutral or acid solution.
- Acids react with bases so that the properties of both are lost to form water and a salt. This is called neutralization. The general equation is

acid + base $\rightarrow$ salt + water

An example is:

$Mg(OH)_2 + H_2SO_4 \rightarrow MgSO_4 + 2H_2O$

- If an acid is known to be a weak solution, you might taste it and note the sour taste.
- Acids react with carbonates to release carbon dioxide; for example,

$CaCO_3 + 2HCl \rightarrow$
$CaCl_2 + H_2CO_3$ (unstable and decomposes)
$\rightarrow H_2O + CO_3\uparrow$

The most common theory used in first-year chemistry is the Arrhenius theory, which states that an acid is a substance that yields hydrogen ions in an aqueous solution. Although we speak of these hydrogen ions in the solution, they are really not separate ions but become attached to the oxygen of the polar water molecule to form the H_3O^+ ion (the hydronium ion). So it is really this hydronium ion we are concerned with in an acid solution.

A table listing common acids and their formulas is given on page 3-4. An explanation of the naming procedures for acids precedes the table.
Bases: Bases may also be defined by some operational definitions that are based on experimental observations. Some of the important ones are as follows.

- Bases are conductors of electricity in an aqueous solution.

EXHIBIT 3.2
Degrees of Ionization
of Common Bases

Completely or Nearly Completely Ionized	Slightly Ionized
Potassium hydroxide	Ammonium hydroxide
Sodium hydroxide	(All others)
Barium hydroxide	
Strontium hydroxide	
Calcium hydroxide	

EXHIBIT 3.1
Degrees of Ionization
of Common Acids

Completely or Nearly Completely Ionized	Moderately Ionized	Slightly Ionized
Nitric	Oxalic	Hydrofluoric
Hydrochloric	Phosphoric	Acetic
Sulfuric	Sulfurous	Carbonic
Hydriodic		Hydrosulfuric
Hyrobromic		(Most others)

Their degree of conduction depends on their degree of ionization. *See* **Exhibit 3.2** of the common bases and their degrees of ionization.

■ Bases cause a color change in indicators. Litmus changes from red to blue in a basic solution, and phenolphthalein becomes pink from its colorless state.

■ A base reacts with an acid to neutralize each other and form a salt and water.

■ Bases react with fats to form a class of compounds called soaps. Earlier generations used this method to make their own soap.

■ Aqueous solutions of bases feel slippery, and the stronger bases are very caustic to the skin.

The Arrhenius theory defines a base as a substance that yields hydroxide ions (OH^-) in an aqueous solution. Some bases have common names; for example:

Sodium hydroxide = lye, caustic soda

Potassium hydroxide = caustic potash

Calcium hydroxide = slaked lime, hydrated lime water

Ammonium hydroxide = ammonia water, household ammonia

Much of the sodium hydroxide produced today comes from the Hooker cell electrolysis apparatus. When an electric current is passed through a salt water solution, hydrogen, chlorine and sodium hydroxide are the products. The formula for this equation is

$$2NaCl + 2HOH \xrightarrow[\text{energy}]{\text{electrical}} H_2\uparrow + Cl_2\uparrow + 2NaOH$$

Broader Acid-Base Theories

Besides the common Arrhenius theory of acids and bases discussed for aqueous solutions, two other theories are widely used. They are known as the Brønsted-Lowry theory and the Lewis theory.

The Brønsted-Lowry theory (1923) defines acids as proton donors, and bases as proton acceptors. These definitions agree with the aqueous solution definition of an acid giving up hydrogen ions in solution, but go beyond to other cases as well. An example is dry HCl gas reacting with ammonia gas to form the white solid NH_4Cl:

$$HCl(g) + NH_3(g) \rightarrow NH_4^+Cl^-(s)$$

The HCl is the proton donor or acid, and the ammonia is a Brønsted-Lowry base, which accepts the proton.

The terminology "conjugate acids and bases" is used in the Brønsted-Lowry theory. In an acid-base reaction, the original acid gives up its proton to become a conjugate base. In other words, after losing its proton, the acid is capable of gaining a proton, thus qualifying as a base. The original base accepts a proton, so it is now classified as a conjugate acid since it could release this newly acquired proton and behave like an acid. Some examples are given below:

$$HCl + NH_3 \longrightarrow NH_4^+ + Cl^-$$
acid   base   conjugate acid   conjugate base

$$HC_2H_3O_2 + H_2O \longrightarrow H_3O^+ + C_2H_3O_2^-$$
acid   base   conjugate acid   conjugate base

The Lewis theory (1916) of acids and bases is defined in terms of the electron-pair concept. This is probably the most generally useful concept of acids and bases. According to the Lewis definitions, an acid is an electron-pair acceptor and a base is an electron-pair donor. An example is the formation of ammonium ions from ammonia gas and hydrogen ions:

Notice that the hydrogen ion is in fact accepting the electron pair of the ammonia, so it is a Lewis acid. The ammonia is donating its electron pair, so it is a Lewis base.

Acid Concentration Expressed as pH

Frequently, acid and base concentrations are expressed in a system called the pH system. The pH can be defined as $-\log [H^+]$, where $[H^+]$ is the concentration of hydrogen ions expressed in moles per liter. The logarithm is the exponent of 10 when the number is written in the base 10. For example,

$100 = 10^2$ so logarithm of 100, base 10 = 2

$10,000 = 10^4$ so logarithm of 10,000, base 10 = 4

$0.01 = 10^{-2}$ so logarithm of .01, base 10 = -2

The logarithms of more complex numbers can be found in a logarithm table.

Problem
Find the pH of a 0.1 molar solution of HCl.

Since HCl ionizes almost completely into H^+ and Cl^-, the $[H^+] = 0.1$ mole/liter.
By definition,
pH = $-\log [H^+]$
So
pH = $-\log [10^{-1}]$
The logarithm of 10^{-1} is -1.
So
pH = $-(-1)$
The pH then = 1.

Since water has a normal H^+ concentration of 10^{-7} mole/liter because of the slight ionization of water molecules, the pH of water is 7 when the water is neither acid nor base.
The normal pH range is from 1 to 14.

Acid	Neutral	Base
1 ←	→ 7 ←	→ 14

Naming Acids

A binary acid (that is, an acid with only two elements) uses the prefix *hydro-* in front of the stem or full name of the nonmetallic element and adds the ending *-ic*. Examples are *hydro*chlor*ic* acid (HCl) and *hydro*sulfur*ic* acid (H_2S).

A ternary acid usually contains hydrogen, a non-metal, and oxygen. Since the amount of oxygen often varies, the most common form of the acid in the series uses merely the stem of the nonmetal with the ending *-ic*. The name of an acid containing one less atom of oxygen than the most common acid has the ending *-ous*. An acid containing one more atom of oxygen than the most common acid uses prefix *per-* and the ending *-ic*. The name of an acid containing one less atom of oxygen than the *-ous* acid has the prefix *hypo-* and the ending *-ous*.

You can remember the names of the common acids and their salts by learning the following simple rules:

Rule
-ic acids form *-ate* salts.

Example
Sulfuric acid forms sulfate salts.

Rule
-ous acids form *-ite* salts.

Example
Sulfurous acid forms sulfite salts.

Rule
hydro-(stem)-*ic* acids form *-ide* salts.

Example
Hydrochloric acid forms chloride salts.

When the name of the ternary acid has the prefix *hypo-* or *per-*, that prefix is retained in the name of the salt (hypochlorous acid and sodium hypochlorite).

(*See* **Organic Acids**, under **Organic chemistry**; *see* **Table J** in **Exhibit 3.13**, page 3-66, for relative strengths.)

Acid-base indicators   *See* **Indicators**.

Activation energy   The energy necessary to get a reaction going by increasing the energy of the reactants so that they can combine. Notice in Figs. 1 and 2 below how the activation energy is identified in an exothermic reaction and an endothermic reaction.

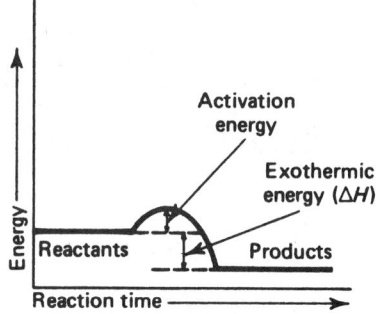

Fig. 1   Activation Energy in an Exothermic Reaction

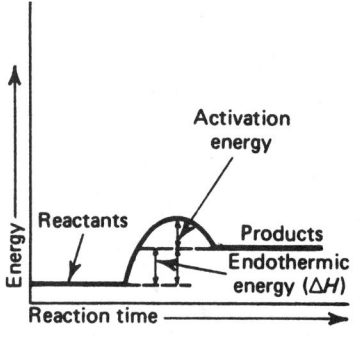

Fig. 2   Activation Energy in an Endothermic Reaction

Alcohols   A class of organic compounds that have a hydroxyl group, OH, attached to a carbon atom. The simplest alcohols are alkanes that have one or more hydrogen atoms replaced by the hydroxyl group, —OH. This is called its functional group.

Common Acids and Bases

Acids, Binary		Acids, Ternary		Bases	
Name	Formula	Name	Formula	Name	Formula
Hydrofluoric	HF	Nitric	HNO_3	Sodium hydroxide	NaOH
Hydrochloric	HCl	Nitrous	HNO_2	Potassium hydroxide	KOH
Hydrobromic	HBr	Hypochlorous	$HClO$	Ammonium hydroxide	NH_4OH
Hydriodic	HI	Chlorous	$HClO_2$	Calcium hydroxide	$Ca(OH)_2$
Hydrosulfuric	H_2S	Chloric	$HClO_3$	Magnesium hydroxide	$Mg(OH)_2$
		Perchloric	$HClO_4$	Barium hydroxide	$Ba(OH)_2$
		Sulfuric	H_2SO_4	Aluminum hydroxide	$Al(OH)_3$
		Sulfurous	H_2SO_3	Iron II hydroxide	$Fe(OH)_2$
		Phosphoric	H_3PO_4	Iron III hydroxide	$Fe(OH)_3$
		Phosphorous	H_3PO_3	Zinc hydroxide	$Zn(OH)_2$
		Carbonic	H_2CO_3	Lithium hydroxide	LiOH
		Acetic	$HC_2H_3O_2$		
		Oxalic	$H_2C_2O_4$		
		Boric	H_3BO_3		
		Silicic	H_2SiO_3		

Methanol is the simplest alcohol. Its structure is

$$
\begin{array}{c}
H \\
| \\
H-C-OH \\
| \\
H
\end{array}
\quad \text{methanol or wood alcohol}
$$

The laboratory preparation of methanol is

$$CH_3Cl + NaOH \rightarrow NaCl + CH_3OH$$

chloromethane   methanol
(methyl chloride)   (methyl alcohol)

For many years methanol, wood alcohol, was obtained industrially by the destructive distillation of wood. Today it is made by the hydrogenation of oxides of carbon in the presence of a suitable catalyst.

$$CO + 2H_2 \xrightarrow[\substack{300-400°C \\ 200 \text{ atm}}]{\text{catalyst}} CH_3OH$$

Methanol is a colorless, flammable liquid with a boiling point of 65°C. It is miscible with water, is exceedingly poisonous, and can cause blindness if taken internally. It can be used as a fuel, as a solvent, and as a denaturant to make ethyl alcohol unsuitable for drinking.

Ethanol is the best known and most used alcohol. Its structure is

$$
\begin{array}{c}
H \quad H \\
| \quad | \\
H-C-C-OH \\
| \quad | \\
H \quad H
\end{array}
\quad \text{ethanol}
$$

(Notice that the alcohol names are derived from the alkane names by replacing the *-e* ending with *-ol*.) The common names of ethanol are ethyl alcohol and grain alcohol.

The laboratory preparation of ethanol is:

$$
\begin{array}{c}
H \quad H \\
| \quad | \\
H-C-C-H \\
| \quad | \\
H \quad H
\end{array}
\xrightarrow{Cl_2}
\begin{array}{c}
H \quad H \\
| \quad | \\
H-C-C-Cl \\
| \quad | \\
H \quad H
\end{array}
\xrightarrow{NaOH}
\begin{array}{c}
H \quad H \\
| \quad | \\
H-C-C-OH \\
| \quad | \\
H \quad H
\end{array}
$$

ethane   chloroethane   ethanol

Simple sugars can be converted to ethanol by the action of an enzyme (zymase) found in yeast.

$$C_6H_{12}O_6 \rightarrow 2C_2H_5OH + 2CO_2\uparrow$$

sugar   ethanol

After fermentation, the alcohol is distilled off. Grains, potatoes, and other starch plants, which can be treated with an acid-water solution to form sugars, can be converted into ethyl alcohol or "whiskey."

The usual process for producing industrial alcohol consists of treating ethene (or ethylene) with concentrated H_2SO_4 and then hydrolyzing the resulting ethyl hydrogen sulfate to ethanol.

$$C_2H_4 \xrightarrow{H_2SO_4} C_2H_5HSO_4 \xrightarrow{H_2O} C_2H_5OH + H_2SO_4$$

Ethanol is a colorless, flammable liquid with a boiling point of 78°C. It is miscible with water and is a good solvent for a wide variety of substances (these solutions are often referred to as "tinctures").

Isomeric alcohols have similar formulas but different properties because of their differences in structure. If the —OH is attached to an end carbon, the alcohol is called a primary alcohol. If the —OH is attached to a "middle" carbon, the alcohol is called a secondary alcohol. Some examples are as follows.

$$
\begin{array}{c}
H \ H \ H \\
| \ | \ | \\
H-C-C-C-OH \\
| \ | \ | \\
H \ H \ H
\end{array}
\xleftrightarrow{\text{isomers}}
\begin{array}{c}
H \ H \ H \\
| \ | \ | \\
H-C-C-C-H \\
| \ | \ | \\
H \ OH \ H
\end{array}
$$

1-propanol   2-propanol
propyl alcohol   isopropyl alcohol

$$
CH_3-CH_2-CH_2-\overset{\displaystyle H}{\underset{\displaystyle H}{C}}-OH
\xleftrightarrow{\text{isomers}}
CH_3-CH_2-\overset{\displaystyle H}{\underset{\displaystyle OH}{C}}-CH_3
$$

1-butanol   2-butanol,
(sometimes called   isobutyl alcohol
n-butanol or normal butanol)
butyl alcohol

(The number in front of the name indicates to which carbon the —OH ion is to be attached.)

Phenols are alcohols derived from the aromatic hydrocarbons. Some important examples of phenols and alcohols that have multiple —OH groups are shown below.

Aldehydes   A group of organic compounds containing the formyl group, CHO. The functional group of an aldehyde is the formyl group.

$$
-C\overset{\displaystyle O}{\underset{\displaystyle H}{\big\Vert}}
$$

Phenols and Some Other Alcohols

Structure	Name	Properties and Uses
	Phenol, carbolic acid hydroxybenzene	Slightly acidic, extremely corrosive, poisonous; used to make synthetic resins, plastics, drugs, dyes, and photographic developers; good disinfectant
	Ethylene glycol, 1,2-ethanediol	Colorless liquid, high boiling point, low freezing point; used as permanent antifreeze in automobiles.
	Glycerine, glycerol, 1,2,3-propanetriol	Colorless liquid, odorless, viscous, sweet taste; used to make nitroglycerine, resins for paint, and cellophane.

The general formula is RCHO, where R represents a hydrocarbon radical.

Aldehydes can be prepared by the oxidation of an alcohol. This can be done by inserting a hot copper wire into the alcohol. A typical reaction is

methanol (methyl alcohol) → methanal (formaldehyde)

The middle structure is an intermediate structure, but since two hydroxyl groups do not stay attached to the same carbon, it changes to the aldehyde by a water molecule "breaking away."

The aldehyde name is derived from the alcohol name by dropping the *-ol* and adding *-al*.

Ethanol forms ethanal (acetaldehyde) in the same manner.

Alkali metals   Another name for the Group 1 (or IA) metals in the periodic chart, based on the fact that they react with water to form alkali or basic solutions. For example.

$$2Na + 2H_2O \rightarrow 2NaOH + H_2\uparrow$$

Alkane series of hydrocarbons   *See* **Organic chemistry**.

Alkylation   The process of combining a saturated alkane with an unsaturated alkene to form a chain hydrocarbon. *See* **Organic chemistry** for more information.

Alkyl group   When a hydrogen atom is removed from an alkane, the carbon and hydrogen portion that remains is called an alkyl group. Alkyl groups do not exist on their own: they must be attached to something, such as a carbon chain. *See* **Organic chemistry** for more information and formulas.

Alkyne series of hydrocarbons   *See* **Organic chemistry**.

Allotropic forms   Forms of an element that have different structures and consequently different properties and energy content. For example, *see* **Carbon**.

Alloy   A substance that contains a mixture of elements and has metallic properties (e.g., brass is an alloy of two metals, copper and zinc, whereas steel is an alloy of iron and carbon with or without other metals).

Alpha particle   A subatomic particle made up of helium nuclei. ^4_2He, positively charged 2^+. Some properties are as follows.

■ Emission reduces the atomic number by 2, the atomic weight by 4 amu (atomic mass units).
■ High energy, relatively low velocity.
■ Average speed is about one-tenth the speed of light.
■ Range: about 5 cm in air.
■ Shielding needed: stopped by the thickness of a sheet of paper or by skin.
■ Interactions: produces about 100,000 ionizations per centimeter; repelled by the positively charged nucleus; attracts electrons, but does not capture them until its speed is much reduced.

Amine   A compound containing the —NH$_2$ or amino group. Under the proper conditions, the amino group can replace a hydrogen in a hydrocarbon compound to form an amine. For examples *see* **Organic chemistry**.

Amino acids   The organic acids that contain one or more amino groups. The simplest uncombined amino acid is glycine, or amino acetic acid, NH_2CH_2—COOH. See structural formula below. More than 20 amino acids are known, about half of which must be supplied in the human diet because they are needed to make up the body proteins.

glycine or amino acetic acid

For more background, *see* **Organic chemistry**.

Ammonia   One of the oldest known compounds of nitrogen. In times past, it was prepared by distilling leather scraps, hoofs, and horns.

It can be prepared in the laboratory by heating an ammonium salt with a strong base. For example,

$$Ca(OH)_2 + (NH_4)_2SO_4 \rightarrow CaSO_4$$
$$+ 2H_2O + 2NH_3\uparrow$$

Industrial methods include the Haber process, which combines nitrogen and hydrogen.

$$3H_2 + N_2 \rightarrow 2NH_3$$

and the destructive distillation of coal that gives off NH_3 as a by-product.

Ammonia is a colorless, pungent gas that is extremely soluble in water; it is lighter than air and has a high critical temperature (the critical temperature of a gas is the temperature above which it cannot be liquefied by pressure alone).

Because ammonia can be liquefied easily and has a high heat of vaporization one of its applications is as a refrigerant. A water solution of ammonia is used as a household cleaner to cut grease. Another use of ammonia is as a fertilizer.

Ammonium hydroxide   A water solution of ammonia plus water, NH_4OH, a weak base. *See* **Acids and bases** for acid-base theory.

Amphoteric, or **amphiprotic**   A term describing a compound that can act either as a proton donor (Brønsted acid) or as a proton acceptor (Brønsted base). Water can exhibit this behavior. How water behaves depends on the ions present. In the case of HCl and H_2O water acts as a base in accepting a proton from the HCl. In the case of NH_3 and H_2O, water donates a proton to produce the NH_4^+ (ammonium ion) and therefore acts as a Brønsted acid.

Angstrom (Å)   An obsolete unit. One angstrom is equal to 1×10^{-10} meter or 0.1 nanometer. *See* **Metric System**, under **Measurements**, for more units of measurement.

Anion   The ion in an electrolyzed solution that migrates to the anode. *See* **Electrochemical reactions**.

Anode   The positive terminal of an electrolytic cell. *See* **Electrochemical reactions**.

Aromatic compounds   The group of carbon compounds that form in unsaturated ring structures. The simplest compound of the aromatic series is benzene (C_6H_6). The basic formula of this series is C_nH_{2n-6}.

The benzene is a resonance structure represented by

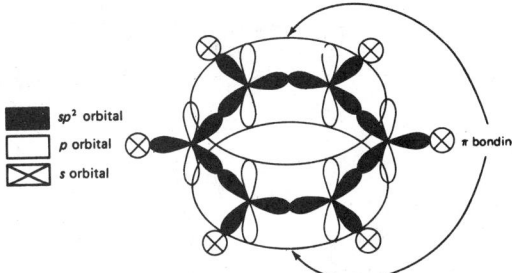

Note: The carbon-to-carbon bonds are neither single nor double bonds but hybrid bonds. This type of bonding is called resonance.

The orbital structure can be represented by

■ *sp²* orbital
□ *p* orbital
⊠ *s* orbital
⊗ *π* bonding

Most of the aromatics have an aroma, thus the name aromatic.

The C_6H_5 group is a radical called phenyl. This is the benzene structure with one hydrogen missing. If the phenyl radical adds a methyl group, the compound is called toluene or methyl benzene. The abbreviation for the toluene structure is

Two other members of the benzene series and their structures are

$C_{10}H_8$ naphthalene

$C_{14}H_{10}$ anthracene

As with chain compounds, the IUPAC system of naming benzene derivatives involves numbering the carbon atoms in the ring in order to pinpoint the locations of the side chains. However, if only two groups are substituted in the benzene ring, the compound formed will be a benzene derivative having three possible isomeric forms. In such cases, the prefixes *ortho-*, *meta-*, and *para-* (abbreviated as *o-*, *m-*, and *p-*) are used to name the isomers. In the ortho structure, the two substituted groups are located

on adjacent carbon atoms. In the meta structure, they are separated by one carbon atom. In the para structure, they are separated by two carbon atoms.

orthoxylene   metaxylene   paraxylene

Arrhenius theory   Most common acid theory used in first-year chemistry. The Arrhenius theory states that an acid is a substance that yields hydrogen ions in an aqueous solution. Although we speak of these hydrogen ions in the solution, they are really not separate ions but become attached to the oxygen of the polar water molecule to form the H_3O^+ ion (the hydronium ion). So it is really this hydronium ion we are concerned with in an acid solution. For more information on acid theory, *see* **Acids and bases**.

Atomic structure   Around 1805, John Dalton proposed some basic assumptions about atoms. Some of these ideas dated back to the ancient Greeks:

- All matter is made up of very small, discrete particles called atoms.
- All atoms of a particular element are alike, but are different from the atoms of any other element.
- Atoms unite in chemical changes to form compounds. A particular compound is always made up of the same kinds of atoms and always has the same number of each kind of atom.
- Chemical reactions involve reorganization of atoms—changes in the way they are bound together. The atoms themselves are not changed in a chemical reaction.

Basic Electrical Charges
The discovery of the electron as the first subatomic particle is credited to J. J. Thomson (England, 1897). He used an evacuated tube connected to a spark coil, as shown in Fig. 3. As the voltage across the tube was increased, a beam of light became visible. This was referred to as a cathode ray. Thomson found that the beam was deflected by both electrical and magnetic fields. From this, he concluded that the cathode rays are made up of very small, negatively charged particles, which he named electrons.

In 1909, Robert Millikan (United States) did his famous oil drop experiment to determine the mass/charge ratio of electrons. This resulted in the determination that the mass of an electron is 9.11×10^{-28} g.

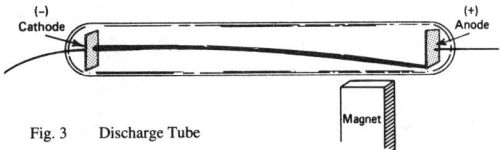

Fig. 3   Discharge Tube

Ernest Rutherford (England, 1911) performed a gold foil experiment (Fig. 4) that had tremendous implications for atomic structure.

CHEMISTRY

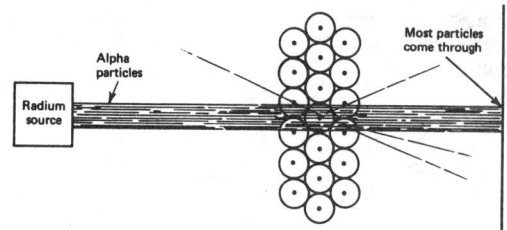

Fig. 4   Rutherford Experiment

Alpha particles (helium nuclei) passed through the foil with few deflections. However, some deflections (1 per 8000) were almost directly back toward the source. This was unexpected and suggested an atomic model with mostly empty space between a nucleus, in which most of the atom's mass is located and which is positively charged, and the electrons that define the volume of the atom.

Further experiments showed that the nucleus is made up of still smaller particles called protons. Rutherford realized, however, that protons, by themselves, could not account for the entire mass of the nucleus. He predicted the existence of a new nuclear particle that would be neutral and would account for the missing mass. In 1932, James Chadwick (England) discovered this particle, the neutron.

Exhibit 3.3 lists the basic particles of the atom.

Bohr Model
In 1913, Niels Bohr proposed his model of the atom. This pictured the atom as having a dense nucleus that was positively charged and electrons in specific circular orbits around this nucleus. The closer to the nucleus, the less energy an electron needed in one of these orbits, but it had to gain energy to go from one orbit to another that was further away from the nucleus.

Because of its simplicity and general ability to explain chemical change, the Bohr model still has some usefulness today.

Components of Atomic Structure
Today the number of subatomic particles identified as discrete units has risen to well over 30. In fact, in the last two decades it has become apparent that even the protons and neutrons are composed of smaller particles, called *quarks*. Nevertheless, the three types of particles listed in Exhibit 3.3 are the most commonly cited.

When these components are combined, we show the protons and neutrons in the nucleus and the electrons in the shells, or principal energy levels (*see*

Electronic Structure, below). Since the actual mass expressions would be very small numbers, the mass of atoms is expressed relative to a particular atom of carbon; for carbon this number is 12 atomic mass units. This is referred to as the atomic mass (formerly, "atomic weight"). The number of protons and neutrons in the nucleus is called the mass number and corresponds to the atomic mass rounded off to the nearest whole number. The atomic number is the number of protons found in the nucleus. An English scientist, Henry Moseley, first determined these numbers from studies of X-ray spectra.

If atoms of the same element with identical atomic numbers have different masses, they are called isotopes. This difference in mass is due to a difference in the number of neutrons in the nucleus.

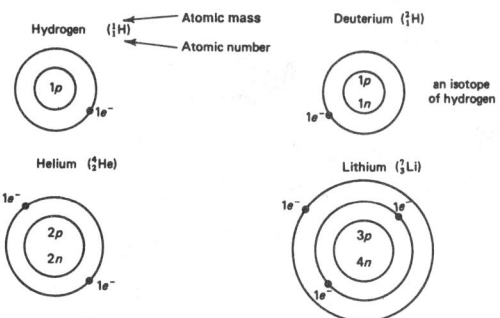

Fig. 5   Some Representative Atoms and Isotopes

The occurrence of isotopes for many of the elements explains why the atomic mass is not a whole number but a decimal number. Isotopes occur in relatively the same percentages in any sample of an element, so the atomic mass is the average mass of the atoms of this element, taking into consideration the percentage of each isotope in a sample of the element.

Electronic Structure
The electrons of each atom are arranged at several different principal energy levels, also called "orbitals" or "shells" (*see* chart below). The outermost shell contains no more than eight electrons, a principle sometimes called the "octet rule."

Principal Energy Level	Letter Designation	Maximum Number of Electrons
1	K	2
2	L	8
3	M	18
4	N	32
5	O	32

EXHIBIT 3.3
Basic Particles of the Atom

Particle	Charge	Actual Mass	Relative Mass Compared to Proton	Discovery
Electron	$-(e^-)$	9.109×10^{-28} g	1/1837	J. J. Thomson, 1897
Proton	$+(p^+)$	1.673×10^{-24} g	1	J. J. Thomson, early 1900s
Neutron	$0\ (n^0)$	1.675×10^{-24}g	1	J. C. Chadwick, 1932

Atomic Configurations of the First 21 Elements

Element	Atomic No.	Mass No.	Number of Protons	Number of Neutrons	Number of Electrons	Electrons in Principal Energy Levels			
						K	L	M	N
Hydrogen	1	1	1	0	1	1			
Helium	2	4	2	2	2	2			
Lithium	3	7	3	4	3	2	1		
Beryllium	4	9	4	5	4	2	2		
Boron	5	11	5	6	5	2	3		
Carbon	6	12	6	6	6	2	4		
Nitrogen	7	14	7	7	7	2	5		
Oxygen	8	16	8	8	8	2	6		
Fluorine	9	19	9	10	9	2	7		
Neon	10	20	10	10	10	2	8		
Sodium	11	23	11	12	11	2	8	1	
Magnesium	12	24	12	12	12	2	8	2	
Aluminum	13	27	13	14	13	2	8	3	
Silicon	14	28	14	14	14	2	8	4	
Phosphorus	15	31	15	16	15	2	8	5	
Sulfur	16	32	16	16	16	2	8	6	
Chlorine	17	35	17	18	17	2	8	7	
Argon	18	40	18	22	18	2	8	8	
Potassium	19	39	19	20	19	2	8	8	1
Calcium	20	40	20	20	20	2	8	8	2
Scandium	21	45	21	24	21	2	8	9	2

Drawings like those in Fig. 5 give valuable aid in determining oxidation numbers, metallic, nonmetallic, and inert elements; chemical reactivity, and the periodic arrangement of the elements.

The atomic configuration of the first 21 elements are shown above.

Oxidation Number and Valence

Each atom attempts to have its outer shell complete and accomplishes this by borrowing, lending, or sharing its electrons. The electrons found in the outermost shell are called valence electrons. The absolute number of electrons gained, lost, or borrowed is referred to as the valence of the atom. When these electrons are lost or partially lost by sharing, the valence number is assigned a + sign for that element and is called its oxidation number. If valence electrons are gained or partially gained by an atom, its valence is assigned a minus sign for its oxidation numbers.

Example

$_{17}$Cl = ●)2)8)7 ← valence electrons

This picture can be simplified to Cl:, showing only the valence electrons as dots. This is called the *Lewis dot structure* of the atom. To complete its outer shell to eight electrons, Cl must borrow one from another atom. Therefore, its valence number is 1. When electrons are gained, we assign a minus sign to this number, so the oxidation number of chlorine is –1.

Example

$_{11}$Na = ●)2)8)1 ← valence electron

Na • (Lewis dot structure)

Since Na tends to lose this electron, its oxidation number is +1.
Some other general rules for oxidation numbers are as follows.
- Atoms of free elements have an oxidation number of zero.
- Hydrogen has an oxidation number of +1 except in metallic hydrides, where it is –1.
- Oxygen has an oxidation number of –2 except in peroxides, where it is –1. In combination with fluorine, the number is +2.

Metallic, Nonmetallic, and Inert Atoms

On the basis of atomic structure, atoms are classified as metals if they tend to lend electrons, as nonmetals if they tend to borrow electrons, and as inert if they tend neither to borrow nor to lend electrons and have complete outer shells.

The term metalloid is used for elements that can lend, borrow, and share electrons.

Atomic Spectra

The Bohr model was based on a simple postulate. Bohr applied to the hydrogen atom the concept that the electron can exist in certain energy levels without an energy change but that, when the electron changes its state, it must absorb or emit the exact amount of energy required to bring it from the initial state to the final state. The ground state is the lowest energy state available to the electron. The excited state is any level higher than the ground state. The formula for changes in energy (ΔE) is

$$\Delta E_{electron} = E_{final} - E_{initial}$$

When the electron moves from the ground state to an excited state, it must absorb energy. When it moves from an excited state to the ground state, it emits energy. This release of energy is the basis for atomic spectra. (*See* Fig. 6.)

Although its derivation is not shown, the most important equation to come from Bohr's model is the expression for the energy levels available to the electron in the hydrogen atom:

$$E = -\left(\frac{2\pi^2 m e^4}{h^2}\right)\frac{Z^2}{n^2}$$

where m is the mass of the electron, e is the charge of the electron, h is Planck's constant, n is an integer (the larger the value of n, the larger the orbit radius), and Z is the nuclear charge. When the appropriate values for m, e, and h have been substituted into this equation, it becomes

$$E = -2.178 \times 10^{-18}\,\mathrm{J}\left(\frac{Z^2}{n^2}\right)$$

By use of this formula, the values for the principal energy levels were calculated and are shown in Fig. 6.

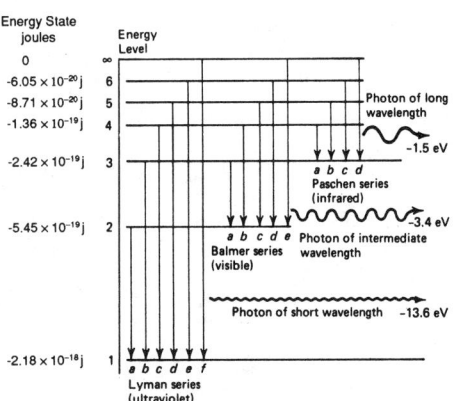

Fig. 6   Atomic Spectra Chart

When energy is released in the "allowed" values, it has the form of discrete radiant energy called photons. Each of the first three levels has a particular name associated with the emissions that occur when an electron reaches its ground state on that level. The Lyman series consisting of ultraviolet radiation, is made up of emissions that occur when an electron cascades from a higher level than the first level down to $n = 1$. Note in Fig. 6 that the next two higher levels are the Balmer (for $n = 2$) and Paschen ($n = 3$) series, respectively.

When the light emitted by energized atoms is examined with an instrument called a spectroscope, the prism or diffraction grating in the spectroscope disperses the light to allow an examination of the spectra or distinct colored lines. Since only particular energy jumps are available in each type of atom, each element has its own unique emission spectra made up of only the lines of specific wavelength that correspond to its atomic structure.

Problem

Hydrogen can have an electron drop from the $n = 4$ to $n = 2$ level. What visible spectral line in the Balmer series will result from this emission of energy?

$$\Delta E_{evolved} = E_{n=2} - E_{n=4}$$

From Fig. 6, $E_4 = -1.36 \times 10^{-19}$ J, $E_2 = -5.45 \times 10^{-19}$ J

$$\Delta E_{evolved} = -5.45 \times 10^{-19}\,\mathrm{J} - (-1.36 \times 10^{-19}\,\mathrm{J}) = -4.09 \times 10^{-19}\,\mathrm{J}$$

(The fact that ΔE is negative indicates that energy was released.)

The formula for the relationship of ΔE to the emission frequency is

$$\Delta E = \frac{h\ (\text{Planck's constant})\ c\ (\text{velocity of light})}{\lambda\ (\text{wavelength})}$$

Substituting, we get

$$-4.09 \times 10^{-19}\,J = \frac{\left(6.626 \times 10^{-34}\,\mathrm{Js}\right)\left(2.9979 \times 10^8\,\mathrm{m/s}\right)}{\lambda}$$

Solving for λ gives

$$\lambda = \frac{\left(6.626 \times 10^{-34}\,\cancel{\mathrm{Js}}\right)\left(2.9979 \times 10^8\,\mathrm{m/\cancel{s}}\right)}{4.09 \times 10^{-19}\,\cancel{J}}$$

$$= 4.87 \times 10^{-7}\,\mathrm{m}$$

This is in the blue-green area of the spectrum.

Visible light spectra include wavelengths as shown below:

7.6×10^{-7} m	$4.0 + 10^{-7}$ m
760 nm	400 nm (nanometers) or 10^{-9} m
7600 Å	4000 Å (angstroms) or 10^{-8} cm

← Increased wavelength (λ)

Increased frequency (f) →

For electromagnetic radiation,

Frequency = $\dfrac{\text{velocity of light}}{\text{wavelength}}$

Red-orange-yellow-green-blue-violet

← Progression of colors →

For a depiction of a partial atomic spectrum for hydrogen, see Fig. 7.

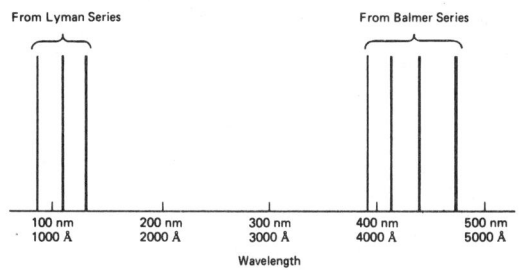

Fig. 7   Partial Atomic Spectrum for Hydrogen

The right-hand group is in the visible range and is part of the Balmer series. The left-hand group is in the ultraviolet region and belongs to the Lyman series.

Investigating spectral lines like these can be used in the identification of unknown specimens.

Mass spectroscopy is another tool used to identify specific atomic structures. This is based on the concept that differences in mass cause differences in the degree of bending that occurs in a beam of ions passing through a magnetic field. This is shown in Fig. 8.

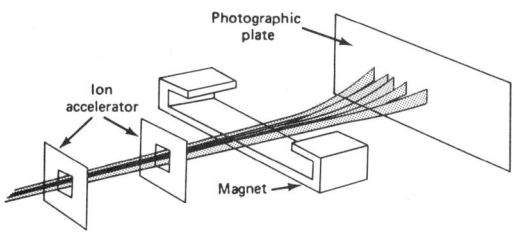

Fig. 8   Mass spectroscope

The intensity on the photographic plate indicates the amount of each particular isotope. Other collectors may be used in place of the photographic plate to collect and interpret these data.

The Wave-Mechanical Model
In the 1920s, a more mathematical model of the atom was developed through the work of such men as de-Broglie, Heisenberg, and Schrödinger. Their work in quantum mechanics described a probability picture of where the electrons at each energy level might best be found. This region of greatest probability is sometimes referred to as an electron cloud. Unlike the previous model, the wave-mechanical model does not attempt to explain the path an electron travels. De-Broglie attributed wave properties to the electron, and these were confirmed later by experimentation.

Each electron orbital in this model of the atom may be described by a set of four quantum numbers. They give the position with respect to the nucleus, the shape of the orbital, its spatial orientation, and the spin of the electron in the orbital.

The principles of the wave-mechanical model are summarized in Exhibit 3.4.

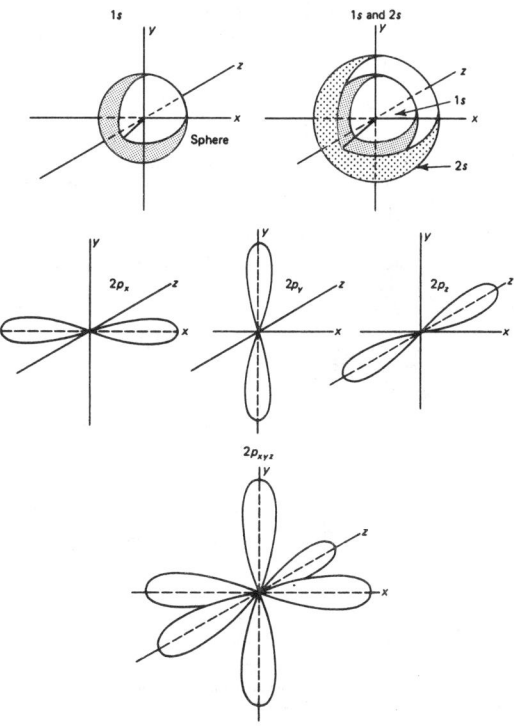

Fig. 9   Atomic Orbital Shapes

EXHIBIT 3.4
Quantum Numbers Used in The Wave-Mechanical Model of the Atom

Principal quantum number 1, 2, 3, 4, 5, etc.	Average distance of the orbital from the nucleus; 1 is closest to the nucleus and has the least energy. These numbers correspond to the shells in the older model of the atom. They are called energy levels.
Secondary or azimuthal quantum number *s, p, d, f* (in order of increasing energy)	The shape of the orbital. The number of possible shapes is limited by the principal quantum number. The first energy level has only one possible shape, the *s* orbital. The second has two possible, *s* and *p*.
Magnetic quantum number *s* = 1 space-oriented orbital *p* = 3 space-oriented orbitals *d* = 5 space-oriented orbitals *f* = 7 space-oriented orbitals	Figure 9 shows the *s*-orbital shape, which is a sphere. The *p* orbitals have dumbbell shapes with three possible orientations on the axis shown. The number of spatial orientations of orbitals is referred to as the magnetic quantum number. The possible orientations are listed.
Spin quantum number +spin −spin	Electrons are assigned one more quantum number, called the spin quantum number, which describes the spin in either of two possible directions. Each orbital can be filled by only two electrons, having opposite spins. This is referred to as the Pauli exclusion principle. Therefore each orbital in Fig. 10 can hold only two electrons.

It is important to remember that, when there is more than one orbital at a particular energy level, such as three p orbitals or five d orbitals, only one electron will fill each orbital until each has one electron. After this, pairing will occur with the addition of one more electron to each orbital. This is called Hund's rule of maximum multiplicity and is shown in Exhibit 3.5, where each slant line indicates an electron: $\emptyset$.

If each orbital is shown in an energy diagram as a $\bigcirc$, we can show the relative energies as in Fig. 10. If this drawing represented a ravine with the energy levels as ledges onto which stones could come to rest only in numbers equal to the circles for orbitals, then pushing stones into the ravine would cause the stones to lose their kinetic energy as they dropped to the lowest level available to them. Much the same is true for electrons.

Sublevels and Electron Configuration
The sublevels do not fill up in numerical order; the pattern of filling is shown on the right side of Fig. 10. In the first instance of this, $4s$ fills before $3d$. (*See* Fig. 10.)

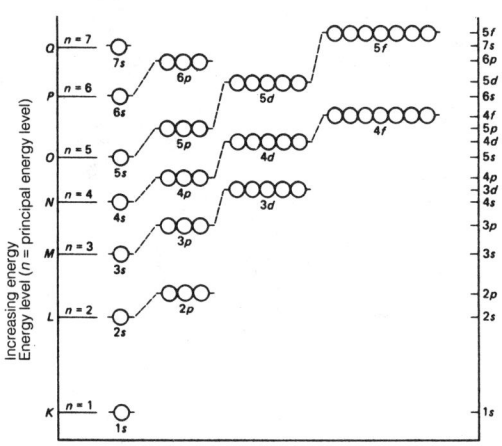

Fig. 10   Approximate Relative Energy Levels of Sublevels

$_{19}$K $1s^2, 2s^2, 2p^6\ 3s^2, 3p^6, 4s^1$

$_{20}$Ca $1s^2, 2s^2, 2p^6, 3s^2, 3p^6, 4s^2$

$_{21}$Sc $1s^2, 2s^2, 2p^6, 3s^2, 3p^6, 4s^2, 3d^1$
                              (note $4s$ filled before $3d$)

There is a more stable configuration to a half-filled or filled sublevel, so at atomic number 24 the $3d$ sublevel becomes half-filled by taking a $4s$ electron;

$_{24}$Cr $1s^2, 2s^2, 2p^6, 3s^2, 3p^6, 3d^5, 4s^1$

and at atomic number 29 the $3d$ becomes filled by taking a $4s$ electron.

$_{29}$Cu $1s^2, 2s^2, 2p^6, 3s^2, 3p^6, 3d^{10}, 4s^1$

In place of the electron configuration notation, electron dot notation may be used; this shows only the chemical symbol surrounded by dots to represent the electrons in the incomplete outer shell, for example,

K• $4s^1$ for potassium (K)

$\overset{\bullet}{\underset{\bullet}{\text{:As}}}$• $4s^2, 4p^3$ for arsenic (As)

• Sr • $5s^2$ for strontium (Sr)

$\overset{\bullet\bullet}{\underset{\bullet\bullet}{\text{:I}}}$• $5s^2, 5p^5$ for iodine (I)

$\overset{\bullet\bullet}{\underset{\bullet\bullet}{\text{:Rn:}}}$ $6s^2, 6p^6$ for radon (Rn)

(The electron configurations are given in the lower left corner of each box of the Periodic Table of the Elements. *See* **Exhibit 3.15**, pages 3-70 to 3-71.

Transition Elements and Variable Oxidation Numbers
The elements in which a d sublevel is filled with electrons after two electrons are in the s sublevel of the next major shell are often referred to as the transition elements. The first examples of these are the elements after calcium, atomic number 20, and before gallium, atomic number 31. The electron configurations of these transition elements are the same in the $1s$, $2s$, $2p$, $3s$, and $3p$ sublevels. It is the fill-

---

EXHIBIT 3.5
Orbital Notations

Chemical symbol	Atomic No.	Orbital Notation			Electron Configuration Notation
		1s	2s	2p	
H	1	$\emptyset$	$\bigcirc$	$\bigcirc\ \bigcirc\ \bigcirc$	$1s^1$
He	2	$\otimes$	$\bigcirc$	$\bigcirc\ \bigcirc\ \bigcirc$	$1s^2$
Li	3	$\otimes$	$\emptyset$	$\bigcirc\ \bigcirc\ \bigcirc$	$1s^2, 2s^1$
Be	4	$\otimes$	$\otimes$	$\bigcirc\ \bigcirc\ \bigcirc$	$1s^2, 2s^2$
B	5	$\otimes$	$\otimes$	$\emptyset\ \bigcirc\ \bigcirc$	$1s^2, 2s^2, 2p^1$
C	6	$\otimes$	$\otimes$	$\emptyset\ \emptyset\ \bigcirc$	$1s^2, 2s^2, 2p^2$
N	7	$\otimes$	$\otimes$	$\emptyset\ \emptyset\ \emptyset$	$1s^2, 2s^2, 2p^3$
O	8	$\otimes$	$\otimes$	$\otimes\ \emptyset\ \emptyset$	$1s^2, 2s^2, 2p^4$
F	9	$\otimes$	$\otimes$	$\otimes\ \otimes\ \emptyset$	$1s^2, 2s^2, 2p^5$
Ne	10	$\otimes$	$\otimes$	$\otimes\ \otimes\ \otimes$	$1s^2, 2s^2, 2p^6$

Maximum electrons in orbitals at a particular sublevel:
s = 2(one orbital) d = 10(five orbitals)
p = 6(three orbitals) f = 14(seven orbitals)

ing of the 3d and changes in the 4s sublevels that are of interest. These are shown in the table below.

Electron Configurations for Transition Elements from Sc Through Zn

Element	Atomic No.	$1s^2, 2s^2, 2p^6, 3s^2, 3p^6$	3d	4s
Scandium	21		1	2
Titanium	22		2	2
Vanadium	23	All	3	2
Chromium	24	the	5	1*
Manganese	25	same	5	2
Iron	26		6	2
Cobalt	27		7	2
Nickel	28		8	2
Copper	29		10	1*
Zinc	30		10	2

The asterisk (*) shows where a 4s electron is drawn into the 3d sublevel. This occurs because the 3d and 4s sublevels are very close in energy and there is a state of greater stability in half-filled and filled sublevels. Because of this, chromium gains stability by the movement of an electron from the 4s sublevel into the 3d sublevel to give a half-filled 3d sublevel. It then has one electron in each of the five orbitals of the 3d sublevel. In copper, the movement of one 4s electron into the 3d sublevel gives the 3d sublevel a completely filled configuration.

That the electrons in the 3d and 4s sublevels are so close in energy levels leads to the possibility that some or all of the 3d electrons are involved in chemical bonding. With the variable number of electrons available for bonding, it is not surprising that transition elements can exhibit variable oxidation numbers. An example is manganese, with possible oxidation numbers of +2, +3, +4, +6, and +7, which correspond to the use of none, one, two, four, and five electrons, respectively, from the 3d sublevel.

The transition elements in the other periods of the periodic table show this same type of anomaly, as they have d sublevels filling in the same manner.

B **Bases** Since acid and base theories are interrelated, bases are covered under **Acids and bases**.
Basic anhydride A metallic oxide that reacts with water to form a basic solution, such as sodium hydroxide or calcium hydroxide. Common examples of this reaction are

$$Na_2O + H_2O \rightarrow NaOH \overset{aq}{\rightarrow} Na^+ + OH^-$$

$$CaO + H_2O \rightarrow Ca(OH)_2 \overset{aq}{\rightarrow} Ca^{2+} + 2OH^-$$

Benzene See **Aromatic compounds**.
Beta particle A fast-moving electron associated with radioactivity and having the following properties:
■ Ejected when a neutron decays into a proton and an electron.
■ High velocity, low energy.
■ Range: 30–40 ft.
■ Shielding needed: stopped by 1 cm of aluminum or thickness of average book.
■ Interactions: weak owing to high velocity, but produces about 100 ionizations per centimeter.
For more information, see **Nucleonics**.

Binary acid An acid that uses the prefix *hydro-* in front of the stem or full name of the nonmetallic element and adds the ending -*ic*. Examples are hydrochloric acid (HCl) and hydrosulfuric acid (H_2S). See **Acids and bases**.
Binary compound A compound consisting of two elements. The metallic element is placed first and the nonmetallic second. See **Naming Compounds**, under **Formulas, writing and calculations of**.
Bohr theory A planetary concept of atomic structure named after Niels Bohr, its originator. See **Atomic structure**.
Boiling point The temperature at which under given conditions of pressure the vapor pressure of the liquid phase equals the outside pressure and the substance boils.

The vapor pressure-temperature relation can be plotted on a graph for a closed system. (*See* Fig. 11.) When a liquid is heated in an open container, the liquid and the vapor are not in equilibrium and the vapor pressure increases until it becomes equal to the pressure above the liquid. At this point the average kinetic energy of the molecules is such that they are rapidly converted from the liquid to the vapor phase within the liquid as well as at the surface. The temperature at which this occurs is known as the boiling point.

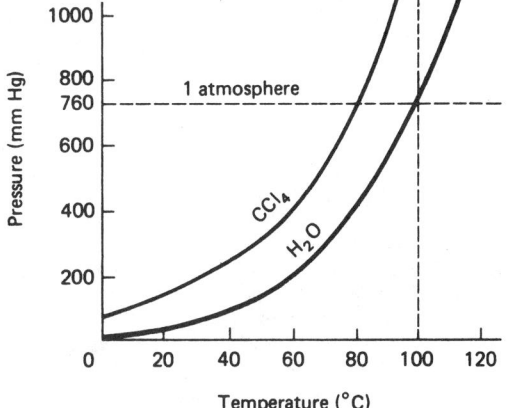

Fig. 11   Vapor Pressure-Temperature Relationship

Bond energy See **Bond Dissociation Energy**, under **Enthalpy**.
Bonding Some elements show no tendency to combine either with like atoms or with other kinds of elements. They are said to be monoatomic molecules; examples are He, Ne, and Ar. A molecule is defined as the smallest particle of an element or a compound that retains the characteristics of the original substance. Water is a triatomic molecule since two hydrogen atoms and one oxygen atom must be combined to have the substance water with its characteristic properties. When atoms do combine to form molecules, there is a shifting of valence electrons, that is, the electrons in the outer energy level of each atom. This results in a usual completion of the outer energy level of each atom. This more stable form may be achieved by the gain or loss of electrons or the sharing of pairs of electrons. The resulting at-

traction of the atoms involved is called a chemical bond. When a chemical bond forms, energy is released; when this bond is broken, energy is absorbed.

Ionic Bonds

When the electronegativity values (shown in chart form in **Exhibit 3.7**, page 3-24) of two kinds of atoms differ by 1.7 or, especially, by more, the more electronegative atom will borrow the electrons it needs to fill its outer energy level and the other kind of atom will lend electrons until it, too, has a complete outer energy level. Because of this exchange, the borrower becomes negatively charged and the lender becomes positively charged. They are now referred to as ions, and the bond or attraction between them is called an ionic or electrovalence bond. These ions do not retain the properties of the original atoms. An example can be seen in Fig. 12.

These ions do not form an individual molecule in the liquid or solid phase but are arranged into a crystal lattice or giant ion-molecule containing many of these ions. Ionic solids like this tend to have high melting points and do not conduct a current of electricity until they are in the molten state.

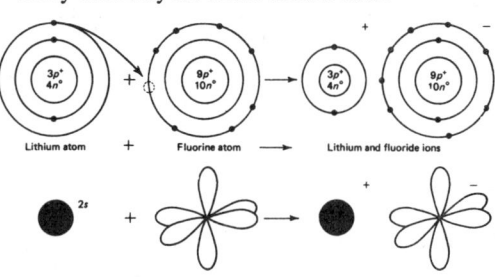

Fig. 12   Ionic Bonds

Covalent Bonds

When the electronegativity difference between two or more atoms is zero or very small (no greater than about 0.5), they tend to share the valence electrons in the respective outer energy levels. This is called a nonpolar covalent bond; for example, using electron-dot notation,

$$\overset{\bullet\bullet}{\underset{\bullet\bullet}{F}}\!\bullet \quad \bullet\,\overset{\bullet\bullet}{\underset{\bullet\bullet}{F}}\!\bullet \quad \longrightarrow \quad \overset{\bullet\bullet}{\underset{\bullet\bullet}{F}}\!\bullet\overset{\bullet\bullet}{\underset{\bullet\bullet}{F}}\!\bullet$$

fluorine atoms → fluorine molecule

These covalently bonded molecules do not have an electrostatic charge as do ionically bonded substances. In general, covalent compounds are gases, liquids having fairly low boiling points, or solids that melt at relatively low temperatures. Unlike ionic compounds, they do not conduct electrical currents.

When the electronegative difference is between 0.5 and 1.7, there will not be an equal sharing of electrons between the atoms involved. In this case, the bond is called a polar covalent bond; for example,

$$H\overset{\circ\circ}{\underset{\circ\circ}{\bullet Cl}}\!\circ$$
hydrogen chloride

• hydrogen electron
∘ chlorine electrons

$$H\overset{\circ\circ}{\underset{\bullet\bullet}{\bullet O}}\!\circ$$
water H

• hydrogen electron
∘ oxygen electrons

Notice the electron pair in the bond is shown closer to the more electronegative atom. Because of this unequal sharing, the molecules shown are said to be polar molecules, or dipoles. There are cases of polar covalent bonds existing in nonpolar molecules. Some examples are CO_2, CH_4, and CCl_4. (*See* Fig. 13.)

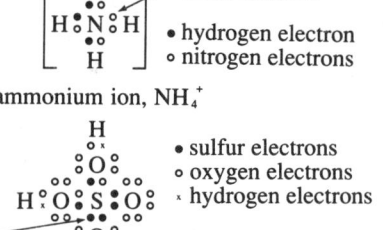

$$\overset{\circ\circ}{\underset{\circ\circ}{O}}\!\bullet\bullet C\bullet\bullet\overset{\circ\circ}{\underset{\circ\circ}{O}}$$
carbon dioxide, CO_2

$$H\overset{\bullet\bullet}{\underset{\bullet\bullet}{C}}H$$
methane, CH_4

carbon tetrachloride, CCl_4

Fig. 13   Covalent Bonds

In all these examples the bonds are polar covalent bonds, but the important thing is that they are symmetrically arranged in the molecule. This results in a nonpolar molecule.

In the covalent bonds described so far, the shared electrons in the pair were contributed one each from the atoms bonded. There are cases in which both electrons for the shared pair are supplied by only one of the atoms. These are called coordinate covalent bonds. Two examples are NH_4^+ and H_2SO_4. (*See* Fig. 14).

both electrons from the nitrogen atom
• hydrogen electron
∘ nitrogen electrons

ammonium ion, NH_4^+

• sulfur electrons
∘ oxygen electrons
× hydrogen electrons

both electrons from the sulfur atom

sulfuric acid molecule, H_2SO_4

Fig. 14   Coorindate Covalent Bonds

Metallic Bonds

In most metals, one or more of the valence electrons become detached from the atom and migrate in a "sea" of free electrons among the positive metal ions. The strong attraction between these differently charged particles forms the metallic bond. Because of this firm bonding, metals usually have high melting points; show the properties of hardness, ductility (can be stretched into wire), and malleability (can be flattened into sheets); and are good conductors of electricity and heat.

Double and Triple Bonds

To achieve the octet structure, which is an outer shell resembling the noble gas configuration of eight electrons, it is necessary for some atoms to share two or even three pairs of electrons. Sharing two pairs of electrons produces a double bond, for example,

$$\overset{\times}{\underset{\times}{O}}\!\overset{\times\times}{:}\!C\!:\!\overset{\times\times}{\underset{\times}{O}}\!\overset{\times}{}$$

carbon dioxide

which may also be shown as

O=C=O

In the line formula, only the shared pair of electrons is indicated by a bond (—). The sharing of three electron pairs results in a triple bond, for example,

H ⁚ C ⁚⁚ C ⁚ H

acetylene

which may also be shown as

H—C≡C—H

It can be assumed from these structures that there is a greater electron density between the nuclei involved and hence a greater attractive force between the nuclei and the shared electrons. Experimental data verify that greater energy is required to break double bonds than single bonds, and triple bonds than double bonds. Also, since these stronger bonds tend to pull atoms closer together, the atoms joined by double and triple bonds have smaller interatomic distances and greater bond strengths, respectively.

Boyle's law   *See* **Gas laws.**

Brønsted-Lowry acid-base theory   *See* **Acids and bases.**

Buffer solutions   Equilibrium systems that resist changes in acidity and maintain constant pH when acids or bases are added to them. A typical laboratory buffer can be prepared by mixing equal molar quantities of a weak acid, such as $HC_2H_3O_2$, and its salt, $NaC_2H_3O_2$. When a strong base, such as NaOH, is added to the buffer, the acetic acid reacts (and consumes) most of the excess OH^- ion. The OH^- ion reacts with the H^+ ion from the acetic acid, thus reducing the H^+ ion concentration in this equilibrium:

$$HC_2H_3O_2 \rightleftarrows H^+ + C_2H_3O_2^-$$

This reduction of H^+ causes a shift to the right, forming additional $C_2H_3O^-$ ions and H^+ ions. For practical purposes, each mole of OH^- added consumes 1 mole of $HC_2H_3O_2$ and produces 1 mole of $C_2H_3O_2^-$ ions.

When a strong acid, such as HCl, is added to the buffer, the H^+ ions react with the $C_2H_3O_2^-$ ions of salt and form more undissociated $HC_2H_3O_2$. This does not alter the $H+$ ions concentration. Proportional increases and decreases in the concentrations of $C_2H_3O_2^-$ and $HC_2H_3O_2$ do not significantly affect the acidity of the solution.

 **Calorimetry**   Problems related to the exchange of heat energy, usually in a calorimeter. A calorimeter is a container that is well insulated from outside sources of heat or cold so that most of its heat is contained in the vessel. If a very hot object is placed in a calorimeter containing some ice crystals, we can find the final temperature of the mixture mathematically and check it experimentally. To do this, certain behaviors must be understood. Ice changing to water and then to steam is not a continuous and constant change of temperature as time progresses. In fact, the chart would look as shown in Fig. 15.

From this graph, you see that heat is being used at 0°C and 100°C to change the state of water, but not its temperature. A single gram of ice at 0°C needs 80 calories, or 3.34×10^2 joules, to change to water at 0°C. This is called its heat of fusion. Likewise, en-

ergy is being used at 100°C to change water to steam, not to change the temperature. A gram of water at 100°C absorbs 540 calories, or 2.26×10^3 joules, of heat to change to 1 gram of steam at 100°C. This energy, called the heat of vaporization, absorbed at the plateaus in the curve is being used to break up the bonding forces between molecules by increasing their energy content so that a specific change of state can occur.

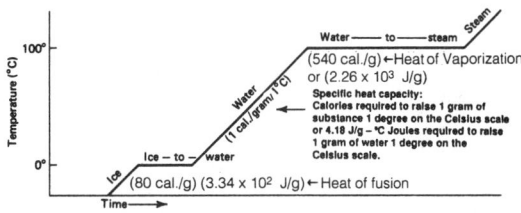

Fig. 15   Changing Ice to Steam

Problem

How much heat is needed to change 100 grams of ice at 0°C to steam at 100°C?
To melt 100 g of ice at 0°C:

$$100 \, g \times \frac{80 \, cal}{1 \, g} = 8000 \, cal = 8 \, kcal$$

To heat 100 g of water from 0°C to 100°C:

$$100 \, g \times \overbrace{(100-0)°C}^{\text{temperature change}} \times \frac{1 \, cal}{1 \, g \times 1°C} = 10,000 \, cal$$
$$= 10 \, kcal$$

To vaporize 100 g of water at 100°C to steam at 100°C:

$$100 \, g \times \frac{540 \, cal}{1 \, g} = 54,000 \, cal = 54 \, kcal$$

Total heat = 8 + 10 + 54 = 72 kcal

To express the answer in joules, use the joule equivalents or the following conversion:

$$72 \, kcal \times \frac{1000 \, cal}{1 \, kcal} \times \frac{4.18 \, joules}{1 \, cal} = 3.01 \times 10^5 J$$

Carbon   An element having 12 protons in its nucleus and occurring in three natural allotropic structural forms. These are diamond, graphite, and amorphous (although some evidence shows the amorphous forms do have some crystalline structure).

The diamond form has a close-packed crystal structure that gives it its property of extreme hardness. In it each carbon is bonded to four other carbons in a tetrahedron arrangement:

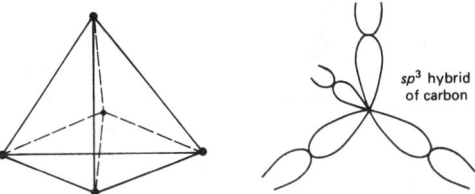

sp^3 hybrid of carbon

It has been possible to make synthetic diamonds in machines that subject carbon to extremely high pressures and temperatures. Most of these diamonds are used for industrial purposes, such as dies.

The graphite form is made up of planes of hexagonal structures that are weakly bonded to the planes above and below. This explains graphite's slippery feeling and makes it useful as a dry lubricant. Its structure can be seen below. Graphite also has the property of being an electrical conductor.

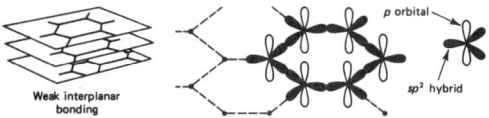

Some of the amorphous forms of carbon, that is, those not having a definite crystalline structure, are charcoal, coke, bone black, and lampblack.

Carbon dioxide (CO_2)   A widely distributed gas that makes up 0.04% of the atmosphere.

Laboratory Preparation
The usual laboratory preparation consists of reacting calcium carbonate (marble chips) with hydrochloric acid, although any carbonate or bicarbonate and any common acid could be used. The gas is collected by water displacement or air displacement. (*See* Fig. 16.)

The test for carbon dioxide consists of passing it through limewater, $Ca(OH)_2$. If CO_2 is present, the limewater turns cloudy because of the formation of a white precipitate of finely divided $CaCO_3$:

$$Ca(OH)_2 + CO_2 \rightarrow CaCO_3\downarrow + H_2O$$

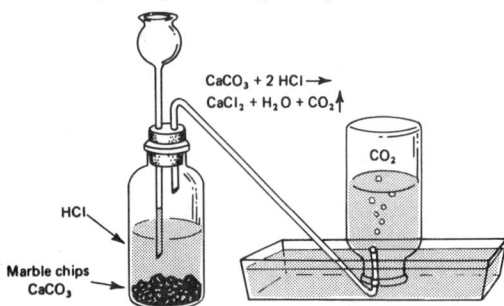

Fig. 16   Laboratory Preparation of Carbon Dioxide

Continued passing of CO_2 into the solution will clear the cloudy condition because the insoluble $CaCO_3$ becomes soluble calcium bicarbonate, $Ca(HCO_3)_2$:

$$CaCO_3\downarrow + H_2O + CO_2 \rightarrow Ca^2{+}(HCO_3)_2{}^-$$

This reaction can easily be reversed with increased temperature or decreased pressure. This is the way stalagmites and stalactites form on the floor and roof, respectively, of a cave. The groundwater containing calcium bicarbonate is deposited on the roof and floor and decomposes into solid calcium carbonate formations.

Important Uses
■ Since CO_2 is the acid anhydride of carbonic acid, it forms the acid when reacted with soft drinks, thus making them "carbonated" beverages:

$$CO_2 + H_2O \rightarrow H_2CO_3$$

■ Solid carbon dioxide (–78°C), or "dry ice," is used as a refrigerant because it has the advantages of not melting into a liquid but sublimes and absorbs three times as much heat per gram as ice in the process.

■ Leavening agents are usually made up of a dry acid-forming salt, dry baking soda ($NaHCO_3$), and a substance to keep these ingredients dry, such as starch or flour.

Carboxyl group   *See* **Organic Acids**, under **Organic chemistry**.

Catalyst   A substance that is used to either slow or speed a reaction but that does not permanently change itself. An example of this concept can be shown in the preparation of oxygen from potassium chlorate ($KClO_3$).

In this preparation, manganese dioxide (MnO_2) is often used. This compound is not used up in the reaction and can be shown to have the same composition as it had before the reaction occurred. The only effect it seems to have is that it lowers the temperature needed to decompose the $KClO_3$ and thus speeds the reaction. Substances that behave in this manner are referred to as catalysts.

A catalyst can also be used to slow a reaction. The mechanism by which a catalyst does this is not completely understood in all cases, but it is known that in some reactions the catalyst does change its structure temporarily. The effect of a catalyst is shown in the reaction graphs in Figs. 17 and 18.

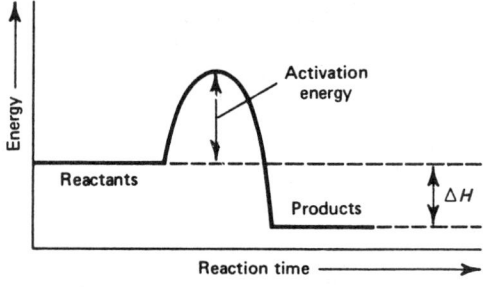

Fig. 17   Reaction Without Catalyst

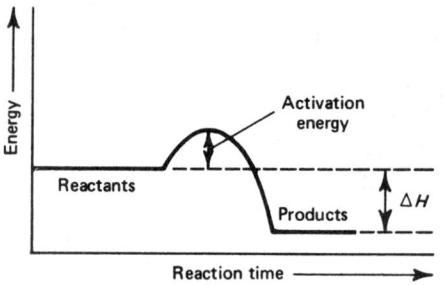

Fig. 18   Reaction With Catalyst

Cathode   The negatively charged pole in an electrolytic cell. *See* **Electrochemical reactions**.

Cation   A positively charged ion that exists in a solution and is attracted to the cathode. *See* **Electrochemical reactions**.

Celsius temperature scale   *See* **Temperature scales**.

Centigrade temperature scale   *See* **Tempera-**
ture scales.
Centimeter   A metric unit of measure that equals
1/100 of the length of a meter. *See* **Measurements**
for details.
Charles' law   *See* **Gas laws**.
Chemical calculations   (Stoichiometry and the
mole concept)

Formula Mass and Molecules
When the formula mass of a molecule or compound
is determined by the addition of its component
atomic masses and expressed in grams, it is called
the gram-formula mass. An example is $CaCO_3$:

$$
\begin{array}{l}
1\ Ca = 40 \\
1\ C = 12 \\
\underline{3\ O = 48 = (3 \times 16)} \\
CaCO_3 = 100\ \text{formula mass} \\
100\ g = \text{gram-formula mass}
\end{array}
$$

The gram-formula mass is called the *gram-molar
mass*, or one *mole*, of that material. The term gram-
molecular mass can also be used when it is known
that the material is a molecular substance, not an
ionic lattice such as NaCl or NaOH.

Gas Volumes and Molecular Mass
Because the volume of a gas may vary depending on
the conditions of temperature and pressure, a standard
is set for comparing gases. The standard conditions of
temperature and pressure (abbreviated STP) are 0°C
and 760 mm of mercury pressure (or 760 torr).
The molecular mass of a gas expressed in grams
and under standard conditions occupies 22.4 liters.
This is an important relationship to remember! The
22.4 liters is referred to as the gram-molecular volume (gmv). Two men are associated with this relationship.
Gay-Lussac's law states that, when only gases are
involved in a reaction, the volumes of the reacting
gases and the volumes of the gaseous products are in
ratio to each other as small whole numbers. This law
may be illustrated by the following cases:

1 vol hydrogen + 1 vol chlorine = 2 vols
hydrogen
chloride
2 vols hydrogen + 1 vol oxygen = 2 vols steam

Avogadro's law, which explains Gay-Lussac's,
states that equal volumes of gases under the same
conditions of temperature and pressure contain
equal number of molecules. This means that 1 mole
of any gas at STP occupies 22.4 liters; so,

32 g O_2 at STP occupies 22.4 liters
2 g H_2 at STP occupies 22.4 liters
44 g CO_2 at STP occupies 22.4 liters.

Density and Molecular Mass
Since the density of a gas is usually given in
grams/liter of the gas at STP, we can use the gram-
molecular volume to molecular mass relationship
to solve two types of problems.

Problem 1

Find the molecular mass of a gas when the density is
given as 1.25 g/liter.

Knowing that 1 mole of a gas occupies 22.4 liters
at STP, we can solve this problem by multiplying
the mass of 1 liter by 22.4 liters/mole.

$$
\frac{1.25\ g}{\text{liter}} \times \frac{22.4\ \text{liters}}{1\ \text{mole}} = 28\ g/\text{mole}
$$

We can also find the density of a gas if we know the
molecular mass. Since the molecular mass occupies
22.4 liters at STP, dividing the molecular mass by
22.4 liters will give the mass per liter, or the density.

Problem 2

Find the density of oxygen at STP.

Oxygen is diatomic in its molecular structure.

O_2 = molecular mass of 2×16 or 32 g/mole

32 g/mole occupies 22.4 liters

Therefore,

$$
\frac{32\ g}{1\ \text{mole}} \div \frac{22.4\ L}{1\ \text{mole}} = \frac{32\ g}{1\ \text{mole}} \times \frac{1\ \text{mole}}{22.4\ L} = 143\ g/\text{liter}
$$

We can find the density of a gas, then, by dividing
its molecular mass by 22.4 liters.

Mass-Volume Relationships

Problem

How many liters of oxygen (STP) can you prepare
from the decomposition of 42.6 grams of sodium
chlorate?

Step 1. Write the balanced equation for the reaction.

$2NaClO_3 \overset{\Delta}{=} 2NaCl + 3O_2\uparrow$

Step 2. Write the given quantity and the unknown
quantity above the appropriate substances.

42.6 grams x liters
$2NaClO_3 \overset{\Delta}{=} 2NaCl + 3O_2$

Step 3. Calculate the equation mass or volume for
each substance that has something indicated above
it, and write the result below the substance. Note
that the units above and below *must* match.

42.6 grams x liters
$2NaClO_3 \overset{\Delta}{=} 2NaCl + 3O_2$
213 grams   67.2 liters

($2 \times$ molecular mass (3×22.4 liters)
  of $NaClO_3$)

Step 4. Form the proportion.

$$
\frac{42.6\ g}{213\ g} = \frac{x\ \text{liters}}{67.2\ \text{liters}}
$$

Step 5. Solve for x.

$x = 13.4$ liters O_2

This problem can also be solved using methods
other than the proportion method shown above.
An alternative is to proceed from step 3 by what
is called the *factor-label method*. The reasoning is as
follows. Since the equation shows that 213 grams
of reactant produces 67.2 liters of the required product, multiplying the given amount by this equality

(so that the units of the answer are correct) will give the same answer as above. So step 4 would be

$$42.6 \text{ grams NaClO}_3 \times \frac{67.2 \text{ liters O}_2}{213 \text{ grams NaClO}_3}$$
$$= 13.4 \text{ liters O}_2$$

Still another method of solving this problem is called the *mole method*. Steps 1 and 2 are the same. Then,

Step 3. Determine how many moles of substance are given.

$$42.6 \text{ g} \div \frac{106.5 \text{ g}}{1 \text{ mole NaClO}_3} = 0.4 \text{ mole NaClO}_3$$

The equation shows that 2 moles NaClO$_3$ makes 3 moles O$_2$. So 0.4 mole NaClO$_3$ will yield

$$4 \text{ mole NaClO}_3 \times \frac{3 \text{ moles O}_2}{2 \text{ moles NaClO}_3} = 0.6 \text{ mole O}_2$$

Step 4. Convert the moles of O$_3$ to liters.

$$0.6 \text{ mole O}_2 \times \frac{22.4 \text{ liters O}_2}{1 \text{ mole O}_2} = 13.4 \text{ liters O}_2$$

Mass-Mass Problems

Problem

How many grams of oxygen can be obtained by heating 100 grams of potassium chlorate?

Step 1. Write the balance equation for the reaction.

$2KClO_3 \rightarrow 2KCl + 3O_2$

Step 2. Write the given quantity and the unknown quantity above the appropriate substances.

$$\begin{array}{ccc} 100 \text{ g} & & x \text{ g} \\ 2KClO_3 & \rightarrow 2KCl + & 3O_2 \end{array}$$

Step 3. Calculate the equation mass for each substance that has something indicated above it, and write the result below the substance. Note that the units above and below *must* match.

$$\begin{array}{ccc} 100 \text{ g} & & x \text{ g} \\ 2KClO_3 & \rightarrow 2KCl + & 3O_2 \\ 245 \text{ g} & & 96 \text{ g} \end{array}$$

Steps 4 and 5 may be done using the *proportion method*.

Step 4. Form the proportion.

$$\frac{100 \text{ g}}{245 \text{ g}} = \frac{x \text{ g}}{96 \text{ g}}$$

Step 5. Solve for x.

$x = 39.3$ g of O$_2$

If you use the *factor-label method*, you would proceed from step 3 as follows.

Step 4. The equation indicates that 245 g KClO$_3$ yields 96 g of O$_2$. Therefore, multiplying the given quantity by a factor made up of these two quantities, arranged appropriately so that the units of the

answer remain uncanceled, gives the answer to the problem:

$$100 \text{ g KClO}_3 \times \frac{96 \text{ g O}_2}{245 \text{ g KClO}_3} = 39.3 \text{ g O}_2$$

The *mole method* may also be used. To solve this problem you would proceed as follows after steps 1 and 2.

Step 3. Determine how many moles of substance are given.

$$100 \text{ g KClO}_3 \times \frac{1 \text{ mole KClO}_3}{122.5 \text{ g KClO}_3} = 0.815 \text{ mole KClO}_3$$

The equation obtained in step 1 shows that 2 moles of KClO$_3$ yields 3 moles of O$_2$. So 0.815 mole KClO$_3$ yields

$$0.815 \text{ mole KClO}_3 \times \frac{3 \text{ moles O}_2}{2 \text{ moles KClO}_3}$$
$$= 1.22 \text{ moles O}_2$$

Step 4. Convert the moles of O$_2$ to grams of O$_2$:

$$1.22 \text{ mole O}_2 \times \frac{32 \text{ g O}_2}{1 \text{ mole O}_2} = 39 \text{ g O}_2$$

Volume-Volume Problems

This type of problem involves only volume units and therefore can make use of Gay-Lussac's law: "When gases combine, they combine in simple whole number ratios." These simple numbers are the coefficients of the equation.

Problem

What volume of NH$_3$ is produced when 22.4 liters of nitrogen are made to combine with a sufficient quantity of hydrogen under the appropriate conditions?

Step 1. Write the balanced equation for the reaction.

$N_2 + 3H_2 \rightarrow 2NH_3$

Step 2. Write the given quantity and the unknown quantity above the respective substances.

$$\begin{array}{ccc} 22.4 \text{ L} & & x \text{ L} \\ N_2 + & 3H_2 \rightarrow & 2NH_3 \end{array}$$

Step 3. Set up a proportion using the coefficients of the substances that have something indicated above them as denominators:

$$\frac{22.4 \text{ L}}{1 \text{ L}} = \frac{x \text{ L}}{2 \text{ L}}$$

Step 4. Solve for x.

$x = 44.8$ L

If you use the *factor-label method*, you would proceed from step 2 as follows.

Step 3. The equation obtained in step 1 shows that 1 volume of N$_2$ will yield 2 volumes of NH$_3$. Therefore, multiplying the given quantity by a factor made up of these two quantities, appropriately arranged so that the units of the answer remain uncanceled, will solve the problem.

$$22.4 \text{ liters N}_2 \times \frac{2 \text{ liters NH}_3}{1 \text{ liter N}_2} = 44.8 \text{ liters NH}_3$$

The *mole method* may also be used. To solve this problem you would proceed as follows.

Step 3. The given quantity is converted to moles:

$$22.4 \text{ liters N}_2 \times \frac{1 \text{ mole N}_2}{22.4 \text{ liters N}_2} = 1 \text{ mole N}_2$$

The equation shows that 1 mole of N_2 will yield 2 moles of NH_3. Therefore, using this relationship will yield

$$1 \text{ mole N}_2 \times \frac{2 \text{ moles NH}_3}{1 \text{ mole N}_2} = 2 \text{ moles NH}_3$$

Convert the moles of NH_3 to liters of NH_3:

$$2 \text{ moles NH}_3 \times \frac{22.4 \text{ liters NH}_3}{1 \text{ mole NH}_3} = 44.8 \text{ liters NH}_3.$$

Chemical changes   Changes in the composition and structure of reactants, resulting in new atomic structure(s) in the products. Chemical changes are always accompanied by adsorption or liberation of energy. If the energy released from the formation of a new structure exceeds the chemical energy in the original substances, energy is given off, usually in the form of heat or light or both. This is called an exothermic reaction.

If, however, the new structure needs to absorb more energy than is available from the reactants, the reaction is endothermic. The two types of reactions are shown graphically in Figs. 19 and 20.

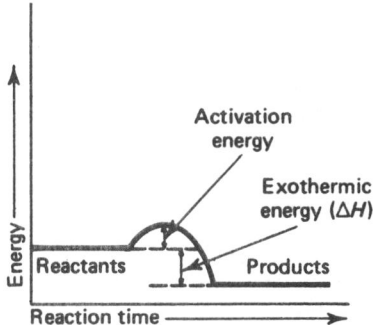

Fig. 19   An Exothermic Reaction

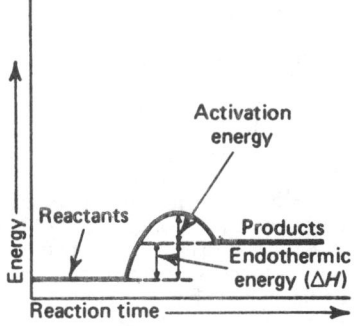

Fig. 20   An Endothermic Reaction

Notice that in Figs. 19 and 20 the term "activation energy" is used. The activation energy is the energy necessary to get the reaction going by increasing the energy of the reactants so they can combine. You know that you have to heat paper before it burns. This heat raises the energy of the reactants so that the burning can begin; then enough energy is given off from the burning so that an external source of energy is no longer necessary.

Chemical properties   Properties observed when a substance reacts or does not react with other substances. Some common examples are as follows: iron rusts in moist air, nitrogen does not burn, gold does not rust, sodium reacts with water, silver does not react with water, and water can be decomposed by an electric current.

Colligative properties   Properties that depend primarily on the concentration of particles, not the type of particle. There is usually a direct relationship between the concentration of particles and the effect recorded. An example is the changing of the freezing point of water by the addition of sodium chloride.

Colloids   Particles in a mixture that are usually larger than ions and smaller than suspension particles; basically they range from about 1 nm to 200 nm in diameter. They cannot pass through semipermeable membranes, and they stay suspended in the mixture. They are visible when a strong beam of light is passed through the mixture.

Combined gas law   *See* **Gas laws**.

Compounds   A compound is a substance made up of two or more elements that are chemically combined. Because of this it has a definite composition and large quantities are homogeneous throughout, as in water and carbon dioxide. The properties of a compound are distinct and different from the properties of the individual elements of its makeup.

Compounds, composition of   *See* **Composition Considerations** under **Formulas, writing and calculations of**.

Concentration   *See* **Solutions**.

Conjugate acid-base   *See* **Acids and bases**.

Conservation of mass and energy, law of   A rule based on a relationship between the concept of mass and energy discovered by Einstein. This law states that matter and energy are interchangeable under special conditions. The conditions have been created in nuclear reactors and accelerators, and the law has been verified. This relationship can be expressed by Einstein's famous equation,

$$E = mc^2$$

Energy = mass × (velocity of light)^2

Conservation of matter, law of   The rule that the sum of the masses of the reactants on the left side of a balanced equation must equal the sum of the masses of the products on the right side, because matter can neither be created nor destroyed.

Covalent bonding   *See* **Bonding**.

Critical conditions   Temperature and pressure. There are conditions for particular substances when it is impossible for the liquid or gaseous phase to exist. Since the kinetic energy of a molecular system is directly proportional to the Kelvin temperature, it is logical to assume that there is a temperature at which the kinetic energy of the molecules is so great that the attractive forces between molecules are insufficient for the liquid phase to remain. The temperature above which the liquid phase of a substance cannot exist is called its *critical temperature*. Above its critical temperature, no gas can be liquefied, regardless of the pressure applied. The minimum pressure required to liquefy a gas at its critical temperature is called its *critical pressure*.

Dalton's atomic theory   *See* **Atomic structure**.

Dalton's law of partial pressure *See* **Gas laws**.

Definite composition, law of   The rule that, every time a particular compound forms, it forms in the same percentage composition. *See* **Formulas, writing and calculations of** for how to determine the percentage composition.

Density   The relationship of mass to a unit volume. It can be shown by the formula $D = m/V$.

Diffusion of gas   *See* **Gases**; **Graham's law of diffusion** under **Gas laws**.

Dilute solutions   *See* **Solutions**; **Graham's law of diffusion** under **Gas laws**.

Distillation   A process of separation of a liquid mixture by taking advantage of varying boiling points. An example is the distillation of water.

The process of distillation involves the evaporation and condensation of the water molecules. The usual apparatus for the distillation of any liquid is shown in Fig. 21.

This method of purification removes any substance that has a boiling point higher than that of water. Dissolved gases or liquids that boil off before the water can be removed by discarding any distillate that forms at a temperature below that of the boiling point of water.

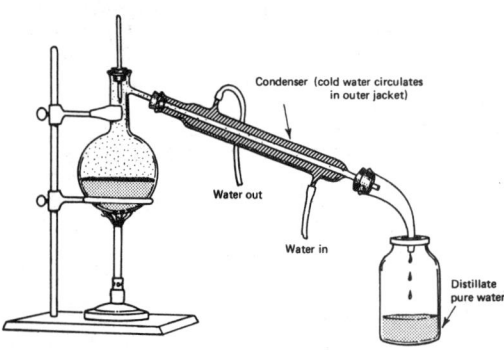

Fig. 21   Distillation of Water

When water contains bicarbonates of Ca, Mg, or Fe it is said to have carbonate hardness, formerly called "temporary" hardness. Such hardness may be removed by boiling since heat causes the bicarbonate to decompose to a carbonate precipitate. This can cause detrimental boiler scales in industrial boilers if not removed.

***d* orbitals**   *See* **Atomic structure**.

Electrochemical reactions (electrochemistry)   In the early 1830s, Michael Faraday discovered that the water solutions of certain substances conduct an electric current. He called these sub-

stances electrolytes. Our definition today of an electrolyte is much the same. It is a substance that dissolves in water to form a solution that conducts an electric current.

The usual apparatus to test for this conductivity is a light bulb placed in series with two prongs that are immersed in the solution tested. (See Fig. 22.)

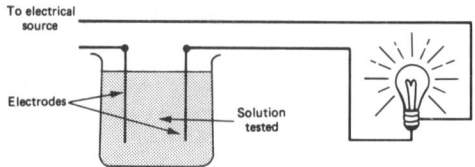

Fig. 22   Apparatus to Test Conductivities of Electrolytes

Using this type of apparatus, we can classify solutions as good, moderate, or poor electrolytes. If they do not conduct at all, they are called nonelectrolytes. The table below classifies some common substances in regard to their conductivities.

Conductivities of Various Water Solutions

Good	Poor	Nonelectrolyte
Sodium chloride	Acetic acid	Sugar
Hydrochloric acid	Ammonium hydroxide	Benzene

The reason that these substances conduct with varying degrees is related to the number of ions in solution.

Ionic lattice substances, such as sodium chloride, are dissociated by the water molecules so that the individual positive and negative ions are dispersed throughout the solution. This process is called *dissociation*.

In the case of a covalently bonded substance the degree of polarity determines the extent to which it will be ionized. The water molecules, which are polar themselves, can help weaken and finally break the polar covalent bonds by clustering around the substance. When the ions are formed in this manner, the process is called *ionization*. Substances that are nonelectrolytes are usually bonded so that the molecule is a nonpolar molecule. The polar water molecule cannot orient itself around the molecule and cause its ionization.

Let us see how the current is carried through the apparatus shown in Fig. 22. The electricity causes one electrode to become positively charged and one negatively charged. These are called the anode and the cathode, respectively. If the solution contains ions, they will be attracted to the electrode with the charge opposite to their own. This means that the positive ions migrate to the cathode, so they are referred to as cations. The negative ions migrate toward the positive anode, so they are called anions.

When these ions arrive at the respective electrodes, the negative ions give up electrons and the positive ions accept electrons, and there is a completed path for the electric current. The more highly ionized the substance, the more current flows and the brighter the light bulb glows. It was the Swedish chemist Arrhenius who proposed a theory to explain the behavior of electrolytes in aqueous solutions.

Oxidation-Reduction (Redox)

Reactions in which electrons are both gained and lost by respective reactants. Half-reactions show each of these processes. The reaction showing the loss of electrons is called *oxidation* and the one showing the gain of electrons is called *reduction*. The relative strength of metals and nonmetals to take part in these reactions is shown in Exhibit 3.6, called the Electromotive Series.

From this chart you notice that zinc is above copper and, therefore, more active. This means zinc can displace copper ions in a solution of copper sulfate.

$$Zn^0 + Cu^2 + SO_4^{2-} \rightarrow Cu^0 + Zn^{2+} + SO_4^{2-}$$

The zero indicates ⟶ The zinc ion
the zinc ——————— carries a 2+
atom is neutral   charge

The Zn atom must have lost two electrons to become Zn^{2+} ions:

$$Zn^0 \rightarrow Zn^{2+} + 2e^- \text{ (electrons)}$$

At the same time, the Cu^{2+} must have gained two electrons to become the Cu^0 atom:

$$Cu^{2+} + 2e^- \text{ (electrons)} \rightarrow Cu^0$$

These two equations are called half-reactions. The loss of electrons by the Zn atom is called oxidation. The gain of electrons by the Cu ion is called reduction. It is important to remember that the gain of electrons is reduction and the loss of electrons is oxidation.

The metal elements that lose electrons easily and become positive ions are placed high in the electromotive series. The metal elements that lose electrons with more difficulty are placed lower on the chart.

The energy required to remove electrons from metallic atoms can be assigned numerical values called electrode potentials.

These voltages depend on the nature of the reaction, the concentration of reactants and products, and the temperature. Throughout this discussion, we use standard concentrations, that is, all ions or molecules in aqueous solution are at a concentration of 1 molar. Furthermore, all gases taking part in the reactions are at 1 atmosphere pressure, and the temperature is 25°C. The voltage measured under these conditions is called standard voltage.

The electrode potentials are shown in the last column of Exhibit 3.6. Notice that hydrogen is used as the standard, with an electrode potential of zero. These values help you predict what reactions will

EXHIBIT 3.6
Electromotive Series

Standard Half-cell Voltages

Element			Oxidation Electron Reaction		Electrode Potential* E^0_{ox} (V)
Potassium			$K \rightarrow K^+$	$+e^-$	+2.93
Calcium			$Ca \rightarrow Ca^{2+}$	$+2e^-$	+2.87
Sodium	Increasing	Increasing	$Na \rightarrow Na^+$	$+e^-$	+2.71
Magnesium	tendency	tendency	$Mg \rightarrow Mg^{2+}$	$+2e^-$	+2.37
Aluminum	for	for	$Al \rightarrow Al^{3+}$	$+3e^-$	+1.67
Zinc	atoms	ions	$Zn \rightarrow Zn^{2+}$	$+2e^-$	+0.76
Iron	to	to gain	$Fe \rightarrow Fe^{2+}$	$+2e^-$	+0.44
Tin	lose	electrons	$Sn \rightarrow Sn^{2+}$	$+2e^-$	+0.14
Lead	electrons	and	$Pb \rightarrow Pb^{2+}$	$+2e^-$	+0.13
Hydrogen	and	form	$H_2 \rightarrow 2H^+$	$+2e^-$	0.00
Copper	form	atoms	$Cu \rightarrow Cu^{2+}$	$+2e^-$	−0.34
Mercury	positive	of the	$2Hg \rightarrow Hg_2^{2+}$	$+2e^-$	−0.79
Silver	ions	metal	$Ag \rightarrow Ag^+$	$+e^-$	−0.80
Mercury			$Hg \rightarrow Hg^{2+}$	$+2e^-$	−0.85
Gold			$Au \rightarrow Au^{3+}$	$+3e^-$	−1.50

*A measure in volts of the tendency of atoms to gain or lose electrons.

Activity of Nonmetals

Element			Reduction Electron Reaction	E^0_{red}(V)
Fluorine	Increasing tendency	Increasing tendency	$F_2 + 2e^- \rightarrow 2F^-$	+2.85
Chlorine	for atoms to gain	for ions to lose	$Cl_2 + 2e^- \rightarrow 2Cl^-$	+1.36
Bromine	electrons and form	electrons and form	$Br_2 + 2e^- \rightarrow 2Br^-$	+1.06
Iodine	negative ions	atoms	$I_2 + 2e^- \rightarrow 2I^-$	+0.53

occur and how readily they will occur. These reactions are called voltaic cell reactions. The following examples will clarify the use of electrode potentials.

If magnesium reacts with chlorine, we can write the equation

$$Mg + Cl_2 \rightarrow MgCl_2$$

The two half-reactions with the electrode potentials would be

Oxidation half-reaction:	Mg	$\rightarrow Mg^{2+} + 2e^-$	$E^0 = +2.37$ V
Reduction half-reaction:	$Cl_2 + 2e^- \rightarrow 2Cl^-$		$E^0 = +1.36$ V
Net reaction:	$Mg + Cl_2$	$\rightarrow Mg^{2+} + 2Cl^-$	$E^0 = +3.73$ V

In this reaction, E^0 is a positive number. This indicates that the reaction occurs spontaneously.

You should also note that the total number of electrons lost in oxidation is equal to the total number of electrons gained so that the net reaction (arrived at by adding the two reactions) does not contain any electrons.

Another example is sodium reacting with chlorine:

$$2Na + Cl_2 \rightarrow 2NaCl$$

The two half-reactions would be

Oxidation half-reaction:	2Na	$\rightarrow 2Na^{2+} + 2e^-$	$E^0 = +2.71$ V
Reduction half-reaction:	$Cl_2 + 2e^- \rightarrow 2Cl^-$		$E^0 = +1.36$ V
Net reaction:	$2Na + Cl_2$	$\rightarrow 2Na^+ + 2Cl^-$	$E^0 = +4.07$ V

Note: The electrode potentials E^0 are *not* multiplied by the coefficients in calculating the E^0 for the reaction.

Again, the E^0 for this reaction is positive and the reaction is spontaneous. The next example shows a negative E^0.

Copper metal placed in an acid solution would be

Oxidation:	Cu	$\rightarrow Cu^2 + 2e^-$	$E^0 = -0.34$ V
Reduction:	$2H^+ + 2e^- \rightarrow H_2$		$E^0 = 0.00$ V
Net reaction:	$Cu + 2H^+ \rightarrow Cu^2 + H_2$		$E^0 = -0.34$ V

Since E^0 is negative, we know the reaction will not take place.

You notice that in Exhibit 3.6 the oxidation reactions with their E^0 values are shown for the metals. If you must use the reduction reaction of one of these metals, the equation must be reversed and the sign of E^0 changed. An example of this is placing a piece of copper into a solution of silver ions:

Oxidation:	$Cu \rightarrow Cu^2 + 2e^-$	$E^0 = -0.34$ V
Reversed to show reduction	$2Ag^+ + 2e^- \rightarrow 2Ag^0$	$E^0 = +0.80$ V
	$Cu + 2Ag^+ \rightarrow Cu^{2+} + 2Ag^0$	$E^0 = +0.46$ V

This reaction would occur spontaneously since E^0 is positive.

For a complete list of standard electrode potentials, *see* **Table L** in **Exhibit 3.13**, page 3-67.

Non-standard-state Cell Potentials

You are undoubtedly aware that the voltage of a battery does not remain constant. After the battery is in use, the voltage begins to decrease. The reason is related to the changes in concentration of the reactants and products that are causing the electron flow. The assumed concentration of 1 molar solutions was

the basis of the voltaic standard voltages given earlier. A German scientist, Walter Nernst, developed a mathematical relationship that enables us to calculate the cell voltage and direction of a spontaneous reaction at other than standard-state concentrations. For a general oxidation-reduction reaction

$$a\,A + b\,B \rightleftarrows c\,C + d\,D$$

the Nernst equation has the form

$$E_{cell} = E^0_{cell} - \frac{0.059}{n} \log \frac{[C]^c[D]^d}{[A]^a[B]^b}$$

where E^0_{cell} is the standard-state cell voltage, n is the number of electrons exchanged in the equation for the reaction, and 0.059 is a constant at 298 K. The concentrations are all in molarity. Concentrations of solids and liquid solvents are considered constant and are not included in the expression.

Notice from this mathematical expression that if the concentrations of the reactants increase or if the product is decreased, the voltage will increase ($E > E^0$). If the concentrations of the products are increased or the concentrations of reactants decreased, the voltage will decrease ($E < E^0$).

Problem   Calculate the cell voltage of

$$Zn(s) \mid Zn^{2+}\ (0.001\ M) \parallel Ag^+\ (0.1\ M) \mid Ag(s)$$

(Each side of the $\parallel$ represents the half-reaction characters, with the concentration when appropriate.)

The reactions would be

Cathode reduction reaction:	
$2Ag^+ + 2e^- \rightarrow 2Ag(s)$	$E^0 = +0.80$ V

Anode oxidation reaction:	
$Zn(s) \rightarrow Zn^{2+} + 2e^-$	$E^0 = +0.76$ V

Cell:	
$2Ag^+ + Zn(s) \rightleftarrows Zn^{2+} + 2Ag$	$E^0 = +1.56$ V

Substituting the known values in the Nernst equation, solve for the E_{cell}:

$$E_{cell} = E^0_{cell} - \frac{0.059}{n} \log \frac{\left[Zn^{2+}\right]}{\left[Ag^+\right]^2}$$

$$E_{cell} = 1.56 - \frac{0.059}{0.2} \log \frac{\left[10^{-3}\right]}{\left[10^{-1}\right]^2}$$

$$= 1.56 - 0.03 \log 10^{-1}$$

$$= 1.56 + 0.03$$

$$= 1.59 \text{ V}$$

Electrolytic Cells

Reactions that do not occur spontaneously can be forced to take place by supplying energy with an external current. These reactions are called electrolytic reactions. Some examples of this type of reaction are electroplating, electrolysis of salt solution, electrolysis of water, and electrolysis of molten salts. An example of this setup is shown in Fig. 23.

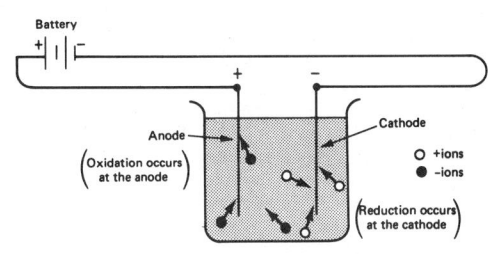

Fig. 23   Electrochemical Reactions

If this solution contained Cu^{2+} ions and Cl^- ions, the half-reactions would be

Anode half-reaction:		
Oxidation	$2Cl^- \rightarrow Cl_2\uparrow + 2e^-$	$E^0 = -1.36$ V
Cathode half reaction:		
Reduction	$Cu^{2+} + 2e^- \rightarrow Cu^0$	$E^0 = +0.34$ V
Net reaction:	$Cu^2 + 2Cl^- \rightarrow Cu^0 + Cl_2\uparrow$	$E^0 = -1.02$ V

(Notice that the E^0 for this reaction is negative so an outside source of energy must be used to make it occur).

Another electrolysis example is the electrolysis of a water solution of sodium chloride. This water solution contains chloride ions that are attracted to the anode and set free as chlorine molecules. The cathode reaction is somewhat more complicated. Although the sodium ions are attracted to the cathode, they are not set free as atoms. Remember, water can ionize to some extent and the electromotive series shows that the hydrogen ion is reduced more easily than the sodium ion. Therefore, hydrogen, not sodium, is set free at the cathode. The reaction can be summarized like this:

Cathode reaction:	$2H_2O + 2e^- \rightarrow H_2\uparrow + 2OH$
Anode reaction:	$2Cl^- \rightarrow 2e^- + Cl_2$
Net reaction:	$2H_2O + 2Cl^- \rightarrow H_2\uparrow + Cl_2\uparrow + 2OH^-$

Another example of electrolysis is the decomposition of water by using an apparatus like the one shown in Fig. 24. The solution in this apparatus contains distilled water and a small amount of H_2SO_4. The reasons for adding H_2SO_4 is to make the solution an electrolyte since distilled water alone does not conduct an electric current. The solution therefore contains ions of H^+, HSO_4^-, and SO_4^{2-}.

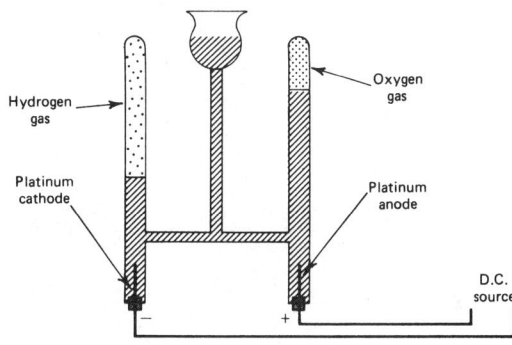

Fig. 24   Electrolysis of Water

The hydrogen ions (H^+) migrate to the cathode where they are reduced to hydrogen atoms and form hydrogen molecules (H_2) in the form of a gas. The SO_4^{2-} and HSO_4^- migrate to the anode but are not oxidized since the oxidation of water occurs more readily. These ions are then merely spectator ions. The oxidized water reacts as shown in the half-reaction below.

The half-reactions can be shown as follows:

Cathode reaction:		
Reduction	$4H^+ + 4e^-$	$\rightarrow 2H_2\uparrow$
Anode reaction:		
Oxidation	$2H_2O \rightarrow O_2\uparrow + 4H^+ + 4e^-$	
Net reaction:	$2HOH \rightarrow 2H_2\uparrow + O_2\uparrow$	

Notice that the equation shows 2 volumes of hydrogen gas are released but only 1 volume of oxygen gas is liberated.

Applications of Electrochemical Cells
One of the most common voltaic cells is the ordinary "dry cell" used in flashlights. Its makeup is shown in Fig. 25(a), along with the reactions. The automobile lead storage battery is also a voltaic cell. When it discharges, the reactions are as shown in Fig. 25(b).

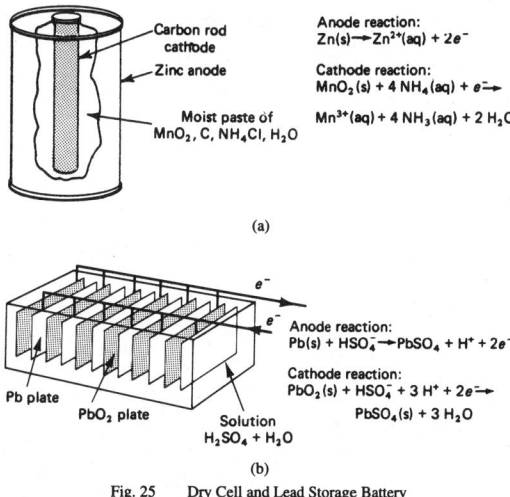

Fig. 25   Dry Cell and Lead Storage Battery

Quantitative Aspects of Electrolysis
The amounts of products liberated at the electrodes of an electrolytic cell are related to the quantity of electricity passed through the cell and to the electrode reactions.

In electrolysis, 1 mole of electrons is called a *faraday* of electric charge. In the reaction of electrolysis of molten NaCl, 1 faraday will liberate 1 mole of sodium atoms.

Cathode reactions: $Na^+ + e^- \rightarrow Na(s)$

At the same time, 1 mole of Cl^- ions at the anode will form 1 mole of chlorine atoms and thus $\frac{1}{2}$ mole of chlorine molecules.

If the metallic ion has been Ca^{2+}, 1 faraday would release only $\frac{1}{2}$ mole of calcium atoms since each calcium ion requires two electrons, as shown here:

$$Ca^{2+} + 2e^- \rightarrow Ca(s)$$

Problem

How many faradays are required to reduce 2.93 g of nickel ions from melted $NiCl_2$?

The reaction is

$$Ni^{2+} + 2e^- \rightarrow Ni(s)$$

The 2.93 g represents

$$2.93 \text{ g} \times 1 \text{ mole}/58.7 \text{ g} = 0.05 \text{ mole}$$

Since the equation shows that it takes two electrons to change each nickel ion into a nickel atom, then it will take 2 F (faradays) per mole. Then 0.05 mole × 2 F/mole = 0.1 F.

Electrolysis *See* **Electrochemical reactions**.

Electrolytic cells *See* **Electrochemical reactions**.

Electromotive series *See* **Electrochemical reactions**.

Electronegativity A number that measures the relative strength with which the atoms of an element attract valence electrons in a chemical bond. This electronegativity number is based on an arbitrary scale from 0 to 4. In general, a value less than 2 indicates a metal.

EXHIBIT 3.7
Electronegativities of the Elements

H						
2.1						
Li	Be	B	C	N	O	F
1.0	1.5	2.0	2.5	3.0	3.5	4.0
Na	Mg	Al	Si	P	S	Cl
0.9	1.2	1.5	1.8	2.1	2.5	3.0
K	Ca	Ga	Ge	As	Se	Br
0.8	1.0	1.7	1.8	2.0	2.4	2.8
Rb	Sr	In	Sn	Sb	Te	I
0.8	1.0	1.7	1.8	1.9	2.1	2.5
Cs	Ba	Tl	Pb	Bi	Po	At
0.7	0.9	1.8	1.8	1.9	2.0	2.2
Fr	Ra					
0.7	0.9					

Notice in Exhibit 3.7 that the electronegativity decreases down a group and increases across a period. The lower the electronegativity number, the more electropositive an element is said to be. The most electronegative element is in the upper right corner—F. The most electropositive is in the lower left corner of the chart—Fr.

Electrons *See* **Atomic structure**.

Electrovalence *See* **Electrochemistry**.

Element A substance that is made up of only one kind of atom. All atoms in an element have the same number of protons and electrons. Slightly more than 100 elements are known; singly or in combination, they constitute all matter. For a complete list of the elements, *see* **Exhibit 3.14**, page 3-68.

Empirical formula The simplest ratio formula that describes the basic mathematical relationship among the individual components. For example, the

empirical formula for acetylene is CH. However, its molecular formula, C_2H_2, represents the actual molecular mass of acetylene. Benzene, with a molecular formula of C_6H_6, has the same empirical formula (1:1 ratio) as acetylene.

Endothermic reaction versus exothermic reaction A reaction is *endothermic* if the heat content of the product(s) is higher than that of the reactants. If, on the other hand, the heat content of the product(s) is less than that of the reactants, the reaction is called *exothermic*. This change of heat content can be designated ΔH. The heat content H is sometimes referred to as the enthalpy. Every system has a certain amount of heat, which changes during the course of a physical or chemical change. The change in heat content ΔH is the difference between the heat content of the products and that of the reactants. The equation is

$$\Delta H = H_{products} - H_{reactants}$$

If the heat content of the products is greater than the heat content of the reactants, ΔH is a positive quantity ($\Delta H > 0$) and the reaction is endothermic. If, however, the heat content of the products is less than the heat content of the reactants ΔH is a negative quantity ($\Delta H < 0$) and the reaction is exothermic. For more information, *see* **Enthalpy**.

Energy levels *See* **Atomic structure**.

Enthalpy In general, all chemical reactions either liberate or absorb heat. The origin of chemical energy lies in the position and motion of atoms, molecules, and subatomic particles. The total energy possessed by a molecule is the sum of all the forms of potential and kinetic energy associated with it.

The energy changes in a reaction are due, to a large extent, to the changes in potential energy that accompany the breaking of chemical bonds in reactants to form new bonds in products.

The molecule may also have rotational, vibrational, and translational energy, along with some nuclear energy sources. All these make up the total energy of molecules. In beginning chemistry, the greatest concern in reactions is the electronic energy involved in the making and breaking of chemical bonds.

Since it is virtually impossible to measure the total energy of molecules, the energy change is usually in terms of the experimental data that we deal with in reactions. This change in quantity of energy is known as the change in enthalpy (heat content) of the chemical system and is symbolized by ΔH.

Changes in Enthalpy

Changes in enthalpy for exothermic and endothermic reactions can be shown graphically as in Figs. 26 and 27.

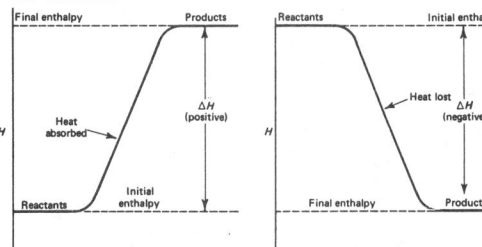

Fig. 26 Enthalpy Change: Exothermic Reaction

Fig. 27 Enthalpy Change: Endothermic Reaction

Notice that the ΔH for an endothermic reaction is positive, and that for an exothermic reaction is negative. It should also be noted that changes in enthalpy are always independent of the path taken to change a system from the initial state to the final state.

Since the quantity of heat absorbed or liberated during a reaction varies with the temperature, scientists have adopted 25°C and 1 atmosphere pressure as the standard-state condition for reporting heat data. In some college textbooks, $\Delta H°$ is given in kilojoules (kJ). Whether you use kcal or kJ, the method of solving enthalpy problems does not change. The conversion factor is 1 kcal = 4.18×10^3 kJ.

To calculate the enthalpy of a reaction, it is necessary to write an equation for the reaction. The standard enthalpy change, designated by $\Delta H°$, for a given reaction is usually expressed in kilocalories and depends on how the equation is written. For example, here is the equation for the reaction of hydrogen with oxygen expressed in two ways:

$$H_2(g) + \tfrac{1}{2}O_2(g) \rightarrow H_2O(g) \quad \Delta H^0 = -57.8\,\text{kcal}$$

$$2H_2(g) + O_2(g) \rightarrow 2H_2O(g) \quad \Delta H^0 = -115.6\,\text{kcal}$$

Experimentally, the ΔH^0 for the formation of 1 mole of $H_2O(g)$ is −57.8 kcal. Since the second equation represents the formation of 2 moles of $H_2O(g)$, the quantity is twice −57.8, or −115.6 kcal. It is assumed that the initial and final states are measured at 25°C and 1 atmosphere, although the reaction occurs at a higher temperature.

Problem

How much heat is liberated when 40.0 g of $H_2(g)$ reacts with excess oxygen (g)?
The reaction equation is

$$H_2(g) + \tfrac{1}{2}O_2(g) \rightarrow H_2O(g) \quad \Delta H^0 = -57.8\,\text{kcal}$$

This represents 1 mole of 2 g or H(g) forming 1 mole of $H_2O(g)$:

$$40\,\text{g} \times \frac{1\,\text{mole}}{2\,\text{g}} = 20 \text{ moles of hydrogen}$$

Since each mole gives off − 57.8 kcal, then

$$20 \text{ moles } \times \frac{-57.8\,\text{kcal}}{1\,\text{mole}} = -1156 \text{ kcal}$$

Notice that the physical state of each participant must be given since the phase changes involve energy changes.

Additivity of Reaction Heats
Chemical equations and ΔH^0 values may be manipulated algebraically. Finding the ΔH for the formation of vapor from liquid water shows how this can be done:

$$H_2(g) + \tfrac{1}{2}O_2(g) \rightarrow H_2O(g) \quad \Delta H^0 = -57.8 \text{ kcal}$$

$$H_2(g) + \tfrac{1}{2}O_2(g) \rightarrow H_2O(l) \quad \Delta H^0 = -68.3 \text{ kcal}$$

Since we want the equation for $H_2O(l) \rightarrow H_2O(g)$, we can reverse the second equation. This changes the sign of ΔH.

$$H_2O(l) \rightarrow H_2(g) + \tfrac{1}{2}O_2(g) \quad \Delta H^0 = -68.3 \text{ kcal}$$

Adding

$$H_2(g) + \tfrac{1}{2}O_2(g) \rightarrow H_2O(g) \quad \Delta H^0 = -57.8 \text{ kcal}$$

yeilds

$$H_2O(l) + H_2(g) + \tfrac{1}{2}O_2(g) \rightarrow$$

$$H_2(g) + \tfrac{1}{2}O_2(g) + H_2O(g) \quad \Delta H^0 = 10.5 \text{ kcal}$$

Simplification gives a net equation of

$$H_2O(l) \rightarrow H_2O(g) \quad\quad \Delta H^0 = 10.5 \text{ kcal}$$

The principle underlying the preceding calculations is known as *Hess's law*. This principle states that, when a reaction can be expressed as the algebraic sum of two or more other reactions, the heat of the reaction is the algebraic sum of the heats of these reactions. This is based upon the first law of thermodynamics, which, simply stated, says that the total energy of the universe is constant and cannot be created or destroyed.

This allows calculations of ΔH values that cannot be easily determined experimentally. An example is the determination of the ΔH of CO from the ΔH_r (the subscript *r* stands for "reaction") of CO_2.

$$C(s) + O_2(g) \quad \rightarrow CO_2(g) \quad \Delta H_r^0 = -94.0 \text{ kcal}$$

$$CO(s) + \tfrac{1}{2}O_2(g) \rightarrow CO_2(g) \quad \Delta H_r^0 = -67.6 \text{ kcal}$$

The equation wanted is

$$C(s) + \tfrac{1}{2}O_2(g) \quad \rightarrow CO(g)$$

To get this, we reverse the second equation and add it to the first:

$$C(s) + O_2(g) \rightarrow CO_2(g) \quad\quad \Delta H_r^0 = -94.0 \text{ kcal}$$

$$CO_2(g) \rightarrow \tfrac{1}{2}O_2(g) + CO(g) \quad \Delta H_r^0 = +67.6 \text{ kcal}$$

Addition yields

$$C(s) + \tfrac{1}{2}O_2(g) \rightarrow CO(g) \quad\quad \Delta H^0 = -26.4 \text{ kcal}$$

This relationship is shown schematically in Fig. 28.

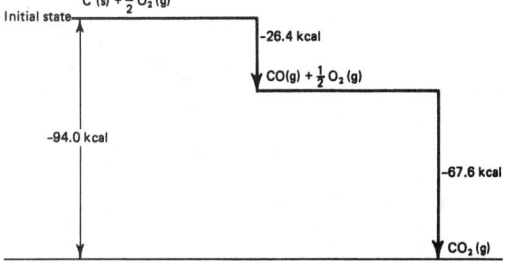

Fig. 28   Schematic Representation of Hess's Law

Standard heats of formation (enthalpy) are designated ΔH_r. Some commonly used standard heats of formation are listed in **Table E** in **Exhibit 3.13**, page 3-64.

An alternative (and easier) method of calculating enthalpies is based on the concept that ΔH is equal to the difference between the total enthalpies of the reactants and products. This can be expressed as

$\Delta H_r^0 = \Sigma$ (sum of) ΔH_f^0 (products) $- \Sigma$ (sum of) ΔH_f^0, (reactants)

Problem 1

Calculate ΔH_r^0 for the decomposition of sodium chlorate:

$$NaClO_3(s) \rightarrow NaCl(s) + \tfrac{3}{2}O_2(g).$$

Step 1. Obtain ΔH_f^0 for all substances.

$NaClO_3(s) = -85.7$ kcal/mole

$NaCl(s) \quad = -98.2$ kcal/mole

$O_2(g) \quad = 0$ kcal/mole (all elements = 0)

Step 2. Substitute these values in the equation.

$\Delta H_r^0 = \Sigma \Delta H_f^0$ (products) $- \Sigma \Delta H_f^0$ (reactants)

$\Delta H_r = -98.2 + 85.7$ kcal

$\Delta H_r = -12.5$ kcal

Problem 2

Calculate ΔH_r for this oxidation of ammonia:

$4NH_3(g) + 5O_2(g) \rightarrow 6H_2O(g) + 4NO(g).$

The individual ΔH_f^0 values are

4 mol $NH_3 \quad = 4 \text{ mol}\left(\dfrac{-11 \text{ kcal}}{\text{mol}}\right) = -44.0$ kcal

$5O_2(g) \quad = 0$

6 mol $H_2O(g) = 6 \text{ mol}\left(\dfrac{-57.8 \text{ kcal}}{\text{mol}}\right) = -346.8$ kcal

4 mol $NO(g) \quad = 4 \text{ mol}\left(\dfrac{21.6 \text{ kcal}}{\text{mol}}\right) = 86.4$ kcal

Substituting these in the ΔH_r equation gives

$\Delta H_r = [-346.8(6H_2O) + 86.4(4NO)]$

$\quad - [-44.0(4NH_3) + 0(5O_2)]$

$\quad = -216.4$ kcal

Bond Dissociation Energy

The same principle of additivity applies to bond energies. Experimentation has found average bond energies for particular bonds. Some of the more common are shown in the following table.

Bond Energies

Bond	Energy (kcal/mole)	Bond	*Energy (kcal/mole)
H—H	104	O=O	119
C—H	99	O—H	111
C—C	83	C—O	86
C=C	146	C=O	177
C≡C	200	H—F	135
O—O	35	H—Cl	103
N—N	39	H—Br	87
Cl—Cl	58	H—I	71

*To use kilojoules, multiply kcal/mole by 4.18×10^3 kJ/kcal.

Problem

Find the bond energy H_{be} for ethane.

$$Ethane = \quad H-\underset{\underset{H}{|}}{\overset{\overset{H}{|}}{C}}-\underset{\underset{H}{|}}{\overset{\overset{H}{|}}{C}}-H$$

and has six C—H bonds and one C—C bond.

$H_{be} = 6E_{C-H} + 1E_{C-C} = 6(99 \text{ kcal})$

$\quad + 1(83 \text{ kcal}) = 677$ kcal

Enthalpy from Bond Energies

A reaction's enthalpy can be approximated through the summation of bond energies; for example,

$H_2(g) + Cl_2(g) = 2HCl(g)$

Bonds Broken	Energy Absorbed (kcal)	Bonds Formed	Energy Evolved (kcal)
H—H	104.2		
Cl—Cl	57.8	2 H—Cl	206.0
Totals	162.0 kcal		206.0 kcal

The difference between heat evolved and heat absorbed is $206.0 - 162.0 = 44.0$ kcal. Since more heat is evolved than absorbed, it is represented as -44.0 kcal. This is for 2 moles of HCl, or -44 kcal divided by $2 = -22$ kcal mole. This answer is very close to the experimentally determined ΔH_f. See **Equilibrium, chemical** for further information.

Entropy An expression of the state of disorder of a system. One of the driving forces of reactions is the need for a greater degree of disorder, for example, the intermixing of gases in two connected flasks when a valve is opened to allow the two isolated gases to travel between the two flasks. Since temperature remains constant throughout the process, the total heat content cannot have changed to a lower energy level and yet the gases will become evenly distributed in the two flasks. The system has thus reached a higher degree of disorder or entropy. See **Equilibrium, chemical** for further information.

Equations, chemical A systematic way of expressing a chemical reaction in which the reactants appear to the left of an arrow and the products to the right:

Reactants $\rightarrow$ products

Chemical formulas are used for both sides, and then, by the use of coefficients, if needed, the number of atoms of each type is balanced (made equal) on both sides of the arrow; for example,

$HCl + NaOH \rightarrow NaCl + H_2O$ coefficients of 1 understood
$2Na + 2H_2O \rightarrow 2NaOH + H_2$ coefficients needed to balance

Redox Equations

In general, many chemical equations are so simple that the process of writing them (once the reactants and products are known) can be carried out by mere inspection. On the other hand, many redox (oxidation/reduction) reactions are of such complexity that the process of writing the equations by trial and error is time consuming. In these cases the operation can be done by limiting the change involved to the actual electron shift and balancing that—an operation that can usually be done without difficulty.

That part of the process being accomplished, the remainder of the equation can easily be adjusted to it. There are several methods by which this can be done, and a number of techniques for each method. We will show two methods: the electron shift method and the ion-electron method.

The electron shift method involves these steps:

1. The molecular formulas are written in a statement of the reaction, and the oxidation states are assigned to the elements.

$$\overset{+1\ -1}{HCl} + \overset{+4\ -2}{MnO_2} = \overset{+1\ -2}{H_2O} + \overset{+2\ -1}{MnCl_2} + \overset{0}{Cl_2}$$

2. Inspection shows that the oxidation state of the manganese atoms has changed from +4 to +2 and that the oxidation state of the chlorine atoms that emerge from the action as a free element has changed from −1 to 0:

$$1(Mn^{4+} + 2e^+ = Mn^{2+})$$
$$2(Cl^{1-} \qquad = Cl^0 + 1e^-)$$

3. The reason for multiplying the two half-reactions by 1 and 2 is to balance the electrons gained with the electrons lost.
4. It appears that $1Mn^{4+} + 2Cl^{1-} = 1Mn^{2+} + 2Cl^0$.
5. Placing these coefficients in the equation gives

$$2HCl + 1MnO_2 = ?*H_2O + 1MnCl_2 + Cl_2.$$

6. From the numbers thus established, the remaining coefficients can easily be deduced. Two *more* molecules of HCl are required to furnish the chlorine for $MnCl_2$, and the two atoms of oxygen in MnO_2 form $2H_2O$.
7. The final equation is: $4HCl + MnO_2 = 2H_2O + MnCl_2 + Cl_2$.

Now consider a more complicated reaction. Only the elements that show a change in oxidation state are indicated.

$$\overset{-1}{HCl} + \overset{+7}{KMnO_4} = H_2O + KCl + \overset{+2}{MnCl_2} + \overset{0}{Cl_2}$$

The electron change is:

$$5\left(Cl^{-1} \qquad = Cl^0 + 1e^-\right)$$
$$1\left(Mn^7 + 5e^- \qquad = Mn^{2+}\right)$$

Therefore, $5HCl + 1KMnO_4 = \tfrac{5}{2}Cl_2 + 1MnCl_2$

5 atoms of chlorine equal $\tfrac{5}{2}Cl_2$ molecules

Multiplying by 2 to avoid fractions gives

$$10HCl + 2KMnO_4 = 5Cl_2 + 2MnCl_2$$

Substituting in the original equation,

$$10HCl + 2KMnO_4 = ?*H_2O + ?*KCl + 2MnCl_2 + 5Cl_2$$

*It is not known as yet what this coefficient will be.

For the remainder of the coefficients, $2KMnO_4$ produces $2KCl$ and $8H_2O$; $2KCl + 2MnCl_2$ calls for six additional molecules of HCl. So finally the expression becomes

$$16HCl + 2KMnO_4 = 8H_2O + 2KCl + 2MnCl_2 + 5Cl_2$$

The second method, the ion-electron method, is more complex but seems to represent the true mechanisms of such reactions more closely. In this method, only units that actually have individual existence (atoms, molecules, or ions) in the particular reaction being studied are taken into consideration. The principal oxidizing agent and the principal reducing agent are chosen from these (by a method to be indicated later), and the electron loss or gain of these two principal actors is then determined by taking into consideration that since electrons can neither be created nor destroyed, electrons lost by one of these actors must be gained by the other. This is accomplished by using two separate partial equations representing the changes undergone by each of the two principal actors.

Probably the best way to show how the method operates will be to follow in detail the steps taken in balancing an actual oxidation-reduction reaction.

Example

Assume that the equation

$$K_2CrO_4 + HCl \rightarrow KCl + CrCl_3 + H_2O + Cl_2$$

is to be balanced.

1. Determine which of the substances present are involved in the oxidation-reduction. This is done by listing all substances present on each side of the arrow and then crossing out those that appear on both sides of the arrow without any portion being changed in any way.

$$\cancel{K^+}, CrO_4^{2-}, H^+, Cl^-, \rightarrow \cancel{K^+}, Cl^-, Cr^{3+}, H_2O, Cl_2$$

Note that Cl^- is not crossed out, although it appears on both sides because some of the Cl^- from the left side appears in a changed form, namely, Cl_2, on the right. The two substances on the left side that are *not* crossed out are those involved in the oxidation-reduction. If, as in this case there are more than two, disregard H^+, OH^-, or H_2O; this will leave the two principal actors.

2. Indicate in two as yet unbalanced partial equations the fate of each of the two active agents; thus,

$$CrO_4^{2-} \rightarrow Cr^{3+}$$
$$Cl^- \rightarrow Cl_2$$

3. Balance these equations chemically, inserting any substance necessary.

$$CrO_4^{2-} + 8H^+ \rightarrow Cr^{3+} + 4H_2O$$
$$2Cl^- \rightarrow Cl_2$$

In the upper partial equation, H^+ had to be added in order to remove the oxygen from the CrO_4^{2-} ion.

H⁺ is always used for this purpose in acid solutions. If the solution is basic, H_2O must be used for the purpose; thus,

$$CrO_4^{2+} + 4H_2O \rightarrow Cr^{3+} + 8OH^-$$

4. Balance these equations electrically by adding electrons *on either side* so that the total electrical charge is the same on the left and right sides; thus,

$$CrO_4^{2+} + 8H^+ + 3e^- \rightarrow Cr^{3+} + 4H_2O$$
$$2Cl^- \qquad\qquad \rightarrow Cl_2 + 2e^-$$

5. Add these partial equations. But before we add we must realize that electrons can neither be created nor destroyed. Electrons are gained in one of these equations and lost in the other. *Those gained in the one must come from the other.* Therefore we must multiply both of these equations through by numbers so chosen that the number of electrons gained in the one will be the same as the number lost in the other; thus,

$$2[CrO_4^{2+} + 8H^+ + 3e^- \rightarrow Cr^{3+} + 4H_2O]$$
$$3[2Cl^- \qquad\qquad \rightarrow Cl_2 + 2e^-]$$

Adding the multiplied equations, we get

$$2CrO_4^{2-} + 16H^+ + 6Cl^- \rightarrow 2Cr^{3+} + 8H_2O + 3Cl_2$$

This sum tells us all that really happens in the oxidation-reduction, but if a conventionally balanced equation is desired (for problem purposes, for example), it can be obtained by carrying the coefficient into the original skeleton equation; thus,

$$2K_2CrO_4 + 16HCl \rightarrow 4KCl + 2CrCl_3 + 8H_2O + 3Cl_2$$
$$\uparrow$$
(4 inserted by inspection)

Example

Note that, since this takes place in the basic solution, H_2O was used to remove oxygen in the upper partial.

Note also that in the second partial it was necessary to *add* oxygen and that this was done by means of OH⁻ ion.

If the solution had been *acid*, then H_2O would have been used for this purpose; thus,

$$I^- + 3H_2O \rightarrow IO_3^- + 6H^+ + 6e^-$$

In general, you will meet three types of partial equations:

1. Where electrons only are needed to balance, as in the second partial of the first example above.
2. Where oxygen must be removed from an ion. In acid solution, H⁺ is used for this purpose as in the first partial of the first example above. In basic solution, H_2O is used for this as in the first partial of the second example above.
3. Where oxygen must be added to an ion. In basic solution, OH⁻ is used for this as in the second partial of the second example above. In acid solution, H_2O is used for this, as in

$$SO_3^{2-} + H_2O \rightarrow SO_4^{2-} + 2H^+ + 2e^-$$

Equilibrium, chemical In some reactions no product is formed to allow the reaction to go to completion, that is, the reactants and products can still interact in both directions. This can be shown as

$$A + B \rightleftarrows C + D$$

The double arrow indicates that C and D can react to form A and B, while A and B react to form C and D.

The reaction is said to have reached *equilibrium* when the forward reaction rate is equal to the reverse reaction rate. Notice this is *not* a static condition but a dynamic one. This must be pointed out because in appearance the reaction seems to have stopped. An example of an equilibrium is a crystal of copper sulfate in a saturated solution of copper sulfate. Although the crystal seems to remain unchanged to the observer, there is actually an equal exchange of crystal material with the copper sulfate in solution. As some solute comes out of solution, an equal amount is going into solution.

To express the rate of reaction in numerical terms, we can use the *law of mass action*, which states that the rate of a chemical reaction is proportional to the product of the concentrations of the reacting substances. The concentration is expressed in moles of a gas per liter of volume or moles of solute per liter of solution. Suppose, for example, that 1 mole/liter of gas A_2 (diatomic molecule) is allowed to react with 1 mole/liter of another diatomic gas B_2, and they form a gas AB; let R be the rate for the forward reaction forming AB. The bracketed symbols $[A_2]$ and $[B_2]$ represent the concentrations in moles per liter for these diatomic molecules. Then $A_2 + B_2 \rightarrow 2AB$ has the rate expression

$$R \propto [A_2] \times [B_2]$$

where $\propto$ is the symbol for "is proportional to." When $[A_2]$ and $[B_2]$ are both 1 mole/liter, the reaction rate is a certain constant value k_1 at a fixed temperature.

$$R = k_1 \qquad k_1 \text{ is called the rate constant}$$

For any concentration of A and B, the reaction rate is

$$R = k_1 \times [A_2] \times [B_2]$$

If $[A_2]$ is 3 moles/liter and $[B_2]$ is 2 moles/liter, the equation becomes

$$R = k_1 \times 3 \times 2 = 6k_1$$

The reaction rate is six times the value for 1 mole/liter concentration of both reactants.

At the fixed temperature of the forward reaction, AB molecules are also decomposing. If we designate this reverse reaction as R', then, since

$$2AB \text{ (or } AB + AB) \rightarrow A_2 + B_2$$

two molecules of AB must decompose to form a molecule of A_2 and one of B_2. Thus the reverse reaction in this equation is proportional to the square of the molecular concentration of AB.

$$R' \propto [AB] \times [AB]$$

or

$$R' \propto [AB]^2$$

and

$$R' \propto k_2 \times [AB]^2$$

where k_2 represents the rate of decomposition of AB at the fixed temperature. Both reactions can be shown in this manner:

$A_2 + B_2 \rightleftarrows 2AB$ (note double arrows)

When the first reaction begins to produce AB, some AB is available for the reverse reaction. If the initial condition is only the presence of A_2 and B_2 gases, then the forward reaction will occur rapidly to produce AB. As the concentration of AB increases, the reverse reaction will increase. At the same time, the concentrations of A_2 and B_2 will be decreasing and consequently the forward reaction rate will decrease. Eventually the two rates will be equal, that is, $R = R'$. At this point, equilibrium has been established, and

$$k_1[A_2] \times [B_2] = k_2[AB]^2$$

or

$$\frac{k_1}{k_2} = \frac{[AB]^2}{[A_2] \times [B_2]} = K_c$$

The convention is that k_1 (forward reaction) is placed over k_2 (reverse reaction) to get this expression. Then k_1/k_2 can be replaced by K_c which is called the equilibrium constant for this reaction under the particular conditions and expressions of molar concentrations. Table K in Exhibit 3.13 shows various equilibria constants at specific conditions. (To distinguish between equlibria expressed in molar concentration from those using partial pressures of gases, K_c and K_p are used respectively.)

In another general example,

$$a\,A + b\,B \rightleftarrows c\,C + d\,D$$

the reaction rates can be expressed as

$$R \propto k_1[A]^a \times [B]^b$$

$$R' \propto k_2[C]^c \times [D]^d$$

Note that the values of k_1 and k_2 are different, but that each is a constant for the conditions of the reaction. At the start of the reaction, [A] and [B] will be at their greatest values, and R will be large; [C], [D], and R' will be zero. Gradually R will decrease and R' will become equal to R. At this point the reverse reaction is forming the original reactants just as rapidly as they are being used by the forward reaction. Therefore no further change in R, R', or any of the concentrations will occur.

If we set R' equal to R, we have

$$k_2 \times [C]^c \times [D]^d = k_1 \times [A]^a \times [B]^b$$

or

$$\frac{[C]^c \times [D]^d}{[A]^a \times [B]^b} = \frac{k_1}{k_2} = K_c$$

We see that, for the given reaction and the given conditions, K_c is the equilibrium constant. If K_c is large, it means that equilibrium does not occur until the concentrations of the original reactants are small and those of the products large. If K_c is small, it

means that equilibrium occurs almost at once and relatively little product is produced.

The equilibrium constant K_c has been determined experimentally for many reactions and is printed in chemical handbooks. (*See* **Tables J** and **K** in **Exhibit 3.13**, page 3-66.)

Suppose we find the K_c for reacting H_2 and I_2 at 490°C to be equal to 45.9. Then the equilibrium constant for the reaction

$H_2 + I_2 \rightleftarrows 2HI$ at 490°C is

$$K_c = \frac{[HI]^2}{[H_2][I_2]} = 45.9$$

Problem 1

At a temperature of 490°C, 3 moles of H_2 and 3 moles of I_2 are introduced into a 1 liter box. Find the concentration of each substance in the box when equilibrium is established.

Initial conditions:

$[H_2] = 3$ moles/liter
$[I_2]\ = 3$ moles/liter
$[HI] = 0$ mole/liter

The reaction proceeds to equilibrium, and

$$K_c = \frac{[HI]^2}{[H_2][I_2]} = 45.9$$

At equilibrium, then,

$[H_2] = (3 - x)$ moles/liter

where x is the number of moles of H_2 that are in the form of HI at equilibrium,

$[I_2] = (3 - x)$ moles/liter

(the same x is used since 1 mole of H_2 requires 1 mole of I_2 to react to form 2 moles of HI, and [HI] $= 2x$ moles/liter

so

$$K_c = \frac{(2x)^2}{(3-x)(3-x)} = 45.9$$

If

$$\frac{(2x)^2}{(3-x)^2} = 45.9$$

then taking the square root of each side gives

$$\frac{2x}{3-x} = 6.77$$

Solving for x:

$$x = 2.32$$

Substituting this x value into the concentration expressions at equilibrium we have

$[H_2] = (3 - x) = 0.68$ mole/liter
$[I_2]\ = (3 - x) = 0.68$ mole/liter
$[HI] = 2x = 4.64$ moles/liter

The crucial step in this type of problem is setting up your concentration expressions from your knowledge of the equation. Suppose that this problem had been as follows.

Problem 2

Find the concentrations at equilibrium for the same conditions as in Problem 1 except that only 2 moles of HI are injected into the box.

$[H_2]$ = 0 mole/liter
$[I_2]$ = 0 mole/liter
$[HI]$ = 2 moles/liter

At equilibrium,

$[HI]$ = $(2 - x)$ moles/liter

(For every mole of HI that decomposes, only $\frac{1}{2}$ mole of H_2 and $\frac{1}{2}$ mole of I_2 are formed.)

$$[H_2] = \tfrac{1}{2}x$$

$$[I_2] = \tfrac{1}{2}x$$

$$K_c = \frac{(2-x)^2}{(x/2)^2} = 45.9$$

Solving for x gives

$x = 0.456$

Then, substituting into the equilibrium conditions.

$$[HI] = 2 - x = 1.54 \text{ moles/liter}$$

$$[I_2] = \tfrac{1}{2}x = 0.228 \text{ mole/liter}$$

$$[H_2] = \tfrac{1}{2}x = 0.228 \text{ mole/liter}$$

Le Châtelier's Principle
A general law, Le Châtelier's principle, can be used to explain the results of applying any change of condition (stress) on a system in equilibrium. It states that if a stress is placed upon a system in equilibrium, the equilibrium is displaced in the direction that counteracts the effect of the stress. An increase in concentration of a substance favors the reaction that uses up that substance and lowers its concentration. A rise in temperature favors the reaction that absorbs heat and so tends to lower the temperature. These ideas are further developed below.

Effects of Changing Conditions
The effect of changing the concentrations: When a system at equilibrium is disturbed by adding or removing one of the substances (thus changing its concentration), all the concentrations will change until a new equilibrium point is reached with the same value of K_c.

If the concentration of a reactant in the forward action is increased, the equilibrium is displaced to the right, favoring the forward reaction. If the concentration of a reactant in the reverse reaction is increased, the equilibrium is displaced to the left. Decreases in concentration will produce effects opposite to those produced by increases.

The effect of temperature on equilibrium: If the temperature of a given equilibrium reaction is changed, the reaction will shift to a new equilibrium point. If the temperature of a system in equilibrium is raised, the equilibrium is shifted in the direction that absorbs heat. Note that the shift in equilibrium as a result of temperature change is actually a change in the value of the equilibrium constant. This is different from the effect of changing the concentration of a reactant; when concentrations are changed, the equilibrium shifts to a condition that maintains the same equilibrium constant.

The effect of pressure on equilibrium: A change in pressure affects only equilibria in which a gas or gases are reactants or products. Le Châtelier's law can be used to predict the direction of displacement. If it is assumed that the total space in which the reaction occurs is constant, the pressure will depend on the total number of molecules in that space. An increase in the number of molecules will increase pressure; a decrease in the number of molecules will decrease pressure. If the pressure is increased, that reaction will be favored that lowers the pressure, that is, that decreases the number of molecules.

An example of using these principles is the Haber process of making ammonia. The reaction

$$N_2 + 3H_2 \rightleftharpoons 2NH_3 + \text{heat} \qquad \text{(at equilibrium)}$$

If the concentrations of the nitrogen and hydrogen are increased, the forward reaction is increased. At the same time, if the ammonia produced is removed by dissolving it into water, the forward reaction is again favored.

Since the reaction is exothermic, the addition of heat must be considered with care. Increasing the temperature causes an increase in molecular motion and collisions, thus allowing the product to form more readily. At the same time, the equilibrium equation shows that the reverse reaction is favored by this increased temperature so a compromise temperature of about 500°C is used to get the best yield.

An increase in pressure will cause the forward reaction to be favored since the equation shows that four molecules of reactants are forming two molecules of products. This tends to reduce the increase in pressure by forming more ammonia.

Equilibria in Heterogeneous Systems
The examples so far have been of systems made up of only gaseous substances. The expression of the K_c of systems is changed with the presence of other phases.

Equilibrium constant for systems involving solids: If the experimental data for the reaction

$$CaCo_3(s) \rightleftharpoons CaO(s) + CO_2(g)$$

are studied, it is found that at a given temperature an equilibrium is established in which the concentration of CO_2 is constant. It is also true that the concentrations of the solids have no effect on the CO_2 concentration as long as both solids are present. Therefore the K_c, which would conventionally be written as

$$K_c = \frac{[CaO][CO_2]}{[CaCO_3]}$$

can be modified by incorporating the concentrations of the two solids. This can be done since the concentration of solids is fixed by the density. The K_c becomes a new constant K:

$K = [CO_2]$

Any heterogeneous reaction involving gases does not include the concentrations of pure solids. As another example, K for the reaction

$NH_4Cl(s) \rightleftarrows NH_3(g) + HCl(g)$

is

$K = [NH_3][HCl]$

Ionization constants: When substances that do not ionize completely are placed in solution, an equilibrium is reached between the substance and its ions. The mass action expression can be used to derive an equilibrium constant for this condition. It is called the ionization constant. For example, an acetic acid solution ionizing is shown as

$HC_2H_3O_2 + H_2O \rightleftarrows H_3O^+ + C_2H_3O_2^-$

$$K = \frac{\left[H_3O^+\right]\left[C_2H_3O_2^-\right]}{\left[HC_2H_3O_2\right]\left[H_2O\right]}$$

The concentration of water in moles/liter is found by dividing the weight of 1 liter of water (which is 1000 grams at 4°C) by its gram-molecular weight, 18g, giving H_2O a value of 55.6 moles/liter. Since this number is so large compared with the other numbers involved in the equilibrium constant, it is practically constant and is incorporated into a new equilibrium constant, designated K_i. Then the new expression is

$$K_i = \frac{\left[H_3O^+\right]\left[C_2H_3O_2^-\right]}{\left[HC_2H_3O_2\right]}$$

Ionization constants have been found experimentally for many substances and are listed in chemical tables. The ionization constants of ammonia and acetic acid are about 1.8×10^{-5}. For boric acid $K_i = 5.8 \times 10^{10}$, and for carbonic acid $K_i = 4.3 \times 10^{-7}$.

If the concentrations of the ions present in the solution of a weak electrolyte are known, the value of the ionization constant can be calculated. Also, if the value of K_i is known, the concentrations of the ions can be calculated.

A small value for K_i means that the concentration of the un-ionized molecule must be relatively large compared with the ion concentrations. A large value for K_i means that the concentration of ions is relatively high. Therefore the smaller the ionization constant of an acid the weaker is the acid. Thus, for the three acids referred to above, the ionization constants show that the weakest of these is the boric acid and the strongest, the acetic acid. It must be remembered that in all cases in which ionization constants are used, the electrolytes must be weak in order to be involved in ionic equilibria.

Ionization constant of water: Since water is a very weak electrolyte, its ionization constant can be expressed as

$2H_2O \rightleftarrows H_3O^+ + OH^-$

(Equilibrium constant) $K = \dfrac{\left[H_3O^+\right]\left[OH^-\right]}{\left[H_2O\right]^2}$

(since $[H_2O]^2$ remains relatively constant, it is incorporated into K_w);

(Ionization constant) $K_w = [H_3O^+][OH^-]$
$$= 1 \times 10^{-14} \text{ at } 25°C$$

From this expression, we see that for distilled water $[H_3O^+] = [OH^-] = 1 \times 10^{-7}$. Therefore the pH, which is $-\log [H_3O^+]$, is

$pH = -\log[1 \times 10^{-7}]$

$pH = -[-7] = 7$ for a neutral solution

The pH range of 1–6 is acid, and the pH range of 8–14 is basic.

Problem 1

This problem incorporates the entire discussion of ionization constants, including finding the pH.

Calculate (a) the $[H_3O^+]$ (b) the pH, and (c) the percentage dissociation for $0.100M$ acetic acid at 25°C. The symbol K_a is used for the ionization of acids. K_a for $HC_2H_3O_2$ is 1.8×10^{-5}.

(a) For the reaction

$H_2O(l) + HC_2H_3O_2 (l) \rightleftarrows H_3O^+ (aq)$
$$+ C_2H_3O_2^- (aq)$$

and

$$K_a = \frac{\left[H_3O^+\right]\left[C_2H_3O_2^-\right]}{\left[HC_2H_3O_2\right]} = 1.8 \times 10^{-5}$$

Let x = number of moles/liter of $HC_2H_3O_2$ that dissociate and reach equilibrium. Then,

$[H_3O^+] = x$, $[C_2H_3O_2^-] = x$,
$$[HC_2H_3O_2] = 0.1 - x$$

Substituting in the expression for K_a gives

$$K_a = 1.8 \times 10^{-5} = \frac{(x)(x)}{0.10 - x}$$

Since weak acids, like acetic, at concentrations of $0.01M$ or greater dissociate very little, the equilibrium concentration of the acid is very nearly equal to the original concentration, that is,

$0.10 - x \cong 0.10$

Because of this, the expression can be changed to

$$1.8 \times 10^{-5} = \frac{(x)(x)}{0.10}$$

$$x^2 = 1.8 \times 10^{-6}$$

$$x = 1.3 \times 10^{-3} = \left[H_3O^+\right]$$

(b) Substituting this in the pH expression gives

$pH = -\log [H_3O^+] = -\log [1.3 \times 10^{-3}]$

$pH = 3 - \log 1.3$

$pH = 2.9$

(c) The percentage of dissociation of the original acid may be expressed as

$$\% \text{ dissociation} = \frac{\text{moles/liter that dissociate}}{\text{original concentration}} \times 100$$

$$\% \text{ dissociation} \times \frac{1.3 \times 10^{-3}}{1.0 \times 10^{-1}} \times 100 = 1.3\%$$

Solubility products: A saturated solution of a substance has been defined as an equilibrium condition between the solute and its ions. For example,

$$AgCl \rightleftarrows Ag^+ + Cl^-$$

The equilibrium constant would be

$$K = \frac{[Ag^+][Cl^-]}{[AgCl]}$$

Since the concentration of the solute remains constant for the temperature, the [AgCl] is incorporated into the K to give the K_{sp}, called the *solubility product* constant:

$$K_{sp} = [Ag^+][Cl^-] = 1.2 \times 10^{-10} \qquad \text{at } 25°C$$

This setup can be used to solve problems in which the ionic concentrations are given and the K_{sp} is to be found or the K_{sp} is given and the ionic concentrations are to be determined.

Problem 2

By experimentation it is found that a saturated solution of $BaSO_4$ at 25°C contains 3.9×10^{-5} mole/liter of Ba^{2+} ions. Find the K_{sp} of this salt.

Since $BaSO_4$ ionizes into equal numbers of Ba^{2+} and SO_4^{2-}, the barium ion concentration will equal the sulfate ion concentration. So the solution is

$$BaSO_4 \rightleftarrows Ba^{2+} + SO_4^{2-}$$
$$K_{sp} = [Ba^{2+}][SO_4^{2-}]$$

Therefore,

$$K_{sp} = (3.9 \times 10^{-5})(3.9 \times 10^{-5}) = 1.5 \times 10^{-9}$$

Problem 3

If the K_{sp} of radium sulfate, $RaSO_4$, is 4×10^{-11}, calculate its solubility in pure water.

Let x = moles of $RaSO_4$ that dissolve per liter of water. Then, in the saturated solution,

$[Ra^{2+}] = x$ moles/liter

$[SO_4^{2-}] = x$ moles/liter

$$RaSO_4(s) \rightleftarrows Ra^{2+} + SO_4^{2-}$$

$[Ra^{2+}][SO_4^{2-}] = K_{sp} = 4 \times 10^{-11}$

Let $x = [Ra^{2+}]$ and $[SO_4^{2-}]$. Then,

$(x)(x) = 4 \times 10^{-11}$

$x = 6 \times 10^{-6}$ mole/liter

Thus the solubility of $RaSO_4$ is 6×10^{-6} mole per liter of water, giving a solution of $6 \times 10^{-6}M$ in Ra^{2+} and $6 \times 10^{-6}M$ in SO_4^{2-}.

Common Ion Effect

When a reaction has reached equilibrium and an outside source adds more of one of the ions that is already in solution, the result is to cause the reverse reaction to occur at a faster rate and reestablish the equilibrium. This is called the common ion effect. For example, in the equilibrium reaction

$$NaCl(s) \rightleftarrows Na^+ + Cl^-$$

the addition of concentrated HCl (12M) adds H^+ and Cl^- both at a concentration of 12M. This increases the concentration of the Cl^- and disturbs the equilibrium. The reaction will shift to the left and cause some solid NaCl to come out of solution.

The "common" ion is the one already present in an equilibrium before a substance is added that increases the concentration of the ion present. This consequently reverses the solution reaction and decreases the solubility of the original substance, as shown in the above example.

Factors Related to the Magnitude of K_c

Relation of minimum energy (enthalpy) to maximum disorder (entropy): Some reactions are said to go to completion because the equilibrium condition is achieved when practically all the reactants have been converted to products. At the other extreme, some reactions reach equilibrium immediately with very little product being formed. These two examples are representative of very large K_c values and very small K_c values, respectively. Essentially two driving forces control the extent of a reaction and determine when equilibrium will be established. These are the drive to the lowest heat content, or enthalpy, and the drive to the greatest randomness or disorder, which is called entropy. Reactions with negative ΔH values (enthalpy or heat content) are exothermic, and reactions with positive ΔS values (entropy or randomness) are proceeding to greater randomness.

The second law of thermodynamics states that the entropy of the universe increases for any spontaneous process. This means that the entropy of a system may increase or decrease but that, if it decreases, then the entropy of the surroundings must increase to a greater extent so that the overall change in the universe is positive. In other words,

$$\Delta S_{universe} = \Delta S_{system} + \Delta S_{surroundings}$$

The following is a list of conditions in which ΔS is positive for the system:
1. When a gas is formed from a solid, for example,
   $$CaCO_3(s) \rightarrow CaO(s) + CO_2(g)$$
2. When a gas is evolved from a solution, for example,
   $$Zn(s) + 2H^+(aq) \rightarrow H_2(g) + Zn^{2+}(aq)$$
3. When the number of moles of gaseous product exceeds the moles of gaseous reactant, for example,
   $$2C_2H_6(g) + 7O_2(g) \rightarrow 4CO_2(g) + 6H_2O(g)$$
4. When crystals dissolve in water, for example,
   $$NaCl(s) \rightarrow Na^+(aq) + Cl^-(aq)$$

Looking at specific examples, we find that in some cases endothermic reactions occur when the products provide greater randomness or positive entropy. For example,

$$CaCO_3(s) \rightleftarrows CaO(s) + CO_2(g)$$

The production of the gas and thus greater entropy might be expected to take this reaction almost to completion. However, this does not occur because another force is hampering this reaction. It is the absorption of energy, and thus the increase in enthalpy, as the $CaCO_3$ is heated.

The equilibrium condition, then, at a particular temperature, is a compromise between the increase in entropy and the increase in enthalpy of the system.

The Haber process of making ammonia is another example of this compromise of driving forces that affect the establishment of an equilibrium. In the reaction

$$N_2(g) + 3H_2(g) \rightleftarrows 2NH_3(g) + heat$$

the forward reaction to reach the lowest heat content and thus release energy cannot go to completion because the force to maximum randomness is driving the reverse reaction.

These factors can be combined in an equation that summarizes the change of free energy in a system. This is designated ΔG. The relationship is

$$\Delta G = \Delta H - T \Delta S \qquad (T \text{ is in kelvins, K})$$

The sign of ΔG can be used to predict the spontaneity of a reaction at constant temperature and pressure. If ΔG is negative, the reaction is (probably) spontaneous; if ΔG is positive, the reaction is improbable; and if ΔG is 0, the system is at equilibrium and there is no net reaction.

The ways in which the factors in the equation affect ΔG are shown in this table:

ΔH	ΔS	Will it Happen?	Comment
Exothermic (−)	+	Yes	No exceptions
Exothermic (−)	−	Probably	At low temperature
Endothermic (+)	+	Probably	At high temperature
Endothermic (+)	−	No	No exceptions

This drive to achieve a minimum of free energy may be interpreted as the driving force of a chemical reaction.

Esters A class of organic compounds made by reacting an appropriate organic acid and alcohol. For this reason esters are often compared to inorganic salts because their preparations are similar. The functional group is RCOO—R. To make a salt, you react the appropriate acid and base. To make an ester, you react the appropriate organic acid and alcohol. For example,

ethanoic acid / ethanol / ethyl ethanoate (ethyl acetate)

The name is made up of the alkyl radical of the alcohol and the acid name in which -ic is replaced with -ate.

The general equation is

$$\overset{*}{R}O-H + R^1CO-OH \rightarrow R^1COO\overset{*}{}R + HOH$$
Alcohol / acid / ester

Esters usually have a sweet smell and are used in perfumes and flavor extracts. Some common esters are listed in the following table.

Common Esters

Name	Formula	Characteristic Odor
Ethyl butyrate	$C_3H_7COOC_2H_5$	Pineapple
Amyl acetate	$CH_3COOC_5H_{11}$	Banana, pear
Methyl salicylate	$C_6H_4(OH)COOCH_3$	Wintergreen
Amyl valerate	$C_4H_9COOC_5H_{11}$	Apple
Octyl acetate	$CH_3COOC_8H_{17}$	Orange
Methyl anthranilate	$C_3H_4(NH_2)COOCH_3$	Grape

Some esters found in the seeds of plants and the bodies of animals are fats. Stearin is such an ester.

stearic acid / glycerol / glycerol stearate (stearin)

Some other examples of esters are

Olein or glyceryl oleate = $(C_{17}H_{35}COO)_3C_3H_5$

Butyrin or glyceryl butyrate = $(C_3H_7COO)_3C_3H_5$

Soap can be made using a fat (like stearin) and lye (sodium hydroxide). This saponification reaction is

$$(C_{17}H_{35}COO)_3C_3H_5 + 3\ NaOH$$
stearin / lye

$$\rightarrow 3\ C_{17}H_{35}COONa + C_3H_5(OH)_3$$
soap / glycerine
(sodium stearate)

Ethers When a primary alcohol, such as ethanol, is dehydrated with sulfuric acid, an ether forms. The functional group is R—O—R^1. R^1 may be the same hydrocarbon group, as shown below:

ethanol + ethanol → ethoxyethane (ethyl ether) or (diethyl ether)

or a different hydrocarbon group:

ethoxypropane (ethyl propyl ether)

The ether name is made up of the first radical's stem, then -oxy, and then the alkane name for the second radical.

Exothermic reaction A reaction in which the energy content of the products formed is less than that of the reactants, and therefore energy usually in the form of heat and light, is released from the reaction. For more information see **Endothermic reaction versus exothermic reaction; Enthalpy.**

Exponential notation (scientific) When students must do mathematical operations with numerical figures, the scientific notation system is very useful. Basically this system uses the exponential means of

CHEMISTRY

expressing figures. With large numbers, such as 3,630,000, move the decimal point to the left until only one digit remains to the left (3.630000) and then indicate the number of moves of the decimal point as the exponent of 10 (3.63×10^6). With very small numbers like 0.000000123, move the decimal point to the right until only one digit is to the left (0000001.23) and then express the number of moves as the negative exponent of 10 (1.23×10^{-7}).

With numbers expressed in this exponential form, you can now use your knowledge of exponents in mathematical operations. Remember: in multiplications you add exponents and in division you subtract the exponents of 10.

Examples

Multiplications: $(2.3 + 10^5)(5.0 \times 10^{-12})$. Multiplying the first number in each, you get 11.5 and the addition of the exponents gives 10^{-7}. Now changing to a number with only one digit to the left of the decimal point gives you 1.15×10^{-6} for the answer.

Try these:

$(5.1 \times 10^{-6})(2 \times 10^{-3}) = 10.2 \times 10^{-9}$
$= 1.02 \times 10^{-8}$
$(3 \times 10^5)(6 \times 10^3) = 18 \times 10^8 = 1.8 \times 10^9$

Divisions:

$(1.5 \times 10^3) \div (5.0 \times 10^{-2}) = 0.3 \times 10^5 = 3 \times 10^4$
$(2.1 \times 10^{-2}) \div (7.0 \times 10^{-3}) = 0.3 \times 10^1 = 3$

(Notice that in division the exponents of 10 are subtracted.)

F

Fahrenheit scale *See* **Temperature scales**.
Faraday *See* **Electrochemical reactions**.
Fission *See* **Nucleonics**.
Formulas, writing and calculations of From knowledge of oxidation numbers and valence and understanding atomic structure, it is possible to write chemical formulas. Exhibit 3.8 is a list of oxidation numbers often encountered in a first-year chemistry course.

General Observations
- The symbols of the metals have + signs; those of the nonmetals and the radicals *except* the ammonium radical have – signs.
- When an element exhibits two possible oxidation states, the lower state can be indicated with the suffix *-ous* and the higher one with *-ic* . However, the preferred method of indicating this difference is to use the Roman numeral of the oxidation state in parentheses after the name of the element, for example, iron(II) for the +2 oxidation state of iron. (The terms *ferrous iron* and *ferric iron*, which represent the older system, are still in common use.)
- A radical is a group of elements that act like a single atom in the formation of a compound. The bonds within these radicals are predominantly covalent, but the groups of atoms as a whole have an excess of electrons when combined and thus are negative ions.

EXHIBIT 3.8
Oxidation Numbers

	Monovalent 1		Bivalent 2		Trivalent 3		Tetravalent 4		5	
Metals Cations (+)	Hydrogen	H	Barium	Ba	Aluminum	Al	Carbon	C	Arsenic (ic)	As
	Potasium	K	Calcium	Ca	Gold (auric)	Au	Silicon	Si	Phosphorus (ic)	P
	Sodium	Na	Cobalt	Co	Arsenic (ous)	As	Manganese (ic)	Mn	Antimony (ic)	Sb
	Silver	Ag	Magnesium	Mg	Chromium	Cr	Tin (stannic)	Sn	Bismuth (ic)	Bi
	Mercury (ous)	Hg	Lead	Pb	Iron (ferric)	Fe	Plantinum	Pt		
	Copper (ous)	Cu	Zinc	Zn	Phosphorus (ous)	P	Sulfur	S		
	Gold (aurous)	Au	Mercury(ic)	Hg	Antimony (ous)	Sb				
	Ammonium[a]	(NH$_4$)	Copper(cupric)	Cu	Bismuth (ous)	Bi				
			Iron (ferrous)	Fe						
			Manganese (ous)	Mn						
			Tin (stannous)	Sn						
Nonmetals Anions (–)[b]	Fluorine	F	Oxygen	O	Nitrogen	N	Carbon	C		
	Chlorine	Cl	Sulfur	S	Phosphorus	P				
	Bromine	Br								
	Iodine	I								
Radicals (–)	Hydroxide	(OH)	Carbonate	(CO$_3$)	Borate	(BO$_3$)	Ferrocyanide	[Fe(CN)$_6$]		
	Bicarbonate	(HCO$_3$)	Sulfite	(SO$_3$)	Phosphate	(PO$_4$)				
	Nitrite	(NO$_2$)	Sulfate	(SO$_4$)	Phosphite	(PO$_3$)				
	Nitrate	(NO$_3$)	Tetraborate	(B$_4$O$_7$)	Ferricyanide	[Fe(CN)$_6$]				
	Hypochlorite	(ClO)	Silicate	(SiO$_3$)						
	Chlorate	(ClO$_3$)	Chromate	(CrO$_4$)						
	Chlorite	(ClO$_2$)	Oxalate	(C$_2$O$_4$)						
	Perchlorate	(ClO$_4$)								
	Acetate	(C$_2$H$_3$O$_2$)								
	Permanganate	(MnO$_4$)								
	Bisulfate	(HSO$_4$)								

[a] Radical
[b] Last syllable of nonmetal is changed to *-ide* in binary compound.

When you attempt to write a formula, it is important to know whether it actually exists. For example, one can easily write the formula of carbon nitrate, but no chemist has ever prepared this compound. Here are the basic rules for writing formulas with three examples carried through each step:

1. Represent the symbols of the components, placing the positive part first, and then the negative part.

Sodium chloride	Calcium oxide	Ammonium sulfate
NaCl	CaO	NH_4SO_4

2. Indicate the respective oxidation numbers above and to the right of each symbol. (Enclose radicals in parentheses for the time being.)

$$Na^{1+}Cl^{1-} \qquad Ca^{2+}O^{2-} \qquad (NH_4)^{1+}(SO_4)^{2-}$$

3. For each symbol, write a subscript number equal to the oxidation number of the other element or radical. This is the same as the mechanical criss-cross method.

$$Na_1{}^{1+}\!\!\diagdown\!\!Cl_1{}^{1-} \quad Ca_2{}^{2+}\!\!\diagdown\!\!O_2{}^{2-} \quad (NH_4)_2{}^{1+}\!\!\diagdown\!\!(SO_4)_1{}^{2-}$$

Since the positive oxidation number shows the number of electrons that may be lost or shared and the negative oxidation number shows the number of electrons that may be gained or shared, you must have just as many electrons lost (or partially lost in sharing) as are gained (or partially gained in sharing).

4. Now rewrite the formulas, omitting the subscript 1, the parentheses of the radicals that have the subscript 1, and the plus and minus numbers.

$$NaCl \qquad Ca_2O_2 \qquad (NH_4)_2SO_4$$

5. As a general rule, the subscript numbers in the final formula are reduced to their lowest terms. There are, however, certain exceptions, such as hydrogen peroxide (H_2O_2), and acetylene (C_2H_2). For these exceptions, you must have more specific information about the compound.

The only way to become proficient at writing formulas is to memorize the oxidation numbers of common elements (or learn to use the periodic chart group numbers) and practice writing formulas.

Naming Compounds

A binary compound consists of two elements. The name of the compound also includes the two elements, the second name having its ending changed to -*ide*, such as NaCl = sodium chloride or AgCl = silver chloride. If the metal has two different oxidation numbers, this can be indicated by the use of the suffix -*ous* for the lower one and -*ic* for the higher one. However, the more modern way is to use a Roman numeral after the name to indicate the oxidation state.

Examples

$FeCl_2$ = ferrous chloride or iron(II) chloride
$FeCl_3$ = ferric chloride or iron(III) chloride

If elements combine in varying proportions, thus forming two or more compounds with different compositions, the name of the second element may be preceded by a prefix, such as mono- (one), di-

(two), tri- (three), or pent- (five). Some examples are carbon dioxide, CO_2; carbon monoxide, CO; diphosphorus trioxide, P_2O_3; and diphosphorus pentoxide, P_2O_5. Notice that, when these prefixes are used, it is not necessary to indicate the oxidation state of the first element in the name since it is given indirectly by the prefixed second element.

A ternary compound, consisting of three elements, is usually made up of an element and a radical. To name a ternary compound, you merely name each component in the order of positive first and negative second.

Composition Consideration

The chemical formula is an indication of the makeup of a compound in terms of the kinds of atoms and their relative numbers. It also has some quantitative applications. By using the atomic masses assigned to the elements, we can find the formula mass of a compound. If we are sure that the formula represents the actual makeup of one molecule of the substance, the term molecular mass may be used as well. In some cases the formula represents an ionic lattice and no discrete molecule exists, as in table salt, NaCl, or the formula merely represents the simplest ratio of the combined substances, not a molecule of the substance, such as CH_2. (This is the simplest ratio of carbon and hydrogen united to form the actual compound ethylene, C_2H_4.) This simplest ratio formula is called the empirical formula, and the actual formula is the true formula. The formula mass is determined by multiplying the atomic mass (in whole numbers) by the subscript for that element in the formula. For example, $Ca(OH)_2$ means (one calcium atomic mass + two hydrogen and two oxygen atomic masses = formula mass):

1Ca	(atomic mass = 40) = 40
2O	(atomic mass = 16) = 32
2H	(atomic mass = 1) = 2

Formula mass $Ca(OH)_2 = 74$

For Fe_2O_3,

2Fe	(atomic mass = 56) = 112
3O	(atomic mass = 16) = 48

Formula mass $Fe_2O_3 = 160$

Percentage Composition

It is sometimes useful to know what percentage of the total mass of a compound is made up of a particular element. This is called finding the percentage composition. The simple formula for this is

$$\frac{\text{Total mass of the element in the compound}}{\text{Total formula mass}} \times 100\%$$

= Percentage composition of that element

To find the percentage composition of calcium in calcium hydroxide, using the values obtained above, we set up the formula as

$$\frac{Ca = 40}{\text{Formula mass} = 74} \times 100\% = 54\% \text{ calcium}$$

To find the percentage composition of oxygen in calcium hydroxide,

$$\frac{O = 32}{\text{Formula mass } = 74} \times 100\% = 43\% \text{ oxygen}$$

To find the percentage composition of hydrogen in calcium hydroxide,

$$\frac{H = 2}{\text{Formula mass } = 74} \times 100\% = 2.7\% \text{ hydrogen}$$

Problem

Find the percentage composition of Cu and H_2O in the compound $CuSO_4 \cdot 5H_2O$ (the dot is read "with").

First, we calculate the formula mass:

$$
\begin{array}{ll}
1Cu & = 64 \\
1S & = 32 \\
4O & = 64 \quad 5(4 \times 16) \\
5H_2O & = 90 \quad 5(5 \times 18) \\
\hline
& 250
\end{array}
$$

and then find the percentages. Percentage Cu:

$$\frac{Cu = 64}{\text{Formula mass } = 250} \times 100\% = 26\%$$

Percentage H_2O:

$$\frac{5H_2O = 90}{\text{Formula mass } = 250} \times 100\% = 36\%$$

When you are given the percentage of each element in a compound, you can find the empirical formula as shown below.

Example

Given that a compound is composed of 60.0% Mg and 40.0% O, find the simple formula of the compound.

1. It is easiest to think of 100 mass units of this compound. In this case, the 100 mass units are composed of 60 mass units of Mg and 40 mass units of O. Since you know that 1 unit of Mg is 24 mass units (from its atomic mass) and, likewise, 1 unit of O is 16, you can divide 60 by 24 to find the number of units of Mg in the compound and divide 40 by 16 to find the number of units of O in the compound.

$$
\begin{array}{cc}
Mg & O \\
24\overline{)60} & 16\overline{)40} \\
2.5 \text{ units Mg} & 2.5 \text{ units O}
\end{array}
$$

2. Now, since we know formulas are made up of whole-number units of the elements, which are expressed as subscripts, we must manipulate these numbers to get whole numbers. This is usually accomplished by dividing the numbers by the smallest quotient. In this case the quotients are the same, so we divide by 2.5.

$$
\begin{array}{cc}
Mg & O \\
2.5\overline{)2.5} & 2.5\overline{)2.5} \\
1 & 1
\end{array}
$$

Our simple formula, then, is one Mg and one O. Therefore, MgO is the empirical, or simplest, formula.

Free energy *See* **Bonding.**
Fusion, atomic *See* **Nucleonics.**

Fusion, heat of The amount of calories needed to convert 1 gram of a substance from the solid to the liquid phase at standard pressure. For example, *see* **Calorimetry**.

G **Gamma rays** A type of electromagnetic radiation that has no electrical charge and exhibits the following properties:

Beta particles and gamma rays are usually emitted together; after a beta is emitted, a gamma ray follows.

Arrangement in nucleus is unknown; same velocity as visible light.

Range: no specific range.

Shielding needed: about 5 in. of lead.

Interactions: weak of itself; gives energy to electrons, which then perform the ionization.

Gases, characteristics and properties of *See* **Gas laws** (e.g., **Graham's, Boyle's** and **Charles'**), for detailed quantitative relationships. For the solution of problems involving gas volumes, *see* **Chemical calculations**.

General Characteristics of Gases

Kinetic-molecular theory has been arrived at, by indirect observations, to explain the forces between molecules and the energy they possess. There are three basic assumptions to the kinetic theory:

1. Matter in all its forms (solid, liquid, and gas) is composed of extremely small particles. In many cases these are called molecules. The space occupied by the gas particles themselves is ignored in comparison with the volume of the space they occupy.

2. The particles of matter are in constant motion. In solids, this motion is restricted to a small space. In liquids, the particles have a more random pattern but still are restricted to a kind of rolling over one another. In a gas, the particles are in continuous, random straight-line motion.

3. When these particles collide with each other or with the walls of the container, there is no loss of energy.

Particular Properties of Gases

As the temperature of a gas is increased, its kinetic energy is increased and this increases the random motion. At a particular temperature not all the particles have the same kinetic energy, but the temperature is a measure of the average kinetic energy of the particles. A graph of the various kinetic energies would resemble a normal bell-shaped curve with the average found at the peak of the curve as shown in Fig. 29.

When the temperature is lowered, the gas reaches a point at which the kinetic energy can no longer overcome the attractive forces between the particles (or molecules) and the gas condenses to a liquid. The temperature at which this condensation occurs is related to the type of substance the gas is composed of and the type of bonding in the molecules themselves. This relationship of bond type to the condensation point (or boiling point) is pointed out in the section on bonding.

That gases are moving in a random motion so that they may move from one position to another is referred to as diffusion. You know that if a bottle of perfume is opened in one corner of a room, the sub-stance—that is, its molecules—will move or diffuse to all parts of the room in time. *See* **Gas laws**.

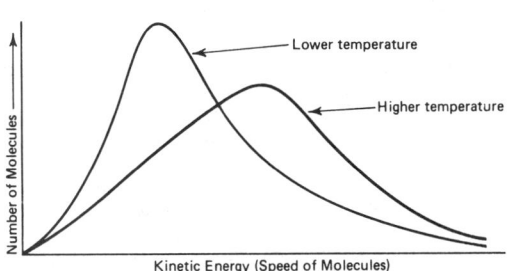

Fig. 29   Molecular Speed Distribution in a Gas at Different Temperatures

Gas laws   Laws that relate the behavior of gases to specific conditions and/or the changes that occur as these conditions are altered.

- **Boyle's law** One of the gas laws describing the relationship of volume and pressure when the temperature is held constant. (*See* Fig. 30.)

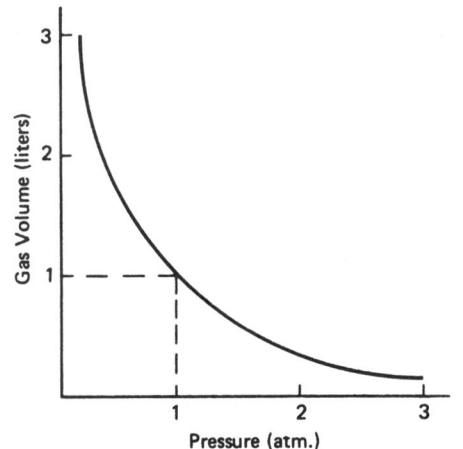

Fig. 30   Graphic Relationship—Boyle's Law

Robert Boyle, a seventeenth century English sci-entist, found that the volume of a gas decreases when the pressure on it is increased, and vice versa, when the temperature is held constant. Boyle's law can be stated as follows:

If the temperature remains constant, the volume of a gas varies inversely as the pressure changes. Then,

$$P_1V_1 = P_2V_2 \qquad \text{at constant temperature}$$

The pressure may be expressed in various units: 1 standard atmosphere (atm) = 760 mm Hg = 760 torr = 101,325 pascals (Pa). The torr is named in honor of Evangelista Torricelli, and the pascal, the SI sys-tem unit of pressure, is named after Blaise Pascal. In the United States, mm Hg and the torr are most com-monly used.

Problem

Given the volume of a gas as 200 mL at 800 torr pressure, calculate the volume of the same gas at 765 torr. Temperature is held constant.

If you know that this *decrease* in pressure will cause an *increase* in the volume, then you know that 200 mL must be multiplied by a fraction (made up of the two pressures) that has a larger numerator than the denominator. So,

$$200 \text{mL} \frac{800 \text{torr}}{765 \text{torr}} = 209 \text{mL}$$

Or you can use the formula

$$P_1V_1 = P_2V_2.$$

Then,

$$V_2 = V_1 \times \frac{P_1}{P_2}$$

$$V_2 = 200 \text{mL} \times \frac{800 \text{torr}}{765 \text{torr}} = 209 \text{mL}$$

- **Charles' law** A gas law that describes the rela-tionship of the volume and temperature of a gas when the pressure is held constant. (*See* Fig. 31.)

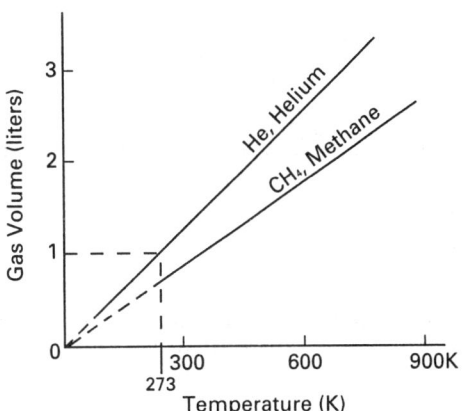

Fig. 31   Graphic Relationship—Charles' Law

Plots of V versus T for two representative gases. The dashed line represents extrapolation of the data into regions where gas would become liquid or solid. Extrapolation shows each gas, if it remained gaseous, would reach zero vol-ume at −273.15°C.

Jacques Charles, a French chemist of the early nineteenth century, discovered that, when a gas un-der constant pressure is heated from 0°C to 1°C, it expands 1/273 of its volume. It also contracts this amount when the temperature is dropped 1 degree to −1°C. Charles reasoned that if a gas at 0°C were cooled to −273°C, its volume would be zero. Actually, all gases are converted into liquids before this temperature is reached. By using the Kelvin scale to rid the problem of negative numbers, Charles' law can be stated as follows:

If the pressure remains constant, the volume of a gas varies directly as the absolute temperature. Then,

$$\frac{V_1}{T_1} = \frac{V_2}{T_2} \text{ at constant pressure}$$

Problem

The volume of a gas at 20°C is 500 mL. Find its volume at standard temperature if pressure is held constant.
Convert temperatures:

$$20°C = 20 + 273 = 293 \text{ K}$$
$$0°C = \ \ 0 + 273 = 273 \text{ K}$$

If you know that cooling a gas decreases its volume, then you know that 500 mL will have to be multiplied by a fraction (made up of the Kelvin temperatures) that has a smaller numerator than the denominator. So,

$$.500 \text{ mL} \times \frac{273 \text{K}}{293 \text{K}} = 465 \text{ mL}$$

Or you can use the formula

$$\frac{V_1}{T_1} = \frac{V_2}{T_2}$$

So,

$$\frac{500 \text{ mL}}{293 \text{K}} = \frac{X \text{ mL}}{273 \text{K}}$$

$$X \text{ mL} = 465 \text{ mL}$$

- **Combined gas law** A combination of Boyle's and Charles' laws into one expression. It can be shown as

$$\frac{P_1 V_1}{T_1} = \frac{P_2 V_2}{T_2}$$

Problem

The volume of a gas at 780 torr pressure and 30°C is 500 mL. What volume would the gas occupy at STP?

You can use reasoning to determine the kind of fractions the temperatures and pressures must be to arrive at your answer. Since the pressure is going from 780 torr to 760 torr, the volume should increase. The fraction must then be 780/760. Since the temperature is going from 30°C (303 K) to 0°C (273 K), the volume should decrease; this fraction must be 273/303. So,

$$500 \text{ mL} \times \frac{780 \text{ torr}}{760 \text{ torr}} \times \frac{273 \text{K}}{303 \text{K}} = 462 \text{ mL}$$

Or you can use the formula

$$\frac{P_1 V_1}{T_1} = \frac{P_2 V_2}{T_2}$$

Solve for

$$V_2 = V_1 \times \frac{P_1}{P_2} \times \frac{T_2}{T_1}$$

$$V_2 = 500 \text{ mL} \times \frac{780 \text{ torr}}{760 \text{ torr}} \times \frac{273 \text{K}}{303 \text{K}} = 462 \text{ mL}$$

- **Ideal gas** In the use of the gas laws, we have assumed that the gases involved were "ideal" gases. This means that the molecules of the gas were not taking up space in the gas volume and that no intermolecular forces of attraction were serving to pull the molecules closer together. You will find that a gas behaves like an ideal gas at low pressures and high temperatures, which move the molecules as far as possible from conditions that would cause condensation. In general, pressures below a few atmospheres will cause most gases to exhibit sufficiently ideal properties for the application of the gas laws with a reliability of a few percentage points, or better.

- **Universal gas law** This gas law is the combination of these variables into the universal gas equation, $pV = nRT$, where n is the amount of gas in moles, R is the universal gas constant, T is temperature in kelvin units, and p and V are usually expressed in atmospheres and liters respectively. Under these conditions $R = 0.08206$ L atm/K mol. This law is often referred to as the Ideal gas law, too.

Problem

A sample of hydrogen gas (H_2) has a volume of 8.56 L at a temperature of 0°C and a pressure of 1.5 atm. Calculate the number of moles of H_2 present in this gas sample.
Solving $PV = nRT$ for n gives

$$n = \frac{PV}{RT}$$

The values are $P = 1.5$ atm, $V = 8.56$ L, $R = 0.08206$ L atm/K mol, and 0°C = 273 K.

Then

$$n = \frac{(1.5 \text{ atm})(8.56 \text{ L})}{\left(0.08206 \frac{\text{L atm}}{\text{K mol}}\right) 273 \text{K}} = 0.57 \text{ mol}$$

Two other laws that relate gaseous behavior to surrounding conditions are:

- **Dalton's law of partial pressure** When a gas is made up of a mixture of different gases, the total pressure of the mixture is equal to the sum of the partial pressures of the components. The partial pressure of any of the gases in the mixture is the pressure of that individual gas if it alone occupied the volume.

$$P_{\text{total}} = P_{\text{gas 1}} + P_{\text{gas 2}} + P_{\text{gas 3}} + \cdots$$

Problem

A mixture of gases at 760 torr pressure contains 65% nitrogen, 15% oxygen, and 20% carbon dioxide by volume. What is the partial pressure of each gas?

$0.65 \times 760 = 494$ torr pressure of N_2
$0.15 \times 760 = 114$ torr pressure of O_2
$0.20 \times 760 = 152$ torr pressure CO_2

- **Graham's law of diffusion** A law that relates the rate at which a gas diffuses to the type of molecule in the gas. It can be expressed as follows: The rate of diffusion of a gas is inversely proportional to the square root of its molecular mass. Hydrogen, with the lowest molecular mass, can diffuse more rapidly than other gases under similar conditions.

Problem

Compare the rate of diffusion of hydrogen to that of oxygen under similar conditions.
   The formula is

$$\frac{\text{Rate A}}{\text{Rate B}} = \frac{\sqrt{\text{molecular mass of B}}}{\sqrt{\text{molecular mass of A}}}$$

Let A be H_2 and B be O_2 :

$$\frac{\text{Rate } H_2}{\text{Rate } O_2} = \frac{\sqrt{32}}{\sqrt{2}} = \frac{\sqrt{16}}{\sqrt{1}} = \frac{4}{1}$$

Therefore hydrogen diffuses four times as fast as oxygen.

Gay-Lussac's law *See* **Gas Volumes and Molecular Mass,** under **Chemical Calculations**.

Graham's law of diffusion *See* **Gas laws**.

Gram *See* **Measurements**.

Half-cell *See* **Electrochemical reactions**.

Half-life *See* **Nucleonics**.

Heat of formation The number of calories evolved or absorbed when a mole (gram-formula mass) of that compound is formed by the direct union of its elements. A positive number indicates heat is absorbed; a negative number indicates heat is evolved. (For mathematical treatment, *see* **Reactions, types of**.)

Henry's law The law that relates the solubility of gases as a direct proportion to the pressure.

Hess's law of heat summation *See* **Additivity of Reaction Heat**, under **Enthalpy**.

Heterogeneous mixture A mixture (that is, a substance with variable composition) that has regions with varying properties. Sand in water, dust suspended in air, and iced tea with ice cubes are examples of heterogeneous mixtures.

Homogeneous mixture A mixture (that is, a substance with variable composition) that has the same properties throughout. Some sugar totally dissolved in water fits this definition, as do most solutions and alloys.

Hund's rule of maximum multiplicity *See* **Atomic structure**.

Hybridization and the VSEPR model Data have shown that bond angles for atoms in molecules with *p* orbitals in the outer shell do not always conform to the expected 90° separation of an *x, y, z* axis orientation. This variation can be expressed by electrostatic repulsion between valence electron charge clouds or by the concept of hybridization.

The electrostatic repulsion, referred to as the valence shell electron pair repulsion (VSEPR), uses as its basis the fact that like charges will orient themselves in such a way as to diminish the repulsion between them.

- Mutual repulsion of two electron clouds forces them to the opposite sides of a sphere. This is called a linear arrangement. For example, BeF_2.

180°

- Minimum repulsion between three electron pairs occurs when each is at the vertex of an equilateral triangle inscribed in a sphere. This is called trigonal planar. For example, BF_3.

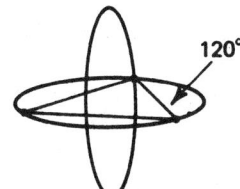 

120°

- Four electron pairs are farthest apart at the vertices of a tetrahedron inscribed in a sphere. This is called a tetrahedral shape. For example, CH_4.

 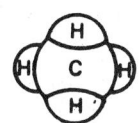

- Mutual repulsion of six identical electron clouds directs them to the corners of an inscribed regular octahedron. This is said to have octahedral geometry. For example, SF_4.

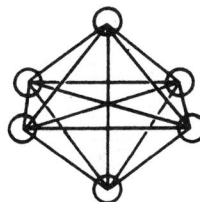 

These same configurations can also be arrived at through the concept of hybridization. Briefly stated, this means that two or more pure atomic orbitals (usually *s, p,* and *d*) can be mixed to form two or more hybrid atomic orbitals that are identical. This concept can be illustrated as follows:

- *sp* Hybrid orbitals. Beryllium fluoride spectroscopic measurements reveal a bond angle of 180° and equal bond lengths:

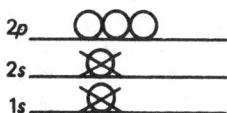

F—Be—F

The ground state of beryllium is:

2p <u>◯◯◯</u>

2s <u>⊗</u>

1s <u>⊗</u>

To accommodate the experimental data we theorize that a *2s* electron is excited to a *2p* orbital; then the two orbitals hybridize to yield two identical orbitals called *sp* orbitals. Each contains one electron but is capable of holding two electrons (see below):

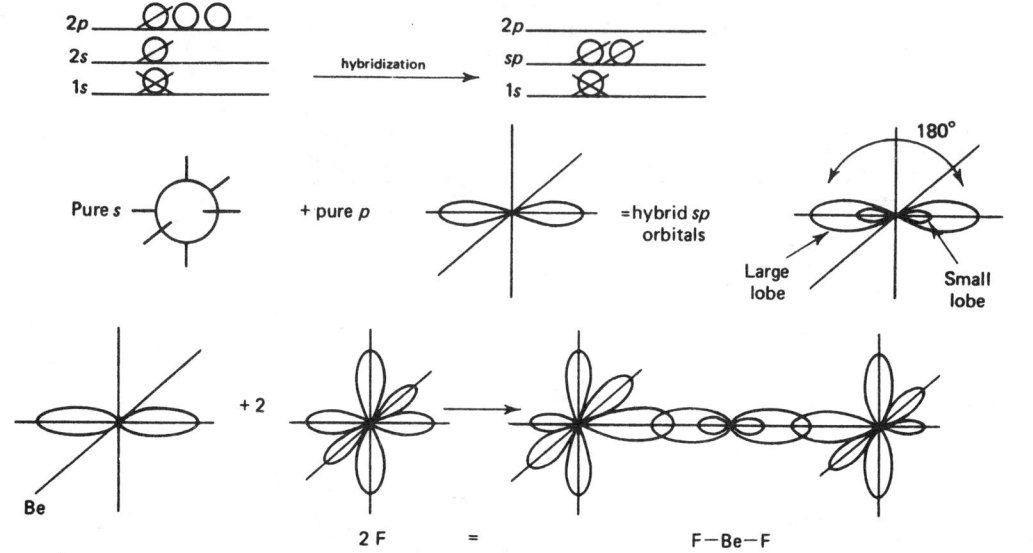

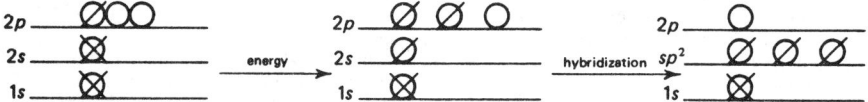

- **■** *sp²* Hybrid orbitals. Boron triflouride has bond angles of 120° of equal strength. To accommodate these data the boron atom hybridizes from its ground state of $1s^2 2s^2 2p^1$ to $1s^2$ and three sp^2 orbitals in a trigonal pattern.

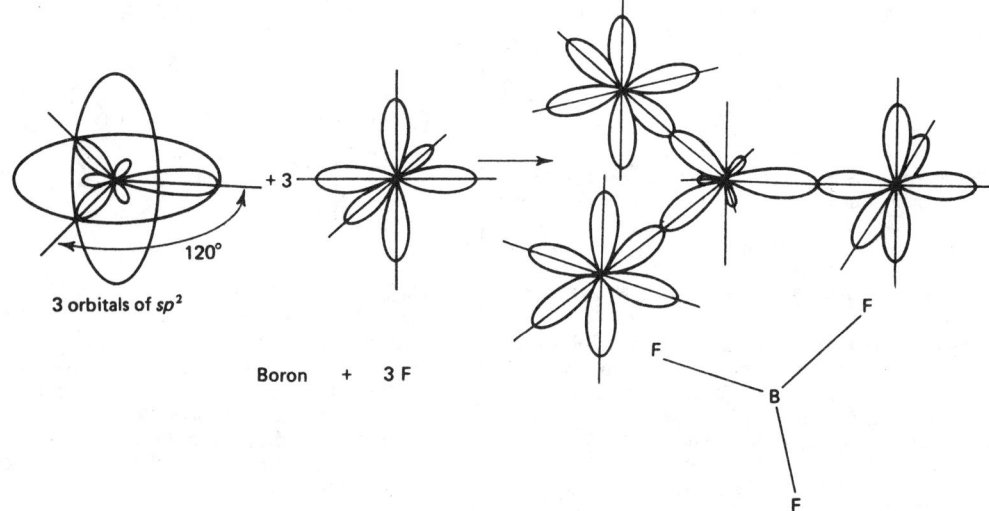

■ sp^3 Hybrid orbitals. Methane, CH_4, can be used to illustrate this hybridization. Carbon has a ground state of $1s^2 2s^2 2p^2$. One $2s$ electron is excited to a $2p$ orbital, and the four involved orbitals then form four new identical sp^3 orbitals:

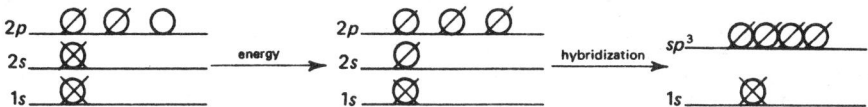

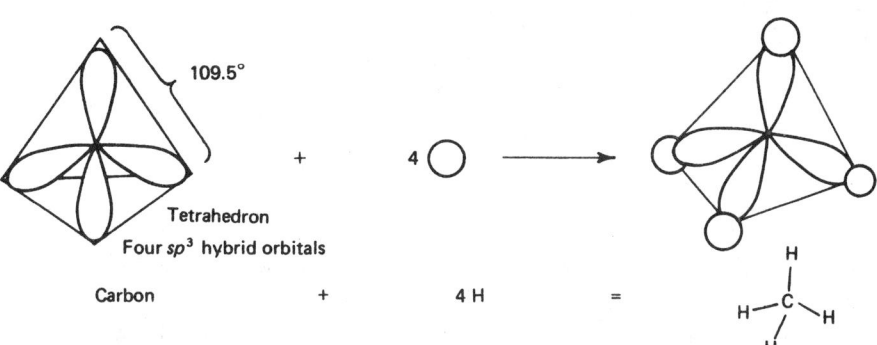

Carbon   +   4 H   =

In some compounds in which only certain sp^3 orbitals are involved in bonding, distortion in the bond angle occurs because of unbonded electron repulsion. Two examples are water, H_2O:

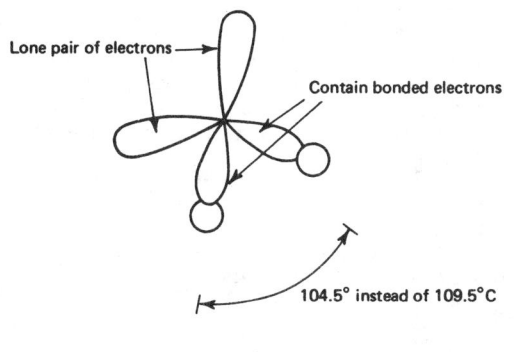

and ammonia, NH_3:

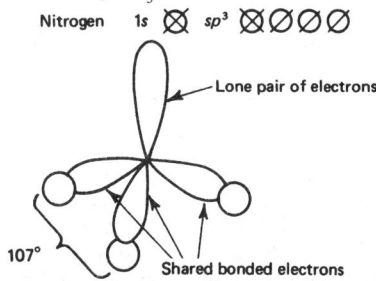

■ sp^3d^2 Hybrid orbitals. These orbitals are formed from the hybridization of an s and a p electron promoted to d orbitals and transformed into six equal sp^3d^2 orbitals. The spatial form of SF_6 is an example.

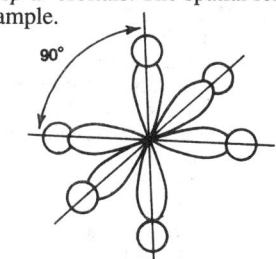

EXHIBIT 3.9
Summary of Hybridization

Number of Bonds	Number of Unused Electron Pairs	Type of Hybrid Orbital	Angle between Bonded Atoms (°)	Geometry	Example
2	0	sp	180	Linear	BeF_2
3	0	sp^2	120	Trigonal planar	BF_3
4	0	sp^3	109.5	Tetrahedral	CH_4
3	1	sp^3	90–109.5	Pyramidal	NH_3
2	2	sp^3	90–109.5	Angular	H_2O
6	0	sp^3d^2	90	Octahedral	SF_6

Hydrocarbons *See* **Organic chemistry**.

Hydrogen bond A proton or hydrogen nucleus has a high concentration of positive charge. When a hydrogen atom is bonded to a highly electronegative atom, its positive charge will have an attraction for neighboring electron pairs. This is called a *hydrogen bond*. The more strongly polar the molecule, the more effective the hydrogen bonding is in binding the molecules into a larger unit. This causes the boiling points of such molecules to be higher than those of similar nonpolar molecules. Good examples are water and hydrogen fluoride. (*See* Fig. 32).

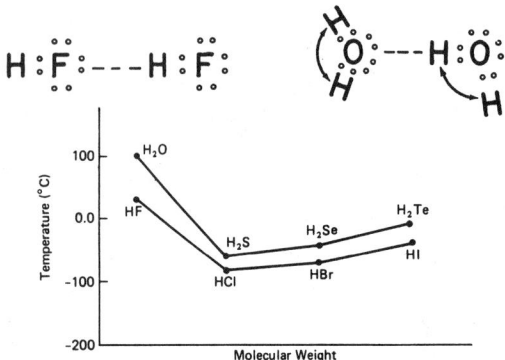

Fig. 32   Boiling Points of Hydrogen Compounds with Similar Electron Dot Structures

Hydroxides *See* **Acids and bases**.

Ideal gas *See* **Gas laws**.

Indicators Chemicals used to indicate the pH of solutions. Some indicators can be used to determine pH because of their color change somewhere along this pH scale. Some common indicators and their respective color changes are given below in Exhibit 3.10. Here is an example of how to read Exhibit 3.10: At pH values below 4.5, litmus is red; above 8.3, it is blue. Between these values, it is a mixture of the two colors.

Ionic bonding *See* **Bonding**.

Ionization energy Atoms hold their valence electrons with different amounts of energy. If enough energy is supplied to one outer electron to remove it from its atom, this amount of energy is called the first ionization energy. With the first electron gone, the removal of succeeding electrons becomes more difficult because of the imbalance between the positive nuclear charge and the remaining electrons.

The lowest ionization energy is found with the least electronegative atom. Study Figs. 33 and 34 carefully, and notice the patterns established.

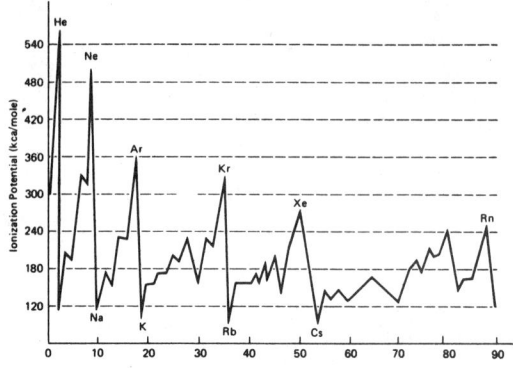

Fig. 33   Atomic Number versus Ionization Potential
(Note trend for identified atoms)

Element		Atomic Number	First Ionization Energy (eV)	Second Ionization Energy (eV)	
Group 1	Li	3	5.39	75.7	Third
	K	19	4.34	31.8	Ionization Energy (eV)
Group 2	Be	4	9.32	18.2	154
	Mg	12	7.64	15.1	80.3

Fig. 34   Sample Ionization Energies for Second and Third Electron Removal

For the ionization energies of the various elements, see **Table I** in **Exhibit 3.13**, page 3-65.

Isomers Compounds having the same molecular formula but different arrangements of atoms. *See* **Organic chemistry** for examples.

Isotopes Forms of the same element that differ in the number of neutrons in the nucleus.

For more information and examples, *see* **Components of Atomic Structure**, under **Atomic structure**.

IUPAC International Union of Pure and Applied Chemistry, an organization that has established standard rules for the naming of all compounds.

Ketones An organic compound recognized by the functional group

$$R-\underset{\underset{O}{\|}}{C}-R^1$$

The simplest ketones can be formed by slightly oxidizing secondary alcohols. The R^1 indicates that this radical need not be the same as R. An example, using the same radical is

---

EXHIBIT 3.10
Some Common Indicators

Indicator	pH Range of Color Change	Color below Lower pH	Color above Higher pH
Methyl orange	3.1–4.4	Red	Yellow
Bromthymol blue	6.0–7.6	Yellow	Blue
Litmus	4.5–8.3	Red	Blue
Phenolphthalein	8.3–10.0	Colorless	Red

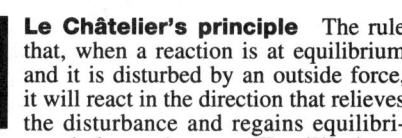

propanol-2
(isopropyl alcohol)

2-propanone
(acetone)

The name of the ketone in the IUPAC system has an ending -*one* with a digit indicating the carbon that has the double-bonded oxygen. Another method of naming a ketone is to name the radicals on either side of the ketone structure and use the word ketone. This would be dimethyl ketone.

Kinetic-molecular theory   *See* **General Characteristics of Gases**, under **Gases**.

L **Le Châtelier's principle**   The rule that, when a reaction is at equilibrium and it is disturbed by an outside force, it will react in the direction that relieves the disturbance and regains equilibrium. For more information, *see* **Equilibrium, chemical**.

Lewis acid-base theory   *See* **Acids and bases**.

Liquids   In a liquid, the volume of the molecules and the intermolecular forces between them are much more important than in a gas. When you consider that in a gas the molecules constitute far less than 1% of the total volume, but in the liquid state the molecules constitute 70% of the total volume, it is clear that in a liquid the forces between the molecules are more important. Because of this decreased volume and increased intermolecular interaction, a liquid expands and contracts only very slightly with a change in temperature and lacks the compressibility typical of gases.

Kinetic Energy of Liquids

A liquid is a phase of matter that has a definite volume and takes the shape of the container. Even though the volume of space between molecules in a liquid has decreased and the mutual attraction forces between neighboring molecules can have great effects on the molecules, they are still in motion. This motion can be verified under a microscope when colloidal particles are suspended in a liquid. The particle's zigzag path indicates molecular motion and supports the kinetic-molecular theory.

Increases in temperature increase the average kinetic energy of molecules and the rapidity of their movement. This is shown graphically in Fig. 35. The molecules in the sample of cold liquid have, on the average, less kinetic energy than those in the warmer sample. Hence the temperature reading T_1, will be less than the temperature reading T_2. If a particular molecule gains enough kinetic energy when it is near the surface of a liquid, it can overcome the attractive forces of the liquid phase and escape into the gaseous phase. This is called a *change of phase*. When fast-moving molecules with high kinetic energy escape, the average energy of the remaining molecules is lower; hence the temperature is lowered.

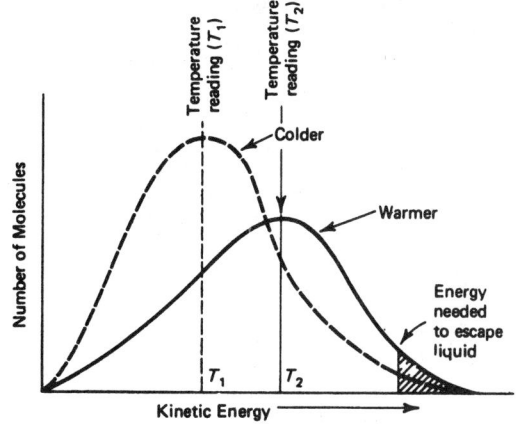

Fig. 35   Distribution of the Kinetic Energy of Molecules

M **Mass**   The quantity of matter that a substance possesses. Depending on the gravitational force acting on it, a unit of weight is assigned to it. Although weight can then vary, the mass of the body is a constant and can be measured by its resistance to a change in position or motion.

Matter   Anything that occupies space and has mass.

Measurements   The student of chemistry must be able to use the correct measurement terms accurately and to solve problems that require mathematical skill, as well as proper terminology, for their correct solution. This section reviews these topics.

Metric System

The metric system of measurement is the one most often used by scientists all over the world.

The Systeme Internationale (in French) or the SI system, is based on the metric system and used by most scientists worldwide. The basic prefixes used in SI systems are listed in Exhibit 3.11.

A unit of length used especially in expressing the length of light waves, is the angstrom, abbreviated as Å and equal to 10^{-8} cm. Now being replaced by the nanometer. 1 Å = 0.1 nanometer.

EXHIBIT 3.11
Metric System Prefixes Used in the SI System

Prefix	Multiples	Scientific Notation	Abbreviation
mega-	1,000,000	10^6	M
kilo-	1,000	10^3	k
hecto-	100	10^2	h
deka-	10	10^1	da
deci-	0.1	10^{-1}	d
centi-	0.01	10^{-2}	c
milli-	0.001	10^{-3}	m
micro-	0.000,001	10^{-6}	μ
nano-	0.000,000,001	10^{-9}	n

CHEMISTRY

Metric units and equivalents:

Length
10 millimeters (mm) = 1 centimeter (cm)
100 cm = 1meter (m)
1000 m = 1 kilometer (km)

Volume
1000 milliliters (mL) = 1 liter (L)
1000 cubic centimeters (cm^3) = 1 liter
1 mL = 1 cm^3

Mass
1000 milligrams (mg) = 1 gram (g)
1000 g = 1 kilogram (kg)

Some equivalents to the English system:
2. 54 cm = 1 inch
1 meter = 39.7 inches (10% longer than a yard)
1 ounce = 28.35 grams
1 pound = 454 grams
2.2 pounds = 1 kilogram
1 quart = 0.946 liter
1.06 quarts = 1 liter (5% larger than a quart).

The metric system standards were chosen as natural standards. The meter was first described as the distance marked off on a platinum-iridium bar but now can be reproduced as 1,650,763.73 times the wavelength of an isotope of krypton where it is excited to give off an orange-red spectral line.

There are some interesting relationships between volume and mass units in the metric system. Since water is most dense at 4°C, the gram was intended to be 1 cubic centimeter of water at this temperature. This means, then, that

1000 cm^3 = 1 liter of water @ 4°C

1000 cm^3 of water weighs 1000 g @4°C

therefore,

1 liter of water @ 4°C weighs 1 kg

and

1 mL of water @ 4°C weighs 1g

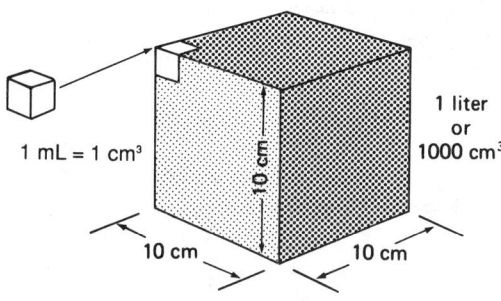

1 mL = 1 cm^3

10 cm

1 liter
or
1000 cm^3

10 cm   10 cm

Factor-Label Method of Conversion
When you are working on problems that involve numbers with units of measurement, it is convenient to use this method so that you do not become confused in the operations of multiplication or division. For example, if you are changing 0.001 kilogram to milligrams, you set up each conversion as a fraction so that all the units will factor out except the one you want in the answer.

$$1 \times 10^{-3} \, \text{kilogram} \times \frac{1 \times 10^3 \, \text{grams}}{1 \, \text{kilogram}}$$

$$\times \frac{1 \times 10^3 \, \text{milligrams}}{1 \, \text{grams}} = 1 \times 10^3 \, \text{mg}$$

Notice that the kilogram is made the denominator in the first fraction to be factored with the original kilogram unit. The numerator is equal to the denominator but is expressed in smaller units. The second fraction has the gram unit in the denominator to be factored with the gram unit in the preceding fraction. The answer is in milligrams since it is the only unit remaining; it assures you that the correct operations have been performed in the conversion.

Metals   *See* **Periodic table**.
Metric system   *See* **Measurements**.
Mixtures   A substance made up of two or more distinct types of particles not chemically united; for example, salt and iron filings, oxygen and nitrogen, gold and silver.
Molality   (abbreviated m) The expression of the number of moles of a solute dissolved in 1000 grams of water. *See* **Solutions** for further explanation and examples.
Molarity   (abbreviated M) The expression of the number of moles of a solute dissolved in 1 liter of solution. *See* **Solutions** for examples.
Mole concept   The concept that one gram-formula mass of a substance contains 6.02×10^{23} particles and, if a gas, occupies 22.4 liters of volume at STP. For example, $2O_2 = 64$ g = 2 moles of $O_2 = 44.8$ liters at STP. For use in solutions, *see* **Volumetric analysis**. For use in problems, *see* **Chemical calculations**.

N   **Nernst equation**   *See* **Non-standard-state Cell potentials**, under **Electrochemical reactions**.
Neutrons   Subatomic particles that have zero charge and are found generally in the nuclei of atoms. *See* **Atomic structure** for further details.
Normality   The number of gram-equivalent mass units of solute in a liter of solution. *See* **Solutions** for further explanation.
Nucleonics   The branch of physical science that deals with the constituents of and all the changes in the atomic nucleus. It began with the discovery of radioactivity in 1896 (less than 2 months after Röntgen published an announcement of the discovery of X-rays). Röntgen had pointed out that the X-rays came from a spot on a glass tube where a beam of electrons, in his experiments, was hitting, and that this spot simultaneously showed strong fluorescence. It occurred to Becquerel and others that X-rays might in some way be related to fluorescence (emission of light when exposed to some exciting agency) and to phosphorescence (emission of light after the exciting agency is removed).

Becquerel accordingly tested a number of phosphorescent substances to determine whether they emitted X-rays while phosphorescing. He had no success until he tried a compound of uranium; he found that the uranium compound, whether or not it was allowed to phosphoresce by exposure to light, continuously emitted something that could penetrate lightproof paper and even thicker materials.

He found that the compounds of uranium and the element itself produced ionization in the surrounding air. Thus either the ionizing effect, as indicated by the rate of discharge of a charged electroscope, or the degree of darkening of a photographic plate could be used to measure the intensity of the invisible emission. Moreover, the emission from the uranium was continuous and perhaps even permanent and required no energy from an external source. Yet, probably because of the current interest and excitement over X-rays, Becquerel's work received little attention for some 2 years following his discovery, until early in 1898 when the Curies entered the picture (Pierre Curie was one of Becquerel's colleagues in Paris). Their painstaking efforts in isolating several other radioactive compounds resulted in the isolation of polonium and radium.

The Nature of Radioactive Emissions

While the early separation experiments were in progress, an understanding was slowly being gained of the nature of the spontaneous emission from the various radioactive elements. Becquerel thought at first that it was simply X-rays, but it was soon found that there are three different kinds of radioactive emission, now called alpha particles, beta particles, and gamma rays. We now know that the alpha particles are positively charged particles of helium nuclei, the beta particles are streams of high-speed electrons, and the gamma rays are high-energy radiations similar to X-rays.

Methods of Detection of Alpha, Beta, and Gamma Rays

All methods of detection of these radiations rely on their ability to ionize. A number of methods are in common use.

- *Photographic plate.* The fogging of a photographic emulsion led to the discovery of radioactivity. If this emulsion is viewed under a high-power microscope, it is seen that beta and gamma rays cause the silver bromide grains to develop in a scattered fashion. However, alpha particles, owing to the dense ionization they produce, leave a definite track of exposed grains in the emulsion. Hence not only is the alpha particle detected, but also its range (in the emulsion) can be measured. Special emulsions are capable of showing the beta-particle tracks.
- *Scintillation counter (see* Fig. 36). A fluorescent screen (e.g., ZnS) will show the presence of electrons and X-rays, as we have already seen. If the screen is viewed with a magnifying eyepiece, small flashes of light, called scintillations, will be observed. By observing the scintillations, one can not only detect the presence of alpha particles, but can also actually count them.
- *The cloud chamber.* One of the most useful instruments for detecting and measuring radiation is the Wilson cloud chamber. Its operation depends on the well-known fact that moisture tends to condense around ions (the probable explanation for some formation of clouds in the

sky). If an enclosed region of air is saturated with water vapor (this is always the case if the water is present) and the air is cooled suddenly, it becomes supersaturated, that is, it contains for the instant more water vapor than it can hold permanently and a fog of water droplets develops around the ions in the chamber.

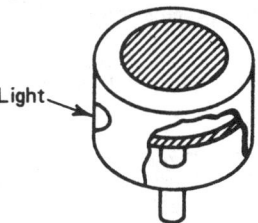

Fig. 36   Scintillation Counter

For example, an alpha particle traveling through such a supersaturated atmosphere supplies a trail of ions on which water droplets will condense. This trail is thus made visible. These trails are usually photographed by a camera that operates whenever a piston moves downward, causing the air to expand and cool.

- *The bubble chamber.* This device utilizes a liquid, such as ether, ethyl alcohol, pentane, or propane that is superheated to well above the boiling point. When the pressure is released quickly, the liquid is in a highly unstable condition, ready to boil violently. An ionizing particle passing through the liquid at this instant leaves a trail of tiny bubbles that may be photographed.
- *The electroscope (see* Fig. 37). One of the simplest and one of the first devices used in work on radioactivity consists of two thin gold leaves that are charged by a battery with the same type of charge. Radioactive materials produce ions in proportion to their radioactivities. A negatively charged electroscope becomes discharged when ions in the air take electrons from the electroscope, causing the leaves to gradually collapse.

Fig. 37   Electroscope

- *The Geiger counter.* This instrument is perhaps the most widely used at the present time for counting individual radiation emissions. It consists of a fine wire of tungsten mounted along the axis of the tube, which contains a gas at reduced pressure. A difference of potential of about 1000 V is applied in such a way as to make the metal tube negative with respect to the wire. The voltage is high enough so that the electrons produced are accelerated by the electrical field. Near the wire, where the field is strongest, the accelerated particles produce more ions, positive ions going to the walls, negative ions being collected by the wire. Any particle that will produce an ion gives rise to the same avalanche of ions, so the type of particle cannot be detected. However, it is possible to detect each individual particle.

Source of Radioactivity

The nuclei of uranium, radium, and other radioactive elements are continually disintegrating. It should be emphasized that spontaneous disintegration produces radon. The time required for half of the material to disintegrate is called its *half-life*. (See **Table F** of **Exhibit 3.13** for a list of other common radiotypes and their respective half-life figures.)

For example, for radium, we know that, on the average, half of all the radium nuclei present will have to be disintegrated to radon in 1590 years. In another 1590 years, half of this remainder will decay, and so on. When the radium atom disintegrates, it loses an alpha particle, which eventually becomes a neutral helium atom upon gaining two electrons. The remainder of the atom is the gas known as radon.

This process of half-life decay can be expressed in an equation as shown

$$X = X_0 \left(\tfrac{1}{2}\right)^{T/H}$$

Where X_0 = starting mass
 X = remaining mass
 T = time that elapsed (in same units as half-life)
 H = half-life

Example: Strontium-85 has a half-life of 65.2 days. If you start with 10 grams of Sr-85, how much will be left after 130.4 days?

Making the appropriate substitutions in the equation, we have
 $X = 10g \left(\tfrac{1}{2}\right)^{130.4/65.2}$
 $X = 10g \left(\tfrac{1}{2}\right)^2$
 $X = 10g \left(\tfrac{1}{4}\right) = 2.5$ grams
   (Amt. of Sr-85 left)

Such a conversion of an element to a new element (because of a change in the number of protons) is called a transmutation. This transmutation can be produced artificially by bombarding the nuclei of a substance with various particles from a particle accelerator, such as the cyclotron.

The following uranium-radium disintegration series shows how a radioactive atom may change when it loses each kind of particle. Note that an atomic number is shown by a subscript ($_{92}$U), and the isotopic mass is shown by a superscript (^{238}U). The alpha particle is designated by the Greek symbol α and the beta particle by β.

$$^{238}_{92}\text{U} \xrightarrow{-\alpha} {}^{234}_{90}\text{Th} \xrightarrow{-\beta} {}^{234}_{91}\text{Pa} \xrightarrow{-\beta} {}^{234}_{92}\text{U} \xrightarrow{-\alpha} {}^{230}_{90}\text{Th} \xrightarrow{-\alpha}$$

$$^{226}_{88}\text{Ra} \xrightarrow{-\alpha} {}^{222}_{86}\text{Rn} \xrightarrow{-\alpha} {}^{218}_{84}\text{Po} \xrightarrow{-\alpha} {}^{214}_{82}\text{Pb} \xrightarrow{-\beta} {}^{214}_{83}\text{Bi} \xrightarrow{-\beta}$$

$$^{214}_{84}\text{Po} \xrightarrow{-\alpha} {}^{210}_{82}\text{Pb} \xrightarrow{-\beta} {}^{210}_{83}\text{Bi} \xrightarrow{-\beta} {}^{210}_{84}\text{Po} \xrightarrow{-\alpha} {}^{206}_{82}\text{Pb} \quad \text{(stable)}$$

For a list of other symbols used in nuclear chemistry, *see* **Table H** in **Exhibit 3.13**, page 3-65.

Particle Lost	Weight Change	Atomic Number Change
Alpha (α)	Loses 4 amu	Decreases by 2
Beta (β)	None	Increases by 1

The stability of an atom seems to be related to binding energy. The binding energy is the amount of energy released when a nucleus is formed from its component particles. If you add the mass of the components and compare this sum to the actual mass of the nucleus formed, there will be a small difference in these figures. This difference in mass can be converted to its energy equivalent using Einstein's equation, $E = mc^2$, where E is the energy, m is the mass, and c is the velocity of light. It is this energy that is called the binding energy.

It has been found that the lightest and heaviest elements have the smallest binding energy per nuclear particle and thus are less stable than elements with intermediate atomic masses, which have the greatest binding energy.

The relationship of even-odd number of protons to the number of neutrons affects the stability of a nucleus. Many stable nuclei have even numbers of protons and neutrons; stability is less frequent in nuclei that have even numbers of protons and odd numbers of neutrons, or vice versa. Only a few stable nuclei are known that have odd numbers of protons and neutrons.

Nuclear Energy

Since Einstein predicted that matter could be converted to energy over a half-century ago, scientists have tried to unlock this energy source. This prediction was verified in 1932 by Cockcroft and Walton, who produced small quantities of helium and a tremendous amount of energy from the reaction

$$^7_3\text{Li} + {}^1_1\text{H} \rightarrow 2\,{}^4_2\text{He} + \text{energy}$$

In fact, the energy released was almost exactly the amount calculated from Einstein's equation.

In 1942, Fermi and his coworkers discovered a sustained chain reaction of fission could be controlled to produce large quantities of energy. This led to the development of the nuclear fission bomb, which brought World War II to an end and initiated the nuclear arms race.

Conditions for fission may be described as follows. When fissionable material, such as ^{235}U, is bombarded with a "slow" neutron, fission occurs, giving off different fission products. An example of such a reaction is shown in Fig. 38.

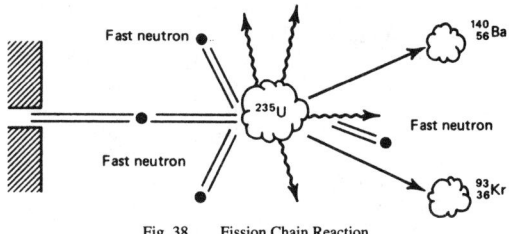

Fig. 38   Fission Chain Reaction

As long as one of the released neutrons produces another reaction, the chain reaction will continue. If each fission starts more than one, the reaction becomes tremendously powerful in a very short time. This occurs in the atomic bomb.

To obtain the neutron "trigger" for this reaction, neutrons must be slowed so that they do not pass through the nucleus without effect. This "slowing down" or moderating is best done by letting fast neutrons collide with many relatively light atoms, such as hydrogen, deuterium, and carbon. Graphite, paraffin, ordinary water, and "heavy water" (containing deuterium instead of ordinary hydrogen) are all suitable moderators.

Nuclear fission can be made to occur in an uncontrolled explosion or in a controlled nuclear reactor. In both cases enough fissionable material must be present so that once the reaction starts, it can at least sustain itself. This amount of fissionable material is called the *critical mass*. In the atomic bomb, the number of reactions increases tremendously, whereas in a reactor the rate of fissions is controlled.

The typical nuclear reactor or "pile" is made up of the following kinds of material:

* Fissionable material—sustains the chain reaction
* Moderator—slows fission neutrons
* Control rods (cadmium or boron steel rods)—absorb excess neutrons and control rate of reaction
* Concrete encasement—provides shielding from radiation

Many variations of this basic reactor have been developed as reactors have become more efficient. Many U. S. cities now receive some of their electrical power from a nuclear power station.

Nucleus *See* **Atomic structure.**

 **Organic chemistry**   Organic chemistry may be defined simply as the chemistry of the compounds of carbon. Since Friedrick Wöhler synthesized urea in 1828, chemists have synthesized thousands of carbon compounds in areas of dyes, plastics, textile fibers, medicines and drugs. The number of organic compounds has been estimated in the neighborhood of a million and constantly increasing.

The carbon atom (atomic number 6) has four electrons in its outermost shell, which show a tendency to be shared (electronegativity of 2.5) in covalent bonds. By this means, carbon bonds to other carbons, hydrogens, halogens, oxygen, and other elements to form the many compounds of organic chemistry.

Hydrocarbons
A hydrocarbon, as the name implies, is a compound containing only carbon and hydrogen in its structure. The simplest hydrocarbon is methane, CH_4. This type of formula, which shows the kinds of atoms and their respective numbers, is called an empirical formula. In organic chemistry this is not sufficient to identify the compound it is used to represent. A good example of this is C_2H_6O. This formula could denote a structure called either an ether or an ethyl alcohol. For this reason, a structural formula is used to indicate how the atoms are

arranged in the molecule. The ether of C_2H_6O looks like

$$H-\overset{\overset{\displaystyle H}{|}}{\underset{\underset{\displaystyle H}{|}}{C}}-O-\overset{\overset{\displaystyle H}{|}}{\underset{\underset{\displaystyle H}{|}}{C}}-H$$

whereas the ethyl alcohol is represented by the structural formula

$$H-\overset{\overset{\displaystyle H}{|}}{\underset{\underset{\displaystyle H}{|}}{C}}-\overset{\overset{\displaystyle H}{|}}{\underset{\underset{\displaystyle H}{|}}{C}}-OH$$

For this reason, then, structural formulas are more often used in organic chemistry. Methane could be

$$H-\overset{\overset{\displaystyle H}{|}}{\underset{\underset{\displaystyle H}{|}}{C}}-H$$

Alkanes
Methane is the first member of a hydrocarbon series called the alkanes (or paraffin series). The general formula for this series is C_nH_{2n+2} where n is the number of carbons in the molecule. The following table provides some essential information about this series. Since many of the other organic structures use the stem of these alkane names, you should learn these names and structures well.

Notice that, as the number of carbons in the chain increases, the boiling point also increases. The first four alkanes listed are gases at room temperature; the subsequent compounds are liquid, becoming more viscous with increasing length of the chain.

Since the chain is increased by a carbon and two hydrogens in each subsequent molecule, the alkane series is referred to as an homologous series.

The alkanes are found in petroleum and natural gas. They are usually extracted by fractional distillation, which separates the compounds by varying the temperature so that each vaporizes at its respective boiling point. Methane, which forms 90% of natural gas, can also be prepared in the laboratory by heating soda lime (containing NaOH) with sodium acetate:

$$NaC_2H_3O_2 + NaOH \rightarrow CH_4\uparrow + Na_2CO_3$$

When the alkanes are burned with sufficient air, the compounds formed are CO_2 and H_2O, for example,

$$2C_2H_6 + 7O_2 \rightarrow CO_2\uparrow + 6H_2O\uparrow$$

The alkanes can be reacted with halogens so that hydrogens are replaced by a halogen atom:

$$H-\overset{\overset{\displaystyle H}{|}}{\underset{\underset{\displaystyle H}{|}}{C}}-H + Br_2 \longrightarrow H-\overset{\overset{\displaystyle H}{|}}{\underset{\underset{\displaystyle H}{|}}{C}}-Br + HBr$$

Some common substitution compounds of methane are

$$H-\overset{\overset{\displaystyle H}{|}}{\underset{\underset{\displaystyle H}{|}}{C}}-Cl \qquad Cl-\overset{\overset{\displaystyle H}{|}}{\underset{\underset{\displaystyle Cl}{|}}{C}}-Cl \qquad Cl-\overset{\overset{\displaystyle Cl}{|}}{\underset{\underset{\displaystyle Cl}{|}}{C}}-Cl$$

| methyl chloride | chloroform | carbon tetrachloride |
| monochloromethane | trichloromethane | tetrachloromethane |

Alkanes

Name	Formula	Number of Structural Isomers	Structure	Boiling Point (°C)
Methane	CH_4	1	$H-\overset{\displaystyle H}{\underset{\displaystyle H}{C}}-H$	−162
Ethane	C_2H_6	1	$H-\overset{H}{\underset{H}{C}}-\overset{H}{\underset{H}{C}}-H$	−89
Propane	C_3H_8	1	$H-\overset{H}{\underset{H}{C}}-\overset{H}{\underset{H}{C}}-\overset{H}{\underset{H}{C}}-H$	−42
n-Butane	C_4H_{10}	2	$H-\overset{H}{\underset{H}{C}}-\overset{H}{\underset{H}{C}}-\overset{H}{\underset{H}{C}}-\overset{H}{\underset{H}{C}}-H$	0
n-Pentane	C_5H_{12}	3	$H-\overset{H}{\underset{H}{C}}-\overset{H}{\underset{H}{C}}-\overset{H}{\underset{H}{C}}-\overset{H}{\underset{H}{C}}-\overset{H}{\underset{H}{C}}-H$	36
n-Hexane	C_6H_{14}	5	$CH_3-CH_2-CH_2-CH_2-CH_2-CH_3$	69
n-Heptane	C_7H_{16}	9	$CH_3-CH_2-CH_2-CH_2-CH_2-CH_2-CH_3$	98
n-Octane	C_8H_{18}	18	$CH_3-CH_2-CH_2-CH_2-CH_2-CH_2-CH_2-CH_3$	126
n-Nonane	C_9H_{20}	35	$CH_3-CH_2-CH_2-CH_2-CH_2-CH_2-CH_2-CH_2-CH_3$	151
n-Decane	$C_{10}H_{22}$	75	$CH_3-CH_2-CH_2-CH_2-CH_2-CH_2-CH_2-CH_2-CH_2-CH_3$	174

When an alkane hydrocarbon has an end hydrogen removed, it is referred to as an alkyl radical. The respective name of each is the alkane name with the -ane replaced by -yl:

Alkane	Alkyl Radical	Compound
methane	methyl	methyl bromide
$H-\overset{H}{\underset{H}{C}}-H$	$H-\overset{H}{\underset{H}{C}}-$	$H-\overset{H}{\underset{H}{C}}-Br$
butane	butyl	butyl chloride
$H-\overset{H}{\underset{H}{C}}-\overset{H}{\underset{H}{C}}-\overset{H}{\underset{H}{C}}-\overset{H}{\underset{H}{C}}-H$	$H-\overset{H}{\underset{H}{C}}-\overset{H}{\underset{H}{C}}-\overset{H}{\underset{H}{C}}-\overset{H}{\underset{H}{C}}-$	$H-\overset{H}{\underset{H}{C}}-\overset{H}{\underset{H}{C}}-\overset{H}{\underset{H}{C}}-\overset{H}{\underset{H}{C}}-Cl$

One method of naming a substitution product is to use the alkyl radical name for the respective chain and the halide as shown above.

Another method, called the IUPAC method, uses a prefix of the name and number of the substitution group and a digit that denotes the carbon atom to which the group is attached along with the alkane name, for example,

$H-\overset{H}{\underset{H}{C}}-\overset{H}{\underset{H}{C}}-\overset{H}{\underset{H}{C}}-Cl$ 　　 $H-\overset{H}{\underset{H}{C}}-\overset{Cl}{\underset{H}{C}}-\overset{H}{\underset{H}{C}}-H$

1-monochloropropane 　　 2-monochloropropane

$H-\overset{H}{\underset{H}{C}}-\overset{H}{\underset{H}{C}}-\overset{H}{\underset{H}{C}}-\overset{H}{\underset{Br}{C}}-\overset{H}{\underset{H}{C}}-H$

2-monobromopentane

(Notice that you number the carbons from the end of the chain that gives you the smallest digit or sum of digits).

Starting with propane in the alkane series, it is possible to get a ring form (cycloalkane) by attaching the two chain ends. This reduces the number of hydrogens by two.

cyclopropane

Since all the alkane series are made up of single covalent bonds, this series and all such structures are said to be saturated. If the hydrocarbon molecule contains double or triple covalent bonds, it is referred to as unsaturated.

Alkene Series (Unsaturated)
The alkene series has a double covalent bond between two adjacent carbon atoms. The general formula of this series is C_nH_{2n}. In naming these compounds the suffix of the alkane is replaced with the suffix -ene, for example,

$H-\overset{H}{C}=\overset{H}{C}-H$

ethene (common name: ethylene)

$H-\overset{H}{C}=\overset{H}{C}-\overset{H}{\underset{H}{C}}-H$

propene (common name: propylene)

The bonding is more complex in the double covalent bond than in the single bonds in the molecule. Using the orbital pictures of the atom, we can show this as

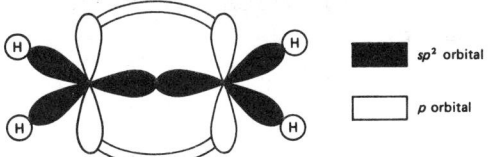

■	*sp²* orbital
☐	*p* orbital

The two *p* lobes attached above and below constitute *one* bond called a pi (π) bond. The *sp²* orbital bonds between the carbons and with each hydrogen are referred to as sigma (σ) bonds.

Alkyne Series (Unsaturated)
The alkyne series has a triple covalent bond between two adjacent carbons. The general formula of this series is C_nH_{2n-2}. In naming these compounds, the alkane suffix is replaced with a *-yne* suffix, for example,

$$H - C \equiv C - H$$

ethyne (common name acetylene)

$$H-C\equiv C-\overset{\overset{\displaystyle H}{|}}{\underset{\underset{\displaystyle H}{|}}{C}}-H$$

propyne

The orbital structure can be shown as:

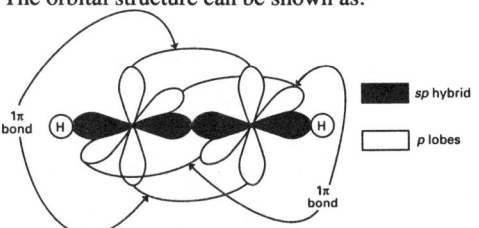

■	*sp* hybrid
☐	*p* lobes

The bonds formed by the *p* orbitals and the one bond between the *sp* orbitals make up the triple bond. *See* **Pi bonds and sigma bonds**.

Additions to Alkenes and Alkynes
Unsaturated alkenes and alkynes can add to their structures by breaking the double or triple bond present. For example,

$$H-\overset{\overset{\displaystyle H}{|}}{C}=\overset{\overset{\displaystyle H}{|}}{C}-H \ + \ Br_2 \ \longrightarrow \ H-\overset{\overset{\displaystyle H}{|}}{\underset{\underset{\displaystyle H}{|}}{C}}-\overset{\overset{\displaystyle Br}{|}}{\underset{\underset{\displaystyle H}{|}}{C}}-H$$

1,2-dibromoethane
(ethylene dibromide)

The 1,2- means that on the first and second carbons in the chain, a bromine atom is bonded. 1,1-Dibromoethane would be

$$H-\overset{\overset{\displaystyle Br}{|}}{\underset{\underset{\displaystyle Br}{|}}{C}}-\overset{\overset{\displaystyle H}{|}}{\underset{\underset{\displaystyle H}{|}}{C}}-H$$

An addition to ethyne could be

$$H-C\equiv C-H \ + \ Br_2 \ \longrightarrow \ H-\overset{\overset{\displaystyle Br}{|}}{\underset{\underset{\displaystyle Br}{|}}{C}}-\overset{\overset{\displaystyle Br}{|}}{\underset{\underset{\displaystyle Br}{|}}{C}}-H$$

Alkadienes have two double covalent bonds in each molecule. The *-ene* indicates the double bond, and the *di-* indicates there are two such bonds. The names of this type are also derived from the alkanes so butadiene has four carbons and two double bonds.

$$\underset{H}{\overset{H}{\diagdown}}C=\overset{\overset{\displaystyle H}{|}}{C}-\overset{\overset{\displaystyle H}{|}}{C}=C\underset{\diagdown H}{\overset{\diagup H}{}}$$

(1,3-Butadiene is a more precise name that indicates the double bonds follow the first and third carbons.) This compound is used in making synthetic rubber.

Aromatics
The aromatic compounds are unsaturated ring structures. The simplest compound of the aromatic series is benzene (C_6H_6). The basic formula of this series is C_nH_{2n-6}. The benzene structure is a resonance structure represented as

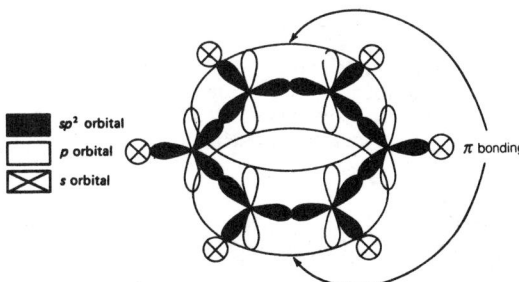

Note: The carbon-carbon bonds are neither single nor double bonds but hybrid bonds. This is called *resonance.*

The orbital structure can be represented as:

■	*sp²* orbital
☐	*p* orbital
⊠	*s* orbital

π bonding

Most of the aromatics have an aroma, thus the name *aromatic.*

Changing Hydrocarbons
■ *Isomerization* is the process of changing the structure of a compound but retaining the same formula. For example, in the chain hydrocarbons, butane is the first compound that can have two different structures or isomers for the same formula.

n-butane   isobutane

This isomerization can be shown by the equation

butane   isobutane

The isomers have different properties, both physical and chemical, from those of the normal structure.

■ *Cracking* is the process by which long chains of hydrocarbons may be made into more useful smaller molecules. This is done under proper conditions of temperature and pressure and often in the presence of a catalyst. For example,

$$C_{16}H_{34} \rightarrow C_8H_{18} + C_8H_{16}$$

hexadecane   octane   octene

Notice that the products formed by cracking a saturated hydrocarbon of the alkanes are a saturated hydrocarbon and an unsaturated alkene.

Alkylation is the combining of a saturated alkane with an unsaturated alkene. For example,

Notice that the product formed by alkylation is a useful chain of hydrocarbon without the previous double bond.

■ *Polymerization* refers to the combination of two or more unsaturated molecules to form a larger chain molecule. For example,

2,4,4-trimethyl-1-pentene

In the product name, 2,4,4-trimethyl-1-pentene, the first three numbers indicate the carbons with the trimethyl (three methyl radicals) attached—one each. The 1 in the middle indicates that the first carbon has the double bond attaching it to the next carbon. In numbering compounds of the alkenes and alkynes, you always number the carbon atom from the end that has the double or triple bond.

■ *Hydrogenation* is the process of adding hydrogens to an unsaturated hydrocarbon in the presence of a suitable catalyst. It is often used to make liquid unsaturated fats into solid saturated fats. For hydrocarbons, for example,

2-methylpropene   2-monomethylpropane

■ *Dehydrogenation* is the removal of hydrogens from a chain molecule in the presence of a catalyst to form an unsaturated molecule. For example,

$$CH_3{-}CH_2{-}CH_2{-}CH_3 \rightarrow$$
$$CH_2{=}CH{-}CH_2{-}CH_3 + H_2$$

butane   1-butene

■ *Aromatization* occurs when hydrocarbons of the alkane series with six or more carbons in the chain are made to form an aromatic hydrocarbon with the loss of hydrogen. This must be done at high temperatures and with a suitable catalyst. For example,

$$CH_3{-}CH_2{-}CH_2{-}CH_2{-}CH_2{-}CH_2{-}CH_3 \rightarrow$$

heptane

toluene

Alcohols

The class of organic compounds in which one or more hydrogen atoms of a hydrocarbon have been replaced by an –OH group.

The –OH group is called the functional group. Methanol is the simplest alcohol. Its structure is

methanol (common name: wood alcohol)

The laboratory preparation of methanol is:

$$CH_3Cl + NaOH \rightarrow NaCl + CH_3OH$$

chloromethane   methanol
(methylchloride)   (methyl alcohol)

For many years methanol was obtained industrially by the destructive distillation of wood. Today it is made by the hydrogenation of oxides of carbon in the presence of a suitable catalyst.

$$CO + 2H_2 \xrightarrow[\substack{300{-}400\,°C \\ 200\ atm}]{catalyst} CH_3OH$$

Ethanol is the best known and most used alcohol. Its structure is

$$H-\underset{\underset{H}{|}}{\overset{\overset{H}{|}}{C}}-\underset{\underset{H}{|}}{\overset{\overset{H}{|}}{C}}-OH$$

ethanol (common names: ethyl alcohol, grain alcohol)

(Notice that the alcohol names are derived from the alkanes by replacing the *-e* ending with *-ol.*) *See also* **Alcohols**.

Aldehydes

The functional group of an aldehyde is

$$-C\overset{\overset{\displaystyle O}{\|}}{\underset{\diagdown}{}}_{H}$$

the formyl group. The general formula is RCHO, where R represents a hydrocarbon radical.

Aldehydes can be prepared by the oxidation of an alcohol. This can be done by inserting a hot copper wire into the alcohol. A typical reaction is

$$H-\overset{\overset{H}{|}}{\underset{\underset{H}{|}}{C}}-OH \overset{\text{mild oxidizing}}{\underset{\text{agent}}{+ [O]}} \longrightarrow \left[H-\overset{\overset{H}{|}}{\underset{\underset{OH}{|}}{C}}-OH \right] \longrightarrow H-C\overset{\overset{O}{\|}}{\underset{\diagdown}{}}_{H} + H_2O$$

methanol
(methyl alcohol)

methanal
(formaldehyde)

The middle structure is an intermediate structure, but since two hydroxyl groups do not stay attached to the same carbon, it changes to the aldehyde by a water molecule "breaking away."

The aldehyde name is derived from the alcohol name by dropping the *-ol* and adding *-al.*

Ethanol forms ethanal (acetaldehyde) in the same manner.

Organic Acids

The functional group of an organic acid is

$$-C\overset{\overset{\displaystyle O}{\|}}{\underset{\diagdown}{}}_{OH}$$

the carboxyl group. The general formula is R—COOH.

Organic acids can be prepared by the mild oxidation of an aldehyde. The simplest acid is methanoic acid, which is present in ants, bees and other insects. A typical reaction is

$$H-C\overset{\overset{O}{\|}}{\underset{\diagdown}{}}_{H} + [O] \longrightarrow H-C\overset{\overset{O}{\|}}{\underset{\diagdown}{}}_{OH}$$

methanal
(formaldehyde)

methanoic acid
(formic acid)

Notice that the name is derived from the alkane stem by adding *-oic.*

Ethanal can be oxidized to ethanoic acid:

$$H-\overset{\overset{H}{|}}{\underset{\underset{H}{|}}{C}}-C\overset{\overset{O}{\|}}{\underset{\diagdown}{}}_{H} + [O] \longrightarrow H-\overset{\overset{H}{|}}{\underset{\underset{H}{|}}{C}}-C\overset{\overset{O}{\|}}{\underset{\diagdown}{}}_{OH}$$

ethanal

ethanoic acid
(acetic acid)

Acetic acid, as ethanoic acid is commonly called, is a mild acid that, in the concentrated form, is called glacial acetic acid. Glacial acetic is used in many industrial processes, such as making cellulose acetate. Vinegar is a 4% to 8% solution of acetic acid that can be made by fermenting alcohol.

$$C_2H_5OH + O_2 \rightarrow CH_3COOH + H_2O$$

ethanol

ethanoic acid
(acetic acid)

One of the aromatic acids is benzoic acid, with a carboxyl group replacing one of the hydrogens:

$$\text{benzoic acid}$$

Summary of Oxygen Derivatives

functional group

$$R-H \rightarrow R-Cl \rightarrow R-OH \rightarrow R^1CHO \rightarrow R^1-COOH$$

hydrocarbon　chlorine　alcohol　aldehyde　acid
substitution
product

(ending *-ol*)　(ending *-al*)　(ending *-oic*)

For more organic structures, *see* **Esters**; **Ethers**; **Ketones**.

Amines and Amino Acids

Amines

The radical NH_2^- is called the amide ion or the amino group. Under the proper conditions, this ion can replace a hydrogen in a hydrocarbon compound. The resulting compound is called an amine; for example,

$$H-\overset{\overset{H}{|}}{\underset{\underset{H}{|}}{C}}-NH_2 \quad \text{or}$$

methyl amine

aniline

Amino Acids

Amino acids are organic acids that contain one or more amino groups. The simplest uncombined amino acid is glycine, or amino acetic acid, NH_2CH_2-COOH. More than 20 amino acids are known, about half of which must be supplied in the human diet because they are needed to make up the body proteins.

Oxidation-reduction reactions *See* **Electrochemical reactions**.

P

Percentage composition *See* **Formulas, writing and calculations of.**
Periodic table

History

The history of the development of a systematic pattern for the elements includes the work of a number of scientists, such as John Newlands, who in 1863 proposed the idea of repeating octaves of properties.

Dmitri Ivanovitch Mendeleyev in 1869 proposed a table containing seventeen columns and is usually given credit for the first periodic table since he arranged elements in groups according to their atomic weights and properties. In a revision of his table in 1871, he rearranged some elements and proposed a table of eight columns, obtained by splitting each of the long periods into a period of seven elements, an eighth group containing the three central elements (such as Fe, Co, Ni), and a second period of seven elements. The first and second periods of seven were later distinguished by use of the letters a and b attached to the group symbols, which are Roman numerals. This nomenclature of periods (Ia, IIa, and so on) appears slightly revised in the present periodic tables, even in the extended form. It is interesting to note that Lothar Meyer proposed a similar arrangement about the same time.

Mendeleyev's table had the elements arranged by atomic weights with recurring properties in a periodic manner. Where atomic weight placement disagreed with the properties that should occur in a particular spot in the table, he gave preference to the element with the correct properties. He even predicted elements for places that were not yet occupied in the table. These predictions proved to be amazingly accurate.

Periodic Law

Moseley stated, after his work with X-ray spectra in the early 1900s, that the properties of elements are periodic functions of their atomic numbers, thus changing the basis of the periodic law from atomic mass to atomic number. This is the present statement of the periodic law.

The Table

The horizontal rows of the periodic chart are called periods or rows. There are seven periods, each of which begins with an atom having only one valence electron and ends with a complete outer shell structure of an inert gas. The first three periods are short periods consisting of two, eight, and eight elements respectively. Periods 4 and 5 are long periods of 18 elements each; period 6 has 32 elements, and period 7 is incomplete with only 23 elements, most of which are radioactive and do not occur in nature.

The vertical columns of the periodic chart are called groups or families. The elements in a group exhibit similar or related properties. The older Roman numeral group number gives an indication of the number of electrons probably found in the outer shell of the atom and thus an indication of one of its possible valence numbers.

In newer periodic charts the vertical groups are merely numbered from 1 to 18 as shown in Exhibit 3.12. A number of charts still carry both designations.

Properties Related to the Periodic Chart

Metals are found on the left of the chart, with the most active metal in the lower left corner. Nonmetals are found on the right side, with the most active nonmetal in the upper right-hand corner of the chart. The noble or inert gases are on the far right. Since the most active metals react with water to form bases, the group I metals are called alkali metals. As you proceed to the right, the base-forming property decreases and the acid forming properties increase. The metals in the first two rows are the light metals, and those in the lower rows are called heavy metals.

EXHIBIT 3.12
Periodic Chart, Showing Properties

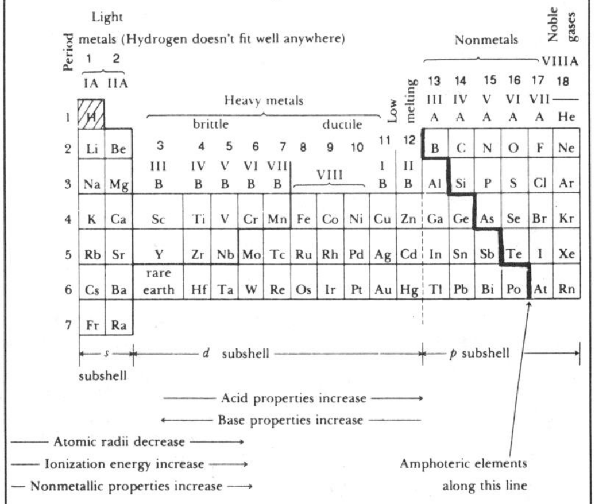

The elements found along the dark line in the periodic chart are called metalloids. They are elements that have certain characteristics of metals and other characteristics of nonmetals. Some examples of metalloids are boron, silicon, arsenic, and tellurium. Study Exhibit 3.12 because it summarizes many of these properties.

A complete periodic table is in Exhibit 3.15 at the back of this section.

Atomic Radii in Periods

The atomic radius is one-half of the distance between the nuclei in a molecule that consists of identical atoms. Since each period increases the number of electrons in the outer shell as you go from left to right in that period, the corresponding increase in the nuclear charge due to the additional protons pulls the electrons more tightly around the nucleus. This attraction more than balances the repulsion between the added electrons and the other electrons, and the radius is generally reduced. An inert gas has a slight increase because of the electron repulsion in the filled outer shell.

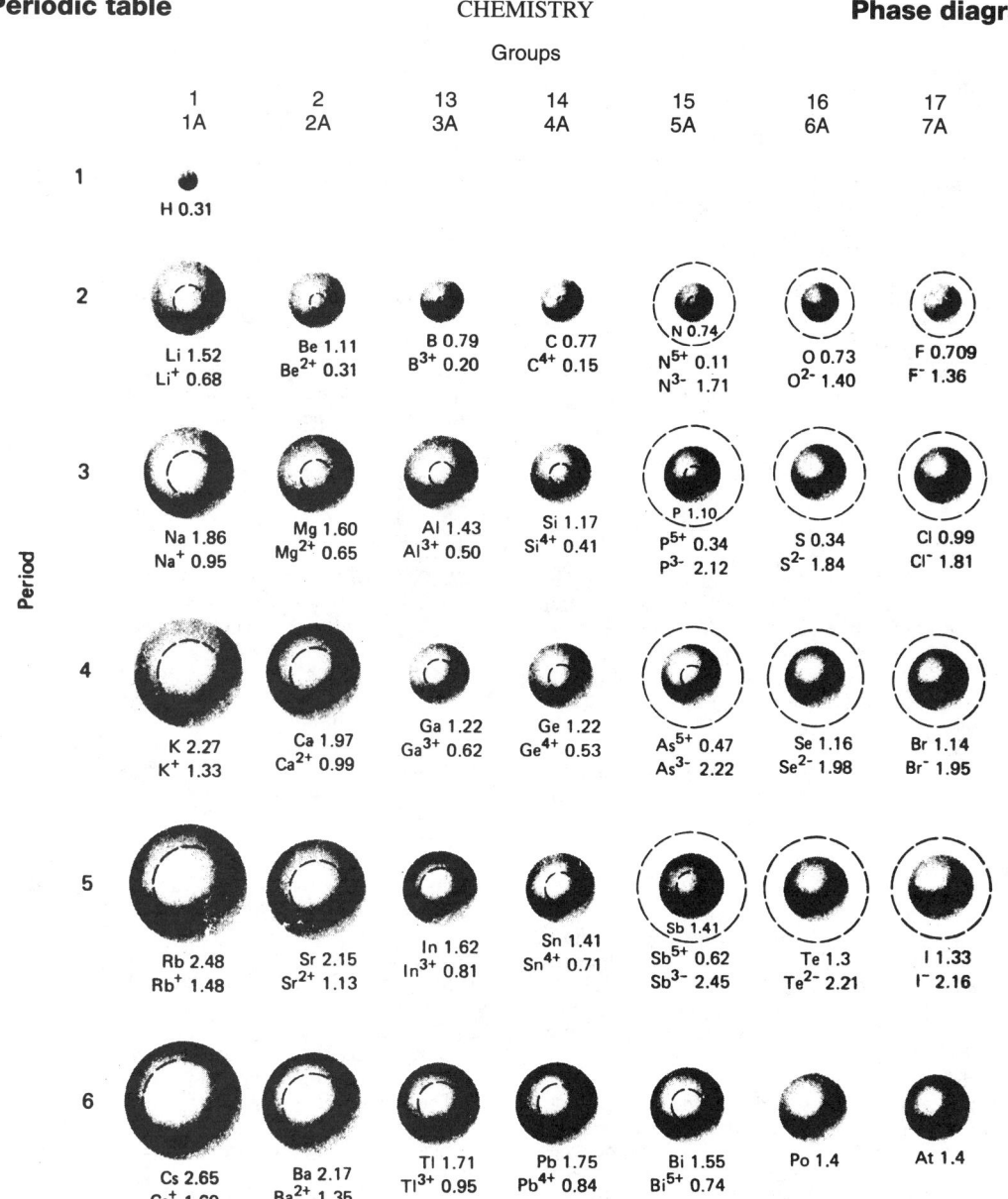

Fig. 39   Representation of Relative Atomic and Ionic Radii (dashed lines are ionic representations)

Atomic Radii in Groups

For a group of elements, the atoms of each successive member have another outer shell in the electron configuration and the electrons there are held less tightly by the nucleus. This is so because of their increased distance from the nuclear positive charge and the shielding of this positive charge by all the intermediate electrons. Therefore the atomic radius increases down a group (*see* Fig. 39).

Ionic Radius Compared to Atomic Radius

Metals tend to lose electrons in forming ions. With this loss of negative charge, the positive nuclear charge pulls in the remaining electrons closer and thus reduces the ionic radius below that of the atomic radius.

Nonmetals tend to gain electrons in forming ions. With this added negative charge, which increases the inner electron repulsion, the ionic radius is increased beyond the atomic radius. (*See* Fig. 39.)

See also **Electronegativity**; **Ionization energy**.

pH   *See* **Acids and bases**.

Phase diagrams   The simplest way to discuss a phase diagram is to use an example, such as Fig. 40.

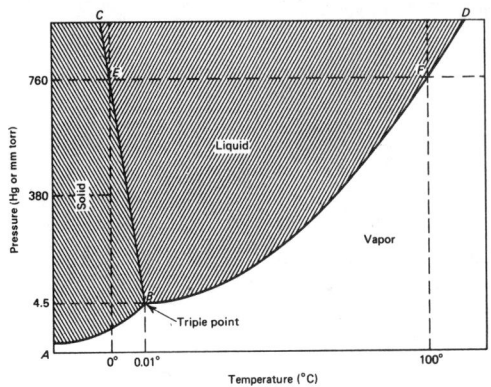

Fig. 40   Partial Phase Diagram for Water
(distorted somewhat to distinguish the triple point from the freezing point)

A phase diagram ties together the effects of temperature and also pressure on the phase changes of a substance. In Fig. 40 the line BD is essentially the vapor-pressure curve for the liquid phase. Notice that at 760 torr (the pressure for 1 atm) the water will boil (change to the vapor phase) at 100°C (point F). However, if the pressure is raised, the boiling point temperature increases, and if the pressure is less than 760 torr, the boiling point decreases along the BD curve down to point B.

At 0°C the freezing point of water is found along the line BC at point E for pressure at 1 atm or 760 torr. Again, this point is affected by pressure along the line BC so that, if pressure is decreased, the freezing point is slightly higher up to point B, or 0.01°C.

Point B represents the point at which the solid, liquid, and vapor phases may all exist at equilibrium. This point is known as the triple point. It is the only temperature and pressure at which three phases of a pure substance can exist in equilibrium with one another in a system containing only the pure substance.

Photons   *See* **Atomic structure**.

Pi bonds and sigma bonds   When bonding occurs between s and p orbitals, each bond is identified by a special term. A *sigma bond* is a bond between s orbitals, or an s orbital and another orbital, such as a p orbital. It includes bonding between hybrids of s orbitals, such as sp, sp^2, and sp^3.

In the methane molecule, the sp^3 orbitals are each bonded to hydrogen atoms. These are sigma bonds.

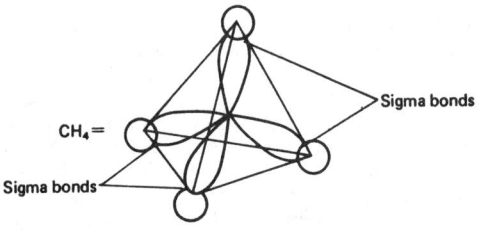

When two p orbitals share electrons in a covalent bond, this is called a *pi bond*. For example,

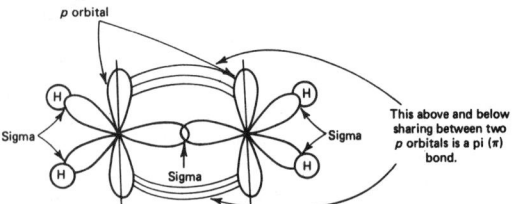

Polar molecules   *See* **Atomic structure**.
p orbitals   *See* **Atomic structure**; **Hybridization and the VSEPR model**.
Proton   A positively charged, subatomic particle usually found in the nucleus of an atom. *See* **Atomic structure** for further explanation.

Quantum number   *See* **Atomic structure**.

Radioactivity   *See* **Nucleonics**.
Reaction rates   The measurement of reaction rate is based on the rate of appearance of a product or disappearance of a reactant. It is usually expressed in terms of a change in concentration of one of the participants per unit time.

Experiments have shown that for most reactions the concentrations of all participants change most rapidly at the beginning of the reaction; that is, the concentration of the product shows the greatest rate of increase, and the concentrations of the reactants the highest rate of decrease, at this point. This means that the rate of a reaction changes with time. Therefore a rate must be identified with a specific time.

Factors Affecting Reaction Rates
Five important factors control the rates of chemical reactions:
1. The nature of the reactants. Some elements and compounds, because of the bonds broken or formed, react more rapidly with each other.
2. The surface area exposed. Since most reactions depend on the reactants coming into contact, the surface exposed proportionally affects the rate of the reaction.
3. The concentrations. The reaction rate is usually proportional to the concentrations of the reactants.
4. The temperature. A temperature increase of 10°C above room temperature usually causes the reaction rate to double or triple.
5. The catalyst. Catalysts can either speed or slow the rate of a reaction. For more information, *see* **Catalyst**.

Collision Theory of Reaction Rates
This theory makes the assumption that, for a reaction to occur, there must be collisions between the reacting species. This means that the rate of reaction depends on two factors: the number of collisions per unit time and the fraction of these collisions that are successful because enough energy is involved.

There is a definite relationship between the concentrations of the reactants and the number of collisions. Graphically, the reaction

$$A + B \rightarrow AB$$

can be examined as the concentration is changed.

 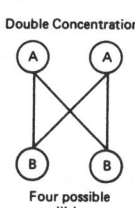 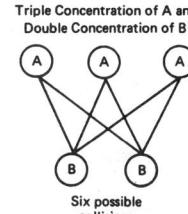

This shows that the number of collisions, and consequently the rate of reaction, are proportional to the product of the concentrations. Simply stated, then, the rate of the reaction is directly proportional to the concentrations.

Reaction Rate Law

The relationship between the rate of a reaction and the masses (expressed as concentrations) of the reacting substances is summarized in the law of mass action. This states that the rate of a chemical reaction is proportional to the product of the concentrations of the reactants. For a general reaction between A and B, represented by

$$aA + bB \rightarrow \cdots$$

the rate law expression is

$r \propto [A]^a[B]^b$ (the brackets represent "concentration of")

or, inserting a constant of proportionality that mathematically changes the expression to an equality, we have

$$r = k[A]^a[B]^b$$

Here k is called the specific rate constant for the reaction at the temperature of the reaction.

The exponents a and b may be added to give the total reaction order. For example,

$$H_2(g) + I_2(g) \rightarrow 2HI(g)$$
$$r = k[H_2]^1[I_2]^1$$

The sum of the exponents is $1 + 1 = 2$, and therefore we have a second-order reaction.

Reactions, types of The many kinds of reactions you may encounter can be classified into four basic types: combination, decomposition, single replacement, and double replacement.

The first type, *combination*, can also be called *synthesis*. This means the formation of a compound from the union of its elements. Some examples of this type are

$$Zn + S \rightarrow ZnS$$
$$2H_2 + O_2 \rightarrow 2H_2O$$
$$C + O_2 \rightarrow CO_2$$

The second type of reaction, *decomposition*, can also be referred to as *analysis*. This means the breakdown of a compound to release its components as individual elements or compound. Some examples of this type are

$$2H_2O \rightarrow 2H_2 + O_2 \quad \text{(electrolysis of water)}$$
$$C_{12}H_{22}O_{11} \rightarrow +12C + 11H_2O$$
$$2HgO \rightarrow 2Hg + O_2$$

The third type is called *single replacement* or *single displacement*. This type can best be shown by some examples in which one substance is displacing another. Some examples are

$$Fe + CuSO_4 \rightarrow FeSO_4 + Cu$$
$$Zn + H_2SO_4 \rightarrow ZnSO_4 + H_2\uparrow$$
$$Cu + 2AgNO_3 \rightarrow Cu(NO_3)_2 + 2Ag$$

The last type of reaction is called *double replacement* or *double displacement* because there is an actual exchange of "partners" to form new compounds. Some examples of this are

$$AgNO_3 + NaCl \rightarrow AgCl + NaNO_3$$
$$H_2SO_4 + 2NaOH \rightarrow Na_2SO_4 + 2H_2O$$
$$\text{(neutralization)}$$
$$CaCO_3 + 2HCl \rightarrow H_2CO_3 + CaCl_2$$
$$\qquad \qquad \downarrow \text{(unstable)}$$
$$\qquad \qquad H_2O + CO_2\uparrow$$

Predicting Reactions

One of the most important topics in chemistry is the understanding of why reactions take place. Taking each of the above types of reactions, let us see how a prediction can be made concerning how the reaction gets the driving force to make it occur.

Combination

The best source of information to predict a chemical combination is the heat of formation table. (*See* **Table E** of **Exhibit 3.13**, page 3-64). A heat of formation table gives the number of calories evolved or absorbed when a mole (gram-formula mass) of that compound is formed by the direct union of its elements. In this book a positive number indicates heat is absorbed and a negative number indicates that heat is evolved. It makes some difference whether the compounds formed are in the solid, liquid, or gaseous state. Unless otherwise indicated (g = gas; l = liquid), the compounds are in the solid state. The values given are in kilocalories (1 kilocalorie is equal to 1000 calories). The amount of heat needed to raise the temperature of 1 gram of water 1 degree on the Celsius scale is 1 calorie. The symbol ΔH is used to indicate the heat of formation. *See* **Endothermic reaction versus exothermic reaction**.

If the heat of formation is a large number preceded by a minus sign, the combination is likely to occur spontaneously and the reaction is *exothermic*. If, on the other hand, the number is small and a negative or a positive number, heat will be needed to get the reaction to go at any noticeable rate. For example,

$$Zn + S \rightarrow ZnS + 48.5 \, kcal \qquad \Delta H = -48.5 \, kcal$$

This means that 1 mole of zinc (65 grams) reacts with 1 mole of sulfur (32 grams) to form 1 mole of zinc sulfide (97 grams) and releases 48.5 kilocalories of heat.

Similarly,

$$Mg + \tfrac{1}{2}O_2 \rightarrow MgO + 143.84 \text{ kcal}$$
$$\Delta H = -143.84 \text{ kcal}$$

indicates that the formation of 1 mole of magnesium oxide requires 1 mole of magnesium and ½ mole of oxygen with the release of 143.84 kilocalories of heat. Notice the use of the fractional coefficient for oxygen. If the equation had been written with the usual whole-number coefficients, 2 moles of magnesium oxide would have been released:

$$2Mg + O_2 \rightarrow 2MgO + 2(+143.84) \text{ kcal}$$

Since, by definition, the heat of formation is given for the formation of 1 *mole*, this thermal equation shows 2 × (−143.84) kcal released.

Another example is

$$H_2(g) + \tfrac{1}{2}O_2(g) \rightarrow H_2O(l) + 68.32 \text{ kcal}$$
$$\Delta H = -68.32 \text{ kcal}$$

In combustion reactions the heat evolved when 1 mole of a substance is completely oxidized is called the *heat of combustion* of the substance. So, in the equation

$$C(g) + O_2(g) \rightarrow CO_2(g) + 94.05 \text{ kcal}$$
$$\Delta H = -94.05 \text{ kcal}$$

the ΔH is the heat of combustion of carbon. Because the energy of a system is conserved during chemical activity, this same equation could be arrived at by adding the following equations:

$$C(s) \quad + \tfrac{1}{2}O_2(g) \rightarrow CO(g) \qquad \Delta H = -26.41 \text{ kcal}$$
$$CO(g) + \tfrac{1}{2}O_2(g) \rightarrow CO_2(g) \qquad \Delta H = -67.64 \text{ kcal}$$
$$\overline{C(s) \quad + \quad O_2(g) \rightarrow CO_2(g) \qquad \Delta H = -94.05 \text{ kcal}}$$

Decomposition

The prediction of decomposition reactions uses the same source of information, the heat of formation table. If the heat of formation is a high exothermic (ΔH is negative) value, the compound will be difficult to decompose since this same quantity of energy must be returned to the compound. A low heat of formation indicates decomposition would not be difficult such as the decomposition of mercuric oxide with $\Delta H = -21.68$ kcal/mole:

$$2HgO \rightarrow 2Hg + O_2 \qquad \text{(Priestley's method of preparation)}$$

A high positive heat of formation indicates extreme instability of a compound, and it can explosively decompose.

Single Replacement

A prediction of the feasibility of this type of reaction can be based on a comparison of the heat formation values of the original compound and of the compound that is formed. For example, in a reaction of zinc with hydrochloric acid, 2 moles of HCl have $\Delta H = 2 \times -22.06$ kcal and the zinc chloride has $\Delta H = -99.40$.

$$Zn + 2HCl \rightarrow ZnCl_2 + H_2\uparrow$$

(*Note:* $\Delta H = 0$ for elements.)

$$2 \times -22.06$$
$$-44.12 \text{ kcal} \neq -99.40 \text{ kcal}$$

This replacement leaves an excess of 55.28 kcal of heat given off, so the reaction would occur.

In this next example, $-220.5 - (-184.0) = -36.5$ excess kilocalories to be given off as the reaction occurs:

$$Fe + CuSO_4 \rightarrow FeSO_4 + Cu$$
$$-184.0 \text{ kcal} \quad -220.5 \text{ kcal}$$

Another simple way of predicting single replacement reactions is to check the relative positions of the two elements in the electromotive chart (*see* **Exhibit 3.6**, page 3-21). If the element that is to replace the other in the compound is higher on the chart, the reaction will occur. If it is below, there will be no reaction.

Double Replacement

For double replacement reactions to go to completion, that is, proceed until the supply of one of the reactants is exhausted, one of the following conditions must be present: an insoluble precipitate is formed, a nonionizing substance is formed, or a gaseous product is given off.

To predict the formation of an insoluble precipitate, you should have some knowledge of the solubility of compounds. The table below gives some general solubility rules.

Solubilities of Compounds

Soluble	Except
Na⁺	
NH₄⁺ } compounds	
K⁺	
Acetates	
Bicarbonates	
Chlorates	
Chlorides	Ag^+, Hg^+, Pb ($PbCl_2$ soluble in hot water)
Nitrates	
Sulfates	Ba, Ca (slight) Pb

Insoluble	
Carbonates, phosphates	Na, NH₄, K compounds
Sulfides, hydroxides	Na, NH₄, K, Ba, Ca

(A table of solubilities such as **Table C** of **Exhibit 3.13**, page 3-63, could also be used as reference.)

An example of this type of reaction is given in its complete ionic form:

$$(K^+ + Cl^-) + (Ag^+ + NO_3^-) \rightarrow AgCl\downarrow + (K^+ + NO_3^-)$$

The silver ions combine with the chloride ions to form an insoluble precipitate, silver chloride.

In a reaction like this, however:

$$(K^+ + Cl^-) + (Na^+ + NO_3^-) \rightarrow K^+ + NO_3^- + Na^+ + Cl^-$$

a mixture of the ions would be shown in the final solution.

Another reason for a reaction of this type to go to completion is the formation of a nonionizing product, such as water. This weak electrolyte keeps its component ions in molecular form and thus removes the possibility of reversing the reaction. All neutralization reactions are of this type:

$$(H^+ + Cl^-) + (Na^+ + OH^-)$$
$$\rightarrow H_2O + Na^+ + Cl^-$$

This example shows the ions of the reactants, hydrochloric acid and sodium hydroxide, and the non-electrolyte product water with sodium and chloride ions in solution. Since the water does not ionize to any extent, the reverse reaction cannot occur.

The third reason for double displacement to occur is the evolution of a gaseous product. An example of this is calcium carbonate reacting with hydrochloric acid:

$$CaCO_3 + 2HCl \rightarrow CaCl_2 + H_2O + CO_2\uparrow$$

Another example of a compound that evolves a gas in sodium sulfite with an acid:

$$Na_2SO_3 + 2HCl \rightarrow 2NaCl + H_2O + SO_2\uparrow$$

In general, acids with carbonates or sulfites are good examples of this type of equation.

Hydrolysis Reactions

Hydrolysis reactions are the opposite of neutralization reactions. In hydrolysis the salt and water react to form an acid and a base. For example, if sodium chloride is placed in solution, this reaction occurs to some degree:

$$(Na^+ + Cl^-) + H_2O$$
$$\rightarrow (Na^+ + OH^-) + (H^+ + Cl^-)$$

In this hydrolysis reaction the same number of hydrogen ions and of hydroxide ions is released so that the solution is neutral. However, if Na_2CO_3 is dissolved, we have

$$(2Na^+ + CO_3{}^{2-}) + 2H_2O$$
$$\rightarrow (2Na^+ + 2OH^-) + H_2CO_3$$

The H_2CO_3 is written together because it is a slightly ionized acid or, in other words, a weak acid. Since the hydroxide ions are free in the solution, the solution is basic. Notice that this was the salt of a strong base and a weak acid that formed a basic solution. This generalization is true for this type of salt.

If we use the salt of a strong acid and a weak base, the reaction would be

$$(Zn^{2+} + 2Cl^-) + H_2O$$
$$\rightarrow (2H^+ + 2Cl) + Zn(OH)_2$$

In this case the hydroxide ions are held in the weakly ionizing compound and the hydrogen ions are free to make the solution acidic. In general, then, the salt of a strong acid and a weak base forms an acid solution by hydrolysis.

A salt of a weak acid and a weak base forms a neutral solution since neither hydrogen ion nor hydroxide ion will be present in excess.

Redox reactions   *See* **Electrochemical reactions**.
Reduction   *See* **Electrochemical reactions**.
Resonance structures   It is not always possible to represent the bonding structure by either Lewis

dot structure or line drawing because data about the bonding distance and bond strength lie between possible drawing configurations and really indicate a hybrid condition. To represent this, the possible alternatives are drawn with arrows between them. Classic examples are sulfur trioxide and benzene.

Sulfur trioxide resonance structures:

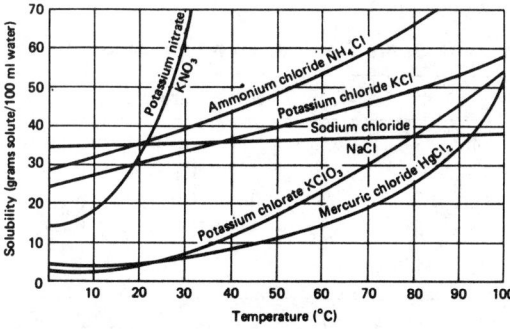

Benzene resonance structures:

Reversible reactions   *See* **Equilibrium, chemical**.

Saturated compounds   Organic compounds that have all bonds as single bonds. *See* **Organic chemistry** for further explanation.

Saturated solution   A solution that holds all the solute it can hold in solution at that temperature and pressure.

Sigma bonds   *See* **Pi bonds and sigma bonds**.

Solute   The substance that is being dispersed into solution. *See* **Solutions** for further explanation.

Solutions   Water is often referred to as the "universal solvent" because of the number of common substances that dissolve in water. When substances are dissolved in water to the extent that no more will dissolve at that temperature, the solution is said to be saturated. The substance dissolved is called the *solute*, and the dissolving medium is called a *solvent*. To give an accurate statement of a substance's solubility, three conditions are mentioned: the amount of solute, the amount of solvent, and the temperature of the solution. Since the solubility varies for each substance and for different temperatures, a student must be acquainted with the use of solubility curves, such as those shown in Fig. 41.

Fig. 41   Solubility Curves

Problem

A solution contains 20 grams of $KClO_3$ in 200 grams of H_2O at 80°C. How many more grams of

$KClO_3$ can be dissolved to saturate the solution at 90°C?

Reading the solubility curve at 90° and up to the graph line for $KClO_3$, you find that 100 grams of H_2O can dissolve 48 grams. So 200 grams could hold (2×48) grams, or 96 grams. Therefore 96 g – 20 g = 76 g $KClO_3$ can be added to the solution.

General Rules of Solubility

- All nitrates, acetates, and chlorates are soluble.
- All common compounds of sodium, potassium, and ammonium are soluble.
- All chlorides are soluble except those of silver, mercury(ious) and lead. (Lead chloride is noticeably soluble in water.)
- All sulfates are soluble except those of lead, barium, strontium, and calcium. (Calcium sulfate is slightly soluble.)
- The normal carbonates, phosphates, silicates, and sulfides are insoluble except those of sodium, potassium, and ammonium.
- All hydroxides are insoluble except those of sodium, potassium, ammonium, calcium, barium, and strontium.

These solubilities are summarized in **Table C** of **Exhibit 3.13**, page 3-63. Some general trends of solubility are shown in the table below. Additional solubility curves for some common compounds are given in **Table B** of **Exhibit 3.13**, page 3-63.

Summary of Types of Solutes and Relationship of Type to Solubility

Generally speaking, solutes are most likely to dissolve in solvents with similar characteristics, that is, ionic and polar solutes dissolve in polar solvents and nonpolar solvents.

It should also be mentioned that polar molecules that do not ionize in aqueous solution (e.g., sugar, alcohol, or glycerol) have molecules as solute particles; polar molecules that partially ionize in aqueous solution (e.g., ammonia or acetic acid) have a mixture of molecules and ions as solute particles; and polar molecules that completely ionize in aqueous solution (e.g., hydrogen chloride and hydrogen iodide) have ions as solute particles.

Water Solutions

Water molecules must overcome the forces that hold molecules or ions together to make them go into solution. This mechanism of the actual process is complex. To make sugar molecules go into solution, the water molecules must overcome the forces holding the solid sugar molecule together. The water molecules cluster around the sugar molecules, pull them off, and disperse, forming the solution.

For an ionic crystal, such as salt, the water molecules orient themselves around the ions (which are charged particles) and again must overcome the forces holding the ions together. Since the water molecule is polar, this orientation around the ion is an attraction of the polar ends of the water molecule. For example,

Once surrounded, the ion is insulated to an extent from other ions in solution because of the dipole property of water. The water molecules that surround the ion differ in number for various ions, and the whole group is called a hydrated ion. This process is called *hydration*, and the number of water molecules associated with a particular ion is called the *hydration number*. This number varies, depending on the size and charge of the ion, but it is often 4 or 6. In general, polar substances and ions dissolve in polar solvents and nonpolar substances such as fats dissolve in nonpolar solvents (e.g., gasoline). The process of going into solution may be exothermic if energy is released in the process, or endothermic if energy from the water is used up to a greater extent than energy is released in freeing the particle.

When two liquids are mixed and they dissolve in each other, they are said to be completely miscible. If they separate and do not mix, they are said to be immiscible.

Some General Trends of Solubility and Factors that Affect the Rate of Solubility

	Temperature Effect	Pressure Effect
Solid	Solubility usually increases with temperature increase	Little effect
Gas	Solubility usually decreases with temperature increase	Solubility varies in direct proportion to the pressure applied to it: *Henry's law*

Factors that Affect the Rate of Solubility	
Pulverizing	increase surface exposed to solvent, thus increasing rate of solubility
Stirring	brings more solvent that is unsaturated into contact with solute
Heating	increases molecular action and gives rise to mixing by convection currents (this heating affects the solubility as well as the rate of solubility)

Two molten metals may be mixed and allowed to cool. This gives a "solid solution" called an alloy.

Expressions of Concentration

There are general terms and very specific terms used to express the concentration of a solution.

The general terms and their definitions are as follows.

Dilute	= small amount of solute is dispersed in the solvent.
Concentrated	= large amount of solute is dissolved in the solvent.
Saturated	= the solution is holding all the solute possible at that temperature. This is not a static condition; that is, some solute particles are exchanging places with some of the undissolved particles, but the total solute in solution remains the same. This is an example of equilibrium.
Unsaturated	= more solute can go into solution at that temperature. The solvent has further capacity to hold more solute.
Supersaturated	= sometimes a saturated solution at a higher temperature can be carefully cooled so that the solute does not get a chance to come out of solution. At a lower temperature, then, the solution will be holding more solute in solution than it should for saturation and is said to be supersaturated. As soon as the solute particles are jarred or a "seed" particle is added to the solution to act as a nucleus, they rapidly come out of the solution, which then reverts to the saturated state.

It is interesting that the words *saturated* and *concentrated* are not synonymous. In fact, it is possible to have a saturated dilute solution when the solute is only slightly soluble and a small amount of it makes the solution saturated, while its concentration remains dilute.

The more specific terms used to describe concentration involve mathematical calculations. The term percentage concentration is based on the percentage of solute in the solution by weight. The general formula is

$$\frac{\text{No. of grams of solute}}{\text{No. of grams of solution}} \times 100\% = \% \text{ concentration}$$

Problem

How many grams of NaCl are needed to prepare 200 grams of a 10% salt solution?

10% of 200 grams = 20 grams of salt

You could also solve the problem using this formula and solving for the unknown quantity:

$$\frac{x \text{ g solute}}{200 \text{ g solution}} \times 100\% = 10\%$$

$$x \text{ g solute} = \frac{10}{100} \times 200 = 20 \text{ g solute}$$

The next two expressions depend on the fact that, if the formula mass of a substance is expressed in grams, it is called a gram-formula mass or 1 mole. Gram-molecular mass can be used in place of gram-formula mass when the substance is really of molecular composition, not ionic like NaCl or NaOH. The definitions and examples are as follows:

■ *Molarity* (abbreviated M) is defined as the number of moles of a substance disolved in 1 liter of solution.

Example

A 1 molar H_2SO_4 solution has 98 grams of H_2SO_4 (its gram-formula mass) in 1 liter of the solution.

■ *Molality* (abbreviated m) is defined as the number of moles of solute dissolved in 1000 grams of solvent.

Example

A 1 molal solution of H_2SO_4 has 98 grams of H_2SO_4 dissolved in 1000 grams of water. This, you will notice, gives you a total volume greater than 1 liter, whereas the molar solution had 98 grams in 1 liter of solution.

The next expression of concentration is used less frequently and depends on knowledge of gram-equivalent mass. This can be defined as the amount of a substance that reacts with or displaces 1 gram of hydrogen or 8 grams of oxygen. A simple method of determining the number of equivalents in a formula is to count the number of hydrogens or find the total positive oxidation numbers since each +1 charge can be replaced by a hydrogen.

Examples

In H_2SO_4 (gram-formula mass = 98 g), there are two hydrogens so the gram-equivalent mass will be

$$\frac{98 \text{ g}}{2} = 49 \text{ g}$$

In Al_2SO_4 (gfm = 150g), there are two aluminums, each of which has a +3 oxidation number, making a total of +6. The gram-equivalent mass will be

$$\frac{150 \text{ g}}{6} = 25 \text{ g}$$

This idea of gram-equivalent mass is used in the definition of the next means of expressing concentration, namely, the normality of a solution.

■ *Normality* (abbreviated N) is defined as the number of gram-equivalent masses of solute in a liter of solution.

CHEMISTRY

Problem

If 49 grams of H_2SO_4 is mixed with enough H_2O to make 500 ml of solution, what is the normality?

Since normality is expressed for a liter, we must double the expression to 98 g of H_2SO_4 in 1000 ml of solution. To find the normality we find the number of gram-equivalents in a liter of solution. So,

$$\frac{98 \text{ g (no. of grams in 1 liter of solution)}}{49 \text{ g (gram-equivalent mass)}}$$

$$= 2 \ N \text{ (normal)}$$

Dilution

Since the expression of molarity gives the quantity of solute per volume of solution, the amount of solute dissolved in a given volume of solution is equal to the product of the concentration times the volume. Hence 0.5 liter of 2 M solution contains

$M \times V =$ amount of solute (in moles)

$$\frac{2 \text{ moles}}{\text{liter}} \times 0.5 \text{ liter}$$

$$= 1 \text{ mole (of solute in 0.5 liter)}$$

Notice that volume units must be identical.

If you dilute a solution with water, the amount or number of moles of solute present remains the same, but the concentration changes. So you can use the expression

before　after

$M_1V_1 \ = \ M_2V_2$

This expression is useful in solving problems involving dilution.

Problem

If you wish to make 1 liter of solution that is 6 M into a 3 M solution, how much water must be added?

$$M_1V_1 = M_2V_2$$

6 $M \times$ 1 liter = 3 $N \times$? liters

Solving this expression, you find that ? liters = 2 liters, which is the total volume of the solution after dilution. This means that 1 liter of water had to be added to the original volume of 1 liter to get a total of 2 liters for the dilute solution volume.

Solvent　The dispersing media of a solution. *See* **Solutions** for further explanation.

s orbitals *See* **Atomic structure.**

Standard conditions of temperature and pressure　In dealing with the gas laws, a student must know what is meant by standard conditions of temperature and pressure (abbreviated STP). The standard pressure is defined as the height of mercury that can be held in an evacuated tube by 1 atmosphere of pressure (14.7 pounds per square inch). This is usually expressed as 760 torr (or mm Hg). Standard temperature is defined as 273 K or absolute (which corresponds to 0° Celsius).

States of matter　The three states in which matter occurs: solid, liquid, and gas. A solid has both a definite size and a definite shape. A liquid has a

definite volume but takes the shape of the container. A gas has neither a definite shape nor a definite volume. These states of matter can often be changed by the addition of heat energy. An example is ice changing to liquid water and finally steam.

Structural formula　*See* **Organic chemistry.**
Subatomic particles　*See* **Atomic structure.**

T　**Temperature scales**　The Celsius or centigrade scale is based on the freezing point of water at 0° and the boiling point of water at 100° under 1 atm of pressure. The corresponding points on the Fahrenheit scale are 32° and 212°. The absolute or Kelvin scale, which measures temperatures in units called kelvins (K), reads 273 K and 373 K, respectively. Note that in Kelvin notation the degree sign is omitted.

You can change from one system to another as shown in Fig. 42 and the formulas below.

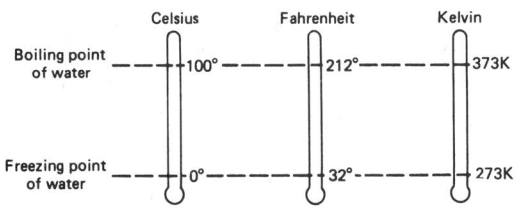

Fig. 42　　Temperature Scales

Conversion formulas:

$$°F = \tfrac{9}{5}°C + 32°$$

$$°C = \tfrac{5}{9} (°F–32°)$$

$$K = °C + 273°$$

Examples

$30°C = ?°F$ 　　$°F = \tfrac{9}{5} (30°) + 32° = 86°$

$68°F = ?°C$ 　　$°C = \tfrac{5}{9} (68° - 32°) = 20°$

$10°C = ?K$ 　　$K = 10 + 273$ 　$= 283$

Titration　*See* **Volumetric analysis.**
Transition elements　*See* **Periodic table.**

U　**Universal gas law**　*See* **Gas laws.**
Unsaturated compounds　Organic compounds that contain one or more double or triple bonds. *See* **Organic chemistry** for further explanation.

Unsaturated solutions　Solutions that do not contain the maximum amount of solute in a given amount of solution at a given temperature.

V　**Valence**　*See* **Atomic structure.**
van der Waals forces　The weak attractive forces between molecules, named for the Dutch physicist Johannes van der Waals. These forces become apparent only when the molecules approach one another closely (usually at low temperatures and high pressure). They are due to the way the positive charges of one molecule attract the negative charges of another molecule because of their distribution at any given instant.

Compounds of the solid state that are bound mainly by this type of attraction have rather soft crystals, are easily deformed, and vaporize easily. Because of the low intermolecular forces, the melting points are low and evaporation takes place so easily that it may occur at room temperature. Examples are iodine crystals and mothballs (paradichlorobenzene and naphthalene).

Vaporization, heat of   The amount of heat needed to convert 1 gram of a substance from the liquid to the gaseous state at standard pressure.

Volumetric analysis   The use of volume measurements to determine the concentrations of "unknown" solutions or solids. Knowledge of the concentrations of solutions and the reactions they take part in are used in these determinations.

Burets

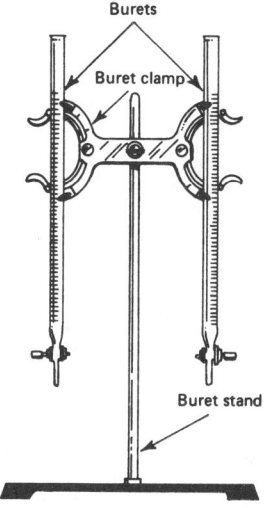

Buret clamp

Buret stand

Fig. 43   Buret Setup for Titration

A common example of a volumetric analysis uses acid-base reactions. If you are given a base of known concentration, say 0.10 M NaOH, and you want to determine the concentration of an HCl solution, you could titrate (*see* Fig. 43) the solutions in the following manner.

First, introduce a measured quantity, 25.0 ml, of the NaOH into a flask by using a pipet or buret. Next, introduce 2 drops of a suitable indicator. Since NaOH and HCl are considered a strong base and a strong acid, respectively, an indicator that changes color in the middle pH range would be appropriate. Litmus solution would be one choice. It is blue in basic solution but changes to red when the solution becomes acidic. Slowly introduce the HCl until the color change occurs. This is called the endpoint.

Suppose 21.5 ml was needed to produce the color change; the reaction that occurred was

$$H^+(aq) + OH^-(aq) \rightarrow H_2O$$

until all the OH^- were neutralized, and then the excess H^+ caused the litmus paper to change color. To solve the question of the concentration of the NaOH, this equation is used:

$$M_{acid} \times V_{acid} = M_{base} \times V_{base}$$

Substituting the known amounts in this equation gives

$$x\, M_{acid} \times 21.5\ \text{mL} = 0.1\ M \times 25.0\ \text{mL}$$
$$x = 0.116\ M$$

Problem 1

Find the concentration of acetic acid in vinegar if 21.6 ml of 0.20 M NaOH is needed to titrate a 25 ml sample of the vinegar.

Using the equation

$$M_{acid} \times V_{acid} = M_{base} \times V_{base}$$

we have

$$x\, M \times 25\ \text{mL} = 0.2 \times 21.6\ \text{mL}$$
$$x = 0.173\ M_{acid}$$

Another type of titration problem involves a solid and a titrated solution.

Problem 2

A solid mixture contains NaOH and NaCl. If a 0.100 g sample of this mixture required 10 ml of 0.100 M HCl to titrate the sample to its endpoint, what is the percentage of NaOH in the sample?

Since

$$\text{Molarity} = \frac{\text{no. of moles}}{\text{liter of solution}}$$

then

$$M \times V = \frac{\text{no. of moles}}{\text{liter of solution}} \times \text{liter of solution}$$
$$= \text{no. of moles}$$

Substituting the HCl information in the equation, we have

$$\frac{0.100\ \text{mole}}{\text{liter of solution}} \times 0.010\ \text{liter of solution}$$
$$= 0.001\ \text{mole}$$

(*Note:* this is 10 mL expressed in terms of a liter.) Since 1 mole of HCl neutralizes 1 mole of NaOH, 0.001 mole of NaOH must be present in the mixture.

$$1\ \text{mole NaOH} = 40.0\ \text{g}$$

So

$$0.001\ \text{mole} \times 40.0\ \text{g/mole} = 0.04\ \text{g NaOH}$$

Therefore 0.04 g of NaOH is in the 0.1 g sample of the solid mixture. The percentage is 0.04 g/0.1 g × 100 = 40%

In the explanations given to this point, the reactions that took place were between monoprotic acids and monobasic bases. This means that each mole of acid had 1 mole of hydrogen ions available, and each mole of base had 1 mole of hydroxide ions available, to interact in this reaction until the endpoint was reached.

$$H^+ (aq) + OH^- (aq) \rightarrow 2H_2O$$

Let's look at an example where this is not true.

Problem 3

A drop of indicator is added to 20.0 mL of an aqueous solution of calcium hydroxide, $Ca(OH)_2$, that is used in a titration. (The volume of the drop can be ignored because it is so much smaller than the volume of the solution.) The solution turns color after 25.0 mL of a standard 0.050 M HCl solution is added. What was the original concentration of the $Ca(OH)_2$ solution?

The balanced equation for the reaction gives the mole relationship

$$\underbrace{2HCl}_{2 \text{ moles}} + \underbrace{Ca(OH)_2}_{1 \text{ mole}} \rightarrow CaCl_2 + 2H_2O$$

The mole relationship here is that the number of moles of acid is twice the number of moles of base.

moles of acid = 2(moles of base)
                $\uparrow$
              mole factor

Since

M_a (molar concentration of acid)
    $\times V_a$ (volume of acid in liters) = moles of acid

and

M_b (molar concentration of base) ×
    V_b (volume of base in liters) = moles of base

we can substitute these products into the mole relationship:

$$M_a V_a = 2 M_b V_b$$

$$M_b = \frac{M_a V_a}{2 V_b}$$

$$M_b = \frac{0.050 \text{ mole/liter} \times 0.0250 \text{ liter}}{2 \times 0.0200 \text{ liter}}$$

$$M_b = 0.0312 \text{ mole/liter}$$

 **Wave-mechanical model**   *See* **Atomic structure**.

 **X-rays**   *See* **Nucleonics**.

Additional Reference Tables   EXHIBIT 3.13

Table A   Densities and Boiling Points of Some Common Gases

Name		Density (grams/liter at STP*)	Boiling Point (at 1 atm) (K)
Air	—	1.29	—
Ammonia	NH_3	0.771	240
Carbon dioxide	CO_2	1.98	195
Carbon monoxide	CO	1.25	82
Chlorine	Cl_2	3.21	172
Hydrogen	H_2	0.0899	20
Hydrogen chloride	HCl	1.64	188
Hydrogen sulfide	H_2S	1.54	212
Methane	CH_4	0.714	109
Nitrogen	N_2	1.25	77
Nitrogen (II) oxide	NO	1.34	121
Oxygen	O_2	1.43	90
Sulfur dioxide	SO_2	2.93	263

*STP is defined as 273 K or 0 °C and 1 atm or 760 torr (mm Hg).

Table B   Solubility Curves

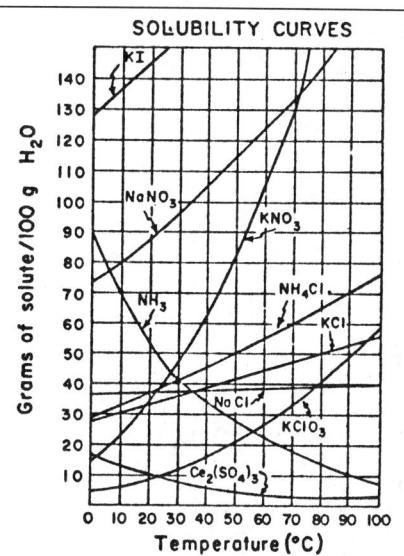

SOLUBILITY CURVES

Table C   Table of Solubilities in Water

i—nearly insoluble
ss—slightly soluble
s—soluble
d—decomposes
n—not isolated

	acetate	bromide	carbonate	chloride	chromate	hydroxide	iodide	nitrate	phosphate	sulfate	sulfide
Aluminum	ss	s	n	s	n	i	s	s	i	s	d
Ammonium	s	s	s	s	s	s	s	s	s	s	s
Barium	s	s	i	s	i	s	s	s	i	i	d
Calcium	s	s	i	s	s	ss	s	s	i	ss	d
Copper (II)	s	s	i	s	i	i	d	s	i	s	i
Iron (II)	s	s	i	s	n	i	s	s	i	s	i
Iron (III)	s	s	n	s	i	i	s	s	i	ss	d
Lead	s	ss	i	ss	i	i	ss	s	i	i	i
Magnesium	s	s	i	s	s	i	s	s	i	s	d
Mercury (I)	ss	i	i	i	ss	n	i	s	i	ss	i
Mercury (II)	s	ss	i	s	ss	i	i	s	i	d	i
Potassium	s	s	s	s	s	s	s	s	s	s	s
Silver	ss	i	i	i	ss	n	i	s	i	ss	i
Sodium	s	s	s	s	s	s	s	s	s	s	s
Zinc	s	s	i	s	s	i	s	s	i	s	i

Table D   Selected Polyatomic Ions

$[Ag(NH_3)_2]^+$	diamine silver	MnO_4^{2-}	manganate
CH_3COO^-	acetate	NH_4^+	ammonium
CN^-	cyanide	NO_2^-	nitrite
CO_3^{2-}	carbonate	NO_3^-	nitrate
$C_2O_4^{2-}$	oxalate	OH^-	hydroxide
ClO_3^-	chlorate	PO_4^{3-}	phosphate
CrO_4^{2-}	chromate	SCN^-	thiocyanate
$Cr_2O_7^{2-}$	dichromate	SO_3^{2-}	sulfite
Hg_2^{2+}	mercury (I)	SO_4^{2-}	sulfate
MnO_4^-	permanganate	$S_2O_3^{2-}$	thiosulfate

Table E   Standard Energies of Formation of Compounds at 1 atm and 298 K

Compound	Heat (Enthalpy) of Formation (kcal/mole)(ΔH_f^0)	Free Energy of Formation (kcal/mole)(ΔG_f^0)
Aluminum oxide $Al_2O_3(s)$	−399.1	−376.8
Ammonia $NH_3(g)$	−11.0	−4.0
Barium sulfate $BaSO_4(s)$	−350.2	−323.4
Calcium hydroxide $Ca(OH)_2(s)$	−235.8	−214.3
Carbon dioxide $CO_2(g)$	−94.1	−94.3
Carbon monoxide $CO(g)$	−26.4	−32.8
Copper (II) sulfate $CuSO_4(s)$	−184.0	−158.2
Ethane $C_2H_6(g)$	−20.2	−7.9
Ethene $C_2H_4(g)$	12.5	16.3
Ethyne (acetylene) $C_2H_2(g)$	54.2	50.0
Hydrogen fluoride $HF(g)$	−64.2	−64.7
Hydrogen iodide $HI(g)$	6.2	0.3
Iodine chloride $ICl(g)$	4.2	−1.3
Lead (II) oxide $PbO(s)$	−52.4	−45.3
Magnesium oxide $MgO(s)$	−143.8	−136.1
Nitrogen (II) oxide $NO(g)$	21.6	20.7
Nitrogen (IV) oxide $NO_2(g)$	8.1	12.4
Potassium chloride $KCl(s)$	−104.2	−97.6
Sodium chloride $NaCl(s)$	−98.2	−91.8
Sulfur dioxide $SO_2(g)$	−71.0	−71.8
Water $H_2O(g)$	−57.8	−54.6
Water $H_2O(l)$	−68.3	−56.7

Sample equation:

$$2Al(s) + \tfrac{3}{2}O_2(g) \rightarrow Al_2O_3(s)$$

Table F   Selected Radioisotopes

Nuclide	Half-life	Particle Emission
^{14}C	5730 y	β^-
^{60}Co	5.3 y	β^-
^{137}Cs	30.23 y	β^-
^{220}Fr	27.5 s	α
^3H	12.26 y	β^-
^{131}I	8.07 d	β^-
^{40}K	1.28×10^9 y	β^+
^{42}K	12.4 h	β^-
^{32}P	14.3 d	β^-
^{226}Ra	1600 y	α
^{90}Sr	28.1 y	β^-
^{235}U	7.1×10^8 y	α
^{238}U	4.51×10^9 y	α

y = years; d = days; h = hours; s = seconds

Table G Heats of Reaction at 1 atm and 298 K

Reaction	ΔH (kcal)
$CH_4(g) + 2O_2(g) \rightarrow CO_2(g) + 2H_2O(l)$	-212.8
$C_3H_6(g) + 5O_2(g) \rightarrow 3CO_2(g) + 4H_2O(l)$	-530.6
$CH_3OH(l) + \frac{3}{2}O_2(g) \rightarrow CO_2(g) + 2H_2O(l)$	-173.6
$C_6H_{12}O_6(s) + 6O_2(g) \rightarrow 6CO_2(g) + 6H_2O(l)$	-669.9
$CO(g) + \frac{1}{2}O_2(g) \rightarrow CO_2(g)$	-67.7
$NaOH(s) \xrightarrow{H_2O} Na^+(aq) + OH^-(aq)$	-10.6
$NH_4Cl(s) \xrightarrow{H_2O} NH_4^+(aq) + Cl^-(aq)$	$+3.5$
$H^+(aq) + OH^-(aq) \rightarrow H_2O(l)$	-13.8

Table H Symbols Used in Nuclear Chemistry

electron	$_{-1}^{0}e$	β^-
positron	$_{+1}^{0}e$	β^+
proton	$_{1}^{1}H$	p
alpha particle	$_{2}^{4}He$	α
neutron	$_{0}^{1}n$	n
gamma radiation		γ

Table I Ionization Energies and Electronegativities

IA							0
313 H 2.1	First Ionization Energy (kcal/mole of atoms) Electronegativity						567 He
	IIA	IIIA	IVA	VA	VIA	VIIA	
124 Li 1.0	215 Be 1.5	191 B 2.0	260 C 2.5	336 N 3.0	314 O 3.5	402 F 4.0	497 Ne
119 Na 0.9	176 Mg 1.2	138 Al 1.5	188 Si 1.8	254 P 2.1	239 S 2.5	300 Cl 3.0	363 Ar
100 K 0.8	141 Ca 1.0	138 Ga 1.6	187 Ge 1.8	231 As 2.0	225 Se 2.4	273 Br 2.8	323 Kr
96 Rb 0.8	131 Sr 1.0	133 In 1.7	169 Sn 1.8	199 Sb 1.9	208 Te 2.1	241 I 2.5	280 Xe
90 Cs 0.7	120 Ba 0.9	141 Tl 1.8	171 Pb 1.8	185 Bi 1.9	Po 2.0	At 2.2	248 Rn
Fr 0.7	Ra						

Table J Relative Strengths of Acids in Aqueous Solution at 1 atm and 298 K

Conjugate Pairs		K_a
Acid	Base	
$HI \rightarrow H^+ + I^-$		very large
$HBr \rightarrow H^+ + Br^-$		very large
$HCl \rightarrow H^+ + Cl^-$		very large
$HNO_3 \rightarrow H^+ + NO_3^-$		very large
$H_2SO_4 \rightarrow H^+ + HSO_4^-$		large
$H_2O + SO_2 \rightarrow H^+ + HSO_3^-$		1.7×10^{-2}
$HSO_4^- \rightarrow H^+ + SO_4^{2-}$		1.3×10^{-2}
$H_3PO_4 \rightarrow H^+ + H_2PO_4^-$		7.1×10^{-2}
$Fe(H_2O)_6^{3+} \rightarrow H^+ + Fe(H_2O)_5(OH)^{2+}$		6.0×10^{-3}
$HF \rightarrow H^+ + F^-$		6.7×10^{-4}
$HNO_2 \rightarrow H^+ + NO_2^-$		5.1×10^{-4}
$Cr(H_2O)_6^{3+} \rightarrow H^+ + Cr(H_2O)_5(OH)^{2+}$		1.0×10^{-4}
$CH_3COOH \rightarrow H^+ + CH_3COO^-$		1.8×10^{-5}
$Al(H_2O)_6^{3+} \rightarrow H^+ + Al(H_2O)_5(OH)^{2+}$		1.0×10^{-5}
$H_2O + CO_2 \rightarrow H^+ + HCO_3^-$		4.4×10^{-7}
$H_2S \rightarrow H^+ + HS^-$		1.0×10^{-7}
$H_2PO_4^- \rightarrow H^+ + HPO_4^{2-}$		6.3×10^{-8}
$HSO_3^- \rightarrow H^+ + SO_3^{2-}$		6.2×10^{-8}
$NH_4^+ \rightarrow H^+ + NH_3$		5.7×10^{-10}
$HCO_3^- \rightarrow H^+ + CO_3^{2-}$		4.7×10^{-11}
$HPO_4^{2-} \rightarrow H^+ + PO_4^{3-}$		4.4×10^{-13}
$HS^- \rightarrow H^+ + S^{2-}$		1.3×10^{-13}
$OH^- \rightarrow H^+ + O^{2-}$		$< 10^{-36}$
$NH_3 \rightarrow H^+ + NH_2^-$		very small

Table K Constants for Various Equilibria at 1 atm and 298 K

$H_2O = H^+(aq) + OH^-(aq)$	$K_w = 1.0 \times 10^{-14}$
$CH_2COO^-(aq) + H_2O = CH_3COOH(aq) + OH^-(aq)$	$K_b = 5.6 \times 10^{-10}$
$NH_3(aq) + H_2O = NH_4^+(aq) + OH^-(aq)$	$K_b = 1.8 \times 10^{-5}$
$CO_3^{2-}(aq) + H_2O = HCO_2^-(aq) + OH^-(aq)$	$K_b = 2.1 \times 10^{-4}$
$Ag(NH_3)_2^+(aq) = Ag^+(aq) + 2NH_3(aq)$	$K_c = 6.3 \times 10^{-4}$
$N_2(g) + 3H_2(g) = 2NH_3(g)$	$K_c = 6.7 \times 10^5$
$H_2(g) + I_2(g) = 2HI(g)$	$K_c = 3.5 \times 10^{10-1}$

Compound	K_{sp}	Compound	K_{sp}
AgCl	1.6×10^{-10}	$PbCl_2$	1.6×10^{-5}
AgBr	7.7×10^{-13}	$PbCrO_4$	1.8×10^{-14}
AgI	1.5×10^{-16}	PbI_2	1.4×10^{-8}
$BaSO_4$	1.1×10^{-10}	ZnS	1.6×10^{-23}

Table L   Standard Electrode Potentials

Ionic Concentrations 1 M Water at 298 K, 1 atm

Half-Reaction	E^0 (V)
$F_2(g) + 2e^- \rightarrow 2F^-$	+2.87
$MnO_4^- + 8H^+ + 5e^- \rightarrow Mn^{2+} + 4H_2O$	+1.52
$Au^{3+} + 3e^- \rightarrow Au(s)$	+1.50
$Cl_2(g) + 2e^- \rightarrow 2Cl^-$	+1.36
$Cr_2O_7^{2-} + 14H^+ + 6e^- \rightarrow 2Cr^{3+} + 7H_2O$	+1.33
$MnO_2(s) + 4H^+ + 2e^- \rightarrow Mn^{2+} + 2H_2O$	+1.28
$\frac{1}{2}O_3(g) + 2H^+ + 2e^- \rightarrow H_2O$	+1.23
$Br_2(l) + 2e^- \rightarrow 2Br^-$	+1.06
$NO_3^- + 4H^+ + 3e^- \rightarrow NO(g) + 2H_2O$	+0.96
$\frac{1}{2}O_2(g) + 2H^+(10^{-7}M) + 2e^- \rightarrow H_2O$	+0.82
$Ag^+ + e^- \rightarrow Ag(s)$	+0.80
$\frac{1}{2}Hg_2^{2+} + e^- \rightarrow Hg(l)$	+0.79
$Hg^{2+} + 2e^- \rightarrow Hg(l)$	+0.78
$NO_3^- + 2H^+ + e^- \rightarrow NO_2(g) + H_2O$	+0.78
$Fe^{3+} + e^- \rightarrow Fe^{2+}$	+0.77
$I_2(s) + 2e^- \rightarrow 2I^-$	+0.53
$Cu^+ + e^- \rightarrow Cu(s)$	+0.52
$Cu^{2+} + 2e^- \rightarrow Cu(s)$	+0.34
$SO_4^{2-} + 4H^+ + 2e^- \rightarrow SO_2(g) + 2H_2O$	+0.17
$Sn^{4+} + 2e^- \rightarrow Sn^{2+}$	+0.15
$2H^+ + 2e^- \rightarrow H_2(g)$	0.00
$Pb^{2+} + 2e^- \rightarrow Pb(s)$	−0.13
$Sn^{2+} + 2e^- \rightarrow Sn(s)$	−0.14
$Ni^{2+} + 2e^- \rightarrow Ni(s)$	−0.25
$Co^{2+} + 2e^- \rightarrow Co(s)$	−0.28
$2H^+(10^{-7}M) + 2e^- \rightarrow H_2(g)$	−0.41
$Fe^{2+} + 2e^- \rightarrow Fe(s)$	−0.44
$Cr^{3+} + 3e^- \rightarrow Cr(s)$	−0.74
$Zn^{2+} + 2e^- \rightarrow Zn(s)$	−0.76
$2H_2O + 2e^- \rightarrow 2OH^- + H_2(g)$	−0.83
$Mn^{2+} + 2e^- \rightarrow Mn(s)$	−1.18
$Al^{3+} + 3e^- \rightarrow Al(s)$	−1.66
$Mg^{2+} + 2e^- \rightarrow Mg(s)$	−2.37
$Na^+ + e^- \rightarrow Na(s)$	−2.71
$Ca^{2+} + 2e^- \rightarrow Ca(s)$	−2.87
$Sr^{2+} + 2e^- \rightarrow Sr(s)$	−2.89
$Ba^{2+} + 2e^- \rightarrow Ba(s)$	−2.90
$Cs^+ + e^- \rightarrow Cs(s)$	−2.92
$K^+ + e^- \rightarrow K(s)$	−2.92
$Rb^+ + e^- \rightarrow Rb(s)$	−2.93
$Li^+ + e^- \rightarrow Li(s)$	−3.00

Table M   Physical Constants

Name	Symbol	Values
Speed of Light	c	3.00×10^8 meters/s
Avogadro's Number	N_A	6.02×10^{23} per mole
Universal Gas Constant	R	$\begin{cases} 0.0821 \text{ liter} \cdot \text{atm/mole} \cdot \text{K} \\ 1.99 \text{ cal/mole} \cdot \text{K} \\ 8.31 \text{ joule/mole} \cdot \text{K} \end{cases}$
Planck's Constant	h	$\begin{cases} 6.63 \times 10^{-34} \text{ joule} \cdot \text{s} \\ 1.58 \times 10^{-37} \text{ kcal} \cdot \text{s} \\ 1.60 \times 10^{-19} \text{ coulomb} \end{cases}$
Charge of Electron	e	

Molal freezing point depression constant for $H_2O = 1.86°C$

Molal boiling point elevation for $H_2O = 0.52°C$

Atomic Mass Unit	1 amu $= 1.66 \times 10^{-24}$g
Heat Equivalent	1 kcal $= 4.18 \times 10^3$ joule
Volume Standard	1 liter $= 1.00 \times 10^3$ cm^3
Angstrom Unit	1 Å $= 1.00 \times 10^{-10}$ meter
Electron Volt	1 eV $= 1.60 \times 10^{-19}$ joule

Table N   Vapor Pressure of Water

°C	torr (mm Hg)	°C	torr (mm Hg)	°C	torr (mm Hg)	°C	torr (mm Hg)
0	4.6	19	16.5	26	25.2	60	149.4
5	6.5	20	17.5	27	26.7	70	233.7
10	9.2	21	18.7	28	28.3	80	355.1
15	12.8	22	19.8	29	30.0	90	525.8
16	13.6	23	21.1	30	31.8	100	760.0
17	14.5	24	22.4	40	55.3	105	906.1
18	15.5	25	23.8	50	92.5	110	1074.6

EXHIBIT 3.14
Alphabetical List of Elements

Name	Symbol	Atomic Number	Atomic Weight	Valence
Actinium	Ac	89	227[a]	3
Aluminum	Al	13	26.98	3
Americium	Am	95	243[a]	3
Antimony	Sb	51	121.75	3, 5
Argon	Ar	18	39.948	0
Arsenic	As	33	74.9216	5, ±3
Astatine	At	85	210[a]	
Barium	Ba	56	137.34	2
Berkelium	Bk	97	247[a]	3, 4
Beryllium	Be	4	9.01504	2
Bismuth	Bi	83	208.980	3, 5
Boron	B	5	10.81	3
Bromine	Br	35	79.903	±1, 5
Cadmium	Cd	48	112.40	2
Calcium	Ca	20	40.08	2
Californium	Cf	98	251[a]	3
Carbon	C	6	12.011	±4, 2
Cerium	Ce	58	140.12	3, 4
Cesium	Cs	55	132.906	1
Chlorine	Cl	17	35.453	±1, 5, 7
Chromium	Cr	24	51.996	2, 3, 6
Cobalt	Co	27	58.9332	2, 3
Copper	Cu	29	63.545	1, 2
Curium	Cm	96	247[a]	3
Dysprosium	Dy	66	162.50	3
Einsteinium	Es	99	254[a]	

EXHIBIT 3.14 (continued)

Name	Symbol	Atomic Number	Atomic Weight	Valence
Erbium	Er	68	167.26	3
Europium	Eu	63	151.96	2, 3
Fermium	Fm	100	257[a]	
Fluorine	F	9	18.9984	−1
Francium	Fr	87	223[a]	1
Gadolinium	Gd	64	157.25	3
Gallium	Ga	31	69.72	3
Germanium	Ge	32	72.59	4
Gold	Au	79	196.967	1, 3
Hafnium	Hf	72	178.49	4
Helium	He	2	4.0026	0
Holmium	Ho	67	164.93	3
Hydrogen	H	1	1.0080	1
Indium	In	49	114.82	3
Iodine	I	53	126.9044	−1, 5, 7
Iridium	Ir	77	192.22	3, 4, 6
Iron	Fe	26	55.847	2, 3
Krypton	Kr	36	83.80	0
Lanthanum	La	57	138.91	3
Lawrencium	Lr	103	257[a]	
Lead	Pb	82	207.19	2, 4
Lithium	Li	3	6.941	1
Lutetium	Lu	71	174.97	3
Magnesium	Mg	12	24.312	2
Manganese	Mn	25	54.9380	2, 3, 4, 6, 7
Mendelevium	Md	101	256[a]	
Mercury	Hg	80	200.59	1, 2
Molybdenum	Mo	42	95.94	3, 5, 6
Neodymium	Nd	60	144.24	3
Neon	Ne	10	20.182	0
Neptunium	Np	93	237.0482	3, 4, 5, 6
Nickel	Ni	28	58.71	2, 3
Niobium (Columbium)	Nb	41	92.906	3, 5
Nitrogen	N	7	14.0067	−3, 2, 5
Nobelium	No	102	254[a]	
Osmium	Os	76	190.2	4, 6, 8
Oxygen	O	8	15.9994	−2
Palladium	Pd	46	106.4	2, 4
Phosphorus	P	15	30.9738	±3, 5
Platinum	Pt	78	195.09	2, 4
Plutonium	Pu	94	244[a]	3, 4, 5, 6
Polonium	Po	84	210[a]	2, 4
Potassium	K	19	39.10	1
Praseodymium	Pr	59	140.91	3
Promethium	Pm	61	145[a]	3
Protactinium	Pa	91	231.036	5
Radium	Ra	88	226.026	2
Radon	Rn	86	222[a]	0
Rhenium	Re	75	186.2	−1, 4, 7
Rhodium	Rh	45	102.906	3, 4
Rubidium	Rb	37	85.466	1
Ruthenium	Ru	44	101.1	3, 4, 6, 8
Samarium	Sm	62	150.35	3
Scandium	Sc	21	44.956	3
Selenium	Se	34	78.96	−2, 4, 6
Silicon	Si	14	28.086	4
Silver	Ag	47	107.870	1
Sodium	Na	11	22.9898	1
Strontium	Sr	38	87.62	2
Sulfur	S	16	32.064	−2, 4, 6
Tantalum	Ta	73	180.948	5
Technetium	Tc	43	99[a]	7
Tellurium	Te	52	127.60	−2, 4, 6
Terbium	Tb	65	158.92	3
Thallium	Tl	81	204.39	1, 3
Thorium	Th	90	232.038	4
Thulium	Tm	69	168.934	3
Tin	Sn	50	118.69	2, 4
Titanium	Ti	22	47.90	3, 4
Tungsten	W	74	183.85	6
Uranium	U	92	238.04	3, 4, 5, 6
Vanadium	V	23	50.941	2, 4, 5
Xenon	Xe	54	131.30	0
Ytterbium	Yb	70	173.04	2, 3
Yttrium	Y	39	88.905	3
Zinc	Zn	30	65.38	2
Zirconium	Zr	40	91.22	4

[a] = mass number of most stable isotope

EXHIBIT 3.15

Periodic Table of the Element.

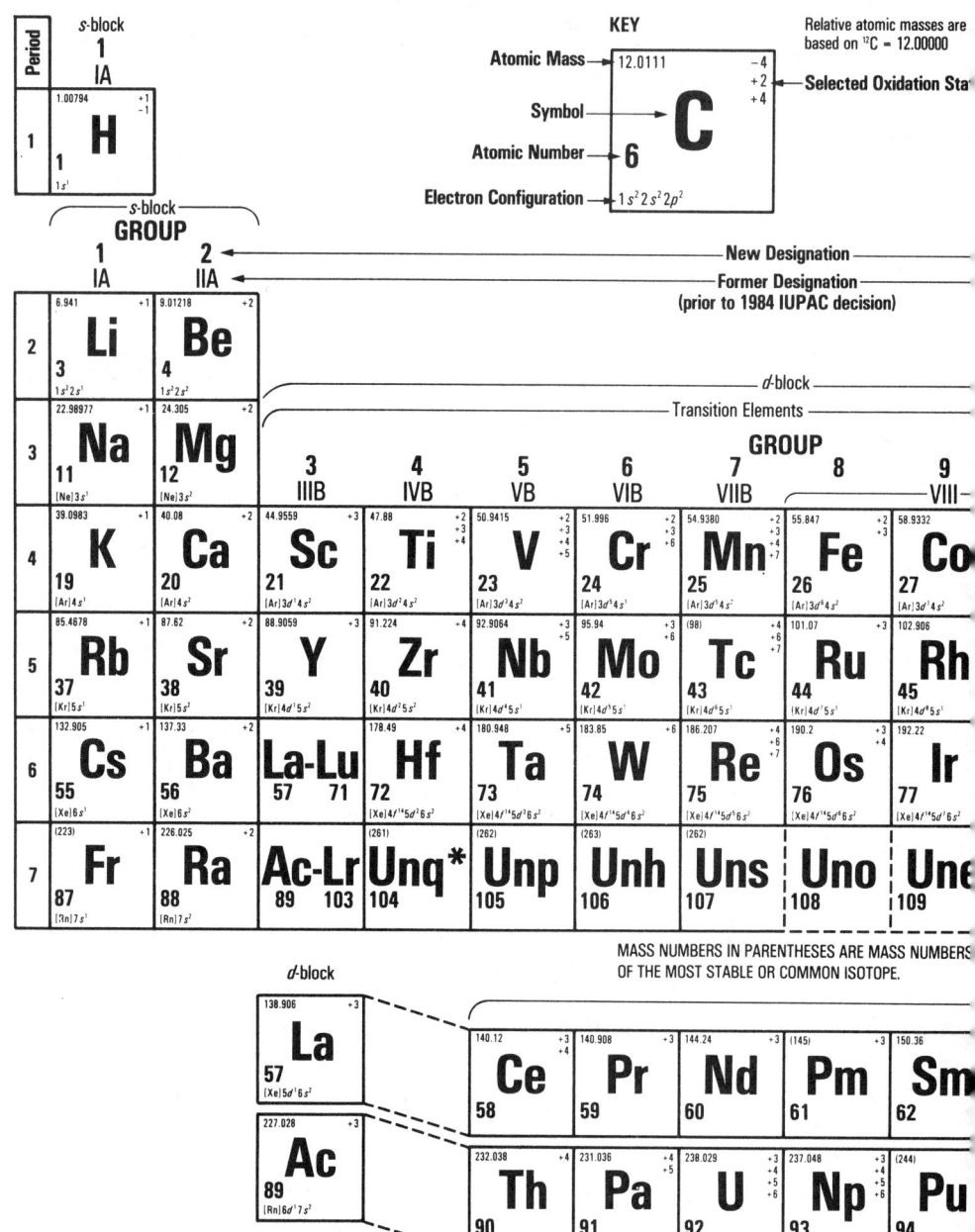

MASS NUMBERS IN PARENTHESES ARE MASS NUMBERS
OF THE MOST STABLE OR COMMON ISOTOPE.

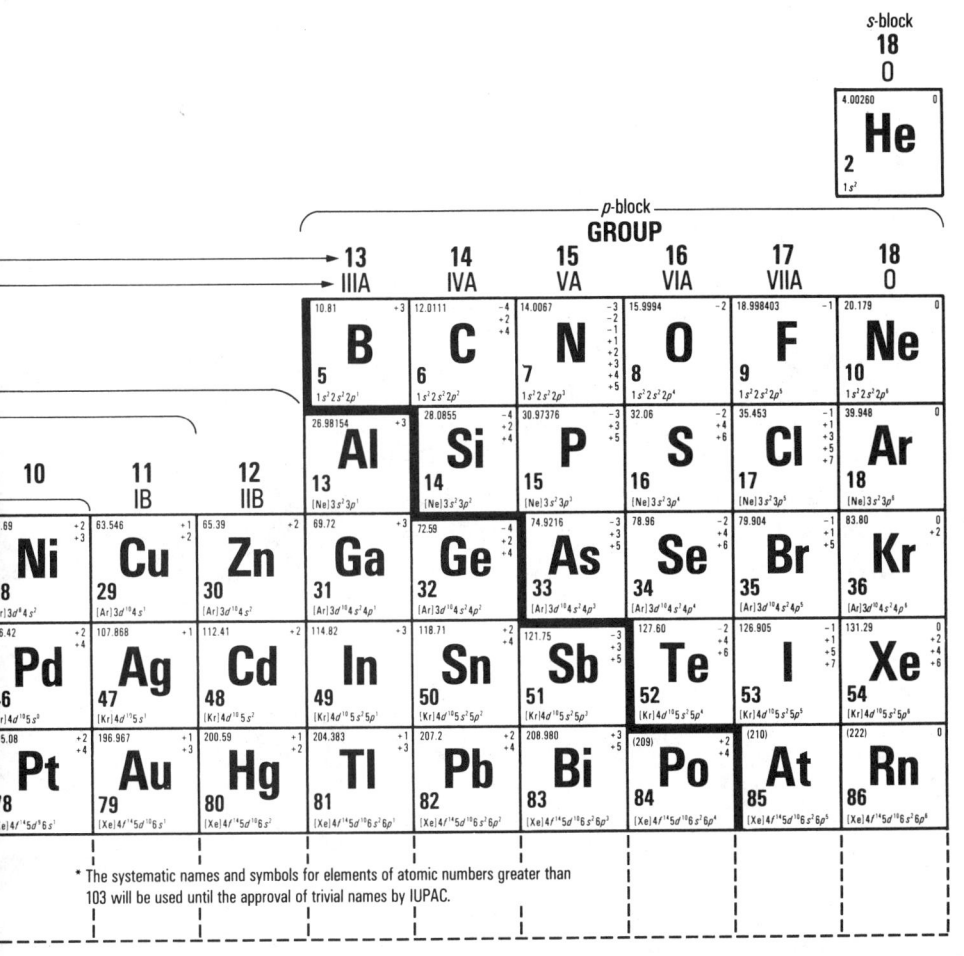

s-block
18
0

4.00260	0
He	
2	
$1s^2$	

— *p*-block —
GROUP

13 IIIA	**14** IVA	**15** VA	**16** VIA	**17** VIIA	**18** 0
10.81 +3 **B** 5 $1s^2 2s^2 2p^1$	12.0111 −4,+2,−1,+4 **C** 6 $1s^2 2s^2 2p^2$	14.0067 −3,−2,−1,+1,+2,+3,+4,+5 **N** 7 $1s^2 2s^2 2p^3$	15.9994 −2 **O** 8 $1s^2 2s^2 2p^4$	18.998403 −1 **F** 9 $1s^2 2s^2 2p^5$	20.179 0 **Ne** 10 $1s^2 2s^2 2p^6$
26.98154 +3 **Al** 13 $[Ne]3s^2 3p^1$	28.0855 −4,+2,+4 **Si** 14 $[Ne]3s^2 3p^2$	30.97376 −3,+3,+5 **P** 15 $[Ne]3s^2 3p^3$	32.06 −2,+4,+6 **S** 16 $[Ne]3s^2 3p^4$	35.453 −1,+1,+3,+5,+7 **Cl** 17 $[Ne]3s^2 3p^5$	39.948 0 **Ar** 18 $[Ne]3s^2 3p^6$

10	**11** IB	**12** IIB					
N.69 +2,+3 **Ni** 8 $3d^8 4s^2$	63.546 +1,+2 **Cu** 29 $[Ar]3d^{10}4s^1$	65.39 +2 **Zn** 30 $[Ar]3d^{10}4s^2$	69.72 +3 **Ga** 31 $[Ar]3d^{10}4s^2 4p^1$	72.59 −4,+2,+4 **Ge** 32 $[Ar]3d^{10}4s^2 4p^2$	74.9216 −3,+3,+5 **As** 33 $[Ar]3d^{10}4s^2 4p^3$	78.96 −2,+4,+6 **Se** 34 $[Ar]3d^{10}4s^2 4p^4$	79.904 −1,+1,+3,+5 **Br** 35 $[Ar]3d^{10}4s^2 4p^5$
							83.80 0,+2 **Kr** 36 $[Ar]3d^{10}4s^2 4p^6$
6.42 +2 **Pd** 6 $[Kr]4d^{10}5s^3$	107.868 +1 **Ag** 47 $[Kr]4d^{10}5s^1$	112.41 +2 **Cd** 48 $[Kr]4d^{10}5s^2$	114.82 +3 **In** 49 $[Kr]4d^{10}5s^2 5p^1$	118.71 +2,+4 **Sn** 50 $[Kr]4d^{10}5s^2 5p^2$	121.75 −3,+3,+5 **Sb** 51 $[Kr]4d^{10}5s^2 5p^3$	127.60 −2,+4,+6 **Te** 52 $[Kr]4d^{10}5s^2 5p^4$	126.905 −1,+1,+5,+7 **I** 53 $[Kr]4d^{10}5s^2 5p^5$
							131.29 0,+2,+4,+6 **Xe** 54 $[Kr]4d^{10}5s^2 5p^6$
95.08 +2 **Pt** 8 $[Xe]4f^{14}5d^9 6s^1$	196.967 +1,+3 **Au** 79 $[Xe]4f^{14}5d^{10}6s^1$	200.59 +1,+2 **Hg** 80 $[Xe]4f^{14}5d^{10}6s^2$	204.383 +1,+3 **Tl** 81 $[Xe]4f^{14}5d^{10}6s^2 6p^1$	207.2 +2,+4 **Pb** 82 $[Xe]4f^{14}5d^{10}6s^2 6p^2$	208.980 +3,+5 **Bi** 83 $[Xe]4f^{14}5d^{10}6s^2 6p^3$	(209) +2,+4 **Po** 84 $[Xe]4f^{14}5d^{10}6s^2 6p^4$	(210) **At** 85 $[Xe]4f^{14}5d^{10}6s^2 6p^5$
							(222) 0 **Rn** 86 $[Xe]4f^{14}5d^{10}6s^2 6p^6$

* The systematic names and symbols for elements of atomic numbers greater than
103 will be used until the approval of trivial names by IUPAC.

— *f*-block —

51.96 +2,+3 **Eu** 63	157.25 +3 **Gd** 64	158.925 +3 **Tb** 65	162.50 +3 **Dy** 66	164.930 +3 **Ho** 67	167.26 +3 **Er** 68	168.934 +3 **Tm** 69	173.04 +2,+3 **Yb** 70	174.967 +3 **Lu** 71	Lanthanoid Series
(243) +3,+4,+5,+6 **Am** 95	(247) +3,+4 **Cm** 96	(247) +3,+4 **Bk** 97	(251) +3 **Cf** 98	(252) **Es** 99	(257) **Fm** 100	(258) **Md** 101	(259) **No** 102	(260) **Lr** 103	Actinoid Series

COMPUTERS AND ELECTRONIC MEDIA

INTRODUCTION

A computer is a machine that stores a set of instructions (a program) for processing data and then executes those instructions when requested. Computers have many applications for businesses, researchers, and students.

A computer system consists of hardware (the physical components of the system) and software (the instructions for the machine to follow). The hardware consists of a unit that reads instructions and determines how to execute them (called the central processing unit, or CPU), a unit where data can be stored for later retrieval (called the memory), and devices for input (where the computer obtains information from the outside world) and output (where the computer presents information to the outside world). A keyboard is an example of an input device; printers and CRT screens (called monitors) are output devices. Some devices (such as disk drives and cassette tape units) can be used for both input and output. Computers can transmit and receive data from other computers by sending signals over telephone lines. A device called a modem can be connected to a computer to transform signals from the computer into signals that can be transmitted over the telephone line.

Modern digital computers are made of electronic components. The first electronic computer, built in 1947, was a huge machine consisting of vacuum tubes. Transistors replaced the vacuum tubes in computers built during the 1950s, making it possible to build computers that were smaller, more reliable, and less expensive. The development of integrated circuits, consisting of many electronic components on a single silicon chip, has made it possible to make computers even smaller and less expensive. This section contains descriptions of many of the electronic components that make up computers.

Computers can be classified into categories based on size and capacity. Supercomputers are very fast computers with large memories used at research laboratories. Mainframe computers are the large computers typically used in businesses and other organizations. A single mainframe computer can be used simultaneously by many different people working at terminals. Minicomputers are smaller than mainframe computers but can still support multiple users. Microcomputers, first built in the mid-1970s, are computers where the entire CPU is contained on a single integrated circuit (called a microprocessor). Microcomputers are small enough and inexpensive enough for individuals to be able to afford them. The development of more powerful microprocessor chips has made it possible to steadily increase the speed and memory capacity of microcomputers. (*See* pages 9-23 and 9-24 for more information on the history of computers.)

Computers can execute many different types of software (programs). To begin with, a computer must have a basic software system called the operating system that allows it to start operation and then read in other software. Application software packages perform tasks such as word processing, data base management, spreadsheets, graphics, interactive learning, or communication. Some software is designed for a single purpose; other software can be used for a much wider variety of purposes. General-purpose packages provide more flexibility, but they can be more complicated to learn because you need to specify exactly what you want done.

As computers became more common, increased effort was directed towards making them more user-friendly. An important step was the development of a Graphical User Interface (GUI), where the user can see menus of choices on the screen, often in the form of icons (pictures), and can point to items with a mouse. Macintosh computers and the program Microsoft Windows provide a GUI for their users. These computers allow the display of graphics mixed with text, and the appearance of the text itself can be altered by changing its size or style. These capabilities led to the development of desktop publishing systems in the mid 1980s, where the computer is used for the page layout process.

The graphics capabilities of microcomputers has greatly expanded, allowing users to see high-resolution color pictures on the screen and explore other types of visual information, such as maps. Also, computers have developed improved sound capabilities. For example, it is possible to obtain a multimedia encyclopedia, which contains text, pictures, and sound. These capabilities require computers with large storage capacity, so CD-ROMs became an increasingly common way of storing computer information.

Many computer programs exist for specialized purposes, such as performing accounting for a business, performing statistical calculations, designing electronic circuits, forming models of the economy, making graphs, or creating architectural designs. Computers also can be used as an interactive teaching tool: presenting information on the screen, asking questions, reading in the answers from a student, informing the student whether the answer was correct, and then moving on to new information at the pace the student can handle. The most advanced type of computer programs fit within the category of artificial intelligence, which consists of programs where a computer simulates human thinking. For example, artificial intelligence includes the study of ways to make a computer understand human languages, such as English. However this is a very difficult problem that has not been solved.

You may write your own computer programs if you learn a computer programming language such as BASIC, Pascal, or LISP. In order to use a programming language, you must have available a compiler or interpreter for that language. Programming languages generally include these features:

- provisions for operations on data, such as arithmetic calculations or manipulations of strings of characters.
- the use of variables to represent data.
- iteration, making it possible for a set of instructions to be executed repeatedly, either a fixed number of times or else indefinitely until a particular condition is met.
- arrays, a collection of many data items which have one name and are identified with subscripts.

■ the ability to write subprograms (subroutines or procedures), making it possible to write complicated programs as different modules (otherwise it would be difficult for people to write long programs).

When writing a computer program, it is best to plan the program carefully. Develop a strategy for solving the problem. (A clearly specified procedure for solving a particular problem is called an algorithm.) Then proceed to write the program. A large program should be designed as a collection of smaller modules because it is easier for a person to understand the program in that form. Some languages, such as Pascal, are designed so that programs consist of subparts (called procedures).

Computer programs often have errors (called bugs), and debugging a program is one of the parts of programming. Bugs can be either syntax errors (meaning that the program does not follow the rules that determine which statements are legal in that language) or logic errors (meaning that the program does not accomplish what it is intended to accomplish).

The section that follows includes brief descriptions of several computer programming languages, as well as more detailed descriptions of two common languages: BASIC and Pascal.

Algorithm An algorithm is a sequence of instructions that tell how to solve a particular problem. An algorithm must be specified exactly, so there can be no doubt about what to do next, and it must have a finite number of steps. A computer program is an algorithm written in a language that a computer can understand, but the same algorithm could be written in several different languages. An algorithm can also be a set of instructions for a person to follow. (*See* **Flowchart**.) A set of instructions is not an algorithm if it does not have a definite stopping place, or if the instructions are too vague to be followed clearly. The stopping place may be at variable points in the general procedure, but something in the procedure must determine precisely where the stopping place is for a particular case. If you study the game of tic-tac-toe long enough, you will be able to develop an algorithm that tells you how to play an unbeatable game. However, some problems are so complicated that there is no algorithm to solve them.

Ampere An ampere (or amp, for short) is the unit for measuring electric current. A current of 1 ampere means that 6.25×10^{18} electrons are flowing by a point each second. A group of 6.25×10^{18} electrons has a charge of 1 coulomb, so 1 ampere = 1 coulomb per second.

Analog computer An analog computer is a computer in which information is stored in a form that can vary smoothly between certain limits rather than having discrete values. (By way of contrast, *see* **Digital computer**.) A slide rule is an example of an analog computer, because it represents numbers as distances along a scale. All modern, programmable computers are digital. Analog computer circuits are used in certain kinds of automatic machinery, such as automotive cruise controls and guided missiles. Also, a fundamental analog computer circuit called the *operational amplifier* is used extensively in audio, radio, and TV equipment.

Apple Apple is one of the largest personal computer manufacturers. The Apple II, introduced in 1977, was one of the earliest popular microcomputers. A wide range of software was written for the Apple II and its followers. In 1984, Apple introduced the Macintosh, the first widely used computer with a graphical user interface. The company, located in Cupertino, California, was founded by Steve Jobs and Steve Wozniak, who began work in a garage.

Array An array is a collection of data that is given one name. An array is arranged so that each item in the array can be located when needed. An array is made up of a group of elements, which may be either numbers or character strings. Each element can be identified by a set of numbers known as subscripts, which indicate the row and column in which the element is located. The dimension of an array is the number of subscripts needed to locate a particular element. For example, it takes two subscripts to identify an element in a two-dimensional array.

Artificial intelligence Artificial intelligence (AI) is the branch of computer science that deals with using computers to simulate human thinking. Artificial intelligence is concerned with building computer programs that can solve problems creatively, rather than simply working through the steps of a solution designed by the programmer. For an example, consider computer game playing. Some games, such as tic-tac-toe, are so simple that the programmer can specify in advance a procedure that guarantees that the computer will play a perfect game. With a game such as chess, however, no such procedure is known; the computer must use, instead, a *heuristic*, that is, a procedure for discovering and evaluating good moves. One possible heuristic for chess would be for the computer to identify every possible move from a given position, and then evaluate the moves by calculating, for each one, all the possible ways the game could proceed. Chess is so complicated that this would take an impossibly long time (on the order of millions of years with present-day computers). A better strategy would be to take shortcuts. Calculating only five or six moves into the future is sufficient to eliminate most of the possible moves as not worth pursuing. The rest can be evaluated on the basis of general principles about board positions. In fact, an ideal heuristic chess-playing machine would be able to modify its own strategy on the basis of experience; like a human chess player, it would realize that its opponent is also following a heuristic and try to predict her behavior.

One of the main problems of AI is how to represent knowledge in the computer in a form such that it can be used rather than merely reproduced. In fact, some workers define AI as the construction of computer programs that utilize a *knowledge base*. A computer that tells you the call number of a library book is not displaying artificial intelligence; it is merely echoing back what was put into it. Artificial intelligence would come into play if the computer used its knowledge base to make generalizations about the library's holdings or construct bibliographies on selected subjects. Computer vision and robotics are important areas of AI. Although it is easy to take the image from a TV camera and store it in a computer's memory, it is hard to devise ways to make the computer recognize the objects it "sees." Likewise, there are many unsolved problems associated with getting computers to move about in three-dimensional space—to walk, for instance, and to find and grasp objects—even though human beings do these things naturally.

Another unsolved problem is natural language processing—getting computers to understand speech, or at least typewritten input, in a language such as English. In the late 1950s it was expected that computers would soon be programmed to accept natural-language input, translate Russian into English, and the like. But human languages have proved to be more complex than was expected, and progress has been slow. The English-speaking computers of *Star Wars* and *2001* are still some years away.

The important philosophical question remains: Do computers really think? Artificial intelligence theorist Alan Turing proposed a criterion that has since become known as the *Turing test*: a computer is thinking if a human being, connected to it by teletype, cannot tell whether he is communicating with a machine or with another person. In response Terry Rankin has pointed out that it makes little sense to build a machine whose purpose is to deceive human beings. Increasing numbers of AI workers are taking the position that computers are not artificial minds, but merely tools to assist the human mind, and that this is true no matter how closely they can be made to imitate human behavior.

ASC The ASC function in many versions of BASIC calculates the ASCII code number associated with a given character. (*See* **ASCII**.) For example, ASC("A") is 65 because the ASCII code of the character "A" is 65 (expressed in decimal).

ASCII ASCII is a standard code for representing characters as binary numbers, used on most microcomputers, computer terminals, and printers. ASCII stands for American Standard Code for Information Interchange.

Assembly language An assembly language is a computer language in which each statement corresponds to one machine language statement. Assembly languages are more cumbersome to use than regular (or high-level) programming languages, but they are much easier to use than pure machine languages, which require that all instructions be written in binary code.

Babbage, Charles Charles Babbage was a nineteenth century inventor who designed several devices, such as the "analytical engine," that included concepts that were later used in computers. However, the technology of his day was not capable of building everything he designed.

Backtracking Backtracking is a problem-solving technique applicable to certain types of problems. Here is how it works. First, start making educated guesses about what moves you should make to reach a solution. If you reach a situation where no allowable moves are left, then you must backtrack, that is, you must undo your last move and look for alternative solutions. If necessary you may need to backtrack several steps back. The programming language Prolog uses backtracking extensively. *See* **Prolog**.

Backup copy A backup copy of a program or set of data is another copy of that program or those data that can be referred to if the original is lost. When working with a microcomputer, you should make backup copies of important disks and store them away from the working copies. On large computer systems, tape drives are often used to store backup copies of disk files.

Bar code A bar code is a pattern of wide and narrow bars, printed on paper or a similar material. A computer reads the bar code by scanning it with a laser beam or with a wand that contains a light source and a photocell. The most familiar bar code is the Universal Product Code, used with cash registers in supermarkets, but bar codes have been utilized to encode many kinds of data, including complete programs for some programmable calculators. Circular bar codes are sometimes used on boxes or pieces of luggage that may be scanned from many different directions.

BASIC BASIC is one of the easiest computer languages to learn, and one of the most popular languages for beginning students and for people with microcomputers. It was designed as an interactive language by John Kemeny and Thomas Kurtz in the 1960s. Since then many different versions of BASIC have been developed for different machines. Many computers are sold with the BASIC language already included.

Here are some features of most BASIC systems:

1. Each BASIC statement must be preceded by a line number. For example:

```
10  X = 25.5
20  PRINT X
```

Here 10 and 20 are line numbers. To execute the program, type RUN. To see the program displayed on the screen, type LIST. The command SAVE causes a program to be stored on a disk or tape, and the command LOAD causes the program to be read from the disk or tape into the computer's memory. However, the exact form of these two commands varies with different computers.

2. Some versions of BASIC require that numeric variable names be only one or two characters long. Many current versions, however, allow longer variable names, making it easier to give meaningful names to variables. A dollar sign, $, placed at the end of the variable name indicates that the variable is a character string variable.

3. Arithmetic operations in BASIC are as follows: $\wedge$ or ** exponentiation, * multiplication, / division, + addition, and – subtraction. In evaluating arithmetic expressions, operations surrounded by parentheses are done first, then exponentiations, then multiplications and divisions, and finally additions and subtractions. An assignment statement is of the form

```
LET  X = expression
```

To execute this statement, the computer will calculate the value of the expression and assign that value to the name X. In most versions of BASIC the word LET is optional.

4. Input-output is handled as follows: The statement INPUT X,Y causes the computer to stop, type a question mark, and then wait for you to type in two values. It will call the first value X and the second value Y.

The statement READ A will cause the computer to look at the top of the data stack and assign that value to A. A data stack is created with a DATA statement, such as DATA 10, 15, 16.04, 30. The first time the computer hits a READ statement, such as READ A, it will give A the value 10. The next time it encounters a READ statement, such as READ B, it will give B the value 15.

The PRINT statement is used for output. The statement PRINT X, Y causes the values of X and Y to be displayed on the screen. The statement PRINT "WORD" causes the character string WORD to be printed. When a comma is used between the items in a print statement, the computer will space the items apart by a standard amount. When a semicolon is used in place of the comma, the computer will jam the items together.

In some versions of BASIC the LPRINT command works exactly the same as PRINT except that the output is directed to a printer instead of to the screen.

5. The GOTO command tells the computer to jump to the indicated statement number. For example, the command GOTO 50 will cause the computer to jump to statement 50 and start executing at that point. The word IF is used to indicate conditional actions. For example:

```
100 IF X<0 THEN PRINT "X IS LESS
THAN 0"
```

or

```
110 IF A=10 THEN GOTO 500
```

Loops can be constructed using FOR and NEXT statements. For example:

```
10 FOR I = 10 TO 20 STEP 2
```

statements in middle, such as:

```
20 J = SQR(I)
30 PRINT I, J
```

```
100 NEXT I
```

This setup will cause the computer to execute the statements in the middle six times. The first time it will use the value I = 10, then the value I = 12, then I = 14, and so on through I = 20.

6. The sizes of arrays are defined with the DIM statement. For example, DIM A(25) defines A to be a one-dimensional array with 25 elements, and DIM B(6,18) defines B to be a two-dimensional array with 6 rows and 18 columns. Each element in the array can be identified by using subscripts, written in parentheses. For example, B(2,1) is the element of B located in row 2, column 1.

7. Subroutines can be defined in BASIC by using the statement GOSUB. Upon reaching the statement GOSUB 150, the computer will jump to statement 150 and start executing there. When the computer reaches a RETURN statement, it knows it has reached the end of the subroutine, so it will jump back to the statement immediately following the original GOSUB statement.

8. Comments can be inserted in a program by using the keyword REM (short for REMARK) at the beginning of the statement. When the computer comes to a statement such as

```
30 REM THIS REMARK IS HERE TO HELP
40 REM ME UNDERSTAND THIS PROGRAM
```

it will completely ignore it and proceed to the next statement.

BASIC is often the best language if you have a simple program that you would like to type and run quickly. Most BASIC systems use interpreters, rather than compilers. This means that a program can be run quickly and easily. Just type RUN, and the program starts executing immediately. However, interpreted programs generally run through much slower than do compiled programs. Therefore, if you have a long program that needs to be executed often but does not require frequent changes, you probably will prefer a compiled language.

Many BASIC versions provide extensive graphics and sound-generation capabilities. However, the details of these commands vary greatly for different machines.

This article has described features of traditional versions of BASIC, such as Microsoft's BASICA or GWBASIC. More recent versions of BASIC, such as Microsoft's Quick BASIC or Visual BASIC, contain many advanced features.

Baud   A baud is a unit that measures the speed of data transmission; 1 baud equals 1 bit per second. Typically data can be transmitted along telephone lines at a rate of 300, 1,200, 2,400, or 9,600 baud.

BBS   A BBS (bulletin board service) is a computer that allows users to log in from remote terminals, exchange messages, and (usually) download programs. Many BBSs are run by microcomputer hobbyists and can be accessed free of charge by dialing a telephone number.

Binary numbers   Binary (base-2) numbers are written in a positional number system that uses only two digits: 0 and 1. Binary numbers are well suited for use by computers, since many electrical devices have two distinct states: on and off. Writing numbers in binary requires more digits than writing numbers in decimal, so binary numbers are cumbersome for people to use.

Each digit of a binary number represents a power of 2. The rightmost digit is the 1's digit, the next digit to the left is the 2's digit, and so on.

Decimal	Binary
$2^0 = 1$	1
$2^1 = 2$	10
$2^2 = 4$	100
$2^3 = 8$	1000
$2^4 = 16$	10000

The table shows some numbers written in binary and decimal form.

Decimal	Binary	Decimal	Binary
0	0	11	1011
1	1	12	1100
2	10	13	1101
3	11	14	1110
4	100	15	1111
5	101	16	10000
6	110	17	10001
7	111	18	10010
8	1000	19	10011
9	1001	20	10100
10	1010		

Bit   Bit is a shorthand term for "binary digit." There are only two possible binary digits: 0 and 1. (*See* **Binary numbers**.) Bits are represented in computers by two-state devices, such as flip-flops. A byte is the number of bits (usually 8) that stand for one character. One kilobyte (K) is 1,024 bytes. A computer memory is a collection of physical objects that can represent bits. The size of a computer memory is the number of bits it can represent, usually measured in Ks.

Bitmap   A bitmap is the representation of a graphical image as a pattern of 1's and 0's. Each digit represents one pixel of the image, which is either white or black. The quality of the image improves as the number of bits in the image increases, because there will be greater resolution. For example, an image one square inch in size requires 300^2 = 90,000 bits if it is to take full advantage of the resolution of a 300-dot-per-inch laser printer. You can see that a bitmap image of an entire page would fill a large amount of the computer's disk space. *See also* **Scanner**.

Boolean algebra   Boolean algebra is the study of operations carried out on variables that can have only two values: 1 (true) and 0 (false). Boolean algebra was developed by George Boole in the 1850s; it was useful originally in applications of the theory of logic, and has become of tremendous importance in that area since the development of the computer.

Boot   To boot a computer is to start it up.

Borland International   Borland International, an influential manufacturer of microcomputer software, was founded by Philippe Kahn and is headquartered in Scotts Valley, California. Its first products were Turbo Pascal, an extremely popular Pascal compiler released in 1984, and Sidekick, a set of IBM PC utilities that are always resident in RAM and can be called up at any time, even in the middle of another task. Later products include the spreadsheet Quattro Pro.

Buffer   A buffer is a device for the temporary storage of data that is located between two other devices of differing speeds. For example, the main computer is much faster than a printer output device, so the output from the computer will be sent to the buffer before it is sent to the printer.

Bug   A bug is an error in a computer program. Bugs can be either syntax errors, meaning that the rules of the programming language were not followed, or logic errors, meaning that the program does not do what it is supposed to do.

Bus   The bus is the main communication avenue in a computer. It consists of a set of parallel wires to which the CPU, the memory, and all input-output devices are connected. The bus contains one wire for each bit needed to give the address of a device or a location in memory, plus one wire for each bit of data to be transmitted in a single step (usually 8, 16, or 32 bits), and additional wires that indicate what operation is being performed.

Byte   A byte is the amount of memory space needed to store one character, which is normally 8 bits. A computer with 8-bit bytes can distinguish $2^8 = 256$ different characters. *See* **Kilobyte**; **Megabyte**.

C   is a programming language developed at Bell Laboratories in the 1970s. C is a general-purpose language like Pascal, but, unlike other general-purpose languages, it gives the programmer complete access to the machine's internal (bit-by-bit) representation of all types of data. This makes it convenient to perform tasks that would ordinarily require assembly language, and to perform computations in the most efficient way of which the machine is capable.

Capacitance   The capacitance of a capacitor is a measure of how much electric charge can be stored on the capacitor. *See* **Capacitor**.

Capacitor   A capacitor is a device for storing an electric charge on two conducting plates separated by an insulating material. The symbol for a capacitor is shown in the figure. The capability of a capacitor to store charge is measured in a unit called the farad. If a capacitor is connected to a direct-current (DC) circuit, a negative charge will develop on one plate and a positive charge will develop on the other plate. No current will flow. If the capacitor is connected to an alternating-current (AC) circuit, current will flow because the capacitor will alternately be charged first in one way and then in the other. The higher the AC frequency, the easier it will be for current to flow through the capacitor.

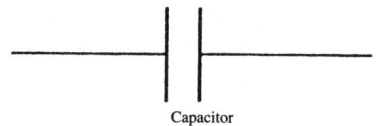

Capacitor

CD-ROM   CD-ROM stands for compact disk read-only memory, which refers to the use of compact disks (similar to audio compact disks) as a computer storage medium. In an audio CD, sound is "digitized" by representing it as a series of numbers corresponding to the amplitude of the sound at a particular time. The binary code for these numbers is then etched in the form of small pits on an aluminun disk about 4½ inches in diameter that is covered with a transparent plastic coating. To play the music, the compact disk is inserted in a player that uses a laser to detect which spots on the disk are reflective. In contrast, a traditional record represents sound in analog form, in which the height of the groove corresponds to the amplitude of the sound.

A computer CD uses the same principle to store

information, which may be text, pictures, or sound. Computer CDs have capacities of several hundred megabytes. They are "read-only" because the user cannot store information on the disks; they can only be used to retrieve information stored on them by the supplier.

For example, the information in an encyclopedia can be stored on a disk, and with appropriate retrieval software a user may read the text, easily look up cross-references, look at pictures or maps, and perhaps listen to sound.

Central processing unit   *See* **CPU**.

Character   A character is any symbol that can be stored and processed by a computer. For example, A, 3, : are computer characters. The ASCII coding system is one way of representing characters on a computer. *See* **ASCII**.

Chip   *See* **Integrated circuit**.

**CHR$**   The function CHR$ in many versions of BASIC calculates the character associated with the given ASCII code. For example, CHR$(65) is "A" because the ASCII code of the character "A" is 65. The CHR$ function is the inverse of the ASC function. If N = ASC(X$), then X$ = CHR$ (N).

Circuit   A circuit is a complete path for an electric current. A circuit must contain a power source, such as a battery or a generator. Electrons will flow from the negative power supply terminal through a conducting medium (such as copper wire) to the positive power supply terminal. A useful circuit must also contain some sort of switch to determine whether or not it will be on, and some device that has resistance, known as the load. A circuit with no load is called a short circuit.

Circuit diagram   A circuit diagram is a schematic picture of an electronic circuit, using symbols to represent electronic components. The purpose of the diagram is to make it as easy as possible for people to trace the flow of current, rather than to exactly reproduce the physical locations of the components in the real circuit. (*See* **Electronic components**.)

Clock   1. The clock of a computer is a circuit that generates a series of evenly spaced pulses. All the switching activity in the computer occurs while the clock is sending out a pulse. Between pulses the electronic devices in the computer are allowed to stabilize. A computer with a faster clock rate is able to perform more operations per second. Powerful computers are now capable of performing an operation every 10 to 20 nanoseconds, and a microprocessor can perform an operation in less than 0.5 microsecond. The clock speed of a computer is often given in megahertz (MHz), where 1 MHz = 1,000,000 cycles per second. The fastest mainframe computers have a clock speed of about 50 MHz.   2. A real-time clock is a circuit within a computer that keeps track of the date and time. Some computers have real-time clocks that run even when the computers are turned off.

Closed   A switch is closed when it is turned on, that is, when it is set so that current can flow through it (see figure).

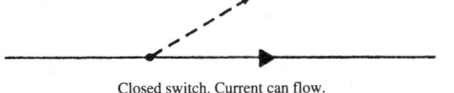

Closed switch. Current can flow.

COBOL   COBOL is a programming language for business data processing, developed in the early 1960s by several computer manufacturers and the U.S. Department of Defense. COBOL statements resemble English sentences, and the structure of the program requires that some documentation be included. COBOL programs are long and wordy, but easy to read; this readability makes it easy for programmers other than the original author to make corrections or changes. A COBOL program consists of the Identification Division, which gives some mandatory documentation, such as the program name; the Environment Division, which describes the machine environment; the Data Division, for data structures and input-output formats and the Procedure Division, for the algorithm.

Coding   Coding is the process of writing an algorithm or other problem-solving procedure in a computer programming language.

Compiler   A compiler is a computer program that translates FORTRAN, Pascal, or a similar high-level programming language into machine language. It contrasts with an interpreter, which executes high-level-language statements as it reads them. The high-level-language program fed into the compiler is called the source program; the generated machine language program is the object program.

Conductor   A conductor is a material in which electric current can flow. In order for a material to be a conductor the electrons must not be too tightly bound to their atoms.

Copy-protected disk   A copy-protected disk cannot be copied by the software normally used to copy disks on a particular computer. The purpose of copy-protecting disks is to prevent unauthorized duplication of copyrighted software. Copy protection is usually achieved by changing the size of the sectors in some of the tracks.

Coulomb   A group of 6.25×10^{18} electrons has a charge of 1 coulomb. (*See* **Ampere**.)

CPU   The CPU (central processing unit) is the part of a computer where arithmetic and logical operations are performed and instructions are decoded and executed. The CPU controls the operation of the computer. A microprocessor is an integrated circuit that contains a complete CPU on a single chip.

Crash   A computer is said to crash when a hardware failure or a program error causes the computer to become inoperable. A well-designed operating system contains protection against inappropriate input, so that a user's program will not be able to cause a system crash.

CRT   CRT stands for cathode ray tube, which is a device whereby electrons are sprayed onto a viewing screen, under the direction of magnetic fields, to form patterns. Examples of CRTs include television screens and computer monitors.

Current   A current is a flow of electrons through a conductor. Current is measured in amperes, 1 ampere = 6.25×10^{18} electrons per second.

Cursor   The cursor is the symbol on a computer terminal that shows you where on the screen the next character you type will appear. Cursors often appear as blinking dashes or rectangles. Many computers have cursor movement (arrow) keys that allow you to move the cursor vertically or horizontally around the screen. This ability is essential for text-editing purposes such as word processing. If you are working with a computer equipped with a mouse, you can use the mouse to move the cursor quickly around the screen.

Cybernetics Cybernetics is the study of how complex systems are controlled. It includes the comparative study of the operations of computers and of the human nervous system.

Data Data are factual information. Data is the plural of the word *datum*, which means "a single fact." Data processing is the act of using data for making calculations or decisions.

Data base A data base is a collection of data stored on a computer storage medium, such as a disk, that can be used for more than one purpose. For example, a firm that maintains a data base containing information on its employees will be able to use the same data for payroll, personnel, and other purposes. *See* **Data base management**.

Data base management Data base management is the task of storing data base and retrieving information from those data. There are three aspects of data base management: entering data, modifying or updating data, and presenting output reports. In a well-designed data base system the user needs to know only the nature of the information that is available and the type of questions that must be asked, without having to know about the physical arrangement of the data on a storage medium (such as a disk or tape). Many mainframe computers are used by businesses for data base management purposes. Several programs are available for microcomputers that perform data base functions, such as dBASE IV, Paradox, and Access, and some data management capabilities are provided with integrated programs such as Lotus 1-2-3. Some examples of data base applications include maintaining employee lists and preparing payrolls, maintaining parts order lists and keeping track of inventories, maintaining customer lists and preparing bills for credit customers, and keeping track of the students at a school. Information in a data base system is generally stored in several different files. For example, a business will often have a file of regular customers and a file of employees. Each file consists of a series of records, with each record containing information on an individual case, such as one person or one transaction. Each record consists of several fields, with each field containing an individual data item. For example, in an employee file there would be one record for each employee, and there would be a field containing the person's name, a field for the address, a field for the Social Security number, and so on. A data base management system must make provisions for adding new records (e.g., when an employee is hired), for deleting unneeded records (e.g., when an employee retires), and for modifying existing records. Some fields (such as the Social Security number) will not change; other fields (such as year-to-date pay) must be changed frequently. When you create a file with a microcomputer data base program, you first need to define the structure of the records in that file. You must state how many fields will be in each record, what the label for each field will be, what type of

data (numeric or character data) will be stored in the field, and what the width of the field will be. The program will make it as easy as possible for you to enter the data by placing carefully labeled prompts on the screen to tell you where to type each individual field. Each data base program has its own commands for adding new records, modifying existing records, or deleting records. The main purpose of a data base management system is to make it possible to obtain meaningful information from the data contained in the data base. A data base program can respond to brief queries on the screen, or it can present detailed printed reports in a format chosen by the user. Here are some general functions that a data base management system should be able to fulfill:

1. Sort the records according to the order indicated by one specific field (e.g., sort in alphabetic order by name, or in numeric order by zip code). You should be able to designate a secondary field along which sorting will occur when there are ties in the primary field. For example, if you are sorting the records by the number of months the customers are overdue in their payments, you probably would like the names of all people one month overdue in alphabetic order, then the names of all people two months overdue in alphabetic order, and so on.

2. Set up selection criteria that allow you to examine only the records that meet a specific condition. For example, you may wish to look only at customers who live in your city, or you may wish to look at all employees whose job title is either "delivery driver" or "warehouse worker."

3. Count the number of records that meet a specific condition. For example, you may wish to count the number of employees who have been with the company for more than 10 years.

4. Perform calculations, such as computing the total amount owed on overdue accounts, or the year-to-date pay for each employee.

5. Connect together information from more than one file. For example, a data base system might contain an employee file that lists the job classification for each employee. A separate file for each job classification would contain information on wages, fringe benefits, and work schedules that apply to all workers in that classification.

Decimal number A decimal number is a number expressed in ordinary base-10 notation, using the digits 0, 1, 2, 3, 4, 5, 6, 7, 8, 9.

Dedicated system A dedicated system is a system designed to fulfill only one function. For example, a dedicated word processor is a computer system designed only for word processing.

Desktop publishing A desktop publishing system makes it possible for a microcomputer user to perform typesetting and page layout tasks. A desktop publishing system must contain these elements:

1. a computer with adequate memory and hard disk space (a graphical user interface is preferred);

2. a large monitor (for extensive desktop publishing work, it is best to have a monitor large enough to show an entire page at once);

3. a desktop publishing program, such as Aldus PageMaker; and

4. a printer, preferably a laser printer.

A scanner is also helpful. A desktop publishing system is most helpful if you need to prepare a newspaper, newsletter, brochure, or other document in which you would like an esthetic layout of text, possibly mixed with drawings and pictures.

Consider how the page layout task would have been done in pre-desktop publishing days. The text would have to be typeset into columns of the appropriate size (likely by a professional printer). Then the pages would have to be laid out by cutting and pasting the text to the proper locations. It would be necessary to separately paste in headlines and drawings. Blank spaces would be left for photographs, which would be added later at the professional print shop.

A desktop publishing program allows the user to design the page layout on the screen. Text can be moved to the proper locations, and the size and style of type can be changed as necessary. Photographs read in with a scanner can be shown in the proper place. With a graphical user interface, a mouse can be used to move items around, and the screen will show you the appearance of the printed page (WYSIWYG, or "what you see is what you get") Finally, camera-ready masters can be produced by a laser printer, which can be used for the reproduction process.

Diagnostic message   A diagnostic message is a message the computer prints in case of an error to help the programmer identify the cause of the error.

Digital computer   A digital computer represents information in discrete form, as opposed to an *analog computer*, which allows representations to vary along a continuum. For example, the temperature of a room might be any value between 0° and 100° Fahrenheit. An analog computer could represent this as a continuously varying voltage between 0 and 100 volts. A digital computer, on the other hand, would have to represent it as a decimal or binary number with a specific number of digits (e.g., 68.80 or 68.81). All modem general-purpose computers are digital. Analog computer circuits, however, are frequently used in industrial control equipment. (*See also* **CD-ROM**.)

Digital Equipment Corporation   Digital Equipment Corporation is a large manufacturer of microcomputers and minicomputers. Digital has manufactured several popular minicomputers, including the PDP-8, introduced in 1965, and the PDP-11, introduced in 1970. Digital introduced the first computer in the line of VAX 32-bit superminicomputers in 1977. The company is located in Maynard, Massachusetts.

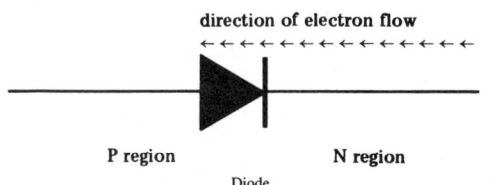

direction of electron flow

P region   N region

Diode

Diode   A diode is a device that allows electric current to pass in one direction, but not in the other (see the figure). A diode is forward biased when the voltage applied to it is the right way for current to flow; otherwise it is reverse biased. The symbol for

a diode is a small arrow. Electrons flow in the direction opposite the way that the arrow points. Diodes are formed by joining two types of doped semiconductors: P type, with a deficiency of free electrons (and an excess of holes), and N type, with a surplus of free electrons. (*See* **Semiconductor**.) The place where the two regions are joined is called the junction.

If a negative voltage is applied to the N region, the electrons will be driven away from the negative voltage and toward the junction. When a positive voltage is applied to the P region, the holes will be driven away from the positive voltage and toward the junction. At the junction, the electrons from the N region will jump into the holes from the P region, with the result that current can flow across the diode (see the figure). If a negative voltage is applied to the N region, then the free electrons in the N region will be pulled away from the junction. Likewise, a negative voltage applied to the P region will pull all the holes away from the junction. The result is that no current flows across the junction, so the diode does not conduct at all. The only way to make current flow would be to apply a large enough voltage to the P region so that electrons are broken out of their crystal structure. This effect is called breakdown, and once it happens most diodes are ruined. Diodes come with ratings that indicate the maximum reverse bias voltage they can withstand before breaking down. Suppose that the current is turned off. What keeps the extra electrons in the N region from filling up the holes in the P region? If the electrons did that, the N region would acquire a net positive charge, and the P region would acquire a net negative charge. Then all the electrons would be repelled from the P region and attracted back to the N region. Each of the phosphorus atoms in the N region contains 15 protons, while each silicon atom contains 14 protons. If the N region as a whole is to remain electrically neutral, it must contain one free electron for every phosphorus atom. Diodes are used in rectifier circuits and in some logic circuits. Transistors consist of three semiconductor regions separated by two junctions. A special type of diode is the light-emitting diode (or LED), which is used for the readout on some calculators.

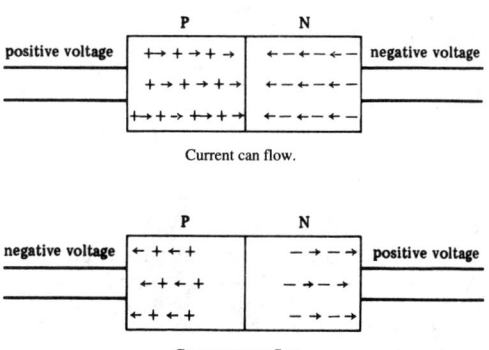

Current can flow.

Current cannot flow.

Disk   A magnetic disk is a computer memory device. Large computers store information on large disk packs consisting of several disks joined together on one spindle. Microcomputers use floppy disks (diskettes) or hard disks. The most common sizes for diskettes are the 5¼ and 3½ inch. A hard disk is usually mounted in the computer and cannot be removed. The part of the computer that reads and writes the disk is known as the disk drive. The iron oxide on the disk consists of microscopically small needles, each of which acts like a tiny bar magnet. Information is stored by magnetizing these needles. The read-write head, which skims the surface of the disk, can either generate a magnetic field to magnetize the needles, or detect the magnetic field of needles that are already magnetized. The binary digits 0 and 1 are represented by changes in the direction of magnetization. Data on disks are stored in many concentric circles each of which is called a track. Each track is divided into sectors, which are the amount of data that the computer reads into memory in a single step. On a multilayer disk pack, the set of tracks in corresponding positions on different layers is known as a cylinder. The directory of a disk is a special area in which the computer records the names and locations of all the files on the disk. In some operating systems, such as MS-DOS and UNIX, the user can create many directories on a single disk. As a typical example, the 5¼-inch floppy disks for the IBM PC have 40 tracks on each of two sides, and each track contains nine 512-byte sectors; with allowances for space taken up by the directory, the capacity of the disk is about 360 kilobytes. Hard disks with capacities ranging from 20 to 200 megabytes are available for the same computer; hard disks for mainframe computers have capacities as large as 2.5 gigabytes (more than 2.5 billion bytes). Data stored on a magnetic disk cannot be read as quickly as data stored in the main memory of the computer, but disk storage has larger capacity and is not erased when the computer is turned off. Storing data on magnetic tape is even cheaper than using disks, but retrieving data from tape storage takes longer because the computer cannot jump from one location on the tape to another without going through all the tape in between.

Documentation   A written description of a computer program is known as documentation. Documentation falls into several categories: 1. internal documentation, consisting of comments within the program. Internal documentation is addressed mostly to future programmers who may have to make corrections or other modifications; 2. on-line documentation, that is, information that is displayed as the program runs or that can be called up with a command such as HELP; 3. reference cards containing easily forgotten details for quick reference; 4. reference manuals, setting out complete instructions for the program in a systematic way; and 5. tutorials, serving as introductions for new users.

DOS   DOS (disk operating system) has been used by many computer manufacturers as a name for various operating systems, including an early operating system for IBM 360; the disk operating system for the Apple II (Apple DOS), MS-DOS, developed by Microsoft for 16-bit microcomputers, and PC-DOS, a version of MS-DOS commonly sold with the IBM PC.

Dot matrix printer   A dot matrix printer forms characters as a pattern of dots. The quality of the printing depends on the number of dots per unit

area; more dots indicates a higher quality of print. For contrast, see **Ink jet printer**; **Laser printer**.

Double density   A double-density floppy diskette is recorded in a format that puts twice as many bits into a given area as the earlier single-density format. See **Disk**.

Down   A computer system is down when it is not available to users for some reason, such as when it malfunctions or when it is being tested.

Download   To download is to transmit a file or program from a central computer to a smaller computer or a computer at a remote site.

E   **Edit**   To edit a file is to examine it and make changes in it, usually with the aid of an editor.

Editor   An editor is a computer program that enables the user to sit at a console or terminal, view the contents of a file, and add material or make other changes. *Full-screen editors* use the entire screen as a "window" through which to look at the file; the user can move the cursor around and type anywhere on the screen, or perform scrolling, that is, move the window up or down relative to the contents originally on the screen.

Electron   An electron is a subatomic particle with a negative electric charge. An atom is made up of a nucleus (consisting of protons and neutrons) surrounded by an orbiting cloud of electrons. Two objects with negative charges will repel each other, but an object with a negative charge will be attracted to an object with a positive charge. An electric current is a flow of electrons.

Electronic components   The basic electronic components that make up computers are wires, transistors, diodes, resistors, capacitors, and inductors. Their schematic symbols are shown in the figure. An integrated circuit is a device consisting of many transistors and other circuit elements on a single silicon chip.

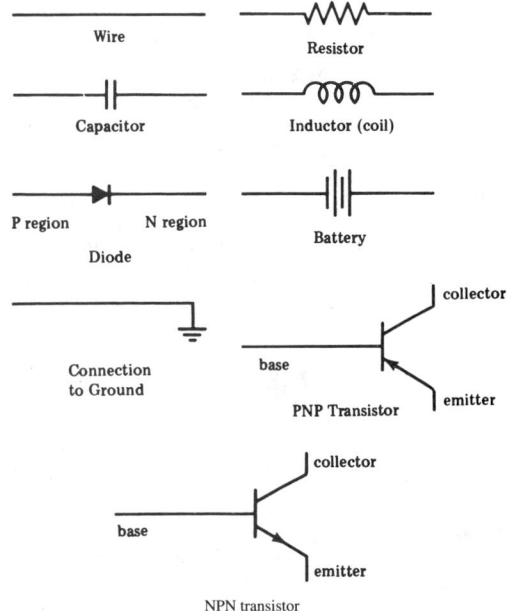

Wire

Resistor

Capacitor

Inductor (coil)

P region   N region

Diode

Battery

Connection to Ground

base

collector

emitter

PNP Transistor

base

collector

emitter

NPN transistor

Electronic mail   An electronic mail system allows a person to type a message at one computer or terminal and then send that message to someone at another terminal or computer. The message will be stored until the receiver chooses to read it.

Electrostatic printer   A printer that prints by using an electric charge to deposit toner on paper, in the same way as a Xerox copier is known as an electrostatic printer.

Elite   An elite typewriter prints 12 characters per inch.

Epson   Epson is a prominent Japanese manufacturer of dot matrix printers, distributed in the United States by Epson America, Inc., of Torrance, California. The Epson MX-80 printer received wide acceptance during the early 1980s and set many standards to which other manufacturers now adhere. Epson printers are capable of many special effects, including dot-by-dot graphics.

Execute   To execute an instruction is to do what the instruction says to do. A computer alternates between a fetch cycle, when it locates the next instruction, and an execute cycle, when it carries the instruction out.

F   **Farad**   The farad is the unit of measure of capacitance. A 1-farad capacitor will store a charge of 1 coulomb when 1 volt is applied across it. Real capacitors range in value from about 10 picofarads (10×10^{-12} farad) to 250,000 microfarads (0.25 farad).

Feedback   Feedback occurs when a control device uses information about the current state of the system to determine the next control action. For example, when a thermostat controls the temperature in a house, it needs to know the current temperature in the house before it decides whether to turn on the furnace.

Field   A group of adjacent characters is called a field. For example, in a company payroll system the information about a single individual can be stored as one record. Each record will be divided into several fields. One field will contain the employee's name, another field, his Social Security number; a third field, his salary or rate per hour; and so on.

File   A file is a collection of information stored by a computer. Microcomputers typically store files on floppy disks or hard disks. A file might consist of a computer program, the text of a document stored by a word processing file, or a collection of data records stored by a data base program.

First-generation computers   First-generation computers are the computers that were built in the late 1940s and early 1950s, using vacuum tubes.

Flowchart   A flowchart is a chart consisting of symbols and words that completely describe an algorithm (i.e., how to solve a problem). Each step in the flowchart is followed by an arrow that indicates which step to do next. Flowcharts can also be used to represent procedures that contain loops. "Start" and "stop" statements are written with ovals, action statements are written with squares; and decision statements are written with diamonds. A decision statement asks a yes or no question. If the answer is yes, the path labeled

"yes" is followed; otherwise the other path is followed. Writing a flowchart often helps to solve a complex programming problem, because it enables you to see where all the branches and loops go. An algorithm written in flowchart form is very versatile, since it can be translated into many different computer programming languages. The flowchart below describes how to solve the quadratic equation $ax^2 + bx + c = 0$

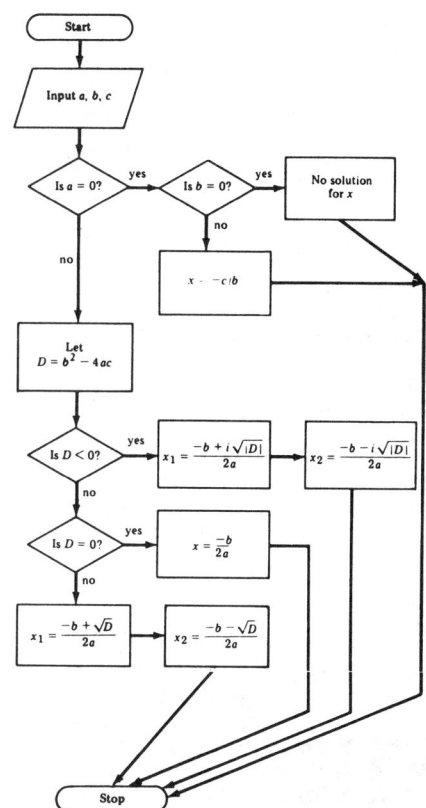

Font   A font is a complete set of characters (letters, numbers, and other symbols) in a particular typeface, style, and size. Many word processing programs and desktop publishing systems allow the user to use more than one font in a document. *See also* **Typeface**.

FORTRAN   FORTRAN, developed by IBM in the late 1950s, was the first major programming language that allowed programmers to describe calculations by means of mathematical formulas. For example

D = (A + B)*C

is an example of a FORTRAN expression to add the values of the variables A and B, multiply by C, and then store the result as D.

Fourth-generation computers   Fourth-generation computers are built around integrated circuits with a large-scale integration. Some people view these computers as being advanced third-generation computers.

Function key   *See* **Programmable function key**.

 **GOSUB** The BASIC statement GOSUB causes the computer to jump to the subroutine that begins at the specified statement number. When the computer reaches the keyword RETURN at the end of the subroutine, it will jump back to the statement immediately following the original GOSUB statement. *See* **BASIC**; **Subroutine**.

GOTO The GOTO expression in BASIC causes the computer to jump to the specified statement number. *See* **BASIC**.

Graphical user interface A graphical user interface (GUI) is a way of communicating with a computer that uses visual feedback to the user as much as possible. Features of a GUI include the use of icons to represent commands and options, pulldown menus that appear when called for and then disappear when no longer needed, and the use of a mouse to move a pointer around the screen. By pointing to the appropriate icons for menu items and clicking a mouse button, various commands can be activated. It is also possible to use the mouse in drawing programs.

The first widely used computer with a GUI was the Apple Macintosh introduced in 1984. The release of Microsoft Windows 3.0 in 1990 provided a widely used GUI for IBM PC-compatible computers. *See* **Windows**.

The graphical user interface on the Macintosh provided an important tool in the growth of desktop publishing. Because the screen of a GUI computer is always in graphics mode, it is possible to change the style of type in a document and have the change be visible on the screen. (This feature is sometimes known as WYSIWYG, "what you see is what you get.") Also, it is possible to blend illustrations with the text.

Graphics Computer graphics is the use of computer output devices, such as screens and plotters, to produce pictures. A plotter is a device that draws on paper, usually by moving a pen from point to point.

 **Hard copy** A hard copy is a printout on paper of computer output.

Hard disk A hard disk is a storage medium using rigid aluminum disks coated with iron oxide. Hard disks have much greater storage capacity than floppy disks; hard disks with a capacity of 40 megabytes or more are available for microcomputers. The read-write head travels across the disk on a thin cushion of air without ever actually touching the disk. However, hard disks have the disadvantage that they are usually built into the machine and cannot be removed, as can floppy disks. *See* **Disk**.

Hardware The hardware in a computer system consists of all the physical elements in the computer, such as integrated circuits, wires, and terminals.

Henry The henry is the unit of measure of inductance. One henry is the inductance of a circuit in which an electromotive force of one volt is produced by a current in the circuit that varies at the rate of one ampere per second.

Hewlett-Packard Hewlett-Packard, located in Palo Alto, California, produces a wide range of electronic instruments and the LaserJet series of laser printers.

Hexadecimal A hexadecimal number is a number written in base-16. A hexadecimal system consists of 16 possible digits, labeled by 0, 1, 2, 3, 4, 5, 6, 7, 8, 9, A (= 10), B (= 11), C (= 12), D (= 13), E (= 14), and F (= 15). For example, the number A4C2 in a hexadecimal means $10 \times 16^3 + 4 \times 16^2 + 12 \times 16^1 + 2 \times 16^0 = 42,178$.

High-level language A high-level language is a computer programming language designed to allow people to write programs without having to understand the inner workings of the computer. BASIC, PL/I, FORTRAN, and Pascal are examples of high-level languages.

Hole A hole is a place where an electron is missing from the crystal structure of a P-type semiconductor. A hole acts as a moving positive charge. (*See* **Semiconductor**.)

 **IBM** IBM (International Business Machines) is the largest computer manufacturer. IBM made office equipment long before the 1950s, when it started making computers. A decade later, IBM had about 80% of the computer market with such models as the IBM 360 computer. The company continues to make popular mainframe computers, such as the 4300 series. In 1981 IBM introduced the IBM PC, which quickly became one of the most popular microcomputers. Now many other companies produce software or peripherals designed to be used with the IBM PC, and several companies produce computers designed to run the same programs as the IBM PC. The headquarters of IBM is in Armonk, New York.

IC *See* **Integrated circuit**.

Icon An icon is a picture that represents a particular command on a computer with a graphical user interface. To execute the command you point to the command with the mouse and push a button.

IF In many programming languages the keyword IF is used to specify an action that is to be executed only if a specified condition is true.

Inductance The inductance of an inductor, or coil, is a measure of the strength of the magnetic field that is generated when a current is passed through that inductor. *See* **Inductor**.

Inductor

Inductor An inductor is a coil of wire that can store energy in the form of a magnetic field. When a current flows in a wire, a magnetic field forms around the wire. When the current is turned off, the magnetic field collapses. A moving magnetic field generates an electric current, so as the magnetic field collapses it will briefly cause a current to flow in the direction opposite the original current flow. The magnetic field of a single wire will be very small, but the field can be made much stronger by wrapping the wire around an iron core many times. The symbol for an inductor is a little coil (see the figure). The strength of the magnetic field that an inductor will generate is measured in a unit called the henry. In a direct-current circuit, the inductor acts like a resistor. The amount by which the inductor resists current flow in an alternating-current circuit

COMPUTERS AND ELECTRONIC MEDIA

increases as the frequency increases. Each time the current changes direction, the collapsing magnetic field generates a reverse current.

Ink jet printer   An ink jet printer forms images by firing tiny jets of ink at the paper. It provides an economical alternative to the laser printer for home use. It is quieter and provides higher quality output than the dot matrix printer. *See also* **Laser printer**.

Input   The input to a computer is the data that are fed into the computer for it to process. (Note that the terms input and output are always used from the computer's point of view.) The input data may be either numbers or character strings (e.g., a list of names). The computer receives input through an input device, such as a keyboard, or from a storage device, such as a disk drive.

Insulator   An insulator is a material in which all the electrons are tightly bound to their atoms, so electric current cannot flow through an insulator. A material in which current can flow is called a *conductor*.

Integrated circuit   An integrated circuit is an electronic device consisting of many miniature transistors and other circuit elements on a single silicon chip. The first integrated circuits were developed in the late 1950s, and since then there has been continued improvement. The number of components that can be placed on a single chip has been steadily rising. The advantages of integrated circuits include the fact that they are very small (less than ¼-inch square), their internal connections are more reliable, they consume much less power, they generate much less heat, and they cost less than similar circuits made with separate components. Integrated circuits are classified by their level of complexity. "Small-scale integration" refers to circuits containing fewer than 10 logic gates; "medium-scale integration," to circuits containing 10–100 gates; and "large-scale integration," to circuits with more than 100 gates. The pattern of components to be placed in an integrated circuit is first mapped out by a computer. It is necessary to add impurities to the silicon crystal to create either P-type or N-type regions. (*See* **Semiconductor**.) An evaporated metal is engraved on the circuit by photographic techniques in the places where electric conducting paths are needed. Integrated circuits are mass produced by making many identical circuits at the same time from a single wafer of silicon. Each circuit must be individually tested, however, because a single defect in the crystal can completely ruin the circuit. The ultimate integrated circuit is the microprocessor, which is a single chip that contains the complete arithmetic and logic unit of a computer.

Integrated software   An integrated software package is a program that combines several functions in one program. For example, Lotus 1-2-3 is an integrated program that combines spreadsheet calculations, data management operations, and graphics. The advantage of an integrated program stems from the fact that the transfer of information from one application to another is easier than it would be if a separate program were used for each application.

Intel   Intel produces the microprocessors used in IBM PC-compatible computers. *See* **Microprocessor**.

International Business Machines   *See* **IBM**.

Interpreter   An interpreter for a particular programming language is a program that executes a program written in that language by reading it one line at a time and doing the specified operations immediately. A program running under an interpreter will generally not run as fast as a program that has been translated by a compiler.

J   **Jacket**   A floppy disk is encased in a stiff plastic jacket that contains holes giving the disk drive access to the information on the disk. The disk should never be removed from the jacket.

Junction   The junction is the part of a diode or transistor where two opposite types of semiconductor material meet. *See* **Diode**; **Transistor**.

K   **Kilobyte**   One kilobyte represents 2^{10} = 1,024 bytes. Computer memories are measured in kilobytes (K); 1 K of memory stores approximately 1,000 characters. *See* **Memory**.

Kirchhoff's law   Kirchhoff's law states that the sum of the voltages across the devices in a series circuit is equal to the total voltage applied to that circuit (see the figure).

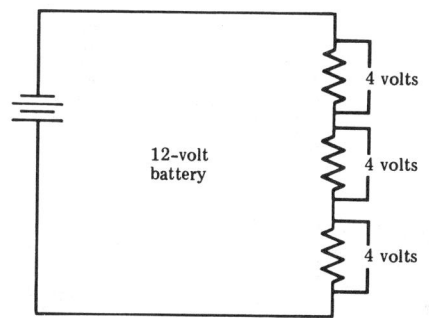

L   **Landscape**   Paper is printed in landscape mode when it is wider than it is tall (similar to a landscape painting). For contrast, *see* **Portrait**.

Laser printer   A laser printer uses a laser beam to generate an image, then transfers it to paper electrostatically. (*See* **Electrostatic printer**.) A laser printer is the best choice for a computer that is used extensively for word processing or desktop publishing. Laser printers commonly have a resolution of 300 dots per inch. For more economical alternatives, *see* **Ink jet printer**; **Dot matrix printer**.

LCD   LCD (liquid crystal display) is the type of display found on many portable computers and digital watches.

LED   The acronym LED stands for light-emitting diode. An LED device will light up when the proper current is passed through it. The display on many calculators is made of LEDs.

Light-emitting diode   *See* **LED**.

Liquid crystal display   *See* **LCD**.

LISP   LISP (short for list processor) is a computer programming language typically used in artificial intelligence work because of the ease with which it handles complex data structures.

Load   To load is to transfer information from an auxiliary storage device into a computer.

LOG   In many versions of BASIC and other languages, the function LOG(X) calculates the natural logarithm of X (that is, the logarithm to the base e). However, in some versions, LOG(X) is the common logarithm and LN(X) is the natural logarithm.

LOGO   LOGO is a computer programming language designed to teach programming to children. It allows the programmer to give commands to a "turtle" that moves around the screen. *See* **Turtle**.

Loop   A loop in a computer program is a set of statements that are to be executed repeatedly. For example, the BASIC program

```
10 FOR I = 1 TO 5
20     PRINT I, I∧2
30 NEXT I
```

contains a loop. Statement 20 will be executed five times, first with I equal to 1, then with I equal to 2, and so on. The output from the program will look like this:

```
1    1
2    4
3    9
4    16
5    25
```

Lotus 1-2-3   Lotus 1-2-3, an integrated software package produced by Lotus Development Corp. has become one of the best selling business decision-making tools. Lotus 1-2-3 combines the functions of a spreadsheet program with data management capabilities and graphics.

Machine language   A machine language contains instructions that a computer can execute directly. Machine language statements are written in a binary code and each statement corresponds to one machine action.

Macintosh   The Macintosh, a computer introduced by Apple in 1984, contains several innovative features, including a microprocessor with some 32-bit capabilities and a graphical user interface (GUI). The Macintosh became popular because it is well-suited for graphics-oriented tasks, such as desktop publishing.

Magnetic bubble memory   Magnetic bubble memory can be used in the same way as RAM but does not go blank when power to it is turned off. At present, bubble memories are more expensive than disks; they are used in very lightweight, portable computers when a disk drive would be too bulky or too fragile.

Mainframe computer   A mainframe computer is a large computer occupying a specially air-conditioned room and supporting typically 100 to 500 users at a time. The IBM 370 and IBM 3081 are examples of mainframe computers.

Matrix printer   A matrix printer forms letters and other symbols by patterns of dots. *See* **Dot matrix printer**.

Megabyte   A megabyte (MB) is an amount of computer memory equal to $2^{20} = 1,048,576$ bytes; 1 MB of memory stores slightly more than 1 million characters. *See* **Memory**.

Memory   The memory is the space within a computer where information is stored while being actively worked on. Most microcomputers have a small amount of read-only memory (ROM), containing the built-in programs that start the operation of the computer when it is turned on, and a large amount of random-access memory (RAM) for the user's programs and data. Except for ROM, memory goes blank when the computer is turned off; any data in it must be copied to disk or tape if they are to be saved. The memory requirements of a computer are dictated by the software that is to run on it. In th early 1980s, 64 K (that is, 64 kilobytes) was a common size for a microcomputer memory. As more advanced software became common, the memory requirements increased, so by the end of the decade 640 K was a minimum amount for a business microcomputer memory. In the early 1990s, as Windows became common, the typical memory size increased to 4 or 8 megabytes.

Menu   A menu is a list of choices that appears on the screen while a particular program is being executed. By typing the number or letter that corresponds to a particular command option, you can cause that command to be executed. The presence of menus in a program makes it easy for people to use the program because they don't need to memorize all the commands. By looking at the menu they can see all their options.

Microcomputer   A microcomputer is a computer whose CPU consists of a single integrated circuit known as the *microprocessor*. Ordinarily, a microcomputer is used by only one person at a time. All home computers are microcomputers. *See* **Integrated circuit**; **Microprocessor**.

Microprocessor   A microprocessor is an integrated circuit ("chip") that contains the complete central processing unit (CPU) of a microcomputer. The original IBM PC was built around the Intel 8088 processor. Subsequently, Intel introduced more advanced processors that could operate at greater speeds: the 80286, the 80386, and the 80486.

Macintosh computers are built around the Motorola 68000 family of processors: the 68020, 68030, and 68040. Microprocessors are commonly described as "8 bit," "16 bit," or the like. The number can refer either to the number of bits in each internal data register or to the number of bits on the data bus; these two numbers are often, but not always, the same. Other things being equal, larger registers and a larger bus enable the processor to do its work faster. Clock speed is also important. The *clock* is the oscillator that causes the microprocessor to proceed from one step to the next in executing instructions. (Each machine instruction takes several clock cycles.) Clock speed is measured in megahertz (MHz); 1 MHz is 1 million cycles per second. Higher clock speeds result in faster computation—but only if exactly the same machine instructions are being executed.

Microsoft, Inc.   Microsoft, one of the leading software-producing companies, was founded by William Gates and Paul Allen in 1975, when they wrote a version of BASIC. Microsoft produces Microsoft BASIC, which is one of the most popular versions of BASIC. The company also produces

IBM PC BASIC, IBM PC DOS, the operating system MS DOS, the spreadsheet program Excel, and the word processing program Microsoft WORD, as well as compilers for several other computer languages and other systems software. In 1990 Microsoft introduced Version 3.0 of Windows, a much improved version of an earlier product that provided a graphical user interface for computers in the IBM PC line. Windows 3.0 rapidly became a best-seller, and many other software makers wrote programs to operate within the Windows environment. The company is located in Redmond, Washington.

Minicomputer A minicomputer is a computer intermediate in size between a mainframe computer and a microcomputer; two examples are the Digital Equipment Corporation VAX and the IBM System/3. A minicomputer typically occupies a large area within a room and supports 10 to 100 users at a time. Minicomputers are typically used by medium-sized businesses and academic institutions.

Mnemonic A mnemonic is a device that helps you remember something. For example, the expression "Spring forward, fall back" helps you remember which way to adjust your clocks in the spring and the fall for daylight savings time. A *mnemonic variable name* is a variable name that helps the programmer remember what the variable means. For example, in a Pascal payroll program the variable to represent the hours worked could be named X312W17HK, but it would be much better to give the variable a mnemonic name such as HOURS.

Modem A modem is a device that connects to a computer and a telephone line and makes it possible to send signals from that computer to another one. The computer needs to operate a communication program, which contains a set of commands for sending and retrieving data. With the use of a modem it is possible for a microcomputer to be connected to another microcomputer, a mainframe computer, a BBS, or a nationwide information service.

Monitor 1. A monitor is a computer program that supervises the activity of other programs. 2. A device similar to a television set that accepts video signals from a computer and displays information on its screen is known as a monitor. The monitor itself does no computing at all.

Mouse A mouse is a special computer input device, connected by a wire to the computer. The mouse has a roller on its bottom designed to roll along the desk top beside your computer. When you move the mouse with one hand, the pointer will move along the screen in the same direction in which the mouse is being moved. A mouse can be useful when working with word processing editing programs, graphics programs, or spreadsheet programs, when it is helpful to be able to move the cursor quickly around the screen. *See* **Graphical user interface**.

MS-DOS MS-DOS (short for Microsoft disk operating system) is one of the most commonly used operating systems on microcomputers. When first operating a computer using MS-DOS, the computer will typically ask for the date and time, and then it will display a prompt such as

A > or A :

This prompt indicates that disk drive A is the default drive, which means that the computer will look for files on the disk in drive A unless it is given an explicit drive designation with the file name. Some often used MS-DOS commands include DIR, which displays a directory of the files on a disk; FORMAT, which prepares a new blank disk so that data can be stored on it; COPY, which copies one file to another; and TYPE, which displays a file on the screen.

Network A network is a system in which different computers are linked together. A local area network (LAN) links computers in the same or adjacent buildings together. A wide-area network links computers over a wide area—in some cases worldwide.

Local area networks are very valuable in office situations in which different computer users need to share the same data. Typically one computer (called the server) is responsible for administering the network. The other computers in the network are connected to the servers either directly or through the other computers in the network, depending on the topology (or arrangement) of the network. Novell Netware is a popular choice of software to administer the network. The network administrator determines the degree of access to the data on the hard disk of the server. Some files allow read/write access (meaning that office workers can update information in the file); other files allow read-only access (as with program files, with which you do not want each individual user to modify the program); other files may allow no access at all (as with confidential data).

Networks are also valuable because they allow users to send electronic mail to each other and to share access to hardware devices, such as printers.

NEXT The keyword NEXT in BASIC is used to mark the end of a loop. For example, the statement NEXT J tells the computer that it has reached the end of the loop that uses J as the counter variable. *See* **Loop**.

Numeric keypad A numeric keypad is a separate set of keys beside the main alphabetic keypad that contains the digits 0 to 9 and a decimal point key. The digits are arranged in the same way as they are on an adding machine. If you have to type large quantities of numeric data, a numeric keypad is quicker to use than the number keys on the regular keypad.

Ohm The ohm is the unit of measure of electric resistance. If an object has a resistance of 1 ohm, then an applied voltage of 1 volt will cause a current of 1 ampere to flow through the device. *See* **Ohm's law**.

Ohm's law Ohm's law states that the current that will flow through a circuit element is equal to the voltage applied across that element divided by the resistance of that element: $I = V/R$, where I = current, in amperes; V = voltage, in volts; and R = resistance, in ohms.

Open A switch is open when it is turned off (see the figure).

Open switch. Current cannot flow.

Operating system An operating system is a program that controls a computer and makes it possible for users to enter and run their own programs. No application programs can run in the absence of an operating system. For an example of an operating system commonly used on microcomputers, *see* **MS-DOS**.

Operations research Operations research is concerned with the development of mathematical models of repetitive human activities, such as those involved in traffic flow, assembly lines, and military campaigns. Operations research makes extensive use of computer simulation.

Optical character reader An optical character reader is a device that can recognize typed or handwritten characters on paper. *See* **Scanner**.

Output The output from a computer is the information that the computer generates as a result of its calculations. Computer output may be printed on paper, displayed on a terminal, or stored on magnetic tapes or disks.

P **Parallel** Two electronic circuit elements are connected in parallel if the electric current will reach the same destination by flowing through either element. The figure shows two resistors connected in parallel.

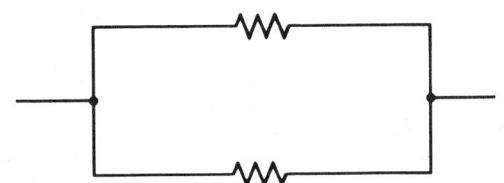

Pascal Pascal, a programming language developed by Niklaus Wirth, is designed to encourage programmers to write modular and well-structured programs. Pascal has become one of the most popular languages for microcomputers, and there are several common versions. Here are some of its features:

1. The first word in a Pascal program is PROGRAM, followed by the program name. The first line normally includes the words (INPUT, OUTPUT). The first part of the program is a declaration section for constants, variables, procedures, and functions. Every variable used in a Pascal program must be declared. The action part of the program starts with the word BEGIN, and the program concludes with the word END, followed by a period. Statements are separated from each other by semicolons.

2. Pascal provides four standard data types: real, integer, Boolean, and char. Integer variables can take on only values that are whole numbers or the negatives of whole numbers. Real variables can take on numeric values that include fractional parts, such as 23.432. Boolean variables are logic variables that can only have two possible values: true or false. Char variables can take on single character values. Here is an example of a declaration section:

```
VAR
   count, total : INTEGER;
   average : REAL
   error : BOOLEAN;
   c : CHAR;
```

3. An assignment statement in Pascal looks like this:

```
x : = 3;
```

Note that a colon followed by an equals sign is the symbol used for assignment. This statement will cause the variable *x* to take on the value 3. For integers and real numbers, + means addition, – means subtraction, * means multiplication, and ** means exponentiation (although exponentiation is not available on all Pascal versions). Division for real numbers is represented by /. There are two separate division commands for integers. The expression of a DIV b will be the quotient of *a* divided by *b*, ignoring the remainder. The expression a MOD b will be the remainder when *a* is divided by *b*. For example, 14 DIV 5 is 2, and 14 MOD 5 is 4.

4. The two input commands are READ and READLN. If you are using Pascal interactively, the statement READ(x) will cause the computer to stop and wait for you to type a value for *x* at the keyboard. READLN (which stands for "readline") works the same way except that after a READLN is executed the computer will start looking at the next data line when it reaches the next input statement. The two output commands are WRITE and WRITELN. The command WRITE(x); causes the value of the variable *x* to be displayed. The command WRITE ('Hello'), causes the word *Hello* to be displayed. The command WRITE (x:6) causes the value of *x* to be displayed in a field that is six characters wide, and the command WRITE(x:7:3) causes the value of x to be displayed in a field that is seven characters wide with three characters to the right of the decimal point displayed. After a WRITE command is executed, the output from subsequent output statements will be displayed on the same line. After a WRITELN statement, the output from subsequent output statements will be displayed on a new line.

5. The IF/THEN/ELSE statement can be used to control the actions of a program. For example:

```
IF x > 0 THEN WRITELN ('x is positive')
ELSE WRITELN ('x is negative');
```

If you would like more than one action to be executed if the condition is true, you may form a compound statement that starts with the word BEGIN and concludes with the word END. For example:

```
IF x > 0 THEN
   BEGIN
     WRITELN ('The value of x is
     positive'); WRITELN ('The square root
     of x is'.SQRT(x)) END;
```

Pascal provides for three types of loops; RE-PEAT, WHILE, and FOR loops. Each of the following program segments causes the numbers from 1–10 to be printed:

```
number  : = 0
REPEAT
 number : = number + 1;
 WRITELN(number);
UNTIL number > = 10;
. . .
number : = 1;
WHILE number < = 10 DO
 BEGIN
  WRITELN(number);
  number : = number + 1
 END;
. . .
FOR number : = 1 TO 10 DO WRITELN(number);
```

6. Arrays are declared by listing the highest and lowest allowable values for their subscripts. For example, the declaration

```
VAR zipcodes : ARRAY [1 . . 20] OF INTEGER;
```

defines zip codes as being a 20-element one-dimensional array, and the declaration

```
VAR table : ARRAY [0 . . 10, 0 . . 15] OF REAL;
```

defines table as being a two-dimensional array with 11 rows (labeled 0–10) and 16 columns (labeled 0–15).

7. One of the most valuable features of Pascal is the capability it provides for writing modular programs. A procedure is a mini Pascal program defined in the declaration section of the main program. The procedure can be executed from the main program simply by listing its name. A procedure may have parameters, and any variables that are declared within the procedure are local to that procedure. Pascal also provides for functions that return values to the calling program.

8. A special feature of Pascal is that it provides the capability for the programmer to define new data types that can be used in addition to the four standard data types. Pascal also allows the programmer to define sets, and then perform a set operation such as union or intersection. By using a structured data type called a record, it is possible to organize related data of different types.

9. Comments in Pascal begin with a left brace, { and end with a right brace, }. On some systems comments begin with (* and end with *). A Pascal program can be very readable if it consists of several procedures that all have meaningful mnemonic names.

Password A password is a secret character string that is required to log onto a computer system, thus preventing unauthorized persons from obtaining access to the computer.

Personal computer A personal computer is designed to be used by only one person, either at home or in a business setting. The term *personal computer* includes some microcomputers that are too large and expensive to be referred to as home computers. One of the first personal computers was the Digital Equipment Corporation PDP-8, a minicomputer often used in scientific laboratories in the early 1970s.

Pica 1. A pica typewriter prints 10 characters per inch. 2. In typesetting, a pica is ⅙ inch, or 12 points.

Pitch The pitch of a printer is the number of characters per inch. In fixed pitch type every character has the same width. With proportional pitch type, some characters are wider than others.

Pixel A picture on a CRT screen is made up of tiny elements called pixels. For example, a typical screen in medium resolution mode consists of a 320 by 200 pixel array. You can draw pictures on the screen by controlling the color of each pixel.

PL/I (PL/1) PL/I is a very powerful programming language developed by IBM in the early 1960s to accompany its System/360 computer. The name stands for programming language one (I) and is also written as PL/I.

Point In typesetting, a point is ½ inch.

Portrait Paper is printed in portrait mode when it is taller than it is wide (similar to a portrait painting). For contrast, see **Landscape**.

Postscript Postscript is a graphical command language for output devices, such as laser printers. Many application programs are designed so that they send Postscript code to the printer, which directs the printer to print text and graphics provided that the printer is Postscript compatible.

Program A program is a set of instructions for a computer to execute. A program can be written in a programming language, such as BASIC or Pascal, or in an assembly language. You may write your own programs if you know a programming language, or you may buy prewritten programs that perform standard tasks, such as word processing or financial calculations. The programs that direct a computer are called software.

Programmable function key A programmable function key is a key on a computer keyboard whose function depends on the software being run. In many cases, programmable function (PF) keys can be defined as equivalent to combinations or sequences of other keys. For example, in IBM PC BASIC, the command KEY 1, "CLS" + CHR$(13) defines function key 1 as equivalent to typing CLS followed by a carriage return [represented by CHR$(13)].

Prolog Prolog, short for programming in logic, is a computer programming language used for writing computer programs that model human thinking. A Prolog program gives the computer facts about the problem, plus rules by means of which other facts can be inferred. The computer can then respond to queries by checking those facts and rules.

Prompt The prompt is a symbol that appears on a computer terminal screen to signal to the user that the computer is ready to receive input. Different programs use different prompts.

Punched card A punched card is a cardboard card on which holes can be punched according to a particular pattern that can be read by a computer. Standard punched cards are 7⅜ inches long and 3¼ inches high. Each card contains 80 columns and 12 rows. Each column represents one letter, number, or other symbol, depending on the pattern of holes in that column. The holes are usually punched on the cards by a keypunch machine, which has a keyboard like a typewriter. Since most people have trouble reading punched-card hole language, most keypunch machines print the symbol stored in each column at the top of the column. The computer reads the cards when they are passed through a card reader, which can flip through cards at a rate of up to 1,000 cards per minute. Each card passes between a light source and a row of solar cells, which detect the location of the holes in the card. The pattern of holes is thus transformed into a pattern of electric signals. The card reader sends these signals to the computer, where they are translated into machine instructions. In the 1960s punched cards were the dominant way of feeding programs into computers. As interactive terminals became more readily available, punched cards became obsolete. It can be a nuisance to carry a deck of punched cards around, and the cards cannot be read by the card reader if they are folded, spindled, mutilated, or wet.

Radio Shack   Radio Shack is a division of Tandy, Inc., which has made a variety of different computers sold under the name TRS-80 or Tandy. The TRS-80 Model I (introduced in 1977) was one of the earliest popular microcomputers and Radio Shack was one of the first companies to establish an extensive chain of retail computer stores.

RAM   RAM is an acronym for random-access memory, which is a memory device whereby any location in memory can be found, on average, as quickly as any other location. A computer's RAM is its main memory where it can store data, so the size of the RAM (measured in kilobytes) is an important indicator of the capacity of the computer. *See* **Memory**.

Random-access memory   *See* **RAM**.

READ   The READ command in BASIC causes the computer to take the top item in the data stack and assign its value to a specified variable name. A data stack is created with the DATA statement. For example, after executing statement 100 in this sequence:

```
110 READ X, Y, Z
110 DATA 10, 105, 50
```

X will have the value 10, Y will have the value 105, and Z will have the value 50.

Read-only memory   *See* **ROM**.

Real time   The term real time refers to the actual amount of time consumed by an operation, rather than just the amount of computer time. (On a time-sharing computer, programs do not consume computer time when the computer is working on something else.) (*See* **Timesharing**.) Real-time programming is programming in which the proper functiomng of the program depends on the amount of real time consumed. For instance, computers that control automatic machinery must often both detect and introduce time delays of accurately determined lengths.

Resistance   The resistance of an electronic component is a measure of how difficult it is for electric current to flow through the component. Resistance

is measured in a unit called the ohm. *See* **Ohm's law**; **Resistor**.

Resistor   A resistor is an electronic component with a fixed amount of resistance to the flow of electric current. The symbol for a resistor is a zigzag line (see the figure). Resistance is measured in a unit called the ohm. If V measures the voltage across the resistor, and R measures the resistance, then the current (I, measured in amperes) that will flow through the resistor can be found from Ohm's law: $I = V/R$.

Resistor

ROM   ROM is an acronym for read-only memory. A ROM contains computer instructions that do not need to be changed, such as the instructions for calculating arithmetic functions. The computer can read instructions out of ROM, but no data can be stored in ROM.

Scanner   A scanner is a device that can read information from a piece of paper and convert it into electronic signals that can be stored in a computer. For example, a desktop publishing system can use a scanner to read photographs into the computer, which are stored as bitmap images. They can then be used in documents. Note that the image may occupy a large amount of disk space, perhaps one megabyte or more. Software is available that can process the image if desired, for example by increasing the contrast.

However, suppose you have scanned a page of text, but you now would like to edit it with your word processor. In this case the scanned image is not helpful by itself; you need to convert it into a text file. (Another advantage of converting it into a text file is that it will occupy much less disk space. The ASCII code for the letter A requires only eight bits, whereas a bitmap image of a letter A may require dozens of hundreds of bits, depending on the size of the image.) Character recognition software is available to perform this task, but it is a complicated job for software to observe a bitmap image of a particular letter and recognize what letter it is. The task is further complicated because letters may be written in different typefaces, they may be tilted, or they may even be handwritten. Although the capability of character recognition software is improving, it is not 100 percent perfect. You can see why it will never achieve perfect recognition. Some handwriting is so illegible that even people are unable to recognize the letters. *See* **Bitmap**.

Second-generation computers   The term second-generation computers refers to computers made with transistors in the 1950s and 1960s.

Sector   A sector is a part of track on a disk. For example, a typical floppy disk system partitions the disk into 40 circular tracks with each track having 10 sectors. *See* **Track**; **Disk**.

Semiconductor   A semiconductor is a material that is neither a good conductor nor a good insulator. Semiconductor devices, such as diodes, transistors, and integrated circuits, are the essential parts that make it possible to build small, inexpensive electronic machines. The most common semiconductor material is silicon. Each atom in a silicon crystal contains four outer-level (or valence) electrons. A pure silicon crystal is not a very good conductor, because these electrons will normally stay bound to their atoms. An N-type semiconductor region is formed by adding a bit of impurity to the pure silicon. This process is known as doping. The impurity added is a material such as phosphorus, where each atom has five valence electrons. The result is a crystal very much like the original one, except that there are now a few extra electrons floating around (one for each atom of phosphorus that was added). The whole crystal is called an N-type region, because it contains free negative charges. If an impurity with only three valence electrons, such as boron, is added to the silicon crystal, gaps are left in the crystal structure because there are not enough electrons to fill all the spaces in the crystal. Each gap is called a hole. Even though a hole is nothing but the absence of an electron, it can be thought of as carrying a mobile positive charge. A semiconductor region with an excess of holes is called a P-type semiconductor region. Electric current can flow in an N-type region in much the same way that it flows in a regular conductor. In a conductor, the current is made up of outer-level valence electrons that are not too tightly bound to their atoms. When a negative voltage is applied to one end of the N region and a positive voltage is applied to the other, the loose electrons will be repelled by the negative voltage and attracted by the positive voltage. Current can flow in the P-type region, but the process is quite different. If a negative voltage is applied to one end of the P-type region, the electrons will be repelled. However, the P-type region does not contain any mobile electrons. What an electron can do is jump into one of the holes. This process creates a new hole where the original electron used to be. We can think of the hole itself as moving toward the negative voltage, carrying a positive charge with it. A semiconductor diode is formed by joining a P-type region and an N-type region. A transistor consists of a thin layer of one type of semiconductor between two layers of the opposite type. A semiconductor integrated circuit is made by placing many P and N regions on a single chip, so as to form a complex circuit containing many miniature transistors and other circuit elements.

Series   Two electronic components are connected in series if they are joined one right after the other (see the figure).

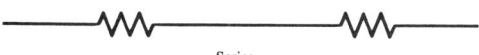

Series

Silicon   Silicon is the primary material used to make semiconductor devices. Each atom in a silicon crystal contains 14 protons and 14 electrons. Ten of the electrons are tightly bound to the nucleus, while the outer four valence electrons can be dislodged relatively easily. (*See* **Semiconductor**.)

Simulation   Simulation is the process of representing one system by another. In computer science, simulation means representation of the real world by a mathematical model solved by a computer. A mathematical model of population growth can simulate a real population. A *deterministic* simulation occurs when the future path of the system is exactly determined by the parameters of the system. A *Monte Carlo* simulation occurs when probabilities are known and a selection of random numbers is used to guide the system.

Software   The software of a computer system is the set of programs that tell the computer what to do. The term software is contrasted with hardware, which refers to the actual physical machines that make up a computer system. The hardware by itself is of little value without the instructions that tell it what to do. Common types of software available for microcomputers include programming language interpreters and compilers (which allow you to write your own software in languages such as BASIC and Pascal), word processing programs, and financial decision-making packages such as spreadsheets, data base management programs, and games. You may also obtain software designed to fulfill a specific task, such as maintaining a firm's general ledger or solving a particular type of scientific problem.

Spreadsheet   One of the most common types of software with business applications are electronic spreadsheet programs, such as Lotus 1-2-3 or Excel. A spreadsheet consists of an array of cells. Each cell can contain a data item, such as a numeric value, formula, or text. By moving the pointer to different cells it is possible to design a table consisting of information such as the monthly sales volume for a company. Spreadsheets are very valuable if you want to ask questions of the following form: "What happens if quantity X changes?" Move the pointer to the cell containing the value of X, enter the new value, and then the program will automatically recalculate the values in all of the other cells that depend on X. Spreadsheet programs need to have commands for saving a spreadsheet as a disk file so you may retrieve it for later use. They also must have commands for printing the spreadsheet. Many also have built-in graphics procedures that make it possible to draw graphs of the data contained in the spreadsheet.

String   A string (or *character string*) is a group of characters stored in a computer. For example, the surname of the first president can be stored as a string 10 characters long: "WASHINGTON." In BASIC character string variable names end in a dollar sign, $. Here are three examples of character string variables:

```
P1$ = "WASHINGTON", P2$ =
"ADAMS", P3$ = "JEFFERSON"
```

Subroutine   A subroutine is a set of instructions, given a particular name, that will be executed when the main program calls for it. In BASIC, a subroutine is labeled by the statement number of its first line and is executed when a GOSUB command is reached.

Subscript   A subscript is a number or letter used to identify a particular element in an array. In mathematics, subscripts are written below the main line, as in x_1, or a_{23}. In most computer languages, however, subscripts are surrounded by parentheses, as in X(l) or A(J). *See* **Array**.

Syntax   The syntax of a programming language is the set of rules that specify how the language symbols can be put together to form meaningful statements. Syntax rules are like grammar rules. If a program violates the language syntax rules, a syntax error has occurred.

Tape   Magnetic tape can be used to store information in a form that can be easily read by a computer. Magnetic tape is much the same as ordinary tape recorder tape. It is much cheaper to store information on tape than in the computer main memory or on a disk memory device, but a longer time is required to locate a particular data item if it is stored on tape. Mainframe computers make extensive use of tape storage, and tape backup units are available for microcomputer hard disks. *See* **Memory**.

Terminal   A computer terminal is an input-output device whereby a user is able to communicate directly with a computer. A terminal must have a keyboard, so that the user can type in instructions and input data, and a means of displaying output, such as a CRT (television) screen or a typewriter.

Texas Instruments (TI)   A manufacturer of semiconductors and computers, TI is headquartered in Dallas, Texas. Jack S. Kilby developed the first working integrated circuit ("silicon chip") at TI in 1958, making it possible to miniaturize electronic equipment to a degree far beyond earlier expectations. Currently, TI produces parts for practically all makes of computers, as well as a number of micro- and minicomputers of its own.

Third-generation computers   The term third-generation computers refers to computers made with integrated circuits. Current computers built with circuits that have large-scale integration are often called *fourth-generation computers.*

Timesharing   Timesharing is a way of running more than one program on the same computer at the same time, so that, for example, the computer can serve many users at different terminals simultaneously. Timesharing is based on the idea that a computer spends most of its time waiting for things to happen. Almost all input-output devices (printers, card readers, disks, etc.) operate much more slowly than the CPU itself; the extreme case is a terminal or console, where the computer may spend minutes or hours waiting for someone to type something. In a timesharing system, more than one program is loaded into memory at once, and when the computer is unable to proceed with one program, it jumps to another. In practice, the computer does not stay on one program more than a fraction of a second even if there is nothing to wait for; to do so would prevent other, possibly shorter, programs from being executed. Also, programs that are not executed are frequently "rolled out" of memory (i.e., copied to disk) to make memory space available to programs that are actually running.

Track   Data that are recorded on a disk are arranged in many concentric circles, each of which is called a track. *See* **Disk**.

Tractor feed   A tractor feed is a mechanism that uses toothed gears to pull the paper forward in a computer printer. The teeth fit into the feed holes in the side of the paper.

Transistor   A transistor is an electronic device formed by sandwiching a thin layer of semiconductor material between two layers of the opposite type of semiconductor. A PNP transistor has a thin layer of N-type semiconductor between two P-type regions. An NPN transistor has just the opposite construction. (*See* **Semiconductor**.) The symbol for a transistor is shown in the figure. The middle

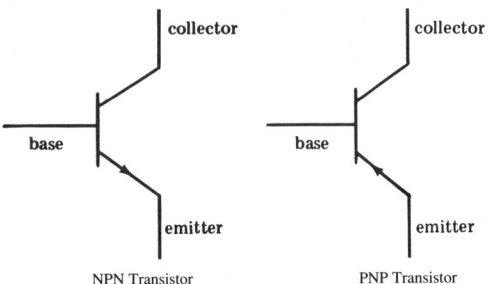

NPN Transistor   PNP Transistor

section is called the base, and the other two regions are the emitter and the collector. The base-to-emitter voltage controls the collector-to-emitter current. In radios, transistors are used as amplifiers. The output signal, measured at the collector, is much larger than the input signal, which is applied to the base. In computers, transistors are used as switches. The nature of the voltage applied to the base determines whether or not the current will flow from the collector to the emitter. Consider an NPN transistor with the emitter connected to ground (0 volt), and the collector connected to a large positive voltage (see the figure). (A PNP transistor works in exactly the same way, except that all voltage polarities are reversed.) If a positive voltage is now applied to the base, the base-emitter junction will be forward biased. This means that the base-emitter junction will act like a conducting diode. (*See* **Diode**.) Electrons in the emitter and holes in the base will be driven toward the junction. The result is that electrons will flow from the emitter to the base. So far, this is exactly what happens in a regular

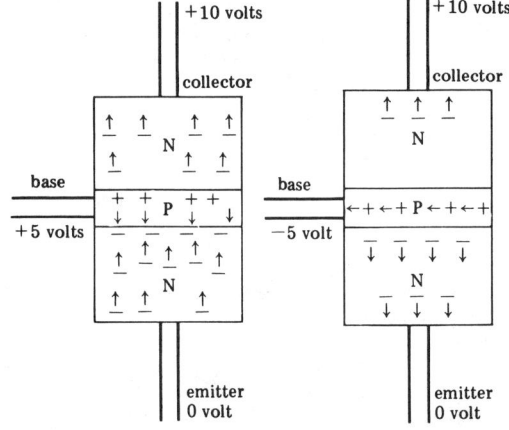

diode. The difference between a transistor and a diode is due to the fact that the base in the transistor is very thin. Some of the electrons that are pushed into the base will be pushed so hard that they travel all the way across the base to the collector. These electrons make up a current flow from the emitter to the collector. An amplifier transistor is designed so that the current flow from the emitter to the collector is actually much greater than the current flow from the emitter to the base. In computers, transistors act as switches (see the figure). If a positive voltage is applied to the base, current will flow from the emitter to the collector, and the transistor acts like a switch that is on (or closed). If a negative voltage is applied to the base, the base emitter junction is reverse biased, causing the flow of electrons from the emitter to the base to stop.

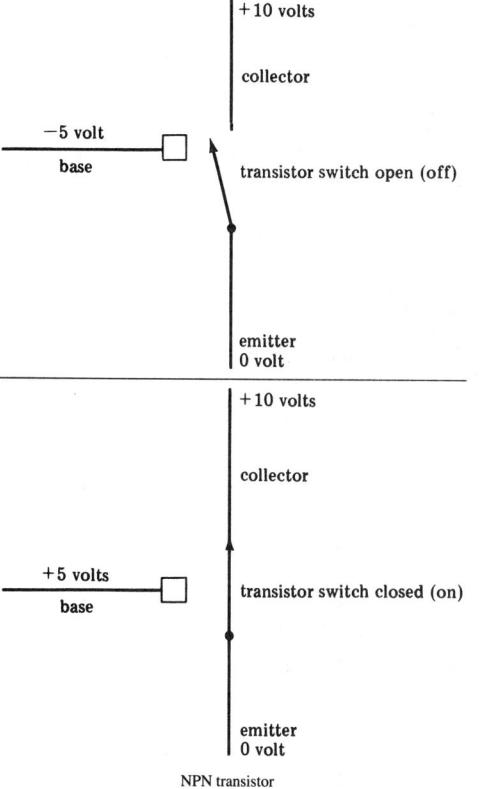

NPN transistor

Since no more electrons are being driven into the base, there are no electrons to sneak across the base into the collector. This means that the current from the emitter to the collector stops, so the transistor acts like a switch that is off (or open). This type of transistor is called a bipolar, or junction, transistor. Another type of transistor is the field-effect transistor.

Turtle   A turtle is a device used for computer-controlled graphics in some computer systems, especially those using the LOGO language. The computer gives commands to the turtle, telling it when to move in certain directions and when to raise or lower its paintbrush. By giving the proper commands, a programmer can draw many kinds of patterns. Some LOGO systems use an actual mechanical turtle that moves along the floor and draws pictures on large pieces of paper. Other systems use imaginary turtles that move around the screen. *See* **LOGO.**

Typeface   A typeface is a set of characters of a particular design. Typefaces of the same design with different weights (plain and bold) and different slants form a typeface family. Exhibit 4.1 shows examples of three typeface families: Times Roman, Helvetica, and Courier. A set of characters of the same typeface and same size is called a font.

One important task in desktop publishing is to select typefaces with a pleasing appearance. Characteristics to look for include the following:

- Is the type fixed pitch or proportional pitch? Fixed pitch means that all letters are the same width, which was the only choice available on a typewriter or early computer. This is still the best choice for text in which the characters must line up, as in a financial table. For most text, it improves the appearance to use proportional pitch, which means that some letters (such as "W") are wider than other letters (such as "I").
- Does the type have serifs? Serifs are ornaments at the ends of the letters. (Type without serifs is called sans serif.) For most text, type with serifs is easier to read. Sans serif type is often used for headlines.

The size and style of a typeface can also be adjusted. Size is usually measured in points (1 point is ½ inch). Italics and boldface are styles that are used for emphasis or other special purposes.

With early microcomputer printers there was no choice of different fonts. The computer would send the code for a letter to the printer, and the printer would make that letter in the only way it knew how. Now, the graphical description of the characters of a font may be stored in the printer memory itself, in a cartridge that plugs into the printer, or as software on a disk. Some fonts are stored as bitmaps, which means that the pattern of dots required to make each character is stored. In other cases, the memory stores only the geometric descriptions needed to design the font, which makes the font scalable: that is, it can be reduced or enlarged. *See* **Bitmap; Pitch.**

UNIX   UNIX is a computer operating system developed by Bell Labs. *See* **Operating system.**

Upload   To upload is to transmit a file to a central computer from a smaller computer or a computer at a remote location.

User-friendly   A user-friendly computer program is designed to be easy for people to use. In the days when computers were operated only by specialists, little attention was paid to making programs user-friendly. However, when computers became more popular, it became very important to write programs that could be easily understood by the people who use them. The most important requirement for making a program user-friendly is a clear, understandable manual that explains how the program works. Other features that can help make a program user-friendly are menus that clearly list the available choices, and command names that are easy to remember. However, a program should not contain so many on-screen explanatory messages that it becomes cumbersome to use for people who have already learned how the program works. *See* **Graphical user interface.**

EXHIBIT 4.1
Samples of Various Typefaces

Times Roman
Proportional pitch, with serifs
24 point 18 point
14 point 12 point 10 point 9 point
ABCDEFGHIJKLMNOPQRSTUVWXYZ
abcdefghijklmnopqrstuvwxyz 1234567890
Plain **Boldface** *Italic*

Helvetica
Proportional pitch, with serifs
24 point 18 point
14 point 12 point 10 point 9 point
ABCDEFGHIJKLMNOPQRSTUVWXYZ
abcdefghijklmnopqrstuvwxyz 1234567890
Plain **Boldface** *Italic*

Courier
Fixed pitch (all letters same width)
24 point 18 point
14 point 12 point 10 point 9 pt
ABCDEFGHIJKLMNOPQRSTUVWXYZ
abcdefghijklmnopqrstuvwxyz 1234567890
Plain **Boldface** *Italic*

Vacuum tube A vacuum tube is an electronic component consisting of electrodes placed inside an evacuated glass tube. Vacuum tubes work by using electric and magnetic fields to control the movements of electrons that have been emitted by one of the electrodes. A CRT (cathode ray tube) television screen is one example of a vacuum tube. The vacuum tubes originally used in computers performed the same type of functions that semiconductor diodes and transistors perform now. A vacuum tube diode consists of two electrodes: a cathode, which emits electrons, and an anode, or plate, which collects electrons. The diode will conduct electricity only when a positive voltage is applied to the plate and a negative voltage is applied to the cathode. A vacuum tube triode contains an electrode called the grid, located between the cathode and the plate. The flow of electrons from the cathode to the plate is controlled by the electric field of the grid. (Simi-larly, the current flow from the emitter to the collector in a transistor is controlled by the voltage applied to the base.) Vacuum tube triodes can be used for amplification and logic functions. The first electronic digital computer, the ENIAC, consisted of 18,000 vacuum tubes. The disadvantages of vacuum tube computers are that they are very big, consume a great deal of power, and generate a lot of heat. Also, it is necessary to constantly replace burned-out tubes.

Valence A valence electron is an electron that is only loosely connected to its atom; hence it can be dislodged easily. (*See* **Conductor**; **Semiconductor**.)

VGA VGA is a standard high-quality graphics mode for IBM PC-compatible computers. It provides a screen resolution of 640 by 480 pixels. More recent computers provide even higher resolution (1,024 by 768 pixels) in a mode known as Super VGA.

Volt The volt is the unit of measure of electric potential. If a potential of 1 volt is applied to a resistor with a resistance of 1 ohm, then a current of 1 ampere will flow through the resistor. (*See* **Ohm's law**.) One volt can also be defined as 1 joule/coulomb, where a joule is a measure of energy: 1 joule = 1 (kilogram) (meter)^2/(second)^2.

Windows Microsoft Windows is a program that provides a graphical user interface for IBM PC-compatible computers. It was the release of Version 3.0 of Windows in 1990 that led to the widespread use of the Windows environment.

Information on the screen is presented in the form of various windows, which all have similar features. This provides consistency in the user interface for different software products. A window has these general features (see the figure):

- A title bar describes the window. The window can be moved by dragging the title bar (that is, using the mouse to move the pointer to the title bar, holding down the left mouse button, and moving the mouse until the window is moved to the desired location).
- A window can be resized by dragging the right, left, or bottom edges of the window.
- Often all the text or graphics does not fit in the window at the same time. The hidden part can be revealed by "scrolling" the window. Imagine that the window itself is a small opening placed over a large piece of paper. If you move the window up, down, left, or right, you can see the rest of the imaginary paper. The window can be scrolled by dragging the scroll boxes with the mouse.
- The maximize button causes the window to take over the entire screen. This is helpful when you are working with a particular application.
- The minimize button causes the window to shrink to an icon. This is helpful if you want to place one program on hold while you work with another. This can be reversed by double-clicking on the icon (that is, moving the mouse pointer to the icon and pressing the left mouse button twice in rapid succession).
- The upper left corner of a window has a small box (the control menu box). If you click on this box, you see a menu that presents various options, such as closing the window.
- Many windows have menu bars that contain words that are headings for various pulldown menus. To activate one of these menus, use the mouse to move the pointer to the heading and press the left button. A menu of further choices will appear; select the one you want by moving the pointer with the mouse. Different windows provide different menu choices, depending on the program you are using. However, some menu choices are common: for example, many windows have a "file" menu that is used for such options as saving and loading data from disk files, and a "help" option, which provides more information about the program.
- When a Windows application needs to communicate with the user, it usually does this

in the form of a dialog box. Dialog boxes vary depending on the use, but they may contain a text box for the user to type in information and various options for you to select with the mouse. A dialog box typically has one button marked "OK," which you should click when you have made your selection and are done with the box. Often there is another button marked "Cancel" for you to click if you have changed your mind and have decided that you don't want any action done.

When you start a Windows session, you see a window called program manager, which contains various icons representing program groups. If you double-click on one of these icons, then a window opens that contains icons for various programs. Double-click on one of these icons to activate that program.

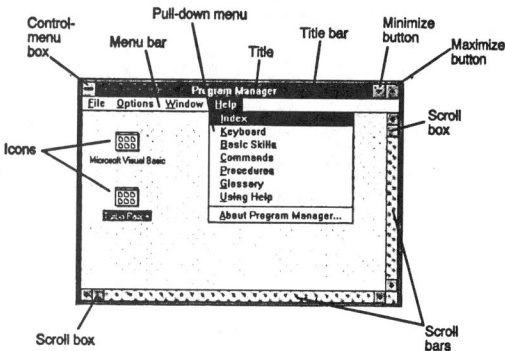

A Window in Microsoft Windows

Word A word is a group of bits stored in a computer memory. The number of bits in a word depends on the type of computer being used. A minicomputer typically may use words that are 16 bits long. Large computers may use words that are up to 64 bits long.

Word processing The use of a computer for word processing makes it possible to solve two common writing problems: 1. People make mistakes when they type. If you are typing on paper, then it is cumbersome to erase mistakes and make corrections. 2. People often need to improve their original draft of a document. If you are typing on paper and want to make a revision, it is necessary to retype the whole page (both the part that needs to be revised and the part that you want to leave the same).

In order to use a computer for word processing, you need a word processing program (such as WordStar, WordPerfect, or Microsoft Word). Each program has its own special features, so you will have to learn the specific commands for the version you are using. The following discussion considers some of the features typically found on word processing systems. As you type your document, the characters you type will appear on the screen. If you want to correct a mistake, simply backspace and type over the mistake. If you want to insert new letters between some existing letters, set the program for insert mode so that the new letters will push the existing letters out of the way instead of erasing them. A symbol called the cursor tells you where on the screen the next character you type will appear. You can move the cursor around the screen by using the arrow keys or a mouse. In most cases the document will be too long to fit on the screen, so you need to be able to move backward and forward through the document. As you type your document, the characters you type are stored in the computer's memory. However, the computer's memory becomes blank if the power to the computer is turned off so you will need to store your document on a disk (or other auxiliary storage device, such as tape) if you intend to work on it again at a later time. The word processing program will have instructions for how to accomplish this. When you are finished with the document then you will need to instruct the computer to print it. Word processing programs typically include several special features, such as word wrap (meaning that the cursor will automatically jump to the next line after you have filled up one line), justification (meaning the right-hand margin will automatically be aligned), find and replace (causing the computer to locate all occurrences of a particular set of characters and change them to something else), block move or copy (causing a block of text to be moved from one location to another, or copying a block from one location to another), automatic page numbering, and special printing features such as underlining or boldfacing.

Word processing programs often come with spelling checker programs, which will identify words that are not included in a list of standard words. This makes it possible to catch misspelled words and typographical errors. However, some proper names, technical terms, and obscure words will show up as misspelled words because they are not included in the standard list. Many programs allow you to add words to the standard list. More seriously, a spelling checker program will not catch a word spelled correctly but used inappropriately, for example using "form" when the word should have been "from." *See also* **Desktop publishing**.

EARTH AND SPACE SCIENCE

Aa　A basaltic lava containing little gas and having low viscosity.

Absolute age　The actual time, in years, at which a geologic formation was laid down. *See* **Radioactive dating**.

Absolute zero　This is –273.15°C, the lowest possible temperature. *See also* **Kelvin scale**, Physics section, page 20-26.

Acid rain　Rain with low pH, produced by combination of rain water with atmospheric pollutants, chiefly oxides of sulfur and nitrogen. Acid rain causes damage to the life of lakes and forests.

Adhesion　The attraction between a liquid and a solid. Water seeping into the ground, for example, forms a thin layer on the surface of the soil particles. *See* **Subsurface water**.

Adiabatic lapse rate　The rate at which air cools as it rises. The cooling results from the expansion of the air as it rises into regions of lower pressure. The lapse rate varies from about 0.6°C per l00 m for saturated air to 1°C per 100 m for dry air.

Adiabatic temperature change　The change in temperature of air without the addition or removal of heat. When air expands because the pressure is reduced, its temperature drops. Conversely, compressing air without adding heat makes it warmer.

Aerobic bacteria　Bacteria that can survive and reproduce only in the presence of oxygen. They play an important role in converting plant remains into humus.

Air　The mixture of gases composing the earth's atmosphere. Dry air is mainly nitrogen (78%), oxygen (21%), and argon (0.9%). The important gas carbon dioxide makes up only about 0.03% of the air, and the rest represents a number of other gases. In addition, water vapor in the air can be anywhere from 0 to about 3%.

Air mass　A large body of air with the same temperature and humidity characteristics. Air masses are classified according to their origin. The table gives the characteristics of the four kinds of air masses in North America.

Name	Symbol	Character	Source
Continental polar	cP	Cold, dry	Canadian arctic
Maritime polar	mP	Cold, moist	North Atlantic and Pacific
Continental tropical	cT	Warm, dry	Mexico and south east United States
Maritime tropical	mT	Warm, moist	Caribbean and South Pacific

The movement of air masses controls the local weather. The boundary between two air masses is called a front. (*See* **Front**.)

Air pressure　*See* **Atmospheric pressure**.

Albedo　The fraction of the radiant energy incident on a planet that is reradiated into space. A white surface, for example, has a high albedo.

Alluvial fan　A wedge shaped mass of sediment deposited at the base of an upland region. Alluvial fans are usually found in desert regions, where they are formed by intermittent rivers.

Alpha decay　*See* Physics section, page 20-2.

Alpha particle　A helium nucleus produced in radioactive decay. *See* Physics section page 20-2, *see also* **Radioactivity**.

Alpine glaciation　Erosion by the action of valley glaciers. When the glacier melts and retreats, it leaves a topography characterized by a broad, flat-bottomed valley with a river meandering in it. At the edges of the valley, waterfalls (hanging valleys) flow down into the valley. At the head of the valley, where there was once the snowfield that produced the glacier, is a deep, bowl-shaped depression call a cirque. It may be occupied by the kind of lake called a tarn. The sharp peaks between cirques are called horns; a ridge between cirques is an arête. The floor of the valley contains erratic boulders and various kinds of moraines. *See* **Glacial deposits**.

Altitude of stars　The distance of a celestial object above the horizon, measured in degrees. The zenith is at 90°. Also called elevation.

Amplitude of earthquake　The height of an earthquake wave at any given location, as measured by a seismograph. *See* **Earthquake**.

Anaerobic bacteria　Bacteria that can or must live in the absence of oxygen. They are considered pollutants in water but play a valuable role in the conversion of plant remains to humus.

Andromeda galaxy, or M31　A spiral galaxy, the galaxy closest to ours, and very much like it.

Anemometer　An instrument for measuring the speed of the wind. It consists of three half-spherical cups, mounted on the ends of short arms that are attached to a central axle. The wind catches in the concave side of the cups, causing the whole apparatus to rotate. Wind speed is measured by the rate of rotation.

Aneroid barometer　A barometer that measures air pressure by its effect on a sealed air chamber.

　　The chamber has one surface corrugated in a pattern of concentric circles. This surface is pressed into the trapped air when the outside pressure rises. The center of the corrugated surface is linked to a dial that records the position of the corrugated surface. Pressure is indicated by the position of that surface.

Angle of repose　*See* **Gravitational erosion**.

Annual motion of stars　The shift of position of the stars in the sky, moving them about 1° west every day, so that they complete a full circuit in a year. This shift is a result of the revolution of the earth around the sun.

Annular drainage　A pattern of stream flow in which the stream tends to form a circular path around the hill. It happens when there is a layer of less resistant rock in the hill.

Antarctic circle　The latitude line at 66½° south, marking the farthest south that the sun is overhead. At the winter solstice, December 21, the sun is overhead at noon at this latitude and is above the horizon for 24 hours.

Anthracite　*See* **Coal**.

Anticline　In a folded rock formation, an arch like structure in which the sides slope downward and away from the center. *See* **Syncline**.

Anticyclone　*See* **High-pressure system**.

Aphelion　The point in its orbit at which a planet is farthest from the sun and thus moving most slowly. The earth's aphelion occurs on July 5, when the distance from the sun is 152 million km.

Apogee   The point in the orbit of the moon or other satellite of the earth at which the satellite is farthest from the earth.

Apollo program   The space exploration program in which American astronauts investigated the moon. The twelve men who landed on the moon performed a number of experiments and brought back samples of soil and rock.

Astronaut James Irwin approaches the Rover on the moon's surface, July 30, 1971.

Apparent motion   The change of position of celestial bodies as viewed and measured from the earth as a point of reference. The fixed stars have an apparent motion in which they appear to revolve around the earth in about 365 days (*see also* **Annual motion of stars**). The sun, moon, and planets have much more complex apparent motions.

Aquifer   A layer of porous rock confined between layers of impervious rock and emerging at the surface in a region of substantial rainfall. The porous rock is charged with water where it emerges at the surface and can carry water for many miles. An aquifer can be tapped to produce artesian wells, supplying water even in areas where there is no rainfall at all.

Arctic circle   The line of latitude at 66½° north that marks the farthest north the sun is overhead. At the summer solstice, June 21, the sun is overhead at noon at this latitude and is above the horizon for 24 hours.

Arête   A ridge between cirques; *see* **Alpine glaciation**.

Arroyo   A steep-sided gulley produced by the intermittent rivers in an arid region.

Artesian well   A well dug into an aquifer.

Asteroid, or planetoid or minor planet A rocky object traveling in orbit around the sun. There are thousands of asteroids in a belt between Mars and Jupiter. They vary in size up to 1020 km (Ceres). It is likely that this asteroid belt represents an early stage in the formation of a planet. Every planet began as an asteroid belt. The asteroids in the other nine belts consolidated into planets, but those in the belt between Mars and Jupiter did not. *See* **Bode's law**.

Asthenosphere   The middle, semiliquid layer of the earth's mantle, in which convection currents flow. They carry heat to the surface and move the continents (*see* **Continental drift**).

Astrology   The belief that human events are strongly influenced by the planets. It begins by defining twelve signs of the zodiac, corresponding to the twelve constellations that lie along the ecliptic. A horoscope is an individual analysis of personality and offer of advice based on the position of the sun in the zodiac at the time of the individual's birth. Although astrology in the past performed a valuable service in promoting the study of the skies, it is now known to have no validity.

Astonomical unit (AU)   The mean distance from the earth to the sun, used as a unit for expressing distance in the solar system. It is equal to 149,597,970.7 km.

Atmosphere   The earth's gaseous envelope. The lowest 10 km of the atmosphere make up the troposphere, in which clouds can form and changes in the weather occur. Above that, to about 50 km, is the stratosphere. *See also* **Air**; **Atmospheric pressure**; **Humidity**.

Atmospheric pressure   The force per unit area exerted on all surfaces by the atmosphere. At sea level, the pressure varies from about 950 to 1050 mb (millibars). Standard atmospheric pressure, defined as a reading of 760 mm on a mercury barometer, is 1013.2 mb. This corresponds to a force of about 2 tons on each square foot of surface.

Atmospheric pressure decreases with altitude at a rate (in the lower atmosphere) of about 100mb/km. The altimeter of an airplane is a barometer that uses this principle to measure the altitude above sea level.

Pressure also depends on humidity. Because water vapor has a lower density than air, the higher the humidity, the lower is the pressure.

The local variations in atmospheric pressure are an important parameter for analyzing and predicting weather. They are measured several times a day and plotted on weather maps (*see* **Isobar**; **High-pressure system**; **Low-pressure system**).

For methods of measuring atmospheric pressure, *see* **Mercury barometer**; **Aneroid barometer**.

Atoll   A ring of coral islands in the ocean (*see* **Coral reef**). Accumulating coral increases the total weight of an oceanic island, forcing it to sink into the earth's crust. When it sinks so far that the central island is completely under water, only the coral ring remains above the surface. There is a lagoon of quiet water within the ring.

Aurora   Flashes of light appearing in the sky in the polar regions. They are produced by the flow of charged particles from the sun striking the upper atmosphere. Auroras are seen in high northern and southern latitudes because the particles are deflected toward the poles by the earth's magnetic field.

Avalanche   A massive downslope movement of snow or loose rock, often triggered by an earthquake.

Azimuth The distance around the horizon, measured in degrees clockwise from north. The position of a celestial object in the sky is given in terms of its azimuth and altitude.

Bailey's beads A string of lights seen at the time of a total eclipse of the sun. They are produced by the light of the sun's margin passing through irregularities on the surface of the moon.

Barnard's star The second nearest star to earth, notable because of its high proper motion of over 10˝ (seconds) of arc per year.

Barometer A device for measuring atmospheric pressure. *See* **Mercury barometer; Aneroid barometer.**

Barycenter The combined center of mass of a two-body system. It is located on a line between centers, at a point such that the product of the mass of a body and its distance to the barycenter is the same for both bodies. We usually say that the moon revolves around the earth, but in fact, both the moon and the earth revolve around their barycenter, which is 4700 km from the center of the earth on the side toward the moon. The earth wobbles. Also, not the earth, but the barycenter of the earth-moon system is in elliptical orbit around the sun.

Basalt Dark-colored igneous rock of high density and fine texture. *See* **Extrusive rock.** The word is also used to refer to the general class of mafic rocks. *See* **Mafic rock.**

Basalt-eclogite hypothesis A theory that explains the uplift of geosynclines to form a new continent. The rock of the lower crust, down to the Moho at 10–30km, is basalt. Below the Moho is the upper mantle. There the great pressure has transformed the basalt into a denser material, eclogite. As sediments pile up on the surface, the pressure below increases, and more of the basalt turns into eclogite. This adds eclogite to the mantle, so the level of the Moho rises. Since the eclogite is more dense than basalt, the volume of material under the crust decreases and the surface subsides. This allows more sediment to accumulate to form a geosyncline.

A geosyncline lifts up to form mountains because of the intense heat deep in the mantle. This heat converts eclogite into basalt. In converting to a material of lower density, the rock expands and pushes upward on the overlying sedimentary layers.

Base level The lowest level to which a stream can flow, usually sea level. In some cases, a large lake can serve as base level. Also, some streams flow into salt lakes or playa lakes below sea level.

Basin and Range Province A region of the western United States, in Nevada, Arizona, and Utah in which the earth's crust is stretched. This has resulted in a series of faults that produce north-south ridges alternating with deep valleys. *See* **Fault-block mountain.**

Batholith *See* **Intrusion.**

Bathyscaph A submarine vessel used to explore the deepest parts of the ocean.

Beaufort scale A scale (*see* **Exhibit 5.1**) invented for the purpose of estimating wind speed on the basis of the appearance of the sea.

EXHIBIT 5.1
The Beaufort Wind Scale

Number	Name	Knots	Sea Condition
0	calm	>1	smooth
1	light air	1–3	ripples, no crests
2	light breeze	4–6	small, glassy wavelets
3	gentle breeze	7–10	large wavelets, breaking
4	moderate breeze	11–16	small, longer waves; white horses
5	fresh breeze	17–21	longer waves; many white horses; some spray
6	strong breeze	22–27	large waves; many foam crests; spray
7	near gale	28–33	white foam blown in streaks; spindrift
8	fresh gale	34–40	high, long waves; foam in streaks; spindrift
9	strong gale	41–47	high waves; rolling; dense foam; much spray
10	whole gale; storm	48–55	heavy rolling; high waves, overhanging crests
11	violent storm	55–63	small ships lost behind high waves; crests blown into foam
12–17	hurricane	64+	air filled with foam and spray; sea white with driving spray

Bedrock The solid rock that underlies all the loose material on the surface. In mountainous regions, bedrock is on the surface, whereas in other places it is covered by sediments and weathered fragments that may be very deep.

Beta decay *See* Physics section, page 20-4.

Beta particle A high-energy electron emitted in the decay of radioactive nuclei. *See* **Radioactivity;** *see also,* Physics section, page 20-41.

Big bang The standard model for the origin of the universe. The universe is now expanding (*see* **Expanding universe**); extrapolating back in time indicates that all the matter of the universe was concentrated in one place about 15–20 billion years ago and then started to separate. Current theory analyzes events following the first 10^{-33} second of the expansion.

At the start, the universe contained many kinds of particles that no longer occur in nature. They are created today in high-energy particle accelerators. By the time the universe was 1 second old most of these had disappeared. The temperature was down to 10^{10}K, and the universe was a mixture of protons, neutrons, electrons, photons, positrons, and neutrinos. Particles combined to form nuclei in another 100 seconds, when the temperature was 10^9K. Some deuterium and a lot of helium formed, but about

75% of the protons remained isolated as hydrogen nuclei. It took another half-million years for electrons and nuclei to join to form atoms, and the temperature was 3000 K.

With the disappearance of free electrons, matter was dispersed sufficiently for photons to escape from the mixture. The universe became transparent. At age 1 billion years, the formation of stars and galaxies began.

See **Cosmic background radiation** for a description of a remarkable bit of supporting evidence.

Big crunch A hypothetical end to the universe, suggesting that it will stop expanding and start to contract. It is suggested that the universe will eventually collapse into nothing.

Binary star A complex of two stars held together by gravitational attraction and revolving around their barycenter. They often appear as a single star, but the nearer binary stars can be resolved by a good telescope. It is possible that a majority of stars are binary.

A spectroscopic binary can be detected by a study of its spectrum. Periodic slight shifts of the spectral lines due to the Doppler effect indicate that the system has a member that is in orbit, so that it is alternately approaching and receding. An eclipsing binary is a system in which one member is darker than the other. When the dark member moves in front of its brighter neighbor the luminosity of the system lessens. A certain pattern of periodic change is characteristic of eclipsing binaries.

Bituminous coal Soft coal, the third stage in coal formation. See **Coal**.

Black dwarf A small, highly dense star that has ceased to shine. A white dwarf has exhausted all its nuclear fuel and shines only because it has not yet cooled. When it cools, it will turn into a black dwarf.

Black hole A celestial object of such extraordinary mass and density that it has an enormously powerful gravitational field. The field is so strong that nothing can escape, not even light. It draws into itself all nearby objects, which continue to add to its mass. A black hole in space can be detected by the radiation produced by materials being drawn into it. There is now evidence to suggest the presence of a black hole at the center of our galaxy.

Bode's law The rule that expresses the regularity of the distances of the planets from the sun: Neglect Mercury and assign the value of 0.3 AU (astronomical units) to Venus. Then, to find the orbital radius of any planet, take the orbital radius of the one next closest to the sun, double it, and add 0.4 AU. The law works well for all planets, except that there is a planet missing between Mars and Jupiter. The search for a planet in that orbit led to the discovery of the asteroid belt where the missing planet should be.

Butte A flat-topped, steep-sided hill composed of horizontal strata in a highly dissected landscape.

C **Calcite** An extremely common mineral, calcium carbonate ($CaCO_3$). When pure, it forms transparent crystals known as Iceland spar. Calcite forms several kinds of rocks; see **Chalk**; **Coquina**; **Limestone**; **Marble**.

Caldera A large, circular depression at the top of a volcano, formed either by explosion or by collapse of the volcano.

Calendar The accepted means of ordering the year by designation of days, months, and so on. Every culture has its calendar, and all are based on the motions of heavenly bodies. Some, such as the Hebrew calendar, are defined by the phases of the moon and are called lunar calendars.

The current calendar in worldwide use is a modification of the Julian calendar, adopted by Julius Caesar. The Julian calendar used a year that is just 365¼ days long. Each month represents, approximately, one lunar cycle, divided into four parts to form the weeks. Since none of these cycles is commensurate with any other, many compromises were necessary. The extra quarter-day was accommodated by making every fourth year 366 days long.

The Julian calendar overestimated the number of days in a year; it is actually 365.242199. Because of this error, the date of the vernal equinox steadily slipped back. By 1582, it had changed from its original value of March 25 to March 11. Pope Gregory XIII then established the Gregorian calendar which we now use. It dropped 10 days from the calendar to set the date of the vernal equinox at March 21. It also eliminated the accumulation of error by deleting the leap years in all century years except those that are divisible by 400.

Calorie See Physics section, page 20-5.

Capillary action The process by which water rises by contact with a solid. In a blotter, for example, water is drawn up into fibers. Smaller fibers have a larger surface area and produce the most effective capillary action.

To take another example, in a tube placed upright in a pan of water, the water rises into the tube by capillary action. The force lifting the water is provided by adhesion to the walls of the tube and cohesion of the water column. Adhesive force is more effective in narrower tubes. The water stops rising when adhesion is balanced by gravity. See **Subsurface water**.

Capillary fringe The region in the soil just above the zone of saturation, in which water rises by capillary action. The smaller the particles, the higher the water rises, but the zone is usually only a few centimeters thick.

Caprock A layer of rock resistant to erosion. Erosion of the softer rocks underneath undercuts the caprock. The result is a landscape of flattopped hills bounded by cliffs. This is a characteristic landscape in arid regions, where the caprock is usually limestone. See also **Butte**.

Carbonation The action of carbonic acid on other substances. Carbonic acid forms when carbon dioxide reacts with water:

$$CO_2 + H_2O \rightarrow H_2CO_3 \text{ (carbonic acid)}$$

Carbonation is an important agent of chemical weathering. Carbonic acid is a weak acid, but it reacts quite well with the mineral calcite, turning it into a soluble material. Calcite is the mineral that makes up some of the most common rocks on earth: limestone, marble, some coral, and the coquina that is formed from cemented seashells. It is also a common binding material in sandstones and conglomerates. In damp climates, decaying vegetation produces carbon dioxide, which combines with water. *See* **Karst topography**.

Carbon-14 dating   See **Radiocarbon dating**.

Carbon dioxide   A gas, formula CO_2, that makes up about 0.03% of the air. It is produced in nature by animal respiration, decay of plants, fires, and volcanoes. Green plants remove it from the air, using the carbon to manufacture organic chemicals. It is an important agent of weathering; *see* **Carbonation**.

Celestial equator   The projection of the earth's equator onto the celestial sphere. This is a circle in the sky that is directly overhead at all points on the equator.

Celestial sphere   The sky as it appears from earth. The sphere has a set of coordinates by which astronomers specify the locations of the stars and other celestial objects. Each fixed star has definite, nearly unchanging coordinates.

The celestial north pole is directly above the earth's North Pole, and the celestial equator is above the earth's equator. Each position on the celestial sphere is specified by declination and right ascension. Declination is latitude, expressed as the angular distance from the equator, positive for north and negative for south. Right ascension is longitude, expressed as the time distance east or west from the position of the sun at the vernal equinox. Each hour of right ascension corresponds to an angular distance of 15° east of the zero meridian of right ascension. Because of the earth's rotation, the celestial sphere rotates around the earth once every 24 hours.

Celsius scale   *See* Physics section, page 20-6.

Centrifugal force   A force, detectable in a rotating frame of reference, exerted outward from the center of rotation. It is important to note that the force is detectable only within the rotating frame. It is correct, for example, to note that the earth bulges at its equator because a centrifugal force pushes its equatorial regions outward. The statement is made from a frame of reference attached to the rotating earth.

It is not correct to use the concept of centrifugal force in connection with the revolution of the earth around the sun, since this is described from a frame of reference attached to the sun. The correct statement is that the gravitational force of the sun, acting centripetally, pulls the earth out of its straight-line path and into an elliptic orbit. *See also* Physics section, page 20-6.

Centripetal force   Any force acting on an object in a direction perpendicular to its velocity. The effect of a centripetal force is to change the direction of velocity without affecting its speed. In the case of the earth in orbit around the sun, the centripetal force acting on the earth is the sun's gravity. This pulls the earth out of its straight-line path and into orbit. If the gravitational force were exactly centripetal, the orbit would be a circle. *See also* Physics section, page 20-6.

Cepheid variable   A large yellow star that varies in magnitude with a period of a few days, rising rapidly to peak luminosity and dropping slowly to a minimum. This class of star is important because there is a definite, known relationship between its absolute magnitude and its period of variation.

The relationship between absolute magnitude and period was found by studying Cepheid variables in the Large Magellanic Cloud. Since the stars were all in the cloud, they were all approximately the same distance away, so the apparent magnitude was a good indication of absolute magnitude. The Cepheid variables in other, nearby galaxies could then be used to determine the distance to the galaxy. The period of variation of the star gave its absolute magnitude, so a measurement of apparent magnitude gave the distance. For an explanation of how this works, *see* **Magnitude**.

Ceres   The largest asteroid, with a diameter of 1025 km.

Chalk   A soft limestone composed of calcite, formed from accumulations of the shells of microscopic oceanic organisms.

Chemical compound   A substance consisting of atoms combined in definite proportions into molecules, or of ions in a definite ratio. The composition of a compound is represented as its chemical formula. The formula H_2O specifies that the molecule is composed of two atoms of hydrogen (H) and one atom of oxygen (O). A typical ionic compound is calcium carbonate, $CaCO_3$. A crystal of calcium carbonate is composed of equal numbers of calcium ions bearing a double positive charge (Ca^{2+}) and carbonate ions bearing a double negative charge (CO_3^{2-}). The formula for the carbonate ion indicates that it contains 1 atom of carbon and 3 of oxygen.

Chemical sedimentary rock   A rock composed of a single mineral that has precipitated out of solution. *See* **Dolomite**; **Gypsum**; **Halite**; **Limestone**.

Chemical weathering   Chemical conversion of rock due to the action of natural forces. The chief agents of chemical weathering are oxygen, water, and atmospheric gases.

Certain minerals, when exposed to air, react with oxygen and change their chemical composition. This can easily be seen in a freshly broken rock, which is often a different color on the surface than in the interior. Iron-containing minerals characteristically turn red when exposed to air and water. Water reacts further with hematite to form a yellow compound.

The carbon dioxide in the air is produced in the respiration of animals, by volcanoes, by fire, by decay in the soil, and by many industrial processes. Nitrogen and sulfur oxides are produced by burning of coal and oil. All these oxides form acids when they combine with water. The acids can alter many different minerals. Calcite rocks, such as limestone, marble, coquina, and calcite-bound sandstones, are rapidly dissolved by the acidic water.

In a rock, some of the minerals are more subject to weathering than others. In granite, for example the feldspar is reduced chemically to clay. This releases the quartz as separate grains.

Chinook   A hot, dry wind produced when air descends on the leeward side of a mountain. It produces desert climates, such as those in the Great Basin of the United States.

Chromosphere   *See* **Sun**.

Cinder cone   *See* **Volcano**.

Circumstellar dust   A concentration of interstellar dust in the neighborhood of a star. It is found most commonly around red giants, which eject material from the surface. *See* **Stellar evolution**.

Cirque   A bowl-shaped depression, high in a mountain, formed by erosion under a snowfield. *See* **Alpine glaciation**.

Cirque-and-horn topography   A high-mountain landscape formed at the head of valley glaciers; *see* **Alpine glaciation**.

Cirrus   *See* **Clouds**.

Clastic sedimentary rocks   Rocks formed by the cementing of sediments that were produced by weathering. The sediments, if small enough can be compacted together to form rock by the weight of overlying sediments. Larger particles can be cemented into rock by minerals, such as calcite and hematite, precipitated out of water.

Clastic sedimentary rocks are stratified, forming layers with the older rocks below the younger ones, and often contain fossils. The relative ages of the fossils can be determined by their positions in the layers. The rocks are classified according to the size of the particles. Conglomerates have particles larger than 3 mm; sandstone particles range from 0.06 to 3 mm, and rocks with still smaller particles are called shale.

Cleavage   The tendency of certain crystalline minerals to break in flat planes, corresponding to planes within the crystal. The angles between cleavage planes are a useful clue to the identity of the mineral. Halite, for example, cleaves along three mutually perpendicular planes.

Climate   The average weather of a region over a period of many years. Climates are characterized chiefly by the pattern of annual changes in temperature and precipitation.

Latitude provides the primary classification of types of climate. Polar climates, in the extreme south and north, are those in which the average monthly temperature never rises above 10°C. In tropical climates, the zone around the equator, average monthly temperatures are never below 18°C. Between these are the midlatitude climates, where there is a distinct seasonal variation between summer and winter. Elevation produces a secondary effect, for at high altitudes polar climates can be found at much lower latitudes.

Seasonal variations in temperature are mitigated by nearness to large bodies of water. Since water has a high specific heat, it does not change temperature quickly. The result is that regions near the ocean or very large lakes have a characteristic marine climate in which the summers are not as hot or the winters as cold as they are farther inland.

Ocean currents also modify temperature. The warm Gulf Stream, flowing to northern Europe, makes that region warmer than corresponding latitudes in Canada. The cold Humboldt Current, flowing from the south polar region, keeps the west coast of South America cool.

The amount of precipitation in a given region is determined primarily by the landform. Where prevailing winds blow from the ocean, there is considerable precipitation. Mountains have a far-reaching effect. Winds rising on the windward side of the mountain form dense clouds as they rise and produce a humid climate. As the air descends on the leeward side, it becomes dry. Deserts are usually found on the leeward side of mountains. *See* **Gulf Stream**; **Humboldt Current**.

Clouds   Masses of water droplets or ice crystals above ground level. Clouds are formed by rising air currents. As air currents rise, the air cools (*see* **Adiabatic temperature change**). When the temperature reaches the dew point, the water vapor condenses onto dust particles in the air. The droplets thus formed make up clouds. As condensation continues, the droplets grow. They also grow by uniting with each other. When the droplets are large enough to fall through the rising air currents, they decend as rain.

If the relative humidity is low, the dew point may be below 0°C. There is then no condensation until the air is below the freezing point. The vapor turns directly into ice crystals (*see* **Sublimation**). Precipitation falls as snow. This happens frequently, at all times of the year. The snowflakes melt before reaching the ground unless the air is cold at lower levels.

Clouds are classified according to their form. There are four main categories, with many intermediates. The fluffy, cottony clouds that often occur in fair weather are called cumulus clouds. The thin, feathery clouds at very high altitudes (up to 10 km) are made of ice crystals and are known as cirrus clouds. As cirrus clouds thicken and migrate to lower levels, they form solid layers known as stratus clouds. When they arrive at still lower altitudes and produce rain, they are called nimbus clouds. Thunderstorms are formed in the very tall, violent clouds of the kind called cumulonimbus (*see* **Thunderstorm**).

Cluster of galaxies   A group of galaxies separated from other such groups by enormous regions of empty space. The Milky Way galaxy is a member of a cluster known as the local group, which contains 21 galaxies in a region 3 million light-years in diameter.

Cluster variable   A kind of variable star of the RR Lyrae type, with periods of less than a day, which are very common in globular clusters.

Coal   The compacted remains of plants that died and left their bodies in stagnant water. When partially decayed, the remains form a fibrous material called peat. Pressure compacts this material into a soft, brown rock called lignite. Continued compaction produces a darker, black material called bituminous, or soft coal. Hard coal, anthracite, is the final result of the process.

All these materials are used as fuel, and all produce pollution problems. The hardest coal, anthracite, burns the cleanest, but even this substance releases quantities of sulfur oxides and fly ash into the air.

Cohesion   The force that holds similar molecules together. When it is strong enough the material is solid. Cohesion in liquids is strong enough to prevent a column of liquid from breaking apart unless counteracting forces are quite great. *See* **Capillary action**.

Cold cloud   A mass of interstellar dust and molecules that absorbs light from stars and reradiates it in the infrared and radio regions. The material contains various organic molecules, e.g., ethyl alcohol. Cold clouds are an early stage in the formation of stars.

EARTH AND SPACE SCIENCE

Cold front   *See* **Front**.

Color Index   A system of classifying stars according to color as a means of identifying their temperature. The radiation from the star is measured at various wavelengths, and a formula is applied to yield an index. An index of zero indicates a surface temperature of about 10,000 K; values range from +2.0 for cold, red stars to –0.4 for hot, blue stars. *See* **H-R diagram**.

Comet   A celestial object made of ice and rocks, orbiting the sun. Some comets return to the neighborhood of the earth at regular intervals such as the 76-year period of Halley's comet. Others are in open orbit and travel around the sun once before escaping into outer space. As a comet approaches the sun, particles streaming from the sun cause the ice to evaporate, and it forms a long tail pointing away from the sun.

The comets we see apparently come from a tremendous agglomeration of comets, called Oort's Cloud, in orbit around the sun at distances far beyond the farthest planet. Perturbations due to other stars can disturb their orbits, causing a comet to fall from the cloud toward the sun.

Compaction   The binding of fine sediments into rock as a result of pressure. *See* **Clastic sedimentary rocks**.

Compressional wave   *See* **Longitudinal wave**, Physics section, page 20-29.

Condensation   The phase transition in which a vapor turns into a liquid. When the air temperature drops, a point is reached at which the water vapor turns to liquid on any solid surface in contact with the air. *See* **Dew point**; **Precipitation**; **Relative humidity**; **Sublimation**.

Conduction   The passage of heat through a material, with no movement of matter. A spoon placed in hot coffee, for example, becomes hot at the other end. Metals conduct heat well, but most nonmetals do not. Much of the heat that flows outward from the center of the earth moves by conduction through the solid core and the solid crust. However, *see also* **Convection**.

Conglomerate   *See* **Clastic sedimentary rocks**.

Constellation   A recognizable pattern formed by stars in the sky, and given a name. Although constellations are convenient for identifying regions of the sky, they have no other significance.

Constructional forces   Forces in the earth's interior that produce deformations of the crust. *See* **Continental drift**; **Earthquake**; **Isostasy**; **Seafloor spreading**; **Volcano**.

Contact   A boundary between two different kinds of rock. Examples include the interface between a lava flow and the underlying rock, the boundary of an intrusion, and the border of a sedimentary deposit with an older surface.

Contact metamorphism   An alteration in the chemical composition and crystal structure of rock as a result of heating by contact with magma. Such metamorphosed rock is found adjacent to igneous intrusion.

Continental accretion   Growth of a continent by adding material at its edge. The material may come from sediments carried by streams from the interior of the continent. Also, if there is a subduction zone at the edge of a continent, as at the western border of North America, the moving continental plate may carry material and deposit it at the edge of the continent.

Continental divide   A line of maximum elevation separating two drainage basins. The continental divides of the United States separate the whole country into three basins.

Continental drift   The theory, now well established, that the continents are large masses of rock resting on solid plates that float on the underlying magma and move around (*see* **Plate tectonics**).

The geography of the Atlantic Ocean provides persuasive evidence for continental drift. North America, Greenland, South America, Europe, and Africa seem to fit together like pieces of a jigsaw puzzle. The theory is substantially bolstered by finding matching geologic formations on the two sides of the Atlantic. These include mountain ranges, mineral deposits, fossils, and glaciated valleys. The evidence is that the Atlantic Basin opened up about 100 million years ago. Accurate measurements show that the continents are moving apart at the rate of a few centimeters a year.

The climates of continental regions in ages past show that the continents have moved. A half billion years ago, continental glaciers covered parts of Africa, India, Australia, and South America, which are now tropical. Coal deposits show that Antarctica and Spitzbergen were once tropical. Such fundamental changes in climate can only be the result of a change in latitude.

Consideration of all the evidence indicates that about 200 million years ago all the major land masses were combined into a single supercontinent, centered somewhere around the South Pole. It has been named Pangaea. The present continents resulted from the breakup of Pangaea and the movement of the separate land masses in different directions.

Continental glacier   A sheet of ice covering a large part of a continent. There are now two such glaciers on earth, one in Greenland and the other in Antarctica.

Some 95% of Greenland is covered by ice, in many regions well over a kilometer thick. It forms there because it snows heavily in the interior, and it is never warm long enough in the summer to melt the snow. The snow piles up and compacts into ice. It flows outward toward the sea in all directions. Antarctica shows the same pattern.

Surface erosion and deposition show that there have been many periods ("ice ages") in which continental glaciers were much more extensive. Most of Canada and the northern U.S. show signs of glaciation: erratic boulders, drumlins, kames, eskers, kettle lakes, moraines, and so on. The farthest recent advance of the ice, about 12,000 years ago, covered all of Canada with a sheet of ice. Its southernmost limit is marked by the Missouri, Ohio, and Mohawk rivers.

Continental growth   The formation of new continental rock, as described by a set of theories to explain the currently observed geologic properties of continents. It is found, for example, that a continent's rocks are of many different ages. This implies that rock has been added from time to time. Often, younger rock is at the periphery. *See* **Continental accretion**.

Material removed from the center of continents is deposited in the bordering oceans, forming geosynclines. The crust sags beneath the weight as more and more sediments are added. At some point, the geosyncline stops subsiding and is lifted above the surface, forming new continental rock.(*See* **Geosyncline**.) The new rock forms mountains; *see* **Basalt-eclogite hypothesis**; **Isostasy**; **Uplift**.

Continental shelf   The region of shallow water extending into the sea at the edge of a continent. *See* **Seafloor topography**.

Continental shield   Ancient igneous rocks forming the central core of a continent.

Continental slope   The steep-sloping sea bottom between the continental shelf and the deep ocean. *See* **Seafloor topography**.

Contour interval   On a contour map, the vertical distance between successive contours.

Contour lines   Lines drawn on a map connecting points of equal elevation.

Contour map   A map in which elevations are represented by contour lines. The slope of the surface is greatest where the contour lines are closest together.

Convection   A process by which heat is transferred in an upward direction by the movement of a fluid. Any time a liquid or gas is warmer at the bottom than at the top, the warmer material rises. The reason is that it has expanded, so that its density is lower.

Wind is the result of differential heating of the air, producing convection currents. Planetary winds are worldwide air movements due to the difference between polar and tropical air. *See* **Planetary winds**. Local weather conditions result largely from convection currents in the atmosphere; *see* **Pressure systems**.

Differential heating of the ocean results in the massive movement of water. *See* **Ocean currents**.

Convection cell   A region in which a fluid, heated at the bottom, forms a closed circulatory pattern. Rising fluid diverges into two horizontal paths at the top. Fluid in adjacent cells converges to form a descending column.

The movement of tectonic plates is apparently due to convection cells in the mantle. The source of heat is the radioactive elements in the earth's interior. Divergence at the top of the fluid magma moves two plates apart, and new crust is formed in the space (*see* **Seafloor spreading**). In a convergence zone, the floating plates are forced together, and one plate plunges under the other (*see* **Subduction zone**).

Convergence zone   A region in which the currents of two adjacent convection cells join to form a single current.

Copernicus, Nicholaus (1473–1543)   Polish astronomer who first described the then known universe as a system in which the sun is at the center and the planets revolve around it.

Coquina   A sedimentary rock of calcite, composed of broken pieces of shells of clams, oysters, and other shellfish, and coral.

Coral reef   An underwater ridge formed by the action of colonial organisms related to the jellyfish. The animal builds a small calcareous external skeleton, and the accumulation of these skeletons for many years produces an enormous ridge in clear, shallow, warm water. The coral reefs, or fringing reefs, are found only offshore in the tropics. There is usually a quiet lagoon between the reefs and the coast of the continent or the oceanic island. *See also* **Atoll**.

Core   The central hot, dense part of the earth, with a diameter of about 3500 km. It apparently consists chiefly of iron and nickel. The inner core, 1250 km in radius, has the properties of a solid. The rest, the outer core, is liquid. For information about how the core is explored, *see* **Earthquake waves**.

Coriolis effect   The change in direction of a moving object due to the rotation of the earth. The effect is observable in both the atmosphere and the ocean. *See* **High-pressure system**; **Low-pressure system**; **Ocean currents**.

Corona   *See* **Sun**.

Coronagraph   An instrument for studying the sun's corona by creating an artificial eclipse. It consists of a telescope with an opaque disk in its focal plane just large enough to blot out the body of the sun.

Cosmic background radiation   Microwaves uniformly distributed throughout the universe. They provide evidence for the big bang model of the universe. When the universe cooled to 3000 K, it became transparent. It emitted the characteristic black-body radiation at that temperature (*see* **Radiation**; *see also* **Radiation**, Physics section, page 20-41). Expansion cooled the universe, and it now has the background radiation at frequencies expected at 3 K.

Cosmological principle   The assumption of cosmologists that, on a large scale, the universe is uniform everywhere. Recent evidence suggests that it may not be true.

Crab nebula   An expanding mass of gas, the remnant of a supernova of the year 1054. It is a strong source of infrared, X-ray, and radio emission. The star remaining at its center is a pulsar.

Craton   A large region of old, undeformed sedimentary rocks covering a continental shield.

Cretaceous period   The final period of the Mesozoic era; it ended with a massive extinction of life, including the disappearance of the dinosaurs.

Crust   The solid outer layer of the earth, consisting of a layer of basalt overlaid, on the continents, with granitic rocks. It is about 10 km thick under the oceans and up to 30 km under the continents. Its boundary with the underlying mantle is called the Moho.

Crystal   A solid material in which the molecules or ions are arranged in regular patterns so that the bulk material forms a mass with flat surfaces. The form of a crystal is an important clue to the chemical identity of minerals. Pure quartz, for example, can be recognized by its six-sided crystals. Crystals form when a material solidifies, either from a melt or by precipitation from solution. The slower the growth of crystals, the larger they become.

Cumulus   *See* **Clouds**.

Cyclone   *See* **Low-pressure system**. The word is also used in a nonscientific context to mean a hurricane or a tornado.

Dark matter Invisible material that is thought to make up most of the matter in the universe. Its nature is completely unknown, but its existence is inferred from gravitational effects.

Dark nebula *See* **Nebula**.

Declination *See* **Celestial sphere**.

Deficit The difference between potential and actual evapotranspiration. *See* **Water budget**.

Deformation A change due to a process such as faulting, folding, tilting, and volcanism, that distorts the older shapes of the rock formations in the earth's crust.

Degenerate matter Matter in which enormous pressure has crushed atoms together so hard that all the electrons have been stripped from the nuclei and the nuclei can approach each other quite closely. The density of degenerate matter is so great that a ton of it would occupy only about 5 cm³. This is the state of matter in a white dwarf.

Delta The sedimentary deposit formed at the mouth of a river owing to the loss of stream velocity when the river enters the sea. It is often triangular in form. The coarsest sediments in a delta are found closest to shore, where there is still some current to carry the finer sediments farther out. *See also* **Deposition**.

Dendritic drainage Drainage in which the stream forms a random pattern of smaller and smaller branches. It occurs where there is no special region of weakness in the underlying bedrock.

Density *See* Physics section page 20-9. Density is an important property in the identification of minerals. A geologist in the field can determine the density of a rock with no other instrument than a spring scale calibrated in grams. Suspending the rock from the scale gives its mass. Its volume in cubic centimeters is the difference between its mass and the scale reading when the rock is immersed in water.

Density is a function of temperature. Nearly all materials expand when heated. This increases the volume without changing the mass. The result is a decrease in density.

Units in the metric system are defined so that the density of pure water at 4°C is exactly 1g/cm³. Water is unusual in that its density decreases as it is cooled below that temperature, so that it has its maximum density at 4°C.

Density current The flow of a dense sediment-water mixture to spread out under a layer of lower density. It occurs in lakes when the balance of sediments at the bottom is suddenly upset by an influx of heavy sediments.

Deposition The accumulation of sediments that have been carried by erosion from one place to another. Examination of the sediments can yield information about the kind of erosion process involved. In still water, the deposited sediments form layers of different kinds of particles. *See* **Vertical sorting**.

Sediments deposited by rivers are not sorted vertically except where there is deep, quiet water. If there is turbulence or the water is shallow, the particles are of mixed sizes. Maximum size depends on the velocity and rate of flow of the river. Large sedimentary particles indicate some combination of high velocity and large volume. Particles carried by rivers become rounded as they move.

Stream-borne sediments ultimately reach the sea. In the absence of current, the sediments are deposited at or near the mouth of the river. Typically, the deposit forms a broad, triangular mass of sediment called a delta. There is often considerable horizontal sorting in a delta. A large delta blocks the outlet of the river, and the main channel breaks up to send the water into the sea through several distributaries. In a delta, new channels form frequently as old channels are blocked.

Sediments deposited by glaciers, as in moraines or eskers, are completely unsorted and may contain large boulders as well as fine silt (*see* **Glacial deposits**). The particles of wind-blown deposits tend to be of uniform size (*see* **Wind deposits**).

Depression A region of low atmospheric pressure. *See* **Low-pressure system**.

Destructional forces Processes that reduce rock to finer material and deposit it at lower levels. Their general tendency is to level the landscape. Agents of destruction are gravity, weathering, rivers, glaciers, waves, and wind.

Deuterium Hydrogen-2, the isotope of hydrogen containing a proton and a neutron in the nucleus. Deuterium is an intermediate product in the hydrogen-burning nuclear fusion process in which four protons combine to form a helium nucleus. *See* **Nuclear fusion**, Physics section, page 20-35.

Dew point The temperature at which water vapor condenses out of the air, forming dew. It depends only on the absolute humidity, the amount of moisture per unit volume of air. As air cools, its ability to hold water vapor diminishes. (*See* **Saturation vapor pressure**.) When the relative humidity reaches 100%, the air is saturated and the vapor condenses onto any surface.

One method of determining the dew point uses a sling psychrometer and a dew point temperature chart. A sling psychrometer consists of two thermometers, one of which has its bulb wrapped in gauze. The gauze is made wet, and the whole apparatus is swung around in a circle to keep moisture from accumulating around the wet bulb. As the water evaporates, it cools the bulb of the thermometer. The chart gives the dew point in terms of known values of temperature and depression of the wet bulb.

Dike *See* **Intrusion**.

Dinosaurs A group of animals that dominated the earth during the Mesozoic era, from 190 to 65 million years ago. They are traditionally classified as reptiles, but current information is that they were highly active and warm blooded, in contrast to the slow-moving reptiles. Many, but not all, were extraordinarily large. They gave rise to the birds in the middle Jurassic. The dinosaurs died out at the end of the Mesozoic.

Dip The angle of downward inclination of a sedimentary rock layer. It is measured perpendicular to the strike line.

Discontinuity A boundary line between two distinctly different systems. The Mohorovicic discontinuity (Moho) is the border between the earth's crust and its mantle. Within the crust, a discontinuity marks the boundary between one sedimentary system and another deposited on top of it.

Divergence zone   A region on the boundary between two convection cells where the flow separates into two streams, one in each cell.

Divide   A region of high elevation separating the drainage basins of two rivers.

Dolomite   A rock composed of a single mineral, a calcium magnesium carbonate. It is formed by precipitation when streams carrying the mineral in solution flow into salt water.

Doppler effect   The shift of frequency of a wave due to the relative motion of the source and the observer. *See also* Physics section, page 20-10.

In astronomical systems, the frequency shift of the light observed is used as an indication of the speed of a star in the radial direction, that is, toward or away from the observer. Motion toward the observer causes a blue shift, a change toward shorter wavelengths. A red shift, a change toward longer wavelengths, indicates motion away from the observer.

Doppler frequency shifts can detect the rotation of a star. When a star rotates, one side of it approaches us and is blue shifted and the other side is red shifted. The result is that all the spectral lines are broadened. In observing a rotating galaxy, Doppler shifts can be measured directly on the two sides of the galaxy.

For the use of the Doppler shift in determining the velocity and distance of galaxies, see **Expanding universe**.

Double star   *See* **Binary star**.

Draconid shower   A meteor shower emerging from the constellation Draco on or about October 9. On this date every year, the earth encounters the debris left by a comet.

Drainage basin   A region in which all the precipitation flows into a given river and its tributaries. For example, all water that is carried to the ocean by the Hudson River comes from the rain and snow that fell in the Hudson River drainage basin. *See* **Continental divide**.

Drainage density   The ratio between the total length of all the stream channels in a region and the area drained.

Drainage divide   *See* **Divide**.

Drainage pattern   The general pattern formed by streams. It is determined primarily by the nature of the underlying bedrock. *See* **Annular drainage**; **Dendritic drainage**; **Radial drainage**; **Trellis drainage**; **Underground drainage**.

Drumlin   *See* **Glacial deposits**.

Dry-bulb thermometer   *See* **Dew point**.

Dynamic equilibrium   A situation in which opposing tendencies neutralize each other in such a way that there is no apparent change. For example, the uplifting of a mountain may be exactly balanced by the rate at which the mountain is eroded.

E **Earth**   The third planet, about 93 million miles (1.48×10^8 km) from the sun. It is approximately spherical, with a radius of about 6400 km. Because of its spin, it is about 0.3% wider at the equator than along the axis between its poles. The age of the earth has been measured by studying the radioactivity of rocks. Each radioactive element decays at a definite rate into other elements. The ratio of the amount of the parent element and that of its offspring can be used to determine the age of the

rock. Several different measurements of this kind agree in giving the age of the earth at about 4.5 billion years. *See* **Half-life**, Physics section, page 20-22; **Radioactivity**, Physics section, page 20-41; **Radioactive dating**, page 5-31.

The earth was formed by the aggregation of materials due to their gravitational attraction. The heat generated by impact melted the material, and the lighter substances rose above the more dense materials. The materials of the earth are arranged in layers according to density. Air, with the lowest density, is the outside layer; the central core has the highest density. The layers are as follows.

The *atmosphere* is the gaseous outer layer. Its density falls gradually with height, shading off into outer space at about 1000 km. For details, *see* **Atmosphere**.

The *hydrosphere* includes the oceans, lakes, rivers, and ice caps. It covers about 70% of the surface to an average depth of 4 km. *See* **Ocean**.

The *lithosphere* is the solid rock, forming a shell about 100 km thick. The outer part, the crust, is completely solid, from 10 to 30 km thick. Below that is the mantle, mixed solid and liquid rock. *See* **Crust**; **Mantle**; **Moho**.

The *core is* the central part, of several layers. *See* **Core**.

Earthquake   A violent shaking of the earth due to slippage of the crust along a fault. The crust is subject to strains due to isostatic movement, causing the crust to bend out of shape. When the strain reaches the breaking point, the crust cracks. Since a fault is a zone of weakness, the break is most likely to occur there. Repeated earthquakes at a fault may move one side of the fault higher than the other or cause a lateral shifting of one side with respect to the other. *See* **Fault**.

An earthquake produces waves in the earth that appear to originate at some point below the surface, called the focus of the earthquake. The focus lies between 60 and 450 km below the surface. The point at the surface directly above the focus is called the epicenter of the earthquake.

The strength of an earthquake is measured in terms of the Richter scale. The zero point on the scale is a barely noticeable motion at the epicenter. The scale is logarithmic, so 1 represents 10 times the amplitude of 0; 2 is 100 times, 3 is 1000 times, and so on.

Most earthquakes occur at the boundaries between tectonic plates. Main centers of activity are the subduction zones at the borders of the Pacific Ocean, the mid-Atlantic Ridge, the Mediterranean Basin, and other plate boundaries.

Earthquake waves   Shock waves produced by earthquakes, which travel through the earth's crust and interior. They can be detected at great distances from the source by an instrument that measures the shaking of the crust (*see* **Seismograph**).

There are two main categories of waves, and both are produced by earthquakes. *See* **Longitudinal wave**, Physics section, page 20-29; **Transverse wave**, page 20-50; **Earth's interior**, page 5-12.

For example, a seismograph record shows two kinds of waves arriving at the seismograph at different times. Both started when the earthquake occurred, but they travel at different speeds. A longitudinal wave called the primary or P wave arrives first. Some time later, a transverse wave, the secondary or S wave, arrives.

For the use of earthquake waves to explore the structure of the earth, *see* **Earth's interior**.

Earthshine The dim light seen on the face of the moon when it is new, or nearly new. At this point, the sun is behind the moon. The light gets to the moon by reflecting from the surface of the earth.

Earth's interior The central zone of the earth. The composition of the interior of the earth is studied by analysis of the distribution of earthquake waves. The waves must obey certain rules: in passing from one material into another, the waves abruptly change direction; in going through a material in which the density changes gradually, they follow curved paths; S waves are transverse, so they can travel only in a solid.

Earthquake waves reveal the structure of the earth's interior. P and S waves curve as they travel through the mantle because of the increasing density of the mantle at greater depths. Both kinds of waves can be detected by seismographs up to a distance of 11,400 km. P waves can also be detected at distances greater than 16,000 km. They have passed through the earth's core, and were bent at the core-mantle boundary. S waves, being transverse, cannot go through the core, indicating that the core is liquid. *See* **Core**.

Eccentricity *See* **Ellipse**.

Eclipse *See* **Lunar eclipse**; **Solar eclipse**.

Ecliptic The path of the sun across the celestial sphere. As the earth revolves around the sun, the position of the sun against the sky changes on an annual cycle. The ecliptic is the path as it would be seen against the stars if we could see them in the daytime. The planets and the moon are always found in a band surrounding the ecliptic, called the zodiac. There are 12 constellations in the zodiac, and they form convenient references for stating the locations of the planets. The equinoxes occur when the sun is at the points where the ecliptic crosses the celestial equator.

Eclogite An igneous rock identical in chemical composition to basalt. It is formed from basalt when extremely high pressures rearrange the crystalline structure of basalt. *See* **Basalt-eclogite hypothesis**.

Einstein telescope An X-ray telescope in orbit around the earth. Since X-rays are absorbed in the atmosphere, the only way to study the X-ray emission of stars and galaxies is to get above the atmosphere. Rockets were used, but they operate for only a few minutes and can give no real image. The Einstein telescope uses a complex set of reflecting surfaces to form a real image of the sky and transmit it back to earth. It operated from 1978 to 1981 and made thousands of important discoveries.

Electromagnetic energy The energy of electromagnetic waves. This is the kind of energy that comes to earth from the sun, through outer space. *See* **Insolation**.

Electromagnetic waves *See* Physics section, page 20-14; **Electromagnetic spectrum**, Physics section, page 20-14.

The waves of most interest to the earth are those that come to us from the sun and can penetrate the atmosphere. *See* **Infrared rays**; **Light**; **Ultraviolet rays**.

Electron *See* Physics section, page 20-14.

Element A substance composed of only one kind of atom. Ninety-two different elements are found in nature, and several others have been produced artificially. Each element is characterized by its atomic number, which is equal to the number of positively charged protons in its nucleus, and to the number of electrons outside the nucleus.

The following are some of the important elements of the earth:

By mass, oxygen makes up 47% of the earth's crust, 18% of the atmosphere and (as a component of water) 88% of the hydrosphere. There is very little oxygen in the interior.

Silicon is the second most abundant element in the crust making up 28%. It is a major component in all granitic rocks. Quartz, an exceedingly abundant mineral, is silicon dioxide. *See* **Silicate minerals**.

Iron is the main component of the earth's core and is also present in the crust. Metallic elements, in order of their abundance in the crust are aluminum, iron, calcium, sodium, potassium, and magnesium.

Ellipse A geometric curve like a flattened circle. The longest diameter is called the major axis and the shortest diameter is the minor axis. An ellipse has two foci. It is constructed in such a way that every point on the curve meets the condition that the sum of its distances to the two foci is a constant. The eccentricity of an ellipse is a parameter that tells how flat it is. Eccentricity is defined as the distance between foci divided by the major axis. A circle is an ellipse with zero eccentricity.

When a planet is in orbit around the sun, the path of the planet is an ellipse with the sun at one focus. Aphelion and perihelion occur at opposite ends of the major axis.

El niño A warm ocean current flowing every few years, eastward from New Guinea to the coast of Peru. It disrupts the usual flow of the Humboldt Current and causes major climatic changes in many parts of the world.

Emergent shoreline The surface features of the coastline produced by the uplift of the land mass or a drop in sea level. The shoreline is usually a straight and regular sandy beach. Sandbars are raised out of the sea to become offshore islands, sandy and parallel to the coast. The lagoon between the islands and the continent may be dotted with low, sandy islands. Low-lying coastal plains turn into salt marsh.

Emission nebula *See* **Nebula**.

Energy *See* Physics section, page 20-15.

Energy-mass equivalence *See* **Mass-energy**, Physics section, page 20-31.

Entrenched meanders Meanders that have cut a deep channel as the land level rises, so that the rivers flow at the bottom of a steep valley in a plain.

Epicenter *See* **Earthquake**.

Epicycles In the geocentric model of the solar system, the circles within circles within circles that were invented to explain the apparent motions of the planets.

Epoch *See* **Geologic time scale**.

Equator The line around the earth marking points halfway between the poles; the position of zero latitude.

Equatorial countercurrent   A large water current flowing eastward in the center of the Pacific Ocean.

Equilibrium   *See* **Graded stream**.

Equinox   The moment when the earth, in its orbit around the sun, is in such a position that the noon sun is directly overhead at the equator. The spring or vernal equinox occurs on March 21, the first day of spring; the fall or autumnal equinox is the first day of fall, September 22 or 23. *See* **Seasons**.

At the equinoxes, the sun is on the horizon at the poles for the full 24 hours. All other points on earth have just 12 hours of daylight (neglecting atmospheric refraction of the sunlight).

Era   *See* **Geologic time scale**.

Erosion   The constant wearing away of the earth's surface as a result of processes that transport loose material and deposit it in a different place. A number of different agents of erosion are known.

Gravity   Most erosional processes move materials downhill. Some processes, such as landslides and hillside creep move soil downhill without involving any other agent. *See* **Gravitational erosion**.

In temperate and tropical climates, the main agents of erosion are *rivers* and *streams*. In due time every mountain is worn down by its rivers. *See* **Stream aging**; **Stream erosion**.

Valley glaciers   cut valleys with characteristic shapes and features. *See* **Alpine glaciation**.

Wind   is an effective agent only in desert climates. *See* **Wind erosion**.

Waves   are an effective erosion agent on seashores. *See* **Wave erosion**.

See also **Density current**; **Deposition**.

Erratic boulder   A boulder made of rock different from the bedrock on which it lies. It was carried to its present location by a glacier.

Escape velocity   *See* Physics section, page 20-16.

Escarpment   A cliff, the free face of a vertical or nearly vertical slope.

Esker   *See* **Glacial deposits**.

Estuary   A long, lagoonlike bay at the mouth of a river, caused by invasion of the sea into the river valley. It results from a rise in sea level or a fall in the level of the land.

Eutrophication   Excessive chemical pollution of a lake by runoff of fertilizing chemicals. This produces overgrowth of algae. When the algae decay, the decay processes use up the oxygen in the lake, causing the death of animal life.

Evaporation   The change from liquid to vapor. Evaporation of water from the surface of lakes, rivers, the ocean, and wet soil adds water vapor to the atmosphere.

The rate of evaporation is controlled by a number of variables. The more surface area, the greater is the rate of evaporation. Droplets of spray, as from breaking waves or rapidly flowing water, have a great deal of surface area for their volume, so they evaporate quickly. Evaporation is faster at higher temperatures.

Water evaporates faster when the air above the surface is low in vapor. At any given temperature, there is a limit to the amount of moisture the air can hold. Evaporation stops when the amount of vapor in the air is at the limit. The air is then said to be saturated, and the relative humidity is 100%. *See* **Dew point**.

Evaporite   A sedimentary rock formed by precipitation from a body of water that evaporates. Examples are halite and gypsum.

Evapotranspiration   Conversion of water to vapor by a combination of evaporation from open surfaces and transpiration from the leaves of plants.

The rate of evapotranspiration is limited by climatic factors and by the amount of water available in the soil. Potential evapotranspiration is the rate at which evapotranspiration occurs if plenty of water is available. It is greatest in summer, when insolation is greatest. In winter, the energy available to produce evapotranspiration is low, and the rate diminishes. If the soil freezes, there is no evapotranspiration.

Actual evapotranspiration may be less than potential evapotranspiration, and occurs when the amount of water in the soil is low. For example in a desert in summer, the potential evapotranspiration is enormous. If there is no water in the soil, however, the actual evapotranspiration is zero. *See* **Water budget**.

Event horizon   The limit of a black hole. Anything that is inside the event horizon cannot escape. *See* **Black hole**.

Evolution   The gradual change in the characteristics of organisms from generation to generation. The study of fossils makes important contributions to an understanding of the course of evolution.

Evolutionary processes increase the number of species in the world. A single species divides into two species, each of which may undergo extensive evolutionary change. Repeated branching of this kind has produced all the existing and extinct kinds of living things, starting with one or a few kinds about 3 billion years ago.

Exfoliation   The breakup of a rock in layers more or less parallel to the surface. It is thought to result when a rock expands because of reduced pressure when overlying material is removed.

Expanding universe   The doctrine that the whole universe is undergoing a steady, uniform expansion. It is based on the observation that the light from all the galaxies is red shifted, indicating that they are all moving away from us. Further, studies of nearby galaxies showed that their radial velocity is proportional to their distance from us. This is called the Hubble law, after its discoverer. If all the galaxies are moving apart and the rate of separation is greater at greater separation, the whole universe must be expanding.

The Hubble law makes it possible to use the red shift to determine the distances of the galaxies. The ratio of radial velocity to distance from us is a constant called the Hubble constant. It is about 17 km/s for each million light-years distance of the galaxy. The red shift of a galaxy can give its radial velocity; this and the Hubble constant tell us how far away the galaxy is. For example, if the red shift shows that a galaxy is receding at 10,000 km/s, its distance from us is

$$\frac{10,000 \text{ km/s}}{17 \text{ km/s}/10^6 \text{ light-years}} = \frac{590 \text{ million}}{\text{light-years}}$$

The farthest galaxies detected are receding at 60% of the speed of light, or 180,000 km/s. Applying the Hubble constant tells us that these galaxies are 11 billion light-years away. The mysterious objects called quasars are even further away (*see* **Quasar**).

Extinction　The disappearance of a species from the earth. This is a normal part of the evolutionary process, and every extinction prepares the way for the evolution of something new. However, the present situation is alarming because the rate at which species are dying out is far greater than at any time in the past. The reason is that human activity has pre-empted most of the world, leaving only a small part of the earth as undisturbed natural habitat.

Extrusion　The production of new rock on the surface of the earth as a result of molten lava rising up from deep in the interior. Volcanoes are the source of extrusions. *See* **Igneous rocks**.

Extrusive rock　Rock formed by the solidification of lava flows. Since lava cools rapidly, extrusive rocks are either noncrystalline or are made of very tiny crystals.

Some extrusive rocks have a spongy texture because the lava from which they formed contains trapped air. If light in color (sialic), they are called pumice, if dark (mafic), scoria.

Obsidian is a glasslike extrusive rock that has cooled so rapidly that it has not formed crystals.

Two important extrusive rocks made of very tiny crystals are basalt (dark, mafic) and rhyolite (light, sialic).

F **Fahrenheit scale**　*See* Physics section, page 20-16.

Fault　A crack in the bedrock along which the rock on one side has moved with respect to the rock on the other. Faults are produced by earthquakes and are lines of weakness along which earthquakes occur repeatedly.

Fault-block mountain　A mountain formed when the crust breaks into a series of blocks because of extensive faulting. Some blocks rise, and others fall. The result is horst and graben topography—high elevations (horsts) alternating with depressions (grabens).

Feldspar　*See* **Silicate minerals**.

Fiord　*See* **Submergent shoreline**.

Fireball　A large, bright meteor.

Floodplain　A broad, flat plain through which an old river meanders. *See* **Stream aging**.

Focus of earthquake　*See* **Earthquake**.

Folded mountain　A mountain formed when lateral pressures cause the crust to bend into a series of folds, forming anticlines and synclines.

Fossil　Remains or imprint of an ancient animal or plant. Fossils are found in sedimentary rocks. They can give detailed knowledge of the anatomy of organisms that lived many millions of years ago.

The relative ages of fossils can be found from the sequence of the sedimentary rocks in which they are found. Undisturbed sediments are horizontal, with the older sediments below the younger. Geologists have established a complete history of the earth's past by comparing fossils and sedimentary rocks in all parts of the world. *See* **Geologic time scale**.

The absolute ages of fossils are found by study of the radioactivity in igneous rocks adjacent to the sedimentary layers. *See* **Radioactive dating**.

The San Andreas Fault seen on Carizzo Plain in California

Foucault pendulum　A heavy bob at the end of a long wire suspended from an extremely low friction bearing. If set in motion, the pendulum swings for many hours. It is found that the plane in which it swings rotates with a period of 24 hours. This is considered evidence for the earth's rotation in space.

Fracture of minerals　The characteristic pattern in which a pure mineral breaks, used as a clue to identification; opposed to cleavage, in which breakage is along flat planes. Quartz, for example, fractures in a shell-like pattern.

Fraunhofer lines　Dark lines in a bright spectrum. The sun's light, for example, contains all visible wavelengths. As it passes through the solar atmosphere, some of the colder gases absorb light at particular wavelengths. This produces dark lines in the spectrum, which indicate the chemical nature of the cold gases that absorbed the light.

Fringing reef　An offshore coral reef.

Front　The boundary between two air masses. Fronts are regions of low pressure characterized by clouds and precipitation.

A cold front occurs when a cold air mass, usually coming from the north, pushes in under a warm air mass. A cold front moves fast and causes the warm air to rise rapidly. Tall cumulus clouds form, frequently producing thunderstorms. As the front passes, the cold air moves in and temperatures drop sharply.

In a warm front, a warm air mass is moving into a region of colder air. At the front, the warm air climbs slowly over the cold air. High, thin clouds form and become lower and thicker, perhaps over a period of several days. Rain or snow will be gentle and may continue for a day or more. If air mass movement stops for a while, forming a stationary front, rainy weather may continue for days.

An occluded front forms when a fast-moving cold air mass passes right through a warm mass and into another mass of colder air. The warm air is lifted completely off the ground. Heavy rain or snow follows.

Frost action   *See* **Physical weathering**.

Gabbro   *See* **Igneous rocks**.

Galaxy   A tremendous aggregation of stars. The number of galaxies in the range of the observable universe is in the millions. They have several different forms. The most common kind is the elliptic galaxy, which is spherical or ellipsoid. Many elliptic galaxies are small, so that only the nearest can be seen. However, they range widely in size, and some are giants.

Spiral galaxies are large and bright, so more of them are visible than elliptics. A spiral galaxy has a nucleus, resembling an elliptic galaxy, at the center of an enormous disk. The disk contains a large number of star clusters and several long arms. The rotation of the galaxies gives the arms a spiral shape. The entire galaxy is surrounded by a halo of stars, many of them aggregated into globular clusters.

A few galaxies are irregular in shape. The two galaxies closest to us, the Magellanic Clouds, are of this type. For information about the galaxy to which the sun belongs, *see* **Milky Way galaxy**.

Galilean satellites   The four largest satellites of Jupiter, discovered by Galileo. *See* **Jupiter**.

Galileo (spacecraft)   A planetary probe launched in 1989. It swung around Venus in 1990, sending back pictures. In 1995 it will take many close-up pictures of Jupiter.

Galileo Galilei   Sixteenth-century physicist and astronomer. Using a telescope, he discovered the moons of Jupiter, the phases of Venus, sun spots, and so on, and provided the critical evidence that the planets orbit the sun.

Gamma radiation   Extremely short wavelength electromagnetic waves. *See* **Radioactivity**, Physics section, page 20-41.

Gegenschein   *See* **Zodiacal light**.

Geocentric model   The ancient model of the universe, also called the Ptolemaic system, in which the earth is at the center. In this model, the stars are on a large sphere that rotates around the earth once a day. The sun, moon, and planets are each on their own sphere. The spheres have different radii, and each rotates at its own speed around the earth. In addition, each planet makes a circular path, known as an epicycle, on its own sphere.

Geologic column   The composite record of geologic time as represented in sedimentary deposits. Each sedimentary series contains a part of this column. Deposits in different parts of the world are correlated by the use of index fossils. By making such correlations, geologists have been able to produce a single linear time sequence for the whole world.

Geologic time scale   The time frame used to refer to geologic events. As shown in Exhibit 5.2, the 4.5 billion year history of the earth is divided into eras and subdivided into periods and epochs.

Geosyncline   An enormous mass of sedimentary material, as much as 15 km thick, but thinner at the edges. It forms as a result of deposition of sediments in shallow water. As the sediments pile up, the crust subsides, so that deposits of great thickness can form.

Geosynclines are the main source of new bedrock added to continents. *See* **Basalt-eclogite hypothesis; Uplift**.

Geothermal energy   Usable energy obtained from the earth's internal heat. In regions where there are geysers and hot springs, water is pumped down into the crust, where it turns into steam that is used to run electric generators.

Geyser   A hot spring that shoots water into the air at intervals.

Giant   An enormous star, with a diameter a thousand times as much as the sun's. Giants are comparatively cool (3000 K at the surface) and have a density substantially lower than that of air at sea level. For the origin and history of these stars, *see* **Stellar evolution**.

Glacial age   *See* **Ice age**.

Glacial deposits   Sedimentary features deposited by glaciers. Most of them are of the kind called till, which is an unsorted sediment containing particles of all sizes ranging from fine flour to large boulders. Till accumulates in moraines, which are of several kinds. A terminal moraine is formed at the end of a glacier, when it melts and deposits its load of sediment. Lateral moraines are deposits at the sides of a glacier. A medial moraine is a deposit at the center of a glacier, formed when two glaciers run together and combine their lateral moraines. A ground moraine is a deposit of material scattered along the bed of the glacier.

Glaciers characteristically produce several other depositional features. Drumlins are oval hills formed under the glacier. They usually occur in clusters, lined up generally with the direction of movement of the ice. An esker is a winding ridge formed in the bed of a tunnel under a glacier. A kame is a cone-shaped hill of sand and gravel deposited at the foot of a receding glacier.

A well-sorted glacial deposit called an outwash plain is formed well below the foot of a glacier. It is formed of sand and finer particles carried away from the glacier by the meltwater.

Glacial trough   The broad, U-shaped valley formed by erosion by a valley glacier. *See* **Alpine glaciation**.

Glaciated landscape   *See* **Alpine glaciation**.

Glacier   A large mass of flowing ice. Glaciers form wherever the amount of snow falling during the winter is more than the amount that melts in the summer. The result is an accumulation, year by year, of deep deposits of snow. Pressure of the upper deposits converts the lower parts into solid ice. Pressure forces the ice to flow out of the snow field by a process of regelation. *See* **Continental glacier; Valley glacier**.

Globular cluster   A spherical group of many thousands of stars. Over a hundred globular clusters are known in space around the Milky Way galaxy, distributed uniformly. They are quite far away, and only a few are bright enough to be seen with the naked eye.

Gneiss   *See* **Metamorphic rocks**.

Graben   *See* **Fault-block mountain**.

Graded bedding   A succession of seasonal sedimentary deposits showing annual bands. In shallow, quiet water, deposits from streams are sorted vertically, with larger particles below the smaller. Each seasonal deposit forms a graded bed.

Graded stream   A river that is exactly in equilibrium, neither fast enough to erode nor slow enough to deposit sediment in its bed.

Granite   An intrusive rock consisting of interlocked crystals of quartz, feldspar, and mica or hornblende. Since the rock is rich in silicon and aluminum, it is low in density and is sialic. The word *granite* is sometimes used to designate the whole class of sialic rocks.

Gravitation   The primary cause of most erosion processes. It directly causes avalanches, hillside creep, and mass wasting, and keeps rivers and glaciers moving downhill.

It is the only force acting at astronomical distances; it keeps planets in orbit and galaxies together.

EXHIBIT 5.2   Geologic time scale, showing

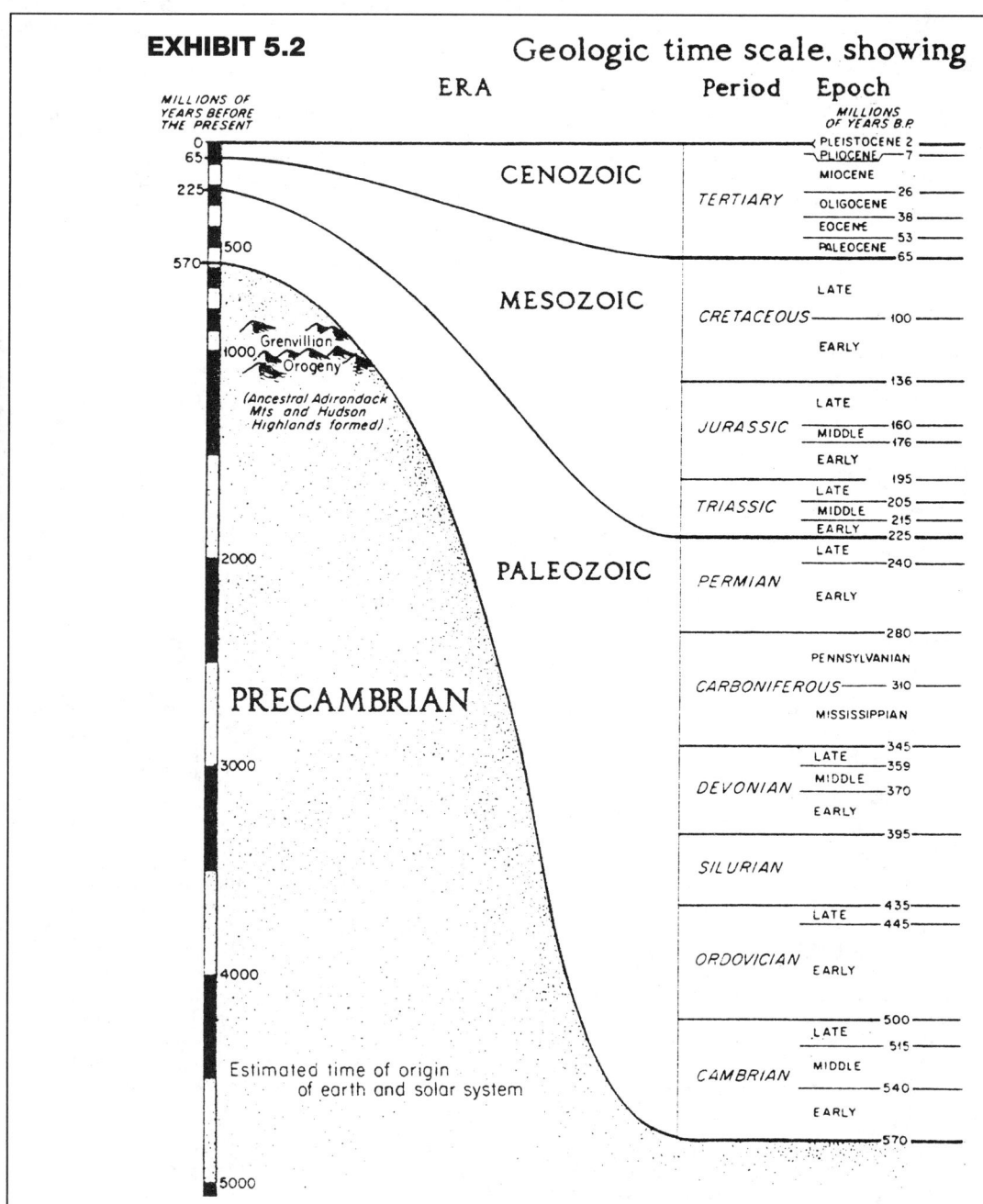

The moon's gravity produces tides and distortions of the earth's crust.

Gravitation is also responsible for the aggregation of matter in space that forms planets and stars. It keeps these astronomical bodies intact. It is the intense gravitational force of very large bodies that causes stars to collapse and heat up to the temperatures needed to produce thermonuclear reactions. *See also* **Gravitational force**, Physics section, page 20-22; **Gravitational energy**, Physics section, page 20-20.

Gravitational erosion The movement of soil downhill under the influence of gravity only. There is a limit to how steeply any loose material can be piled up. For example, when a pile of sand is deposited from a hopper, the sand piles up until the sides of the sand pile make a certain definite angle with the horizontal. Any additional sand slides

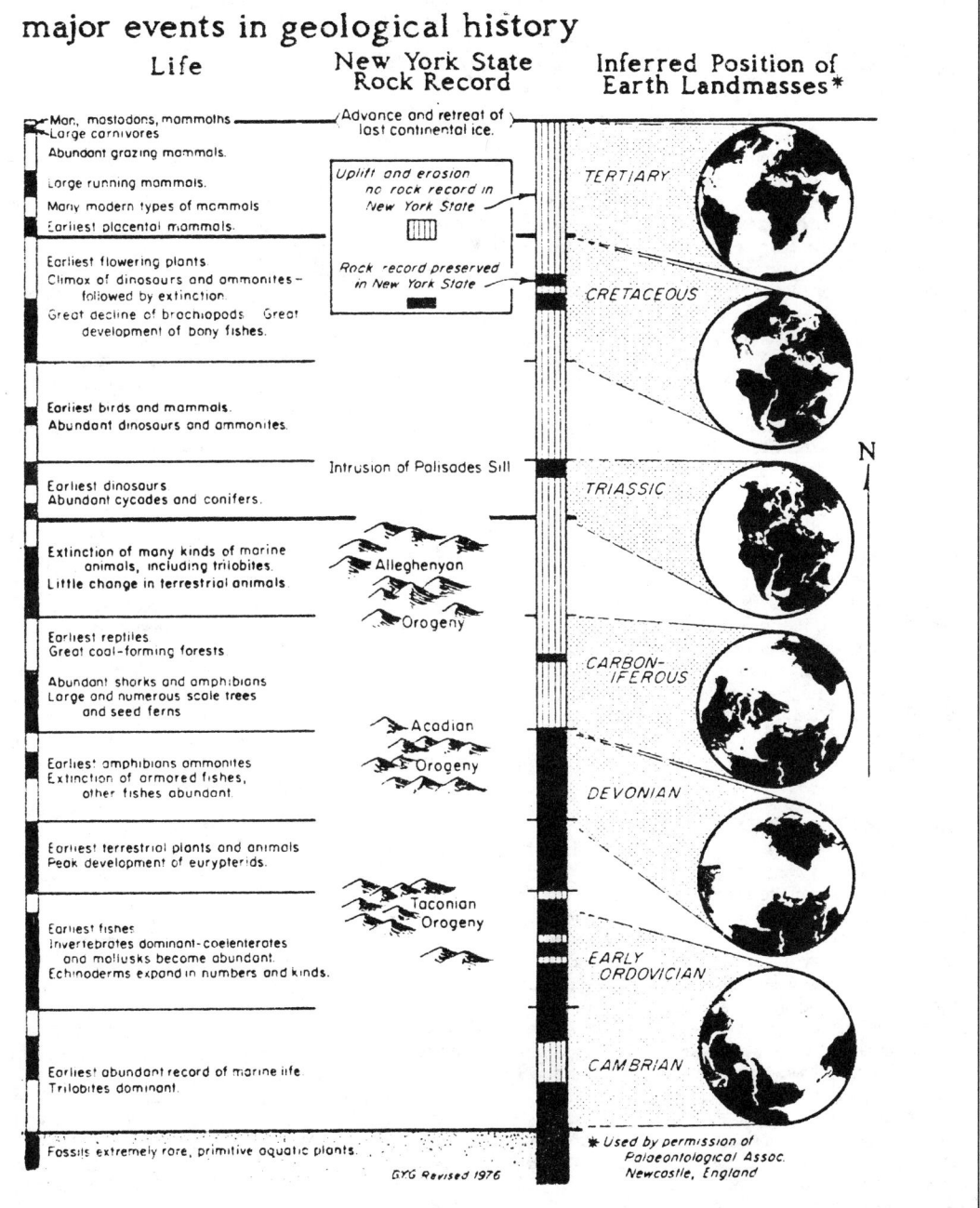

major events in geological history

Life   New York State Rock Record   Inferred Position of Earth Landmasses*

Man, mastodons, mammoths
Large carnivores
Abundant grazing mammals.

Large running mammals.
Many modern types of mammals
Earliest placental mammals.

Earliest flowering plants.
Climax of dinosaurs and ammonites – followed by extinction.
Great decline of brachiopods. Great development of bony fishes.

Earliest birds and mammals.
Abundant dinosaurs and ammonites.

Earliest dinosaurs
Abundant cycades and conifers.

Extinction of many kinds of marine animals, including trilobites.
Little change in terrestrial animals.

Earliest reptiles.
Great coal-forming forests.

Abundant sharks and amphibians
Large and numerous scale trees and seed ferns

Earliest amphibians ammonites
Extinction of armored fishes, other fishes abundant.

Earliest terrestrial plants and animals
Peak development of eurypterids.

Earliest fishes.
Invertebrates dominant - coelenterates and mollusks become abundant.
Echinoderms expand in numbers and kinds.

Earliest abundant record of marine life.
Trilobites dominant.

Fossils extremely rare, primitive aquatic plants.

Advance and retreat of last continental ice.

Uplift and erosion no rock record in New York State

Rock record preserved in New York State

Intrusion of Palisades Sill

Alleghenyan
Orogeny

Acadian
Orogeny

Taconian
Orogeny

TERTIARY

CRETACEOUS

TRIASSIC

CARBON-
IFEROUS

DEVONIAN

EARLY
ORDOVICIAN

CAMBRIAN

N

* Used by permission of Palaeontological Assoc. Newcastle, England

GYG Revised 1976

down. The greatest angle at which a material can pile up is called its angle of repose. The angle of repose for dry earth materials is about 35°. Water in the soil reduces the angle of repose.

If soil is piled up at its angle of repose, heavy rainfall may make the angle of repose smaller. The soil is then piled up beyond its angle of repose, and it becomes unstable. The result may be a massive flow of loose material downhill. This is a landslide. Large landslides can be disastrous, wiping out towns and killing thousands of people.

Soil may move downhill imperceptibly, over a period of years. Rain loosens the particles and they settle at a slightly lower level. This is called hillside creep.

Gravitational lens A galaxy that produces a lens-like action when its strong gravitational field bends light rays. The effect was first noted when two very distant galaxies, close to each other, seemed to be identical. It turned out that they were two images of the same galaxy. The light from the galaxy had passed another galaxy, which acted as a gravitational lens.

Gravitational potential energy The energy due to the separation in space of objects attracted to each other by the force of gravity. Since any two objects attract each other through gravitational force, separating them stores energy. In outer space, two meteoroids can attract each other. As they rush toward each other, their gravitational potential energy changes to kinetic energy. When they collide, it becomes heat. This process, repeated many times, aggregated enough material to form the earth, with its hot interior. *See also* **Stellar evolution**.

In geologic systems, gravitational potential energy plays a major role. Anytime anything is lifted off the earth, its potential energy increases. Water in a mountain has more potential energy than the same water in the sea. As the water flows downhill, its potential energy is converted into kinetic energy, which does the work of erosion. In a hydroelectric plant, water is dammed to store its potential energy. This is converted into electric energy by allowing the water to turn the turbines that run the generators. *See also* **Gravitational energy**, Physics section, page 20-20.

Great Barrier Reef An enormous coral reef off the east coast of Australia.

Great Rift Valley A long, deep valley, running from the Red Sea southward into east Africa, formed by a fault.

Greenhouse effect The warming of the earth due to the difference in wavelength between incoming and outgoing radiation. Since the earth is not as hot as the sun, the electromagnetic wave energy it radiates is at longer wavelengths, in the infrared. The infrared rays are blocked by carbon dioxide and other gases in the air, so their energy is not lost into outer space. The amount of lost energy depends critically on the amount of greenhouse gases in the air. As the amount rises, more of the infrared rays are trapped, so the surface temperature of the earth increases. Since industry produces large amounts of carbon dioxide by burning fuel, there is a secular trend toward higher temperatures.

Greenwich time The time at the arbitrary zero of longitude, at the observatory in Greenwich, England. Greenwich time is a convenient point of reference for astronomical work.

Ground moraine *See* **Glacial deposits**.

Groundwater The water in the zone of saturation, where the spaces between particles are filled with water. *See* **Subsurface water**.

Gulf Stream An ocean current, formed from water flowing westward from north Africa. It is warmed in the Caribbean and flows out of the Gulf of Mexico across the Atlantic to northern Europe.

Gypsum A rock composed entirely of calcium sulfate ($CaSO_4$). It is an evaporite, precipitated from solution when water carrying the mineral in solution evaporates. Gypsum is processed into plaster of Paris.

H

Hail *See* **Precipitation**.

Half-life *See* Physics section, page 20-22. The reliability of half-lives makes it possible to use them to date the geologic past. *See* **Radioactive dating**.

Halite A mineral, sodium chloride (NaCl), which is common table salt. It is an evaporite formed by precipitation when a salt-laden body of water evaporates.

Hanging valley A waterfall in which a river flows into a glacial trough. *See* **Alpine glaciation**.

Hardness A property useful in the identification of minerals. The criterion for hardness is that a harder mineral can leave a scratch on a softer mineral. *See* **Moh scale**.

Heat *See* Physics section, page 20-22.

Heliocentric model The model of the universe in which the sun is at the center and the planets, including the earth, revolve around the sun. Originally, the stars were also considered heliocentric, but we now know that they are not. *See* **Solar system**.

Helium The second element of the periodic table of elements; its nucleus has two protons and two neutrons. It is the second most abundant element in the universe, after hydrogen. Much of it was produced in the big bang, but radioactive decay keeps increasing the quantity (*see* **Radioactivity**, Physics section, page 20-41). The first nuclear fusion reaction in stars produces helium from hydrogen, in the second reaction, helium forms carbon. *See* **Nuclear fusion**; **Stellar evolution**.

Hematite A mineral, an oxide of iron (Fe_2O_3). It is an important ore.

High-pressure system, or anticyclone A region of the atmosphere in which the barometric pressure is higher than in surrounding regions. In a "high," air descends and the surface winds blow outward from the center. Because of the Coriolis effect, they spiral clockwise in the Northern Hemisphere and counterclockwise in the Southern Hemisphere. Since air becomes drier as it descends, highs are regions of fair weather. As a high approaches, the barometer rises, foretelling fair weather.

Hillside creep *See* **Gravitational erosion**.

Horn A peak between cirques; *see* **Alpine glaciation**.

Horoscope *See* **Astrology**.

Horst *See* **Fault-block mountain**.

Hot spot An active volcanic center. It is anchored in the asthenosphere, and forms a series of volcanoes as the crustal plate moves over it.

H-R diagram (Hertzsprung-Russell diagram) A chart (*see* **Exhibit 5.3**) on which the properties of stars are plotted. The ordinate is the luminosity, and the abscissa is the spectral class. Spectral class depends on temperature, which is noted on another abscissa scale at the top.

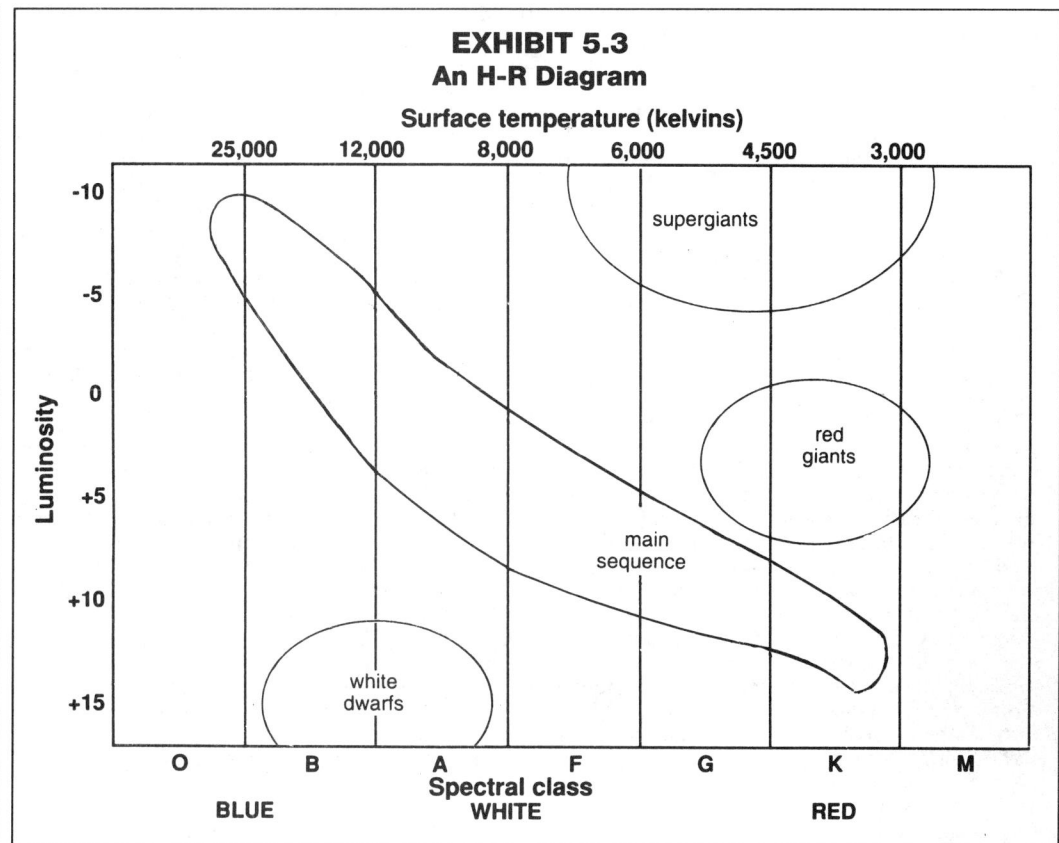

EXHIBIT 5.3
An H-R Diagram

Surface temperature (kelvins)

H-R diagram showing luminosity (vertical axis, from -10 to +15) versus spectral class (horizontal axis O B A F G K M) and surface temperature (25,000 to 3,000 kelvins), with regions labeled supergiants, red giants, main sequence, and white dwarfs. Spectral classes marked BLUE, WHITE, RED.

When a star first forms by the aggregation of smaller particles, the heat generated raises the temperature. At about 100 million degrees, hydrogen fusion begins and the star enters the main sequence. Its position on the main sequence depends entirely on its mass. Type O stars are the most massive, more than 100 times the mass of the sun. They burn extremely hot and blue, and use up their hydrogen quickly, in a few million years. The smallest stars, some not much bigger than Jupiter, are type M. They are much cooler, are red in color, and use their hydrogen much more slowly. They stay on the main sequence for billions of years.

When a star has used up its hydrogen, other reactions begin, and the star leaves the main sequence. What happens next depends on the mass of the star. *See* **Stellar evolution**.

Hubble constant   *See* **Expanding universe**.

Hubble law   *See* **Expanding universe**.

Humboldt Current, or Peru Current   A cold ocean current flowing northward off the west coast of South America. *See* **El niño**.

Humidity   The amount of water vapor in the air. It is highly variable, up to about 60 g/m³. *See also* **Relative humidity**.

Humus   Organic matter in the soil produced from the decay of plants and animals. Since it is this decay that provides essential nutrients for plant growth, abundant humus produces fertile soil. Humus, because of its spongy texture, is also valuable for its capacity to hold water.

Hurricane, or typhoon   A violent tropical cyclonic storm. Hurricanes form in a low-pressure system over warm, tropical water. Rising moist air condenses, releasing large amounts of latent heat of vaporization. This heat promotes evaporation at the surface, and the amount of warm moist air increases. Surface barometric pressure at the center of the storm drops rapidly, and inflowing winds pick up speed. A storm is called a hurricane if the wind speed exceeds 120km/hour. When the storm reaches the shore, the winds can do enormous amounts of damage. *See* **Latent heat**, Physics section, page 20-27.

Hydrogen   The first element in the periodic table of elements; its nucleus is a proton. Hydrogen makes up about 75% of the universe. It is the most common constituent of interstellar matter. It is the fuel for the first nuclear fusion reaction when a star forms; *see* **Nuclear fusion; Stellar evolution**.

Hydrosphere   The layer of water, including oceans, lakes, and rivers, that lies over the earth's crust.

Hygrometer   An instrument for measuring relative humidity. It consists of a hair that controls the position of a needle against a scale. When the humidity is high, the hair lengthens slightly.

I **Ice age**   A geologic period in which large parts of the earth's surface were covered by continental glaciers. Evidence of such past glaciation can be found all over the world, including Canada and the northern United States. The evidence is of two kinds: deposition and erosion. Depositional features include erratic boulders, which can be moved only by a glacier, as well as kames, eskers, drumlins, and various kinds of moraines. Long Island (New York), for example, is largely formed of a terminal moraine.

When a contintental glacier, a kilometer or more thick, moves across a river valley, it erodes the valley into a characteristic form. It planes down the surface of the far side of the valley, giving it a more gentle slope than it would otherwise have. Bedrock on this side may have deep striations, grooves cut by rocks carried along at the bottom of the glacier. The bedrock may also have a polished appearance, as though it were sandpapered. The near side of the valley is extremely steep. It is undercut by the glacier, and has accumulations of talus at its base.

There have been many periods of continental glaciation. The most recent is the Pleistocene, which ended about 10,000 years ago. In this period, glaciers over a kilometer thick covered much of Canada and the United States during four separate episodes. Sculpturing by these glaciers formed the terrain that produced most of the lakes and rivers in the region.

Ice cap   A large mass of ice in the colder, polar regions; a continental glacier. There are three on earth: Antarctica, Greenland, and (on water) North Polar. Mars also has ice caps.

Igneous rocks   Rocks formed by the cooling of molten rock. Magma solidifying inside the crust forms intrusive rocks, and lava solidifying on the surface forms extrusive rock.

Igneous rocks are classified according to two main criteria: composition and grain size. Mafic rocks are dark in color and high in density and are composed mainly of iron and magnesium minerals. Sialic rocks are light in color and low in density and contain much aluminum and silicon. *See* table below.

The grain size of igneous rocks is an indication of the rate of cooling. Rocks that cool quickly, as in lava flows, have a very fine grain size. Intrusive rocks cooling deep in the crust are coarsely grained. Four kinds of igneous rock represent the extreme characteristics:

Granite: sialic, coarse grained
Rhyolite: sialic, fine grained
Gabbro: mafic, coarse grained
Basalt: mafic, fine grained

Scheme for Igneous Rock Identification

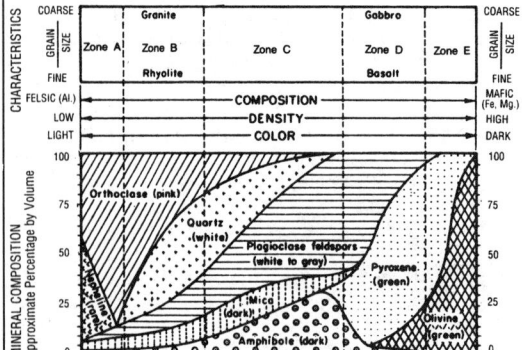

Index fossil   A fossil that can be used to determine the comparative date of a sedimentary layer. To be useful for dating, a fossil needs two properties: the organism must have lived for a comparatively short period of time, and it must be widespread over a large region of the earth. If two identical index fossils are found in different regions, the layers in which they occur must be of the same age.

Inertia   *See* Physics section, page 20-24.

Infiltration   The process by which water penetrates spaces in the soil. *See* **Permeability**; **Porosity**.

Infrared astronomy   The study of celestial objects by examination of the infrared rays they emit. Some cool objects produce no visible light at all and are detected only in the infrared range of wavelengths. They can be photographed on films sensitive to infrared. The longer infrared rays, up to about 1 mm, cannot pass through the earth's atmosphere. Infrared studies of the sky in this wavelength range are done by a telescope in orbit at an altitude of 900 km.

Infrared rays   Electromagnetic waves with wavelengths in the range 0.7 µm (micrometers) to 1 mm. All infrared rays are too long to be visible. The energy of the sun comes to the earth in the form of electromagnetic waves, and about half is infrared. *See* **Insolation**; **Radiation**.

Insolation   The transfer of electromagnetic energy from the sun to the earth. The total solar energy arriving at the earth is about 3.7×10^{21} cal/day. About half of the earth's insolation is in the infrared, the rest is visible and ultraviolet.

The intensity of insolation depends primarily on the angle at which the sun's rays strike the earth. Insolation is most intense when the rays are perpendicular to the surface. If the rays make a small angle, they spread out over a larger area, so the intensity is less. The angle of insolation depends on three parameters:

Latitude: At higher latitudes, the sun's rays strike at smaller angles. The rays are never vertical north of 23½° north latitude, or south of 23½° south. At the poles, the angle is zero at the equinoxes.

Season: Summer is the season when the sun is highest in the sky and its rays are most nearly vertical. In winter, in either hemisphere, the rays strike at a low angle.

Time of day: The sun is low at sunrise and highest at midday.

The intensity of insolation is also affected by the clarity of the atmosphere. X-rays and ultraviolet rays are absorbed high in the atmosphere, and infrared is taken up by carbon dioxide and other gases with large molecules. *See* **Greenhouse effect**.

Much of the incident radiation does not warm the earth because it is reflected. Clouds, ice, and water are good reflectors. *See* table below.

Insolation Budget

Fate of incident radiation	Percent
Reflected by clouds	25
Absorbed by atmosphere	19
Reflected at surface	6
Absorbed at surface	50
	100

Interferometry A technique of improving the resolution of radio telescopes by using the interaction of two or more telescopes. Resolution depends on the size of the receiving antenna. Two smaller antennas 1 km apart have the same resolution as a single antenna 1 km wide. The output of the two antennas is fed into a computer, which makes use of the phase difference of the two signals to produce a high-resolution image. (*See* **Resolution**.)

The largest interferometric system now in use is the very large array in New Mexico. It consists of 27 movable radio telescopes, in an array 36 km across. It can produce the same resolution of a 20 cm wave as a visible-light telescope made of a mirror 9 cm wide. Plans are in operation for a set of radio telescopes with a baseline extending across half the earth.

Intermittent stream A stream that flows only after the infrequent rains of an arid region.

International date line A line, mostly along the 180° meridian, marking the change of day as it is passed. Suppose you are in Fiji, at longitude 178° east on a Wednesday. You start to travel westward at the speed of light. Every time you go 15°, you have to set your clock back an hour. By the time you reach 179° west, you have set it back 24 hours, and it is Tuesday. The correction is made when you pass the 180° meridian, the international date line. You have moved your clock back 24 hours, but on passing the international date line, you move your calendar ahead 1 day to compensate. When you get back to Fiji, it is Wednesday.

Interplanetary dust The collection of micrometeoroids, a few micrometers in diameter, orbiting the sun.

Interstellar medium The material in the vast, empty spaces of the universe. It consists of an extremely tenuous gas, far rarer (emptier) than the best vacuum on earth. It is a gas with only about one atom per cubic centimeter. There are also some micrometer-sized grains, or dust particles, no more than 50 per cubic kilometer.

In some regions, the interstellar material is more concentrated. These regions are called nebulas. For details, *see* **Nebula**.

Intrusion A mass of igneous rock formed by magma flowing upward and solidifying within the earth's crust. A dike is an intrusion that cuts across pre-existing layers; a sill lies between layers. A very large intrusion is called a batholith.

Intrusive rock *See* **Igneous rocks**.

Ion *See* Physics section, page 20-25.

Ionization The removal or addition of one or more electrons to an atom or a molecule to give it an electric charge. In the earth's atmosphere, the ultraviolet rays of the sun ionize the air at a high altitude. *See* **Ionosphere**.

Ionosphere A layer of the atmosphere, in the altitude range from 40 to 60 km, in which the absorption of solar radiation produces extensive ionization of atmospheric gases. In absorbing much of the sun's ultraviolet radiation, the ionosphere protects life on earth.

The ionosphere plays a part in the transmission of radio waves on earth. Short waves can reflect from the ionosphere and so can be sent to remote regions even though they tend to travel in straight lines.

Island arc A linear group of oceanic, volcanic islands, formed on the landward side of an oceanic trench.

Isobar A line on a weather map that joins points of equal barometric pressure. Isobars form a series of closed curves surrounding each low and each high.

Isostasy The theory that accounts for the uplift of mountains. It is based on the granitic nature of the main mass of continental rock. The continental rock rests on a base of basaltic rock that is a continuous crust over the whole earth, including the ocean floor. Under the basalt layer is the semiliquid mantle rock. The Moho is the boundary between the basalt layer of the crust and the mantle.

The theory of isostasy states that each block of the crust floats on the mantle. The continents float higher because they are mainly granite, which has a lower density than basalt. As sediment piles up in a geosyncline, it sinks into the mantle. The displaced mantle rock flows beneath the continents. The continents are losing mass by erosion, so they rise as the mantle flows in. This accounts for the uplift processes that build mountains. *See* **Uplift**.

Isotherm A line drawn on a weather map through points of equal temperature.

Isotope *See* Physics section, page 20-25.

J **Japan Current** A warm oceanic current flowing across the northern Pacific from the Sea of Japan to the Pacific Northwest of the United States and Canada.

Jet stream A fast-moving stream of air, 6–12 km high in the atmosphere. Wind speeds can be as high as 300 km/hour. Jet streams play a significant role in the control of local weather.

Joint A crack in bedrock, usually resulting from reduction in pressure as deep-lying rocks rise toward the surface.

Jupiter The fifth planet, 780 million km from the sun. It is the largest planet, a giant, with a radius of 70,000 km. It rotates very rapidly for its size, with a period of 10 hours, it revolves around the sun once every 11 years. It has been photographed by space probes, which showed considerable detail of the dark and light bands that cross the planet. They are features of a highly active atmosphere. The outstanding feature is the great red spot, a persistent vortex larger than the earth. Jupiter, like the sun, is 98% hydrogen and helium.

Voyager I discovered that Jupiter has a thin, faint ring, made of very tiny particles. It also has sixteen known satellites. Four of them, the Galilean satellites, are quite large and easily seen with a small telescope. The satellite Io is one of the oddest bodies in the solar system. It has many highly active volcanoes and is probably completely liquid inside.

In 1992 the planetary probe Ulysses made detailed studies of the gas belt around Jupiter. It consists mainly of oxygen and sulfur, apparently from volcanoes on the satellite Io. It also studied Jupiter's strong gravitational field.

Next to the sun and the moon, Jupiter is the brightest object in the sky, with apparent magnitude –2.5. It is often seen high in the sky, and some of its surface features, such as the great red spot and many of its satellites, can be seen with a moderate-sized telescope.

Kame　*See* **Glacial deposits**.

Karst topography　The typical landscape of a limestone region in a humid climate. With decaying vegetation producing acid, the groundwater can dissolve the limestone. The drainage system moves completely underground. The underground rivers carve out large caverns with stalagmites and stalactites. When a cavern roof collapses, a sinkhole forms. Repeated collapse may leave a natural bridge standing.

Kelvin temperature　*See* **Kelvin scale**, Physics section, page 20-26.

Kepler's laws　The laws of the motion of the planets, developed by Johannes Kepler in the seventeenth century as a generalization of many years of observation. He summarized his results in the form of three laws:

1. The planets revolve in elliptic orbits with the sun at one focus.
2. A line drawn from the planet to the sun sweeps out equal areas in equal time intervals. Stated algebraically, the law says that a planet's velocity is inversely proportional to its distance from the sun.
3. For every planet, the square of its orbital period is proportional to the cube of its average distance from the sun. In other words, the fraction T^2/R^3 is the same for all planets of the solar system. The value of this constant can be found by using the values for the earth: $T = 365.24$ days; $R = 149,700,000$ km.

When Newton developed his theory of mechanics, he incorporated Kepler's laws into a more general physics.

Kettle　A depression in an outwash plain formed when a block of ice is left behind by a receding glacier. When the ice melts, it leaves a kettle. This may be filled with water to form a kettle lake.

Kinetic energy　The energy that anything has because of its movement. It is equal to $\frac{1}{2}mv^2$, where m is mass and v is velocity. *See also* Physics section, page 20-26.

When a rock or a mass of water moves downhill, it loses potential energy. As it speeds up, it gains kinetic energy. The kinetic energy of moving water is lost as the water does the work of erosion: carrying sediments, eroding stream banks, and weathering the rocks in the river. A landslide is a sudden conversion of potential into kinetic energy, which can do a great deal of damage.

In windstorms, it is the kinetic energy of the air that does damage. The energy comes from the potential energy stored in pressure differences in the atmosphere. Ultimately, the energy comes to the earth by insolation.

The surface of the moon is pitted with craters. The energy for the production of these craters comes from the kinetic energy of meteorites striking the surface. The earth's surface also has craters of this sort, such as the meteor crater in Arizona. In the original formation of the earth, many such particles came together, attracted by their mutual gravitation. As they approached each other, their potential energy of gravitation was converted into kinetic energy. On impact, the kinetic energy became thermal energy. Enough thermal energy was produced to melt the entire mass.

Lagoon　A body of quiet salt water isolated from the open sea by islands. The islands may be a fringing reef, an atoll, or the offshore islands of an emergent coastline.

Lake effect　The influence of a large lake on local climatic conditions. The high specific heat of the water tends to mitigate large temperature ranges, so winters are warmer and summers cooler. Because of the ample supply of atmospheric moisture, regions near lakes tend to have more rain and snow than others.

Landscape　The surface features of a region. A mountain landscape is at high elevation and is characterized by jagged peaks and steep valleys. A plain is a flat stretch of country at low elevation. A region of low hills with all their crests at about the same elevation is a plateau. Limestone may produce a unique kind of landscape; *see* **Karst topography**.

Landscapes are changed by erosion; *see* **Alpine glaciation**; **Stream aging**.

Landslide　*See* **Gravitational erosion**.

Large Cloud of Magellan　An irregular galaxy, the nearest galaxy to ours.

Latent heat　The heat released or absorbed in a change of phase. *See also* Physics section, page 20-27.

The energy released by evaporation of water vapor in the atmosphere may be converted into the kinetic energy of strong winds. *See* **Hurricane**.

Lateral moraine　*See* **Glacial deposits**.

Latitude　Distance north or south of the equator, measured in degrees. The latitude at the equator is 0. Going north and traversing one quarter of the earth's surface, one reaches the North Pole, so the latitude there is 90° north. Similarly, the latitude at the South Pole is 90° south.

Lava　Magma that reaches the earth's surface emerging through volcanoes. It hardens to form extrusive igneous rock.

Leaching　The process by which water, running off or percolating through the soil, dissolves minerals and removes them from the soil. In humid climates, most of the calcium and magnesium minerals are leached out of the soil.

Light　The visible part of the electromagnetic spectrum, consisting of waves with lengths in the range $450 - 720 \times 10^{-9}$ m. This is a very small part of the whole spectrum. The color of light is a function of the way the human eye reacts to it. It is determined chiefly by the wavelength of the light. The visible spectrum looks violet at the short-wave end and red at the long-wave end. White light, such as that from the sun, is a mixture of all visible frequencies. *See also* **Electromagnetic spectrum**, Physics section, page 20-14.

Lightning　A high-power electric spark that discharges the charge separation between clouds and ground or between two clouds.

Light-year　The distance that light, traveling at 3.0×10^8 m/s, travels in a year. It is the common unit of distance used in astronomy, equal to about 9.5×10^{15} m.

Lignite　*See* **Coal**.

Limestone　A rock composed of the single mineral calcite, calcium carbonate ($CaCO_3$). Calcite precipitates when streams carry it in solution into saltwater.

Deposits of calcite are also formed by certain microscopic organisms with calcareous shells. Compaction and cementing of these deposits forms limestone.

Limestone is highly soluble in acidified water. In humid regions, limestone forms a unique kind of landscape (*see* **Karst topography**). In dry regions, on the contrary, it is highly resistant to erosion and often forms the caprock at the top of a mesa.

Lithosphere   *See* **Earth**.

Local group   *See* **Cluster of galaxies**.

Lodestone   *See* **Magnetite**.

Longitude   Angular distance east or west of the prime meridian. Longitude is marked on maps in terms of meridians, which are north-south lines from pole to pole. The prime meridian, arbitrarily designated as 0 of longitude, is the meridian that passes through Greenwich, England. Halfway around the world, east or west, it reaches the 180° meridian in the Pacific Ocean (*see* **International date line**). Other longitudes are given in degrees east or west of 0.

Longitudinal wave, or compressional wave   *See* Physics section, page 20-29.

Sound waves and the P waves produced by earthquakes are longitudinal.

Longshore current   *See* **Wave deposits**.

Low-pressure system, or cyclone   A region of the atmosphere in which the barometric pressure is lower than in the surrounding regions. "Lows" form at fronts, where the air is rising. Surface winds rush into the center of a low. Because of the Coriolis effect, they spiral in, counterclockwise in the Northern Hemisphere and clockwise in the Southern Hemisphere. The rising air results in the formation of clouds and stormy weather. As a low approaches, a falling barometer foretells stormy weather.

Luminosity   The brightness of a star. *See* **Magnitude**.

Lunar eclipse   An eclipse in which the earth comes to a position between the moon and the sun, thus preventing the sun's light from reaching the moon. Lunar eclipses occur only during the full moon, when the bright side of the moon faces the earth. A lunar eclipse is partial when the earth's shadow covers only part of the moon. Total eclipses of the moon occur, on the average, about once a year.

Lunar orbiter   An artificial satellite of the moon, a station on the way to the moon's surface. To land people on the moon, they are first put into orbit around the moon. They descend from the orbiter to the moon, and return to the orbiter for the trip home.

Luster   A characteristic property of minerals representing the way light reflects from their surface. Some examples are the metallic luster of pyrite, the glassy luster of quartz, the pearly luster of some micas, the dull luster of talc, and the silky luster of asbestos.

M

Mafic rock   Dark, high-density rock composed chiefly of iron and magnesium minerals. It contains little or no quartz and feldspar. Mafic rock underlies all the oceans and lies under the granitic rocks of the continents. It forms the upper layer of the earth's mantle. Basalt is mafic and the word *basalt* is frequently used as a general term for all mafic rocks.

Magellanic Clouds   Two irregular galaxies near earth.

Magma   The molten rock under the earth's crust. Magma exists in local concentrations called magma chambers, some 20 km or more below the surface, where temperatures are 600°C and higher. There are mafic and sialic magmas, and many of them contain dissolved gases. *See* **Intrusion**; **Volcano**.

Magnetic declination   The difference between a compass reading and true geographic north.

Magnetic reversal   The process by which the earth's magnetic field changes direction. The reversal is abrupt (on a geologic time frame) and occurs at intervals varying from less than 100,000 to over 1 million years. The cause is not known. *See* **Seafloor spreading**.

Magnetism of rocks   A property of igneous rocks that can be used to determine the past history of the earth's magnetic field. The earth's field magnetizes the rocks as they solidify, and the direction of the magnetization indicates the direction of the earth's field at the time when the rocks formed. *See* **Seafloor spreading**.

Magnetite, or lodestone   The iron oxide ore (Fe_3O_4) that can become a strong, permanent magnet.

Magnitude   A scale for expressing the brightness of stars. Apparent magnitude is the apparent brightness of the stars. A very bright star is a star of first magnitude, and dimmer stars are of second, third, and so on. The scale adopts the star Aldebaran as the standard for first magnitude. For each successively higher magnitude number, the amount of light received is smaller by a factor of 2.5. The very brightest stars have negative magnitude; the brightest is Sirius, magnitude −1.5. The apparent magnitude of a star depends mainly on two factors: the rate at which it emits light (its luminosity) and its distance from earth.

The absolute magnitude expresses the luminosity of a star. It is defined as the apparent magnitude a star would have if it were at a distance of 10 parsecs, which is 32.6 light-years. If both the absolute magnitude and the apparent magnitude of a star are known, its distance can be calculated. Luminosity, and thus the absolute magnitude of a star, can often be found by a study of its spectrum.

Main sequence   *See* **H-R diagram**.

Mantle   The part of the earth, about 2900 km thick, that lies between crust and the core. The interface between crust and mantle is called the Moho. The mantle is in three layers. The upper layer is solid rock, about 100 km thick. It contains hot spots, where magma chambers form. Below this solid layer is the asthenosphere a layer of semiliquid material about 250 km thick. Convection currents in the asthenosphere are probably the force that moves tectonic plates. Between the asthenosphere and the core, the mantle is dense and solid.

Marble   A metamorphic rock consisting chiefly of calcite. It forms from limestone exposed to great pressure.

Mariana trench   The deepest part of the ocean, to 35,800 feet. It is in the Pacific near the Philippines.

Maritime climate   Climate influenced by proximity to the sea. Such climates generally lack extremes of temperature, are humid, and may be locally influenced by warm or cold ocean currents.

Mars   The fourth planet, 250 million km from the sun. It is not much over half the size of the earth, with a radius of 3600 km. It rotates with a period of 24½ hours; it revolves around the sun once every 687 days. Its atmosphere, mostly carbon dioxide, is extremely thin, so the surface is easily seen.

The surface of Mars has been photographed at close range by several space probes, some of which landed on the surface. It has a permanent polar ice cap, made of water ice, in the north. Furthermore, a large ice cap of frozen carbon dioxide appears at either pole in the winter. There are many active volcanoes, and a large part of the planet is covered with lava flows. The surface, in places, is carved by canyons and dry river beds, indicating that there was once a great deal of running water. There is no longer, and water is now confined to the ice cap.

The Mars observer space probe will arrive there in 1993, and will spend a year in orbit. It will make detailed maps of the surface, study the soil, weather, and geology, and test to see whether there is a magnetic field, which has not so far been found.

Mars has two small, irregularly shaped satellites, the larger only 28 km in its largest diameter. They move rapidly because they are very close to the surface. The larger satellite completes an orbit every 8 hours, so the "month" is less than the "day."

In the sky, Mars is often nearly as bright as Jupiter and can be seen as often. It can be identified by its reddish color.

Mosaic of the Schiaparelli hemisphere of Mars. This mosaic is composed of about 100 Viking Orbiter images acquired in 1980.

Mass wasting   The process by which rock, loosened by weathering, falls or slides downhill.

Meander   A wide curve in the path of a river. *See* **Stream aging**.

Mercury   (1) The first planet, 43 million km from the sun. It is the smallest planet, with a radius of only 2400 km. It takes 59 days to rotate on its axis and 88 days to complete an orbit. Since it is so close to the sun, its daytime temperature is very high, up to about 700 K, but it drops to 100 K at night. There is no significant atmosphere.

Space probe pictures of Mercury show the surface to be pitted and cratered, like the surface of the moon. There are also lava flows.

The sun is always directly over the equator on Mercury, and the poles are very cold. Radar studies in 1991 suggest that there are polar ice caps.

Because it is so close to the sun, Mercury is not easy to find. It can be seen as a very bright star for about a week every Mercury year, but only just after sunset or before sunrise.

(2) A metallic element, liquid at room temperature. Because of its great density (13.6 g/cm³) it is used in making barometers. It is also used in high-quality thermometers because of its uniform expansion when heated. Its oxide is a red mineral called cinnabar.

Mercury barometer   An instrument for measuring atmospheric pressure. It consists of a vertical glass tube about 80 cm long, with the upper end sealed. It is filled with mercury and the lower end is then immersed in an open dish of mercury. Because there is no air in the tube, the pressure of the atmosphere, exerted through the open dish, holds up the mercury in the tube. Pressure is measured by the height of the mercury in the tube above the open surface. A standard atmosphere is defined as the pressure when the mercury stands at 760 mm.

Meridian   See **Longitude**.

Mesa   A flat-topped hill. It is formed by erosion of an uplifted plain when there is a caprock layer that is highly resistant. When the hill is small, it is called a butte.

Metamorphic rocks   Rock that has been changed from sedimentary or igneous by the action of heat or pressure. When rocks metamorphose, they change their crystalline structure without melting or undergoing chemical change.

Marble is recrystallized limestone. It is often fairly pure calcite.

Slate is metamorphosed shale. Pressure causes mineral crystals to form in thin layers perpendicular to the direction of the pressure. This gives slate a definite layered structure.

Schist is a more highly metamorphosed form, usually from slate. Crystals of mica, for example, can grow quite large in thin layers, so that the whole rock is banded.

Quartzite is a hard, compact rock consisting almost entirely of quartz. It forms from sandstone.

Gneiss is a rock with wide bands, usually of quartz, formed by the metamorphosis of granite, conglomerate, or other kinds of rocks.

Meteor   A bright streak of light appearing suddenly in the sky as a result of a meteoroid burning up on entering the earth's atmosphere. *See also* **Meteorite**; **Meteoroid**. There are about 25 million meteors bright enough to be seen on the average dark, moonless night, but they are visible only to a nearby observer. The number may be much greater on nights of meteor showers. Some showers occur on about the same date every year. The Perseid shower, on August 11, is the result of a mass of meteoroids that were strewn into space by the disintegration of a comet.

Meteorite　A meteoroid that was not completely destroyed on entering the atmosphere and that falls to earth. There are two main varieties: iron and stony. Iron meteorites are nearly pure iron, with other metals alloyed with it. Stony meteorites are chiefly silicates. They are of all sizes. The largest ever found weighed about 60 tons. There is evidence that extremely large meteorites sometimes strike the earth. The meteor crater in Arizona is 1300 m across and 180 m deep. It was formed by a large iron meteor that struck the earth about 25,000 years ago and disintegrated, scattering fragments of iron up to 7 km from the crater.

Meteoroid　Particles of stone or metal traveling in random orbits around the sun. Most of them have masses of under a gram, but some are extremely large. They are probably of two kinds: remains of the original structure of the solar system and debris from the disintegration of comets. A meteoroid that enters the atmosphere burns up, producing a streak of light called a meteor. A meteoroid that survives to reach the ground is called a meteorite.

Midocean ridges　Large ranges of extrusive rock formed at the center of oceans. *See* **Seafloor spreading**.

Milky Way　A diffuse, glowing band of light in the sky, visible on very dark nights. With a good telescope, it can be resolved into millions of separate stars. *See* **Milky Way galaxy**.

Milky Way galaxy　The galaxy to which the sun belongs. It is a flattened, rotating disk with spiral arms, about 100,000 light-years in diameter and made up of some 10^{11} stars. It appears as a band in the sky because in that direction, we are looking along the plane of the galaxy. The sun is a star in one of the spiral arms. Moving at about 200 km, the sun completes an orbit around the center of the galaxy in about 250 million years.

In addition to the stars in the main body of the galaxy, there are hundreds of star clusters in the space around it. The galaxy also contains masses of interstellar dust. The center of the galaxy is obscured by dust.

Millibar　A unit of pressure, equal to 100 N/m^2 (newtons per square meter). A standard atmosphere is 1013.2 mb.

Mineral　A naturally occurring substance with a definite chemical composition and physical structure. Rocks are composed of minerals. Minerals are identified by a set of physical characteristics: color, cleavage, fracture, luster, hardness, streak, density, crystalline structure, and chemical composition. A few minerals make up the largest part of the earth's crust. Most of them are compounds of silicon, oxygen, and metals, *see* **Silicate minerals**. There are a few nonsilicate rock-forming minerals.

Carbonates form enormous masses of rock in the form of limestone, marble, coquina, chalk, and others. Calcite is calcium carbonate, $CaCO_3$. When pure, it forms soft, transparent crystals with a glassy luster that cleave in three planes. Dolomite, $MgCa(CO_3)_2$, is the other common carbonate. Carbonates are not found in igneous rocks, since they are chemically destroyed by high temperatures.

Sulfates of calcium are common as evaporites. *See* **Gypsum**.

Two halides, also formed by evaporation, are widespread. Halite is NaCl, ordinary table salt. Fluorite is CaF_2, calcium fluoride. It forms cubic crystals, usually purple in color.

Moh scale　A group of 10 minerals used as a standard of hardness. In order of increasing hardness, they are:

1. talc	6. orthoclase
2. gypsum	7. quartz
3. calcite	8. topaz
4. fluorite	9. corundum
5. apatite	10. diamond

Moho　The Mohorovicic discontinuity, the boundary between the crust and the mantle of the earth. It was discovered by study of the P and S waves produced by shallow earthquakes. One set goes directly through the crust, and the other is refracted when it passes across the Moho into the denser rocks of the mantle.

Monsoon　A period of very wet and stormy weather in Southeast Asia.

Moon　The earth's satellite. It has a diameter of 3476 km, about 0.3 that of the earth, and orbits the earth at an altitude of 380,000 km. A complete orbit takes about 29½ days. Since the moon rotates on its own axis in the same time, one side of the moon always faces the earth.

The mean density of the moon is 3.3 g/cm^3 about the same as the earth's crust. The rocks are chemically similar to basalt. Large, flat areas, called maria (Latin *mares*, *maria*, sea) are covered with lava, although there are no volcanoes. The source of the heat that melted the rocks is in doubt. Many areas of the surface are pitted with craters, produced by the impact of meteors.

Moraine　*See* **Glacial deposits**.

Mountain building　Uplift process that produces mountains. Several kinds of processes each produce a different kind of mountain.

Fault-block mountains, like the Sierra Nevada, are the result of crustal movement in which the crust is broken into pieces and piled up in a jumbled fashion. Strata are usually flat but are found at all angles to the horizontal.

In *folded mountains*, such as the Appalachians, the crust is not broken but is extensively deformed into folds. The rock is metamorphic.

Erosional mountains, as in the Colorado Plateau, are the result of stream erosion of a plateau. The rock may be horizontal layers of sedimentary rock, or it may be an uplifted peneplain. Streams cut into the plateau, leaving mountains between their valleys.

Volcanic mountains, like Hawaii and the mid-Atlantic Ridge, are built by extrusion.

Mountain range　A linear series of mountains, extending on a continental scale. Near the west coast of the Americas, a series of ranges extends the entire length of both continents: Aleutian Islands, Canadian Coast Range, Cascades, Sierra Nevada, Sierra Madre, Andes. The ranges paralleling the shore are intimately associated with offshore trenches. *See* **Subduction zone**.

EARTH AND SPACE SCIENCE

Neap tide   *See* **Tides**.

Nebula   A cloud of intergalactic dust, consisting of up to several thousand micrometer-sized grains per cubic kilometer of space. They may be classified into three kinds.

A *dark nebula* absorbs light and obscures parts of the sky, including the center of our galaxy.

A *reflection nebula* appears bright because it reflects the light from nearby stars.

An *emission nebula* emits light. It does so by fluorescence; it absorbs ultraviolet radiation from a nearby star and re-emits it in the visible range.

For description of a planetary nebula, *see* **Nova**.

A "spiral nebula" is not a nebula. Improvements in telescopes showed that these objects consist of many stars. They are galaxies.

Neptune   The eighth planet, 4.5 billion km from the sun. It is a large planet, with a radius of 25,000 km; its period of rotation is not accurately known but appears to be about 18 hours. It is so far from the sun that it takes 165 years to complete an orbit.

The 1989 visit to the planet by the space probe *Voyager* revealed that it was surrounded by three rings, as well as six small satellites in addition to the two large ones already known. Its atmosphere is composed of hydrogen, helium, and methane, and the winds in it blow at speeds up to 1500 miles an hour. A dark spot in the atmosphere is a cyclonic storm. There is a strong magnetic field, tilted at 50° to the axis of rotation.

Neptune cannot be seen with the naked eye. It was found because it was looked for. In 1845, John Couch Adams in England and Jean Joseph Leverrier in France independently suggested the existence of a planet beyond Uranus and predicted its exact location. It was found there. The prediction was based on the perturbations in the orbit of Uranus. In the 150 years that Uranus had been known, its orbit was off the calculated value by 2′ (minutes) of arc, even after allowing for the gravitational effects of Jupiter and Saturn. This deviation was the datum that predicted the existence and location of Neptune.

Neutrino   *See* Physics section, page 20-34.

Since neutrinos are produced in many kinds of nuclear reactions, they flow in enormous numbers out of stars. There is a tremendous flux of neutrinos in the universe. Most of the neutrinos that strike the earth pass right through and come out the other side. Nevertheless, extremely delicate experiments have detected them. The nature and numbers of neutrinos in the universe are critical questions for cosmology. If neutrinos have rest mass and if there are enough of them, their gravitational effect would be sufficient to slow the expansion of the universe and make it start to contract.

Neutron   *See* Physics section, page 20-34.

Neutron star   A star in which pressure is so enormous that all atomic structure is collapsed, so the star consists of nothing but neutrons closely packed together. Density is as much as a billion times as high as that of a white dwarf, so that a piece of a neutron star the size of a pinhead would have a mass of 100 million tons. A neutron star is the final stage of the evolution of a star with a mass of two or three times that of the sun, too large to become a white dwarf and too small to become a black hole.

A neutron star is seen in the sky as a pulsar, a star that emits radio waves in short, rapid pulses. The pulses occur with periods ranging from a thousandth of a second up to about 3 seconds. These pulses are thought to be a kind of lighthouse effect; the star emits its radio energy steadily in a narrow beam. The pulse effect is due to the beam's arriving at our radio telescopes once in each rotation.

Newton's laws   *See* Physics section, page 20-34.

Nimbus   *See* **Clouds**.

Nitrogen   A gaseous element, making up 78% of the earth's atmosphere.

Noon   The moment of the day at which the sun is directly over the meridian, that is, directly north or south of the observer. Before noon, the time is A.M., ante meridian, or before the meridian. After noon is post meridian, P.M.

North magnetic pole   The S pole of the earth's magnetic field. It is located in northern Canada at 79° N latitude; 71° W longitude. *See also* **Magnetism of earth**, Physics section, page 20-30.

Nova   A star that suddenly emits a burst of light, remaining unusually bright for days or weeks. The best theory so far is that a star that will become a nova is a white dwarf belonging to a binary system—very hot, but small. Its companion star ejects matter, which is attracted to the white dwarf. There, the temperature is so high that the new material, which is not degenerate, undergoes nuclear fusion. The sudden burst of energy blows the material off the surface with a flash of light. The material blown out of a nova is sometimes visible as an expanding shell around the star, called a planetary nebula.

See also **Supernova**.

Nuclear fission   *See* Physics section, page 20-34.

Nuclear fusion   Production of energy by combining small nuclei into larger nuclei. *See* also Physics section, page 20-35.

In star formation, nuclear fusion of the kind called hydrogen burning begins when the temperature reaches about a million kelvins. Several different reactions may occur, involving such intermediates as deuterium, lithium, and beryllium nuclei, but the overall result is always

$$4 \text{ hydrogen-1} \rightarrow \text{helium-4} + \text{neutrino} + \text{gamma photon}$$

When temperatures reach 100 million K, the process called helium burning can take place. It is called the triple-alpha process because three helium nuclei are involved:

$$3 \text{ helium-4} \rightarrow \text{carbon-12} + \text{gamma photon}$$

Nucleus   *See* Physics section, page 20-35.

Oblate spheroid   A sphere slightly flattened along one diameter. The earth and other rotating bodies have this shape, flattened at the poles because the equatorial regions bulge.

Obsidian   A dark, mafic extrusive rock with a glassy texture.

Ocean   The saltwater mass that covers 72% of the earth's surface. The ion content of the ocean increases as dissolved minerals are carried to the sea by rivers. The present concentration is about 3.5% dissolved matter. Two ions—sodium (Na^+) and chloride (Cl^-)—constitute ordinary salt, about 85% of the mineral matter in the sea. Most of the rest is sulfate (SO_3^{2-}), magnesium (Mg^{2+}), calcium (Ca^{2+}), potassium (K^+), and bicarbonate (HCO_3^-).

The depth of the ocean increases from the edge of the continent to the deepest parts of the sea, where the floor may be very irregular. *See* **Seafloor topography**.

Great mountain ridges mark many parts of the ocean floor; *see* **Seafloor spreading**. Deep trenches are found where one tectonic plate is moving under another; *see* **Subduction zone**.

In the ocean, large quantities of water flow for great distances, producing a wide influence on climate and biota. *See* **Ocean currents**.

Ocean currents   Movement of large amounts of water streaming through the ocean. Surface currents flow to depths of 2 km or so, driven by prevailing winds. The direction of these currents is strongly influenced by the Coriolis effect. Surface currents may be warm or cold and have a great effect on climate.

In the Southern Hemisphere, vast regions of open ocean have counterclockwise currents. The flow of water in the South Pacific carries cold antarctic water northward along the west coast of South America (Humboldt Current). The water is cold enough to allow penguins to live at the equator, in the Galapagos Islands. The water warms as it flows westward in the equatorial region. Then it turns south and warms Australia and New Zealand. A similar flow in the South Atlantic cools the west coast of Africa and warms the east coast of South America. There is a third massive counterclockwise flow in the Indian Ocean.

In the Northern Hemisphere, circulation tends to be clockwise. However, there is not as much open ocean, and the currents are much more complex. The Gulf Stream is a warm surface current that flows out of the Caribbean to the west coast of Europe. It makes regions of Western Europe considerably warmer than places at the same latitude in North America. The Labrador Current is cold water flowing south between Greenland and North America. Clockwise flow in the north Pacific brings warm water (Japan Current) to the west coast of North America.

The vertical movement of water produces deep currents in the ocean. Water moves vertically as more dense water sinks below the less dense. The higher density is produced by the colder temperatures and by a higher salt concentration. In the Mediterranean, for example, the climate is dry and a higher evaporation rate makes the water saltier than in the Atlantic. Mediterranean water sinks and flows out along the bottom into the Atlantic, being completely replaced by inflowing Atlantic water once every 75 years.

Ocean trench   *See* **Seafloor topography**; **Subduction zone**.

Oort's Cloud   *See* **Comet**.

Orbit   *See* Physics section, page 20-36.

Organic sedimentary rocks   Rocks formed from the remains of organisms. Chalk and some other forms of limestone are deposits of shells of microscopic marine animals. *See also* **Coal**.

Original horizontality   The principle that sediments are laid down in horizontal layers. The strata of sedimentary rocks may be variously folded, tilted, and fractured owing to processes that lift the layers after they are formed.

Orogeny   Mountain building.

Orographic effect   The influence of mountains on climate. When prevailing winds strike a mountain range, they rise on the windward side; pressure and temperature drop, forming clouds and rainy weather. On the leeward side, the winds descend becoming hotter. The windward side of the mountain range has a humid climate, and the leeward side is usually a desert.

Outcrop   Bedrock penetrating to the surface through the soil layers. By studying outcrops, geologists deduce the properties of the bedrock.

Outwash plain   A broad, flat area consisting of fine particles carried away from the front of a glacier by meltwater.

Oxbow lake   *See* **Stream aging**.

Oxidation   In rocks, the chemical alteration of minerals by combining with the oxygen of the air. *See* **Chemical weathering**.

Ozone   A form of oxygen with three atoms per molecule instead of the usual two.

Ozone layer   A layer of ozone gas 15–35 km above the earth. Produced by the action of sunshine on oxygen, it protects life on earth by blocking ultraviolet radiation.

P   **Pangaea** The supercontinent of 200 million years ago in which all the large land masses were aggregated. *See* **Continental drift**.

Parallel of latitude   An imaginary circle drawn around the earth, parallel to the equator, to mark latitude.

Parsec   A measure of distance used in astronomy, equal to 3.26 light-years.

Partial pressure   That part of the total pressure of a mixed gas due to any given constituent. In dry air at a pressure of 1 atm, for example, the partial pressure of the oxygen is 152 mm, of nitrogen 600 mm, and of other gases about 8 mm, a total of 760 mm.

The partial pressure of the water vapor in the air is known as vapor pressure. It varies considerably. *See* **Humidity**; **Saturation vapor pressure**.

Particle shape   The geometric form of particles of sediment. Shape has a great influence on settling rate. A broad, flat particle exposes a great deal of surface to the water in which it is settling, so it descends much more slowly than a round particle of the same mass. When a batch of mixed sediments is dumped into water, the rounder particles are found at the bottom of the sedimentary layer. *See also* **Porosity**.

Particle size   The physical dimensions of a particle of sediment. Size influences settling rate, since larger particles fall through water faster than smaller particles. When a mixed batch of sediment is dumped into water, the sedimentary deposit is sorted vertically, with the larger particles on the bottom. Colloidal particles, which are extremely small, may not settle out at all.

In a stream, the maximum size of the particles that can be carried depends entirely on the stream velocity. Sedimentary deposits in the ocean or a lake thus give an important clue to the velocity of the stream that carried the sediment and thus also to the landform in which the stream flowed.

See also **Porosity**; **Chemical weathering**; **Physical weathering**.

Peat   *See* **Coal**.

Peneplain   A low-lying plain that is the result of a long period of erosion. A peneplain may be uplifted to form a plateau and subsequently dissected by rivers to form an erosional mountain range.

Perigee   The point in the orbit of the moon or an earth satellite at which it is closest to the earth.

Perihelion   The point in a planet's orbit at which the planet is closest to the sun and is thus moving fastest. The earth's perihelion occurs on January 4, when the distance to the sun is 148 million km. *See also* **Aphelion**.

Period   The length of time for a repeated process to make one full cycle. Thus, the period of the earth's rotation is 24 hours, and the period of its revolution 365.24 days.

For a completely different meaning, *see* **Geologic time scale**.

Permeability   The rate at which water can pass through material. For example, bedrock that has many cracks allows water to sink into it rapidly and is therefore highly permeable.

Sand is a highly permeable material because the particles are not very small and there are large, interconnected spaces between them. At the other extreme is clay, which has extremely tiny particles that cling together and close the air spaces when wet.

The permeability of soil influences the fate of water that strikes the surface. Water infiltrates rapidly into a permeable soil. On level ground, the water may form puddles that infiltrate slowly or not at all if the soil is impermeable. If the ground slopes, water falling on impermeable soil runs off faster than it can infiltrate.

Perseid   A meteor shower coming out of the constellation Perseus that occurs about August 11 every year.

Peru Current   *See* **Humboldt Current**.

Phases of matter   The physical condition of a substance that defines its boundaries. In the solid phase, an object has a definite shape of its own and this determines its boundaries. In the liquid phase, the material settles into its container until its upper boundary is a flat, level surface. In the gas phase, there is no boundary, and the substance spreads out to fill whatever container it is in.

Phases of the moon   Stages in the changing appearance of the moon as seen from earth. At any moment, the half of the moon that faces the sun is bright, and the other half is dark. When the bright half is facing the earth, we see the moon as a complete disk, and the phase is called "full." When the dark half is facing the earth, the moon may not be visible at all, the phase is "new." The moon has a 29½ day cycle.

Photon   A particle of light or other electromagnetic radiation. *See also* Physics section, page 20-38.

Phylum   Any of the main divisions of the animal kingdom (for example, Mollusca, Arthropoda).

Physical weathering   Reduction in particle size by natural means, with no chemical change.

Frost produces physical weathering because of a peculiar property of water. When it freezes into ice, it expands. Thus, if water seeps into cracks in rocks and then freezes, its expansion can widen the crack and split the rock.

The roots of plants, penetrating into cracks in rocks, can exert large forces. As the plants grow and the roots thicken, they can widen cracks. Lichens growing on bare rocks have rootlike structures that can penetrate the smallest cracks. *See* **Exfoliation**; **Pressure unloading**.

Rock that has formed deep inside the crust experiences a release of pressure when it is uplifted. It thus expands and cracks.

In coastal areas, salt water can get into cracks. When the water evaporates, salt crystals grow and can split the rocks. *See also* **Exfoliation**.

In deserts, sand blown by wind can abrade rocks, breaking the rock down into smaller particles.

Pillow lava   Rounded mounds of extruded rock formed by lava flows from underwater volcanoes.

Plains   *See* **Landscape**.

Planet   A dark body revolving around a star. The only planets definitely known are those in orbit around the sun. Other stars are so far away that any planets around them cannot be seen. However, the theory of star formation suggests that many stars are surrounded by planetary systems. The motion of a planet around a star causes a slight wobble in the star's position. There have been claims that this wobble has been found, but they have never been confirmed.

Nine known major planets orbit the sun. Most of them have one or more satellites in orbit around them. The following chart is a summary of some of the features of the planets. For further information, look under the name of each planet.

Name	Orbital Radius (AU)	Diameter (km)	Number of Satellites
Mercury	0.39	4,880	0
Venus	0.72	12,102	0
Earth	1.00	12,756	1
Mars	1.52	6,794	2
Jupiter	5.20	143,200	16
Saturn	9.52	120,000	17
Uranus	19.16	51,800	15
Neptune	29.99	49,500	8
Pluto	39.37	2,600	1

Note that there is some question about the numbers of satellites because additional small satellites, not visible from earth, have been found by planetary exploration vehicles.

Planetary motion   *See* **Gravitation**; **Kepler's laws**. *See also* **Newton's laws**, Physics section, page 20-34; **Orbit**, page 20-36.

Planetary nebula   A ring or shell of gas ejected from a star. *See* **Nova**.

Planetary winds   Prevailing winds that blow consistently in zones that cover the entire earth. They are produced by convection currents in the troposphere. Heated air rises in the equatorial region; cold air descends at the poles. Along the surface, planetary winds blow from the poles toward the equator. They are deflected from the north-south line and broken up into several convection cells because of the Coriolis force.

The general distribution of pressure zones and planetary winds at the equinoxes is as follows. In the equatorial regions, rising air currents produce low pressure and no prevailing winds. North of the equatorial zone, northeast trade winds blow steadily: in the Southern Hemisphere, the trade winds blow from the southeast. The high-pressure regions at about 30° (north and south) are the windless "horse latitudes." At still higher latitudes the prevailing westerlies blow, and near the poles the winds are again from the east.

Planetoid   *See* **Asteroid**.

Plateau   *See* **Landscape**.

Plate tectonics   The theory that explains major structural changes in the earth's crust on the basis that the crust consists of a number of separate solid plates that move around, floating on the underlying mantle.

The continents, consisting of low-density sialic rocks, rest on the mafic plates that form the main mass of the crust. Evidence for the motion of continents shows that the plates of the crust are moving. *See* **Continental drift**.

Extrusion processes in the ocean floor constantly add to the tectonic plates by building enormous undersea mountain ranges. *See* **Seafloor spreading**.

As the plates move, they collide, and one plate slips under another. This produces a region of active mountain building. *See* **Subduction zone**.

The most widely accepted theory to account for plate movement is that the plates are carried by the flow of the magma under the crust. *See* **Convection cell**.

Playa lake   A temporary lake formed in desert regions during the infrequent periods of rain. It is fed by temporary streams and drains only by evaporation.

Pluto   The ninth planet, averaging 5.9 billion km from the sun. Its orbit is highly eccentric, and at perihelion it is closer to the sun than Neptune. Next to Mercury, it is the smallest planet, with a radius of about 3000 km; it rotates with a period of 6.4 days and revolves around the sun once every 248 years. Pluto is so far away that it looks like a star, and no surface features are known. However, one satellite has been detected. Pluto is the only planet that has not been visited by a space probe.

Polaris   The north star. A Cepheid variable star varying from magnitude 2.5 to 2.6 with a period of 4 days, lies practically at the zenith above the earth's North Pole. Consequently, its position in the sky does not change during the night, and its elevation above the horizon is always equal to the latitude of the observer.

Pollution   The artificial introduction of undesirable materials into the air, water, and soil. Water is being polluted by a large number of human activities:

Waste dumping: Rivers are used for the purpose of carrying away soluble wastes of industrial plants and human sewage. Sewage improperly treated, contains many kinds of bacteria that spread disease in epidemic fashion. Chemical wastes are frequently poisonous or carcinogenic. Recently, both kinds of dumping in highly populated regions have even produced serious pollution problems in adjacent parts of the ocean.

Heat dumping: Stream water is being used to cool industrial plants and electric generating plants. The water returned to the stream is often so warm that it does extensive damage to the living organisms in the stream.

Runoff: Chemicals used as insecticides, herbicides, and fertilizers in farms are washed into the rivers and the water table. Dangerous materials are leached out of solid waste dumps and wind up in the subsurface water.

Air is also being polluted by automobile exhaust and smokestack gases. These also wind up in the water, as they are washed out of the air by rain.

Porosity   The percentage of open space in a soil, determining the amount of water that can be held. Round particles of uniform size, such as those of sand or gravel, leave a lot of space, and their porosity is around 35% regardless of the size of the particles. Sediments of mixed sizes have low porosity, perhaps 10–25%, because the small particles fill in the spaces between the larger particles. Clay consists of flat particles; porosity is high when the deposit is fresh, but the grains tend to settle out in horizontal layers, reducing the porosity to 10% or less. Porous rocks, such as sandstone, can serve as valuable reservoirs of underground water; *see* **Aquifer**.

Potential evapotranspiration   *See* **Evapotranspiration**; **Water budget**.

Precambrian   Roughly, the first 4 billion years of the earth's history. After the first 2 billion years or so, the first life appeared, probably in a form something like bacteria. By the end of the Precambrian, most of the modern phyla of animals were represented in the oceans.

Precession   The wobble of a rotating object, such as a top that is slowing down. The earth's axis is tilted at an angle of 23½° from the plane of its orbit. While maintaining this angle, the axis changes the direction of its tilt. It makes a complete precession cycle every 26,000 years. Thus Polaris will again be the north star 26,000 years from now.

Precipitation   (1) Atmospheric water that reaches the ground. When heat is removed from the air, the air cools until it reaches the dew point. The continued removal of heat causes a change of phase into the liquid form (condensation). However, if the partial pressure of the water vapor in the atmosphere is less than 4.58 mm of mercury, the water vapor turns into the solid phase at a dew point somewhere below 0°C (sublimation). Precipitation takes a number of different forms. *Dew* is water vapor condensed onto solid surfaces. It usually forms during the night, or early in the morning, when temperatures drop to the dew point. On cold, dry nights, the dew point is not reached until the temperature drops below 0°C and the vapor sublimes to form *frost*. *Rain* is droplets of water. As rising air currents carry air into colder regions, the temperature drops to the dew point and water condenses onto dust particles to form clouds. As the droplets continue to grow, they become heavy enough to fall through the rising air. If the air is fairly dry so that the partial pressure of the water vapor is low, there is no condensation; if the temperature drops far enough, the vapor sublimes into *snow*. Much of the rain that reaches the ground forms as snow and melts on the way down. *Sleet* is rain that falls through a cold layer of air and freezes into ice pellets on the way down. It is often accompanied by *freezing rain,* which falls as rain and freezes on striking a cold surface. *Hail* forms in violent thunderclouds, usually in the summer when warm air rises rapidly. Water droplets are carried upward into cold regions, where they freeze. The ice may be carried upward many times, acquiring a new layer of ice each time. Eventually, the hailstone becomes heavy enough to fall through the rising air to the ground.

(2) The process of a substance in solution forming solid particles.

Pressure   *See* Physics section, page 20-40; *see also* **Atmospheric pressure**.

Pressure gradient   The rate at which pressure changes from one region to another. Isobars close together indicate a high pressure gradient. Large pressure gradients produce strong winds. On a weather map, a hurricane appears as a small region ringed with closely crowded isobars.

Pressure systems   Regions of the atmosphere in which barometric pressure is a minimum or maximum. *See* **High-pressure system**; **Low-pressure system**.

Pressure unloading   The reduction in pressure as deep layers of rock are lifted by force from below. As the pressure is reduced, the rock cracks in many places. *See* **Exfoliation**.

Primary waves or P waves   *See* **Earthquake waves**.

Prime meridian   The arbitrary zero meridian. *See* **Longitude**.

Proper motion   The visible change in position of a star in the sky, that is, its motion perpendicular to our line of sight to it. It is always so small that it can be detected only by comparing photographs taken 20 years apart. Almost all proper motions of stars are less than 1" of arc per year.

Proton   *See* Physics section, page 20-40.

Psychrometer   An instrument for measuring atmospheric humidity. *See* **Dew point**.

Pulsar   *See* **Neutron star**.

Pumice   A sialic extrusive rock with a spongy texture. It forms when lava is blown out of a violent volcano that contains much trapped gas.

Q **Quartz**   *See* **Silicate minerals**.
Quasar   A mysterious source of enormous amounts of energy in the farthest reaches of the universe. Quasars were discovered when their radio waves were detected and have since been detected visually. Their red shifts show them to be traveling away from us at speeds approaching the speed of light. Applying the Hubble law implies that they are a billion light-years or more away. This means that we see them as they were a billion years ago. The furthest quasar, 15 billion light years away, shows us a structure that formed shortly after the birth of the universe.

Considering the great distance of these objects and their apparent magnitude, it is clear that they produce enormous amounts of energy. The energy is in all parts of the spectrum, from X-rays to radio waves. Quasars are hundreds of times as luminous as observable galaxies. The best guess is that these objects are the nuclei of some sort of supergalaxy that no longer exists in the universe.

R **Radar astronomy**   Measurement of distances to nearby planets by the use of radar. A device sends out a radio wave and measures distance by the length of time the wave takes to return after being reflected. Radar astronomy has added a great deal of accuracy to the measurement of distances within the solar system.

Radial drainage   A stream pattern in which the main streams flow radially outward from the top of a hill. This is the pattern on a hill unless there is a layer of weaker rock in the hill.

Radial velocity   The speed of a star along a line toward or away from the observer. *See* **Doppler effect**.

Radiation   The process by which electromagnetic waves carry energy from one place to another. The transferred energy is a form of heat, since the direction and the amount of energy transferred depend on temperature.

All objects warmer than their surroundings cool by emitting infrared radiation. Objects colder than their surroundings absorb radiation and warm. The amount of energy transferred in this way depends on the difference in temperature. The hotter an object, the more energy it radiates.

Temperature also determines the wavelength of the radiation emitted. Objects that are only slightly warm radiate longwave infrared rays. A moderately hot object at 500 K (= 227°C) emits a great deal of energy at the shorter wavelength infrared. If the temperature rises from 500 to 1000 K, the energy output is sixteen times greater, and many objects radiate some energy in the visible range. They are then said to be "red hot." At 2000 K (the filament of an incandescent lamp) the entire visible spectrum is emitted, as well as a small amount of ultraviolet. The object is "white hot." At still higher temperatures, much of the energy is in the ultraviolet.

Astronomers find the surface temperatures of stars by studying the wavelengths of the light they emit. The temperature corresponds to a particular value of the wavelength at which energy radiated is a maximum. The hottest visible stars are blue and emit substantial amounts of ultraviolet light. The coldest visible stars are red, but invisible stars that emit only in the infrared have also been found. *See* **Stellar temperature**; *see also* **Radiation**, Physics section page 20-41.

Radiation pressure   The force exerted on matter by electromagnetic waves. It is extremely small and can be effective only in the deep vacuum of outer space. Radiation pressure pushes a stream of particles away from the sun (*see* **Solar wind**). It is also responsible for the tail of a comet. When a comet is near the sun, heat vaporizes some of its ice and radiation pressure from the sun pushes the vapor out, forming the tail.

Radiative balance The condition in which the earth radiates into space the same amount of energy it receives from the sun. Heat from internal radioactivity makes a very small contribution. If the earth were in radiative balance, its temperature would remain constant.

In fact, the earth is never in radiative balance. It receives more energy than it radiates during the day, and the reverse is true at night. There is also an annual cycle, due to the change in seasons. On average, the gains and losses approximately balance out over the year. For reasons that are not well understood, there is also a 20 year cycle. Geologic evidence indicates that there are also long-range changes in the average temperature; *see* **Ice age**.

Radioactive dating The process of determining the actual date of a geologic formation by comparing the abundance of a radioactive material with that of its decay product. Since the half-life of the isotope is known, the amount of decay that has taken place indicates how long the material has been there. (*See* **Half-life**, Physics section, page 20-22.)

Dating is done on single crystals of an igneous rock. The assumption is that when the rock is molten, all materials are uniformly dispersed. After a crystal forms, the decay products are trapped in the crystal along with the parent compound. For example, uranium-235 decays with a half-life of 710 million years. It decays through eleven short-half-life intermediates to form lead-207, which is stable. To date an igneous rock, a single crystal containing uranium-235 is analyzed for the amounts of uranium-235 and lead-207 in it. The amount of lead-207 in ordinary lead is subtracted, so the rest must have been formed by the decay of uranium-235. If this number of atoms equals the number of atoms of uranium-235, half of the uranium-235 has decayed, and the age of the crystal is 710 million years.

Other radioactive processes used in dating are uranium-238 to lead-206 (4.5 billion years), thorium-232 to lead-208 (13.9 billion years), rubidium-87 to strontium-87 (50 billion years), and potassium-40 to argon-40 (1.3 billion years). *See also* **Radiocarbon dating**.

Radioactivity The breakdown of certain unstable atomic nuclei. *See also* Physics section page 20-41. Radioactivity inside the earth is the main continuing source of heat that produces volcanic and tectonic activity. However, it has little effect on surface temperatures, which are dominated by insolation and reradiation. *See also* **Radioactive dating**.

Radio astronomy The study of celestial objects by analysis of the radio waves they produce (*see* **Radio telescope**). Quasars and pulsars were discovered by radio telescopes, and they have supplied much information about the sun and other stars.

Radiocarbon dating A method of dating organic remains by their content of radioactive carbon.

Carbon-14 is formed in the atmosphere continuously by the bombardment of nitrogen atoms with cosmic rays. It decays back to nitrogen-14 with a half-life of 5770 years. The decay is balanced by the formation of new carbon-14, so that there is always a steady level in the atmosphere.

The carbon-14 is oxidized to carbon dioxide, and photosynthesis incorporates it into plants. As long as a plant is alive, the ratio of carbon-12 to carbon-14 is the same as in the atmosphere. When the plant dies, the carbon-14 continues to decay. Thus, the remains of plants, or of animals that ate them, can be dated by the ratio of carbon-12 to carbon-14. The method is accurate and useful for remains up to 50,000 years old.

Radio telescope A device for receiving radio waves from outer space. It consists of a large parabolic reflector (a "dish") that intercepts the wave and focuses it onto a small receiver. The signals are then analyzed electronically. A great deal of information about stars and galaxies can be obtained from the radio waves they emit.

An important limitation to the use of radio telescopes is that they have poor resolution because the waves have such large wavelengths (*see* **Resolution**). A way around this problem is to use the telescopes in groups (*see* **Interferometry**).

Rain *See* **Precipitation**.

Rain shadow A region that has little or no rainfall because it lies on the leeward side of a mountain range.

Raised beach A steplike surface feature at the margin of an emerging continent. The horizontal surface was once at the edge of the sea, where it was eroded level by wave action. Uplift raises it to a higher position.

Recharge Replenishment of the water table by precipitation. *See* **Water budget**.

Red Giant *See* **Stellar evolution**.

Red Shift *See* **Expanding Universe**; **Doppler effect**.

Reflection nebula *See* **Nebula**.

Regelation Solidification of supercooled water to form ice as a result of release of pressure. High pressure lowers the melting point of ice, so that it melts at temperatures below the usual freezing point. A glacier is able to flow because of this special property of water. The weight of a large mass of ice causes melting at points of contact with surrounding rock. The meltwater flows around the rock and refreezes.

Relative age The age of a sedimentary layer compared with that of other layers. In undisturbed sediments, the older layers are below younger layers. The relative ages of sediments all over the world have been combined into a single system. *See* **Geologic column**; **Geologic time scale**. The absolute ages of sedimentary layers are found by radioactive dating of adjacent igneous rocks. *See* **Radioactive dating**.

Relative humidity The amount of moisture in the air relative to the amount the air can hold at the given temperature. This can be expressed as the ratio of absolute humidity to humidity at saturation. For example, at a temperature of 20°C, air is saturated when it holds 17.3 g of vapor per cubic meter. If, at that temperature, the absolute humidity is 9.5 g/m³, then

$$\text{Relative humidity} = \frac{\text{absolute humidity}}{\text{humidity at saturation}}$$
$$= \frac{9.5 \text{ g/m}^3}{17.3 \text{ g/m}^3}$$
$$= 0.55 = 55\%$$

Relative humidity can also be calculated on the basis of vapor pressure (*see* **Saturation vapor pressure**). At 20°C the air is saturated at a vapor pressure of 23.4 mb. If the actual vapor pressure at that temperature is found to be 4.5 mb, then

$$\text{Relative humidity} = \frac{\text{vapor pressure}}{\text{saturation vapor pressure}}$$
$$= \frac{4.5 \text{ mb}}{23.4 \text{ mb}}$$
$$= 0.19 = 19\%$$

As a practical matter, relative humidity can be measured by determining the temperature and the dew point. *See* **Dew point**.

Relief   The degree of difference between high and low elevations exhibited by a landscape. Mountains have high relief; plains have very low relief.

Residual sediment   A sediment that has not been transported. It has weathered out of the bedrock on which it lies.

Resolution   The degree of detail in an image. Resolution is ultimately limited by the size of the objective lens or mirror of a telescope and the wavelength of the light or other radiation being studied. The larger the objective lens and the smaller the wavelength, the higher the resolution of the image will be. Thus, even with an ordinary telescope, resolution is better in the violet than in the red.

A large mirror for a telescope has two advantages: it produces an image with high resolution and it gathers a large amount of light. There are many ways to compensate for low light-gathering power, such as electronic image intensification and long photographic exposure. Resolution can be enhanced slightly by electronic processing of the image, but only within a very narrow limit. Enlarging an image with poor resolution does not make more detail available: the image becomes larger and fuzzier.

Retrograde motion   The motion of a planet through the sky when it appears to reverse its direction for a period of time. The planets, in general, move in eastward paths against the background of fixed stars. However, when the earth is moving eastward between Jupiter and the sun, Jupiter appears to be moving retrograde, to the west.

In the old geocentric model of the solar system, retrograde motion was accounted for on the assumption that the paths of the planets include small circles within circles, or epicycles. The heliocentric model dispensed with epicycles, accounting for retrograde motion on the basis of the relative motions of the earth and the planet.

Rhyolite   *See* **Extrusive rock**.

Richter scale   *See* **Earthquake**.

Right ascension   *See* **Celestial sphere**.

Rock   Solid matter making up the crust of the earth. Rocks are composed of substances called minerals, that have definite chemical and physical structures. *See* **Igneous rocks; Metamorphic rocks; Sedimentary rocks**.

Rock cycle   The series of changes through which the rock passes as a result of erosion, melting, and metamorphosis. Igneous rocks can be converted into sediments, which may then erode further or cement into sedimentary rock. Any rock can be metamorphosed by exposure to heat and pressure deep within the crust. At still deeper levels any rock can be melted. The magma can then be intruded or extruded to form new igneous rock.

Rock-forming minerals   Minerals that are the chief components of common and widespread kinds of rocks. About 90% of the lithosphere is made of a few minerals: feldspar, quartz, mica, calcite, hornblende, augite, garnet, magnetite, olivine, and pyrite. *See* **Silicate minerals**.

Runoff   Precipitated water that flows over the surface without infiltrating into the soil. Runoff is greatest when the underlying substrate is saturated or impervious. A steep slope promotes rapid runoff.

S

Sandstone   *See* **Clastic sedimentary rocks**.

Sargasso Sea   A region of the Atlantic Ocean bounded by the Gulf Stream to the north and the Equatorial Current to the south. The water is stagnant, warm, and salty. It contains many unique life-forms, including enormous masses of the seaweed *Sargassum*.

Saturation vapor pressure   The greatest possible partial pressure of water vapor at given temperature. If water is kept in a closed container, it evaporates until the air above the water is saturated; that is it can hold no more vapor. The partial pressure of the water vapor is then the saturation vapor pressure. The warmer the air, the more water will evaporate before saturation is reached.

Saturation vapor pressure varies with temperature. At 100°C the saturation vapor pressure is 1 atm (= 760 mm mercury = 1013 mb). This means that at that pressure, liquid water and water vapor, unmixed with air, are in equilibrium. In other words, this is the normal boiling point of water.

Below 0°C air may be saturated over ice. Thus, if ice is kept in a closed container at −10°C, the air is saturated at a partial pressure of 2.6 mb.

Saturn   The sixth planet, 1400 million km from the sun. It is a giant planet, with a radius of 60,000 km; it spins rapidly, turning every 10 hours, and revolves around the sun once every 30 years. Saturn, like Jupiter, is made mainly of hydrogen and helium. Its specific gravity is only 0.7, the lowest of any planet. Its hydrogen-helium atmosphere has many small vortices and hurricane-force winds blow all the time.

Saturn's most spectacular feature is its bright rings. Photographs from space probes showed the rings to have a complex structure, as they consist of hundreds of thousands of fine ringlets. They are composed mainly of pieces of water ice, mostly microscopic but some as large as 10 km. There are also rocks in the rings. Gravitational interactions between the rings and the seventeen known satellites produce on-going changes in the structure of the rings.

Saturn's largest satellite, Titan is almost as big as Mercury. It is the only satellite in the solar system known to have its own atmosphere. This is mostly nitrogen, with a little methane. Since the temperature is only 27 K, there must also be liquid nitrogen on the surface.

Saturn is not a bright feature in the sky because it is so far away. It has been known since antiquity, however, and its rings were seen when the first small telescopes were turned heavenward.

Photograph of Saturn taken by *Voyager 2* on July 21, 1981 from 21 million miles away.

Schwartzchild radius   The event horizon (that is, the limit) of a black hole. *See also* **Black hole**.

Scoria   A porous mafic extrusive rock produced when lava is blown explosively out of a gas-rich volcano.

Seafloor spreading   The process by which tectonic plates move apart in the deep sea. The divergent boundaries between plates are marked by enormous underwater mountain ranges. The mid-Atlantic Ridge runs north-south for 21,000 km down the center of the Atlantic Ocean, emerging at the surface in Iceland and the Azores. The ridge is an active center of volcanic activity and shallow earthquakes. Lava spewed out of the ridge adds to the edges of the tectonic plates as they move apart.

The best evidence for seafloor spreading is found in the direction of magnetization of the rock of the tectonic plates. The earth's magnetic field reverses at irregular intervals, and the direction of the field is recorded in the extruded lava. The rock outside the ridge forms a series of strips, parallel to the ridge. The direction of magnetization in these strips alternates, pointing north in one strip and south in the next. Further, the pattern of magnetic change is the same on both sides of the ridge. The youngest rock is closest to the ridge.

The mid-Atlantic Ridge is one part of a worldwide system of such ridges. It connects with a ridge that passes around the southern tip of Africa, into the Indian Ocean, and from there into the Pacific.

Seafloor topography   The form of the bottom of the sea. Characteristically, the seafloor slopes gently at the edge of a continent, forming the continental shelf. At the continental slope, up to about 100 km from the edge of the continent, the slope suddenly steepens. In the continental slope, there are many deep, V-shaped submarine canyons. Some of the canyons are drowned river valleys, but the deeper canyons were probably cut in the seafloor by turbidity currents.

At the base of the continental slope, massive sedimentary deposits form the continental rise. This is a flat surface that slopes steeply to the abyss, the deep sea. The abyss is largely flat, but it is broken in many places by hills and seamounts formed of deposits from submarine volcanoes. Some of the seamounts, called guyots, are flat on top, having been eroded to sea level before subsiding into the sea.

Tectonic action produces certain characteristic features on the seafloor; *see* **Seafloor spreading**; **Subduction zone**. Another feature is island chains, such as the Hawaiian Islands. These are volcanoes erupting on the ocean bottom. The chain is formed because the crust moves over a hot spot in the mantle. The hot spot produces volcanoes.

Seasons   The annual cycle of changes in the weather. Each season lasts 3 months. The seasons in the Northern Hemisphere are as follows.

Spring starts at the spring equinox, March 21. On that day, there are 12 hours of daylight all over the the world and the sun is over the equator. During spring, the sun moves farther north and the length of the day increases. As the angle of insolation increases the weather becomes warmer.

Summer begins at the summer solstice, June 21. On that day, the sun is at its farthest north position, the duration of daylight is greatest, and the angle of insolation is at a maximum. During summer, the sun moves farther south, but accumulation of heat continues.

Autumn or fall begins at the autumnal equinox, September 22 or 23. Daylight is back to 12 hours, and the sun is over the equator. The decreasing insolation angle brings cooling of the weather.

Winter starts at the winter solstice, December 21 or 22, when the sun is at its southernmost position and the duration of daylight is a minimum. During winter, daylight and the angle of insolation gradually increase, until there are once again 12 hours of daylight at the spring equinox.

In the Southern Hemisphere, the entire pattern of change of seasons is opposite to that in the Northern Hemisphere.

Secondary waves, or S waves   *See* **Earthquake waves**.

Sedimentary rocks   Rock formed by the consolidation of sedimentary deposits. *See* **Clastic sedimentary rocks** for rocks formed by mechanical weathering. For rocks formed from chemically deposited sediments, *see* **Dolomite**; **Gypsum**; **Halite**; **Limestone**.

Sedimentation   The depositing of earth materials that have been transported from one place to another. An example is the sediment deposited on the inside of a meander; *see* **Stream aging**. The most widespread deposits are those made at the mouth of a river.

Other agents of erosion also move material from one place to another. *See also* **Alpine glaciation**; **Glacial deposits**; **Wave deposits**; **Wind deposits**.

Seismic sea wave   *See* **Tsunami**.

Seismic waves   *See* **Earthquake waves**.

Seismograph   An instrument for measuring the vibrations in the crust of the earth. A seismograph is solidly anchored in bedrock so that it shakes when the earth shakes. Its key feature is a large mass that is suspended from a spring, is free to pivot, and does not move with the rest of the instrument. The photosensitivepaper vibrates with the earth, so the light reflected from the mirror on the mass produces a pattern of vibration on the paper.

The vibrations of the crust at any location provide clues to the origin and nature of earthquakes anywhere in the world; *see* **Earthquake waves**. They are also the main source of information about the structure of the earth; *see* **Earth's interior**. Geologists exploring for oil and other minerals investigate the structure of the crust by setting off an explosion and studying the output of a seismograph some distance away.

Seyfert galaxy   A spiral galaxy with luminosity, mostly in the infrared, a hundred times normal. No explanation for this is known.

Shale   *See* **Clastic sedimentary rocks**.

Shear waves   *See* **Earthquake waves**; **Transverse wave**, Physics section, page 20-50.

Shield volcano   *See* **Volcano**.

Shooting star   The popular name for a **meteor**.

Shoreline landscape   The general appearance of the land bordering the ocean. Unless the land is rising or falling, the shoreline is dominated by the deposition of sediments; *see* **Wave deposits**. For the typical landscape of the shore of a rising landmass, *see* **Emergent shoreline**. For a sinking sea border, *see* **Submergent shoreline**.

Sialic rock   Low-density, light-colored rock consisting mainly of minerals rich in silicon and aluminum, with little or no magnesium and iron. Sialic rocks make up the core of the continents. Since their density is comparatively low, they float on top of the mafic rock of the lower crust and mantle. Granite is a common sialic rock, and the word *granite* is often used to indicate the entire class of sialic rocks.

Sidereal day   The period of the earth's rotation as measured with reference to the fixed stars. *See* **Solar day**.

Sidereal year   The period of the earth's revolution as measured with reference to the fixed stars. See **Solar year**.

Silicate minerals   Minerals consisting of silicon and oxygen in combination with other elements. The group includes about 60% of all minerals, and they make up by far the largest part of the crust of the earth.

The fundamental unit cell of all silicate minerals is a tetrahedron, or a four-sided pyramid. The four corners of the pyramid are occupied by oxygen atoms, and there is a silicon atom in the center. Silicate minerals can be divided into families according to the way these cells join with each other and other elements to form crystals.

Isolated tetrahedra are minerals in which the unit cells are separate from each other. The crystal is held together by metallic ions between the cells. In the dark green minerals of the olivine group, the metals are almost entirely iron and magnesium. The garnets, which come in many colors, also have aluminum, chromium, calcium, and manganese in their structure.

Chains are minerals in which the unit cells are bound together into long chains. Each unit cell is firmly bonded to two adjacent cells. The bond is an oxygen atom shared by the two cells. Metallic ions join the chains together, weakly. Some of the members of this group, such as asbestos tend to break into long, thin fibers. Hornblende, pyroxenes, augite, and jade belong here. They are rich in magnesium and iron and are a chief component of all mafic igneous rocks.

Sheets are minerals in which each unit cell is bound to three others by shared oxygen atoms, so that a large number of cells are joined together into a sheet. Adjacent sheets are held together by weak bonds, consisting of ions of sodium, potassium, and calcium. The micas show this structure by cleaving into very thin, flat sheets. The banding of metamorphic rocks is often produced by crystallized micas.

Networks are minerals in which each unit cell shares all its oxygen atoms with four adjacent cells, forming a three-dimensional structure. The feldspars are the most abundant minerals in the crust. They are often found in well-formed crystals that cleave along two planes. Metallic ions such as sodium, potassium, calcium, and aluminum, are found substituting for the silicon in many cells. Colors can be white, pink, or greenish, depending on the metallic ions present. Since feldspars weather into clay when exposed to water, they are not often found in water-deposited sediments.

Quartz (silicon dioxide, SiO_2), when pure, forms hard, glassy, six-sided crystals that fracture. It is a network in which every cell is bound to four others at its corners, so no other metals are present. Quartz is a component of all granites and gneisses. Sand and sandstone are often fairly pure quartz. Quartz occurs in a wide variety of forms, some of which are gemstones, such as rock crystal, amethyst, jasper, and opal.

Sill   *See* **Intrusion**.

Sinkhole   *See* **Karst topography**.

Soil   Loose surface material. A *transported soil* is a sedimentary deposit; *see* **Deposition**. A *residual soil* is a soil that has formed by the weathering of the rock on which it rests.

Soil formation starts with the weathering of the bedrock, reducing it to small fragments. Lichens can grow on the bare rock. This promotes weathering. The decay of lichens adds organic material, or humus, to the soil. Mosses and grasses then grow and decay, to increase the humus content of the soil. Humus generates acid, which contributes to the weathering of the rock. The uppermost layer is then called topsoil. It is black in color and able to support a luxurious growth of plants.

In a mature soil, there is a layer of subsoil below the topsoil. This contains some humus and minerals leached out of the topsoil by infiltrating water. As weathering of the bedrock continues, all the layers deepen.

A number of kinds of soil are recognized. In a *forest soil*, abundant rainfall leaches calcite and other soluble minerals out of the topsoil, leaving it rich in iron and aluminum. A *desert soil*, in contrast, is rich in soluble minerals. *Grassland soil* is found in semi-humid prairies, where soluble minerals have leached to a lower level, but one that can still be reached by the roots of grasses. *Tropical soil* is characteristic of the warm, extremely humid tropical rain forests. The soil is poor in minerals because of effective leaching; it is poor in humus because organic matter is rapidly destroyed by bacteria.

Solar constant   The amount of radiation coming from the sun, measured at the outside of the atmosphere. It is about 140,000 J/m^2 (joules per square meter) per second.

Solar day   The interval between successive moments when the sun is on the meridian. Because of the earth's revolution around the sun, the length of the solar day varies by about 15 minutes during the year. Our clocks define 24 hours as the average length of the solar day throughout the year, called the mean solar day (*see* **Time**).

The sidereal day, measured from a fixed star instead of the sun, is 4 minutes shorter than the solar day. The reason is that the earth is revolving around the sun. In the course of a year, it makes one full revolution more as measured from the stars than as measured from the sun. One revolution in a year amounts to 4 minutes every day.

Solar eclipse   A conformation of celestial bodies in which the moon comes between the sun and the earth. The disk of the moon and the disk of the sun, as viewed from earth, are about the same size, so the moon can completely block the sun. If only part of the sun's disk is obscured, the eclipse is called partial; if the face of the sun is completely covered, the eclipse is total. Since the moon's shadow on the earth is small, the total eclipse can be seen from only a small part of the earth.

A solar eclipse occurs only when the moon is new, that is, the phase at which the moon, in its orbit, might come between the sun and the earth.

On the average, this happens about once every eighteen lunar orbits. *See* **Phases of the moon**.

Solar flare   An intensely bright spot on the solar surface, lasting from a few minutes to a few hours. A flare pours out charged particles and also releases enormous amounts of energy in the ultraviolet and X-ray ranges. The mechanism is unknown.

Solar system   The sun and all the objects held to it by gravitational attraction. Aside from the nine major planets and their satellites, the following objects are part of the solar system:

A large number of minor planets; *see* **Asteroid**.

Masses of ice and rocks, orbiting the sun in very long, elliptic orbits; *see* **Comet**.

Stony or metallic chunks wandering through space; *see* **Meteoroid**. *See also* **Planet**.

Solar wind   A stream of particles, mostly protons and electrons. flowing out of the sun. It is driven by radiation pressure and is especially strong during solar flares, when it may disrupt radio communication by disturbing the ionosphere. *See also* **Aurora**.

Solar year, or tropical year   The time interval between two successive spring equinoxes. It is equal to 365.24 days (*see* **Calendar**).

The sidereal year, measured with respect to the fixed stars, is 20 minutes longer than the solar year. The reason is the precession of the earth's rotation. This precession goes through a complete 360° cycle every 26,000 years. The result is that the number of revolutions every 26,000 years is one complete revolution less if measured from the stars than if measured from the sun. One revolution per 26,000 years gives the difference of 20 minutes per year.

Solstice   The moment when the earth's axis makes its greatest angle with respect to the line drawn from the sun. The summer solstice occurs every year on June 21. The noon sun is then directly overhead at the Tropic of Cancer, 23½° north latitude. This the first day of summer (*see* **Seasons**). Daylight lasts 24 hours at all points north of the Arctic Circle, 66½° north latitude. South of the Antarctic Circle, there is no daylight.

The winter solstice, on December 21 or 22, is the reverse. The sun is overhead at noon on the Tropic of Capricorn; the length of daylight is 24 hours south of the Antarctic Circle, and there is none at all north of the Arctic Circle. *See also* **Equinox**.

Source region   The part of the world in which an air mass has formed. *See* **Air mass**.

Specific gravity   The density of a material compared with the density of water. Thus, a mineral with a specific gravity of 2.6 has a density 2.6 times as great as that of water. Since the density of water is 1 g/cm^3, the specific gravity of anything is a dimensionless number equal to the density of the substance in grams per cubic centimeter.

Spectral class   An old way of classifying stars according to the kinds of spectra they produce. The spectra differ in their Fraunhofer lines, produced by absorption of selected wavelengths in the cooler outer layer of the stars. It is now known that the different spectral classes represent different surface temperatures. *See* **Stellar temperature**; **H-R diagram**.

Spectrograph   An instrument for recording spectra; a spectroscope with film.

Spectroscope   An instrument for studying spectra. Although prisms have been used for breaking white light into its component wavelengths, they have long since given way to a superior device, the diffraction grating. This consists of a mirrored surface ruled with a great many fine lines. The light is reflected from the surface at an angle that depends on its wavelength. A good spectroscope can spread out the entire visible spectrum to several meters. Measurements of wavelength accurate to parts per million are routine.

Spectrum   *See* Physics section, page 20-46.

The spectrum of a star yields enormous amounts of information, including temperature (*see* **Stellar temperature**), velocity and rotation (*see* **Doppler effect**), chemical composition (*see* **Fraunhofer lines**), and magnetic field (*see* **Zeeman effect**).

Speed of light   The speed of all electromagnetic waves in a vacuum. It is the ultimate speed; nothing travels faster. Particles with no rest mass, such as photons and perhaps neutrinos, can exist only at this speed. Its value is 2.998×10^8 m/s.

EARTH AND SPACE SCIENCE

Spring tide *See* **Tides.**

Stalactite An icicle-shaped feature hanging down from the roof of a limestone cave. It is formed and grows as water, laden with limestone in solution, drips down. As the water evaporates the limestone comes out of solution. *See* **Karst topography.**

Stalagmite A conical structure pointing up from the floor of a limestone cave. *See also* **Stalactite.**

Star path The apparent path of a star across the sky. The path is the result of the earth's rotation so it is circular. Since the northern end of the earth's axis points approximately to Polaris this star does not move during the night, and the paths of all other stars form circles around Polaris.

Station model The standard form of presentation of data taken at a weather station. A weather station reports the following information, which appears on the station model: amount of cloud cover, barometric pressure, recent change in pressure, precipitation, wind direction and velocity, visibility, present weather, temperature, and dew point.

Stellar evolution The sequence of stages through which a star goes during its lifetime. A star begins life as a large amount of interstellar gas and dust. The material is drawn together by mutual gravitational attraction. The force of impact converts the gravitational energy of the material to thermal energy. When the temperature reaches about a million degrees at the center, the star enters the main sequence as nuclear fusion begins. Most of the star is hydrogen; the fusion process converts this to helium. The energy released keeps the temperature high enough to continue the nuclear fusion (*see* **Nuclear fusion**; **H-R diagram**).

On the H-R diagram, most stars lie in the region labeled main sequence. The length of time a star takes to attain the main sequence depends on its mass. If the mass is 0.1 solar mass, the condensation stage takes 100 million years and the star reaches the main sequence when it is quite cool and not very bright. At the other extreme (top of the diagram), a star with 100 times the mass of the sun reaches the main sequence in 10,000 years and becomes extremely bright and hot.

In stars of the main sequence, energy is obtained from the nuclear fusion reaction in which hydrogen is converted into helium. A dust cloud turns into a star on the main sequence when its temperature reaches a million degrees and the hydrogen-burning reaction starts. A star spends most of its life on the main sequence. During that time, helium is added to the core. The core of main sequence stars consists almost entirely of helium. The core keeps growing, it is surrounded by a shell in which the hydrogen-to-helium reaction takes place. Outside this shell, the rest of the star is mainly hydrogen.

When the core grows to a certain size, its gravity is so strong that it collapses. The energy it releases pushes the outer part of the star to an enormous size. Its surface temperature drops. The star leaves the main sequence and becomes a red giant. When the sun reaches this stage, in another 5 billion years it will be large enough to swallow the earth.

Hydrogen burning continues to add helium to the core. As more and more mass is added to the helium core, it becomes compressed so much that the tem-

perature reaches 100 million degrees and a new fusion process begins. Three helium nuclei combine to form carbon. This is a process like that in a bomb, and the core explodes in only a few hours. The star then collapses, forming a new core made of carbon and oxygen. This is surrounded by a shell of burning helium, which is surrounded by a shell of burning hydrogen. The star returns to the red giant stage.

What happens next depends on the size of the star. In smaller stars, which began at the lower end of the main sequence, hydrogen burning adds helium, and helium burning continues to add carbon to the core. Eventually the star casts off much of its outer material into space, and the core collapses completely into degenerate matter. With no nuclear reactions going on, the star is extremely hot and has a density of hundreds of tons per cubic centimeter. It is a white dwarf.

Larger stars burn faster and leave the main sequence more quickly. The enormous gravitational forces in their center can make the carbon-oxygen core hotter than is possible in smaller stars. At about 600 million degrees, new fusion reactions start. The carbon and oxygen form new reaction shells inside the helium-burning shell. A whole series of shells develops, until the star consists of an iron core surrounded by a series of shells, each with a different nuclear reaction. In the largest stars, the pressure may be so great that the iron core collapses until its nuclei are jammed together. The sudden drop in pressure makes the whole star explode. The star becomes a supernova.

The subsequent history of the star depends on the mass remaining. Smaller remnants become white dwarfs; those between 1.4 and 3 solar masses become neutron stars, still larger stars become black holes.

Stellar temperature The temperature of the outer layer of a star, which is far lower than the internal temperatures. The surface temperature determines the spectral class to which the star belongs and its position on an H-R diagram.

The absorption spectrum of the outer layers of a star gives a direct measurement of the surface temperature. As light from the star passes through the outer layers, some wavelengths are absorbed more strongly than others, producing a dark-line spectrum. Each dark line represents the absorption of specific photons by the outer layer. The higher the temperature, the greater is the absorption of the high-energy (short-wavelength) photons. Thus, the relative strengths of the lines provide the clue to the temperature.

Storage The amount of water in the soil. *See* **Water budget.**

Strata Layers of sedimentary rock. The nature, form, thickness, and shape of the strata are the chief clues to the geologic history of a region. Strata laid down in the ocean are always horizontal. They are composed of sediments carried down by streams. A conglomerate rock containing large pebbles indicates that the streams flowed rapidly, so that large particles could be carried. On the other hand, a deposit of limestone, which is carried in solution, indicates an old river flowing through level country. If no uplift of land intervenes, sedimentary rocks are graded, with conglomerate on the bottom and limestone on top. This is an indication of the reduction by erosion of the adjacent land mass. The thickness of the sediments is a clue to the size of the original land mass.

An alteration in this ideal sequence tells of tectonic events. If a layer of sandstone tops a limestone layer, the streams must have been rejuvenated by uplift of the land. The layers themselves may have been altered. Sedimentary rocks that have been subjected to repeated earthquakes show many fault lines, and the layers are tilted at various angles or even completely inverted. Folding and metamorphosis of the rock tell of past intervals of enormous lateral pressure.

Stratus   *See* **Clouds.**

Streak   The color of the powder of a mineral, used as a clue to identification. The color is found by rubbing the mineral on a piece of unglazed porcelain so that it leaves a streak mark. The color of the streak may be quite different from the color of the mineral. Hematite, for example, may be red or black, but its streak is always reddish brown.

Stream aging   The changes in the form of rivers and valleys as a result of erosion by the river. Three main stages can be identified.

Youthful streams are characteristic of mountainous regions, but in some cases are also found at low elevations. They flow rapidly in fairly straight lines between steep valley walls. They may carry very large particles, and boulders and cobbles in their beds create rapids. Where they undercut the bed into softer rocks, they have waterfalls.

Mature streams occur where the surrounding mountains have been worn down to low hills. Stream velocity is slower because the river is not as far above its base level. The valley is wide, and the river winds between gently sloping roundtopped hills. The curves in the river are called meanders. Because the velocity is so low, the river cannot carry particles larger than sand.

An *old river* winds in wide meanders across a floodplain. The plain is covered with sediments that the river deposited in its previous paths. The river periodically rises and floods the whole plain, leaving deposits of silt. There is no sloping hill on its banks; the hills are far away at the edge of the floodplain. Meanders may be so great that the path closes on itself, giving the river a shorter path. The isolated bend in the river becomes an oxbow lake.

Meanders convert mature rivers to old rivers. As the water flows around the bend, it cuts under the bank on the outside of the curve. On the inside of the curve, the velocity is low and the river drops its sediments. There is a sandbar at every inside curve. As the river cuts its bank, the meander becomes wider and moves downstream. The floodplain is formed from the fine sediments left behind in the old stream channel. In its old age, the river has shortened its channel by cutting through the narrow neck of land at the base of one meander. It has left an oxbow lake.

Stream discharge   The volume of water passing a given point in a river per unit time. Most streams have a certain base level of flow, measured in cubic meters per second. The rate of discharge increases during precipitation as a result of runoff.

It continues to be high after rain, since water continues to enter the river as groundwater seeps in through the banks. There is also much annual variation. In desert climates streams dry up completely during the dry season.

Stream erosion   The work of a stream in transporting sediments to lower levels. Hillside creep continually adds sediments to rivers. The amount and kind of erosion depend on the velocity of the water and on the discharge rate, the amount of water carried per unit time.

Rivers flow faster wherever the land slopes more steeply. Water flows fastest at the center of the stream, where it is unimpeded by contact with the banks or stream bed. In a large river, more water flows unimpeded and the average velocity is greater than in a small river. In the bed of the river, however, the velocity is determined only by the slope of the bed.

The size of the particles a river can carry depends on the river velocity. Ionic materials are carried in solution, and their transport does not depend on the river velocity. The finest silt particles are in suspension and can also be carried by even the slowest rivers. Larger particles rest on the stream bottom and move downstream by bouncing along the bottom.

As particles bounce along the bottom of a river, they are constantly abraded. This rounds the particles and converts the pebbles and cobbles into silt.

Stream gradient   The slope of a river bed. The steeper the gradient is, the faster the flow of water and the greater the rate of erosion. On the average, the gradient of a stream is high in its upper reaches and becomes smaller and smaller as the river nears the sea. Gradient changes with age; youthful rivers have a high gradient, but the gradient of an old river may approach zero.

Stream pattern   The various ways in which streams form patterns of flow. *See* **Annular drainage; Dendritic drainage; Radial drainage; Trellis drainage; Underground drainage.**

Stream velocity   The speed of the water, determined by the stream gradient. For a discussion of the influence of velocity, *see* **Stream erosion.**

Strike   The direction of a horizontal line on the bedding plane of a rock formation. *See* **Dip.**

Subduction zone   A region where one tectonic plate is moving into another and plunging beneath it. The typical picture of a subduction zone is found along the west coast of North America.

Some distance offshore, there is a deep trench in the ocean bottom, running parallel to the shore. These ocean trenches are the deepest parts of the ocean, reaching down to 10 km or more. The plunging plate produces earthquakes, some of them with deep foci. The plunging end of the plate eventually joins the mantle. Collisions with the overriding plate exert upward forces, and earthquakes lift new mountain ranges parallel to the edge of the continent. Through the faults thus produced, magma rises in volcanic eruptions.

Earthquakes and volcanoes are the spectacular features that mark the subduction zones of the world. The major earthquake zones are found along the west coast of the Americas, the east coast of Asia and the Pacific islands, and the Mediterranean

EARTH AND SPACE SCIENCE

Basin. These regions mark the boundaries between tectonic plates.

Sublimation   The phase transition of solid to vapor or vice versa. If the partial pressure of water vapor in the atmosphere is less than 4.58 mm of mercury, water does not normally exist as a liquid. It is either solid or vapor. Heat added to ice when the pressure is that low changes the ice directly into water vapor. *See also* **Precipitation**.

Submarine canyon   *See* **Seafloor topography**.

Submergent shoreline   The surface features of the sea border when the landmass is subsiding. Typically, the shoreline tends to become quite irregular as the sea invades the land to the level of a contour. River valleys become tidal estuaries, hilltops become islands, and ridges become promontories or peninsulas. Good harbors are most often found on submergent shorelines. If the land is eroded by valley glaciers, submergence converts the valleys into steep-sided bays often many kilometers long, called fiords.

Some submergent shorelines are different. If the original landmass was a flat plain, the submergent shoreline is quite straight.

Subsurface water   Water held in the soil. It is held in three zones: the zone of saturation, the capillary fringe, and the zone of aeration. Consider what happens to water falling onto a perfectly dry soil. The first water adheres to the surface of soil particles in the upper layer, leaving air spaces between the grains. Additional water infiltrates through these air spaces to moisten the soil particles lower down. The *zone of aeration* becomes deeper, from the top down.

When the zone of aeration reaches impervious bedrock, water can infiltrate no farther. It begins to fill the spaces between the soil particles, producing a *zone of saturation*. As more water enters, the zone of saturation deepens, rising into the zone of aeration. If the zone of saturation reaches the surface, the surface is muddy and no more water can enter.

Water in the zone of saturation is called groundwater, and its upper surface is the water table. If a well is dug into the water table, water flows out of the zone of saturation into the well.

There is another layer between the water table and the zone of aeration. It is called the capillary fringe. Water rises into this region from the water table by capillary action. The fringe is anywhere from a centimeter to a meter thick, depending on the size and shape of the soil particles. The soil is saturated in this region, but water does not flow out of it into a well.

Sun   Our star. It is a smallish star on the main sequence, where it will remain for another 10 billion years. The visible diameter is 1.4 million km, about 109 times the diameter of the earth. Its mass is about 75% hydrogen and 23% helium: the rest is just about every known element. As a main sequence star, it receives its energy from a thermonuclear reaction that turns hydrogen into helium at the rate of 600 million tons per second. The reaction occurs deep inside the sun, where the temperature reaches several million degrees.

Radiation from the sun's interior cannot penetrate its atmosphere, so we can see only the radiation from the atmosphere. The luminous part of the atmosphere is a layer some 250 km thick called the photosphere. It is made of many elements, all in gas phase, with a pressure of only a few pascals. The temperature of the visible photosphere is about 6800 K, or 11,700°F.

The photosphere is surrounded by a transparent layer of gases up to 3000 km thick, called the chromosphere. It is visible only during a total eclipse. Outside this, also visible during an eclipse, is the corona. It has an extremely low density and high temperature and is several million kilometers thick.

Sunspots   Spots in the photosphere that are about 1500 K cooler than the surrounding material. They usually last a few days. On the average, the number of sunspots reaches a maximum every 11 years.

Supernova   A star that suddenly flares up, increasing its luminosity by a factor of hundreds of millions. Supernovas occur in the Milky Way galaxy about once every 30–50 years and last from several months up to a few years. A large part of the star is blown off into space. It is thought that a supernova is produced when too much material falls into the degenerate core of a large red giant. The pressure becomes too great for the degenerate electrons to support the extra material, and the star collapses in a few seconds. This releases an enormous amount of gravitational energy, which blows the outer part of the star into space.

Surplus   *See* **Water budget**.

Syncline   In a folded rock system, a troughlike structure in which the sides slope upward away from the center. *See also* **Anticline**.

T **Talus**   Accumulated rock debris at the bottom of a steep slope or cliff.

Tectonic forces   The forces within the crust of the earth that produce deformation and faulting. They are the chief causes of mountain building.

Tectonic plates   The large, continent-sized pieces of the earth's crust. *See* **Plate tectonics**.

Temperate climate   Hot, dry summers and cool, moist winters.

Temperature   The property of a system that determines the direction of heat transfer. By definition, heat always travels of itself from a system of higher temperature to a system of lower temperature. No heat is transferred between systems of equal temperature. For methods of measuring temperature, *see* **Thermometer**, Physics section, page 20-48.

The temperature of stars is determined by studying the light they emit. *See* **Radiation**.

Tephra   *See* **Volcano**.

Terminal moraine   *See* **Glacial deposits**.

Terrace   *See* **Wave erosion**.

Thermometer   *See* Physics section, page 20-48.

Thunder   Violent sound waves produced by lightning.

Thunderhead   A cumulonimbus cloud in which a thunderstorm develops.

Thunderstorm   A violent storm characterized by thunder and lightning. It begins with a rapid and substantial upward flow of air, as occurs in a deep low at a cold front. Condensation within the air produces a cloud that grows rapidly into a turbulent cumulonimbus cloud, or thunderhead, that is several kilometers deep. Within the cloud, rising air currents separate electric charge, so that the upper part of the cloud becomes positive and the lower part negative. The accumulated electric charge discharges—within the cloud, to a different cloud, or to the ground. This is a lightning bolt. The sudden heating of the air produces the thunder.

Tidal wave   A misnomer for **tsunami**.

Tides   The daily cycle of rise and fall of local sea level. The water level of the ocean is highest in two regions: the side toward the moon and the side opposite the moon. The reason for the tide is that the moon's gravitational pull is strongest on the parts nearest the moon. The direct high tide (facing the moon) occurs because the moon is pulling the water away from the earth. The indirect high tide (opposite the moon) is the result of the fact that there the earth is closer to the moon than the sea is; the earth is pulled away from the sea.

As the earth turns, the direct high tide faces the moon. Because the moon is also moving, the full cycle of two high tides takes 23 hours and 10 minutes instead of 24 hours. The actual moment of high tide is rarely when the moon is directly overhead because the flow of the water is strongly modified by local conditions of sea bottom and coastline.

The sun also has an influence on the tides. It is not as strong as the moon's influence because the sun is so far away. At the time of the new moon the sun and the moon are on the same side of the earth. This is the time of spring tide, when the high tide is highest and the low tide is lowest. Another spring tide occurs when the moon is full and the sun is acting on the indirect high tide. When the moon is in its quarter phases, the sun is 90° away from the moon in the sky, and the tidal range is least. This is called the neap tide.

Till   An unsorted glacial deposit, as in a moraine. *See* **Glacial deposits**.

Time   The order of events, as measured by clocks. A clock can be any device that operates cyclically. Conventional time is measured by the rotation of the earth.

Local time is based on the length of the day. Roughly, a day is the time elapsed between one noon and the next, where noon is defined as the moment when the sun is on the meridian. That time period is divided into 24 hours. Practically, this definition must be modified to take account of the fact that the length of the solar day varies throughout the year (*see* **Solar day**). The length of the day is defined as the mean solar day.

Since the location of the sun in the sky changes throughout the day, local time is not the same everywhere. An arbitrary standard called Greenwich mean time (GMT) is adopted. This is the local time at the zero meridian, passing through the astronomical observatory in Greenwich, England. Local time differs from GMT according to longitude. Since the earth rotates eastward, local time is later than GMT at points east of the Greenwich meridian, at a rate of 1 hour for each 15° longitude. This rate of time variation with longitude amounts to 360° in 24 hours.

For practical purposes, local time is not useful because it differs so much from place to place. The world is therefore divided into standard time zones. Each zone covers approximately 15° of longitude, deviating somewhat for convenience. Standard time is taken as constant throughout each zone and changes abruptly by 1 hour in passing from one zone to the next.

Topographic map   *See* **Contour map**.

Tornado   A cyclonic storm of small size and extreme violence. Tornados often occur in groups, along the line of a cold front where there are thunderstorms. A tornado starts as a funnel-shaped vortex descending from a cloud. The vortex is usually several hundred meters across, and the winds in it may reach 500 km/hour. Pressure at the center is extremely low, perhaps several hundred millibars lower than the surrounding pressure.

During the hour or so that a tornado lasts, it can do enormous damage. The fierce winds can blow down a house. Additional damage is done because of the extremely low pressure at the center of the tornado. The pressure difference between the air inside and the air outside the house can cause the roof to blow off.

Transit   The passage of an inferior planet, Mercury or Venus, across the face of the sun.

Transpiration   The process by which water vapor passes into the atmosphere from the leaves of plants. It is an important part of the atmospheric water cycle. *See* **Water budget**.

Transported sediment   *See* **Deposition**.

Transverse wave   *See* Physics section, page 20-50.

Trellis drainage   A stream pattern found in regions where the underlying rock is folded and eroded. The streams follow the outcrops of the less resistant rock.

Trench   *See* **Subduction zone**.

Tropical storm   A cyclonic storm developed over warm, tropical water, which may develop into a hurricane. *See* **Hurricane**.

Tropical year   *See* **Solar year**.

Tropic of Cancer   The northernmost latitude reached by the sun when it is directly overhead, 23½° north. *See* **Solstice**.

Tropic of Capricorn   The southernmost latitude reached by the sun when it is directly overhead, 23½° south. *See* **Solstice**.

Tsunami   A wave in the ocean produced by underwater earthquakes or landslides. Tsunamis are usually not noticed at sea, but become steeper and higher when they reach shallow water. When they break on shore, they can do enormous damage.

Turbidity current   A flow of unstable sediments along the sea bottom. Sand may pile up on the continental shelf until it reaches an unstable condition. Any slight disturbance then causes a sudden collapse of the accumulation, and the sediments flow down the continental slope and settle in the deep sea.

Typhoon   *See* **Hurricane**.

U

Ultraviolet rays   Electromagnetic waves with wavelengths shorter than visible light, from about 3×10^{-9} to 4.5×10^{-7} m. The sun's energy is rich in ultraviolet rays, and they are capable of doing much damage to the skin and may produce cancer. Most of the sun's UV light is filtered out by a layer of the atmosphere called the ozone layer.

Without this protection, much of the life on earth would be destroyed. Currently there is concern that the ozone layer is being damaged by the introduction of various chemicals into the atmosphere, particularly the chlorinated hydrocarbons.

Unconformity A boundary between two distinctly different geologic series of sediments. For example, a geologist may trace a series of horizontal sediments into the crust and reach a point at which the series suddenly stops. This point rests on the upper surface of a series of folded rocks. This indicates that the folded rocks were eroded down and the horizontal sediments subsequently deposited on top of the older rock. An unconformity represents a gap, of unknown duration, in the geologic record.

Underground drainage A system in which streams are all underground. It occurs in limestone regions where the rock has been eroded chemically. *See also* **Karst topography**.

Uplift The rising of mountains. An important cause of uplift is apparently the conversion of eclogite into basalt under a geosyncline (*see* **Basalt-eclogite hypothesis**).

A whole set of phenomena is associated with uplift; *see* **Continental drift**; **Earthquake**; **Isostasy**; **Seafloor spreading**; **Volcano**. For the usual results of rapid uplift, *see* **Mountain building**.

Uranus The seventh planet, 2.9 billion km from the sun. It is a large planet, with a radius of 24,000 km; its period of rotation is not accurately known but appears to be about 16½ hours. It is so far from the sun that it takes 84 years to complete an orbit. The tilt of its axis from its orbital plane is 84°, so that its south pole sometimes points almost directly at the sun or at us. We sometimes see it almost directly over its poles. It is the only planet that spins toward the west instead of the east.

Uranus, like the other giant planets, is surrounded by an atmosphere of hydrogen and helium. There is also considerable methane in the atmosphere, which gives it a greenish color. It has five satellites visible from earth. When a space probe took a close look at Uranus in January 1986, it found a world quite different from anything else in the solar system. Winds blow at 350 km/hour in its atmosphere, which is marked by colored bands. Its magnetic field is tilted at 55° from its axis, so its north magnetic pole is nowhere near its north geographic pole.

The space probe found a system of icy rings, but these are different from those of other planets in that they contain good-sized boulders. It also found eleven additional satellites, some of them embedded in the rings. Several of the satellites are extremely strange, one is smooth on the surface although everything around it is pitted with meteor craters. Another satellite is practically split in half by a deep fault.

Uranus is visible, but it is so far away that it is easily mistaken for a star. It was discovered in 1781.

Urban heat island A city region in which the temperatures are usually higher than in surrounding areas. Cities produce extra heat by burning fuel, and reradiation into space is inhibited by atmospheric pollution and a high carbon dioxide concentration.

Usage *See* **Water budget**.

Valley glacier A glacier formed high in a mountain. It begins in a snow field, high enough on a mountain that the snow does not melt completely during the summer. The snow accumulates year by year. The weight of accumulated snow compresses the lower layers to form ice grains and, ultimately, solid ice. The glacier flows down a valley by a process of regelation, producing a characteristic kind of erosion called alpine glaciation.

Van Allen layer A belt of charged particles, mostly electrons, surrounding the earth. The belt is doughnut-shaped, is centered 3000 km above the equator and extends out about 15,000 km. The particles are entrapped by the earth's magnetic field.

Vapor pressure *See* **Partial pressure**.

Vein A mineral deposit left by precipitation from solution and formed in a crack in the bedrock.

Venus The second planet, 109 million km from the sun. It is almost as big as the earth, with a radius of 6100 km; it rotates very slowly, taking 243 days to turn once, it revolves around the sun once every 224 days, so its year is shorter than its day. The surface is covered by a dense fog. The Pioneer space probes found that the lower atmosphere is clear up to 32 km and consists mostly of carbon dioxide. Above that level, the fog is a layer of sulfuric acid vapor 12 km thick. The upper layer sustains winds up to 200 km/hour.

In 1991, the Magellan space probe mapped the surface of Venus, using radar to penetrate the atmosphere. The planet has many active volcanoes, and there are extensive lava plains, as well as mountains up to 7 miles high. The surface also has enormous craters, produced by meteorite impacts.

Because it is closer to the sun than the earth, Venus is never seen during the middle part of the night. However, it is often the brightest object in the sky when it appears in the hours after dusk or before dawn. Like the moon, Venus has phases. When it is on the other side of the sun from us, it is full. As it comes toward us, it goes through quarter and crescent phases, and its apparent size increases greatly.

Vertical sorting Formation of layers of sediment characterized by differences in the size and shape of the particles. Particles settle faster if they are larger, denser, or rounder than others. If the water is fairly deep and quiet, they form graded beds on the bottom.

Volcanic ash Rock and dust blown into the atmosphere by a violent volcanic eruption. The ash sometimes spreads very widely over distant parts of the earth. A deposit of ash can serve as a useful time marker in a sedimentary bed, since the deposit occurred at the same time in widely different regions.

Volcanic glass Obsidian.

Volcanic neck The remnant, after erosion, of an old volcano. The lava solidified in the central pipe of a volcano may be much harder than the rest of the cone. When the cone has been eroded away, the central lava core stands as an isolated peak. The Devil's Tower in Wyoming is one of the largest volcanic necks.

Volcano A vent in the crust through which magma from the mantle is extruded. The extruded material is either lava or tephra. Lava flows as a viscous

EARTH AND SPACE SCIENCE

liquid from the top and sides of the volcano. Tephra is material blown violently out of the top of the crater. It cools quickly and descends to the earth in the form of ash and solid rocks called volcanic bombs. Magma containing water vapor or other gases produces tephra as the gases expand when rising to the surface. Volcanic cones are classified into three types.

A *cinder cone* is made of tephra. Characteristically, it is a small volcano with a wide crater at the top and steep sides. Tephra, blown out the top, piles up along the sides at its angle of repose.

A *shield volcano,* such as the ones that make up the Hawaiian Islands, has a broad, flat shape. It is formed by lava overflowing from an enormous crater or running out through cracks in the flanks of the cone. These cones may be many kilometers wide at the base and can grow to great height with only gentle slopes down the sides.

Composite cones, such as Etna and Mount St. Helens, are made of alternate layers of lava and tephra. They can grow to large size but are not as large as the largest shield volcanoes. The characteristic shape is a fairly steep, often concave profile, sloping to a point at the top with a crater in it. The lava of the crater can gradually solidify until much of the central pipe is solid. Internal pressure cannot be released until it reaches tremendous values. Then, the entire mountain may explode. The most violent volcanic eruptions are tephra eruptions of composite volcanoes.

 **Water budget** The input and usage of water of a given region, analyzed on a monthly basis. It is a reflection of the climate. Water budget is analyzed in terms of the following parameters.

Income is the total amount of precipitation during the month. It is expressed as the equivalent depth of liquid water that falls, in millimeters.

Storage is the water in the zone of aeration of the soil, where it is accessible to plants. On the average, the most water that can be kept in storage is equivalent to 100 mm of precipitation.

Evapotranspiration is the process that removes water from the soil by direct evaporation and by transpiration through the leaves of plants.

Potential evapotranspiration is the amount of evapotranspiration, limited only by climatic factors, that would occur if there were unlimited water in storage. *Actual evapotranspiration* may be less than potential evapotranspiration, since evapotranspiration must stop when storage water is exhausted.

Based on these parameters, four stages in the water budget process can be identified.

Surplus occurs if additional precipitation falls on the land when the storage is full. Any precipitation falling when the storage is at 100 mm will run off the surface or find its way into rivers through the groundwater.

Usage is the stage during which evapotranspiration is greater than precipitation, so that water is withdrawn from storage.

A period of *deficit* occurs when storage drops to zero. During any month when there is no water in storage, evapotranspiration is equal to precipitation and all the water that comes in goes out. A desert is in a constant state of deficit.

Recharge occurs when there is room for more water in storage and precipitation is greater than evapotranspiration. The excess income adds to storage.

Water cycle The changes through which water enters the earth's atmosphere and hydrosphere The main features are as follows.

Evapotranspiration converts water in the land and sea into vapor in the air.

Condensation converts the vapor into the droplets and ice particles in clouds.

Precipitation returns the water to the land and sea.

Runoff and *infiltration* carry the water, through rivers, back to the sea.

Water gap A valley cut across a ridge by a stream. A water gap can exist only when the stream is there before the ridge. As the ridge is uplifted by tectonic processes, the river cuts through it as fast as it rises.

Water supply The availability of water for human use. Water is made available by several methods.

Rivers are the chief source of usable water. They are often dammed to impound a large quantity of water in a reservoir.

Gravity wells are wells dug into the groundwater. This is a practical source of water wherever the water table is not too far below the surface.

Artesian wells tap a water supply deep in the bedrock. They are dug into an aquifer, which is a layer of porous rock, such as sandstone, between two layers of impervious rocks, such as shale. If the porous layer outcrops in a humid region, water can flow into it and be conducted for large distances. Artesian wells even provide water to oases in the middle of the Sahara Desert.

Desalination provides fresh water for islands and desert regions by removing the salt from seawater. This is a very expensive process, not suitable for very large scale use.

Glaciers, melted, provide water for some towns and cities in northern and mountainous regions.

Water table The upper surface of the zone of saturation. To obtain groundwater, a well must be dug through the water table into the zone of saturation.

Wave deposits Sediments deposited by coastal waves. When waves break on a beach, the water flows back under the incoming water, creating an undertow. This carries sand, especially the finer particles, out to sea. They are deposited under the line of breakers, creating a sandbar. If the shoreline emerges, the sandbar becomes a line of offshore islands.

The waves do not usually come in directly toward the shore. They have a component of motion parallel to the shore, called a longshore current. This carries sand consistently in one direction along the shore. The sand may be deposited at the mouth of a bay, forming a sand spit. Continued action of this kind may build a bar across the entire mouth of the bay. A lagoon formed this way eventually becomes filled with sediments from the land and turns into a salt marsh.

Wave erosion Abrasion of shorelines by sand carried in by wave action, and transport of the sand. Wherever waves strike a seaside cliff or rocky shore, they carve the rock. They can undercut coastal cliffs, creating caves and leaving large freestanding masses of bedrock in the shallow water. Since the breaking waves do the work, the shore is cut only as far down

EARTH AND SPACE SCIENCE

as sea level. As the wave-cut cliff is cut back from the shore, it leaves a flat, rocky shelf behind, called a terrace.

Wavelength   *See* **Wave**, Physics section, page 20-51.

Weathering   Processes that reduce large pieces of rock to smaller particles. *See* **Chemical weathering**; **Physical weathering**.

Weather map   A map showing the weather conditions at a particular moment. The simplest weather maps contain limited information, such as local temperatures and wind direction and velocity at many points. They always indicate the pressure patterns by the use of isobars. Fronts are generally shown as well. Meteorologists use weather maps to help in making forecasts.

Wet-bulb thermometer   *See* **Dew point**.

Wind   The horizontal movement of air. Air is set into motion by pressure differences, so the wind blows out of a high-pressure region and into a low. Its velocity depends largely on the pressure gradient.

Wind deposits   Particles carried and deposited by the wind. Wind deposits occur on a small scale on seashores, but are chiefly characteristic of deserts, where there are large quantities of wind and few obstructions.

Only the smaller particles can be carried by the wind, so a wind deposit contains nothing larger than sand grains. The grains are carried by bouncing along the ground. This gives them a rounded shape and a frosted surface. If there is slight irregularity on the ground the sand grains drop to the ground as they go over the top onto the leeward side. The pile of sand grows, and it eventually forms a dune. Dunes always migrate downwind because sand grains blow over the windward face of the dune and drop down over the top into the leeward side.

Wind erosion   A process of sandblasting, wind blows loose sand against bedrock and wears it away. This is effective only in desert climates, where sand lies loose on the surface. Since the blowing sand is usually no more than 1 m above ground level, wind erosion tends to undercut the bedrock where it strikes.

Wind vane   A device, usually arrow shaped, for indicating the direction of the wind. It is usually pivoted at the center of gravity and exposed to the wind on top of a building. The wind exerts its largest force on the tail of the arrow, so the device swings around until its head is pointed in the direction from which the wind comes.

Wind velocity   The speed of the wind, in miles or kilometers per hour. To learn how it is measured, *see* **Anemometer**.

 **Zeeman effect**   The splitting of a line of a spectrum due to the presence of a strong magnetic field. In the gas where the line is produced, a magnetic field separates an energy level within the atoms into two or more levels. This shows up in the spectrum as a double or triple line.

Zenith   The point on the celestial sphere directly overhead.

Zodiac   The twelve constellations in line around the ecliptic.

Zodiacal light   A faint band of light sometimes seen stretching across the sky around the ecliptic. It is due to the reflection of sunlight from particles in space. The light is sometimes concentrated in a space directly opposite the sun; it is then known as *gegenschein* (German, "shining against").

Zone of aeration   *See* **Subsurface water**.

Zone of saturation   *See* **Subsurface water**.

EXHIBIT 5.4
Earth Science Reference Tables and Charts

PROPORTIONS

Kepler's harmonic law of planetary motion
: (Period of Revolution)^2 $\propto$ (mean radius of orbit)^3 : $T^2 \propto R^3$

Universal law of gravitation
: Force $\propto \dfrac{\text{mass}_1 \times \text{mass}_2}{(\text{distance between their centers})^2}$: $(F \propto \dfrac{m_1\, m_2}{d^2})$

Potential energy
: Potential Energy $\propto$ mass $\times$ acceleration due to gravity $\times$ height : PE

Kinetic energy
: Kinetic Energy $\propto$ mass $\times$ (velocity)^2 : $(KE \propto mv^2)$

EQUATIONS

Per cent deviation from accepted value
: Deviation (%) $= \dfrac{\text{difference from accepted value}}{\text{accepted value}} \times 100$

Circumference of a circle
: Circumference = 2π radius : $(C = 2\pi r)$ Note: $\pi = 3.14$

Volume of a sphere
: Volume $= \dfrac{4}{3}\pi$ (radius)^3 : $(V = \dfrac{4}{3}\pi r^3)$

Volume of a rectangular solid
: Volume = length $\times$ width $\times$ height : $(V = lwh)$

Density of a substance
: Density $= \dfrac{\text{mass}}{\text{volume}}$: $(D = \dfrac{m}{v})$

Eccentricity of an ellipse
: Eccentricity $= \dfrac{\text{distance between foci}}{\text{length of major axis}}$: $(e = \dfrac{d}{L})$

Gradient
: Gradient $= \dfrac{\text{change in field value}}{\text{change in distance}}$

Relative humidity
: RH(%) $= \dfrac{\text{vapor pressure of dewpoint temp}}{\text{vapor pressure of dry-bulb temp}} \times 100$

Latent Heat $\begin{vmatrix} \text{solid} \longleftrightarrow \text{liquid} \\ \text{liquid} \longleftrightarrow \text{gas} \end{vmatrix}$
: Heat (cal) = mass $\times$ heat of fusion
: Heat (cal) = mass $\times$ heat of vaporization

Heat energy (lost or gained)
: Heat (cal) = mass $\times$ temp change $\times$ specific heat

PHYSICAL CONSTANTS

RADIOACTIVE DECAY DATA

Radioactive Element	Disintegration	Half-life
Carbon 14	$C^{14} \rightarrow N^{14}$	5.6×10^3 years
Potassium 40	$K^{40} \rightarrow Ar^{40}$	1.4×10^9 years
Uranium 238	$U^{238} \rightarrow Pb^{206}$	4.5×10^9 years
Rubidium 87	$Rb^{87} \rightarrow Sr^{87}$	6.0×10^{10} years

PROPERTIES OF WATER

Heat of fusion of water	= 80 cal/g
Heat of vaporization of water	= 540 cal/g
Density of water (3.98°C)	= 1.00 g/ml

ASTRONOMY MEASUREMENTS

Measurement	Earth	Sun	Moon
Mass (m)	5.98×10^{24} kg	1.99×10^{30} kg	7.35×10^{22} kg
Radius (r)	6.37×10^3 km	6.96×10^5 km	1.74×10^3 km
Average density	5.52 g/cm³	1.42 g/cm³	3.34 g/cm³

SPECIFIC HEATS OF COMMON MATERIALS
(in cal/g C°)

Water	= 1.0
Ice	= .5
Water Vapor	= .5
Dry Air	= .24
Basalt	= .20
Granite	= .19
Iron	= .11
Copper	= .09
Lead	= .03

EARTH AND SPACE SCIENCE

ECONOMICS
AND BUSINESS

Ability-to-pay principle   A tax theory according to which taxes should be levied according to the taxpayer's capacity to pay. Progressive income taxes are based on the ability to pay principle. *See* **Benefit principle**; **Progressive taxes**.

Absolute advantage   In international economics, the capability of one producer to produce a given good or service using fewer resources than any other producer. Not as important in determining trade patterns as comparative advantage. *See* **Comparative advantage**.

Accelerated depreciation   Any one of a number of allowed methods of calculating depreciation that permit greater amounts of deductions in earlier years than permitted under the straight-line method, which assumes equal depreciation during each year of the asset's life.

Accelerationist theory   The economic theory that holds that unemployment cannot be permanently reduced through inflation. *Contrast with* **Phillips curve**.

Accelerator   In economics, the proposition that a firm's investment responds to its growth in output. If the rate of growth of output falls, say, from 4% to 2%, firms reduce their investment even though output continues to increase.

Accounting principles   Rules and guidelines of accounting. They determine such matters as the measurement of assets, the timing of revenue recognition, and the accrual of expenses. The "ground rules" for financial reporting are referred to as Generally Accepted Accounting Principles (GAAP). To be "generally accepted," an accounting principle must have "substantial authoritative support" such as by promulagation of a Financial Accounting Standards Board (FASB) pronouncement. Accounting principles are based on the important objectives of financial reporting. An example of an accounting principle is accrual.

Accrual accounting   Accounting method whereby income and expense items are recognized as they are earned or incurred, even though they may not have been received or actually paid in cash. The alternative is cash basis accounting.

Actuarial science   Branch of knowledge dealing with the mathematics of insurance, including probabilities. It is used in ensuring that risks are carefully evaluated, that adequate premiums are charged for risks underwritten, and that adequate provision is made for future payments of benefits.

Ad valorem   Latin for according to value. An ad valorem tax is assessed on the value of goods or property; not on the quantity, weight, extent, etc.

Affirmative action   Steps taken to correct conditions resulting from past discrimination or from violations of a law, particularly with respect to employment.

AFL-CIO   The largest labor union in the United States. The AFL-CIO was formed in 1955 when the AFL, or American Federation of Labor, founded in 1881, merged with the CIO, or Congress of Industrial Organizations, formed in 1935 as a splinter group of the initial AFL.

Agency shop   Situation in which an employer may hire any worker without regard for whether the worker belongs to a union, but once hired the worker must either join or pay dues to a union as a condition for retaining his or her job. *See* **Closed shop**; **Open shop**; **Union shop**.

Aggregate demand   The total amount of goods and services demanded by consumers, firms, and the government at different price levels in a given period of time. Keynesian economics focuses on aggregate demand, in particular on the effect of government fiscal and monetary policies in affecting the aggregate demand. *See* **Aggregate supply**; **Fiscal policy**; **Keynesian economics**; **Monetary policy**.

Aggregate demand curve   The aggregate demand curve describes the relationship between price levels and the sum of the quantity of output that consumers (for consumption), firms (for investment), and governments are willing to purchase. The aggregate demand curve shows a negative relationship between the price level and quantity of output demanded: the higher the price level, the less output will be demanded. Together with the aggregate supply curve, the aggregate demand curve can be used to determine the equilibrium level of real GDP and the equilibrium price level. *See* **Aggregate supply curve**.

Aggregate supply   In macroeconomics, the total amount of goods and services supplied to the economy at alternative price levels in a given period of time. Aggregate supply is at the center of supply-side economics, which espouses policies designed to increase the aggregate supply of goods and services. *See* **Aggregate demand**; **Laffer curve**; **Marginal tax rate**; **Supply-side economics**.

Aggregate supply curve   The aggregate supply curve describes the relationship between price levels and the quantity of output that firms are willing to provide. The aggregate supply curve shows a positive relationship between the price level and quantity of output supplied: the higher the price level, the more output will be supplied. Together with the aggregate demand curve, the aggregate supply curve can be used to determine the equilibrium level of real GDP and the equilibrium price level. *See* **Aggregate demand curve**.

Agribusiness   Large-scale production, processing and marketing of food and nonfood farm commodities and products. Agribusiness is a major commercial business. California has the largest concentration of agribusiness in the United States.

Alien corporation   Company incorporated under the laws of a foreign country regardless of where it operates. Alien corporation can be used as a synonym for the term foreign corporation. However, foreign corporation also is used in U.S. state law to mean a corporation formed in a state other than that in which it does business.

Allocation of resources   Central subject of economics: manner in which scarce factors of production are apportioned among producers, and in which scarce goods are apportioned among customers.

Amortization
1. Reduction of a debt by periodic charges to assets or liabilities, such as payments on mortgages.
2. In accounting statements, the systematic write-off of costs incurred to acquire an intangible

asset, such as patents, copyrights, goodwill, organization, and expenses.

Analytical review   Auditing process that tests relationships among accounts and identifies material changes. It involves analyzing significant ratios and trends for unusual change and questionable items. Included in the analytical review process are: (1) reading important documents and analyzing their accounting and financial effects; (2) reviewing the activity in an account between interim and year end, especially noting entries out of the ordinary; (3) comparing current period account balances to prior periods as well as to budgeted amounts, noting reasonableness of account balances by evaluating logical relationships among them (i.e., relating payables to expenses, accounts receivable to sales).

Annuity   Contract sold by life insurance companies that builds investment value tax-deferred and guarantees that at a future time, typically retirement, payments will be made to the beneficiary, called the annuitant. The payments may be fixed (fixed annuity) or variable (variable annuity) and may extend for life or some specified period.

Antitrust acts   Federal statutes that regulate trade in order to maintain competition and prevent monopolies. *See* **Clayton Anti-trust Act of 1914**; **Sherman Anti-trust Act of 1890**.

Applied economics   Use of principles and results of theoretical economic study in the real world, particularly in the formulation of governmental economic policy. *See also* **Keynesian economics**.

Appreciation   In general, any increase in the market value of an asset. When used in international finance, appreciation occurs when a flexible exchange rate changes so that it takes more of a foreign nation's currency to purchase a unit of the domestic nation's currency, or, conversely, when a unit of the domestic nation's currency can purchase more of the foreign currency. *Contrast* **Depreciation**.

Arbitrage   Financial transaction involving the simultaneous purchase in one market and sale in a different market with a profitable price differential. True arbitrage positions are riskfree.

Arm's length transaction   Transaction among parties, each of whom acts in his or her own best interest. Transactions between the following parties would, in most cases, not be considered arm's length: a husband and wife; a father and son; a corporation and one of its subsidiaries.

Assets   Anything owned that has value. *See* **Balance sheet**; *contrast with* **Liabilities**.

Audit   Inspection of the accounting records and procedures of a business, government unit, or other reporting entity by a trained accountant, for the purpose of verifying the accuracy and completeness of the records. It may be conducted by a member of the organization (internal audit) or by an outsider (independent audit). A CPA audit determines the overall validity of financial statements. A tax (IRS) audit determines whether the appropriate tax was paid. An internal audit generally determines whether the company's procedures are followed and whether embezzlement or other illegal activity occurred.

Automatic stabilizers   Certain taxes and forms of government expenditures that fluctuate automatically with business conditions in such a way as to combat the business cycle. The prime example of an automatic stabilizer is unemployment insurance: after a reduction in economic activity, unemployment insurance payments automatically rise, thereby offsetting and reducing some of the initial downturn in spending.

B | **Balanced-budget multiplier** A proposition from Keynesian economics that asserts that a simultaneous increase in government spending financed by an equal increase in taxes raises the real gross domestic product by an amount equal to the increase in government spending. Conversely, a decrease in spending matched by a reduction in taxes leads to an equal decrease in the real GDP. Therefore, the balanced-budget multiplier equals 1.0.

Balance of payments   The system of recording all of a country's economic transactions with the rest of the world during a particular time period. The balance of payments is typically divided into subaccounts, such as the capital and current accounts. The current account covers imports and exports of goods; the capital account covers movements of investments. These subaccounts may show a deficit or surplus; the overall balance of payments, however, will not be in surplus or deficit since every dollar spent on foreign items is returned to buy U.S. goods or securities. *See also* **Balance of trade**.

Balance of trade   The difference over a period of time between the value of a country's imports, such as automobiles and stereos, and its exports of merchandise, such as foodstuffs and computers. When a country exports more than it imports, the balance of trade is in surplus and the country is said to have a favorable balance of trade; when imports predominate the balance of trade is in deficit and is called unfavorable. However, an unfavorable balance of trade does not necessarily mean the country is in a weak economic condition since a strong economy can often lead to increased imports.

Balance sheet   Financial report showing the status of a company's assets, liabilities, and net worth on a given date. The fundamental accounting equation featured on a balance sheet is that assets are equal to liabilities and net worth. Unlike an income statement, which shows the results of operations over a period of time, a balance sheet shows the state of affairs at one point in time. In other words, a balance sheet is a snapshot, not a motion picture. *See* **Assets**; **Income statement**; **Liabilities**; **Net worth**.

Balloon payment   Final payment on a loan when that payment is greater than the preceding installment payments and pays the loan in full. For example, a debt requires interest-only payments annually for five years, at the end of which time the principal balance (a balloon payment) is due.

Bankruptcy   State of insolvency of an individual or an organization, that is, an inability to pay debts. There are two kinds of legal bankruptcy under U.S. law: Chapter 7 or involuntary, when one or more creditors petition to have a debtor judged insolvent by a court; and Chapter 11, or voluntary, when the debtor brings the petition. In both cases the objective is an orderly and equitable settlement of obligations.

Barter   Trade of goods or services directly without use of money. Barter is inefficient compared with

ECONOMICS
AND BUSINESS

trade utilizing money since a barter transaction requires "a double coincidence of wants"; that is, both sides of the transaction must desire what the other person is willing to trade. Although rare in developed countries, during times of extreme inflation barter may become the preferred mode of commerce. Barter is more common in less developed economies.

Base period   Particular time in the past used as the yardstick or starting point when measuring economic data. A base period is usually a year or an average of years; it can also be a month or other time period.

Base year   Particular time in the past used as a yardstick for measuring economic data. For example, the rate of inflation is determined by measuring current prices against those that prevailed in a base year; the real GDP is calculated by valuing the current year's output at prices that prevailed during a base year.

Base-year analysis   Analysis of trends in economic data using parameters from a specified year. Expressing data such as the gross national product in constant dollars uses price levels of a specific base year so as to eliminate the effect of inflation upon the data.

Bear market   Prolonged period of falling prices. A bear market in stocks is usually brought on by the anticipation of declining economic activity, and a bear market in bonds is caused by rising interest rates. *See also* **Bull market**.

Benefit principle   A tax theory that states that taxes should be levied according to the benefits the taxpayer derives from the government expenditures financed by the taxes. For instance, the benefit principle holds that highways should be constructed and maintained through tolls and gasoline taxes paid by those who use the highways. *Contrast with* **Ability-to-pay principle**.

Beta   *See* **Volatility**.

Black Friday   Sharp drop in a financial market. The original Black Friday was September 24, 1869, when a group of financiers tried to corner the gold market and precipitated a business panic followed by a depression. The panic of 1873 also began on Friday, and Black Friday has come to apply to any debacle affecting the financial markets.

Black market   The illegal sale of merchandise. For example, during wars, black markets spring up for restricted goods in short supply. In many countries, black markets for foreign exchange exist owing to government restrictions on the prices that will be paid for foreign currencies, such as the U.S. dollar.

Black Monday   October 19, 1987, when the Dow Jones Industrial Average plunged a record 508 points following drops the previous week, reflecting investor anxiety about inflated stock price levels, federal budget and trade deficits, and foreign market activity. Program trading was a contributing factor.

Blind entry

1. Entry that reveals only its classificatory identity, appropriate debit and credit amounts, and does not include an explanatory description of the transaction.
2. Posting to a ledger account not documented by a journal or other source record.

Blind trust   Trust where assets are not disclosed to their owner. This prevents the underlying asset owner, while in an official public capacity, from being charged with favoring companies in which he owns stock.

Blue chip   Informal term for the common stock of a big, high-quality company with a tradition of profit growth and regular dividends.

Blue-collar   Worker line employee performing a type of work that often requires a work uniform, which may be blue in color, hence blue-collar. Blue-collar workers range from unskilled to skilled employees. They are not exempt from hour and wage laws and therefore must be paid overtime for working more than 40 hours per week.

Blue-sky law   State law regulating the sale of corporate securities through investment banking companies; enacted to prevent the sale of securities of fraudulent enterprises.

Boilerplate

1. Standardized or preprinted form for agreements.
2. Standardized language, as on a printed form containing the terms of a lease or sales contract, often phrased to the advantage of the party furnishing the form, with the expectation that the contract will be signed without being carefully examined.

Bond   A government or corporate security that obligates the issuer to pay the bondholder a specified sum of money, usually at specific intervals, and to repay the principal amount of the loan at maturity. Bondholders have an IOU from the issuer but, unlike the owners of stock, do not have ownership privileges.

Bonded goods   Goods brought into a country that are placed in a bonded warehouse until all duties are paid.

Book value   Value of individual assets, or of a company's stock calculated as original cost less allowances for depreciation. Book value may vary from current market value although accounting principles require that assets be carried at the lower of cost or market values.

Borrowed reserves   Funds borrowed by commercial banks from a Federal Reserve bank for the purpose of maintaining the required reserve ratios. The commercial banks pay interest on these loans; the interest rate is known as the discount rate. *See* **Discount rate**; **Discount window**; **Required reserve ratio**.

Bottom line

1. Net income after taxes.
2. Expression as to the end-result of something. An example is the sales generated from an advertising campaign.

Bridge loan   Short-term loan that is made in expectation of intermediate- or long-term loans, also called a swing loan. The interest rate on the bridge loan is generally higher than on longer term loans. An example would be a temporary loan that is made to permit a closing on a building purchase prior to a closing on long-term mortgage financing.

Brookings Institution   Nonprofit organization in Washington, D.C., which produces scholarly studies of significant economic and political issues and problems.

Budget Estimate of revenues and expenditures for a specified period.

Built-in stabilizers *See* **Automatic stabilizers**.

Bull market Prolonged period of rising securities prices. *See also* **Bear market**.

Business Commercial enterprise, profession, or trade operated for the purpose of earning a profit by providing a good or service. Businesses can be organized as proprietorships, partnerships, or corporations.

Business cycle Recurring periods of expansion and contraction in economic activity with effects on inflation, growth, and employment. A complete business cycle extends from a peak, when the real GDP is at its maximum relative to its trend, to a recession, during which the real GDP falls below its trend, to the trough, where the GDP is at its minimum relative to its trend, to an expansion, when the GDP grows above its trend until it reaches the next peak. Business cycles are irregular, but generally average between two and five years in length.

Buyout Purchase of at least a controlling percentage of a company's stock to take over its assets and operations. A buyout can be accomplished through negotiation or through a tender offer. *See also* **Leveraged buy out**.

By-product Residue arising at various stages in the production of a principal commodity. The by-products of the meat packing industry are glue and hair, for example. Certain industries produce toxic by-products that can become environmental hazards.

Cafeteria benefit plan Arrangement under which employees may choose their own employee benefit structure. For example, one employee may wish to emphasize health care and thus would select a more comprehensive health insurance plan for the allocation of the premiums, while another employee may wish to emphasize retirement and thus allocate more of the premiums to the purchase of pension benefits.

Calendar year Continuous period beginning January 1 and ending December 31. *See also* **Fiscal year**.

Call option *See* **Option**.

Capacity Ability to produce during a given time period, with an upper limit imposed by the availability of space, machinery, labor, materials, or capital. Capacity may be expressed in units, weights, size, dollars, man hours, labor cost, etc. Typically, there are five different concepts of capacity.

Capital In economics, capital is factories, machines, and other man-made inputs into the production process. Economists differentiate between capital—the actual inputs—and the funds used to finance the purchase of the capital. In business, capital refers to the amount of money invested in an enterprise. In personal finance, it usually means the funds, sometimes called principal, put in financial investments, as distinguished from the interest and dividends earned by the capital. *See also* **Working capital**.

Capital account The balance of payments account that keeps track of short—(under one year) and long-term investment funds flowing between the reporting country and foreign countries. Examples of subaccounts include bank deposits, currency holdings, securities transactions, loans, bond issues sold abroad, and direct investment in foreign plant and equipment. A positive capital account balance means more funds have flowed into the reporting country than outward.

Capital asset

1. Asset purchased for use in production over long periods of time rather than for resale. It includes (a) land, buildings, plant and equipment, mineral deposits, and timber reserves; (b) patents, goodwill, trademarks, and leaseholds; and (c) investments in affiliated companies.
2. In taxation, property held by a taxpayer, except cash, inventoriable assets, merchandise held for sale, receivables, and certain intangibles.
3. Fixed asset usually consisting of tangible assets such as plant and equipment and intangible assets such as a patent.

Capital expenditure An acquisition or an improvement (as distinguished from a repair) that will have a life of more than one year. *See* **Capital improvement**.

Capital flight Movement of large sums of money from one country to another to escape political or economic turmoil or to seek higher rates of return. The United States is perceived as a safe haven for capital.

Capital gain The amount by which the market value of a capital asset or security investment exceeds its purchase price. Gains are said to be realized when the asset is sold and unrealized when simply held. Long-term capital gains, defined by the holding period, have at times been subject to favorable tax treatment by the Internal Revenue Service. *See also* **Capital loss**.

Capital goods Goods, such as industrial buildings, machinery, and equipment used in the production of other goods, as well as highways, office buildings, and government installations. In the aggregate such goods influence the country's productive capacity.

Capital improvement Betterment to a building or equipment that extends its life or increases its usefulness or productivity. The cost of a capital improvement is added to the basis of the asset improved and then depreciated, in contrast to repairs and maintenance, which are expensed currently.

Capital intensive Requiring large investments in capital assets. Motor-vehicle and steel production are capital intensive industries. To provide an acceptable return on investment, such industries must have a high margin of profit or a low cost of borrowing. The term capital intensive is sometimes used to mean a high proportion of fixed assets to labor.

Capitalism Economic system with four major traits: (1) private ownership of property exists; (2) property and capital provide income for the individuals and firms that accumulated and own it; (3) individuals and firms are relatively free to compete with others for their own economic gain; (4) the profit motive, that is, the search for profits, is basic to economic life. Although no nation is an example of a pure capitalist society, the United States is organized primarily along capitalist lines. *See also* **Price system**; *contrast with* **Socialism**.

Capital loss   Loss from the sale of a capital asset.

Caps   Limitations, especially those placed on the extent of interest rate or payment adjustments associated with adjustable-rate mortgages. An *annual adjustment* cap places a ceiling on the amount the interest rate can be changed during one year. A *life-of-loan* cap places a ceiling on the interest rate over the loan term. A payment cap limits the amount of change in the monthly payment amount from year to year.

Carrot and stick   Strategy often used in negotiations where one side offers the other something it wants while threatening negative sanctions if the other side does not comply with its requests. Thus a union could offer wage concessions in exchange for better work-rule provisions while threatening to strike if no accommodation can be reached.

Carrying costs   Expenses incurred because a firm keeps inventories, also called *holding costs.* They include interest foregone on money invested in inventory, storage cost, taxes, and insurance. The greater the inventory level, the higher the carrying costs. Term also applies generally to any out-of-pocket costs incurred while an investor has a position. Also called cost of carry.

Cartel   A group of businesses or nations that agree to influence prices by regulating production and marketing of a product. The goal of a cartel is to operate similarly to a monopoly, although most cartels have less control over their industry than would a monopoly. A number of nations, including the United States, have laws prohibiting cartels. The most famous contemporary cartel is the Organization of Petroleum Exporting Countries (OPEC), which has managed to restrict oil production and raise the price of oil. *See* **Monopoly**.

Cash basis accounting   Method of recognizing revenue and expenses when cash is received or disbursed rather than when earned or incurred. Individual taxpayers generally use the cash basis. *Contrast with* **Accrual accounting**.

Cash cow   Business that generates a continuing flow of cash. Such a business usually has well-established brand names whose familiarity stimulates repeated buying of the products. Stocks that are cash cows have dependable dividends.

Cash flow   The cash a company generates from its operations and other activities, such as borrowing money, selling assets, or issuing new stock. The Statement of Cash Flows included in annual reports analyses all changes affecting cash in the categories of operations, investments, and financing. Depending on whether more cash comes in or goes out, we speak of positive or negative cash flow. A business with more assets than liabilities can still go bankrupt if its cash flow is inadequate to meet obligations. In investing, cash flow means net income plus non-cash charges like depreciation, indicating the company's ability to pay dividends.

Caveat emptor   Latin phrase meaning "let the buyer beware." Often this implied that sellers would not be held responsible for defective merchandise. This theory of liability evolved in the past, when goods were simpler and buyers were as able as sellers to judge the quality of an item. Today it is gradually being supplanted by the theory that sellers are liable for harm caused by their goods, particularly when the items are complicated so that the seller has a distinct information advantage over the buyer about the good in question.

Caveat venditor   Latin phrase meaning "let the seller beware." Also known as Caveat subscriptor. This generally implies that sellers rather than buyers will be responsible for defective or harmful merchandise. This is particularly so whenever the seller is held to have superior information relative to the buyer about the qualities and uses of the good being sold.

Central bank   Country's bank that (1) issues currency; (2) administers monetary policy, including open-market operations; (3) holds deposits representing the reserves of other banks; and (4) engages in transactions designed to facilitate the conduct of business and protect the public interest. In the United States, the Federal Reserve System is the central bank.

Certificates of deposit (CD)   Debt instruments issued by banks and savings institutions in various denominations and with fixed maturities ranging from a few weeks to several years. Interest rates are set competitively and premature withdrawals are subject to penalties.

Certified public accountant (CPA)   Accountant who has passed certain exams, achieved a certain amount of experience, reached a certain age, and met all other statutory and licensing requirements of the U.S. state where he or she works. In addition to accounting and auditing, CPAs prepare tax returns for corporations and individuals.

Ceteris paribus   Latin phrase meaning "all other things equal." In other words, when the term "ceteris paribus" is used, it implies that only the factors explicitly mentioned change; all other relevant factors are held constant.

Channel of distribution   Means used to transfer merchandise from the manufacturer to the end user. Intermediaries in the channel are called middlemen. Those who actually take title to the merchandise and resell the goods are *merchant middlemen.* Those who act as broker but do not take title are *agent middlemen.* Merchant middlemen include wholesalers and retailers. Agent middlemen include manufacturer's representatives, brokers, and sales agents. Channels normally range from 2-level channels without intermediaries to 5-level channels with 3 intermediaries. For example, a caterer who prepares food and sells it directly to the customer is in a 2-level channel. A food manufacturer who sells to a restaurant supplier, who sells to individual restaurants, who then serve the customer, is in a 4-level channel.

Chief executive officer (CEO)   Officer who has ultimate management responsibility for an organization. The CEO reports directly to a board of directors, which is accountable to the company's owners. The CEO, usually the chairman of the board or president, appoints other managers to assist in carrying out the responsibilities of the organization.

Clayton Anti-trust Act of 1914   An amendment to the Sherman Anti-trust Act of 1890, the Clayton

Act is a major piece of antitrust legislation that prohibits interlocking directorates, exclusive selling contracts, and price cutting designed to destroy competition. The Clayton Anti-trust Act exempted labor unions from the Sherman Act's prohibition of "combinations in restraint of trade."

Clearinghouse
1. Association, usually formed voluntarily by banks, to exchange checks, drafts, or other forms of indebtedness held by one member and owed to another. Its object is to settle balances between the banks of a city or region with a minimum of inconvenience and labor.
2. In a stock or commodities exchange, an organization to facilitate settlement of the debits and credits of its members with each other.

Closed economy Self-sufficient economic system in which all production and consumption is contained within itself; no commerce (exporting or importing) outside the system itself exists.

Closed shop Organization in which workers are required to be in a union before they can be hired. For all practical purposes, closed shops were made illegal by the Taft-Hartley Act of 1947. *See* **Agency shop**; **Open shop**; **Union shop**.

Closely held corporation Corporation most of whose voting stock is held by a few shareholders; differs from a closed corporation because enough stock is publicly held to provide a basis for trading. Also, the shares held by the controlling group are not considered likely to be available for purchase.

Collective bargaining Process of settling labor disputes by negotiation between the employer and representatives of employees.

Collusive oligopoly Industry containing few producers (oligopoly), in which producers agree among one another as to pricing of output and allocation of output markets among themselves. Cartels, such as OPEC, are collusive oligopolies.

Command economy Economy in which supply and price are regulated or imposed by a central non-market authority. Prime examples are genuine communist economies.

Commercial bank Most common and most unrestricted type of bank, allowed the most latitude in its services and investments. Insurance for depositors may be provided by the Federal Deposit Insurance Corporation.

Commercial paper Short-term debt obligations with maturities ranging from 2 to 270 days issued by banks, corporations, and other borrowers to investors with temporarily idle cash.

Commodity Any tangible good; product that is the subject of sale or barter. Bulk goods such as grains, metals, and foods are traded on a commodities exchange or on the spot market.

Common stock Units of ownership of a corporation. Owners of common stock typically are entitled to vote on the selection of directors and other important matters, as well as to receive dividends on their holdings. In the event the corporation is liquidated, the claims of preferred stockholders, bondholders, and other creditors take precedence over those of common stockholders.

Communism In theory, anticapitalist proposals of Karl Marx and his followers that communal ownership of the means of production is preferable; in practice, economic systems in which production facilities are state-owned and production decisions are made by official policy and not directed by market action.

Company union Labor union usually considered to be very sympathetic to the management of the company where it is located. It therefore may not represent the true interests of its members since it could be compromised by the company.

Comparative advantage The ability to produce a good or service at a lower relative cost than other competitors. In other words, a nation has a comparative advantage in producing those items it does best compared with other nations. Comparative advantage is the cornerstone of international trade: Nations export goods and services in which they have a comparative advantage and import those goods and services in which they have a comparative disadvantage. Comparative advantage is different from absolute advantage. *See* **Absolute advantage**.

Complements Two goods or services that go together, such as peanut butter and jelly. When the price of one goes up, less of both will be demanded; if the price of one falls, more of both will be demanded. *Contrast* **Substitutes**.

Compulsory arbitration Forceful submission of a labor dispute to a neutral third party such as a government body or the American Arbitration Association for resolution; also called *binding arbitration*. This method has been strongly resisted by labor unions and employers who prefer to rely on collective bargaining and associated economic pressure, such as strikes and lockouts, to reach a settlement of such disputes.

Computer conferencing Bringing participants together at different locations to exchange information and discuss problem situations. Conference members can take part in a discussion by computer terminal whenever they wish.

Concentration ratio Measure of competitiveness within an industry. A "four-firm concentration ratio" is commonly formed by adding together the market shares of the four largest firms within the industry. It is generally believed that high concentration ratios are associated with low degrees of competition. Therefore, many economists advocate that the government take action to reduce the concentration in concentrated industries.

Conflict of interest Inconsistency between the interests of a person, such as a public official, in connection with the performance of his duties. Examples are: a judge who decides a zoning case on land he owns; a law firm that represents both plaintiff and defendant.

Conglomerate Corporation composed of companies in a variety of unrelated businesses. An example of a conglomerate would be a company with different branches that manufacture automobile tires, candy, and computers.

Congress of Industrial Organizations (CIO) Labor union formed in 1935 by John L. Lewis as the result of a division with the American Federation of Labor. The major point of dispute was the attempt by Lewis to organize unions on an industry-wide basis rather than the traditional concept followed by the American Federation of Labor. The two organizations merged in 1955.

Conservatism

1. Accounting: Understating assets and revenues and overstating liabilities and expenses. Expenses are recognized sooner, revenues later. Hence reported earnings are lower. Conservatism holds that in financial reporting it is preferable to be pessimistic rather than optimistic since there is less chance of financial readers being hurt relying on the financial statements. Excessive conservatism may result in misguided decisions.
2. Business: cautious and careful attitude, such as not taking excessive risk. An example is a portfolio manager who invests in safe securities.
3. Politics: limited government spending, resulting in lower taxes.

Consolidated balance sheet One that shows the financial position of an affiliated group of companies as though they constituted a single economic unit. The effect of intercompany relationships and the results of intercompany transactions will have been eliminated in the consolidation process. *See also* **Consolidated financial statement**.

Consolidated financial statement Financial statement that brings together all assets, liabilities, and other operating accounts of a parent company and its subsidiaries.

Consortium Group of companies formed to promote a common objective or engage in a project of benefit to all members. The relationship normally entails cooperation and a sharing of resources, sometimes even common ownership.

Constant dollars Dollars of a base year, used as a gauge in adjusting the dollars of other years in order to ascertain actual purchasing power. Sometimes called "inflation adjusted dollars" or "real dollars." *See* **Base year**; **Nominal**; **Real**.

Constant returns to scale A term used in the economic theory of the firm. Constant returns to scale occurs when the long-run average total cost stays the same as output expands. This results when a proportional increase in all inputs causes output to expand by the same proportion. *See* **Decreasing returns to scale**; **Increasing returns to scale**.

Consumer goods Goods bought for personal or household use, as distinguished from capital goods, which are used to produce other goods.

Consumerism Public concern over the rights of consumers, the quality of consumer goods, and the honesty of advertising. The ideology came into full focus in the 1960s after President John F. Kennedy introduced the Consumer Bill of Rights, which stated that the consuming public has a right to be safe, to be informed, to choose, and to be heard. Fuel was added to the fire in 1966 with the publication of Ralph Nader's book *Unsafe at Any Speed,* which attacked portions of the automotive industry. When corruption of government officials in the Watergate scandal of the seventies, and inflation and widespread consumer disenchantment with the quality of many American products were combined with the greater sophistication brought about by consumer advocates, consumerism became a powerful, action-oriented movement. The primary concern of this

force is to fulfill and protect the rights of consumers articulated by President Kennedy more than two decades ago.

Consumer price index (CPI) Price index that measures the cost of goods and services purchased by a "representative" consumer. The CPI is reported monthly by the U.S. Bureau of Labor Statistics. Many pension and wage contracts are tied to changes in the CPI, thereby giving protection against inflation and reduced purchasing power. Also known as the "cost-of-living index."

Consumer surplus The maximum consumers are willing to pay for a good or service minus what they actually pay for the item.

Consumption Household spending on goods and services. Consumption spending accounts for by far the largest fraction of total spending in the economy, about 60% of total spending, that is, 60% of the gross national product. *See* **Gross national product**.

Conversion cost Cost of moving from one kind of equipment or production process to another. Conversion cost is high when converting from a manual system to a computerized system. It includes the cost of new equipment plus training.

Convertible security Corporate security, usually a bond or preferred stock, that is exchangable for another security, usually common stock, at a prestated price. Convertibles pay less income than a straight bond or preferred stock but somewhat higher income than straight common stock and have capital gains potential.

Cooling-off period

1. Interval (usually 20 days) between the filing of a preliminary prospectus with the Securities and Exchange Commission and the offer of the securities to the public.
2. Period during which a union is prohibited from striking, or an employer from locking out employees. The period, typically 30 to 90 days, may be required by law or provided for in a labor agreement.

Cooperative

1. Type of corporate ownership of real property whereby stockholders of the corporation are entitled to use a certain dwelling unit or other units of space. Special income tax laws allow the tenant stockholders to deduct interest and property taxes paid by the corporation; also known as co-op.
2. Organization for the production of marketing of goods owned collectively by members who share the benefits, for example, agricultural cooperative.

Corporate veil Using a corporation to disguise or protect a person's actions. Courts will often pierce the corporate veil to try the underlying person.

Corporation Legal entity, chartered by a U.S. state or by the federal government. It has three chief distinguishing features: (1) limited liability—owners can lose only what they invest and no more; (2) easy transfer of ownership through the sales of stock; (3) continuity of existence. Although a small minority of businesses are organized as corporations, owing to the advantages of limited liability and ease of obtaining funds, corporations account for the overwhelming majority of business within advanced economies. *See* **Limited liability**, **Partnership**; **Proprietorship**.

Correction   Reverse movement, usually downward, in the price of an individual stock, bond, commodity, or index. If prices have been rising on the market as a whole and then fall dramatically, this is known as a *correction within an upward trend*.

Cost accounting   Branch of accounting concerned with providing detailed information on the cost of producing a product.

Cost-benefit analysis   Method of measuring the benefits from a decision, calculating the cost of the decision and then proceeding with the action if the benefits outweigh the costs. It is often said that the government should use cost-benefit analysis when deciding on its projects. Although the basic principle behind cost-benefit analysis is not very controversial, controversy often surrounds a particular calculation of the costs and benefits involved in a project.

Cost-effectiveness   Ability to generate sufficient value to offset an activity's cost. The value can be interpreted as revenue in the case of a business. Public relations is cost effective if it generates new and retains old business.

Cost of capital   Rate of return that a business could earn if it chose another investment with equivalent risk, that is, the opportunity cost of the funds employed as the result of an investment decision. Cost of capital is also calculated using a weighted average of a firm's costs of debt and class of equity.

Cost-of-living adjustment (COLA)   Automatic adjustment of wages or other payments designed to offset changes in the cost of living, usually as measured by the consumer price index. This protects the real purchasing power of the contracts. *See* **Real wage**.

Cost-plus contract   Contract under which the contractor receives payment for total costs plus a stated percentage or amount of profit. A *cost-plus percentage* contract gives the contractor no incentive to economize; on the contrary he would be better off by spending more. A *cost-plus fixed-fee* contract is a more reasonable contract.

Cost-push inflation   Inflation caused by rising costs of productive inputs, such as labor or petroleum, which are passed on by businesses in the form of higher prices. The higher prices then cause inflation. *See also* **Demand-pull inflation**.

Council of Economic Advisors   Group of economists appointed by the president of the United States to provide counsel on economic policy.

Countercyclical policy   Government economic policies designed to dampen the effects of the business cycle. During the inflation of the early 1980s, the action by the Federal Reserve Board to raise interest rates was a countercyclical policy designed to reduce demand and thus end inflationary expansion.

Coupon   The interest rate of an interest-bearing bond. Term comes from once prevalent bearer bonds with actual coupons to be clipped and cashed. The coupon, a stated percentage of a bond's face value, may differ from the same bond's yield, which is the relationship of the coupon to market price.

Craft union   Union of skilled tradespeople sharing comparable trade skills. Most of these unions are organized on a local basis, but are often affiliated with the AFL-CIO. The opposite of a craft union is an industry-wide union, such as the United Auto Workers or the United Rubber Workers.

"Creative accounting"   Management's attempt to "fool around" with its accounting in order to overstate net income. Examples of income management include selling off low-cost basis assets to report gains, unjustifiably lengthening the expected life of an asset to reduce expense (e.g., depreciable life), and underaccruing expenses (e.g., bad debt provisions). To financial statement users, "creative accounting" has a negative connotation.

Creeping inflation   Slow but inexorable continuing inflation that though it seems tolerable in the short run, nonetheless leads to significant long-run price increases. A sustained inflation of 2% per year will cause prices to increase over fivefold in a century.

Critical path method (CPM)   Planning and control technique that optimizes the order of steps in a process given the costs associated with each step. Manufacturing industry uses CPM to plan and control the complete process of material deliveries, paper work, inspections, and production.

Crowding out   Theory that increases in government borrowing—particularly federal government borrowing—raise interest rates, thereby causing individuals and business to defer their borrowing plans. These private sector participants are said to be "crowded out" of financial markets by the government.

Crown jewels   In corporate mergers and acquisitions, target company's most desirable properties, the disposal of which reduces its value and attractiveness as a takeover candidate.

Current account   The balance of payments account that keeps track of the goods and services that flow out of (exports) and into (imports) the domestic country. When the current account is negative, that is, domestic residents have purchased more from foreigners than they have sold to them, the current account is said to be "in deficit." In other words, when the current account is in deficit, imports have exceeded exports.

Cycle billing   Sending invoices to customers systematically throughout the month rather than billing all customers on the same day each month, thus spreading work evenly over time.

Cyclical demand   Demand that varies cyclically over time, usually in response to some effect of season or business cycle. Demand for electricity and Christmas ornaments is seasonally cyclical; demand for housing is affected by the effects of the business cycle upon interest rates.

Cyclical unemployment   Unemployment caused by a downturn in the business cycle.

Data base   Storehouse of related data records independently managed apart from any specified program or information system application. It is then made available to a wide variety of individuals and systems within the organization. In essence, it is an electronic filing cabinet providing a common core of information accessible by a program. An example is a data base of inventory items.

Debenture　Unsecured bond backed only by the integrity and general financial strength of the issuer. *See* **Bond.**

Debt instrument　Written promise to repay a debt; such as a bill, bond, banker's acceptance, note, certificate of deposit, or commercial paper.

Decentralization　Essential decision making and policy formulation done at several locations throughout an organization. The objective is to give decision-making authority to those most directly responsible for the outcome of those decisions, with first-hand experience and knowledge about the issues involved.

Decreasing returns to scale　A term used in the economic theory of the firm. Decreasing returns to scale occurs when the long-run average total cost rises as output expands. In this case, a proportional increase in all inputs causes the output to expand by a smaller proportion. *See* **Constant returns to scale; Increasing returns to scale**.

De facto corporation　Corporation existing in fact, but without the actual authority of law.

Deficit financing　Borrowing by a government agency to make up for a revenue shortfall. Deficit financing stimulates the economy for a time but eventually can become a drag on the economy by pushing up interest rates.

Deficit spending　Excess of government expenditures over government revenue, creating a shortfall that must be financed through borrowing.

Deflation　Actual decline in the prices of goods and services. For instance, prices falling at 3% per year are deflating. Deflation is the reverse of inflation and pertains to decreases in prices; it should not be confused with disinflation, which simply refers to a reduction in the inflation rate.

Deflator　Statistical factor or device designed to adjust the difference between values unaffected by inflation, called real or constant values, and the value as affected by inflation, called nominal or dollar values. *See* **Constant dollars; Real GDP**.

Demand　Economic expression of desire, and ability to pay, for goods and services. Demand is neither need nor desire; the essence of demand is the willingness to exchange value (goods, labor, money) for varying amounts of goods or services, depending upon the price asked.

Demand curve　A curve that shows the relationship between the price of a good or service and the quantity demanded. Demand curves almost always trace out a negative relationship between the price and quantity demanded: A higher price reduces the quantity demanded. A demand curve, together with a supply curve, can be used to determine the equilibrium price and quantity produced of a good or service. *See* **Equilibrium market price; Giffen good; Supply curve**.

Demand deposit　An account at a financial institution, such as a bank, which, without prior notice to the institution, can be immediately withdrawn by check or cash withdrawal. Also informally called "checking accounts." Demand deposits make up the largest fraction of the nation's M1 money supply. *See* **M1**.

Demand-pull inflation　Price increases occurring when the supply of goods and services is not adequate to meet the demand. Often said to result from an excess of demand. *See* **Cost-push inflation**.

Demonetization　Withdrawal from circulation of a specified form of currency. For example, the Jamaica Agreement between major International Monetary Fund countries officially demonetized gold starting in 1978, ending its role as the major medium of international settlement.

Deposit multiplier　*See* **Money multiplier**.

Depreciation　(1) In national income accounting, depreciation is the consumption of capital during production—i.e., the wearing out of plant and capital goods. (2) In business accounting, the law encourages replacement of capital assets by permitting the recovery of cost through tax-deductible charges for depreciation. Acceptable depreciation methods range from straight-line, where equal annual charges are taken over the estimated useful life of the asset, to various methods of accelerated depreciation, where a higher proportion of cost is written off in early years with greater tax benefits. (3) In international finance, depreciation is the decline in the foreign exchange price of one currency relative to another. That is, it takes more of the domestic currency to purchase a unit of a foreign nation's currency.

Depression　Economic condition characterized by a severe recession, that is, a severe curtailment in business activity. The Great Depression of the 1930s was marked by unemployment rates near 25% of the labor force. Although political observers frequently assert that opposition policies have resulted in a "depression," most economists reserve the use of this term to exceptionally deep recessions.

Deregulation　A policy of greatly reducing government regulations, generally advocated as a means to allow freer markets to create a more efficient marketplace so the consumer is better served.

Devaluation　Lowering of the value of a country's currency relative to gold and/or the currencies of other nations. The opposite is *revaluation.*

Direct marketing　Selling via a promotion delivered individually to the prospective customer. Direct marketing differs from general marketing in that the result of a promotion is measurable in terms of response; also, direct marketing is largely dependent upon the use of customer files and lists. Frequently associated with mail order, direct marketing also includes a variety of promotion media such as door-to-door selling, videotex services, newspaper inserts, telemarketing, *take-one* cards, and package inserts. Direct marketing is a more personal type of promotion than advertising. The direct marketer selects the individuals who will receive the promotion, and is the direct recipient of the response, if any. The response may be a purchase, an inquiry, or a referral that can be traced directly back to the individual. Through the use of lists, computer files, and data bases, the fourth "P" of marketing, *place,* is brought to the individual consumer. Direct marketing is utilized by virtually every type of business and organization. However, the primary users are magazine publishers, catalog houses, political campaign organizations, and financial institutions.

Discount rate   The interest rate the Federal Reserve charges commercial banks for loans. *See also* **Discount window**.

Discount window   Place in the Federal Reserve where banks go to borrow funds at the discount rate. Borrowing from the Fed is a privilege, not a right, and banks are discouraged from using the privilege except when they are short of reserves.

Discretionary income   Spendable income remaining after the purchase of physical necessities, such as food, clothing, and shelter, as well as the payment of taxes. Marketers of goods other than necessities must compete for the consumer's discretionary dollars by appealing to various psychological needs, as distinguished from physical needs. When the economy weakens, goods normally purchased with discretionary income are the first to show reduced sales volumes. An expensive perfume will not sell during a depressed economic period, but people will continue to buy food and pay rent.

Discretionary policy   Government economic policy that is not automatic or built into the system. The Federal Reserve Board's implementation of its power to add to or subtract from the money supply and to set the discount rate are examples of discretionary policies.

Discretionary spending power   Government spending capability that is not mandated by law or required automatically within the system.

Diseconomies   Costs resulting from an economic process that are not sustained by those directly involved in the process; also called *negative externalities*. Many types of pollution are diseconomies in that those who pollute do not pay the costs resulting from it and, therefore, neither do their customers.

Disinflation   Slowing down of the rate at which prices increase—usually during a recession, when sales drop and retailers are not always able to pass on higher prices to consumers. Not to be confused with deflation, when prices actually drop.

Disposable income   The after-tax income left available for households to spend on consumption or to save.

Diversification   Reducing risk by putting assets in the securities of different companies or in several categories—common stocks, bonds, and precious metals, for instance. Standard advice from most financial analysts is to diversify so that one bad choice does not wipe out the value of an entire portfolio.

Diversified company   Company that has many products and services serving several markets. A company may attempt to manufacture the products itself, or it may acquire or merge with an ongoing organization. The advantages of diversification include being better able to weather business cycles since some product lines or services may be countercyclical. *See also* **Conglomerate**.

Divestiture
1. Loss or voluntary surrender of a right, title, or interest.
2. Remedy by which the court orders the offending party to rid itself of assets before the party would normally have done so. This remedy is sometimes used in the enforcement of the antitrust laws, whereby a corporation must shed a part of its business to comply with the law.

Dividend   Distribution of earnings to shareholders in the form of money, stock, scrip, or, rarely, company products or property. The amount is decided by the board of directors and is usually paid quarterly. Taxpayers must declare dividend income in the year dividends are received. Mutual funds pay their own dividends, usually quarterly or monthly, using dividend and interest income earned from the fund's investments.

Dollar cost averaging   Buying a mutual fund or securities using a consistent dollar amount of money each month (or other period). More securities will be bought when prices are low, resulting in lowering the average cost per share.

Domestic corporation   Corporation doing business in the U.S. state in which it is incorporated. In all other U.S. states, its legal status is that of a foreign corporation.

Double-entry bookkeeping   Record of transactions that require entries in at least two accounts. Every transaction is reflected in offsetting debits and credits. For instance, when a telephone bill is accrued at year end, (1) telephone expense must be recorded and (2) accrued expenses payable must be increased.

Dow Jones Industrial Average   *See* **Stock index**.

Downside risk   Estimate of an investment's possible decline in value and the extent of the decline, taking into account the total range of factors affecting market price.

Downturn   Shift of an economic or stock market cycle from rising to falling. The economy is in a downturn when it moves from expansion to recession, and the stock market is in a downturn when it changes from a bull market to a bear market.

Dumping   Selling goods abroad below cost in order to eliminate a surplus or to gain an edge on foreign competition. Dumping by foreigners is illegal in the United States and most other countries.

 **Earned income**   Income from personal services. Earned income generally includes wages, salaries, tips, and other employee compensation. Compensation includes items that can be excluded from gross income, such as lodging, or meals furnished for the employee's convenience. Earned income also includes any net earnings from self-employment. Pension and annuity payments are not included.

Easy money   State of the money supply when the Federal Reserve allows ample funds to build in the banking system, thereby making loans easier to get. This sort of policy is often said to lead to lower unemployment, higher growth rates of real GDP, and higher inflation rates. *Contrast* **Tight money**.

Econometrics   Use of computer analysis and statistical techniques to describe in mathematical terms the relationship between key economic forces. Econometric models are statistically estimated, numerical relationships between different factors in the economy. They are often used to forecast the outcomes of proposed government policies .

Economic indicators   Key statistics showing the state of the economy. Among indicators classified as

ECONOMICS AND BUSINESS

leading rather than lagging, are the average work-week, weekly claims for unemployment insurance, new orders, vendor performance, stock prices, and changes in the money supply. *See also* **Lagging indicators**.

Economic profit   A payment in excess of what is necessary to get something done. *See* **Normal profit**.

Economics   The study of how people choose among alternative uses of their scarce resources. Macroeconomics studies the aggregate economy; microeconomics deals with smaller economic units, such as individual firms, consumers, and industries.

Economic sanctions   Internationally, restrictions upon trade and financial dealings that a country imposes upon another for political reasons, usually as punishment for following policies of which the sanctioning country disapproves.

Economic system   Basic means of achieving economic goals inherent in the economic structure of a society. Major economic systems are capitalism, socialism, and communism.

Effectiveness lag   The time it takes from the start of a government policy until it affects the economy.

Efficiency   In economics, when people produce all that can be produced, given their resource endowment. To produce more of one good or service, an efficient economy must produce less of other goods or services. An efficient economy is producing on the production possibility curve. *See* **Production possibilities curve**.

Elastic demand   When the price elasticity of demand for a product exceeds 1.0. In this case, an increase in the price of the good reduces the total amount spent on the good; a decrease in the good's price raises the total amount spent. *See* **Elasticity**; **Price elasticity of demand**; *contrast* **Inelastic demand**.

Elasticity   Responsiveness of one variable to another; both changes are expressed as percentages. For instance, the price elasticity of supply is the percentage change in the quantity supplied for every 1% change in the price; the income elasticity of demand is the percentage change in the quantity demanded induced by a percentage change in real income.

Engel's law   Observation, by 19th-century economist Ernst Engel, that as family income rises, the proportion of it devoted to expenditures for food declines.

Enterprise zone   Designated area within which businesses enjoy very favorable tax credits and other advantages, such as planning exceptions. Enterprise zones are generally found in derelict inner urban districts that have experienced significant employment declines.

Equity   In investments, ownership interest—stock as opposed to bonds. In lending, the difference between the amount an asset, such as a borrower's home, could be sold for and the claims, such as mortgages, against it.

Equation of exchange $MV = PQ$, where M is the money stock, V the velocity of money, P the price level, and Q the real GDP. The equation of exchange is a cornerstone of the quantity theory. *See* **Quantity theory of money**; **Velocity**.

Equilibrium   In general terms, a situation in which there is no automatic tendency toward change. For instance, the equilibrium price for a firm to charge is the price that yields the maximum profit. At any other price, the firm is sacrificing profits and so will soon change the price. At the profit maximizing price, no forces are automatically set in motion for the firm to change its price. *See* **Equilibrium market price**.

Equilibrium market price   The price at which the quantity demanded equals the quantity supplied. Also termed the "market clearing price," for at this price all the goods or service supplied is purchased—taken off the market—by demanders.

Ergonomics   Science of designing machines and equipment for the dynamics and needs of human physiology to increase productivity and comfort.

Escalator clause   Provision in a contract allowing cost increase to be passed on. In an employment contract, an escalator clause might call for wage increases to keep employee earnings in line with inflation. In a lease, an escalator clause could obligate the tenant to pay for increases in fuel or other costs.

Eurocurrency   Money deposited by corporations and national governments in banks away from their home countries, called *Eurobanks*. The terms Eurocurrency and Eurobanks do not necessarily mean the currencies or the banks are European, though more often than not that is the case. The Eurodollar is only one of the Eurocurrencies, though it is the most prevalent. Also known as *Euromoney*.

Eurodollar   U.S. dollar held as a deposit in a European commercial bank (Eurobank). Eurodollars were created after World War II by U.S. defense and foreign aid expenditures. Since the dollar was then backed by gold, it became a popular reserve currency in Europe and it is still commonly used for settling international transactions. Most Eurodollars are now created by the purchase of European goods by Americans.

European Economic Community (EEC)   Economic alliance formed in 1957 by Belgium, France, Italy, Luxembourg, The Netherlands, and West Germany to foster trade and cooperation among its members. Trade barriers were gradually abolished and import duties were standardized with non-EEC countries. Membership was subsequently extended to Great Britain, Ireland, and Denmark (1973); Greece (1984); and Spain and Portugal (1986).

European Monetary System (EMS)   Proposed agreement among European Economic Community members to limit fluctuations in exchange rates among their currencies within an agreed set of bounds.

Excess profits tax   Extra federal tax placed on the earnings of a business. Such tax may be levied in times of national emergency, such as wartime, and is designed to increase national revenue. It is distinguishable from a *windfall profits tax*, designed to prevent excessive corporate profit in special circumstances.

Excess reserves   Reserves held by banks above the amount they are legally required by the Federal Reserve to keep on hand. Banks generally try to minimize the amount of their excess reserves since excess reserves have no return. *See* **Federal**

Reserve System; **Required reserve ratio**; **Required reserves**.

Exchange rate　Price at which one country's currency can be converted into another's. The exchange rate between the U.S. dollar and the British pound is different from that between the dollar and the West German mark, for example. Most exchange rates float freely and change slightly each trading day; some rates are fixed and do not change as a result of market forces.

Excise tax　Federal or state tax on the sale or manufacture of a commodity, usually a luxury item, for example, federal and state taxes on alcohol and tobacco.

Expansion　Period of time during which the real GDP is growing vigorously. Expansions bridge the trough of the business cycle with its peak. Most expansions last between 1½ and 4 years. *See* **Business cycle**.

Expenditure multiplier　The number by which an initial increase in spending must be multiplied to give the final increase in the real GDP. The expenditure multiplier is important in the Keynesian analysis of macroeconomics. In particular, Keynesian analysis concludes that the expenditure multiplier exceeds 1.0, so that an increase in government spending or investment spending leads to a larger increase in real GDP. For instance, if the expenditure multiplier equals 8, a $10 billion increase in government spending causes an $80 billion increase in the real GDP. The expenditure multiplier in the simple Keynesian model equals 1 divided by (1 - marginal propensity to consume). Also called the government spending multiplier, the investment multiplier, and the spending multiplier. *See* **Balanced-budget multiplier**; **Keynesian economics**; **Tax multiplier**.

Export-Import Bank (EXIMBANK)　Bank set up by Congress in 1934 to encourage U.S. trade with foreign countries. Its activities include (1) financing exports and imports; (2) granting direct credit to non-U.S. borrowers to help finance the purchase of U.S. exports; and (3) providing export guarantees, insurance against commercial and political risk, and discount loans.

Exports　Goods or services shipped outside a country. *Contrast* **Imports**.

Externalities　*See* **Negative externalities**; **Positive externalities**.

F　**Factoring**　Form of financing whereby accounts receivable are purchased from a manufacturer by a financial company, called a factor. The factor earns the difference between the face amount of the collected receivable and the discounted price paid to buy it. Factoring is commonly used to finance seasonal businesses, such as those in the garment industry, with a long lead time between manufacture and retail sale.

Factor of production　Any input used to produce output. The main factors of production are (1) land—all forms of natural resources, including farmland, mines, oil wells, forests, and so on; (2) labor—all human effort, such as unskilled labor, the talents of an athlete, or the skills used by a surgeon; (3) capital—includes all man-made inputs, such as

factories, machinery, highways, and transportation equipment.

Fair market value　Price at which an asset or service passes from a willing seller to a willing buyer. It is assumed that both buyer and seller are rational and have a reasonable knowledge of relevant facts.

Fair trade　Term used in retailing that refers to an agreement between a manufacturer and retailers that the manufacturer's product be sold at or above an agreed-upon price. In many states, fair-trade agreements were incorporated into and enforceable by state laws. However, in 1975, Congress passed the Consumer Goods Pricing Act, which prohibits the use of resale price maintenance laws in interstate commerce. This act has worked effectively to eliminate fair-trade arrangements.

Fascism　Doctrine; collection of concepts; and dictatorship by government of a country, often involving hostile nationalistic attitudes, racism, and private economic ownership under rigid government control. A fascist regime is often militarily belligerent.

Favorable trade balance　Situation where the value of a nation's exports is in excess of the value of its imports.

Feasibility study　Determination of the likelihood that a proposed product or development will fulfill the objectives of a particular investor. For example, a feasibility study for a proposed housing subdivision should (1) estimate the demand for housing units in the area; (2) estimate the absorption rate for the project; (3) discuss legal and other considerations (4) forecast cash flows; and (5) approximate investment returns likely to be produced.

Featherbedding　Work rules requiring payment to employees for work not done or not needed. One variation is for a union to preserve existing jobs by prohibiting the use of new technology.

Fed　*See* **Federal Reserve System**.

Federal Deposit Insurance Corporation (FDIC)　Federal agency established in 1933 that insures (within limits) funds on deposit in member banks. Prior to the creation of this agency, depositors had no guarantee that they would get back their funds if the bank in which the funds were deposited failed. This frequently led to "runs" on weak banks during which all depositors tried simultaneously to withdraw their deposits from the bank. Such runs have been greatly reduced by the presence of FDIC insurance. In 1989, Congress passed savings and loan association bailout legislation that reorganized FDIC into two insurance units: The *Bank Insurance Fund (BIF)* continues the traditional FDIC functions with respect to banking institutions; the *Savings Association Insurance Fund (SAIF)* insures thrift institution deposits, replacing the *Federal Savings and Loan Insurance Corporation (FSLIC)*, which ceased to exist.

Federal funds　Funds deposited by commercial banks at Federal Reserve banks, including funds in excess of bank reserve requirements. Banks may lend federal funds to each other on an overnight basis at the federal funds rate.

Federal funds rate　Interest rate charged by banks with excess reserves when loaned to other banks needing overnight loans to meet reserve requirements. The federal funds rate is an important interest rate in the economy since it is continuously monitored by the Federal Reserve. The Federal Reserve often tries to influence and keep the federal funds rate with the bounds it has determined for its policies.

Federal Open Market Committee (FOMC)　The key committee in the Federal Reserve System. The FOMC sets monetary policy for the Federal Reserve. It is composed of the seven Federal Reserve Board governors, the president of the New York Federal Reserve regional bank, and, on a yearly rotating basis, four of the presidents of the other eleven Federal Reserve regional banks. The chairman of the FOMC is one of the governors. The chairman is appointed by the president of the United States and confirmed by the Senate.

Federal Reserve Board　Governing board of the Federal Reserve System. Its seven members are appointed by the president of the United States subject to Senate confirmation and serve 14-year terms. One term expires every two years. The terms are set at 14 years in an attempt to remove this position from "short-run" political influence.

Federal Reserve System　System established in 1913 to regulate the U.S. monetary and banking system. The Federal Reserve System (the Fed) is composed of 12 regional Federal Reserve banks and all commercial banks that have elected to become part of the system. The Federal Reserve Board oversees the entire system. *See also* **Discount rate**; **Federal Open Market Committee**; **Federal Reserve Board**; **Monetary policy**; **Open market operations**.

Federal Trade Commission (FTC)　Federal agency established in 1914 to foster free and fair business competition and prevent monopolies and activities in restraint of trade.

Fiat money　A money that is not backed by gold or any other valuable good. In other words, a money whose value in exchange as money vastly exceeds its value as a commodity. (For example, the value of the paper used in a dollar bill falls far short of its value as a dollar bill.) Most currencies today, such as the dollar, are fiat monies.

Fiduciary　Person, company, or association holding assets in trust for a beneficiary. The fiduciary is legally responsible for investing money prudently for the beneficiary's financial well-being. Executors of wills and estates, receivers in bankruptcy, and trustees who administer assets for underage or incompetent beneficiaries are examples of fiduciaries. Most states have laws regulating fiduciary investments and preventing fiduciaries from acting in their own interests.

Financial future　Futures contract based on a *financial instrument.* Such contracts usually move under the influence of interest rates. As rates rise, contracts fall in value; as rates fall, contracts gain in value. Examples of instruments underlying financial futures contracts are U.S. Treasury bills and notes, Government National Mortgage Association (Ginnie Mae) pass-throughs, foreign currencies, and certificates of deposit.

Financial market　Market for the exchange of capital and credit in the economy. Examples of financial markets are stock markets, bond markets, commodities markets, and foreign exchange markets.

Financial planner　Professional who analyzes personal financial circumstances and prepares a program to meet financial needs and objectives. Financial planners, who may be accountants, bankers, insurance agents, lawyers, real estate or securities brokers, or independent practitioners, should have knowledge of wills and estate planning, retirement planning, taxes, insurance, family budgeting, debt management and investments. Some sell financial products, whereas others simply advise. Several organizations accredit financial planners.

Financial statement　Written record of the financial status of an individual, association, or business organization. The financial statement includes a balance sheet and an income statement (or operating statement or profit and loss statement) and may also include a statement of changes in working capital and net worth.

Firm　General term for a business, corporation, partnership, or proprietorship.

First in, first out (FIFO)　Method of inventory valuation in which cost of goods sold is charged with the cost of raw materials, semi-furnished goods, and finished goods purchased "first" and in which inventory contains the most recently purchased materials. In times of rapid inflation, FIFO inflates profits, since the least expensive inventory is charged against cost of current sales, resulting in *inventory profits.* As a consequence, last-in, first-out (LIFO) inventory valuation has become a more popular method, since it reduces current taxes by eliminating inventory profits.

Fiscalist　Economist who prefers that government affects the economy by raising and lowering taxation and/or government spending; contrasts with monetarist.

Fiscal policy　Federal taxation, spending, and debt policies designed to level the business cycle, achieve full employment, and keep the inflation rate low. Fiscal policy is set by the actions of the Congress and president. Fiscal policy is administered separately from monetary policy, although the goals are the same.

Fiscal year　Any continuous 12-month period used by a business or government as its accounting period. *See also* **Calendar year**.

Fixed costs　Costs incurred by a firm that do not change as the firm's output increases or decreases. For example, the rent that a firm must pay on its premises is a fixed cost since the rent must be paid for the length of the contract regardless of the amount the firm produces. Ultimately the rental contract will come up for renewal, at which time the rent becomes a variable rather than a fixed cost. *See* **Variable cost**.

Fixed exchange rate　A foreign exchange rate between the currencies of countries that is pegged by government actions. At the Bretton Woods International Monetary Conference in 1944, a system of fixed exchange rates was set up, which lasted until the early 1970s, when it was replaced with a system of flexible exchange rates. *See* **Flexible exchange rate**.

Flexible exchange rate　System in which a country's foreign exchange rate between its currency and the currencies of different countries is free to move in response to market forces. *Contrast with* **Fixed exchange rate**.

Flextime   Scheduling concept that allows for non-traditional work hours to be employed on a systematic basis. Hours can be arranged for different times or periods of time to accommodate such aspects as efficiency, traffic, motherhood, disabilities, continuous operations, etc.

Float

1. Amount of funds represented by checks that have been issued but not yet collected.
2. Time between the deposit of checks in a bank and payment. Due to the time difference, many firms are able to "play the float," that is, to write checks against money not presently in the firm's bank account.
3. The issue of new securities, usually through an underwriter.

Floating exchange rate   *See* **Flexible exchange rate**.

Foreign exchange   Instruments employed in making payments between countries—paper currency, notes, checks, bills of exchange, and electronic notifications of international debits and credits.

Foreign exchange rate   Price at which one country's currency can be converted into another's. Under the current system of flexible exchange rates, these values change from day to day. *See* **Fixed exchange rate**; **Flexible exchange rate**.

Foreign trade zone   Separate, enclosed place near a port where goods may be brought for storage, inspection, packaging, or other processes; also called *free trade zone*. No duties are assessed while the goods are in the foreign trade zone.

401(k) plan   Plan that allows an employee to contribute pretax earnings to a company pool, which is invested in stocks, bonds, or money market instruments; also known as a salary reduction plan. The contributions as well as earnings on them are only taxed when withdrawn. Annual contributions are limited to $7000.

Free enterprise   Conduct of business without direct government interference; conducting business primarily according to the laws of supply and demand; risking capital for the purpose of making profit.

Free market   Market in which there is little or no control or interference by government or by any other powerful economic force or entity, such as a monopoly, cartel, or collusive oligopoly.

Free port   Port where no duties are imposed on ships that load or unload.

Functional obsolescence   Decline in value due to changing tastes or technical innovation.

Future   Common name for a futures contact, an agreement to buy or sell a specific amount of a commodity at a particular price on a stipulated future date. Futures originated as ways for farmers to protect (hedge) their crops against adverse price changes. Traded on various commodities exchanges composing the futures market, futures are widely used for hedging purposes, for financial speculation, and for investment purposes. Futures are traded on a wide variety of agricultural and mineral commodities as well as currencies and financial instruments, including stock indexes.

GDP   *See* **Gross domestic product**.

GDP gap   The difference (gap) between actual and full employment output. *See* **Inflationary gap**.

General ledger   Formal ledger containing all the financial statement accounts of a business. It contains offsetting debit and credit accounts. Certain accounts in the general ledger, termed *control accounts,* summarize the details booked on separate subsidiary ledgers.

Generally Accepted Accounting Principles (GAAP)   Conventions, rules, and procedures that define accepted accounting practice, including broad guidelines as well as detailed procedures.

General partner   In a partnership, a partner whose liability is not limited. All partners in an ordinary partnership are general partners. A limited partnership must have at least one general partner.

Giffen good   A good or service whose demand decreases—rather than increases—when its price goes down. Conversely, the demand will increase when its price increases. This is the case when the item is a strongly inferior good so that the income effect of a higher price, which motivates an increase in demand, outweighs the substitution effect from the increase in price—which motivates a decrease in demand. Giffen goods apparently do not occur or are very scarce in reality. *See* **Income effect**; **Inferior good**; **Substitution effect of a price change**.

GNP   *See* **Gross domestic product**.

Golden handshake   Early retirement incentives given to an employee by a firm. The nature of the incentives varies from an acceleration of retirement benefits to a direct cash award.

Golden parachute   Lucrative contract given to top executives of a company. It provides lavish benefits in case the company is taken over by another firm, resulting in the loss of the job. A golden parachute might include generous severance pay, stock options, or a bonus payable when the executive's employment at the company ends.

Gold fixing   Daily determination of the price of gold by selected gold specialists and bank officials in London, Paris, and Zurich. The price is fixed at 10:30 A.M. and 3:30 P.M. London time every business day according to the prevailing market forces of supply and demand.

Gold standard   Monetary system under which units of currency are convertible into fixed amounts of gold. Such a system is said to be anti-inflationary. The United States has been on the gold standard in the past but was taken off in 1971. *See also* **Hard currency**.

Government spending multiplier   *See* **Expenditure multiplier**.

Grandfather clause   Provision included in a new rule that exempts from the rule a person or business already engaged in the activity coming under regulation.

Graveyard shift   Work shift in the middle of the night; third shift in a manufacturing operation. The graveyard shift usually begins at midnight and ends at 8 A.M., although there are variations.

Great Society   Set of economic and social programs advocated by President Lyndon Johnson, with the objectives of eradicating poverty, increasing employment, improving environmental and urban conditions, and fostering rapid economic growth.

Gresham's law   Theory in economics that holds that bad money drives out good money. The "bad money", which is overvalued or mutilated, is spent and the "good money", which is fully valued or intact, is hoarded and thereby driven from use as a mechanism of exchange. This law is named for Sir Thomas Gresham, who was master of the mint in the reign of Queen Elizabeth I.

Gross domestic product (GDP)   The value of all goods and services produced by a country. It is distinguished from gross national product (GNP), which includes net income from abroad. Effective November 1991 the U.S. Department of Commerce decided to use GDP rather than GNP in official economic statistics on the theory that GDP provides a better guide to changes in domestic production and is a better tool than GNP for steering economic policy. The majority of industrial economies in the world favor GDP.

Gross national product (GNP)   *See* **Gross domestic product (GDP)**.

Hard currency   Currency recognized internationally to be relatively stable in value and readily acceptable in most international transactions. Examples of hard currency are the U.S. dollar, the Swiss franc, and the West German mark.

Hard goods   Durable merchandise such as televisions, appliances, hardware, furniture, or recording equipment. *See also* **Soft goods**.

Heavy industry   Traditional production industries in the auto, steel, rubber, petroleum and raw material areas, that require high capitalization and the production of large quantities of output. Heavy industry employs many people and is often beset by environmental impacts.

Hedge   Strategy used to offset business or investment risk. A perfect hedge is one eliminating the possibility of future gain or loss. Also called *hedging*.

High-yield bond   Bond that has a credit rating below the lowest investment grade, which is BBB. Such bonds are issued by companies lacking long records of stable sales and earnings and having questionable balance sheet strength. They pay a higher yield to compensate for the greater risk of default. Term is often used synonymously with junk bond, although bond professionals feel the latter has a pejorative connotation not warranted by the generally good payment performance of these issues.

Historical cost   Accounting principle requiring that all financial statement items be based on original cost or acquisition cost.

Horizontal merger   The combination into one business of two companies that sell similar products. For instance, the purchase of J.C. Penney by Sears would be a horizontal merger. Horizontal mergers are often deemed likely to lead to increased market concentration and adverse economic behavior. At the limit, a horizontal merger could produce a monopoly or near monopoly. Therefore, horizontal mergers are usually carefully scrutinized by government agencies, such as the

Federal Trade Commission. *See* **Concentration ratio**; **Federal Trade Commission**; **Monopoly**; **Vertical merger**.

Horizontal union   Craft union whose organization includes all workers in a particular craft or skill throughout an industry, region, or country.

Human capital   Skills and ability acquired by people through schooling and on-the-job training.

Hyperinflation   Inflationary episode in which the currency becomes virtually worthless. The classic example is Germany in the mid 1920s, when it eventually cost billions of marks to mail a letter or buy bread.

Implementation lag   The time it takes between the government's recognition that a particular economic policy is desirable and when the policy is put in place.

Import quota   An imposed limit upon the quantity of a good or service that may be brought into a country or economy over a period of time. Quotas may be imposed by governments or producers themselves.

Imports   Good or service that is produced outside the country in which it is consumed. *Contrast* **Exports**.

Incentive pay   Wage system that rewards a worker for productivity above an established standard. A variation of the piece-rate system developed by Frederick W. Taylor, incentive pay is based on a bonus given to the worker or workers who exceed a given standard production rate within a defined period of time.

Income effect   In microeconomics, the effect on the quantity demands of a good or service when real income changes. If an increase in income results in an increase in the quantity demanded, the good is called a normal good; if the increase in income causes the demand for the good to fall, the good is said to be an inferior good. *See* **Giffen good**; **Inferior good**; **Normal good**; **Substitution effect of a price change**.

Income elasticity of demand   The percentage change in the quantity demanded of a good or service caused by a 1% change in real income.

Income policy   General term for attempts by the government to stabilize wages and prices and lower inflation through "voluntary cooperation" of firms and unions or by using price and wage controls that make it illegal to raise prices and wages above set limits. *See* **Tax-based income policy**.

Income statement   Financial report that gives a firm's operating results, such as net income or loss, for a specific period of time. The fundamental accounting equation used in preparing an income statement is that revenue minus expenses equals profit or loss. *See* **Balance sheet**.

Income tax   Annual tax on income levied by the federal government and by certain state and local governments. There are two basic types: the personal income tax, levied on incomes of households and unincorporated businesses, and the corporate income tax, levied on the net earnings of corporations. Income taxes account for more than half of the federal government's total revenue. The personal income tax is designed to be progressive, that is, to take a higher percentage of higher incomes than lower incomes. *See* **Marginal tax rate**; **Progressive taxes**; **Regressive taxes**.

Increasing returns to scale   A term used in the economic theory of the firm. Increasing returns to scale occurs when long-run average total cost falls as output expands. In this case, a proportional increase in all inputs causes output to expand by a larger proportion. *See* **Constant returns to scale**; **Decreasing returns to scale**.

Independent union   Union that is not affiliated with the AFL-CIO. The United Mine Workers and the Teamsters are two of the largest independent unions. *See also* **Unaffiliated union**.

Index   Statistical composite that measures changes in stock or bond prices or the economy, often expressed in percentage changes from a base year or from the previous month. For instance, price indices, such as the consumer price index or producer price index, try to measure what happens to average prices. Thus, by the early 1980s the consumer price index had climbed from a value of 100 in 1967 to the low 300s, meaning that the basket of goods the index is based on had risen in price more than 200%. *See* **Base year**; **Consumer price index**; **Inflation rate**; **Producer price index**.

Individual Retirement Account (IRA)   Tax-deferred fund into which individual employees can contribute up to $2000 annually. Income level and eligibility for an employee pension plan determine whether or not the employee's contribution is tax-deductible.

Industrialist   Individual involved in the business of industry. The term evolved from the early industrial period, when large trusts and monopolies were formed by a group of business people referred to as industrialists.

Industrial Revolution   Period marking the introduction of mass production, improved transportation, technological progress, and the industrial factory system. In the United States this period is generally agreed to have begun at the time of the Civil War (1861–1865).

Industrial union   Organization of all crafts within an industry under one union. The CIO under the leadership of John L. Lewis used the industrial union concept to organize General Motors, United States Steel, and Ford Motor Company. Industrial unionism was the basis of the original break from the AFL, which organized by craft.

Industry standard   Orderly and systematic formulation, adoption, or application of standards used in the industrial sector of the economy. An industrial standard is a generally accepted requirement to be met for the attainment of a recurrent industrial objective. In the automotive industry, standardized tire sizes are an example.

Inelastic demand   When the price elasticity of demand for a product is less than 1.0. In this case, an increase in the price of the good raises the total amount spent on the good; a decrease in the good's price lowers the total amount spent. *See* **Elasticity**; **Price elasticity of demand**; *contrast* **Elastic demand**.

Infant industry argument   Claim that developing sectors of the economy need protection against international competition while they establish themselves. In response to such pleas, the government may enact a tariff or quota to stifle foreign competition. *See* **Quota**; **Tariff**.

Inferior good   A good or service that people demand less of when their incomes increase. Hamburger is an example: When poorer people find that their income has increased, they buy less hamburger and more steaks. *Contrast* **Normal good**.

Inflation   General rise in the prices of goods and services. Inflation is measured using a price index. *See* **Cost-push inflation**; **Demand-pull inflation**; **Index**; **Inflation rate**.

Inflationary gap   When the aggregate demand for goods and services exceeds the aggregate supply, thus causing prices to rise if the economy is at full employment (also known as demand-pull inflation) or bringing about increases in production and reductions in unemployment if the economy is not at full employment.

Inflationary spiral   Episode of inflation in which price increases occur at an increasing rate, and currency rapidly loses value.

Inflation rate   Rate of change of prices, that is, the growth rate of the price level. Two primary U.S. indicators of the inflation rate are the consumer price index and the producer price index, which track changes in prices paid by consumers and by producers. The inflation rate can be calculated on an annual, monthly, or other basis. *See* **Base year**; **Consumer price index**; **Index**; **Producer price index**.

Injections   Term used in Keynesian analysis of the aggregate economy, an injection is any form of spending other than consumption, such as investment and government spending. *See* **Keynesian economics**; *contrast* **Leakages**.

Insider   As defined by the *Securities Act of 1934,* corporate director, officer, or shareholder with more than 10% of a registered security, who through influence of position obtains knowledge that may be used primarily for unfair personal gain to the detriment of others. The definition has been extended to include relatives and others in a position to capitalize on inside information.

Institutional investor   Organization that trades large volumes of securities. Some examples are mutual funds, banks, insurance companies, pension funds, labor union funds, corporate profit-sharing plans, and college endowment funds.

Interest rate   Cost of borrowing funds, or return from saving funds, expressed as a percentage rate per time, usually one year. For instance, the interest rate on a car loan may be 11% per year.

International cartel   Cartel that operates internationally. The best-known example in recent years has been the Organization of Petroleum Exporting Countries (OPEC). *See* **Cartel**.

International Monetary Fund (IMF)   Organization set up by the Bretton Woods Agreement in 1944. The primary focus of the IMF is on lowering trade barriers and stabilizing foreign exchange rates. The IMF also helps developing nations pay their international debts; when it does so, it often imposes guidelines aimed at lowering inflation, lowering imports, and raising exports. *See* **Foreign exchange rate**.

Inventory The value of a firm's raw materials, work in process, supplies used in operations, and unsold finished goods.

Investment (1) When used in macroeconomics or national income accounting, refers to the purchase of additional capital goods, that is, to the purchase of the actual goods themselves. (2) When used in finance or more casually, refers to the use of funds to try to earn additional funds. For instance, investment in the stock market may refer to the purchase of stock in order to profit from increases in the price of the stock bought.

Investment company Firm registered with and regulated by the Securities and Exchange Commission (SEC) under the Investment Company Act of 1940 that, for a management fee, invests the pooled funds of small investors in securities appropriate for its stated investment objectives. Investment companies are popularly known as mutual funds.

Investment multiplier *See* **Expenditure multiplier**.

Invisible hand The economic theory; first advanced by Adam Smith in 1776, that people seeking only their own economic welfare will ("as if by an invisible hand") advance the total economic well-being of society. This is often used by advocates of laissez-faire policies to justify deregulation. *See* **Deregulation**; **Laissez-faire**.

Itinerant worker Worker who continually moves from job to job. Itinerant workers are often used for harvesting agricultural crops, and they move from harvest to harvest.

J-curve In economics, description of an expected turnaround in an activity such as foreign trade. The former trend continues for a while, then bottoms out and turns up the right side of the J.

Job sharing Dividing responsibilities and hours of one job between two people. Job sharing is an alternative to layoffs in that both employees can at least have part-time work until economic conditions improve.

Joint Economic Committee of Congress (JEC) Joint House and Senate committee that concerns itself with significant economic matters. It also is charged with keeping abreast of significant economic developments in order to keep Congress informed about them.

Joint venture Agreement by two or more parties to work on a project together. A joint venture, which is usually limited to one project, differs from a partnership, which forms the basis for cooperation on many projects.

Journeyman Skilled tradesperson who has completed a prescribed apprenticeship in a particular craft. The status of journeyman indicates that an individual has mastered all the specific skills of the craft.

Junk bond *See* **High-yield bond**.

Keogh Plan Tax-deferred pension account designated for employees of unincorporated businesses or for persons who are self-employed, either full-time or part-time.

Keynesian economics Body of macroeconomic thought originated by the British economist John Maynard Keynes (1883–1946), whose landmark book, *The General Theory of Employment, Interest and Money,* was published in 1935. Keynes believed that active government intervention (monetary policy and particularly fiscal policy) in the marketplace was the only method of ensuring economic growth and stability. He held that insufficient demand causes unemployment and that excessive demand causes inflation. Keynesian economics has had a great influence on the public economic policies of industrial nations, including the United States. *See* **Fiscal policy**; **Macroeconomics**; **Monetarist**; **Monetary policy**; **Quantity theory of money**; **Supply-side economics**.

Kinked demand curve An economic theory that asserts that firms in an oligopoly face a demand curve with a "kink": If a firm raises its price, no other firm will match the increase so that the initial firm will lose most of its customers. Thus, demand above the equilibrium price is very elastic. However, if the firm lowers its price, all the other firms will match the decrease so that the original firm will not gain many new customers. Therefore, demand below the equilibrium price is very inelastic. *See* **Oligopoly**; **Price elasticity of demand**.

Kondratieff cycle or **Kondratieff wave** Theory of the Soviet economist Nikolai Kondratieff, in the 1920s, that the economies of the Western capitalist world are prone to major up-and-down "supercycles" lasting 50 to 60 years.

Labor force The total number of employed workers and unemployed workers searching for work. In the United States, data on the labor force are released monthly by the U.S. Bureau of Labor Statistics.

Labor intensive Activity in which labor costs are more important than capital costs. Deep-shaft coal mining and computer programming are labor intensive.

Labor-Management Relations Act Taft-Hartley Act of 1947. The Taft-Hartley Act amended the Wagner Act of 1935. Major provisions are (1) It outlawed the closed shop. (2) It instituted an eight-day cooling-off period for strikes threatening the national health or safety. (3) Unions cannot use union monies for national elections. (4) It allowed suits for breach of contract against unions. (5) It outlawed unfair labor practices by unions.

Labor union Association of workers for the purpose, in whole or in part, of bargaining, on behalf of workers, with employers about the terms and conditions of employment.

Laffer curve Curve named for the U.S. economist Arthur Laffer that shows the relationship between marginal tax rates and the government's total tax revenue. Laffer asserted that government tax revenues will increase if marginal tax rates are cut. The basic idea is that the reduction in marginal tax rates will increase the incentive to work and earn income, thereby raising the government's total tax revenues. The Laffer curve is a cornerstone of supply-side economics. *See* **Marginal tax rate**; **Supply-side economics**.

Laggard industry One that lags behind the rest of the economy in output, employment, and contributions to the gross domestic product (GDP). A laggard industry in one nation may not be one in another nation.

Lagging indicators   Series of indicators that follow or trail behind aggregate economic activity. Six lagging indicators are currently published by the government: unemployment rate, business expenditures, labor cost per unit, loans outstanding, bank interest rates, and book value of manufacturing and trade inventories.

Laissez-faire   Economic doctrine that minimal interference of government in business and economic affairs is best. Adam Smith's path-breaking book, *The Wealth of Nations* (1776), described this in terms of an "invisible hand" that would provide for the maximum good of all. The laissez-faire period in U.S. history was ended by the beginning of the twentieth century, when large monopolies were broken up by government action. Keynesian economics advocates a rejection of laissez-faire. The movement toward deregulation of business in recent years is to some extent a return to laissez-faire policies. *See* **Invisible hand**; **Keynesian economics**.

Last in, first out (LIFO)   Method of inventory valuation whereby the most recent goods purchased or manufactured are considered the first ones sold. It shows a lower profit during rising prices than would the First-in, first-out (FIFO) method.

Law of comparative advantage   Principle of economics that nations and people are better off when they produce the goods and services in which they have a comparative advantage and trade for the other goods and services they want. *See* **Comparative advantage**.

Law of demand   Principle of economics that, all other things being equal, the quantity demanded and the price of a product are negatively related: More is demanded at a lower price; less is demanded at a higher price.

Law of diminishing marginal returns   Principle of economics that after some point, as a firm adds more and more units of an input, the input's marginal physical product diminishes; that is, the additional units of the input add less to total output than before.

Law of diminishing marginal utility   Principle of economics that as people consume more of a good in a given time period, its marginal utility declines; that is, the additional units of the good add less to the good's total utility. *See* **Marginal utility**.

Law of increasing relative price   Principle of economics that as more of a good or service is produced, its opportunity cost rises.

Law of supply   Principle of economics that, all other things being equal, the quantity supplied and the price of a product are positively related: More is supplied at a higher price; less is supplied at a lower price.

Leading indicators   An index released monthly by the U.S. Commerce Department designed to help predict the future course of economic conditions. During an expansion, a general rule of thumb says to expect a recession in the future if the index of leading indicators falls for three consecutive months. In a recession, the same rule of thumb predicts an expansion in the future after the index has risen for three consecutive months. *See* **Business cycle**; **Expansion**; **Recession**.

Leakages   A term used in Keynesian analysis of the aggregate economy. Leakages include any allocation of income not spent directly on goods and services, such as savings and taxes. *See* **Keynesian economics**; *contrast* **Injections**.

Lease   Contract granting use of real estate, equipment, or other fixed assets for a specified time in exchange for payment, usually in the form of rent. The owner of leased property is called the lessor, the user the lessee.

Letter of credit   Instrument or document issued by a bank guaranteeing the payment of a customer's drafts up to a stated amount for a stated period. It substitutes the bank's credit for the buyer's credit and eliminates the seller's risk. It is used extensively in international trade.

Leverage   In general: the use of borrowed funds to enhance return or value without increasing investment. Operating leverage refers to the extent to which a business's costs are fixed rather than variable; the more operating leverage a firm has, the more sales it needs to break even, but the more profitable it becomes after that point. Financial leverage refers to the amount of long-term debt a firm has in relation to its equity. Shareholders benefit from financial leverage to the extent the return on borrowed funds exceeds the cost of borrowing.

Leveraged buy out (LBO)   In general, the takeover of a company, financed by using borrowed funds. Most often, the target company's assets serve as security for the loans taken out by the acquiring company or group, which then repays the loans out of the profits of the acquired company or by selling its assets. In recent years, many leveraged buy outs have been financed through issuing high-yield bonds. *See* **High-yield bond**.

Liabilities   Claim by others on the assets of a company or individual. If assets are what are owned, liabilities are what are owed. Casually equivalent to "debt."

Lien   A creditor's claim against property. For example, a mortgage is a lien against a house; if the mortgage loan is not paid, the house can be seized and sold to satisfy the debt. Liens may be granted by courts to satisfy judgments. A mechanic's lien attaches to buildings and structures until contractors and suppliers are paid in full.

Limited liability   A feature of the corporate form of business organization that means each owner of the business is not liable for the debts of the company beyond the amount he or she invested in the company. Therefore, if a company goes bankrupt owing its creditors $100 million, the owners of the business are not personally liable for the debt.

Limited partner   Member of a partnership whose liability for partnership obligations is limited to the investment in the partnership. A limited partner is not allowed to take active part in the management of the partnership. Limited partnerships have always been useful for tax shelters. However, under the Tax Reform Act of 1986, limited partnerships are ruled *passive investments* and their tax benefits are severely limited. General partners have unlimited joint and several liability, and manage the partnership.

Line and staff organization   Delineation of organizational authority between management personnel (staff) having overall planning and direction responsibilities and operational personnel (line) having direct job performance responsibilities. Staff is advisory to the line function.

Liquidity   The ease with which an asset, such as a bond or a stock, can be converted into money: the easier this conversion, the more liquid is the asset.

Long run   In microeconomics, the period of time it takes for a firm to change all its inputs, including its plant size and its equipment. The long run varies between firms in different industries: it takes less time for a hot dog vendor to change all of his or her inputs than for General Motors. *See* **Short run**.

Lorenz curve   A diagram that indicates the distribution of income among income groups. The percentage of the population is shown on the horizontal axis, and the percentage of income is on the vertical axis. If there were complete equality of income, the Lorenz curve would be a 45° line.

M1   The most popular measure of the money supply. Ml includes only cash held by the public plus checking accounts. Also called the narrow money supply.

M2   Called the broad measure of the money supply, M2 is an alternative measure of the money supply that contains more assets than M1. Included in M2 are all the assets in M1 plus savings accounts, time deposits under $100,000, money market mutual fund shares, and a few other minor assets. *See* **M1**; **Money**.

Macroeconomics   Study of a nation's economy as a whole as well as the forces that shape the nation's aggregate economic condition. The effects of government monetary and fiscal policies on such factors as unemployment, gross domestic product, and inflation are a prime concern of macroeconomics.

Malthusian Law of Population   Proposition by the early 19th-century philosopher Thomas Malthus that economic growth occurs more slowly than population growth and that, therefore, general prosperity is impossible. Malthus did not reckon with the very rapid increases in productivity brought on by industrialization.

Managed currency   Currency whose international value and exchangeability is heavily regulated by its issuing country.

Managed economy   Economy in which considerable government intervention takes place in order to direct economic activity. Socialist and communist economies are managed much more than capitalist economies, which rely more upon market forces to direct economic activity.

Management by Objective (MBO)   Planning and control method of management that seeks congruence between management and employee goals. Performance goals are jointly agreed upon by management and the employee and subsequently evaluated.

Management Information System (MIS)   System providing uniform organizational information to management in the areas of control, operations, and planning. MIS usually relies on a well-developed data management system, including a data base for helping management reach accurate and rapid organizational decisions.

Marginal   When used in economics, generally refers to "a change in" or "an additional unit of" whatever factor or variable is being discussed. For example, marginal cost refers to a change in cost caused by producing an additional unit of output.

Marginal cost   The increase or decrease in costs that result by producing either one unit more or less output. Determining marginal cost is important to the firm's decision whether to expand or contract output.

Marginal efficiency of capital   Annual percentage yield earned by the last additional unit of capital; that is, the return a firm earns by increasing its capital by a unit. The marginal efficiency of capital measures the return from additional investment; the interest rate is the cost of making an investment. As long as the marginal efficiency of capital of an additional investment exceeds the interest rate, firms will make the investment in new capital. *See* **Investment**.

Marginal physical product (MPP)   The addition to total output due to an added unit of an input.

Marginal propensity to consume (MPC)   The proportion of additional disposable income (expressed as a decimal) that will be consumed, rather than saved, by a consumer or the entire economy. If 90 cents of an additional dollar of income will be consumed, then the MPC = 0.90. The MPC plays a key role in Keynesian economics since the MPC affects the size of the expenditure and tax multipliers. *See* **Expenditure multiplier**; **Keynesian economics**; **Marginal propensity to save**; **Tax multiplier**.

Marginal propensity to save (MPS)   The proportion of additional disposable income (expressed as a decimal) that will be saved, rather than spent on consumption, by a consumer or the entire economy. If 10 cents of an additional dollar of income will be consumed, then the MPS = 0.10. The marginal propensity to save plus the marginal propensity to consume equal 1.0, since from an additional one dollar of disposable income, the amount saved plus the amount spent on consumption must equal 1 (dollar). The MPS is important in Keynesian analysis of macroeconomics. *See* **Keynesian economics**; **Marginal propensity to consume**.

Margin requirement   The percentage by which the value of securities bought with borrowed money must exceed the amount of the loan. The Federal Reserve Board imposes an initial margin requirement on customers of securities brokers and dealers. Margin maintenance requirements are imposed by the National Association of Securities Dealers and the New York Stock Exchange as well as by brokerage firms themselves.

Marginal revenue (MR)   The change in total revenue caused by selling one additional unit of output. For a firm in a perfectly competitive industry, the marginal revenue equals the price of the product; for a firm in a monopoly industry, the marginal revenue is less than the product's price.

Marginal revenue product (MRP)   The addition to total revenue when one additional unit of an input (such as capital or labor) is employed.

Marginal tax rate   Amount of tax imposed on an additional dollar of income. In the U.S. progressive income tax system, the marginal tax rate increases as income increases. Supply-side economists hold that this reduces the incentive to be productive and discourages business investment. In urging that marginal tax rates be cut for individuals and businesses, they argue that the resulting increased work effort and business investment would improve economic conditions. *See* **Laffer curve; Progressive taxes; Supply-side economics**.

Marginal utility   The additional satisfaction (utility) a consumer receives from the consumption of one more unit of a good or service.

Market   In economics, a place where products or services are bought and sold, directly or through intermediaries. Also called the marketplace.

Market aggregation   In economic theory, combining supply and cost factors of individual producers in order to create supply and cost factors for an entire market.

Market index   Numbers representing weighted values of the components that make up the index. A stock market index, for example, may be weighted according to the prices and number of outstanding shares of the various stocks.

Marxism   Political, social, and economic theories of Karl Marx. Applied Marxism, in an economy, results in either a communist economy or a heavily socialist economy.

Mature economy   Economy of a nation whose population has stabilized or is declining, and whose economic growth is no longer robust. Such an economy is characterized by a decrease in spending on roads or factories and a relative increase in consumer spending.

Member bank   A commercial, privately owned bank that is a member of the Federal Reserve System. All nationally chartered banks must be members of the Federal Reserve System; state-chartered banks have a choice of whether they will apply to become members.

Mercantilism
1. Seventeenth and eighteenth century economic policy under which trading nations generated wealth and power by exporting manufactured goods in exchange for gold.
2. In modern times, second-rate status of nations having a heavy dependence on imported manufactured goods.

Merchant bank   Financial institution that engages in investment banking, advising clients in mergers and acquisitions, and a variety of other services including security portfolio management. The venerable merchant banks are European, such as Rothschild and Hambro, but with relaxed regulation and increased multinational activity, many American banks now engage in merchant banking.

Merger   Combination of two or more companies into one surviving firm. *See* **Horizontal merger; Vertical merger**.

Micro accounting   Term connoting the accounting for a person, company, or government agency, as distinguished from *macro accounting,* which is the accounting for aggregate economic activities of a nation. Micro accounting also applies to the accounting and reporting of financial information of subunits of the entity.

Microeconomics   The study of the behavior of basic economic units, such as companies, industries, or households. Microeconomics is concerned with the factors that determine relative prices (rather than the overall inflation rate) and the level of production in one industry or of one firm (rather than total gross domestic product). *See* **Macroeconomics**.

Minimum efficient scale   The level of output for a firm in which the long-run average cost is at its minimum.

Mixed economic system, mixed economy   Economy in which both market forces and government intervention and direction are used to determine resource allocation and prices. The U.S. economy is a mixed economy; although it relies to a great extent upon markets, government also regulates some of the private economy.

Monetarist   A school of economic thought that believes that the money supply is the key to the business cycle ups and downs in the economy. Such monetarists as Milton Friedman think that the money supply has far more impact on the economy's future course than the level of federal spending. This stands in contrast to Keynesian economics. Also in contrast to Keynesian economics is the monetarist belief that the Federal Reserve should forego an active monetary policy in favor of slow but steady growth in the money supply. *See* **Federal Reserve System; Fiscal policy; Keynesian economics; Monetary policy**.

Monetary base   Essentially all the cash in the economy. More formally, the monetary base equals the cash (currency plus coins) held by the public plus the reserves that banks keep at the Federal Reserve. Banks can, at their wish, withdraw these reserves in the form of currency.

Monetary policy   Federal Reserve decisions about changes in the money supply designed to stabilize the economy and smooth the business cycle. It is generally believed that Federal Reserve actions to increase the growth rate of the money supply and/or lower interest rates spur economic growth, lower unemployment, and raise inflation. The reverse occurs when the Federal Reserve lowers the growth rate of the money supply and/or raises interest rates. *See* **Discount rate; Easy money; Open market operations; Required reserve ratio; Tight money**.

Money   Generally defined by economists as the asset that serves as the medium of exchange, serves as a store of value, and is used as the unit of account. Many assets either fulfill these criteria or come close. Thus there are several alternative definitions, such as M1 and M2, of which assets are money. *See* **M1; M2; Near money**.

Money multiplier   The factor by which small changes in bank reserves are translated into large changes in the money supply. For example, through an open market operation a bank receives $200,000 of additional reserves when the required reserve ratio is 10%. The bank is thus required to keep $20,000 in the form of reserves. The remaining $180,000 becomes a loan, which is deposited in the borrower's bank. When the borrower's bank sets aside $18,000 as required reserves, it is then free to loan out the remaining $162,000 to another borrower. Carried to its limit, the initial $200,000 could lead to an ultimate increase of $2,000,000 in bank deposits and hence in the money supply. In this case, the money multiplier is 10, since the $200,000 of reserves creates 10 times $200,000, or $2,000,000, worth of additional money.

Money supply   The total stock of money in the economy. Too much money in relation to the output of goods tends to push prices and inflation up; too little lowers prices and inflation. In the United States, the money supply is managed by the Federal Reserve. *See* **Federal Reserve System**; **Money**.

Monopolistic competition   An industry structure characterized by freedom to enter or exit the industry and many different sellers, each selling a slightly different product. The fast-food industry is often used as an example of a monopolistically competitive industry. *Contrast* **Monopoly**; **Oligopoly**; **Perfect competition**.

Monopoly   The control of the production of a good or service by one firm. Monopoly, which is characterized by lack of competition, leads to high prices and a general lack of responsiveness to the desires of consumers. Antitrust laws enacted in the late nineteenth and twentieth centuries have outlawed most of the flagrant monopoly practices in the United States. *See* **Cartel**; **Natural monopoly**; **Oligopoly**; **Perfect competition**.

Monopsony   Market situation in which there is only a single consumer of the good produced.

Multiplier   *See* **Balanced-budget multiplier**; **Expenditure multiplier**; **Money multiplier**.

Municipal bond   Debt instrument issued by a state or local governmental entity. Municipal bonds and other municipal instruments, called "munis," are exempt from federal income taxes (as well as state and local income taxes in the issuer's jurisdiction) provided their ultimate purpose is public (financing general government needs or special projects with a public purpose, such as a sewer system) and not private or "non-essential," such as a sports stadium or a trade or convention facility. General obligation bonds are backed by the full faith and credit of the issuer, which includes its taxing power, whereas revenue bonds are repayable from the income of the project they finance. Some munis are insured against default by private companies to enhance their credit ratings.

Mutual fund   *See* **Investment company**.

N **National Association of Securities Dealers (NASD)**   Organization of stock brokerage firms dealing in the over-the-counter market. Operating under the supervision of the SEC, the NASD's basic purposes are to standardize practices, establish and enforce ethical standards and equitable rules, and represent brokerage firms in their dealings with government and the investment communities.

National bank   Commercial bank whose charter is approved by the U.S. Comptroller of the Currency rather than by a state banking department. National banks are required to be members of the Federal Reserve System and to belong to the Federal Deposit Insurance Corporation.

National debt   The total debt owed by the federal government. The national debt is made up of debt obligations, such as treasury bills, treasury notes, and treasury bonds. In the late 1980s, the national debt was over $2 trillion dollars.

National income accounts   Statistical aggregates calculating the nation's total production of goods and services, as well as the nation's total income. The most important of these are the gross domestic product, the value of all the goods and services produced; the net domestic product; the GDP minus the total amount of depreciation; and disposable income, the total income individuals have left after taxes to spend or save. National income accounts were first developed during the 1930s and 1940s.

Nationalization   The takeover of a private company's assets or operations by a government. The company may or may not be compensated for the loss of its assets. In developing nations, an operation is typically nationalized if the government believes the company is exploiting the host country and/or exporting too high a proportion of the profits. In developed countries, industries are often nationalized when they need government subsidies to survive. *Contrast* **Privatization**.

National Labor Relations Act (NLRA)   Wagner Act (1935). Federal statute establishing collective bargaining by (1) creating the National Labor Relations Board, (2) providing NLRB-supervised elections, (3) outlawing unfair labor practices by employers, and (4) authorizing the NLRB to conduct unfair labor practice hearings.

National wealth   Sum total of the value of all of the capital and goods held within a nation.

Natural monopoly   An industry in which the most efficient producer is a monopoly; technically defined as an industry with falling average variable costs throughout the range of possible levels of production. Most public utilities are considered examples of natural monopolies. Since the most efficient producer will be a monopoly, natural monopolies are often granted a charter by the government to ensure that they face no competition. Once granted this charter, the company is then regulated by the government in an attempt to limit the price it would otherwise charge and increase the amount of output it would otherwise produce.

Natural rate of unemployment   The level of unemployment to which the economy tends in the absence of temporary policies and temporary shocks. These temporary events can cause the actual unemployment rate to diverge from the natural rate of unemployment.

Near money   Assets that are easily convertible into cash. Some examples are government securities and bonds close to their redemption date.

Negative cash flow   Situation in which a business spends more cash than it receives through earnings or other transactions in an accounting period.

Negative externalities   Activities that impose uncompensated costs upon others not participating in the activity. For example, acid rain from a coal-burning utility plant in the Midwest that kills trees in the East inflicts a negative externality upon the owners of the trees. Also called external diseconomies. *Contrast* **Positive externalities**.

Negative relationship A mathematical relationship that can exist between two variables. X and Y are negatively related if an increase (decrease) in X causes a decrease (increase) in Y. The demand curve is an example in economics of a negative relationship: a higher price results in a lower quantity demanded. *Contrast* **Positive relationship**.

Net domestic product A measure of aggregate economic activity derived by subtracting total depreciation from the gross domestic product.

Net worth Amount by which assets exceed liabilities. In general terms, net worth measures what would be left over if all assets were sold at their carrying value and all debts paid. For a corporation, net worth is also known as "stockholders' equity."

New Deal Collection of political and economic policies and programs promulgated by the first two administrations of the presidency of Franklin D. Roosevelt. The New Deal policies were aimed at combating the economic miseries of the Great Depression.

New York Stock Exchange (NYSE) Oldest (1792) and largest stock exchange in the United States, located at 11 Wall Street in New York City; also known as the *Big Board*. The common stocks of more than 1,600 companies are traded and companies must meet the exchange's stringent listing requirements. Bonds, prefered stock, warrants, options, and rights are also traded on the NYSE.

Nominal The stated or face value of a security as opposed to its market value. When used in an economic context, signifies a variable measured in terms of dollars rather than measured in terms of goods or purchasing power. Nominal variables do not make allowance for inflation and the corresponding decrease in the purchasing power of the dollar. *Contrast* **Real**.

Nominal interest rate The interest rate in terms of dollars, without adjusting for inflation. This is contrasted with the real interest rate, which adjusts for inflation. The interest rates quoted in financial markets are generally nominal interest rates. *See* **Real interest rate**.

Nominal wage The number of dollars earned for an hour's work. The nominal wage is measured in units of dollars, or currency. Contrasted with this is the real wage, which is measured in terms of the goods or services that may be purchased with an hour's work. *See* **Real wage**.

Nonprofit organization Association that is allowed to exist without paying income taxes. Most nonprofit organizations are in a socially desirable business (hospital, educational institution, charity) and those so qualified by the Internal Revenue Service may receive contributions that are tax deductible to the donor.

Normal good A good that people demand more of when their income increases. Also called a Superior good. *Contrast* **Inferior good**.

Normal profit A profit just sufficient to cause a firm to remain in business. In other words, a profit that just covers the owner's opportunity cost of investing in one line of business rather than another. For example, if $100,000 can be invested in a video rental store or saved in a savings account yielding 10%, the video rental store must return at least 10% (the normal profit) to cover the opportunity cost of investing in it rather than saving the funds in the savings account. Any return over 10% represents an economic profit. *See* **Economic profit**.

Obsolescence Process by which property becomes useless, not because of physical deterioration, but because of changes outside the property, notably scientific or technological advances.

Okun's law An empirical generalization used in macroeconomics: for every 2% real GDP is below its full-employment level over a year, the unemployment rate will rise by approximately 1%.

Oligopoly A market situation in which a small number of selling firms control the market supply of a particular good or service and hence its price. Because each firm in an oligopoly knows any change in its market share will be reflected in the sales of the other firms, there tends to be a high degree of interdependence among firms; each firm must make its price and output decisions with a regard to the responses of the other firms in the oligopoly. An oligopoly can be perfect—when all the firms produce an identical good or service (cement)—or imperfect—when each firm's product has a different identity but is essentially similar to the others (cigarettes).

Open economy Economy in which foreign investment, imports, and exports are easy to accomplish and play a substantial role in economic life.

Open market operations (OMO) The purchase or sale of government securities by the Federal Reserve System. These transactions are carried out by the Securities Department of the Federal Reserve Bank of New York under the instructions of the Federal Open Market Committee. The purchase of government securities increases the reserves of the banking system and thereby results in an increase in the money supply; the sale of government securities has the opposite impact. Open market operations are perhaps the most important of the three basic ways the Federal Reserve conducts it monetary policy. *See* **Federal Reserve System**; **Monetary policy**.

Open shop Enterprise that employs workers without regard to whether they are members of a labor union. *See* **Agency shop**; **Closed shop**; **Union shop**.

Open union Union that admits any qualified worker to its membership without requiring the payment of an initiation fee, high dues, examinations, or any other practice designed to discourage membership.

Opportunity cost A fundamental concept in economics. The opportunity cost of an item or action is the value of the next best alternative that had to be sacrificed to pursue the selected item or action.

Option The right, but not the obligation, to buy or sell property that is granted in exchange for an agreed-upon sum. If the right is not exercised after a specified period, the option expires and the option buyer forfeits the money. In finance, the term refers to a contract covering an underlying security, such as stocks, commodities, or stock indexes. A *call* gives its buyer the right to buy 100 shares of the underlying security at a fixed price before expiration, which may be three to twelve months or more away.

The opposite of a call is a put, which grants the right to sell. The price of an option is called a *premium*. Most puts and calls are never exercised; they are actively traded on exchanges as their premiums rise or fall reflecting the relationship between the exercise price and the market price of the underlying security.

Overhead   Expenses of running a business that are not directly associated with a particular product or service sold—for example, rent, heat, and employee benefits as opposed to labor and materials. Also called *indirect costs* and *burden.*

Pareto's law   Theory that the pattern of income distribution is constant, historically and geographically, regardless of taxation or welfare policies, also called *law of the trivial many and the critical few* or *80-20 law.* Thus, if 80% of a nation's income will benefit only 20% of the population, the only way to improve the economic lot of the poor is to increase overall output and income levels. Pareto is also credited with the concept, called *Paretian optimum* or *Pareto optimality,* that resources are optimally distributed when an individual cannot be moved into a better position without putting someone else into a worse position.

Partnership   A form of organizing a business in which two or more people agree to pool their funds and share in the profits and losses. Partnerships are common in service organizations, such as accounting and law. Unlike the owners of corporations, general partners can be personally liable for all the debts incurred by their company. *See* **Corporation**; **General partner**; **Limited liability**; **Proprietorship**.

Paternalism   Management method assuming ultimate responsibility for employee welfare in such areas as benefit decisions, job assignments, and promotions. The term is also pejorative in the sense that management assumes inferior status for employees.

People intensive   Process requiring many people to complete, not easily automated. A hospital is an example of a people-intensive organization.

Perfect competition   The market condition in which no single buyer or seller has the power to alter the market price of a good or service by its actions. Characteristics of a perfectly competitive market are (1) a large number of buyers and sellers; (2) a homogeneous (identical) product; (3) awareness among all participants of all prices and volumes; (4) freedom of entry and exit. Perfect competition exists only as a theoretical ideal. *See* **Monopoly**; **Oligopoly**.

Perfect (pure) monopoly   Market dominated by a single producer, where no competition of any kind to that producer can arise.

Periodic audit
1. Audit for an intermediate period (e.g., one month, three months).
2. Audit carried out at specified intervals within the year.

Peter principle   Theory that people rise in their career in every hierarchy to the level of their own incompetence; based on the book *The Peter Principle and Why Things Always Go Wrong* by Lawrence J. Peter. Work in organizations is accomplished by those employees who have not yet reached their level of incompetence.

Petrodollar   Dollar paid to oil-producing countries and deposited in Western banks.

Phillips curve   An empirically estimated relationship between the inflation rate and the unemployment rate. The Phillips curve purports to show a negative relationship: When the inflation rate increases, the unemployment rate decreases. Until the early 1970s, economists assumed that the Phillips curve relationship made impossible the combination of high inflation and high unemployment. The experience of that decade forced economists to revise their use of the Phillips curve and allow for the possibility that the curve may shift from one period to the next. *See* **Natural rate of unemployment**.

Pigou effect   Effect of price changes upon the real value of privately held money balances. A decrease in the price level increases the buying power of money that people have, and so increases their consumption and thus has an expansionary effect upon the economy.

Planned economy   Economy in which government planning dominates the direction of economic activity, and market forces are not allowed to do so to any considerable degree. Socialist and, especially, communist economies are planned economies, while capitalist economies are much less so.

Portfolio   Any group of investments designed to reduce risk through diversification. Portfolios aim to eliminate "specific or unsystematic" risk (for example, a particular stock's falling in price because of financial difficulties) and do not reduce systematic or market risk (the risk common to all securities in a given category, the risk of a falling stock market, for example).

Positive externalities   When an activity creates a benefit for others who do not pay for the benefit. Also called external economies. *Contrast* **Negative externalities**.

Positive relationship   Mathematical relationship that can exist between two variables. X and Y are positively related when an increase (decrease) in X causes an increase (decrease) in Y. The supply curve is an example of a positive economic relationship: A higher price leads to an increase in the quantity supplied. *Contrast* **Negative relationship**.

Precautionary demand for money   A term used in Keynesian analysis of the demand for money, refers to the demand for money due to the fact that unforeseen events can occur that necessitate the use of money, such as an unexpected medical emergency or a sale. Often the precautionary demand for money is said to be influenced by people's income. *See* **Keynesian economics**; **Speculative demand for money**; **Transaction demand for money**.

Preferred stock   Part of the equity of a corporation that enjoys priority over common stock in the distribution of dividends and of assets in liquidation. Preferred issues are normally non-voting and pay a fixed dividend, although some are adjustable.

Present value   Value of dollars to be received in the future (called future dollars) in terms of what they are worth today. A dollar to be received in the future is worth less than a dollar received today because the dollar received today can be invested and yield additional interest income.

Price ceiling   A law imposed by the government prohibiting the price of a product from going above a certain level. Price ceilings are often instituted to try to guarantee that demanders will be able to afford items deemed necessary. Frequently price ceilings give way to shortages and black markets. *See* **Black market; Shortage**.

Price discrimination   A situation that occurs when a supplier sells the same good or service to two different demanders for a different price, even though the cost of providing the good or service to the demanders is the same.

Price-earnings ratio (P/E ratio)   Statistic that equals market price per share divided by earnings per share. It is a good ratio to use in evaluating the investment possibility of a company. A steady decrease in the P/E ratio reflects decreasing investor confidence in the growth potential of the entity. Some companies have high P/E multiples reflecting high earnings growth expectations. Young, fast-growing companies often have high P/E stocks with multiples over 20. A company's P/E ratio depends on many factors such as risk, earnings trend, quality of management, industry conditions, and economic factors.

Price elasticity of demand   A measure of the responsiveness of the demand for a product to a change in its price. The price elasticity of demand is the absolute value of the percentage change in the quantity demanded caused by a 1% change in the price, that is, the absolute value of the percentage change in the quantity demanded divided by the percentage change in price. *See* **Elasticity**.

Price elasticity of supply   A measure of the responsiveness of the supply of a product to a change in its price. The price elasticity of supply is the percentage change in the quantity supplied caused by a 1% change in the price, that is, the percentage change in the quantity supplied divided by the percentage change in price. *See* **Elasticity**.

Price floor   Government-set minimum price. It is illegal to sell the product below the price floor. Often the goal of the price floor is to guarantee that the producers receive an adequate income.

Price index   Index that traces the change in price of a market basket of goods over time, that is, an index that shows how the price of a "representative" good changes with time. *See* **Consumer price index; Producer price index**.

Price support   Government-set minimum price guaranteed to suppliers. If the market price falls below the price support, the government makes up the difference. Price supports can be used to try to give suppliers adequate income.

Price system   Reliance upon prices to decide what and how much of each good will be produced, determine the rate of economic growth, and set the distribution of income. Capitalist societies generally rely upon the price system. *See* **Capitalism**.

Prime rate   Interest rate charged by banks to their most credit-worthy customers. This rate often receives publicity when it changes.

Private good   A good or service that is purchased and consumed by one individual. *Contrast* **Public good**.

Private sector   The part of the economy comprising households and firms owned by individuals. This stands in contrast to the public sector, which is the governmental part of the economy.

Privatization   Sale of government-owned and government-operated industries or companies to the private sector. *Contrast* **Nationalization**.

Producer price index (PPI)   Measure of change in wholesale prices (formally called the wholesale price index). The PPI is compiled by the U.S. Bureau of Labor Statistics and released on a monthly basis. *See* **Consumer price index; Price index**.

Production function   The relationship between the inputs and the resulting output of a product. The production function is an engineering relationship; it takes no account of the prices of the inputs or of the price of the output. It is concerned only with the amounts of the inputs and output.

Production possibilities curve   A graph showing the various maximum combinations of goods and services a firm or an economy is capable of producing. Also called Product transformation curve.

Productivity   Measured relationship of the quantity and quality of units produced and the labor per unit of time. For example, an increase in productivity is achieved through an increase in production per unit of labor over time.

Product transformation curve   *See* **Production possibilities curve**.

Profit and loss statement   *See* **Income statement**.

Progressive taxes   Tax system in which those with higher incomes pay taxes at higher rates than those with lower incomes. The U.S. income tax is an example since households with higher incomes generally face higher marginal tax rates than households with lower incomes. *See* **Marginal tax rate**; *contrast* **Regressive taxes**.

Property taxes   Government taxes levied on property, particularly real estate. Property taxes are the major component of the revenue raised by most local governments.

Proprietorship   One of the methods used to organize businesses. A proprietorship is an unincorporated business owned by a single person. The individual proprietor has the right to all the profits from the firm and is also responsible for all the firm's liabilities. *See* **Corporation; Partnership**.

Protect, protection, protectionism, protectionist   Economic policies designed to restrict imports of goods that compete with domestic producers. Protectionists advocate protectionism in order to protect domestic producers from foreign competition.

Prudent-man rule   Standard adopted by some U.S. states to guide those with responsibility for investing the money of others. Such fiduciaries (executors of wills, trustees, bank trust departments, and administrators of estates) must act as a prudent man or woman would be expected to act, with discretion and intelligence, to seek reasonable income, preserve capital, and, in general, avoid speculative investments. *See* **Fiduciary**.

Public choice   Economic theory of how governments behave. The basic axiom is that individuals within the government will seek to advance their own welfare rather than necessarily advancing society's overall well-being.

ECONOMICS AND BUSINESS

Public domain

1. All lands and waters in the possession of the United States, and all lands owned by the several states, as distinguished from lands possessed by private individuals or corporations.
2. Information, the source of which is available to anyone and is not subject to copyright.

Public good　A good or service whose consumption by one person does not diminish its consumption by others and whose consumption cannot be limited only to those who pay for it. National defense is the classic example of a public good. Frequently public goods must be provided by the government since private producers have little incentive to produce items that can be consumed by people who do not pay for them. *Contrast* **Private good**.

Public sector　The part of the economy comprised of governmental enterprises. This stands in contrast to the private sector, which are households and firms owned by individuals.

Pump priming　Economic policy of increasing government expenditures and/or reducing taxes in order to stimulate the economy to higher levels of output. Pump priming measures are supposed to be temporary, existing only until the economy spontaneously develops and sustains growth on its own.

Purchasing power of the dollar　This measures how many goods and services may be purchased with a dollar. In the presence of inflation, the dollar loses purchasing power since the prices of goods and services are rising. *See also* **Constant dollars**; **Nominal**; **Real**.

Pure capitalism　Economic system in which principles of capitalism operate unfettered by any limiting factor such as government control or interference. By inference, government performs little except those functions that cannot be performed by any other entity.

Put option　*See* **Option**.

Pyramiding

1. Use of financial leverage paper profits from an investment to finance purchases of additional investments.
2. Building of a business through a dealership network designed primarily to sell dealerships rather than useful products.
3. Fraudulent business practice in which the chain of distribution is artificially expanded by an excessive number of distributors selling to other distributors at progressively higher wholesale prices, ultimately resulting in unnecessarily inflated retail prices.

Q　**Quantity demanded**　The amount of a good buyers are willing and able to purchase at a given price. Quantity demanded should be distinguished from demand. Quantity demanded refers to the amount that buyers demand at a particular price; demand refers to the amount wanted and able to be purchased at all prices.

Quantity supplied　The amount of a good producers are willing and able to sell at a given price. Quantity supplied should be distinguished from supply. Quantity supplied refers to the amount that sellers will produce at a particular price; supply refers to the amount produced at all prices.

Quantity theory of money　Economic theory that relies on the equation of exchange ($MV = PQ$, where M is money, V is velocity, P is the price level, and Q is the real GDP) to derive its predictions. At its simplest level, quantity theory advocates assume the velocity of money and the real GDP are fixed, deriving the result that increases in the supply of money proportionally raise the price level. The simple quantity theory was the hallmark of most macroeconomic theories prior to the advent of Keynesian economics. In a more sophisticated form, it has enjoyed a renaissance in recent years. *See* **Equation of exchange**; **Keynesian economics**; **Monetarist**; **Velocity**.

Quota　A quantitative limit, usually governmentally imposed, on the amount of a good or service that may be imported in a given time period. A quota imposes a physical limit on the amount imported: 10 million units and no more, for example. *See* **Tariff**.

R　**Random walk**　Economic theory about the movement of stock prices that asserts that past price changes are of no use in forecasting future price movements. Most economists believe this theory is correct; many stock market analysts dispute it by contending that there are predictable patterns in the prices of stocks.

Rate of return on investment　Annual percentage return after taxes that actually occurs or is anticipated on an investment. For example, if $100,000 is invested in a stock and the after-tax return on it for the year is $8,000, the rate of return is 8%. The term Total Return includes any capital gains or losses.

Rational expectations　Specifically, an economic term for expectations that are, on average, correct and are based upon the best available information. More generally, a name often given to a school of macroeconomic thought that holds that government monetary policy cannot affect the real GDP or unemployment. According to this school, monetary policy affects only the inflation rate. *See* **Keynesian economics**; **Macroeconomics**; **Monetarist**; **Monetary policy**.

Reaganomics　General collection of conservative, free-market economic policies favored by President Ronald Reagan and his administration.

Real　When used in an economic context, signifies a variable measured in terms of actual goods and services rather than in terms of dollars. Real variables adjust for inflation. *See* **Constant dollars**; **Purchasing power of the dollar**; *contrast* **Nominal**.

Real business cycle　A theory in macroeconomics that the main causes of the business cycle are from real sources, such as changes in tax rates or technology, rather than from changes in the money supply. The real business cycle approach stands in contrast to the monetarist view that fluctuations in the money supply are the prime cause of business cycles. *See* **Business cycle**; **Macroeconomics**; **Monetarist**.

Real earnings　Wages, salaries, and other earnings, corrected for inflation over time so as to produce a measure of actual changes in purchasing power.

Real GDP   The gross domestic product corrected for inflation by valuing the outputs using base year prices. The real GDP attempts to strip away the influence of changing prices on the GDP. Also called the GDP in constant dollars. *See* **Base year**.

Real income   Income of an individual, group, or country adjusted for changes in purchasing power caused by inflation. For instance, if the cost of a market basket increases from $100 to $120 in ten years, reflecting a 20% decline in purchasing power, salaries must rise by 20% if real income is to be maintained.

Real interest rate   The percentage increase in purchasing power, that is, in real goods and services, that borrowers pay back to lenders. The real interest rate equals the nominal rate of interest minus the inflation rate. *See* **Nominal interest rate**; **Real**.

Real wage   The wage paid to workers corrected for inflation; the real wage measures the number of goods and services a worker can buy with an hour's work. *Contrast* **Nominal wage**.

Recession   Downturn in economic activity, commonly defined as at least two consecutive quarters of decline in a country's real GDP. A recession bridges the period between a peak and a trough in the business cycle. A severe and long-lasting recession is called a depression. *See* **Business cycle**; **Depression**; *contrast* **Expansion**.

Recognition lag   The time it takes for the government to realize that a particular economic policy is called for.

Recovery   Another term for expansion, used more commonly in the past. *See* **Expansion**.

Regressive taxes   Tax system that results in the rich paying a lower percentage of their income as taxes than do the poor. *Contrast with* **Progressive taxes**.

Relative price   The dollar price of a good compared to the dollar price of another good. The relative price of good *A* indicates how much of good *B* (rather than how many dollars) must be given to obtain one more unit of good *A*.

Renewable natural resource   Natural resource that can be replaced over time and, so, is not used up irrevocably. Petroleum is not renewable; solar energy is (because it is always there) and forest products can be (because they can be regrown).

Rent   When used in economics, refers to any payment to a factor of production in excess of the factor's opportunity cost. For instance, a ball player who earns $300 000 a year and whose next best opportunity would pay $40,000 a year is receiving a rent of $260,000 a year.

Required reserve ratio   The fraction of various deposits commercial banks must keep on hand as reserves, either as currency within the bank or on deposit at the Federal Reserve System. The Federal Reserve sets the required reserve ratios, which vary according to the type of deposit. Demand deposits face a higher required reserve ratio than do time deposits. *See* **Demand deposit**; **Federal Reserve System**; **Required reserves**; **Time deposit**.

Required reserves   The amount of reserves a depository institution, such as a bank, is legally mandated to keep on hand. Reserves include cash kept on the premises and deposits kept at the Federal Reserve. The amount of required reserves is determined by applying the various required reserve ratios—the fraction of a deposit that must be kept as reserves—to the total amount of that type of deposit. For instance, if the required reserve ratio for demand deposits is 14%, a bank must keep $14 from every $100 of demand deposits as reserves. *See* **Required reserve ratio**.

Restraint of trade   In common law and as used in antitrust laws, illegal restraints interfering with free competition in commercial transactions, which tend to restrict production, affect prices, or otherwise control the market to the detriment of consumers of goods and services.

Retained earnings   Profits kept to accumulate in a business after dividends are paid. Contrary to popular illusion, retained earnings are not necessarily kept in the form of cash. Instead, they are often invested in more capital, inventory, or other aspects of the business.

Right-to-work law   Outlawing a union shop in states that have adopted it, according to section 14(b) of the Taft-Hartley Act. It prohibits agreements requiring membership in a union as a condition of continued employment of a person who was not a member when hired.

Rollover
1. To replace a loan or debt with another.
2. To change the institution that invests one's pension plan, without recognition of taxable income.

S **Safe Harbor Rule**   Provision enacted as part of the Economic Tax Recovery Act of 1981 to guarantee sale/leaseback treatment to certain transactions if specific requirements are met. The purpose of this provision was to make it easier for loss companies to "sell" their tax benefits accruing on new asset purchases by entering into sale/leaseback transactions with profitable companies. The intent was to generate an immediate cash flow for such loss companies, rather than deferring the benefits through carryover provisions.

Sale and leaseback   Form of lease arrangement in which a company sells an asset to another party—usually an insurance or finance company, a leasing company, a limited partnership, or an institutional investor—in exchange for cash, then contracts to lease the asset for a specified term.

Sales journal   Special book in which credit sales are recorded. The total columns of the sales journal are posted as a debit to accounts receivable and a credit to sales. Separate columns may exist to classify sales by category (e.g., product line).

Savings   The portion of disposable income not spent on consumption. *See* **Consumption**; **Disposable income**.

Savings and loan association   A financial institution that obtains the bulk of its deposits from consumers and invests the majority of its assets in home mortgages.

Scale
1. Economics: Amount of production, as in economy or diseconomy of scale.
2. Labor: Wage rate for specific types of employees.

For example, the union scale for carpenters is $20.00 per hour.

3. Modeling: Proportional relationship between the dimensions of a drawing, plan, or model and the dimensions of the physical object it represents.

Scrip (1) In general: receipt, certificate, or other representation of value recognized by both payer and payee. Scrip is not currency, but may be convertible into currency. (2) Securities: temporary document that is issued by a corporation and that represents a fractional share of stock resulting from a change in the way a company's invested capital is broken down and distributed. Scrip certificates may be aggregated or applied toward the purchase of full shares. Scrip dividends are sometimes paid by companies short of cash.

Seasonality Variations in economic activity that recur with regularity as the result of changes in climate, holidays, vacations, tax deadlines, or other seasonal factors. For instance, the retail toy industry, which sells the vast majority of its production between Thanksgiving and Christmas, is subject to seasonality in its sales.

Secondary market Exchanges and over-the-counter markets where securities are traded subsequent to original issuance, which took place in the primary market. Proceeds of secondary market sales go to the selling dealers and investors, not to the companies that originally issued the securities.

Securities and Exchange Commission (SEC) Federal agency empowered to regulate and supervise the selling of securities, to prevent unfair practices on security exchanges and over-the-counter markets, and to maintain a fair and orderly market for the investor.

Self-correcting mechanism The means by which an economy achieves full employment with any government intervention. Generally, Keynesian economists believe the self-correcting mechanism is fairly slow; monetarists and advocates of the rational expectations approach usually think it fairly rapid. In large part, this difference accounts for the Keynesian preference for governmental intervention and the suggestion of the monetarist and rational expectations approach to forego governmental intervention. See **Keynesian economics**; **Monetarist**; **Rational expectations**.

Selling short Sale of a borrowed security by an investor who expects the price will drop. When the price falls, the investor profits by buying the security (at the lower price) and returning the security to whomever it was initially borrowed from.

Shareholder See **Stockholder**.

Sherman Anti-trust Act of 1890 The law that declared illegal "every contract, combination in the form of trust or otherwise, or conspiracy, in restraint of trade or commerce" in the United States. The Sherman Act was the first important law in the United States designed to protect the public against agreements by producers to regulate the flow of goods and services in order to raise their prices.

Shop steward Most immediate representative of local union in a plant or department. Generally elected by fellow employees, the shop steward handles grievances, collects dues, solicits new members, and so on. A shop steward usually continues to work at his job and handles union matters on a part-time basis, frequently on the employer's time.

Shortage When the quantity demanded of a good or service exceeds the quantity supplied. This is caused by the price of the item being below the equilibrium market price. Contrast **Surplus**.

Short run In economics, the period of time when a firm can change the quantity employed of some of its inputs, but not all of the inputs. The short run differs for firms in different industries since, for example, it takes an electric utility longer to build a nuclear power plant than for a florist to grow new flowers. See **Long run**.

Shutdown price The price beneath which the firm will close its operations rather than continue to produce.

Silicon Valley Area in California where a significant amount of high-tech research is conducted. Silicon is a component in advanced computer chips.

Silver standard Backing of a currency by guaranteeing its exchangeability for silver. U.S. silver certificates had been backed by silver.

Simplified employee pension plan (SEP) Type of pension plan in which both the employee and the employer contribute. The Tax Reform Act of 1986 limits annual employee deferrals to $7000 in 1987, and provides for inflation-related increases in later years.

Single-entry bookkeeping Accounting system that does not use balancing debits and credits. Transactions are recorded in just one account.

Skill intensive Occupation or job requiring a highly skilled work force. Examples of skill-intensive work include machinists, computer programmers, tool and die makers, and cooks.

Small business According to the U.S. Department of Commerce, a business employing fewer than 100 people. Small businesses play a disproportionately important role in innovation as well as in the economic and employment growth in the United States.

Smokestack industry Heavy industry, typified by the steel and auto industries. The term originates in the fact that these industries usually have large smokestacks for their operations. U.S. smokestack industries are facing intense international competition.

Socialism The method of organizing an economy so that the government owns most, if not all, of the nation's capital. The state then runs most, if not all, of the nation's businesses. Contrast **Capitalism**.

Soft currency Funds of a country that are not acceptable in exchange for the hard currencies of other countries. Soft currencies, such as the Soviet Union's ruble, are fixed at unrealistic exchange rates and are not backed by gold, so that countries with hard currencies, like U.S. dollars or British pounds, are reluctant to buy them.

Soft dollars Brokerage industry term for commission-generating business directed to a firm owed money in lieu of direct cash payment.

Soft goods Merchandise that is soft to the touch, such as clothing and other textile goods; considered in the merchandising industry to be nondurable goods. See also **Hard goods**.

Soft money
1. In a proposed development or an investment, money contributed that is tax deductible.
2. Sometimes used to describe costs that do not physically go into construction, such as interest during construction, architects' fees, and legal fees.

Soil bank   Land held out of agricultural production in an effort to stabilize commodity prices and promote soil conservation. Subsidies to farmers participating in the soil bank program are provided by the U.S. Department of Agriculture.

Sole proprietor   Unincorporated business with one owner having all the net worth. In the event the business fails, the owner is *personally* liable for all debts incurred.

Sovereign risk   Risk that a foreign government will default on its obligations because of a change in national policy. Relevant when making loans to foreign countries.

Special drawing rights (SDRs)   Assets first issued by the International Monetary Fund in 1970 for use in the place of gold and other foreign reserves. SDRs are designed for use by countries in settling their transactions with other, foreign, countries. *See* **International Monetary Fund**.

Speculative demand for money   A term used in Keynesian analysis of the demand for money, it refers to the demand due to the fact that holding money is sometimes safer than holding other interest-bearing assets. The speculative demand for money is often said to be influenced by the interest rate: The higher the interest rate, the greater the opportunity cost of holding money, so the less money will be demanded. *See* **Keynesian economics**; **Precautionary demand for money**; **Transaction demand for money**.

Spending multiplier   *See* **Expenditure multiplier**.

Spillover   Effects of economic activity or process upon those who are not directly involved in it. Odors from a rendering plant are negative spillover effects upon its neighbors; the beauty of a homeowner's flower garden is a positive spillover effect upon neighbors.

Split   Short for split-up, the increase in a corporation's number of outstanding shares of stock without any change in the shareholder's equity or the aggregate market value at the time of the split. Thus, a 2-for-1 split results in twice as many shares at half the market value. The usual purpose of a split is to make shares more affordable to more investors. Reverse splits, or split-downs, are rare.

Stagflation   Period of time when inflation and unemployment are simultaneously rising. Such an event was deemed impossible by the early, simple use of the Phillips curve; when it occurred in the 1970s economists were forced to revise their use of the Phillips curve. *See* **Phillips curve**.

Stagnation   Period of no, or slow, economic growth.

Standard of living   Sum total of amenities, quality, and quantity of goods and services consumed by consuming units within an economy.

Standard & Poor's 500 stock index   *See* **Stock index**.

Statement of condition   *See* **Financial statement**.

Steel-collar worker   Use of robots as employees on a production line. It symbolizes the replacement of the blue-collar worker.

Stock   Ownership of a corporation represented by shares that are a claim on the corporation's earnings and assets. *See* **Common stock**; *contrast* **Bond**.

Stockholder   Individual or organization with an ownership position in a corporation. Stockholders must own at least one share of stock. Stockholders are generally entitled to vote for the members of the board of directors and also to receive dividends as paid by the company.

Stockholders' equity   *See* **Net worth**.

Stock index   Indicators used to measure and report value changes in representative stock groupings. The most well known are the Dow Jones Industrial Average, which includes the prices of thirty actively traded blue-chip stocks, and Standard & Poor's Composite Index of 500 Stocks, which includes 500 stocks representing about 80% of the market value of all the stocks traded on the New York Stock Exchange. Both the Dow Jones Average and Standard & Poor's 500 try to measure the performance of the stock market as a whole. *See* **Stock market**.

Stock market   General term referring to the organized trading of securities through various exchanges. The largest stock market is the New York Stock Exchange, located in Manhattan.

Straight-line method of depreciation   Depreciation method whereby an equal amount of the asset's cost is considered an expense for each year of the asset's useful life.

Street name   Phrase describing securities held in the name of a broker or another nominee instead of a customer. Since the securities are in the broker's custody, transfer of the shares at the time of sale is easier than if the stock were registered in the customer's name and physical certificates had to be transferred.

Structural unemployment   Unemployment caused by changes in demand or technology seriously affecting certain industries, occupations, or areas of the country so that only with high costs can the unemployed workers relocate and/or retrain for new careers.

Subsidiary company   Company whose voting stock is more than 50% owned by another firm. A subsidiary company is part of another company.

Subsidy   Payment or other favorable economic stimulus (such as remission of taxation) given by government to certain individual or groups of economic entities, usually to encourage their continued existence, growth, development, and profitability. In the United States, subsidies are given to the agricultural industry, the very poor, and many other groups.

Substitutes   Two goods or services that compete with each other, for example, butter and margarine. When the price of one good goes up, the quantity demanded of the other good rises; if the price of one good falls, the quantity demanded of the other good decreases. *Contrast* **Complements**.

Substitution effect of a price change   A lower relative price for a good or service means the opportunity cost of buying the good or service falls, which encourages demanders to increase their purchases of the item in question. *See* **Income effect**.

Substitution law   Economic proposition that no good is absolutely irreplaceable, that at some set of prices, consumers will substitute other goods for it.

Sunset industry   Mature industry at the end of the product life cycle. For example, the buggy whip industry was a sunset industry.

Sunshine law   State or federal law, also called *government in the sunshine law,* that requires most meetings of regulatory bodies to be held in public and most of their decisions and records to be disclosed.

Superior good   *See* **Normal good**.

Supply curve   A curve showing the relationship between the price of a good or service and the quantity that suppliers are willing to supply. Supply curves generally show a positive relationship between the price and the quantity supplied: The higher the price, the greater will be the quantity supplied. A supply curve, together with a demand curve, can be used to establish the equilibrium market price and the quantity of a good or service. *See* **Demand curve**; **Equilibrium market price**.

Supply-side economics   Theory of macroeconomics contending that drastic reductions in marginal tax rates will stimulate productive investment in new capital equipment and increased work effort, thereby improving overall economic conditions. Supply-side economics stands in contrast to Keynesian economics: supply-siders believe that governmental policies should focus on work and investment incentives, that is, the supply side of markets. Keynesian economics asserts that governmental policies should concentrate on ensuring adequate demand for output. *See* **Keynesian economics**; **Laffer curve**; **Marginal tax rate**.

Surplus   When the quantity supplied exceeds the quantity demanded. This occurs when the price is above the market equilibrium price. *See* **Equilibrium market price**; *contrast* **Shortage**.

Sweatshop   Place of employment having unacceptable working conditions. Sweatshops are commonly characterized by low pay, poor working conditions, safety violations, and generally inhumane treatment of employees.

Sympathetic strike   Strike by workers with no direct dispute against management to display solidarity with another striking union. Sympathy strikes give added power to labor by presenting a united front.

Syndicate   Group of individuals or companies that has formed a joint venture to undertake a project that the individuals would be unable or unwilling to pursue alone.

Synergy   Action of a combined enterprise to produce results greater than the sum of the separate enterprises. For example, a merger of two oil companies, one with a superior distribution network and the other with more reserves, would have synergy and would be expected to result in higher per share than before.

T **Taft-Hartley Act**   Popular name for the Labor-Management Relations Act of 1947, the stated purpose of which is to protect employers' rights to resist unionization and restrict union activities. It imposes on unions many of the conditions for good faith bargaining that were imposed on management by earlier laws.

Tariff   Federal tax on imports or exports. When the tax is imposed to protect domestic producers from foreign competition, it is called a "protective tariff."

Tax-based income policy (TIP)   A policy calling for the government to increase taxes on firms and workers who raise prices too much and reduce taxes for those who keep their prices within guidelines. Tax-based income policies are designed to try to reduce the inflation rate.

Tax haven   Foreign country providing significant, permanent tax breaks to individuals and companies operating within it. In a tax haven country, foreigners may receive income or own assets and pay very low taxes. Many companies are situated or have subsidiaries in tax havens for tax avoidance reasons. There are two objectives for establishing a subsidiary in a tax haven: (1) a subsidiary can operate as a legitimate operation and generate profits while simultaneously enjoying the tax advantages; and (2) a parent may establish a subsidiary in a tax haven for the purpose of tax avoidance only. The major purpose is to shift income from a country with high taxes to a tax haven country by using a subsidiary as an intermediary.

Tax incidence   The determination of the economic entity that actually ends up paying a particular tax. For instance, some or all taxes upon producers are often added to the price of the good(s) or service(s) produced so that the incidence of the tax actually falls upon the consumer.

Tax multiplier   The amount by which a change in taxes alters the real GDP. For instance, if a $10 billion increase in taxes lowers the real GDP by $50 billion, the tax multiplier is 5. At its simplest level, the Keynesian approach to macroeconomics calculates that the tax multiplier will equal—(marginal propensity to consume) divided by (1—marginal propensity to consume). *See* **Expenditure multiplier**; **Keynesian economics**; **Marginal propensity to consume**.

Tax Reform Act of 1986   Landmark federal law that lowered tax rates, curtailed tax shelters, shifted a part of the overall tax burden from individuals to corporations, and modified *the alternative minimum tax* (AMT). With regard to the latter, the alternative minimum tax, already in place, was made more generally applicable to individuals and was extended to corporations.

Tax shelter   Any device by which a taxpayer can reduce his tax liability by engaging in activities that provide him with deductions or credits that he can apply against his tax liability. In such cases, the activities engaged in are said to shelter the taxpayer's other income from tax liability. Most tax shelters were curtailed by the Tax Reform Act of 1986.

Telecommunications   Transmission of messages by telephone, telegram, or television.

Tender offer   Public offer to buy, for cash, securities or both, the shares of a corporation, usually at a higher price (called a premium) than the current market price.

Theory of games   A mathematical treatment of the situation in which one player's actions may have an influence on another player's actions. The theory of games is often used in trying to understand the behavior of firms within an oligopolistic industry structure. *See* **Oligopoly**.

Tieabout hypothesis   The economic theory that smaller governments and greater mobility of citizens and firms between cities, states, and nations produce more efficient government since governments must compete to retain citizens and firms.

Tight money   When credit is difficult to obtain, usually because of the monetary policy of the Federal Reserve. Tight money is frequently said to lead to higher unemployment, reduced growth in the real GDP, and lower inflation. *Contrast* **Easy money**.

Time deposit   Savings account held in a financial institution for a fixed term or with the understanding that the banks may require notice before the depositor can withdraw the funds. Although banks are authorized to require 30 days' notice of withdrawal from savings accounts, this requirement is generally waived for passbook savings accounts.

Tokenism   Formalistic compliance with affirmative action legislation by hiring a small (token) number of people to comply with requirements for having representatives of impacted groups. Tokenism is a formalistic affirmative action compliance policy.

Total revenue   Total dollar volume of sales over a given time period, usually one year or one quarter. This equals the price of the product(s) times the quantity sold.

Trade barrier   Any form of governmental or operational activity or restriction which renders importation of some goods into a country difficult or impossible. Tariffs are an example; so is the plethora of regulations and inspections that hamper importation of automobiles into Japan.

Trade deficit or surplus   Excess of imports over exports (for a trade deficit) or of exports over imports (for a trade surplus), resulting in a negative or positive balance of trade. The trade deficit is one part of the current account. Factors influencing the balance of trade include the country's exchange rate, production advantages in key manufacturing areas, and whether the country can produce enough of certain products to completely satisfy the domestic demand for them. *See* **Balance of payments**; **Current account**.

Trade-off   The typical situation when satisfying more of one need means satisfying less of another.

Trade union   Association of workers to promote and protect the welfare, interests, and rights of its members—also called *labor union*.

Traditional economy   Economy dominated by methods and techniques that have strong social support even though they may be old-fashioned or out of date.

Transaction demand for money   A term used in Keynesian analysis of the demand for money, it refers to the demand due to the fact that money can be used to purchase goods and services. Often the transaction demand for money is said to be influenced by people's income. *See* **Keynesian economics**; **Precautionary demand for money**; **Speculative demand for money**.

Transfer payment   Payment by the government (or, less often, by firms) to persons in exchange for neither goods nor services supplied. Social Security payments are transfer payments since the recipients do not supply anything to the government in exchange for the payments. Wages paid to judges are not transfer payments since, in exchange for the payment, the judge supplies his or her services to the government.

Treasury bill (T-bill)   Debt issued by the U.S. Treasury with a maturity of one year or less. The key distinction between a T-bill and other Treasury obligations is the T-bill's year or shorter maturity. The U.S. Treasury borrows—issues debt—when the federal government is running a deficit, that is, spending more than it receives in taxes. Currently, the minimum denomination of a T-bill is $10,000. *See* **Treasury bond**; **Treasury note**.

Treasury bond   Debt issued by the U.S. Treasury with a maturity of 10 years or longer. Currently, the longest maturity being issued is 30 years. The key distinction between a Treasury bond and other Treasury obligations is the Treasury bond's 10 year or longer maturity. Treasury obligations are backed by the full faith and credit of the U.S. government. Non-treasury government obligations issued by U.S. government agencies (called government or agency securities) have the indirect backing of the government. The U.S. Treasury borrows by issuing, in part, Treasury bonds, when the federal government is running a deficit, that is, spending more than it receives in taxes. Currently, the minimum denomination of a Treasury bond is $1000. *See* **Treasury bill**; **Treasury note**.

Treasury note   Debt issued by the U.S. Treasury with a maturity of more than one year but less than 10 years. The key distinction between a Treasury note and other Treasury obligations is the maturity span of the Treasury note between one and 10 years. The U.S. Treasury issues Treasury notes when the federal government is running a deficit, that is, spending more than it receives in taxes, so that the government needs to borrow to finance its expenditures. Currently, the minimum denomination of a Treasury note is $1000. *See* **Treasury bill**; **Treasury bond**.

Treasury stock   Stock reacquired by the issuing company and held in its treasury, available to be retired or resold.   It is issued but not outstanding and cannot be voted or pay dividends.

Trial balance   In accounting, one of the first steps in closing the books at year-end. All accounts are listed; debits and credits are totaled and should balance.

Trickle down   Theory that economic growth can best be achieved by letting investors and businesses flourish, since their prosperity will ultimately trickle down to middle and lower income people, who will benefit by increased economic activity.

Trust   Fiduciary relationship in which a party, called a trustee, holds title to property for the benefit of another party, called a beneficiary.

Turnaround   Favorable reversal in the fortunes of a company, a market, or the economy at large. Stock market investors speculating that a poorly performing company is about to show a marked improvement in earnings might profit handsomely from its turnaround.

ECONOMICS AND BUSINESS

Turnkey   Any project constructed or manufactured by a company where the company ultimately turns it over in finished form to the client that will use it, so that all the user has to do is turn the key, so to speak, and the project is underway. The term is used of housing projects, computer systems, utility plants, and other projects.

U **Unaffiliated union**   Union not affiliated with the AFL/CIO. The United Mine Workers and the Teamsters are two of the largest unaffiliated unions. *See also* **Independent union**.

Unbalanced growth   Economic growth in which certain sectors of the economy grow faster than others, thus causing economic dislocations or economically risky overreliance of the economy upon certain sectors.

Underground economy   Portion of the economy that goes largely undetected by taxing authorities. Transactions usually are barter or in cash and include both illegal activities and activities that would be legal except for their unrecorded nature.

Unemployment   The state of being without paid work, although willing and able and actively seeking work.

Unemployment rate   The fraction of the labor force who are unemployed. Defined as the total number of unemployed workers divided by the labor force, which equals the total number of unemployed workers plus the total number of employed workers. The unemployment rate is a key macroeconomic variable since it is intimately related to the nation's aggregate economic well-being.

Unfavorable balance of trade   Value of a country's imports exceeding value of its exports. The United States has had an unfavorable balance of trade throughout the early and middle 1980s.

Union   Employee association designed to promote employee rights and work-related welfare.

Union shop   A situation in which an employer may hire any worker without regard for whether the worker belongs to a union, but once hired the worker must join the union as a condition for retaining his or her job. *See* **Agency shop**; **Closed shop**, **Open shop**.

Utility   When used in economics, the satisfaction a consumer attains from his or her consumption of goods and services. Also used informally to describe the securities of public utilities companies.

V **Value added tax (VAT)**   A tax levied on the value added to a product at each stage of its manufacturing cycle as well as at the time of purchase by the ultimate consumer. For example, a steel company would pay a tax on the iron it purchases to make steel; an automobile manufacturer would pay a tax on the steel it bought to make a car; finally, the consumer would pay a tax on the car when it was purchased. The value-added tax is a major source of revenue for countries in the European Common Market but is not used in the United States.

Variable annuity   *See* **Annuity**.

Variable cost   Costs incurred by a firm that change with the level of production. Wages, the expense of raw materials, and depreciation of the firm's capital equipment are all examples of variable costs because they will change with changes in the amount of output produced. *Contrast* **Fixed costs**.

Velocity   Velocity measures how many times a dollar is spent in a given period of time. For example, a dollar spent on a pizza may be paid to an employee who uses the dollar to buy a book. The dollar may next be used to pay another worker who uses the dollar to buy paint, and so on. Velocity is an important component in the equation of exchange. *See* **Equation of exchange**; **Quantity theory of money**.

Venture capital   Important source of financing for start-up companies or others embarking on new or turnaround ventures that entail some investment risk but offer the potential for above-average future profits; also called risk capital. Prominent among firms seeking venture capital in the 1980s are those classified as emerging-growth or high-technology companies.

Vertical merger   Combination into one business of firms at different stages of production. For instance, the purchase by General Motors of one of its steel suppliers would be a vertical merger. Vertical mergers generally do not pose the major threat of creating a monopoly and so are often easier to consummate than horizontal mergers. *Compare* **Horizontal merger**.

Vertical union   Labor union consisting of many crafts and unskilled occupations within the same industry. The CIO under the leadership of John L. Lewis was instrumental in creating industrial unions causing vertical unionization in industries, as opposed to the horizontal craft union policy of the AFL.

Vesting   Entitlement of a pension plan participant (employee) to receive full benefits at normal retirement age (or a reduced benefit upon early retirement), whether or not the participant still works for the same employer. The Employee Retirement Income Security Act of 1974 (ERISA) mandates vesting under certain specific rules.

Volatility   Tendency of a security, comodity or market to rise or fall sharply in price within a short-term period. An individual stock's volatility is related to that of the overall market using the Beta coefficient (called "Beta" for short).

W **Wage stabilization**   When wages cease to change rapidly; also a collection of policies intended to bring about an end to inflationary wage increases.

Wagner Act   Legislation of 1935 that significantly strengthened labor's bargaining power; also called National Labor Relations Act. The Act created the National Labor Relations Board (NLRB), and prohibited antilabor practices by management. In 1937, the Supreme Court declared the Wagner Act constitutional.

Wall Street   Common name for the financial district at the lower end of Manhattan in New York City where major stock exchanges and other financial institutions are located.

Warrant   Short for subscription warrant, a security usually issued together with a bond or preferred stock, that entitles the holder to buy an amount of common stock at a specified price for a stated period of years or for perpetuity. Warrants are freely transferable and traded on the major exchanges.

Wasting asset
1. Fixed asset, other than land, that has a limited useful life and is therefore subject to depreciation.
2. Natural resource that diminishes in value because of: extractions of oil, ores, or gas, the removal of timber; or similar depletion.

Wealth The net value of all the assets a person owns. Correctly calculated, wealth should include the value of a person's skills, that is, the value of all future earnings from these skills. *See* **Human capital**.

Welfare state Country in which government provides considerable services to its population, particularly in the areas of medical care, minimum income guarantees, and retirement pensions.

Wetback Illegal Mexican immigrant who crossed the Rio Grande river into the United States for work. An individual who employs wetbacks is employing illegal Mexican immigrants.

White-collar worker Classification for employees performing nonmanual work, which includes the majority of employees in the United States today. White-collar workers are those employees who work in clerical, administrative, and professional nonmanual occupations.

Windfall profit Profit that occurs suddenly as a result of an event not controlled by the person or company profiting from it.

Workers Compensation Acts Statutes that in general establish liability of an employer for injuries or sicknesses that arise out of and in the course of employment. The liability is created without regard to the fault or negligence of the employer. Benefits generally include hospital and other medical payments and compensation for loss of income. If the injury is covered by the statute, compensation thereunder will be the employee's only remedy against his employer.

Working capital Current assets less current liabilities, properly called *net working capital*. Working capital is a measure of a company's liquidity. Sources of working capital are (1) net income, (2) increase in noncurrent liabilities, (3) increase in stockholders' equity, and (4) decrease in noncurrent assets.

Work papers Documents prepared or obtained by the auditor in performing an examination of a client's financial records. The work papers may be called into court and may be subject to examination by the IRS when they relate to tax pool analysis. Included in the work papers are schedules, analyses, transcriptions, memos, and confirmation results related to balance sheet and income statement items. The work papers serve as the basis of the work performed and support the auditor's opinion. Upon review of the work papers, a reviewer can determine the quality of the work performed.

Yankee Bond Market Dollar-denominated bonds issued in the United States by foreign banks and corporations. The bonds are issued in the United States when market conditions there are more favorable than on the Eurodollar bond market or in domestic markets overseas.

Year-to-date (YTD) Accumulation of accounts from the start of the fiscal year to the latest available period. Sales, purchases, and profits for any current week or month may be displayed year-to-date.

Yield curve Graph showing how interest rates change with the time left before a security matures. This is commonly plotted with the interest rate on the vertical axis and the time to maturity on the horizontal axis. The resulting diagram shows whether short-term interest rates are higher or lower than long-term interest rates.

Zero-base budgeting (ZBB) Method of setting budgets for corporations and government agencies that requires a justification of all expenditures, not only those that exceed the prior year's allocations. Thus all budget lines are said to begin at a zero base and are funded according to merit.

Zero coupon security Security that makes no periodic interest payments but instead is sold at a deep discount from its face value. The buyer of such a bond receives the rate of return by the gradual appreciation of the security, which is redeemed at face value on a specified maturity date. For tax purposes, the Internal Revenue Service maintains that the holder of a zero-coupon bond owes income tax on the interest that has accrued each year.

Zero economic growth When national income neither grows nor falls. A few groups advocate zero economic growth as a solution to problems of pollution, resource depletion, and so on.

Zero population growth (ZPG) Forecast of no further increase in the population of the United States. Demographers study fertility rates to determine whether the United States will incur ZPG; economic and business implications are significant.

Zone of employment Physical area within which injuries to an employee are compensable by workers' compensation laws. It denotes the place of employment and surrounding areas, including the means of entrance and exit, that are under control of the employer.

GOVERNMENT

Abolitionist Before the American Civil War, one who believed in the doing away with slavery. (*See also* **Abolition**, page 10-2)

Abrogation The destruction or annulment of a former law by an act of legislation, by usage, or by constitutional authority.

Absentee voting A provision of many democracies that allows those who may have problems recording their vote at the polling booth the opportunity to vote. Examples include postal voting, special voting booths, and proxy voting.

Absolute monarchy A form of government in which the head of state occupies his or her position as a hereditary right and exercises complete control over the affairs of government; a limited, or *constitutional,* monarchy is one in which the head of state has powers that are limited by law or custom and his or her duties are largely ceremonial.

Acquittal The clearing of a person of a crime he or she has been charged with. A finding of not guilty.

Act A bill that has been approved by a legislature and has also passed through any other procedure required by the constitution of a country. (For example, in the United States an act may be subject to Supreme Court review for its constitutionality.) Lawyers commonly refer to acts as statutes.

Action The legal demand for one's rights to be asserted in court.

Adjourn To stop a meeting.

Adjournment sine die To adjourn without setting a date for reconvening.

Adjudication The application by courts of legal rules to a particular set of facts.

Administration The term that applies to those in charge of management of the executive department. (For example, the Clinton Administration.)

Administration bill One proposed to the Congress by the President, often as part of the President's legislative program.

Adversary system The system of trial practiced in the United States and some other countries in which each of the opposing parties has full opportunity to present and establish its opposing arguments before a court.

Advice and consent Under Article II, Section 2 of the United States Constitution, the advice and consent of the Senate is needed in two situations: a two-thirds vote is necessary to approve foreign treaties, while a majority vote is necessary to confirm the appointment of ambassadors, Supreme Court justices, and heads of Cabinet departments.

Affidavit A written or printed declaration or statement of facts, made voluntarily, and confirmed by an oath.

Affirm When a higher court declares that a lower court's decision was valid and correct.

Affirmative action Policies designed to incorporate ethnic and racial minorities, including women, into political, economic, and social institutions. First use of the term was in 1961 in an executive order issued by President John F. Kennedy.

Aggression Attack or invasion of territory of another country.

Agrarian parties Political groups or organizations that claim to represent the interests of the agricultural sectors of the population. (For example, the Grange.)

Alien Someone who is not a citizen of a country. An alien is a person within the meaning of the due process clause of the United States Constitution.

Allegiance Obligation of obedience to a government.

Alliance A union or association of two or more countries, formed by a league or treaty for reasons of common interest.

Ambassador A public officer or representative of one government commissioned to conduct international business with a foreign government.

Amendment A change or revision. A provision in the United States Constitution allowing for change with time. A provision that has been added to the Constitution. *See* The Constitution of the United States, pages 10-91 to 10-105.

American Revolution The successful revolt of the American colonies against English rule which resulted in the establishment of the United States.

Amnesty An act of pardon or forgiveness, usually granted by a government, to a person or group of persons.

Anarchy A political outlook that rejects forms of authority. Lack of government and law. Anarchists support a social order based on voluntary cooperation between individuals and groups.

Anti-Federalists Originally those who opposed the Federal Constitution drafted in Philadelphia in 1787. Advocates of state power as opposed to strong central government.

Appeal The request for a review. In law, an appeal is the resorting to a superior court to review the decision of a lower court. The superior court is said to have appellate jurisdiction.

Appeasement The act of giving in to a potential enemy in the hope that further aggression will be avoided.

Appellate jurisdiction The authority of a court to review the decisions of a lower or inferior court; to hear and decide cases on appeal.

Apportionment Determining the number of representatives that a state, country, or other subdivision may send to a legislature. Based on the population of given area.

Appropriation act A legislative act authorizing the expenditure of public funds for specified purposes.

Appropriations Funds set aside for a particular use. The term is usually applied to governmental expenditures.

Arbitration The settlement of a dispute by a hearing before one or more persons chosen by the conflicting parties. It is agreed in advance that the disputing parties will abide by the arbitrator's award.

Aristocracy The theory and practice of government rule by a special class or caste of persons making up an elite. Common historical usage implies an inherited nobility.

Armistice The suspension or cessation of hostilities between belligerent nations for a considerable time. Usually negotiations for a durable peace are anticipated by the participating parties.

Arraignment In criminal practice, to bring the prisoner to court in person to answer a charge.

Articles of Confederation   The first formal Constitution of the United States, ratified in 1781. The Articles were replaced by the Constitution in 1789. *See also* History of the United States section, page 10-5.

Assembly   The lower or more numerous branch of a legislature.

Assembly, right of   Right guaranteed by the First Amendment of the United States Consitution. The right of a collection of persons to meet together, peacefully, for purposes including the protest of governmental policies and the promotion of ideas.

Assessed value   The value placed on a property by local government for real estate tax purposes. Generally less than *market* value, the price for which the property could be sold.

Association of Southeast Asian Nations (ASEAN)   Organization of nations of Southeast Asia, including Indonesia, Malaysia, Philippines, Singapore, and Thailand, formed in 1967 to promote economic, social, and cultural cooperation and development.

Attorney General   Head of the Department of Justice with responsibility for advising the president and others on legal matters.

Authorization bill   A legislative enactment that authorizes a program and often limits the funds needed to finance it. Normally passed prior to a related appropriations bill, which actually makes money available, sometimes less than the amount authorized.

Autocracy   Literally, self-rule; rule or government by an individual who is not held responsible for his or her actions through any normal political process.

Autonomy   Limited independence; self-government without sovereign power.

B **Baby boomer**   One of the unusually large number of individuals born during the years after World War II, roughly 1945–1965.

Bail   The amount of money or property held by the court to ensure that a person will show up for his or her trial.

Balance of power   A situation in which nations possess sufficient political, economic, and military power to prevent others from achieving a dominant advantage in world affairs; an equilibrium between states so that, in a time of crisis, neither side will attack the other.

Balance of trade   A measure of a country's exports and imports; a favorable balance is said to exist if exports exceed imports, an unfavorable balance exists if imports exceed exports.

Ballot   Method of voting, usually in secret, by written or printed tickets or slips of paper, or voting machine.

Barrio   A Spanish word meaning "neighborhood." A section of a city in the United States inhabited predominantly by people of Spanish background.

Belligerent   A country that is at war or is openly supporting another country at war.

Bicameral   The organization of the legislative body into two distinct groups of members, selected on different bases, and usually for different terms; called *houses* in English-speaking countries, elsewhere they are usually called *chambers;* the lower house is usually selected by broad popular vote (U.S.

House of Representatives), the upper may represent political subdivisions within a country (U.S. Senate); although they deliberate and vote separately, both houses must pass most measures to be enacted; a bicameral structure is thought to prevent the passage of poorly considered legislation.

Bilateral   Two-sided, as opposed to unilateral, one-sided, or as compared to multilateral, many-sided action or treaty.

Bill   A proposed law under consideration by a legislative body; when passed it becomes a law.

To obtain a copy of a bill, resolution, committee report or public law, call or write your legislator. You may also write directly to the House or Senate.

For House measures (H.R. –) or Public Laws (P.L. –), write: House Document Room, B-18 House Annex II, Washington, DC 20515 or call 202-225-3456.

For Senate measures (S. –) or Public Laws (P.L. –), write: Senate Document Room, B-4 Hart Building, Washington, DC 20510. (Telephone requests are not accepted.)

Bill of attainder   A law that punishes a specific person without the benefit of a trial. A bill of attainder is prohibited by the United States Constitution in Article I, Section 9.

Bill of Rights   A listing of fundamental rights guaranteed to the people against infringement by the government; the first ten amendments to the U.S. Constitution.

Bi-metallism   Backing a nation's currency with both gold and silver.

Black Code   A series of laws severely restricting the rights of African-Americans during the Reconstruction period and after, largely in southern states.

Black power   A political and social movement arguing that African-Americans should exercise control over their own destiny. Assumes that the group needs political and economic power to achieve its goals. The concept has since been adopted by several racial, ethnic, and other groups.

Bloc   A group of political parties temporarily joined to work for the same goal.

Blue-collar worker   An individual who works in industry or in a factory. Generally refers to the working class.

Blue laws   Laws regulating entertainment, work, and business on Sundays. Laws written to enforce moral behavior.

Board of Estimate   Local government board in some large cities responsible for determining tax rates and budgets.

Body politic   A social compact or agreement by which the group covenants with each member, and each member with the whole group, that certain laws shall govern for the common good. (For example, the Mayflower Compact.)

Boondoggle   The expenditure of public money on usually worthless public projects.

Bourgeoisie   The middle class. Particularly, merchants and industrialists in that period when nobility was the upper class. Bourgeois refers to one who is a member of the middle class.

Boycott   A refusal to conduct business with a particular person or group of persons in order to obtain acceptance of certain conditions.

EXHIBIT 7.1
How a Bill Becomes a Law*

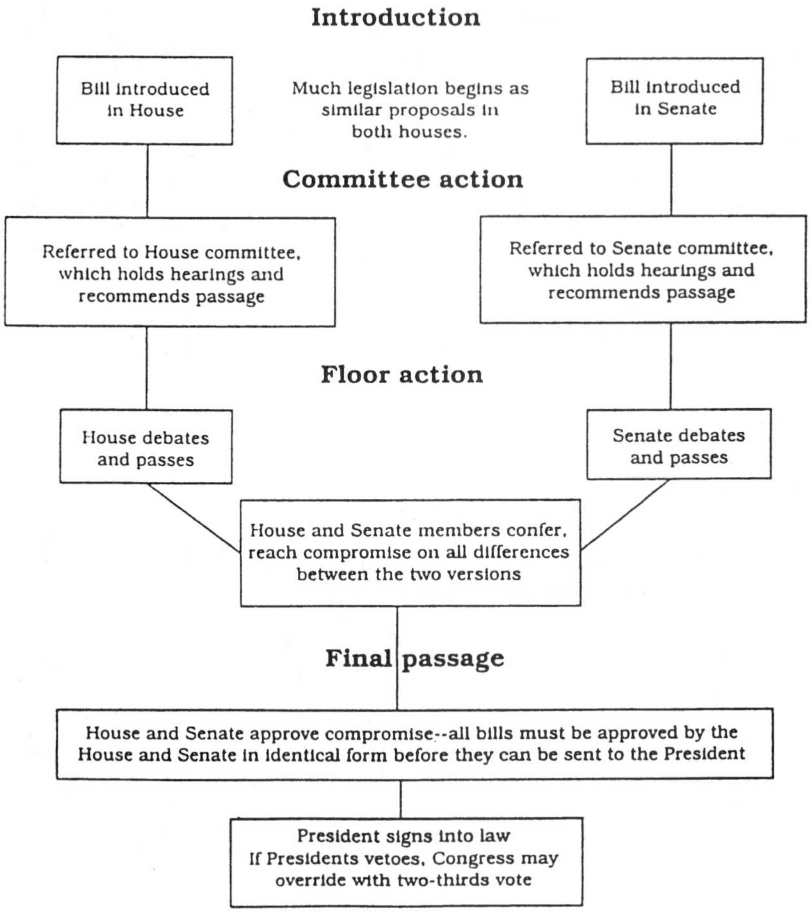

Introduction

| Bill Introduced in House | Much legislation begins as similar proposals in both houses. | Bill Introduced in Senate |

Committee action

| Referred to House committee, which holds hearings and recommends passage | | Referred to Senate committee, which holds hearings and recommends passage |

Floor action

| House debates and passes | | Senate debates and passes |

House and Senate members confer, reach compromise on all differences between the two versions

Final passage

House and Senate approve compromise--all bills must be approved by the House and Senate in identical form before they can be sent to the President

President signs into law
If Presidents vetoes, Congress may override with two-thirds vote

*Source: Reprinted by permission of the National Association of Towns and Townships.

GOVERNMENT

Brinkmanship   A term coined in respect to the foreign policy approach of Secretary of State John Foster Dulles, and used since to describe a gambler's attitude in the management of foreign affairs. Dulles said that one must be prepared to go to the "brink," presumably atomic war, if a nation were to be taken seriously in international affairs.

Budget   A financial statement that estimates and limits future expenses by noting anticipated income and expenses. In the United States, the legislative branch and its committees play a leading role in budgetary decision making.

Budget, Capital   Part of a local budget used for physical improvements and the purchase of major equipment. Financed through long-term debt or state or federal grants.

Bundestag   The lower house of the Federal Republic of Germany; the upper house is known as the *Bundesrat.*

Burden of proof   In the law of evidence, the necessity or duty of proving a fact or facts in dispute. In the United States, where a criminal is presumed innocent until proven guilty, the prosecutor has the burden of proof.

Bureaucracy   Permanent administrative agencies of government designed to carry out public policy; commonly used in a negative sense to connote unresponsiveness or an unreasoning devotion to rules.

 **Cabinet**   Composed of the heads of major administrative departments who, as a group, discuss whatever matters the President decides to bring to their attention; among its members in the U.S. government are the Attorney General and the Secretaries of State, Treasury, Defense, Interior, Agriculture, Commerce, Labor, Transportation, Education, and others. *See* **Exhibit 7.4**, page 7-19.

Canon Law   Laws, rules, or ordinances of the church.

Capital The chief city of a state or nation. The seat of government. Money or property used for the production of wealth.

Capitalism An economic system in which most of the means of producing and managing goods and services are privately owned and operated in competition with others for a profit.

Capital offense A crime for which the death penalty may be imposed.

Capitation tax Tax on the basis of population. To be distinguished from taxes on merchandise.

Capitol Hill The location of the Capitol Building in Washington, D.C. Commonly used to refer to the U.S. Congress.

Caribbean Community and Common Market (Caricom) Association of island nations in the Caribbean, established in 1973, to coordinate foreign policy and improve cooperation in economic, social, and cultural areas.

Cartel A business monopoly that extends beyond national boundaries.

Caucus A meeting of partisans, commonly members of the same political party, to plan strategies or nominate candidates.

Caveat A warning to be careful, to beware.

Cede To give up. Usually used in the context of land.

Censorship The practice of putting restrictions on or suppressing the expression of information, opinion, ideas, or the arts.

Censure A formal declaration of disapproval. An expression by a legislative body condemning the actions of a member.

Census A periodic official count of people of a state, nation, or other political subdivision. The census is taken every ten years in the United States and a primary purpose of the census is to reapportion legislative districts.

Central Intelligence Agency (CIA) The government agency responsible for gathering and analyzing foreign intelligence for the United States.

Certiorari An order commanding judges of a lower court to certify the record of a case for judicial review by an appellate court. Certiorari is most commonly used to refer to the Supreme Court of the United States, which uses the method to choose the cases it wishes to hear.

Chargé d'affaires An embassy official ranking just below the ambassador who takes charge when the ambassador is not available.

Charter A document issued by a government or ruler granting rights and privileges to an individual or group. (For example, charters were granted to the founders of the 13 American colonies in the 17th century, whether companies or proprietors.)

Checks and balances An organizational arrangement that enables each of the coordinate branches of a government to exercise some degree of control over the others, for example, the power of the chief executive to veto acts of the legislature. This system enables the legislative, executive, and judicial branches to exercise limited control over the others and thereby protect itself against encroachments on its authority.

Chief Justice The presiding judge of the United States Supreme Court. *See also* **Exhibit 10.5**, page 10-71.

Chilling effect Any law or practice that has the effect of discouraging an individual, or group of individuals, from exercising their constitutional rights.

Citizen A member of a country who owes allegiance to it and is entitled to its protection; citizenship may be obtained by birth within the country, by birth outside the country if parents are citizens and by naturalization, a process in which applications must meet qualifications established by law.

City charter An outline for a municipal corporation that prescribes the form of city government, powers and duties of municipal officials, and other details concerning procedures and powers; a state legislature may pass a special act that constitutes the charter for a particular city, or it may grant "home rule," in which the city adopts its own charter subject to the constitution and laws of the state.

City government Three major forms, with variations, exist in the United States: (1) *the mayor-council plan* is based on the idea of separation of powers and checks and balances; the powers are divided between an elected mayor and an elected council; both "strong" mayor and "weak" mayor plans exist; (2) nominate in a *commission plan* a commission of usually three to five elected members head administrative departments and as a group are responsible for policy and legislation; and (3) in a *council-manager plan* an elected council determines policy and hires or fires a professional manager who advises the council and implements policy.

Civil disobedience A type of lawbreaking used to demonstrate the injustice of a particular law or policy. Used primarily to bring attention to the matter.

Civil law The body of law, distinguished from criminal law, that prescribes the rights and duties of private persons in their various relationships.

Civil rights The rights guaranteed an individual in state and national laws and constitutions against infringement by other individuals or the government; most notable is the Bill of Rights and the Fourteenth Amendment, which indicates that no state shall deprive any person of life, liberty, or property without due process of law or deny any person within its jurisdiction the equal protection of the laws; political scientists identify *substantive* rights, such as freedom of press, speech, and religion, and *procedural* rights, such as protection against unreasonable search and seizure or other rights associated with judicial process.

Civil service The civilian as distinguished from the military personnel of government.

Civil Service Commission Created by Congress in 1883 to establish a merit system by which appointments to federal jobs were made on the basis of qualifications, rather than political favors.

Clear and present danger Based on the Supreme Court decision (*Schenck* v. *United States* 1919) that no restrictions should limit free speech unless there is a "clear and present danger" of substantial evil.

Clericalism A term used to describe the influence religious groups may have on political systems. Primarily used to describe the role of the Catholic church in countries where Catholicism has been dominant.

Cloture A method of ending debate, usually a filibuster, in the Senate by vote of three-fifths of all Senators. After cloture is invoked, all debate and procedural matters must end within a specified period of time.

Coalition A combination of individuals or parties, usually needed to obtain a majority vote.

Code A collection of laws and regulations. Many states have official codes of all laws in force and the federal government has a code of all federal statutes and regulations.

Cold War A term used to describe the intense competition since the end of World War II between the United States and the Soviet Union in which each has sought to strengthen its position by gaining geopolitical advantages through alliances, military power, intrigue, and other ways; characterized by hostility in diplomacy, economics, politics, and other spheres but with an absence of actual warfare. With the break-up of the former Soviet Union, the Cold War is generally considered over.

Collective action Term generally used to refer to the action taken by members of a group with a common interest. The action's purpose is to further the common interest. (For example, industrial collective action to secure protection against foreign competition.)

Collective bargaining Settlement of labor-management disputes by discussion between representatives of the workers and the employer.

Collective security An association of nations with the purpose of providing greater protection from aggression. (For example, NATO.)

Colonial government, types of Three types of colonies existed prior to the Revolutionary War; (1) *charter or self-governing,* these were Connecticut and Rhode Island, which governed themselves under a charter granted by the King to the settlers; (2) *proprietary,* these were Pennsylvania, Maryland, and Delaware, where the King granted land and governing authority to an owner who was often obligated to respect the King's wishes; and (3) *royal,* these were subject to direct control by the King who was represented by a governor.

Comity Courtesy, respect. In general, the principle of comity is that the courts of one state or jurisdiction will respect the laws of another state or jurisdiction. Also used in the relationship between state and federal courts.

Command economy A system in which the national government controls all aspects of economic activity and directs the production and distribution of goods for the country.

Committee of the whole The entire membership of a legislative chamber sitting as a committee under procedural rules that differ from and are more informal than the rules of procedure in accordance with which the chamber ordinarily transacts its business.

Committee system In legislatures, committees consider bills, resolutions, and other items of legislative business having to do with the matters over which the committee has been given jurisdiction. (For example, House Ways and Means Committee considers bills dealing with financial matters.)

Common law Rules of law developed through a process of judicial decision and adherence to established precedent with respect to spheres of individuals and group activity unregulated by the provision of written laws; in the event of conflict between statutory stipulation and the rules of common law, the former prevails; originates with judicial decision and precedent and becomes widely accepted, or common.

Commonwealth of Independent States (CIS) The arrangement formed in 1991 among republics of the former Soviet Union. There is no central government, and decisions are made by a joint council of republican leaders.

Commonwealth of Nations Originally the British Commonwealth of Nations, a loose association of 50 independent nations that were once part of the British Empire. The symbolic head of the Commonwealth is the British monarch.

Communism An economic system based on production of goods and services and the ownership of property by the community; as a government, characterized by government control and planning and, historically, limitation of civil rights.

Compact An agreement between persons, states, or nations. A contract between parties.

Compelling state interest Term used to describe an action of a state, or the federal government, which is justified even though it appears to violate a constitutional protection. The serious need for the "state action" allows the constitutional infringement.

Compromise A settlement in which both sides give up something in order to reach an agreement.

Compulsory voting Although most democracies consider voting a voluntary civic duty, some countries require voting and failure to do so is punishable by a fine. (For example, Australia, Belgium, Greece.)

Concurrent Acting in conjunction with each other. Certain powers of the states and the federal government are said to be concurrent when both have the authority. (For example, taxation.)

Concurrent powers Powers that are exercisable by both the national government and the states; for example, the power to tax.

Confederation A league of friendship. Usually brought together for mutual support. *See* **Articles of Confederation**, page 10-5.

Conference committee A committee created to iron out differences between the two houses of a bicameral legislature in regard to the bills each has passed concerning a particular problem.

Congressional Record Started in 1873, a daily recording of the proceedings of Congress.

Congressional Representative A member of Congress, most frequently applied to members of the House of Representatives.

Conscientious objector One who is opposed to participation in war, usually for religious reasons.

Conscription The draft. Compulsory enrollment for military service.

Consensus Agreement. A set of beliefs, values, and norms shared by individuals at a given time.

Conservative A person who generally supports established procedures and conditions and resists efforts to change; people who favor limiting government involvement in social and other programs.

Conservative Party A major political party in Great Britain.

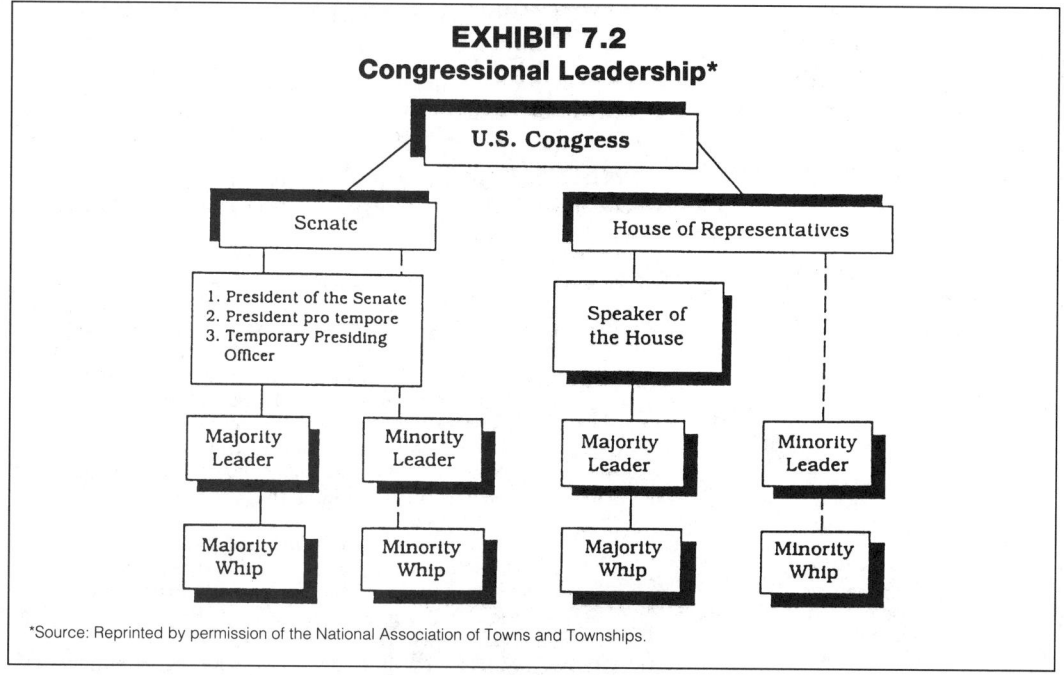

EXHIBIT 7.2
Congressional Leadership*

*Source: Reprinted by permission of the National Association of Towns and Townships.

Conspiracy   A combination of two or more persons brought together for the purpose of committing an illegal act.

Constituency   A territorial division and its population, which forms a key element in the election of a representative.

Constitution   The fundamental laws and principles, written and unwritten, that outline the organization of a government; in the United States the Constitution went into effect in 1789 and consists of seven articles, the first three outlining the powers and responsibilities of the legislative, executive, and judicial branches and the remaining articles setting forth relations between the states, the amending process, some general provisions, and the ratification process; the first ten amendments often called the Bill of Rights, were adopted by Congress in 1791; there have been twenty-six amendments to date; among the basic principles of the U.S. Constitution are the following: (1) the basic law of the land is the Constitution, it describes how the government is organized and operates, what can and cannot be done, and how Constitutional changes may be made; (2) federal system, a union of states in which each agrees to share the authority of governing with a central government, this has resulted in a division of powers between the states and the national government; (3) democratic-republican form, ultimate decision-making power resides with the people; however, representatives are elected to conduct the affairs of governing; and (4) separation of powers, the power to govern is divided among the legislative branch, which has primary responsibility for passing laws, the executive branch, which is primarily responsible for administering the laws, and the judicial branch, which is primarily responsible for interpreting the law. *See* The Constitution of the United States, pages 10-91 to 10-105.

Constitutional convention   A group of delegates or representatives of the people responsible for framing or revising a constitution. Original convention for the framing of the United States Constitution took place in Philadelphia in 1787. Article V of the United States Constitution provides that a constitutional convention may be called if agreed to by two-thirds of the states. *See also* History of the United States section, page 10-15.

Constitutional law   Both the law pertaining to the written document entitled the constitution and all those matters dealing with the organization of government and its relationship to the citizen.

Containment policy   Name given to U.S. foreign policy during the Cold War, a policy whose goal was to prevent the spread of communism.

Contempt   A willful disregard for public authority. In its most common usage, contempt of court is any act to hinder or obstruct a court in the administration of justice.

Continental Congress   Group of representatives elected by the colonies; government for the United States during the American Revolution, 1775–1781. *See* **Continental Congress, First**, page 10-15.

Contract   An exchange of written or spoken promises between two or more parties to do or not do a particular thing or group of things. Contracts are legally enforceable.

Conventions, national party   A meeting of a political party attended by delegates from the states for the purpose of adopting a party platform and nominating candidates for President and Vice President.

Copyright   The exclusive legal right of ownership to a literary, musical, or artistic work.

EXHIBIT 7.3
Standing Committees of the Congress

House Committees

Agriculture
Appropriations
Armed Services
Banking, Finance, and Urban Affairs
Budget
District of Columbia
Education and Labor
Energy and Commerce
Foreign Affairs
Government Operations
House Administration
Interior and Insular Affairs
Judiciary
Merchant Marine and Fisheries
Post Office and Civil Service
Public Works and Transportation
Rules
Science and Technology
Small Business
Standards of Official Conduct
Veterans' Affairs
Ways and Means

Senate Committees

Agriculture, Nutrition, and Forestry
Appropriations
Armed Services
Banking, Housing, and Urban Affairs
Budget
Commerce, Science, and Transportation
Energy and Natural Resources
Environment and Public Works
Finance
Foreign Relations
Governmental Affairs
Judiciary
Labor and Human Resources
Rules and Administration
Small Business
Veterans' Affairs

Coroner   A public official charged with the responsibility of investigating suspicious deaths.

Corporation   A firm operating under a government charter that allows it by law to act as a single person with all the rights of a person under the law. A corporation is usually composed of two or more persons who share ownership.

Corpus delicti   The object upon which a crime has been committed. (For example, body of a murdered person.)

Council-manager plan   *See* **City government**, page 7-5.

Counsel   Attorney, lawyer, or counselor.

County   A subdivision of a state that has varying governmental powers.

Coup d'état   Seizure of power by an individual or group, normally with little or no violence, it is usually carried out by a military officer or group, or by

a person or group of persons who already have some position in the government.

Court   An organ of government, federal, state, or local, that provides the function of the application of the laws to controversies brought before it. The objective of the court is the administration of justice.

Court-martial   A military court for trying and punishing offenses committed by members of the armed forces.

Crime   A legally forbidden act considered an offense against the public for the commission of which punishment is imposed; divided into two categories: felony, which is a serious offense usually punishable with a year or more in prison, and misdemeanor, which is a less serious offense usually punishable with a fine of less than 1 year in jail.

Crown   A concept in the law of Great Britain and other Commonwealth countries, such as Australia, New Zealand, and Canada. The Crown is the legal entity representing the organs of the central government.

Cruel and unusual punishment   Punishment that is so unfitting for the crime that it is a shock to the moral sense of the population. Prohibited by the Eighth Amendment of the United States Constitution.

D

Dark horse   A person who is given little chance of winning, commonly associated with presidential candidates.

Declaration of Independence   A document adopted by the Second Continental Congress on July 4, 1776, explaining why the colonists were breaking their political ties with Great Britain; it suggests the purposes of government and lists the actions by the King and Parliament that have denied basic human rights, thereby causing the colonists to "declare that these United Colonies are, and of right ought to be, free and independent states." *See also* History of the United States section, pages 10-20 to 10-22.

De facto/De jure   A de facto (in fact) government is one that is actually in control of a country but has not established its legitimate government; a de jure (in law) government is the legitimate government, which has established its legitimacy by long continuance, by constitutional procedures, or by recognition by other states. Also applied to situations, as in de facto segregation as opposed to de jure segregation.

Deficit   The amount by which expenditures are greater than revenues. Deficit spending by a government occurs when spending excedes income and it is necessary to borrow funds.

Delegate   An individual who is authorized by either election or appointment to make laws or decisions in the group's behalf. A representative of a group to a meeting or a convention.

Delegation of power   The granting of power by one organ of government to another; also the conferment of power to agencies of government by constitutional provision.

Democracy   Rule by the people; government by the consent of the governed, either directly as in town meetings or indirectly through the election of representatives; based on the principles of individual dignity, majority rule, liberty, equal rights, and equal opportunities.

GOVERNMENT

1870 woodcut showing the first Democratic donkey, a symbol invented by cartoonist Thomas Nast.

Democratic Party   A major U.S. political party that traces its origin to the Democratic-Republican Party led by Thomas Jefferson; many members today emphasize their support of "the common person" and tend to favor using the federal government to advance social and economic programs.

Depression   A low point of an economy's cycle. Time of unemployment and financial collapse. In U.S. history, 1929 marked the beginning of the Great Depression.

Desegregate   To put an end to separation due to race. Usually accomplished by a judicial order.

Despotism   A type of government where the power is in the hands of a single individual. There is no division of powers in the ruling of the country. The ruling figure is known as the despot.

Détente   A period of time, or a policy, of lessening tensions between two hostile nations.

Dictator   A leader with absolute power; a ruler who orders others without respect to constitutional limitations.

Diet   The national legislative assembly of Japan and other countries.

Diplomacy   The practice of conducting relations between nations to maintain or advance national interests.

Diplomatic recognition   Government acceptance of another government's right to represent its people. Used to express approval or disapproval of another government.

Direct democracy   The form of government where the people vote directly on issues. In Greece in the 5th century B.C. all citizens were entitled to vote in the General Assembly. Seventeenth- and 18th-century America experienced direct democracy in town meetings. Today, most governmental decision-making by the people is done through representative democracy.

Discrimination   Unfair treatment of a group of people due to race, sex, nationality, religion, etc. Majority's denial of rights to certain minority groups.

Disfranchisement   The taking away of the right to vote in public elections.

Displaced person   One who is uprooted from his or her native land and forced to move elsewhere. Reasons usually involve war or political oppression.

Dissent   A term commonly used to denote the disagreement of one or more judges of a court with the majority's decision.

District of Columbia   The seat of the federal government of the United States. The Constitution makes the District of Columbia subject to the exclusive jurisdiction of Congress.

Divine law   Those laws attributed to God.

Divine right   The doctrine that the ruler's right to rule derives from God.

Dollar diplomacy   A type of economic policy whereby the United States sought to insure its investment abroad, particularly in Latin America, by using military power or the threat of military power. *See also* History of the United States section, page 10-23.

Domicile   The permanent residence of a person. Determines where a person may exercise the privilege of voting and other legal rights.

Double jeopardy   Being tried twice by the same government for commission of the same crime.

Due process   As interpreted by the Supreme Court, the due process clauses of the Fifth and Fourteenth Amendments prohibit the national government and the states from depriving any person of life, liberty, or property by unreasonable, arbitrary, or capricious action.

Duty   A type of tax, usually levied on imports into a country.

E **Edict**   A formal order. A public proclamation issued by a government leader or governmental authority.

Elastic Clause   Article I, Section 8 of the U.S. Constitution, which grants Congress the power "to make all laws which shall be necessary and proper" for carrying out its legislative powers; also referred to as the "necessary and proper" clause.

Election   The choosing of government officials by those qualified to vote.

Election campaign   The time period before an election when the candidates and the political parties attempt to win votes for the upcoming election.

Electoral college   A body of individuals selected for the purpose of choosing an official; for example, the presidential electors from each state, collectively considered, who select the President of the United States.

Electorate   The members of the population who, as qualified voters, have the right to vote for public officers.

Emancipation   The act of setting free. (For example, Lincoln's Emancipation Proclamation of 1863, setting free all slaves within states which were still in rebellion.)

Emergency powers   In democracies, the right of the executive to suspend normal legislative procedure, and in some cases, certain rights of the citizens in an emergency situation. In the United States

Constitution, Article II, Sections 2 and 3 allow the President powers that can be utilized in time of war, natural disasters, rebellion, and strikes. Like other actions by the executive branch, these powers are subject to review by the Supreme Court.

Emigration   The leaving of one country to reside in another.

Eminent domain   The power of a government to take private property for public use, subject in the United States to the payment of just compensation.

Empire   Many lands and diverse peoples under the control of one ruler or nation.

Entente   An agreement temporarily uniting two or more countries, usually informal and unsigned.

Enterprise zone   An area designed to attract business and industry by offering a variety of tax benefits and other incentives to encourage investment, usually established to attract businesses to economically disadvantaged areas.

Entitlement   A government program in which those individuals who qualify receive funds or benefits based on a specific formula. Once enacted, entitlement programs are available to all those who meet the criteria.

Entrapment   The act of those working for the state to induce a person to commit an illegal act, and then to institute a criminal prosecution against that person.

Enumerated powers   Powers listed in Article I, Section 8 of the United States Constitution. These powers are not denied to the national government or reserved to the states or the people.

E pluribus unum   The motto of the United States, "out of many, one."

Equal protection of the laws   Based on the Fourteenth Amendment of the U.S. Constitution which prohibits arbitrary, unreasonable, and invidious discrimination against individuals or classes of individuals; "no State shall make or enforce any law which shall abridge the privileges or immunities of citizens of the United States; nor shall any State deprive any person of life, liberty, or property, without due process of law; nor deny to any person within its jurisdiction the *equal protection of the laws*."

Espionage   Spying. The gathering of information usually involving the national defense by a hostile nation.

Ethnic group   Composed of individuals having a common culture, race, or place of origin. Especially members of a racial or national minority within a larger community.

European Community (EC)   An association of Western European nations, originally members of an economic organization called the Common Market or European Economic Community. By the early 1990s it had moved toward establishing political as well as economic union with plans to share resources and eliminate internal taxes and other barriers between the countries.

Evidence   Proof presented at a trial through the testimony of witnesses, writings, exhibits, documents, etc. to convince the jury or the court of the validity of an argument or contention.

Exclusionary rule   When evidence is seized in violation of constitutional protections, usually in violation of the Fourth Amendment's protection against unreasonable search and seizure, the evidence must be excluded at trial.

Executive   The function of administering or carrying out the policies of a government; also, an official empowered to direct and control the administration of policies; one of the three major departments of government that is responsible for executing the laws; the principal official in a country, the President.

Executive agreement   An agreement between the President and another country, not requiring the approval of the Senate as with a treaty.

Executive pardon   Authorized by Article II, Section 2 of the United States Constitution, the executive pardon is an act of grace by the President relieving an individual from punishment for a crime he or she has committed.

Executive privilege   The right of the President to not disclose certain information. Usually the information concerns national security, but may also apply to domestic policy affairs. The executive privilege is subject to judicial review. (For example, President Nixon had to disclose contents of certain recordings after claiming executive privilege.)

Executive session   The consideration of official business in secret session.

Exit polling   The practice of polling voters as they leave the polling place to determine quickly the trends in an election.

Ex officio   By reason of holding a particular office; for example, the mayor of a city is made an ex officio member of the city planning commission.

Expatriation   When one lives in a foreign country, either voluntarily or as an exile.

Ex post facto law   A law that is given retroactive effect, being made applicable to action taken prior to, as well as after, its enactment. Such laws are forbidden by the Constitution.

Express powers   Those powers specifically listed in the Constitution given to the national government or one of the branches of government.

Extradition   The returning of a person suspected of committing a crime from one state or country to another.

Extraterritoriality   The operation of laws upon a person beyond the boundaries of the enforcing nation.

F **Fairness Doctrine**   Federal requirment that radio and television stations present important issues so that all the major points of view are fairly represented.

Fascism   A totalitarian system of government controlled by one highly organized party that demands adherence to the regime's political, economic, and social beliefs and uses force and arbitrary power to enforce its desires; characterized by suppression of opposition, centralized government control of private enterprise, extreme nationalism, racism, and militarism.

Favorite son   Candidate for presidency who has support from his or her own state or region but little elsewhere.

Federal   Pertaining to the national government of the United States.

Federal Bureau of Investigation (FBI)   Part of the Department of Justice, responsible for investigating violations of federal law except those involving currency, taxes, and postal laws, which are handled by other federal agencies.

Federalism   A system of government with a constitutional division of powers between a central government and the major political subdivisions of a body politic; both the central government and the major political subdivisions derive their powers from the same source, that is, the constitution; under the U.S. Constitution, this power is divided between the states and the national government.

Federalist Papers   First published in 1787, the *Federalist Papers* were a grouping of 85 essays authored by Alexander Hamilton, James Madison and John Jay promoting the adoption of the Constitution. *See also* History of the United States section, page 10-32.

Federal Reserve System   A central banking system in the United States of twelve district banks under the supervision of a board of governors; the district banks serve as "banker's banks," hold and transfer funds, and seek to provide fluidity and stability to the banking system.

Federation   An organization of states or countries in an association or league.

Felony   A crime of a more serious nature than a misdemeanor. Generally, a felony is an offense receiving a punishment of imprisonment for more than one year.

Feminism   The view that women have the same political, economic, and social rights as men.

Feudalism   The political, social, and economic system prevalent in Europe from about the 9th to 15th centuries, in which land was held under an overlord to whom the landholder owed homage, armed service, and various duties. Powerful landholders often controlled vast areas and had considerable control over the lives of those beneath them. Any political or social system similar to medieval feudalism.

Filibuster   A "minority group" strategy of prolonging debate and resorting to various delaying tactics until a legislative chamber withdraws a measure from consideration.

Fireside chats   Originally radio talks given by President Franklin D. Roosevelt. Now frequently used to describe a media address in which the President presents his proposals directly to the American people.

First Amendment freedoms   The opening Article of the United States Constitution's Bill of Rights. Included are the "open society" rights of freedom of press and speech, the guarantees against any official establishment of religion or any prohibition on its free exercise and, finally, the rights to assemble peacefully and to petition the government. This was ratified in 1791.

Fiscal policy   Financial policy of a government particularly in regard to the management of its debts and the money supply.

Forensic   Belonging to courts of justice. Suitable for public debate.

Fourteen Points   President Wilson's statement of war aims delivered to Congress during World War I. Among the points were freedom of the seas, self-determination of subject peoples, reduction of armaments and, most importantly, at least to President Wilson, a league of nations to keep the peace in the post-war world.

Franchise   The right to vote. A special right granted by a government. Also, the right to market a product or service.

Franking privilege   The right members of Congress have to send mail to their constituents without paying postage.

Freedom of Information Act   Act passed by Congress in 1966 which established a general right of public access to federal government records. The act is designed to prevent abuse of federal agencies by requiring them to make public certain information about their operations.

Full faith and credit   Article IV of the Constitution requires each state to recognize and accept the legislative acts and judicial proceedings of every other state; for example, a marriage, will, or contract in one state must be recognized in all others.

Fundamental Orders of Connecticut   Compact of 1639 in the Connecticut River towns of Hartford, Windsor, and Wethersfield known as the first written constitution in America. *See also* History of the United States section, page 10-35.

Fundamental rights   The more important private rights of an individual that should be protected against infringement. In the United States, fundamental rights are those rights which have their origin in the express terms of the United States Constitution.

Gay rights   A movement seeking the elimination of discrimination against homosexuals.

Gender   The classification by sex, male or female.

General Agreement on Tariffs and Trade (GATT)   A treaty setting rules for international trade. It provides a forum for settling disputes and negotiating changes.

General election   A regular recurring statewide or national election at which the voters decide who will take office.

General strike   A form of work stoppage by wage earners implemented to paralyze the economic system of a nation in an attempt to gain economic or political change.

General Welfare Clause   The provision of Article I, Section 8 of the United States Constitution that allows Congress to tax and pay debts for the "general welfare of the United States."

Genocide   The deliberate murder, or attempted murder, of a whole people. The extermination of a people may be based upon racial, ethnic, religious, cultural, economic, or political factors.

Gentrification   A process in which a neighborhood changes as more affluent individuals move into less affluent neighborhoods and make improvements that have the effect of increasing housing and living costs, making the neighborhood too expensive for the people who were living there before the process started.

Gerrymander   The division of a state into political subdivisions to secure a majority for a given political party in elections. Intentional arrangement of voting districts for this purpose is unlawful.

GOVERNMENT

Ghetto   A part of a city where people of one minority group, commonly African-American, live together.

Glasnost   Policy of *openness* instituted by Mikhail Gorbachev, 1985–1991, to reform the stagnating political and economic system in the Soviet Union. *See* **Perestroika**, page 7-18.

Good Neighbor Policy   Part of the New Deal's foreign policy, aimed at strengthening and improving United States ties with Latin America. *See also* History of the United States section, page 10-37.

GOP   The initials for "Grand Old Party," a term for the Republican party.

Governor   The elected executive of each American state.

Grandfather Clause   A provision in a new law that exempts some from its regulations. Used by some of the southern states after the Civil War to restrict the voting privileges of blacks. *See also* History of the United States section, page 10-38.

Grand jury   A jury of 12 to 23 members whose duty is to receive complaints and accusations in criminal cases, hear the evidence, and grant an indictment where they are satisfied that there is probable cause that a crime was committed and that the accused ought to go to trial. If no probable cause is found, the result is dismissal.

Great Society   A term used to describe the legislative program of President Lyndon B. Johnson in which he proposed to extend voting rights, provide support for health and education, and advance other domestic causes. *See also* History of the United States section, page 10-38.

Grievance   A complaint.

Gross National Product (GNP)   The total market value of the output of all goods and services of a country for the period of one year. The amount includes sales of goods and services to individuals, corporations, and governments and includes the excess of exports over imports.

Group of Seven (G–7)   An organization of the major industrial democracies—Canada, France, Germany, Italy, Japan, the United Kingdom, and the United States—that meets periodically to discuss economic issues.

Guarantee Clause   Article IV, Section 4 of the United States Constitution provides that the federal government guarantees to every state a republican form of government and the protection of the federal government in the event of domestic violence.

Guerilla   One who carries on or assists with irregular war. Guerilla warfare involves the weaker side using methods of their own choice and constantly trying to benefit from the element of surprise. Guerilla warfare was used quite effectively by the North Vietnamese in the Vietnam War to help achieve American withdrawal.

Guild   An association of men, women, or both in the same trade or craft formed for mutual aid and protection.

Habeas corpus, writ of   An order issued by a court to an officer who has taken an individual into custody, directing that the arrested individual be brought before the court and that the officer show cause for the arrest and detention.

Head of state   Leading figure in a political system, sometimes ceremonial. Many times a monarch or president. The head of state is not necessarily the head of government.

Hearsay   Evidence in a judicial proceeding that is secondhand; not coming from the personal knowledge of the witness.

Hegemony   Leadership, paramount influence, or military and economic overlordship of one nation over another, or over other nations or regions.

Heresy   An offense against religion. An opinion going against church doctrine.

Home rule   A system of permitting local units to devise their own forms of government and to be free from external control in matters of local concern; the practice that allows cities to conduct local public affairs with a minimum of interference from state officials.

Homicide   The act of one human being taking the life of another.

Hopper   A box in which a bill to be considered by a legislative body is placed. When a member of Congress introduces a bill, it is said to be thrown into the *hopper*.

Hostage   A civilian seized by a group or individual and held captive to force negotiations, payments, or changes in policy, a technique frequently used by terrorists. *See* **Terrorism**, page 7-23.

House of Burgesses   First representative Assembly in the English colonies, Jamestown, Virginia, 1619.

House of Commons   The lower house of Parliament in Great Britain; members elected by voters and serve terms up to 5 years or until an election is called for by the Prime Minister; the leader of the majority party serves as the Prime Minister.

House of Lords   The upper house of Parliament in Great Britian; members serve for life with the vast majority entitled to their position by heredity and others appointed by the monarch upon recommendation by the Prime Minister.

House of Representatives   The name of the lower house of Congress. Also the name of a similar body in the legislative branch of most states.

Human rights   A large but ill-defined group of rights that are rooted in moral beliefs; the U.S. Declaration of Independence refers to these self-evident truths: "that all men are created equal, that they are endowed by their Creator with certain unalienable Rights, that among these are Life, Liberty and the Pursuit of Happiness"; a human right becomes a *civil right* when it is enacted into law.

Hyphenated Americans   Americans of foreign birth or recent ancestry, such as Italian-Americans or Chinese-Americans.

Ideology   A system of values based on political, economic, and social beliefs that are fundamental to an individual or national way of life; a set of beliefs.

Illegal   Against or not authorized by the law.

Immigration   The coming into a country for permanent residence.

Immunity   Exemption or freedom from something burdensome. According to state and federal laws, a witness may be granted immunity from prosecution for his or her testimony in grand jury proceedings.

Impeachment The formal presentation of charges against a public official for the purpose of bringing about his or her subsequent trial and, if convicted, removal from office; at the national level the power of impeachment is vested in the House of Representatives and the power to try an impeached officer is granted to the Senate.

Imperialism A government foreign policy of annexing territory by force or political pressure, or gaining political, economic, or military control over weaker lands.

Implementation The conversion of intentions into actions.

Implied powers Powers inferred from one or more express grants of authority in the Consitution; powers that exist because the Constitution authorizes Congress to make "all laws which shall be necessary and proper, for carrying into execution the foregoing powers..."

Impoundment The refusal of the President of the United States to spend funds appropriated by law. This may occur when a president disagrees with a program that has been enacted by the legislature. Its constitutionality remains in question.

Inalienable rights Rights that cannot be surrendered. The Declaration of Independence announced that "all men were created equal" and "endowed by their Creator with certain inalienable Rights," more specifically "to Life, Liberty and the pursuit of Happiness."

Inauguration Ceremony at which an official is sworn into office.

Income Money or other gain received by an individual, corporation, etc. for labor or services, or from property or investments. Common classes of income include salaries, wages, business profits, dividends, interest, rents, royalties, alimony, annunities, etc.

Incumbent The person currently holding an elected office.

Indictment A written accusation prepared by a grand jury, indicating that there is sufficient evidence to bring the accused person to trial.

Indirect election When an office holder, such as the President of the United States, has been elected by a designated body of persons (electoral college), who in turn have been elected by an even larger electorate (eligible voters).

Industrial Revolution The phase of economic development in a country characterized by a change from home to factory production.

Inflation An economic condition in which there is a decline in the value of money and an increase in the prices for goods and services. Thought to be caused by excessive increases in the money supply and/or expansion of credit.

Infrastructure The basic structures, or foundation, upon which a country depends for its economic existence and growth. Among these are transportation and communication systems, power plants, water and sewer systems, and education.

Inherent powers Powers not granted by another authority. Powers not listed in the Constitution, but which are necessarily in the government by reason of its role as a government. The conducting of foreign affairs includes inherent powers.

Initiative A procedure by which voters petition for a new law, which becomes effective if approved by a majority of those voting on the proposition of a subsequent election.

Injunction A court order requiring a person to do, or stop doing, something that is a violation of law or that would cause irreparable damage to private rights or property.

Insurgent A rebel. One who rises in revolt against authorities.

Insurrection A rebellion of citizens in resistance to their government. The American Civil War sometimes is referred to as an insurrection.

Integration Bringing together or making as one. Applied especially to blacks and whites in a number of social areas.

Interest group A coherent group with special interests that it seeks to have government serve; when such a group is organized and uses the methods of pressure politics to attain its ends, it is called a *pressure group*.

Internal Revenue Service (IRS) An agency under the Department of the Treasury that is responsible for collecting taxes and protecting against fraud; sources of revenues include personal and corporate income taxes, excise, estate, and gift taxes.

Internal security In the United States, the branches of the central government such as the Central Intelligence Agency and the Federal Bureau of Investigation, which protect the country from subversive activities.

International Court of Justice The main judicial body of the United Nations. Created in 1946, the Court consists of 15 judges appointed by the General Assembly and the Security Council. The Court's decisions are made under international law.

International Criminal Police Organization (Interpol) An organization of more than 145 nations originally established in 1923 and designed to promote mutual assistance and cooperation in law enforcement.

Internationalism An ideology that emphasizes the unity of the world's peoples and deplores restrictive national boundaries and competing national governments.

Interposition The doctrine that state governments may place their authority between the federal government and the state's citizens, thus preventing the enforcement of an unconstitutional act of Congress. The concept is based on the Tenth Amendment of the United States Constitution reserving powers to the states not delegated to the central government.

Interrogation In criminal law, the questioning by authorities of one suspected of criminal activity.

Interstate commerce Commercial traffic of property or persons between two states.

Interstate Commerce Commission Commission established by Congress in 1887 as part of the Interstate Commerce Act to regulate those engaged in interstate commerce.

Intrastate commerce Commerce within a state.

Isolationism A foreign policy which discourages alliances and compacts with other nations.

Item veto The power of a chief executive to veto parts of a bill, usually only items in appropriation acts. Also called *line item veto*.

GOVERNMENT

J **Jacksonian democracy** Historical identification of the United States political system between approximately 1820 and 1850. Period of rapid westward expansion and economic growth. Universal white male voting rights, the two-party system, and the presidential nominating system were included in American political developments. The followers of Jackson became known as the Democratic Party and their opponents were known as the Whigs.

Jeffersonian democracy Counterpart of Hamiltonian ideology of government during the infant stage of American governmental development. Emphasis on decentralization of power. Faith in the "educated" masses and concern for individual freedoms. Ideologies of Jeffersonian democracy can be traced forward to the Democratic Party, and later the Populist and Progressive political movements in American political history.

Jim Crow law A law enforcing segregation, or restricting the rights of African-Americans.

Jingoism Exaggerated or blustering nationalism; chauvinism; belief in an overaggressive foreign policy.

Joint committee A committee composed of members of both houses of a bicameral legislature.

Judge An officer appointed or elected to preside and to administer the law in a court of justice.

Judgment The official and final decision of a court of law.

Judicial The branch of government related to the courts and their decisions concerning the legality of laws and acts.

Judicial activism Judicial philosophy in which judges are instrumental not only in a judicial capacity, but also in a legislative and executive manner. Judicial activism is based on a loose interpretation of the Constitution.

Judicial review The doctrine that the judicial branch has the right of final decision concerning the constitutionality of governmental action whenever the issue of constitutionality is necessarily involved in the settlement of a legal controversy; the power of the Supreme Court to declare legislative or executive acts unconstitutional. *See Marbury v. Madison*, page 7-15 and page 10-53.

Judicial self-restraint The counter-philosophy to judicial activism, which believes that judges should refrain from allowing their personal views or ideas to affect decisions. Strict adherence to existing precedent and statutory law and avoidance of expansion of constitutional doctrine through implication.

Judiciary One of the three main departments of the U.S. Government, consisting of a Supreme Court and such inferior courts as Congress may from time to time establish, such as customs and patent appeals courts, courts of claims, customs courts, and tax courts; the Supreme Court has (1) original jurisdiction in which it hears cases involving states or diplomatic representatives, and (2) appellate jurisdiction in which the Court hears appeals from lower courts.

Junta A Spanish word that means, literally, council; often used to mean a small group, usually of military officers, which seizes power in a coup d'état and carries on a dictatorial government.

Jurisdiction The right to exercise official authority over individuals or territory.

Jurisprudence The philosophy, or science, of law.

Jury A group of impartial people who are sworn to hear evidence and make a decision based on the facts submitted to them; a trial jury, or *petit* jury, generally consists of twelve people.

Justice, Department of An administrative department of the federal government headed by the Attorney General; provides legal advice, investigates violations of federal law, conducts selected cases before the Supreme Court, and oversees U.S. attorneys and federal prisons.

 **Keynesian economics** Ideas of John Maynard Keynes, British economist. Essentially, Keynes believed in government spending during depression periods and retrenching with economy budgets and high taxation during periods of boom. *See also* Economics and Business section, page 6-18.

Keynote speech The address that opens a presidential nominating convention and sets forth the major ideas and themes of the party.

KGB A body, created in 1918 and attached to the Council of Ministers of the Soviet Union, that performed intelligence and police actions dealing with espionage, treason, terrorism, and other anti-state activities.

Knesset The Israeli parliament.

L **Labor Party** A major political party in Great Britain, organized to protect and advance the rights of workers.

Labor union Organization of workers to improve their wages and working conditions.

Laissez-faire Literally, leave be or let alone; the doctrine that government should limit its activities to the protection of life and property and take no part in economic processes.

Lame duck An officeholder who is finishing a term of office that will be assumed by another.

Law Rule or regulation prescribed by authority and having a binding force. Laws in a society set standards for human conduct, and those who go against them are subject to the prescribed punishment. Consult *How Our Laws Are Made*, available free from your U.S. Representative or from the U.S. Government Printing Office, Washington, D.C. 20402.

Lawyer An individual studied in legal issues with the authority to practice law.

League of Arab States (The Arab League) An organization of Arab nations created in 1945 and intended to foster cooperation and mediate disputes. It sometimes represents Arab states in international negotiations.

League of Nations International organization created after World War I to promote international cooperation and to achieve international peace and security. The refusal of the United States to join the League harmed its effectiveness. The League of Nations was replaced in 1946 by the United Nations. *See also* History of the United States section, page 10-49.

Left-wing Individuals or groups whose views are considered liberal or, in extreme cases, radical. The terms "left" and "right" originated in a meeting of the National Assembly in Paris in 1789 in which the more revolutionary members sat on the left of the speaker's rostrum and the less revolutionary on the right.

Legal tender   Any kind of money that is declared official by an act of government.

Legislative committees   In the United States Congress, legislative committees are groups within the House of Representatives and the Senate which are used primarily as fact-finding bodies to obtain information concerning a bill of their particular area of expertise. Through debate, gathering of information from witnesses, and investigation, the committee will prepare a piece of legislation for full debate in the branch of the legislature in which the committee exists. (For example, Ways and Means Committee of the House of Representatives.)

Legislature   One of the three main departments of the U.S. Government, consisting of a House of Representatives and a Senate, whose principal function is making the laws; Article I, Section 8 of the U.S. Constitution lists the powers of Congress; both houses of Congress possess similar lawmaking authority, with the exception that only the Senate has the authority to ratify treaties with foreign nations, and only the House of Representatives has the power to originate bills for raising revenues; the Constitution provides that the House choose its own Speaker and that the Vice President of the United States be the presiding officer of the Senate; both houses select other officers, with the Senate choosing a president pro tempore to preside in the absence of the Vice President; each house determines its own rules of procedure and must keep and publish a journal of its proceedings; in addition to its lawmaking function, members of Congress may conduct investigations, try impeachments and determine the qualifications of its own members, approve or reject presidential appointments and treaties, choose a President from among the three highest candidates if none has a majority, and represent the people from their district or state.

Leninism   The ideology of the Russian revolutionary leader (1870–1924) that the workers of the society would rise in revolution and that eventually the "State" would wither away in a classless communist society.

Letters of Marque and Reprisal   Provided for in Article I, Section 8 of the United States Constitution authorizing private citizens to capture and destroy ships and goods of enemy nations without being guilty of piracy. No longer effective.

Libel   A written statement that is untrue and damaging to a person's reputation.

Liberal   A person who is generally open to ideas that challenge traditions and existing institutions; one who tends to favor government action in social, economic, and other matters.

Libertarian   An individual, and a political party, that advocates minimal government involvement in the lives of citizens.

Liberty   Personal rights and their enjoyment. Freedom from restraints except for those that are mandated by law.

Litigation   To settle a legal dispute in a court of law. The act of adversaries using a court of law and its rules to settle a legal suit.

Lobbyist   An individual or agent of an interest group who endeavors to influence the determination of public policy by presenting information to individual legislators, legislative committees, and other public officials or by resorting to other techniques of persuasion.

Locke, John   English philosopher and political theorist (1632–1704). Locke's writing on natural individual rights and political systems through the consent of the governed were employed by the founding fathers of the American republic in both the Revolutionary period and the formation of our own constitutional form of government.

Log-rolling   The practice in which one member in a legislative body helps another in passing laws of local or personal interest in exchange for the same favor.

Loyalty oath   Oath that declares an individual's support of his or her government. The United States Constitution requires oaths of certain political figures in Article II, Section I and Article VI, Clause 3.

**Machiavelli**   Italian politician, historian, and political theorist (1469–1527). The political doctrine most often credited to Machiavelli is that "the end justifies the means," taken from his most known work, *The Prince.*

Machine   An entrenched political party organization, normally headed by a political *boss.*

Madison, James   American statesman (1751–1836). Commonly known as "Father of the Constitution," a title well-deserved as he was probably the best studied in political institutions among those at the Constitutional Convention. Madison maintained the complete records of the convention and co-authored the *Federalist Papers* with Alexander Hamilton and John Jay. Instrumental in the passing of the first ten amendments to the Constitution, the Bill of Rights. Member of Congress, secretary of state (1801–1809), and president (1809–1817).

Magistrate   One who administers judicial functions.

Magna Carta   Great Charter signed in 1215 that listed the rights of nobles and the limits on the king of England.

Majority leader   Leader of the majority political party in the legislature; responsible for planning political strategy, guiding debate, maintaining party discipline, and speaking for the party in taking positions for or against the executive; actual power may depend on personality, political know-how, and other intangible factors; the *minority leader* heads the political party in the minority.

Malice   A condition of one's mind that results in a person doing a wrongful act to another without justification. Intentional doing of a wrongful act.

Mandamus   A writ from a court commanding the performance of a particular act.

Mandate   A vote of confidence from the people. Also, a mandate referred to a colony held in trust by a major power under the League of Nations (1919–1946).

Marbury* v. *Madison   Landmark case in American constitutional history in 1803, that established the right of the Supreme Court to decide on the constitutionality of an act of Congress. Commonly referred to as the establishment of judicial review. *See also* History of the United States section, page 10-53.

Marking up a bill   The review and revision of a bill, section by section, by a congressional committee or subcommittee before a vote.

Marshall Plan   Introduced in 1947 as the European Recovery Program by U.S. Secretary of State George Marshall, the plan originally offered financial assistance to all war-torn European nations. Rejected by the Communist nations, it served to strengthen Western European nations whose economies had been destroyed during World War II and were therefore targets for Communism.

Martial law   The establishment of military control over a civilian population in an emergency situation, with the consequence that military decrees supersede civilian law and military courts replace civilian courts in the area where martial law has been proclaimed.

Marxism   Developed in the writings of German thinker Karl Marx (1818–1883) and most complete in *The Communist Manifesto* and *Das Kapital*. Marx professed that the State was nothing else than an organization, or "executive committee," of the ruling classes. He saw all history as class history and saw society as divided into the bourgeoisie, which controlled the capital, and the proletariat, which sold its labor for wages. Marx advocated the organization of workers into an economically forceful unit (trade unions) and a politically potent force (revolutionary movement) with the end result being the overthrow of the bourgeoisie and the development of a socialist system of government and economics.

Mayflower Compact   An agreement signed by the free adult males aboard the Mayflower in 1620 to govern themselves by making laws for the Puritan colony.

Mayor-council plan   *See* **City government**, page 7-5.

McCarthyism   Making accusations, especially of disloyalty, on the basis of inadequate evidence; refers to the time period (1946–1955) when Wisconsin Senator Joseph McCarthy was the leading figure of a movement exploiting the fear of Communist subversion in the United States.

Mediation   A third person comes into negotiations between two parties with the intention of helping to settle the dispute. The decision of the mediator is usually not binding on the parties.

Medicaid   A federal program that provides medical care for needy people who are not eligible for Medicare.

Medicare   A federal program that provides health care for persons over the age of 65.

Megalopolis   A large urban area heavily populated and usually including many cities. (For example, New York City and surrounding areas.)

Mercantilism   The practice of achieving a favorable balance of trade (exports exceeding imports) through government acts to benefit the commercial interests of the country. (For example, English Navigation Acts of the 1680s.)

Merit system   The employment of civil service workers on the basis of merit as determined by a

civil service examination, as opposed to appointments based on patronage. *See* **Spoils system**, page 7-22.

Metropolitan area   A densely populated region, predominantly urban in character, that has developed a substantial degree of unity in its social and economic life.

Military regime   The substitution of military for civilian control of the State. Top political decisions are made primarily by members of the military establishment.

Miranda Rule   After a person suspected of a crime has been taken into custody and before questioning begins, he or she must be informed of the following: right to remain silent, statements made may be used against the individual, right to an attorney, and that if the individual cannot afford an attorney, one may be provided. *Miranda v. Arizona,* 384 U.S. 436 (1966).

Misdemeanor   A crime of a less serious nature than a felony. Generally a misdemeanor is an offense receiving a punishment of a fine or a jail term of less than one year.

Mistrial   A trial that cannot stand in law because of error. The trial has been invalidated.

Monarchy   System of government with a king or queen as a ruler. Types of monarchies include aristocratic, absolute, and constitutional.

Monetary policy   Government control of the economy by expanding or contracting the money supply.

Monopoly   Control of all the production or sale of a commodity by a single person or business group; complete monopoly rarely exists except when it is created by government action; in economics, monopoly is used to mean control of enough of a commodity to be able to set prices arbitrarily.

Montesquieu   French political writer and thinker (1689–1755). Inspired by John Locke, Montesquieu believed in the separation of powers between the executive, legislative, and judicial branches of government and saw the system of checks and balances as the key to preservation of a working government.

Moratorium   A period of suspended activity. Delay or postponement of an action or proceeding.

Most Favored Nation Clause   A common treaty provision that grants to the recipient all privileges granted to any other nation by the granting nation. It often applies to trade agreements. The general design of such clauses is to establish the principle of equality of international treatment.

Municipality   An incorporated city or town.

N   **National debt**   Amount of money owed by the government of a nation.

National interest   A combination of the security, economic, and ideological concerns of a nation. The pursuit of policies that seek national benefits and advantages.

Nationalism   A patriotic sentiment or feeling for one's country.

Nationalize   The transfer of property or services from private individuals to a national government.

National Register of Historic Places   A listing of districts and sites of significance in American history or architecture. Listing in the National Register allows the Interior Department to grant funds to improve the property.

National Security Council   Part of the executive office of the President, responsible for coordinating military actions and advising the President on all aspects of national security.

Naturalize   The process of converting an alien into a citizen; applicants must meet qualifications established by law, including minimum age of 18, continuous lawful residence in the United States for 5 years, ability to read, write, speak, and understand English, good moral character, no disqualifying political beliefs, and a knowledge of U.S. history and government.

Natural law   Rules that seem to be true and are argued to be true because they are either rational or because they are ordained by God. Necessary rules of human conduct.

Natural rights   Rights of mankind which are distinguished from positive rights, or positive law. Natural rights grow out of natural law; positive rights are rights that have been created by a government in the form of laws or statutes.

Nazism   *See* **Fascism**, page 7-10.

Necessary and Proper Clause   Provision of the United States Constitution, Article I, Section 8, which authorizes Congress to make all laws necessary and proper to carry out their foregoing listed powers. Sometimes referred to as the "elastic clause."

Negligence   The failure to do something that a reasonable person would do, or the doing of something that a reasonable or prudent person would not do.

Negotiation   The practice of settling disputes by means other than resorting to armed force. Judicial, arbitrational, or diplomatic methods of dispute settlement. The settling of disputes by discussion and compromise.

Neutral   The state of a country when it neither allies itself nor assists another country at war.

New Deal   Term used by President Franklin D. Roosevelt during his first campaign for election in 1932; used to describe the wide-ranging series of social and economic reforms advocated during the Roosevelt presidency. *See also* History of the United States section, page 10-57.

New Federalism   Parts of President Richard Nixon's and President Ronald Reagan's domestic programs that centered on returning some power to the states at the expense of the national government under the assumption the federal government had grown too large and unresponsive to local needs.

New Freedom   Slogan for domestic reform program of President Woodrow Wilson.

New Frontier   The domestic and foreign policy programs of President John F. Kennedy.

New Nationalism   Slogan for the reform program of President Theodore Roosevelt.

Nolo contendere   A plea used by defendants in criminal cases that literally means "I will not contest it." The pleading of *nolo contendere* has a similar legal effect to pleading guilty.

Nomination   The naming of a candidate for office, usually by a political party; nominations may be obtained through a direct primary in which members of a political party vote to select a candidate, by selection of a caucus or convention, by filing a petition, or by a self-announcement of candidacy.

Nonviolent   A peaceful kind of protest connected with Martin Luther King.

North Atlantic Treaty Organization (NATO)   A mutual defense alliance formed in 1949 by the United States and Western Europe to protect Western Europe from attack; expanded to include additional countries in the Atlantic area, the alliance has been weakened in recent years by political conflicts. Its purposes and functions have been undergoing a reexamination since the end of the Cold War.

Notice   In a legal use of the word, a person has notice if he or she knows a fact, should know it, or has been given notification of it.

Nuclear proliferation   The spread of nuclear weapons around the world.

Nullification   The doctrine that state governments have the right to declare acts of the federal government unconstitutional and to prevent their enforcement within the state.

O   **Oath**   The solemn affirmation that one will do something, such as perform the duties of an office or tell the truth in a court.

Obiter dicta   The parts of an opinion of a court that are not necessary to the decision and, therefore, are not to be regarded as precedent for future decisions.

Obscenity   A literary, musical, artistic, or other expression or action that is said to be indecent and to have no redeeming social value.

Oligarchy   Government by a few; a regime in which all political power is held by a relatively small group, usually self-appointed; the term is applied both to such a government and to the group holding power.

Ombudsman   A public official who hears and seeks to resolve complaints against the government from citizens or consumers.

Open Door   American foreign policy in regard to the Far East that was initiated by Secretary of State John Hay in 1899. The policy sought equal commercial opportunity for all nations and the abolition of restrictive spheres of influence, particularly in China. *See also* History of the United States section, page 10-59.

Opinion polls   A survey of potential voters to determine their mood and attempt to determine the outcome of the election. Opinion polls started to play a part in American politics in the 1930s when the Gallup poll predicted the election of President Roosevelt in 1936.

Ordinance   Another name for a rule or a law. Usually issued by a municipality.

Organization of African Unity (OAU)   An organization of 50 African countries formed in 1963 to coordinate economic, defense, cultural, and social policies, and to end colonialism in Africa.

Organization of American States (OAS)   An organization of 35 nations in North, Central, and South America, formed in 1948 to deal with a wide vriety of problems facing the countries of the Western Hemisphere.

Organization of Petroleum Exporting Countries (OPEC)   Created in 1960 to set world oil prices by controlling production and to advance the interests of its members when dealing with the major industrialized oil-consuming nations.

Original jurisdiction The original jurisdiction of a court consists of the kind of cases that may be brought before that court prior to consideration by any other tribunal; authority to hear a case in the first instance.

Override A common usage is that of Congress's power to overturn a presidential veto by a two-thirds vote of both the Senate and the House of Representatives .

P

PAC *See* **Political Action Committees**, below.

Pacifism Doctrine that opposes war. Political, religious, or moral objection to war.

Pardon A grant of exemption from the legal consequences of a crime before trial, during trial, or after trial and conviction; a pardon frees the individual from whatever disabilities have been incurred as a consequence of criminal behavior.

Parliament The legislative assembly of Great Britain.

Parliamentary government A system of government in which the executive and legislative functions are combined and headed by a Prime Minister and Cabinet, who hold office as representatives of the majority party for as long as they maintain the confidence of a majority in the Parliament; to lose a vote of confidence results in the resignation of the governing officials and the call for another election.

Parole The conditional release from prison of a convict before the expiration of his or her sentence.

Patent An exclusive right granted to a person who makes scientific or industrial discoveries. Granted by the government and conveying a right.

Patronage The privilege of a political party organization or party leader of directing the appointment of public officials or employees as rewards for support in political campaigns; it easily degenerates into a spoils system. *See* **Spoils system**, page 7-22.

Penal Anything that relates to or contains a penalty.

Perestroika Policy of *restructuring* instituted by Mikhail Gorbachev, 1985–1991, to reform the stagnating political and economic system in the Soviet Union. (*See* **Glasnost**, page 7-12.) The policy had the unintended effect of promoting new freedoms and nationalism.

Perjury Telling a lie while under oath.

Petit jury The ordinary jury for trial of a criminal or civil case. To be distinguished from a grand jury.

Petition In a constitutional sense, a written plea from an individual or organized group protesting some wrong, either personal or societal, in hopes of gaining a redress. Right protected by the First Amendment of the United States Constitution.

Pigeonhole To file away undesirable or controversial legislative proposals so that they will not be considered.

Plaintiff The person who brings a civil suit. The party who complains or sues.

Platform A statement of principles adopted by political parties at national conventions as a basis for appealing for public support, a *plank* refers to a specific subject in the platform.

Pleading The process whereby parties in a legal suit bring forth their claims and defenses. Usually takes the form of a complaint by one side and then an answer by the opposing side.

Plebiscite A special election in which an unauthorized act of government or seizure of power in a coup d'état is referred to the voters for approval; similar to, but not identical with, a referendum.

Plurality More votes than any other competing candidate, that is, the most votes regardless of the proportion of the total number of votes cast for the several candidates competing for a particular office.

Plutocracy Government by the wealthy. A group of wealthy people who control or influence the government.

Pocket veto The indirect veto by the President of a bill by the decision not to sign the bill within 10 days if, before the 10 days have elapsed, Congress has adjourned.

Police power The power of a government to restrict individual freedom of action and the use of property in order to safeguard or promote the general welfare; the power of the government to impose limits on personal liberty and property rights for the protection of public safety, health, and morals, for example, the power to force individuals to be vaccinated.

Police state Usually an essential element of a totalitarian government where the police, as an arm of the government, have a wide and unquestionable discretion in regard to law. (For example, Nazism during the 1930s in Germany.)

Policy The general course by which a government is guided in public affairs.

Politburo Central organ of the Communist Party in the former Soviet Union's political structure. The Politburo is the functional equivalent of the Cabinet in the government of the United States.

Political Action Committees Commonly known in United States politics as PACs. Groups formed, not part of a political party, to raise financial support for candidates of their choice with the hope of having influence if the candidate is elected. (For example, National Conservative Political Action Committee, NCPAC.)

Political party A voluntary organization that seeks to gain control of the government by placing its members in office; also offers criticism of opposing parties, nominates candidates, conducts election campaigns, persuades people to register and vote, defines issues, provides information to the public, and helps voters act collectively to shape governmental policies.

Political science An academic study of political organizations and the operations of government institutions.

Polity A society or institution with an organized government, state, or body politic.

Poll tax A tax that must be paid before a person is allowed to vote. Poll taxes as a prerequisite to voting in federal elections are prohibited by the Twenty-fourth Amendment of the United States Constitution. Also unconstitutional in state elections.

Populist Originally, a member of a movement promoting agrarian interests and suspicious of the Eastern establishment, particularly banks and large corporations. An individual who sees domestic and social issues as class differences and supports the poor and working people against big business.

Pork barrel   Government appropriations for projects in local districts that provide jobs or confer special benefits to the district and are useful for an officeholder's re-election.

Positive law   Law actually made for a governmental legal system. Laws and statutes of a society. To be distinguished from natural law.

EXHIBIT 7.4
Order of Presidential Succession

(To succeed to the presidency a person also must meet those Constitutional requirements.)
1. The Vice President
2. Speaker of the House
3. President pro tempore of the Senate
4. Secretary of State
5. Secretary of the Treasury
6. Secretary of Defense
7. Attorney General
8. Secretary of the Interior
9. Secretary of Agriculture
10. Secretary of Commerce
11. Secretary of Labor
12. Secretary of Health and Human Services
13. Secretary of Housing and Urban Development
14. Secretary of Transportation
15. Secretary of Energy
16. Secretary of Education
17. Secretary of Veterans' Affairs

EXHIBIT 7.5
Requirements for Office

President of the United States

Elected for a 4-year term. Cannot be elected more than twice or serve more than 10 years. Must be a natural citizen, at least 35 years old, and a resident of the United States for at least 14 years.

Vice President of the United States

Same requirements as for President.

United States Senator

Elected for a 6-year term. Two senators are elected from each state. Must be 30 years old, a citizen of the United States for at least 9 years, and an inhabitant of the state he or she represents at the time of the election.

United States Representative

Elected for a 2-year term. Must be a citizen of the United States for at least 7 years, at least 25 years old, and an inhabitant of the state he or she represents at the time of the election.

EXHIBIT 7.6
Presidential Elections: Major Third Political Parties

Year	Candidate	Party	Percent of Total Vote
1832	William Wirt	Anti-Masonic	8.0
1848	Martin Van Buren	Free Soil	10.1
1856	Millard Fillmore	Know-Nothing	21.4
1860	John C. Breckinridge	Democratic Secessionist	18.1
1860	John Bell	Constitutional Union	12.6
1892	James B. Weaver	Populist	8.5
1912	Theodore Roosevelt	"Bull Moose" Progressive	27.4
1912	Eugene V. Debs	Socialist	6.0
1924	Robert M. LaFollette	Progressive	16.0
1948	Strom Thurmond	States' Rights "Dixiecrats"	2.4
1968	George Wallace	American Independent	13.5
1980	John Anderson	National Unity	7.0
1992	Ross Perot	United We Stand	19.0

Power of attorney   Authorization for one person to act as another's agent or attorney. Power of attorney may be specialized or general in nature.

Preamble   An introduction to a document, as in the United States Constitution.

Precedent   A decision of a court that is considered an example to follow in a later case of the same nature.

Precinct   A small area within a city, comparable to a neighborhood, for purposes of voting in elections or for administering a police department.

President   The chief executive of the United States; to be constitutionally eligible for the presidency, an individual must be a natural-born citizen of the United States, at least 35 years old, and a resident of the United States for 14 or more years; the term of office is 4 years, and no person may be elected more than twice; an extremely powerful official whose preeminent role in the governmental process is attributable to a combination of legal authority and various extralegal factors, including the need for leadership, partisan politics, and the disposition of the general public to support the only national official to be chosen by the entire country; has legislative power that includes the responsibility of providing information concerning the "State of the Union," recommending measures for consideration by Congress, and the power to veto bills passed by the Congress; has political power based on popular support, prestige, persuasive abilities, support of pressure groups, and the power to reward or punish legislators through various political actions; has power as the chief administrator of the national government, the principal determiner of its foreign policy, and the civilian commander-in-chief of its armed forces; charged with the duty of enforcing national laws, possesses important powers of appointment and removal, shares treaty-making power with the Senate, and is authorized to grant pardons and issue reprieves.

President of the Senate Under the Constitution, the Vice President of the United States has this title and presides over the Senate.

President pro tempore A member elected by the Senate to preside when the President of the Senate, who is also the Vice President of the United States, is absent.

Pressure group Any organized group of individuals that endeavors to influence the course of government action by bringing pressure to bear on public officials.

Presumption of innocence A principle of American criminal law that states that one is innocent until proven guilty and it is the State's burden to prove the accused guilty beyond a reasonable doubt.

Primary An election within a political party to nominate candidates for office or delegates to a convention; voters in a *closed* primary must be members of the particular political party; nonaffiliated voters may also participate in an *open* primary.

Prime Minister The chief executive in a parliamentary form of government; the head of a council of ministers.

Prior restraint In American constitutional law, it is prohibited by the First Amendment to prohibit a publication before it is published. To do so would be prior restraint of freedom of press. Three exceptions to the prohibition of prior restraint are if the writings appear to represent a "clear and present danger," are obscene, or invade the zone of personal privacy.

Privy Council Governmental body in England appointed by the Crown that at one time functioned as the Cabinet in the United States. In current times, the Privy Council only meets in full on ceremonial occasions.

Probable cause The situation that exists when the facts and circumstances make the probability of something more likely than less. Probable cause is necessary to arrest or search without a warrant.

Probation In criminal law to allow one convicted of a crime to go free while his or her prison sentence is suspended during good behavior, generally under the supervision of a probation officer.

Procedural due process Rights guaranteed by the Fourteenth Amendment including right to counsel, confrontation of witnesses, notice, and hearing. Protective of property and liberty interests.

Proclamation A public announcement of an official policy.

Progressive Movement Term used to describe the period of reform in American politics during the first two decades of the 20th century.

Progressive tax A tax that increases as wealth or income increases so that those with greater wealth pay a larger percentage in taxes. An example is the graduated income tax. A regressive tax, in contrast, is one under which all pay the same amount, thereby requiring those with limited resources to pay a greater percentage of their income or wealth. An example is the state sales tax.

Proletariat Class of persons made up by unskilled workers. The lower class of people in a population without capital or property.

Propaganda Ideas, beliefs, and information (true or otherwise) spread by an organized group or government. Used to change an attitude or belief in certain directions.

Prosecutor A public officer whose duty is the prosecution of criminal proceedings on behalf of the people.

Protective tariff A duty imposed on imports for the purpose of protecting domestic industries or producers, as opposed to a revenue tariff, which is enacted to raise funds.

Protectorate A country protected by a more powerful state which shares in its government.

Purge The process of removing undesirables. To free a state or party of disloyal elements.

Pursuit of happiness The right of personal freedom including freedom of contract, freedom of occupation, liberty of thought, and enjoyment of home and family.

Q

Quarter A soldier's place, lodging. To give soldiers a place to sleep and meals to eat in a citizen's home. The Second Amendment to the United States Constitution forbade the quartering of soldiers in the homes of citizens during times of peace, and during war it would be permissable only in a manner prescribed by law.

Quash To make void. To annul.

Question time In Parliamentary systems of government, notably Great Britain, the period when government ministers respond to questions from members of the House of Commons.

Quorum The number of members in a legislative body needed to officially conduct business.

Quota A number or proportion assigned to each group.

R

Racism The doctrine that some races are inherently superior to others because of supposed cultural and intellectual inheritance.

Radical One who demonstrates a hostility to established interests. Groups on both the "left" and the "right" who favor changes in the basic structure of society.

Random sampling A process of interviewing an unstructured group within the population.

Ratification The confirmation of a bill, law, or action. (For example, a treaty with a foreign nation must be ratified by two-thirds of the Senate.)

Reactionary One who favors a return to an older, more conservative way of life.

Reaganomics Policy followed during administration of President Ronald Reagan to stimulate economic activity by reducing taxes and government regulations, particularly on businesses and wealthy individuals.

Reapportionment An adjustment or realignment in legislative districts according to population shifts and changes. Article I, Section 2 provides for a national census every ten years for this purpose.

Rebellion Resistance to the operations of a government by force and arms.

Recall An election held for the purpose of enabling voters to remove an official prior to expiration of his or her legal term; the filing of a petition demanding this type of election is prerequisite.

Recess   The suspension of official business by a legislative body. Differs from *adjournment* in that it does not end a legislative session.

Recession   An economic decline or slight depression.

Redress of grievances   A remedy for the people's complaints about a problem in government. Used in the First Amendment to the United States Constitution, "to petition the Government for a redress of grievances."

Referendum   Generally, the referring of a question, such as a tax increase, a bond issue, or a constitutional amendment, to the voters for decision directly by their votes.

Religious right   A general term applied to politically active conservatives professing fundamentalist Christian religious beliefs.

Remedy   In law, a right to which an injured party is entitled.

Reparations   Payment in compensation for damages usually caused as a result of war or a war-connected activity.

Representative   *See* **Congressional Representative,** page 7-6.

Republic   A government in which citizens elect representatives to determine laws and policies.

Republican Party   A major U.S. political party that traces its origin to the slavery issue in the 1850s and Abraham Lincoln; many members today tend to favor the rights of states, as opposed to the federal government, and individual freedom from government regulation. *See also* History of the United States section, page 10-64.

Reserve Clause   A concept based on the Tenth Amendment, which states that powers not delegated to the United States "are reserved to the States respectively, or to the people."

Resolution   A formal expression of Congress's opinion. Not a law in that it does not have a permanent affect on the subject matter of the resolution.

Revenue   Government income from all sources, but primarily taxes, such as income, corporate, property, sales, estate and gift, excise, customs duties, and others.

Reverse discrimination   The idea that some action or effort to compensate for the effects of past discrimination against minorities results in discrimination against the majority.

Revolution   The overthrow of the existing government, usually by force and violence, with widespread participation.

Rider   An amendment to a bill, usually on an unrelated subject and of a controversial nature, passage of the main bill also results in passage of the rider.

Right-wing   Individuals or groups whose views are considered conservative or in extreme cases, reactionary.

Rule of Law   A fundamental principle of American and British legal systems and constitutional government. It involves three points: (1) the absolute supremacy of law over arbitrary power—no person is above the law, not even the chief executive; (2) equality before the law; and (3) the constitution as the supreme law of the land and the protective force of inherent or natural rights.

Run-off election   A second election, usually between the two top candidates. Usually held after an election in which several candidates ran for an office and none received a majority of the votes cast.

S **Search warrant**   A judicial writ or order authorizing a search and describing the place to be searched and the person or things to be seized; legal permission obtained by a police officer from a court to enter and search a building and take persons, papers, or other effects into custody; the Fourth Amendment protects "the right of the people to be secure in their persons, houses, papers, and effects, against unreasonable searches and seizures."

Secretariat   The whole group of secretaries and civil servants who conduct the routine business of an international organization, such as the United Nations.

Sectionalism   Devotion to the interests of a state or some particular section of the country over and above the interests of the nation as a whole.

Sedition   Communication or agreement that encourages disrespect for the law and advocates the overthrow or reformation of the existing form of government.

Segregation   The policy or practice of separating racial or ethnic groups, particularly African-Americans from whites in the United States; facilities and practices that were supposedly "separate but equal" came under widespread criticism and protest in the 1960s and sparked a civil rights movement that resulted in substantial change.

Select committee   A temporary committee established by Congress to study a problem or conduct an investigation.

Selectmen   Local officials, generally found in the New England town meeting form of government, who are responsible for town affairs between annual meetings.

Self-determination   The right of a people to control their political destiny. Enunciated during World War I by Woodrow Wilson, who declared it to be the right of every nation that "wishes to live its own life" and "determine its own institutions."

Self-incrimination   The revelation of facts by an individual that may result in criminal proceedings against him or her; based on the Fifth Amendment of the Constitution, which states that no person "shall be compelled in any criminal case to be a witness against himself"; a person may waive this right and testify if he or she so chooses.

Senate   The name of the upper house of Congress. Also the name of a similar body in the legislative branch of most states.

Senator   A member of the upper legislative body in the United States; each state elects two Senators who serve overlapping terms of 6 years.

Senatorial courtesy   The senatorial practice of withholding consent to presidential appointments to federal positions located in a state if the Senators of that state, members of the President's party, object to the appointees; consent may also be withheld if a Senator belonging to the presidential party objects to a nominee who is a resident of the Senator's state.

Seniority rule   A rule generally adhered to by both houses of Congress and by various state legislatures in designating committee chairmen; that is, the majority member of longest continuous service on a committee becomes chair of that committee; seniority as determined by length of continuous House or Senate membership also receives consideration, along with sundry other factors, in making assignments to standing committees.

Separate but equal doctrine First held in the Supreme Court case of *Plessy v. Ferguson,* 163 U.S. 537 (1896) stating that separation of races was permissible if the facilities were of equal quality. Overturned by *Brown v. Board of Education,* 347 U.S. 483 (1954).

Separation of church and state The requirement rooted in the Constitution and judicial decisions that the government cannot promote a particular religion or interfere with the practice of religion.

Separation of powers An organizational arrangement featured by the distribution of powers among two or more mutually independent and coordinate branches of government, with each branch free to exercise its powers without being under obligation to submit to the dictates of the other branches; the separation into legislative, executive, and judicial branches normally results in a system of *checks and balances.*

Session The annual meeting of Congress. A new session begins each January 3. Each Congress is composed of two sessions, corresponding with the terms of office of the members of the House of Representatives. The 100th Congress, for example, was held 200 years after the government began.

Shield law A law designed to protect reporters from having to reveal their sources of information.

Slander False statements that damage another person's character or reputation; when written it is known as *libel.*

Social contract A political theory that holds that people originally existed in a *state of nature* without law or government and that they entered into a solemn "social compact," which created a state in which the individual gave up some personal liberty in exchange for security and the benefits of law and order; the English philosopher John Locke postulated that the people entered into a "social contract" with a ruler who was bound to rule honestly and justly; failing to do so he or she broke the contract and thereby released the people from obligations of allegiance and they were justified in removing him or her; the earliest known example of a body politic being created this way is the Plymouth Colony, when the settlers wrote the Mayflower Compact to "associate themselves together into a civil body politic"; from the social contract idea grew the belief in government by the consent of the governed that today forms the philosophical bases of many democratic nations.

Socialism A doctrine characterized by government ownership and operation of the means of production and distribution, with all members of the society sharing the work and the products.

Social mobility Movement within a society composed of different social classes.

Social Security A contributory social insurance system paid to participants who have retired or are disabled or to their surviving dependents.

Social stratification A society composed of a number of social levels, based primarily on economic measurement.

Solidarity The binding together of peoples with interest in a similar cause. Polish labor organization led by Lech Walesa that led to overthrow of Poland's Communist government.

Sound bite Message of a political candidate that conveys a favorable impression in a few seconds. Often intended for television news programs.

Southeast Asia Treaty Organization (SEATO) A military alliance formed in the 1950s to contain the spread of communism.

Sovereignty An independent state with supreme authority within its borders, the power of a nation to act without interference or control by another.

Soviet A governing council officially elected by and representing the people in the former Soviet Union; there were thousands of local *soviets;* the highest level of government was known as the *Supreme Soviet,* which was a bicameral body composed of an upper house, the *Soviet of Nationalities,* with equal representation from each of the Republics, and the *Soviet of the Union,* representing the general population; in practice, the Supreme Soviet did not deliberate or debate but listened to reports and endorsed decisions made by the Communist Party leadership.

Speaker The presiding officer of the lower house in a legislative body, the House of Representatives, for example; retains all the rights of a regular member and has considerable power as a result of decisions regarding legislative procedures.

Speedy trial Guaranteed to the accused by the Sixth Amendment of the United States Constitution.

Sphere of influence A geographic area in which a nation seeks to dominate to the point of securing preferential treatment of a political, economic, and even social nature.

Split ticket A ballot that is cast for candidates of two or more political parties.

Spoils system A practice in which a political party that wins an election removes officeholders identified with the opposition and replaces them with its own loyal supporters; ability to discharge official responsibilities is given secondary, if any, consideration; opposite of a merit system.

Square Deal The name given to the domestic program of President Theodore Roosevelt.

Stalinism Ruthless dictatorship. Complete control of political and economic power, often accompanied by the inhumane elimination of competitors or opponents. Relating to Joseph Stalin, the general secretary of the Communist Party of the former U.S.S.R. (1922–1953).

Standing A person's right to bring a lawsuit because he or she is directly affected by the issues raised.

Standing committee A permanent committee in the Congress.

Star Chamber A secret session without a jury in which a person is tried or otherwise condemned as a result of cruel proceedings or the use of torture.

Stare decisis Literally, "let the decision stand." The practice of basing judicial decisions upon similar cases decided in the past.

State, Department of An administrative department of the federal government, it is the chief adviser to the President for foreign affairs; responsible for developing and implementing foreign policy, sends and receives diplomatic representatives, maintains trade and cultural relations, issues passports, and handles other matters involving foreign nations.

State of the Union Address An annual report, required by the Constitution, given by the President to the Congress.

States rights In a federal system of government, these are the rights and powers reserved to the states. (For example, control of intrastate commerce.)

Statute Law established by a legislative body with the approval of the executive (or passed over a veto). Distinct from *common law*, which has been established by custom, tradition, or precedent; *constitutional law*, or the law embodied in the basic governing document; and *ordinances*, the rules established by local subdivisions of a state.

Statute of Limitations A period of time allowed for bringing a lawsuit or charging someone with a crime.

Strict construction The legal philosophy that the Constitution should receive a close or rigid reading and interpretation.

Strike A general refusal to work by a body of workers in hopes of forcing the employer to concede to demands.

Subpoena A writ or order commanding a person to appear in court, usually as a witness, under penalties for disobedience of the order.

Woman flag bearer in a parade for women's suffrage.

Substantive due process Constitutional guarantees prohibiting arbitrary deprivation of life, liberty, or property.

Suffrage The right to vote in an election; the U.S. Constitution states, in the Fifteenth Amendment, that the right to vote shall not be denied "on account of race, color, or previous condition of servitude"; in the Nineteenth Amendment, shall not be denied on account of sex; and in the Twenty-sixth, shall not be denied to anyone 18 years old or older.

Summit meeting A meeting of heads of state concerning issues of mutual concern. Originally referred to United States-Soviet meetings, now commonly applied to any significant meeting of high government or corporate officials.

Summons A notification to the named person that an action has been commenced against him or her in court and that he or she is required to appear, on the day named, and answer the complaint.

Sunset clause A clause within the law that states that the law, unless renewed, will end by a specified date.

Sunshine law A law requiring that meetings of government agencies be open to the public.

Superpower A country with overwhelming power to make war; commonly refers to the United States.

Supremacy Clause Article VI of the United States Constitution states that all laws made in pursuance of the Constitution and all treaties made under the authority of the United States shall be the "supreme law of the land."

Supreme Court Judicial branch of the United States federal government. Created by Article III of the Constitution granting it both original and appellate jurisdiction.

Tariff A tax on imports, normally imposed to raise revenue or increase the cost of imports and thereby protect domestic producers from foreign competition.

Tax A compulsory payment, levied on a person's income, property, or some other value according to law, for the support of the government or to promote a social or economic objective.

Taxing power Power of the federal, state, and local governments. Added in 1913, the Sixteenth Amendment to the United States Constitution allowed the government to impose an income tax.

Territory A part of the United States, not admitted as a state, but with a separate legislature, and with executive and judicial officers appointed by the president.

Terrorism The use of violence or threats to achieve political objectives by intimidating others, undertaken by those with extremely strong religious or political beliefs and who may welcome martyrdom in pursuit of their goals.

Testimony Evidence given by a competent witness, under oath; as distinguished from evidence derived from writings and other sources.

Theocracy A government in which power is concentrated in the hands of religious officials who often claim to rule with divine guidance.

Think tank Research organizations generally devoted to public policy research and often used by political candidates and public officials.

Titular   Having a title that implies authority, but with little or no discretion in the exercise of authority; the Queen of Great Britain is the titular ruler; in the United States, a defeated candidate for President is the titular head of his or her political party.

Tocqueville, Alexis de (1805–1859)   French historian whose nine-month visit to the United States in 1831 and 1832 resulted in his work *Democracy in America*, which deals with social conditions and governmental systems, and the advantages of democracy on American intellect, feelings, manners, politics, and ways of life.

Tort   An injury or wrong committed, either with or without force, to the person or property of another.

Totalitarian   A government under the complete, or total, control of one party or group; a dictatorship.

Town meeting   Often considered the purest form of democracy, the town meeting was the earliest form of self-government in England's American colonies. The gathering of the residents of a township to discuss policy decisions, physical improvements and needs, and financial concerns.

Traditional society   A community that places great importance on preserving customs and values and often lacks modern technology.

Treason   A violation of allegiance owed to one's country; Article 3, Section 3 of the U.S. Constitution states that "treason against the United States, shall consist only in levying War against them, or in adhering to their Enemies, giving them Aid and Comfort. No Person shall be convicted of Treason unless on the Testimony of two Witnesses to the same overt Act, or on Confession in open Court."

Treasury, Department of   An administrative department of the federal government responsible for managing national finances; collects duties and taxes, coins money, oversees the national banking system, and has custody of public funds.

Treaty   A formal agreement between two or more states of the world community; classified as *bilateral* if between two countries, *multilateral* if more than two countries, entered into for the purpose of making, changing, or ending defense, trade or other agreements; in the United States negotiated by the authority of the executive branch and must be ratified by a two-thirds vote of the Senate; the President may also reach agreement with foreign governments by negotiating an *executive agreement,* which does not require congressional approval and, as might be expected, may meet with congressional opposition.

Trespass   An unlawful interference with a person's property or rights.

Trial   The examination of the facts of a case in court to determine who is in the right.

Trustee system   Trust territories were formally known as mandates under the League of Nations. The trustee system was established under the United Nations Trusteeship Council to govern areas toward self-government in the best interests of their inhabitants.

Tyranny   Rule of an oppressive or unjustly severe government. Under the rule of a tyrant. Arbitrary and despotic form of government.

EXHIBIT 7.7
United Nations Organization

General Assembly   The assembly of all member nations, each having one vote. It meets in annual sessions, and special sessions can be called by the Secretary General when requested by a majority of members or by the Security Council. The General Assembly approves the budget for the U.N. and decides what proportion of the expenses each member will bear.

Security Council   A council of 15 members. Five—China, France, Russia, the United Kingdom, and the United States—are permanent members. The remaining 10 are elected by the General Assembly for two-year terms. The Council is responsible for maintaining international peace and security.

Economic and Social Council   A council of 54 members, elected by the General Assembly for three-year terms, responsible for economic, social, cultural, educational, health, and related matters.

Secretariat   The Secretary General, elected by the General Assembly, is the chief administrative officer of the U.N.

International Court of Justice (World Court)   The principal judicial organ of the U.N., it deals with cases submitted to it by member nations and gives advisory opinions. Its decisions do not set precedents. If one party fails to abide by the court's decision, the other party may appeal to the Security Council.

U   **Unanimous**   Agreement by all, without dissent.

Underground   A term used figuratively to describe a political group that operates secretly or as a conspiracy in defiance of law or government authority. Also used to describe economic activities, as in underground economy, conducted without the knowledge or consent of a government, often to avoid payment of taxes.

Unicameral   A legislative body with one house; Nebraska is the only state having a unicameral legislature, established in 1934, many unicameral city councils exist in the United States.

Unitary system of government   A political system that concentrates the power of governing at one level, as opposed to a federal system that divides power between the national and state governments; state governments are unitary systems since, with few exceptions, they possess authority to create units of local government and prescribe the nature and extent of their powers.

United Nations   An international organization of nations formed in 1945 and now headquartered in New York City; its purpose is to promote international peace and security, maintain observance of international law, and promote economic and social progress; more than 140 nations are represented in the General Assembly; the five major powers—United States, Russia, Great Britain, the People's Republic of China, and France—have permanent representation on the Security Council, where they may veto any proposal; many functions are conducted by U.N. agencies: Food and Agriculture Organization (FAO), United Nations Educational, Scientific, and Cultural Organization (UNESCO), the World Health Organization (WHO), and others.

United States Attorney Appointed by the President for each federal judicial district to, among other duties, prosecute all offenses against the United States.

Unwritten constitution Commonly accepted conventions that modify a written constitution; originating in common law and customs; the President's Cabinet may be said to be part of the unwritten constitution.

Urbanization The movement of people from rural areas to the cities, generally associated with industrialization.

V **Vagueness doctrine** A principle of constitutional law that requires that a law must be clear in its purpose and must inform a person of what is commanded or prohibited.

Venue The particular county, city, or geographical area in which a court with jurisdiction may hear and determine a case.

Verdict In practice, the formal decision or finding made by a jury, reported to the court.

Veto power The power of a chief executive to disapprove legislative acts within a designated period of time following their submission to the chief executive for consideration; a veto is suspensive, if the legislature may override it, otherwise it is absolute; the constitutional power of the President to refuse to sign a bill passed by Congress preventing it from becoming a law; the action is taken by the President returning the bill without his or her signature and with objections to the house in which it originated; however, if a bill is not signed by the President *and* he or she does not return it within 10 days while Congress is in session, it becomes a law without the signature; if Congress adjourns during this time the bill dies; Congress may override a presidential veto by repassing the same bill by a two-thirds vote in each house.

Vice President Second highest executive official, elected with the President for the same term of office and must meet the same qualifications; succeeds the President in case of the latter's death, removal, resignation, or inability; presides over the Senate and, by invitation of the President, assumes other responsibilities.

Virtual representation Doctrine that professes that even if one does not have the vote, he or she is represented by a legislature that is sensitive to the needs of the population. A claim by the British in response to American colonial complaints of no representation.

Vote Suffrage. An expression in the political process of one's will or choice.

W **Ward** A political subdivision within a city, generally for the purpose of electing members of the local legislative body; a low-level politician who performs chores for a political boss may be called a *ward heeler* as a derogatory term.

War on Poverty A call issued by President Lyndon B. Johnson that led to passage by Congress of the Economic Opportunity Act; objectives included the improvement of the economy, increased educational and job opportunities, rehabilitation of local communities, and assistance for the disadvantaged.

War powers The powers given by the Constitution to the executive and legislative branches to wage war; "The President shall be commander-in-chief of the army and navy of the United States, and of the militia of the several States when called into the actual service of the United States," according to the Constitution; congressional authority in military matters is indicated by its expressly granted powers to declare war, grant letters of marque and reprisal, and make rules concerning captures on land and water, to raise and support armies, to provide and maintain a navy, to make rules for the government and regulation of the land and naval forces, to provide for calling forth the militia to execute the laws of the Union, suppress insurrections, and repel invasions, to provide for organizing, arming, and disciplining militia; when invoked during a national emergency, these powers enable the national government to do many things not expressly authorized by the Constitution, such as the establishment of compulsory military service, and when the United States is engaged in war, the powers of the national government, by implication, come close to being unlimited; an example is the placement of U.S. citizens of Japanese extraction in "war relocation centers."

Warrant A document issued by a court that gives someone authority to do something.

Watergate A term used to refer to the illegal break-in at the Democratic Party Headquarters in the Watergate complex in Washington, D.C. and the ensuing coverup by administration officials, including President Richard Nixon, which eventually led to a congressional investigation and Nixon's resignation as President. Newly created terms ending in "gate" are now commonly applied to political controversies or illegalities (e.g., Irangate).

Welfare state A society with a form of government that takes responsibility of protecting and promoting the well-being of all its citizens. Support includes coverage for disease, sickness, old age, occupational accidents, and unemployment.

Whip A member of a legislative body whose function is seeing to it that party members are in attendance on occasions when crucial voting occurs; serves as contact person between the leaders of the party and the rank and file party members.

Whistle blowers Government or corporate employees who report to the public about irregularities in their departments or businesses.

White-collar worker An individual who works in a clerical, office, or professional occupation.

White paper An official policy statement on an existing problem issued by government or political officials.

Winner take all In presidential elections, the awarding of all of a state's electoral votes to the candidate with the most popular votes.

Witness   One who testifies to what he or she has seen, heard, or otherwise observed.

World Bank and International Monetary Fund (IMF)   Created at the end of World War II to help war-torn countries rebuild and to promote economic growth throughout the world. As part of the Economic and Social Council of the U.N., the World Bank and the IMF today primarily lends money to less developed countries.

Writ   A legal paper or court order commanding the person to whom it is directed to perform or refrain from performing a specific act.

Write-in   A vote cast for a person whose name is not listed on the ballot by writing his or her name.

Writ of habeas corpus   An order directing an official to deliver a prisoner to court with an explanation of the reasons for the prisoner's detention. If the court finds the reasons inadequate, it may order the prisoner's release.

Writ of mandamus   A court order commanding a public official to perform a duty associated with his office.

Xenophobia   A fear or hatred of foreigners.

Zoning   The practice of dividing land in a city into specific districts, or zones, and restricting the type of building or activity that is permissible, the principal types of zones are commercial, industrial, and residential and various combinations; zoning regulations may also regulate building design, density, installation of sewer and water systems, and other environmental factors.

GOVERNMENT

EXHIBIT 7.8
Government-related Abbreviations and Acronyms

AA	Administrative Assistant; Alcoholics Anonymous
ACLU	American Civil Liberties Union
ADA	Americans for Democratic Action; Americans with Disabilities Act
AFL-CIO	American Federation of Labor and Congress of Industrial Organizations
AID	Agency for International Development
AMTRAK	National Railroad Passenger Corporation
BLS	Bureau of Labor Statistics
BOE	Board of Estimate; Board of Education
CAB	Civil Aeronautics Board
CEA	Council of Economic Advisers
CHOB	Cannon House Office Building
CIA	Central Intelligence Agency
CO	Certificate of Occupancy
COPE	Committee on Political Education (AFL-CIO)
CORE	Congress of Racial Equality
CDBG	Community Development Block Grants
CU	Consumers Union of the United States
D, Dem.	Democrat
DC	District of Columbia
DEA	Drug Enforcement Agency
DIA	Defense Intelligence Agency
DOD	U.S. Department of Defense
DOE	U.S. Department of Energy; U.S. Department of Education
DOT	U.S. Department of Transportation
DSOB	Dirksen Senate Office Building
EC	European Community
EPA	Environmental Protection Agency
FAA	Federal Aviation Administration
Fannie Mae (FNMA)	Federal National Mortgage Association
FAO	Food and Agriculture Organization of the United States
FBI	Federal Bureau of Investigation
FCC	Federal Communications Commission
FHA	Federal Housing Administration
Freddie Mac	Federal Home Loan Mortgage Corporation
FTC	Federal Trade Commission
GAO	General Accounting Office
GATT	General Agreement on Tariffs and Trade
Ginnie Mae (GNMA)	Government National Mortgage Association
GNP	Gross National Product
GSA	General Services Administration
HSOB	Hart Senate Office Building
HSS	U.S. Department of Health and Human Services
HUD	U.S. Department of Housing and Urban Development
I, Ind.	Independent
ICC	Interstate Commerce Commission
ILO	International Labor Organization
IMF	International Monetary Fund
IRS	Internal Revenue Service
JCS	Joint Chiefs of Staff
LHOB	Longworth House Office Building
LWV	League of Women Voters
MC	Member of Congress
MP	Member of Parliament
MSA	Metropolitan Statistical Area
NAACP	National Association for the Advancement of Colored People
NASA	National Aeronautics and Space Administration
NATO	North Atlantic Treaty Organization
NEH	National Endowment for the Humanities
NLRB	National Labor Relations Board
NOW	National Organization for Women
NRC	Nuclear Regulatory Commission
NSC	National Security Council
OAS	Organization of American States
OECD	Organization for Economic Cooperation and Development
OMB	Office of Management and Budget
PAC	Political Action Committee
PILOT	Payment in lieu of taxes
R, Rep.	Republican
REIT	Real Estate Investment Trust
RFP	Request for Proposals
RHOB	Rayburn House Office Building
RSOB	Russell Senate Office Building
RTC	Resolution Trust Corporation
SALT	Strategic Arms Limitations Talks
SBA	Small Business Administration
SCLC	Southern Christian Leadership Conference
SDI	Strategic Defense Initiative
SEC	Securities and Exchange Commission
TVA	Tennessee Valley Authority
UNRRA	United Nations Relief and Rehabilitation Administration
VA	Veterans Administration
VISTA	Volunteers in Service to America
WHO	World Health Organization
WIC	Women and Infant Children

HEALTH AND MEDICINE

PUBLISHER'S NOTE: The material presented in this Health and Medicine section is for informational purposes only. Nothing in this section should be construed as endorsing any product, or representing or intending to represent medical advice to the reader. The only source for this type of information should be your personal health-care provider.

DIET AND NUTRITION

Nutrients

Many of us grew up believing that people got sick from what they *didn't eat*. This is still true in much of the world, where people are starving. In the United States, however, people are more likely to be suffering from illnesses that are caused by *eating the wrong things*. Health problems that have been linked to diet include heart disease, high blood pressure, some kinds of cancer, and weight problems. People who eat a balanced diet, one that includes all the necessary nutrients and fiber, and avoids too much fat and salt, are more likely to live long and healthy lives.

The National Academy of Sciences has developed a set of recommended dietary allowances (RDAs) for 20 nutrients, including calories. These RDAs are shown in Exhibit 8.1. In general, you can get enough of all of these nutrients by eating a variety of healthy foods, without taking vitamin or mineral supplements.

The following discussion provides a guide to the basic nutrients found in food—you will learn how each substance works in your body and contributes to good health.

Proteins

Protein is the basic building block of every cell in the body. In addition, protein is used to make blood, form antibodies that fight infection, and supply energy. You need protein in your diet every day. About 15 to 20 percent of your daily calories should come from protein.

Proteins are composed of materials known as amino acids. The body makes some of these, but others, called essential amino acids, must be obtained ready-made from food. The nutrient value of any food protein is determined by the number of essential amino acids it contains. Proteins that supply the most of these compounds are rated highest in biological value, and best meet the body's needs.

The most common sources of "high-quality" protein are meat, fish, poultry, eggs, milk, and dried peas and beans. Unfortunately, many of these sources are also high in fat and cholesterol (see pages 8-3 to 8-4). However, fish, poultry without the skin, low-fat dairy products, and dried peas and beans provide high-quality protein without too much fat.

HEALTH AND MEDICINE

EXHIBIT
Food and Nutrition Board, National Academy
Recommended Dietary
Designed for the maintenance of good nutrition of

Category	Age (years) or Condition	Weight[b] (kg)	(lb)	Height[b] (cm)	(in)	Protein (g)	Fat-Soluble Vitamins Vita-min A (μg RE)[c]	Vita-min D (μg)[d]	Vita-min E (mgα-TE)[e]	Vita-min K (μg)
Infants	0.0–0.5	6	13	60	24	13	375	7.5	3	5
	0.5–1.0	9	20	71	28	14	375	10	4	10
Children	1–3	13	29	90	35	16	400	10	6	15
	4–6	20	44	112	44	24	500	10	7	20
	7–10	28	62	132	52	28	700	10	7	30
Males	11–14	45	99	157	62	45	1,000	10	10	45
	15–18	66	145	176	69	59	1,000	10	10	65
	19–24	72	160	177	70	58	1,000	10	10	70
	25–50	79	174	176	70	63	1,000	5	10	80
	51+	77	170	173	68	63	1,000	5	10	80
Females	11–14	46	101	157	62	46	800	10	8	45
	15–18	55	120	163	64	44	800	10	8	55
	19–24	58	128	164	65	46	800	10	8	60
	25–50	63	138	163	64	50	800	5	8	65
	51+	65	143	160	63	50	800	5	8	65
Pregnant						60	800	10	10	65
Lactating	1st 6 months					65	1,300	10	12	65
	2nd 6 months					62	1,200	10	11	65

[a] The allowances, expressed as average daily intakes over time, are intended to provide for individual variations among most normal persons as they live in the United States under usual environmental stresses. Diets should be based on a variety of common foods in order to provide other nutrients for which human requirements have been less well defined.

[b] Weights and heights of Reference Adults are actual medians for the U.S. population of the designated age, as reported by NHANES II. The median weights and heights of those under 19 years of age were taken from Hamill et al. (1979). The use of these figures does not imply that the height-to-weight ratios are ideal.

No single cereal grain, vegetable, or fruit supplies all the essential amino acids, though each provides some protein. By combining cereal and vegetable foods with a little meat or other source of animal protein, you can improve the protein value of your meal. Examples of such combinations include rice and beans, peanut butter and bread, cereal with milk, rice and fish, and spaghetti with meat sauce.

Vegetarians may have a problem getting enough protein in their diets, particularly if they do not eat either dairy products or eggs. It is difficult to plan a vegetarian diet so that it includes enough of the nutrients that are often scarce in vegetables, such as vitamins and minerals.

Carbohydrates

Carbohydrates are the starches and sugars that supply most of our energy needs. The energy from carbohydrates allows other nutrients, such as proteins, to be used to build tissue, not to produce energy.

Foods such as bread, cereal, and potatoes are a form of starch known as "complex carbohydrates." Table sugar (sucrose) and honey are referred to as "simple sugars." Foods rich in simple sugars fill you up with carbohydrates without giving you the other nutrients that you need. Complex carbohydrates, on the other hand, are a very important part of any diet. They provide a wide range of vitamins, minerals, fiber, and even protein. Of your total calories, 10 to 15 percent should come from simple sugars, and 40 percent from complex carbohydrates.

Good sources of complex carbohydrates include grains (wheat, oats, corn, and rice), products made from grains (noodles, flour, macaroni, spaghetti, grits, breads, and breakfast cereals), white potatoes, sweet potatoes, and dried beans and peas. Fruits, cane and beet sugars, jellies, jams, candy and other sweets, honey, molasses, and syrups are concentrated sources of simple sugars.

Fats

Fats are a concentrated source of energy and provide more than twice the energy in carbohydrates or proteins. They are also rich in vitamins A, D, E, and K. Certain fats are essential for your body to function properly. They make up part of the structure of body organs; form a protective cushion around vital structures; provide an essential fatty acid, linoleic acid; and, by serving as a source of energy, allow protein to be used for cell building. Each day, no more than 30 percent of your total calories should come from fat.

THREE TYPES OF FATS

Saturated fats are animal fats from red meat (beef, lamb, pork) or whole-milk dairy products (milk, butter, cream, cheese, ice cream). Because these fats can raise your blood cholesterol levels (see page 8-4), and contribute to heart disease, you should limit your daily intake of foods containing saturated fats to 10 percent of your total calories.

8.1
of Sciences—National Research Council
Allowances,[a] Revised 1989

practically all healthy people in the United States

Water-Soluble Vitamins							Minerals						
Vita-min C	Thia-min	Ribo-flavin	Niacin	Vita-min B6	Fo-late	Vitamin B12	Cal-cium	Phos-phorus	Mag-nesium	Iron	Zinc	Iodine	Sele-nium
(mg)	(mg)	(mg)	(mg NE)[f]	(mg)	(µg)	(µg)	(mg)	(mg)	(mg)	(mg)	(mg)	(µg)	(µg)
30	0.3	0.4	5	0.3	25	0.3	400	300	40	6	5	40	10
35	0.4	0.5	6	0.6	35	0.5	600	500	60	10	5	50	15
40	0.7	0.8	9	1.0	50	0.7	800	800	80	10	10	70	20
45	0.9	1.1	12	1.1	75	1.0	800	800	120	10	10	90	20
45	1.0	1.2	13	1.4	100	1.4	800	800	170	10	10	120	30
50	1.3	1.5	17	1.7	150	2.0	1,200	1,200	270	12	15	150	40
60	1.5	1.8	20	2.0	200	2.0	1,200	1,200	400	12	15	150	50
60	1.5	1.7	19	2.0	200	2.0	800	800	350	10	15	150	70
60	1.5	1.7	19	2.0	200	2.0	800	800	350	10	15	150	70
60	1.2	1.4	15	2.0	200	2.0	800	800	350	10	15	150	70
50	1.1	1.3	15	1.4	150	2.0	1,200	1,200	280	15	12	150	45
60	1.1	1.3	15	1.5	180	2.0	1,200	1,200	300	15	12	150	50
60	1.1	1.3	15	1.6	180	2.0	1,200	1,200	280	15	12	150	55
60	1.1	1.3	15	1.6	180	2.0	800	800	280	15	12	150	55
60	1.0	1.2	13	1.6	180	2.0	800	800	280	10	12	150	55
70	1.5	1.6	17	2.2	400	2.2	1,200	1,200	320	30	15	175	65
95	1.6	1.8	20	2.1	280	2.6	1,200	1,200	355	15	19	200	75
90	1.6	1.7	20	2.1	260	2.6	1,200	1,200	340	15	16	200	75

[c] Retinol equivalents. 1 retinol equivalent = 1 µg retinol or 6 µg β-carotene.
[d] As cholecalciferol. 10 µg cholecalciferol = 400 IU of vitamin D.
[e] α-Tocopherol equivalents. 1 mg d-α tocopherol = 1 α-TE.
[f] 1 NE (niacin equivalent) is equal to 1 mg of niacin or 60 mg of dietary tryptophan.

Other types of fats, polyunsaturated and monounsaturated, may actually help to lower the blood cholesterol level when they are substituted for saturated fats. Polyunsaturated fats are found in corn, cottonseed, sesame, soybean, and safflower oil and in many fish. Good sources of monounsaturated fats are olive oil, peanut oil, cottonseed oil, and canola oil. Of your total calories, 10 percent should come from polyunsaturated fats, and 10 percent from monounsaturated fats.

Cholesterol
Cholesterol is a fatlike substance found in every cell of the body. Everyone has cholesterol, but people who eat excessive amounts of fat may have high levels of cholesterol in their blood. There the excess cholesterol accumulates and builds up deposits called plaque on the walls of the blood vessels. People with high cholesterol levels are more likely to suffer from heart disease and high blood pressure.

There are two kinds of cholesterol. Cholesterol attaches to proteins in the blood called lipoproteins. Low-density lipoproteins (LDLs) carry cholesterol that builds up plaque, so LDL-cholesterol is considered "bad" cholesterol. High-density lipoproteins (HDLs), on the other hand, carry cholesterol to the liver, where the body can get rid of it; therefore HDL-cholesterol is regarded as "good" cholesterol.

Mineral Elements
For normal growth and function, the body requires many minerals. Calcium and iron are particularly important during the growing years. Sufficient amounts of calcium ensure that the bones will grow properly. Milk and dairy products are the richest sources of calcium. Vitamin D helps the body absorb calcium; that is the reason why vitamin D is added to milk. Iron is an important part of the red blood cells. Without enough iron, a person will be weak and anemic. Lean cuts of meat, poultry, fish, and enriched cereals are all good sources of iron.

Sodium (common table salt) helps the body retain water. In excess, salt can lead to high blood pressure and can increase the risk of heart attack or stroke. Of our dietary sodium, 75 percent comes from the processing and/or manufacturing of food, 10 percent represents the natural sodium content of food, and 15 percent is added during cooking or at the table. Many processed

EXHIBIT 8.2
Function, Sources, and Nutritional Risks of the Major Minerals

Mineral	Functions	Good Sources	Nutritional Risks	
			Inadequate Intake	Excessive Intake
Calcium	Growth and maintenance of bones and teeth; blood clotting; contraction of muscles	Dairy products: milk, cheese, yogurt; spinach, chard, mustard greens, broccoli; sardines	Rickets (abnormal bone growth) in children; osteoporosis (porous bones that break) in adults	Deposits of calcium in the body; decreased absorption of magnesium, zinc, and iron
Phosphorus	Growth and maintenance of bones and teeth; metabolism of carbohydrates, protein, and fat; storage and release of energy; firing of nerves	Liver; yeast; dairy products; nuts, seeds; tofu; oatmeal; eggs; soft drinks	Weakness; loss of appetite; poor formation of bones and teeth; cramps and weakness in muscles	Imbalance of the calcium-to-phosphorus ratio, which may cause a deficiency of calcium
Sodium	Fluid balance	Table salt; cured meats; food in brine solution	Muscular weakness and cramps; low blood pressure headaches	Fluid retention, causing swelling of hands and feet; high blood pressure; heart disease
Potassium	Fluid balance; muscle contraction; nerve function; maintenance of normal heartbeat; release of energy from carbohydrates, proteins, and fats	Fruits and vegetables; whole grains; yeast; meats; dairy products; molasses	Abnormal heartbeat; muscle cramps, weakness, lethargy, abdominal pain	Abnormal heartbeat; muscular paralysis

EXHIBIT 8.2 (continued)
Function, Sources, and Nutritional Risks of the Major Minerals

Mineral	Functions	Good Sources	Nutritional Risks	
			Inadequate Intake	Excessive Intake
Zinc	Formation of genetic material (DNA and RNA); component of many enzymes; normal bone formation; absorption of B vitamins	Liver; wheat germ; eggs; nuts; oysters; whole grains; some legumes; bran	Poor growth; failure to mature sexually; poor wound healing and appetite	Nausea, vomiting, fever, anemia; premature birth; skin rash
Iodine	Formation of thyroid hormones that help control metabolism, growth, and energy production	Iodized salt; seafood	Goiter (enlarged thyroid gland); mental retardation; protruding abdomen, swollen features in newborns when mother deficient	Potentially could cause iodine poisoning; thyroid gland disease
Iron	Synthesis of homoglobin (protein in the blood that carries oxygen); part of several enzymes	Liver, red meat; yeast; dark green, leafy vegetables; egg yolk; apricots, prunes; molasses; enriched and whole-grain cereals	Anemia; weakness	Heart, liver, and pancreas disease
Copper	Formation of hemoglobin; part of several enzymes	Oysters; nuts, seeds; cocoa powder; oatmeal; liver; milk	Abnormal blood count; bone disease	Nausea, vomiting, diarrhea; headache
Fluoride	Formation of strong bones, teeth	Fluoridated water, seafood	Tooth decay; osteoporosis	Stained teeth; brittle bones

foods—foods that are bought already prepared—are high in salt. You can cut way down on the amount of salt you eat just by cooking your own food instead of relying on canned or frozen food, and by using herbs and spices, rather than table salt, for flavoring.

Exhibit 8.2 provides additional information regarding essential minerals.

Vitamins
Vitamins play a major role in body processes. They aid in the release of energy from foods, promote the growth and development of tissue, and are essential to the proper functioning of nerves and muscles. Diseases caused by lack of vitamins were a serious problem in the past when fresh fruits and vegetables were hard to get. Today, such diseases are relatively uncommon in the United States because many foods that people eat regularly are rich in vitamins.

Whole grain and enriched cereals and breads contain much vitamin B. Vitamins A and D are present in fortified milk, and vitamin C is in citrus fruits. Vegetable oils contain lots of vitamin E.

Sometimes young people don't get enough of vitamins A and C. Vitamin A is particularly important

for healthy skin and good vision. A good source of vitamin A is carrots. Vitamin C, also called ascorbic acid, plays a role in bone formation, wound healing, and the maintenance of healthy gums. Citrus fruits such as oranges and grapefruit are rich in vitamin C.

Exhibit 8.3 provides additional information regarding essential vitamins.

Fiber
Fiber consists of the parts of plant foods that the body doesn't digest. This material furnishes bulk, or roughage, that is essential for the normal functioning and health of the intestinal tract. Good sources of fiber include fresh fruit (with the skin on), vegetables, and baked goods and cereals made with whole-grain flours.

Water
Water is essential for life. A person can live for days, even weeks, without food, but only a few days without water. About two-thirds of the human body is made up of water; it is the medium of all body fluids and products. Everyone requires a regular and liberal intake of water.

EXHIBIT 8.3
Function, Sources, and Nutritional Risks of the Major Vitamins

Vitamins	Functions	Good Sources	Nutritional Risks	
			Inadequate Intake	Excessive Intake
A	Night and color vision; healthy skin; growth and repair of tissue; proper bone development	Liver; yellow fruits and vegetables; egg yolk; butter; dark green, leafy vegetables; fish and liver oils	Night blindness; rough, dry skin; retarded growth; dry eyes	Headaches; joint and bone pain; loss of hair; dry skin; fatigue; abnormal growth; liver damage
D	Calcium absorption from the intestine; bone mineralization; proper tooth formation	Fortified milk products; fish-liver oil; butter; egg yolks	Rickets (abnormal bone growth) in children; osteomalacia (porous bone) in adults; muscular weakness	Calcium deposits in tissues; nausea, vomiting, loss of appetite; elevated blood cholesterol
E	Antioxidant (prevents breakdown of fats and oils by oxygen); muscle formation; maintenance of red blood cell membranes	Vegetable oils, margarine; whole grain cereals; wheat germ; soy-beans, sprouts; nuts	Breakdown of red blood cells; nerve damage	Headache; blurred vision; skin rash
K	Blood clotting	Green, leafy vegetables; cabbage, cauliflower; soybeans	Impaired blood clotting	Unknown
B₁ **(Thiamin)**	Metabolism of carbohydrates for energy; growth and repair of tissue—especially nerves, heart, and muscle	Whole-grain cereals and breads; yeast; wheat germ; liver, pork products; legumes	Beriberi: muscle weakness, confusion, enlargement of the heart, loss of appetite	Unknown
B₂ **(Riboflavin)**	Metabolism of carbohydrate, protein, and fat for energy; growth and repair of tissue	Liver; dairy products; eggs; whole-grain cereals and breads; salmon	Cracks in the skin around the lips and corners of the mouth; sensitivity to light	Unknown
B₃ **(Niacin)**	Metabolism of carbohydrate, protein, and fat for energy	Liver; whole grain cereals and breads; yeast; peanut butter	Pellagra; skin discoloration, confusion, swollen tongue, irritability, dermatitis, diarrhea, loss of appetite, insomnia	Flushing or itching of the skin; abnormal heartbeat; high blood sugar; ulcers
B₆ **(Pyridoxine)**	Metabolism of protein; absorption of fat; formation of red blood cells	Whole grain cereals and fruits; seeds and nuts	Skin changes such as dermatitis and eczema; dizziness; sores on the mouth, tongue, and lips; anemia; numbness; convulsions	Disorders of the nervous sytem. Dependency can develop on high doses, and deficiency symptoms can occur when intake is reduced to normal levels.

EXHIBIT 8.3 (continued)
Function, Sources, and Nutritional Risks of the Major Vitamins

Vitamins	Functions	Good Sources	Nutritional Risks	
			Inadequate Intake	Excessive Intake
B$_{12}$	Metabolism of carbohydrate, protein, and fat; synthesis of genetic code (DNA and RNA); formation of red blood cells	Liver; milk; eggs	Pernicious anemia; red tongue; irritability, drowsiness, depression	Unknown
C	Synthesis of collagen (substance that holds cells together); formation of connective tissue in skin, bones, muscles; protection against destruction of vitamins A, E, thiamin, and riboflavin by oxygen	Citrus fruits; vegetables; potatoes	Scurvy: bleeding gums, abnormal blood clotting, weight loss, weakness, poor wound healing, irritability	Dependency can develop on high doses, and deficiency symptoms of scurvy may occur when intake is reduced to normal levels.

Weight Control

Your Weight

How much a person should weigh depends on many factors, including the size of his/her frame (small, average, large), sex, and height. There are no universally accepted definitions of the terms "overweight" and "obesity." Overweight is frequently defined as a body weight from 10 to 20 percent higher than the usual weight for persons of the same sex and height. Obesity is an excessive accumulation of body fat. It is best defined as a body weight that is 20 percent or more above the desirable weight for women of a specific height and type of frame, and 25 percent or more above the desirable weight for men.

You can get an idea of what your weight should be from Exhibit 8.4. Remember to subtract one pound for each year by which you are younger than 25.

Daily Calorie Needs

A calorie is a unit used to express the heat or energy value of food. Calories are obtained from three sources:

- Carbohydrate yields 4 calories per gram.
- Protein yields 4 calories per gram.
- Fat yields 9 calories per gram.

A certain number of calories are required by the body for its day-to-day activities. The daily calorie need is the number of calories used by the body each day to maintain its present weight. The number of calories required by an individual depends upon that person's sex, size, age, and activity level.

You can estimate the approximate number of calories you need each day by a simple formula. Take the midpoint of your desirable weight range, and multiply this figure by 18 for a man and by 16 for a woman. The answer is the approximate number of calories used daily by an adult of average activity.

For example, Exhibit 8.4 shows that the desirable weight for a 25-year-old, small-framed man 5 feet 9 inches tall is about 140 pounds. If his activities are average, he will use 140×18, or about 2,520, calories per day.

If you are very active, your calorie needs will be much higher than predicted by the above formula. Similarly, if you are relatively inactive, you will need fewer calories.

Basic Weight-Control Facts

The basics of weight control are simple: we can control the amount of food we eat, our activity level, or both. If we take in more calories than we expend in energy, we gain weight. People who weigh too much simply eat more calories than they use each day for growth or other activities. Leftover calories are stored as fat. On the other hand, if we expend more calories in energy than we eat, we lose weight. If we use up the same number of calories we take in, our weight remains unchanged.

About 3,500 extra calories are required to produce a pound of body fat. This means that 3,500 fewer calories should get rid of a pound of body fat. Cutting 500 calories a day from your diet will generally lead to a safe and sensible weight loss of one pound a week and will not leave you so hungry that you can't think about anything but food. If you are severely overweight or have medical problems, have a doctor and/or a registered dietitian supervise your diet.

If you don't want to decrease the amount of food you eat, then increase the number of calories you burn through more activity and exercise. Whether you wish to lose weight, gain weight, or simply maintain your current weight, exercise is beneficial. Even daily activities such as moderate walking, making beds, gardening, and carpentry can provide useful exercise.

Exhibit 8.5 indicates the calorie expenditures required for various activities.

EXHIBIT 8.4
1983 Metropolitan Height and Weight Tables

Weights at ages 25–59 based on lowest mortality. Weight in pounds according to frame (in indoor clothing weighing 5 lbs. for men and 3 lbs. for women; shoes with 1" heels).

MEN

Height Feet	Inches	Small Frame	Medium Frame	Large Frame
5	2	128–134	131–141	138–150
5	3	130–136	133–143	140–153
5	4	132–138	135–145	142–156
5	5	134–140	137–148	144–160
5	6	136–142	139–151	146–164
5	7	138–145	142–154	149–168
5	8	140–148	145–157	152–172
5	9	142–151	148–160	155–176
5	10	144–154	151–163	158–180
5	11	146–157	154–166	161–184
6	0	149–160	157–170	164–188
6	1	152–164	160–174	168–192
6	2	155–168	164–178	172–197
6	3	158–172	167–182	176–202
6	4	162–176	171–187	181–207

WOMEN

Height Feet	Inches	Small Frame	Medium Frame	Large Frame
4	10	102–111	109–121	118–131
4	11	103–113	111–123	120–134
5	0	104–115	113–126	122–137
5	1	106–118	115–129	125–140
5	2	108–121	118–132	128–143
5	3	111–124	121–135	131–147
5	4	114–127	124–138	134–151
5	5	117–130	127–141	137–155
5	6	120–133	130–144	140–159
5	7	123–136	133–147	143–163
5	8	126–139	136–150	146–167
5	9	129–142	139–153	149–170
5	10	132–145	142–156	152–173
5	11	135–148	145–159	155–176
6	0	138–151	148–162	158–179

Copyright 1983 Metropolitan Life Insurance Company
Reprinted Courtesy of Metropolitan Life Insurance Company.

Planning a Day's Food

There are five basic food groups:
- Milk, yogurt, and cheese group.
- Meat, poultry, fish, dry beans, eggs, and nuts group.
- Vegetable group.
- Fruit group.
- Bread, cereal, rice, and pasta group.

The recommended daily number of servings of each food group are graphically illustrated in Exhibit 8.6, "Food Guide Pyramid." Note that you should restrict your consumption of fats, oils, and sweets.

What counts as one serving? Exhibit 8.7 summarizes current U.S. government advice.

Exhibit 8.8 shows that the *exact* number of recommended servings of the five food groups depends on a person's age, sex, and activity level. How many servings of each group do *you* need?

When you choose among various foods, keep in mind that some are more beneficial to your health than others. For example, skim milk is better for you than whole milk because it contains less fat and also has a slightly higher calcium content.

Exhibit 8.9 summarizes some "recommended" and "not recommended" choices from the various food groups. Try to stick with the "recommended" items.

Purchasing Food Wisely

New government legislation requires that labels on all food products contain specific information on dietary content. The guidelines cover nearly every health and nutrition claim that could be made by a food manufacturer, and detail what information food labels should contain, down to the size of the print. For example, food can be described as "light" or "lite" on the label only if it has 50 percent less fat than other foods to which it is compared. The word "more" can be used only if a food product contains 10 percent more of a given ingredient than other goods of the same type.

The back panel of the label must tell you the number of grams of components, such as fat or cholesterol, a product contains, and also express that number as a percentage of the recommended total amount of fat or cholesterol the average consumer should eat in a day. Each label must list percentages of suggested fat and cholesterol daily intakes for both 2,000-calorie daily diets with 65 grams of fat and 2,500-calorie diets with 80 grams of fat.

The new labels also contain information on vitamins A and C, along with the minerals iron and calcium. Information regarding other vitamins and minerals, however, is no longer required.

EXHIBIT 8.5
Approximate Energy Expenditure by a Healthy Adult Weighing About 150 Pounds

Activity	Calories per hour
Lying quietly	80–100
Sitting quietly	85–105
Standing quietly	100–120
Walking slowly, 2½ mph	210–230
Walking quickly, 4 mph	315–345
Light work, such as ballroom dancing; cleaning house; office work; shopping	125–310
Moderate work, such as cycling, 9 mph; jogging, 6 mph tennis; scrubbing floors; weeding garden	315–480
Hard work, such as aerobic dancing; basketball; chopping wood; cross-country skiing; running, 7 mph; shoveling snow; spading garden; swimming, "crawl"	480–625

© 1988 The ServiceMaster Company L.P.

EXHIBIT 8.6
Food Guide Pyramid

A Guide to Daily Food Choices

Fats, Oils, & Sweets
USE SPARINGLY

KEY
■ Fat (naturally occurring and added)   ▼ Sugars (added)
These symbols show that fat and added sugars come mostly from fats, oils, and sweets, but can be part of or added to foods from the other food groups as well.

Milk, Yogurt, & Cheese Group
2–3 SERVINGS

Meat, Poultry, Fish, Dry Beans, Eggs, & Nuts Group
2–3 SERVINGS

Vegetable Group
3–5 SERVINGS

Fruit Group
2–4 SERVINGS

Bread, Cereal, Rice, & Pasta Group
6–11 SERVINGS

SOURCE: U.S. Department of Agriculture/U.S. Department of Health and Human Services

EXHIBIT 8.7
What Counts As One Serving?

Breads, Cereals, Rice, and Pasta
1 slice of bread
½ cup of cooked rice or pasta
½ cup of cooked cereal
1 ounce of ready-to-eat cereal

Vegetables
½ cup of chopped raw or cooked vegetables
1 cup of leafy raw vegetables

Fruits
1 piece of fruit or melon wedge
¾ cup of juice
½ cup of canned fruit
¼ cup of dried fruit

Milk, Yogurt, and Cheese
1 cup of milk or yogurt
1½ to 2 ounces of cheese

Meat, Poultry, Fish, Dry Beans, Eggs, and Nuts
2½ to 3 ounces of cooked lean meat, poultry, or fish
Count ½ cup of cooked beans or 1 egg or 2 tablespoons of peanut butter as 1 ounce of lean meat (about ⅓ serving).

Fats, Oils, and Sweets
LIMIT CALORIES FROM THESE, especially if you need to lose weight.

The amount you eat may be more than one serving. For example, a dinner portion of spaghetti would count as two or three servings of pasta.

EXHIBIT 8.8
How Many Servings Do You Need Each Day?

	Women & some older adults	Children, teen girls, active women, most men	Teen boys & active men
Calorie level*	about 1,600	about 2,200	about 2,800
Bread group	6	9	11
Vegetable group	3	4	5
Fruit group	2	3	4
Milk group	**2–3	**2–3	**2–3
Meat group	2, for a total of 5 ounces	2, for a total of 6 ounces	3, for a total of 7 ounces

*These are the calorie levels if you choose lowfat, lean foods from the 5 major food groups and use foods from the fats, oils, and sweets group sparingly.

**Women who are pregnant or breastfeeding, teenagers, and young adults to age 24 need 3 servings.

EXHIBIT 8.9
Guide to Good Food

	Recommended	*Not Recommended*
MILK AND MILK PRODUCTS	**Milk** Buttermilk (skim or low-fat) Chocolate milk (1–2%) Low-fat or skim milk (fluid, evaporated, or powdered)	**Milk** Buttermilk (from whole) Chocolate milk (from whole) Evaporated (from whole) Whole
	Cheese Low-fat cheese (less than 15% fat) Low-fat (1–2% fat) cottage cheese Mozzarella, part skim milk Ricotta, part skim milk Skim-milk cheese	**Cheese** Blue cheese Cheddar Cream Creamed cottage cheese Mozzarella, whole milk Parmesan Ricotta, whole milk Swiss
	Yogurt Nonfat, plain Low-fat, fruited, flavored, or frozen	**Yogurt** Whole, plain or fruited
	Miscellaneous Ice milk	**Miscellaneous** Butter Half and half Ice cream Cream (light, sour, and whipping)
MEAT OR MEAT ALTERNATIVES	**Beef (Choice or Good)** Chuck Flank steak Ground (lean, 10% fat) Round, bottom or top Rump, all cuts	**Beef (Prime)** Brisket Canned Corned Ground (15–20% fat) Roast, rib Sausage
	Lamb Leg Rib, chop or roast	**Lamb** Breast Ground Mutton
	Luncheon Meat Thin-sliced lean meat Turkey franks, turkey ham, turkey pastrami	**Luncheon Meat** Bologna Bratwurst Frankfurters, beef and pork Salami
	Fish and Shellfish Any fresh or frozen fish or seafood Tuna, canned in water	**Organ Meat (high in cholesterol)** Liver Sweetbreads
	Pork Canadian bacon Leg, whole rump Ham, center or rump Loin, rib or chop Ribs, center or shank	**Pork** Country-style ham Deviled ham Loin, back ribs Pork, ground Sausage Spare ribs
	Veal Cutlets Leg Loin Rib Shank Shoulder	**Veal** Breast

EXHIBIT 8.9 (continued)
Guide to Good Food

Recommended	*Not Recommended*
Poultry Chicken Cornish hen Turkey	**Poultry** Duck, domestic
Meat Alternatives Peas or beans, dried Egg white or egg substitute	**Egg (high in cholesterol)** Egg yolk

BREADS, CEREALS, AND OTHER GRAINS

Recommended	*Not Recommended*
Breads French or Italian Pita Pumpernickel Raisin Rye Whole wheat White Bagel, small Bun, hamburger, hot dog Cornbread English muffin Muffin Pancake Roll, plain Tortilla, corn or wheat Waffle	**Breads** Biscuit Butter roll Cheesebread Croissants Doughnut Egg bread Sweet roll
Cereal Barley, cooked Bulgar, cooked Bran flakes Cold cereal Hot cereal Grits, cooked Corn meal, dry	**Cereal** Cereals, presweetened Cereals with coconut
Pasta Macaroni Noodles Lasagna Spaghetti	**Pasta** Noodles, egg Noodles, chow mein
Crackers Arrowroot Bread sticks Graham Matzo Pretzels, no salt Pretzel sticks, no salt Rye wafers Saltines, low sodium Soda Wheat	**Crackers** Cheese puffs Corn chips Potato chips Tortilla chips Other commercial crackers
Starchy Vegetables Corn Dried beans, peas, and lentils Hominy Peas Potato Pumpkin Rice (white/brown) Sweet potato Winter squash	**Starchy Vegetables** Beans seasoned with bacon or ham hocks Creamed corn Fried rice Potatoes, French fried

EXHIBIT 8.9 (continued)
Guide to Good Food

	Recommended	*Not Recommended*
	Miscellaneous	**Miscellaneous**
	Bread crumbs	Pies
	Corn starch	Popcorn, buttered and salted
	Popcorn, air-popped	
FRUITS AND JUICES	Fresh fruits and juices except as prepared at right	Fruit pie filling
		Fruit roll ups
		Fruit in sugar syrup, light
		Fruit in sugar syrup, heavy
		Fruit whips
		Sweetened juices
VEGETABLES	All vegetables except as prepared at right	**Fried Vegetables**
		Vegetables with Sauces
		Vegetables in butter sauce
		Vegetables in cream sauce
		Vegetables in cheese sauce
FAT	Avocado	Butter
	Margarine	Bacon, bacon fat
	Nuts	Chocolate
	Olives	Coconut
		Cream
		Lard
		Hydrogenated vegetable oils
	Oil	**Oil**
	Canola	Coconut
	Corn	Palm
	Cottonseed	
	Olive	
	Peanut	
	Safflower	
	Sesame	
	Soybean	
	Sunflower	
	Walnut	
	Salad Dressing	**Salad Dressing**
	Caesar	Blue cheese
	French	Creamy
	French, low-calorie	Green Goddess
	Italian	Salad dressings
	Italian, low-calorie	with sour cream
	Mayonnaise	or cheese
	Mayonnaise, light	Tartar sauce
	Thousand Island	
	Thousand Island, low-calorie	
	Vinegar and oil	
MISCELLANEOUS	Angel food cake	Cake (with icing)
	Cakes and cookies made with recommended ingredients	Cupcakes (with icing)
		Ice cream
		Pies, fruit
	Fruit ice	Sugar
	Gelatin, sweetened	Honey
	Sherbet	Jams
		Jellies

EXHIBIT 8.10
Fast Food Guide

Restaurant	Nutrient						
	Calories	Protein (grams)	Carbohydrates (grams)	Fat (grams)	Saturated Fat (grams)	Cholesterol (milligrams)	Sodium (milligrams)
Burger King							
Apple Pie	305	3	44	12	4	4	412
Breakfast Bagel Sandwich	387	17	46	14	5	268	780
✓ Cheeseburger	317	17	30	15	7	48	651
✓ Chicken Tenders	204	20	10	10	2	47	636
French Fries, Regular	227	3	24	13	7	14	160
French Toast Sticks	499	9	49	29	5	74	498
✓ Hamburger	275	18	29	12	6	37	509
Scrambled Egg Plate	468	15	33	30	NA	370	808
Specialty Chicken Sandwich	688	26	56	40	8	82	1423
Vanilla Shake	321	9	49	10	NA	NA	205
Whopper	628	27	46	36	12	90	880
✓ Whopper, Jr.	322	15	30	17	6	41	486
Dairy Queen							
Chicken Breast Fillet	608	27	46	34	NA	78	725
Chicken Nuggets	276	16	23	18	NA	39	505
Dipped Cone, Regular	340	6	42	16	NA	60	100
Fish Fillet	430	20	45	18	NA	40	674
Float	410	5	82	7	NA	20	86
Hot Dog	280	11	21	16	NA	45	830
Malt, Regular	760	14	134	18	NA	50	260
"Mr. Misty," Regular	250	0	63	0	NA	10	10
Shake, Regular	710	14	120	19	NA	50	260
✓ Single Hamburger	360	21	33	16	NA	45	630
✓ Soft Ice Cream	140	3	22	4	NA	10	45
Sundae, Regular	310	5	56	8	NA	70	120
Domino							
✓ Cheese Pizza	376	22	56	10	5.5	19	483
Deluxe Pizza	498	27	59	20	9.3	40	954
Pepperoni Pizza	460	24	56	18	8.4	28	825
Veggi Pizza	498	31	60	19	10.2	36	1035
Jack in the Box							
Apple Turnover	401	4	45	24	10.8	15	350
✓ Beef Fajita Pita	333	24	27	14	5.9	45	635
Breakfast Jack®	307	18	30	13	5.2	203	871
✓ Cheeseburger	315	15	33	14	5.7	41	746
Chef Salad	295	32	3	18	9.4	107	812
✓ Chicken Fajita Pita®	292	24	29	8	2.9	34	703
✓ Hamburger	267	13	28	11	4.1	26	556
Jumbo Jack®	584	26	42	34	11.0	73	733
✓ Regular Taco	191	8	16	11	5.2	21	406
Super Taco	288	12	21	17	8.0	37	765
Taco Salad	503	34	28	31	13.4	92	1600
Kentucky Fried Chicken							
Biscuit	232	4	27	11	2.9	1	539
✓ Cole Slaw	119	1	13	7	1.0	4	197
✓ Corn on the Cob	176	5	32	3	1	1	21
Extra Crispy Breast	354	27	14	21	5	93	842
Drumstick	173	13	6	11	3	65	346
Kentucky Fries	244	3	31	12	3	2	139
Kentucky Nuggets, 6 pieces	276	17	13	17	4	71	840
✓ Mashed Potatoes and Gravy	71	2	12	2	0.5	1	342

*NA = Not Available; ✓ = Best Choices

EXHIBIT 8.10 (continued)
Fast Food Guide

Restaurant	Nutrient						
	Calories	Protein (grams)	Carbohydrates (grams)	Fat (grams)	Saturated Fat (grams)	Cholesterol (milligrams)	Sodium (milligrams)
Original Recipe							
Breast	283	28	9	15	4	93	672
✓ Drumstick	146	13	4	9	2	67	275
Long John Silver							
Battered Fish, 1 piece	150	12	9	8	1.8	30	510
✓ Chicken Plank, 1 piece	110	8	6	6	1.4	15	320
Children's Meal 1 fish, fries, and 1 hushpuppy	440	16	49	20	4.9	30	590
2 planks, fries, and 1 hushpuppy	510	20	52	24	5.9	30	730
✓ Clam Chowder	140	11	10	6	1.8	20	590
✓ Coleslaw	140	1	20	6	1.0	15	260
✓ Corn on the Cob	270	6	38	14	2.6	5	95
Crispy Fish Sandwich	600	29	60	28	6.3	30	1220
✓ Garden Salad	140	8	9	8	NA	5	330
✓ Homestyle Fish, 1 piece	125	7	9	7	1.6	20	200
Ocean Chef Salad	250	24	19	9	0.7	80	1340
McDonald's							
Apple Pie	260	2	30	15	6	5	240
Big Mac	560	25	43	32	10	103	950
✓ Cheeseburger	310	15	31	14	5	53	750
Chicken Nuggets	290	19	14	16	4	65	520
Egg McMuffin	290	18	28	11	4	226	740
✓ English Muffin with Butter	170	5	27	5	2	9	270
Fish-O-Filet	440	14	38	26	5	50	1030
French Fries, Regular	220	3	26	12	5	9	110
✓ Hamburger	260	12	31	10	4	37	500
McDonald Cookies	290	4	47	9	2	0	300
Scrambled Eggs	140	12	1	10	3	399	290
✓ Garden Salad	110	7	6	7	3	83	160
Vanilla Shake	360	10	56	10	5	41	170
Taco Bell							
Beef Burrito	397	23	38	17	7.4	57	926
Bean Burrito	356	13	54	10	2.9	9	888
Burrito Supreme	407	18	45	18	7.7	33	796
✓ Chicken Fajita	225	14	20	10	3.7	44	619
Encharito	382	20	31	20	9.3	54	1243
✓ Pintos and Cheese	190	9	19	9	3.6	16	642
Soft Taco	228	12	18	12	5.4	32	516
✓ Steak Fajita	234	15	19	11	4.8	14	485
✓ Taco	183	10	11	11	4.6	32	276
Taco Salad	941	36	63	61	19.0	80	1662
✓ Tostada	243	9	27	11	4.1	16	596
Wendy's							
✓ Chef Salad	180	15	10	9	NA	120	140
Chicken Breast Filet Sandwich	430	26	41	19	NA	60	705
Chili	230	21	16	9	NA	50	960
French Fries	310	4	38	15	NA	15	105
Frosty	400	8	59	14	NA	50	220
✓ Garden Salad	102	7	9	5	NA	0	110
✓ Kid's Hamburger	260	13	30	9	NA	30	510
✓ Plain Potato	250	6	52	2	NA	trace	60
Wendy's Big Classic	580	24	47	34	NA	80	1015

*NA = Not Available; ✓ = Best Choices

EXHIBIT 8.11
Not-So-Fast-Food Fare

	Calories	Grams of fat*	Milligrams of sodium†
APPETIZERS			
Denny's Chicken Strips (4 oz)	240	10	600
Denny's Mozzarella Sticks (1 stick)	88	7	206
Ponderosa's Breaded Zucchini (4 oz)	102	1	584
Ponderosa's Chicken Wings (2 pieces)	213	9	610
Red Lobster's Bayou-Style Seafood Gumbo (6 oz)	180	5	800
Red Lobster's Shrimp Cocktail (6 large shrimp with shrimp sauce)	120	2	460
SOUPS			
Big Boy's Cabbage Soup (cup)[a]	37	0	623
Country Kitchen's Old-Fashioned Calico Bean Soup	<400	NA	>1000
Denny's Cheese Soup (1 bowl)	309	22	898
Denny's Split Pea Soup (1 bowl)	231	5	1519
Shoney's Clam Chowder (6 fl oz)	94	5	66
Shoney's Vegetable Beef Soup (6 fl oz)	82	2	1254
The Olive Garden's Minestrone (6 fl oz)	45	<1	220
SIDE DISHES			
Ponderosa's Potato Wedges (3.5 oz)	130	6	171
Ponderosa's Stuffing (4 oz)	230	11	800
Red Lobster's Rice Pilaf (4 oz)	140	3	390
The Olive Garden's Breadsticks (1)	70	2	365
SALADS			
Big Boy's Chicken Breast Salad with Dijon	391	11	415
Chili's Caribbean Chicken Salad	374	7	NA
Country Kitchen's Grilled Chicken Breast Salad	<400	NA	<1000
Denny's Chef Salad	492	20	1370
Denny's Taco Salad (includes fried tortilla shell)	953	50	2628
Perkins's Mini Chef Salad	238	11	1883
T.G.I. Friday's Garden Cobb Salad	320	10	NA
T.G.I. Friday's Salad & Baked Potato	400	5	NA
The Olive Garden's Garden Salad	230	15	560
SANDWICHES			
Values are for sandwiches only unless otherwise indicated; no fries, coleslaw, etc. are included.			
Big Boy's Breast of Chicken with Mozzarella Sandwich	404	13	421
Big Boy's Turkey Pita Sandwich	224	5	833
Country Kitchen's Barbecued Pork Sandwich	<400	NA	>1000
Denny's Club Sandwich	590	20	582
Perkins's Cajun Chicken Pita Sandwich (includes fruit cup)	429	12	432
Red Lobster's Broiled Fish Fillet Sandwich	300	10	450
Ruby Tuesday's Open-Faced Chicken Breast Sandwich	458	16	616
Shoney's Reuben Sandwich	596	35	3873
Shoney's Shoney Burger	498	36	782
T.G.I. Friday's Fresh Vegetable Baguette	290	11	NA
T.G.I. Friday's Gardenburger	390	8	NA
ENTREES			
Big Boy's Cajun Cod[b]	364	12	461
Big Boy's Chicken 'n Vegetable Stir Fry[b]	562	14	750
Big Boy's Spaghetti Marinara[b]	450	6	761
Big Boy's Vegetable Stir Fry[b]	408	10	703
Chili's Chicken Fajitas	557	9	NA
Chili's Grilled Chicken Platter	742	21	NA
Denny's Catfish (2-4 oz)[c]	576	0	460

* Someone following an 1,800-calorie diet should average a maximum of 60 grams of fat a day.

† The National Academy of Sciences recommends a sodium limit of 2,400 milligrams a day.

[a] All Big Boy dishes listed are Big Boy Health Smart menu items.

[b] Includes dinner salad (no dressing), bread, and margarine.

[c] Entree only

[d] Salad, salad dressing, and bread not included; values based on accompaniments of 4 oz steamed broccoli and 6 oz rice.

EXHIBIT 8.11 (continued)
Not-So-Fast-Food Fare

	Calories	Grams of fat*	Milligrams of sodium†
ENTREES			
Denny's Chicken Fried Steak (2 pieces, without gravy)[c]	252	15	422
Denny's Liver with Bacon and Onions (2 slices)[c]	334	15	516
Perkins's Cajun Chicken Dinner[d]	516	10	867
Perkins's Lemon Chicken Dinner[d]	517	10	868
Perkins's Orange Roughy[d]	364	6	891
Ponderosa's Chopped Steak (4 oz)[c]	225	16	150
Ponderosa's New York Strip (10 oz)[c]	314	15	1420
Ponderosa's Sirloin Tips (5 oz)[c]	473	8	280
Ponderosa's Steak Kabobs (3 oz, meat only)[c]	153	5	280
Red Lobster's Bay Platter (shrimp, scallops, pollock, and rice)	500	20	1820
Red Lobster's Seafood Lover's Sampler (crab, shrimp, scallops, pollock, and crab legs)	650	27	1800
Red Lobster's Shrimp Scampi	310	23	250
Ruby Tuesday's Steamed Vegetable Plate	404	2	138
Shoney's Baked Fish[c]	170	1	1641
Shoney's Country Fried Steak[c]	449	27	1177
Shoney's Hawaiian Chicken[c]	262	7	593
Shoney's Italian Feast[c]	500	20	369
T.G.I. Friday's Pacific Coast Chicken	320	13	NA
The Olive Garden's Baked Lasagna (lunch item)	330	18	1030
The Olive Garden's Eggplant Parmigiana (lunch item)	220	14	720
The Olive Garden's Veal Parmigiana	590	40	1120
The Olive Garden's Veal Piccata	230	16	150
DESSERTS			
Big Boy's Frozen Yogurt Shake	184	0	127
Big Boy's No-No Frozen Dessert	75	0	36
Ponderosa's Chocolate Mousse (1 oz)	78	4	18
Ponderosa's Spiced Apple Rings (4 oz)	100	0	20
Shoney's Apple Pie A La Mode	492	23	574
Shoney's Carrot Cake	500	26	476
Shoney's Hot Fudge Sundae	451	22	226
Shoney's Strawberry Pie	332	17	247
BREAKFAST ITEMS			
Denny's Cinnamon Roll	450	14	750
Denny's Eggs Benedict (1)	658	36	2197
Denny's French Toast (2 slices with butter and powdered sugar)	729	56	275
Denny's Waffle (1 waffle)	261	10	62
Perkins's Denver Omelette (with muffin & fruit cup)	511	17	1125
Perkins's Harvest'Cakes with Reduced Calorie Syrup (stack of 5)	533	10	2300
Perkins's Seafood Omelette (with muffin & fruit cup)	549	16	925
Shoney's Country Gravy (¼ cup)	82	7	255
Shoney's Grits (¼ cup)	57	3	62
Shoney's Home Fries (¼ cup)	53	2	24
Village Inn's Fresh Veggie Omelette	413	17	1367
Village Inn's Granola & Fruit with Yogurt and Blueberry Muffin	860	27	758
Village Inn's Low Cholesterol Fruit & Nut Pancakes	332	10	1287

* Someone following an 1,800-calorie diet should average a maximum of 60 grams of fat a day.

† The National Academy of Sciences recommends a sodium limit of 2,400 milligrams a day.

[c] Entree only

[d] Salad, salad dressing, and bread not included; values based on accompaniments of 4 oz steamed broccoli and 6 oz rice.

All calorie and fat figures have been rounded to the nearest whole number. Consumers should be aware that the figures are not "engraved in stone." The calorie and fat content of a steak, for instance, will vary depending on a particular piece's proportions of protein, fat, and water and whether it's cooked rare or well-done.

Reprinted with permission from the August 1992 issue, *Tufts Diet & Nutrition Letter*, 53 Park Place, New York, NY 10007.

Eating Out

"Fast food" has become a national favorite. Fortunately, you can make healthful choices even when you go out to eat. Exhibit 8.10, "Fast Food Guide," allows you to make the best choices, in terms of good nutrition, from the menus of several popular restaurants. These "good picks" are indicated by check marks.

In "sit-down" restaurants, the choice is a bit more difficult, because of the different types of menu items from which to select. Exhibit 8.11 shows the nutritional content of many appetizers, soups, side dishes, salads, sandwiches, entrees, desserts, and breakfast items served by popular national restaurants. In deciding what to order, try to pick the items that are lowest in grams of fat and milligrams of sodium.

Suggestions for Those Who Want to Lose Weight

If you are trying to lose weight, here are a few helpful suggestions:

1. Record everything you eat, including snacks, so that you can keep track of your calories.
2. Don't eat while you are doing something else. In this way you can avoid eating when you are not actually hungry.
3. Sit down while eating.
4. Don't eat too fast. Give your body a chance to notice that it has had enough to eat.
5. Eat meals and snacks only in the parts of your home intended for eating.
6. Don't try to lose weight too fast. A sensible goal is one pound a week.
7. Don't try to lose too much weight. Be aware of the danger of anorexia nervosa (see page 8-19).

Suggestions for Those Who Want to Gain Weight

If you are very much underweight, you should see your doctor and/or a registered dietitian before starting any type of a diet. Choose familiar foods that appeal to you. If you prefer, eat regular meals at the same time each day. Instead, you may find that frequent, small meals or between-meal snacks along with regular meals work better for you. In any case, eat more of the higher calorie foods. Take larger portions of foods, and enjoy seconds (as long as you are hungry).

GLOSSARY OF MEDICAL TERMS

Abdomen   The part of the body between the chest and the pelvis; the belly, including the stomach, liver, intestines, and other organs called the viscera.

Abortion   Termination of pregnancy; expulsion or removal of the embryo or fetus before it has reached full development and can normally be expected to be capable of independent life. It may be spontaneous or induced.

Abscess   An accumulation of pus that results from a breakdown of tissues (a common problem being tissue breakdown around a tooth, producing an "abscessed tooth").

Achilles tendon   The large tendon that connects the calf muscles to the heelbone.

Acne   An inflammatory disease of the sebaceous glands of the skin, usually on the face and upper body, characterized by papules, pustules, comedones (blackheads) and in severe cases by cysts, nodules, and scarring. The most common form—acne vulgaris—usually affects persons from puberty to young adulthood. Treatment includes topical and oral antibiotics, topical vitamin A derivatives, dermabrasion, and cryosurgery.

Acquired Immune Deficiency Syndrome (AIDS)   A serious, often fatal condition in which the immune system breaks down and does not respond normally to infection. The victim commonly develops Kaposi's sarcoma and recurrent severe infections. The disease became epidemic in the early 1980s, affecting almost exclusively male homosexuals, intravenous drug users, and hemophiliacs. It has now spread to heterosexual populations and is known to be transmitted through sexual contact or the use of contaminated drug apparatus. The cause has been identified as a virus (human immunodeficiency virus, HIV). No treatment has yet proved effective. *See also* **Kaposi's sarcoma**; **AIDS**, page 2-3.

Acquired immunity   Any form of immunity (insusceptibility to a particular disease) not innate but obtained during life. It may be natural, actively acquired by the development of antibodies after an attack of an infectious disease (for example, chicken pox) or passively acquired, as when a mother passes antibodies against a specific disease to a fetus through the placenta or to an infant through colostrum; or it may be artificial, acquired through vaccination.

Acupuncture   A method of producing analgesia or treating disease by inserting very thin needles into specific sites on the body along channels, called meridians, and twirling, energizing, or warming the needles; it is used by practitioners of traditional medicine in China.

Acute   (1) Coming on suddenly and severely; (2) sharp, as an acute pain. *Compare* **Chronic**.

Addiction   A condition of strong or irresistible dependence on the use of a particular substance (for example, heroin, alcohol) such that abrupt deprivation of the substance produces characteristic withdrawal symptoms.

Addison's disease   A disease caused by failure of function of the cortex of the adrenal gland, resulting in deficiency of adrenocortical hormones and disturbance of the normal levels of glucose and minerals in the body. Symptoms, often gradual in onset, include weakness, anorexia, fatigue, increased pigmentation, weight loss, and reduced tolerance to cold. Treatment includes administration of adrenocortical hormones and maintenance of normal levels of glucose and electrolytes in the blood. Many people with Addison's disease wear a MedicAlert ID; also called Addison's syndrome.

Adenoid   Lymphatic tissue in the back of the nasal passage, on the wall of the nasopharynx. Adenoids may become enlarged and cause difficulty in breathing through the nose after repeated infection.

Adhesion   A bond of fibrous tissue that causes normally separate structures to stick together. Adhesions are most common in the abdomen, where they frequently follow surgery, injury, or inflammation. If they cause pain or other symptoms or interfere with normal functioning, surgical intervention is necessary.

Adipose tissue   A type of connective tissue containing many fat cells. It forms a layer under the skin and serves as an insulating layer and as an energy reserve.

Adolescence   The period between puberty and adulthood, marked by extensive physical, psychological, and emotional changes.

Adrenaline   *See* **Epinephrine**.

Advance directives   Conversations, written directions, living wills, and durable powers of attorney that indicate to health-care providers an individual's wishes as to the medical interventions to be made or withheld if he/she were to lose the capacity to make decisions. *See also* **Durable power of attorney**; **Living will**.

Afterbirth   The fetus-supporting material (placenta and fetal membranes) expelled from the mother's uterus after a baby is born.

AIDS   *See* **Acquired Immune Deficiency Syndrome**.

Albumin   A water-soluble protein found in most animal tissues. Determination of the types and levels of albumin in the blood, urine, and other body tissues and fluids is the basis of many diagnostic tests. The constant presence of albumin in the urine usually indicates kidney disease.

Alcoholics Anonymous   An international organization established as a support group for persons who want to free themselves, by means of self-help and other programs, from dependence on or addiction to alcohol. A member is expected to acknowledge his/her drinking problem, to attend meetings regularly, to share experiences and difficulties, and to try to maintain sobriety "one day at a time." Even after prolonged abstinence, members do not consider themselves cured; rather, they refer to themselves as "recovering alcoholics."

Alcoholism   A chronic condition in which alcoholic drinks are taken to excess, leading to a breakdown in health and inability to function properly; dependence on or addiction to alcoholic beverages such that abrupt deprivation leads to withdrawal symptoms. Alcoholism may occur at any age; its cause is unknown but hereditary and biochemical as well as cultural and psychosocial factors are believed to play important roles. The consequences of alcoholism include impaired intellectual functioning, physical skills, memory, and judgment; peripheral abnormalities in nerve function; esophageal and gastrointestinal problems; impaired liver function, sometimes leading to cirrhosis of the liver; and damage to the heart muscle. Impaired emotional, social, and often economic/professional functioning also affects the self, family, and community. Alcoholism in pregnant women is also thought to damage the growth and development of the fetus (fetal alcohol syndrome). Acute withdrawal symptoms include tremor, anxiety, hallucinations, and in severe cases delirium tremens. Treatment includes psychotherapy, often in groups such as Alcoholics Anonymous, and the use of certain drugs (for example, Antabuse) that cause vomiting if alcohol is ingested.

Alimentary canal   The digestive tube through which food passes and is digested and absorbed. It extends from the mouth to the anus and includes the mouth, pharynx, esophagus, stomach, small intestine, and large intestine; also alimentary tract. *See also* **Digestive system**.

Allergy   A hypersensitivity reaction to the presence of an agent (allergen) that is intrinsically harmless such as animal hairs, dust, pollen, or substances in certain foods. Symptoms vary widely but may include bronchial congestion, the appearance of a rash (often itchy), vomiting, edema, conjunctivitis, runny nose or serious systemic reactions leading to anaphylactic shock and possibly death. Allergies are very common, affecting probably more than 15% of the U.S. population. Allergies are diagnosed through skin tests (patch test, scratch test) and other laboratory procedures. Treatment is avoidance of the allergen, if possible; the use of antihistamine drugs to relieve the symptoms; desensitizing injections in some cases (for example, hay fever); and other measures. *See also* **Anaphylaxis**; **Hay fever**.

Alzheimer's disease   A progressive loss of mental ability and function, often accompanied by personality changes and emotional instability. It is a common disorder, affecting both men and women; it usually starts between ages 50 and 60 often with memory lapses and changes in behavior; it progresses to include symptoms of confusion, restlessness, inability to plan and carry out activities and sometimes hallucinations and loss of sphincter (for example, bladder) control. The cause is unknown but plaques and neurofibrillary tangles are commonly found in the brain tissue. There is no cure, with treatment aimed at alleviating the symptoms. Also called senile dementia.

Amenorrhea   Abnormal stoppage or absence of the menstrual flow. It may be caused by congenital abnormality of the reproductive tract or by hormonal dysfunction, malnutrition, marked change in the amount of body fat (as occurs in strenuous exercise programs), severe trauma, or emotional upset. Primary amenorrhea is arbitrarily defined as delay of onset of the menstrual flow (menarche) beyong age 18. Secondary amenorrhea refers to cessation of menstruation in a woman who has previously menstruated. Treatment involves correction of the underlying cause and hormone therapy if necessary.

Amnesia   Loss of memory, due to injury to the brain or severe emotional trauma. There are several kinds of amnesia, including anterograde amnesia, retrograde amnesia, and transient global amnesia.

Amniocentesis   The taking of amniotic fluid by needle puncture through the abdominal wall of the pregnant woman to aid in the diagnosis of fetal abnormalities (for example, Down syndrome, Tay-Sachs disease). The test cannot be performed until about the 15th or 16th week of pregnancy and is recommended when a hereditary pattern in the family or the mother's age (over 35) increases the chance of fetal defects.

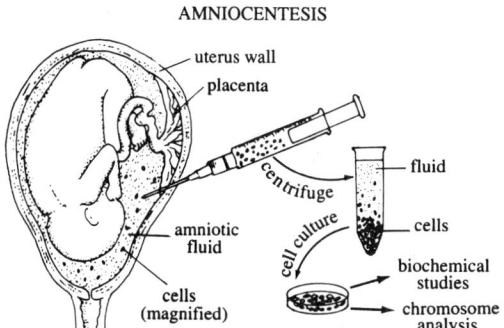

AMNIOCENTESIS

uterus wall
placenta
centrifuge
amniotic fluid
cell culture
cells (magnified)
fluid
cells
biochemical studies
chromosome analysis

Amniotic sac　Thin-walled bag that contains the fetus and amniotic fluid during pregnancy.

Amphetamine　A central nervous system stimulant used to treat narcolepsy and some forms of depression and attention-deficit disorders. It alleviates fatigue, promotes alertness, and decreases appetite. Overdosage causes gastrointestinal complaints, rapid heart rate, restlessness, sleeplessness, and in very high doses hallucinations and feelings of panic. It has a high potential for abuse, resulting in tolerance and dependence. Slang name: speed.

Analgesic　A pain-relieving substance (for example, aspirin, acetaminophen).

Anaphylaxis　A strong allergic reaction to the ingestion or injection of a substance (for example, penicillin, shellfish) to which a person has become sensitized by previous exposure. Symptoms may include localized swelling and itching, breathing problems, and in severe cases shock and even death.

Anemia　A condition in which the hemoglobin content of the blood is below normal limits. It may be hereditary, congenital, or acquired. Basically anemia results from a defect in the production of hemoglobin and its carrier, the red blood cell (for example, production of abnormal hemoglobin, misshapen red blood cells, or inadequate levels of hemoglobin); increased destruction of red blood cells; or blood loss (for example, in hemorrhage after injury or in excessive menstrual flow); the most common cause is a deficiency in iron, an element necessary for the formation of hemoglobin. Symptoms vary with the severity and cause of the anemia but may include fatigue, weakness, pallor, headache, dizziness, and anorexia. Treatment also depends on the cause and severity and may include an iron-rich diet, iron supplements, blood transfusions, and the correction or elimination of any pathological conditions causing the anemia. There are several types of anemia, including aplastic anemia, pernicious anemia, sickle-cell anemia, and thalassemia.

Anesthesia　Absence of sensation, especially that of pain. In general anesthesia, which is administered before a major operation (for example, removal of a lung), total unconsciousness results from injection or inhalation of anesthetic drugs. In local anesthesia loss of sensation is confined to a given small part or area of the body (for example, the tissues surrounding a tooth to be extracted). In regional anesthesia loss of sensation is produced in a specific area of the body (for example, in the pelvic area during

childbirth by an epidural anesthetic). In topical anesthesia loss of sensation is confined to the surface skin or mucous membranes (for example, benzocaine solution sprayed on the skin). Anesthesia may also be produced by hypnosis, acupuncture, and nerve damage (as in leprosy).

Anesthetic　A drug (for example, procaine hydrochloride [Novocain]) that causes temporary loss of sensation.

Aneurysm　A saclike widening in a blood vessel; it occurs most often in the aorta but can also occur in other blood vessels. Aneurysms are usually caused by atherosclerosis or hypertension, sometimes by trauma, infection, or other factor. An aneurysm may rupture, causing hemorrhage, or it may lead to the formation of thrombi and/or emboli that may block an important blood vessel. Common types of aneurysms include aortic aneurysm and cerebral aneurysm. Treatment includes use of drugs to reduce the force of cardiac contraction, analgesic and antihypertensive drugs if indicated, and, in some cases, surgical removal of part of the aorta or affected artery.

ANEURYSM OF THE ABDOMINAL AORTA

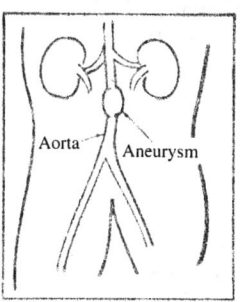

Aorta
Aneurysm

Angina pectoris　Chest pain, often accompanied by a feeling of choking or impending death; the pain typically radiates down the left arm. It is usually caused by a lack of oxygen to the heart muscle, resulting from atherosclerosis of the coronary arteries; attacks are precipitated by exertion, exposure to cold, or stress. Pain is relieved by rest and use of drugs (for example, nitroglycerine) to dilate the coronary arteries.

Angioplasty　Surgery done on arteries, veins, or capillaries; a technique in which a balloon is inflated inside a blood vessel to flatten any plaque (patch) that obstructs it and causes it to become narrowed (used especially to open coronary arteries).

Anorexia nervosa　An emotional disorder, occurring most commonly in adolescent females, characterized by abnormal body image and fear of obesity and prolonged refusal to eat, leading to emaciation, amenorrhea, and other symptoms and sometimes resulting in death. Treatment includes psychotherapy and nourishment.

Antacid　A chemical that reduces acidity (for example, sodium bicarbonate), especially one taken to relieve "upset stomach."

Antibiotic　A drug (for example, penicillin), derived from a microorganism or produced synthetically, that destroys or limits the growth of a living organism, especially a disease-producing bacteria (for example, *Streptococcus*) or fungus.

Antibody　A complex molecule (immunoglobulin) that is produced by lymph tissue in response to the presence of an antigen (such as a protein of bacteria or other infecting organism) and that neutralizes the effect of that foreign substance.

Antigen　A substance (for example, a toxin) or organism (for example, an amoeba) that, when entering the body, causes the production of an antibody that reacts specifically with the antigen to neutralize, destroy, or weaken it. The presence of certain antigens is the criterion for typing in the ABO blood grouping system and is important in tissue cross-matching for transplants (for example, the HLA antigen in kidney transplants).

Antihistamine　A drug, used to treat allergies, hypersensitivity reactions, and colds, that works to reduce the effects of histamine (for example, chlorpheniramine maleate [Coricidin]).

Anti-inflammatory　A drug that counteracts or reduces inflammation (for example, aspirin).

Antiseptic　An agent (for example, soap) that slows or stops the continuing growth of microorganisms but may not actually kill them.

Antitoxin　A drug or other agent (for example, antivenin) that prevents or limits the effect of a microorganism's poison (toxin).

Anxiety attack　An acute episode of intense anxiety and feelings of panic, accompanied by symptoms such as palpitations, breathlessness, sweating, gastrointestinal complaints, and feelings of imminent disaster. The attacks usually occur suddenly, may last from a few seconds to an hour or more, and may occur infrequently or several times a day. Treatment includes reassurance; the use of anxiolytic and ataraxic drugs; sedation, if necessary; and often psychotherapy to alleviate the underlying causes.

Aorta　The main trunk of the arterial blood circulatory system from which all other arteries (except the pulmonary) branch. This large artery stems from the heart at the left ventricle, passes upward (ascending aorta) toward the neck, arches (aortic arch) and loops and descends downward (descending aorta) along the left side of the vertebral column through the chest region (thoracic aorta), through the diaphragm to the abdomen (abdominal aorta) where it divides into two iliac arteries. Major arteries (for example, carotid, coronary) branch from the aorta transporting the aorta's freshly oxygenated blood to the various organs of the body. The aortic valve, situated between the left ventricle and the aorta, prevents blood from flowing back from the aorta into the heart.

Aplastic anemia　A deficiency of the formed elements (for example, red blood cells, white blood cells) of the blood due to a failure of the cell-producing machinery of the bone marrow, caused by a neoplasm or, most commonly, by exposure to toxic chemicals, radiation, or certain drugs.

Appendicitis　Inflammation of the vermiform appendix. Symptoms are pain in the abdomen, generally but not exclusively on the right side, nausea, vomiting, low-grade fever, and elevated white blood cell counts. Treatment is appendectomy.

Appendix　The apparently functionless wormlike or fingerlike attachment to the first part of the large intestine in the lower right abdomen.

Arteriogram　An X-ray of an artery filled with a contrast medium.

Arteriosclerosis　A disorder of the arteries, common with advancing age and in certain diseases (for example, hypertension), characterized by calcification, loss of elasticity and hardening of the walls of the arteries, resulting in decreased blood flow, especially to the brain and extremities. Symptoms include intermittent limping, memory deficits, headache, and dizziness. There is no specific treatment, but moderate exercise, a low-fat diet, and avoidance of stress are generally recommended.

Artery　A vessel that carries blood away from the heart to the other tissues throughout the body. Except for the pulmonary artery (which carries blood to the lungs), arteries carry oxygen rich blood. Most arteries are named for the body part they traverse or reach (for example, the femoral artery courses along the femur). *See also* **Aorta**.

Arthritis　Inflammation of a joint that may cause swelling, redness, and pain. There are several types of arthritis, the most common of which are gout (gouty arthritis), osteoarthritis, and rheumatoid arthritis.

Artificial Insemination (AI)　Introduction of sperm into the female birth canal by means of an instrument (for example, a slender tube and syringe) to increase the likelihood of conception. The sperm specimen may be provided by the woman's husband (AIH) or partner or by an anonymous donor (AID).

Artificial respiration　An emergency procedure for maintaining a flow of air through the pulmonary system, using mechanical means or hand pressure, to aid a person whose breathing has stopped (for example, because of drowning, injury, or drugs) or is otherwise not controlled. *See* **Cardiopulmonary resuscitation**.

Asbestos　A fiberlike, fire-resistant mineral commonly used as an insulator and roofing material, it is now implicated in causing lung disease (asbestosis) even when inhaled in small amounts and for a limited time and as a carcinogen.

Asphyxia　A condition in which insufficient or no oxygen reaches the tissues, thereby threatening the life of the organism. Common causes are drowning, electric shock, inhaling poison gas, and choking.

Aspirin　Acetylsalicylic acid, a drug commonly used to relieve pain and reduce fever and inflammation; it may also (in prescribed amounts) prevent blood clotting and help prevent strokes, heart attacks, and cataracts. Side effects include stomach discomfort and gastrointestinal bleeding; for these reasons buffered aspirins are available. Accidental overdosage of aspirin is a common form of poisoning, especially among children.

Asthma　A respiratory disorder characterized by recurrent episodes of difficulty in breathing, wheezing (especially on expiration), cough, and thick mucus production, usually caused by a spasm or inflammation of the bronchial airways. Attacks are precipitated by exposure to an allergen (for example, pollen, dust, food), strenuous exercise, stress, or infection. Asthma is most common in childhood (occurring more often in boys) and has a strong hereditary factor. Treatment involves the use of bronchodilators and elimination of the causative agent. Also called bronchial asthma.

Astigmatism   A defect in vision in which the light rays cannot be focused properly on the retina because of abnormal curvature of the cornea or lens of the eye; corrective lenses improve vision.

Asymptomatic   Without symptoms.

Atherosclerosis   A common disorder of the arteries in which plaques of material (mostly cholesterol and lipids) form on the inner arterial walls, making them thick and nonelastic and narrowing the opening of the vessel, thus causing decreased flow of blood to those organs supplied by the artery. Common with aging, a frequent complication of hypertension, obesity, and diabetes, and associated with some hereditary metabolic disorders, atherosclerosis is an important cause of heart disease. In some cases segments of occluded arteries may be surgically bypassed (as in coronary bypass surgery). Preventive measures include a low-fat diet, exercise, and avoidance of smoking and stress.

ATHEROSCLEROSIS

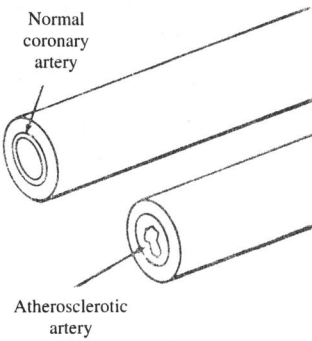

Normal coronary artery

Atherosclerotic artery

Athlete's foot   A fungal infection (ringworm) of the foot, generally starting between the toes causing itching. Later, bacteria may replace the fungus and cause the skin between the toes to turn white, crack, and peel off. Treatment is by antifungal preparations.

Atrophy   A decrease in size of a part or organ, resulting from a wasting away of tissue, as may occur, for example, in disease or from lack of use.

Auditory canal   The tubelike structure that leads from the outside of the ear to the eardrum; also called auditory meatus.

Aura   A sensation, as light, halos, or warmth, that may signal the start of a migraine or an epileptic attack.

Autism   Abnormal withdrawal into oneself, marked by severe communication problems, short attention span, inability to interact socially, and extreme resistance to change. Children with autism are extremely difficult to teach.

Autoimmune disease   Any of a large group of diseases marked by an abnormality of the functioning of the immune system that causes the production of antibodies against one's own tissues and other body materials. Autoimmune diseases include systemic lupus erythematosus, rheumatoid arthritis, and other collagen diseases; and idiopathic thrombocy-

topenic purpura, autoimmune leukopenia, and other hemolytic disorders.

B   **Bacterium**   Any of a large group of small, unicellular microorganisms (class Schizomycetes) found in the soil, water, and air, some of which cause disease in humans and other animals. Bacteria are generally classified as rodshaped (bacillus), spherical (coccus), comma-shaped (vibrio), or spiral (spirochete).

TYPES OF BACTERIA

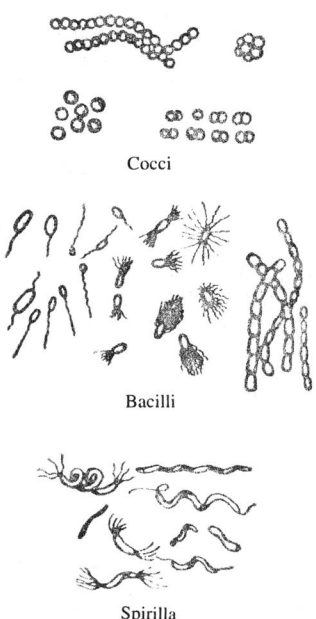

Cocci

Bacilli

Spirilla

Barbiturate   A drug (for example, phenobarbital) that depresses brain and spinal cord activity and was once widely used to treat convulsions and produce sedation. Barbiturates are potentially habit forming and have largely been replaced by safer drugs.

Behavior modification   A technique for changing undesirable behavior into acceptable behavior, generally by rewarding appropriate responses and ignoring or punishing inappropriate behavior. *Compare* **Biofeedback**.

Benign   Mild, noncancerous, and/or not spreading, as of a disease or growth, especially a benign tumor. *Compare* **Malignant**.

Bile   A thick, yellow-green-brown fluid made by the liver, stored in the gallbladder, and discharged into the upper part of the digestive tract (duodenum), where it breaks down fats, preparing them for further digestion. Also called gall.

Biofeedback   A technique, apparently learnable, that enables a person to manipulate ordinarily involuntary processes, such as heartbeat and blood pressure, through concentration and knowledge (feedback) of bodily effects or responses as they occur and are monitored by special machines that provide visual and/or auditory data.

Biopsy   The removal of a small amount of tissue and/or fluid from a living body and its examination by microscopic and/or other analytical methods to establish or confirm the presence of a disease, to follow its course, and/or to estimate its outcome. The specimen is usually obtained by suction through a needle, but other methods and instruments, including surgery, are also used.

Birth control   *See* **Contraception**.

Birth control pill   *See* **Oral contraceptive**.

Birth defect   An abnormality that is present at birth. It may be the result of a genetic abnormality or of an abnormality during pregnancy or the birth process. A cleft palate, resulting from incomplete development and union of the parts forming the palate, is an example of a birth defect. Also called congenital defect.

Bisexual   (1) Having both male and female gonads; (2) having the drives and characteristics of both sexes; (3) participating in or desiring sexual contact with persons of both sexes.

Bladder   (1) The urinary bladder, a muscular and membranous sac that stores urine. Urine produced in the kidneys passes through the ureters into the bladder; sphincters control the release of urine from the bladder through the urethra and out of the body; (2) any saclike fibrous and membranous organ that holds liquids secreted into it for later passage to another part of the body or out of the body, as in the gallbladder, which stores bile.

Blister   A vesicle filled with serum; a collection of fluid below the skin, usually resulting from a burn.

Bloat   Swelling or filling with gas, as in abdominal distension.

Erythrocytes   Leukocytes
Red blood cells   White blood cells

Platelets

The two major types of blood cells: erythrocytes and leukocytes. Platelets, necessary for blood coagulation, are sometimes considered blood cells.

Blood   A fluid tissue that is pumped by the heart through arteries, capillaries, and veins carrying oxygen and nutrients to body cells and carbon dioxide and other waste products away from body cells. Human blood is composed of a pale yellow fluid called plasma in which are suspended red blood cells, white blood cells, platelets, and a variety of chemicals, including hormones, proteins, carbohydrates, and fats. Adult males have about 70 ml/kg of body weight, women about 65 ml/kg.

Blood bank   A unit or department, usually associated with a hospital or laboratory, that collects, processes and stores blood for use in blood transfusions and other purposes.

Blood cell   Any of two types of cells—red blood cells (erythrocytes) and white blood cells (leukocytes)—found in human blood. Platelets, though not true cells, are also sometimes included.

Blood coagulation   The process by which liquid blood is changed into a semi-solid mass, a blood clot. It can occur in an intact blood vessel but usually starts with an injury and the exposure of blood.

Platelets clump at the wound site and chemical changes in the blood lead to the formation of a fibrin meshwork and the trapping of blood cells into a clot. Also called blood clotting.

Blood count   The enumeration of red blood cells (erythrocytes), white blood cells (leukocytes) and sometimes platelets found in an accurately diluted one cubic millimeter sample of blood. Erythrocytes normally number 4.5 million (women) to 5 million (men), leukocytes 5,000 to 10,000, and platelets 150,000 to 450,000. Changes from the normal numbers usually indicate disease and are used as an aid to diagnosis.

Blood group   The classification of blood, based on the presence or absence of certain antigens on the surface of red blood cells, used to determine compatibility for transfusions. There are many systems for classifying blood; the most commonly used is the ABO blood group system.

Blood pressure   The force of blood on the walls of the arteries resulting from the squeezing effect of the heart's left ventricle (systole), with residual maintenance (diastole) as the heart chambers relax and expand. Abbreviated BP, blood pressure is usually measured, using a sphygmomanometer placed at the brachial artery in the arm, as the force needed to raise a column of mercury and expressed in millimeters (mm) of mercury (Hg) as a fraction, the upper number representing the systolic pressure, the lower number the diastolic pressure. Blood pressure varies with age, sex, condition of the arteries, force of the heart muscle contraction, emotional state and general health of the arteries and heart. Adult blood pressure is usually considered normal at about 120/80 mm Hg; in children it is lower. High blood pressure is termed hypertension; low blood pressure, hypotension.

Blood test   Any of several techniques used to determine if the cellular makeup (for example, blood count), chemical levels (for example, amount of glucose), or other factors (for example, capillary blood coagulation time) are within normal limits or to ascertain if disease-producing organisms or their products, alcohol, drugs, or poisons are present.

Blood transfusion   The administration of whole blood or its components to replace blood lost through surgery, disease, or injury. Blood typing is the first step to ensure that the donor's and the recipient's blood match in the transfusion of whole blood.

Blood typing   A technique for determining a person's blood type or group. In typing for the commonly used ABO blood group system, blood cells are matched with serum known to be type A or type B, and the blood type is determined by whether clumping of the cells occurs.

Blood vessel   Any of the network of tubes that transport blood throughout the body, including arteries, veins, arterioles, and venules.

Bone marrow   Specialized soft tissue found within bone. Red bone marrow, widespread in the bones of children and found in some adult bones (for example, sternum, ribs), is essential for the formation of mature red blood cells. Fat laden yellow bone marrow, more common in adults, is found primarily at the ends of long bones.

Booster injection   A supplementary dose ("booster shot") of a vaccine or other immunizing

substance, given to raise or restore the presumably waning effectiveness of a previous dose.

Botulism Severe and often fatal form of food poisoning resulting from eating food (usually canned or otherwise preserved) containing the microorganism *Clostridium botulinum*, which produces a toxin (botulin) that causes fatigue followed by marked disturbances in vision, muscle weakness, and often fatal respiratory complications. Hospitalization and use of antitoxin are required.

Bowel The intestines, especially the large intestine.

Brain The mass of nervous tissue in the skull; the main part of the central nervous system, the primary center for regulating body activities. The brain includes the two hemispheres of the cerebrum, the cerebellum, the pons, and the medulla oblongata, each part with specialized functions. The brain is covered by protective membranes (meninges) and has cavities (ventricles) containing fluid.

Brain death Irreversible unconsciousness with total loss of brain function, usually determined by loss of reflex activity and respiration and fixed, dilated pupils while the heart continues to beat. In the United States, legal definitions of brain death vary from state to state, but usually electrical activity of the brain must be shown to be absent on at least two electroencephalograms taken 12 to 14 hours apart.

Brain scan A painless diagnostic procedure using radioactive isotopes to examine the brain and localize and identify possible lesions or other abnormalities. *See also* **CAT scan**.

Breast cancer One of the most common malignancies in women in the United States, with several known risk factors, including a family history of breast cancer, early menarche, late menopause, having no children or having them late in life, exposure to ionizing radiation, obesity, hypertension, chronic cystic disease of the breast, and possibly a high-fat diet. Early symptoms are usually detected by the woman during breast self-examination and include a small painless lump, thick or dimpled skin, or a change in the nipple; later symptoms include nipple discharge, pain, and swollen lymph glands in the armpit area. Diagnosis is made by physical examination, mammography, and laboratory examination of tumor cells obtained through biopsy. Treatment depends on the location and size of the tumor and whether it has spread to other areas and may be lumpectomy or some type (for example, radical or simple) of mastectomy, often followed by chemotherapy and/or radiotherapy. Since early diagnosis and treatment greatly improve the rate of cure, women are advised to practice regular breast self-examination. (*See* figure, page 8-24.)

Bronchial asthma *See* **Asthma**.

Bronchitis Inflammation of the bronchial tubes. Acute bronchitis, a common disorder often following an upper respiratory infection, is characterized by cough, fever, and chest pain. Treatment is by pain and fever reducers, steam inhalation and antibiotics, if indicated. Chronic bronchitis, bronchial inflammation that is persistent, often caused by cigarette smoking, exposure to other irritants, or recurrent infections, is characterized by mucus secretions, cough, and frequently increasing difficulty in breathing.

Bunion A swelling and thickening of the joint where the big toe joins the foot, displacing the big toe toward the other toes. Caused by chronic irritation from ill-fitting shoes, bunions may become painful and require surgery.

Bursitis Inflammation of a bursa (a fluid-containing, membrane-lined cavity located in connecting tissues, usually in the vicinity of joints, where friction would otherwise occur) often precipitated by injury, infection, excessive trauma or effort, or arthritis or similar condition and characterized by pain and often limited mobility. Treatment is by analgesics, anti-inflammatory agents, immobilization of the affected area, and in some cases the use of corticosteroid injections at the affected site.

Cancer An abnormal, malignant growth of cells that invade nearby tissues and often spread (metastasize) to other sites in the body, interfering with the normal function of the affected sites. Although the basic cause of cancer remains unknown, most forms of cancer can be traced to a specific causal or precipitating factor, as, for example, cigarette smoking, exposure to cancer-producing chemicals or ionizing radiation, or overexposure to the sun; viruses are associated with some cancers and genetic (familial) susceptibility plays a role in certain forms of the disease. The incidence of different types of cancer varies greatly with age, sex, ethnic group, and geographic location. In the United States cancer is second to heart disease as a cause of death with breast cancer and lung cancer leading the statistics. The parts of the body most often affected by cancer are the breast, lungs, colon, uterus, oral cavity, and bone marrow. Major signs of cancer include a change in bladder or bowel habits; a sore that does not heal; a persistent cough or hoarseness; unusual bleeding or discharge; thickening or lump in the breast or other part of the body; indigestion or difficulty in swallowing; and change in a wart or mole. The treatment of cancer may involve surgery, the irradiation of affected parts, and/or the use of chemotherapy. The prognosis depends on the type and site of the cancer, the promptness of initial treatment, and other factors; about one-third of those patients with newly diagnosed cancers are ultimately permanently cured. *See also* **Breast cancer**; **Carcinoma**; **Leukemia**; **Lymphoma**; **Sarcoma**.

Capillary (1) A tiny blood vessel, connecting arterioles and venules. Through the one-cell-layer-thick walls (approximately 0.008 mm diameter) of capillaries oxygen and nutrients are passed from arterioles to body tissues and carbon dioxide and other wastes are passed from body tissue to venules; (2) any other small, hairlike tube for carrying lymph or other material.

Carbon monoxide poisoning A toxic condition caused by the inhalation and absorption of carbon monoxide gas. The carbon monoxide combines with hemoglobin, displacing oxygen, and causes loss of oxygen to body tissues. Symptoms include headache, shortness of breath, confusion, drowsiness, unconsciousness, and if continued, death. Treatment involves removal of the carbon monoxide environment and the administration of oxygen.

Carcinogen A specific substance or chemical that gives rise to a cancer; a cancer-forming agent.

Carcinoma A malignant growth of cells (epithelial cells) that arises in the coverings and linings of the body parts (for example, skin and mucous membranes) and in glands; these cells tend to invade adjacent tissues and to spread (metastasize) to other parts of the body via the lymphatic channels and/or bloodstream. *Compare* **Leukemia**; **Lymphoma**; **Sarcoma**.

Cardiac arrest A sudden cessation of cardiac output and blood circulation, usually caused by ventricular fibrillation or other serious abnormality in function of the ventricles of the heart, and leading to oxygen lack, buildup of carbon dioxide, acidosis, and, if untreated, to kidney, lung, and brain damage and death. Treatment is by immediate cardiopulmonary resuscitation (CPR). Also called cardiopulmonary arrest.

Cardiac arrhythmia Abnormal rate of electrical activity in the heart, caused by malfunction of impulse-conducting fibers in the heart or inability of the heart to respond to stress.

Cardiac monitor A device for continual observation of the function of the heart. It may include electrocardiograph, oscilloscope, and other recordings of heart function; there may be an alarm to alert medical personnel to abnormal changes.

Cardiogram Electronic recording of the rhythm and changes in the heart. Also called electrocardiogram.

Cardiopulmonary resuscitation (CPR) An emergency procedure, consisting of external cardiac massage and artificial respiration, used as the first treatment for a person who has collapsed, is unresponsive, has no pulse, and has stopped breathing. The purpose is to restore blood circulation and prevent death or brain damage due to lack of oxygen. CPR may be performed as a one- or two-person

How to examine your breasts

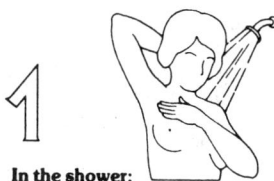

In the shower:

Examine your breasts during bath or shower; hands glide easier over wet skin. Fingers flat, move gently over every part of each breast. Use right hand to examine left breast, left hand for right breast. Check for any lump, hard knot or thickening.

Before a mirror:

Inspect your breasts with arms at your sides. Next, raise your arms high overhead. Look for any changes in contour of each breast, a swelling, dimpling of skin or changes in the nipple.

Then, rest palms on hips and press down firmly to flex your chest muscles. Left and right breast will not exactly match—few women's breasts do.

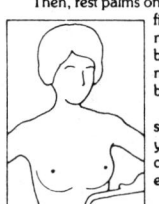

Regular inspection shows what is normal for you and will give you confidence in your examination.

Lying down:

To examine your right breast, put a pillow or folded towel under your right shoulder. Place right hand behind your head—this distributes breast tissue more evenly on the chest. With left hand, fingers flat, press gently in small circular motions around an imaginary clock face. Begin at outermost top of your right breast for 12 o'clock, then move to 1 o'clock, and so on around the circle back to 12. A ridge of firm tissue in the lower curve of each breast is normal. Then move in an inch, toward the nipple, keep circling to examine *every part of your breast*, including nipple. This requires at least three more circles. Now slowly repeat procedure on your left breast with a pillow under your left shoulder and left hand behind head. Notice how your breast structure feels.

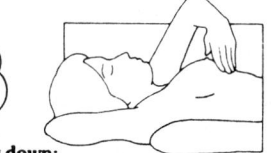

Finally, squeeze the nipple of each breast gently between thumb and index finger. Any discharge, clear or bloody, should be reported to your doctor immediately.

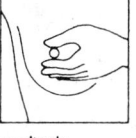

American Cancer Society

technique. Currently, the American Heart Association recommends that laypeople be taught only the one-person method, which involves cardiac compressions at a rate of 80 to 100 per minute, with two artificial breaths interspersed between every 15 compressions. As a rule, CPR should not be performed by untrained individuals, though emergency dispatchers have successfully given instructions over the phone to people at the bedside of cardiac arrest victims. A portion of every CPR class is dedicated to teaching the treatment of airway obstruction. *See also* **Heimlich maneuver**.

Cardiovascular system   Body parts, including the heart and blood vessels, involved in the pumping of blood and transport of nutrients, oxygen, and waste products throughout the body.

Carrier   A person, generally in apparent good health, who harbors organisms that can infect and cause disease in others. Probably the most notorious carrier was Typhoid Mary.

Cartilage   Tough supporting connective tissue serving to protect and connect body parts; it is found chiefly in body tubes (for example, trachea) and joints. (In the embryo the parts of the skeleton that develop into bone.) Cartilage has no nerves or blood supply of its own.

CAT (Computerized Axial Tomography) scan   A method for examining the body's soft tissues (for example, the brain) using X rays, with the beam passing repeatedly (scanning) through a body part, and a computer calculating tissue absorption at each point scanned, from which a visualization of the tissue is developed. The technique enables the radiologist to study normal structures as well as detect tumors, fluid buildup, dead tissue, and other abnormalities.

Cataract   An eye disorder in which the lens becomes less transparent (more opaque) so that light rays cannot reach the retina and there is progressive painless loss of vision. Most cataracts are caused by degenerative changes after age 50, but some may be caused by trauma to the eye or exposure to certain chemicals; some are hereditary and some congenital (due perhaps to viral infection during pregnancy). Treatment is removal of the lens and use of special contact lenses or eyeglasses or the implantation of an intraocular lens (IOL); in children soft cataracts may be removed by fragmentation (via ultrasound) and drainage.

Cathartic   An agent that promotes evacuation of the bowel, especially fluid evacuation by stimulating peristalsis (for example, senna, aloe products); by increasing the bulk or fluidity of the feces (for example, magnesium sulfate, magnesium hydroxide); or by lubricating the intestinal wall (for example, mineral oil). *Compare* **Laxative**.

Catheter   A flexible, usually rubber or soft plastic, tube inserted into the body for removing or instilling fluids for diagnosis or treatment purposes. In its most common use a catheter is inserted through the urethra into the bladder to withdraw urine and empty (for example, before surgery) or irrigate the bladder.

Cauterize   To destroy tissue for medical reasons (for example, the removal of a wart) by burning with a hot iron, electron current, or chemical.

Cell   An individual living unit, the basic unit of structure for tissues and organs, composed of an outer membrane, a main mass, and a nucleus, which controls the cell's metabolism and reproduction.

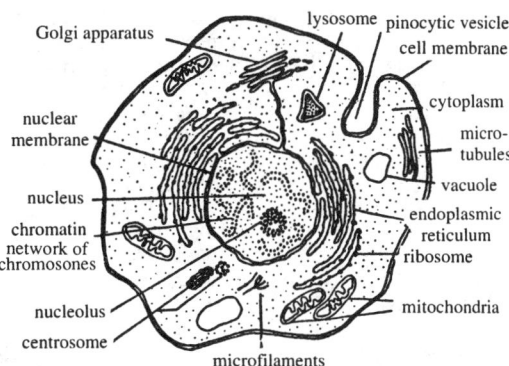

TYPICAL CELL

Golgi apparatus — lysosome — pinocytic vesicle — cell membrane — cytoplasm — micro-tubules — vacuole — endoplasmic reticulum — ribosome — mitochondria — nuclear membrane — nucleus — chromatin network of chromosones — nucleolus — centrosome — microfilaments

Cellulose   The basic constituent (a polysaccharide) of plant fiber, providing bulk necessary for proper intestinal function. Fruit, bran, and green vegetables provide cellulose.

Celsius   Pertaining to a temperature scale in which the freezing point of water is 0 degree and the boiling point is 100 degrees, as compared with 32 degrees and 212 degrees, respectively on the Fahrenheit scale. The name, commonly abbreviated as C, honors Anders Celsius, who devised it. Also called centigrade.

Central nervous system   One of the two main divisions of the human nervous system (the other being the peripheral nervous system), consisting of the brain and the spinal cord, made up of gray matter (mostly nerve cells and associated parts) and white matter (mostly nerve fibers), and containing protective cerebrospinal fluid. The main coordinating and controlling center of the body, the central nervous system processes information to and from the peripheral nervous system.

Cerebral hemorrhage   Flow of blood from a ruptured blood vessel in the brain; causes include high blood pressure, head injuries, and aneurysm. Symptoms, which depend on the site of the bleeding and the type of blood vessel involved, may include numbness and diminished mental function, or, if severe, coma and death. *See also* **Cerebrovascular Accident**.

Cerebral palsy   Loss or deficiency of muscle control due to permanent, nonprogressive brain damage occurring before or at the time of birth. Symptoms include difficulty in walking, poor coordination of the limbs, lack of balance, speech or other sense organ difficulties, and sometimes mental retardation. Treatment depends on the difficulties present and may include leg braces, speech therapy, and antispasmodic or muscle-relaxing drugs.

Cerebrovascular Accident (CVA)   An abnormal condition in which hemorrhage or blockage of the blood vessels of the brain leads to oxygen lack and resulting symptoms—sudden loss of ability to move a body part (as an arm or parts of the face) or to speak, paralysis, weakness, or, if severe, death. Usually only one side of the body is affected. Physical therapy and speech therapy can result in some degree of recovery. Also called stroke.

Cervix   The neck or necklike part of an organ, especially the neck of the uterus, that part of the uterus that extends into the vagina; dilation of the cervix permits the passage of the fetus in childbirth.

Cesarean section   Surgical incision through the abdomen and uterus for removal of a fetus, performed when conditions (for example, maternal hemorrhage, premature separation of the placenta, fetal distress, baby too large for passage through mother's pelvis) for normal vaginal delivery are deemed hazardous for mother or baby. The rate of Cesarean deliveries in the United States has recently increased. Hazards include those of major surgery for the mother and the possibility of too-early birth of the baby. Also called Caesarean; C-section.

Change of life   Colloquial for menopause.

Chemotherapy   The treatment of disease by chemical agents. The term includes the use of drugs (for example, antibacterials, antifungals) to harm or kill disease-causing microorganisms but most commonly refers to the use of drugs to treat cancer. Anticancer (antineoplastic) drugs generally inhibit the proliferation of cells and include alkylating agents (for example, chlorambucil), antimetabolites (for example, fluorouracil), periwinkle plant derivatives (for example, vincristine), antineoplastic antibiotics (for example, adramycin, mithramycin), and radioactive isotopes (for example, iodine-131, phosphorus-32, gold-198). All these agents are associated with side effects, the most common of which are nausea and vomiting, suppression of bone marrow function, and loss of hair. Medications are available to alleviate some side effects.

Chickenpox   An acute contagious disease, caused by herpes varicella zoster virus, characterized by a rash of vesicles on the face and body. Chickenpox is a common childhood disease; it is usually mild in otherwise healthy children but may be serious in babies, children weakened by other diseases, and in adults. After an incubation period of two to three weeks, the disease usually begins with slight fever and malaise, after which itchy macules develop often first on the back and chest; followed by fluid-containing vesicles that break easily and become encrusted. Treatment consists of fever-reducing drugs, lotions to relieve itching, and rest. No vaccine against chickenpox is available; one attack usually confers life-long immunity, but the virus lays dormant in nerve cells, sometimes to be reactivated, causing shingles. Also called varicella. *See also* **Herpes zoster**.

Child abuse   The physical, emotional, or sexual maltreatment of a child, often resulting in serious and often permanent injury or impairment and sometimes in death. Abuse may be overt, as in severely beating a child, or covert, as in depriving a child of needed affection and emotional support. The abuser may be a parent, a sibling (often older and stronger), another relative, or an unrelated adult. Child abuse occurs at all socioeconomic levels (though it is probably reported more often among the poor, who visit hospital clinics or social agencies) and involves children and parents of all ages, but certain factors are thought to increase the risk. Especially at risk are parents who are very young and/or emotionally unstable, who were themselves abused as children, or who are involved in marital strife or are undergoing other extreme stress (e.g., unemployment); and children who are very young (particularly in cases of beating and physical abuse), who are difficult by temperament, or who have emotional or physical handicaps.

Chinese restaurant syndrome   A group of symptoms—headache, a tingling and burning sensation, and sometimes a feeling of facial pressure—caused by eating food containing monosodium glutamate (MSG), which is often used in Chinese cooking. Many restaurants have now stopped using MSG in their food.

Chiropractic   A system of diagnosis and treatment based on the belief that many diseases are caused by pressure on nerves due to misalignments (subluxations) of the spinal column and that such diseases can be treated by correction (for example, by massage) of the misalignment.

Chronic   Long-lasting or frequently recurring (for example, pain). *Compare* **Acute**.

Cilia   (1) Eyelashes; (2) hairlike projections from a cell, especially in the upper respiratory tract, where cilia move particles of dust or other materials.

Circulatory system   Network of channels through which a fluid passes around the body, especially, the network of arteries and veins transporting blood in the body.

Circumcision   Surgical removal of the foreskin (prepuce) of the penis widely performed on newborn boys (required in the Jewish and certain other religions) though its medical benefit is not proved and some risks (for example, injury to the urethra, hemorrhage) are associated with the procedure.

Cirrhosis   A chronic diseased condition of the liver in which fibrous tissue and nodules replace normal tissue, interfering with blood flow and normal functions of the organ, including gastrointestinal functions, hormone metabolism, and alcohol and drug detoxification. A chief cause of cirrhosis is chronic alcoholism, and hepatitis and other infections may also be responsible. Symptoms include nausea, flatulence, light-colored stools, and abdominal discomfort. Treatment is by rest, a protein-rich diet, and abstinence from alcohol. If untreated, liver and kidney failure and gastrointestinal hemorrhage can occur, leading to death.

Clot   A clump of material formed out of the contents of a fluid, as of blood. *See* **Blood coagulation**.

Coagulation   The clotting process. *See* **Blood coagulation**.

Cobalt   A metallic element, the radioactive isotope of which (^{60}Co) is used in the treatment of cancer. Cobalt is contained in vitamin B_{12}.

Cocaine   A white, crystalline powder, derived from the leaves of the coca plant or prepared synthetically, and used widely as an anesthetic. Cocaine is also a drug of abuse, used for its stimulating properties. Adverse reactions, especially when used illicitly, include restlessness, euphoria, tremors, stroke, and myocardial infarction. Cocaine is addictive and is associated with death due to heart attacks and cardiovascular accidents (strokes), even in young people.

Codeine   A chemical (alkaloid), derived from opium or morphine, used as a pain reliever and cough suppressant. Side effects include nausea, constipation, and drowsiness; if taken in large amounts or for a long period, it is potentially addictive.

Coitus   The sexual union of a man and a woman in which the penis is inserted into the vagina, usually accompanied by excitement and often orgasm and ejaculation.

Cold   Infection involving the nasal passages and upper part of the breathing system (not including the lungs) and marked by such symptoms as a runny nose, watery eyes, and a sore throat. Caused by one of many different viruses, a cold may be treated with rest, decongestants, and increased fluids, but usually not with antibiotics, which do not affect viruses. Also called common cold.

Cold sore   A "fever blister" caused by herpes simplex virus, occurring on the skin or mucous membranes (for example, at the corner of the mouth).

Colic   (1) Acute pain in the gut, especially intestinal pain with spasms (cramps); acute pain associated with passage of a stone or spasm of smooth-muscle tube or other organ, as in the passage of gallstones (biliary colic) or kidney stones (renal colic); (2) in infants, recurrent (usually daily, often at the same time of day) episodes of persistent crying, usually accompanied by signs of abdominal distress; it may be caused by intestinal gas (from air swallowed with food), though other explanations (for example, neurological immaturity) have also been proposed.

Colitis   Inflammation of the colon, either episodic and functional (irritable bowel syndrome, spastic colon) or more serious chronic and progressive bowel disease (for example Crohn's disease, ulcerative colitis). Irritable bowel attacks, often precipitated by stress, are characterized by colicky pain and constipation or diarrhea; they are treated by stress avoidance and a bland diet. Chronic diseases lead to ulceration of intestinal tissue, bleeding, severe diarrhea, and other complications.

Colon   The segment of large intestine from the cecum to the rectum.

Colostomy   The surgical creation of an opening (stoma) in the abdominal wall to allow material to pass from the bowel through that opening rather than through the anus. A colostomy may be temporary, to allow an inflamed area of the intestine to heal, or it may be permanent, as in cancer of the colon or rectum.

Colostrum   First fluid given off by the mother's breasts just before or after the birth of her baby; it contains white blood cells, protective antibodies, protein, and fat in a thin, yellow fluid.

Coma   A state of profound unconsciousness from which one cannot be aroused, resulting from drug action, toxicity (as in nephritis), brain injury, or disease.

Communicable disease   Any disease transmitted from one person or animal to another, either directly through body discharges (for example, nasal droplets, sputum, feces) or indirectly through substances or objects (for example, contaminated drinking glasses, toys, bed linens) or vectors (for example, flies, mosquitoes, ticks). Communicable diseases include those caused by viruses, bacteria, fungi, and parasites. Also called contagious disease.

Compress   A pad, usually of cloth or gauze (sometimes hot, cold, or medicated), applied with pressure to an inflamed part or to a wound to help control bleeding or to keep parts from protruding through a wound.

Compression bandage   A strip of cloth wrapped around a part to stop hemorrhage, immobilize the part, or keep fluid from collecting in a limb.

Conception   (1) Fertilization of the female egg cell (ovum) by a male sperm cell; the beginning of pregnancy; (2) the originating of a new idea; (3) a concept.

Concussion   A violent jarring or shaking, as from a severe blow or shock, especially one to the head. A concussion may cause a limited period of unconsciousness.

Condom   A thin sheath, usually of rubber or plastic, placed over the penis and used during coitus as a protection against sexually transmitted diseases (for example, AIDS) and as a reasonably effective contraceptive.

Congenital   Present at birth. A congenital anomaly (abnormality) may be inherited, acquired during pregnancy, or inflicted as the result of the birth process.

Conjunctivitis   Inflammation of the mucous membrane lining of the eyelids and the front of the eye, caused by bacterial or viral infection, allergy, or irritation. The eyes look pink; the eyelids are stuck together in the morning, and there is discomfort, but usually not pain. Treatment depends on the cause. Also called pinkeye.

Connective tissue   Material that supports and binds other tissues and parts of the body; it includes skin, bone, tendons, ligaments, and interlacing fibrils. Many diseases of connective tissue are difficult to cure, for example, lupus erythematosus, rheumatoid arthritis, and sarcoidosis.

Constipation   Difficulty in having bowel movements because of loss of muscle tone in the intestine, very hard stools, or other causes (for example, diverticulitis, intestinal obstruction). An increase in roughage (fruits, vegetables, bran) in the diet along with plenty of water often helps this condition.

Contact dermatitis   A skin rash resulting from exposure to an irritant such as an alkali or acid or to a substance to which one has an allergic response (for example, poison ivy). *See also* **Rhus dermatitis**.

Contact lens   A small, curved, glass or plastic lens placed on the eye to correct vision. The lens is fitted to the individual's eye and made to float on a tear film. Contact lenses must be inserted carefully and periodically removed and cleaned. Soft contact lenses, made of a hydrophilic plastic, are more comfortable and can be worn for longer periods than glass contact lenses.

Contamination   The inclusion, intentionally or accidentally, of unwanted substances or factors; pollution.

Continence   (1) Self-restraint or moderation, as in eating or in sexual activity; (2) the ability to hold urine and feces and to voluntarily control their passage from the body.

Contraception   A process or technique for the prevention of pregnancy. Methods include total abstinence from coitus; coitus interruptus (withdrawal); periodic abstinence or rhythm (refraining from coitus during a woman's fertile time, the time around ovulation, which is determined by the calendar method or by determination of basal temperature); the use of mechanical devices to block sperm from moving up the female genital tract (including the condom, diaphragm, intrauterine device [IUD], cervical cap, sponge); biochemical methods (birth control pill or oral contraceptive, hormonal injections); chemical means (spermicidal creams, jellies, foams, and suppositories); and sterilization (vasectomy in men, tubal ligation in women).

Contraction   (1) A shortening, or tension increase, as in muscle action; a persistent abnormal shortening; (2) in labor, rhythmic tightening of the upper uterine musculature that decreases the size of the uterus and pushes the fetus through the birth canal; uterine contractions typically begin mildly and then increase in severity and frequency, sometimes coming at a rate of one every two minutes and lasting about one minute.

Contusion   A bruise; a superficial, nonlacerating injury from a blow.

Convalescence   A period of recovery from injury, illness, or surgery, generally the time after the crisis has passed until health is regained.

Convulsion   A sudden, involuntary and violent contraction of a group of muscles, sometimes with loss of consciousness; sometimes caused by high fever in otherwise healthy infants and young children, or it may occur in a seizure disorder (for example, epilepsy) or following head injury.

Corn   Horny mass of epithelial cells overlying a bone, usually on the toes and resulting from chronic pressure (for example, from ill-fitting shoes). Treatment includes paring or peeling of the hard tissue and relief of the pressure.

Cornea   The outer, transparent portion of the eye, consisting of five layers through which light passes to the retina.

Corneal transplant (graft)   Replacement of a diseased or damaged cornea with one taken from a donor eye, usually from a person who recently died.

Coronary artery   One of a pair of arteries that branch from the aorta and supply the heart. Any malfunction or disease of these arteries (coronary artery disease such as coronary atherosclerosis) can seriously affect the heart (for example depriving it of necessary oxygen and nutrients).

Coronary bypass   A type of open-heart surgery in which a prosthesis or section of a blood vessel (for example, the saphenous vein) is grafted onto a coronary artery and connected to the aorta to bypass a diseased or blocked section of the coronary artery in an effort to improve the blood supply to the heart, decrease the work load of the heart, and relieve angina. The operation was introduced in the 1960s and has been widely used since, but the possible risks of thrombosis or closure of the graft and the benefits of alternative methods of treatment have made the operation somewhat controversial.

Coronary occlusion   An obstruction of a coronary artery, caused by a blood clot or progressive atherosclerosis.

Cortisone   A hormone of the adrenal cortex that functions in carbohydrate metabolism and which, as a drug, is used to treat inflammatory conditions.

CPR   *See* **Cardiopulmonary resuscitation**.

Crab louse   A body louse (*Phthirus pubis*) that infects the hair of the genital region and is often transmitted venereally.

Crack   Street term for an illicit preparation of cocaine that is far more potent, addictive, and dangerous than the typical nasally inhaled powder form. Crack has precipitated strokes and heart attacks in young, previously healthy individuals, sometimes resulting in death.

Cranial nerves   The 12 pairs of nerves, each pair having sensory or motor functions, or both, that extend from the brain without passing through the spinal cord. (The XIth pair arises from both the brain and the upper spinal cord.) The 12 pairs of nerves are: olfactory, optic, oculomotor, trochlear, trigeminal, abducens, facial, vestibulocochlear (acoustic), glossopharyngeal, vagus, (spinal) accessory, hypoglossal.

Cranium   The skull; specifically the bony enclosure of the brain; it is composed of eight bones (frontal, occipital, sphenoid, ethmoid, two temporal and two parietal).

Crib death   *See* **Sudden Infant Death Syndrome**.

Cryosurgery   The use of extreme cold (for example, liquid nitrogen) to destroy unwanted tissue (for example, warts, cataracts, skin cancer). The cooling agent is applied by means of a metal probe; temperatures as low as −160°C can be achieved.

C-section   *See* **Cesarean section**.

Culture   A deliberate growing of microorganisms in a solid or liquid medium (for example agar, gelatin).

Curettage   The scraping of a cavity, especially the inside of the uterus or other surface, either to remove a tumor or other unwanted material or to obtain a sample of tissue for analysis.

Cyst   (1) A closed, fluid-filled sac embedded in tissue (as in the breast) that is abnormal or results from disease; (2) an anatomically normal sac (for example, the gallbladder or the dacrocyst, the tear sac in the eye).

Cystic fibrosis   An inherited disease, usually recognized in infancy or early childhood, in which the glands, especially those of the pancreas, lungs, and intestines, become clogged with thick mucus. The sweat is typically salty, containing high levels of sodium and chloride. Respiratory infections are common and can lead to death. Life expectancy has improved markedly and many victims now reach adulthood. Also called fibrocystic disease of the pancreas; mucoviscidosis.

Cystitis   Inflammation of the urinary bladder and ureters, characterized by pain, urgency and frequency of urination, and blood in the urine. More common in women, it may be caused by bacterial infection, stones, tumor, or trauma. Treatment depends on the cause and may include increased fluid intake and antibiotics.

D and C   *See* **Dilatation and Curettage**.

Decongestant   A drug (for example, epinephrine) that reduces congestion; decongestants may be applied as nasal sprays or drops or taken by mouth.

Defecation   The passage of feces out of the body; bowel movement.

Defibrillation The stopping, usually by electric shock, of heart muscle contractions that are out of normal rhythm (are fibrillating). In this common emergency procedure, a defibrillator delivers an electric shock (of preset voltage) to the heart through the chest wall in an attempt to restore normal heart rhythm.

Deformity Condition in which the body in general or any part of it (for example, the hand) is misshapen, distorted, or malformed. A deformity may result from injury, disease, or birth defect (for example, Arnold-Chiari deformity in which part of the brain protrudes through the skull).

Degeneration Physical and/or mental decline that involves tissue and cellular changes and the loss of specialized function; the extreme result is death of the parts involved and loss of their function.

Degenerative disorder Any of several conditions that lead to progressive loss of function (for example, chorea, parkinsonism).

Dehydration Extreme loss of water from the body tissues, often accompanied by imbalance of sodium, potassium, chloride, and other electrolytes in the body. Dehydration may occur in prolonged diarrhea, vomiting, or perspiration and is of more concern in infants and young children. Symptoms include thirst, dry skin, cracked lips, and dry mouth. Treatment involves restoring the fluid and electrolyte balance either by having the person drink liquids or by the intravenous administration of water and salts.

Déjà vu A sense that what one is seeing or experiencing has been encountered before, when actually it has not. Déjà vu occurs in normal persons but is more frequent in certain disorders (for example, some forms of epilepsy).

Delirium A usually brief state of incoherent excitement, confused speech, restlessness, and hallucinations. It may occur in high fever, ingestion of certain toxic substances and drugs, nutritional deficiencies, endocrine imbalance, or severe stress (for example, postoperative) or mental illness. Treatment includes bed rest, quiet, the use of drugs to quiet the patient, and treatment of the underlying cause. *Compare* **Dementia**.

Delirium Tremens (DTs) Acute and severe (sometimes fatal) mental disturbance caused by prolonged and excessive alcohol intake or by withdrawal from alcohol use after prolonged drinking. Symptoms include loss of appetite and restlessness, followed by excitement, disorientation, sweating, shaking, anxiety, extreme perspiration, and terrifying hallucinations. The acute episode, a medical emergency, is followed by sleep and convalescence, sometimes plagued by complications such as respiratory infections, heart failure, and extreme fatigue. Treatment includes use of sedative drugs and adequate nutrition (usually including vitamin supplements).

Dementia A progressive state of mental decline, especially of memory function and judgment, often accompanied by disorientation, stupor, and disintegration of the personality. It may be caused by certain metabolic diseases, drug intoxication, or injury, in which cases it is often reversible once the underlying cause is treated. In other cases it is caused by a disease (for example, Alzheimer's disease), brain injury, or degeneration brought about by aging (senile dementia) that causes irreversible changes. *Compare* **Delirium**.

Depilatory A chemical or other agent that removes hair.

Depressant A drug that decreases or slows the function or activity of a body part or system (for example, a cardiac depressant slows the heartbeat).

Depression (1) In anatomy, a hollow or depressed area, a downward placement, (2) in physiology, a decrease in function or activity; (3) in psychology, a dejected state of mind with feelings of sadness, discouragement, and hopelessness, often accompanied by reduced activity and ability to function, unresponsiveness, apathy, and sleep disturbances. The condition may be mild and temporary, a sign of emotional disorder, or severe and long-lasting and a sign of serious psychosis. Treatment depends on the severity of the condition and may include psychotherapy, use of antidepressant drugs, and occasionally the use of electroshock therapy. Evidence indicates that a tendency toward some forms of depression may be inherited. *See* Psychology, 21-8.

Dermatitis Acute or chronic inflammation of the skin, which becomes red and itchy and may develop blisters or other eruptions. There are many causes, including allergy, disease (for example, eczema), and infection. Treatment depends on the cause.

Dermatology The medical specialty concerned with the skin and its development, function, diseases, and treatment.

Detached retina Separation of the retina from the choroid in the back of the eye, usually resulting from internal changes in the eye, sometimes from severe injury. Symptoms include the sensation of flashing lights as the eye is moved and the appearance of floating spots in front of the eye. Treatment is by cauterization or other surgery.

Detoxification Process of removing a poison (toxin) or neutralizing its effect, normally a function of the liver.

Deviated septum An abnormal shift in position of any wall-like part that separates two chambers, most often referring to the nasal cavity. Deviated nasal septum is a common condition, causing symptoms of obstructed nasal passages, sinusitis, recurrent infection, nosebleeds, and difficulty in breathing. Treatment is by surgery.

Diabetes mellitus A complex and chronic disorder of metabolism due to total or partial lack of insulin secretion by the pancreas (specifically by the beta cells of the islets of Langerhans in the pancreas) or to the inability of insulin to function normally in the body. Symptoms include excessive thirst and urination, weight loss, and the presence of excessive sugar in the urine and the blood. The disease is common and evidence suggests that the incidence is increasing. There are two major forms: generally more severe, inherited, juvenile diabetes and usually less severe adult, or late-onset, diabetes, which usually appears between the ages of 40 and 60; in adult diabetes a hereditary predisposition may be triggered by obesity, severe stress, pregnancy, menopause, or other factors. There is no cure for diabetes mellitus. Treatment depends on the severity of the disease; mild forms may be managed with diet alone, but other cases require the use of drugs to lower blood sugar levels (oral antidiabetics) or injections of insulin. Severe and/or untreated cases frequently lead to serious complications, including premature atherosclerosis, often affecting the legs and leading to ulcers of the feet; kidney disorders; and eye disorders, sometimes leading to blindness. *See also* **Diabetic coma; Insulin shock.**

Diabetic coma A condition that can occur in diabetes mellitus as a result of failure to take prescribed insulin or the presence of some stress (for example, infection, surgery) that increases the need for insulin. Warning signs include great thirst, headache, nausea, and vomiting. If left untreated, the condition can lead to death. Treatment includes the administration of insulin and steps to correct dehydration and electrolyte imbalances. *Compare* **Insulin shock.**

Dialysis (1) A method, involving a semipermeable membrane, used to separate smaller particles from larger ones; (2) a medical procedure for filtering waste products from the blood of some kidney-disease patients or for removing poisons or drugs.

Diaphragm (1) The muscular partition that divides the chest from the abdomen and functions in respiration, moving downward during inspiration (breathing in) to increase the volume of the thoracic (chest) cavity and moving upward during expiration (breathing out) to decrease the volume; (2) a rubber or plastic dome-shaped cup that fits over the cervix of the uterus and that is used, with spermicidal jelly, as a contraceptive; it acts as a barrier to the passage of sperm upward in the female reproductive tract.

Diarrhea The frequent passage of loose, watery stools (the stools may contain mucus, blood, or excessive fat), sometimes accompanied by nausea, vomiting, abdominal cramps, and feelings of malaise and weakness. Diarrhea may be a symptom of a viral or bacterial infection (mild or severe), food poisoning, disorder of the colon (for example, colitis), gastrointestinal tumor, metabolic disorder, or other abnormal condition. Untreated, it can lead to dehydration, electrolyte imbalance, and weakness. Treatment depends on the cause, but the symptom itself may be treated with an antidiarrheal drug (for example, Lomotil).

Diastole The period between two contractions of the heart, when the chambers widen and fill with blood. On heart muscle contraction (systole), the blood is pumped through the heart and into the arteries. (In blood pressure readings, diastole is the second [or lower] number given.)

Digestion The process of breaking down food, by mechanical (for example, chewing, churning) and chemical (for example, the action of enzymes) means, into substances that can be absorbed and used by the body.

Digestive system Those parts of the body that function in a coordinated manner for the digestion and absorption of food. Included are the digestive tube and accessory organs (for example, gallbladder, liver) that secrete enzymes used in the digestion of foods.

Dilatation and Curettage (D & C) Dilatation of the cervix of the uterus and scraping of the endometrium (lining) of the uterus. It is a common procedure, usually performed using local anesthetic, to remove uterine tissue for examination and diagno-

sis, to stop prolonged or heavy bleeding, to remove the products of conception (a method of abortion), to remove retained fragments of the placenta after childbirth or abortion, and to remove small tumors.

Diphtheria An acute, contagious infection caused by the bacterium *Corynebacterium diphtheriae*, which produces a toxin affecting the whole body, and characterized by severe inflammation of the throat and larynx with production of a membrane lining the throat, along with fever, chills, malaise, brassy cough, and, in some cases (especially if untreated or unusually severe), by impaired function of the heart muscle and peripheral nerves. More common in children and once epidemic in many parts of the world, it is now rare in the United States because of routine immunization (DPT) against the disease. Treatment is by diphtheria antitoxin, antibiotics, rest, increased fluid intake, and tracheostomy, if necessary.

Diploid Pertaining to an individual or cell that has two complete sets of homologous chromosomes, one set from each parent; the diploid chromosome number is found in somatic (body) cells, not in gametes (sex cells), and is characteristic for each species, being 46 in normal human body cells.

Disc A flattened, rounded part, especially referring to the cushioning tissues between the vertebrae.

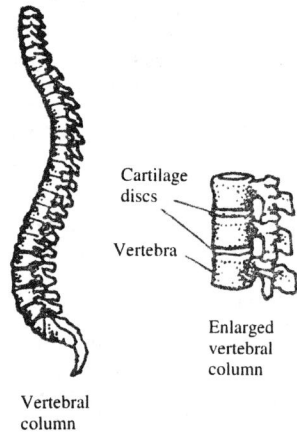

Discs separate and cushion the vertebrae.

Diuretic A drug that promotes the production and excretion of urine; it is commonly used in the treatment of edema, hypertension, and congestive heart failure. There are several types of diuretics, including thiazides (for example chlorothiazide [Diuril] and hydrochlorothiazide [Esidrix]), loop diuretics (furosemide [Lasix]), and others (spironolactone [Aldactone]). Several adverse reactions are common to diuretics, chiefly electrolyte (especially sodium and potassium) imbalances.

Diverticulitis Inflammation of an abnormal sac (diverticulum) at a weakened point in the digestive tract, especially the colon. Symptoms include cramp like abdominal pain, fever, and diarrhea or constipation. Treatment is by rest, antibiotics; severe cases may require surgery.

Douche Introduction of a jet of water or special fluid into or around a given part, especially the vagina, to cleanse or free the part from odor-causing contents, or to treat pelvic or vaginal infection.

Down syndrome　A congenital defect, usually caused by the presence of an extra No. 21 chromosome (trisomy) and characterized by mental retardation (the I.Q. averages 50 to 60); oblique placement of the eyes; a small head, flattened at the back; a large, furrowed tongue; short stature; bowel defects; and heart abnormalities. This syndrome, the most common of the chromosomal abnormalities, is associated with advanced maternal age, especially over 35 (1 in 80 offspring of women over 40 are affected); it can be detected through amniocentesis. Care of a Down syndrome child involves both the prevention of physical problems (for example, respiratory infections, to which these children are especially prone) and long-range programs to promote mental and motor skills.

Durable power of attorney　A legal document that allows a competent patient to designate a surrogate, typically a relative or close friend, to make medical decisions if the patient loses his/her decision-making capacity. The surrogate should base decisions on the patient's previously expressed preferences, if known, or what is considered to be in the patient's best interest, if his/her wishes are not known.

Dysentery　Intestinal inflammation caused by bacteria, protozoa, parasites, or chemical irritants and marked by abdominal pain; frequent, bloody stools; and rectal spasms. Treatment includes replacement of lost fluids and sometimes antibiotics.

Dyslexia　An impairment of the ability to read in which letters and words are reversed. Dyslexia, which affects more boys than girls, is usually linked to a central nervous system disorder, although some experts believe that it represents a complex of problems, possibly including visual defects, impaired hearing, stress, and inadequate instruction.

Dyspepsia　Stomach upset; a disorder of the digestive function, marked by vague discomfort, heartburn, or nausea.

Dysplasia　A general term for any abnormal change or development, as in the shape or size of cells.

E**CG**　Abbreviation for electrocardiogram.

Ectopic pregnancy　An abnormal pregnancy, occurring in about 2% of all pregnancies, in which the fertilized egg (embryo) implants outside of the uterus, most often (90%) in the Fallopian tube (tubal pregnancy) but occasionally in the ovary (ovarian pregnancy) or abdominal cavity (abdominal pregnancy). As the embryo develops the tube ruptures or other complications arise, usually causing hemorrhage and requiring immediate surgery. Also called extrauterine pregnancy.

Eczema　An inflammation of the skin that usually produces itching and the development of small blisterlike formations that release fluid and then form a crust. It may be caused by contact with a specific irritant or occur without apparent cause.

Edema　The abnormal collection of fluid in spaces between cells, especially just under the skin or in a given cavity (for example, peritoneal cavity) or organ

(for example, the lungs [pulmonary edema]). Causes include injury, heart disease, kidney failure, cirrhosis, and allergy. Treatment depends on the cause.

EEG　Abbreviation for electroencephalogram.

Ego　Term used by Freud and now generally accepted to mean the self, especially the conscious self. *Compare* **Id**; **Superego**.

Ejaculate　The sperm-containing fluid (semen) emitted during ejaculation.

Ejaculation　The sudden discharge of semen during coitus, masturbation, or nocturnal emission. The fluid volume of each ejaculation is between 2 and 5 milliliters, and it contains between 50,000,000 to 150,000,000 spermatozoa. The sensation of ejaculation is called orgasm.

EKG　Abbreviation for electrocardiogram (the preferred abbreviation is ECG).

Electrocardiogram　A graphic recording, produced by an electrocardiograph, of the electrical activity of the heart. Commonly referred to as an ECG (or EKG), it allows the detection of abnormalities in the transmission of the cardiac impulse through the heart muscle and serves as an important aid in the diagnosis of heart ailments.

ELECTROCARDIOGRAM (ECG)

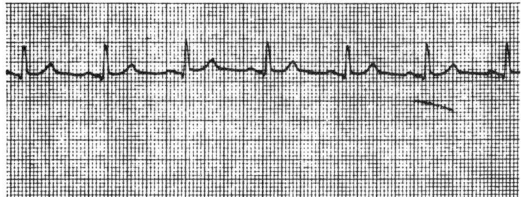

Electroencephalogram (EEG)　A graphic recording, produced by an electroencephalograph, of the electrical activity of the brain. Electroencephalograms are helpful in detecting and locating brain tumors and in diagnosing epilepsy.

Electrolysis　(1) An electrical action that causes a chemical (for example, a salt) to break down into simpler forms; (2) the passing of an electric current into a hair root to remove superfluous or unwanted hair.

Electrolyte　A chemical (element or compound) in the body that when dissolved produces ions, conducts an electric current, and is itself changed in the process. The proper amount and equilibrium of certain electrolytes (for example, calcium, sodium, potassium) in the body is essential for normal health and functioning.

Electrolyte balance　Equilibrium between electrolytes in the body that is essential for normal functioning, with a deficiency or excess of a particular electrolyte usually producing characteristic symptoms. The normal electrolyte balance may be disturbed by many abnormal conditions, including prolonged diarrhea or vomiting, kidney malfunction, malnutrition, or disturbed activity of the adrenal cortex, pancreas, pituitary, or other gland.

Embolism　Blockage of a blood vessel, especially an artery, by an embolus. Treatment depends on the nature of the embolus, the degree of obstruction and the blood vessel affected.

Emphysema Abnormal condition of the lungs in which there is overinflation of the air sacs (alveoli) of the lungs leading to a breakdown of their walls, a decrease in respiratory function, and in severe cases, increasing breathlessness. Emphysema appears to be associated with chronic bronchitis, cigarette smoking, and advancing age; one form that occurs early in life is related to a hereditary lack of an enzyme. Early symptoms of emphysema include dyspnea, cough, rapid heart rate; advanced cases are marked by signs of oxygen lack (restlessness, weakness, confusion) and frequently by complications of pulmonary edema and congestive heart failure. Breathing exercises, drugs such as bronchodilators and the prevention of respiratory infections may be helpful; severe cases may require oxygen.

Endocarditis Inflammation of the membrane (endocardium) lining the inside of the heart and the heart valves, caused by bacterial infection or occurring as a complication of another disease (for example, rheumatic fever). Symptoms include fever, and changes in heart rhythms; damage to heart valves may occur. Treatment consists of bedrest, antibiotics, and surgery, if necessary, to treat damaged valves.

Endometriosis A condition marked by the presence, growth, and function of endometrial tissue outside of its normal location, the lining of the uterus, in such sites as the uterine walls, the Fallopian tubes, the ovaries, and other sites within the pelvis or, rarely, outside it. Endometriosis is fairly common (estimated 15% of women), especially in childless women and women who have children late in life. Symptoms depend on the size and location of the displaced tissue but commonly include painful menstruation, painful coitus, and sometimes painful urination and defecation and premenstrual staining. Endometriosis is a common cause of infertility. Treatment includes analgesics to relieve pain, hormones to decrease the size and number of lesions, and, in severe cases, surgery.

Endometrium The mucous membrane lining of the uterus, which, under hormonal control, changes in thickness and complexity during the menstrual cycle and if pregnancy does not occur is mostly shed during menstruation.

Endorphin Any of several naturally occurring chemicals (proteins) in the brain believed to be involved in reducing or eliminating pain and in enhancing pleasure. Studies show that acupuncture may induce activation of endorphins. *Compare* **Enkephalin.**

Endoscopy Viewing the inside of a body cavity by means of a special instrument (endoscope), inserted usually through a natural body opening (for example, the mouth, vagina, urethra) but sometimes through an incision.

Enkephalin Any of a group of brain chemicals (proteins) that influence mental activity and behavior (sometimes grouped with the endorphins as "natural opiates"). Evidence shows that these chemicals influence the body's immune system and help fight disease. *Compare* **Endorphin.**

Epicardium The innermost of the two layers of the pericardium, the membranous covering of the heart.

Epidermis The superficial, outer layers of the skin that contain numerous nerve endings but no blood vessels. Made up of squamous epithelium tissue, the epidermis is divided into an outer stratum corneum containing dead cells that are sloughed off as new cells from the inner stratum germinativum push upward; other layers are also sometimes found, especially in thick skin (for example, the palms and soles).

Epilepsy A neurological disorder characterized by recurrent episodes (ranging from several times a day to once in several years) of convulsive seizures, impaired consciousness, abnormal behavior, and other disturbances produced by uncontrolled electrical discharges from nerve cells in the brain. Trauma to the head, brain tumor, chemical imbalances, and other factors may be associated with epilepsy, but in most cases the cause is unknown. Treatment depends on the severity and frequency of episodes. Common types of epilepsy are grand mal epilepsy and petit mal epilepsy.

Epinephrine (1) A hormone of the adrenal medulla that acts as a powerful stimulant in times of fear or arousal and has many physiological effects, including increasing breathing, heart, and metabolic rates to provide quick energy, constricting blood vessels, and strengthening muscle contraction; (2) a synthetic drug used in the treatment of bronchial asthma to reduce bronchial spasm and dilate air passageways and during surgery to reduce blood loss by constricting blood vessels. Also called adrenaline.

Episiotomy An incision made to enlarge the opening of the vagina during a difficult birth. The purpose is to make the delivery easier or to hasten it, and to avoid stretching and tearing adjacent muscle and tissue.

Epstein-Barr virus The virus that causes infectious mononucleosis; in parts of Africa it is associated also with a type of lymphoma.

Erection A state of rigidity, especially of the penis, which becomes enlarged and elevated when its tissues fill with blood, usually as a result of sexual arousal but also occurring normally during sleep and as a result of physical stimulation. Erection of the penis enables the organ to enter the vagina during coitus.

Erythrocyte A mature red blood cell, which contains the pigment hemoglobin, the main function of which is to transport oxygen to the tissues of the body. A red blood cell is a biconcave disc with no nucleus. It is the main cellular element in the blood; in one cubic milliliter of blood there are usually 4,500,000–5,000,000 erythrocytes in males, 4,000,000–4,500,000 in females.

Estrogen A general term for the female hormones (including estradiol, estrone, estriol) produced in the ovaries (and in small amounts in the testes and adrenals). In women estrogen functions in the menstrual cycle and in the development of secondary sex characteristics (for example, breast development in adolescence). As a synthetic preparation, sold under many trade names, estrogen drugs are used to treat menstrual irregularities, to relieve symptoms of menopause, to treat cancer of the prostate, and in oral contraceptives. Long-term use of estrogen has been associated with some blood-clotting disorders and some forms of cancer and is controversial.

Eustachian tube The mucous membrane-lined tube that connects the nasopharynx and the middle ear, it allows pressure in the inner ear to be equalized with that of the atmosphere. Increased pressure in the tube, occurring, for example, in a plane that is ascending, can usually be relieved by swallowing. Also called auditory tube.

Euthanasia Deliberately causing the death of a person who is suffering from an incurable disease, either actively by the use of artificial means (for example, drugs) or passively by withholding treatment necessary for the prolongation of life.

F **Fallopian tube** Either of two tubes or ducts, each of which extends from the uterus to the region of an ovary. The tube serves as passage for the movement of an ovum from the ovary (after ovulation) to the uterus and for the movement of sperm from the uterus upward toward the ovary. Fertilization normally occurs in the Fallopian tube. Also called oviduct.

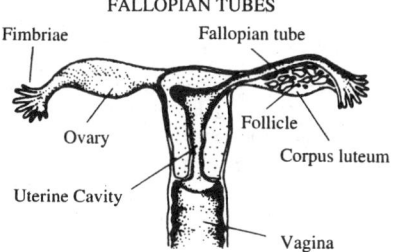

FALLOPIAN TUBES

Fimbriae
Fallopian tube
Ovary
Follicle
Corpus luteum
Uterine Cavity
Vagina

Feces The material discharged from the bowel in defecation. Formed in the colon, feces consist of water, undigested food residue, bacteria, and mucus. Also called stool.

Fetus The live offspring while it is inside the mother (in utero), in humans, from the beginning of the third month of pregnancy until birth.

Fever A rise in the temperature of the body. Normal body temperature is 98.6° Fahrenheit (37.0° Celsius) taken orally, somewhat higher rectally. A rise in temperature can sometimes be caused by severe stress, strenuous exercise, or dehydration, but fever is most often a sign of infection (bacterial, viral, or other) or other disease. Fever is often accompanied by headache, chills, and feeling of malaise; high fevers can cause delirium and convulsions (especially in young children). The onset, course, and duration of a fever vary with the cause; certain diseases are associated with characteristic rising and falling curves that may aid in diagnosis. *Compare* **Temperature**.

Fever blister A cold sore caused by a herpes virus. *See* **Herpes simplex**.

Fiber (1) A long, threadlike structure (for example, a nerve fiber); (2) food content (cellulose) that adds roughage to the diet.

Fiberoptics The technique in which thin, flexible, glass or plastic fibers in special instruments called fiberscopes are used to view inner parts of the body; the fibers transmit light and relay a magnified image of the body part.

Fiberscope A flexible instrument containing light-carrying glass or plastic fibers used to view internal body structures. Fiberscopes are especially designed for examination of particular body parts. For example, the bronchoscope is designed for viewing the tracheal and bronchial region; the gastroscope is designed for viewing the interior of the stomach; the duodenoscope is designed for viewing the duodenum.

Fibrocystic disease of the breast A common condition among women, characterized by the presence of one or more cysts in the breast. The cysts are benign but should be watched carefully for any changes in size or consistency; women with fibrocystic breast disease have a higher-than-average likelihood of developing breast cancer later in life. In many cases no treatment is necessary; in other cases aspiration of the cyst, with or without biopsy, is performed. Some investigators believe that consumption of caffeine (for example, in coffee, soft drinks) in large amounts is associated with fibrocystic breast disease.

Fibroid tumor A benign tumor (fibroma) containing fibrous tissue, especially that of the uterus. Fibroid tumors of the uterus are common and in many cases do not require treatment; if, however, they cause discomfort or hemorrhage, surgical removal is necessary.

Fibroma A nonmalignant tumor of connective tissue.

Flatulence An abnormal amount of abdominal gas, causing distension of the stomach or intestine and sometimes discomfort.

Fluoroscopy A technique in which a special device (fluoroscope) allows the immediate projection of X-ray images of the body onto a special fluorescent screen. It eliminates the need for taking and developing X-ray photographs.

Food allergy A hypersensitivity reaction to a substance—an antigen, most often a protein—ingested in food. Symptoms may include rhinitis, diarrhea, nausea, vomiting, itchy skin eruptions, bronchial asthma, colitis, and other signs. Foods commonly associated with allergic reactions in sensitized people include eggs, wheat, milk, fish and other seafoods, citrus fruits and tomatoes, and chocolate.

Food poisoning Acute illness caused by eating food containing toxic substances (for example, insecticide) or organisms (bacteria and fungi, especially certain mushrooms) and the toxins produced by them. The bacteria most commonly responsible for food poisoning are *Clostridium botulinum*, *Salmonella*, and *Staphylococcus*; the mushrooms are *Amanita* species. Symptoms vary with the type of poison and may range from mild abdominal discomfort, nausea, and diarrhea to severe symptoms including paralysis, coma, and death. *See also* **Botulism**; **Gastroenteritis**.

Frostbite Tissue change, especially of the fingers, toes, ears, or nose, caused by freezing, generally because of prolonged exposure to very cold weather. The affected parts turn white and become numb. Gentle warming in tepid water, without rubbing, is the appropriate first aid measure. Severe freezing results in the death of the tissues, necessitating amputation of the affected part.

G **Gallbladder** A pear-shaped organ, about 8 centimeters (3 inches) long and located on the lower surface of the liver, that is a reservoir for bile. Bile produced in the liver passes (through the hepatic duct) to the gallbladder, where it is stored; the presence of food, especially fats, in the duodenum and hormonal influences cause the gallbladder to contract, releasing the bile to the common bile duct for transport to the duodenum. The gallbladder is a common site of stone formation (cholelithiasis) and inflammation (cholecystitis).

Gallstone   A stonelike mass (calculus) in the gallbladder or in its duct.

Gamma globulin   *See* **Immune gamma globulin.**

Gangrene   Tissue death resulting from lack of nutrition when the blood supply to the affected part is decreased or lost because of disease (for example, diabetes), injury, blood clot, tourniquet, frostbite, severe burn, or bacterial infection. The arms and legs are most commonly affected.

Gastritis   Inflammation of the lining of the stomach characterized by loss of appetite, nausea, vomiting, and discomfort after eating. Acute gastritis is caused by the ingestion of an irritating substance (for example, aspirin, too much alcohol) or by bacterial or viral infection; chronic gastritis is often a symptom of gastric (peptic) ulcer, stomach cancer, pernicious (chronic) anemia, or other disorder.

Gastroenteritis   Inflammation of the stomach and intestines. Symptoms include abdominal discomfort, loss of appetite, nausea, vomiting, and sometimes diarrhea. Causes include bacterial or viral infection, the ingestion of toxic or irritating substances, allergic reactions to specific foods (for example, milk intolerance), and other disorders.

Gastroscopy   Visual examination of the stomach (especially the upper part of the stomach) by means of a flexible, fiberoptic instrument (gastroscope) inserted through the esophagus; photographs may be taken and specimens removed for analysis.

General anesthesia   An agent, usually given by inhalation or intravenous injection, that produces unconsciousness and complete loss of sensation throughout the body; it is used for major surgery (for example, removal of a lung or of the stomach). *Compare* **Local anesthesia.**

Genetic counseling   The process of determining the risk of a particular genetic disorder occurring within a family and providing information and advice based on that determination; used to help couples in family planning and in the care of children affected or thought to be affected with a particular genetic disorder. An accurate diagnosis is essential and may require special biochemical and cell studies; a careful and complete family medical history is also needed. The subjects of prenatal diagnosis (*see* **Amniocentesis**), artificial insemination, sterilization, and termination of a pregnancy may be included in the counseling, depending on the particular disease and circumstances involved.

Genetic engineering   The process of altering and controlling the genetic makeup of an organism through manipulation and recombination of the genetic material, DNA.

Genetic screening   The process of analyzing a specific group of people to detect the presence of or susceptibility to a particular disease or diseases. Examples include the screening of all infants for phenylketonuria and the screening of certain racial or ethnic groups who have a high incidence of a particular disease, such as sickle-cell anemia among blacks and Tay-Sachs disease among Ashkenazic and Sephardic Jews. *See also* **Genetic counseling**.

Genital herpes   *See* **Herpes genitalis**.

Genitalia   The male or female reproductive organs, especially the external ones. Also called genitals.

Gentian violet   An agent with antibacterial, antifungal, and anthelmintic properties used to treat pinworms and infections of the skin and vagina.

Geriatrics   A medical specialty that deals with the problems of aging and the diagnosis and treatment of diseases affecting the aged.

Germ   (1) A microorganism, especially one that causes disease; (2) a unit from which a structure or part originates (for example, germ layer, the layer from which new tissue develops).

German measles   *See* **Rubella**.

Gestation   The period of time in humans and other viviparous animals from fertilization of the ovum to birth; the length of pregnancy. In humans, gestation averages 266 days, or about 280 days from the first day of the last menstrual period. *See also* **Pregnancy**.

Gingivitis   Condition in which the gums are red, swollen, and bleeding. It most commonly results from poor oral hygiene and the development of bacterial plaque on the teeth, but it is also common in pregnancy and may be a sign of another disorder (for example, diabetes mellitus, vitamin deficiency).

Gland   Any of numerous organs in the body (for example, thyroid gland), each of which is made up of specialized cells that secrete or excrete materials unrelated to their own metabolism but needed by the body. There are two main types of glands: endocrine, or ductless, glands, which secrete hormones directly into the bloodstream; and exocrine, or duct, glands, which release materials into ducts or onto adjacent epithelial surfaces. Included among the exocrine glands are sweat glands, sebaceous glands, and tear glands.

Glaucoma   A disease in which elevated pressure in the eye, due to obstruction of the outflow of aqueous humor, damages the optic nerve and causes visual defects. Acute (angle-closure) glaucoma is an hereditary disorder with the iris blocking the flow of aqueous humor; symptoms, which may occur suddenly, include dilated pupil, red eye, blurred vision, and severe eye pain, sometimes accompanied by nausea and vomiting; if untreated—by special eye drops or surgery—angle-closure glaucoma may result in permanent blindness within a few days. The much more common open-angle, or chronic, glaucoma, also hereditary, is one of the leading causes of blindness in the United States. Caused by blockage of the canal of Schlemm, it produces symptoms very slowly with gradual loss of peripheral vision over a period of years, sometimes with headache, dull pain, and blurred vision. Treatment involves the use of special eye drops. Glaucoma can also occur as a congenital defect or as a result of another eye disorder.

Glucose   Simple sugar, which is the major energy source in the body. Ingested in certain foods, especially fruits, and produced by the breakdown of other carbohydrates, glucose is absorbed into the blood from the intestines; excess amounts are stored in the form of glycogen, chiefly in the liver. Determination of glucose levels in the blood is important in the diagnosis of many disorders, including diabetes mellitus. Pharmaceutical preparations of glucose (for example, dextrose) are widely used in medicine.

Goiter   An enlargement of the thyroid gland at the front of the neck; it may be caused by deficiency of iodine in the diet, by tumor, or by overactivity (Graves' disease) or underactivity of the thyroid gland. Treatment depends on the cause; it often involves surgical removal of all or part of the thyroid gland.

Gonad   A gland that produces sex cells (gametes); in males the gonads are the testes; in females, the ovaries.

Gonadotropins   Hormones that stimulate the function of the gonads.

Gonorrhea   A common sexually transmitted disease caused by the bacteria *Neisseria gonorrhoeae* and transmitted through contact with an infected person or with secretions containing the bacteria. Symptoms include painful urination and burning, itching, and pain around the urethra and in women the vagina, accompanied by a greenish yellow, pus-containing discharge. If untreated, the infection spreads, especially in women, infecting the reproductive organs, causing inflammation of the liver, and, if widespread, leading to septicemia and polyarthritis, with painful lesions in joints and tendons and infection of the conjunctiva of the eye that can lead to blindness. Treatment is by antibiotics.

Gout   A disease in which a defect in uric acid metabolism causes the acid and its salts to accumulate in the blood and joints, causing pain and swelling of the joints (especially the big toe area), accompanied by fever and chills. The disease is more common among men than women and usually has a genetic basis. If untreated, the disease causes destructive tissue changes in the joints and kidneys. Treatment includes a purine-free diet and use of drugs to reduce inflammation and to increase the excretion of uric acid salts or decrease their formation. Also called gouty arthritis.

Graft   A tissue or organ that is taken from one site and transplanted to another site on the same person (autograft), as in transplanting thigh skin to the arm to replace badly burned skin, or that is taken from one person and inserted in another, as in a kidney transplant. *See also* **Transplant**.

Grand mal   (1) An attack, suffered in epilepsy, during which the patient becomes unconscious, develops bluish discoloration (cyanosis) of the skin and lips due to oxygen lack, and experiences convulsions; (2) a type of epilepsy characterized by recurrent grand mal attacks. *Compare* **Petit mal**.

Graves' disease   Protrusion of the eyeballs (exophthalmos) combined with enlargement of the thyroid gland (goiter). Symptoms may include nervousness and weight loss, rapid pulse rate (tachycardia), increased rate of metabolism, and anemia. *See* **Goiter**; **Hyperthyroidism**.

Gynecology   The medical specialty concerned with the health care of women, including function and diseases of the reproductive organs. It combines both medical and surgical concerns and is usually practiced in combination with obstetrics.

 **Hallucination**   The perception of something that is not actually present; it may be visual (seeing objects that are not present), auditory (hearing noises that are not present), olfactory (smelling things that are not present), gustatory (tasting things that are not present), or tactile (feeling touch sensations that are not present). Hallucinations are a common symptom of severe mental illness (for example, schizophrenia); they also occur after injury to the head, in delirium accompanying severe illness, in delirium tremens, and from the use of hallucinogens.

Hallucinogen   A substance—for example, LSD (lysergic acid diethylamide), mescaline, phencyclidine, angel dust—that excites the central nervous system, producing hallucinations (false perceptions); mood changes; increases in pulse, blood pressure, and body temperature; dilation of the pupils of the eyes; and other physiological and psychological changes.

Hamstring muscle   Any of three powerful muscles at the back of the thigh.

Hardening of the arteries   *See* **Arteriosclerosis**.

Hashish   A drug prepared from the Indian hemp plant, *Cannabis sativa*, that produces euphoria, distorted perceptions, and sometimes hallucinations.

Hay fever   A type of allergy, with symptoms of sneezing, runny nose, and watery eyes, that occurs seasonally on exposure to pollen. Antihistamines are frequently used to alleviate the symptoms; if the specific allergen can be identified, desensitization may be possible.

Health Maintenance Organization (HMO)   A system of health care whereby members pay a specified fee entitling them to comprehensive care, often including both in-hospital and out-patient services. Most HMOs limit the choice of physicians and hospitals to either their own institutions and employees or those that have specifically contracted to provide care to member patients.

Hearing   The sense of receiving and interpreting sounds. Sound waves enter the outer ear, cause vibrations of the eardrum and bones of the middle ear, and are transmitted to the inner ear from which they are transmitted along the auditory nerve to the brain for interpretation.

Hearing impairment   A decrease or limitation in sensitivity to sound.

Heart   The muscular, roughly cone-shaped organ that pumps blood throughout the body. Lying behind the sternum between the lungs, it is about the size of a closed fist, about 12 centimeters (5 inches) long, 8 centimeters (3 inches) wide at its broadest upper part, and about 6 centimeters (2¼ inches) thick and weighs about 275 to 345 grams (10–12 ounces) in males, 225 to 275 grams (8–10 ounces) in females. Under outer epicardium membranes, the heart wall—myocardium—consists of cardiac muscle; the innermost layer—the endocardium—is continuous with lining of the blood vessels. The heart is divided into left and right sides by a septum; each side has an upper atrium (auricle) and lower ventricle. Through coordinated nerve impulses and muscular contractions, initiated in the sinoatrial node of the right atrium, the heart pumps blood throughout the body. Deoxygenated blood, carried to the heart by the vena cava, flows into the right atrium and passes into the right ventricle, from which it flows through pulmonary arteries to the lungs, where it gives up its wastes and becomes freshly oxygenated. The oxygenated blood then passes through the pulmonary veins into the left atrium and from there into the left ventricle. From the left ventricle it is pumped throughout the body. The heart normally beats about 70 times per minute. It is nourished by coronary blood vessels.

Heart attack   Popular term for a disruption of the normal function of the heart. *See* **Myocardial infarction**.

Heartburn   A painful, burning sensation in the chest, below the sternum, resulting from irritation in the esophagus most often due to backflow of acidic stomach contents into the esophagus. It is often a symptom of hiatal hernia, peptic ulcer, or other disorder. Also called pyrosis.

Heart failure   Inability of the heart to pump enough blood to maintain normal body requirements. It may be caused by congenital defects or by any condition (for example, atherosclerosis of coronary arteries, aortic stenosis, myocardial infarction) that damages or overloads the heart muscle. Symptoms include edema, shortness of breath, and feelings of faintness. Treatment depends on the specific cause of the heart malfunction and on the age and general condition of the patient.

Heart murmur   An abnormal heart sound. Some heart murmurs are benign and of no significance; others are signs of abnormal heart function.

Heart rate   The number of heart contractions (beats) per minute. Normal adult heart rate is about 70–72 beats per minute; an abnormally rapid heart rate (over 100 beats per minute in an adult) is tachycardia; an abnormally slow rate (below 60 beats per minute in an adult) is bradycardia. Children normally have a heart rate faster than an adult. *See also* **Pulse**.

Heart valve   Any of four structures (two semilunar valves, the mitral valve, and the tricuspid valve) within the heart that by closing and opening control blood flow in the heart and permit flow in only one direction.

Heat exhaustion   Condition characterized by dizziness, nausea, weakness, muscle cramps, and pale, cool skin caused by overexposure to intense heat and depletion of body fluids and electrolytes. It is most common in infants and the elderly. Recovery usually occurs with rest, replacement of water and electrolytes, and removal from the intense heat. Also called heat prostration. *Compare* **Heatstroke**.

Heatstroke   A severe, sometimes fatal, condition caused by prolonged exposure to intense heat and failure of the body's temperature-regulating capacity. Symptoms include high body temperature; rapid heartbeat; red, hot, dry skin; confusion; and possibly convulsions and loss of consciousness. Treatment includes cooling of the body, fluid and electrolyte replacement, and sedation. Also called sunstroke. *Compare* **Heat exhaustion**.

Heimlich maneuver   An emergency procedure to help a person who is choking because food or other material is lodged in the trachea. The rescuer should hold the choking person from behind and place one fist, thumb side in, against the victim's abdomen, in the midline immediately above the navel. The other hand should be placed over the fist. Quick upward thrusts are then administered to force the obstruction out of the trachea. A maximum of five thrusts should be tried, but each individual thrust should be delivered with sufficient force as to attempt to clear the airway by itself. Vomiting or internal organ damage can result from this maneuver, though the risks are lessened if the rescuer has been properly trained by the American Red Cross or by the American Heart Association in cardiopulmonary resuscitation.

HEIMLICH MANEUVER

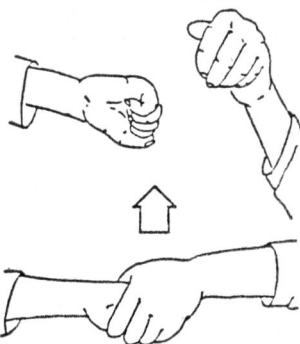

Note: This diagram is not intended for instructional purpose.

Hematoma   A localized collection of blood, usually clotted, in an organ, space, or tissue due to escape of blood from a blood vessel, often the result of trauma; when the hematoma occurs near the skin surface, it causes discoloration (for example, a black eye).

Hemoglobin   The complex compound, containing the non-protein, iron-containing pigment heme and the protein globin, found in red blood cells (erythrocytes) that transports oxygen to cells throughout the body and carries carbon dioxide away from body cells. In the high oxygen concentration of the lungs, hemoglobin binds with oxygen to form oxyhemoglobin. In the tissues of the body, the oxygen is given off and the hemoglobin combines with carbon dioxide to form carboxyhemoglobin, which is carried back to the lungs. There the carbon dioxide is given off and more oxygen picked up for transport to the body cells. Normal hemoglobin concentration in blood is 13.5 to 18 grams per deciliter for males, 12 to 16 for females.

Hemolysis   Breakdown of red blood cells and the release of hemoglobin. It occurs normally at the end of the life span of a red blood cell; abnormally in certain allergic reactions, on exposure to certain bacteria and venoms, in hemodialysis, and in certain other conditions.

Hemophilia   An inherited disorder characterized by excessive bleeding and occurring only in males. Several forms of the disease—including hemophilia A and hemophilia B (also called Christmas disease)—occur; in all forms one of the factors necessary for normal blood coagulation is missing or present in abnormally low amounts. Greater than usual blood loss in dental extractions and simple injuries and bleeding into joint areas commonly occur; severe internal hemorrhage is less common.

Treatment involves administration of missing blood coagulation factors in some cases and transfusions to replace lost blood.

Hemorrhage The loss of a large amount of blood during a short time, either externally or internally. The bleeding may be from an artery (the blood flows in spurts and is bright red), from a vein (the blood flows slowly and is dark), or from a tiny vessel or capillary (the blood oozes). External bleeding may be controlled by pressure, elevation, and ice on the wound; a tourniquet is a last resort. Internal bleeding requires prompt medical attention. Loss of large amounts of blood can lead to shock and death.

Hemorrhoid Swelling of a vein or veins (varicosity) in the lower rectum or anus, either internal, above the anal sphincter, or external, outside the anal sphincter. Often associated with constipation, straining to defecate, pregnancy, or prolonged sitting, hemorrhoids are often painful and sometimes bleed with defecation. Treatment includes topical agents to shrink and anesthetize the hemorrhoids, compresses, and, if severe, ligation or surgical excision.

Hepatitis An inflammation of the liver, characterized by jaundice, loss of appetite, abdominal discomfort, an enlarged and abnormally functioning liver, and dark urine. It may be caused by bacterial or viral infection, infestation with parasites, alcohol, drugs, toxins, transfusions of incompatible blood, or as a complication of another disease (for example, infectious mononucleosis) and may be mild and brief or prolonged and severe, even life-threatening.

Hereditary Pertaining to transmission from parents to offspring; inherited (for example, an hereditary disorder, a disorder that is passed from parents to offspring).

Hernia Protrusion of an organ through an abnormal opening in the muscular wall surrounding the organ area. It may be congenital or acquired as a result of injury, muscular weakness, or disease. Common types of hernia include hiatal hernia, inguinal hernia, and umbilical hernia.

Herniated disc Rupture of the fibrocartilage of the disc between vertebrae of the spinal column, occurring most often in the lumbar region. With the ruptured disc there is a lack of cushioning between the vertebrae above and below and resultant pressure on spinal nerves, causing pain. Also called slipped disc; ruptured intervertebral disc.

Heroin A strongly addictive drug made from morphine; it has no medical uses in the United States but is widely abused.

Herpes Any of a group of viruses that cause painful blister-like eruptions on the skin. *See* **Herpes genitalis**; **Herpes simplex**; **Herpes zoster**.

Herpes genitalis An infection, caused by type 2 herpes simplex virus, usually transmitted by sexual contact, characterized by recurrent attacks of painful eruptions on the skin and mucous membranes of the genital area. Symptoms include fever, malaise, urinary problems, painful coitus, swelling of lymph glands in the inguinal area, and lesions on the glans or foreskin of the penis in males and lesions on the vagina and cervix, sometimes with a discharge from the cervix, in females. Treatment is aimed at relieving symptoms; there is no cure. Also called genital herpes.

Herpes simplex An infection, caused by herpes simplex virus, that usually affects the skin and nervous system, producing small, transient, sometimes painful blisters on the skin and mucous membranes. Herpes simplex 1 (HS1) most commonly affects the facial region, especially the area near the mouth and nose. Symptoms include tingling and burning, followed by blisterlike eruptions that dry and crust before healing. Treatment involves keeping the area clean to prevent secondary infection and topical use of drying medications. Also called cold sore. Herpes simplex 2 (HS2) commonly affects the genital region. *See also* **Herpes genitalis**.

Herpes zoster An infection with herpes zoster virus, usually occurring in adults, and characterized by blisterlike eruptions along the course of an inflamed nerve. Symptoms include pain—chronic or intermittent, mild or severe—along the course of the lesions, sometimes with fever, malaise, and headache. Treatment is symptomatic and includes cold compresses and calamine applications on the lesions. Complications, occurring most often in the elderly, include postherpetic neuralgia, which may last for months. Also called shingles.

Hiatus hernia Protrusion of part of the stomach through the diaphragm. It is a common disorder and in many cases produces no symptoms. Symptoms, when present include gastroesophageal reflux (heartburn), the flow of acid stomach contents into the esophagus. Also called hiatal hernia.

High blood pressure *See* **Hypertension**.

Holistic medicine A system of medical care based on the concept that a person is an integrated entity, more than the sum of his/her physiological, mental, psychological, and social parts.

Hormone A complex chemical produced and secreted by endocrine (ductless) glands that travels through the bloodstream and controls or regulates the activity of another organ or group of cells—its target organ. (For example, growth hormone released by the pituitary gland controls the growth of long bones of the body.) Secretion of hormones is regulated by feedback mechanisms and neurotransmitters.

Host (1) An organism in which another, usually parasitic, organism lives; (2) the recipient of a transplanted organ or tissue.

Hotflash A transient feeling of warmth experienced by some women during menopause; the frequency and severity of the flashes vary widely.

Hydrogen peroxide A clear liquid compound (H_2O_2) applied in water solution to cleanse wounds and as a mouthwash.

Hydrophobia (1) Rabies; (2) an irrational fear of water. *See* **Rabies**.

Hyperglycemia Higher-than-normal amount of glucose in the blood, most often associated with diabetes mellitus but sometimes occurring in other conditions. *Compare* **Hypoglycemia**.

Hypertension A common disorder, often with no symptoms, in which the blood pressure is persistently above 140/90 mg Hg. Causes of hypertension include adrenal and kidney disorder, toxemia of pregnancy, and thyroid disorders, but in most cases—essential hypertension—the cause is unknown, though obesity, hypercholesterolemia, and high sodium levels are predisposing factors. Symptoms, when present, include headache, palpitations, and easy fatiguability. Severe hypertension damages the cardiovascular system and frequently results in heart disorders. Treatment is by diuretics, vasodilators, central nervous system depressants and inhibitors, and ganglionic blocking agents (beta blockers, for example, propranolol). Adequate rest and a low-sodium, low-fat diet are also usually advised. *Compare* **Hypotension**.

Hyperthyroidism Overactivity of the thyroid gland due to tumor, overgrowth of the gland, or Graves' disease.

Hyperventilation A ventilation rate in the lungs that is greater than demanded by body needs, the result of too frequent and/or too deep breathing; often associated with emphysema; asthma; hyperthyroidism; central nervous system disorders; increased metabolic needs from fever, infection, or exercise; or acute anxiety or pain. The carbon dioxide level in the blood decreases and the oxygen level increases. Symptoms include faintness, tingling of the fingers and toes, and, if continued, chest pain and respiratory alkalosis.

Hypnosis A passive, sleeplike state in which perception and memory are altered, and the person is more responsive to suggestion and has more recall than usual; used in psychotherapy and in medicine to induce relaxation and relieve pain. Susceptibility to hypnosis varies widely. *See* Psychology, 21-14.

Hypoglycemia A lower-than-normal level of glucose in the blood, usually resulting from administration of too much insulin (in diabetes mellitus), excessive insulin secretion from the pancreas, or poor diet. Symptoms include headache, weakness, anxiety, personality changes, and, if severe and untreated, coma and death. Treatment is by administration of glucose.

Hypotension Blood pressure that is abnormally low; it may result from hemorrhage, excessive fluid loss, heart malfunction, Addison's disease, or other disorder. In some people blood pressure drops when they rise from a horizontal position (orthostatic hypotension). Mild, transient hypotension may cause light-headedness and syncope. Severe hypotension leads to inadequate blood circulation and shock. *Compare* **Hypertension**.

Hypothermia (1) A condition in which the body temperature is below 35° Celsius (95° Fahrenheit), most often occurring in the elderly or very young who are exposed to excessive cold; symptoms include pallor, slow, shallow respiration, and slow, faint heartbeat; (2) deliberate reduction of body temperature to slow metabolic rate and lower oxygen demands for therapeutic reasons or certain surgical procedures.

Hypothyroidism Decreased activity of the thyroid gland.

Hysterectomy Surgical removal of the uterus, done to remove tumors or to treat hemorrhage, severe pelvic inflammatory disease, or a cancerous or precancerous condition. In a total hysterectomy, the uterus and cervix are removed; in a radical hysterectomy, the ovaries, oviducts, uterus, cervix, and associated lymph nodes are removed.

Ibuprofen A nonsteroid, anti-inflammatory drug used in the treatment of arthritis and available in nonprescription strength for relief of mild to moderate pain. Adverse effects include gastrointestinal disturbances and skin irritation.

ICU Abbreviation for intensive care unit.

Id In psychoanalysis, the unconscious; the unconscious part of one's psyche, the source of instincts and drives, based largely on the tendency to avoid pain and to pursue pleasure.

Immune gamma globulin Immunizing agent made from pooled human plasma, used for immunization against certain infectious diseases (for example, measles, poliomyelitis) and to treat immunodeficiencies (for example, hypogammaglobulinemia). Adverse reactions include pain and inflammation at the injection site. Also called immune globulin.

Immune system The complex interactions that protect the body from pathogenic organisms and other foreign invaders (for example, transplanted tissue), including the humoral response, chiefly involving B cells and the production of antibodies, and the cell-mediated response, chiefly involving T cells and the activation of specific leukocytes. The organs involved include the bone marrow, the thymus, and lymphoid tissue.

Immunization The process by which resistance to an infectious disease is induced or increased.

Immunodeficiency An abnormal condition in which some part of the body's immune system is inadequate, and consequently resistance to infectious disease is decreased. Immunodeficiency may be congenital or acquired. *See* **Acquired Immune Deficiency Syndrome (AIDS)**.

Immunoglobulin Any of five classes of structurally distinct antibodies, produced in lymph tissue in response to the invasion of a foreign substance. The five major kinds are immunoglobulin A, D, E, G, and M. Also called immune serum globulin. *See also* **Antibody**; **Antigen**.

Impetigo A bacterial (usually streptococcal and/or staphylococcal) infection of the skin, common in children and very contagious, in which localized skin redness develops into fluid-containing small blisters that gradually crust and erode. Treatment is by topical and sometimes oral antibiotics, careful washing, and steps to prevent the spread of the infection.

Implant To attach a part of tissue to a host (for example, to insert a tooth); the part of tissue inserted into a host for repair of a damaged part (for example, a blood vessel graft) or for therapeutic reasons (for example, pacemaker inserted in the chest).

Impotence (1) Weakness; (2) the inability of the male to achieve erection of the penis or, less commonly, to ejaculate. Impotence may be organic, due to disease (for example, diabetes mellitus) or ingestion of certain drugs; or psychogenic. *Compare* **Sterility**.

Incontinence The inability to control urination and/or defecation.

Incubation period The time between exposure to a disease-causing organism and the appearance of the symptoms of the disease (for example, the 2– to 3–week interval between exposure to the chickenpox organism and the appearance of symptoms).

Incubator (1) A special transparent device that provides a controlled environment (for example, a particular temperature) for a premature or low-birth-weight infant; (2) a laboratory device for the cultivation of eggs or microorganisms.

Indigestion *See* **Dyspepsia**.

Induction of labor In obstetrics, the artificial starting of the childbirth process by puncturing the amniotic sac surrounding the fetus or by administration of drugs (oxytocin) to stimulate contractions of the muscles of the uterus. Labor may be induced to speed childbirth in cases of maternal or fetal distress or electively (for example, to avert the possibility of a woman delivering outside of a hospital).

Infection (1) The invasion of disease-producing microorganisms into a body where they may multiply, causing a disease; (2) a disease caused by disease-producing microorganisms (for example, certain bacteria).

Infectious hepatitis *See* **Viral hepatitis**.

Infectious mononucleosis An acute infection, caused by the Epstein-Barr virus and most common among young people; it is not highly contagious. Symptoms include fever, swollen lymph glands, sore throat, enlarged spleen and liver, abnormal liver function, fatigue, and malaise. Treatment is symptomatic, including bed rest to prevent spleen rupture or other spleen or liver complications. One attack usually confers immunity. Also called glandular fever; kissing disease; mono.

Infertility The condition of being unable to bear young—in a woman, an inability to conceive; in a male, an inability to impregnate. Female infertility may be due to a defective ovum, an ovulation disorder, a blockage of the Fallopian tubes, a uterine disorder, or a hormonal imbalance; in a male, infertility may be due to a lower-than-normal number of sperm produced or to sperm with abnormal shape or motility. Many cases of infertility can be corrected through surgery, drugs, or other medical procedures.

Inflammation Response of the tissues of the body to irritation or injury, characterized by pain, swelling, redness, and heat. The severity, specific characteristics, and duration of the inflammation depends on the cause, the particular area of the body affected, and the health of the person.

Influenza An acute, contagious, virus-caused infection of the respiratory tract; symptoms usually begin suddenly and include fever, sore throat, cough, muscle aches, headache, fatigue, and malaise, and often signs of the common cold (watery eyes, runny nose). Treatment is symptomatic and includes rest, pain relievers and fever reducers, and increased fluid intake. The disease usually subsides within a week; complications (for example, bacterial pneumonia) usually affect only the very young, the old, or those weakened by another condition. Several strains of the virus have been identified and new strains emerge at intervals, often named for the geographic region in which they are first discovered (for example, Asian flu). Also called flu; grippe.

Informed consent Permission obtained from a patient (or in the case of a child or an adult incapable of making decisions, another authorized person) for the performance of a particular procedure or test, after being told (and understanding) fully the risks, options, and expected results. Informed consent, usually in a signed statement, is generally required before any invasive procedure (for example, surgery or diagnostic procedures in which instruments are inserted into the body), before admission to any experimental or research study, and in certain other situations.

Injection The act of inserting a liquid into the body forcefully by means of a syringe; the fluid may be injected into a vein (intravenous), muscle (intramuscular), under the skin (subcutaneous), or into the skin (intradermal).

Insemination The introduction of semen into the vagina either during coitus or through other techniques. *See* **Artificial insemination**.

Insomnia A condition characterized by difficulty falling asleep or staying asleep or by seriously disturbed sleep (for example, frequent short awakenings). It may result from a variety of psychological and physical causes; treatment depends on the cause and condition of the person.

Insulin (1) A hormone secreted by the beta cells of the islets of Langerhans of the pancreas; it regulates the metabolism of glucose and, secondarily, intermediary processes in the metabolism of carbohydrates and fats. Inadequate insulin levels lead to too-high glucose levels and other disturbances of metabolism, often associated with diabetes mellitus; (2) a drug made from the natural hormones used to treat diabetes mellitus.

Insulin shock An abnormal physiological state in which the blood glucose level is too low; it may be caused by an overdose of insulin, decreased food intake, or excess exercise. Symptoms include sweating, trembling, nervousness, irritability, and pallor; if not corrected, it can lead to convulsions and death. Treatment requires the administration of glucose. *See also* **Hypoglycemia**. *Compare* **Diabetic coma**.

Intensive Care Unit (ICU) A hospital unit in which patients with life-threatening conditions are provided with constant care and close monitoring, and often involving the use of sophisticated machines for caring for and maintaining the patient.

Intercourse *See* **Coitus**.

Internal medicine That branch of medicine concerned with the function of internal organs and the diagnosis and treatment of disorders affecting these organs.

Intestinal flu Inflammation of the stomach and intestine caused by a virus; symptoms include abdominal discomfort, nausea, vomiting, and diarrhea. *See also* **Gastroenteritis**.

Intestine That part of the alimentary canal extending from the pyloric opening of the stomach to the anus. It is divided into two major parts; the small intestine (made up of the duodenum, jejunum and ileum), where most digestion and absorption of food occurs; and the large intestine (consisting of the cecum; appendix; ascending, transverse, and descending colons; and the rectum), where water is absorbed from material passing from the small intestine. Waves of muscular contractions—peristalsis—propel material through the intestine.

Intrauterine device (IUD) A contraceptive device, made up of a bent plastic or metal (a coil, loop, or other shape) inserted through the vagina into the uterus where it functions to prevent pregnancy. Complications of IUD use include infection, undetected expulsion, perforation of the uterus, bleeding, and pain. *See also* **Contraception**.

Intravenous   Into or within a vein.

Intravenous feeding (IV)   The administration of nutrients through a vein.

In vitro   Pertaining to an artificial condition, as within a test tube or other laboratory apparatus.

Iodine   A nonmetallic element that is an essential nutrient (in small amounts) and is used in antiseptics, in radioisotope scanning procedures, and in certain treatments of thyroid cancer.

Ipecac   A drug used to induce vomiting in some types of poisoning and drug overdose. Adverse effects include gastrointestinal irritation, or, if vomiting does not occur and the ipecac is retained, cardiac abnormalities.

Iron   A metallic element essential for hemoglobin synthesis in the body and used in various drugs.

Iron-deficiency anemia   A type of anemia caused by lack of adequate iron to synthesize hemoglobin. Symptoms include fatigue and weakness.

Irrigation   Washing out of a body part by water or other fluid.

IUD   Abbreviation for intrauterine device.

IV   Abbreviation for intravenous, especially intravenous feeding.

J **Jaundice**   A yellowing of the skin and whites of the eyes caused by an accumulation of the bile pigment bilirubin in the blood. Jaundice is a symptom of many disorders, most commonly obstruction of the ducts (biliary tract) that carry bile to the intestine, as by a gallstone; disease of the liver, due to infection, alcoholism, poisons, or other factors; and anemia in which there is excessive destruction of red blood cells. Also called icterus.

Jet lag   Condition marked by fatigue, sleep disturbances, and sluggish body functions, caused by disruption of the body's normal circadian (daily) rhythm as a result of traveling through several time zones.

Joint   The point where two or more bones meet. A joint may be immovable (fibrous), as those of the skull; slightly movable (cartilaginous), as those connecting the vertebrae; or freely movable (synovial), as those of the elbow and knee. Also called articulation.

Jugular veins   Any of several veins in the neck that drain blood from the head and empty into larger veins leading to the heart.

K **Kaposi's sarcoma**   A malignant neoplasm that starts as soft purplish or brownish spots on the feet and then spreads from the skin to the lymph nodes and internal organs. Until the early 1980s it occurred almost exclusively among older Jewish, Italian, and black men, but after that time it increased in incidence and is now one of the common manifestations of acquired immune deficiency syndrome (AIDS).

Ketone   Any of a group of organic chemicals derived by oxidation of alcohol and containing a carbon-oxygen group. Among the ketones are acetone and acetoacetic acid.

Kidney   Either of two bean-shaped excretory organs that filter wastes (especially urea) from the blood and excrete them and water in urine and help to regulate the water, electrolyte, and pH balance of the body. The kidneys are located in the dorsal part of the abdominal cavity, one on each side of the vertebral column. Each kidney, about 11 centimeters (4.5 inches) long, 6 centimeters (2.5 inches) wide, and 2.5 centimeters (1 inch) thick consists of an outer cortex and inner medulla and contains one million or more filtering units, called nephrons. Blood passes through tufts of capillaries (glomeruli) in the nephrons, where it is filtered; the filtrate then passes through tubules, where some substances (for example, sugar, some salts) are selectively reabsorbed, into collecting ducts. The final product—known as urine—passes out of the kidney through tubes known as ureters and is carried to the bladder. The function of the kidney is controlled by hormones, especially the antidiuretic hormone (ADH) produced by the pituitary gland. The kidney is subject to inflammation, infection, the formation of stones (urinary calculi), and other disorders.

Kidney failure   *See* **Renal failure**.

Kidney stone   *See* **Urinary calculus**.

Kyphosis   An abnormality of the vertebral column in which there is increased convex curvature in the upper spine, giving a hunchback or humped back appearance. Mild cases are often self-limiting and asymptomatic; severe or progressive cases may cause back pain and are sometimes treated with special back braces. *Compare* **Lordosis**; **Scoliosis**.

L **Labor**   The process by which a baby is born and the placenta is expelled from the uterus. Labor has three stages; the first, or stage of dilation, characterized by contractions of the uterine wall and dilatation of the opening of the cervix; the second, or stage of expulsion, during which the baby is born; and the third, or afterbirth stage, in which the placenta is expelled. The average duration of labor is about 13 hours in first pregnancies (12 hours in first state, 1 hour in second, few minutes in third); about eight hours in subsequent pregnancies.

Laceration   A wound with a jagged edge, resulting from a tearing or scraping action.

Lactation   (1) The synthesis and secretion of milk by the mammary glands of the breast; (2) the time during which an infant or child is nourished with breast milk.

Lactic acid   (1) A chemical formed by the process of glycolysis; during strenuous exercise it may accumulate in muscle cells; (2) the acid formed by the action of certain bacteria on milk and milk products.

Lactose intolerance   A disorder, due to a defect or deficiency of the enzyme lactase, resulting in an inability to digest lactose and symptoms of bloating, flatulence, abdominal discomfort, nausea, and diarrhea on ingestion of milk and milk products.

Lamaze method of childbirth   A method of psychophysical preparation for childbirth, developed by the French obstetrician Fernand Lamaze in the 1950s, that is now the most widely used method of natural childbirth. In classes during pregnancy and in practice sessions at home, the pregnant woman, usually with the help of a coach (called a "monitrice"), learns the physiology of pregnancy and childbirth, techniques of relaxation, concentration, and breathing, and exercises certain muscles to promote control during labor and childbirth.

Large intestine   That portion of the digestive tract containing the cecum; appendix; ascending, transverse, and descending colons; and the rectum.

Laryngitis   Inflammation of the mucous membrane of the larynx and swelling of the vocal cords, characterized by loss or hoarseness of voice, cough, and sometimes difficult breathing. It may be acute, caused by bacterial or viral infection or irritation (for example, from irritating fumes); or chronic, from excessive use of the voice or excessive smoking or long-term exposure to irritants. Treatment depends on the cause, but usually includes rest of the voice, a moist atmosphere, and the avoidance of irritants. (In young children spasm of the larynx and difficulty in breathing may result.)

Larynx   The organ that contains the vocal cords and is responsible for sound production; it is part of the air passageway connecting the pharynx and the trachea, and it produces a bump—the Adam's apple—in front of the neck.

Laser   Acronym for Light Amplification by Stimulated Emission of Radiation; an instrument that produces a very thin beam of light—of one wavelength—with radiation intense enough to be used surgically to destroy tissue or to separate parts.

Laughing gas   See **Nitrous oxide**.

Laxative   An agent that promotes bowel evacuation by a mild action, by increasing the bulk of the stool or softening it, or by lubricating the intestinal tract. *Compare* **Cathartic**.

Lead poisoning   A toxic condition caused by inhaling or ingesting lead or lead compounds (for example, in some paints). Acute poisoning causes gastrointestinal disturbances, mental disturbances, and paralysis of the extremities, sometimes followed by convulsions and collapse. Chronic poisoning causes irritability, anorexia, and anemia, and often progresses to produce acute symptoms.

Learning disability   Any of several abnormal conditions of children or adults who, although having at least average intelligence, have difficulty in learning specific skills—for example, reading (dyslexia) or writing (dysgraphia)—or have other problems associated with normal learning procedures. It may result from psychological or organic causes or from slow development of motor skills, but in many cases the cause is unknown.

Legionnaire's disease   Acute pneumonia caused by the bacterium *Legionella pneumophilia*; symptoms include muscle pain, fever, cough, chills, and chest pain. Treatment is by the antibiotic erythromycin. *See also* Biology, page 2-32.

Lens implant   An artificial clear plastic lens implanted in the eye, usually when the natural lens has been removed because of a cataract but sometimes to treat other eye abnormalities.

Lesion   General term for any visible, local abnormality of tissue, such as an injury, wound, boil, sore, rash.

Leukemia   One of the major types of cancer; a malignant neoplasm of blood-forming tissues, characterized by abnormalities of the bone marrow, spleen, lymph nodes, and liver and by rapid and uncontrolled proliferation of abnormal numbers and forms of leukocytes (white blood cells). Leukemia may be acute, rapidly progressing from signs of fatigue and weight loss to extreme weakness, repeated infections, and fever; or it may be chronic, progressing slowly over a period of years. Leukemia is usually classified according to the type of white blood cell that is proliferating abnormally. Treatment involves chemotherapy, blood transfusions, antibiotics to control infections, and sometimes, bone marrow transplants. Also called cancer of the blood.

Leukocyte   A white blood cell. There are five types of leukocytes: three granulocytes with granules in the cytoplasm—neutrophils, basophils, and eosiniphils—and two agranulocytes, lacking granules in the cytoplasm—lymphocytes and monocytes. An important part of the body's defense mechanism, leukocytes phagocytose bacteria and fungi and function in allergic reactions and the response to cellular injury.

Libido   The sexual drive; for psychoanalytic theory, *see* Psychology, page 21-16.

Ligament   A shiny, usually whitish, band of fibrous connective tissue that binds joints together and connects bones and cartilage. *Compare* **Tendon**.

Ligation   Tying with silk thread, wire, or other filament a blood vessel or duct; it is done to prevent bleeding (for example, during surgery) or to prevent passage of material through a duct (for example, to prevent fertilization from occurring in the Fallopian tube). *See also* **Tubal ligation**.

Liniment   A preparation (usually containing an alcohol or oil) applied to the skin to relieve discomfort.

Liver   One of the largest and most complex organs of the body, located in the upper right part of the abdominal cavity. The liver weighs about 1 pound (1.6 kg) in males, a little less in females; is dark reddish-brown, soft, and solid; is divided into four lobes; and is supplied by two blood systems, the hepatic artery, bringing freshly oxygenated blood to the liver and the hepatic portal vein (part of the portal blood system) carrying nutrients from the stomach and intestines to the liver. The liver has numerous functions; it is a site of protein, carbohydrate, and fat metabolism; it helps regulate the level of blood sugar, converting excess glucose into glycogen and storing it; it secretes bile, which is stored in the gallbladder before its release into the intestinal tract; it synthesizes substances involved in blood clotting (for example, fibrinogen); it produces plasma proteins; it synthesizes vitamin A; it detoxifies poisonous substances; and it breaks down worn out erythrocytes (red blood cells).

Liver cancer   A malignant neoplastic disease of the liver occurring most often as a metastasis from another cancer. Primary liver cancer is common in parts of Africa and Asia, where it is often associated with aflatoxins, but is rare in the United States, often associated with cirrhosis of the liver. Symptoms include loss of appetite, weakness, bloating, jaundice, and enlarged, tender liver and mild upper abdominal discomfort. The lesions often metastasize through the portal and lymphatic systems. Treatment depends on the nature and extent of the neoplasm; it may involve removal of a primary tumor and/or chemotherapy.

Living will　A legal document whereby a person directs health-care providers as to the medical care to be given if he/she becomes terminally ill and is incapable of making decisions. In many states, these documents are legally enforceable.

Local anesthesia　The administration of a local anesthetic agent to induce loss of sensation in a small area of the body. It may be applied topically, as in spraying on the skin before removing a small lesion; or it may be injected subcutaneously. Brief dental and surgical operations are the most common indications for use. *Compare* **General anesthesia**.

Lockjaw　A common term for tetanus, during the late stages of which the jaw muscles sometimes spasm.

Lordosis　(1) The normal curvature of the cervical (neck) and lumbar spine seen from the side as an anterior concavity; (2) an increased degree of curvature.

Lower respiratory tract　That part of the respiratory tract that includes the left and right bronchi and the lungs.

Lumpectomy　Surgical removal of a tumor without removal of much surrounding tissue or nearby lymph nodes; performed in some cases of breast tumor and other tumors.

Lung　Either of a pair of highly elastic, spongy organs in the chest that are the main organs of respiration, inhaling air from which oxygen is taken and exhaling carbon dioxide. The lungs are composed of lobes, the right with three, the left with two. The lobes are divided into lobules, each of which contains blood vessels, lymphatics, nerves, and ducts connecting the alveoli, or air spaces, where the actual oxygen-carbon dioxide exchange takes place.

Lung cancer　One of the most common types of cancer. Predisposing factors include cigarette smoking and exposure to asbestos, vinyl chloride, coal products, and other industrial and chemical products. Symptoms include cough, difficulty in breathing, blood-tinged sputum, and repeated infections. Treatment depends on the type, site, and extent of the cancer and may include surgery, chemotherapy, and radiation.

Lyme disease　Acute inflammatory disease, thought to be caused by a tick-borne bacterium, that affects one or more joints (especially the knees and other large joints), causing heat, swelling, and skin redness, often accompanied by chills, fever, and malaise. Cardiac abnormalities and neurologic complications sometimes occur. Preventive measures include wearing protective clothing (long-sleeved shirt, and pants tucked into boots) in wooded areas and examination of the body for ticks after possible exposure. Treatment is by pain relievers (for example, aspirin), antibiotics (tetracycline, penicillin), and sometimes corticosteroids.

Lymph　A thin fluid that bathes the tissues of the body, circulates through lymph vessels, is filtered in lymph nodes, and enters the blood system through the thoracic duct at the junction of the subclavian vein and jugular vein. It contains chyle and leukocytes (mostly lymphocytes), but otherwise is similar to plasma.

Lymphatic system　A network of capillaries, vessels, ducts, nodes, and organs that help maintain the fluid environment of the body and help to protect the body by producing lymph and conveying it around the body. Lymphatic capillaries unite to form lymph vessels, which have numerous valves to control lymph flow and nodes to filter the lymph. The lymphatic vessels lead to two large vessels; the thoracic duct and right lymphatic duct, both in the neck, from which the lymph drains into the bloodstream. Specialized lymph organs include the spleen, thymus, and tonsils.

LYMPH CIRCULATION

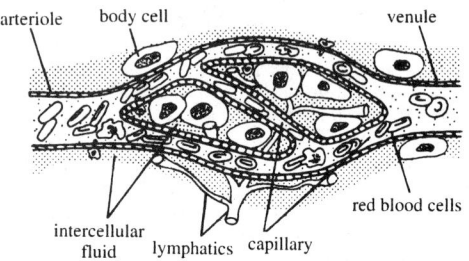

arteriole　body cell　venule

red blood cells

intercellular fluid　lymphatics　capillary

Lymph node　Any of the many small structures that filter lymph and produce lymphocytes. Lymph nodes are concentrated in several areas of the body, such as the armpit, groin, and neck. Also called lymph gland.

Lymphoma　A neoplasm of lymph tissue, usually malignant; one of four major types of cancer. Lymphomas differ widely in the types of cells affected and the prognosis; general characteristics include enlarged lymph nodes, weakness, fever, weight loss, and malaise followed by enlargement of the spleen and liver. Types of lymphomas include Burkitt's lymphoma and Hodgkin's disease. Treatment is usually by chemotherapy and radiotherapy.

Lysergic Acid Diethylamide (LSD)　Hallucinogen; drug that produces illusions, hallucinations, distorted perceptions, feelings of panic, depression, or paranoia, and widespread physical symptoms (for example, increased body temperature and blood pressure, dilation of the pupils, muscle weakness). Psychological dependence may occur. The drug is not used therapeutically but is a drug of abuse. Treatment of LSD intoxication involves attempts to calm the person and the use of tranquilizers and barbiturates. Also called acid.

M **Malaise**　A vague feeling of weakness or illness; often an early sign of illness.

Malaria　A serious infectious illness characterized by recurrent episodes of chills, fever, headache, anemia, muscle ache, and an enlarged spleen. It is caused by *Plasmodium* protozoa, transmitted from human to human through the bite of an infected *Anopheles* mosquito or through blood transfusions or infected hypodermic needles; it is largely confined to tropical and subtropical areas. Treatment is by chloroquine, or in hard to treat cases, a combination of quinine, sulfonamides, and other drugs. Prevention includes removal of swampy areas where *Anopheles* mosquitos breed, the use of insecticides and mosquito netting, and the use of antimalarial drugs when traveling in malaria areas.

Malignant Worsening or progressing toward death, especially a cancer that is invasive and metastatic (spreading). *Compare* **Benign.**

Malignant tumor A tumor that tends to grow and spread to other body parts, in most cases leading to death unless treated.

Malnutrition A state of poor nutrition, resulting from an insufficient, excessive, or unbalanced diet or from impaired ability to absorb and assimilate foods.

Malpractice Negligent or incorrect performance of professional duties; in medicine, the term refers specifically to care rendered patients by health-care providers and institutions. Generally, four prerequisites are necessary to establish a valid claim for medical malpractice: (1) a provider-patient relationship existed; (2) negligent care was rendered; (3) the patient suffered damage or harm; and (4) the damage or harm done to the patient was a direct result of the negligent care.

Mammography Procedure in which the soft tissues of the breast are X-rayed to detect benign or malignant tumors. Periodic mammography is generally recommended for women thought at high risk for breast cancer and in certain other situations.

Marijuana Drug, made from the dried leaves of the *Cannabis sativa* plant, which, when smoked, provides a sense of euphoria often accompanied by changes in mood, perception, memory, and fine motor skills. The drug has been used to help relieve the nausea associated with cancer chemotherapy. Street names include pot, grass, and weed.

Mastectomy The surgical removal of one or both breasts to remove a malignant tumor.

Modified radical mastectomy—the removal of a breast with the underlying pectoralis minor muscle and some adjacent lymph nodes (the major chest muscle—pectoralis major—is not removed).

Radical mastectomy—surgical removal of a breast, underlying chest muscles (both pectoralis major and pectoralis minor), lymph nodes in the armpit area, and fat and other tissues in the surrounding area.

Simple mastectomy—the removal of a breast with the underlying chest muscles and adjacent lymph nodes and tissues left intact.

Measles An acute, contagious, viral disease, occurring primarily in children who have not been immunized and involving the respiratory tract and a spreading rash. Highly contagious, measles is spread by direct contact with droplets from the nose, mouth, or throat of infected persons, often in the prodromal stage. After an incubation period of about two weeks, fever, malaise, cough, loss of appetite, and photophobia (intolerance to light) develop, followed by characteristic blue-centered, small red spots on the membranes of the tongue and mouth (Koplik's spots). Two or three days later the characteristic rash appears, starting as pinkish spots in the head region and spreading to a red maculopapular rash over the trunk and extremities. Fever to 103° Fahrenheit (39.5° Celsius) or higher and inflammation of the pharynx and trachea occur. About five days later the lesions flatten, become brownish and fade, and the fever subsides. Treatment includes pain relievers, fever reducers, rest, and lotions (for example, calamine) to soothe the skin and relieve itching. Complications include otitis media, pneumonia, laryngitis, and occasionally encephalitis. One attack provides life-long immunity. Prevention is by immunization with live measles vaccine, usually done when the child is 1 to 1½ years old; or, in those unvaccinated and exposed to the disease, passive immunization with immune globulin.

Medicaid The federally and state-funded program of health care for needy persons, regardless of age. Five basic services are provided: inpatient hospital, outpatient hospital, laboratory and X-ray, skilled nursing home, and physician. In each state, income and assets criteria determine eligibility.

Medicare The federally administered system of health insurance, available to persons aged 65 and over, whether working or retired. Part A, Hospital Insurance, provides some protection against the costs of hospitalization, certain related inpatient institutional care, and home care. Part B, Supplementary Medical Insurance, in return for payment of a monthly fee that is adjusted annually, covers part of physicians' fees and certain other services (for example, X-ray and laboratory tests, radiotherapy, and medical equipment used at home, such as an oxygen tent or a wheelchair). Although Medicare is unquestionably helpful, many elderly persons consider it advisable to have private health insurance as well.

Melanoma Any of several malignant neoplasms, primarily of the skin, consisting of melanocytes. Most melanomas develop from a pigmented nevus (mole); any change in color or shape of such a mark suggests melanoma. Prognosis depends on the location, depth, and size of the lesion, and on the general health of the patient.

Membrane A thin layer of tissue that covers an organ or lines a cavity or part (for example, the pleura is a membrane enclosing the lung).

Menarche The first menstruation, usually occurring between the ages of 9 and 16.

Meninges Three connective tissue membranes that protect and enclose the brain and spinal cord. The outer layer is the tough, thick dura mater; the middle layer, the delicate, spiderweblike arachnoid; the inner layer, the highly vascularized pia mater. The inner two layers are collectively the leptomeninges; the cerebrospinal fluid circulates between them.

Meningitis Inflammation of the meninges, most commonly due to bacterial infection, but sometimes caused by viral or fungal infection, spreading tuberculosis, neoplasm, or chemical irritation. Symptoms include headache, stiff neck, fever, nausea, vomiting, and intolerance to light and sound, often followed by convulsions and delirium. Treatment depends on the cause; bacterial meningitis is treated by antibiotics; viral, fungal, or other forms of meningitis are more serious and difficult to treat.

Menopause The cessation of menstruation, usually occurring naturally between the ages of 45 and 55. The term is also used to refer to that stage of a woman's life during which gradual hormonal changes, sometimes accompanied by vasomotor symptoms, such as hot flashes, and other signs (for example, dryness of vaginal membranes and palpitations), lead to the cessation of menstrual periods. The production of gonadotropins from the pituitary and estrogens from the ovaries gradually decreases; ovulation ceases, and menstrual periods stop. The periods may become scanty and irregular in occurrence, there may be episodes of heavy bleeding, or cessation may be abrupt. Emotional disturbances may result from hormonal imbalances during the period, but many of the symptoms once believed due to menopause cannot be reliably attributed to it. Also called climacteric; change of life.

Menses   The flow of blood and other material from the uterus during menstruation.

Menstrual cycle   The recurring cycle, beginning at menarche and ending at menopause, in which the endometrial lining of the uterus proliferates in preparation for pregnancy and when pregnancy does not occur is shed at menstruation. The average menstrual cycle is 28 days, with day 1 the first day of menstrual flow, but the length of the cycle varies greatly among women.

Menstruation   The discharge of blood and uterine material from the vagina at intervals of about a month during a woman's reproductive years. Also called catamenia. *See also* **Menses**; **Menstrual cycle**.

THE MENSTRUAL CYCLE

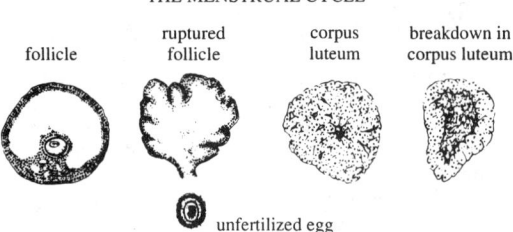

follicle   ruptured follicle   corpus luteum   breakdown in corpus luteum

unfertilized egg

Changes in the Ovary

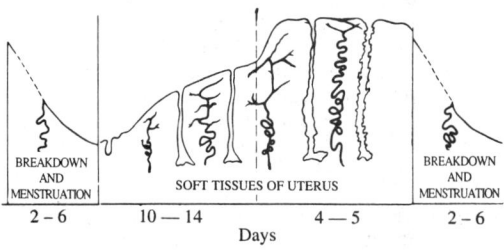

BREAKDOWN AND MENSTRUATION   SOFT TISSUES OF UTERUS   BREAKDOWN AND MENSTRUATION

2 – 6   10 — 14   4 — 5   2 – 6

Days

Changes in the Uterus Wall

Metabolism   The combined chemical and physical processes that take place in the body involving the distribution of nutrients and resulting in growth, energy production, elimination of wastes, and the performance of other body functions.

Metastasis   The spread of a tumor from its site of origin to distant sites, usually through the bloodstream, through the lymphatic system, or across a cavity such as that contained in the peritoneum.

Methadone   A synthetic narcotic pain-reliever used in the treatment of opiate (especially heroin) addicted persons and sometimes to relieve severe pain. Adverse effects include drowsiness, gastroin-

testinal disturbances, respiratory and circulatory depression, and the potential for addiction.

Microbiology   That branch of biology concerned with the study of microorganisms, including bacteria, viruses, rickettsiae, fungi, and protozoa.

Microorganism   A very small organism, usually visible only with the help of a microscope; included among microorganisms are bacteria, viruses, rickettsia, fungi, and protozoa.

Midwife   A person who assists women in labor and childbirth.

Migraine   A recurring vascular headache, occurring more frequently in women. The cause is unknown but the pain is associated with dilation of extracranial blood vessels; attacks are often triggered by allergic reactions, menstruation, alcohol, or relaxation after a period of stress. A typical attack, which may last from several hours to several days, starts with a prodromal episode of visual disturbances (for example, aura or flashing lights), numbness, tingling, vertigo, or other sensations, followed by the onset of severe usually unilateral pain, sometimes accompanied by nausea, vomiting, photophobia (intolerance to light), irritability, and fatigue. Ergotamine preparations that constrict cranial arteries are helpful if taken at the onset of an attack; aspirin does not usually provide relief. Also called megrim; hemicrania.

Milk of magnesia   A laxative and antacid, containing magnesium hydroxide; it is used to treat constipation and acid indigestion.

Mineral oil   A laxative and stool softener used to treat constipation. Adverse effects include possible laxative dependence, fat-soluble vitamin deficiency, and abdominal cramps.

Miscarriage   A spontaneous (non-induced) abortion.

Mite   Any of a group of small arachnids (relative of spiders and ticks), some of which cause local skin irritation and itching in humans.

Mitral valve   One of four valves of the heart; it is situated between the left atrium and left ventricle and allows blood to flow from the left atrium to the left ventricle but prevents backflow. It consists of two flaps or cusps. Also called biscuspid valve; left atrioventricular valve.

Mono   *See* **Infectious mononucleosis**.

Morning sickness   Nausea and vomiting that are common in pregnancy, usually occurring in the morning but sometimes at other times during the day; morning sickness often disappears after the first 3 or 4 months of pregnancy. Symptomatic relief is often provided by eating small, frequent meals that prevent the stomach from being empty.

Morphine   A narcotic analgesic used to relieve pain. Adverse effects include respiratory depression, cardiovascular abnormalities, and the potential for dependence.

Motor nerve   A nerve that conducts impulses from the brain or spinal cord to muscles or organs of the body.

Motor neuron   A nerve cell that makes up the pathway between the brain or spinal cord and an effector organ—a muscle or gland.

Mouth-to-mouth resuscitation   *See* **Cardiopulmonary resuscitation**.

Mucous membrane   A thin sheet of tissue that covers or lines parts of the body. It consists of a layer of epithelium overlying thicker connective tissue. It protects underlying organs, secretes mucus, and absorbs water and solutes.

Mucus Viscous secretions of mucous membranes and glands, containing mucin, water, white blood cells, and salts.

Multiple sclerosis A progressive disease in which nerve fibers of the brain and spinal cord lose their myelin cover. It begins usually in early adulthood and progresses slowly with periods of remission and exacerbation. Early symptoms of abnormal sensations in the face or extremities, weakness, and visual disturbances (for example, double vision) progress to abnormal reflexes, tremors, difficulty in urination, emotional instability, and difficulty in walking, leading to increasing disability. There is no specific treatment; corticosteroids and other drugs are used to treat symptoms.

Mumps An acute viral disease characterized by swelling of the parotid glands, most likely to affect nonimmunized children, but it may occur at any age, sometimes producing a severe illness in adults. After early symptoms of fever, malaise, headache, and low-grade fever, earache, parotid gland swelling, and fever to 104° Fahrenheit (40° Celsius) occur, sometimes with salivary gland enlargement, and, in postpubertal males, swelling and tenderness of the testes. Complications include mumps, meningitis, arthritis, and nephritis. Treatment includes rest and drugs to relieve pain and reduce fever. Prevention is by immunization with attenuated live-virus vaccine, routinely given at 15 months of age.

Muscle A kind of vascular, conductive, and elastic tissue, composed of fibers that can contract, causing movement of parts and organs. There are three basic kinds of muscle; skeletal muscle, which is striated in appearance, controls voluntary movements, responds quickly to neural stimulation, and is paralyzed if innervation is lost; smooth muscle, which is not striped in appearance, comprises the musculature of all visceral organs, responds slowly to stimulation, and controls involuntary movement; and cardiac muscle, which is striped in appearance, but does not respond as quickly as skeletal muscle and which continues to contract if it loses its neural stimuli.

Muscle relaxant A drug that reduces the contractility of muscle fibers by blocking the transmission of nerve impulses at neuromuscular junctions, by increasing the time between contractions of fibers, by decreasing the excitability of the motor end plate, by interfering with nerve synapses in the central nervous system, or by interfering with calcium release from muscle or by other actions; the drugs are used to treat muscle spasm and as adjuncts to anesthesia for certain surgical procedures.

Muscular dystrophy Any of a group of hereditary diseases of the muscular system characterized by weakness and wasting of groups of skeletal muscles, leading to increasing disability. The various forms differ in age of onset, rate of progression, and mode of genetic transmission; the most common is Duchenne's muscular dystrophy.

Duchenne's muscular dystrophy—the most common of the muscular dystrophies (approximately 50%), is an X-linked recessive disease (affecting only males) with symptoms first appearing around the age of 4. Progressive wasting of leg and pelvic muscles produces a waddling gait and abnormal curvature of the spine, progressing to inability to walk and confinement to a wheelchair (usually by age 12), often accompanied by progressive weakening of cardiac muscle. There is no specific treatment and death, usually from heart disorders, often results by age 20. Also called pseudohypertrophic dystrophy.

Myotonic muscular dystrophy—a severe form of muscular dystrophy characterized by drooping eyelids, facial weakness, difficulty with speech, and weakness of the hands and feet spreading to arms, shoulders, legs, and hips. Also called myotonia atrophica; Steinert's disease.

Limb-girdle muscular dystrophy—a form of muscular dystrophy (autosomal recessive disease) characterized by progressive muscular weakness beginning in either the shoulder or pelvic girdle.

Myocardial infarction A heart attack; the death of an area of heart muscle due to interruption of its blood supply through occlusion of the coronary arteries by atherosclerosis or an embolus. Typical signs include crushing, viselike pain in the chest that may radiate to the arm, especially the left arm, and neck region; shortness of breath; faintness; anxiety; and an ashen appearance; there are also often irregular heart rhythm, demonstrable on an electrocardiogram; weak pulse; and low blood pressure. Treatment involves cardiopulmonary resuscitation, if necessary; oxygen, if necessary; and drugs to control heart rhythm, anticoagulants, sedatives, and analgesics; close monitoring to guard against complications and prevent ventricular fibrillation or cardiac arrest is essential. Prognosis depends on the extent of heart damage, but most patients are able to return to normal life with some limitations regarding diet, activity, and stress.

Myocardium The thick, muscular middle layer of the heart wall, composed almost entirely of cardiac muscle. (The other layers are the outer epicardium and inner endocardium.)

Myopia Nearsightedness; a defect in vision caused by elongation of the eyeball or an error in refraction so that the image comes to a focus in front of the retina; it can be corrected by concave lenses.

**Narcotic** A drug, derived from opium or produced synthetically, that relieves pain, induces euphoria and other mood changes, decreases respiration and peristalsis, constricts the pupils, and produces sleep. Narcotic drugs are addictive after repeated use. Narcotic drugs used for pain relief include morphine and meperidine (Demerol) and codeine; heroin and other narcotics are common street drugs.

Nasal decongestant A drug that provides temporary relief of nasal symptoms associated with the common cold, rhinitis, and upper respiratory infections. Most contain an antihistamine and vasoconstrictor, and many are sold without prescription. Prolonged use may lead to dependency.

Nasal sinus Any of numerous cavities in the skull lined with a mucous membrane continuous with the nasal membrane; among the nasal sinuses are the frontal sinuses; ethmoidal sinuses, and maxillary sinuses. *See* **Sinusitis**.

Natural childbirth Labor and childbirth with little or no medical intervention and the mother given minimal or no drugs to relieve pain or aid the birth process. It is considered the safest for the baby, but certain conditions (for example inadequate birth canal, fetal distress, illness in the mother) may make it impossible. *See also* **Lamaze method of childbirth**.

Nephritis Inflammation of the kidney.

Nerve One or more bundles of fibers that connect the brain and spinal cord (central nervous system) with the rest of the body. Sensory nerves transmit impulses (afferent impulses) from the sense organs and other organs of the body to the brain and spinal cord. Motor nerves transmit impulses (efferent impulses) from the brain and spinal cord to the glands, muscles, and other organs of the body. A nerve consists of an epineurium enclosing bundles (fasciculi) of fibers; each fasciculus contains microscopic nerve fibers, each enclosed in a neurolemmal sheath. *See also* **Nervous system**.

Nervous breakdown Colloquial for a mental condition that disrupts normal functioning.

Nervous system The extensive network of cells specialized to conduct information in the form of impulses that controls, regulates, and coordinates all functions of the body. It is divided into the central nervous system, made up of the brain and spinal cord, and the peripheral nervous system, which includes the cranial nerves, spinal nerves, and the autonomic nervous system. The basic unit of the nervous system is the neuron, or nerve cell.

Neuritis Inflammation of a nerve, producing pain, loss of sensation, defective reflexes, and muscular atrophy. It can result from many causes.

Neurology That branch of medicine concerned with the structure, function, and diseases of the nervous system.

Neurosis An inefficient way of thinking or behaving, that may be manifested by depression, anxiety, defense mechanisms, compulsion, phobias, or obsessions and which produces psychological pain or discomfort. The perception of reality is usually not impaired and behavior remains within socially accepted limits. *Compare* **Psychosis**; *see* page 21-18.

Neurosurgery Any surgery involving the brain, spinal cord, or peripheral nerves.

Nicotine A poisonous alkaloid found in tobacco, thought responsible for the dependence of regular smokers on tobacco. In small doses nicotine stimulates the nervous system, causing an increase in pulse rate, a rise in blood pressure, and a decrease in appetite. In large doses, it is a depressant, slowing the heartbeat and leading to respiratory depression.

Nitroglycerin A coronary vasodilator used in the treatment of angina pectoris. Adverse effects include headache, flushing, and low blood pressure.

Nitrous oxide A gas used as an anesthetic. Nitrous oxide produces light anesthesia and is used in minor surgery, childbirth, and dentistry, but not alone for major surgery. In small doses it sometimes produces exhilaration and is called laughing gas.

Nongonococcal urethritis An infectious disease of the urethra, usually caused by the *Chlamydia trachomatis* parasite and sexually transmitted. Symptoms are painful urination and discharge from the penis in males, and erosion of the cervix in females. A fetus passing through the birth canal of an infected mother may develop infection of the nasopharynx and eyes. Treatment is by tetracyclines or erythromycin.

Nuclear magnetic resonance (NMR) A diagnostic technique in which an electromagnetic field stimulates atomic nuclei within the patient's body, causing these nuclei to release energy that is recorded with sensitive receivers. The technique is much more accurate than X-ray films for showing certain abnormalities in the body.

Nutrient A substance that must be supplied by the diet to provide for normal health of the body, for energy and for growth. Nutrients include proteins, fats, carbohydrates, vitamins, and minerals.

O **Obesity** The condition of being overweight; an increase in the amount of fat in the subcutaneous tissues of the body. The most common cause is overeating, often beginning in early childhood. Various disease conditions (especially thyroid, pituitary, and other endocrine gland problems) can also contribute to obesity. Treatment involves diet and sometimes counseling. Rarely, drug therapy or surgical treatment is recommended.

Obstetrics That branch of medicine concerned with the care of women during pregnancy, childbirth, and the immediate postpartum period; it is often practiced in conjunction with gynecology.

Occlusion (1) A blockage or closing off of a vessel or passageway in the body, as in a clot occluding a blood vessel; (2) the manner in which the teeth in the opposing jaws meet in biting.

Occupational therapy A division of physical therapy in which handicapped or convalescing people learn and use, under the direction of a trained therapist, skills for daily life activities and for specific occupations with the goal of providing recreation and exercise and maximizing the capabilities of the person.

Ointment A semisolid preparation, usually containing a drug, applied externally, as, for example, an anesthetic or antibacterial ointment applied to a skin irritation.

Oncology The medical specialty and treatment concerned with the study of tumors.

Operating Room (OR) A room in a health-care facility where surgical procedures requiring anesthesia are performed.

Ophthalmology The medical specialty concerned with the eye: its development, structure, functions, defects, diseases, and treatment. *Compare* **Optometry**.

Opiate A drug that contains opium, is derived from opium, or is produced synthetically and has opiate-like characteristics. Opiates are central nervous system depressants; they relieve pain and suppress cough. Included among them are morphine, codeine, and heroin.

Optic nerve Either of a pair of cranial nerves that arise in the retina and transmit visual impulses from the eye to the visual cortex of the brain; second cranial nerve.

Optometry The practice of testing the eyes for visual acuity and prescribing corrective lenses or other visual aids. *Compare* **Ophthalmology**.

Oral contraceptive A pill containing a combination of estrogen and progestin preparations that inhibits ovulation and thus prevents conception. It is a highly effective contraceptive if taken as directed and is generally acceptable to users and has several useful side effects, including relief of dysmenorrhea, the regularization of menstrual cycles, and the relief of acne. However, oral contraceptives have been associated with side effects, some serious, that make them unadvisable for some women. Serious adverse effects include an increased tendency to develop thromboembolus disorders (for example, a stroke); less serious side effects experienced by many women include weight gain, breakthrough bleeding, breast tenderness, and depression. The use of oral contraceptives is generally not recommended for women with a history of breast or pelvic cancer, undiagnosed vaginal bleeding, cardiovascular disease, liver disease, renal disease, thyroid disorders, diabetes, and generally women over 35 who smoke. Also called the pill.

Orthopedics That branch of medicine concerned with the musculoskeletal system (bones, joints, muscles, ligaments, tendons) and the treatment of disorders affecting it.

Osteoarthritis The most common form of arthritis, occurring mostly in the elderly and characterized by degenerative changes in the joints. Symptoms of pain after exercise or use, joint stiffness, and swelling develop, causing disability especially when they affect the hip, spine, or knee. The cause is unknown but may involve many factors, sometimes aggravated by stress. Treatment includes rest, heat, anti-inflammatory drugs, injection of corticosteroids into the joint areas, and, if severe, surgery. *Compare* **Rheumatoid arthritis**.

Osteopathy A treatment system that uses all the usual forms of medical therapy, including drugs and surgery, but places greater emphasis on the relationship of organs and the musculoskeletal system, using manipulation to correct structural problems.

Osteoporosis Abnormal loss of bony tissue, causing fragile bones that fracture easily; pain, especially in the back; and loss of stature. The condition is common in postmenopausal women and also occurs in persons immobilized, given steroid therapy for a long period, or having certain endocrine disorders. Postmenopausal osteoporosis is sometimes treated with estrogen preparations.

Ovary One of a pair of female gonads, or sex organs, located in the lower abdomen. Under the influence of follicle-stimulating hormone (FSH) and luteinizing hormone (LH) from the pituitary gland an ovum is released from a follicle on the surface of the ovary at roughly monthly intervals during a woman's reproductive life. The ovum then enters the Fallopian tube (oviduct) for possible fertilization and for passage to the uterus.

Over-the-counter drug A drug that is sold without a prescription.

Ovulation The expulsion of an ovum (egg) from the ovary after the rupture of a Graafian follicle in the ovary under the influence of pituitary and ovarian hormones. Ovulation typically occurs midway in the menstrual cycle, 14 days after the first day of the last menstrual period, and is sometimes marked by a sharp pain in the lower abdomen on the side of the ovulating ovary.

P **Pacemaker** (1) An electrical (battery operated) device used to maintain a normal heart rhythm by stimulating the heart muscle to contract. Some pacemakers stimulate the heart at a fixed rate; others stimulate the heart muscle on demand, sensing when heart contractions fall below a minimum rate; (2) the sinoatrial node of the heart, that part of the heart that regulates heartbeat.

Pack To treat the body or any part of it by wrapping it (for example, with blankets or sheets), applying compresses to it, or stuffing it (for example, gauze in a wound or tampon in a body opening) to provide therapy (for example, cold ointment), or to absorb blood.

Palate The structure that is the roof of the mouth and floor of the nasal cavity; it is divided into the hard palate and the soft palate.

Palpitation Rapid, strong beating of the heart, associated with emotional arousal and certain heart abnormalities. *See* **Tachycardia**.

Palsy A condition associated with paralysis, as, for example, Bell's palsy or cerebral palsy.

Pancreas A compound gland, about 6 inches (15 centimeters) long, lying behind the stomach. It is both an exocrine gland, secreting pancreatic juice, which contains several digestive enzymes, into the pancreatic duct that unites with the common bile duct opening into the duodenum; and an endocrine gland, secreting the hormones insulin and glucagon from its islets of Langerhans directly into the bloodstream.

Papanicolaou test A method of examining stained cells shed by mucous membranes, especially those of the cervix, used for early diagnosis of cancer and precancerous changes in cells. In its most common use, a smear of cervical cells is obtained during a routine pelvic examination. Also called pap test.

Pap test *See* **Papanicolaou test**.

Paralysis An abnormal condition characterized by loss of sensation or loss of muscle function; it may be congenital or result from injury, disease, or poisoning. *See also* **Paraplegia**; **Quadriplegia**.

Paramedical Pertaining to health-related activities or personnel supplemental to physicians and nurses and their activities; for example, ambulance attendants are paramedical personnel.

Paranoia A mental disorder characterized by delusions of persecution, often organized into an elaborate and logical system of thinking and often centered on a specific theme, such as job persecution or a financial matter. Suspiciousness, hostility, and resistance to therapy are often characteristic of the paranoid person.

Paraplegia Paralysis of the lower limbs, sometimes accompanied by loss of sensory and/or motor function in the back and abdominal region below the level of the injury; it most often occurs as a result of trauma (for example, automobile accident or sports accident), but may also be congenital (for example, spina bifida) or acquired as a result of alcoholism, syphilis, or disease affecting the spinal cord or associated nerves. Treatment depends on the cause and extent of damage; it may include surgery (for example, laminectomy); use of special immobilization devices; and the administration of pain-relieving drugs and drugs to prevent infection, especially of the bladder. *Compare* **Quadriplegia**.

Parapsychology The study of psychic phenomena, such as extrasensory perception, clairvoyance, and mental telepathy. *See* Psychology, page 21-20.

Parasite An organism that lives in or on another organism—the host—obtaining nourishment from it.

Parkinsonism A slowly progressive neurological disorder characterized by resting tremor, shuffling gait, stooped posture, rolling motions of the fingers, drooling, and muscle weakness, sometimes with emotional instability. It most often occurs after the age of 60 and its cause is unknown, but it may occur in young people as a result of encephalitis, syphilis, or certain other diseases. Treatment is by levodopa, and occasionally, in severe cases, by surgery. Also called Parkinson's disease.

Paroxysm (1) A sudden, violent attack, especially a seizure or convulsion; (2) a marked increase in symptoms.

Parturition The process of giving birth.

Passive immunity A type of acquired immunity in which antibodies against a particular disease or against several diseases are transmitted naturally, through the placenta to an unborn child or through colostrum to a nursing infant; or artificially, through the administration (usually by injection) of antiserum. Passive immunity is not permanent.

Patch test A skin test for identifying an allergen. A paper or cloth patch containing suspected allergens (for example, pollen, animal hair) is applied to the skin; the appearance of red, swollen skin or any rash when the patch is removed—usually 1 or 2 days later—usually indicates allergy to that particular substance.

Pathology The study of disease, its causes and effects, especially the observable effects of disease on body tissues.

PCP Abbreviation for phencyclidine hydrochloride.

Pediatrics That branch of medicine concerned with the development of children and the diagnosis and treatment of diseases and disorders affecting children.

Pelvic Inflammatory Disease (PID) An inflammatory condition of the female pelvic organs, often associated with bacterial infection. Symptoms include lower abdominal pain, fever, and foul-smelling vaginal discharge. Treatment is by antibiotics; pain-relieving drugs, if necessary; and, if an abscess develops, surgical drainage. Severe or recurrent attacks often lead to scarring of the Fallopian tubes, sometimes causing infertility.

Pelvis The lower part of the trunk of the body, composed of the right and left hip bones (the innominate bone, made up of the ilium, ischium, and pubis), the sacrum and the coccyx; it protects the lower abdominal organs and provides for the attachment of the legs. The pelvis is usually lighter and wider in females than in males.

Penicillin Any of a group of antibiotics, including ampicillin, oxacillin, penicillin G, and penicillin V, known under many trade names (for example, Pen-

abar, Pen-Vee K, Pentids) derived from *Penicillium* fungus or produced synthetically, which are used to treat a wide variety of bacterial infections. Some members of the penicillin family are effective administered orally; others must be given by injection. Some forms are inactivated by the enzyme penicillinase produced by certain bacteria; others, including cloxacillin and oxacillin, are penicillinase-resistant. Hypersensitivity reactions, manifested by rash, fever, bronchospasm, and other symptoms, occur in some people given penicillin, and a small number develop a serious reaction leading to anaphylactic shock. *See also* **Anaphylaxis.**

Penis The external reproductive organ of the male that contains the urethra through which urine and semen pass. Most of the organ is composed of erectile tissue that becomes engorged under conditions of sexual excitement, causing the penis to become erect; it is then capable of entering the vagina during coitus and discharging semen in ejaculation. Urination occurs without erection.

Peptic ulcer A circumscribed erosion in or loss of the mucous membrane lining of the gastrointestinal tract. It may occur in the esophagus (esophageal ulcer), stomach (gastric ulcer), duodenum (duodenal ulcer), or jejunum (jejunal ulcer), the stomach and duodenum being the most common sites. It may result from excess acid production or from a breakdown in the normal mechanisms protecting the mucous membranes and is often associated with stress, the intake of certain drugs (for example, corticosteroids and certain anti-inflammatory agents). Symptoms include gnawing pain, often worse when the stomach is empty, after certain foods, or when the patient is under stress. Treatment includes avoidance of tobacco, alcohol, and irritating foods; drugs to decrease acidity (for example, cimetidine); and a diet of small, frequent meals; if the ulcer perforates the wall of the gastrointestinal tract and hemorrhage occurs, surgery is usually required.

Pericardium The double-layered sac surrounding the heart and large vessels entering and leaving the heart. The inner serous pericardium contains a layer that adheres to the surface of the heart and a layer that lines the inside of the outer fibrous pericardium. The fibrous pericardium is tough and comparatively inelastic; it protects the heart and inner membranes. Between the two layers is the pericardial space, containing pericardial fluid that lubricates the membrane surfaces and allows easier heart movement.

Periodontics That branch of dentistry concerned with the diagnosis and treatment of diseases of the tissues surrounding the teeth.

Peristalsis Rhythmic, wavelike contractions of the smooth musculature of the digestive tract that force food through the tube and wastes toward the anus.

Peritoneum Serous membrane that covers the entire abdominal wall (parietal peritoneum) and envelops the organs contained in the abdomen (visceral peritoneum).

Peritonitis Inflammation of the peritoneum caused by bacteria or irritating substances (for example, digestive enzymes) introduced into the abdominal cavity by a puncture wound, by surgery, by a ruptured abdominal organ, or through the bloodstream. A ruptured appendix is the most frequent cause, but peritonitis can also result from perforated peptic ulcer or rupture of the spleen or Fallopian tubes (as in ectopic pregnancy), or from other conditions. Symptoms include abdominal distension and pain, nausea, vomiting, rebound tenderness, chills, fever, rapid heart rhythm, and if untreated, electrolyte imbalance, shock, and heart failure. Treatment involves control of the infection, usually with antibiotics, repair of any perforation; withdrawal of fluid from the abdominal cavity, if necessary; and maintenance of fluid and electrolyte balance.

Pernicious anemia   A type of anemia characterized by defective red blood cell production, the presence of megaloblasts (excessively large red blood cells) in the bone marrow, and deterioration of nerve tissue in the spinal cord. It is caused by a lack of intrinsic factor (essential for the absorption of vitamin B_{12}) or by a deficiency of vitamin B_{12} in the diet. Symptoms include pallor, anorexia, weight loss, fever, weakness, and tingling of the extremities. Treatment includes the administration of vitamin B_{12}, folic acid, and iron.

Personality disorder   Any of a group of mental disorders characterized by maladaptive and usually rigid patterns of behavior.

Petit mal   A form of epilepsy characterized by brief (usually momentary) episodes of unconsciousness, sometimes accompanied by muscular spasm, twitching, or loss of muscle tone. Treatment to prevent attacks includes anticonvulsants. *Compare* **Grand mal**.

Phagocyte   A cell that surrounds, engulfs, and digests microorganisms and cellular debris. Fixed phagocytes, including macrophages, do not circulate in the blood but are found in the liver, bone marrow, spleen, and other areas. Free phagocytes, such as leukocytes, circulate in the blood.

Phallus   The penis.

Pharynx   The throat; muscular tube extending from the base of the skull to the esophagus that serves as a passageway for food from the mouth to the esophagus and for air from the nose and mouth to the larynx. It is divided into the nasopharynx, oropharynx, and laryngopharynx, and it connects with the Eustachian tubes, the posterior nares, the mouth, the larynx, and the esophagus.

Phencyclidine hydrochloride (PCP)   A hallucinogenic drug now rarely used in medicine. Street name: angel dust.

Phenobarbital   A barbiturate used as a sedative to treat anxiety and as an anticonvulsant to treat some forms of epilepsy. Adverse effects include drowsiness, skin reactions, interaction with many other drugs, and possible development of dependence.

Phenotype   The observable characteristics of an organism that are the result of genetic makeup and environmental factors.

Phlebitis   Inflammation of the wall of a vein, most often occurring in the legs. Thrombosis commonly develops. Treatment includes rest and support of the area (for example, by elastic stockings), anti-inflammatory drugs, and analgesics.

Phlegm   Thick mucus of the respiratory passages.

Phobia   An anxiety disorder characterized by irrational and intense fear of an object (for example, a dog), an activity (for example, leaving the house), or physical conditions (for example, height). The intense fear usually causes tremor, panic, palpitations, nausea, and other physical signs. Types of phobia include agoraphobia (fear of open or public places), claustrophobia (fear of being confined in closed rooms or small spaces), zoophobia (irrational and excessive fear of animals), and pyrophobia (excessive fear of fire). Treatment includes desensitization therapy and other techniques of behavior therapy. *See also* Psychology, page 21-21.

Photosensitivity   Abnormal sensitivity of the skin to the sun caused by a disorder (for example, albinism) or the result of certain drugs (for example, tetracycline, phenothiazines).

Physical therapy   (1) Treatment by physical means; (2) the health profession that is concerned with health promotion, prevention of physical disabilities, and rehabilitation of persons disabled by pain, disease, or injury; and is involved with evaluating patients and treating them through the use of physical therapeutic measures, as opposed to medicines, surgery, or radiation.

Pigment   A substance giving color, including blood pigments (for example, hemoglobin), retinal pigments (for example, rhodopsin) and melanin found in the skin and iris of the eye.

Piles *See* **Hemorrhoid**.

Pinkeye   *See* **Conjunctivitis**.

Pituitary gland   A small endocrine gland attached to the hypothalamus that releases many hormones controlling many body activities and influencing the activity of many other endocrine glands. It is divided into anterior and posterior portions, each with separate functions.

Placebo   An inactive substance (for example, distilled water or sugar) or less-than-effective dose of a harmless substance prescribed and administered as if it were an effective dose of a needed drug; used as a control in tests of drug efficacy and to treat certain patients who do not need or should not be given a drug they request.

Placenta   Highly vascular fetal organ through which the fetus absorbs oxygen, nutrients, and other substances from the mother and excretes carbon dioxide and other wastes. It forms around the eighth day of gestation as the blastocyst becomes implanted in the wall of the uterus. At the end of pregnancy the placenta weighs about one sixth the weight of the infant. Its maternal side is rough, divided into lobules, and has fingerlike chorionic villi that project into the uterine wall. The fetal side is smooth, covered with the fetal membranes. The placenta is expelled after the birth of the child in the third stage of labor. Also called afterbirth.

Plantar wart   A wart occurring on the sole that, because of pressure, develops a callous ring around its soft center and becomes painful. Treatment includes cryosurgery, electrodesiccation, and application of topical acids.

Plaque   (1) A flat, raised patch on the skin or mucous membrane; (2) a deposit of atherosclerosis; (3) a deposit of saliva and bacteria found on teeth that encourages the development of caries.

Plasma   Acellular, colorless, fluid part of blood and lymph which contains water, electrolytes, glucose, fats, proteins, and bile and in which erythrocytes, leukocytes, and platelets are suspended. In addition to carrying the cellular elements, plasma helps maintain the fluid-electrolyte and the acid-base balances of the body and helps transport wastes. *Compare* **Serum**.

Plastic surgery   That branch of surgery concerned with the alteration, reconstruction, and replacement of body parts to correct a structural or cosmetic defect.

Platelet   A disc-shaped small cellular element in the blood, essential for blood clotting. Normally 200,000 to 300,000 platelets are found in one cubic centimeter of blood.

Pleura   A delicate membrane covering the lungs and the inner surface of the chest; it is divided into the visceral pleura, which covers the lungs, and the parietal pleura, which lines the chest wall and covers the diaphragm. Between the two layers of the pleura is a small space (pleural space) containing fluid that acts as a lubricant.

Pleurisy   Inflammation of the pleura, especially the parietal layer of the pleura, marked by difficulty in breathing and sharp pain. Causes include pneumonia, tuberculosis, and cancer of bronchi. Treatment depends on the cause.

Pneumocystosis   Infection with the organism *Pneumocystis carinii*, usually occurring only in infants or immunosuppressed persons (for example, those with acquired immune deficiency syndrome—AIDS); usually involves the lungs (pneumonia) and is characterized by fever, cough, rapid breathing, and cyanosis (bluish discoloration of the skin due to lack of oxygen). This form of pneumonia may be fatal. Current treatment includes pentamidine and sulfa drugs; other agents are being tried experimentally.

Pneumonia   Inflammation of the lungs, usually caused by infection with bacteria, (especially pneumococcus), viruses, fungi, or rickettsiae. Symptoms include fever, chills, headache, cough, chest pain, and, as the disease progresses, difficult and painful breathing, the production of thick, purulent sputum, rapid pulse, and sometimes gastrointestinal complications. Treatment depends on the cause; it often includes antibiotics, analgesics, expectorants, rest, fluids, and oxygen.

Podiatry   That medical specialty concerned with the diagnosis and treatment of diseases and disorders of the feet.

Poison ivy   *See* **Rhus dermatitis**.

Poison oak   *See* **Rhus dermatitis**.

Poison sumac   *See* **Rhus dermatitis**.

Poliomyelitis   An infectious disease that affects the central nervous system. It is caused by the polio virus and was once epidemic in many parts of the world, but now is largely prevented by vaccination with Salk or Sabin vaccines. Many infections are asymptomatic; some produce only mild symptoms of fever, malaise, headache, and gastrointestinal upsets; others cause paralysis, most often of the lower limbs. Treatment is largely symptomatic. Also called polio; infantile paralysis.

Polyp   A growth or nodule, usually benign, most commonly arising from a mucous membrane (for example, in the nose, ear or uterus).

Pore   A small opening, as the openings of the sweat glands in the skin.

Portal system   A system of veins that drains blood from abdominal organs (the digestive organs, pancreas, spleen, and gallbladder) and transports it to the liver.

Postnasal drip   Discharge of nasal mucus into the posterior pharynx, caused by infection (for example, common cold, influenza, sinusitis) or allergy and usually associated with a feeling of nasal and throat obstruction and with unpleasant taste and odor. Treatment includes agents to constrict nasal vessels; irrigation of sinuses, if necessary; surgical correction of nasal polyps or deviated septum, if indicated; allergy treatment; and/or antibiotics.

Postpartum   Pertaining to the few days following childbirth. *See* Psychology, page 21-21.

Precancerous   Pertaining to a growth that is not malignant but probably will become so if left untreated.

Pregnancy   Gestation; the period during which a woman carries a developing fetus in the uterus from the time of conception to the birth of the child. Pregnancy lasts 266 days from the day of fertilization but is usually calculated as 280 days from the first day of the last menstrual period. The fertilized ovum, or zygote, implants in the wall of the uterus and undergoes growth and development, nourished and protected by the placenta that forms from embryonic and maternal tissue in the uterus. Pregnancy involves changes in virtually every system of a woman's body, including an increase in total blood volume and cardiac output, an increase in kidney filtration and in urination; enlargement of the breasts and changes in the color of the nipple area as the breasts prepare to provide milk for an infant; skin changes, sometimes including chloasma; gastrointestinal changes, often manifested as heartburn, nausea, vomiting, and constipation; increased nutritional needs and weight gain (20 to 25 pounds or more); and numerous endocrine changes, including increased thyroid and adrenal function and the release of hormones from the placenta.

Premature infant   An infant born prior to 37 weeks gestation regardless of birth weight. A premature infant is usually of low birth weight, has incompletely developed organ systems, and appears scrawny, with little subcutaneous fat, a large head, and pinkish, translucent skin. The cause of prematurity is unknown in many cases, but in some is associated with toxemia, multiple pregnancy, chronic disease, trauma, or poor nutrition. The prognosis depends on the maturity of the various organ systems of the infant's body and on the postnatal care given, with the best care being provided in intensive care neonatal units. Treatment involves maintenance of stable body temperature and respiration, provision for adequate fluid and nutrient intake, and prevention of infection.

Premature Ventricular Contraction (PVC)   Irregularity of the cardiac rhythm. Isolated PVCs may not be significant, but frequent, recurrent PVCs usually indicate heart abnormality and may be a precursor of ventricular fibrillation and cardiac arrest.

Premenstrual tension (PMT)   A poorly understood syndrome of tension, irritability, edema, headache, mastalgia (breast pain), bloating, appetite changes, and changes in muscular coordination occurring in many women several days before the onset of the menstrual flow.

Progesterone   Hormone produced by the corpus luteum of the ovary, the placenta during pregnancy, and in small amounts by the adrenal cortex; it prepares the uterus for a fertilized egg. Natural and synthetic progesterones and progestational compounds (for example, norethindrone) are used in oral contraceptives and in drugs to treat abnormal uterine bleeding.

Prognosis   Prediction of the probable outcome of a disease based on what is known about the usual course of the disease and on the age and general health of the patient.

Prostaglandin   Any of a group of hormonelike fatty acids produced in small amounts in many body tissues, including the uterus, brain, and kidneys, and in semen. Prostaglandins act on target organs to produce wide-ranging effects. They affect capillary action; endocrine, nervous system, and smooth muscle functions; and many other body functions, including contractions of the uterus and regulation of blood pressure. Aspirin and certain other analgesics (nonsteroidal anti-inflammatory agents) are believed to act by interfering with the synthesis or reaction of certain prostaglandins.

Prostate   Firm, chestnut-sized gland in males at the neck of the urethra that produces a secretion that is the fluid part of semen.

Prosthesis   An artificial device attached to the body to aid its function or replace a missing part; included among prostheses are artificial limbs, hearing aids, and implanted pacemakers.

Psoriasis   A chronic skin disorder characterized by periods of remissions and exacerbations of dry, scale-covered red patches; occurring especially on the scalp, ears, genitalia, and skin over bony prominences; a type of arthritis may occur with the skin disorder. Treatment includes corticosteroids, ultraviolet light treatments, and the use of medicated creams and shampoos.

Psychiatry   That branch of medicine concerned with the study of the mind and the diagnosis, treatment, and prevention of mental, emotional, and behavioral disorders.

Psychoanalysis   A branch of psychiatry, founded by Sigmund Freud, in which the processes of the mind are studied through techniques such as dream interpretation and free association to bring repressed conflicts into the consciousness, analyze them, and adjust behavioral patterns related to them.

Psychology   The study of mental activity, especially as it relates to behavior.

Psychosis   A major mental disorder in which the person is usually detached from reality and has impaired perceptions, thinking, responses, and interpersonal relationships. Most people with a psychosis require hospitalization; treatment involves the use of psychoactive drugs and psychotherapy. *Compare* **Neurosis**.

Psychotherapy   The treatment of mental disorders by psychological, not physical, techniques. There are many approaches to psychotherapy, including behavior modification, psychoanalysis, and group therapy.

Puberty   The time at which sexual maturity occurs and reproductive function becomes possible. It is characterized by the development of secondary sexual characteristics, such as breast development in girls and deepening voice in males, and by the start of menstruation in girls. The changes are brought about by pituitary gland-stimulated increases in sex hormones.

Pulmonary   Pertaining to the lungs or respiratory system.

Pulmonary artery   The artery that carries deoxygenated blood from the right ventricle of the heart to the lungs for oxygenation. The artery leaves the heart and passes upward before dividing, one branch going to each lung. *See also* **Pulmonary circulation**.

Pulmonary circulation   The system of blood vessels transporting blood between the heart and the lungs. Deoxygenated blood leaves the right ventricle by way of the pulmonary artery, which divides, sending branches to each lung. The deoxygenated blood gives off its carbon dioxide and takes in oxygen in the alveoli of the lungs. The freshly oxygenated blood is then transported by the pulmonary vein to the left atrium of the heart where it enters the systemic circulation for transport throughout the body.

Pulmonary embolism   The blockage of a pulmonary artery by foreign matter or a thrombus (blood clot); it is characterized by difficult breathing, sharp chest pain, shock, and bluish discoloration of the skin, and if untreated, by pleural effusion, heart rhythm abnormalities, and frequently death. Predisposing factors include prolonged immobilization, especially associated with surgery or childbirth; blood vessel wall damage; and factors increasing the tendency of the blood to clot. Treatment is by removal of the embolus, oxygen, cardiac massage, and the use of anticoagulants.

Pulmonary vein   Either of two blood vessels one leaving each lung, that return oxygenated blood to the left atrium of the heart.

Pulse   Regular, rhythmic beating of an artery resulting from the pumping action of the heart. The pulse is easily detected on superficial arteries (for example, the radial artery) and corresponds to each beat of the heart. The average adult pulse at rest is 60 to 80 beats per minute, but this may change with illness, emotional stress, exercise, or other factors. *See also* **Heart rate**.

Pupil   The circular opening in the center of the iris, lying behind the anterior chamber and cornea and in front of the lens, through which light passes to the lens and retina. The diameter of the pupil changes with muscle action of the iris in response to changes in light and other stimulation.

Purulent   Producing or containing pus.

Pus   Thick yellowish or greenish fluid, containing dead white blood cells, bacteria, and dead tissue, formed at an infection site.

Quadriplegia   Paralysis affecting all four limbs and the trunk of the body below the level of spinal cord injury. Trauma is the usual cause. *Compare* **Paraplegia**.

Quarantine   Isolation of people with communicable diseases or people exposed to communicable diseases during the period of contagion in an effort to prevent the spread of the disease.

R **Rabies** An acute, often fatal, viral disease affecting the brain and spinal cord, transmitted to humans by the bite of infected animals, especially dogs, skunks, bats, foxes, and raccoons. After an incubation period that may range from a few days to one year, symptoms of fever, malaise, headache, and muscle pain are followed after a few days by severe and painful muscle spasms, especially of the throat, delirium, difficulty in breathing, paralysis, coma, and death. The disease may be prevented in those bitten by an animal suspected of being rabid by a series of injections of human rabies vaccine combined with rabies immune globulin.

Radiation Electromagnetic energy emitted in the form of rays or particles, including gamma rays, X rays, ultraviolet rays, visible light, and infrared radiation. Some of these radiation forms are used in medicine for diagnosis (for example, X rays) and treatment (for example, use of radioactive elements, such as radium, in cancer treatment).

Radiation sickness An abnormal condition caused by exposure to ionizing radiation, as, for example, from exposure to nuclear bomb explosions or from exposure to radioactive chemicals in the workplace. Symptoms and prognosis depend on the amount of radiation, the exposure time, and the part of the body affected. Low-to-moderate dose causes nausea, vomiting, headache, and diarrhea, sometimes followed by hair loss and bleeding. Severe exposure causes sterility, damage to the fetus in pregnant women and in many cases the development of cataracts, some forms of cancer, and other diseases. Severe exposure can cause death within hours.

Radiation therapy The treatment of disease, especially certain forms of cancer, by the use of radiation given off by special machines or by radioactive isotopes. The radiation interferes with the division (mitosis) of cells and the synthesis of DNA in the cells. Many cancer cells are destroyed by radiation; the major disadvantage is possible damage to cells and tissues in nearby areas.

Radiology That branch of medicine concerned with radioactive substances and their use in diagnosis and treatment.

Rapid Eye Movement (REM) A period of sleep characterized by rapid eye muscle contractions, detectable by electrodes placed over the skin near the eyes, and during which dreaming occurs. REM sleep periods, lasting from a few minutes to about 30 minutes, alternate with nonrapid eye movement (NREM) periods during sleep.

Rectum The last portion of the large intestine, about 5 inches (12–13 centimeters) long, connecting the sigmoid colon and the anus. Feces are stored in the rectum before defecation.

Red blood cell *See* **Erythrocyte**.

Reflex An involuntary function or movement of a part in response to a particular stimulus (for example, the knee-jerk reflex).

Regression A return to an earlier condition, especially the retreat of an adult into childlike behavior.

Regurgitation (1) The return of swallowed food into the mouth; (2) the backflow of blood through a defective heart valve.

Rehabilitation The restoration of an individual or of a part of the body to normal function after injury, disease, or other abnormal state.

Rejection (1) In medicine, an immunological response whereby substances or organisms that the system recognizes as foreign are not accepted, as in the body's attack against an invading microorganism (for example, bacteria) or rejection of a transplanted organ; (2) in psychiatry, denying attention or affection to another person.

Relapse To show again the signs of a disease from which the patient had appeared to have recovered; the recurrence of a disease after apparent recovery.

REM Abbreviation for rapid eye movement.

Remission Partial or complete disappearance of or lessening of the severity of the symptoms of a disease; it may be spontaneous or the result of therapy; temporary or permanent.

Renal calculus *See* **Urinary calculus**.

Renal failure The inability of the kidneys to excrete wastes and function in the maintenance of electrolyte balance. Acute renal failure—characterized by the inability to produce urine and an accumulation of wastes, is often associated with trauma, burns, acute infection, or obstruction of the urinary tract; its treatment depends on the cause and, often includes antibiotics and reduced fluid intake. Chronic kidney failure—which may occur as a result of many systemic disorders, causes fatigue and sluggishness, diminished urine output, anemia, and often complications of hypertension and congestive heart failure; treatment depends on the cause, often involving the use of diuretics, restricted protein intake, and if it cannot be otherwise treated, hemodialysis.

Reproductive system The organs and tissues involved in the production and maturation of gametes and in their union and subsequent development to produce offspring. In the male the reproductive system includes the testes, vas deferens, prostate gland, seminal vesicles, urethra, and penis. In the female it includes the ovaries, Fallopian tubes, uterus, vagina, and vulva. The reproductive system is under the control of numerous hormones secreted by the pituitary gland, the sex organs (ovaries and testes), and the adrenal glands.

Resistance The degree of immunity or resistance to a disease that the body possesses; the degree to which a disease-causing microorganism is unaffected by antibiotics or other drugs, as in penicillin-resistant bacteria.

Respiratory failure Inability of the heart and lungs to maintain an adequate level of gaseous exchange. Treatment involves correction of any underlying cardiac or lung disorder, administration of oxygen, maintenance of clear airways, the use of bronchodilators, and other measures.

Respiratory tract The organs and structures associated with breathing, gaseous exchange, and the entrance of air into the body. It includes the nasal cavity, pharynx, larynx, and trachea (the upper respiratory tract) and the bronchi, bronchioles, and lungs (lower respiratory tract) and associated muscles.

Resuscitation The act of reviving a person or returning him/her to consciousness through the use of cardiopulmonary resuscitation and similar techniques.

Retina   The multilayered, light-sensitive membrane of the eyeball that receives images of objects and transmits visual impulses through the optic nerve to the brain for interpretation. The outer part of the retina, next to the choroid, contains the pigment rhodopsin; the inner layers, continuing to the vitreous body, contain rods and cones (light-sensitive nerve cells) and their associated ganglia and fibers.

Reye's syndrome   A poorly understood syndrome involving abnormal brain function and fatty infiltration of internal organs, especially the liver. It occurs chiefly in children following an acute viral infection (especially viruses associated with influenza and chickenpox); an association with aspirin intake has also been observed. Vomiting and confusion typically occur about a week after the viral infection, sometimes leading to disorientation, seizures, coma, and respiratory arrest. The cause is unknown and there is no specific treatment. Intensive monitoring of all vital functions and correction of any imbalances, along with antibiotics, improve the prognosis.

Rheumatoid arthritis   A chronic, destructive disease characterized by joint inflammation. It usually begins in early middle age, most often in women, and is marked by periods of remission and exacerbation. Symptoms are varied, often including fatigue; low-grade fever; loss of appetite; morning stiffness; tender, painful swelling of two or more joints, most commonly the joints of the fingers, ankles, feet, hips and shoulders; and small subcutaneous nodules near joints. There is no cure; treatment includes rest, pain-relieving drugs, exercises to maintain joint mobility, and anti-inflammatory agents (for example, indomethacin, phenylbutazone), and, if other measures are not successful, corticosteroids. *Compare* **Osteoarthritis**.

Rh factor   An antigen present in the erythrocytes (red blood cells) of about 85% of people; it is called Rh factor because it was first identified in the blood of rhesus monkeys. Those persons having the factor are designated Rh-positive; those lacking the factor, Rh-negative. Blood for transfusions must be classified for Rh factor, as well as for ABO classification, to prevent possible incompatibility reactions. If an Rh-negative person receives Rh-positive blood hemolysis and anemia can result; a similar reaction can occur if an Rh-positive fetus (the fetus having inherited the Rh factor from the father) is exposed to antibodies to the factor by an Rh-negative mother.

Rh incompatibility   Lack of compatibility between two blood samples because one contains Rh factor and the other does not.

Rhus dermatitis   Type of contact dermatitis resulting from contact with plants of the genus *Rhus*, including poison ivy, poison oak, and poison sumac.

Ringworm   Any of several fungal infections of the skin often characterized by ringlike skin lesions, including athlete's foot and jock itch.

Rocky Mountain spotted fever   An infectious disease caused by *Rickettsia rickettsii* and occurring throughout North and South America. It is characterized by fever, headache, muscle pains, mental confusion, and red patches that spread from the wrist and ankles over the trunk of the body; abdominal distension and hemorrhage sometimes occur. Treatment is with the antibiotics chloramphenicol and tetracycline.

Roseola   A benign illness of infants and young children, characterized by abrupt, high fever; mild sore throat; and, a few days later, a faint, patchy, pinkish rash that lasts for a few hours to a few days. Treatment involves fever-reducing agents (for example, aspirin, acetaminophen) and, if convulsions occur in association with high fever, anticonvulsants.

Rubella   A contagious viral disease characterized by fever, mild symptoms of upper respiratory infection, and a diffuse fine red rash lasting for a short period, usually three or four days. The disease is usually mild and self-limiting; however, if contracted by a woman in early pregnancy it may cause serious damage to the fetus. There is no treatment; prevention is by rubella vaccine, usually given to children as part of a normal immunization program; the vaccine should not be given to a pregnant woman or one who plans to become pregnant within three months. Also called three-day measles; German measles.

Sabin vaccine   An oral vaccine, consisting of live attenuated poliovirus, given to provide immunity to poliomyelitis. It is given as part of the recommended immunization schedule for infants, usually in two or three doses, before the age of 6 months with an added dose at 18 months and 4 or 5 years. Also called trivalent live oral poliomyelitis vaccine (TOPV). *Compare* **Salk vaccine**.

Saline   Containing a salt, especially sodium chloride; a solution containing sodium chloride as a plasma substitute and to correct electrolyte imbalances.

Saliva   Clear fluid, containing water, mucin, the enzyme ptyalin, and salts, secreted by the salivary glands and mucous glands of the mouth and serving to moisten food, aid in chewing and swallowing, and start the digestion of starches.

Salivary gland   Any of three pairs of glands that secrete saliva into the mouth. The parotid salivary glands secrete a serous fluid; the sublingual salivary glands a mucous fluid; and the submandibular glands a fluid with both serous and mucous components.

Salk vaccine   A vaccine consisting of inactivated poliovirus injected subcutaneously to provide immunity to poliomyelitis. It is used for infants, children with deficient immune systems, and unvaccinated adults. Also called IPV.

Salmonella   A genus of gram-negative rod-shaped bacteria, some of which cause typhoid fever and some forms of gastroenteritis in humans.

Sarcoma   A malignant neoplasm arising in bone, muscle, or other connective tissue.

Scabies   A contagious disease caused by the itch mite (*Sarcoptes scabiei*) and characterized by itching and skin irritation, often leading to secondary infection. Treatment includes scabicides and antihistamines to relieve itching. All contacts, bedding, and clothing must be treated to prevent spread and reinfestation.

Schizophrenia   Any of a group of mental disorders characterized by gross distortions of reality, withdrawal from social contacts, and disturbances of thought, language, perception, and emotional response. Symptoms are highly varied and may include apathy, catatonia or excessive activity, bizarre actions, hallucinations, delusions, and rambling speech. Some cases are mild; others severe, requiring prolonged or permanent hospitalization. There is no known cause; a combination of hereditary or genetic predisposition factors together with psychological, biochemical, and sociocultural factors is throught to be responsible in many cases. Treatment includes use of tranquilizers, antidepressants, and psychotherapy. *See* Psychology, pages 21-24, 21-25.

Sciatica   Pain felt in the back and down the back and outer part of the thigh and leg due to compression on sacral spinal nerve roots or the sciatic nerve, often associated with degeneration of an intervertebral disc. Treatment is by rest; intractable cases may require surgery.

Sclerosis   A condition characterized by hardness of tissue, resulting from inflammation, mineral deposits, or other causes.

Scoliosis   An abnormal lateral or sideward curve to the spine; it is common in childhood, caused by congenital malformations, poliomyelitis, unequal limbs, or other factors. Early treatment involving surgery, casts, exercises, and braces may prevent progression.

Scratch test   A skin test for identifying an allergen. A small amount of a solution containing a suspected allergen is placed on a scratched skin area; if redness and wheal formulation develop, allergy to that particular substance is indicated.

Scrotum   The pouch of skin containing the testes and parts of the spermatic cords below the abdomen. It is divided into two lateral portions by a ridge that continues ventrally to the undersurface of the penis and dorsally to the perineum. Because it holds the testes away from the abdomen, the scrotum allows the production of sperm at a temperature lower than that of the abdomen.

Sebaceous gland   Any of numerous sebum-secreting organs in the dermis throughout the body (except the palms and soles), especially abundant on the scalp, face, nose, mouth, and ears. In most cases the sebum is secreted into hair follicles but in some places (for example, the labia minora, lips) it is secreted onto the surface. The sebum oils the hair and skin, helps retain body heat, and prevents sweat evaporation.

Seborrhea   Any of several conditions in which there is over-activity of the sebaceous glands and the skin becomes oily.

Sebum   Secretion of the sebaceous glands, containing fat and cellular debris. With sweat, it moistens and protects the skin.

Sedative   An agent that decreases activity and excitability, relieves anxiety, and calms the person. Some sedatives have a general effect; others affect the activities of certain organs (for example, intestines or vasomotor system). *See* page 21-25.

Semen   The thick, whitish secretion discharged from the male urethra during ejaculation. It contains spermatozoa and secretions of the prostate gland, seminal vesicles, and other glands. Also called seminal fluid.

Senile dementia   A mental disorder of the aged, resulting from atrophy and degeneration of the brain, with no signs of cerebrovascular disease. Symptoms,

which are generally slowly progressive, include loss of memory, periods of confusion and irritability, confabulation, and poor judgment. Also called senile psychosis. *Compare* **Alzheimer's disease**.

Serum   Clear thin, sticky fluid of blood; like plasma, it contains no cells or platelets; unlike plasma, it also contains no fibrinogen.

Sex hormone   A steroid hormone responsible for sexual development and reproductive function. The main female sex hormones are estrogens and progesterone; the male sex hormones are androgens (including testosterone).

Sexual intercourse   *See* **Coitus**.

Sexually Transmitted Disease (STD)   Communicable disease transmitted by sexual intercourse or genital contact; examples are gonorrhea, syphilis, herpes genitalis, Chlamydia trachomatis, and acquired immune deficiency syndrome (AIDS). Formerly called venereal disease.

Shock   An abnormal state, usually an alarm reaction to trauma, characterized by reduced cardiac output, circulatory insufficiency, low blood pressure, rapid heartbeat, and pallor.

Sickle cell anemia   A hereditary blood disease, occurring mostly in blacks, in which abnormal hemoglobin (hemoglobin HbS) causes red blood cells to become sickle-shaped, fragile and nonfunctional, leading to anemia. Persons inheriting the trait from only one parent may show few symptoms; those inheriting it from both parents have chronic anemia, an enlarged spleen, lethargy, weakness, blood clot formation, and joint pain.

Sign   An observable indication of a disease.

Sinusitis   Inflammation of one of the paranasal sinuses, occurring as a result of an upper respiratory infection, an allergic response, a change in atmospheric pressure, or a defect of the nose. As sinus secretions accumulate, pain, fever, tenderness, and headache develop, serious complications include spread of the infection to the bone or brain. Treatment is by antibiotics (if infection is present), decongestants, steam inhalation, and in some chronic cases, surgical drainage.

Skeleton   The framework of the body, made up of 206 bones that provide structure and form for the body, protect delicate internal organs, provide for the attachment of muscles, produce red blood cells, and serve as blood reservoirs. The skeleton is divided into two major parts: the axial skeleton, which includes the skull, vertebral column, breastbone, and ribs; and the appendicular skeleton, which includes the pectoral (shoulder) girdle (clavicle and scapula) and the pelvic (hip) girdle and the upper and lower appendages (arms and legs).

Skin   The outer covering of the body, the largest organ of the body. It protects the body from injury and invasion by microorganisms, helps (through hair follicles and sweat glands) maintain body temperature, serves as a sensory network, lubricates and waterproofs the exterior, and serves as an organ of excretion. The skin consists of an outer layer: the epidermis, and an inner layer: the dermis, which contains nerve endings, hair follicles, glands, lymph vessels, and blood vessels. Also called cutis.

Skin cancer   A tumor of the skin. Skin cancer is the most common and most curable malignancy.

There has been a dramatic increase in the number of cases of skin cancer in recent years, thought due to overexposure to the sun and other ultraviolet rays (such as in tanning booths). People who are susceptible to sunburn should use sun blocking creams whenever they are exposed to strong sunlight. Treatment depends on the location and extent of the tumor; it may involve surgery, radiotherapy and/or chemotherapy. *See also* **Melanoma.**

Skin graft   A portion of skin cut and removed from one area of the body and used to cover a part that has lost its skin, due to burns, injury, or other cause. A skin graft is usually taken from another part of the body of the same person (autograft), but sometimes from another person (homograft) as a temporary measure.

Skull   The bony skeleton of the head, consisting of the cranium, made up of 8 bones that contain and protect the brain; and the facial skeleton, consisting of 14 bones.

Slipped disc   *See* **Herniated disc.**

Small intestine   The longest part of the digestive tract, about 24 feet (7 meters), extending from the pylorus of the stomach to the ileocecal junction. It is divided into the duodenum, jejunum, and ileum; it is a major site of food digestion and absorption of nutrients.

Smallpox   A highly contagious viral disease characterized by fever, weakness, and a pustular rash. The disease was once widespread, but since 1979 has been abated throughout the world as a result of vaccination programs. Also called variola.

Socialization   The process by which a person learns to adapt to and be productive within the expectations and standards of a group or society.

Sodium bicarbonate   An antacid used in the treatment of indigestion and gastric acidity. Adverse effects include electrolyte imbalance.

Spasm   Sudden, involuntary muscle contraction; a sudden constriction of a blood vessel or other hollow organ.

Specimen   A small sample of something; a part of a whole intended upon analysis to reveal characteristics of the whole (for example, a urine specimen used for urinalysis).

Sperm   *See* **Spermatozoon.**

Spermatocide   A chemical that kills sperm; found in many contraceptive creams, jellies, and foams. Also called spermicide.

Spermatozoon   The male sex cell that fertilizes an ovum. It develops in the seminiferous tubules of the testis. Tadpolelike, it is tiny (about 1/500 inch) with a head, neck, and tail.

Sperm count   Estimate of the number of spermatozoa in an ejaculate; used as an indication of male fertility. An ejaculate normally contains between 300,000,000 and 500,000,000 spermatozoa; significantly lower numbers usually indicate sterility.

Sphincter   A circular band of muscle that constricts or closes an opening in the body, as the pyloric sphincter, separating the lower part of the stomach from the duodenum.

Spina bifida   A relatively common congenital defect in which there is a malformation of the posterior portion of a vertebra; unless the defect affects a large area or spinal cord material protrudes, there are few or no symptoms. The condition can be diagnosed by amniocentesis at about the 16th week of pregnancy.

Spinal column   *See* **Vertebral column.**

Spinal cord   A major part of the central nervous system that conducts sensory and motor impulses to and from the brain and is a site of reflex activity. It is a cylindrical tube, extending from the base of the brain through the vertebral canal to the upper part of the lumbar region. It has an inner core of gray matter, containing mostly nerve cells, surrounded by white matter with nerve fibers. The entire cord is surrounded by meninges (protective membranes). From it arise 31 spinal nerves.

Spinal curvature   Abnormality in curvature of the vertebral column. *See* **Kyphosis; Lordosis; Scoliosis.**

Spleen   Large, dark-red, oval organ situated on the left side of the body between the diaphragm and stomach. It is part of the lymphatic and reticuloendothelial systems, functioning to destroy worn out erythrocytes and platelets, to produce leukocytes, lymphocytes, and other cells involved in immune responses; it also stores blood and produces red blood cells before birth.

Sprain   An injury to ligaments around a joint, causing pain, swelling, and skin discoloration. The severity of symptoms and degree of immobility depend on the site of injury and extent of damage of tissues. Treatment includes support, rest, and cold compresses at the time of injury.

Staphylococcal infection   Infection with pathogenic species of *Staphylococcus* bacteria; usually characterized by abscess formation. Common staphylococcal infections include carbuncles, furuncles, and some forms of food poisoning.

Sterility   (1) pertaining to a living organism: state of being unable to reproduce; (2) pertaining to a nonliving object: state of being free from disease-causing microorganisms.

Sterilization   (1) A surgical procedure in which a woman or man is rendered incapable of reproducing; in males the procedure is a vasectomy; in females, a form of tubal ligation. (2) a means of rendering objects free of microorganisms that may produce disease by boiling, subjecting to steam in an autoclave, or by use of disinfectants and antiseptics.

Stillbirth   Birth of a fetus that shows no signs of life (for example, respiration, heartbeat, or movement).

Stimulant   An agent, such as a drug, that activates or increases the activity of a body part or system. Amphetamines and caffeine are central nervous system stimulants.

Stomach   An expandible, sac-like organ that forms part of the digestive tract between the esophagus and the duodenum. It is located below the diaphragm in the right upper part of the abdomen, partly under the liver. The stomach receives partly digested food from the esophagus through the cardiac sphincter. In the stomach the food is churned by muscular layers of the stomach and mixed with the secretions of the gastric glands, chiefly hydrochloric acid and the enzyme pepsin. The semiliquid mass then passes through the pyloric sphincter to the duodenum.

Stone   A hard mass. *See* **Gallstone; Urinary calculus.**

Stool Feces.

Strep throat Streptococcal infection of the oral pharynx and tonsils, producing fever, sore throat, chills, lymph node enlargement, and occasionally gastrointestinal disturbances. Treatment is by antibiotics, usually penicillin or erythromycin, and analgesics. Complications include sinusitis, ear infection, or, if inadequately treated, rheumatic fever.

Streptococcus A genus of bacteria, many species of which produce disease in humans, including tonsillitis, pneumonia, and urinary tract infections. Some strains of *Streptococcus* bacteria have become resistant to penicillin.

Streptomycin An antibiotic used to treat tuberculosis and many other bacterial infections. Adverse effects include ear and kidney damage.

Stress Any factor—physical (for example, infection), emotional (for example, anxiety), or other—that requires a change in response or affects health in any way, especially, having an adverse effect on the functioning of the body or any of its parts. Continual stress brings about widespread neurological and endocrine responses that over a period of time lead to changes in the functioning of many body organs, often leading to disease (for example, hypertension and allergic responses).

Stress test Test that measures the function of a system when it is subjected to controlled amounts of stress. For example, the treadmill test measures the effect of stress on cardiovascular and respiratory function; the fetal stress test measures the adequacy of fetal-placental function and the condition of the fetus.

Stricture Narrowing of any tubular structure (for example, esophagus, ureter) caused by inflammation, the presence of a tumor, pressure from an adjacent organ, or muscle spasm.

Stroke *See* **Cerebrovascular Accident**.

Stye Bacterial (often staphylococcal) infection of a gland at the base of an eyelash, characterized by a pus-filled cyst, redness, pain, and other signs of inflammation; also: sty.

Styptic A substance used as an astringent, often to control bleeding.

Subcutaneous Beneath the skin, as in a subcutaneous injection.

Sudden Infant Death Syndrome (SIDS) Unexpected and sudden death of an apparently healthy infant during sleep with no autopsy evidence of disease. It is the leading cause of death in infants between 2 weeks and 1 year of age. The cause is unknown, but certain risk factors have been identified: prematurity; low birth weight; male sex; winter months; mothers who are very young, smoke, or are addicted to a drug; and recent mild upper respiratory infection. Also called crib death.

Superego In psychoanalysis, part of the psyche that functions as a conscience and for the formation of ideals; it forms as parental and societal standards are incorporated into a child's mind.

Suppository A mass of material that melts when placed in the vagina, urethra, or rectum; it can be used to deliver drugs, especially in babies or those with vomiting conditions.

Suture (1) A natural seam or border in the skull formed by the close joining of bony surfaces; (2) material (for example, silk, catgut, wire) used for surgical stitches; (3) to stitch torn or cut edges together with suture material.

Symptom A subjective indication of a disease (for example, a feeling of nausea); it may or may not be accompanied by an objective sign (for example, vomiting).

Syndrome A complex of signs and symptoms presenting a clinical picture of a disease or disorder.

Syphilis A sexually transmitted disease caused by the *Treponema pallidum* spirochete; it is transmitted by sexual contact or through the placenta (congenital syphilis). Symptoms occur in stages; primary stage: chancre filled with spirochetes, most often in anal or genital region, but can occur elsewhere; secondary stage: malaise, nausea, vomiting, fever, bone and joint pain, rash, and mouth sores; third stage: soft tumors, called gummas, that ulcerate and then heal, leaving scars; they may form anywhere in the body and may or may not be painful. Various parts of the body, including the heart, nervous system, and lungs, may be damaged, leading to death. These three stages occur over a prolonged period, often stretching 15 or more years before the third stage takes hold. As a result of congenital syphilis, a child may be born blind or deformed. Treatment is by penicillin, often in very large doses for a prolonged period.

Systole The contraction of the heart, especially of the ventricles, driving blood into the aorta and pulmonary artery.

Tachycardia Abnormally rapid heart rate—in an adult over 100 beats per minute. Heart rate normally increases in response to fear and excitement and also in conditions where there is lack of oxygen, as in congestive heart failure, hemorrhage, or shock.

Tapeworm infection Intestinal infection caused by a species of parasitic tapeworm, usually caused by eating raw or undercooked meat or fish that is an intermediate host to the tapeworm or its larva. Symptoms include diarrhea and weight loss; diagnosis is made when worms and eggs are found in the stool.

Tartar Hard deposit that forms on the teeth and gums.

Tay-Sachs disease An inherited disease (autosomal recessive disease) characterized by progressive mental and physical degeneration and early death. It is caused by a lack of the enzyme hexosaminidase, which results in an accumulation of sphingolipids in the brain. The disease occurs almost exclusively among Ashkenazic and Sephardic Jews. Symptoms appear by age 6 months, after which there is progressive degeneration with blindness, the development of a cherry red spot on the retina, spasticity, dementia, and death before the age of 4. There is no treatment. The disease can be diagnosed prenatally through amniocentesis.

T cell A small, circulating lymphocyte that matures in the thymus and is the chief agent of cell-mediated immunity, involved particularly in transplant rejection and delayed allergic reactions.

Tear duct A duct, such as the lacrimal duct or the nasolacrimal duct, that transports tears.

Teething Physiological process of the eruption of deciduous (baby) teeth through the gums, usually extending from 4 to 6 months to about 30 months when all 20 milk teeth have appeared. Discomfort in the gum area may occur, and symptoms of drooling, biting of hard objects, and irritability are common.

Telepathy The supposed ability of one person to know the thoughts of another; the communication of thought from one person to another by nonphysical means.

Temperature In humans and other animals, a measure of the heat associated with the metabolism of the body. Normal human temperature taken orally is considered to be 98.6° Fahrenheit (37° Celsius), but it may vary from person to person, and even in the same person, depending on the time of day and level of activity.

Temple Region of the head in front of and above each ear.

Tendon One of many whitish, glistening fibrous bands of tissue that connect muscle to bone; tendons are inelastic and strong and occur in various thicknesses and lengths. *Compare* **Ligament**.

Tennis elbow Painful inflammation on the tendon at the outer border of the elbow, caused by overuse of lower arm muscles. Treatment is by rest, anti-inflammatory medications, and, if necessary, corticosteroid injections.

Tension headache Pain, chiefly at the back of the head and often spreading forward, occurring as a result of tensing the body as a response to overwork, strong emotion, or psychological stress.

Testicular cancer Malignant neoplasm of the testes, occurring most often in men between the ages of 20 and 35, often affecting an undescended testis and more frequently the right testis. In its early stages testicular cancer is often asymptomatic, and it may metastasize, later causing urinary and pulmonary symptoms and an abdominal mass. Treatment depends on the nature of the tumor and includes surgery (orchidectomy), radiation and/or chemotherapy.

Testis Either of a pair of male gonads, or sex glands, that produces sperm and secretes androgens. The adult testes, each about 1½ inches (4 centimeters) long and oval-shaped, are suspended in the scrotum below the abdomen. Each testis consists of many hundred seminiferous tubules where sperm develop. The sperm pass from there through efferent ducts to the epididymis, after which they pass into the vas deferens for movement toward the penis. Also called testicle.

Testosterone A male sex hormone, produced chiefly in the testes, but also in small amounts in the adrenal glands and in the ovaries of women. It is responsible for the development of male secondary sex characteristics (for example, deep voice and facial hair). Preparations of testosterone are used in the treatment of deficiency conditions, breast cancer in women, and certain other conditions. Adverse effects of the use of these preparations include fluid retention, masculinization in women, and acne.

Test-tube baby A baby born as a result of fertilization occurring outside the woman's body. Ova

are removed from a woman's body (usually using a laparoscope) and mixed with sperm in a culture medium. If fertilization occurs, the fertilized egg is then implanted in the woman's uterus and pregnancy continues.

Tetanus An acute and serious infection of the central nervous system caused by a toxin produced by the *Clostridium tetani* bacterium. The bacterium, common in the soil, especially in farm areas, infects wounds with dead tissue, as in a puncture wound, laceration, or burn. Symptoms include fever, headache, irritability, and painful spasms of the muscles, causing lockjaw and laryngeal spasm, and, if untreated, leading to muscle spasm of virtually every organ. Prompt and thorough cleaning of wounds is important to prevent the disease. Treatment of the disease includes use of tetanus toxoid and antibiotics, maintenance of an airway if laryngeal spasm occurs, control of muscle spasms, and sedation. Also called lockjaw.

Tetrahydrocannabinol (THC) The active principle in hemp-plant derivatives such as marijuana and hashish. Considered a mild hallucinogen, THC causes sensory and perceptual disturbances, euphoria and other mood changes, decreased motor coordination, and various physiological changes, including alterations in pulse rate, respiration rate, and pupil size. THC is a drug of abuse but has also been used to relieve the nausea and vomiting associated with chemothereapy for cancer.

Thorax The bone and cartilage cage, formed in the front by the sternum and rib cartilage and in the back by the thoracic vertebrae and dorsal parts of the ribs, that encloses the lungs, heart, esophagus, and other structures. Also called chest.

Thrombolytic therapy Administration of a drug with the intention of causing dissolution of an abnormal blood clot, such as in the coronary (myocardial infarction) or pulmonary (pulmonary embolism) arteries. Available agents include streptokinase, urokinase, tissue plasminogen activator (TPA), and APSAC (a derivative of streptokinase). These preparations may be given either by intravenous injection or directly into the blocked artery. In suitable candidates with acute myocardial infarction, these agents are considered first-line therapy.

Thrombosis A condition in which a blood clot (thrombus) forms within a blood vessel. Thrombosis in an artery supplying the brain results in a stroke (cerebrovascular accident); in an artery supplying the heart in a myocardial infarction; in veins thrombophlebitis. A thrombus may also move from its site of origin. *See* **Embolism**.

Thyroid gland A large endocrine gland situated at the base of the neck. It consists of two lobes, one on each side of the trachea, connected by an isthmus. Under the influence of thyroid-stimulating hormone (TSH) released from the anterior pituitary gland, the thyroid secretes the hormone thyroxin into the bloodstream; it is essential for normal growth and development in children and normal metabolic rates in adults. Disorders of the thyroid include goiter, myxedema, and cretinism.

Tic A repeated, largely involuntary, spasm or twitch. *See* Psychology, page 21-27.

Tick   A blood-sucking parasite, some species of which cause diseases in humans, including Lyme arthritis, Rocky Mountain spotted fever, and tularemia. *See* **Lyme disease**.

Tine test   A tuberculin skin test in which a disc bearing tuberculin antigen is used to puncture the skin. The development of hardened skin around the area indicates active disease or previous exposure and the need for further testing.

Tissue   A collection of cells specialized to perform a particular function. The cells may be all of the same type (for example, in nervous tissue) or of different types (for example, in connective tissue). An aggregate of tissues with a specific function is an organ.

Tonsillitis   Inflammation or infection of a tonsil. Acute tonsillitis, often caused by bacterial, especially streptococcal, infection, produces sore throat, fever, headache, enlarged lymph glands in the neck region, and difficulty in swallowing. Treatment is by rest, fluids, and antibiotics. Surgery (tonsillectomy) is sometimes performed to prevent recurrent streptococcal attacks.

Tourniquet   A device, as a tight bandage or rubber tube, pressed on an artery to stop the flow of blood in a hemorrhage; used only when other measures cannot be used or have not succeeded.

Toxic   (1) Pertaining to a poison; (2) pertaining to a disease that is progressive; (3) harmful.

Toxic shock syndrome (TSS)   A serious acute infection caused by toxins elaborated by certain strains of *Staphylococcus aureus*; it most often occurs in menstruating women using high-absorbency tampons but also occasionally occurs in nonmenstruating women, men, and children. Onset is sudden with fever, headache, reddish skin, sore throat, and gastrointestinal disturbances; low blood pressure and renal and liver abnormalities may follow, leading to death.

Trait   A characteristic, especially an inherited characteristic.

Tranquilizer   A drug that produces a calming effect, lessening anxiety and tension. Most tranquilizers induce drowsiness and can cause dependence.

   Major tranquilizer—a drug, usually a derivative of phenothiazine or butyrophenone, used to treat psychotic conditions in which a calming effect is desired. *See also* Psychology, page 21-27.

   Minor tranquilizer—any of several drugs, including diazepam (Valium) and chlordiazepoxide (Librium), used to relieve anxiety, tension, and irritability; many also reduce skeletal muscle spasm.

Transfusion   The introduction of whole blood or components of blood (for example, plasma, platelets, or packed erythrocytes) from one person (the donor) or from pooled material into the bloodstream of another (the recipient). Donor and recipient blood must be compatible.

Transplant   (1) To transfer an organ or tissue from one person (the donor) to another (the recipient) or from one body part to another to replace a diseased organ or to restore normal function. The organs most commonly transplanted are the skin and kidneys; corneal, bone, cartilage, and vessel transplants also occur, and, rarely, heart and liver transplants. The major problem with donor-recipient transplants is the tendency of the recipient's body to reject the transplanted tissue as foreign; donor and recipient are carefully matched by blood typing and tissue typing procedures (the best donors are identical twins) to minimize the chances of rejection. (2) Any organ or tissue transferred from one person to another or from one part of the body to another part.

Trauma   (1) Physical injury caused by accident, violence, or disruptive action (for example, a fracture); (2) severe emotional shock.

Trench mouth   Infection of the mouth and gums marked by ulcers on the mucous membranes; it often occurs as a secondary infection in malnourished or debilitated people. Treatment depends on the cause, the primary illness, and health of the person.

Trichinosis   Infestation with the parasitic roundworm *Trichinella spiralis*, transmitted by eating undercooked meat, especially pork. Symptoms vary greatly in severity and include nausea, diarrhea, abdominal pain, and fever, sometimes progressing to muscle pain, tenderness, and stiffness as the roundworm larvae migrate from the intestinal tract to the muscles, where they become encysted. There is no specific cure; treatment is aimed at alleviating symptoms. Once all the larvae become encysted completely, symptoms usually disappear.

Trimester   One of the three periods, each of approximately three months, into which pregnancy is divided.

Tubal ligation   A sterilization procedure in which both Fallopian tubes are ligated (tied) in two places and the intervening space removed or crushed so that the tube is effectively blocked and conception cannot occur. It is a common method of contraception.

Tubal pregnancy   A type of ectopic pregnancy in which the conceptus implants in the Fallopian tube; it is the most common type of ectopic pregnancy (about 90%), with prior injury to the tube and pelvic infection predisposing factors. Symptoms occur as the embryo grows and ruptures the tube and include sudden sharp pain on one side of the abdomen and bleeding, but diagnosis is often difficult. Treatment is removal of the products of conception and removal or repair of the ruptured tube.

Tuberculin test   A test to determine past or present infection or exposure to tuberculosis based on a skin reaction to the injection, scratching, or puncturing of the skin with tuberculin, a purified protein derivative of the tuberculosis bacterium.

Tuberculosis   A chronic infection with *Mycobacterium tuberculosis*, transmitted by inhalation or ingestion of droplets; it usually affects the lungs but may also affect other organs. Early symptoms include fever, loss of appetite, fatigue, and vague chest pain; later, night sweats, difficulty in breathing, production of purulent sputum, and signs of severe lung involvement occur. Treatment is by antituberculosis drugs (for example, isoniazid) and antibiotics, rest, and proper nutrition. There has been a significant increase in tuberculosis cases in recent years. Many of these new cases are caused by organisms that are resistant to standard therapy. For this reason, physicians are using combinations of standard drugs, as well as experimental agents, to control the disease.

Tumor   A growth of tissue, characterized by uncontrolled cell proliferation. A tumor may be benign or malignant; localized or invasive. Also called neoplasm.

Tunnel vision Condition in which peripheral sight is diminished and vision is limited to that area in front of the eyes.

Ulcer A circumscribed lesion of the skin or mucous membrane of an organ formed by the necrosis of tissue resulting from an infectious, malignant, or inflammatory process. Some types of ulcers are decubitus ulcers (bedsores) and peptic ulcers.

Ultrasonography A process by which the reflection of high-frequency sound waves is used to develop an image (sonogram) of a structure; used in medicine to study fetal growth and detect abnormalities, and to study the heart and many other organs.

Ultrasound Sound waves at very high frequencies, used in the technique of ultrasonography to aid diagnosis. *See also* **Ultrasonography**.

Umbilical cord Flexible cordlike structure that connects the fetus to the placenta during pregnancy. It contains arteries that carry blood to the placenta and a vein that returns blood to the fetus and the remains of the yolk sac and allantois. In the newborn it is usually about 24 inches (60 centimeters) long.

Unconscious Unaware of one's surroundings; unable to respond to sensory stimuli.

Urethra A small, tubular structure that drains urine from the bladder, passing it to the outside. In women it is very short, located behind the pubis between the clitoris and the vaginal opening; in men it is much longer, passing from the bladder through the prostate gland into the penis, and serving as the passageway for semen during ejaculation.

Urethritis Inflammation of the urethra, usually with symptoms of painful urination. It is most commonly caused by bladder or kidney infection and is treated with antibacterials and pain relievers.

Urinalysis Analysis of urine by physical, chemical, or microscopic means to reveal color, turbidity, pH, and the possible presence of microorganisms, blood, pus, or crystals, or abnormal levels of ketones, proteins, sugar, and other compounds. Urinalysis is an important aid in diagnosing urinary system disorders, metabolic disorders, and other conditions.

Urinary calculus A stone formed in any part of the urinary system (kidney, ureter, bladder); some are small enough to pass in the urine, with or without pain; others must be removed surgically.

Urinary tract infection Any infection of the organs of the urinary system; it is more common in women than in men and is most often caused by bacteria. Symptoms include frequency, burning pain on urination, and sometimes blood or pus in the urine. Treatment is by antibacterials and pain-relievers. Types of urinary tract infections are cystitis, urethritis, and pyelonephritis.

Uterus That part of the female reproductive system specialized to allow the implantation, growth, and nourishment of a fetus during pregnancy. The nonpregnant uterus is a hollow, pear-shaped organ, about 3 inches (7.5 centimeters) long, suspended in the pelvic cavity by ligaments. Its upper end is connected to the Fallopian tubes; its lower end narrows into a neck, or cervix, that opens into the vagina. The uterus has an inner mucous layer, the en-

dometrium, which undergoes cyclic changes during the menstrual cycle and helps form the placenta in pregnancy; a muscular layer, the myometrium, contractions of which expel a child during labor and childbirth; and an outer connective tissue, parametrium, that extends into the broad ligament.

Vaccination The introduction of attenuated (weakened) or killed viruses or microorganisms (or occasionally of substances extracted from these agents) into the body to induce immunity by causing the production of specific antibodies. Vaccination has abated smallpox throughout the world; has decreased the incidence of poliomyelitis and diphtheria to very low levels in North America and Europe; and is also available against other diseases, including measles and mumps.

Vaccine A preparation of attenuated or killed disease-producing viruses or microorganisms (or of substances extracted from them) administered orally or by injection to induce active immunity to a specific disease.

Vagina A muscular tube lined with mucous membrane that forms the lower part of the female reproductive tract, situated behind the bladder and in front of the rectum and extending from the vaginal opening to the cervix of the uterus. It receives the penis during coitus, ejaculation of semen usually occurring in the upper vagina, from where the sperm move upward to fertilize an ovum. The vagina is normally sufficiently elastic to allow the passage of a child.

Vaginitis Inflammation of the vagina, often producing pain, itchiness, burning on urination, and increased, sometimes foul-smelling discharge. It may be caused by infection (for example, candidiasis), poor hygiene, dietary deficiency, or local irritation (for example, from a contraceptive). Treatment depends on the cause.

Valve A structure, usually a flap or fold of tissue, found in some tubes and tubular organs that restricts the flow of fluid in them to one direction only. Valves are important structures in the heart, veins, and lymph vessels.

Varicose vein A swollen, tortuous vein with abnormally functioning valves. It is a common condition, usually affecting the veins of the legs; it is more common in women than men and often associated with congenitally weak valves, pregnancy, obesity, or thrombophlebitis. Symptoms include pain, muscle cramps, and a feeling of heaviness in the legs. Elevation of the legs and the use of elastic stockings often help. Severe cases may require surgical intervention.

Vasectomy A surgical procedure to render a male sterile by severing the vas deferens. Potency is not affected.

Vein Any of many vessels that carry blood to the heart; it may be part of the pulmonary venous system, portal system, or (most veins) the systemic venous system. All veins except the pulmonary vein carry deoxygenated blood from the tissues of the body to the vena cava and heart. The walls of veins are thinner and less elastic than the walls of arteries and contain valves that maintain the flow of blood toward the heart.

Vena cava Either of two large veins returning deoxygenated blood from the peripheral circulation to the right atrium of the heart.

Venereal disease (VD) *See* **Sexually Transmitted Disease**.

Venom A toxic fluid secreted by some snakes and other animals, including certain fish and insects, and transmitted in their bites or stings. Some venoms produce local irritation and swelling at the site of the bite or sting; others produce systemic, sometimes fatal, effects, usually focused on the circulatory or nervous system.

Ventricle (1) Either of the two lower chambers of the heart. The left ventricle receives oxygenated blood from the pulmonary vein through the left atrium and pumps it to the aorta from which it passes throughout the body. The thinner-walled right ventricle receives deoxygenated blood from the venae cavae through the right atrium and pumps it through the pulmonary artery to the lung for the exchange of gases; (2) any of four fluid-filled cavities in the brain containing cerebrospinal fluid.

Ventricular fibrillation A serious disturbance in cardiac rhythm, characterized by disorganized impulse conduction and ventricular contraction. Unconsciousness occurs and death may follow within minutes if defibrillation and other life-saving measures are not immediately provided.

Vertebra Any of the 33 bones of the spinal column (vertebral column, or backbone), including 7 cervical (neck region), 12 thoracic (chest region), 5 lumbar, 5 sacral (fused), and 4 coccygeal (fused). Except for the first two—the atlas and axis—each vertebra consists of a centrum, or body, from which the neural arch, enclosing a cavity through which the spinal cord passes, and processes for the attachment of muscles arise. The vertebrae are connected by ligaments and separated by intervertebral discs, which cushion adjacent vertebrae.

Vertebral column The firm, flexible, bony column that is the longitudinal axis and chief supporting structure of the human body, extending from the base of the skull to the coccyx (tailbone). It consists of 26 separate bony parts: 7 cervical vertebrae, 12 thoracic vertebrae, 5 lumbar vertebrae, a sacrum (composed of 5 fused sacral vertebrae), and a coccyx (composed of 4 fused coccygeal vertebrae). The vertebrae, which serve for the attachment of muscles, are separated by intervertebral discs. The vertebral column normally has several curves, most visible from a lateral view: a cervical curve, convex ventrally; a thoracic curve, concave ventrally; a lumbar curve, convex ventrally; and a pelvic curve, concave ventrally.

Viral hepatitis A form of hepatitis, inflammation of the liver, caused by one of the hepatitis viruses. Symptoms include anorexia, headache, fever, pain in the region of the liver, malaise, jaundice, and diarrhea with the stools clay-colored. Treatment includes rest, the avoidance of fatigue, and a low-fat, high-protein diet; the person is usually advised to abstain from alcohol for a year after the attack. Severe infection, especially with hepatitis B, can cause permanent damage to liver tissue and result in hepatic coma and death.

Viral pneumonia Infection of the lung or lungs caused by a virus. *See* **Pneumonia**.

Virus A small particle that is not living and does not exhibit signs of life but which can reproduce itself within a living cell. A virus particle is called a virion; it consists of a nucleic acid (DNA or RNA) core and a protein coat, called a capsid. A virus reproduces by infecting a host cell, and taking over the nucleic acid of that host cell, making more virus nucleic acid and protein. As new virus particles develop, the host cell bursts, releasing the new virus particles. Viruses are responsible for many human diseases.

Vitamin Any of a group of organic compounds that in very small amounts are esssential for normal growth, development, and metabolism. They cannot be synthesized in the body (with a few exceptions) and must be supplied by the diet. Lack of sufficient quantities of any of the vitamins produces a specific deficiency disease. Vitamins are generally classified as water-soluble or fat-soluble. The water-soluble vitamins are vitamin B complex and vitamin C; the fat-soluble vitamins are vitamins A, D, E, and K.

Viviparous Bearing live offspring, not eggs; characteristic of most mammals and also of some fishes and reptiles.

Vocal cord Either of two folds of tissue, each containing an elastic tissue known as the vocal ligament, that protrudes from the sides of the larynx forming a narrow slit in the larynx, called the glottis. As air is exhaled through the larynx the vocal cords vibrate, producing sound. Movements of the tongue, lips, jaws, and accessory mouth structures mold the column of air passing through the glottis, producing sounds of different intensity and pitch.

Voice box *See* **Larynx**.

 **Wart** A small benign, often hard, growth in the skin, caused by a virus, and more common in children and young adults. Warts frequently disappear spontaneously but may be treated by cryosurgery (usually using liquid nitrogen), electrodesiccation, application of certain chemicals (for example, salicylic acid), and removal by curette. Also called verruca.

Wheeze An abnormal, high-pitched sound heard through a stethoscope in an airway blocked by mucus, tumor, muscle spasm, or pressure. It occurs in asthma, in chronic bronchitis, and unilaterally in the presence of a foreign body or growth in the airway.

White blood cell *See* **Leukocyte**.

Whole blood Blood that has not been modified or altered, except for the addition of an anticoagulant; used in blood transfusions. Various components of whole blood may be separated out and used to replace a missing or deficient factor in the blood of persons with certain diseases (for example, certain clotting factors, separated out and given to hemophiliacs.

Wisdom tooth Any of the last four teeth on each side of the upper and lower jaws. They are the last teeth to erupt, usually between the ages of 16 and 21, and often cause pain and dental problems.

 **Xeroradiography** A photoelectric process for producing an X-ray image that uses lower radiation and shorter exposure time than conventional X-ray techniques; it is used chiefly to detect breast tumors.

HISTORY OF TECHNOLOGY

Introduction

Technology refers to the ways in which people use discoveries to satisfy needs and desires and to alter the environment to improve their lives. From the very beginning of human life on earth, people have had to work to obtain food, clothing, and shelter. Throughout human history, men and women have invented tools, machines, materials, and techniques to make their work easier. They also discovered power sources such as water power and electricity to increase their work rate. Technology, therefore, involves the use of tools, machines, techniques, and sources of power to make work easier and more productive. It is the human activity that changes the material world to satisfy human needs. As such, technology comprises the vast body of knowledge and devices by which humans have progressively mastered their natural environment over the centuries.

Of course, when we speak of technology today we are looking at it in a much narrower sense. Generally, we are referring to industrial technology, or the technology that began about 200 years ago with the development of power-driven machines, growth of the factory system, and mass production of goods and that created the basis for our modern society. Today we often say that we live in an age of technology meaning that the pace of invention and change has increased with amazing rapidity. In fact, the rate of change in science and technology has become so increasingly swift that according to one estimate, 90 percent of all the scientists who had ever lived were alive and active in the 1970s. This increased scientific activity has brought new ideas, processes, and inventions in an ever-growing amount.

This brings us to another characteristic of modern technology, its relationship to science. Today, science and technology are closely related. Many modern technologies such as nuclear power and space flight depend on science and the applications of scientific knowledge and principles. Each advance in pure science creates new opportunities for the development of new designs and ways of making things to be used in daily life, and in turn, technology provides science with new and more accurate instruments for its investigations and research. This has been a recent phenomenon, however, with its beginnings in the 16th century. Before then, science and technology were separate fields with separate identities. Science involved the ideas and investigations of philosophers who sought knowledge of the natural and physical world. Technology was carried on by craftspeople who could not make use of the speculations of scientists in solving technological problems such as the milling of wheat or the tanning of leather.

The scientific revolution that began in the 16th century was the first time that science and technology began to work together. Thus, Galileo, who made revolutionary discoveries in astronomy and physics, also built an improved telescope and patented a system of lifting water. Francis Bacon favored experimental science and suggested that scientists learn the methods of craftspeople while craftspeople learn more about science. Bacon, Descartes, and other scientists envisioned a time when humans could master the environment. Ever since, science and technology have

grown closer together. However, it was not until the 19th century that technology truly was based on science and inventors began to build on the work of scientists. For example, Thomas Edison built on the early experiments of Faraday and Henry in his invention of the first practical system of electrical lighting. So too, Edison carried on his investigations until he found the carbon filament for the electric light bulb in a research laboratory he started in Menlo Park, New Jersey. This was the first true modern technological research.

It is generally agreed that 'Man is a toolmaking animal.' In a sense the history of technology is the history of "man," or all humankind. One of the major determining characteristics of human behavior is the fashioning of tools. This is a pattern of innovation requiring thought rather than a pattern of instinctive behavior characteristic of other animal species. It is this ability to apply technological methods that separates humans from animals. Humans have technology, while other animals do not. Since toolmaking is an important aspect of human nature, the history of technology is the history of humans. Thus, we must begin our investigation of technology at the very beginning of human history.

Stone Age Technology
(to ca. 3000 B.C.)

Until about 10,000 years ago, humans lived in small communities, wandering from place to place to obtain food by hunting, fishing, and gathering nuts, berries, and plants. Then, some human communities began to lead a more settled life as they learned to farm and domesticate animals. This period of transition from the Paleolithic, or Old Stone Age, to agriculture and settled communities is called the Neolithic, or New Stone Age. It is also known as the Neolithic Revolution because of the great increase in technology and the great changes in the social and political organization of humans. It was these changes that in time led to the rise of civilization around 3000 B.C. Let us look at the beginnings of human technology in the Old Stone Age and the important developments that occurred in the New Stone Age that helped make it possible for the first civilizations to arise.

Tools

This period of prehistory is called the Stone Age because humans made tools of stone. They turned stones into tools by shaping them to serve specific purposes and to carry out special tasks. Early people's tools were sharp, jagged-edged rocks used for cutting, scraping, and chopping. They made them by flaking and polishing hard, fine-grained stones such as flint, sandstone, and volcanic rock. These early tools were made by striking a small rock with another rock, chipping away pieces of the tool to make a sharp edge. Over the many centuries of existence, humans made important advances in technique in the use of stone. At first, tools were simple hand-held stones, but in time, they became more complex until eventually wooden handles were added. Over the centuries, as humans improved their stone-working techniques, they created many kinds of tools and weapons using pointed-flaked stones. Among them were the stone-headed spear, the harpoon, and the arrow. Further evidence of their great ingenuity in creating tools and weapons is shown in the development of slings, throwing sticks, blowguns, bird snares, fish and animal traps, and nets, as well as fishhooks, and harpoons made of bone. These tools, however, were all devised to help humans hunt and to gather food.

The Neolithic Revolution brought faster developments in technology as humans began to settle down and discovered agriculture. Prehistoric farmers who lived in the New Stone Age developed many new tools to make their work easier. These tools included sickles to cut grain, grinding stones to grind grain into flour, and axlike tools called celts. Sometime before 3000 B.C., farmers invented a wooden plow that could be pulled by oxen. It enabled them to turn over more soil than they could by using their older hand plows. Irrigation techniques also became established in the river valleys of Egypt and Mesopotamia. Irrigation ditches and canals were dug and in Egypt a crude lift called a shadoof, which consisted of a leather bucket, was used to raise water from the Nile to the valley above.

In the Neolithic Period, humans began to use new substances such as clay and brick to improve their lives. They learned to make pottery which enabled them to boil and store water more easily than the animal skins or bark containers used in earlier times. Building techniques also became more developed, evidence of which are the tombs, burial mounds, and religious structures, of which many were built of sun-dried brick. This material also began to be used in building dwellings. Neolithic people also began to make fabrics from plant fibers, which took the place of animal skins. Important new tools not concerned with farming were developed including the potter's wheel, bow drill, pole lathe, and the wheel itself. Finally, manufacturing developed in this period as people used the techniques for grinding corn, baking clay into pottery, and spinning and weaving textiles. Other processes such as dyeing, fermenting, and distilling were also employed. Many of these were developing into specialized crafts by the time the first civilizations appeared. So too, metal workers were beginning to learn techniques for extracting and working softer metals such as gold, silver, copper, and tin.

Sources of Power and Transportation

An important development of the Old Stone Age was the use of fire by humans. This was the first power source available to humans although it was only used to cook foods and as a defense against wild animals. Human muscle power remained the primary source of power until the New Stone Age when humans began to make use of domesticated animals such as the ox and donkey as sources of power.

Important improvements were made in transportation and communication in the New Stone Age. Paleolithic people traveled on foot and carried their belongings strapped to their backs. Eventually, they learned to make sledges from logs, poles, and rawhide which they used to drag heavy loads. In later times, they built sledges with runners that slid more easily along the ground. With the development of agriculture and permanent settlements, trade began to grow. The need for better transportation led Neolithic people to use the donkey and ox which had been domesti-

cated for farm work as pack animals. Then, harnesses were invented so that the animals could be used to pull sledges.

Water transportation also developed in the Old Stone Age as humans built rafts of logs or reeds. In later times, they learned to fashion dugouts and canoes that were propelled by paddles or poles. By the end of the Neolithic Period, the sail which harnessed wind to power small boats had appeared. It is thought that the Egyptians invented sailboats in about 3200 B.C. These early ships were simple vessels with a small sail rigged in the bow and could sail only before the prevailing wind. They had fixed sails which were of use only when the wind was blowing in the direction the ship wanted to go. With the invention of the wheel in the New Stone Age around 3500 B.C., most likely in Mesopotamia, the first wheeled vehicles appeared.

The First Civilizations
(ca. 3000–500 B.C.)

It must be remembered that these developments took place over thousands of years of human development of which we have no written record and that they occurred first in only small areas in the world. The Neolithic Revolution began in four great river valleys that exhibited certain characteristics, namely, a warm climate and an annual flood of the river that left fertile soil. These were the river valleys of the Nile in Egypt, the Tigris and Euphrates in Mesopotamia, the Hwang in China, and the Indus in India. Here, men and women in the New Stone Age first developed agriculture, domesticated animals, developed irrigation techniques, and began manufacturing. Their increased food supply led to population growth and resulted in a momentous series of social and political changes that gave rise to the first civilizations.

The technological changes discussed above occurred very slowly over a long period and were in response to only the most basic human needs, the need for food and shelter. However, about 5,000 years ago in the four river valleys, a cultural transformation took place that created new needs and resources and led to a great increase in technological innovation. This was the creation of the first cities.

Craftspeople, Merchants, and Transportation

Around 3500 B.C. some farm villages developed into cities. This probably occurred first in the Tigris-Euphrates Valley in the lower part of Mesopotamia (what is today Iraq). Cities developed in the Nile Valley about 3000 B.C., in the Indus Valley in about 2500 B.C., and in China about 1500 B.C. Just as technological progress in agriculture had made Neolithic villages possible, new advances in agriculture in the New Stone Age led to the development of cities. The invention of new farm tools, methods of cultivation, irrigation, and animal raising led to an increased food supply. A plentiful food supply meant that many people could stop farming. They became city dwellers and were able to pursue other jobs. Some of them became craftspeople making tools, pottery, and other items that they sold. As city life became more complex, a class of merchants came into being to sell the products made by others. Advances in transportation made it possible for this merchant class to exist. These advances which occurred between 3000 and 500 B.C. involved improvements in sailing vessels and wheeled vehicles.

By 3000 B.C. the Egyptians were able to build sailing ships that could put out to sea. These ships, unlike earlier ones, had a definite shape and had a large rectangular sail rigged amidships. They could sail before and across the wind but needed to be rowed to travel into the wind. These ships sailed the Mediterranean and Red seas on short trading trips. Between 2000 and 1000 B.C. peoples who lived along the Mediterranean developed larger, stronger ships. The Phoenicians had a large fleet of merchant ships that traveled the length of the Mediterranean by 1000 B.C. Yet, without navigational instruments, travel was slow and difficult and the ships generally stayed within sight of land. These ships were steered using oars at the stern and since wind could not always be relied on, many had teams of oarsmen who rowed.

The first wheeled vehicles were built in Mesopotamia about 3500 B.C. but were not widely used until about 3000 B.C. These first vehicles were four-wheeled carts pulled by oxen. Each wheel was a wooden disk made from three rectangular boards. The first spoked wheels appeared between 2000 and 1500 B.C. These were used by chariots which were light enough to be pulled by horses. These horse-drawn chariots were the fastest vehicles in ancient times.

Metalworking and the Bronze Age

Among the many craftspeople were metalworkers who used metals that were found in metallic form, especially soft metals such as gold and copper that could be worked by beating and hammering. Then, it was discovered that certain metals could be extracted from ore. Most likely, the first to be found was malachite, which, when placed in a strong fire, could be reduced to copper. This led to the search for other ore, the development of metallurgy, the end of the Stone Age, and the beginning of the early Metal Age. Since soft metals could only be used in decorative items or coins, ways were sought to harden copper so that tools and weapons could be made. Eventually, alloying in which copper was fused with other metals to make bronze was discovered. Copper mixed with tin created a hard, yellow metal that could be cast into shapes when molten. Bronzesmiths soon used the techniques of coppersmiths and goldsmiths of heating metal in a crucible over a fire and casting it into molds made of stone or clay to make ax or spear heads or other shapes. Metalworkers using copper and later bronze, which became the most important material of the early civilizations, turned out useful tools such as plows, hoes, sickles, and axes.

Agriculture, Manufacturing, and Building

Many improvements were made in this period in the production of food. In the Nile Valley, the people developed the technique of basic irrigation, or ponding back the annual floodwater of the Nile for as long as possible. In Sumer, engineers channeled water from the river although this system was not as successful as in the Nile Valley since salt built up in the soil causing infertility. Both irrigation systems depended on engineering skills in building dikes, embankments, canals, underground aqueducts to prevent water evaporation,

and water-raising devices such as the shadoof. Many new products such as wines, oils, and cosmetics were manufactured. Presses were devised to make the wines and oils, while the potter's wheel was widely used to spin clay into shapes.

In building, technological developments were mainly in the ability to construct large-scale structures. Sun-dried brick remained the primary building material in Mesopotamia but now it was used to construct massive temples called ziggurats. Builders in Egypt used stone to construct the massive pyramids and temples. Stones were pulled on rollers and raised up the structure by ramps and balanced levers. Stones up to 200 tons could be moved by placing them on sleds and having hundreds of workers heave them on palm-fiber ropes. As cities grew, large public buildings were constructed, including temples for worship, and storehouses for grain and weapons, as were roads and aqueducts to carry water. For example, the Babylonians and Assyrians paved streets and built bridges across large rivers.

Although most of these innovations may seem like simple devices to us, they sparked great changes in the way people lived. The invention of the brick mold made it possible to make sun-dried bricks a uniform size and shape and also to produce them quickly. A plentiful supply of bricks in turn made it possible to build dwellings, huge temples, and other structures. The wheel and sail made travel over great distances possible, enlarging the scope of human experience, and made trade with far-off places possible. Traders became the instrument by which technological knowledge was transmitted in the ancient world. Metal tools of copper made carpentry possible while metal weapons would enable some groups to conquer others and create great empires. Once civilization was firmly established, the introduction of a new technological innovation—the working of iron— led to great new changes and made possible the great classical civilizations of Greece and Rome.

Greece and Rome
(500 B.C.–500 A.D.)

In comparison with the Greeks' and Romans' contributions in the fields of philosophy, law, government, literature, and art, their contributions in technology were limited. Nonetheless, they were responsible for many technological innovations and invented many new mechanical devices. Although they showed great ingenuity in engineering, their work was largely based on earlier discoveries and generally did not involve dramatic new innovations.

Ironworking

The mastery of ironworking was the major technological contribution of Greece and Rome. Although a technique for working iron was developed about 1000 B.C. somewhere in Asia Minor, it was the Greeks and Romans who improved techniques for turning iron ore into its metal form and for fashioning it into tools and weapons. Turning iron ore into its metal form required great heat and furnaces had to be constructed that could maintain this intensive heat for hours. In this period, this was achieved by placing the ore into a hot deep fire of charcoal. The carbon in the charcoal slowly combined with the oxygen in the iron ore and escaped as gas. The fire was not hot enough to melt the resulting iron but it softened it into a small spongy ball of iron. This was taken from the furnace and hammered into a solid block or bar. Repeated heating and forging forced out impurities leaving good wrought iron. Later, the wrought iron bars were shaped by reheating them and hammering them into shape. In time, ironmakers learned to intensify the fire by blowing on it through a hollow tube and, eventually, foot bellows were used to force air into the fire. Iron was a great improvement over bronze because it was more abundant and it was harder and stronger. Iron could be heated, hammered, and tempered into extremely hard, sharp knives and sword blades. The Romans learned ironworking techniques from the Greeks and developed them to a high degree of perfection.

Agriculture

With the mastery of ironworking came the invention of the iron plow, making it possible for farmers to plow more deeply and to cultivate heavier soil. As the Roman Empire grew, the small farms increased in size and became highly specialized, with most of them raising wheat. The Romans introduced to Europe advanced farming techniques developed in the Middle East such as the ox-drawn plow and irrigation. However, the Romans also developed many new farming methods. They began the two-field system, the practice of allowing half a field to lay fallow or unplanted each year so that nutrients and moisture were restored to the soil. They developed systems of crop rotation, built terraces up mountain sides enabling them to grow grapes and olives along the steep Mediterranean shore, and began the selective breeding of plants and livestock. Irrigation canals and huge storage granaries were constructed by Roman engineers. In the drier parts of the empire, extensive irrigation systems were built which utilized a scoop wheel, that is a wheel with iron buckets attached all around it, to raise water.

Inventions, Building, and Manufacturing

The Greeks and Romans invented many ingenious mechanical devices. The Greeks developed the catapult, water clock, compound pulley, and other hoisting devices. Somewhere in the eastern Mediterranean region about 2,000 years ago the waterwheel was invented, making it possible to lift water for irrigation and to grind grain using water power rather than human muscle power. The great Archimedes of Syracuse was responsible for the screw, pulley. and lever. Alexandrian engineers made mechanical devices such as pumps, compressed-air engines and even what may be regarded as the first steam turbine. Although these inventions were not made use of, they can be considered the first machines.

The Romans were responsible for introducing rotary motion. Examples of this included a treadmill to power cranes and other heavy lifting devices and a rotary water-raising device for irrigation which was a scoop wheel powered by a treadmill. The Romans were the first to use waterwheels to provide power and by the end of the Roman era, there were many watermills in use.

Although they constructed splendid buildings, the Greeks did not produce any technological innovations in building. The Romans, however, were important innovators in building. They used fired brick and tile in addition to stone and developed cement. Roman engineers were probably the first to use concrete as a building material. This was a vast improvement over construction solely with stone and marble because concrete was cheaper, easier to obtain, and more adaptable to a variety of forms. The Romans were probably the best architects and construction engineers of ancient times. From the Greeks they learned classic styles using columns and pediments; but they added many developments of their own. The Romans contributed the arch (learned from the Etruscans), vault, and dome. By combining arches, they were able to create massive structures with vaulted dome roofs. They built aqueducts, tunnels, bridges, and the largest and most complex buildings the world had ever seen.

Greeks and Romans continued to manufacture crafts such as pottery, glass, textiles, and leather and their improvements in these were in the perfection of style. Although the Romans invented siege catapults that depended on torsion and tension power, the rest of their military equipment was not technologically superior and included swords and iron tipped spears.

Transportation

As in earlier times, the sailing ship remained the primary method of long-distance travel. The Greeks made improvements in sailing ships including the building of two masted vessels and increased the number of sails from one to four. They also began to develop a fighting ship, equipped with a ram in its bow. Moreover, cargo ships relying entirely on the wind without oarsmen were developed. By 400 B.C., 300 ports dotted the Mediterranean and several thousand ships from various countries traveled the sea. The Romans took over the Greek cargo and fighting ships and added little that was new. However, the Romans built the largest fleet of cargo ships in the ancient world. Their chief technological contribution was in their remarkably built roads, running throughout the empire and paved over long stretches. Although roads were not new, most earlier roads were little more than dirt tracks. The Romans were the first people to construct an extensive system of paved roads. The best Roman roads were 16–20 feet wide and 3–6 feet thick with a base consisting of several layers of crushed stone and gravel. The roads were then paved with stone blocks. These roads were used mainly to transport troops and military supplies but they also were an important communication link between Rome and its provinces and facilitated trade within the empire. By 200 A.D., more than 50,000 miles (80,000 kilometers) of paved roads connected Rome and its empire.

The Middle Ages
(800–1500 A.D.)

The period after the decline of the Roman Empire in the West is called the Middle Ages. This long period is usually divided into three parts. The earliest period until the year 1000 is the Early Middle Ages, the period from about 1000–1300 is the High Middle Ages, while the years between 1300 and 1500 are the Late Middle Ages. Each of these periods saw distinct changes in the way people lived and the rate of technological change increased steadily.

In the Early Middle Ages, Europe was overrun by invading groups of people, including the various Germanic tribes, Vikings, and Muslims, causing great disruption and a general decline in civilization. Many of the achievements of Greco-Roman civilization were forgotten and by the 800s most people lived on isolated feudal manors that were largely self-sufficient. Roads fell into disrepair, trade dwindled almost to a standstill, and towns and cities ceased to exist, as did governmental institutions.

However, around the year 1000, as the invasions ended and political stability returned, great changes took place creating a dynamic new era. In this period of the High Middle Ages, Europe underwent an enormous economic revival that saw the reestablishment of commerce and trade, the growth of cities, and experimentation and growth in all fields of human endeavor. In part, this process involved the rediscovery of the knowledge and achievements of ancient Greece and Rome. Thus, in the High Middle Ages, technological progress was characterized by the preservation, recovery, and modification of earlier achievements. However, by the Late Middle Ages, some important technological innovations had occurred.

Discovering how certain innovations came about in the Middle Ages in Europe raises a problem since few records were kept. Many inventions from this period were developed independently and earlier in other civilizations of Asia, such as China, India, and Persia. Consequently, it is not possibie to tell whether a particular invention was a case of spontaneous invention in two or more areas or if it was transmitted in some unknown way from the Asian society where it originated first. It must be remembered that in the earlier years this was a period of isolation, especially in Europe, and there was little contact among peoples in Asia and Europe. Consequently, it seems likely that some of the key inventions of the period, such as the windmill and gunpowder, developed independently in each society. Others, however, were transmitted to Europe.

While Europe lay in chaos in the Early Middle Ages, many African and Asian civilizations were experiencing dynamic development and technological innovation. Medieval Europe's closest eastern neighbor was the Byzantine Empire, the eastern half of the Roman Empire that lasted for 1,000 years past the collapse of the western empire. Here, the traditions of Greco-Roman civilization endured and became available to Europe through its traders, especially the Italian city-states of Venice and Genoa. Although the Byzantine Empire was not responsible for many technological innovations, it served as a transmission point between Europe and the civilizations of Islam, India, and China.

As Islam spread from the 7th century on, it created an empire in southwestern Asia and North Africa bound by religious and cultural ties. The Arabs assimilated the scientific and technological achievements of the Greco-Roman world and added their own innovations. This vast body of knowledge became available to Europe through the Moors in Spain, Arabs in Sicily and the Holy Land, and trade with North Africa. Islam also helped to transmit some of the technology of India and China. By the year 1000, Chinese civilization had developed many techniques and crafts, including silk working, gunpowder, iron casting, papermaking, windmills, and porcelain, that were unknown in Europe. Although Europe acquired many technological innovations from Asia and Africa during the period of the Middle Ages, it transformed itself from an agricultural society with a subsistence economy into a dynamic society with growing trade, industry, and cities. This transformation was largely a technological achievement.

Sources of Power

New sources of power developed in this period were one of the reasons for this great achievement. Several inventions made it possible to use horses in place of oxen as a source of energy. Before the appearance of the rigid horsecollar in about the year 800, horses wore a harness that fit across the neck and could choke the animal if it pulled a heavy load. The rigid horsecollar shifted the weight to the horse's shoulders enabling it to pull four or five times as much weight as before. It made it possible to harness a horse to a heavy plow. Horses soon replaced oxen as the primary work animals. Horses had more stamina than oxen and could work harder and longer. The iron horseshoe, which appeared in Europe in about 1000, protected horses' hooves from damage, enabling them to travel farther and faster. Before the invention of the horseshoe, horses often suffered damaged hooves if they traveled long distances at high speed. Shortly after 1000, the whiffletree, a pivoted crossbar at the front of a wagon to which a horse team's harnesses are attached, came into use. This invention, which equalized the pull of the horses, enabled a wagon to be pulled by a team of them.

The harnessing of wind and water power were two other great technological achievements. As you remember, the Romans began to use water power during the later empire and some of their techniques probably survived. However, the first type of watermill to be used in northern Europe was the Norse mill, which was a horizontally mounted watermill that directly drove a pair of grindstones using no gears. This type of mill required a strong stream of water to turn the wheel at high speed to maintain an adequate grinding speed without gearing the upper millstone. Later, medieval mill builders began adding elaborate gearing mechanisms. At first, watermills were used to grind grain but in later years they were used to saw wood, crush vegetable seeds for oil, and perform many other tasks.

Windmills were also introduced to Europe, probably in the late 1100s. Although the first windmills were developed in Persia, it seems likely that they were not transmitted to Europe but developed there independently, especially since the two differed in design. Windmills were widely used in the Middle Ages, especially in England, Spain, and the Netherlands. In time, both windmills and watermills were used in mining, ironmaking, lumber sawing, paper-making, and in the cloth industry.

The medieval interest in mechanical devices led to the development of the mechanical clock. The oldest of these clocks, dating from 1386, is in Salisbury Cathedral in England and is driven by weights controlled by a swinging arm that engages with a gear wheel. Clocks run by springs date from the 1400s. These made it possible to make smaller mechanisms and prepared the way for the portable clock.

Agriculture
These new sources of power made it possible for medieval farmers to increase their productivity. Moreover, new tools and farming techniques also contributed to increased food production in the High Middle Ages. Among the most important new farm tools was a type of wheeled heavy plow that made it possible to farm the moist, heavy soils of northern Europe, thereby bringing a vast area of new farmland into production. The earlier, smaller light plows used in southern Europe could not cut deeply into these heavier soils. New methods of cultivation, especially the three-field system, which replaced the two-field system, also improved farming. In the two-field system, half the land was planted with winter wheat while the other half was left fallow to restore the nutrients. In the new method, one third of the land was planted in winter wheat, another third in oats and vegetables in the spring, and a third was left fallow. With two thirds of the land in use instead of only half, by the 12th century crop production doubled and in some areas even tripled. The introduction of new crops such as oats, beans, and peas also improved people's diets and enriched the soil with nitrates. European farmers also continued to improve plants and livestock by selective breeding.

Manufacturing, Crafts, and Building
The manufacture of cast iron is one of the great technological achievements of the Middle Ages. In the 1400s, for the first time, a blast furnace was developed that could reduce iron ore to its liquid form, making it possible to pour the molten metal into molds. This new blast furnace used a bellows driven by a waterwheel to provide a continuous blast of air, raising the furnace temperature. Being able to cast the iron made it possible to manufacture large items such as cannons in great quantities. (Gunpowder, invented in Asia, had reached Europe around 1200.)

While traditional craft industries such as ropemaking, leatherworking, and metalworking continued to expand in the growing towns, new crafts such as soapmaking began. Soap manufacturing was the first industrial process to make widespread use of coal as fuel. The development of the coal industry was another important innovation of this period. At first, mining techniques were primitive and involved obtaining coal near the earth's surface. Later, mining techniques progressed allowing miners to probe deeper into the earth. Techniques of shafting, pumping, using treadmills, animal power, and waterpower and conveying the ore from mines in trucks were developed. Important technological innovations in building produced the wonderful Romanesque and Gothic building styles used in this period. Medieval engineers constructed tall masonry buildings that let in natural light by using the cross-rib vault and the flying buttress.

Transportation and Communications
The Middle Ages witnessed important technological achievements in sea transportation as the design and construction of ships improved greatly. In the 500s, the triangular lateen sail came into use. Unlike rectangular sails, the lateen sails worked when ships sailed into the wind. Around 1300, the first ships to use a rudder rather than steering oars in the bow were built. Rudders could steer bigger ships and by the 1400s shipbuilders were making ships four times as large as before. These ships had a rudder and most had three masts and three sails.

By about 1200, northern European shipbuilders had developed a broad sturdy ship called a cog which was used for 200 years as the standard merchant and war vessel. These ships had one large sail, could stand up to rough seas and high winds, and had deep wide hulls to hold bulky cargo. Around 1300, the new steering apparatus—the rudder—was added to the cog. In the same period, shipbuilders in the Mediterranean area began to increase the use of the triangular lateen sails on their smaller, lighter ships. During the 1400s, they combined the best features of the cog with their lighter, lateen-rigged ships, producing two-, and in time, three-masted vessels.

Important new navigational instruments were developed in the Middle Ages. The magnetic compass allowed sailors to navigate their ships even if the sky was overcast, and the astrolabe measured the angle of the sun or a star above the horizon, from which the position of the ship could be calculated. These improvements in ships and instruments as well as improvements in construction and equipment such as better ropes, sails, and navigational charts made it possible for ships to make ocean voyages. These in turn led to the voyages of discovery in the 1400s and 1500s and the beginning of the expansion of European power.

Transportation on land was still primarily on foot or horseback although horse-drawn wagons came into increased use. There was some experimentation in bridge building and canal construction. Lock gates were used in 1180 on a canal built to connect Bruges, located in present-day Belgium, to the sea.

One of the most important technological innovations of the Middle Ages was the invention of printing from movable metal type. Printing from wood blocks or engravings had existed for centuries, but movable type made printing much faster because it was much easier to arrange ready-made letters than to carve letters into wood. Accordingly, in the mid-1400s printing replaced handwriting as the main way to produce books.

Johannes Gutenberg is generally considered the inventor of printing in Europe. Movable type had been used previously in Asia, but Europeans apparently did not know about it. Gutenberg put together several separate inventions to create a workable system for manufacturing metal type, printing from it, and reusing it. For the first time, it was easy to produce many identical copies of one book. Printing spread ideas and improved communication throughout Europe.

Beginning of the Modern Period (1500–1750)

During the Middle Ages, technological change was marked by slow but substantial development. The period between 1500 and 1750 witnessed a greatly increased pace of technological change that was associated with the important social, political, economic, and religious changes occurring in Europe. These changes included the creation of the modern nation state, the splitting of Christendom by the Protestant Reformation, the Renaissance and the accompanying scientific revolution, the Commercial Revolution, and overseas expansion which profoundly altered Europe and was accompanied by changes in technology. The overseas voyages of exploration and expansion in this period were made possible by improvements in navigation, instruments, and ships. Europe's colonization of the Americas was made possible by the development of superior weaponry. Iron cannons mounted on the light maneuverable European ships gave the Europeans a decisive advantage over other peoples of the world. It was the combination of these political, economic, social, and technological changes that paved the way for the Industrial Revolution that began in the 1750s and the creation of the modern world.

By 1400 the medieval pattern of civilization was dissolving and by 1650 a new pattern had come into being. This new pattern was created by the many political, social, and economic forces that interacted in these years. However, the primary force was economic. The relatively static agrarian economy of the Middle Ages gave way to a dynamic commercial economy. Economic change in turn produced social, political, and technological changes.

The Commercial Revolution

From the late 1400s to about 1750, the economic life of western Europe changed greatly. This transformation was caused by an explosion of trade as merchants began to sell their goods far and wide and to seek new markets. By the mid-1400s, the greatly increased trade caused European merchants to develop new trade and business practices that were to transform the economy of Europe. So great was the change that it is called the Commercial Revolution.

This was not a revolution in how products were manufactured, for they continued to be made by traditional handicraft methods. Instead, it was a revolution in the way goods were bought and sold. The Commercial Revolution was basically a change from the localized town-centered economy of the later Middle Ages to one that involved an entire country. Also, trade became worldwide. In some cases, developments that had already begun such as the use of money and banking services simply sped up. Standardized systems of money came into being making economic transactions more stable and reliable. This in turn encouraged the growth of international commerce and the rise of banks. New types of business organizations such as the joint stock company were created. Merchants began to increase their trade networks and search for markets far from their home base. This was a change from the Middle Ages when there were few surplus goods and most were sold a short distance from where they were produced.

The woolen cloth industry in Britain was one of the first industries in which the new trade practices were used. Since the 1300s, the woolen cloth industry had been controlled by local town guilds that limited production, set standards and prices, and controlled the local market. Some merchants looking for opportunities for profit sought to evade guild restrictions and decided to have cloth made outside of the towns. They took the wool to farmers whom they paid to spin and weave local woolen cloth in their homes. This system of production was called the domestic system and it continued to be used until the Industrial Revolution. Other items such as buttons, gloves, knives, and clocks were also made this way.

Once a steady supply of wool cloth became available, merchants found new markets, thereby tremendously increasing the volume of trade. Because of the need for increased supplies of cloth the process of cloth manufacture was partially mechanized with the use of spinning wheels and weaving looms. Pressures to increase productivity led to some technological innovations by the early 1700s, but early attempts at devising spinning machines were not successful.

The Scientific Revolution

Much of the importance of the Renaissance lay in the scientific revolution that accompanied it. During the 1500s and 1600s, the way in which the people of Europe viewed themselves and the universe underwent a dramatic change that is known as the Scientific Revolution. It involved the work of a succession of great astronomers, physicists, and mathematicians whose discoveries undermined many ideas that had been accepted without question since the time of ancient Greece. A whole new system of ideas and theories was created based on direct observation of nature and a belief in the power of reason.

During the Middle Ages the authority of Aristotle in the natural world, Ptolemy in astronomy, and Galen in medicine were accepted almost without question. However, beginning in the 1500s, their authority was challenged and scientists set out by observation and experiment to explain the natural world. The revolution in science began with Copernicus, who found that the orbits of the planets could be described much more simply and accurately by placing the sun instead of the earth at the center of the solar system. Galileo's discovery of satellites orbiting Jupiter helped win adherents for Copernicus' theory by showing that not everything went around the earth. Later, Johannes Kepler realized that the orbits were elliptical, not circular, and formulated three mathematical laws of planetary motion. In the mid-1600s, Sir Isaac Newton showed that Kepler's laws were the direct result of gravity extending over an unlimited distance. Ever since Newton, the story of science has been one of continuous acceleration in the growth of knowledge.

Chemistry began in the bubbling cauldrons of medieval alchemists seeking vainly to transform base metals into gold. By the 1600s, however, chemistry had become a science, largely due to the work of Robert Boyle. Using a scientific approach, he identified more than a dozen chemical elements. Progress was also made in biology. William Harvey explained the function of the heart and the circulation of blood, Anton van Leeuwenhoek invented a microscope and described the existence of bacteria and microbes.

Technology was of great importance to the Scientific Revolution and rapid strides were made in developing new instruments to carry out research. Along with optical devices, such as telescopes and microscopes, measuring instruments of various kinds were invented. Moreover, scientists such as Bacon and Boyle wanted to learn to master nature and use science for practical advantage to humankind. They believed that science could be used to raise the material standard of living. This emphasis on the practical applications of science first advocated in the 1600s began the wedding of science, or the search for truth, with technology, or the creation of material goods and control over nature.

Central to the great achievements in the 1600s and 1700s was the development of the scientific method that became the cornerstone of the Scientific Revolution. Its requirement for explanation based on carefully planned experiments, observation of results. and the formulating of general laws led to a questioning attitude toward traditional practices and beliefs and demonstrated the power of the human mind to achieve control over nature and solve the mysteries of the universe.

Transportation

Many new developments occurred in the field of transportation. Road building techniques were improved and the first large-scale canal, the Languedoc Canal, between the Mediterranean and the Bay of Biscay in France was completed in 1692. It was 500 miles (240 kilometers) long, consisting of 100 locks, a tunnel, three large aqueducts and a large reservoir. Hundreds of canals were built in Europe from the late Middle Ages to the 1700s. And during the 1700s, England and France constructed the first well-paved roads since Roman times. By the 1600s, most people used horsedrawn wagons to haul goods locally but they were seldom used on long hauls because of the poor roads. Until the 1800s horse-drawn boats, barges, and ships were the chief means of long-distance inland transport. Animals pulled these vessels along the banks of rivers and canals with ropes.

The greatest improvements, however, were made in sea transportation probably as an outgrowth of the great expansion in commerce and desire for trade. It was the great desire for trade with Asia on the part of the European nations that led to the voyages of exploration in the 1400s and 1500s. Before such voyages could be undertaken, however, better sailing ships and instruments as well as more knowledge of the geography of the world were needed. Consequently, mapmakers began to study shorelines more carefully, draw more precise maps, draw lines of latitude, and mark the distance North and South of the equator. Better navigational instruments also helped to make long sea voyages possible. Among the most important were the compass and the astrolabe which had been developed earlier. The quadrant, which was used to measure the altitude of a star from the horizon was improved, and in the mid-1700s a clock to keep accurate time at sea was developed, enabling sailors to determine longitude by comparing local solar time to the time at the prime meridian. *See also* **Prime Meridian** page 5-30; **Solar day,** page 5-35.

By 1500 the Europeans had developed better ships. These three-masted ships were square-rigged vessels with a mainmast in the middle of the ship, a foremast in the forward part of the ship, and a mizzenmast in the back. It was this type of ship that was used by such explorers as Columbus and Magellan. In the mid-1500s a new type of ship known as a galleon appeared that was used as both a warship and a cargo ship. Galleons were large vessels with their foremast and mainmast carrying two or three sails and they could carry heavy guns. In the 1600s and 1700s, larger and larger ships that used more sails to increase their speed were built for trade with India, Africa, and Asia.

These improved ships made long sea voyages possible and led to the European discovery of America. Moreover, the superior arms developed by advanced European technology enabled them to conquer thriving civilizations such as that of the Aztecs. Overseas expansion had tremendous consequences for Europe resulting in economic expansion and thriving Capitalism. Accelerated trade and production caused increased wealth and in time led European civilization to become the dominant world civilization. As new products from India, Asia, Africa, and the Americas began to flow into Europe new manufacturing techniques had to be developed. New industries such as sugar refining and tobacco processing were started, further stimulating growth, expansion, and trade.

Iron Production, Mining, and Sources of Power

In this period, experiments were carried out involving the use of coal instead of charcoal to smelt and process cast iron into wrought iron. The first success came in 1709 when Abraham Darby used coal to melt iron ore in an enlarged and improved blast furnace. Other industries such as glassmaking, brickmaking, and pottery manufacturing were using coal as a fuel. Besides mining for coal and iron, other mining activities were expanded between 1500 and 1750. Metals such as tin and lead were mined and the manufacturing of brass was begun.

A new source of power, steam, was developed in this period. The theoretical basis for steam power came from the scientific research of Robert Boyle, Otto von Guericke, and Denis Papin. Although Thomas Savery developed a steam engine in 1698, the first commercially successful steam engine was built by Thomas Newcomen. Newcomen's engine came into use in the 1720s and it was used in the British coal mines to pump water out of the deep mines. However, the Newcomen engine had serious faults in that it wasted heat and used a great deal of fuel. Water and wind remained the chief sources of power for industry in this period but many uses would be found for the steam engines in the 1800s.

Agriculture

Tremendous strides were made in agriculture in the early 1700s and the great changes became collectively known as the Agricultural Revolution. This was a prelude to the Industrial Revolution and helped to make it possible. Prior to this, the European voyages of discovery also affected agriculture as new crops and livestock were introduced to Europe. From the native peoples of the Americas, Europeans learned of cocoa, corn, peanuts, peppers, squash, potatoes, tobacco, and tomatoes, and many of these crops helped to increase the food supply of Europe.

The Agricultural Revolution was the result of a series of discoveries and inventions that made farming more productive. The most important developments of the Agricultural Revolution involved improved methods for growing crops, advances in breeding livestock, and the invention of new farm machines. Although the Agricultural Revolution began in the Low Countries (what are today Belgium and the Netherlands) where farmers discovered new ways to increase the fertility of the soil, it was in Great Britain that the new and efficient agricultural methods were put into effect. This was largely the result of the enclosure movement that began in the 1400s and led to the establishment of larger, more efficient farms. As you recall, grain growing reduces the nutrients in the soil, so medieval farmers allowed their fields to lie fallow in alternate years. In the 1500s, Dutch farmers began planting crops such as peas, beans, and clover to improve soil fertility and they also began heavily manuring and adding minerals to the soil. Increased soil fertility meant greater crop production and also led to increased farm animal production. For example, cattle feeding on the nutritious clover and grasses grew larger and fatter, yielding more beef and milk as well as more manure to fertilize fields and produce still greater crop yields.

In the early 1700s, the Agricultural Revolution was brought to Britain and Viscount Charles Townshend and Jethro Tull helped to spread the new ideas. Townshend used techniques such as heavy manuring, adding minerals to the soil, and rotating crops. His experiments with crop rotation resulted in the four-field rotation system, which enabled farmers to grow crops on all their land each year and not leave any land fallow. Before the four-field system, farmers could not raise enough to feed their livestock through the winter. Consequently, animals had to be slaughtered in the fall and their meat preserved with salt. Now farmers could produce fresh meat all year. Tull invented the seed drill, a device that set seeds in the ground at just the right depth and space for best growth. He also invented a horse-drawn hoe that broke up and loosened the soil so plants could grow better. Robert Bakewell set up scientific breeding programs that produced cattle with more meat, sheep with finer wool, and cows with better milk.

Although the technological innovations of the period between 1500 and 1750 were not truly outstanding, except for the steam engine, they made the period of the Industrial Revolution, which was marked by tremendous innovation, possible. In Britain, especially, a political and social environment open to invention was created in this period. Other factors including the buildup of vast commercial resources and capital and the use of new agricultural products and raw materials also contributed to the beginning of the Industrial Revolution. Moreover, the superior techniques developed in Europe enabled the Europeans to expand their influence over the world. The superiority of their technology made it possible for the Europeans to penetrate all areas of the globe and spread their civilization.

The Industrial Revolution
(1750–1900)

A major change in the way people live, work, and think began about 250 years ago, and in many ways is still going on today. This change, which is termed the Industrial Revolution, involved the replacement on a massive scale of human and animal power with power from machines. It brought factory production and mass production of standardized items by machine that made manufactured goods cheap and abundant for the first time. It brought the harnessing of new energy sources from steam and later electricity. Transportation and communication improved immensely and constant change and material progress became a fact of life. Industries grew with self-generating momentum as each new invention or new technological advance brought yet another new invention or advance as the pace of industrialization quickened.

The Industrial Revolution began in Great Britain in about 1750 because conditions there were right for change. After 1600, the British economy became the most highly developed in Europe and Britain was Europe's leading manufacturing and trading nation. Capital for investment in new industry was abundant, and banking and investment were highly developed. Britain had relatively good roads and many canals for the cheap transport of raw materials and finished goods. More important, coastal and river trade was well developed and all the major population centers could be reached by cheap water-borne transport. Rising demand for manufactured goods from Britain's colonies and overseas markets helped to expand the British economy. Moreover, it had large deposits of coal and iron and a technologically advanced iron and metals industry. Population increases and efficient agricultural production provided a large labor supply. Finally, an atmosphere conducive to innovation encouraged skilled engineers, scientists, and technicians to experiment with new methods and invent new machines. As Britain became the world's leading commercial and trading power, the demand for British manufactured goods increased tremendously but the production methods of the time could not keep up with the demand for goods. The stage was set for the introduction of new, more efficient means of manufacturing.

The Textile Industry
The first industry to become industrialized in Great Britain was the cotton textile industry. In 1733, James Kay patented the flying shuttle, a device that sped up the weaving process, so that a weaver could double the amount of cloth produced in a day. To meet the demand for thread which was spun one at a time on a spinning wheel, James Hargreaves invented the spinning jenny in 1764 which enabled workers to produce up to 24 threads at a time. The water frame invented by Richard Arkwright in 1769 was the first machine to replace human hand power in weaving with another

power source. At first, powered by a waterwheel, the water frame produced strong cotton threads on hundred of spindles. With Samuel Crompton's mule in 1779, the water frame was perfected so that many hundreds of fine, high-quality threads suitable for weaving fine fabrics could be spun at the same time. Edmund Cartwright's power loom mechanized and sped up the weaving process still more.

Since the new machines required water power, many early cotton mills were built on swift-flowing streams in the North and West of England. These were the world's first factories and the factory system soon became the dominant way of working, replacing the domestic system. The large new power-driven machines were installed in a large centralized factory where workers came to perform their tasks.

Steam Power
The first cotton mills used water power to operate their machinery but this limited the number of sites where factories could be located. A new source of energy was needed and this was found in steam power. As you remember, crude steam engines were invented by Savery and Newcomen and were used to pump out the water that seeped into and flooded the coal mines. These crude engines used coal to heat water, creating steam that drove large pistons, which operated the pumps. Steam became the principal power source for the machines developed in the Industrial Revolution because of the work of James Watt who patented an efficient steam engine. Over 20 years, Watt perfected the steam engine so that by the 1780s, it had begun to replace water power as the chief source of energy used in manufacturing.

In the years after Newcomen and Watt, the main improvement was the development of engines capable of using high-pressure steam. In the late 1700s and early 1800s, Richard Trevithick designed and built the first high-pressure steam engine capable of using 30 pounds of pressure. Other improvements included the compound engine, which used the steam twice or more at descending pressures until it was used up, and in 1884, the steam turbine, invented by Sir Charles Parsons. This high-speed engine, was a major technological innovation and was an economical source of power to turn electric generators by allowing steam to pass through the blades of a series of rotors of increasing size. The steam energy was turned into very rapid circular motion that was ideal for generating electricity. Although improvements were made in the construction and size of turbines, the basic principles have remained the same, and steam turbines are still the main source of electric power except in mountainous areas where water turbines are used to generate hydroelectric power.

This advance in power technology was one of the outstanding features of the Industrial Revolution. When it began, the sources of energy that were available were human and animal power and wind and water power. The advent of steam power did not merely replace these sources of power, it transformed them. Besides the development of the steam engine. waterwheels and windmills were improved. By the mid-1800s, new designs made it possible to increase the speed of the waterwheel thereby preparing the way for the water turbine, which is still an efficient method

of producing power. Nonetheless, steam became the major power source of the Industrial Revolution.

The Iron Industry
As you recall, in the early 1700s, a British ironmaker, Abraham Darby, discovered that coke, produced by heating coal to drive out impurities, could be substituted for charcoal in iron production and that coal could also be used to heat the furnace. However, since the iron smelted with charcoal could be worked more easily, ironmakers did not switch over to the coke method. Then in 1750, Darby's son developed a process that made iron produced with coke as easy to work as iron produced with charcoal. After 1760, coke smelting spread throughout Britain. In 1760, John Seeton invented a blast furnace that could smelt iron quickly and cheaply. Another improvement came in 1784, when Henry Cart devised a new process called puddling that produced pure and workable iron in large quantities very cheaply. He also invented steam-driven rolling mills that made it possible to roll iron into useful shapes using steam-driven machine power in a factory. In the 1800s, wrought iron, which is purer and less brittle than cast iron, was developed as a material for making the boilers of steam engines, which had to be strong, lightweight, and made of materials that could be bent into shape and riveted in place. These qualities also made wrought iron ideal as a building material for bridge girders and arches in railroad stations.

As in the cotton textile industry, invention followed invention in an accelerating pace in the iron industry. Iron production, like textile production, turned into an industrial process where the bulk of the labor was done by machines and products were produced cheaply and in quantity. By 1800, iron that could be used to build machines and the steam engines to power the machines was inexpensive and abundant. In 1797, Henry Maudsly invented a metal lathe that could cut metal parts of machines accurately to a thousandth of an inch. This invention led to the machine tooling industry, which made it easier to make all kinds of machines. Machine operations in factories began to be applied to many industries and industrial processes, whereby machines that were driven by steam power did most of the work and thus took over almost all manufacturing.

Transportation
In the 1600s, roads in most of Europe were so poor—little more than dirt tracks—that overland travel was difficult. For example, the 200 mile trip by horse-drawn coach from London to York in England took more than a week. Realizing how important transportation was in the 1700s, people built a number of surfaced roads and canals that connected widely separated areas in Great Britain, including a series of turnpikes constructed between 1751 and 1771. Until the early 1800s, waterways were the cheapest way to transport coal, iron, and other heavy freight in Britain. Consequently, British engineers widened and deepened many streams to make them navigable and built canals to link cities and to connect the coalfields with rivers. In the early 1800s, two Scottish engineers, John Loudon McAdam and Thoman Tilford, made important advances in road construction. McAdam

devised the macadam type of road surface which consists of crushed rock packed in layers while Tilford originated a technique of using large flat stones for road foundations. These road-building methods made land travel faster and enabled manufactured goods to be delivered more efficiently.

Improvements continued to be made in sailing ships in this period. Packet ships that sailed across the Atlantic between Europe and the United States on regular schedules, whether or not they were fully loaded, were introduced in 1818. However, the swiftest and most beautiful of all were the clipper ships, which first appeared in the 1840s. Designed for speed, the clippers had slender hulls and many sails, with as many as six rows to a mast; some ships had 35 sails. At top speed, they could make 20 knots.

The major innovation of this period, however was the use of steam power to drive ships. The steam engine revolutionized water transportation as ships no longer had to depend upon uncertain winds. In 1787, John Fitch, an American inventor demonstrated the first workable steamboat. The first commercially successful steamboat was built in 1807 by another American, Robert Fulton. Within a few years, steamboats became common on British rivers and by the mid-1800s steam powered ships were carrying raw materials and manufactured goods across the Atlantic.

Also in the late 1700s, British shipbuilders began to build ships of iron instead of wood. These ships were lighter, stronger, safer, and cheaper to build. The *Vulcan,* the first all-iron sailing ship was launched in Great Britain in 1818. By the late 1800s, steel was replacing wood and iron in most shipbuilding. In 1836, a propeller that could drive steamboats more efficiently than a paddle wheel was invented. As ships changed from wood to steel and from paddle wheel to propellers, new types of engines and new sources of power were developed. During the late 1800s, the one-cylinder steam engine was replaced by the two-cylinder compound engine, which created more power and lessened the use of coal. In the 1890s, Charles A. Parsons designed a marine steam turbine that was more powerful and efficient than the steam engine.

Railroads

The growth of the Industrial Revolution depended on industry's ability to transport raw materials and finished goods over long distances. Even with good water transport and paved roads, this need outstripped available resources as the Industrial Revolution progressed. This problem of transportation was solved by putting the new power source—the steam engine—on wheels. Horse-drawn cars that moved on wooden rails had long been used in British coal mines. Once practical steam engines were available, it was not long before a steam engine was used to pull cars on rails. Steam locomotives were built as early as 1802 but it was not until 1825 that George Stephenson built the first steam locomotive that could successfully move heavy loads long distances. Stephenson and a group of investors built a railway line between the English mining towns of Darlington and Stockton. Railways became a great success and businesspeople rushed to invest in them. By 1845, every large city and industrial region in Britain was linked by rail lines. Railroads

further reduced the cost of goods by providing cheap transport. Even bulky materials such as metal ore and coal could be transported cheaply by rail to urban factories and then sent as finished goods to British cities and ports. Railroads became an essential part of the vast expansion of production in the Industrial Revolution and helped to make it possible for the Industrial Revolution to develop rapidly in Great Britain.

Agriculture

Agriculture also continued to improve in the 1800s as new farm machines were introduced. In the United States, inventors began to work on machines to harvest and process the large amounts of grain that were produced. In 1834, Cyrus McCormick patented the reaper, the first successful harvesting machine. Also in 1834, John and Hiram Pitts patented a thresher. Inventors also began working on a combine which was a combined harvester and thresher but these were not widely used until the early 1900s. The steel plow invented by John Deere in 1837 helped to increase grain production, especially in the United States. The steel plow worked much better than cast iron or wooden plows in the thick soils of the Midwest. In the 1800s, the food packing and canning industries were developed. Refrigeration techniques were introduced in the years after 1850 making it possible to transport meat and other perishables in refrigerated ships all over the world.

The Spread of the Industrial Revolution

The second phase of the Industrial Revolution began in the 1850s and picked up momentum as industrialization spread to other nations in Europe and North America. In this new phase, Britain's role as the leading industrial power was challenged as new industrial powers like Germany and the United States took the lead in developing new technology. Industrialized nations were transformed as new industries grew up including steel, chemicals, electricity, petroleum, and the machines dependent on petroleum fuels like automobiles and, later, aircraft. Much of the technology we still use today became common during this later phase of the Industrial Revolution.

The Steel Industry and Industrialization in Other Fields

The first phase of the Industrial Revolution involved the cotton, textile. and iron industries. During the second phase, steel production became much more important than iron production. Before the 1850s, steel, which is harder, less brittle than iron, and more adaptable, was difficult and expensive to make. Then Henry Bessemer invented a process for making high-grade steel cheaply. When this process was perfected in the 1870s, the steel industry took off. Steel became the primary building material, being used in beams for skyscrapers, cables for bridges, machinery, and ships. In fact, steel production was so important that a nation's wealth was often measured by the amount of steel it produced.

Using steam engines, iron, and steel, British manufacturing introduced power-driven machinery in many industries. The production of shoes, clothing, and furniture became mechanized as did printing and papermaking. Moreover, some new inventions and processes had important byproducts that developed into separate industries. Coke, a byproduct of coal, was used to smelt iron. Then it was discovered that the gases released from the coal in making coke could be burned to give light. By the 1850s, gas was piped into cities and used to light streets and homes.

Closely linked with the iron and steel industry was the advent of mechanical engineering as the demand for steam engines and other large machines increased. The engineering workshops that developed in the 1800s helped to increase the mechanization of industry and transportation. These workshops produced looms, locomotives, and other machines and also made great innovations in the machine tools that made these machines. The lathe developed into an all metal, power-driven machine capable of more accurate work than the former hand or foot operated wooden framed lathes. Drilling and slotting machines, milling and plowing machines, and a steam hammer were among the many new machines invented to make machines. In the late 1800s, manufacturers began to specialize in producing certain types of machines with some producing vehicles while others produced machines to meet a particular industry's needs.

Electricity

Electricity was another important technological development in this phase of the Industrial Revolution. Electricity is an extremely flexible form of energy that can be transported over great distances away from its generation source, by wire, to light cities and run machines. It can be generated by using water power or using coal or other fuels. It was Michael Faraday's discoveries about electricity ln 1831 that established the principles of electrical generation. Others took his discovery and used it to develop the dynamo, or electric generator. Driven by a steam engine or by water power, the dynamo transformed mechanical power into electrical energy which could run machines in factories. The first practical generators were built in the 1870s, and in the 1880s, transformers were introduced, which allowed electricity to be transported cheaply at high voltage and then converted to a lower voltage for use. Electricity soon became the primary energy source in the industrial world.

Long before this, people had observed electricity and its connection with magnetism but they did not put the knowledge to practical use. Not until 1800 did Alessandro Volta find a way to provide a steady flow of electric current when he built the first battery. Soon after, André Ampère worked out the principles governing the magnetic effect of an electric current. Samuel Morse put the work of Volta and Ampère to practical use by sending electricity over a wire at the other end of which was a machine that clicked when the electricity was switched on or off. Morse worked out a system by which patterns of clicks could represent letters of the alphabet, thereby inventing the telegraph. Inventors then tried to find a way to carry electricity under the sea through cables. A cable was constructed across the English Channel in the 1850s but it was not until 1866 that Cyrus Field and a group of Americans laid a cable across the Atlantic Ocean.

In the 1870s, inventors began to experiment with electrical devices. Alexander Graham Bell completed work on the telephone in 1876. By 1905, there were 10 million phones in the United States alone. At the same time, Thomas Alva Edison perfected the incandescent light bulb as well as systems for making electricity for lighting available in the home and work place. He also invented the phonograph and the movie projector. By 1900, there were 2 million buildings using electric lights. Phonograph music and film shows in theaters became available. Then in 1895 Guglielmo Marconi developed radio, a way to send messages through space without wires.

Petroleum

Petroleum that seeped out to the earth's surface was a novelty called "rock oil" and was used as a medicine in the mid-1800s. However, chemists soon found that products such as paint solvent, kerosene, and lubricating oil, could be made from it. In 1859, an American, Edwin L. Drake, drilled the first successful oil well in Titusville, Pennsylvania. This soon led to the search for oil all over the world. At first, oil was used mainly to distill kerosene to fuel oil lamps. Oil from which the kerosene had been extracted was considered a waste product until it was found that other components of petroleum could be burned in internal combustion engines. The invention of the gasoline engine in 1885 spurred the development of the oil industry. In the late 1800s, large oil companies were formed to supply the world's need for gasoline to run engines and kerosene to light homes.

Transportation

The second phase of the Industrial Revolution saw dramatic new developments in transportation. The expansion of railroads was an important characteristic of the later stage of the Industrial Revolution as railroads were built all over the industrial world. Electricity revolutionized public transportation in the industrial cities making it possible to build electrically run tramways, elevated railways, and subways. It also made elevators in tall buildings possible. However, electricity could not run road vehicles not attached to cables or rails. Attempts to harness the steam engine to road vehicles were not successful because steam engines require bulky boilers that need to be started well ahead of time to build up a head of steam.

The internal combustion engine, which derives power from the expansion of the burning fuel itself rather than steam, appeared in the 1800s and made automobiles possible. An engine that burned coal gas was built by Etienne Lenoir in Paris in 1860, but it was too expensive to run. Then in 1878 a German inventor, Nikolaus Otto, refined the coal-gas engines and they were installed in small industries replacing steam boilers. However, these gas engines used gas supplies that were piped to towns and this meant they could only be used in buildings. When it was found that liquid fuels derived from oil in the form of gasoline could be used it became possible to put the engine on wheels. It was the internal combustion engine powered by gasoline that made the introduction of the automobile possible. In 1885, Gottlieb Daimler, a German engineer, developed a practical internal combustion engine that could be fueled by gasoline. Along with Karl Benz, he put this new engine on wheels, thereby devising the world's first practical automobile. In the 1890s, Rudolph Diesel developed an internal combustion engine that could be used to power large trucks and ocean-going vessels to carry heavy loads. Automobiles changed the way people in the industrial world lived with suburbs becoming easier to reach and convenient travel a fact of life for many people. In 1903, Orville and Wilbur Wright used gasoline power to make the first successful airplane flight, thus beginning still another new industry. Air travel, however, did not become common until well into the 20th century.

Advances in Science

New experimental methods and technological advances made possible by the Industrial Age transformed the study of biology, chemistry, and physics and opened new frontiers of knowledge and of scientific experimentation and exploration. Major advances were made in the fight against disease that prepared the foundation for the modern practice of medicine. In 1796, Edward Jenner discovered that if people were inoculated (deliberately infected) with a mild disease called cowpox, they became immune to the killer disease smallpox. At the time, no one knew why inoculation worked. Then, in the 1860s to 1880s, Louis Pasteur determined that numerous diseases, as well as fermentation, were caused by microscopic organisms (bacteria, which he called germs or microbes); that germs could be killed by heating (pasteurization); and that in some cases inoculation with germs could make a person immune to a disease by causing the body to create substances (now called antibodies) to protect itself. A German physician, Robert Koch, made discoveries that reinforced the connection between germs and disease discovered by Pasteur. In 1882, he isolated the germ that caused tuberculosis.

Between 1800 and 1900, public health services were established in many nations and sanitation became an important part of the fight against disease. Modern sewer systems were built and clean water supplies became available. Improvements in sanitation and the identification of the organisms that caused infectious diseases and their methods of transmission helped to reduce the death rate from infectious diseases. There were also dramatic improvements in surgery. In 1871, Joseph Lister introduced a carbolic acid spray that successfully prevented infection during operations. New forms of anesthesia were introduced and, in 1897, x-rays were discovered.

Chemistry also made important advances in the 1800s and many of the products that were discovered stimulated economic development and encouraged the growth of new industries. The invention of new metal alloys made possible the production of different kinds of metals for specialized industrial purposes. A new process for manufacturing soda ash was responsible for greater efficiency and cost savings in the production of soaps, textiles, and paper products. Other achievements included the development of synthetic dyes, the production of inexpensive paper and rayon from wood pulp, and the development of the first plastics.

The Industrial Revolution dramatically changed the way that goods were produced and the way in which people lived. It led to the creation of large industries and in the beginning caused harsh working conditions and great dislocation. In time, however, it brought great material progress, eventually improving the lives of people in the industrialized world. It also brought increasing urbanization and new business forms, such as corporations, and new business methods. The Industrial Revolution also changed people's outlook as they came to believe in progress as the keynote to the future. The world was changing rapidly. Railroad lines and other forms of transportation enabled people to travel and manufactured goods to be shipped all over the world. New discoveries by chemists and the introduction of electricity stimulated the development of new industries. Technological advances created new jobs and made new products, such as bicycles, typewriters, telephones, and vacuum cleaners, available to many people. By 1900, technology and progress had become synonymous and science was seen as an endless source of new ideas and inventions.

The Industrial Revolution also made people realize that technology had become an important social and cultural influence. This awareness can be seen in the development of patent legislation and technical education and in the growth of professional organizations of engineers and other specialized groups. Moreover, as technology took on increasing importance, it became an important subject of discussion. Some saw it as offering hope for increasing social progress and democracy while others saw it as an evil responsible for the harsh working conditions and the urban ills of the late 1800s and early 1900s. Nonetheless, it was recognized that technology was an important feature of the new industrial society it had helped to create and it would continue to be an important influence in the shaping of the 20th century. No one, however, could predict the dramatic increase in technology, science, and knowledge that came in the 20th century.

Technology from 1900 to 1945

The Industrial Revolution brought with it large-scale production, machine power, and a climate of technological change as each industry witnessed invention after invention that increased production. Yet the great strides of the Industrial Revolution pale when compared to the technological achievements of the 20th century. Modern technology has advanced at a dizzying pace and in the years since 1900 the world has witnessed the advent of the airplane, rocket, space flight, electronics, nuclear power, antibiotics, insecticides, and many other inventions. Technology has also led to important political changes in the world. In the 1900s, the United States rather than Great Britain became the technological leader and as a consequence also became the world's most powerful nation. The two world wars fought in the 20th century also had important technological consequences as exemplified by the rapid development of the airplane and the development of the tank and the atomic bomb. They quickened the pace of technological development as states and private industry undertook the support of scientific research and innovation. Large research teams were organized and sponsored by governments and industrial corporations to develop and apply new techniques. To deal with this vast technological innovation we shall take the year 1945 as a dividing point.

Power Sources and Industrial Innovation

Before the development of nuclear power in 1945, there were no major innovations in fuel and power sources. Instead, the years between 1900 and 1945 witnessed improvements in the sources of power that already existed. The internal combustion engine was steadily improved to meet the needs of airplanes and automobiles, while the high-compression Diesel engine was further developed and used in trucks and tractors. By the 1890s, electricity was being generated on a large scale. In the 1900s there was an enormous expansion of electrical power generation and distribution as larger and larger production plants using steam, coal, or oil fired burners were created. Moreover, the distance over which electricity could be transmitted dramatically increased as did the efficiency of transmission. Electricity and the internal combustion engine remained the major sources of power for industry and transportation.

Although iron and steel remained the dominant materials of the industrial age, many new materials were created in the 20th century. By alloying iron and steel with other metals, important new materials were created. Silicon steel, which is highly magnetic, was produced as were the first stainless steels, alloys of steel with chromium and nickel. A new metal, aluminum, also became extremely important because its light weight and strength made it adaptable for aircraft construction and other uses.

The chemical industry made great strides in the 1900s as it created many new useful substances. Plastics, or substances produced by chemical reactions and then molded or pressed into permanent shapes, became commercially important as did artificial fibers. The first artificial textiles were made from rayon but later research led to the development of nylon which is extremely strong and flexible. Chemists succeeded in replacing many natural materials with artificially produced ones. The first of these was synthetic rubber, invented in 1893 but not widely used until the 1940s.

Increased chemical knowledge also led to the creation of the modern pharmaceutical industry. Aspirin was developed in 1899 when chemists successfully turned salicylic acid into acetylsalicylic acid. Sulfa drugs were introduced and the discovery of penicillin by Alexander Fleming eventually led to the production of the first antibiotic drugs. A host of advances in medical technology including blood transfusions, x-rays, and radium therapy have proved to be especially beneficial.

Agriculture

After 1900, science and technology helped to make agriculture increasingly productive by providing farmers with new sources of power, by producing improved plants and livestock breeds, and by developing new agricultural chemicals. In the early 1900s the first gasoline-powered tractors powerful enough to pull a plow appeared in the United States. Later, in the 1920s, all-purpose tractors were introduced that could be used to power a variety of new farm machinery from combines to cotton pickers. In time,

tractors replaced work animals and steam-powered machines on most U.S. farms. The extension of electricity to farms gave farmers a useful source of power to make farm work easier and more productive. The development of genetics in the 1900s made it possible to greatly improve plant and livestock varieties by scientific breeding. Plant varieties that produced high yields were developed as were improved cows that produced more milk and chickens that grew twice as fast as earlier breeds on half the feed. Chemistry produced synthetic fertilizers, insecticides, herbicides, and chemical disease controls such as fungicides, which have helped to increase production.

Transportation

Transportation changed more dramatically between 1900 and 1945 than in any other period of history. The main reason for the changes was the availability of new sources of power. The last major advance in steam engines was the replacement of piston engines with steam turbines, introduced in 1884 by Sir Charles Parsons and used to power the large ocean liners of the early 1900s. Soon, internal combustion engines replaced steam engines because they used less fuel. In 1892, Rudolph Diesel invented an especially fuel-efficient engine that did not use spark plugs; instead it ignited the fuel using heat generated by compression. Diesel engines were the main power source for the submarines of World War I, and they saw extensive civilian use soon afterward.

Henry Ford's introduction of assembly line mass production of automobiles led to dramatic production increases and made automobiles widely available. By 1923, production reached almost 2,000,000 cars a year. This, however, was not a period of great technological innovation, as automobiles maintained their basic designs from the 1890s. Although improvements such as the self-starter were added, producing autos in quantity was the major innovation. Automobiles became the chief means of transportation in the United States during the 1920s.

The airplane is truly an invention of the 1900s with the first successful flight by the Wright brothers in 1903. It was World War I that stimulated aircraft construction and development, transforming the manufacture of aircraft into an important industry. The small fragile wooden aircraft were soon transformed into metal framed and skinned aircraft. The first commercial airlines began service in Europe in 1919 and in many other parts of the world in the 1920s. In this period, airplanes were powered by gasoline engines and propellers. In the late 1930s, German engineers built the first planes with jet engines but these early jet aircraft were warplanes.

World War II again greatly stimulated improvements in aircraft design with the creation of the helicopter and the German V-l flying bomb, a pilotless aircraft. Rockets which were developed as a weapon during the war took on special significance in the years after 1945. The principle of rocket propulsion was already known and Robert H. Goddard had built experimental liquid fuel rockets in 1926. A group of German scientists spurred on by the war created the V-2 rocket which was propelled by burning a mixture of alcohol and liquid oxygen and reached a height of 100 miles.

Communications

Spectacular developments in communication have gone hand in hand with the great developments in transportation. Many significant inventions used in communications such as the typewriter, the linotype for setting lines of print, the rotary press and photography were products of the 1800s although they were vastly improved in the 1900s. Motion picture photography, however, was a creation of the 1900s and became widely available after World War I.

The greatest advance in communication was radio, which uses invisible electromagnetic waves to carry signals. Radio waves were predicted mathematically by James Clerk Maxwell in 1864 and demonstrated in the laboratory by Heinrich Hertz in 1881. By 1901 Guglielmo Marconi was using them to send messages in Morse code across the Atlantic Ocean.

Radio took a big step forward in 1906, when Lee De Forest invented a vacuum tube (thermionic valve) that could amplify weak signals by causing a strong electric current to mimic the variations in a weaker one. This made it possible to receive much weaker radio signals. Tubes also made it possible to generate purer radio waves (thus reducing interference) and to modulate radio waves with sound. Radio broadcasting to the general public began in the 1920s. Other outgrowths of radio technology included tape recording, radar, and television.

In the period between 1900 and 1945, technology had a tremendous impact on the lives of people throughout the world. The automobile and electric power greatly changed how people lived in this period. These inventions added to the ongoing process of urbanization and led to a virtual revolution in everyday daily life through the mass production of household goods and appliances. The rapid development of transportation and communication facilities including the airplane, movies, and radio made the world seem smaller and meant that what happened in one part of the world would have repercussions all over.

Technology After 1945

Today we live in an age of science and technology. The groundwork for this new age was laid by the Scientific Revolution of the 1600s and the Industrial Revolution of the 1700s. Beginning about 1940, spurred on by wartime pressures and massive government support, science and technology were combined on a massive scale for the first time in history. In a very short time, this combination of science and technology produced such great changes that some began to use the term revolution, referring to the new age of science and technology as "the Second Industrial Revolution" or "the Revolution of Science and Technology." In these years, nuclear power became a fact of life, while striking advances were made in engineering, chemicals, medical technology, transportation, and communications. Developments in the field of electronic engineering have brought computers, remote control, and instant communication. At the same time, humans have been able to explore beyond the earth for the first time, since space travel became possible starting in the 1960s.

Before World War II, as we have seen, major advances had been made in science in both Europe and America. Scientists working by themselves or with a few colleagues in the laboratories of universities or large industries had achieved important discoveries and breakthroughs. However, during and after the war, scientific research became more and more a carefully organized team effort. This began in 1939, when the U.S. government committed funds to the exploration of atomic energy. During the war, this exploration turned into a massive effort known as the Manhattan Project that involved thousands of scientists, engineers, and workers in the development of an atomic bomb. The success of this venture showed the effectiveness of organized research and prompted the government and private industry to spend more and more on scientific research and development. As a result of this organized scientific activity, knowledge began to accumulate at such an enormous rate that many began to speak of a "knowledge explosion." It was estimated that the amount of knowledge available was doubling every decade.

Even more important, each advance opened up new horizons for science and led to further progress in technology. New industries were created as thousands of new products became available. Among the products of the new technology were radar, antibiotics, jet aircraft, atomic weapons, nuclear reactors, space travel, solar energy, computers, lasers, and robots to name only a few. Today, the pace of change has accelerated and new technologies are being developed so rapidly that their effects are hard to foresee.

Space Travel

Perhaps the most dramatic technical advances have occurred in the realm of outer space where exploration has produced discoveries and inventions that will forever change the way people live, learn, and interact. The dream of space travel is as old as history, but in the 20th century the dream became reality with astonishing swiftness. As you recall, the first airplane flight occurred in 1903 and in 1926, Dr. Robert Goddard launched the first liquid-fueled rocket, which traveled 200 feet. During World War II, German scientists developed large rockets that were capable of carrying one-ton bombs a hundred miles into space and striking the earth 300 miles away.

After World War II, the superpower rivalry between the United States and the Soviet Union stimulated rocket research and development. Both nations realized that large rockets could be used to attack an enemy from thousands of miles away, and that satellites put into orbit around the earth by rockets, could transmit messages or spy on other countries.

The exploration of space began with a race between the United States and the Soviet Union. The United States was taken by surprise in 1957 when the Soviets launched the first artificial satellite, Sputnik, but the Americans managed to orbit a satellite of their own less than a year later. The first long space flights, the first woman in space, and the first space walk were all Soviet achievements. Meanwhile, in the 1960s, the United States conducted a manned space program in three stages: Project Mercury, to put men in space; Project Gemini, to develop better spacecraft; and Project Apollo, to land men on the moon. In 1961, Alan Shapard became the first American in space, and in

1962, John Glenn was the first to orbit the earth. By the mid-1960s the Americans took the lead in the "space race," and with the flight of *Apollo 11* in July 1969, the American astronauts Neil Armstrong and Edwin Aldrin became the first human beings to walk on the moon.

The United States made a few more flights to the moon in the early 1970s, but subsequent space exploration has been done by unmanned probes. The *Mariner* voyages to Mars, the *Voyager* mission to the outer planets, and the Soviet probes of Venus, to name only a few, have revolutionized our knowledge of the solar system. Since 1990 the Hubble Space Telescope has been photographing all parts of the universe with an image quality greater than is possible from any observatory on earth.

Manned flights have concentrated on putting space to practical use. The U.S. space shuttle, first used in 1981, enables astronauts to conduct experiments in space, launch satellites at low cost, and even catch and repair existing satellites. The Soviet (now Russian) *Mir* space station has been occupied by many different astronauts over a period of years. Meanwhile, thousands of communication satellites are in use, launched by France, India, China and many other countries.

Satellites are used not only for global communication, but also for TV broadcasting and even navigation. The Global Positioning System (GPS) uses satellites to enable anyone, anywhere on earth, to determine their precise latitude and longitude using a special computerized receiver. Positions are accurate to within a few yards. In the late 1990s it is expected that GPS receivers will be used widely on boats, cars, and aircraft and will replace other forms of navigation.

Electronic Communication

Television revolutionized U.S. life in the 1950s. The invention that made television possible was the cathode ray tube (CRT, "picture tube"), a vacuum tube with a screen that is scanned by an electron beam to produce a visible image. Other crucial inventions were the iconoscope (a light-sensitive CRT used in TV cameras) and the coaxial cable (which can carry high frequency signals without distortion).

TV broadcasts began in the 1930s, but World War II tied up technical resources and the real growth of TV began around 1949. The cultural impact of TV came from its ability to deliver the same entertainment and advertising to the entire nation at once, thus creating the expectation that people everywhere should look alike, talk alike, and act alike.

Telephone communication has advanced greatly since 1945. By the mid-1950s, almost all telephone exchanges were automatic: users could dial local numbers for themselves without the aid of an operator. Direct dialing was extended to long-distance calls in the 1960s and overseas calls in the 1970s.

Today, the worldwide telephone system can justifiably be called the world's largest machine. Its parts are linked together not only by wire cables, but also by radio, satellites, and fiber optics (cables that transmit light rather than electricity and can carry many signals at once with no interference or crosstalk).

In the 1980s, cellular telephones came into wide use. These require no connection to wires because they are linked by radio to the nearest antenna tower. Mobile radiotelephones had existed since the 1950s, but they required the user to be within a few miles of a particular tower. Cellular phones, by contrast, divide the country into cells, each served by its own tower, and cellular phones are automatically "handed off" from one cell to the next as the user moves around. Thus, cellular phones work almost anywhere.

Computers and Microelectronics

The electronic computer has affected life more than any other invention since the automobile. Although machines for performing mathematical calculations had existed since ancient times, it was not until the 1940s that these machines became electronic rather than mechanical. An important advance was John von Neumann's realization, in the 1940s, that a computer could store in its memory not only the numbers to be worked on, but also a program of instructions telling it what calculations to perform. This made computers tremendously more versatile.

The first commercially available programmable computer, UNIVAC, was patented in 1951. It nearly filled a room and contained hundreds of miles of wire. It relied on thousands of vacuum tubes, each of which consumed lots of power and was prone to failure. Vacuum tube computers ran slowly and broke down every few hours.

The invention of the transistor in 1947 made computers much more practical. A transistor does the same work as a vacuum tube, but consumes much less power and is much more reliable, in fact, it never wears out in normal use. (*See* **Transistor**, page 4-20.) By the mid-1960s, transistors were widely used not only in portable radios and tape recorders, but also in room-sized computers that handled large scientific or financial calculations. For the first time, accounting and record keeping could be done automatically, by machine; computer-printed bank statements, invoices, and mass mailings became a familiar part of the business scene.

The next major invention was the integrated circuit (IC), a combination of several transistors on a single chip of silicon. An ordinary transistor is made by adding impurities to a silicon crystal in three places. In 1958, Jack Kilby of Texas Instruments realized that by adding impurities in more than three places, he could make a single silicon chip into several transistors plus other interconnecting components. The first commercial ICs, in the early 1960s, were little more than double or triple transistors, but the number of components on each chip steadily increased, exceeding 1 million by the late 1980s.

In 1971, Intel Corporation introduced the microprocessor, an IC containing the entire central processing unit (CPU) of a computer. The same year, Intel also introduced a computer memory IC, and it became possible to build small, cheap microcomputers.

The impact of microprocessors was immense. Computers were suddenly much smaller, cheaper, and easier to use. This led to new computer applications.

The computers of the 1950s and 1960s had been so large and expensive that they were used only for large computations that could not be done any other way. But the late 1970s saw the advent of the personal computer, a device no larger than a typewriter and only slightly more expensive. Personal computers were used for word processing, simple bookkeeping, video games, and other tasks for which older computers would never have been cost effective. Microprocessors also provided computerized control functions in other kinds of equipment, such as automobile engines, video tape recorders, "intelligent" thermostats, and even wristwatches. *See* **Microprocessor,** page 4-14.

Robots

In the industrial world of tomorrow most of the physical work will be performed by robots guided by computers. Robots can be designed and programmed to analyze and modify production automatically without human intervention. Robot automation is already widely used in Japan, Germany, and the United States, particularly in the automotive industry where robots fit the parts of an automobile together on the assembly line, paint the body, and test the components to see that they work properly. Often, robots perform jobs that humans cannot do at all, such as working with dangerous materials or making millions of precise movements or measurements over and over without error or variations. Automated robots can make goods faster, better. and cheaper than people using old-style machinery.

Lasers

In 1960, C. H. Townes, A.L. Schawlow, and T. H. Maiman invented the laser, a device that produces beams of synchronized light waves. Its uses were extremely varied—a perfect example of the engineering applications of a scientific discovery. Lasers were used in surgery to weld damaged tissue in the eye, to burn away skin growths, and to repair decayed parts of teeth. Lasers helped engineers to build straight tunnels and pipelines and enabled manufacturers to cut precisely into hard substances such as diamonds. Lasers transmitted radio, television, and telephone signals and made it possible to show three-dimensional pictures on a television or film screen. One specialized use was holography, a process for making three-dimensional photographs of objects. Infrared lasers form images in computer printers and retrieve optically encoded data from compact disks.

Plastics

As you recall, the first synthetic substances called plastics were developed by chemists in the 1880s. Some of these substances were widely used such as celluloid to make movie films. However, it was not until after 1945 that plastics came into widespread daily use. They were used in kitchen equipment, construction of buildings, and manufacture of objects ranging from toys to cars. Plastics altered the appearance and manufacture of most objects people use daily from toothbrushes to telephones. Plastics are manufactured in many different forms with varied characteristics. For example, glass fiber has been molded into rigid shapes for car and ship bodies. Synthetic fibers also have come into wide use as they were made into easy-care fibers for clothing, furniture, and other uses.

Energy and Transportation

Automobiles and aircraft continued to advance after 1945. Cars became faster, more comfortable, and cheaper. Jet aircraft, using gas turbine engines with no propellers, came into wide use in the 1960s and made it possible to travel to any part of the world quickly and at relatively low cost. Air travel superseded railways and ships as the main mode of long-distance travel. Most passenger jets travel at about 600 mph, just below the speed of sound, but supersonic (faster than sound) passenger travel became available on some routes in 1976.

Meanwhile, concern has arisen about the world's supply of petroleum. A gasoline shortage in 1973 made Americans suddenly realize that petroleum will not necessarily always be abundant, and there was a sudden push to make cars more fuel-efficient. This push paid off; typical cars of the 1990s get three times as many miles per gallon as the luxury cars of the late 1960s. Moreover, by burning less gas, they produce less air pollution. It is not clear whether gasoline will still be widely available 50 or 100 years from now; the search for other sources of power is continuing.

In some ways the most promising source of energy is nuclear power, of which there are two forms: fission (splitting large atoms, such as uranium) and fusion (combining small ones, such as hydrogen). Both processes release gigantic amounts of energy from small amounts of fuel. Nuclear fission was the source of energy in the bombs dropped on Hiroshima and Nagasaki in 1945. Subsequently, nuclear fission reactors have been built in many countries; they use a controlled nuclear reaction to heat water, making steam, which drives turbines to generate electricity. In 1954, the United States launched the first nuclear-powered submarine, the *Nautilus*, and, in 1959, he first nuclear-powered ship, the *Savannah*.

A serious disadvantage of fission is that the fuel used for the reaction, and the reaction by-products, are radioactive and therefore dangerous. Fusion lacks these disadvantages; neither the fuel nor the products of fusion need be radioactive. Practical fusion reactors have not yet been developed, however, and are not expected for many years to come. As of the mid-1990s, intensive research is continuing.

"Natural" sources of energy, such as windmills and solar power, have attracted much interest since the 1970s, but a serious drawback is the limited amount of energy available in any particular place. In the short run, the solution to the world's energy problems is not merely increasing the supply, but also reducing the demand for energy by making existing technology more energy efficient. There have been remarkable successes; for example, the air conditioners of 1990 use only half as much energy as those of 1970, and microwave ovens consume far less energy than any earlier form of cooking.

Medical Research

Advances in science and technology were accompanied by important breakthroughs in medicine. As you recall, Alexander Fleming discovered penicillin, which stopped the growth of disease-carrying bacteria, in 1928. In later years, other substances were found that had similar effects. Streptomycin, which attacked penicillin-resistant bacteria, was discovered in 1944. In the years after 1945, these antibiotics transformed the fight against disease as they cured illnesses that were previously untreatable and made surgery safer from infection. Genetic research led to the discovery of DNA, the essential component of genes, and the understanding of the genetic code, or how a gene is structured. This breakthough made possible new research into viruses, bacteria, and human cells and made it possible to reproduce life forms in the laboratory.

Besides great scientific strides, the postwar era ushered in a "machine age" in medicine. Today hospitals rely heavily on computers. Monitoring devices first designed to measure the effects of weightlessness on astronauts are now used in hospitals. These devices consist of tiny sensors to measure pulse, heartbeat, and breathing. In intenslve care units, information from sensors is fed into a computer at a central nursing station. Advances in medical technology have been used in surgery. The first kidney transplant took place in 1952. The pacemaker developed in the 1960s improved heart care and the first successful heart transplant was done in 1968. Advances since 1970 include microsurgery, which makes it possible to repair tiny defects in the body and even reattach severed limbs; improved understanding of the body's immune system; and successful drug treatment of mental illnesses such as depression and schizophrenia.

Agriculture

Since 1945, farming has been transformed to meet the increased demand for more food and scientific farming has come into use. Scientists have discovered ways to produce seeds that yield more rice and wheat than ever before. This effort to use new seeds and farming methods such as increased use of chemical fertilizers to increase world food production is known as the "green revolution." Today, farming has become increasingly mechanized. Farmers use electric motors to run milking machines, irrigation pumps, and other farm machinery. They also use electronic and automated equipment such as devices that fill feed troughs and collect and grade eggs automatically. Some farmers use computers to solve problems and to obtain information from computer services at agricultural colleges or farm information centers. New food-producing techniques such as agriculture hydroponics to farm the sea and seabed are being explored. Also, technology has been applied to food processing and has resulted in freeze-drying and irradiation as methods of preservation.

The Effects of Technology

Modern technology has had a tremendous effect on the lives of people throughout the world. Inventions such as the automobile influenced where people lived and worked and how they spent their leisure time. Radio and television changed people's entertainment habits and brought them information about world events as they happened while the telephone revolutionized communications. Today, technology has brought goals into reach that few would have dreamed were possible 100 years ago. Humans have the capability to conquer hunger, cure and prevent many diseases, and transport goods and people swiftly and easily all over the world. Even space travel has become a reality.

Over the centuries of human history, technology has benefited people by increasing their production of goods and services, reducing the amount of labor needed to produce goods and services, making labor easier, and bringing higher living standards. Technology has made a tremendous increase in the production of goods and services possible and today workers can produce many more goods than workers of 100 years ago. For example, in the 1800s, people and animals provided the work force on American farms while today machines do most of the work. Machines have reduced the amount of labor needed to produce goods, thereby increasing worker productivity and giving them more leisure time. In the 1800s, factory workers toiled 12–16 hours a day, 6 days a week, and vacations were unheard of. Today, most American and European workers work 8 hours a day, 5 days a week, and have paid holidays and vacations. Technology has also made work easier as machines perform most of the laborious functions that used to be done by hand. Finally, the increased production of goods has produced high living standards in the world's industrialized nations where people are better fed, clothed, and housed than ever before in history. Technology has also increased our life span as better health care, nutrition, and sanitation have helped to eliminate and control disease.

Despite the many benefits technology has brought, it also has created serious problems. Although technology has enabled people in the industrialized nations of the world to live better and fuller lives, only a small part of the world's population enjoys the full benefits of modern technology. Moreover, the industrialized nations have been plagued by the undesirable side effects of technology such as air and water pollution. These side effects are largely the result of the fact that most technological innovations were put into use without any consideration or realization of possible harmful side effects. Thus, the advent of the automobile opened up wondrous new possibilities but as more and more automobiles came onto the roads, traffic, noise, and air pollution from exhaust fumes also came in its wake.

Among the most unwelcome effects of technology have been environmental pollution and the depletion of the world's natural resources. Today, most industrialized nations face problems of air, water, soil, and noise pollution. Although automobile exhaust and factory smoke and waste are the chief culprits, the products as well as the processes of industrialization also contribute to pollution. Thus, some chemical insecticides pollute the soil and water and also endanger plant and animal life. Power plants that burn coal and oil to generate electricity spew tons of pollutants into the air. The increased production techniques brought by technology have also led to a great depletion of the world's natural resources. As power production increases to meet ever-increasing production demands, the supply of fuels is rapidly decreasing. Many fear we are in danger of running out of oil and other resources that are not replaceable.

Other serious challenges have been created by technology. Perhaps the most important is controlling nuclear energy. Nuclear weapons threaten the very existence of our world. Although nuclear energy has been put to productive uses such as nuclear power plants to generate electricity, these too have proved to be dangerous. Events such as the Chernobyl disaster show that nuclear power plants can endanger human life if radiation leaks into the air. Moreover, disposing of nuclear waste which remains dangerous for thousands of years is a troublesome problem that still awaits solution. Still another serious challenge is the world's growing population which is a direct result of medical technology and its new drugs and techniques. As life expectancy goes up and the birth rate rises, population increases cause serious problems in the poorer developing nations where hunger and poverty remain a fact of life.

Milestones in Land Transportation

5000 B.C.   Humans used oxen, donkeys, and other animals as pack animals. Simple wooden sleds were the first primitive vehicles and were drawn by animals.

3500 B.C.   The wheel was invented, most likely in Mesopotamia. The first wheeled vehicles were four-wheeled carts and each wheel was a wooden disk made from 3 rectangular boards.

2500 B.C.   Wheeled vehicles were widely used. Chariots drawn by two horses yoked to a central pole appeared.

2000–1500 B.C.   The first spoked wheels appeared.

300s B.C.–200 A.D.   The Romans built the first extensive system of paved roads. At its height, their empire had 50,000 miles (80,000 kilometers) of well-kept roads.

1 A.D.   The Chinese invented the horsecollar enabling animals to carry much heavier loads. This did not appear in Europe until the 800s.

800s   The rigid horsecollar appeared in Europe enabling horses to carry heavy loads.

900s   The iron horseshoe came into use in Europe.

1000s   The whiffletree appeared making it possible for wagons to be pulled by teams of horses.

1100s   The first traveling carriages were built. In the 1400s carriages with suspension systems became known as coaches.

1500s   The earliest railroads were installed in coal mines, first in Germany, then in Britain. Raised wooden rails were used and people drew trucks along them.

1600s   Passenger wheeled vehicles were greatly improved and small private carriages and coaches were widely used.

1657   A regular cross-country service for travelers was started in England, using vehicles called stagecoaches.

1662   The first city coach line opened in Paris.

1700s   British inventors developed the steam engine.

1804   Richard Trevithick invented the first steam locomotive. On its first demonstration it traveled at 5 mph, carrying 10 tons of iron ore and 70 passengers in 5 wagons.

1810   Two Scots improved road-building techniques. Thomas Telford's method involved the use of three separate layers of stone. John McAdam devised a method that was simple and inexpensive—a single, thick layer of fine stone chips was surfaced with asphalt or concrete.

1825   The first successful steam-operated railroad began operating in England. The Stockton-Darlington railway line carried both passengers and freight.

1830   The world's first passenger railroad opened, the Liverpool-Manchester line. The Baltimore & Ohio was the first railroad in America to adopt steam power. It used the *Tom Thumb* engine, the first steam locomotive built to burn coal.

1831   The first railroad service in the United States began. It ran out of Charleston on the South Carolina Railroad.

1857   Steel rails first used in Britain.

1860   Etienne Lenoir of France invented the first practical internal combustion engine, which used the expansion of burning gas instead of steam.

1863   London's first subway opened.

1865   The first rail of America's Union Pacific, the world's first transcontinental railroad, was laid.

1869   The first transcontinental railroad in the United States was completed. George Westinghouse patented the air brake making high-speed train travel possible.

1878   Nikolaus Otto, a German inventor, developed an internal combustion engine that used only one-fifth the fuel of Lenoir's and it became a commercial success.

1879   Werner von Siemens demonstrated the first electric railroad (300 yards long) at the Berlin Trade Exhibition.

1885   Two Germans developed successful gasoline engines and the automobile. Karl Benz built a three-wheeled carriage while Gottlieb Daimler devised a motorcycle.

1888   John B. Dunlop of England patented the pneumatic (air-filled) tire. F.J. Sprague of the United States invented the electric street railway.

1890   London's subway began using electric trains.

1892   Rudolf Diesel patented the diesel engine.

1893   The first 100-mph railroad run was made by the American Locomotive *999*. Charles and Frank Duryea built the first successful gasoline-powered automobile in the United States.

1895   The Baltimore & Ohio railroad operated the first successful electric locomotive.

1896   Henry Ford produced his first successful car. Its 2-cylinder, 4-hp engine had a maximum speed of 25 mph.

1898   The first public subway in the United States was opened in Boston.

1902   First appearance of the high-performance 35-hp Mercedes. It had all the features of a modern automobile—a four-cylinder engine, pressed-steel chassis, honeycomb radiator, and gear stick.

1903   An electrically powered German locomotive set a speed record when it reached a speed of 130 mph.

1904   The New York City subway opened.

1907   C.S. Rolls and Sir Henry Royce built the first vehicle to outclass the Mercedes. Called the "Silver Ghost," it was produced almost unchanged until after World War II.

1908   Production began on the first truly mass-produced car, Henry Ford's Model T.

1925   The first diesel-electric locomotive began regular railroad service in the United States.

1950 The British Rover Company made the first turbine car. In 1953, it set the first speed record for its class—151 mph.

1964 Japan's Tokaido Line, the world's most highly automated intercity rail system, began service between Tokyo and Osaka. Trains travel up to 150 mph and carry up to 1,000 passengers each. Express trains make the 320-mile run in three hours.

1969 The first high-speed trains in North America began service: an experimental 85-mph train linking Boston and New York, a 120-mph unit between New York and Washington, and Canada's 90-mph Rapido, linking Toronto and Montreal. Although tested at speeds up to 170 mph, they are limited to speeds of half this because of tracks built in an earlier era. The French Aerotrain began service on the 75-mile run between Paris and Orleans.

1976 Britain introduces high-speed diesel trains that travel at an averge speed of 125 mph.

1983 The French TGV (*Train à Grande Vitesse*) set a world speed record reaching 170 mph. It regularly makes the 264-mile Lyon-Paris run at an average speed of 132 mph.

1987 Japan and West Germany tested prototype trains with top speeds of up to 250 mph.

Milestones in Water Transportation

10,000 B.C. Humans devised the first vessel which was a floating log that they straddled and guided with their feet and hands. Later they lashed together several logs to make a raft.

8000–7000 B.C. Rafts of materials such as logs or reeds were built. Dugouts and canoes were fashioned. These early crafts were propelled by paddles or poles.

5000 B.C. The first ship was the dugout canoe, a log in which a cavity was scooped out.

3200 B.C. Sailboats were invented by the Egyptians.

3000 B.C. Egyptian ships became the first seagoing vessels. They had a double, ladderlike mast supported by stays and at the stern were 3 steering oars. When the wind was not blowing, the mast was lowered and oarsmen rowed.

1200 B.C. The Phoenicians developed keeled sailing ships. They built a large fleet of merchant ships and for 500 years were the greatest merchant sailors in the world. Their ships used square sails but were driven mainly by oars.

500 B.C. The Greeks used galleys for warships but by 700 B.C. they built two-banked galleys (two rows of oarsmen on each side—one above the other). Later they invented the trireme, which carried 3 rows of oarsmen on each side, one above the other, and could go 168 miles in 24 hours. Their merchant ships were broader, with a single square sail, and no oarsmen. They built the first ships with 2 masts and eventually developed a simple 4-sail rig.

100 A.D. The rudder was invented in China.

500s The triangular lateen sail appeared. Unlike the widely used square sails, lateen sails worked well when ships sailed into the wind.

800 Square-rigged Viking long ships were the finest ships in Europe at this time. Long and lean, they had a sharply upturned bow and carried a single square sail on a mast about 40 feet high. The largest ships carried 30 oars on each side and had room for 240 men.

1100 Chinese and Mediterranean navigators developed the magnetic compass, which enabled sailors to navigate out of sight of land.

1200 Shipbuilders in northern Europe introduced a broad sturdy ship called a cog. By 1300, cogs had a rudder to steer rather than steering oars. In the Mediterranean area, shipbuilders increased the use of lateen sails, from small boats with 1 mast to large galleys with 3 masts.

1400–1500 The 3-masted ship made the voyages of discovery possible; 2- and 3-masted carracks combining the best features of the cog and the lateen-rigged sailing ships were developed.

1450 The carrack was the most used merchantship in the 15th century. A carrack of average size was about 125 × 34 feet. A smaller and more graceful type of carrack was the caravel.

1501 The invention of portholes by Descharges de Brest meant that mounted guns and naval artillery were used on ships for the first time.

1550 Galleons, big ships with a high sterncastle and 2 or 3 sails on the foremast and mainmast and 1 or 2 sails on the mizzenmast, came into use. They were used as both war and merchant ships. The East India Company built its own ships for the trade with India called "East Indiamen." They were merchantships armed like warships against possible attacks and carried 4-masts.

1620 The submarine was invented by Cornelius Drebbel, a Dutch physicist.

1776 David Bushell of the United States built an early submarine. Called the *Turtle,* it submerged when the ballast was filled with tanks of water.

1783 In France the Marquis Claude de Jouffroy d'Abbans built and sailed the first paddle-driven steamboat, called *Pyroscaphe* ("fire ship"), on the Saone River.

1790 In the United States, John Fitch's steamboat *Experiment* began passenger service between New York and Trenton, New Jersey but the venture failed.

1807 In the United States, Robert Fulton's steamboat *Clermont* started regular service on the Hudson River between New York City and Albany. It was 150 feet long with two 15-foot paddle-wheels and a 20 hp engine and traveled at a speed of almost 5 mph.

1812 The United States introduced frigate ships—fast, slender-hulled warships with four light sails attached to each of 3 masts. Some had as many as 50–60 guns and an additional deck.

1816 The Black Ball line began regular transatlantic service between New York and Liverpool. The ships were called packet ships because they transported packets of mail.

1819 The *Savannah,* built in the United States was the first steamship to cross the Atlantic. It took 26 days but the engines were used only half the time.

1833 Isaac McKim built the first American clipper, called the *Ann McKim.*

1836 The screw propeller was patented by two inventors—first in England by Francis Smith and then

6 weeks later in the United States by John Ericson, a Swedish engineer.

1838　Two English ships, *Sirius* and *Great Western,* became the first to cross the Atlantic entirely under steam, in 19 and 15 days, respectively.

1843　The ship *Great Britain,* built by British engineer Isambard Kingdom Brunel, became the first large iron ship to be driven by a screw propeller and the first screw-driven steamer to cross the Atlantic Ocean.

1845　Donald McKay launched *The Rainbow,* the first true clipper ship. Fastest of all the sailing ships, clippers were 3 masted, with a low slender hull and a vast area of sail (up to 5–6 sails on each mast).

1852　American-built clipper ships, especially those of Donald McKay, began to set speed records. The *Champion of the Seas* covered 465 miles in 24 hours. Steamships took another 25 years to beat this record.

1894　Sir Charles Parsons' ship *Turbinia* became the first to be fitted with a new type of engine, the steam turbine.

1907　The liner *Mauretania* was launched. The *Mauretania* and the *Lusitania* were the first giant express liners to use turbines and the first ships to reduce transatlantic traveling time to 5 days.

1932　The giant French liner *Normandie* was launched. Run by turboelectric power, it was the first of the 1,000-foot liners and for some years the biggest ship in the world.

1954　The U.S. Navy launched the world's first nuclear-powered ship, the submarine *Nautilus.*

1959　The United States launched the world's first nuclear powered merchant ship, the *Savannah.*

1959　The first Air Cushion Vehicle (ACV), invented by Christopher Cockerell, was tested. A mixture of boat and airplane, the hovercraft skims over the water on a cushion of compressed air forced beneath the vehicle by high-volume fans.

1960　America's nuclear-powered *Triton* was the first submarine to go around the world underwater without surfacing.

1980　Japan launched *Shin-Aitoku Maru,* a 1,750-ton tanker that was the first sail-assisted commercial ship in 50 years.

1983　German engineer Ortwin Fries invented the hinged ship which is designed to bend into a V-shape and suck up oil spills into its twin hulls.

Milestones in Air Travel

1783　Sebastian Lenormand was the first person to use a parachute. He jumped from the Tower of the Montpellier Observatory in France.

1783　Joseph Montgolfier and his brother Etienne perfected the hot-air balloon and then built the first lighter-than-air balloon that carried a person. Pilatre de Rozier, a French physician, became the first man to leave the ground in a balloon that rose to 84 feet. A month later, the first free flight was made when de Rozier and the Marquis d'Arlandes traveled over Paris and the Seine for a distance of 5½ miles. Only 10 days later, Jacques Alexandre Charles and M.N. Robert ascended in a hydrogen balloon of their own design and construction covering 27 miles in 2 hours.

1797　Andre Garnerin of France was the first person to use a parachute to jump from a balloon, at a height of 3,000 feet.

1804　Using the principles of air resistance, Sir George Cayley of England began constructing model gliders, which became the prototype for later airplanes.

1842　Based on Cayley's research, W.S. Henson of England designed the first complete steam-powered airplane, called the "Aerial Steam Carriage," which was a 150-foot span monoplane.

1853　Sir George Cayley of Britain built the first man-carrying glider.

1884　The first practical dirigible, *La France,* was flown by Captains C. Renard and A.C. Krebs.

1890　Clément Ader achieved short hopping flights of 150 feet with steam-powered aircraft but the pilot had no control over the aircraft's movements.

1895　David Schwartz built two rigid airships of aluminum which became plentiful in the 1880s for the first time. This light metal became important in the development of aircraft.

1896　Samuel P. Langley, an American, successfully flew his model aircraft *Aerodrome* for 90 seconds, covering half a mile. It was a 2-hp monoplane with a steam engine.

1898　Count Ferdinand von Zeppelin of Germany designed a giant rigid airship. It was 400 feet long, had two 16-hp Daimler engines, and contained 400,000 cubic feet of hydrogen.

1903　Wilbur and Orville Wright made the first successfully powered, controlled, and sustained airplane flight on December 17 at Kitty Hawk, North Carolina. Their biplane *Flyer* spanned more than 40 feet and was outfitted with a 4-cylinder, 16-hp gasoline engine. The Wrights made and designed every part of the plane themselves. Of the four flights made that day, the first, by Orville, covered 120 feet in 12 seconds while the fourth, by Wilbur, covered 852 feet in 59 seconds.

1907　The twin-rotor type helicopter designed by Paul Cornu was the first manned helicopter to make a free flight. It reached a height of 5 feet.

1909　Louis Blériot made the first successful flight across the English Channel. His 24-hp Mark XI monoplane, which was constructed of glued wood and sailcloth, took 37 minutes to fly the 31 miles.

1910　The huge zeppelins, constructed around a rigid metal framework instead of the earlier balloons, went into passenger service for the first time. They carried 35,000 passengers in 4 years and were used for bombing and reconnaissance in World War I. In the 1920s and 1930s they provided the first regular transatlantic passenger services.

1911　Glenn Curtiss piloted and co-designed the first practical seaplane. The world's first twin-engined plane—the British *Short Tandem-Twin,* appeared.

1914　The German airship *Hindenburg* (an 803-foot long zeppelin) was the largest ever built.

1915　The German Fokker E monoplane, the first true fighter plane, was introduced.

1918　By the end of World War I there were specialized aircraft of many kinds—from transports to light fighters and heavy bombers—that could travel over 150 mph and cruise above 2,000 feet. The world's first scheduled airmail service was established between New York City, Philadelphia, and Washington, D.C.

1919 In a converted bomber, a Vickers Vimy twin-engined biplane, two British aviators, John Alcock and Arthur Brown, became the first to fly nonstop across the Atlantic. They covered the 1,890 miles between Newfoundland and Ireland in 16 hours 27 minutes.

1923 Juan de la Cierva of Spain built the first practical rotating-wing aircraft by fitting a large, horizontal, overhead rotor driven by an engine and airscrew to the fuselage of an Avro 504 trainer. It was the flapping rotor that later made helicopter development possible. J. A. Macready and Oakley G. Kelly made the first nonstop transcontinental flight. In a Fokker T-2, they covered the 2,520 miles from New York to San Diego in 26 hours 50 minutes 3 seconds.

1927 Charles Lindbergh of the United States made the first nonstop transatlantic solo flight from New York to Paris, in a single-engine monoplane called the *Spirit of St. Louis.* He flew the 3,610 miles in 33 hours 30 minutes at an average speed of 107.4 mph.

1929 The *Graf Zeppelin* became the first airship to fly around the world. lt took 21 days 7 hours 43 minutes.

1930 Frank Whittle of England patented the design for the aircraft jet propulsion engine that was put into wide use 10 years later.

1932 Amelia Earhart was the first woman to make a solo crossing of the North Atlantic. She flew from Newfoundland to Ireland in 15 hours 18 minutes.

1933 Wiley Post, an American, made the first solo flight around the world. He covered 15,596 miles in 7 days 18 hours 49 minutes flying time.

1939 Igor Sikorsky invented the first practical helicopter, the single-rotor VS-300. The Heinkel Company of Germany built and flew the first jet-propelled airplane. It was capable of reaching 435 mph.

1941 Igor Sikorsky made the first helicopter flight of more than 100 minutes. Britain's first jet was a Gloster aircraft, with engines designed by Sir Frank Whittle.

1944 The German firm Focke-Wulf designed one of the earliest VTO (vertical take-off) models—a fighter that climbed 25,000 feet a minute and traveled, after leveling off, at 620 mph.

1949 In a U.S. Boeing B-50 bomber, Capt. James Gallagher and a crew of 18 made the first nonstop flight around the world. At an average speed of 239 mph they covered 22,500 miles in 94 hours 1 minute, after being refueled in the air 4 times.

1952 British Overseas Airways, using the de Haviland *Comet 1,* began the world's first scheduled jet airliner passenger service.

1953 Lt. Col. Marion Carl of the United States broke the altitude record by flying a rocket-powered plane, the Douglas Skyrocket, to 83,235 feet. Three months later, Scott Crossfield, using the same plane, made the first flight at 1,327 mph, nearly twice the speed of sound.

1955 The American Boeing 707 was the first of the "big jets." It was able to travel 4,000 miles at 600 mph, carrying up to 202 passengers.

1957 *Sputnik I,* launched by the Soviet Union, was the world's first successful artificial satellite.

1958 The United States sent its first satellite, *Explorer I,* into orbit.

1961 Yuri Gargarin of the Soviet Union became the first person to fly in outer space when he made a single-orbit flight around the earth. A month later Alan B. Shepard of the United States made a 302-mile suborbital flight in the Mercury capsule *Freedom 7.*

1962 John Glenn became the first American to orbit the earth. He completed 3 orbits in 5 hours 55 minutes.

1963 Valentina Tereshkova of the Soviet Union became the first woman in space. Joseph Walker, an American test pilot, flew the rocket-powered X-15 to a record altitude of 354,200 feet.

1964 The Soviet Union's *Voskhod I* became the first spacecraft to carry a team of astronauts—a crew of 3.

1965 Aleksei Leonov became the first person to "walk" in space, during the March flight of *Voskhod 2.* Three months later, astronaut Edward H. White became the first American to accomplish this, on the *Gemini 4* flight.

1966 Both the Soviet Union and the United States succeeded in soft-landing unmanned spacecraft on the moon. The crew of the U.S. *Gemini 8* achieved the first "linkup" in space by successfully docking their capsule with an orbiting unmanned *Agena* target vehicle.

1968 In September, the Soviet Union's *Zond 5* became the first unmanned craft to go around the moon and return to earth. On Christmas Eve, the 3-man crew of America's *Apollo 8* became the first human beings to make a flight around the moon.

1969 The British-French supersonic jet transport *Concorde 001* made its first test flight. In July, *Apollo 11* astronauts Neil Armstrong and Edwin Aldrin became the first men to walk on the moon.

1970 Boeing introduced the widebodied 747 which carries up to 490 passengers, thereby beginning the era of jumbo jets.

1971 The Soviet Union launched the first space station, *Salyut 1.* It was manned for 23 days but the crew of 3 died on their return flight.

1973 The first U.S. space station, *Skylab l,* was launched.

1975 The first international space docking was carried out by the Russian *Soyuz 19* and the U.S. *Apollo 18.*

1976 The *Concorde* began passenger service. It crosses the Atlantic in less than three hours, flying at speeds of more than 1,000 mph.

1981 The first reusable space vehicle, the space shuttle *Columbia,* made its first flight.

1983 Sally Ride became the first U.S. woman in space during a flight of the space shuttle *Challenger.*

1986 The space shuttle *Challenger* exploded shortly after lift-off, killing its crew of 7.

1988 Space shuttle flights resumed.

History of the Computer

1642 Blaise Pascal, a French scientist and philosopher, built the first successful digital calculating machine. This first adding machine could only count.

1671–1694 Gottfried Wilhelm Leibniz, a German mathematician, invented in 1671 and completed in 1694, a more advanced adding machine. Called the "Stepped Reckoner," it could count, multiply, divide, and extract square roots.

1835 Charles Babbage, an English inventor, formulated and drew up plans for a device called the "analytical engine," the world's first computer.

1859 George Boole, an English logician and mathematician, developed symbolic logic, the basis of what is now called Boolian algebra and binary switching, upon which modern computing is based.

1886–1890 Herman Hollerith, an American statistician, invented the punched card and in 1890 developed a tabulating machine to use punched cards to classify and count the data for the U.S. census.

1930 Vannevar Bush, an American scientist, developed a large electromechanical analog computer.

1939–1944 Herman Aiken of Harvard with IBM engineers constructed a fully automatic calculator.

1942 John Atanasoff and Clifford Berry of Iowa State University constructed the first electronic digital calculator. John Von Neumann at Princeton designed a computer that stored programs and used binary numbers.

1946 Presper Eckert and John W. Mauchly at the University of Pennsylvania invented and developed ENIAC (Electronic Numerical Integrator and Calculator), the first all-electronic digital computer.

1951 UNIVAC 1 was introduced, the first computer to handle both numerical and alphabetic information with ease. It was the first mass produced computer.

1956 A logical and algebraic language called FORTRAN for programming computers was introduced.

1958 Jack Kilby of Texas Instruments built the first working integrated circuit (IC) from a chip of silicon.

1960 Transistors began to be used in computers, replacing tubes.

1964 BASIC, a simplified form of FORTRAN for students, was introduced at Dartmouth College.

1971 Pocket calculators were introduced. The Intel Corporation introduced a microprocessor, an entire computer processor on a silicon chip.

1977 Apple, Commodore, and Tandy introduced affordable personal computers.

1982 IBM introduced its Personal Computer (PC), whose design was not patented and was easily "cloned" (copied) by other manufacturers. IBM PC clones soon dominated the personal computer market.

1984 Apple introduced its Macintosh personal computer, with a windowed screen display modeled on that of the slightly earlier Xerox Star.

1990 Networks of fast microcomputers rivaled the power of the fastest large computers, and the future of large computers began to be debated.

EXHIBIT 9.1
Some Important Inventions and Discoveries

Invention or Discovery	Origin	Date
adding machine (addition, multiplication)	Leibniz	1670s
adding machine (addition only)	Pascal	1642
AIDS (acquired immuno-deficiency syndrome)	U.S. Centers for Disease Control, Pasteur Institute, Paris	1981
air brake	Westinghouse	1869
air-conditioning	Carrier	1911
aircraft, fighter	Germany	1915
aircraft, jet, first practical	Various	1940–41
aircraft, jet, passenger service	British Overseas Airways Company	1952
airplane, first successful controlled flight	Wright brothers	1903
airplane, glider	Cayley	1853
airplane, supersonic, commercial passenger	British Airways	1976
airship, lighter than air	Zeppelin	1898
anesthesia, with ether	Long	1842
anesthesia, with ether, public demonstration	Morton	1846
antibiotic, penicillin	Fleming	1928
antimatter, antielectrons observed in laboratory	Anderson	1932
antiseptic surgery	Lister	1865
aspirin (acetylsalicylic acid)	Hofmann	1893
atom, as basic unit of chemistry	Dalton	1808
atom, structure of, nucleus and electrons	Rutherford	1911
automobile, mass-produced (Model T)	Ford	1908
automobile, three-wheeled	Benz	1885
bacteria	Leeuwenhoek	1670s
Bakelite	Baekeland	1909
balloon, as aircraft	Montgolfier brothers	1783
barometer	Torricelli	1643
battery	Volta	1800
bicycle	MacMillan	1840
blast furnace	Unknown	1400s

Invention or Discovery	Origin	Date
Boolean algebra	Boole	1859
brakes, hydraulic	Loughead	1918
bubble chamber, to observe subatomic particles	Glaser	1951
calculator, microelectronic, pocket-sized	Various	1971–73
calculus, differential and integral	Leibniz	1748
calculus ("fluxions")	Newton	1687
cash register	Ritty	1879
cell, as basic unit of all living things	Schwann, Schleiden	1838
celluloid, (first plastic)	Hyatt	1869
chariot	Unknown	2000–1500 B.C.
circulation of blood	Harvey	1628
clock, mechanical	Various	1300s
clock, with pendulum	Huygens	1656
cloud chamber, to observe subatomic particles	Wilson	1911
computer, analog	Bush	1927
computer, digital, all-electronic	Eckert, Mauchly	1946
computer, digital, in commercial use	UNIVAC	1951
computer, digital, fully programmable	Von Neumann	1942
computer, digital, mechanical	Babbage	1835
computer, digital, microelectronic	Apple, Tandy, Commodore	1977
computer, language BASIC	Kemeny, Kurtz	1964
computer, language FORTRAN	IBM	1958
computer, langugage Pascal	Wirth	1971
computer logic	Boole	1859
cotton gin	Whitney	1793
dialysis (artificial kidney machine)	Kolff	1943
diamond, synthetic	General Electric	1955
DNA, structure	Watson, Crick	1953
economics, first scientific study	Smith	1776
electromagnetism	Oersted	1820
electromagnetism, early studies	Faraday, Henry	1831
electromagnetism, theory developed	Maxwell	1864
electron, charge measured accurately	Millikan	1923
electron, mathematical theory of orbits, etc.	Schrödinger	1926
electron, as part of atom	Bohr	1913
electron, as particle of electricity	Thomson, Townsend	1896–98
elevator (for passengers)	Otis	1857
engine, internal combustion, burning coal gas	Lenoir	1860
engine, internal combustion, burning gasoline	Daimler	1885
engine, internal combustion, four-cycle	Otto, Langen	1876
engine, internal combustion, no spark plugs	Diesel	1892
engine, jet	Whittle	1930
evolution, biological	Darwin	1859
eyeglasses	Various	1200s
facsimile (fax) machine	Bain	1843
facsimile (fax) machine, microelectronic	United States, Japan	1980s
fan, electric	Wheeler	1882
food, quick-frozen	Birdseye	1920
galaxies, recognized as such	Hubble	1924
gas, for lighting	Various	1850s
generator, electric, in laboratory	Faraday	1831
generator, electric, in practice	Various	1870s
genetics, first scientific study	Mendel	1865
geological history, first scientific study	Lyell	1830
geometry, first systematic study	Euclid	ca. 300 B.C.
germ theory of disease	Pasteur	1860s
governor, on steam engine	Watt	1788
gravity, accurate mathematical model	Newton	1687
gunpowder, in Europe	Unknown	ca. 1200

Invention or Discovery	Origin	Date
heart, artificial, implanted in human	Jarvik	1982
heart-lung machine	Gibbon	1953
heart transplant	Barnard	1968
helicopter, first practical	Sikorsky	1941
heredity, first scientific study	Mendel	1865
homeostasis (self-regulation of living organism)	Bernard	1865
horsecollar, rigid, to pull heavy load	Various	ca. 800
horsecollar, to hitch horse to heavy load	China	ca. 1
horseshoe, first use in Europe	Various	ca. 1000
hovercraft	Cockerell	1959
hypodermic syringe	Pravaz	1853
insulin	Banting, Best	1921
integrated circuit	Kilby	1958
iron, cast	Unknown	1400s
iron, first use	Asia Minor	ca. 1000 B.C.
irrigation, of farm crops	Unknown	Before 3000 B.C.
isotopes, of neon	Thomson	1912
jet engine	Whittle	1930
kidney machine	Kolff	1943
laser	Townes, Schawlow, Maiman	1960
lenses	Various	1200s
light, carbon arc	Davy	1809
light, electric	Edison	1879
light, refraction of	Snell	1621
lock, pin-tumbler	Yale	1865
locomotive, steam	Trevithick	1804
logarithms	Stifel	1544
logarithms, published tables	Napier	1614
loom, power	Cartwright	1786
loom, water-powered (water frame)	Arkwright	1769
loom, to weave designs automatically	Jacquard	1804
medicine, first scientific approach	Hippocrates	400s B.C.
Metric System	France	1790s
microcomputer, commercial, in wide use	Apple, Tandy, Commodore	1977
microorganisms	Leeuwenhoek	1670s
microprocessor	Intel Corp.	1971
microscope, compound	Janssen	1590
microscope, electron	Various	1930s
microscope, first extensive scientific use	Leeuwenhoek	1670s
microwave oven	United States	1950s
molecules, as fixed combination of atoms	Dalton	1808
motion picture camera	Marey	1888
motion picture projector	Edison	1891
motion pictures, with sound	Edison	1913
motorcycle	Daimler	1885
motor, electric	Faraday	1822
mutations, genetic	de Vries	1901
neutron	Chadwick	1932
nuclear energy, controlled fission	Fermi	1942
nuclear weapons, used in warfare	United States	1945
oil well, first successful	Drake	1859
oxygen	Priestley, (one of several discoverers)	1774
paper	Cai Lun	105
paper, first use in Europe	Various	1400s
parachute	Lenormand	1783
pavement, macadam	McAdam	1810
penicillin	Fleming	1928

Invention or Discovery	Origin	Date
periodic table	Mendeleyev	1868
phonograph	Edison	1877
phonograph, electronic	Maxfield	1925
photocopying, dry (xerography)	Carlson	1938
photocopying machine	Graffin	1900
photography, color	Lumière brothers	1904
photography, dry plates	Maddox	1871
photography, first use	Niepce	1826
photography, roll film	Eastman	1889
photons	Planck	1900
planetary motion, laws of	Kepler	1609
plastic, Bakelite	Baekeland	1909
plastic, celluloid	Hyatt	1869
plow, cast iron	Newbold	1797
plow, steel	Deere	1837
plow, wooden, pulled by oxen	Unknown	Before 3000 B.C.
positron, antielectron	Anderson	1932
pressure cooker	Papin	1680
printing, from movable type, China	Bi Sheng	1045
printing, from mass-produced movable metal type	Gutenberg	1455
propeller, for ship	Smith, Ericson	1836
psychoanalysis	Freud	1895
psychology, experimental, first studies	Wundt	1879
pulsars	Hewish, Bell	1967
pump, piston type	Ctesibius	200s B.C.
pump, screw type	Archimedes	200s B.C.
punched card, counted and sorted by machine	Hollerith	1890
quantum theory	Planck	1900
radar	Watson-Watt	1936
radioactivity	Becquerel	1896
radio, communications across Atlantic	Marconi	1901
radio, first practical use	Marconi	1895
radio, FM	Armstrong	1933
radio waves, in laboratory	Hertz	1881
radio waves, predicted mathematically	Maxwell	1864
railway, commercial service	England	1825
railway, transcontinental, completed	Union Pacific	1869
reaper (harvesting machine)	McCormick	1834
refraction of light	Snell	1621
refrigeration, to make ice	Perkins	1834
refrigerator	Goss	1913
relativity theory	Einstein	1905
rifle	Germany (?)	ca. 1500
road, paved	Rome	200s B.C.
robots, in science fiction	Čapek	1921
robots, practical	United States	1960s
rocket	Goddard	1926
rubber, vulcanized	Goodyear	1839
sailboat	Egypt	ca. 3200 B.C.
satellite, artificial	Soviet Union	1957
seaplane	Curtiss	1911
seed drill (for planting)	Tull	ca. 1700
sewing machine	Howe	1846
ship, clipper	Various	1840s
ship, frigate	U.S. Navy	1812
ship, nuclear-powered, civilian	United States	1959
ship, nuclear-powered, submarine	U.S. Navy	1954
ship, sailing	Egypt	ca. 3000 B.C.
ship, sailing, into wind	Various	500–600
ship, steam-powered, crossing Atlantic	United States	1819
shuttle, flying (for weaving)	Kay	1733
silicon chip integrated circuit	Kilby	1958
slide rule	Mannheim	1859

Invention or Discovery	Origin	Date
solar battery	Pearson, Chapin, Fuller	1954
solar system, earth-centered theory	Ptolemy	100s
solar system, sun-centered theory	Copernicus	1543
space station	Soviet Union	1971
space travel, first human in space	Leonov	1961
space travel, to moon	Armstrong, Aldrin	1969
spacecraft, reusable	United States	1981
spinning jenny	Hargreaves	1764
spinning wheel	Germany	1200s
stagecoach, scheduled service	England	1657
starter, electric for automobile	Kettering	1911
steamboat, early experiment	Papin	ca. 1680
steamboat, passenger	Fitch	1790
steamboat, passenger, commercial success	Fulton	1807
steam engine	Newcomen	1712
steam engine, condensing	Watt	1765
steam turbine	Parsons	1884
steel, process for making efficiently	Bessemer	1870s
submarine	Drebbel	1620
submarine, nuclear-powered	U.S. Navy	1954
submarine, practical	Bushnell	1776
telegraph	Morse	1837
telephone	Bell	1876
telescope	Lippershey	1608
telescope, first scientific use	Galileo	ca. 1610
television, iconoscope tube for TV camera	Zworykin	1923
tire, air-filled	Dunlop	1888
tractor, gasoline-driven	Various	1900–10
tractor, steam-driven	Cugnot	1769
transistor	Bardeen, Brattain, Shockley	1947
transplant, human heart	Barnard	1968
trigonometry	Ptolemy	100s
tuberculosis, bacteria identified	Koch	1882
typesetting machine, Linotype	Mergenthaler	1884
typewriter	Sholes, Glidden, Soulé	1868
vaccination, smallpox, using related disease	Jenner	1796
vaccine, measles	Enders	1963
vacuum cleaner	McGaffey	1869
vacuum cleaner, electric	Spangler	1907
vacuum tube, diode, to detect radio signals	Fleming	1904
vacuum tube, triode to amplify signals	De Forest	1906
virus, tobacco mosaic	Ivanovsky	1892
vitamins	Hopkins	1906
vulcanization of rubber	Goodyear	1839
washing machine	King	1851
waterwheel	Rome, Mesopotamia	ca. 100 B.C.
wheel, on ox cart	Mesopotamia	3500–3000 B.C.
wheel, with spokes	Unknown	2000–1500 B.C.
whiffletree (to hitch horses to wagon)	Various	ca. 1000
windmill, first use in Europe	Various	1100s
windmill, with tail to keep it facing wind	Lee	1745
X rays	Roentgen	1895
xerography, Xerox machine	Carlson	1938

HISTORY OF THE UNITED STATES

AAA *See* **Agricultural Adjustment Act.**

ABC Conference The ABC powers (Argentina, Brazil, and Chile) met with the United States at Niagara Falls, Canada, during the spring of 1914 to help prevent war between the United States and Mexico. The tension arose over the arrest of unarmed American marines who had gone ashore for supplies at Tampico, Mexico. President Woodrow Wilson refused to accept the apology extended by General Victoriano Huerta of Mexico and ordered the U.S. Marines to occupy Veracruz, Mexico's chief port. War seemed imminent, but Huerta fled the country and was replaced by Venustiano Carranza. The new government was quickly recognized by the United States.

Abolition The movement to abolish slavery in the United States gained momentum after the Missouri Compromise of 1820. Radical abolitionists, led by William Lloyd Garrison of Massachusetts, demanded the immediate emancipation of all slaves. Moderates wished to compensate the slave owners. Militants like John Brown resorted to violence. Brown murdered five proslavery men in Kansas. Later, at Harper's Ferry in what is now West Virginia, he tried to start an armed insurrection of slaves. *See* **John Brown's Raid.**

Abrams v. United States (250 U.S. 616, 1919) During World War I Congress passed two espionage and sedition acts outlawing utterances detrimental to the war effort. Abrams and others were convicted under these acts for throwing "subversive" leaflets from a roof in New York and were sentenced to twenty years' imprisonment. Justice Oliver Wendell Holmes dissented from the Supreme Court decision sustaining the conviction. In his dissent, Holmes describes the "clear and present danger" theory. He went on to say: "In this case sentences of twenty years' imprisonment have been imposed for the publishing of two leaflets that I believe the defendants had as much right to publish as the Government has to publish the Constitution of the United States now vainly invoked by them."

Adams, Abigail (1744–1818) Wife of President John Adams and influential first lady in his administration, she was an early and persuasive advocate of equality of the sexes. She was the mother of John Quincy Adams, sixth president of the United States.

Adams, Charles Francis (1807–1866) He was the son of President John Quincy Adams, was graduated from Harvard in 1825, and practiced law in Boston. He served in Congress 1856–61 and resigned when appointed by President Lincoln as minister to England. This post was of crucial importance during the Civil War. He performed his diplomatic services with great skill, resolving the *Trent* affair and issues involving warships built in England for the Confederacy. He also helped arbitrate the *Alabama* claims after the war.

Adams, John (1735–1826) Harvard graduate and attorney, he acted as defense counsel for the British soldiers who were charged with murder in the "Boston massacre" case. A member of the Continental Congress (1774–78), he served on the committee that drafted the Declaration of Independence. He also played a key role in drafting the Massachu-

setts Constitution of 1780. He was one of the three negotiators (with Benjamin Franklin and John Jay) of the Peace Treaty of 1783 with England, was minister to Great Britain (1785–88), first vice president of the United States in the administration of George Washington, and second president of the United States (1797–1801). *See also* Presidents of the United States section, beginning on page 10-83.

Adams, John Quincy (1767–1848) Like his father, he was a Harvard graduate, an attorney, and president (sixth) of the United States. He served as minister to the Netherlands, Prussia, Russia, and Great Britain and was chairman of the commission that negotiated the Treaty of Ghent (1814), ending the War of 1812. As secretary of state in the administration of James Monroe (1817–25), he played a principal role in formulating the Monroe Doctrine (1823). As president (1825–29), he sponsored internal improvements in the national interest. After his defeat for re-election in 1828 by Andrew Jackson, he served in the House of Representatives (1831–48), where he steadfastly opposed the extension of slavery in the territories of the United States and led the opposition to the "rap rule" prohibiting discussion in the House on antislavery petitions. *See also* Presidents of the United States section, beginning on page 10-83.

Adams-Onis Treaty (1819) Jackson's virtual conquest of Florida and the revolutionary activities in Central and South America of Bolivar, San Martin, and O'Higgins formed a favorable setting for this treaty. By its terms Spain ceded Florida to the United States; the United States assumed claims in Florida against Spain to a total of $5 million; the United States gave up all claims to Texas; and the "Spanish step line" from the mouth of the Sabine River to the 42nd parallel at the Pacific Coast marked the limits of Spanish territory in North America.

Adamson Railway Labor Act (1916) This act was passed when President Woodrow Wilson urged Congress to avert an imminent railroad strike. The act provided the same pay for an eight-hour day as for the previous ten-hour day, plus time-and-a-half for overtime. The president was given the power to take over the railroads if, for military reasons, he thought it necessary.

Adams, Samuel (1722–1803) A leading revolutionary in the independence movement, he mounted opposition to the Sugar Act (1763), the Stamp Act (1765), and the Townshend Acts (1767). He helped organize the Sons of Liberty and was a leader of the Boston Tea Party (1773) and a signer of the Declaration of Independence (1776). He opposed compromise and urged immediate independence from Great Britain. He served as governor of Massachusetts (1794–97).

Addams, Jane (1860–1935) Social reformer and peace activist, she was the founder of Hull House (1889), which she described in her book, *Twenty Years at Hull House* (1930). The settlement provided such services as health care, classes in English, and other educational and cultural activities, including art, music, and drama. Her peace activities included chairing the International Congress of Women at The Hague in 1915, at which she helped found and became first president of the Women's International League for Peace and Freedom.

Affirmative Action   In 1965, President Lyndon B. Johnson signed an executive order directing that employers on federal contracts must take "affirmative action" to hire qualified women and members of minorities. In the Alan Bakke case involving admission to a California medical school, the Supreme Court in 1978 struck down a rigid quota system but upheld the general principle of affirmative action.

AFL   *See* **American Federation of Labor**.

AFL-CIO   *See* **American Federation of Labor and Congress of Industrial Organizations**.

Afro-American Unity, Organization for (1964) Malcolm X broke with the Black Muslims over the idea of total separation of the races. His new organization advocated a union of all non-white peoples everywhere to fight for equality with whites.

Agassiz, Jean Louis Rodolphe (1807–1873) An eminent geologist and zoologist, he came to the United States from Switzerland in 1846. At Harvard University, he established the Harvard Museum of Comparative Zoology (1859) and carried out field work in Brazil, at Lake Superior, and in California. He opposed Charles Darwin's theory of evolution through natural selection. As a teacher and lecturer he exerted considerable influence in the advancement of science.

Agricultural Adjustment Act (AAA) (1933) The first farm relief measure passed by the New Deal, it adopted the principle of restricting production by paying farmers to reduce crop acreages.

By its provisions farmers were paid not to raise livestock and to destroy acreage already planted in order to decrease production by about 30 percent. The money paid to cooperating farmers came from taxes levied on food processors. In 1936 (*United States* v. *Butler*) the Supreme Court declared the law unconstitutional.

When the act was declared unconstitutional, crop restrictions were accomplished by the Soil Conservation and Domestic Allotment Act of 1936. This latter act in turn was superseded by a second Agricultural Act in 1938. Under these laws, (1) farmers were paid to follow soil conservation practices for the benefit of the nation—payments were made to farmers to plant soil-building crops in place of market staples; (2) a program of acreage allotments and (3) one of marketing quotas were prepared in order to keep surpluses down; and (4) farmers were given commodity loans to support prices and to withhold surpluses from the market. Desirable prices for different staples were determined by the principle of "parity," one of restoring the farmers' equality of purchasing power to that of other groups.

***Alabama* claims**   During the Civil War, naval vessels, including the raider *Alabama*, were built in Britain for the Confederacy, contrary to international law since Britain was a declared neutral. These ships were permitted to "escape" and wrought heavy damage on Union merchant shipping. At the war's end, the United States claimed direct and collateral damages (based on the prolongation of the war) amounting to over a billion dollars. An international tribunal consisting of representatives from Brazil, Italy, and Switzerland along with the United States and Great Britain settled the claims (August 25, 1872) with an award to the United States of $15,500,000.

Alaska Purchase (1867)   Russia was ready to sell Alaska, which was very remote from Moscow and too difficult to protect from possible aggression by Great Britain. Secretary of State Seward negotiated its purchase for $7,200,000. The Senate, mindful of Russia's pro-Union stand during the Civil War, quickly ratified the treaty. Newspapers ridiculed the purchase as "Seward's folly," "Seward's icebox," and as an "Arctic wasteland," but accessible wealth in fish, furs, timber, and precious minerals abounded in Alaska.

Albany Congress (1754)   Seven colonies and the friendly Iroquois attended. The imminence of the Seven Years' War (1756–63) led to the call for the meeting. Benjamin Franklin's Albany plan provided for a grand council of delegates from each colony and a president-general appointed by the king. It would regulate native American affairs and maintain a common armed force. The colonies rejected this plan as it encroached upon their individual powers. The Parliament disapproved because such a plan might be turned against England.

Albany Plan of Union   *See* **Albany Congress**.

Alcott, Louisa May (1832–1888)   An author, she lived in Boston and served as a nurse with the Union army during the Civil War. She edited a children's magazine, *Merry's Museum*. Alcott is best known for her many novels, especially *Little Women*, whose characters Jo, Amy, Beth, and Meg were drawn from her own family. Her many works, which appeared during the 1870s and 1880s, were (and some still are) widely read.

Aldrich-Vreeland Act (1908)   This act created the National Monetary Commission to study banking and currency systems; the Commission made recommendations to Congress that were embodied in the Federal Reserve Act of 1913. The Aldrich-Vreeland Act also provided for the issuance of emergency currency.

Algeciras Conference (1906–1907)   French "peaceful penetration" of Morocco with British approval offended Germany. A French-German clash could become a major war. At Kaiser Wilhelm's request President Theodore Roosevelt asked for a conference, which met at Algeciras, Spain. The outcome was a diplomatic defeat for Germany as a modified French encroachment on Moroccan sovereignty continued. That the United States had intervened in a European quarrel to help avert war caused an uneasy U.S. Senate to state that the involvement was not to be interpreted as any modification of the "traditional American foreign policy" of isolation.

Alger, Horatio (1834–1889)   Born in Revere, Massachusetts, and a graduate from Harvard Divinity School, he served for a brief period as a Unitarian minister, then went to New York where he served as a social worker among the poor. He turned to writing novels in which the heroes were poor boys (such as he knew in his work) who invariably rose from rags to riches. He wrote more than a hundred books on this theme, and his name became a symbol of effort and determination leading inevitably to success.

Alien and Sedition Acts   In 1798 John Adams, leader of the Federalists, was president and Thomas Jefferson, leader of the Democratic-Republicans, was vice president. England and France were at war. The Federalists sided with England; the Democratic-

Republicans with France. Anti-British émigrés from Ireland and from France were arriving in the United States in large numbers. Claiming a national emergency, the Federalists, who controlled Congress, enacted the Alien and Sedition Laws, which Adams quickly signed into law. The Alien Act authorized the president to expel from the country any alien whom he considered dangerous to the public peace and safety. The Sedition Act made it a crime "to publish false, scandalous, or malicious writing against the government, either house of Congress, or the President." A new Naturalization Act extended the period of residence in the United States to fourteen years (instead of the previous requirement of two years) before an alien could become a citizen. To counter these acts, Jefferson and Madison drafted the Kentucky and Virginia Resolutions. The Alien and Sedition Acts expired with the fifth Congress, March 3, 1801. In 1802 Congress restored the two-year residence requirement for citizenship.

Allen, Ethan (1737–1789) Born in Litchfield, Connecticut, he settled in Vermont. He led the Green Mountain Boys in the capture of Fort Ticonderoga from the British (1775). He attempted to invade Canada but was captured and later released. When Congress refused his petition to grant statehood to Vermont, he entered into negotiations with the British to make Vermont a province of Canada. The charge of treason was not proved, and Allen settled in Burlington, Vermont. He is recognized as a founder of that state.

Alliance for Progress (1961) This agreement extended economic and educational assistance to Latin American nations on condition they would take steps to modify their political structure to achieve land reform, tax reform, more representative government, and greater political stability. Such changes were vastly difficult because Havana, Moscow, and Beijing encouraged native Communist parties to create revolutions. Also, many of the people of Latin America had never known prosperity or self-government, and those in authority in Latin American nations often saw the program as a threat to their wealth and power. President Kennedy considered this plan one of his major goals. *See* **Peace Corps**.

Alliance, Treaty of (1778) Victory at Saratoga (October 1777) persuaded France that alliance with the United States would serve French interests. France sought revenge against England for the treaties of Utrecht (1713) and Paris (1763) and also saw a possibility of strengthening its position in the West Indies. When this treaty became effective the United States and France would come to the other's aid whenever either was at war with England. This agreement was "from the present time and forever." This clause caused embarrassment in President Washington's administration and prompted his famous advice against permanent, entangling alliances.

Allies In World War I, the term "the Allies" referred to France, Great Britain, Russia, and the other nations that fought on their side. These included Italy, the United States, Belgium, Japan, Greece, Portugal, Serbia, and Montenegro. The other side—consisting of Germany, Austria-Hungary, Turkey, and Bulgaria—was called the Central Powers.

Altgeld, John Peter (1847–1902) His parents came to America from Germany shortly after he was born, and he grew up on a farm in Ohio. He served in the Union army and worked in a chemical factory, on a railroad gang, and as a farmhand in Missouri. After studying law, he went to Chicago and entered politics. He ran for Congress in 1884 and for the U.S. Senate the following year. He lost both times but was elected superior court judge in 1886. In 1892 he won the governorship of Illinois, the first Democrat to hold this office in forty years. He showed strong sympathy for labor and the underdog and granted a pardon, supported by an 18,000-word paper, to three men imprisoned in connection with the Haymarket riots. Altgeld played a leading role in the 1896 Democratic convention that nominated William Jennings Bryan. The platform, which he helped draft, contained his views in the statement: "As labor creates the wealth of the country, we demand the passage of such laws as may be necessary to protect it in all its rights." In 1901 he entered a law partnership with Clarence Darrow.

Amendments to the Constitution *See* The Constitution of the United States, beginning on page 10-91.

America First Committee Americans were divided as to what course to follow with respect to World War II in Europe. Most accepted the leadership of President Franklin Delano Roosevelt in helping Britain hold back the Nazi tide. A sizable minority, however, organized the America First Committee, which secured the adherence of the national hero Charles A. Lindbergh, in a strenuous but ultimately futile national campaign to prevent the United States from getting involved in any war.

American Federation of Labor (1881) First named the Organized Trades and Labor Unions, it reorganized in 1886 as the American Federation of Labor (AFL) with Samuel Gompers, its first president, remaining in office thirty-seven years. He restricted union aims to immediate economic gains, such as collective bargaining, wages, and hours. The members of the federation were craft unions. Although it dominated the labor field for about forty years, its membership, restricted largely to skilled workers, represented only a small fraction of wage earners. In 1955 the AFL merged with the CIO to become the AFL-CIO.

American Federation of Labor and Congress of Industrial Organizations (AFL-CIO) After many years of controversy within the labor movement, a merger was effected between the rival factions the American Federation of Labor, headed by George Meany, and the Congress of Industrial Organizations, headed by Walter Reuther. The merger, called the AFL-CIO, took place in 1955, with Meany becoming president and Reuther vice president. The new organization, with its seventeen million members in organized labor, wielded great power. *See* **Taft-Hartley Act**.

American System A nationalist economic program originated by Henry Clay and favored by the Whigs, it called for protective tariffs, a national bank, internal improvements (roads and canals) through federal aid, and the sale of public lands to produce revenue.

Amistad **case** The Spanish ship *Amistad*, bound for the United States, left Cuba in 1839 with a cargo of fifty-four African slaves. Led by Cinque, the slaves murdered the captain and three of the crew and headed the vessel northward, arriving at Long Island, where they were taken into custody by a U.S. warship. The blacks were imprisoned at New London, Connecticut. Spain demanded they be surrendered to be tried for piracy. Southern Senators insisted they be tried for murder. Abolitionists came to their legal defense. The case reached the Supreme Court in 1841. The blacks were represented by 74-year-old John Quincy Adams, whose eloquence so impressed the Court that the defendants were freed and permitted to return to Africa.

Amnesty Act (1872)   The constitutions of the "sinful ten" ex-Confederate states, formed under military occupation provided for in the Reconstruction Acts, granted suffrage to freedmen and denied it to many whites prominent in the Confederate armed forces. This Amnesty Act removed the suffrage restrictions against whites except for about 500 men who had held important posts in the Confederate forces or government.

Anaconda Plan   The plan proposed by General Winfield Scott at the outbreak of the Civil War for defeating the Confederacy. The plan called for capturing the Mississippi and Tennessee rivers, thus breaking the Confederacy in pieces and then crushing each of the parts. The name refers to the anaconda snake, which crushes its victims to death.

Anarchism   A political philosophy opposed to organized government, which it considers an instrument of oppression used by the ruling classes. Some anarchists advocated various forms of violence to achieve their goals.

Anthracite coal strike (1902)   In May, John Mitchell led 140,000 miners on strike in Pennsylvania. By October a coal famine had set in. George Baer, representing the mine operators, refused to bargain with Mitchell. President Theodore Roosevelt held that heating homes throughout the Northeast was more important than the issues between miners and operators. He invited Baer and Mitchell to the White House to negotiate. Baer walked out of the meeting in a huff, but when President Roosevelt threatened to operate the mines with the army, Baer, under orders from J. P. Morgan, negotiated with Mitchell.

Union and Confederate forces at the Battle of Antietam in 1862, a victory for the Union army.

Antietam, Battle of (1862)   September 17, 1862, was the bloodiest day of the Civil War as the armies of Robert E. Lee and George B. McClellan clashed near Sharpsburg, Maryland. Lee's plan was frustrated when an order describing his plan fell into Union hands. Each side sustained some 13,000 casualties, but Lee was forced to retreat and McClellan failed to follow up his advantage.

ANZUS Treaty (1952)   The treaty united Australia, New Zealand, and the United States in a regional defensive alliance against aggression in the Pacific area. The Korean War stimulated its formation to defend against or to forestall Chinese Communist aggression. NATO, OAS, SEATO, and CENTO were formed with a similar purpose in other regions.

Aroostook War (1838)   Since the Treaty of Paris, 1783, disagreement over our northeastern boundary was a constant irritant. Maine and New Brunswick, then Nova Scotia, and the United States called out troops and appropriated money to settle the issue by force. President Van Buren arranged a truce while the problem was referred to a commission. Settlement was eventually made by the Webster-Ashburton Treaty in 1842.

Arthur, Chester A.   *See* Presidents of the United States section, beginning on page 10-83.

Articles of Confederation   On a resolution of Richard Henry Lee of Virginia on June 3, 1776, the Continental Congress in Philadelphia appointed a committee to "prepare a plan of confederation of the colonies." In July the committee, headed by John Dickinson of Pennsylvania, reported to Congress "Articles of Confederation and Perpetual Union." On November 15 the articles were adopted by the Congress and sent to the states for ratification.

Articles of Confederation ratified (1781)   By November 1777, the Articles of Confederation were approved by the Second Continental Congress and submitted to the states. They were to become the new government only after all thirteen states had ratified them. Maryland withheld ratification until all states with claims to western lands agreed to give such lands to the United States government. The agreement was reached, and in March 1781 Maryland's ratification brought the Articles of Confederation into effect. The land ordinances culminating in the Northwest Ordinance of 1787 were the happy results of Maryland's action.

Articles of Confederation, weaknesses   The articles that served as the instrument of national government from March 1, 1781, to March 4, 1789, had the following weaknesses: (1) there was no chief executive; (2) there was no judicial department; (3) a majority of nine votes was required to pass important laws; (4) Congress could requisition taxes from the states but could not force their collection; (5) Congress could requisition men into the armed forces but could not draft men into the service of the United States; (6) the members of Congress were paid by their states, and a state could recall any of its delegates at any time; (7) Congress was not given exclusive power to regulate interstate and foreign commerce; (8) Congress was not given the power to issue paper money; (9) treaties made by the United States could be nullified by the action of the states; (10) amending the Articles of Confederation required the unanimous vote of the thirteen states.

Astor, John Jacob (1763–1848)   Born in Germany, he left for London in 1780 and came to

America in 1783. He entered the fur business and established companies throughout the West and in Canada. His investments in Far East shipping and New York real estate yielded substantial returns. Astor also established Astoria near the mouth of the Columbia River in Oregon for fur trading with Canada. His company maintained offices not only throughout America but also in Europe and Asia. Toward the end of his life he was known as the richest man in the United States, leaving an estate valued at $20 million, a fabulous sum at that time.

Atlantic Charter (1941)   Conferences aboard warships off Newfoundland between President Franklin Roosevelt and Great Britain's Prime Minister Winston Churchill resulted in the following declarations: (1) no territorial gains are sought by the United States or Britain; (2) territorial adjustments must conform to the wishes of the people involved; (3) people have a right to choose their own government; (4) trade barriers should be lowered; (5) there must be disarmament; (6) there must be freedom from fear and want; (7) there must be freedom of the seas; (8) there must be an association of nations.

Atom bomb   During World War II Albert Einstein and others advised President Franklin D. Roosevelt that it was theoretically possible to derive enormous energy instantaneously from atomic fission. A secret project with the code name Manhattan was funded, and scientists were enlisted in a frantic effort to make an atom bomb before the enemy succeeded in doing so. The first atom bomb was successfully detonated in the New Mexico desert at Alamogordo on July 16, 1945. Shortly thereafter, on August 6, an atom bomb was dropped from a U.S. warplane, destroying the Japanese city of Hiroshima, killing or wounding 400,000 people. A second atom bomb was dropped three days later on Nagasaki, causing equal devastation and forcing Japan to surrender.

Atomic Test Ban Treaty (1963)   The United States and the USSR agreed not to conduct nuclear tests in space, in the atmosphere, or underwater. Underground tests were not banned as there was no satisfactory way to detect them without inspection, which Russia would not accept. Contamination from underground testing is at a minimum. India and Communist China have not ratified the treaty, but over a hundred other nations have.

Audubon, John James (1785–1851)   American ornithologist and artist, he was born in Haiti, educated in France, and came to America in 1803, where he engaged in the study of birds and in making striking drawings of his subjects. He went to England in 1826 and teamed up with a London engraver to produce the pioneer work *Birds of America*, which established his reputation. The work contained detailed figures of more than 500 species. The Audubon Society adopted his name in recognition of his contributions to ornithology.

B **Bacon's Rebellion** (1676)   In 1675, Jamestown's frontier settlers asked Governor Berkeley for protection against attacks by native Americans. He refused, claiming that indiscriminate retaliation punished peaceful natives. Many settlers believed Berkeley's real motive was the protection of his fur trade with the natives. Nathaniel Bacon, without authorization, led a force that wiped out a native village. Civil war followed between Bacon's rebels and Berkeley's militia. Bacon died, and the rebellion collapsed. Berkeley executed over twenty rebels in defiance of orders from King Charles II to pardon them. Recalled by the King, Berkeley died in 1677, a few weeks after his arrival in England.

Baker v. Carr (369 U.S. 186, 1962)   In a landmark case, the Supreme Court held that states must reapportion their election districts to make them approximately equal in population. It established the principle of "one man, one vote," basing its decision on the clause of the Fourteenth Amendment, ". . . nor shall any State . . . deny to any person within its jurisdiction the equal protection of the laws." The case of *Wesberry* v. *Sanders*, decided two years later, applied the same principle to the districts for congressional elections in which gross disparities existed in many states. For example, in Texas one district had nearly a million in population, and another had 200,000. Thus a voter in the latter had five times the voting power as one in the former.

Balance of payments   This phrase refers to the difference in the value of goods and services bought and those sold by a nation. An unfavorable balance represents payments in excess of receipts and ultimately may have to be settled by payments of gold.

Ballinger-Pinchot controversy (1910)   Gifford Pinchot, chief forester in the Department of Agriculture, charged that Secretary of the Interior Richard A. Ballinger abused the power of his office by releasing government lands rich in coal to private interests and by permitting private interests to acquire water power sites on western land that had been set aside by the federal government for conservation. President Howard Taft sided with Ballinger, forcing Pinchot, an appointee of Theodore Roosevelt, to resign. Ballinger resigned a year later because of unfavorable public reaction.

Baltimore crisis (1891)   Secretary of State Blaine and our minister to Chile, Patrick Egan, aided the government of Chile in its unsuccessful attempt to quell a rebellion. The USS *Charleston* seized a rebel ship carrying arms. The eventual rebel victory inspired anti-American demonstrations, and in Valparaiso, two sailors from the USS *Baltimore* were killed. The new Chilean government rejected U.S. protests, but when President Benjamin Harrison sent a war message to Congress, Chile apologized and paid an indemnity of $75,000.

Bank of the United States (1791)   Whether Congress had the right to establish this bank was the first substantial issue leading to the formation of two major political parties under the Constitution. Was the bank "necessary" within the meaning of the implied powers clause of the Constitution? The Federalists, advocating "loose construction" of the Constitution, pushed the bill through Congress over the opposition of Jefferson's Democratic-Republicans with their "strict construction." It was a private bank (80 percent of its stock in private hands; 20 percent owned by the United States), which by law performed functions for and received privileges from the government.

Bank of the United States (Second) (chartered 1816)   The expiration of the first BUS was followed by five years of unstable currency, unstable state bank notes, and wild fluctuation of war prices (War of 1812). These circumstances resulted in a reversal by the Republican party of its antibank stand. It established the Second BUS, patterned after the First BUS. The Clay-Biddle maneuver, making the BUS the major issue of the presidential campaign of 1832, brought forth Jackson's veto of the bill to recharter it. Jackson's re-election began his "war on the bank," which caused its steady decline until it expired in 1836.

Barbary States of North Africa　　Algiers, Morocco, Tripoli, and Tunis required the United States to pay tribute for "protection" of trading vessels from pirates. In 1801, the ruler of Tripoli increased the amount of tribute and declared war. Jefferson dispatched warships to the Mediterranean. The skill and daring of U.S. Navy Lieutenant Stephen Decatur forced Tripoli to sign a treaty (1805) abandoning the demand for tribute. The phrase ". . . to the shores of Tripoli" in the Marines' anthem derives from this action. Tribute to the other Barbary States continued until 1816. With the United States at war with England (War of 1812), the ruler of Algiers declared war on the United States and proceeded to seize American vessels and enslave their crews until increased tribute was paid. Congress authorized naval action. Captain Stephen Decatur again prevailed and forced Algiers, Tunis, and Tripoli to yield. Tribute was renounced, and American vessels in the Mediterranean were freed from the depredations of the Barbary States.

Barnburners　　An antislavery faction split the Democratic party in New York in 1848 and caused the Whigs to elect General Taylor as president. The loyal Democrats in this election were nicknamed the "hunkers." The name "barnburners" was applied to the antislavery faction when the opposition charged that they were willing to burn down the Democratic barn to rid themselves of the proslavery rats.

Barton, Clara (1821–1912)　　At the outbreak of the Civil War, she left the teaching profession and organized nursing and relief services for disabled Union soldiers. During the Franco-Prussian War (1870) she served in Europe with the International Red Cross. Back in the United States, she organized the National Society of the Red Cross (1881), serving as its first president. Her proposal to add peacetime disaster relief to the International Red Cross agenda was adopted at Geneva in 1884.

Bataan, battle of (1942)　　The Bataan Peninsula in the Philippines was the scene of an American military disaster early in World War II. The Japanese cut off all relief to the beleaguered American and Filipino soldiers and forced them to march without food or water (death march) to a jungle prison. On orders from President Roosevelt, General Douglas MacArthur left the troops and escaped to Australia. As he departed he uttered the prophetic words "I shall return."

Bay of Pigs (1961)　　President Kennedy had said, "There will not, under any circumstances, be an invasion in Cuba by the United States' armed forces." Cuban refugees (not U.S. forces) were being trained and equipped in Guatemala by the United States. On April 17 this force landed at the Bay of Pigs on Cuba's south shore. Castro's nine-plane air force sunk their supply ships. About 400 were killed and 1200 captured. On May 1, dictator Castro jubilantly announced Cuba to be a member of the Russian-Chinese Communist camp.

Beecher, Henry Ward (1813–1887)　　Antislavery preacher and editor and gifted orator, he drew huge audiences. He urged civil disobedience of the Fugitive Slave Law, defended the union in the face of hostile audiences in England during the Civil War, and advocated women's suffrage. His sister, Harriet Beecher Stowe, wrote the famous antislavery novel *Uncle Tom's Cabin*.

Bell, Alexander Graham (1847–1922)　　Inventor of the telephone (1876), the photophone for transmission of sound by light, and improvements on the phonograph, Bell was born in Scotland, came to America in 1870, and became an American citizen in 1882. His wife Mabel G. Hubbard had been deaf from childhood, and Bell was interested in education of the deaf. The Bell Telephone Company was founded in 1877.

Bennington, battle of (1777)　　As Burgoyne's army moved south into New York from Canada, he sent a detachment of some 700 men into what is now Vermont in order to capture military supplies at Bennington. A battle ensued at which American militiamen under General John Stark destroyed virtually the entire invading unit.

Berlin Blockade (June 24, 1948, to May 17, 1949)　　On June 24, Russia blocked traffic by highway, waterway, and railway to and from Berlin except for the Soviet sector. Over two million people were thus cut off from supplies. The United States, with some British aid, established the airlift Operation Vittles, which did the impossible: it kept planes taking off and landing on an average of one every five minutes around the clock for almost ten months, including the winter. The blockade was then lifted. This test of strength reassured the West Germans and informed the Russians that force would not settle the German question the Soviet way.

Berlin crisis (1961)　　Khrushchev announced that Russia would make a treaty with East Germany, after which the United States would have to deal directly with East Germany about the Western Zone in Berlin. President Kennedy would not recognize East Germany and said, "We...will not permit the Communists to drive us out of Berlin...." The July total of persons fleeing from East to West Germany reached 30,000. In August the wall was built. Vice President Johnson and General Clay went to Berlin to assure the West Germans of support. With the exodus from East Germany stopped by the wall, Khrushchev accepted the status quo and the crisis faded.

Big Four　　Term applied to the national leaders who first dominated the Versailles Conference after World War I. They were Woodrow Wilson (United States), Lloyd George (Britain), Georges Clemenceau (France), and Vittorio Emanuele Orlando (Italy).

Big stick　　President Theodore Roosevelt stated his policy in international affairs with the expression "speak softly and carry a big stick." He was perceived as following this policy in 1903 when he dispatched U.S. naval units to help the province of

Panama gain independence from Colombia. The latter had been dragging its feet in granting civil rights across Panama. The United States promptly recognized the independence of Panama. In a matter of weeks, Panama negotiated a treaty giving the United States a right of way to build a canal across Panama for a passageway joining the Atlantic and Pacific oceans.

Bill of attainder   Punishment of an individual by a legislative process used formerly in England for political reasons and used in the place of judicial processes requiring evidence of guilt; the Constitution denies this power to Congress.

Bill of Rights (1791)   The Constitution would have been rejected by the states had there been no pledge by Federalist leaders to prepare a bill of rights for adoption as amendments. Massachusetts, New Hampshire, Virginia, and North Carolina ratified the Constitution with the reservation that such amendments would follow immediately. President Washington referred to the promised bill of rights in his inaugural address of April 1789. The first Congress proposed the first ten amendments (Bill of Rights), which were ratified by December 1791. Their purpose was to prevent encroachments by the federal government upon the powers of the states.

Bimetalism   A policy of backing paper money with both gold and silver that could work if both metals were accepted at a fixed ratio. After 1873, however, the advocates of silver (chiefly miners of silver and farmers who wanted cheap money to help them repay their debts and to increase the cost of their crops) agitated for increased government minting of silver. As the value of silver declined relative to gold, the latter currency began to disappear. Ultimately the United States would have to go off the gold standard. The election of 1896 centered on this issue. With the defeat of William Jennings Bryan, the advocates of silver had to give way. Bimetalism did not work. Gold was then established as the single backing for U.S. currency.

Black codes   Laws passed by the Southern states immediately after the Civil War to regulate behavior of the former slaves, these codes were seen as laws that virtually amounted to involuntary servitude expressly forbidden by the Thirteenth Amendment.

Black Friday   A stock and gold market crisis, September 24, 1869, it was caused by the attempt of the speculators Jay Gould and Jim Fisk to corner the national gold supply. Many businessmen who needed gold to meet their obligations were forced to pay exorbitant prices or were driven into bankruptcy. When President Grant became aware of what was happening, he ordered the Treasury to sell gold, but much damage had been done in the interim.

Black Hawk War (1832)   Disagreement over the validity of the alleged transfer of vast native American lands in Illinois, Wisconsin, and Missouri to the United States resulted in war. Black Hawk, chief of the Sauk and Fox, led his people into the disputed territories searching for food and an area to settle that would be suitable for raising corn. Several skirmishes culminated in the battle of Bad Axe River, Wisconsin, where the natives were almost annihilated. Abraham Lincoln served as captain of the Illinois militia in the Black Hawk War.

Black, Hugo LaFayette (1886–1971)   Born in Alabama, he served in the U.S. Senate 1927–37. Black was appointed associate justice of the U.S. Supreme Court by President Franklin D. Roosevelt in 1937 and served on the Court thirty-four years. His record on the Court is contained in the nearly 1000 opinions he wrote. This record displays an absolute adherence to the Bill of Rights and an insistence that the Fourteenth Amendment made the entire Bill of Rights applicable to the states. On freedom of speech, he explained his position in these words: "My view is, without deviation, without exception, without any ifs, buts, or whereases, that freedom of speech means that you shall not do something to people, either for the views they have or the views they express or the words they speak or write."

Blacklist   A list of names or firms with which one refuses to do business; this is a weapon formerly used by management to prevent the employment of union organizers and members.

Bland-Allison Act (1878)   The act was the government's response to cheap-money advocates who had vigorously protested the "crime of '73." (*See* **Crime of '73**.) "Silver Dick" Bland, representative from Missouri, introduced a bill for unlimited (free) coinage of silver at the ratio of 16:1. Senator Allison of Iowa amended the bill to limit the amount of silver purchased to $2–4 million per month at the market price.

Bleeding Kansas   Under provisions of the Kansas-Nebraska Act of 1854, the question of slavery in these two territories was to be decided by the residents themselves on the principle of popular sovereignty. Kansas at once became a battleground between proslavery and antislavery factions. Rival governments were set up. Violence ensued. In 1856, proslavery men resorted to arson and pillage against Free-soilers. This was followed by the Potawatomie Massacre in which a party of abolitionists, led by John Brown, murdered five proslavery men. Intermittent fighting continued until the Civil War, when Kansas came into the Union as a free state (1861).

Blockade   The isolation of an enemy by military force, usually naval patrols, to cut off commerce with the rest of the world; a "paper blockade" is one not actually in effect in the vicinity of the enemy coastline.

Blue Eagle   The National Recovery Act of 1933 was one of the first pieces of federal legislation under Franklin D. Roosevelt's New Deal. The act established codes of fair competition with which businesses were asked to comply. Those who agreed were permitted to display the NRA Blue Eagle, signifying their membership for public approval.

Bonus Bill (1817)   The bill was introduced by Representative Calhoun to provide highways linking the East and the South with the West. Most of the money was to come from earnings of the 20 percent shareholdings of the government in the Second Bank of the United States. Calhoun pointed to the "general welfare" clause and to the power "to establish post roads" as Constitutional justification for such legislation. Although President Madison approved the purpose of the bill, he vetoed it because he thought it unconstitutional. The bill derived its name from the fact that funding of the federal highways was to come in part from the $1,500,000 "bonus" paid to the U.S. government by the Second Bank of the United States for its twenty-year charter (1816–36).

Bonus marchers Mounting unemployment during the Great Depression of the 1930s led to a march on Washington, D. C., by more than 10,000 veterans of World War I. They had a veteran's bonus of $1000 payable in twenty years. Congress passed a bill in 1931 over President Hoover's veto requiring payment of half the bonus immediately. The bonus marchers came to Washington, D.C., from all over the country demanding payment of the other half. They camped in open spaces near the White House. Hoover ordered General Douglas MacArthur to disperse the veterans. Serving under him was Dwight Eisenhower. MacArthur used tear gas, tanks, and some gunfire to break up the veterans' "bonus army."

Boone, Daniel (1734–1820) He was a pioneer, frontiersman, and legendary hero. Born near Reading, Pennsylvania, Boone moved to the mountains of North Carolina, served in the French and Indian War, and was for a time a captive of the Shawnee. He established a fort at Boonesborough, Kentucky, having previously led a party through the Cumberland Gap. His last years were spent in Missouri, where he received a land grant.

Engraving by Paul Revere depicting the Boston Massacre.

Boston Massacre (1770) On March 5, an altercation between a British sentry and a civilian attracted a crowd. Captain Preston with ten British soldiers came to the sentry's aid. Epithets, snowballs, and other missiles flew as the soldiers stood with fixed bayonets. Someone, not Captain Preston, shouted "fire!" Five civilians were killed, six others wounded.

John Adams and Josiah Quincy, both anti-English, served as lawyers for the soldiers. Two were convicted of manslaughter and set free after being branded on the hand. This mild sentence was a strong indication that the crowd was more at fault than Captain Preston and his squad of soldiers.

Boston Tea Party (1773) Three tea ships at Griffin's Wharf had their cargoes dumped into the harbor during the night of December 16. This raid, carried out by Boston Whigs and Sons of Liberty disguised as native Americans, was arranged by Sam Adams. England's reaction was the passage of the Intolerable Acts, a series of punitive measures that united the colonies and brought them closer to rebellion. Attempts to import tea and collect the tax failed in New York City, Philadelphia, and Charleston, but no other port held a tea party such as Boston's.

The Boston Tea Party

Boxer uprising (1900) The Boxers, a nationalist organization intent upon driving the "foreign devils" out of China, killed over 200 foreigners during the spring and summer of 1900. In Peking the German ambassador was murdered, and the personnel of the several legations barricaded themselves in the British Embassy awaiting rescue, which arrived after several weeks. U.S. troops from comparatively nearby Philippines formed the major part of the international relief force of about 5000. Secretary of State John Hay rejected the idea of partitioning China and persuaded the other nations to accept a cash indemnity.

Boycott A concerted movement, as of labor or consumers, to refuse to do business with an adversary in order to force the adversary to yield to specific demands. The term may also be applied to show social or political disapproval.

Bradford, William (1590–1657) He was one of the Pilgrims who went from England to Holland seeking religious freedom. The Pilgrims, including Bradford, came to America in 1620 on the *Mayflower*. They founded their colony at Plymouth, Massachusetts, and chose William Bradford as their governor, a position he held off and on for the first three crucial decades of the colony's existence. His *History of Plymouth Plantation* is not only a classic account of these trying years but a distinguished literary work.

Brain trust The term is applied to a team of able advisors, including a large number of university professors, who helped Roosevelt formulate the New

Deal reforms. Among those whose ideas were sought by President Roosevelt and who constituted his "brain trust" were Rexford G. Tugwell, Adolphe A. Berle, Jr., and Raymond Moley, all members of the Columbia University faculty.

Brandeis, Louis D. (1856–1941) Born in Louisville, Kentucky, he practiced law in Boston. Brandeis made a reputation using economic and social data in advocating public causes. His nomination to the Supreme Court in 1916 by President Woodrow Wilson met determined opposition. On the bench he served with distinction, often allied in judgment with Justice Oliver Wendell Holmes. Brandeis retired from the Court in 1939. Brandeis University at Waltham, Massachusetts, founded in 1948 under Jewish sponsorship, bears the name of the justice.

Bretton Woods Conference The conference met in July 1944 in the White Mountains of New Hampshire with representatives of forty-four nations present. The International Monetary Fund was established to help promote trade and the International Bank for Reconstruction and Development to aid nations devastated by World War II. The United States contributed $8.8 billion (about 25 percent) for the fund and $9.1 billion (about 35 percent) for the bank. The USSR was invited but did not attend the conference.

Brown v. Board of Education of Topeka (347 U.S. 438, 1954) In this momentous Supreme Court decision, the Warren Court unanimously reversed the "separate but equal" ruling of *Plessy v. Ferguson* (1896). The Court's holding that separate could not be equal was based on evidence presented by Thurgood Marshall and other counsel as well as on amicus curiae briefs presented in behalf of the plaintiff showing psychological scars inflicted on black children by racial segregation.

Bryan, William Jennings (1860–1925) Political leader and orator, Bryan was three times (1896, 1900, and 1908) unsuccessful Democratic candidate for president of the United States. His advocacy of the coinage of silver, epitomized in the memorable speech at the 1896 Democratic convention in which he charged that the country's financial interests were crucifying the people on a "cross of gold," pitted the farmers of the West against the bankers and industrialists of the eastern cities. Bryan helped Woodrow Wilson gain the Democratic nomination for president in 1912. Wilson chose him for secretary of state, but Bryan resigned in 1916 in opposition to Wilson's foreign policy, which he forsaw as leading to American intervention in World War I. At Dayton, Tennessee, in 1925, Bryan served as chief counsel in prosecuting John T. Scopes, a biology teacher, who had taught his students the theory of evolution, which Bryan, a religious fundamentalist, opposed. Counsel for the defense was the great trial lawyer Clarence Darrow. The trial attracted worldwide interest.

Buchanan, James *See* Presidents of the United States section, beginning on page 10-83.

Bull moose party (1912) In 1911, Senator Robert M. LaFollette of Wisconsin organized the National Republican Progressive League, which soon announced that LaFollette was the logical candidate for president of the United States. The Republican

convention at Chicago in 1912, however, renominated President Taft with 561 votes to 107 and 41 for Theodore Roosevelt and LaFollette, respectively. The Progressives shouted fraud, bolted the convention, and two months later held their own convention. Amid great enthusiasm and to the tune of "Onward Christian Soldiers," Roosevelt was nominated. He declared himself fit and "feeling like a bull moose," ready for the fray.

Bull Run, battle of (1861, 1862) Yielding to political pressure, Union forces under General Irvin McDowell began a "march on Richmond" on July 21, 1861. His army was engaged by Confederate forces under General Pierre G. T. Beauregard. The Union army nearly prevailed, despite the determined stand of General Thomas J. Jackson, who hence earned the nickname "Stonewall," when reinforcements led by General Joseph E. Johnston arrived and drove the Union troops back to Washington, D.C., in a rout. At the second battle of Bull Run (generally referred to as Manassas Junction in the South), August 29–30, 1862, Lee's Confederate troops supported by Jackson and General James Longstreet drove the Union armies led by General John Pope and inadequately supported by General George B. McClellan and Fitz-John Porter back to Washington, D.C. The war was to go on for two more years before armies under General Ulysses S. Grant could successfully move on Richmond.

Bunker Hill, battle of (June 17, 1775) To prevent the British from occupying Dorchester Heights overlooking Boston, 1200 American colonial troops under Colonel William Prescott secretly took positions on Breed's Hill during the night of June 16. Sir William Howe was astonished at the sight, easily visible from the British ships in the harbor. Because of the tide, the landing of British troops was delayed until noon. By that time the colonials had 1600 men on the hill. The attacking force numbered 2400. Two frontal attacks failed. The third succeeded only because the defenders' ammunition gave out. British casualties included many officers and totaled about 1050, over three times the colonial losses. The results strongly bolstered the morale of the American colonial forces, who proved they could stand up to the best troops the British had.

Burlingame Treaty (1868) The treaty established formal friendly relations with China. It provided free immigration between the United States and China, recognized China's complete sovereignty within its own borders, and placed China on the "most favored nation" basis for treatment of its nationals in the United States. The treaty was negotiated for the United States by Anson Burlingame, who had been U.S. minister in China and was well regarded there. Chinese immigration was encouraged at this time to provide labor in the mines and on railroad construction in the West.

Burr, Aaron (1756–1836) Born in Newark, New Jersey, he studied law and served in the American Revolution, becoming a lieutenant colonel at the age of twenty-one. Burr practiced law in New York City, where he became active in politics as a Democratic-Republican. He was attorney general of New York (1789–91) and U.S. Senator (1791–97). Burr tied with Jefferson in the presidential election of 1800 and became vice president when the House chose Jefferson. He killed his foe Alexander Hamilton in a pistol duel in 1804. Burr became involved in a conspiracy in the Southwest for which he was charged with treason. The trial was conducted in Richmond by Chief Justice Marshall (1807). Burr was acquitted, went to Europe (1808–12), and then returned to practice law in New York City.

Bush, George *See* Presidents of the United States section, beginning on page 10-83.

Byrd, Richard Evelyn (1888–1957) Graduated from the U.S. Naval Academy (1912), he became commander of U.S. air forces in Canada. Byrd was leader of a U.S. Navy polar expedition in 1925 and made a flight over the North Pole the following year, winning the Congressional Medal of Honor. He established a base at "Little America" in the Antarctic region and flew over the South Pole in 1929. Byrd made successive trips to the Antarctic (1933–47), gathering scientific data and conducting a geologic survey of the entire South Pole region for the U.S. Navy.

Cairo Conference (1943) This was a summit meeting of President Franklin D. Roosevelt, Prime Minister Winston Churchill, and Generalissimo Chiang Kai-shek during World War II to make joint decisions about postwar Asia. Japan would be required to surrender unconditionally. It would have to return all territories taken since the outbreak of World War I, including Manchuria and Formosa (Taiwan). Korea was to become independent.

Calhoun, John C. (1782–1850) Born in South Carolina, he graduated from Yale in 1804 and practiced law in South Carolina. Calhoun served in the House of Representatives (1811–17), where he was a spokesman for slavery and a "war hawk" in the War of 1812. He was secretary of war in President Monroe's cabinet (1817–25) and vice president under John Quincy Adams (1825–29) and under Andrew Jackson (1829–32), when he resigned in personal and political conflict with Jackson. South Carolina returned him to the U.S. Senate (1832–44), and President John Tyler of Virginia appointed him secretary of state. During his incumbency he secured the annexation of Texas. In 1845 he again returned to the Senate, where he served until his death in 1850. Calhoun was a staunch advocate of states' rights. In 1828 he wrote "South Carolina Exposition and Protest" against the tariff, a philosophical disquisition on the right of a state to nullify a federal law. A dying man, he was wheeled into the Senate (March 4, 1850) to hear his colleague, Senator Mason of Virginia, read his speech on the Compromise of 1850 in which he raised grave questions about the threat to slavery and to the South.

Camp David Accord In August 1978, less than a year after President Anwar Sadat of Egypt addressed the Israeli Parliament in Jerusalem, President Jimmy Carter met at the presidential retreat at Camp David in Maryland with Sadat and Prime Minister Menachem Begin of Israel. The Camp David summit conference with three heads of state, each with his coterie of advisors, produced a series of tentative agreements concerning Israeli occupation of the Sinai peninsula, the west bank of the Jordan, the Gaza strip, the status of the PLO (Palestinian Liberation Organization), and the status of Jerusalem. These agreements, called the Camp David Accord, were approved by the governments of both Egypt and Israel. A treaty of peace between the two nations that had fought four wars (1948, 1956, 1967, and 1973) was signed on the lawn of the White House on March 26, 1979.

Cannonism, revolt against (1910) Representative "Uncle Joe" Cannon of Illinois was speaker of the House during President Taft's administration. He seized extraordinary powers, such as appointing members of all House committees and making himself chairman of the House Rules Committee, which decided which bills were to be submitted to Congress. He alone could determine the flow of legislation. Representative George Norris led a coalition of insurgent Republicans and Democrats that changed the House rules so that the Speaker could not serve on the Rules Committee. "Uncle Joe's" power was broken.

Cardozo, Benjamin N. (1870–1938) He graduated from Columbia University and practiced law in New York City and served on New York State's highest court, the Court of Appeals, 1917–32, the last five years as its chief judge. In 1932 President Herbert Hoover appointed him to the U.S. Supreme Court, where he was associate justice until his death in 1938. His opinions both for the court and in dissent, as well as his books on jurisprudence, including *The Nature of the Judicial Process* (1921), *The Growth of the Law* (1924), and *The Paradoxes of Legal Science*, are distinguished both for their insights and for their literary quality.

Carnegie, Andrew (1835–1919) He came to the United States from Scotland in 1848. From his first job, for which he earned $1.20 a week, he advanced as telegrapher with the Union forces during the Civil War. After the war he was in the iron and oil businesses and in 1873 began his spectacular career in the steel industry, fostering the steady growth of steel production in the United States. The Carnegie Steel Company was sold in 1901 to become the core of the giant United States Steel Corporation. He then retired to establish charitable trusts, notably the Carnegie Institution of Washington, the Carnegie Foundation for the Advancement of Teaching, and the Carnegie Endowment for International Peace, as well as substantial contributions to libraries throughout the world.

***Caroline* affair** (1837) A band of Canadian rebels took refuge on Navy Island on the Canadian side of the Niagara River. U.S. sympathizers used the steamboat *Caroline* to supply them. On the night of December 29, Canadian soldiers crossed to the American side of the river and set the *Caroline* afire and adrift. In this raid one American was killed. The following May 29, Americans burned the British steamboat *Sir Robert Peel* while it was tied to a pier on the U.S. side of the St. Lawrence River. The northeastern frontiers on both sides of the border seemed eager for a confrontation. *See* **Aroostook War.**

Carpenter's Hall The building was lent to the First Continental Congress as a meeting place (September 5, 1774) by the Carpenter's Guild. Located at 320 Chestnut Street in Philadelphia, the building, which was constructed in 1770, has been designated a U.S. landmark.

Carpetbaggers A derogatory term applied to Northern politicians, businessmen, and others who migrated to the South during Reconstruction to take advantage of opportunities to advance their own fortunes. The name implies that they were down-and-outers who could put all their belongings in a piece of hand luggage called a carpetbag.

Carter, Jimmy (James Earl) *See* Presidents of the United States section, beginning on page 10-83.

Carver, George Washington (1824–1943) Born of slave parents near Diamond Grove, Missouri, he learned to read at the age of twenty and received a B.S. and M.S. in chemistry from Iowa State College. Carver became head of the department of agricultural research at Tuskegee Institute, Alabama, where he carried on research making significant discoveries in the use of peanuts and sweet potatoes, from which he derived medicines, dyes, plastics, and other products. In 1940 he made a grant of his life's savings to establish the Carver Foundation for Chemical Research.

Casablanca Conference (1943) This was a meeting between Roosevelt and Churchill at Casablanca, Morocco, to plan military strategy for the conquest of Europe. From the meeting came the decision to demand an "unconditional surrender" of the Axis powers. Other decisions included sending aid to the eastern front to aid the USSR in weakening the Nazi war machine. Plans for the invasion of Sicily and Italy were made at this conference to strike at what Churchill called "the soft underbelly of the Axis."

Cass, Lewis (1782–1866) He moved from his native New Hampshire to Ohio, where he studied law and served in the legislature. Cass enlisted in the army and led troops under Harrison in defeating the British and native Americans in the West during the War of 1812. He was governor of Michigan Territory (1813–31), secretary of war in Jackson's cabinet (1831–36) during the Black Hawk War, minister to France (1836–42), and senator from Michigan (1845–48), supporting the "manifest destiny" policy for acquisition of Texas and Oregon. Cass was also Democratic candidate for president in 1848, U.S. senator in 1848–57, and secretary of state in Buchanan's cabinet (1857–60). He urged Buchanan to send reinforcements to Fort Sumter and resigned when the president refused to do so.

Cather, Willa (1876–1947) Her family moved from Virginia when she was a child to Nebraska, where she graduated from the University in 1895. She taught school, wrote for the Pittsburgh *Daily Leader* (1878–1901), and was editor of *McClure's Magazine* (1907–12). Cather turned to writing novels and produced several brilliant works, including *Oh, Pioneers!* (1913), *My Antonia*, (1918), and *Death Comes for the Archbishop* (1927). The latter is a sensitive portrayal of missionary work of the Catholic Church in native American and Spanish New Mexico.

Caucus An informal political meeting; up to 1824 caucuses of members of Congress nominated presidential candidates.

Central Intelligence Agency (CIA) After the attack on Pearl Harbor it was decided to establish a federal agency to gather intelligence information around the world so that we would never again be caught unaware. In 1947 the CIA was established by Congress. Its funding, personnel, and modus operandi are not a matter of public record. It is known that it helped overthrow the Premier of Iran in 1953, the government of Guatemala in 1954, and the Socialist Allende government of Chile in 1973. One of its high-altitude planes, a U-2, was shot down over the Soviet Union in 1960. It backed the disastrous Bay of Pigs attempt to overthrow the Castro government of Cuba in 1961. A U-2 spy plane took aerial photographs in 1962 showing missile sites in Cuba installed by the Soviets. These posed nuclear threats to the United States and led to the **Missile Crisis in Cuba** (*see* page 10-54). During the 1970s, several CIA employees were convicted of crimes related to the Watergate break-ins. Although it is barred by its charter from engaging in domestic operations, a special committee appointed by President Ford in 1975 found that the CIA was engaged in "plainly unlawful" domestic spying in violation of the civil rights of American citizens. CIA operations are clandestine, but the mining of Nicaragua's harbors was brought to the International Court of Justice at The Hague in the Netherlands and the United States was charged with violations of international law. The Iran-Contra hearings in Congress (1987) disclosed the active participation of the CIA in aiding the Contras at the time when Congress had voted to cut off all aid.

Central Treaty Organization (CENTO) Also known as the Baghdad Pact, it was initiated in 1954 by Secretary of State John Foster Dulles to prevent the spread of Soviet Communism in the Middle East. The original members were Iran, Iraq, Pakistan, and Turkey. CENTO received support from the United States.

Chancellorsville, battle of (May 2–4, 1863) In a major engagement in Virginia during the Civil War, Union forces under General Joseph (Fighting Joe) Hooker were outflanked by Lee's great subordinate General Thomas J. (Stonewall) Jackson and driven back in their attempt to march on Richmond. Jackson was mistakenly shot at dusk by one of his own men and died several days later, a serious loss to the Confederacy. The Union suffered 17,000 casualties in this campaign and the Confederates 13,000.

Chase, Solomon P. (1808–1873) Born in New Hampshire, he graduated from Dartmouth and went to Ohio, where he practiced law and defended runaway slaves. In the U.S. Senate (1849–55) he opposed both the Compromise of 1850 and the Kansas-Nebraska Act of 1854 for their recognition of the right of slavery to spread to the territories of the United States. He served as Republican treasurer of Ohio (1855–60). Lincoln appointed him secretary of the treasury, and in that capacity Chase created the National Banking System. He resigned from the cabinet in a controversy with Seward. Then Lincoln appointed him chief justice of the U.S. Supreme Court. He presided over the trial of Jefferson Davis and over the impeachment trial of President Andrew Johnson.

Chávez, César (b. 1927) In 1963, César Chávez, a Mexican-American who had himself been a migrant farm worker, emerged as a leader of the exploited Mexican workers. He established the United Farm Workers Organizing Committee and led the union of farm laborers in a strike against the powerful grape growers of California. After a five-year struggle during which he was on a 25-day fast to prevail upon his members to renounce violence, the union won contracts providing for an increase in pay and better working conditions.

Chesapeake-Leopard affair (1807) In June the British frigate *Leopard* stopped the U.S. frigate *Chesapeake* off the Virginia coast to reclaim four alleged deserters. Captain Barron of the *Chesapeake*, denying he had deserters aboard, refused to permit a search. Heavy fire from the *Leopard* killed three Americans, wounded several, and extensively damaged the ship. The British took four men from the *Chesapeake*, one deserter and three Americans. Captain Barron was disciplined for neglect in not having his ship ready for battle. England offered reparations to President Jefferson, but the "war hawks" used this incident to create a war fever.

Chinese Exclusion Act (1882) Under the Burlingame Treaty of 1868, Chinese laborers were granted immigration rights, but by 1880 sentiment against this cheap labor caused a reversal of the policy. The act of 1882 abrogated the previous arrangement and excluded immigrants from China for a period of ten years. The spirit of the law was violated when the act was renewed in 1892 and in 1902 with no terminal date. In 1943, with Chinese forces fighting as our allies, Congress reinstated Chinese immigration. Under existing quota laws, 105 immigrants from China were legally admitted to the United States.

Civilian Conservation Corps (CCC) (1933) A relief agency organized by the New Deal and administered by the War Department, it provided employment for young men in conservation work projects; most of their wages were paid to their parents on relief.

Civil Rights Act (1957) The act set up a six-person Civil Rights Commission to protect the individual's right to the "equal protection of the law" and particularly to prevent the right of suffrage being denied on account of race or color. Federal courts were authorized to grant injunctions in support of the Civil Rights Commission. Under this act the black vote in the southern states increased appreciably.

The Civil Rights Act of 1964 prohibited discrimination in voting, public education institutions, hiring and promotion of workers, hotels, restaurants, theaters, gas stations, and other public facilities. The act received strong support from President Lyndon B. Johnson. *See also* **Voting Rights Act** (1965).

Civil Works Administration (CWA) (1933) The CWA employed people on government jobs on which the payroll, not materials, was the major expense. People were given jobs similar to those they had previously held. Much of the activity was make-work, derisively called boondoggling, but its supporters considered pay for work was far better than a cash dole in maintaining the morale of the recipients. This program, participated in by federal, state, and local governments, was merged with the Federal Emergency Relief Act (FERA) in 1934.

Clark, George Rogers (1752–1818) Clark carried the Revolutionary War into the West as far as the Mississippi River. His exploits in capturing British posts at Kaskaskia, Cahokia, and Vincennes gave the Americans control of what is now south-ern Illinois between the Mississippi, Ohio, and Wabash rivers. This campaign gave substance to our claim, recognized in the Treaty of Paris, 1783, of the Mississippi River as our western border.

His older brother William was co-captain of the famous Lewis and Clark expedition (1804–06), which explored the West at the request of President Jefferson. *See* **Lewis and Clark Expediton**.

Clay, Henry (1777–1852) Born in Virginia where he studied law, he moved to Lexington, Kentucky. Clay was speaker of the House of Representatives (1811–20 and 1823–25), candidate for president 1824, 1832, and 1844, and helped negotiate the Treaty of Ghent (1814) with Great Britain, ending the War of 1812. He was secretary of state in John Quincy Adams' administration and U.S. senator from Kentucky 1831–42 and 1849–52. His sponsorship of the Compromise of 1820, the Compromise Tariff of 1833, and especially the Compromise of 1850 earned him the title "the Great Pacificator."

Clayton Anti-trust Act (1914) This was a major part of President Wilson's domestic program. Provisions against monopolies forbade: (1) interlocking directorates among large competing corporations; (2) ownership of stock by any corporation in a competing corporation; and (3) price cutting below cost to eliminate a competitor. To favor labor it provided that (1) labor unions and other nonprofit mutual help associations are exempt from the antitrust laws; (2) only when there is a danger of irreparable damage to property may injunctions be used in labor disputes; and (3) boycotts, peaceful picketing, and peaceful strikes are legal.

Clayton-Bulwer Treaty (1850) The major terms of this treaty with England were (1) both nations agree not to colonize or control any republic of Central America; (2) neither nation would seek exclusive control of any isthmian canal; (3) if a canal were built through the isthmus the area would be protected by both England and the United States to assure its neutrality and security; and (4) any canal through the isthmus must be open to the use of all nations on the same terms.

Clemens, Samuel Langhorne (1835–1910) Assumed name Mark Twain, he grew up in Missouri. Clemens worked as a printer and later as a licensed pilot on Mississippi steamboats and worked as a miner, newspaper reporter, and lecturer. He is best known as a humorist and novelist, especially for *The Innocents Abroad* (1865), *The Adventures of Tom Sawyer* (1876), *Life on The Mississippi* (1883), and *The Adventures of Huckleberry Finn* (1884). Beneath the surface of adventure and humor in these and other of his works there is a strong current of social criticism, ever a universal element that gives considerable substance to his work.

Cleveland, Grover *See* Presidents of the United States section, beginning on page 10-83.

Clinton, DeWitt (1769–1828) A New Yorker prominent in politics and a graduate of Columbia University, he was a member of the New York Bar and served in the New York Assembly and Senate. Clinton resigned from the U.S. Senate to become mayor of New York City (1803). He was chiefly responsible for creating the New York public school system. Clinton ran against Madison for president in

1812, and was governor of New York in 1817–23 and 1825–28. He is best remembered for his sponsorship of the Erie Canal, completed in 1825.

Clinton, George (1739–1812)   He studied and practiced law in New York, was a member of the Second Continental Congress that adopted the Declaration of Independence and brigadier general in the Continental army during the Revolutionary War. He served as governor of New York during the formative years of its independence for seven 3-year terms (1777–95 and 1801–1804). He was vice president one term under Jefferson (1805–1809) and one under Madison (1809–13). He was the uncle and sponsor of DeWitt Clinton.

Clinton, Bill (William Jefferson) (b. 1946)   Born in Hope, Arkansas, Clinton graduated from Georgetown University (1968), was a Rhodes Scholar at Oxford University in England (1968–70), and earned a law degree from Yale University in 1973. He ran unsuccessfully for the U.S. House of Representatives in 1974 and was a professor at the University of Arkansas Law School from 1974 to 1976. After a term as Arkansas Attorney General (1976–78), at age 32 he became the nation's youngest governor. Defeated for re-election, he practiced law for two years, then was elected governor again in 1982 and was re-elected in 1984, 1986, and 1990. On January 20, 1993, Clinton, a Democrat, became the 42nd president of the United States. *See also* Presidents of the United States section, beginning on page 10-83.

Coal Strike (1902)   *See* **Anthracite coal strike**.

Cold war   A term widely used after 1947 in reference to the developing hostility between the United States and Russia. The alliance of the United States, Great Britain, and the USSR broke down after World War II, culminating in two military alliances—the North Atlantic Treaty Organization (NATO), 1949, and the Warsaw Pact, 1955.

Colonies in America (1607–1733)   *See* **Exhibit 10.1**.

Columbus, Christopher (1451–1506)   Although he was not the first European to reach the New World, his exploration subsequently led to the European colonization. Born in Genoa, Italy, Columbus went to sea before he was ten. At twenty-five a ship on which he was sailing was wrecked by pirates off the coast of Portugal. He became captain of a Portuguese ship. His decision to sail across the Atlantic to the East was not supported by King John of Portugal, so he went to Spain and there he won the approval of King Ferdinand and Queen Isabella. On his first voyage westward he was at sea six weeks before his three ships reached land at San Salvador on October 12, 1492. They thought they were in India. Columbus made three more transatlantic voyages (1493, 1498, and 1502). He explored much of the Caribbean, including the shore of South America, but never knew he had discovered two continents—North and South America.

Committee of Public Information   This was a U.S. propaganda agency created by Congress in 1917 to mobilize public opinion behind the war effort. It was headed by the journalist George Creel.

Committee to Re-elect the President   A committee headed by Attorney General John N. Mitchell to re-elect President Nixon in 1972, it masterminded the break-in of the Democratic Party national headquarters at the Washington, D.C., Watergate Hotel Complex and committed other illegal acts and "dirty tricks." It received illegal contributions from several corporations, including $400,000 from the International Telephone and Telegraph Corporation (ITT) and $527,500 from the Associated Milk Producers, Inc.

Committees of Correspondence (1772)   Sam Adams persuaded Boston to form a committee to record examples of British "infringements" and "violations" of colonial rights. Other towns throughout Massachusetts were to do the same. The resulting propaganda was sent to the other colonies. Within two years, eleven colonies had effective committees cooperating to keep resentment against England at a high pitch.

Common Sense   A pamphlet written by Thomas Paine and published January 9, 1776, it sold 120,000 copies within three months and a total of 500,000 copies. It urged immediate independence of the American colonies from Great Britain. Coupled with its vigor and sharpness in saying what the people wanted to hear was an idealistic plea to make America the one place in the world where freedom and love of humanity could flourish. *Common Sense* did much to make the Second Continental Congress and the people ready for the Declaration of Independence.

Compromise of 1850   Daniel Webster, with prestige in the North, aided Clay, a national figure from Kentucky, to push through Congress a series of agreements that delayed the outbreak of the Civil War. The major provisions were (1) California became a free state; (2) Texas got $10 million for accepting a reduction in size; (3) any states formed from the territories of New Mexico and Utah would decide by popular vote whether to be free or slave states, but while New Mexico and Utah were territories there would be no restrictions on slavery; (4) no slave trading would be allowed in the District of Columbia; and (5) a fugitive slave law satisfactory to the South was passed.

Confederate States of America   A government organized at Montgomery, Alabama, February 8, 1861, by seven states that seceded from the Union. Mississippi, Alabama, Florida, South Carolina, Georgia, Louisiana, and Texas were later joined by Virginia, Arkansas, Tennessee, and North Carolina. These eleven states constituted the Confederate States of America (1861–65).

Congressional Reconstruction Act (1867)   A series of reconstruction acts divided ten ex-Confederate states, not including Tennessee, into five military districts, each under a major general. Martial law was enforced by federal troops. The governments established under Lincoln's 10 percent plan were abolished, and new constitutional conventions and elections were held in each state. Provisions of the Fourteenth Amendment were part of the reconstruction program. Under these acts the "crime of reconstruction" suppressed southern whites and maintained the supremacy of the Republican Party. Lincoln's fears that a congressional reconstruction plan would be punitive were fully realized.

Congress of Industrial Organizations (CIO)   This was an aggressive nationwide labor union led in the early years by John L. Lewis. The initials CIO originally stood for the Committee for Industrial Organization, within the American Federation of Labor. In 1938 it became an independent labor union following the principle of industry-wide unionism rather than craft-based unionism. *See also* **American Federation of Labor and Congress of Industrial Organizations (AFL-CIO).**

Connecticut Plan The Constitutional Convention (1787) faced a serious disagreement between the large and small states over representation in Congress. The large states favored the Virginia plan, which called for representation based on population. The small states insisted on the New Jersey plan of equal representation for all states. Roger Sherman presented the Connecticut Plan, which was accepted. There was to be a Senate in which each state was to have two members and a House of Representatives in which population would determine the number of members from each state.

Conservation The preservation of our natural resources of soil, water, forests, minerals, wild life, wilderness, and grandeur, conservation as a major national policy was promoted by President Theodore Roosevelt. New Deal conservation measures under President Franklin D. Roosevelt included the Tennessee Valley Authority (1933), the Civilian Conservation Corps (1937), and the Agricultural Adjustment Act (1938). Conservation is a continuing concern of every administration and is strongly supported by citizen voluntary associations, such as the Sierra Club, Wilderness Society, the Nature Conservancy, and the Natural Resources Defense Council.

Constitutional Convention (1787) The convention got underway May 25 in Independence Hall, Philadelphia. Rhode Island was not represented among the fifty-five delegates who registered. Regular attendance during the four months of meetings numbered between thirty and thirty-five members. Washington was chosen chairman of the convention so that his prestige could count heavily in winning ratification of the Constitution. Madison's notes, published in 1840 shortly after his death, give carefully recorded details of the convention proceedings as well as accounts of conflicting views there expressed. The convention completed its work of drawing up a constitution for the United States, and adjourned September 17, 1787.

The Constitution went into effect on June 21, 1788, when it was ratified by New Hampshire, the ninth state to do so. By May 29, 1790, when Rhode Island voted for ratification, all of the original 13 states had joined. (Virginia was tenth, New York was eleventh, and North Carolina was twelfth.) *See* **Exhibit 10.2**.

Contadora The Contadora process was an effort by four Caribbean sponsoring countries—Colombia, Mexico, Panama, and Venezuela—to mediate among five Central American nations where much national and international tension existed: Nicaragua, El Salvador, Costa Rica, Honduras, and Guatamala. In July 1983,the presidents of the four Contadora states, the name taken from the island where they met, stated that their aims included effective control of the regional arms race, the withdrawal of all foreign advisors, and the prohibition of the use of the territory of one state to plan military or political activities that would cause instability in other states.

Continental Congress, First (1774) The congress met in Carpenter's Hall, Philadelphia. Only Georgia was not represented. King George III was petitioned to repeal all regulatory laws passed since 1763, and the time for another meeting for consideration of his reply was set for May 10, 1775. Meanwhile trade in English goods was boycotted, the use of English products was drastically curtailed, Massachusetts operated under a new government to sidestep the King's Council and governor, and colonial militia began drilling on many a village green.

Continental Congress, Second (1775) The congress was held in Independence Hall, Philadelphia. Lexington and Concord had been the king's reply to the First Continental Congress. Washington was appointed commander in chief, committees were formed to draw up a Declaration of Independence and a permanent form of government, and Canada was invited to join the rebellion. This congress acted as the government without a constitution until the adoption of the Articles of Confederation in March 1781.

Conway cabal Thomas Conway, an Irish colonel who had served in the army of France, was appointed in September 1778 inspector general of the Continental armies. He wrote a letter to General Horatio Gates attacking George Washington. The latter reacted sternly to what appeared to be part of a conspiracy to have him removed. Gates denied any connection with this move. Conway resigned his post and apologized to Washington before returning to France.

Coolidge, Calvin *See* Presidents of the United States section, beginning on page 10-83.

Cooper, James Fenimore (1789–1851) Novelist and historian, he served for a time in the U.S. Navy and then resigned and proceeded to write a series of five frontier novels known as "The Leather-Stocking Tales" recounting the life of his hero Natty Bumppo, who lived and fought among the native Americans. He lived in Europe (1826–33). Upon his return he settled in Cooperstown, New York, where he wrote a *History of the Navy of the United States of America*. Among his lesser known works are travel tales of Europe and social criticisms of American provincialism.

Cooper, Peter (1791–1883) A manufacturer, he invented a machine for cloth shearing, designed the first steam locomotive (called Tom Thumb) built in the United States, made the first structural iron for fireproof buildings in his mill at Trenton, New Jersey, and was the first U.S. iron manufacturer to use the Bessemer converter. He invested heavily in Cyrus Field's Atlantic cable and was president of the New York, Newfoundland, and London Telegraph Company. Cooper ran for president in 1876 on the Greenback party ticket. He established Cooper Union in New York City as an educational center "for the advancement of science and art."

Copperheads Northern Democrats, also called peace Democrats, who opposed the Lincoln administration in its war efforts against the seceded Southern states. A leading "copperhead," Congressman Clement L. Vallandigham of Ohio, was arrested in 1863 for "declaring sympathy for the enemy." President Lincoln ordered him banished to the Confederacy.

EXHIBIT 10.1
Early Colonies in America (1607–1733)

Colony	Date Place Founder	Type a) When founded b) In 1775	Pertinent Bits Of Information
Virginia	1607 Jamestown London Co.	a) Charter to stock company b) Royal	
Plymouth	1620 Plymouth Pilgrims	a) Self-governing b) Royal	Leyden, Holland Wm. Brewster— first leader Separatists Miles Standish— military leader Wm. Bradford— early governor
New Hampshire	1623 Portsmouth John Mason	a) Mass. claimed it; the title was obscure. Charles II made it royal in 1679. b) Royal	Very weak settlement. Southern towns taken over by Mass.
Maine	1623 Portland Sir Ferdinando Gorges	a) Proprietary, claimed by Mass. b) Royal	Became part of Mass. in 1691
New York	1624 Albany and New Amsterdam Dutch	a) Proprietary in 1664 when the Duke of York took it for England. b) Royal	N.Y. Harbor and the Hudson River separated the English colonies. This was an intolerable situation to the empire-minded British.
New Jersey	1624 Part of New Netherlands with N.Y. Dutch	a) Same as N.Y. b) Royal	For a period it was divided into East and West Jersey. For several years New York's governor also governed N.J. although the courts and the legislature were separate. Not until 1738 was N.J. definitely a separate, unified colony.
Massachusetts	1630 Boston Mass. Bay Co.	a) Charter to stock company b) Royal	
Maryland	1634 St. Mary's Province Cecilius Calvert the 2nd Lord Baltimore	a) Proprietary b) Proprietary	Started as a Catholic colony. The Toleration Act of 1649 gave freedom of religion to all who believed in the Trinity. Granted to protect Catholics from interference by other Christians.

EXHIBIT 10.1 (continued)
Early Colonies in America (1607–1733)

Colony	Date Place Founder	Type a) When founded b) In 1775	Pertinent Bits Of Information
Rhode Island	1636 Providence Roger Williams	a) Self-governing b) Self-governing	Freedom for all religious and for non-believers. Anne Hutchinson
Connecticut	1636 Hartford Thomas Hooker	a) Self-governing b) Self-governing	Fundamental Orders in 1639 was the first written constitution in the New World. Davenport's colony at New Haven became part of Conn. in 1662.
Delaware	1638 Wilmington Swedes	a) Proprietary after conquest by England in 1664. b) Proprietary	First settled by Swedes.
North and South Carolina	1665 Albemarle Eight Noble Lords	a) Proprietary b) Royal	Albemarle Sound and Charleston Harbor where the earliest settlements were made are 300 miles apart. They had little contact with each other. Started with an impractical government based on John Locke's ideas. There was almost continual political strife. North and South Carolina became separate colonies in 1711.
Pennsylvania	1638 Philadelphia Wm. Penn	a) Proprietary b) Proprietary	Quaker settlement. Also many Germans (Pennsylvania Dutch). In the buying of the land from the Indians and allowing complete religious freedom Pa. followed the good example of R.I. Penn's colony was called "The Holy Experiment." After 1700 it had a unicameral (one-house) legislature.
Georgia	1733 Savannah James Oglethorpe	a) Proprietary b) Royal	A mismanaged attempt at human rehabilitation. Many debtors and other unfortunates were among the first settlers. The prohibition of the rum trade and slavery during the first decade was an economic mistake. It had the unenviable location to serve as a buffer between Spanish Florida and the Carolinas.

EXHIBIT 10.2
States in the Union

State	Date Constitution was Ratified
1. Delaware	December 7, 1787
2. Pennsylvania	December 12, 1787
3. New Jersey	December 18, 1787
4. Georgia	January 2, 1788
5. Connecticut	January 9, 1788
6. Massachusetts	February 6, 1788
7. Maryland	April 28, 1788
8. South Carolina	May 23, 1788
9. New Hampshire	June 21, 1788
10. Virginia	June 25, 1788
11. New York	July 26, 1788
12. North Carolina	November 21, 1789
13. Rhode Island	May 29, 1790

State	Admitted to the Union
14. Vermont	March 4, 1791
15. Kentucky	June 1, 1792
16. Tennessee	June 1, 1796
17. Ohio	March 1, 1803
18. Louisiana	April 30, 1812
19. Indiana	December 11, 1816
20. Mississippi	December 10, 1817
21. Illinois	December 3, 1818
22. Alabama	December 4, 1819
23. Maine	March 15, 1820
24. Missouri	August 10, 1821
25. Arkansas	June 15, 1836
26. Michigan	January 26, 1837
27. Florida	March 3, 1845
28. Texas	December 29, 1845
29. Iowa	December 28, 1846
30. Wisconsin	May 29, 1848
31. California	September 9, 1850
32. Minnesota	May 11, 1858
33. Oregon	February 14, 1859
34. Kansas	January 29, 1861
35. West Virginia	June 20, 1863
36. Nevada	October 31, 1864
37. Nebraska	March 1, 1867
38. Colorado	August 1, 1876
39. North Dakota	November 2, 1889
40. South Dakota	November 2, 1889
41. Montana	November 8, 1889
42. Washington	November 11, 1889
43. Idaho	July 3, 1890
44. Wyoming	July 10, 1890
45. Utah	January 4, 1896
46. Oklahoma	November 16, 1907
47. New Mexico	January 6, 1912
48. Arizona	February 14, 1912
49. Alaska	January 3, 1959
50. Hawaii	August 21, 1959

English General Lord Cornwallis surrenders at Yorktown.

Cornwallis, General Lord   (1738–1805)   He was commander of British forces in the American Revolutionary War. The defeat of his army of 8000 troops by combined American and French land and naval forces in October 1781 was the last major engagement of the war. The surrender of Cornwallis led to the decision of the British government to end the war and offer peace negotiations.

Corrupt bargain   In the election of 1824 the electoral vote was split among four candidates: Andrew Jackson of Tennessee, 99; John Quincy Adams of Massachusetts, 84; William Crawford of Georgia, 41; and Henry Clay of Kentucky, 37. Since no one had a majority, the Twelfth Amendment to the Constitution required that the House of Representatives choose the president from the top three. Henry Clay was now out of the running and used his influence in the House to secure the election of Adams. When Adams became president and appointed Clay secretary of state, Jackson and his followers, who believed he should have been selected by the House to be president, charged that Clay and Adams had made a "corrupt bargain." Historians generally regard this charge as having little merit.

Court-packing bill   During the first term of President Franklin D. Roosevelt, a number of New Deal laws passed by Congress and signed by the president were declared unconstitutional by the Supreme Court. On his re-election in 1936, FDR sent to Congress a proposal that would give him authority to appoint one new justice to the Court for every one (not to exceed six) who had reached the age of seventy and failed to retire. Potentially, this would have given him authority to increase the Court membership to fifteen by recommending the appointment of six new members. The proposal was hotly contested. Its opponents described it as a "court-packing bill." The proposal was rejected by a vote of 10 to 8 in the Senate Judiciary Committee and by the entire Senate by a vote of 70 to 22. *See* **Supreme Court and Franklin Delano Roosevelt**.

Crane, Stephen   (1871–1900)   Author and newspaper correspondent, he is best known for his Civil War novel *The Red Badge of Courage* (1895), a fictional account of the mental and emotional experience of the young New York farm boy Henry Fleming, an infantryman with the Union forces in the battle of Chancellorsville.

Crédit Mobilier   (1872)   This corporation let contracts for the many jobs that went into building the Union Pacific Railroad. It bought building materials and supplies to sell to the UP. Prices charged for services and materials were exorbitant. By "milking" the UP, the dividends of the Crédit Mobilier climbed to 625 percent. Bribes paid to congressmen blossomed into laws giving tremendous land grants and liberal loans to the UP. Among the more prominent congressmen owning stock in Crédit Mobilier were Representatives Ames of Massachusetts, Brooks of New York, Garfield of Ohio, Colfax of Indiana, and Senator Wilson of Massachusetts.

Crime of '73   In 1873, an act of Congress discontinued the coinage and use of silver as money. The act was passed in recognition that silver was no longer being used by people as money. By 1876, however, the increased production of silver led the silver mining interests and the advocates of cheap money to demand that the U.S. government resume the minting of silver coins. They referred to the act of 1873 demonitizing silver as "the crime of '73."

Crittenden compromise (1861)   Proposals made by Senator Crittenden of Kentucky to bring the seceded states back into the Union by protecting their interests in slavery by "permanent amendments" to the Constitution, the plan included a provision for the extension of slavery to new territories south of 36°30'. This was unacceptable to the Republicans.

"Cross of gold" speech   At the Democratic national convention of 1896, William Jennings Bryan of Nebraska delivered a speech advocating the free coinage of silver in opposition to the Republicans, who favored the gold standard. When he concluded his oration with the challenge ". . . you shall not crucify mankind upon a cross of gold," the convention went wild and nominated thirty-six-year-old Bryan as their presidential standard bearer.

Custer's last stand at Little Big Horn on June 25, 1876.

Cumberland Road   Authorized by Congress in 1806, the Cumberland Road was the first to be built with federal funds. Begun in 1811, it extended from Cumberland, Maryland to Wheeling, West Virginia, and was widely used by Easterners heading West. The road was later extended across Illinois to Vandalia, within 100 miles of St. Louis. In the East the road was linked with Baltimore, providing a major travel artery from the Atlantic to the Mississippi.

Custer's last stand   At the battle of the Little Big Horn (Montana), June 25–26, 1876, General George A. Custer and his 264 cavalrymen were totally annihilated by a superior force of native Americans led by Crazy Horse and Sitting Bull. Custer was known to the natives as an implacable foe dedicated to their extinction.

D

Darrow, Clarence (1857–1938) Prominent Chicago trial lawyer and labor advocate, he defended the two "thrill killers" in the sensational Leopold-Loeb case. He faced William Jennings Bryan in the trial of Thomas Scopes, who taught evolution, contrary to Tennessee law, in 1925, and defended Dr. Ossian Sweet and his brother, who were black, in a Detroit case marked by racism.

Dartmouth College Case (1819) New Hampshire passed a law changing Dartmouth College, a private institution, to Dartmouth University, a state institution. Trustees opposed to this change contended through their lawyers, one of whom was Daniel Webster, that the original charter of 1769 was a contract between the king and the trustees and that it was still a contract between New Hampshire and the trustees. This position, accepted by the Supreme Court, made the state law unconstitutional as it violated Article I, Section 10, "no state shall pass any law impairing the obligation of contracts." The inviolability of contracts was greatly strengthened.

Davis, Jefferson (1808–1889) He graduated from West Point (1828) and fought in the Black Hawk War (1832) and in the Mexican War (1846), being wounded at the battle of Buena Vista. He was Democratic congressman from Mississippi (1845–46), U.S. senator (1847–51) and (1857–61), defeated for governor (1851), and secretary of war under President Pierce (1853–57). Davis served as the only president of the Confederate States of America (February 18, 1861, to April 24, 1865). He was imprisoned after the war (1865–67), indicted for treason, and released on bail but never tried. He then traveled abroad and returned to his home in Mississippi, where he wrote *The Rise and Fall of the Confederate Government* (1881).

Dawes Act (1887)   The act was a plan to break up native American tribes by granting land ownership to individual natives. Each head of family got 160 acres plus 40 more for each minor child. Each single adult and orphan got 80 acres. If the land was good only for grazing, the allotments were doubled. In order to encourage living on the land it was provided that the native owners would not sell their land during the first 25 years. Natives included under the Dawes Act had the full rights of United States citizens.

D-Day (June 6, 1944)   Operation Overlord was the greatest naval military maneuver of all time. Over two million men trained in England for months for the invasion of the Continent across the Channel. The operation included bombardment by air of the entire French-Belgian coastline; 4000 troop ships; 600 fighting ships; 176,000 troops; 11,000 planes; and glider planes dropping paratroops behind enemy lines. The Supreme Commander of the Allied Expeditionary Forces, General Eisenhower, directed the invasion and prolonged attack. By July a million troops had crossed into France, and by September more than two million.

Debs, Eugene V. (1855–1926)   Socialist party candidate for president (1900, 1904, 1908, 1912, and 1920), Debs was raised and educated in Indiana, where he worked five years on the Terre Haute and Indianapolis Railroad (1870–75). In 1893 he organized the American Railway Union. He served a six-month prison term for his part in the Pullman strike of 1894. His outspoken opposition to U.S. participation in World War I in violation of the Espionage Act brought him a conviction and sentence of ten years in prison, but he was pardoned in 1921 by President Harding, who feared that he might become a martyr if he were to die behind bars. Debs rejected communism and remained a Socialist to the end of his life.

Decatur, Stephen (1779–1820)   He received his first naval commission as midshipman in 1798 and served in the West Indies during the naval war with France. In a famous exploit during the war with Tripoli (1804), he led a boarding party to recapture and burn the frigate *Philadelphia* to deny its use to the enemy. In the War of 1812 he commanded the *President* and the *United States*, which scored a victory over the British *Macedonian*. After the war he led a squadron to the Mediterranean, where he compelled Tripoli and other Barbary States to make compensation for piracy against American merchantmen. At a dinner given in his honor he uttered the famous toast, "Our country! In her intercourse with foreign nations may she always be in the right; but our country, right or wrong." He was killed in a duel near Blandenbur, Maryland, with James Barron, a fellow naval officer, on March 22, 1820.

Declaration of Independence (*See* text following)   On June 7, 1776, the Second Continental Congress, meeting at Independence Hall in Philadelphia, heard Richard Henry Lee, delegate from Virginia, make a motion to the effect that the United Colonies "are and of right ought to be independent states." The motion was seconded by John Adams of Massachusetts. It was discussed for four days, and then it was agreed that a formal vote be postponed until July 1. A committee was appointed to prepare a formal declaration. The committee consisted of Thomas Jefferson (Virginia), Benjamin Franklin (Pennsylvania), John Adams (Massachusetts), Robert Livingston (New York), and Roger Sherman (Connecticut). The members asked Jefferson to draft the declaration. He agreed and worked on it from June 11 to June 28. He later said, "I turned to neither book nor pamphlet while writing it." Franklin and Adams made a few changes. Members of Congress made others before it was approved July 2 and formally adopted July 4, 1776.

The Declaration falls into three main divisions. First there is a statement of the "natural rights" of human beings. This is packed into four not very long sentences. Next is a long list of complaints about the king and a statement or two about the humble patience of the American colonies under such treatment; and finally, there is the declaration that the colonies are now independent states.

The Declaration was proclaimed in Philadelphia July 8 and was read the next day before Washington's troops in New York. By resolution of Congress the Declaration of Independence was engrossed on parchment and the fifty-five delegates affixed their signatures on August 2 and the following days.

Declaration of Independence (text)
The Declaration of Independence
In Congress, July 4, 1776
THE UNANIMOUS DECLARATION OF THE THIRTEEN UNITED STATES OF AMERICA
When, in the Course of human events, it becomes necessary for one people to dissolve the political bands which have connected them with another, and to assume among the powers of the earth, the separate and equal station to which the Laws of Nature and of Nature's God entitle them, a decent respect to the opinions of mankind requires that they should declare the causes which impel them to the separation.

We hold these truths to be self-evident, that all men are created equal, that they are endowed by their Creator with certain unalienable Rights, that among these, are Life, Liberty, and the pursuit of Happiness. That, to secure these rights, Governments are instituted among Men, deriving their just powers from the consent of the governed, that, whenever any Form of Government becomes destructive of these ends, it is the Right of the People to alter or to abolish it, and to institute new Government, laying its foundations on such principles, and organizing its powers in such form, as to them shall seem most likely to effect their Safety and Happiness. Prudence, indeed, will dictate that Governments long established, should not be changed for light and transient causes; and, accordingly, all experience hath shewn, that mankind are more disposed to suffer, while evils are sufferable, than to right themselves by abolishing the forms to which they are accustomed. But, when a long train of abuses and usurpations, pursuing invariably the same Object, evinces a design to reduce them under absolute Despotism, it is their right, it is their duty, to throw off such Government and to provide new Guards for their future security. — Such has been the patient sufferance of these Colonies; and such is now the necessity which constrains them to alter their former Systems of Government. The history of the present King of Great Britain is a history of repeated injuries and usurpations, all having in direct object the establishment of an absolute Tyranny over these States. To prove this, let Facts be submitted to a candid world. — He has refused his Assent to Laws the most wholesome and necessary for the public good.

He has forbidden his Governors to pass Laws of immediate and pressing importance, unless suspended in their operation till his Assent should be obtained; and when so suspended, he has utterly neglected to attend to them.

He has refused to pass other laws for the accommodation of large districts of people, unless those people would relinquish the right of Representation in the Legislature, a right inestimable to them and formidable to tyrants only.

He has called together legislative bodies at places unusual, uncomfortable, and distant from the depository of their Public Records, for the sole purpose of fatiguing them into compliance with his measures.

He has dissolved Representative Houses repeatedly, for opposing with manly firmness his invasions on the rights of the people.

He has refused for a long time, after such dissolutions, to cause others to be elected; whereby the Legislative Powers, incapable of Annihilation, have returned to the People at large for their exercise; the State remaining, in the meantime, exposed to all the dangers of invasion from without, and convulsions within.

He has endeavored to prevent the population of these States; for that purpose, obstructing the Laws for Naturalization of Foreigners; refusing to pass others to encourage their migrations hither, and raising the conditions of new Appropriations of Lands.

He has obstructed the Administration of Justice by refusing his Assent to Laws for establishing Judiciary Powers.

He has made Judges dependent on his Will alone, for the tenure of their offices, and the amount and payment of their salaries.

He has erected a multitude of New Offices, and sent hither swarms of Officers to harass our People, and eat out their substance.

He has kept among us, in times of peace, Standing Armies, without the Consent of our legislatures.

He has affected to render the Military independent of, and superior to, the Civil Power.

He has combined, with others, to subject us to a jurisdiction foreign to our constitution, and unacknowledged by our laws; giving his Assent to their Acts of pretended legislation:

For quartering large bodies of armed troops among us:

For protecting them by a mock Trial, from Punishment, for any Murders which they should commit on the Inhabitants of these States:

For cutting off our Trade with all parts of the world:

For imposing Taxes on us without our Consent:

For depriving us, in many cases, of the benefits of Trial by Jury:

For transporting us beyond Seas to be tried for pretended offenses:

For abolishing the free System of English Laws in a neighboring Province, establishing therein an Arbitrary government, and enlarging its Boundaries, so as to render it at once an example and fit instrument for introducing the same absolute rule into these Colonies:

For taking away our Charters, abolishing our most valuable Laws, and altering, fundamentally, the Forms of our Governments:

For suspending our own Legislatures, and declaring themselves invested with Power to legislate for us in all cases whatsoever.

He has abdicated Government here, by declaring us out of his Protection, and waging War against us.

He has plundered our seas, ravaged our Coasts, burnt our towns, and destroyed the lives of our people.

He is, at this time, transporting large Armies of foreign mercenaries to compleat the works of death, desolation, and tyranny, already begun with circumstances of Cruelty & perfidy scarcely paralleled in the most barbarous ages, and totally unworthy of Head of a civilized nation.

He has constrained our fellow Citizens, taken Captive on the high Seas, to bear Arms against their Country, to become the executioners of their friends and Brethren, or to fall themselves by their Hands.

He has excited domestic insurrections amongst us, and has endeavored to bring on the inhabitants of our frontiers, the merciless Indian Savages whose known rule of warfare, is an undistinguished destruction of all ages, sexes and conditions.

In every stage of these Oppressions, We have Petitioned for Redress, in the most humble terms; our repeated Petitions have been answered only by repeated injury. A Prince, whose character is thus marked by every act which may define a Tyrant, is unfit to be the ruler of a free people.

Nor have We been wanting in attentions to our British brethren. We have warned them, from time to time of attempts made by their legislature to extend an unwarrantable jurisdiction over us. We have reminded them of the circumstances of our emigration and settlement here. We have appealed to their native justice and magnanimity, and we have conjured them by the ties of our common kindred to disavow these usurpations, which would inevitably interrupt our connections and correspondence. They too have been deaf to the voice of justice and of consanguinity. We must, therefore, acquiesce in the necessity, which denounces our Separation, and hold them, as we hold the rest of mankind, Enemies in War, in Peace Friends.

We, therefore, the Representatives of the United States of America, in General Congress, Assembled, appealing to the Supreme Judge of the world for the rectitude of our intentions, do, in the Name, and by Authority of the good People of these Colonies, solemnly publish and declare, That these United Colonies are, and of Right ought to be, Free and Independent States; that they are Absolved from all Allegiance to the British Crown, and that all political connection between them and the State of Great Britain is, and ought to be, totally dissolved: and that, as Free and Independent States, they have full Power to levy War, conclude Peace, contract Alliances, establish Commerce, and to do all other Acts and Things which Independent States may of right do. And, for the support of this Declaration, with a firm reliance on the Protection of Divine Providence, we mutually pledge to each other our Lives, our Fortunes, and our sacred Honor.

The foregoing Declaration was, by order of Congress, engrossed, and signed by the following members:

John Hancock

New Hampshire	North Carolina
Josiah Bartlett	William Hooper
William Whipple	Joseph Hewes
Matthew Thornton	John Penn
Massachusetts Bay	James Smith
Samuel Adams	George Taylor
John Adams	James Wilson
Robert Treat Paine	George Ross
Elbridge Gerry	Delaware
Francis Hopkinson	Caesar Rodney
John Hart	George Read
Abraham Clark	Thomas M'Kean
Pennsylvania	Maryland
Robert Morris	Samuel Chase
Benjamin Rush	William Paca
Benjamin Franklin	Thomas Stone
John Morton	Charles Carroll,
George Clymer	of Carrollton
Rhode Island	Virginia
Stephen Hopkins	George Wythe
William Ellery	Richard Henry Lee
Connecticut	South Carolina
Roger Sherman	Edward Rutledge
Samuel Huntington	Thomas Heyward, Jr.
William Williams	Thomas Lynch, Jr.
Oliver Wolcott	Arthur Middleton
New York	Georgia
William Floyd	Button Gwinnett
Philip Livingston	Lyman Hall
Francis Lewis	George Walton
Lewis Morris	
New Jersey	
Richard Stockton	
John Witherspoon	
Thomas Jefferson	
Benjamin Harrison	
Thomas Nelson, Jr.	
Francis Lightfoot Lee	
Carter Braxton	

Resolved, That copies of the Declaration be sent to the several assemblies, conventions, and committees, or councils of safety, and to the several commanding officers of the continental troops; that it be proclaimed in each of the United States, at the head of the army.

Declaratory Act (1766)   The act was passed by Parliament at the same time it repealed the Stamp Act. It asserted the right of Parliament to make any laws to hold the colonies and Britain together. It was a complete rejection of the "taxation without representation is tyranny" cry from America and colonial arguments holding that Parliament had no right to levy revenue and internal taxes.

De Lome letter   In a private letter written to a friend, the Spanish minister to the United States, De Lome, wrote disparagingly of President McKinley; the letter was stolen from a post office in Havana and released by Cuban revolutionists in order to stir up American opinion against Spain in 1898.

Deposit, right of   The farmers of the Ohio and Mississippi valleys shipped a million dollars worth of corn, wheat, tobacco, cotton, and meat products to New Orleans, where it was taken from riverboats and placed on oceangoing vessels. The right to deposit these goods in New Orleans prior to transshipment had been guaranteed for three years by the Pinckney Treaty of 1795, but the farmers believed they had secured it permanently. Late in 1802 the Spanish governor in New Orleans withdrew this right, which meant American shippers would have to pay for the privilege of deposit. To regain the right of deposit, Jefferson sent James Monroe to France (the latter had acquired New Orleans and the Louisiana Territory from Spain) to negotiate for the right of deposit. It was during these negotiations that Napoleon suddenly offered to sell the entire Louisiana Territory to the United States.

Dewey, Commodore George (1837–1917)   Graduate from the U.S. Naval Academy (1858), he served under Farragut at the Battle of New Orleans (1862). As commodore of the U.S. Asiatic fleet he led his squadron 600 miles to Manila Bay when he learned of the declaration of war against Spain in 1898. His ships scored a major victory there, destroying eight Spanish warships, thus ensuring U.S. possession of the Philippines. Dewey was acclaimed a national hero and invested by Congress with the new rank admiral of the navy.

Dewey, John (1859–1952)   Philosopher, educator, and sociopolitical activist, he was born in Vermont and received his doctorate in philosophy at Johns Hopkins University. He taught at the Universities of Michigan, Minnesota, and Chicago. At the latter university he headed a new division, the school of education as well as the campus experimental school where his progressive education teaching methods were developed. In 1905 he came to Columbia University, where he remained for the rest of his life. He was founder of the American Association of University Professors (AAUP), the college teachers' union. Dewey's writings in education, such as *Democracy and Education* (1915), and in philosophy, notably *Philosophy and Civilization* (1931), had great influence worldwide.

Dickinson, John (1732–1808)   Born in Maryland, he was a member of the Delaware Assembly (1760–62) and the Pennsylvania Assembly (1762–65 and 1770–76). His pamphlet *Letters from a Farmer in Pennsylvania to the Inhabitants of the British Colonies* was conciliatory in tone but firm in its opposition to the Townshend Acts. As a delegate to the First Continental Congress from Pennsylvania and to the Second Continental Congress from Delaware he sent conciliatory petitions to the king of England. He refused to sign the Declaration of Independence but was a delegate from Delaware to the Constitutional Convention and signer of that document. Dickinson College in Carlyle, Pennsylvania, of which he was the founder, bears his name.

Dingley Tariff of 1897   Tariff rates on wool reached a new high, averaging over 50 percent. Hides were removed from the free list. Protectionism was accepted as policy by the McKinley administration.

Direct primaries   Elections held to permit the voters to choose party candidates instead of leaving their nomination to political machines.

Dix, Dorothea Lynde (1802–1887) Social worker and reformer, she operated a school for girls in Boston. A chance event, teaching a Sunday school class in a women's prison, opened her eyes to ghastly conditions, including insane inmates living in filthy, unheated rooms. Reform in mental health care and in the treatment of prisoners and paupers became her career. During 1840–41 she visited every prison, almshouse, and house of correction in Massachusetts. Her *Memorial to the Legislature of Massachusetts* (1843) exposed conditions of the treatment of the mentally ill. She followed this with similar investigations in states throughout the East, South, and Midwest. Her reports resulted in major reforms in the treatment of the mentally ill, handicapped, and imprisoned. During the Civil War she was appointed supervisor of army nurses. In 1881, six years before her death, she retired to Trenton State Hospital in New Jersey, a model mental hospital she had helped establish.

Dixiecrats Nickname for the States' Rights party, it was made up of insurgent Democrats of the South who bolted from the Democratic party in 1948 and nominated Governor Strom Thurmond of South Carolina as their presidential candidate.

Dixon-Yates contract (1954) A federal agreement under President Eisenhower to purchase electric power from a private syndicate instead of expanding the TVA generating facilities, the contract was abandoned because of public protest against the large profits it would have given a private utility at the expense of taxpayers.

Dollar diplomacy The policy of using national diplomacy to promote the business interests of American citizens in foreign countries, it was employed especially by the Taft administration in the Caribbean area and in China.

The policy was supported by armed intervention in the Dominican Republic in 1905 and in succeeding years in Cuba, Honduras, Nicaragua, Haiti, and Costa Rica. The policy was reversed by Franklin D. Roosevelt's "good neighbor policy" in 1933.

Dominion of New England (1685–1688) A union of New England, New York, and New Jersey formed by James II, who appointed Sir Edmund Andros as royal governor over the Dominion.

Dorr's Rebellion (1841) Rhode Island was governed under its original charter, obtained from Charles II in 1663, limiting suffrage to male property holders. Under the leadership of Thomas W. Dorr, a convention met in Providence (October 1841) and formed the "People's Constitution" providing for white manhood suffrage. The legislature reaffirmed the "Landholder's Constitution." In the ensuing election one party elected Dorr as governor; the other inaugurated Samuel W. King. President Tyler prepared to send federal troops to support King. Dorr's followers attempted to seize the Rhode Island state arsenal. When this failed, Dorr's rebellion collapsed. Dorr attempted to flee the state, then returned, gave himself up, and was sentenced to life imprisonment but was released a year later (1845). A new constitution with greatly liberalized voting rights was adopted in 1843.

Dos Passos, John (1896–1970) This author is best known for his *U.S.A.* trilogy, which uses stream of consciousness, newspaper items, songs, and biographic sketches to give an impressionistic history of the United States during the early twentieth century. The trilogy consists of *The 42nd Parallel* (1930), *1919* (1932), and *The Big Money* (1936). Written during the Great Depression, the novels depict an image of America in turmoil.

Frederick Douglass

Douglass, Frederick (1817–1895) Born a slave, Douglass escaped from Baltimore and settled in New Bedford, Massachusetts, where he worked as a common laborer although he had learned to read as a house slave. At an antislavery convention in 1841 he spoke so eloquently that he was hired as a lecturer for the society. He fled to the British Isles to escape being captured and returned as a fugitive slave. On his return in 1847 he bought his freedom and founded the abolitionist newspaper *North Star*, which he edited. As an advisor to John Brown, he fled to Canada and then to England after Brown's capture and execution. During the Civil War, Douglass helped enlist blacks into the Union regiments. After the war he held federal offices in the District of Columbia and served as U.S. consul general to Haiti (1889–91).

Douglas, Stephen A. (1813–1861) He went west from his native Vermont at the age of twenty and settled in Illinois, where he studied law and became a state legislator and judge. After two terms in the House of Representatives (1843–47), he was elected to the U.S. Senate where he served until his death. Known as the "Little Giant," he confronted Abraham Lincoln in a series of seven debates (the Lincoln-Douglas debates) in Illinois in a contest for the Senate seat, which he won. His doctrine of "popular sovereignty," further refined in the "Freeport doctrine" for determining the status of slavery in the territories, lost him the support of the South. This split the Democratic party for which he was the candidate for president in 1860 and resulted in the election of the Republican candidate, Abraham Lincoln. Douglas supported Lincoln's policy of taking all measures necessary to save the Union.

"Doves" and "hawks" These terms came into common use during the War in Vietnam (1964–73). As opposition to the war grew, those who sought a negotiated peace with the Communist government in Hanoi came to be called "doves"; those who urged stepping up the war for fear that the loss of Vietnam to the Communists would lead to the overthrow of neighboring governments (the domino theory) came to be called "hawks." The terms are now widely used to distinguish those who oppose (doves) and those who favor (hawks) military force to attain political objectives in international affairs.

Draft riots (1863) The first Union conscription act went into effect March 3, 1863. All men aged twenty to forty-five became liable to conscription but could provide a substitute or pay $300 to avoid military service. The poor thus believed themselves discriminated against and the blame for the draft was placed on blacks, who were victims of draft riots, which broke out in New York City. Over a period of four days (July 13–16), hundreds, chiefly free blacks, lost their lives and $1 million in property was destroyed. Several regiments of Federal troops were detached from Meade's army, which was pursuing Lee after Gettysburg, and sent to New York to restore order.

Drago Doctrine (1902) After Britain, Germany, and Italy jointly blockaded Venezuela in an effort to collect debts owed them, the foreign minister of Argentina, Louis M. Drago, announced a policy that no European power might use force against any American nation to collect debts. This policy, in accord with the spirit of the Monroe Doctrine, was supplanted by the Roosevelt Corollary to the Monroe Doctrine in 1904.

Dred Scott case (1857) The Supreme Court ruled that the black man Dred Scott was not a citizen and had no right to bring his case to court. Two lower courts had reached this same decision. The Supreme Court went on to explain, however, that neither Congress nor territories could legislate on slavery; only states, according to the Tenth Amendment, could do so. The North considered these remarks of the Court unofficial and obiter dictum. The South considered these opinions a formal, legal decision. Scott's plea for freedom was based on his residence for extended periods in the "free" territory of Wisconsin and the free state of Illinois.

Dreiser, Theodore (1871–1945) A novelist, his realism and social criticism projected him into the forefront of twentieth century American writers. After graduation from Indiana University, he worked as a reporter in Chicago, St. Louis, and Pittsburgh before coming to New York, where his first novel, *Sister Carrie* (1900), provoked censorship because of its sexual frankness. His trilogy *The Financier* (1912), *The Titan* (1914), and *The Stoic* (1947) is based on the career of the industrialist Charles T. Yarkes. His best known work, *An American Tragedy* (1925), involved the drowning of an unmarried pregnant woman by her lover.

DuBois, William Edward Burghardt (1868–1963) Born and raised in Great Barrington, Massachusetts, DuBois attended Fiske University in Tennessee and then went to Harvard University for his second B.A., his M.A., and, after two years study at the University of Berlin, his Ph.D (1896). While on the staff of the University of Pennsylvania he produced a sociological study entitled "The Philadelphia Negro." At Atlanta University he produced a series of annual studies (1897–1915) on various aspects of black life and culture. In 1903 he wrote a classic work, *The Souls of Black Folk*, which contained a challenge to Booker T. Washington's status as spokesman for the black community. DuBois left Atlanta to assume a leading role in the newly formed National Association for the Advancement of Colored People (NAACP). In his later years he devoted his energies to the idea of Pan-Africanism. In 1935 he published a major work based on ten years of research, *Black Reconstruction in America, 1860–1880*. In 1961, two years before his death at ninety-five, he joined the Communist party, left the United States, and went to live in Ghana, where he was well received.

Dulles, John Foster (1888–1959) He entered the prominent law firm of Sullivan and Cromwell in 1911 and headed that firm from 1927 until his death. Dulles specialized in international law and held various posts with the federal government, including delegate to the United Nations (1946–50), advisor to the State Department (1950–53), and finally secretary of state (1953–59) in the Eisenhower administration. In that capacity he traveled over 500,000 miles as the major architect of U.S. foreign policy seeking the "liberation" of countries in the Soviet bloc. He forced Britain and France to abandon the Suez Canal attack (1956), formulated the Eisenhower Doctrine for preserving peace in the Middle East (1957), and was willing to go to the brink of war in the Berlin crisis of 1958.

Dumbarton Oaks Conference (August–October, 1944) In Washington, D.C., the United States, Great Britain, the USSR, and China drew up a charter that was to serve as a starting point from which to work at the San Francisco Conference to be held later. Concerning their rights on the Security Council of the Proposed United Nations, the big powers were unable to reach definite conclusions, except that they would each insist on a veto. The USSR was inclined to have the veto enable a member to keep any issue from coming before the council for discussion. The Russian position here closely paralleled the position taken by the United States under the Root formula for our entrance into the World Court.

Dunbar, Paul Laurence (1872–1906) Black American poet of the first rank, he was born in Dayton, Ohio, of slave parents. He wrote in both classic English and in dialect expressing his understanding of the black experience and his love for his people in both pathos and humor. His collected poems include *Lyrics of Lowly Life* (1896), *Lyrics of the Hearthside* (1899), *Lyrics of Love and Laughter* (1903), and *Lyrics of Sunshine and Shadow*. Dunbar died of tuberculosis at the age of thirty-four.

Dunne, Finley Peter (1867–1936) One of the greatest humorist writers in our history, he was born in Chicago, and went to work as office boy on the Chicago *Telegram* after leaving high school. He became city editor of the Chicago *Times* at twenty-one and editor of the Chicago *Evening Post* editorial page four years later. Dunne began to write weekly humorous articles and in 1893 created his famous character Mr. Martin Dooley, an Irishman and a bachelor who, from behind the bar of his small saloon on Archery Road, explained to Hennessy (Dooley's straight man), in a deep brogue, all the events of the day and more. In more than 700 short dialect pieces, including "Some Army Appointments," "The Dreyfus Case," "Americans Abroad," "The Future of China," and "The Supreme Court Decisions," he wrote with keen insight, often biting irony, and always raucus humor. His work was read at cabinet meetings. Presidents sought to keep in his good graces. His first authorized collection, *Mr. Dooley in Peace and in War* (1898), sold at the rate of 10,000 copies a month.

A photograph of refugees from the Dust Bowl in 1936.

Dust Bowl   A semi-arid high plains area subject to serious wind erosion in years of drought; the area straddles parts of Texas, Oklahoma, Colorado, and Kansas.

E   **Eakins, Thomas** (1844–1916)   Realistic painter and Dean of the Pennsylvania Academy of Fine Arts, he painted people of all walks of life as they were at their work. His painting of President Hayes was rejected because it showed him at his desk in shirt-sleeves. His masterpiece of Walt Whitman caused the poet to say Eakins painted what was, not what he thought ought to be. His students carried on and expanded the style of realism well into the twentieth century.

Eastman, George (1854–1932)   He formed Eastman-Kodak Company in Rochester (1892), capitalizing on inventions he had made in photography. His company became the world's largest manufacturer of photographic supplies. Employee loyalty was secured by a liberal policy of welfare and profit sharing. He made substantial bequests to the University of Rochester, the Eastman School of Music in the same city, the Massachusetts Institute of Technology (MIT), and Tuskegee and Hampton Institutes and established a professorship in American studies at Oxford.

Eaton affair (1831)   Secretary of War Eaton married Peggy O'Neale, a barmaid of unquestionable appeal and questionable character. The cabinet wives, led by Mrs. Calhoun, refused to accept Mrs. Eaton socially. President Jackson brought this problem to a Cabinet meeting, where only Van Buren joined him in urging acceptance of Mrs. Eaton. To emphasize his stand, Van Buren resigned with Secretary of War Eaton. Jackson called for the resignation of all other cabinet members except the postmaster general. Van Buren had maneuvered himself closer to Jackson while deepening the split between Calhoun and Jackson.

Eddy, Mary Baker Morse (1821–1910)   Founder of the Christian Science religion, which developed in 1866 when she recovered her health after reading of the healings of Jesus as described in the New Testament. Her book *Science and Health with Key to the Scriptures* (1875) is the basis of the religion. The mother church, the First Church of Christ, Scientist, was established in Boston in 1892. Christian Science churches throughout the world are branches of this church. Healing is at the heart of the religion. Periodicals published by the church include the *Sentinel*, the *Christian Science Journal*, and the widely read daily *Christian Science Monitor*, which contains at least one article in a foreign language.

Thomas A. Edison

Edison, Thomas Alva (1847–1931)   An inventor who was granted more than 1000 patents. While employed by the Western Union Telegraph Company in 1869, he made his first invention, an electrographic vote recorder. He established research laboratories at Menlo Park, New Jersey, in 1876 and moved to larger quarters at Orange, New Jersey, the following years. He hired assistants who worked with him as teams to produce practical inventions. These included the incandescent electric lamp (his company, the Edison General Electric Company, became the giant General Electric Company), the phonograph (1877), an improved motion picture projector, and the storage battery, the electric dynamo, electric locomotive, dictaphone, and mimeograph.

Edwards, Jonathan (1703–1758) Theologian and philosopher, he was influential in the religious revival known as the Great Awakening of the 1730s and 1740s. He was pastor of the Presbyterian Church at Northampton, Massachusetts until 1750 and later at Stockbridge, where he was missionary to the native Americans. He was appointed president of the College of New Jersey (Princeton) in 1757 but died shortly thereafter. His philosophical-theological works—*The Nature of True Virtue, Original Sin,* and *Freedom of the Will*—written in the last years of his life, exerted considerable influence among intellectuals on both sides of the Atlantic.

Eggheads A nickname for intellectuals, it came to take on a derisive connotation as used by the opponents of Adlai Stevenson in the 1952 campaign.

Albert Einstein

Einstein, Albert (1879–1955) Born in Germany he received his doctorate from the University of Zurich in Switzerland working in theoretical physics and developing his special theory of relativity. In 1905 he arrived at the equation $E = mc^2$, the basis of atomic energy. This implied that 1 pound of helium, if turned into energy, would light a 10-watt electric light bulb for 100 million years. In 1921 he was awarded the Nobel Prize in Physics. When Hitler threatened the Jews, Einstein left Germany and came to the United States, accepting a post at the Institute for Advanced Study at Princeton. On August 2, 1939 he sent a historic letter to President Roosevelt stating that it was possible to produce a weapon of unprecedented destructive potential by releasing the energy of the atom. His special theory of relativity (1905) was followed by the general theory of relativity (1915). In the United States in 1953 he developed his unified field theory. He was an active Zionist and, in 1948, was offered but did not accept the presidency of the new state of Israel. Einstein was also an accomplished violinist.

Eisenhower Doctrine (1957) The doctrine stated that the United States would use armed force upon request of any Middle East nation that was under threat of imminent or actual aggression. Congress also appropriated $200 million for the president to use to develop the economic or military power of such a nation. The Sixth Fleet was stationed in the Mediterranean. In 1957, Lebanon asked for help to put down a coup stirred up by Syria and Egypt. About 14,000 Marines restored order and Lebanese authority, after which Egypt and Syria agreed to let Lebanon alone.

Eisenhower, Dwight D. *See* Presidents of the United States section, beginning on page 10-83.

Elastic clause *See* **Enumerated powers**.

Election of 1992 President George Bush ran for re-election and said he would do anything necessary to win. In the Republican primaries he was opposed by Pat Buchanan, a television and newspaper political commentator, representing the religious right. Bush and his running mate Vice President Dan Quayle were nominated by the Republican National Convention in Houston, Texas, on August 17.

Candidates for the Democratic party nomination included former Senator Paul Tsongas of Massachusetts, Senator Tom Harkin of Iowa, former Governor Jerry Brown of California, Senator Bob Kerry of South Dakota, and Governor Bill Clinton of Arkansas. Clinton secured enough delegates in the Democratic primaries by June 2 to insure his nomination. He was nominated for president at the Democratic National Convention in New York City on July 16 and chose Senator Albert Gore, Jr., of Tennessee as his running mate. The next day, as Clinton and Gore left on a campaign bus tour of eight states, polls showed that Clinton had a substantial lead.

A third candidate, H. Ross Perot, entered the race as an independent promising to eliminate the federal budget deficit and to end the gridlock in Congress. His popular appeal posed a challenge to the major parties until his sudden announcement on July 16 that he was dropping out of the campaign. On October 1 he reentered the race. His followers had succeeded in placing his name on the ballot as an independent in all 50 states.

Three 90-minute televised debates were held in October involving Bush, Clinton, and Perot, as well as a debate between the three vice-presidential candidates—Quayle, Gore, and retired Vice Admiral James Stockdale (Perot's running mate).

As Election Day approached, polls showed Bush closing the gap but Clinton retaining the lead. Perot, who had spent $60 million of his own money on the campaign, chiefly on half-hour television ads, was still an uncertain factor.

Results of the Election: Bill Clinton was elected 42nd president of the United States. He won 33 states and the District of Columbia. Bush won 18 states.

	Electoral Vote	Popular Vote	% Popular Vote
Clinton	370 (270 needed to win)	43,728,375	43
Bush	168	38,167,416	38
Perot	0	19,237,247	19

103rd Congress (1993–95)

	Democrat	Republican	Independent
Senate:	57	43	0
House of Reps.:	261	173	1 (Socialist)

Women in the Senate 103rd Congress (1993–95)

Barbara Boxer (D., California)—former member of the House of Representatives

Carol Moseley Brawn (D., Illinois)—former Cook County official, the first black woman to serve in the U.S. Senate

Diane Feinstein (D., California)—former Mayor of San Francisco, elected to the U.S. Senate

Nancy Kassenbaum (R., Kansas)—term in U.S. Senate not expired

Barbara Milkuski (D., Maryland)—re-elected to the U.S. Senate

Patty Murray (D., Washington)—former state senator, elected to the U.S. Senate

Electoral college　*How the President and Vice President Are Elected by the Electoral College*

The president is elected by a simple majority vote of the electoral college. Each state has as many votes in the electoral college as it has members in Congress. The District of Columbia has as many electoral votes as any state having the least number of such votes.

The day popularly known as election day is the first Tuesday after the first Monday in November. A presidential election occurs every fourth year, always falling on the years with a date evenly divisible by four. The political parties hold conventions in each state, usually in the spring, to nominate the members of the electoral college. Whichever party polls the largest vote in the state has thereby elected its nominees to the electoral college. The electoral college members meet, usually in their state capitals, on the first Monday after the second Wednesday in December and cast their votes for President. By custom, not by constitutional provision, the electors vote for the candidate of their party, which results in all the electoral votes of any state going to the candidate with the largest popular vote in that state. The list of votes is signed and sealed by the governor of the state and sent to the president of the U.S. Senate, the vice president. On January 6 a joint session of Congress is held at which the vice president presides and the ballots are counted. Technically, this is the election of the president. If January 6 is a Sunday, the election is held the following day.

The electoral college members vote for president and vice president on separate ballots. The president and vice president must come from different states. The procedures for election of president and vice president are identical unless the electoral college fails to give a majority vote to any candidate. In that case the procedures differ from that point on.

How the President and the Vice President Are Elected When the Electoral College Fails to Reach a Decision

If no candidate for the president receives a majority of the electoral votes, the election goes to the House of Representatives. There each state has one vote. The members of the House from each state have to caucus, hold a meeting, and decide how to cast their one vote. Two-thirds of the total number of states must be present, and it takes a majority of all the states to elect the president. The House is restricted in its choice to the *top three* candidates who received the most votes in the electoral college.

If no candidate for vice president gets a majority of the electoral vote, the election goes to the Senate. There each senator has one vote. Two-thirds of the total number of senators must be present, and it takes a majority of all the senators to elect the vice president. The Senate is restricted in its choice to the *top two* candidates who received the most votes in the electoral college.

No matter what the circumstances of the election, the president and the vice president must be from different states.

When circumstances arise during an election for which there is no provision in the Constitution or other law, it will be the duty of Congress to find some way out of the tangle. This occurred during the disputed election of 1876. *See* The Constitution of the United States: Amendments Xll; XX section 3; XXIII; XXIV; and XXV.

Elkins Act (1903)　The act strengthened the Interstate Commerce Act of 1887 by forbidding rebates to shippers. Railroads were not to deviate in any detail from the published rates. Federal courts could issue injunctions to enforce the law. The act was sponsored by President Theodore Roosevelt.

Elliot, Charles William (1834–1926)　After graduating from Harvard University (1853), he taught mathematics and chemistry there for two years before going to study in Europe. Upon his return he was appointed professor of chemistry at MIT, where he remained (1865–69) until his appointment to the presidency of Harvard. His forty years in this post were marked by a number of educational innovations, notably the elective system for students and sabbaticals for staff. The university was expanded to include the graduate schools of arts and sciences, applied science, and business administration. As chairman of the National Education Association's Committee on Secondary School Studies, his report issued in 1892 exerted great influence on secondary school academic curriculum. Elliot also edited the *Harvard Classics* (known as the "five-foot shelf").

Emancipation Proclamation (1862)　This provided that all slaves in those states and parts of states in rebellion on or after January 1, 1863, were to be free. Slavery in the four loyal states was not affected by this proclamation. For greater effectivness Lincoln held back the announcement of this policy until after the Union victory at Antietam in September 1862.

Other nations now knew for the first time that a Union victory meant the end of slavery in the United States. Lincoln said slavery must die that the Union might live.

Embargo (1807)   Jefferson's response to England's seizures of American shipping and other violations of our rights (*see Chesapeake-Leopard affair*) was an embargo on all American shipping bound for a foreign port. No foreign vessel was allowed to take on cargo at an American port. Jefferson believed England's need for American goods was greater than our need for its trade. The resistance of American shippers to the embargo coupled with too few officials to enforce it resulted in widespread smuggling. England did not change its policy. American shipping was headed for disaster.

Emergency Quota Act of 1921   After World War I, during a period of economic recession, there was intense opposition to immigration. By an immigration act in 1921, Congress limited the number of immigrants who could be admitted from any country annually to 3 percent of the number of persons from that country who were living in the United States in 1910 as established by the census of that year.

Emerson, Ralph Waldo (1803–1892)   Influential American philosopher, lecturer, essayist, and poet, for a time Emerson served as a Unitarian minister. In America he formed close associations with Longfellow, Hawthorne, Margaret Fuller, Oliver Wendell Holmes, and particularly with Thoreau. In Europe he formed intellectual associations with Carlyle, Coleridge, and Wordsworth. He was a leading transcendentalist as well as an active abolitionist. Among his publications were *Essays* (1841 and 1844), *Poems* (1847), *Addresses and Lectures* (1849), and ten volumes of his *Journals,* edited and published posthumously by his son Edward Waldo Emerson.

Enterprise zones   An idea that gained support during the Reagan administration, it was designed to encourage economic development in poor urban areas by giving tax breaks and other preferences to business establishments.

Enumerated powers   The principle that a government may exercise only those powers granted to it by its founders, as in the American Constitution. In the U.S. Constitution the powers of Congress are enumerated in Article I, Section 8. This section also contains the "elastic clause," which gives Congress the power "to make all laws which shall be necessary and proper for carrying into execution" the enumerated powers.

Environmental Protection Agency   Established as an independent agency of the federal government in 1970 to serve as the public's advocate of a livable environment, its mandate includes the regulation of air and radiation programs, water programs, hazardous waste disposal, pesticide and toxic waste control, and research for technological control of all forms of pollution. The agency came under severe criticism in the early 1980s for alleged "foot-dragging" in the performance of its mission.

Equal Rights Amendment (ERA)   An Equal Rights Amendment was introduced in Congress in 1923 and every year thereafter until 1948, but failed to pass. During the ensuing years the measure was bottled up in the Judiciary Committee of the House of Representatives. It was finally forced out of committee in 1970 and passed with an overwhelming vote in the House. Two years later it was approved by the necessary two-thirds vote in the Senate and sent to the states for ratification by the state legislatures. The amendment read as follows:

Section 1. Equality of rights under the law shall not be denied or abridged by the United States or by any state on account of sex.

Section 2. The Congress shall have the power to enforce this article by appropriate legislation.

Approval by three-fourths of the states, as required by Article V of the Constitution for ratification of amendments, proved difficult to attain.

The original time limit for ratification was March 22, 1979 (seven years after it was submitted by Congress to the states). The deadline was extended to June 30, 1982, but by that date it had failed to be ratified since only 35 of the necessary 38 (three-fourths of the 50 states) had voted approval.

Era of good feeling   This was a period of strong nationalism from 1816 into the 1820s during which there was an absence of strife between political parties. James Monroe was president during this period.

Ericsson, John (1803–1889)   Inventor and engineer, he was born and grew up in Sweden, where he served in the engineering and surveying units of the naval and military forces while still a teenager. In London (1826–38) he developed the screw propeller for navigation. In the United States he designed and built a new type of ironclad fighting ship, the *Monitor,* for the Union navy in 1861. The victory of the *Monitor* over the *Virginia* (*Merrimac*) at Hampton Roads, March 9, 1862, revolutionized naval warfare by making wooden fighting ships obsolete. He continued to design and build iron warships for the Union navy until the end of the Civil War. His body was taken back to Sweden for burial.

Erie Canal (1825)   New York State financed the construction of this first great east-west highway in the United States. This 363-mile canal with eighty-two locks provided the most comfortable, quickest, and least expensive route. Barges made the trip from New York City to Buffalo in five days. The canal drew traffic from the Ohio River-Great Lakes region to New York City away from its previous route down the Ohio and Mississippi rivers to New Orleans. The Northeast and the West were drawn closer together economically and politically.

Ervin, Sam (1896–1985)   U.S. Senator from North Carolina, he presided over the televised hearings seeking the facts about the break-in at Democratic Headquarters in the Washington, D.C., Watergate Hotel Complex during the night of June 17, 1972. The Ervin committee consisted of seven members—four Democrats and three Republicans. The committee held its first hearing May 17, 1973, and by August 9 had taken over 7000 pages of testimony. Ervin's previous experience in the U.S. Senate since 1954 and prior to that as a judge in North Carolina (1935–54), coupled with the high regard in which his Senate colleagues held him and his unflagging devotion to the Constitution, made him the natural member of the Senate to preside over the hearings. *See also* **Watergate and the Nixon administration**.

Esch-Cummins Act (1920)   The act is also known as the Railroad Transportation Act of 1920. It returned the railroads to private operation. Its more important provisions follow: (1) $200 million was appropriated to re-establish railroad properties and equipment to their prewar condition; (2) a $300 million revolving fund was set up to aid financially weak railroads; (3) a Railway Labor Board was created to settle disputes between labor and management; (4) railroads were to be consolidated into fewer systems; and (5) The Interstate Commerce Commission could evaluate railroad property and fix rates to yield a fair return.

Escobedo v. Illinois (1964)   Police did not permit Escobedo to call his lawyer while they interrogated him and secured his confession of murder. The Supreme Court reversed the ruling of the Illinois court and ordered Escobedo released from prison, where he was serving a twenty-year term. The Supreme Court ruled that advice of counsel was necessary to protect defendant's constitutional right against self-incrimination as provided in the Fifth Amendment.

Espionage Act (1917)   War hysteria caused Congress to enact the Espionage Act of June 15, 1917. Penalties as high as a fine of $10,000 and twenty years' imprisonment could be imposed for interfering with the draft or causing insubordination in the armed services. The postmaster general was empowered to exclude from the mails any material he considered seditious (treasonable). The act was upheld by the Supreme Court in *Schenck* v. *United States* (1919).

Essex decision (1805)   American ships with cargoes from the French and Spanish West Indies stopped at American ports, landed their cargoes, paid customs, and reloaded the cargoes destined for France, which was at war with England. This procedure constituted legal neutral commerce according to British law. This policy was reversed in the *Essex* case, however, when a British court ruled that such "broken" voyages, which were from their origin destined for a belligerent port, were illegal and subject to seizure. From 1805 on, seizure of American ships greatly increased.

Established churches   Official or government churches in the colonies in which tithes were collected from all citizens for their support during this time of union of church and state. The disestablishment of the churches brought the separation of church and state.

European Cooperation Administration   *See* **Marshall Plan**.

Evarts, William Maxwell (1818–1901)   Graduated from Yale and from Harvard Law School and admitted to the New York Bar in 1841, he represented the federal government during the Civil War in arguing that captured vessels were prizes of war. He successfully defended President Johnson in the impeachment trial in the Senate and served as U.S. attorney general 1868–69. He represented the United States at Geneva in presenting the *Alabama* claims against Britain. He was chief counsel for Hayes in the disputed election of 1876, secretary of state (1877–81) and U.S. senator from New York (1885–91).

Everson v. Board of Education (1947)   Hugo L. Black wrote the majority in the 5 to 4 decision of the Supreme Court upholding a New Jersey statute authorizing local school districts to reimburse parents of children attending parochial schools for the cost of transportation to and from school. The decision, based on the "child welfare" principle, stated that the law as applied "does no more than provide a general program to help parents get their children, regardless of their religion, safely and expeditiously to and from accredited schools." In the same decision, Black declared: "No tax in any amount, large or small, can be levied to support religious activities or institutions."

Excise tax   An internal revenue tax applied to sales of specific items rather than general sales taxes; examples are taxes on the sale of liquor and tobacco products.

Explorers of the American Continent   *See* **Exhibit 10.3**.

Exposition and Protest (1828)   Reacting to the protective tariff of 1828, which was regarded in South Carolina as harmful to the plantation economy dependent on exports, Vice President John C. Calhoun published anonymously the "Exposition and Protest." It argued that the tariff act of 1828 was unconstitutional and therefore subject to nullification by any of the states. Acting on this theory, South Carolina passed the Nullification Act of 1832.

Ex post facto law   This is a law imposing penalties for an act committed before the law was passed and legal at the time it was committed. The Constitution provides in Article I, Section 9: "No bill of attainder or *ex post facto law* shall be passed."

Extraterritoriality   Claimed by countries for their citizens, exempting them from the laws of certain foreign countries in which they may be residing or doing business, these privileges were enjoyed in China by citizens of the United States, Britain, France, Japan, and other powers well into the twentieth century.

Fair Deal   Name given to the social policies of Harry S Truman's administration, based on an extension of Roosevelt's New Deal, it included full employment, expanding Social Security, stronger civil rights legislation, and housing for low-income people.

Fair Employment Practices Committee (FEPC)   This was a committee established during World War II by Congress to prevent discrimination in hiring. Attempts to make this procedure permanent failed in the Congress, but it was adopted by many of the states.

Fair Labor Standards Act (1938)   The act set minimum wages and maximum hours and forbade the employment of children under sixteen in business establishments engaged in or that affected interstate commerce. Time-and-a-half was paid for overtime (over forty hours per week). Farm laborers, domestic servants, and professional workers were exempted from this act. The act was also known as the Wages and Hours Law.

Farm Credit Administration (1933)   The FCA helped farmers to refinance mortgages over a longer period of time at lower interest rates. It also eased the burden of farm loans by consolidating several existing farm agencies.

EXHIBIT 10.3
The Explorers

The explorers are grouped according to the nation sponsoring the expedition. Within each national group the listings are in chronological order.

Explorers often worked for nations other than their own. For example, Amerigo Vespucci we may call an Italian. He thought of himself as a citizen of Florence. His first exploration was in the service of Spain and his second in the service of Portugal. Henry Hudson was English but he worked for the Netherlands. Both Cabots, father and son, were citizens of Venice but they explored for England.

1000	Leif Ericson *(Norway)*	Atlantic coast from Nova Scotia to R.I. First European to land in America.
1488	Bartholomeu Dias *(Portugal)*	Rounded southern tip of Africa, the Cape of Good Hope. Turned back.
1498	Vasco da Gama *(Portugal)*	Rounded the Cape of Good Hope. Crossed Indian Ocean to India. Started continuous trade by sea between Europe and the Far East.
1501	Amerigo Vespucci *(Portugal)*	Second trip. Sailed along much of the eastern coast of South America. On his first trip in 1499, working for Spain, he had sailed along much of the northern coast. Both trips together gave geographers a good idea of the size of the continent from north to south.
1492	Christopher Columbus *(Spain)*	Aug. 3, 1492 the Santa Maria, Pinta, and Nina sailed from Palos. On Oct. 12th they arrived at the Bahama Islands. Columbus called the island San Salvador (probably Watling Island). He explored the islands of Cuba and Haiti (Hispaniola).
1493	Christopher Columbus *(Spain)*	Explored the Leeward Islands and Puerto Rico. Made the settlement of Santo Domingo on the island of Haiti headquarters for further explorations.
1498	Christopher Columbus *(Spain)*	Explored the Island of Trinidad and the nearby coast of South America.
1502	Christopher Columbus *(Spain)*	Coast of Central America from Panama to Honduras.
1499	Amerigo Vespucci *(Spain)*	See above—1501—Vespucci
1513	Ponce de Leon *(Spain)*	Explored Florida searching for the "fountain of youth."
1513	Vasco Nuñez de Balboa *(Spain)*	Saw the Pacific Ocean from the Isthmus of Panama on Sept. 25, 1513. This led to the idea that North and South America might be about as wide as Panama.
1519–1521	Hernando Cortez *(Spain)*	Conquered the Aztec Indians of Mexico under their king, Montezuma. Great wealth in gold and silver shipped to Spain.

1519–1522	Ferdinand Magellan *(Spain)*	First circumnavigation of the world. Left Spain Sept. 20, 1519; killed in the Philippines April 27, 1521. Expedition returned to Spain Sept. 6, 1522. Claimed Philippines for Spain.
1530–1536	Francisco Pizarro *(Spain)*	Conquered the Inca Indians of Peru and founded a settlement at Lima.
1539–1542	Hernando de Soto *(Spain)*	Explored the Gulf Coast from Florida to the Mississippi River. Went into what is now Georgia, Alabama, Mississippi, Arkansas, and Oklahoma. Died of fever and buried in the Mississippi River.
1540–1542	Francisco Vásquez de Coronado *(Spain)*	Discovered the Grand Canyon of Arizona. Also explored New Mexico, the Panhandle area of Texas, and Kansas.
1524	Giovanni da Verrazano *(France)*	Explored the coast from Carolina to Nova Scotia. Also entered New York Harbor and Narragansett Bay.
1534	Jacques Cartier *(France)*	Explored the St. Lawrence Gulf and River to Montreal.
1608–1615	Samuel de Champlain *(France)*	Went up the St. Lawrence and through the Great Lakes to Lake Huron. Discovered Lake Oneida and Lake Champlain. Made eleven trips. Established fur trade with the Indians. The "Father of New France."
1673	Pere Marquette & Louis Joliet *(France)*	Explored Mackinac Strait, Lake Michigan, Green Bay, Wisconsin River, and Mississippi River to the Arkansas River.
1682	Robert Sieur de La Salle *(France)*	Went from the Great Lakes to the Mississippi River and down to its mouth.
1497	John Cabot *(England)*	Sailed along the coast from Newfoundland to Maine.
1498	John Cabot *(England)*	Sailed from Newfoundland to Chesapeake Bay.
1509	Sebastian Cabot *(England)*	Explored northeast coast.
1577–1580	Sir Francis Drake *(England)*	Second circumnavigation of the world.
1609–1611	Henry Hudson *(Netherlands)*	Explored the Hudson River and Hudson Bay. A mutinous crew set him adrift in Hudson Bay in June 1611.

HISTORY OF THE
UNITED STATES

Farmers' Alliances   In the 1880s farmers' alliances were formed in various parts of the country. A Northern alliance and a Southern alliance differed over the admission of blacks but agreed to press for easier credit, regulation of railroad rates, and tariff reduction. The alliances went out of existence in 1892 when they met with other groups in Omaha, Nebraska, and formed the Populist Party.

Farragut, David Glasgow (1801–1870)   During a lifetime in the U.S. Navy, Farragut rose from midshipman at the age of nineteen to admiral fifty-six years later. In the interim he had served on the frigate *Essex* during the War of 1812 in the Pacific, established the Navy Yard at Mare Island, destroyed the Confederate fleet at New Orleans in 1862, achieved a victory at Mobile, Alabama, the following year where he uttered the oft-quoted statement "Damn the torpedoes, full speed ahead," and after the Civil War led a squadron on a tour of Europe.

Federal Farm Board (l932)   This agency was created under the Agricultural Marketing Act passed by Congress under the Hoover administration; it promoted the organization and lent money for agricultural marketing cooperatives as a means of price relief to distressed cotton and wheat farmers; it failed and was abolished in 1933.

Federal Farm Loan Act (1916)   The act set up twelve Farm Loan Banks to serve members of farm loan associations. A Federal Farm Board of five members administered the system, which enabled farmers to arrange long-term loans at lower interest rates than were available to them at other banks. Farmers could borrow amounts up to 50 percent of the value of their land and 20 percent of the value of the improvements thereon.

Federal Housing Administration (FHA) (l934)   An agency established under the New Deal to guarantee private home mortgages and provide funds to promote housing construction.

Federalist Papers   A series of eighty-five political essays written in 1787 and 1788 to persuade the people of New York to ratify the U.S. Constitution. Although the papers were signed "Publius," it is known that the authors were Alexander Hamilton, James Madison, and John Jay. The papers, later published in book form as *The Federalist*, are to this day one of the most lucid and insightful analyses of the theory and practice of government as envisaged by the authors of the Constitution.

Federal Reserve Act (1913)   Sometimes called the Glass-Owen Bill, this act established twelve Federal Reserve Banks in Boston, New York, Philadelphia, Cleveland, Richmond, Atlanta, Chicago, St. Louis, Minneapolis, Kansas City (Missouri), Dallas, and San Francisco. All banks under the National Banking Act of 1863 were made member banks of the Federal Reserve System. Other banks could join. A Federal Reserve Board, now a Board of Governors, appointed by the president supervised the system. Regulation of the rediscount rate is a key stabilizing factor in the board's influence on credit.

Federal Trade Commission (FTC) (1914)   The commission is a bipartisan body of five members appointed by the president for seven-year terms. Its jurisdiction extends over large corporations, except for banking and transportation. Its "cease and desist" orders curb unfair trade practices, the most common of which are deceptive labeling, adulteration of products, and conspiracies to fix prices. It assists corporations in avoiding violations and is useful in advising the government of infractions of antitrust laws.

Fenians   A secret organization of Irish-Americans during the Civil War period, who invaded Canada in 1866 in a plan to exchange Canada for Irish independence. The United States arrested some of its leaders to indicate to Britain that it was not in support of the movement. The death of its leader, John O'Mahoney, in 1877 brought about the decline of the Fenians.

Fermi, Enrico (1901–1954)   An Italian-born physicist, he was awarded the Nobel Prize in 1938 for work in uranium fission, a forerunner of the atom bomb. He came to the United States in 1939 to escape seizure by the Fascists. Fermi actively participated in making the first atom bomb. He was professor of physics at Columbia University 1939–45 and at the University of Chicago 1945–54. He discovered the element neptunium.

Field, Cyrus West (1819–1892)   He made a fortune in the papermaking business and spent it on the project for which he is known, the Atlantic cable. With the support of New York bankers, he raised $1,500,000 with which a telegraph cable was laid on the floor of the Atlantic Ocean from Newfoundland to Ireland, completed in 1858. The cable ceased working, but with the determined efforts of Field it was relaid successfully after the Civil War.

Field, Marshall (1835–1906)   He started as a clerk in a dry goods store at the age of seventeen in Pittsfield, Massachusetts, and eventually became proprietor of Marshall Field & Company in Chicago, at the time (1881–1906) the largest wholesale and retail dry goods store in the world, with his own factories as a major source for his merchandise. He founded the Chicago Manual Training School, donated the site for the University of Chicago, and provided funds for the Field Museum of Natural History on the site of the Chicago World's Fair of 1893.

Field, Stephen Johnson (1816–1899)   He graduated from Williams College, practiced law in New York, went to California during the gold rush of 1849, and was elected to the state legislature when California entered the Union in 1850. He served in the California Supreme Court (1857–63), the last four years as chief justice, and was appointed to the U.S. Supreme Court by President Lincoln in 1863. Field served thirty-four years, longer than any justice except William O. Douglas (thirty-six). His dissents mark him as a judge with courage and insight, particularly in the slaughterhouse cases (1873) and in the Chinese immigration case.

Fifty-four forty or fight   This cry was raised by American expansionists, particularly in the West, over the Oregon Territory dispute with Britain. The claim included the entire Oregon Territory to the southern border of Alaska, 50° 40' north latitude. President Polk had been elected on a platform calling for "the reoccupation of Oregon." War was looming with Mexico, however, and a proposal was made by Britain to extend to the sea the boundary line established at 49° north latitude to the Rockies by the treaty of 1818. The Oregon Treaty of 1846 accepted the 49th parallel as our northern boundary to the Pacific.

Filibuster   This term has two distinct meanings: (1) an unauthorized military expedition of adventurers against another country in time of peace; (2) obstructive parliamentary tactics employed by a minority to prevent passage of unwanted legislation—it usually takes the form of long pointless speechmaking.

A filibustering expedition took place in 1851 when some 500 Americans led by a Venezuelan general left New Orleans secretly and attempted to seize Cuba. A filibuster in the second meaning of the term occurred in 1964, when southern senators prevented the Civil Rights Act of that year from coming to a vote for three months.

Fillmore, Millard   *See* Presidents of the United States section, beginning on page 10-83.

"Fire-eaters"   Southern extremists who favored secession in the decade preceding the Civil War.

Fish, Hamilton (1808–1893)   He was governor of New York (1849–50), U.S. senator from New York (1851–57), and secretary of state in Grant's two administrations (1869–77) when he negotiated the settlement of the *Alabama* claims against Britain. He resolved a crisis with Spain in 1873 over the *Virginius*, an arms-running ship illegally flying the U.S. flag in a foray in Cuba, secured a commercial treaty with Hawaii (1875), and tried unsuccessfully to obtain for the United States the rights to an interocean canal in either Colombia or Nicaragua.

Fletcher v. Peck (1810)   This case is the first in which the Supreme Court declared a state law unconstitutional. By bribery of Georgia legislators, speculators obtained land grants along the Yazoo River. A later legislature canceled these grants, which had been obtained by fraud. The Supreme Court, Chief Justice Marshall presiding, held that the law canceling the original grants violated the Constitutional provision forbidding a state to impair the obligation of contracts. Issuing land grants was legal and a valid contract. The Court refused to consider why the Georgia legislature made the grants.

Flexner, Abraham (1866–1959)   He was an educator influential in the reform of medical education resulting from his books *Medical Education in the U.S. and Canada* and *Medical Education in Europe*, where he studied after taking an M.A. at Harvard University (1906). Another of his influential works was *Universities—American, English, German* (1930), favoring traditional academic education and criticizing the elective system. He helped direct bequests of the Rockefellers, Carnegie, and Eastman toward educational purposes. He was the first director and moving force of the Institute for Advanced Study at Princeton, New Jersey, with which Albert Einstein was associated after he came to the United States.

Foraker Act (1900)   The act set up a government for Puerto Rico. A governor general with a veto and a council of eleven were appointed by the president of the United States. Five of the council members were Americans who served as department heads,

and the other six were Puerto Ricans. This council also served as the upper house of the legislature, which had an assembly elected by popular vote.

Force Bill (1833)   The bill approved President Jackson's use of whatever force was necessary to execute the laws. Passage of this bill by 31 to 1 in the Senate and 149 to 47 in the House showed South Carolina and Calhoun how little support they had for the state's action in passing the Nullification Act against protective tariffs.

However, another bill signed by President Jackson the same day, known as Clay's compromise tariff, reduced the rates to satisfy South Carolina and make nullification unnecessary. The South Carolina convention also "nullified" the Force Bill, which would, in any case, no longer be involved.

Ford, Gerald R.   *See* Presidents of the United States section, beginning on page 10-83.

Ford, Henry (1863–1947)   He left school at the age of fifteen and worked as a machinist and sawmill operator. He built his first automobile in 1892 and organized the Ford Motor Company in 1903. By 1909 he was mass-producing the model-T motor car on an assembly line. Ford introduced innovations in labor relations, including an eight-hour day with a minimum wage of $15 per day and a profit-sharing plan for his employees. During World War I he sent a group of idealists to Europe in a "peace ship," which he chartered in an attempt to bring the war to an end by mediation. He was an unsuccessful candidate for the U.S. Senate in 1918. In 1936 he and his son Edsel established the Ford Foundation, which made substantial bequests to schools and colleges through its subsidiary, the Fund for the Advancement of Education.

Henry Ford in his first car, built in 1892.

Four freedoms   In a speech to Congress on January 6, 1941, prior to U.S. entry into World War II, President Franklin D. Roosevelt attained moral leadership of the world in declaring four essential universal freedoms. These he enumerated as (1) freedom of speech, (2) freedom of religion, (3) freedom from want, and (4) freedom from fear. He specified that the latter could only be attained by "a world-wide reduction of armaments."

Fourteen points   This was a statement of American war aims as announced by President Wilson in January 1918 and accepted by Germany as the basis of the Armistice in November 1918. The fourteenth point called for the establishment of the League of Nations.

France, undeclared war with (1798–1799) President John Adams' reaction to the XYZ affair was to prepare for war, to wage war, but not to declare war. He appointed Washington commanding general. Congress created the Department of the Navy and declared the Treaty of Alliance (1778) with France at an end. Clashes occurred between American and French naval units, but most of the activity was in West Indian waters, where about 200 American privateers drove French merchantmen off the seas. These hostilities continued for over a year, but there was no declaration of war.

Frankfurter, Felix (1882–1965)   An immigrant to the United States from Austria at the age of twelve, Frankfurter earned his B.A. degree from the College of the City of New York and L.L.B. with highest honors from Harvard Law School. He taught at Harvard Law School (1914–39). He wrote *The Case of Sacco and Vanzetti* (1927), reviewing all the evidence and the trial procedure and concluding that the defendants were improperly convicted, tried, sentenced, and executed. In 1939 President Roosevelt appointed him to the Supreme Court on which he served until his retirement in 1962. On the Court he repudiated the position of Justices Black and Douglas that the rights granted in the First Amendment are absolute, holding instead that they were to be balanced against the rights of the government. He likewise denied the protection of the Bill of Rights to those who advocated overthrow of the government by force.

Franklin, Benjamin (1706–1790)   One of the founding fathers of the republic, Franklin's gamut of accomplishments is unique in human annals. He was statesman, scientist, author, editor, publisher, inventor, innovator, diplomat, counselor, and citizen of the world. Franklin was born in Boston. He went to live in Philadelphia at the age of seventeen. His contributions are: He owned and edited the *Pennsylvania Gazette*; published annually *Poor Richard's Almanack*, containing many original aphorisms and observations on the human condition; invented the Franklin stove; demonstrated the identity of lightning and electricity; established a circulating library in Philadelphia; drafted the first plan for union of the colonies in 1854 (the Albany plan); served as postmaster general of the colonies; was a member of the Second Continental Congress and served on the committee to draft the Declaration of Independence; helped make the Treaty of Alliance with France (1778), which brought substantial French aid in the War of Independence; participated in the negotiation of the Treaty of Peace with Great Britain (1783); and was an influential member of the convention that drew up the Constitution of the United States.

Freedman's Bureau   Established by Congress to aid distressed refugee former slaves and other destitute people in the South after the Civil War, the agency distributed clothing, established hospitals and schools, and provided transportation. It was un-

popular among many whites in the South and was disbanded in 1872.

Chappel's portrait of Benjamin Franklin.

Freeport Doctrine   This was the position taken by Douglas in his debate with Lincoln at Freeport, Illinois, that, if the people of a territory wish, they could exclude slavery by failing to enact local regulations for its protection. He said this could be done in spite of the Dred Scott decision, which held that it was legal to take slaves into the territories.

This doctrine, which was repudiated in the South divided the Democratic party and led to the election of Lincoln on the Republican ticket in 1860.

Frémont, John C. (1813–1890)   He was engaged in a number of explorations in the West that caused him to be known as "the Pathfinder." He helped in the conquest of California. Frémont was U.S. senator from that state (1853–54) and candidate for president for the newly formed Republican party (1856). Appointed major general of Union forces in the West at the outbreak of the Civil War, he was relieved of this command for freeing slaves contrary to Lincoln's orders. He was territorial governor of Arizona (1878–83). Frémont was married (1841) to Jessie Benton, daughter of Senator Thomas Hart Benton of Missouri.

French and Indian War (1754–1763)   England pushed France off the continental North America. Initial French victories at Great Meadows (1754), Fort Duquesne (1755), and Fort William Henry (1757) ended when Pitt the Elder took over the British War Ministry. Thereafter the French were defeated at Fort Louisbourg, Fort Frontenac, and Fort Duquesne (1758), Fort Niagara and Fort Quebec (1758), and Montreal (1760). *See* **Paris, Treaty of (1763)**.

Fugitive Slave Law (1850)   This law amended the original law of 1793. It provided measures whereby the federal government would assume responsibility for the return of fugitive slaves to their owners. An affidavit by the claimant was to be accepted as proof of ownership. Bystanders were required to aid in the capture and return of fugitives. Obstruction of the law was punishable by a fine of $1000 and a prison term of six months. If a slave escaped through the negligence of a marshal, the latter might be sued for the value of the lost slave. Testimony of fugitives claiming to be free was not admissable as evidence. As might have been expected, abolitionists refused to abide by this law which gave rise to incidents of violence.

Full Employment Act (1964)   The act provides for two committees, one an Executive Committee of Economic Advisors to inform the president on the employment situation, the other a Congressional Joint Committee on Economics to initiate legislation when so advised by the president. Both committees function as fact-finding and advisory bodies. The act was passed during the political campaign of 1964 with full support of the Democratic party and some Republicans, but not the standard bearer, Barry Goldwater.

Fuller, Sarah Margaret (1810–1850)   A leading nineteenth century feminist, Fuller conducted a program of conversations for women (1839–44) on literature, education, mythology, and philosophy. These became the basis for her best known work, *Woman in the Nineteenth Century*, published by Horace Greeley in 1845. With Ralph Waldo Emerson she edited the transcendentalist journal *The Dial* (1840–42). She came to know many of the great literary figures of her time, including Poe, Thoreau, Carlyle, and the Brownings. In Italy she participated in the Mazzini revolution and bore a son to the Marquis Angelo Ossoli. She died with her son and husband in a shipwreck while crossing the Atlantic.

Fulton, Robert (1765–1815)   He spent his early years in the United States as a draftsman and artist, went to London in 1786, and remained in Europe (including France) for twenty years during which he turned to civil engineering and navigation. He invented a machine for sawing marble, and a spinning machine. He designed and built cast iron bridges, a submarine mine and torpedo, and a submarine, but these were apparently ahead of their time. Back in the United States he designed and built a steam-powered boat, the *Clermont*, which completed a successful voyage from New York to Albany and back in 1807. In 1814 he constructed for the U.S. government a paddle-wheel steam warship, which the navy did not activate.

Fundamentalism   This is a term applied primarily in religion to those who adhere to traditional orthodox teachings. Christian fundamentalism accepts a literal interpretation of the Bible as containing revealed truth from God. Fundamentalist preachers have used television to spread their teaching. In Iran, fundamentalism is the orthodox religion of Shi'ite Islam as taught and applied by the late powerful religious leader Ayatollah Ruhollah Khomeini.

Fundamental Orders of Connecticut (1639)   This was the first written constitution in America.

It provided for a representative government with an elected governor, six assistants, and an assembly. Thomas Hooker, founder of Hartford in 1636, was probably the leader in having this constitution adopted by the settlements at Hartford, Windsor, and Wethersfield.

Gadsden Purchase (1853)   This purchase of an area of about 30,000 square miles south of the Gila River might well be considered a delayed completion of the Guadalupe-Hidalgo Treaty of 1848. The $10 million paid to Mexico was a most generous price, which several members of Congress considered an appropriate gesture to compensate Mexico for its losses in the war. The area contained a pass through the Rockies suitable for a railroad. The purchase of this territory, which now constitutes the southern part of Arizona and New Mexico, was negotiated by James Gadsden, U.S. minister to Mexico.

Gag Rule adopted (1836)   By resolution, the House and Senate annually ruled that all petitions to Congress about slavery would be tabled without consideration. Every year ex-President John Quincy Adams, representative from Massachusetts, protested the resolution as a violation of the Constitution and the rights of his constituents. Deplorable as was the acrimonious argument in Congress over slavery, the method used to avoid it was worse. Congress discontinued the gag resolutions in 1844. The term "gag rule," has also been applied to the Bush administration ruling that prohibited abortion counseling in family planning clinics that receive federal funds.

Gallatin, Albert (1761–1849)   He came to the United States from Switzerland in 1780. Member of Congress (1795–1801), he served as secretary of the treasury under Jefferson and Madison (1801–14). He was one of the commissioners who negotiated the Treaty of Ghent, restoring peace with Great Britain after the War of 1812. He was U.S. minister to France (1816–23) and to England (1826–27) and president of the National Bank of New York City (later Gallatin Bank) from 1831 to 1839. A leading American ethnologist, Gallatin published extensive studies of the native American and founded the American Ethnological Studies in 1842.

Garfield, James A.   *See* Presidents of the United States section, beginning on page 10-83.

Garrison, William Lloyd (1805–1879)   He was an abolitionist, newspaper editor, and publisher. After editing several newspapers, Garrison founded his own, *The Liberator*, dedicated to the abolition of slavery. The first edition of the paper appeared January 1, 1831, and carried his statement: "On this subject [slavery] I do not wish to...speak...with moderation...I will not retreat a single inch—and *I WILL BE HEARD*." In 1833 Garrison organized the American Anti-Slavery Society. Opposition to abolitionism was so strong in the North that Garrison was dragged through the streets of Boston and barely escaped with his life (1835). He continued to publish *The Liberator* for 35 years. After the Civil War he devoted himself to other causes, including the plight of native Americans and Chinese, the prevention of cruelty to animals, and free trade.

Garvey, Marcus Mosiah, Jr. (1887–1940) Born in Jamaica, he traveled throughout Central America and Europe working at various jobs while still a young man. For a time he attended London University. On returning to Jamaica he founded the Universal Negro Improvement Association (UNIA) in 1914. He came to New York two years later and went on a speaking tour of the United States. In 1918 he founded the successful newspaper *Negro World* and revived the UNIA in Harlem and other cities. He organized business enterprises run by blacks, such as the steamship company Black Star Line. He started a "back to Africa" movement. He was imprisoned for fraudulent use of the mails, pardoned by President Coolidge, and deported as an undesirable alien. Dr. William DuBois ridiculed the UNIA movement. In 1964 the Jamaican government transferred Garvey's remains from his London grave to the Marcus Garvey National Shrine in Jamaica.

Gaspee (1772) On June 9 the British revenue ship *Gaspee* was led onto a sandbar while pursuing a smuggler. That night armed men in small boats from Providence surrounded the *Gaspee,* forced the crew ashore, and burned the ship. This exploit was observed by many, but all attempts to identify the participants were futile. The Rhode Islanders approved the ship burning, and the Sons of Liberty were ready to deal effectively with informers. The sandbar in the Providence River is now called Gaspee Point.

General Agreement on Tariffs and Trade (GATT) (1947) It was originally signed at Geneva, Switzerland, by twenty-three nations, including the United States. Membership increased to seventy-seven by 1970. The members agree to eliminate trade barriers, reduce tariffs, and abide by agreements on international trade.

Genêt affair (1793) During the French Revolution, England and France were at war. France sent "Citizen" Edmund Genêt to the United States to get help under the Alliance of 1778. Genêt proceeded to outfit American ships to prey on British commerce and organized an attempt to detach Florida and Louisiana from Britain's ally, Spain. Americans were hostile to England, but when Genêt appealed to them over President Washington's head they turned against him. A new, more radical government had come into power, and Genêt's return to France would have meant certain death. Washington allowed him to remain in the United States. Genêt married New Yorker George Clinton's daughter and settled down to the life of a gentleman farmer.

Geneva Summit Conference (1955) President Eisenhower met with British Prime Minister Eden, French Premier Fauré, and Russian Premier Bulganin. Eisenhower proposed an exchange of "complete blueprints" of military facilities and acceptance of photographic reconnaissance by air over each nation's territory. Russia rejected both ideas. All agreed, however, that the production and control of atomic weapons, limitation of armaments, German unification, and European security were proper subjects for negotiation. No definite commitments were made, but this conference changed the harsh tone of Stalin, who died in 1953, to a more agreeable note and gave rise to the hopeful outlook called "the spirit of Geneva."

Gentlemen's agreement (1907–1908) In an agreement reached between the United States and Japan by an exchange of notes, Japan refused to issue passports to immigrants to the United States and the San Francisco School Board rescinded its order segregating Japanese children.

A novel entitled *Gentleman's Agreement* by Laura Z. Hobson published in 1974, dealt with a totally different subject, anti-semitism among the wealthy in a New England town near Stamford, Connecticut.

George, Henry (1839–1897) Tax reform was the most notable idea in his *Progress and Poverty* (1879), which pointed out that ground rent—rent for space exclusive of man-made improvements thereon—arises only because a developing community adds value to space. George advocated that all such increased value of land be taken from the owner in taxes because the added value belonged to the community that had created it. The income from such taxation might be enough to pay all expenses of government and hence the idea became known as "the single tax." The most economic use of land would be encouraged by such a tax, and speculation in land would be eliminated. George's tax theories, in modified form, are in effect in some cities.

Gerrymander To organize legislative and congressional districts in such a way as to secure the greatest number of districts with a majority of voters favorable to the party doing the redistricting.

Abraham Lincoln's Gettysburg Address.

Gettysburg Address (November 19, 1863) At the dedication of the cemetery at Gettysburg, the principal speaker was Edward Everett, former president of Harvard, who spoke for two hours. Lincoln's brief remarks, however, were soon perceived to be a classic. The president's profound dedication opened with the words "Four score and seven years ago...." and closed with the resolve "that these dead shall not have died in vain; that this nation, under God, shall have a new birth of freedom; and that government of the people, by the people, for the people, shall not perish from the earth."

Gettysburg, battle of (July 1–3, 1863)   In a major three-day battle fought in Pennsylvania, Lee's Confederate forces of 75,000 men were turned back by Union armies of 88,000 under General George G. Meade, who failed to pursue the retreating Confederates. Losses for the Union were 3155 dead, some 20,000 wounded or missing; for the Confederacy, 3903 dead, some 24,000 wounded or missing. The battle is often considered the turning point of the Civil War. Major fighting thereafter was confined to the South.

Ghent, Treaty of (1814)   The treaty ended the War of 1812. It provided for "status quo ante bellum"—all was to be as before the war. Impressment was not mentioned; neither was any settlement made for losses in American shipping due to British action during the Napoleonic Wars. Boundary disputes were left for consideration later by commissions to be established.

Gibbons, James (1834–1921)   Ordained a Roman Catholic priest (1861) in Baltimore, bishop in 1868 (the youngest bishop at the time), and archbishop in 1877, he was named a cardinal (the second in the United States) in 1885. During the Civil War he was chaplain at Fort McHenry. At Rome in 1887 he spoke for the Knights of Labor, winning papal assurance that the organization would not be banned as a secret society in either the United States or Canada. He dedicated the Catholic University of America in Washington, D.C., in 1888 and served as its chancellor until his death. He was firm in his dedication to American ideals.

Gibbons v. Ogden (1824)   The New York legislature granted a franchise to Fulton and Livingston for the exclusive right to navigate steamboats in New York waters. Ogden had his license to operate from Fulton and Livingston. Gibbons, with a license from the United States, was operating between New York City and Hoboken, New Jersey. Gibbons challenged the constitutionality of the Ogden license. Chief Justice Marshall ruled that commerce included navigation, not merely buying and selling. The lower Hudson River and waters between New York City and Hoboken were interstate waters under federal authority. The New York State franchise was pronounced void.

G.I. Bill of Rights (1944)   Enacted during World War II as the Servicemen's Readjustment Act, the act provided for college or vocational education of World War II veterans largely at the expense of the federal government. It also entitled veterans to unemployment insurance for a year and provided loans for homes and for businesses. Servicemen in World War II were called G.I.'s because the supplies and equipment they received while in the armed services were stamped with the letters "G.I.," meaning "government issue." Some benefits of the original act were extended to veterans of the Korean War.

Goethals, George Washington (1858–1928)   He attended the College of the City of New York and the U.S. Military Academy (West Point), from which he was graduated and commissioned in 1880. As lieutenant colonel of engineers, he was assigned by President Theodore Roosevelt to supervise the construction of the Panama Canal, a difficult task that he discharged with such skill as to become known as "the builder of the Panama Canal." He served as governor of the Canal Zone (1914–16). He retired as major general in 1916 but was recalled to active duty during World War I to serve as assistant quartermaster general in charge of supply and transportation of all military personnel.

Gold rush   With the discovery of gold (January 24, 1848) near Sacramento, California, the news spread like wildfire, attracting prospectors from all over the world. Clipper ships brought adventurers from the East around Cape Horn to the gold fields in 100 days. Others came overland, crossing the Rockies and the High Sierras via Donner Pass. Even Europe and Australia yielded gold-hungry contingents to swell the ranks of the "forty-niners." The trip from the East by wagon trains often took five months. By 1850 California was ready for statehood. By 1853, $65 million in gold had been taken from the streams and hills of California.

Gold miners during the Gold Rush of 1849.

Gompers, Samuel (1850–1924)   He worked as a cigarmaker's apprentice in London, where he was born. He came to the United States at the age of thirteen and joined the Cigar Makers Union the following year. In 1880 he became president of the American Federation of Labor, which he helped organize. He served as president (except for one year) until his death. His leadership kept the union from becoming involved in politics. The policy he espoused was striving to improve the wages, hours, and working conditions of union members organized on the basis of crafts (carpenters, brick layers, machinists, etc.). He helped secure the support of organized labor for the national war effort in World War I.

Good Neighbor Policy, (1933)   In his first inaugural address, Franklin D. Roosevelt said, "In the field of world policy I would dedicate this nation to the policy of the good neighbor...." Some definite moves in this direction were (1) the Seventh Pan-

American Conference of 1933, at which the United States agreed that no nation had the right to intervene in the external or internal affairs of another; (2) the abrogation in 1934 of the Platt Amendment, except for the naval base at Guantanamo; and (3) the adoption in 1935 of reciprocal tariff agreements as the established policy of the United States.

Gore, Al (Albert), Jr. (b. 1948) Born in Washington, D.C., where his father Albert Gore, Sr., was a member of the House of Representatives and later U.S. senator (1952–70), the younger Gore graduated from Harvard in 1969 with a B.A. cum laude in government. He served in Vietnam as a reporter with the 20th Engineers, and after his return, was a reporter on the Nashville Tennessean. He was elected to the House of Representatives in 1976, 1978, 1980, and 1982, and to the U.S. Senate in 1984. Deeply concerned about the environment, he is the author of a 1992 book entitled *Earth in the Balance*, in which he describes in detail the earth's plunge toward self-destruction and offers a blueprint of strategies for saving the planet.

Grandfather clause This refers to laws of Louisiana, Alabama, Georgia, South Carolina, North Carolina, Virginia, and Oklahoma passed between 1895 and 1910. These laws extended suffrage to poor whites while denying it to blacks and thus circumvented the Fifteenth Amendment. They provided that any man whose ancestors could vote as of January 1, 1867, had suffrage rights even though he owned no property, paid no taxes, and had no formal education. In 1915 the Supreme Court declared these laws unconstitutional in the *Guinn* v. *United States* case.

Grangers In 1867, Oliver H. Kelley founded an organization of Midwest farmers known as the National Grange of the Patrons of Husbandry. Other granges sprang up during the 1870s and 1880s. These farmers' associations were at first chiefly social, with elements of cooperation in problems of marketing, storing, and shipping their products. The granges found a common problem in the exorbitant prices charged by railroads, particularly when a town was served by only one road. In Illinois and other states the granges developed enough political power to get the legislature to limit the rates the railroads could charge. The law was challenged in Illinois and upheld by the Supreme Court in *Munn* v. *Illinois* (1876). This decision was modified ten years later in the case of *Wabash* v. *Illinois*. By the end of the 1880s the granges had ceased to be a political or economic force.

Grant, Ulysses S. *See* Presidents of the United States section, beginning on page 10-83.

Great Awakening An evangelical religious revival that began in the 1730s with the preaching of Jonathan Edwards, the movement was characterized by personal conversion, often expressed in emotional outburst. The revival was spread from Georgia to Maine by the itinerant preacher George Whitfield; in Virginia through the ministry of Samuel Davies; and by others during the 1740s and 1750s among Baptists, Presbyterians, and Congregationalists.

Great Compromise (1787) The decision by the delegates at the Constitutional Convention to have a two-house legislature—a Senate in which the states would have equal representation and a House of Representatives in which the states would be represented according to population—this compromise was proposed by Roger Sherman from Connecticut and is sometimes called the Connecticut Compromise. Prior to the adoption of this proposal, the convention was deadlocked between the Virginia plan calling for representation according to population favored by the large states and the New Jersey plan for equal representation favored by the small states.

Great Depression The stock market crash of October 24, 1929, ushered in the greatest economic crisis in American history. The depression continued despite determined efforts of the New Deal until the demands for goods and services created by World War II brought prosperity back to farms and factories after ten years of suffering. During the Great Depression over 5000 banks closed their doors. Millions lost their savings, their farms, and their homes. In 1933 more than one-fourth of the labor force, some 15 million workers, were unemployed. Bankers and brokers committed suicide. Young people, many of whom had never worked roamed the country riding freight trains. The railroads actually added empty cars to cut down the deaths and injuries of the young vagrants. In *The Grapes of Wrath*, John Steinbeck describes the futile efforts of the Okies and Arkies who migrated in jalopies from their abandoned farms on the plains seeking a better life in California.

Great Migration This term is applied primarily to the large-scale migration of Puritans from England to America from 1620 to 1640; it is also used in reference to the great westward movement following the War of 1812.

Great Society In an address at Ann Arbor, Michigan, in the spring of 1964, President Lyndon B. Johnson proposed the Great Society, with the government taking a leading role in improving the quality of life for all Americans. In his State of the Union message in January, Johnson promised an "unconditional war on poverty." His program included VISTA (the domestic Peace Corps); a Job Corps for school dropouts; Upward Bound, designed to help bright youngsters go to college; a Neighborhood Youth Corps for the unemployed; and the Head Start program for preschool education for underprivileged children. Other goals of the Great Society included a concerted attack on crippling diseases, war on crime and delinquency, increased support for public education, and the guarantee of civil rights for all.

Greeley, Horace (1811–1873) Born in Vermont where he started his career in newspaper work, he came to New York in 1831 and three years later founded a weekly journal, *The New Yorker*. In 1841 he founded the influential New York *Tribune* with which his name is associated in history. The newspaper served as a medium for the advocacy of anti-slavery views, feminism, labor unions, temperance, a protective tariff, and homestead legislation to encourage settlement of the West. The expression "Go West, young man" said to have originated with Greeley, expressed his confidence in the opportunities available in the West. He helped found the new Republican party and supported Lincoln for president in 1860 on a platform opposed to the extension of slavery. Greeley withheld support from Lincoln in 1864 because he thought Lincoln could not win re-election. In 1872 he ran unsuccessfully against Grant as candidate of the Liberal Republican party.

Selling apples in New York City during the Great Depression of the 1930s.

Greenback Labor party   The party was organized by representatives of farmers and labor at a convention in Toledo, Ohio, in 1878, attended by delegates from twenty-eight states. Its platform called for the issuing of more paper money (greenbacks) to make it easier for farmers to pay their debts to banks. Its labor-related program demanded the reduction of hours for industrial workers and restriction of Chinese immigration, which competed with native labor. The party polled over one million votes in 1878 and elected fourteen members to Congress. This was the high point under the leadership of James B. Weaver of Iowa. In the election of 1880, Weaver, the party's candidate for president, received 308,000 votes. In 1884 Benjamin F. Butler of Massachusetts, former Civil War general and foe of the South, was the party's last presidential candidate.

Guadalcanal (1942)   On August 7, eight months after Pearl Harbor, the first major offensive against Japan began with marines landing in the Solomon Islands at Guadalcanal, where they took the airport and named it Henderson Field. This began an island-hopping campaign toward Japan via the Gilberts, the Marshalls, the Marianas, Leyte Gulf, the Philippines, Iwo Jima, and Okinawa. This offensive lasted into June 1945. On August 6, 1945, the first atom bomb hit Hiroshima.

Guadalupe-Hidalgo Treaty (1848)   The major terms of this treaty concluding the Mexican War were (1) the Rio Grande River was accepted as the boundary of Texas; (2) the Territory of New Mex-

ico, including what is now all of the states of New Mexico, Arizona, Utah, Nevada, and part of Oklahoma, Kansas, Colorado, and Wyoming, was ceded to the United States; (3) California was ceded to the United States; and (4) the United States paid Mexico $15 million and assumed claims against Mexico of $3.25 million.

H **Habeas corpus**   A legal writ by which an arrested person may demand his freedom unless sufficient cause can be shown to justify holding him for trial.

Hale, Nathan (1755–1776)   With the British in control of New York, General Washington was anxious to get information about their forces. Nathan Hale, a young captain, agreed to go to Long Island as a spy. Hale was a graduate of Yale who was teaching school in Connecticut when he enlisted in the Continental army of Washington. He was about to return when he was captured by the British, who found concealed in the sole of his shoe notes written in Latin. He was sentenced to death. Just before he was hanged (September 22, 1776) he uttered the immortal words, "I only regret that I have but one life to lose for my country."

Hamilton, Alexander (1755–1804)   Born in the British West Indies, Hamilton came to New York at the age of seventeen to study at Columbia College. He organized an artillery company and fought in the Revolutionary War. With the rank of lieutenant colonel he served as Washington's private secretary. As delegate from New York to the Constitutional Convention (1787), he advocated a strong central government. He was the major author of the Federalist Papers, which helped secure ratification of the Constitution by New York and other states. As Washington's first secretary of the treasury his financial program, which was approved, placed the new nation on a firm footing. Political differences with Jefferson (secretary of state) gave rise to the first political parties, with Hamilton leader of the Federalists. Differences with Vice President Aaron Burr culminated in a duel in which Hamilton was fatally wounded.

Hancock, John (1737–1793)   Merchant and statesman, he played a leading part in the American Revolution. He graduated from Harvard in 1754 and ten years later had become head of the largest trading firm in Boston. When the British seized his sloop *Liberty* for allegedly violating customs, he was defended by John Adams. He was delegate from Massachusetts to the Second Continental Congress, was elected president of that body, and was first to sign the Declaration of Independence. In 1780 Hancock became the first governor of Massachusetts and served nine 1-year terms. In 1788 he presided over the Massachusetts convention that ratified the Constitution.

Harding, Warren G.   *See* Presidents of the United States section, beginning on page 10-83.

Harlan, John Marshall (1833–1911)   A Kentucky slaveholder, Harlan fought for the Union in the Civil War and supported the Civil War Amendments (Thirteenth, Fourteenth, and Fifteenth). Republican President Hayes appointed him to the Supreme Court in 1877. He served on the Court until 1911, during a period when he was often a lone dissenter as in *Plessy* v. *Ferguson* (1896), which laid down the "separate but equal" doctrine that held sway until 1954 when *Brown* v. *Board of Education* established Harlan's view as the law of the land. Harlan's dissents include not only civil rights decisions but also cases involving the protection of workers, regulation of railroads, sustaining the first federal income tax, and other litigation in which his minority views later prevailed.

Harrison, Benjamin *See* Presidents of the United States section, beginning on page 10-83.

Harrison, William Henry *See* Presidents of the United States section, beginning on page 10-83.

Harris, Townsend (1804–1878)   He fought successfully for the establishment of the free College of the City of New York (1847). After Perry forced Japan to open its doors to American traders, Harris, who had previously made trading voyages in the Pacific, was named consul general to Japan and negotiated the first commercial agreement with Japan in 1857.

Hartford Convention (1814)   The New England states sent delegates to protest the War of 1812. This convention opposed "Mr. Madison's war" by proposing changes in the Constitution to make a declaration of war more difficult, break the "Virginia dynasty" of presidents, and safeguard the future of the Federalist party. Its resolutions were on their way to Congress when the news broke of Jackson's victory at New Orleans and the signing of the Treaty of Ghent. Victory and peace overwhelmed the Hartford protesters, whose actions, although wholly legal, were commonly denounced as traitorous.

Hatch Act (1887)   A federal law creating the state agricultural experiment stations.

Hatch Act (1939)   A federal law passed to prevent corrupt political practices its main effect was to prevent political campaigning by federal civil service employees. As amended in 1940 it sought to limit campaign contributions and expenditures in federal election campaigns.

Hawaiian monarchy overthrown (1893)   The McKinley tariff removed all advantages to Hawaii in its sugar trade with the United States. The Hawaiian economy was severely damaged. Queen Liliuokalani assumed dictatorial powers to rebuild Hawaiian trade away from dependence upon the United States. Sanford Dole, an American planter in Hawaii, John Stevens, U.S. minister at Honolulu, and marines from the USS *Boston* deposed the queen and requested the annexation of Hawaii by the United States. President Cleveland blocked this attempt, but under McKinley a joint resolution of Congress annexed the Hawaiian Islands on July 7, 1898.

Hay-Bunau-Varilla Treaty (1903)   Later in the same year that the Hay-Herran Treaty with Colombia failed to materialize, Secretary of State Hay concluded an almost identical treaty with Philippe Bunau-Varilla, representative of the new Republic of Panama. The only significant point of difference in this treaty was that the leased strip of land across Panama was to be 10 miles wide instead of 6. *See* **Panama Canal**.

Hayes, Rutherford B. *See* Presidents of the United States section, beginning on page 10-83.

Hay-Herran Treaty (1903)   Secretary of State Hay and the Colombian Minister Herran drew up an agreement whereby the United States acquired a ninety-nine year renewable lease on a 6 mile-wide strip of land across Panama. The United States was to pay $10 million and, after nine years, an annual rental of $250,000. The Senate ratified this agreement, but, much to President Theodore Roosevelt's dismay, the Colombian Senate refused to ratify the treaty. *See* **Hay-Bunau-Varilla Treaty**; **Panama Canal**.

Hay, John M. (1838–1905)   He practiced law in Springfield, Illinois. Lincoln brought him to Washington to serve as one of his private secretaries. After Lincoln's assassination he held diplomatic posts in Europe before returning to the United States in 1870. McKinley appointed him secretary of state in 1898, and Theodore Roosevelt kept him on in that office until 1905. Hay published a number of works in poetry and fiction but is best known as coauthor with John G. Nicolay of the ten-volume *Abraham Lincoln: A History*.

Haymarket Riot (1886)   Against instructions from Mayor Harrison of Chicago, the police chief and 180 officers advanced to break up a crowd of about 3000 gathered to protest police brutality at the McCormick Harvester Company the previous day. A dynamite bomb killed seven officers, and the return fire by police took a heavier toll. Eight labor leaders were convicted, four of whom were executed. Six years later Governor Altgeld pardoned those in prison. He said that the "malicious fury" shown by Judge Gary during the trial made a farce of justice. The massacre unjustly and seriously hurt labor unions.

Hay-Pauncefote Treaty (1901)   Secretary of State John Hay reached an agreement with foreign minister Pauncefote of England with respect to the building of a future canal across the Isthmus of Panama. Britain gave up its right, acquired in the Clayton-Bulwer Treaty of 1850, for joint responsibility in policing any future Panama canal. In return, the United States gave assurances that ships of all nations would be allowed to use the canal on equal terms.

Headright   A land grant in colonial Virginia given originally to those who paid the passage of an immigrant; usually 50 acres.

Henry, Patrick (1736–1799)   A leading advocate of independence, Henry was a prominent lawyer and gifted orator in western Virginia. As a member of the Virginia legislature, he challenged Britain's right to enforce the Staub Act of 1765. At the Virginia convention, which was convened at his urging in 1715, he concluded an address with the oft-quoted words "give me liberty or give me death." Henry served in the Continental Congress (1774–76), helped draft the Virginia Constitution, and was governor of Virginia (1776–79 and 1784–86).

Hepburn Act (1906)   This act gave the Interstate Commerce Commission its first real power. It forced railroads to obey its orders. If railroads protested the commission's decisions by court action, the decisions were in effect while litigation proceeded. The jurisdiction of the commission was enlarged to cover bridges, terminals, ferries, sleeping cars, and express companies.

Hill, James J. (1838–1916)   He started as a clerk in a steamship company and grew in wealth and influence until he was known in the Northwest as "the Empire Builder." He was responsible for developing the Great Northern Railroad and, along with J. P. Morgan, held major interests in the Northern Pacific Railroad. In a key Supreme Court case his Northern Securities Company, a holding company, was ordered dissolved because it was in violation of the Sherman Anti-trust Act (*Northern Securities Company* v. *United States*, 1904).

Hiroshima and Nagasaki (1945)　About 4 square miles were laid waste and about 160,000 people killed and injured by the first atom bomb, which released over Hiroshima energy equivalent to the explosion of about 20,000 tons of TNT. Nagasaki was hit on August 9, three days later. On August 10 Japan indicated willingness to surrender. Allied terms were accepted on August 14 (V-J Day).

Holmes, Oliver Wendell, Jr. (1841–1935) Holmes was the son of Dr. Oliver Wendell Holmes, the "Autocrat of the breakfast table," and Amelia Lee Jackson Holmes, the daughter of Justice Jackson of the Massachusetts Supreme Court. He attended Harvard College (1857–61). Before graduation he had enlisted in the Twentieth Massachusetts Volunteers in which he saw active service for three years with the army of the Potomac and was three times seriously wounded. He attended Harvard Law School (1864–66), was admitted to the bar (1867), and practiced law until 1881, when his book *The Common Law* was published, leading to a full-time appointment to the Harvard Law School faculty. He was associate justice of the Supreme Judicial Court of Massachusetts (1882–89) and chief justice (1889–92). President Theodore Roosevelt appointed him associate justice of the Supreme Court of the United States in 1902, and he served on the Court until his retirement in 1932. He wrote almost 2000 judicial opinions. His infrequent dissenting opinions caught the imagination of lawyers and lay people. His minority views in many cases have prevailed.

Home Owners Loan Corporation (HOLC) (1933) An emergency home refinancing agency created to prevent loss of homes by foreclosure.

Homestead Act (1862)　Westward expansion of our population continued during the Civil War. Prospectors were seeking gold and silver, California and Oregon were attracting new settlers, and many were going west to escape the draft. The Homestead Act stimulated this westward movement by offering 160 acres to any head of a family. The land could be his (or hers) if he lived on it for five years, or he could buy it at $1.25 an acre after he had lived on it for six months. A registration fee of about $30 was charged. The purpose of the act was frustrated to a degree by land companies and other speculators buying the better land at $1.25 an acre for resale. The provisions of residence and of being the head of a family were so fraudulently administered that the effect of the law was to encourage speculation more than homesteading.

Homestead Strike (1892)　A cut in wages plus the refusal of Henry Frick, general manager of Carnegie Steel, to negotiate with the union precipitated a strike. Frick hired a private force of 300 Pinkerton "police," who shot it out with the armed strikers. Ten were killed. The Pinkertons surrendered, but later the Pennsylvania State Militia broke the strike.

The large-scale use by a corporation of strikebreakers and a private armed force were new tactics on the American labor scene.

Hoover, Herbert　*See* Presidents of the United States section, beginning on page 10-83.

Hopkins, Harry Lloyd (1890–1946)　He attended Grinnell College in Iowa and moved to New York City, where he was a social worker and met Franklin D. Roosevelt. He was a trusted advisor and close friend of President Roosevelt. Hopkins was the federal administrator of Emergency Relief (1933); WPA administrator (1935–38); Lend-lease Act administrator (1941); special presidential envoy on delicate foreign missions during World War II; and impartial chairman of the cloth and suit industry from 1945 to his death.

Houston, Sam (1793–1863)　He moved from Texas to Tennessee (1807). He lived with the Cherokee Indians, fought under Jackson in the War of 1812, and studied law. Houston was a congressman from Tennessee (1823–27) and governor of Tennessee (1827–29). He resigned when his wife left him and went to live with the Cherokees. Sent by Jackson to Texas to make a treaty with the native Americans (1832), he stayed on to command the army that fought Mexico for Texan independence, which was achieved as a result of his brilliant victory at San Jacinto (1836). He was president of the Republic of Texas (1836–38) and (1841–44), senator from the new state of Texas (1846–59), and governor of Texas (1859–61). He was deposed for refusing to have Texas join the Confederacy but was permitted to live peaceably in his state. The new city of Houston was named for him when it was founded in 1836.

Hughes, Charles Evans (1862–1948)　He studied at Brown University (1881) and Columbia Law School (1884). He was governor of New York (1906–10) and associate justice of the U.S. Supreme Court (1910–16). He ran for president of the United States on the Republican ticket in 1916 and lost to Wilson in a closely contested election, 277 to 254 in the electoral college, with California casting the deciding votes. He was secretary of state (1921–26) and chief justice of the U.S. Supreme Court (1930–41). A moderate on social legislation, he nevertheless presided over the so-called "nine old men" who invalidated much of the early New Deal program.

Humphrey, Hubert H. (1911–1978)　His lifelong liberal political views stem from the time his family lost their home during the Great Depression. He left college to work in his father's drugstore. Later he graduated from the University of Minnesota. He was elected mayor of Minneapolis in 1945 and re-elected by the largest plurality ever recorded in that city. He was the first Democrat from Minnesota ever elected to the U.S. Senate (1948), where he was a regular sponsor of social legislation. A founder of the Americans for Democratic Action (ADA), he was a strong sponsor of arms control. Humphrey was vice president under Lyndon B. Johnson (1964–68), and Democratic candidate for president against Nixon in 1968.

Hundred days　President Franklin D. Roosevelt called Congress into special session on March 5, 1933, the day after his inauguration. Congress remained in session until June 16, the first "hundred days" of Roosevelt's first term. The legislation enacted during this session, touching all aspects of American economic life, was virtually a peaceful revolution. Included were the Emergency Bank Relief Act, Federal Security Act, Steagall (Banking) Act, Agricultural Adjustment Act, National Industrial Recovery Act, Civilian Conservation Corps, Tennessee Valley Authority, Home Owners Loan Act, and Federal Emergency Relief Act.

Hutchinson, Anne Marbury (1591–1643)   Born and raised in England, the daughter of an Anglican clergyman, Anne became interested in theology. She was married in 1612 and bore fifteen children during the next twenty years. She came to America in 1634 after her religious mentor John Cotton was forced to leave England over disagreement with Anglican church authorities. Anne began to hold meetings in her home preaching liberal doctrines, including feminism. This led to controversy with church authorities, and she was banished from the Massachusetts colony and excommunicated from the church in 1638. She and her family moved to Portsmouth, Rhode Island. Again embroiled in religious controversy, she moved with her six youngest children (her husband having died) to the Dutch colony of New Netherlands in 1642, settling at present-day Pelham Bay Park in the Bronx where, the following year, she and five of her children were massacred by native Americans.

Immigration Act (1924)   In 1924 the percentage and the census date used to determine quotas were changed to lessen the number of immigrants from southern and eastern Europe, where quotas were usually filled, while making little difference to western and northern Europeans, whose quotas were rarely totally used. The 1924 law specified 2 percent on the census of 1890 (for example, see **Immigration, Emergency Quota Act**). The total of all quotas was cut from 357,000 to 164,000.

In 1929 the law was further modified by a *National Origins* formula. A total annual immigration maximum was set at 150,000. Asians were excluded. Quotas did not apply to Western Hemisphere nations. All other nations had a quota based on the number of Americans who traced their origin to that nation. In 1952, the *McCarran-Walters Act* modified the 1929 law by including Asians in the formula. Some provisions were also added to keep out "subversives" and to expel immigrants belonging to "communist or communist-front" organizations. The *Immigration Act of 1965* discontinued quotas based on national origin. Preference is extended to those who have relatives living in the United States. The basis factor of selection is the occupation of the applicant. The *Refugee Act of 1980* was passed to admit refugees on a systematic basis for humanitarian reasons. The 1985 ceiling was set at 70,000 refugees. Immigration to the United States was numerically limited to 270,000 annually, with no more than 20,000 from any one country. The Immigration Act of 1990, signed into law by President Bush on November 29, raised the number of immigrants entering the United States annually to 700,00 exclusive of refugees.

Immigration, Emergency Quota Act (1921)   This first quota law allowed 3 percent on the census of 1910. For example, if the census of 1910 showed 10,000 persons in the United States who had been born in X nation this law gave that nation a quota of 300. The total allowed to enter the United States from quota nations was 357,000.

Immigration legislation   Our immigration policy evolved through piecemeal legislation starting with the **Chinese Exclusion Act** of 1882 see page 10-13 and the **Gentlemen's agreement** with Japan (*see* page 10-36). To stem the tide of immigration after World War I, an immigration quota law was passed (*see* **Immigration, Emergency Quota Act**) followed by a basic law in 1924 (*see* **Immigration Act**; **Quotas, immigration**).

Implied powers   Powers of Congress not directly granted by the Constitution but permitted by the elastic clause which gives Congress the power "To make all laws . . . necessary and proper" for executing the powers expressly granted.

Impressment of seamen   With working conditions and pay better on American than British ships, seamen often deserted the latter to join the former. British naval vessels would stop American ships on the sea, board the ships, and remove "deserters." Americans were thus sometimes seized and "impressed" into service in the British Navy or Merchant Marine. (*See* **Chesapeake-Leopard affair**.) Impressment of American seamen was cited by President Madison as an American grievance in the War of 1812.

Income Tax (1895)   This tax was included in the Wilson-Gorman Tariff. By a 5 to 4 decision (*Pollack v. Farmers' Loan & Trust Company*), the Supreme Court earlier had declared a tax on incomes to be a direct tax, not apportioned among the several states according to their respective populations. Article I, Section 9, forbids any such federal tax. The income tax violated the letter of the Constitution but not its purpose, which was to prevent inequitable taxation of the people of one state compared with those of another. In 1913 the Sixteenth Amendment made the income tax constitutional.

Indentured servants   Immigrants in colonial times voluntarily or involuntarily entered into contracts to sell their labor for a period of years in return for payment of their ship passage to America. The period of indenture varied from two to seven years.

Independence Hall   The hall, first built as the Pennsylvania State House in 1735, was used by the Continental Congress, which approved and signed the Declaration of Independence in 1776, and by the Constitutional Convention, which prepared the U.S. Constitution during the summer of 1787. The Liberty Bell is inside the hall. The hall contains memorabilia of the American Revolutionary era.

Independent Treasury   Also called the subtreasury system, it is the practice of depositing federal revenues in government offices in lieu of banks of any kind. In government offices the money could not be lent or used by bankers as reserves upon which paper money could be issued. The subtreasury system, established in 1840 by President Van Buren, reduced the capacity of private banks for expanding credit. The system was replaced in 1913 by the Federal Reserve Act.

Indian Affairs, Bureau of   Established in 1824 the Bureau was assigned to the Department of the Interior in 1849. It has functioned as a ward of native Americans to assist them in education and in making adjustments to an economic and cultural society alien to their traditional way of life. Native American resentment of the attitude of the Bureau manifested itself in 1972, when militant members of the American Indian Movement (AIM) seized the Bureau's building in Washington, D.C.

Indian Reorganization Act (1934)   The policy of the Dawes Act was reversed. Tribal life was to be recognized as a normal and viable mode. Native Americans were no longer to be urged to adapt to the "individual" American norm.

Industrial Workers of the World (IWW)   The IWW was a radical labor organization founded in Chicago in 1905. Its members, called "the Wobblies," were recruited originally from the mines and lumber camps of the West but later joined by textile workers in the East. It was led by William "Big Bill" Haywood, who hoped to build an industrial union of both skilled and unskilled workers powerful and militant enough to overthrow the capitalist system. It conducted a strike marked by violence in the textile industry in Lawrence, Massachusetts, in 1912, when it was at the peak of its power with 75,000 members. The IWW opposed U.S. entry into World War I, and its leader Haywood was imprisoned for obstructing recruitment during the war. The IWW dissolved soon after.

Inflation   When prices rise faster than income, the purchasing power of the dollar is reduced, bringing about the economic condition known as inflation. During World War II dwindling of consumer goods (a large percentage of production went into military supplies and equipment) coupled with a rapid rise in employment and income threatened to produce runaway inflation. To meet this challenge the government set up an Office of Price Administration to control prices and ration scarce commodities, such as meat and gasoline. The attempt to limit price increases on a voluntary basis during the Ford administration when WIN (whip inflation now) buttons were distributed proved unsuccessful.

Initiative and referendum   Processes by which voters may directly vote upon laws; intended to give law-making power to the voters since state and local legislative bodies are not always fully responsive to the popular will.

Injunction   A court order forbidding some action; frequently used as a weapon against organized labor except as outlawed. Violation of an injunction may result in assessment of heavy penalties for "contempt of court."

Insular cases   A series of Supreme Court decisions made after 1900 related to the status of colonies and territories outside the U.S. mainland. These cases recognized liberal powers of Congress to apply or refuse provisions of the Constitution in these possessions. In broad outline, the incorporated territories of Hawaii and Alaska, which were destined for statehood, were entitled to be governed under constitutional guarantees. The unincorporated island (insular) areas— Puerto Rico, the Philippines, the Virgin Islands, and Samoa—were to enjoy lesser privileges but their people were entitled to basic constitutional guarantees of life, liberty, and protection of property.

Interstate Commerce Commission (1887)   The commission was established by the Interstate Commerce Act. Members of the commission, at first five and now eleven, are appointed by the president with the consent of the Senate. Ineffective in its early years, the commission has since been given adequate powers through reinforcing acts of Congress, chief among them the Elkins Act of 1903, Hepburn Act of 1906, Mann-Elkins Act of 1910, Esch-Cummins Act of 1920, and Motor-Carrier Act of 1935.

Intolerable Acts (1774)   They provided for (1) closing the port of Boston; (2) appointing members of the Massachusetts Council by the king; (3) forbidding town meetings without the governor's consent; and (4) trying in England any officials charged with a capital crime. Parliament also extended Quebec, with its French population and Catholic religion, to the Ohio River into areas claimed by Massachusetts, Connecticut, and Virginia. Although the Quebec Act was not specifically a penalty for Boston's Tea Party, New England and Virginia strongly resented it. To them it was another punitive act of Parliament along with the Intolerable Acts. The response of the American colonies was the calling of the First Continental Congress in 1774.

Inventions—U.S.   *See* **Exhibit 10.4**.

Iran-Contra affair   In late November 1986, an item in a newspaper in Lebanon revealed that the U.S. government had been engaged in a covert operation selling arms to Iran in order to secure the release before the November 1986 senatorial elections of U.S. hostages held in Lebanon. Profits from the sale were alleged to have been diverted to the "Contras" fighting in Nicaragua, contrary to U.S. Law. A joint U.S. Senate-House committee, headed by Senator Daniel K. Inouye of Hawaii, held hearings during the spring of 1987 to get the facts. Key cabinet officers and others who had knowledge of these actions were questioned. A key witness who requested immunity as a condition of giving testimony that might incriminate him was Lieutenant Colonel Oliver L. North, who was deeply involved in these affairs while he was assigned to the National Security Council.

Testimony at the hearings disclosed that high U.S. government officials had provided the Contras with private and international sources of funds for conducting military operations against the Nicaraguan government. President Reagan was aware that Robert C. (Bud) McFarlane, his National Security Advisor from October 1983 to December 1985, had solicited and obtained monthly contributions of $1 million from King Fahd of Saudi Arabia. Elliot Abrams, Assistant Secretary of State for Inter-American Affairs, obtained a $10 million contribution from the oil-rich Middle East kingdom of Brunei.

In its final report, the majority concluded: "It was the President's policy—not an isolated decision by [Oliver] North or Poindexter—to sell arms secretly to Iran and to maintain the Contras 'body and soul,' the Boland amendment (outlawing aid to the Contras) notwithstanding." Evidence was presented of a deal to trade 4,000 American anti-tank missiles for five American hostages held in Lebanon.

On March 4, 1987, President Reagan, in a public statement, said: "A few months ago I told the American people I did not trade arms for hostages. My heart and best intentions still tell me that's true, but the facts and the evidence tell me it's not." Three weeks later he added: "It sort of settled down to just trading arms for hostages." In November 1986 elections the Republicans lost control of the Senate. A release of the hostages prior to the election might have affected election results.

An independent counsel, Lawrence E. Walsh, was appointed to investigate possible criminal activities involved in the affair, and after more than six years of probing, indictments were obtained. One defendant, former Secretary of Defense Casper W. Weinberger, was charged with obstruction of justice, giving false testimony to Congress, and other felonies. His trial was set for January 5, 1993. On December 24, 1992, President Bush granted a "full, complete unconditional pardon" to Weinberger and five other defendants. In a statement on the pardons Walsh said: "The Iran-Contra cover-up, which has continued for more than six years, has now been completed with the pardon of Caspar Weinberger."

Iraqgate   Loan guarantees made by the Bush administration to Iraq enabled Saddam Hussein to purchase more than $5 billion in grain. The loans were negotiated through the Atlanta branch of Banco Nazionale del Lavoro, Italy's largest bank. Instead of going to Iraq, the grain shipments were regularly diverted to other countries where money for the sales was used by Iraq to obtain military technology, develop nuclear weapons, secure missiles and armament of mass destruction, and build a formidable capability for aggressive warfare.

A tip on irregularities in the loans led to an FBI raid on the Atlanta bank in August 1989, when thousands of records were seized. Representative Henry B. Gonzales, chairman of the House Banking, Finance and Urban Affairs Committee, charged that the CIA failed to cooperate in the investigation of the bank. Federal Judge Marvin H. Shoob made similar charges against both the CIA and the Justice Department, as did Senator David L. Boren, chairman of the Senate Intelligence Committee. In October 1992 CIA officials admitted they had misinformed prosecutors in Atlanta but said they did so at the urging of the Justice Department.

With pressure mounting, Attorney General William P. Barr appointed a friendly former federal judge, Frederick Lacey, to conduct an investigation. Lacey found no irregularities and reacted angrily at charges that the investigation was less than rigorous.

On December 10, 1992, President-elect Bill Clinton indicated that after his inauguration he would consult with his attorney general about appointing a special prosecutor to conduct an investigation. A key question on which Iraqgate hinges is: Did Bush administration officials cover up efforts to help Iraq build up its military capabilities in the years before the invasion of Kuwait?

Irrepressible conflict   In a speech at Rochester, New York (1858), U.S. Senator William H. Seward spoke of the growing hostility between North and South over slavery as an "irrepressible conflict." Whether armed conflict was inevitable and "irre-

EXHIBIT 10.4
Important 19th and 20th Century Inventions

Industry

1831	Colt Revolver: Samuel Colt
1831	Electric Dynamo: Michael Faraday
1837	Rubber: Charles Goodyear
1879	Electric Light Bulb: Thomas A. Edison
1895	X-Ray: Wilhelm Roentgen
1907	Radio Vacuum Tube: Lee De Forest
1909	Bakelite (Plastic begins synthetics revolution): Lee Backeland
1912	Cellophane: Jacques Brandenberger
1926	Liquid Fuel Rocket: Robert Goddard
1934	Synthetic Superpolymer (Nylon): Wallace Carothers
1937	Mark I (computer): Howard Aiken
1942	Controlled Nuclear Fission: Enrico Fermi
1940s	Electric Computer: American Industry
1951	Power Producing Nuclear Fission: United States Atomic Energy Commission
1960	Demonstration of Laser Action: Theodore Maiman

Agriculture

1793	Cotton Gin: Eli Whitney
1797	Iron Plow: Charles Newbold
1834	Reaper: Cyrus McCormick
1868	Modern Steel Plow: James Oliver

Mining and Smelting

1851	New method of making steel from iron: William Kelly
1856	Bessemer Process: Henry Bessemer, used blast of hot air to remove impurities from molten iron.

Transportation and Communication

1807	Steamboat: Robert Fulton
1830	Locomotive: George Stevenson
1831	Screw Propellor: John Ericsson
1844	Telegraph: Samuel Morse
1867	Sleeping car: George Pullman
1872	Air brake: George Westinghouse
1876	Telephone: Alexander Graham Bell
1895	Automobile: developed by Henry Ford
1896	Motion Pictures: C. F. Jenkins
1903	Airplane: Wright Brothers
1906	Radio: R. A. Fessenden
1942	Jet Planes: Lockheed Company
1951	Television: J. L. Baird and C. F. Jenkins
1951	Transistor: William Shockley and Bell Telephone Team
1975	Video Home System (VHS)

pressible" depends on one's world view, but events such as John Brown's attempted armed insurrection were rapidly catapulting the country to civil war, and whether it might have been avoided or not, the terrible war came.

Irving, Washington (1783–1859)   Best known as an author, Irving was also a lawyer and served on several diplomatic missions for the United States. He attained prominence with his comic *History of New York by Diedrich Knickerbocker* (1809). He lived in Europe (1815–32), where he wrote *The Sketch Book* (1820) containing the "Legend of Sleepy Hollow" and the ingratiating "Rip Van Winkle." From England he went to Germany, France, and Spain, where he served (1826–29) on the U.S. Embassy staff. There he wrote historical works on Spain. He later served on the U.S. Embassy staff in London (1829–32) and again in Spain (1842–46).

Isolationism   The American policy of avoiding "entangling alliances" with European nations, it was dominant after World War I when American membership in the League of Nations was turned down in the Senate. The policy reappeared before Pearl Harbor when a group called "America First," headed by Colonel Charles A. Lindbergh, sought to keep America neutral in the war launched by Hitler.

American Marines raise the flag on Iwo Jima in February, 1945.

Iwo Jima, battle of (1945)   The U.S. Marines took this island south of Japan in a prelude to a planned invasion. The heavily fortified island was staunchly defended by its Japanese garrison, who took 20,000 American casualties, including more than 4000 dead in twenty-six days of fighting. The symbolic raising of the American flag by four marines on the top of Mount Suribachi was photographed by Joe Rosenthal of the Associated Press to become perhaps the most representative visual memento of the war.

J   **Jackson, Andrew**   *See* Presidents of the United States section, beginning on page 10-83.
Jackson State College   At Jackson State college in Mississippi, an institution with a predominantly black student body who were protesting the invasion of Cambodia in May 1970, the state highway patrol fired into a dormitory, killing two students.

Jackson, Thomas J. "Stonewall" (1824–1863)   He graduated from the U.S. Military Academy (West Point) in 1846. After serving as a major in the Mexican War, he taught artillery tactics and natural philosophy at the Virginia Military Institute in Lexington, Virginia, where he was known as a devoutly religious man and an extremely conscientious instructor. He was commissioned brigadier general in the Confederate army and became known as Stonewall Jackson because it was said his troops stood like a "stone wall" at the first battle of Bull Run. He was promoted to major general and served under Lee as a brilliant tactician, successfully defeating superior Union forces in a series of engagements during the spring and summer of 1862. At Chancellorsville (May 2, 1863) he forced a Union retreat but was fatally wounded by his own troops, who mistook him for the enemy at dusk. Lee was distraught and said "I have lost my right arm."

Jamestown (1607)   Prominent in its tragic history were Captain John Smith, Lord De La Warr, Governor Dale, John Rolfe, Nathaniel Bacon, and Governor Berkeley. Its ups and downs were marked by disease and fires, famine, the tobacco trade, the introduction of slavery to America, the House of Burgesses in 1619, the massacre by native Americans in 1622, and Bacon's Rebellion in 1676. In 1698 the exhausted settlement moved a few miles from the James River to Williamsburg. The original site of Jamestown contains little more than an historical marker.

Jay-Gardoqui Treaty (1789)   Jay represented the United States; Gardoqui represented Spain. They agreed that Spain's exclusive right to navigate the Mississippi River be recognized for thirty years. In return, Spain's European and West Indian ports were to be open to American shipping. Congress voted 7 to 5 for the treaty, only two short of the nine votes required under the Articles of Confederation. That a majority of the states were willing to sacrifice the interests of the Southwest for an advantage to the Northeast intensified sectional ill will.

Jay, John (1745–1829)   Born in New York City, he graduated from King's College (Columbia) in 1764 and was admitted to the New York Bar four years later. A member of the First and Second Continental Congresses (1774–76) and president of the Congress (1778–80), he was chairman of the committee that drew up the first constitution of New York State (1777). Member of the delegation that negotiated the treaty of peace with Great Britain (1783), he was also Secretary of Foreign Affairs (1784–90). His treaty with Spain, the Jay-Gardoqui agreement of 1785, failed to gain approval in Congress. He wrote five of the Federalist Papers advocating adoption of the Constitution by the states. First Chief Justice of the United States (March 4, 1789), he was sent to England and negotiated the Jay Treaty of 1794. He resigned from the Supreme Court to become governor of New York (1795–1801).

Jay Treaty (1795)   The impressment of American sailors, the continued presence of British fur traders within our northern borders, and the incitement of native Americans were major irritants. In spite of the Treaty of Paris (1783), American debtors had not paid British creditors nor had Loyalists been paid for their confiscated properties. The Jay Treaty said nothing about impressment and left debts and

Loyalist issues for future settlement, but did promise that British subjects would leave the Great Lakes fur region within a year. Washington and the Senate accepted this humiliating treaty; it was better than war.

Jefferson, Thomas   *See* Presidents of the United States section, beginning on page 10-83.

Jim Crow laws   Passed chiefly in the 1890s to deprive the blacks of a degree of equality they had gained upon emancipation, the laws provided for strict segregation of the races in schools, restaurants, transportation facilities, sports arenas, and other public places. In *Brown* v. *Board of Education* (1954), the Supreme Court held what blacks had always known, that "separate" could not be equal and that segregation relegated blacks to second-class citizenship.

John Birch Society   A semi-secret political organization founded in 1958 by Robert Welch, Jr., a candy manufacturer, this political action group, named after a member of a U.S. intelligence team killed in 1945 by Chinese communists, advocated an extreme rightist program, including taking the United States out of the United Nations, abolishing the federal income tax, repeal of Social Security legislation, and rejecting the authority of the Supreme Court. The society attained publicity during the 1960s when the Wyoming legislature was, for a time, under its influence.

John Brown's Raid (1859)   On October 16, John Brown with eighteen men and boys seized the federal arsenal at Harper's Ferry, Virginia. After two days, ten of his band, including two of his sons, were killed or dying. The survivors surrendered to Colonel Robert E. Lee. Brown and four of his followers were hanged in early December. The raid was a futile attempt on the part of Brown and the abolitionists who financed him to free the slaves.

Johnson Act (1934)   An act of Congress against European nations that had defaulted on debts arising out of World War I, it prohibited such nations from marketing bond issues in the United States. Sponsored by Senator Hiram W. Johnson of California, the act was also known as the Foreign Securities Act.

Johnson, Andrew   *See* Presidents of the United States section, beginning on page 10-83.

Johnson, Joseph Eggleston (1807–1891)   He graduated from the U.S. Military Academy (1829) and served in the Mexican War, where he was five times wounded. He was brigadier general at the outbreak of the Civil War. He chose to go with the Confederate army, where he received the same rank. He drove back Union forces at the first battle of Bull Run (1861). He served in Congress (1879–81) and as federal commissioner of railroads (1885–90).

Johnson, Lyndon B.   *See* Presidents of the United States section, beginning on page 10-83.

Joint-stock company   Trading companies, forerunners of present-day corporations, organized for single trading ventures by selling stock to members; used in founding the early colonies in America.

Jones, John Paul (1747–1792)   Born in Scotland, where he entered the merchant marine, he came to the United States in 1773 and was commissioned a lieutenant in the Continental navy at the outbreak of war with Britain. His ship *Alfred* was the first to carry the flag with thirteen stripes but still had the union jack in the canton, which was replaced by stars in June 1777. His ship was manned in part by black slaves, who were liberated after the war. He commanded the sloop *Raugen* operating out of Brest, Belgium, preying on British merchantmen. At the request of Franklin, who was representing the states in Paris, Jones was put in charge of a small fleet. Jones renamed the flagship *Bonhomme Richard* after Benjamin Franklin (who called himself Poor Richard) and defeated the British frigate *Serapis* (September 23, 1779), despite the latter's heavier armament. After the war Jones served for a time as rear admiral in the Russian navy. He resigned in 1789. His remains were brought back from Paris for burial at the U.S. Naval Academy.

Judicial review   The doctrine that a court may pass upon the constitutionality of legislation; the right was assumed by the Supreme Court under Chief Justice Marshall.

Judiciary Act (1789)   The Act established a Supreme Court of six judges, provided thirteen district courts and three circuit courts, and created the office of attorney general. This act set up our federal judiciary system. A clause of the law granting the Supreme Court the right to issue writs of mandamus was declared unconstitutional in the *Marbury* v. *Madison* decision in 1803.

Kanagawa Treaty (1854)   President Fillmore sent Commodore Matthew C. Perry to Japan with a task force that sailed November 24, 1852, and arrived in Tokyo harbor belching black smoke. Perry delivered a letter from the president to the emperor on July 14, 1853. He returned the following year with seven warships. The Japanese were duly impressed and signed a treaty at Kanagawa to open their ports of Shimoda and Hakodate to U.S. trade and to guarantee the safety of shipwrecked U.S. seamen.

Kansas-Nebraska Act (1854)   This bill, pushed by Stephen Douglas, divided the Nebraska Territory at the 40th parallel into Kansas and Nebraska. The issue of slavery was to be settled by vote of the settlers in each territory. All the area had been made free from slavery by the Missouri Compromise of 1820. This reopening of the slave controversy shattered what was left of the major parties, Whigs and Democrats, whose members regrouped as Northerners against slavery and Southerners for slavery. This new political alignment pointed away from compromise toward civil war.

Kearney, Dennis (1879)   Kearney organized the California Workingman's party in San Francisco. He blamed most of labor's ills, especially low wages and unemployment, on the competition from Chinese laborers. Claiming that the beef eater could not compete with the rice eater for jobs, Kearneyite groups used violence against the Chinese. Congress responded by passing the Chinese Exclusion Act in 1882.

Kearsarge* v. *Alabama (1864)   Union merchant vessels were constantly under attack by Confederate armed raiders. Most powerful of these was the cruiser *Alabama*, built for the Confederacy in England. After destroying fifty-eight merchant ships, *Alabama* put in at Cherbourg, France, for repairs. U.S.S. *Kearsarge* had followed her and was lying in wait outside the harbor. Captain John A. Winslow had orders to track down and destroy *Alabama*, although the two ships were equally matched in maneuverability and firepower. On the morning of June 19, *Alabama* suddenly made for the open sea. *Kearsarge* promptly engaged it and sank it in an action that lasted little more than an hour.

Kellogg-Briand Pact (1928) Often called the Pact of Paris, this pact was proposed by French Foreign Minister Briand to Secretary of State Kellogg, who then suggested a multilateral, instead of bilateral, pact. The treaty, soon signed by over sixty nations, renounced war as an instrument of national policy. Headlines proclaimed "War Outlawed." There was no force to back it up except for considerable moral influence of world opinion. It was a suitable declaration of intentions for the tenth anniversary of the cease fire ending World War I. It proved futile in preventing World War II, however.

Kennedy assassination (November 22, 1963, at Dallas, Texas) President and Mrs. Kennedy were seated in the rear seat of an automobile with the top down. Texas Governor Connally and Mrs. Connally were seated directly in front of them. The presidential motorcade, formed at the city airport, was nearing downtown Dallas. Happily enthusiastic crowds lined the street. At 12:30 P.M. two shots were fired, both hit the president, wounding him in the head and neck and causing death within half an hour. The second shot also seriously wounded Governor Connally, who recovered several weeks later. The bullets were fired from an upper window in the Texas Book Depository Building, used for storage space by the Dallas school department. Two hours after the shooting, Lee Harvey Oswald was arrested. He repeatedly denied killing the president. Oswald was shot and killed while in custody. The Warren Commission reported that all evidence pointed to Oswald as the lone assassin.

Kennedy, John F. *See* Presidents of the United States section, beginning on page 10-83.

Kennedy, Robert Francis (1925–1968) He left Harvard to join the navy in 1944. He returned to Harvard, where he played football and received an A.B. in 1948, and an L.L.B. from the University of Virginia in 1951. In the U.S. Department of Justice criminal division, he worked for the Senate subcommittee on investigations (1953). He became chief counsel (1954) to the Senate permanent committee on investigations. He was attorney general in John F. Kennedy's administration (1961–63), Democratic senator from New York (1965–68), and candidate for president (1968), winning primaries in Indiana, Nebraska, and California, where he was assassinated June 6, 1968.

Kent, James (1763–1847) Admitted to the New York Bar in 1785, he was professor of law at Columbia (1794–98 and 1824–26) and member of the New York State judiciary (1798–1823), where he exercised a major influence in formulating judicial procedure and establishing legal principles. His major written work, *Kent's Commentaries on the American Law*, helped integrate British common law and American law as modified by constitutional and statutory principles. The *Commentaries* served as basic legal authority well into the twentieth century.

Kent State University On April 20, 1970, President Nixon, without consulting Congress, ordered American troops into Cambodia where Vietnamese troops were operating. Passions flared up among American college students throughout the country, who were well aware that over 40,000 Americans had already lost their lives and 250,000 wounded in the longest and most unpopular war in our history. The National Guard was called out to face a crowd on the campus of Kent State University in Ohio on April 30, 1970. The guardsmen fired into the crowd, killing four and wounding many.

Kentucky and Virginia Resolutions (1798) Passed by these two Republican-dominated state legislatures condemning and denying the constitutionality of the Alien and Sedition Acts, these resolutions were the first formal statement of the doctrines of states rights and nullification. The resolution adopted by the Kentucky legislature was drawn up by Jefferson. A somewhat less extreme view was expressed in a resolution drawn up by Madison and adopted by the legislature of Virginia.

An 1861 cartoon depicting King Cotton.

King Cotton In 1858, Senator Hammond of South Carolina had declared: "You dare not make war upon cotton! . . . Cotton is king." This expressed the view, widely held in the South, that the need for cotton to feed British mills was so great that Britain would go to war to keep southern cotton flowing freely to Britain. Although there was an element of truth in this view, it was not nearly enough to bring Britain to war on the side of the Confederacy

King, Martin Luther, Jr. (1929–1968) King, the son of a minister and grandson on his mother's side of a minister, grew up in Atlanta where he attended all-black elementary school and high school. After graduating from Morehouse College in Atlanta, he studied theology at the Crozer Seminary in Pennsylvania and then took his doctorate in theology at Boston University. He went to Alabama to become pastor of the Dexter Avenue Baptist Church in Montgomery, the capital city. He led the bus boycott that culminated in 1956 with integration of the buses, having been imprisoned in the meantime. This demonstration of nonviolent protest, despite provocation and violence of the opposition, continued in his leadership of the newly formed Southern Christian Leadership Conference (SCLC) in 1957. In 1958 he wrote *Stride Toward Freedom*. In 1963 he was imprisoned for leading nonviolent civil disobedience activities to attain desegregation. While in prison, he wrote "Letter From a Birmingham Jail." The following year he wrote *Why We Can't Wait*. On August 28, 1963, he addressed a crowd of a quarter of a million people, repeating the classic refrain "I Have a Dream." He opposed the escalation of the Vietnam War. While on the balcony of a motel in Memphis, Tennessee, where he was participating in a strike of sanitation workers, he was assassinated by one bullet fired by James Earle Ray, an escaped convict, on April 4, 1968. In 1964 he had been awarded the Nobel Peace Prize. His birthday, January 15, was declared a national holiday in 1984.

Martin Luther King Jr.

Kissinger, Henry Alfred (b. 1923)　Born in Germany, he came to the United States in 1938, became a U.S. citizen in 1943, and received an A.B. from Harvard (1950), an M.A. (1952), and a Ph.D. (1954). He joined the Harvard faculty in 1951 and became a full professor in 1962. He served as the assistant for national security affairs to Presidents Nixon (1969–74) and Ford (1974–75). He was secretary of state under Nixon (1973–74) and Ford (1974–77). He has been a member of the Georgetown University faculty since 1977; founder of Kissinger Associates, Inc., in New York City and analyst on ABC News; and author of a number of books on history and foreign relations. He was awarded the Nobel Prize for Peace in 1973 in connection with the end of the Vietnam War. He was

also awarded the Presidential Medal of Freedom in 1977.

Kitchen cabinet　The name given by President Jackson's foes to friends of the president, including several influential newspaper publishers whom Jackson consulted in preference to his regular cabinet in making policy decisions, the term implies that they came in through the back door and met in secret.

Knights of Labor (1869)　This organization was founded by Uriah S. Stephens. By the 1880s its membership was about 700,000, with Terence Powderly as its president. Men, women, blacks, whites, aliens, the well-educated, the illiterate, the skilled, agrarian workers, industrial workers, and clerks formed its 6000 local unions. Political goals, such as the graduated income tax, temperance, abolition of child labor, and cooperatives, supplemented the usual economic demands for more pay, fewer hours, and other improvements in working conditions. This heterogeneous mass with a complex program lacked cohesive strength. It disintegrated under undeserved and violent public reaction against all organized labor caused by the Haymarket Riot of 1886.

Know-Nothing party　Originally called the Order of the Star Spangled Banner, it adopted the name American party and ran ex-President Millard Fillmore as its unsuccessful candidate in the election of 1856. It acquired the name because it was rooted in secret societies, such as the Sons of '76, whose members when questioned would reply "I know nothing." The members were anti-Catholic and opposed the immigration of the Irish, who were coming to the United States in large numbers in the 1840s. The party split over the slavery issue and ceased to exist when war came in 1861.

Korean War (1950–1953)　North Korea attacked across the 38th parallel on June 25. The U.N. Security Council, with Russia absent, voted sixteen hours later 9 to 0 to support South Korea. President Truman had already assured Secretary-General Trygve Lie of U.S. support, but it was important that the action be officially a U.N. move. Public announcement of actual U.S. support of South Korea came on June 27, many hours after U.S. naval and air units had been ordered into action.

Korea, which had been occupied by Japan since 1910, was freed during World War II only to be divided by the 38th parallel into a Russian zone north of 38° and an American zone south. With the coming of war in 1950, U.S. forces under General Douglas MacArthur drove the North Korean forces to the border of Manchuria. In November 1950, Chinese forces swarmed across the border, driving the U.N. armies (chiefly U.S.) back to the 38th parallel. Contrary to orders from President Truman, General MacArthur attempted to provoke all-out war with China. Truman removed him from command and put General Matthew B. Ridgway in his place. The fighting continued until July 1953, when a truce was signed restoring the 38th parallel as the boundary between the two Koreas.

Ku Klux Klan　An organization of ex-Confederates founded as a secret society at Pulaski, Tennessee, in December 1865 to oppose Congressional reconstruction. Former Confederate General Nathan B. Forrest became the leader with the title "Grand

Wizard." To maintain white supremacy, the Klan used violence and intimidation against the former slaves. Congress passed Ku Klux Klan Acts in 1870 and 1871 to enforce the provisions of the Fourteenth and Fifteenth amendments. The Klan was revived in 1915 with an expanded program including anti-Semitism and anti-Catholicism. It spread throughout the country, attaining considerable influence during the 1920s. A skeleton organization still exists and surfaces from time to time despite legislation barring the order in many states.

La Follette, Robert M. (1855–1925) He was born and raised on a Wisconsin farm, practiced law, and was elected district attorney in 1880 and 1882 on a Republican ticket although opposed by politicians in his own party. He served three terms in the House of Representatives (1885–91) but was defeated in the 1890 election. He attacked the political bosses, who refused him the nomination for governor. He was finally nominated and won in 1900. He was reelected in 1902 and 1904 and elected to the U.S. Senate in 1906, where he remained until his death. He supported Wilson's reform measures, such as the Clayton Anti-Trust Act of 1914. He opposed the League of Nations. He ran for president in 1924 as the Progressive party candidate supported by organized labor.

LaGuardia, Fiorello H. (1882–1947) He did newspaper work in Arizona and Florida, served as U.S. consul in Hungary and Italy, studied law at New York University, and was admitted to the New York Bar in 1910. He was elected to Congress (1917) as a Republican. He joined the U.S. Air Force and served on the Italian front in World War I. He was president of the New York City Board of Aldermen (1920–21), member of Congress (1922–32), and cosponsor of the Norris-LaGuardia Anti-injunction Act. He was defeated for re-election in 1932 by a coalition of Democratic and Republican political bosses. He organized the Fusion party and was elected Mayor of New York City in 1933, 1937, and 1941. He proved to be a colorful, dynamic, incorruptible mayor, easily outmaneuvering the Tammany machine. He secured the adoption of a new city charter (1938). He tried unsuccessfully to get a commission in the Air Force in World War II but served as chief of the U.S. Office of Civilian Defense. He was director of the U.N. Relief and Rehabilitation Administration (UNRRA) in 1946.

Landrum-Griffin Act (1959) The act restricted secondary boycotts, particularly union refusal to handle "hot cargo"; union practices in elections and meetings that deprived union members of control over their officers; and picketing in situations in which the union was engaged in organizing the employees of a business.

Lansing-Ishii Agreement (1917) Secretary of State Lansing objected to Japan's intent to take Shantung and other German possessions in the Far East. When Japan and the United States were partners in World War I this difference was smoothed over, but not resolved, by an agreement easily subject to opposing interpretations. The agreement said in part that the United States recognized that "territorial propinquity creates special relations between countries, and consequently, the government of the United States recognizes that Japan has special interests in China, particularly in the part to which her possessions are contiguous."

League of Nations Proposed by President Woodrow Wilson at the end of World War I, it became part of the Treaty of Versailles (1919). The League Covenant (constitution) provided for a council composed of the great powers and an assembly composed of all members. The United States did not join the League because Wilson could not get the necessary two-thirds vote of the Senate. The United States cooperated with the League on economic matters and on efforts to attain disarmament. The League disbanded when it failed to prevent World War II and was replaced after the war by the United Nations.

Lecompton Constitution (1857) A constitution for Kansas, which was about to seek admission as a state, was submitted to a vote of the people of Kansas. They could vote for the constitution "with slavery" or "without slavery." But "without slavery" meant those slaves already in Kansas and their descendants would remain slaves. There was no way to create a free Kansas. Most antislavery voters ignored the election; proslavery voters approved the constitution "with slavery" by an overwhelming margin. President Buchanan recommended its acceptance, but Congress rejected this Lecompton fraud.

Lee, Richard Henry (1732–1794) He was best known for having introduced the resolution on June 7, 1776, in the Second Continental Congress calling for a declaration of independence from Britain. Congress approved the resolution and appointed a committee of five (including Thomas Jefferson) to draft the declaration. As a member of the Virginia House of Burgesses, Lee had opposed the Sugar Act of 1764. He originated the plan (with Patrick Henry and Thomas Jefferson) in 1773 for committees of correspondence among the colonies. He was president of Congress (1784–85), opposed ratification of the Constitution by Virginia, and was influential in securing a Bill of Rights to the Constitution.

Lee, Robert Edward (1807–1870) He graduated from the U.S. Military Academy at West Point (1829), served in the Mexican War (1846–48) and was Superintendent of West Point (1852–53). He declined Lincoln's offer to command the U.S. Army at the outbreak of the Civil War and chose to command the armies of Virginia. Lee became commander of the Confederate army of northern Virginia and in the final phases of the war was commander of all Confederate forces. Despite skillful use of his forces, he was finally overwhelmed by Grant and signed surrender papers at Appomattox Court House in Virginia on April 9, 1865. He served as the president of Washington University, renamed Washington and Lee University, in Lexington, Virginia (1865–70).

Lehman, Herbert H. (1878–1963) Member of the New York banking firm of Lehman Brothers, he became lieutenant governor of New York (1928–32) and governor (1932–42). A New Deal Democrat, he sponsored liberal social legislation in New York, including a labor relations act, a minimum wage law, and an unemployment insurance statute. He filled a one-year unexpired term as U.S. senator from New York (1950–51) and was elected to a full six-year term (1951–57). In the Senate he was an outspoken foe of McCarthyism and challenged the senator from Wisconsin to prove his allegation of communists in the State Department. Despite Lehman's close personal and political association with Roosevelt, he openly opposed the latter's "court-packing proposal" as not in the best interest of our system of government. From 1943 to 1946 Lehman served as the first director of the U.N. Relief and Rehabilitation Administration (UNRRA).

Confederate General Robert E. Lee.

Lend-Lease Act (1941)   Britain had reached the point where it had spent all its money and exhausted its credit, so Congress passed "An Act to Promote the Defense of the United States" (lend-lease). It permitted the president to "sell, transfer, exchange, lease, or otherwise dispose of" war equipment to any nation for use in the interests of the United States. Hitler attacked Russia three months later, whereupon lend-lease was extended to our new ally. Lend-lease was proposed by Roosevelt and approved by Congress (March 1941) despite fierce opposition by a Senate minority

Lewis and Clark Expedition (1804–1806)   President Jefferson sent Meriwether Lewis and William Clark to explore the Louisiana Territory just purchased from France. They were instructed to penetrate to the Pacific Coast. By way of the Missouri, Snake, and Columbia Rivers the expedition of about forty reached the West Coast in November 1805. Captain Robert Gray had entered the mouth of the Columbia River in 1792 and named it. Lewis and

Clark, Captain Gray, and American settlers in the area constituted our claim to Oregon, which was recognized by England with the boundary settlement made in 1846. The Lewis and Clark expedition left St. Charles, Missouri, on May 21, 1804. and arrived safely back in St. Louis on September 23, 1806. They spent the winter of 1805–06 on the Pacific Coast, having crossed the Rockies and gone well beyond the Louisiana Territory. They brought back important information about the geography of the American continent and of its native inhabitants.

The Lewis and Clark expedition on the Columbia River.

Lewis, John L. (1880–1969)   He started working in the coal mines at the age of sixteen. A gifted speaker and militant labor leader, he became legislative representative of the American Federation of Labor and president of the United Mineworkers (UMW), 1920–1960. He became vice president of the AFL in 1934 but left the following year to form the Congress of Industrial Organizations (CIO). An early supporter of President Roosevelt, he opposed him in the 1940 election and resigned from the presidency of the CIO when Roosevelt won the election. He later broke with Philip Murray, the new head of the CIO, and took the UMW out of that organization (1942). He led a national coal strike in 1946 in which the U.S. government took control of the mines but granted most of the strikers' demands.

Lexington, battle of (April 19, 1775)   The first battle of the Revolution was fought at Lexington, Massachusetts, more than a year before independence, between British troops and colonial militia ("minutemen") who held up the British march to Concord where they intended to seize military supplies of the colonial militia. During the night before the battle, Paul Revere had ridden through the countryside alerting the men, eight of whom were to die in the battle. In his "Concord Hymn," Ralph Waldo Emerson immortalized their deed by writing that they "fired the shot heard round the world."

Liberal Republicans   A faction which left the Republican Party in 1872 to support the Democratic nominee, Horace Greeley.

Liberator, The   *See* **Garrison, William Lloyd**.

Liberty Party   An antislavery, third party that nominated a presidential candidate in 1840.

Lincoln, Abraham *See* Presidents of the United States section, beginning on page 10-83.

Lincoln assassination (April 14, 1865) Lincoln sat in a theater box watching a play. The assassin, a demented actor named John Wilkes Booth, sneaked up behind and shot Lincoln once in the head at 10:15 P.M. Booth jumped to the stage, shouted "sic semper tyrannis" (thus always to tyrants) and fled to Virginia, where he was apprehended and shot. The President died at 7:30 A.M. on April 15. At the same time as the attack on Lincoln another conspirator attacked and seriously wounded Secretary of State William H. Seward in his home. Nine conspirators were caught, of whom four were hanged, four imprisoned, and one freed by the verdict of the jury.

Lincoln-Douglas debates (1858) Senator Douglas, Democrat, was running for re-election to the U.S. Senate from Illinois. Lincoln, a Republican, opposed him. The debates centered on the legal status of slavery in the territories. To win re-election, Douglas had to please an antislavery Illinois constituency, yet he could not afford to alienate southern Democrats if he was to run for President and win two years later. His **"Freeport Doctrine"** (see page 10-34) won the senatorship in 1858 and was a factor in his defeat in the presidential election of 1860. These debates brought national stature to Lincoln. At Freeport, Lincoln had asked Douglas how he could support both the Dred Scott decision and popular sovereignty. Douglas was forced to reply that slavery could not exist where local law was opposed. The South would not accept this, and the Democratic party was split.

Little Rock, Arkansas (1957) By an injunction, a state court forbade integration in the high school as a measure to prevent public disorder. A federal district court set aside the state court's injunction and re-established integration as had been ordered by the local school board. Governor Faubus called out the National Guard to "maintain order," which really meant to keep black students from entering the high school. A conference between Governor Faubus and President Eisenhower failed to resolve the issue. The President sent troops to Little Rock. The black pupils went to school, and the orders of the federal court were obeyed.

National Guard soldiers stand watch at Central High School in Little Rock, Arkansas in 1957.

Livingston, Robert R. (1746–1813) He practiced law in New York. Member of the Continental Congress, he was one of the committee of five appointed to draft the Declaration of Independence. He helped draft the Constitution of the State of New York (1777). He was chief justice of New York and in that capacity administered the oath of office to President Washington in New York City (April 30, 1789). First secretary of foreign affairs under the Articles of Confederation (1781–83), he urged ratification of the Constitution. Jefferson appointed him minister to France, where he negotiated the Louisiana Purchase (1803), giving us all the territory to the Rockies. He joined with Robert Fulton in the venture of the steamboat *Clermont*, named for Livingston's estate, and with Fulton obtained a monopoly of steam navigation on the Hudson River, which was voided by the Supreme Court in the case of *Gibbons* v. *Ogden* in 1824.

Lobbying Practice of individuals and pressure groups of seeking by various means to influence the vote of members of governmental bodies.

Locofocos A faction that gained control of the Democratic party in New York in 1835, they opposed the Bank of the United States and favored "hard money" against the paper money with which their wages were paid. Their influence was in back of the institution of the Independent Treasury System by President Van Buren. The name was given to them derisively for lighting candles with "locofoco" matches when the Tammany Democrats turned off the gaslight.

Log-rolling A practice of vote-trading by legislators in support of each other's favorite laws.

Long drive, the Before the Civil War, cattle were driven from Texas to markets in the North and West. In 1846 a herd was driven from Texas to Ohio. Two years later 500 cattle were driven across the desert and mountains to California. After the Civil War, cattle were driven north to cities on the newly built railroads: Sedalia, Missouri, Abilene, Kansas; Cheyenne, Wyoming, and Ogallala, Nebraska. The drivers were cowboys. Between 1866 and 1888 more than five million head of cattle were marketed by way of the long drive.

Longfellow, Henry Wadsworth (1807–1882) After studying foreign languages in Spain, Italy, and Germany (1826–29), he joined the faculty of Bowdoin College, his alma mater, and later Harvard. He became one of America's best known poets. Many of his works were based on history, including *Evangeline,* 1847 (native American hero); *The Courtship of Miles Standish,* 1858 (the Pilgrims); *Ballads and Other Poems,* 1841, which includes "The Village Blacksmith" and "The Wreck of the Hesperus"; and *Tales of a Wayside Inn,* 1863–94, which includes "Paul Revere's Ride."

Long, Huey Pierce (1893–1935) He traveled throughout Louisiana as a salesman (1910–14), passed the bar examination after eight months at Tulane University Law School, and was elected to the State Railroad Commission (later Public Service Commission) in 1918, 1921, and 1924, serving as chairman in 1921–26. He bought a mansion in Shreveport. He was convicted of criminal libel in 1921. He was an unsuccessful candidate for governor in 1924, but was elected governor in 1928. He was nicknamed "Kingfish." Impeached by the legislature in 1929, he barely escaped removal from office. He was elected to the U.S. Senate in 1930 but stayed on as governor for another year for political reasons. He became an open foe of President Roosevelt in 1933. He founded a national organization of political clubs called "Share the Wealth." He promised every family enough government money to buy a house, car, and radio, pensions for the old, and tuition scholarships for the young. The money was to come from the liquidation of huge fortunes. He announced his candidacy for President in August 1935. He was assassinated in the Louisiana State capitol the following month, having established a virtual dictatorship in Louisiana.

Los Angeles riots   On March 3, 1991, four white Los Angeles policemen stopped Rodney King, a black motorist, forced him to lie down, kicked him and beat him more than 50 times with their nightsticks. By chance the incident was videotaped from the window of a nearby residence. The police officers involved were easily identified on the tape shown that night on national television. King sustained a fractured skull, broken leg, and other serious injuries. Twelve days later, the four officers were indicted for assault with dangerous weapons. The Los Angeles Police Commission suspended Police Chief Daryl Gates but the City Council overruled this action and Gates refused to resign.

The ensuing trial was held in April 1992 in Simi Valley, a community made up primarily of white commuters, 45 miles from Los Angeles. Ten of the twelve jurors were white, one was Hispanic, and one Asian. After viewing the tape and listening to other evidence, the jury on April 29 rendered its verdict and acquitted the four defendants. News of the acquittal spread rapidly throughout Los Angeles and the nation. Rioting, arson, and looting engulfed the Los Angeles area from April 29 to May 4. More than 50 people were killed and 600 buildings were destroyed by fire. Damage was estimated at over $1 billion. The violence spread to other cities, including Miami, Atlanta, San Francisco, and Las Vegas. President Bush sent units of the army and marines to Los Angeles, where they remained for two weeks before order was fully restored. Police Chief Gates resigned June 26, 1992, and was replaced by Willie Williams, a black, who had been police commissioner in Philadelphia. In April 1993, a Federal jury verdict convicted two of the four police officers of civil rights violations.

Louisiana Purchase Treaty (1803)   Robert Livingston, U.S. minister to France, assisted late in the negotiations by James Monroe, arranged the terms of the treaty. The American offer to buy New Orleans was countered by Napoleon's offer to sell the whole Louisiana Territory. The United States eagerly accepted. It paid $10 million, gave assurance that Spanish subjects in Louisiana would become U.S. citizens, and agreed that eventually states from the area would enter the Union. This treaty doubled the area of the United States, guaranteed control of most of the length of the Mississippi River, and avoided having a powerful empire on the western border.

Lowell, James Russell (1819–1891)   The leading man of letters of his time, he succeeded Longfel-

low as Professor of French and Spanish at Harvard (1856–86). He had received his B.A. degree there in 1838 and his law degree two years later. Lowell contributed articles to the *National Anti-Slavery Standard.* Several volumes of poetry published in 1848 established his pre-eminence in literature. He was the first editor (1857–61) of the *Atlantic Monthly* and continued to write poetry and essays until his death. He served as minister to Spain (1877–80) and to England (1880–85).

Loyalists   Term for Americans who remained loyal to Great Britain during the Revolutionary War. The patriots called them Tories, the name of King George's staunch supporters in England. About one-third of the people in the colonies remained loyal to the king. These included rich and poor, and they were found in all the colonies, particularly in New York, New Jersey, and Georgia. Benjamin Franklin's son William, the governor of New Jersey, was a loyalist. About 80,000 loyalists left the country during the war or at its end. Many went to Canada or back to England. The British government compensated them for their loss of land and other property during the war.

***Lusitania* sunk** (1915)   On May 7 at 2 P.M. off the Irish coast, Captain Schweiger, in command of the German submarine U20, wrote in his log, "Right ahead appeared four funnels and two masts of a steamer. Clean bow-shot from 700-meter range. Shots hit starboard side right behind bridge. An unusually heavy detonation follows . . . . In the front appears the name *Lusitania* in gold letters." The ship sank in eighteen minutes with a loss of 1198 of its 1924 passengers and crew on board. This catastrophe, which took 128 American lives, aroused strong anti-German feeling in the United States. The *Lusitania* was a British passenger liner, carrying troops and munitions as well as American civilians. The sinking was used by pro-British propagandists to turn American opinion against Germany.

Lyon, Mary (1797–1849)   She attended seminaries (high schools) in Amherst and Ashfield, Massachusetts and was a teacher (1831–34). She devoted herself to establishing a school for girls of moderate means (1834–37). She opened Mount Holyoke Female Seminary (later Mount Holyoke College) at South Hadley, Massachusetts (1837). Mount Holyoke is the oldest continuing college for women in the United States. Mary Lyon was its first president (1837–49). Under her leadership the college offered an academic program similar to that offered at men's colleges, such as Amherst. Most of the early graduates became teachers in the United States and abroad.

M **MacArthur, Douglas** (1880–1964)   He graduated from the U.S. Military Academy in 1903, served in the Philippines (1903–04) and in Japan (1905–06), was aide-de-camp to President Theodore Roosevelt (1906–07), and commanded the Forty-second (Rainbow) Division in World War I and was twice wounded in action. He became superintendent of West Point as brigadier general in 1920. He served in the Philippines (1922–30). He was chief of staff (1930–35). He retired from the U.S. Army (1937) but was recalled for active duty (July 1941) as commander of U.S. forces in the Far East. He resisted the Japanese in the Philippines. He was ordered to

General Douglas MacArthur.

escape to Australia, saying "I shall return," which he did as supreme allied commander of forces in the Southwest Pacific. As a five-star general, he accepted the surrender of the Japanese forces on the deck of the battleship *Missouri* on September 2, 1945. He commanded the occupational forces in Japan (1945–51) He was supreme commander of U.S. forces in the Korean War (1950–51) until he was removed by President Truman on April 10, 1951.

Macon's Bill (1810)   This was the third attempt (*See* **Embargo**; **Non-Intercourse Act**) to force England and France to respect the rights of neutrals on the high seas. All embargoes were lifted. With the nation (either England or France) that stopped molesting our shipping, we would continue trading; but, after ninety days, we would reimpose an embargo on the other nation. France (Napoleon) repealed its restrictions, but England continued to enforce its orders in council against neutral shipping. This situation brought the United States much closer to the War of 1812.

Madison, James   *See* Presidents of the United States section, beginning on page 10-83.

Manifest destiny   The phrase was first used in advocating the annexation of Texas in 1845. It meant that it was the God-given mission of the United States to occupy all the territory from the Atlantic to the Pacific. The phrase achieved national currency and was repeated in connection with the acquisition of the territory won from Mexico in the 1846–48 war and of the Oregon Territory in the Northwest.

Mann-Elkins Act (1910)   The act extended the authority of the Interstate Commerce Commission to include telephone, telegraph, and cable communication. It also made more effective the enforcement of the long-short-haul clause of the original Interstate Commerce Act of 1887.

Marbury v. Madison (1803)   Federalist "midnight" appointee Marbury asked the Supreme Court for a writ of mandamus that would order Republican Secretary of State Madison to give him his commission as a justice of the peace. Federalist President John Adams had approved this commission, but it had not been delivered to Marbury. Federalist Chief Justice Marshall found the provision of the Judiciary Act of 1789 authorizing such a writ to be unconsti-

tutional because it extended the original jurisdiction of the Court as set in the Constitution. Marbury failed to get his job, but a Federalist judge established a precedent for judicial review of the laws of Congress—a battle won by Republicans but a war won by Federalists.

Marshall, George Catlett (1880–1959) Graduate of Virginia Military Institute (VMI) in Lexington, Virginia, where his memorial library is now located, he served with the First Army in France during World War I and was appointed chief of staff of armed forces (1939–45) and five-star general (1944). He supervised Allied strategy in World War II. He was ambassador to China in 1945 and secretary of state (1947–49). He proposed the Marshall Plan in a commencement address at Harvard (June 1947) to rescue Europe from economic chaos (*see* **Marshall Plan**). It was approved by Congress in 1948. He formulated the Truman Doctrine (1947) for aid to Greece and Turkey and any other nation "resisting attempted subjugation by armed minorities or by outside pressures." He served as secretary of defense (1950–51) and was awarded the Nobel Prize for Peace (1953).

Marshall, John (1755–1835)   He served as an officer in the War of Independence, practiced law in Richmond, Virginia, was a member of Congress 1789–1800, and was appointed by John Adams to chief justiceship of the U.S. Supreme Court, a position he held for thirty-four years (1801–35). A Federalist, he helped, by his decisions, to strengthen the power of the federal government. In *Marbury* v. *Madison* (1803), he established the principle of judicial review of acts of Congress by federal courts.

Marshall Plan (1947)   The plan set up a committee on European economic cooperation to plan "political and social conditions in which free institutions can exist." Twenty-two nations meeting in Paris considered the offer of the United States to underwrite a receivership for war-devastated Europe. Russia denounced the idea as an "imperialistic plot." Sixteen nations joined this European Recovery Plan (ERP). Four years and $17 billion later, a once prostrate Western Europe, ripe for absorption into the communist orbit, had been transformed into prosperous nations with representative governments, many of them members of NATO.

Maryland Religious Toleration Act (1649) Lord Cecil Calvert, the second Lord Baltimore, acquired a charter in 1632 from King Charles I to found Maryland. Jesuit missionaries and many Catholics were among the early settlers, which made Maryland the most Catholic of the English colonies. Friction between Catholics and Anglicans coupled with boundary disputes with Virginia were ever-present problems. In 1649 the Religious Toleration Act granted freedom of religion to all who believed in the Trinity. This attempt to subdue Catholic-Protestant friction had little effect. In 1654 the Toleration Act was repealed.

Mason and Dixon line   The boundary line between Pennsylvania and Maryland drawn by two English surveyors, Charles Mason and Jeremiah Dixon, whose work (1763–69) settled a boundary dispute between the two states. The line was extended in 1784 to become the northern boundary of Delaware and western Virginia. The Mason and

Dixon line and the Ohio River came to be recognized as the dividing line between slave and free territory. It is still referred to as the line separating North and South. Technically, the line was 39° 43'26.3" north latitude.

Maximilian affair   Emperor Napoleon III attempted to set up a French empire in Mexico during the Civil War in violation of the Monroe Doctrine and over the protests of the United States. He placed the Archduke Ferdinand Maximilian on the throne in Mexico in 1864. At the end of the Civil War, U.S. troops were dispatched to the Mexican border, while the Mexicans, led by Benito Juarez, took steps to regain control over their country. Napoleon III withdrew his troops, the hapless Maximilian foolishly decided to remain in Mexico and was captured and executed (1867).

Mayflower Compact   An agreement aboard the ship *Mayflower* in 1620 by the Pilgrim settlers at Plymouth, it pledged colonists to abide by the democratic principle of majority rule.

McCarran Act (1951)   This act was also called the Internal Security Act. It required communist and communist-front organizations to register with the attorney general. Their members could not become citizens and, if already citizens, could be denaturalized in five years. They were also subject to special restrictions of employment by defense industries and government. The law passed over President Truman's veto. Vague terms, such as "communist front," made court interpretation difficult and enforcement uneven. In retrospect the law appeared more futile than wise and also seemed to reflect a bit of hysteria.

McCarran-Walters Act (1952)   The act modified the 1929 quota formula by including Asians. It left national origin as the basic factor of selection. Procedures were established to prevent entrance into the United States of subversives, particularly those connected with communist or communist-front organizations.

McCarthyism   A term designating ruthless, reckless, and unfair charges , like those used by Senator Joseph McCarthy, against one's enemies.

McClellan, George B. (1826–1885)   Graduated from West Point (1846), he resigned from the army (1857) to do engineering work for the railroads. He returned to the army as major general in Ohio. He served in the East, 1861–62, but was removed from command for being too cautious. He ran for president as a Democrat against Lincoln in 1864. He resided in Europe 1864–68. He was chief engineer of the New York City Department of Docks (1870–72) and governor of New Jersey (1878–81).

McCormick, Cyrus Hall (1809–1884)   He designed and developed the agricultural reaper at his farm near Walnut Grove, Virginia, which is now a national museum. He made improvements in the reaper (1832–40) and set up his own manufacturing plant at Chicago (1847), introducing modern methods of production and distribution, including labor-saving devices, mass production, deferred payments, advertising testimonials, and field trials. The widespread introduction of the McCormick reaper revolutionized American agriculture.

McCulloch v. Maryland (1819)   Cashier McCulloch of the branch of the Second Bank of the United States located in Baltimore refused to pay a state tax levied with intent to force the bank out of business. The case came before the Supreme Court, which ruled that Congress had the power to establish the Bank of the United States, and therefore any state law threatening its effectiveness or existence was in violation of Article VI of the Constitution. This article directs judges to declare null and void any state law contrary to a law made in pursuance of the Constitution of the United States. Marshall's decision strengthened the federal government.

McKinley assassinated (1901)   An anarchist under the delusion that he had a mission to kill "Czar McKinley" shot the President on September 6. The tragedy occurred at the Pan-American Exposition in Buffalo, New York. McKinley died September 14. Czolgosz, an American citizen, was electrocuted.

McKinley, William   *See* Presidents of the United States section, beginning on page 10-83.

Meat Inspection Act (1906)   The secretary of agriculture was authorized to order meat inspection at abattoirs and meat-packing establishments and condemn any found unfit for human consumption. The act was supported by President Theodore Roosevelt and by a public that was outraged by the disclosures contained in Upton Sinclair's novel *The Jungle*, published in 1906, depicting the marketing of poisoned and refuse-ridden foods.

Mercantilism   The prevailing economic theory applied in Europe during colonial times; called for the exercise of numerous economic powers and controls by the state, contrasts with later economic philosophy of laissez-faire or free enterprise.

Merit system   The civil service system by which public employees are chosen upon a basis of qualifications rather than by political influence.

Mexican War (1846–1848)   U.S. expansionists' desire to acquire California from Mexico and Mexico's resentment at U.S. annexation of Texas (1845) broke out into armed conflict over the territory between the Nueces and Rio Grande Rivers in 1846. President Polk had dispatched American forces to the disputed territory under General Taylor. Another army under General Stephen W. Kearny headed for California, where forces under Captain John C. Frémont overthrew Mexican rule. A third army under General Winfield Scott moved on Mexico City from the coastal port of Veracruz. By the ensuing Treaty of Guadalupe-Hidalgo (February 2, 1848), the United States acquired about one-half of Mexico, including Texas and California, and agreed to pay Mexico $15 million plus assuming $3,250,000 in claims of American citizens against Mexico.

Missile Crisis in Cuba (1962)   On October 22, President Kennedy announced that Russia had placed intermediate-range ballistic missiles and jet bombers in Cuba. He demanded their removal and placed an air-sea blockage around Cuba. Five days later Khrushchev agreed to the removal on condition that the United States would not invade Cuba. Kennedy accepted this condition provided the United States could have on-site inspection to verify removal of the bombs. The blockade continued while the missiles and planes were removed, but on-site inspection was not allowed. This confrontation seemed perilously close to nuclear war.

Missile gap This term was much used in the early 1960s to refer to the alleged lag in American missile development and production compared with that of Russia.

Missouri Compromise (1820) Maine and Missouri entered the Union as a free and a slave state, respectively. The Louisiana Territory south of 36°30' was made slave, north of it, except Missouri, free. Representative Tallmadge proposed restrictions on slavery in Missouri that, although not adopted, started heated debate. Southern congressmen claimed Congress could not attach conditions when admitting states; Northern congressmen claimed it could. This sectional difference over slavery was a political issue that was not yet entangled with moral concepts. It aroused no significant public attention, but to Congressman Cobb of Georgia it foreshadowed "a fire that only seas of blood could extinguish."

The famous Civil War battle of the *Monitor* and the *Merrimac*.

Molly Maguires A secret, criminal labor organization operating in the anthracite coal fields of Pennsylvania in the 1870s, it was eventually suppressed.

Monitor and Merrimac (March 9, 1862) The Confederate navy had rebuilt the former Union warship *Merrimac* and renamed it *Virginia*. The vessel, now equipped with a powerful ram and an iron coat, sailed out of Norfolk on March 8, 1862, and made directly for the federal squadron at Hampton Roads. Before the day was over the ram had sunk the U.S.S. *Cumberland*, forced the U.S.S. *Congress* into shallow water, where it was stranded, and forced its surrender, and drove the U.S.S. *Minnesota* ashore. The next morning *Virginia (Merrimac)* was suddenly confronted by a new type of fighting ship, *Monitor*, an ironclad vessel with a revolving turret designed for the Union navy by the Swedish naval engineer John Ericson. The two ships slugged it out for two hours. *Virginia* returned to port never to fight again. *Monitor* became a prototype for many similar ships. It went down in a gale in the Atlantic after the war.

Monroe Doctrine (1823) British Foreign Secretary George Canning suggested that the United States join England in telling European powers not to colonize further in Central and South America. Secretary of State John Quincy Adams advised President Monroe to accept the idea but to announce it as an independent American policy. On December 2, President Monroe stated in his annual message that interference by a European power with the independence of a republic in the Western Hemisphere would be an "unfriendly" act. At the same time he said it was a policy of the United States not to interfere with the internal affairs of European nations. Monroe's message also warned the European powers that the United States would consider it "dangerous to our peace and safety" if they were to attempt "to extend their system to any portion of this hemisphere."

Monroe, James *See* Presidents of the United States section, beginning on page 10-83.

Montevideo Conference (1933) A Pan-American Conference at Montevideo, Uruguay, where President Roosevelt declared his opposition to armed intervention in inter-American affairs.

Monticello The home Jefferson designed and built is situated on a mountaintop overlooking Charlottesville, Virginia. It is owned and operated as a patriotic shrine by the Thomas Jefferson Memorial Foundation and is open to the public. Jefferson's grave at Monticello is marked by a tombstone on which is engraved the inscription he wrote: "Here was buried Thomas Jefferson, author of the Declaration of American Independence, of the Statute of Virginia for Religious freedom and father of the University of Virginia." Jefferson was the founder, architect, and builder of the buildings of the University of Virginia, also located at Charlottesville. President Bill Clinton, whose middle name is Jefferson, symbolically began his bus trip at Monticello to his inauguration.

Morrill Land Grant Act (1862) The act gave to each state the proceeds from the sale of 30,000 acres of public land for each member it had in Congress. The money went to support vocational college courses in agriculture and the mechanical arts. In some instances established colleges added these vocational courses, but in most cases new colleges were founded.

Morris, Robert (1734–1806) He came to America from England at the age of thirteen and became a successful merchant in Philadelphia. A member of the Continental Congress (1775–78) and signer of the Declaration of Independence, he served as superintendent of finance during the War of Independence. As a delegate to the Constitutional Convention (1787), he supported a strong national government. He was senator from Pennsylvania (1789–95). He lost his fortune in land speculation and was in a debtor's prison in Philadelphia (1798–1801).

Morse, Samuel Finley Reese (1791–1872) He went to London to study painting (1811–15) and returned to Boston, then went to Charleston and New York working as a portrait painter and was president (1826–42) of the National Academy of Design, which he helped found. He began to experiment with electricity as a means of transmitting signals. He devised the code of dots and dashes that became known as the Morse code. He received an appropriation from Congress of $30,000 in 1834 to construct a telegraph line from Washington, D.C., to Baltimore. It was over this line in 1844 that his message "what hath God wrought" was successfully transmitted using the Morse code. His telegraph played an important role in communications during the Civil War.

HISTORY OF THE UNITED STATES

Muckrakers   A nickname given by Theodore Roosevelt to journalists who actively exposed, after 1900, the wrongdoings of big business. The so-called muckrakers included such famous writers as Ida M. Tarbell, Lincoln Steffens, and Upton Sinclair.

Mugwumps   Reform Republicans who supported Cleveland in the election of 1884, they considered themselves too good to support the regular Republican candidate James G. Blaine so they were derisively dubbed "mugwumps," a native American word meaning "great man."

Muscle Shoals Bill   A measure introduced in 1928 and 1931 by Senator George Norris of Nebraska providing for federal operation of the dam at Muscle Shoals, Alabama, for the production of low-cost fertilizer, the project was finally realized in 1933 through the creation of the TVA. The bill. vetoed by Coolidge in 1928 and by Hoover in 1931, was approved as the Tennessee Valley Authority by President Franklin Roosevelt in 1933.

N **Nast, Thomas** (1840–1902)   A political cartoonist, he exposed the corruption of the Tweed Ring (Tammany Hall) in New York City. He used the elephant to represent the Republican party, the donkey for the Democratic party, and the vicious tiger for Tammany. His effective use of the cartoon to demolish his target added the word *nasty* to the English language.

National Banking Act (1863)   The act had as an immediate purpose the raising of money for the Civil War by supplying a ready market for government bonds. Banks buying U.S. bonds received bank notes, paper currency, up to 90 percent of the value of the bonds. Banks purchasing bonds under this law had to have one-third of their capital in such bonds. The act taxed state bank notes out of existence and thus ended much of the chaos in the currency system. Even with many modifications, however, this system was never satisfactory. It was replaced by the Federal Reserve System in 1913.

National Banking Crisis (1933)   On March 5, the day after his inauguration, Franklin D. Roosevelt declared a four-day bank holiday that stopped all activities of the Federal Reserve System and other banks, loan associations, and credit unions. Most such institutions had been closed a day or two earlier through the action of several state governors. On March 9, Congress passed the Emergency Banking Relief Act, which confirmed the "bank holiday" and provided for reopening of the banks as soon as examiners found them sound. Over 5000 banks opened within three days. Almost all banks were solvent, and those that were not were reorganized.

National Defense Education Act (1958)   The act provided about $575,000,000 for educational purposes. In many cases federal funds were available to institutions only when matched by state funds. Some of the grants provided loans of up to $1000 to college students at 3 percent interest; fellowships for graduate students planning to teach; grants to schools and colleges for facilities required in the science and language fields; and grants for the use of movies, radio, and television for teaching purposes.

National Labor Relations Board   This is the agency created in 1935 under the Wagner Act to administer laws affecting labor-management relations in interstate commerce. The two main functions of the Board are to prevent unfair labor practices and to determine employee representation in collective bargaining. The board was created by the National Labor Relations Act (known as the Wagner Act).

National Organization for Women (NOW)   This organization was founded by Betty Friedan in 1966. Her book, *The Feminine Mystique*, published in 1963, was the opening gun in the modern militant women's liberation movement. A "women's strike for equality" was organized by NOW as a nationwide movement, resorting to strikes, boycotts, and demonstrations in the 1960s and 1970s to attain equality with men in all aspects of life.

Deep-rooted resentments came to the surface as the "women's liberation" movement gained momentum. Women sought equal pay for equal work, equal opportunity for promotion, the right to maternity leave without loss of job or seniority, advancement to positions of responsibility and authority in government, in industry, and in the professions, recognition of the value of work in the home, participation of men in the duties and responsibilities traditionally performed by women, recognition in textbooks of women's role in history, and a more positive image in the media to replace the traditional sex symbol.

NOW has continued to agitate for women's rights, particularly for the adoption of the Equal Rights Amendment. The organization, headed by Molly Yard in 1989, includes both women and men in its membership. Its agenda comprises a broad spectrum of social reforms including affordable child care, lesbian and gay rights, pay equity, keeping abortion and birth control legal, greater research on women's diseases such as breast cancer, and reducing military expenditures.

National Recovery Administration (1933)   The National Industrial Recovery Act (NIRA) mobilized business and labor to restore prosperity. Under General Hugh Johnson hundreds of codes, each for a different type of business, were written. Most businesses joined this voluntary program and displayed the NRA symbol, the Blue Eagle. After some initial success, this gigantic "planned economy" bogged down in red tape and disorder. In 1935 the Supreme Court (*Scheckter* v. *United States*) declared the NRA unconstitutional because it invaded spheres restricted to states, gave legislative powers to the code makers, and unreasonably stretched the commerce clause of the Constitution. The act provided for a National Recovery Administration (NRA).

NATO, *See* **North Atlantic Pact.**

Navigation Acts   Laws enacted by the British Parliament to implement the mercantilist theory of government control over economic relations between mother country and colonies.

Neutrality Acts (1935–1939) *1935 Neutrality Act* This was a reaction to Italy's attack upon Ethiopia. It provided that, after the president formally recognized that a war was in progress, American citizens could not sell arms to belligerents.

1937 Neutrality Acts The Spanish conflict broke out in July 1936, but the previous neutrality laws did not apply to civil wars. So in January 1937, Congress placed an embargo on munitions to either side. This was a strange action. The normal procedure would have been to continue trade as usual with the government of Spain, in this case the Loyalists, and ignore the rebels unless and until they won the war. This embargo kept munitions from the Loyalists while the rebels got massive help from Germany and Italy. Our action was not only irregular, but against our own interests. In May, another neutrality act gave the President discretion in the use of embargoes and forbade travel by U.S. citizens on ships of belligerents. This act was aimed at the renewed Sino-Japanese conflict.

Revision of 1939 This was a "cash-and-carry" plan. All embargoes were lifted so that any ships could come to American ports, pay cash, and carry away anything they could buy. Here, finally, was a "neutrality" law that served our purposes. The British and French had control of the seas so their merchant marines enjoyed a near monopoly of this cash-and-carry trade. This was America's first step toward becoming the "arsenal of democracy."

New Deal Franklin D. Roosevelt promised a New Deal to people suffering from an unprecedented economic depression. Upon his election to the presidency, Roosevelt moved swiftly to fulfill his promise. Almost every aspect of the nation's economic, social, and political life was transformed or regenerated. The physical rehabilitation of the country was undertaken through the Civilian Conservation Corps (CCC), the Tennessee Valley Authority (TVA), and the Soil Conservation Service. Relief for the unemployed came through the Public Works Administration (PWA), the Work Progress Administration (WPA), and the National Youth Administration (NYA). The Agricultural Adjustment Act (AAA), the National Industrial Recovery Act (NIRA), the National Labor Relations Act (NLRA), the Federal Deposit Insurance Corporation (FDIC), the Social Security Act, the Securities and Exchange Commission (SEC), and other legislation from the period of 1933–39 show how pervasive the New Deal was in restructuring and rehabilitating a country suffering from economic woes.

New England Confederation (1643) The members of this first union among the colonies were Massachusetts, Plymouth, Connecticut, and New Haven. Massachusetts dominated the Confederation, whose purpose was to maintain more effective protection against the native Americans and to check encroachment by the Dutch of the Hudson River Valley. Rhode Island, despised by Puritan Massachusetts as "the Lord's debris," was not permitted to join the Confederation. The organization continued rather ineffectively until 1684.

New Harmony In 1825, Robert Owen, an English industrialist turned philanthropist and socialist, established New Harmony in Indiana. By late 1825 about 1000 men, women, and children were ready to try a utopian socialist economy. Their constitution, in effect by February 1826, provided equal ownership of property, equal obligation of labor, freedom of speech, and freedom of action. Lack of effective central authority and emphasis on freedom of individual action produced chaos akin to anarchy. In fifteen months the social-economic experiment collapsed. Most other similar well-intentioned experimental communities slid down the same path to failure.

Newlands Reclamation Act (1902) The act provided that money from the sale of semiarid public lands in sixteen western states be used for constructing and maintaining irrigation projects. The irrigated land was to be sold to settlers on a ten-year payment plan, and the income from such sales was to expand the projects by transforming semiarid grazing land worth a few cents an acre into citrus, sugar beet, and vegetable farms worth hundreds of dollars per acre.

New Netherland Under Peter Stuyvesant this Dutch colony with its government at New Amsterdam had been plagued by wars with the native Americans. Tariff and boundary disputes with the English aggravated the general adverse economic conditions throughout the colony. When the English sailed into the harbor on a mission of conquest in 1664, Director-General Peter Stuyvesant could organize no resistance. He surrendered to the Duke of York, and New Amsterdam became New York.

New Orleans, Jackson's victory (1815) On January 8 a force of over 7500 troops under General Sir Edward Pakenham made a frontal attack against about 7000 men under General Andrew Jackson. Withering cannon fire won decisively for the Americans, whose losses in killed and wounded were 71 compared with 2000 for the British. The Treaty of Ghent, ending the War of 1812, was signed December 24, 1814, but the news had not reached the United States by the time the battle of New Orleans was fought.

Nixon, Richard M. *See* Presidents of the United States beginning on page 10-83, and page 10-78.

Non-Intercourse Act (1809) This act, passed a few days before the end of Jefferson's second term, lifted all embargoes on American shipping except those bound for French and British ports. A slight increase in U.S. shipping resulted, but there was no modification of the violation of American rights on the high seas.

Norris, George William (1861–1944) He grew up on a small farm in Ohio, studied law in Indiana, and practiced in Nebraska. He was a judge (1896–1902), in the House of Representatives (1903–13), and senator from Nebraska (1913–43). He advocated a graduated income tax and conservation. He opposed U.S. entry into World War I but supported entry into World War II. A Republican, he supported Franklin D. Roosevelt in 1932, 1936, and 1940. He supported the New Deal agricultural acts. He saw his bill, the Norris-LaGuardia Anti-injunction Act, enacted into law in 1932, a major victory for organized labor. He was the major force in the enactment of the Twentieth (Lame Duck) Amendment to the Constitution in 1932. He shepherded the Tennessee Valley Authority (TVA) Act through the Senate.

Norris-LaGuardia Anti-Injunction Act (1932) The act restricted the use of court injunctions in labor disputes; outlawed the yellow dog contract in which a worker agreed, as a condition of employment, not to join a union; and declared it to be a public policy that labor have the right to organize and bargain collectively without interference by employers.

North Africa Campaign (1942) In June the Germans took Tobruk, thus threatening Alexandria and the Suez Canal. Operation Torch was planned as an Anglo-American offensive to be launched by October. British forces fought westward from El Alamein while Anglo-American forces landing at Oran, Algiers, and just west of Tunis squeezed the Germans onto Cape Bon, where 275,000 surrendered on May 7, 1943. U.S. Generals Patton and Bradley with England's Field Marshal Montgomery under the command of Eisenhower carried Operation Torch to success over the brilliantly fought campaign of the German General Rommel.

North Atlantic Pact (1949) The pact set up NATO (the North Atlantic Treaty Organization) a strictly military alliance, to "secure the principles of democracy, personal freedom, and political liberty." Its immediate purpose was to discourage Russia from aggressive action in Western Europe. Sole possession of the atom bomb by the United States helped buy time required for the Marshall Plan to succeed and NATO to develop. Twelve nations formed NATO in April; later three others joined (Belgium, Britain, Canada, Denmark, France, Greece, Iceland, Italy, Luxembourg, the Netherlands, Norway, Portugal, Turkey, West Germany, and the United States). General Eisenhower was NATO's first commander.

Northern Securities Case (1904) J. P. Morgan, James J. Hill, and W. Averell Harriman merged their railroads into the Northern Securities Company, which served the northwest quarter of the United States. By a 5 to 4 vote the Supreme Court declared the merger violated the Sherman Anti-trust act. The railroads claimed that the merger would result in lower costs and better service. If this merger were legal, the Court reasoned, it would also be legal for one company to operate all the railroads of the United States. Such a private monopoly they contemplated as intolerable.

Northwest Ordinance (1787) The Land Ordinances of 1784 and 1785 set a precedent for admitting new states. The area almost enclosed by the Great Lakes and the Mississippi and Ohio rivers was surveyed into townships 6 miles square. One section (1 square mile) in each township was reserved to support public education. Slavery was prohibited. Trial by jury and freedom of worship were guaranteed. Most important of all, new states were to enter the Union on an equal basis with the original thirteen. Between 1803 and 1848, Ohio, Indiana, Illinois, Michigan, and Wisconsin became states.

NRA *See* **National Recovery Administration**.

Nuclear Test Ban Treaty (1963) The treaty, ratified by the Senate 80 to 19, specified that the signers (United States of America, USSR, and Great Britain) will not conduct a nuclear test in the atmosphere, in space, or underwater. Tests underground were not banned since there was no way to detect them without an inspection system and the parties could not agree on an inspection system. Over a hundred nations signed the treaty, not including the nuclear powers France and China.

Nullification Ordinance (1832) Following the logic of the Kentucky Resolution as expanded by Hayne and Calhoun, South Carolina nullified the Tariff of 1832. All protective tariffs, claimed South Carolina, were unconstitutional because they were taxes not intended to "pay the debts," "provide for the common defense,"or "provide for the general welfare."

Nuremberg War Crimes Trials (1945–1946) A series of trials of twenty-two leading Nazis accused of committing crimes against the laws of war and humanity and plotting aggressions contrary to treaty pledges. Associate Justice Robert H. Jackson of the U.S. Supreme Court was a special prosecutor at the trials. Nineteen of the accused were convicted: twelve were sentenced to be hanged and seven to jail terms.

Nye Committee (1934) The committee investigated the munitions industry as it operated during World War I. Manufacturers of armaments and the banks that financed them made large profits as they sold to all nations, thus stimulating armament races among them. These "merchants of death" were charged with having used pressure to get the United States into World War I. The Nye Committee findings strengthened the influences of isolationists during the middle 1930s, an influence reflected in the neutrality acts from 1935 to 1937. The scramble of corporations for business is probably an almost negligible factor as a cause of war.

O **Office of Price Administration (OPA)** An agency created in 1942 to administer price controls after the outbreak of World War II, it had the power to place ceilings on all prices except farm commodities and to ration scarce supplies of such goods as automobile tires, sugar, coffee, and gasoline; various other food items were rationed later.

Ohio Idea (1868) This was a proposal to redeem Civil War bonds with greenbacks. Although adopted first by the Democrats, it got lip service in the Midwest from both major parties. The issue was used for its vote-getting appeal, but neither party seriously pressed for legislation to implement this inflationary policy.

Okinawa, battle of (1945) In a major battle (March 22 to June 22, 1945), U.S. forces gained control of the large island of Okinawa, only 350 miles from the Japanese homeland. Over 100,000 Japanese, many in suicide missions, were killed in the battle, which ended in a victory for U.S. forces with losses of 11,260 killed and 33,000 wounded. Okinawa was to be a major staging area for Operations Olympic and Coronet, the invasion of Japan. The detonation of an atomic bomb over Hiroshima (August 6, 1945) and Nagasaki (August 9) forced the surrender of Japan without the invasion.

Old Hickory This is the affectionate name given to General Andrew Jackson at the battle of New Orleans by his victorious troops, January 8, 1815. *See* **New Orleans, Jackson's victory**.

Omnibus states (1889–1890) North Dakota, South Dakota, Montana, and Washington entered the Union in 1889. Idaho and Wyoming entered in 1890. These "omnibus states," with twelve senators and six representatives, made a political prize worth a political price. The Republican party paid the price; it supported the Sherman Silver Act in return for support for the McKinley Tariff.

Open Door Policy (1899)   The Opium War, 1842, started European "spheres of influence" around Chinese ports. By 1899 additional infringements on Chinese sovereignty by England, Germany, France, Russia, and Japan had occurred. America's acquisition of the Philippines stimulated its interest in Far Eastern trade. Secretary of State John Hay appealed to all nations with spheres of influence to give up their respective localized trade advantages in exchange for freedom to trade in all Chinese ports subject only to normal regulation by China. The acceptance of Hay's suggestion opened the doors (ports) of China to all nations on the same basis.

Oregon Treaty (1846)   England claimed that Canada extended as far south as the 42nd parallel; the United States claimed as far north as 54°40'. After years of agreed-upon joint occupation, the final settlement placed the boundary at the 49th parallel from the Rockies to the West Coast. Vancouver Island, which extends south of 49°, was given to Britain.

Organization of American States (OAS)   A collective defense system organized in 1947 at Rio de Janeiro by the United States and Latin America under the Rio Treaty. The charter (constitution) of the OAS was signed by the twenty-one republics of the Western hemisphere (the United States and the nations to the south) in 1948. The headquarters of the OAS is at the Pan-American Union building in Washington, D.C.

Oriental immigration stopped (1882)   By treaty the United States could "regulate, limit, or suspend" but not prohibit Chinese immigration. In 1882, Congress, in response to pressure from the Pacific Coast area, suspended for ten years the privilege of Chinese to enter the United States. Renewal of the "suspension" for another ten years however, was interpreted by China as a prohibition and therefore an insult to their people as well as a violation of the treaty agreement. *See* **Chinese Exclusion Act**.

Ostend Manifesto (1854)   Instructions from Secretary of State Marcy led to a conference at Ostend, Belgium, of Soulé, Mason, and Buchanan our ministers to Spain, France, and England, respectively. The conference brought forth a brash manifesto about Cuba. The most outrageous statement was, "But if Spain, dead to the voice of her own interest, and actuated by stubborn pride and a false sense of honor, should refuse to sell Cuba to the United States, then, by every law, human and divine, we shall be justified in wresting it from Spain...." Foreign and domestic protests resulted in Soulé's resignation and the recall of Mason and Buchanan.

Otis, James (1725–1783)   He practiced law in Massachusetts. Otis argued against the legality of writs of assistance (search warrants) used by royal customs officials in seeking to enforce the Sugar Act of 1733. He urged colonial representation in Parliament and proposed calling the Stamp Act Congress (1765) in which he participated. He was incapacitated by a blow on the head from a royal tax collector (1769).

Owen, Robert (1771–1858)   A successful textile manufacturer in England, he was concerned with the welfare of his employees. He came to the United States in 1825 and founded a utopian colony at New Harmony, Indiana, with about 1000 people. The idealistic commune broke down in chaos, failing to bring about the millennium eagerly sought by its founder.

P **Paine, Thomas** (1737–1809)   Born of Quaker parents near London and raised in poverty, he met Franklin, who gave him a letter of recommendation. He came to Philadelphia in 1774. He wrote the famous pamphlet *Common Sense* in January 1776, urging American independence. He served in the American army during the War of Independence. He returned to Europe in 1787. He wrote *The Rights of Man* (1791–92), calling for radical reforms in British government. He went to France (1792) and was imprisoned during the French Revolution. He wrote *The Age of Reason* (1794–96). He returned to America in 1802 and died in poverty.

Panama Canal   The canal across Panama permits oceangoing vessels to move between the Atlantic and Pacific Oceans without going around Cape Horn. The canal was built (1904–14) after President Theodore Roosevelt had helped Panama to gain independence from Colombia. The U.S. Army engineers, headed by George N. Goethals, constructed the canal. The right of way for the canal had been granted by Panama in the Hay-Bunau-Varilla Treaty, whereby the United States agreed to pay Panama $10 million plus a yearly rental fee for a "perpetual" lease of a 10-mile-wide strip (the Canal Zone) over which the canal was built. By treaty (1978), the United States agreed to turn the canal over to Panama on December 31, 1999, and the latter agreed to maintain the neutrality of the area. *See* **Hay-Herran Treaty**.

Pan-American Conference (1889)   Secretary of State Blaine called this conference in Washington D.C. Eighteen nations sent delegates. Blaine's purpose was to increase U.S.-Latin American commerce by reciprocal trade favors. Coffee, hides, molasses, and tea were allowed free entry to the United States as long as the nations exporting these products accepted U.S. goods free or with a moderate revenue duty. This first conference is significant as the forerunner of the Pan-American Union and the Organization of American States.

Pan-American Union   Originally the International Union of American Republics, it was organized at a meeting in Washington, D.C. (1889–90). The name was changed to the Pan-American Union in 1910. It is housed in the Pan-American Union Building in Washington D.C., where the twenty-one republics comprising the union met from time to time. In 1948 the members created the Organization of American States (OAS).

Paris, Treaty of (1763)   The treaty ended the French and Indian War (Seven Years War). Its terms put France out of North America and India: (1) England got all of Canada it had not previously taken by the Treaty of Utrecht, 1713. (2) England got all lands in North America as far west as the Mississippi River—except New Orleans. Spain gave Florida to England in exchange for Cuba, which England had taken during the war. (3) Spain got from France all land west of the Mississippi River and also New Orleans, which was on both sides of the Mississippi. (4) France was given fishing rights off Newfoundland. (5) France left India; England stayed.

Paris, Treaty of (1783)   The major provisions were as follows: (1) the independence of the United States of America was recognized, (2) the U.S. northern border was set at the St. Croix River, St. Lawrence watershed, 45th parallel, St. Lawrence River, Great Lakes to the Mississippi River, (3) the U.S. western border was fixed at the Mississippi River south to the 31st parallel; (4) the U.S. southern border was fixed along the 31st parallel from the Mississippi River to the St. Mary's River to the Atlantic Ocean; (5) Congress recommended that debts between British and Americans be valid as of before the war; and (6) Congress recommended that property confiscated from Loyalists be paid for or returned.

Paris, Treaty of (1898)   Spain accepted the terms in December 1898, and the U.S. Senate ratified the treaty in February 1899, by a vote of 57 to 27, just one vote over the required two-thirds majority. The major provisions were as follows: (1) Spain gave up all claims to Cuba; (2) Spain ceded the Philippines to the United States for $20 million; and (3) Spain ceded Puerto Rico and Guam to the United States.

Patroon   Dutch colonizers awarded large land grants in New Netherland in return for bringing settlers to America; settlers became tenants of the patroons.

Pauling, Linus (b. 1901)   Professor of chemistry and chemical engineering at California Institute of Technology (CIT) since 1931, he was awarded the Nobel Prize in Chemistry (1954) for discoveries in chemical bonding and awarded the Nobel Prize for Peace (1963) for leadership in bringing about the halting of testing nuclear weapons aboveground. Founder and director of the Linus Pauling Institute of Science and Medicine at Palo Alto, California, for research in cancer, AIDS, and other diseases he is the author of *Vitamin C and the Common Cold* (1970), *Vitamin C, the Common Cold, and the Flu* (1976), with Dr. Evan Cameron *Cancer and Vitamin C* (1979), and *How to Live Longer and Feel Better* (1986), a work on the prevention and treatment of common ailments through regular consumption of harmless food supplements.

Peace Corps   Established by Congress in 1961 at the request of President John F. Kennedy. During the first year about 3000 volunteers worked in Asian, African, and Latin American nations. Peace Corps members live with the people, sharing their standard of living. They are taught the native language. Their pay is $75 per month, deposited in the United States, and they receive traveling and living expenses. Members vary in age from 18 to over 60; however, young men and women, many college graduates, predominate. This comparatively inexpensive person-to-person program has developed good will and built the capacity for self-help in hundreds of communities.

Pearl Harbor (1941)   At 7:55 A.M. on December 7 (1:20 P.M. Washington, D.C. time), Japanese planes and submarines hit Pearl Harbor. Nineteen battleships were put out of commission, only four of

which were restored to service. About 170 U.S. planes were destroyed, most of them while on the ground. Civilian deaths were under a hundred, but servicemen killed totaled about 2400. The wounded numbered about 1300. The Japanese lost about fifty planes and three submarines. On December 8 Congress declared war by a unanimous vote in the Senate and with only one negative vote in the House.

Headline in *The New York Times* announcing the Japanese attack on Pearl Harbor on December 7, 1941.

Peary, Robert Edwin (1856–1920)   Commissioned in the U.S. Navy Corps of Engineers (1881), he explored Greenland while on leave (1886). He led a scientific expedition to Greenland (1891–92) and made a voyage to the Polar Sea (1898–1902). He made two more trips to the Polar region, being the first to reach the North Pole on April 6, 1909. The last part of the trip was made by dog-drawn sled assisted by Eskimos.

Pendleton Act (1883)   The act was the first significant attack on the spoils system. It set up a Civil Service Commission and placed about 10 percent of federal employees on the merit system. The president was empowered to add positions to the merit list. States were encouraged to pass similar legislation. The assassination by a disappointed office seeker of President Garfield in 1881 made this reform inevitable.

Perkins, Frances (1880–1965)   A member of Roosevelt's famous "brain trust," Frances Perkins was the first woman to hold a cabinet post. She became Secretary of Labor, a newly created department. It was during the New Deal period that labor began an era of great gains. With the strong support of President Roosevelt, Frances Perkins, and public opinion, landmark labor legislation was passed, such as the Wagner (National Labor Relations) Act, the Social Security Act, and the Fair Labor Standards Act. Perkins also served under President Truman as a member of the Civil Service Commission (1946–53).

Perot, H. Ross (b. 1930)   Born in Texas, Perot graduated from the U.S. Naval Academy at Annapolis. He founded Electronic Data Systems in 1962 and sold it in 1984 for $2.4 billion. He ran for president as an independent in 1992, receiving 19 percent of the popular vote but no electoral votes. During the campaign, Perot focused on the federal budget deficit and on the need to reform election financing. He promised, if elected, to step down after serving one term. *See* **Election of 1992**.

Perry, Commodore Matthew C. (1794–1858)   In 1853 and again in 1854, Perry displayed naval strength and diplomatic skill to reverse Japan's policy of isolation. U.S. battleships in Tokyo Bay and discussions with the emperor yielded a treaty

(Kanagawa) providing for the proper treatment of shipwreck victims, trade, and facilities for provisioning foreign ships. This marks the beginning of Japan's modernization and its rise as a dominant power in Asia.

Perry, Oliver H. (1785–1819) He served in the Naval War with France (1797–99) and in the Mediterranean (1802–18) against Tripoli. During the War of 1812 he was in command of naval forces on Lake Erie, where he defeated the British fleet (1813) and sent General William Henry Harrison the oft-quoted message: "We have met the enemy and they are ours." For this important victory he received the thanks of Congress and was acclaimed a national hero.

Pershing, John J. (1860–1948) His lifelong career with the U.S. Army commenced at his graduation from West Point (1886), where he taught military tactics (1897–98). He fought in wars against native Americans in the Southwest, served in the Philippines, commanded the expedition against Pancho Villa in Mexico (1916), and was appointed by President Wilson to command the American forces in France during World War I. After the war he was promoted to full general and was army chief of staff (1921–24).

Persian Gulf War In August 1990, armed forces of Iraq overran and occupied Kuwait. When President Saddam Hussein refused to pull out, U.S. armed forces were dispatched to the area in operation "Desert Shield" to help Saudi Arabia protect itself against any further Iraqi aggression. On November 29, 1991, the UN Security Council authorized the use of force if Iraq did not pull out of Kuwait by January 15, 1991. By then U.S. armed forces in the Persian Gulf area numbered nearly half a million. On January 12, the U.S. Senate, by a vote of 52–47, and the House of Representatives, by a vote of 250–183, authorized the use of U.S. armed forces to expel Iraq from Kuwait. The British Parliament and the French National Assembly followed in a few days with similar votes for the use of their troops in the Gulf.

On the night of January 16, 1991, an all-out attack led by the U.S. Air Force was launched on targets in Kuwait. French, British, Canadian, and Saudi Arabian planes participated in the attack. Token forces from 23 other nations were sent to help expel the Iraqis. The operation, labeled "Desert Storm", was supervised by General Colin Powell, chairman of the U.S. Joint Chiefs of Staff, with all Allied forces under the command of U.S. General H. Norman Schwarzkopf.

Iraq destroyed Kuwaiti oil storage facilities, causing an oil slick 60 miles long and 20 miles wide inflicting severe environmental contamination and destruction of wild life.

An Allied ground offensive involving 200,000 troops began on February 24. Iraqi resistance was much weaker than anticipated, and Allied operations were suspended on February 27. The next day Iraq announced a cease-fire. Saddam Hussein survived defeat and remains in power in Iraq.

On April 10, 1992, the Pentagon reported that Allied combat deaths in the Gulf War were approximately 220.

Philippine base closing As a result of the Spanish-American War (1898–99) the United States acquired the Philippine Islands from Spain. At Subic Bay, 42 miles from Manila, the largest overseas U.S. naval base was constructed in 1899 along with a naval air station and an air force base. When the Philippines gained their independence in 1946, (See **Tydings-McDuffie Act, 1934**), the base was leased on a renewable basis by the United States. Pressure against the lease increased as part of the world-wide movement against imperialism after World War II. The lease that expired in 1992 was not renewed by the Philippine government. In formal ceremonies November 24, 1992, the U.S. flag was lowered and the final contingent of 700 marines, of what had been a force of over 12,000 men and women, left the base.

Philippine Insurrection (1899–1902) Emilio Aguinaldo led native forces in support of Dewey's capture of Manila. He expected independence for the Philippines after the expulsion of Spain. As it became clear that rule by the United States was to replace rule by Spain, Aguinaldo became a popular and effective leader of the Filipino rebellion. Atrocities were common during the long, drawnout guerrilla warfare. Aguinaldo was captured in March 1901, but the rebellion continued for another year. Americans killed totaled over 4000 and Filipinos about 600,000.

Pierce, Franklin See Presidents of the United States section, beginning on page 10-83.

Pike, Zebulon M. (1799–1813) He led an army expedition from St. Louis into the northern part of the Louisiana territory to seek the sources of the Mississippi River (1805–06) at the same time that the Lewis and Clark party was exploring the western part. Later he explored New Mexico and Colorado, where the 14,000-foot peak in the Rocky Mountains bears his name. He was commissioned a brigadier general during the War of 1812 and was killed in an assault on York (Toronto).

Pinchot, Gifford See **Ballinger-Pinchot controversy**.

Pinckney Treaty (1795) The treaty is also called the San Lorenzo Treaty. Spain accepted the 31st parallel and St. Mary's River, set in the Treaty of Paris, 1783, as America's southern border. Free navigation of the Mississippi River and the right to deposit goods at New Orleans for transshipment without payment of duties were included. This very favorable treaty with Spain helped to soften the anger felt over the Jay Treaty with England of the same year.

Platt Amendment (1901) The amendment was incorporated by Cuba, with considerable reluctance, into its constitution. It had been prepared by the Congress of the United States and its major provisions were as follows: (1) Cuba must make no treaty endangering its independence; (2) Cuba must not borrow money beyond its capacity to repay; (3) the United States must be permitted to intervene in Cuba whenever disorder threatens "life, property, and individual liberty"; and (4) the United States may buy or lease coaling and naval stations in Cuba. In 1934 the United States abrogated all terms of the Platt Amendment except that granting the naval base established at Guantanamo.

Plessy v. Ferguson (1896)   Plessy, an "octoroon" (a person of one-eighth black ancestry), had been fined $25 for riding in the white section of a railway coach. He claimed the separation law was unconstitutional. The Supreme Court ruled that laws requiring separation of blacks and whites in public places do not imply inferiority of either race. If facilities are approximately equal, segregation does not violate the equal protection of the laws guaranteed by the Fourteenth Amendment. This judicial reasoning prevailed until reversed by *Brown* v. *Topeka Board of Education* in 1954.

Plurality   The votes polled by the leading candidate, not necessarily a majority of all votes cast.

Point Four Program (1949)   President Truman, in his inaugural address of 1949, as a fourth point in a program designed to make underdeveloped nations able to help themselves, urged extending technical know-how and capital equipment as basic to self-development. The stress was on building capacity to produce, rather than merely providing relief. This technical and economic assistance blossomed into expenditures totaling several billions and affecting scores of nations.

Polk defeated Clay (1844)   Clay and Van Buren expected to be presidential candidates on the Whig and Democratic tickets, respectively. Both publicly stated opposition to the annexation of Texas because it would excite sectional hostility over slavery and lead to war with Mexico. The Democratic convention passed over Van Buren and nominated Polk, who came out for annexing Texas and Oregon. Clay modified his stand on Texas, a shiftiness that dampened enthusiasm among his supporters. James Birney, Liberty party nominee, cut Clay's vote in New York and Michigan so that Polk became the first "dark horse" candidate to win the presidency.

Polk, James K.   *See* Presidents of the United States section, beginning on page 10-83.

"Popular sovereignty"   The solution offered by Douglas to the controversy over slavery in the territories, it proposed to leave the decision regarding slavery to the residents of the territory.

Populist party organized (1891)   Surpluses of cereal crops, cotton, and silver forced agrarian and mining communities into poverty. A People's party (Populists) was organized to protest this "suffering amidst plenty" about which the two major parties were silent. In 1892 the Populist presidential candidate, James B. Weaver, got over one million votes and twenty-two electoral votes. Their platform blamed "governmental injustice" for breeding "two great classes—tramps and millionaires." This famous Omaha Platform foreshadowed future changes by advocating a graduated income tax, direct election of senators, eight-hour working day, Australian ballot, extension of the merit system, and restriction of immigration.

Portsmouth, Treaty of (1905)   Negotiations to end the Russo-Japanese War appealed to Russia, which was faced with revolution, and to Japan, whose victories in war had endangered its financial stability. They accepted President Theodore Roosevelt's invitation to confer at Portsmouth, New Hampshire. The settlement gave Japan control of Korea, Manchuria, and the Laiotung Peninsula and also possession of the southern half of the island of Sakhalin. Japan was denied its demand for a huge cash indemnity. The peacemaker, Roosevelt, got the ill will of both Japan and Russia, but was awarded the Nobel Peace Prize in 1906.

Potsdam Conference (1945)   President Truman, Churchill (later replaced by Attlee), and Stalin met six weeks after Germany's surrender. The decisions made included the following: (1) "unconditional surrender" to be demanded of Japan; (2) peace treaties to be arranged with Austria, Bulgaria, Finland, Hungary, and Rumania; (3) a tribunal to be established to try war criminals; (4) Germans in Czechoslovakia, Hungary, and Poland to be deported to Germany; and (5) Germany's economy to be kept primarily agricultural. During this conference Truman got word that an atom bomb had been successfully tested. Hiroshima was destroyed four days after the conference adjourned.

Powderly, Terence Vincent (1849–1924)   Railroad worker and machinist, he joined the Knights of Labor and became president of the Knights in 1879. Membership grew rapidly from 9000, reaching a peak of 700,000 in 1886. Elected on the Greenback-Labor party ticket to three terms as mayor of Scranton, Pennsylvania (1878–84), he opposed strikes and favored arbitration. He joined the Republican party and became immigration commissioner (1897–1902). He also served in the Labor Department (1921–24).

Powell, John Wesley (1834–1902)   He enlisted in the Union army and lost his right arm at the battle of Shiloh. He was a professor of geology and a museum curator. He was the first white man to explore the Green and Colorado Rivers, a 900-mile journey, as leader of an expedition (1869). He made further explorations (1871–75) and served as director of the U.S. Geological Survey (1880–94). He was head of the Bureau of Ethnology for the Smithsonian Institution from 1879 to 1902.

Presidential Succession Act (1947)   The act fixed the succession to the presidency from vice president to Speaker of the House, to temporary chairman of the Senate, to cabinet heads in order of the seniority of the departments. Critics of this order point out that a Speaker of the House is frequently not of the same party as the late president and vice president and also that the House would soon elect another speaker, thus raising the question whether he (or she) or the temporary chairman of the Senate was next in line. The Twenty-fifth Amendment to the Constitution (1967) provides for succession to the presidency in the case of disability of the president.

Proclamation Act (1763)   The act included a provision establishing a line from Canada to Florida along the Appalachian divide. Territory west of this line was reserved for native Americans. Pontiac's War emphasized the necessity of placating the native Americans. The colonists mistook the line as an attempt to "hem them in." There was no way to enforce observance of the line, and it did nothing to abate the westward movement of settlers. Colonials already in the Ohio Valley paid no attention to the king's order "forthwith to remove themselves."

Proprietors   English individuals or groups awarded land for settling colonists on it; the proprietor became the landlord and the settlers his tenants.

Public (elementary) schools (1647)   All Massachusetts towns of fifty families were required to provide a teacher to instruct in reading and writing. Towns of a hundred families must have a Latin grammar school. These facilities could be private or tax supported. Concern over one's ability to read the Bible was an important factor in the early development of organized education.

Public Works Administration (PWA) (1933)   The PWA, headed by Secretary of the Interior Harold L. Ickes, made contracts with private firms for the construction of public works, such as post office buildings, schools, conservation projects, power plants, bridges, dams, and aircraft carriers. Between 1933 and 1939, some $6 billion had been spent and over half a million unemployed had been put to work under the PWA.

Pulitzer, Joseph (1847–1911)   He came to the United States from Hungary in 1864, served with the Union army, studied law, and was elected to the Missouri Legislature (1869). He was police commissioner of St. Louis (1870–72). He purchased the St. Louis *Post* and the *Dispatch* and combined them (1878). He purchased the New York *World* (1883) and established the New York *Evening World* (1887). He left a $2 million bequest to Columbia University to establish a school of journalism. He also provided for annual Pulitzer Prizes for outstanding achievements in journalism, literature, history, biography, poetry, music, and related fields.

Pullman strike (1894)   A wage cut precipitated the strike, which spread from Chicago to the Pacific Coast. It was effective and orderly under the leadership of Debs, founder of the American Railway Union. In spite of protests from the mayor of Chicago and the governor of Illinois, federal troops were sent to Chicago on July 2 to enforce a federal injunction ordering Debs not to (1) obstruct the mail, (2) destroy property, or (3) direct the strike. Because Debs directed the strike—albeit to keep it peaceful—he was arrested. Subsequent violence was suppressed by federal troops. The injunction was so unfair in this situation that even conservative newspapers deplored its use.

Pure Food and Drug Act (1906)   Along with the Meat Inspection Act of the same year (prompted by disclosure of filthy and dangerous meat products in *The Jungle* by Upton Sinclair), this act provided for federal inspection of meat products shipped from one state to another and forbade the manufacture, sale, or transportation of adulterated foods or poisonous patent medicines. An addition to the law (1911) made it illegal to use false or misleading advertising. Subsequent additions, such as the Wheeler-Lea Act of 1938, enlarged the scope of Federal supervision by adding cosmetics and providing more severe penalties for violations. Federal law now requires packaged foods, drugs, and cosmetics to be labeled with a detailed listing of contents, including artificial color, flavor, and/or preservatives.

Q   **Quarantine speech** (1937)   On October 5 in Chicago, President Franklin Roosevelt attacked recent neutrality legislation by asserting that it aided the aggressors. It was obvious that he had in mind the Spanish Civil War then raging and Japanese aggression in China. He urged a "worldwide quarantine" against aggressors and thereby dropped all pretense of neutrality. This definitely partisan position startled the people of the United States, but the president proved to be only a little ahead of public opinion, which soon caught up with him.

Quartering Act (1765)   The act required the colonial governor to quarter troops in inns and unused buildings when no barracks were available. Boston had many British soldiers and few barracks. The Sons of Liberty, other patriots, and the Boston Whigs were usually able to keep unused buildings unfit for barracks. British soldiers were frequently forced to encamp on Boston Common. Parliament allowed the Quartering Act to expire in 1770, but a new one was enacted in 1774 requiring the colonists to provide food and lodging for British soldiers sent to America. This procedure is prohibited by the Bill of Rights, the Third Amendment, of the U.S. Constitution.

Quebec Act (1774)   Parliament extended the boundaries of the Province of Quebec south to the Ohio River and west to the Mississippi and granted religious freedom to the French Catholics in this region. The act alarmed the English colonists because it threatened to wipe out the claims of Virginia, Massachusetts, and Connecticut to the territories south and west of the Great Lakes and also because it seemed designed to strengthen Catholicism in this territory.

Quebec, fall of (1759)   General Wolfe defeated General Montcalm on the Plains of Abraham. This British victory over the French decided the outcome of the French and Indian War in North America. This was part of the Seven Years' War (1756–63) being fought in Europe and India as well as in America. As a result of this victory, England acquired all of Canada from France by the Treaty of Paris (1763), making the battle of Quebec one of the decisive battles of history.

Quotas, immigration   The Emergency Quota Act of 1921 introduced the principle of quotas by providing that immigration from any country in Europe was restricted each year to 3 percent of the number of persons from that country living in the United States in 1910. The immigration act of 1924 further restricted immigration from Europe by making the quota 2 percent and basing it on the 1890 population. *See also* **Immigration legislation**.

R   **Randolph, Asa Philip** (1889–1979)   Randolph was born in Florida. His parents were descendants of Virginia slaves. He came to New York City at the age of twenty-two and joined the Socialist party. He went to Chicago, where because of his labor and Marxist sympathies, he was asked to organize the porters and employees of the Pullman Company. A gifted speaker, he persuaded 53 percent of the employees to join the Brotherhood of Sleeping Car Porters. In 1917 the union negotiated the first contract between an American corporation and a black union. Elected first president of the

National Negro Congress (1936), he urged President Franklin Roosevelt to integrate the armed forces in World War II. His threatened march on Washington, D.C., caused Roosevelt to set up a Fair Employment Practices Committee (1941). He caused President Truman to end racial discrimination in the armed forces (1948). He was awarded the Medal of Freedom by President Johnson in 1964.

Randolph, John (1773–1833) He served intermittently in the House of Representatives (1799–1829) and in the Senate (1825–1827). He was at first a Jeffersonian, but he defected over the secret attempt to acquire Florida. He opposed Clay's American System—chartering the Second Bank of the United States and tariff and internal improvements at Federal expense—as unconstitutional. He was U.S. minister to Russia for a short time under Jackson.

Rankin, Jeanette P. (1880–1973) Born on a ranch near Missoula, Montana, Rankin was the first woman to be elected to the House of Representatives (1916) after stumping the state for women's suffrage, which was approved in a statewide referendum in Montana in 1914. She voted against the U.S. declaration of war in 1917. She introduced the Nineteenth (women's suffrage) Amendment, which was ratified in 1920. With Jane Addams and Florence Kelley she founded the Woman's International League for Peace and Freedom (WILPF) in Zurich, Switzerland (1919). Elected to Congress again in 1940, she cast the only vote against declaring war on the Axis after the attack on Pearl Harbor (1941). She made seven trips to India (1946–71) to study the nonviolent methods of Gandhi. She led a women's march on Washington, D.C. (January 1968), in opposition to the Vietnam War.

Rayburn, Sam (1882–1961) Born in Tennessee, he moved with his family to Texas in 1887. He was a member of the U.S. House of Representatives (1913–61) and Speaker of the House for 17 years (1940–46, 1949–53, and 1956–61). He sponsored New Deal legislation and strongly supported the war effort in World War II. A close friend of Lyndon B. Johnson, he sponsored Johnson's effort to get the Democratic nomination for President in 1960 and urged him to accept the vice presidential nomination and run with John F. Kennedy.

Reagan, Ronald *See* Presidents of the United States section, beginning on page 10-83.

Reciprocal Trade Agreements Act (1934) The tariff policy of the New Deal provided for the negotiation of tariff agreements with separate nations. Secretary of State Hull made trade agreements with many Latin American nations as well as other countries. The treaties reduced tariff duties to promote trade and thereby helped combat economic nationalism.

Reconstruction (1865–1877) This was the twelve-year period between the end of the Civil War and the removal of all federal troops from the former Confederate states. The political and economic rehabilitation of the South after the devastating war were the problems of Reconstruction. The Lincoln plan of restoring the states to the Union was rejected by the radical Republicans who controlled Congress. They impeached and almost succeeded in removing President Johnson, who tried to apply this plan. In-

stead, the South was divided into five districts under the control of federal troops. The Thirteenth, Fourteenth, and Fifteenth Amendments to the Constitution were adopted. With the rise of the Ku Klux Klan and the removal of federal troops after the election of 1877, the rights granted to the former slaves by the Fourteenth and Fifteenth Amendments were generally withdrawn in practice by the white majority.

Reconstruction Finance Corporation (RFC) (1932) Established by Congress at the request of President Hoover, the RFC was the Republican solution to the mass unemployment of the depression. Hoover assured the nation that "prosperity is just around the comer." The RFC advanced some $2 billion in loans to state and local governments and to banks, railroads, farm mortgage associations, and large corporations in order to provide jobs and stimulate the economy. The depression worsened, however, and the Republicans were swept out of office in the election of 1932.

Reed, Walter (1851–1902) He studied medicine at the University of Virginia and at Bellevue Hospital in New York. He entered the U.S. Army Medical Corps and served in Arizona, returning East in 1881. He was stationed near Johns Hopkins Medical School and began experiments with vaccines. Soldiers in the Spanish-American War (1898) were dying of yellow fever. Reed was appointed head of an Army commission to fight this deadly disease. His experiments proved that the mosquito was the cause. On his grave in Arlington National Cemetery is the inscription "He gave to man control over that dreadful scourge, Yellow Fever."

Referendum A form of direct legislation whereby certain measures are required to be submitted to the decision of the voters, usually because of a failure to act by a legislative body.

Reparations Payments assessed usually against a defeated nation held responsible for war damage.

Republican party (organized 1854) Resentment at the passage of the Kansas-Nebraska Bill sparked the formation of the Republican (GOP) party at Ripon, Wisconsin. Its first adherents organized to prevent the spread of slavery into the territories. Many Free-Soilers, Northern Democrats, and Northern Whigs joined to back John C. Frémont in the presidential campaign of 1856. Their second presidential candidate, Abraham Lincoln, won in 1860.

Resumption Act (1875) The act provided for redemption of greenbacks in gold beginning January 1, 1879. This sound money program of the Republican party reduced the amount of greenbacks in circulation and restored confidence in this fiat paper money. Protests against the act led to demands for "free silver," an issue of high political controversy until the Klondike gold rush of 1898 and the Gold Standard Act of 1900.

Revere, Paul (1735–1818) He learned the silversmith craft in his father's Boston shop, fought in the French and Indian War, joined the Sons of Liberty, and opposed the Stamp Act (1765). He carried messages for the Committees of Correspondence and participated in the Boston Tea Party (1773). He rode to Lexington to warn of the approach of British troops (April 18, 1775) and served as colonel in the

War of Independence. His shop made armaments for the troops. He built the first rolling mill in America after the war.

John S. Copley's portrait of Paul Revere.

Right of deposit   The right of American shippers to store goods in New Orleans free of customs duties while awaiting reloading for shipment on oceangoing vessels was guaranteed by a treaty with Spain in 1795. When it was withdrawn in 1802, Jefferson started negotiations to buy New Orleans and ended up with the Louisiana Purchase.

Riis, Jacob A. (1849–1914)   Born in Denmark, he emigrated to the United States in 1870. He worked on the *South Brooklyn News* and bought the newspaper. He worked as a police reporter for the *New York Tribune*. He became a crusader for improved conditions for the poor. Settlement House on New York City's East Side was named the Jacob A. Riis Settlement. He fought for improved health laws, better public schools, and child labor laws. He advocated public kindergartens, vocational education, and public parks and playgrounds. He was one of the founders of the Boy Scouts.

Roanoke Island   (1585–1587)   Expeditions equipped by Sir Walter Raleigh landed at Roanoke Island (Albermarle Sound, North Carolina). Each group stayed only a few months. A third settlement in 1587 was "lost" sometime previous to August 1591. The first English child native to the present United States, Virginia Dare, was born here on August 18, 1587.

Robinson-Patman Act (1936)   The act, also known as the Anti-price Discrimination Act, outlawed the practice of chain stores purchasing goods at lower prices than other retailers, thus permitting the former to drive the latter out of business and establish monopolies. The law was to be enforced by the Federal Trade Commission.

Rockefeller, John D. (1839–1937)   He entered the oil business in Pennsylvania and organized the Standard Oil Company (1867), which was incorporated (1870) with himself as President. He drove competitors out of business. The giant Standard Oil Company of New Jersey, which controlled the various Rockefeller interests, was held to be in violation of the Sherman Anti-trust Act and was ordered dissolved by the Supreme Court in 1911. The $1 billion Rockefeller fortune established charitable trusts, including the Rockefeller Institute for Medical Research, the General Education Board, the Rockefeller Foundation, and a substantial endowment to the University of Chicago in 1892.

Roosevelt, Anna Eleanor (1884–1962)   Born into the aristocracy of privilege, Roosevelt became the champion of the poor, the underprivileged, the minorities, and the dispossessed of the world. She married her distant cousin Franklin D. Roosevelt and bore their six children, but the marriage (as her childhood) was not a happy one. Yet, as the first lady of her country, she helped further the causes of equal rights for women and civil rights for blacks. Her influential newspaper column, *My Day,* was widely circulated and read. President Truman appointed her U.S. delegate to the U.N. General Assembly, where she helped secure the adoption of the Universal Declaration of Human Rights. Her brief biography in *American Reformers* closes with the statement: "In every respect she was one of the most remarkable personalities of the twentieth century, leaving her mark on almost every important political and social cause that occurred during her lifetime."

Roosevelt Corollary   An interpretation and enlargement of the Monroe Doctrine by Theodore Roosevelt, it asserted the right of the United States to intervene in Latin American nations to require them to meet their financial obligations to creditor nations. Roosevelt first applied this corollary to the Monroe Doctrine in 1904 when he sent armies into the Dominican Republic to force that country to pay its foreign debts and thus remove grounds for possible foreign occupation of territory in the Western Hemisphere. The Roosevelt Corollary was again applied in Nicaragua (1909), Haiti (1915) the Dominican Republic (1916), and again in Nicaragua (1926). The Good Neighbor Policy announced by Franklin D. Roosevelt in 1933 constituted a reversal of this policy.

Roosevelt, Franklin Delano   *See* Presidents of the United States section, beginning on page 10-83.

Roosevelt, Theodore   *See* Presidents of the United States section, beginning on page 10-83.

Root, Elihu (1845–1937)   He practiced law in New York. He was secretary of war (1899–1904), secretary of state (1905–19), U.S. senator from New York (1909–15), and president of the Carnegie Endowment for International Peace (1910–25). He was awarded the Nobel Prize for Peace (1912). He helped write the covenant of the Permanent Court of International Justice and secured U.S. membership in the court under a formula acceptable to the court and to the U.S. Senate. *See also* **Root-Takahira Agreement**.

Root-Takahira Agreement (1908)   Also known as the **Gentlemen's agreement** (*see* page 10-36), this executive agreement was made to subdue Japanese resentment concerning U.S. immigration laws and California's anti-Japanese land laws. It was reached while the U.S. fleet was on a world tour (December 1907 to February 1909) and received an enthusiastic welcome at Yokohama. The major terms provided that (1) the United States recognize Japan's dominance in Korea and South Manchuria; (2) Japan recognize United States sovereignty in the Philippines; and (3) both nations respect the Open Door Policy in China.

Rosenberg case   Julius and Ethel Rosenberg, born in New York City, were convicted (April 1951) of passing classified information about America's atom bomb to the Soviets. Their appeals failed to overturn the conviction, and both were executed (1953). They are the only Americans ever executed in peacetime for espionage. Their two sons (raised by the Meeropol family) have endeavored to reopen the case, alleging that their parents were victims of McCarthyism's pervasive influence during the early 1950s. The Soviets exploded their first atom bomb in September 1949.

Rum, Romanism, and rebellion   In an election address on behalf of James G. Blaine, Republican candidate for president in 1884, the Reverend Samuel D. Burchand referred to the Democratic party as the party of "rum, Romanism, and rebellion." Blaine, who was present, failed to repudiate this slur on the Catholics. The New York press featured this slogan, causing defection of the Irish Catholic voters from the Republican party, the loss of New York, and the election of the Democratic candidate Grover Cleveland.

Rush-Bagot Agreement (1818)   Richard Rush of the United States and Charles Bagot of England concluded arrangements for no war vessels or armaments on the Great Lakes, except for police action. This was the beginning of a series of agreements resulting in a demilitarized United States-Canadian border. The 5000-mile unfortified boundary between the United States and Canada (including Alaska) is the only one of its kind in the world.

Rush, Benjamin (1745–1813)   He studied medicine in the United States and in the United Kingdom and returned to Philadelphia in 1769. Signer of the Declaration of Independence, he led the fight in Pennsylvania for ratification of the Constitution. He was treasurer of the U.S. Mint (1797–1813) and taught medicine at the University of Pennsylvania. A pioneer in psychiatry, he wrote a text on diseases of the mind (1812).

S   **Sacco-Vanzetti case** (1921)   Nicola Sacco, a shoe-factory employee, and Bartolomeo Vanzetti, a fish peddler, were executed in 1927 after conviction of robbery and murder in a payroll holdup in South Braintree, Massachusetts. Judge Webster Thayer presided at the trial. Both men were Italian immigrants, radicals, and draft dodgers. Neither the $15,776 payroll nor the getaway car was traced to the accused. Many thought public hysteria against radicals, not guilt, explained the verdict. Throughout Europe and Latin America the trial became a cause célèbre. The fairness of the trial and the verdict is as much in doubt now as when it happened. In his book

The Case of Sacco and Vanzetti, Felix Frankfurter, professor of law at Harvard and later a justice on the Supreme Court, wrote: "Judge Thayer's opinion stands unmatched for discrepancies between what the record discloses and what the opinion conveys." On July 19, 1977, Governor Dukakis of Massachusetts, which had executed Sacco and Vanzetti, vindicated the victims by official proclamation.

Saint Augustine (1565)   This Spanish garrison has had a continuous existence since its founding by Menendez. It is the oldest community in the United States.

Saint Lawrence Seaway Act (1954)   The act established the St. Lawrence Seaway Development Corporation to construct a channel for ocean traffic into the Great Lakes. Hydroelectric power was also to be developed for both Canada and the United States. In June 1959, Queen Elizabeth of Great Britain and President Eisenhower officially opened the Seaway, which permitted oceangoing shipping to penetrate inland 2342 miles to Duluth on Lake Superior. The waterway accommodates ships up to 750 feet in length, 72 feet beam, and 27 feet draft.

"Salutary neglect"   Describes the economic freedom the English colonies were allowed by the failure to enforce mercantilist controls.

Sanctions   The application of economic or other measures against a nation to force it to obey international law.

Sandinistas   They led an uprising in Nicaragua in 1979 that ousted the repressive military regime of Anastasio Somoza, which had been supported by the United States. The leaders of the new leftist regime, headed by Daniel Ortega, call themselves Sandinistas, after General Sandino, who led a liberal insurrection against the dictatorial Chamarro government in 1926.

San Francisco Conference (1945)   Delegates from fifty nations drew up the charter of the United Nations. Over strong opposition, the United States, Russia, Great Britain, France, and China insisted on having veto power on the Security Council. Other than this one defeat, the smaller nations made a great many changes in the Dumbarton Oaks version of a UN charter, which had been drawn up the previous year by the big powers. A month after the conference adjourned, the United States joined the United Nations when the Senate accepted the charter by a vote of 89 to 2.

Saratoga, battle of (1777)   For ten days preceding his surrender at Saratoga, Burgoyne had been hard-pressed in several engagements. Arnold and Morgan were chiefly responsible for these successes, although Gates was in command. The British forces were in retreat when they were surrounded at Saratoga by colonial forces about three times their number.

Saturday Night Massacre (October 20, 1973)   The Department of Justice had appointed Archibald Cox, a Harvard law professor, in May 1973 and assured him a free hand as special prosecutor in the Watergate break-in affair. When Cox attempted to secure the White House tapes, Nixon ordered Attorney General Richardson to fire Cox. Richardson refused and resigned. Deputy Attorney General Ruckelshaus refused to fire Cox and was fired. Solicitor General Robert Bork, third in line, agreed to perform as requested, was appointed acting attorney general, and fired Cox. These events, known as the Saturday Night Massacre, occurred on October 20, 1973. On June 24, 1974, the Supreme Court ruled, in a unanimous decision, that Nixon was obliged by law to deliver the tapes to the new special prosecutor. On August 9, 1974, Nixon resigned as President.

Scalawags These were white Southerners who cooperated fully with the radical Republicans and sometimes used their superior knowledge and abilities to seize as much power and steal as much money as they could by gaining high office in the "reconstructed" state governments. This occurred during the Reconstruction years following the Civil War.

Schurz, Carl (1829–1906) He came to the United States from Germany in 1852 and served in the Union army, attaining the rank of major general. He was U.S. senator from Missouri (1869–75), secretary of the interior (1877–81), and an editor of the *New York Evening Post* and *The Nation* in the 1880s and *Harper's Weekly* during the 1890s. He was a leading Republican during this era.

Scopes Trial (1925) John Scopes, a public school teacher in Dayton, Tennessee, taught the theory of evolution and thus violated the state law that forbade teaching any "theory that denies the story of the divine creation of man as taught in the Bible." William Jennings Bryan won the case for Tennessee in spite of the wit, barbs, and talent of the defendant's counsel, Clarence Darrow. The trial, conducted in a circus atmosphere, was pathetic and possibly funny. The state supreme court upheld the constitutionality of what it called "a bizarre case." The rest of the world called it "the monkey trial."

Seal Controversy (1889) Before the United States purchased Alaska in 1867, the Bering Sea was exclusively Russian waters. After the purchase other nations considered the Bering Sea international waters and hunted seals there. The United States, claiming the Bering Sea to be exclusively American waters, seized Canadian vessels. Great Britain and the United States submitted the dispute to arbitration in Paris by commissioners representing France, Sweden, and Italy. Their decision in 1893 declared the Bering Sea international waters, assessed damages against the United States for the seized ships, and established hunting restrictions to prevent the extinction of the seals.

Secession (1860–1861) Four days after the election of Lincoln (November 6, 1860), the South Carolina Legislature called into session a special convention that met in Columbia, South Carolina, and voted unanimously (December 20) that "the union now subsisting between South Carolina and the other states...is hereby dissolved." Ten states followed South Carolina's lead: Mississippi, January 9, 1861; Florida, January 10; Alabama, January 11; Georgia, January 19; Louisiana, January 26; Texas, February 1; Virginia, April 17; Arkansas, May 6; Tennessee, May 7; and North Carolina, May 20. These eleven states made up the Confederate States of America. They established their capital at Montgomery, Alabama (later moved to Richmond, Virginia), and chose Jefferson Davis of Mississippi as their president.

Securities and Exchange Commission (SEC) (1934) The supervision of the stock market (Wall Street) was taken from the Federal Trade Commission and placed under the authority of the Securities and Exchange Commission. Strict control over all stock exchanges, brokers, and dealers was established. Buying securities on margin came under far tighter regulations. Descriptions of securities offered for sale had to contain all pertinent information, accurately stated. False advertising and inadequate information, prevalent before the 1929 crash, were made illegal.

Selective Service Act (1940) The act was the first peacetime draft in our history. Over 16 million men, twenty-one to twenty-five years old, registered, and before November the first draftees were inducted. A few men resisted the law as a violation of the "involuntary servitude" of the Thirteenth Amendment. The courts upheld the law, however, as not requiring involuntary servitude within the meaning of those words as used in the Constitution. It was also pointed out that Congress had the power to "raise and support armies." By September 1940, national necessity and, after Pearl Harbor in 1941, overwhelming public opinion demanded the draft.

Separatists A group of Puritans who favored complete separation from the Church of England and the independence of each congregation. The colony of Plymouth was founded by the Separatist Pilgrims in 1620.

Seward, William H. (1801–1872) He practiced law in Auburn, New York, was a member of the New York State Senate (1830–32), governor of New York (1838–42), and member of the U.S. Senate (1848–60). He opposed the Compromise of 1850, saying there was a "higher law" than the U.S. Constitution and because he opposed slavery. He called the struggle over slavery an "irrepressible conflict" in an 1858 speech. He unsuccessfully sought the Republican party nomination for president in 1856 and 1860. Lincoln appointed him secretary of state (1861). He successfully negotiated the *Trent* affair and the *Alabama* claims with Britain. He was seriously wounded in his home at the time Lincoln was assassinated in the same conspiracy. He successfully negotiated the purchase of Alaska (1867), which was ridiculed as "Seward's folly." The Senate refused to ratify his treaty for the purchase of the Danish West Indies or to support his efforts to acquire the Hawaiian Islands.

Shays' Rebellion (1786) Captain Daniel Shays and his "army" had central and western Massachusetts in turmoil from August to February, 1786–87. His men, many of them Revolutionary War veterans, were about to lose their farms to creditors for unpaid taxes and mortgages. Courts were forcefully prevented from holding sessions. The rebellion collapsed when the Massachusetts militia captured most of Shays' men at Petersham. More than six months of armed bands roving about the state had brought no aid from the U.S. government. Captain Shays was condemned to death but later pardoned.

Sherman Anti-trust Act (1890) Both major parties had promised laws to suppress the power of corporations to enlarge profits at the expense of the peoples' welfare. This law made illegal "Every contract, combination in the form of trust or otherwise, or conspiracy, in restraint of trade or commerce among the several states, or with foreign nations...." Ineffective for several years because the courts gave interpretations favorable to business of "conspiracy," "restraint," "commerce," and "trust," the law's significance was that it reflected the government's concern about the public welfare as affected by private business.

Sherman Silver Purchase Act (1890) A victory for the inflationists and advocates of the use of greater amounts of silver money, the law required the treasury to purchase and coin 4,500,000 ounces of silver per month and pay for it with legal tender treasury notes redeemable in gold.

Sherman, William Tecumseh (1820–1891) Graduated from the U.S. Military Academy at West Point (1840), he served in the Mexican War (1846–47). He was in the banking business in San Francisco, practiced law in Kansas, and was superintendent of the military academy at Alexandria, Louisiana (1859–61). In the Civil War he commanded a brigade at the first battle of Bull Run (July 1861). He became Major General after Shiloh (1862) and commanded troops under Grant at Vicksburg. He was commander of Union forces in the West after March 1864. He took Atlanta (September 1) and Savannah (December 21) and received the surrender of J. E. Johnston at Durham, North Carolina, on April 26, 1865. He succeeded Grant in command of military forces, 1869–84. Efforts to have him run for president in 1884 were rebuffed in the classic definitive comment: "If nominated, I will not run; if elected I will not serve."

Sit-down strike A labor weapon used by the CIO in 1937 and 1938; instead of maintaining pickets outside plants to prevent strikebreakers from replacing strikers, the strikers remained in possession of the plant.

Slidell Mission Polk's appointment of John Slidell to go to Mexico to bargain for the cession of New Mexico, California, and the disputed boundary of Texas in return for American assumption of debt claims against Mexico and a large payment of cash. The Mexican government refused to enter into discussion with Slidell.

Smith, Alfred E. (1873–1944) He grew up in poverty on the Lower East Side of New York City and became a factor in Tammany politics. He served in the New York State legislature, 1903–15. As majority leader of the assembly he sponsored reform legislation. He was governor of New York for four 2-year terms (1919–21 and 1923–29). He ran for president of the United States in 1928 as Democratic candidate against Hoover. At first he supported Franklin D. Roosevelt's New Deal, but then organized the Liberty League in opposition. He was the first Catholic to run for president on a major party ticket.

Social Security Act (1935) The major provision of this act is the Old Age and Survivor's Insurance Program. A payroll tax of about 3 percent, half paid by the employer and half by the employee, financed retirement payments beginning at age 65. Other provisions involving joint federal-state action include

unemployment insurance, aid to the blind, crippled, and destitute; aid to delinquent children; maternity and infant care; public and health work, and vocational rehabilitation. Increases in the tax rates and benefits have been frequent. In 1950 the Truman administration added nearly ten million beneficiaries by broadening the old age insurance benefits of the 1935 act. Attempts by the Reagan administration to curtail the so-called entitlement benefits of Social Security were overwhelmingly rebuffed in Congress.

Soil Conservation and Domestic Allotment Act of 1936 Act of Congress to restrict farm production by making benefit payments to farmers to plant part of their land in soil-building crops.

"Solid South" Term applied to the one-party (Democratic) system of the South following the Civil War; followed to preserve white supremacy.

Sons of Liberty A secret organization of patriots whose radical program attracted followers in Boston, New York, and other colonial cities, they took to the streets in opposition to the Stamp Act (1765), forcing all royal stamp agents in the colonies to resign. Their leaders included Samuel Adams in Boston, the merchant Isaac Sears in New York, and Paul Revere, who made engravings of the Boston Massacre of 1770 for the Sons of Liberty.

"Sooners" Term applied to landseekers around 1890 who tried to enter Oklahoma sooner than the deadline for the "runs" to begin.

Southeast Asia Treaty Organization (SEATO) In November 1954, SEATO was formed. Eight nations combined under a pledge to meet any threat of armed aggression by united action. They "meet in order to agree on the measures which should be taken for common defense." They have established headquarters at Bangkok, the capital of Thailand, where a secretariat functions. There is a small armed force at SEATO's command, but its effectiveness as a military power rests in the willingness of the United States to lead and the others to follow, whenever a crisis arises. In view of our action in Korea this may be a substantial deterrent to aggression; but it has none of the immediate striking force of NATO. The members of SEATO are the United States, Great Britain, France, Australia, New Zealand, Thailand, Pakistan, and the Philippines.

Southern Christian Leadership Conference (SCLC) Founded in 1957 in Atlanta by Martin Luther King, Jr., to fight segregation, it supported civil disobedience—the refusal to obey unjust laws—such as nonviolent sit-ins, boycotts, and protest marches. The conference worked primarily in the South. After the assassination of Martin Luther King, Jr., the SCLC chose the Reverend Ralph David Abernathy as its leader.

Spanish-American War (1898) Public opinion in the United States sided with revolutionists in Cuba who were opposing the brutal Spanish rule in the island. After riots in Havana, the USS *Maine*, which had been dispatched to Cuba to protect American life and property, was destroyed by an explosion of unknown origin. A declaration of war against Spain soon passed Congress. The U.S. Asiatic fleet under Commodore George Dewey steamed from Hong Kong to Manila, where it destroyed the Spanish fleet. Land forces in Cuba defeated the Spanish regulars, forcing the blockaded fleet to try to run the American fleet, which proceeded to destroy the Spanish warships. At the Treaty of Paris (October 1898), Spain ceded the Philippine Islands to the United States for $20 million, granted independence to Cuba, and ceded Puerto Rico and Guam to the United States.

Specie Circular (1836)   This circular was issued by President Jackson. It limited payment to the United States for public lands to gold and silver (specie) or certain paper money of equal soundness. As many land companies and banks were unable to meet their payments in such currency, they were forced into bankruptcy. Although not the basic cause of the panic of 1837, the Specie Circular precipitated it.

Spoils system   This is the practice of victorious political parties of removing officeholders of the opposition party and giving their jobs to supporters of the ruling party. In a speech in the U.S. Senate (1831), William Learned Marcy of New York justified the practice in the oft-quoted phrase "to the victor belong the spoils." President Jackson applied the system in U.S. national politics on a relatively large scale.

Square Deal   President Theodore Roosevelt promised a "square deal" to all—employees, workers, farmers, traders, ranchers. All would enjoy "equal opportunity and reward." It was the forerunner of Woodrow Wilson's "New Freedom" and the ideological grandfather of Franklin D. Roosevelt's "New Deal."

Squatter   A settler who appropriates land for himself without first securing title.

"Squatter sovereignty"   A solution proposed by Lewis Cass to the controversy over slavery in the territories, it proposed to allow residents of a territory to decide whether it would be slave or free.

Stalwarts   In 1880 the Republican party was split between two factions—the Stalwarts, led by Senator Roscoe Conkling of New York, who favored the spoils system, and the opposition, whom they labeled Halfbreeds. Conkling tried to have Grant nominated for a third term but had to compromise on General James A. Garfield of Ohio. His running mate, Chester A. Arthur, was a leading Stalwart, Arthur succeeded to the presidency six months after Garfield's inauguration when the President succumbed to an assassin's bullet. Arthur yielded to the demand for an end to the spoils system and signed the Pendleton Civil Service Reform Act in 1883.

Stamp Act (1765)   The act was part of the Grenville program. It levied taxes of 1¢ to $10 on items originating in the colonies (wills, insurance policies, newspapers, playing cards, etc.). An internal tax to raise revenue was declared by James Otis to be beyond the jurisdiction of Parliament. "Taxation without representation is tyranny" expressed the popular view.

Stamp Act Congress (1765)   The Congress met in New York City at the call of Massachusetts. Nine colonies (Massachusetts, South Carolina, Rhode Island, Connecticut, New Jersey, Delaware, New York, Pennsylvania, and Maryland) sent delegates. Their petition to the king and Parliament

asserted that only their own assemblies could levy revenue taxes.

Stanford, Leland (1824–1893)   He practiced law in New York, went into business in California (1852) and was elected governor of California (1861) and kept that state in the Union. He joined with Collis P. Huntington and others in organizing the transcontinental Central Pacific Railroad Company in 1861, of which he remained president until his death. He was also a director of the Southern Pacific Railroad. He served as U.S. senator from California (1885–93). He founded Leland Stanford Junior University (1885) in memory of his son. The substantial endowment he gave enabled the university to become a major national institution of higher learning, often called "the Harvard of the West."

Stanton, Elizabeth Cady (1815–1902)   Married to an abolitionist, she herself decided to struggle for "the emancipation of women from the dogmas of the past, political, religious, and social." With Lucretia Mott, she dominated the first women's rights convention at Seneca Falls, New York, in July 1848. She wrote tracts on temperance, antislavery, education, and especially women's rights. She worked closely with Susan B. Anthony for women's suffrage. She was president of the New York State Suffrage Society and first president of the National Women's Suffrage Association (1890–92).

Stephens, Alexander Hamilton (1812–1883)   He practiced law in Georgia and was a member of Congress (1843–59). A moderate on slavery, he was elected vice president of the Confederate States of America (February 1861). He served in Congress (1873–82) and was elected governor of Georgia (1882).

Stevens, Thaddeus (1792–1868)   Born in Vermont, he moved to York, Pennsylvania. He practiced law and held strong antislavery convictions. He was a member of the Pennsylvania Legislature during the 1830s, a member of Congress (1848–53), and active in the new Republican party. He served in Congress as a Republican (1859–68), where he headed the powerful Ways and Means Committee. A leading advocate of stern measures against the South, opposing Lincoln's "charity for all," he led in imposing military Reconstruction of the South and in impeachment proceedings against President Johnson. With Senator John Bingham, he was a chief architect of the Fourteenth Amendment to the Constitution.

Stimson Doctrine (1932)   In 1931 Japan occupied Manchuria and established a puppet state that called itself Manchukuo. Japan claimed Manchukuo established itself by revolution. Investigation by the League of Nations confirmed outright Japanese conquest, a confirmation that brought about Japan's withdrawal from the league. By the Stimson Doctrine, the United States declared it would recognize no change in sovereignty brought about by external force. Secretary of State Stimson urged economic sanctions against Japan, but neither President Hoover nor the League of Nations was ready to risk war in Asia.

Stimson, Henry L. (1867–1950)   He practiced law in New York City, was U.S. attorney for the Southern District of New York (1906–1909), and secretary of war in the Taft cabinet (1911–13). He served as a colonel of artillery in France in World War I and was governor general of the Philippines (1927–29), secretary of state (1929–33) and secretary of war in Franklin D. Roosevelt's cabinet (although he was a lifelong Republican) from July 1940 to September 1945. *See* **Stimson Doctrine**.

Stock market crash (1929)   A five-to seven-year period of speculation in securities preceded the Wall Street stock market crash of October 29. In two weeks stock prices fell $30 billion, and in three years and nine months they fell a total of $74 billion. The inauguration of President Franklin Roosevelt and the "bank holiday" coincided with the low point, March 1933, of the worst depression in our history. A slow irregular recovery found ten million unemployed in 1939. World War II began in Europe in September 1939, bringing "war prosperity."

Stowe, Harriet Beecher (1811–1896)   Born in Litchfield, Connecticut, the daughter of a Congregational minister, she married a professor of biblical literature. She started to write to help support her family. She began to write *Uncle Tom's Cabin* as a serial for an abolitionist newspaper. The complete novel, published in 1852, sold over 300,000 copies the first year and was eventually translated into fifty-two languages. The story portrays the evils of slavery and contains the Christian message of the hero Uncle Tom, who is released through death into salvation and freedom. Stowe published a sequel, *A Key to Uncle Tom* (1853), in which she describes the sources of the story in answer to criticism that it is a totally distorted account of slavery. Stowe continued to write, chiefly on the subject of women's moral influence in molding the home and family.

Strategic Arms Limitation Talks (SALT)   The first SALT agreement (1972) between the United States of America and the USSR approved by the Senate provided for a limitation on ABM (antiballistic missiles) and a freeze of long-range nuclear missiles at existing levels. The agreement was for a five-year period, but both sides agreed to abide by it after 1977 if the other side did. In 1979, President Carter and Soviet leader Leonid Brezhnev signed SALT II, agreeing to limit the number of strategic weapons, but the Senate refused to ratify the agreement. Relations with the Soviets worsened with the invasion of Afghanistan in December 1979. Despite the failure to ratify SALT II, both sides continued to abide by the terms of the agreement. In 1986 the Reagan Administration repudiated the agreement.

Suez Crisis (1956)   After withdrawal of British troops from the Suez Canal area, Egypt denied Israeli ships use of the canal. To no avail Egypt's dictator, Nasser, was urged to operate the canal for ships of all nations on equal terms, as had always been done. Israeli forces invaded Egypt to the canal, where they were joined by British and French airborne troops. At the United Nations the United States and Russia condemned this aggression. At the request of the United Nations, British, French, and Israeli forces withdrew from Egypt. When the canal reopened, Israeli ships were still excluded from its use.

Sugar Act (1764)   The act reduced taxes on rum, molasses, sugar, and spirits from the non-British West Indies. The original higher taxes had been levied in 1733 but rarely collected under the policy of "salutary neglect." This reduction brought no rejoicing because Grenville, the new chancellor of the exchequer, gave every evidence that he intended to collect the taxes. Salutary neglect had ended.

Sumner, Charles (1811–1874)   Graduated from Harvard College and Law School, he opposed the extension of slavery. He helped found the Free-Soil party, advocated the civil rights of blacks in Massachusetts, and was U.S. senator from Massachusetts (1851 until his death in 1874). An outspoken opponent of slavery, he sought repeal of the Fugitive Slave Act. He protested against the Kansas-Nebraska Act of 1854, which led to the formation of the Republican party. Insulting remarks about Senator Butler of South Carolina led to an assault on him (while he was seated at his desk) by Senator Brooks of South Carolina, who used a cane on him. It took 3½ years for Sumner to recover and return to the Senate (1856–59). He became the spokesman in the Senate for the moral sentiment of civil rights for blacks. He sought to have education and land provided to blacks. He supported Horace Greeley against Grant in 1872. His proposal to outlaw racial discrimination in public accommodations, transportation, schools, churches, and cemeteries was well ahead of his time.

Supreme Court and Franklin Delano Roosevelt (1937)   Invalidation by the Court of the NRA and AAA irked President Roosevelt, who had won re-election supported by all but two states. He proposed a reorganization of the Court that would permit an additional judge on the Court for every one thereon who had reached seventy years of age until the total membership of the Court reached fifteen. This proposal was a dud; his own party, the press, and the people disapproved. However, a series of pro-New Deal decisions and Roosevelt replacements of retiring justices transformed the Supreme Court to the President's liking long before his death in April 1945. The proposal was denounced by its foes as a "court-packing" device. *See* **Court-packing bill**.

Supreme Court and segregation (1954)   The withdrawal of federal troops from the South after the election of 1876 restored white supremacy. Provisions of the Fourteenth and Fifteenth Amendments extending to blacks the same civil rights enjoyed by whites were ignored. In 1896, in *Plessy* v. *Ferguson,* the "separate but equal" facilities for blacks and whites were declared constitutional. In 1954, however, in *Brown* v. *Board of Education of Topeka, Kansas,* a unanimous Supreme Court ruled, "Separate educational facilities are inherently unequal." Thus, segregated schools violated the "equal protection of the laws" clause of the Fourteenth Amendment.

Supreme Court appointments (1981–1992)   With the retirement of Justice Potter Stewart from the Supreme Court in 1981, President Reagan nominated Sandra Day O'Connor of the Arizona Supreme Court. She was confirmed by the Senate and sworn in September 25, 1981, the first woman to serve on the Supreme Court. Five years later, additional openings came. Chief Justice Warren E. Burger retired in 1986, and President Reagan's nominee for the chief justiceship, Justice William H. Rehnquist, was confirmed by the Senate. The vacancy brought about by Justice Rehnquist's move to the chief justiceship was filled when the Reagan nominee, Judge Antonin Scalia of Virginia, was confirmed.

After the retirement of Justice Lewis F. Powell, Jr., in 1987, President Reagan nominated Judge Robert Bork of the U.S. Court of Appeals for the District of Columbia to fill the vacancy. Judge Bork had been a professor of law at Yale University. A staunch conservative, he had frequently criticized the Supreme Court in his writings and speeches. After three weeks of televised hearings, the Senate Judiciary Committee recommended 9 to 5 that the nomination be rejected. The full Senate then voted 58 to 42 against confirmation.

Reagan's next nominee, Douglas Ginsburg, met with opposition when it was disclosed that he had used marijuana when he was a judge. He asked to have his name withdrawn. The name of Judge Anthony M. Kennedy of California was then submitted to the Senate and he was promptly confirmed.

Judge William Brennan, senior member on the Court, announced on July 20, 1990, that he was retiring after 33 years on the Court. President Bush submitted the name of Judge David H. Souter of New Hampshire, who was serving on the U.S. Court of Appeals in Boston. The nomination was confirmed by the Senate September 27, 1990.

Justice Thurgood Marshall resigned in 1991 after 24 years on the Supreme Court. President Bush sent to the Senate the name of Clarence Thomas, a U.S. Circuit Court judge. Televised hearings before the Senate Judiciary Committee disclosed sharp differences as to his qualifications. The hearings were complicated by testimony from Anita Hill, a professor of law at the University of Oklahoma, charging that she had been sexually harassed by Judge Thomas when she was on his staff at the Department of Education and at the Equal Employment Opportunity Commission. Thomas adamantly denied the charges. The Committee voted 7 to 7, thus submitting no recommendation. The Senate confirmed the nomination 52 to 48. On March 19, 1993, Justice

Byron R. White declared that he would retire prior to the beginning of the new court term in October. His 31-year career on the Supreme Court would come to an end leaving a vacancy for President Clinton to fill. *See* **Exhibit 10.5**.

Syndicalism   Radical trade union movement and philosophy advocating use of violent, direct action such as sabotage and general strikes.

Taft-Hartley Act (1947)   This was a comprehensive labor law that modified the labor policies established by the Wagner Act. Although the Wagner Act strengthened unionism vis-à-vis management, the Taft-Hartley law included various provisions intended to regulate union practices. The act outlawed the closed shop (only union members may be hired) but permitted the union shop (nonunion members may be hired but they must subsequently join the union). It provided a sixty-day "cooling off" period at the end of a contract during which no strike may be called. The president may order an additional 80-day cooling off period if he (or she) is of the opinion that the strike may be dangerous to the national health and safety. The act declared mass picketing, secondary boycotts, and featherbedding to be unfair labor practices and forbade contributions by unions to political campaigns.

Taft, William H.   *See* Presidents of the United States section, beginning on page 10-83.

Tallmadge Amendment   An amendment to the Missouri statehood bill to prohibit the introduction of slaves into Missouri and providing for emancipation of slaves born after the admission of Missouri; intended to make Missouri a free state but failed to pass.

Tariffs   *See* **Exhibit 10.6**.

Taylor, Zachary   *See* Presidents of the United States section, beginning on page 10-83.

Tea Act (1773)   A Parliamentary act that gave the British East India Company a virtual monopoly over the sale of tea in America, it was resented both because it was a precedent for British monopolies in America and because it retained an import duty on tea bought by the Americans. When the colonial merchants recognized the danger of being driven out of the tea business, they joined the radicals. Leaders throughout the colonies prevented the landing of tea cargoes. In Boston, Samuel Adams organized the well-known Boston Tea Party (1773), and other seaports followed their example of destroying the tea. Consumers turned to coffee and chocolate.

Teapot Dome scandal (1924)   Presidents Taft and Wilson had set aside oil reserves for the navy at Teapot Dome, Wyoming, and Elk Hills, California. President Harding transferred supervision of these reserves from the Navy Department to the Interior Department. Secretary of the Interior Albert Fall, in a secret, illegal, and corrupt deal, leased Elk Hills and Teapot Dome to oilmen Edward Doheny and Harry Sinclair, respectively. Secretary Fall was convicted of accepting a bribe of $100,000, and the Supreme Court ordered the leases cancelled. Secretary of the Navy Denby and Attorney General Daugherty resigned during the scandal.

Teheran Conference (November 28 to December 1, 1943)   A major summit conference between

---

EXHIBIT 10.5
Chief Justices
of the Supreme Court

John Jay, New York	1789–1795
John Rutledge, South Carolina	1795
Oliver Ellsworth, Connecticut	1795–1799
John Marshall, Virginia	1801–1835
Roger B. Taney, Maryland	1836–1864
Salmon P. Chase Ohio	1864–1873
Morrison R. Waite, Ohio	1874–1888
Melville W. Fuller, Illinois	1888–1910
Edward D. White, Louisiana	1910–1921
William H. Taft, Ohio	1921–1930
Charles E. Hughes, New York	1930–1941
Harlan F. Stone, New York	1941–1946
Fred M. Vinson, Kentucky	1946–1953
Earl Warren, California	1953–1969
Warren E. Burger, Minnesota	1969–1986
William Rehnquist, Arizona	1986–

Joseph Stalin, Franklin D. Roosevelt, and Winston Churchill took place during World War II at Teheran, the capital of Iran. Plans were made for joint action to destroy the Nazi war machine "by land, sea, and air."

Teller Amendment (1898) The declaration of war by Congress against Spain (April 19, 1898) contained a clause known as the Teller Amendment, stating that the United States had no intention of annexing Cuba and that control of the island would be returned to its people at the end of the war.

Tennessee Valley Authority *See* **TVA**.

Tenure of Office Act (1867) Passed by the radical Republicans in Congress as a challenge to President Johnson, the act required the president to secure the consent of the Senate before removing any appointees that had been confirmed by the Senate. Its intent was to protect Secretary of War Edwin M. Stanton, who was acting as an informer behind Johnson's back. Johnson dismissed Stanton as expected, and Congress countered with impeachment proceedings, citing the removal of Stanton as "a high crime and misdemeanor."

Tet Offensive In late January 1968, during Tet, the Vietnamese New Year, a massive, carefully planned offensive was unleashed by the Vietnamese forces. Twenty-seven South Vietnamese cities including the capital, Saigon, came under concerted attack. In March 1968 President Lyndon Johnson announced that he would not be a candidate for re-election.

EXHIBIT 10.6
Tarriffs

1789 This tariff is sometimes referred to as Hamilton's 10 percent tariff. It was a revenue tariff with rates from 5 to 15 percent. Hamilton wished to establish the principle of protection even though there was little to protect and no strong protectionist sentiment. His *Report on Manufactures* showed that he was looking to the future, but Congress would not follow his lead.

1828 This Tariff of Abominations resulted from political maneuvering under southern leadership, principally Calhoun's. High rates on raw materials as well as on finished products meant many would lose as much as they gained by the tariff. A few disgruntled senators who normally favored protection might vote against this abominable bill and, if so, their vote added to the Southern bloc might defeat the bill. This plan failed as the Senate voted 26 to 21 for the bill. Rates were higher than ever, and the South was a victim of its own scheme. The next move would be South Carolina's Nullification Act.

1846, Walker When Clay's Compromise Tariff of 1833–42 expired, the Whigs passed a tariff at protective levels, but in 1846 the Democrats reversed the trend with the Walker Tariff, which lowered rates and increased the number of items on the free list. This trend continued until the Civil War.

1861, Morrill From 1833, Clay's Compromise Tariff to the Civil War rates continued on a downward trend. The Morrill Tariff reintroduced protectionist rates, which continued on their upward trend until the Underwood-Simmons Tariff of 1913.

1890, McKinley This tariff gave American manufacturers the protection they wanted. The average ad valorum rate was about 50 percent. Reciprocal provisions with Latin America were included (*see* **Pan-American Conference**). American sugar growers were given a 2¢ per pound bounty (*see* **Hawaiian monarchy overthrown**). Wheat and corn, major export crops, were protected for reasons making some political but no economic sense. The Republican party pledged support for the Sherman Silver Act to the western states, especially the five Omnibus states, in return for their support of the McKinley tariff.

1894, Wilson-Gorman This tariff slightly reduced the high tariff rates of the McKinley Tariff of 1890. It contained an income tax provision that was declared unconstitutional by the Supreme Court.

1897, Dingley This tariff was even more protective than the McKinley Tariff of 1890. It reversed the Democratic downward direction of the Wilson-Gorman Tariff of 1894 to re-establish the Republican highly protective rates. This super-protective trend in tariffs was not checked until the Underwood Tariff of 1913.

1909, Payne-Aldrich The extremely protective rates (57 percent) of the Dingley Tariff of 1897 were reduced to about 37 percent. President Taft had requested a much greater reduction, but Senator Aldrich of Rhode Island engineered over 800 changes in the bill before it passed. These super-protective rates were a major factor in the Republican party split into Progressives, led by Norris and LaFollette against the Old Guard.

1913, Underwood This first substantial reduction of the tariff since the Civil War (Morrill Tariff) cut rates about 28 percent below the preceding Payne-Aldrich Tariff. By appeals to the people in speeches, by addresses to Congress, and by twisting congressmen's arms through patronage, Wilson pressured a reluctant legislature to give him the tariff he requested. The first income tax after the adoption of the Sixteenth Amendment was part of this tariff bill.

1922, Fordney-McCumber This tariff was a Republican defense against a not yet developed, but expected, postwar flow of European products to America. Europe's only path to recovery and payment of war debts was an increase in exports. The tariff was more protective than any previous tariff. New U.S. industries developed during the war, especially chemicals, received special attention. A new feature allowed the president, on the advice of the Tariff Commission, to raise or lower rates as much as 50 percent. Retaliatory tariffs sprang up throughout the world so that foreign trade became increasingly difficult.

1930, Hawley-Smoot President Hoover had asked for a downward revision of the rates in the Fordney-McCumber Tariff. What Congress passed was an upward revision due largely to the influence of Senator Grundy, a recent president of the Manufacturers Association of Pennsylvania. A petition of about 1000 economists urged Hoover to veto the bill, but the president wished to avoid a serious interparty fight and he hoped to modify several rates through the Tariff Commission. No such modifications developed.

Texas, Republic of, independence (1836)   Friction over slavery and the growing number of Americans in Texas led to repressive measures by Mexico. On March 2, Texas declared her independence. The twelve-day siege at the Alamo ended in a massacre on March 6 of the Texan rebels. On April 21, however, Sam Houston led the Texans to victory at San Jacinto over Mexican General Santa Anna. Mexico refused to honor the agreements forced on Santa Anna, but nevertheless on October 22 Sam Houston became the first president of the Republic of Texas.

Theocracy   Rule by religious leaders, as in early Massachusetts.

Tilden, Samuel J. (1814–1886)   He practiced law in New York City and made a fortune in railroad practice. He instituted reforms as chairman of the state Democratic committee, helping to oust New York City's corrupt Tweed Ring. He was governor of New York (1874–76) and Democratic candidate for president, beating Hayes by a majority of 250,000 but losing the election to the Republican-controlled electoral commission. He left a fortune that helped found the New York Public Library.

Tippecanoe, battle of (1811)   The gifted Chief Tecumseh organized the tribes east of the Mississippi into a formidable alliance whose objective was to drive the white hordes back and halt their relentless attack on the native Americans. General William Henry Harrison (later President Harrison) defeated Tecumseh's force at the battle of Tippecanoe, in present-day western Indiana. The native American retreat marked the end of their challenge to settlement of the old Northwest.

Tonkin Gulf episode (1964)   President Johnson had secretly ordered U.S. Navy ships to cooperate with the South Vietnamese in raids along the coast of North Vietnam. Two American ships were reportedly fired upon at the Gulf of Tonkin by the North Vietnamese. Johnson requested and received passage of a congressional resolution (Tonkin Gulf Resolution) permitting him to use force in Southeast Asia. This made it possible for one President to escalate the war in Asia without congressional approval. The resolution was repealed by Congress in June 1971.

Townshend Acts (1767)   These were import duties on tea, glass, paper, lead, and paint. Since the taxes were external, the American colonials admitted Parliament's right to levy them, but only if used to regulate trade in the empire. These acts stated as their purpose the raising of revenue to pay some of the costs of civil government in the colonies. Colonial protests in the form of Dickinson's *Farmer's Letters* and a boycott greeted these new taxes.

Trade Agreement Act of 1934   Applied to the principle of reciprocal tariffs. Permitted the president to raise or lower existing tariffs up to 50 percent without Senate approval.

Trade Expansion Act of 1962   Authorized tariff cuts up to 50 percent to promote trade with Common Market countries. Led to expansion of European-American trade resulting from the Kennedy round of tariff negotiations concluded in 1967.

Transcendentalism   An optimistic, liberal philosophy of Emerson and other New England intellectuals before the Civil War; emphasized the dignity of the common man; held that intuition transcended experience.

Trent affair (1861)   Confederate agents James Mason and John Slidell ran the Union blockade to Havana, Cuba. They boarded the British ship *Trent,* which was stopped on the high seas by the U.S.S. *San Jacinto* commanded by Captain Wilkes. Mason and Slidell were taken to Boston and imprisoned. Secretary of State Seward advised Lincoln that Wilkes' action was illegal. England sent 8000 troops to Canada. Lincoln released Mason and Slidell, who were allowed to proceed to London and Paris, respectively, to represent the Confederate government.

The fall of the Alamo to Santa Anna's forces.

Triangular trade   In order to raise money to pay for the import of British manufactured goods (chiefly textiles and tools), the colonies sold their products (chiefly fish, flour, and lumber) in the West Indies in exchange for sugar, molasses, or rum. Sometimes these products went directly to England, where currency could be obtained; sometimes to Africa, where slaves were secured and returned for cash sales. A variety of triangular voyages resulted. These were called "triangular trade."

Tripoli, War with (1801–1805)   The United States along with European powers paid tribute annually to Morocco, Algiers, Tripoli, and Tunis to avoid piratical raids on commerce and seizure of people for ransom. President Jefferson reversed this policy. He sent the *Philadelphia* and *Constitution* with several smaller ships to blockade these ports on the Barbary Coast. By 1805 treaties brought piracy almost to a halt. By 1815 Commodore Preble and Stephen

Decatur, among others, had ended piracy off the North African coast.

Truman Doctrine (1947)   The doctrine declared that either "direct or indirect aggression undermines the foundations of international peace and hence the security of the United States." Guerrilla forces from Albania, Bulgaria, and Yugoslavia infiltrated Greece to a dangerous degree. Russia threatened Turkey over control of the Dardanelles. The UN response to Greek pleas was blocked by the Soviet veto. On March 12 Truman started substantial military equipment and advisors flowing into Greece and Turkey. Russia's push toward the Mediterranean was stopped, and Communist party strength in France, Italy, and Greece subsided. The cold war was on in earnest.

Truman, Harry S   *See* Presidents of the United States section, beginning on page 10-83.

Trust   A device used to create business monopolies. Under it, competing corporations surrender voting stock to a board of trustees in return for trust certificates. The trustees then operate the separate companies as a unit for purposes of price-fixing and other policies.

Tubman, Harriet (around 1821–1913)   Born a slave in Maryland, Harriet Tubman did heavy field work for the first twenty-five years of her life. When two of her sisters were sold to a slave trader to be taken to the deep South, Harriet determined to escape. She set out alone, carrying only a small package of food. She followed the North Star during the night and slept in barns during the day. She made her way to Philadelphia in 1846 and found work in a hotel. She learned about the "underground railroad," often the homes of Quakers who helped fugitive slaves. She determined to return to her former plantation and rescue her family, risking her freedom and her life. On her first trip back she rescued her sister and two children. She made nineteen trips in all, freeing over 300 slaves, including nearly all her brothers and sisters. Determined efforts were made to capture her. Rewards as high as $12,000, a huge sum in those days, were offered for her dead or alive. She was never caught. During the Civil War she served the Union both as a nurse and as a spy. She was called the Moses of her people.

Turner's, Nat, rebellion (1831)   This black preacher led about sixty-five slaves on plantation raids in Southampton, Virginia. Over fifty whites were killed. The resulting manhunt by whites left about a hundred blacks dead and Turner, with twenty of his band, was held for trial and execution.

TVA (1933)   The government hydroelectric plant and two munition factories on the Tennessee River at Muscle Shoals, Alabama, used in World War 1, were reactivated under President Franklin D. Roosevelt for peacetime purposes. Electric power was generated to serve parts of seven states. The munitions factories were converted to fertilizer plants. The Tennessee Valley Authority administered this multipurpose operation, which developed electric power, irrigation, river navigation, flood control, preservation of wild life, fisheries, soil improvement, pest controls, and chemical fertilizers. The electric power from the TVA was a major factor in developing the atom bomb at Oak Ridge during World War II.

Tweed Ring   Tammany boss William Marcy Tweed and his associates plundered the city treasury through padded bills, false vouchers, kickbacks, and bribery. His crimes were revealed in *The New York Times* and graphically depicted in brilliant cartoons of Thomas Nast. Tweed offered Nast a huge sum of money if he would go to Europe. The Tweed Ring was broken when the leader was brought to trial and convicted (1872). Tweed died in jail.

Twenty-seventh Amendment (1992)   A twenty-seventh amendment became part of the U.S. Constitution on May 7, 1992. The amendment, originally proposed by James Madison and approved by Congress in 1789 for submission to the states, reads; "No law, varying the compensation for the services of the Senators and Representatives, shall take effect until an election of Representatives shall have intervened." Ratification was completed May 7 when the legislature of Michigan, the thirty-eighth state to approve the amendment, voted favorably, thus satisfying the constitutional requirement of approval by the legislatures of three-fourths of the states. Under this amendment, a law increasing the salaries of members of Congress cannot go into effect until after a new Congress is elected.

Tydings-McDuffie Act (1934)   The act provided for granting independence to the Philippines by 1945. The native legislature was to frame a constitution subject to approval by the president of the United States. This was done by 1935 when the Philippine Commonwealth, with Manuel Quezon as its first president, started its trial run toward complete independence. In World War II the Japanese occupied the Philippines from May 1942 to December 1944, but, with a delay of only one year, the birthday of the Philippine Republic was officially celebrated on July 4, 1946. The act provided for the retention of U.S. naval bases in the Philippines. *See* **Philippine base closing.**

Tyler, John   *See* Presidents of the United States section, beginning on page 10-83.

U-2 Incident (1960)   On May 1, a U.S. espionage plane, a U-2, was shot down in central Russia near Sverdlovsk. The pilot, Francis Powers, was alive and the equipment of the plane recognizable. Knowing no details, the United States suggested that the plane had been on a routine weather observation flight and had been blown off course. Detailed pictures from Russia made attempts at deception more embarrassing than the truth. On the opening day of the summit conference at Paris, May 16, Khrushchev brusquely demanded an apology from Eisenhower. The president refused, and the conference broke up before it got under way. On January 1, 1961, Khrushchev, anxious to resume negotiations with the United States, announced that the USSR was dropping its complaint over the U-2 incident.

Un-American Activities Committee   Established by the House of Representatives in 1938 under the chairmanship of Martin Dies of Texas, it was known as the Dies Committee. Its official name was the House Committee to Investigate Un-American Activities. The House voted in 1945 to make it a permanent committee. It recommended the dismissal of 3800 government employees. The

Department of Justice investigation resulted in bringing charges against thirty-six government employees.

Uncle Tom's Cabin   *See* **Stowe, Harriet Beecher**.

Slaves on their way to freedom at a station on the Underground Railroad.

Underground railroad   These were systems of stations organized in the Northern states to aid runaway slaves escape from the South and gain their freedom in Canada. By 1830 an organized underground railroad existed in fourteen Northern states. Fugitive slaves were hidden in houses and barns, called stations, along escape routes extending into Canada.

United Mine Workers (UMW)   Organized in 1890, the UMW, under its president, John Mitchell, conducted a major coal strike in 1902. President Theodore Roosevelt forced the mine owners to negotiate, and the UMW won recognition plus a 10 percent raise. John L. Lewis, who was president from 1920 to 1960, helped organize the Congress of Industrial Organizations (CIO), which merged with the AFL in 1955 to form the American Federation of Labor and Congress of Industrial Organizations (AFL-CIO), but Lewis later took the UMW out of this organization. With nearly half a million members, the union was able to use the strike weapon to make gains for its members, even challenging to disrupt the war effort during World War II.

United Nations   Delegates from fifty nations assembled at San Francisco (April–June 1945) and drafted the charter (constitution) of the United Nations. The charter was ratified by the required number of nations (including the U.S. Senate) and went into effect on October 24 (UN Day). It provided for a general assembly in which each member nation has one vote, a security council of eleven members, including five permanent members (United States, USSR, Great Britain, France, and China), an economic and social council, an international court of justice, a trusteeship council, and a secretariat (administrative department) headed by a secretary-general.

Urban riots   The summers of 1966 and 1967 brought large-scale rioting ("a long hot summer") in Brooklyn, Buffalo, and Rochester in New York State; in Los Angeles, California; in Chicago, Illinois; in Cleveland and Toledo, Ohio; and in Detroit, Michigan. By far the most serious destruction of life and property was in Los Angeles and Detroit. The life and property cost in Los Angeles was thirty-five

killed and many millions of dollars lost by fire; in Detroit forty were killed and there was even greater property damage than in Los Angeles. Detroit's terror flared for five nights, July 23–27, 1967.

A few statistics give some concept of the scope of this largest riot in our history. Detroit officials reported 1364 fires during the five nights. The men called upon to suppress the violence included 4200 city police, 600 state troopers, 6000 National Guards, and 4700 army paratroopers. There were 800 buildings torn down because they had been made unsafe by fire. Buildings destroyed by fire numbered in the thousands. Over 3000 arrests were made. *See* **Los Angeles riots**.

U.S. Embassy at Teheran seized   (hostages held November 4, 1979) The shah (ruler) of Iran left his country, which was in a state of revolution on January 16, 1979. The Ayatollah Khomeini, an exiled religious leader, returned from Paris and took control in February. He was particularly bitter against the United States because the shah had been admitted there for medical treatment. He decided to hold the hostages until the United States returned the shah to stand trial in Iran. All members of the Iranian diplomatic corps in the United States were protected and permitted to return safely to their country. The U.S. hostages were said to be in the hands of an independent group of militants, most of them students. On April 24, 1980, an unsuccessful attempt, in which eight members of the U.S. armed forces died, was made to rescue the hostages. The hostages were subjected to medieval cruelties. The fifty-two hostages were released January 20, 1981, when Ronald Reagan was inaugurated as president.

V **Vallandigham, Clement** (1820–1871) In the North, opponents of "Lincoln's war" were called "copperheads." Their leader was a congressman from Ohio by the name of Clement Vallandigham. Under an 1862 order from President Lincoln that all persons "affording aid and comfort to rebels" would be subject to martial law, Vallandigham was tried by a military court and sentenced to prison for the duration of the war. Lincoln commuted the sentence to banishment and Vallandigham was escorted behind enemy lines. The South had no use for him, and he made his way to Canada. Meanwhile, he was nominated as the Democratic candidate for governor of Ohio and conducted his campaign from Canada. Although not elected, he polled a substantial vote. He returned to Ohio during the war and continued to defy "King Lincoln" but was not further prosecuted.

Valley Forge   During the bitter cold winter of 1777–78, Washington's army was encamped at Valley Forge, Pennsylvania, 20 miles west of Philadelphia, while the British forces under General William Howe benefited from the relative warmth and comfort of the city. Washington's army, poorly supplied, lacked warm clothing and adequate food.

Van Buren, Martin   *See* Presidents of the United States section, beginning on page 10-83.

Veblen, Thorstein B. (1857–1929)   Son of Norwegian immigrants, Veblen graduated from Carleton College in Minnesota. Later he studied philosophy at Johns Hopkins in Baltimore and at Yale, where he received a Ph.D. but could not find a job. He then enrolled at Cornell University to study economics and secured a position as a fellow at the University of Chicago. His first and greatest book, *The Theory of the Leisure Class* (1899), presented a new view of economic development and served as a challenge to traditional economics. It exercised considerable influence among liberals in the social sciences.

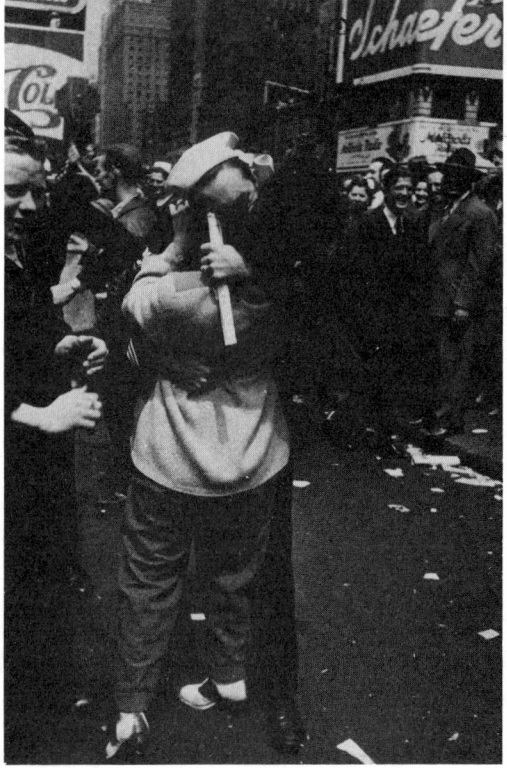

New Yorkers celebrating V.E. Day, the end of World War II in Europe in 1945.

V.E. Day (May 8, 1945)   Victory in Europe was achieved on this day with the unconditional surrender of the remainder of German military forces to the Allies. Russian and American troops had previously met at the Sebe River. The instrument of surrender was signed by Field Marshal Jodl in the Allied Headquarters at Reims and was formally ratified the next day in Berlin.

Venezuelan Boundary Crisis (1895)   A boundary dispute between British Guiana and Venezuela existing since 1840 flared hotly in 1885 when Britain extended its claims to include an area where new discoveries of gold had been made. President Cleveland urged arbitration to avoid a violation by England of the Monroe Doctrine. Lord Salisbury, British Foreign Minister, asserted that the Monroe Doctrine had no international status. After diplomatic tempers cooled, the dispute was arbitrated. Any parts of the disputed area occupied by either party for the last fifty years were awarded to that party.

Venezuelan debt controversy (1902)   Germany, England, and Italy bombarded ports of

Venezuela after prolonged less forceful approaches to reach agreement on debts owed by Venezuela had failed. President Theodore Roosevelt had advised the European nations that attempts to collect debts that did not result in seizure of Venezuelan territory did not violate the Monroe Doctrine. The bombardment caused Venezuela to request arbitration, and the European powers accepted the suggestion of Secretary of State John Hay to submit the financial problem to The Hague Tribunal. This incident brought about the Drago Doctrine.

Versailles Treaty (rejected 1920)   President Wilson played a role in framing this treaty, which contained the Covenant of the League of Nations. An effective statesman on the world scene, Wilson had nevertheless been inept in his relations with Congress. The Senate's rejection of the treaty reflected the personal antagonism between Wilson and Republican Senator Lodge and also the aftermath of the unusually bitter congressional campaign of 1918. While "taking the issue to the people," Wilson suffered a severe stroke in September 1919. Harding's election in 1920 made the entrance of the United States into the League of Nations a lost cause.

Vicksburg, battle of (May 22 to July 4, 1863)   The march to Vicksburg from the land side entailed a series of battles over a period of three weeks. Grant's army of 20,000 outfought larger Confederate forces over a distance of about 200 miles in enemy territory, and on May 22, 1863, the siege of Vicksburg began. The Confederate garrison under Pemberton held out under a brutal bombardment and two major assaults until July 4, when he surrendered with his 30,000 troops, who were on the point of mutiny through lack of food. Aside from prisoners, the casualties were about equal, between 9000 and 10,000. Lincoln had found a general who could win and stick at it until he ran the enemy right into the ground.

Vietnam   France was in control of Indo-China (Laos, Cambodia, and Vietnam) for a century before World War II. The Japanese occupied Indo-China during World War II. When the French returned after the war they were faced with the Vietminh, communist armies led by Ho Chi Minh that had fought the Japanese invaders. The Vietminh defeated the French army at Dien Bien Phu in 1954. A Geneva agreement divided Vietnam at the 17th parallel. In the North, the communist government was recognized with its capital at Hanoi. In the South the French set up a government based in Saigon. Free elections were to be held in 1956 to unite the country, but they were never held. Communist guerrilla forces in the South threatened to overthrow the Saigon government. President Kennedy sent in 2000 U.S. "military advisers" and increased the number to 15,500 before he was assassinated. President Johnson committed U.S. ground forces but could not defeat the Vietnamese even though he increased the number of troops to over 500,000. The war became increasingly unpopular, and Johnson knew he could not be reelected in 1968. Nixon, claiming to have a "secret" plan to end the war, was elected in 1968. The war went on. Nixon sent troops into Cambodia. It was learned that he had secretly authorized bombing Cambodia with over 3500 air raids since 1969. The plan was to turn the fighting over to the South Vietnamese as American troops were withdrawn. South Vietnam was unable to stem the tide from the North. On April 29, 1975, the last Americans, military and civilian, were evacuated from Vietnam, which was then under control of the Hanoi government just as it would have been in 1956 had the United States accepted the decisions of the Geneva Conference.

Villa's raids (1916)   Pancho Villa, a hero to many of the poorer people of Mexico, a revolutionary to President Carranza, and a bandit in American opinion, had led raids resulting in the killing of eighteen American engineers working in Mexican mines and, at another time, in the murder of seventeen U.S. citizens in Columbus, New Mexico. With the reluctant consent of President Carranza, Wilson sent General John J. Pershing into Mexico with a cavalry unit to catch Villa. After a ten-month pursuit proved futile, the U.S. troops were recalled. Villa was eventually killed by one of his Mexican enemies.

Virgin Islands   These islands in the eastern Caribbean were purchased by the United States from Denmark in 1917 during World War I for $25,000. Negotiations that had previously failed were consummated to prevent the islands from being taken by Germany. Of some fifty islands, the larger St. Thomas, St. John, and St. Croix are tourist favorites. Other sources of income are sugar and rum.

Virginia and Kentucky Resolutions   *See* **Kentucky and Virginia Resolutions**.

Virginia Plan   Introduced at the Constitutional Convention by Edmund Randolph of Virginia, the plan called for a bicameral (two-house) legislature with representation in each house based on population. This favored the large states. The New Jersey plan, introduced by William Patterson of New Jersey, proposed a bicameral legislature with each state having equal representation in each house. The Connecticut Plan, which was eventually accepted, was introduced by Roger Sherman of Connecticut. It proposed a bicameral legislature with representation to be based on population in the lower house (House of Representatives) and equal representation in the upper house (Senate). Once this issue was resolved the convention moved forward with its work.

Virginia's first legislature (1619)   An assembly of twenty-two men, two chosen from each town, "hundred," or plantation, met with Governor Yeardley and his council at Jamestown. This was the House of Burgesses, the first representative government in the New World.

V-J Day (September 2, 1945)   The instruments of surrender, signifying victory over Japan, were signed this day on the battleship *Missouri* in Tokyo Bay. General Douglas MacArthur accepted the surrender of Japan. Truman had warned the Japanese of a new weapon (the atom bomb) that would unleash horrible destruction of life if they carried on further resistance. The warning was not heeded, and the first bomb was dropped on Hiroshima on August 6, 1945, killing or wounding 180,000 people. A second bomb fell on Nagasaki three days later, killing or wounding 80,000 people. The Japanese then agreed to lay down their arms on condition that the emperor be permitted to remain as nominal ruler. MacArthur became the actual ruler of Japan during the next seven years.

Volstead Act (1920-1933)   The Eighteenth Amendment to the Constitution was proposed in late 1917, ratified in 1919, and put into effect on January 16, 1920. It outlawed the "manufacture sale, or transportation of intoxicating liquors." The Volstead Act, passed in 1920 over President Wilson's veto, defined the word *intoxicating* to mean any beverage containing over one-half of 1 percent alcohol. The Eighteenth Amendment was repealed in 1933 by ratification of the Twenty-first Amendment.

Volunteers in Service to America (VISTA)   It was organized in 1965 as the domestic counterpart to the Peace Corps. Volunteers receive training in accomplishing a special mission associated with people living in poverty. Assignments include working with children, the elderly, native Americans; and working in migrant labor camps, with the mentally ill, and in depressed rural areas.

Voting Rights Act (1965)   The act, sponsored by President Lyndon Johnson, was signed into law on August 6, 1965. It outlawed literacy tests and provided for registration of black voters by federal agents in states or counties that had less than 50 percent of its eligible voters registered on November 1, 1964. This provision automatically applied to Alabama, Georgia, Louisiana, Mississippi, and South Carolina, as well as many counties in North Carolina and Virginia. President Johnson hailed the law as finally putting the Fifteenth Amendment into effect.

Wabash decision (1886)   The state of Illinois set maximum railroad freight rates within the state. This was to protect shippers dependent on one railroad from rates set according to the "all the traffic will bear" practice of rate making. As rates set for Illinois would affect rates charged in other states, the Supreme Court ruled the Illinois laws unconstitutional because they regulated interstate commerce, a power reserved to the federal government. The Supreme Court commented upon the need for remedial legislation, which stimulated Congress to pass the Interstate Commerce Act in 1887.

Wade-Davis Bill (1864)   The bill provided that a seceded state could re-enter the Union only after a majority of its white male citizens took an oath of allegiance to the United States and the state submitted a constitution acceptable to Congress. Since the bill was passed during the last days of the session, Lincoln was able to kill it by a pocket veto. It was clear that a political struggle between the President and Congress over a reconstruction policy was under way.

Wagner Act (1935)   The act set up the National Labor Relations Board (NLRB) to make labor's right to organize effective. Elections in shops and industries were supervised to determine which union, if any, employees wished to join. Company unions were made illegal. Employers' attempts to discourage union membership through hiring or firing policies, persuasion by speech or press, and refusal to bargain collectively with union representatives were forbidden. It was a completely prolabor law intended to equalize the bargaining power of labor with that of management. Under its protection Big Labor came into being. *See* **National Labor Relations Board**.

War Hawks (1812)   Henry Clay was leader of the War Hawks. He made the most of his position as Speaker of the House to fan the war spirit. John C. Calhoun of South Carolina, Felix Grundy of Tennessee, Richard Johnson of Kentucky, and Langdon Cheves of South Carolina were other leading War Hawks. They were motivated by hatred of England or by ambition for expansion, or both. Clay thought a few Kentucky riflemen could capture Canada. There was talk of taking Florida and Mexico. The members of Congress clamoring for war represented the inland areas. They blamed the wars with native Americans upon the Canadians. At any given moment in history, what a people believe can be more influential and more important than what is true. The period preceding the War of 1812 was such a time.

War Production Board   The agency created by executive order in 1942 to oversee the production of war equipment and allocate materials between war and civilian needs.

Warren, Earl (1891–1974)   His parents were immigrants from Scandinavia who settled in California in 1889. Earl Warren, their only child, was raised in a family of very modest means, his father being a railroad worker. Earl, too, worked at menial railroad jobs but managed to get a college education at Berkeley. He went on to study law, getting his J.D. degree in 1914. He enlisted in the army during World War I. After his discharge he began a fifty-year career in public service—district attorney, state attorney general, and Republican governor of California (1943–53). He ran for vice president of the United States on the unsuccessful ticket of Republican candidate Thomas E. Dewey in 1948. He was appointed chief justice of the United States in 1953, a position he held until his retirement in 1969. He presided over decisions of great national import, including the school desegregation case *Brown* v. *Board of Education of Topeka, Kansas* (1954); *Baker* v. *Carr* (1962), the "one man, one vote" decision that required redistricting to establish equal state (and later federal) election districts; *Escobedo* v. *Illinois* (1964), reasserting the Fifth Amendment right against self-incrimination in criminal actions; and *Miranda* v. *Arizona*, further guaranteeing the rights of arrested persons when being interrogated by the police. At the request of President Lyndon Johnson, Warren reluctantly headed the commission of inquiry into the circumstances of the assassination of President Kennedy.

Washington, Booker T. (1856–1915)   Born a slave in Virginia, he became a national spokesman for his race. He advocated education and self-improvement of blacks. After graduating from Hampton Institute, Virginia, he opened the Tuskegee Institute in Alabama in a rundown building with a handful of students and developed it into a renowned educational institution. He urged his students to become skilled workers. Unlike his later rival, W. E. B. DuBois, he opposed agitation and confrontation and was willing to postpone the day of racial equality. His attitude was that slow and steady wins the race. Booker T. Washington's autobiography, *Up From Slavery*, is the best known of his many books. Under Washington's leadership Tuskegee's growth was financed by northern industrialists, including Andrew Carnegie, H. H. Rogers

of Standard Oil, and George Peabody. Washington was awarded an honorary degree from Harvard (1896), received President McKinley at Tuskegee (1898), and dined at the White House with President Theodore Roosevelt (1901).

Washington Conference (1921–1922)   The conference was presided over by Secretary of State Charles Evans Hughes. The agreements reached were as follows: (1) the United States, Great Britain, Japan, France, and Italy (five-power pact) limited their naval vessels of 10,000 tons and over in the ratio of 5:5:3:1.75:1.75; (2) the United States, Great Britain, Japan, and France (four-power pact) would settle disputes arising in the Far East by peaceful means; (3) all these powers plus Belgium, China, the Netherlands, and Portugal (nine-power pact) would respect China's political and territorial integrity; (4) Shantung was returned from Japan to China; and (5) asphyxiating gases were outlawed.

Washington, George   *See* Presidents of the United States section, beginning on page 10-83.

Watchful Waiting (1913)   In February 1913, President Madero of Mexico was assassinated by colleagues of Huerta, who then became president. When President Wilson took office he refused recognition of Huerta and blockaded Veracruz to prevent the delivery of arms shipments. This was the "watchful waiting." On April 9, 1914, American sailors were arrested at Tampico for trespassing in a restricted area but were soon released. Huerta refused to apologize, and U.S. Marines seized Veracruz on April 21. The ABC Conference at Niagara Falls, Canada, paved the way for the U.S. evacuation of Veracruz, Huerta's leaving Mexico, and the election of Carranza as President of Mexico. *See* **ABC Conference**.

Watergate, and the Nixon administration (1972–1974)   On June 17, 1972, at 2:30 A.M., five men were arrested in the Washington, D.C., Watergate Hotel Complex. They had broken into the national headquarters of the Democratic Party.

A seven-member Senate committee formed to investigate how presidential campaigns, particularly the campaign in 1972, had been conducted began hearings on May 17, 1973, and by August 9 had taken over 7000 pages of testimony. Most of these hearings were televised.

Witnesses before the Ervin Committee gave conflicting accounts of phone conversations and conferences. Since they had been taped, Senator Ervin, speaking for his committee, asked the president to make these tapes available to the committee. The president refused.

A special prosecutor, Archibald Cox, was appointed by President Nixon with a promise of full authority to prosecute cases without interference. Cox soon found that conflicting testimony in several cases could not be resolved without access to the tapes that President Nixon would not release. Cox went to the U.S. Court of Appeals, asking it to order the President to deliver them.

On October 20, 1973, a "bomb" dropped. President Nixon told Attorney General Richardson to fire Cox. Richardson refused to do so and resigned. The president then instructed Deputy Attorney General Ruckelshaus to fire Cox. He also refused, and Nixon fired him. The president told Solicitor General Robert

Bork to fire Cox. He did. This became known as the Saturday Night Massacre.

The Committee to Re-elect the President had received illegal contributions from several corporations. A few of their names were household words: American Airlines ($55,000), Goodyear Tire & Rubber Company ($40,000), and Gulf Oil ($100,000). As of February 1974, litigation was in process concerning contributions by ITT ($400,000) and Associated Milk Producers, Inc. ($527,500).

On June 24, 1974, a unanimous vote of the Supreme Court decided that President Nixon was legally obligated to deliver the requested tapes to Special Prosecutor Jaworski. Only six days later, the House Judiciary Committee voted to recommend that the House impeach Nixon on three charges: (1) obstruction of justice; (2) abusing his authority and violating his oath of office; and (3) subverting the Constitution by defying eight subpoenas for tapes in order to block impeachment.

He was told the House would impeach him by an overwhelming vote and the Senate would probably find him guilty by a wide margin over the two-thirds vote required. In a televised address President Nixon announced his resignation to take effect the following day, August 9, 1974.

Meanwhile Vice President Spiro Agnew, who was charged with bribery and extortion while governor of Maryland and vice president of the United States, plea-bargained his way out of jail by resigning as vice president. The penalty imposed by the court was a fine of $10,000 and three years' probation.

This resignation brought the Twenty-fifth Amendment into operation. President Nixon submitted the name of Gerald R. Ford, member of the House of Representatives from Michigan for 25 years as the new vice president. Ford was 60 years old, a conservative Republican, and considered by members of both houses of Congress as a suitable choice. He took the oath of office on August 9, 1974.

On his thirty-first day in office, September 8, President Ford granted Richard Nixon a "full, free and absolute pardon." Ford's press secretary, J. F. terHorst, resigned in protest. Shock and dismay were reactions from many members of Congress. An eventual pardon had been considered likely, but not until guilt had been legally established.

Webster-Ashburton Treaty (1842)   The treaty settled the border between Maine and New Brunswick. It also established the line from Lake Superior up the Pigeon River, through a chain of lakes and along the Rainey River to the Lake of the Woods. These settlements ended a long period of ill feeling associated with the Canadian border.

Webster, Daniel (1782–1852)   Born in Massachusetts, he graduated from Dartmouth College in New Hampshire (1801). He was elected to Congress from New Hampshire (1813–17). He moved to Boston, where he practiced law, appearing before the Supreme Court in the landmark cases *Dartmouth College* v. *Woodward, McCulloch* v. *Maryland,* and *Gibbons* v. *Ogden.* A member of the House of Representatives from Massachusetts (1823–27) and the U.S. Senate (1827–41 and 1845–50) and secretary of state (1841–43 and 1850–52), he was one of the greatest orators in American history. He defended the Union against Senator Hayne of South Carolina in an all-day oration on the floor of the Senate in which the stirring peroration starting with the words "when my eyes shall be turned to behold for the last time the sun in heaven...let their last feeble glance...behold the gorgeous ensign of the republic..." and ending with the stirring sentiment "Liberty *and* Union, now and forever, one and inseparable." In his last speech in the Senate, the famous Seventh of March (1850) address, he supported the Compromise of 1850 even though it made major concessions to slavery. *See also* **Webster-Hayne debates.**

Webster-Hayne debates (1830)   A debate in Congress over the sale of public lands brought a clash between the Northeast and the South over the nature of the Union. Hayne of South Carolina said that states created the Union. The South had insisted upon the Tenth Amendment's specifically and emphatically limiting federal power and recognizing states' rights. Nullification was clearly a power residing with the states. Webster insisted "We the people" established the Constitution with its primary purpose "to form a more perfect union," a purpose impossible to realize if each state could interpret federal law and the Constitution as it saw fit.

Wheeler-Rayburn Act (1935)   This act, also called the Public Utilities Holding Company Act prohibited holding companies beyond the second degree in interstate public utilities. The enforcement of this act was under the Securities and Exchange Commission for financial structure and policies, under the Federal Power Commission for electric power, and under the Federal Trade Commission for gas. Many holding companies were forced to reorganize.

Whiskey Rebellion (1794)   The excise tax on whiskey bore heavily on the corn farmers of Western Pennsylvania, who were forced to change corn into whiskey in order to get it to markets in New York and Philadelphia. They resisted the tax by attacks on federal marshals and tax collectors. Federal troops numbering 15,000 suppressed the disorders, which lasted about four months. President Washington backed Secretary of the Treasury Hamilton in the collection of this tax. It was a demonstration that our new government could and would collect taxes, a feat neither England nor the government under the Articles of the Confederation had been able to do. Washington himself took command of the troops at Reading, Pennsylvania, before dispatching them west to suppress the rebellion.

Whitney, Eli (1765–1825)   Graduated from Yale in 1792, he went to Georgia to study law. He observed slaves picking seeds from cotton by hand. Having learned mechanical crafts in his father's metal shop, he devised a cotton gin (engine) that enabled one worker to produce 50 pounds of cleaned cotton in a day. This made cotton a profitable crop and vastly increased the demand for and value of slaves in the South. The cotton gin was patented in 1794. Whitney was forced to spend his income on legal efforts to suppress patent infringements. Back in New Haven, Whitney secured a contract to produce 10,000 rifles for the federal government. He introduced the revolutionary manufacturing idea of interchangeable parts for which he designed precision

HISTORY OF THE UNITED STATES

machinery. Unskilled workers could now produce the muskets to specifications.

Wildcat banks   State-chartered banks that followed unsound banking practices by issuing paper money not sufficiently backed up by reserves of specie.

Willard, Emma Hart (1787–1870)   A pioneer in the education of women, she began teaching in 1804. She opened a school for boys and girls in her father's home. She taught in a Middlebury, Vermont, seminary for girls. She married Dr. Willard and opened a female college in her home (1814). She wrote *Plan for Improving Female Education* (1819), secured a grant from Troy, New York, and opened a female seminary (college) in September 1821, with the curriculum including the sciences, mathematics, history, modern languages, philosophy, household management, and nonsectarian religious studies. The Troy Female Seminary attracted students from all over the country. Many were granted loans to finance their education, repayable when they took teaching positions.

Williams, Roger (1603–1683)   This pastor of Plymouth and Salem offended Massachusetts Puritans by insisting that enforcement of the Ten Commandments was not a responsibility of the civil government. He further angered Massachusetts officialdom by asserting that the land claimed in their charter had been stolen from the native Americans. Threatened with exile to England, he fled to Narragansett Bay to establish the Providence Plantations in 1636 (Rhode Island). He maintained friendly relations with the native Americans, granted complete religious freedom, and set up a most liberal government. Official recognition was given Rhode Island by charter in 1644.

Wilmot Proviso (1846)   Introduced by David Wilmot, representative from Pennsylvania, the proviso forbade slavery in any territory the United States might gain by the Mexican War then going on. The proviso passed the House but had no chance of passing the Senate. Consideration of the Wilmot bill set off stormy debates over slavery and the right of Congress to legislate thereon; it also split Congress into factions defending and attacking the Mexican War itself.

Wilson at Versailles (1919)   Wilson's influence prevented Clemenceau from getting the Saar and German Rhineland for France, kept Orlando from getting Fiume for Italy, and the Poles from annexing East Prussia. Wilson agreed to give Shantung to Japan if it would soon be returned to China, as it finally was in 1921. The Monroe Doctrine was specifically excluded from interpretation by the League of Nations. In order to get the league's covenant written into the Versailles Treaty, Wilson accepted some terms neither he nor the American people approved. Such inequities, Wilson stated, could be corrected through the league as time proved them unwise.

Wilson's "Fourteen Points" (1918)   The points were part of an address he gave before Congress on January 8. It outlined the "only possible" program to prevent war. The major principles included (1) open covenants; (2) freedom of the seas; (3) removal of barriers to international trade; (4) reduction of armaments, (5) self-determination of peoples; and (6)

an association of nations. His call for an association of nations was his fourteenth point, and he emphasized it as the most important of all.

Wilson, Woodrow   *See* Presidents of the United States section, beginning on page 10-83.

Winthrop, John (1588–1649)   He practiced law in London, came to Salem as president of the Massachusetts Bay Company in 1630 with 700 Puritans, settled in Boston, served as governor or deputy governor of the "Bible Commonwealth" (1629–49) and was first president of the New England Confederation (1643). His two-volume work, *The History of New England*, a classic of English literature and history, based on the journal he kept during the years 1630–44, was published in 1825–26.

Works Progress Administration (WPA) (1935)   The largest and most comprehensive of the New Deal relief agencies, it promoted a great variety of programs to provide jobs and incomes for the unemployed.

World Court   Located at The Hague in the Netherlands, the court was originally established in 1921 as the judicial branch of the League of Nations. It became the judicial agency of the United Nations in 1945 as the International Court of Justice. The court consists of fifteen members, each serving for a term of nine years, elected by the general assembly and the security council. All members of the United Nations are also members of the International Court of Justice. The United States is a member with the proviso, known as the Conally Amendment, that the United States will decide whether a matter falls within the jurisdiction of the court.

World War I (1914–1918)   The war, which started in the summer of 1914 when a Serbian (Yugoslav) patriot assassinated the heir to the Austro-Hungarian throne, ultimately involved many of the world's nations from all continents. The Allies consisted of England and its empire, France, Italy, Russia, Belgium, Serbia, Montenegro, Rumania, Greece, Portugal, Japan, and later (April 6, 1917) the United States. The Central Powers consisted of Germany, Austria-Hungary, the Ottoman Empire (Turkey), and Bulgaria. President Wilson urged Americans to remain impartial "in thought as well as in action." He ran for re-election in 1916 on the platform "he kept us out of war." The fear of a German victory changed America's attitude, however, and Congress responded to Wilson's call by declaring war on Germany on April 6, 1917. The United States sent 2 million troops to France and brought about the downfall of the imperial German and Austro-Hungarian governments. Wilson declared that we were fighting "to make the world safe for democracy" and that the United States sought no material gains. U.S. military forces in Europe were commanded by General John J. Pershing. Personnel losses were 117,000 killed, 204,000 wounded, and 4500 prisoners and missing. The fighting ceased on November 11, 1918 (Armistice Day). The peace treaties were signed at Versailles (France) on June 18, 1919. Because the League of Nations was part of the treaty, however, the U.S. Senate refused to ratify the treaty by the required two-thirds vote.

World War II (1939–1945)   Hitler's Nazi armies invaded Poland on September 1, 1939. Britain and

France declared war on Germany on September 3. Russia attacked Poland from the east on September 17, occupied the Baltic States by October 10, and attacked Finland on November 30. Germany attacked Russia on June 22, 1941. Japanese naval and air forces made a surprise attack on the U.S. naval base at Pearl Harbor in Hawaii on December 7, 1941. It was now all-out war between the Allies—United States, Great Britain, and Russia (France was defeated by the Nazis in June 1940 with Italy attacking from the South)—versus the Axis—Germany, Japan, and Italy. The United States was involved in the war in Europe (including North Africa) and in Asia, including the entire Pacific Ocean. Major diplomatic decisions were made jointly by Franklin D. Roosevelt (United States), Winston Churchill (Great Britain), and Joseph Stalin (USSR). Overall war strategy was planned under the leadership of General George C. Marshall. Commander of all U.S. forces in Europe and Africa was General Dwight D. Eisenhower. In the Pacific the commander of U.S. forces was General Douglas MacArthur. A major naval and air battle was won by U.S. forces under Admiral Chester W. Nimitz at Midway Island on June 3–6, 1942. U.S. troops under General Eisenhower in conjunction with British troops invaded North Africa (October 1942) and drove the German and Italian troops out of that continent. Italy was then invaded from the south (July 1943). The USSR broke the back of the German invasion at Stalingrad (September 1942). The carefully prepared invasion of Europe from England was launched under General Eisenhower on D-Day, June 6, 1944, when Allied forces landed on the beaches of Normandy in France. The end of the war in Europe came with the German surrender on May 7, 1945 (V-E Day). The war in the Pacific consisted of island battles, including Iwo Jima and Okinawa, with fierce resistance from the Japanese. After atom bombs were dropped on Hiroshima (August 6, 1945) and Nagasaki (August 9, 1945), the Japanese surrendered on August 14, 1945. Official surrender took place on September 2, 1945 (V-J Day). U.S. casualties in World War II were 292,000 killed, 672,000 wounded, and 140,000 prisoners or missing.

Wounded Knee, battle of (December 29, 1890) This was more of a slaughter than a battle. The Sioux were performing their sacred Sun Dance, which had been outlawed by the federal government. At Wounded Knee in South Dakota, they were attacked by federal troops who ordered them to stop and then proceeded to kill some 200 men, women, and children. The men fought back killing twenty-nine of the invaders. In 1973 members of the American Indian Movement occupied the village of Wounded Knee and held it for two months as a symbol of their past grievances and demand for restitution.

Wright, Wilbur (1867–1912) and **Orville** (1871–1948) Brothers who pioneered in aviation, they manufactured bicycles at Dayton, Ohio. They became interested in aeronautics and studied on their own, constructed a motor-powered aircraft, and tested it at Kitty Hawk, North Carolina, where, on December 17, 1903, Orville piloted the plane and stayed aloft fifty-nine seconds, traveling 852 feet. Returning to Dayton they perfected the craft and, by the end of 1905, they flew 24 miles in thirty-eight minutes. The following year they obtained a patent for their invention. The U.S. Army conducted tests and accepted the craft in 1909. The Wright brothers organized a company in 1909 and began the manufacture of airplanes.

Writs of Assistance (1761) These writs were general search warrants issued by colonial courts to officers looking for smuggled goods. James Otis denounced such warrants as lacking in specific identification of the place to be searched and other details common to search warrants. He claimed such warrants to be unconstitutional and a denial of "the natural rights of man." Many colonial courts agreed with Otis.

 **XYZ affair** (1797) The French government, the corrupt Directory, was angered by the Jay Treaty with England and refused to receive Charles Coatesworth Pinckney when he arrived in France in December 1796. President Adams then appointed a three-man commission consisting of Pinckney and John Marshall (Federalists) and Elbridge Gerry (Republican) to attempt to secure a treaty of commerce and friendship with France. Instead of negotiating with this commission, the French foreign minister Tallyrand sent three agents to meet with the Americans. These agents, designated by the commission as X, Y, and Z, demanded a U.S. loan to France and a bribe of $240,000. The demands were rejected and commissioners Marshall and Gerry were recalled, leaving Pinckney in France to avoid giving France an excuse for declaring war on the United States. When Adams reported the French demands to Congress (designating their agents as X, Y, and Z), a wave of anger swept through the nation. The cry was "millions for defense but not one cent for tribute." There followed an undeclared naval war between France and the United States (1798–1800).

 **Yalta Conference** (1944) Franklin Roosevelt, Churchill, and Stalin agreed that (1) Russia would start a front against Japan; (2) liberated states would freely choose representative governments, (3) the San Francisco Conference on a United Nations would convene April 5, 1945; (4) Germany would be jointly occupied by the United States, Russia, England, and France; (5) Russia would occupy northern Korea and the United States would occupy southern Korea; (6) the Kurile Islands and southern Sakhalin would belong to Russia; (7) Poland would lose its eastern third to Russia but be extended westward at Germany's expense, and (8) the Ukraine and Byelo-Russia would have separate membership in the United Nations.

Yellow Dog contract In the 1890s, employers began to require prospective employees to sign an agreement that they would not join a union if employed by the company. These were dubbed "yellow dog" contracts by the unions, but the provision was upheld by the courts. The yellow dog contract was outlawed by the Norris-LaGuardia Anti-injunction Act of 1932.

"Yellow" journalism Newspapers made sensational to attract readers; associated originally with the use of yellow ink, particularly in the first comic strip, "The Yellow Kid."

Yorktown (1781) When Cornwallis settled his forces at Yorktown, he assumed British sea power controlled Chesapeake Bay and that Lafayette's forces were too weak to be a threat. A French fleet was soon to control the bay, however, while reinforcements were gathering under Steuben, Rochambeau, De Grasse, and Washington. Lafayette's weak force grew to 16,000 men under Washington. With his 8000 men, Cornwallis was hemmed in. Several attacks and counterattacks ended in the surrender of Cornwallis on October 17. Peace negotiations dragged on until September 1783, when the Treaty of Paris was ready for presentation to the U.S. Congress.

Young, Brigham (1801–1877) His family moved from Vermont to western New York and settled near Palmyra, where Joseph Smith, founder of the Mormon Church, published *The Book of Mormon.* Young was converted to the Mormon faith in 1832. By 1838 he had become a senior leader of the church. Upon the death of Joseph Smith (1844), Young became a leader of the church and guided the mass migration of the members to the Great Salt Lake in Utah (1847) and was first governor of the territory of Utah (1849–57). When he was removed by President Buchanan because of his advocacy and practice of polygamy, Young remained in effect the leader of the colony, and his administrative genius laid the groundwork for the survival and growth of the Mormon Church.

Young Plan (1929) The treaty of Versailles named Germany as the guilty party for World War I and required Germany to pay reparations to the Allies. An Allied Reparations Commission fixed the amount of reparations at $132 billion (1925). Germany defaulted (1923), and President Coolidge named a commission headed by Charles G. Dawes to investigate.

The resulting Dawes Plan (1924) scaled down the payments and set up a schedule. Germany's failure to meet the terms of the Dawes Plan brought about further negotiations. A new commission, headed by the American financial expert Owen D. Young, met in Paris (February 1929). The Young Plan reduced the amount of reparations to some $8 billion payable over fifty-eight and a half years at 5½ percent interest and set up a Bank for International Settlements whose profits would pay the reparations of the final twenty-two years. At the Lausanne Conference (1932), over 90 percent of the Young Plan reparations were cancelled, and with the advent of Hitler as German Chancellor the following year, all German reparations for World War I were renounced.

Zenger trial (1735) New York's colonial governor, William Cosby, had aroused opposition by his arbitrary acts. The *New York Weekly Journal,* printed by Peter Zenger, represented Cosby's political opponents. It stated that Cosby was arbitrary and tyrannical. Zenger was charged with seditious libel. Andrew Hamilton, Zenger's lawyer, claimed that true statements were not libelous. The judge ruled that publication itself was libel regardless of the truth. The jury rejected the court's ruling, believed the statements published to be true, and declared Zenger not guilty. This was a big step toward freedom of the press.

Zimmerman note The Zimmerman note (1917), intercepted by the British and released by the State Department on March 1, influenced public opinion against Germany. This message from Germany to Mexico promised Mexico the return of Texas, New Mexico, and Arizona if Mexico would enter the war against the United States and invite Japan to do the same. Zimmerman was foreign secretary of Germany.

PRESIDENTS OF THE UNITED STATES

l. George Washington (1732–1799): President 1789–1797

Washington's public service before he became president:

> Lieutenant colonel in the French and Indian War (1753–56)
>
> Virginia delegate to the First and Second Continental Congresses (1774 and 1775)
>
> Head command of the Continental armies in the Revolution (1775–83)
>
> Virginia delegate to the Annapolis Convention (1786)
>
> Chairman of the Constitutional Convention (1787)

Washington as president:

1789   Congress established offices of Secretary of State, Secretary of Treasury, Postmaster General, and Attorney General.

Washington sought to keep party strife at a minimum. He appointed Jefferson, leader of the strict constructionists of the Constitution, and Hamilton, leader of the loose constructionists, as secretary of state and of treasury, respectively. In 1794, John Jay, a New York Federalist, and James Monroe, a Virginian Democratic-Republican, were sent to London and Paris, respectively, to represent the United States. In his farewell address he warned that political party strife was a constant danger.

1789   Judiciary Act

1789   Tariff, excise taxes, sale of public lands

These were the chief sources of revenue for what then seemed to be a tremendous federal debt.

1790   Assumption Bill

Passed by logrolling in association with the location of the permanent capital no farther north than the Potomac River.

1791   Bill of Rights ratified

Some states demanded assurance of this action as a condition for their ratification of the Constitution.

1791   Bank of the United States (BUS)

1793   Citizen Genêt and Washington's neutrality proclamation

1794   Whiskey Rebellion in Pennsylvania—*See* page 10-79.

1795   Jay Treaty with England

1795   Pinckney Treaty with Spain

1796   Farewell Address

Washington opposed permanent entangling alliances and expounded upon the "baneful effects of the spirit of party." The foreign policy advice was a basic guide for over a century, and the danger that political parties in their struggle for power may destroy the nation is always with us.

2. John Adams (1735–1826): President 1797–1801

Adams' public service before he became president:

> One of the most effective writers against the Stamp Act
>
> Defended the British soldiers involved in the Boston Massacre
>
> Massachusetts delegate to both the First and Second Continental Congresses
>
> Helped to negotiate the Treaty of Paris, 1783
>
> Vice president under Washington

Adams as president (Federalist):

1797   XYZ affair—*See* page 10-81.

1798   Alien Act, Sedition Act, Naturalization Act—*See* **Alien and Sedition Acts**.

These excuses to protect the United States from non-existent revolutionary Jacobin dangers were really aimed to lessen the influence of the Democratic-Republican Party. They boomeranged against the Federalists and Jefferson was elected.

1798   Kentucky and Virginia Resolutions—*See* page 10-47.

3. Thomas Jefferson (1743–1826): President 1801–1809

Jefferson's public service before he became president:

> Member of the Virginia House of Burgesses
>
> Wrote "A Summary View of the Rights of British America" in 1774
>
> Virginia delegate to the Second Continental Congress, 1775–76
>
> Wrote the Declaration of Independence
>
> Governor of Virginia, 1779–81
>
> U.S. Minister to France, 1785–89
>
> Secretary of state, 1789–93
>
> Leader of the Republican party (Democratic-Republican)
>
> Vice president under Adams
>
> Wrote the Kentucky Resolutions
>
> Author of the Statute of Virginia for Religious Freedom

Jefferson as president (Democratic-Republican):

1803   *Marbury* v. *Madison*

1804   Louisiana Purchase

1804   Twelfth Amendment

1804–06   Lewis and Clark expedition

1807   Embargo Act

1809   Non-Intercourse Act

4. James Madison (1751–1836): President 1809–1817

Madison's public service before he became president:

> Member of the Second Continental Congress from Virginia, 1775–81
>
> A leading force in arranging the Mount Vernon, Annapolis, and Philadelphia Constitutional Conventions
>
> Author of several issues of the Federalist Papers
>
> Secretary of state under Jefferson
>
> Author of the Virginia Resolution against the Alien and Sedition Acts

Madison as president (Democratic-Republican):

1810   Macon Act

1811   William Henry Harrison defeated Tecumseh at Tippecanoe

1812–15   War of 1812 (Treaty of Ghent)
1814   Hartford Convention
   Marked the end of the Federalist party as a national influence.
1816   Second Bank of the United States (BUS)

5. James Monroe (1758–1831): President 1817–1825
Monroe's public service before he became president:
   Revolutionary War record:
   Fought at White Plains, Trenton (wounded), Brandywine, Germantown, and Monmouth
   Made a major during the winter at Valley Forge
   Member of the Virginia Legislature
   U.S. Senator
   U.S. minister to France (1794–96)
   Governor of Virginia
   Special envoy to France at the time of the Louisiana Purchase (1803)
   U.S. minister to England (1803–06)
   Secretary of state under Madison (1811–17) and also secretary of war (1814-15)

Monroe as president (Democratic-Republican):
1817–23   Era of Good Feeling—*See* page 10-28.
   National pride soared at the news of the Treaty of Ghent and Jackson's victory at New Orleans. The disintegration of the Federalist party meant no organized opposition to government policies.
1818   Rush-Bagot Agreement
1819–24   Marshall's decisions (*McCulloch* v. *Maryland, Dartmouth College* v. *Woodward,* and *Gibbons* v. *Ogden*)
1819   Adams-Onis Treaty
1820   Missouri Compromise—*See* page 10-55.
1823   Monroe Doctrine
1824   First sectional tariff

6. John Quincy Adams (1767–1848): President 1825–1829
Adams' public service before he became president:
   U.S. minister to the Netherlands (1794–96)
   U.S. minister to Prussia (1797–1801)
   U S. minister to Russia (1809–14)
   U S. minister to Great Britain (1815–17)
   Secretary of state under President Monroe

Adams as president (National Republican):
1825   Erie Canal—*See* page 10-28.
1828   Tariff of Abominations
1828   Calhoun's "Exposition and Protest"
1828   Noah Webster's dictionary
   This accepted authority on words greatly aided in building national unity by checking the development of provincial dialects.

7. Andrew Jackson (1767–1845): President 1829–1837
Jackson's public service before he became president:
   U.S. senator from Tennessee (1797)
   Judge of the Tennessee Supreme Court (1798–1804)
   Major general and hero at the battle of New Orleans (1815)
   Led the conquest of Florida (1818)
   Military governor of Florida (1823)
   U.S. senator from Tennessee (1823–25)

Jackson as president (Democrat):
1829–41   Jacksonian democracy
   Reforms and movements for the people's benefit marked this period. The first President of truly "common-folk" family background inspired these developments, although Jackson himself did not lead them and even disapproved of some of them.
1832   Tariff
1832   South Carolina's Nullification Act
1832   Veto of the recharter of the Second Bank of the United States
1833   Force Bill
1833   Clay's Compromise Tariff
1836   Specie Circular
1837   Gag Rule adopted by Congress—*See* page 10-35 for new "gag rule" application under the Bush administration.

8. Martin Van Buren (1782–1862): President 1837–1841
Van Buren's public service before he became president:
   U S. Senator from New York (1821–28)
   Governor of New York (1829)
   Secretary of state under Jackson (1829–32)
   Vice president under Jackson (1833–37)

Van Buren as president (Democrat):
1836–44   Gag Rule in effect
1837   Panic
1840   Independent or Sub-Treasury System

9. William Henry Harrison (1773–1841): President March 4 to April 4, 1841
Harrison's public service before he became president:
   Governor of the Indiana Territory (1801–12)
   In command at the battle of Tippecanoe (1811)
   Defeated the British in Canada (Thames River, 1813)
   U.S. Senator from Ohio (1825–28)

Harrison as president (Whig):
1841   Died one month after inauguration, April 4

10. John Tyler (1790–1862): President 1841–1845
Tyler's public service before he became president:
   Member of Congress from Virginia (1816–21)
   Governor of Virginia (1825–27)
   U.S. Senator from Virginia (1827–36)

Tyler as president (Democrat elected on a Whig ticket):
1842   Webster-Ashburton Treaty
1844   Telegraph (Baltimore to Washington, D.C.)

11. James K. Polk (1795–1849): President 1845–1849
Polk's public service before he became president:
   Member of the House of Representatives from Tennessee (1825–39)
   Speaker of the House (1835–39)
   Governor of Tennessee (1839–41)

Polk as president (Democrat):
1845   Texas entered the Union
1846   Oregon boundary settled at the 49th parallel
1846–48   Mexican War (Guadalupe-Hidalgo Treaty)
1846   Wilmot Proviso versus Calhoun-Davis Treaty

12. Zachary Taylor (1784–1850): President 1849–1850

Taylor's public service before he became president:
U.S. Army (1808–48)
Defeated Santa Anna at Buena Vista (1847)

Taylor as president (Whig):
1849   California gold rush ("forty-niners")

13. Millard Fillmore (1800–1874): President 1850–1853

Fillmore's public service before he became president:
Member of the House of Representatives (1833–35; 1837–43)
Vice president under Taylor

Fillmore as president (Whig):
1850   Compromise of 1850 (Omnibus Bill)
1850   Clayton-Bulwer Treaty
1852   *Uncle Tom's Cabin*

14. Franklin Pierce (1804–1869): President 1853–1857

Pierce's public service before he became president:
Brigadier general under General Scott in the Mexican War
Member of the House of Representatives from New Hampshire (1833–37)
Member of U.S. Senate from New Hampshire (1837–42)

Pierce as president (Democrat):
1853   Gadsden Purchase
1853   Matthew Perry opened Japan to world trade
1854   Kansas-Nebraska Act—*See* page 10-46.
1854   Ostend Manifesto
1856–58 Violence in Kansas

15. James Buchanan (1741–1868): President 1857–1861

Buchanan's public service before he became president:
Member of Congress from Pennsylvania (1820–31)
U.S. minister to Russia (1832–33)
U.S. Senator from Pennsylvania (1835–45)
Secretary of state under Polk (1845–49)
U.S. minister to Great Britain (1853–56)
Helped draft Ostend Manifesto (1854)

Buchanan as president (Democrat):
1857   Taney's Dred Scott Decision
1858   Lincoln-Douglas debates
1859   John Brown at Harper's Ferry
1861   Morrill Tariff

16. Abraham Lincoln (1809–1865): President 1861–1865

Lincoln's public service before he became president:
Member of Illinois State Legislature (Whig) (1835–42)
Member of U.S. House of Representatives (1846–48)

Lincoln as president (Republican):
1861–65 Civil War
1862   Homestead Act
1862   Morrill Act encouraged establishment of land-grant colleges
1863   Emancipation Proclamation (in effect January 1, 1863; issued September 22, 1862)—*See* page 10-27.
1863   National Banking Act
1865   Lincoln assassinated by John Wilkes Booth, April 14, 1865

17. Andrew Johnson (1808–1875): President 1865–1869

Johnson's public service before he became president:
Democratic congressman from Tennessee (1843–53)
Governor of Tennessee (1853–57)
Democratic senator from Tennessee (1857–62)
Military governor of Tennessee (1862–64)
Vice president in Lincoln's second term (43 days)
The only Southern senator to support the Union during the Civil War

Johnson as president (Republican):
1865   Thirteenth Amendment
1866   Field's Atlantic cable (Newfoundland to Ireland)
1867   Tenure of Office Act
1867–68 Reconstruction Acts
1867   Purchase of Alaska
1868   Fourteenth Amendment
1868   Johnson's impeachment and trial

18. Ulysses S. Grant (1822–1885): President 1869–1877

Grant's public service before he became president:
Captain in the Mexican War
"Unconditional surrender" Grant at Forts Henry and Donelson
After Vicksburg and Chattanooga in supreme command of Union army
Forced Lee's surrender at Appomattox (April 9, 1865)

Grant as president (Republican):
1869   Union Pacific and Central Railroads join at Promontory, Utah
1870   Fifteenth Amendment
1872   *Alabama* claims settled at Geneva Tribunal
1872   Crédit Mobilier scandal broke
1872   Tweed Ring
1873   Panic
1875   Whiskey Ring
1877   *Munn* v. *Illinois*
1877   Electoral Commission elected Hayes

19. Rutherford B. Hayes (1822–1893): President 1877–1881

Hayes' public service before he became president:
Member of Congress from Ohio (1865–67)
Governor of Ohio for three terms (1868–72; 1874–76)

Hayes as president (Republican):
1877   Federal troops withdrawn from the South
1878   Bland-Allison Act passed over Hayes' veto

20. James A. Garfield (1831–1881): President March 4 to September 19, 1881

Garfield as president (Republican):
1881   Garfield assassinated by Julius Guiteau, September 19, 1881

21. Chester A. Arthur (1830–1886): President 1881–1885

Arthur's public service before he became president:

Quartermaster general of New York during the Civil War

Collector of customs duties at the Port of New York

Vice president March 4–September 19, 1881

Arthur as president (Republican):
1882   Chinese Exclusion Act
1883   Pendleton Act
1883   Pendleton Act

22. Grover Cleveland (1837–1908): President 1885–1889
Cleveland's public service before he became president:

Assistant district attorney of Erie County, New York (1863)
Sheriff of Erie County, New York (1864)
Mayor of Buffalo, New York (1881–82)
Governor of New York (1882–84)

Cleveland as president (Democrat):
1886   Presidential Succession Act
1886   Knights of Labor reached its peak membership and the American Federation of Labor (AFL) founded
1886   Haymarket Square riot
1886   *Wabash Railroad* v. *Illinois*
1887   Cleveland versus Congress on tariff and the surplus
1887   Interstate Commerce Act

23. Benjamin Harrison (1833–1901): President 1889–1893
Harrison's public service before he became president:
Officer in the Civil War (Indiana Regiment)
U S. Senator from Indiana (1881–87)

Harrison as president (Republican):
1889–90   Washington, Montana, North Dakota, South Dakota, Wyoming, and Idaho entered the Union (Omnibus states)
1889   Pan-American Conference
1889–91   Incidents involving Secretary of State Blaine with Germany, Italy, England, and Chile
1890   Logrolling involving the McKinley Tariff and the Sherman Silver Act
1890   Sherman Anti-trust Act

24. Grover Cleveland (1837–1908) *See* first administration, 1885–1889
Second administration: President 1893–1897 (Democrat)
1893   Panic
1893   The gold reserve and the Morgan deal
1894   Wilson-Gorman Tariff
1894   Pullman strike
1895   Venezuelan boundary dispute

25. William McKinley (1843–1901): President 1897–1901
McKinley's public service before he became president:
Officer in the Union army at Antietam and other battles
Member of the House of Representatives from Ohio (1876–81; 1883–90)
Governor of Ohio (1891–95)

McKinley as president (Republican):
1897   Dingley Tariff

1898   Spanish-American War (Treaty of Paris)
1898   Hawaiian Islands annexed
1899   First Hague Conference
1900   Open Door Policy
1900   Boxer Rebellion
1900   Governments set up in the Philippines and Puerto Rico
1901   Platt Amendment for Cuba
1901   McKinley assassinated by Leon Czolgosz (September 6), six months into his second term as president

26. Theodore Roosevelt (1858–1919): President 1901–1909
Theodore Roosevelt's public service before he became president:
Assemblyman in the New York State Legislature (1882–84)
U S Civil Service commissioner (1889–95)
New York City Police commissioner (1895–97)
Assistant secretary of the navy (1897–98)
Organized and led the Rough Riders in the Spanish-American War (1898)
Governor of New York (1898–1900)
Vice president during the six months of McKinley's second term (1901)

Theodore Roosevelt as president (Republican):
1901–03   Panama Canal Zone acquired
The Hay-Pauncefote Treaty, the Hay-Herran Treaty, the revolt of Panama from Colombia, and the Hay-Bunau-Varilla Treaty were major moves in this acquisition—*See* page 10-40.
1902   Newlands Reclamation Act
1902   Coal strike
1903   Department of Commerce and Labor established
1904   Venezuelan debt controversy
1904   Northern Securities case
1904   Roosevelt Corollary to the Monroe Doctrine
1905   Receivership of the Dominican Republic
1905   Portsmouth Treaty
1906   Algeciras Conference
1906   Pure Food and Drug Act
1906   Hepburn Act
1907   Second Hague Conference (Drago Doctrine)
1907   "Gentlemen's agreement" with Japan
1908   Root-Takahira Agreement with Japan

27. William H. Taft (1857–1930). President 1909–1913
Taft's public service before he became president:
U.S. solicitor general under Harrison (1890–92)
Judge of U.S. Circuit Court (1892–1900)
Head of commission to organize government of the Philippines (1900)
First governor general of the Philippines (1901–04)
Secretary of war under Theodore Roosevelt (1904–08)

Taft as president (Republican):
1909   Payne-Aldrich Tariff
Rhode Island's Senator Aldrich and two successive speakers of the House, "Uncle Joe" Cannon and

Champ Clark, defeated Taft's efforts toward tariff reform.

1910 Ballinger-Pinchot controversy—*See* page 10-6.

Public opinion erroneously concluded that Taft was not supporting conservation. Actually, Taft's conservation record was excellent. He persuaded Congress to set up the Bureau of Mines to watch over government mineral sites, added tremendous tracts of timber in the Appalachians, and initiated conservation of oil lands.

1911 Antitrust suits against Standard Oil Company of New Jersey and the American Tobacco Company ("rule of reason" introduced)

1913 Sixteenth Amendment

28. Woodrow Wilson (1856–1924): President 1913–1921

Wilson's public service before he became president:
    President of Princeton University (1902–10)
    Governor of New Jersey (1910–12)

Wilson as president (Democrat):
1913 Seventeenth Amendment
1913 Underwood Tariff
1913 Federal Reserve Act (Glass-Owen Bill)
1913–14 "Watchful waiting" with Mexico

The assassination of the Mexican president, Madero, by supporters of General Huerta, Wilson's refusal to recognize Huerta as president of Mexico, the arrest of U.S. Marines at Tampico, the occupation of Veracruz by the United States, the ABC Conference at Niagara Falls, Canada, and the election of Carranza as president of Mexico were the major items in United States-Mexican relations.

1914 Clayton Antitrust Act
1915 *Lusitania* sunk
1916 Sussex Pledge made (broken February 1, 1917)
1917–18 World War I—*See* page 10-80.

On the home front the Liberty Loans, Adamson Act, Emergency Fleet Corporation, War Industries Board, Lever Food and Fuel Act, and the Overman Act were major aspects of the war effort.

On the fighting front America's greatest contributions occurred at Château-Thierry, Belleau Wood, Second Battle of the Marne, the Somme, Ypres, Saint Mihiel, and the final ictory push in the Meuse-Argonne section from September 26 to November 11.

On the idealogical front President Wilson's "fourteen points" speech of January 8, 1918, had tremendous immediate impact. Such ideas as open diplomacy, freedom of the seas, reduction of trade barriers, reduction of armaments, self-determination of peoples, and an association of nations remain vital.

1917 Virgin Islands purchased from Denmark
1919 Eighteenth Amendment
1919 "Red scare" and Attorney General Palmer
1919 Versailles Treaty and the League of Nations
1920 Esch-Cummins Act (Transportation Act of 1920)
1920 Nineteenth Amendment

29. Warren G. Harding (1865–1923): President 1921–1923

Harding's public service before he became president:

Senator in the Ohio Legislature (1900–04)
Lieutenant governor of Ohio (1904–06)
U.S. senator from Ohio (1915–21)

Harding as president (Republican):
1921–22 Washington Naval Conference
1922 Fordney-McCumber Tariff

30. Calvin Coolidge (1872–1933): President (1923–1929)

Coolidge's public service before he became president:
    Mayor of Northampton, Massachusetts (1910–11)
    Lieutenant Governor of Massachusetts (1916–18)
    Governor of Massachusetts (1919–20)
    Vice president of the United States (1921–23)

Coolidge as president (Republican):
1924 Teapot Dome and Elk Hills scandals exposed
1925 Ambassador Morrow set pattern to end extensive foreign ownership of oil properties in Mexico
1927 Veto of the McNary-Haugen Bill
1928 Kellogg-Briand Pact (Pact of Paris)

31. Herbert Hoover (1874–1964): President (1929–1933)

Hoover's public service before he became president:
    Headed war relief in Belgium
    Food administrator in World War I
    Secretary of commerce under Harding and Coolidge

Hoover as president (Republican):
1929 National Origins Immigration Act
1929 Panic and depression
1930 Boulder Dam (Hoover Dam)
1930 Hawley-Smoot Tariff
1932 Stimson Doctrine
1933 Twentieth Amendment

32. Franklin D. Roosevelt (1882–1945): President 1933–1945

Franklin Roosevelt's public service before he became president:
    State senator in New York (1911–13)
    Assistant secretary of the navy (1913–20)
    Governor of New York (1928–32)

Franklin Roosevelt as president (Democrat):
1933 Civilian Conservation Corps (CCC) Reforestation Act
1933 Agricultural Adjustment Act (AAA)
1933 National Industrial Recovery Act (NRA)
1933 Federal Securities Act
1933 Gold standard modified
1933 Tennessee Valley Authority (TVA)
1933 Good Neighbor Policy (Platt Amendment abrogated)
1933 Twenty-first Amendment
1934 Dollar devalued
1935 Works Progress Administration (WPA)
1935 National Labor Relations Act (Wagner-Connery Act)—*See* **Wagner Act**, page 10-77.
1935 Social Security Act
1935–39 Neutrality Acts—*See* page 10-56.
1937 Roosevelt's Supreme Court reorganization plan
1937 *Panay* incident
1938 The second AAA

1940 Fifty "overage" destroyers transferred to England in exchange for air bases in the Western Hemisphere

1940 Selective Service Act (first peacetime draft in United States)

1940 Roosevelt elected for third consecutive term

1941 Lend-Lease Act—*See* page 10-50.

1941 United States occupied Greenland for Denmark

1941 Iceland welcomed U.S. occupation

1941 Atlantic Charter

1941 Pearl Harbor (December 7)

The next day the United States declared war on Japan. On December 11 Germany and Italy declared war on the United States.

1942 MacArthur driven from Corregidor as Japan took Philippines (May 6)

In December 1944, MacArthur reoccupied the Philippines after Japanese sea power had been broken in the battle of Leyte Gulf—*See* **World War II**, page 10-80.

August 1942–June 1945 Island hopping in the Pacific

The major hops were Guadalcanal (Solomons); Tarawa and Makin (Gilberts); Kwajalein and Eniwetok (Marshalls); Saipan and Guam (Marianas); Iwo Jima; and Okinawa.

1942–43 African campaign

American Generals Eisenhower and Patton cooperated with the British General Montgomery. The British worked westward from Egypt while the Americans worked eastward from Casablanca on the Moroccan coast. The German and Italian forces under Rommel (the Desert Fox) were relentlessly pushed between two superior forces until they were trapped in Tunisia, where a quarter of a million troops surrendered on May 13, 1943. The North African coast was thus a base for an attack on Italy. In September General Mark Clark invaded Italy at Salerno.

1943–46 International conferences planned for winning the war and building the peace

The more important meetings were at Casablanca (January 1943), Moscow (October 1943), Cairo (November 1943) Teheran (November 1943), Bretton Woods (July 1944), Dumbarton Oaks (August 1944), and Yalta (February 1945).

1944 General Eisenhower made Supreme Commander at Headquarters of Allied Expeditionary Forces in London (SHAEF)

1944 D-Day, June 6

33. Harry S Truman (1844–1972): President 1945–1953

Truman's public service before he became president:
    Captain in the field artillery in World War I
    Judge of Jackson County Court in Missouri (1922–34)
    U.S. senator from Missouri (1934–44)
    Vice president (1945)

Truman as president (Democrat):

1945 San Francisco Conference (April)

1945 V-E Day (May 6)

1945 United States joined the United Nations (July 28)

1945 Atom bombs dropped on Hiroshima (August 6) and on Nagasaki (August 9)

1945 V-J Day (August 15)

1946 Philippines became independent (July 4)

1947 Truman Doctrine

1947 Marshall Plan (European Recovery Plan, ERP)

1947 Taft-Hartley Act

1947 Presidential Succession Act

1948–49 Berlin Airlift (June 24 to May 17)

1949 North Atlantic Treaty Organization (NATO)

1950–51 Korean War (June to June)—*See* page 10-48.

Negotiations for exchange of prisoners dragged on into 1953 before a truce, not peace, was arranged.

1951 Twenty-second Amendment

34. Dwight D. Eisenhower (1890–1969): President 1953–1961

Eisenhower's public service before he became president:
    Assistant military advisor to the Philippines (1935–39)
    Chief of War Plans Division in Office of Chief of Staff (1942)
    Chief of Operations Divisions in Office of Chief of Staff (1942)
    Commander of invasion of North Africa (1942)
    Commander of invasion of Europe-SHAEF (Supreme Headquarters Allied Expeditionary Forces) (1944)
    Chief of staff (1945)
    President of Columbia Univeristy (1948–51)
    Supreme commander of allied powers in Europe SHAPE (Supreme Headquarters Allied Powers in Europe) (1951)

Eisenhower as president (Republican):

1953–55 Taiwan, Quemoy, and Matsu

1954 *Brown* v. *Board of Education, Topeka, Kansas*

1954 Substantial support in money and supplies for France in Indo-China

1954 Southeast Asia Treaty Organization (SEATO)

1956 Suez Crisis

1957 Eisenhower Doctrine

1957 Race in space began (Sputnik I orbited the earth)

1959 Alaska and Hawaii became states

1959 St. Lawrence Seaway opened

1960 U-2 incident wrecked summit conference

35. John F. Kennedy (1917–1963): President 1961–1963

Kennedy's public service before he became president:
    Distinguished record in Pacific theater of World War II (1941–45)
    Member of the House of Representatives from Massachusetts (1947–53)
    Member of the Senate from Massachusetts (1953–61)

Kennedy as president (Democrat):

1961 Twenty-third Amendment

1961 Peace Corps

1961 Alliance for Progress

1961 Bay of Pigs, Cuba

1961 Berlin Wall built

1962 *Baker* v. *Carr*
1962 United States guaranteed South Vietnam protection from aggression
1962 Cuban missile crisis
1963 Nuclear Test Ban Treaty
1963 Kennedy assassinated by Lee Harvey Oswald (November 22)

36. Lyndon B. Johnson (1908–1973): President 1963–1969
Johnson's public service before he became president:
   Member of the House of Representatives from Texas (1937–49)
   Commander in U.S. Navy—distinguished war record (1941–45)
   Member of the Senate from Texas (1949–61)
   Minority leader (1953–55)
   Majority leader (1955–61)
   Vice president (1961–63)

Johnson as president (Democrat):
1964 *Wesberry* v. *Sanders*
1964 Civil Rights Act
1964 Twenty-fourth Amendment
1964 Economic Opportunity Act (began official War on Poverty)
1965–66 Massive military and air-sea support for South Vietnam
1965 Immigration Act
1965 Twenty-fifth Amendment proposed
1966 Medicare (effective July 1)

37. Richard M. Nixon (b. 1913): President 1969–1974
Nixon's public service before he became president:
   Officer in the U.S. Navy (1942–46)
   Member of the House of Representatives from California (1947–51)
   Member of the Senate from California (1951–53)
   Vice president 1953–61

Nixon as president (Republican):
1969 Moon landings by American astronauts in Apollo 11 and Apollo 12
1969 Massive protests against war in Vietnam, troop withdrawals begin
1972 Nixon visits China
1972 Nixon visits USSR, signs Strategic Arms Limitation Treaty (SALT I)
1973 Senate Select Committee televised hearings on the Watergate scandal begin May 17, shocking revelations; White House counsel John Dean testifies that Nixon took part in a cover-up—*See* page 10-78.
1973 Vice President Spiro Agnew resigns (October 11); Nixon submits name of Gerald Ford who is confirmed by Congress and sworn in December 6.
1974 Nixon resigns August 8; Ford is sworn in as president August 9

38. Gerald R. Ford (b. 1913): President 1974–1977
Ford's public service before he became president:
   Lieutenant commander in U.S. Navy during World War II
   Member of the House of Representatives from Michigan (1949–74)
   Republican leader of the House (1966–74)
   Member of the Warren Commission investigating the assassination of President Kennedy

Appointed vice president after resignation of Spiro Agnew (1973–74)

Ford as president (Republican):
1974 Ford grants Nixon a "full, free and absolute pardon" for any crimes he may have committed; the pardon granted one month after Ford took office
1974 Ford in Asia: meets Soviet leader Brezhnev in a détente move in Vladivostok, then visits Japan and South Korea

39. James E. (Jimmy) Carter (b. 1924): President 1977–1981
Carter's public service before he became president:
   Graduated from Annapolis Naval Academy
   Aide to Admiral Rickover (Nuclear Submarine Program)
   Member of the Georgia Senate
   Governor of Georgia (1971–75)

Carter as president (Democrat):
1978 Panama Canal Treaties; United States terminates lease of Canal Zone as of December 31, 1999, retains defense rights
1978 Carter holds meetings at Camp David (the presidential retreat in Maryland) with Begin of Israel and Sadat of Egypt; peace accords are drawn up for Middle East
1979 Formal signing of treaty in Washington bringing peace between Egypt and Israel
1979 SALT II (Strategic Arms Limitation Treaty) negotiated by Carter and Brezhnev
1979 Nuclear power plant at Three Mile Island near Harrisburg, Pennsylvania, overheats and releases radioactive gasses
1979 (November 4) A mob led by militant students occupies the U.S. embassy in Teheran (Iran) and holds fifty-two Americans as hostages
1980 Rescue efforts (April 24) abandoned; eight Americans die in the effort; hostages treated cruelly; finally released January 20, 1981, after a 444-day ordeal, just as Reagan is being sworn in as president

40. Ronald Reagan (b. 1911): President 1981–1989
Reagan's public service before he became president:
   Captain in U.S. Air Force (1942–45)
   Governor of California (1967–74)

Reagan as president (Republican):
1980 (November) Reagan wins in landslide—Electoral College: Reagan 489, Carter 49; Republicans gain control of Senate first time in 30 years
1981 Budget priorities: sharp increase in defense expenditures with decrease in social programs; unbalanced budget leads to deficits reaching over $200 billion annually by 1986
1981 Supply-side economics: cut taxes drastically; business will expand and produce vast supplies of consumer goods
1981 Appointment of Justice Sandra Day O'Connor (first woman) to U.S. Supreme Court
1982 Cold war resumed: president makes public reference to USSR as "The focus of evil in the modern world''; ratification of SALT II blocked but terms observed
1983 Attempt to overthrow government of Nicaragua; military aid to "Contras"; CIA mining of Nicaraguan harbors revealed contrary to international law

1983 Grenada invaded by 6000 U.S. troops; leftist government overthrown

1983 Marine barracks in Lebanon destroyed by suicide attack; 242 U.S. Marines die; U.S. forces withdrawn

1984 Congress defeats request for military aid to the Contras

1985 Six U.S. astronauts die as space shuttle explodes (January 28)

1985 Reagan-Gorbachev summit meeting in Geneva

1985 Gramm-Rudman-Hollings law for balanced budget

1986 Income Tax Reform Act

1986 House approves $100 million aid for Contras

1986 U.S. war planes bomb Tripoli

1986 Supreme Court appointments: William H. Rehnquist, chief justice; Antonin Scalia, associate justice

1986 Reagan presses SDI (Strategic Defense Initiative), called Star Wars

1986 Reagan and Gorbachev summit meeting in Iceland

1986 Election November 4, 1986; Republicans lose control of Senate to Democrats 55 to 45

1986 Iran-Hostage-Contra scandal breaks (November)

1987 Congressional hearings on Iran-Contra affair dominate the news, Reagan popularity affected

1987 Robert Bork's nomination to the Supreme Court rejected

1987 Trade deficit causes concern. The total deficit for 1986 is reported as a record $169.78 billion

1987 Reagan and Gorbachev sign Intermediate-Range Nuclear Forces (INF) Treaty

1988 Judge Anthony Kennedy becomes Supreme Court justice

1988 Plant-closing bill becomes law

41. George Herbert Walker Bush (b. 1924): President 1989–1993

Bush's public service before he became president:
     U.S. Navy pilot in World War II
     Graduated from Yale University, 1948
     Member of House of Representatives from Texas, 1966–1970
     U.S. Ambassador to United Nations, 1971–73
     Head of U.S. Liaison Office in Beijing (China), 1974–75
     Director of Central Intelligence Agency (CIA), 1976–77
     Vice president, 1981–89

Bush as president (Republican):

1989 U.S. forces invade Panama to overthrow Manuel Noriega

1990 Judge David H. Souter confirmed as Supreme Court justice

1991 Desert Storm: U.S. forces combine with 29 other nations to drive Iraq out of Kuwait

1991 Judge Clarence Thomas appointed to Supreme Court

1991 Los Angeles riots; more than 50 die

1992 Twenty-seventh Amendment added to Constitution

1992 U.S. troops in Somalia

1993 Bombing raids on Iraq because of noncompliance with terms of UN cease-fire agreement

42. William (Bill) Clinton (b. 1946): President 1993 to present

Clinton's public service before he became president:
     Arkansas attorney general (1976–78)
     Governor of Arkansas (1979–81; 1983–93)

Clinton as president (Democrat)

1992 November Clinton wins presidency—Electoral College vote: Clinton 370, Bush 168, Perot 0.

The Constitution of the United States

General objectives of the Constitution

WE THE PEOPLE of the United States, in Order to form a more perfect Union, establish Justice, insure domestic Tranquility, provide for the common defence, promote the general Welfare, and secure the Blessings of Liberty to ourselves and our Posterity, do ordain and establish this CONSTITUTION for the United States of America.

ARTICLE I · LEGISLATIVE DEPARTMENT

A bicameral Congress

SECTION 1. All legislative Powers herein granted shall be vested in a Congress of the United States, which shall consist of a Senate and House of Representatives.

Selection and term of Representatives

SECTION 2. ¹The House of Representatives shall be composed of Members chosen every second Year by the People of the several States, and the Electors in each State shall have the Qualifications requisite for Electors of the most numerous Branch of the State Legislature.

Qualifications of Representatives

²No person shall be a representative who shall not have attained to the Age of twenty five Years, and been seven Years a Citizen of the United States, and who shall not, when elected, be an Inhabitant of that State in which he shall be chosen.

Apportionment of Representatives among states—see Section 2 of Fourteenth Amendment: a decennial census; maximum and minimum size of House

³[Representatives and direct Taxes shall be apportioned among the several States which may be included within this Union, according to their respective Numbers, which shall be determined by adding to the whole Number of free Persons, including those bound to Service for a Term of Years, and excluding Indians not taxed, three fifths of all other Persons.].* The actual Enumeration shall be made within three Years after the first Meeting of the Congress of the United States, and within every subsequent Term of ten Years, in such Manner as they shall by Law direct. The Number of Representatives shall not exceed one for every thirty Thousand, but each State shall have at Least one Representative; and until such enumeration shall be made, the State of New Hampshire shall be entitled to chuse three, Massachusetts eight, Rhode-Island and Providence Plantations one, Connecticut five, New-York six, New Jersey four, Pennsylvania eight, Delaware one, Maryland six, Virginia ten, North Carolina five, South Carolina five, and Georgia three.

Filling of vacancies

⁴When vacancies happen in the Representation from any State, the Executive Authority thereof shall issue Writs of Election to fill such Vacancies.

Choice of Speaker and other officers; sole power of impeachment

⁵The House of Representatives shall chuse their Speaker and other Officers; and shall have the sole Power of Impeachment.

Composition of Senate; see Seventeenth Amendment for selection of Senators.

SECTION 3. The Senate of the United States shall be composed of two Senators from each State, [chosen by the Legislature thereof,]** for six Years; and each Senator shall have one Vote.

Terms of Senators— overlapping

²Immediately after they shall be assembled in Consequence of the first Election, they shall be divided as equally as may be into three Classes. The Seats of the Senators of the first Class shall be vacated at the Expiration of the second Year, of the second Class at the Expiration of the fourth Year, and of the third Class at the Expiration of the sixth Year, so that one third may be chosen every second Year; [and if Vacancies happen by Resignation, or

NOTE:—This text of the Constitution follows the engrossed copy signed by Gen. Washington and the deputies from 12 States. The superior number preceding the paragraphs designates the number of the clause; it was not in the original.

*The part included in heavy brackets was changed by section 2 of the fourteenth amendment.

**The part included in heavy brackets was changed by section 1 of the seventeenth amendment.

Vacancies—see Seventeenth Amendment

otherwise, during the Recess of the Legislature of any State, the Executive thereof may make temporary Appointments until the next Meeting of the Legislature, which shall then fill such Vacancies].*

Qualifications

³No Person shall be a Senator who shall not have attained to the Age of thirty Years, and been nine Years a Citizen of the United States, and who shall not, when elected, be an Inhabitant of that State for which he shall be chosen.

Vice President to preside; choice of other officers

⁴The Vice President of the United States shall be President of the Senate, but shall have no Vote, unless they be equally divided.

⁵The Senate shall chuse their other Officers, and also a President pro tempore, in the Absence of the Vice President, or when he shall exercise the Office of President of the United States.

Trial of impeachments by Senate; penalties if impeached and convicted.

⁶The Senate shall have the sole Power to try all Impeachments. When sitting for that Purpose, they shall be on Oath or Affirmation. When the President of the United States is tried, the Chief Justice shall preside: And no Person shall be convicted without the Concurrence of two thirds of the Members present.

⁷Judgment in Cases of Impeachment shall not extend further than to removal from Office, and disqualification to hold and enjoy any Office of honor, Trust or Profit under the United States: but the Party convicted shall nevertheless be liable and subject to Indictment, Trial, Judgment and Punishment, according to Law.

Times, places and manner of holding Congressional elections.

SECTION 4. ¹The Times, Places and Manner of holding Elections for Senators and Representatives, shall be prescribed in each State by the Legislature thereof; but the Congress may at any time by Law make or alter such Regulations, except as to the Places of chusing Senators.

Congressional sessions— see Twentieth Amendment

²The Congress shall assemble at least once in every Year, and such Meeting shall [be on the first Monday in December,]** unless they shall by Law appoint a different Day.

Judging elections and qualifications; size of a quorum; expulsion of members of Congress

SECTION 5. ¹Each House shall be the Judge of the Elections, Returns and Qualifications of its own Members, and a Majority of each shall constitute a Quorum to do Business; but a smaller Number may adjourn from day to day, and may be authorized to compel the Attendance of absent Members, in such Manner, and under such Penalties as each House may provide.

Rules of proceedings and keeping of journal.

²Each House may determine the Rules of its Proceedings, punish its Members for disorderly Behavior, and, with the Concurrence of two thirds, expel a Member.

³Each House shall keep a Journal of its Proceedings, and from time to time publish the same, excepting such Parts as may in their Judgment require Secrecy; and the Yeas and Nays of the Members of either House on any question shall, at the Desire of one fifth of those Present, be entered on the Journal.

Adjournment

⁴Neither House, during the Session of Congress, shall, without the Consent of the other, adjourn for more than three days, nor to any other Place than that in which the two Houses shall be sitting.

Compensation and immunities of members of Congress

SECTION 6. ¹The Senators and Representatives shall receive a Compensation for their Services, to be ascertained by Law, and paid out of the Treasury of the United States. They shall in all Cases, except Treason, Felony and Breach

---

*The part included in heavy brackets was changed by clause 2 of the seventeenth amendment.

**The part included in heavy brackets was changed by section 2 of the twentieth amendment.

of the Peace, be privileged from Arrest during their Attendance at the Session of their respective Houses, and in going to and returning from the same; and for any Speech or Debate in either House, they shall not be questioned in any other Place.

Limitations on appointment of members of Congress to civil offices; no national office-holder to be a member of Congress

²No Senator or Representative shall, during the Time for which he was elected, be appointed to any civil Office under the Authority of the United States, which shall have been created, or the Emoluments whereof shall have been encreased during such time; and no Person holding any Office under the United States, shall be a Member of either House during his Continuance in Office.

Origin of revenue bills

SECTION 7. ¹All Bills for raising Revenue shall originate in the House of Representatives; but the Senate may propose or concur with Amendments as on other Bills.

Veto power of President: overriding of veto

²Every Bill which shall have passed the House of Representatives and the Senate, shall, before it become a Law, be presented to the President of the United States; If he approve he shall sign it, but if not he shall return it, with his Objections to that House in which it shall have originated, who shall enter the Objections at large on their Journal, and proceed to reconsider it. If after such Reconsideration two thirds of that House shall agree to pass the Bill, it shall be sent, together with the Objections, to the other House, by which it shall likewise be reconsidered, and if approved by two thirds of that House, it shall become a Law. But in all such Cases the Votes of both Houses shall be determined by Yeas and Nays, and the Names of the Persons voting for and against the Bill shall be entered on the Journal of each House respectively. If any Bill shall not be returned by the President within ten days (Sundays excepted) after it shall have been presented to him, the Same shall be a Law, in like Manner as if he had signed it, unless the Congress by their Adjournment prevent its Return, in which Case it shall not be a Law.

³Every Order, Resolution, or Vote to which the Concurrence of the Senate and House of Representatives may be necessary (except on a question of Adjournment) shall be presented to the President of the United States; and before the Same shall take Effect, shall be approved by him, or being disapproved by him, shall be repassed by two thirds of the Senate and House of Representatives, according to the Rules and Limitations prescribed in the Case of a Bill.

Enumerated powers of Congress:

SECTION 8. ¹The Congress shall have Power To lay and collect Taxes, Duties Imposts and Excises, to pay the Debts and provide for the common Defence and general Welfare of the United States; but all Duties, Imposts and Excises shall be uniform throughout the United States;

Taxation

Borrowing of money

²To borrow Money on the credit of the United States;

Regulation of commerce

³To regulate Commerce with foreign Nations, and among the several States, and with the Indian Tribes;

Naturalization and bankruptcy

⁴To establish an uniform Rule of Naturalization, and uniform Laws on the subject of Bankruptcies throughout the United States;

Coining of money; weights and measures

⁵To coin Money, regulate the Value thereof, and of foreign Coin, and fix the Standard of Weights and Measures;

Punishment of counterfeiting

⁶To provide for the Punishment of counterfeiting the Securities and current Coin of the United States;

Postal service

⁷To establish Post Offices and post Roads;

Patents and copyrights

⁸To promote the Progress of Science and useful Arts, by securing for limited Times to Authors and Inventors the exclusive Right to their respective Writings and Discoveries;

Creation of courts

⁹To constitute Tribunals inferior to the supreme Court;

Piracies and high seas felonies

¹⁰To define and punish Piracies and Felonies committed on the high Seas, and Offences against the Law of Nations;

Declaration of War

¹¹To declare War, grant Letters of Marque and Reprisal, and make Rules concerning Captures on Land and Water;

Provide armed forces and for calling forth and organizing the militia

¹²To raise and support Armies, but no Appropriation of Money to that Use shall be for a longer Term than two Years;

¹³To provide and maintain a Navy;

¹⁴To make Rules for the Government and Regulation of the land and naval Forces;

¹⁵To provide for calling forth the Militia to execute the Laws of the Union, suppress Insurrections and repel Invasions;

¹⁶To provide for organizing, arming, and disciplining the Militia and for governing such Part of them as may be employed in the Service of the United States, reserving to the States respectively, the Appointment of the Officers, and the Authority of training the Militia according to the discipline prescribed by Congress;

Congress to govern the District of Columbia and other places owned by national government

¹⁷To exercise exclusive Legislation in all Cases whatsoever, over such District (not exceeding ten Miles square) as may, by Cession of particular States, and the Acceptance of Congress, become the Seat of the Government of the United States, and to exercise like Authority over all Places purchased by the Consent of the Legislature of the State in which the Same shall be, for the Erection of Forts, Magazines, Arsenals, dock-Yards, and other needful Buildings;—And

Necessary and proper (elastic) clause

¹⁸To make all Laws which shall be necessary and proper for carrying into Execution the foregoing Powers, and all other Powers vested by this Constitution in the Government of the United States, or in any Department or Officer thereof.

Express limitations on national government— Congress in particular

SECTION 9.   ¹The Migration or Importation of such Persons as any of the States now existing shall think proper to admit, shall not be prohibited by the Congress prior to the Year one thousand eight hundred and eight, but a Tax or duty may be imposed on such Importation, not exceeding ten dollars for each Person.

²The Privilege of the Writ of Habeas Corpus shall not be suspended, unless when in Cases of Rebellion or Invasion the public Safety may require it.

³No Bill of Attainder or ex post facto Law shall be passed.

Express limitations on national government— Congress in particular

*⁴No Capitation, or other direct, Tax shall be laid, unless in Proportion to the Census or Enumeration herein before directed to be taken.

⁵No Tax or Duty shall be laid on Articles exported from any State.

⁶No Preference shall be given by any Regulation of Commerce or Revenue to the Ports of one State over those of another: nor shall Vessels bound to, or from, one State be obliged to enter, clear, or pay Duties in another.

⁷No Money shall be drawn from the Treasury, but in Consequence of Appropriations made by Law; and a regular Statement and Account of the Receipts and Expenditures of all public Money shall be published from time to time.

⁸No Title of Nobility shall be granted by the United States: And no Person holding any Office of Profit or Trust under them, shall, without the Consent of the Congress, accept of any present, Emolument, Office, or Title, of any kind whatever, from any King, Prince, or foreign State.

Express limitations on states

SECTION 10.   ¹No State shall enter into any Treaty, Alliance, or Confederation; grant Letters of Marque and Reprisal; coin Money; emit Bills of Credit;

---

*See also the sixteenth amendment.

make any Thing but gold and silver Coin a Tender in Payment of Debts; pass any Bill of Attainder, ex post facto Law, or Law impairing the Obligation of Contracts, or grant any Title of Nobility.

²No State shall, without the Consent of the Congress, lay any Imposts or Duties on Imports or Exports, except what may be absolutely necessary for executing it's inspection Laws: and the net Produce of all Duties and Imposts, laid by any State on Imports or Exports, shall be for the Use of the Treasury of the United States; and all such Laws shall be subject to the Revision and Controul of the Congress.

³No State shall, without the Consent of Congress, lay any Duty of Tonnage, keep Troops, or Ships of War in time of Peace, enter into any Agreement or Compact with another State, or with a foreign Power, or engage in War, unless actually invaded, or in such imminent Danger as will not admit of delay.

ARTICLE II · EXECUTIVE DEPARTMENT

Executive power vested in President; term of office—see Twenty-second Amendment

SECTION 1. ¹The executive Power shall be vested in a President of the United States of America. He shall hold his Office during the Term of four Years, and, together with the Vice President, chosen for the same Term, be elected as follows:

Selection of Presidential electors and number per state

²Each State shall appoint, in such Manner as the Legislature thereof may direct, a Number of Electors, equal to the whole Number of Senators and Representatives to which the State may be entitled in the Congress: but no Senator or Representative, or Person holding an Office of Trust or Profit under the United States, shall be appointed an Elector.

Replaced by Twelfth Amendment

[The Electors shall meet in their respective States, and vote by Ballot for two Persons, of whom one at least shall not be an Inhabitant of the same State with themselves. And they shall make a List of all the Persons voted for, and of the Number of Votes for each; which List they shall sign and certify, and transmit sealed to the Seat of the Government of the United States, directed to the President of the Senate. The President of the Senate shall, in the Presence of the Senate and House of Representatives, open all the Certificates, and the Votes shall then be counted. The Person having the greatest Number of Votes shall be the President, if such Number be a Majority of the whole Number of Electors appointed; and if there be more than one who have such Majority, and have an equal Number of Votes, then the House of Representatives shall immediately chuse by Ballot one of them for President; and if no Person have a Majority, then from the five highest on the List the said House shall in like Manner chuse the President. But in chusing the President, the Votes shall be taken by States, the Representation from each State having one Vote; A quorum for this Purpose shall consist of a Member or Members from two thirds of the States, and a Majority of all the States shall be necessary to a Choice. In every Case, after the Choice of the President, the Person having the greatest Number of Votes of the Electors shall be the Vice President. But if there should remain two or more who have equal Votes, the Senate shall chuse from them by Ballot the Vice President.]*

Congress to determine the time of choosing electors and the casting of electoral votes

³The Congress may determine the Time of chusing the Electors, and the Day on which they shall give their Votes; which Day shall be the same throughout the United States.

Required qualifications of President

⁴No Person except a natural born Citizen, or a Citizen of the United States, at the time of the Adoption of this Constitution, shall be eligible to the Office of President; neither shall any Person be eligible to that Office who shall not

---

*This paragraph has been superseded by the twelfth amendment.

have attained to the Age of thirty five Years, and been fourteen Years a Resident within the United States.

Succession to the Presidency; also see the Twenty-fifth Amendment

⁵In Case of the Removal of the President from Office, or of his Death, Resignation, or Inability to discharge the Powers and Duties of the said Office, the Same shall devolve on the Vice President, and the Congress may by Law provide for the Case of Removal, Death, Resignation or Inability, both of the President and Vice President declaring what Officer shall then act as President, and such Officer shall act accordingly, until the Disability be removed, or a President shall be elected.

Compensation of the President

⁶The President shall, at stated Times, receive for his Services, a Compensation, which shall neither be encreased nor diminished during the Period for which he shall have been elected, and he shall not receive within that Period any other Emolument from the United States, or any of them.

Presidential oath of office

⁷Before he enter on the Execution of his Office, he shall take the following Oath or Affirmation:—"I do solemnly swear (or affirm) that I will faithfully execute the Office of President of the United States, and will to the best of my Ability, preserve, protect and defend the Constitution of the United States."

Powers of the President: Commander in Chief

Granting of pardons and reprieves

SECTION 2. ¹The President shall be Commander in Chief of the Army and Navy of the United States, and of the Militia of the several States, when called into the actual Service of the United States; he may require the Opinion, in writing, of the principal Officer in each of the executive Departments, upon any Subject relating to the Duties of their respective Offices, and he shall have Power to grant Reprieves and Pardons for Offences against the United States, except in Cases of Impeachment.

Treaty-making with advice and consent of Senate

Appointment of officials with advice and consent of Senate; appointment of inferior officers by President alone if Congress so provides

²He shall have Power, by and with the Advice and Consent of the Senate, to make Treaties, provided two thirds of the Senators present concur; and he shall nominate, and by and with the Advice and Consent of the Senate, shall appoint Ambassadors, other public Ministers and Consuls, Judges of the supreme Court, and all other Officers of the United States, whose Appointments are not herein otherwise provided for, and which shall be established by Law: but the Congress may by Law vest the Appointment of such inferior Officers, as they think proper, in the President alone, in the Courts of Law, or in the Heads of Departments.

Temporary filling of vacancies

³The President shall have Power to fill up all Vacancies that may happen during the Recess of the Senate, by granting Commissions which shall expire at the End of their next Session.

Make recommendations to Congress and provide information

Call special sessions of Congress

Receive ambassadors and other public ministers

Enforce the laws

SECTION 3. He shall from time to time give to the Congress Information of the State of the Union, and recommend to their Consideration such Measures as he shall judge necessary and expedient; he may, on extraordinary Occasions, convene both Houses, or either of them, and in Case of Disagreement between them, with Respect to the Time of Adjournment, he may adjourn them to such Time as he shall think proper; he shall receive Ambassadors and other public Ministers; he shall take Care that the Laws be faithfully executed, and shall Commission all the Officers of the United States.

Civil officers, including President and Vice President, to be removed from office if impeached and convicted

SECTION 4. The President, Vice President and all civil Officers of the United States, shall be removed from Office on Impeachment for, and Conviction of, Treason, Bribery, or other high Crimes and Misdemeanors.

ARTICLE III · JUDICIAL DEPARTMENT

Structure of national judiciary

SECTION 1. The judicial Power of the United States, shall be vested in one supreme Court, and in such inferior Courts as the Congress may from time to

Tenure and compensation of judges	time ordain and establish. The Judges, both of the supreme and inferior Courts, shall hold their Offices during good Behaviour, and shall, at stated Times, receive for their Services, a Compensation, which shall not be diminished during their Continuance in Office.

Jurisdiction of the national judiciary

SECTION 2.   ¹The judicial Power shall extend to all Cases, in Law and Equity, arising under this Constitution, the Laws of the United States; and Treaties made, or which shall be made, under their Authority;—to all Cases affecting Ambassadors, other public Ministers and Consuls;—to all Cases of admiralty and maritime Jurisdiction;—to Controversies to which the United States shall be a Party;—to Controversies between two or more States;—between a State and Citizens of another State;*—between Citizens of different States,—between Citizens of the same State claiming Lands under Grants of different States, and between a State, or the Citizens thereof, and foreign States, Citizens or Subjects.

Original and appellate jurisdiction of the Supreme Court

²In all Cases affecting Ambassadors, other public Ministers and Consuls, and those in which a State shall be Party, the supreme Court shall have original Jurisdiction. In all the other Cases before mentioned, the supreme Court shall have appellate Jurisdiction, both as to Law and Fact, with such Exceptions, and under such Regulations as the Congress shall make.

Jury trial in criminal cases other than impeachment

³The Trial of all Crimes, except in Cases of Impeachment, shall be by Jury; and such Trial shall be held in the State where the said Crimes shall have been committed; but when not committed within any State, the Trial shall be at such Place or Places as the Congress may by Law have directed.

Definition of treason and requisites for conviction

SECTION 3.   ¹Treason against the United States, shall consist only in levying War against them, or in adhering to their Enemies, giving them Aid and Comfort. No Person shall be convicted of Treason unless on the Testimony of two Witnesses to the same overt Act, or on Confession in open Court.

Punishment for treason

²The Congress shall have Power to declare the Punishment of Treason, but no Attainder of Treason shall work Corruption of Blood, or Forfeiture except during the Life of the Person attainted.

ARTICLE IV · RELATION OF THE STATES TO EACH OTHER

Interstate obligations: full faith and credit, privileges and immunities of citizens, rendition of fugitives from justice

SECTION 1.   Full Faith and Credit shall be given in each State to the public Acts, Records, and judicial Proceedings of every other State. And the Congress may by general Laws prescribe the Manner in which such Acts, Records and Proceedings shall be proved, and the Effect thereof.

SECTION 2.   ¹The Citizens of each State shall be entitled to all Privileges and Immunities of Citizens in the several States.

²A Person charged in any State with Treason, Felony, or other Crime, who shall flee from Justice, and be found in another State, shall on Demand of the executive Authority of the State from which he fled, be delivered up, to be removed to the State having Jurisdiction of the Crime.

Obsolete

³[No Person held to Service or Labour in one State, under the Laws thereof, escaping into another, shall, in Consequence of any Law or Regulation therein, be discharged from such Service or Labour but shall be delivered up on Claim of the Party to whom such Service or Labour may be due.]**

Admission of new states

SECTION 3.   ¹New States may be admitted by the Congress into this Union; but no new State shall be formed or erected within the Jurisdiction of any other State; nor any State be formed by the Junction of two or more States, or Parts

---

*This clause has been affected by the eleventh amendment.
**This paragraph has been superseded by the thirteenth amendment.

of States, without the Consent of the Legislatures of the States concerned as well as of the Congress.

²The Congress shall have Power to dispose of and make all needful Rules and Regulations respecting the Territory or other Property belonging to the United States; and nothing in this Constitution shall be so construed as to Prejudice any Claims of the United States, or of any particular State.

SECTION 4.   The United States shall guarantee to every State in this Union a Republican Form of Government, and shall protect each of them against Invasion; and on Application of the Legislature, or of the Executive (when the Legislature cannot be convened) against domestic Violence.

ARTICLE V · AMENDMENTS

The Congress, whenever two thirds of both Houses shall deem it necessary, shall propose Amendments to this Constitution, or, on the Application of the Legislatures of two thirds of the several States, shall call a Convention for proposing Amendments, which, in either Case, shall be valid to all Intents and Purposes, as Part of this Constitution, when ratified by the Legislatures of three fourths of the several States, or by Conventions in three fourths thereof, as the one or the other Mode of Ratification may be proposed by the Congress; Provided, [that no Amendment which may be made prior to the Year One thousand eight hundred and eight shall in any Manner affect the first and fourth Clauses in the Ninth Section of the first Article; and]* that no State, without its Consent, shall be deprived of its equal Suffrage in the Senate.

ARTICLE VI · GENERAL PROVISIONS

¹All Debts contracted and Engagements entered into, before the Adoption of this Constitution, shall be as valid against the United States under this Constitution, as under the Confederation.

²This Constitution, and the Laws of the United States which shall be made in Pursuance thereof; and all Treaties made, or which shall be made, under the Authority of the United States, shall be the supreme Law of the Land; and the Judges in every State shall be bound thereby, any Thing in the Constitution or Laws of any State to the Contrary notwithstanding.

³The Senators and Representatives before mentioned, and the Members of the several State Legislatures, and all executive and judicial Officers, both of the United States and of the several States, shall be bound by Oath or Affirmation, to support this Constitution; but no religious Test shall ever be required as a Qualification to any Office or public Trust under the United States.

ARTICLE VII · RATIFICATION OF
THE CONSTITUTION

The Ratification of the Conventions of nine States, shall be sufficient for the Establishment of this Constitution between the States so ratifying the Same.

DONE in Convention by the Unanimous Consent of the States present the Seventeenth Day of September in the Year of our Lord one thousand seven hundred and Eighty seven and of the Independence of the United States of America the Twelfth . IN WITNESS whereof We have hereto subscribed our Names.

George Washington
President and Deputy from Virginia

[Signed also by the deputies of twelve States.]

---

*Obsolete.

New Hampshire
John Langdon
Nicholas Gilman

Massachusetts
Nathaniel Gorham
Rufus King

Connecticut
William Samuel Johnson
Roger Sherman

New York
Alexander Hamilton

New Jersey
William Livingston
David Brearley
William Paterson
Jonathan Dayton

Maryland
James McHenry
Daniel Carroll
Dan of St. Thomas Jenifer

Virginia
John Blair
James Madison, Jr.

North Carolina
William Blount
Hugh Williamson
Richard Dobbs Spaight

Pennsylvania
Benjamin Franklin
Robert Morris
Thomas FitzSimons
James Wilson
Thomas Mifflin
George Clymer
Jared Ingersoll
Gouverneur Morris

Delaware
George Read
John Dickinson
Jacob Broom
Gunning Bedford, Jr.
Richard Bassett

South Carolina
John Rutledge
Charles Pinckney
Charles Cotesworth Pinckney
Pierce Butler

Georgia
William Few
Abraham Baldwin

Attest: **William Jackson**, Secretary

RATIFICATION OF THE CONSTITUTION

The Constitution was adopted by a convention of the States on September 17, 1787, and was subsequently ratified by the several States, on the following dates: Delaware, December 7, 1787; Pennsylvania, December 12, 1787; New Jersey, December 18, 1787; Georgia, January 2, 1788; Connecticut, January 9, 1788; Massachusetts, February 6, 1788; Maryland, April 28, 1788; South Carolina, May 23, 1788; New Hampshire, June 21, 1788; Virginia, June 25, 1788; New York, July 26, 1788; North Carolina, November 21, 1789; Rhode Island, May 29, 1790.

ARTICLES IN ADDITION TO, AND AMENDMENT OF, THE CONSTITUTION OF THE UNITED STATES OF AMERICA, PROPOSED BY CONGRESS, AND RATIFIED BY THE LEGISLATURES OF THE SEVERAL STATES PURSUANT TO THE FIFTH ARTICLE OF THE ORIGINAL CONSTITUTION

ARTICLE I*

Freedom of religion, speech, press, and assembly

Congress shall make no law respecting an establishment of religion, or prohibiting the free exercise thereof; or abridging the freedom of speech, or of the press; or the right of the people peaceably to assemble, and to petition the Government for a redress of grievances.

ARTICLE II

Militia and the right to bear arms

A well regulated Militia, being necessary to the security of a free State, the right of the people to keep and bear Arms, shall not be infringed.

ARTICLE III

Quartering of soldiers

No Soldier shall, in time of peace be quartered in any house, without the consent of the Owner, nor in time of war, but in a manner to be prescribed by law.

———

*Only the 13th, 14th, 15th, and 16th articles of amendment had numbers assigned to them at the time of ratification.

ARTICLE IV

Unreasonable searches and seizures prohibited

The right of the people to be secure in their persons, houses, papers, and effects, against unreasonable searches and seizures, shall not be violated, and no Warrants shall issue, but upon probable cause, supported by Oath or affirmation, and particularly describing the place to be searched, and the persons or things to be seized.

ARTICLE V

Indictment by grand jury; no double jeopardy; due process of law; no self-incrimination; compensation for taking property

No person shall be held to answer for a capital, or otherwise infamous crime, unless on a presentment or indictment of a Grand Jury, except in cases arising in the land or naval forces, or in the Militia, when in actual service in time of War or public danger; nor shall any person be subject for the same offence to be twice put in jeopardy of life or limb; nor shall be compelled in any criminal case to be a witness against himself, nor be deprived of life, liberty, or property, without due process of law; nor shall private property be taken for public use, without just compensation.

ARTICLE VI

Guarantee of basic procedural rights in criminal prosecutions, e.g., jury trial, confrontation of witnesses

In all criminal prosecutions, the accused shall enjoy the right to a speedy and public trial, by an impartial jury of the State and district wherein the crime shall have been committed, which district shall have been previously ascertained by law, and to be informed of the nature and cause of the accusation; to be confronted with the witnesses against him; to have compulsory process for obtaining Witnesses in his favor, and to have the Assistance of Counsel for his defence.

ARTICLE VII

Jury trial in common law suits

In Suits at common law, where the value in controversy shall exceed twenty dollars, the right of trial by jury shall be preserved, and no fact tried by a jury, shall be otherwise reexamined in any Court of the United States, than according to the rules of the common law.

ARTICLE VIII

Excessive bail or fines, cruel and unusual punishments prohibited

Excessive bail shall not be required, nor excessive fines imposed, nor cruel and unusual punishments inflicted.

ARTICLE IX

Retention of rights by the people

The enumeration in the Constitution, of certain rights, shall not be construed to deny or disparage others retained by the people.

ARTICLE X

Reserved powers of the states

The powers not delegated to the United States by the Constitution nor prohibited by it to the States, are reserved to the States respectively, or to the people.

ARTICLE XI

Immunity of states from suits by citizens or aliens in national courts

The Judicial power of the United States shall not be construed to extend to any suit in law or equity, commenced or prosecuted against one of the United States by Citizens of another State, or by Citizens or Subjects of any Foreign State.

ARTICLE XII

Replaces third paragraph of Section 1, Article II.

The electors shall meet in their respective states and vote by ballot for President and Vice-President, one of whom, at least, shall not be an inhabitant of the same state with themselves; they shall name in their ballots the person

Principal provision requires
separate ballots for
President and Vice
President and a majority
electoral vote. Procedure
to be followed if no
candidate obtains a
majority

voted for as President, and in distinct ballots the person voted for as Vice-President, and they shall make distinct lists of all persons voted for as President, and of all persons voted for as Vice-President, and of the number of votes for each, which lists they shall sign and certify, and transmit sealed to the seat of the government of the United States, directed to the President of the Senate;—The President of the Senate shall, in presence of the Senate and House of Representatives, open all the certificates and the votes shall then be counted;—The person having the greatest number of votes for President, shall be the President, if such number be a majority of the whole number of Electors appointed; and if no person have such majority, then from the persons having the highest numbers not exceeding three on the list of those voted for as President, the House of Representatives shall choose immediately, by ballot, the President. But in choosing the President, the votes shall be taken by states, the representation from each state having one vote; a quorum for this purpose shall consist of a member or members from two-thirds of the states, and a majority of all the states shall be necessary to a choice. [And if the House of Representatives shall not choose a President whenever the right of choice shall devolve upon them, before the fourth day of March next following, then the Vice-President shall act as President, as in the case of the death or other constitutional disability of the President.]* The person having the the greatest number of votes as Vice-President, shall be the Vice-President, if such number be a majority of the whole number of Electors appointed, and if no person have a majority, then from the two highest numbers on the list, the Senate shall choose the Vice-President; a quorum for the purpose shall consist of two-thirds of the whole number of Senators, and a majority of the whole number shall be necessary to a choice. But no person constitutionally ineligible to the office of President shall be eligible to that of Vice-President of the United States.

ARTICLE XIII

Slavery and involuntary
servitude prohibited

SECTION 1.   Neither slavery nor involuntary servitude, except as a punishment for crime whereof the party shall have been duly convicted, shall exist within the United States, or any place subject to their jurisdiction.

SECTION 2.   Congress shall have power to enforce this article by appropriate legislation.

ARTICLE XIV

Definition of United States
and state citizenship;
no state abridgment of
privileges and immunities of
United States citizens;
no state denial of due
process of law or equal
protection of the laws
to any person

SECTION 1.   All persons born or naturalized in the United States, and subject to the jurisdiction thereof, are citizens of the United States and the State wherein they reside. No State shall make or enforce any law which shall abridge the privileges or immunities of citizens of the United States; nor shall any State deprive any person of life, liberty, or property, without due process of law; nor deny to any person within its jurisdiction the equal protection of the laws.

Apportionment of
Representatives among the
states according to
population, excluding
untaxed Indians. Provision
for reduction of
representation under
specified circumstances

SECTION 2.   Representatives shall be apportioned among the several States according to their respective numbers, counting the whole number of persons in each State, excluding Indians not taxed. But when the right to vote at any election for the choice of electors for President and Vice President of the United States, Representatives in Congress, the Executive and Judicial officers of a State, or the members of the Legislature thereof, is denied to any of the male inhabitants of such State, being twenty-one years of age, and citizens of the United States, or in any way abridged, except for participation in rebellion, or other crime, the basis of representation therein shall be reduced in the proportion which the number of such male citizens shall bear to the whole number of male citizens twenty-one years of age in such State.

HISTORY OF THE
UNITED STATES

Disqualification from office-holding by officials who, having taken an oath to support the Constitution, engage in rebellion against the United States

SECTION 3. No person shall be a Senator or Representative in Congress, or elector of President and Vice President, or hold any office, civil or military, under the United States, or under any State, who, having previously taken an oath, as a member of Congress, or as an officer of the United States, or as a member of any State legislature, or as an executive or judicial officer of any State, to support the Constitution of the United States, shall have engaged in insurrection or rebellion against the same, or given aid or comfort to the enemies thereof. But Congress may by a vote of two-thirds of each House, remove such disability.

Validity of public debt incurred for suppressing rebellion not to be questioned. All indebtedness incurred in support of rebellion illegal and void

SECTION 4. The validity of the public debt of the United States, authorized by law, including debts incurred for payment of pensions and bounties for services in suppressing insurrection or rebellion, shall not be questioned. But neither the United States nor any State shall assume or pay any debt or obligation incurred in aid of insurrection or rebellion against the United States, or any claim for the loss or emancipation of any slave; but all such debts, obligations and claims shall be held illegal and void.

SECTION 5. The Congress shall have power to enforce, by appropriate legislation, the provisions of this article.

ARTICLE XV

Right of citizens to vote not to be denied because of race, color, or previous condition of servitude

SECTION 1. The right of citizens of the United States to vote shall not be denied or abridged by the United States or by any State on account of race, color, or previous condition of servitude.

SECTION 2. The Congress shall have power to enforce this article by appropriate legislation.

ARTICLE XVI

Congress empowered to levy income taxes without apportionment among states on a population basis

The Congress shall have power to lay and collect taxes on incomes, from whatever source derived, without apportionment among the several States, and without regard to any census or enumeration.

ARTICLE XVII

Popular election of Senators for six year terms by persons qualified to vote for members of the most numerous branch of the state legislature

The Senate of the United States shall be composed of two Senators from each state, elected by the people thereof, for six years; and each Senator shall have one vote. The electors in each State shall have the qualifications requisite for electors of the most numerous branch of the State legislatures.

Procedure for filling vacancies in Senate

When vacancies happen in the representation of any State in the Senate, the executive authority of such State shall issue writs of election to fill such vacancies: *Provided*, That the legislature of any State may empower the executive thereof to make temporary appointments until the people fill the vacancies by election as the legislature may direct.

This amendment shall not be so construed as to affect the election or term of any Senator chosen before it becomes valid as part of the Constitution.

ARTICLE XVIII

Prohibition Amendment; repealed by Twenty-first Amendment

SECTION 1. After one year from the ratification of this article the manufacture, sale, or transportation of intoxicating liquors within, the importation thereof into, or the exportation thereof from the United States and all territory subject to the jurisdiction thereof for beverage purposes is hereby prohibited.

SECTION 2. The Congress and the several States shall have concurrent power to enforce this article by appropriate legislation.

SECTION 3. This article shall be inoperative unless it shall have been ratified as an amendment to the Constitution by the legislatures of the several States, as provided in the Constitution, within seven years from the date of the submission hereof to the States by the Congress.*

ARTICLE XIX

Right of citizens to vote not to be denied because of sex

The right of citizens of the United States to vote shall not be denied or abridged by the United States or by any State on account of sex.

Congress shall have power to enforce this article by appropriate legislation.

ARTICLE XX

Ending of terms of President, Vice President, Senators, and Representatives

SECTION 1. The terms of the President and Vice President shall end at noon on the 20th day of January, and the terms of Senators and Representatives at noon on the 3d day of January, of the years in which such terms would have ended if this article had not been ratified; and the terms of their successors shall then begin.

Beginning of required annual Congressional sessions

SECTION 2. The Congress shall assemble at least once in every year, and such meeting shall begin at noon on the 3d day of January, unless they shall by law appoint a different day.

Procedure to be followed if President elect has died or no President has been chosen or qualified by beginning of the Presidential term. This amendment also deals with other contingencies

SECTION 3. If, at the time fixed for the beginning of the term of the President, the President elect shall have died, the Vice President elect shall become President. If a President shall not have been chosen before the time fixed for the beginning of his term, or if the President elect shall have failed to qualify, then the Vice President elect shall act as President until a President shall have qualified; and the Congress may by law provide for the case wherein neither a President elect nor a Vice President elect shall have qualified, declaring who shall then act as President, or the manner in which one who is to act shall be selected, and such person shall act accordingly until a President or Vice President shall have qualified.

SECTION 4. The Congress may by law provide for the case of the death of any of the persons from whom the House of Representatives may choose a President whenever the right of choice shall have devolved upon them, and for the case of the death of any of the persons from whom the Senate may choose a Vice President whenever the right of choice shall have devolved upon them.

SECTION 5. Sections 1 and 2 shall take effect on the 15th day of October following the ratification of this article.

SECTION 6. This article shall be inoperative unless it shall have been ratified as an amendment to the Constitution by the legislatures of three-fourths of the several States within seven years from the date of its submission.

ARTICLE XXI

The Eighteenth Amendment establishing prohibition repealed

SECTION 1. The eighteenth article of amendment to the Constitution of the United States is hereby repealed.

---

*Repealed by section 1 of the twenty-first amendment.

SECTION 2.   The transportation or importation into any State, Territory, or possession of the United States for delivery or use therein of intoxicating liquors, in violation of the laws thereof, is hereby prohibited.

SECTION 3.   This article shall be inoperative unless it shall have been ratified as an amendment to the Constitution by conventions in the several States, as provided in the Constitution, within seven years from the date of the submission hereof to the States by the Congress.

ARTICLE XXII

No person may be elected to Presidency for more than two terms

SECTION 1.   No person shall be elected to the office of the President more than twice, and no person who has held the office of President, or acted as President, for more than two years of a term to which some other person was elected President shall be elected to the office of the President more than once. But this article shall not apply to any person holding the office of President when this Article was proposed by the Congress, and shall not prevent any person who may be holding the office of President, or acting as President, during the term within which this Article becomes operative from holding the office of President or acting as President during the remainder of such term.

SECTION 2.   This article shall be inoperative unless it shall have been ratified as an amendment to the Constitution by the legislatures of three-fourths of the several States within seven years from the date of its submission to the States by the Congress.

ARTICLE XXIII

Allocation of presidential electors to District of Columbia

SECTION 1.   The District constituting the seat of Government of the United States shall appoint in such manner as the Congress may direct:

A number of electors of President and Vice President equal to the whole number of Senators and Representatives in Congress to which the District would be entitled if it were a State, but in no event more than the least populous State; they shall be in addition to those appointed by the States, but they shall be considered, for the purposes of the election of President and Vice President, to be electors appointed by a State; and they shall meet in the District and perform such duties as provided by the twelfth article of amendment.

SECTION 2.   The Congress shall have power to enforce this article by appropriate legislation.

ARTICLE XXIV

Right of citizens to vote in national elections not to be denied because of failure to pay taxes

SECTION 1.   The right of citizens of the United States to vote in any primary or other election for President or Vice President, for electors for President or Vice President, or for Senator or Representative in Congress, shall not be denied or abridged by the United States or any State by reason of failure to pay any poll tax or other tax.

SECTION 2.   The Congress shall have power to enforce this article by appropriate legislation.

ARTICLE XXV

Succession to the Presidency and Vice Presidency in case of vacancies

SECTION 1.   In case of the removal of the President from office or of his death or resignation, the Vice President shall become President.

SECTION 2.   Whenever there is a vacancy in the office of the Vice President, the President shall nominate a Vice President who shall take office upon confirmation by a majority vote of both Houses of Congress.

SECTION 3.   Whenever the President transmits to the President pro tempore of the Senate and the Speaker of the House of Representatives his written declaration that he is unable to discharge the powers and duties of his office, and until he transmits to them a written declaration to the contrary, such powers and duties shall be discharged by the Vice President as Acting President.

Presidential disability: procedure for determining when and for how long disability exists. Vice President to act as President for duration of disability

SECTION 4.   Whenever the Vice President and a majority of either the principal officers of the executive departments or of such other body as Congress may by law provide, transmit to the President pro tempore of the Senate and the Speaker of the House of Representatives their written declaration that the President is unable to discharge the powers and duties of his office, the Vice President shall immediately assume the powers and duties of the office as Acting President.

Thereafter, when the President transmits to the President pro tempore of the Senate and the Speaker of the House of Representatives his written declaration that no inability exists, he shall resume the powers and duties of his office unless the Vice President and a majority of either the principal officers of the executive department or of such other body as Congress may by law provide, transmit within four days to the President pro tempore of the Senate and the Speaker of the House of Representatives their written declaration that the President is unable to discharge the powers and duties of his office. Thereupon Congress shall decide the issue, assembling within forty-eight hours for that purpose if not in session. If the Congress, within twenty-one days after receipt of the latter written declaration, or, if Congress is not in session, within twenty-one days after Congress is required to assemble, determines by two-thirds vote of both Houses that the President is unable to discharge the powers and duties of his office, the Vice President shall continue to discharge the same as Acting President; otherwise, the President shall resume the powers and duties of his office.

ARTICLE   XXVI

Citizens eighteen years or older not to be denied suffrage because of age

SECTION 1.   The right of citizens of the United States, who are eighteen years of age or older, to vote shall not be denied or abridged by the United States or by any State on account of age.

SECTION 2.   The Congress shall have power to enforce this article by appropriate legislation.

ARTICLE   XXVII

A vote of Congress to increase the salaries of its members goes into effect only after a new Congress is elected.

No law varying the compensation for the services of the Senators and Representatives shall take effect until an election of representatives shall have intervened.

CHRONOLOGY OF AMERICAN

Political and Governmental	Military and Special Events	American Foreign Relations
	I. PERIOD OF EXPLORATION	
1000 Most highly developed Pre-Columbian governments in America were those of Incas in Peru and Aztecs in Mexico.		
	1482 Portugal refused to support Columbus in proposed westward voyage.	
	1492 Columbus made first voyage to America.	
	1497 Cabot claimed North American coast for England.	
	1500 Cabral discovered Brazil.	
	1513 Balboa discovered the Pacific by crossing Isthmus of Panama.	
	1513 Ponce de Leon explored Florida.	
	1519–1521 Cortes conquered Aztecs.	
	1512–1522 Magellan circumnavigated the globe.	
	1524 Verazzano explored Canada.	
	1531–1535 Pizarro conquered Incas in Peru.	
	1533–1541 Cartier explored along St. Lawrence River.	
	1539 De Soto began exploration in North America.	
	1540–1542 Coronado explored present southwestern United States.	
	1565 St. Augustine, Florida, founded.	
	1585–1587 Raleigh sent expeditions to colonize Roanoke Island.	
	1607 Jamestown founded.	
	1608 Quebec founded	
1609 Virginia received new charter.	**1609** Santa Fe founded.	
1619 First legislature in Virginia.		
1624 Virginia became royal colony.	**1624** New Amsterdam (N.Y.) founded.	
	1630 Massachusetts Bay Colony founded.	
	1634 Maryland settled.	
	1636 Roger Williams settled Providence.	
	1636 Hooker settled Connecticut.	
	1638 Delaware settled.	
1639 Fundamental Orders of Connecticut.		
1643 New England Confederation organized.		

HISTORY AND CIVILIZATION

Economic and Technological	Cultural and Intellectual	Parallel Events in World History	

AND COLONIZATION, TO 1763

Economic and Technological	Cultural and Intellectual	Parallel Events in World History	
		1000	Leif Ericson discovered Vinland.
		1095–1291	The Crusades fought.
		1460	Prince Henry of Portugal died.
		1487	Diaz rounded Cape of Good Hope.
		1493	Treaty of Tordesillas fixed Line of Demarcation.
		1498	Vasco Da Gama sailed to India.
		1517	Luther's Theses published.
		1519–1556	Charles V reigned in Europe.
		1534	Henry VIII established Anglican church.
		1577	Drake began circumnavigation of globe.
		1588	Spanish Armada defeated.
		1598	Edict of Nantes.
1612	Rolfe introduced superior variety of tobacco to Virginia.			
			1618–1648	Thirty Years' War.
1619	First slaves brought to Virginia.			
		1620	Pilgrims introduced congregational churches to America.	
			1628	Charles I signed Petition of Right.
		1636	Harvard University founded.	
		1639	Baptist church first organized in Rhode Island.	
			1642–1646	Civil War in England.
			1643–1715	Louis XIV reign.

Political and Governmental	Military and Special Events	American Foreign Relations
	1664 New Netherland captured by Duke of York.	
	1670 Charleston founded.	
	1675 King Phillip's War.	
1676 Governor Berkeley recalled to England.	**1676** Bacon's Rebellion.	
1679 New Hampshire made separate colony.		
	1681 Pennsylvania granted to William Penn.	
	1682 LaSalle claimed the Mississippi for France.	
1688 Dominion of New England.		
	1690–1697 King William's War.	
	1691 Plymouth absorbed by Massachusetts.	
	1702–1713 Queen Anne's War.	
1729 North Carolina made separate colony.		
	1733 Georgia settled.	
	1744–1748 King George's War.	
1751 Georgia became royal colony.		
1754 Albany Congress.	**1754–1763** French and Indian War.	
	1755 Braddock's defeat.	

Economic and Technological	Cultural and Intellectual	Parallel Events in World History
	1647 Public elementary schools established by law in Massachusetts.	
	1649 Maryland Religious Toleration Act passed.	
1651 First navigation act passed.		
1660 Enumerated Commodities Act passed.		**1660** Charles II crowned King of England.
		1685 James I became King of England.
		1685 Edict of Nantes revoked in France.
		1689 William of Orange crowned King of England, in Glorious Revolution; Bill of Rights.
		1689–1697 War of League of Augsburg.
	1692 Witchcraft trials at Salem.	
	1693 William and Mary College founded.	
1696 Navigation Act passed.		
1697 Triangular trade began.		**1697** Treaty of Ryswick.
1699 Woolens Act passed.		
1700 Rice became Carolina export staple.		
	1701 Yale founded.	
		1702–1713 War of Spanish Succession.
	1704 *Boston News Letter* published.	
		1713 Peace of Utrecht.
		1715–1774 Louis XV reigned in France.
1732 Hat Act passed.	**1732** *Poor Richard's Almanac* began.	
1733 Molasses Act.		
	1735 Zenger Trial.	
	1740 Great Awakening centered about this time.	**1740–1748** War of Austrian Succession.
1747 Franklin began experiments with electricity.		
		1748 Treaty of Aix-la-Chapelle.
1750 Iron Act passed.		
		1756–1763 Seven Years' War.
		1758 William Pitt Prime Minister.

Political and Governmental		Military and Special Events		American Foreign Relations	
		1759	Fall of Quebec.		
		1760	British take Montreal.		
1761	Writs of assistance protested by James Otis.				
1763	Proclamation Act established Indian reserve in the West.				

II. ERA OF THE AMERICAN REVOLUTION

Political and Governmental		Military and Special Events		American Foreign Relations	
1763	Paxton Boys.	1763	Pontiac's War.		
1764	Sugar Act.				
1765	Stamp Act.	1765	Stamp Act Congress.		
1765	Quartering Act and repeal of Stamp Act.				
1766	Declaratory Act.				
1767	Townshend Acts.				
		1768–1771	Regulator movements.		
		1769	Spanish colonize California.		
1770	Townshend Acts repealed except tea tax.	1770	Boston Massacre.		
1772	Committees of Correspondence organized.	1772	Gaspée burned.		
1773	Tea Act.	1773	Boston Tea Party.		
1774	Intolerable Acts and Quebec Act.	1774	Lord Dunmore's (Indian) War in Kentucky.		
1774	First Continental Congress met.				
1775	Second Continental Congress met.	1775	Battles of Lexington, Concord, and Bunker Hill.		
1776	Declaration of Independence.	1776	Washington lost Battle of Long Island.		
		1776–1783	American Revolution.		
1777	Articles of Confederation submitted to states.	1777	Battle of Saratoga.		
		1777–1778	Washington at Valley Forge.		
		1778	British land at Savannah.	1778	Treaty of Alliance with France signed.
		1778–1779	Clark captured British posts in the Northwest Territory.		
1781	Articles of Confederation ratified.	1781	Cornwallis captured at Yorktown.		
				1783	Treaty of Paris recognized American independence.
1785	Land Ordinance enacted.			1785	Jay-Gardoqui Treaty negotiated but failed ratification.
		1786	Shays' Rebellion.		
1787	Northwest Ordinance enacted.				
1787	Constitutional Convention met at Philadelphia.				
1788	Constitution ratified.				

Economic and Technological	Cultural and Intellectual	Parallel Events in World History
		1760–1820 Reign of George III.

AND THE CONFEDERATION, 1763–1789

Economic and Technological	Cultural and Intellectual	Parallel Events in World History
		1763 Treaty of Paris.
1764 Parliament forbade colonial paper money by Currency Act.		
		1770 Lord North made Prime Minister in England.
		1774–1792 Louis XVI reigned in France.
1775 First American submarine built.		
	1776 Thomas Paine wrote *Common Sense*.	**1776** Adam Smith published *Wealth of Nations*.
1784 Depression in America.	**1784** Methodist church in America organized.	

Political and Governmental	Military and Special Events	American Foreign Relations
		III. EARLY NATIONAL
1789 Washington inaugurated president.		
1789 Judiciary Act.		
1790 National capitol moved to Philadelphia.		
1791 Whiskey Tax.		
1791 Bill of Rights.		
1791 Vermont, first state admitted.		
1792 Kentucky admitted.		
		1793 Washington proclaimed neutrality; Citizen Genet's recall demanded.
	1794 Whiskey Rebellion.	**1794** Jay Treaty.
	1795 Treaty of Greenville ended Indian wars in northwest.	**1795** Pinckney Treaty.
1797-1811 John Adams president		**1797** XYZ Affair.
1798 Alien and Sedition Acts; Kentucky and Virginia Resolutions.	**1798–1799** Undeclared naval war with France.	
1800 Capitol removed to Washington.		**1800** Alliance with France abrogated.
1800 Jefferson elected president.		**1800** Louisiana transferred to France.
	1801–1805 War with Tripoli.	
1803 Marbury v. Madison.		**1803** Louisiana Purchase Treaty.
1804 12th Amendment ratified.	**1804** Hamilton-Burr duel.	
	1804–1806 Lewis and Clark Expedition.	
		1805 Essex decision.
	1806 Burr expedition.	**1806** Berlin decrees.
	1807 Chesapeake-Leopard Affair.	**1807** Embargo Act.
		1809 Non-intercourse Act
1810 Fletcher v. Peck.		**1810** Macon's Bill.
	1812 War begun against Great Britain.	
1814 Hartford Convention.	**1814** British burned national capital.	**1814** Treaty of Ghent ended War of 1812.
	1815 Jackson's victory at New Orleans.	
	1818 Rush-Bagot Agreement.	
1819 McCulloch v. Maryland; Dartmouth College case.		**1819** Adams-Onis (Florida) Treaty.
1820 Missouri Compromise.		

Economic and Technological	Cultural and Intellectual	Parallel Events in World History
PERIOD, 1789–1828		
1789 First tariff act.		**1789** French Revolution began.
1790 Slater built first textile mill.		
1791 Bank of the United States chartered.		
1793 Cotton gin invented.		**1793** Louis XVI beheaded.
		1793–1794 French "Reign of Terror."
1794 Lancaster Turnpike completed.		
	1797 Great Revivals began.	
		1799 Napoleon became First consul.
		1803 Napoleon renewed war in Europe.
		1804 Napoleon made Emperor.
1807 Embargo stimulated rise of American manufacturing.		
1807 Clermont steamed up the Hudson.		
1808 Foreign slave trade became illegal.		
		1810–1822 Wars for Latin America independence.
1811 National Road begun.		
	1815 U.S. population 9 million.	**1815** Battle of Waterloo and Congress of Vienna.
	1815–1860 New England literary renaissance.	
1816 Second Bank of the U.S. chartered; protective tariff passed.		
1817 Bonus Bill vetoed.	**1817** American Colonization society organized.	
1817 Erie Canal begun.		
1819 Panic.		
1819 Cast iron plow.		
1820 Land Law revised.		
1820 New England ships became more active in California coastal trade.		

Political and Governmental	Military and Special Events	American Foreign Relations
1821 Missouri admitted.	**1821** Stephen F. Austin began colonization of Texas.	
	1821 Santa Fe trade begun.	
		1823 Monroe Doctrine announced.
1824 Adams defeated Jackson.		
1824 Gibbons v. Ogden.		
1826 Antimasons organized.		**1826** Panama Congress.
		1827 Joint occupation of Oregon renewed.
1828 Tariff of Abominations.		

IV. JACKSONIAN

1830 Webster-Hayne debates.		
1831 Jackson reorganized Cabinet as result of Eaton affair.		
1832 Protective tariff maintained; Nullification Ordinance; Nullification Proclamation.	**1832** Year of several fur expeditions to the Far West.	
1832 Jackson vetoed Bank Bill; Jackson reelected.	**1832** Black Hawk's War.	
1833 Force Bill and Compromise Tariff.		
	1834 Rev. Lee started mission in Oregon.	
1836 Specie circular issued.		**1836** Republic of Texas won independence
1836 Gag rule adopted.		
1837 Independent treasury defeated.	**1837** Caroline Affair.	**1837** Texan independence recognized.
	1837-1842 Seminole War	
	1838 Aroostook War.	
1840 Harrison elected, first Whig president.		
1841 Harrison died; Tyler became president.	**1841** First pioneer settlers traveled overland to California.	
		1842 Webster-Ashburton Treaty.
		1842 Commod. Jones seized Monterey, California.
	1843 Large migration to Oregon.	
1844 Polk defeated Clay for president.		
		1845 Texas annexed.
		1845 Slidell mission sent to Mexico.
1846 Wilmot Proviso first introduced.	**1846–1848** Mexican War.	**1846** Oregon Treaty.

Economic and Technological	Cultural and Intellectual	Parallel Events in World History
		1822 Latin American independence completed.
1825 Erie Canal completed.	**1825** Robert Owen founded New Harmony colony.	
1827 Baltimore & Ohio Railroad chartered.		

DEMOCRACY, 1828–1850

1830 *Tom Thumb* locomotive made trial run on B & O Railroad.	**1830** Mormon church organized.	**1830** July Revolutions; Louis Phillippe became king of France.
	1831 Garrison began publication of *The Liberator.*	
	1831 Nat Turner Rebellion.	
		1832 First English Reform Bill.
	1833 Oberlin College founded.	
1835 Colt revolver patented.		
1835–1836 Speculative boom and inflation.		
1837 Business panic followed by long depression.		**1837** Rebellion in Canada.
1837 Deere's steel plow.		
1841 Preemption Act.		
1842 Courts recognized right of collective bargaining.		
1844 Morse constructed first telegraph line.		
	1845 Poe published *The Raven.*	
1846 Walker Tariff.		**1846** Repeal of English Corn Laws.
1846 Howe invented sewing machine.		
1846 Ether used in surgery.		

Political and Governmental	Military and Special Events	American Foreign Relations
	1847 Mormons began colonization of Utah.	
	1847 Scott marched to Mexico City.	
1848 Taylor elected president.	**1848** Gold discovered at Sutter's mill.	**1848** Treaty of Guadalupe Hidalgo.
1849 Department of Interior established.	**1849** California Gold Rush.	

V. SECTIONAL STRIFE AND

Political and Governmental	Military and Special Events	American Foreign Relations
1850 Taylor died in office and was succeeded by Filmore.		**1850** Clayton-Bulwer Treaty.
1850 Compromise of 1850; California admitted.		
1852 Pierce inaugurated as president.		
		1853 Gadsden Purchase Treaty.
1854 Kansas-Nebraska Act; Republican Party organized.		**1854** Admiral Perry negotiated treaty with Japan.
		1854 Ostend Manifesto.
	1856 Proslavery forces burned Lawrence, Kansas	
1857 Buchanan inaugurated as president.	**1857** Senator Sumner assaulted by Preston Brooks.	
1857 Dred Scott.		
1857 Lecompton constitution refused by Kansas.		
1858 Lincoln-Douglas debates.		
	1859 John Brown's Raid	
1860 Lincoln elected president.	**1860–1861** Southern states seceded.	
1861 Lincoln inaugurated.	**1861** Ft. Sumter surrendered; Civil War began; Battle of Bull Run.	**1861** Mason and Slidell taken from the *Trent*.
1861 Proposals of Peace Convention ignored.		**1861** Napoleon III intervened in Mexico.
1862 Emancipation Proclamation issued.	**1862** Battle of Antietam.	
1862 Homestead Act.		
	1863 Vicksburg taken by Grant; Lee defeated at Gettysburg.	
1864 Lincoln vetoed Wade-Davis Bill.	**1864** Wilderness Campaign; Sherman's march through Georgia.	

VI. RECONSTRUCTION

Political and Governmental	Military and Special Events	American Foreign Relations
1865 Lincoln assassinated; Johnson became president.	**1865** Lee surrendered at Appomattox.	
1865 13th Amendment ratified.	**1865–1885** Last Indian wars fought.	
1866 Civil Rights Bill passed.	**1866** Race riots in the South.	**1866** Maximilian executed in Mexico.

Economic and Technological	Cultural and Intellectual	Parallel Events in World History
		1848 Revolutions in Europe; Communist Manifesto.

CIVIL WAR, 1850–1865

Economic and Technological	Cultural and Intellectual	Parallel Events in World History
1850 First federal land grant to subsidize railroad building.	**1850** U.S. population reached 23 million.	
1851 Singer developed first practical sewing machine.		
	1852 *Uncle Tom's Cabin* published.	
		1854–1856 Crimean War.
	1855 Amana colony settled in Iowa.	
1857 Business panic.	**1857** *Helper's Impending Crisis* published.	
1857 First overland stage line operated to California.		
1859 Oil industry began with "Drake's Folly."		**1859** Darwin published *Origin of the Species.*
1859 Pike's Peak and Comstock mining booms.		
1860–1861 Pony Express.		
1861 Transcontinental (Pacific) Telegraph.		**1861** Russia emancipated serfs.
1861 Morrill Tariff.		
1862 Union Pacific and Central Pacific railroads chartered.	**1862** Morrill Land Grant College Act.	
1863 National Banking Act passed.		
1864 First Pullman car built.		

PERIOD, 1865–1877

Economic and Technological	Cultural and Intellectual	Parallel Events in World History
1866 National Labor Union organized.		
1866 Atlantic cable operated successfully.		

Political and Governmental	Military and Special Events	American Foreign Relations
1867 Congressional Reconstruction Acts passed.		**1867** Alaska Purchase.
1868 14th Amendment ratified.		**1868** Burlingame Treaty with China.
1868 Johnson impeachment.		
1869 Grant inaugurated.	**1869** "Black Friday" gold conspiracy.	
1870 15th Amendment ratified.	**1870** Legal Tender cases.	
1870–1871 Enforcement acts passed against KKK.		
	1871 Tweed Ring prosecuted.	**1871** U.S. arrested Fenian leaders.
		1871 Treaty of Washington.
1872 Amnesty Act.	**1872** Crédit Mobilier scandal exposed.	
1872 Greeley defeated by Grant.		
1873 "Salary Grab" Act.	**1873** Spain captured the *Virginius* in Cuba.	
1873 Grant began second term.		
1875 Greenback Party organized.		**1875** Hawaiian Reciprocity Treaty.
1876 Hayes inaugurated as president. Southern Reconstruction ended.		

VII. THE CONSERVATIVE

Political and Governmental	Military and Special Events	American Foreign Relations
1879 Denis Kearney active in California.		
1881 Garfield became president; assassinated; Arthur succeeded to presidency.		
1883 Pendleton Act created Civil Service Commission.		
1885 Cleveland inaugurated.		
1886 Wabash Decision.	**1886** Haymarket Riot.	
1887 Interstate Commerce Commission created.		
1889 Harrison inaugurated as president.	**1889–1890** Omnibus states admitted in the West.	**1889** First Pan-American Conference.
1889 Department of Agriculture created.		**1889** Fur Seal Controversy began.
	1890 American frontier substantially closed.	
1891 Populist Party organized.		**1891** *Baltimore* crisis with Chile.

Economic and Technological		Cultural and Intellectual		Parallel Events in World History	
1867	Farmers' Grange organized.			1867	Second Reform Bill adopted in Britain.
1867	Abilene, Kansas, first "cowtown" built.				
1868	"Ohio Idea" proposed by Democrats in the election.				
1869	First transcontinental railroad completed.	1869	Resurgence of temperance movement.		
1869	Knights of Labor organized.				
				1871	Prussian victory over France in Treaty of Frankfurt; Germany united.
1872	Westinghouse airbrake put in use.				
1873	Business panic.	1873	Kindergarten introduced.		
1873	Silver demonetized in "Crime of '73."				
1873	Carnegie concentrated energies in steel business.				
1874	Large-scale manufacture of barbed wire began.	1874	WCTU organized.		
1875	Resumption Act passed.				
1876	Bell invented the telephone.				

ERA, 1877–1901

Economic and Technological		Cultural and Intellectual		Parallel Events in World History	
1877	National railroad strike.				
1878	Twine binder invented.				
1878	Bland-Allison Act.				
1879	Gold standard resumed.	1879	Henry George published *Progress and Poverty*.		
1879	Standard Oil trust organized.	1879	Christian Science founded.		
1881	American Federation of Labor began.				
		1882	Oriental immigration stopped.		
1883	Three more transcontinental railroads completed.			1883	Germany, Italy, and Austria form Triple Alliance.
1883	Downturn in cattle boom began.				
1886	Decline of Knights of Labor.				
1887	Hatch Act began establishment of agricultural experiment stations.	1887	Dawes Act.		
1890	Sherman Silver Purchase Act, McKinley Tariff, and Sherman Anti-Trust Acts passed.				

Political and Governmental		Military and Special Events		American Foreign Relations	
1893	Cleveland began second term.			1893	Hawaiian monarchy overthrown.
1895	Income tax declared unconstitutional.			1895	Venzuelan boundary crisis.
1896	Hardest fought election in American politics.				
1897	McKinley inaugurated.				
		1898	Spanish-American War.	1898	Treaty of Paris signed with Spain; Hawaii annexed.
		1899–1902	Philippine Insurrection.	1899	Open Door Policy announced; First Hague Conference.
1900	McKinley reelected.	1900	Boxer Uprising.		
1900	Foraker Act established government in Puerto Rico.				

VIII. THE PROGRESSIVE

Political and Governmental		Military and Special Events		American Foreign Relations	
1901	McKinley assassinated; Roosevelt became president.			1901	Platt Amendment imposed on Cuba; Hay-Pauncefote Treaty negotiated.
1902	Newlands Reclamation Act.	1902	Insurrection in Philippines suppressed.	1902	Venezuelan debt controversy and Drago Doctrine.
1903	Department of Commerce and Labor created.			1903	**Hay-Herran Treaty with Colombia not ratified; Hay-Bunau-Varilla Treaty with Panama**
				1903	Alaskan Boundary dispute settled.
1905	Roosevelt began second term.			1905	Roosevelt helped negotiate Treaty of Portsmouth.
1906	Pure Food and Drug Act.			1906–1907	Algeciras Conference.
				1907	Second Hague Conference.
1908	National Conservation Commission.			1908	Root-Takahira Agreement.
1909	Taft inaugurated as president.			1909–1913	"Dollar Diplomacy" of Taft administration.
1910	Revolt against "Cannonism."				
1912	"Bull Moose" party in presidential election.	1912	Arizona and New Mexico admitted.	1912	Panama Canal Tolls Act.
1913	Wilson inaugurated as president.			1913	"Watchful Waiting" policy adopted against Huerta.
1913	16th and 17th Amendments added.				
1913	Department of Labor made separate.				

Economic and Technological		Cultural and Intellectual		Parallel Events in World History	
1892	Homestead strike.			1892	Dual Alliance of France and Russia formed.
1893	Business panic, followed by severe depression.				
1894	Pullman strike; Coxey's Army; Wilson Tariff Act.			1894–1895	Sino-Japanese War.
				1895	Cuban war for independence began.
				1895	Jameson Raid in South Africa.
1896	Klondike gold rush began.	1896	Plessy v. Ferguson permitted segregated schools.		
		1896	Marconi invented wireless telegraphy.		
1897	Dingley Tariff.				
				1889–1902	Boer War.
1900	Gold Standard Act.	1900	U.S. population 75 million.		

ERA, 1901–1914

1902	Anthracite coal strike.			1902	British-Japanese alliance.
1903	Wright brothers first successful flight.				
1903	Elkins Act.				
1904	Northern Securities case decided.			1904–1905	Russo-Japanese War.
				1905	Revolution in Russia.
1906	Construction of Panama Canal began.				
1906	Hepburn Act.				
1907	Brief money panic.				
1907	First radio broadcast.				
1908	Model "T" Ford developed.				
1909	Payne-Aldrich Tariff.				
1910	Mann-Elkins Act.			1910	Madero led revolution in Mexico.
1913	Underwood Tariff and Federal Reserve Acts passed.			1913	Huerta led counter-revolution in Mexico.

Political and Governmental	Military and Special Events	American Foreign Relations

IX. THE WILSON ADMINISTRATION

Political and Governmental	Military and Special Events	American Foreign Relations
1914 Clayton Anti-Trust Act passed and Federal Trade Commission created.	**1914** American marines captured Vera Cruz.	
1916 Wilson reelected by narrow vote.	**1916** Marines sent to Santo Domingo. **1916** Villa led border raid against Columbus, New Mexico.	
		1917 U.S. declared war on Germany.
		1917 Lansing-Ishii Agreement.
		1917 Virgin Islands purchased from Denmark.
	1918 American Expeditionary Force active in battles on the Western Front.	**1918** Wilson announced Fourteen Points.
1919–1920 Congressional debates over Treaty of Versailles. Treaty rejected.		**1919** Wilson at Versailles Peace Conference.
1920 Presidential election, a "solemn referendum," and Republican landslide.		
1920 Merchant Marine Act passed.		

X. THE CONSERVATIVE

Political and Governmental	Military and Special Events	American Foreign Relations
1921 Harding inaugurated.		**1921** Separate American peace made with Germany, Austria, and Hungary.
1921 Sacco-Vanzetti case began.		
		1921–1922 Washington Conference.
1923 Harding died; Coolidge succeeded to presidency.		
1923 Farm "bloc" became important factor in Congress.		
1924 Adjusted compensation ("bonus") voted for veterans.		**1924** Dawes Plan adopted.
1924 Teapot Dome scandal.		
1924 LaFollette won 5 million votes in presidential election.		
1925 Coolidge began second term.		
1927 Coolidge vetoed McNary-Haugen Bill.		**1927** Morrow initiates friendly policy toward Mexico.
1928 Coolidge again vetoed McNary-Haugen farm relief.		**1928** Kellogg-Briand Pact; failure of Geneva Disarmament Conference.
1929 Hoover inaugurated as president.		**1929** Young Plan negotiated.

Economic and Technological	Cultural and Intellectual		Parallel Events in World History

AND WORLD WAR I, 1913–1921

Economic and Technological	Cultural and Intellectual		Parallel Events in World History
1914 Panama Canal completed.			**1914** Assassination of Archduke Ferdinand caused outbreak of World War I.
	1915 "Grandfather" clauses declared unconstitutional.		**1915** British ship *Lusitania* sunk.
1916 Federal Farm Loan Act and Adamson Railway Labor Acts passed.			**1916** French ship *Sussex* sunk.
			1917 Mexico adopted new constitution.
	1918–1919 Influenza epidemic caused 500,000 deaths in U.S.		
	1919 18th Amendment ratified and Volstead Act passed.		
	1919–1920 "Big Red Scare."		
1920 Esch-Cummins Act returned railroads to private ownership.	**1920** 19th Amendment gave vote to women.		

REPUBLICAN ERA, 1921–1933

Economic and Technological	Cultural and Intellectual		Parallel Events in World History
	1920s Decade of revolt against Victorianism in manners and morals.		
1921 Primary postwar depression.	**1921** Emergency Immigration Act passed.		
1922 Fordney-McCumber Tariff Act.			**1922** Mussolini rose to power.
	1924 Basic immigration law passed.		
	1924 Ku Klux Klan reached climax.		
1925 Rust Brothers invent cotton picking machine.	**1925** Scopes trial.		
1926 Radio came into popular use.	**1926** Sinclair Lewis published *Elmer Gantry.*		
1927 Lindbergh solo flight to Paris.			
1928 "Talking pictures" introduced.			
1929 Stock market crash precipitated Great Depression.			
1929 Agricultural Marketing Act created Federal Farm Board.			
1929 Hawley-Smoot Tariff.			

Political and Governmental	Military and Special Events	American Foreign Relations
		1931 Hoover declared moratorium on international debts.
	1932 "Bonus army" driven out of Washington.	**1932** Stimson Doctrine.

XI. THE NEW

Political and Governmental	Military and Special Events	American Foreign Relations
1933 FDR inaugurated in depth of Great Depression.		**1933** Roosevelt launched "Good Neighbor" Policy.
1933 20th ("Lame Duck") Amendment ratified; 21st (prohibition repeal) Amendment ratified.		
1933 Numerous New Deal relief, recovery, and reform measures passed: CCC, FERA, CWA, FCA, AAA, NRA, USES, TVA, HOLC, FDIC, and SEC (1934).		
		1934 Platt Amendment abrogated.
		1934 Nye Committee investigated munitions industry; Johnson Act against debt defaulters.
1935 "Second New Deal" begun: WPA created, Wagner Act, Wheeler-Rayburn Social Security established.	**1935** Last marines withdrawn from Haiti and Nicaragua.	**1935–1937** Neutrality Act passed.
1936 Soil Conservation Act; Merchant Marine Act.		
1936 Presidential election Democratic landslide; Roosevelt sought reform of Supreme Court.		
1937 Roosevelt began second term.		**1937** Roosevelt delivered "Quarantine speech" against aggressor nations.

XII. WORLD WAR II AND

Political and Governmental	Military and Special Events	American Foreign Relations
		1939 Mutual security policies adopted at Panama City and Havana.
		1939 U.S. canceled treaty of 1911 with Japan.
		1939 Revision of Neutrality Acts permitted aid to Allies.
	1940 Selective Service Act passed.	
1941 Roosevelt began third term.	**1941–1942** Battle of the Atlantic against German submarines at its worst.	**1941** Atlantic Charter announced by Roosevelt and Churchill; Lend-Lease Act passed.
	1941 Attack on Pearl Harbor brought U.S. into World War II.	
	1942 U.S. began counterattacks against Japan and Germany by invasions of Guadalcanal and North Africa	
		1943 Casablanca Conference demanded "unconditional surrender;" Moscow Conference agreed to formation of UNO.

Economic and Technological	Cultural and Intellectual	Parallel Events in World History
	1930s Decade of the Great Depression and its blighting economic and social effects.	**1931** Japan invaded Manchuria.
1932 Home Loan Bank Act.		

DEAL, 1933–1939

1933 National banking crisis.		**1933** Hitler came to power in Germany.
1934 Reciprocal Trade Agreements Act.		
1934 Tydings-McDuffie Act provided for Phillippine independence.		
1935 Gold Clause Act nullified gold clauses in contracts.		**1935** Italy invaded Ethiopia.
1935 Drought and "dust bowl."		
1936–1939 Sulfa drugs.	**1936** *Gone with the Wind* published.	**1936** Germany reoccupied Rhineland.
		1936 Rome-Berlin Alliance.
		1936 Spanish Civil War began.
1937–1938 Depression renewed; severe strikes occurred as labor sought union recognition.		**1937** Japan opened war against China.
1938 Fair Labor Standards Act.		**1938** Germany annexed Austria, later Czechoslovakia.
		1939 German-Soviet nonaggression pact.

THE COLD WAR PERIOD

1939–1952 Discovery and use of antibiotics.	**1939** Steinbeck published *The Grapes of Wrath*.	**1939** World War II began with Nazi invasion of Poland.
		1940 Nazis overran western Europe.
		1941 Hitler began invasion of Russia.
		1941 Japan won wide ranging victories over the Pacific and Far East.
		1943 Italy surrendered.

HISTORY OF THE UNITED STATES

Political and Governmental		Military and Special Events		American Foreign Relations	
		1944	June 6 "D-Day" invasion of Normandy; Dec.-Jan., Battle of the Bulge.	**1944**	Yalta Conference on disposal of defeated powers and other problems.
		1944–1945	Philippines reoccupied.		
1945	Roosevelt began 4th term and died soon thereafter; Truman succeeded to presidency.	**1945**	May, Germany defeated. August, Japan surrendered.	**1945**	April, UNO charter drawn up at San Francisco; Potsdam Conference.
1946	Atomic Energy Commission created; Republican won mid-term election; demobilization.	**1946**	Overhasty demobilization of armed forces; peacetime conscription adopted.	**1946**	International war crimes trials began.
1947	Presidential Succession Act.	**1947**	Department of Defense formed by merger of War and Navy departments.	**1947**	Peace treaties signed with minor powers.
				1947	Truman Doctrine applied in Greece and Turkey.
				1947	Marshall Plan (ECA) adopted by Congress.
1948	Presidential victory of Truman.	**1948**	Berlin blockade began; ended in 1949.		
1949	Truman began second term; Fair Deal.	**1949**	European rearmament under NATO.	**1949**	North Atlantic Pact; Point Four program.
1949	Communists convicted under Smith Act.				
1950	McCarran Act against communists.	**1950**	Korean War began.	**1950s**	Decade of recurring diplomatic crises.
1951	22nd Amendment (anti-third term) ratified.	**1951**	McArthur recalled by Truman.	**1951**	Peace treaty with Japan.
1952	Eisenhower carried Republicans to victory.	**1952**	ANZUS Treaty.		
1953	Eisenhower inaugurated.	**1953**	Korean War ended in truce.		
1953	Department of HEW created.				
1954	St. Lawrence Seaway Act passed.	**1954**	Indo-China War ended by Geneva conference.		
		1955	SEATO formed.		
		1955	Geneva Summit Conference.		
		1956	Suez War.		
1957	Eisenhower began second term.			**1957**	Eisenhower Doctrine approved by Congress.
		1958	Alaska admitted.		
		1958	Communist China shelled Quemoy and Matsu; American troops landed in Lebanon		
		1959	Hawaii admitted.		

Economic and Technological		Cultural and Intellectual		Parallel Events in World History	
1945	Atomic Age began with successful bombing of Hiroshima and Nagasaki.			1945	Russia declared war on Japan.
1946	Year of prolonged strikes and inflation.				
1946	Congress passed Full Employment Act.				
1947	Taft-Hartley Act.			1947	Cominform organized.
1947	Television came into wide use.				
				1948	Israel wins independence
				1949	Indonesian independence recognized.
				1949	Republic of West Germany formed.
				1949	Russia exploded her first atomic bomb.
		1950	Social Security Act liberalized.	1950	Communists completed victory in China.
		1950s	Decade of the "Beat Generation," the "affluent society," and mass culture.		
1952	Truman confiscated steel industry during long strike.	1952	McCarran-Walters Act revised immigration law.		
1953	Reciprocal Trade Agreements Act extended throughout Eisenhower administration.				
1953	Slight recession.				
1954	Capital goods boom began.	1954	Supreme Court ruled separate schools unconstitutional; Social Security liberalized again.	1954	Sovereignty of West Germany recognized.
		1955	Labor fought for guaranteed annual wage; CIO-AFL merger.	1955	Peace treaty with Austria signed.
				1956	Hungarian revolt crushed by Soviets.
		1957	Civil Rights Act; Little Rock violence over school integration.	1957	Russia launched Sputnik I.
1958	Economic recession.	1958	National Defense Education Act, federal funds for science, math, languages, libraries.		
1959	Landrum-Griffin Act to regulate labor unions.			1959	Castro came to power in Cuba.

Political and Governmental		Military and Special Events		American Foreign Relations	
				1960	U-2 incident.
1961	Kennedy inaugurated.	1961	Bay of Pigs disaster in Cuba.	1961	Crisis over Berlin.
1961	23rd Amendment ratified.			1961	Alliance for Progress began in Latin-America; Peace Corps established.
1962	Kennedy clashed with steel industry.	1962	Crisis with Russia over missiles in Cuba.	1962	Almost all trade with Cuba banned.
1962	Midterm elections endorsed Kennedy administration.				
1963	Kennedy tax reforms delayed in Congress.			1963	Atomic test-ban treaty signed with Russia.
1963	Nov. 22, Kennedy assassinated; Johnson succeeded to Presidency.				
1964	24th Amendment (anti-poll tax) ratified; Supreme Court requires reapportionment of state legislatures; Johnson elected president over Goldwater.	1964	Escalation of war in Vietnam.		
1965	Johnson announces "The Great Society."	1965	Further escalation of war in Vietnam; U.S. Marines land in Dominican Republic.	1965	Immigration Act ended quotas based on national origin.
				1965–1966	Massive U.S. military aid to South Vietnam.
1966	25th Amendment ratified.				
1967	25th Amendment ratified, dealing with presidential disability.				
1967–1968	Long, hot summers of urban rioting.				
1968	Assassination of Dr. Martin Luther King Jr., civil rights leader; and Senator Robert F. Kennedy, candidate for President.			1968	Vietnam crisis pushed Johnson away from reelection attempt.
1968	Report of the National Advisory Commission on Civil Disorders.				
1968	Richard Nixon elected president; Spiro Agnew as vice president.				
1969	Increased protests against war in Vietnam; U.S. troop withdrawals begun.	1969	U.S. put first man on the moon.		

XIV.

Political and Governmental		Military and Special Events		American Foreign Relations	
		1970	Vietnamization of Indochina conflict begun.		
1971	26th Amendment ratified, lowering voting age to 18.				
1972	Watergate break-in at Democratic national headquarters.			1972	Nixon visited China, ending 22 years of hostility.
				1972	Nixon's visit to Moscow produced Strategic Arms Limitation Treaty (SALT).

Economic and Technological	Cultural and Intellectual	Parallel Events in World History

THE 1960s

Economic and Technological	Cultural and Intellectual	Parallel Events in World History
	1960 Stronger civil rights act passed.	
		1961 Russians built Berlin wall.
1962 John Glenn rocketed into orbit; stock market panic and recovery.	**1962** Integration violence at Jackson, Mississippi.	
1963 Johnson won tax reductions from Congress.	**1963** National integration crisis worsened.	**1963** Rift between Russia and China widened.
	1964 Civil Rights Act of 1964 passed.	**1964** Khrushchev deposed as Soviet leader.
1965 Johnson's "War on Poverty," curtailed by rising Vietnam costs.		
1966 Medicare Act went into operation.		
	1967 New Metropolitan Opera House, New York, with giant murals by Marc Chagall.	**1967** Israel defeated Arab states in six-day war; Jerusalem reunited.
	1968 Fair Housing Act barred racial discrimination in sales and rentals of most housing.	
	1969 Woodstock, New York music and art fair attracted 300,000 enthusiasts.	

THE 1970s

Economic and Technological	Cultural and Intellectual	Parallel Events in World History
1971 Amtrack established to restore adequate passenger rail service.	**1971** Publication of Pentagon Papers revealed Vietnam policy making procedures.	**1971** People's Republic of China admitted into United Nations.
	1971 Two "new" galaxies discovered adjacent to earth's galaxy, the Milky Way.	
	1971 Cigarette advertising banned from U.S. television.	

Political and Governmental	Military and Special Events	American Foreign Relations
1973 Agnew forced to resign over income tax evasion; Representative Gerald Ford of Michigan named new vice president.	**1973** U.S.—North Vietnam cease-fire agreement; U.S. troops withdrawn.	
1974 Top Nixon aides indicted for Watergate-related crimes; the president also named "unindicted co-conspirator."		
1974 Facing impeachment, Nixon resigned; Ford became president.		
1974 Ford pardoned Nixon one month after starting office.		
	1975 All of Vietnam fell under Communist control.	
1976 James E. Carter, former Democratic Governor of Georgia, elected President.	**1976** U.S. Bicentennial widely celebrated.	
	1976 Two U.S. spacecraft touched-down on surface of Mars.	
		1978 Panama Canal treaties signed, ending U.S. operation and control.
		1978 Carter brought Egypt's Sadat and Israel's Begin to peace conference.
	1979 Major nuclear power plant failure at Three Mile Island, Pennsylvania.	**1979** U.S. embassy and hostages seized at Teheran, Iran.

XV.

1980 Ronald Reagan unseated President Carter in landslide election victory.		**1980** Aborted attempt to rescue American hostages by helicopter.
1981 Sandra Day O'Connor named first female Supreme Court Justice.		

	Economic and Technological		Cultural and Intellectual		Parallel Events in World History
1973	Mid-East oil producers boycotted shipments to U.S.; other nations friendly to Israel.			1973	Yom Kippur War, fourth between Arabs and Israel since 1948.
1973-1974	Apollo space ships docked with Skylab; much information collected.				
1974	OPEC (Organization of Petroleum Exporting Countries) quadrupled world crude oil prices. Expensive nuclear power plants begun.				
		1975	Brooklyn's Bobby Fischer gave up world chess championship.		
1976	Conrail combined ailing northeast railroads to revitalize freight service.	1976	Episcopal Church approved ordination of women as priests and bishops.		
		1976	Increased concern that spray can gases damage earth atmosphere's ozone layer.		
1977–1980	High inflation and large government expenditures hurt Carter's reelection chances.			1977	President Sadat of Egypt visited Israel to discuss peace.
				1979	Moslem fundamentalists overthrew monarchy in Iran.
				1979	Soviet troops invaded Afghanistan, chilling détente.
				1979	Nicaraguan Sandinistas ousted repressive military regime of Anastasio Somoza.

THE 1980s

	Economic and Technological		Cultural and Intellectual		Parallel Events in World History
		1980	Alaska Lands Conservation Act doubled area of U.S. national parks.	1980–1984	Civil War in El Salvador pitted President Duarte against leftist insurgents.
		1980s	Social changes noted from 1970s on — Americans more aware of needs and problems of senior citizens and the handicapped; number of women employed in medicine and the sciences grew dramatically; and 40% of population increase was in three states of Texas. Florida, and California.	1980	Iran-Iraq war started; replaced Israel as main Arab problem.
		1980s	School reform movement focused national attention on the importance and purposes of effective instruction.		
		1980s	Epidemic spread of AIDS sparked medical research for treatment and cure.		
1981	Congress cut social programs: Medicare, food stamps, college student loans, mass transit.				

Political and Governmental	Military and Special Events	American Foreign Relations
	1983 CIA mined Nicaraguan harbors.	**1983** U.S. arms aid to anti-*Sandinista contras* to topple Nicaraguan government.
	1983 U.S. troops invaded eastern Caribbean island of Grenada.	
		1983 Loss of 241 U.S. marines in Beirut, Lebanon, terrorist attack.
1984 Reagan and Bush easily reelected over Walter Mondale.		
1985 Congress passed Gramm-Rudman Act requiring reductions in government spending (Balanced Budget Act).		**1985** Reagan paid controversial visit to German military cemetery at Bitburg.
	1986 Explosion of shuttle *Challenger* shelved U.S. manned space program.	
	1986 U.S. warplanes bombed Tripoli, Libya to punish open support of terrorist.	
	1986 Reagan proposed Star Wars (Strategic Defense Initiative) research and deployment plan.	
1987 Iran-contra scandal exposed arms for hostages deal; illegal covert activities.	**1987** U.S. Navy began escorting Kuwaiti oil tankers through Persian Gulf.	**1987** U.S.-USSR treaty to ban, destroy many nuclear missiles in Europe.
1987 Reagan's Supreme Court nominations of Robert Bork and Douglas Ginsburg defeated.	**1987** Bicentennial of U.S. Constitution sparked renewed study of our basic law.	
1988 George Bush and Dan Quayle were elected to the presidency and vice presidency.	**1988** Terrorists killed nine tourists on a cruise in the Aegean Sea.	**1988** U.S.A. and Canada reached a free trade agreement.
1988 Congress overrode Reagan's veto of the Civil Rights Bill.	**1988** Lieutenant Colonel Higgins, an American army officer, kidnapped in Lebanon and later murdered.	
1989 George Bush inaugurated as the 41st president.	**1989** American troops invaded Panama to capture General Manuel Noriega, resulting in damage and harm to population.	**1989** President Bush and Mikhail Gorbachev, President of the USSR, met on a ship off the coast of Malta for a summit conference.
		1989 Berlin Wall torn down, allowing free travel in Germany.

Economic and Technological		Cultural and Intellectual		Parallel Events in World History	
1981	Reagan administration advocated supply-side economics and higher military spending.				
1981–1984	Reaganomics led to doubling of the national debt.				
				1982	Israeli invasion of Lebanon forced out Arafat's PLO terrorists.
				1984	Drought and poverty caused widespread famine in Africa.
1985	Previously world's largest creditor.	**1985**	Televised Live Aid concerts involved millions widespread in famine relief for Africans.	**1985**	Americans and Europeans kidnapped and held hostage in Lebanon.
				1985	Mikhail S. Gorbachev became the new general secretary of the Soviet Communist Party. He called for "glasnost" (openness) and "perestroika" (restructuring) at home and for détente with the United States.
				1986	Corazon Aquino defeated dictator Ferdinand Marcos for Philippine presidency.
1987	U.S. trade gap hit all-time high in October ($17.6 billion).	**1987**	Nobel Peace Prize to Costa Rican President Oscar Arias for peace plan for Central America.		
1987	October Stock market crash raised fears of unemployment in 1988.				
		1988	Supreme Court declared private club restrictions unconstitutional.	**1988**	Palestinians rioted against Israeli control of Gaza; West Bank demanded self-government.
		1988	Benazio Bhutto became first Islamic woman to be Prime Minister of Pakistan.		
1989	Space shuttle *Atlantis* launched a spacecraft on its trip to planet Jupiter.	**1989**	Ronald Brown became first African-American chairman of the National Democratic Committee of the U.S.A.	**1989**	Emperor Hirohito of Japan died at age 87, to be succeeded by his son.
1989	*Voyager II* spacecraft submitted amazing report on planet Neptune.	**1989**	Salman Rushdie's book *Satanic Verses* banned. The Ayatollah sentenced him and his publishers to death. Many protests by other countries; Rushdie forced into hiding.	**1989**	Thousands of Chinese students took over Central Square in Peking to protest actions by government. Many killed by military police.

Political and Governmental	Military and Special Events	American Foreign Relations
		XVI.
1990 Democrats retain control of the House of Representatives and the Senate.	**1990** General Noriega surrendered to American troops in Panama.	**1990** Western Alliance ended Cold War and began plans for joint action with USSR and East Germany.
1990 Inquiry began into the role of five U.S. senators in the failure of savings and loan banks.		
1991 Clarence Thomas became 106th Justice of the Supreme Court.	**1991** Persian Gulf War fought.	**1991** International Conference on Global Warming, a threat to life on Earth, held in Geneva, Switzerland.
	1991 Los Angeles riots occurred after trial resulting from beating of Rodney King.	
1991 Haitians who entered U.S.A. were detained at Guantanamo Bay for return to Haiti because they were said to be economic, not political refugees.		
1992 Unemployment in the U.S.A. increased to over 7 percent, the worst in five and one-half years.	**1992** U.S. naval base in Philippines closed.	**1992** United Nations requested Libya to extradite two suspects in 1988 bombing of Pan Am flight 103, which crashed in Scotland.
1992 President Bush went to the Far East to try to obtain trade agreements that would benefit Americans.		**1992** Chilean arms shipment to Croatia declared in violation of U.N. ban on such shipments. Material intercepted in Budapest, Hungary.
1992 Data from 1990 census challenged. Secretary of Commerce Mosbacher will release correct figures, upon which the allocation of representatives in Congress is based.		
1992 CORE (the Congress of Racial Equality) accused of fraud in preparing amnesty applications for aliens under the 1986 Immigration Reform and Control Act. Suit entered by the Federal Immigration Bar Association.		
1992 Bill Clinton and Al Gore were elected to the presidency and vice presidency. *See* **Election of 1992**, page 10-26, for detailed discussion.		
1993 Bill Clinton inaugurated as 42nd president.	**1993** World Trade Center in New York City bombed by terrorists.	
	1993 President Clinton ordered bombing of Iraqi intelligence center in retaliation for plot to assassinate former president George Bush.	

Economic and Technological		Cultural and Intellectual		Parallel Events in World History	

THE 1990s

1990	Human gene therapy was administered for the first time. The patient was a 4-year-old girl and the procedure involved recombinant DNA.			**1990**	Iraq occupied Kuwait.
1990	Microsoft introduced Version 3.0 of Windows, providing a graphical user interface for PCs.				
		1991	First time an asteroid in space, *Gaspra*, was photographed.	**1991**	Boris Yeltsin became the first popularly elected president of Russia.
		1991	Law professor Anita Hill accused Judge Clarence Thomas of sexual harassment.	**1991**	East and West Germany reunited.
1992	The federal budget deficit was the focus of Ross Perot's campaign for the presidency.	**1992**	First joint U.S.-Japan space shuttle mission took place.	**1992**	Formal end to Cold War proclaimed by George Bush and Boris Yeltsin.
		1992	MADD (Mothers Against Drunk Driving) movement continued to grow into powerful lobbying group.	**1992**	Council of U.N. supported use of military to make sure aid reached civilians in Bosnia.
		1992	A Florida boy won the legal right to "divorce" his parents so that his foster parents could adopt him.		
		1992	Miami emerged as center for Latin-American art.		
		1992	Film *JFK* stirred reaction that may lead to release of Warren Commission files relating to assassination of President John F. Kennedy.		
		1992	Space Shuttle *Atlantis* launched its first spy satellite.		
1993	Slow economic growth as U.S. gradually emerged from recession.	**1993**	Holocaust memorial museum opened in Washington, D.C.	**1993**	Czechoslovakia split into Slovakia and the Czech Republic.
1993	"Voicemail" became the norm in offices across the U.S.	**1993**	The use of DNA evidence in legal cases became more common.		

HISTORY OF THE WORLD

Aachen Formerly known as Aix-la-Chapelle. An historic spa, later industrialized, located in Germany. In the Roman period, it was a watering place and was named Aquae Grani. By 470 the Franks had driven the Romans out and established themselves there. Under Frankish emperor Charlemagne, it became the capital of the Frankish Empire. Charlemagne built his palace here and most of his successors were crowned here until 1531. In the 1600s Aachen declined in importance.

Abbadides (Abbadids) Arab Muslim dynasty that briefly ruled Seville, Spain (1023–1091). They were in power from the collapse of the caliphate of Cordoba to the occupation of Seville by the Almoravides.

Abbasids Dynasty of Muslim caliphs who ruled the Empire of the Caliphate (750–1258). The Abbasids were the second great dynasty of the Islamic Empire who based their claim to rule on descent from Abbas, uncle of Mohammed. In 750, the Abbasids led by Abu Al-Abbas overthrew the Umayyads, the first Islamic ruling dynasty and transferred the capital of the empire from Damascus to Baghdad. The dynasty reached its peak during the reign of Harun Al-Rashid (786–809) and Mamun (813–833) when the Islamic empire experienced a golden age of culture. In later years, corruption and stagnation resulted in the decay of the empire and after 1000, it became fragmented.

Abd-al-Hamid II (1842–1918) Ottoman sultan. He replaced his liberal brother, Murad V, on the Ottoman throne in 1876, declared him insane, and abolished his constitution. He attempted to block Western ideas, to control the nation with an iron hand, and to turn back the clock. This finally led to a coup in 1908 by young army officers demanding a constitution and a homogeneous nation. Hamid was deposed in 1909 and his brother Muhammed V (r.1909–1918), was placed on the throne—in name only, for the government was actually controlled by an organization known as the Young Turks.

Abdullah, king of Jordan (Abdullah ibn Hussein) (1882–1951) First king (1946–1951) of newly independent Jordan. During the Arab-Israeli War (1948 and 1949), he took the West Bank of the Jordan River and subsequently annexed the territory. He was assassinated in 1951.

Abelard, Peter (1079–1142) An important scholastic philosopher who became a brilliant and highly influential teacher at the University of Paris in the 1100s. After a tragic love affair with Heloise, he entered a monastery. His theological writings met with ecclesiastical condemnation in 1122 and 1141 and he was excommunicated by the pope. Abelard's book *Sic it Non* (*Yes and No*) raised many questions about church doctrine. He sought to foster thought and inquiry for he believed that "By doubting we come to inquiry and by inquiry we perceive the truth."

Aberhard, William (1878–1943) Canadian politician who advocated social credit, or cash payments to citizens by the government. He helped to organize the Social Credit party in Alberta and served as Alberta's premier (1935–1943), but was unable to implement his programs.

Abraham In the Old Testament, the first Hebrew patriarch. According to the biblical account, in about 1800 B.C. he led the Hebrews who were originally herders from Ur into Canaan.

Absolutism Government under which the ruler has unlimited power. The development of absolutism is closely associated with the emergence of modern nation states in the late 1400s and replaced feudalism as the form of government. However, it dates back to ancient times where it was practiced by the tyrants in Greek city-states and in the neighboring Oriental empires.

Abu-al-Abbas (as-Saffah) (722–754) Muslim caliph (750–754), founder and first caliph of the Abbasid dynasty who overthrew the Umayyad caliph.

Abu Bakr The father-in-law of Mohammed who became the first caliph or successor to Mohammed. He was an early follower of Mohammed and accompanied him on the flight from Mecca in 622. Selected by Mohammed as his successor, Abu Bakr continued the Prophet's work and was responsible for conquering Arabia and beginning the compilation of the Koran.

Acadia Former French colony in North America. It included what are now the coastal Canadian provinces of Nova Scotia, New Brunswick, and Prince Edward Island, as well as parts of Maine.

Achaeans Indo-European people who invaded the Greek peninsula from the north around 2000 B.C. They intermixed with the local population as they conquered new territory and eventually extended their conquests over the Peloponnesus, or southern half of Greece. Warrior kings ruled walled cities that were built at Mycenae, Thebes, and other locations in southern Greece. The civilization of the Achaeans is called Mycenaean and it was built on the achievements of the earlier Minoan civilization. According to the *Iliad* and the *Odyssey*, two famed epic poems by Homer, around 1250 B.C. under the leadership of the king of Mycenae, the Achaeans attacked Troy and destroyed it in the ensuing Trojan War. Frequent warfare among the rival Mycenaean kingdoms caused the civilization's decline and it was destroyed by Dorian invadors, illiterate Greek-speaking people. The collapse of this civilization in about 1100 B.C. ushered in a period called the Dark Ages which lasted until about 800 B.C.

Achaemenids Ancient Persian dynasty founded in the 7th century B.C. that included the founder of the Persian Empire, Cyrus the Great and provided kings of the empire from 550–330 B.C.

Achilles Legendary Greek hero of Homer's *Iliad* and prominent Greek warrior in the Trojan War. After hearing a prophecy of his death at Troy, his mother dipped him in the river Styx to make him immortal, but the heel by which she held him was not touched by the water. Odysseus persuaded him to go to the Trojan War. The *Iliad* recounts his quarrel with Agamemnon, his withdrawal from the fighting, his grief over the slaying of his friend Patroclus by Hector, and how he avenged the death of Patroclus by slaying Hector. Achilles was himself killed by Paris who wounded him in the heel with a poisoned arrow.

Acropolis The fortified, elevated citadel, or hilltop fortress around which life revolved in the Greek city-states. The famed Athenian Acropolis, a hill about 260 feet high, was covered during the time of Cemon and Pericles with the Parthenon and other buildings that are considered great architectural works.

The Acropolis in Athens.

Actium, battle of   Here the forces of Octavian who later became Augustus defeated the forces of Antony and Cleopatra in 31 B.C. By his victory, Octavian became the sole ruler of the Roman Empire.

Act of Settlement   Passed by Parliament in 1701, it provided that if Queen Anne (the Protestant daughter of James II who was overthrown in the Glorious Revolution and succeeded by William and Mary) who came to the throne after the deaths of William and Queen Mary, died without an heir, the throne was passed to the House of Hanover upon the succession of King George I.

Act of Supremacy   Two acts of Parliament that gave the English king supreme authority over the Church of England and thus broke ties with Rome. The first, in 1534, made Henry VIII head of the church in England, and the second, in 1559, vested this authority in Elizabeth I.

Act of Union   In 1707, it merged the separate governments of England and Scotland into one kingdom known as Great Britain. The Scottish Parliament was abolished and Scots were given seats in the House of Lords and the House of Commons.

Addis Ababa   The capital city of Ethiopia. It was founded by Menelik II in 1889. It was the capital of Italian East Africa (1936–1941).

Addison, Joseph (1672–1719)   Well-known English essayist, poet, and dramatist. Addison is best remembered for his essays on manners and morals and literary critiques. His style combined wit, elegance, and clarity. Addison's essays appeared in three literary journals, *The Tatler*, *The Spectator*, and *The Guardian*. Addison was also a Whig politician who served as a member of Parliament and held various government posts.

Adelard of Bath   A 12th-century English scholastic philosopher famed for his scientific studies. He introduced Arabic works in science, mathematics, and philosophy that influenced medieval thought, especially that of medieval scholastic scholars who sought to synthesize traditional Christian thought with the new secular learning.

Adenauer, Konrad (1876–1967)   In 1949, when Great Britain, the United States, and France combined their three occupied German zones into the German Federal Republic of West Germany, Konrad Adenauer the leader of the Christian Democrats was elected as chancellor. He had been mayor of Cologne from 1917, a member of the legislature of the Rhine province, had ordered Nazi flags removed from Cologne when Hitler visited it in 1933, was removed as mayor by Goering, and was twice jailed by the Nazis. At the age of 73 "der Alte," the Old One, was elected chancellor in 1949, and the Western allies replaced military governors with civilians.

Adowa, battle of   In March of 1896 Italian invading forces fought the Ethiopian forces of Emperor Menelik II at Adowa in Ethiopia. Menelik's army defeated the Italians who were greatly outnumbered thereby insuring the independence of Ethiopia and allowing Menelik to go forward with his program to modernize and strengthen his nation.

Adrianople, battle of   In 378 A.D., scene of the Visigoth victory over the Romans led by Emperor Valens. Two years earlier in 376 A.D. the Visigoths, driven by their fear of the invading Huns, had crossed the Danube River and received permission to settle within the borders of the Roman Empire. Abuse at the hands of Roman officials caused the Visigoths to revolt and they marched against Constantinople. At Adrianople, the Emperor Valens sought to stop the advancing Visigoths but he was killed and his army was defeated.

Adrianople, Treaty of   Ended the Russo-Turkish War of 1828 and 1829. Under the terms of the treaty Russia secured the mouth of the Danube and the eastern coast of the Black Sea from Turkey. Autonomy was given to Serbia and promised to Greece.

Aegean Civilization   Term used for the cultures of pre-Hellenic Greece. Minoan civilization was the rich culture of Crete. Mycenaean civilization was the culture of mainland Greece.

Aeneid   A famous epic written by Virgil between 30 and 19 B.C. describing the mythical origin of Rome and glorifying Rome's greatness. The poem tells of the wanderings of Aeneas and the Trojans, their arrival in Italy, and their victory over the Latins and Rutulians.

Aeschylus (524–456 B.C.)   Greek poet of Athens who wrote tragedies, one on the great victory at Salamis in 480 B.C., where he fought, and another the story of Agamemnon, a Greek leader of the Trojan War, the Persians, and Oresteia.

Aetolian League   A military federation created in western Greece in the 4th century B.C. to oppose the Achaean League and the Macedonians. In 200 B.C., it fought with the Romans and defeated Philip V of Macedon. Afterwards, the Aetolians tired of Roman interference in their affairs and they joined the Seleucid king, Antiochus III against the Romans. Their defeat in the ensuing conflict caused the League to lose power and pass into oblivion.

African National Congress   Major political force in the Union of South Africa. Led by Nelson Mandela, it is moving the current white-dominated government toward the elimination of all vestiges of apartheid and toward black majority rule. *See* **Apartheid**; **Mandela, Nelson**.

Afrikaners   Term used to refer to the white descendants of the Dutch farmers who settled in South Africa in the late 17th century. The Afrikaner language, a dialect of Dutch is called Afrikaans.

EXHIBIT 11.1
Independence Comes To Africa*

Country	Year of Independence	From
South Africa	1931	Britain
Sudan	1956	Britain & Egypt
Ghana	1957	Britain
Guinea	1958	France
Cameroon	1960	France
Central Africa Empire	1960	France
Chad	1960	France
Congo (People's Republic of)	1960	France
The Congo (Democratic Republic of—Zaire)	1960	Belgium
Dahomey (Benin)	1960	France
Gabon	1960	France
Ivory Coast	1960	France
Malagasy Republic (Madagascar)	1960	France
Mali	1960	France
Mauritania	1960	France
Niger	1960	France
Nigeria	1960	Britain
Senegal	1960	France
Somalia	1960	Italy & Britain
Togo	1960	France
Upper Volta	1960	France
Sierra Leone	1961	Britain
Burundi	1962	Belgium
Rwanda	1962	Belgium
Uganda	1962	Britain
Kenya	1963	Britain
Malawi	1964	Britain
Tanzania**	1964	Britain
Zambia	1964	Britain
Gambia	1965	Britain
Rhodesia	1965	Britain
Botswana	1966	Britain
Lesotho	1966	Britain
Equatorial Guinea	1968	Spain
Swaziland	1968	Britain
Guinea-Bissau	1974	Portugal
Mozambique	1975	Portugal
Angola	1975	Portugal
Cape Verde Islands	1975	Portugal
Comoro Islands	1975	France
Sao Tomee Principe	1975	Portugal
Djibouti	1977	France
Namibia	1990	South Africa

*   Liberia and Ethiopia already independent.
** Tanzania was formed by the union of Tanganyika and Zanzibar.
    Tanganyika gained independence in 1961 and Zanzibar in 1963.

Agamemnon   In Greek legend the king of Mycenae, brother of Menelaus, and leader of the Greeks in the Trojan War. The *Iliad* recounts the quarrel between Agamemnon and Achilles.

Age of Pericles   Period in Athenian history (461–429 B.C.). When Pericles ruled Athens and the city-state reached the height of its power and prosperity.

Age of Reason   *See* **Enlightenment**.

Agincourt   Famous battle of the Hundred Years' War in which the army of King Henry V of England routed the French forces in October of 1415. Although the French knights outnumbered the English by three or four to one, the English employed foot soldiers with longbows who were able to cut down the charging French knights. The battle demonstrated once again that the new method of fighting had outdated the feudal method of mounted, heavily armored knights on horseback.

Agra   City in India which is famed as the site of the Taj Mahal. Akbar the Great made Agra the capital of the Mogul Empire in the 1560s. Shah Jahan, a descendant of Akbar the Great had the Taj Mahal built as a tomb for his beloved wife in the 1600s.

Aguinaldo, Emilio (1869–1964)   Filipino revolutionary. He led the Philippine revolt against the Spanish during the Spanish-American War. Aguinaldo helped American troops drive the Spanish out of Luzon and then immediately declared the Philippines to be a republic. When the United States would not grant independence, Aguinaldo led military action against American troops throughout 1899. In 1900 the United States declared local self-government for the Philippines, and the last of Aguinaldo's followers surrendered in 1902.

Ahriman The evil spirit, representing darkness in the ancient Zoroastrian religion of the Persian Empire.

Ahura Mazda The Wise Lord, or supreme god, who stood for truth, goodness, and light in the ancient Zoroastrian religion of the Persian Empire. Ahura Mazda was believed to be the creator of the world and as the lord of good and light was constantly at war against Ahriman and the gods of evil. Zoroaster believed that at the end of the world Ahura Mazda and the forces of good would triumph.

Aix-la-Chapelle, Treaty of The scene of three congresses held in the years 1668, 1748, and 1818. The first congress of 1668 drew up the treaty that ended the War of Devolution between France and Spain. Under its terms, France kept its conquest in Flanders but restored Franche Comté to Spain. The second congress held in 1748 ended the War of Austrian Succession between the forces of France, Prussia, and Spain on the one side and England, Austria, and the Netherlands on the other side. The terms of this treaty generally restored the prewar boundaries but gave Silesia to Prussia and awarded Parma, Piacenza, and Guastalla to Philip V of Spain. The congress of 1818 was a meeting of the Quadruple Alliance of Great Britain, Austria, Prussia, and Russia and an attempt by the Alliance to govern Europe.

Ajanta Site of caves in the Ajanta Hills in India carved by Buddhist monks between 200 B.C. and 700 A.D. and used as temples and living quarters for a Buddhist order. During the Gupta Empire, artists decorated the cave walls with brilliant colored paintings illustrating episodes in Buddha's life. These Ajanta cave paintings are the best preserved examples of Gupta art in existence.

Akbar (1542–1605) Great mogul emperor (1556–1605). The reign of Akbar, the grandson of Babur, founder of the Mogul Empire, is considered the golden age of the Mogul Empire. An outstanding administrator, scholar, and artist, Akbar was the equal of contemporary monarchs such as Elizabeth I of England and Suleiman the Magnificent of the Ottoman Empire. The central purpose of Akbar's administration was to unite the Hindus and Moslems. Thirty percent of the officials of the government were Hindu, and he even attempted to found a new religion known as the Divine Faith that would combine both faiths. Despite his tolerance and wisdom, another of Akbar's main objectives was the expansion of the empire, and it was during his era that the empire reached its greatest size, extending from central Asia to southern India, and from Persia to the Ganges.

Akhenaton (Ikhnaton) (Amenhotep IV) (d. 1362 B.C.) Egyptian pharaoh who ruled from about 1379–1362 B.C., famed for attempting to change Egypt's polytheistic religion to monotheism. His new religion was centered on a single supreme sun god, Aton. Akhenaton's religious reforms roused strong opposition from the Egyptian priests who favored the worship of the chief Egyptian god, Amon and it received few followers. Religious conflict caused serious divisions within Egypt during Akhenaton's reign and after his death the new religion died out.

Akkadians A group of people who originally lived as nomads on the Arabian peninsula and then settled in the Tigris-Euphrates valley in Akkad. In about 2350 B.C. under the ruler Sargon, they conquered Sumer, the first civilization to arise in Mesopotamia. A less advanced people, the Akkadians adopted the more advanced Sumerian civilization and expanded Sumerian trade, thereby spreading Sumerian civilization throughout Mesopotamia. Akkadian rule was brief and following the death of Sargon, civil war broke out and eventually led to the rise of a new ruling group, the Amorites.

Alaric (370–410) King of the Visigoths (395–410), a Germanic tribe, which was an ally of Roman Emperor Theodosius. After the death of Theodosius, Alaric led his troops in rebellion against the empire and his attempted invasions of Italy were halted by Stilicho in 402 and 403. In 403, Alaric invaded Italy again and in 410 he captured and plundered the city of Rome. Afterwards, the Visigoths moved into what is today Spain and established a kingdom there.

Albertus Magnus (1200–1280) A 13th-century scholastic philosopher, scientist, and theologian who taught at universities in Germany and in Paris. He is probably best known as the teacher of Thomas Aquinas. Albert who was known as a great naturalist wrote on botany, zoology, and chemistry. In the *Summa Theologiae* he tried to reconcile the thought of Aristotle with that of Christianity maintaining that it was possible to gain knowledge both through faith and reason.

Albigenses A religious group centered in southern France in the 12th and 13th centuries considered to be heretical by the Christian Church. They denied the truth of the birth, death, and resurrection of Jesus Christ and believed in the existence of two creators, one of good and one of evil. In 1208, Pope Innocent III called for a crusade against the group and a merciless war to hunt them down was waged for the next 20 years until the sect finally disappeared.

Albuquerque, Alfonso (1453–1515) The second governor of the Portuguese colonies in India (1506–1515), who was the founder of the Portuguese trading empire in the East in the early 1500s. He occupied Goa in 1510 and from here proceeded to seize important points along the trade routes. He captured the Strait of Malacca, the gateway to the Moluccas and the spice trade. Albuquerque also took Ormuz at the entrance to the Persian Gulf, which gave Portugal control of the Indian Ocean.

Alchemy An ancient body of learning that sought to find out how matter was constituted and attempted to change base metals into gold. Alchemists searched for a miraculous philosopher's stone that had the power to change lead into gold, cure disease, restore youth, and prolong life. Alchemy is thought to have originated in ancient China or Egypt and was later influenced by the Greeks and Arabs. It reached Europe in the 12th century through the Muslims and in time gave rise to modern chemistry.

Alcibiades (450–404 B.C.) Athenian statesman and military leader. Regarded as both brilliant and unscrupulous, he rose to prominence during the Peloponnesian War (431–404 B.C.), when Athenian power was declining. He rallied the Athenians to an alliance against Sparta and a disastrous campaign in Sicily in 415 B.C. Falsely charged with defacing sacred statues, he fled to Sparta. He aided the Spartans until forced to flee to Persia in 411 B.C. Recalled to Athens in 411 B.C., he led the Athenian fleet to victories against the Spartans and recovered Byzantium in 408 B.C. But when the Athenian fleet was defeated by Lysander in 406 B.C., he was exiled.

Alcuin (735?–804) An 8th-century Anglo-Saxon (English) scholar and monk who was considered the intellectual leader of northern Europe in the late 8th century. Charlemagne asked him to come to the Frankish court to establish schools and oversee the revival of learning. Alcuin was the central force in the cultural and intellectual reform known as the Carolingian renaissance.

Aldrin, Edwin (b. 1930) American astronaut who, along with Neil Armstrong, became the first person to land on the moon on July 20, 1969.

Alembert, Jean (1717–1783) An 18th-century French mathematician, physicist, and philosopher who edited the scientific articles in Diderot's famed *Encyclopedia.*

Alexander I (1777–1825) Russian czar (1801–1825). After defeats at Austerlitz and Friedland, he submitted to Napoleon's Continental System, under the Treaty of Tilst in 1807. He later repulsed Napoleon's invasion of Russia in 1812, marched into Paris in 1814, and, by his defeat of Napoleon, became one of the most important rulers in Europe. In his early years, he instituted many liberal reforms. After 1814, however, he formed the Holy Alliance and support for conservative and reactionary policies, especially those of Metternich.

Alexander II (1818–1881) Russian czar (1855–1881). Shortly after his accession, he negotiated an end to the Crimean War (1835–1856) and instituted many liberal reforms, including the Edict of Emancipation of 1861 which abolished serfdom and the limited local government of the Zemstvo. His reforms, however, failed to prevent the rise of revolutionary and terrorist movements in the 1860s, and his attempts to suppress them led to his assassination. During his reign he brutally suppressed a Polish rebellion in 1863, formed the Three Emperors' League, extended Russian territories in central Asia, and engaged in the Russo-Turkish Wars (1877 and 1878).

Alexander III (Orlando Bandinelli) (d. 1181) Italian-born pope (1159–1181). With help from the Lombard League, he managed to assert papal authority over Holy Roman Emperor Frederick I and forced him to sign the Treaty of Vienna in 1177. He also opposed Henry II of England, canonized Thomas à Becket, and received Henry's penance for Becket's murder.

Alexander III (1845–1894) Russian czar (1881–1894). He became czar after his father's assassination and instituted reactionary policies and censorship. The power of the Zemstvos was sharply curtailed, national minorities were forced to undergo Russification, and religious minorities were persecuted.

Alexander Nevsky (1220–1263) Russian prince and military hero. He defeated the Swedes at the Battle of the Neva in 1240 and the Teutonic Knights.

Alexander the Great (Alexander III) (356–323 B.C.) Macedonian king (336–323 B.C.), successor to his father Philip II. One of the world's greatest conquerors, he created a vast empire extending from Greece to northern India, and, by his conquests, helped spread Greek civilization throughout the ancient world. Soon after becoming king, Alexander crushed revolts in Thrace, Illyria, and Thebes. His rule in Greece thus established, he began his epic military expedition (334–324 B.C.) with some 37,000 soldiers and the initial objective of conquering Persia. He met and defeated the Persians at the battles of Granicus in 334 and Issus (in Syria, 333), laid siege to and finally took Tyre in 332 to complete conquest of Phoenicia, marched unopposed into Egypt (332 and 331), and there founded the great city of Alexandria in 332. He again defeated the Persians at the Battle of Gaugamela in 331, sent Persian king Darius II into flight, and sacked the Persian capital of Persepolis in 331. He continued eastward to Media in 330 and central Asia, where he conquered the Scythians in 329. Despite open discontent in his army (over his acceptance of Persian manners), Alexander invaded India in 327. After the Battle of Hydaspes in 326, he took control of Punjab and, his men, unwilling to go farther, returned to Persia in 324. He subsequently consolidated Macedonian control of his conquests and attempted to integrate Greeks and Persians by, among other things, ordering his soldiers to marry Persian women. He died shortly after a prolonged banquet in 323.

Alexandra (1884–1925) Queen consort of English king Edward VII (m. 1863) and mother of King George V.

Alexandra Feodorovna (1827–1918) Last czarina of Russia, consort of Nicholas II (1894–1918). Her unfailing loyalty to the hated Rasputin and her disastrous meddlings in politics helped bring about the Russian Revolution. A Hessian princess, she came under Rasputin's sway when he seemed able to control her son's hemophilia. While Nicholas was at the front in World War I, she took control of the government in 1915 and began replacing government ministers with favorites of Rasputin. This discredited the government and opened the way for the October Revolution in 1917. She was shot, with Nicholas and her children, by revolutionaries.

Alexandria Egypt's second largest city. Founded in 332 B.C. by Alexander the Great, it became one of the largest and greatest cities of antiquity. The Ptolemies ruled their Egyptian-based empire from there (323–330 B.C.), and it became a principal center of both Hellenistic and Jewish culture.

Alexius I Comnenus (1048–1118) Byzantine emperor (1081–1118). Alexius restored the crumbling Byzantine Empire that, when he took power, was threatened by invasions and internal dissent. He defended against Norman invasions (1081–1085), contained the Seljuk Turks, repulsed invasions by a tribe of nomadic Turks in 1091, and put down rebellions in Crete and Cyprus. His request for aid from the West against the Turks resulted in proclamation of the First Crusade in 1096.

Alfonso I (Henriques) (1111?–1185)   First king of Portugal (1139–1185). He engaged in wars (1128–1139) against the Moors and rulers of León and Castile to establish an independent kingdom. He was crowned after his victory over the Moors at Ourique on July 25, 1139. He continued fighting and captured Lisbon in 1147.

Alfonso II (the Fat) (1185–1223)   King of Portugal (1211–1223). He helped defeat the Moors at Las Navas de Tolosa in 1212. He quarreled with the church and was excommunicated by Honorius III.

Alfonso III (1210–1279)   Portuguese king (1248–1279). He completed the unification of Portugal by driving the Moors from Algarve in 1249. He instituted political, financial, and commercial reforms.

Alfonso IV (1291–1357)   King of Portugal (1325–1357). He aided Alfonso XI of Castile in his victory over the Moors at Tarifa in 1340. His approval of the murder of his daughter-in-law, Inés de Castro, led to a revolt by his son (later Pedro I).

Alfonso V (the African) (1432–1481)   Portuguese king (1438–1481). He won major victories against the Moors in North Africa but failed to advance his wife's claim to Castile. He was decisively defeated by rival claimants, Queen Isabella and King Ferdinand, at the Battle of Toro in 1476.

Alfonso VI (1030–1109)   Christian king of León (1065–1109) and Castile (1072–1109). His advances into Muslim territories brought about the takeover of Muslim Spain by the Almoravids. El Cid was active during Alfonso's reign.

Alfonso VI (1643–1683)   Portuguese king (1656–1683). Mentally impaired, he let Count Castelho Melhor rule. He was ousted by his wife and his brother, later Peter (Pedro) II. During Alfonso's reign, Spain recognized Portugal's independence in 1668.

Alfonso VII (1104–1157)   King of León and Castile (1126–1157). He warred frequently against the Muslims but was unable to prevent Alfonso I from establishing an independent Portugal in 1139.

Alfonso VIII (the Noble) (1155–1214)   Spanish king of Castile (1158–1214). He was defeated by Muslim Almohades, and Castile was invaded by León and Navarre. He recovered and later led allied Spanish forces to a major victory over the Moors at Las Navas de Tolosa in 1212.

Alfonso X (the Wise) (1221–1284)   Spanish king of Castile and León (1252–1284). He conquered Cádiz and Cartagena from the Moors, sought unsuccessfully to become Holy Roman Emperor (1257–1275), and encouraged culture and learning.

Alfonso XI (the Avenger) (1311–1350)   Spanish king of Castile and León (1312–1350). He led the Spanish to victory over the Moors at the Battle of Algeciras, now in Morocco in 1344.

Alfonso XII (1857–1941)   King of Spain (1874–1885), son of Isabella II. Forced into exile in 1868, by a revolution, he was proclaimed king in 1874. He returned to Spain in 1875, restored order, and consolidated the power of the monarchy.

Alfonso XIII (1886–1941)   King of Spain (1886–1931). His reign was marked by political and social instability. He supported the military coup of Primo de Rivera in 1923 and went into exile in 1931 with the establishment of the Second Republic.

Alfred the Great (849–899)   Ruler of the kingdom of Wessex, his forces defeated the Danes in 886 and they withdrew to the eastern third of England which was called the Danelaw. All of England then accepted Alfred's rule and he was king from 871–889. Alfred was a cultured leader as well as a wise ruler.

Allende, Salvador (1908–1973)   Chilean politician. In 1970 Salvador Allende became the Western Hemisphere's first constitutionally elected Marxist president. Allende advocated state ownership of resources, abolition of minority class privileges, and a "republic of the working class." He promised to govern with traditional Chilean "democratic decency." By September 1973 Allende was dead, thousands were arrested, and constitutional Marxism and 45 years of democratic government in Chile had ended.

Alliance for Progress   Inter-American economic assistance program. The United States established this aid program in 1961 to bolster South American countries against communism and to effect social and economic reforms. Funding was sharply reduced after 1971.

Allies, World War I   One of the opposing sides in World War I that reflected the Alliance system consisting of the Triple Entente nations of France, Britain, and Russia.

Allies, World War II   One of the opposing sides in World War II that came to include Britain, France, the United States, the Soviet Union, China, and 43 other nations.

Almohades (Almohads)   Muslim sect and dynasty of Berber Muslims that ruled Morocco and Muslim Spain in the 12th and 13th centuries.

Almoravides (Almoravids)   Berber Muslim dynasty, rulers of an empire in North Africa and Muslim Spain in the 11th and 12th centuries.

Amenhotep IV   *See* **Akhenaton.**

Amnesty International   An international organization that monitors human rights violations. It received the Nobel Prize for Peace in 1977. With headquarters in London, there are 700,000 members in more than 150 countries.

Amon   The most important of the Egyptian gods who was frequently represented as a ram or a human with a ram's head.

Amorites   A group of people who attacked the river valley cities of Mesopotamia in about 2000 B.C. They built the village of Babylon on the Euphrates River which grew into a great city-state. Their greatest king, Hammurabi, established an empire in Mesopotamia by 1700 B.C.

Amritsar Massacre   In 1919 at Amritsar, India, troops under British command fired on unarmed Indian nationalist protesters, killing some 400 and wounding about 1200. The massacre strengthened the anti-British movement in India.

Anabaptists   Christian sects that arose in Europe during the 16th-century's Protestant Reformation. Anabaptists generally rejected infant baptism in favor of adult baptism, favored separation of the church and state, and opposed the use of force.

Anarchism   Theory that advocates complete individual freedom, especially from control by government or other outside authority. Based on the belief that such restrictions corrupt humans.

Anaxagoras (500–428 B.C.)   Greek philosopher who taught in Athens. Among his students were Pericles and, it is believed, Socrates. He was banished for his teachings on the physical nature of the universe.

Anaximander (611–547 B.C.)   Greek philosopher whose teachings are said to prefigure the development of astronomy and the theory of evolution. One of the earliest Western philosophers, he attempted to provide a systematic explanation of the nature of the universe and all things in it.

Anaximenes (6th century B.C.)   Greek philosopher. He held that air was the primary substance of the universe and that all matter was composed of air but different in density.

Ancien Régime   Term for the political and social order in France up to the outbreak of the French Revolution, in 1789.

Andropov, Yuri (1914–1984)   Successor to Brezhnev who continued to work to strengthen the Soviet economy and defenses. After his death in 1984, Chernenko came to be the leader of the Soviet Union.

Angevin   Another name for the Plantagenet kings of England (1154–1399), the first three of whom were also counts of Anjou (thus Angevin).

Angkor Wat   Ruins of a great temple of the ancient Khmer Empire of Cambodia.

Anglo-Saxons   Name given to Germanic-speaking peoples made up of three different Germanic tribes, the Angles, Saxons, and Jutes who settled in England at the end of Roman rule and formed several small kingdoms there.

Anne (1665–1714)   Last Stuart ruler who was queen of England, Scotland and Ireland (1702–1707), and later first queen of Great Britain (1707–1714). Her reign, one of transition to parliamentary government, was dominated by the War of Spanish Succession (1702–1713). None of Anne's children survived her and, by the Act of Settlement in 1701, George I of the House of Hanover, succeeded to the throne. Her reign was marked by intellectual awakening, popularization of Palladian architecture, and by growth of empire, constitution, and of the political power of the press.

Annexation   Act by which a nation or a state declares sovereignty over territory formerly outside its borders.

Anschluss   Term applied to the project of union between Austria and Germany. Forbidden by the peace treaties of 1919, it became a reality when Hitler annexed Austria to Germany in 1938.

Antony (Antonius, Marcus) (Marc Antony) (83–30 B.C.)   Roman soldier, political leader, and ally of Julius Caesar. A courageous soldier, he served with Caesar in Gaul in 54 B.C., became a tribune in 49 B.C., and joined Caesar in the civil war against Pompey in 48 B.C., in which Pompey was defeated. He became consul with Caesar in 44 B.C. and, after Caesar's assassination, forced the conspirators to flee Rome. Antony for a time opposed both the Senate and Caesar's heir, Octavian (later Augustus Caesar). But after gaining the support of Lepidus, Antony came to terms with Octavian, and the three (Octavian, Antony, and Lepidus) formed the Second Triumvirate, with Antony ruling Asia. His alliance with

Cleopatra, and, his dissolute life-style, alienated both Octavian and the Senate. Octavian attacked and defeated Antony at Actium in 31 B.C. and, when Octavian pursued him to Alexandria, both Antony and Cleopatra committed suicide.

Apartheid   Policy followed in South Africa that involves separation of the races politically and economically. South Africa is in effect a compartmentalized society in which each racial group, white and native, lives separately, has separate kinds of work, separate levels of wages, and separate standards of education. The policy of apartheid or separation is not a new one. The Dutch settlers of the 18th and 19th centuries believed in "baasskap" or boss-hood, simply white domination. The modern form of apartheid is the result of conditions that developed in the 1920s and 1930s.

Appeasement   The making of concessions to an aggressive potential enemy in the hopes of avoiding trouble and usually made from weakness rather than from strength. This policy was followed by the Western democracies in the 1930s in response to the aggressive acts of Hitler and Mussolini in order to maintain peace.

Aquinas, Thomas (1225–1274)   Italian theologian and philosopher. Dominican friar and one of the great medieval scholars, determined to reconcile Aristotle's reasoning with church faith. Aquinas maintained that faith and reason were not in conflict with one another but led to a greater understanding of God. By "reason" he meant Aristotelian logic and precise definitions of words and concepts. In his 22-volume *Summa Theologica,* a sort of encyclopedia of all theology, he set out to prove that all scientific knowledge agreed with church beliefs, taking up each point in church doctrine and proving it.

Aquino, Corazon (b. 1933)   President of the Philippines (1987–1992). Mrs. Aquino (widow of Benigno Aquino, an opponent of Ferdinand Marcos) was chosen by the United Nationalist Democratic Organization to oppose Marcos in the 1986 election. She had the support of the Roman Catholic church and a large part of the population. She became president after a disputed election and as a result of a nonviolent popular revolution. *See* **Marcos, Ferdinand Edralin**.

Arafat, Yasir (b. 1929)   Leader of the Palestinian Liberation Organization (PLO) who has called for the establishment of a Palestinian state on the West Bank.

Archimedes (287–212 B.C.)   The foremost Greek mathematician and physicist of the age. He showed the ratio of pi, 3.1416, of the diameter of a circle to its circumference, invented pulleys, the lever, the law of specific gravity, and the spiral screw inside a cylinder to raise water.

Aristarchus (310–230 B.C.)   Greek scientist who determined that the earth and planets revolving around the sun, measured almost exactly the solar year and lunar month. Mistakenly he believed that the earth was the center of the universe, an error accepted until Copernicus (1473–1543) proved the contrary.

Aristophanes (444–380 B.C.)   The most famous Greek comic writer, he made fun of many aspects of Athenian life, its leaders, and its assemblies in *The Clouds* and *The Frogs*.

Aristotle (384–322 B.C.) Macedonian Greek philosopher and scientist, one of the great thinkers of all time. His works in philosophy, science, ethics, and esthetics had a major influence on the development of civilization in the West. Aristotle studied under Plato at the Academy in Athens and later tutored Alexander the Great. Returning to Athens in 335, he opened a school (the Lyceum) and taught there until just before his death. His works, lost in the West after the fall of Rome, were reintroduced by Arab scholars in the 9th century and formed the basis of Scholasticism. In his time, Aristotle stressed the importance of observation, the necessary correlation of theory to fact, and the value of logic. *See also* Philosophy section, page 19-3.

Arkwright, Richard (1732–1792) English inventor whose construction of a spinning machine known as the water frame in 1769, which used water power to run it, was an early step in the Industrial Revolution.

Armada, Spanish A great fleet of 130 ships launched by Philip II of Spain against England in 1588 to stop English attacks by the so-called sea dogs against Spanish ships and to wipe out the Protestant "heresy" in England. The Armada was defeated by a combination of smaller, quicker, English ships and a storm that destroyed many Spanish ships. Only half of the Spanish ships returned to Spain and its defeat marked the beginning of the decline of Spanish sea power.

Armstrong, Neil (b. 1930) American astronaut who in the Apollo II mission became the first person to walk on the moon in July, 1969.

Arthur A legendary, early British king around whom a great body of medieval stories known as Arthurian legend developed. The first references to him appear about 600 A.D. and place him as a British leader of the Celts who fought against the Anglo-Saxon invaders. According to *Historia* (1137) by Geoffrey of Monmouth he was a conquerer of Western Europe who headed a magnificent court.

Aryans Indo-European people who originally came from the region between the Black and Caspian seas, north of the Caucasus and invaded India in about 1500 B.C., destroying the ancient Indus Valley civilization that flourished in Mohenjo-Daro and Harappa. Between 1500 and 1000 B.C., they conquered the Indus Valley and then spread eastward until they controlled northern India. What is known about the Aryans comes from Vedas, or religious books. Eventually they settled down and became the ruling class turning the conquered Indian people into a subjected laboring class.

Ashanti, empire of (Asante) African kingdom in what is now central Ghana. The Ashanti people occupied the region by the 13th century and, in the second half of the 1600s, King Osei Tutu created the empire, with his capital at Kumasi. The Ashanti continued to expand their empire, supplying the British and Dutch with slaves from conquered peoples in the 1700s. Wars with the British in the 1820s, 1860s, and 1870, led first to a British takeover in 1896, then annexation to the British Gold Coast colony in 1901.

Ashikaga The second of three shogunates to rule Japan between 1185 and 1868. After the end of the Kamakura shogunate in 1333, one noble, Ashikaga Tokauji won power and had himself made shogun in 1338, establishing his family as Japan's second line of military rulers. The Ashikaga family ruled Japan until 1568 but they were never able to control the powerful nobles and warfare was almost continuous. During this period of rule, feudalism continued to be the system of government in Japan.

Asoka (273–232 B.C.) Indian emperor who was the grandson of Chandragupta, founder of the Maurya dynasty and brought the Maurya Empire to the height of its power. One of the greatest rulers of ancient India, he brought nearly all India under one empire for the first time in history. However, after his bloody conquests, Asoka, remorseful for the suffering he had inflicted, converted from Hinduism to Buddhism and abandoned wars of conquest. Though tolerant of all faiths, he made Buddhism the state religion of India and built numerous monasteries. He sent Buddhist missionaries throughout India and its adjacent lands and as far as Syria, Egypt, and Greece. India prospered and art flourished under the reign of Asoka but after his death the Mauryan Empire swiftly declined.

Assad, Hafez-al (b. 1928) A military officer who became president of Syria and encouraged Syrian economic and military development.

Assurbanipal (d. 626 B.C.) King of the Assyrians under whom the Assyrian Empire reached its height in about 6600 B.C. In his capital of Nineveh, he built a library containing 22,000 cuneiform tablets written in Babylonian, Assyrian, and Sumerian.

Assyrians One of the many groups of people who conquered the land of Mesopotamia in ancient times. They are known for the introduction of cruelty as a political policy, the use of iron for warfare, and the deliberate preservation of the achievements of the past. From the highland region north of Nineveh, the Assyrians, who had for 1,000 years maintained predominance in their region, moved southwards. In 910 B.C., they captured Babylon, moved into the Mediterranean land of Syria, and by 700 B.C. under Sargon II (who took the name of the conqueror of the Tigris-Euphrates area nearly 2000 years earlier) were in possession of the entire Fertile Crescent, including Syria, Egypt, Phoenicia, and Israel, making Nineveh their capital. The Assyrians were unskilled in administration, and after only 150 years of rule, were conquered by the Chaldeans.

Atahualpa (d. 1533) The last ruler of the great Inca Empire who was taken prisoner by the Spanish conquistador Francisco Pizarro in 1532 and put to death.

Atatürk, Kemal (1881–1938) Mustafa Kemal or Kemal Pasha was a Turkish soldier, statesman, and president (1923–1938), considered the founder of modern Turkey. He was a leading figure in the Young Turks and other nationalist groups from 1908. By 1921 he headed a nationalist army, which repulsed a Greek invasion between 1919 and 1922 and subsequently overthrew the sultan in 1922. He abolished the sultanate and during his long term as president of the republic, he instituted many reforms aimed at westernizing Turkey.

Athens   Historic city capital of Greece. Athens was a focal point of ancient Greek culture, noted as a center of the arts and learning. Many of the temples and other buildings of the ancient city remain as classic works of architecture. The democratic form of government developed in the city-state of Athens is considered the forerunner of modern democracy. Athens rose as the dominant city-state in ancient Greece during the 5th century B.C. Its power was broken by its archrival, Sparta, during the Peloponnesian War at the end of the 5th century. Athens continued for a time as a cultural center, but it never again attained its former greatness.

Atlantic Charter   Document signed in August, 1941 in which the United States and Great Britain announced their basic aims for a peace settlement. President Roosevelt and Prime Minister Churchill met on shipboard off the Newfoundland shore in order to set down clearly their objectives for future peace. In it, they pledged their countries to the spread of democratic principles; it established 18 points similar to Wilson's Fourteen Points of World War I and also stipulated that a "permanent system of general security" should be established at the end of the war (the origins of the United Nations).

Attila (406?–453 A.D.)   King of the Huns from about 433–453 and known as the Scourge of God. In 451, he led his forces into Gaul but he was defeated by the combined forces of Germanic tribes and a Roman army. In 452, he invaded northern Italy but abandoned his plan to take Rome according to some because of the plea of Pope Leo I but more likely because of hunger and disease. His death in 453 ended the Hun threat to the empire but the Germanic invasions continued.

Attlee, Clement (1883–1967)   The leader of the British Labour party whose victory in the general election of 1945 against Churchill and his coalition government made him the prime minister. This gave the party the opportunity to implement its policy of nationalization, the state ownership of the means of production and distribution, under his leadership. The government nationalized the Bank of England, coal mines, railroads, trucking industry, and docks in 1947. People who held shares in these enterprises exchanged them for government bonds. These businesses were then operated by government boards, for the nation and not for private profit.

Augsburg, peace of (1555)   A temporary settlement of conflicts caused by the Reformation within the Holy Roman Empire, on the German states. According to this settlement, the prince of each German state within the empire was to decide which religion—Lutheranism or Catholicism—would be followed in his lands. Most southern German rulers remained Catholic while most in the north chose Lutheranism.

Augustine, Saint (354–430 A.D.)   One of the earliest and greatest Christian thinkers who is considered a church father. Born in North Africa, he converted to Christianity and became a bishop in Roman Africa. Augustine's most famous works are *The City of God* and *Confessions*.

Augustus (63 B.C.–14 A.D.)   The first Roman emperor originally known as Octavian, he was a grandnephew of Julius Caesar who adopted him and made him his heir. After Caesar was assassinated he gained power in Rome and formed the Second Triumvirate in 43 B.C. with Marc Antony and Lepidus. Lepidus was forced to retire, and the Roman world was divided between Octavian ruling in the West and Antony in the East. After differences with Antony, he persuaded the Senate to declare war against him and Cleopatra at Actium in 31 B.C. The republic came to an end and Octavian made himself the ruler of the Roman world. Octavian was given the title Augustus by the Senate and he began the period known as the Pax Romana, or Roman Peace.

Aurangzeb (1618–1707)   Mogul emperor of India (1658–1707). The last Mogul emperor to control all of India, Aurangzeb was a man of great courage and talent. However, he was also a fanatical Moslem, determined to conquer the entire peninsula and to convert all his subjects to Islam. The Hindus naturally objected, and Hindu princes organized the Mahratha Confederacy, with its power centered around the city of Poona. In his attempt to conquer the south of India, Aurangzeb over-extended his resources and ultimately the viceroys of the empire broke away, establishing independent principalities in Hyderabad, Mysore, Bengal, and Oudh.

Auschwitz   Located in Poland, one of the most infamous concentration camps of World War II (with Dachau, Buchenwald, Treblinka, and others). Three million Jews, other minorities, and political opponents to the Third Reich were murdered here or died of disease and starvation.

Austerlitz, battle of   Here, in 1805, Napoleon won a great victory over the Russian army under Emperor Alexander I and the Austrian army under Francis I, thereby forcing Austria out of the war. Russia continued the war but was forced to withdraw its troops from Austria.

Austrian Succession, War of the (1740–1748)   This complex war involved the major European powers in a general and largely indecisive conflict. The war broke out after the death of Holy Roman Emperor Charles in 1740, a member of the powerful Hapsburg family. It was fought over succession to the vast Hapsburg family domains (centered in Austria), although other political rivalries were involved (notably between France and Britain). Long before his death, Charles had issued the Pragmatic Sanction of 1713, naming his daughter, Maria Theresa, as heir to the Hapsburg lands (but not the imperial title). During his lifetime, Charles labored tirelessly to win general support in Europe for her succession. But on Charles's death, Maria was seen as too weak to retain control of the domains, and rival claimants disputed her succession. When war broke out, France, Prussia, Spain, Bavaria, and Saxony took up arms against Austria, ruled by Maria. Britain under George II sided with Austria. An ongoing war between Britain and Spain (War of Jenkins' Ear) spread to French and British colonies (King George's War in North America) and later to Britain (second revolt of the Jacobites). Exhaustion, not decisive victory, eventually ended the war. Maria was recognized as heir to Hapsburg domains and her husband, Francis I, was elected Holy Roman Emperor. Prussia (the real winner) won Silesia from Austria and emerged as a major power.

Austro-Hungarian monarchy *See* **Dual monarchy.**

Austro-Prussian War (Seven Weeks' War) War (June 15–August 23, 1866) between Prussia (with Italy) and Austria (with Hanover, Bavaria, and most other German states). The war resulted in Austria's exclusion from the German Confederation (reorganized as the North German Confederation) and thus opened the way to the eventual unification of Germany under Prussian domination. The war was precipitated by Prussian Chancellor Bismarck to gain those ends for Prussia.

Austro-Turkish War A war (1682–1699) between Austria (and her allies) and the Ottoman Empire. The Turks sued for peace and agreed to the Treaty of Karlowitz in 1699.

Authoritarianism Political system based on blind submission of individuals to a central authority, either a single leader or a small group of them.

Autocracy System of government in which a single ruler has absolute power over the entire government.

Averröes (1126–1198) Important Spanish-Muslim philosopher of the 12th century also known as ibn-Rushd. From a family of religious scholars and judges, he became chief judge of Cordova. His commentaries on Aristotle's writings were important to medieval Christian philosophers and his attempts to reconcile Greek methods of logic with Islamic doctrine greatly replaced medieval scholastic philosophers.

Avicenna (980–1037) Preeminent Muslim scholar known in Arabic as ibn-Sina who was a poet, doctor, scientist, and philosopher. He wrote about every field of knowledge relying on the work of Aristotle. His *Canon of Medicine*, based on Greek knowledge, was used by physicians in Muslim and Christian lands.

Avignon City in France that became the residence of the popes, beginning with Pope Clement V, during the period known as the Babylonian Captivity (1309–1377). It was also used by several antipopes during the Great Schism which lasted from 1378–1408. It remained the property of the papacy until 1791 when it was annexed by France.

Axis powers One of the opposing sides in World War II, consisting of a coalition of nations headed by Germany, Italy, and Japan. The Axis was first formed in 1936 with an Italo-German accord and became a full alliance in 1939. In 1940 Japan joined with the Berlin Pact to which several Eastern European nations also acceded.

Axum A trading empire in sub-Saharan Africa that began its rise in the 1st century A.D. Located in the north corner of the Ethiopian highlands, Axum or the Kush Empire, was the great ivory market of northern Africa. During the 2nd and 3rd centuries A.D. its power rose, and by the 4th century it had conquered Meroe, a rival trading empire, and burned the city to the ground. During the 4th century Axum became Christian (the Coptic church) with strong political and religious links with Byzantine Egypt.

Ayacucho Located in South Peru the defeat of the Spanish by Bolivar's forces under the leadership of

Sucre here in 1824 won the independence of Peru and marked the triumph of the independence movement in South America.

Ayub Khan, Mohammed (1909–1974) Pakistani politician and president (1958–1969), General Ayub Khan seized power in Pakistan in 1958, imposed martial law, and ruled as a dictator. Under his rule, Pakistan made progress in land redistribution and industrial development. However, in 1969, riots and protests caused him to resign and the government was turned over to army leaders.

Azikiwe, Nnamdi (b. 1904) Nigerian statesman. A nationalist leader in Africa in the 1930s. From Nigeria, he was educated in America and returned to Africa in 1934, where he edited a newspaper in the Gold Coast. In 1937 he went back to Nigeria to publish the *West African Pilot* which spread ideas of self-determination and independence. He was elected to the premiership of East Nigeria (1954–1959). In 1960 he was appointed to the largely honorary office of governor-general.

Aztecs An Indian nation of warriors, merchants, and organizers, who were probably the first Americans to use swords. Their religion was bloody and warlike with human sacrifice being the basis for the faith. Trade was a prestige profession, and the civilization flourished. Tenochtitlán, their capital, was a remarkable city with a population of around 300,000 and a system of canals. Wandering Aztecs reached Ananhuac about 1200 A.D. and learned a great deal from their predecessors, the Toltecs. In 1325 the Aztecs founded Tenochtitlán and gained a foothold in central Mexico. In 100 years they were the strongest tribe in the valley, and by 1440, under Montezuma I, they had moved east and south and controlled most of central Mexico in a confederation of tribes. Between 1519 and 1521 Hernando Cortés and 400 Spanish troops defeated them.

B **Babur** (Babar, Baber) (1483–1530) The founder of the Mogul Empire, Babur was a Turk from what is today Russian Turkestan, who claimed descent from both Genghis Khan and Tamerlane. In 1504 he established a small kingdom in Afghanistan. From here, at the head of the 12,000 Moslems he swept down on India, conquered Delhi in 1526, and made it his capital. He then proceeded to conquer most of northern India and these conquests formed the Mogul Empire.

Babylon City in ancient Mesopotamia located on the Euphrates River that was the center of Babylonia. Under Hammurabi it reached greatness, but was later destroyed by Sennacherib. Once again under Nebuchadnezzar, in about 526 B.C. it reached a height of luxury and was famed for its Hanging Gardens, considered one of the wonders of the world. After its capture by the Persians in 538 B.C., the city declined.

Babylonian Captivity Period when the papacy was moved from Rome to Avignon and the French king controlled the papacy. In the late 13th century, French king Philip IV, objected to the pope's contention that Philip could not tax the French clergy. The pope finally gave in, but the conflict resulted in Philip's securing the election of a French clergyman as pope and the moving of the papal court from

Rome to Avignon in France. For nearly 70 years (1309–1377) the popes lived in Avignon in what was called the Babylonian Captivity, in reference to the time when King Nebuchadnezzar of Babylon took the people of Judah as captives to Babylon. In 1378 an Italian clergyman was elected pope by the College of Cardinals while the French cardinals elected their man at Avignon. A third pope was finally elected in 1409 A.D. at the Council of Pisa where 500 prelates and delegates from the states of Europe attempted to resolve the problem. Finally in 1417 A.D. the Council of Constance was able to secure the election of a pope, which ended the Great Schism in the church.

Bacon, Francis (1561–1626) Famous 17th-century scientist and philosopher from England who formalized the inductive method of acquiring knowledge and emphasized the usefulness of knowledge. *See also* Philosophy section, page 19-4.

Bactria A kingdom established in northwestern India by the Bactrian Greeks descendants of Greek soldiers who came with Alexander the Great when he invaded the Persian Empire and India. In the 2nd century B.C., Bactrian king Demetrius established this kingdom and encouraged the blending of Greek and Indian civilization. Around 30 B.C., the Bactrians were defeated by a new wave of invaders.

Balboa, Vasco Nuñez de (1475–1519?) Spanish conquistador who discovered the Pacific Ocean in 1513.

Baldwin, Stanley (1867–1947) British statesman. As prime minister (1923 and 1924, 1924–1929, and 1935–1937) he obtained passage of the Trade Disputes Act in 1927, which limited the power of unions, and played a role in the abdication of Edward VIII in 1936. He opposed British rearmament in the face of the increasing German military threat.

Balfour Declaration Issued in 1917 by Arthur Balfour, the British foreign secretary, after the British captured Palestine from Turkey. It announced that it was England's intention to establish a national home for the Jews in Palestine "without prejudicing the rights of non-Jews." At this time the Arabs in Palestine numbered about 700,000, whereas the Jews were a minority of about 70,000.

Baltic states Name for former countries of Lithuania, Latvia, and Estonia, which were located east of the Baltic Sea. The territory was under Russian rule from the 1700s. After World War I and the Baltic War of Liberation, the three independent countries were formed in 1918 but were retaken by Russia in 1940 and incorporated into the U.S.S.R. They have become independent since 1991, with the collapse of communism in the Soviet Union.

Bandaronaike, Mrs. Sirimavo (b. 1916) Elected in 1960 in Sri Lanka, she became the world's first woman prime minister (1960–1965). During her first administration the country suffered from inflation and rising unemployment. She was ousted in 1965, but was returned to power in 1970. In 1972 Ceylon became a "socialist democracy" as the Republic of Sri Lanka. She was voted out of office in 1977 and the next year Sri Lanka adopted a presidential form of government.

Bantu A diverse people of Africa, related primarily by similarities in their languages. Bantus occupy al-most all of southern Africa below the Congo River. It is believed that Bantus originally occupied homelands in east-central Africa and spread (1st century B.C.?) south from there.

Bao Dai (b. 1913) Last Vietnamese emperor (1925–1945). Emperor of Annan who was proclaimed the ruler of all Indochina by the Japanese on the eve of their defeat in 1945. His puppet government could not retain its position against a nationalist government proclaimed by Ho Chi Minh, an old revolutionary leader with Communist ties, who proclaimed the independence of Indochina as the Republic of Vietnam in 1949.

Barbarian invasions Name given to the conquest of portions of the western Roman Empire by tribes from the north. By the 4th century A.D. Rome's power had declined, allowing Germanic tribes to seize and settle in northern Roman provinces. The Visigoths crossed the Danube in 376 and, led by Alaric, sacked Rome in 410. His successor, Ataulf, sought to fuse Roman elements into a Visigothic kingdom. Rome was nearly sacked in 451 by the Huns under Attila, and was sacked in 455 by the Vandals under Gaiseric. The Germanic tribes under Odoacer deposed in 476 Romulus Augustulus, last Roman emperor of the West, and the Western empire ceased to exist. Other groups to seize Roman territory included the Ostrogoths, Burgundians, and the Franks.

The destruction of the Bastille in Paris on July 14, 1789.

Bastille Famous French prison in Paris that was stormed on July 14, 1789 by a Parisian mob marking the outbreak of the French Revolution.

Batista, Fulgencio (1901–1973) An army sergeant who in 1934 led a revolt in Cuba and set up puppet presidents. Batista set up a new constitution in 1940 and easily won the presidential election for a four-year term. Batista was sent into exile in 1944 but returned and in 1952 organized his army followers, seized power, and established a brutal dictatorship. Opposition to him grew, and he was over-thrown by Fidel Castro.

Battle of Britain   Took place during World War II and was the greatest air attack in history up to that time. On June 19, 1940 Hitler commenced air attacks that increased in intensity until 1,000-plane raids were mounted daily. German strategic error and British radar, plus the incredible work of an overworked air force, finally forced Germany to substitute submarine warfare.

Battle of the Bulge   The last desperate German counterattack of World War II to stop the Allied advance into Germany that began on December 16, 1944 in northern France. The battle lasted a month and the Allies launched a counteroffensive that wiped out German gains and were able to advance into Germany.

Becket, Thomas à (1117–1170)   English martyr and archbishop of Canterbury, he first served as the chancellor of Henry II. Against his wishes, Henry II made him archbishop and the two men soon opposed one another over the issue of royal authority over the church, especially Henry's plan to transfer the trials of clergy accused of crimes from church to royal courts. In 1170, Thomas was murdered in the cathedral by supporters of the king.

Bedouin   Nomadic peoples of Arabia who spoke the Semitic language of Arabic and became converts to Islam.

Begin, Menachem (1913–1992)   Leader of Israel's Likud Party, he was prime minister from 1977–1983. In 1978 he was awarded the Nobel Prize for Peace for concluding a peace treaty with Egyptian president Anwar Sadat. *See* page 11-109.

Behistun inscription   A large cliff rock that contained writing in three languages—Persian, Susian (a Persian dialect), and cuneiform Babylonian and enabled scholars to decipher the cuneiform writing of Mesopotamia. From a list of known Persian cuneiform signs, it was possible to read the Persian and thus in turn, the Babylonian.

Benedict, Saint (d. 547)   Italian monk of the 6th century who founded the Benedictine Order. He established the first Benedictine monastery at Monte Cassino in 529 and created the Rule of St. Benedict, a set of rules to govern monastic life that served as a guide for other religious orders.

Benes, Eduard (1886–1948)   Czech statesman who served as president of Czechoslovakia (1935–1938) and after the Munich pact headed the Czech provisional government in London. After the war, he was once again elected president of Czechoslovakia in 1946 but resigned after the Communist coup d'état of 1948.

Ben-Gurion, David (1886–1973)   First prime minister of Israel when the nation came into being in 1948. He founded a Zionist movement in Russia, emigrated to Palestine in 1905, and was exiled from Palestine in 1914 because of his views. He spent several years in the United States, returned to Palestine, and served as secretary of the General Federation of Labor until 1935. From then on he was the leader of the MAPAI, the Israeli Labor party.

Benin, kingdom of   Former West African kingdom located in what is now Nigeria. A powerful kingdom even before the advent of Portuguese exploration of Africa in the 1200s, it began trade with Portugal in the late 15th century and remained a power in the region until the 18th century when it began its decline. The kingdom fell to British control in the late 19th century.

A 16th century sculpture depicting African warriors.

Bentham, Jeremy (1748–1832)   English philosopher who was the founder of utilitarianism, a theory that holds that the good of society and its laws is to ensure the greatest good for the greatest number of people. He believed that monarchy should be abolished, and that literate adults should have the right to vote. Since each individual is concerned with his own welfare and happiness, the best interests of the community are served by individualism or complete laissez-faire, in which every person is left free to satisfy his self-interest. *See also* Philosophy section, page 19-4.

Berlin Blockade   In the spring of 1948 Stalin decided to drive the West out of Berlin, and he closed all rail, land, and water routes to the city. The Russians expected that the Allies would be unable to supply the 2.5 million inhabitants of West Berlin but a massive airlift was the West's answer to this threat. For nearly 11 months, from June 1948 to May 1949, planes flew night and day, saving Berlin by bringing in over 2.5 million tons of food and coal. Stalin finally surrendered and lifted the blockade.

Berlin Conference   A conference held in Berlin in 1884 and 1885 to settle the conflicting claims of the European powers over the lands of Africa. The main problem discussed was the Belgian claim to the Congo that conflicted with that of several other nations. Agreements here, along with those made over the following years, divided Africa among the European nations.

Berlin Wall Barrier erected by the Communist government of East Germany in 1961 to stop the escape of their citizens to the West. In November 1989, as part of a democratization movement throughout Eastern Europe, openings were made in the Wall and it ceased to be a symbol of political separation and repression. *See* **East European Revolution.**

Bernard of Clairvaux, Saint (1090–1153) French cleric, a mystic, and in his day one of the most prominent figures in the Roman Catholic church. A Cistercian monk, he founded the monastery at Clairvaux in 1115 and spent the rest of his life as its abbot. Nevertheless, he gained great influence in the church by his eloquence, his widespread reputation as a pious and devoted churchman, and his influence with the popes of the day.

Bessemer, Henry (1813–1898) An English engineer who discovered a process for making steel by removing carbon from molten iron, resulting in the reduction of the cost of steel by nearly 85 percent.

Bethmann-Hollweg, Theobald von (1856–1921) German statesman. As chancellor of Germany (1909–1917), he did not want war, but his policies contributed to the outbreak of World War I. His attempts to bring about a mediated end to the war led to his forced resignation.

Bhagavad-Gita Sanskrit poem that forms the last 18 chapters of *The Mahabharata*, the longest epic poem in world literature. The theme is religious and the Gita stresses that doing one's moral duty or dharma, is the highest fulfillment in life. Krishna, the human incarnation of the god Vishnu tells of the alternate paths of salvation, which include salvation through the performance of action appropriate to one's station in life, salvation through the attainment of knowledge of the Supreme Being, and salvation through faith and devotion to a personal god, especially Krishna.

Bhutto, Benezir (b. 1953) Prime Minister of Pakistan (1988–1990). The first female leader of a Muslim nation in modern times, she was dismissed in 1990.

Bhutto, Zulfikar Ali (1928–1979) Pakistani political leader. His policies helped to cause the secession of East Pakistan and the ensuing war in 1971. As president (1971–1973) and prime minister (1973–1977), he opposed secession and the formation of Bangladesh but was forced to recognize its independence in 1974. He was overthrown by General Zia (*see* page 11-135) in 1977. Charged with plotting the assassination of a political foe, he was imprisoned and executed in 1979.

Bill of Rights, English Famous document of the English constitution adopted in 1689, it recognized the results of 17th-century struggle between Parliament and the Stuart monarchy. Its principles were accepted by King William and Queen Mary in the Declaration of Rights as a condition for ascending to the throne after the overthrow of James II in the bloodless Glorious Revolution of 1688. Among the principles established by the Bill of Rights was that the monarch was subject to the laws of Parliament and that all English subjects had certain civil and political rights.

Bismarck, Otto von (1815–1898) German statesman who served as chancellor of Germany (1871–1890) and was responsible for the unification of Germany. In 1862, King William I of Prussia appointed Otto von Bismarck as chief minister of state, a man whose policy was to influence European affairs for the next 25 years. Bismarck's first problem was to persuade the independent states of Germany to unite, give up their sovereignty, and accept the leadership of Prussia. He was also convinced that Austria was Prussia's rival for control of Germany, and knew that sooner or later a showdown would take place between the two. The great questions of the day, he said, are not to be decided by speeches but by "blood and iron." Between 1862 and 1866, despite opposition from German liberals, he built up the strength of the Prussian army and his blood and iron policy resulted in three wars, against Denmark, Austria, and France, each success contributing to final unification of Germany under Prussian leadership. With unification completed in 1871, the king of Prussia was crowned Kaiser William I, Emperor of the Germans, and Bismarck became chancellor of the German Empire. His policies included the prevention of a European coalition against Germany that was carried out through the creation of the Dual Alliance in 1879 between Germany and Austria and the Triple Alliance of 1882 that included Italy. Bismarck instituted social security reforms providing workers with protection against sickness, accidents, and old age and waged a battle known as "Kulturkampf" to subordinate the Catholic church to the state. He was dismissed by Kaiser William II who wanted to carry out his own policies.

Black Death An infectious epidemic disease caused by a bacterium that is transmitted to humans by fleas from infected rats. Bubonic plague, the most common form, is characterized by very high fever, chills, delirium, and enlarged painful lymph nodes (buboes) but there are also pneumonic that affects the lungs and septicemic that infects the blood. In the black form of plague, hemorrhages turn black, giving the term "Black Death" to the disease. The earliest known visitation of the plague to Europe occurred in Athens in 430 B.C. A disastrous epidemic occurred in Rome in the 3rd century in which 5,000 persons are reported to have succumbed daily. However, the most widespread epidemic began in Constantinople in 1334 and rapidly spread throughout Europe. In less than 20 years the Black Death killed as much as three quarters of the population of Europe and Asia. The great plague of London in 1665 is recorded in many works of literature. Quarantine measures helped to contain the disease somewhat but serious epidemics continued to occur even in the 19th century. The disease is still prevalent in many parts of Asia.

Blanc, Louis (1811–1882) French Socialist who outlined his ideal of a new social order on the principle "From each according to his abilities, to each according to his needs." He advocated the establishment of a system of social workshops controlled by the workers as the first stage in achieving this goal. He organized the first Socialist party in France in the 1840s and was a leader in the revolution of 1848. As a member of the provisional government he established social workshops but the plan was sabotaged. Afterwards his role in an insurrection of the workers caused him to flee to England where he remained until 1871. He returned to France where he became a member of the National Assembly and later a leader of the left in the Chamber of Deputies.

Blitzkrieg German term, meaning "lightning war" used to describe the German battle tactic in World War II of using massive numbers of airplanes and mechanized forces in sudden assaults on opposing forces.

Bloody Sunday The spark that set off the Revolution of 1905 in Russia. On January 9, 1905, a priest, Father Gapon, led 200,000 unarmed workers to the palace gates in St. Petersburg in order to demand an eight-hour day, a minimum wage of a ruble a day, and a constituent assembly. The workers were fired upon by the guards, and over 500 were killed and thousands wounded. Bloody Sunday united the dissatisfied bourgeois, proletariat, and peasants. By the end of 1905, 1,500 governmental officials had been assassinated, peasants had seized estates, a strike committee had been set up by Leon Trotsky, and one of the most complete general strikes in history followed. The life of the country came to a standstill. Soviets (councils) of workers were established all over Russia and pressed the demand for a representative assembly. The czar finally gave in and by the October Manifesto granted a legislative duma, but Nicholas maintained control of foreign policy.

Blum, Leon (1872–1950) French Socialist who headed the first Popular Front Government that was elected in 1936 and consisted of a coalition of Socialists, Radical Socialists, and Communists. This Popular Front government passed many labor reforms but conservative opposition to Blum's fiscal policies forced him to resign in 1937. Blum served as premier once again for two months in 1946 and 1947.

Boer War (1899–1902) The culmination of friction between the Dutch settlers and the British in South Africa. In 1834 Britain had abolished slavery throughout the empire, including Cape Colony at the southern tip of Africa, acquired from the Netherlands in 1815, but inhabited by Dutch settlers called Boers or farmers since 1660. The Boers resented interference with their slave system of native Africans, and moved out from British jurisdiction in a vast trek across the Vaal and the Orange rivers to form two independent Boer republics, the Orange Free State and the Transvaal (South African) Republic. Between 1852 and 1887 British policy fluctuated between recognition of the two republics and acquisition of them. In 1891 the Transvaal Republic was regarded, contradictorily, as being independent and under the sovereignty of Great Britain. The discovery of gold and diamonds in the republics, essentially "farmer" republics uninterested in mineral wealth, led to a great influx of adventurers who expected Great Britain to protect and extend their rights and interests. Cecil Rhodes, the imperialist and diamond-mine owner, who became prime minister of Cape Colony, decided to use the discontent as a means to take over the Boer republics for Great Britain. His attempt to take over the Transvaal Republic led to the Boer War, in which the Boers were finally defeated, and agreed to accept British control for the time being in return for eventual self-government.

Boleyn, Anne (1507–1536) Queen consort of King Henry VIII of England and the mother of Queen Elizabeth I. She became Henry's second wife when he divorced Katharine of Aragon to marry her but the marriage was generally unpopular in England. Henry soon tired of Anne and after she failed to produce a male heir to the throne he decided to marry Jane Seymour. Anne was brought to trial in 1536 for adultery and condemned to death.

Bolívar, Simón (1783–1830) Leader of the South American Revolution of the 1800s who was known as the "Liberator." Beginning in 1810, Bolívar resisted the Spanish, and finally freed Colombia, Venezuela, and Ecuador by 1822 and made them the new nation of El Gran Colombia which in a few years broke up into the three separate countries. While Bolívar was freeing the northern part of the continent, José de San Martín of Argentina, tried to free the Viceroyalty of Río de la Plata, and succeeded in winning its independence in 1816. Bolívar crossed the mountains and took Quito in northern Peru and met San Martín in 1822 to discuss joint operations. San Martín turned over his command to Bolívar and in 1824 Bolívar freed Peru.

Bolsheviks One of the two main branches of Marxist Socialism in Russia from 1903–1918, the other being the Mensheviks. In 1903, when the Russian Social Democratic party split into two factions, the Bolsheviks led by Lenin advocated immediate revolution and the establishment of a dictatorship of the proletariat. In the Russian Revolution of 1917 the Mensheviks cooperated with the government established under the leadership of Kerensky but this regime was overthrown by the Bolsheviks in 1917. After the outbreak of warfare, the Bolsheviks won control and Lenin became the leader of the Soviet Union. The Bolsheviks became the Russian Communist party in 1918.

Bonaparte, Joseph (1768–1844) Brother of Napoleon who made him king of Naples in 1806 and king of Spain in 1808. Unsuccessful in defending his throne in the Peninsular War, he was forced to abdicate in 1813.

Bonaparte, Louis Napoleon *See* **Napoleon III**.

Bonaparte, Napoleon *See* **Napoleon I**.

Boniface, Saint (675–754?) An 8th-century English monk, his missionary work brought him the name "Apostle of Germany." He is known for converting pagan Germany to Christianity under the protection of Charles Martel of the Franks. He founded many bishoprics and monasteries and he was made archbishop of Mainz in 745.

Boniface, VIII (1235–1303) Thirteenth-century pope whose conflict with King Philip IV of France was the principle feature of his papacy. When Philip IV demanded that the clergy pay taxes he issued a papal bull in 1296 that said that the clergy could not be taxed without the consent of the pope. Philip struck back by cutting off the contributions of the French church to the pope. In a papal bull issued in 1302, Boniface advanced the principle that the pope was supreme in both spiritual and temporal matters and that princes were subject to the pope's authority in both. In response, Philip IV sent an envoy to Italy who held the pope prisoner. He was soon released but died a month later.

Book of the Dead　Egyptian religious text probably from the 6th and 7th centuries B.C. that contained charms, prayers, and formulas.

Bourbons　Royal family of France originally of France. Its branches also ruled in Spain, the two Sicilies, and Parma. The first of the Bourbon family to become king of France was Henry IV (1589–1610), who was succeeded by his son Louis XIII, and his grandson Louis XIV. Louis XIV's descendants ruled France, except during the French Revolution and the Napoleonic Era (1792–1814), until Charles X was deposed in 1830. The line of Bourbon-Spain came to rule Spain with the accession of Philip V, a grandson of Louis XIV, to the Spanish throne in 1700. The last Bourbon king on the Spanish throne was Alfonso XIII who was deposed in 1931.

Bourgeoisie　Originally, French merchants and craftsmen in medieval times, who, as a class, occupied the economic and social middle ground between landowners and peasants. With the breakup of feudal society, the rise of capitalism, and the advent of the Industrial Revolution, the bourgeoisie came to include a wide range of groups of entrepreneurs, such as bankers, factory owners, merchants, and professionals.

Boxer Rebellion　Another phase in the revolutionary process in China, it was symptomatic of the growing unrest and the increasing antiforeignism and was the last desperate effort to drive out the foreigners. Led by a group that called itself the Fists of Righteous Harmony, the rebellion that broke out in 1900 was supported quietly by the throne. It was directed against all foreigners and any Chinese who had come under the influence of the West (particularly Christians). The foreign legations in Peking were attacked, and 242 Westerners were killed as well as several thousand Chinese converts. The Western governments immediately sent an allied army (the greatest number of men to relieve the legations was sent by Japan—80,000). With this, the movement collapsed. The effects of the Boxer Rebellion included the demand of indemnity of $333,000,000, the foreign occupation of 13 places around Peking, and the punishment of many officials. The rebellion convinced many of the most conservative bureaucrats that change had to come about in China and reforms by the Manchus (1901–1910) were instigated. Schools were established, the examination system was abolished, and students were sent abroad to study. A new army was created, a constitution was drafted in 1908, provincial assemblies were put into operation in 1909, and a national assembly in 1910. Earlier reforms in China had been within the Confucian system but these reforms were not, and the Manchus soon found that drastic change was undermining the very foundations of their government.

Braganza　Braganza ruling house of Portugal (1640–1910) and Brazil (1822–1889). The family was founded by Alfonso (d. 1451), the illegitimate son of Portuguese King John I. The first member of

the royal line was John IV, who ruled the newly independent Portugal (1640–1656). The line of rulers lasted until the ouster of Manuel II in 1910 and formation of the republic. The Braganza family also provided rulers of Brazil for a time in the 19th century.

Brahma　Supreme god. *See* **Hinduism**.

Brandt, Willy (1913–1992)　German statesman. Former mayor of West Berlin and foreign minister he became chancellor of West Germany in 1969. He continued the policy he had initiated as foreign minister, that of Ostpolitik, or the "Eastern Policy" of seeking normal relations with Eastern Europe, particularly with the Soviet Union. In Moscow he and Premier Kosygin signed an agreement. Although he received the Nobel Peace Prize for his Ostpolitik, Brandt met stiff opposition at home and in May 1974, Brandt abruptly announced his resignation, ostensibly because a close personal aide was arrested and confessed that he was an East German spy on Brandt's staff.

Brest-Litovsk, treaty of　Separate peace treaty in World War I signed by Soviet Russia and the Central Powers on March 3, 1918. Under the harsh treaty, Russia agreed to the evacuation of the Ukraine, Finland, the Baltic states, Poland, and the Transcaucasus. It lost three-quarters of its iron and coal, one-quarter of its arable land, one-quarter of its population, and one-third of its manufacturing and also had to pay a large war indemnity. Since Russia concluded a separate peace, almost all the countries of the world broke diplomatic relations, but Lenin adhered to it in order to save the Russian Revolution.

Brezhnev, Leonid (1906–1982)　Russian Communist leader. In 1964, he replaced Khrushchev as first secretary of the Communist party, while Aleksei Kosygin became premier. Brezhnev rose to power first as a Red Army political commissar and briefly as a member of the Communist party Central Committee. Under Khrushchev, Brezhnev was put in charge of the virgin lands program, in 1956 he was reinstated in the Central Committee, and in 1957 he was made a full member of the Presidium. In 1960 he was given the honorary title of Soviet president, but he resigned in 1963 to give full attention to the secretariat. By this time he was slated as Khrushchev's successor. Although Brezhnev and Kosygin shared power, by the 1970s, Brezhnev had emerged as the undisputed head of the Soviet Union. His policies included encouragement of Soviet economic growth, maintaining Soviet security, and détente with the West. At his death in 1982, he was succeeded by Yuri Andropov.

Briand, Aristide (1862–1932)　French statesman who served as premier of France ten times between 1909 and 1921. As French foreign minister in the years between 1925 and 1932 he was the chief architect of the Locarno Pact of 1925 which improved relations between Germany and the former Allies in World War I and the Kellogg-Briand Pact of 1928 in which 62 nations agreed to renounce war as an instrument of foreign policy. In 1926, Briand shared the Nobel Peace Prize with Gustav Stresemann of Germany.

British East India Company　British trading company that controlled commercial and political affairs in India in the 18th and 19th centuries. Chartered in 1600 by Queen Elizabeth I to gain a share of the Asian spice trade, the company focused on India after 1623. In India, the company defeated the Portuguese in 1612 and was granted political powers in India in 1668 by Charles II. The French were finally expelled from India between 1751 and 1760 by Robert Clive and the company took control of Bengal in 1765, making it the dominant power in India. British government intervention in India was affected by the Regulating Act of 1773 and the East India Act of 1784. The government took over all administrative functions after the Indian Mutiny or Sepoy Mutiny of 1857.

British North America Act   Legislation (March 29, 1867) by which the British Parliament united Upper and Lower Canada (Ontario and Quebec), Nova Scotia, and New Brunswick to form the Dominion of Canada. The act also provided a constitutional framework for governing the dominion until 1982, when constitutional power was formally transferred to Canada.

Bronze Age   Period in the late Neolithic Age that marked the beginning of what historians called civilization. In this period, bronze replaced copper and stone as the main material used in tools and weapons. The first knowledge of bronze-working was discovered in southwestern Asia about 5,000 years ago, at about the same time the world's first civilization arose here.

Brutus, Marcus (85–42 B.C.)   Known as the principal assassin of Julius Caesar. Originally he sided with Pompey in the power struggle with Caesar, but Caesar later pardoned him and gave him an administrative office. He joined Cassius in the plot against Caesar in 44 B.C. and supported the Republican cause. After his forces were defeated by those of Marc Antony and Octavian he committed suicide.

Bubonic plague   See **Black Death**.

Buddhism   One of the great religions of the world, it is based on the teachings of Gautama Buddha. According to legend, Gautama was born in 563 B.C. into the second caste of India, the warrior, and brought up in the luxury of warrior aristocrats. At the age of 29, while on a journey, Gautama is reported to have seen an old man, a sick man, a dead man, and an ascetic. This worried him, for he could not understand why there should be so much misery in the world. For six years he sought a solution, trying all the Hindu methods, such as asceticism and mortification of the flesh, in order to understand God. Finally, he seated himself under the sacred Bodhi tree and meditated for 49 days, until he achieved enlightenment and became known as Buddha, the enlightened one. For the next 45 years of his life he traveled, preached, and spread his religion. Buddhism maintained many Hindu doctrines such as reincarnation, the doctrine of karma, and renunciation of the world, but Buddha disagreed with the methods of achieving these objectives. He did not believe in mortification of the flesh or in caste distinctions, since all people were to him equal in spiritual potential. The core of Buddha's teachings were the Four Noble Truths: suffering is universal, the cause of all suffering is selfish desire and cravings, the cure to the problem of suffering therefore is to eliminate all selfish desire, and the way to do this is to follow the Noble Eightfold Path. The Noble Eightfold Path for eliminating selfish desire consists of right views or knowledge, the right ambition, right speech, right conduct, right means of livelihood, right effort or self-discipline, right thoughts, right meditation or concentration. The achievement of enlightenment is the fundamental aim for the Buddhist as it is for the Hindu. Once one achieves enlightenment, he is said to have reached Nirvana and is finally released from the wheel of death and rebirth. In time, Buddhism divided into two sects. Hinayana, the Lesser Vehicle, is the original faith, relying solely on one's own introspection and faith to achieve enlightenment. It became the dominant form of Buddhism in Ceylon, Burma, Thailand, and Cambodia. Mahayana, the Greater Vehicle, is the Chinese adaptation of Buddhism, and the primary difference is that it relies on other Buddhas and gods to achieve enlightenment or Nirvana. It incorporates the use of saints called bodhisattvas praying to them for aid. Gradually more emphasis was put on good works than on contemplation. Mahayana Buddhism became the dominant form in China, Japan, Vietnam, and Korea. Buddhism in 272 B.C. was the state religion of India; by 65 A.D. it had spread to China and by 600 A.D. it was introduced into Japan and became the state religion during the 700s. By 800 A.D. the faith had spread all over the Far East, but 100 years before that date it had died out in India. The main reason for its demise in India was its renunciation of the caste system, which challenged the existing social structure. *See also* Religion section, pages 22-4 and 22-13.

Bülow, Bernhard Heinrich Martin, Fürst von (1849–1929)   German statesman. As chancellor of Germany (1900–1909) he attempted to strengthen Germany's position as a world power, but instead his policies strengthened the Triple Entente of Britain, France, and Russia.

Burke, Edmund (1729–1797)   A British statesman and political writer. A member of the Whig party, Burke was sympathetic to the American colonies in 1774 and 1775. Though he championed many liberal and reform causes, Burke believed that political, social, and religious institutions reflected the wisdom of the ages. His opposition to the French Revolution, based on the fear that violent change would cause disorder and bring about tyranny, made him the spokesman of European conservatives. Burke's writings had important influence on conservatives in England, the United States, and France.

Bushido   Term meaning "way of the warrior" and a code of conduct in Japan identified with Samurai warriors. The code developed from feudal times and stressed personal honor and, above all, loyalty to the feudal lord. Formulated during the Kamakura shogunate during the 12th–14th centuries, it became the code of the Daimyo and Samurai in the 17th century. In the 19th century the code was made the basis for fierce loyalty to the emperor and governed Japanese life until the end of World War II.

Buxar, battle of   This battle in 1764 brought the rich province of Bengal completely under control of the East India Company, giving it a strong base from which to conquer the rest of India. In 1765

Robert Clive obtained from the Newab of Bengal the right to administer the revenues (known as dewani) of Bengal, Bihar, and Orissa, and this meant that the East India Company had in effect become a sovereign power on the mainland of India.

Byzantine Empire　The eastern half of the Roman Empire that survived after the decline and collapse of the Roman Empire in the West. The emperor Diocletian divided the Roman Empire into East and West and moved his court to Asia Minor making it the center of the Roman Empire instead of Rome. In 330 A.D. Roman emperor Constantine founded a new capital city for the empire called Constantinople, which became the center of the new Byzantine Empire that developed out of the eastern Roman Empire and outlived the western Roman Empire by 1,000 years. Byzantium became enormously rich as the great center of trade from every quarter of the compass. Envied for its great wealth, Byzantium maintained a carefully recruited and well-trained army with its own medical ambulance corps, highly skillful intelligence service, and skilled diplomats to negotiate. The empire was Roman in its law and centralized organization, but Greek in culture, language, and emperors. The government was authoritarian and highly centralized. The church was headed by a Patriarch who was simply one of a number of bishops singled out and appointed by the emperor, and therefore always dismissable by the emperor. The cultural contribution of Byzantium was that of preserving, during the several centuries in which knowledge of Greek disappeared from Europe, Greek masterpieces and making copies of them, printing of books, building of great libraries and a university, and the preservation of the works of Plato, Aristotle, Homer, and Sophocles. Despite attack by the Persians, the Seljuk Turks in the 11th century, and the Crusaders in 1204, the empire survived until 1453 when it was overwhelmed by the Ottoman Turks—the so-called fall of Constantinople.

C　**Cabot, John** (1450–1498)　Italian navigator who explored for England. His voyage to North America in 1497 gave England its claims in the "New World."

Cabral, Pedro (1460–1526)　Portuguese navigator who accidentally reached the coast of Brazil that he claimed for Portugal in 1500. When destined for India he was blown off course and forced westward.

Caesar, Augustus　*See* **Augustus**.

Caesar, Julius (102–44 B.C.)　Great Roman statesman and general. Caesar strengthened Rome's control over the empire by replacing the Roman oligarchy with a dictatorship and by pacifying Italy and the provinces. He extended the empire throughout Gaul and devised the Julian calendar, the basis of the modern calendar. Caesar aligned himself with the popular party during his early career and, in 60 B.C., sought the consulate of Rome. Frustrated by Senate opposition, he formed the first Triumvirate with Crassus and Pompey and thus became consul in 59 B.C. He was then named proconsul of Gaul and Illyricum in 58 B.C. and became a military hero as commander of Roman armies in the Gallic Wars (58–51 B.C.) Crassus' death ended the triumvirate

Julius Ceasar.

in 53 B.C. and set Pompey, now sole consul, against Caesar. In 49 B.C. Caesar led his armies from Gaul against Pompey. Crossing the Rubicon, he marched unopposed to Rome, and was made dictator. Caesar emerged victorious from the ensuing military exploits between 49 and 45 B.C. in the provinces against Pompey's army and in 44 B.C. was named dictator for life. But his dictatorial powers had aroused bitter resentment in Rome. On the Ides of March (March 15) of 44 B.C. Caesar was assassinated by a band of conspirators that included Brutus, Cassius, and Casca.

Caligula (12–41 A.D.)　The third of the Claudian emperors of the Roman Empire, the line beginning with Caesar Augustus (Octavian), considered the first emperor of Rome. He succeeded Tiberius as emperor but suffered from insanity and his rule was marked by senseless cruelty and despotism. His rule (37–41 A.D.) ended with his assassination and he was succeeded by Emperor Claudius.

Caliph　The successor to Mohammed, the founder of Islam, who was the religious and political head of the state. The first caliph was Abu Bakr (632–634) father-in-law of Mohammed who conquered Arabia. He was followed by Umar, Uthman, and Ali who were descendants of Mohammed and are called the Orthodox Caliphs. Their reign was broken in 661 when Muawiya took the caliphate by force and established the Umayyad dynasty. The Abbasid line later replaced the Umayyads. Later rival caliphates were set up in Baghdad, Cordova, Spain, and Cairo, Egypt. In 1258 invading Mongols, under a nephew of Genghis Khan, captured and destroyed Baghdad. These Ottoman Turks seized control of the eastern Moslem world, became themselves fierce converts to Mohammedanism, captured Constantinople in 1453, and threatened all Europe. The Turkish sultans in Constantinople retained their supremacy as caliphs until 1908 A.D. Since then there has been no recognized official head of the Moslem world. The caliphate was officially dissolved in Turkey by the National Assembly in 1924.

Calvin, John (1509–1564) Famous French Protestant leader of the Reformation who preached the doctrine of predestination; that God, who knows the past, the present, and the future, must always know which people will be saved and which shall be eternally damned. Calvin became the virtual dictator of the city of Geneva, which became a theocracy, a state ruled by a church, since only those whom Calvin regarded as the faithful could vote and hold office in Geneva. Being a dictator, Calvin suffered no opinion but his own, with a consequence that during five years "heretics" were executed and over 70 were banished. Nevertheless, for both religious and political reasons Calvinism flourished and spread into England and France where Calvin's followers were known as Huguenots. The present-day Presbyterian, Congregational, and other religious denominations contain the basic features of Calvinism laid down by Calvin in his *Institutes of Religion*: simple worship, bible readings, sermon, prayers, and hymns.

Camp David Accord *See* History of the United States section, pages 10-11.

Canaan Name by which the land west of the Jordan River, including Syria and the mountainous districts (inhabited by the Amarites in ancient times) was known. According to biblical tradition, Abraham was bidden by God to leave Chaldea and lead the Hebrews into Canaan, which became their land, known as Palestine.

Canossa Located in north-central Italy. It was the scene in 1077 of penance by Henry IV, the Holy Roman Emperor, who supposedly waited barefoot for 3 days outside the castle walls before Pope Gregory VII lifted his ban of excommunication against him.

Canterbury Tales Collection of stories written in the English vernacular by Geoffrey Chaucer (1340–1400 A.D.), one of the great medieval writers, portraying the people of the countryside of England and describing a cross section of lower and middle class people.

Canute (999–1035) Danish king who invaded England in 1015 and ruled it as part of a larger kingdom that included Denmark and Norway. Canute lived in England most of the time, ruling the kingdom well, but his successors did not share his talents and the kingdom did not last.

Capet, Hugh (938–996) A French noble who was chosen to be king by an assembly of nobles after the death in 987 of the last Carolingian king of France. As king he ruled only a small region around the city of Paris but he founded a line of kings called the Capetians who ruled France for over 300 years.

Capetians French royal house named for Hugh Capet who ruled France from 987 until 1328 when the throne passed to the house of Valois. When the Capetians succeeded to the throne of France, the royal possessions were modest in comparison with those of the Dukes of Normandy, Brittany, Aquitaine, Guienne, Champagne, and Gascony. Feudal obligations of these vassals to their king were little more than a gesture. The Capetian monarchs strengthened their possessions and power whenever the opportunity was favorable. They established primogeniture, the succession of estates to the eldest son, in place of election of a successor by the nobles. Through the efforts of the Capetian kings, France developed a strong central government under a powerful monarch by the early 1300s and the land owned by the English king in France was diminished to parts of the provinces of Aquitaine and Gascony.

Carbonari Italian secret society that was active in the Italian nationalist movement of the 1800s and involved in revolts. One of its members was Mazzini who created Young Italy, a society dedicated to uniting their country into a democratic republic.

Carlsbad decrees Resolutions adopted at a conference of ministers of the German states called by Metternich in response to a flurry of discontent among university students in 1819. These measures provided for press censorship, supervision of the universities, and suppression of liberal agitation.

Carolingian dynasty Dynasty of Frankish rulers, established in the 7th century by Pepin. They ruled as mayors of the palace under the Merovingian kings until Pepin the Short made himself king in 751 A.D. His son, Charlemagne who was crowned emperor in 800, brought the dynasty to its height. The Carolingian Empire was divided up by the Treaty of Verdun of 843 and members of the dynasty continued as kings in Germany until 911 and in France until 987.

Carranza, Venustiano (1859–1920) Mexican revolutionary and political leader. Carranza joined Madero in his revolt in 1910 against Diaz, and then fought Huerta when he overthrew Madero in 1913. Carranza headed the provisional government between 1914–1917 and during this time successfully countered uprisings by Villa and Zapata. He accepted the constitution of 1917 and served as president (1917–1920).

Carthage Former Phoenician colony founded in Tunisia in 800 B.C. By 264 B.C. when it first came into conflict with Rome, it was governed along much the same lines, but with the advantage of permanent military leaders instead of elected consuls. Its power was based on trade and commerce in the Mediterranean and it founded colonies in North Africa, Spain, and western Sicily. Carthage posed a threat to expanding Rome, particularly when during a civil war in Messina (the northeastern tip of Sicily) the Carthaginians responded to an appeal by Messina for assistance. This incident was the beginning of the Punic Wars, so named from the Roman term for the Phoenician people of Carthage. Carthage was eventually defeated in the Punic Wars (264–241 B.C., 218–201 B.C., and 149–146 B.C.) and the city itself was destroyed in 146 B.C.

Cartier, Sir Georges Etienne (1814–1873) Canadian statesman. A leading French-Canadian advocate of federation, he became joint prime minister of Canada (1858–1862) with Sir John Macdonald and later served in the government of unified Canada.

Cartier, Jacques (1491–1557) French navigator who first explored the Gulf of St. Lawrence and discovered the St. Lawrence River, starting France on its control of Canada.

Cartwright, Edmund (1743–1823) Inventor of the power loom during the period of the Industrial Revolution in England.

Cassius, Gaius (d. 42 B.C.) A Roman noble who supported Pompey in his power struggle with Julius Caesar, by whom he was later pardoned. He joined the plot to assassinate Caesar and was defeated with Brutus by Marc Antony's forces at the Battle of Philippi.

Caste system Hereditary social class system established under Hinduism probably by the Aryans who invaded and came to dominate India by 1500 B.C. Caste is similar to strict class distinction but is more restricted, for people marry only within their caste, associate only with people of their caste, and live according to the rules, ceremonies, and rituals of their particular caste. There were four major castes in India—the Brahmin or priestly caste, the Kshatriuas or warrior, the Vasiya or merchant, and the Sudra or laboring caste. There were, however, thousands (perhaps 7,000) of subcastes, and the division was made on professional or occupational lines. The castes were not socially or religiously equal. The Brahmin was the elite. All caste was a matter of birth. The untouchable was below and outside of caste and could not be associated with. The only jobs they were allowed were those the Hindu would consider unclean, such as tanning, latrine duty, and street cleaning. Today caste and untouchability are officially abolished.

Castlereagh, Lord (1769–1822) British foreign minister who helped to organize the "concert of Europe" against Napoleon and represented Great Britain at the Congress of Vienna in 1814 which met to redraw the map of Europe after Napoleon's defeat. He advocated moderate terms for France and favored a policy of balance of power with a return of conservative governments in Europe.

Castro, Fidel (b. 1926) Leader of the 1959 revolution in Cuba that overthrew Fulgencio Batista, the dictator who came to power in 1934. The new revolutionary government headed by Castro became an openly Communist regime after he declared he was a Marxist.

Catherine I (1684–1727) Ruled as empress of Russia (1725–1727). A Livonian servant girl she became Peter the Great's second wife. After his death Peter's palace guards chose her as his successor and she ruled ably.

Catherine II (the Great) (1729–1796) Ruled as empress of Russia (1762–1796). Formerly Princess Sophie, a minor German princess, she married Peter III in 1744. After a palace revolt that deposed Peter in 1762 she was proclaimed empress. With no legitimate title to the throne, she won over the nobility by exempting them from taxation and mili-

tary service. Her foreign policy was predatory, expansionist, and politically unsound. By this time Poland was no longer the power it had once been. Enfeebled by political anarchy, and open to attack from all sides because it was a plain without defensive frontiers, it presented its neighbors with the opportunity to dismember it. In three grabs between 1772 and 1795 Russia, Austria, and Prussia dismembered it completely. While Russia added some 180,000 square miles to its own territory, it also brought 6 million discontented Poles into the Russian Empire, and at the same time obliterated the buffer state between Prussia and Russia. Land had been acquired at the expense of political safety.

Catherine de Medici (1519–1589) A member of the Italian Medici family who became queen of France when she married King Henry II and was regent for her son Charles IX. She was involved in the plot against Protestants that became the massacre of Saint Bartholomew's Day in 1572.

Catherine of Aragon (Katherine) (1485–1536) Daughter of Ferdinand and Isabella of Spain, she was the first wife of Henry VIII and queen of England. Unable to produce a male heir, Henry's interest waned and he divorced her to marry Anne Boleyn.

Catherine of Valois (1401–1437) The daughter of King Charles VI she married King Henry V of England and became queen. She later married Owen Tudor and it is from their union that the line of Tudor kings descended.

Caudillo Term for a leader who is a political boss with a strong military following. It is used especially in reference to South American leaders who came to power after the revolution for independence.

Cavour, Camillo Benso (1810–1861) Chief architect of Italian unification in the 1800s under Victor Emanuel II. As prime minister of the Kingdom of Sardinia, he drove the Austrians out of Lombardy in 1859. In 1860 other areas in central Italy joined Sardinia by plebiscite. In 1861 the Kingdom of Italy was proclaimed under the ruler of Sardinia, Victor II.

Cellini, Benvenuto (1500–1572) Great Renaissance artist from Florence known especially for his work in silver and gold.

Central Powers Name applied to Germany and its allies during World War I. In addition to Germany, the Central Powers included Austria-Hungary, Bulgaria, and the Ottoman Empire.

Chaeronea, battle of Famous battle of 338 B.C. in which Philip of Macedon defeated the Athenians and became the master of Greece.

Chaldeans A Semitic group of people who overthrew the Assyrians in Mesopotomia in 612 B.C. and took over most of their empire under Nebuchadnezzar who ruled from the city of Babylon between 605 and 562 B.C., the Chaldeans conquered most of the lands of the Fertile Crescent. They made important advances in science and astronomy and were famed for their magnificent city of Babylon which was the site of the famous Hanging Gardens. Their empire fell to the Persians in 539 B.C.

Chamberlain, Neville (1869–1940) British prime minister in 1937 who became the symbol of the policy of appeasement toward Germany and Italy. He signed the Munich Pact of 1938 which gave up the

Sudetenland (of Czechoslovakia) to Hitler saying that he had achieved "peace in our time."

Champlain, Samuel de (1567–1635)　French explorer and the founder of New France. He established a colony in Quebec, discovered Lake Champlain, and extended French claims from Canada, west to Wisconsin.

Champollion, Jean-François (1790–1832) French Egyptologist who deciphered Egyptian hieroglyphics by using the Rosetta Stone.

Chandragupta I (d. 330 A.D.)　Indian king and the founder of the Gupta dynasty.

Chandragupta II (d. 415 A.D.)　The most famous of the Gupta rulers of India. The Gupta Empire reunited most of northern India from about 320–535 A.D. and under Chandragupta II the empire reached its greatest height. The period of the Gupta dynasty is known as the high point of India's classical period. Medicine, literature, and the arts (particularly sculpture) flourished. Great universities were established, and mathematicians and astronomers were as accurate and advanced as their contemporaries in the rest of the world. The decimal, the zero, and Arabic numerals all originated in India.

Chandragupta Maurya (d. 286? B.C.)　Indian emperor and founder of the Maurya dynasty. After the death of Alexander the Great, the first in Indian history to unite all northern India under one effective imperial authority. The Mauryan Empire was a police state with an efficient revenue system, taxing trade and land and controlling all mines.

Charlemagne. The first Holy Roman Emperor.

Charlemagne (771–814 A.D.)　King of the Franks who was crowned emperor of the Romans in 800 A.D. by Pope Leo III, thereby beginning the so-called Holy Roman Empire. He expanded his empire until it included what is modern France, Holland, Belgium, Switzerland, Austria, West Germany, North Spain, and some land farther eastwards. Charlemagne aspired to exert the authority of the former Roman emperors, and tried to maintain personal control throughout his empire by *missi dominici*, men sent by the king (a layman and a clergyman who traveled in pairs as royal inspectors). These men also exercised judicial powers, instituted the "sworn inquest," forerunner of the grand jury

that gave information under oath to traveling judges, later to become the basis of the English jury system. Charlemagne was a patron of learning and brought the famous English scholar and churchman Alcuin to conduct his school at Aachen. After Charlemagne's death his empire broke up, and with it the revived Roman Empire.

Charles I (1600–1649)　English king (1625–1649). His firm belief in the divine right of kings and consequent struggles with Parliament resulted in the English Civil War between 1642 and 1649. Charles's marriage to the unpopular French Catholic Henrietta Maria and his wars against Spain and France only added to his differences with Parliament. The struggle began soon after his accession and was characterized by bold maneuvers on both sides: Parliament refused Charles money grants until he agreed to end arbitrary practices; Charles briefly relented, agreeing to the Petition of Right in 1628, then dissolved Parliament in 1629 and ruled without it, raising money by a variety of means. Charles's need for money prompted the calling of the Short and Long Parliaments in 1640, which in turn resulted in the English Civil War. Defeated, Charles was tried and executed in 1649.

Charles I (1863–1908)　Portuguese king (1889–1908). Charles vied with Britain and Japan for African colonial territories and contended with unrest at home. A revolt in 1906 prompted him to grant Prime Minister João Franco dictatorial powers. This resulted in a revolt in 1908 and in his assassination.

Charles I (1887–1922)　Last ruler of the Austro-Hungarian Empire (1916–1918), successor to Emperor Francis Joseph. He acceded during World War I and tried to open negotiations for peace in 1916. He likewise failed in a plan to keep the dual monarchy united, and in 1918 Hungary and Czechoslovakia declared independence.

Charles II (Charles the Bald) (823–877)　King of the West Franks (France) (843–877) and emperor of the West (875–877). He agreed to the redivision of the empire by the Treaty of Verdun of 843 and the Treaty of Mersen of 870. He then succeeded to the imperial crown in 875.

Charles II (1630–1685)　English king (1660–1685), successor (after the English Restoration) to his father, Charles I. His restoration in 1660 brought a period of relative stability after the fall of the Protectorate. Following the English Civil War, he invaded England but was defeated by Cromwell in 1651 and fled to the Continent where he remained until his restoration. Though he favored Catholicism and religious toleration, he was forced by public sentiment and acts of the Cavalier Parliament to accept strict laws of uniformity. His reign was marked by a gradual increase in the power of Parliament, the rise of political parties, advances in colonization and trade, and the brilliant restoration period of culture.

Charles II (1661–1700)　Last Spanish Hapsburg king (1665–1700). His reign was marked by the continued decline in Spain's power, the War of Devotion, and the War of the Grand Alliance. His choice of Philip of Anjou (Philip V) as successor led to the War of Spanish Succession (1701–1714).

Charles III (Charles the Fat) (839–888)　Frankish emperor of the West (881–887) and king of the East

HISTORY OF THE WORLD

(882–887). He briefly reunited Charlemagne's empire (885–887) but proved a weak ruler.

Charles III (Charles the Simple) (879–929) French king (893–923). He ended Norse raids by ceding territory to them (now part of Normandy), and added Lorraine to the French kingdom in 911.

Charles III (1716–1788) Spanish king (1759–1788). An "enlightened despot," he instituted many beneficial administrative reforms. His reign was marked by defeat in the Seven Years' War (1756–1763) and Spain's participation in the American Revolution.

Charles IV (Charles the Fair) (1294–1328) French king (1322–1328). The last of the Capetian kings, won a part of Aquitaine from the English in 1327 who then controlled the territory.

Charles IV (1316–1378) German king (1346–1378). Elected Holy Roman emperor in opposition to Louis IV in 1346, he succeeded him in 1347, but was not crowned until 1355.

Charles IV (1748–1819) Spanish king (1788–1808). A weak ruler, he relied on de Godoy to run the government. His reign was marked by two invasions by the French (1794–1807) and domination by Napoleon. He was forced to abdicate in 1808.

Charles V (Charles the Wise) (1337–1380) French king from (1364–1380). As regent for his father (1356–1360), he put down the Jacquerie revolt. As king, he ruled France during its recovery from the early phase of the Hundred Years' War (1337–1453). He consolidated the power of the monarchy, strengthened the military, instituted reforms, and regained almost all the territories lost to the English.

Charles V (1500–1558) Spanish king (1516–1556), as Charles I, and Holy Roman emperor (1519–1556), as Charles V. A Hapsburg, he was one of the most powerful European kings, ruling over a vast inherited empire that included much of Europe and all of Spain's New World possessions. Charles's reign was marked by involvement in the Italian Wars (1494–1559) against France and by attempts to stop Luther and the Protestant Reformation. Charles abdicated in 1556 in Spain to his son Philip II and in the Holy Roman Empire to Ferdinand I.

Charles VI (Charles the Well-Beloved) (Charles the Mad) (1368–1422) French king (1380–1422). He suffered fits of insanity and could not rule by himself. His reign was marked by war between the Armagnacs and Burgundians, the English invasion of France in 1420, and the Treaty of Troyes in 1420.

Charles VI (1685–1740) Austrian Holy Roman emperor (1711–1740), and last of the direct Hapsburg line. A pretender to the Spanish throne, he precipitated the War of Spanish Succession (1700–1714). His accession as emperor in 1711 soon ended this conflict, though he again warred against Spain as a member of the Quadruple Alliance (1718–1720). In wars with the Ottoman Empire (1716–1718, 1736–1739), he won and then lost territory in Hungary and Serbia. He lost the War of Polish Succession (1733–1735). His attempt to ensure succession of his daughter Maria Theresa to Hapsburg domains (by the Pragmatic Sanction of 1713) led to the War of Austrian Succession (1740–1748).

Charles VII (Charles the Well-Served) (1403–1461) French king (1422–1461). From the time of the Siege of Orleans in 1429 to the Battle of Castillon in 1453, he gradually forced the English out of France and thus finally ended the Hundred Years' War (1337–1453). He also issued the Pragmatic Sanction in 1438.

Charles VII (Charles Albert) (1697–1745) Holy Roman emperor (1742–1745). On the death of Charles VI, he became embroiled in the War of Austrian Succession (1740–1748) and died before peace was restored.

Charles VIII (1470–1498) French king (1483–1498). He initiated the Italian Wars (1494–1559) with an abortive invasion of Italy, in which he hoped to conquer the kingdom of Naples.

Charles IX (1550–1574) French king (1560–1574). The Wars of Religion began during his reign. Under pressure from his mother, Catherine de Medici, he ordered the massacre of St. Bartholomew's Day in 1572, in which thousands of Huguenots were killed.

Charles X (1757–1836) French king (1824–1830). He took part in the counterrevolutionary Wars of the Vendée. As king he vainly tried to reestablish the ancien régime. His last prime minister, de Polignac, provoked the July Revolution of 1830.

Charles Martel (680?–741) Frankish mayor of the palace who united all of the Merovingian kingdoms under his rule. He halted the Muslim advance in Europe at the famed battle of Tours in 732.

Chartists British reform movement in the period 1838–1858, which took its name from the People's Charter. The Chartists, regarded as radical agitators because of their dangerous program, were comprised of workers and some members of the middle-class who demanded six major reforms, universal suffrage, secret ballot, equal voting districts, elimination of property qualifications for members of Parliament, payment of members, and annual elections.

Chaucer, Geoffrey (1340–1400 A.D.) Great medieval writer who is known for the *Canterbury Tales*.

Chernenko, Konstanten Ustinovich (1911–1985) Soviet leader who came to power after the death of Yuri Andropov in 1984 (*see* page 11-8). He was considered the last of the "old guard" Soviet rulers and, after his death, was followed by Mikhail Gorbachev (*see* page 11-45).

Chernobyl accident Worst nuclear accident in history, it occurred about 60 miles from Kiev (Ukraine) in April 1986. Explosions at a nuclear power plant released a huge cloud of radioactive dust and gas. An undetermined number of people died and hundreds of thousands were exposed to varying degrees of radiation as winds spread the dust over Ukraine and Belarus. Traces went as far north as Scandinavia and as far west as France.

Chiang Kai-shek (1887–1975) Chinese general and leader of the nationalists (1928–1948). The chief aide of Sun Yat-Sen in the Revolution of 1911 he became prominent in the Kuomintang party in 1923. After Sun Yat-Sen's death in 1925, Chiang, as head of the military forces, rivaled for power with Wang Ghing-Wei, a leftist who was the

EXHIBIT 11.2
Rulers of China

Imperial Dynasties
Dynasty

2205–1766 B.C.	Hsia
1766–1122 B.C.	Shang
1122–221 B.C.	Chou
221–206 B.C.	Ch'in
206 B.C.–9 A.D.	Han, Earlier
25–220 A.D.	Han, Later
220–264	Wei
265–317	Chin (Western)
317–419	Chin (Eastern)
420–479	Sung (Liu Sung)
479–502	Ch'i (Tsi)
502–557	Liang
557–589	Ch'en (Chen)
589–618	Sui
618–907	T'ang (Tang)
618–626	Emperor Kao-tsu
627–649	Tai-tsung, son of Kao-tsu
650–683	Kao-tsung, son of Tai-tsung
684–704	Wu-hou, consort of Tai-tsung
713–755	Ming-huang
756–762	Su-tsung, son of Ming-huang
763–779	Tai-tsung
750–804	To-tsung

Dynasty

907–1125	Liang
923–936	T'ang
936–946	Chin
947–950	Han
951–960	Chou
960–1127	Sung (all China)
1127–1280	Sung (in South China) (Mongol invasion of China 1127–1280)

Dynasty

1206–1280	Yüan (in North China)

Emperor

1260–1294	Kublai Khan

Dynasty

1280–1368	Yüan (over all China)
1368–1644	Ming

Emperor

1368–1398	Hung-wu
1403–1424	Yung-lo
1426–1435	Hsan-te
1488–1505	Hung-hsi
1522–1566	Chia-ching
1573–1619	Wan-li

Dynasty

1644–1912	Ch'ing or Ta Ch'ing (Manchu)

Rulers of Ch'ing Dynasty
Emperor

1644–1661	Shih-tsu (Shun-chih)
1662–1722	K'ang-hsi, son of Shih-tsu
1723–1735	Yung-cheng, son of K'ang-hsi
1736–1796	Ch'ien-lung, son of Yung-cheng

Emperor

1796–1820	Jen-tsung, Chia-ch'ing, son of Ch'ien-lung
1820–1850	Hsan-tsung, Tao-kuang, son of Jen-tsung, Chia-ch'ing
1851–1861	Wen-tsung, Hsien-feng, son of Hsan-tsung, Tao-kuang
1862–1875	Ki-tsiang, T'ung-chih, son of Wen-tsung, Hsien-feng

Regent

1862–1873	Tsu-hsi, wife of Wen-tsung, Hsien-feng

Emperor

1875–1908	Tsai-tien, Kuang-hs, cousin of Ki-tsiang, T'ung-chih

Regent

1898–1908	Tz'u-hsi

Emperor

1908–1912	P'u-yi, Hsan-t'ung, nephew of Tsai-tien, Kuang-hs (Emperor of Manchukuo in 1934)

Republic

1912	Provisional President Sun Yat-sen
1912–1913	Provisional President Yüan-Shih-k'ai
1913–1916	President Yan-Shih-k'ai
1916–1917	President Li-Yan-hung
1917–1925	Head of Government Sun Yat-sen in Canton
1917–1918	President Feng Kuo-chang
1918–1922	President Hsu Shih-chang
1921–1923	President Li-Yan-hung
1923–1924	Provisional President Ts'ao K'un
1924–1926	President Tuan Ch'i-jui
1927–1931	President (in Nanking) Chiang Kai-shek
1932–1943	President Lin Sen
1939–1945	Prime Minister H. H. Kung (Kung Hsiang-hse)

Taiwan (Formosa)

1949–1975	President Chiang Kai-shek
1975–1978	President Yen Chia-kan
1978–1988	President Chiang Ching-kuo

Chinese People's Republic

1949–1976	Chairman Mao Tse-tung
1949–1976	Prime Minister and Foreign Secretary Chou En-lai
1976	Prime Minister Deng Xiaoping
1959–1966	President Liu Shao-chi
1976–1981	Prime Minister Hua Kuo-feng
1976–1981	Chairman Hua Kuo-feng
1977–1987	Chairman, Communist Party Deng Xiaoping Advisory Commission
1980–	Prime Minister Zhao Ziyang
1981–1987	Secretary-General, Hu Yaobang Communist Party
1987–	Secretary-General, Zhao Ziyang Communist Party

new chairman of the government. In March of 1926 Chiang carried through a coup d'état for leadership of the party. In the summer of 1926 the campaign against the warlords for the reunification of China under Chiang's direction was begun. His quest for power turned out to be a three-way struggle—Chiang versus the Communists and Chiang versus the warlords. By the end of 1928 Chiang had taken the role of leadership, Nanking was declared the new capital of the new China, and most of China had been unified. Chiang continued as the leader of China through World War II during which he fought both the Japanese and the Chinese Communists. After the war, a civil war erupted which saw the victory of the Communists forcing Chiang to flee to Taiwan where he established the Nationalist government.

Ch'in dynasty (221–206 B.C.) The Ch'in is famous for its contribution to China's political unity. The ruler called himself Chin Shih (first) Huang (emperor) Ti (deity of the Shang dynasty), and it was he who was solely responsible for the determined effort to unify and establish a central government over all China. He standardized weights, measures, and the writing system and laid out a network of roads. It is from the word "Ch'in" that China is named. The price paid for unification was heavy. No freedom of thought was allowed, all books were burned except those on agriculture, medicine, and divination, and those who disagreed with the state were killed either by being buried alive or by forced labor on the Great Wall (completed in 204 B.C.).

Chinese civil war War (1945–1949) that culminated a long struggle between Kuomintang (nationalist) Chinese and the Communist Chinese for control of China. The civil war is generally considered to have begun in 1945, soon after the end of World War II. But Communist and Nationalist forces had been fighting in China intermittently since 1927.

Chinese examination system A system of civil service examinations long in use in the Chinese Empire. Candidates were tested in their knowledge of the Confucian classics. The system began around 124 B.C. under Han Emperor Wu Ti (156–87 B.C.), and was expanded in the T'ang and Sung dynasties. The system helped maintain the stability of China for over 2,000 years, and was not abolished until 1905 amid a movement to modernize China.

Chinese Revolution of 1911 Uprising that succeeded in overthrowing the last (Ch'ing, or Manchu) dynasty of Chinese emperors and establishing a Chinese Republic.

Ch'ing dynasty (Manchu) Last dynasty of China, that ruled from 1644–1912. The dynasty was established by the Manchus, a people from Manchuria North of China, under Emperor Ch'ien Lung (1736–1796). The Manchus invaded and conquered China, but did not change its ways. China's imperial government remained essentially the same, although the Manchus set up a dyarchy in which there was one Manchu and one Chinese for every post. They attempted to maintain their dynastic identity and not be absorbed as the Mongols had been by Chinese culture. They forbade intermarriage between Manchu and Chinese, retained Manchuria, as an exclusive preserve for themselves, limited the army to Manchurians, and increased further the absolutism of the emperor. The Chien-Lung period (1736–1795) was the height of Manchu power. China stood in marked contrast to Europe at the time and was certainly its equal if not its superior. It was also a period of great physical extension—the Tarim Basin area, Manchuria Mongolia, Tibet, all were under China's control, and even raids into Nepal were conducted. The Ch'ing strongly opposed foreign trade but were forced in a series of wars in the 19th century to open China and the European powers soon carved China into spheres of influence. Efforts to reform and strengthen China under the Manchus failed and they were overthrown by a rebellion in 1911.

Chivalry Code of moral and ethical conduct that developed during feudal times in Europe in the Middle Ages. Central to the code was the feudal knight, who exhibited the ideal qualities of piety, loyalty to his feudal lord, courtesy and courtly affection for ladies of the court, and valor on the field of battle. Chivalry flourished in the 12th and 13th centuries, especially during the Crusades. It declined as an ideal of conduct by the 15th century when military campaigns were more openly waged for gain than for reasons of honor or religious duty.

Chou dynasty (1125–255 B.C.) This was the longest dynasty in China, and it controlled the area from north of the Yellow River to south of the Yangtze River. It was noted for its political organization, essentially feudalistic, in which local lords and princes received land holdings in return for homage and service to their overlord. In time the local rulers became virtually independent, China experienced political chaos and decentralization resembling European feudalism. By 720 B.C. the reign of the Chou was weak, and power was distributed among principalities similar to feudal states. But there was more uniformity of culture than there was in Europe. This was also the outstanding creative period of Chinese thought, as it was in many areas of the world; it corresponds in time with the height of Greek culture, the Hebrew prophets, and the flowering of Buddhism in India.

Chou En-lai (1898–1976) Chinese Communist leader, premier (1949–1976) and foreign minister (1949–1976). A founder of the Chinese Communist party, he served (1924–1927) with other Communists in the Kuomintang's nationalist revolution. During the subsequent civil war between 1927 and 1949 in which the Kuomintang turned against the Communists, he participated in the Long March. A leading Communist official thereafter, he helped bring the Communists to power in 1949. Later, as foreign minister, he headed delegations to the Geneva and Bandung conferences. He is said to have exercised a moderating influence during the Cultural Revolution and to have been responsible for the Sino-American rapprochement in the 1970s.

Christianity General term used to describe the religion that arose in Palestine in the 1st century A.D. from the life and teachings of Jesus Christ and that has spread to nearly every part of the world. Historically, it has been the predominant religion in the West for many centuries and had an enormous influence on the development of Western civilization, especially in literature, art, architecture, and music. Christianity is based on the New Testament, which records the acts and teachings of Jesus, and the Old Testament is regarded as sacred and authoritative Scripture. Christian doctrine was further refined by a series of "creeds" promulgated in the course of early church history. Together these beliefs attempted to reflect Jesus Christ's own revelations about God and the salvation of humankind. Apostles chosen by Jesus constituted the early leadership of the church, or "assembly" of his followers. The church perpetuated the teachings of Jesus, claimed the authority to interpret them authentically, and administered the sacraments, believed to have been established by Jesus for the spiritual benefit of the faithful. However, disagreements among Christians about Jesus' teachings occurred as early as New Testament times. Major doctrinal crises usually resulted in "little churches" that split off from the main church and maintained "heresies," such as arianism, monophysitism, nestorianism, donatism, and so on. These were condemned by the main tradition, and most of the dissident Eastern and African churches had split from the church by the end of the Council of Chalcedon in 451 A.D. Bitter disputes over such issues as Iconoclasm caused the final split in 1054 between the Roman Catholic and eastern Orthodox churches. Some centuries later, Christianity was again divided by the Protestant Reformation, which followed Luther's rebellion in 1517 against the authority of the church. Protestantism arose from this split and became, with the Roman Catholic church, one of the three main branches of Christianity.

Winston S. Churchill.

Churchill, Sir Winston Leonard Spencer (1874–1965)　British statesman, author, and prime minister (1940–1945, 1951–1955). He is regarded as one of the outstanding figures of the 20th century for his brilliant leadership of Britain during World War II. A soldier and well-known journalist by the time he was elected to Parliament in 1900, he was a Conservative party member throughout most of his ca-

reer. He served in a variety of government posts, including first lord of the admiralty (1911–1915), colonial secretary (1921–1922), and chancellor of the exchequer (1924–1929). Churchill recognized and spoke out against the threat of Nazi Germany and was next appointed to the admiralty in 1939. He became prime minister in 1940 when Chamberlain's government was ousted for its handling of the war with Germany. During the war years, he rallied the British to the war effort, lobbied for help from the United States, and helped write the famous Atlantic Charter of 1941. Churchill was out of power (1945–1951), though he spoke vigorously against the menace of the U.S.S.R. (coining the phrase "iron curtain"). Prime minister again in 1951, he retired in 1955 but continued as a member of Parliament until 1964.

Cicero (106–43 B.C.)　Roman orator, politician, and philosopher who gave his name to the first great period of Latin literature. His *Orations* reveal the cross-currents of Roman politics and are a useful source of material for historians. *See also* Philosophy section, page 19-5.

Cistercians　Order of Roman Catholic monks founded in 1098 in France by Saint Robert. An outgrowth of the Benedictine order, the Cistercians were reformers. They rebelled against the laxity that had overtaken the Benedictine order by returning to the strict, ascetic life of the first Benedictines. Saint Bernard of Clairvaux influenced the development of the order, being largely responsible for its rapid spread during the 12th century. By the 14th century, however, it weakened and declined.

City-state (Greek polis)　A city and surrounding lands governed as an autonomous state by its citizens. Though city-states appeared in other civilizations, they were especially important in the history of ancient Greece. Such city-states as Athens, Sparta, and Thebes came to dominate whole regions of Greece.

Clairvaux, Saint Bernard of (1090–1153) French cleric, and one of the most prominent figures in the Roman Catholic church in his day. A Cistercian monk, he founded the monastery at Clairvaux in 1115 and spent the rest of his life as its abbot. He gained great influence in the church and advised popes and kings.

Claudius (10 B.C.–54 A.D.)　Roman emperor who as the nephew of Emperor Tiberius was placed on the throne by soldiers after the murder of Emperor Caligula. During his reign, the empire was consolidated and renewed. He added Britain to the empire and is said to have been poisoned by his fourth wife, Agrippina.

Cleisthenes (ca. 510 B.C.)　An Athenian ruler and political reformer who made a significant contribution to democracy by replacing family tribal political divisions with 10 new electoral districts from each of which 50 members were chosen by lot annually to constitute the Council of 500, or Boule, which handled the long-range problems of foreign policy, finance, and war. A Board of Strategoi, or Generals, was elected annually, one by each of the 10 tribes. This system assured the political equality of all citizens.

Clemenceau, Georges (1841–1929)　French premier (1906–1909) who was important in helping to win the Allied victory in World War I. He opposed President Wilson at the Versailles Peace Conference after the war believing that the treaty was too lenient toward Germany.

Clement V (1264–1314) French archbishop whose election as pope was arranged by the French king Philip IV. He established the papal residence at Avignon in France beginning the so-called Babylonian Captivity. He was dominated by Philip IV and did his bidding.

Clement VII (1478–1534) A member of the Medici family, he was pope from 1523–1534. He ignored the problems the Reformation posed for the church and struggled with Henry VIII of England refusing to grant him a divorce from his first wife Catherine of Aragon.

Cleopatra (69 B.C.) Queen of Egypt who led a revolt against her younger brother that was supported by Julius Caesar and won her the kingdom. After Caesar's death she married Marc Antony and their forces threatened the Roman Empire. Octavian who later became Augustus defeated their forces at Actium in 31 B.C., after which she and Antony committed suicide.

Clermont, council of Church council held in 1095 at Clermont, France in which Pope Urban II preached the First Crusade. The Byzantine Empire was at that time being reduced by Muslim conquests and Emperor Alexis I requested aid from the pope. At the council, Urban II urged French knights to take up the cause, citing Muslim persecutions, the Muslim capture of the Holy Land, and the possible material gain of such a venture.

Clive, Robert (1725–1774) British soldier and statesman who was the military leader of the East India Company in India. His victories against the French opened India to the influence and later the control of Great Britain. He gained control of Bengal where he served as governor and from this power base began to extend British control over other parts of India including Behar, Orissa, and Calcutta.

Clovis (466–511) Frankish king and founder of the Merovingian dynasty he conquered most of Gaul (France) and southwestern Germany. It was during his reign (481–511 A.D.) that unification of the Frankish kingdom was achieved partly through military and political skill but also because his conversion to Christianity won him the support of the Roman Catholic church. Under succeeding Carolingian kings, who followed the Merovingians, the kingdom was expanded into an empire that by 800 A.D. included many former Roman territories.

Code of Hammurabi A collection of 282 laws during the reign of Hammurabi, king of Babylonia. The code controlled aspects of life in Babylon such as dealing with agriculture, commerce, wages, hours, working conditions, property rights, marriage, and so forth. The laws regarding justice involved "an eye for an eye" concept of punishment.

Colbert, Jean Baptiste (1619–1683) French financial minister under Louis XIV and his chief adviser after 1661. He favored the policy of mercantilism, protected industries with subsidies and tariffs, regulated prices, built a modern road and canal network, developed the navy, and encouraged colonization.

Cold War State of tension between two nations that does not involve actual warfare. It came to be used to describe the tension that developed after World War II between the world powers—the United States and the former Soviet Union. It led to the formation of opposing alliance systems. The Cold War ended in 1989, as the U.S.S.R. lost control of Eastern Europe (*see* **East European Revolution**) and the Communist party lost control of the former Soviet Union in December 1991.

Columbus, Christopher (1451?–1506) A Genovese who is famed as the discoverer of America. His studies of geography led him to believe that the East could be reached by sailing westward. Rebuffed by Genoa and Venice, he finally gained royal support from the Spanish rulers in 1492 and sailed from Spain in three ships, Santa María, Pinta, and Nina. He landed on San Salvador in 1492. His reception in Spain was enthusiastic. On a second expedition in 1493 his discoveries included Puerto Rico, the Virgin Islands, and Jamaica. During a third voyage in 1498, he discovered the mouth of the Orinoco in Venezuela. His administration of a colony in Haiti resulted in his return to Spain in chains. A fourth expedition in 1502 reached the coast of Honduras but was forced back by hardships.

Christopher Columbus, the first mariner to believe that the East Indies could be reached by sailing westward across the Atlantic. He did not know the Americas stood in the way.

Comecon Council for Mutual Economic Assistance, an organization established by the Soviet Union in 1949 to improve trade between the U.S.S.R. and its European satellite states.

Cominform Communist Information Bureau established in 1947 to coordinate Communist party activities throughout Europe. It was a Europe-wide espionage, foreign policy, and economic coordination center until it was dissolved in 1956.

Comintern The Communist International established by Lenin in 1919 to promote revolutionary Marxism. Although its aim was world revolution it was the means by which the U.S.S.R. maintained control over the international Communist movement.

Commercial Revolution   Term used to refer to the changes in European economic life in the period between 1500 and 1750. During the 16th and 17th centuries European nations reaped the rewards of the age of exploration. Trading and colonization increased, and capitalism expanded until it encompassed all economic life. This period, which was little more than the extension of earlier developments but on a vaster scale, is usually referred to as the Commercial Revolution. Trade and commerce increased as new sources of raw materials and new markets opened. The growth of capitalism, the accumulation of funds to invest in large trading enterprises, brought a demand for money to keep up with growing business. Gold and silver poured into Europe from the New World, encouraged business and increased prices.

Committee of Public Safety   The revolutionary or emergency government of France established by Robespierre after he suspended the Constitution during the French Revolution. It was set up by the Jacobins who were radicals. Composed of about 12 members, this group had almost unlimited powers.

Common law   Developed in England and unlike Roman law, it is a body of law that is not codified, or explicitly written down. Decisions of royal justices were collected in Year Books as the basis or precedents for future decisions on similar issues, and thus became "common" to all parts of England, based not upon statutes but upon custom.

Common Market: European Economic Community   *See* page 11-38.

Communard   Term used to refer to members of the short-lived Paris commune established in March of 1871. It was formed after an uprising by socialists and radical republicans opposed to peace with Germany and the conservative new Third Republic. In May government troops suppressed the commune killing 25,000 communards in the fighting.

Communism   Political philosophy based upon the principle of collective ownership of both property and means of production. Communists view history from the perspective of class struggle and seek to establish a classless society, in its most ideal form a "dictatorship of the proletariat." The idea of a communal society, a fundamental element of Communist thought, dates back to the ancient Greeks and was advanced by Plato in his philosophical work *The Republic*. Thomas More in his famous work *Utopia* (1516) promoted the idea of a communal society. The Industrial Revolution and the severe economic hardships suffered by workers gave rise to socialism in the late 18th and early 19th century. Modern communism then emerged from the Socialist movement (*see* **Socialism**), first as a radical wing of socialism and finally in the early 1900s as a separate and distinct ideology of revolution and collective ownership. Modern communism is based on the writings of Karl Marx and Friedrich Engels in the *Communist Manifesto*. The fundamental rivalry between Communist and capitalist societies has been a factor in world history since the creation of the first Communist state in the U.S.S.R., in 1917. Communism collapsed as the political ideology of most Eastern European nations (*see* page 11-34) in 1989 and was abandoned even by the former Soviet Union in 1991. Most party remnants became part of a regular multiparty system. The former Soviet Union became known as the Commonwealth of Independent States in 1991.

Concert of Europe   Agreement that grew out of the Quadruple Alliance in which Russia, Austria, Prussia, Great Britain, and France agreed to act together to preserve peace in Europe and to maintain the territorial settlement of the Congress of Vienna. It was a form of international government by concert, or agreement, and crises were to be settled by conferences.

Concordat of Worms   Agreement concluded in 1122 between Henry V, emperor of the Holy Roman Empire and the pope by which the problem of lay investiture was resolved. The emperor agreed to permit the church to elect church officials and to invest them with the spiritual church robes and emblems; the emperor must be present at the ceremonies, and he had the right to give to the new church officials their secular powers and fiefs, and to receive their homage as their temporal overlord. This division of authority was clearly not the final answer to the problem, which was not to be resolved so simply.

Confucianism   Chinese philosophy based on the teachings of Confucius (King Fu-tzu 551–479 B.C.). The main purpose of Confucius' philosophy and teachings was to bring social order into an era of political chaos and confusion and to return to the days of the founders of the Chou dynasty. The code became the most successful of all systems of conservatism, lasting 2,000 years as the chief ideology of the world's largest country. Confucius believed that only through harmonious relations among individuals could true harmony between humans and nature be reached. His teaching is less a religion and more a code of behavior or morals, based essentially upon the relationships of individuals. Confucius did not formulate theories about the nature of the universe, the after-life, or immortality. He was concerned with the codes of behavior by which people could live together in peace. The universe was governed by laws that regulated the stars and the seasons and thus maintained a balance. It was the duty of individuals to act similarly, because order would prevail if all people, rulers and ruled, respected the laws, set good examples for each other, and tried to live together in harmony. Each person was to assume a specific place in society, with specific duties and modes of conduct. This was accomplished by a system of superiors and inferiors. The Five Relationships of superiors over inferiors were prince over subject, father over son, husband over wife, elder brother over younger brother, and friend over friend. The classes in society were ordered on the Confucian idea of a hierarchy of worth: first, scholars; second, farmers; third, artisans; fourth, merchants; fifth, slaves. Confucianism placed great emphasis on an intellectual and landed elite, and depreciated the value of anyone in commerce or manufacturing.

Congress of Berlin   Meeting of European powers called in 1878 to renegotiate the Treaty of San Stefano and deal with British and Austro-Hungarian dissatisfaction with terms forced on the Ottoman Empire by Russia after the Russo-Turkish War (1877–1878). Headed by Otto von Bismarck, the meeting resulted in the Treaty of Berlin which cost Russia much of what it had gained in the earlier treaty. Austria-Hungary was to occupy Bosnia and Herzegovina; Britain was to occupy Cyprus; and Montenegro, Serbia, and Romania were recognized as independent. An autonomous Bulgaria (much smaller than that sought by Russia) was created under Ottoman sovereignty. Russia gained control over Ottoman territories in Asia and the Balkans.

Congress of Vienna Meeting held in 1815 after the defeat of Napoleon redrew the map of Europe and attempted to return Europe to the period before the French Revolution by restoring conservative governments, establishing a balance of power, and a concert of Europe. The leaders of the Congress were Prince Metternich, chancellor of Austria, Lord Castlereagh, foreign secretary of Great Britain, Czar Alexander I of Russia, King Frederick William III of Prussia, and Talleyrand, the representative of the losing side, France. The doctrine of legitimacy (or that monarchs who were legitimately entitled to their thrones be restored) advanced by Talleyrand was followed. France was restricted to its boundaries of 1792 and the Bourbons were restored in the person of Louis XVIII. France was now accepted as a member in good standing of the European nations but with barriers against possible future expansion: the kingdom of the Netherlands (Belgium and Holland), the kingdom of Prussia in the Rhineland, the kingdom of Sardinia in the South, and the North Italian States under the jurisdiction of Austria. Austria was restored, with the exception of its former possession of the Austrian Netherlands (Belgium), but was compensated with several Italian states and duchies—the Tyrol, the Illyrian provinces, Milan, Parma, Modena, Tuscany. The Germanic states were reduced to a loose confederation of 38 states under the presidency of Austria. Russia received much of Poland as an integral part of its territory, so that Poland, which had disappeared by 1795 under the successive seizures by Austria, Prussia, and Russia, now reappeared, even if only as a province of Russia. Great Britain retained the useful colonial outposts it had won during the war: Malta, Tobago in the West Indies, Cape Colony in Africa, Honduras in Central America, and Guiana in South America. As a further guarantee for future peace, the four nations of Great Britain, Russia, Austria, and Prussia formed the Quadruple Alliance, a political alliance designed to prevent another major war. In 1818 France was also admitted. On the surface, the peace of Europe was restored and the map of Europe remained unchanged for 35 years, and no major war occurred. But underneath this apparent calm the growing demand of the people of Europe for their own national states and for liberal governments caused several revolutions.

Congress party *See* **Indian National Congress.**

Concentration camps *See* **Auschwitz.**

Conservatism Belief in preserving the stability of the existing order. Conservatives oppose broad reforms (though not necessarily all reform) that may cause upheavals of the social or political system and thus often oppose liberalism. Conservatism of the 19th century, a reaction against the French Revolution (1789–1799), was articulated in the works of Edmund Burke and others. It was characterized by support for rule by the king and the propertied class and opposed liberal republicanism of the rising bourgeoisie. In modern times, conservatism has come to favor such things as freedom from the regulation of business and opposes extension of the welfare state.

Conservative party Major British political party formed in 1832, a coalition of middle-class interests. Though it represents a conservative viewpoint, the party has traditionally favored moderate social and political reforms. The successor to the Tory party, it was formed after passage of the Reform Bill of 1832.

Constantine Roman emperor who ruled the western half of the empire starting in 312 and became sole emperor of a united empire in 324 A.D. He named the capital of the empire Byzantium, which was later renamed Constantinople, and issued the Edict of Milan in 313 A.D., which granted toleration for Christians in the empire.

Consulate French government (1799–1804) established after the overthrow of the Directory in the coup d'état of 18 Brumaire. Under the Consulate, three consuls—one of whom was Napoleon—ruled France, until Napoleon's assumption of the title "emperor" in 1804.

Containment Policy adopted by the United States in 1947 in response to Russian expansionism in the period after World War II. The aim of this policy was to confine, or contain, Communist influence to its existing territorial limits.

Continental system Attempt by Napoleon Bonaparte to exclude British trade from Europe between 1806 and 1813 in the hope of undermining British trade and its economy and thereby weakening Britain. British naval superiority enabled it to break the system and it eventually collapsed.

Copernicus, Nicolaus (1474–1543) Polish astronomer, considered the founder of modern astronomy. His Copernican theory of a heliocentric universe in which the earth turns on its own axis and revolves around the sun met with opposition because it contradicted the long-accepted Ptolemaic theory that the earth was the center of the universe.

Cordeliers Political club formed in 1790 during the French Revolution. Officially known as the Society of the Friends of the Rights of Man and of the Citizen, it was founded to denounce abuses of power. It soon became a formidable political power under the leadership of Danton and others. The Cordeliers were involved in the deposing of King Louis XVI, and later, under the more radical influence of Hébert and Marat, brought down (1792 and 1793) the moderate Girondists.

Coronado, Francisco Vásquez de (1510–1544) Spanish explorer who sought to find the fabled Seven Cities of Gold in America. His expedition opened up the southwest.

Cortés, Hernando (1485–1547) Spanish conquistador who with an expedition of 400 men between 1519 and 1521 defeated the Aztecs and brought Mexico into the Spanish empire.

Council of Constance   Council of the Catholic church held between 1414 and 1418 to end the Great Schism that had produced three rival popes.

Counter-Reformation   Catholic response in the 1500s to the Protestant Reformation. With much of northern Europe becoming Protestant, the Catholic church set out to reform its own internal abuses and to wage an active fight on behalf of its basic faith. The Catholics refer to this as the Catholic Reformation; the Protestants call it the Counter-Reformation. From Spain came the essential and necessary missionary spirit. Ignatius Loyola (1491–1556) a soldier, became a militant crusader for the Catholic church and founded the Society of Jesus, a new monastic order that participated actively in the world. They were the active missionaries of the Counter-Reformation, prepared to intrigue and to use force whenever necessary. The Holy Office, or Inquisition, was the chief agent of the church for the repression of heresy. Holding secret trials and turning condemned heretics over to the secular government to be burned, it maintained a brutal reign of terror and successfully stamped out all heresy in Italy and Spain. It had little success north of the Alps, and by the end of the 16th century both it and the Counter-Reformation had spent their force.

Coup d'état   A sudden change of government, usually started by a group within the existing government. Not a revolution, in which a great part of a nation may be engaged. Examples: Suharto in Indonesia, restricting Sukarno's power; the ousting of Nkrumah from Ghana.

Crassus, Marcus Licinius (d. 53 B.C.)   Roman who served as consul with Pompey in 70 B.C. later he joined the First Triumvirate with Julius Caesar and Pompey. He ruled the province of Syria for the empire and undertook a campaign against the Carthians in which he was defeated at Carrbae in 53 B.C.

Crecy, battle of   At this site in 1346, Edward III of England defeated Philip VI of France in an important battle of the Hundred Years' War. It was the first time that English footsoldiers using longbows were employed in warfare and they decimated the French knights on horseback.

Crimean War   In 1853 Nicholas I sent the Russian army to invade the Turkish provinces of Moldavia and Wallachia. War between Russia and Turkey ensued, and in 1854 France and Britain entered on Turkey's side. The Crimean War was disastrous for all concerned, and incompetence, intrigue, lack of supplies, and inferior equipment led to a Russian defeat. In 1856 Alexander II asked for peace.

Cro-Magnon people   So named after the caves in France where their remains were first discovered. They either replaced or dominated and absorbed the earlier Neanderthal people. They were clearly of the *Homo sapiens* type, the first of modern humans, the inventor of more tools, flintheaded weapons such as the harpoon and spear, and probably the bow and arrow. Cro-Magnon people discovered how to make fire and, in addition, showed considerable skill in portraying animals on cave walls. They used bones, antlers, and ivory for specialized tools, invented the use of the awl and thread, and apparently gave some attention to burial ceremonies. They grew no food,

domesticated no animals, and lived as nomadic food gatherers.

Cromwell, Oliver (1599–1658)   Leader of the Puritans in Parliament who opposed King Charles I and his supporters known as Royalists or Cavaliers. They wanted the powers of the king to be curbed and their action led to civil war and revolution in England. Cromwell organized his forces into an army that the Cavaliers could not match and after two defeats in battle, Charles I surrendered in 1646. Cromwell's army controlled Parliament, which became known as the Rump Parliament. The Rump Parliament abolished both the monarchy and the House of Lords, proclaimed England a Commonwealth, and appointed a special court to try Charles I for treason. He was condemned and beheaded early in 1649. Cromwell took over the reins of power and became essentially a military dictator. He was given the title of Lord Protector, which he held from 1653 until 1658. This period of the Commonwealth is often called the Protectorate and there was almost as much friction between him and Parliament as there had been between the Stuart kings and Parliament. The old resentment of central power reappeared and Cromwell was forced to dissolve Parliament. He ruled alone during most of the Commonwealth period. *See* **English Civil War**; **Protectorate**.

Cromwell, Richard (1626–1712)   Son of Oliver Cromwell, he succeeded him as Lord Protector after his death in 1658. Unable to win the support of the army and Parliament, the Commonwealth came to an end in 1660 when Parliament invited Charles II, the son of Charles I, to rule.

Crusaders celebrate their capture of Jerusalem from the Muslims in 1099.

Crusades   The military campaigns of feudal Christendom against the Islamic peoples who held the Holy Land of Palestine between 1096 and 1254. With the rise of Islam came the occupation of the Holy Land by the Arabs. Generally, they did not interfere with pilgrimages to the Holy Land, but in the 11th century the Seljuk Turks occupied Asia Minor and seriously threatened the Byzantine Empire. Called upon by the Byzantine emperor to give assistance, Pope Urban II in 1095 called for a holy crusade against the infidel, and in 1096 the

First Crusade of the total eight was launched. Religious enthusiasm, the blessing of the church, opportunity for obtaining landed estates, and the desire of the church to reduce local fighting between groups of barons, all stimulated the crusading movement. The first expedition of enthusiastic but ill-trained and poorly led people was a failure. But the official First Crusade in 1096 under trained leaders resulted in the capture of Jerusalem and Asia Minor, and the establishment of the Christian kingdom of Jerusalem, a strip of land roughly 500 miles long and 50 miles wide, from the borders of Egypt to the Euphrates River. This kingdom of Jerusalem, which was divided into the kingdom itself and three great fiefs called Antioch, Tripoli, and Edessa, lasted for nearly 100 years. Two centuries of Crusades did not achieve the basic purpose of retrieving the Holy Land from the infidels, although secondary influences were significant. Spain finally drove the Muslims out of the peninsula, and Christians in Eastern Europe were able to hold back subsequent attempted Muslim invasions. The Crusades had many lasting effects on Europe, chief of which was broadening people's outlook, as they came into contact with other lands and other customs and also the weakening of feudalism. The Crusades also accelerated trade and brought the Europeans into contact with the philosophy, science, and culture of the Islamic world.

Cultural Revolution   Name given to the period between 1965 and 1968 when Mao Tse-tung sought to reassert Maoist doctrine, renew the revolutionary spirit, and purge China of "The Four Olds"–old thought, old culture, old customs, and old habits. Led by the Red Guard, millions of young followers of Mao organized in military-style units, the Cultural Revolution caused great upheaval and chaos in China. Because of its severe disruption to the Chinese economy and life it was halted in 1968.

Cuneiform   Wedge-shaped writing developed in the lower Tigris-Euphrates Valley probably by the Sumerians. It was written with a stylus on a piece of clay that was later baked to make a permanent record. It was used by the people of all the Sumerian empires until the Persians conquered the region.

Curie, Pierre (1859–1906) and **Curie, Marie Sklodowska** (1867–1934)   French scientists and codiscoverers of radium and polonium. After A. Becquerel discovered radioactivity, Marie began her own investigations. She was joined by Pierre in 1898, and in that year they jointly isolated radium and polonium. With Becquerel they were awarded the 1903 Nobel Prize in Physics. Following Pierre's death, Marie continued work on radium and received the 1911 Nobel Prize in Chemistry.

Curzon, Lord (1859–1925)   British statesman who as governor-general of India (1899–1905) put through many useful reforms. Establishing rural banks, reorganizing agriculture, strictly enforcing measures against British soldiers who abused Indians, and encouraging the study of Indian history were all to his credit. However, his lack of understanding of Indian attitudes caused many of his reforms to be resented. Later, he served as Britain's foreign secretary, presiding at the Lausanne Conference (1922 and 1923) and paving the way for the Dawes Plan.

Cyril (d. 869)   Greek Christian missionary from the Byzantine Empire who with his brother Methodius, also a missionary, sought to convert the Slavs to Christianity in the 800s. Since the Slavs had no written language, Cyril created a modified Greek alphabet that became known as the Cyrillic alphabet.

Cyrus the Great (d. 529 B.C.)   Persian king (550–529 B.C.) who began the Persian conquests in Mesopotamia, or the Middle East, and created the first modern empire in history. He conquered the Medes, Lydians, and Chaldeans. This empire extended from the Indus to the Mediterranean and from the Caucasus to the Indian Ocean.

D

Da Gama, Vasco (1469–1524)   Portuguese navigator who made the first sea voyage to India and returned home with a cargo of spices. His voyage made it possible for Portugal to dominate the spice trade and break the Venetian monopoly of trade with the East.

Da Vinci, Leonardo (1452–1519)   Italian painter, sculptor, architect, and inventor who is considered the great example of Renaissance genius. *See also* Art section, page 1-21.

Daimyo   Title of the great feudal lords in Japan who owned vast estates. By the 16th century, they controlled most of Japan and although they owed allegiance to emperor and shogun, the daimyo were virtually independent sovereigns in their territories. They were brought under the power of the shogunate in 1603 and they were forced to turn their lands over to the emperor by the Meiji government in 1869.

Daladier, Edouard (1884–1970)   French politician who served as premier three times—1933, 1934, and 1938–1940. He signed the Munich Pact, which gave the Sudetenland of Czechoslovakia to Nazi Germany.

Dalai Lama   Spiritual leader of the people of Tibet. Fled to exile in India in 1959 when Chinese Communists invaded and occupied Tibet. He won the 1990 Nobel Prize for Peace.

Danelaw   In 9th- and 10th-century England, it meant the area in northeastern England that the Vikings, called Danes by English, were forced to remain after the Saxon armies, under the English king Alfred the Great, defeated them. It was in this area that Danish law prevailed.

Dante Alighieri (1265–1321)   Italian poet whose work *The Divine Comedy* is considered the highest literary expression of medieval thought. He broke with tradition by writing in the vernacular Italian rather than in Latin and by stressing happiness on earth.

Danton, Georges Jacques (1759–1794)   A leader of the French Revolution who championed the extreme left in the National Assembly and played an important role in overthrowing the monarchy in 1792. As head of the provisional government and minister of justice he set up the Revolutionary Tribunal and dominated the first Committee Of Public Safety in 1793. He came into conflict with Robespierre the leader of the extremists, lost his influence, and in 1794 was arrested and sent to the guillotine.

Darius I (the Great) (549–486 B.C.) Persian king (521–486 B.C.) A member of the Achaemenid dynasty, he proved to be a great ruler. He extended the Persian Empire into northern India and Europe, and in battle against the Scythians he invaded Macedonia and Thrace in 515 B.C. He was, however, unsuccessful in his efforts against the Greek city-states during the Persian Wars. Noted as a great builder and administrator, he created an effective administrative organization based on a system of satrapies.

Darius II (Darius Nothus) (d. 404 B.C.) Persian king (423–404 B.C.) who spent much time suppressing revolts, he formed an alliance with Sparta against Athens in 412 B.C., and lost Egypt in 410 B.C.

Darius III (Condomannus, Darius) (d. 330 B.C.) Last king of Persia's Achaemenid dynasty (336–330 B.C.). He was defeated by Alexander the Great at Granicus in 334, Issus in 333, and Gaugamela in 331.

Darwin, Charles (1809–1882) British naturalist whose scientific investigations led him to formulate the theory of evolution that he set forth in *On The Origin of Species*. Darwin's theory concluded the following: humans were descended from a lowly organism; evolution involves "natural selection," that is in the struggle to survive in nature only the fittest survive; and this "fitness" will be handed down to those capable of surviving. This theory of the survival of the fittest was carried over by others into general human affairs and became known as "Social Darwinism" or the Darwinian theory applied to society.

David (d. 973 B.C.) Second king of Israel (1013–973 B.C.), one of the great figures in the Old Testament. A heroic figure for both Christians and Jews, David is the subject of such famous biblical narratives as the David and Goliath story. Many of the psalms are also attributed to him. David succeeded Saul as king of the Hebrews, after first serving and then warring against him. As king, David forged the confederation of Hebrew tribes into a unified kingdom and fixed his capital at Jerusalem.

Dawes Plan Plan presented by American banker Charles G. Dawes to the Allied Reparation Committee in April 1924 that provided for a reduction in German reparations payments and stabilization of German finances. It enabled Germany to meet the Versailles Treaty obligation between 1924 and 1929.

D-Day Code name for the first day of Operation Overlord in World War II when Allied forces landed on the French coast at Normandy on June 6, 1944 in the largest seaborne invasion in history. Under the command of Dwight Eisenhower, 120,000 Allied assault-forces crossed the English Channel and landed on five beaches on the coast of Normandy where they secured beachheads and began the invasion of Nazi-occupied France.

Dead Sea Scrolls Ancient scrolls (ca. 100 A.D.) discovered in 1947 in caves near the northwestern shore of the Dead Sea. They have been a source of controversy and are reputed to contain material about the beginnings of the Christian religion.

Decembrist Revolt Conspiracy of military officers in St. Petersburg who attempted to overthrow the tsarist government in December 1825 and to establish a more representative government. Nicholas I severely punished the plotters and the revolt influenced his reign which proved to be especially repressive.

Declaration of the Rights of Man French document drafted by Sieyes in 1789 and instituted by the National Assembly that was a statement of democratic principles and rights, containing the basic ideas of John Locke, Rousseau, and many of the principles stated in the U.S. Declaration of Independence and Bill of Rights. All officials were responsible to the people, who were to enjoy proper legal trials, the rights of liberty and property, and participation in lawmaking. It asserted the equality of all people, the sovereignty of the people, and the inalienable rights of the individual to "liberty, peace, and security."

de Gaulle, Charles (1890–1970) French general and politician who, when France fell to German invasion in June 1940, fled to England with other French citizens and organized the Free French Movement. In London, de Gaulle established the Free French National Committee to serve as a government-in-exile with himself as head. In 1944, when Allied forces were approaching Paris, de Gaulle led his troops into Paris as its liberator and as head of the Free French, took over the government, named a cabinet, and governed by executive decree. In 1946 de Gaulle, who disliked working with the three political parties, resigned and retired to his country home. Between 1945 and 1948 French politics were extremely unstable, and the Communists were often the largest single party. In May 1958, however, the French army leaders seized power in Algeria and demanded the return of de Gaulle. In June de Gaulle took over the government on his own conditions. In September a new constitution was ratified that gave dominant power to the president, who would be elected for a 7-year term, could dissolve Parliament, and, in emergency, could assume the powers of a dictator. The Fifth Republic was proclaimed. De Gaulle became the national "arbiter" of France, guiding its course to unify the nation and bring France to its natural destiny of "greatness" by a more independent foreign policy and by developing its nuclear capacity. In 1965 the French people elected de Gaulle to a second 7-year term as president. They were fearful that without a strong leader France might again experience political chaos. In 1969 de Gaulle demanded a referendum to support his demand for a new constitution that would reduce the power of the Senate. French voters rejected his proposal and he immediately resigned and went into seclusion until his death in November 1970.

De Klerk, Fredrik Willem (b. 1936) Leader of the Union of South Africa since 1989. He has worked with the blacks in South Africa to create a more democratic government and has eliminated apartheid as a part of the reform process. *See* **Apartheid**.

Delhi Sultanate First Muslim empire in India that ruled between 1206 and 1526. It was founded by Muhammed of Ghor, an Afghan general, who took Delhi in 1192 and whose Muslim armies conquered much of northern India. At his death, Aybeh, or Qutb ud-Din, one of his generals set up a sultanate at Delhi. It was known as the "slave dynasty" because he and some of his successors were former military slaves and ruled until 1290. It was succeeded by the Khalji dynasty, which ruled until 1320, brought almost the entire subcontinent under the Delhi sultanate's sway, and steadily repulsed the Mongols. Revolts and a loss of territory began in the Tughluq dynasty (1325–1398). With the capture of Delhi by Tamerlane in 1398, the sultanate disintegrated. Only local rulers remained until the establishment of the Mogul Empire in the 16th century.

Delian League   A confederation of Greek city-states formed in 477 B.C. as a defensive measure against the possibility of future Persian attacks. Ships and money were contributed by the member states. The League became the foundation of the Athenian Empire, for in 454 B.C. the treasury was moved from Delos to Athens. Athens used force to prevent secession from the League (in 482 B.C. Lesbos attempted to revolt and as punishment its people were sold into slavery), and spent the tribute on the beautification of the Athenian state.

Democracy   Form of government based on rule by the people, though that rule may be exercised in various ways. The classic example of early democracy is that of the ancient Greek city-state Athens. It was a direct democracy, in which all citizens participated in government by their vote. That system worked because the total number of citizens was small and a large part of the populace (slaves and women) was denied citizenship. Athenian democracy, and the democratic assemblies of the early Roman republic, represented short-lived experiments in government by the people. Both gave way to imperial forms of government and it was not until the 18th and 19th centuries that the democratic form of government began to flourish. The gradual ascendancy of parliamentary government in Britain, the American Revolution, and the French Revolution were important in its implementation and rapid spread during the 18th–20th centuries. Modern democracy is generally a representative democracy: government is run by representatives of the people elected and fully accountable to them. This form of government is often accompanied by a constitution that empowers the government and enumerates the rights of the people (constitutional democracy).

Demosthenes (384?–322 B.C.)   Athenian and the greatest Greek orator. A professional speech writer, he turned to politics in 355 B.C. By his speeches he warned the Athenians against King Philip of Macedon, who was becoming a threat to their liberty. Later he struggled against the pro-Macedonian faction in Athens.

Deng Xiaoping (Teng Hsiao-p'ing)   (b. 1902) Chinese Communist leader. As general secretary of the Chinese Communist party (1956–1967) he worked closely with Mao Tse-tung. Purged in 1967 during the Cultural Revolution, he was rehabilitated and became first deputy prime minister in 1977. He used his political acumen to name supporters to key posts and, as a result, was the chief policymaker throughout the 1980s. He stepped down from all party positions in 1987 but in 1993 still remains the most influential force in China.

Descartes, René (1596–1650)   French philosopher, mathematician, and scientist whose teachings

are known as Cartesian. The developer of coordinate geometry, he believed that nature could be reduced to a mathematical formula and advanced "the principle of systematic doubt." *See also* Philosophy section, page 19-7.

De Soto, Hernando (1500–1542)   Spanish explorer who led an expedition to Florida, explored what is now the southern United States, and is believed to be the first white man to cross the Mississippi River.

Détente   Diplomatic term that means the relaxation of tensions between countries. The term is used for the improved relations between the United States and the Soviet Union that began in 1969 and culminated in the SALT talks and an agreement on arms reduction in 1973. The heyday of détente was from 1972–1978. After that, the Soviet involvement in Afghanistan and the repression by the Polish government threatened to revive the Cold War.

De Valera, Eamon (1882–1975)   Irish statesman who in the 1920s led the movement to seek complete independence from Great Britain. He was the president of Sinn Fein (1917–1926), founded the extreme republican group Fianna Fáil in 1924, served as prime minister (1937–1948, 1951–1954, 1957–1959) and as president (1959–1973) of Ireland.

Dias, Bartholomeu (1450?–1500)   Portuguese navigator who was the first European to round the Cape of Good Hope in 1486 thereby opening the sea route to India.

Díaz, Porfirio (1830–1915)   Mexican general who was a mestizo and in 1876 seized dictatorial power. For more than 30 years he ran Mexico on the theory that the nation's salvation would be the capital and skills of foreign investors. Díaz was dictator of Mexico (1877–1911). One percent of the population owned 70 percent of the land; Catholicism was the state religion, church and state worked hand in hand, the Indian had no rights and had been forced into peonage, and foreign companies controlled most of the natural resources of the country. In 1910, a revolution against Díaz broke out.

Diderot, Denis (1713–1784)   French philosopher and a leading figure of the Enlightenment whose life work was editing the *Encyclopedia*, a 28-volume work summarizing the views of the leaders of the Enlightenment and attempting to encompass all human knowledge.

Diem, Ngo Dinh (1901–1963)   Leader in South Vietnam who declared himself the first president of the Republic of Vietnam in 1954. He restored order to South Vietnam but refused to hold elections and suppressed all opposition. His repressive measures eventually led to a coup in 1963 in which Diem was assassinated.

Dien Bien Phu   Final defeat of the French forces by the Vietminh under Ho Chi Minh in 1954 which caused the French to withdraw from Vietnam.

Diocletian (284–305 A.D.)   Roman emperor who helped stabilize the empire over the military anarchy of the 3rd century. Diocletian more than doubled the number of provinces to 101, grouped these into 13 dioceses, or administrative units, grouped into four Prefectures: Gaul and Britain; Italy, Spain, and Africa; the Danubian provinces and the Balkans; and the eastern provinces. He divided the empire into two halves with two co-emperors and two subordinate assistant Caesars who would eventually succeed the Augustus or emperor. Diocletian himself took over the eastern half of the Empire and assigned the western half to Maximian. Upon Diocletian's retirement in 305 A.D., civil war disrupted the empire until Constantine made himself ruler of the western empire in 312 A.D.

Directory　Government of France between 1795 and 1799 following the fall of Robespierre. Power was held by five directors assisted by a legislature made up of a council of 500 and a council of 250 called the Council of Ancients. The Directors were generally inefficient, guilty of corruption, and soon sank low in the public esteem, while the army demonstrated its successes and even won acclaim for its victories against France's enemies. The Directory was overthrown and replaced by the Consulate of Three, of which Napoleon Bonaparte was to become the leader.

Disraeli, Benjamin (1804–1881)　British statesman who as leader of the Tory or Conservative party served as prime minister of England several times in the 1800s alternating with Gladstone, the leader of the Liberal party. His Reform Bill of 1867 doubled the number of voters in England and his second ministry saw an aggressive foreign policy that added foreign territories to the British Empire. His policy of increased democracy and imperialism revitalized the Conservative party. He was also famous as a novelist.

Divine right　Royalist doctrine asserting that a king's power came from God and that the ruler was accountable only to God, not to the people. It reached its height in Europe in the 17th century. It was largely ended by England's Glorious Revolution and the French Revolution.

Dollfuss, Engelbert (1892–1934)　Austrian statesman who became chancellor in 1932 and declared a dictatorship along Italian Fascist lines in 1934. He was assassinated by Austrian Nazis attempting a takeover.

Domesday Book　A comprehensive record of property in England compiled in 1086 ordered by William the Conqueror in order to maintain his authority, evaluate his possessions, and ensure the collection of taxes due. Commissioners were sent to each country to take a complete census, to establish the size and value of all land holdings and everything they possessed, including the number of mills, farm animals, and so on.

Dorians　A group of Greek invaders who swept down from the North and overwhelmed Mycenae about 1100 B.C. occupying the Peloponnesus and Crete. The Dorians were illiterate and their arrival initiated a period of confusion and decline known as the Greek Dark Ages.

Draco (ca. 621 B.C.)　Chief archon of Athens in 621 B.C. he established a code of law that was extremely severe (the death penalty was given for stealing a cabbage). It was important, however, because it took punishment for a crime out of private hands and placed it under the control of the state.

Drake, Sir Francis (1540?–1596)　English navigator and adventurer, regarded as the greatest of Elizabethan seamen. From 1572, Drake undertook

a number of raiding missions against the Spanish colonies in the Americas, which made him rich and famous. On one such expedition (1577–1580) he became the first Englishman to circumnavigate the earth. In 1588 he served as vice-admiral against the Spanish Armada.

Dravidians　Name of ancient people who inhabited the Indian subcontinent before the coming of the Aryans. A short dark-skinned people, they lived in the first Indus valley civilization that was centered in Harappa and Mohenjo-Daro. Today, the Dravidians live primarily in southern India and speak the Dravidian language.

Dreyfus affair　Controversy over the French army's refusal to recognize the false conviction of Captain A. Dreyfus for treason. The affair dominated French political life from Dreyfus' conviction in 1894 to his final exoneration in 1906. Dreyfus, an Alsatian of Jewish background, was convicted on the evidence of a document that he supposedly wrote, offering military intelligence to the German military attaché. Later it was discovered that Major F. Esterhazy had written the document. Esterhazy was acquitted by a court-martial in 1898, prompting E. Zola, a supporter of Dreyfus, to publish his open letter *J'Accuse*, accusing the judges of acquitting Esterhazy in order to protect the army. In 1898 it was learned that another document apparently incriminating Dreyfus was, in fact, forged by Major Hubert Henry. Dreyfus was retired, but, incredibly, was once again convicted. In order to settle the matter, President E. Loubet pardoned Dreyfus in 1899 and in 1906 a court of appeals exonerated him. He was reinstated in the army. The affair polarized French society for more than a decade.

Druids　Ancient Celtic priests and teachers. Knowledge of them comes chiefly from Roman writers, notably Julius Caesar.

Dual monarchy (Austro-Hungarian Monarchy)　System established in 1867 whereby the Austrian Empire was divided into the Austrian and the Hungarian kingdoms. The two states were united in the person of the Austro-Hungarian monarch who ruled through ministries in Austria and Hungary. The ministers of war, foreign affairs, and finance were combined. Because of this plan, Austrian Emperor Francis Joseph was crowned king of Hungary on June 8, 1867.

Dubcek, Alexander (1921–1992)　Czechoslovakian political leader whose liberal reforms led to the Soviet invasion of Czechoslovakia in 1968. In 1967 he became the first secretary of the Communist party. His subsequent easing of censorship, rehabilitation of political prisoners, and program of democratization alarmed the Soviet Union, which with other Warsaw Pact countries invaded Czechoslovakia. Dubcek was forced to make political concessions to the Soviets and his reform program was gradually dismantled.

Duma　Russian legislative body that was created by Czar Nicholas II after the 1905 revolution. The Duma served as the lower house of the Russian legislature until the revolution of 1917.

Dunkirk　Site of the heroic evacuation between May 19 and June 4, 1940 of some 340,000 British and French troops trapped by the advancing Germans early in World War II. The two-pronged German invasion of Belgium encircled the British and French divisions by May 20 and an attempted Allied breakout to the South was defeated. With the Germans closing in and their only escape being to cross the English Channel, the British organized (May 29) what became an armada of transports and civilian craft, and every available boat was pressed into service. The success of the evacuation was in large part due to the Royal Air Force, which provided air cover for the evacuation.

Dürer, Albrecht (1471–1528)   German artist. Considered one of the great artists of the German Renaissance. He adapted styles of the Italian Renaissance painters and was noted for his use of classical forms and for his technical mastery. He was famed for his woodcuts and engravings as well.

Durham, John George Lampton, 1st earl of (1792–1840)   British statesman. As governor-general of Canada in 1838, he assumed near-dictatorial powers in dealing with French-Canadian resistance in Lower Canada. He was author of the *Report on the Affairs of British North America*, which was called the Durham Report and called for unification of Canada politically by granting what amounted to virtual self-government and geographically by building roads and canals.

Dutch East India Company   Dutch colonial trading company (1601–1798) that advanced and protected Dutch commercial and colonial interests from the Cape of Good Hope to the Strait of Magellan.

Duvalier, François (Papa Doc) (1907–1971)   Haitian dictator. Elected president in 1957, he declared himself president for life in 1964, and suppressed all opposition through terrorism.

Dyarchy (Diarchy)   Governmental system introduced by the British to India in 1919. It gave control of certain parts of the government to local officials while keeping the major control in British hands. It sought to develop Indian self-rule by stages.

East European Revolution   Series of events between 1989 and 1991 that brought an end to the Communist governments in East European nations. It also refers to the end of control of Eastern Europe by the Soviet Union during this period. This led to the independence of Bulgaria, Czechoslovakia, Hungary, Poland, and Romania, and resulted in a peaceful (velvet revolution) breakup of Czechoslovakia into two entities: Czech Republic and Slovakia. The collapse of the independent Communist government led to violence between ethnic and religious groups in the former Yugoslavia, which was broken up into the independent states of Slovenia, Croatia, and Serbia. The province of Bosnia and Herzegovina exploded into an atrocity-filled civil war in 1992–93, including charges of genocide (*see* **Ethnic cleansing**). For maps and statistical information about Eastern Europe, *see* the World at a Glance section.

Easter Rebellion   Revolt in Ireland in 1915 against British rule. Led by Pearse, the rebellion broke and was suppressed only after bitter fighting in the streets. The subsequent execution of Pearse and others helped bring down the Asquith govern-

ment and paved the way for creation of the Irish Free State.

Eastern Question   Broad term referring to the series of international conflicts and crises in the 19th and 20th centuries brought on by the breakup of the Ottoman Empire. Control of the Eastern European territories of the Ottoman Empire was of key importance to various European powers, notably Russia, whose interest in the region dated from the 1500s. In the 1800s, competing interests and the growing instability of the region led to a series of shifting alliances among European powers to take over or prevent the takeover of various parts of the region. The crises were numerous and included the Russo-Turkish Wars, the War of Greek Independence, the Crimean War, the Bosnian Rebellion, the Bosnian Crisis, and the Balkan Wars. The Eastern Question ended with World War I and the collapse of the Ottoman Empire.

Eden, Robert Anthony (1897–1977)   British statesman. He was prime minister (1955–1957), but was forced to resign after he ordered military intervention in the Suez Canal crisis in 1956.

Edgar (Eadgar) (943?–975)   King of the English (959–975), he supported reforms of the English monasteries which brought about a return to strict observance of the Benedictine rule. He was formally crowned king in 973, at Bath, in the first coronation for a king of all England.

Edict of Emancipation   Edict issued in Russia on March 3, 1861 by Alexander II, freeing the serfs.

Edict of Milan   Decree (313 A.D.) that granted religious toleration of Christians within the Roman Empire. Issued by Constantine, emperor of the West, and Licinius, emperor of the East, it established a lasting policy of toleration within the empire.

Edict of Nantes   Declaration granting religious toleration in France in 1598. King Henry IV attempted to restore peace between the Protestant Huguenots and Catholics by granting Protestants greater freedom. By the edict, Huguenots were allowed the same civil and social rights as Catholics, though they were not allowed to hold religious services in Paris.

Edward I (1239–1307)   English king (1272–1307), who consolidated the power of the crown at the expense of the barons and the clergy. He conquered and annexed Wales in 1284. From 1290 until his death, he was involved in wars to control Scotland. By various statutes, he limited the authority of church courts to clerical matters, and, by the Statutes of Westminster he limited the power of the feudal lords. He also convened the Model Parliament in 1295.

Edward II (1284–1327)   King of England (1307–1327), who succeeded his father, Edward I. He was a weak ruler and his wife, Isabella, with de Mortimer, deposed him.

Edward III (1312–1377)   English king (1327–1377), who succeeded his father, Edward II. He seized the regency controlled by his mother and R. de Mortimer, 1st earl of March, and began the long series of wars with France known as the Hundred Years' War (1337–1453). His reign saw the rising power of the Commons in Parliament, the ravages

EXHIBIT 11.3
Rulers of England and Great Britain

Saxon and Danish Rulers

828–839	Egbert, King of Wessex
839–858	Ethelwulf, King of Wessex, son of Egbert
858–860	Ethelbald, King of Wessex, son of Ethelwulf
860–866	Ethelbert, King of Essex, son of Ethelwulf
866–871	Ethelred I, King of Wessex and Kent, son of Ethelwulf
871–899	Alfred the Great, King of Wessex and Overlord of England, son of Ethelwulf
899–924	Edward the Elder, King of Angles and Saxons, son of Alfred
924–940	Athelstan, King of Angles and Saxons, son of Edward
940–946	Edmund I, King of England, brother of Athelstan
946–955	Edred, King of England, brother of Athelstan
955–958	Edwy, son of Edmund I
959–975	Edgar, brother of Edwy
975–978	Edward the Martyr, son of Edgar
978–1016	Ethelred II the Unready, brother of Edward
1016	Edmund II Ironside, son of Ethelred II
1016–1035	Canute, son of Sweyn Forkbeard
1035–1040	Harold I Harefoot, son of Canute
1040–1042	Hardicanute, son of Canute
1042–1066	Edward the Confessor, son of Ethelred II
1066	Harold II, brother-in-law of Edward

House of Normandy

1066–1087	William I the Conqueror
1087–1100	William Rufus, son of William the Conqueror
1100–1135	Henry I Beauclerc, son of William the Conqueror

House of Blois

1135–1154	Stephen, nephew of Henry I

House of Anjou (Plantagenet)

1154–1189	Henry II, grandson of Henry I
1189–1199	Richard I Coeur de Lion, son of Henry II
1199–1216	John Lackland, son of Henry II
1216–1272	Henry III, son of John
1272–1307	Edward I Longshanks, son of Henry III
1307–1327	Edward II, son of Edward I
1327–1377	Edward III, son of Edward II
1377–1399	Richard II, grandson of Edward III

House of Lancaster

1399–1413	Henry IV Bolingbroke, grandson of Edward III
1413–1422	Henry V, son of Henry IV
1422–1461	Henry VI, son of Henry V
1470–1471	Henry VI (restored)

House of York

1461–1470	Edward IV, great-great-grandson of Edward III
1471–1483	Edward IV (restored)
1483	Edward V, son of Edward IV
1483–1485	Richard III, brother of Edward IV

House of Tudor

1485–1509	Henry VII, son-in-law of Edward IV
1509–1547	Henry VIII, son of Henry VII
1547–1553	Edward VI, son of Henry VIII
1553	Jane (Lady Jane Grey, Queen for 9 days)
1553–1558	Mary I, daughter of Henry VIII
1558–1603	Elizabeth I, daughter of Henry VIII

House of Stuart

1603–1625	James I, son of Mary, Queen of Scots
1625–1649	Charles I, son of James

Commonwealth

1653–1658	Oliver Cromwell, Lord Protector
1658	Richard Cromwell, Lord Protector, son of Oliver Cromwell

House of Stuart (Restored)

1660–1685	Charles II, son of Charles I
1685–1688	James II, son of Charles I
1689–1702	William III of Orange and Mary II, daughter of James II (joint rulers)
1702–1714	Anne, sister of Mary

House of Hanover

1714–1727	George I, great-grandson of James I
1727–1760	George II, son of George I
1760–1820	George III, grandson of George II
1820–1830	George IV, son of George III
1830–1837	William IV, son of George III
1837–1901	Victoria, granddaughter of George III

House of Saxe–Coburg–Gotha

1901–1910	Edward VII, son of Victoria

House of Windsor

1910–1936	George V, son of Edward VII
1936	Edward VIII, son of George V
1936–1952	George VI, brother of Edward VIII
1952	Elizabeth II, daughter of George VI

of the Black Plague (1348 and 1349, 1362, 1369), and the resultant labor shortages that helped end serfdom.

Edward IV (1442–1483)   King of England (1461–1470, 1471–1483), who led the Yorkist party against the Lancastrians in the Wars of the Roses between 1455 and 1485 and, after being forced to flee England in 1470, returned to depose Henry VI.

Edward V (1470–1483)   King of England in 1483 who was arrested and believed murdered by his uncle, the duke of Gloucester. The duke thereupon succeeded him as Richard III.

Edward VI (1537–1553)   English king (1547–1553) who succeeded his father, Henry VIII as a young boy and therefore his regents, E. Seymour and John Dudley (1532?–1588), duke of Northumbria, administered the kingdom. During Edward's reign, Protestant reforms were introduced to the newly created Church of England. Dudley arranged for Edward to name Lady Jane Grey to succeed him.

Edward VII (1841–1910)   English king (1901–1910), who succeeded his mother, Queen Victoria. As king he promoted Anglo-French relations in 1904.

Edward VIII (1894–1972)   King of England (1936), who abdicated the throne when objections within the government to his proposed marriage with the twice-divorced Wallis Warfield Simpson threatened a constitutional crisis. Thereafter known as the duke of Windsor.

Edward the Confessor (d. 1066)   King of England (1042–1066). On Edward's death, Norman claims to the throne resulted in the Norman Conquest.

Egbert (d. 839)   King of Wessex (802–839). By his victory over the English kingdom of Mercia, he ended Mercia's domination of Wessex and thus began the rise of Wessex as the dominant power in England.

Egypt (Arab Republic of Egypt)   Country located in northeastern Africa. Civilization developed in the fertile Nile valley in extremely ancient times and had reached a high degree of organization by 3100 B.C. At that time a unified kingdom was created by joining Lower Egypt (essentially, the region of the Nile delta in the north) and Upper Egypt (region south of Cairo). Ancient Egyptian civilization flourished for nearly two millennia thereafter (about 2700–1000 B.C.) before beginning the period of final decline. Egyptian history up to Alexander's conquest in 332 B.C. in general divided into 30 dynasties. Alexander the Great's conquest of Egypt marked the beginning of continuous domination of foreign powers that lasted into the 20th century. During that time the Egyptians absorbed first Hellenic Greek, then Roman, and finally Muslim cultural influence from their rulers. Modern Egypt has played an important role in Mideast affairs. Until the late 1970s it was the leading center of Arab unity and of opposition to Israel. Then in 1978 and 1979 Egypt became the first Arab nation to establish diplomatic relations and enter into formal peace agreements with Israel.

Egyptian-Israeli Peace Treaty   Treaty signed in 1979 by Egyptian President Sadat and Israeli Prime Minister Begin. The agreement formally ended the state of war that had existed between the two countries for some 30 years and established diplomatic relations.

Einhard (Eginhart) (770–840)   Frankish historian who was a favorite in the court of Charlemagne and wrote the biography *Life of Charlemagne.*

Eleanor of Aquitaine (1122?–1204)   Queen consort of Louis VII of France (1137–1152) and Henry II of England (1152–1189). For supporting her sons in a revolt against Henry, she was imprisoned by him. She was adviser to her sons King Richard I and King John of England.

Elizabeth (Petrovna, Elizabeth) (1709–1762)   Became empress of Russia (1741–1762) by overthrowing young Ivan VI. Advised by her chancellor, Bestuzhev-Ryumin, she rid Russia of German influence and opposed Prussia in the Seven Years' War.

Queen Elizabeth I of England.

Elizabeth I (1533–1603)   English queen (1558–1603), whose reign saw a period of increasing commercial activity, England's rise as a naval power, the beginnings of English exploration and colonization in the New World, and a period of great literary activity. The dominant aspect of her reign, however, was the restoration of Protestantism and her struggle with Catholics at home and abroad. She reestablished the Church of England and the subsequent Catholic rebellions and plots against Elizabeth resulted in increasingly repressive measures against them. Her anti-Catholic policies and encouragement of raids by English privateers on Spanish shipping finally provoked Philip II of Spain to mount an unsuccessful attempt to invade England and end Protestantism there. *See* **Armada, Spanish.**

Elizabeth II (b. 1926)   Became British queen in 1952, successor to her father, George VI. She entered the direct line of succession upon abdication of her uncle, Edward VIII in 1936. Though her role is largely symbolic and ceremonial, Elizabeth enjoys great popularity with her subjects.

Elizabethan Age   Period of English history spanning the reign of Elizabeth I (1558–1603). England enjoyed many years of general peace and prosperity and rose as a great naval power during this period, but it was most remarkable as a golden age of English literature. Shakespeare, Spenser, and Marlowe all belong to this time.

Emigrés   French royalist sympathizers who fled France during the revolution. Many joined Prince de Condé in setting up court at Koblenz, and most returned on restoration of the monarchy in 1814.

Ems Dispatch   Telegram sent to Prussian chancellor Otto von Bismarck by King Wilhelm I of Prussia on July 13, 1870. The French ambassador had sought assurances from Wilhelm that no member of his family would seek the Spanish throne. Wilhelm refused to give such an assurance and then telegraphed a report of his conversation with the ambassador to Bismarck. Bismarck, who wanted a test of strength with France, edited the telegram to make it appear that France had been insulted and published it. Consequenlly, France declared war beginning the Franco-Prussian War.

Enclosure movement   The fencing in, or enclosing of, common lands (lands formerly used by all those in a village) into individual holdings. This movement carried out by English landlords began in England in the 1500s and continued into the 1700s. Its purpose was to combine scattered lands into large landholdings that were efficient for large scale farming. However, it also resulted in forcing small farmers to give up their livelihood and move to the cities.

Encyclopedists (Encyclopédistes)   Name of a group of writers who produced the *Encyclopédie*, a great French encyclopedia of science, arts, and trades, which was important in advancing the ideas of the Enlightenment. The work was edited by Alembert and Diderot.

Engels, Friedrich (1820–1895)   German socialist philosopher who, as a collaborator with Marx, helped found modern communism. He collaborated with Marx to write the *Communist Manifesto*.

English Civil War (Great Rebellion)   Armed conflict from 1642 and 1649 between forces of the English Parliament and those of the monarchy, under Stuart king Charles I. The war was caused by a series of political and religious problems. The absolutism of King Charles (and of James I before him) brought an ongoing struggle for power between the king and Parliament to a head. Attempts to impose religious uniformity aroused Puritans and Independents against the government as well. In general, the war pitted the Royalists, composed of the aristocracy, the Anglicans, and the Catholics, against Parliamentarians, including the gentry, merchants, and artisans. During the war Oliver Cromwell emerged as the leading figure of the parliamentary army and the army became a stronghold of Puritan settlement. Cromwell became leader of the government under the Commonwealth and Protectorate created after the monarchy was abolished. The monarchy was reestablished in 1660. *See* **Cromwell, Oliver**.

Enlightened despot   Monarch whose power, though absolute, was theoretically based on the rule of reason. The doctrine of enlightened despotism arose during the 18th-century Enlightenment.

Enlightenment (Age of Reason)   Intellectual movement of the 18th century centered in France but extending throughout Europe and to America. Characterized by a belief in rationalism, science, and natural laws, it fostered new views that challenged accepted religious, political, and social doctrines. The Enlightenment was in part an outgrowth of the 17th-century advances in science and philosophy.

Entente Cordiale   The special understanding reached between Britain and France in 1904. By the agreement, France was given a free hand in Morocco, while British control of Egypt was recognized. Spheres of influence in Africa, Thailand, and the Pacific were better defined. Russia joined the pact in 1907 making it the Triple Entente.

Enver Pasha (1881–1922)   Turkish general. A young Turk, he was a leader in the 1908 revolt to restore the liberal 1876 constitution. He became minister of war, helped bring Turkey into World War I as a German ally, and, during the war, became virtual ruler of Turkey. He fled Turkey after the war.

Epicureanism   Greek school of philosophy founded by Epicurus after 306 B.C. It held that the chief aim of life was to experience pleasure and avoid pain. Epicurus himself taught that such an end was to be achieved by prudence and moderation, but this aspect of his teaching was not always observed by his followers. *See also* Philosophy section, page 19-8.

Erasmus (Desiderius) (1466?–1536)   Dutch theologian and one of the great humanist scholars. He traveled widely throughout Europe and, through his critical and satirical works, became a leading figure among the circle of humanist thinkers. After refusing to join Luther's movement for radical reforms, he opposed him openly. Among Erasmus' many important works are his edition of the *New Testament*, *The Praise of Folly*, and *Colloquies*.

Eratosthenes (275–195 B.C.)   Greek scientist, astronomer, and poet who was the first to measure the earth's circumference and tilt of its axis.

Eric the Red (ca. 10th century)   Norse explorer who after being exiled from Iceland explored Greenland and founded the first colony there in 986.

Estates-General   French national assembly in which the chief estates—clergy, nobility, and commons—were represented as separate bodies. Originating in the king's council, or Curia Regis, the French States-General was first summoned in 1302 by Philip IV. Its powers were never clearly defined and its main function was to approve royal legislation. Though it acquired jurisdiction over taxes, it was eclipsed by the growth of royal power. Thus, the Estates-General was seldom convened after 1500 and did not meet at all from 1614–1789. The States-General of 1789 was called by Louis XVI as a last resort to solve the government's financial crisis. It first met on May 5, 1789, and it became immediately evident that the third estate (commons) and the liberals among the clergy and nobles intended to transform it from a consultative into a legislative assembly. The third estate (with 50% of total delegates) rejected the customary voting procedure (by estates) and insisted that balloting should proceed by head. In June, the third estate forced the issue by openly defying the king and declaring themselves the National Assembly. Louis XVI accepted the accomplished fact.

Ethnic cleansing   The forcible removal of Bosnian Muslims by Serbians from towns and villages in Bosnia and Herzegovina. This action has been condemned as genocide by many nations, especially the United States and Great Britain. *See* **East European Revolution**.

Etruscans   Ancient people who established a flourishing civilization in northern Italy between the 8th and 4th centuries B.C. They are believed to have emigrated to Italy from the Near East around the 12th century B.C. They initiated trade with the Greeks, and their navy virtually dominated the Mediterranean in the 7th and 6th centuries B.C. They ruled Rome, as the legendary "Tarquin kings," but were expelled around 509 B.C., according to tradition. The Romans defeated them decisively and began the gradual subjugation of the Etruscan cities (completed by 282 B.C.). The Romans borrowed freely from Etruscan civilization, and the Latin alphabet is derived from the earlier Etruscan writing system.

Euclid (ca. 300 B.C.)   Greek mathematician famous for his *Elements*, a collection of theorems and problems that formed the basis of geometry.

Euripides (480?–406 B.C.)   One of the three great tragic poets (with Sophocles and Aeschylus) of ancient Greece. He is said to have written 92 plays of which 18, definitely attributed to him, survive. Among his extant works are *Cyclops*, *Orestes*, and *Electra*.

European Economic Community (Common Market)   West European economic association. It was formed in 1958 and its original members were Belgium, France, Italy, Luxembourg, The Netherlands, and West Germany. Its goals were to establish the economic union of member nations and eventually to bring about political union. It has sought to eliminate internal tariffs, institute a uniform external scale of tariffs, achieve free movement of labor and capital from one nation to another, abolish obstructions to free competition, and establish collective trade and transportation policies. In 1973, Great Britain, Ireland, and Denmark joined the organization. The Maastricht Treaty, signed in December 1991, is the latest attempt to make the idea of a United States of Europe a reality. As of this writing, in 1993, the treaty has not been ratified by all the member states.

Existentialism   Modern school of philosophy concerned with human beings' relationship to the world around them. It teaches that the actual existence of humanity holds the clue to the meaning of being. Existentialism stems from Kierkegaard's revolt against the rationalism of Hegel.

Exodus   The escape in about the 13th century B.C. by the Jews from their enslavement in Egypt. It is an event of great significance in biblical history and is described in the second book (Exodus) of the Old Testament. The book narrates the flight from Egypt under Moses' guidance and includes the crossing of the Red Sea, the trek through the wilderness, and the giving of the Ten Commandments on Mt. Sinai.

 **Fabian Society**   English Socialist society, founded in 1883 by Frank Podmore and Edward Pease to gradually advance the Socialist cause from within the existing government framework. Fabians did not advocate revolutionary methods for change. They helped organize a labor-oriented committee in 1900, which later became the British Labour party.

Faisal (1906–1975)   Saudi Arabian king (1964–1975). A leading figure in the Arab world, he led Saudi Arabia against Israel in the Arab-Israeli War of 1967. He was assassinated by his nephew.

Faisal I (Faysal I) (Feisal I)   King of Syria (1920) and Iraq (1921–1933). A leader of the Arab nationalist movement, he was a key figure in the Arab revolt against Ottoman rule during World War I. Crowned king of Syria in 1920, he was deposed by the French in the same year but became king of Iraq with support of the British.

Faisal II (Faysal II) (Feisal II) (1935–1958)   Last king of Iraq (1939–1958), who was killed during the revolution that ended the monarchy there.

Falange   Spanish political party that became the ruling party of Spain under General Francisco Franco. Organized in 1933 by José Antonio Primo de Rivera, it became the party of Spanish fascism. Falangists took part in the Spanish Civil War (1936–1939), and, after 1937, the group was taken over by Franco. Franco made it the official party under his dictatorship and it continued in power until recent times.

Falkland Islands War   Brief war in 1982 between Argentina and Britain over possession of the Falkland Islands. Following years of unsuccessful negotiations with Britain for possession of the islands, the Argentines invaded and took control. A British naval task force arrived and took several Argentine strongholds on the islands. After surrounding the main Argentine contingent it forced nearly 10,000 Argentine troops to surrender.

Fanfani, Amintore (b. 1908)   Italian statesman. A left-wing Christian Democrat, he held numerous government positions and was a leading force in Italian politics in the 1950s and 1960s.

Faraday, Michael (1791–1867)   English scientist, famous for his contributions to the study of electricity and magnetism.

Far East   Term that generally refers to the eastern portion of the Asian continent. It includes eastern Siberia, Mongolia, China, Korea, and Japan and is sometimes also meant to include the countries of southeast Asia.

Farouk I (Faruk I) (1920–1965)   Egyptian king (1936–1952). His unpopular policies and Egypt's defeat by Israel in 1948 led to his overthrow by Naguib and Nasser.

Fascism   Political movement for totalitarian government that began in Italy in 1919 under the leadership of Mussolini. Fascism is sometimes used more restrictively to refer to the Italian movement, the parallel German movement being distinguished as National Socialism (Nazism). Fascism is characterized by subservience of the individual to the state, extreme nationalism, elitism, formation of the corporative state, militarism, and imperialism. Fascism in

Italy developed amid the post World War I chaos bred by labor unrest and attempts at Communist and Socialist takeover. Mussolini's Fascist party, with the backing of many conservative elements, took control of the Italian government in 1922 after the famous March on Rome. The Fascist party remained the ruling party of Italy until the end of World War II.

Fashoda Incident Diplomatic crisis in 1898 between Britain and France over claims to the Sudan. Defying British claims, the French sent a military contingent from the Congo and occupied Fashoda (now Kodok). The British, under Lord Kitchener, arrived two weeks later. The French government, fearing all-out war, withdrew its forces a month and a half later, and subsequently dropped claims to the region in 1899 in return for British concessions in the Sahara.

Fatima (606?–632) Daughter of Muhammad and wife of Ali. An important figure in Islamic religion, she is by tradition the forebear of the Fatimid dynasty.

Fatimid (Fatimite) Muslim dynasty that ruled an empire in North Africa (909–1711). The Fatimids claimed the Muslim caliphate as descendants of Muhammad's daughter Fatima. The dynasty was founded by the Syrian Said ibn Husayn. He was proclaimed the Mahdi following rebellions in northwestern Africa and Sicily in 909 and ruled there in opposition to the Abbasid caliphs. The Fatimids subsequently reached their greatest power under el-Moizz (reigned 935–975) who conquered Egypt, Palestine, and part of Syria, and built Cairo. The empire began to disintegrate after his reign.

February Revolution Revolution in France in 1848 that brought about the abdication of King Louis Philippe and creation of the short-lived Second Republic. The king's increasingly reactionary policies, opposition to his unpopular minister Guizot, and widespead unemployment caused by a severe economic slump resulted in the revolt. The provisional government was a coalition of moderate Republicans, led by de Lamartine, and Socialist Republicans, led by L. Blanc. It subsequently recognized "the right to work," created the national workshops to ease unemployment, and proclaimed universal male suffrage. The workshops soon failed, however, and mass demonstrations by Socialist Republicans aroused fears of a Communist takeover. Moderates were thus victorious in elections for the new National Assembly, and, in the face of new unrest, moved to dissolve the national workshops. This precipitated the bloody uprising known as June Days. The assembly promulgated a new constitution and Louis Napoleon (later Napoleon III) was elected president. Soon after taking office, Napoleon seized power.

Fenian movement Irish nationalist movement. A secret revolutionary group organized in 1858 to achieve complete Irish independence from Britain, it included groups in both Ireland and America. It actively harassed the British in Britain, Ireland, and America in the 1860s and 1870s. It was eventually replaced by the Sinn Fein movement.

Ferdinand I (Ferdinand the Great) (d. 1065) Spanish king of Castile (1035–1065) and León (1037–1065). He brought much of Spain under his control and began the expulsion of the Moors.

Ferdinand I (1345–1383) Portuguese king (1367–1383) who waged three successive wars to gain the Castilian throne and each time suffered a humiliating defeat.

Ferdinand I (1503–1564) Holy Roman emperor (1558–1564), who negotiated the Peace of Augsburg in 1555.

Ferdinand II (1578–1637) Holy Roman emperor (1619–1637), king of Bohemia and Hungary. His reign was marked by the Thirty Years' War, in which he attempted to put down a series of rebellions by Protestants which began just after his succession to the Bohemian throne in 1618.

Ferdinand III (1199–1252) King of Castile (1217–1252) and León (1230–1252) who united Castile with León and recaptured most of Spain from the Moors.

Ferdinand III (1608–1657) Holy Roman emperor (1637–1657). A series of defeats at the hands of Protestants forced him to agree to the Peace of Westphalia in 1648, ending the Thirty Years' War.

Ferdinand V (Ferdinand the Catholic) (1452–1516) Spanish king who through marriage and conquest, pursued the unification of the Spanish kingdoms into what is now modern Spain. He married Isabella I of Castile in 1469 and from 1474 they ruled Castile jointly. He conquered Granada from the Moors, began the Italian Wars against France, conquered Naples in 1504, and annexed most of the kingdom of Navarre in 1512. His reign saw the voyage of Columbus in 1492 and the acquisition of rich possessions in the New World. With Isabella, he also instituted the Inquisition and expelled the Jews in 1492 and the Moors in 1502.

Ferdinand VI (1784–1833) Spanish king (March–May 1808, 1814–1833), who was forced from the throne by Napoleon and imprisoned until 1814. Ferdinand resumed control after Napoleon's ouster from Spain, but his rule was harsh and repressive.

Fertile Crescent Ancient Middle Eastern region stretching from the Nile to the Euphrates in parts of modern Egypt, Israel, Lebanon, Syria, Jordan, and Iraq. The site of some of the earliest settlements in human history. The region has been conquered numerous times.

Feudalism System based on the exchange of land and services that was prevalent in medieval Europe between the 8th and 14th centuries. By this system, a feudal lord granted lesser nobles (vassals) rights to lands (fiefs) within his domains and guaranteed them protection from attack. In return, the vassals swore their loyalty to the feudal lord and provided a specified number of warriors for his army and agreed to provide certain services. Vassals, in turn, subdivided their fiefs (subinfeudination), and thus became lords to vassals of progressively smaller fiefs. At the bottom of this complex structure was the feudal manor, which was formed by serfs and which by its agricultural output provided the economic base for the feudal system. The feudal system is generally thought to have arisen in Europe in the Frankish kingdom of Charlemagne between the 8th and 9th centuries and was a response to the widespread disorder caused by the invasions of the Germanic tribes, Muslims, and Vikings. From there, it was spread by Frankish conquests to Spain, Italy, and Germany. It was transplanted to England by the Normans under William the Conqueror. The rise of powerful monarchs and the growth of a new middle class among other factors, helped bring about a gradual decline of feudalism. By the 14th century it had largely disappeared. Other cultures also experienced periods of feudalism, notably Japan (10th–19th centuries).

Fief In feudalism, land granted by a lord to a vassal in return for the vassal's knightly service and allegiance. The fief was the cornerstone of feudal society.

Fifth Republic Name given the new government of France established with the election in 1958 of Charles de Gaulle as president.

Five Dynasties Chinese historical period between the end of the T'ang dynasty in 907 and the beginning of the Sung dynasty in 960. Five successive short-lived dynasties tried but failed to establish authority. Corruption and anarchy reigned instead, and northern China also suffered famine and floods.

Five-year Plan In the U.S.S.R., name given economic programs designed to increase industrial and agricultural growth through establishment of quotas or goals. The first plan was established in 1928 by Joseph Stalin. The plans did not generally achieve the goals.

Flagellants Christian sect originating in 13th-century Europe and practicing self-punishment (whipping) as a means to avoid God's wrath.

Flanders Historic country located along the North Sea coast and now divided between Belgium and France. Flanders became the leading center of the cloth industry in Europe in the 13th century and its major cities (Ghent, Ypres, and Bruges) prospered as free communes in manufacturing and trade. Industrialization and prosperity during the 13th and 14th centuries brought a period of rebellion against French domination, alliance with England during the Hundred Years' War, and conquest by the dukes of Burgundy. Flanders passed to the Hapsburgs in 1477, came under control of the Spanish Hapsburg kings in 1506, and unsuccessfully rebelled against Spanish rule between 1576 and 1584. After 1714, parts of Flanders passed to various powers until 1830, when the final disposition between Belgium and France was completed.

Fleming, Sir Alexander (1881–1955) Scottish bacteriologist who with Sir Howard Florey discovered penicillin.

Florence Historic city (pop. 457,000), located in central Italy. In the 14th and 15th centuries, Florence was not only a great center of Renaissance art and humanist studies but also a leading banking center and a birthplace of modern capitalism. In ancient times Florence was first an Etruscan, then a Roman town, and rose to importance in the 12th century. Florence was ruled by the famous Medici family between 1434 and 1737. In 1737, the Hapsburg-Lorraine family succeeded the Medici and ruled Florence until it was absorbed into the unified kingdom of Italy (1860).

Foch, Ferdinand (1851–1929) French general and in 1918, commander of Allied armies in World War I who was largely responsible for the final defeat of the Germans in 1918.

Forbidden City Chinese fortress city located within the city of Peking, so-called because most Chinese were forbidden to enter. It was the site (1421–1911), of the emperors' palaces.

Forum Roman meeting place. It was a large, centrally located open-air place in which Roman citizens would gather for festivals, speeches, elections, or other public events.

Fourier, Charles (1772–1837) French social philosopher. He advocated the organization of society based on the phalanx, a communal unit of 1,620 people. His philosophy fostered numerous attempts at communal societies, including the Brook Farm experiment in the United States.

Fourier, Jean Baptiste Joseph, Baron (1768–1830) French mathematician and physicist noted for his contributions in the field of mathematical physics.

Fourth Republic Name given to the French government established in 1946 after World War II.

Francis I (1494–1547) French king (1515–1547). Much of his reign was spent in conflict with Holy Roman Emperor Charles V. During his reign the French Renaissance flowered and Cartier explored North America.

Francis I (1708–1765) Holy Roman emperor (1745–1765). As duke of Lorraine (1729–1737), he ceded his duchy to Poland to end the War of Polish Succession. His marriage in 1736 to Maria Theresa, a stronger personality and Hapsburg heiress, led to his accession as coregent of Austria and Holy Roman emperor during the War of Austrian Succession.

Francis II (1544–1560) French king (1559 and 1560). The Guise family effectively ruled France during his short reign and used their power to persecute the Huguenots (Protestants).

Francis II (Francis I of Austria) (1768–1835) Last Holy Roman emperor (1792–1806) and king of Bohemia and Hungary. He was also first emperor of Austria (Francis I, 1804–1835). A determined opponent of the French Revolution and of Napoleon, he was several times defeated by the French in battles between 1793 and 1806. In 1806 he was compelled to sign the Treaty of Pressburg, which dissolved the Holy Roman Empire.

Franciscans Originally a religious order founded in Italy in 1209 by Saint Francis of Assisi. The order was founded on rules written by Saint Francis stressing a life of poverty, religious devotion, and dedication to helping others.

Francis Ferdinand (1863–1914) Austrian archduke (1875–1914) who was the heir to the Austrian throne and whose assassination at Sarajevo on June 28, 1914 touched off World War I.

Francis Joseph (1830–1916) Emperor of Austria (1848–1916) and king of Hungary (1867–1916). An absolutist, Francis was forced to yield to constitutional reform in 1867 and creation of the Dual Monarchy after a series of military reversals. He allied himself with the Central Powers in World War I.

Franco, Francisco (1892–1975) Spanish general and dictator. He took part in the military revolt in 1936 at the outset of the Spanish Civil War and later that year became leader of the rebel government.

With the aid of German and Italian troops, he brought the Civil War to an end in 1939.

Franco-Prussian War   War (1870 and 1871) between France and Prussia (with allied German states). The war brought about the unification of the German states under Prussian domination and thus achieved the long-sought goal of Prussian minister Otto von Bismarck. France suffered a humiliating defeat soon after and the consequences of the war were far-reaching: France rebelled against the monarchy and established the Third Republic in 1870, Germany was unified in 1871, and French power over continental Europe ended.

Frankfurt, Treaty of   French-German treaty that ended the Franco-Prussian War in 1871. France was forced to yield disputed territories in Alsace and Lorraine, to pay a five-billion-franc indemnity, and to suffer German occupation until these terms were met.

Franks   Germanic tribe that formed a powerful empire in Gaul after the fall of the Roman Empire. By the 3rd century A.D. the Franks began a series of invasions into Gaul. Clovis I united the several Frankish tribes (5th century A.D.), adopted Christianity, and conquered much of Gaul from the Romans. He established the Frankish Empire, which flourished under the Merovingian dynasty and later the Carolingian. The Franks reached their height under the rule of Charlemagne (in the 9th century) whose empire was divided and eventually became France and Germany.

Frederick I (Frederick Barbarossa) (1123–1190)   Holy Roman emperor (1155–1190), whose reign was marked by attempts to pacify warring German nobles and by several unsuccessful attempts to gain control over Lombardy. He was killed during the Third Crusade.

Frederick I (1657–1713)   First Prussian king (1701–1713). By promising Prussian military aid in the oncoming War of the Spanish Succession, he won permission from Leopold I to create the kingdom of Prussia in 1701.

Frederick II (1194–1250)   Holy Roman emperor (1220–1250) king of Germany (1212–1220), Sicily (1197–1250), and Jerusalem (1229–1250). His attempts to unify Italy and Germany, largely unsuccessful, were opposed vigorously by the Lombard League. While conducting the Fifth Crusade, he crowned himself in 1229, king of Jerusalem. Because of his unceasing struggles with the papacy, the German nation was weakened.

Frederick II (Frederick the Great) (1712–1786)   Prussian king (1740–1786). Under Frederick's leadership, Prussia evolved from a small Germanic state into an international power. A brilliant military tactician, Frederick seized portions of Silesia in the War of Austrian Succession. Almost defeated in the Seven Years' War (1756–1763), Frederick emerged victorious when his admirer Peter III assumed the Russian throne and took Russia out of the war. Frederick promulgated civil, legal, and penal reforms and internal improvements such as roads and canals. A patron of the arts, he enjoyed a long correspondence with Voltaire. (*See* page 11-130.) Frederick increased Prussian domains through the First Partition of Poland in 1772 and engaged in the War of

Bavarian Succession (1778 and 1779) to prevent Prussia's rival, Austria, from gaining power within the Holy Roman Empire.

Frederick William (Frederick the Great Elector) (1620–1688)   Elector of Brandenburg (1640–1688). Frederick negotiated an armistice to the Thirty Years' War and built a strong army in the interim, ensuring him fair treatment in the Peace of Westphalia. He unified Prussia and secured its sovereignty through a treaty in 1657 with Poland.

Frederick William I (1688–1740)   Prussian king (1713–1740), who was a strong ruler. He instituted many reforms and built the Prussian army into a powerful fighting force.

Frederick William II (1744–1797)   Prussian king (1786–1797). Though he was not considered an exceptional leader during his reign, Prussia continued its territorial expansion, notably at the expense of Poland through the partitioning of it.

Frederick William III (1770–1840)   King of Prussia (1797–1840). A weak king, he was dominated by Napoleon, but he allied himself with Russia and declared war in 1813 on France. After the Congress of Vienna, he alienated his people by joining the reactionary Holy Alliance.

Frederick William IV (1795–1861)   Prussian king (1840–1861). His reign was marked by a brief rebellion in 1848 and by his involvement in unsuccessful plans to unify Germany.

French East India Company   French colonial trading organization established in 1664 by Colbert to protect French trade interests. It was successful for a time in India under J. Dupleix, less so in America, and was abolished in 1769.

French Revolution   The prolonged political and social struggle between 1789 and 1799 in France that involved the overthrow of the monarchy and establishment of the First Republic. The revolution was caused by a number of factors, chief among them resentment against the ancien régime, the old social order dominated by the king and his nobles, and a prolonged crisis over government finances. The ideas of the Enlightenment and the recent success of the American Revolution also helped provide a climate for the revolution. The revolution began as an attempt to create a constitutional monarchy and in this early phase the moderates dominated the revolution. But by late 1792, the demands for long-overdue reforms resulted in the proclamation of the republic. The republic was consumed by the violence of the revolution. Attacks by other European nations only multiplied effects of the bitter factional struggles, riots, and counterrevolutionary uprisings. The chaos helped bring the extreme radicals to power and touched off the bloody Reign of Terror. The French succeeded in mustering powerful armies and were victorious against their foreign enemies. However, several attempts to form a stable republican government failed and ended in creation of the Consulate, a dictatorship led by the military leader, Napoleon.

French Revolutionary Wars   Series of wars between 1792 and 1802 between France and various European powers, notably Austria and Britain. (The wars against France between 1803 and 1815 are called the Napoleonic Wars.) The French Revolutionary Wars were sparked by the European monarchs' disapproval of the new revolutionary government, by attempts to restore the monarchy in France, and by the desire of some revolutionary factions to demonstrate the strength of their new government. To defend France, the revolutionary government created what became a powerful army and the wars quickly became a vehicle for the expansion and aggrandizement of France. Britain, which became France's most stubborn enemy, retained supremacy of the seas. The wars brought Napoleon to power in France, gained France considerable territory and influence in Europe, and brought on the final collapse of the Holy Roman Empire in 1806.

Freud, Sigmund (1856–1939) Austrian neurologist and founder of psychoanalysis. Freud pioneered the use of free association in the treatment of psychological problems and explored the effect of childhood impressions and repressed feelings on later behavior. His theories had a major influence on other scientists working in the field, including Adler and Jung. Both Adler and Jung, however, disagreed with Freud's emphasis on the importance of sexuality as a motivating force in behavior, and they developed their own followings. *See also* Psychology section, pages 21-11, 21-12.

Frobisher, Sir Martin (1535?–1594) English navigator who led three exploratory voyages (1576, 1577, 1578) to Canada's northern coast in an unsuccessful attempt to find a northwest passage.

Froissart, Jean (1333?–1400?) French courtier and chronicler whose chronicles of the 14th century provide a valuable and lively account of the times.

Fronde Two major rebellions (1648–1653) by French nobles brought about for the most part by their opposition to the growing power of the monarchy of Louis XIV.

Frontenac, comte de Palluau et de (Louis de Buade) (1620–1698) French governor of New France (1672–1682, 1689–1698). He defeated the warring Iroquois Confederacy in 1696, and during the war between England and France he successfully defended the colony against British attack.

Fuad I (Ahmed Fuad Pasha) (1868–1936) Egyptian king (1922–1936), the first to reign after Egypt's independence from Britain. He was made sultan in 1917 and became king when Egypt was declared nominally independent in 1922.

Fujiwara family Family of Japanese nobles that virtually ruled Japan from the 9th–12th centuries. The Fujiwaras rose to power under Nakatomi (later Kamatari) Fujiwara (d. 669), and gained dominance under Yoshifusa Fujiwara (804–872), but were defeated by the Minamoto and Taira families in the 12th century.

Gagarin, Yuri Alekseyevich (1934–1968) Soviet astronaut and national hero. The first man to travel in space (April 12, 1961), he orbited for about one and one half hours aboard his spacecraft, Vostok 1, and reached a maximum orbit of 188 miles above the earth.

Galen (Galenus, Claudius) (130–200 A.D.) Greek physician. Sometimes considered the founder of experimental physiology, he was regarded as the principal medical authority well into medieval times.

Galerius (Gaius Galerius Valerius Maximianus) (d. 311 A.D.) Roman emperor (305–310 A.D.) of the Eastern Empire, successor with Constantius I (in the West) to Diocletian.

Galileo (properly, Galileo Galilei) (1564–1642) Italian mathematician, physicist, and astronomer. One of the world's great scientists, he is regarded as the founder of the experimental method, which is the cornerstone of modern science. He discovered the law of pendulums as a student and first won notice by his invention of the hydrostatic balance in 1586. He later experimented (1589–1592) with falling bodies and disproved the Aristotelian theory that objects of different weights fall at different speeds. His researches confirmed his belief in the Copernican theory and he openly supported in 1613 this heliocentric theory. It was condemned by the church in 1616 as dangerous and Galileo was warned by church authorities against supporting it. He was subsequently tried and sentenced to house arrest by the Inquisition. He continued his scientific work, however.

Gallic Wars Series of campaigns conducted by Julius Caesar between 58 and 51 B.C. leading to the Roman conquest of Gaul. The campaigns gave Caesar immense power and prestige. As commander of a strong army he was able to contest Pompey's authority as leader of Rome.

Gallipoli Campaign (Dardanelles Campaign) Allied military operation in Turkey during World War I. The Allies attempted to wrest control of the Dardanelles from Turkey in order to better supply Russia. After an unsuccessful naval attempt to force the straits, British and French troops landed on both sides of the straits, notably on the Gallipoli peninsula. The operation became a disaster in which 55,000 Allied troops were lost before the evacuation (December 1915–January 1916).

Gambetta, Léon (1838–1882) French political leader. After the fall of the Second Empire in 1870, he organized a provisional government of national defense, dramatically escaped from Paris in a balloon, and was virtual dictator of France for five months (1870 and 1871). One of the founders of the Third Republic and shapers of its constitution in 1875, he served briefly as premier (1881 and 1882).

Gandhi, Indira (1917–1984) Indian prime minister (1966–1977, 1980) and daughter of Nehru. Facing a challenge to her 1972 election, she declared a state of emergency in 1975 and suspended the 1976 election. She was unseated as prime minister the following year (July 25, 1977) but after new elections she was returned to power several years later (January 14, 1980). She was assassinated in New Delhi (1984) by two of her own bodyguards. The assassins belonged to the Sikh religious minority, which had been in violent confrontation with the government.

Gandhi, Mohandas Karamchand (1869–1948) Indian political leader and national hero who became a symbol of nonviolent protest and of India's independence movement. Educated in both India and Britain, he remained overseas until 1914. His nonviolent campaigns of civil disobedience (called satyagraha) against various laws soon propelled him to the leadership of the movement for Indian home rule, as well as the Congress party. During the 1930s, the pattern of Gandhi's mass nonviolent protests and subsequent arrests continued. But Gandhi only gained prestige (he was called Mahatma, or "great soul") and he was able to wrest major concessions from the British rulers of India. During the early part of World War II, he began demanding India's complete independence from Britain. This he tried to achieve by refusing Indian support for the British war effort against the Japanese, a tactic that resulted in his internment until 1944. He vigorously supported Britain's postwar plans to grant India's independence, though he was unsuccessful in opposing the partition of India and creation of Pakistan in 1947. He was assassinated (January 30, 1948) by a Hindu fanatic.

Gandhi, Rajiv (1944–1991)   Grandson of Nehru (*see* page 11-85) and son of Indira Gandhi. He succeeded his mother after her assassination in 1984, becoming prime minister. He resigned in 1989, and during the election campaign of 1991, he was assassinated.

Gang of Four   Four leading figures of the Cultural Revolution in China (1966–1969) who were put on trial (November 20, 1980) along with other radicals. They were charged with a variety of abuses during the Cultural Revolution, including the deaths of some 34,000 people. The leading figure among the four was Chiang Ch'ing, Mao Tse-tung's wife; the trial marked her fall from power.

Garibaldi, Giuseppe (1807–1882)   Italian soldier and hero of the Risorgimento, or unification of Italy. While in his twenties, he was involved in an unsuccessful revolt in 1835 in Italy and fled to South America, where he became famous as a leader of the rebel forces in Uruguay (1842–1846). Garibaldi returned to Italy and joined his friend Mazzini in establishing a revolutionary republic in Rome in 1849. Having given up his hopes for an Italian republic, he was willing in 1860 to serve the interests of Victor Emmanuel II to further the unification of Italy. That year he undertook his famous conquest of the Kingdom of Two Sicilies with the Expedition of the Thousand.

Gaul   Ancient name for the area once inhabited by Celts, roughly comprising modern France. Roman Gaul included also parts of northern Italy and flourished as a center of Roman civilization until the collapse of the Western empire in 476 A.D. Thereafter, it came under control of the Franks.

Gaullists   French political term. Gaullists were the supporters of the nationalistic policies of French General (later president) de Gaulle (*see* page 11-31). The term was employed to describe de Gaulle's followers during the period of his leadership of the Free French and it was retained to describe the political party organized after 1945 and dominant after the foundation of the Fifth Republic.

General Agreement on Tariffs and Trade (GATT)   Created after World War II, GATT attempts to develop worldwide trade policy and avoid economic conflict between the nations of the world. *See also* History of the United States section, page 10-36.

Genghis Khan (orig. name Temujin) (1167?–1227)   Mongol conqueror, who, as leader of notoriously savage Mongol armies, created a vast Asian empire.

He succeeded in conquering other Mongol tribes and in organizing them in 1206 into a confederacy. With his capital at Karakorum (in the modern Mongolian People's Republic), he invaded (1213–1218) and conquered northern China. From 1218–1224 he extended his empire in the West, conquering parts of what are now northern India, Iran, Iraq, and southern Russia. By the time of his death, the empire extended from the Korean peninsula in the East to the Black Sea in the West. The empire was subsequently divided among his sons.

Geoffrey of Monmouth (1100–1154)   English clergyman and writer. He was author of *Historia Regum Britanniae* (1135), a fanciful account of British kings that contained the first account of the legendary King Arthur and widely influenced British literature.

George I (1660–1727)   German-born elector of Hanover and king of Great Britain (1713–1727), the first of the Hanoverian kings and successor to Queen Anne. An unpopular king, he succeeded under the 1701 Act of Settlement.

George II (1683–1760)   German-born elector of Hanover and king of Great Britain (1727–1760), a member of the Hanover family, and successor to his father, George I.

George III (1738–1820)   King of Great Britain (1760–1820), a member of the Hanover family, and successor to his grandfather, George II. Under his reign Britain enjoyed a period of economic prosperity and cultural activity. At the same time the king's policies led to political instability at home and the American Revolution abroad.

George IV (1762–1830)   King of Great Britain (1820–1830), a member of the Hanover family, and successor to his father George III. His reign saw a marked decline in the influence of the monarchy.

George V (1865–1936)   King of Great Britain (1910–1936), successor to his father, Edward VII. He played a moderating role in the crises during his reign and guided Britain through World War I.

George VI (1895–1952)   King of Great Britain (1936–1952), successor to his brother Edward VIII. He is noted for his efforts to shore up British morale during World War II. He was succeeded by his daughter Elizabeth II.

German Confederation   A loose confederation (1815–1866) of 35 independent German kingdoms and four free cities formed largely for mutual defense. It was dominated by Austria, and its history was marked by a growing rivalry between Austria and Prussia. Following the destruction of the Holy Roman Empire by Napoleon and the subsequent fall of his French-based empire, the German states were left largely unprotected. The German Confederation was therefore created at the Congress of Vienna in 1815 and a German diet under Austrian presidency was formed. The diet, briefly supplanted between 1848 and 1850 by the Frankfurt Parliament, survived until the Austro-Prussian War of 1866 and the formation of the North German Confederation.

German East Africa   Name of a former German colony in East Africa. The region was first explored by the Germans in 1884 and was declared a protectorate in 1885. In 1891 the German government took direct control of the colony, overcame native rebellions and developed it. Following World War I, it was divided in 1919 between Britain and Belgium, becoming Tanganyika and Ruanda Urundi, respectively.

German Unification   The rejoining of East and West Germany (separated after World War II) in 1991, has created a new and very powerful economic and political factor in European diplomatic and military affairs. This created a nation of more than 80 million people with a per capita GNP of more than $24,000, making this the most populaced, industralized state in Europe. *See also* World at a Glance section.

Germanic laws   German tribal laws. These were the unwritten, customary laws of the Germanic peoples prior to their contact with Rome. They dealt predominantly with family and property rights and codes of justice and punishment, and were regarded as personal and tribal law, not territorial.

Gestapo   Notorious Nazi secret police organization officially responsible for internal security within the Third Reich. Formed in 1933, the Gestapo had the power to arrest enemies of the state without judicial review. The Gestapo terrorized the German populace and became a primary element in Hitler's persecution of the Jews, sending millions of them to concentration camps where they were systematically murdered.

Ghazan, Mahmud (1271–1304)   Mongol ruler of Persia (1295–1304). Ghazan was the first Mongol ruler to convert to Islam, which he made the state religion of Persia. He extended his domains to include Syria.

Gharnavids   Turkish dynasty that ruled vast areas in modern Afghanistan, Iran, and northern India (977–1186). Its most notable sultan was Mahmud who reigned from 998–1030. Its first capital was Ghazni, Afghanistan, and then Lahore, India. Conquests by the Seljuk Turks in 1040 brought on the decline of this empire.

Gibraltar (Rock of Gibraltar)   One of the ancient Pillars of Hercules, it is a British crown colony and strategic fortress at the western approach to the Mediterranean. Taken by the Moors in 711, it was reconquered by the Spanish in 1462. The English captured it in 1704 during the War of Spanish Succession and have held it ever since.

Gilbert, Sir Humphrey (1539?–1583)   English navigator and soldier. He reached Newfoundland in 1583 on an exploratory voyage to North America and claimed it for England.

Gilgamesh   Legendary king important in Babylonian mythology who, on the death of his friend Enkidu, sought a plant that would make him immortal. The king's exploits are recounted in the *Epic of Gilgamesh*. One version was unearthed from the ruins of the library of Assyrian King Ashurbanipal, who ruled in the 7th century B.C. This written version of the legend is thought to date from 2000 B.C., and has attracted special interest because of its account of a universal flood that supposedly once engulfed humankind.

Girondists   French political group that played an important role in the early stages of the French Revolution. Composed of well educated, moderate republicans, the group dominated the Legislative Assembly between 1791 and 1792. The decline of the Girondists began with the overthrow of the constitutional monarchy in 1792 and the formation of the revolutionary National Convention. The Convention was dominated by radical Jacobins, called Montagnards, who had the support of the working class. The Girondists' moderate policies and open opposition to the Montagnards put them in disfavor with the populace. Hostility toward Girondists culminated in the execution of many of the party's leaders at the outset of the Reign of Terror.

Giscard d'Estaing, Valery (b. 1926)   French political leader. Giscard d'Estang served as finance minister for C. de Gaulle and G. Pompidou before becoming president in 1974. He was defeated in 1981 by Socialist F. Mitterand.

Giza, pyramids of   Egyptian pyramids. These three pyramids built about 2613–2500 B.C., are located near the city of Giza on the western banks of the Nile. They are included among the ancient Seven Wonders of the World. Khufu built the oldest (and largest, over 480 feet high), Khafre the second (over 470 feet high), and Menkaure the third (over 355 feet high).

Gladiators   Professional fighters of ancient Rome who were pitted against one another or wild animals in armed combat, often to the death. Gladiators provided a popular form of entertainment in the Roman world from about 264 B.C. to about 405 A.D. and fights were performed in arenas before large crowds.

Gladstone, William Ewart (1809–1898)   One of the greatest British statesmen of his century and prime minister (1868–1874, 1880–1885, 1886, 1892–1894). He entered Parliament in 1833 as a Conservative and held a number of government posts as a Conservative before changing his affiliation and becoming Liberal party leader in 1867. His many accomplishments included civil service reform, an end to paid military commissions, institution of the secret ballot, a system of national public education, and Irish land reforms.

Glasnost   The policy of openness created by Mikhail Gorbachev in the late 1980s in the U.S.S.R. Some attribute the end of communism in the U.S.S.R. in part to the forces set in motion by the policy of glasnost.

Glorious Revolution (Bloodless Revolution)   In English history the period between 1688 and 1689 that saw the overthrow of King James II, the crowning of William of Orange and his wife Mary II, and the final recognition of parliamentary supremacy. James II's Catholicism and the birth of his Catholic son and heir, James Edward, aroused a united Whig and Tory opposition to his rule. Parliament offered the English throne to the Dutch prince William and his wife Mary, James II's Protestant daughter. William landed at Torbay in England in 1688 with some 14,000 men and James fled to France after his armies deserted him. The throne was offered to William and Mary under the conditions set forth in the British Bill of Rights in 1689. These conditions, which assured parliamentary supremacy, were accepted and the two were crowned as joint rulers in 1689.

Gnosticism   Religious movement, important in the early history of Christianity, which promised personal salvation through revelation of mystical knowledge. Gnosticism fused elements of many religious, philosophical, and mythical systems of the ancient world and, though the many gnostic sects varied widely in their beliefs, they generally believed in a world-creator, religious dualism, and Docetism. Gnosticism came to be regarded as a heresy by the Christian church and by the 6th century most gnostic sects had disappeared.

Godwin (Godwine) (d. 1053)   English nobleman, earl of Wessex. He helped Edward the Confessor gain the throne in 1042 but was later exiled by him in a dispute in 1051. Godwin launched a successful invasion of England in 1052, forcing Edward to restore his lands.

Goebbels, Joseph Paul (1897–1945)   German propaganda minister in Hitler's Third Reich. A loyal ally to Hitler from 1926, Goebbels was instrumental in his rise to power. As propaganda minister (1933–1945), he skillfully manipulated the mass media to maintain Hitler's power and to forward the planned extermination of millions of Jews.

Golden Horde   Mongol kingdom established by Batu, grandson of Genghis Khan, in 1256 and ruled by his descendants until 1502. Their empire consisted of most of Russia.

Good Emperors, the   Name given to the Roman emperors who reigned during the years 96–169 A.D. They were Nerva, Trajan, Hadrian, Antoninus Pius, Marcus Aurelius, and Lucius Aurelius Verus.

Gorbachev, Mikhail Sergeyvich (b. 1931)   Communist party leader who became president of the Soviet Union in 1985. His policies of glasnost (*see* page 11-44) and perestroika (*see* Government section, page 7-18) and other factors, such as agricultural failure, industrial stagnation, and rising nationalism, helped cause the breakup of the U.S.S.R. and the fall from power of the Communist party in 1991. Following a failed coup by former Communist officials in August 1991, Gorbachev could not stop the breakup of the former Soviet Union. In December 1991, his office ceased to exist and he resigned.

Gordon, Charles George (1833–1885)   British soldier and colonial administrator. He became famous as a military commander in China during the Taiping Rebellion (1860–1865) and gained further honors in pacifying the Sudan (1873–1880). In 1874 he was sent back to the Sudan and was killed in the Battle of Khartoum.

Göring, Hermann Wilhelm (Goering) (1893–1946)   German military and political leader, one of Hitler's chief lieutenants. When Hitler came to power in 1933 he was made prime minister and air minister. He set up the Gestapo and concentration camps, and in the late 1930s mobilized Germany for war.

Gothic   Medieval artistic and architectural style in Europe from the 12th–15th centuries. Originating in France, it supplanted the Romanesque style. Gothic art was flowing, mystical, individualistic, and tended toward the naturalistic. Gothic architecture was characterized by height, high vaulted ceilings, tracery between large (often stained glass) windows, and flying buttresses. There was increasing emphasis on decorative detail toward the end of the movement. The most famous example of Gothic architecture is the Cathedral of Notre-Dame in France. The Gothic styles gave way to the Renaissance forms.

Goths   Germanic tribes. An ancient Teutonic people, they included the Ostrogoths and the Visigoths. The Ostrogoths established an empire in the region of the Ukraine. After the fall of their empire, in 370 A.D. to the Huns, they joined the Huns in conquest. After the Huns were forced back, the Ostrogoths, when they traveled westward, invaded Italy and overthrew Odoacer in 493. The Visigoths moved into the Roman Empire in the 4th century A.D., sacked Rome in 410, then turned westward to Gaul and Spain. In Gaul they were defeated by Frankish King Clovis in 507 and were defeated in Spain in 711 by Muslim invaders from North Africa.

Government of India Acts   British laws passed by Parliament (1773–1935) to govern India. The first act (1773–1830), also known as the East India Company Acts, regulated the British East India Company. Later acts transferred in 1858 power to the crown, and finally paved the way for Indian self-government.

Gracchus, Caius Sempronius (d. 121 B.C.)   Roman tribune (123 and 122 B.C.). Elected tribune on the death of his brother, Tiberius Gracchus, he continued his brother's agrarian reforms. The reforms aroused opposition among the aristocrats and he was killed following the defeat for a third term as tribune.

Gracchus, Tiberius Sempronius (d. 133 B.C.)   Roman tribune in 133 B.C. As tribune he formulated the Sempronian Law, designed to eliminate the widespread poverty of Romans by redistributing public lands to them. Subsequent opposition to his plan in the Senate resulted in a riot in which he was killed.

Great Colombia (Gran Colombia)   Former South American republic. Established in 1822 by Bolívar, it consisted of parts of modern Colombia, Panama, Venezuela, and Ecuador. It lasted until 1830, when Venezuela and Ecuador established their independence.

Great Fear   Name given to panics in July and August of 1789 among the rural peasants in France during the early phase of the French Revolution. Peasants, who had stopped paying taxes to local land aristocrats, were overcome by unfounded rumors that the aristocrats had hired brigands to attack them. This prompted a series of peasant revolts that brought an end to the taxes.

Great Leap Forward   Chinese Communist campaign (1958 and 1959) to increase agricultural and industrial output by reorganizing the populace into communes. The government hoped to take advantage of China's great manpower reserves by this new system. The program ended in failure in 1960.

Great Trek   Emigration between 1835 and 1840, by 14,000 Afrikaners (Boers) from Cape Colony into the African interior. Opposed to British policies, especially those favoring natives, the Afrikaners moved northward, battled with native peoples, and finally established the Afrikaner republic of Natal in 1839.

Great Wall of China   Celebrated defensive wall built (214–204 B.C.) by Ch'in dynasty Emperor Shih Hwang-ti and added to by succeeding rulers. The 1,500-mile-long, 25-foot-high wall failed to prevent invasions from the North.

Greek Civil War   Civil war between Communist and rightist factions in Greece between 1944 and 1949. Following the withdrawal of Nazi occupation forces, Communist guerrillas attacked both rightist guerrilla forces and the British occupation army. By the Varkizoi Agreement (January 14, 1945), a short-lived government was established. Government instability and widespread unrest, however, led to new fighting (May 1946). The Communist faction was finally defeated, with American and British aid, by October 1949.

Greek fire   Flammable substance used by the Byzantines in warfare from the 7th century. This secret mixture ignited on contact with water and was used effectively against Arab fleets in naval battles.

Greek Independence, War of   The Greek revolt between 1821 and 1832 against the Ottoman Empire. After centuries of Turkish domination, Greeks in the Peloponnesus rebelled in 1821 and proclaimed Greek independence in 1822. The revolt attracted popular support in Europe and the Turks were forced to seek aid from Egypt in 1824. The Egyptians and Turks soon occupied much of the southern Peloponnesus, but their advance was slowed by the intervention of the European powers. The London Conference of 1830 and 1831 of European powers set the final terms of Greek independence. The Ottoman Turks recognized the independent kingdom of Greece by the Treaty of Constantinople in 1832.

Gregorian Calendar   Reformed calendar, instituted by Pope Gregory XIII in 1582. A reformation of the Julian calendar, it established the 365-day year with a leap year of 366.

Gregory I, Saint (Gregory the Great) (540–604) Italian-born pope (590–604). A doctor of the church, he was a celebrated church administrator, noted for his reforms in both church organization and liturgy. He promoted spiritual supremacy of the pope, established the authority of the pope in temporal matters, began the Christianization of Britain in 596, and encouraged the spread of monasticism.

Gregory VII, Saint (orig. Hildebrand) (1020–1085) Italian-born pope (1073–1085). One of the great church reformers in the face of powerful opposition, Gregory undertook reforms to end widespread church corruption. In 1073 he called reform synods, condemned clerical marriage and simony, and appointed legates to oversee enforcement of church laws. His battle for reform focused on lay investiture, which he banned in 1075 and which set German Emperor Henry IV against him. He twice excommunicated Henry.

Gregory IX (Segni, Ugolino di) (1147?–1241) Italian-born pope (1227–1241). A pope of forceful disposition, he twice excommunicated Holy Roman Emperor Frederick II (1227 and 1239) and organized the office of the Inquisition in 1233.

Gregory of Tours, Saint (538?–593) French historian and bishop. He wrote the *History of the Franks*, still regarded as an important historical resource.

Grenville, George (1712–1770)   British statesman. As chief minister (1763–1765) under King George III, he put through the Revenue Act of 1764 and the Stamp Act of 1766, both of which served to stir up sentiment for rebellion in the American colonies.

Grey, Lady Jane (1537–1554)   English queen for nine days in 1553, successor to Edward VI. Soon after being crowned, she acceded to Mary I's claim to the throne and was later sentenced for treason.

Gromyko, Andrei Andreyevich (1909–1989) Became Soviet foreign minister in 1957 and a member of the Soviet Central Committee in 1956. He was appointed U.S. ambassador (1943–1946), he became deputy foreign minister in 1946, and delegate to the United Nations in 1946. As foreign minister, he pursued Cold War policies against Western powers. During the 1970s he played an important part in the Nixon-Brezhnev summit talks.

Guayaquil Conference   Strategy meeting in July of 1822 between leaders of the South American independence movement. Bolívar and San Martín met at this Ecuadorian coastal city to discuss joining forces against Spain. They failed to reach an agreement and Bolívar continued to fight alone.

Guelphs and Ghibellines   Two opposing political factions prominent during the struggle for control of northern and central Italy between the 13th and 15th centuries. The Guelphs supported the pope and the Ghibellines the German Holy Roman emperors. The rivalry led to numerous local wars during this period and in Florence a long civil war that ended in 1266 with the expulsion of the Ghibellines. By the 14th century after the power of Holy Roman emperors declined in Italy and the papacy was removed to France, the rivalry was important only in local political struggles.

Guerrero, Vicente (1783?–1831)   Mexican revolutionary and president (1829). From 1810 he led revolutionary forces and became a celebrated guerrilla fighter. After 1822, he joined forces with Santa Anna in toppling Iturbide and became vice president under Guadalupe Victoria. Guerrero was overthrown in 1829 by his vice president, Anastasio Bustamente.

Guevara, Che (Guevara de la Serna, Ernesto) (1928–1967)   Argentinian-born Communist revolutionary leader. An important figure in Castro's Cuban revolution in 1959, he became a renowned leader of revolutionary movements in Latin America.

Guilds (gilds)   Medieval European merchant and craft associations. Guilds originated in Europe in the 11th century as merchants' associations, formed to protect traveling merchants from bandits. Merchants' guilds became powerful, both economically and politically in the 12th and 13th centuries. They were completely displaced, however, by the rise of the craft guilds and disappeared by the 14th century. The craft guilds, composed of workers in a particular craft, declined in the 15th century as a result of internal disputes and other problems.

Gupta dynasty   Dynasty of rulers of India (320–550 A.D.). Guptas ruled over an empire that at one time included northern and parts of central India.

The dynasty was founded by Chandragupta I and the empire was greatly expanded by Samudragupta. Chandragupta II was the greatest of all Gupta rulers. Indian art and commerce flourished under the Guptas until the empire was overrun by the Huns in the 5th century.

Gutenberg, Johann (1400–1468?) German generally regarded as the inventor (in the West) of the method of printing with movable type. It is believed that Chinese and Korean printing techniques, invented earlier and similar to Gutenberg's, were unknown to Europeans.

H **Habeas corpus** Writ issued by a court to one who has imprisoned another, calling for the person detained to be produced before the court for a specific purpose. It is used largely to prevent false imprisonment.

Hadrian (76–138 A.D.) Roman emperor (117–138 A.D.). An energetic ruler, Hadrian fortified the empire's boundaries and built Hadrian's Wall, a defensive stone wall to protect the northern border of Roman territories in Britain against invading tribes.

Hagia Sophia (Santa Sophia) Former cathedral at Constantinople, considered a masterpiece of Byzantine art and one of the world's most magnificent buildings. Built as a Christian church by Byzantine emperor Justinian I, it became a mosque in 453 after the Turks conquered Constantinople and now is a museum.

Hague, the Capital of the Netherlands. Originally a town that grew up around a palace built by Count William of Holland in 1250, it became one of the important diplomatic centers of Europe by the 17th century. Since the first Hague Conference in 1899, the city has been associated with advancement of international justice. The International Court of Justice is located here.

Haile Selassie (Tafari Makonnen) (Ras Tafari) (1891–1975) Emperor of Ethiopia (1930–1974) who worked to modernize his country and bring it into the world political arena. He led the unsuccessful defense against the invading Italian army in 1935 and with British help regained his throne in 1941. He was deposed in 1974 in a military coup.

Hakluyt, Richard (1552?–1616) English geographer. His many books on voyages of discovery helped promote exploration and colonization of North America by the English.

Halifax, Edward Frederick Lindley Wood, 1st earl of (1881–1959) English statesman. He was viceroy of India (1926–1931), foreign secretary (1938–1940), and ambassador to the United States (1941–1946). As foreign secretary he was a staunch supporter of Chamberlain's appeasement policy toward the Nazis.

Halley, Edmund (1656–1742) English astronomer and mathematician. Though noted for a variety of discoveries relating to heavenly bodies, he is known best for calculating accurately the return in 1758 of the comet now named after him.

Hammarskjöld, Dag (1905–1961) Swedish statesman and secretary general of the United Nations (1953–1961). Noted as an able and active peacemaker, he played an important role in easing the Suez Crisis in 1956 and in maintaining Mideast stability during the crisis in Lebanon in 1958. He was killed in an airplane crash while attempting to mediate an end to the civil war that broke out in the Congo in 1960.

Hammurabi (1792–1750 B.C.) Babylonian credited with bringing Mesopotamia under one rule, he is known best for his comprehensive legal code covering economic, familial, criminal, and civil codes of conduct.

Han dynasty Chinese dynasty. Founded by Liu pang (later known as Han Kao Tsu), it succeeded the Ch'in dynasty and ruled China (202? B.C.–220 A.D.). Many characteristic features of Chinese culture were established in this period. The Han unified China, repealed many harsh laws, promoted education and culture, and spread Confucianism. A paid bureaucracy and the Chinese Examination System were instituted during this period, and a distinctive artistic style also emerged. Wu Ti was one of the most notable rulers. Wang Mang briefly interrupted the reign of the Han (9–23 A.D.) by his revolt.

Han-fei-tzu (d. 233 B.C.) Chinese philosopher. His advocacy of authoritarianism and complete obedience to the emperor gained great influence in the Ch'in dynasty. He is credited with the philosophy known as legalism.

Hannibal (247–182? B.C.) Carthaginian general during the Second Punic War (218–201 B.C.). His attack on a city allied to Rome, precipitated in 218 B.C. the Second Punic War. In one of history's most celebrated military maneuvers, he led an army of 40,000 soldiers with a supply train of elephants out of Spain and across the Alps to invade Rome itself. He gained major victories over the Romans at Lake Trasimeno in 217 and Cannae in 216 but was unable to take the city. Recalled in 203 to defend Carthage from Roman attack, he was defeated at Zama in 202. He later joined Syrian King Antiochus in wars against Rome, but was defeated in 182.

Hanno (5th century B.C.) Carthaginian navigator who led a fleet of ships along the West coast of Africa for the purpose of establishing new colonies. He eventually founded 7 colonies and may have reached Sierra Leone.

Hanover, House of German ruling family of Hanover. Descended from the Guelphs, the line acceded to the British throne, through the Act of Settlement in 1701, through George I. Succeeding Hanoverian rulers of England were George II, George III, George IV, and William IV. Upon the accession of Queen Victoria in 1837 the two kingdoms were separated, Victoria being unable by Hanoverian law to accede to the throne of Hanover.

Hanseatic League Once powerful federation of cities between the 13th and 17th centuries, mainly located in what is now northern Germany. It sought to establish trade monopolies and protect its concerns against piracy, robbery, and intervention by foreign governments. The cities of Lubeck and Hamburg founded the league in 1241. It eventually included over 100 other cities and virtually controlled trade in the Baltic and North Sea regions. The league established great trading depots, including the Steelyard in London, Bruges, Bergen, and Novgorod. The league reached the zenith of its power with conquest of the Danes and the Treaty of Stralsund in 1370. The league gradually declined thereafter because it was unable to resist the Dutch in the Baltic region, the growing power of other European kingdoms, internal struggles among member cities, and the change in trading patterns brought about by the discovery of the New World.

Han Yu (han Wên-kung) (768–824) Chinese official, essayist, and poet. A Confucian, he was an outspoken critic of Taoism and Buddhism, and was once exiled from the emperor's court for his views.

Hapsburg (Habsburg) One of the major dynasties of European rulers (13th–20th centuries). Members of the Hapsburg House became rulers of Austria, the Holy Roman Empire, and Spain. The line can be traced to the 11th-century counts of Hapsburg, and in 1273 Rudolf I founded the imperial line. Elected king of the Germans in 1273, he acquired Austria in 1278 and made it a hereditary possession in 1282. The Hapsburgs ruled as kings of the Germans (rulers not crowned as "emperor" by the pope) with interruptions until 1452, when Frederick III was crowned Holy Roman emperor. Thereafter the title remained in the family until the empire fell to Napoleon in 1806. By advantageous marriages and inheritances of family domains, Hapsburg rulers vastly increased their holdings and reached the height of their power in the 16th century under Emperor Charles V, who was also Spanish King Charles I. The Hapsburg line was divided on his death into Spanish (rulers 1504–1700) and Austrian lines. The Austrian line (known as Hapsburg-Lorraine after 1740) ruled the Holy Roman Empire to 1806 and Austria, Hungary, and Bohemia until 1918.

Hara, Kei (Hara, Takashi) (1856–1921) Japanese statesman and prime minister (1918–1921). He built his Seiyukai party into a Western-style political machine and became the first Japanese prime minister to form a cabinet according to parliamentary principles.

Harappa Early civilization that existed in India between 2500 and 1500 B.C. This civilization, believed to be that of the Dravidians, reached a high level of development and was overcome by the Ayans who invaded India in 1500 B.C. Two of its cities, Mohenjo-Daro and Harappa, have been discovered.

Hardenberg, Prince Karl August von (1750–1822) Prussian statesman. As chancellor from 1810, he guided Prussia through the turbulent years of the Napoleonic Wars and was responsible for many political and social reforms.

Hargreaves, James (d. 1778) English inventor who devised the spinning jenny in 1764.

Harmhab (Horemheb) Egyptian pharaoh (1350–1315 B.C.) and founder of the 19th dynasty. He restored worship of the traditional god Amon and brought about a return of prosperity.

Harold II (1022?–1066) Last Saxon king of England in 1066. Chosen heir by Edward the Confessor, Harold ruled less than a year before his defeat by William, duke of Normandy, at the Battle of Hastings, in which he was killed.

Harsha (590?–647?) Indian ruler (606–647). An able commander, he united all of northern India into an empire that lasted throughout his reign.

Harun-al-Rashid (Harun ar-Rashid) (764–809) Fifth Abbasid caliph (786–809) and most famous of the dynasty. He reigned during the height of the Islamic Empire, which then included southwestern Asia and northern Africa. His exploits and the splendor of his court at Baghdad are celebrated in *The Thousand and One Nights*.

Harvey, William (1578–1657) English physician who was the first to identify correctly the function of the heart and blood circulation. He published his findings in 1628.

Hasan (Hassan) (624–669) Islamic ruler, the 5th caliph in 661, and a grandson of Muhammad. He was proclaimed caliph on the death of his father Ali but soon relinquished the title to Muawiyah, who challenged his succession.

Hassan II (b. 1929) Became Moroccan king in 1961. Hassan suspended Morocco's constitution in 1965, but continued unrest forced him to yield to reforms in 1971 and a larger role for Parliament.

Hastings, battle of English-Norman battle in October of 1066 in which English King Harold II was defeated and killed by the invading forces of William (the Conqueror), duke of Normandy. William moved on to London, where he was crowned king in December. This battle is widely regarded by historians as the most important event in British history, marking the start of Norman influence in England.

Hatshepsut (d. 1481 B.C.) Egyptian queen, wife of Thutmose II. A woman of unusually great power, she ruled Egypt during the reign of her husband, and also as regent for Thutmose III. She brought a period of peace to Egypt.

Hausa States (Haussa States) Group of former African states located in what is now northern Nigeria. Conquered many times during their history, they were taken over in the early 1900s by the British and incorporated into the protectorate of Nigeria.

Havel, Vaclav (b. 1936) Czechoslovak literary figure whose popularity brought him into political prominence. With the collapse of communism (*see* page 11-27) and the East European Revolution (*see* page 11-34), he became the negotiator for dissidents. At the formation of the new non-Communist Republic of Czechoslovakia in 1989, he became its first president. He resigned the presidency when the country divided into two independent states in 1992. In 1993, he was elected Czech president.

Hawkins, Sir John (Hawkyns, Sir John) (1532–1595) English seaman and admiral. The first Englishman to engage in the slave trade in 1562, he directed reconstruction of the English fleet and took part in the battle against the Spanish Armada.

Heath, Edward Richard George (b. 1916) British politician. A conservative, Heath entered Parliament in 1950 and held a variety of posts in the governments of Eden, Macmillan, and Douglas-Home. As prime minister between 1970 and 1974, he succeeded in gaining British entry into the Common Market in 1972. However, increasing economic troubles and conflict in northern Ireland led to his defeat.

Hébert, Jacques Réne (1755–1794) French journalist and revolutionary. A Jacobin and a leader of the sans-culottes (*see* page 11-110), he was involved in the storming of Tuileries Palace in 1792 and the overthrow of the monarchy. Soon after he became a member of the Commune of Paris, he was arrested in May 1793 for aiding the radical movement to oust the (moderate) Girondists from the National Convention. His sans-culotte supporters won his release soon after, however, and in June 1793 Hébert was involved in the riot by working-class radicals that forced the expulsion of Girondists from the National Convention. With the Jacobins now in power, Hébert attempted to force the revolution into ever more extreme measures through his control of the sans-culottes, who had forced in September 1793 institution of the Reign of Terror. He was opposed from mid-1793 by Danton and Robespierre, and in 1794 Hébert was arrested and guillotined.

Hector Trojan hero. The son of Priam, he slew the Greek Patroclus in the Trojan War, and was, in turn, slain by Achilles.

Hedonism Philosophical doctrine, derived in part from the Greek Cyrenaics, that holds that human pleasure is the highest good.

Hegel, Georg Wilhelm Friedrich (1770–1831) German idealistic philosopher, one of the most influential 19th-century thinkers. Hegel held ultimate reality to be absolute spirit or mind, and hence held that "whatever is rational is real and whatever is real is rational." All things tend to the complete and perfect design of the mind by a logical process which Hegel called the "dialectic." In this process an original tendency, or "thesis," gives rise to its opposite tendency, an "antithesis." Both are then resolved into a higher unity, a "synthesis." Hegel analyzed all reality in terms of this dialectic, and it became a favorite tool of subsequent philosophers.

Hegira (hejira) Name for Muhammad's flight in 622 from Mecca and journey to Medina, a pivotal event in the history of Islam. Under a system developed by Omar, 2nd caliph, all events of the Muslim era are dated from the beginning of the lunar year (July 16, 622) in which the hegira occurred. Muhammad was driven from Mecca for opposing the local polytheistic religion and, once in Medina, established himself in that city.

Heian period Period of Japanese history between 794 and 1185 marked by the rise of Buddhism, development of the manorial system, and control of the imperial court by the Fujiwara clan.

Helen (Helen of Troy) Celebrated beauty in Greek mythology who was the cause of the Trojan War. The wife of Spartan King Menelaus she was taken by Paris (or fled with him) to Troy. Troy was besieged by an army of Greeks and, after its fall, Helen was reconciled with her husband.

Hellenic League League of Greek city-states except for Sparta formed in 338 B.C. by Philip of Macedonia. After Philip's death in 336, several of these cities rebelled, only to be suppressed by Alexander the Great in 335. After Alexander's death in 323, Athens led in creating a new league, which was destroyed in 322 by the Macedonians under Antipater. Later Hellenic Leagues were revived in 303 by Demetrius I and by Antigonus III in 224.

Hellenism Name applied to the culture of the ancient Greeks, especially that of Athens at its height in 5th century B.C. It is also applied to the works of those who later adopted Hellenic values and principles. The Hellenistic Age, a time when Greek culture spread throughout the eastern Mediterranean, is generally dated from the death of Alexander the Great to the rise of Augustus in Rome (323–330 B.C.).

Helots Spartan slaves. Considered state property, they were assigned to both agricultural and military tasks. Because of their huge numbers, Helot revolts were greatly feared by the Spartans.

Henry I (Henry the Fowler) (876?–936) German king (919–936), and founder of the Saxon line. He added Lotharingia (Lorraine) to the German kingdom in 925, put an end to Magyar raids, and reasserted the authority of the monarchy.

Henry I (1008–1060) Capetian king of France (1031–1060). He put down various rebellions and later warred unsuccessfully against William, duke of Normandy.

Henry I (Henry Beauclerc) (1068–1135) King of England (1100–1135). Henry obtained the crown while his older brother, Robert, duke of Normandy, was away on crusade. Henry subsequently defended the crown against an invasion in 1101 of England by Robert and later took Normandy from Robert in 1106. Henry's efforts to arrange the succession of his daughter, Matilda, resulted in a civil war during the reign of his successor, Stephen.

Henry II (973–1024) Holy Roman emperor (1014–1024) and German king (1002–1024). The last Saxon emperor, he recaptured most of the German land taken by Polish king Boleslaus I and extended his influence throughout Italy.

Henry II (1133–1189) King of England (1154–1189). The grandson of Henry I, son of Matilda and husband of Eleanor of Aquitaine, Henry founded the Plantagenet line. He restored order to strife-torn England, reformed its laws, and established the supremacy of royal courts over local justices. He defined church-state relations with the Constitutions of Clarendon, but his arguments with Thomas à Becket led indirectly to the latter's murder. Henry consolidated English holdings in northern England, Ireland, and Scotland. He was the father of Richard I and John I.

Henry II (1519–1559) King of France (1547–1559), son of and successor to Francis I. Regarded as a weak ruler, he instituted repressive measures against Protestants, added Calais to French domains in 1558, and negotiated an end to the Italian Wars.

Henry III (Henry the Black) (1017–1056) German king and Holy Roman emperor (1046–1056). His reign marked the height of the Holy Roman emperor's power. His efforts to reform the church, however, did not succeed.

Henry III (1551–1589) French king (1574–1589). As duke of Anjou, he aided his mother Catherine de Médicis in planning the St. Bartholomew's Day Massacre in 1572. His reign was marked by the Wars of Religion that raged in France between the Catholics and Huguenots, and by the War of the Three Henrys (1585–1589).

Henry IV (1050–1106) Holy Roman emperor (1056–1106). His reign was marked by a long and unsuccessful struggle with the pope over lay investiture. His struggle with the church began in 1075 when he appointed a number of bishops. Condemned by Pope Gregory VII for the action, Henry declared the pope deposed in 1076, only to be himself declared deposed by the pope. Faced with a rebellion against the crown, Henry was forced to submit to the pope and was absolved after doing penance at Canossa in 1077. However, the German nobles elected Rudolf of Swabia as anti-king and a civil war ensued (1077–1080), from which Henry emerged victorious. Gregory in the meantime again deposed Henry, who in turn made Clement III antipope. Henry then invaded Italy between 1081–1083 and drove Gregory into exile, where he died. The reforming popes who succeeded Gregory supported revolts against Henry.

Henry IV (Henry of Bolingbroke) (Henry of Lancaster) (1367–1413) English king (1399–1413), a son of John of Gaunt, and the first of three kings of the House of Lancaster. He led a successful rebellion against King Richard II in 1399 after which he claimed the crown for himself. His reign was marked by rebellions, including those in Wales and Scotland, and the crown's worsening financial troubles.

Henry IV (1553–1610) First Bourbon king of France (1589–1610). His reign marked the end of the Wars of Religion (1562–1598). Henry was raised a Protestant and, as Henry of Navarre, became nominal leader of the Protestants (Huguenots) in the Wars of Religion after 1569. In 1584, he became heir to the French throne (by the accession of Henry III and death of his heir). However, the Catholic League bitterly opposed the possible accession of a Protestant, and provoked the War of the Three Henrys. Henry was successful in this war and, in 1589, became king by the death of Henry III. Henry converted to Catholicism in 1593, which ended the opposition. He then instituted a policy of reconciliation that resulted in the Edict of Nantes, establishing religious toleration. Henry's subsequent reign was marked by a period of general stability and rebuilding.

Henry V (1081–1125) Holy Roman emperor (1106–1125), and last of the Salian dynasty. The struggle over investiture continued in his reign and when Henry lost the support of his bishops, as well as the nobles, he was forced to accept a compromise measure, the Concordat of Worms in 1122.

Henry V (1387–1422) English king (1413–1422). Allying England with the Burgundians, Henry reopened the Hundred Years' War and led the English to victory in the Battle of Agincourt in 1415. He conquered Normandy and Rouen and concluded the Treaty of Troyes in 1420, by which he agreed to marry Catherine of Valois, daughter of French king Charles VI. Charles acknowledged him rightful heir to the French throne.

Henry VI (1421–1471) King of England (1422–1461, 1470 and 1471), the last Lancastrian king of England. Completely unfit to rule, he lost all English territories in France except for Calais. A period of insanity (1453–1454) led to the appointment of Richard, duke of York, as lord protector, and his recovery led to the long struggle for the throne between the Houses of York and Lancaster in the Wars of the Roses.

Henry VII (orig. Henry Tudor) (1457–1509) English king (1485–1509), founder of the Tudor dynasty. During the period of civil war called the Wars of the Roses, Henry (of the House of Lancaster) was a leading contender for the throne. Henry landed in England in 1485, defeated Richard III at Bosworth Field, and was crowned king in 1486. By his marriage to Edward IV's daughter, Elizabeth, he united the Houses of York and Lancaster and founded the Tudor line. This also ended the Wars of the Roses. His reign saw the beginnings of English overseas exploration.

Hans Holbein's painting of King Henry VIII of England.

Henry VIII (1491–1547) English king (1509–1547). The early years of Henry's reign were marked by participation with the Holy League from 1511 in war against France and by the defeat of invading Scottish armies. Henry received in 1521 the title "Defender of the Faith" from Pope Leo X for his book, written in answer to Luther and the emerging Protestant movement. By 1529, however, Henry fell afoul of the church through his efforts to divorce his first wife Catherine of Aragon. Henry's excommunication in 1534, and finally passage of the Act of Supremacy resulted in the creation of the Church of England. In subsequent years, Henry dealt ruthlessly with any opposition, Catholic or Protestant, to this position as supreme head of the church in England. Events of Henry's later reign included the continuing struggle with the French, a defeat of Scottish forces that resulted in the death of King James V, and a series of new wives that brought the total to 6 by the time of his death.

Henry the Navigator (1394–1460) Portuguese prince. The success of the exploratory voyages along the African coast, which he sponsored, laid the foundation for the Portuguese colonial empire.

Heraclitus (535–475 B.C.) Greek philosopher, an early proponent of a metaphysical philosophy. He believed permanence to be an illusion and the only reality was constant change.

Hercules (Heracles) (Herakles) Hero of great strength and courage in Greek and Roman mythology, son of Zeus and Alcmene. Hercules undertook his famous 12 tasks to repent the murder of his wife and children, committed in a fit of madness.

Herodotus (484?–425 B.C.) Greek historian. Herodotus traveled widely throughout the known world, settling in southern Italy. He is remembered for his richly detailed history of the Persian Wars, and is often called the "father of history."

Herod the Great (73?–4 B.C.) King of Judaea (37–4 B.C.). Herod was made king of Judaea by the Roman Marc Antony in 39 B.C. and took possession of the kingdom 2 years later. He put down revolts in the early part of his reign and in succeeding years Judaea enjoyed a period of great prosperity. He constructed many public buildings and, though he had converted to Judaism, he promoted Hellenism. According to the Bible, he was in power at the time of Jesus' birth and ordered the massacre of the Innocents.

Herriot, Edouard (1872–1957) French statesman. He headed the Radical (Socialist) party from 1919 until his death and was premier three times (1924–1925, 1926, 1932).

Hertz, Heinrich Rudolph (1857–1894) German physicist. He discovered radio waves in 1886 and thereby proved J. Maxwell's electromagnetic theory of light and heat. The unit of frequency, the hertz, is named for him.

Herzl, Theodor (1860–1904) Austrian-born founder of modern Zionism. The Dreyfus case convinced Herzl that acceptance of Jews in Europe was impossible. He subsequently wrote *The Jewish State*, a pamphlet in which he advocated creation of a separate Jewish state.

Hess, Rudolf (1894–1987) German Nazi leader. He created a sensation in 1941 when on his own initiative he flew to Scotland apparently for the purpose of negotiating peace between Britain and Germany. He was sentenced to life imprisonment during the Nuremberg trials.

Hidalgo y Costilla, Miguel (1753–1811) Mexican priest and national hero. He organized and led between 1810 and 1811 an army of Mexicans in a nearly successful rebellion against Spanish rule. His revolt marked the opening of the Mexican Revolution.

Hideyoshi (Toyotomi) (1536?–1598) Japanese soldier and, as the emperor's chief minister, dictator from 1585–1598. He completed the unification of Japan in 1590, instituted numerous civil reforms, and launched an unsuccessful invasion in China in 1592.

Hieroglyphics A system of picture-writing used by the ancient Egyptians from 3400 B.C. Hieroglyphic writing died out by 500 A.D., and meaning was lost until it was deciphered in the early 1800s through the use of the Rosetta Stone.

Himmler, Heinrich (1900–1945) German National Socialist leader and one of the most powerful men in Hitler's Third Reich. Notorious for his ruthlessness and cruelty, he headed the SS (state police unit) and the Gestapo (secret police) and ran the concentration camps in which millions died. *See* **Gestapo**.

Hindenburg, Paul von (1847–1934) German field marshal and president of the Weimar Republic (1925–1934). The commander of German armies during World War I he emerged as a national hero despite Germany's defeat. In 1933, he appointed Hitler as his chancellor and thus opened the way for Hitler's takeover of the German government.

Hinduism Religion practiced by the majority of the people of India. Hinduism in its modern form evolved in stages from ancient Vedism in 1500 B.C. to Brahmanism, and finally (2nd century B.C.) to early Hinduism. During its long development Hinduism has absorbed doctrines, rites, and practices from numerous other religions and sects and has spawned a great number of Hindu sects. Generally, however, Hinduism is characterized by acceptance of the Vedas (sacred texts), adherence to the caste system, belief in cycles of life, death, and rebirth of the individual, and the promise of escape from this cycle through enlightenment.

Hipparchus (Hipparchos) (2nd century B.C.) Important early Greek astronomer. He is believed to have compiled the first star catalogue and discovered subtle changes in the equinoxes caused by the wobble in the earth's rotation.

Hippocrates (460–370 B.C.) Greek physician, frequently called the "father of medicine." The Hippocratic Oath, still administered to all new physicians, reflects his medical ethics.

Hirohito (1901–1989) Emperor of Japan from 1926–1989. His reign was marked by wars against China from the 1930s and Japan's participation in World War II. He accepted unconditional surrender in 1945 and a new constitution making him a constitutional monarch in 1946.

Hiroshima Japanese city, the target of the first atomic bomb (August 6, 1945). The bombing virtually destroyed the city, hastened the end of World War II, and marked the beginning of the age of nuclear warfare.

Hitler, Adolf (1889–1945) Austrian-born German dictator (1933–1945) and founder of the National Socialist party (Nazis). He started the National Socialist party in 1921 and turned it into a nationalistic, paramilitary group. He failed in 1923 in his attempt to seize power in Bavaria (Munich Beer Hall Putsch), was arrested, and while in jail wrote *Mein Kampf* (My Struggle), an explanation of his political ideas. The Nazi party grew rapidly during the Great Depression, largely because of Hitler's ability to play on hatred of the Jews and Communists in the name of German nationalism. The party's strength in the Reichstag increased greatly as a result, though Hitler lost the 1932 presidential election to von Hindenburg. Von Hindenburg named Hitler as his chancellor in 1933, however, and Hitler soon after began to consolidate his power. He succeeded in gaining emergency powers, and in banning the Communists. He then won passage of the Enabling Act (March 23, 1933), which established the Third Reich. Following von Hindenburg's death in 1934 Hitler became sole ruler of Germany and embarked on his program of expanding German power. At the same time, he began his program of the "Final Solution" (*see* **Holocaust**). He occupied the Rhineland in 1936, annexed Austria in 1938, occupied Czecho-slovakia in 1939, and invaded Poland in 1939. The last action provoked the outbreak of World War II. Despite his remarkable early successes, the tide of the war was clearly against him by 1944. It is believed that he committed suicide in his Berlin bunker in 1945.

Adolph Hitler salutes a labor movement parade in Nuremberg, Germany in 1934.

Hittite Empire   Once powerful kingdom in Meso-potamia (Asia Minor) (1600–1200 B.C.). The Hittites are believed to have discovered the technique of tempering iron and thus figure in the beginnings of the Iron Age. The Hittite peoples first appeared (1800 B.C.) in what is now central Turkey in a migration from the East. They established the Old Kingdom (1600–1400 B.C.) and during this period Hittite rulers gradually expanded their domains throughout Turkey and into northern Syria. The Hittite ruler Mursilis I attacked Babylon (1590) and thereby ended the rule of the Amorite kings. The empire reached its greatest power [especially under Suppiluliumas I (1380–1340)] during the New Kingdom (1400–1200), when it dominated Meso-potamia. Some time around 1200 B.C. invasions by Phrygian, Thracian, and Assyrian peoples caused the sudden collapse of the Hittite empire. By 700 B.C. the Assyrians had absorbed the last vestiges of the Hittite empire.

Hizbollah   Terrorist organization made up primarily of Palestinian nationalists. It is headquartered in Lebanon, supported by Syria and Iran, and has as its main target Israel.

Hobbes, Thomas (1588–1679)   British philosopher. A theorist in both natural and political philosophy. He formulated a mechanistic view of human actions, and his writings on free will and the social contract had an enormous influence on the development of political philosophy.

Ho Chi Minh (pseud. of Nguyen That Thanh) (1890–1969)   Vietnamese Communist leader. During World War II, he organized the Viet Minh movement for Vietnamese independence and his guerrilla units fought the Japanese. After the war in 1945, he proclaimed Vietnam a republic, of which he became president (1945–1954). He was soon embroiled in the Indochina War (1946–1954) and the republic was divided into South and North Vietnam. As president of North Vietnam (1954–1969), he organized the National Liberation Front and the Vietcong guerrilla armies, which fought in the South during the Vietnam War (1960–1975).

Hohenstaufen   Family of German nobles and rulers of the Holy Roman Empire between 1138 and 1254. The family originated in the 11th century with a Swabian count, Frederick (d. 1105). The first Hohenstaufen emperor was Conrad III, crowned in 1138. The Hohenstaufen rulers were opposed by the Guelphs and, by their involvement in Italy, eventually brought about the downfall of the family. The family became extinct by the death in 1254 of Conrad IV, the execution of Conrad in 1268, and the execution of Frederick's illegitimate son, Enzio in 1272.

Hohenzollern   Family of German nobles that ruled Prussia (1415–1871), brought about a united Germany (1871–1918), and created a line of Romanian kings (1866–1947). The family was begun by the 11th-century counts of Zollern. Following the death of Frederick of Hohenzollern in 1200, the family split into Franconian and Swabian lines. The fortunes of the Franconian line grew around control of Brandenburg, of which Frederick I became elector in 1417. Thereafter the line increased its power and domains and in 1701 Frederick I was crowned king of the new kingdom of Prussia. After the unification of Germany in 1871, the Franconian rulers ruled as German kaisers until the establishment of the Weimar Republic in 1918. The Swabian line later split into the Hohenzollern-Hechingen and Hohenzollern-Sigmaringen lines. The latter division produced princes and then kings of Romania (1866–1947).

Hojo   Family of Japanese feudal nobles. As regents for a line of weak shoguns and puppet emperors, they were in effect the rulers of Japan between about 1219 and 1333.

Holocaust   The systematic persecution of Jews, other ethnic minorities, and political opponents of the Nazis from 1933 to 1945. Concentration camps were established, slave labor was used, and during the war, Hitler declared a "final solution," and the camps became extermination sites. It is estimated that upwards of 12 million people died, of which at least 6 million were Jewish. In 1993, the United States dedicated a Holocaust Memorial Museum in Washington, D.C. See **Hitler, Adolf**.

Holy Alliance   League formed in 1815 by Russian czar Alexander I, Austrian king Francis I and Prussian king Frederick William III. The league was largely an agreement in which the monarchs swore to uphold Christian principles in their kingdoms. A part of the general European realignment after the fall of Napoleon's empire, it was eventually joined by all Christian European rulers except British king George IV. The alliance itself had little direct impact, but it became a symbol of conservative reactionary policies by which monarchs maintained social order and that characterized European politics until the mid-19th century.

Holy Land   Name applied to the Middle Eastern region of Palestine. It is so called because of its historical associations with the Christian, Islamic, and Jewish religions.

Holy Roman Empire   Political entity in central Europe from the 10th–19th centuries, which gave rise to the modern states of Germany and Austria. Its history is complex and begins with the Carolingian Empire of Charlemagne. Charlemagne's empire was from 800 considered the successor state to the western Roman empire (defunct since 476) and embraced much of Europe. But it was divided in 843 and central authority soon died out in the two major divisions, the eastern kingdom (roughly, modern Germany) and the western kingdom (roughly, modern France). Otto I restored control in the East and in 962 was crowned emperor of the Romans by the pope. The Holy Roman Empire was thus founded as the reconstituted western Roman empire. In subsequent centuries the empire was torn by struggles with the popes and by the rising power of the princes. In the 13th century the Holy Roman emperors gave up their claims to control Italy and in the 14th century they lost effective control over the princely states within the empire. They had direct rule over only their personal domains, though in the case of the Hapsburg emperors who ruled from the 15th century this amounted to considerable territory. The Protestant Reformation, wars with the Ottoman Turks, and with France further weakened the empire in the next centuries. Its final collapse was brought on by the French Revolutionary Wars at the end of the 18th century.

Homer   Ancient Greek poet who is generally regarded as the author of two of the greatest epic poems in Western literature, the *Iliad* and the *Odyssey*.

Home Rule   Irish movement for self-government. Formed in 1870 by Isaac Butt and led by Parnell to 1890, the movement included demands for a separate Irish parliament and land reform. Two Home Rule bills (1886, 1893) were backed by W. Gladstone's British Liberal party, but they failed to overcome conservative opposition in Parliament. A third Home Rule bill was finally passed in 1912, but implementation was delayed by the outbreak of World War I. During the war, radical Irish Republicans came to the fore, and, with the declaration of Irish independence by the Dail Eireann in 1918, the Irish Republican Army went into armed rebellion against the British government. The Irish Free State (later the Republic of Ireland) was created in 1921.

Hooke, Robert (1635–1703)   English physicist and inventor. He is credited with discovering the law of elasticity in solids now called Hooke's law, and with being the first to use the biological term "cell."

Horace (Flaccus, Quintus Horatius) (65–8 B.C.)   Roman poet, one of the great lyric poets of all time. His works reflect the temper of the Augustan Age and his mastery of poetic form.

Horthy, Miklós von Nagybanya (1868–1957)   Hungarian admiral and head of state (1920–1944). He defeated the Communist revolutionaries and was named regent to the deposed emperor, Charles I.

Horthy later refused to allow Charles to retake the throne and he ruled Hungary himself until he was arrested by Hitler.

Hottentots   A South African people who controlled a large part of South Africa before the arrival of European settlers. They are now divided among several tribes, and their pastoral culture is largely dispersed.

Houphouët-Boigny, Félix (b. 1905)   Leader of the Ivory Coast since it achieved independence in 1960. He has maintained a pro-Western policy.

Howard, Catherine (1521?–1542)   Fifth queen of English king Henry VIII. Married to the king shortly after his divorce from Anne of Cleves in 1540, she was convicted of adultery the following year and was beheaded.

Hsia   Legendary first dynasty in traditional Chinese history that is said to have reigned from 1994–1523 B.C. (2205–1766 B.C., by traditional dating). It was succeeded by the Shang dynasty. Archaeological evidence indicates the existence of an early Hsia state in the Yellow River Valley in northeastern China. The potter's wheel, bronze weapons, and chariots are believed to have been in use during the Hsia period. Yu is the legendary founder of the dynasty.

Hsiung-nu   Asian people who established an empire in Manchuria, Mongolia, and Siberia in the 3rd century B.C. They raided northern China for several centuries and established several dynasties, but declined in importance by the 5th century A.D. The Great Wall of China was completed to control their advance.

Hsüan T'ung (P'u Yi, Henry) (1905–1967)   Last emperor of China (1908–1912). He ruled under the name of Hsüan T'ung, and was later emperor of the Japanese Manchurian puppet state of Manchukuo under the name of K'ang Té.

Hsün-tzu (298–230 B.C.)   Chinese philosopher. He promoted the teachings of Confucius and stressed the benefits of culture in overcoming humankind's basic evil nature.

Huang-Hsing (1871–1916)   Chinese general. As Sun Yat-sen's representative in China during the 1911 revolution, he played a key role in the toppling of the Chinese imperial dynasty. He served as Sun's prime minister and was a founding member of the Kuomintang.

Huang Ti (Yellow Emperor) (Shen Yen Huang Ti)   The third of China's legendary early emperors who, according to tradition, reigned in the third millennium B.C. Many fundamental elements of China's civilization are credited to him, including mathematical calculations, the calendar, money, the use of bamboo, and the study of medicine, among others. He is, with Lao-tze, considered the founder of Taoism.

Huáscar (d. 1533)   Emperor of the Incas in Peru. On his father's death in 1525, he succeeded to the larger portion of an empire divided between his brother Atahualpa and himself. He lost the empire to his brother in 1532 and was later secretly murdered by him.

Hudson, Henry (d. 1611)   English navigator in English and Dutch service. Seeking the northwest passage for the Dutch East India Company, he explored the Hudson River in 1609. On another attempt financed by the English, he discovered and explored what became known as Hudson Bay in 1610.

Huerta, Victoriano (Huerta, Vicente García de la) (1854–1916) Mexican general who overthrew President Madero and became military dictator between 1913 and 1914. After seizing power, Huerta was faced with numerous attempts at counterrevolution as well as the opposition of President Wilson of the United States. Huerta finally fled Mexico.

Huguenots French Protestants, important in French history during the 16th and 17th centuries. Followers of Calvin, Huguenots first suffered persecution at the hands of the French Catholic monarchy shortly after the beginning of the Protestant Reformation in 1517. Despite executions and massacres, the movement spread to the French nobility, where it became interrelated with the struggle for political power. Bitter rivalry led to such events as the Conspiracy of Amboise in 1560, the St. Bartholomew's Day Massacre in 1572, and the Wars of Religion between 1562 and 1598. A period of toleration followed the Edict of Nantes in 1598 and ended with Huguenot uprisings in the 1620s when King Louis XIII attempted to suppress Protestantism. By the Peace of Alais in 1629, Huguenots lost their political power, and, under Louis XIV, the Edict of Nantes was revoked in 1685. This led to a mass exodus of most Huguenots from France. Civil rights of Huguenots were not restored until 1787. By the Declaration of the Rights of Man in 1789 they were granted religious equality.

Hulagu Khan (Hulegu o Hulaku) (1217–1265) Mongol ruler, grandson of Genghis Khan, and founder of the Il-Khan dynasty. Sent to put down a revolt by the Persians, he defeated and executed Caliph Mustasim, destroyed the Islamic capital of Baghdad in 1258, and set up his khanate, which lasted until 1335.

Humanism Philosophy or attitude that places people and human values, welfare, and creativity at the center of consciousness. Humanism was the philosophy that, beginning in the 14th century was a central feature of the Renaissance in Italy, and spread over the rest of Europe in the following three centuries. It represented a shift from the medieval view of the world as an adjunct to God's creation and fostered a new emphasis on the study of humans and the world as objects in themselves. It looked to Greek and Roman models in art, literature, and thought. In modern times, Humanism has come to mean an agnostic philosophy that regards humans as "the measure of all things," as opposed to religious beliefs.

Humbert I (Umberto 1) (1844–1900) Italian king (1878–1900). Under his reign Italy joined in the Triple Alliance in 1882 and prosecuted the Ethiopian War (1895–1896).

Humbert II (Umberto II) (1904–1983) Last king of Italy in 1946. A referendum held shortly after his succession created a republic and stripped him of his powers.

Hunan Army (Hsiang Army) Chinese regional army organized in 1852 in the province of Hunan by Tséng Kuo-fan. Its purpose was to help bring an end to the Taiping Rebellion. At its peak the force numbered approximately 125,000 men.

Hundred Days Period in French history from March 20 to June 28, 1815 during which Napoleon returned from exile and attempted to reestablish his empire. Escaping exile on the island of Elba, he landed in the south of France on March 1, 1815 and marched north with a small force. By the time he reached Paris on March 20, 1815, he had rallied France behind him and forced King Louis XVIII to abdicate. Once again emperor, he was opposed from March 25 by a new coalition of nearly all the other European nations. Napoleon's forces were victorious in the battles of Ligny and Quatre Bras June 16, but were completely crushed at the great Battle of Waterloo on June 18. Soon after, Napoleon surrendered to the British, and King Louis was restored on June 28, ending the Hundred Days period.

Hundred Years' War Series of related wars (1337–1453) between England and France. The conflict stemmed from English claims to the French throne (based on descent from the Norman conquerer, William I) and the long rivalry over territories on the Continent that were then English possessions. Just before war broke out, France and England were vying for the lucrative wool and cloth trade of Flanders, and English king Edward III was concerned about protecting the English held duchy of Guienne (in modern France). Edward touched off the war by invading France to take the crown by force. The protracted war that followed was fought mainly in France and devastated the country. The outbreak of the Black Plague only added to the loss of life on both sides. The consequences of the war were far-reaching. English presence on the Continent was all but ended; and the ravages of war contributed to the decline of feudalism, the rise of a middle class, and the emergence of a strong monarchy.

Hungarian Revolution of 1956 Brief but bloody rebellion between October 23 and November 14, 1956 against Russian domination in Hungary. The revolt was caused by a series of factors, including the movement for reform in Poland, the denunciation of Stalinism by Khrushchev, and the Soviet-aided ouster in July, 1956 of the repressive regime of Matyas Rakosi in Hungary. The revolt was sparked when Hungarian forces fired on people demonstrating in Budapest in support of Polish reform and in opposition to Soviet presence in Hungary. Nagy, who as premier had earlier (1953–1955) introduced reforms in Hungary, was restored to power and János Kádár formed a countergovernment and called for Soviet assistance. Russian forces entered Hungary on November 4 and the rebellion was crushed by November 14. Kádár was installed as the new head of the government.

Huns Nomadic people of Asia, notorious for their military skills and savagery, who in the 5th century A.D. threatened the Roman Empire. Skilled horsemen and archers, they appeared in eastern Europe in about 370 A.D., and, fighting in roving bands (hordes), they conquered the Alani, Ostrogoths, and Visigoths. Victories over the latter two peoples caused great migrations eastward. In the 5th century A.D. the Huns occupied eastern and central Europe and had reached the borders of the eastern Roman Empire. By 432 A.D. a single king of the Huns, Rugilas (Rua or Roas), was exacting tribute from the Romans. His successor, Attila the Hun, launched three invasions into the empire (441, 447, 451). On the first he advanced into the eastern empire and threatened Constantinople. On the second he again attacked the eastern empire and passed through the Balkans into Greece. On the third he attacked the western empire and unsuccessfully attempted to take Gaul. After he was defeated by a combined force of Romans and Visigoths at the Battle of Chalons in 451, however, he invaded and briefly ravaged Italy. His death in 453 was soon followed by disintegration of his kingdom and the Huns as a unified people.

Husein ibn-Ali (Husayn ibn-'Ali) (1856–1931) Arabian king (1917–1924). Emir of Mecca (1908–1916) under the Turks, he led the Arab revolt against the Turks in 1916 during World War I and proclaimed himself king of Arabia in 1917. He was defeated in a war with Ibn Saud in 1924 and went into exile.

Hussein ibn Talal (b. 1935) Became Jordanian king in 1935. During his reign he has maintained a generally moderate stance in the Arab-Israeli conflicts, although he joined with the Arabs in the war of 1967. He successfully put down a revolt by Palestinian guerrillas in Jordan in 1970. He supported the Arab cause in the Yom Kippur War of 1973. Relations became strained with the United States because of his opposition to the Camp David Accord (*see* History of the United States section, page 10-11) and, in 1991, his failure to condemn Iraqi aggression in the Persian Gulf War (*see* page 11-96).

Hussein, Saddam (b. 1937) Iraqi politician, member of the Baith party since 1957. He became president and virtual dictator in 1979. He launched the invasion of Iran in 1980 (*see* **Iran-Iraq War**), but was forced to accept a cease-fire in 1988. In 1990, he invaded Kuwait, causing a worldwide embargo and eventually the Persian Gulf War (*see* page 11-96), which ended with Iraq's defeat and withdrawal from Kuwait. U.N. sanctions remained in force while the United Nations inspected Iraqi sites of nuclear and chemical weapons.

Huss, John (1369–1415) Czech religious reformer. A Catholic priest, he was excommunicated and later burned at the stake for advocating the teachings of Wycliffe (*see* page 11-134). His death led to Hussite Wars between 1419 and 1434.

Hyksos Invaders of ancient Egypt who were probably a Semitic people. They invaded and conquered Egypt during the Middle Kingdom and took the kingship. They ruled as kings of Egypt (1675–1550 B.C.) and introduced the horse and chariot to Egypt. The Hyksos kings were finally defeated in 1570 B.C. by Amasis I.

I **Ibáñez (del Campo), Carlos** (1877–1960) President of Chile (1927–1981). He was popular in the pre-Depression era for implementing labor and education reforms.

Ibn Battutah (1304?–1378?) Muslim traveler and writer. He visited countries from Morocco (his birthplace) to China from around 1325, describing his travels in detail in his book *Rihlah* (*Travels*). He is considered one of the most reliable authorities on his times.

Ibn Khaldun (1334–1406) Arab historian, philosopher, and statesman. Born in Tunis, he served as a Muslim judge in Cairo. Considered the greatest of the Arab historians, he provided a description of Arab culture in his *Muqaddiman* (*Introduction*), as well as a philosophy of history explaining the rise and fall of civilization.

Ibn Saud (1888–1953) Saudi Arabian king and founder in 1932 of the modern Saudi state. By 1922 he had firm control of the Nejd and then conquered the Hejaz (1924 and 1925), of which he became king in 1926. In 1932 he changed the name of this kingdom to Saudi Arabia. He introduced a stable, nationalistic form of government and put an end to tribal wars. His decision to open the country to oil exploration led to the discovery of one of the world's largest oil fields.

Ibn Zuhr (Avenzoar) (1090–1162) Islamic physician, born in Seville, and a leading medical authority of his day.

Ibrahim Pasha (1789–1848) Egyptian general. He was the conqueror of Arabia and Syria for his father Muhammad Ali, the ruler of Egypt; but was obliged to evacuate some of his conquests when Western powers came to the aid of a faltering Ottoman Empire. He briefly succeeded his father as viceroy of Egypt before his death.

Iconoclastic Controversy Religious dispute. The Iconoclasts of the Byzantine Empire opposed the use of images or icons in religious worship on the grounds that icons were sacrilegious. Emperor Leo III denounced the use of icons in 726 and in subsequent years icon worshipers and iconoclastics were alternately persecuted. The controversy raged throughout the 8th and 9th centuries, and was denounced in 787 by the Second Council of Nicaea, which decreed that icons could be venerated but not worshiped. The controversy was ended in 843 with the restoration of icon worship during the reign of Emperor Michael III.

Idris I (1890–1983) The king of Libya from its independence in 1951 until he was deposed by a coup d'état in 1969. He was a leader of the Senussi sect in Cyrenaica before becoming king.

Ignatius of Loyola, Saint (1491–1556) Spanish religious leader. He entered military service, and was wounded at Pamplona in 1521. While convalescing he conceived the idea of becoming a soldier for Christ. At the University of Paris he formed the nucleus of Jesus, a religious order for men organized along military lines. After approval by the pope in 1540, the Jesuits with Ignatius as their first general organized the most effective Catholic response to the Reformation, dominated and revolutionized European education, and became the largest religious order of modern times.

Igor (1150–1202) Russian prince and legendary hero. His defeat in a battle in 1185 inspired the first work of Russian literature, *The Song of Igor's Campaign* (1187).

Ikeda, Hayato (1899–1965) Moderate Japanese statesman who was prime minister (1960–1964). He played a large part in Japan's amazing economic recovery following World War II.

Ile-de-France French region and former province located around Paris. It was the center of the French monarchy's lands from which the modern nation of France evolved.

Iliad **and** *Odyssey*   Two celebrated Greek epic poems, believed to have been written in the 9th century B.C. by Homer. In ancient Greece they were revered as sources for moral and spiritual guidance. In modern times they are considered among the greatest masterpieces of Western literature. The *Iliad* tells the story of the Trojan War fought to return Helen to her husband, Spartan king Menelaus. The *Odyssey* narrates the adventures of Odysseus, a Greek hero during his return to Ithaca after the Trojan War.

Il-Khan   Mongol dynasty that reigned from 1258 to 1353 in Persia (modern Iran). Between 1253 and 1258, the Mongol Hulagu Khan conquered this territory, including the Islamic capital of Baghdad, and founded the Il-Khan dynasty. The dynasty reached its height under Mahmud Ghazan (1295–1304), who became the first Mongol to convert to Islam (Sunni). In subsequent years internal unrest broke the Il-Khan's power and brought their rule to an end in 1353.

Imhotep (2980–2950 B.C.)   Egyptian sage. Imhotep was revered as the architect of the first step pyramid, as a doctor, and adviser to Third Dynasty kings. He was elevated to deity status after his death.

Imperialism   In general, the rule over or control of one state by another. More specifically, "imperialism" is used in either of two ways, referring to ancient and modern forms. Ancient imperialism is the process by which early empires were created. This involved military conquest and, to one degree or another, political domination. Ancient imperialism led to creation of the Macedonian, Persian, Roman, Chinese, and numerous other empires. Modern imperialism is the policy by which nations built colonial empires beginning in the 15th and 16th centuries. Modern imperialism was at first spurred on by the rewards of increased trade and mineral riches in the Americas, the Indies, and later Africa. However, the industrial age brought new motivations. The great colonial empires of the 18th and 19th centuries were exploited for raw minerals and also served as ready markets for the vast quantities of finished goods produced by the industrial nations. Competition between the great colonial powers, notably the British, French, Dutch, Portuguese, and later the Germans, led to instability and frequent wars during the 19th century. In the 20th century, however, the rise of nationalism brought new resistance to this form of imperialism and resulted in independence movements within the colonies. The years after World War I, and especially those following World War II, saw the breakup of colonial empires as most former colonies won their independence.

Inca   South American Indian people and their vast empire in the Andes region, which at the time of the Spanish conquest in the 1500s extended from Ecuador to northern Chile. According to legend, the empire was founded (1100 A.D.) by Manco Capac at what is now Cuzco, Peru. It expanded slowly until the early 15th century when a period of rapid conquests began. The empire reached its zenith under the rule of Huayna Capac (1492–1525), who divided the empire between his sons, Atahualpa and Huáscar. The two subsequently warred against each other

and, when the Spanish conquistador Pizarro arrived in South America in 1532, Atahualpa had just defeated his brother. After being received by Atahualpa on friendly terms, Pizarro captured and executed him in 1533, entered Cuzco, and with his small force easily subjugated this empire of 10–12 million people. At the time of the Spanish conquest the Incas had a well advanced civilization organized in a rigid hierarchy, over which the emperor ruled with absolute (and divine) authority. Inca society was based on agricultural production and its religion centered on sun worship. They were great builders and constructed magnificent cities such as Machu Picchu, and a system of roads, irrigation, and mountainside terraces. There was also extensive mining and advanced metallurgy. Under the Spanish, the Inca religion was forcibly suppressed, a colonial government was installed, and the native population was drawn away from agriculture for work in the mines and colonial towns.

Indian Councils Act   British reform act for the government of India enacted in 1909. It provided for increased Indian self-government in the form of a representative legislature. An earlier act of the same name in 1861 reorganized India's executive administration.

Indian National Congress (Congress party)   Political party in India. Founded in 1885, it became a vehicle for the Indian independence movement in the early 20th century. The party was taken over in 1917 by militants such as Tilak and Besant and, under the leadership of Gandhi, it organized the passive-resistance campaigns (satyagraha) against British domination that continued to the 1940s. The party was disbanded in 1942 by the British but reorganized in 1945 and became the ruling party of independent India in 1947. It was led (1947–1964) by Nehru until his death and continued as the ruling party under I. Gandhi. Opposition to Mrs. Gandhi, however, finally split the party in 1969 into the New Congress party, supporting Mrs. Gandhi, and the Old Congress party, supporting Morarji R. Desai. Desai succeeded Mrs. Gandhi as prime minister between 1977 and 1980 under the banner of a new Janata party. In 1980, Mrs. Gandhi was returned to power as prime minister, at the head of her faction of the Congress party.

India-Pakistani wars   Conflicts between India and Pakistan in the years after the British partition of the Indian subcontinent on August 15, 1947. War broke out in 1971 over the independence of East Pakistan. Pakistan lost the war and East Pakistan became Bangladesh (*see* World at a Glance section). Tension continues over the Muslim state of Kashmir, occupied by India and Pakistan.

Indochina war (French Indochina War)   War (1945–1954) fought by Vietnamese Communists and Nationalists against occupying armies, most notably the French. Following the Japanese defeat in World War II, British and Chinese forces occupied the region. At the same time, however, Communist Nationalist leader Ho Chi Minh proclaimed the Democratic Republic of Vietnam and began a war against the British and Chinese. French troops reoccupied Indochina in 1946 and, after the breakdown of an agreement granting the Vietnamese

republic a large measure of autonomy, fighting resumed in 1946. This time it was between the French
and the Communist Nationalist (Vietminh) forces
under Vo Nguyen Giap. Heavy fighting continued
through 1947. Ater failing to come to terms with
Ho Chi Minh, the French supported creation of an
independent Vietnam with Bao Dai as emperor. The
Vietminh continued fighting, however, drove the
French from northern Vietnam, conquered parts of
Laos, and broke French military strength at Dien
Bien Phu in 1954. Geneva Conference accords
signed July 21, 1954 ended the war, provided for
partition of Vietnam, and promised elections for reunification by 1956. The United States, which had
been aiding the Bao Dai regime since 1950, did not
sign the accord and thus opened the way for its involvement in the Vietnam War.

Indo-European　Name applied to the large family
of languages of Europe and southern and southwestern Asia, believed to have evolved from a common
parent language, Proto-Indo-European, spoken
sometime before 2000 B.C. Indo-Iranian languages
such as Persian and Sanskrit are members, as well as
the Celtic, Germanic, Greek, Romance, and Slavic
languages of Europe.

Indulgence　Catholic theological term for the pardon and remission of temporal punishment due to
sin. In the early church, severe penances were imposed upon penitent sinners. As time went on, the
church relaxed the actual penalty, granting an "indulgence" instead by which the penitent received the
same merit as if he had actually performed the
penance. Abuses which crept into the granting of
indulgences, specifically the buying and selling of
them, was one of the issues which led to the revolt of
Luther in 1517 at the time of the Reformation.

Indus Civilization (Mohenjo-Daro civilization)
Ancient civilization that flourished in the Indus
River Valley (2500–1500 B.C.). Excavations at Mohenjo-Daro and Harappa in modern Pakistan have
revealed a civilization as advanced as those of ancient Egypt and Mesopotamia.

Industrial Revolution　Period between about
1750 and 1850 that saw industry become the predominant force in European economic and social
life. This era was marked by the shift from agricultural and cottage-industry forms of production to
the factory system, the great increase in the use of
machinery for production, a population shift that
created great urban centers, and the marked dependence of laborers on their employers. The
Industrial Revolution began in the British cotton
textile industry and is generally dated from
1750–1850. Though the use of machinery was not
unknown and though some factories were operating before 1750, this period saw the gradual
changeover to an industrial society in Britain.
Traditionally, certain inventions are associated
with the beginning of industrialism, incuding
Watt's steam engine, Kay's flying shuttle,
Hargreaves' spinning jenny, Crompton's spinning
mule, and Edmund Cartwright's power loom. In
succeeding years the Industrial Revolution spread
to other countries: France after 1830, Germany
after 1850, and the United States principally after
1860.

Industrial Revolution: Women workers engaged in power loom weaving in a
textile factory in the 1840s.

Innocent III (orig. Lotario di Segni) (1161–1216)
Italian-born pope (1198–1216). Under Innocent's
reign, the papacy achieved its greatest power. Continuing the policies of Gregory VII regarding supremacy of the pope over secular rulers, Innocent
became involved in struggles with European kings
to enforce his authority. He vied with Holy Roman
Emperor Otto IV, excommunicated him in 1210,
and finally crowned Frederick II in his place in
1215. In England, he forced acceptance of his favorite as archbishop of Canterbury and thereby began a struggle with King John. He excommunicated
John in 1209, ultimately forcing John in 1213 to accept the sovereignty of the pope and to agree to pay
him tribute. In addition to asserting papal authority
over these and other European sovereigns, Innocent
also preached the Fourth Crusade, promoted the Albigensian Crusade, and called the great Fourth Lateran Council.

Inquisition　Name of two historic Roman Catholic
tribunals. 1. The Medieval Inquisition was established in 1233 by Pope Gregory X in response to
the spread of heretical sects, such as the Albigenses
and Waldenses in northern Italy, southern France,
and Germany. Judges of the Inquisition were chosen
from among the Dominicans to try and judge cases
of heresy, then considered intolerable by civil and
ecclesiastical authorities alike. If found guilty of
heresy, the heretic was turned over to secular authorities for punishment. Though burning at the
stake was the ultimate penalty for unrecanted heresy, this penalty was uncommmon in medieval
times. The usual punishment was penance, fine, or
imprisonment. During the Catholic Reformation, the
functions of the Medieval Inquisition were assigned
to the Holy Office in 1542. It was active against
Protestantism and heard charges of heresy against
Galileo in what became a famous trial. 2. Spanish
Inquisition. This was a quasi-ecclesiastical tribunal
established in 1478 by King Ferdinand and Queen
Isabella primarily to examine converted Jews, and
later converted Muslims, and punish those who were
insincere. Pope Sixtus IV reluctantly approved the
Spanish Inquisition, which was largely controlled by
the Spanish monarch. The Spanish Inquisition was
much harsher than the Medieval Inquisition and the
death penalty was more often exacted.

Instrument of Government　English constitution
under which Oliver Cromwell ruled England as lord

protector between 1653 and 1657. It vested executive authority in the lord protector and a council of state, created a unicameral Parliament, and disenfranchised all Catholics and rebels.

International First (1864–1881): Socialist labor federation founded at London, on September 28, 1864 that quickly came under the domination of Karl Marx. It was called the International Workingmen's Association. While its express purpose was to foment a Socialist workers' revolution, it failed to play an active role in labor unrest of the period. Split in 1876 by a power struggle between Marx and the anarchist M. Bakunin, it was largely defunct by 1881. Second (1889–1914): Loose federation of Socialist groups and labor unions founded at Paris, in 1889. Though committed to an eventual Socialist revolution, the group generally supported parliamentary democracy. The chief aim of the International, however, was its opposition to war, and the outbreak of World War I split the organization along national lines. Third (Communist International): *See* **Comintern**.

International Court of Justice United Nations judicial body organized in 1945 and superseding the Permanent Court of International Justice, the judicial arm of the League of Nations. The court is based at the Hague and consists of 15 judges selected by the U.N. Security Council and the General Assembly.

International Monetary Fund International organization, conceived in 1944 at the Bretton Woods Conference and associated with the United Nations as a specialized agency in 1945 to help provide stability of international exchange rates and aid member nations in international transactions.

Intifadeh Started in 1985 as a Palestinian uprising on the West Bank and Gaza. The purpose of the uprising has been to gain greater freedom and political voice for Palestinians living in the occupied territories.

Inukai, Ki Tsuyoshi (1855–1932) Japanese politician, president of the Seiyukai party (1929–1932), and prime minister (January–May 1932). His assassination marked the rise of military and the end of party control of the Japanese government.

Investiture Controversy Power struggle in the 11th and 12th centuries between the Holy Roman Empire and the papacy. The controversy centered on the rift beginning in 1075 between Henry IV and Pope Gregory VII over "lay investiture" and was not finally settled until the Concordat of Worms was issued in 1122. At the time of the controversy, bishops and other clerics had both secular and clerical powers over ecclesiastical domains. Both the emperor and the pope were involved in their installation (investiture), a practice known as lay investiture. The practice led to abuses of the clerical offices, and reacting to a movement for reform, Pope Gregory abolished lay investiture in 1075. In the struggle that followed, Henry was excommunicated, civil war between factions of rebellious nobles broke out (over this and other issues) within the Holy Roman Empire, and Henry attacked Rome (1081 and 1082). Under Emperor Henry V, the controversy continued until a compromise was finally arranged with Pope Calixtus II in the Concordat of Worms of 1122.

Ionia Ancient district of Asia Minor on the Aegean Sea in modern western Turkey. Colonized by the Ionian Greeks (1000 B.C.), it was taken by Croesus (6th century B.C.) and then by the Persians under Cyrus the Great. The Ionian revolt against Persia resulted in the Persian Wars. The Ionian cities fell to Alexander the Great in 334 B.C. and later to Rome, and were destroyed as Greek cities by the Ottoman conquest in the 1400s.

Ionian School Early school of Greek philosophy, composed of philosophers who were active in the 6th and 5th centuries B.C. in Ionia. They held divergent views, though in general they attempted to explain the world around them in terms of matter and physical forces. Among the thinkers of this school were Thales, Anaximander, Anaximenes, Anaxagoras, Heracleitus, and Diogenes of Apollonia.

Ionic order Greek architectural style. The Ionic is one of the major styles of early Greek architecture. It is characterized by slender fluted columns topped by a scroll-shaped capital, and had developed by the 6th century B.C.

Iqbal, (Sir) Muhammad (1873–1938) Indian poet, philosopher, and political leader. He urged the establishment of an independent Muslim state, and is considered the spiritual father of modern Pakistan.

Iran-Iraq War (1980–1988) Also called the Gulf War, this conflict raged for several years. Started by Iraq, the issue was a border dispute as well as a religious one. The conflict ended partly as a result of the efforts of the Secretary General of the United Nations Pérez de Cuéllar. *See page 11-96.*

Irish Free State Name used by the Republic of Ireland from 1922 to 1937; that is, during the period that Ireland had dominion status within the British Empire.

Irish Home Rule Movement *See* **Home Rule**.

Irish Land Acts Legislation passed (1870–1903) for the benefit of Irish tenant farmers. The acts, initiated by Gladstone, were designed to curtail landlord abuse and provide incentives for peasant proprietorship.

Irish Republican Army (IRA) Irish nationalist organization dedicated to the creation of a single unified Irish state. Organized from the elements dispersed during the Easter Rebellion of 1916, it became the political arm of the Sinn Fein party, and opposed dominion status after the creation of the Irish Free State in 1922. It declined after its former supporter Eamon De Valera took over the Irish government and because of its opposition to the Allies in World War II, and was eventually outlawed by both Irish governments. In 1969, it launched new terrorist measures in northern Ireland and even into Great Britain in the mid 1970s, continuing through 1993.

Iron Age Period in the development of human culture in which iron came to be used predominantly for making tools and weapons. The Iron Age, which succeeded the Bronze Age, began at various times in various locations. Widespread use of iron is generally thought to have begun in the Near East and it is the Hittites who are credited with discovering the technique of tempering iron. Following the breakup of the Hittite Empire in 1200 B.C., ironworking techniques were spread through Europe and Asia Minor.

By the 5th century B.C., the use of iron was well established in Europe.

Iron Curtain   Name applied to the Soviet Union's policy of limiting Western information and influence within its borders and those of its Eastern European satellites after World War II. The term was coined by Winston Churchill and used in a speech at Fulton, Missouri on March 6, 1946.

Irredentism   Originally an Italian nationalist movement that aimed to add to Italy all territories inhabited by Italian-speaking people not included at the time of the unification of Italy (1870 and 1871). These included the Trentino, Trieste, Istrai, Fiume, and parts of Dalmatia, most of which Italy finally acquired after World War I.

Isabella I   (Isabella the Catholic) (1451–1504) Queen of Spain. Queen of Castile, with her husband Ferdinand V she united most of Spain, instituted the Inquisition, expelled the Jews in 1492, and drove the Moors from Granada in 1492. She financed the expedition of Columbus that discovered the Americas.

Isaurian   Dynasty of Byzantine emperors that ruled from 717–802. The line was founded by Leo III and the last reigning member of the line was Empress Irene, who was forced to abdicate in 802.

Ishtar   Leading goddess of the ancient Assyrian and Babylonian religions. She was revered as the goddess of love, sex, and war, and as the Earth Mother, or Mother Goddess.

Islam   One of the world's three great monotheistic religions, with Christianity and Judaism. Islam is the newest of the three and was founded by the prophet Muhammad in the 7th century A.D. Muslims believe Muhammad was the last of the prophets (i.e., Adam, Noah, Abraham, Moses, and Jesus) sent by Allah (God). They exult in their submission to and praise of Allah. The Islamic faith, derived from the earlier Judaic and Christian faiths, is based on the Koran, the revelations of Allah to Muhammad; the Sunna, collections of sayings of Muhammad compiled in the 9th century; and the principle called Ijma, by which long-established practices are simply accepted as legitimate. The prophet Muhammad during his lifetime laid the foundations of the great Muslim theocratic state, the Empire of the Caliphate. After his death, the empire was rapidly expanded to include domains stretching from India, across the Mideast, and into North Africa and served to spread the Muslim faith throughout these regions. A dispute over the succession of the caliph in the 7th century gave rise to the two main divisions in the Muslim world: the Sunni (orthodox) and Shi'ite sects. *See also* Religion, page 22-9.

Ismail I   (1486–1524) Shah of Persia (1501–1524), founder of Safavid dynasty. Established the Shi'ite form of Islam as the state religion, thus incurring the special enmity of the Sunni Turks and Uzbeks, with whom he warred unceasingly.

Ismail Pasha   (1830–1895) Egyptian ruler under Ottoman sovereignty (1863–1879). The Suez Canal was completed during his rule, but his improvement schemes plunged Egypt into debt, and he was forced to sell his canal shares to Britain in 1875 and put Egypt's finances under the control of foreign bondholders.

Israel, kingdom of   Originally, the Old Testament kingdom of the Hebrews ruled by Saul, David, and Solomon. Following the rebellion in 933 B.C. by Jeroboam I, the kingdom was divided. The northern part, which was thereafter called Israel, included lands of the 10 northern tribes. The southern part, called Judah, included the lands of the tribes of Benjamin and Judah. The kingdom of Israel was overrun in 721 by Assyrians under Sargon II, and many of the inhabitants were carried off. They became known as the Ten Lost Tribes.

Itagaki, Taisuke   (1837–1919) Japanese statesman. He played a major role in the 1868 Meiji Restoration, founded the Jiyuto (Liberal) party, and worked to bring constitutional reforms to the government.

Ito, Hirobumi, Prince   (1841–1909) Japanese statesman and premier (1886–1888, 1892, 1898, 1900, and 1901). He tried to introduce Western ideas learned while on government missions to the United States and Europe, and drafted the constitution of Japan in 1889.

Iturbide, Agustín de   (1783–1824) Mexican military leader. He led in the Mexican independence movement and, as Agustín I, ruled as emperor (May 1822–March 1823).

Ivan III   (Ivan the Great) (1440–1505) Grand duke of Moscow (1462–1505). He broke the power of Novgorod, exploited divisions between the Tatars of the Golden Horde, and captured part of the Ukraine from Lithuania. He laid the groundwork for a strong Russian monarchy.

Ivan IV   (Ivan the Terrible) (1530–1584) Grand duke of Moscow from 1533 and first czar of Russia (1547–1584). Notorious for cruelty and erratic behavior later in his reign, he nevertheless greatly expanded Russian domains and consolidated the power of the monarchy at the expense of the Boyars. He summoned the first national assembly in 1566, began Russia's expansion to the East by conquering Kazan and Astrakhan, and engaged in the long, unsuccessful Livonian War (1557–1582). Siberia was also conquered.

Ivan V   (1666–1696) Czar of Russia (1682–1696). Physically and mentally unfit to rule, he was nominal coruler with Peter I under his sister Sophia's regency. He retained his title after Peter's succession in 1689 but never actively ruled.

Ivan VI   (1740–1764) Czar of Russia (1740 and 1741). A nominal ruler, he was deposed as an infant by Elizabeth, daughter of Peter I, and imprisoned until his assassination more than 20 years later.

Iyeyasu   (Tokugawa) (Ieyasu) (1542–1616) Japanese soldier and ruler. Iyeyasu aided Hideyoshi's unification of Japan. He subsequently made himself daimyo and shogun, and virtual ruler of Japan. He was the founder of the Tokugawa shogunate, which ruled Japan until 1867.

 **Jacobins**   Political club that rose to prominence as a faction during the French Revolution. Under the leadership of Robespierre, the group dominated the revolutionary government between 1793 and 1794 and was responsible for the Reign of Terror. The club began in 1789 as a group of moderate deputies to the National Assembly though by 1790

bourgeois moderates had swelled their ranks and made the club an important pressure group. Following the overthrow of the king in 1792, the club admitted Montagnards, and began to espouse more democratic than radical, revolutionary aims. They opposed and ousted the Girondists in 1793 over the prosecution of the French Revolutionary Wars, set up the revolutionary dictatorship, and oversaw the Reign of Terror. The Jacobins fell from power with Robespierre's overthrow on 9 Thermidor (July 27, 1794) and thereafter the club was suppressed.

Jacobites   Supporters of English king James II (and his heirs in the Stuart line) after the Glorious Revolution of 1688. Considerable support for James remained after his exile in 1688 and was kept alive between 1688 and 1746 by Roman Catholics and disaffected Tories. Jacobites were especially active in Scotland and two unsuccessful rebellions were organized there (1715, 1745).

Jacquerie   Revolt in May and June 1358 by French peasants during the Hundred Years' War (1337–1453). Peasants in northern France rebelled when French nobles demanded increased taxes despite the fact that the countryside had recently been pillaged by English mercenary soldiers. Led by Guillaume Cale and E. Marcel, the peasants sacked and burned castles. They were defeated less than a month later, however, and thousands were massacred by the vengeful nobles.

Jagatai (d. 1242)   Mongol conqueror and a son of Genghis Khan. He joined in his father's great wars of conquest and, following the death of Genghis Khan did not oppose the succession of his younger brother, Ogadai, as grand khan. In the division in 1227 of the Mongol Empire among the heirs of Genghis Khan, Jagatai gained vast domains corresponding roughly to Turkistan and Afghanistan.

Jagiello (Jagello) (Jagellon)   Dynasty that ruled in Bohemia, Hungary, Lithuania, and Poland in the 14th–16th centuries (in Poland from 1386–1572). The dynasty was founded by Jagiello, duke of Lithuania, who took the name Ladislas I of Poland and was a major force in European affairs.

Jainism   Indian religion. Arising in the 6th century B.C. as a reaction to the rigidity of the Vedic religion, Jainism was by tradition established by 24 saints, or religious figures, the last being Vardhamana Mahavira. It taught a rigid form of asceticism, a reverence for all living things, and the performance of good acts as means for escaping the cycle of rebirth and achieving Nirvana. At first quite distinct from Hinduism, Jainism eventually incorporated elements of Hinduism. Today many prominent Indians practice Jainism.

James I (1394–1437)   King of Scotland (1406–1437). By breaking the power of the nobility and the Highland clans, James established strong monarchical rule in Scotland.

James I (James VI) (1566–1625)   Scottish king of England (1603–1625), successor to Elizabeth I and first of the Stuart line in England. James first succeeded his mother, Mary Queen of Scots, to the Scottish throne (under a regency) in 1567 and then succeeded to the English throne. During his reign in England, war with Spain was ended and relations between James and the Parliament deteriorated

seriously. This last helped bring on the English Civil War some years later.

James II (1430–1460)   King of Scotland (1437–1460). He reestablished the strong monarchy created by James I.

James II (1633–1702)   English king (1685–1688). His overthrow during the Glorious Revolution of 1688 established the supremacy of the Parliament in England. His penchant for autocratic methods and efforts to promote Catholicism, prepared the way for the Glorious Revolution. But it was the birth in 1688 of his son and (Catholic) heir that finally precipitated the revolt. James was succeeded by his daughter Mary and her Protestant husband, William III.

James IV (1473–1513)   King of Scotland (1488–1513). He unified Scotland and allied it with France against Henry VIII of England.

Janissaries (Janizaries)   A special elite corps of the army of the Ottoman Empire, noted for its military successes in the 15th and 16th centuries. Members of the corps were procured by taking the children of Ottoman Christian subjects and training them. By the 18th century they had become involved in Ottoman politics. Opposing reform, they revolted in 1826, were defeated, and the organization was dissolved.

Jaurès, Jean (1859–1914)   French Socialist leader who helped to found the unified French Socialist party in 1905.

Jenkins's Ear, War of   War (1739–1743) between England and Spain. The war was soon absorbed by the larger conflict of the War of Austrian Succession.

Jenner, Edward (1749–1823)   English physician. From 1796 he pioneered the use of vaccination to prevent smallpox, a major step in the development of the science of immunology.

Jeremiah (Jeremias) (650–570 B.C.)   One of the major Hebrew prophets, whose activities and prophecies are recorded in the Old Testament.

Jihad   Islamic religious term meaning holy war. Muslims believe that if they die in a proclaimed holy war, they will go to heaven.

Jimmu Tenno (660 B.C.)   Legendary first emperor of Japan. Believed to have been a direct descendant of the sun goddess, he is regarded as founder of the dynasty of Japanese emperors that still reigns today.

Jinnah, Muhammad Ali (1876–1948)   Indian Muslim statesman. He served as head of the Muslim League (1934–1948), led the struggle to establish Pakistan, and served as its first governor-general (1947 and 1948).

Joan of Arc (Jeanne d'Arc) (1412–1431)   French saint and heroine during the Hundred Years' War. A visionary, the young girl became convinced she had a divine mission to aid the French dauphin Charles (later Charles VII) against the English. After persuading Charles to give her troops, she raised the Siege of Orléans in 1429 and won the Battle of Patay. Shortly after Charles's coronation, however, she failed in her siege of Paris and was captured. Turned over to an ecclesiastical court, she was tried as a heretic and was burned at the stake.

Jodl, Alfred (1890–1946)   German general. During World War II, Jodl was Hitler's chief of the armed forces operation staff and a key adviser.

Joffre, Joseph Jacques Césaire (1852–1931) French general and marshal of France. He was commander-in-chief of the army in World War I (1914–1916), and his tactics led to the French victory at the 1914 Battle of the Marne.

John (1167?–1216) King of England (1199–1216). The youngest son of Henry II, he succeeded his older brother, Richard I. He quarreled with the church and saw his kingdom placed under a papal interdict in 1208. He abused feudal custom and was forced by his barons to sign the Magna Carta, England's first grant of general liberties, in 1215. During his reign England lost most of its domains in France.

John I (John the Great) (1357–1433) Portuguese king (1385–1433). During his reign, John concluded an alliance with England and began the period of Portuguese overseas colonization. One of John's sons was Prince Henry the Navigator.

John II (John Comnenus) (1088–1143) Byzantine emperor (1118–1143). John occupied himself with regaining lost Byzantine lands and influence. He was successful against the Magyars, Serbs, Petchenegs, and Roger II of Sicily, but was forced to yield trading privileges to Venice.

John II (John the Good) (1319–1364) King of France (1350–1364). Captured by the English in the Battle of Poitiers in 1356 during the Hundred Years' War, he was released in return for hostages. When one hostage escaped, John returned voluntarily to England, where he died.

John II (John the Perfect) (1455–1495) King of Portugal (1481–1495), successor to his father. He curbed the power of the nobility, made peace with Spain, and sponsored colonizing expeditions. Bartholomeu Dias rounded the Cape of Good Hope in 1488 during his reign.

John III (John the Fortunate) (1502–1557) King of Portugal (1521–1557). Portuguese influence in Brazil, India, Macao, and the Spice Islands was expanded during John's reign. Domestically, he instituted the Inquisition and involved the Jesuits in higher education. The Portuguese overseas empire reached its height during his reign.

John IV (d. 1656) King of Portugal (1640–1656). John expelled the Spanish from Portugal in 1640 and became king. He also ousted the Dutch from Brazil in 1654 and allied himself with France against Spain in order to protect his interests. He was the first king of the Braganza line.

John V (John Palaeologus) (1332–1391) Byzantine emperor (1341–1347, 1355–1376, 1379–1391). He recognized the sovereignty of the Ottoman Turks, who had captured large parts of the empire. He tried to heal the Christian schism between East and West in order to secure Western help against the Turks.

John V (1689–1750) King of Portugal (1706–1750). John inherited the War of Spanish Succession but eventually made peace with France and Spain. Enriched by gold from Brazil, his court was an elegant center of culture.

John VI (1769–1826) King of Portugal (1816–1826). He was forced to rule from Brazil (1807–1821) because of the Napoleonic Wars and French occupation. He was also forced to recognize Brazilian independence in 1825 under his son Dom Pedro I.

John XXIII (Roncalli, Angelo Giuseppe) (1881–1963) Pope from 1958–1963, he was a highly popular figure in the history of the modern church. He was noted for promoting peace and social reforms to aid the poor, seeking cooperation with other religious denominations, and convening the Second Vatican Council.

John of Gaunt (1340–1399) Duke of Lancaster from 1362 and son of King Edward III of England. In effect he ruled in England during the last years of his father's reign and during the early reign of Richard II. He was the ancestor of the Tudor kings.

John Paul II (b. Wojtyla, Karol) (b. 1920) Polish born, he became pope in 1978. John Paul II was the first non-Italian pope to be elected in nearly half a century. He has made numerous journeys abroad.

Johnson, Samuel (1709–1784) English literary figure who was renowned for his conversation as well as for his writings. His pioneering *Dictionary of the English Language* was published in 1755. In 1763, he began his association with his most famous biographer, Boswell.

Joliet, Louis A French fur trapper who explored parts of North America along with Jacques Marquette, he traveled down the Great Lakes, the Wisconsin River, and the Mississippi River.

Jonson, Ben (1572–1637) English Elizabethan playwright, critic, and poet. Considered to be the second-ranking English playwright after his friend Shakespeare.

Joseph I (1678–1711) Holy Roman emperor (1705–1711). King of Hungary (1687–1711). In the War of the Spanish Succession, he successfully fought France but unsuccessfully supported the claim of his brother Charles (later Charles VI) to the Spanish throne.

Joseph II (1741–1790) Holy Roman emperor (1765–1790) and first of the Hapsburg-Lorraine line. An enlightened despot, Joseph initiated many social and administrative reforms, although most did not last beyond his reign. Dominated by his mother, Maria Theresa, during the first years of his reign, he undertook a broad plan to modernize the empire after her death. He abolished serfdom in 1781 and granted peasants basic rights, abolished monasteries, reduced the clergy, issued the Edict of Toleration, and attempted to centralize government of the diverse territories within the empire. This last reform led to revolts in Hungary and the Austrian Netherlands. His reign also saw the War of Bavarian Succession, territorial acquisitions from the first Partition of Poland, and participation of Austrian forces in the Russo-Turkish War (1787–1792).

Joséphine (Marie Joséphine Rose Tascher de la Pagerie) (1763–1814) Empress of France and wife of Napoleon Bonaparte (1796–1809).

Joule, James Prescott (1818–1889) English physicist, noted for his discovery of the law of conservation of energy. The electrical unit of measure is named after him.

Juan Carlos I (b. 1938) Became Spanish king in 1975, successor to General Francisco Franco. The son of the Carlist pretender Don Juan, he was designated in 1954 by Franco as the next ruler of Spain. Juan Carlos succeeded to the throne in 1975, after Franco's death. He withstood an attempted military coup in which Spanish Civil Guardsmen stormed the Parliament and took many of the country's leaders hostage.

Juárez, Benito (1806–1872) Mexican national hero and president (1858–1861). He took part in the overthrow of Santa Anna, and, as minister of justice, reduced the power of the church and army in what is called the Ley Juárez. He emerged victorious in the War of the Reform (1858–1861) and then led the opposition government during the brief reign of Emperor Maximilian (1864–1867). After Maximilian's fall, he was elected president (1867–1872) twice.

Judah Southern part of the kingdom of Israel, a separate Israelite kingdom after the northern part seceded (933 B.C.).

Judaism One of the world's three great monotheistic religions. Modern Judaism is actually rabbinic Judaism, which developed (from 1st century A.D.) from the religion of the Jews of ancient Palestine. This forerunner of Judaism also gave rise to Christianity. Rabbinic Judaism arose after the destruction of the second Temple at Jerusalem. Rabbis (teachers) replaced the priests as religious leaders, the autonomous synagogues replaced the Temple as the center of worship, and prayer and study of the Torah were substituted for the sacrificial rites of the Temple. The Judaic tradition evolved by the rabbis governed both religious and secular life and preserved Jewish culture during the many centuries in which the Jews were dispersed in various foreign lands.

Juliana (b. 1909) Queen of the Netherlands (1948–1980). She stepped down in favor of her daughter Beatrix (b. 1938), who became queen in April 1980.

Julian Calendar Calendar instituted (46 B.C.) by Julius Caesar, dividing the year into 12 months and making it 365 days, 11 hours in length. It was superseded by the Gregorian calendar in most of Europe in 1582, although the change was not made in England until 1752 and in Russia until after 1917.

Julian Emperors The four emperors who ruled after Augustus from 14–68 A.D. who were related in some way to Julius Caesar. They included Tiberius, Caligula, Claudius, and Nero.

Julius II (1443–1513) Pope (1503–1513). He returned the Papal States to church control and joined in the Holy League against France. He was a great patron of the arts, commissioning his own portrait by Raphael, the initial building of St. Peter's in 1506 by Bramante, and the Creation frescoes on the ceiling of the Sistine Chapel by Michelangelo.

July Revolution Rebellion in July 1830 in France that resulted in the forced abdication of Charles X and the crowning of Louis-Philippe. A victory for the upper bourgeoisie over the aristocracy, the rebellion was brought about by Charles's attempt to restore the absolutist Ancien Régime. It was sparked by his selection of the unpopular Ultra royalist de Polignac to head the government. To overcome opposition to de Polignac in the Chamber of Deputies, Charles issued the July Ordinances of July 26, dissolving the chamber, changing the electoral system, and imposing press censorship. Riots broke out in Paris, Charles abdicated, and Louis-Philippe was chosen king in August by the deputies.

June Days Revolt between June 23 and 26, 1848 by workers in Paris, France, during the early months of the Second Republic. Though workers had supported the February Revolution of 1848, unemployment and failure of the work-relief program (national workshops) failed to ease the workers' discontent. A mass protest on May 15 in which workers briefly took over the National Assembly, resulted in the decision to dismantle the national workshops. The ensuing revolt engulfed Paris in bloody street fighting and brought down the interim government. General Louis Cavaignac was granted dictatorial powers to restore order, and finally put an end to the fighting.

Jung, Carl Gustav (1875–1961) Swiss psychologist. One of his early works, *The Psychology of Dementia Praecox* (1906), led to a collaboration with Freud. Jung broke with Freud in 1913 after publishing *The Psychology of the Unconscious* (1912). He developed the theory of personality types, extroverted and introverted, and of the collective unconscious. *See also* Psychology section, page 21-16.

Junkers Members of the landlord ruling class in Prussia. In German politics they formed the party of reaction and defense of landed interests and supported Bismarck prior to the Franco-Prussian War (1870 and 1871).

Juno Chief goddess in the Roman religion, wife and sister of Jupiter, and guardian of women and marriage. She corresponds to the Greek goddess Hera.

Junta Governmental committee. A junta is a council that exercises administrative powers, usually in a political emergency or after the overthrow of a government.

Justinian I (483–565 A.D.) Byzantine emperor (527–565 A.D.). One of the great rulers of the late empire, he is especially remembered for the legal codex, *Corpus Juris Civilis* compiled at his direction. His reign saw expansion of the empire, including reconquest of Africa from the Vandals (533–548) and Italy from the Ostrogoths (535–554). Many public buildings were constructed during his reign, including the Hagia Sophia.

Jutes Ancient Germanic people, possibly from the area near the mouth of the Rhine, who invaded England in the 5th century A.D. and settled in Kent and on the Isle of Wight.

Juvenal (Decimus Junius Juvenalis) (1st–2nd century A.D.) Leading Roman satirical poet whose 16 verse satires described the follies and vices of Roman life and served as models for later writers.

 **Kaaba** (Caaba) Sacred shrine in the Great Mosque at Mecca and the major site of pilgrimage for the followers of Islam. Muslims face toward it when praying.

Kadet (Constitutional Democratic party) Russian political party founded in 1905. A party of moderation, it was continually undermined by more radical groups and ceased to function after 1917.

Kafirs (Kaffirs) Term originally applied by Muslims to all unbelievers. Adopted by the European settlers of South Africa, it was applied to the Bantu-speaking native peoples of the area.

Kali   Hindu goddess, also known as the Black One. The consort of Shiva, she was goddess of death and destruction and was worshiped by the Thugs.

Kalidasa (5th century? A.D.)   Indian dramatist, considered to be the greatest Sanskrit writer and perhaps the greatest writer in India's history. The drama *Sakuntala* is his best-known work.

Kalinin, Mikhail Ivanovich (1875–1946)   Russian politician. Official head of the Soviet Union (1919–1946), he was chairman of the Soviet central executive committee (1919–1938) and of the Presidium (1938–1946).

Kalmucks (Kalmycks)   Nomadic people of Mongolian stock occupying the region of the lower Volga River in the U.S.S.R. The Kalmucks migrated to the region in the 1600s from Chinese Turkistan and were at first allies for the expanding Russian Empire. In the 1700s they were made vassals, however, and Russian oppression forced the Kalmucks into their disastrous journey back to China, most in 1771. Of the 300,000 that began the trek, the majority were killed in attacks by Russians, the Kazakh, and Kirghiz peoples. Those that reached Chinese Turkistan settled in Sinkiang, northwestern China. The remaining Kalmucks in Russia were exiled to Siberia after World War II for collaborating with the Germans. They were released from exile in 1957.

Kamakura Shogunate   Period in Japanese history from 1192–1333 when members of the Minamoto clan ruled Japan as shoguns. Minamoto Yoritomo, operating from Kamakura (North of Kyoto) crushed the rival clans of Taira and Fujiwara and was named shogun by the emperor in 1192. Yoritomo thus established the long period of rule by the shoguns and the warrior class. Imperial administration was quickly undermined during the Kamakura period and replaced by that of the shoguns. Following Yoritomo's death in 1199, however, the Hojo clan came to power as regents and became effective rulers under the Minamoto shoguns. The Hojo clan (and the Kamakura shogunate) remained in power until Emperor Daigo II led a successful revolt in 1333 in which he ended the Kamakura rule. He reigned until 1336, when he in turn was ousted, thereby beginning a period of wars that brought the Ashikaga shoguns to power. During the Kamakura shogunate, the feudal system was established, foreign trade flourished, the Zen and Pure Land sects of Buddhism were introduced to Japan, and there was a cultural flowering as well.

Kamehameha I (Kamehameha the Great) (1758?–1819)   Hawaiian king who united and ruled all the Hawaiian Islands (1810–1819) and established the Kamehameha dynasty of Hawaiian rulers.

Kamenev, Lev Borisovich (1883–1936)   Russian Communist leader. He was a member, with Stalin and Zinoviev, of the triumvirate that succeeded Lenin and opposed L. Trotsky. He was executed in the Stalinist purge of the 1930s.

Kamikaze   Japanese word meaning "divine wind." It was originally applied to the typhoon that destroyed a Mongol invasion fleet in 1281. In World War II it was applied to the Japanese suicide pilots who tried to fly their bomb-loaded planes into American ships.

Kammu (737–806)   Emperor of Japan and founder of Kyoto, the capital of Japan until 1868. A strong ruler, he diminished the power of the Buddhists and brought peace to Japan's northern borders.

Kanagawa, Treaty of (Perry Convention)   Treaty of March 31, 1854 between Japan and the United States. The treaty was secured by Commodore Perry, who had sailed to Japan (1853 and 1854) with a fleet of American warships to end Japanese isolationism. It secured good treatment for American sailors, opened two ports to trade and established an American consulate at Shimoda. It was the model for later treaties with other Western powers.

Kanem-Bornu   African empire that flourished in the region around Lake Chad from the 9th–19th century. It reached its height in the 16th and 17th centuries.

K'ang-hsi (1654–1722)   Chinese emperor (1661–1722). He extended China's rule to Taiwan, Tibet, and Outer Mongolia, and encouraged the teaching of Western mathematics and astronomy.

K'ang Sheng (1899–1975)   Chinese political leader. An active Communist since the 1920s, he was a member of the Central Committee and the Politburo and was one of the most powerful leaders in China.

Kaniska (Kanishka) (78?–103? A.D.)   Ruler of northern India and the most famous Kushan king. He was an ardent Buddhist and may have introduced the belief to China. Trade with the Romans was fostered during his reign.

Kant, Immanuel (1724–1804)   German philosopher. His metaphysical work *Critique of Pure Reason* expressed his theories of what humans could know. His *Critique of Practical Reason* (1788) gave his ethical beliefs, and his *Critique of Judgment* (1790) combined and completed his philosophies. He engineered a revolution in philosophy by focusing on what the human mind could subjectively know rather than upon what was objectively "out there."

Kao Kang (1902–1955)   Chinese Communist leader. He was one of the most powerful political figures in the Communist government until his purge in 1955 from the party.

Kao Tsu (Liu Pang) (256–195 B.C.)   Chinese emperor (202?–195 B.C.). Originally a peasant named Liu Pang, he seized power when the Ch'in dynasty collapsed. He established the Han dynasty, which created the administrative system that characterized Chinese rule until 1911.

Karageorge (b. George Petrovic) (1752?–1817)   Serbian patriot who led the Serbian uprising against the Turks in 1804. He was named hereditary leader of the Serbs in 1808, and founded the Karageorgevich dynasty that ruled Serbia (1842–1858), and the kingdom of Serbs, Croats, and Slovenes (later Yugoslavia) (1903–1945).

Karolyi, Mihàly, Count (1875–1955)   Hungarian statesman who sought Hungarian autonomy within the Austro-Hungarian Empire. After World War I, he briefly served as president of the Hungarian Republic in 1919 before the rise of Kun.

Kassem, Abdul Karim (1914–1963)   Iraqi political and military leader. After leading a successful revolt in 1958 against the Iraqi monarchy he became the first premier of the Iraqi Republic, but was overthrown and executed by the Baath party in 1963.

Kassites Ancient people, possibly originating in western Iran, who conquered Babylonia and ruled there from the 18th–12th century B.C.

Kaunda, Kenneth (David) (b. 1924) Zambian political leader who led the Zambian independence movement and became Zambia's first president in 1964.

Kay, John (1704–1764) English inventor of the flying shuttle in 1733, a major advance in the development of mechanical weaving.

Keitel, Wilhelm (1882–1946) German field marshal and chief of staff of the German high command during World War II.

Kellogg-Briand Pact (Pact of Paris) International agreement of 1928 declaring an end to war as an instrument of national policy. Initiated by U.S. Secretary of State Kellogg and French Foreign Minister Briand, the pact was originally signed in Paris by 15 nations and ultimately was subscribed to by 62. The pact was rendered ineffective by the lack of means of enforcement, by provisions that allowed defensive wars, and wars to defend allies.

Kent, kingdom of Ancient English kingdom. Founded by the Jutes in the 5th century A.D., it rose to power in the 6th century under Aethelbert, but in the 9th century became part of the kingdom of Wessex.

Kenyatta, Jomo (1894–1978) Kenyan political leader and statesman. He was a leader in the Kenyan independence movement and became first president of the Republic of Kenya in 1964–1978.

Kepler, Johannes (1571–1630) German astronomer, author of three laws describing planetary motion, now known as Kepler's laws. Kepler's work contributed to the later work of Newton.

Kerensky, Aleksandr Feodorovich (1881–1970) Russian revolutionary. He took part in the February Revolution of 1917 that toppled the czarist government, and served as premier of the Provisional Government from July until the Bolshevik October Revolution.

Keynes, John Maynard, 1st baron of Tilton (1883–1946) British economist whose views have influenced the economic policies of many governments, notably Roosevelt's New Deal. He wrote *The General Theory of Employment, Interest, and Money*, which advocated government intervention in solving the unemployment problems.

KGB Russian political security police force. Its name comes from the Russian "Committee for State Security." Created in 1954, it functioned as an espionage agency as well as a force against internal subversion and domestic dissidence. It ceased to exist with the collapse of the former U.S.S.R. *See* **Communism**.

Khanate of Khiva Former khanate in south-central Asia, ruled by the Uzbeks. It flourished from the 1500s until its conquest by Russia in 1873. The area is now part of the independent republics of Turkmenistan and Uzbekistan since December 25, 1991.

Khartoum, battle of Battle in 1885 between British forces and the forces of the Mahdi, at Khartoum, Sudan. The British were besieged at Khartoum and were finally overwhelmed, and British

general Charles Gordon and all his garrison were killed.

Khazars (Chazars) Turkic people who ruled a powerful empire (6th–10th century) located west of the Volga and north of the Black Sea in what was formerly southeastern U.S.S.R. The Khazar Empire controlled trade between Byzantium and the East and between the Arab Empire and Slavic peoples to the north. By the 8th century the Khazar ruling class had embraced Judaism and entered into close relations with the Byzantines. The empire fell in 965 to invading Russian armies and thereafter ceased to be a power.

Khmer Empire Ancient empire of southeast Asia located in what are now Cambodia and Laos. Established in the 6th century it rose to prominence in the 9th–15th centuries, during which time Buddhism, Hinduism, Sanskrit literature, and other elements of Indian culture flourished in the region. The empire reached its height in the 12th and 13th centuries when the cities of Angkor Wat and Angkor Thom were built. Its decline began in the 14th century with repeated invasions by Annamese and Thais.

Khmer Rouge Cambodian Communists. Supported by the Vietcong, the insurgent group overthrew the government of Lon Nol in 1975, and, after a bloody rule, was in turn overthrown by a Vietnamese-backed faction in 1978.

Khomeini, Ruhollah, Ayatollah (1900–1989) Iranian religious leader, a Muslim Shi'ite, and virtual dictator of Iran from January 31, 1979 as a result of the Iranian revolution. He instituted a puritanical and repressive regime, increasingly dominated by religious leaders. Declining to take responsibility for actual government, even though his power was absolute, he contributed to increasing turmoil and chaos, especially after Iraq's military attack on Iran on September 22, 1980.

Khrushchev, Nikita Sergeyevich (1894–1971) Russian Communist leader, first secretary of the Communist party of the Soviet Union (1953–1964) and premier (1958–1964). A member of the ruling Politburo from 1959, he won the power struggle that erupted after Stalin's death in 1953 and that year replaced Malenkov as the party's first secretary. His long tenure during the Cold War era was marked by his de-Stalinization program in 1956, Russian intervention in the Hungarian Revolution in 1956, erection of the Berlin Wall in 1961, the U-2 incident, failed Five-Year Plans, and the Cuban missile crisis in 1962. His ouster in 1964 was brought on by failures in the Cuban crisis, agricultural production, as well as deteriorating relations with China.

Khufu (Cheops) (2589–2566 B.C.) Ancient Egyptian king of the 4th dynasty. He built the great pyramid at Giza.

Khyber Pass Steep mountain pass on the border of Pakistan and Afghanistan. It has long been a commercial route to India as well as an invasion route for such conquerors as Alexander the Great and Tamerlane.

Kido Koin (Kido Takayoshi) (1833–1877) Japanese statesman. He helped to overthrow the Japanese shogunate in 1866 and restore imperial rule. He subsequently helped to end feudalism in Japan and institute constitutional government.

Kierkegaard, Søren (1813–1855) Danish philosopher and religious writer whose works had a tremendous influence on the development of modern Existentialism. Kierkegaard opposed the philosophical system of the dialectic advanced by Hegel and held that people's existence must be governed by their own conscious choice. He also advanced the theory that in religion "truth is subjectivity." *See also* Philosophy section, page 19-12.

Kim Il-sung (Kim Song Ju) (b. 1912) Leader of the Democratic People's Republic of Korea (North Korea) since 1948. In 1972 he took the title of president and made his son his heir.

Kindi (Al-Kindi) (9th century) Arab philosopher. He translated Aristotle's work into Arabic and attempted to reconcile Aristotelian and Neoplatonist thought. His extensive writings dealt with medicine, astrology, and mathematics.

King (William Lyon), MacKenzie (1874–1950) Prime minister and leader of the Liberal party in Canada during most of the years from 1920 to 1948. He kept Canada's English and French populations united during World War II and the postwar period.

Kitchener, Horatio Herbert, 1st earl (1850–1916) British field marshal and statesman. He conquered the Sudan and reoccupied Khartoum in 1898, and was chief of staff in the South African War. As secretary of war (1914–1916), he greatly expanded Britain's military forces.

Knights Hospitallers (Knights of St. John) (Knights of Jerusalem) (in full Order of the Hospital of St. John of Jerusalem) Important religious and military order founded in about 1099 in Jerusalem by Gerard de Martignes. Dedicated to the healing and protection of pilgrims to the Holy Land, the order grew rich and powerful during the Crusades. Grateful knights, healed at the order's hospital, made bequests of money and land, while the knights of the order undertook military operations in its name. The misfortunes of the Crusaders and the rise of Turkish power, however, forced the order to relocate several times after the fall of Jerusalem in 1187: to Acre in 1189, to Cyprus in 1291, to Rhodes in 1310, which they conquered, and to Malta in 1530. The order declined in importance after being driven out of Rhodes. Napoleon's conquest of Malta in 1798 effectively brought the order to an end. In 1879 it was reorganized and revived as a charitable organization.

Knights Templars (Templars) (Knights of the Temple of Solomon) Important religious military order founded about 1119 during the Crusades by Hugh de Payens at Jerusalem to protect Christian pilgrims from Muslim attacks. It subsequently grew into a powerful army in service against the Muslims and, through bequests, gained considerable wealth and lands in Europe. After the failure of the Crusades, the Templars became a powerful banking group and thereby aroused opposition by the European nobility. French King Philip IV, with consent of Pope Clement V, began persecutions in 1307 of the Templars. By 1314, its property had been confiscated, and the order ceased to exist.

Knox, John (1514–1572) Scottish reformer and founder of the Church of Scotland. With the beginning of the Scottish Reformation in 1557, Knox returned to Scotland in 1559 to lead the fight against

Catholic armies. Following the establishment of the Church of Scotland, Knox and others wrote the *First Book of Discipline* setting forth the basic organization of the church.

Koch, Robert (1843–1910) German bacteriologist, a leading figure in the founding of bacteriology. His contributions include the discovery of the organisms causing anthrax in 1876 and those causing tuberculosis in 1882.

Koguryo Ancient Korean kingdom, founded between the 2nd and 1st centuries B.C. In 668 it was overrun by the Chinese T'ang and Korean Silla dynasties, and was incorporated into the kingdom of Silla.

Kohl, Helmut (b. 1930) Chancellor of West Germany since 1983. He presided over Germany's economic boom, which was slowed in the late 1980s by the unification with the former German Democratic Republic (East Germany). *See* **East European Revolution; German Unification**.

Koran (Quran) The sacred book of Islam. A compilation of the revelations received by Muhammad during his lifetime, it is one of the world's most influential books and the major unifying force in the Islamic religion. The authorized version was written in 650 by Muhammad's secretary, Zaid ibn Thabit, by order of the caliph Uthaman. Divided into 114 chapters (suras), the Koran sets forth religious doctrine and codes concerning conduct of the followers of Islam. Accepted as the word of God, the Koran is above doubt or criticism in the Islamic world.

Korean War War (1950–1953) between the North Koreans, backed by the Communist Chinese, and the South Koreans, backed by U.N. peace forces (principally U.S. troops). Korea was ravaged by the war and there were some 4 million casualties (2 million of them civilians). The war was caused by various factors, including the Communists' desire to reunite Korea under their rule and the rise of Cold War tensions between Communist and non-Communist nations. Korea had been divided at the end of World War II, with Soviet forces occupying the territory north of the 38th parallel, and U.S. forces to the south of it. Plans to reunite the country were never instituted. A Communist government was established in the North and a pro-Western government evolved in the South. Thus the Communist invasion of the South in 1950 became a part of the larger Cold War between the Communists and the United States and its Western allies.

Koryo Korean kingdom (935–1392) from which the name Korea is derived. During its existence the Korean peninsula was unified.

Kosciusko, Thaddeus (1746–1817) Polish general and champion of Polish independence. He fought with distinction against the British in the American Revolution, then fought unsuccessfully in Poland against the Russians (1792–1793). After the second Partition of Poland in 1793, he led a rebellion in 1794 against both Russian and Prussian forces. This led to the third Partition of Poland and his imprisonment (1794–1796).

Kossuth, Louis (Lajos) (1802–1894) Hungarian revolutionary, one of the leading figures in the Hungarian Revolution of 1848. He led the Republic of

Hungary briefly in 1849, but was forced to resign in the face of Russian and Austrian intervention.

Kosygin, Aleksey Nikolayevich (1904–1980) Russian statesman who succeeded Khrushchev as premier (1964–1980). He played a major role in Soviet economic planning. As premier, he shared power with Brezhnev for a time but was gradually overshadowed.

Kremlin Triangular citadel in Moscow, once a fortress, and was the seat of the government of the former U.S.S.R. Originally constructed in 1156 and modified considerably thereafter, the Kremlin is surrounded by a wall topped by 20 towers. Inside are numerous buildings that were once cathedrals, armories, and palaces, now used for government purposes. The center of czarist government until 1792, when Peter the Great made St. Petersburg capital, it became the seat of the revolutionary government in 1918. Since December 1991 it is the seat of the Russian government.

Krishna One of the leading Hindu divinities, the 8th incarnation of Vishnu.

Kublai Khan (1215–1294) Mongol emperor (1260–1290). He was founder of the Mongol Yüan dynasty in China. He ruled China and nominally controlled a vast Mongol empire that stretched across Asia. His military expeditions against Korea and Burma were successful, but he failed in his attacks on Japan between 1274 and 1281. He was a great builder, and the splendor of his court was recorded by Marco Polo.

Kulturkampf German Chancellor O. Bismarck's struggle between 1871 and 1883 to assert government control over the Roman Catholic church. Precipitated by the declaration in 1870 of papal infallibility (which expanded papal powers at the expense of secular leaders), conflict between the church and state governments broke out in Germany and other European countries. In Germany, Bismarck had, by 1872, taken steps to limit Catholic influence, including expulsion of the Jesuits. He instituted the May, or Falk, Laws (May 1873), which further limited church powers, and then mandated in 1875 civil marriage services. Resistance by German clergymen and the Catholic Center party's 1878 election victory forced Bismarck to moderate.

Kun, Béla (1886–1939) Hungarian Communist leader who briefly headed a Soviet republic in Hungary in 1919. Later a leader of the Comintern, he became a victim of the Stalinist purges of the 1930s.

Kuomintang (KMT) Chinese Nationalist political party, the ruling party in China (1928–1949). Following the Communist takeover in 1949 on the mainland, the KMT formed the opposition government in Taiwan. Organized in 1912 as a political party after the Chinese Revolution of 1911, it was led by Sun Yat-sen and called for parliamentary government. Banned in 1913, the party organized opposition governments between 1917 and 1923 under Sun and then joined in 1923 with the Chinese Communist party (CCP). The KMT launched in 1926 the Northern Expedition and, by 1928, after breaking with the CCP the previous year, took control of the government. Civil war between the Nationalists and the Communists raged almost continuously thereafter until the CCP expelled the KMT in 1949.

Kushan Empire Empire established over much of northern India, Afghanistan, and territories to the North from 78–220 A.D. by the Kushanas, a people from central Asia. They declined at about the time of the rise of the Sassanidae.

Kwang Hsu (1872–1908) Emperor of China (1875–1908). After assuming authority in 1889, he issued several edicts to institute reform in China during the "hundred days of reform." His aunt Tz'u Hsi soon resumed the regency, ending Kwang's rule.

Labor unions Organizations of workers for improvement of pay, benefits, and working conditions. Unions are the chief manifestation of the labor movement, which rose in response to the new economic and social order brought about by the Industrial Revolution. Early unions in Europe date from the 1700s and were at first suppressed by law. During the 1800s unions generally won legal recognition and greatly increased their memberships.

Labour party British political party, founded in 1900 by a coalition of trade unions with participation by members of the Fabian Society. Though openly committed to Socialist ideals since 1918, the party has traditionally favored specific legislative programs over ideology. The party formed its first government between 1922 and 1924 under Ramsay MacDonald, who again led the government between 1929 and 1931. The Labour party joined the coalition government under Churchill during World War II and, after a major victory at the polls in 1945, formed the government of Clement Attlee (1945–1951). During Attlee's ministry, major Socialist programs were enacted, including nationalization of railroads, banks, mines, and utilities, and establishment of a national health plan. Ousted by the conservatives, the Labour party returned to power under Wilson (1964–1970, 1974–1976) and under Callaghan (1976–1979).

Ladislaus I (1040–1095) King of Hungary (1077–1095). One of Hungary's national heroes, he defended the country against the Poles, Russians, and Tatars and conquered Croatia.

Ladislaus II (Jagiello) (1350?–1434) King of Poland (1386–1434). Ladislaus, grand duke of Lithuania, married Polish Queen Jadwiga, became king, and thereby founded the Jagiello dynasty. During his reign, he warred against the Teutonic Knights and, by his victories made Poland a great power.

Lafayette, Marie Joseph Paul Yves Roch Gilbert du Motier, marquis de (La Fayette) (1757–1834) French soldier and political leader, a hero of the American Revolution and the early French Revolution. During the French Revolution, he was a prominent member of the bourgeois faction; served in the Assembly of Notables, the States-General, the National Assembly (vice president, 1789); and drafted the Declaration of the Rights of Man in 1789. He fell from prominence when, frightened by the growing extremism of the revolution, he ordered the Paris National Guard to fire on a mob in July of 1791. Under threat of trial for his opposition to radical republicanism, he defected to Austria in 1792. Returned to France by Napoleon in

1799, he lived quietly until the July Revolution of 1830 when he helped install King Louis Philippe.

Laissez-faire Economic theory popular during the 18th and 19th centuries, which assumed an underlying natural order in economic systems. Thus, it was believed, individuals left to their own initiative (i.e., free from government regulation) would naturally produce the greatest good for themselves and society as a whole. Adam Smith and John Stuart Mill became the leading exponents of the doctrine in Britain, where it appealed to the commercial interests of the Industrial Revolution.

Lao-tze (Lao-tzu) (604–531 B.C.) Chinese classical philosopher. The reputed founder of Taoism, he preached conformity to the Tao, or eternal spirit of right conduct, and is considered one of the great figures of Chinese history.

La Salle, Robert Cavelier, sieur de (1643–1687) French explorer in North America. He claimed the Mississippi Valley region for France in 1682 and named it Louisiana.

Las Casas, Bartolomé de (1474–1566) Spanish missionary and historian. He worked to improve the treatment of South American Indians by the Spanish, helped bring about the New Laws of 1542, and wrote the *Historia General de las Indias*.

Lateran Councils Councils of the Roman Catholic church at Rome. First (9th ecumenical): Convened by Pope Calixtus II in 1123 it reaffirmed decisions of the Concordat of Worms regarding the Investiture Controversy. Second (10th ecumenical): Convened in 1139 by Pope Innocent II, it ended the schism created by election of antipope Anacletus II (reigned 1130–1138), and forbade marriage by monks, nuns, and other clerics. Third (11th ecumenical): Convened in 1179 by Pope Alexander III, it came after restoration of peace between the pope and Holy Roman Emperor Frederick I. The council ordered that the pope be elected solely by the college of cardinals (by a two-thirds majority) and proclaimed the Albigensian Crusade. Fourth (12th ecumenical): Convened in 1215 by Pope Innocent III, it is considered one of the great councils. It instituted many lasting organizational and procedural reforms, proclaimed the Crusades to recover the Holy Land, defined the doctrine of transubstantiation, and established the Easter Duty. Fifth (18th ecumenical): Held (1512–1517) under Popes Julius II and Leo X, the council opposed attempts to revive conciliarism and issued the Concordat of 1516, providing for a settlement of disputes between the pope and French king Louis XII.

Lateran Treaty Agreement on February 11, 1929 between Italy and the papacy, settling the Roman Question. During the unification of Italy, the kingdom of Italy seized control of the Papal States and the city of Rome. The new government offered the pope compensation for the territories taken and rights to the Vatican and Lateran. But the pope refused and thus created the Roman Question. Negotiations began in 1926 and the final agreement was reached in 1929. It provided for creation of Vatican City as an independent state, establishment of Roman Catholicism as the state religion in Italy, and a large financial compensation to the church for loss of the Papal States.

Latin America Term used to refer to the Spanish and Portuguese-speaking countries south of the southwest border of the United States, including Mexico and the nations of Central America and South America.

Latin Empire of Constantinople Feudal empire centered at Constantinople between 1204 and 1261. It was established by leaders of the Fourth Crusade after they captured the Byzantine capital of Constantinople in 1204 and divided various Byzantine lands among themselves and their Venetian bankers. Viewed as a Western intrusion, in Eastern lands, it began to decline soon after its creation. The empire suffered the hostility of the local population, incursions of the Bulgars and Turks, and resistance by the Byzantine emperors, who retired across the Bosporus to form the empire of Nicaea. The empire lapsed after Byzantine emperor Michael VIII retook Constantinople in 1261.

Latin Kingdom of Jerusalem Kingdom established in 1099 in Palestine and Syria by leaders of the First Crusade. A feudal kingdom, it included the cities of Jerusalem, Acre, and Tyre and controlled Antioch, Edessa, and Tripoli. Subsequent crusades were unsuccessful against the Muslims, and Jerusalem fell in 1187 to Saladin. Thereafter Muslim armies made further conquest and expelled the last Christian forces from the region by the capture of Acre in 1291.

Latins Ancient people that inhabited Latium, a plain in what is now central Italy. Romans were Latins and Rome was one of the early Latin cities established in the region. The cities formed confederations to resist the Etruscans and Samnites and Rome gradually emerged as the dominant power.

Latin Wars Wars (340–338 B.C.) in which a number of Italian cities sought equality with Rome. With their defeat by Rome, some of these states were made into colonies, others into states dependent upon Rome, and others ceded land for settlement by the Romans.

Laurier, Sir Wilfrid (1841–1919) Canadian statesman and first French-Canadian prime minister (1896–1911). A leader of the Liberal party, he worked to develop the Canadian West.

Lausanne, Treaty of 1. Treaty on October 18, 1912 concluding the Italo-Turkish War. The treaty called for Turkey's withdrawal from Tripoli. 2. Treaty on July 24, 1923 that formally ended hostilities of the Greco-Turkish War (1920–1922) and modified terms of the Treaty of Sèvres. By it Turkey regained control of the Dardanelles, eastern Thrace, and other territories, including Smyrna.

Laval, François Xavier de (Laval-Montmorency, François Xavier) (1623?–1708) French cleric, the first Catholic bishop in Canada. He founded the seminary of Quebec in 1663, which became Laval University.

Laval, Pierre (1883–1945) French politician. As premier of the Vichy government during World War II (1942–1944), he instituted forced labor and other harsh measures in France.

Lavalleja, Juan Antonio (1786–1853) Uruguayan revolutionary. He led a group, known as the Thirty-three Immortals, and declared Uruguayan independence from Brazil in 1825.

Lavoisier, Antoine Laurent (1743–1794) French chemist. He explained the role of oxygen in combustion.

Law, Andrew Bonar (1858–1923) British statesman. He succeeded Arthur Balfour as Conservative party leader in the House of Commons (1911–1915), where he opposed Irish Home Rule. He became prime minister (1922 and 1923).

Lawrence, Charles (1709–1760) British general and governor of Nova Scotia (1756–1760). He was largely responsible for the deportation of French colonials from Acadia (in Canada) after the British took over this French colony.

Lawrence, Thomas Edward (Lawrence of Arabia) (1888–1935) English soldier and author. During World War I, he led the Arab troops of Faisal I in revolt against the Turks and described his adventures in *The Seven Pillars of Wisdom* (1926).

League of Nations International organization (1919–1946) formed to maintain peace and security in the post-World War I world. Though the league generally failed in its aims during the 1930s, it provided a foundation for the U.N. organization that succeeded it. Provided for by the Paris Conference of 1919 (largely due to American president Wilson's efforts) and the Treaty of Versailles of 1919, the league consisted of a secretariat, council, assembly, and the Permanent Court of International Justice. Original members included the World War I Allies and neutral nations, which were later joined by other nations. The United States, however, did not join because of isolationist sentiment in Congress. This and the provision for unanimous assent in both the assembly and council seriously weakened the league. Though it was generally successful in social and economic matters, it failed to effectively promote disarmament. Then, beginning with Japan's occupation of Manchuria in 1931, the inability of the league to prevent armed aggression by Japan, Italy, and Germany followed in the 1930s, and with the outbreak of World War II, the league collapsed. It was officially dissolved in 1946.

Leakey, Louis Seymour Bazett (1903–1972) British archaeologist and anthropologist. He is noted for his controversial interpretations of extremely ancient humanoid fossils, which indicated that forerunners of humans were much older than previously thought. His wife, Mary Leakey, discovered in 1959 the noted Zinjanthropus fossil remains (believed 1.75 million years old) in the Olduvai Gorge, Tanzania. Leakey subsequently discovered in 1961 a more direct ancestor of humans, the *Homo habilis*.

Leclerc, Charles Victor Emmanuel (1772–1802) French general, Napoleon's brother-in-law. He died of yellow fever contracted while putting down a revolt in Haiti led by Toussaint L'Ouverture.

Lee Kuan Yew (b. 1923) Became first prime minister of the Republic of Singapore in 1959.

Leeuwenhoek, Antony van (1632–1723) Dutch scientist. Using microscopes he made himself, he became the first to describe accurately bacteria, protozoa, red corpuscles, spermatozoa, striped muscle, and many other microscopic cells and organisms.

Legalism A Chinese philosophy of government dating from the 2nd century B.C. One of its leading exponents was the scholar Itan Fei-tzu who favored a highly efficient, strict, and powerful government with a ruler with absolute power. Legalism was put into practice by Shih Huang-Ti. He was the founder of the Ch'in dynasty but the dynasty lasted only a short time. However, the highly centralized government created by the Ch'in under the influence of the legalist philosophy was a long-lasting feature of Chinese government.

Legion Unit of the Roman army. It was in use from about 400 B.C. to the time of the German invasions and, though its composition and organization varied through this period, generally consisted of 4,000–6,000 infantrymen arranged in 8 ranks. Other units, such as cavalry, were also part of the legion.

Legislative Assembly Name of the national representative body of revolutionary France (1791 and 1792). Dominated by the moderate Girondists, it was replaced by the National Convention after the overthrow of the monarchy. During the Second Republic, the name was revived for the assembly, which sat for 2 years (1849–1851).

Leibniz, Gottfried Wilhelm, baron von (Leibnitz) (1646–1716) German philosopher and mathematician. Leibniz developed new notations for calculus and a theory of infinitesimal calculus that predated Newton's findings by 3 years.

Leicester, Robert Dudley, earl of (1532?–1588) English courtier who won the favor of Queen Elizabeth I but did not succeed in marrying her. A member of the Puritan sect, he opposed Catholics in England and advocated war with Spain.

Leif Ericson (1000?) Norse explorer, son of Eric the Red. On a voyage to Greenland, he apparently went off course and landed somewhere in North America, which he called Vinland. He wintered there and then went on to Greenland. By another account, he first went to Greenland and then sailed westward on a voyage of discovery.

Leipzig, battle of (Nations) Major defeat in 1813 for Napoleon during the Napoleonic Wars. The battle resulted in the loss of Germany and Poland.

Lenin, Nikolai (pseud. of Ulyanov, Vladimir Ilich) (1870–1924) Russian Communist leader, a central figure in the Russian Revolution, and founder of the Bolsheviks. On the outbreak of the Russian Revolution of 1917, Lenin's return to Russia was arranged by the Germans, who were counting on the revolution to eliminate Russia from participation in World War I. In Russia, Lenin opposed the provisional government, advocating instead a dictatorship of the proletariat. Lenin's Bolshevik faction gradually gained control of the Soviets in ensuing months and finally ousted the provisional government in the October Revolution of 1917. Lenin became dictator and, aided by Stalin, Trotsky, and others, arranged the Treaty of Brest-Litovsk in 1918 with Germany, turned Russian factories over to workers, ended private ownership of land, nationalized banks, and introduced other radical reforms. Consolidating his position, Lenin successfully opposed attempts at counterrevolution between 1918 and 1921 and crushed his political opponents. By the time of his death in 1924, he ruled virtually without opposition and had succeeded in laying the foundations of the Russian Communist state.

Lenin proclaims the Soviet Republic.

Leninism   Term applied to the political, economic, and social theories advanced by Lenin. His theories were built on the teachings of Karl Marx and included a new perception of imperialism. Lenin held that imperialist powers would, in their exploitation of underdeveloped regions, come into conflict with each other and thereby sow the seeds of their own destruction. Leninism was also marked by its authoritarian temper, especially in its concept of the revolutionary party as an elite, highly disciplined organization.

Leo I, Saint (400–461 A.D.)   Italian-born pope (440–461). One of the important popes of the early church. He actively opposed heresy and his doctrines regarding the two natures of Jesus in one person were adopted at the Council of Chalcedon.

Leo III, Saint (d. 816)   Italian-born pope (795–816). He crowned Charlemagne as Roman emperor in 800, thus re-creating the Roman Empire in the West and establishing the tradition by which the pope conferred imperial authority on the emperor.

Leo III (the Isaurian) (680–741)   Byzantine emperor (717–741) and founder of the Isaurian dynasty. He defeated the last Arab siege of Constantinople (717 and 718) and began the long controversy over iconoclasm in 726.

Leo VI (Leo the Wise) (Leo the Philosopher) (866–912)   Byzantine emperor (886–912) whose compilation of imperial law, the *Basilica*, was adopted as the Byzantine Empire's legal code.

Leo X (Medici, Giovanni de') (1475–1521)   Italian-born pope (1513–1521). His main interest was in the arts. He excommunicated M. Luther in 1521 for initiating a protest against the sale of indulgences during his reign and thus figured in the beginning of the Protestant Reformation.

Leo XIII (Pecci, Gioacchino) (1810–1903)   Italian-born pope (1878–1903). He helped end the anti-Catholic Kulturkampf in Germany and worked to end friction between the papacy and secular governments elsewhere.

Leonardo da Vinci (1452–1519)   Italian painter, sculptor, architect, engineer, and scientist who was one of the greatest figures of the Renaissance and who is today remembered as the archetypal "Renaissance man" for his multifaceted genius.

Leonidas (d. 480 B.C.)   King of Sparta (491–480 B.C.). He became a Spartan hero when he led the unsuccessful defense of the pass of Thermopylae in 480 B.C. against invading Persians during the Persian Wars. He and his force of 300 Spartans were killed in the battle.

Leopold II (1747–1792)   Holy Roman emperor (1790–1792), successor to his brother, Joseph II. An enlightened despot, he repealed many of his brother's reforms, which were then precipitating rebellion in Hapsburg domains. He subsequently joined Prussia in the Declaration of Pillnitz, a cause of the French Revolutionary Wars (1792–1802).

Leopold II (1835–1909)   King of Belgium (1865–1909). He sent explorer H. Stanley to the Congo, which he later used to base his claim on the region. The Congo Free State was recognized to be under his personal control in 1885 until reports of this ruthless exploitation of the natives forced the Belgian government to take it over in 1908.

Lepanto, battle of   Naval victory on October 7, 1571 for Christian allies of the Holy League over the Ottoman navy. Little more than a temporary setback for the Ottoman Turks, the battle marked the first major defeat of the Turks by Christian forces.

Lepidus, Marcus Aemilius (d. 13 B.C.)   Roman statesman. With Mark Antony and Octavian, a member of the second triumvirate (43–36 B.C.) that ruled Rome after the assassination of Julius Caesar. He was forced from power in 36 B.C. after attempting to revolt against Octavian.

Lesseps, Ferdinand Marie, vicomte de (1805–1894)   French diplomat and engineer. He originated the idea of the Suez Canal and directed its construction (1859–1869). His Panama Canal project ended in scandal and a French government inquiry.

Lettres de cachet   French warrants. These secret letters were used to imprison or exile personal enemies of the king or nobility (from the 17th century). They were outlawed by the National Assembly in 1789.

Levant   Term used for those countries on the eastern shore of the Mediterranean, from Egypt to Greece. It sometimes also refers to the former French Levant states, Syria and Lebanon.

Leyte gulf, battle of (Philippine Sea, battle of)   Major World War II victory for the United States in battle against the Japanese on October 23–25, 1944. Considered one of the greatest sea and air battles, the victory enabled the United States to reconquer the Philippines.

Liberalism   Generally, a philosophy that advocates maintaining the freedom of individuals from outside restraints. It is characterized by a belief in the fundamental goodness and rationality of humankind and belief in continuing change as a means to perfect the order of things. Thus it often arises in opposition to conservatism. Fueled by ideas of the Enlightenment, liberalism flourished in the 18th–19th centuries as a movement toward greater personal liberty, toward restrictions on government powers, and toward such persuasive doctrines as laissez-faire economics. By the 20th century however, the focus of liberalism had been changed by disparity between industrialists' wealth and the lot of the worker. Thus in modern times, liberalism became concerned with freeing the individual from economic and social restraints. To do this, liberals have sought to institute government programs to provide basic protections for the individual, such as social security, welfare, and other minimum-maintenance programs.

Liberal party   British party that, with the Conservative party, was one of the two major parties in that country between 1832 and 1931. Formed from the Whig party after the Reform Bill of 1832, the Liberal party embraced many progressive social-reform causes including extension of the franchise and Home Rule for Ireland. At the same time, it favored laissez-faire capitalism and free trade. The party placed many prime ministers in office, such as Gladstone, Asquith, and, during World War I, Lloyd George. The party declined from the 1920s vis-à-vis the Labour party because of its adherence to laissez-faire doctrines. It finally split in 1931 and thereafter became a minor party. A revival in the 1970s brought back to it the votes of about 15 percent of the electorate.

Liberal Union   British political party formed in 1886 by disaffected members of the Liberal party. They opposed the policies of W. Gladstone.

Li Hung-chang (1823–1901)   Chinese statesman. He commanded forces against the Taiping Rebellion (1861–1864), founded the Chinese navy, and became the dominant figure in Chinese foreign affairs after 1872. He worked to improve relations with the West and to modernize China.

Liliuokalani (1838–1917)   Queen of the Hawaiian Islands (1891–1893). She succeeded her brother King Kalakaua and was deposed for trying to resist changes in the constitution.

Lin Piao (1907–1971)   Chinese Communist general and politician. After the Long March (1934 and 1935), he became commander of Communist forces in the northeast against Chiang Kai-shek's Nationalist army. He became heir apparent to Mao Tse-tung after replacing Liu Shao-ch'i in 1966 as second-in-command of the Chinese Communist party.

Li Po (Li Tai Po) (700–762)   Chinese T'ang dynasty poet, considered one of China's greatest.

Lister, Joseph, 1st baron (1827–1912)   English surgeon, founder of antiseptic surgery.

Litvinov, Maxim Maximovich (1876–1951)   Russian Communist diplomat. As commissar of foreign affairs between 1930 and 1939, he sought cooperation with Western nations against the Axis Powers. He was ambassador to the United States (1941–1943).

Liu Shao-ch'i (1898–1974)   Chinese Communist leader. A recognized authority on party organization, he was head of state between 1959 and 1968 and heir apparent under Mao Tse-tung. He was ousted during the Cultural Revolution.

Livingstone, David (1813–1873)   Scottish missionary and explorer. Arriving in Africa as a medical missionary in 1841, Livingstone explored its interior, and his discoveries included Victoria Falls and the Zambezi River.

Livy (59 B.C.–17 A.D.)   Great Roman historian Sponsored by Emperor Augustus, Livy wrote the collection of 142 books known as the *Annals of Rome*, which cover the history of Rome from its founding in 753–9 B.C. Thirty-five books are extant and fragments and summaries of all but two remain.

Li Yuan (565–635)   Chinese emperor (618–627) and founder of the T'ang dynasty. An official in the Sui dynasty government, he led a revolt in 617 that put him in power.

Lloyd George, David, 1st earl of Dwyfor (1863–1945)   Controversial, Welsh-born, British statesman, and liberal prime minister (1916–1922). After ousting Asquith, he became prime minister and, during his term of office, helped bring the United States into World War I, played a major role in negotiating the Treaty of Versailles, and set up the Irish Free State.

Locarno Pact   Agreement signed on October 16, 1925 at Locarno, Switzerland, by Germany and other European powers, guaranteeing the post-World War I borders of the Rhineland, Belgium, France, and Germany. A major step in Germany's reentry to postwar world affairs, the agreement was preceded by several treaties between individual signatories and eventually led to Germany's acceptance into the League of Nations. The pact was denounced by Hitler and was finally broken when the Germans demilitarized the Rhineland in 1936.

Locke, John (1632–1704)   English philosopher who founded British empiricism. His doctrines on natural rights influenced the writing of the Declaration of Independence and the Constitution of the United States. In his *Essay Concerning Human Understanding*, he described the human mind and the process by which it acquires knowledge through the five senses. Natural rights, he believed, included the rights of property, the pursuit of happiness, and religious toleration. Locke held that governments were social compacts and should be based on natural laws. His philosophy greatly influenced the thinking of the 18th-century Enlightenment and provided a philosophical basis for the American and French Revolutions. *See also* Philosophy section, page 19–13.

Lollardy   English church reform movement that began in the 1300s at Oxford. Some Lollard doctrines are said to have presaged those of the Reformation. Started by John Wycliffe, the movement spread throughout England. Persecutions began in 1399 under Henry IV and, after two rebellions were suppressed (1414, 1431), the movement went underground, surviving until the rise of the Reformation in the 1500s. Lollard doctrines, as set forth in their *Twelve Conclusions* (1395) and elsewhere, include: condemnation of the papacy; belief in primacy of the Scriptures; denial of transubstantiation; opposition to war; and condemnation of sacramentals, confession, pilgrimages, clerical celibacy, and other practices of the Catholic church.

Lombard League   Alliance formed in 1167 by the Lombard cities in northern Italy against Holy Roman Emperor Frederick I (Barbarossa). Following attempts by Frederick to enforce his authority over the cities, they formed the league with the support of Pope Alexander III and successfully resisted Frederick's armies. By the Peace of Constance in 1183, Frederick guaranteed the cities their freedom and the league ceased to be important. It was reactivated in 1226 to defend against attacks by Holy Roman Emperor Frederick II. Cities in the league included Milan, Venice, Mantua, Padua, and Brescia.

Lombards, kingdom of   Kingdom in Italy formed in the 6th century by Germanic tribes known as the Lombards. Led by Aloin, these tribes migrated south and conquered (568–572) most of the north and parts of central and southern Italy. After a period of initial instability, the kingdom flourished (7th and 8th centuries) with its center at Pavia. Frankish conquest of the kingdom was provoked by Lombard invasions of the Papal States. The Franks, under Pepin the Short, invaded Lombard domains in 751 to aid Pope Stephen II. When Lombard king Desiderius again attacked Rome in 772, Charlemagne completely conquered the Lombard kingdom and ended its existence as an independent state.

Long March   Heroic march undertaken between 1934 and 1935 by the remnants of the Chinese Communist army during the Chinese Civil War. When Chinese Nationalists surrounded their base in southeast China, about 100,000 Communist soldiers broke out of the trap on October 15, 1934. During their subsequent 6,000-mile march to a new base in Shensi province in northwest China, the Communists crossed rugged terrain and were harried by Nationalist forces. Mao Tse-tung became leader of the Chinese Communist party during the march, and, by the time the Communists reached Shensi, over half had died or been killed.

Long Parliament   Name for the English Parliament that sat from November 1640 to March 1660 during the English Civil War period. Called by Charles I to raise money, the Parliament refused, and civil war broke out soon after. After Charles's defeat, the Parliament was purged of 143 members, mostly Presbyterians believed to be royalist sympathizers who were forcibly removed. Reduced to 60 members, it thereafter became known as the Rump Parliament. Later, Charles I was tried and executed by the Parliament, which was twice dissolved for intervals by Oliver Cromwell and was succeeded by the Convention Parliament.

Lon Nol (b. 1913)   Cambodian military leader. He was premier between 1966 and 1967, and took control of the government after overthrowing Prince Sihanouk in 1970. Reverses in the civil war with Communist Khmer Rouge guerrillas eventually drove him from office in 1975.

Lost tribes of Israel   Ten tribes of Israel that were exiled from there by Assyrian king Sargon in 722 B.C. Their fate is unknown, but several theories assert that they became the ancestors of various peoples, including the Anglo-Saxons, American Indians, and Ethiopians.

Lothair I (795–855)   Carolingian emperor in title (840–855), a successor to his father, Louis I, and grandson of Charlemagne. His defeat at Fontenoy in 841 marked the end of his attempts to reunite the Carolingian Empire under his rule. By the Treaty of Verdun in 843, he became ruler of Lotharingia, the middle portion of the divided empire.

Lothair II (1075–1137)   Holy Roman emperor (1133–1137). He was elected to succeed Henry V, and his was the first case in which an elective monarchy came to power over a rival, hereditary claimant.

Lotharingia   Kingdom created by the division of the Carolingian Empire into three parts. Lotharingia (then also called Francia Media) was the middle of the three kingdoms established by the Treaty of Verdun in 843 and was first ruled by Emperor Lothair I. At its greatest extent, it included what are now The Netherlands, Belgium, Luxembourg, the region of Lorraine in France, and Italy.

Louis I (Louis the Pious) (778–840)   Carolingian emperor (814–840), successor to his father, Charlemagne. His reign was marked by revolts by his sons over his plans to divide the empire among them. They deposed and later restored him twice, once in 830 and again in 833. His reign marked the end of the unified Carolingian Empire.

Louis I (1838–1889)   Portuguese king (1861–1889). His reign was marked by political unrest and numerous changes of ministries. Under his rule, slavery was abolished in Portuguese colonies.

Louis II (d. 875)   Frankish king of what is now Italy (844–875), nominal emperor of the Carolingian Empire. Louis spent most of his reign holding the invading Arabs in check in southern Italy.

Louis II (Louis the Stammerer) (846–879)   Frankish king (877–879) of the West (France) Frankish kingdom, successor to his father, Charles II (the Bald).

Louis III (863–882)   Frankish king (879–882) of the West (France). He ruled jointly with his brother Carloman, and turned back the Norman invasion at Saucourt in 881.

Louis V (967–987)   King of France (986 and 987). The last Carolingian king of France, he was succeeded by Hugh Capet, founder of the Capetian line.

Louis VI (Louis the Fat) (1081–1137)   King of France (1108–1137). He fought several wars with King Henry I over English territories on the Continent and strengthened royal authority.

Louis VII (Louis the Young) (1120–1180)   King of France (1137–1180). He annulled his marriage to Eleanor of Aquitaine in 1152, who subsequently married Henry II of England. This gave rise to Henry's claims to Aquitaine and a long series of wars between Louis and Henry. Louis aided Henry's sons in a revolt against their father (1173 and 1174) but gained no territories from it.

Louis VIII (1187–1226)   King of France (1223–1226). He invaded England in 1216 at the invitation of the barons, then rebelling against King John, but withdrew in 1217 after the accession of Henry III eroded his support among them.

Louis IX (Saint Louis) (1214–1270)   King of France (1226–1270). His mother, Blanche of Castile, was his regent to 1234 and, later, his close adviser. He was defeated and captured on the Seventh Crusade and settled territorial disputes with Henry III of England by the Treaty of Paris in 1259. His reign was marked by a period of peace and prosperity.

Louis X (1289–1316)   King of France (1314–1316). He was forced to grant charters to the nobles to gain their support. He was dominated by Charles of Valois.

Louis XI (1423–1483) French king (1461–1483). As king, he succeeded in overcoming the rebellious nobles and thereby laid the basis for an absolute monarchy in France.

Louis XII (1462–1515) King of France (1498–1515), known as "the Father of the People" for his benevolent rule. His foreign policy was dominated by attempts to conquer parts of Italy in the Italian Wars.

Louis XIII (1601–1643) French king (1610–1643). His reign was marked by the strong leadership of his ministers, Cardinal de Richelieu and Mazarin, who centralized royal authority and laid the foundation for absolutism in France. Rebellions by French Protestants (Huguenots) were quelled and France joined in the Thirty Years' War from 1635.

Louis XIV, the famous Sun King of France, known for his statement "I am the state."

Louis XIV (The Sun King) (1638–1715) French king (1643–1715). Louis' reign marked the height of absolutism in France, and, by his expansionist policies, he embroiled the country in a costly series of wars. During Louis' minority, France was weakened by the ongoing Thirty Years' War (1618–1648) and rebellions known as the Fronde (1648–1653). Louis took power in 1661 on the death of the powerful minister Cardinal Mazarin, continued the process of centralizing authority in his own hands, and fostered a period of commercial prosperity. With the royal finances restored and the army strengthened, Louis set out on the first of his wars to enlarge French domains. Within France, Louis' reign was marked by his arbitrary use of the *lettres de cachet* and his growing intolerance of Protestants (Huguenots), which ended in his revocation of the Edict of Nantes in 1685.

Louis XV (1710–1774) French king (1715–1774). Louis was a weak and (at his death) unpopular ruler. The financial difficulties that arose during his reign helped bring on the French Revolution (1789–1799). Made king at 5, he attained his majority in 1723. The government, however was largely run by Fleury between 1726 and 1743. Louis' reign was marked by the following: the War of Polish Succession (1733–1735), acquisition of the duchy of Lorraine in 1735, the War of Austrian Succession (1740–1748), and the disastrous Seven Years' War (1756–1763), which cost France its Canadian and Indian colonies.

Louis XVI French king (1774–1792). He was overthrown during the French Revolution. Louis was an ineffective ruler and failed in attempts at fiscal and administrative reform, put forward by such ministers as Turgot and Necker. The extravagance of the court and French support (1778–1781) for the American Revolution helped bring the government to near bankruptcy. Thereafter, Louis' reign was swept up in the events of the French Revolution.

Louis XVII (1785–1795?) Titular king of France during the French Revolution. The son of Louis XVI, he was imprisoned with the royal family in 1792. After his father's execution, Louis was for a time the symbol of royalist hopes. He died in prison.

Louis XVIII (1755–1824) French king (1814–1824), crowned after the fall of Napoleon. Following the outbreak of the French Revolution, he fled France in 1791 and actively promoted counterrevolutionary plots. He was made king of France in 1814, partly through the efforts of Talleyrand. His reign began the Restoration Period (1814–1830).

Louis Philippe (Citizen King) (1773–1850) King of the French (1830–1848), successor to Charles X by the July Revolution of 1830. Once a liberal supporter of the French Revolution, Louis Philippe lived in exile from 1793 until the Restoration. He joined the liberal opposition to the monarchy, and was later chosen king by Thiers, Lafayette, and other bourgeois leaders of the July Revolution. Though it began in a liberal spirit, his reign gradually became absolutist. Workers' rebellions, demands for enfranchisement of the lower bourgeoisie, and the struggles between Legitimists and Bonapartists eventually culminated in the February Revolution of 1848. The king abdicated in February of 1848 and fled to England.

Louis the Child (893–911) Frankish king (899–911) of the East (Germany). Louis was the last German Carolingian ruler.

Louis the German (804–876) Frankish king (843–876) of the East (Germany). He was allotted a portion of the divided Carolingian Empire by his father, Louis I. Louis joined with his brother, Charles the Bald, to block Lothair I's attempt to reunite the Carolingian Empire under his rule. Louis and Charles forced Lothair to accept the divided empire by the Treaty of Verdun in 843.

Lower Canada Name applied (1791–1841) to the Canadian region comprising present-day Quebec. Settled primarily by the French, it was joined with Upper Canada by the Act of Union in 1841 and became known as Canada East. With the confederation of Canada in 1867 it became Quebec.

Lower Egypt Region of Egypt usually considered to include the Nile delta and valley. A rich fertile region, it was united with Upper Egypt by Egyptian King Menes in 3100 B.C.

Lublin, union of Agreement on July 1, 1569 between Poland and Lithuania, merging the two kingdoms into a federated state under a single monarch. King Sigismund II, king of Poland and Lithuania, pressured Lithuanian nobles into accepting formal unification, which lasted to the end of the 18th century.

Luddites Bands of workers in England who attempted between 1811 and 1812 to destroy textile machinery. Fostered by low wages and unemployment, the movement began in 1811 in Nottingham with night raids on textile factories to destroy equipment. The movement spread to other industrial areas, and in 1812 harsh repressive measures were enacted to put an end to it. A brief resurgence of the movement in 1816 was similarly dealt with.

Lumumba, Patrice Hemery (1925–1961) Political leader of Zaire (then called the Congo). He worked for its independence from Belgium and was its first prime minister in 1960. He was murdered after being deposed in the unrest that followed independence.

Lusitania British ship that was torpedoed and sunk by a German submarine on May 7, 1915, with a loss of 1,195 lives. This incident was a factor in the U.S. entry into World War I.

Luther, Martin (1483–1546) German religious leader, father of the Protestant Reformation, and founder of Lutheranism. While a professor (1511–1546) at the University of Wittenberg, in Saxony, he arrived at his fundamental doctrine of personal salvation through faith alone. This doctrine ultimately put him in conflict with the widespread church practice of selling indulgences, and, on October 31, 1517, he nailed his famous Ninety-five Theses to the door of the church in Wittenberg to protest this practice. Thereafter, Luther found wide support for his protest, refused to recant in 1518, burned a papal bull condemning his views in 1520, was thereupon excommunicated, and called before the Diet of Worms in 1521. During this period, he expanded the scope of reforms he sought. After the Diet of Worms ordered his arrest, Luther was given protection (1521 and 1522) by the Elector Frederick III. He returned to Wittenberg, however, to try to prevent splits within the growing Reformation movement. The remainder of his years were spent in voluminous writing and in disputes with leaders of new sects spawned by his beliefs, including Zwingli and Calvin.

Lutheranism The branch of Protestant Christianity based on the teachings of Luther. Lutheranism stems from Luther's famous Ninety-five Theses which sparked the Protestant Reformation. Luther's doctrine stressed that human salvation comes from faith alone, through the redeeming sacrifice of Jesus Christ; that the Scriptures constitute the one necessary guide to truth; and the sacraments are valid only as aids to faith. Luther denied the sacrificial character of the Catholic Mass, and the Lutheran churches formed according to his doctrines abolished clerical celibacy, had communion administered under both kinds (bread and wine), and retained only the two sacraments of Baptism and the

Lord's Supper. The Lutheran churches, organized around individual local congregations, were at first established state churches in the German principalities. Lutheranism also became the established church in Denmark, Finland, Norway, and Sweden.

Luxemburg, Rosa (1870?–1919) German revolutionary. She was a founder of the Spartacus party which became the German Communist party.

Lvov, Prince Georgi Yevgenyevich (1861–1925) Russian statesman. A member of the first Duma in 1905, he was head of the revolutionary Provisional Government (March–July 1917). He resigned in favor of Kerensky.

Lycurgus In Greek tradition, the Spartan leader whose reforms of Spartan government and society created the characteristically militaristic Spartan way of life. He may have ruled in the 7th century B.C.

Lydia Ancient country of Mesopotamia in what is now northwest Turkey. The tyrant Cyges founded the Mermnadae dynasty (685–546 B.C.), which built a powerful Lydian empire of great wealth. The Lydians are believed to have originated the use of coined money during this time. Croesus, the last ruler of independent Lydia, was defeated by Cyrus the Great of Persia in 546 B.C. Lydia later became a province under the Romans.

Lysander (d. 395 B.C.) Spartan military leader. He was admiral of the Spartan fleet that defeated Athens at Notium in 407 B.C. and that ended the Peloponnesian War by taking Athens in 404 B.C.

M **Maastricht Treaty** *See* **European Economic Community**.

Macao (Macau) Portuguese province at the mouth of the Canton River in China. Settled by Portugal in 1557, it was a major port until the rise of Hong Kong in the 1800s.

Maccabees (Hasmoneans) Family of Jewish rulers and patriots that ruled Palestine in the 2nd to 1st centuries B.C.

MacDonald, James Ramsay (1866–1937) English statesman, first British Labour party prime minister (1924, 1929–1931, 1931–1935).

Macdonald, Sir John Alexander (1815–1891) Canadian statesman. He played a major role in the union of the Canadian provinces as the Dominion of Canada in 1867 and was its first prime minister (1867–1873, 1878–1891).

Macedonia European region on the Balkan Peninsula consisting of parts of Greece, Yugoslavia, and Bulgaria. Under Philip II (359–336 B.C.), ancient Macedon came to dominate Greece. Seat of the Macedonian Empire under Alexander the Great, it later was conquered by the Roman, Byzantine, and Ottoman empires. Various claims to the region led to the Balkan Wars (1912 and 1913) and the division of the region, largely between Greece and Yugoslavia.

Macedonian Wars Four wars between the Kingdom of Macedonia and Rome that resulted in complete domination of Greece by Rome.

Machiavelli, Niccolò (1469–1527) Italian statesman, author, and philosopher. A Florentine diplomat, he wrote *The Prince*, which contained his thoughts on the methods by which a prince may acquire and make use of political power. It is thought that he used Borgia as the model for his cynical, ruthless prince. *See also* Philosophy section, page 19-13.

Machu Picchu　Ancient Incan city, located in the Andes mountains of Peru. First discovered in 1911 by Hiram Bingham, it is one of the major pre-Columbian archaeological sites.

Mackenzie, Sir Alexander (1764?–1820)　Canadian explorer. He charted the course of the Mackenzie River in 1789 and made the first transcontinental journey across America north of Mexico in 1793.

Mackenzie, William Lyon (1795–1861)　Canadian journalist and political insurgent. He led an unsuccessful attempt in 1837 to take over the government of Toronto.

MacMahon, Marie Edmé Patrice Maurice de (1808–1893)　French marshal and statesman. A monarchist, he was the second president (1878 and 1879) of the French Third Republic (1870–1940).

Macmillan, Maurice Harold (b. 1894)　British statesman. As prime minister (1957–1963), he sought to improve relations with the United States after the Suez Canal crisis, but failed to gain Great Britain's entry into the Common Market.

Madero, Francisco Indalecio (1873–1913)　Mexican president (1911–1913). He was a leader in the revolution against President Díaz. Unsuccessful as a reform president, he was arrested and murdered by order of Huerta.

Magellan, Ferdinand (1480–1521)　Portuguese navigator and explorer. Sponsored by Spanish King Charles I (later Holy Roman Emperor Charles V), Magellan set out in 1519 to find a western sea route to the Molucca Islands (Spice Islands). He sailed the strait that bears his name, and discovered the Philippines. Though he died in the Philippines in 1521, his expedition continued west, becoming the first to circumnavigate the globe.

Maginot Line　Network of fortifications on the French-German frontier that was supposedly impregnable to any German assault. During World War II the Germans bypassed the line, attacking through Belgium, thus rendering the line useless.

Magna Carta (Magna Charta)　English charter, important in the development of British constitutional law and a symbol (mainly by later interpretations) of basic liberties. Angered by King John's heavy taxation and abuses of power, the barons and the church united to force him (by threat of civil war) to sign the document at Runnymede on June 19, 1215. Originally written to guarantee rights of the nobility, it contained provisions for church freedom, trial by jury, habeas corpus, and matters of minor import.

Magnus I (Magnus the Good) (1024–1047)　King of Norway (1035–1047) and Denmark (1042–1047). He succeeded Danish king Harthacanute in 1042, thereby joining Norway and Denmark. He attempted to press Harthacanute's claim to the English throne but was unsuccessful.

Magyars　People, living primarily in Hungary, who speak the Hungarian language of the Finno-Ugric family. Descended from nomadic peoples who migrated from the Urals in the 5th century, they also include groups living in Romania, Yugoslavia, Czechoslovakia, and the Ukraine.

Mahayana　A leading form of Buddhism, practiced in China, Japan, Korea, and Tibet and noted for its more liberal treatment of Buddhist doctrine.

Mahdi　In Islam, a leader who will appear at the end of the world to save true believers. Although this is not mentioned in the Koran, there have been several claimants to the title.

Mahdi, Muhammad Ahmed (Muhammad Ahmed) (1843?–1885)　Muslim leader who claimed he was the Mahdi. He led a successful revolution against the Egyptian occupation of the Sudan, and defeated the British at Khartoum in 1885.

Maimonides (Maimon, Moses ben) (1135–1204)　Spanish-born Jewish philosopher, considered one of the greatest influences on Jewish thought.

Maipu, battle of　Battle on April 5, 1818, near Santiago, Chile. Here San Martín defeated Spanish royalist forces and gained independence for Chile.

Majapahit Empire (Madjapahit) (Modjopahit)　Hindu kingdom that flourished in Java from the 13th to the 15th century. The Majapahit period is regarded as a golden age in the history of Java. The kingdom was centered in eastern Java though its extent at the height of its power is uncertain.

Major, John (b. 1943)　Prime minister of Great Britain, elected in 1990. Supported the United Nations in the Persian Gulf War (*see* page 11-96). He has maintained close ties with the United States.

Malenkov, Georgi Maksimilianovich (1902–1989)　Soviet statesman and Communist leader. He became premier and party secretary briefly, in 1953, after the death of Stalin that year but was forced to resign as premier, following a policy struggle with Khrushchev.

Malthus, Thomas Robert (1766–1834) English economist. His *An Essay on the Principle of Population* contended that population would always increase faster than means of subsistence.

Mamelukes　Warrior class that provided rulers of Egypt from 1250 until the conquest by Ottoman Turks in 1517. Of Asian stock, Mamelukes were first used as slaves and then as warriors by the Muslim rulers of Egypt.

Manchukuo　Puppet state established in 1932 in Manchuria by the Japanese. Its nominal ruler was Henry Pu Yi, last Ch'ing emperor. It ceased to exist in 1945 when Manchuria was returned to China after World War II.

Manco Capac (d. 1544)　Inca ruler. Kept prisoner by Pizarro, he escaped in 1536, raised an army, and laid siege to Cuzco. Defeated, he continued to fight in the mountains, but was murdered by followers of another rebel leader.

Mandarin　Formerly, a Chinese imperial official. The dialect spoken by Chinese officials was known as Mandarin Chinese and in its modern form is the most widely used dialect in China.

Mandate　Designation for a colonial territory placed under the control of another power by the League of Nations. The system of mandates was used after World War I to provide for those former German and Turkish territories (including Iraq, Palestine, Syria, and Southwest Africa) that were deemed unable to govern themselves.

Mandela, Nelson (b. 1918)　Leader of the African National Congress (ANC). A symbol of the majority black quest for political equality and resistance to the white minority's policy of apartheid (*see* page 11-8). He was imprisoned from 1962 to 1990. He was released from a life sentence in 1990 to signal a moderation in the government's policy. As president of the ANC, he has been negotiating with President F. W. De Klerk (*see* page 11-31) to empower the black majority.

Manichaeism (Manichaeanism) Religious sect founded in Persia on the 3rd century A.D. teachings of Mani. It drew on Gnosticism, Zoroastrianism, and Christianity. Manichaeism was a dualistic religion that held the universe was divided into the forces of God and light and the forces of Satan and evil. Humans had both, the spirit being light and goodness, the body itself being evil. The sect spread rapidly for a time, though by the 6th century it had largely disappeared in the West.

Manitoba Canadian province. First settled in the 17th century by the Hudson's Bay Company it was contested by the British and French in the French and Indian Wars, and was ceded to Britain by the Treaty of Paris in 1763. It became a province in 1870.

Manorial system (Seignorial system) Medieval economic system in which a lord gave a peasant the right to tend land on his estate in return for a fixed payment. The system, derived from feudalism, flourished in Europe in the 11th to the 15th centuries, and similar systems arose elsewhere, notably in Japan.

Mansa Musa King of the empire of Mali (1312–1332). During his reign the Mali Empire, located in West Africa, reached the height of its power. In 1304, Mansa Musa left his capital at Timbuktu and made a pilgrimage across the Sahara to Mecca, displaying the great wealth of Mali along the way. He supported education, the arts and building, and made Timbuktu an important center of Muslim learning.

Mansur (Al Mansur) (d. 775) Second Abbasid caliph (754–775), successor to his brother Abu al-Abbas. He founded the city of Baghdad in 762.

Manuel I (Emanuel I) (1469–1521) Portuguese king (1495–1521). During his reign Portugal became a major commercial power through the voyages of discovery of da Gama and Cabral.

Manuel II (1889–1932) Portuguese king (1908–1910). He succeeded to the throne after his father and brother were assassinated and was deposed by the republican revolution.

Manzikert, battle of Byzantine-Turkish battle in 1071 at Manzikert, now in Turkey. Some 70,000 Seljuk Turks detroyed an army of 40,000 under Byzantine emperor Romanus IV. The battle led to the fall of Asia Minor to the Turks.

Mao Tse-tung (1893–1976) Chinese Communist leader, founder and first chairman of the People's Republic of China (1949–1959). Mao was a founding member of the Chinese Communist party. After the split between the Nationalist Kuomintang and the Communists, Mao led an abortive peasant revolt known as the Autumn Harvest Uprising in 1927. Continuing to oppose the Kuomintang, Mao helped to set up the Kiangsi Soviet in southeastern China and became its chairman in 1931. Nationalist military successes against the Communists

forced the Red Army to make its famed Long March of some 6,000 miles to Shensi province in northwestern China. There, Mao established Communist control in the region and began the long struggle against Nationalist Kuomintang (*see* **Chinese civil war**) and the invading Japanese (1937–1945) during World War II. The last phase of the civil war with the Nationalists broke out soon after World War II, and in 1949 the Communists established control over China. Mao, who had become chairman of the Chinese Communist party (CCP) in 1935, became chairman of the new People's Republic of China in 1949. In following years Mao sought to establish communism in China independently of the Russian model and sought to adapt Marxist ideology to Chinese society. In order to build the Chinese economy, Mao instituted the Great Leap Forward in 1958; a disastrous economic experiment that led to the rise of Liu Shao-ch'i as chairman of the republic. Mao retained his position as chairman of the CCP. The struggle between Liu and Mao led to the Cultural Revolution in 1966, and by 1970 Mao was once again undisputed leader of China, remaining so until his death. Mao's writings, especially those dealing with the revolutionary movement and guerrilla tactics, achieved a tremendous influence in China and in other countries, especially among radicals in the developing nations.

Mao Tse-tung, chairman of the Communist party in China, 1959.

Maquis French guerrilla forces that fought against German occupation forces during World War II.

Marat, Jean Paul (1743–1793) French revolutionary leader.

Maratha kingdom (Mahrattas) (Maharashtra) Kingdom in west-central India that rose to power in the period between the fall of the Mogul Empire and British conquest of India (in the 18th and 19th centuries).

Maratha wars   Series of three wars (1775–1818) in India between the British and the Maratha Confederacy, resulting in the fall of the Maratha Confederacy and British domination in India.

Marathon, battle of   Battle in 490 B.C. in which Athenian and Plataean forces under Miltiades defeated the Persian army of Darius I. This great battle of the Persian Wars ended the first Persian expedition against the Greek mainland.

Marcellus, Marcus Claudius (268–208 B.C.) Roman general. Five times consul of Rome, he was called "the sword of Rome." He conquered Syracuse (212 B.C.), and died while fighting against Hannibal.

March on Rome   Fascist insurrection in 1922 led by Mussolini, by which fascism came to power in Italy. Fascist forces threatened to seize power in Rome and elsewhere and began massing their followers for the insurrection, planned for October 28. After King Victor Emmanuel III refused to declare martial law, Prime Minister Luigi Facta resigned, crippling the Italian government. Mussolini then was asked on October 29 to form a government by the king to avert a civil war. Mussolini's new government gave him, on November 25, dictatorial powers until December 31, 1923.

Marconi, Guglielmo, Marchese (1874–1937) Italian physicist. He pioneered wireless telegraphy and was the first to transmit radio signals across the Atlantic in 1901.

Marcos, Ferdinand Edralin (1917–1990) Became president of the Philippines in 1966. Pursuing a policy of close ties with America and hostility to communism, he declared martial law in 1972 and maintained strict authoritarian control of his country. He was forced from power in 1987. He and his wife, Imelda, lived in exile in Hawaii until his death.

Marcus Aurelius (orig. Marcus Aurelius Antoninus) (121–180 A.D.) Roman emperor (161–180 A.D.) and famous exponent of Stoicism. Though he ordered persecutions of Christians, his rule was otherwise considered wise and humane.

Marduk   Ancient Babylonian god. God of all Babylonia, he was also the leading god of the city of Babylon.

Marengo, battle of   Battle on June 14, 1800 in which the French under Napoleon defeated the Austrians. The victory secured northern Italy for France during the French Revolutionary Wars.

Margaret (1353–1412) Queen of Denmark, Norway, and Sweden. She married Norwegian king Haakon VI, overthrew Swedish king Albert, and established in 1397 the Kalmar Union.

Margaret of Anjou (1430?–1482) Queen consort to English king Henry VI (m. 1445). She was a leader of the Lancastrians against the Yorkists during the Wars of the Roses.

Maria Theresa (1717–1780) Austrian archduchess and queen of Hungary and Bohemia (1740–1780), consort of Holy Roman Emperor Francis I. She succeeded her father Charles VI as ruler of Austrian Hapsburg domains by the law of pragmatic sanction. Her succession resulted in the War of Austrian Succession (1740–1748).

Marie Antoinette (1755–1793) French queen (1774–1793), wife of King Louis XVI, and an important figure in events leading to the French Revolution. She was the daughter of Austrian Holy Roman Emperor Francis I. Her unpopularity in France helped undermine the credibility of the monarchy. This was due in part to her Austrian heritage, extravagance, association with dissolute courtiers, and influence over her indecisive husband. She was taken prisoner during the storming of Tuileries in 1792 and guillotined in 1793.

Marie de Médicis (1573–1642) Queen consort (m. 1600) of French king Henry IV of France and regent (1610–1617) for their son, Louis XIII. She depleted the treasury and formed an alliance with Spain before being exiled by her son.

Marie Louise (1791–1847) Empress of France (1810–1815), second wife of Napoleon I, mother of Napoleon II, and daughter of Holy Roman Emperor Francis II.

Maritime Provinces   Name for the Canadian Atlantic provinces of New Brunswick, Nova Scotia, and Prince Edward Island.

Marne, battle of the   1. Allied victory in 1914 over German forces advancing on Paris during World War I. The battle marked the failure of the German Schlieffen Plan. 2. Allied victory in 1918 over German forces during World War I. The battle marked the turning point of World War I in favor of the Allies.

Marquette, Jacques (1637–1675) French missionary explorer. He and Louis Joliet (1645–1700) discovered and charted the course of the Mississippi River in 1673.

Marshall Plan (European Recovery Program) American program (1948–1952) that successfully aided the recovery of Western European nations after World War II.

Marx, Karl (1818–1883) German economist and philosopher, considered the founder and premier theorist of modern socialism and international communism.

Marxism   Collective term applied to the political, economic, and social theories advanced by Marx and Engels in such works as the *Communist Manifesto* and *Das Kapital*. Marx's theories greatly influenced the Socialist movement of the late 19th century and are considered the theoretical foundation for modern international communism. In his writings, Marx advanced the doctrine of dialectical materialism, the idea that the history and structure of civilization have been determined by economic systems operating during each stage of development. As each system developed, he asserted, new economic forces arose and inevitably led to the system's replacement. Thus, feudalism was replaced by capitalism, and capitalism was fated to be replaced by socialism and, ultimately, communism. A key element of Marxist doctrine is the view of all history as the history of class struggle, of the ruling elite pitted against the working class. According to Marx, this would eventually lead to crisis, in which the working class would rise up against the capitalist order, seize the means of production, and establish communal ownership through a "dictatorship of the proletariat." With the abolishment of the ruling class, all class struggle, hence all history, would come to an end. Finally, when a rational economic system was evolved, the structure of the political state would wither away. Marx's theories had a profound influence on the development of Socialist movements and were the basis for the Bolshevik political movement led by Lenin. The Bolsheviks' success in establishing the first Communist state in Russia in 1917 contradicted Marx's conviction that the first Communist uprising would take place in a modern industrialized nation. The massive political bureaucracy created under Lenin, and Stalin, also contradicted Marxist doctrine. Subsequent modifications of capitalism, such as the workers' vastly higher standard of living and the rise of a managerial class, have also brought some of Marx's principal tenets into question. However, Marxism as a body of political thought remains, in name if not in practice, the official political dogma of the world's Communist nations. In the late 1980s and early 1990s, Marxism lost its political influence in Eastern Europe and the former Soviet Union. *See* **Communism**; **East European Revolution**. *See also* Philosophy section, page 19-15.

Mary I (Mary Tudor) (1516–1558)   English queen (1553–1558), daughter of Henry VIII and Catherine of Aragon. Her marriage in 1554 to Spanish king Philip II caused great opposition. She briefly reestablished Roman Catholicism between 1555 and 1559 in England and persecuted Protestants.

Mary II (1662–1694)   English queen (1689–1694). After James II, her father, was forced into exile by the Glorious Revolution of 1688, Mary became joint sovereign with her husband William of Orange (William III).

Mary Queen of Scots (Stuart, Mary) (1542–1587) Scottish queen (1542–1567). Her life was marked by controversy and intrigue. She was named queen shortly after birth. Her early life was spent in France. She returned in 1561 to Scotland and married her unpopular cousin Lord Darnley in 1565, to strengthen claims to the English throne. After her husband's murder, generally attributed to the Earl of Bothwell, she married Bothwell in 1567. This led to a Scottish revolt, Mary's forced abdication in 1567, and her escape to England in 1568. As an heir to the throne and a threat to Queen Elizabeth, Mary was kept under guard in England. After several plots by Catholics to overthrow Elizabeth in favor of Mary, Mary was implicated in a scheme and was beheaded.

Masaryk, Jan (1886–1948)   Czech statesman and diplomat. He became foreign minister in 1940 in the government in exile in London during World War II, and remained in office after the Communist takeover in 1948.

Masaryk, Thomas Garrigue (1850–1937)   A founding father of Czechoslovakia and its first president (1918–1935). With Benes, he organized a de facto government of Czechoslovakia, which won the support of the Allies. When independent Czechoslovakia was formed after World War I, Masaryk was elected president (1918, 1920, 1927, 1934) and instituted a major land-reform program.

Massacre of Saint Bartholomew's Day   Massacre of French Protestants (Huguenots) that started in Paris on August 24, 1572 and marked the beginning of renewed fighting in the Wars of Religion. The massacre was a result of the continuing reli-gious and political rivalry between Protestants and Catholics (led by the Guise family). The Guise family and Catherine de Médicis, mother of King Charles IX, sought to check the rising influence of Coligny, a Protestant. When an attempt to assassinate Coligny failed, Catherine persuaded King Charles to order the death of Huguenot leaders then in Paris for the wedding of Henry of Navarre (later Henry IV). A general massacre of Protestants broke out in Paris and spread to the countryside. Thousands were killed by the time the persecution was halted in October.

Matriarchy   Social system in which family descent is traced through the mother's lineage. Such societies have been observed in Pacific islands, African tribes, and in some American Indian cultures.

Matsuoka, Yosuke (1880–1946)   Japanese statesman. As foreign minister (1940 and 1941) he helped establish the Axis alliance with Germany and Italy in 1940.

Maurya empire   Ancient Indian empire (4th–2nd centuries B.C.) of the Maurya dynasty rulers. The first great Indian empire, it united nearly the whole Indian subcontinent (and part of Afghanistan) and saw the development of a flourishing Indian culture. The empire was founded by Chandragupta I. The kingdom reached its greatest expansion under the rule of Asoka who established Buddhism as the state religion. Following his reign, the empire entered into decline and by 185 had broken up into petty kingdoms.

Maximilian (1832–1867)   Austrian archduke and emperor of Mexico (1864–1867). Unpopular with the Mexicans, he was opposed by Juárez. Supported for a time by French troops sent by Napoleon III, he refused to abdicate after their withdrawal in 1867, and was captured and shot.

Maximilian I (1459–1519)   Holy Roman emperor (1493–1519). He greatly expanded the hereditary Hapsburg domains, often at the expense of the interests of the Holy Roman Empire. He also ensured Hapsburg succession in Spain by the marriage of his son Philip to heiress Joanna (Charles V was their son).

Maya   Group of related Central American Indian tribes, living in the Yucatan peninsula, southern Mexico, Guatemala, and Belize. The origin of Maya is uncertain, but by the 1st millennium B.C. they had already begun to establish an advanced culture. The Mayan civilization was based on agriculture, and each community retained political independence under the rule of a local hierarchy of priests and political chieftains. Mayan cities centered around royal houses and religious temples built on pyramidal structures. The Maya devised an extremely accurate calendar, a vigesimal (base 20) number system, a complex pantheon of gods and religious ceremonies, and a system of hieroglyphic writing that has yet to be deciphered. Their culture is noted for its advances in the arts, architecture, astronomy, and mathematics.

May Fourth Movement   Mass movement in China in the early 20th century sparked by intellectuals who sought government reform and modernization of Chinese society. The movement, beginning as early as 1915, was precipitated by the government's inability to check Japanese expansionism. But among intellectuals it fostered a broad attack on traditional Chinese society and culture and helped to introduce Western ideologies.

Mazarin, Jules (Mazarini, Giulio) (1602–1661) French cardinal and statesman. He succeeded Cardinal Richelieu as minister of France in 1642 under King Louis XIII and remained powerful during the regency of Anne of Austria.

Mazzini, Giuseppe (1805–1872) Italian revolutionary and political writer. He campaigned for a united Italy under a republican government, founded the Young Italy Movement in 1831, and was a leader in the short-lived Roman Republic of 1849. He aided Garibaldi in his efforts to unify Italy and later refused to take part in the monarchical government established in 1861.

Mboya, Tom (Mboya, Thomas Joseph) (1930–1969) Kenyan political leader. A leader in the Kenyan independence movement.

McClure, Sir Robert John Le Mesurier (1807–1873) British naval officer. As commander of a ship in an Arctic expedition (1850–1854), he was the first to complete a northwest passage, culminating the long search for a sea route from the Atlantic to the Pacific Ocean by way of the Arctic.

McNaughton, Andrew George Latta (1887–1966) Canadian army officer. He was commander of Canadian forces in England during World War II.

Medici Italian family, rulers of Florence from the 15th to the 18th century, and world-famous patrons of the arts who transformed Florence into a treasure house of European art.

Meiji restoration Period of modernization and Westernization in Japan (1868–1912). During this period Japan developed its industry and became a world power. The period began with restoration of power to the emperor, Mutsuhito (reign name, Meiji), after the centuries-long rule by Tokugawa shoguns. The emperor abolished feudalism, made Tokyo the capital, modernized government administration, and acceded to a new constitution. The government thereafter consisted of an upper and lower (elected) house, a premier, and a group of elder statesmen (Genro). During this period, which ended in 1912 with Meiji's death, Japan engaged in the Sino-Japanese War (1894 and 1895) and the Russo-Japanese War (1904 and 1905).

Meir, Golda (Mabovitch, Goldie) (Myerson, Goldie) (1898–1978) Israeli political leader and prime minister (1969–1974). She was a founder of Israel, and as prime minister she made a concerted though unsuccessful effort to achieve peace in the Middle East. The Fourth Arab-Israeli War was fought during her administration.

Mencius (371?–288? B.C.) Chinese Confucian philosopher who had a major role in the development of Confucianism. He is called the second sage, after Confucius. His *Book of Mencius* states that humans are innately good, holds family duty to be the foundation of society, and stresses the need for rulers to be concerned for the common people.

Mendel, Gregor Johann (1822–1884) Austrian biologist. He formulated Mendel's Law on dominant and recessive genes, and discovered the male

cell's role in fertilization. His studies ignored in his lifetime, were later rediscovered and form the basis for modern genetics.

Mendès-France, Pierre (1907–1982) French statesman. A Radical Socialist, he was premier (1954 and 1955) when France declared an armistice with Indochina. He was forced from office because of his liberal policy toward Algeria.

Mendoza, Antonio de (1490?–1552) Spanish colonial administrator and first viceroy of New Spain (1535–1550). His 15-year administration was just and fair to the Indians and helped stabilize the Mexican territory.

Menelaus Mythical Greek king of Sparta. He was the husband of Helen, whose abduction was the cause of the Trojan War. He fought under his brother, Agamemnon.

Menelik II (1844–1913) Ethiopian emperor (1889–1913). Menelik consolidated power, built a new capital at Addis Ababa, and established a strong central government. His armed forces crushed an Italian invasion attempt (1895 and 1896), at the Battle of Aduwa, insuring Ethiopian independence. Menelik expanded Ethiopia's territory, and worked to modernize his empire.

Menes (ca. 3100 B.C.) Egyptian king. He united Upper and Lower Egypt and founded the 1st dynasty. He also is said to have founded the ancient capital of Memphis.

Mensheviks Russian revolutionary party. The Mensheviks, opposed to Lenin's Bolsheviks, sought to form a party of the masses (rather than a revolutionary elite), believed there was a necessary transition period before creating the Socialist state, and were willing to work with bourgeois elements during this time to achieve their goal. The Mensheviks were formed by a split caused by Lenin in 1903 in the Russian Social Democratic Workers' party. The Social Democratic party was permanently split into two factions in 1912 and thereafter the Mensheviks were often divided by internal dissent. They dominated the provisional government of Russia after the February Revolution of 1917 but were ousted from power by the Bolsheviks in the October Revolution and were officially suppressed by the Bolsheviks after 1922.

Mercantilism Economic policy and theory that dominated European financial and governmental thinking from the 16th to the 18th century. It argued that governmental regulation of a nation's industry and trade was necessary, that exports were preferable to imports or to equal trade, that large populations and armies were beneficial to a nation, and that a country's true wealth was determined by its possession of gold and silver.

Mercia, kingdom of Ancient Anglo-Saxon kingdom comprising much of central England. Settled in the 6th century by Angles, it was overcome and divided in 1886 by invading Danes in the East and Alfred of Wessex in the West.

Merovingians Frankish dynasty and empire (5th–8th centuries) in Western Europe. The rise of the Merovingians from their kingdom on the Rhine began with the rule of Clovis I (481–511). He united the Salian and Ripuarian Franks, accepted Christianity in 496, and, by his conquests, created a vast empire that included most of Gaul. His empire was divided by his four sons at his death. Merovingian territories were briefly united again under the rule of Clotaire II and Dagobert I (613–639, inclusive). Already weakened by the many bitter internal wars, the Merovingian rulers after Dagobert lost all real power to the noblemen. Called the "do-nothing" kings, these kings ruled in name only and the mayors of the palace (supposedly in the king's service) held actual power. Charles Martel greatly expanded his power as mayor of the palace, and his son, Pepin the Short, finally overthrew the last Merovingian king, Childeric III, in 751. He thus founded the Carolingian Empire.

Mesopotamia   Historic region located in what is now Iraq. An important center of early civilization, the area is the fertile plain surrounding the Tigris and Euphrates rivers. The earliest towns in the region were located in the North (5th millennium B.C.), though the first important cultures eventually rose in the South, notably Sumer. There followed the dynasty of Ur, the Akkadian Empire, the first and second Babylonian Empires, and the Assyrian Empire. Thereafter the region succumbed to other powers, beginning with the Persians, Macedonians, and Romans.

Methodism   Protestant Christian religious movement in Britain and America, based largely on the teachings of Wesley. The movement began in 1729 in Oxford, England, when Wesley, his brother Charles, Whitefield, and others began to hold meetings for religious study. Adopting elements advanced by the Moravian church, the group began a program of evangelism, and by their actions were barred from participation within the Church of England.

Metternich, Prince Klemens Wenzel Nepomuk Lothar von (1773–1859) Austrian statesman, was the leading European statesman (1815–1848), whose conservative policies helped maintain political stability in post-Napoleonic Europe. As Austrian foreign minister between 1809 and 1848, he helped form the Quadruple Alliance, which finally defeated Napoleon in 1813. Thereafter he sought to maintain the balance of power in Europe and to preserve the stability of the monarchies against liberal movements. He made Austria the dominant power in the German Confederation, helped create the Holy Alliance, took part in formulating the Carlsbad Decrees, and was a leading figure at the congresses of Vienna (1814 and 1815). Metternich was forced out of power by the liberal revolutions of 1848, brought on in part by the repressive measures he advocated to maintain order.

Mexican Revolution   Period of political and social turmoil in Mexico following the overthrow of Díaz by Madero in 1911. Madero subsequently headed a popular movement that sought to implement reforms in Mexico. But his rule was ineffective and he was in turn overthrown by General Huerta. Huerta's reactionary rule led to revolts headed by Carranza, Villa, and Zapata, and he was forced from office in 1914. Carranza became president, though his rule was challenged by Villa and Zapata, who continued armed resistance. Under Car-

ranza, Mexico established the Constitution of 1917. Reform came slowly, however, and Mexico remained politically volatile for many years.

Michael (1596–1645) Russian czar (1613–1645), founder of the Romanov dynasty. His election ended the Time of Troubles. During his reign Russia made peace with Sweden and Poland.

Michael (b. 1921) Romanian king (1927–1930, 1940–1947). He overthrew the dictatorship of I. Antonescu in 1944 and supported the Allies in World War II. He was forced into exile by the Communist takeover in 1947.

Michelangelo (Buonarroti) (1475–1564) Italian artist, one of the towering figures of the Italian Renaissance. A gifted poet, painter, and sculptor, he is celebrated for such masterpieces as his statues of David and Moses, and the *Pietà* (1497). His painting of the Sistine Chapel took four years to complete (1508–1512). *See also* Art section, page 1-23.

Middle Ages   Period in European history from the 5th to the 15th century between the fall of the Roman Empire and the discovery of the New World by Columbus in 1492. It was the transition period from the ancient cultures to those of the modern world, and its beginning phase is sometimes referred to as the Dark Ages. The Middle Ages were marked by the rise of the church, by the spread and collapse of feudalism, and by the formative stages of many of the modern European states.

Middle East   Term denoting the countries of southwestern Asia and northeastern Africa, including parts of Turkey, Syria, Israel, Jordan, Iraq, Iran, Lebanon, all of the Arabian peninsula, Egypt, and Libya.

Middle Kingdom   Period in ancient Egyptian history, lasting from the latter half of the 11th dynasty to the 12th dynasty (2000–1786 B.C.). It followed the First Intermediate Period, which began with the rule of Amenemhet I and ended with the rule of Amenemhet IV. Egypt enjoyed commercial prosperity during this period, which also saw the rule of the pharaohs as feudal lords, the transfer of the capital from Thebes to Ithowe, the conquest of lower Nubia, and a golden age of Egyptian literature and arts. The Middle Kingdom was followed by the Second Intermediate Period and the coming of the Hykos.

Mill, John Stuart (1806–1873) British philosopher and political economist. He further developed the utilitarian doctrines established by Bentham and the elder Mill, and formulated principles of inductive reasoning. His works include *A System Of Logic* and *On Liberty*.

Milvian Bridge   Roman bridge, over the Tiber where Constantine defeated Maxentius in 312 A.D., and thus became sole ruler in the western Roman Empire. Here, too, he saw the vision of a cross in the sky that led him to adopt Christianity. Constantine soon after brought about toleration of Christianity in the empire.

Minamoto Yoritomo (1147–1199) Japanese shogun (1192–1199), founder of the Kamakura shogunate. He participated in the rebellion against the Taira clan and later set up the feudal system and the shogunate, by which Japan was ruled until the 19th century.

Ming Dynasty of native Chinese emperors (1368–1644) who greatly expanded the Chinese Empire. Under its rulers the empire came to include all or parts of Vietnam, Burma, Turkistan, Korea, and Mongolia. Hung-Wu, founder of the dynasty, came to power in 1368 and ousted the Mongols of the Yuan dynasty in 1371. During the long reign of the Ming emperors the Chinese civil service was reinstituted, Confucianism was state-supported, exploratory voyages as far West as Arabia were made in the years between 1405 and 1433, European settlements were established in the 1500s at Canton and Macao, Christian missionaries arrived, and the arts, especially ceramics and architecture, flourished. A succession of weak rulers, heavy taxes, and dissent among factions in government led to peasant revolts and the fall of the dynasty in 1648 to the Ch'ings (Manchus).

Minoan civilization Bronze Age culture that developed on Crete (3000–1000 B.C.). One of the ancient Greek Aegean civilizations, it was for a time a major maritime power in the Mediterranean. By 1500 B.C. the Minoans had a well-developed written language and had become skilled in working ceramics and bronze. The Minoan capital at Cnossus with its luxurious palace, was twice destroyed (and rebuilt) in the second millennium B.C., possibly by earthquakes and/or invasions by the Mycenaeans. The palace was destroyed a last time in 1400 and, soon after, the Minoan civilization disappeared. This civilization is generally divided into three periods: Early Minoan (3000–2200 B.C.), Middle Minoan (2200–1500 B.C.), and Late Minoan (1500–1000 B.C.). The Mycenaean civilization predominated after the fall of the Minoans.

Minseito Japanese political party formed in 1927. A centrist party, it had ties with Japanese business interests and sought better relations with the West. The Minseito was a major party in the years before World War II. The party was dissolved in 1940 after the militarists came to power. A new Democratic party, formed after World War II, absorbed much of the Minseito party's membership.

Miranda, Francisco de (1750–1816) Venezuelan revolutionary. He fought the Spanish, briefly gained Venezuelan independence in 1810, and ruled with dictatorial powers. He was forced to surrender to the counterattacking Spanish in 1812 and died in prison.

Mithraism Major religion of the ancient world, widespread within the Roman Empire shortly before adoption of Christianity in the 3rd century A.D. Roman Mithraism, which in some ways resembled Christianity, was concerned with the battle between good and evil, and held out the promise of immortality to its followers. Worship of the god Mithras flourished in Persia in the 5th century B.C. and subsequently spread throughout the Mediterranean world. In Greece it became one of the Mystery religions and in Rome it flourished by the 2nd century A.D. With the official adoption of Christianity, Mithraism was suppressed in the Roman Empire and soon disappeared.

Mittérand, François (b. 1916) Became French president in 1981. A Socialist, Mittérand won a clear victory over former President Giscard d'Estaing and, in subsequent elections for the National Assembly, his party's candidates won by wide margins. In office, Mitterand increased the taxes of business and the wealthy and raised the minimum wage by 10 percent.

Model Parliament Two representative bodies that figured in the development of the British Parliament 1. Assembly convened in 1265 during the Barons' War (1263–1267) by Simon de Montfort. Present were two citizens (burgesses) from each city and two knights from each shire in England. 2. Assembly convened in 1295 by King Edward I. Representatives of the higher clergy, knights, burgesses, and lower clergy attended.

Mogul (Mughal) Muslim dynasty that ruled in India from the 16th–19th centuries. The Mogul Empire was at its height from the 16th to the early 18th centuries and was noted for its efficient administrative organization and for its great contributions in the fields of art, architecture, and literature. The Mogul Empire was founded by Baber, who established Mogul power in India. Other notable Mogul rulers were Akbar (ruled 1556–1605), who greatly expanded Mogul power; his son Jahangir (ruled 1605–1627), Shah Jahan (ruled 1628–1658), who expanded Mogul power into Deccan and who built the Taj Mahal at Agra; and Aurangzeb (ruled 1658–1707), under whose rule the Mogul Empire reached its height and began its decline. Aurangzeb was unable to halt the rising strength of the Marathas, and after his death in 1707 the empire began to divide into a group of provinces. In the 18th century British influence in the region also began to increase, and the empire was further weakened. Its last ruler, Bahadur Shah II (ruled 1837–1857) was emperor in title only. After the failure of the Indian Mutiny (Sepoy Mutiny) of 1857, he was deposed by the British and the empire ceased to exist.

Molotov, Vyacheslav Mikhailovich (orig. Skriabin) (1890–1986) Russian statesman. As foreign minister, he was chief Russian spokesman for international affairs during and after World War II. A hard-line Stalinist, he tried unsuccessfully to depose Khrushchev in 1957 and was expelled from the Communist party in 1964.

Moltke, Helmuth von (1800–1891) Prussian field marshal. As chief of the general staff (1858–1888), he was responsible for Prussian successes in the war against Denmark in 1864, the Austro-Prussian War in 1866, and the Franco-Prussian War (1870 and 1871).

Monasticism Religious movement in which individuals seek spiritual perfection by living apart from the general society. Monks generally live communally in their monasteries (though in some monastic movements they live as hermits). Their lives are strictly regulated by the monastic rule and worship is the central focus of their existence. Monasticism has been part of various religions, including Christianity (Western and Eastern), Hinduism, Buddhism, Islam, and Jainism. In the Western Christian church, monasticism generally arose in the 6th century and acquired its characteristic form from the teachings of St. Benedict. Thereafter, monasticism spread throughout Europe and spawned many important orders.

Mongol Empire   Great Asian Empire founded in the 1200s by the Mongol conqueror Genghis Khan. After uniting the Mongol tribes under him in 1206, Genghis Khan invaded northern China and subdued Korea. He next led his fierce bands westward, conquered Khorezm, the region of modern Iran and Iraq, part of Russia, and raided northern India. On his death in 1227 Genghis' son Ogadai became the imperial ruler (great khan), and each of his other sons ruled a part of the empire (khanate). In the West, Mongols under Batu Khan conquered Russia and there established in 1241 the Khanate of the Golden Horde, or Kipchak Empire, that ruled Russia until the 15th century. In Persia, the Mongol conqueror Hulagu Khan established the Il-Khan dynasty, which ruled there (1258–1353). Kublai Khan became great khan in 1260 and moved the Mongol capital to China, where he built a splendid city. He founded the Yüan dynasty, which ruled China until the rise of the Ming dynasty in 1368. Under Tamerlane (reigned 1360–1405), the Mongols of the Timurid Empire, in central Asia, rose to importance for a time. Finally, the Mongol conqueror Baber established the Mogul dynasty in India (1526–1707). From the 15th century, however, the history of the empire was one of decline and power struggles between tribal factions. Finally, Mongolia itself was conquered by the Manchus (17th and 18th centuries).

Monotheism   Religious doctrine. Monotheism holds that there is only one God, as opposed to polytheism, which recognizes many gods.

Montcalm, Louis Joseph de (1712–1759) French general. He was commander of the French forces in Canada during the French and Indian War. He successfully defended French territories against the British until his defeat and death at the Battle of the Plains of Abraham.

Montezuma (Moctezuma) (1480?–1520) Aztec emperor (1502–1520). A despotic and unpopular ruler, he was taken hostage by the Spanish ruler Cortés. He was killed during the Aztec uprising against the Spanish.

Montfort, Simon de (1160–1218) Norman crusader. He led the Albigensian Crusade in southern France and was killed at the siege of Toulouse.

Montfort, Simon de, earl of Leicester (1208–1265) English statesman and soldier. Formerly an adviser to Henry III and leader of his forces during revolts in Gascony, Montfort broke with the king and became leader of the barons during the Barons' War. Following his victory at Lewes in 1264, he became virtual ruler of England and summoned the Model Parliament. He was finally defeated and captured at the Battle of Evesham.

Montgomery, Bernard Law, 1st viscount Montgomery of Alamein (1887–1976) Noted British field marshal during World War II. He defeated Rommel's forces at el-Alamein in Africa in 1942 and forced their surrender in 1943. He took part in the invasion of Sicily in 1943 and Italy, and played a major role in the Normandy invasion of 1944 and the subsequent Allied drive to Germany.

Moors   Originally, a mixed Arab and Berber people living in the Roman province of Mauretania. They became zealous converts to Islam in the 8th century and, led by Tarik (ibn Ziyad), invaded the Iberian peninsula in 711. There they conquered the Visigoths and ranged into France, where their advance was checked in 732 by Charles Martel at Poitiers. All of Spain, save the northern Christian part, was subsequently constituted as a Muslim caliphate under Abd ar-Rahman I. With its capital at Córdoba, the caliphate prospered and many centers of commerce and Muslim culture were established. The Moors were slowly driven from the Iberian peninsula in the Christian reconquest (in the 11th–15th centuries), and many Moors resettled in North Africa. Those that remained in Spain were persecuted under the Inquisition and were finally expelled in 1609.

More, Sir Thomas (1478–1535) English author, statesman, and Roman Catholic saint. More wrote his famous *Utopia* and served as lord chancellor to Henry VIII (1529–1532). His refusal to endorse Henry's Act of Supremacy, creating the Church of England, led to his resignation and eventual execution. *See also* Philosophy section, page 19–15.

Moscow Declaration   Agreement of October 30, 1943 by the Soviet Union, Britain, the United States and China on the need to establish an international peace-keeping organization. It was one of the preliminary agreements that led to formation of the United Nations.

Moses (14th and 13th centuries B.C.) Great Hebrew prophet and religious leader. Knowledge of his life is based on biblical accounts, according to which he was raised in the Egyptian court. He fled Egypt after becoming a shepherd, received his call from Yahweh (God) to rescue the Hebrews. He returned to Egypt and demanded that the pharaoh (possibly Ramses II) release his people. Moses finally led his people out of Egypt (*see* **Exodus**) and across the desert to Mt. Sinai where he received the Ten Commandments. He then led the Hebrews on the 40-year journey to the Holy Land (Canaan), during which there was much hardship and dissent. When the Hebrews reached the edge of the Holy Land at the Jordan River, Moses climbed Mt. Pisgah to view it and then disappeared. Moses is traditionally regarded as the author of the first five books of the Old Testament (Genesis, Exodus, Leviticus, Numbers, and Deuteronomy), known collectively as the Pentateuch.

Mosley, Sir Oswald Ernald (b. 1896) British politician. He founded the British Union of Fascists in 1932. He conducted an anti-Jewish campaign and supported the Nazis, which resulted in his confinement (1940–1943).

Most-favored-nation clause   Provision in treaties for international trade. It stipulates that the two participating nations will grant each other all commercial concessions (such as favorable import duties) that have been extended to other nations.

Mountain, the (Montagnards) French extremist faction in the National Convention during the French Revolution. They opposed (and eventually defeated) the more moderate Girondists, eventually took control of the Jacobins, and became the controlling force behind the Reign of Terror. Principal figures in the group were Robespierre and Danton.

Mountbatten, Louis, 1st earl Mountbatten of Burma (1900–1979) British admiral and statesman. As supreme Allied commander in southeast Asia (1943–1946), Mountbatten defeated the Japanese in Burma. He was last viceroy of India in 1947 and chairman of the chiefs of defense staff (1959–1965).

Muawiya (d. 680)　He once served as Muhammad's secretary and later became governor of Syria. In the first Muslim Civil War he contested the succession of Ali to the caliphate and, after Ali's death in 661, deposed his successor, Hassan. Muawiya thus founded the Umayyad dynasty.

Mubarak, Hosni (b. 1929)　Became Egyptian president in 1981, successor to Anwar Sadat upon his assassination. By his visit in 1982 to Saudi Arabia, Mubarak established the first high-level contact with that country since the split between Egypt and its Arab neighbors over the Camp David accords.

Muhammad (570?–632)　Arabian prophet and religious leader, founder of Islam. *See* **Islam**.

Muhammad II (1430–1481)　Ottoman sultan (1451–1481), called the Conqueror. He captured Constantinople bringing the Byzantine Empire to an end. He made Constantinople his capital, and took Greece, most of Serbia, and the Aegean Islands.

Muhammad Ali (Mehemet Ali) (Muhammad Ali Pasha) (1769–1849)　Egyptian viceroy (1805–1848), considered the founder of the modern Egyptian state.

Mukden incident　Incident on September 18, 1931 used by Japan as a pretext for its invasion of Manchuria. Following an attempt to sabotage the Japanese-controlled South Manchurian Railway, Japanese troops occupied nearby Mukden. With the arrival of more troops from Korea, the Japanese army began to actively take over the territory. Chiang Kai-shek's Nationalist armies, then occupied in civil war with the Communists, were unable to oppose the Japanese, and by February conquest of Manchuria was complete. Thereupon, the Japanese created the puppet state of Manchukuo.

Müller, Hermann (1876–1931)　German statesman and political leader in the Weimar Republic. He was chancellor (1920, 1928–1930) and, during his second term, negotiated the Young Plan and brought an end to French occupation of the Rhineland in 1929.

Mulroney, Brian (b. 1939)　Prime minister of Canada since 1984, leader of Conservative party. He has maintained Canadian unity by giving concessions to Quebec. Cosigner with the United States and Mexico of the North American Free Trade Agreement (NAFTA).

Munich Pact (Agreement)　Pact on September 30, 1939 between Germany and other European powers providing for the German annexation of the western Czechoslovakian territory of Sudetenland. The pact was rendered meaningless when Hitler invaded Czechoslovakia in March 1939.

Munich Putsch (Beer Hall Putsch)　Hitler's unsuccessful attempt in 1923 to seize power in Bavaria and, ultimately, to take control of the Weimar Republic. As leader of the National Socialist (Nazi) party, Hitler joined with the extremist General Ludendorff in a badly organized attempt to incite a right-wing revolution in Munich. Hitler had hoped

to capitalize on Germany's severe economic crisis, but his plan soon failed.

Murad I (1326?–1389)　Ottoman sultan (1360–1389) By his conquests, he made the Byzantine Empire a vassal state, consolidated Ottoman control over Anatolia, extended Ottoman domains into the Balkans, and established the Ottoman capital at Edirne (formerly Adrianople) in 1362. He laid the foundations of the administrative system of the later Ottoman Empire and formed the military corps known as the Janissaries.

Murat, Joachim (1767–1815)　French marshal and king of Naples (1808–1815). Murat was one of Napoleon's most able cavalry commanders and distinguished himself in Napoleon's Italian, Egyptian, Peninsular, and Russian campaigns. He helped Napoleon seize power and again joined him in the Hundred Days' campaign.

Muslim League (orig. All-India Muslim League)　Political organization founded in 1906 in India. Formed by Aga Khan III for the protection of Muslims' rights, the group broke away from the predominantly Hindu Indian National Congress and demanded a separate Muslim state in 1940. Led by (Muhammad Ali) Jinnah, it won the creation of Pakistan in 1947 and became the dominant political party in the new state. The league had split into factions by the 1960s and declined after the 1970 elections.

Mussolini, the dictator of Italy, surrounded by Italian officers in the 1930s.

Mussolini, Benito (1883–1945)　Italian Fascist dictator. The preeminent leader of Italian fascism, he organized the first Fascist party in 1921 and orchestrated the Fascist militia's march on Rome in 1922 and by it became head of the Italian government. Thereafter his rule was marked by the institution of his dictatorship. Ousted from power in 1943, he headed a German-backed opposition government until his execution in 1945.

Mycenaean civilization   Ancient Aegean civilization that flourished on the Greek mainland (1600–1200 B.C.). The Mycenaeans entered Greece from the north in the 2000 B.C. They were in regular contact with Minoans on Crete, and they incorporated many elements of Minoan civilization into their own culture. The period of their cultural and commercial domination of the region lasted from 1400–1100 B.C., when the Dorian Greeks displaced the Mycenaeans. The epics of Homer are now regarded as giving a vivid picture of Mycenaean civilization at its height.

N **Naboplassar** (7th century B.C.)   Babylonian king (625–605 B.C.). He ended Assyrian control of Babylonia and thus founded in 625 the Chaldean Empire. He warred against Necho II of Egypt.

Nagano, Osami (1880–1947)   Japanese admiral. Nagano ordered and organized the 1941 Japanese attack on Pearl Harbor which brought America into World War II.

Nagarjuna (150–250 A.D.)   Indian Buddhist philosopher. Nagarjuna founded the Madhyamika (Middle Path) school of Buddhism, and was especially noted for his concept of "emptiness."

Naguib, Muhammad (b. 1901)   Egyptian general and political leader. He took part in the Egyptian revolution of 1952 that deposed King Farouk I and became premier of the new military regime. In 1954 he was removed from power and replaced by Nasser.

Nagy, Imre (1896–1958)   Hungarian Communist premier. Nagy was premier (1953–1955) but was forced out by Soviet pressure.

Naples, kingdom of   Former kingdom in Italy. The kingdom of Naples, often united with Sicily, dominated southern Italy from the Middle Ages until 1860. Roger II unified the region and declared himself king of Sicily and Apulia in 1130. Because the area was of strategic naval and commercial importance, it became the focus of frequent power struggles. At various times the region was ruled by Normans, Hohenstaufens, Angevins, Spanish, and the Bourbons. The area was united with the rest of Italy by Garibaldi in 1860.

Napoleon I (Napoleon Bonaparte) (1769–1821) Emperor of the French (1804–1814). One of the great conquerors of all time and a gifted administrator as well, Napoleon created a short-lived French empire that included virtually all of continental Europe. By his conquests, he helped to spread liberal reforms instituted in France and thereby affected the subsequent development of modern Europe. Napoleon served with the republican army during the French Revolutionary Wars and was given command of the republican army in Italy in 1796. He quickly reorganized the units under his command into an effective fighting force, and his Italian campaign (1796–1797) was overwhelmingly successful. Napoleon's campaign in Egypt (1798–1799) proved disastrous. At the same time, France's armies on the Continent suffered serious reverses, and the revolutionary government was on the verge of collapse.

Napoleon returned to France and, with the aid of his brother, Lucien Bonaparte, and Joseph Sieyes, overthrew the Directory in 1799. Napoleon was given dictatorial powers as head of the consulate. He consolidated his position and from 1800–1802 brought the French Revolutionary Wars to a successful conclusion. In the following years he instituted reforms in education, law—notably the Napoleonic Code— and government. He was crowned emperor in 1804. With the empire thus established, Napoleon set about creating a nobility and a court. He ultimately named rulers to various states (notably Spain, Holland, Naples, and Sweden). But when he made himself king of Italy (1805), the British (already at war with him) and other powers organized against him and the Napoleonic Wars broke out. Napoleon enjoyed his greatest military successes during these wars and by about 1808 he had extended French control throughout the Continent. But his invasion of Russia proved disastrous. The defeat cost Napoleon his empire. One by one former allies joined the coalition of powers against him and by 1814, the Napoleonic Wars had come to a close. Napoleon abdicated in 1814, and was exiled to the island of Elba. Napoleon's final defeat did not come until 1815, however. In that year he returned to France and began his famous Hundred Days in which he attempted to reestablish his empire. Utterly defeated at Waterloo, Napoleon again abdicated in 1815 and lived out the rest of his life in exile on the island of St. Helena.

Napoleon Bonaparte, First Consul of France in 1803, at age 34.

Napoleon II (1811–1832) Titular king of Rome. He was the son of Napoleon and Marie Louise. After his father's 1815 abdication, he was brought to his mother's land, Austria, where he remained a virtual prisoner until he died of tuberculosis. He was used as a pawn by Metternich in bargaining with France.

Napoleon III (1808–1873) Emperor of the French, nephew of Napoleon I and son of Louis Bonaparte. After two unsuccessful attempts to seize power, he was elected French president in 1848. He proclaimed himself emperor in 1852 and inaugurated the Second Empire. His foreign and domestic policies were popular until 1860, when he was forced to liberalize his government. He was captured during the Franco-Prussian War (1870 and 1871), deposed, and died in exile.

Napoleonic Wars Wars fought between 1803–1815 by Napoleon I of France against various European powers. The Napoleonic Wars followed an earlier series of wars, the French Revolutionary Wars. The French Revolutionary Wars had helped bring Napoleon to power and made France the most powerful nation on the European continent. But Napoleon was unable to match the British navy, and the British remained a continuing threat to his dominance of Europe. Mutual distrust finally resulted in declaration of war between France and Britain in 1803 and, in the years following, various coalitions of European states tried unsuccessfully to defeat Napoleon. Napoleon soon extended his French empire across nearly all of continental Europe. But his ill-fated invasion of Russia in 1812 proved to be his undoing. Defeated in 1814, Napoleon was forced into exile. He returned to power briefly during his famous Hundred Days only to meet his final defeat at Waterloo.

Nasser, Gamal Abdel (1918–1970) Egyptian statesman. Nasser assisted the 1952 coup d'état that ended the monarchy. He also ousted General Naguib in 1954, naming himself prime minister. He was elected and served as president of Egypt (1956–1958) and of the United Arab Republic (1958–1970). Strongly Muslim and nationalistic, he seized control of the Suez Canal in 1956 provoking the Suez crisis, established an alliance with the U.S.S.R., and fought the June 1967 war against Israel. During his tenure he was the foremost symbol of Arab nationalism and resistance to Western domination.

National Assembly The legislative assembly into which the States-General constituted themselves in June 1789, during the French Revolution. The aim was to prepare a constitution (hence it is also called the Constituent Assembly). The National Assembly ultimately brought about creation of a constitutional monarchy in 1791 and was superceded by the Legislative Assembly.

National Convention French legislative body (1792–1795). Successor to the Legislative Assembly during the French Revolution. Convened after the suspension of King Louis XVI, the National Convention established the republic and condemned Louis to death. It came under the control of the Jacobins, and then of Robespierre, who promoted the Reign of Terror. The Thermidorian

reaction in the Convention brought this bloody period to an end. The National Convention was replaced by the Directory.

Nationalism Political or social movement in which the individual's primary loyalty is given to the state. Arising with the formation of modern nation states, nationalism became a major influence in the history of Europe in the 17th and 18th centuries. Later it became a driving force in movements by national groups against imperial rule. Extreme nationalism also contributed to the rise of fascism in Italy and National Socialism (Nazism) in Germany.

National Socialism (Nazism) Political movement in Germany, the German counterpart of Fascist movements that arose in Europe and elsewhere after World War I. National Socialism shared with other Fascist movements the characteristics of extreme nationalism, militarism, determination to create a totalitarian state, formation of an elitist class, unswerving obedience to a single leader, and nationalistic expansionism. Hitler, leader of the German Fascists, outlined many of the doctrines of National Socialism in his book, *Mein Kampf*. Racism was a particularly strong element in the German movement and centered on a fanatical belief in the existence of a "master race," composed of Germanic peoples. *See* **Hitler, Adolf**; **Nazi party**.

Natural rights Philosophical concept. Natural rights are inherent rights that cannot be taken away by a government. They are expressed in the Declaration of the Rights of Man and the Declaration of Independence, and in the writings of such thinkers as J. Locke and T. Paine.

Navigation Acts English legislation (14th–19th centuries) designed to limit carrying trade to ships of England and English colonies. The first Navigation Act was passed in 1381 but could not be implemented because of a lack of ships. The era of an effective act dates from 1651, when a law aimed primarily at Dutch shipping began the practice of "enumerating" goods that could be shipped to England or its colonies only in Dutch ships. It contributed to the outbreak of the first Dutch War (1652–1654). Enforcement of the acts, especially the 1664 act, by which English colonies could receive European goods shipped only via England, also contributed to unrest in the American colonies. These laws were especially effective during the 17th and 18th centuries, and English-carrying trade tonnage increased during this period. The acts were all eventually repealed (1849 and 1854).

Nazi party (National Socialist German Workers' party) German political party, the instrument of Hitler's rise to power, and the organ through which he exercised totalitarian control of the German state (1933–1945). Founded in 1919 as the German Workers' party, it was renamed and reorganized by Hitler along paramilitary lines (by creating the SS, or Nazi storm troops). He took complete control of it in 1921, and, with the aid of Goering, Hess, and (later) Goebbels, began to establish the Nazi themes.

Neanderthal A widespread group of Paleolithic (Old Stone Age) people who lived from about 100,000–40,000 years ago. Named for the valley in Germany where their remains were first found, the remains of Neanderthal people have also been found in Europe, Asia, and Africa. They were short, powerfully built, with heavy jaws, thick eyebrow ridges, and large noses. They lived in caves, wore clothes of animal skins, knew the use of fire, and buried their dead with tools and food (thereby exhibiting religious beliefs). Neanderthal people disappeared and were eventually replaced by Cro-Magnon people. *See also* History of Technology section.

Near East   Term sometimes applied to the areas around the eastern Mediterranean, the southwestern parts of Asia, and northeast Africa. Today it is more often designated as the Middle East.

Nebuchadnezzar (630–562 B.C.) King of Babylon (605–562 B.C.). In 586 B.C., he destroyed Jerusalem while putting down a revolt there and exiled most of its inhabitants to Babylon (Babylonian captivity). He rebuilt most of the temples in his land and made Babylon, with its Hanging Gardens, one of the most beautiful cities in the ancient world.

Necker, Jacques (1732–1804)   Swiss-born French statesman and financier. As director of finances and the treasury in prerevolutionary France he tried but failed to restore fiscal soundness to the old regime. He was one of those who recommended calling the States-General, and his dismissal by Louis XVI was one of the causes of the seizure of the Bastille on July 14, 1789.

Nefertiti (1372–1350 B.C.)   Egyptian queen. She was the wife of Akhenaton and influenced his religious reforms.

Nehru, Jawaharlal (1889–1964)   Indian statesman, a leader in the movement for India's independence, and India's first prime minister (1947–1964). He joined the nationalist movement for Indian independence from Britain led by M. Gandhi in 1919. With Gandhi's help, he became president in 1929 of the Indian National Congress, and was reelected three times. When Indian independence was granted in 1947, he became prime minister and minister of foreign affairs. He adopted a policy of nonalignment in international matters and promoted a domestic program of industrialization and socialization. He sought reorganization of the separate Indian states along linguistic lines. His administration was marked by conflict with Pakistan over Kashmir and by a Chinese invasion of India in 1962.

Nelson, Horatio (Viscount Nelson) (1758–1805) English admiral and national hero. His ships destroyed the French fleet in 1798 at the Battle of the Nile, stranding Napoleon's army in Egypt. At Trafalgar, in 1805, his fleet annihilated a numerically superior French-Spanish fleet ending Napoleon's hopes of subduing Britain. Nelson was killed at Trafalgar.

Neolithic period (New Stone Age)   Period of prehistory from about 8000–3000 B.C. in which humans perfected stone-working techniques, improving tools and weapons by grinding and polishing stone. This period is characterized by the domestication of plants and animals, the rise of settled villages, and the emergence of pottery and weaving as elaborate crafts. The principal achievement was the cultivation of crops and domestication of animals which resulted in a more settled, less nomadic existence and the establishment of permanent villages. A reliable

food supply led to population increase, specialization of labor, and in time created changes that led to the rise of civilization. *See also* History of Technology section.

Neoplatonism   Philosophical school developed especially by Plotinus in Alexandria and Rome in the 3rd century A.D. Based on Plato's teaching and containing elements of Oriental philosophy and mysticism, it was the last of the great pagan schools of thought. It taught belief in the One, a comprehensive deity, who gave the Logos (divine word) to individuals through emanation. Its influence declined after Justinian closed the Academy at Athens in 529 A.D., but it influenced both medieval and modern philosophy.

Neo-Pythagoreanism   Philosophical movement that developed in the 1st century A.D. It incorporated elements of the philosophy advanced in the 6th century B.C. by Pythagoras, greatly emphasizing the mystical elements while borrowing from Jewish and Hellenistic philosophy.

Nero (Claudius Caesar) (37–68 A.D.)   Roman emperor (54–68 A.D.). His reign went well until cruelty, vanity, and instability surfaced and he murdered his mother in 59 A.D. and his wife in 62 A.D. He blamed the Christians for the fire that destroyed much of Rome in 64 A.D. (which he was popularly believed to be responsible for) and he began their persecution. He rebuilt the city, creating the Mammoth Golden House as his palace. In 68 A.D., the legions and the Praetorian Guard revolted, and Nero committed suicide.

Nestorianism   Christian movement (5th century A.D.) which held that Jesus Christ had two distinct personalities—divine and human—linked by a moral union. Advanced by Nestorius, this view was condemned by the Council of Ephesus in 431 A.D. which held that Jesus had both human and divine natures but was one person. Though Nestorianism declined in the West it spread through the Middle East, Persia, India, and China, reaching its height from the 7th–10th centuries in the form of the Nestorian church.

Neustria   Western part of the Merovingian Frankish kingdom, located in what is now northwestern France and including Paris. Formed by Clovis I in the 6th century when he divided his domains among his descendants, Neustria was involved in dynastic wars with the neighboring Frankish kingdom of Austrasia.

New Brunswick   Eastern Canadian province, one of the Maritime Provinces. Although explored in 1525 by the Portuguese, it was settled by the French under Champlain and the sieur de Monts in 1604. Under the French, the area of Nova Scotia and New Brunswick was called Acadia, and when the British gained control after the French and Indian War both territories were known as Nova Scotia. Many Loyalists from New England settled there after the American Revolution, and it became a separate province in 1784. In 1867, it joined with other provinces to form the Dominion of Canada.

New Economic Policy (NEP)   Russian Communist economic policy that allowed limited free enterprise such as small businesses and sale of surpluses by peasants. Instituted by Lenin in 1921, to relax tensions and gain support for the regime, it followed the earlier period of "war communism" characterized by forced requisitions of goods, confiscation of capital, nationalization, etc. The NEP was replaced by the first Five-Year Plan in 1928.

Newfoundland Island off the eastern coast of Canada, which with Labrador forms the 10th Canadian province. It was discovered in 1497 by J. Cabot. It became a province in 1949.

New Granada New Granada was a Spanish colonial viceroyalty in South America. It included what is now Colombia, Ecuador, Panama, and Venezuela. Originally part of the viceroyalty of Peru, it was created as the separate viceroyalty of New Granada in the 18th century.

Ne Win, U (Thakin Shu Maung) (b. 1911) Burmese military and political leader. As a military commander he played a leading role in achieving Burma's independence from Britain in 1948. In 1962 he overthrew the government of U Nu and established a military junta that dominated Burmese politics in the next decades. He remained in power until 1981.

New Kingdom (New Empire) Period of ancient Egyptian history (1580–1085 B.C.), which included the 18th–20th dynasties. The New Kingdom began after the overthrow of the Hyksos. Thebes was made capital. The pharaohs centralized power in their own hands and by their conquests brought the Egyptian empire to its greatest extent (parts of Asia included). During this period such pharaohs as Thutmose I and Thutmose III proved themselves great conquerors. Many temples were built and the pharaoh Akhenaton briefly established a monotheistic religion in Egypt. After the reign of Ramses III (1198–1167), the priests at Thebes gained power and thus brought about ancient Egypt's decline. The New Kingdom was followed by a period of domination by various foreign peoples that led finally to the reduction of Egypt to a Roman province.

New Spain Spanish viceroyalty (1535–1821) consisting of Mexico, what is now the southwestern United States, and Central America south to Panama. Spain's possessions among the Caribbean Islands, Florida, and the Philippines were also once administered as part of the viceroyalty. New Spain ceased to exist after Mexico won its independence in 1821.

Newton, Sir Isaac (1642–1726) English mathematician and physicist. Newton discovered laws of motion and universal gravitation, calculus, and the variations of the light spectrum. His findings were published in the *Principia* (1687) and *Opticks* (1704). Today Newton and Leibnitz share the credit for the discovery of calculus, but Newton's laws of motion and universal gravitation are considered among the greatest syntheses in the history of human thought. They dominated science until replaced by the theory of Einstein in the 19th century.

Nguyen Cao Ky (b. 1930) South Vietnamese military and political leader. He served as commander of the United States-backed South Vietnam air force (1963–1965). In 1967 he became vice president under Nguyen Van Thieu, whom he unsuccessfully attempted to oppose in the 1971 elections.

Nguyen dynasty Vietnamese dynasty, founded in 1820 by Nguyen Anh. The dynasty nominally ruled after the French occupation of Indochina, until 1945.

Nguyen Van Thieu (b. 1923) South Vietnamese (Republic of Vietnam) political leader. President (1967–1975) during the years of major American involvement in the Vietnam War, he was unable to check the Communist advance following the withdrawal of the United States in 1973.

Nicholas I (1796–1855) Czar of Russia (1825–1855). Acceding despite the Decembrist Conspiracy, Nicholas suppressed the Polish uprising of 1830 and 1831 and helped Austria subdue Hungary in 1849. His attempt to expand into Ottoman domains led to the Crimean War.

Nicholas II (1868–1918) Last Russian czar (1894–1917). An ineffective and autocratic ruler, Nicholas was greatly influenced by his wife Alexandra, who was in turn dominated by Rasputin. Russia's defeat in the Russo-Japanese War (1904 and 1905) led to the Revolution of 1905 and Nicholas was forced to establish a duma in 1906. He took command of the army in World War I in 1915, leaving Alexandra to govern. Under Alexandra, government at home became chaotic and this, with failures in the war, led to the Russian Revolution of 1917. Nicholas and his family were shot by revolutionaries in 1918.

Nietzsche, Friedrich Wilhelm (1844–1900) German philosopher who proposed new values in place of what he regarded as the decadent slave morality of Christianity in *Beyond Good and Evil* (1886). One of his new values involved the "superman" who would achieve by asserting a "will to power." Nietzsche developed this idea in *Thus Spake Zarathustra* (1883–1885). He predicted the "death of God" in his *Joyful Wisdom* (1910), among other works. His ideas influenced the Nazis, although Nietzsche was an anti-state individualist and not anti-Semitic.

Nihilism Nineteenth-century movement among the Russian intelligentsia that advocated the overthrow of all order and authority. Given its name in the novel by I. Turgenev, *Fathers and Sons* (1861), the movement embraced both those who wanted to overthrow existing governments by force and terror and those who sought to throw off personal moral restraints.

Ninety-five Theses Martin Luther's historic document posted on the church door in Wittenberg, Germany, on October 31, 1517, a date that is now considered the beginning of the Protestant Reformation. The theses not only protested the selling of indulgences in the Roman Catholic church, but advanced Luther's opinions on doctrines of the faith, which proved to be unacceptable to church authority. Originally the theses were posted only to invite debate from other Catholic theologians. They later came to be considered the inauguration of the Reformation.

Nineveh Ancient city. Nineveh was the capital of the Assyrian empire, located near modern Mosul, Iraq. Sennacherib and Ashurbanipal greatly contributed to its glory by their buildings and sculptures. The fabulous royal library of Nineveh was organized by Ashurbanipal. The city fell to a coalition of Babylonians, Medes, and Scythians in 612 B.C.

Nkrumah, Kwame (1909–1972)　Ghanaian states-man. Nkrumah led strikes against British domina-tion of Ghana, which achieved independence under his leadership. He later became its first prime min-ister in 1951 and president in 1960.

Nobel, Alfred Bernhard (1833–1896)　Swedish inventor and industrialist. Nobel invented dynamite, though he was a pacifist. With his fortune he estab-lished the coveted Nobel prizes, awarded yearly to scientists, writers, and peacemakers.

Nok Culture　An early West African people who thrived between 700 B.C. and 200 A.D. in what is now northern Nigeria. Archaeologists have discov-ered that they lived in semi-independent villages and were among the first to master the art of iron work-ing. Their culture declined and disappeared after 200 A.D.

Noncooperation Movement　Indian protest movement organized between 1920 and 1922 by Gandhi as a reaction to the British Amritsar Massacre in 1919. The movement involved boy-cotting British institutions and goods. An outbreak of violence brought the movement to an end though Gandhi later used nonviolent protests (satyagraha) against the British to gain India's independence.

Nonproliferation Treaty　Treaty (July 1, 1968) in which nuclear powers agreed to prevent the spread of nuclear-weapons technology to nations that did not then possess such capabilities. The treaty was signed by the United States, Britain, the Soviet Union, and numerous nonnuclear countries.

Norman Conquest　English historical period in-augurated in 1066. One of the formative eras in Eng-lish history, it began with the defeat of English king Harold II by William the Conqueror, duke of Nor-mandy, at the Battle of Hastings. Thereafter the cus-toms, laws, and language of the Normans were introduced in England. William replaced the English nobles with his Norman followers and established the feudal system in England.

Normandy Invasion (Operation Overlord)　World War II Allied invasion. On D-Day, June 6, 1941, Al-lied land, naval, and air troops invaded the northern shores of Nazi-held France. They established beach-heads (Utah, Omaha, Gold, Juno, Sword) in five key areas by the next day, opening the area for other Al-lied troops. The invasion signaled the beginning of the end of the Nazi war effort. The invasion, the largest amphibious landing in history, was overseen and executed by General D. Eisenhower. Some 800,000 combat troops had been massed in Britain for the operation. Over 4,000 ships, under the com-mand of the British admiral Sir Bertram Ramsay, were used in the invasion; about 5,000 fighters and almost 6,000 bombers were used to provide air sup-port. British field marshal Montgomery was in com-mand of Allied ground forces during the invasion.

Norodom Sihanouk (b. 1922)　Cambodian king (1941–1955). Following the French withdrawal from Indochina in 1954, he established the People's Socialist Community, abdicated the throne in favor of his father (Prince Norodom Suramarit), and be-came prime minister. He became head of state again after his father's death in 1960, but was unsuccess-ful at maintaining neutrality during the Vietnam War and was overthrown in 1970 by a rightist coup.

Norsemen (Northmen) (Normans)　Scandinavian Vikings who, from the 8th century, raided and colo-nized such diverse territories as England, Ireland, France, and Russia. Vikings also colonized Iceland and Greenland and even visited "Vinland" (North America). Norsemen from what is now Denmark were called Danes and attacked England as early as 787. The major assault by Norsemen on France came about 845. In 912, French king Charles III gave the Norse leader Rollo the area around Rouen. This was the beginning of the duchy of Normandy. In Russia, the Norsemen were known as Varangians, and one of them, Rurik, established at Novgorod in 862 the dynasty that ruled in Russia until 1598. In the same period, strong rulers such as Harold I and Canute began to organize Norse homelands into the Scandi-navian nations of Norway, Denmark, and Sweden.

North Africa　Geographical designation. This term identifies the African countries south of the Mediter-ranean and north of the Sahara Desert. It generally includes Morocco, Algeria, Tunisia, Libya, and, sometimes, Egypt.

North Africa, campaign of　Series of military ac-tions in North Africa (between 1940 and 1943) dur-ing World War II. The turning point came in 1942 in the Battle of El Alamein. The British, now under command of Field Marshal Montgomery, forced German General Rommel to retreat. Outwitting British attacks, he fell back to southern Tunisia. New Allied forces, commanded by General Eisen-hower, landed in the west in 1942 in Algeria. They pushed into Tunisia and guaranteed the German de-feat, but only after heavy fighting. When the Axis forces finally surrendered in 1943 more than 250,000 troops were taken prisoner. The Axis defeat in North Africa was a major victory for the Allies.

North Atlantic Treaty Organization (NATO)　Alliance formed after World War II by the Atlantic nations of Europe and North America to counter po-tential Soviet bloc threats. The treaty was originally signed April 4, 1949, and members included Bel-gium, Canada, Denmark, France, Great Britain, Ice-land, Italy, Luxembourg, The Netherlands, Norway, Portugal, and the United States. Greece and Turkey joined in 1952 and West Germany in 1955. With the end of the Cold War (*see* page 11-26), the mili-tary purpose ended. NATO continues to exist, re-defining its role.

Northeast Boundary Dispute　American-Cana-dian border controversy. Due to the vagueness of the 1783 Treaty of Versailles, the border between Maine and New Brunswick was unclear. After the Aroostook War, America and Britain decided to set-tle the matter permanently through the Webster-Ashburton Treaty of 1842.

Northern War (Great War)　Fought (1700–1721) by Sweden under Charles II and Russia under Peter I (the Great). Russia was supported by Denmark, Saxony, Poland, Prussia, and Hanover. The original belligerents (Russia, Poland, and Denmark) sought to break Swedish hegemony in the Baltic region. Charles prolonged the war by proving a far better warrior than expected, but Sweden was ultimately defeated. The Northern War, concurrent with the War of Spanish Succession in southern Europe, marked the rise of Russian power in the Baltic.

North German Confederation An alliance of 22 German states north of the Main River under the leadership of Prussia. Formed in 1866 after the Austro-Prussian War, it succeeded the German Confederation that had been dominated by Prussia's rival, Austria. The new confederation lasted between 1866 and 1871, when Prussian minister Bismarck achieved his goal of creating a unified empire of all German states under Prussian domination (and excluding Austria). Bismarck thereby created the modern German state.

Nostradamus (Notredame, Michel de) French physician and astrologer. His symbolic rhymes have come to be regarded by some as prophecies for the world's future and its ending.

Nova Scotia One of the Maritime Provinces of eastern Canada. The French founded the first settlement in 1605, but there was constant conflict with the English for control of the area known as Acadia. In 1755, England gained control and expelled the French Acadians. The Colony of Nova Scotia entered the Canadian Confederation in 1867.

November Insurrection Unsuccessful Polish rebellion (1830 and 1831) against Russian domination of the Congress Kingdom of Poland. It began on November 29, 1830 after the French July Revolution and rebels seized control of Warsaw. Czar Nicholas was deposed as king on January 25, 1831 and the numerically superior Russian army advanced into Poland in February. The Russians attacked Warsaw in September after several battles and the Polish army withdrew to Prussia, where it surrendered on October 5.

Novgorod Russian city located in northwest Russia. The foundation of the Russian state dates from 862 when the inhabitants of Novgorod asked Rurik to rule them. At its height in the 14th century, Novgorod boasted rich fairs, factories, and churches. It came under the control of Moscow in 1478.

Nubia Ancient region of northeastern Africa that was for many centuries ruled by Egypt. By the 8th century B.C. Nubia had become independent and conquered Egypt. The Nobatae formed the next powerful kingdom of the area and converted to Christianity. After the Muslim takeover in the 14th century, the area became divided into small states.

Nuclear Test-Ban Treaty Treaty signed in Moscow on August 5, 1963 between the United States, Britain, and the Soviet Union, banning nuclear-weapons tests in the atmosphere, in outer space, and under water. It provided for no international enforcement machinery, nor, since France and China did not sign, did it include all nuclear powers.

Numidia Ancient North African country, situated roughly in modern Algeria. Masinissa became ruler after allying himself with Rome in the Punic Wars and was the leader during Numidia's golden age. Under King Juba I, Numidia fell to Rome in 46 B.C. but enjoyed a long period of prosperity until the invasion of the Vandals in 428. It was later conquered by the Muslims.

Nuremberg trials War-crimes trials held after World War II in Nuremberg, Germany, for the purpose of trying leaders of the Nazi party. The trials were conducted by a special international tribunal. Twenty-four Nazi leaders were indicted, including Goring, Keitel, von Ribbentrop, Rosenberg, Hess, and Schacht. The tribunal held 403 public sessions (November 20, 1945–October 1, 1946), heard hundreds of witnesses, and utilized captured German documents to prove the charges of war crimes and crimes against peace and humanity (notably the slaughter of the Jews). Two defendants, including H. Goring, committed suicide. The trials were controversial, but the tribunal argued that all the violations were of international laws recognized prior to World War II and that Nazi crimes against the Jews required a unique response.

Nurhachi (1559–1626) Manchurian tribal chief and founder of China's Ch'ing (Manchu) dynasty (1644–1912). After uniting Manchuria, he began the conquest of the Chinese empire, which his son, Dorgon, completed.

Nyerere, Julius (b. 1922) First president of the United Republic of Tanzania (from 1964). He founded the Tanganyika National Union political party in 1954, became the first prime minister and then president when Tanganyika became independent in 1961, and effected the union of Tanganyika and Zanzibar as Tanzania in 1964.

OAS *See* **Organization of American States.**

Obregón, Álvaro (1880–1928) Mexican general and president (1920–1924). Obregón supported Carranza against Huerta, F. Villa, and Zapata, but eventually deposed Carranza. As president, he advocated education and land reforms and improved relations with the United States.

Oceania (Oceanica) Pacific Islands. This is the collective name for the thousands of islands in the central and South Pacific Ocean. Ethnically they are divided into Australasia, Melanesia, Micronesia, and Polynesia.

Ockham, William of (Occam) (1285–1349) English Franciscan philosopher. He opposed the Aristotelian realism of Thomas Aquinas, holding that universal ideas exist only in the thinking mind. In philosophy he was a nominalist whose ideas contributed to the decline of scholasticism and eventually to the Protestant Reformation.

October Manifesto Manifesto issued on October 30, 1905, by Russian Czar Nicholas II. Issued in response to the Russian Revolution of 1905, it guaranteed civil liberties and called for establishment of a duma, which would have the power to confirm all legislation. The manifesto would have turned the Russian government into a constitutional monarchy, but it was only partially enacted.

October Revolution (November Revolution) The coup d'état of October 24–25, 1917 (October in the Old Style Julian Calendar that was used in Russia until 1918; by our dating and New Style—November 6–7, 1918) under the leadership of Lenin, took control of the Russian Revolution. The revolution began with the February Revolution, the abdication of Czar Nicholas II in 1917, and the formation of a provisional government dominated by Socialists (eventually headed by A. Kerensky).

Octobrists (Union of October 17) Russian conservative political party. It sought enactment of constitutional reforms based on the October Manifesto issued by Czar Nicholas II. Formed in 1906, the party was dissolved during the 1917 Russian Revolution.

Oda Nobunaga (1534–1582) Japanese military leader. He was the first Japanese commander to arm his troops with muskets. With his allies Hideyoshi Toyotomi and Ieyasu, he unified most of Japan.

Oder-Neisse Line Polish-German frontier established by the Soviet Union, Great Britain, and the United States at the 1945 Potsdam Conference. Poland was compensated at Germany's expense for the Soviet acquisitions on her eastern border. These controversial borders were not recognized by West Germany until 1971.

Odoacer (Odovacar) (435–493 A.D.) German chieftain and mercenary in Roman service who deposed the last Western Roman emperor, Romulus Augustus, in 476 A.D. He was the virtual ruler of Italy until assassinated by an Ostrogothic king, Theodoric, acting for the Byzantines.

Odysseus (Ulysses) Greek mythical king and warrior. His adventures in the Trojan War were related in Homer's *Iliad*, and his long trip back to Ithaca recounted in Homer's *Odyssey*.

Ogadai (1185–1241) Mongol ruler (1229–1241), successor to his father, Genghis Khan. He conquered northern China in 1243 and sent armies, under Batu Khan, westward into Russia, where they sacked Kiev in 1240 and thereby ended Russian resistance. Ogadai built the Mongol capital city of Karakorum.

O'Higgins, Bernardo (1778–1842) Chilean soldier and statesman. He became leader of the revolutionary forces in Chile in 1813 and helped defeat the Spaniards at Chacabuco in 1817. He was named supreme dictator and proclaimed Chilean independence on February 12, 1818. He was the first president of Chile, until 1823, when he was deposed for his reforms.

Old Kingdom (Pyramid Age) One of the three great divisions of ancient Egyptian history (with the Middle and New Kingdoms), the period during which the great pyramids were built. Generally this period may be taken to include dynasties 3rd–6th, though sources vary (1st–6th and 3rd–8th are also given). Dates vary as well, though 2700–2200 B.C. is a good guideline. The Egyptian capital was at Memphis. Among the notable rulers of this period are Zoser, Snefru, Jhufu, Menkaure, and Pepi.

Oleg (d. 912) Early Russian ruler. He was a Viking leader and the reputed founder of Kievan Russia. Oleg expanded his realm of Novgorod, inherited from Rurik, to include Kiev, which then became the capital of a Kievan-Novgorodian state in 882. His treaties with the Byzantine Empire (907–911) opened Russia to Greek, Christian, and cultural penetration.

Olympic Games Religious athletic games. These ancient Greek games were held (776 B.C.–393 A.D.) at Olympia once every four years and were called an Olympiad to honor Zeus. They were revived in 1896, and are now held in a different world city every four years.

Omar (Umar) (581–644) Second Muslim caliph. A father-in-law of the prophet Muhammad, he at first opposed Islam, but was converted by 618. He chose Abu Bakr as the first caliph to succeed to the authority of the prophet in 632, and succeeded him in 634. During his caliphate, Arab armies advanced into Syria, Egypt, and Persia. He established the administration and taxation of the subsequent empire.

Ontario East-central Canadian province. The area was first explored by the French in the early 17th century, although settlement (by Britain and France) was delayed because of wars with the Iroquois Indians. British claims to the region were upheld by the Treaty of Paris in 1763, and Ontario was joined to the province of Quebec in 1774. Ontario and Quebec entered the Dominion of Canada as separate provinces in 1867.

OPEC *See* **Organization of Petroleum Exporting Countries.**

Open door International diplomatic term applied to the policy of a country that trades with all other nations on an equal basis. The term was first used in the 1890s by the United States, which sought to trade with China at a time when such nations as Britain, Russia, France, Japan, Italy, and Germany all demanded special trade concessions from the Chinese. The policy was advanced (1899 and 1900) to the major nations by U.S. Secretary of State J. Hay. Hay declared it to be in effect in 1900.

Opium War Name given to two 19th-century wars between China and European powers. The first war (1839–1842) began when China attempted to enforce its ban on the importation of opium and seized British-owned opium in Canton. Britain soon defeated China and forced it to cede Hong Kong to Britain, open several ports to British trade, and pay an indemnity. The second war (1856–1860) began after Chinese boarded the British ship *Arrow*. France joined Britain in a new war against China. Soon defeated China agreed to the Treaty of Tientsin (1858), which opened a number of new ports to European trade and secured rights of interior travel in China, rights for Christian missionaries, residence in Peking for foreign diplomats, and legalization of the opium trade. China's opposition to the agreements led to new conflict and the occupation in 1860 of Peking and burning of the imperial summer palace. The conflict ended with the Conventions of Peking in 1860, which granted still further concessions.

Organization of American States (OAS) International organization, founded in 1948 to promote military, economic, and cultural cooperation. Its member nations include the United States and most of the nations of Latin America. Cuba was expelled from the OAS in 1962.

Organization of Central American States Central American association, organized in 1951 to promote regional and economic unity. Its member states include Costa Rica, El Salvador, Guatemala, Honduras, and Nicaragua.

Organization of Petroleum Exporting Countries (OPEC) International group formed in 1960 to promote the interests of countries that supply the world market with oil. When the group was founded, member nations were largely at the mercy of the great international oil companies, which controlled all-important (in times of plentiful supply) systems of distribution and marketing. But as oil consumption began to outstrip production in the late 1960s, producing countries began to get the upper hand. By cutting back their production, OPEC members found they could effectively force the great industrial powers to pay any price for oil they demanded. The huge price increases it put into effect in 1973 signaled the ascendancy of OPEC as a dominant force in the world oil industry. Membership now includes oil-producing countries in the Middle East, Africa, and South America. In the 1980s, OPEC found it difficult to maintain unity over the price and supply of oil due to an economic slump, the Iran-Iraq War (*see* page 11-58), and the Persian Gulf War (*see* page 11-96).

Orlando, Vittorio Emmanuele (1860–1952) Italian statesman. As premier (1917–1919), he was one of the "Big Four" at the Versailles Peace Conference in 1919, which formally ended World War I.

Orléans, siege of Historic siege of Orléans, France (between 1428 and 1429) by the English during the Hundred Years' War. The English, supporting the claims of English king Henry VI to the French throne, laid siege to Orléans, controlled by the supporters of the French dauphin Charles VII. The English brought the city to near surrender when Joan of Arc, who had gained the permission of Charles to raise an army, entered the city and lifted the siege. The English defeat marked the turning point in the Hundred Years' War.

Orsini Roman family that from the 12th century held great political and religious power in Rome and Italy.

Orthodox Eastern church Collective name for the family of Christian churches that exist largely in the Middle East, Eastern Europe, and Russia. All the Orthodox churches accept the authority of the first seven ecumenical councils of the Catholic church but do not accept later councils. They also do not recognize the authority of the Roman Catholic pope as supreme head of the church nor the practice of mandatory celibacy for priests. The origins of the Orthodox church can be traced to the late Roman Empire. As the empire weakened and was divided into the Western Empire and the Eastern Empire, so too did the early Christian church suffer a growing division. The Western church developed along Latin lines and adapted Roman political and civil patterns, while the Eastern church retained a traditional Greek heritage. The separation between the two parts of the Christian world occurred slowly from the 5th–11th centuries, and became a complete schism in 1054 when Pope Leo IX excommunicated Michael Cerularius, patriarch of Constantinople, and all his followers.

Osei Tutu (d. 1712) West African leader, founder and first ruler of the Ashanti nation. The nation was created from a confederacy of West African kingdoms in what is now Ghana.

Osman I (Othman I) (1259–1326) Turkish leader, founder of the Ottoman Empire. Declaring himself emir in 1299, Osman greatly extended his holdings, largely through conquest of territory from the Byzantine Empire.

Ostracism Greek political banishment imposed by Athenians on those disrupting local stability. The banishment lasted 10 years.

Ostrogoths (East Goths) Germanic tribe. The Ostrogoths were the Eastern tribes of the Goths, the Visigoths being their Western counterparts. They were believed to have originated in southern Russia. After being conquered by the Huns in 370 A.D., they joined with them against the Visigoths and pushed westward into the Roman Empire. After Attila's death in 453 A.D., many Ostrogoths settled in Hungary. Others continued into Italy, where their leader, Theodoric, defeated Odoacer and became king in 493. They were finally subjugated by the Byzantine general Narses in 552 and were absorbed into other cultures.

Otto I (Otto the Great) (912–973) German king (936–973) and Holy Roman emperor (962–973). Otto became king at the end of a period in which the East Frankish kingdom—created by the Treaty of Verdun—had broken up into petty states. As German king, Otto succeeded in extending his authority over rebellious German dukes by force of arms and by using the church to strengthen his rule. The pope crowned Otto emperor in 962, and concluded an agreement to regulate relations between the pope and the emperor. Otto's coronation is thus usually taken as the beginning of the Holy Roman Empire and its long, often troubled alliance with the church.

Ottoman Empire Former empire established in the 13th century by the Osmanli (Ottoman) Turks. Formed from the territories once ruled by the Seljuk Turks, the empire expanded its holdings at the expense of the Byzantine Empire. The Ottoman conquest of Constantinople in 1453 marked the end of the Byzantine Empire. The Ottomans then advanced into Europe, creating an empire that stretched from the Balkans (southeast Europe), across the Near East and into North Africa. By the early 18th century the empire began to disintegrate, and during the 19th century the Eastern Question became a major concern of European powers. The empire was finally dismembered at the end of World War I.

Ovid (Naso, Publius Ovidius) (43 B.C.–18 A.D.) Roman poet, considered one of the great poets of antiquity.

Owen, Robert (1771–1858) British manufacturer and reformer. A successful textile manufacturer, he instituted reforms in child employment, education, health, and hygiene. His progressive ideas were adopted by several experimental communities, including one at New Harmony, Indiana.

P **Pact of Steel** Treaty (May 22, 1939) between Germany and Italy, confirming the German-Italian alliance. The treaty obligated each to enter any war in which the other was engaged. Thus Italy joined Hitler in World War II (June 10, 1940) and ultimately broke the treaty by reaching a separate peace with the Allies on September 3, 1943.

Páez, José Antonio (1790–1873) Venezuelan revolutionary and statesman. He aided Bolívar in the fight for South American independence from Spain. Later, however, he led the movement to separate Venezuela from Bolívar's Great Colombia in 1831.

Páez was president (1831–1835), (1839–1843), and dictator (1861–1863) of Venezuela.

Pahlevi, Mohammed Reza Shah (1919–1980) Shah of Iran. He ascended the throne in 1941, after his father, Reza Shah Pahlevi was deposed by British and Soviet military intervention. He was forced to leave the country briefly in 1953. He was restored with American and British help and subsequently attempted to promote social and economic reforms. The shah, generally pro-Western in attitude, launched projects to modernize his country, but was often beset by financial and political instability. He was overthrown in 1979 by a Muslim fundamentalist revolution that brought Ayatollah Khomeini to power.

Pahlevi, Reza Shah (1877–1944)   Shah of Iran (1925–1941). An army officer, he led a coup d'état in 1921 becoming prime minister of the new regime in 1923. He changed the name of Persia to Iran. Virtually a dictator, Reza Khan deposed Ahmed Shah, the last shah of the Kajar (or Qajar) dynasty in 1925, and was proclaimed shah of Iran. He changed his name to Reza Shah Pahlevi, thus founding the Pahlevi dynasty. He introduced many reforms, reorganizing the army, government administration, and finances. He abolished all special rights granted to foreigners, thus gaining real independence for Iran. Reza Shah was forced to abdicate in favor of his son, Mohammed Reza Shah in 1941.

Palaeologus   Byzantine ruling dynasty. This Greek family ruled the Byzantine Empire from 1261–1453, when the Turks brought the empire to an end. Emperor Michael VIII became the first ruler of the line when he ousted the crusader kings of the Latin Empire of Constantinople and thereby restored the Byzantine Empire. The last ruler of the family, Constantine XI, was killed defending Constantinople against the Turks.

Paleolithic (Old Stone Age)   The earliest period of human development and the longest phase of human history, dating from about 500,000 years ago to 6000 B.C. Life was sustained by gathering food and hunting. Roughly chipped axes were the basic tools. It is believed that during this period fire was developed and language evolved.

Palestine   Historic region on the east coast of the Mediterranean, including modern Israel and the part of Jordan east of the Jordan River. Palestine is considered a Holy Land by the Jews, Christians, and Muslims, and the historic center of the region is Jerusalem. Palestine, inhabited since very ancient times, is the scene of many of the events recounted in the Bible. The region was controlled by various powers of the ancient world though it remained a Jewish homeland until late in the Roman era. Palestine subsequently fell to the Muslims in the 7th century A.D. Palestine remained in Muslim hands until the 20th century, though by the end of the 19th century Jews had already begun again to colonize the region. The movement to create a Jewish homeland in Palestine after World War I resulted in serious clashes between Arabs and Jews there. The conflict between Arabs and Israelis continued after the creation of Israel in 1948 and has contributed to Mideast instability into the 1980s and 1990s.

Palestine Liberation Organization (PLO)   Arab political and terrorist organization. Founded in 1964, the PLO is made up of various Arab guerrilla groups dedicated to reclaiming Palestinian homelands now occupied by Israel. The group has been involved in a bitter guerrilla war with the Israelis, and their activities have included airplane hijackings, terrorist bombings, massacres of Israeli civilians, and skirmishes with Israeli military forces. Since 1964 the PLO has been headed by Yasir Arafat, whose guerrilla organization (Al Fatah) dominates the PLO. The PLO was formally recognized by the United Nations in 1974. In 1988 Arafat renounced the use of terrorism and, as a result, the United States agreed to meetings. The progress of these meetings has been slowed by continued terrorist activity and Israeli reaction, especially the Israeli expulsion of over 400 Palestinians to Southern Lebanon.

Pan-Germanism   German nationalist movement, organized in 1894. It called for the political unification of all German-speaking people. The movement was used to justify Germany's expansionist policies and after World War I figured in Hitler's National Socialist program.

Pankhurst, Emmeline Goulden (1857–1928) British feminist, who founded the Women's Social and Political Union in 1903 to promote women's suffrage.

Pan-Slavism   Slavic unity movement. This movement arose in the 19th century and stressed the common culture and history of the various Slavic peoples, then divided between Austrian and Ottoman empires. Pan-Slavism figured in Russian imperial policy, contributed to the outbreak of the Russo-Turkish War (1877 and 1878), and was a factor in Russia's alliance with Serbia against the Austrians in the years before World War I.

Papacy   The system of government of the Roman Catholic church, which is headed by the pope (bishop of Rome), who is considered the successor to St. Peter and vicar of Christ. The pope is considered infallible by the Roman Catholic church in matters of faith or morality and is head of independent Vatican City. Early popes played an important role in the spread of the Christian church and in resolving the many doctrinal disputes of that era. In medieval times popes were the central figures in the great struggles for power between the church and European monarchs. Later they instituted the Catholic Reformation and, gradually forced to relinquish their secular powers, came to focus on spiritual concerns. In modern times, the popes have been especially active in adapting the church to the rapidly changing modern world.

Papal States   Former territory over which the pope had direct temporal rule (756–1870). The size of the territory varied throughout its history but at its greatest extent it included a wide swath across central Italy.

Papen, Franz von (1879–1969)   German politician. As Hindenburg's chancellor, he facilitated the rise of the Nazi party by lifting the ban on their paramilitary troops and later helped bring Hitler to power.

Papineau, Louis Joseph (1786–1871)   French-Canadian political leader. He stirred his followers in Lower Canada to rebellion against British rule in 1831, shortly before the revolt led by W. Mackenzie broke out. *See* **Mackenzie, William Lyon.**

EXHIBIT 11.4
Popes
The First Bishops of Rome

41?–67? A.D.	St. Peter	536–537	St. Silverius
67?–79?	St. Linus	537?–555	Vigilius
79?–91 ?	St. Anacletus or Cletus	556–561	Pelagius I
91–?100	St. Clement I (Clement of Rome)	561–574	John III
100–?107	St. Evaristus	575–579	Benedict I
107–?116	St. Alexander I	579–590	Pelagius II
116–?125	St. Sixtus I	590–604	St. Gregory I the Great
125–?136	St. Telesphorus	604–606	Sabinian
136–?140	St. Hyginus	607	Boniface III
140–?154	St. Pius I	608–615	St. Boniface IV
154–?165	St. Anicetus	615–618	St. Deusdedit or Adeodatus I
165–174	St. Soterus	619–625	Boniface V
174–189	St. Eleutherius	625–638	Honorius I
189–198	St. Victor I	638–640	Severinus
198–217	St. Zephyrinus	640–642	John IV
217–222	St. Calixtus or Callistus I	642–649	Theodore I
222–230	St. Urban I	649–653	St. Martin I
230–235	St. Pontian	654–657	St. Eugene I
235–236	St. Anterus	657–672	St. Vitalian
236–250	St. Fabian	672–676	Adeodatus II
251–253	St. Cornelius	676–678	Donus
251–?258	Novatianus (anti-pope)	678–681	St. Agatho
253–254	St. Lucius I	682–683	St. Leo II
254–257	St. Stephen I	683–685	St. Benedict II
257–258	St. Sixtus II	685–686	John V
258–268	St. Dionysius	686–687	Conon
268–274	St. Felix I	687–692	Paschal I
274–283	St. Eutychian	687	Theodorus (anti-pope)
282–296	St. Caius	687–701	St. Sergius I
296–304	St. Marcellinus	701–705	John VI
308–309	St. Marcellus I	705–707	John VII
309?	St. Eusebius	708	Sisinnius
310?–314	St. Miltiades or Melchiades	708–715	Constantine I
314–335	St. Sylvester I	715–731	St. Gregory II
336	St. Mark	731–741	St. Gregory III
337–352	St. Julius I (Rusticus)	741–752	St. Zachary
352–366	Liberius	752	Stephen II
355–365	Felix II (anti-pope)	752–757	St. Stephen III
366–367	Ursinus (anti-pope)	757–767	St. Paul I
366–384	St. Damasus I	767–768	Constantine II (anti-pope)
384–399	St. Siricius	768	Philippus
399–401	St. Anastasius I	768–772	Stephen IV
401–417	St. Innocent I	772–795	Adrian I
417–418	St. Zosimus	795–816	St. Leo III
418–419	Eulalius (anti-pope)	816–817	Stephen V
418–422	St. Boniface I	817–824	St. Pascal I
422–432	St. Celestine I	824–827	Eugene II
432–440	St. Sixtus III	827	Valentine
440–461	St. Leo I the Great	827–844	Gregory IV
461–468	St. Hilary	844	John (anti-pope)
468–483	St. Simplicius	844–847	Sergius II
483–492	St. Felix III (II)	847–855	St. Leo IV
492–496	St. Gelasius I	855	Anastasius (anti-pope)
496–498	Anastasius II	858–867	St. Nicholas I the Great
498–514	St. Symmachus	867–872	Adrian II
498–505	Laurentius (anti-pope)	872–882	John VIII
514–523	St. Hormisdas	882–884	Marinus I
523–526	St. John I	884–885	St. Adrian III
526–530	St. Felix IV (III)	885–891	Stephen VI
530–532	Boniface II	891–896	Formosus
530	Dioscorus (anti-pope)	896	Boniface VI
532–535	John II	896–897	Stephen VII
535–536	St. Agapetus I	897	Romanus

Anti-pope: Pope set up in opposition to the elected pope

EXHIBIT 11.4 *(continued)*

897	Theodore II
898–900	John IX
900–903	Benedict IV
903	Leo V
903–904	Christopher
904–911	Sergius III
911–913	Anastasius III
913–914	Landus
914–928	John X
928	Leo VI
929–931	Stephen VIII
931–935	John XI
936–939	Leo VII
939–942	Stephen IX
942–946	Marinus II
946–955	Agapetus II
955–964	John XII
964–965	Leo VIII
964	Benedict V (anti-pope)
965–972	John XIII
973–974	Benedict VI
974–983	Benedict VII
983–984	John XIV
984–985	Boniface VII (anti-pope)
985–996	John XV
996–999	Gregory V
997–998	John XVI (anti-pope)
999–1003	Sylvester II
1003	John XVII
1003–1009	John XVIII
1009–1012	Sergius IV
1012–1024	Benedict VIII
1012	Gregory (anti-pope)
1024–1032	John XIX
1032–1044	Benedict IX
1044–1045	Sylvester III (anti-pope)
1045	Benedict IX
1045–1046	Gregory VI
1046–1047	Clement II
1047–1048	Benedict IX (anti-pope)
1048	Damasus II
1049–1054	St. Leo IX
1055–1057	Victor II
1057–1058	Stephen X
1058–1059	Benedict X (anti-pope)
1058–1061	Nicholas II
1061–1073	Alexander II
1061–1064	Honorius II (anti-pope)
1073–1085	St. Gregory VII
1080–1100	Clement III (anti-pope)
1087	Victor III
1088–1099	Urban II
1099–1118	Pascal II
1100	Theodoric (anti-pope)
1102	Albertus (anti-pope)
1105–1111	Sylvester IV (anti-pope)
1118–1119	Gelasius II
1119–1124	Calixtus or Callistus II
1118–1121	GregoryVIII (anti-pope)
1124	Celestine (anti-pope)
1124–1130	Honorius II
1130–1143	Innocent II
1130–1138	Anacletus II (anti-pope)
1138	Victor IV (anti-pope)

1143–1144	Celestine II
1144–1145	Lucius II
1145–1153	Eugene III
1153–1154	Anastasius IV
1154–1159	Adrian IV
1159–1181	Alexander III
1159–1164	Victor V (anti-pope)
1164–1168	Pascal III (anti-pope)
1168–1178	Calixtus or Callistus III (anti-pope)
1178–1180	Innocent III (anti-pope)
1181–1185	Lucius III
1185–1187	Urban III
1187	Gregory VIII
1187–1191	Clement III
1191–1198	Celestine III
1198–1216	Innocent III
1216–1227	Honorius III
1227–1241	Gregory IX
1241	Celestine IV
1243–1254	Innocent IV
1254–1261	Alexander IV
1261–1264	Urban IV
1265–1268	Clement IV
1271–1276	Gregory X
1276	Innocent V
1276	Adrian V
1276–1277	John XXI
1277–1280	Nicholas III
1281–1285	Martin IV
1285–1287	Honorius IV
1288–1292	Nicholas IV
1294	St. Celestine V
1294–1303	Boniface VIII
1303–1304	Benedict XI
1305–1314	Clement V
1316–1334	John XXII
1328–1334	Nicholas V (anti-pope)
1334–1342	Benedict XII
1342–1352	Clement VI
1352–1362	Innocent VI
1362–1370	Urban V
1370–1378	Gregory XI
1378–1394	Clement VII (anti-pope)
1394–1423	Benedict XIII (anti-pope)
1378–1389	Urban VI
1389–1401	Boniface IX
1404–1406	Innocent VII
1406–1415	Gregory XII
1409–1410	Alexander V
1410–1415	John XXIII (anti-pope)
1417–1431	Martin V
1424?–1429	Clement VIII (anti-pope)
1431–1447	Eugene IV
1439–1449	Felix V of Savoy (last anti-pope)
1447–1455	Nicholas V
1455–1458	Calixus or Callistus III (Borgia)
1458–1464	Pius II
1464–1471	Paul II
1471–1484	Sixtus IV
1484–1492	Innocent VIII
1492–1503	Alexander VI
1503	Pius III

EXHIBIT 11.4 *(continued)*

1503–1513	Julius II	1689–1691	Alexander VIII
1513–1521	Leo X	1691–1700	Innocent XII
1522–1523	Adrian VI	1700–1721	Clement XI
1523–1534	Clement VII	1721–1724	Innocent XIII
1534–1549	Paul III	1724–1730	Benedict XIII
1550–1555	Julius III	1730–1740	Clement XII
1555	Marcellus II	1740–1758	Benedict XIV
1555–1559	Paul IV	1758–1769	Clement XIII
1559–1565	Pius IV	1769–1774	Clement XIV
1566–1572	St. Pius V	1775–1799	Pius VI
1572–1585	Gregory XIII	1800–1823	Pius VII
1585–1590	Sixtus V	1823–1829	Leo XII
1590	Urban VII	1829–1830	Pius VIII
1590–1591	Gregory XIV	1831–1846	Gregory XVI
1591	Innocent IX	1846–1878	Pius IX
1592–1605	Clement VIII	1878–1903	Leo XIII
1605	Leo XI	1903–1914	St. Pius X
1605–1621	Paul V	1914–1922	Benedict XV
1621–1623	Gregory XV	1922–1939	Pius XI
1623–1644	Urban VIII	1939–1958	Pius XII
1644–1655	Innocent X	1958–1963	John XXIII
1655–1667	Alexander VII	1963–1978	Paul VI
1667–1669	Clement IX	1978	John Paul I
1670–1676	Clement X	1978–	John Paul II
1676–1689	Innocent XI		

Papyrus　Reed plant once widely cultivated by the ancient Egyptians and used by them to make writing paper (from 3500 B.C.).

Paris, Treaty of　1. Treaty of 1763 between Britain, France, and Spain ending the Seven Years' War (1756–1763) and the subsidiary French and Indian War in the colonies. The treaty marked the ascendancy of Britain as the leading colonial power. By its terms Britain received French holdings in Canada, America (east of the Mississippi), Grenada, the Grenadines, and Senegal. Britain received Florida from Spain and returned Cuba and the Philippines to Spain, while Spain got all of the Louisiana Territory west of the Mississippi from France. Britain gave France Guadeloupe, Martinique, Miquelon, and St. Pierre. Britain also restored some French possessions in India. 2. Treaty of 1783 between the United States, Britain, and other European powers ending the American Revolution (1775–1783). By its terms Britain recognized American independence. U.S. boundaries were fixed (at the Mississippi in the West), Spain reacquired Florida and Minorca from Britain, and France got Senegal and Tobago. 3. Treaty of 1814 between France and the allied powers who had defeated Napoleon. The terms of the treaty were not harsh and included a return of France to its borders of 1792, restoration to France of most of its colonies taken by Britain, and the loss of Malta to Britain. No indemnity was imposed and a congress was to be held at Vienna to work out final arrangements 4. Treaty of 1815 between France and the victorious European allies after Napoleon's defeat at the end of his Hundred Days. Harsher terms were imposed and included a large indemnity, a return to the borders of 1790, and payment of expenses for an army to occupy northern France. 5. Treaty of 1856 between Russia and the allies (Ottoman Turks, Britain, France, and Sardinia) ending the Crimean War. Russia returned Kars and regained Sevastopol, ceded the mouth of the Danube and part of Bessarabia, and abandoned claims to protect Christians within the Ottoman Empire. The Black Sea was declared neutral.

Paris Peace Conference　Conference between 1919 and 1920 of Allied leaders at the end of World War I to determine peace terms to be imposed on Germany and the other Central Powers. It resulted in the Treaty of Versailles with Germany, in the Treaty of Saint-Germain with Austria, and the Treaty of Neuilly with Bulgaria.

Park Chung Hee (1917–1979)　South Korean president (1963–1979). He rose to power through the military and participated in the 1961 military coup against the civilian government. Elected president in 1963, he subsequently consolidated his power and instituted a police state in Korea. During his administration, border clashes with North Korea subsided and the economy improved. Park was assassinated in 1979.

Parlement　A French royal court under the Ancien Régime. There were parlements in Paris and 14 provincial cities. They combined the functions of a department of justice and appellate court, had no legislative powers, but did enjoy a certain "right of remonstrance" against royal acts.

Parliament　Legislative assembly. In Britain, Parliament consists of the reigning monarch, the House of Lords, and the House of Commons. Power rests largely with the House of Commons, the monarch being sovereign in name only and the House of Lords having lost much of its power in 1911. The origins of the British Parliament can be traced to the 13th-century royal feudal council, the Curia Regis, which gave rise to the House of Lords and to the irregular assemblages of the knights and burgesses, which gave rise to the House of Commons. Though a forerunner of Parliament (King Edward III's Model Parliament) was convened in 1295, the basic structure of Parliament did not appear until the 14th century. Thereafter, Parliament began a long struggle for supremacy over the English monarchs, usually relying on its control of finances to force concessions. Parliament finally established its supremacy over the monarchs by the Glorious Revolution of 1688, and thereafter the monarchs' involvement in government steadily diminished.

Parliament Act   British act of 1911 by which the House of Lords lost its veto power over parliamentary legislation. It was passed amid a political crisis caused by the opposition by the House of Lords to proposed tax on the wealthy to fund a social insurance program. The bill was advanced in 1909 by D. Lloyd George.

Parnell, Charles Stewart (1846–1891)   Leading figure in the Irish Home Rule movement in the late 1800s. *See* **Home Rule.**

Parthia   Ancient Asian country, located in what is now modern Iran. The territory was part of the Assyrian, Persian, Macedonian, and Seleucid empires before Arsaces founded the Parthian kingdom in 247 B.C. At its peak in the 1st century B.C., the Parthian Empire extended from the Euphrates River to the Indus River and from the Oxus River to the Indian Ocean. The empire was taken over in 226 A.D. by Ardashir I, founder of the Sassanidae Empire.

Partition(s) of Poland   Three successive divisions of Polish territories in the 18th century that resulted in complete dismemberment of Poland.

Pasteur, Louis (1822–1895)   French chemist whose work led to the germ theory of disease. He discovered the process of pasteurization and used vaccination against anthrax in sheep in 1881 and against rabies in 1885.

Pathet Lao (Lao Country)   Laotian Communist political and military organization. Formed in 1950, the group fought the French in the 1950s, later participated in a Laotian coalition government, and, from 1961, fought a bitter civil war against the American backed Laotian government. With the withdrawal of U.S. forces from southeast Asia, the Laotian government forces surrendered and the Pathet Lao took control in 1975.

Patricians   Members of the Roman upper class. The patricians represented the wealthy, educated privileged classes of ancient Rome. For many years only they could hold public office. By the 3rd century B.C., however, this distinction between the patricians and the plebeians (lower class) was eliminated. Members of the new ruling aristocracy, composed of both patricians and office-holding plebeians, were called nobles.

Paul I (1754–1801)   Russian emperor (1796–1801). On gaining the throne, he reversed many of his mother's reforms (Catherine II), alienated the nobility by taking steps to centralize power, and, by his inconsistent foreign policy, managed to isolate Russia during the period of the French Revolutionary Wars.

Paul III (Farnese, Alessandro) (1468–1549)   Italian-born pope (1534–1549). He sanctioned the Society of Jesus (Jesuits) in 1540, initiated the Catholic Reformation, and called the Council of Trent in 1545.

Paul, Saint (d. 67 A.D.)   Christian missionary and saint. Originally a Pharisee called Saul of Tarsus, he persecuted Christians until a vision and a miracle converted him. He then became a zealous missionary to the Gentiles and a founder of many churches. His epistles (letters) to his followers are included in the New Testament. His writings greatly influenced subsequent church doctrine.

Pax Romana   Roman peace. Period of stability (27 B.C.–180 A.D.) from the beginning of Augustus' reign until the death of Marcus Aurelius that the Roman Empire enjoyed peace, and orderly government.

Peasants' Revolt   Popular uprising in England in 1381 over a variety of grievances, including the poll tax and the Statute of Labourers in 1351, which held down wages of a work force then decimated by the plague. Led by Wat Tyler, the rebels marched on London, took the Tower of London, and beheaded the Archbishop of Canterbury. During a meeting at Mile End, the rebels forced King Richard II to make concessions, including an end to serfdom, forced labor, and restrictions on trade. Tyler was killed at London soon afterward, however, and the revolt collapsed. Richard then rescinded the Mile End concessions.

Peasants' War   Revolt (1524–1526) by the peasants and townspeople in southern Germany and Austria against the repressive policies of the nobles and clergy. Inspired in part by the Reformation and the teachings of such leaders as Luther and H. Zwingli, the peasants and poor townspeople formed armies to force religious and political concessions demanded by such rebel leaders as Munzer. Luther denounced the movement, and it was ruthlessly crushed in Germany in 1525. In Austria the disorders lasted until 1526.

Pedro I (1798–1834)   First emperor of Brazil (1822–1831). Pedro declared Brazilian independence from Portugal on Sept. 7, 1822 and accepted a liberal constitution in 1824. Later forced to abdicate to his son, Pedro II, he returned to Portugal, ousted King Miguel and restored his daughter Maria II.

Pedro II (1825–1891)   Emperor of Brazil (1831–1889), successor to his father Pedro I. A man of great learning, he worked for reform. The abolition of slavery in Brazil, effected with his support in 1888, was widely opposed by landowners.

Peel, Sir Robert (1788–1850)   British statesman, prime minister (1834 and 1835, 1841–1846), and founder of the Conservative party. A Tory member of Parliament in his early years, after his first ministry fell, he saw the need for reform, issued his Tamworth Manifesto, and formed the Conservative party. During his second ministry, he introduced an income tax and repealed the Corn Laws.

Peloponnesian League   Confederation of Greek city-states organized and dominated by Sparta in the 6th century B.C. as a military alliance.

Peloponnesian War   War (431–404 B.C.) between Sparta and Athens (and respective allied city-states) for control of Greece. Before the war Sparta held sway over most of the city-states of inland Greece (through the Peloponnesian League), while Athens controlled the Delian League, a maritime empire extending out over the Aegean. Sparta had a superior land army and Athens had a powerful navy. The two city-states had long been rivals and the intricate system of alliances with other city-states meant that even local conflicts could erupt into a general war. Although Athens entered the war with the riches of the Delian treasury to support its war effort, Sparta ultimately emerged victorious. Athens never regained its former power, and Sparta for a time became the undisputed power in ancient Greece.

Peloponnesus Peninsula of Greece forming the southern part of the country. It is almost completely separated from mainland (central) Greece by the Gulf of Corinth. In ancient times, its major cities included Sparta and Corinth.

Peninsular War Series of military campaigns between 1808 and 1814 conducted by British, Portuguese, and Spanish forces against the French in the Iberian Peninsula during the Napoleonic Wars. The Peninsular War was prompted by the French invasion of Portugal following Portugal's refusal to join Napoleon's Continental System. The French army (1771–1813), forced Portuguese king John VI to flee to Brazil and French forces invaded Spain and occupied Madrid. The Peninsular War came to an end with Napoleon's abdication in 1814.

Pepin of Heristal (d. 714) Ruler of the Franks (687–714). He became mayor of the palace in 680 of the Frankish kingdom and ruled the kingdom. He was father of Charles Martel and grandfather of Charlemagne.

Pepin the Short (714?–768) First Carolingian king of the Franks (751–768). He had himself crowned as king of the Franks in 751. In return for papal consent to his crowning, he protected Rome from the Lombards and turned over conquered Italian territories to the pope in what is called the Donation of Pepin in 756. These lands formed the basis for the Papal States.

Pepys, Samuel (1633–1703) English administrator and famous diarist. His diary (1660–1669) provided a vivid account of the English Restoration period.

Peres, Shimon (b. 1923) Israeli Socialist politician, leader of the Labor party since 1977, alternated as prime minister with Yitzhak Shamir (*See* page 11-113) from 1984 to 1989. Named prime minister in 1992, but was replaced by Yitzhak Rabin (*see* page 11-103).

Perestroika *See* Government section, page 7-18.

Pérez de Cuéllar, Javier (b. 1920) Peruvian diplomat, U.N. Secretary-General from 1982 to 1991. He oversaw the end of the Iran-Iraq War in 1988 and independence for Namibia in 1989. He also led U.N. actions against Iraqi invasion of Kuwait (*See* **Persian Gulf War**) and obtained release of Western hostages held in Lebanon.

Pergamum Ancient city in northern Asia Minor, the capital of the kingdom of Mysia, and one of the greatest cultural centers of the Hellenistic civilization.

Pericles (495–429 B.C.) Athenian statesman and general. Pericles became the leader of Athens, he ended the war with Persia in 448 B.C., asserted Athenian domination over member states of the Delian League, and arranged a truce with Sparta in 445 B.C. In this period of peace Pericles strengthened the Athenian navy, instituted reforms that

strengthened the Athenian democracy, patronized the arts, and embarked on a great program of building that glorified Athens.

Perón, Juan Domingo (1895–1974) Argentine president (1946–1955, 1973 and 1974) and nationalist. During the early part of his presidency, he and his wife Eva were popular with the workers and were able to make many economic and political changes, in a reform program called the Perónísmo. His regime became increasingly totalitarian and anti-clerical, however, and he was deposed in 1955. He lived in Spain until his brief return to power in 1973.

Perón, María Estela Martínez de (Isabel Perón) (b. l931) President of Argentina (1974–1976). The second wife of Juan Perón, she was his vice president (1973 and 1974) and succeeded him after he died in office. She was ousted by a military coup.

Perón, María Eva Duarte de (Evita) (1919–1952) Argentine political leader, the wife of President Juan Perón. Popular with the masses, she wielded great political power during her husband's first term. She effected many reforms, including voting rights for women.

Persia Historic empire of ancient origins centered in modern Iran and at times extending well into southwest Asia. Persia began its rise to prominence in about the 7th century B.C. and by the 6th century B.C. had become the dominant power of the ancient near eastern world. After the 5th century B.C., the power and fortunes of the empire rose and fell. Persia was conquered variously, notably by the Macedonian Greeks and the Muslims, and its vast domains were greatly reduced. Persia nevertheless developed a distinctive culture that drew on Greek, Muslim, and other influences. After a long period of control by Arab Muslims and Turkic peoples, Persia again emerged in the 16th century as an independent empire.

Persian Gulf War The war began with Iraq's unprovoked invasion of Kuwait on August 2, 1990. A United Nations Security Council deadline to withdraw went unheeded. United States-led allied forces, carrying out U.N. directives, then liberated Iraqi-held Kuwait. Under the military command of U.S. general Norman Schwarzkopf, Iraqi forces were defeated in six weeks (January 17–February 28, 1991), with an estimated loss of 100,000 Iraqi soldiers, 480 allied troops, and many thousands of civilians in Iraq and Kuwait. *See also*, History of the United States section, page 10-61.

Persian Wars Series of military campaigns conducted by the Persians against the Greeks beginning in 499 B.C. The wars were sparked by revolt of the Ionian Greeks against Persian rule in 499. The cities of Athens and Eretria aided the Ionian Greeks, but the revolt was crushed in 494 by Persian king Darius. Darius then sent a large force to punish Athens and Eretria. The Persians took Macedon and Thrace in 492, but their fleet was badly damaged by storms and they were obliged to withdraw. A second expedition occupied Eretria, but while attempting to advance upon Athens, the Persians were defeated at Marathon in 490, by an Athenian force led by Miltiades. Darius gathered a massive third expeditionary force, but died in 486 before it could move against Greece. The expedition was conducted by his son and successor, Xerxes I, who landed in Greece in 480. The Persians were delayed at Thermopylae by a small Spartan force under Leonidas, and although the Persians took Athens, their navy was destroyed at Salamis in 480. Xerxes returned to Persia but left an army in Greece under Mardonius. The Greek victory over Mardonius at Plataea in 479, and destruction of the Persian fleet at Mycale that year marked the end of Persia's military campaigns against mainland Greece. After 479, sporadic fighting between the Greeks and Persians continued until a peace was concluded in 449. The wars between Persia and the Greek city-states resulted in the decline of Persian power and the rise of Greek power.

Pétain, Henri Philippe (1856–1951)　French marshal. Though a hero at Verdun in World War I, Pétain collaborated with the Nazis and became head of the French Vichy government during World War II.

Peter (d. 64? A.D.)　Apostle, pope, and saint. According to the Bible, Peter was a fisherman of Galilee who was originally known as Simon. In the Roman Catholic church, he is considered the first pope.

Peter I (Peter the Great) (1672–1725)　Russian czar (1682–1725). Peter's reign was dominated by his efforts to modernize and westernize Russia. He brought Russia into the European sphere, created the first Russian navy, took measures to control the nobility, improved the position of women, reduced the power of the clergy, and imported Western technology. Other events of his reign included Russo-Turkish Wars, and the Northern War with Sweden (1700–1721). He also created a new capital city, St. Petersburg.

Peter II (1648–1706)　King of Portugal (1683–1706). Peter concluded the treaty of Lisbon of 1683, by which Spain recognized Portugal's independence, and failed in his attempts to keep Portugal out of the War of Spanish Succession.

Peter II (1715–1730)　Czar of Russia (1727–1730). Only 11 at his accession, he was manipulated by the Dolgoruki family. They arranged the arrest of Catherine's former adviser, Menshikov, and moved the capital (1728) to Moscow.

Peter III (1717–1786)　King of Portugal (1777–1786). He was crowned with his niece, Maria I, and the two ruled jointly. Both were unfit for rule, however, and the government was run by others.

Peter III (1728–1762)　Czar of Russia in 1762. Soon after taking power, Peter removed Russia from the Seven Years' War and alienated both the church and the nobles. His wife thereupon conspired his overthrow on June 9, 1762 and succeeded him as Catherine II (the Great). Peter was killed a short time later.

Peter V (1837–1861)　King of Portugal (1853–1861). He ended slavery in Portuguese territories in 1858, promoted education and the beginnings of industrialization.

Peter the Hermit (1050–1115)　French religious leader. By his preaching, he won over thousands to the First Crusade and led one of the ill-equipped bands of zealous citizens to Byzantium. His follow-

ers were largely wiped out in the early stages of fighting in Asia Minor.

Petition of Right　English parliamentary act of 1628. A part of the power struggle between Charles I and Parliament, it was intended to stop abuses of power by Charles. It included an end to arbitrary arrest and imprisonment, the quartering of soldiers in civilian homes, taxation without parliamentary approval, and the use of martial law in peacetime. Charles agreed to it in June 1628 in return for money grants he needed to prosecute his foreign wars, then promptly violated it. Nevertheless, the petition is important in English constitutional law.

Petrarch, Francesco (Petrarca, Francesco) (1304–1374)　Italian Renaissance poet and scholar, Petrarch was one of the greatest scholars and lyric poets of his age and proved to be a major influence in spreading Greek ideals, humanism, and other elements of early Renaissance thought.

Pharaoh　Title of Egyptian kings. The title, meaning, "the great house," was bestowed on all kings of ancient Egypt from the time of the New Kingdom.

Philip I (1052–1108)　Capetian king of France (1060–1108). Throughout his reign Philip struggled to prevent the union of England and Normandy, which would overpower France.

Philip II (382–336 B.C.)　Macedonian king (359–336 B.C.), whose conquest of Greece laid the foundation for the great Macedonian Empire established by his son, Alexander the Great. From 357 B.C., Philip embarked on his program of expansion by war and alliances and defeated his last opponents in Greece (Athens and Thebes) in the Battle of Chaeronea in 338 B.C. He was killed while preparing to invade Persia.

Philip II (Philip Augustus) (1165–1223)　French king (1179–1223). Philip was the first powerful Capetian king and more than doubled his domains by conquering parts of Flanders and by taking English possessions on the Continent (Angevin domains). By his victory at the Battle of Bouvines in 1214, he established France as a major power. He also instituted administrative reforms and allowed prosecution of the Albigensians.

Philip II (1527–1598)　King of Spain (1156–1198) and Portugal (1580–1598, as Philip I). He succeeded his father, Holy Roman Emperor Charles V, to the Spanish throne and had earlier received from him the Spanish Netherlands, Milan, Naples, and Sicily. Philip married English Queen Mary I in 1554 and, after her death in 1558, was refused by Elizabeth I. Under Philip, Spain emerged as the dominant power in Italy after the Italian Wars and enjoyed victories against the Ottoman Turks. But Philip's efforts to defend Catholicism (sometimes combined with his political aims) led to trouble at home and abroad. Within the empire, persecutions by the Inquisition were increased, resulting in a revolt in the Spanish Netherlands. The revolt ended in the independence of the United Provinces. Philip's conflicts with Protestants in other countries brought war against England and the disastrous defeat of the Spanish Armada which resulted in the decline of Spain as a military power. He also involved Spain in the French Wars of Religion, which, combined with his other foreign wars, seriously weakened the finances of the empire.

Philip III (Philip the Bold) (1245–1285)   King of France (1270–1285). He died during the retreat from an unsuccessful attack on the Spanish kingdom of Aragon.

Philip III (1578–1621)   King of Spain (1598–1621), Philip also ruled Naples, Sicily, and Portugal (as Philip II), though he was content to let his favorites do the actual governing. The Moriscos were expelled during his reign, in 1609.

Philip IV (Philip the Fair) (1268–1314)   Capetian king of France (1285–1314). Philip's reign was marked by his successful struggle against the church. Early in his reign, Philip's need for money to prosecute foreign wars caused him to impose a tax on the clergy. Pope Boniface VIII opposed the tax in 1296 but was forced to concede. Philip next arrested a bishop and thereby renewed the dispute with Boniface. To resolve the matter, Philip convened (1302 and 1303) a council of nobles, clergy, and others (the first French States-General). When Boniface answered by threatening Philip with excommunication Philip had him arrested. Boniface died soon afterward and Philip secured the election of Pope Clement V. Thereafter, Clement cooperated with Philip, and moved the papacy to Avignon in 1309. *See* **Babylonian Captivity**.

Philip IV (1605–1665) Spanish king (1621–1665). His reign was marked by his willingness to let his ministers govern and by Spain's decline as a European power.

Philip V (1294–1322)   French king (1317–1322). Philip strengthened local militias and instituted other administrative reforms.

Phlip V (1683–1746)   Spanish king (1700–1746). First Bourbon king of Spain. His succession resulted in the War of Spanish Succession and loss of territories by the Peace of Utrecht. Philip's early attempts to retake lost territories in Italy failed when the Quadruple Alliance was formed against him. His later involvement in the wars of Polish Succession and Austrian Succession, however, won Naples, Sicily, Parma, and Piacenza for Spain.

Phlip VI (1293–1350)   French king (1328–1350). First king of the Valois line. His reign was marked by the beginning of the Hundred Years' War (1337–1453) and the outbreak of the Black Plague (1348 and 1349) in France.

Philippine Insurrection   An outgrowth of the Philippine Revolution and the Spanish-American War. Filipino leader Aguinaldo refused to accept the Treaty of Paris in 1898, by which Spain ceded the Philippines to the United States, and continued to fight for Filipino independence. Aguinaldo was captured in 1901 and the war ended a year later.

Philippine Revolution   Filipino war for independence from Spain (1896–1898). The war was led by Aguinaldo. After the outbreak of the Spanish-American War, Aguinaldo helped American Commodore Dewey occupy Manila in 1898 and established a provisional government. However, the Treaty of Paris in 1898 ceded the Philippines to the United States, and Aguinaldo led the Philippine Insurrection against American control.

Philosophes   Name given to the writers, philosophers, social critics, and political scientists of the Enlightenment who popularized the use of reason in human affairs.

Phoenicia   Ancient name applied to the narrow coastal region bordering the eastern Mediterranean roughly contiguous with modern Lebanon. The Phoenicians were related to the Canaanites and had established themselves as traders and sailors by the 25th century B.C. Early on they came under the influence of the Egyptians, with whom they traded. Although never a unified country, Phoenicia saw the rise of several important cities, notably Byblos, Sidon, Tyre and Tripoli. Phoenician traders founded settlements throughout the Mediterranean, such as on the islands of Rhodes and Cyprus and at Utica and Carthage. Later, Phoenicia gained independence as Egyptian power began to decline around the 12th century B.C. During this period Phoenician traders ranged widely through the Mediterranean. The Phoenicians were known for their metalwork, glasswork, woven cloth, and fabric dyed with a color known as Tyrian purple. Their greatest innovation, however, was their alphabet, which was adopted by the Greeks and eventually replaced the older system of hieroglyphic writing. Phoenicia came under Persian domination in the 6th century B.C. and was conquered by Alexander the Great in the 4th century B.C. Under the Macedonian rule much of the region was Hellenized and Phoenician culture underwent a decline. Phoenicia ceased to exist when the area was incorporated into the Roman province of Syria in 64 A.D.

Physiocrats   French intellectuals in the 1700s who developed the first complete system of economics. Led by François Quesnay, they emphasized that land was the ultimate source of all wealth, advocated a single tax on it, extolled free trade and laissez-faire, and stressed the importance of natural laws.

Piast   Polish dynasty. The Piasts were Poland's first dynasty, ruling from the 11th century to 1370, when they were replaced by the Jagiello line. Branches of the family, however, continued in Bohemia for several more centuries.

Picts   Ancient people of Scotland. They frequently invaded Roman-held Britain and established a kingdom in Scotland that flourished in the 8th century.

Pilsudski, Joseph (1867–1935)   Polish general and politician. A lifelong fighter against Russia for Polish independence, he declared Poland a republic in 1918 and became its first president. He dominated Polish politics, both in and out of office, into the 1930s.

Pinochet Ugarte, Augusto (b. 1915)   Became Chilean military leader and president in 1973. As commander-in-chief of the army he directed the successful coup against his predecessor, President Allende in 1973. He resigned in 1992.

Pisa, Council of   Roman Catholic church council. It was called in 1409 to heal the papal schism that had resulted in the naming of two rival popes, Gregory XII in Rome and Benedict XIII in Avignon. The council deposed both and elected a third pope, Alexander V. Far from ending the schism, the council complicated matters by establishing three papal claimants. The Council of

Constance (1414–1418) ultimately forced all three to resign and elected Martin V.

Pisistratus (605–527 B.C.) Tyrant of Athens (560–556, 554–527 B.C.). Pisistratus established Athenian hegemony in Ionia, sponsored extensive pubic building, passed important land laws, and commissioned a definitive edition of Homer.

Pitt, William (the Elder), 1st earl of Chatham (1708–1778) British statesman, and noted orator, called "the Great Commoner." His vigorous foreign policies during the Seven Years' War (1756–1763), led to French defeats in India, Africa, and North America, and to Britain's emergence as the world's greatest colonial power. He entered Parliament in 1735 and, called by George II to serve as secretary of state, he effectively became the prime minister (1756–1761) for most of the war in which Britain stripped France of most of its colonial empire.

Pitt, William (the Younger) (1759–1806) British prime minister (1783–1801, 1804–1806) Pitt led Britain through the French Revolutionary and early Napoleonic wars. As prime minister starting in 1783, he attempted to reorganize government finances in order to reduce the national debt, lowered customs duties, revised the British East India Company's role in India's government in 1784, created Upper and Lower Canada by his Constitution Act in 1791, and organized Britain (and various foreign coalitions) for war after the start of the French Revolutionary Wars. He returned in 1804 to form his second ministry after the outbreak of the Napoleonic Wars and organized the Third Coalition against Napoleon in 1805.

Pius VII (Barnaba Chiaramonti) (1740–1823) Pope. He signed the Concordat of 1801 with Napoleon and took part in his coronation in 1804. His later opposition to Napoleon led to French annexation of the Papal States in 1809. Pius excommunicated Napoleon but became the emperor's virtual prisoner.

Pius IX (Mastai-Ferretti, Giovanni Maria) (1792–1878) Pope (1846–1878). His reign was the longest in Catholic history. During his pontificate the Papal States and Rome passed to Italy in 1870.

Pizarro, Francisco (1476–1541) Spanish conqueror of the Incas of Peru. He accompanied Balboa when he discovered the Pacific Ocean in 1513.

Plain, the In the French Revolution, the amorphous, moderate party that occupied the lower seats in the National Convention chamber. It was distinguished from the more radical representatives of the Montagnard who occupied the higher seats.

Planck, Max (1858–1947) German physicist. He originated the modern quantum theory in 1900 which revolutionized modern physics.

Plantagenets The kings of England between 1154 and 1485. The name is thought to derive from the broom worn in the cap of the founder of the dynasty, Geoffrey of Anjou. Also known as Angevins.

Plato (427?–347 B.C.) Ancient Greek philosopher. One of the great philosophers of all time. He became a pupil of Socrates, whose ideas and use of the dialectic (Socratic method) in pursuing truth later played an important role in Plato's writings. After Socrates' trial and execution in 399 B.C., Plato left Athens. He returned to Athens in 388 B.C. and founded the Academy, an institution devoted to the investigation of scientific and philosophical truth, which flourished until the 6th century A.D., when it was closed by Justinian. Plato is known best for his writings, among them the *Republic, Apology, Symposium, Phaedo, Meno,* and the *Laws.* All of his writings take the form of dialogues, and many of them contain the character of Socrates as a leading figure. They are noted for their use of the dialectic, the technique of questioning all beliefs and assumptions in an attempt to come to a larger or more general truth or conception of reality. Plato's system of philosophy was based on the concept of a body of unchangeable and archetypal Ideas, of which the world's objects or appearances are mere approximations. The greatest of these Ideas was the Idea of the Good. The quest for the Good would ultimately lead humans to harmony with the state and the universe. Plato's writings had enormous influence in the growth of Western civilization, and his writings retain a position of eminence in both Western philosophy and Western literature. In addition, his writings provide the primary source of knowledge of Socrates' teachings. *See also* Philosophy section, page 19-19.

Plebeians (plebs) In Roman history, the general body of citizens, as opposed to the aristocratic patricians. Originally excluded from all officeholding, by 287 B.C. they had achieved virtual political equality, although social distinction continued to be maintained.

Plebiscite System of government by which questions are submitted to direct national vote instead of being determined by parliamentary representatives.

PLO *See* **Palestine Liberation Organization.**

Pogrom Attack on minority groups carried out with the connivance or toleration of the authorities. "Pogrom" is derived from the Russian word for riot or devastation. Pogroms against Jews began in Russia in 1881 following the assassination of Czar Alexander II and continued sporadically until the Russian Revolution.

Poincaré, Raymond (1860–1934) French president (1913–1920) and three times premier (1912 and 1913, 1922–1924, 1926–1929). A conservative nationalist, he ordered France's occupation of the Ruhr in 1923 after Germany failed to pay war reparations.

Polignac, Auguste Jules Armand Marie, prince de (1780–1847) French royalist statesman. He became the principal minister to King Charles X. His ordinances of 1830 dissolving the chamber of deputies and muzzling the press led to the July Revolution and Charles's downfall.

Polish Corridor Territory along the Baltic awarded to Poland by the Treaty of Versailles (1919). Since it divided East Prussia from the rest of Germany, it was the cause of great friction between Poland and Nazi Germany. The dispute led ultimately to the German invasion of Poland and the opening of World War II.

Politburo Soviet governmental body. The Politburo was the policy-making and administrative arm of the Communist party of the Soviet Union and therefore of all Soviet Russia. The first Politburo was created by the Bolsheviks shortly before the 1917 revolution, and included Lenin, Trotsky, and

Stalin. After the revolution the Politburo was dissolved, but it was reestablished in 1919. Stalin abolished it in 1952, replacing it with the Presidium. The Politburo was restored in 1966. It generally included 11 or 12 members, and its meetings were secret. President Gorbachev downgraded its power in 1991 and, with the breakup of the U.S.S.R. in December 1991, the Politburo ceased to exist.

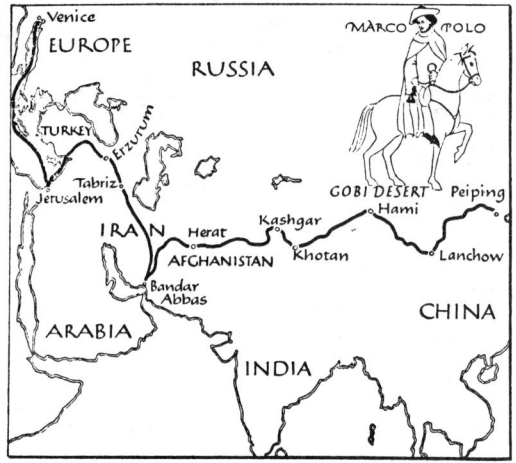

A map showing explorer Marco Polo's route on his journey from Venice to China.

Polo, Marco (1254?–1324?) Venetian traveler in China. His book, known in English as *The Travels of Marco Polo,* was one of the earliest and most important sources of Western knowledge of Asia. In 1271, he accompanied his father and uncle on a trip across central Asia. They reached Peking and the court of Mongol emperor Kublai Khan in 1275. Polo became a favorite of the emperor and performed missions for him. He returned to Europe via Persia in 1292 and arrived in Venice in 1295.

Polytheism Belief in many gods, as opposed to the monotheism of Christianity, Judaism, and Islam. In polytheism, each god tends to become identified with a function, such as fire, storm, death, etc., and each tends to become personified.

Pompeii Ancient Roman city. Situated at the foot of Mount Vesuvius near modern Naples, it was damaged by an earthquake in 63 A.D., and then completely covered over by the eruption of Vesuvius in 79 A.D. Rediscovered in 1748, it has become a major source of our knowledge of Roman civilization.

Pompey (106–48 B.C.) Roman general and statesman. Pompey gained important victories in Africa, Italy, Spain, and Gaul. In 70 B.C. he was elected consul along with Marcus Licinius Crassus. Together, Pompey, Crassus, and Caesar formed the First Triumvirate in 61 B.C. The rivalry between Caesar and Pompey intensified in 54 B.C. In 49 B.C., Caesar crossed the Rubicon, invaded Italy, and defeated Pompey at Pharsalus in 48 B.C. Pompey fled to Egypt, where he was murdered.

Pompidou, Georges Jean Raymond (1911–1974) French premier (1962–1968) and president of the Fifth Republic (1969–1974). A wartime protégé of de Gaulle, he later became prominent as both banker and politician, and helped draft the constitution of the Fifth Republic.

Ponce de Léon, Juan (1460–1521) Spanish explorer. He founded the oldest settlement in Puerto Rico (1508 and 1509), and discovered Florida in 1513.

Popular Front Political coalitions in Europe formed by liberals, moderates, Socialists, and Communists during the 1930s. These coalitions were aimed at blocking the then growing Fascist movement, and Popular Front coalitions gained control of governments in France and Spain during the 1930s.

Portsmouth, Treaty of Treaty concluded in 1905 between Russia and Japan at Portsmouth, New Hampshire, ending the Russo-Japanese War. By its terms Russia recognized Japan as the dominant power in Korea and ceded Port Arthur, the Liaotung Peninsula, and southern Sakhalin Island to Japan. Both powers agreed to restore Manchuria to China.

Potsdam Conference (Berlin Conference) Allied meeting in 1945 at Potsdam, near Berlin, after Germany's surrender in World War II. Present at the conference were American President Truman, Russian Premier Stalin, and Great Britain's prime ministers, first Churchill and later (from July 26, after he had succeeded Churchill as prime minister) Attlee. The resulting Potsdam Agreement outlawed Nazism in Germany, placed Germany's eastern provinces under the control of Russia and Poland, decentralized the German economy, set terms for reparations, and agreed to try war criminals.

Praetorians (Praetorian Guard) Special military force organized in 27 B.C. by Roman emperor Augustus to guard the emperor. As the only military force allowed in Rome, they acquired great power, even making and deposing emperors. Septimius Severus reorganized them in 193 A.D. and Constantine finally abolished them in 312 A.D.

Pragmatic Sanction Royal decree on issue of major importance to the state. The most famous of these sanctions was that issued by Holy Roman Emperor Charles VI in 1713. Lacking male heirs, Charles decreed that succession to the vast Hapsburg family domains would be continued through his daughter Maria Theresa. Charles worked tirelessly to secure acceptance of the sanction by European rulers. Nevertheless Charles's death in 1740 marked the beginning of the War of Spanish Succession over Maria Theresa's accession. The Treaty of Aix-la-Chapelle in 1748 ending the war confirmed the Pragmatic Sanction of 1713.

Praxiteles (370–330 B.C.) Ancient Greek sculptor. Considered one of the greatest classical artists.

Prefect (praefect) In ancient Roman government, a class of officers and magistrates to whom authority was delegated. The prefects of the city ruled it in the absence of the consuls, and the praetorian prefects, commanding the praetorians, sometimes functioned as virtual prime ministers of the emperors.

Prester John Legendary Christian ruler. According to 12th-century accounts originating with the crusaders, Prester John ruled a vast Christian land first thought to be in Asia and later in Africa.

Pretoria Convention Agreement in 1881 between Britain and the Transvaal, amid the continuing conflict with the Boers. The agreement granted the Transvaal self-government subject to British sovereignty and control over foreign relations. It did not last.

Pretorius, Andries Wilhelmus Jacobus (1799–1853) Boer leader. He was a leader of the Great Trek from the British-dominated Cape Colony to Natal. Continuing to oppose the British, he went into the Transvaal in 1848 and was instrumental in establishing Transvaal independence.

Pretorius, Martinus Wessel (1819–1901) Boer statesman. He was elected first president of the South African Republic (the Transvaal) and president of the adjoining Orange Free State in 1859 but was unable to unite the two.

Priestley, Joseph (1733–1804) English scientist and theologian. Priestley conducted important scientific investigations into the nature of electricity and discovered oxygen.

Prime minister (premier) The head of a parliamentary form of government who serves under the head of state (king or president). In Britain, the prime minister has broad powers, including responsibility for policy making, administrative functions, and appointment of Cabinet ministers and other lesser government officers. The prime minister, a member of Parliament and usually the leader of the majority party, is responsible to Parliament and must resign in the event the government cannot carry the parliamentary majority. Under other systems of parliamentary government, the president (as head of state) is invested with the real responsibility of governing and the prime minister has only minor functions.

Primo de Rivera, Miguel (1879–1930) Spanish general and dictator. After a successful coup d'état in 1923, he became the virtual military dictator of Spain (1923–1930). His authoritarian regime provoked widespread opposition and he was forced to resign.

Primogeniture In inheritance law, the right of the eldest son to inherit exclusively. In England and Western Europe primogeniture prevented the division of estates and enhanced the power of the landed aristocracy.

Prince Edward Island A Maritime Province of Canada. The island was discovered in 1534 by Jacques Cartier. First settled by the French in the early 18th century, it was ceded to the British in the Treaty of Paris in 1763. It became a province in 1769, and entered the Canadian confederation in 1873.

Princip, Gavrilo A Serbian nationalist who assassinated Archduke Francis Ferdinand, the heir to the Austrian throne, in Sarajevo on June 28, 1914. This was the spark that ignited World War I.

Principality of Antioch One of the most powerful Crusader States (11th–13th centuries). Crusaders conquered the city of Antioch and surrounding territory (located in what is now southeastern Turkey) from the Muslims in 1098 during the First Crusade. It survived until the Mameluke conquest in 1268.

Privateering The use of specially commissioned, privately operated ships by belligerents to prey upon enemy shipping in time of war. From the 13th century, privateering was used to supplement a country's naval strength. The heyday of privateer-

ing came in the 16th–17th centuries, when such English privateers as J. Hawkins and F. Drake pursued Spanish shipping and the French government commissioned many privateers to prey on English shipping.

Privy Council In English history, the council of the king's principal advisers. It held executive, legislative, and judicial powers during its heyday. It diminished in importance with the decline of the king's actual political power.

Progressive Conservative party (Conservative party) Major Canadian political party. Like its Liberal party counterpart, it is a broad-based coalition rather than an ideologically oriented party. It held power briefly from 1957–1963.

Proletariat The working class, without property and living entirely from the sale of their labor. In Marxist theory, the proletariat is believed to be created by the capitalist system. Marxists further hold that the proletariat would, by historical necessity, eventually resort to revolution to seize power from the capitalists.

Protagoras (480–410 B.C.) Greek Sophist philosopher, adversary of Socrates. He promoted the slogan "Man is the measure of all things," i.e., that truth is subjective and relative to the individual.

Protectionism System of protecting a nation's domestic industry by levying duty (tariffs) upon competing products imported from abroad. These duties increase the price of the imported goods by comparison with the domestically produced article.

Protectorate In international relations, an arrangement whereby a stronger state undertakes to protect a weaker state, called a protectorate. Theoretically, the protectorate retains its sovereignty, unlike a colony.

Protectorate English government established (1653–1659) after the English Civil War and the execution of Charles I. In 1649 England was declared a commonwealth under the rule of the Rump Parliament, although Oliver Cromwell, who was controlling the army, wielded the real power. Cromwell dissolved the Rump Parliament in 1653 and established the Nominated, or Barebones, Parliament. After its failure he accepted the Instrument of Government, by which he became, in 1653, lord protector of the commonwealth of England, Scotland, and Ireland. From then until his death Cromwell was virtual dictator in England. *See* **Cromwell, Oliver.**

Protestantism One of three main branches of Christianity, with Roman Catholicism and Eastern Orthodoxy. Protestantism grew out of the Reformation in the 16th century, and there are numerous Protestant churches that grew out of the reform movement. The two main branches are Lutheranism and Calvinism. The characteristic doctrine of the original Protestant movement was justification by faith alone, not by church dispensations or by good works. Renewed emphasis on the teachings of the Bible and a general movement away from liturgy were also characteristic. In the years after the start of the Reformation, new Protestant churches sprang up and existing ones split into diverse sects.

Proudhon, Pierre Joseph (1809–1865) French Socialist and theorist. His theory of "mutualism," in which social groups would bargain within the framework of agreed principles, greatly influenced later radical movements.

Provisional government   Russian government formed after the fall of the czar in March 1917. Headed by Kerensky, it governed Russia until the October Revolution.

Ptolemy (Claudius Ptolemaeus) (2nd century A.D.) Ancient Alexandrian astronomer, mathematician, and geographer. He formulated the geocentric Ptolemaic system.

Ptolemy I (d. 283 B.C.) Egyptian king (305–285 B.C.).   A Macedonian, Ptolemy was one of Alexander the Great's most successful generals. After Alexander's death in 323 B.C., he quarreled with other generals over the empire's division, and became satrap of Egypt. He engaged in warfare to protect and expand his holdings. He named himself Egypt's king in 305 B.C. and established Alexandria as a center of culture and commerce, founded its famed library, planned Egypt's government, and began the Ptolemaic dynasty.

Punic Wars   Three major wars between Rome and Carthage resulting in the subjugation of Carthage and Rome's acquisition of territories beyond the Italian peninsula in the western Mediterranean. In the First Punic War (264–241 B.C.), fought for control of Sicily, the Romans defeated Carthage by sea power. In the Second (218–201 B.C.), Hannibal of Carthage achieved the extraordinary military feat of crossing the Alps and reaching the Po Valley with 30,000 troops. He won every battle until, at last, he was defeated at the battle of Zama. After the Third Punic War (149–146 B.C.), Rome captured and destroyed Carthage, burning the city to the ground, selling its people into slavery, and plowing the land with salt in order to destroy its fertility. During these three wars Rome annexed Sicily, Corsica, Sardinia, Spain, and parts of North Africa.

Purge Trials   Series of political trials (1936–1938) in the Soviet Union. They were held to eliminate opponents or potential rivals to the rule of Stalin. The trials continued the process by which Stalin virtually swept away all the old Bolshevik leaders and consolidated his power over every facet of Soviet life, including the Communist party.

Pythagoras (582–507 B.C.)   Greek philosopher and mathematician. Pythagoras and his school taught that all relationships could be expressed in numbers, and that numbers were the true essence of life. Many theories developed by the Pythagoreans are still employed today in geometry. *See also* Philosophy section, page 19-19.

Pytheas (4th century B.C.)   Greek navigator and geographer who explored the western coastline of Europe, who was the first Greek to visit the British Isles, and who may have sailed as far north as Iceland.

Pythian Games   Ancient Greek games. They originally featured musical contests in honor of Apollo at Delphi; athletic contests were added in imitation of the Olympic Games after 582 B.C.

Q **Qaddafi, Muammar al-** (b. 1942) Radical Arab nationalist, Libyan revolutionist, and dictator since 1969. He led the military coup in 1969 to overthrow King Idris I, and set himself up as ruler of Libya. His reign has been marked by anti-Western policies, the closing of American bases in Libya, government confiscation of Italian and Jewish property, nationalization of foreign-owned oil facilities, a proposed union with Egypt in 1973, and then border wars with Egypt in 1977. Qaddafi's support for Arab terrorist groups, such as the PLO (Palestine Liberation Organization), and Muslim revolutionaries, such as Ayatollah Khomeini, has led to the growing isolation of Libya. In 1987 U.S. President Reagan ordered aircraft raids on Tripoli and Benghazi in retaliation for alleged Libyan ties to terrorist attacks. The United Nations imposed limited sanctions in 1992 after Libyan agents were linked to the 1988 Pan Am flight 103 explosion over Lockerbie, Scotland.

Quadruple Alliance   1. Alliance in 1718 formed by Austria, France, Great Britain, and The Netherlands against Spain. The alliance was established after Spanish king Philip V attempted to overturn the terms of the Peace of Utrecht by seizing Sardinia and Sicily. 2. Alliance formed in 1815 by Austria, Great Britain, Prussia, and Russia after their defeat of Napoleon. The alliance was made to enforce the conditions of the Treaty of Paris of 1815 and to prevent further French military ventures. In 1818 France was admitted to the alliance.

Quebec   Canadian province. First discovered and explored by J. Cartier, and later by S. de Champlain. The region, named New France, became a French colony in 1663. The British gained control of it by the Treaty of Paris of 1763. In 1791, the area now known as Ontario was made a separate colony called Upper Canada, and Quebec became known as Lower Canada. Although Quebec and Ontario were subsequently reunited in 1841, they entered the confederation of Canada as separate provinces in 1867.

Quebec Act   British parliamentary law of 1774 establishing a permanent government for Canada. The act replaced the temporary administration set up by the Proclamation of 1763, extended Quebec's territory south to the Ohio River, and provided for religious tolerance of Roman Catholics.

Quebec Campaign   Unsuccessful military expedition (1775 and 1776) by the American colonials against Canada during the American Revolution. Two American contingents were sent against Canada with the ultimate goal of taking Quebec. The force under General B. Montgomery first captured Montreal in 1775. It later joined a force under Colonel Arnold in an unsuccessful attack on strongly fortified Quebec on December 31, 1775.

Quebec Conference   1. Meeting in Quebec, Canada in 1864 that laid the foundations for an independent dominion of Canada. Thirty-three delegates from the various provinces of British North America drew up a draft constitution called the Quebec Resolutions, or Seventy-two Resolutions. This formed the basis of the 1867 British North America Act creating modern independent Canada. 2. Conference in 1943 attended by American President Roosevelt, British Prime Minister Churchill, Canadian Prime Minister Mackenzie King, and Chinese Foreign Minister Soong. The conference formulated tentative plans for Allied landings in Europe. 3. Meeting between American President Roosevelt and

British Prime Minister Churchill in 1944 at which strategy for defeating Germany was discussed. It was decided to advance against Germany on two fronts rather than make a single effort to take Berlin.

Quesnay, François (1694–1774) French economist and physician. A pioneer in the development of economic theory, he was the leader of the physiocrats.

Quetzalcoatl Ancient Mexican god. Represented as a feathered serpent, he was involved in the cult of human sacrifice. Revered as a god who gave the people corn, weaving, and the calendar, he figured in Aztec and Toltec cultures.

Quisling, Vidkun (1887–1945) Norwegian puppet prime minister (1940–1945). A Fascist, he served as prime minister under German occupation of Norway during World War II. His name became a byword for "traitor."

R **Ra** (Re) Egyptian god of the sun and creation. Depicted as sailing across the sky in a celestial barge, he fought the powers of darkness each night.

Rabelais, François (1490–1553) French Renaissance humanist and satirist. A learned monk and physician, he celebrated Renaissance ideals in his great satirical work *Gargantua and Pantagruel.*

Rabin, Yitzhak (b. 1922) Prime minister of Israel and leader of the Labor party 1974–1977. Succeeded Shimon Peres (*see* page 11-96) in 1992 and fulfilled his promise to talk directly with Palestinian Arabs.

Racine, Jean Baptiste (1639–1699) French poet and dramatist, considered a master of French classical tragedy.

Raffles, Sir Thomas Stamford (1781–1826) British colonial administrator. He was one of the founders of Britain's empire in the Far East and acquired Singapore for Britain in 1819.

Rafsanjani, Hojatoleslam Ali Akbar Hashemi (b. 1934) Iranian cleric and politician. Speaker of Iranian Parliament 1980, he became president in 1989. With the death of Ayatollah Khomeini (*see* page 11-64), he became the most powerful figure in Iran. He has attempted to moderate Iran's strident anti-Western stance.

Raj Indian term most commonly used to refer to the British from 1858–1947.

Rajputs People of northwest India who traditionally considered themselves members of the Hindu warrior class. The Rajputs were organized in a clan system and were powerful from the 7th century to the early 17th century, when they became subjects of the Moguls. They rose again briefly in the 18th century after the fall of the Moguls, only to be subjugated by the Marathas and then the British.

Raleigh, Sir Walter (Ralegh) (1552?–1618) English courtier, adventurer, and poet. A favorite of Elizabeth I, he organized the ill-fated Roanoke Colony and was involved in other unsuccessful colonizing ventures.

Ramakrishna (1836–1886) Indian religious seer and mystic, founder of worldwide religious movement based on his belief in a universal religion.

Ram Mohan Roy (Ray, Rammohan) (1774–1833) Indian thinker and reformer. He advocated

a reaffirmation of Hindu culture but supported some aspects of Western culture, notably education. He was instrumental in abolishing suttee, or sacrifice of a widow on her husband's funeral pyre.

Rama Tiboti (Ramathibodi I) (1312–1369) Thai warrior-king and lawgiver. In 1350, he established a unified Thai state (Siam), which his descendants, the Ayutthaya dynasty, ruled until 1767. He also drafted a legal code that was not changed significantly until the 19th century.

Ramayana With the *Mahabharata,* one of the two most important Hindu Sanskrit texts. Written in 300 B.C. it chronicles the life of Rama, the ideal man and king.

Ramses II (Rameses II) (d. 1237 B.C.) Egyptian pharaoh (1304–1237 B.C.), named "the Great." His reign was marked by a period of great prosperity, the building of temples at Karnak, Luxor, and Abu Simbel, and increased slavery (possibly including the Hebrews).

Ramses III (Rameses III) (d. 1167 B.C.) Egyptian pharaoh (1198–1167 B.C.) He defended Egypt against invaders from Libya and the "sea peoples," including the original Philistines then colonizing Palestine.

Ranjit Singh (Runjeet Singh) (1780–1839) Maharaja of the Punjab. Making himself the principal leader of the Sikhs (from 1801), he founded the Sikh kingdom by conquering Afghan and Pathan territories in northern India.

Rasputin, Grigori Yefimovich (1872–1916) Russian peasant mystic who had great influence in the court of Czar Nicholas II. He gained the favor of Czarina Alexandra because he was able to relieve the suffering of her hemophiliac son, Alexis. When Nicholas went to the front during World War I, Rasputin's corrupt influence hastened the collapse of the czarist government, leading to the Russian Revolution of 1917. A group of noblemen plotted his assassination.

Rathenau, Walter (1867–1922) German statesman and industrialist. He organized the German economy both for World War I and for reparation payments afterward and ended the postwar German isolation by helping to engineer the Treaty of Rapallo.

Reciprocity The principle or policy by which two or more nations grant each other equal treatment, usually in international trade, which generally results in a mutual lowering of import duties.

Reconquista Name for the drive by Spanish Christians to recapture the Iberian peninsula from the Muslims. During the Muslim invasions of the early 8th century Christians were only able to maintain control over small kingdoms in northern Spain. By the 11th century, Spanish Christians began an active campaign to expand these domains and retake the peninsula. They had largely succeeded by the 13th century. The last Muslim stronghold Granada, was conquered by King Ferdinand in 1492.

Reforma, la Period in Mexican history (1854–1876) characterized by liberal reforms directed mainly against special privileges of the army and the church. It began with announcement of the liberals' Plan of Ayutla in 1854 and the ouster of the dictator Santa Anna in 1855. There followed a succession of liberal presidents (most notably Juárez), revolts and civil wars, and the brief restoration of the monarchy under Maximilian. Reform legislation enacted included abolishing church and military courts, forcing the sale of church-owned secular lands, a liberal constitution curtailing military and church power, and confiscation of church lands.

Reformation Religious reform movement that arose in the 16th century. It began as a reaction to practices within the Roman Catholic church that some held to be either unsupported by scriptural teaching or simply corrupt and abusive usurpations of authority. The movement ultimately gave rise to the various Protestant churches. Although earlier movements for church reform had arisen in Europe, the Reformation dates from 1517, when Martin Luther issued his Ninety-five Theses. Other religious dissidents, such as John Calvin, also spread the movement for reform, which was fueled by religious zeal, the new spirit of Renaissance Humanism, and social changes resulting from the growth of a prospering mercantile class.

Reform Bills Series of laws that enlarged the British electorate and removed voting inequities. A bill in 1832 increased the representation of large towns proportionally and increased the electorate 50 percent by eliminating certain voter qualifications. The 1856 act again redistributed parliamentary seats according to population and again doubled the body of eligible voters. The bill in 1884 enabled nearly all males to vote. In 1918, suffrage was extended to all over the age of 30, regardless of sex, and the voting age was lowered to 21 in 1928.

Reform movement of 1898 Short-lived reform movement in China during the reign of Emperor Kuang Hsu. China's defeat in the Sino-Japanese Wars (1894 and 1895) and the attempts by Western powers to exploit China gave rise to sentiment for Westernizing Chinese culture. Scholar and reformer K'ang Yu-wei gained the emperor's confidence and persuaded him to issue sweeping reforms of traditional Chinese society. The movement was cut short, however, by a coup led by Empress Dowager Tzu Hsi.

Regency British historical and cultural period (1811–1820). It spanned the regency of George, prince of Wales, who came to power as regent after his father, George III, went insane. It was marked by the end of the Napoleonic Wars, dissolute courtly life, interest in antiquity and Oriental artifacts, and a flowering of the arts. Romantic literature, including the work of Keats, Byron, Shelley, and Sir Walter Scott, flourished in this period, which also saw the development of distinctive styles in the decorative arts and architecture.

Regulating Act British parliamentary legislation passed in 1773 reorganizing the British East India Company. Its object was to improve the government of Bengali domains, and it represented the first British government intervention in the company's administration of India. The British government took over complete administrative control by 1858.

Reichstag Legislative assemblies of the Holy Roman Empire and German successor states. The Holy Roman emperor began to meet with city representatives in 1100. The meetings became formal assemblies after 1250 and exerted legislative power until 1648, playing only a ceremonial role after that date. An elected Reichstag was established by the German Empire (1871–1918), and was continued under the Weimar Republic between 1919 and 1933. The Reichstag surrendered its power to Hitler by the Enabling Act in 1933, and was reduced to ceremonial functions during the Third Reich. It was replaced after World War II by the Bundestag in West Germany.

Reichstag Fire The burning of the Reichstag building in Berlin on the night of February 27, 1933. Hitler blamed the fire on the Communists, however, and used the incident to justify his assumption of dictatorial powers.

Reign of Terror Period during the French Revolution. Instituted in September 1793, and directed by the Committee of Public Safety, the Terror was intended to crush all opposition to the revolution. The period also saw the rise of Robespierre as virtual dictator of France, enactment of the laws of Maximum (establishing price controls and forbidding hoarding), institution of universal conscription and reorganization of the army. Toward the end of the Terror, even allies of Robespierre (including followers of Hébert and Danton) fell victim to the guillotine. Finally, popular reaction against the Terror resulted in the overthrow of Robespierre in 1794 and the subsequent Thermidorean reaction.

Religion, Wars of Series of civil wars (1562–1598) in France between the Catholics, led by the powerful Guise family, and the French Protestants, known as Huguenots. The civil wars revolved around religious differences but were further complicated by struggles among the nobility for political power. The wars culminated in the accession of the Huguenot leader, Henry of Navarre (as Henry IV), to the French throne in 1589. In an attempt to resolve the continuing struggle, he converted to Catholicism in 1593 and finally ended the wars by the Edict of Nantes in 1598, granting religious toleration to the Protestants.

Remus Legendary co-founder of Rome (traditionally 753 B.C.). Remus and his twin brother, Romulus, founded the town that became Rome.

Renaissance Transition period in Europe from medieval to modern culture. The Renaissance is generally viewed as a rebirth or reawakening of learning and the arts, which began in Italy in the 1300s and then spread throughout Europe. The Renaissance period may be broadly divided into the Italian Renaissance of the 1300s and 1400s and the Northern Renaissance (centers outside Italy) of the 1400s and 1500s. It may also be divided into Early (1400–1490), High (1490–1520), and Late (1520–1600) periods, though these dates may vary. Central to the Renaissance period was the rise of Humanism, a movement placing new emphasis on individuals and on the temporal (as opposed to secular) world about them. Humans became "the measure of all things" and the individual accomplished in a wide variety of pursuits, became a Renaissance ideal. The intellectual "rebirth" of the Renaissance had wide ramifications. There was a sudden emphasis on education, particularly study of the Greek and Roman classics. In literature and philosophy, it was people and the world about them that became the center of attention. In the arts, interest shifted from idealized religious themes to more worldly conceptions, and advances were made in areas of technical concern (perspective, use of color, study of human anatomy). In architecture, Renaissance designers adapted earlier classical forms and medieval Gothic styles were gradually abandoned. Advances in science during the Renaissance helped prepare the way for the 17th-century revolution in science. The Renaissance in Italy began in Florence, and thereafter spread to Venice, Rome, and other cities. The great cultural flowering in Italy, as elsewhere, was aided by wealthy patrons.

Reparations   Payments required of a defeated nation for war damages, especially those imposed on Germany after World War I and World War II.

Republic   Form of government in which power is vested in officers who represent the public and who govern in accordance with established laws for the sake of the common good. The government of the United States is a federal republic.

Resistance   Underground political paramilitary forces that grew inside the countries occupied by Germany during World War II.

Restoration   1. Period in English history (1660–1688) that included the reigns of Charles II and James II. It began with the restoration of the monarchy under Charles after the experiment in republican government failed (*see* **Protectorate**). Under James II, anti-Catholic sentiment and reaction against his absolutism quickly brought about the Glorious Revolution of 1688 and the end of the Restoration period. 2. Period in French history (1814–1830) that began with Napoleon's fall from power and restoration of the Bourbon monarchs. Largely through the efforts of Talleyrand, Louis XVIII assumed power after Napoleon's first abdication in 1814, in what is called the First Restoration. His rule was interrupted by Napoleon's Hundred Days, however, and the Second Restoration began after Napoleon's second abdication in 1815. The Restoration period included the reigns of Louis and his successor, Charles X. It was marked by France's recovery from its defeat under Napoleon and growing friction between the royalist and republican factions. The Restoration was ended in 1830 when these tensions culminated in the July Revolution.

Revolution   Fundamental change in political institutions, leadership, and social structure, often accompanied by violence. Classic examples are the American, French, Russian, and Chinese revolutions.

Revolutions of 1848   Revolutions in Europe sparked by the French February Revolution of 1848, which overthrew French king Louis Philippe. Soon after the February Revolution, uprisings in Vienna, Prague, Venice, and other cities marked the beginning of a general uprising of national groups within the control of Hapsburg, Austria. Austrian emperor Ferdinand was forced to make constitutional concessions in Austria, Hungary, and Bohemia, and was faced with a rising movement for independence in Italy. The revolutions led to Ferdinand's abdication in December 1848 and the accession of his nephew as Francis Joseph I. The uprisings in Bohemia and Italy began to fail in 1848. In 1849, Francis Joseph,

with Russian aid, crushed the revolution in Hungary and forced many of its leaders, including Kossuth, to flee. In Germany the uprisings led to establishment of the liberal Frankfurt Parliament, which sought to reform the German Confederation into a unified state. The Parliament, after much deliberation, adopted a new constitution in 1849 and offered the crown to Prussian king Frederick William IV, who declined.

Rhee, Syngman (1875–1965)   First president of South Korea (1948–1960). He ruled South Korea as a popular but authoritarian president, until forced from office on election-rigging charges.

Rhodes, Cecil John (1853–1902)   British South African statesman and financier. He worked for the extension and consolidation of southern African territories under British domination.

Ribbentrop, Joachim von (1893–1946)   German diplomat and Nazi foreign minister (1938–1945). He concluded the Russo-German nonaggression pact of 1939, which paved the way for Hitler's attack on Poland (the immediate cause of World War II).

Ricci, Matteo (1552–1610)   Italian Jesuit missionary in China. By mastering the Chinese language and classics, he was able to interpret Christianity and the West for the Chinese literati and thus introduced them to European culture.

Richard I (Richard Coeur de Lion) (Richard the Lion-Hearted) (1157–1199)   King of England (1189–1199). He joined his brothers in a rebellion (1173 and 1174) against their father, Henry II, and defeated him in another clash in 1189. He joined Philip II of France on the Third Crusade in 1190, shortly after becoming king. He conquered Cyprus and with Philip took Acre in 1191, but was forced into a treaty with Saladin after failing to take Jerusalem. On his way back to England he was captured in Austria and held for ransom until 1194 by Holy Roman emperor Henry VI. He then returned to England, put down a revolt by his brother John, and spent the remainder of his reign fighting Philip II in France.

Richard II (1367–1400)   King of England (1377–1399). Conflicts with his barons eventually led to his overthrow by his cousin, Bolingbroke, duke of Lancaster, who became Henry IV. He was the son of Edward the Black Prince.

Richard III (1452–1485)   Last Yorkist king of England (1483–1485). He took the throne from his brother, Edward IV, eliminating the latter's young sons, until he was defeated and killed in the Battle of Bosworth Field that ended the Wars of the Roses.

Richelieu, Armand Jean du Plessis, duc de (1585–1642)   French cardinal and chief minister (1624–1642) to Louis XIII. His domestic policy aimed at weakening the power of the nobility and Huguenots to establish the central absolute authority of the monarchy. His foreign policy sought to end Hapsburg power. He formed alliances with Protestants during the Thirty Years' War (1618–1648) and finally brought France into it in 1635 against the Hapsburg powers. The wars wrecked French finances but marked the country's ascendancy as a major power.

Riel's rebellions   Two brief revolts in western Canada against the government. Both were led by

Louis Riel. In 1869 and 1870, Riel organized the Metis (half European, half Indian) of the Red River area into a provisional government, in order to prevent Canada from taking over the land that until then had been administered by the Hudson's Bay Company. The government crushed the revolt, but gave Red River its own provincial government, and Riel led a second revolt (1884 and 1885) on behalf of the Metis of Saskatchewan, but was captured and hanged.

Risorgimento Italian nationalistic movement resulting in a unified Italian state in 1861. In the early 19th century, during the post-Napoleonic period in Europe, sentiment for unification of Italy, at that time divided and dominated by foreign powers, arose. The Carbonari, as well as other secret societies, and Mazzini's nationalistic movement (Young Italy) were formed and, by the mid-1800s, the unification movement had gained momentum.

Robert I (Robert the Bruce) (1274–1329) Scottish king (1306–1329) and hero of Scottish independence. Following a struggle for leadership of the Scottish nationalists, Robert was crowned king of Scotland in 1306 in defiance of the English. He was decisively defeated by the English at the Battle of Methven in 1306. He ultimately defeated the English at the famous Battle of Bannockburn. The English recognized Scottish independence by the Treaty of Northampton in 1328.

Robespierre, Maximilien François Marie Isidore de (1758–1794) French revolutionary. As a lawyer and head of the Jacobins, he was known as "the Incorruptible." He became a member of the National Convention. There, as a leader of the radical Montagnards, he played an important role in ousting the moderate Girondists in 1793 from power, and thus in altering the course of the revolution. He next joined and dominated the Committee of Public Safety and through it became the leading power behind the Reign of Terror, which he ultimately used to eliminate even his former allies. He was finally ousted in the coup of 9 Thermidor (July 27, 1794) and was tried and executed the following day.

Roentgen, Wilhelm Conrad (Röntgen) (1845–1923) German physicist. He discovered X rays in 1895.

Röhm, Ernst (Roehmm, Ernst) (1887–1934) German National Socialist leader. An early Nazi party member and organizer of the storm troops, he was a potential rival to Hitler. He was executed without trial on Hitler's orders during the Blood Purge.

Rollo (Rou) (Hrolf) (860–932) Norman chieftain, founder of the duchy of Normandy. He invaded and conquered the land around the mouth of the Seine (now in France). He was granted rule over it in 911 by French king Charles III in return for accepting vassalage and baptism.

Roman Catholic church One of the three major branches of Christianity (with Protestant and Orthodox Eastern churches). It is a worldwide union of churches recognizing the primacy of Rome. The authority of the popes is traditionally believed to derive from the continuous line of popes (bishops of Rome) succeeding St. Peter. The church claims to be the one true apostolic Christian church, maintaining its supremacy in doctrinal questions that created other branches of Christianity. The early years of the church, following the crucifixion of Jesus Christ, were marked by the rapid spread of Christianity, persecution and then toleration by the Romans, the growing isolation of Rome and the Western church from the Eastern church (centered at Constantinople) after the fall of the Western Roman Empire in 476 A.D., and finally the alliances between the popes at Rome and the kings of Europe from the 8th century. In the following centuries of the Middle Ages, the church became a powerful force in European politics and culture. For a time popes were able to command the submission of the great European monarchs. The struggle between the popes and the Holy Roman emperors, however, gradually eroded that power and, by the 15th and 16th centuries papal power was overshadowed by the absolutist monarchs in Europe. Meanwhile the split between the Western and Eastern halves of the Christian world continued to widen, until finally the Schism of 1054 resulted in a complete break and formation of the Orthodox Eastern church. A second great division of the Christian world occurred in the 16th century. The Protestant Reformation resulted in the creation of a host of new Christian sects and forced the Roman Catholic church to institute the sweeping reforms of the Catholic Reformation.

Roman Empire Name of the Roman state after Augustus assumed imperial powers in 27 B.C. and thus formally ended the republic. The empire was later divided into the Western Roman Empire and Eastern Roman Empire in 286 A.D. by Diocletian. Through much of the subsequent period it was governed by co-emperors of the East and West. The death of Theodosius I marked the beginning of the permanent division in 395 A.D. of the empire. The Western Roman Empire, unable to withstand the barbarian invasions ceased to exist in 476 A.D. with the death of Emperor Romulus Augustus. The Eastern Roman Empire survived as the Byzantine Empire, and thus the Carolingian Empire in the 8th century is sometimes regarded as the successor state to the Western Roman Empire.

Romanesque Style of medieval art and architecture that reached its height in the 11th and 12th centuries. In architecture it was characterized by the use of rounded arches and massive walls. It gave way to the Gothic style. The Romanesque movement in art, centered in France, represented a fusion of Roman, Carolingian, Byzantine, Teutonic, and other influences and was marked by its concern for powerful imagery and grand conception.

Romanov Russian royal dynasty. The Romanovs ruled Russia from 1613 until the revolutions of 1917. They traced their royal lineage to Anastasia Romanovna, first wife of Ivan the Terrible. They came to power after the Time of Troubles when Michael Romanov became czar. The line ended during the Russian Revolution with the assassinations of Nicholas II and his family.

Roman Republic Name of the ancient Roman state from the time the Romans gained independence in 509 B.C. from the Etruscan Tarquin kings to the accession of Augustus as Roman emperor in 27 B.C.

EXHIBIT 11.5
Roman Emperors

27 B.C.–14 A.D.	Augustus		251–253	Gallus
14–37	Tiberius		253	Aemilian
37–41	Caligula		253–259	Valerian
41–54	Claudius		259–268	Gallienus
54–68	Nero		268–270	Claudius II Gothicus
68–69	Galba		270	Quintillus
69	Otho		270–275	Aurelian
69	Vitellius		275–276	Tacitus
69–79	Vespasian		276	Florian
79–81	Titus		276–282	Probus
81–96	Domitian		282–283	Carus
96–98	Nerva		283–285	Carinus
98–117	Trajan		283–284	Numerian
117–138	Hadrian		284–305	Diocletian
138–161	Antoninus Pius		286–305; 306–308	Maximian
161–180	Marcus Aurelius			
161–169	Lucius Verus		305–306	Constantius I Chlorus
180–192	Commodus		305–311	Galerius
193	Pertinax		306–307	Severus
193	Didius Julianus		306–312	Maxentius
193–211	Septimius Severus		308–313	Maximinus Daia
209–211	Geta		311–324	Licinius
211–217	Caracalla		331–337	Constantine I the Great
217–218	Macrinus		337–340	Constantine II
218–222	Heliogabalus (Elagabalus)		337–350	Constans
222–235	Alexander Severus		337–361	Constantius II
235–238	Maximinus Thrax		361–363	Julian the Apostate
238	Gordian I Africanus		363–364	Jovian
238	Gordian II		364–375	Valentinian I (in the West)
238	Balbinus		364–378	Valens (in the East)
238	Pupienus Maximus		375–383	Gratian (in the West)
238–244	Gordian III Pius		375–392	Valentinian II (in the West)
244–249	Phillip the Arab		379–395	Theodosius I the Great
249–251	Decius		383–388	Magnus Maximus
251	Hostilian		392–394	Eugenius

Roman Emperors In West

395–423	Honorius
421	Constantius III
423–425	Johannes
425–455	Valentinian III
455	Petronius Maximus
455–456	Avitus
457–461	Majorian
461–465	Libius Severus
467–472	Anthemius
472	Olybrius
473	Glycerius
473–475	Julius Nepos
475–476	Romulus Augustulus

Roman Emperors In East

395–408	Arcadius
408–450	Theodosius II
450–457	Marcian
457–473	Leo I
473–474	Leo II
474–491	Zeno

Roman Senate   Roman governmental body. Formed in the 6th century B.C. as an advisory council appointed by the kings of Rome, it evolved into a powerful legislative body that lasted until the end of the Roman Empire. Originally composed of patricians, the Senate gradually came to include wealthy plebeians. It wielded great power in financial, administrative, military, and religious affairs until the end of the 2nd century B.C., when corruption and the rise of two antagonistic political factions within the Senate weakened its ability to govern. The Senate lost much of its power after the assassination of Julius Caesar in 44 B.C.

Romanticism   Movement in literature and the arts that arose in the 18th and 19th centuries as a reaction to the extreme rationalism of the Enlightenment and the strictures of classicism in the arts. The movement began in Germany and England in the late 18th century and thereafter spread to other countries. Its aims were various and often conflicting, but generally were characterized by opposition to rationalism and social conventions; belief in the natural individual and natural beauty, and in the primacy of human emotions, self-expression, and individualism, and an interest in mystical, medieval, and Oriental themes.

Rome (empire) Great empire of ancient times that for several centuries dominated the Mediterranean world. The history of ancient Rome can be broadly divided into two epochs, the Roman Republic (509–27 B.C.) and the Roman Empire (27 B.C.–476 A.D.). The rise of Rome began with the subjugation of the Italian peninsula (largely completed in the 3rd century B.C.). Acquisition of overseas territories began with the Punic Wars (3rd and 2nd centuries B.C.) in which the great Carthaginian Empire was destroyed and its territories were absorbed by Rome. Thereafter the Romans expanded their domains through various conquests, uniting under their rule an empire that encircled the Mediterranean and extended northward into the British Isles. Roman culture, laws, and customs were spread throughout the empire and greatly influenced the subsequent development of civilization in the West. The decline of the empire began at about the end of the 2nd century A.D. and the following centuries were marked by the breakdown of authority and political chaos, worsening economic problems, oppressive taxation, and finally the destructive invasions by various barbarian peoples. The Western Roman Empire collapsed before the barbarian hordes in 476 A.D., which is traditionally considered the end of the Roman Empire. However, the Eastern Roman Empire continued for many centuries thereafter as the Byzantine Empire.

Rommel, Erwin (1891–1944) German field marshal during World War II. After performing brilliantly in France in 1940, he became the near legendary German commander of the Afrika Korps in the North African Campaign. He was commander in northern France when the Allies landed in 1944. Rommel was forced to take poison after discovery of his part in the plot against Hitler's life.

Romulus Legendary founder and king of Rome. He and his brother Remus built the town in 753 B.C.

Romulus Augustulus (5th century A.D.) Last Roman emperor of the West (475 and 476 A.D.). He was deposed by the German conqueror Odoacer.

Roses, Wars of the Dynastic wars between 1455 and 1485 in England between the houses of York (white rose insignia) and Lancaster (red rose insignia). They fought over rival claims to the English throne. The claimants in both houses were descendants of Edward III, though the Lancastrians had been in power since 1399. However, the Yorkist position was strengthened by discontent over the ineffective rule of Henry VI, English losses in France during the Hundred Years' War (1337–1453), heavy taxes, and disorders such as Cades' Rebellion. In the last phase of the wars, Henry Tudor (Lancaster) defeated and killed Richard (Yorkist) at the Battle of Bosworth Field in 1485 and was crowned Henry VII. This ended the wars. Henry further cemented the peace by marrying Elizabeth of York in 1486 and by quelling the last Yorkist revolts.

Rosetta Stone Inscribed basalt stone that provided the key to deciphering ancient Egyptian hieroglyphics. Found in 1799 by Napoleon's troops near Rosetta, Egypt, the stone bore inscriptions in Greek, Egyptian demotic, and hieroglyphics. Champollion finally deciphered the ancient writings in 1821.

Rothschild, Meyer Amschel (1743–1812) Founder of the Rothschild banking dynasty. Originally a Frankfort money-changer, he capitalized on his position as adviser to the landgrave of Hesse-Kassel and, through his sons, founded Rothschild banks in London, Paris, Vienna, and Naples.

Rothschild, Nathan Meyer (1777–1836) Founder of the London branch of the famous Rothschild banking dynasty. He was noted for helping the British subsidize their allies in the fighting against Napoleonic France.

Roundheads Name of the party of Parliamentarians that opposed Charles I in the English Civil War (1642–1649). They were so named because of their short haircuts. The Royalists wore their hair long in the then fashionable ringlets.

Rousseau, Jean Jacques (1712–1778) Swiss-born French author and philosopher. A highly controversial figure in his lifetime, he influenced both the development of Romanticism and the political thought of the French Revolution. *See also* Philosophy section, page 19-20.

Rudolf I (Hapsburg, Rudolf of) (1218–1291) German king (1273–1291), and first of the Hapsburg line of emperors. His election ended the Interregnum in the Holy Roman Empire. His wars against Ottocar II of Bohemia, a rival for the crown, helped restore eastern German lands, and he consolidated the rule over lands central to his family dynasty (notably Austria). He was never crowned Holy Roman emperor.

Rump Parliament Phase of England's Long Parliament (1640–1660) that began in 1648 following expulsion of members unacceptable to the rebel army in the so-called Pride's Purge. These expelled members were recalled in 1660, restoring the Long Parliament. It voted its own dissolution in March 1660 after providing for the convening of the Convention Parliament. This paved the way for the English Restoration.

Rurik Dynasty of Russian noblemen and czars that ruled Russia until 1598. The line was founded by Rurik (d. 879) and his brothers, Scandinavian adventurers called Varangians, who gained control of Novgorod in 862. Rurik's successor later gained control of the Russian princely states, notably Moscow, and thus came to control the empire. Beginning with Ivan III, who ended Tatar control of the region in 1480, succeeding members of the line enlarged and consolidated their control over Russian domains. Ivan IV (the Terrible) was the first ruler to proclaim himself czar and Fedor I was the last ruler of the Rurik family. He was succeeded by Boris Godunov, whose reign ended in the Time of Troubles and the rise of the Romanov dynasty.

Russian Civil War War (1918–1922) between the Bolshevik Red Army and counterrevolutionary (White Army) forces, variously aided by the Germans, French, British, Japanese, and Americans. The Bolshevik takeover during the Russian Revolution coalesced opposition to the Communists (as the Bolsheviks called themselves since 1918) and a number of border territories proclaimed independence. The Red Army led by Trotsky won, and by 1922 most of the former Russian territories had been regained, and with the Communist government in firm control, the Union of Soviet Socialist Republics was proclaimed.

Russian Revolution of 1905   Rebellion in Russia that led to the establishment of a constitutional monarchy and paved the way for the Russian Revolution of 1917. Czar Nicholas II's reign was marked by increased repression and protest against it, calls for reform by the zemstvos, and widespread discontent over losses in the Russo-Japanese War. The unrest finally culminated in Bloody Sunday in which soldiers fired on a peaceful protest in 1905. This incident galvanized opposition to the czarist regime and resulted in widespread strikes and uprisings. By October the revolt had reached a fever pitch and Nicholas was forced to issue the October Manifesto, in which he acceded to rule by a constitution, promised creation of the Duma (a legislative body), and named Count Witte prime minister. Order was restored soon after, though the arrest of rebel leaders provoked some further protests.

Russian Revolution of 1917   Name applied to the political uprising in Russia in which the monarchy was overthrown and the Bolsheviks under Lenin came to power. The Revolution of 1917 was actually two revolutions: the February Revolution, which led to the overthrow of the czar and end of the Romanov dynasty; and the October Revolution, which brought the Bolsheviks to power in Russia. The revolution had far-reaching consequences. It brought into being the world's first Communist state and resulted in sweeping reform of Russian society.

Russo-Japanese War   Brief war (1904 and 1905) between Russia and Japan, an outgrowth of rivalry over control of Manchuria and Korea. After negotiations failed, largely because of Russian intransigence to produce a settlement, Japan launched a surprise attack in February 1904 on the Russian stronghold of Port Arthur. The Japanese finally took Port Arthur in January 1905 and inflicted a decisive defeat at the Battle of Mukden in March 1905. The final blow came when Russia's Baltic fleet, attempting to relieve Russian forces in the East, was intercepted and destroyed at Tsushima in May 1905 by a Japanese naval force. The Treaty of Portsmouth in 1905 ended the war in a humiliating defeat for Russia. Russia conceded territories (including Port Arthur) to Japan, though it retained control of northern Manchuria. The war marked the emergence of Japan as a major power.

Russo-Turkish Wars   Wars fought by Russia and the Ottoman Empire (16th–19th centuries) that resulted in Russian conquest of Ottoman domains between the Black Sea and the Balkans. Concern over Russian expansionism and the general decline of the Ottoman Empire eventually brought direct involvement by other European powers in the 19th century (*see also* **Eastern Question**.)

S **Sabines**   Ancient people who lived in the Sabine Hills near Rome. The Sabines were conquered by the Romans in 290 B.C. and became Roman citizens in 268 B.C.

Sadat, Anwar el (1918–1981)   Egyptian president (1970–1981) and statesman, noted for securing the first Arab peace treaty with Israel. In 1952 he aided his fellow officer and longtime friend Nasser in overthrowing King Farouk and served in several posts during Nasser's rule. Made vice president in 1969, he succeeded to the presidency on Nasser's death in 1970. He ordered Russian military advisers to leave Egypt and launched the Arab-Israeli War of 1973 against Israel. After the war Sadat engaged in a search for a negotiated peace in the Mideast which eventually led to his historic trip to Jerusalem in 1977 to address the Israeli Knesset. Peace talks between Israel and Egypt, in which the United States took part, led to the Egyptian-Israeli Peace Treaty of 1979 (*see* page 11-36). Opposition within Egypt to Sadat's rule culminated in Sadat's assassination in 1981 by a group of disaffected Muslim fundamentalists within the army. He shared the 1978 Nobel Prize for Peace with Israel's Menachem Begin.

Safavids   Persian Muslim dynasty (1501–1736). It was founded by Ismail I, who conquered and subdued large areas of Persia, added several Iraqi territories, and proclaimed Shi'ite Islam as the state religion. Under the military leadership of Abbas I (ruled 1587–1629), the Safavids defeated Turkey, expanded Persia's territories, ended Portuguese encroachment, established trade with the West, and became an international power. The dynasty began a slow decline at the death of Abbas I and ended with the rule of Abbas III (1732–1736), who was overthrown by Nadir Shah.

Saint Bartholomew's Day, massacre of   *See* **Massacre of Saint Bartholomew's Day.**

Saladin (1137?–1193)   Muslim sultan and military leader, noted for his chivalry in battle against the Crusaders, founder of the Ayyubid dynasty. He ended Fatimid control in Egypt in 1171. He extended his control over Damascus, and began to subdue local rulers throughout Syria and Palestine. Saladin took Jerusalem in 1187, thereby ending the Latin Kingdom of Jerusalem. This prompted the unsuccessful Third Crusade after which Saladin permitted Christians access to Jerusalem.

Salamis, battle of   Naval battle in 480 B.C. between the Greeks and the Persians during the Persian Wars. It was fought in the straits between the island of Salamis and the Greek mainland. The Greeks under Themistocles won the battle, one of the most celebrated encounters of history. Themistocles lured the superior Persian navy (600 ships to over 360 Greek vessels) into the narrow straits, and thus made it impossible for the Persians to maneuver. The Greeks subsequently sank 200–300 Persian ships, losing only about 40.

Salazar, Antonio de Oliveira (1889–1970)   Dictator of Portugal (1932–1968). Made premier in 1932, he instituted a new constitution in 1933 which turned Portugal into a corporate state and gave Salazar dictatorial powers. Although a number of Salazar's reform measures were successful, he was unable to substantially reduce poverty and illiteracy in Portugal. He is credited with making the country financially stable.

Salian dynasty   Line of German emperors that ruled the Holy Roman Empire (1024–1125). During its tenure, the investiture controversy with the papacy broke out.

Salic law   Rule of succession in some European royal houses forbidding females to succeed to family titles. Supposedly dating to Frankish times, it was invoked by the French, English, and Spanish monarchies.

SALT *See* **Strategic Arms Limitation Talks**, page 10-70.

Samanids Persian dynasty that ruled (819–999) after the Arab Muslim conquest of Iran. The dynasty greatly advanced Persian literature, art, and architecture.

Samudragupta (d. 380 A.D.) Indian emperor (330–380 A.D.) of the Gupta dynasty, successor to his father, Chandragupta I. He expanded Gupta control over much of northern India. A poet and musician as well as warrior and conqueror, he was considered a model of the ideal Hindu ruler.

Samurai Japanese warrior class. The samurai rose in the 12th century during Japan's feudal period and played a major role in Japanese life. As highly skilled warriors, they were instrumental in establishing the shoguns as real rulers in Japan in the 12th century and provided the basis for the shoguns' power in subsequent centuries. During the long, peaceful reign of the Tokugawa shoguns (17th–19th centuries), the samurai gradually moved into bureaucratic posts. After the Meiji Restoration in 1868, the class was abolished with feudalism.

San Martín, José de (1778–1850) South American revolutionary leader. He played a major part in the liberation of Argentina, Peru, and Chile from Spanish rule. He led an army across the Andes to defeat the Spanish in Chile in 1817 and deferred to Bolívar in 1822, who then became the leader of the South American independence movement.

Sans-culotte French term meaning "without knee breeches," applied to the more radical supporters of the French Revolution, especially the lower classes. It derived from the long trousers adopted by the lower classes to replace knee breeches, considered aristocratic. *See* **Hébert, Jacques René**.

Sanskrit Sacred language of the Hindu religion. Long used by Indian religious scholars and the upper caste, it developed from the earlier Verdic language. Though technically a dead language, it continues to be used in the scholarly and literary fields.

San Stefano, Treaty of Treaty of 1878 between Russia and the Ottoman Turks ending the Russo-Turkish War of 1877 and 1878. This treaty was subsequently altered by the Congress of Berlin in 1878.

Santa Anna, Antonio López de (1794–1876) Mexican general and statesman. He fought with Iturbide in securing Mexican independence in 1821 but helped to overthrow Iturbide in 1823. He followed a policy of supporting, then helping to overthrow, subsequent leaders. His victory over the Spanish at Tampico in 1829 helped him gain the presidency in 1833. His ruthless treatment of Texans at the Alamo and Goliad aided the Texan independence movement and contributed to his defeat by Sam Houston at San Jacinto and the loss of Texas. Forced from office in 1836, Santa Anna returned to power (1839–1844, 1846 and 1847) but was again removed from office after his defeats in the Mexican War. He returned to power once more in 1853 but was exiled two years later.

Saracens Name applied in the Middle Ages to the Muslim enemies of Christendom. Originally referring to northern Arabian raiders, it eventually was applied to all Muslims, whether Arabs, Moors, or Turks.

Sardinia, kingdom of European kingdom formed in 1720 for Duke Victor Amadeus II of Savoy after Sicily passed to Austrian control. The kingdom included Sardinia, Savoy, Piedmont, and Nice, and in the 18th and 19th centuries it grew to include other territories. It became the center of the movement to unify Italy in the 19th century and was given control of territories conquered by Garibaldi in 1860. In 1861, Sardinian king Victor Emmanuel II became king of Italy, and the House of Savoy became the ruling house of Italy.

Sargon (d. 605 B.C.) Ancient Assyrian king (721–705). He was also known as Sargon II. He consolidated the Assyrian Empire, defeating and resettling conquered weaker peoples. He conquered Babylon and Samaria and destroyed the northern kingdom of Israel in 721 B.C.

Sargon (Sharrukin) (2800? B.C.) Ancient Mesopotamian ruler. From Akkad, he defeated Sumer and established the first great Semitic Empire. His empire of Akkad included the area later ruled by Babylonia.

Saskatchewan Province of western Canada. Members of the Hudson's Bay Company settled the area in 1774 and controlled it until 1869, when it became part of Canada's Northwest Territories. Extension of the railroad in 1882 into Saskatchewan brought more settlers, and the last Indian rebellion was put down in 1885. Saskatchewan became a province in 1905.

Sassanidae (Sassanids) (Sassanians) Last ancient Persian dynasty to rule before the Arab conquest of Persia in 651. The dynasty was founded by Ardashir I in 226 A.D. The Sassanidae promoted a revival of native Persian arts and letters and made Zoroastrianism the state religion. The last Sassanidae ruler died in exile in 651.

Sato, Eisaku (1901–1975) Japanese prime minister (1964–1972). He held important government posts during Japan's post-war period. As prime minister, he signed a treaty with the United States reestablishing Japan's control over Okinawa. He shared the 1974 Nobel Prize for Peace.

Satrap Name given provincial governors of the ancient Persian Empire. In general, a satrap administered the province, collected taxes, and was the supreme judge.

Satsuma Revolt Rebellion by samurai warriors in 1877 led by General Saigo to try to reassert their historic position. The revolt was in response to the reforms of the Meiji government that deprived the samurai of their economic and military privileges. Government forces crushed the rebellion.

Saud (1902–1969) Saudi Arabian king (1953–1964). Forced to yield some of his powers to an executive council headed by his brother Faisal in 1958, he was deposed by Faisal in 1964, and died in exile.

Saul First king (11th century?) of the ancient Israelites. In the Bible, he was noted for his prowess in battle and for his jealousy of his successor, David, whom he tried to destroy.

Savonarola, Girolamo (1452–1498) Italian Dominican religious reformer. He enthralled Florence with his sermons, noted for their moral rigor. He challenged papal authority and later was repudiated and executed by the Florentines.

Savoy, House of European royal dynasty. Founded in the 11th century by Humbert I, the White-Handed, it first dominated the French Swiss-Italian Alpine region, then spread to Piedmont. Made a ducal family of the Holy Roman Empire in 1416, it eventually came to rule vast areas of France, Switzerland, and Italy. After receiving the kingdom of Sardinia in 1720, their support of Italian unification led to the creation in 1861 of the kingdom of Italy, with the House of Savoy as its royal family. The House of Savoy remained the ruling house of Italy until 1946, when a republic was established.

Saxons Germanic peoples whose influence grew as the Roman Empire declined. The Saxons conducted numerous raids of piracy along the coasts of northern Germany, Gaul, and Britain, and, with the Angles, many Saxons settled in Britain in the 6th century. On the Continent, their constant warfare against the Franks ended with their defeat in the 9th century and their forced conversion to Christianity by Charlemagne.

Sayyid dynasty Dynasty that ruled India's Delhi sultanate (1414–1451). The four sultans of the dynasty were barely able to maintain themselves and eventually gave way to the Lodi dynasty.

Schism 1. Schism of 1054. Final division of the Christian church into the Roman Catholic (Western) church and the Orthodox Eastern church. 2. Great Schism. Division in the Roman Catholic church (1378–1417) in which two rival lines of popes emerged. To end the schism, the Council of Pisa was convened in 1409 and declared against the then-reigning popes in Rome and France. In 1410 the council installed John XXIII as pope. John succeeded in winning widespread support and then called the Council of Constance in 1414. Gregory XII in Rome resigned and the council deposed both John XXIII and Benedict XIII, then reigning in France. Pope Martin V was elected and the schism was ended.

Schlieffen, Alfred, Graf von (1833–1913) German field marshal. As head of the German general staff (1891–1905) he devised the Schlieffen plan in 1895, the strategy later attempted by Germany in World War I. This plan was to crush French resistance in a war by a massive, lightning attack from the north through Belgian and Dutch territory (ignoring their neutrality). The plan also called for an attack by relatively light forces concentrated in the south against France and in the east against Russia. The plan failed during World War I because the forces attacking through Belgium and Holland were not strong enough. However, in World War II Germany brilliantly executed the basic plan.

Schliemann, Heinrich (1822–1890) German archaeologist who excavated the ruins of ancient Troy.

Schmidt, Helmut (b. 1918) West German chancellor (1974–1982). A Social Democrat, he served as minister of defense (1969–1972), minister of finance (1972–1974), and succeeded Willy Brandt as chancellor. He oversaw the rapid economic expansion of West Germany. He was succeeded by Helmut Kohl (*see* page 11-65) in 1983.

Scholasticism Medieval Christian philosophical and theological movement that arose in the 11th century. It embraced various schools of thought that were, in general terms, concerned with questions of reconciling faith and reason and it stimulated a renewed interest in ancient Greek philosophy. Earlier Christian thinkers, notably St. Augustine (through his writings on Platonism) helped set the stage for medieval Scholasticism. In the 11th century St. Anselm founded the movement and in his writings used reason to better understand belief ("faith seeking understanding"). The works of Aristotle (translated from Arabic) became available for the first time in Christian Europe by the 13th century and had a tremendous impact on medieval scholastic thinkers. Albertus Magnus began the synthesis of Aristotelianism and Christian theology, but St. Thomas Aquinas, one of the greatest thinkers of the Christian church, brought it to full development.

Schopenhauer, Arthur (1788–1860) German philosopher. A successor of Kant in the idealist school, he saw will rather than mind as the fundamental principle of existence and developed a philosophy based on this idea. His most important work was *World as Will and Idea.*

Schuman, Robert (1886–1963) French statesman and prime minister (1947–1963). As foreign minister (1948–1953) he proposed the Schuman plan for pooling European coal and steel resources. This move toward European cooperation eventually led to the formation of the European Common Market.

Schuschnigg, Kurt von (b.1897) Austrian statesman. As prime minister (1934–1938) he strove to prevent Austria's takeover by Germany in 1938.

Schweitzer, Albert (1875–1965) Alsatian theologian, philosopher, and medical missionary in Africa. Renouncing fame as a scholar and musician, he founded a medical mission (Lambaréné Hospital) in Africa, illustrating his philosophical principle of "reverence for life."

Scipio Ancient Roman patrician family. They were distinguished by their patronage of Greek culture but even more by family members who were outstanding Roman leaders during the 3rd and 2nd centuries B.C.

Second Coalition, War of the War (1798–1802) conducted by a coalition of European nations against France, the last phase of the French Revolutionary Wars. On December 24, 1798, the monarchies of Russia and Britain, in agreement with Naples, Portugal, Austria, and the Ottoman Empire, formed the Second Coalition to oppose Napoleon's expansionism. Russia and Britain agreed to drive France from The Netherlands, Austria was to combat Napoleon in Germany, and Switzerland and combined Austro-Russian forces were to expel the French from Italy. The coalition was only partially successful before Russia withdrew in 1799, and France subsequently regained some of its earlier losses. The conflict was ended by the Treaty of Amiens in 1802, which also closed the French Revolutionary Wars.

HISTORY OF THE WORLD

Second Empire French government under the rule of Emperor Napoleon III (1852–1870). Originally chosen as president of the Second Republic in 1848, Napoleon III declared himself emperor in 1852. He followed Napoleon I's tradition of autocratic rule and expansionism. However, France's humiliation in the Franco-Prussian War of 1870 led to his overthrow and declaration of the Third Republic.

Second Republic French government (1848–1852) formed after the abdication of King Louis Philippe in the February Revolution of 1848 and establishment of the provisional government of Louis Blanc. Louis Napoleon, nephew of Emperor Napoleon, was elected president of the republic. Though the Second Republic had a constitution and a legislature, its rule was brief. Louis Napoleon overthrew his own government, proclaimed himself Emperor Napoleon III in 1852, and declared the Second Empire.

Second Republic Spanish republican government (1931–1939) formed after the ouster of King Alfonso XIII. A constitution was promulgated and church property was confiscated, but the moderate policies followed by President Zamora brought attacks from both the right and left. He was ousted in the 1936 elections by the Popular Front (a coalition of republicans, Communists, syndicalists, and Socialists). Soon after their president, Azaña, took office, the Spanish Civil War broke out. The Second Republic was replaced by Franco's Nationalist government at the end of the war in 1939.

Seleucid Kingdom (Seleucid Empire) Hellenistic empire of Asia Minor. The Seleucid dynasty (312–364 B.C.) was centered in Syria and ruled over vast areas of Asia Minor that had been captured by Alexander the Great. The dynasty was founded by the Macedonian Seleucus I, one of Alexander's generals, following Alexander's death. In the division of Alexander's empire, Seleucus was given Babylonia. He rapidly added territories that extended from Syria to the Indus River. Subsequent Seleucid rulers were instrumental in spreading Greek culture throughout Asia Minor. However, the empire was gradually reduced and was limited to Syria and Cilicia by the time of its absorption by Rome in 64 B.C.

Seleucus I (d. 280 B.C.) Macedonian general and from 312 B.C, first of the Seleucid rulers of the eastern portions of Alexander the Great's empire. His rule extended over Syria, Asia Minor, Mesopotamia, and Persia. He founded Antioch as his capital.

Self-Strengthening movement Chinese movement begun in 1861 to adopt elements of Western civilization in order to strengthen the Ch'ing (Manchu) dynasty against both internal forces and further aggression by Western nations. The movement began to decline in the 1870s.

Seljuks Turkish dynasty that ruled much of western Asia and Asia Minor from the 11th–13th centuries. Originally an Asiatic nomadic people the Seljuks converted to Islam in the 11th century and soon created a vast empire after taking power in the empire of the Caliphate.

Semite A member of an ethnic group speaking a Semitic language. As early as 2500 B.C. the Semites began to migrate from the Arabian Peninsula. Semitic peoples include the ancient Akkadians, Assyrians, Aramaeans, Israelites and Phoenicians, and the modern Arabs and Jews.

Seneca, Lucius Annaeus (Seneca the Younger) (3 B.C.–65 A.D.) Roman Stoic philosopher, statesman, and dramatist, considered the leading literary figure of his day. Tutor and adviser to Nero, he held great power during Nero's early reign (54–62 A.D). Eventually, conflicts with the emperor led to his retirement and he was finally ordered by Nero to commit suicide. Seneca's writings had a profound influence on later literature, notably Elizabethan drama.

Sennacherib (d. 681 B.C.) Ancient Assyrian king (705–681 B.C.), successor to his father, Sargon II. He is noted for the rebuilding of Nineveh, the destruction of Babylon in 689 B.C., and the siege of Jerusalem in 701 B.C.

Separatists Factions of English Christians who tried to remove themselves from the authority of the Church of England. The principal Separatists were Brownists, Pilgrims, Baptists, and the Society of Friends.

Sepoy Rebellion (Indian Mutiny) Widespread revolt (1857 and 1858) by native Indian troops known as sepoys serving in the British East India Company army. The revolt brought about the transfer of authority in India from the company to the British crown in 1858 and later became a symbol for Indian nationalists. Resentment against East India Company rule had been building for some time, particularly over the company's annexation of native lands and its failure to respect native customs. Hindus and Muslims alike were offended by the introduction of cartridges that were removed to be greased with cow and pig fat and this sparked the mutiny. Indian troops rebelled on May 10, 1857 at Meerut and the bloody revolt (involving massacres of British army officers and European civilians) spread rapidly throughout northern and central India. British forces retook Delhi in September 1857 and Lucknow in March 1858. The revolt was effectively crushed in 1858, though some fighting continued into 1859. As a result of the uprising, the (titular) ruler of the Mogul Empire, Bahadur Shah II, was banished by the British. This formally ended the existence of the Mogul Empire.

Serf In feudalism, a peasant laborer bound to the land owned by a lord. The serf owed payment, usually a portion of crops, and services to the lord in return for protection and use of the land.

Seven Hills of Rome The seven hills upon which the city of Rome was built. The original city of Romulus was built on the Palatine hill. The other hills are Capitoline (which became the principal one and site of the palaces of the Caesars), Quirinal, Viminal, Esquiline, Caelian, and Aventine.

Seven Wonders of the World Seven greatest man-made works of the ancient world. Lists varied but usually included the pyramids of Egypt, the Hanging Gardens of Babylon, the Colossus of Rhodes, the statue of Zeus at Olympia, the Temple of Artemis at Ephesus, the Pharos lighthouse of Alexandria, and the Mausoleum at Halicarnassus.

A king distributing royal charters to his vassals.

Seven Years' War   War fought (1756–1763) in Europe and in colonial domains in other parts of the world. The American phase of the war was called the French and Indian War. The war evolved from two separate ongoing struggles between European powers: the rivalry between Prussia and Austria (which had been humiliated by Prussia in the War of Austrian Succession 1740–1748) and the colonial rivalry between Britain and France (in Canada, America, India, and elsewhere). The war itself pitted Prussia, Britain, and Hanover against Austria and France. Austria and France were joined variously by Sweden, Russia, Saxony, and Spain. The war began in 1756 and Prussia and Britain eventually emerged victorious. Prussia was confirmed as a leading European power and Britain became the chief colonial power, having stripped France of nearly all its colonial possessions.

Sévres, Treaty of   Treaty of 1920 between the Allies and the Ottoman Turks, concluded at Sévres, France, after World War I. By its terms the Ottoman Empire was abolished and Turkey was forced to renounce all non-Turkish possessions. The Dardanelles were internationalized and demilitarized. Palestine and Mesopotamia became British mandates, Syria became a French mandate, and Hejaz and Armenia became independent kingdoms. The treaty was rejected by the nationalists led by Kemal Atatürk and was superseded by the Treaty of Lausanne in 1923.

Seymour, Jane (1509?–1537)   Third queen of English king Henry VIII. She gave birth to his only son (who became King Edward VI) and died a few days later.

Shah Jahan (1592–1666)   Fifth Mogul emperor of India (1628–1658). Many great buildings, notably the Taj Mahal, were built during his reign.

Shakespeare, William (Shakespere) (1564–1616)   English poet and playwright, considered the greatest of all dramatists.

Shamir, Yitzak (b. 1915)   Israeli politician, leader of Herut party. Prime minister 1983–1984. Alternated as prime minister with Shimon Peres (*See* page 11-96) from 1984 to 1989.

Shang   Chinese dynasty, also called the Yin. The Shang ruled northern China (1766–1122 B.C.). It is the earliest Chinese dynasty to be historically verified by archaeological evidence and written inscriptions. The Shang period saw great advances in bronze casting, pottery, weaving, and agriculture. It appears that ancestor worship and human sacrifice were practiced and the Shang rulers had a highly organized system of government.

Shen Nung   Legendary Chinese emperor, believed to have been born in 2800 B.C. He was the second of China's mythical great emperors and is said to have taught the Chinese farming skills and to have established an agricultural society.

Shih Huang Ti (Ch'in Shi Huang Ti) (255–210 B.C.)   Chinese emperor (247/6–210 B.C.) who first unified the empire and built the Great Wall of China. Following his accession as king of the Ch'in Kingdom of northwestern China, he annexed 6 other Chinese kingdoms to create in 221 B.C. the Ch'in Empire. He thereupon abolished the old feudal order, divided his empire into 36 military districts, established a centralized administration, and instituted uniform standards in weights and measures, laws, and written language. He was a builder and, in addition to the Great Wall, ordered construction of roads and canals. His struggle with the Confucian scholars (supporters of the old feudal order) led to the Burning of the Books in 213 B.C. and the eventual rise of the Han dynasty.

Shi'ites   Muslim sect, one of the two major divisions of Islam, the other being the Sunni. The Shi'ites originated in Persia as partisans of Ali, son-in-law of Muhammad, after the first Muslim Civil War. They opposed the Omayyad dynasty supported by the Sunni. The Shi'ites believe that a Mahdi will appear at the millennium. Shi'ism is the official religion of Iran and also has followers in India, Iraq, Yemen, Pakistan, and Oman. In the 1980s they became a political force in the Arab world. They control the government of Iran (*see* **Khomeini, Ruhollah, Ayatollah**). They have been connected to terrorism outside the Arab world. *See also* Religion section, page 22-19.

Shimabara Rebellion   Japanese insurrection (1637–1688) in which the predominantly Catholic population of Shimabara rose against unjust taxation. More than 100,000 troops failed to quell the rebellion and a Dutch gunship had to be called in. The rebellion caused further Christian persecution and led Japan's leaders to adopt a policy of isolation.

Shimonoseki, Treaty of   Treaty of 1895 between China and Japan ending the First Sino-Japanese War. By its terms China, who had lost the war, accepted Korean independence and ceded Taiwan, the Pescadores islands, and Port Arthur and the Liaotung Peninsula to Japan. Japan subsequently returned Port Arthur and the Liaotung Peninsula after European protests.

Shinto   Indigenous religion of Japan that is more a way of life than a formal dogma. Its major divinities are Amaterasu, the sun goddess and her brother Susanowo, the storm god, but all objects contain a holy spirit call kami. Ancestor worship and pilgrimages to shrines are important aspects of Shinto, which literally means "the way of the gods." The Japanese emperor was considered divine as a direct descendant of Amaterasu. This belief was promoted until 1946 when Emperor Hirohito disavowed his divinity.

Shiva (Siva)   The four-armed Hindu god of destruction. With Brahma (creation) and Vishnu (preservation), he is one of the 3 major gods of Hinduism.

Shogun   Military leaders who were the real rulers of Japan (1192–1867). Shogun was the title of the imperial military commander, and in 1192 the emperor appointed Minamoto Yoritomo shogun. Yoritomo gained control over the government, and in subsequent centuries the shoguns, as well as the warrior class they controlled, ruled Japan. The emperor was sovereign in title only. Under the shoguns, Japan remained locked in a rigid feudal system. The emperors did not regain power until the Meiji Restoration in 1868, which marked the end of feudalism in Japan and the beginning of the movement toward modernization. The shogunate itself was hereditary and was held successively by the following families: Kamakura shogunate (Minamoto family) (1192–1333), Ashikaga shogunate (1338–1578), and Tokugawa shogunate (1603–1867).

Short Parliament   Fourth English Parliament in the reign of King Charles I. Convened April 1640 by Charles to provide aid for a war against the Scottish Covenanters, it refused to do so until the king had replied to its grievances. It was dissolved in May and followed by the Long Parliament (*see* page 11-71).

Shotoka, Prince (d. 629 A.D.)   As regent (592–629 A.D.) for his aunt Empress Siuko, Prince Shotoka reorganized the Japanese government and began to strengthen the central government with the Seventeen Article Constitution of 604 A.D. which declared the supremacy of the emperor, took away inherited government offices, and appointed officials by merit following the Confucian system in China. Shotoka sent Japanese missions to China and they brought Chinese culture and the Buddhist religion back to Japan. Prince Shotoka's policies were continued in the mid 600s by the Saika reforms.

Siegfried Line   Line of fortifications built along Germany's western frontier in the 1930s. It corresponded to the French Maginot Line and succeeded in slowing down the Allied offensive in World War II.

Sieyès, Emmanuel Joseph (1748–1836)   French revolutionary statesman. He played a major role in the early years of the French Revolution, drafted the Declaration of the Rights of Man and later helped organize the coup d'état that overthrew the Directory.

Sikhs   People of northwest India, followers of a religion founded in the 15th century by Nank. Fusing Hindu and Muslim beliefs, the Sikhs worship one God and employ meditation and exercise to attain the realization of God. They revere their guru (teacher) and accept as their only religious text the Adi Granth, largely a collection of hymns by the early gurus. They came to control much of the Punjab in the 18th century but were defeated by the British in the Sikh Wars of the 19th century.

Sikh Wars   Two 19th-century wars between the Sikhs and the British. 1. The first Sikh war (1845 and 1846) was sparked by a Sikh invasion into British India and culminated in the defeat of the Sikhs and British annexation of Kashmir. 2. The second Sikh war (1848 and 1849) was caused by an uprising and resulted in a British victory and the annexation of the Punjab.

Silesian Wars   1. The first Silesian war (1740–1742) was fought between Prussia and Austria for possession of Silesia. It was begun by the invasion of Silesia by Prussian king Frederick II, in alliance with Bavaria, France, and Saxony. Austria was defeated, and by the Treaty of Breslau in 1742 Prussia gained possession of much of Silesia. 2. The second Silesian war (1744 and 1745) was begun by Frederick II, who crossed Saxony and invaded Bohemia. He captured Prague but was forced back into Saxony. The war was ended by the Treaty of Dresden in 1745 between Austria and Prussia, and Frederick retained possession of Silesia.

Silk Road (Silk Route)   Ancient trade route across Asia from the Roman Empire to China. Roughly the same route was followed by Marco Polo in his travels.

Silla, kingdom of   Ancient kingdom of Korea which arose (1st and 2nd centuries A.D.) in eastern Korea. With the kingdoms of Koguryo and Paekche, it was one of the 3 early Korean kingdoms and later unified the peninsula under native Korean rule for the first time in 670. An administrative bureaucracy, influenced by Chinese patterns, was set, and Buddhism flourished. The Silla rulers were supplanted by the Koryo dynasty in 935.

Simpson, Sir George (1792–1860)   Scottish-born Canadian explorer. Simpson explored Canada for the Hudson's Bay Company and made an overland journey (1841 and 1842) across the northern part of the world.

Sinan (1489?–1587?)   Foremost Ottoman architect, who designed and built more than 300 structures. He built the mosques of Suleiman I at Constantinople and Selim II at Adrianople.

Sinn Fein   Irish Nationalist political party of Ireland, whose name means "We Ourselves." Originally a movement founded in 1899 by Griffith, it sought to gain independence from England. It gathered momentum after the Easter Rebellion of 1916 under the leadership of De Valera. After De Valera withdrew in 1927 to enter the Dail of the Irish Free State, Sinn Fein declined in importance and eventually became the political arm of the Irish Republican Army (IRA).

Sino-French War   Undeclared war (1883–1885) between France and China arising from French expansion into Vietnam. China claimed Vietnam as a protectorate, and after France declared a protectorate over Annam in 1883, China sent troops to Vietnam.

Soon defeated, China was forced to recognize French interests in Annam and Tonkin in 1885.

Sino-Japanese War   1. War (1894 and 1895) between China and Japan over control of Korea. The Japanese, having a modern, well-equipped army, easily invaded Shantung and Manchuria and forced the Chinese to sue for peace. By the Treaty of Shimonoseki of 1895, the Chinese agreed to pay a large indemnity, to cede vast areas (including Taiwan) to Japan, to grant trade privileges to Japan, and to recognize the nominal independence of Korea. Japan emerged from the conflict as a major international power. 2. War (1937–1945) between China and Japan. Following its occupation of Manchuria (1931 and 1932), Japan pressed the Chinese for further concessions. The ongoing civil war between Chinese Nationalists and Communists made it all but impossible to resist the growing threat of an invasion by Japan. In 1936, the Nationalists and Communists agreed to form a common front against the Japanese, and in July 1937 hostilities broke out. Japan quickly occupied Peking and Tientsin, and soon after took Shanghai and the capital of Nanking. The Japanese continued their rapid advance over the eastern portions of China, taking cities and other strategic points while the Chinese pursued a scorched-earth policy and waged a bitter guerrilla war from within. China declared war on the Axis powers in 1941, after the Japanese attack on Pearl Harbor, and the fighting in China thus became part of World War II. In 1942–1944, despite an increase in aid from the United States and Britain and the diversion of Japanese forces to fighting elsewhere, the Chinese were unable to gain the initiative, though they slowed the Japanese advance and inflicted some serious defeats. In fact, it was not until the spring of 1945, just before the Japanese surrender, that the Chinese were able to mount a successful offensive.

Sivaji (Shivaji) (Grand Rebel) (1627–1680)   Indian ruler, founder of the Maratha kingdom. He expanded his domains at the expense of the Mogul Empire.

Six Dynasties   Name given to the period in China between the fall of the Han dynasty in 220 A.D. and the beginning of the Sui in 581 A.D. The era was marked by political disintegration but also by such cultural advancements as the introduction of Buddhism and Taoism, medical and scientific study, and the use of coal, tea, and gunpowder. It was named after the six dynasties that ruled during the following periods: the Wu (222–280 A.D.), the eastern Ch'in (317–419), the Liu-Sung (420–479), the southern Ch'i (479–502), the Liang (502–557), and the Ch'en (557–581).

Sixteen Kingdoms   Name applied to a group of dynasties, all but 3 non-Chinese, that ruled in northern China from 304–439 A.D.

Slave dynasty   First dynasty of the Delhi Sultanate in northern India. It ruled between 1209 and 1290 and was so named because its founder, Qutbud-Din Aibak, was once a slave.

Slavery   Age-old institution of involuntary servitude, now eliminated in nearly every part of the world. Mention of slavery has been found in writings of the Babylonians, Hebrews, Egyptians, and other ancient peoples and it was common among the Greeks and Romans. After the fall of Rome, slavery in the medieval European states was generally replaced by the feudal institution of serfdom. It continued in the Muslim states, however. European involvement in slavery was renewed in the 15th century with the beginnings of overseas exploration and colonization, and slaves were used mainly in colonial domains. The Portuguese took the first Negro slaves from West Africa in the 1440s, and in the 16th century, Spain and England also began trading them (France, Denmark, and American colonials started in the 17th century). By the late 17th century, the English dominated the slave trade. The prime market for slaves was in the New World colonies. The Spanish began importing large numbers of slaves into South America after native Indian slaves proved too rebellious. In North America the first slaves were introduced in 1619 at Jamestown, Virginia, and, though slaves were later sent to other British colonies in the Americas, it was in the South that they became an integral part of the plantation economy. Active slave trade by European powers continued throughout the 18th century. But by the beginning of the 19th century, abolitionists were already mounting their campaign to bring about its end. Slavery ended in the United States with the passage of the Thirteenth Amendment in 1865. *See* The Constitution of the United States, page 10-91.

Smith, Adam (1723–1790)   Scottish economist and philosopher. Smith's famous book, *Wealth of Nations* (1776), greatly influenced economic theory. It argued for laissez-faire doctrines such as free trade and held that the "invisible hand" of individual competition would ultimately work to the public benefit.

Smith, Ian Douglas (b. 1919)   Rhodesian politician. A white supremacist, he became prime minister in 1964 and unilaterally declared Rhodesia's independence from Britain in 1965. His white Rhodesian government subsequently resisted international pressures, including economic boycott, and ruled until 1980, when blacks came to power and renamed the country Zimbabwe.

Smuts, Jan Christiaan (1870–1950)   South African soldier and statesman. He fought the British in the Boer War but later was instrumental in forming the Union of South Africa in 1910. He was prime minister (1919–1924, 1939–1948).

Social contract   Agreement or bond by which human beings move from a state of nature to form society. This theory was first advanced by Thomas Hobbes and John Locke.

Social Darwinism   Discredited 19th-century social philosophy based on the Darwinian theory of evolution. It held that human societies, like animal species, were subject to the law of "survival of the fittest."

Social Democratic party of Germany   German political party. Founded in 1863 as a Marxist workers' party, it became a formidable power in Germany during the early 1900s. It was suppressed in 1933 by Hitler and reorganized after World War II. However, it was unable to successfully challenge the coalition of Christian Democrat and other parties until after 1959, when it eliminated Marxist ideology and broadened its appeal as a people's party. Since the 1970s the party has formed coalition governments in Germany under Brandt and Schmidt.

Socialism   Politico-economic doctrine. Socialism seeks to replace the competitive capitalist system with a cooperative society, in which means of production and distribution are owned either by the government or collectively by the people. A response to the hardships and social injustice bred by the Industrial Revolution, socialism dates primarily from the works of such thinkers as Babeuf, Saint-Simon, Fourier, and Owen. Babeuf, sometimes called the first Socialist theorist, sought to advance economic egalitarianism during the French Revolution. Saint-Simon postulated government control of the economy and industry, while Fourier and Owen believed in decentralizing society into small collectives. New elements of class struggle and the necessity of revolution were added to Socialist thought by way of Marx and Engels' *Communist Manifesto* (1848). For the rest of the 19th century and into the early 20th, the doctrinal dispute over revolutionary socialism versus evolutionary socialism divided Socialists and ultimately brought about the permanent split between Democratic Socialists (advocates of gradual change) and Communists (advocates of revolutionary change). Though many other issues divided Socialists in the early 1900s, the triumph of the Bolsheviks in the Russian Revolution of 1917 resulted in the complete separation of revolutionaries (now Communists) from the Socialist movement. Thereafter, Democratic Socialists gradually gained power in European countries (especially after World War II), notably in Britain (*see* **Labour party**), Germany (*see* **Social Democratic party of Germany**), and, in the 1980s, France.

Society of Jesus (Jesuits)   Roman Catholic religious order, founded in 1534 by St. Ignatius of Loyola and approved in 1540 by Pope Paul III. The Jesuits played an important role in the Catholic Reformation and also established many schools in Europe.

Socrates (470?–399 B.C.)   Greek philosopher. One of the great philosophers of ancient Greece, whose life and teachings have made a profound impression on Western thought. Socrates spent much of his life in the public places of Athens conducting discussions, or dialogues, with his fellow citizens. He developed a mode of inquiry known as the dialectic, or Socratic method, by which the truth of a given statement is tested by a series of questions. His purpose was to gain knowledge, the basis of virtue, or right conduct. Eventually he was accused of impiety and corruption of youth and was sentenced to death. With his disciples by his side, he committed suicide by drinking hemlock. Socrates wrote nothing, and our knowledge of his life and teachings comes mainly from the writings of his disciple Plato. *See also* Philosophy section, page 19-21.

Solidarity   *See* **Walesa, Lech**.

Solomon   Great king of ancient Israel (973–933 B.C.), renowned for his wisdom. He encouraged trade and thereby brought on a period of great commercial prosperity. He also built lavish cities and constructed the first Temple of Jerusalem.

Solon (638–599 B.C.)   Athenian statesman who laid the foundations of democracy in Athens. Elected archon (chief magistrate) in 594 B.C. amid a social crisis caused by the widespread indebtedness of the populace to the aristocracy, he instituted his economic reforms called Seisachtheia. He ended the practice of securing loans with personal liberty (serfdom resulted from failure to pay), annulled all debts contracted in this manner, restricted exports, and reformed the currency. He also reformed the Athenian constitution, allowing all free men to participate in the assembly for the first time. The power of the Areopagus was limited and a council of Four Hundred was created to represent the propertied class. Solon also introduced a new law code to replace the harsh Draconian Code.

Solzhenitsyn, Aleksandr Isayevich (b. 1918) Russian writer and a leading dissident against the excesses of the Soviet system. He received the Nobel Prize in Literature in 1970. He was exiled to the West in 1974 when the Soviet Union revoked his citizenship for criticizing the government. In 1976 he settled in the United States. His citizenship was restored in 1990.

Somoza, Anastasio (1896–1956)   President of Nicaragua (1936–1947, 1951–1956). As head of the army from 1933, he ruled the country even when out of office. He established his family's rule in Nicaragua, which lasted until 1979.

Songhai, empire of   Ancient African empire in the Niger Valley of the Sudan. Founded by Berbers in about 700 A.D. and converted to Islam, the empire reached its height under Askia Muhammad I (1493–1528) with Timbuktu its chief city. The invasion of Moorish troops from Morocco in 1591 destroyed the empire.

Sophia (1630–1714)   Electress of Hanover, and granddaughter of James I of England. Her son became George I of England by the Act of Settlement.

Sophia Alekseyevna (1657–1704)   Regent of Russia (1682–1689), daughter of Czar Alexis. She ruled during the minority of her brother Ivan V and half-brother Peter I (Peter the Great).

Sophists   Greek philosophical school that flourished from the 5th century B.C. Skeptical about the possibility of knowing truth, the Sophists opposed philosophical doctrine and instead taught the art of rhetorical persuasion. Protagoras was the first prominent Sophist. *See also* Philosophy section, page 19-22.

Sophocles (496–406 B.C.)   Greek tragedian who is ranked with his contemporaries Aeschylus and Euripides as one of the greatest tragic poets. He made several innovations in Greek drama and wrote over 120 plays.

South Africa Act   British act (effective May 31, 1910) that created the Union of South Africa by uniting the British possessions of Cape, Natal, Transvaal, and Orange River. The act also provided a constitution and its provisions established white supremacy there.

Southeast Asia Treaty Organization (SEATO) Alliance created by a treaty in 1954 by the United States, Australia, France, New Zealand, Pakistan, the Philippines, Thailand, and Britain. It was intended to bolster the region's defenses after the

French withdrawal from Indochina. The Vietnam War disrupted the alliance and it held its final joint exercises in 1976.

Souvanna Phouma (b. 1901)   Laotian statesman. He was frequently premier during the years of civil war from 1951. Forced to the right by the gains of the Communist Pathet Lao, he relied heavily on American aid during the Vietnam War years. Nevertheless, the Communists took control in 1974 and 1975.

Soviet   Council and basic elective political unit of the modern Soviet Union's government. Dominated by the Communist party, soviets are arranged in a hierarchy ranging from local to national jurisdiction and are charged with legislative and executive functions. The first soviets were organized by rebels during the 1905 revolution; during the 1917 revolution the soviets formed in all of Russia's major cities, rivaled the Russian Provisional Government for power.

Spaak, Paul-Henri (1899–1972)   Belgian statesman and socialist. The Belgian foreign minister at various times from 1938 until his death, he served as premier (1938 and 1939, 1947–1950) and became the first U.N. General Assembly president in 1946.

The Spanish army in a parade in Madrid.

Spanish Civil War   War (1936–1939) between republican (leftist) and nationalist (rightist) forces in Spain that brought General Franco to power in 1939. With the establishment of the Second Spanish Republic in 1931, moderate republicans (liberals, moderate Socialists) gained power. In the first, unsettled years of the republic they were opposed by the nationalists, then consisting of the aristocracy, royalists, the church, military, and Fascists. However, extremist factions on both sides came to the fore and, after civil war broke out in 1936, they played a major role in the continuing struggle. The republican faction was split by conflicts between Communists, anarchists, and radical Socialists. These disputes ultimately contributed to their downfall, despite considerable aid provided by the Soviets. The nationalists, on the other hand, were quickly unified under the leadership of Franco and were supplied with troops and material by Fascist Italy and Nazi Germany.

Spanish Succession, War of   A war (1701–1714) fought in Europe to determine the succession to the Spanish throne on the death of Spanish king Charles II. (Related fighting in the American colonies was known as Queen Anne's War.) French king Louis XIV, seeking to greatly enhance French power on the Continent, supported the accession of his grandson Philip of Anjou. This was opposed by England, which feared French political and economic domination of Europe, and by Holy Roman emperor Leopold I, who championed the claims of his son, Archduke Charles. A third claimant was Bavarian Prince Joseph Ferdinand. Attempts to find a negotiated settlement began after the War of the Grand Alliance (1689–1697) with the First and Second Partition treaties. They failed after the death of Charles II and the accession of Philip as Philip V. England then formed the Grand Alliance against France and the war began. Most fighting occurred outside Spain.

Sparta   City-state of ancient Greece. Founded in about 1100 B.C. by the Dorians, Sparta became, by the 6th century B.C. one of the most powerful city-states in Greece. Its dominance of the Peloponnesus and support of oligarchies against democracies led to its famous rivalry with Athens. Sparta finally defeated Athens in the Peloponnesian War and Sparta became the leading power in Greece. It remained so until its defeat by Thebes in 371 B.C. Sparta eventually fell under Macedonian, then Roman rule, and was destroyed by the Goths in 395 A.D.

Spartacus (d. 71 B.C.)   Thracian-born Roman gladiator who led the slaves in the Servile War in Italy (73–71 B.C.).

Spartacus League   Militant German Socialist organization. Protesting against World War I, the Spartacists split from the German Social Democratic party in 1916. They later allied themselves with the Russian Bolsheviks in 1919 and thus became the German Communist party. Party leaders Liebknecht and Luxemburg were murdered after they organized a general strike in Berlin in 1919.

Speer, Albert (1905–1981)   German architect and Nazi official. He organized German war production, bringing it to its peak in 1944.

Speke, John Hanning (1827–1864)   British explorer. He discovered Lake Victoria, one of the sources of the Nile River.

Spencer, Herbert (1820–1903)   English philosopher. An early advocate of evolution, he and Huxley helped bring about acceptance of Darwin's theory of evolution.

Sputnik   The world's first artificial satellite launched in 1957 by the Russians as the first of 10 satellites in the Sputnik series.

SS (Schutzstaffel) (Black Shirts)   Nazi military corps formed in 1929. Commanded by Himmler, it eventually became the instrument of Nazi party control in Germany and occupied territories. By the end of World War II the SS had grown to 35 divisions responsible for domestic and international security and included the Gestapo, the armed Waffen SS units, and concentration camp guards.

Stalin, Joseph Vissarionovich (1879–1953)   Soviet Communist leader, originally surnamed Dzhugashvili. Stalin became general secretary of the Central Committee in 1922 after the Bolsheviks came to power in the Revolution of 1917. In the power struggle after Lenin's death, Stalin defeated Trotsky, Zinoviev, Kamenev, and Bukharin to become virtual dictator of the Soviet Union and the Communist party. In 1928, Stalin instituted a new policy of industrialization and collectivization of agriculture. Resistance by kulaks, or farmers, to collectivization led to untold misery and death. Failures in Stalin's Five-Year Plan caused further hardship. The 1930s saw the Purge Trials, by which Stalin eliminated all potential opponents, and the signing of a nonaggression pact with Germany in 1939. Stalin's hopes of keeping Russia out of World War II ended with the German invasion of the Soviet Union in 1941, and his inability to deal at first with the invasion contributed to the Red Army's disastrous early losses. He subsequently acted as commander-in-chief of the victorious Soviet forces, although his role as military leader is disputed. Stalin's participation in Teheran in 1943 and Yalta in 1945 conferences established the Soviet Union as one of the major world powers, and led to Soviet domination of Eastern Europe after the war. In the late 1940s and early 1950s he became the leading Communist figure in the Cold War and further increased his tyrannical rule. After his death in 1953, a power struggle led to the rise of Khrushchev.

Joseph Stalin, who came to power in the Soviet Union after Lenin's death.

Stalingrad, battle of   Important turning point of World War II during which the Russians gained the offensive against the Germans. More than 500,000 Germans attacked and largely destroyed Stalingrad in September 1942, but the Russians continued to hold out and by November 1942, had surrounded the Germans, who were eventually forced to surrender in February 1943. Hundreds of thousands

were killed and wounded on both sides in this bloody battle.

Stanley, Sir Henry Morton (1841–1904)   British-born American reporter and explorer. Stanley's diverse activities included fighting for both sides in the American Civil War, newspaper reporting, finding the missing Dr. Livingstone in Africa, and colonizing the Congo and Uganda.

Star Chamber   English royal court. An outgrowth of the king's council, it eventually included civil and criminal matters in its jurisdiction, and for a time it was a popular expedient to common-law courts. Under the Stuart kings (notably Charles I), however, the court became a device for asserting royal powers. It was abolished in 1641 soon after by the Long Parliament.

State   Term applied to the political organization of a society, or the form or institution of government ruling the affairs of a society.

States-General *See* **Estates-General**.

Stephen (1097–1154)   King of England (1135–1154). Forced to acknowledge Matilda, the daughter of Henry I, as legitimate heir, Stephen nevertheless claimed the throne on Henry's death. Matilda invaded England in 1139 and, after capturing Stephen at Lincoln in 1141, reigned for six months. Stephen regained the throne and drove Matilda out of England in 1148, though he was unable to restore order in his domains.

Stoicism   Philosophical school founded in 300 B.C. at Thens by Zeno of Citium. It arose in opposition to Epicureanism, spread among the Greeks, and after the 2nd century B.C. became influential among the Romans. Stoicism was derived from the teachings of Cynics. Stoics held that all reality is material and that God, or reason, is the universal working force. Thus, living according to nature or reason was to come into harmony with the divine order of the universe. The ideal, virtuous life was to be achieved by exercising wisdom and restraint, by casting off passion and desire, and by right conduct and devotion to duty.

Stone Age   Stage in the development of human culture beginning about 2.5 million years ago and lasting until the beginning of the Bronze Age, or roughly about 3500 B.C. (in the Near East). Dating varies widely according to region and particular culture, and an essentially Stone Age culture exists even today among some primitive peoples. The Stone Age is characterized by the use of stone (along with wood and bone) for tools and implements, and is commonly subdivided into the Paleolithic and Neolithic states. The Paleolithic (Old Stone Age) period is the earliest and lasted until about 8000–6000 B.C. The Neolithic (New Stone Age) period is generally taken to begin with the advent of domestication of animals, cultivation of food plants, and development of village culture. It ends with the appearance of metal weapons and tools. The term Mesolithic (Middle Stone Age) usually refers to a stage of cultural development in northwestern Europe, from 8000–3000 B.C. *See also* History of Technology section.

Stonehenge   Famous prehistoric stone structure near Salisbury, in southern England. Built and added to between the 18th and 14th centuries B.C., it was apparently used for religious purposes, though not by the Druids, as is popularly believed. The structure is made up of large stones arranged in concentric circles about a central altar stone.

Strathcona, 1st baron (1820–1914)   Canadian financier and statesman. He became governor of the Hudson's Bay Company (1889–1914) and was a leading figure in the company that completed the Canadian Pacific Railway.

Streicher, Julius (1885–1946)   German Nazi leader, a vicious anti-Semite who used his newspaper, *Der Stürmer,* to spread hatred of the Jews.

Stresemann, Gustav (1878–1929) German statesman. As foreign minister of the Weimar Republic, he succeeded in pursuing a policy of conciliation with Germany's former enemies and arranged Germany's admission to the League of Nations.

Stuart (Stewart)   Royal family of Scotland and England (reigned 1603–1714). The family originated in the 11th century and from the 12th century the Stuarts were hereditary stewards of Scotland. The first Stuart king of Scotland was Robert II (1371–1390). The Stuart claim to the English throne stemmed from the marriage of Scottish king James IV to English king Henry VII's daughter, Mary Tudor. Their granddaughter, Mary Queen of Scots, was mother of Scottish King James VI, who became King James I (1603–1625), first Stuart king of England. Thereafter the Stuarts reigned (or claimed the throne) during the tumultuous period of the English Civil War, Restoration, and the Glorious Revolution. The Act of Settlement in 1701 excluded the Stuarts from the throne, but descendants of the Stuart line ruled until the Hanovers came to power in 1714.

Sucre, Antonio José de (1795–1830)   A South American revolutionary. He was Bolívar's chief lieutenant and participated in fighting against the Spanish in Peru, Bolivia, Ecuador, and Colombia and commanded in the Battle of Ayacucho. He was first president of Bolivia (1826–1828).

Suez Canal   Canal in Egypt. An important commercial waterway connecting the Mediterranean Sea and the Red Sea. Built by a private French company (1859–1869) under the supervision of F. de Lesseps, it passed to the British after they established control over Egypt in 1882.

Suharto (b. 1921)   Became president of Indonesia in 1967. He led the army in putting down a Communist-influenced coup d'état in 1965. From then on he effectively controlled the government, though Sukarno remained president. Suharto finally became president in 1967 and was reelected in 1973.

Sui   Chinese dynasty (581–618) that reunited China after the Six Dynasties period. The Sui emperors were Yang Chien (541–604) and his son, Yang Kuang (d. 618). They began construction of a canal system, called the Grand Canal, and refortified the Great Wall. The dynasty was overthrown and the succeeding T'ang dynasty adopted many of the Sui governmental systems.

Sukarno (1901–1970)   Indonesian statesman, president (1949–1967), and leader of the nationalists in the fight for independence from the Dutch (1945–1949). After becoming president he consolidated his power, dissolved the assembly in 1959,

and made himself dictator. At the same time, he sought closer relations with the Communists, particularly the Chinese. An attempted Communist coup, however, resulted in a takeover by the Indonesian army and Sukarno's ouster.

Suleiman I (Suleyman I) (1494–1566)   Sultan of the Ottoman Empire (1520–1566). He was known as "the Magnificent" and "the Lawgiver" for his expansion of the empire, his patronage of the arts, and his many reforms. His conquests include Belgrade in 1521, Rhodes in 1522, southern Hungary in 1526, and parts of Persia, Iraq and Tripoli by 1551. His navy, under the command of Barbarossa, terrorized the Mediterranean. During his reign, Suleiman also formed what became a long-standing alliance with France against the Hapsburg rulers of Europe.

Suleiman II (1642–1691)   Ottoman sultan (1687–1691). Through his minister, Mustafa Kuprili, he introduced liberal reforms. His reign was marked by the Austro-Turkish War.

Sulla, Lucius Cornelius (138–78 B.C.)   Roman general and politician. Sulla seized power in 83 B.C. and made himself dictator for life. He began the systematic murder of thousands of his opponents. At the same time, he instituted a program of governmental reforms, notably those to restore the power of the Senate. He resigned unexpectedly in 79 B.C.

Sully, Maximilien de Béthune, duc de (1560–1641)   French financier and statesman. A close friend of Henry IV, be became finance minister by 1598 and restored the royal treasury, which had been seriously depleted by the Wars of Religion.

Sultan   Islamic term applied at first to spiritual leaders of the Islamic community and later to Muslim rulers wielding political authority.

Sumer   Ancient civilization of southern Mesopotamia from roughly the 4th–3rd millennium B.C. to the beginning of the 2nd millennium B.C. Though an extensive village culture existed in the region by the 5th millennium B.C., the formation of Sumerian cities and the rise of Sumerian culture did not begin until the 4th–3rd millennium. From that time, such cities as Eridu, Erech, Lagash, Larsa, and Ur flourished as commercial and cultural centers and rivaled one another for control of neighboring lands. In the 24th century B.C., however, the Semitic people of northern Mesopotamia, the Akkadinas, conquered Sumer and made it part of their empire. The Akkadinas absorbed and thus spread much of the Sumerian culture (including cuneiform writing) before they were, in turn, conquered in the 22nd century B.C. by invaders from the north. Thereafter, the Sumerians enjoyed a brief resurgence under the leadership of such cities as Lagash and notably, Ur. But dynastic struggles and invasions by neighboring peoples brought on their final decline in the 20th century B.C. During their ascendancy, the Sumerians developed the first writing system (cuneiform) in the Near East, the first written civil law code, commercial and banking systems, skills in pottery-making and metalworking, and agricultural and military technology. The fall of Sumerian civilization was followed by the rise of Babylonia.

Sung   Chinese dynasty and historic period (960–1279), which followed the Five Dynasties period. One of the great epochs of Chinese history, it was marked by commercial prosperity, a cultural flowering, administrative reforms, and technological innovations. The dynasty was founded by Chao K'uang-yin (reigned 960–976). With its capital at Kaifeng, the Sung dynasty was not seriously threatened until 1127. At this time, invasions by nomadic Jurchen tribes from the north forced Sung rulers to move their capital to Lin-an (now Hangchow) in the South. Thus, the Sung dynasty is usually divided into northern Sung (960–1127) and southern Sung (1127–1279). The Sung dynasty was finally conquered in 1279 by the invading Mongols under Kublai Khan, who replaced it with the Yuan dynasty. Sung rulers instituted administrative reforms, many of which were aimed at centralizing power and also fostered the growth of schools and a great government bureaucracy. Commercial prosperity came as a result of increased trade, notably with India, Persia, and the Arabs. The Sung period was further marked by the increase in printing (with movable type by the 11th century), a revival of Confucianism and the writings of Chu Hsi, the compilation of great encyclopedias and histories, and a golden age of Chinese landscape painting and ceramics. It also saw the use of gunpowder and the magnetic compass for navigation.

Sunga Dynasty that ruled North India between 185 and 73 B.C. It succeeded the Maurya Empire. During the rule of this dynasty Brahmanical Hinduism reemerged as the official state religion, after a temporary eclipse by Buddhism.

Sunnites (Sunnis) Traditional or orthodox sect of Islam, adhered to by over three-quarters of all Muslims. They accept the actual succession of the early Muslim caliphs, while the other major sect, the Shi'ites, say that Ali (the fourth) was the first true successor Muhammad. The Sunnites also accept the Sunnah as the legitimate body of Muslim traditions. *See also* Religion section, page 22-20.

Sun Yat-sen (1866–1925) Chinese revolutionary, the father of the Chinese republic, and leader of the Nationalist Kuomintang until his death. Sun led an abortive revolt at Canton in 1895 and for the next 16 years worked in exile to promote revolution in China. He returned to China during the Revolution of 1911 and served for a few months as president of the provisional government (1911 and 1912). Next he led an abortive revolt in 1913 against the dictatorial regime of Yuan Shih-k'ai and fled China until 1917. Sun became president of the Nationalist government at Canton in 1923, formed an alliance with the Chinese Communists, and reorganized the Nationalist Kuomintang with the help of Russia.

Svoboda, Ludvik (1895–1979) Czechoslovakian general and president (1968–1975). Svoboda was a military hero in both World War I and World War II. As president, he obtained the release of the political prisoners taken in the Russian invasion of 1968.

Syndicalism Theory of government holding that power of the state should be primarily concentrated in the hands of organized labor unions. Influenced by Proudhon and Sorel, it flourished especially in France, Spain, Italy, and Latin America before World War I. It declined with the spread of Communist-dominated unions.

 **Tacitus** (55?–117 A.D.) Roman historian. Tacitus served in many military and governmental posts before becoming consul in 97 A.D. He quickly gained a reputation as an eloquent speaker, then turned to writing. His works include *Germania,* a history of early German tribes and two major works on Roman history, the *Histories* and the *Annals.*

Tagore, Sir Rabvindranath (1861–1941) Indian poet and philosopher. Tagore sought to combine elements of East and West in his works. He was the first Asiatic to win the Nobel Prize in Literature in 1913.

Taika Reforms Series of reform measures carried out in the mid-600s to establish a stronger government in Japan modeled after that of China under the Tang dynasty. All land in Japan was made the property of the imperial government which allotted it to peasants to farm. The reforms included a new tax system, roads, and reorganizing the country in provinces administered by governors appointed by the imperial government.

Taiping Rebellion Uprising (1850–1864) against the Manchu dynasty of China, a precursor to the Nationalist and Communist movements. Its leader was Hung Hsiu-ch'uan (1814–1864) who believed he was the younger brother of Jesus Christ. A new religion was formed around his teachings in the late 1840s and gained support among the peasants and workers in Kwangsi. It was loosely based on Christianity, opposed Confucianism, and advocated radical reforms, such as communal ownership of property and equality of women. Beginning in 1850 with a few thousand followers, the rebels soon gathered support and eventually mustered a highly organized army of 1 million zealous troops. The rebels succeeded in capturing Nanking in 1853 and made it their capital. The failure of subsequent expeditions and internal dissent weakened the movement, however. An attempt to take Shanghai in 1860 was stopped by the "Ever-Victorious Army" organized by Europeans. A Manchu army under Tseng Kuo-fan besieged Nanking (1862–1864) and finally captured the city in 1864. Hung committed suicide and the revolt was broken. Nevertheless, it had seriously weakened the Manchu government and paved the way for later rebellions and the final collapse of the Manchu dynasty.

Taira family Japanese military clan, or family also called Heike. Founded in the 9th century, it reached its height in the 12th century but was defeated in 1185 by the Minamoto clan.

Taisho (Yoshihito) (1879–1926) Japanese emperor (1912–1926). During his reign, Japan joined the Allies in World War I and became firmly established as a great power. His son, the future emperor Hirohito, became regent in 1921.

Tale of the Genji Written in about the year 1000 by Lady Murasaki Shikubu, it is the world's first novel and is considered one of the masterpieces of Japanese literature.

Talleyrand, Charles Maurice de (Talleyrand-Périgord) (1754–1838) French statesman and diplomat. His persuasive skills brought him high advisory and diplomatic positions under the Directory,

Napoleon, Louis XVIII, and Louis Philippe. He represented France at the Congress of Vienna (1814 and 1815), skillfully limiting the demands of other countries upon France, and restoring many European borders to their Napoleonic status.

Talmud   Written compilation of the oral laws of the Jews, after the Old Testament, the most important Judaic text. It consists of the Mishna, the text of the laws; and the Gemara, commentary.

Tamerlane (Timur) (1336–1405)   Mongol conqueror. A Muslim and self-proclaimed descendant of Genghis Khan, he gained firm control of the throne of Samarkand (in modern Soviet Turkistan) by 1369. Thereafter he led his army of Turks and Mongols in a series of campaigns that vastly expanded his domains. He warred against Persia, and by 1387 had extended his empire to the Euphrates River. Crossing the Euphrates in 1392, he advanced northward to conquer the Caucasus region. India was invaded next in 1398 and the Delhi Sultanate was ruthlessly destroyed, during which time Tamerlane ordered the massacre of tens of thousands. Turning westward again, Tamerlane captured Baghdad in 1401, attacked the Egyptian Mamelukes in Syria, and defeated the Ottoman Turks in Asia Minor. Tamerlane died before launching his planned invasion of China and on his death the empire he had created was divided among his heirs.

Tamil   Ancient Dravidian dialect, spoken mainly in Madras, India.

T'ang   Dynasty of Chinese rulers (618–907). The dynasty was founded after the overthrow of the Sui dynasty by Li Yuan. T'ang rulers greatly expanded the empire, and at its height, under Emperor Hsuan Tsung (ruled 712–756), it included parts of Korea, Manchuria, Mongolia, Tibet, and Turkistan. Trade was stimulated, and in the ensuing period of prosperity the arts, particularly poetry and sculpture, flourished. Confucianism enjoyed a resurgence and was officially adopted by the state. The civil service system was further refined. However, the empire was weakened by an unsuccessful revolt (755–763) led by An Lu-shan, a Turkish general. In subsequent years, provincial warlords gained power and ultimately overthrew the T'ang rulers.

T'ang Hsuan Tsung (685–762)   Chinese emperor of the T'ang dynasty. During his reign China reached the peak of its power and prosperity, though the T'ang dynasty's decline began soon after.

T'ang T'ai Tsung (600–649)   Chinese emperor (626–649). Second emperor of the T'ang dynasty. Considered the founder of the dynasty, he consolidated the empire, drove out the Turks, and encouraged art and literature.

Tantras   Collection of Hindu and Buddhist holy books that include information on such topics as religious rituals, traditions, and the practice of yoga. They date from the 6th or 7th century.

Taoism   Major Chinese religious and philosophical system. Taoism was, by tradition, founded by Lao-Tze in the 6th century B.C. According to Taoism, human beings can find Tao (the Way) by following a policy of nonaction, or passivity. The Way is the natural course of all events in the world, and the human path to happiness is through elimination of desire, ambition, and struggle, which go contrary to all nature. Taoism was in part a reaction to the organized system of ethical conduct advanced by Confucianism. By the 5th century A.D., it was an organized religion. A hierarchy of gods was developed and ways to increase longevity and achieve immortality were sought. Taoist religion has been an important influence in China, especially in the arts.

Tarik (ibn Ziyad) (ca. 711)   Berber general. Tarik led the first Muslim invasion of Spain in 711, conquering much of the Iberian Peninsula and firmly establishing Moorish influence there.

Tatars (Tartars)   Turkic-speaking peoples of the former U.S.S.R. living near the Volga River region and numbering some 6 million. The name once referred to Mongols and other Asiatic people who invaded Europe, some of whom merged to form the Golden Horde, a powerful force in Russia.

Tay Son Rebellion   Vietnamese uprising (1771–1788) led by three brothers from Tay Son, Vietnam. They overthrew the ruling dynasties governing Vietnam, defeated the Chinese sent to support the rulers, and unified the country. During their brief rule (1788–1793) they attempted to introduce social reforms.

Teheran Conference   Allied conference of 1943 at Teheran, Iran, during World War II. Attended by President Roosevelt, British Prime Minister Churchill, and Soviet Premier Stalin, it coordinated strategy involving the Allied invasion of Western Europe.

Ten Kingdoms   Independent kingdoms that rose in southern China in the period (907–960) between the end of the T'ang and the rise of the Sung dynasties.

Tennis Court Oath   Oath sworn on June 20, 1789 by members of the Third Estate during the early stages of the French Revolution. The delegates to the Estates-General had on June 17 formed the National Assembly, and, finding themselves barred from their meeting place, convened at a tennis court, where they swore not to disband until a constitution had been granted the country. Their determination led King Louis XVI to direct the clergy and nobility to join the National Assembly on June 27.

Tenochtitlán   Ancient capital city of the Aztecs, which stood on the site of present-day Mexico City. Founded in 1325, it was captured and largely razed in 1521 by Cortés.

Ten Years' War   Cuban revolt against Spanish rule (1868–1878). It was led by Carlos Manuel de Céspedes, who called for the gradual emancipation of slaves and universal suffrage. He also favored Cuban independence, although not all the insurrectionists agreed. After 10 years of brutal fighting, which left about 200,000 Cubans and Spanish dead, the insurrection was defeated. The Treaty of El Zanjón in 1878 made liberal promises, most of which were not kept.

Tet Offensive   Major offensive in February 1968 by the Vietcong and North Vietnamese regulars during the Vietnam War. The combined Communist forces staged attacks in more than 100 cities throughout South Vietnam (including Saigon), thus proving their continued strength and embarrassing American military leaders. Fighting lasted a month at the city of Hue and Communist losses were heavy, but the offensive proved a major propaganda victory.

Tetzel, Johann (1465–1519)   German Dominican monk. His granting of indulgences in return for donations to a building fund sparked Luther's initial challenge to the Catholic church.

Teutonic Knights (German Order)   Catholic military order founded in 1190 at Acre by German nobles during the Third Crusade. In the 13th century the order moved to Europe, became a powerful force, and gained control of Prussia. Through the 14th century, the order expanded its holdings and power, and many of its cities became members of the Hanseatic League. Its continued attacks on Poland and Lithuania led to the order's defeat in the Battle of Tannenberg in 1410 and its subsequent decline. The order was dissolved in 1525 by Grand Master Albert of Brandenburg.

Tewfik Pasha (1852–1892)   Khedive of Egypt (1879–1892). Egyptian opposition to Western influence during his rule led to military intervention by the British in 1882, who took virtual control of Egypt.

Tewkesbury, battle of   English battle on May 4, 1471, the final battle of the Wars of the Roses. There the Yorkists under King Edward IV defeated the Lancastrians led by Margaret of Anjou and Prince Edward.

Thales (636–546 B.C.)   Greek philosopher, considered the first Western natural philosopher. One of the Seven Wise Men of Greece, he held that all things were based on one element—water.

Thanom Kittikachorn (b. l911)   Thai army general and prime minister (1963–1973). He restored parliamentary democracy under a new constitution in 1968, but his seizure of power through a military takeover in 1971 led to his ouster in 1973.

Thant, U (1909–1974)   Burmese diplomat. As secretary-general of the United Nations (1962–1971) he helped find peaceful solutions to the Cuban missile crisis in 1962 and the conflicts in the Congo after 1962 and Cyprus in 1964. He was also influential in resolving the India-Pakistan War of 1965.

Thatcher, Margaret (b. 1925)   Became British prime minister in 1979. A Conservative, she was elected amid a worsening economic crisis in Britain and later oversaw the British victory in the Falkland Islands War. She stepped down as prime minister and Conservative party leader in November 1990, and was succeeded by John Major.

Themistocles (525–460 B.C.)   Athenian statesman and naval commander. Themistocles urged the strengthening of the Greek navy and defeated the Persians at Salamis in 480 B.C.

Theocracy   Form of government in which God is the ultimate authority and laws evolve as from God, through priests or clergy. Thus, priests act as both spiritual and secular rulers of the state.

Theodora (500–548 A.D)   Byzantine empress (527–548 A.D.), wife of Emperor Justinian. She had great influence during Justinian's rule and played a key role in saving the throne during the Nika riot in 532 A.D.

Theodoric the Great (454–526 A.D.)   Ostrogothic king of Italy (493–526). Acting in behalf of Byzantine Emperor Zeno, Theodoric led his Gothic army in an invasion of Italy from 488. By 493 he had captured Ravenna and killed Odoacer, the German

chieftain who had overthrown the last Western Roman emperor in 476. He subsequently ruled over Italy as king, though he was nominally in the service of the Byzantines.

Theodosian Code   Compilation of Roman laws from the reign of Constantine to that of Theodosius II, under whom it was issued in 438 A.D. It was later used in compiling the Justinian Code.

Theodosius I (Theodosius the Great) (346?–395 A.D.)   Roman emperor of the East (379–395). He defeated the Goths in the East and convened the Second Council of Constantinople in 381.

Theodosius II (401–450 A.D.)   Roman emperor of the East (408–450 A.D.). He left the actual ruling to his sister Pulcheria and his wife Eudocia. He authorized the Theodosian Code and negotiated with Attila the Hun.

Thermidor   Eleventh month of the French Revolutionary calendar. The coup d'état of 9 Thermidor (July 27, 1794) brought down Robespierre and ended the Reign of Terror. The coup was carried out by a hastily organized coalition of factions in the National Convention, following a speech by Robespierre on July 26 in which he denounced certain unnamed enemies. Robespierre and others were guillotined July 28 and the Thermidorian reaction, as it was called, was swift. The machinery of the Reign of Terror was dismantled, the radical Jacobins were suppressed, and the moderates came into control. The Thermidorian period ended with the establishment of the Directory in 1795.

Thermopylae   Historic Greek pass linking northern and southern Greece. Here a small force of Spartans under Leonidas made a heroic but unsuccessful stand in 480 B.C. against the vastly superior army of Persian king Xerxes during the Persian Wars.

Thiers, Louis Adolphe (1797–1877)   French statesman and historian. Thiers served in several ministerial positions under King Louis Philippe, opposed Emperor Napoleon III and the Franco-Prussian War, and after the war became president of the Third French Republic (1871–1873).

Third Coalition, War of the (1805)   Early phase of the Napoleonic Wars fought by a coalition of England, Austria, Russia, and Sweden against France and Spain. Napoleon defeated the Austrians in the Battle of Ulm, suffered a naval defeat by the British in the Battle of Trafalgar, and defeated the Austrians and Russians in the Battle of Austerlitz, thus crushing the coalition.

Third Reich   Name given the German government (1933–1945) under the rule of Hitler and the Nazi party. *See* **Hitler, Adolf**; **National Socialism**; **Nazi party**.

Third Republic   Name given the French government established in 1870 after the fall of the Second Empire in the Franco-Prussian War. It was succeeded in 1940 by the Vichy government during World War II.

Third World   Term applied to the less developed and often politically nonaligned countries of Africa, Asia, and Latin America.

Thirty Tyrants   1. Name given the group of 30 Athenians who ruled Athens (404 and 403 B.C.) under Spartan domination after the Peloponnesian War. They were overthrown by Thrasybulus.

2. Name given the group of pretenders to the Roman throne who rose during the reigns of Emperors Valerian and Gallienus. (253–268 A.D.).

Thirty Years' War Series of interrelated conflicts (1618–1648) that ultimately led to the end of Hapsburg dominance in Europe, the crippling of the Holy Roman Empire, and the emergence of France as the leading power in Europe. The war, which left Germany devastated, began in Bohemia as a reaction to imperial repression of Protestantism and quickly spread to other Hapsburg domains in the Holy Roman Empire. Denmark and Sweden, each in turn, joined the conflict against the Hapsburgs. In the final phase of the conflict, France entered the war in a successful move to break the power of the Holy Roman Empire. Peace negotiations (1645–1648) culminated in the Treaty of Westphalia in 1648, which ended the Thirty Years' War. Its terms were favorable to France and Sweden and left the house of Hapsburg and the Holy Roman Empire severely crippled. France became the dominant power in Europe.

Three Emperors' League Alliance (1873–1877, 1881–1887) of Germany, Austria-Hungary, and Russia, originated by German chancellor Bismarck, to preserve peace between Russia and Austria-Hungary and to isolate France. It was disrupted by the Russo-Turkish War (1877 and 1878) but was secretly renewed in 1881.

Three Kingdoms Period in Chinese history (220–280 A.D.) during which three kingdoms ruled China after the fall of the Han dynasty. They were the Wei, which ruled in the North; the Wu, which ruled in the South; and the Shu Han, which ruled in the West. Wei conquered Shu Han in 264 A.D. and established the Chin dynasty. The dynasty then conquered the Wu in 280 A.D. and reunited China.

Thucydides (460–400 B.C.) Greek historian. wrote *The History of the Peloponnesian War* (covering the years 431–411), which is noted for its accuracy, impartiality, and (then) novel examination of human character in relation to the events of the war.

Thugs (Phansigars) Indian religious sect. Devoted to the goddess Kali, the Thugs dressed as religious mendicants or merchants and killed their victims, usually travelers, as offerings to her. They were suppressed by the British in the 1800s.

Thutmose I (Thothmes I) (d. 1512 B.C.) Egyptian king (1526–1512). He secured control of the Nile Valley as far as its fourth cataract, on whose rocks he inscribed records of his victories. He also sent military expeditions deep into Syria.

Thutmose II (Thothmes II) Ancient Egyptian king (1512–1504 B.C.). He married his half-sister Hathsepsut, who quickly overpowered him and ruled in his stead.

Thutmose III (d. 1450 B.C.) Egyptian king (1504–1450 B.C.). The regency of his aunt, Queen Hathsepsut, ended in 1482, and he began the conquests that made Egypt a great power. He added Syria, Kadesh, Mitanni, and part of the Sudan to his empire. He erected many monuments and temples and brought Egypt great wealth and prosperity.

Tiananmen Square (Beijing, China) Public square, it was the scene in 1989 of bloody student demonstrations for democratic reform. Sparked by the death on April 15 of a party reformer, Hu Yao-

Pang, crowds of up to 100,000 a day defied orders and occupied the square. On the night of June 3–4, heavily armed government troops attacked and killed approximately 1,000 people. Thousands more were arrested and some leaders fled abroad.

Tiberius (42 B.C.–37 A.D.) Second Roman emperor (14–37 A.D.), successor to his stepfather Augustus. He ruled ably in the early years of his reign but later, under the influence of Sejanus, became a tyrant.

Tigris and Euphrates Rivers rising in Turkey and flowing through southwestern Asia to join in southern Iraq. The ancient region of Mesopotamia encompassed this river system, and gave rise to such early civilizations as Sumer, Akkad, Babylonia, Assyria, and Chaldaea.

Tilak, Bal Gangadhar (1856–1920) Indian Nationalist leader. He negotiated the Lucknow Pact in 1916, which unified Hindus and Muslims against British rule in India.

Timurids Turkish dynasty (15th century) descended from Tamerlane. Upon Tamerlane's death, the empire, comprising domains extending from India to Persia (modern Iran), was divided into Eastern and Western sections and distributed between his sons. Shah Rokh (ruled 1405–1447), given the Eastern half of the empire, quickly reunited much of the territory. He sparked a literary and cultural movement, established a library at his capital Herat, and encouraged trade. After his death, the empire fell into anarchy and eventually disintegrated into local dynasties. Baber, one of these rulers, founded the Mogul Empire in India.

Tito (Josip Broz) (1892–1980) President of Yugoslavia (1953–1980) and Communist leader. He became leader of the Communist party in Yugoslavia in 1937. During World War II, he led the partisans in guerrilla fighting and, from 1945, headed the Yugoslav government. He pursued policies independently of the Soviet Union and was expelled from the Cominform in 1948. Thereafter, he maintained relations with Western and Communist powers, as well as with nonaligned countries. His regime was one of the most liberal in the Communist world.

Togo, Heihachiro, Count (1847–1934) Japanese admiral. In the Russo-Japanese War, he defeated the Russians at Port Arthur in 1904 and at the Battle of Tsushima in 1905—the first defeat of a European power by Asians.

Tojo, Hideki (1884–1948) Japanese general and wartime premier (1942–1944). Tojo helped instigate the attack on Pearl Harbor in 1941 and led Japan's war effort until 1944.

Tokugawa Last shogunate of Japan (ruled 1603–1867). Founded by Ieyasu, who came to power in 1603 after the death of Hideyoshi, the shogunate ruled by means of a centralized feudal government. The capital was moved from Kyoto to Edo (now Tokyo) and the reign of the Tokugawa family was marked by a period of peace, prosperity, and cultural flowering. Nearly all foreign trade was ended and Confucianism was promoted. The Tokugawa shoguns were ousted from power during the Meiji Restoration.

Toltec Ancient people of Mexico, warriors who dominated central Mexico from 900 A.D. to the rise of the Aztecs (in the 12th and 13th centuries). Toltecs were skilled in building, metallurgy, and the arts. They are believed to have worshiped the sun and practiced human sacrifice.

Tordesillas, Treaty of   Treaty of 1494 between Spain and Portugal dividing between them the newly discovered lands in the Americas and the East. The treaty generally followed a papal bull issued by Alexander VI, allotting the Americas to Spain and Africa, and Asia to Portugal. But it fixed the dividing line farther west, giving Portugal a claim to Brazil.

Tory   Name of a once-powerful English political party. It was originally applied to Catholic king James II's supporters, who believed in the divine right and absolutist powers of the king. After the Glorious Revolution of 1688, the party represented the rural gentry and generally favored a powerful monarchy, religious uniformity, and noninvolvement in foreign wars. The party was powerful under Queen Anne (reigned 1702–1714) but was effectively dissolved as a party under George I, because of its ties with the Jacobites. A new Tory party formed under the leadership of William Pitt and remained in power from 1783–1830. However, the party's reactionary policies during this period, coupled with passage of the Reform Bill of 1832, resulted in the breakup of the party in the 1830s. Tory factions reemerged in the Conservative party.

Totalitarianism   Form of authoritarian government in which the state attempts to control every aspect of the life of its citizens. The term was first used to describe the Fascist regime in Italy, the Nazi regime in Germany, and the Communist regime in the Soviet Union.

Toussaint L'Ouverture, François Dominique (1744–1803)   Haitian revolutionary leader. As the leader of a band of rebels, he sided with the French in 1794 and drove out the British and Spaniards. He fell afoul of Napoleon in 1801, however, when he sought greater independence from France.

Trafalgar, battle of   Naval battle in 1805 between Britain and France, fought during the Napoleonic Wars, off Cape Trafalgar, Spain. It established British naval superiority for the rest of the century and ended Napoleon's plans to invade England. Twenty-seven British ships under Admiral Nelson defeated a fleet of 33 French and Spanish ships commanded by Villeneuve. The French lost 20 ships, the British none. But Nelson was killed by a French sniper.

Trajan (53–117 A.D.)   Roman emperor (98–117 A.D.), successor to Nerva. Born in Spain, he was the first non-Italian emperor. He conquered Dacia and much of Parthia in the East. He encouraged building and constructed Trajan's Forum in Rome and Trajan's bridge (the first bridge across the Danube).

Trent, Council of   Important council of the Roman Catholic church, held three sessions (1545–1547, 1551 and 1552, 1562 and 1563) under two popes, Paul III and Pius IV. It met in response to the Protestant Reformation, and all doctrinal disputes raised by Protestants were answered. The council's far-reaching results included reforms and definitions concerning the sacraments, the Scriptures, church dogma, duties of the clergy, and other

subjects. The council marked the beginning of the Catholic Reformation.

Tribune   Ancient Roman government official. Originally military officers, tribunes by the 5th century B.C. had assumed governmental functions, notably as protectors of the rights of the plebeians. Tribunes were elected by the plebs, usually 10 in number, and gradually gained control (by their veto power) over the Roman Senate. They had relatively little power during the Roman Empire.

Trident Conference (Anglo-American Conference)   Secret wartime conference of World War II in Washington, D.C. in 1943. President Roosevelt, Prime Minister Churchill, and their combined chiefs of staff planned the opening of a second front in Europe (Normandy invasion).

Triple Alliance   1. Alliance formed in 1668 by England, The Netherlands, and Sweden to oppose French aggression during the reign of French king Louis XIV. The alliance was short-lived, as Louis soon secured an agreement (Treaty of Dover) with England. 2. Alliance formed in 1717 by France, Great Britain, and The Netherlands, primarily to oppose Spain and secure the provisions of the Peace of Utrecht. In 1718 the alliance was joined by Austria, and thus became the Quadruple Alliance. 3. Alliance formed in the late 19th and early 20th centuries by Germany, Austria-Hungary, and Italy. It was opposed by the Triple Entente consisting of France, Russia, and Great Britain. The two power blocs—Triple Alliance and Triple Entente—continued to dominate European politics up to the eve of World War I.

Triumvirate   In ancient Rome, a board of three government officials appointed to carry out a specified task. The term was applied to the alliance between Caesar, Pompey, and Crassus (formed 60 B.C.). This was the First Triumvirate. The Second Triumvirate consisted of Octavian (later Augustus), Antony, and Lepidus, and resulted in reforms that gave the triumvirs dictatorial powers. It was organized in 43 B.C.

Trojan War   Legendary war between the Greeks, led by Agamemnon, and the city of Troy, defended by Hector and others. It is believed to have had its roots in a real conflict that took place in 1200 B.C. The mythical battle began when Trojan prince Paris kidnapped Helen, wife of King Menelaus of Sparta. For 10 years the Trojans and the invading Greeks fought many heroic but inconclusive battles. Finally, the Greeks built a large wooden horse, ostensibly a gift for the Trojans. A number of Greek warriors hid inside it and the Greeks embarked their ships, pretending to sail home. The Trojans wheeled the horse inside the city and that night the warriors opened the gates of Troy for their fellow Greeks, who then conquered the city. The war inspired many poems and stories, most notably Homer's *Iliad* and *Odyssey*.

Trotsky, Leon (pseud. of Bronstein, Lev Davidovich) (1879–1940)   Russian Communist leader. He was a chief theorist, a leader in both the 1905 and 1917 revolutions, and Lenin's commissar for foreign affairs. In the latter capacity he arranged the Treaty of Brest-Litovsk with Germany. He next became war commissar, rebuilding the Russian army. Trotsky and his archrival, Stalin struggled for power after Lenin's death in 1924. Stalin eventually stripped Trotsky of his influence and expelled him from Russia in 1929. Trotsky spent the rest of his life in exile, writing and preaching revolution.

Troubadours   Medieval lyric poets who composed in the dialect of Provence, *langue d'oc*, in southern France. They flourished between the 11th and the 13th centuries and greatly influenced subsequent European literature.

Troyes, Treaty of   Treaty in 1420 between England and France. An attempt to settle the Hundred Years' War (1337–1453). English king Henry V was to marry the daughter of Charles VI and thereby become successor to the French throne. But the disinherited French dauphin (later Charles VII) resisted the settlement with the aid of Joan of Arc.

Truce of God   Decree issued by the church in the Middle Ages that forbade fighting on weekends and holy days. Gradually more days were added until there were only 80 days a year when fighting was legal. These restrictions could not be strictly enforced.

Trudeau, Pierre Elliott (b. 1919) French Canadian Liberal party leader and prime minister (1968–1979, 1980–1984). He was noted for his championship of liberal domestic programs and for a more independent foreign policy. His administration was marked by the rise of French separatism and ongoing attempts at constitutional reform. He was defeated in 1984 by Brian Mulroney.

Trujillo, Molina, Rafael Leonidas (1891–1961) General and dictator of the Dominican Republic (1930–1961). His rule was marked by ruthless suppression of opposition, which ultimately led to his assassination.

Trusteeship   Method of governing territories. It was established in 1946 by the U.N. to replace the former League of Nations mandates. By the mid-1970s, nearly all the U.N. trusteeship territories had become independent nations and U.N. members.

Tseng Kuo-fan (1811–1872) Chinese general and government administrator under the Ch'ing dynasty. Tseng was successful in suppressing the Taiping Rebellion and conciliating the Western powers. He gave the declining Chinese imperial government a new lease on life.

Tshombe, Moise Kapenda (1919–1969) Congolese leader. Tshombe led Katanga in secession (1960–1963) from the newly independent Congo Republic, was said to be implicated in the murder of Lumumba, and was finally exiled in 1963. He returned to become premier (1964 and 1965) of a reunited Congo Republic, but soon after was accused of treason and fled.

Tudor   Dynasty of English rulers (reigned 1485–1603). The family was of Welsh origins. Its rise to power began with Owen Tudor (d. 1461), who fought in the service of Henry V, wed Henry's widow (Catherine of Valois), and supported his Lancastrian stepson Henry VI in the Wars of the Roses. Owen Tudor's grandson (Henry Tudor) became Henry VII after the Lancastrian victory at Bosworth Field in 1485 and thus founded the Tudor dynasty. The subsequent Tudor reign saw the rise of England as a naval power, creation of the Church of England, and increased powers of the monarchy.

Tull, Jethro (1674–1741) English agriculturist and inventor. He influenced English agriculture through his invention of a seed drill that planted seeds in a straight row.

Tupac, Amaru (1742?–1781) Peruvian Indian revolutionary. Taking the name of an ancestral Inca leader, he led Peruvian Indians in a revolt (1780 and 1781) to improve their lot. He was captured and executed.

Tupper, Sir Charles (1821–1915) Canadian statesman. As premier of Nova Scotia (1864–1867), he helped bring that province into the Dominion. He was instrumental in building the Canadian Pacific Railway and was briefly the federal prime minister in 1896.

Turgot, Anne Robert Jacques (1727–1781) French economist and statesman. A Physiocrat (*see* page 11-98) he was controller of finance (1774–1776) and attempted by drastic reforms to restore the royal treasury. He was opposed by Queen Marie Antoinette, however, and his ouster continued the financial crisis that contributed to the outbreak of the French Revolution.

Tutankhamen (Tutenkhamon) (d. 1352 B.C.) Egyptian pharaoh (1361–1352). He restored the traditional god Amon to prominence after the religious revolution of Ikhnaton. His world-famous tomb was discovered in 1922.

The golden funeral mask of the Egyptian pharoah Tutankhamen.

Tutu, Archbishop Desmond (b. 1931) Anglican cleric, archbishop of Capetown, head of South African Angelican Church. A world-renowned opposition leader to apartheid, he won the Nobel Prize for Peace in 1984. *See also* **Apartheid**.

Twelve Tribes of Israel   In the Bible, the Hebrew tribes that settled in the Promised Land after the Exodus. The tribes were named after Jacob's offspring.

Two Sicilies, Kingdom of the   Name of the kingdoms of Sicily and Naples, which included all of southern Italy below the Papal States and which were variously ruled separately and jointly from the 11th–19th centuries. The Kingdom of the Two Sicilies was founded by the Normans, who conquered Sicily and the southern Italian Peninsula (kingdom of Naples) from the Byzantines, Muslims, and Lombards. The territory passed to the Hohenstaufen Holy Roman emperors in the 12th century. Under them, southern Italy became a prosperous commercial center from which Greek and Arab culture spread to Europe. The French nobleman Charles of Anjou conquered Sicily and the kingdom of Naples in 1266 after the Hohenstaufen line died out, but he was driven out of Sicily in 1282 after the Revolt of the Sicilian Vespers. The Spanish House of Aragon then took control of Sicily in 1302, while the kingdom of Naples remained in the hands of the French Angevin line. A long series of wars between Sicily and Naples ensued, with the Spanish Aragonese finally winning both kingdoms in 1442. Spanish rule was broken by the War of Spanish Succession (1701–1714) and the brief rule of the Austrian Hapsburgs. By 1735, however, the Spanish Bourbons were again in firm control of both Sicily and Naples. Napoleon gained Italy at the end of the 18th century. Spanish rule was restored in 1815, and from 1816 the kingdoms of Sicily and Naples were ruled jointly as the Kingdom of the Two Sicilies. The Kingdom of the Two Sicilies was finally conquered in 1860 by Garibaldi, and was joined with northern states to form the kingdom of Italy in 1861.

Tyler, Wat   (d. 1381)   English rebel leader. He led the Peasants' Revolt in 1381.

Tyrant   In Greek history, a ruler who usurped or acquired power by illegal means. The term was originally not connected with oppressive rule. Tyrants especially appeared during the 7th–5th centuries B.C. and often favored the populace against the aristocrats. Instances of their misrule after the 5th century gradually gave the term its modern meaning.

Tz'u Hsi   (Tzu Hsi) (1834–1908)   Dowager empress of China (1861–1908) and regent for most of that period. She came to power by bearing the emperor's only son, T'ung Chih. As regent for him and his successors, she steadfastly resisted reforms and played a role in the Boxer Rebellion.

U   **Ulbricht, Walter**   (1893–1973)   East German Communist leader. A founder of the German Communist party, he became deputy premier of the German Democratic Republic in 1949 and was secretary general of the Social Unity party (1950– 1971). He ordered the building of the Berlin Wall in 1961.

Umar   (Omar) (581–644)   Second Muslim caliph (634–644). A father-in-law of the prophet Muhammad, he chose Abu Bakr as the first caliph to succeed to the authority of the prophet in 632, and succeeded him in 634. During his caliphate, Arab armies advanced into Syria, Egypt, and Persia. He established the administration and taxation of the subsequent empire.

Umayyad   (Omayyad)   Muslim dynasty that ruled (661–750) the empire of the caliphate. The Umayyads held power after the first four orthodox caliphs, so-called because the legitimacy of their reigns is unquestioned. The Umayyads, however, took power after Muawiya, founder of the dynasty, deposed Caliph Hasan in 651. The accession of the Umayyads thus gave rise to the split between the majority Sunni Muslim sect (which accepts the Umayyad legitimacy) and the Shi'ite sect (which denies it). The Umayyads established their capital at Damascus, continued the expansion of the empire of the caliphate (Spain was conquered), established effective systems of communication, and instituted administrative reforms. Internal unrest mounted toward the end of their reign and a successful revolt in 750 brought the Abbasid dynasty to power. Following the revolt, members of the Umayyad family were massacred. Only one is known to have escaped (Abd ar-Rahman I) and he established the Umayyad dynasty in Spain (in power 755–1031).

United Arab Republic   Name designating the political union between Egypt and Syria (1958–1961). Yemen also joined the union in 1958. Intended to be the nucleus of the United Arab States, it broke up after a coup d'état in Syria and Syria's subsequent withdrawal in 1961.

United Front   Union formed twice between the Chinese Communist party and the Kuomintang (1924–1926, 1936–1945). The second alliance was established to achieve a common front against the Japanese invaders.

United Nations   (U.N.)   International body formed during World War II by the nations allied against the Axis. The term was first used by President Roosevelt, and the concept of a permanent body to deal with international problems posing a threat to world peace gained momentum with the Moscow Declaration in 1943, the Dumbarton Oaks Conference in 1944, and the Yalta Conference in 1945. A meeting of the Allied nations at the San Francisco Conference led to signing on June 26 and ratification on October 24 of the United Nations Charter. The charter provided for several structures within the organization, the leading ones being the Secretariat, the Security Council, and the General Assembly. All members of the U.N. are represented in the General Assembly, which makes decisions on political, budgetary, trusteeship, and administrative questions. The Security Council includes 15 members, 5 of which the United States, the People's Republic of China, Great Britain, France, and the former U.S.S.R.—are permanent members. The remaining 10 are elected to the council by the General Assembly. The Security Council deals with matters of international security, and in important decisions the affirmative votes of the permanent members are necessary. Hence, U.N. action frequently has been halted during crises with an effective veto by a member within the Security Council. The Secretariat deals largely with administrative matters involving the U.N. From the 1950s, the membership of the U.N. has grown susbstanially to more than 150 members.

Upanishads   Philosophical commentaries forming the last section of the Hindu Vedas. The Upanishads are the basis for the Vedanta system of philosophy.

Upper Canada   Name applied (1791–1841) to the Canadian region comprising present-day Ontario. Settled primarily by the British, it was joined with Lower Canada by the Act of Union in 1841 and became known as Canada West. With the confederation of Canada in 1867, it became the province of Ontario.

Urban II (Eudes of Lagery) (Odo of Lagery) (1042–1499)   Pope (1088–1099). He continued Gregory VII's reform movement, strengthened the papacy, and, through his preachings, helped to inspire the First Crusade.

Urban VI (Prignano, Bartolomeo) (1318?–1389)   Pope (1378–1389). His election and subsequent actions alienated the French cardinals. They denied his election and elected Clement VII, thus beginning the Great Schism.

Urdu   Indo-Iranian language. The official language of Pakistan. Urdu is spoken by more than 25 million people and has a classical literature dating from the 14th century.

Uthman (Othman) (d. 656)   Third Muslim caliph (644–656), successor to Omar, and son-in-law of Muhammad. He continued Muslim conquest and expanded the power of the caliphate. His establishment of an official version of the Koran led to his assassination and a resulting struggle for leadership.

Utilitarianism   School of moral philosophy in the 1800s whose main adherents were James Mill, John Stuart Mill, and Jeremy Bentham. Bentham's theory was based on the principle that the greatest happiness of the greatest number is the criterion of the highest good. The utilitarians were a strong force for reform in the first half of the 19th century and their doctrines helped to shape the Liberal party in Britain.

Utrecht, Peace of   Two series of treaties (1713–1715) (one between France and other European countries and the other between Spain and other European countries), that ended the War of Spanish Succession. In the first series France concluded treaties in 1713 with England, The Netherlands, Savoy, Prussia, and Portugal. By these treaties France acknowledged the accession of Queen Anne to the English throne and ceded to England the Hudson Bay territory, Newfoundland, Nova Scotia, and St. Kitts. The treaties also included French cession of the Spanish Netherlands to Austria by treaty with The Netherlands. France recognized the king of Prussia, and signed peace with Portugal. In the second series of treaties (July 1713–February 1715), Spain signed treaties with England, Savoy, The Netherlands, and Portugal. Spain ceded Gibraltar and Minorca to England and granted England the right to sell slaves in Spanish America. It ceded Sardinia to Savoy and received acknowledgment of Philip V's succession (the cause of the war), signed a peace with the Dutch, and in 1715 made peace with Portugal.

Utrecht, Union of   Union of provinces in the Low Countries that became independent of Spanish rule in 1579 and that later became the modern state of The Netherlands.

V   **Valens** (328–378 A.D.)   Roman emperor of the East (364–378 A.D.). Valens defeated the Visigoths, then allowed them to settle in the empire. They rebelled and destroyed the Roman army at the Battle of Adrianople. There Valens was killed and the Eastern empire was rendered defenseless.

Valois   French royal house, a branch of the Capetians, who ruled France (1328–1589), beginning with Philip VI. The first half of their reign was marked by the Hundred Years' War and by challenges from the nobility. However, the Valois rulers ably met both threats, consolidated their power, and established their sole right of taxation. The direct line ended with the death of Charles VIII in 1498. It continued with the houses of Valois Orléans and Valois Angoulême until the advent of Henry IV and the Bourbons in 1589.

Vandals   Germanic tribe. Fleeing the Huns in the early 5th century A.D., they embarked upon their own campaign of conquest, sweeping through Gaul and into Spain. Led by Gaiseric, they crossed into North Africa in 420 and eventually captured Carthage in 439 A.D. Rome recognized Gaiseric's rule 3 years later and the Vandals began their pirate attacks upon Mediterranean shipping. From there they raided Sicily and southern Italy, and sacked Rome in 455 A.D. Aryan Christians, they vigorously persecuted other Christian sects. The power of the Vandals declined after Gaiseric's death in the late 5th century and was finally broken by Byzantine General Belisarius in 533 A.D.

Vassal   In feudal society, the holder of a fief, or landed estate granted by an overlord in return for feudal services.

Vatican Councils   1. The First Vatican Council (1869 and 1870), or 20th ecumenical council of the Catholic church, was convened in 1869 at the Vatican by Pope Pius IX. It was interrupted by the capture of Rome in 1870 by Italian troops. The council upheld the pope as supreme leader of the Catholic church and promulgated the dogma of papal infallibility when speaking *ex cathedra* on matters of faith or morals. 2. The Second Vatican Council (1962– 1965), or 21st ecumenical council of the Catholic church, was convened in 1962 at the Vatican by Pope John XXIII and continued by Pope Paul VI. The council issued 16 documents through which it sought to promote a spiritual renewal within the Catholic church. It invited representatives from both Protestant and Eastern Orthodox churches to observe the proceedings. Its principal accomplishments included modification of the liturgy of the Mass, support for the spirit of ecumenism and condemnation of anti-Semitism. Its wide-ranging reforms have had a major impact on the church.

Vaucreuil-Cavagnal, Pierre François de Rigaud, marquis de (1698–1765)   Last French governor of New France (1755–1760). After the defeat of General Montcalm, he surrendered New France to Britain in 1760.

Veda   Sacred Indian texts. Among the oldest examples of ancient Indian literature, the Veda include texts of hymns, poetry, and prose that state the essential beliefs, laws, mythology, prayers, and rituals of Hinduism. They originated with the Aryans, who entered India in 1500 B.C. The Veda are divided into four primary groupings: the Samhitas, containing hymns and liturgies; the Brahmanas, prose explanations of sacrificial ceremonies; Aranyakas, instructions for meditations; and the Upanishads, mystical writings.

Vendée, Wars of the   French royalist insurrections. From 1793–1832, the French region of the Vendée frequently attempted counterrevolutions to defeat the French Republic and restore the monarchy. The peasants of the Vendée first rebelled against conscriptions by the French government in March 1793. They were joined by displaced nobles, who spread the revolt throughout the summer and fall but were defeated in December 1793. The harsh treatment of defeated counterrevolutionaries by the republicans led to a second Vendée insurrection in 1794. Smaller royalist revolts in the Vendée took place in 1799, 1815, and 1832.

Venezuela Boundary Dispute   Prolonged territorial dispute between Great Britain and Venezuela over the boundary between Venezuela and British Guiana. The disagreement continued through much of the 19th century but took on added meaning when gold was discovered in the disputed area. In 1887, the nations broke off diplomatic ties. In 1895, American Secretary of State Olney invoked the Monroe Doctrine and demanded arbitration. Britain at first refused but eventually yielded to avoid conflict with the United States. In 1899, an arbitration panel awarded most of the disputed territory to Britain.

Venezuela claims   Financial claims pressed upon Venezuela in the early 20th century. During the rule of Venezuelan President Castro, Venezuela fell into a complicated financial tangle. In 1902, France, Great Britain, Germany, and Italy demanded swift repayment of outstanding loans to Venezuela, pressing their claims by sending gunboats to blockade Venezuelan ports. After they bombarded several port cities, the United States intervened as unofficial arbitrator. The matter was referred to the Hague Tribunal in 1904, which ruled that Venezuela must repay the belligerent countries before settling its debts with neutral nations. Venezuela fulfilled its obligations in 1907.

Verdun, Treaty of   Treaty in 843 by which the Carolingian Empire was divided among the three sons and heirs of Emperor Louis I (the Pious). After the death of Louis I in 840, the empire was rent by warfare among his sons Louis the German, Charles II (the Bald), and Lothair I. By the treaty, Lothair retained the title of emperor and received much of Italy, Alsace-Lorraine, Burgundy, and the Low Countries. This narrow, middle part of the empire, was called Lotharingia (or Francia Media). Louis the German received territory east of the Rhine, which formed the basis for modern Germany. Charles II received the western territory of the empire, which evolved into modern France.

Vergennes, Charles Gravier, comte de (1717–1787)   French statesman. Appointed foreign minister in 1774 by King Louis XVI, he formed the alliance between France and the American colonists during the American Revolution. He negotiated the Treaty of Paris in 1783.

Vergil (Virgil) (70–19 B.C.)   Greatest of Latin poets. His major work was the *Aeneid.*

Versailles, Treaty of   Treaty on June 28, 1919 ending World War I. Its provisions, the result of the Paris Peace Conference, were primarily drawn up by American President Wilson, British Prime Minister Lloyd George, French Premier Clemenceau, and Italian Prime Minister Orlando. Germany was not consulted. The treaty also made provision for establishment of the League of Nations. Germany's colonies became mandates of the League of Nations, and Alsace Lorraine was returned to France. In addition, Germany was forced to accept responsibility for the war, agreed to huge reparation payments and surrender of equipment, limited its army to 100,000 troops, relinquished vast land holdings to Poland (including the Polish Corridor), and agreed to demilitarization of the Rhineland. The United States did not ratify the treaty, but its provisions were implemented and helped to cause the early rise of Hitler and Nazism. Hitler subsequently broke the treaty's provisions.

Vespucci, Amerigo (1454–1512)   Italian navigator. He explored the east coast of South America, which he considered to be a new continent. The name "America" is derived from his name.

Vestal   Ancient Roman priestess who tended the perpetual fires in the Temple of Vesta, goddess of the hearth. The vestal virgins were chosen from prominent Roman families and were bound by a vow of chastity. They enjoyed great privileges and influence in Roman life.

Viceroy   Governor of a province, territory, or country by authority of a king or sovereign. Rulers of Spanish territories in the Americas were viceroys, and British viceroys governed Ireland and British India.

Vichy   French government headed by Marshal Pétain, established during World War II after the French-German armistice in June 1940. It controlled that part of France not occupied by Germany, and its policies were generally favorable to Germany. It continued to exist until 1944.

Victor Emmanuel II (1820–1878)   King of Sardinia (1849–1861) and first king of a united Italy (1861–1878). As king of Sardinia he appointed Count Cavour as prime minister and encouraged the efforts of Garibaldi.

Victor Emmanuel III (1869–1947)   Italian king (1900–1946). He brought Italy into World War I on the side of the Allies. He refused to oppose the rise of fascism and supported the government of Mussolini.

Victoria (1819–1901)   Queen of Great Britain and Ireland (1837–1901) and empress of India (1876–1901). She succeeded her uncle William IV to the English throne, but she was prevented by the Salic law from succeeding to the Hanoverian throne, thus separating the two crowns. Her prime ministers included Melbourne, Peel, Palmerston, Disraeli, and Gladstone. During her reign, the British Empire reached its peak. Britain established its rule in India, struggled with the question of Home Rule in Ireland, remained neutral during the American Civil War, and fought the Crimean War. Victoria's strict personal moral values greatly enhanced the prestige of the monarchy and gained her enormous popularity. She put her stamp on an entire era of English history, which came to be known as the Victorian Age.

Official Jubilee portrait of Queen Victoria of Great Britain.

Fighting tactics of the Vikings, who invaded Europe in the 9th and 10th centuries.

Viet Cong (Viet-Nam Cong-San) Communist guerrilla forces that fought in South Vietnam (1954–1975) to overthrow the government of South Vietnam and reunify Vietnam under Communist rule. The Viet Cong, aided by troops and material from the north, successfully fought a long and bloody guerrilla campaign against the army of the Republic of South Vietnam and later against the American armed forces sent to aid the South Vietnamese. They formed the National Liberation Front in 1968, which in turn joined with other groups to form the Provisional Revolutionary Government (PRG). The PRG took part in the cease-fire negotiations in Paris in 1973 but, after American withdrawal from Vietnam, the Viet Cong and North Vietnamese regular forces completed the conquest of South Vietnam in 1975.

Viet Minh Popular name for Viet Nam Doc Lap Dong Minh, a coalition of Communist and Nationalist groups that fought for Vietnamese independence from French rule. It was formed and led by Ho Chi Minh.

Vietnamization American policy during the Vietnam War. Implemented by the Nixon administration (early 1970s), it called for a gradual increase in South Vietnamese participation in the war. American military involvement was to be reduced at the same time, until the South Vietnamese took over all fighting.

Vietnam War War fought (1960–1975) by Communist and non-Communist forces for control of South Vietnam. It ended in a Communist victory (and in the reunification of North and South Vietnam), despite heavy involvement by American forces (1965–1973). The Vietnam War was an outgrowth of the earlier Indochina War.

Vikings Norse raiders and adventurers who sailed from their homelands in Scandinavia to attack and pillage European coastal settlements between the 9th and 11th centuries.

Villa, Francisco (Pancho Villa) (Arango, Doroteo) (1877?–1923) Mexican bandit and revolutionary, a leading figure in the revolts against Díaz (1910 and 1911) and Huerta (1913 and 1914). Villa's raid on Columbus, New Mexico in 1916 led to the American punitive expedition into Mexico by General Pershing.

Vishnu One of the three principal gods of Hinduism. He is revered as the preserver of the world and restorer of the moral order.

Visigoths (West Goths) Germanic tribe, the western branch of the Goths. The Visigoths left the Black Sea region in the 3rd century A.D. and harassed the Roman Empire's border region of Dacia. The Visigoths were allowed to settle in the empire to escape the Huns, but soon rebelled against its excessive taxation. They crushed Emperor Valens at Adrianople in 37 A.D. and, under Alaric I, sacked Rome in 410 A.D. They were allowed to rule large areas of Gaul and Spain, and in 475 A.D., their leader Euric declared independence. His son Alaric II was defeated and killed by Clovis in 507. The Visigoths then settled around Toledo, and finally capitulated to the invading Muslims in 711.

Vizier In the Ottoman Empire, the most important minister under the sultan. The term was first adopted in the 14th century and was applied to provincial, administrative, and military figures.

Vladimir I (Saint Vladimir) (956–1015) Grand duke of Kiev (980–1015) and first Christian ruler of Russia. He consolidated Kiev and Novgorod into a single realm and ordered the conversion of his people to Greek Orthodox Christianity.

Voltaire, François Marie Arouet de (1694–1778) French author and historian, one of the foremost figures of the Enlightenment. He was known as a poet, playwright, and wit. Imprudent talk and witty lampoons against authority first brought him a stay in the Bastille and then exile in England, prompting his *Letters Concerning the English,* which popularized the ideas of Newton and Locke. An outstanding historian, he is best known today for such books as *Candide* and his *Philosophical Dictionary,* a forceful work supporting the ideas of the Enlightenment.

Vo Nguyen Giap (b. 1912) Vietnamese general and government minister. A Communist, he became commander of the Viet Minh in 1946 and defeated the French at Dien Bien Phu in 1954. He played a strategic role in the Tet Offensive of 1968 during the Vietnam War.

W Wafd Egyptian nationalist political party founded in 1918. "Wafd" means "delegation," and the name was applied to the party because its founders demanded an Egyptian "delegation" (to work for Egyptian independence) in the post-World War I peace process. Although several times declared illegal, the party was Egypt's major organized political force from 1923, and it clashed frequently with King Faud and his successor, Farouk. Opposed to Germany, it came to power with British support during World War II and returned to power again in 1950, this time agitating for further revisions of Anglo-Egyptian treaties. The Egyptian revolution in 1952 and dissolution of the political parties brought an end to the Wafd.

Wahabi Muslim reform movement founded by Muhammad ibn Abd al-wabia in the 18th century. It became the religion of the Saudi rulers and is thus an influential sect in modern Saudi Arabia. It is a puritanical movement that advocates living by the Koran and rejects the excesses of luxury and elaborate worship.

Waldenses (Waldensians) Religious group centered in Piedmont (Italy) and Dauphiné (France) from the 12th century. The Waldenses sought a life of poverty and gospel simplicity. They eventually drifted into what became heresy to the Roman Catholic church, denying purgatory, the papacy, prayers for the dead, and some of the sacraments. They emphasized a simple biblicism and criticized the ecclesiastical abuses of the day. Often persecuted, they nevertheless continued to survive. Most Waldensians accepted the Reformation and became, in effect, another Swiss Protestant church in 1532.

Waldheim, Kurt (b. 1918) Fourth secretary-general of the U.N. (1972–1982), replacing U Thant of Burma. A career diplomat, he was Austria's U.N. representative (1965–1968), foreign minister (1968–1970), and was elected president of Austria in 1986. He was succeeded by Thomas Klestli in June 1992.

Walesa, Lech (b. 1943) Polish labor leader, he founded Solidarity, an industrial trade union, and led widespread strikes that gained concessions in 1980. The union was outlawed in 1981 but reinstated in 1988. He won the Nobel Prize for Peace in 1983, and was elected president in 1990.

Walpole, Robert 1st earl of Orford (1676–1745) British statesman and Whig leader, generally regarded as the first British prime minister. Walpole supported the succession of Hanoverian King George I in 1714, which restored the Whigs to power, and thereafter began his ascendancy. In 1721, he was appointed first lord of the treasury and chancellor of the exchequer. Thereafter he remained in power until 1742, and by his astute handling of Parliament and skillful distribution of royal patronage helped lay the foundations for the office of prime minister. His purge of opposition elements in his ministry in 1733 established his firm control over the Cabinet. Walpole is especially noted for his accomplishments in the area of finance. He also endeavored to promote trade and reduce tariffs, and sought to keep Britain out of war. Unable to escape involvement in the War of Austrian Succession, Walpole was ousted from power in 1742 after military reverses.

Wang An-shih (1021–1086) Chinese poet, Confucian scholar, and government administrator. As chief minister for Emperor Shen Tsung, he carried out financial reforms, established an agricultural loan program, levied an income tax, and organized a militia.

Wang Ching-wei (1885–1944) Chinese political leader. He was a supporter of Sun Yat-sen and after Sun's death in 1925 challenged Chiang Kai-shek for control of the Kuomintang. He served as premier of Japanese-controlled China (1938–1944).

Wang Mang (45 B.C.–23 A.D.) Chinese Han dynasty official who seized the throne and ruled as emperor (9–23 A.D.). His many radical governmental and land reforms were opposed by the aristocracy, which rebelled and restored the Han dynasty.

Warlord Regional military commanders in China who, between 1916 and 1949, often functioned as independent rulers in the areas they controlled. Chinese President Yuan Shi-k'ai had relied on military force to rule and, after his death in 1916, many of his former generals took control of their military territories, especially in the north. In the south, Chiang Kai-shek consolidated Nationalist rule and by his Northern Expedition, regained control over warlords. Many warlords retained local control, however, and were not finally eliminated until the Communist victory in 1949.

Warring States Period (481–221 B.C.) in Chinese history. This period brought an end to the long reign of the Chou dynasty (ruled 1122–221 B.C.) and was marked by the rise of a number of petty kingdoms. Corruption was widespread and wars between the states were frequent. Despite the chaotic nature of this period, some of the great thinkers in Chinese history flourished then (notably Mencius) and helped establish doctrines that would later dominate Chinese culture.

Warsaw Treaty Organization (Warsaw Pact) Defensive alliance between the U.S.S.R. and its

Eastern European satellites, created by a treaty signed in Warsaw in 1955 to counterbalance NATO. The Warsaw Pact countries consisted of Albania (until 1968), Bulgaria, Czechoslovakia, East Germany, Hungary, Poland, Romania, and the U.S.S.R. With the collapse of communism (*see* page 11-27), and the East European Revolution (*see* page 11-34) the Warsaw Pact ended in 1992.

Warsaw Uprising　Rebellion in which the Polish underground army briefly recaptured and held Warsaw against the Germans (August–October 1944). The Poles were defeated by German reinforcements while the Soviet Army remained idle just across the Vistula. Thus, any potential Polish military opposition to postwar Soviet domination of Poland was eliminated.

Washington, Treaty of　Agreement on May 8, 1871 between Britain and the United States that settled the Alabama claims and regulated navigation in the St. Lawrence and the Great Lakes. It was the first treaty in which Canada was recognized as a distinct entity.

Waterloo, battle of　Final battle of the Napoleonic Wars, fought on June 18, 1815 at this Belgian village south of Brussels, and famous as Napoleon's military demise. The battle turned into a rout and Napoleon was compelled to retreat with heavy losses (25,000 French casualties plus those taken prisoner; 23,000 allied casualties). Napoleon abdicated for his second and last time on June 22.

Watt, James　(1736–1819)　Scottish inventor. He devised numerous improvements in and additions to the steam engine of Thomas Newcomen. Watt's improved engine was a milestone in the Industrial Revolution.

Weimar Republic　German republic (1919–1933) created after Germany's defeat in World War I. The new government was created on July 31, 1919 amid social unrest (notably uprising by Communists) and severe economic problems. Subsequent years were characterized by chronic parliamentary instability, a period of inflation, and mass unemployment, all of which eventually led to Hitler's rise to power in 1933.

Weizmann, Chaim　(1874–1952)　Russian-born scientist, Zionist leader, and Israeli statesman. A leader in the Zionist movement, Weizmann helped to negotiate the Balfour Declaration and was the first president of Israel (1948–1952).

Wellington, Arthur Wellesley, 1st duke of　(1769–1852)　British soldier and statesman. He commanded British, Portuguese, and Spanish forces in the Peninsular War, defeated Napoleon in the Battle of Waterloo, and served as prime minister of Great Britain (1828–1830).

Wessex　Saxon kingdom, once located in southern England, and a part of the Anglo-Saxon Heptarchy. Founded by Saxon invaders in the late 5th century A.D., it rivaled the other Anglo-Saxon kingdoms for control of territories until the 9th century Danish invasion. Under the leadership of Aethelred I and Alfred the Great, Wessex alone withstood the Danish armies. Then, by reconquering Danish holdings by 927, the kings of Wessex made themselves masters of all England.

Westminster Conference　Meeting held in London (1866 and 1867) to plan the union of Canadian provinces. Resolutions of the conference were incorporated into the British North America Act of 1867.

Westminster, Statute of　English laws, the first three of which were enacted under Edward I. 1. Westminster I in 1275 put long-unwritten laws into legal, written forms, most notably equal legal protection for the poor. 2. Westminster II in 1285 concerned land tenure and entailments. 3. Westminster III in 1290 ended the subinfeudation of land by making a new owner responsible to the prime overlord, not the subholder. 4. Statute, passed by Parliament in 1931, recognizing the autonomy of member nations within the United Kingdom. It created the British Commonwealth of Nations.

Westphalia, Peace of　Treaty on October 24, 1648 ending the Thirty Years' War. The treaty marked the end of the period of religious wars in Europe that arose from the Protestant Reformation. The major participants in the treaty were Sweden and France on the one side and the Holy Roman Empire and Spain on the other. The treaty seriously weakened the Holy Roman Empire by recognizing the sovereignty of the individual German states within its domains. This was an important victory for France, which had sought to break the power of the Hapsburg Holy Roman emperors. The treaty also recognized the independence of The Netherlands and the Swiss Confederation. Among the various territorial adjustments stipulated in the treaty were those awarding Alsace to France and West Pomerania to Sweden. Other provisions of the treaty related to religious settlements. In general, a policy of toleration was instituted in the German states and Calvinism was recognized.

Weyler y Nicolau, Valeriano　(1838–1930)　Spanish general. He was captain-general of Spanish forces in Cuba (1896 and 1897), and his harsh treatment of Cuban rebels caused a wave of protest from America just before the Spanish-American War.

Whig　Name used to denote what was variously a political party and a faction in England (in the 17th–early 19th centuries). The Whig faction emerged in 1679 as a group opposing the succession of the Catholic Stuart king James II. James was finally deposed by Whigs and his former Tory supporters in the Glorious Revolution of 1688. Thereafter Whigs became identified with the interests of the landowning aristocracy and the wealthy middle class. Whig leaders, notably Sir Robert Walpole, dominated the government during the reigns of George I and George II (1714–1760). During the period from 1760–1784, Whig and Tory factions ceased to be identifiable as distinct groups and appointments were made on the basis of personal and family influence. In 1784, however, the emergence of a new Tory party (under William Pitt the Younger) helped coalesce opposition factions into a new Whig party. The Whigs then advanced the interests of industrialists, religious dissenters, and others who favored reforms. The Whig party ceased to exist in the 19th century and many of its members joined the emerging Liberal party, forming the party's conservative wing.

White Lotus Rebellion　Chinese rebellion. The White Lotus was a Buddhist cult that opposed domination by the Manchus of the Ch'ing dynasty. From

1796–1804, they conducted a guerrilla revolt in the mountains of central China in protest against their poverty and excessive taxation. The imperial forces were hindered for several years by corruption within the army, but they eventually put down the rebellion. However, the revolt revealed the declining power of the Manchus and paved the way for other revolts in the 1800s that ended in the overthrow of the Ch'ing dynasty.

White Revolution   Reform movement in Iran during the 1950s and 1960s, instituted by Mohammed Reza Shah Pahlevi and his advisers. It aimed especially at land reforms, and an Office of Land Reform was established on August 20, 1960. Ultimately, however, the "revolution" failed to gain popular support and the shah was forced to abdicate by the Islamic revolution in 1979. *See* **Pahlevi, Mohammed Reza Shah**.

White Volunteer Army   Russian armies formed in the winter of 1917 and 1918 in the peripheral areas of the former Russian Empire to combat the Bolshevik regime established under Lenin. Though aided by 14 allied nations, they lacked unified leadership and necessary supplies and were unable to prevail against the Red Army.

Wilhelmina (1880–1962)   Queen of The Netherlands (1890–1948). Forced into exile in Britain during World War II, she encouraged Dutch resistance to German occupation.

William I (William the Conqueror) (1027–1087) English king (1066–1087) and duke of Normandy (1035–1087). With the help of French king Henry I, he established his rule in Normandy in 1047, then later repulsed two French invasions of Normandy (1054, 1058). In 1051, on a visit to his cousin, English king Edward the Confessor, he is thought to have received a promise of the English throne. On Edward's death, however, the crown passed to Harold, earl of Wessex. William secured the pope's support for his claim and raised an army. Invading England in 1066, he defeated and killed Harold in the Battle of Hastings, marched on London, and was crowned king on Christmas Day. The English resisted his rule and William spent several years crushing rebellions, seizing estates, and redistributing lands to his Norman supporters. He brought the church under his control and firmly established feudalism in England. William authorized the compilation of the Domesday Book in 1085, a complete survey of England. His son Robert succeeded him as duke of Normandy, and his son William as king of England. William the Conqueror was an able administrator, a ruthless and intelligent military commander, and one of the greatest leaders of his time. His conquest of England radically altered the history of England and of Western Europe.

William I (the Silent, Prince of Orange) (1533–1584) Prince of Orange and Count of Nassau. In 1568 he led the rebellion of The Netherlands against the rule of Philip II of Spain.

William I (1772–1843)   First king of The Netherlands (1815–1840). Commerce and industry flourished under his rule, but his treatment of Belgium, then part of The Netherlands, led to its secession in 1830.

William I (1797–1888)   King of Prussia (1861–1888) and first German emperor (1871–1888). He appointed Otto von Bismarck prime minister of Prussia in 1862, and thereafter followed a militaristic policy that finally established Prussian dominance over a unified Germany.

William II (William Rufus) (d. 1100)   King of England (1087–1100), successor to his father William I the Conqueror. His rule was ruthless and he made many enemies. He conducted wars in Scotland, Wales, and Normandy, and maintained Norman rule over England.

William II (1859–1941)   King of Prussia and German emperor (1888–1918). His support of Austria-Hungary against Serbia contributed to the outbreak of World War I and increased military control of the government. With Germany's defeat, he abdicated.

William III (William of Orange) (1650–1702) Stadtholder of the United Provinces of The Netherlands (1672–1702) who became king of England (1689–1702) by the Glorious Revolution. He ruled jointly with his wife Queen Mary II, promoted Protestantism, fiscal and parliamentary reform, and led campaigns against Louis XIV in the war of the Grand Alliance. He defeated James II at the Battle of the Boyne in Ireland, thereby ending James' attempt to retake the English throne.

William IV (1765–1837)   British king (1830–1837). He opposed parliamentary reform, but reluctantly accepted passage of the Reform Bill of 1832.

Wilson, Sir James Harold (b. 1916)   British statesman. A leader of the Labour party, he served twice as prime minister (1964–1970, 1974–1976). His government was marked by trouble with white-ruled Rhodesia, serious economic problems, and unrest in Ireland.

Windsor, House of   From 1917 the official surname of the royal family of Britain. It replaced the family name of Wettin and dynastic name of Saxe-Coburg-Gotha. This change was effected by George V during World War I.

Wingate, Orde Charles (1903–1944)   British general. During World War II he organized and led the Chindits, or Wingate's Raiders, a guerrilla unit that fought against the Japanese in Burma.

Witenagemot (Witan)   King's council that existed in England in Anglo-Saxon times. It consisted mainly of the nobles and bishops, and advised the king on land grants, taxes, and other matters.

Witt, Jan de (1625–1672)   Dutch statesman and patriot. As grand pensionary he led Holland in the Dutch Wars and was instrumental in forming the Triple Alliance of 1668 and negotiating the Treaty of Aix-la-Chapelle.

Wittelsbach   Name of the family dynasty that ruled Bavaria (1180–1918). In addition to providing Bavarian kings, the line also produced a king of the Germans (Rupert of the Palatinate, 1400–1410) and two Holy Roman emperors (Louis IV of Bavaria, 1314–1337; Charles VII, 1742–1745).

Wolfe, James (1727–1759)   British commander in the French and Indian War. He led British forces in the capture of Quebec in 1759 from the French, thereby ensuring British dominance in Canada.

Wolsey, Thomas (1475–1530)   English statesman and Catholic cardinal. As lord chancellor of England

(1515–1529), he was the leading force in English politics during the early reign of King Henry VIII.

Woman suffrage　The right of women to the vote. The movement for woman suffrage arose in many countries in the 19th and 20 centuries. In the United States, woman suffrage began with a declaration of women's rights issued on July 19, 1848 by Mott, Stanton, and other feminists. The movement gained momentum with the formation in 1869 of the National Woman Suffrage Association, which sought woman suffrage through a constitutional amendment; and the American Woman Suffrage Association, which sought it through state legislation. Both factions merged in 1890 to form the National American Woman Suffrage Association. A number of states eventually granted woman suffrage and national woman suffrage was established in 1920, by the 19th Amendment to the Constitution. In Great Britain, the movement for woman suffrage began as a part of the Chartist movement. In the early 20th century the movement became more militant under the leadership of Emmeline Pankhurst and others. Women received equal voting rights with men in Britain in 1928.

World War I　Worldwide conflict (1914–1918) fought between the Allies (France, Britain, Russia, Italy, United States, and others) and the Central Powers (Germany, Austro-Hungarian Empire, Ottoman Empire, and others). The bloodiest, most widespread war the world had known up to that time, World War I resulted in over 30 million casualties, left much of Europe in ruin, and revolutionized modern warfare. Among the causes of World War I were the rise of nationalist movements in Europe (especially in Serbia), hardening of alliances between various European powers (Triple Alliance and Entente), colonial rivalries in Africa and elsewhere, the continuing instability of the Balkan Peninsula region (Austrian annexation of Bosnia and Herzegovina in 1908), Balkan Wars (1912 and 1913), and the gradual collapse of the Ottoman Empire (Eastern Question). The spark that touched off World War I was the assassination of Austrian Archduke Ferdinand by a Serbian nationalist in 1914. The war quickly spread to many different fronts and eventually involved all the major Western powers. World War I saw the rise of bloody trench warfare (especially on the Western Front), the mechanization of warfare (tanks, planes, and motorized vehicles used), and the advent of chemical warfare. It also brought drastic political changes. Russia's staggering losses on the Eastern Front helped bring down the czarist government in 1917 and led to creation of the first Communist state. The Ottoman Empire, long in decline, finally collapsed under the strains of war and was dismembered. The war also broke up the Austro-Hungarian Empire, giving rise to the independent states of Austria, Hungary, Czechoslovakia, and Yugoslavia (as it was later called). The German surrender finally ended the war in 1918. Initially, the tremendous destruction caused by the war gave wide support to the newly created League of Nations and international efforts to end wars. But the war had set in motion great social and economic changes. Coupled with German resentment at the harsh peace terms imposed by the Allies, these changes helped pave the way for the outbreak of World War II.

World War II　Worldwide conflict (1939–1945) involving all of the great powers and many of the lesser states as well. The combatants were divided into two opposing groups: the Allies (led by Britain, the United States, France, and [after 1941] the U.S.S.R.), and the Axis powers (led by Germany, Russia [to 1941], Italy, and Japan). The war resulted in widespread destruction and suffering and cost many millions of lives. In addition, millions of others (notably Jews and Poles) died in Nazi death camps or were made slave laborers. The mechanization of warfare reached new levels in World War II and the airplane emerged as an important weapon in war on land and at sea. Finally, the use of atomic bombs by the United States at the end of the war introduced the age of nuclear warfare. The causes of World War II are rooted in the economic, social, and political chaos of Europe following World War I. The economic collapse in Germany after the war and the harsh peace terms imposed by the Allies fostered German resentment and gave birth to Hitler's Nazi party. Fascism, under Mussolini, was also born of the postwar chaos in Italy. The rise of militaristic, totalitarian regimes was further aided by fear of the Communists and by a new economic collapse in the late 1920s and early 1930s (the Great Depression helped bring Hitler to power in Germany). It was Hitler who, after clearly adopting a militaristic aggressive policy, started World War II by invading Poland in 1939. Though Hitler quickly conquered Continental Europe, his decision to invade the U.S.S.R. in 1941 (until then an ally) proved to be his undoing. After the Japanese began the war in the Pacific Theater, the United States entered the hostilities and Germany was confronted by the combined forces of the United States, the U.S.S.R., and the British Commonwealth, as well as resistance fighters from conquered nations. From about 1942, the tide of the war turned against the Axis powers and the surrender of Nazi Germany in May 1945 was closely followed by the Japanese surrender in September 1945. Treaties were signed at Paris in 1947 by the Allies and Italy, Romania, Hungary, Bulgaria, and Finland. A peace treaty with Japan was signed in 1951.

Worms, Diet of　Imperial diet called in 1521 during the Reformation by Holy Roman Emperor Charles V. It was convened at Worms, Germany, to consider action against Protestant reformer Martin Luther. Luther had already been condemned by Pope Leo X and was given safe conduct to appear before the diet on April 17, 1521. There Luther was asked to repudiate his teachings; on the following day he refused. The subsequent Edict of Worms on May 25 declared Luther a heretic and outlaw and forced him to go into hiding for some months.

Worms, Synod of　1. Synod of German Catholic bishops called in 1076 at Worms, now in West Germany, by Holy Roman Emperor Henry IV. A high point in Henry's conflict with the pope over lay investiture, the synod declared Pope Gregory VII deposed, in response to Gregory's attempt to impose reforms. Gregory subsequently excommunicated and deposed Henry in 1076. 2. Synod of German bishops called in 1122 at Worms to settle the investiture controversy between Holy Roman Emperor Henry V and Pope Calixtus II. The synod formulated the Concordat of Worms. *See* **Concordat of Worms**.

Wu Chao (d. 705 A.D.)   Chinese empress who was the only woman sovereign in China's history (683–705 A.D.). Made empress by her husband Emperor Kao T'ang/Tsung, she took control of the government at his death and ruled in his stead. An excellent administrator, she reorganized the army, oversaw the conquest of Korea, reduced taxes, and used the civil service system to recruit legal officials. Because of her encouragement of Buddhism, it reached the height of its popularity in China during her reign.

Wu Ti (156–87 B.C.)   Emperor (140–87 B.C.) of the Chinese Han dynasty. He greatly expanded the empire (into Vietnam, Korea, and the northern and western border regions), instituted administrative reforms to further strengthen imperial authority, set up the Chinese Examination System, and established Confucianism as the state religion.

Wycliffe, John (Wyclif, John) (1320–1384)   English reformer and theologian whose attacks on church doctrine anticipated the Protestant Reformation. He began the first English translation of the Bible.

Xavier, Saint Francis (1506–1552) Catholic missionary priest, called "the Apostle of the Indies." One of the seven original Jesuits, he converted many thousands in India, Ceylon, the Malay Archipelago, and Japan.

Xenocrates (396–314 B.C.)   Greek philosopher. A disciple of Plato, he succeeded Speusippus as head of the Greek Academy.

Xenophanes (6th century B.C.)   Greek philosopher and poet, a member, and once thought to be the founder of the Eleatic school. He asserted the existence of one God closely identified with the material world.

Xenophon (434 –355 B.C.)   Greek military leader and historian who commanded Greek forces in the service of Persian king Cyrus the Younger. His best-known work, the *Anabasis,* recounts the retreat of the Ten Thousand Immortals following Cyrus' death at Cunaxa in 401 B.C.

Xerxes I (519–465 B.C.)   Persian king (486–465 B.C.), successor to his father, Darius I. He prepared a massive force for the conquest of Greece, but was defeated at Salamis in 480 B.C.

Yalta Conference Allied conference held in 1945 during World War II, at Yalta in the Crimea. Attended by American President Roosevelt, British Prime Minister Churchill, and Russian Premier Stalin, it restated the Allied determination to receive only unconditional surrender in Germany. The conference planned for the postwar occupation of Germany by the four major Allied powers, discussed the postwar reorganization of Europe, and made plans for the San Francisco Conference to establish the United Nations.

Winston Churchill, Franklin D. Roosevelt, and Joseph Stalin at the Yalta Conference held in 1945 to plan the end of World War II.

Yamamoto, Isoroku (1884–1943)   Japanese admiral. He led the attack on Pearl Harbor, thus precipitating American entry into World War II.

Yeltsin, Boris (b. 1931)   President of Russia, 1991. A Communist party member since 1961, he was called up by Gorbachev (*see* page 11-45) to lead the Moscow party but was forced out in 1987. His popular following led to his election to Parliament in 1990 and subsequent elevation to Chairman of Parliament. He took over effective leadership of the U.S.S.R. following a failed coup in August 1991 and became the first popularly elected president of Russia. Economic difficulties have eroded his power. The industrialized nations have pledged over $30 billion in aid. In April 1993, he called for and survived a referendum that asked Russian voters for a vote of confidence.

Yeoman   In English history, a member of a class between the gentry and simple laborers. The term was also applied to servants or retainers of middle rank and to such units as the Yeomen of the Guard, long the personal bodyguard of the king.

Yeomen of the Guard   Personal bodyguard of the sovereign of England, established in 1485 by Henry VII. They are often called beefeaters.

Yi dynasty   Dynasty of rulers of Korea (1392–1910). The dynasty was founded by General Yi Song-gye, who seized power in 1392 with aid from China's Ming rulers. The capital was established at Seoul and Chinese cultural influence was strong (Confucianism was adopted by the state). In subsequent years the dynasty repulsed an invasion by the Japanese in 1592 but was forced to recognize the Manchus as their overlords after an invasion in 1627. From the 17th to the 19th centuries, the Yi rulers imposed a policy of isolationism and it was not until after the Japanese forced them to accept trade relations in 1876 that commerce with Western powers began. Soon after, however, the rise of Japanese influence on the mainland resulted in the takeover of Korea. In 1910 Japan ended the Yi dynasty reign by annexing the kingdom.

Yin-yang   In Chinese philosophy, the two opposite but complementary groups of qualities that form the basis of the world. Yin is represented as earth, dark, female, odd, negative, and passive, and Yang is represented as Heaven, light, male, even, positive, and active.

Yoritomo (1147–1199)   Japanese warrior of the Minamoto clan. He became the first Kamakura shogun of Japan in 1192.

York, House of   Royal house of England, a branch of the Plantagenet family. Its members included three kings, Edward IV, Edward V, and Richard III. Its claims to the English throne in opposition to those of the House of Lancaster resulted in the Wars of the Roses.

York, Richard Plantagenet, 3rd duke of (1411–1460)   English nobleman and claimant to the throne of England. He served as protector (1454 and 1455, 1455 and 1456) during the mental lapses of King Henry IV. His attempts to secure the crown led to the Wars of the Roses. He was recognized as heir apparent in 1460 but was defeated and killed by Margaret of Anjou at the Battle of Wakefield in 1460.

Yoshida, Shigeru (1878–1967)   Japanese statesman. He served as prime minister of Japan five times between 1946 and 1954 and oversaw Japan's recovery from World War II.

Young Italy   Italian movement that sought establishment of a republic of Italy. Founded in 1831 by Mazzini, it was instrumental in the Italian Risorgimento (*see* page 11-106) but declined in importance after 1848.

Young Plan   Second plan adopted for payment of German reparations after World War I, succeeding the Dawes Plan. Put into effect in 1930, it was repudiated by Hitler.

Young Turks   Group of young Turkish revolutionaries who rebelled against Sultan Abdul Hamid II in 1908 and compelled him to restore constitutional government. The term has since been used to designate young factions within larger groups.

Yüan   Chinese dynasty (1260–1368) established in 1260 by Kublai Khan. The Yüan made their capital at Peking, built the Grand Canal, constructed a road and canal system linking the country, and developed a postal system. They also encouraged trade with the West. Marco Polo lived at their court and took tales of their culture back to Europe. However, the Yüan never established rapport with the Chinese natives and were overthrown by the Ming in 1368.

Yüan Shih-kai (1859–1916)   Chinese imperial official and first president of the Republic of China (1912–1916). He ruled harshly and dissolved Parliament in 1914, thus provoking popular revolts. His attempt to establish a new dynasty and restore the empire in 1916 led to his downfall.

Yung-Lo (1360–1424)   Chinese emperor (1403–1424). Third of the Ming dynasty emperors. He led expeditions against the Mongols, annexed Annam, sent ships as far as East Africa, moved the capital from Nanking to Peking in 1421, and brought the Ming Empire to the point of its greatest power and influence.

Zaghlul Pasha, Saad (1860–1927) Egyptian nationalist leader and statesman. As head of the Wafd party he helped lead the movement for Egyptian independence after World War I.

Zaibatsu   Family-owned Japanese financial and economic combines or cartels. They have played an enormous role in Japan's economic development since the Meiji restoration in 1868 and control important segments of Japan's commerce, finance, and industry.

Zangi (1084–1146) Seljuk ruler. He fought successfully against the crusaders, established the Zangi dynasty (1127–1250), and extended his rule over much of Syria, Palestine, and Iraq.

Zapata, Emiliano (1879–1919) Mexican revolutionary. An advocate of agrarian reform, he at first supported but later opposed Madero and his successors. Zapata's army occupied Mexico City three times (1914 and 1915).

Zapotec Indian people of Mexico inhabiting the eastern and southern regions of Oaxaca. Once an independent nation centered at Monte Albán, they enjoyed an advanced civilization reflecting Mayan and Toltec influences. Subsequently allied with the Aztecs, they continued to flourish until the Spanish Conquest.

Zealots   Jewish sect noted for its extreme opposition to Roman rule in Judea. The Zealots played a leading role in the unsuccessful revolt against Rome (66–70 A.D.).

Zemstvo   A local and provincial assembly in czarist Russia. Established in 1864 as one of the major reforms of Alexander II, the Zemstvos produced numerous reforms and improvements before being superseded in 1917 by the Soviets after the Bolshevik Revolution.

Zen Buddhism   Buddhist sect. It was founded in the 5th century A.D. by Bodhidharma, who brought it from India to China. From there it spread to Japan. Zen stresses the awakening (satori) of the wisdom (prajna) that lies dormant within each soul. This wisdom is awakened by meditation and by personal instruction of a master to a pupil. Zen came to be a significant influence in many aspects of Chinese and Japanese life.

Zenobia (d. after 272 A.D.)   Queen of Palmyra. She greatly expanded her realm through conquest in Asia Minor and Egypt before her defeat and capture by Roman emperor Aurelian in 272 A.D.

Zeno of Citium (336–264 B.C.)   Greek philosopher. Zeno studied under the Cynics before establishing his own school at the Stoa Poikile in Athens, from which evolved the name of his philosophy, Stoicism.

Zetkin, Clara (1857–1933)   German feminist and Communist leader. One of the founders of the German Communist party.

Zhukov, Georgi Konstantinovich (1896–1974) Russian general and marshal of the Soviet Union. He played a major role in the Russian defeat of the German offensive in World War II.

Zia, Mohammad ul-Haq (1924–1989)   Ruler of Pakistan after a successful coup against Zulfikar Bhutto (*see* page 11-14) in 1977. He died in a plane crash in August 1988.

Zimmermann Telegram (Zimmermann Note) Telegram sent in 1917 by German Foreign Secretary Arthur Zimmermann to the German ambassador to the United States suggesting an alliance with Mexico in the event of American entry into World War

I against Germany. The telegram, intercepted and made public, helped arouse American sentiment against Germany.

Zinoviev, Grigori Evseyevich (1883–1936) Russian Communist leader who played a leading role in the Soviet government (1917–1926). With Stalin and Kamenev he formed the triumvirate that ruled after the death of Lenin. He also headed the Comintern (1919–1926). He was executed during the Stalinist purges.

Zionism Jewish movement for the establishment and preservation of a Jewish national state in Palestine. The first Zionist council was held in 1897 in Basel, Switzerland under the leadership of Herzl. With the advent of World War I, Great Britain lent its support to the movement through the Balfour Declaration in 1917. World War II reemphasized the need for a Jewish homeland. The U.N. plan for the partition of Palestine resulted in the establishment of a Jewish state in 1948.

Zog I (Ahmed Bey Zogu) (1895–1961) King of Albania (1928–1939). He led Albania into military and financial dependence on Mussolini's Italy and was overthrown after the Italian invasion of Albania.

Zola, Emile (1840–1902) French novelist, a leader of the naturalist movement in France, and one of the greatest French writers of the 19th century. He played a leading role in the Dreyfus Affair.

Zollverein German customs union. Begun in the early 1800s by Prussia, it grew to include all the German states. Its policies were incorporated in 1871 into the German Empire.

Zoroastrianism Ancient Persian religion founded in the 6th century B.C. by Zoroaster. Its teachings center on Ahura Mazda, a god of righteousness, who would battle the evil spirits led by Ahriman until the ultimate victory over evil is achieved. Zoroastrianism was made the state religion of Persia by the Sassanidae in the 3rd century A.D. and is believed to have influenced both Judaism and Christianity. Its few remaining adherents are known as Parsees.

Zwingli, Huldreich or **Ulrich** (1484–1531) Swiss reformer, the leading figure in the Swiss Protestant Reformation. His opposition to Luther's views on the nature of the Eucharist led to great dissension within the Protestant church.

LANGUAGE ARTS

GRAMMAR

Noun

The noun is a naming word. It is used to identify people, places, objects, ideas, emotions—in short, anything that can be named: *John, Harlem, committee, amplification, table, hatred, baseball.*

Nouns can be recognized by their form and their position in the sentence as well as by their naming function. Below are some of the things to look for when you are trying to identify the nouns in a sentence.

1. Most nouns can follow the word *the* or other determiners such as *my, a, this: a truth, his moves, this infiltration.*
2. All nouns can occur before and after verbs: His *moves* dazzled the *spectators. Faith* moves *mountains.*
3. All nouns can follow relationship words called prepositions: *before* winter, *after* Christmas, *in* his adversity.
4. Most nouns can take an *s* or an *es* at the end of the word to express the idea of more than one: *soup, soups; church, churches; debate, debates.*
5. Some nouns can take an apostrophe and an *s* or an apostrophe by itself to express belonging: the *boy's* bicycle; the *boys'* room; *Dickens'* novels.
6. Some nouns can start with a capital letter to indicate the name or the title of some specific thing or person: *Wilson High School, Armando, America, September, Jew, Surgeon General.*
7. Some nouns have endings such as *-ness, -tion, -ity* whose function is to indicate that the word is a noun: *reasonableness, adversity, infiltration.*

Proper and Common

The name or title of an individual, of a person, place, or thing, is usually expressed by a proper noun or nouns. They are always capitalized. When these nouns do *not* refer to the name of a person or thing, they are common nouns and are *not* capitalized. Compare:

I will ask *Mother.*

Yesterday she became a *mother.*

I think that *Crescent City* is in Alberta.

The *city* lay on a crescent in the river.

Among other things, proper nouns name people, continents, countries, provinces, states, counties, parishes, geographic regions, days of the week, months of the year, holidays, festivals (but not seasons): *Christmas, winter, December, Friday, Alberta, The Netherlands, Judge Hernandez.*

Singular and Plural

Most nouns can be singular or plural in form. The usual plural form adds *s* or *es* to the end of the word: *sigh, sighs; fox, foxes; category, categories; calf, calves.* Note the *y* and the *f* change before a plural ending. *Trys** and *Skys** are incorrect forms. There is less consistency with the *f* forms. *Hoofs* is possible; *rooves** is not. It is advisable to have a dictionary at hand when dealing with certain plurals.

Some nouns have irregular plural forms: *child, children; goose, geese; sheep, sheep.* Some nouns borrowed from other languages keep their orignal plural forms: *datum, data; cherub, cherubim; crisis, crises; formula, formulae.* Note that *formula* is used so frequently that the incorrect form *formulas** is being used by some educated speakers. It is advisable to have an up-to-date dictionary on hand when you are faced with foreign plurals.

Some nouns can normally occur in the singular form only: *much dust, much dusts*; more courage, more courages*; less fun, less funs*.* These nouns are called mass nouns or noncountable nouns. Note that some determiners such as *much* and *less* work only with noncountable nouns, although recently there has been a tendency among educated speakers to use *less people** (*people* is a countable noun) rather than *fewer people.*

A few noncountable nouns can appear in the plural form if the idea of a difference of kind is stressed. *There are some new instant coffees on the market. Several wheats grow in Australia.*

Possessive Case

The possessive case of nouns is formed by adding an apostrophe and an *s* to words that do not end with an *s* or a *z* sound: *the boy's room, the children's school;* and by adding only the apostrophe to words that do end with an *s* or a *z* sound: *the boys' room, Dickens' novel.* If, however, the word ending in *s* or *z* sound is a proper noun with only one syllable, an apostrophe and an *s* are added to the word: *Keats's sonnets, Santa Claus's reindeer.*

Care must be taken in forming the possessive form of nouns ending with *y* because although the singular and plural forms sound the same way, they are spelled differently:

the baby's cry [one baby's cry]

the babies' murmurings [the murmurings of several babies]

When possession is shared by two or more nouns, the possessive case is used for the last noun in the series: *Jose, Fred, and Edward's canoe.*

When two nouns refer to the same person, the second noun is in the possessive case:

the mother of the bride's yellow dress [The bride probably wore white. If the phrase sounds awkward, the use of two possessives does not improve it much: *the bride's mother's yellow dress.*] Better: *The yellow dress of the bride's mother.*

Nonanimate things do not normally "possess" anything. The possessive form using the preposi-

---

*Throughout the text, an asterisk will be used to indicate an ungrammatical form in Standard American English.

tion *of* is used in order to express an arrangement or part of nonanimate things:

piles of coats NOT coats'* piles

the edge of the chisel NOT the chisel's* edge

However, writers have long made exception to this rule in such matters as time, money, and transportation: *a day's work, a dollar's worth, the ship's compass*. Today more and more nonanimate things are taking the apostrophe form of the possessive: *the razor's edge, the book's success, education's failure*. Obviously, there is no clear rule about when *the razor's edge* is approved and *the chisel's* edge* is frowned on.

Remember too that when writing creatively you are allowed a certain amount of free rein, which is usually referred to as "poetic license."

Noun Functions

The noun can perform a variety of functions. The functions listed here are discussed in greater detail later in this section.

The noun can work as the subject, object, or complement of a finite verb or verbal.

Being a recent *arrival* [complement of the verbal *being*] from Puerto Rico, *Margarita* [subject of the verb *was*] was proud that she could speak *Spanish* [object of the verb *speak*] as well as English.

The noun can work as the object of a preposition.

Margarita, who came from *Puerto Rico* [object of the preposition *from*], spoke excellent Spanish in her *home* [object of the preposition *in*] and good English at *school* [object of the preposition *at*].

The noun can work after another noun as a modifier or an appositive, as it is also called.

my brother *Charles*

his problem, a damaged *retina*

The noun can work before another noun as a modifier.

a *problem* child   a *noun* clause   a *bottle* opener

The noun can work as a modifier of an adjective or a verb.

They were *battle* weary. [modifier of the adjective *weary*]

They arrived *yesterday*. [modifier of the verb *arrived*]

The noun in the possessive case can work as a determiner introducing another noun.

the *bride's* mother [*The bride's* introduces *mother*. The article *the* belongs to *bride's*, not to *mother*.]

Pronoun

Although a pronoun often takes the place of a noun in a sentence, the pronoun is sometimes a word that lacks specific meaning. Indefinite pronouns like *anyone, something, somebody* mean only that unspecified people or things are referred to.

When pronouns replace other words, they carry the meaning of these replaced words. The replaced words are called the *antecedent* of the pronoun. The antecedent of a pronoun is usually a noun and its modifiers, if any, but sometimes the antecedent can be a whole sentence.

The dog lost *its* bone. [*Its* replaces *the dog*.]

The old man, *who* had his car stolen, was in shock. [*Who* replaces *the old man*.]

Personal

The personal pronouns are distinguished by person, case, and number.

FIRST PERSON (the person speaking or writing)

Case	Singular	Plural
Nominative	I	we
Possessive	my, mine	our, ours
Objective	me	us

SECOND PERSON (the person addressed)

Case	Singular	Plural
Nominative	you	you
Possessive	your, your	your, yours
Objective	you	you

In the third person, pronouns are also distinguished by gender.

THIRD PERSON (the person, place, or thing spoken or written about)

Case	Singular			Plural
	MASCULINE	FEMININE	NEUTER	
Nominative	he	she	it	they
Possessive	his	her, hers	its	their, theirs
Objective	him	her	it	them

Relative

When a sentence is embedded inside another sentence to function as a relative clause, a relative pronoun replaces the repeated noun in order to make the new sentence grammatical.

Magic Johnson, *who* has all the moves, could not be stopped.

The tools *that* he bought yesterday were specked with rust.

Who, whom, whose, that refer to people; *which, of which, that* refer to things. Sometimes the relative pronoun can be omitted altogether: *The tools he bought yesterday were specked with rust.*

Interrogative

The interrogative pronouns *who, whom, whose, which, what*, are some of the words that introduce questions. *Who, whom*, and *whose* indicate that the expected answer will be a person: *what* indicates that the answer will be something nonhuman;

which may be used for either persons or things.

Who was the chairman?   Answer: John

What was he carrying?   Answer: a suitcase

Which girl was hurt?   Answer: Justine

Demonstrative
The demonstrative pronouns *this, these, that, those* indicate nearness to or distance from the speaker, literally or figuratively. The antecedent of the pronoun is usually in another clause or sentence. Sometimes the reference is too general for there to be a specific antecedent.

This is my father, Mr. Rodriguez, and *those* are my children, Juanita and Armando. [The antecedent *Mr. Rodriguez* is literally closer to the speaker than are his children.]

Marcellus would climb trees at night. *This* disturbed his mother. [The antecedent of *this* is the sentence about Marcellus' nocturnal tree-climbing.]

Be gentle to *those* who stay angry. [*Those* has no antecedent, in the normal sense of the word. The reference is limited by the relative clause that follows it.]

Indefinite
The indefinite pronouns are so named because their antecedents are usually vague or unknown. These are such words as *each, all, either, anyone, somebody, everyone, whoever, whatever.* They form the possessive case in the same manner as nouns: *anyone's, somebody else's.*

Intensive and Reflexive
Personal pronouns ending with *self* or *selves* (*myself, ourselves, itself,* etc.) have two functions. The first is to repeat the noun antecedent in order to emphasize and intensify the meaning: *Mary herself was responsible.* The second function is also to repeat the noun antecedent but in a different part of the sentence.

I hurt *myself.* [*Myself* repeats *I*, but it functions as the object and the antecedent *I* functions as the subject.]

Myself should not be used in place of *me*: He is going to the hockey game with Michelle and *myself.** [*Me* should be used.]

Pronoun Case
Case is a form change that denotes the relation of a noun or a pronoun to other words in the sentence. In English, nouns have only one form change that could be called a case change—the apostrophe form (possessive case). (See Possessive Case in the section on Nouns.) Some pronouns have three or four case forms. They are the personal pronouns and the two relative pronouns *who* and *whoever.*

Nominative or Subjective Case
The pronoun forms *I, we, you, it, he, she, they, who, whoever* are in the nominative case. The uses of the nominative case follow:

Expressing a subject:

Jason and *I* are going to the pizza parlor. [*Me** and Jason* and *Jason and me** are not acceptable in the standard dialect.]

I don't know *who* stole the peach tree. [*Who* is the subject of *stole.*]

Give it to *whoever* comes. [*Whoever* is the subject of *comes,* not the object of *to.* The object of *to* is the whole clause *whoever comes.*]

Expressing the subject repeated:

Three members of our club gave woodwind recitals—Glynis, Paul, and *I*. [The subject is repeated by *Glynis, Paul, and I.* This repeated structure is called an *appositive.*]

Expressing the subject when the verb is deleted:

He is more articulate than *she.* [The verb *is* after *she* has been deleted because it is understood, and to repeat it would be redundant.]

He plays as well as *I.* [The verb *play* has been deleted. Many speakers find this construction unduly self-conscious, so they add a word that takes the place of a verb. He *plays as well as I do.*

Coming after the verb be: Some educated speakers find the nominative case after *be* so artificial that they will sometimes prefer to use the objective form of the pronoun.

It was *they* who found the dog. [OBJECTIVE: It was *them* who found the dog.]

That must be *she.* [OBJECTIVE: That must be *her.*]

It is *I.* [OBJECTIVE: It is *me.*]

Objective or Accusative
The pronoun forms *me, us, her, him, them, whom, whomever* are in the objective case. There is no case distinction for *you* and *it* in the objective. The same is true, in English, for all nouns. The uses of the objective case follow:

Expressing the object of a verb, verbal, or preposition:

Shoving *me* before *him,* he forced *me* down the alley.

My brother came between Carlos and *me.* [Sometimes people will say *between Carlos and I** under the mistaken impression that polite people always say *I* rather than *me.*]

Whom were they talking about? [*Whom* is the object of the preposition *about.* In writing, *whom* must always be used in this context. In speaking, *who* is becoming acceptable: *Who were they talking about*?]

Expressing the object repeated:

The police ticketed three members of our group, Garcia, McEwan, and *me.*

Expressing the object when the verb is deleted:

Mr. Anderson did not recommend him as highly as *me.* [*As he did me* is also possible here.]

Expressing the nominal before the infinitive:

We wanted *him* to suffer. [A nominal is a word that is not a noun but functions as one.]

Possessive or Genitive

There are two sets of pronoun forms in the possessive case:

1. my our your her his its their whose
2. mine ours yours hers his its theirs whose

The first set of pronouns function as noun modifiers (*his escape, my wife*) and are called here *possessives*. The second set of pronouns function as nominals (This is *mine*; *Whose* were found?) and are called here *independent possessives*.

As we have seen, nouns (see Possessive Case in the section on nouns) and indefinite pronouns (see Indefinite Pronouns) also have a possessive case.

Functions of Possessives

Possessives function as determiners before nouns.

The meanings usually conveyed by these possessive determiners are possession, connection, the performer of an act, and the classification of a thing.

Whose car was stolen? [The question asks about the possession of a car.]

the *bureau's* lawyers [The bureau does not possess the lawyers so much as the lawyers are connected to the bureau.]

Possessives function in gerund phrases as the introducer of the phrase. They also function as the substitute for the nominative case which expresses the performer of the action. Thus *He was leaving* becomes *his leaving.*

His leaving at dawn upset his father.

The *girl's* singing of Brahms's "Lullaby" was musical. [This gerund phrase must not be confused with a participle phrase, which in the following sentence modifies the nominative case *girl*: *The girl singing in the next room is my sister.*]

There are some exceptions to the rule that gerund phrases are started by a possessive noun or pronoun.

He slipped away without *anybody* in the room noticing him. [The possessive form is not used because it does not immediately precede the gerund.]

Luis saw *him* leaving the parking lot. [After verbs like *see, hear,* and *watch,* the objective form of the pronoun or noun is used.]

Throwing the bola is not easy. [The action is so general that the writer has nobody in particular in mind. Therefore, no noun or pronoun introduces the gerund phrase.]

Functions of Independent Possessives

Independent possessives are nominals; that is, they function as subjects, objects, or complements as nouns do.

I wonder *whose* this is. [*Whose* is the complement of the verb *is*. Note that this *whose* differs from the *who's* in *Who's there?*]

His was a fascinating personality. [*His* is the subject of the verb *was.*]

He's a friend of *Mother's* and *mine.* [*Mother's* and *mine* are the objects of the preposition *of.*]

Verb

The verb is a word or a group of words that usually express an action or a state of being. There are two kinds of verbs that must be distinguished:

1. *The finite verb* works with the subject of the sentence to give a sense of completeness, a sense of a statement having been made.
2. The *nonfinite verb or verbal* works as a nominal (something like a noun) or a modifier. It never works with a subject. It does not give a sense of completeness. Compare:

FINITE	NONFINITE
The documents *had compromised* him.	the *compromising* documents . . .

The authorities *accused* him of fraud. the authorities, *having accused* him of fraud, . . .

The forms and functions of the finite verb are discussed in this section. Nonfinite verbs or verbals are discussed in the section Verbal.

Finite

Finite verbs can be recognized by their form and their position in the sentence. Here are some of the things to look for when you are trying to identify the finite verbs in a sentence:

1. Most finite verbs can take an *ed* or a *d* at the end of the word to indicate time in the past: *cough, coughed; celebrate, celebrated.* A hundred or so finite verbs do not have these regular endings.
2. Nearly all finite verbs take an *s* at the end of the word to indicate the present when the subject of the verb is third person singular: *cough, he coughs; celebrate, she celebrates.* The exceptions are auxiliary verbs like *can* and *must.*
3. Finite verbs are often groups of words that include such auxiliary verbs as *can, must, have,* and *be: can be suffering, will have gone, must eat.*
4. Finite verbs usually follow their subjects: He *coughs.* The documents *had compromised* him. They *will have gone.*
5. Finite verbs surround their subjects when some forms of a question are asked: *Is* he *coughing? Did* they *celebrate?*

Verbs are distinguished by number (singular and plural) and by person (first, second, third). In general, verbs have a different form only in the third person singular of the present tense.

I, you, we, they *move.*

BUT

He, she, it *moves.*

An exception is the verb *to be*, which is more highly inflected:

SINGULAR   I *am*; you *are*; he, she, it *is*

PLURAL   We, you, they *are*

The finite verb can be a one-word verb with an indication of present or past tense: *watch, watched; freeze, froze.*

The finite verb can also be a group of words composed of one or more of the following ingredients:

1. Modal auxiliaries: *will, would, can, must,* etc.
2. Perfect auxiliary: a part of the verb *have* plus an *-en* or an *-ed* ending.
3. Progressive auxiliary: a part of the verb *be* plus an *-ing* ending.
4. Passive auxiliary: a part of the verb *be* plus an *-en* or an *-ed* ending.
5. Main Verb: *watch, tolerate.*

Below is a paradigm or layout of some forms of the finite verb *watch*.

Modal		Perfect	Progressive	Passive
	had	watched		
	was		watching	
	was			watched
	had	been	watching	
	had	been		
could	watch			
could	have	watched		watched
could	be		watching	
could	be			watched
could	have	been	watching	
could	have	been		watched

Mood

A verb may be placed in the indicative, imperative, or subjunctive mood to indicate differences in the intention of the speaker or writer.

The *indicative mood* is used to make an assertion or ask a question.

The horse *galloped* down the street.

Where *are* you *going*?

The *imperative mood* is used for commands, directions, or requests.

COMMAND   *Go* to the store and *order* a typewriter.
DIRECTION   *Turn* right at the next traffic light.
REQUEST   Please *answer* my letter.

Subjunctive Forms. The present and past tense forms of the verb are sometimes used to express matters that are not present or past in the usual sense. They are matters of urgency, formality, possibility, and unreality. The present and past tense forms of the verb used for the subjunctive are not the expected forms. These unexpected forms are called forms of the *subjunctive mood.* (The expected forms are called forms of the *indicative mood.*)

I demand that he *see* me immediately.

I move that the motion *be* tabled.

It was important that she *love* me.

If she *were* to go, there might be trouble.

If he *were* talented, he could make money.

There are ways to express subjunctive meanings other than using past and present forms of the verb. Such auxiliaries as *might* and *should* can also be used: *If you had been presentable, I might have taken you to the party.*

Transitive and Intransitive

Verbs are classified as transitive or intransitive.

A transitive verb (*transit* means to *carry,* as in *rapid transit*) requires an object to complete its meaning. The object of a transitive verb is affected, however slightly, by whatever the verb expresses:

The hammer *struck* the anvil.

Angela *read* the newspaper.

An intransitive verb makes an assertion without requiring any object.

The clock *strikes.*

He *walks* down the street every evening.

A *copulative verb,* a special kind of intransitive verb, is one that connects the subject to a noun, pronoun, or adjective in the predicate.

Sean *is* the president. [*Is* connects *Sean* to *president. Sean* and *president* are the same person. A noun like *president* used after a copulative verb is called a predicate nominative.]

The most frequently used copulative verb is *to be.* Other commonly used copulative verbs are *become, seem, smell, look, grow, feel, sound, get, taste, appear.*

Many verbs are both transitive and intransitive. A good dictionary will indicate the differences in meaning.

Passive Voice

Transitive verbs can be switched from the *active voice* to the *passive voice* by a transformation that changes the form of the verb and moves the object into the subject's position. The old subject, if it stays in the sentence, becomes a prepositional phrase starting with *by.* Thus, *Sandy Koufax won the award* is transformed into *The award was won by Sandy Koufax.*

The passive voice is used to emphasize or direct attention to the receiver of the action, in this case *the award.* The passive voice switches our attention from *Sandy Koufax* to what he received: *the award.*

The passive voice is also used to eliminate the necessity of naming the agent of the action when that agent is unknown or unimportant.

Prison authorities released Alfred Krupp from prison in 1951.

Alfred Krupp *was released* from prison in 1951.

Present and Past Tenses

All main verbs are either in the present tense or the past tense: *watch, watched.* The word *tense* is also used for other forms, such as perfect and progressive forms.

The present tense expresses any time that has some element of the present in it, no matter how small.

This apple *tastes* good. [a present situation]

Apples *taste* good. [a general truth]

In *Hamlet,* the opening scene *takes* place at night. [A play written in the past has a plot summary alive in the present.]

Rita *goes* to Mexico City tomorrow. [The action will occur in the future, but there is a suggestion that the decision to go may have occurred in the present.]

He *uses* lemon in his tea. [a habitual action, past, present, and future]

The past tense excludes the present and covers those events that took place at a definite time or habitually in the past. As with the present tense, the meaning is sometimes reinforced by other words that indicate time.

I *went* down the street yesterday. [a completed event in the past]

Whenever Rock *went* down the street, the people cheered. [a habitual action in the past]

Modal Auxiliaries

Modal auxiliaries, verbs such as *can, could, may, might, must, ought, shall, should, will,* and *would,* always occur as part of verb phrases. Modal auxiliaries express a large variety of ideas and feelings. A few of the more common uses are listed here.

PERMISSION	You *can* put your shirt on now.
	You *may* come in.
ABILITY	I *can* read braille.
	She *could* open the door.
NECESSITY	He *must* see her today.
	He *had* to go to Nairobi.
CONCLUSION	He *must* have seen her.
GENERAL TRUTH	Cats *will* sleep for hours.

Future Time

English has no future tense as does Latin. Instead, English uses modal auxiliaries, present and past tense forms, and adverbials of time to express future time.

He *is going to* lose his mind.

He *is about to* lose his mind.

I *begin* work *tomorrow.*

It's time you *went* to bed.

Shall and Will

To indicate simple futurity, formal usage dictates that *shall* is correct for the first person and *will* and *won't* are correct for the second and third persons.

I (we) *shall* (*shall not*) go.

You *will* (*won't*) go.

He (she, it, they) *will* (*won't*) go.

In recent years, *will* and *won't* have been commonly used for all persons even in relatively formal writing. But the *shall* form has persisted in idiomatic expressions. *Shall we dance?* is certainly more commonplace than the awkward sounding *Will we dance?*

To indicate a promise or determination, *will* is used in the first person: *I* (*we*) *will go.* To express a command or determination, *shall* is used in the second and third persons: *You* (*he, she, it, they*) *shall go.*

Perfect Tenses

A perfect tense is used to talk about an action that occurs at one time but is seen in relation to another time. *I ran out of gas* is a simple statement about a past event. *I've run out of gas* is a statement about a past event that is connected with the present.

I *have waited* for you. [The *present perfect* indicates that the action occurred in the past and was completed in the present.]

Luis *has visited* San Juan several times. [The action occurred frequently in the past so that it has become part of Luis' present experience.]

I *had waited* for you. [The *past perfect* shifts the action further into the past so that it is completed in relation to a later time.]

Mary *had been* out in the canoe all morning when she suddenly fell into the lake. [The *past perfect* indicates that, in the past, one event occurred before the other.]

By sundown he *should have finished the job.* [The *conditional perfect* suggests that something else occurred at a later time to affect the completion of the job.]

By sundown he *will have finished* the job. [The *future perfect* indicates that the event will be completed by a definite time in the future.]

Progressive Tenses

Progressive tenses draw our attention to the continuity of an action rather than its completion. A verb that in its own meaning already expresses a continuity does not need a progressive form. (*I live in Boston* already says it. *I am living in Boston,* the progressive form, says it twice.) But compare *He worked in his cellar* with the progressive form, which stresses the continuity of the action: *He was working in his cellar.* The progressive is often helped out by adverbials that express continuity.

He *is always running* to his mother.

I *must have been painting* the house for days now.

I've been washing the dog. [The combination of perfect and progressive paints a vivid picture of a person deeply involved in a past process of some duration with immediate relevance to the wet present.]

Adjective and Adverb

Adjectives and adverbs identify the distinctive feature of something: the fastness of the horse in *the fast horse*, the fastness of the driving in *He drove fast*, the dishonor of the conduct in *dishonorable conduct*, the dishonor of the behavior in *He behaved dishonorably*.

Recognition

Adjectives and adverbs can be distinguished from each other by their form and their position in the sentence. here are some ways of distinguishing these words.

If a word fits one or both of the following blank positions, it is an adjective, not an adverb:

He was very . . . It was very . . .

He was very *cowardly*. It was very *swampy*.

Some adjectives, of course, do not fit these blanks because they should not be used with the intensifier *very*. (*He was very unique** is incorrect. Since *unique* means one of a kind, there are no real degrees of being *unique*.) More important, however, is that other noun modifiers do not go in these blanks; therefore, this is a useful way to distinguish adjectives from other noun modifiers.

Because she was a *city* dweller, she was very *city*.*[*City* can be a noun modifier, but it is not an adjective.]

Because he was a *jolly, green* giant, he was *green* and *jolly*. [*Green* and *jolly* are adjectives.]

Adjectives and adverbs can sometimes be distinguished by form. Some of the several forms are listed below, including the most important one, which is that most adverbs are adjectives plus *-ly*. (In a few cases both the adjective and the adverb end in *-ly*: *cowardly, hourly*.)

	ADJECTIVE	ADVERB
theory [*noun*]	theoretical	theoretically
differ [*verb*]	different	differently
honor [*noun*]	honorable	honorably

The Article

The most used adjectivals are the articles *a, an,* and *the*. *A* and *an* are called indefinite articles because they single out any one unspecified member of a class. *The* is called a definite article because it specifies a particular member or a particular group of members of a class.

A is used when it immediately precedes a word beginning with a consonant sound: *a book, a tree. An* is used when it immediately precedes a word beginning with a vowel sound: *an apple, an ancient city.*

Functions

Although adjectives and adverbs can perform the same functions as verb complements and modifiers, their functions are usually quite distinct.

NOTE: The sound, not the actual letter, determines the form of the indefinite article: *a university, an R.C.A. television set, and an 8–sided object.*

Adjectives modify a noun or function as the complements of copulative verbs such as *be, seem, feel*.

The *old* man, *tired* and *surly*, waited for the return of his children. [*Old, tired,* and *surly* modify the noun *man*.]

Adverbs modify verbs and other modifiers.

He spoke to her *quietly*. [modifies the verb *spoke*]

Comparison of Adjectives and Adverbs

Adjectives and adverbs have positive, comparative, and superlative forms. The positive form is the basic word: *small, beautiful, lush, loudly*.

For adjectives of one syllable, the comparative is usually formed by adding *-er* to the positive form: *small, smaller, smallest; lush, lusher, lushest*.

For most adjectives of more than one syllable and for most adverbs, the comparative and superlative are formed by combining *more* and *most* with the positive form: *beautiful, more beautiful, most beautiful; loudly, more loudly, most loudly*.

Some adjectives and adverbs do not follow these rules.

Positive	Comparative	Superlative
bad	worse	worst
ill	worse	worst
good	better	best
well	better	best

The *comparative form* indicates a comparison of two things or two groupings of things. Usually the two things or groupings of things are mentioned explicitly in the sentence, but this is not always so.

She ran *faster* than her mother.

After that restful night, he was *more relaxed* when we came to see him.

The *superlative form* is used when more than two things are compared.

She was the *fastest* reader in her family.

She shouted *the most loudly* of them all. [Some writers prefer to express the adverbial by means of an adjective form: *She shouted the loudest of them all.*]

Confusion of Adjectives and Adverbs

Some words like *fast, slow, very, late* function as either adjectives or adverbs.

ADJECTIVE It was a *fast* train. [modifies noun *train*]
ADJECTIVE The clock was *fast*. [complements verb *was*]
ADVERB The horse ran *fast*. [modifies verb *ran*]

When an adjective follows a copulative verb (like *is, feel, look, seem, become, smell*), it complements the verb and is known as a predicate adjective.

The water is (seems, feels, looks, is getting, is becoming) *hot*.

I feel (look, am) *fine, ill, sick, good, bad*.

You look *beautiful*. [not *beautifully*]

Verbal

Verbals are verbs that have lost their subjects, their capacity to indicate definite time, and their capacity to express such ideas as necessity, obligation, and possibility.

Infinitive
The infinitive is the most versatile of the three verbals. It can be both active and passive, perfect and progressive.

To live happily is not so hard. [*present active* form indicating present time]

To be living today is not so bad. [*present progressive active* form indicating a continuous action in the present]

He was pleased *to have been recommended*. [*perfect passive* form indicating two different times in the past]

To have been recommended would have pleased him. [*perfect passive* form indicating that a past action could have happened, but didn't. This is a subjunctive use of the infinitive.]

The *to* in the infinitive is sometimes omitted. Compare: *Ask me to do it, Let me do it*; *He was made to confess, They made him confess*. Note that dropping *to* creates a more informal sentence.

Present Participle
The name of this participle is misleading. It can indicate not only the present but also the past and the future.

Arriving early, they smiled with embarrassment. [The actions are both in the past.]

Arriving tomorrow, they will be met at the airport. [The actions are both in the future.]

The present participle has a perfect form in which the auxiliary *have* plus the *-en* or *-ed* form of the verb is used.

Having arrived early, they decided to wait for their host. [The actions are at different times in the past.]

Gerund. The gerund is a present participle that functions as a noun and therefore names an action or a state of being. Like the infinitive, it may have modifiers and complements.

Swimming is good exercise.

Eating too much is bad for one's health.

Bowling on the green was his favorite sport.

Past Participle
The past participle can indicate past, present, and future meanings.

Thus *deceived*, he will be outraged. [both actions in the future]

Baffled by you attitude, I cannot help you. [both actions in the present]

Baffled by your attitude, I cannot help you. [both [both actions in the past]

The past participle has both perfect progressive forms.

Having been discovered, the thief confessed.

Being watched, he could only pretend to mow the lawn.

Functions of Verbals
Because they have lost their subjects and their tense, verbals never function as do finite verbs. Instead, they function as nominals (structures that behave like nouns) or as modifiers. Usually they carry along with them their own modifiers and verb completions.

When the present participle works as a nominal, it is called a *gerund*. The infinitive working as a nominal is still called an infinitive. Some of the more common uses of the verbal follow:

1. Verbals as *nominals*:

   Being watched made him nervous. [gerund as subject]

2. Verbals as *modifiers of nouns*:

   His desire *to recant* was urgent. [modifies *desire*]

3. Verbals as *modifiers of verbs*:

   He went to the mountains *to meditate*. [modifies *went*]

4. Verbals as *modifiers of adjectives*:

   He was anxious *to cooperate*. [modifies *anxious*]

Prepositions and Conjunctions

Prepositions and conjunctions are relationship words that are used to connect elements in the sentence. Prepositions and the several kinds of conjunctions perform different functions and should be carefully distinguished from each other.

Prepositions and Subordinating Conjunctions
Prepositions and subordinating conjunctions can be distinguished from each other by what follows them and because there are a limited number of subordinating conjunctions.

The preposition is followed by a nominal. The nominal can be a noun, pronoun, gerund phrase, or noun clause.

because of the bad weather [The noun *weather* is the object of the preposition *because of*.]

before leaving home [The gerund phrase *leaving home* is the object of the preposition *before*.]

after what he had done [The noun clause *what he had done* is the object of the preposition *after*.]

The subordinating conjunction is followed by a subject-verb structure with no other relationship word involved. Thus *he had done* can follow a subordinating conjunction, and *what he had done* can follow a preposition.

because the weather was bad [*Because* is a subordinating conjunction introducing the subordinate clause.]

before he left home [*Before* is a subordinating conjunction introducing the subordinate clause.]

Before, after, since, as, until are both preposition and subordinating conjunction depending on what follows: *Since this morning*; *since you went away*.

If, when, while, although *and some others are subordinating conjunctions that can have their subject-verb structures transformed so that they begin to look like prepositional phrases.*

when you were mopping the floor

when mopping the floor

if it is at all possible

if at all possible

although he was very angry

although very angry

Most prepositions and subordinating conjunctions by their function are not easily confused with each other.

Prepositions	Subordinating Conjunctions
in	if
by	why
for	how
beneath	although
because of	because
than	that
except	than
as	as

Despite the sustained campaign of advertising agencies, *like* is still a preposition.

Like* I was saying, it's going to rain. [*As I was saying* is the preferred form.]

Like me, Hans enjoyed soccer.

Samsons smell good *like** a walnut should. [*As a walnut should* is still preferred in the standard dialect.]

Coordinating Conjunctions

Coordinating conjunctions join sentence elements of equal importance. These conjunctions are *and, but, or, nor, for, yet*. They may join a word to another word (bread *and* butter), a phrase to another phrase (into the oven *or* over the fire), an independent clause to another independent clause (He wanted to learn, *but* he hated to study), a dependent clause to another dependent clause (Matilda came in after I arrived *but* before dinner was served).

Coordinating conjunctions are occasionally used effectively to introduce a sentence.

He said he would do it. *And* he did.

She swore that she told the truth. *Yet* she lied.

Correlative Conjunctions

Correlative conjunctions are pairs of words used to join sentence elements of equal importance. They are words like *both . . . and, either . . . or, neither . . . nor, not only . . . but also*.

Either you go now, *or* you stay here forever.

Sentence Connectors

Sentence connectors join whole statements in clause or sentence form. Because some of these relationship words have adverbial forms (*obviously, naturally, unfortunately*), they are sometimes called *conjunctive adverbs*. The most common sentence connectors are *therefore, however, consequently, thus, then, in fact, moreover, nevertheless, so, in addition, meanwhile*. When they join independent clauses, they work with a semicolon. When they relate sentences, a period is used.

We watched his folly develop; *in fact*, we nurtured it.

Joe Louis was a fantastically successful boxer. *However*, he did not emerge from his great career as a rich man.

Unlike coordinating conjunctions, some sentence connectors can be inserted appropriately within the structure of the second statement.

She was not pleased by his skating technique. She was delighted, *however*, by his self-control and poise.

Interjection

Interjections (the word means *thrown in*) are words that do not fulfill any of the functions of the previous parts of speech. They are such words as *yes, no, oh, ah, well, hello*. Although they are frequently used in sentences, they are not properly parts of the sentence structure and are therefore separated from the remainder of the sentences by punctuation marks.

THE SENTENCE AND ITS PARTS

When we are speaking, our sentences can be quite short. One side of a telephone conversation will reveal things like "Yes . . . sure . . . why not . . . OK, about five o'clock." However, usually when we speak and always when we write, our sentences are longer, having a subject and a predicate.

Subject and Predicate

The sentence has two parts. The topic of the sentence is the *subject*. What is said about the subject is the *predicate*. Usually but not always, the subject identifies the agent of the action; that is, it tells us who or what is doing something.

Subject	Predicate
The delegates	arrived this morning.
San Juan	is the capital of Puerto Rico.
Grambling, a small black college in Louisiana,	has produced many outstanding professional football players.
The city	was surrendered to Wallenstein.

[The subject of the sentence is *the city*, but the city didn't do anything. Something was done to the city by persons unspecified. The agent is not expressed in this sentence.]

Positions of Subject and Predicate in Sentence

Nearly always, the subject of the sentence comes first. There are occasions, however, when the subject does not come first.

Occasionally, for purposes of emphasis, the natural word order will be changed so that the predicate comes first.

Pete Rose roared into third base. [no emphasis]

Into third base roared Pete Rose. [emphasis on the predicate, which comes first]

In sentences that ask questions rather than make statements, the subject can come first, but the more usual order is to place the subject inside the verb.

Your mother is coming today?

Is *your mother* coming today?

In sentences that give commands, rather than make statements, again the subject can come first, but, nearly always, the subject and part of the verb are deleted.

You will do as I tell you!

Do as I tell you!

Sometimes, the subject can be moved out of its initial position, and a word that is lexically empty (that is, it has no meaning at all) takes its place.

To see you is nice. [*To see you* is the subject of the sentence.]

It is nice *to see you.* [*To see you* is still the subject of this sentence.]

Forms of the Subject

The subject of the sentence has several forms. The most frequent forms are nouns, proper nouns, and pronouns.

We shall overcome.

Who is on third base?

Marcus Garvey was a charismatic leader.

Those comments annoyed Jack.

Occasionally, larger structures, such as noun clauses, gerund phrases, and infinitive phrases, can function as the subject of a sentence. For convenience, nouns, pronouns, and these larger structures are called *nominals*.

What she did annoyed Jack. [*noun clause* functioning as the subject]

Playing chess amused Jack. [*gerund phrase* functioning as the subject]

To collect every stamp issued by Mexico was Juan's ambition. [*infinitive phrase* functioning as the subject]

Simple and Complete Subjects. The noun or pronoun by itself is the *simple subject*. This subject is important to identify because it controls the form of the verb. The simple subject and the verb form it controls are in italic type in these examples:

One of the ships *is* sinking.

The *mayor*, as well as the councilmen, *has* been implicated.

The noun phrase—that is, the noun and all its modifiers—is the *complete subject* [one of the ships].

Sometimes more than one nominal can be used as the subject of the sentence. The combination of several nominals to express the topic of the sentence is called a *compound subject*.

The *drivers* and the *loaders* have threatened to strike.

Not only the *price* but also the *quality* of their products fluctuates wildly.

What he did and *what he said* were not the same.

Forms of the Predicate

The predicate, what is being said about the topic of the sentence, always has a verb. The verb usually has a verb completion called an *object* or a *complement*. Like the noun or the pronoun, the verb often has modifiers. The predicate of the sentence is, in effect, made up of a verb, a verb completion, and some verb modifiers. The various forms of the predicate depend on the kind of verb involved and the kind of verb completion.

Predicate with a Transitive Verb. The most frequent form of the predicate is one in which the verb expresses some kind of action and is followed by a nominal. This nominal is called the *object*; the verb is called a *transitive verb*.

In the following sentences the verbs *brought*, *tuned*, and *said* are transitive verbs. The nominals functioning as the objects of these verbs are italicized.

They brought *their guitars* with them.

Juanita tuned *the piano*.

After the party Jack said *that they would have to clean the place*.

Some transitive verbs can drop their objects and still make sense. *They have been celebrating* is as grammatical as *They had been celebrating his birthday.*

Some transitive verbs use two verb completions: a *direct object* and another structure called an *indirect object* or a *complement*, to refer to the object and complete the meaning of the verb.

Nouns, pronouns, and prepositional phrases starting with *to* or *for* can function as *indirect objects.*

Eliseo gave twenty pesos *to his brother.*

Eliseo gave *his brother* twenty pesos.

He called *her* a taxi.

Nouns, pronouns, prepositional phrases, adjectives, and verbal phrases can function as *complements.*

He called her a *star.* [The complement *star* refers to the object *her*; they identify the same person. This can easily be confused with the two-object form above: *He called her a taxi.* (*You're a taxi* is not what is meant here!) A lot of bad television jokes are based on this confusion.]

He thought the whole thing a *bad joke.* [The noun *joke* and its modifiers function as the complement.]

They made her *taste the papaya.* [infinitive phrase *(to) taste the papaya* as the complement]

I made him *sick.* [*adjective* as the complement]

They heard their father *leaving the house.* [*participle* phrase as the complement]

He put the book *on the table.* [The prepositional phrase *on the table* functions as the complement.]

Predicate with Copulative Verb. When the verb expresses being, seeming, or becoming, the verb is called a *copulative verb.* These verbs are followed by a nominal, an adjective, or an adverbial. (An adverbial is anything that works like an adverb.)

Not many verbs function as copulatives, but those that do are common and are used frequently; *be, seem, become, remain, appear, look, feel, sound, taste, smell, grow.*

Puerto Rico became *a commonwealth* in 1952. [*noun* as complement]

Her point was *that Joe Louis was the greatest champion of all time.* [*noun clause* as complement]

Juanita will be *at her music teacher's house.* [The *prepositional phrase* is the complement. It is an adverbial telling where.]

The meat smelled *bad.* [The *adjective* is the complement. People sometimes use the adverb *badly* here. This is wrong.]

The careful use of adjectives after verbs marks one of the differences between standard and nonstandard usage.

Predicate with an Intransitive Verb. Some words do not need an object to complete them. These verbs can stand by themselves, or they are com-

pleted by an adverbial that indicates location or direction. The adverbial is called the *complement.* The verb, with or without the complement, is called an *intransitive verb.*

The situation deteriorated. [Nothing completes the verb.]

The clouds vanished. [Nothing completes the verb.]

He lay *down.* [The adverbial *down* completes the verb.]

He sat *on the desk.* [The adverbial *on the desk* is the complement.]

Compound Predicate Verbs and Verb Completions. Sometimes more than one verb or verb completion can occur in the predicate of the sentence. These structures are called the *compound verb*, the *compound object*, or the *compound complement.*

Their Puerto Rican heritage made *Luis and Rosita* proud. [two nouns functioning as the compound object]

Jack *fell* down and *broke* his crown. [two verbs functioning as the compound verb]

His stupid remark made her *angry* and *dangerous.* [two adjectives functioning as the compound complement]

Phrases and Clauses

As we have seen already, words work together in groups that can be moved around as single units.

In the garden was a statue.

A statue was *in the garden.*

These movable groups of words are called *phrases* and *clauses.* A brief listing of the word groups that are recognizable as particular kinds of phrases and clauses follows. Sometimes these word groups are recognizable because of their form, sometimes because of their function.

Phrases. Phrases are groups of words that do not have a subject and finite verb. Within them however, can be inserted other structures that do have subjects and verbs.

A *prepositional phrase* is a preposition followed by a nominal as its object. This phrase has too many functions to be of help in recognizing it.

The speaker was a woman *of extraordinary eloquence.* [The prepositional phrase modifies the noun *woman.*]

A *participial phrase* starts with a present or past participle. It modifies a noun or pronoun that is implicitly involved in the action expressed by the participle.

Holding the dog by its collar, the boy refused to let go. [The participle phrase modifies *the boy*, the person holding the dog.]

A *gerund phrase* is a participial phrase that functions as a nominal.

Using profane language is not permitted here. [The gerund phrase is the subject of the verb *is permitted*.]

An *infinitive phrase* starts with an infinitive. Sometimes the *to* of the infinitive form is omitted. This phrase has too many functions to be of help in recognizing it.

It was our desire *to serve humanity*. [The infinitive phrase functions as the subject of *was*.]

A *noun phrase* is a noun with its determiner and its modifiers. It is the noun phrase, not the noun, that is usually replaced by a pronoun.

The furniture, which they had saved so hard for, had been slashed with a knife. There was no doubt that *it* had been irretrievably ruined. [The noun phrase is the noun, its determinant *the*, and the relative clause modifying *furniture*.]

A *verb phrase* is not easy to define, because grammarians cannot agree on what to recognize as a verb phrase. There are at least three different patterns currently in use. Here we describe the verb phrase as a main verb and its auxiliaries: She *could have been watching* him.

Clauses. Clauses are groups of words that have subjects and finite verbs. Usually clauses are introduced by such relationship words as *who, that, so that, where, but, and, however*. Clauses can stand by themselves, or they can be dependent on other structures.

Independent Clauses. An independent clause can stand by itself. In this case, it starts with a capital letter and ends with a period, a question mark, or an exclamation point. It is called a sentence.

Hold tight!   She's pretty.   Who did it?

An independent clause can be joined to another independent clause by punctuation, coordinating conjunctions, or sentence connectors.

Mrs. Butler spends lavishly; she has an independent income; unfortunately, she has no taste.

Dependent Clauses. Like phrases, dependent clauses function as nominals and as modifiers. A dependent clause can be sometimes recognized by its introductory relationship word or by its function in the sentence.

Noun clauses usually start with *that*, but they can start with relative pronouns like *who* or *what*, or they can start with subordinating conjunctions like *if, when, why, where*, or *how*. Noun clauses function as nominals.

How he escaped was stated in the report.

Knowing *who was cheating* disturbed him greatly.

Adjectival clauses nearly always start with relative pronouns, although these pronouns are sometimes deleted. Adjective clauses modify nouns and pronouns and follow them as closely as possible.

A man *I know* grows tomato plants *that never bear fruit*. [The adjective clauses modify *man* and *plants*. As these clauses identify which man and which plants are being talked about, they are called *restrictive clauses* and are left unpunctuated.]

My brother, *who is not very sentimental*, did visit the Moravian village *where we were born*. [The first adjective clause is set off by commas to indicate that it is *nonrestrictive*; that is, it gives additional information rather than restricting the meaning of the noun.]

Adverbial clauses start with a variety of subordinating conjunctions that usually indicate such meanings as time, place, reason, manner, condition. Adverb clauses function as modifiers of verbs, other modifiers, and sentences.

He was bitter *that she had deserted him*.

We should answer *when she calls*.

Sentence Classification by Clause Type

For easy reference, a sentence can be classified according to the distribution of independent and dependent clauses.

A *simple sentence* is an independent clause (*Facts are stubborn things.*).

A *compound sentence* has two or more independent clauses (*There the wicked cease from troubling, and the weary be at rest.*).

A *complex sentence* has an independent clause and one or more dependent clauses (*When she got there, the cupboard was bare.*).

A *compound-complex sentence* has two or more independent clauses and one or more dependent clauses (*Jack fell down, and Jill came tumbling after because she was too busy watching Jack.*).

Modification

As has been shown in previous sections, subjects, objects, complements, and finite verbs are the basic elements that work together to make up the sentence. *Modifiers*, on the other hand, depend on other structures for their existence in the sentence. In the first example below, the adjective *old* is the complement of the verb. In the second example, the meaning of *old* stays the same, but its function has changed. The adjective *old* now acts as modifier to the noun *man*.

The man is *old*.

The *old* man is tired.

Modifiers of Verbs. Verb modifiers (or *adverbials*, as they are sometimes called) identify the distinctive features of the action of state of being expressed by the verb. These are adverbs, nouns, prepositional phrases, infinitive phrases, and adverbial clauses.

When he spoke, they fell silent. [*adverbial clause* modifying *fell*]

They went to Carnegie Hall *to hear Marian Anderson sing*. [*infinitive phrase* modifying *went*]

Verb modifiers *frequently* occur *after the verb*.

[*adverb of frequency* and *prepositional phrase* modifying *occur*]

Delighted *because she had arrived early*, he opened the champagne. [*adverbial clause* modifying the verbal *delighted*]

They arrived *this morning*. [*noun of time* modifying *arrived*]

Position of Verb Modifiers. Most verb modifiers can move around the sentence without changing their function or meaning: *He raised his hand slowly*; *Slowly he raised his hand*; *He slowly raised his hand*.

Adjectivals. Adjectivals are noun modifiers that identify a large number of distinctive features in the nouns they modify. Short adjectivals, with the exception of adverbs, sit between the determiner and the noun. Determiner and noun are given in italics in the following examples.

the wounded marine *sergeant*

a tall, dark, distinguished *gentleman*

Modifiers of Adjectives and Adverbs. Adjectives and adverbs are often modified by adverbs that indicate the comparative intensity of the quality involved. A man can be *slightly* tired, *somewhat* tired or *very* tired. These adverbs are called *intensifiers*.

She spoke *quite* firmly to him. [adverb somewhat intensified]

He was *rather* quiet when she spoke. [adjective somewhat intensified]

She was *extremely* happy to see him. [adjective very intensified]

As a result, they sang *much* more loudly. [adverb very intensified]

SENTENCE ERRORS

Sentence Fragments

When modifiers or nominals are lengthy, careless writers sometimes allow them to break off from their sentences to stand by themselves. The modifier or nominal left standing alone is called a sentence fragment.

In the following example, an adverbial clause is left standing by itself. *Because he was serving his residency at the overcrowded city hospital.** The reader is left in suspense, asking, "Well, what about it?" The writer may add a new sentence: *He had little leisure time*, but this is not a good repair job. The fragment still stands.

Sentence fragments can be corrected in two ways:
1. by properly relating the large modifier to its noun or verb or relating the large nominal to its verb.
2. by starting all over again and converting the modifier or nominal into a sentence that can stand by itself.

Comma Fault

When the writer uses a comma between two sentences, rather than relating them with a semicolon or a relationship word or separating them with a period, space, and capital letter, the result is called a *comma fault* or *comma splice* and can sometimes be confusing.

Classes will begin on September 19, the year 1984 should be a good one for all of us at Northern State.*

The comma fault is easily repaired by making two sentences out of the spliced sentences. *Classes will begin on September* 19. *The year* 1984 *should be a good one for all of us at Northern State.* If this solution seems too abrupt, then one of the methods of coordinating two sentences should be employed.

We had taken the wrong turning, *and* we found we were heading south instead of west. [coordinating conjunction *and* punctuated with a comma]

We had taken the wrong turning; we found we were heading south instead of west. [*semicolon* relating two sentences with similar content]

We had taken the wrong turning; *thus* we found we were heading south instead of west. [sentence connector *thus* punctuated with a semicolon]

Fused Sentence

The fused sentence is two or more sentences run together with no punctuation or spacing to separate them. As a result, the reader, misled and confused, must reread the sentence and, even then, may not always catch the writer's intent.

With gladness, we see the Christmas season approach Mrs. Dunkeld and I share our joy with you.*

The quick cure for the fused sentence is to make two distinct sentences out of it.

With gladness, we see the Christmas season approach. Mrs. Dunkeld and I share our joy with you.

If the two sentences sound awkward, then the use of relationship words, such as coordinating conjunctions and sentence connectors, may be in order.

With gladness we see the Christmas season approach. Mrs. Dunkeld and I, therefore, share our joy with you.

WRITING WITH CLARITY

Relating significant forms in a sentence and binding together structures and modifiers by word order and relationship words is called agreement.

Subject and Verb Agreement by Number

A verb and its subject are of the same number. The rule for number agreement is not difficult. A singular subject requires a singular verb; a plural subject requires a plural verb. To apply the rule, however, you must be able to do three things: Remember that the subject controls the verb form—do not be distracted by other structures that may stand close to the verb; be able to determine the number of the subject; and finally, know the correct singular and plural forms of the verb.

Subject Controls Number of Verb Form

In the sentence *One of our ships is missing* there is a temptation to let the plural noun *ships*, which stands by the verb, control the verb form because *ships is* sounds peculiar. The temptation must be resisted, for it is the more remote word *one*, the subject of the verb, that controls the number of the verb. There are several circumstances in which another structure may distract the writer from remembering that the subject controls the number of the verb form.

The verb agrees with the subject, not with the elements in the modifier of the subject.

Each of the sofas *is* ninety inches long.

A *swarm* of bees *is* coming toward us.

The verb agrees with the subject, not with the following complement.

The greatest *nuisance is* the refunds we have to make.

The *children* of today *are* the hope of tomorrow. [The complement nouns *refunds* and *hope* do not control the verb form. To do so, they must be moved into the subject position of the sentence to become the subjects of their sentences: The *hope* of tomorrow *is* the children of today.

If for any reason the subject is moved out of the subject position, it will still control the verb form as long as another nominal is not moved into its place.

Ramon and Eduardo are at the jai alai game.

Where *are Ramon and Eduardo*? [The sentence has been transformed into a question, and *Ramon and Eduardo* is still the subject of the sentence.]

There is one exception to the rule. The word *it* can also function as an expletive displacing the subject of the sentence. However, because it is also a singular pronoun, it controls the verb even if the subject is plural. Usually the subject displaced by

it is obviously singular so that it doesn't really matter what controls the singular verb form.

It is rumored *that he is about to resign.*

Number of Noun Subject Controls Verb Form

Most problems in subject-verb agreement occur because the number of the noun or nouns functioning as the subject is not always apparent. *The fish* can be singular or plural despite its singular form. *The news* is always singular despite its plural form.

Some nouns in the plural form can be singular in meaning, or they can be plural in meaning.

Trousers, tongs, wages, tactics, pliers, scissors, odds, and *barracks* are plural in meaning. Therefore they require a plural verb.

The scissors *are* in the lefthand drawer.

Billiards, news, mathematics, linguistics, mumps, and *measles* are singular in meaning. Therefore they require a singular verb.

Measles *is* a communicable disease.

Some nouns in the plural form can be both singular and plural, although in most uses they are plural. Compare:

Politics *has* always attracted persons of talent.

The politics of the situation *are* complicated.

Some nouns that specify an amount of something are singular when the things or people involved are regarded as a unit. In this case, they take a singular verb.

Two plus two *is* four.

Eight pounds of grapes *seems* a lot.

Ten percent of their capital *has* been absorbed already.

Ten percent of the men drafted *are* over thirty. [Here the men are regarded as individuals, not as a unit.]

Collective nouns are usually singular but can be plural. If the collective is regarded as a unit, the collective noun is singular and requires a singular verb.

The orchestra *performs* well under any conductor.

The family *is* coming over this afternoon.

If, however, members of the collective are considered individually, the collective noun is plural and requires a plural verb.

The family *were* informed as soon as they could be reached by telephone. [Members of the family were informed individually by means of several telephone calls.]

Number of Compound Subject Controls Verb Form

A compound subject coordinated by and *is nearly always plural and requires a plural verb form.*

Mink and sable *are* expensive furs.

The senator and his wife *were* warmly received.

If, however, the compound subject refers to just *one* person or thing, then the verb form is singular.

A scholar and a gentleman *is* what he strives to be.

When the compound subject refers to closely related things, it can be singular or plural depending on the closeness of the relationship. In borderline cases, the singular form of the following verb sounds better.

The courage and patriotism of de Gaulle *were* cherished by many Frenchmen in 1940. [The two qualities are related but distinct from each other; so the plural verb form is used.]

The protection and feeding of young fledglings *is* the constant preoccupation of the adult birds. [The two qualities seem so close that the singular verb form is used.]

Singular nouns coordinated by or, either . . . or, neither. . . nor, *or by* not only . . . but also *are regarded as a singular subject and a singular verb form.*

Not only the mother but also the child *was* badly dehydrated.

Either the muffler or the tailpipe *was* replaced.

Neither time nor prosperity *has* softened his heart.

When these coordinating conjunctions join plural nouns, the verb is plural. (*Neither the Saints nor the Packers are going to win this year.*) When these conjunctions join singular and plural nouns, then the verb agrees in number with the closer noun to it.

Neither his advisors nor the President himself *has* acted wisely in this crisis. [*President* is closer to the verb.]

Number of Pronoun Subject Controls Verb Form

Most indefinite pronouns are regarded as singular pronouns and require a singular verb form.

Somebody across the street *is* playing a trombone.

As yet *nobody has* challenged my theory.

Each of the sofas *is* over ninety inches long.

Everybody in the room *was* getting sleepy.

Some of these indefinite pronouns can work as determiners before singular nouns, and although there may be a strong feeling that more than one thing is involved, the verb form is still singular.

Neither idea *was* any good.

Each baby chick *was* inspected to establish its sex.

A few indefinite pronouns such as many, several, *and* few *refer to more than one person or thing. These pronouns are plural and take plural verb forms.*

Several *have* already been tested.

Many *are* called, but few *are* chosen.

The nouns *variety* and *number* also take plural verb forms when they are preceded by *a*. When they are preceded by *the*, they are singular.

A number of horsemen *were* on the hill.

The number of horsemen on the hill *was* not great.

Like collective nouns, some indefinite pronouns can be either singular or plural depending on whether they refer to a quantity or individual units of something.

Some of the cereal *is* wormy.

Some of the apples *are* rotten.

Most of the money *is* gone; so *are* most of the people. [A quantity of money and several people have disappeared.]

The pronoun *none* behaves in a similar fashion; in addition, it can be singular when the meaning of *not one* of the individuals is intended.

Luckily, *none* of the property *was* damaged; *none* of the horses *were* hurt; but *none* of us *is* blameless in this matter.

A relative pronoun can be either singular or plural, depending on the number of its antecedent. Sometimes the antecedent is not easy to find.

She is one of those courageous *women who have* sacrificed their lives for woman's rights. [*Who* can refer in general for its meaning to *she*, *one*, or *women*. Specifically it refers to the plural *women*. Therefore the verb that the pronoun *who* controls is plural.]

Pronoun and Antecedent Agreement

As was pointed out, a pronoun is a word that sometimes lacks specific meaning. Most pronouns depend on another structure for their meaning. The other structure, the antecedent, controls the pronoun with regard to number, person, gender, and the lexical features of people and things. Some of the pronouns controlled by their antecedents are the personal, demonstrative, and relative pronouns.

Number of Antecedent

Collective nouns can be singular or plural depending on whether the collective or the several individuals involved are emphasized. The following pronouns are singular or plural accordingly.

The staff express *its* confidence in *its* medical director. [The staff acted collectively.]

The staff have been airing *their* grievances publicly. [Individual staff members had been complaining.]

NOTE: As regards gender, collective nouns are neuter, requiring the pronouns *it*, *its*, and *which*.

Indefinite pronouns are usually singular but can be plural depending on whether a quantity or individual units are emphasized. The following pronoun is singular or plural accordingly.

Some of the cereal has kept *its* freshness, but *some* of the apples have worms in *their* cores. [The cereal is in quantity, the apples in individual units.]

A compound subject is singular when the coordinator is or *and plural when the coordinator is* and.

The senator and his wife were warmly received after *their* world tour.

Either Vincente or Martin may leave *his* children with us.

When one of the antecedents joined by *or* or *nor* is plural, the pronoun agrees in number with the closer antecedent.

Neither the producer nor the *sponsors* admit *they* were aware of the fraudulent practices.

Neither the sponsors nor the *producer* admits that *he* was aware of the fraudulent practices.

When the antecedent of the pronoun is a large structure like a sentence, the following pronoun is always singular.

Lumsden tried to calm the child's fears. He found *this* more difficult than he had expected.

Person and Gender of Antecedent

As nearly all noun and pronoun antecedents are third person, there is seldom any problem in selecting the correct pronoun to follow them. *Mr. Riggs said that* he *would accept the chairmanship.*

As far as gender is concerned, English bases gender on sexual difference, whereas other European languages use arbitrary gender distinctions in which football is masculine, television is feminine, and a girl can be neuter. In English, a masculine pronoun follows a male antecedent; a feminine pronoun follows a female antecedent; and a neuter pronoun follows nearly all other antecedents. Thus *a girl* is *she, an uncle* is *he,* and *a comb* is *it.*

Traditionally, masculine pronouns have been used to refer to abstract, singular nouns like *mayor, judge, professor, doctor, senator, employer, person,* and *reader:*

A judge must use *his* discretion in such a matter.

Since, today, women have assumed larger roles in many formerly masculine fields, the problem of sexist language arises. It can be solved in several ways:

by using both third person singular pronouns:

A judge must use *his or her* discretion in such a matter.

by using plural forms to avoid the singular human noun:

NOTE: As regards gender, the masculine pronoun has traditionally been used to refer to an indefinite pronoun (like *everyone*); today, however, *his or her* is considered the preferred form to use when an indefinite pronoun is the antecedent: *Everyone is wearing his or her jogging suit to the picnic.*

Judges must use *their* discretion in such matters.

by the sparing use of *you:*

Once the writer has determined his purpose . . .

Once *you* have determined your purpose . . .

by revising the sentence:

The worker should divide his task . . .

The task should be divided . . .

Human or Nonhuman Antecedent

It and *its* are the pronouns used when the antecedent is nonhuman. However, animals whose sex is significant or who are well-known to the speaker can be called *he* or *she,* which are the pronouns used for antecedents that are human.

The relative pronouns *who, whom, that* refer to antecedents that are human (or are familiar animals); *which, that* refer to antecedents that are nonhuman.

He is one of *those who* know all too well that the *memories that* move us fade all too fast. [*Those* is the human antecedent of *who; memories* is the nonhuman antecedent of that.]

Faulty Pronoun Reference

Pronouns lack specific meaning and must have antecedents to give them this meaning. Like dangling modifiers, pronouns can cause confusion if it is not clear to what they are referring. The correction of faulty pronoun reference depends on what kind of fault is involved.

Omission of Antecedent

When the antecedent of a pronoun is omitted, the faulty reference can be corrected by putting the antecedent back into its sentence; by substituting the antecedent for the pronoun; or by rewriting the sentence or sentences.

IMPLIED REFERENCE
Instead of setting a total fee, the orthodontist charged twenty dollars a month until the work was completed, *which* the dental profession considers unethical.

CLEAR
Instead of setting a total fee, the orthodontist charged twenty dollars a month until the work was completed, an arrangement *that* the dental profession considers unethical. [antecedent *an arrangement* stated explicitly]

SIMPLIED REFERENCE
My father wants me to be a doctor, but *this* is a profession that does not appeal to me.

CLEAR
My father wants me to be a doctor, but *medicine* is a profession that does not appeal to me. [antecedent *medicine* replacing its pronoun]

Separation of Antecedent and Pronoun

If a pronoun is too widely separated from its antecedent, the reference of the pronoun may be obscured. This kind of obscurity can be corrected by substituting the antecedent for the pronoun.

OBSCURE
While bathing in the *surf* at Malibu Beach, he was knocked down and almost drowned. *It* was too strong for him.

CLEAR
While bathing in *the surf* at Malibu Beach, he was knocked down and almost drowned. *The surf* was too strong for him.

Anticipating Reference
Anticipatory reference is a word order situation in which the pronoun in a dependent clause comes before its antecedent in the independent clause. If the sentence is short, the result is acceptable: *When I received it, the shirt was stained.* In longer sentences, however, the reader may be kept uninformed too long about the meaning of the pronoun.

OBSCURE
IF *they* are washed gently with warm water and a mild detergent and are then wrapped in a soft, absorbent cloth and left to dry, *these orlon garments* will retain their original shape and texture.

CLEAR
IF *these orlon garments* are washed . . . . *they* will retain . . . .

Errors of Agreement
An antecedent's control of the form of its pronoun is a strong connecting device inside and outside the sentence. If errors of agreement occur, the connection between the antecedent and its pronoun is blurred. The reader knows what is meant, but his or her sense of form is offended.

BLURRED
YOU must keep your *silverware* out of the salty air; *they* will tarnish if you don't.

CLEAR
YOU must keep your *silverware* out of the salty air; *it* will tarnish if you don't. [*Silverware* is a singular collective noun.]

Case

Case denotes the relation of nouns and pronouns to other words in the sentence. There are three relationships or cases:

Nominative Case
The *nominative case* indicates that the noun or pronoun is used as the subject of a verb, as an appositive to a subject noun, or as a predicate noun.

Mary plays the piano. [nominative case, subject of the verb.]

The younger *girl*, *Mary*, plays the piano. [*Mary* is in the nominative case as the appositive to *girl*.]

The girl playing the piano is *Mary*. [*Mary* is in the nominative case because it is a predicate noun used after the copulative verb *is* to refer to *girl*.]

Subject of Verb in Nominative Case.

John is growing taller.

He was born in Vernal, Colorado.

They are studying nuclear physics.

Predicate Noun or Pronoun in Nominative Case. The predicate noun or pronoun stands for the same person or thing as the subject and renames it. Therefore the predicate noun or pronoun is in the same case as the subject, the nominative case.

Mr. Dill is a *sexton*.

They thought that the thief was *I*.

Appositive of a Subject in Nominative Case.

Mr. Daly, my *neighbor*, is a probation officer.

The sponsors, *we who are present here*, must sign the petition.

Objective Case
The *objective case* indicates that the noun or pronoun receives the action of the verb or the verbal, or that it is the object of a preposition. Nouns and pronouns indicate case either by their position in the sentence or by their form. Nouns retain the same form in the nominative and objective cases, but change form to indicate the possessive case: *Mary's*.

Object of a Verb in Objective Case.

He blew the *whistle*.

We thanked *him* for his kindness.

He taught *her* Greek.

Object of Verbal in Objective Case.

Smelling the *coffee*, I jumped out of bed. [*Coffee* is the object of the participle *smelling*.]

Subject of Infinitive in Objective Case.

We hired *her* to demonstrate our products. [*Her* is the subject of the infinitive *to demonstrate*.]

Object of Preposition in Objective Case.

Grandmother's linens will be divided between *you* and *me*. [*You* and *me* are objects of the preposition *between*.]

We will divide the spoils among *us*. [*Us* is the object of the preposition *among*.]

Relative Pronouns. Put the relative pronoun *who* or *whom* in the case demanded by its use in the clause to which it belongs.

Livingston was the man *who* was sent to find Stanley. [*Who* introduces the dependent clause and is in the nominative case because it is the subject of the verb *was sent*.]

Who do you suppose gave him our address? [*Who* is the subject of *gave*, not the obejct of the parenthetical clause *do you suppose*.]

Whom were they talking about? [*Whom* is the object of the preposition *about*.]

Help *whoever* deserves help. [*Whoever* is the subject of the verb *deserves* and is therefore in the nominative case.]

Possessive Case

The *possessive case* usually indicates possession.

I tuned *Mary's* piano.

Put nouns and pronouns in the possessive case when they are used to show the following:

Possession:

Carol's store

Connection:

China's apologists [apologists who represent China]

The performer of an act:

Houdini's escape

Time, measurement, weight:

a day's wages [the wages earned in a day]

a hair's breadth [the width of a hair]

Put a noun or pronoun in the possessive case when it *immediately* precedes a gerund.

Whenever she thinks of *Henry's leaving*, she begins to cry.

I will not take the blame for *somebody's pilfering*.

Dangling Modifiers

A dangling modifier is a dependent structure that is related to the wrong word in the sentence. It is usually caused by the writer's starting a construction and forgetting where he or she is going. As a result, the sentence is momentarily misleading and often ludicrous.

*Coming around the bend in the road,** the church was seen.

In the preceding sentence, the church seems to be coming around the bend, an unusual occupation for an ecclesiastical building. The error is caused by the writer's chopping from the sentence the person who did both the seeing and the coming. The sentence can be repaired by including that person.

Coming around the bend in the road, *he* saw the church.

With Verbals

Most dangling modifiers involve verbals. One way of "undangling" these modifiers is to determine who or what is involved in the action and then make sure that this person or thing is in the sentence and that the modifier stands close to it. Looking through his field glasses, the bird flew away.

Looking through his field glasses, *he saw* the bird fly away.

In some instances, the structure that should be modified is in the sentence, but the modifier, by its position, seems to modify something else.

To provide maximum coverage, you must have a comprehensive *policy*.*

To provide maximum coverage, a *policy* must be comprehensive.

With Prepositional Phrases and Verbals

Verbals embedded inside prepositional phrases can sometimes relate to the wrong structure. *Before baking a cake, the hands should be washed.** Inside the prepositional phrase that functions as a verb modifier, the verbal is relating to the wrong structure, *the hands*.

Before *you* bake a cake, *you* should wash *your* hands.

With Elliptical Clauses

Elliptical clauses are clauses from which words have been deleted: *When eight years old, her father began to teach her Greek.**

The dangling modifier can be corrected by expanding the clause to recover the deleted words. When *she was* eight years old, her father began to teach her Greek.

Misplaced Modifiers

Because word order in English is very important to the functioning of structures, a modifier that gets out of position can cause confusion. A misplaced modifier usually gets that way because too often we write things down in the order in which they entered our minds. Our minds being what they are, the resulting disorder can produce alarming results. Many a joke has been built around the misplacing of modifiers. *For Sale*: 1963 *Volkswagen by elderly gentleman recently rebored and new battery installed.* Obviously, it is the Volkswagen and not the elderly gentleman which has been modified by the reboring and battery installation. The solution, then, is to reorder the sentence so that the modifiers clearly modify the right structure.

Misplaced Verb Modifiers

Most verb modifiers can move with some freedom around a sentence. This freedom can too easily become confusion because a verb modifier can attach itself to the wrong verb or noun. The solution is to bring it back close to its verb.

AMBIGUOUS
JACK threatened to divorce her *often*.

CLEAR
JACK *often* threatened to divorce her.

Misplaced Noun Modifiers

Noun modifiers have fixed positions before and after the noun. If for any reason they are dislodged from their correct positions, confusion and ambiguity result. The sentence must be rearranged to get the noun modifier back into its correct position, or the sentence must be recast.

AMBIGUOUS
He finally got rid of his hiccups by holding his breath, *which had lasted an hour.*

CLEAR
By holding his breath he finally got rid of his hiccups, *which had lasted an hour.*

Noun modifiers that are prepositional phrases can give particular trouble because if they are misplaced, they not only can refer to other nouns but they also can become verb modifiers on the spot.

Double Reference Modifiers
Some structures are so placed that they can refer to the structure before or the structure after them. These squinting modifiers are sometimes completely ambiguous. The use of punctuation to separate the modifier from one of the structures sometimes helps, but it is better to move the squinting modifier to a position from which it looks in one direction only.

AMBIGUOUS
THE doctor said that if my aunt did not move to a warmer climate *within a year* she would be dead. [Must she move within a year, or will she be dead within a year?]

CLEAR
THE doctor said that if my aunt did not move to a warmer climate she would be dead *within a year.*

Misplaced Common Adverbs
In colloquial speech, adverbs like *only, almost, merely, scarcely, just,* and *even* are often misplaced without unduly confusing the listener. *Luigi only had* 20 *with him at the time* is clear in its meaning. In formal writing, however, these adverbs should be placed next to the structures they modify. *Luigi had only $20* . . . .

COLLOQUIAL
He *merely* asked the question because he was curious.

FORMAL
He asked the question *merely* because he was curious.

Faulty Phrase Compounding
Faulty phrase compounding is the careless or too enthusiastic compounding of phrases. Because compounded phrases can be vague or ambiguous and because new compounds are invented all the time by product packagers and others, great care must be exercised in using the essential but often uncontrollable structures.

Below is a list of compounded noun and adjective phrases ranging from those long accepted to those that definitely are to be avoided. Note that the hyphen is used frequently in these compounds. When you are compounding, it is wise to have a good modern dictionary at hand.

Long-accepted, usable noun-phrase-adjective-phrase compounds

roadside cafe	The cafe sits beside a road.
waterproof	Something is impervious to water.
baby-sitter	Someone who sits with or looks after a baby.
fly-by-night operation	The operation has a temporary unreliable character.

Acceptable, recently coined noun-phrase/adjective-phrase compounds

dropout	Someone has dropped out of school or out of organized society.
hang-up	Something has irritated or inhibited someone so that he has become tense.
war-related	Something is related to an activity connected with war-making.
full automated, disk-oriented computer system	A system of machines that can compute automatically is oriented to a (magnetic) disk.

Split Constructions

Because word order is so vital to English, the words of a particular structure should stand together. For emphasis or clarity, a good writer alters the expected flow of words and structures. However, the pointless separation of words within a structure or of closely related structures may cause awkwardness or obscurity. When separation produces either of these effects, the writer should change the order of the words or revise the sentence.

Pointless Separations
The basic elements of a structure, such as preposition and object or auxiliary verb and main verb, can at times be separated by short intruders like *at times,* but the integrity of the structure is threatened by larger interruptions.

The *verb phrase*:

AWKWARD
There stands the house that I *will,* within five years, *purchase and remodel.*

IMPROVED
There stands the house that I will *purchase and remodel* within five years.

The *noun phrase*:

AWKWARD
She's *a talented,* and here I must point out that I have good qualifications to make such a judgment, *intelligent person.*

SOMEWHAT IMPROVED
She is a talented person, and because I think that

my qualifications are good enough to make such a judgment, I would add further that she is also an intelligent person.

The *infinitive* with *to*:

AWKWARD
I hope that you will be able *to* satisfactorily *repair* my television set within a week.

IMPROVED
I hope that you will be able *to repair* my television set satisfactorily within a week.

The *prepositional phrase*:

AWKWARD
He pawed through every garment on the bargain counter, looking *for*, in that welter, *a short-sleeved shirt*.

IMPROVED
In the welter of the bargain counter, he pawed through every garment, looking *for a short-sleeved shirt*.

Mixed Constructions

In speaking, we sometimes start one structure, slide to another structure, forget the first structure, and start all over again. A written court transcript of testimony given under some pressure makes the point well.
When I got to the door, and just as I was going down the steps, it was about seven thirty I think, well maybe seven thirty-five, I don't tell time too well, anyway I was going to get my car fixed and I saw this man coming up to me, he was about my height and he asked me where Seventh Street was, I think he as wearing a rain . . . .
The initial adverb clauses have long been forgotten as the witness, groping for continuity, continues to mix up his constructions.
In writing, we usually have the chance to rewrite, and the mixed constructions should be tracked down and eliminated.

MIXED
I told him to invest in mutual funds if *he can*.

IMPROVED
I told him, "Invest in mutual funds if *you can*."

IMPROVED
I told him to invest in mutual funds if *he could*.

Faulty Comparison

Mistakes are made in writing comparisons because the meanings of the comparative and superlative forms of the adjective pose problems and because elements of a comparison may be wrongly omitted.

Omission of Elements

A comparison is nearly always shortened by the deletion of repeated elements. *She is more beautiful than* her sister (*is*) (*beautiful*). Sometimes the omission of elements from the second half of a comparison can be done badly so that the reader is confused by the ambiguity involved.

COMPLETE COMPARISON

Carla ranks Cole Porter higher than Carla ranks Barry Manilow.*

FAULTY OMISSION
Carla ranks Cole Porter higher than Barry Manilow. [Manilow has become an evaluator of Cole Porter.]

COMPARISON RESTORED
Carla ranks Cole Porter higher than she ranks Barry Manilow.

Comparison Omission

Comparisons should not be approximate. Things being compared should be stated precisely. In the following examples, fuzzy comparisons are made between states and mountains and between filters and cigarettes.

The mountains in Vermont are lower and greener than New Hampshire*.

The mountains in Vermont are lower and greener that the *mountains* in New Hampshire.

Both *as* and *than* are involved when a comparison is made twice.

In the ring, Tag Martin is as ferocious *as*, if not more ferocious *than*, Jack Dempsey was.

Because the structure looks formidable, a writer will often omit the first comparison word *as*.

In the ring, Tag Martin is as ferocious, if not more ferocious *than* Jack Dempsey was.*

The easiest correction is to avoid the structure altogether and write something with roughly the same meaning. *In the ring, Tag Martin is at least as ferocious as Jack Dempsey.*

Comparative and Superlative Forms

The rule is that the comparative form refers to two things; the superlative form refers to more than two things.
The meaning of the comparative form of the adjective, in which an individual is *singled out* to be compared to other members of its group, is made explicit by the use of the word *other*. If this word is omitted the result can be confusing.

CONFUSING
Alaska is bigger than any state in the union. [This comparison implies that Alaska is *not* a state in the union.]

CLEAR
Alaska is bigger than any *other* state in the union.

The superlative form of the adjective is used when an individual is *included* within the members of the group being compared to the individual. When the individual is included in the group, the excluding word *other* should not be used.

CONFUSING
Charlie is the oldest of all the *other* boys in the class. [*All* includes Charlie; *other* excludes Charlie.]

CLEAR
Charlie is the oldest of all the boys in the class.

Omission of Necessary Words

If structures are not unduly separated and each structure is well constructed, writers frequently delete words when they feel confident that the construction of the parts of a sentence is clear: *when assembling the case for the clock*. We know that words like *you are* have been omitted.

We are expected to fill in the gaps and we do (fill in the gaps). In *He had been tried and judged already*, we supply the *had been* for the second verb.

Because the deletion of words can cause awkwardness and misunderstanding, care must be taken in handling deletions. Below are listed some of many situations in which it is wise not to delete words from their structures.

AMBIGUOUS
When he appeared for the hearing, he was accompanied by a friend and advisor. [one or two people?]

CLEAR
When he appeared for the hearing he was accompanied by a friend and *an* advisor. [two people]

INCOMPLETE
He has never expressed trust or loyalty to anyone.

COMPLETE
He has never expressed trust *in* or loyalty to anyone.

INCOMPLETE
He had laughed and been reprimanded for his action.

COMPLETE
He had laughed and *had* been reprimanded for his action.

EMPHASIS AND CONSISTENCY

Emphasis

It is frequently desirable to emphasize an entire sentence, or a single word or a group of words within a sentence. Without the use of emphasis, writing is flat and uninteresting.

Sentence Arrangement
To give prominence to an entire sentence, place it at either the beginning or end of the paragraph.

The roads were hot and dusty. The grass in the meadows was burned to a parched golden brown. Cattle in dried-up river bottoms licked hopefully at gravel and rocks where water had always been before. *It had not rained for weeks, and there would be no rain for two more weeks to come.*

Word Emphasis
To give emphasis to single words or groups of words, pay attention to the arrangement of the

order of the words as they occur in the sentence. Words at the beginning and end of a sentence are likely to attract more attention than words in the middle. Words or phrases placed out of their usual or expected positions also call attention to themselves.

In normal English word order, for example, adjectives precede the nouns they modify. Reversing this order calls particular attention to the adjectives.

NORMAL
The *tired old* judge slumped on the bench.

REVERSED
The judge, *old* and *tired*, slumped on the bench.

In normal word order the flow of a sentence moves from the subject to the verb and concludes with words related to the verb.

John and Barbara were married on a sunny day in May.

[subject]   [verb]   [adverbial modifiers]

The statement is clear, but no part of it is emphasized because the order of the words is exactly what the reader expects. To give prominence to adverbial modifiers, place them at the beginning of the sentence. To emphasize the date, recast the sentence to read:

In May, John and Barbara were married on a sunny day.

To emphasize both the weather and the date, revise the sentence to read:

On a sunny day in May, John and Barbara were married.

Notice how the abnormal word order of this sentence calls attention to the entire sentence and makes it more interesting and emphatic. Journalism employs the technique of altering word order to place special emphasis at the beginning the lead sentence of a news story.

The same principle applies to the position of single words in the sentence.

NORMAL
He drew himself to attention smartly.

EMPHATIC
Smartly he drew himself to attention.

In some sentences, a telling and dramatic effect can be achieved by completely reversing normal word order.

NORMAL
The men marched into battle.

REVERSED
Into the battle marched the men.

CAUTION: Do not try to recast every sentence, or even the majority of sentences, to secure emphasis. Such a procedure defeats its own purpose by producing an effect of strained and artificial writing.

Repetitive Emphasis

When a word or phrase is repeated immediately or soon after its original use, the reader is certain to notice the repetition. Deliberate repetition, therefore, is a certain method for obtaining emphasis, and it creates a dramatic effect.

His father was *weak*, his sister was *weak*, and he was *weak*.

. . . that government of the *people*, by the *people*, for the *people* . . .

Voice Emphasis

The choice of active or passive voice should depend on which element of the sentence is to be emphasized. In a typical sentence containing a transitive verb, such as

John owns a horse.

The use of the active voice emphasizes John's ownership. If the statement is intended to answer a question about the horse, it should be placed in the passive voice:

The horse is owned by John.

In general, if there is no particular problem of emphasis, the active voice is preferable since it is more direct and gives a stronger effect.

Flat and Lively Writing

To give a flat and lifeless effect to writing, the simplest device is to use only simple and compound sentences in normal word order. Writers often do this deliberately to create a pallid atmosphere:

He went into the house. He looked around listlessly for a few minutes and then slumped into a chair. No sound was heard except the ticking of the clock. He rested his head on the back of the chair and gradually fell into a deep and profound sleep.

Compare:

He walked slowly into the house, feeling fatigue gather like a knot behind his neck as he slumped into the armchair. Silence spread around him, broken only by the tick ticking of a clock, pounding inside his head like the beats of a metronome—a pulse of blood in his temples. Gradually a rhythm would form to seduce him into a troubled sleep.

But to indicate distinctions between ideas of greater and lesser importance, place the lesser words and phrases in subordinate positions in the sentence. In the following sentence, nothing is emphasized, and the entire statement is flat:

New York City is on the East Coast, and it is America's largest seaport.

To stress the location of New York City, recast the sentence as follows:

New York City, which is America's largest seaport, is on the East Coast.

To stress the importance of New York City as a seaport, rewrite the sentence:

New York City, which is on the East Coast, is America's largest seaport.

Parallelism and Balance

Two or more ideas that are similar in nature are known as parallel ideas. For effective presentation, express them in parallel form: a noun should be paralleled with a noun, an infinitive with an infinitive, and so on.

PARALLEL NOUNS
They studied *history*, *mathematics*, and *chemistry*.

NOT PARALLEL
They studied about the past, mathematics, and how matter is constituted.

PARALLEL INFINITIVES
He learned *to swim*, *to play* tennis, and *to ride* a horse.

NOT PARALLEL
He learned to play tennis, swimming, and the art of horseback riding.

Consistency

In dealing with any subject, decide in advance on the method of treating the subject and then endeavor to be consistent.

Tense

When writing a narrative, decide on a basic tense and do not change it unless the reference to some prior or subsequent event demands a change.

INCONSISTENT
John *sprang* to his feet when he *heard* the whistle. He *ran* as fast as he could to reach the upper deck. There he *sees* a battleship bearing down on them. [Inconsistent change to present tense]

Number

When discussing a type or a class, decide in advance whether to use the singular or plural number, and do not change it.

INCONSISTENT
The automatic washing *machine* is a great invention. It saves homemakers many hours of drudgery. *These machines are* among the most wonderful inventions of the twentieth century.

CONSISTENT
The automatic washing *machine* is a great *invention*. It saves the homemaker many hours of drudgery. This *machine* is *one* of the most wonderful inventions of the twentieth century.

Person

Decide in advance whether a piece of writing is to be personal or impersonal, and do not change the point of view.

INCONSISTENT
When learning to play a piano, *the student* should remember that great care and precision are essential. *You* should practice simple pieces until they are completely mastered.

In this paragraph, the *you* in the second sentence should be changed to *he or she*.

Tone

Unless you wish to jar the reader by some sudden intrusion, keep the tone and level of writing constant. Informal or chatty writing admits the use of slang or colloquialisms that are out of keeping with formal writing. Notice the absurdity of the following:

The dean exhorted the statutory members of the faculty to redouble their efforts and *get going*.

I get sick and tired of hearing you squawk about your *lassitude*.

Variety

The type of sentence structure appropriate to a given piece of writing depends on the nature of the subject, the purpose of the author, and the anticipated audience. Directions, for example, should be written in simple language and short sentences.

To reach the Denby Road Church:
1. Follow Route 4 to Carmine Street.
2. Turn right and continue to the second traffic signal (Denby Road).
3. Turn left on Denby Road.
4. You will see the church on the righthand side of the street.

Short, direct sentences are also effective in describing action.

The guard raised his gun. He fired. The prisoner's body jerked. Blood poured from the hole in his forehead.

Long wandering sentences create their own moods.

The clouds lay along the horizon in a soft white stream as the sun went down and the sky filled with purple light.

PUNCTUATION

Punctuation is a device used to assist the reader. It takes the place of changes in tone, inflection, and volume, and of pauses, facial expressions, and so on, by which a speaker makes his or her meaning clear.

Terminal Punctuation

Period

The principal use of the period is to indicate the end of sentence that is not a question or an exclamation.

The period is often used for terminal purposes when a sentence is not involved, as after numbers in a list:
1. The President.
2. The Council.
3. The Board of Trustees.

The period is used to terminate most abbreviations:

e.g., i.e., Mr., Dr., Rev., etc.

Three periods are used to indicate the omission of one or more words or even sentences in a quotation:

"I pledge allegiance . . . to the republic . . ."

When the omission occurs after the end of a sentence, the three periods are added after the period that terminates the sentence:

"Shakespeare was born in 1564 . . . . He married Ann Hathaway in 1582."

Question Mark

The question mark is used to terminate a sentence with a direct question.

Who are you? Why? He did?

When enclosed in parentheses, the question mark indicates uncertainty or doubt:

He lived from 1635 (?) to 1680.

Exclamation Point

Use the exclamation point to terminate a strong expression of feeling. Do not use it for indications of mild emotion, and do not use it repetitively, or the dramatic impact will be destroyed.

Nonsense! I don't believe you.

I'll shoot the first man who moves!

Get out of this house at once!

Comma

The comma is the most frequently used (and abused) aid to reading. Most poor users of commas annoy their readers by inserting illogical commas or too many commas. There is no need for uncertainty if the basic principles governing the use of the comma are clearly understood.

In a Series

Use the comma to separate words, phrases, or clauses in a series.

John, Fred, Harry, Frank

Usually the final element in the series is preceded by *and* or *or* to indicate the termination of the series:

John, Fred, Harry, and Frank

The comma before the terminating conjunction (*and* or *or*), although not absolutely essential, is used to prevent confusion because of the not infrequent appearance of *and* within the members of a series:

She shopped at Johnson's, Ward and Nelson's, and French's.

He ate soup, meat and potatoes, and pie.

A single adjectival modifying a noun often defines the noun and does not take a comma: *pine* tree, *drinking* glass, *red* dress. Another adjective preceding such an adjective-noun phrase functions as if it modified the entire phrase and is therefore not separated from the phrase by a comma: *tall* pine tree, *large* drinking glass, *beautiful* red dress.

To call attention to each adjective as individually and separately describing the noun and to add emphasis to a description, use a comma to separate the adjectives:

a tall, dark, distinguished gentleman

To Separate Clauses
Use the comma to separate the independent clauses of a compound sentence when they are joined by a coordinating conjunction. The comma is placed immediately before the conjunction (*and, but, or, nor, for, yet*) to indicate that the conjunction introduces a clause.

The mayor invited the members of the committee to lunch, *and* most of them accepted her invitation.

I haven't succeeded in balancing my checkbook, *yet* I plan to continue writing checks.

When the clauses are very short so that most or all of the sentence can be taken in instantaneously by the eye, the comma is not required.

He sent for her and she came.

To Separate Interjections
Occasionally, words or phrases in a sentence are not integrated in the sentence structure. Separate such nonintegrated words or phrases from the remainder of the sentence by commas.

Oh, I thought so.

Hello, I'm glad to see you.

I tried so hard, *alas*, to do it.

Terms of direct address are normally used as interjections.

John, get the book.

You over there, put on your hat.

Use the comma to set off sentence modifiers like *however, moreover, furthermore, therefore, nevertheless,* and phrases like *on the other hand, in addition, to the contrary.*

However, she caught the train.

He tried, *moreover*, to attain his goal.

On the other hand, he wasted his money.

Use the comma to set off *absolute* phrases. Absolute phrases are not connected to the remainder of the sentence by relating words and are therefore set off by commas.

The river being cold, we did not go swimming.

It seemed sensible, *the weather being warm*, to pack a lunch.

To Set Off Phrases
Since the first element in an English sentence is normally its subject, any phrase or clause of five words or more preceding the subject is concluded with a comma to indicate that the subject is about to appear.

During the long winter of 1881, the king suffered a severe illness.

When I see robins on the lawn, I know that spring is here.

If the phrase is so short that the reader can take in both the phrase and the subject in a single sweep, the comma is not necessary.

In 1881 the king suffered a severe illness.

To Interrupt Word Order
Set off by commas any words, phrases, or clauses that interrupt normal word order. Normally, adjectives precede the nouns they modify, and, normally, subjects are followed by verbs or by modifying phrases or clauses:

The old and respected firm in the city went bankrupt.

If, for purpose of emphasis, the adjectives *old* and *respected* follow the noun *firm*, they are set off by commas:

The firm, old and respected, went bankrupt.

A single comma should never interrupt the natural flow of a sentence, as from subject to verb or from verb to verb completion. But intruding elements of any kind should be indicated by being preceded and followed by commas.

The river, it seems likely, will overflow its banks.

The year of his graduation, 1950, was an eventful one.

She was a tall and, to put it mildly, thin woman.

With Nonrestrictive Elements
Any word, phrase, or clause that is not essential to the meaning of a sentence is called *nonrestrictive*. Set off nonrestrictive elements by commas.

Some words, like "scurrilous," are difficult to spell.

His father, Mr Smith, was ill.

The Homeric epics, the *Iliad* and the *Odyssey*, are long poems.

Be careful to distinguish between such nonrestrictive elements and restrictive elements. Restrictive words, phrases, or clauses are necessary to the meaning of a sentence and are never set off by commas.

Shakespeare's play *Hamlet* is a masterpiece.

The people who sat in the balcony paid less for their seats.

My brother, who sat in the balcony, enjoyed the play. [The location of his seat is not considered essential to the statement being made.]

By insertion or omission of commas, the writer can indicate whether elements are restrictive or not.

His dog Rover is a collie. [The lack of commas indicates that he has several dogs. One of them is named Rover.]

His dog, Rover, is a collie. [He owns only one dog. The name is given but it is not essential.]

When the nonrestrictive element occurs at the end of the sentence, the comma preceding it indicates its relative unimportance.

The president was interviewed by a large group of reporters, who were informally dressed.

With Contrasted Elements
Use the comma to emphasize the contrast between two parts of a sentence.

He wanted to see a psychiatrist, not a lawyer.

His diet was wholesome, not appetizing.

She longed to find happiness, but found misery instead.

To Prevent Misreading
Use the comma to prevent misreading when the sequence of words in a sentence might lead to momentary confusion.

During the summer, days become longer.

Without the comma, the reader might well read *summer days*.

Soon after, the meeting was adjourned.

Without the comma, the reader might read *after the meeting*, and this fragment would have no subject.

The lawyer interviewed John and Fred, and seemed very happy about what they had to say.

In this sentence the two *and*'s occur in close proximity. The first joins the nouns *John* and *Fred*: the second joins the verbs *interviewed* and *seemed*. The comma after *Fred* clarifies the structure of the sentence.

Conventional Uses
Certain uses of the comma have become established by convention.
1. Following the salutation of an informal letter: Dear Mildred,
2. Following the complimentary close of a letter: Yours truly,
3. Separating dates of the month from the year: June 19, 1942
4. Separating parts of an address: Mr. John Smith, 138 Elm Street, Syracuse, N.Y. 13082
5. Separating numbered or lettered divisions or subdivisions: Book III, Chapter 9; or III, 9; or A, d
6. Separating names from distinguishing titles: Frank Jones, Jr. or Edward French, Ph.D.
7. Separating thousands in large figures: 1,497,341
8. Separating a direct quotation from the indication of the speaker: She said, "Be gone!"

Misuse of Comma
Do not annoy the reader by inserting commas where they are not required. Commas are intended to help the reader; unnecessary commas only confuse.

Interrupting Thought
Do not interrupt the normal flow of thought with a comma.

WRONG
The fact that the train had broken down halfway between its point of departure and its destination, was sufficient reason for the passengers to malign the railroad. [The subject is a long clause, but it is entirely clear. It opens the sentence as expected, and it is followed immediately by the verb. Inserting a comma after *destination* merely impedes the flow of thought.]

WRONG
He drove a hard, sharp, painful, bargain. [The comma after *painful* separates the adjective *painful* from the word it modifies.]

And and *Or*
Do not separate words or phrases by *and* or *or*.

WRONG
He went to the office, and opened his mail. [*And* joins the compound verb *went* and *opened*. It does not join two clauses.]

With Conjunctions
Do not place a comma between a conjunction and the word or words it introduces.

WRONG
He was tired but, he refused to stop driving.

WRONG
The lonely woman continued to hope that, her son was still alive.

Semicolon

The semicolon functions midway between the comma and the period as an indication of a pause. It is stronger than the comma and weaker than the period.

With Clauses
The principal use of the semicolon is to mark the dividing point in a compound sentence, the clauses of which are not joined by a coordinating conjunction.

The policeman stood on the corner; he was watching the traffic pattern at the intersection.

The boss had a good sense of humor; nevertheless, she was a strict supervisor.

With Word Groupings
A proliferation of commas in a sentence may lead to confusion. The semicolon, as a stronger mark, is therefore useful in punctuating major elements that themselves contain commas.

He visited several colleges, schools, and institutions; several factories, office buildings, and churches; and a number of public buildings of a miscellaneous nature. [The three major divisions, the first two of which contain commas, are clarified by the use of the semicolon.]

Colon

The colon is principally used to introduce a list (frequently in conjunction with such words as *following* or *as follows*). It should not be used to introduce a short list such as *He raised beans, peas, apples, pears, and plums.*

The gentlemen who contributed to the fund were: John Doe, Frank Smith, Eliot Doolittle, and Ezra Jones.

The principles on which the club was founded are as follows:
1. The establishment of a revolving fund for education.
2. The provision of entertainment for the children.
3. Monthly social meetings for the adults.

Occasionally the colon is used to introduce a single word or phrase to add dramatic significance.

He had only one thing to live for: death.

The colon can be used to introduce a single word, phrase, or clause when it acts as a substitute for the words *as a result.*

The president died: the firm failed.

The colon is used after the salutation of a business letter (Dear Sir: or To Whom It May Concern:) and to divide subdivisions from major divisions as in recording time (12:25) or Biblical references (Genesis 10:3).

Dash

The dash is used to indicate a sharp or sudden break in the normal or expected flow of sentence structure. (In typing, a dash is represented by two hyphens.)

He asked me—what was he thinking?—to marry him.

I hoped that he—. But I'd rather not talk about it.

The dash may be used to separate parenthetical ideas or ideas inserted as an afterthought.

PARENTHETICAL
The New York skyline—especially when viewed for the first time—is a breathtaking sight.

AFTERTHOUGHT
He ran down the hill with the speed of an express train—or so it seemed.

The dash is used in dialogue to describe hesitating or halting speech.

"I mean—I think—I think I mean," he began hesitantly. "I think I mean I'd make a good husband."

Hyphen

The hyphen is used to make a compound word out of two or more words intended to be read as a single unit, sometimes to modify a noun.

The Dartmouth-Brown game

Mr. John King-Smith

A high-pressure salesman

A sugar-coated pill

A holier-than-thou expression

The hyphen is used to indicate that the remainder of a word is to follow when the word is broken at the end of a line. Words may not be divided arbitrarily; they may be broken only between syllables. (Syllables are the parts of a word that are naturally pronounced as units. When in doubt about correct division into syllables, consult a good dictionary.)

The hyphen is used with compound numbers from *twenty-one* to *ninety-nine.*

The hyphen is used to separate dates of birth and death: *John Barton* (1181–1214); scores of games: 13–12; and other figures when the relationship between them is obvious.

Apostrophe

Apart from indicating possession, the apostrophe is principally used to indicate letters in a contraction.

Who's there? She's afraid.

Peter's plum.

The apostrophe is also used to form plurals of numbers and letters for which there is no acceptable plural.

X's

O's

9's

Parentheses and Brackets

Parentheses are used to enclose materials that are so intrusive as to be an annoying interruption of sentence structure.

It is important (importance being understood to be a relative matter) to obey the law.

The law was passed (1) to satisfy the governor, (2) to please the people, and (3) to provide greater safety.

The houses were classified as (a) bungalows, (b) ranch-type houses, (c) split-level houses.

His novel *The Homeward Trail* (1917) was a best-seller.

Brackets are used to enclose additions by the editor to any kind of quoted matter.

"The author [Mark Twain] was known primarily as a humorist."

"He was born in 1835 [?] in a small southern town."

If parentheses and brackets are to be used in a sentence, the parentheses must appear *within* the brackets. In this instance, brackets do not signify an editorial comment, but rather act as double parentheses.

Joan Baez's most famous record ["Mary Hamilton" (1958)] earned a gold record for her.

Quotation Marks

In Titles
Quotations marks are used to indicate titles of *short works*, such as articles in magazines, short stories, one-act plays, essays, short poems, and chapter titles.

"The Raven" [short poem]

"The Murders in the Rue Morgue" [short story]

"Bound East for Cardiff" [one-act play]

Direct Quotations
Quoted material, whether oral or written, is indicated by quotation marks. Only the exact words of the original speaker or writer should be so enclosed. An indirect quotation or a report of the substance of what was said or written should not be enclosed by quotation marks, but should be inserted within the quotation in brackets.

In direct quotations, indications of the speaker (*he said*, *she asked*) are separated from the quotation by a comma or marked off by two commas if reference to the speaker is placed within a sentence.

"Please don't tell my mother," he whined.

The nurse replied, "That's exactly what I intend to do."

"Well, at least," he entreated, "don't tell her everything."

When the indication of the speaker is placed at the end of a quotation that concludes with a question mark or an exclamation mark, the comma is omitted.

"Don't you know enough to stop?" he asked.

"Let me go!" she shrieked.

In quotations other than dialogue, the punctuation and capitalization of quoted matter is reproduced exactly as it was originally written. Note the absence of a comma before the quote in both examples.

The author believes that "Capitalism is here to stay."

The novel reflected the author's "growing concern with the problem of juvenile delinquency."

If the quotation is longer than one paragraph, no end quotation marks are placed at the conclusion of the first paragraph. All succeeding paragraphs are prefaced by quotation marks, and only the final paragraph is concluded with end quotation marks.

Long quotations (ten lines or more) from writings are frequently not enclosed in quotation marks. They are set off from the original writing by indentation. Smaller typeface is customary for printed matter and single spacing for typewritten material.

Double Quotations
Single quotation marks are used to indicate a quotation within a quotation.

"I've just read Shelley's 'Ode to the West Wind,'" she said.

The alternation of double and single quotation marks is continued for the inclusion of quotations within quotations within other quotations. Such complexities should be avoided, of course, but the following is an example of the technique:

"Are you aware," asked the lawyer, "that the defendant precisely stated, 'I did not read "The Bride Said, 'No' " '?"

Be sure that all relevant punctuation stays within the correct set of quotation marks. Note particularly the placement of the question mark as terminal punctuation. See below.

Punctuation Within Quotations
The placing of quotation marks in connection with other punctuation follows the standard procedures instituted by printers for the sake of the physical appearance of the page. Periods and commas are always placed inside end quotation marks.

"I wanted," he said, "to go home."

Colons and semicolons are always placed outside end quotation marks. Other marks are placed where they logically belong—within the quotation if they punctuate the quotation, outside the quotation if they punctuate the sentence of which the quotation is a part.

He called his friend "old frog"; he didn't mean it as an insult.

"How are you?" I asked.

How can I tell that "Whatever is, is right"?

Beware of "the valley of the shadow of death"!

Dialogue
Standard practice in the punctuation of dialogue calls for a new paragraph for each change of speaker. Descriptive or other materials related to the speaker are contained in the same paragraph as the quotation.

"Why did you go to the festival?" Amanda asked, feeling angry and confused.

A particular advantage of this convention is that when only two speakers are involved, the alternation of paragraphs makes it unnecessary to identify each speaker in turn and allows dialogue to be paced more rapidly and without interruption.

"What do you want from me?" Jeanette asked angrily. "Don't I do enough around here already?"

"Like what, for instance?" Hal said. "What do you do?"

"Washing."

"Go on."

"Ironing and cooking and cleaning and listening—listening to you whenever you care to sit me down and talk to me!"

"All right, all right, I get your drift. Don't get so excited."

Italics

Italics is a term used to designate a particular font of printed type in which the letters slant upward to the right as in the word *italics*. In written or typed material, italics are indicated by underlining.

In Titles

Use italics to indicate the titles of novels, full-length plays, long book-length poems, full-length motion pictures, the titles of books in general and the names of newspapers. They are also used to indicate names of magazines or periodical publications of any sort. This usage in conjunction with quotation marks helps to distinguish the complete book from the chapter and the collection from the poem and so on.

Hamlet   A Tale of Two Cities
The Atlantic Monthly   The New York Times

EXCEPTIONS: Through convention, the Bible and the books of the Bible are neither italicized nor put in quotation marks.

For Emphasis

Italics are occasionally used to give emphasis to a particular word or group of words. This usage should be avoided and resorted to only when no other method of stressing the word is available.

"I didn't mean your husband; I meant *you*!"

EXHIBIT 12.1
Table of Proofreading Symbols

ℓ or ɣ or ୨	delete; take it out	*ital*	set in italic (*italic*)
⌒	close up; print as one word	*rom*	set in roman (roman)
ℓ̂	delete and close up	*bf*	set in boldface (**boldface**)
∧ or > or ⅄	caret; insert here *(something)*	⹀ or ⌃ or /or H̲	hyphen
#	insert a space	N̸	en or N/ en dash (1965–72)
eq #	space evenly where indicated	M̸	em or M/ em — or long — dash
stet	let marked text stand as set	∨	superscript or superior (2 as in πr²)
tr	transpose / change order the	∧	subscript or inferior (2 as in H₂O)
/	used to separate two or more marks and often as a concluding stroke at the end of an insertion	⌄ or X	centered (⌄ for a centered dot in p · q)
[	set farther to the left	⌃	comma
]	set farther to the right	∨	apostrophe
⌒	set ae or fi as ligatures æ or fl	⊙	period
=	straighten alignment	; or ;/	semicolon
‖ ‖	straighten or align	: or ⊙	colon
X	imperfect or broken character	or	quotation marks
□	indent or insert em quad space	(/)	parentheses
⁋	begin a new paragraph	[/]	brackets
sp	spell out (set 5 lbs as five pounds)	OK/?	query to author: has this been set as intended?
Cap	set in capitals (CAPITALS)	9	turn over an inverted letter
sm cap or *s.c.*	set in small capitals (SMALL CAPITALS)	*wf*	wrong font; a character fo the wrong size or esp. style
lc	set in Lowercase (lowercase)		

WORDS AND PHRASES FREQUENTLY MISUSED

a—an

He said it was *an* honor to meet you.
It wasn't right for you to call that child *an* urchin.

accept—except

I *accept* your apology.
Everyone *except* John may leave.

adapt—adopt

In a foreign country, you must *adapt* to new customs.
The Grays plan to *adopt* several hard-to-place children.

adverse—averse

He overcame many *adverse* circumstances to win the marathon.
The mayor said he was *averse* to my proposal.

advert—avert

The speaker *adverted* to an earlier talk she had given.
She narrowly *averted* a dangerous fall.

advice—advise

Because of Michael's excellent *advice*, Bob completed a successful business deal.
Michael will *advise* Bob to be daring.

affect—effect

The accident did not *affect* Thomas.
The *effect* on his brother, however, was great.

aggravate—annoy

If you continue to scratch that rash, you will *aggravate* your condition.
Your constant scratching *annoys* me.

all ready—already

Call me when you are *all ready* to go. (each one)
By the time Sue arrived, we had *already* finished dinner.

all together—altogether

The four of us were *all together* at the coffee shop.
This book is *altogether* too long.

allude—refer

In passing the speaker *alluded* to the new technology in business.
The speaker *referred* to statistics that demonstrated the rise of technology in business.

allusion—illusion

T.S. Eliot uses an *allusion* to Greek mythology in that poem.
You have the *illusion* that I enjoy classical music, I don't.

altar—alter

Many a would-be-bride has been left at the *altar*.
Would it be inconvenient for you to *alter* your plans for this weekend?

alumnus(ni)—alumna(ae)

Ted is an *alumnus* of Columbia, and so is Sally Ann, but June and Pete are alumni of Yale.

Mary is an *alumna* of Bryn Mawr, and Gert and Sada are *alumnae* of Sarah Lawrence. (This form is feminine only.)

amiable—amicable

Kindly Dr. Brown is the most *amiable* professor on the faculty.
Management and the union reached an *amicable* settlement.

among—between

The campaign director divided the state *among* his *three* most competent assistants. (any number greater than two)
In many of today's homes, the care of the children is divided *between* the *two* parents.

amount—number

You would not believe the *amount* of time I have spent on this project.
I wish I could reuse the *number* of hours I have spent on this project.

ante—anti

Scarlett O'Hara remembered those *ante*bellum days fondly. (before)
He is heading a new *anti*nuclear committee in our city. (against)

anxious—eager

I am *anxious* about the diagnosis. (to unhappily anticipate)
I am *eager* to see your new car.

anywhere

(There is no such word as anywheres.)

apt—liable

Having a good brain, he is *apt* to get high grades.
Unless it cuts spending, the firm is *liable* to fail.

as—like

Paula looks very much *like* her sister.
Rosemary swims *as* well as Pam does.
Carl looks *as* if he needs a nap.

ascent—assent

The *ascent* to the tower was frighteningly steep.
Before continuing, I await your *assent*.

beside—besides

Linda likes to sit *beside* Ellen at the table.
Who, *besides* Pam, is taking swimming lessons?

born—borne

Our youngest child was *born* last month.
John has *borne* the burden by himself for long enough. (to carry, as in a weight, etc.)

borrow—lend—loan

May I *borrow* your pocket calculator? (take from)
I can *lend* you my mechanical pencil. (give to)
I need a $500 *loan*.
borrow from ("borrow off" is unacceptable)

brake—break

I prefer a bicycle with a foot *brake*. This makes it easier to *brake* for a chipmunk crossing the road.
If you are not careful, you will *break* that dish.

bring—take

"*Bring* the book over here to me." (carry toward)
"When you leave, *take* the book away with you." (carry away)

burst—bust

The balloon got bigger and bigger and finally *burst*.
The sculptor was happy with the *bust* done in marble.

can—may
Some fortunate people *can* arrange their time to include work and pleasure. (possible to do)
You *may* hunt deer only during certain seasons. (need permission for)

capital—capitol—Capitol
Ricardo has 90% of the necessary *capital* for his new business venture.
Trenton is the *capital* of New Jersey.
New Jersey's *capitol* building is in Trenton.
Did you visit the *Capitol* when you were in Washington, D.C.?

cite—sight—site
An attorney often *cites* previous cases that support her argument.
One of the most beautiful *sights* in the country is the Grand Canyon.
The alternative school will be built on this *site*.

coarse—course
I find this *coarse* fabric to be abrasive.
That is an acceptable *course* of action.

complement—compliment
Rice nicely *complements* a chicken dinner.
I'd like to *compliment* you for doing such a thorough job.

continually—continuously
Tom is *continually* late. (always)
The river runs *continuously* through several towns. (from one to the other)

council—counsel
Our neighbor has just been elected to the town *council*.
The troubled man sought his friend's *counsel*.

credible—creditable
Because the defendant had a good alibi, his story seemed *credible*. (believable)
As a result of many hours of hard work, Joe presented a *creditable* report.

currant—current
His unusual recipe called for *currant* jelly.
Because the *current* was swift, the canoe was difficult to maneuver.

desert—dessert
The *desert* is very hot and dry.
More and more young soldiers have been *deserting* the army.
Apple pie is America's favorite *dessert*.

detract—distract
His constant lying *detracts* from his good qualities. (takes away)
The loud noise *distracted* her, making her lose concentration. (averting attention)

die—dye
Eventually, every living thing *dies*.
I'll never *dye* my hair.

different from
My opinion on the subject is *different from* his. (This is the correct form; *different than* is incorrect.)

discover—invent
The builders *discovered* oil on our land. (found)
Whitney *invented* the cotton gin. (began)

discreet—discrete
He was *discreet* in his habits.
Each grain of rice was *discrete*, not clinging to the others.

draw—drawer
Marlene *draws* very well.
She keeps her pads and pencils in the top *drawer* of her desk.

emigration—immigration
The Harlows *emigrated* from England. (coming from)
After *immigrating* to the United States, the Harlows settled in Kansas. (going to)

famous—infamous
John Simpson is a *famous* pianist.
Arthur Jones is an *infamous* car thief.

farther—further
My car can run *farther* on this other brand of gasoline.
I cannot continue this discussion any *further*.

forceful—forcible
Mark is very aggressive and has a *forceful* personality.
To break down a door is one way of making a *forcible* entry.

formally—formerly
Please dress *formally* for the wedding.
I was *formerly* employed by a jewelry company, but I am now working in a bank.

good—well
Maria did a *good* job.
Maria doesn't feel *well*.

grate—great
The continuous harsh and rasping sound *grated* on my nerves.
A *grate* in the sidewalk covered the opening to the sewer.
Ernest Hemingway was considered a *great* writer in his own lifetime.

hanged—hung
He was condemned to be *hanged* by the neck until dead.
The stockings were *hung* by the chimney with care.

healthful—healthy
Orange juice is *healthful*.
If you eat properly and exercise sufficiently, you will be *healthy*.

imply—infer
Although he did not state it directly, the candidate *implied* that his opponent was dishonest.
From the mayor's constructive suggestions, the townsfolk *inferred* that he was trying his best to do a good job.

it's—its
I think *it's* a fine idea!
The dog wagged *its* tail.

later—latter
Sue can finish the report *later* in the week.
I can meet you Tuesday or Thursday. The *latter* [meaning Thursday] would be more convenient.

lead—led
I'll need one more *lead* pipe to complete this plumbing job.
I only enjoy a race when I am in the *lead*.
John was unfamiliar with that route, so Jules *led* the way.

learn—teach
Harriet is having great difficulty with her efforts to *learn* flowcharting.

Leslie is patiently trying to *teach* Harriet how to flowchart.

leave—let

If the customs officer finds nothing wrong with a traveler's baggage, the officer *lets* the traveler *leave* the area.

loose—lose

Eric was excited about his first *loose* tooth.

If you step out of line, you will *lose* your place.

manor—manner

The *manor*, or landed estate, dates back to feudal times in England.

They don't like the *manner* in which you responded to my sincere question.

miner—minor

The coal *miners* were trapped during the cave-in.

The young man was not allowed to enter the bar because he was a *minor*.

moral—morale

Because of Ed's high *moral* standards, he returned the wallet to its owner.

The story of "The Boy Who Cried Wolf" has a *moral* that applies to everyone.

Because the war was *immoral,* the *morale* of the troops was low.

nauseated—nauseous

When we drove past the dead skunk, the car was filled with a *nauseous* odor.

The odor of the dead skunk *nauseated* Sara.

pail—pale

The amount of paint needed to finish the job would fill a one-gallon *pail*.

Because of her long illness, Maria's complexion was very *pale*.

passed—past

We *passed* the Model T on the parkway.

We cannot always try to recapture the *past*.

peace—piece

If we work together, perhaps we can end war and achieve a truly lasting *peace*.

In time, we will be paying an extremely high price for a *piece* of paper.

persecute—prosecute

Older children frequently *persecute* their younger siblings.

You are *prosecuted* if you are put on trial for a crime.

personal—personnel

The items written in a diary are very *personal*.

When applying for a job at a large company, you must go to the *personnel* office.

plain—plane

The meaning is quite *plain* and requires no further explanation.

We rode for miles across the open *plains* of Kansas.

The *plane* landed smoothly.

Please *plane* that wood so that I can build a birdhouse with it.

practicable—practical

Studying computer programming is a *practicable* plan for the future.

Computerizing payroll is a *practical* business decision.

precede—proceed

A preface always *precedes* the body of a book.

Don't let me interrupt you; *proceed* with your work.

principal—principle

A school is as good as the teachers and *principal*.

The *principal* actors in the play remained for a final rehearsal of the second act.

The *principle* upon which many simple machines are based is frequently the lever.

quiet—quite

As the campers lay down for the night, *quiet* settled over the campsite.

That is *quite* a strong accusation.

raise—rise

When we *raise* the flag, we'd like everyone in the audience to *rise*.

sit—set

The chairman requested committee members to *sit* down. (human)

The artist *set* the clay on the workbench and began to create a sculpture. (inanimate)

stationary—stationery

Theater seats are most often *stationary*.

When I write letters, I always use my engraved *stationery*.

sure—surely

I am *sure* Alice will be at the meeting.

Surely, you don't expect me to take notes.

than—then

New York is smaller *than* Wyoming, but Wyoming has a much smaller population *than* New York. (comparison)

First the eastern seaboard was colonized, *then* settlers moved westward. (refers to next)

their—there—they're

When leaving *their* war-torn country, most of the refugees left all *their* possessions behind.

There are no easy answers to the problem of worldwide hunger.

As for the members of Congress, *they're* not always responsible for the wisest decisions.

through—threw

The special crew worked *through* the night to repair the damaged wires.

When the Little League pitcher *threw* the ball, her teammates cheered.

to—too—two

United States presidents often travel *to* foreign countries. (preposition)

Many foreign heads of state visit the United States, *too*. (also)

Two visitors were the late Anwar Sadat and Margaret Thatcher. (number)

vain—vane—vein

The *vain* man peered at his reflection in every window as he strolled down the street.

A rooster is the traditional weather *vane* symbol.

Veins are passageways that carry deoxygenated blood to the heart.

vale—veil

Vale is an uncommonly used synonym for valley.

The mourning woman hid her grief behind her *veil*.

wade—weighed

The smaller children were told to *wade* near the shore.

The clerk *weighed* and priced the fresh vegetables.

waist—waste

If you measure your *waist* before you go to buy a

pattern, you will avoid much confusion.

Don't *waste* precious time gossiping on the phone.

weather—whether

Tomorrow morning the general *weather* conditions will determine the distance of our first day's hike.

Whether or not you wish to pay taxes, you must.

who's—whose

The teacher asked, "*Who's* responsible for clean up today?"

We must determine *whose* turn it is.

writes—rights—rites

Kurt Vonnegut *writes* excellent fiction.

Their attorney explained the family's *rights* in the lawsuit.

The religious *rites* of many tribes are an impressive part of their culture.

your—you're

Where is *your* car parked?

You're attempting something that's too difficult for you.

PREFIXES, ROOTS, SUFFIXES

Prefixes

Prefix	Meaning	Examples of Use
a, an	without; not	amoral; anarchy
amb, ambi	both	ambidextrous; ambiguity
amphi	around; on both sides	amphitheater, amphibious
anti	against	antidote; antipathy
apo	from; away from; off	apology; apostate
bi	two	bisect; bicycle
cata, cath	down; against	catastrophe; cataract; cathode
contra	against; opposed	contradict; controversial
dia	across; through	diagram; diameter
epi, eph	upon; on the outside	epilogue; ephemeral
extra	beyond; outside	extraordinary; extravert
hemi	half	hemisphere; hemistich
hetero	different	heterogeneous; heterodox
hyper	over; above	hyperbole; hypercritical
hypo	under	hypodermic; hypostatic
infra	lower; less than	infrahuman, inframarginal
intra	within	intramural; intracellular
juxta	near; nearby	juxtaposition; juxtatropical
meta	after; beyond	metaphysical; metamorphosis
multi	many; much	multitude; multiply
ob	to; toward; opposite; facing	obstacle; obverse
para, par	by the side of; near	parallel; parable
peri	around	periscope; perimeter
preter	past; before; exceeding	preternatural; predispose
proto	first, earliest form of	protoplasm; prototype
retro	back	retrograde; retrospection
semi	half, almost; twice in a given period	semitropical; semiannual
subter	below; underneath; less than	subterfuge; subterranean
super	over; above	superman; supercilious
supra	above	supraterrestrial; supramolecular
ultra	outside; excessive	ultramarine; ultramodern
vice	one who takes the place of	viceroy; vice president

Latin Roots

Root	Meaning	Examples of use
A		
acr	sharp, acute	acrimonious, acrid
act	to drive	action
aer, air	air	aerial; airplane

ag	to do	agitate
ali	another	alias; alibi
alter	another	alternative; alternate
amat	to love	amatory; amateur
anim	mind; passion; soul	animal; animate
ann	year	annual; anniversary
apt	to fit; to adjust	adapt; aptitude
aqu	water	aqueduct; aquarium
art	art, skill	artist; artisan
aud, audit	to hear	audible; audition
avi	bird	aviary; aviation

B

bell	war	belligerent; bellicose
ben	good; well	benediction; benefactor

C

cad	to fall	cadence
cap	head	captain, capital
cap	to take	captive
cent	one hundred	centipede, century
cid, cis	to cut; to kill	suicide; incision
cit	to summon	incite
civi	city; citizen	civil; civilization
clam, clamat	to cry out	clamor; exclamation
compl, complet	to fill	comply; completion
cor, cord	heart	core, cordial
corp, corpor	body	corpse; corporeal; incorporate
cresc	to grow	crescent; excrescence
cret	grown	concrete; accrete
curr, curs	to run	current; excursion

D

da, don	to give	data; donate
doc	to teach	doctrine
dom	home	domain, domicile
domin	to rule	domineer; dominate

E

er	to wander; go	errand; errant
equ	equal	equation
ev	an age	coeval; medieval

F

fall, fals	to deceive	fallacy; falsify
fam	report	famous; infamy
fin	end	final; finite
fix	to fasten	affix, fixture
flat	blown	inflate, deflate
flect, flex	to bend; bending	deflect; reflexive
flu	to flow	fluency; confluent
fund, fus	to pour	refund; profuse; effusion

G

gen, gener	birth; race; kind	progeny; genesis; generation
gest	to carry; to carry on	gesture; suggest
grad, gress	to step; to walk	graduate; progress
greg	flock; herd	gregarious; aggregate

J

junct	a joining	junction; adjunct

L

labor	to work	laboratory; laborious
lapi	stone	lapidary; lapis lazuli
leg, lect	to read; to choose	legible, select

| loqu, locut | to speak | elocution; loquacious |
| luc | light | lucid; elucidate |

M

mal	bad	malady; malefactor
man	hand	manual; manicure
mar	sea	marine; maritime
mon	to warn	monitor
monit	to remind	admonish
mor, mort	to die	mortal; moribund
mov, mot	to move	movable; motion

O

| omni | all | omnipotent, omnivorous |
| oper | a work | opera; operation |

P

pac	peace	pacific; pacify
pel, puls	to drive	repel, compulsion
pend	to hang	pendant; depend
plen	full	replenish; plenary
pon, posit	to place	position; proponent

R

rat, ratio	reason; plan	ratio; rational
rid, ris	to laugh	deride; risible
rog, rogat	to ask	arrogant; interrogate
rupt	broken	rupture; bankrupt

S

scien	knowing	science; prescience
sed, sess	to sit, to remain seated	sedentary; session
sent, sens	to feel; to think	sensible; sentiment
serv	to serve	servant; servile
sol, solut	to loose	dissolve; solution
sum, sumpt	to take	resume; consumption
surg, surrect	to rise	surge; insurrection

T

tang, tact	to touch	tangible; contact
tempor	time	temporary; extemporize
terr	land; earth	territory; terrace

U

| urb | city | urban; urbanity |

V

vag	to wander	vagabond; vagary
val	to be strong; to have worth	valor; valuable
vinc, vict	to conquer	convince; victory
volv, volut	to roll	revolve; convolution

Greek Roots

Root	Meaning	Examples of use
agogue	leader	demagogue; pedagogue
agon	contest	protagonist
angel	messenger	evangel; archangel
arch	first; chief; commander	patriarch; monarch
astron	star	astronomy
bar, baro	heavy weight	barometer; baritone
bibl, biblio	book	Bible; bibliophile
dem, demo	people	democracy
dendr, dendro	tree; plant	philodendron; dendrite

derm	skin	epidermis; dermatology
dox	opinion	orthodox; paradox
dyna	power	dynamic; dynasty
eu	well; good	euphony; eulogy
gamy	marriage	monogamy; polygamy
gram	written	diagram; epigram
grapho, graphy	to write	graphology; telegraphy
helio	sun	heliograph; heliocentric
melo	song	melody; melodrama
micr, micro	small	microscope; microcosm
mono	one	monologue; monograph
morph	body; form	amorphous; morphology
neo	new	neophyte; neologism
ortho	straight	orthodox; orthopedic
pan	all	panacea
ped, pedi	child	pediatrician
phos, photo	light	photograph; phosphorous
phys, physic	nature	physical; physiology
polis, polit	city; citizen	metropolis; cosmopolite
pseudo	false	pseudo; pseudonym
psych, psycho	soul; mind	psychic; psychologist
pus, pod	foot	octopus; tripod
scope	see; look at	microscope; telescope
spher, sphere	sphere	spherical; atmosphere
tech, techno	skill; art	technology; technical
tele	far	telescope; telepath; telephone
thei, theo	god	pantheism; theology
trop, trope	turning	heliotrope; tropic
typ, type	print; image	typical; prototype

Suffixes

Suffix	Meaning	Examples of use
Noun Suffixes		
age	relating to; relationship	adage; homage
an, ian	belonging to; concerned with	American; agrarian; electrician
ant, ent	agency or instrumentality	servant; agent
ate	office or function	mandate; consulate
action, ition	act or state of	education, recognition
ese	of; relating to	Chinese; journalese
ine	procedure; art	medicine; discipline
ite	native or citizen of	urbanite; Brooklynite
ity	state of being	paucity; sagacity
oid	something like	anthropoid; alkaloid
or	state or quality; agent or doer	ardor; candor; aviator; auditor
ory	a place of; serving for	dormitory; ambulatory
tude	that which is	certitude; beatitude
ure	process, being	creature; procedure
Adjective Suffixes		
aceous, acious	of the nature of	mendacious, herbaceous
ant, ent	doing or being something	ascendant; pleasant; resplendent
ate, ite	possessing or being	desolate; delicate; favorite
cle, cule	little	corpuscle; molecule; animalcule
escent	growing; in a state of	obsolescent; adolescent
il, ile	pertaining to; suited for	utensil; servile; civil
ine	like; characterized by	feline; feminine
ive	having the nature or quality of	positive; negative; active
Verb Suffixes		
esce	to increase; grow; become	effervesce; coalesce
fy	to make; to render	electrify; deify
ize	to render or make	colonize; satirize

FOREIGN TERMS IN ENGLISH

Latin

Note: There are three ways to pronounce Latin: the ancient Roman pronunciation (not accurately reconstructed until the early 1900s), the Italian-like pronunciation used by the Catholic Church, and the English-like pronunciation still used by lawyers. For example, *Caesar* is pronounced *KAI-sahr* in the Roman system, *CHAY-sahr* in the Church, and *SEE-zer* in the English system.

The pronunciations given here are in the English system, except for a few words that occur mainly in Church Latin. Be prepared to hear wide variation in the ways all of these words are pronounced.

A

a fortiori (a for-ti-OR-eye)   For a still stronger reason; all the more. *Example:* We must promote fairness to protect the weak and *a fortiori* to protect ourselves.

ad hominem (ad HOM-i-nem)   Against the person. *Example:* An *ad hominem* argument is an argument that attacks a person's character or qualifications rather than refuting what the person is saying.

alter ego (ALL-ter EE-go)   Another self; a bosom friend. *Example:* Throughout his life, D. H. Lawrence searched for a man who would be his *alter ego*.

amicus curiae (a-MIKE-us CUR-i-ee)   A friend of the court; a person or group who gives advice or presents a brief in a legal case in which he or she is not involved. *Example:* As *amicus curiae* the American Civil Liberties Union presented a brief in the Larsen case.

annus mirabilis (AN-nus mi-RAB-i-lis)   A wonderful year; a year in which great events occur. *Example:* His *annus mirabilis* was 1922, the year he completed the *Quartet in G Minor*, the *Symphony in D Minor*, and his opera *The Tocsin*.

a posteriori (a pos-teer-i-OR-eye)   Reasoning from effect to cause; applied to conclusions drawn from the study of facts. *Example:* Scientific reasoning often works *a posteriori*, going from observations to theories.

C

casus belli (CASE-us BELL-eye)   A reason for declaring war. *Example:* Hitler seldom bothered to find a *casus belli* before attacking a nation.

corpus delicti (COR-pus dee-LICK-teye)   The body of the crime; a legal phrase meaning evidence that a crime has been committed. Sometimes the expression is mistaken to mean the body of the victim. *Example:* Without a *corpus delicti* the district attorney cannot seek an indictment.

E

ex cathedra (ex ka-THEE-dra)   From the throne; by the authority of one's position. Often used in con-nection with the Pope. *Example:* The pronouncement was made *ex cathedra* and must be obeyed.

F

flagrante delicto (fla-GRANT-ee dee-LICK-toe)   While the crime is blazing; in the very act; red-handed. *Example:* Since the cashier was caught *flagrante delicto*, his attorney could not present a defense and was forced to enter a plea for mercy.

H

hic jacet (hick JASE-et)   Here lies; an epitaph. *Example:*
Hic jacet my wife Amanda.
Stranger, do not sigh.
At last she knows peace
And so do I.

Homo sapiens (HO-mo SAY-pi-ens)   Rational man; the biological name for the human species. *Example:* We sometimes forget that *Homo sapiens* is not the only earth dweller.

I

in extenso (in ex-TEN-so)   At full length. *Example:* If he explains his case *in extenso*, the referee will find against him out of sheer boredom.

in extremis (in ex-TREME-iss)   Near death; in the last extremity. *Example:* Hearing that the king was *in extremis*, the priest rushed to the palace to administer the last rites.

infra dignitatem (IN-fra dig-ni-TATE-em)   Colloquially shortened to *infra dig*; beneath one's dignity. *Example:* Believing that explanations were *infra dignitatem*, the royal governor merely issued orders.

in loco parentis (in LO-co pa-REN-tis)   In the place of a parent; acting as one's guardian. *Example:* During his brother's long illness, he acted in *loco parentis* for his nieces and nephews.

in re or *re* (in ree)   In reference to; concerning. *Example:* *In re* the Casson affair, a firm of actuaries has been hired to audit the books for the last five years.

in vacuo (in VACK-yoo-oh)   In a vacuum; without previous reference; without reference to surroundings or regard for reality. *Example:* He is always so preoccupied that he frequently makes remarks *in vacuo* and is annoyed because no one understands him.

in vitro (in VIT-ro)   In glass; in a test tube; in the laboratory. *Example:* As biology becomes more like chemistry, more biological experiments can be done *in vitro* so that animals need not suffer.

in vivo (in VIVE-oh *or* in VEEV-oh)   In a living organism (usually an animal or human). *Example:* Test-tube studies suggest that this drug should kill viruses, but its effectiveness has never been demonstrated *in vivo*.

ipse dixit (IP-see DIX-it)   He himself has said it; an assertion without proof. *Example:* He talks incessantly, and his every statement is delivered as an *ipse dixit*.

L

lapsus linguae (LAP-sus LING-wee)   A slip of the tongue. *Example:* The announcer made an embarrassing *lapsus linguae* and was immediately cut off the air.

M

mirabile dictu (mi-RAB-i-lee DIK-too)   Strange to say; marvelous to relate. *Example:* The mechanic jiggled a lever, and, *mirabile dictu*, the motor started without a cough or a groan.

modus operandi (MO-dus op-er-AND-eye)   Way of operating or working. *Example:* Sherlock Holmes's first step was often to identify the criminal's *modus operandi*.

modus vivendi (MO-dus viv-END-eye)   Manner of living; temporary agreement; a way of coexisting with a person or nation despite fundamental disagreement. *Example:* The United States and Cuba do not cooperate in any way; they have still not found a *modus vivendi.*

N

ne plus ultra (nee plus UL-tra)   Nothing more beyond; perfection. *Example:* The Rolls Royce is the *ne plus ultra* of cars.

O

obiter dictum (O-bit-er DIK-tum)   The plural is *obiter dicta*. An incidental opinion by a judge or critic; not binding; a digression or an aside. *Example:* This book of *obiter dicta* is a delightful supplement to his critiques.

P

passim (PASS-im)   Here and there; applied to words used many times in a piece of writing. *Example:* Surprising rhymes occur *passim* in the first three verses.

pax vobiscum (PAX vo-BEES-kum)   Peace be with you. *Example:* Murmuring *pax vobiscum*, the anchorite genuflected before the queen.

persona non grata (per-SO-na non GRAH-ta)   An unacceptable person; an acceptable person is *persona grata*. These terms are frequently applied to official representatives of a country. *Example:* The American consul is *persona non grata* in Ruritania and will have to be recalled.

prima facie (PRIME-a FACE-ee-a)   On the face of or on the surface; at first view; on first appearance. *Example:* Possession of drugs is *prima facie* evidence of participation in illegal drug traffic.

pro bono publico (pro BO-no PUB-li-co)   For the public good; a favorite signature of those who write letters to editors of newspapers and magazines. *Example: Pro bono* work done by lawyers is work that they do as unpaid volunteers.

pro tempore (pro TEMP-oh-ree)   Often shortened to *pro tem*; temporarily; for the time being. *Example:* He is chairman *pro tem* of the Committee on Good and Welfare.

Q

qua (kway *or* kwah)   As; considered as. *Example:* There is nothing to be said for her hat *qua* hat, but it's a charming theatrical prop.

quid nunc (kwid nunk)   What now; one who is curious to know everything that passes; a gossip. *Example:* For years old Jones was the *quid nunc* on the faculty.

quondam (KWON-dam)   Former. *Example:* Hurricane Goetz, a *quondam* ballet dancer, is a contender for the heavyweight championship in wrestling.

R

rara avis (RARE-a AY-vis)   A rare bird; an unusual specimen; an extraordinary person. *Example:* An honest politician is a *rara avis*.

re   See *in re*

reductio ad absurdum (ree-DUCK-tee-oh ad ab-SUR-dum)   A reduction to an absurdity; carrying an argument or action to logical extremes. *Example:* Many conditions in Huxley's *Brave New World* are a *reductio ad absurdum* of conditions and tendencies already present in the world.

S

sanctum sanctorum (SANK-tum sank-TO-rum)   Holy of holies; innermost temple; the office of an awesome person. *Example:* It was five years before Mr. Bartle invited me into his *sanctum sanctorum* and implied that, if I worked hard, I might be made a member of the firm.

sine qua non (SINE-ee kwah NON)   Without which there is nothing; a prerequisite; an indispensable condition. *Example:* Mutual respect, if not love, is the *sine qua non* of a successful marriage.

stet (stet)   Let it stand. Used in the printing industry to label things that have been marked out by accident and should not be deleted.

sub rosa (sub RO-sa)   Under the rose; privately; confidentially. *Example:* I have been told *sub rosa* that the Joneses are on the verge of separation.

sui generis (SOO-ee JEN-er-is)   Of his, her, its own kind; in a class by itself; unique. *Example:* This book is *sui generis* a masterpiece, but it will not appeal to many.

V

vade mecum (VAY-dee MEE-kum)   Go with me; a manual or handbook; a book carried as a constant companion. *Example:* The Bible is the *vade mecum* of many Christians.

vox populi (VOKS POP-u-leye)   The voice of the people; shortened to *vox pop*. This expression is one half of the expression *Vox populi, vox Dei*, "The voice of the people is the voice of God." *Vox pop* is a favorite signature of letters in newspapers.

French

Note: French has many sounds that are quite unlike English. The pronunciations shown here are only a rough guide.

A

agent provocateur (a-ZHAHN pro-vo-ka-TUHR)   A person who incites another person or an organization like a political party or trade union to commit an illegal act for which they can be punished. *Example:* The union soon suspected him of being an *agent provocateur* and expelled him.

amour-propre (ah-MOOR PROP-r)   Self-esteem; self-love; vanity. *Example:* If you are lacking in *amour-propre*, no one will take you seriously.

au courant (oh koor-AHN)   Up-to-date; well up in or informed in. *Example:* To be *au courant* one must read several newspapers daily.

B

bête noire (BET NWAHR)   A black beast; a pet aversion; a detested person. *Example:* Knowing that Thomas à Becket was the King's *bête noire*, a group of loyal knights murdered him in the cathedral.

bon vivant (bon vee-VAHN)   An epicure; a lover of good living; a man about town. *Example:* Beau Brummel was a famous *bon vivant* of the eighteenth century.

C

chef-d'oeuvre (shay DUH-vr)   Chief work, a masterpiece. *Example: War and Peace* is Tolstoy's *chef-d'oeuvre*.

collage (ko-LAHZH)   A piece of art composed of various materials; wood, cloth, newspaper, etc., an assembly of different fragments (see *montage*).

comme il faut (kohm-eel-FO)   As it ought to be; in good form; proper. *Example:* It is not *comme il faut* for a man to dine without a jacket.

contretemps (kohn-tra-TAHN)   Embarrassing moment. *Example:* The groom's dropping the ring was the first in a series of *contretemps* that made a shambles of the wedding.

coup de grâce (koo duh GRAHS)   A blow of mercy; the death blow; a final decisive stroke. *Example:* We had won a series of naval victories, but the atomic bombing of Hiroshima and Nagasaki was the *coup de grâce* that finished the war.

D

de rigueur (duh ri-GUHR)   In good form or taste; according to strict etiquette. *Example:* In American courtship today, a chaperon is no longer *de rigueur*.

dernier cri (der-nyay kree)   The last word; the latest fashion. *Example:* This gown by Dior is the *dernier cri* from Paris.

déshabillé (dayz-ah-bee-YAY)   Undressed or partly undressed; in negligee. The expression also appears as *en déshabillé*. *Example:* For her to be seen in the garden *en déshabillé* was definitely compromising.

E

enfant terrible (ahn-FAHN teh-REE-bl)   A bad child; a child whose behavior is embarrassing; a person who embarrasses his party or organization by blunt remarks. *Example:* Charles Wilson's inopportune remarks made him the *enfant terrible* of the Eisenhower cabinet.

en rapport (ahn rah-POR)   In harmony; in mutual understanding and sympathy. *Example:* For a satisfactory song recital the singer and the accompanist must be *en rapport*.

F

femme fatale (fahm fa-TAHL)   A woman who lures men to destruction; a female spy; an irresistible beauty. *Example:* In former times the "vamp" was the motion picture conception of the *femme fatale*.

fin de siècle (fahn duh SYEH-kl)   End of the (19th) century; a period free from social and moral traditions; decadent. *Example:* He belongs with the French *fin de siècle* school of writers.

H

hors de combat (or duh kom-BAH)   Out of the combat; incapacitated, disabled. *Example:* Glenway strained a ligament in his first race and was *hors de combat* for the rest of the season.

I

idée fixe (ee-day-FEEKS)   A fixed idea; an obsession. *Example:* Communism is an *idée fixe* with him; he sees communism as the cause of all his troubles.

ingénue (ahn-zhay-NYOO)   An innocent or ingenuous girl, especially as represented on the stage; the actress who plays such a part. *Example:* She is too old to play an *ingénue*, but no one can equal her in such a role.

insouciance (ahn-soo-see-AHNS)   Lack of concern; indifference. *Example:* His is the *insouciance* of the rich who have never known hardship and deprivation.

M

maître d'hôtel (MAY-tra do-TEL)   A steward or butler; a headwaiter. *Example:* To get a desirable table in that restaurant one must give the *maître d'hôtel* a large tip.

mélange (may-LAHNZH)   A mixture; a medley. *Example:* This room is furnished in a *mélange* of Chippendale, Hepplewhite, and Grand Rapids pieces.

ménage (may-NAHZH)   Household; family. *Example:* The expenses of the king's *ménage* amounted to over a million pounds a year.

mise en scène (meez-ahn-SEN)   Stage setting or equipment; the surroundings in which anything is seen. *Example:* He is a fascinating reconteur because of the way he describes the *mise en scène* of a story.

montage (mon-TAHZH)   Arrangement in one composition of pictorial elements borrowed from several sources; a picture made in this way. *Example:* The director of the picture has attempted to achieve effects by the use of *montage*, but the elements do not blend, and the film lacks artistic unity.

N

noblesse oblige (no-BLESS ob-LEEZH)   Nobility obligates; a code of behavior of the aristocracy; the graciousness of the nobility. *Example:* The Rockefeller family's gift to the school is an excellent example of *noblesse oblige*.

nouveau riche (noo-VO REESH)   The newly rich; up-start. *Example:* It took little time for the *nouveau riche* to force his way into society.

P

pièce de résistance (PYESS duh ray-zee-STAHNS)   The main course or dish; the most valuable object in a collection. *Example:* Of all these paintings, the Goya is the *pièce de résistance*, the one most widely admired and coveted.

potpourri (poh-poo-REE)   Mixture; medley; miscellany. *Example:* This stage piece is a boring *potpourri* of song, dance, spectacle, miming, and skits.

Q

qui vive (kee veev)   Who goes there; an alert, usually preceded by "on the." *Example:* The security police are on the *qui vive* for any muttering or complaints that may develop into resistance.

R

raison d'être (ray-ZON DET-r)   Reason for being; justification. *Example:* Many acute and tolerant critics can find no *raison d'être* for Henry Miller's *Tropic of Cancer.*

rapport, see *en rapport.*

rapprochement (rah-prosh-MAHN)   Development of mutual understanding; a term in diplomacy for the establishment of friendly relations between countries. *Example:* For a short while after the death of Stalin, I had some hope for a *rapprochement* between the Soviet Union and the United States.

rendezvous (RAHN-day-voo)   An appointment or engagement of two or more people to meet at a fixed time or place; a place for such a meeting. *Example:* Their midnight *rendezvous* was a small restaurant in the Loop.

riposte (ree-POST)   In fencing, a quick thrust after a parry; a quick answer; repartee. *Example:* In time he learned to curb his tongue and withhold the sharp *riposte.*

S

sang froid (sahn frwah)   Cold blood; self-possession; composure. *Example:* With the utmost *sand froid* the housing inspector admitted that he had accepted favors from the Red Star Construction Company.

soupçon (soop-SOHN)   Suspicion; a bit; a small portion. *Example:* The ragout needs a *soupçon* of sherry.

T

tour de force (toor duh FORCE)   A feat of skill or strength; a trick in music, drama, or literature; an exhibition of great technical or mechanical skill. *Example:* The series of literary parodies in *Ulysses* is a dazzling display, a *tour de force* that shows Joyce's mastery of language and his intimate knowledge of English literature.

V

vis-à-vis (veez-ah-VEE)   Face to face with another; opposite; in reference to; opposed to. *Example:* When he stands *vis-à-vis* his accusers, I am sure that his bravado will disappear.

volte-face (volt FAHSS)   An about-face; a complete reversal of policy, opinion, or attitude. *Example:* It is preposterous to hope that China will execute a *volte-face* and agree to disarmament with inspection and controls.

Italian

A

a cappella (ah kah-PEL-la)   Unaccompanied singing, especially choral music. *Example:* Since the last half of the recital will be sung *a cappella*, the instrumentalists will be able to fill another engagement on the same evening.

adagio (ah-DAH-jo)   Leisurely. *Adagio* describes music that is to be played slowly.

alfresco (ahl-FRESS-ko)   Taking place in the open air; dining out of doors. *Example:* Mozart preferred to dine *alfresco*, under the stars.

allegro (al-LEH-gro)   Merry. *Allegro* describes music that is to be played in a fast and lively manner.

andante (an-DAHN-tay)   Walking along. *Andante* describes music that is to be played at a steady, moderate pace.

B

bolognese (bo-lo-NYAY-zay)   In the style of the city of Bologna. *Example: Spaghetti bolognese* is spaghetti with meat sauce.

bravura (brah-VOOR-ah)   Bravery; a display of spirit and dash. *Example:* The truth is that young Mr. Bixon is incapable of the kind of *bravura* pianism required by the showier compositions of Liszt.

C

cicerone (chee-chay-RO-nay *or* sis-er-OWN)   a guide to a museum or other sights (like the ancient statesman and writer Cicero). *Example:* Our *cicerone* left us at the end of the tour.

con amore (kone ah-MOHR-ay)   With love and devotion; tenderly. *Example:* You will be able to play this passage *con amore* if you slow down slightly.

D

dolce far niente (DOL-chay FAR NYEN-tay)   Sweet inactivity. *Example:* By February, the overworked students were longing for a summer of *dolce far niente.*

dolce vita   See *la dolce vita.*

F

forte (FOR-tay) (abbreviated *f*)   Strong. In music, loud.

fortissimo (for-TIS-si-mo) (abbreviated *fff*)   Extremely strong. In music, extremely loud.

L

la dolce vita (la DOL-chay VEE-tah)   Sweet life; life of pleasure. *Example:* When he got his inheritance, he quit his job and devoted himself to *la dolce vita.*

M

ma non troppo (mah nohn TROP-po)   But not too much. (Used in musical directions; for example, *adagio ma non troppo* means "slow, but not too slow.")

P

pianissimo (pyah-NIS-see-mo) (abbreviated *ppp*)   (Musical term.) Extremely soft.

piano (PYAH-no) (abbreviated *p*)   (Musical term.) Soft.

presto (PRESS-toe)   Rapidly; quickly; a direction in music calling for a fast tempo. *Example:* In the traditional sonata the second movement is usually a *presto* movement.

punctilio (poonk-TEEL-ee-oh)   A fine point; a nice point of behavior or etiquette; fastidiousness; meticulousness. *Example:* The duel was fought with the utmost *punctilio*; neither of the contestants was injured, and their honor was satisfied.

V

vendetta (ven-DET-ta)   A blood feud; from the feuding families of Corsica who avenged the death of relatives. *Example:* The rivalry between the gangs has developed into a *vendetta* in which three youths have already been slain.

SPELLING RULES

There is a widespread belief that English spelling is illogical and ungoverned by rules. This is not true. Most English words are spelled according to established rules. There are exceptions to each rule, but they are not as numerous as is commonly believed.

These spelling rules are simple and easily learned. Even better, you will find that you already know many of them and apply them automatically as you write. Also good news—in some cases two different spellings are acceptable; for example, you may correctly write either *cargos* or *cargoes*, *referenda* or *referendums*, Tom *Williams's* son or Tom *Williams'* son.

If you apply the rules, you will improve your spelling ability greatly, for you will be able to spell correctly two thirds or more of all words.

Forming Plurals

Most nouns add *s* to form the plural.

EXAMPLES: dogs, houses, papers.

Nouns Ending in a Sibilant Sound
(*s*, *ss*, *sh*, soft *ch*, *x*, *z*)
A noun ending in a sibilant sound adds *es*.

EXAMPLES: biases, lasses, dishes, birches, boxes, quizzes.

Nouns Ending in *o*
A noun ending in *o* adds *s* (EXAMPLES: autos, pianos, radios) or *es* (EXAMPLES: heroes, potatoes, tomatoes).

Note: According to Webster, some nouns ending in *o* may add either *s* or *es* to form the plural.

EXAMPLES: buffaloes or buffalos, dominoes or dominos, volcanoes or volcanos. In each case, the first form is preferred.

Nouns Ending in *f* or *fe*
Some nouns ending in *f* add *s*.

EXAMPLES: chiefs, handkerchiefs, roofs, dwarfs.

Some nouns ending in *f* or *fe* change the *f* to *v* and add *s* or *es*:

EXAMPLES: calf, calves; knife, knives; wife, wives.

Nouns Ending in *y*
A noun ending in *y* preceded by a vowel adds *s*.

EXAMPLES: keys, toys, donkeys.

A noun ending in *y* preceded by a consonant or *qu* changes the *y* to *i* and adds *es*.

EXAMPLES: rally, rallies; duty, duties; secretary, secretaries; soliloquy, soliloquies.

Letters, Signs, and Digits
A lowercase letter, a sign, a digit, or an abbreviation with periods adds an apostrophe and s.

EXAMPLES: *x*'s, &'s, 2's Ph.D.'s.

An acronym or other abbreviation without periods, or a date, adds *s* without the apostrophe.

EXAMPLES: IOUs, 1980s.

Certain Words of Latin or Greek Origin
Some words derived from Latin or Greek retain their original plurals.

EXAMPLES FROM THE LATIN: alumnus (male), alumni; radius, radii; bacillus, bacilli; datum, data; erratum, errata; bacterium, bacteria.

Note: For some common Latin-derived nouns ending in *um*, the plural may be formed either by changing the *um* to *a* or by adding *s*.

EXAMPLES: curricula or curriculums, memorandums or memoranda.

EXAMPLES FROM THE GREEK: analysis, analyses; crisis, crises; criterion, criteria; phenomenon, phenomena.

Other Unusual Plurals
A few nouns add *en*, change the vowel, or remain the same.

EXAMPLES: child, children; ox, oxen; man, men; tooth, teeth; goose, geese; sheep, sheep; moose, moose.

Proper Names
Most proper names add *s*.

EXAMPLES: the two Amys, three Jennifers, and four Michaels in my class.

A proper name ending in a sibilant adds *es*.

EXAMPLES: Jones, Joneses; Marsh, Marshes; Larch, Larches; Marx, Marxes; Paz, Pazes.

Forming Possessives

Common Nouns
The possessive case of a *singular* noun is formed by adding an apostrophe and *s*.

EXAMPLES: child's, boss's, lady's, boy's, man's, president's.

A *plural* noun that ends in *s* adds just an apostrophe.

EXAMPLES: bosses', ladies', boys', presidents'.

A *plural* noun that does not end in *s* adds an apostrophe and *s*.

EXAMPLES: children's, men's.

Personal Pronouns

A personal pronoun adds just *s*.

EXAMPLES: its, hers, ours, yours, theirs.

Proper Names

A *singular* proper name adds an apostrophe and *s*.

EXAMPLES: Mary's house, Burns's poems, Dickens's novels, Mr. Richards's lawn.

Exceptions: Two traditional exceptions to this rule are the proper names *Jesus* and *Moses*, which add only the apostrophe.

EXAMPLES: in Jesus' name, Moses' leadership.

Note: When a singular proper name has two or more syllables, some writers prefer the possessive forms *Dickens'* and *Richards'*.

A *plural* proper name adds just an apostrophe.

EXAMPLES: the Adamses' garden, the McKenzies' cat.

Multiple versus Separate Ownership

To indicate ownership by *two or more persons*, an apostrophe and *s* are added only to the last name.

EXAMPLES: Watson and Crick's discovery; Ann, Lisa, and Jerry's dog.

To indicate *separate* ownership, an apostrophe and *s* are added to each name.

EXAMPLES: the secretary's and treasurer's reports, ABC's and CBS's camera crews.

IE or EI

Put *i* before *e*.

EXAMPLES: ach*ie*ve, bel*ie*f, ch*ie*f, fr*ie*nd, misch*ie*f, p*ie*ty, qu*ie*t, rev*ie*w, ser*ie*s, th*ie*very, y*ie*ld.

Exceptions: After *c*, place *e* before *i*: c*ei*ling, perc*ei*ve, rec*ei*ve, rec*ei*pt.

When the sound is *ay*, place *e* before *i*: fr*ei*ght, n*ei*ghbor, v*ei*l, w*ei*gh.

Hint: Memorize this little rhyme which has helped generations of spellers.

> Put *i* before *e*
> Except after *c*
> Or when pronounced *ay*
> As in n*ei*ghbor or w*ei*gh;
> And except s*ei*ze and s*ei*zure
> And also l*ei*sure,
> w*ei*rd, h*ei*ght, and *ei*ther, forf*ei*t and n*ei*ther.

Note: The word *financier* is an exception to the rule that *c* is followed by *ei*.

There are some other words, not included in the rhyme above, in which *e* precedes *i*:

caffeine	Fahrenheit	protein	sovereign
codeine	heifer	seismic	stein

-CEDE, -CEED, -SEDE

The ending *-cede* is more common than *-ceed* or *-sede*.

EXAMPLES: ac*cede*, con*cede*, pre*cede*, re*cede*, se*cede*.

Only three words end in *-ceed*: ex*ceed*, pro*ceed*, suc*ceed*. Notice that they begin with *ex-*, *pro-*, and *suc-*. Here is a mnemonic that will help you remember them. A boxer is a *pro*-fessional. When he retires, he is an *ex*-fighter. Then he has a *suc*-cessor.

Only one word ends in *-sede*: super*sede*.

Adding Prefixes

A prefix is one or more syllables attached to the beginning of a word to change its meaning. When a prefix is added to a word, the spelling of the original word is not changed.

Prefix	Meaning	Example
ab-	away, from	abduct (lead away)
ante-	before	antechamber (a room located before another)
anti-	against	antiseptic (against poisoning)
circum-	around	circumnavigate (sail around)
com-, con,	with, together	concelebrate (celebrate together)
de-	down	demote (put down)
dis-	apart, not	disagreeable
hyper-	over, above, beyond	hyperactive (overactive)
il-, im-, in-, ir-,	not	illogical, immoral, indisposed, irrelevant
inter-	between, among	interview, international
intra-	within	intrauterine (within the uterus)
mis-	bad, wrong	misdeed
non-	not	nonprofessional
over-	in excess	overzealous
per-	through	perambulate (travel through)
post-	after, behind	postgraduate
pre-	before	premedical
pro-	forward, instead of	provide (look forward)
re-	back, again	retaliate (fight back) repel (hurl back)
sub-	under	subway, subtract
super-	over, above	superhuman
trans-	across	transcontinental
un-	not	unnatural, unoccupied

Note: Many spelling errors occur when a prefix ends with the letter with which the word begins. Just add the prefix to the word; don't omit a letter.

> *un* + necessary = unnecessary (*not* unecessary)
> *mis* + step = misstep (*not* mistep)
> *pre* + eminent = preeminent (*not* preminent)

Adding Suffixes

A suffix is one or more syllables attached to the end of a word. Examples of suffixes are *-able*, *-ible*, *-ly*, *-ness*, *-ous*, *-ar*, *-ery*, *-ary*.

With the exception of *-able* and *-ible*, suffixes cause few spelling difficulties. Learn when to add *-able* and when to add *-ible*.

-able

Nouns ending in *-ation* form adjectives by adding *-able*.

Noun	Adjective
admir*ation*	⟶ admir*able*
applic*ation*	⟶ applic*able*
communic*ation*	⟶ communic*able*
damn*ation*	⟶ damn*able*

Some other words that do not end in *-ation* also add *-able* to form adjectives. All of them are common words.

comfort + *able* = comfortable
eat + *able* = eatable
read + *able* = readable
talk + *able* = talkable

There is no hard-and-fast rule covering these words. You will have to learn them individually.

Hint: The suffix *-able* is more common than *-ible*. If in doubt, use *-able*, and you will have more than a fair chance of being correct.

When you want to add *-able* to a word that ends in *e*, how do you spell the new word? Here's the rule: Drop the final *e* unless it is preceded by *c* or *g*. In that case the *e* is needed to retain the soft sound.

admire + *able* = admirable
desire + *able* = desirable
live + *able* = livable
BUT
enforce + *able* = enforceable
change + *able* = changeable

-ible

In words ending in *-ible*, the suffix is often preceded by *ss*.

acce*ss*ible   permi*ss*ible   transmi*ss*ible

Words ending in *-ible* often have a noun form ending in *-ion*.

Noun	Adjective
combust*ion*	⟶ combust*ible*
destruct*ion*	⟶ destruct*ible*
digest*ion*	⟶ digest*ible*
percept*ion*	⟶ percept*ible*
reprehens*ion*	⟶ reprehens*ible*

Most words with stems ending in soft *c* or *g* use *-ible* to retain the soft sound. The word *produce* has the adjective *producible* because adding *-able* would change the pronunciation of *c* from its present soft sound to *k*. Other words in this class are:

conduc*ible*   deduc*ible*   elig*ible*
intellig*ible*   irasc*ible*   reduc*ible*

Note that in these words the final *e* of the stem is dropped:

deduce + *ible* = deducible

When forming adverbs from adjectives ending in *-al*, simply add *-ly* to the original word.

Adjective	Adverb
accident*al*	⟶ accidental*ly*
practic*al*	⟶ practical*ly*
re*al*	⟶ real*ly*

-ous

When adding *-ous* to a noun ending in a consonant, do not change the spelling of the noun.

danger + *ous* = dangerous
hazard + *ous* = hazardous
marvel + *ous* = marvelous
riot + *ous* = riotous
slander + *ous* = slanderous

Exceptions: When *-ous* is added to the noun *disaster* and *wonder*, the *e* is dropped:

disaster + *ous* = disastrous
wonder + *ous* = wondrous

Nouns ending in *f* change the *f* to *v* when *-ous* is added.

grief + *ous* = grievous
mischief + *ous* = mischievous

Nouns ending in *y* drop the *y* and add *e* before *-ous*.

beauty + *ous* = beauteous
pity + *ous* = piteous
plenty + *ous* = plenteous

Nouns ending in *e* drop the *e* before *-ous*.

adventure + *ous* = adventurous
desire + *ous* = desirous
trouble + *ous* = troublous

Occasionally the final *e* is retained before *-ous* to keep the soft sound of *g*.

courage + *ous* = courageous
advantage + *ous* = advantageous
outrage + *ous* = outrageous

-ar

Only a small number of words end in *-ar*. Memorize ten of the most common.

beggar	collar	familiar	liar	regular
calendar	dollar	grammar	peculiar	singular

-ary and -ery

Only two commonly used words end in *ery:* station*ery* and cemet*ery*. If you remember that station*ery* means pap*er*, you will not misspell it. (Anything which is sta-tion*ary* is *at* a place.)

More than 300 words end in *-ary*.

Final Y

Final *y* preceded by a *vowel* remains *unchanged* when a termination is added.

attorney + *s* = attorneys
portray + *ing* = portraying
annoy + *ed* = annoyed
employ + *er* = employer
convey + *ance* = conveyance
betray + *al* = betrayal

Exceptions: lay + *ed* = laid   gay + *ly* = gaily

Final *y* preceded by a *consonant* changes to *i* when a termination is added.

ruby + *s* = rub*i*es
icy + *est* = ic*i*est
mercy + *less* = merc*i*less

tidy + *ness* = tidiness
pity + *ful* = pitiful

Exceptions: Final *y* is retained before *-ing*.

carry + *ing* = carrying
copy + *ing* = copying
tally + *ing* = tallying

Final E

Drop final *e* before a suffix beginning with a *vowel*.

advise + *able* = advisable
large + *est* = largest
love + *er* = lover
desire + *ous* = desirous
ache + *ing* = aching
argue + *ing* = arguing
divine + *ity* = divinity

Exceptions: When a word ends in *oe* or *double e*, the final *e* is not dropped in order to retain the same pronunciation.

canoe + *ing* = canoeing
hoe + *ing* = hoeing

| agree | agree*able* | agree*ing* |
| see | see*able* | see*ing* |

The *e* is retained also in *singeing* (burning) and *dyeing* (coloring) to avoid confusion with *singing* and *dying*.

Note: When *-ing* is added to a word ending in *ie*, the *e* is dropped and the *i* changed to *y* before adding the suffix:

die + *ing* = dying
lie + *ing* = lying
vie + *ing* = vying

Retain final *e* before a suffix beginning with a *consonant*.

coarse + *ness* = coarseness
like + *ness* = likeness
excite + *ment* = excitement
require + *ment* = requirement
hate + *ful* = hateful
care + *less* = careless

Exceptions: *Due*, *true*, and *whole* drop final *e* before *-ly*: duly, truly, wholly.

Some words ending in *e* drop the *e* before *-ment* and *-ful*: argue, argument; judge, judgment; acknowledge, acknowledgment; awe, awful.

Note: The spellings *judgement* and *acknowledgement* are also correct, but the other spellings are preferred.

Words Ending in *-IC*

Words ending in *-ic* and *k* before a suffix beginning with *e*, *i*, or *y* used as a vowel.

| frolic | frolic*k*ed | frolic*k*ing |
| picnic | picnic*k*ed | picnic*k*ing |

Doubling the Final Consonant

When a one-syllable word ends in a single vowel and a consonant, the consonant is doubled before a suffix beginning with a vowel.

One-Syllable Words

| hit | hi*tt*er | hi*tt*ing |
| spin | spi*nn*er | spi*nn*ing |

A word that has more than one syllable ending in a single vowel and consonant, and is accented on the final syllable, doubles the final consonant before a suffix beginning with a vowel.

Words of More Than One Syllable

| occur | compel | commit | omit |
| occu*rr*ed | compe*ll*ing | commi*tt*ing | omi*tt*ing |

Words ending in *-ful* double the *l* when *-ly* is added.

Words Ending in *-ful*

| careful | beautiful | dutiful |
| careful*ly* | beautiful*ly* | dutiful*ly* |

Contractions

To form a contraction, just insert an apostrophe where one or more letters are left out.

I + am = I'm
we + are = we're
can + not = can't
she + would = she'd

Compound Nouns and Adjectives

Numbers and Fractions

Hyphenate the numbers from twenty-one to ninety-nine and fractions used as adjectives.

EXAMPLES: thirty-three, one-half pint of milk.

Self- Words

Hyphenate most *self-* words.

EXAMPLES: self-evident, self-made, self-esteem.

Modifiers of Two or More Words

Hyphenate a compound modifier that *precedes* the noun.

EXAMPLES: four-cylinder car, user-friendly computer, hit-and-run driver.

Exceptions: Do *not* hyphenate a compound modifier that precedes the noun *but:*
a. Consists of an *-ly* adverb and an adjective.

EXAMPLES: carefully designed building, highly paid computer programmer.

b. Includes a comparative or superlative form.

EXAMPLES: a higher salaried executive, the lowest ranked car.

Do *not* hyphenate a compound modifier that *follows* the noun.

EXAMPLES: The dam was well constructed.

COMMONLY MISSPELLED WORDS

A

abandoned
abbey
aberration
abeyance
abridgment
abscess
absence
absurd
abundance
abutting
academy
accede
accent
accessible
acclimate
accommodate
accompany
accumulation
accusation
achievement
acknowledge
acquaint
acquired
acquisition
across
actually
acutely
adage
addressee
adequate
adieu
adjournment
adjunct
advertise
advertisement
advice
advise
advisable
affirmative
aggravate
aggregate
agitation
aisle
alcohol
allege
allies
ambassador
amendment
amplify
ancient
anecdote
anemia
angle
annoyance

annum
anticipate
antipathy
antique
apologetic
apparatus
apparently
appellate
appetite
appreciation
appropriation
approximately
apricot
architecture
arduous
arguing
arouse
arraignment
arrest
article
artificial
ascertain
aspirations
assassination
assessment
assigned
association
assurance
athlete
attach
attempt
attendance
attendants
attorneys
authentic
aversion
awkward
axle

B

baccalaureate
bachelor
bacteria
banana
bankruptcy
beatitude
beleaguered
belligerent
benefit
biased
bimonthly
biscuit
blamable
bookkeeping

bored
boundary
bounteous
broccoli
bungalow
bureau
burglaries
business

C

calendar
cameos
campaign
cancel
candidacy
candle
cannon
canon
capital
capitol (a building)
carburetor
carnage
carriage
category
caucus
cauldron
cavalier
cavalry
cease
cemetery
certified
chagrined
chamois
chancellor
changeable
charitable
chauffeur
chisel
cinnamon
citation
clamorous
classified
clique
clothe
colonel
colossal
column
commandant
commemorate
commenced
commitment
committal
committee
committing
community
comparative
compel
competition
competitors
complacency
conciliatory
conclusively
condemned
confectionery
congenial

congestion
conjunction
connoisseur
conquer
conscience
conscientious
conscious
conscript
consequently
conservatory
consistent
consummation
contagious
contemptible
continually
control
controller
convenient
conversant
cooperate
coronation
coroner
corporal
corral
correlation
correspondence
correspondent
corrugated
corset
countenance
courtesies
criticism
crochet
cronies
crucial
crystallized
currency

D

deceive
decision
declaration
deferred
definite
delegate
deliberate
delicious
delinquent
demurrage
denunciatory
deodorize
derogatory
description
desecration
desert
desirable
despair
dessert (food)
destruction
detrimental
development
digestible
dilapidated
dilemma
dining room

diocese
diphtheria
dirigible
disappear
disappearance
disapprove
discipline
discretion
dispatch
dispensable
dissatisfied
dissatisfy
dissolution
distillery
distinguished
distributor
dormitory
drastically
dual
duchess
duel
duly
dungarees
duped
dyeing
dying

E
economical
economy
ecstasy
eczema
effects
efficient
elaborate
electrolysis
embarrass
embassies
emergency
eminently
emolument
emphasis
emphasize
emphatically
endurance
enormous
enthusiastic
ephemeral
equilibrium
equinoctial
equipped
error
essential
everlasting
exaggerate
exceed
excel
exercise
exhibition
exhortion
existence
extradite
extraordinary
extravagant

F
facilitation
faculties
fallibility
falsify
falsity
fascinated
fatal
feudal
filial
finally
financial
financier
finely
flexible
foggy
foliage
forcible
foreign
foretell
forfeit
forgo
fortissimo
fragrance
fraternally
frightfully
frostbitten
fundamental
furl

G
gallery
galvanized
gelatin
glamour
glimpse
guaranteed
guardian
gout
government
grammar
grandeur
grapevines
grease
grieve
guarantee
guidance
guild
guitar

H
handicapped
harass
hearth
height
heinous
heritage
hideous
hindrance
histrionic
hosiery
hybrid
hygienic
hysterics

I
idiomatic
ignoramus
ignorant
illegitimate
illuminate
illustrative
incompetent
imminent
impartiality
impeccable
impromptu
incongruity
indecent
indictment
ingenuity
ingenuous
inimitable
innocent
innocuous
inoculate
insulation
insurance
integrity
intelligence
intercede
interruption
irreparably
itemized

J
jealous
jeopardy
journal
jovial
judgment
judiciary
jurisdiction

K
kindergarten
kinsman

L
label
laboratory
labyrinth
laceration
lacquer
ladies
larceny
latter
leggings
legitimate
leisure
libel
lieutenant
ligament
lightning
liquidate
literally
loose
lose
losing

lovable
loveliness
lucrative
luxury
lynch

M
macaroni
mackerel
magnificent
maintenance
malice
maneuver
mannequin
manual
marmalade
masquerade
massacre
matinee
mattress
mayonnaise
mechanical
medal
medallion
medicine
medieval
mediocrity
melancholy
memoir
mercantile
mercury
merely
midget
midriff
military
millinery
millionaire
misanthrope
mischievous
misdemeanor
mislaid
misspell
misstep
monarchical
monkeys
monotonous
morale
moribund
mortgage
movable
murmuring
muscle
museum
myriad

N
necessary
negligible
negotiate
nervous
nevertheless
nickel
niece
ninety
ninth

notary
notoriety
nowadays
nuisance

O
obedient
obliged
obstacles
occasionally
occur
occurrence
odyssey
official
omissions
omitted
opportunity
option
ordinance
overwhelming

P
pacifist
pageant
pamphlet
panel
panicky
papal
parachute
paradoxical
parallel
parasite
parliament
parole
partisan
pastime
patient
patronize
pattern
peculiar
penitentiary
people's
perceive
perilous
perjury
permanent
permissible
persevere
personnel
pervade
phrenologist
physical
physician
picnicking
piquancy
pitiful
plagiarism
plague
planned
playwright
pneumonia
policy
politician
portable

portend
portiere
possession
possibilities
post office
postpone
potato
poultry
prairie
preceding
precious
predatory
predilection
preferably
preference
premises
preparation
prescription
prestige
presume
presumptuous
previous
primarily
primitive
principal
principalship
principle
prisoner
privilege
probably
proceed
proffer
profit
proletarian
promissory
promptness
propaganda
proprietor
psychology
publicity
publicly
punctilious

Q
quantities
quartet
questionnaire
queue
quinine

R
rabid
raisin
realize
reasonable
receipted
receipts
receptacle
recognizable
recommend
recompense
reconcile
recruit
refrigerator

regrettable
regretted
rehearsal
relevant
relieve
religious
remodel
renaissance
renascence
repetitious
requisition
reservoir
resilience
resonance
resources
responsibility
responsible
restaurant
rheostat
rhetorical
rheumatism
rhubarb
rhythm
rickety
ridiculous
righteous
roommate
routine

S
Sabbath
sacrilegious
salable
salaries
salient
sandwiches
Saturn
saucy
scenes
scissors
screech
scripture
scrutiny
secretary
seize
senior
serenity
series
session
sieges
significant
silhouette
similar
sincerely
sitting
sobriquet
society
solemn
soliciting
sophomore
soporific
source
sovereign
specialized
specific

specifically
spiritualist
squalor
squirrels
staid
staunch
stationary (fixed)
statutes
steak
strengthen
strenuous
stretch
studying
subsidy
suburb
subversive
succeed
successor
suffrage
summarize
superb
supersede
surfeit
surgeon
symmetrical
sympathy
systematic

T
tableaux (or tableaus)
taciturn
talcum
tantalizing
tariff
taunt
technical
temperament
temperature
temporarily
tenet
tennis
terse
tetanus
thermometer
thesis
thorough
thought
tournament
tragedy
traitor
transaction
transient
transparent
treachery
tremendous
triumph
troupe (theatrical)
truce
tuition
turkeys
twelfth
twins
typewriting
typhoid
tyranny

LANGUAGE ARTS

U
unanimous
unauthorized
unbearable
unconscious
undoubtedly
undulate
unfortunately
uniform
unify
unnecessary
utilize

V
vacancy
vacillate
vacuum
vague
valuing
vegetable
vein
velvet
vengeance
verbal
villain
visible
vivisection
voluntary
voucher

W
warrant
warranted
weather
Wednesday
weird
welfare
we're
whether
wholly
width
wield
wiring
witnesses
woman's
women's
wrapped
wretched

Y
yacht
yoke

Z
zephyr
zucchini

ABBREVIATIONS

A
A.D.	*anno Domini* (the year of the Lord)
abbr.	abbreviation
abr.	abridged, abridgment
acct.	account
ad inf.	*ad infinitum* (to infinity)
ad lib.	*ad libitum* (at will)
AC	alternating currency
AM	amplitude modulation
amp	ampere
anon.	anonymous
app.	appendix
art., arts	article, articles
atm	standard atmosphere

B
b.	born
bal.	balance
B.C.	before Christ
BP	boiling point
bibliog.	bibliography
bk., bks.	book, books
Btu	British thermal unit
bu.	bushel

C
| °C | Celsius |
| ca., c. | *circa* (about) |

cal	gram calorie
Cal	kilogram calorie
C.E.	common era
cf.	compare, confer
ch.	chapter
COD	cash on delivery
copr. or c	copyright
col., cols.,	column, columns
cu.	cubic

D
d.	day
d.	died
db	decibel
DC	direct current
dept.	department
diss.	dissertation
doz.	dozen

E
ea.	each
ed.	edition, editor
e.g.	*exempli gratia* (for example)
et al.	*et alii* (and others)
et seq.	*et sequens* (and the following)
etc.	*et cetera* (and others, and so forth)
ex.	example

F
f., ff.	following page, following pages
°F	Fahrenheit
FM	frequency modulation
fig., figs.	figure, figures
fl. oz.	fluid ounce
ft.	foot
ft lb	foot-pound

G
| g | gram |
| gal. | gallon |

H
h., hr.	hour
ha	hectare
HP	horsepower

I
ibid.	*ibidem* (the same)
id.	*idem* (the same)
i.e.	*id est* (that is)
in.	inch
incl.	inclusive, including, includes
inf.	*infra* (below)
IQ	intelligence quotient

J
| Jr. | junior |

K
K	Kelvin
kg	kilogram
kwh	kilowatt-hour

L

l	liter
l, ll	lines, lines
lb.	pound
loc. cit.	*loco citato* (in the place cited)

M

m	meter
mdse	merchandise
mfg., mfr.	manufacturing, manufacturer
mi.	mile
min.	minute
MP	melting point
MPG	miles per gallon
MPH	miles per hour
ms., mss.	manuscript, manuscripts

N

n.b.	*nota bene* (note well)
n.d.	no date
no., nos.	number, numbers
non seq.	*non sequitur* (does not follow)

O

op. cit.	*opere citato* (in the work cited)
oz.	ounce

P

p., pp.	page, pages
par.	paragraph
pass.	*passim* (throughout), passive
pd.	paid
pH	measure of acidity or alkalinity
pk.	peck
pl.	plural
prep.	preposition
pt.	part
pt.	pint
pub.	published, publication

Q

qt.	quart

R

RF	radio frequency
R.I.P.	*requiescat in pace* (may he/she rest in peace)

S

sec.	second
sec.	section
ser.	series
sic	so (place in brackets to indicate that a seeming mistake was copied from the original material as it appears)
sq., sq	square
Sr.	senior
st.	stanza
std.	standard
STP	standard temperature and pressure
supp.	supplement
syn.	synonym, synonymous

T

trans., tr.	translator, translation, translated by

V

v., vb.	verb
vol., vols.	volume, volumes
v., vs.	*versus* (against)

Y

yd.	yard
yr.	year

LANGUAGE ARTS

SYNONYMS AND ANTONYMS

Note: Antonyms appear in *italics*

Abate   reduce, decrease, diminish; *increase*
Abhor   detest, despise
Abject   wretched, miserable, despicable
Abjure   to swear to give up, avoid, repudiate
Abortive   fruitless, failing, useless
Abrogate   abolish, repeal by law
Absolve   to set free from guilt, exonerate
Abstemious   moderate in eating or drinking, sparing; *gluttonous*
Abstract   theoretical; *substantive*
Abysmal   of low quality, bottomless
Acclaim   applause, admiration
Acclimate   to become accustomed to new surroundings, adapt
Accolade   praise, approval; *reprimand*
Acme   peak, pinnacle, zenith; *nadir*
Acquiesce   to give consent by remaining silent, accede
Acrid   bitter, sharp
Acrimonious   bitter, caustic
Acumen   quickness in seeing and understanding, keen insight, shrewdness
Adage   maxim, proverb, familiar saying
Adamant   stubborn, unyielding; *flexible*
Adjudicate   settle, judge
Adroit   skillful, clever; *clumsy*
Adulation   excessive praise, slavish flattery
Adversary   opponent, enemy, foe; *ally*
Advocate   to speak or write in favor of, recommend publicly
Aegis   shield, protection, sponsorship
Affable   gracious, friendly, *withdrawn*

Afflict   to cause pain or suffering, distress
Affluent   rich; *impoverished*
Alacrity   briskness, quick willingness, speed; *lethargy*
Allay   calm, soothe; *agitate*
Alleged   reported, supposed
Alleviate   ease, lighten; *exacerbate*
Allusion   indirect reference, slight or incidental mention of something
Aloof   distant, apart, reserved; *outgoing, gregarious*
Altercation   quarrel, dispute, fight
Altruism   unselfishness, philanthropy; *cupidity, avarice*
Ambiguous   vague, indefinite; *specific*
Ameliorate   improve, relieve; *exacerbate*
Amicable   friendly, peaceful; *belligerent*
Amnesty   a general pardon
Amoral   unable to distinguish between right and wrong; *moral*
Anarchy   chaos, disorder
Anathema   something greatly detested, a curse
Animosity   ill will, hostility; *friendship*
Anomaly   irregularity, abnormality
Antediluvian   old fashioned, before the flood; *modern*
Antipathy   dislike, distaste, hate
Antiseptic   preventing infection by stopping the growth of disease germs, sterile, barren
Antithesis   exact opposite
Apathetic   unemotional, indifferent; *concerned*
Apropos   fittingly, opportunely
Arbiter   judge, referee
Arbitrary   whimsical, dictatorial
Archaic   out of date, ancient, old-fashioned
Arrears   unpaid debts
Ascertain   discover, verify
Ascetic   severe
Asinine   foolish, silly, stupid
Asperity   harshness of temper
Assiduous   devoted, busy, attentive
Assimilate   to take in and make part of oneself, absorb
Assuage   soothe, irritate
Atonement   amends, expiation
Atrophy   to waste away, degenerate
Atypical   uncharacteristic, abnormal; *conforming*
Audacity   boldness, daring
Augment   to enlarge, increase
Auspicious   with signs of success, favorable
Austere   severe, harsh; *adorned*
Avarice   greed, passion for riches; *altruism, philanthropy*
Avid   eager
Avocation   minor occupation, hobby

Badger   to pester, nag, annoy
Baffle   to hinder someone by being too hard to understand, perplex
Balk   to refuse to move, frustrate
Banal   trivial, meaningless from overuse, commonplace
Barrister   lawyer, attorney, solicitor
Bauble   trinket; *jewel, gem*
Bedlam   confusion, uproar

Belated   late, delayed; *timely*
Belittle   to make seem less important, trivialize; *intensify*
Belligerent   warlike, hostile; *peaceful*
Benediction   blessing; *curse*
Beneficent   kind
Benign   kindly, harmless, gentle; *malignant*
Bequest   legacy, gift
Besiege   surround, hem in
Besmirch   to dim the reputation, soil, stain
Bestial   beastly, brutal; *civilized*
Bias   prejudice
Bigoted   narrow-minded, prejudiced
Bizarre   odd, peculiar, strange
Blasphemy   abuse or contempt for God, profanity
Blatant   loud, showy, conspicuous
Bliss   happiness, pleasure; *hell*
Bogus   fake, counterfeit; *genuine*
Bona fide   genuine; *bogus*
Boorish   rude, bad-mannered
Brash   impudent; *polite, respectful*
Brawn   bulk, muscles
Bucolic   rural, rustic; *urbane*
Buff   follower, fan, devotee
Bulwark   protection
Bumptious   arrogant
Burgeon   grow, flourish; *stifle*

Cabal   clique
Cacophony   harsh sound, discord; *harmony*
Cadaver   corpse, body
Cajole   coax, wheedle
Callous   unfeeling; *sensitive*
Calumny   false accusation, slander; *accolade*
Candor   honesty, openness, frankness; *deceit*
Capitulate   surrender; *resist*
Capricious   flighty, unpredictable, erratic; *constant*
Captious   quarrelsome, argumentative; *accepting*
Carnage   slaughter, bloodshed
Carnivorous   using animals as food, meat-eating; *herbivorous*
Castigate   to correct by punishing, chastise
Caustic   sarcastic, biting, acrimonious; *mild*
Celerity   speed, rapidity; *sluggishness*
Censure   to criticize, rebuke; *approve*
Cessation   stop; *continuance*
Chagrin   feeling of disappointment, humiliation
Charlatan   a fraud, pretender; *authenticity*
Chicanery   trickery, underhandedness; *straight-forwardness*
Chronic   lasting a long time, habitual; *fleeting*
Circuitous   roundabout; *direct*
Circumspect   cautious, prudent; *impulsive*
Clandestine   secret, undercover; *aboveboard*
Cliche   banality, platitude; *originality*
Coalesce   merge, join; *split*
Cogent   forceful, convincing, persuasive; *ineffective*
Cognizant   having knowledge of, aware; *ignorant*
Comatose   unconscious

Commiserate pity, sympathize with
Commodious large, spacious; *cramped*
Complacent smug, self-satisfied; *discontented*
Compunction remorse, regret
Conciliate soothe, reconcile; *exacerbate*
Concoct to prepare by mixing with a variety of ingredients, devise, invent
Condone excuse, pardon; *begrudge*
Congenial having similar tastes and interests, kindred; *incompatible*
Conjecture opinion, guess; *documentation*
Connoisseur an expert; *dilettante*
Connubial having to do with marriage, conjugal
Controversial open to argument, debatable, disputed
Copious ample, abundant, plentiful; *scarce*
Corpulent fat, obese; *slender, lean*
Corroborate to make more certain, confirm, support
Countermand to cancel an order, withdraw
Coup revolution, overturn
Covert secret, hidden; *open, aboveboard*
Credence belief, credit
Criterion standard test, model
Cryptic having a hidden meaning, secret, obscure
Culpable deserving blame, guilty; *innocent*
Cumbersome hard to manage, clumsy, unwieldy
Cupidity greed, avarice; *altruism*
Cursory not thorough, hasty; *comprehensive*
Curtail shorten, reduce, lessen; *expand*
Cynical doubting the sincerity and goodness of others, sneering, sarcastic

Dearth great scarcity, shortage; *abundance*
Debacle sudden downfall or collapse, disaster
Debilitate to make feeble, weaken; *strenghten*
Debonair genial, courteous
Decadence growing worse, decline, decay
Decapitate behead
Decorum good taste in speech or dress, fitness
Decrepit old and feeble, worn-out; *hale, healthy*
Deduce to reach a conclusion by reasoning, infer
Defame to speak evil of, malign; *honor*
Degrade to bring into dishonor, corrupt
Deleterious causing harm, injurious; *salubrious*
Delve to search carefully for information, excavate
Demeanor behavior, manner
Demur object, disapprove
Demure artificially proper, coy, reserved
Denounce condemn; *praise*
Deplete reduce, lessen; *replenish*
Deplorable regrettable, wretched
Depraved corrupt, perverted, debased
Deride scorn; ridicule
Derogatory lowering in honor or estimation, disparaging; *uplifting*
Desolate devastated, barren, solitary, dreary
Despot absolute ruler, oppressor
Destitute impoverished; *affluent*

Desultory jumping from one thing to another without aim or method, unconnected
Deter prevent, stop
Devious trick, roundabout
Devout religious, pious, sincere
Dextrous skillful, clever, deft; *clumsy*
Diatribe bitter speech directed at someone or something, denunciation
Diffident shy; *assertive*
Digress diverge, swerve, stray
Dilettante dabbler, amateur
Diminutive tiny, small
Discern to see clearly, distinguish
Disciple believer in the thought and teaching of a leader, follower
Disconsolate sad, dejected; *elated, cheerful*
Discord disagreement; *harmony, concord*
Discreet cautious, prudent; *imprudent*
Disdain scorn, contempt
Disgruntled in bad humor, discontented; *happy, satisfied*
Disheveled rumpled, messed; *tidy*
Dismantle to take apart, strip
Disparage to speak slightingly of, belittle, discredit; *praise*
Disparity inequality, difference; *similitude*
Disperse scatter; *assemble*
Dissent disagreement; *agreement*
Distraught crazed, distracted
Diverse varied; *alike*
Divulge to make known, reveal
Docile obedient, tame; *disruptive*
Dogmatic opinionated, stubborn
Doleful very sad, mournful, dismal; *exultant*
Dormant in a state of rest or inactivity, asleep; *active*
Dupe one who is easily deceived or tricked, scapegoat
Duplicity trickery, deceitfulness
Duress use of force, compulsion
Dwindle to shrink, diminish; *increase*

Eccentric unusual, odd; *predictable*
Edifice a large or impressive building, structure
Effectuate cause
Efficacy effectiveness
Effrontery shameless boldness, insolence
Egotistical vain, conceited; *modest, unpretentious*
Egregious remarkably bad, outrageous, flagrant
Elapse to slip away, pass
Elicit to draw forth, evoke
Emanate to come forth, emit
Embryonic undeveloped, in the early stages, immature
Emend to free from errors, correct
Eminent outstanding, distinguished, noteworthy
Emulate to strive to equal, imitate
Encomium a formal expression of high praise, eulogy
Enervate to weaken, unnerve; *bolster, support*
Engender produce, create

Enhance to make greater in quality or importance, upgrade; *degrade*
Enigma baffling problem or person, riddle
Enmity hostility, hatred; *friendship, amity*
Ennui feeling of weariness from lack of interest, boredom; *euphoria*
Enormity great size of a problem, immensity
Entourage group of attendants, retinue, followers
Ephemeral short-lived, transitory; *permanent*
Epithet insult
Epitome person or thing that represents the best, embodiment
Equitable just, valid; *unfair*
Erudite scholarly, learned
Esoteric understood only by a select few, secret, private; *public*
Esthetic showing an appreciation of beauty in nature or art, artistic
Evince show manifest, display
Exacerbate worsen, aggravate; *ameliorate*
Excoriate denounce violently, abrade
Exemplary outstanding
Exhort to advise earnestly, urge
Exonerate to free from blame, absolve; *persecute*
Expedite hasten; *prolong*
Exploit to make unfair or selfish use of, utilize
Expunge to remove completely, erase
Extenuating making the seriousness of an offense seem less, weakening
Extinct no longer existing, superseded
Extol to praise highly, commend; *criticize*
Extortion obtaining something by threats or force, extraction
Extraneous foreign, unessential, outside
Extrinsic not essential, external; *intrinsic*
Extrovert one who tends to act rather than think, uninhibited; *introvert*
Exultation great rejoicing, triumph

Fabricate to make up, invent; *document*
Facade outward appearance, face
Facetious being shyly humorous, witty
Facile easily done, adept; *difficult*
Fallacious logically unsound, misleading, deceptive
Fallible error-prone; *perfect*
Falter to draw back, waver; *persevere*
Fastidious dainty in taste, particular, choosy
Fatuous foolish, silly; *rational*
Feasible can be carried out easily, practicable; *impossible*
Feckless futile, ineffective
Feisty touchy, excitable, captious; *phlegmatic*
Fervid full of strong feeling, spirited; *phlegmatic*
Fervor passion
Fester to cause soreness or pain, rankle; *heal*
Fiasco a complete or ridiculous failure, breakdown
Fiat an authoritative order or command, decree
Fickle whimsical, capricious
Fiduciary held in trust, trustee
Flabbergasted speechless

Flagrant shocking, egregious, notorious, scandalous; *respectful*
Flamboyant striking, ornate; *simple*
Fledgling beginner, novice; *expert, authority*
Florid rosy, ruddy
Fluctuate to rise and fall, change; *stabilize*
Formidable hard to overcome, dreaded; *welcomed*
Fortuitous happening by chance, accidental; *premeditated*
Fracas noisy quarrel or fight, uproar
Fray a brawl, fight, battle
Frenetic excessively excited, frenzied; *calm*
Fretful peevish, worried, agitated; *happy*
Frugal avoiding waste, thrifty, economical; *prodigal*
Frustrate to prevent from accomplishing, thwart, foil; *encourage*
Fulsome so much as to be disgusting, overdone
Furtive secretive, stealthy
Futile worthless, useless, abortive; *effective, fruitful*

Galvanize to stir into action, arouse
Garbled confused; *clear, intelligible*
Gargantuan enormous, gigantic; *miniscule*
Garrulous talking too much, wordy; *reticent*
Gaudy cheap and showy, ostentatious; *decorous*
Gaunt having a starved look, emaciated; *rotund*
Germane to the point, pertinent; *irrelevant*
Gesticulate to point to wildly, gesture
Gist main point, essence
Glean to gather information little by little, learn
Gratuity a present in return for favors, tip
Grave serious, solemn; *jocular*
Gregarious fond of being with others, outgoing; *withdrawn*
Grisly frightful, horrible
Grotesque odd or unnatural in shape or appearance, bizarre; *simplex*
Grueling tiring, exhausting; *exhilarating, refreshing*
Guile crafty deceit, cunning
Gullible naive, unsophisticated; *skeptical*

Habitat home, environs
Hackneyed overused, trite; *fresh, original*
Halcyon calm, peaceful; *riotous*
Hapless unlucky, unfortunate
Harass to trouble by repeated attacks, persecute
Harbinger advance notice, forerunner
Haven place of shelter and safety, sanctuary
Havoc great destruction, ruin
Hedonistic pleasure-seeking, indulgent; *ascetic*
Heinous wicked, hateful, despicable
Herculean powerful, challenging
Heterogeneous different in kind, unlike, varied; *homogeneous*
Hirsute hairy
Hoary old, ancient; *newborn*
Hoax a mischievous trick, dupe

Homogeneous same, similar; *heterogeneous*
Hyperbole exaggeration
Hypothesis something assumed because it seems like a true explanation, theory

Idyllic simple, charming
Ignominious shameful, disgraceful
Ilk class, kind, sort
Imbibe to drink, absorb
Immaterial unimportant; *relevent, pertinent*
Imminent about to happen, threaten
Immutable permanent; *changing, flexible*
Impassive unmoved, emotionless; *emotional*
Impeach accuse of wrongdoing, charge
Impeccable irreproachable, faultless; *imperfect*
Impede to stand in the way of, hinder, obstruct
Imperceptible gradual, subtle
Imperturbable not easily disturbed, calm; *excitable*
Impetuous acting with rash energy, hasty; *deliberate*
Impious not showing reverence for God, wicked
Implacable unable to be appeased, unyielding
Implement to carry out a mission, enact, accomplish
Imply to mean without saying, suggest
Importune to annoy with pressing demands, plead
Impregnable unyielding
Impromptu spontaneous, off-hand; *rehearsed*
Improvident wasteful
Inadvertent lax, careless; *planned, intentional*
Inane foolish, silly; *sensible*
Inanimate lifeless, dull; *lively, animated*
Incessant unceasing
Incipient just beginning, commencing
Inclement rough, stormy
Incognito concealing name or position, disguised
Incoherent disconnected, confused; *coordinated*
Incompatible not able to live or work together peaceably, antagonistic
Incorrigible too firmly fixed in bad ways to be reformed, depraved; *reparable*
Incriminate to accuse of a crime, implicate
Incumbent office-holder
Indict to charge formally with a crime, accuse
Indifferent uncaring, neutral; *concerned*
Indigent poor, needy; *affluent*
Indolent lazy, idle; *industrious*
Indulgent giving in to another's whims or wishes, lenient
Inept awkward, inappropriate
Inevitable unavoidable, imminent
Inexorable unyielding, relentless; *flexible*
Ingenious good at inventing, clever
Ingratiate to bring oneself into favor, accept
Inhibit to hold back, restrain
Innocuous harmless; *injurious*
Innovative creative; *stagnant*
Innuendo insinuation, hint
Inordinate much too great, excessive

Insatiable that cannot be satisfied, greedy; *appeasable*
Insidious working secretly or subtlely, wily, shy
Insipid boring, bland; *exciting*
Insolent boldy rude, insulting
Integral necessary to make something complete, essential
Interminable endless, unceasing; *terminative*
Intransigent uncompromising, stubborn; *flexible*
Intrepid very brave, fearless; *cowardly, timorous*
Intrinsic essential, inherent; *extrinsic*
Inundate to flood, deluge
Invalidate to make useless, nullify
Invective violent attack in words, abuse
Inveterate deeply rooted, habitual
Irascible easily angered, irritable
Irate angry, enraged, furious, indignant
Irrevocable cannot be revoked, final
Itinerant traveling, wandering, nomadic
Itinerary route of travel, plan

Jeopardize to put in danger, risk, imperil; *protect*
Jostle to crowd against, shove, push; *restrain*
Jubilant showing joy, rejoicing; *depressed*
Judicious wise, sensible; *intemperate*
Jurisdiction territory over which authority extends, control
Juxtapose put side by side, adjoin; *separate*

Laceration a deep cut, wound
Lackluster dull, boring, uninspired; *stimulating*
Laconic expressing much in few words, concise, pithy; *garrulous, verbose*
Lampoon to ridicule, satirize
Landmark the high point or turning point of a period, historic
Larceny theft
Latent lying hidden and undeveloped, potential; *active, operational*
Laudable praiseworthy, commendable
Lax careless, remiss, negligent, slack; *strict, exact*
Legacy money or property left to someone in a will, bequest
Lethal causing death, fatal
Lethargy drowsiness, indifference, apathy; *enthusiasm*
Levity gaiety, frivolity; *seriousness, sobriety*
Liaison a working relationship, inter-communication
Lithe flexible, supple, limber; *stiff*
Litigation lawsuit
Livid discolored by a bruise, pallid
Loquacious talkative, garrulous; *laconic*
Lucid clear, sane, rational; *opaque*
Lucrative profitable, remunerative
Ludicrous absurd, laughable
Lugubrious very sad, mournful
Lurid sensational, startling

Magnanimous generous in overlooking insult or injury, noble
Maim to cripple, disable, mutilate
Maladjusted poorly-adapted
Malady disease, ailment, sickness
Malcontent dissatisfied, rebellious
Malevolent vicious, evil; *benevolent*
Malignant having an evil influence, harmful; *benign*
Malingerer one who pretends to be ill in order to escape work, shirker; *martyr*
Malleable pliable, yielding, adaptable; *rigid*
Mammoth gigantic, enormous
Mandate an authoritative order, directive
Mandatory authoritatively required, obligatory
Manifold having various forms, diverse
Martial warlike, soldierly; *peacelike*
Martinet strict disciplinarian, stickler
Matriarch mother
Maxim a statement of a general truth, precept
Meander to wander aimlessly, roam; *settle*
Mediate interpose, intervene, settle
Meditate to think deeply and continuously, reflect, ponder
Mendacious false, lying; *honest*
Menial fit for servants, low servile
Mentor advisor, teacher
Metamorphosis change, transformation
Meticulous careful about details, scrupulous; *careless, sloppy*
Mien way of conducting oneself, manner, bearing
Milieu surroundings, environment
Militant ready and willing to fight, combative; *peaceful*
Miniscule rather small, tiny, minute
Mitigate lessen; *exacerbate*
Modish fashionable, stylish; *outmoded, passé*
Morbid gruesome, unhealthy, diseased; *wholesome*
Moribund dying, failing; *lively, prospering*
Motivate arouse, incite
Mundane ordinary, earthy; *spiritual*
Murky obscure with smoke or mist, gloomy
Myopic near-sighted

Nadir the lowest point, bottom; *zenith*
Naive foolishly simple, childlike, ingenuous; *sophisticated, artful*
Nebulous cloudy, vague; *clear, definite*
Nefarious very wicked, villainous, vicious; *saintly*
Neophyte beginner, novice; *professional*
Nirvana perfection, heaven, utopia
Noisome foul-smelling, offensive, toxic
Nomadic wandering, itinerant
Nonchalant indifferent, casual; *concerned*
Nondescript hard to describe, unrecognizable
Nostalgia yearning for the past, homesickness
Noxious harmful to health or morals, pernicious
Nuance subtlety

Obese very fat, corpulent, stout; *slender*

Obfuscate confuse, bewilder
Obliterate to blot out, erase, destroy
Oblivion forgetfulness
Obscure unclear, clouded, ambiguous; *obvious, transparent*
Obsequious excessively willing to serve or obey, fawning, servile
Obsolete no longer in use or practice, old-fashioned; *serviceable*
Obviate to make unnecessary, prevent, eliminate
Occult hidden, mysterious
Odious hateful, disgusting; *pleasurable*
Officious offering unwanted advice, meddlesome; *aloof*
Ominous threatening, sinister, menacing
Omnipotent all-powerful
Onerous burdensome, laborious, oppressive; *inconsequential*
Opulent wealthy, abundant, luxuriant
Orthodox standard; *unconventional*
Ostensible on the surface, apparent
Ostentatious showy, pretentious; *decorous, conservative*
Ostracize to banish, shut out, bar
Oust to force out, eject, dispossess
Overt without attempt at concealment, open; *surreptitious*

Pacify to make peaceful, tranquilize, placate; *enrage*
Palatable tasty, savory; *disagreeable*
Palliate to cover up, excuse, extenuate
Paltry petty, trifling, insignificant
Panacea cure-all
Pandemonium scene of wild disorder, noise, confusion
Paramount dominant, chief, supreme; *trivial*
Parasite one who lives at the expense of others, leech, sponge
Pariah someone despised or rejected by others, outcast
Parochial narrow, limited, provincial
Parsimonious miserly, stingy; *generous, altruistic*
Pathetic pitiful
Paucity scarcity, dearth, insufficiency; *abundance*
Penitent regretful; *unrepentant*
Pensive expressing deep thoughtfulness with some sadness, contemplative
Perfidious treacherous; *faithful*
Perfunctory superficial, indifferent; *thorough, comprehensive*
Pernicious injurious, fatal; *harmless, innocuous*
Perpetrate to do something evil or criminal, commit
Persevere to continue to do something in spite of difficulty, persist
Peruse study, examine
Perverse persisting in error or fault, contrary
Phlegmatic sluggish, dull, apathetic; *excitable*
Pivotal important, crucial; *trivial, trifling*
Plaintiff one who brings suit in a court of law, complainant; *defendant*

Plausible   seemingly true, acceptable; *incredible*
Plethora   overabundance, excess; *dearth*
Plunder   rob, loot
Poignant   sharp or biting to the smell or taste, piercing, moving
Ponder   ruminate, reflect, consider
Potent   convincing, authoritative
Pragmatic   practical; *unrealistic*
Precipitate   to cause to happen before expected, hasten; *deter*
Preclude   prevent
Preeminent   excelling others, dominant, surpassing
Premonition   a forewarning, presentiment
Prestigious   illustrious, influential
Pretext   excuse, fabrication
Prevaricate   to turn aside from the truth, equivocate
Procrastinate   to defer, postpone
Profound   deep, insightful; *superficial, trivial*
Profuse   flowing, generous, lavish; *limited, scant*
Prolific   producing many young or much fruit, abounding; *barren, infertile*
Promulgate   to publish or make known officially, spread
Propensity   natural inclination, tendency
Propitious   favorably inclined, auspicious; *unfavorable*
Proponent   supporter
Propriety   correctness, properness; *inappropriate-ness*
Prosaic   matter-of-fact, commonplace, dull; *poetic*
Provincial   naive, unsophisticated; *worldly*
Provocative   exciting, stimulating; *tiresome*
Proximity   nearness, closeness; *distance*
Prudent   sensible, discreet; *foolhardy extravagant*
Pugnacious   quarrelsome, belligerent; *peaceable*

Qualm   scruple of conscience, uneasiness, misgiving
Quandary   state of perplexity, dilemma
Quell   to put an end to, overcome
Quintessence   pure essence, model

Rabid   unreasonably extreme, fanatical
Rambunctious   noisy, unruly, boisterous; *calm*
Rancor   bitter resentment, ill will; *amity*
Rapacious   grasping, greedy
Raucous   harsh-sounding, hoarse; *mellifluous*
Raze   to tear down, destroy
Rebuke   to express disapproval of, scold
Recant   to withdraw a previous opinion, statement, renounce
Recondite   profound, concealed, esoteric
Redress   to set right, remedy
Redundant   not needed, superfluous
Refute   to show something to be false or incorrect, deny; *confirm*

Rehabilitate   to restore to a good condition, reinstate
Relevant   to the point, pertinent; *irrelevant*
Remiss   negligent, inattentive, slack in meeting one's responsibilities; *careful*
Remorse   sadness, regret
Remote   distant, secluded; *nearby*
Remuneration   reward, payment
Renegade   deserter, traitor; *loyalist, patriot*
Repent   to feel sorry for having done wrong, regret
Replenish   refill
Replete   abundantly supplied, filled
Reprehensible   wicked, blameworthy
Repress   to prevent from acting, subdue
Reprimand   to disapprove severly, scold; *praise*
Repudiate   to refuse to accept, disown
Repugnant   distasteful, objectionable
Repulse   to drive back, repel; *attract, allure*
Rescind   repeal, cancel
Residue   remainder
Respite   time of relief and rest, reprieve
Reticent   reserved in speech, silent; *garrulous, verbose, loquacious*
Retract   withdraw, recede
Revere   worship, honor; *defame*
Revile   to abuse with words, scold
Rigor   strength, thoroughness
Ritual   a system of rites, ceremony
Rue   to be sorry for, regret
Rural   characteristic of the country as opposed to the city, countrified; *urban*

Sagacious   wise, shrewd; *unintelligent*
Salient   standing out, prominent; *hidden, unnoticeable*
Salubrious   healthful
Salutary   beneficial, wholesome; *harmful*
Sardonic   bitterly sarcastic, scornful, mocking
Satire   sarcasm, ridicule
Saturate   to fill full, soak
Scanty   minimal, inadequate; *sufficient, copious*
Schism   a division into hostile groups, split
Scoff   jeer, deride, ridicule
Scowl   to look angry by lowering the eyebrows, frown; *smile*
Scrupulous   conscientious, punctilious; *careless, negligent*
Scrutinize   examine, study; *glance*
Scurrilous   abusive in an indecent way, foul
Sedate   calm, serious; *nervous*
Sensual   indulging too much in the pleasure of the senses, lustful, lewd; *abstinent*
Servile   yielding through fear or lack of spirit, subservient
Simian   apelike, monkeylike
Simulate   to put on a false appearance, pretend
Sinuous   wavy, bending
Site   location
Skirmish   a brief fight, conflict
Slovenly   careless, untidy
Smug   too pleased with one's own goodness or cleverness, complacent
Sojourn   a brief stay, vacation

Solace   comfort or relief, consolation
Solicit   seek, entreat
Soliloquy   talking to oneself, monologue
Somber   gloomy, melancholy; *cheerful*
Sordid   dirty, contemptible
Spontaneous   impromptu, voluntary; *rehearsed*
Sporadic   occurring in scattered instances, occasional; *continual*
Spurious   false, illegitimate; *genuine*
Squander   to spend foolishly, waste; *preserve*
Squeamish   easily shocked, prudish, queasy
Stagnant   inactive, dull, sluggish; *active, flowing*
Stigma   mark of disgrace, stain
Stipulate   to demand as a condition of agreement, contract
Stoic   one who remains calm and represses his feelings, impassive
Strident   shrill, grating, cacophonous; *mellifluous*
Stringent   severe, harsh, strict, rigorous; *lax, lenient*
Stymie   to thwart, frustrate, hinder
Subservient   slavishly polite and obedient, submissive
Subterfuge   trick or excuse used to escape somethng unpleasant, deception
Subtle   artful, crafty, deft; *obvious*
Succinct   expressed briefly and clearly, concise; *verbose*
Succulent   juicy; *dry*
Succumb   to give way, yield, die; *persevere*
Sullen   showing bad humor or anger, gloomy, sulky
Sultry   hot and moist, torrid
Supercilious   scornful, haughty
Superfluous   more than is needed, unnecessary
Surfeit   too much, excess; *shortage, dearth*
Surmise   to infer, guess
Surreptitious   secret, stealthy, clandestine; *authorized, overt*

Taciturn   silent, reticent; *garrulous*
Taint   trace of decay, stain
Tangible   that which can be touched, real, actual; *indefinite*
Tantalize   to torment by holding out hopes that are repeatedly disappointed, tease
Taut   tightly drawn, tense; *lax, relaxed*
Temerity   foolish boldness, recklessness; *cautiousness*
Temper   moderate, soften; *incite*
Tenable   defensible; *untenable*
Tenacious   holding firmly, cohesive, persistent
Tentative   provisional, experimental; *final*
Terse   concise, succinct; *long-winded*
Tether   leash, rope
Therapy   curative treatment, rehabilitation
Thespian   an actor, tragedian
Throng   a crowd, mob
Thwart   to hinder, obstruct, foil
Timorous   fearful, afraid; *brave*
Titanic   enormous; *miniscule*
Torpid   sluggish, lethargic; *energetic*

Totalitarian   dictatorial
Toxic   poisonous; *harmless*
Tractable   docile, manageable; *rebellious*
Traduce   slander
Transgression   sin
Transient   fleeting, temporary, ephemeral; *permanent*
Transpire   to come to pass, happen
Tremulous   quivering, fearful; *dauntless*
Trenchant   keen, penetrating, incisive
Trite   stale ideas or language, hackneyed; *original, fresh*
Truncated   shortened, abbreviated; *unabridged*
Turbulent   disorderly, unruly, boisterous; *peaceful*
Tyro   amateur, beginner, novice; *professional*

Ubiquitous   everywhere at the same time, widespread
Ultimate   most remote or distant, farthest, final
Unconscionable   unscrupulous, unreasonable, excessive
Unctuous   oily in speech or manner, glib
Unilateral   affecting one side only, unilineal; *bilateral, reciprocal*
Unkempt   untidy, messy, slovenly; *meticulous*
Urbane   polished, suave; *unsophisticated*
Usurp   to take and hold by force or without right, supplant
Utopia   an ideal place, heaven, nirvana

Vacillate   to show indecision, hesitate, waver
Valor   bravery, courage; *fear, cowardice*
Vehement   acting with great force, passionate, violent
Vendetta   a blood feud, revenge
Veneer   a thin surface layer, gloss
Venerable   worthy of respect, impressive
Venom   poison, spite, malice
Verbose   wordy, prolix; *terse, succinct*
Vestige   a sign of something which has once existed, trace
Vexatious   annoying
Viable   workable, practical
Vicarious   taking the place of another thing or person, substitute
Vindicate   to clear from criticism, absolve; *implicate*
Virile   manly, masculine; *effeminate*
Virulent   bitterly hostile, poisonous
Vitriolic   sarcastic, caustic
Vivacious   full of life, spirited; *dull, inanimate*
Vociferous   clamorous, noisy
Volatile   changeable, fickle
Voluble   talkative, glib, garrulous; *taciturn, reticent*
Voluminous   massive in terms of writing, large, bulky; *meager, spare*
Voracious   greedy in eating, gluttonus, insatiable
Vulnerable   open to criticism or attack, weakened; *protected, invulnerable*

Wan   sickly, pale

Wane   to decline in power or importance, abate, subside; *wax, increase, revise*
Warranty   promise, pledge, authorization
Wheedle   to persuade by flattery, coax; *dissuade*
Whet   to sharpen, stimulate
Willful   stubborn; *flexible*
Wince   to draw back suddenly as in pain, flinch
Wrest   to take by force, usurp

Zealous   enthusiastic, fervent
Zenith   highest point, summit, peak; *nadir*

HOW TO MAKE A SPEECH

Calming "The Jitters"

People not experienced in speaking to audiences of any size in formal or semiformal situations are often overcome with terror at the prospect of preparing and delivering a speech. A trip to the dentist or a high-wire walk over the Grand Canyon seems a pleasant pastime by contrast.

But this terror can be reduced, or even eliminated, by gathering experience. That is not to say that concern, perhaps even slight apprehension, is not a plus when setting out to deliver a speech: A little nervousness will keep you on your toes and make your presentation more effective. Arrogance and condescension (born from terror) quickly convey themselves to an audience, however. Thus the speaker should be concerned about the task, but not paralyzed with fear.

Speaking is like any other activity. The more you speak in public, the easier the job becomes and the better you are at it. So, painful as it may seem at the outset, you should seize every opportunity to speak that comes your way.

How can you achieve the ideal state of mind so that speaking becomes a pleasure and not a hardship?

First, think of the times when you have been a member of an audience. As you settled back to listen to a speech, you undoubtedly had high hopes of being entertained or informed, or both, and wanted the speaker to do an excellent job.

So this is the first thing to keep in mind: The audience is with you, not against you. They want to hear your message, they want to appreciate your humor—in short, they want to like you and your speech.

Which is not to say there is no such thing as a hostile audience. If you undertook to deliver a talk on Calvin Coolidge as our most successful president to the Democratic National Committee, you would certainly not find the audience receptive. But, then, why would you accept such an assignment in the first place, unless your masochism is at a dangerously high level?

However, there are times when an audience is lukewarm or even potentially hostile, but will at least give your message a hearing. One of the most famous speeches in American history took place in 1896 when the Democratic National Convention was torn between so-called gold and silver wings of the party, with neither side in control. Then William Jennings Bryan delivered the "Cross of Gold" oration, calling on sectional prejudice and the self-pity and self-interest of residents of the Midwest, West, and South. He stampeded the convention and won his party's nomination, running on a platform that he dictated.

So, even if your audience is not wildly supportive at the outset, you can win them over with the appropriate appeal.

Knowing Your Audience

One of the most important rules of good speech-making is know your audience. Many times as an undergraduate, in a speech class or elsewhere on the campus, you will have the opportunity to appear before groups of your fellow students. They constitute a homogeneous sort of audience and one you should know very well; therefore, you should be able to reach them with maximum effectiveness.

In later life, the situation may not be so clear-cut. The corporate executive addressing a meeting of stockholders faces an audience whose members have widely varying educational backgrounds and, perhaps, intellectual levels. He or she must tailor the speech so that it is neither too lowbrow for the well educated nor too highbrow for the others.

How can proper tone be achieved? The primary rule is to select the level of language appropriate to the listeners, unless of course the aim is not to communicate, but to intimidate. Philologists teach us that there are formal, informal, and common levels of speech, but presumably a speaker would resort to the latter only on the rarest of occasions, if ever. Thus the speaker chooses between the two other levels, depending on the constituency of the audience. To one set of listeners there may be innumerable reasons for a course of action; to another there may be many reasons. To the former group, a theory may be pedestrian; to the latter, commonplace.

Equally important, however, is tailoring the content of the speech to the listeners. Those accustomed to receiving information orally are able to assimilate more data in more condensed form than those who are inexperienced listeners.

Hence, if invited to give a speech, the speaker should ascertain exactly what the audience will be like. To be told that the speech will be given to a group of teachers is not sufficient. What kind of teachers? Elementary school? High school? College? Graduate school? Teachers of English? Teacher of biology? Teachers of computer programming? Similarly, an address may be to parents of high school students, 90 percent of whom

LANGUAGE ARTS

go on to college, or to parents who see only 30 percent of their children undertake higher education. The address will have to be quite different, depending on the circumstances.

Presumably when you are invited to speak it is because of *your* expertise in a certain area, and so it is unwise to assume that your listeners are as knowledgeable in this field as you are. Yet the temptation to talk down to the audience must also be avoided. It was Mark Twain who urged speakers never to overestimate the amount of information people have, but never to underestimate their intelligence.

Purpose of Speech

Another significant element that must be taken into account while the speech is still in the planning stage is the purpose of that speech. It may have any one of four functions.

(1) The planners of an event may simply wish someone to stand up and make noises with his or her mouth. For instance, when a new municipal park is opened, it is considered appropriate to have the mayor or the parks commissioner preside over the ceremony and deliver some remarks. Everyone knows what is going to be said about increased recreational opportunities for young and old alike, the foresight of town planners, etc., etc., but a speech is traditional and so a speech is delivered. And what is expected must be given: The mayor would make a bad mistake if he or she used such an opportunity to launch into an attack on the opponents of proposed changes in the zoning ordinance. The listeners want familiar remarks, and familiar remarks are what must be delivered.

(2) The planners may wish to be entertained. The most frequently encountered example of this is the after-dinner speech. Following a three-martini cocktail hour and a heavy dinner with wine, the last thing diners want on their menu is a lengthy, turgid, fact-filled oration. They want their relaxed mood to continue and so they want to be amused. This accounts for the popularity of stage, screen, and television comedians on what is called the rubber-chicken circuit.

(3) You may be asked to transmit information. The prime example of this is the college classroom lecture, described by one cynic as the process by which the notes of the professor become the notes of the students without passing through the minds of either. Realistically, however, the system of supplementing textbook material with information gathered by the professor is standard in most colleges and universities. And there are many other examples of this function of speechmaking, especially in the sort of speech by a superior to his or her subordinates, outlining new procedures, or by an expert informing the general public about the details of his or her work that pertain to them.

(4) A speech may be given to affect the listeners and thus influence their future courses of action. The church sermon tries to teach a moral lesson and thus to cause congregants to adapt their lifestyles to the strictures of a particular faith. The political speech attempts to indicate why a particular party or faction supports the causes it does and so win more widespread acceptance of those causes from actual or potential voters. The sales pitch is calculated to convince the hearers that all of their problems will be solved by the purchase of a particular product, thereby seducing them into purchasing that product.

Length

The next issue you must consider is the length of the speech. Obviously this depends in large part on the content, yet you should not be oblivious to the fact that contemporary auditors have a shorter span of attention than did auditors of, say, a hundred years ago. Indeed, in the days before electronic media became so important in our lives, listening to a speech was frequently an afternoon or evening's entertainment, the equivalent of going to a movie or a play in our day.

In the United States today, the era of the two- or three-hour speech has passed. Even an hour-long address, like that customarily delivered by the keynote speaker at a national convention, is quite rare. Further, recent presidents, when speaking to the nation via the electronic media, have almost invariably confined themselves to a half hour or even less. The precedent for this was established in the 1930s, when President Franklin D. Roosevelt inaugurated what he called "Fireside Chats," delivered over the radio. These brief and rather informal talks replaced the bombastic and extended oratory common to an earlier era.

Generally it can be said that the shorter you make a speech, the more work it entails for you, but the more effective it is apt to be. The story is told of a college president asked to deliver a speech on any subject he chose, of any duration he chose. "If you want a two-hour speech, my fee will be $1000; if you want a 20–minute speech, my fee will be $2000," he said. The implication is clear: If a speaker is allowed to stand up and ramble on about anything that comes into his or her head, the preparation time will be minimal; if the speaker must organize the material carefully, he or she will have to spend time arranging and condensing the information to fit into the more confining limits.

Preparation

A good speaker never relies only on on-the-podium inspiration to get through a speech. The "something will come to me" attitude is dangerous in the extreme, for if the "something" fails to materialize, the speaker is in real trouble.

A way of avoiding this is to write the entire speech and memorize it, but the risk involved here is considerable. If your memory is infallible, then this is a possibility, but if you are capable of forgetting, it is risky. There can be few more embarrassing moments for a speaker reciting from memory than to lose the thread of a thought and then have to pick up the text, leaf through it to find the point at which he or she broke off, and only then resume the speech.

Another way is to read the speech. Sometimes, of

course, this is necessary, for instance, if a government official is outlining a proposal on, say, nuclear disarmament. He is going to be quoted by the electronic media and the newspapers, so it is essential to present the figures with 100 percent accuracy. Often the text of such a speech is written out and mimeographed in advance for presentation to media representatives, but if it is not, there is all the more reason to read the text. Modern technology has made it possible for the text of a speech to be presented line by line on a screen at the lectern so that the speaker can create the illusion that he or she is not reading (but there is a drawback to this, which is treated later).

The ideal way to proceed, once the outline of the speech has been determined, is to compile a set of notes, perhaps on small cards, say, 4 × 6 inches, listing either the principal points to be made or perhaps key phrases that will serve to remind the speaker of those points. Winston Churchill, one of the most effective speakers of the twentieth century, used the latter method, jotting down important groups of words to recall strategic portions of his arguments and filling in the rest of the speech with transitions.

Voice and Gesture

As Churchill so expertly demonstrated, words are the principal weapon in any speaker's arsenal, but there are two other vital elements in speechmaking: the voice and the gesture, which also involve stance and mobility.

Just as the violin or the piano is the musician's instrument, so the voice is the speaker's. A mellifluous and resonant voice can sometimes cover up a feeble argument, and has often done so. Likewise, volume can play a significant role. The story is told of one speaker who wrote this message to himself in the margin of his notes: "Argument weak here. Yell like hell."

As an instrument, the voice is not that complex. The lungs are the bellows that force air through the windpipe into the larynx, the voice box; the passage of air through these vocal cords makes sounds that differ according to the action of muscles, which make the cords vibrate. These sounds are received into the open space of the pharynx and are modified by the palate, tongue, teeth, and lips to produce words.

The principal difficulty most speakers have is with the lungs. Either the person is not breathing properly (i.e., deeply enough) or the speaker is so nervous that the larynx tightens up and the air does not have a free passage. The result is a heightened pitch and, in the worst cases, a shortness of breath that leaves the speaker all but gasping.

Keep in mind that you ought not be fatalistic about the pitch of your voice. To assume that the pitch of your voice is a gift (or a curse) from the gods or an inherited trait and that you can do nothing about changing it is wrong. Rarely do people complain about a voice pitched too low; the objection is most frequently to a high soprano or tenor voice. But the pitch of the voice can be lowered by breathing more deeply. This is the most significant key to greater resonance, and many exercises exist to help you. When you are undressed, take a slow breath as if you were breathing the air into your stomach. Put your thumbs at either side of your waistline, with your fingertips trying to reach each other across the body directly below your ribs. Try to imagine that you are filling your stomach with air. Now give several quick gasps and you will feel your body pressing against your fingertips. This indicates that the muscles of the diaphragm are pressing against the abdominal organs to make room for your expanding lungs. Repeated frequently, this should result in the outward pressure of the body's growing relatively stronger at each quick intake of breath.

An important corollary on the use of the voice is to remember that, because you are speaking for 30 minutes, this does not mean that you must fill the air with your voice for every one of the 1800 seconds involved. It is quite acceptable to pause in your delivery, for the alternative is to fill the spots where pauses may logically occur with meaningless sounds like "er" or "uh."

Almost as important as the words and the voice is platform presence, which involves stance, motion, and gesture. Most of our speech watching and auditing at the present time involves listening to either political speeches or sermons, neither of which provides an ideal model. When a president speaks, he is usually seated behind a desk so that we get, if not a talking head, a talking upper torso; if he is at a press conference, he is standing behind a lectern. Likewise a speaker at a political convention is bound to the lectern because he or she is reading from a Teleprompter; the clergy are confined to the pulpit.

To speak with maximum effectiveness, you should be able to move about—not of course that racing around the dais or stage is the best course, because too much motion can be distracting to the audience. Keeping distractions to a minimum is obviously important, since you hope to keep the listeners' attention focused on the content of the speech. Hence playing with a key chain or rattling coins in your pocket is hardly a valuable technique. However, by using the lectern as a sort of home base and moving around it, you can achieve sufficient mobility and still be able to consult your notes, if need be.

Your audience obviously will be looking at your head more than at your body, so a major question for you is what to let your eyes focus on. Ideally, you will look at all sections of the audience, but you do not want to do this at the expense of looking like a spectator at a tennis match. A good technique is to shift your focus as you shift your position on stage, or as you move from one idea to the next. Some speakers, on the other hand, prefer to focus on a single member of the audience who appears especially receptive, and to speak principally to that individual. Such a person should be in or near the center of the audience, however, not in the front row or, say, way off to the left side, or the majority of the audience will feel left out, a fatal flaw in a speaker.

Your platform presence begins the moment you are introduced, and it is most effective to pause for a moment to look at the audience before you begin to speak: not too long, for you have no wish to look as if you are trying to stare them down or as if you'd forgotten why you are there. A brief sweep of those present should prove worthwhile.

Many speakers are bothered by the problem of what to do with their hands as they talk. If you are at a lectern and are forced to stay there, then there is no problem, because most of the time your hands will be clasping the sides of the lectern. If you are moving around, you may feel the problem more acutely. When you are not gesturing, there is no objection to your clasping your hands in front of you or behind your back or even (if you are wearing a jacket) putting one or both hands in a jacket pocket.

As to gesturing, there are more don'ts than do's. Above all, do not keep your hands constantly in motion, making fluttering, birdlike motions; it is better not to gesture at all than to do this. Second, do not make small, constricted gestures. The sole complaint that was made about President John F. Kennedy's technique as a speaker was that he had the habit of stabbing the air with his right hand, index finger extended; the gesture became monotonous and was always picked up by those who were parodying him as a speaker, principally because it was such a tight movement. Third, do not employ excessively flamboyant or effusive gestures. The day of grandiloquent oratory has passed, and most of us have been conditioned by television watching to expect restrained movements by our speakers. Finally, do not resort to obvious gestures. In delivering a phrase like "between you and me," do not accompany the words with a wide sweep of the arm to take in the entire audience and then with a hand pointed at your own chest. Indeed, as you grow more experienced as a speaker, you may well find that you are no longer concerned about what to do with your hands; having lost your self-consciousness, you will do what comes naturally.

Content

As to the speech itself, clearly the circumstances determine its content. That is, as has already been pointed out, an after-dinner speech differs from a candidate's political address. Yet certain observations can be made about the parts encountered in most speeches.

(1) The introduction. When you are presented to the audience, acknowledge those in attendance in descending order of importance, with the presenter mentioned first, as, for example, "Mr. Chairman, Madam President, members of Alpha Alpha Alpha, ladies and gentlemen." Make it a point to look at the person or persons whose presence you are acknowledging, if you can conveniently do so. A speaker may create a poor impression by reciting this information while looking closely at his or her notes. If you intend to open your remarks with an anecdote or a joke, keep in mind that it must be apropos. Contemporary audiences are far too so-phisticated to react favorably to lines like, "A funny thing happened to me on my way to the banquet tonight." If you do not have a story that fits the situation, leave the comedy to the comedians and get down to business. It almost goes without saying that a story or a joke in bad taste will cause you to lose your audience even before you start.

Do not forget that the first five minutes of your speech will make or break you. If you have not captured your listeners' attention by that time, you probably never will.

Thus it becomes incumbent on you early on to let your auditors know what you are talking about and your point of view on that subject.

(2) The next order of business is to present details of the matter you are discussing. In doing this, it is vital that you present your facts in such a way that they can be assimilated. As has already been suggested, many listeners cannot take in large doses of material presented to them orally. After all, a speech is not an essay on the printed page. With the latter, if the reader misses the point on first reading, the text is still there to be consulted again. Not so with the former: If the listener does not understand on first hearing, there is no opportunity to review. With this in mind, you should reinforce every point you make with a simile, metaphor, or an illustration that vivifies that point and makes it more memorable.

(3) Then you should state what you propose to do about the situation under discussion and what you propose that your listeners should do. If, for example, you are delivering a political speech, you should make it clear that you intend to vote a certain way and urge that the members of the audience would find it wisest to do the same. There is, of course, no law that prohibits your suggesting that there are really no alternatives open to a rational human being. Your objective at this point is to make the strongest statement you can of your position and to impress on your audience that they ought to share that position.

(4) Following that, you should give your reasons for holding the position you do. If there is any historical background, that should be presented first. Then you should offer your arguments, starting with the most compelling and proceeding to the others in descending order of importance. When you are preparing your speech, discard any weak arguments.

(5) Then you should consider the arguments that have been raised against your position and tear them down. Here again there is no regulation mandating that you should state counter arguments completely or forcefully, since your aim is to make them appear inconsequential. That is, if there is one powerful argument against the stand you have taken, you may not wish to mention it at all. As for disposing of the others, a good logic textbook will provide the weapons for your use.

(6) Finally, there is the conclusion. This is the most significant portion of any speech, because most people remember best what they hear last. It is no coincidence that some of America's most famous speeches are famous just because their

endings are so forceful. Consider Daniel Webster's "Second Reply to Hayne," which ends, "Liberty *and* Union, now and for ever, one and inseparable." Or Abraham Lincoln's "Gettysburg Address," which concludes, "government of the people, by the people, for the people shall not perish from the earth." Or, lastly, the aforementioned "Cross of Gold" speech by Bryan, which ends, "You shall not press down upon the brow of labor this crown of thorns, you shall not crucify mankind upon a cross of gold." If media representatives are present, they may pick up a memorable phrase from the beginning or the middle of a speech and feature it, as happened with Franklin Roosevelt's "the only thing we have to fear is fear itself," and John Kennedy's, "Ask not what your country can do for you; ask what you can do for your country." If newspaper, television, and radio reporters are not among your listeners, however, it is best to build toward a climax at the end and save your best phrase for the last. You can be sure your speech has been successful when your audience is walking out at the end saying, "I could have listened to that speaker for hours," not "I thought that speaker would never stop."

LAW

Abandonment The intentional giving up of rights or property with no future intention to regain title or possession.

Abduction The criminal or wrongful act of forcibly taking away another person through fraud, persuasion or violence.

Abortion The premature termination of a pregnancy; may be either spontaneous (miscarriage) or induced. A woman enjoys a constitutional right to have an abortion during the first trimester of her pregnancy. During the second trimester, however, the state may regulate the abortion procedure, and during the third trimester the state may even proscribe abortion except where medically necessary to preserve the health of the mother.

Abrogate To annul, repeal, put an end to; to make a law void by legislative repeal.

Abscond To travel secretly out of the jurisdiction of the courts, or to hide in order to avoid a legal process such as a lawsuit or arrest.

Abstract of title A short history of title to land noting all conveyances, transfers, grants, wills, and judicial proceedings, and all encumbrances and liens, together with evidence of satisfaction and any other facts affecting title.

Accessory A person who aids or contributes to a crime as a subordinate. An accessory performs acts that aid others in committing a crime or in avoiding apprehension. In some jurisdictions an accessory is called an aider and abettor.

Accessory after the fact A person who harbors or assists a criminal knowing that he or she has committed a felony or is sought in connection with a crime.

Accessory before the fact A person who incites, counsels or orders another to commit a crime, but who is not present when it is committed.

Accomplice One who voluntarily joins another in committing a crime. An accomplice has the same degree of liability as the defendant.

Accuse To institute legal proceedings charging someone with a crime.

Accused The person charged with a crime; the defendant.

Acquit To set free from an accusation of guilt by a verdict of not guilty.

Acquittal A legal finding that an individual charged with a crime is not guilty and is therefore set free.

Action A court proceeding wherein one party prosecutes another party for a wrong done, or for protection of a right, or prevention of a wrong.

Act of God A manifestation of the forces of nature, which could not have been prevented or avoided by foresight or prudence. Proof that an injury was caused by an act of God may be used as a defense against negligence, though it will not excuse a contractual duty in the absence of statutory or contractual language to the contrary.

Ad hoc Latin term meaning "for this, for this particular purpose." An ad hoc committee is one commissioned for a special purpose, an ad hoc attorney is one designated for a particular client in a special situation.

Adjourn To postpone; to delay briefly a court proceeding through recess. An adjournment for a longer duration is termed a continuance. The term has a special meaning in the rules of legislatures which adjourn between legislative sessions, but recess for periods, of whatever duration within a single session.

Adjudication The determination of a controversy and pronouncement of judgment.

Administrator Someone appointed to handle the affairs of a person who has died without leaving a will. If the decedent left a will, an executor performs the same function.

Admissible evidence Evidence that may be introduced in court to aid the judge or jury in deciding the merits of a case. Each jurisdiction has established rules of evidence to determine what evidence is admissible. A judge may exclude otherwise admissible evidence when he or she determines that its value is outweighed by such factors as undue consumption of time, prejudice, confusion of issues, or a danger that the jury will be misled. A lurid, gory photograph, for example, depicting the scene of the crime, the weapon used, or the injury to the victim may have very high probative value as to several issues in a criminal trial, but since it may cause undue prejudice in the minds of the jurors, it will be excluded if there is any other way to prove the necessary facts.

Admission The voluntary acknowledgment that certain facts are true, a statement by the accused or by an adverse party that tends to support the charge or claim against him or her but is not necessarily sufficient to establish guilt or liability. In civil procedure, an admission is a pretrial discovery device by which one party asks another for a positive affirmation or denial of a material fact or allegation at issue.

Adopt To agree to, appropriate, borrow, derive from, make use of; the formal process terminating legal rights between a child and his or her natural parents and creating new rights between the child and the adopting parents.

Adoption The legal process by which the parent/child relationship is created between persons not so related by blood. The adopted child becomes the heir and is entitled to all other privileges belonging to a natural child of the adoptive parent.

Adversary Opponent or litigant in a legal controversy or litigation.

Advisory opinion A formal opinion by a judge, court, or law officer upon a question of law submitted by a legislative body or government official but not presented in an actual court case or adversary proceeding. Such an opinion has no binding force as law.

Advocacy The active taking up of a legal cause; the art of persuasion. A legal advocate is a lawyer.

Affidavit A written statement made under oath before an officer of the court, a notary public, or another person legally authorized to certify the statement.

Affirm To approve or confirm; refers to an appellate court decision that a lower court judgment is correct and should stand.

Affirmative action A positive step taken to correct conditions resulting from past discrimination or from violations of a law.

Affirmative action programs Hiring practices and other employment programs adopted to eliminate discrimination in the employment of minority persons. Such programs are required by federal law.

A fortiori   Latin term meaning "with stronger reason." An inference that because a certain conclusion or fact is true, then the same reasoning makes it even more certain that a second conclusion is true. For example: Dan is accused of aiding in a bank robbery in which all of the participants were over six feet tall. One suspect has already been cleared by police because he is only five feet six inches. Since Dan is only five feet two inches, a fortiori he could not have participated in the robbery and will also be cleared.

Age discrimination   The denial of privileges as well as other unfair treatment of employees on the basis of age, which is prohibited by federal law under the Age Discrimination Unemployment Act of 1967. This act was amended in 1978 to protect employees up to 70 years of age.

Agency   A relationship in which one person (agent) acts on behalf of another (principal) with the authority of the latter. *Compare* **Partnership**.

Aggrieved party   One who has been injured or has suffered a loss. A person is aggrieved by a judgment, order or decree whenever it operates prejudicially and directly upon his or her property, or monetary or personal rights.

Aid and abet   To knowingly encourage or assist another in the commission or attempted commission of a crime.

Alias   "Otherwise known as," an indication that a person is known by more than one name. "AKA" and "a/k/a" mean "also known as" and are used in indictments to introduce the listing of an alias.

Alibi   An excuse that proves the physical impossibility that a suspected person could have committed the crime.

Alien   One who is not a citizen of the country in which he lives. A *resident alien* is a person who has been admitted to permanent resident status but has not been granted citizenship. An *illegal alien* is a noncitizen who has not been given permission by immigration authorities to reside in the country in which he is living.

Alimony   Court-ordered payment for the support of one's estranged spouse in the case of divorce or separation.

Allegation   In a pleading, an assertion of fact; a statement of what the contributing party expects to prove.

Amend   To alter. One amends a statute by changing (but not abolishing) an established law. One amends a pleading by adding to or subtracting from an already existing pleading.

American Civil Liberties Union (ACLU)   A national organization, founded in 1920, that seeks to enforce and preserve the rights and civil liberties guaranteed by the federal and state constitutions. Its activities include handling cases opposing allegedly repressive legislation, and publishing reports and informational pamphlets.

Amicus curiae   Latin term meaning "friend of the court." A qualified person who is not a party to the action but gives information to the court on a question of law. The function of an *amicus curiae* is to call attention to some information that might escape the court's attention.

Amnesty   A pardon extended to a group of persons excusing them for offenses against the government.

Annul   To make void; to dissolve that which once existed, as to annul a marriage. Annulment wipes out or invalidates the entire marriage, whereas divorce only ends the marriage from that point on and does not affect the former validity of the marriage.

Answer   The defendant's principal pleading in response to the plaintiff's complaint. It must contain a denial of all the allegations the defendant wishes to dispute, as well as any affirmative defenses by the defendant and any counterclaim against the plaintiff.

Antitrust laws   Statutes that promote free competition by outlawing such things as monopolies, price discrimination, and collaboration, for the purpose of restraint of trade, between two or more business enterprises in the same market. The two major U.S. antitrust laws are the Sherman Act and the Clayton Act.

A posteriori   Latin term that means "from the most recent point of view." Relates to knowledge gained through actual experience or observation, rather than through logical conclusions. *Compare* **A priori**.

Appeal   A request to a higher court to review and reverse the decision of a lower court. On appeal, no new evidence is introduced; the higher court is limited to considering whether the lower court erred on a question of law or gave a decision plainly contrary to the evidence presented during trial. Unless special permission is granted by the higher court to hear an interlocutory appeal, an appeal cannot be made until the lower court renders a final judgment.

Appearance   The required coming into court of a plaintiff or defendant in an action either by himself or through his attorney. An appearance is a voluntary submission to the jurisdiction of the court.

Appellant   The party to a lawsuit who appeals the decision to a higher court. *Compare* **Appellee**.

Appellate Court (Appeals Court)   A court having the authority to review the law applied by a lower court in the same case. In most instances, the trial court first decides a lawsuit, with review of its decision then available in an appellate court.

Appellee   The party prevailing in the lower court who argues, on appeal, against setting aside the lower court's judgment. In some state courts this party is referred to as the respondent. *Compare* **Appellant**.

A priori   Latin term meaning "from the former, from the first." Modern usage has deviated significantly from the Latin. An a priori conclusion or judgment is one that is necessarily true, that is neither proved by nor capable of being disproved by experience, and that is known to be true by a process of reasoning independent of all factual evidence. The term is commonly used to indicate a judgment that is widely believed to be certain or that is introduced presumptively, without analysis or investigation. Thus to accuse someone of having assumed a fact or conclusion *a priori is* often to disparage him or her for having failed to support a judgment through evidence or analysis. *Compare* **A posteriori**.

Arbiter   A person (other than a judicial officer) appointed by the court to decide a controversy according to the law. Unlike an arbitrator, the arbiter needs the court's confirmation of his decision for it to be final.

Arbitration   Submitting a controversy to an impartial person, the arbitrator, chosen by the two parties in the dispute to determine an equitable settlement. Where the parties agree to be bound by the determination of the arbitrator, the process is called *binding arbitration*. In labor law, arbitration has become an important means of settling disputes, and the majority of labor contracts provide for arbitration of disputes over the meaning of contract clauses.

Arbitrator   An impartial person chosen by the parties to solve a dispute between them, who is empowered to make a final determination concerning the issue(s) in controversy, who is bound only by his own discretion, and from whose decision there is no appeal.

Argument   A course of reasoning intended to establish a position and to induce belief.

Arraign   To bring a defendant to court to answer the charge under which an indictment has been handed down.

Arraignment   An initial step in the criminal process in which the defendant is formally charged with an offense, given a copy of the complaint, indictment, information or other accusatory instrument, and informed of his constitutional rights, including the pleas he may enter. Where the appearance is shortly after the arrest, it may properly be called a presentment since often no plea is taken.

Arrest   To deprive a person of liberty by legal authority; in the technical criminal law sense, to seize an alleged or suspected offender to answer for a crime.

Arson   The willful and malicious burning of another's house; sometimes expanded by statute to include acts similar to burning (such as exploding) or the destruction of property other than dwellings.

Articles of impeachment   A formal statement of the grounds upon which the removal of a public official is sought, similar to an indictment in an ordinary criminal proceeding. In the federal system, articles of impeachment are voted by the House of Representatives, with the trial occurring before the Senate.

Articles of incorporation   The document that creates a private corporation, according to the general corporation laws of the state.

Artifice   A fraud or a cunning device used to accomplish some wrong; usually implies craftiness or deceitfulness.

Assault   An attempt or apparent attempt to inflict bodily injury upon another by using unlawful force, accompanied by the apparent ability to injure that person if not prevented. An assault need not result in a touching so as to constitute a battery. Thus, no physical injury need be proved to establish an assault. An assault may be either a civil or criminal offense. Some jurisdictions have defined criminal assault to include battery—the actual physical injuring. *Aggravated assault* is an assault with a dangerous or deadly weapon.

Associate justice   A member of the U.S. Supreme Court, other than the chief justice; the

title held by a judge, other than the presiding judge, on the highest court of some states.

Assumption of risk   In torts, an affirmative defense used by the defendant in a negligence suit claiming that plaintiff had knowledge of an obviously dangerous condition or situation and yet voluntarily exposed himself to the hazard thereby relieving the defendant of legal responsibility for any resulting injury. In contract law, the agreement by an employee to assume the risks of ordinary hazards arising out of his occupation.

At law   That which pertains to or is governed by the rules of law, as distinguished from the rules of equity; according to the rules of the common law. In England, and later in the United States courts of law developed strict rules establishing the kinds of causes of action that could be maintained and the kinds of remedies that were available. Courts of equity established different rules and remedies, partly to mitigate the rigors of the law courts. "At law" and "in equity" thus refer to two different bodies of jurisprudence.

Attachment   A legal proceeding by which a defendant's property is taken into custody and held for payment of a judgment in the event plaintiff's demand is later established and judgment is rendered in his favor.

Attempt   An overt act, beyond mere preparation, moving directly toward the actual commission of a criminal offense. The attempt to accomplish a criminal act is often made a crime itself, separate and distinct from the crime that is attempted.

Attest   To affirm as true; to sign one's name as a witness to the execution of a document; to bear witness to.

Attorney-client privilege   Protection of the confidential communications between a client and his or her attorney from disclosure to any other party; can be waived by the client but not by the attorney.

Attorney General   The chief law enforcement officer of the federal government or of a state government.

Attractive nuisance   The doctrine in tort law that holds that one who maintains something dangerous on his premises that is likely to attract children is required to reasonably protect the children against the dangers of that attraction. Thus, one has a duty to fence swimming pools, to remove doors from discarded refrigerators, to enclose partially constructed buildings, and to be sensitive to other potentially dangerous conditions that attract curious children.

Audit   An inspection of the accounting records and procedures of a business, government unit or other reporting entity by a trained accountant, for the purpose of verifying the accuracy and completeness of the records. It may be conducted by a member of the organization (internal audit) or by an outsider (independent audit).

Auditor   A public officer charged by law with the duty of examining and verifying the expenditure of public funds; an accountant who performs a similar function for private parties.

Autopsy   The dissection of a body to determine the cause of death. It may involve the inspection of important organs in order to determine the nature of a disease or abnormality.

B

Bad debt A debt that is not collectible and is therefore worthless to the creditor; a debt that becomes uncollectible because the debtor is insolvent.

Bad faith Breach of faith; a willful failure to respond to plain, well-understood statutory or contractual obligations; dishonesty in fact in the conduct or transaction concerned.

Bail A monetary or other security given to secure the release of a defendant until time of trial and to assure the defendant's appearance at every stage of the proceedings.

Bail bond The document executed in order to secure the release of an individual in legal custody. The person who puts up bail generally forfeits security given in the event the defendant jumps bail—that is, fails to appear as required for court dates.

Bailiff A court attendant or officer who has charge of a court session. The bailiff keeps order, custody of the jury and custody of the prisoners while in court.

Bankruptcy Popularly defined as insolvency, the inability of a debtor to pay debts as they become due. Technically, however, it is the legal process under the Federal Bankruptcy Act by which assets of the debtor are liquidated as quickly as possible to pay off creditors and to discharge the bankrupt, or free him of his debts, so that he may start anew.

Bankruptcy Court A U.S. district court created specifically to carry out the Federal Bankruptcy Act.

Bar The complete body of attorneys, so called because they are the persons privileged to enter beyond the bar that separates the general courtroom audience from the judge's bench. The *case at bar* refers to the particular action before the court. In procedure, *bar* refers to a barrier to the relitigating of an issue. A bar operates to deny a party the right or privilege of rechallenging issues in subsequent litigation. The prevailing party in a lawsuit can use the favorable decision to bar retrial of the action.

Barrister In England, a legal practitioner whose function is similar to that of an American trial lawyer, although the barrister does not prepare the case from the start. This is done by a solicitor who assembles the materials necessary for presentation to the court and settles cases out of court.

Battery The unlawful touching of or use of force on another person willfully or in anger. Battery may be considered either a tort, giving rise to civil liability for damages to the victim, or a crime.

Bench The court; the judges composing the court collectively; the place where the trial judge sits.

Bench warrant A court order for the arrest of a person; commonly issued to compel a person's attendance before the court to answer a charge of contempt or if a witness or a defendant fails to attend after a subpoena has been duly served.

Beneficiary A person for whose benefit property is held in trust. A person to whom another is in a fiduciary relation, whether the relation is one of agency, trust, guardianship, partnership or otherwise; a person named to receive the proceeds or benefits of an insurance policy; a person named in a will to receive certain property.

Bequeath To give or leave through a will a gift of personal property, as distinguishing from a gift of real property. The term disposition encompasses both a bequest of personalty and a devise of realty.

Bequest A gift of personal property by will. A devise ordinarily passes real estate, and a bequest passes personal property.

Bestiality Sexual intercourse with an animal. Bestiality constitutes a crime against nature.

Bigamy The criminal offense of having two or more wives or husbands at the same time. A bigamous marriage is void.

Bill An order drawn by one person on another to pay a certain sum of money in commercial law, an account for goods sold, services rendered, and work done. In the law of negotiable instruments, any form of paper money. In legislation, a draft of a proposed statute submitted to the legislature for enactment. In equity pleadings, the name of the pleading by which the complainant sets out his or her cause of action.

Bill of lading In commercial law, the receipt a carrier gives to a shipper for goods given to the carrier for transportation. The bill evidences the contract between the shipper and the carrier, and can also serve as a document of title creating in the person possessing the bill ownership of the goods shipped.

Bill of particulars A detailed statement provided in a criminal case, as an amplification of the pleading to which it relates, in order to advise the court, and, more particularly, the defendant, of the specific facts or allegations to which he or she will be required to respond.

Bill of Rights The first ten amendments to the U.S. Constitution, that part of any constitution that sets forth the fundamental rights of citizenship. It is a declaration of rights that are substantially immune from government interference.

Binder A written memorandum of the most important items of a preliminary contract; an insurer's acknowledgment of its contract to protect the insured against accidents of a specified kind until a formal policy can be issued or until the insurer gives notice of its election to terminate.

Blackmail The demanding of money either for performing an existing duty, or for preventing an injury, or exercising an influence; the extortion of things of value from a person by threats of a personal injury, or by threatening to accuse the person of a crime or an immoral conduct, which if true, would tend to disgrace the person.

Blue laws Strict statutes or local ordinances most frequently enacted to preserve observance of the Sabbath by prohibiting commercial activity on Sundays. With increasing frequency, blue laws are being abolished so that people may freely choose activities without regard to societal notions as to appropriate Sunday conduct.

Blue sky laws State laws regulating the sale of corporate securities through investment companies, enacted to prevent the sale of securities of fraudulent enterprises.

Boilerplate Any standardized or preprinted form for agreements. Also, standardized language, as on a printed form containing the terms of a lease or sales contract, often phrased to the advantage of the party furnishing the form, with the expectation that the contract will be signed without being carefully examined.

Bona   Latin term meaning "good, virtuous," also, goods, property.

Bona fide   Latin term meaning "in good faith." Without fraud or deceit; genuine.

Bond   Evidence of a long-term debt that is legally guaranteed as to the principal and interest specified on the face of the bond certificate. The rights of the holder are specified in the bond indenture, which contains the legal terms and conditions under which the bond was issued. Bond debt is secured or guaranteed primarily by the ability of the issuer (borrower) to pay the interest when due and to repay the principal at maturity.

Brain death   The irreversible cessation of brain function; statutory or case law definitions of death are being expanded in many jurisdictions to include this. Among the factors considered are the failure to respond to external stimuli, the absence of breathing or spontaneous movement, the absence of reflex movement, and a flat electroencephalograph reading following a 24-hour observation period.

Breach   Failure to perform some contracted-for or agreed-upon act, or to comply with a legal duty owed to another or to society.

Breach of contract   A wrongful nonperformance of any contractual duty of immediate performance; failing to perform acts promised, by hindering or preventing such performance or by repudiating the duty to perform.

Breach of the peace   Conduct that destroys or menaces public order and tranquility, including violent acts or acts or words likely to produce violence in others. In its broadest sense the term refers to any criminal offense.

Breaking and entering   Two of the elements necessary to constitute a burglary, consisting of the use of physical force, however slight, to remove an obstruction to an entrance. For example, pushing open a door that is ajar, followed by unauthorized entry into a building, is sufficient to constitute the breaking and entering elements of burglary.

Bribery   The voluntary giving of something of value to influence the performance of an official duty.

Brief   A written argument concentrating upon legal points and authorities (i.e., precedents) used by the lawyer to convey to the court (trial or appellate) the essential facts of his or her client's case. This includes a statement of the questions of law involved, the law that should be applied, and the application the lawyer desires made of that law by the court.

Broker   One who for a commission or fee brings parties together and assists in negotiating contracts between them; a person whose business it is to bring buyer and seller together.

Burden of proof   1. The duty of a party to substantiate an allegation or issue, either to avoid dismissal of that issue early in the trial or to convince the court of the truth of that claim and hence to prevail in a civil or criminal suit. 2. The duty of a plaintiff, at the beginning of a trial, to make a *prima facie* showing of each fact necessary to establish the existence of a cause of action; referred to as the duty of producing evidence (also burden of evidence or pro-

duction burden). 3. The obligation to plead each element of a cause of action or suffer a dismissal; referred to as the *pleading burden*.

Burglary   In common law, an actual breaking into a dwelling, with intent to commit a felony. Some statutes have expanded burglary to include any unlawful entry into or remaining in a building or vehicle with intent to commit a crime.

Bylaws   Rules adopted for the regulation of an association's or corporation's own actions. In corporation law, bylaws are self-imposed rules that constitute an agreement or contract between a corporation and its members to conduct the corporate business in a particular way. In the absence of law to the contrary, under common law the power to make bylaws resides in the members or shareholders of the corporation. When used by corporations, the term bylaws deals with matters of corporate structure and machinery as distinguished from regulations which are imposed by a board of directors to deal with problems relating to the day-to-day management.

Canon   One of a body of rules to guide the interpretation of statutes, ordinances, etc. In ecclesiastical law a rule primarily concerning the clergy, but also at times embracing lay members of a congregation.

Capital offense   A criminal offense punishable by death, for which bail is generally unavailable to the defendant.

Capital punishment   Imposition of the death penalty.

Case   An action, cause, suit, or controversy, at law or in equity.

Cause of action   A claim in law and fact sufficient to form the basis of a valid lawsuit, a *right of action* is the legal right to sue, a *cause of action* is the composite of facts that gives rise to a right of action.

Caveat   Latin term meaning "let him beware." A warning or caution. A suggestion to a judicial officer to take care how he or she acts in a particular matter and to suspend the proceeding until the merits of the issue thus raised (the caveat) are determined.

Caveat emptor   Latin for "let the buyer beware." This phrase expresses the rule of law that the purchaser buys at his or her own risk.

Cease and desist order   An order of a court or other body having judicial authority prohibiting the person or entity to which the order is directed from undertaking or continuing a particular activity or course of conduct. Such an order may be issued upon a showing, to a degree of certainty or probability, that the conduct is unlawful or likely to be found unlawful.

Censure   A reproach or reprimand, especially when delivered by a judicial or other official body; the act of pronouncing such a reproach or reprimand.

Certificate of occupancy   A document issued by a local government agency signifying that a building or dwelling conforms to local building code regulations.

Certificate of title   A document indicating ownership, similar to a bill of sale and usually associated with the sale of new motor vehicles.

Certiorari   Latin term meaning "to be informed of." A means of gaining appellate review; a common law writ, issued by a superior court to a lower court, commanding the latter to certify and return to the former a particular case record so that the higher court may inspect the proceedings for irregularities or errors.

Challenge   An objection by a party (or party's lawyer) to the inclusion of a particular prospective juror as a member of the jury that is to hear that party's cause or trial, with the result that the prospective juror is disqualified from the case.

Chancellor   In English law, the name of the chief judge of the court of chancery. In American law, a judge in a court of chancery.

Chancery   The jurisprudence that is exercised in a court of equity; synonymous with equity or equitable jurisdiction.

Chapter 11   Under Chapter 11, a debtor is permitted to postpone all payments on debts so that he or she can reorganize the business. While other bankruptcy proceedings seek to have the debtor's assets sold and to have all the creditors paid to the extent possible, Chapter 11 seeks to give the debtor a breathing spell with the hope that the business will recover and all creditors will be fully repaid. The goal is a plan that specifies how much the creditors will be paid, in what form they will be paid, and other details.

Character witness   A witness who testifies at another person's trial, vouching for that person's high moral character and standing in the community, but who does not have knowledge of the validity of the charges against that person.

Charge   In criminal law, a description of the underlying offense in an accusation or indictment. In trial practice, an address delivered by the court to the jury at the close of the case, telling them the principles of law they are to apply in reaching a decision. The charge may also include instructions given during the trial for the jury's guidance.

Charter   A document issued by the government establishing a corporate entity.

Chattel   Any tangible, movable thing; personal property as opposed to real property; goods.

Chattel mortgage   A mortgage on personal property created to secure the payment of monies owed or the performance of some other obligation. This security device has for the most part been replaced by the security agreements available under the Uniform Commercial Code.

Chief justice   The presiding member of certain courts with more than one judge; especially, the presiding member of the U.S. Supreme Court who is the principal administrative officer of the federal judiciary.

Child support   The amount of money the court requires one spouse to pay to the other who has custody of the children born of the marriage. It may be imposed by the court with or without an award of alimony.

Circuit court   One of several courts in a given jurisdiction; a part of a system of federal courts extending over one or more counties or districts formerly applied to the U.S. courts of appeals. *Compare* **District Court**.

Circumstantial evidence   Indirect evidence; secondary facts from which a principal fact may be reasonably inferred.

Citation   1. A reference to a legal authority, for example, a citation to a statute or case. 2. A writ similar to a summons, in that it commands the appearance of a party in a proceeding. The object of a citation is to give the court proper jurisdiction and to notify the defendant that a suit has been filed.

Cite   1. To summon; to order to appear, as before a tribunal. 2. To make reference to a text, statute, case or other legal authority in support of a proposition or argument; also the reference thus made.

Civil   The branch of law that pertains to suits other than criminal practice and is concerned with the rights and duties of persons in contract, tort, etc.

Civil Action   An action to protect a private right or to compel a civil remedy in a dispute between private parties, as distinguished from a criminal prosecution.

Civil disobedience   Refusal to obey government demands or commands, especially as a nonviolent and usually collective means of forcing concessions from the government.

Civil law   1. Roman law embodied in the Justinian Code and presently prevailing in most western European states, it is also the foundation of the law of Louisiana. 2. The law concerned with noncriminal matters. 3. The body of laws established by a state or nation, as distinguished from natural law.

Civil rights   The nonpolitical rights of all citizens, especially those rights relating to personal liberty. Civil rights differ from civil liberties in that civil rights are positive in nature, and civil liberties, negative; that is, civil liberties are immunities from governmental interference or limitations on governmental action (as in the First Amendment) that have the effect of reserving rights to individuals.

Claim   The assertion of a right to money or property; the sum of facts giving rise to a right that is enforceable in the courts. A claim must show the existence of a right, an injury, and damages. One who makes a claim is the claimant.

Class action   A suit brought by one or more members of a large group of persons on behalf of all members of the group. If the court permits the class action, all members must receive notice of the action and must be given an opportunity to exclude themselves. Members who do not exclude themselves are bound by the judgment, whether favorable or not.

Clear and present danger   In constitutional law, a standard used to determine if one's First Amendment right to speak may be curtailed or punished. If the words are spoken in such circumstances and are of such a nature as to create a clear and present danger that they will bring about certain evils that government has a right to prevent, the government may prohibit or punish the use of those words.

Clerk   An assistant or a subordinate. A *court clerk* is an officer whose duties include keeping records, issuing process, and entering judgment. A *law clerk* is an assistant to a lawyer or a judge, whose primary job is to aid in researching and writing briefs or opinions and in handling cases.

Closing   The consummation of a transaction involving the sale of real estate or of an interest in real estate, usually by payment of the purchase price (or some agreed portion), delivery of the deed or other instrument of title, and finalizing of collateral matters.

Cloture   In legislative assemblies that permit unlimited debate (filibuster), a procedure or rule by which debate is ended so that a vote may be taken on the matter. In the U.S. Senate, a two-thirds majority vote of the body is required to invoke cloture and terminate debate.

Code   A systematic compilation of laws, for example, the Criminal Code (referring to penal laws) and the Motor Vehicle Code (referring to laws relating to motor vehicles).

Codefendant   A defendant who is joined together with one or more other defendants in a single action.

Code of professional responsibility   A set of rules based on ethical considerations that govern the conduct of lawyers; passed by the American Bar Association and adopted by most states, enforced by state disciplinary boards. Some states require lawyers to prove their knowledge of the code by passage of a course or test before being allowed to practice in that state.

Codicil   A supplement to a will, whose purpose is to add to, subtract from, or qualify, modify or revoke the provisions of a prior will. For example: Larry executed his will at a time when his relationship with his brother was at a low point. As the relationship improves, Larry writes a codicil to his will providing that a certain amount of money pass to the brother. The codicil also revokes any statement in the will that specifically denies the brother anything.

Collusion   1. The making of a secret agreement with another to commit fraud or engage in other illegal activity, or in legal activity with an illegal end in mind. 2. An agreement between husband and wife to suppress facts or to make up evidence important to the existence of lawful grounds for divorce.

Comity (comitas)   A rule of courtesy by which one court defers to the concomitant jurisdiction of another, most often used in reference to the long-standing public policy against federal court interference with state criminal proceedings.

Commercial law   The body of law that concerns the rights and obligations of persons in their commercial dealings with one another, such as the Uniform Commercial Code and laws prohibiting unfair trade practices.

Common law   The system of jurisprudence which originated in England and was later applied in the United States, that is based on judicial precedent (court decisions) rather than legislative enactment (statutes) and is therefore derived from principles rather than rules. In the absence of statutory law regarding a particular subject, the judge-made rules of common law are the law on that subject. Thus the traditional phrase "at common law" refers to the state of the law in a particular field prior to the enactment of legislation in that field.

Common-law marriage   One based not upon ceremony and compliance with legal formalities, but upon the agreement of two persons, legally competent to marry, to cohabit with the intention of being husband and wife, usually for a minimum period of seven years.

Community property   All property that a husband and wife acquire by joint effort during marriage. Property owned prior to marriage or acquired by gift or inheritance is considered separate property. Only some states have adopted the community property doctrine.

Commutation   In criminal law, substituting a lesser punishment for a greater one, such as life imprisonment for a death sentence, a shorter term for a longer one. Commutation is the prerogative of the chief executive (president or governor), who possesses the power of executive clemency. A commutation can be granted only after a conviction, whereas other forms of clemency, such as a pardon, can be granted at any time. Also, a commutation merely lessens punishment, while a pardon removes all legal disabilities of a conviction.

Competent   Properly or legally qualified, able; capable of understanding or of acting reasonably. Competent evidence is both relevant and proper to the issue being litigated. A competent court has proper jurisdiction over the person or property at issue. A criminal defendant is competent to stand trial if he is able to consult with a lawyer with a reasonable degree of rational understanding and has a rational as well as a factual understanding of the proceedings against him. An individual is competent to make a will if he understands the extent of his property, the identity of the natural objects of his bounty, and the consequences of making a will.

Complainant   The party who initiates the complaint in an action or proceeding, practically synonymous with petitioner and plaintiff. The appropriate term to use is determined by the nature of the proceeding and the court in which it is instituted.

Complaint   In a civil action, the first pleading of the plaintiff setting out the facts on which the claim is based; the purpose is to give notice to the adversary of the nature and basis of the claim asserted. In criminal law, the preliminary charge or accusation made by one person against another to the appropriate court or officer, usually a magistrate. However, court proceedings, such as a trial, cannot be instituted until an indictment or information has been handed down against the defendant.

Concur   To agree. A concurring opinion agrees with the conclusion of the majority but may state different reasons why such a conclusion is reached.

Concurrent   Existing together; in conjunction with. In criminal law, *concurrent sentence* describes multiple sentences that a convicted defendant is to serve at the same time.

Condemn   1. To take private property for public use, such as the building of a highway, with or without consent but for just compensation. 2. To declare legally useless or unfit for habitation, as an unsafe building. 3. To sentence to death a person convicted of a capital offense.

Confession   An admission of guilt or other incriminating statement by the accused; not admissible at trial unless voluntarily made.

Confidence game   A scheme by which a swindler wins the confidence of his victim and then cheats him of his money by taking advantage of the confidence reposed in him.

Confiscate   1. With regard to acts by a government entity, to take private property without just compensation. 2. To seize goods or property and divest the owner of his or her proprietary rights usually as a result of some violation of the law involving the goods or property seized.

Conflict of interests   An inconsistency between the public interest and the personal interest of a public official that arises in connection with the performance of official duties.

Conjugal rights   The rights of married persons which include companionship, domestic happiness, the comforts of dwelling together, joint property rights, and the intimacies of domestic relations. In prison, a conjugal visitation permits an opportunity for sexual intimacy between the inmate and his or her spouse.

Conscientious objector   A status recognized by U.S. Selective Service ("draft") laws and accorded to one who, in good conscience, because of religious belief, is opposed to war. Such a person may be excused from participation in military service otherwise required by law and may be permitted to substitute community service.

Consideration   Something of value given in return for performance or promise of performance for the purpose of forming a contract; generally required to make a promise binding and to make agreement of the parties enforceable as a contract. Consideration distinguishes a contract from a gift.

Conspiracy   A combination of two or more persons to commit an unlawful act, or to commit a lawful act by unlawful means. A conspiracy to injure another is an actionable tort; it may also be a criminal offense.

Conspirator (Coconspirator)   One involved in a conspiracy; one who acts with another, or others, in furtherance of an unlawful transaction.

Constitution   The fundamental principles of law by which a government is created and a country is administered. In Western democratic theory, a mandate from the people in their sovereign capacity, concerning how they shall be governed. It is distinguished from a statute, which is a rule decided by legislative representatives and subject to limitations of the Constitution.

Constitutional rights   Individual liberties granted by the State or Federal Constitutions and protected from governmental interference.

Construction   An interpretation of something not totally clear. To determine construction of a statute or constitution is to decide the meaning of an ambiguous part of it. *Strict construction* refers to a conservative or literal interpretation of statutes, stressing rigid adherence to terms specified.

Consumer protection   Refers to laws designed to aid retail consumers of goods and services that have been improperly manufactured, delivered, performed, handled or described. Such laws provide the retail consumer with additional protections and remedies not generally provided to merchants and others who engage in business transactions.

Contempt of court   An act or omission tending to interfere with orderly administration of justice, or to impair the dignity of the court or respect for its authority.

Contingent fee   A charge made by an attorney for services rendered to his or her client, recovery of which depends upon a successful outcome of the case. The amount is often agreed to be a percentage of the client's recovery. Such fee arrangements are often used in negligence cases, but it is unethical for an attorney to charge a criminal defendant a fee contingent upon the result.

Continuance   The adjournment or postponement to a specified subsequent date, of an action pending in a court.

Contract   A promise, for the breach of which the law provides a remedy, or the performance of which the law recognizes as a duty; a transaction involving two or more individuals whereby each has reciprocal rights to demand performance of what is promised.

Controlled substance   A drug whose general availability is restricted, any substance that is strictly regulated or outlawed because of its potential for abuse or addiction. Controlled substances include narcotics, stimulants, depressants, hallucinogens, and cannabis.

Contumacy   Willful disobedience to the summons or orders of a court; overt defiance of authority. Contumacious conduct may result in finding of contempt of court.

Convey   In real property law, to transfer property from one to another, by means of a written instrument and other formalities.

Convict   One who has been determined by the court to be guilty of the crime charged; to determine such guilt.

Conviction   The result of a legal proceeding in which the guilt of a party is ascertained and upon which sentence or judgment is founded. The confession of an accused in open court or a verdict that ascertains and publishes the fact of guilt are both sufficient to constitute a conviction.

Copyright   Protection by statute or by the common law giving authors and artists exclusive right to publish their works or to determine who may so publish. When by statute, copyright is exclusively a matter of federal law.

Coroner   A public official who investigates the causes and circumstances of suspicious deaths that occur within his or her jurisdiction and makes a finding in a coroner's inquest.

Corporation   An association of shareholders (or a single shareholder) created under law as an artificial person, having a legal entity separate from the individuals who compose it, with the capacity of continuous existence or succession, and the capacity of taking, holding and conveying property, suing and being sued, and exercising, like a natural person, other powers that are conferred on it by law. A corporation's liability is normally limited to its assets, the shareholders are thus protected against personal liability for the corporation. The corporation is taxed at special tax rates, and the stockholders must pay an additional tax upon dividends or other profits from the corporation. Corporations are subject to regulation by the state of incorporation and by the jurisdictions in which they carry on their business.

Corpus delicti   Latin term meaning "body of the crime." The objective proof that a crime has been committed; sometimes refers to the body of the victim of a homicide, but the term has a broader meaning. The corpus delicti for a robbery, for instance, is the stolen money. For the state to introduce a confession or convict the accused it must prove a corpus delicti, i.e., the occurrence of specific injury or loss and a criminal act as the source of the loss.

Corpus juris Latin for "body of law." A series of texts containing much of the civil and canon ecclesiastical law.

Cosign The act of affixing one's signature in addition to the principal signature of another in order to verify the authenticity of the principal signature.

Counsel 1. Attorney or legal adviser. 2. The advice or aid given with respect to a legal matter. 3. In criminal law, the term may refer to the advising or encouraging of another to commit a crime.

Count A distinct statement of plaintiff's cause of action. In indictments, a count, like a charge, is an allegation of a distinct offense. A complaint or indictment may contain one or more counts.

Counterclaim A counterdemand by the defendant against the plaintiff. It is not a mere answer or denial of the plaintiff's allegation, but asserts an independent cause of action in favor of the defendant.

Counterfeit Forged; fabricated without right; made in imitation of something else to defraud by passing the false copy for genuine.

Court calendar A schedule of cases awaiting disposition in a given court, also referred to as the trial list or the court docket.

Court-martial A military tribunal with jurisdiction over offenses against the law of the service in which the offender is engaged, a proceeding in such a court.

Court of claims The court of the United States, created to determine all presented claims founded upon any law of Congress, upon any regulation of an executive department, or upon any contract, express or implied, with the government of the United States, and also all claims that may be referred to the court by either house of Congress. It has no power over matters in equity.

Court of equity A court having jurisdiction in cases where an adequate and complete remedy cannot be had at law. Courts that are guided primarily by equitable doctrine are said to be courts of equity. Thus, a bankruptcy court is a court of equity. Courts of equity, which arose independent of courts of law in England, have merged with the latter in most jurisdictions of the United States. *See* **Equity**.

Court of law A tribunal with jurisdiction over cases at law. The term applies to courts that administer justice according to federal or state law or common law, as distinguished from courts that follow the principles of equity and are called chancery courts. Law courts and equity courts, however, are generally no longer distinguished and a court of law is any tribunal administering the law.

Court of record A court that, like most modern courts, is required by law to keep a record of its proceedings, including the orders and judgments it enters, and that has the authority to imprison and to levy fines.

Creditor One to whom money is owed by the debtor, one to whom an obligation exists. In its strict legal sense, a creditor is one who voluntarily gives credit to another for money or other property; in its more general sense it is one who has a right by law to demand and recover of another a sum of money on any account.

Crime A wrong that the government has determined is injurious to the public and that may therefore be prosecuted in a criminal proceeding. Crimes include felonies and misdemeanors.

Crime of passion A crime committed under the influence of sudden or extreme passion. That an act was committed in the heat of passion may provide a defense to a charge of murder, since it negates the element of premeditation, a necessary element of murder. *See* **Manslaughter**.

Criminal 1. Done with malicious intent, with a disposition to injure persons or property. 2. One who has been convicted of a violation of the criminal laws.

Cross-examination The questioning of a witness, by a party or lawyer other than the one who called the witness, concerning matters about which the witness has testified during direct examination. The purpose is to discredit or clarify testimony already given so as to neutralize damaging testimony or present facts in a light more favorable to the party against whom the direct testimony was offered.

Cruel and unusual punishment A penalty tantamount to torture, or excessive in proportion to the offense for which it is imposed, or inherently unfair, or by contemporary standards shocking to people of reasonable sensitivity. A punishment not inherently cruel and unusual may become so by the manner in which it is inflicted. Such punishment is prohibited by the Eighth Amendment to the U.S. Constitution.

Culpable Deserving of moral blame or punishment, at fault; having acted with indifference to consequences and to the rights of others.

Custody As applied to property, the condition of holding a thing within one's personal care and control. As applied to persons, such control over a person as will insure his or her presence at a hearing, or the actual imprisonment of a person resulting from a criminal conviction. Custody of children is legal guardianship.

Custody of children The care and control of minor children awarded by the court to one parent in a divorce proceeding. Where parents both make application for joint custody, and circumstances render the arrangement feasible, some courts have awarded custody to both parents so that responsibility for the children is shared. Under a joint custody order, each parent would assume custody of the children for a fixed period, such as for six months or for the school year or for the summer vacation.

D **Damages** Monetary compensation that the law awards to one who has been injured by the action of another; monetary recompense for a legal wrong such as a breach of contract or a tortuous act.

Day in court Refers broadly to the opportunity afforded a party to a lawsuit to be heard by the court.

Deadly weapon Any device capable of causing death or serious bodily injury. An instrument may be intrinsically deadly, as a knife or pistol, or deadly because of the way it is used, as a wrench or hammer.

Death penalty   The ultimate punishment imposed for murder or other capital offenses. The U.S. Supreme Court has determined that the death penalty is not in every instance to be considered unconstitutional, as cruel and unusual punishment.

Debenture   Written acknowledgment of a debt secured only by the general credit or promise to pay of the issuer. Debentures are the common type of bond issued by large, well-established corporations with adequate credit ratings. The written agreement under which the debentures are sold, the indenture, is specific as to maturity date, interest rate, call features and convertibility. Holders of debentures representing corporate indebtedness are creditors of the corporation and entitled to payment before shareholders upon dissolution of the corporation.

Debt   Any obligation of one person to pay or compensate another.

Debtor   One who owes another anything, or is under obligation, arising from express agreement, implication of law, or principles of natural justice, to pay money or to fulfill some other obligation; in bankruptcy or similar proceedings the person who is the subject of the proceeding.

Deceased   One who has died. In property law, the alternate term decedent is generally used. In criminal law, "the deceased" refers to the victim of a homicide.

Deceit   The tort or fraudulent representation of a material fact made with knowledge of its falsity, or recklessly, or without reasonable grounds for believing its truth and with intent to induce reliance on it.

Declaration   In common law, the formal document specifying the plaintiff's cause of action including the facts necessary to sustain a proper cause of action and to advise the defendant of the grounds upon which he or she is being sued.

Decree   The judicial decision in a litigated cause rendered by a court of equity; the determination of a cause in courts of admiralty and probate. It is accurate to use the word judgment for a decision of a court of law and decree from a court of equity, although the former term now includes both.

Deed   An instrument in writing that conveys an interest in land from the grantor to the grantee. Its main function is to pass title to land.

De facto   Latin term meaning "in fact." By virtue of the deed or accomplishment; actually. Used to refer to a situation in which a condition or institution is operating as though it were official or pursuant to law, but which is not legally authorized. Such situations may arise where, for example. an authorizing law is declared invalid, or required legal formalities have not been satisfied. *Compare* **De jure**.

Default judgment   A judgment against a defendant who has failed to respond to a plaintiff's action or to appear at the trial or hearing.

Defeasance   An instrument that negates the effectiveness of a deed or of a will; a collateral deed that defeats the force of another deed upon the performance of certain conditions.

Defendant   In civil proceedings, the party responding to the complaint; one who is sued and called upon to make satisfaction for a wrong complained of by another. In criminal proceedings, the accused.

Defense   A denial, answer or plea disputing the validity of a plaintiff's case, or making some further contention that renders the defendant not liable upon the facts alleged by the plaintiff.

Defraud   To deprive a person of property or interest, estate or right by fraud or deceit.

De jure   Latin term that means "by right, lawful; legitimate." Generally used in contrast to de facto; de jure connotes "as a matter of law," whereas de facto connotes "as a matter of practice not founded upon law."

Deliberation   The process by which the reasons for and against a verdict are weighed by jurors. While such verdict should be the consensus of the judgments of each juror, the purpose of deliberation is to allow opinions to be changed by conference in the jury room.

Denial   A refutation of affirmative allegations contained in the pleading of an adversary. A defendant in his answer must admit, deny or state he has insufficient information upon which to admit or deny the allegations.

De novo   Latin term meaning "new." In a trial de novo, issues of law and issues of fact are reconsidered as if the original trial had never taken place.

Deportation   The transfer of an alien to a foreign country because the deporting government refuses to harbor a person whose presence is deemed inconsistent with the public welfare.

Deposition   A method of pretrial discovery that consists of a stenographically transcribed statement of a witness under oath, in response to an attorney's questions, with opportunity for the opposing party or his or her attorney to be present and to cross-examine. Such a statement is the most common form of discovery and may be taken of any witness (whether or not a party to the action). When taken in the form described, it is called an oral deposition. Depositions may also be taken upon written interrogatories, where the questions are read to the witness by the officer who is taking the deposition.

Detention   Holding of a person charged with a crime following the person's arrest on that charge.

Devise   A gift of real property made by will. In modern usage, the term may also embrace testamentary gifts of personal property.

Directed verdict   A verdict returned by the jury at the direction of the trial judge, by whose direction the jury is bound. In civil proceedings, either party may receive a directed verdict in its favor if the opposing party fails to present a prima facie case or a necessary defense. In criminal proceedings, there may be a directed verdict of acquittal, but not a directed verdict of conviction, which would violate the defendant's constitutional rights to a jury determination of guilt or innocence.

Direct examination   The initial questioning of a witness by the party who called the witness. The purpose is to present testimony containing the factual argument the party is making.

Disbar   To rescind an attorney's license to practice law because of illegal or unethical conduct.

LAW

Discharge To satisfy or dismiss the obligations of a contract or debt; the method by which a legal duty is extinguished.

Discovery Modern pretrial procedure by which one party gains information held by the adverse party, concerning the case, the disclosure by the adverse party of facts, deeds and documents that are exclusively within his or her possession or knowledge and that are necessary to support the other party's position.

Dismissal A cancellation. Dismissal of a motion is a denial of the motion. Dismissal of a complaint or a related count terminates proceedings on the claim asserted in the complaint. Dismissal of an appeal places the parties in the condition as if there had been no appeal, confirming the judgment of the lower court.

Disorderly conduct In its broadest sense, this is conduct that tends to breach the peace, disturb those who see or hear it, or endanger the morals, safety or health of the community.

Disposition 1. The giving up of anything; often used in reference to a testamentary proceeding, as in "the disposition of the estate." 2. Courts "dispose of" cases, i.e., determine the rights of the parties or otherwise terminate the proceedings. 3. In criminal law, the sentence of the defendant is the disposition.

Dispossess To oust, eject or exclude another from the possession of lands or premises, whether by legal process (as where a landlord lawfully evicts a tenant) or wrongfully.

Dissenting opinion A reasoned opinion that differs from that of the majority of the court.

Dissolution In corporation law, the end of the legal existence of a corporation, whether by expiration of charter, decree of court, act of legislature, vote of shareholders or other means.

Distress The act or process by which a person, without prior court approval, seizes the personal property of another in satisfaction of a claim, as a pledge for performance of a duty, or in reparation of an injury.

District attorney The prosecuting officer of a judicial district such as a city or state.

District Court 1. A court, established by the U.S. Constitution, having territorial jurisdiction over a district that may include a whole state or part of it. A district court has original jurisdiction, exclusive of courts of the individual states, over all offenses against laws of the United States, and is a court of general jurisdiction for suits between litigants of different states. 2. An inferior court in several states having limited jurisdiction to try certain minor cases.

Disturbing the peace Any public act that molests inhabitants or that excites fear among normal persons.

Divestiture Loss or surrender of a right or title or interest, a remedy by which the court orders the offending party to rid itself of assets before the party would normally have done so. Divestiture, like restitution, has the purpose of depriving a defendant of the gains of wrongful conduct. It is a remedy sometimes used in the enforcement of the antitrust laws.

Divorce Dissolution of the bonds of marriage.

Docket A list of cases on a court's calendar; a formal record of the proceedings in the court whose decision is being appealed.

Domain Land of which one is absolute owner.

Domicile An individual's permanent home or principal establishment. Residence is not the same as domicile, since a person can have many transient residences but only one legal domicile, which is the home address to which he or she always intends to return for prolonged periods. The domicile of a business is the address where the establishment is maintained or where the governing power of the enterprise is exercised. For purposes of taxation, it is often a principal place of business.

Double jeopardy Prosecution or punishment twice for the same offense, which is prohibited by the U.S. Constitution and by many state constitutions.

Dram Shop Act A legislative enactment imposing strict liability upon the seller of intoxicating beverages when the sale results in the harm of a third party's person, property or means of support.

Driving while intoxicated (D.W.I.) The criminal offense of operating a motor vehicle while under the influence of alcohol or drugs. State law controls both the definition of "operating," such as whether it includes the actual driving of the car or merely sitting in the car, and the level of intoxication needed in order to be found in violation of the law.

Due process of law A phrase introduced into American jurisprudence in the Fifth and Fourteenth Amendments to the U.S. Constitution; the principle that the government may not deprive an individual of life, liberty or property unless certain rules and procedures required by law are followed. The phrase does not have a fixed meaning, but embodies society's fundamental notions of legal fairness. Specifically, the constitutional safeguard of substantive due process requires that all legislation, state or federal, must be reasonably related to a legitimate government objective. The concept of procedural due process guarantees procedural fairness where the government attempts to deprive one of his property or liberty; this requires notice and a fair hearing prior to a deprivation of life, liberty or property.

Duress Refers to conduct that has the effect of compelling another person to do what he or she need not otherwise do. It is a recognized defense to any act, such as a crime, contractual breach or tort, all of which must be voluntary to create liability.

Easement A right, created by an express or implied agreement, to make lawful and beneficial use of the land of another. Such use must not be inconsistent with any other uses already being made of the land.

Embezzlement Fraudulent appropriation for one's own use of property lawfully in his or her possession, a type of larceny that did not exist in common law because it does not involve a trespassory taking; thus, it is a crime created by statute. Embezzlement is often associated with bank employees, public officials or officers of organizations, who may in the course of their lawful activities come into possession of property, such as money, actually owned by others.

Eminent domain   The inherent right of the state to take private property for public use without the individual property owner's consent. Just compensation must be paid to the property owner.

Enjoin   To command or instruct with authority; to suspend or restrain. One may be enjoined or commanded by a court either to do a specific act or to refrain from doing a certain act.

Entrapment   In criminal law, an affirmative defense created either by statute or by court decision in the given jurisdiction that excuses a defendant from criminal liability for crimes induced by trickery on the part of law enforcement officers or other agents of the government.

Equal opportunity   A term to signify an employer's adoption of employment practices that do not discriminate on the basis of race, color, religion, sex or national origin. Such discrimination was outlawed by Title VII of the Civil Rights Act of 1964.

Equal protection of the laws   Constitutional guarantee embodied in the Fourteenth Amendment to the U.S. Constitution, which states in relevant part that "No State shall. . . deny to any person within its jurisdiction the equal protection of the laws." The essential purpose of this constitutional doctrine is to ensure that the laws and the government treat all persons alike, unless there is some substantial reason why certain persons or classes of persons should be treated differently.

Equal Rights Amendment (E.R.A.)   A proposed amendment hoping to eliminate sex as a basis for any decisions made by a state of the United States. This amendment was never ratified by a sufficient number of states to qualify as a constitutional amendment, but the basic premise underlying the proposal has become an accepted standard in many statutes and court decisions.

Equitable distribution   A just division of property among interested parties; the process by which, as part of a dissolution of marriage proceeding under a no-fault divorce statute, the court apportions between husband and wife all assets acquired by either or both of them, whether owned jointly or individually, during the marriage.

Equity   Generally, justice or fairness. Historically, equity refers to a separate body of law developed in England in reaction to the inability of the common law courts, in their strict adherence to rigid writs and forms of action, to consider or provide a remedy for every injury. The king therefore established the court of chancery to do justice between parties in cases where the common law would give inadequate redress. The principle of this jurisprudence is that equity will find a way to achieve a lawful result when legal procedure is inadequate. Equity and law courts are now merged in most jurisdictions, though equity jurisprudence and equitable doctrines are still independently viable.

Escrow   A written instrument, such as a deed, temporarily deposited with a neutral third party (the escrow agent), by the agreement of two parties to a valid contract. The escrow agent will deliver the document to the benefited party when the conditions of the contract have been met. The depositor has no control over the instrument in escrow.

Estate   Technically, the nature and extent of a person's interest in or ownership of land; broadly, estate applies to all that a person owns whether real or personal property.

Evidence   All the means by which any alleged matter of fact, the truth of which is submitted to investigation at judicial trial, is established or disproved. Evidence includes the testimony of witnesses, introduction of records, documents, exhibits, or any other relevant matter offered for the purpose of inducing the trier of fact's belief in the party's contention.

Exclusionary rule   A constitutional rule of law that provides that otherwise admissible evidence may not be used in a criminal trial if it was obtained as a result of illegal police conduct.

Execute   To complete, as a legal instrument; to perform what is required; to give validity to, as by signing and perhaps sealing and delivering. For example, a contract is executed when all acts necessary to complete it and to give it validity as an instrument are carried out, including signing and delivery.

Executive clemency   The power constitutionally reposed in the president, and by most state constitutions, in the governor, to pardon or commute (i.e., reduce) the sentence of one convicted by a court within his or her jurisdiction. *Compare* **Reprieve**.

Executor (or executrix)   A person who either expressly or by implication is appointed by a testator (one who dies leaving a will) to carry out the testator's directions concerning the dispositions made under the will. When the appointee is a woman, she is the executrix.

Exhibit   Any document or object introduced as evidence in court.

Expert witness   A witness having special knowledge, skill or experience in the subject about which he or she is to testify.

Ex post facto   Latin term meaning "after the fact." Refers especially to a law that makes punishable as a crime an act done before the passing of the law and that was innocent when done. An ex post facto law is also one that makes a crime more serious than when it was committed, inflicts a greater punishment, or alters legal rules of evidence to require less or different testimony to convict than the law required when the crime was committed. Such laws violate provisions of the Constitution of the United States, which provide that neither Congress nor any state shall pass an ex post facto law.

Expropriation   The taking of private property for public purpose upon the payment of just compensation, which is recognized as an inherent power of the state over its citizens.

Extenuating circumstances   Unusual factors tending to contribute to the consummation of an illegal act, but over which the actor had little or no control. These factors therefore reduce the responsibility of the actor and serve to mitigate punishment or payment of damages.

Extortion   In common law, the corrupt collection by a public official of an excessive or unauthorized fee; punishable as a misdemeanor. Under modern statutes the offense includes illegal taking of money by anyone who employs threats, or other illegal use of fear or coercion, to obtain money, and whose conduct falls short of the threat to personal safety required for robbery. Extortion is used interchangeably with blackmail and is commonly punished as a felony.

Extradition The surrender by one state to another of an accused or convicted person. A state's chief executive has the right to demand from the asylum state the return of a person who was accused of a crime based upon probable cause. Extradition prevents the escape of fugitives who seek sanctuary in another state. It enables the state in which the offense occurred to swiftly bring the offender to trial.

Eyewitness A person who can testify as to what he or she has experienced by his or her presence at an event.

Failure of issue Termination of one's bloodline. The words are most often used in a will or deed to refer to a condition that operates in the event either no children be born or no children survive the decedent. These words, or the phrase "die without issue," may fix a condition whereby an estate will, in the event of failure of issue, pass automatically to an alternative person or in an alternative manner designated in the will itself.

Fairness doctrine A requirement that broadcasting stations present contrasting viewpoints on controversial issues of public importance. This doctrine imposes two affirmative responsibilities on the broadcaster: 1. To present adequate coverage of controversial public issues and 2. To ensure that this programming presents differing viewpoints so that the public are fully and fairly informed.

Fair trade laws State statutes that permit a manufacturer to establish minimum resale prices that may not be varied by the wholesaler or distributor. Such agreements do not violate the antitrust laws when they are entered into under the provisions of state fair trade laws.

Fair use In federal copyright law, an insubstantial permitted use by another of material protected by copyright.

False arrest Unlawful arrest, unlawful restraint of another's personal liberty or freedom of locomotion. It may be a criminal offense or the basis of a civil action for damages.

False imprisonment As a tort, the intentional, unjustified detention or confinement of a person. Where the restraint is imposed by virtue of one claiming legal authority to do so and an arrest occurs, it will be a false arrest as well as a false imprisonment.

False pretense The statutory crime of obtaining money or property by making false representations of fact; also known as misrepresentation.

Federal Bureau of Investigation (F.B.I.) An agency of the U.S. Department of Justice, charged by law with investigating violations of all laws of the U.S. government, except those expressly assigned to other agencies.

Federal courts The U.S. courts (distinguished from the courts of the individual states), including district courts (general courts of original jurisdiction, which are the federal trial courts), courts of appeals (formerly circuit courts of appeals, which are

principally appellate review courts), and the Supreme Court (the only court created directly by the Constitution, and the court of last resort in the federal system). Other specialized courts in the federal system are court of claims (hears suits involving allowable claims against the U.S. government), court of customs and patent appeals (reviews customs court decisions), and customs court (reviews decisions of the customs collectors).

Felony Generic term employed to distinguish certain high crimes from minor offenses known as misdemeanors; crimes declared to be such by statute or to be "true crimes" by the common law. Statutes often define felony as an offense punishable by imprisonment for more than one year or by death or imprisonment generally. The original common law felonies were felonious homicide, mayhem, arson, rape, robbery, burglary, larceny, prison breach (escape) and rescue of a felon.

Fiduciary A person having a duty, created by his undertaking, to act primarily for the benefit of another in matters connected with his undertaking; one who holds a position of confidence, as, for example, a trustee.

Fifth Amendment The amendment to the U.S. Constitution, part of the Bill of Rights, that establishes certain protections for citizens from actions of the government by providing 1. that a person shall not be required to answer for a capital or other infamous crime unless an indictment or presentment is first issued by a grand jury, 2. that no person will be placed in double jeopardy, 3. that no person may be required to testify against himself, 4. that neither life, liberty nor property may be taken without due process of law, and 5. that private property may not be taken for public use, without payment of just compensation.

Finding The decision of a court on issues of fact. The decision's purpose is to answer questions raised by the pleadings or charges. It is designed to facilitate review by disclosing the grounds on which the judgment rests. Findings of fact are made by a jury in an action at law, or, if there is no jury, they are made by the judge.

Foreclosure Generally, the termination of a right to property; specifically, an equitable action to compel payment of a mortgage or other debt secured by a lien. As to real property, foreclosure is precipitated by nonpayment of the debt or other default under the loan agreement, and leads to the court's order that the property to which the mortgage or lien is attached be sold to satisfy that debt.

Forensic Belonging to the courts of justice; indicates the application of a particular subject to the law. For example, forensic medicine employs medical technology to assist in solving legal problems.

Fourteenth Amendment One of the so-called "Civil War Amendments" to the Constitution in that it was ratified after the Civil War; protects all persons from state laws that attempt to deprive them of "life, liberty or property, without due process of law," or that attempt to deny them equal protection of the laws. The amendment has been used to extend the protection of almost all of the provisions of the Bill of Rights to citizens of every state.

Franchise   1. A special privilege that is conferred by the government upon individuals and that does not of common right belong to the citizens of the country. For example, a municipality may grant to a local bus company a franchise that will give it sole authority to operate buses in the municipality for a certain number of years. 2. The right given to a private person or corporation to market another's product within a certain area. 3. Elective franchise (sometimes called simply "the franchise") refers to the right of citizens to vote in public elections.

Fraud   Intentional deception resulting in injury to another. Fraud usually consists of a misrepresentation, concealment or nondisclosure of a material fact, or at least misleading conduct, devices or contrivance.

Free and clear   Unencumbered. In property law, a title is free and clear if it is not encumbered by any liens or restrictions.

Freedom of Information Act   A federal law requiring that, with specified exceptions, documents and materials generated or held by federal agencies be made available to the public and establishing guidelines for their disclosure.

Friend of the court   A qualified person who is not a party to the action but gives information to the court on a question of law. The function of this person is to call attention to some information that might escape the court's attention. ("Friend of the court" is often referred to by the Latin term *amicus curiae*.)

Full faith and credit   The federal constitutional requirement that the public acts, records and judicial proceedings of one state be respected by each of the other states. Thus, if a judgment is conclusive in the state where it was pronounced, it is equally beyond dispute everywhere in the courts of the United States. The judgment is entitled to full faith and credit when the second court's inquiry discloses that the same questions were properly before the first court and were fully and fairly litigated and finally decided there

G   **Gag order**   A court-imposed order to restrict information or comment about a case. The ostensible purpose of such an order is to protect the interests of all parties and preserve the right to a fair trial by curbing publicity likely to prejudice a jury. A gag order cannot be directly imposed on members of the press because this constitutes an impermissible prior restraint and violates the First Amendment.

Garnishment   Process in which money or goods in the hands of a third person, which are due a defendant, are attached by the plaintiff. It is a statutory remedy that consists of notifying a third party to retain something he has that belongs to the defendant (debtor), to make disclosure to the court concerning it, and to dispose of it as the court shall direct.

Gerrymander   To create a civil division of an unusual shape within a particular locale for improper purpose; to redistrict a state, creating unnatural boundaries and isolating members of a particular political party, in the hope that a maximum number of the elected representatives will be of that political party.

Good cause   Substantial or legally sufficient reason for doing something. For example, if a statute provides for granting a new trial upon a showing of good cause, such good cause might include the existence of fraud, lack of notice to the parties or newly discovered evidence. Motions submitted before a judge, which in essence ask the judge to do something, must be supported by a showing of good cause. On a motion to exclude or suppress evidence for trial, good cause must be shown by example of illegal police conduct in the seizing of the evidence. For the motion to be granted, the judge must be convinced the conduct occurred and is enough to justify exclusion.

Good faith   Total absence of intention to seek unfair advantage or to defraud another party; an honest intention to fulfill one's obligations; observance of reasonable standards of fair dealing. In property law, a good faith purchaser of land pays value for the land and has no knowledge or notice of any facts that would cause an ordinary prudent person to make inquiry concerning the validity of the conveyance.

Grandfather clause   A provision permitting persons engaged in an activity before passage of a law affecting that activity to receive a license or prerogative without the necessity of fulfilling all that is legally required of persons subsequently undertaking the same activity.

Grand jury   A jury to determine whether the facts and accusations presented by the prosecutor warrant an indictment and eventual trial of the accused, called *grand* because of the relatively large number of jurors impaneled (traditionally twenty-three).

Grievance   One's allegation that something imposes an illegal burden, or denies some equitable or legal right, or causes injustice. An employee may be entitled by a collective bargaining agreement to seek relief through a grievance procedure.

Guaranty   A promise to be responsible for the debt, default or miscarriage of another; a warranty or promise to undertake an original obligation; something given as security for the performance of an act or the continued quality of a thing.

Guardian   One who legally has care and management of the person or estate, or both, of an incompetent; an officer or agent of the court who is appointed to protect the interests of minors or incompetent persons and to provide for their welfare, education and support.

H   **Habeas corpus**   Latin term meaning "you have the body." The writ of habeas corpus, known as the great writ, has varied use in criminal and civil contexts. It is a procedure for obtaining a judicial determination of the legality of an individual's custody. Technically, it is used in the criminal law context to bring the petitioner before the court to inquire into the legality of his or her confinement. The writ of federal habeas corpus is used to test the constitutionality of a state criminal conviction. The writ is used in the civil context to challenge the validity of child custody and deportations.

Hearing   A proceeding where evidence is taken to determine an issue of fact and to reach a decision on the basis of the evidence, describes whatever takes place before magistrates sitting without jury. Thus a hearing, such as an administrative hearing, may take place outside the judicial process, before officials who have been granted judicial authority expressly for the purpose of conducting such hearings.

Hearsay rule   A rule that declares not admissible as evidence any statement other than that by a witness while testifying at the hearing and offered into evidence to prove the truth of the matter stated. The hearsay statement may be oral or written and includes nonverbal conduct intended as a substitute for words. The reason for the hearsay rule is that credibility of the witness is the key ingredient in weighing the truth of his statement; so when that statement is made out of court, without benefit of cross-examination and without the witness' demeanor being subject to assessment by the judge or jury, there is generally no adequate basis for determining whether the out-of-court statement is true.

Homicide   Any killing of a human being by the act, agency, procurement, or culpable omission of another. An unlawful homicide, or one resulting from an unlawful act, may constitute murder or manslaughter. Justifiable homicide is the killing of a human being by commandment of the law, in the execution of public justice, in self-defense, in defense of habitation, property or person.

Hostile witness   One whose relationship to the opposing party is such that his or her testimony may be prejudiced against that party.

Hung jury   One whose members cannot reconcile their differences of opinion and that therefore cannot reach a verdict by the degree of agreement required (generally unanimity, but sometimes a substantial majority).

Immaterial   Not material, irrelevant; nothing to do with the case; not significant.

Immunity   Right of exemption from a duty or penalty, benefit granted in exception to the general rule. Immunity from prosecution may be granted a witness to compel answers the witness might otherwise withhold because of the constitutional privilege to avoid self-incrimination.

Impaneling   Selection and swearing in of jurors; listing of those selected for a particular jury.

Impeach   To charge a public official with wrongdoing while in office. Impeachment proceedings against officers of the United States are governed by the Constitution. To impeach the testimony of a witness means to question that witness's honesty.

Inalienable rights   Fundamental rights, including the right to practice religion, freedom of speech, due process and equal protection of the laws, that cannot be transferred to another nor surrendered except by the person possessing them. *See* **Bill of Rights**.

In camera   Latin term meaning "in chambers." In camera designates a judicial act while court is not in session in the matter acted upon. Confidential or otherwise sensitive documents are often examined in camera to determine whether information should be revealed to the jury and so become public record.

Incarceration   Confinement in prison.

Incendiary   Arsonist, one who maliciously sets property on fire; an object capable of starting and sustaining a fire is an incendiary device.

Incest   A criminal offense of sexual intercourse between members of a family, or those between whom marriage would be illegal because of blood relationship.

Incompetency   Inability, disqualification, incapacity. Lack of legal qualifications or fitness to discharge a required duty; lack of physical, intellectual or moral fitness. When a person is adjudicated incompetent, a guardian is appointed to manage the incompetent's affairs, unless the incompetent recovers competency to the satisfaction of the court. An adjudicated incompetent lacks capacity to contract and his contracts are void.

Incriminate   To hold another, or oneself, responsible for criminal misconduct; to involve someone, or oneself, in an accusation of a crime.

Indemnity   1. The obligation to make good any loss or damage another person has incurred or may incur. 2. The right that the person suffering loss or damage is entitled to claim.

Indictment   A formal written accusation, drawn up and submitted under oath to a grand jury by the public prosecuting attorney, charging one or more persons with a crime. The grand jury must determine whether the accusation, if proved, would be sufficient for conviction of the accused, in which case the indictment is indorsed by the foreman. Once an indictment is filed, the matter passes to the Court. Indictments also serve to inform an accused of the offense with which he or she is charged and must be clear enough to enable the accused to prepare an adequate defense. *Compare* **Charge**; **Complaint**; **Information**; **Presentment**.

Indigent   Generally, a person who is poor, financially destitute. In a legal context, a person found by a court to be unable to hire a lawyer or otherwise meet the expense of defending a criminal matter, at which point defense counsel is appointed by the court.

Information   A written accusation of crime signed by the prosecutor, charging a person with the commission of a crime; an alternative to indictment as a means of starting a criminal prosecution. The purpose of an information is to inform the defendant of the charges against him or her and to inform the court of the factual basis of the charges.

Informed consent   Consent given only after full disclosure of what is being consented to; constitutionally required in certain areas where one may consent to what otherwise would be an unconstitutional violation of a right.

Injunction   A judicial remedy awarded to restrain a particular activity; first used by courts of equity to prevent conduct contrary to equity and good conscience. The injunction is a preventive measure to guard against future injuries, rather than one that affords a remedy for past injuries.

Injury   Wrong or damage done to another, either in his person, rights, reputation or property. Legal injury is any damage that results from a violation of a legal right and that the law will recognize as deserving of redress.

Inns of court   Four private societies in England that prepare students for the practice of law and that alone may admit them to the bar; that is, confer the rank of barrister. The four inns of court are Inner Temple, Middle Temple, Lincoln's Inn, Gray's Inn.

Inquest   Judicial inquiry; an inquiry made by a coroner to determine cause of death of one who has been killed, or has died suddenly, under suspicious circumstances, or in prison.

Insider   A person whose opportunity to profit from his or her position of power in a business is limited by law to safeguard the public good. Both federal securities acts and state blue sky laws regulate stock transactions of individuals with access to inside information about a corporation, since the prospect of insider trading may inhibit investment by the general public due to their concern that the price of securities has been artificially inflated or deflated by such trading.

Insider trading   Buying or selling of corporation stock by a corporate officer who profits by his or her access to information not available to the public. Corporate insiders who trade on the basis of non-public corporate information may be exposed to liability under state or federal law because of a policy that everybody should have equal access to information and that insiders should not profit personally from something that belongs to the corporation.

Insolvency   Inability to meet financial obligations as they mature in the ordinary course of business; excess of liabilities over assets at any given time.

Instrument   In commercial law, a written formal document that records an act or agreement and provides the evidence of that act or agreement.

Insufficient evidence   A term usually referred to in a decision by a judge that a prosecutor or other party charged with proving a crime has failed to provide the minimum of evidence necessary to even ask a jury to decide a question of fact.

Interrogation   The process by which suspects are rigorously questioned by police. *See* **Miranda rule**.

Intestate   The condition of having died without leaving a valid will. An intestate estate is property that a testator has failed to dispose of by will.

Issue   As a verb, to put into circulation, as to a buyer. In corporation law, a stock issue is the process by which a corporation authorizes, executes and delivers shares of stock for sale to the public. The term also describes the shares offered by the corporation at a particular time. In the law of real property, the noun issue means descendants. In legal practice, a point of fact or law disputed between parties to the litigation, generally an assertion by one side and a denial by the other.

J   **Judgment**   The determination of a court of competent jurisdiction upon matters submitted to it.
Jurisdiction   1. Power to hear and determine a case; may be established and described with reference to a particular subject or to parties in a particular category, the geographic or political entity governed by a particular legal system or body of laws.

Jurisprudence   The science of law; the study of the structure of legal systems, such as equity, and of the principles underlying that system, a collective term denoting the course of judicial decision, i.e., case law, as opposed to legislation; sometimes a synonym for law.

Jurist   A legal scholar, one versed in law, particularly the civil law or the law of nations; a judge.

Juror   A person sworn as a member of a jury; a person selected for jury duty, but not yet chosen for a particular case.

Jury   A group, composed of the peers of the parties or a cross section of the community, summoned and sworn to decide on the facts in issue at a trial. An ordinary trial jury is called a petit ("petty") jury. Its function is to determine issues of fact in civil and criminal cases and to reach a verdict in conjunction with those findings. While the number of jurors has historically been twelve, many states now permit six-member juries in civil cases, and some states permit six-member juries to hear criminal cases as well.

Justice of the peace   A judicial officer of inferior rank, who presides in a court of statutorily limited civil jurisdiction and who is also a conservator of the peace with limited jurisdiction in criminal proceedings, prosecutions, and commitment of offenders, as fixed by statute.

Juvenile courts   Tribunals designed to treat youthful offenders separately from adults. The purpose of this has been to replace the adversary nature of normal proceedings with concern for the child's well-being.

Juvenile delinquent   A minor who has committed an offense ordinarily punishable by criminal processes, but who is under the age, set by statute, for criminal responsibility.

K   **Kangaroo Court**   A court that has no legal authority and that disregards all the rights normally afforded to persons; its conclusions are not legally binding. This is a slang term referring to a court that is biased against a party and thus renders an unfair verdict or judgment.

Kidnapping   Unlawful carrying away of a person against his or her will; false imprisonment coupled with removal of the victim to another place. Kidnapping was only a misdemeanor in common law, but is a serious felony in the United States.

King's Bench (Queen's Bench)   Court of King's Bench or Court of Queen's Bench (depending on the reigning monarch); the highest English common law court, both civil and criminal, so called because the king or queen formerly presided; now known as the King's Bench or Queen's Bench Division of the High Court of Justice, embracing the jurisdiction of the former Courts of Exchequer and Courts of Common Pleas.

L   **Larceny**   The felonious taking and carrying away of the personal property of another, without the person's consent, by someone who is not entitled to possession, with intent to deprive the owner of the property and to convert it to the use of the taker or another person other than the owner. Larceny is sometimes classified as either grand larceny or petit (petty) larceny, according to the value of the property taken or the method employed.

Law The legislative pronouncement of rules to guide one's actions in society; the total of those rules of conduct put in force by legislative authority or court decisions, or established by local custom.

Leading question A question posed by a trial lawyer that is sometimes improper because it suggests to the witness the answer he or she is to deliver, or in effect prompts answers in disregard of actual memory. For example: In direct examination during the trial, the witness is asked "Isn't it true that you saw Rich standing outside the store waiting for a friend when the robbery occurred?" That question will be objected to as a leading question since it suggests to the witness how he should explain or recall the event, instead of simply inquiring how the event actually took place. However, leading questions are proper as part of cross-examination since the object of such examination is to test the credibility of the statement made during direct examination.

Lease An agreement by the lessor (owner) temporarily to give up possession of property while retaining legal ownership (title); an agreement by the owner-landlord to turn over, for all purposes not prohibited by terms of the lease specifically described premises to the exclusive possession of the lessee for a definite period and for a consideration commonly called rent.

Legacy A disposition by will of personal property; synonymous with bequest but properly distinguished from devise, which is a disposition of real property.

Legal Aid Society State-funded and state-administered offices established throughout the country to deliver legal services to financially needy litigants, that is, those unable to afford to retain private counsel.

Liability An obligation to do or refrain from doing something; a duty that eventually must be performed; an obligation to pay money owed, as opposed to an asset; responsibility for one's conduct, such as contractual liability, tort liability, criminal liability, etc.

Liable Responsible for; obligated in law.

Libel A tort consisting of a false, malicious publication aiming to defame a living person. Printed or written material, signs or pictures that tend to expose a person to public scorn, hatred, contempt, or ridicule may be considered libelous.

License A grant of permission needed to legalize doing a particular thing, exercising a certain privilege or pursuing a particular business or occupation. Licenses may be granted by private persons or by governmental authority.

Lien A charge, hold or claim upon the property of another as security for some debt or charge. The term connotes the right the law gives to have a debt satisfied out of the property to which it attaches, if necessary by the sale of the property.

Limited jurisdiction Refers to courts that are only authorized to hear and decide certain or special types of cases; also known as special jurisdiction. For example: The Court of Claims has limited jurisdiction to only hear claims against the United States based on certain types of violations. A small claims court is limited to a specified dollar amount that it can litigate. *See also* **Jurisdiction**.

Limited liability The limitation placed on the amount an investor of a corporation can lose resulting from a lawsuit against the corporation or other loss suffered by the corporation; the liability for losses that is limited to the amount an investor or shareholder invests in the corporation. The corporation itself also enjoys limited liability inasmuch as the corporation's obligations are always limited to its assets unless, with regard to particular transactions, personal responsibility is assumed by an officer or shareholder of the corporation.

Lineup The police procedure in which a person suspected of a crime is placed in a line with several other persons and a witness to the crime attempts to identify the suspect as the person who committed the crime. The procedure must not be "unduly suggestive," or the identification will not be admissible in a criminal trial.

Litigants The parties actively involved in a lawsuit; plaintiffs or defendants involved in litigation.

Litigation A judicial contest aimed at determining and enforcing legal rights.

Lobbyist One engaged in the business of persuading legislators to pass laws that are favorable, and to defeat those that are unfavorable, to the interests of the lobbyist or of the lobbyist's clients.

Logrolling Refers to schemes by legislators to force passage of desired bills without convincing their colleagues of the merits of their proposals. One type of logrolling is the inclusion under one bill of secondary bills, each of which probably would not be approved if voted on singly.

Loiter To linger for no evident reason, particularly in a public place, around a school or near a transportation facility. There are criminal prohibitions of such behavior as loitering for purposes of begging, gambling, soliciting another to engage in sexual intercourse, or for the purpose of selling or using drugs.

**Magistrate** A public civil officer, invested with some part of the legislative, executive or judicial power. In a narrower sense, the term includes only inferior judicial officers, such as justices of the peace.

Malfeasance The doing of a wrongful and unlawful act; any wrongful conduct that interrupts or interferes with the performance of official duty.

Malice The state of mind that accompanies the intentional doing of a wrongful act without justification and in wanton or willful disregard of the plain likelihood that harm will result.

Malpractice A professional's improper or immoral conduct in the performance of his duties done either intentionally or through carelessness or ignorance; commonly applied to physicians, surgeons, dentists, lawyers and public officers to denote negligent or unskillful performance of duties where professional skills are obligatory on account of the fiduciary relationship with patients or clients.

Mandamus Latin term meaning "we command." A writ issued by a court ordering a corporation, officer, or inferior court to perform an official act or duty required of it by law. For example: A state legislature passes a law which provides that, upon request, a person has the right to see any information the government has on file for that person. Kathy files such a request with the state's attorney general and is refused access to her information. Unless the refusing party can show some compelling need for secrecy, a court will issue a writ of *mandamus* to the holder of the records, directing that person to release the information.

Mandate   A judicial command; an official mode of communicating the judgment of the appellate court to the lower court.

Manslaughter   Unlawful killing of another person without malice aforethought; distinguished from murder (and its possible attendant death penalty) as an explainable, less extreme homicide. Most jurisdictions distinguish between voluntary and involuntary manslaughter. *Voluntary manslaughter* is intentional killing committed under circumstances that, although they do not justify the homicide, reduce its evil intent. A charge of manslaughter is appropriate where the defendant killed the victim in rage, terror or desperation. *Involuntary manslaughter* consists of a homicide resulting from criminal negligence or recklessness.

Maritime law   The traditional body of rules and practices related to business transacted at sea or to navigation, ships, seamen, harbors, and general maritime affairs. It is, and always has been, a body of law separate from every other jurisprudence.

Martial law   Law of military necessity, where the military exercises great control over civilian affairs, generally because of war or civil insurrection. When instituted, martial law represents the unchecked will of the commander, controlled only by consideration of strategy and policy. In the United States the president, as commander in chief of the armed forces, would assume unreviewable discretion were martial law declared.

Material witness   One who can give testimony that might have a bearing upon the outcome of a cause and that no one else is able to give. In criminal law, the term refers particularly to a witness about whom there is reasonable expectation that he or she can give testimony bearing upon the defendant's guilt or innocence.

Memorandum   An informal discussion of the merits of a matter pending in a lawyer's office usually written by a law clerk or junior associate for a senior associate or partner. Also called an Office memorandum.

Memorandum of law   An argument by an advocate in support of his or her position; like a brief but less formal.

Miranda rule   The requirement to inform a person of his privilege against self-incrimination (right to remain silent) and his right to the presence and advice of a retained or appointed attorney before any interrogation by law enforcement authorities. Prior to any questioning, the person must also be warned that any statement he does make may be used as evidence against him. Statements and evidence obtained in violation of this rule, unless these rights have been knowingly waived (and the evidence voluntarily provided), are not admissible in the defendant's criminal trial and are grounds for federal constitutional challenge to any conviction obtained thereby.

Miscarriage of justice   Damage to the rights of one party to an action that results from errors made by the court during trial and that is sufficiently substantial to require reversal.

Misdemeanor   A class of criminal offenses less serious than felonies and sanctioned by less severe penalties.

Misfeasance   The wrongful or injurious performance of an act that might have been lawfully done.

Mistrial   A trial that has been terminated and declared void prior to the jury's returning a verdict (or the judge's declaring his verdict in a nonjury trial) because of some extraordinary circumstance (such as death or illness of a necessary juror or of an attorney), or because of some fundamental error prejudicial to the defendant that cannot be cured by appropriate instructions to the jury (such as the inclusion of highly improper remarks in the prosecutor's summation), or most commonly because of the jury's inability to reach a verdict because it is hopelessly deadlocked in its deliberations (hung jury). Mistrial does not result in a judgment for any party, but merely indicates a failure of trial.

Mitigating circumstances   A set of conditions that, while not exonerating the accused, might reduce the sentence or the damages arising from the offense.

Modus operandi   Latin term meaning "the manner of operation." The means of accomplishing an act, especially the characteristic method employed by a defendant in repeated criminal acts.

Moot court   A fictitious court established to argue hypothetical cases. Law schools form moot courts as an instrument of learning.

Mortgage   In common law, a conveyance of, or granting of a lien upon, real property of a debtor to his creditor, intended as a security for the repayment of a loan, usually the purchase price (or a part thereof) of the property so conveyed or encumbered.

Motion   An application to the court requesting an order in favor of the applicant. Motions are generally made in reference to a pending action and may be addressed to a matter within the discretion of the judge, or may concern a point of law. Motions may be made orally or, more formally, in writing.

Municipal court   A city court that administers the law within the city. These courts generally have exclusive jurisdiction over violations of city ordinances and may also have jurisdiction over minor criminal cases arising within the city and over certain civil cases.

Murder   Unlawful killing of another human being with premeditated intent or malice aforethought. *First degree murder* is unlawful killing that is deliberate and premeditated. *Second degree murder* is unlawful killing of another with malice aforethought but without deliberation and premeditation. Such malice may be in the form of express malice as the actual intention to kill, or of implied malice where there is no intent but, where death is caused by an act which discloses such a reckless state of mind as to be equivalent to an actual intent to kill.

Natural law Law that so necessarily agrees with the nature of human beings, that without observing the maxims, the peace and happiness of society cannot be preserved; that law, knowledge of which may be attained merely by the light of reason, and from the facts of its essential connection with human nature.

Negligence Failure to exercise a degree of care that a person of ordinary prudence (a "reasonable man") would exercise under the same circumstances. The term refers to conduct that falls below the standard established by law for the protection of others against unreasonable risk of harm.

Negotiable instrument A writing signed by the maker or drawer, containing an unconditional promise or order to pay a specific sum, payable on demand or at a definite time, and payable to order or to bearer. A draft, check certificate of deposit, and note may or may not be negotiable instruments, depending upon whether the elements of negotiability are satisfied. An ordinary check issued by an employer to an employee or by a customer to a store is a negotiable instrument.

No fault A system of insurance whereby all persons who are injured in an automobile accident may be compensated for any injuries resulting therefrom, without regard to who was at fault.

Nolo contendere Latin term meaning "I do not wish to contend, fight or maintain (a defense)." A statement that the defendant will not contest a charge made by the government. It admits all facts stated in the indictment for the purposes of a particular case, but it cannot be used as an admission elsewhere, or in any other proceeding, such as a civil suit arising from the same facts.

Nonfeasance In the law of agency, the total omission or failure of an agent to perform a distinct duty that he has agreed with his principal to do; also, the neglect or refusal, without sufficient excuse, to do what is an officer's legal duty to do. Nonfeasance differs from *misfeasance,* which is the improper doing of an act that one might lawfully do, and from *malfeasance,* which is the doing of an act that is wholly wrongful and unlawful.

Notary public A public officer authorized to administer oaths, to attest to and certify certain types of documents, to take depositions, and to perform certain acts in commercial matters. The seal of a notary public authenticates a document. In some jurisdictions an attorney admitted to practice within the jurisdiction can act as a notary public. In many jurisdictions private persons can apply for and receive authority to act as notaries to witness documents.

Note A written paper that acknowledges a debt and promises payment to a specified party of a specific sum, and that describes a time of maturity that is either definite or will become definite.

Not guilty A plea by the accused in a criminal action that denies every essential element of the offense charged. A plea of not guilty on arraignment obliges the government to prove the defendant's guilt beyond a reasonable doubt and preserves the right of the accused to defend against the charge. A jury verdict of not guilty does not mean the jury found the accused innocent, but simply that the state failed to prove its case beyond a reasonable doubt.

Notice Information concerning a fact, communicated by or derived from an authorized person. For example, a defendant might receive notice that a lawsuit has been instituted against him or her.

Nuisance Anything that disturbs the free use of one's property, or that renders its ordinary use uncomfortable. In tort law, a wrong arising from unreasonable or unlawful use of property to the annoyance or damage of another or of the public.

Oath An affirmation of the truth of a statement.

Objection A procedure whereby a party asserts during a trial that a particular witness, line of questioning, piece of evidence, or other matter is improper and should not be continued, and asks the court to rule on its impropriety or illegality.

Obstruction of justice The impeding of those who seek justice in a court, or of those who have duties or powers of administering justice therein; includes attempting to influence, intimidate, or impede any juror, witness, or officer in any court regarding the discharge of his or her duty. Statutes addressing this subject may reach beyond interference with the judicial process and also proscribe interference with police officers and other such administrative officials.

Offense Any violation of law for which a penalty is prescribed, including both felonies and misdemeanors.

Opinion The reason given for a court's judgment, finding or conclusion, as opposed to the decision, which is the judgment itself. When the court is composed of more than one judge or justice, and more than one opinion has been written in a given case, the opinion that expresses the view of the majority of the judges presiding, and thus announces the decision of the court, is referred to as the *majority opinion.* A *concurring opinion* is a view basically in accord with the majority opinion, but written to express a somewhat different perception of the issues, to illuminate a particular judge's reasoning or to expound a principle which he or she holds in high esteem. An opinion that concurs "in the result only" is one that rejects the reasoning and conclusions concerning the law or the facts on the basis of which the majority reached its decision, and that expresses a different view that has coincidentally led the judge or justice to recommend the same disposition as was agreed upon by the majority. A *dissenting opinion* is a view that disagrees with the disposition made of the case by the court with the facts or law on the basis of which the court arrived at its decision, or the principles of law announced by the court in deciding the case. Opinions may also be written that express a dissent "in part."

Ordinance A local law that applies to persons and things subject to the local jurisdiction. Usually it is an act of a city council or similar body that has the same force as a statute when it is duly enacted.

Overrule 1. To overturn or make void the decision of a prior case, generally accomplished in a different and subsequent case, when a court renders a decision that is substantially opposite of the decision made in the prior case. A decision can be overruled only by the same court or a higher court within the same jurisdiction. 2. To deny a motion, objection or other point raised to the court.

Palimony   An award of support like alimony but made to a partner in a dissolved nonmarital relationship. Where the partners had an express contract, founded on consideration other than sexual services, some courts have held the contract enforceable; where no such formal agreement exists, the court may determine whether the conduct of the parties warrants a finding of implied contract or other understanding to support an award.

Paralegal   One not a member of the bar who is employed, usually by a law office, to perform a variety of tasks associated with a law practice, any of which may be performed properly and conveniently by one not trained or authorized to practice law.

Pardon   An exercise of the sovereign prerogative to relieve a person from further punishment and from legal disabilities resulting from a crime of which he or she has been convicted. Its effect is that of relaxing the punishment and blotting out guilt, so that in the eyes of the law the offender is as innocent as if the offense had never been committed.

Parole   In criminal law, a conditional release from imprisonment that entitles the person receiving it to serve the remainder of his term outside prison if he complies with all the conditions connected with his release.

Partnership   1. A contract of two or more persons to place their money, effects, labor and skill, or some or all of them, in lawful business, and to divide the profit and bear the loss in certain proportions. 2. An association of two or more persons to carry on as co-owners a business for profit. Partners are individually liable for the debts of the partnership, and assets individually owned will be used to satisfy any such debt when partnership assets are insufficient. A partnership is not subject to tax; rather the income is divided and taxed as personal income to the individual partners, unlike profits in corporations. The decision whether to form a partnership or to incorporate is generally controlled by the tax consequences.

Party   1. In a judicial proceeding, a litigant (plaintiff or defendant); a person directly interested in the subject matter of a case; one who would assert a claim, make a defense, control proceedings, examine witnesses, or appeal from the judgment. 2. A person or entity that enters into a contract, lease, deed, etc.

Patent   A grant of right to exclude others from the making or selling of an invention during a specified time. It gives its owner a legitimate monopoly.

Penal law   A law to preserve public order that defines an offense against the public and inflicts a penalty for its violation. Statutes that grant a private civil action against a wrongdoer are not considered penal, but remedial, in nature.

Perjury   The criminal offense of making false statements under oath. In common law, only a willful and corrupt sworn statement made without sincere belief in its truth, and made in a judicial proceeding regarding its material matter, was perjury. Today, statutes have broadened the offense so that in some jurisdictions any false swearing in a legal instrument or legal setting is perjury.

Petition   A written application addressed to a court or judge, stating facts and circumstances relied upon as a cause for judicial action, and containing a formal request for relief.

Plagiarism   Appropriation of the literary composition of another and passing off as one's own the product of the mind and language of another. The offense of plagiarism, known in the law as infringement of copyright, comes into being only when the work allegedly copied is protected by copyright.

Plaintiff   The one who initially brings the suit. The one who, in a personal action, seeks a remedy in a court of justice for an injury to, or a withholding of, his or her rights.

Plea   In equity, a special answer relying upon one or more things as a reason for the suit to be dismissed, delayed or barred. At law, broadly, any one of the common law pleadings. Technically, the defendant's or respondent's answer by matter of fact to the plaintiff's petition or complaint. In criminal procedure, the defendant will enter a plea at his arraignment of not guilty, guilty or, in some jurisdictions, nolo contendere or non vult (meaning no contest).

Plea bargaining   The process whereby the accused and the prosecutor negotiate a mutually satisfactory disposition of the case. The defendant may plead guilty to a lesser offense or to only one or some of the counts in a multicount indictment. In return, the defendant seeks concessions on the type and length of the sentence or a reduction of counts against him.

Pleadings   Statements, in logical and legal form, of the facts that constitute plaintiff's cause of action and defendant's ground of defense. Pleadings are either allegations by the parties affirming or denying certain matters of fact, or other statements in support or derogation of certain principles of law, which are intended to describe to the court or jury the real matter in dispute.

Police court   An inferior municipal court with limited jurisdiction in criminal cases. Minor cases can be disposed of by such courts, but otherwise they generally have power only to arraign the accused and set bail.

Police Power   Inherent power of state governments, often delegated in part to local governments, to impose upon private rights those restrictions that are reasonably related to promotion and maintenance of the health, safety, morals and general welfare of the public.

Polygamy   In criminal law, the offense of having more than one husband or wife at one time.

Polygraph   A lie detector; an electromechanical instrument that measures and records certain physiologic changes that it is believed are involuntarily caused by the subject's conscious attempts to deceive the questioner. Once the machine has recorded the subject's responses to the questions, the operator interprets the record and determines whether the subject is lying.

Power of attorney   An instrument in writing by which one person appoints another as his agent and confers upon him the authority to perform certain specified acts or kinds of acts on his behalf. The primary purpose of a power of attorney is to evidence the authority of the agent to third parties with whom the agent deals.

Precedent   A previously decided case recognized as an authority for the disposition of future cases. In common law, precedents were regarded as the major source of law. A precedent may involve a novel question of common law or it may involve an interpretation of a statute. To the extent that future cases rely upon the precedent or distinguish it from themselves without disapproving of it, the case will serve as a precedent for future cases.

Preliminary hearing   A hearing, before indictment, to determine whether probable cause for the arrest of a person existed; a hearing to determine whether there is sufficient evidence to warrant the defendant's continued detention and whether submission of such evidence to the grand jury is warranted.

Premeditation   Forethought. As one of the elements of first-degree murder, the term is often equated with intent and deliberateness.

Presentment   A written accusation of crime by the grand jury upon its own initiative, without consent or participation of a prosecutor, in the exercise of the jury's lawful inquisitorial powers.

Presumption of innocence   The prevailing assumption that the accused is innocent until proven guilty. Because of this presumption, the government bears the burden of proof that the defendant is guilty beyond a reasonable doubt.

Prima facie   Latin term meaning "at first view, on its face." Not requiring further support to establish existence, validity, credibility.

Privileged communication   Communication that occurs in a setting of legal or other recognized professional confidentiality. Designating a communication as privileged allows the speakers to resist legal process to disclose its contents. When communications are termed privileged, a breach by one party of the concurrent confidentiality can result in a civil suit in tort by the other party to the communication. Communications that are privileged may include: 1. communications in the sanctity of the marital relationship; 2. communications between physicians and their patients; 3. communications of psychological counselors and their clients; 4. priest-and-penitent communications; 5. communications between attorney and client, and 6. in some jurisdictions, communications between journalists and their sources.

Probable cause   A requisite element of a valid arrest or search and seizure, consists of knowledge of facts and circumstances sufficient in themselves to warrant belief that a crime has been committed (in the context of an arrest) or that property subject to seizure is at a designated location (in the context of a search and seizure).

Probate   The act of proving that an instrument purporting to be a will was signed and otherwise executed in accordance with the legal requirements for a will, and of determining its validity; the combined result of all procedures necessary to establish the validity of a will.

Probation   The procedure whereby a defendant found guilty of a crime, upon a verdict or plea of guilty, is released by the court without imprisonment, subject to conditions imposed by the court, under the supervision of a probation officer.

Procedure   Legal method; the machinery for carrying on the suit, including pleading, process, evidence and practice. The term thus refers to the mechanics of the legal process—the body of rules and practice by which justice is meted out by the legal system—rather than the substance and content of the law itself.

Proceeding   The succession of events in the process of judicial action; the form in which actions are to be brought and defended, the manner of intervening in suits, of conducting them; the mode of deciding them, of opposing and of executing judgments.

Process   A formal writing (writ) issued by authority of law; any means used by the court to acquire or to exercise its jurisdiction over a person or over specified property; usually refers to the method used to compel attendance of a defendant in court in a civil suit.

Property   Every species of valuable right or interest that is subject to ownership, has an exchangeable value or adds to one's wealth or estate. Property describes one's exclusive right to possess, use and dispose of a thing, as well as the object, benefit or prerogative that constitutes the subject matter of that right.

Prosecution   The act of pursuing a lawsuit or criminal trial; the party initiating a criminal suit, i.e., the state. Where the civil litigant, or the state in a criminal trial, fails to move the case towards final resolution or trial as required by the court schedule, the matter may be dismissed for want of prosecution or for failure to prosecute.

Prosecutor   A public official who prepares and conducts the prosecution of persons accused of crime. In certain cases, the legislature may appoint a special prosecutor to conduct a limited investigation and prosecution. The state prosecutors are usually called district attorneys or county prosecutors. The federal prosecutor is known as the U. S. attorney for a certain federal district. The prosecutor is charged with the duty of seeing that the laws of his or her jurisdiction are faithfully executed and enforced.

Proximate cause   That which in natural and continuous sequence, unbroken by any new independent cause, produces an event, and without which an injury would not have occurred.

Public defender   A lawyer, usually one holding public office, whose duty is to defend accused persons unable to pay for legal assistance.

Quid pro quo   Latin term meaning "something for something." That which a party receives or is promised in return for something the party promises, gives or does.

Rape   An act of unlawful sexual intercourse accomplished through force or threat of force by one party and implying lack of consent and resistance by the other party.

Real property   Land and whatever is erected or growing on it, or affixed to it. Rights issuing out of, annexed to, and exercisable within or about, the land. *Compare* **Chattel**.

Reapportionment   The changing of a legislative district or of the number of seats a state is entitled to in the Congress to more clearly reflect the population of that district or state; an attempt to meet the right of every person to vote on a one-person, one-vote basis.

Reasonable doubt   Refers to the degree of certainty required of a juror before he can make a legally valid determination of the guilt of a criminal defendant. These words are used in instructions to the jury in a criminal trial to indicate that innocence is to be presumed unless the jury can see no reasonable doubt of the guilt of the person charged. The term does not require that proof be so clear that no possibility of error exists; it means that the evidence must be so conclusive that all reasonable doubts are removed from the mind of the ordinary person.

Recess   Temporary adjournment of a trial or hearing after commencement of the trial or hearing. The recess may be short, for lunch, overnight, or for a few days. If it amounts to a substantial delay in the proceedings, it is called a continuance.

Reciprocity   Generally, a relationship between persons, corporations, states, or countries whereby privileges granted by one are returned by the other.

Record   A precise history of a suit from beginning to end, including the conclusions of law thereon, drawn by the proper officer to perpetuate the exact facts. In real property law, to enter in writing in a repository maintained as a public record any mortgage, sale of land, or other interest affecting real property located within the jurisdiction of the government entity maintaining the public record.

Recovery   The establishment of a right by the judgment of a court, though recovery does not necessarily imply a return to whole or normal; the amount of the judgment; the amount actually collected pursuant to the judgment.

Referendum   Referring of legislative acts to the voters for final approval or rejection.

Remand   To send back, as for further deliberation; to send back to the tribunal (or body) from which the matter was appealed or moved. When a judgment is reversed, the appellate court usually remands the matter for a new trial to be carried out consistent with the principles announced by the appellate court in its opinion ordering the remand.

Repeal   Abrogation or annulling of a previous law by the enactment of a subsequent statute, which either expressly declares that the former law shall be revoked, or contains provisions so irreconcilable with those of the earlier law as to abrogate the earlier law by necessary implication.

Reprieve   In criminal law, the postponement of a sentence for an interval in which the execution is suspended.

Res   Latin term meaning "a thing." The subject matter of actions that are primarily *in rem,* that is, actions that establish rights in relation to an object, as opposed to a person. For example, in an action that resolves a conflict over title to real property, the land

in question is the *res.* Tangible personal property can also be a res.

Respondent   In equity cases, the party who answers a pleading.

Restraining order   An order granted without notice or hearing, demanding the preservation of the status quo until a hearing to determine the propriety of injunctive relief, temporary or permanent. A restraining order is always temporary, since it is granted pending a hearing; thus it is often called a temporary restraining order.

Restraint of trade   In common law and as used in the antitrust laws, illegal restraints interfering with free competition in commercial transactions, which tend to restrict production, affect prices, or otherwise control the market to the detriment of consumers of goods and services.

Retainer   Compensation paid in advance to an attorney for services to be performed in a specific case. A retainer may be the whole sum to be charged (plus expenses), but more often is a deposit, with the attorney furnishing a periodic or final statement of how much the client owes for services rendered.

Retraction   The withdrawing of a plea, declaration, accusation, promise, etc.

Retrial   A new trial in which an issue or issues already litigated, and as to which a verdict or decision by the court has been rendered, are reexamined by the same court for some sufficient reason, such as a recognition that the initial trial was improper or unfair as a result of procedural errors. *Compare* **Mistrial**.

Reversal   As used in opinions, judgments and mandates, changing to the contrary the decision of a lower court or other body.

Robbery   Forcible stealing; the taking of property from the person of another by violence or by putting the other person in fear. *Armed robbery* is robbery aggravated by the fact that it is committed by a defendant armed with a dangerous weapon, whether or not the weapon is used in the course of committing the crime.

 **Sanction**   To approve, to reward or punish; a consequence of punishment for violation of accepted norms of social conduct, which may be of two kinds: those that redress civil injuries (civil sanctions) and those that punish crimes (penal sanctions).

Search warrant   An order issued by a judge or magistrate authorizing certain law enforcement officers to conduct a search of specified premises for specified things or persons. In those cases where warrants are required, only a judge or magistrate who has not previously considered the facts giving rise to the application can issue a search warrant, and only upon showing of probable cause that the described item is located in the designated place and that it was involved in the planning or commission of a crime.

Sedition   Illegal action that tends to cause the disruption and overthrow of the government.

Self-defense   The self-protection of one's person, or preservation of members of one's family and, to a lesser extent, one's property, from harm by an aggressor, in a way and under circumstances that the law recognizes as justifying the protective measures. It is a valid defense to a criminal charge or to tort liability.

Self-incrimination, privilege against The constitutional right of a person to refuse to answer questions or otherwise give testimony against himself that will create substantial likelihood of criminal incrimination. The privilege can be displaced by a grant of use immunity, which guarantees that neither the compelled testimony nor any fruits will be used against the witness. Given such immunity, the witness is no longer exposed to the hazard of self-incrimination and thus must respond to questions or provide evidence. It should be emphasized that the privilege against self-incrimination, like all constitutional rights, may be waived. Miranda warnings are generally necessary before such a waiver will be found to qualify a confession as admissible evidence in a criminal trial.

Sentence Punishment ordered by a court for a person convicted of a crime, usually either a noncustodial sentence such as probation or a fine, or a *custodial sentence* such as a term of imprisonment. A *concurrent sentence* is a sentence that overlaps with another as opposed to a consecutive (cumulative) sentence, which runs by itself beginning after or ending before the running of another sentence. A *consecutive sentence* is a sentence that runs separately from one or more other sentences to be served by the same individual. The sentence is cumulative to the extent that it begins after an existing sentence has terminated either by expiration of the maximum term of the existing sentence, or by release from the present sentence through parole. A *suspended sentence* is a sentence whose imposition or execution has been withheld by the court on certain terms and conditions.

Sequester To separate from; to hold aside, as in to sequester assets or to sequester witnesses during a trial.

Sequestration In equity, the act of seizing property belonging to another and holding it until profits have paid the demand for which the property was taken.

In law, the practice of keeping jury members together and guarded from improper contact with people who are not members of the jury throughout the trial and jury deliberations. Juries are sequestered at the discretion of the trial judge when he or she feels sequestration would serve the interests of justice. Sequestration of witnesses is frequently ordered by the court at the request of one of the parties to insure that incourt testimony of each witness will not be colored by what another witness said.

Settlement The conclusive resolving of a matter; especially, a compromise achieved by adverse parties in a civil suit before final judgment, whereby they agree between themselves, thus eliminating the necessity of judicial resolution of the controversy.

Sheriff's sale (judicial sale) A sale of property by the sheriff under authority of a court's judgment and writ of execution in order to satisfy an unpaid judgment, mortgage, lien or other debt of the owner.

Shield laws In the case of news persons, laws designed to protect a journalist's confidential sources of information and to protect other information, notes and materials from disclosure. In the case of rape victims, laws that limit the questions a defendant may ask about the lifestyle of the victim unless those questions can be shown to be essential for a fair trial.

Sine qua non Latin term meaning "without which not." That without which the thing cannot be; an absolutely essential and necessary thing. The following example shows how the term is used in law cases: Tom purchases a new refrigerator. He puts the old one on the street to be carted away but does not remove the door or lock it shut. A child is severely injured when he is trapped inside the refrigerator. The sine qua non is Tom's failure to do something about the door, which made the refrigerator an attractive nuisance.

Slander Spoken words that tend to damage another's reputation. *Compare* **Libel**.

Sodomy Crime against nature, including bestiality and, in many jurisdictions, other acts of unnatural sexual intercourse as defined and proscribed by statute. Sodomy was a common law felony in the United States.

Stare decisis Latin term meaning "to stand by that which was decided." Rule by which common law courts are reluctant to interfere with principles announced in former decisions and therefore rely upon judicial precedent as a compelling guide to decision of cases raising issues similar to those in previous cases. For example: A state supreme court rules that a person's privacy interests demand court protection of telephone toll records from police investigations. Several years later, the issue is brought back to the court. The prosecutor claims that other states allow the records to be used without interference in privacy and that other privacy protections can be employed if necessary. Even if some new members of the court agree with the prosecutor, the court most likely will apply stare decisis and abide by the previous decision.

Statute An act of the legislature, adopted under its constitutional authority, by prescribed means and in certain form, so that it becomes the law governing conduct within its scope. Statutes are enacted to prescribe conduct, define crimes, create inferior government bodies, appropriate public monies, and in general to promote the public welfare.

Statute of frauds The statutory requirement that certain contracts be in writing to be enforceable.

Statute of limitations Any law that fixes the time within which parties must take judicial action to enforce rights or else be thereafter barred from enforcing them. The enactment of such laws derives from the belief that there is a point beyond which a prospective defendant should no longer worry about future possibility of an action against him, that the law disfavors "stale evidence," and that no one should be able to "sit on his rights" for an unreasonable time without forfeiting claims.

Statutory rape The crime of having sexual intercourse with a female under an age set by statute, regardless of whether or not she consents to the act.

Stay A halt in a judicial proceeding where, by its order, the court will not take further action until the occurrence of some event.

Stay of execution   A process whereby a judgment is precluded from being executed for a specific period.

Stipulation   An agreement or concession made by parties in a judicial proceeding or by their attorneys, relating to a matter before the court.

Subpoena   Latin term meaning "under penalty." A legal order issued under the authority of a court to compel the appearance of a witness at a judicial proceeding; disobedience may be punishable as contempt of court.

Suit   Any proceeding in a court of justice by which an individual pursues a remedy that the law affords.

Summons   An order requiring the appearance of the defendant under penalty of having a judgment entered against him for failure to appear. The object of the summons is to notify the defendant that he has been sued.

Suppression of evidence   A decision made by a judge not to allow certain evidence into a criminal trial because the evidence was obtained by illegal or improper means.

Supremacy clause   The popular title for Article VI, Section 2 of the U.S. Constitution, which is the main foundation of the federal government's power over the states, providing that the acts of the federal government are operative as supreme law throughout the union.

Supreme court   The highest appellate court in most jurisdictions and in the federal court system. It is usually the appellate state court of last resort, and in the absence of a federal question, its decisions cannot be reviewed by other courts and must be respected. In some states this court is an inferior court and not the court of last resort. In the federal court system, the U. S. Supreme Court is expressly provided for in the Constitution, which vests judicial power in "one Supreme Court" and such inferior courts as Congress shall establish. It consists of a chief justice and eight associate justices appointed by the president with the advice and consent of the U.S. Senate.

Surrogate   A judicial officer of limited jurisdiction, who has jurisdiction over the probate of wills, the settlement of estates and in some cases adoptions.

Taft-Hartley Act   The popular name for the Labor-Management Relations Act of 1947, whose purpose is to protect employers' rights by broadening their rights to free speech on unionization; by permitting them to disregard unions formed by supervisory personnel; by outlawing the closed shop; by permitting employees to refrain from union activity; by limiting employee elections on whether to unionize to one per year; by prohibiting unions from forcing an employee to join, from forcing an employer to discriminate against non-union employees, from refusing to bargain collectively with the employer, from engaging in wildcat strikes, from charging discriminatory membership fees, and from extracting favors or kickbacks from employers.

Taking the fifth   The popular term given to a person's assertion of his Fifth Amendment right not to give evidence that will incriminate himself.

Tenancy   The right to possess an estate, whether by lease or by title. In general, tenancy refers to any right to hold property. It also refers to holding in subordination to another's title, as in the landlord-tenant relationship.

Tenant   One who holds land by any kind of title or right, whether permanently or temporarily; one who purchases an estate and is entitled to possession, whether exclusive or to be shared with others; one who leases premises from the owner or from a tenant.

Testator (testatrix)   One who makes and executes a testament or will. Testator applies to a man, testatrix to a woman.

Testimony   Statement made by a witness, under oath, usually related to a legal proceeding or legislative hearing; evidence given by a competent witness under oath, as distinguished from evidence derived from writing and other sources.

Title   Ownership; a term used in property law to denote the composite of facts that will permit one to recover or to retain possession of a thing. A "defect" in title is referred to as a cloud on title.

Title search   An investigation of documents in the public record office to determine the state of a title, including all liens, encumbrances, mortgages, etc., affecting the property; the means by which a chain of title is ascertained.

Tort   A wrong; a private or civil wrong or injury resulting from a breach of a legal duty that exists by virtue of society's expectations regarding interpersonal conduct, rather than by contract or other private relationship. The essential elements of a tort are existence of a legal duty owed by the defendant to the plaintiff, breach of that duty, and a causal relation between the defendant's conduct and the resulting damage to the plaintiff.

Trademark   Any mark, word, letter, number, design, picture or combination thereof in any form, which is adopted and used by a person to denominate goods that he makes, is affixed to the goods, and is neither a common or generic name for the goods nor a picture of them, nor is merely descriptive of the goods. Protection from infringement on a trademark is afforded by law.

Trial   A judicial examination of issues between parties, whether they are issues of law or fact, before a court that has jurisdiction over the cause. Trials are governed by established procedures and court rules, and usually involve offering of testimony or evidence.

Trial court   Court of original jurisdiction, where matters are to be litigated first and where all evidence relative to a cause is received and considered. All states differentiate between trial courts and appellate courts. The distinction is that it is the function of the trial court first to determine the facts and the law in a case, with the appellate court acting predominantly as a court of review of law, but not fact.

Tribunal   An officer or body having authority to adjudicate matters.

Trust   1. An entity that holds assets for the benefit of certain other persons or entities. The person holding legal title or interest, who has responsibility for the assets and distribution of the assets or distribution of the income generated by such assets, is the trustee. The beneficiary is the person for whose benefit the trust is created. 2. Any relationship in which one acts as guardian or fiduciary in relation to another's property. Thus, a deposit of money in a bank is a trust, or the receipt of money to be applied to a particular purpose or to be paid to another is a trust.

Trustee   One who holds legal title to property in trust for the benefit of another person, and who is required to carry out specific duties with regard to the property, or who has been given power affecting the disposition of property for another's benefit.

Truth in Lending Act   A federal law, the provisions of which assure individuals applying for commercial credit information relating to the cost of credit, enabling them to decide which credit source offers them the most favorable credit terms. Under this law, the commercial lender must inform the borrower of the dollar amount of the interest charges and the interest rate, computed on an annual basis according to the specified formula, and must afford borrowers who pledge real property as security for the loan a three-day period in which to rescind the transaction.

Unconstitutional   Conflicting with some provision of the constitution. A statute found to be unconstitutional is considered void or as if it had never been, and consequently all rights, contracts or duties that depend on it are void. Similarly, no one can be punished for having refused obedience to the law once it is found to be unconstitutional.

Uniform Commercial Code (UCC)   A code of laws governing various commercial transactions, including the sale of goods, banking transactions, secured transactions in personal property, and other matters. The UCC was designed to bring uniformity in these areas to the laws of the various states. It has been adopted, with some modifications, in all states (except Louisiana) as well as in the District of Columbia and in the Virgin Islands.

Unlawful assembly   A misdemeanor in common law consisting of a meeting of several persons with a common plan that, if carried out would result in a riot; a meeting of persons who intend to commit a crime by open force; a meeting to execute a common design, lawful or unlawful, in an unauthorized manner that is likely to cause a breach of the peace.

Vagrancy   General term for a class of minor offenses, such as idleness without visible means of support, loitering, and wandering around from place to place without any lawful purpose.

Variance   In legal procedure, a discrepancy between what is charged or alleged and what is proved or offered as proof. In zoning law, an exemption from the application of a zoning ordinance or regulation permitting a use that varies from that otherwise permitted. The exception is granted by the appropriate authority in special circumstances to protect against undue hardship wrought by strict enforcement.

Venue   A neighborhood, a neighboring place; synonym for place of trial. Venue refers to the possible or proper place for trial of a suit, among several places where jurisdiction could be established. Venue essentially involves the right of the party sued to have the action heard in a particular judicial district, for reasons of convenience. In a criminal trial where publicity surrounding the crime would virtually preclude fair trial, the court will direct a change of venue, or removal of the proceedings to a different district or county.

Verdict   The opinion rendered by a jury, or a judge where there is no jury, on a question of fact. A verdict differs from a judgment in that a verdict is not a judicial determination, but rather a finding of fact that the trial court may accept or reject and utilize in formulating its judgment.

Vested   Fixed, accrued or absolute; generally used to describe any right or title to something that is not dependent upon the occurrence or failure to occur of some specified future event.

Waiver   An intentional and voluntary surrender of some known right, which generally may either result from an express agreement or be inferred from circumstances.

Wanton   Grossly negligent or careless; with a reckless disregard of consequences.

Ward   One of the sections into which a town is divided for educational or election purposes.

Ward of the court   A person whom the law regards as incapable of managing his or her own affairs, and over whom or over whose property a guardian is appointed.

Warrant   A written order from a competent authority directing the doing of a certain act, especially one directing the arrest of a person or persons, issued by a court, body or official.

Warranty   An assurance by one party to a contract of the existence of a fact upon which the other party may rely, intended to relieve the promisee of any duty to ascertain the fact for himself or herself, and which amounts to a promise to indemnify the promisee for any loss if the fact warranted proves untrue.

White-collar crime   A catch-all phrase connoting a variety of frauds, schemes and commercial offenses by business persons, confidence men and public officials; includes a broad range of nonviolent offenses that have cheating as the central element. Consumer fraud, bribery, and stock manipulation are other examples of white-collar crime.

Will   A person's declaration of how he desires his property to be disposed of after his death. A will may also contain other declarations of the testator's desires as to what is to be done after he dies so long as it disposes of some property.

Witness   1. One who gives evidence in a cause before a court and who attests or swears to facts or gives testimony under oath. 2. To observe the execution of, as that of an instrument, or to sign one's name to it to authenticate it (attest it). *See also* **Hostile witness**; **Character witness**; **Material witness**.

Writ   A legal order issued by an authority and in the name of the state to compel a person to do something therein mentioned. It is issued by a court or other competent tribunal, and is directed to the sheriff or other officer authorized to execute it. In every case the writ itself contains directions for doing what is required.

Writ of execution A routine court order by which the court attempts to enforce the judgment granted a plaintiff by authorizing a sheriff to seize the property belonging to the debtor to satisfy the judgment obtained by the creditor.

Youthful offenders Youths accused of crime who are processed in the juvenile court system, and so are treated as delinquents rather than as adult criminals. The age beyond which an offender is considered an adult for prosecution and punishment purposes has not been uniformly established and so varies from state to state.

Zoning Legislative action, usually on the municipal level, that divides municipalities into districts for the purpose of regulating the use of private property and the construction of buildings within the zones established. Zoning is said to be part of the state police power, and therefore must be for the furthering of the health, morals, safety, or general welfare of the community.

LAW

LIFE SKILLS

CHECKING ACCOUNTS AND AUTOMATED TELLER MACHINES

Checking Accounts

How Fast Will Your Checks Clear?

There you stand, like a kid with his nose pressed against a pet-store window. Your money is romping behind the glass and you can't get at it. Any checks you deposit may be held by your bank until they clear.

If you write a check against deposited funds too soon, it will probably bounce. You'll pay $3 to $30 for the error. To bounce-proof your checks, sign up for overdraft checking. Alternatively, move your account to a small, friendly bank that will honor checks written against uncollected funds—although you'll probably be charged for the service. A *really* friendly bank will waive the fee.

Under federal law, banking institutions must give you access to at least $100 of your deposit on the next business day, and generally *must* clear the rest of your deposit on the following schedule:

1. One business day for federal, state, and local government checks, electronic payments (like direct deposit of a paycheck or Social Security check), postal money orders, cash, personal checks drawn on the same bank, cashier's checks, and certified checks.
2. Two business days for local checks.
3. Five business days for out-of-town checks.
4. On deposits fed into a bank's own ATM machines before noon—two business days, for cash, cashier's checks, and state and local government checks; one day for federal government checks; three days for local checks, and seven days for out-of-town checks. Add one day for deposits made after noon.
5. Seven business days, for all deposits made before noon in ATMs not owned by your bank; eight days for deposits after noon.
6. On deposits made by mail or in the bank's night depository—two days after receipt by the bank for cashier's checks and state and local government checks; three days for local checks, seven days for out-of-town checks.

These rules exist solely to whip reluctant banks into line. Many institutions cheerfully offer one-day clearance for almost all checks. And even the banks that hold your checks for two to eight days might credit interest to your account from the day of deposit.

Is a bank ever allowed to hold checks longer than usual? Absolutely. It needs at least some weapons against the risk of dishonesty and fraud. Expect a delay in drawing against deposited checks if:

1. You're a brand new customer. The bank gets 30 days to take your measure, during which time you might have to wait longer than usual for checks to clear. But even new customers can draw, the next business day, on the first $5,000 of funds from a government, cashier's, or travelers check, or from deposits made electronically. So if you move, transfer your bank account by wire.
2. You repeatedly overdraw your checking account, or are redepositing a check that bounced. In this case, a local check can be held for 7 days and an out-of-town check for 11 days.
3. You deposit more than $5,000 in checks in a single day. Part of your money will be released on the normal schedule; part can be held up to four days longer.

These rules all apply to withdrawals by check or to cash withdrawals through a human teller. Limits are allowed on cash withdrawals through an ATM.

More Check Facts

To cash checks at a branch other than your own, get a signature card.

When you endorse a check (that is, sign your name on the back) it becomes as good as money and can be cashed by anyone who finds it. To prevent that, endorse it with instructions: "Pay to the order of Tiny Tim" or "For deposit only." When accepting an endorsed check from someone else, ask him to write "pay to the order of (you)," so that if you lose it neither of you will be out the money.

Endorse checks on the back, at the left-hand end (when viewed from the front), in the first inch and a half of space. If your signature is anywhere else, the bank may ask you to sign again. Most checks now carry a line to show where your signature goes.

Technically, a check may be good for years. But in practice, the bank might refuse any check that is more than one year old. That is, if the bank notices.

If you write a check and wish you hadn't, call your bank and ask that payment be stopped. Your account should be flagged right away, but you have to follow up with written authorization—usually by filing a stop-check form. The cost: $3. to $20. A stop-payment lasts for a limited period of time but can be renewed. If the check slips through, the bank takes responsibility for it. The stop-check form should spell out the rules.

You can arrange for regular, automatic transfers from your checking to your savings account. Interest on your certificates of deposit can be deposited into either account.

If someone forges your signature on a check and the bank cashes it, you are entitled to 100 percent reimbursement. It doesn't matter that you failed to report that your checkbook was stolen (although you should have). It doesn't matter that you kept your checks with your credit cards, which carry your signature. In most cases, it is the bank's absolute responsibility to guard against forgery. But you have a responsibility, too. If you don't report a forgery within 14 days after the bank mailed your statement, and fraudulent checks continue to be cashed by the same person, the later losses are all yours.

Use a *certified check* when the person you're paying wants a guarantee that the check will be good. The bank certifies that the check will be paid, by withdrawing the money from your account when the check is issued. A *cashier's check* can be used by people with no checking account. You give the money to the bank and it issues a check on its own account. Banks, S&Ls, and money-order companies, and the Post Office also issue money orders, payable to specific people. Keep all receipts. They're your only proof of payment. File them as if they were canceled checks.

Balancing Your Checkbook

Good news: *You don't have to.* The Rockies won't crumble, Gibraltar won't tumble, if you take the bank's word that your balance is right. Personally, I'm not happy unless my checkbook adds up—but that's easy for me to say; I let my husband do it. If you are allergic to arithmetic, here's the minimum you can get away with:

- ■ Enter every deposit and withdrawal on your check register as you go along—not forgetting your dealings with ATMs or money withdrawn when you paid for something with a debit card. You need a running total so you won't overdraw. Also, you don't want to fall below the minimum balance your account requires.
- ■ When the statement comes in, check every deposit and withdrawal against your check register, to be sure that the bank got everything right. If you wait a year or more to report a mistake, the bank might not make good. This system also catches alterations that a dishonest clerk might have made to your check.
- ■ Put a check on each check that was cashed.
- ■ If you have an interest-paying checking account, add the interest the bank paid that month to your checkbook balance. Then subtract all the fees. (These items show on your monthly statement.)

Assuming that nothing feels wildly out of line, it's okay to leave it at that. I don't trust a bank to enter checks correctly but I do trust its addition. (My own addition isn't so hot.)

Every six months or so, purge your math errors. Take the current balance, as reported by your bank; add all new deposits; subtract all uncashed checks; enter the result as the new balance in your checkbook, and start over.

Mind you, I don't recommend that you leave your checkbook a mess. But getting it in balance isn't the end-all of good financial planning.

Automated Teller Machines

The ATM machine is McBanking at its easiest. You insert a card and punch a few buttons. Instantly, you're in touch with your bank account—to confirm your checking-account balance, withdraw or deposit funds, or at some machines, switch money from one account to another. Thanks to these fast-cash machines, you can get money whenever you want: in the middle of a holiday weekend or late on Sunday night. Banks hook up their ATMs to national networks, so funds are even available if you run short while you're out of town.

But ATMs are sometimes a nuisance—for example, when they make mistakes. When you ask for $100, only $70 might show up in the drawer.

Around half of the banks now charge you for using their own ATMs—usually around 25 cents to $1 per transaction. It's sometimes more expensive than visiting the human teller. More than two-thirds of the banks charge if you reach your account through an ATM owned by another institution—maybe 75 cents to $2. The fee is usually for withdrawals. Deposits and balance inquiries may be free.

Most ATMs also accept credit cards. You use them to take out a loan against a line of credit. Debit cards, by contrast, withdraw money directly from your account.

If the Big Attraction of ATMs Is Convenience, the Big Risk Is Crime.

When you slip your card into an outdoor ATM, you're a sitting duck for a cruising crook. He knows that you've just picked up some cash. If he has the time, he might force you at knifepoint to tap your account for even more. Then he might steal your car and drive away.

ATM crime is growing, although no one knows by exactly how much. Banks don't like to report it, for fear of scaring you away. Also, full disclosure of the risks of using ATMs might give victimized customers stronger grounds for suing the banks to recover their losses. So the bankers keep mum.

Under the Electronic Fund Transfers Act, your bank has to reimburse you for all but $50 of an unauthorized withdrawal, provided that you report the loss immediately. So you're covered if a thief swipes your card and drains your account. You are also covered if you're persuaded by a gun in your back to empty out your account. Some institutions have tried to avoid paying customers in this situation, but the law says you're owed.

It is not at all clear, however, that the bank has any liability for your losses if you're knocked on the head as you're leaving the machine. Customers have sued their banks, but most of the cases are settled out of court. In at least one case, a bank argued successfully that the customer was himself negligent for using a poorly lighted ATM at night. Here's how to play it safe with an ATM:

- ■ Don't use ATMs at night, even if they are located on bank property. A survey by the Bank Administration Institute discovered that most ATM crimes take place between 7:00 P.M. and midnight, on bank premises.
- ■ Don't use ATMs in isolated areas at any time.
- ■ Don't use ATMs that are badly lit or readily accessible to a quick-hit thief in an automobile.
- ■ Don't be the only person at an ATM.
- ■ Don't use ATMs that are hidden by shrubbery.
- ■ Don't use a drive-up ATM without first locking the car doors.
- ■ Don't use ATMs that lack a permanent surveillance camera that could identify an assailant. (During a Florida lawsuit, it was discovered that, although a sign at an ATM said the machine was under surveillance, no camera existed.)
- ■ Don't write your personal identification number (PIN) on your ATM card. The PIN tells the

bank machine that you're really you. If your card is lost, that number is an open door into your account.

■ Don't give your PIN to a stranger. If the stranger claims to be a cop or a banker, he's lying. No one but a crook would ask.

TRAVELING ABROAD

Passports

Who Needs a Passport

U.S. citizens need passports to depart from or enter the United States and to enter most foreign countries. Exceptions include short-term travel between the United States and Mexico and Canada. For many Caribbean countries a birth certificate or voter registration card is acceptable proof of U.S. citizenship. However, a valid U.S. passport is the best travel documentation available and, with appropriate visas, is acceptable in all countries. Check with a travel agent or the airlines for specific passport requirements for admission to the country you plan to visit.

Mexico has initiated a new law regarding children traveling alone or with only one parent. If the child travels with one parent, a written, notarized consent must be obtained from the other parent and authenticated at a Mexican consulate. No authorization is needed if the child travels alone and is in possession of an American passport. Children traveling alone with only a birth certificate require authorization from both parents.

When to Apply

Demand for passports becomes heavy in January each year and begins to decline in August. You can help reduce government expenses and avoid delays by applying between September and December. However, even in those months, periods of high demand for passports can occur, so we recommend that you apply several months in advance of your planned departure whenever possible. (Passport agencies will expedite issuance in genuine, documented emergencies.) If you need visas, allow additional time—approximately two weeks per visa.

How to Apply

For your first passport you must present, in person, a completed form DSP-11, Passport Application, at one of the passport agencies listed at the back of this section or one of the several thousand federal or state courts or U.S. post offices that are authorized to accept passport applications. You may be able to find the address of one of these agencies in the government listings of your telephone book.

If you have had a previous passport and wish to obtain another, you may be eligible to apply by mail. Check the qualifications listed under When to Apply by Mail on page 14-5.

What to Bring When You Apply

1. Properly completed Passport Application (DSP-11). Do not sign it.
2. Proof of U.S. citizenship, which can be the following.
   a. Your previously issued passport or one in which you were included. If you are applying for your first passport or cannot submit a previous passport, you must submit other evidence of citizenship.
   b. If you were born in the United States:
   A Birth Certificate. This must show that the birth record was filed shortly after birth and must be certified with the registrar's signature and raised, impressed, embossed, or multicolored seal. You can obtain a certified copy from the Bureau of Vital Statistics in the state or territory where you were born. (Notifications of Birth Registration or Birth Announcements are not normally accepted for passport purposes.) A delayed birth certificate (one filed more than one year after the date of birth) is acceptable provided it shows a plausible basis for creation of the record at a later time.
   Secondary Evidence of Birth. If primary evidence is not obtainable, submit a notice from a state registrar stating that no birth record exists, accompanied by the best secondary evidence possible. This may include a baptismal certificate, a hospital birth record, affidavits of persons having personal knowledge of the facts of your birth, or other documentary evidence such as early census, school, family Bible records, newspaper files, and insurance papers. A personal knowledge affidavit should be supported by at least one public record reflecting birth in the United States.
   c. If you were born abroad:
   A Certificate of Naturalization.
   A Certificate of Citizenship.
   A Report of Birth Abroad of a Citizen of the United States of America (Form FS-240) or
   A Certification of Birth (Form FS-545 or DS-1350).

If you do not have any of the above documentation and are a U.S. citizen, you should take all available proof of citizenship to the nearest U.S. passport agency and request assistance in proving citizenship.

3. Proof of Identity.
You also must establish your identity to the satisfaction of the person accepting your application. The following items generally are acceptable documents of identity if they contain your signature and if they readily identify you by physical description or photograph:
   A previous U.S. passport.
   A Certificate of Naturalization or Citizenship.
   A valid driver's license.
   A government (federal, state, municipal) identification card.
The following documents are not acceptable:
   Social Security card.
   Learner's or temporary driver's license.
   Credit card of any type.
   Any temporary or expired identity card or document.

Any document that has been altered or changed in any manner.

If you are unable to present one of the first four documents to establish your identity, you must be accompanied by a person who has known you for at least two years and who is a U.S. citizen or a permanent resident alien of the United States. That person must sign an affidavit in the presence of the same person who executes the passport application. The witness will be required to establish his or her own identity. You must also submit some identification of your own.

4. Two photographs.

Present two identical photographs of yourself that are sufficiently recent (normally taken within the past six months) to be a good likeness. The photographs should not exceed 2 × 2 inches in size, and the image size from the bottom of the chin to the top of the head (including hair) must be not less than 1 inch or more than 1⅜ inches. Passport photographs are acceptable in either black and white or color.

Photographs should be clear, front view, full-face, and printed on thin white paper with a plain, light (white or off-white) background. Photographs should be portrait-type prints taken in normal street attire without a hat and should include no more than the head and shoulders or upper torso. Dark glasses are not acceptable except for medical reasons. Passport Services encourages photographs where the applicant is relaxed and smiling.

Only applicants who are on active duty in the U.S. Armed Forces and are proceeding abroad in the discharge of their duties may submit photographs in military uniform.

Most vending machine prints are not acceptable for use in passports. Newspaper and magazine prints are not permissible.

Length of Validity and Fees
The U.S. passport period of validity is 10 years. Applicants under 18 years of age continue to be issued 5-year passports, since their appearance changes more quickly. The fee for the l0-year passport is $65. The fee for the 5-year passport is $40.

In addition, a $10 acceptance fee is charged to applicants who are required to apply in person. A personal appearance and the acceptance fee are waived for applicants who meet the qualifications to apply by mail.

You may pay in person by check, bank draft, or money order. You may also pay in cash at a passport agency and at *some, but not all* post offices and clerks of court.

No Inclusion of Family Members in Your Passport
Experience has shown that persons may be inconvenienced or delayed abroad unless they have an individual passport. Therefore, since January 1981, all persons regardless of age or family relationship are required to obtain individual passports in their own name.

Required Appearance for Minors
Any applicant who is between ages 13 and 18 *must* appear in person, accompanied by a parent or legal guardian. For children under the age of 13, a parent or guardian may appear on their behalf.

When to Apply by Mail
You may apply by mail if all of the following are true:
- You have been issued a passport within 12 years prior to your new application.
- You are able to submit your most recent U.S. passport with your new application.
- Your previous passport was issued on or after your 16th birthday.
- You use the same name as that on your most recent passport or you have had your name changed by marriage or court order.

How to Apply by Mail
If you are eligible to apply by mail, obtain form DSP-82, Application for Passport by Mail, from one of the offices accepting applications or from a travel agent and complete the information requested.
- Sign and date the application.
- Attach your previous passport; two identical 2 × 2-inch photographs—which are sufficiently recent (normally taken within the past six months) to be a good likeness—signed in the center on the reverse, and the $55 passport fee. (The $10 acceptance fee is waived for applicants eligible to apply by mail.)
- Include your date of departure to ensure speedy processing of your application.
- If your name has changed, submit the original or certified copy of the court order or marriage certificate that shows the change of name.
- Mail the completed application and attachments to one of the passport agencies listed on pages 14-11 and 14-12 for processing. An incomplete or improperly prepared application will delay issuance of your passport.

If you are being assigned abroad on U.S. government business and wish to apply by mail for a no-fee passport (no-fee regular, official, diplomatic), you must submit the mail-in application form, your authorization to apply for a no-fee passport, your previous passport, and two photographs to the Washington D.C. Passport Agency for processing.

After You Receive Your Passport
Be sure to sign it and fill in the personal notification data page. Your previous passport and the original documents you submitted will be returned to you with your new passport.

Additional Visa Pages
If you require additional visa pages before your passport expires, you can obtain them by submitting your passport to a passport agency listed at the end of this section. You may request a 48-page passport at the time of application if you are planning to travel abroad extensively. There is no charge for extra pages or for a 48-page passport.

Validity of an Altered or Mutilated Passport for Travel
If you mutilate or alter your U.S. passport in any way (other than changing the address and personal notification data), you may render it invalid, cause your-

self much inconvenience, and expose yourself to possible prosecution under the law (Section 1543 of Title 22 of the U.S. Code).

Mutilated or altered passports should be turned in to passport agents, authorized postal employees, or U.S. consular officers abroad.

Loss or Theft of U.S. Passport

Your passport is a valuable document of citizenship and identity which should be carefully safeguarded. Its loss may cause you unnecessary travel complications as well as significant expense.

If your passport is lost or stolen in the United States, report the loss or theft immediately to Passport Services, Department of State, 1425 K Street, N.W., Washington, D.C., 20524 or to the nearest passport agency.

Should your passport be lost or stolen abroad, report the loss immediately to the nearest U.S. embassy or consulate and to local police authorities. If you can provide the consular officer with the information contained in the passport, it will facilitate issuance of a new passport. Therefore, we suggest you photocopy the data page of your passport and keep it in a separate place. In addition, leave the passport number, date, and place of issuance with a relative or friend in the United States. In the event of a lost or stolen passport, this information can be obtained and furnished to the consular officer abroad to assist in verification of the previous passport.

Other Passport Information

Sometimes travelers will depart from the United States with a passport that is about to expire. Travelers should be aware that if you are returning to the United States with an expired passport you are subject to a passport waiver fee of $100 for traveling with an expired passport. The fee is payable to the Immigration and Naturalization Service at the port of entry.

Additional information about this or any other passport-related matter may be obtained from any of the passport agencies listed on the last page of this section.

Visas

A visa is an endorsement or stamp placed in your passport by a foreign government that permits you to visit that country for a specified purpose and a limited time—for example, a 3-month tourist visa. It is advisable to obtain necessary visas before you leave the United States because you will not be able to obtain visas for some countries once you have departed. Apply directly to the embassies or nearest consulates of the countries you plan to visit, or consult a travel agent. Passport agencies cannot help you obtain visas.

Foreign Entry Requirements

Department of State publication M-264, *Foreign Entry Requirements*, gives entry requirements for U.S. citizens traveling to every foreign country and tells where and how to apply for visas and tourist cards. It can be ordered for 50¢ from the Consumer Information Center, Pueblo, Colorado 81009. Note: This publication is updated annually but may not reflect the most current requirements. It is a good idea to verify the latest visa requirements with the embassy or consulate of the country or countries you plan to visit.

Because the visa is usually stamped directly onto one of the blank pages in your passport, you will need to fill out a form and give your passport to an official of each foreign embassy or consulate. You may need one or more photographs. Many visas require a fee. The process may take several weeks for each visa, so apply well in advance of your trip.

Tourist Card

If the country you plan to visit requires a tourist card, you can obtain one from that country's embassy or consulate, from an airline serving the country, or at the port of entry. There is a fee for some tourist cards. Check entry requirements while you are planning your trip.

Proof of Citizenship

Certain countries require only proof of U.S. citizenship to enter and depart the country. In such cases, you may use a current or expired U.S. passport. Sometimes a certified copy of your birth certificate, a naturalization certificate, or a Report of Birth Abroad of a Citizen of the United States is acceptable proof of U.S. citizenship. Remember that no matter what proof of citizenship a foreign country requires, U.S. Immigration has strict requirements for your reentry into the United States. A passport serves this purpose best.

Immunizations

Under the International Health Regulations adopted by the World Health Organization, a country may require International Certificates of Vaccination against yellow fever and cholera. Check your health care records to ensure that measles, mumps, rubella, polio, diphtheria, tetanus, and pertussis immunizations are up-to-date. Medication for malaria and certain other preventive measures are advisable for some travelers. No immunizations are needed to return to the United States.

Pertinent information on vaccination and certificate requirements, U.S. Public Health recommendations, and other health hints for the traveler are included in the publication *Health Information for International Travel,* which is available for $5 from the U.S. Government Printing Office, Washington, D.C. 20402 or may be obtained from your local and state health departments, or physicians. This information is also available on the Centers for Disease Control 24-hour hotline: 404-639-2572. It is not necessary to be vaccinated against a disease to which you will not be exposed and few countries refuse to admit you if you arrive without the necessary vaccinations. Officials will either vaccinate you, give you a medical follow-up card, or in rare circumstances put you in isolation for the incubation period of the disease for which you were not vaccinated. Check requirements before you depart.

If you do need vaccinations, they must be recorded on approved forms such as those included in the booklet PHS-731, *International Certificates of Vaccination as Approved by the World Health Organization.* If your doctor or public health office does not have this booklet, it can be obtained from the Superintendent of Documents, U.S. Government Printing Office, Washington, D.C. 20402, or Government Printing Office bookstores. Keep it with your passport.

Travel Advisories and Warnings

The Department of State issues travel advisories to alert U.S. citizens to conditions abroad that may affect them adversely. A **warning** recommends deferral of travel to all or part of a country. **Caution** advises about unusual security conditions, including the potential for unexpected detention, unstable political conditions, or serious health problems. A caution is not intended to deter travel to a country. A **notice** provides information about situations that do not present a risk but could result in inconvenience.

These advisories are distributed widely throughout the travel industry. If you are traveling to a particular area or country where there may be some concern about existing conditions, you may wish to contact the nearest passport agency, your travel agent or airline, or the Department of State's Citizens Emergency Center at 202-647-5225 to learn of any problems.

Dual Nationality

A foreign country may claim you as a citizen of that country if:

- You were born there.
- Your parent is or was a citizen of that country.
- You are married to a citizen of that country.

If you are in any of the above categories, check your status (including military obligations) before you leave with the embassy or consulate of the country that might claim you as a citizen. In particular, U.S. citizens may have problems in the Middle East, South America, and Africa. Some countries refuse to recognize dual citizenship and do not allow U.S. officials access to arrested Americans.

Organized Programs

Most private programs for vacation, study, or work abroad are reputable and financially sound. However, some may exact exorbitant fees, use deliberately false "educational" claims, and provide working conditions far different from those advertised. Even programs of legitimate organizations can be poorly administered. Be cautious. Before committing yourself or your finances find out about the organization and what it offers.

Student Travelers

Students interested in saving money on transportation and accommodations and in obtaining other discounts may wish to acquire an International Student Identity Card. This I.D. card is available with proof of student status and a small fee from the Council on International Education Exchange, 205 East 42nd Street, New York, New York 10017.

Charter Flights and Airlines

There have been occasions when airlines or companies selling seats on charter flights or tour packages have gone out of business, stranding passengers overseas. Therefore, if you plan to travel on a charter flight, you should consider purchasing trip insurance.

If you are unsure of the stability of the airline, charter company, or tour operator, you should ask your travel agent what recourse you have if the company ceases to operate. Read your contract carefully. Your local Better Business Bureau or the American Society of Travel Agents at 1101 King Street, Alexandria, Virginia 22314, tel. 703-739-2782, can provide more information on a travel company's complaint record.

Customs

Become familiar with U.S. customs regulations. Foreign-made personal articles taken abroad are subject to duty and tax unless you have acceptable proof of prior possession. Documents such as a bill of sale, insurance policy jeweler's appraisal, or receipt for purchase may be considered reasonable proof of prior possession. Items such as watches, cameras, tape recorders, or other articles that may be readily identified by serial number or permanently affixed markings may be taken to the Customs Office nearest you or to the port of departure for registration before departing the United States. The certificate of registration provided will expedite free entry of these items when you return.

Driver's Licenses and Permits

Check with the embassy or consulate of the countries in which you plan to drive for local requirements. If possible, obtain road maps of the countries where you intend to drive. Many countries do not recognize a U.S. driver's license. However, most countries accept an international driver's license. You can obtain one at a local office of an automobile association. You must be at least 18 years of age and will need two passport-size (2×2-inch) photographs and your valid U.S. license. A fee is required.

Certain countries, such as Switzerland, require road permits in lieu of tolls for using their divided highways. Driving on these roads without a permit can lead to fines.

Car rental agencies in other countries usually provide auto insurance, but in some countries the required coverage is minimal. A good rule of thumb when renting a car is to purchase insurance coverage that is at least equivalent to that which you carry at home.

In general, your U.S. auto insurance does not cover you abroad. However, your policy may apply when you drive to countries that neighbor the United States. Even if your policy is valid in Canada or Mexico, it may not meet the minimum requirements. In most of Canada, you must carry at least $200,000 in liability insurance. Mexico requires that if vehicles do not carry theft, third-party liability, and comprehensive insurance, the owner must post a bond that could be as high as 50 percent of the value of the vehicle. If you are uninsured or underinsured for a country, auto insurance can usually be purchased at the border.

Insurance

For travelers who become seriously ill or injured on a trip abroad, getting medical and hospital care can be costly. Make sure your medical insurance policy provides adequate protection for you while overseas. If your health insurance policy does not cover you abroad, you are urged to purchase a temporary health policy that does. There are short-term health and emergency assistance policies designed for travelers. You can find the names of the companies offering them from your travel agent or your health insurance company, or from advertisements in travel publications.

Many international insurance companies now offer trip cancellation, baggage loss, and travel accident insurance for overseas travel. Some major companies that sell travelers checks are making new protection policies available for travelers who purchase their brand of travelers checks. Social Security Medicare programs do not provide payment for hospitals or medical services outside the United States.

Medical Care and Medicines

If you go abroad with preexisting medical problems, carry a letter from your doctor describing your condition, including information on any prescription medicines you must take. You should also have the generic names of the drugs. Leave all medicines in their original labeled containers. These precautions will make customs processing easier, although a doctor's certificate may not suffice as authorization to transport drugs to all foreign countries. To ensure you do not violate the laws of the country or countries you visit, consult the embassy or consulate of those countries for precise information before leaving the United States.

If you have allergies, reactions to certain medicines, or other unique medical problems, consider wearing a "medical alert" bracelet or similar warning.

Should you become ill while you are abroad, contact the nearest U.S. embassy or consulate for a list of local doctors, dentists, medical specialists, clinics, and hospitals. If your illness or injury is serious, the consul can help you find medical assistance from that list and, at your request, will inform your family or friends of your condition. If necessary, a consul can assist in transfer of funds from the United States. Payment of hospital and other expenses is your responsibility. Consular officers cannot supply you with medication.

Several private organizations provide listings of physicians to international travelers. Membership in these organizations is generally free, although a donation is requested. Membership entitles the traveler to a number of traveler's medical aids, including a directory of physicians with their overseas locations, telephone numbers, and fee schedules. The physicians are generally English-speaking and provide medical assistance 24 hours a day. The addresses of these medical organizations can be found in many travel magazines or obtained from a travel agent.

Valuables

Due to the risk of loss, valuables such as jewelry, family photographs, or objects of sentimental value should not be taken abroad. If jewelry is taken, it should be worn on the person, concealed, to prevent the grab-and-run type of theft.

Money

Do not carry large amounts of cash. Take most of your money in travelers checks and remember to record the serial number, denomination, and the date and location of the issuing bank or agency where you purchased them. Keep this information in a safe but separate place so if you lose your travelers checks you will be prepared for quick replacement.

Some credit cards can be used worldwide in certain establishments and may allow you to draw cash advances up to your credit limit or ceiling. It is wise to remove all unnecessary credit cards from your wallet before you leave. Make a list of the account numbers of the major credit cards you plan to take. The best exchange rate usually is obtained on credit card purchases. However, keep track of your credit card purchases so as not to exceed your credit limit. Travelers have been arrested overseas for mistakenly exceeding their credit limit.

Always report the loss or theft of your credit cards or travelers checks immediately to the company and notify local police. If you are staying in one place for a while, consider opening an account for check cashing or other financial transactions at a U.S. bank that has an overseas affiliate. U.S. embassies and consulates cannot cash checks for you.

Make advance arrangements with a relative or friend in case an emergency leaves you short of cash. Major banks and some travel agencies can help you arrange a transfer of funds from your hometown to a foreign bank in most foreign cities.

Before departing the United States, purchase small amounts of foreign currency to use for buses, taxis, phone calls, tips, and other incidentals when you first arrive. You can purchase foreign currency from certain U.S. banks and from foreign exchange firms, or at foreign exchange windows and vending machines at international airports. Remember that foreign exchange windows and banks at foreign airports may be closed when your flight arrives from the United States, so having a small amount of foreign currency with you is a good idea.

Itinerary

Leave a detailed itinerary (with names, addresses, and phone numbers of persons and places to be visited) with family or friends so you can be reached in an emergency, receive mail, or get money in a hurry. Include a photocopy of your passport information page, credit card, travelers check, and airline ticket numbers.

Lodging

Reserve your lodging as far in advance as possible and reconfirm your reservations at each stopover along the way. Many travelers wait until they reach their destination before making hotel reservations. Particularly during peak tourist travel months, you should have a hotel reservation for at least the first night you arrive in a foreign city. Remember you may be tired and if you are unfamiliar with your surroundings, you could have difficulty locating a hotel that is convenient and meets your requirements. However, many train stations and some airports have travel desks that can assist you in finding a hotel when you arrive.

An alternative to hotels and pensions is the youth hostel system, which offers travelers of all ages clean, inexpensive overnight accommodations at 6,000 locations in 70 countries. International regulations require that men and women sleep in separate facilities, though some hostels have family rooms that can be reserved in advance. Curfews are often imposed and membership is often required. For information write American Youth Hostels, P. O. Box 37613, Washington, D.C. 20013-7613.

Mail

Make arrangements to pick up mail or messages if you will be gone for an extended length of time. Some banks and credit card companies handle mail for their customers. General Delivery (Poste Restante) services at post offices in most countries will hold mail for you. U.S. embassies and consulates do not handle private mail.

While You Are Overseas

Dealing with the Unexpected

If you change your travel plans (miss your return flight to the United States or extend your trip), be sure to notify relatives or friends back home. Should you find yourself in an area of civil unrest or natural disaster, let them know you are safe as soon as you can.

Protect Your Passport

Your passport is the most valuable document you will carry abroad. It confirms that you are a U.S. citizen. Guard it carefully. Do not use it as collateral for a loan and do not lend it to anyone. It is your best form of identification when you pick up mail, or check into hotels, embassies, and consulates. It is all right to leave your passport at a hotel reception desk so it may be checked by local police authorities. If your passport is not returned the following morning, or if it is lost or stolen, immediately report the incident to local police and to the nearest U.S. embassy or consulate. Keep the number, date, and place of issuance of your passport in a separate but safe place in case your passport is lost or stolen.

Passport Fraud

Reports show that U.S. passports are being used for many criminal acts, including illegal entry into the United States. This often causes embarrassment to innocent citizens whose names have become associated with illegal activites. To protect the integrity of the U.S. passport and the security of the person bearing it, Passport Services has found it necessary to take special precautions in processing lost passport cases. These precautions may involve some delay before a new passport is issued.

It has been found that the main cause for losing a passport or having it stolen is carelessness. Travelers should be acutely aware of problems that arise abroad when a U.S. passport is lost or stolen. A passport should not be packed in luggage or left in an empty hotel room. It should be carried with you whenever possible. One family member should not carry all the passports for the entire family.

Other Precautions

Coat pockets, handbags, and hip pockets are particularly susceptible to theft. You can prevent a potential theft from occurring by carrying your belongings in a secure manner. Women may wish to carry shoulder bags tucked under the arm and held securely by the strap. Men may want to use their inside coat/front trouser pocket or a money belt instead of a hip pocket. In additon, if you wrap your wallet in rubber bands it is much more difficult to remove without your feeling it. Should you find yourself in a crowded area, such as the subway, marketplace, or at a festival, take special precautions. You may also consider purchasing a belt pouch to foil purse snatchers and pickpockets. Do not make it easy for thieves to pick your pocket!

Money

Local banks generally offer better rates of exchange than hotels, restaurants, or stores. Rates are often posted in windows. Above all, avoid private currency transactions in which you risk being swindled, stuck with counterfeit currency, or subject to arrest. Learn and obey all local currency laws.

Purchases and Mail

Any small items purchased abroad should be mailed personally to your home address or carried in your luggage. This will prevent misaddressed packages, nonreceipt of merchandise, or receipt of wrong merchandise. If you do mail a purchase, be sure to ask about insurance.

Many European countries levy a value added tax (VAT) on the items you buy. If you plan to ship your purchases home, you can sometimes avoid paying this tax. However, in cases where you are required to pay the VAT, you may wish to ask the store clerk for an application to apply for a refund. You can only obtain this refund for those purchases you ship or carry with you. It does not apply to food, hotel bills, or other services. Because the rules for obtaining a refund are somewhat confusing and vary from country to country you should check with the appropriate country's tourist office for specific requirements.

Purchases of Wildlife

Be careful when buying articles made from wild animals or purchasing live wild animals to bring home as pets. Some items, such as those made from elephant ivory, sea turtle shell, crocodile leather, or fur from endangered cat species, and many species of live animals cannot be brought into the United States legally. Your wildlife souvenirs could be confiscated by government inspectors, and you could face other penalties for attempting to bring them into the United States. Do not buy wildlife or wildlife products unless you are sure of being able to bring them back into the country.

Customs

Keep all receipts for items that you buy overseas. They will be helpful in making your U.S. Customs declaration when you return.

Registering with the U.S. Embassy or Consulate

You should register with the nearest U.S. embassy or consulate:

- If you plan to stay in one country for longer than a month. Registration will make it easier to replace a lost or stolen passport or to assist or evacuate you in an emergency. If you are with an escorted tour, make sure registration is taken care of for you. If it is not, or if you are traveling on your own, leave a copy of your itinerary at the nearest U.S. embassy or consulate soon after arrival. Registration makes it easier for consular employees to help you if you encounter difficulties.

- If you are going to a country where there is not U.S. representation (Albania or South Yemen, for example), register in an adjacent country, leave an itinerary, and ask about conditions in the country you plan to visit.
- If you must travel to a country or area that is experiencing civil unrest, has a particularly unstable political climate, or is undergoing a natural disaster such as an earthquake or hurricane.

Help from American Consuls

U.S. consular officers are located at U.S. embassies and consulates in most countries overseas. They are available to advise and help you if you are in any serious trouble.

Consuls are responsive to the needs of U.S. nationals traveling or residing abroad. However, they must devote their priority time and energies to those Americans who are in serious legal, medical, or financial difficulties. Consular employees also provide non-emergency services such as information on absentee voting, selective service registration, travel advisories, and acquisition and loss of U.S. citizenship. They can arrange for the transfer of Social Security and other benefits to beneficiaries residing abroad, provide U.S. tax forms, and notarize documents. They also provide information on procedures to obtain foreign public documents.

Because of the small number of consular officers abroad and the growing number of American travelers, consuls cannot provide routine or commercial-type services. For example, consuls cannot act as travel agents, lawyers, information bureaus, banks, or the police. Please do not expect them to find you employment, get residence or driving permits, act as interpreters, search for missing luggage, or settle disputes with hotel managers, although they can tell you how to get assistance on these and other matters.

Legal Requirements

When you are in a foreign country, you are subject to its laws. Use common sense. Avoid areas of unrest and disturbance. When entering some countries or registering at hotels, you may be asked to fill out a police card listing your name, passport number, destination, local address, and reason for traveling. In some nations, you may be required to leave your passport at the hotel reception desk overnight so it can be checked by local police officials. These are normal procedures required by local laws. If your passport is not returned the following morning, again, report the impoundment, loss, or theft to local police authorities and the nearest U.S. embassy or consulate.

Deal only with authorized outlets when you exchange money or buy airline tickets and travelers checks. Do not deliver packages for anyone unless you are certain they do not contain drugs or other contraband.

Some countries are particularly sensitive about photographs. In such countries, travelers should refrain from photographing police and military installations and personnel; industrial structures, including harbor, rail, and airport facilities; border areas; and in the exceptional event that these should occur during the visitor's stay in the country, scenes of civil disorder or other public disturbances. Taking such photographs may result in detention, confiscation of the camera and film, and imposition of fines. For more information about possible restrictions of this type, U.S. citizens should check with the U.S. embassy or consulate in the country concerned or ask a local police officer or government official.

Become familiar with local regulations before you sell personal effects such as clothing, cameras, and jewelry. Strictly adhere to local laws. The penalties you risk are severe.

Drug Arrests

About 3,000 Americans are arrested abroad each year. One-third of those arrested are held on drug charges. Despite repeated warnings, drug arrests and convictions are still a common occurrence. If you are caught with either soft or hard drugs overseas, you are subject to local—not U.S.—laws. Stiff penalties for possession or trafficking often are strictly enforced. If you are arrested, you will find the following:

- Few countries provide a jury trial.
- Most countries do not accept bail.
- Pretrial detention, often in solitary confinement, may last for months.
- Prisons may lack even minimal comforts—bed, toilet, washbasin.
- Diets are often inadequate and require supplements from relatives and friends.
- Officials may not speak English.
- Physical abuse, confiscation of personal property, degrading or inhumane treatment, and extortion are possible.

If you are convicted, you face a sentence of the following:

- Two to 10 years in most countries.
- A minimum of six years hard labor and a stiff fine in some countries.
- The death penalty in some countries.

Do not get involved with illegal drugs overseas. It can ruin more than your vacation. It can ruin your life!

Legal Aid

If you do have difficulties with the local authorities, remember you are subject to local laws. Unfortunately, what American officials can do is limited by foreign laws, U.S. Laws, and geography. The U.S. government has no funds for your legal fees or other related expenses.

Nevertheless, you should consult a consular officer if you find yourself in a dispute that could lead to legal or police action. Although U.S. consular officers cannot serve as attorneys or give legal advice, they can provide lists of local attorneys and help you find adequate legal representation. It should be noted that the consular attorneys lists, although carefully prepared, are compiled from local bar association lists and responses to questionnaires. Neither the Department of State nor U.S. embassies or consulates can assume any responsibility for the caliber, competence, or professional integrity of the attorneys. Consular officers will do whatever they can to protect your legitimate interests and ensure that you are not discriminated against under local law. They cannot get you out of jail. If you are arrested, ask permission to notify the consular officer at the nearest U.S. embassy or consulate. Under international agreements and practice, you have the right to get in touch with the U.S. consul. If you are turned down keep asking, politely but persistently. If unsuccessful, try to have someone get in touch for you.

When alerted, American officials will visit you, advise you of your rights according to local laws, and contact your family and friends for you if you wish. Consuls can transfer money, food, and clothing to the prison authorities. They will try to get relief if you are held under inhumane or unhealthful conditions or treated less favorably than others in the same situation.

If Destitute
Should you become destitute abroad, the U.S. consul can help you get in touch with your family, friends, bank, or employer and tell you how to arrange for them to send funds for you.

If Ill or Injured
If you are injured or become seriously ill abroad, the consul will help you find medical assistance and inform your family or friends. In an emergency when you are unable to communicate, the consul will check your passport for the name and address of any relative, friend, or legal representative whom you wish to have notified.

Marriages Abroad
Marriages abroad must be performed in accordance with local laws. In many countries, there is a lengthy residence requirement before a marriage may take place. There are also certain documentary requirements. Consult the embassy or consulate of the country in which you plan to marry to learn about these regulations.

U.S. diplomatic and consular officials do not have the authority to perform marriages. In some instances they can provide a Certificate of Witness to a Marriage, which will help establish the validity of a foreign marriage in the United States. However, such a certificate is usually not necessary, because a marriage recognized as valid under the laws of the country where the marriage was performed is usually recognized by most states in the United States.

Births Abroad
A child born abroad to a U.S. citizen parent or parents generally acquires U.S. citizenship at birth. The parent should contact the nearest U.S. embassy or consulate to have a Report of Birth Abroad of a Citizen of the United States of America prepared. This document is recognized as proof of acquisition of U.S. citizenship and is acceptable evidence for obtaining a passport and most other purposes.

Deaths Abroad
When an American dies abroad, the consular officer reports the death to the next of kin or legal representative. A Report of the Death of an American Citizen (Optional Form 180) is prepared by the consular official to provide the facts concerning the death and the custody of the personal estate of the deceased. The consul then obtains family instructions and nec-

essary private funds in order to make arrangements for local burial or return of the body to the United States. Under certain circumstances, a consular officer becomes the provisional conservator of a deceased American's estate and arranges for the disposition of those effects.

When You Return

Return Transportation
Reconfirm your return reservation at least 72 hours before departure. Whenever possible, obtain a written reconfirmation. If you do it by phone, record the time, day, and the name of the agent who took the call. If your name does not appear on the reservations list, you have no recourse and may find yourself stranded.

Departure Tax
Some countries, such as the British Virgin Islands, levy a departure tax on returning travelers at the airport before permitting them to board their returning flight. The departure tax can be as much as $50. You should consult the appropriate airline or a travel agent about this. Make sure you set the departure tax money aside so you have it available when you arrive at the airport to return from your trip.

Immigration and Customs
If a passport was required for your trip, have it ready when you go through Immigration and Customs. It is a good idea to have your baggage packed to make inspection easy. When possible, pack separately the articles you have acquired abroad. Have your receipts handy in case you need to support your customs declaration. If you took other documents with you, such as an International Certificate of Vaccination, a medical certificate, or a Customs certificate of registration for foreign-made personal articles, have them ready also. When returning to the United States by car from Mexico or Canada, have your certificate of vehicle registration handy.

The U.S. Customs Service currently allows each U.S. citizen to bring back $400 worth of merchandise duty free, provided the traveler has been outside the United States for at least 48 hours and has not already used this exemption within 30 days, and provided the traveler brings the purchases into the United States with him/her. The next $1,000 worth of items brought back for personal use or gifts is subject to duty at a flat rate of 10 percent.

Passport Agencies
Apply early for your passport!

Boston Passport Agency
Thomas P. O'Neill Federal Building, Room 247
10 Causeway Street
Boston, Massachusetts 02222
*Recording: 617-565-6698
**Public Inquiries: 617-565-6990

Chicago Passport Agency
Suite 380, Kluczynski Federal Building
230 South Dearborn Street
Chicago, Illinois 60604-1564
*Recording: 312-353-5426
**Public Inquiries: 312-353-7155 or 7163

Honolulu Passport Agency
Room C-106, New Federal Building
300 Ala Moana Boulevard
Honolulu, Hawaii 96850
*Recording: 808-541-1919
**Public Inquiries: 808-541-1918

Houston Passport Agency
Suite 1100, Mickey Leland Federal Building
1919 Smith Street
Houston, Texas 77002
*Recording: 713-653-3159
**Public Inquiries: 713-653-3153

Los Angeles Passport Agency
Room 13100, 11000 Wilshire Boulevard
Los Angeles, California 90024-3614
*Recording: 310-575-7070
**Public Inquiries: 310-575-7075

Miami Passport Agency
3rd Floor, Federal Office Building
51 Southwest First Avenue
Miami, Florida 33130-1680
*Recording: 305-536-5395 (English)
  305-536-4448 (Spanish)
**Public Inquiries: 305-536-4681

New Orleans Passport Agency
Postal Services Building
Room T-12005
701 Loyola Avenue
New Orleans, Louisiana 70013-1931
*Recording: 504-589-6728
**Public Inquiries: 504-589-6161

New York Passport Agency
Room 270, Rockefeller Center
630 Fifth Avenue
New York, New York 10111-0031
*Recording: 212-541-7700
**Public Inquiries: 212-541-7710

Philadelphia Passport Agency
Room 4426, Federal Building
600 Arch Street
Philadelphia, Pennsylvania 19106-1684
*Recording: 215-597-7482
**Public Inquiries: 215-597-7480

San Francisco Passport Agency
Suite 200, 525 Market Street
San Francisco, California 94105-2773
*Recording: 415-744-4444
**Public Inquiries: 415-744-4010

Seattle Passport Agency
Room 992, Federal Building
915 Second Avenue
Seattle, Washington 98174-1091
*Recording: 206-553-7941
**Public Inquiries: 206-553-7945

Stamford Passport Agency
One Landmark Square
Stamford, Connecticut 06901-2767
*Recording: 203-325-4401
**Public Inquiries: 203-325-3538 or 3530

Washington Passport Agency
1425 K Street, N.W.
Washington, D.C. 20524-0002
*Recording: 202-647-0518
**Public Inquiries: 202-326-6020

---

*Twenty-four-hour recording includes general passport information, passport agency location, hours of operation, and information regarding emergency passport services during non-working hours.
**For other questions, call Public Inquiries number.

STUDY AND LEARNING AIDS

How to Study and Take Tests

The Study Process

An average beginning college student has spent over 22,000 hours studying from the time he or she began school until the twelfth grade. This enormous amount of time could have been reduced considerably through dynamic study skills. But most students are never really taught *how* to study. It's a process they are expected to learn on their own.

Efficient studying does not simply consist of reading, underlining, and rereading. Your new study process will consist of reading, writing, thinking, and recalling. It is based on the layered learning process and actually takes less time than your old method of study. It may seem longer at first, but each step takes less time, and because it is so well structured, you will have better recall at test time.

Time and time again students have proved that reading and recalling is much more effective than spending all their time reading and highlighting. The only way to learn the material is to become actively involved in absorbing and integrating it. Study reading is an active process, not a passsive one.

PREPARE BY BROWSING THROUGH TEXTS

Survey to get an overview of the book, turning pages quickly so that you spend about two minutes to gather the information that answers the following questions:

- How is the book organized?
- What are the main subject areas?
- What do I already know about these areas?
- How difficult is the material, and how difficult is its presentation?

Begin to structure your notes around the design of the book. Decide how much material you wish to learn. Draw a chart that will help organize the material. Place the more important information to the left, details to the right. Leave more room under topics and titles that involve more pages. Draw these maps and lines before reading to help your mind organize and store the data better. For an illustration of how you would set up your paper see the box at left.

PREVIEW ASSIGNED CHAPTER

Move quickly, skimming through the chapter much faster than your usual reading rate. Your purpose here is to find out what is important and how it is presented, not to read it. Check all bold-faced headings, turning each into a question you will answer later. Also check copy under the chapter titles, each of the subtitles, and the main ideas. This will only take a few seconds a page, but it will give you important clues to the material and help you later to read it faster, because you will be prepared for new ideas. Look over the visual aids, such as maps, charts, diagrams, illustrations, and pictures to help you grasp each point more quickly. Then read any summaries or questions included at the end of the chapter. Summaries are usually helpful because they include the points the author thought were most important.

Before proceeding with your study, set two goals. Set a comprehension goal: decide how well you need to know the material. Will you be tested? If so, how thoroughly? Set a time goal for your particular section or chapter based upon how well you need to know it. In easy or familiar material, your goal may be fifteen pages an hour. But whatever your goal, make sure that it is only for one chapter or section—setting lengthy or unrealistic goals only leads to discouragement and failure. By achieving both these goals, you will speed your study time greatly.

At this stage you should have in your notes the chapter title, subtitles, and all major ideas. You should already know a lot about the material.

UNDERSTAND, DON'T MEMORIZE

Now is the time to read the chapter as quickly as you can to understand the ideas. After each page

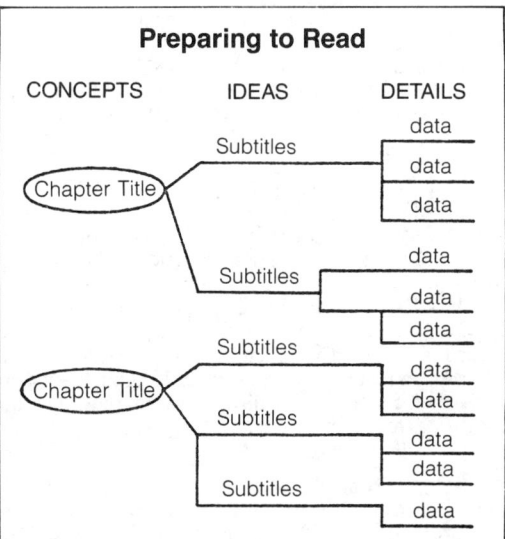

Preparing to Read

CONCEPTS   IDEAS   DETAILS

or major idea, go back to your notes and add the supporting details to them. Do not proceed more than a page without writing something down. This is an important key to textbook comprehension and retention. Respond to the material by continually summarizing it in your notes, using your own words. The old way of studying was to read and forget. Get into the habit of reading and responding. You will find even the most boring books become interesting.

Reduce the use of underlining seemingly important thoughts; do not use highlighter, Magic-marker, or felt-tip pens. Such a study method is premature; you are not in a position to judge what is most important until you've read the entire chapter. It postpones learning; you may simply color the material, rather than understand it. It is permanent; have you ever tried to erase it? It gives all material equal weight. It distracts; have you ever tried to read a used book marked with highlighter? It devaluates the book; it ruins the appearance and resale value of the book.

Instead, use a pencil to mark important ideas. Whenever something looks valuable, put a check mark in the margin, just to the side of the passage. This marks what is important, but is not permanent. Later, during a review you can reevaluate your marks and leave them in place, erase them, or add a second mark for emphasis. This system is one of the most valuable tools you can use. Not only is it flexible, but it is quite inexpensive. Continue reading each chapter, marking what is important with a check and adding to your notes until you are finished.

REVIEW MATERIAL

Go back through the chapter and reread it quickly to refresh your memory. Answer the chapter questions, see relationships, and complete your notes. Look at your notes. Do you now have details to support each main idea? Can you study that chapter from your notes? The answers should be yes. Your goal has been to get the material out of the text into your notes, then into your mind. Textbooks are often wordy and difficult to understand. Put the ideas in your own words and you will learn the material much more quickly.

The following questions can help you evaluate textbooks and other nonfiction works:

- Do you clearly understand the author's goal? If not, check the preface, foreword, and introduction.
- Do you understand how the author has presented his or her material? What do you think is the general method of presentation? What are the main ideas? Minor ones? Check the table of contents for these answers.
- What are the conclusions drawn by the author? Do you agree with them? Why did the author come to those conclusions? If you do not agree, in what areas was the author weak? Were the author's premises weak, or only his or her conclusions?

- How would you compare the author with anyone else you may have read? Is the book up-to-date? What else have you read that either reaffirmed or conflicted with it? In what ways?
- Can you now relate the text material to class lecture notes?

THINK AND RECALL NOTES

Spend time to integrate and remember your material because this is as important as reading it. If your notes are unclear, try rewriting them, basing your organization around the main ideas. Think about the concepts presented in the chapter, and try to explain them in your own words. Practice recalling information with and without your notes. Try to study as much as possible from your notes. They are bound to be more understandable than the text. Do not spend your time reading and rereading your texts. Your exams are a test of your thinking and recalling abilities, not usually your reading skills. So practice thinking and recalling your notes and the text material.

The Study Process

Use this procedure to provide a plan of attack for study.

BROWSE:
Entire book
Note vocabulary, degree of difficulty, style, organization
PREVIEW:
Assigned section
Note main ideas, charts, diagrams, maps, illustrations, formulas, topic sentences, summaries, questions
Write main ideas
READ:
To understand, not to memorize
Respond as you read; write after each section, depending on material
REVIEW AND CHECK:
Notes on chapter; fill in gaps—refresh memory.
Make sure text and notes agree
RECALL:
Chapter or section, first from memory, then double-check from notes; think about your material

---

Reading for Results

As important as reading is to success in school, many students dislike it. Those who do like to read are usually good at it. A conclusion one might reach is that people like to do things they're good at. This section is designed to help you improve your reading so that even if you still dislike some of your texts, at least you'll be able to dislike them for less time. First we discuss rapid reading—an essential for success in school.

NO LIMIT TO READING SPEED

Would it help you if you could read twice as fast as you read now? How about twenty times as fast, and with better comprehension? If that sounds impossible, it's not. The human mind is capable of seeing and understanding material as fast as one can turn pages, and some people do read that fast. John Stuart Mill, Theodore Roosevelt, and John F. Kennedy were all naturally fast readers, as have been many others. They were what are known as gifted readers: those who read very fast with excellent comprehension. Gifted readers come from every walk of life, for reading is a skill not related to age, occupation, heredity, or intelligence. The only reason that you may not read fast now is because your natural gifts may have been smothered in school.

The way reading is taught in most public schools is the same technique used a century ago. Curiously, the average American reads at about the same rate today as 100 years ago. Most people read between 100 and 400 words per minute, the national average. But slow readers are severely penalized throughout life and are simply unable to keep up because of the tremendous volume of reading required today. It is hoped that schools will change their methods of reading instruction so that someday all students will be rapid readers. In theory, the only things that should decide reading rate are the student's background in the subject, the purpose for reading the particular material, and the ability to turn pages. Some readers, tested in difficult textbook material, have read thousands of words per minute with excellent comprehension. That's over a dozen pages per minute. Yet some of these same superreaders used to read at rates of only 200 words per minute. So it is certainly possible for the average reader to increase his or her reading speed considerably.

What limits your reading rate? Poor habits, such as subvocalization (pronouncing words to yourself), regression (going back to reread material already covered), prolonged fixation (stopping and staring at one word), and inefficient eye movement (losing your place and wandering between lines). These poor habits cause tired eyes, boredom, low speeds, and low comprehension. It is not ability that you lack, it is training. Because we are taught to read at 100–400 words per minute, we are led to believe this is our "normal rate." But these rates are no more normal than 10 or 10,000 words per minute. Improving your rate only takes proper training and time.

A book cannot give the kind of help necessary to make a dramatic increase in your reading skills. But, until you can get some professional help from a well-trained, rapid reading instructor, there *are* some positive steps you can take.

HAND READING

As children, we were generally taught not to underline words with our fingertips. But this method actually helps increase speed and comprehension. It builds speed in reading because it prevents unnecessary backing up and rereading, which consumes about one-sixth of your reading time. It also prevents unneeded, prolonged fixations—the habit of staring at one word or phrase for a long period. Reading with your hand on the page improves your comprehension because it directs your attention to a spot instead of allowing your eyes and mind to wander. Simply place your fingertip under the first word and move it along at a comfortable rate, underlining each word. Be sure to pick up your finger at the end of each line, lifting it to begin the next one. Read directly above your fingertip, and watch your rate soar.

HOW TO ADJUST SPEED

Do not read everything at the same rate. You should read light fiction quickly and technical texts at about one-half that rate. When you read easy material, speed up and you will enjoy reading more. A common misconception is that reading faster ruins enjoyment. This is not true. When you were in first grade, you probably read at a rate of 10–50 words per minute. Now you may read 100–500 words per minute, a full ten times faster! Did you lose any enjoyment from books? Of course not, and, in fact, you may enjoy books more now than when you read slowly. Decide upon your purpose and read to seek the level of comprehension you require. When your purpose in reading is entertainment, read faster than usual. If you are responsible for retaining the material, take notes often, reread difficult passages, and read at your maximum rate of comprehension, not to memorize.

SEE YOURSELF AS A GOOD READER

Do you see yourself as a slow reader or as a fast reader? Your actions are consistent with your conception of yourself. Always push yourself, being aware of what you need to get out of the material. Believe you can get what you want, when you want it and you will have no problem achieving your goal. Seeing yourself as a fast reader can become a self-fulfilling prophecy.

Sit back, close your eyes, and picture yourself sitting down at a desk reading rapidly with excellent comprehension. Imagine yourself at a desk or table you know well, moving down the page, not only comprehending what you have read, but quickly recalling it from your notes. Practice this once or twice a day for about two minutes each time. Within several weeks you should see a notable improvement in your reading speed.

RANGE OF VISION

One reason you might read slowly is that you read with a narrow, constricted, "hard focus;" you have disciplined your eyes to see only a couple of words at a time. This severely limits your speed. Your reading focus is different from your usual vision. The difference is easy to explain. What do you see when you look outside your window? Do your eyes focus only on a spot three-quarters of an inch by five-eighths of an inch? What you see is an entire panorama with everything in focus. You should see a page in the same way.

In order to regain your usual range of vision for reading, you will need some practice. This will require the use of both hands and a large book. Flip through the pages of the book quickly, turning them from the top with your left hand and pulling your eyes down the page by brushing down each page with the edge of your right hand. Your fingers should be extended and relaxed. Follow your hand down each page with your eyes, trying to see as many words as possible. Start by brushing each page in two or three seconds, gradually reducing the time spent on each page until you can go as fast as you can turn pages. Pace yourself, starting at twenty pages a minute, slowly increasing to one hundred pages a minute within one to two months. This practice work helps your eyes see more words at a time by preventing zooming in or focusing only on individual words. Practice for five minutes a day for several weeks. Remember that it is unlikely that you'll read faster without practicing. Reading is a skill, and as with any other skill, all the instruction in the world won't help you unless you actually practice what you learn.

Some students are afraid that if they go faster, they'll miss words. But they already know most of the words they are about to see. There are over 600,000 words in our language, but 400 of them compromise sixty-five percent of printed material. These are structure words that have no meaning, but they tie the sentence together. For example, in the second sentence of this paragraph, the structure words are *but, of the, about, to*. Remove those words and the sentence is choppy, but still readable: "They already know most words they are see." Since you've read those 400 words many times, don't let them slow down your reading by dwelling on them.

A famous psychologist, James Cattell, determined through research that our untrained visual capacity is about four words in one-hundredth of a second. That is 400 words a second or 24,000 words per minute that we're capable of seeing and understanding. Australian psychologist John Ross has reported that the human mind can process depth information in 0.0002 seconds. He defines depth information as nonfiction technical material. Some students may wonder whether or not they can comprehend material by reading at a faster rate. You can. Just practice and you'll see results immediately.

Do not worry about understanding everything when you read fast. You can see and understand everything, but merely reading something does not ensure retention. You will retain information by practicing recall, not by reading more slowly. Usually the more slowly you read, the more the mind wanders, with little comprehension and recall.

The ideal level on which to read is a purely mental or intellectual plane: Do not clog or block information in your mind by negative emotions, such as anxiety, worrying, and fear of "not getting it." If you develop an open, positive, "go-for-it" attitude, you'll read much better.

At higher rates of speed it's also helpful to talk to yourself. Discuss aloud the topic of each para-graph for additional clarity and reinforcement. Conceptual vocalization, the skill of thinking out loud, enables you to better process ideas and concepts.

In order to get the comprehension you need at faster speeds, it helps to have an adequate background in the material. You can get background information in several ways: (1) from reading other material on that subject, (2) from personal experience, and (3) from prereading. The purpose of prereading is to become familiar with the main ideas and to organize those ideas into a pattern. This organizing step is crucial to developing speed in reading textbook material.

One other hint that will help you read faster is often overlooked: Hold your book four to six inches farther away from your eyes than usual. Your eyes won't have to work so hard because the farther objects are from your eyes, the less movement it takes to see them all. So be sure your material is at least fifteen inches from your eyes; you'll enjoy increased speed and comprehension, and reduce fatigue.

IMPROVING CONCENTRATION

Readers with the best comprehension are usually fast readers. The more slowly you read, the more chances there are for you to daydream and lose concentration and hence, comprehension. Comprehending well is a process and a habit, not a mystery. Actually, comprehension is a twofold process: (1) perceiving and organizing information, and (2) relating that information to what you already know. Several factors determine the degree of comprehension you'll get from the material you read. Those factors are your background in that subject, your reading skills, and the organization and presentation of that material.

There is virtually no comprehension when the reader does not have the necessary vocabulary and background. Comprehension is largely dependent on how well the reader already knows the subject. Because background increases the vocabulary and subject familiarity, get the most amount of prior knowledge you can. Then processing becomes almost subliminal, it happens so fast. When the reader has an extensive background, there is even a point at which material can be read prior to conscious awareness. Background is the reason a beginning law student might read at 70–200 words per minute, yet a practicing attorney can read the same material much faster. Therefore, the first habit to get into that will build comprehension is to gain the necessary background for that subject. Two excellent ways to accomplish this are listening to lectures and reading other, easier material on the same subject.

GREATER MEANING

Reading is an active process, not passive. Anticipate ideas and read for a purpose—to answer your questions—by actively searching for the information you want. Have questions in mind before you read, not afterward. If you begin reading a book with questions, you'll complete your reading with the answers. Think about the important points and read to understand them. Be confident that you can get what you want, and you will. Do not argue with the author while reading. Save critical analysis for later, so you will not slow yourself down, lose concentration, and miss the flow of the material. Put pencil checks in the margins of the sections you would like to go back to.

UNDERSTANDING, NOT MEMORIZING

In order to have a smooth, continuous flow of information in your mind, don't stop to memorize facts. Save that process for later when you study your notes, and then continue. At all times you should read as rapidly as you can understand the ideas.

CULTIVATE A POSITIVE ATTITUDE

You must care about what you are reading or studying. If you don't, create a need to care. Use positive reinforcement. You might say to yourself, "Once I get this reading done, I'll be able to do something I enjoy more." Don't use negative reinforcement or a self-threat, such as, "If I don't get an *A* in this class, I'll lose my scholarship." If you maintain a strong, receptive attitude, you will find comprehension will be easier because you are not fighting yourself. Fighting reading is much like panicking while swimming. The secret is to relax.

UPGRADE POOR HABITS

It's difficult to comprehend what you read when you are tired, sleepy, depressed, or in pain. Some students complain that their comprehension is poor while doing their reading at three in the morning. At that hour, many couldn't comprehend the morning newspaper. It is critical to be not only alert, but relaxed. Be comfortable and in tune with the subject of the book. Reading posture definitely affects comprehension. Sit at a desk when possible. Study in an upright position with the book flat on the table, fifteen inches or more away. The more stretched out and relaxed your study position, the more you will encourage its usual result—drowsiness, poor concentration, or sleep. If you want comprehension, speed, and retention, sit up alertly and act like you are serious about accomplishing the task.

LAYERED LEARNING PROCESS

The study procedure described in the previous section is an extremely useful tool for comprehension. Basically it involves approaching the material on several levels, and taking notes after each. As a review, here are the steps:

- Browse through the material, becoming aware of its structure, complexity, and organization.
- Prepare and preview the material more slowly, noting bold-faced headings, summaries, subtitles, visual aids, and topic sentences. Add main ideas to your notes. Set your purpose: Exactly

what level of comprehension do you need? How far away is the exam? With your purpose in mind, set a realistic chapter or section goal.
- Read the material, a chapter at a time, moving as quickly as you can understand the ideas. Stop after each page and add details to your main ideas.
- Review your notes and text, filling in gaps, viewing the overall content and organization, and refreshing your memory.
- Think about and recall the information.

ORGANIZE

Your mind seeks organization, logical sequences, and order. Give it a chance to comprehend the material by grouping ideas and details into meaningful blocks. Restructure the material into easy-to-picture thoughts. Use every possible combination of thought pictures that will work. When you perceive the unity and structure of the material you are studying, you will grasp its meaning much faster. Strive toward understanding the structure as well as the details.

WRITE AS YOU READ

Get in the habit of immediately recalling on paper what you have read. Because you will understand each point better, the following point will be that much clearer. Comprehension depends upon understanding each preceding idea. The better you understand and recall one idea, the more likely you will understand the next. Stick to each part of the study process, and you will find comprehension becoming a habit.

Reading Points to Remember

Read for speed

1. Realize that there is no limit to your speed.
2. Read with your hand.
3. Learn to adjust your rates according to material and purpose.
4. See yourself as a good reader.
5. See more words at a time.

Read for comprehension

1. Read quickly to improve concentration.
2. Read actively for greater meaning.
3. Read to understand, not to memorize.
4. Maintain a positive attitude.
5. Upgrade poor physical habits.
6. Use the layered learning process:
   Browse
   Preview
   Read
   Review
   Recall
7. Organize what you read.
8. Write as you read.

Taking Notes

Efficient notes are vital to straight *A*s. Most of your studying should be done from notes taken in class and from the text. Your notes show how well you understand material presented. Students are not usually taught how to take concise, creative notes. Most have to learn from others or through trial and error. Learn the following basics and then use your creativity to develop the formats that work best for you and the subjects in which you are interested.

SUMMARIZE, DON'T DUPLICATE

Your notes should not be a re-creation, but rather a synopsis, a synthesis. Accuracy is your first consideration. But beyond that, try to reconstruct the material in your own words. This is the beauty of good notes: They are more understandable and interesting than a text or lecture. Include as many examples as time or necessity permits.

SHORTHAND

It is time consuming to spell out each word you choose to include in your notes. You can phonetically abbreviate by using the consonants of a word to create a phonetic representation that you will be able to write rapidly and interpret easily for review. Look at the following sentence from a lecture given in a literature class:

Jean-Paul Sartre is a French existentialist who was born in Paris in 1905.

Your notes might read as follows:

Sartre, exis, Paris 1905.

Use as many symbols and abbreviations from math as you can. The following table shows some symbols that can be used for shortcuts in notetaking.

Notetaking Symbols

SYMBOL	EXPLANATION
>	Greater than, more than
<	Less than
=	The same, equals
≠	Not the same, different
X	Times, cross, trans
→	Toward, going
←	From
∴	Therefore, because
∞	Infinity, a great deal
(+)	Positive, good
(−)	Negative, against
c,w/	With
w/o	Without
↓	Down, under, decreasing
↑	Above, up, increasing
$	Dollars, money
Q	Question
A	Answer

TITLES AND HEADINGS

The thoughts and ideas you record will not all be of the same importance. With some practice, you will begin to automatically write more important ideas in larger size print and details in a much smaller size. Such variations will help you remember your notes more easily and make them more fun to take down. Another helpful method is the use of geometric shapes to identify and categorize ideas. The following table shows some examples.

Geometric Key for Use in Notetaking

GEOMETRIC SYMBOL	EXPLANATION
□	Main Ideas: Inserted in square
✓	Main Ideas: Marked with check
✓✓	Important Concepts or Facts to Remember: Marked with two checks
○	Names of People: Circled
▭	Minor Ideas or Details: Inserted in rectangle
△	Reasons, Why, How: Inserted in triangle
→ LETTER SIZE	Relationships or Connecting Ideas: Indicated by arrows and letter size to show subordinate ideas

FORMAT OF SUBJECT

Each subject group has basic characteristics that help you organize your information and thoughts on that particular subject. Notetaking stumps many students because in some textbooks the information on each page is not well organized. Some books may go for a dozen pages without bold-faced headings or changes in organization. Difficulty in studying and taking notes often arises from such textbooks. Fortunately, most textbooks are better written today than they were years ago. Many have chapter summaries, bold-faced headings, and questions to answer. But when you use a book that does not indicate what is important by its format, use the information in the table that follows to help organize your notes and study procedure. It includes the basic formats for three main subject areas.

In order to take notes well, you must be proficient at sorting information. To understand an idea, you need to see its parts as well as its whole. Depending on the subject, the parts are quite predictable. First, find the main idea; it is often in the first two sentences of each paragraph. To do that, look for phrases like "most importantly," "first of all," "it must be emphasized that . . ." Any similar phrase is the author's way of telling you that something important is being said.

Second, find supporting details and examples to explain the main ideas. These usually follow the

Basic Subject Formats for Use in Notetaking

SUBJECT AREA	FORMAT AND STRUCTURE
Social Sciences	
Law	Issues and principles
Political Science	Background information
Sociology	Problems, conflicts
Psychology	Reasoning, procedure
History	Decisions, results
	Conclusions, alternatives
Exact Sciences	
Math	Background, idea description
Biology	Laws, theorems, axioms
Physics	Supportive examples,
Chemistry	approach
	New problems to solve
	Solutions, other applications
Literature	
Novels	Background on author, topic
Plays	Characters
Poetry	Problems, issues defined
	Events, complications
	Crises, problem solved

main idea and often include stories or data, such as names and dates.

Next, isolate the information you need by sorting actual facts from filler data, such as the author's personal experiences and opinions. This is easy because the facts are often proper names, places, or numbers. Once isolated from the facts, the remaining material can often be identified as filler.

Texts often follow a sequence. For example, math texts mights follow this sequence: Background information, statement of laws, axioms, or theorems, examples, problems presented to be solved. When you take notes for a math class, don't simply copy an important theorem. Ensure comprehension by examining the other parts of the sequence of information.

CREATIVE APPROACH

The more unusual and eye-catching your notes are, the more you will enjoy studying them and the easier it will be for you to recall the information contained in them. Don't use a standard outline form. Its two major drawbacks are inflexibility and difficulty in recalling. Use pictures, cartoons, arrows, different colored pens, and different size headings. Helpful, creative notes take very little practice, but if you need some ideas, refer to the samples that follow.

Sample Notes for Chemistry

These notes, based on the format for exact sciences, include subject description, laws, examples, problems to solve, and solutions.

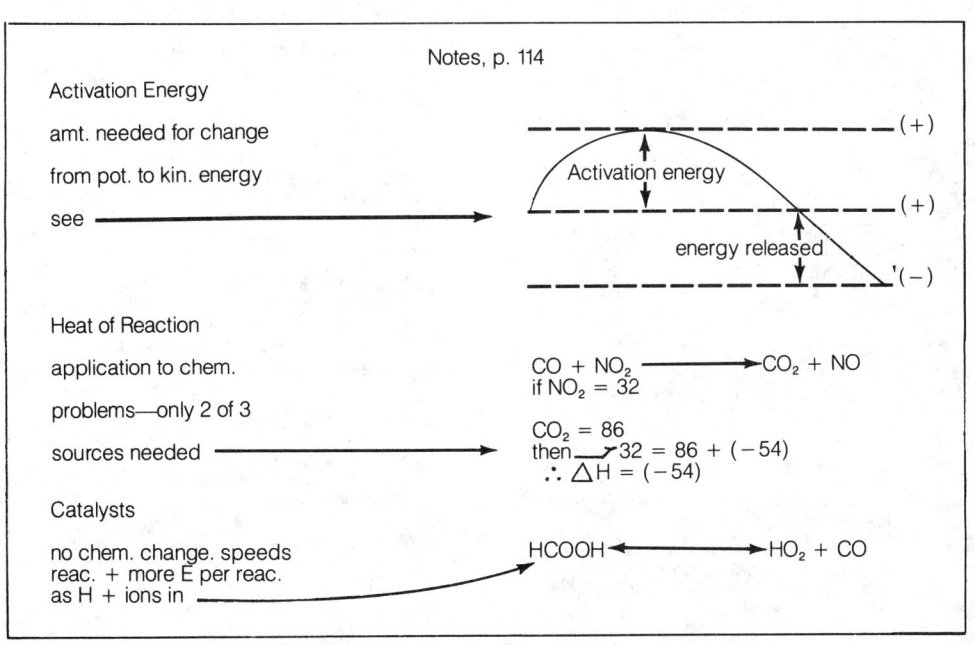

Notes, p. 114

Activation Energy

amt. needed for change

from pot. to kin. energy

see

Activation energy

energy released

Heat of Reaction

application to chem.

problems—only 2 of 3

sources needed

$CO + NO_2 \longrightarrow CO_2 + NO$
if $NO_2 = 32$

$CO_2 = 86$
then $32 = 86 + (-54)$
$\therefore \triangle H = (-54)$

Catalysts

no chem. change. speeds
reac. + more E per reac.
as H + ions in

$HCOOH \longleftarrow HO_2 + CO$

Sample Notes for History

Categorize your information so that you will follow the flow of events better. This format allows a better understanding of details as well as major events.

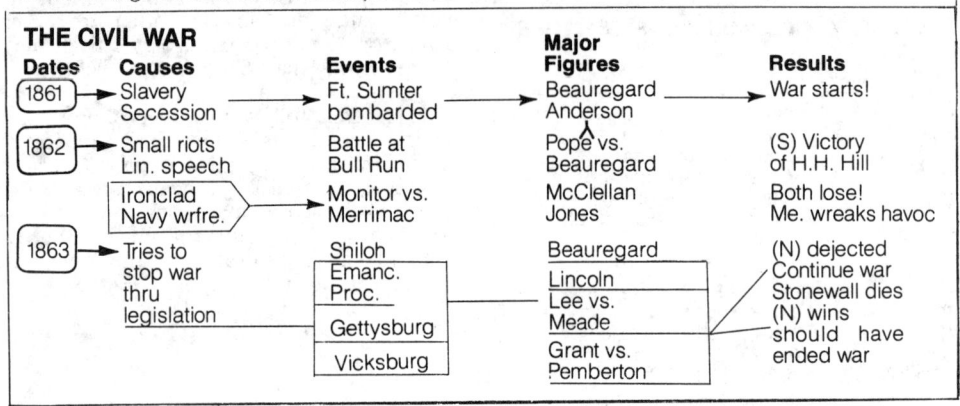

THE CIVIL WAR

Dates	Causes	Events	Major Figures	Results
1861	Slavery Secession	Ft. Sumter bombarded	Beauregard Anderson	War starts!
1862	Small riots Lin. speech	Battle at Bull Run	Pope vs. Beauregard	(S) Victory of H.H. Hill
	Ironclad Navy wrfre.	Monitor vs. Merrimac	McClellan Jones	Both lose! Me. wreaks havoc
1863	Tries to stop war thru legislation	Shiloh	Beauregard	(N) dejected Continue war Stonewall dies
		Emanc. Proc.	Lincoln Lee vs. Meade	(N) wins should have ended war
		Gettysburg		
		Vicksburg	Grant vs. Pemberton	

Sample Notes for Novels

This format includes background on author, characters, settings, problems, events, crises, and solutions.

THE STRANGER, by Albert Camus

AUTHOR 1913–60, Fr. exis., Nobel Prize '57.
Works, inc., THE FALL, THE PLAGUE, THE REBEL.
Believed in decisions, you are what you do, action, commitment, responsibility, true to self.

CHARACTERS

Major — Meursault
Marie
Raymond

Minor — Old Perez
Mother
Celeste
Salamano
Masson
Judge
Prosecutor
Chaplin
Arabs

SETTINGS

General — Algiers
Early 1900s
Very hot

Specific — Beach
Office
Marengo
Jail
Courtroom

MOODS
Methodical → Unresponsive
Tension Lunacy
Frustration Registration

CONFLICTS

Man vs. man
Concern & decision vs. apathy
Meursault vs. normal world
Arabs vs. Raymond
Prosecutors vs. Meursault

EVENTS

Mer. Mom's death
Meur. & Marie, Raymond
Conflicts w/girlfriend &
   Arabs, beach scene

CRISIS

Meursault kills Arab, imprisoned,
trial is farce,
Meursault adjusts to jail life, found
guilty, Chaplin and God rejected,
to be decapitated

SOLUTION

Meursault is reborn, good
feelings at end, a spiritual
rejuvenation

Sample Notes for Philosophy

In these notes, the left-hand side was prepared in advance, from the texts. Then the page of notes is taken to the class lecture so that additional comments can be made on the right-hand side.

Aristotle's Critique of Spartan Constitution

```
BACKGROUND ON ARTIST
  Current society is?
  Scien-philos-astron-
  "A is A," concretes,
  the realistic, specifics

A's ANALYSIS OF S.C.
  (−) pop. mngmnt.
  (−) laws
      property laws
  bribe $
  no election of ovrsrs
  (−) treasury low on $
  (+) excess lifetime offcrs
  (+) must add soldiers


(Q's FOR CLASS)
  implications of his crit.
  justified?
  Compr/contr w/US
    Constit.
  define: "polis"
          "Ephoralty"
```

KEEP NOTES TOGETHER

An ingenious way to learn a subject quickly and with better understanding is to take notes in tandem. Take class lecture notes on a page opposite the notes you took while studying the text.

Ideally, you should read the text and take notes prior to the class lecture. Put your notes on the left-hand side of your paper, leaving the right half for class work. Then when the professor lectures, you will not only understand his or her comments better, but you won't have to write as much. If you keep class and study notes on the same topic together on a page, you will take fewer notes and understand more. Other students in class may be writing frantically while you relax and jot down only an occasional supporting detail. Even if you can't take text notes in advance, bring your lecture notes home and reverse the process.

Steps to Better Recall

PAY ATTENTION

Being aware is the first step to developing better recall. Begin to notice the part of the page on which information is located. Notice how it's presented, and take an extra look at visual aids. Surprisingly, many people do not even know what color their walls and curtains are, what their license plate number is, or even their Social Security number. Knowing these things may not be very important, but learning to be more aware of your surroundings can be very helpful in developing memory skills.

GET INFORMATION RIGHT

Make sure that you correctly understand the data. This sounds like a simple rule, but particularly in the case of remembering statistics, people rarely focus on the numbers themselves. They pay attention to the significance of the numbers. At gatherings where new people are introduced, make sure you understand a person's name and its spelling. Then repeat it for clarification and reinforcement.

DEVELOP A POSITIVE ATTITUDE

Telling yourself you can remember is part of developing a healthy self-image. Faith in yourself relaxes and encourages stronger mental processes through opening previously closed thought channels. We can only do what we believe we can.

THE NEED TO REMEMBER

Most of the time, the incentive to remember information is already there. But every object of memory is made much stronger when you intensify your desire to recall. If you met someone at a party who interested you, your desire to remember

Lecture Note-taking Responsibilities

Responsibility	Objective	Procedure
Listen	Anticipate your purpose	Decide if you need to remember everything in the lecture or only main ideas
		Determine what material you will be responsible for on a test
		Determine if the lecture is a compliment to your reading assignment or new material
	Spend most of your time listening not taking notes	Listen to understand
		Listen for entire ideas
		Summarize ideas
		Determine the main points
		Decide how the main points are being made
	Think and concentrate as you listen	Note examples given
		Decide if you agree with the main points
		Determine if your previous knowledge allows you to interpret the information differently from presentation
		Try to recall the lecture so that you could present the information covered to someone else
Take Notes	Be brief	Write main ideas first Write details if time allows
	Use key words	Write down key words that allow recall of additional information presented
	Use symbols	Take notes using symbols, underlining pictures, cartoons and arrows
	Have extra supplies	Carry spare pens, pencils, and paper
	Review and reorganize	Go over notes; rewrite or add extra information while the material is fresh in your mind

the right name and phone number would be strong. Similarly, when you know you'll be tested on a book, your efforts increase appreciably.

UNDERSTAND

Although it may sound obvious, make sure you thoroughly understand what you want to remember. This rule applies equally to poetry, mathematics, history, sciences, and related fields. If something makes sense, it's much easier to recall.

BE CREATIVE

One of the most powerful ways to recall is to unleash your imagination. Turn your text material into pictures, change names into pictures, exaggerate, and be artistic. Try to put some color into the data; associate the information with sight, sound, taste, and smell.

USE REPETITION

Immediately after a learning activity, preferably within an hour, refresh your memory through a review. We use both long-term and short-term memory, and most of what we take in goes into our short-term memory. For example, when you look up a number in the phone book, you remember it just long enough to dial it. Then you promptly forget it. This is, of course, short-term memory. To transfer memory data to long-term recall, we need to repeat it and use it for reinforcement. The ideal way to study and memorize is to spend six sessions, each lasting one hour, on a subject, rather than six hours straight. In this way data are reinforced sufficiently to be filed in long-term memory.

CREATE MENTAL PICTURES

Often called the key to memorizing, mental pictures enable your mind to work in its more natural state. Usually, your mind stores images and pictures, not words. When you think of milk, do you picture the four letters *m-i-l-k*? Most people picture a glass or carton of milk. By the normal storage system, by creating mental pictures, you can remember data much more easily. Change words and ideas into pictures and simply study the pictures, not the words.

Your memory skills will improve if you practice creating mental pictures about what you want to recall. The more unusual and absurd the mental picture you create, the more likely you will be to recall the word or information associated with it.

Use the following ideas to create vivid mental pictures:

1. Imagine some kind of *action* taking place.
2. Form an image that is *out of proportion*.
3. Create in your mind an *exaggerated version* of the subject.
4. Substitute and *reverse* a normal role. For example, in order to remember to mail a letter, imagine the letter carrying *you* out to the mailbox and stuffing *you* inside.

MEMORY SKILLS BY ASSOCIATION

Probably the simplest method of remembering is by association, the process of recalling one item because another reminded you of it. This system requires no more than some awareness and a quick mental picture. For example, if you wanted to remember to bring a pen to class, simply imagine black, gooey ink all over the door knob where you live. Make a quick but strong mental picture of it. Then when you leave for class, reaching for the door knob will trigger the mental picture of ink, and you'll remember your pen.

Improve your memory skills by practicing word associations using mental pictures. For example, in associating the words *table* and *dance*, first form a clear picture of a table in your mind. Visualize a table that you use frequently, one familiar to you. In order to associate *table* with *dance*, imagine the table, standing up on two legs, dancing wildly, with the other two legs spinning in the air. Because it is such an absurd picture, it will stick in your mind. Each time you think *table*, you will also think *dance*.

Linking words can continue in a similar manner. If you wished to next link the word *dance* to *duck*, for example, you might create a mental picture of a huge, six-foot-tall, all white, overfed, pot-bellied duck dancing and whirling, with feathers flying.

Using the method of linking through mental pictures, you have created a chain of associations: *table* to *dance*, *dance* to *duck*. In this way, you never try to memorize more than one word at a time. The process is all done with mental pictures. The system of forming associations by using the link method will help you to memorize lists of names, places, events, items, or almost anything.

CONTRASTING SUBJECTS

Apparently our subconcious needs time to sort and categorize information for long-term storage and retrieval. To facilitate this process, do not study two similar subjects back to back. Instead, work on a dissimilar subject in the interval. For example, do not follow the study of algebra with calculus, or Spanish with Italian.

INTERFERENCE

Cut down on distractions that might ordinarily follow a study session. It is best to study before a restful, quiet time or even before bed. Then your mind will have time to relax, sort, and store the necessary information.

STUDY WHOLES

Whether the subject is a Shakespearean play or an assignment in anatomy, your mind functions best with complete pictures to remember. Even if you have to memorize only one part of a chapter, become familiar with all of it. For example, if you had to explain to someone why a local beach has low and high tides, it would be much easier if you also discussed how our tides are simply opposite from those on the other side of the world. For some reason our recall varies even within the whole picture we are learning. Use the BEM concept for better recall: We remember material best from the beginning, second best from the end, and our recall is weakest on the middle. Therefore, spend more time on the middle to allow for that tendency.

PRACTICE MATERIAL

Frequently review, repeat, recite, and use the material you wish to remember. Almost any information learned becomes familiar, and even second nature, through usage. Try to integrate the data into daily usage. There is no substitute for practice.

PRACTICE UNDER ALL CONDITIONS

If you practice recalling only under "prime" conditions, information may elude you during test time. When you have critical information to remember, create flash cards on 3×5 inch index cards to take with you. Then whenever you have a break, at mealtime, while relaxing, or in the library, study the cards and practice recalling.

Preparing for Tests

The first and most obvious preparation for taking tests is to study beforehand. But an effective study procedure that will help ensure success is one that is planned from the beginning of the course and carried on, step by step, throughout the school term.

FIRST FEW WEEKS

To ace your tests, start the first week of school. Find out about your instructor. What is his or her favorite topic or author? Is student creativity encouraged, or is the class run by the rules? What kind of classwork is expected? Exactly what will your studying entail? Try to read ahead in your texts. Take notes before you go to class; it saves time and increases your understanding. As you read, ask questions of yourself or bring them to class. Add class lecture notes to your home text notes, always trying to consolidate and unify them.

MIDDLE OF COURSE

Try to study a little every day. This is a lot more effective and less stressful than cramming. Ask questions when you don't understand course material. Don't put them off, or you will forget about them. See your professor for extra help early in the term, not the day before a test. This shows a genuine interest on your part, and the extra contact will pay off at test time. Most important, be sure to introduce yourself and make the most favorable impression you can. In your particular fields of interest, it's also helpful to ask your professor if he or she has any suggested reading material outside of assigned class texts. The secret is to show some genuine interest in your class subject. You'll find that if you approach most subjects with an open mind and a positive attitude, there will be a wealth of material to stimulate and interest you. Allow your interest to extend to your professor. He or she is like anyone else and appreciates the personal touch.

Read as much background material as possible. The more you read about a topic, the greater your understanding of it, and the faster you will be able to read it. Gaining a wide background in a subject area will give you a big edge at test time. Another student may read the text and be able to recall most of it, but you will have the advantage even if you can recall only part of the additional reading you have done. You should also check your notes occasionally to make sure they are familiar and understandable.

LAST WEEK BEFORE EXAM

Find out what kind of exam will be given, and alter your studying accordingly. If an objective test is scheduled, use memory techniques and concentrate on details. For a subjective or essay exam, the best approach is to get a wide background in that subject, stressing ideas rather than details. Concentrate on knowing something about almost everything. Rework your notes into a new format, trying to see the material from new angles. Review sessions are helpful, but only get together with others if they are good students. Otherwise, you will be really "soaked" for information, and learn nothing yourself. A *C* student usually doesn't enlighten an honor student.

LAST FEW DAYS

At this point, start identifying what you don't know. Many students review by going over material they already know well. Often, parts they

don't know are ignored, making their study process ineffective. Don't pat yourself on the back for what you do know: Find out what you don't know. Remember this secret about how to study for tests: If your test is a final, turn to the index of your textbook and start with the first entry. Ask yourself if you understand that term, and continue until you come across an unfamiliar term. Look it up in the text, read about it, then take notes on it so you won't forget again. This system allows you to check yourself on every term, idea, person, and detail in the entire textbook. If your test is only on chapters seven and eight, turn to the table of contents and find out which pages those chapters cover. Suppose those chapters include pages 77–102. Turn to the index again, and start at the beginning again. But this time look down the right side, noting only the terms on pages 77–102. That way you will only study the chapters you will be tested on.

Turn to the end of your text chapters and review the summary or listing of the author's questions.

This can be helpful in directing your study efforts. At many colleges and universities, tests used during previous terms are kept on file in the library. These can be a gold mine because many professors don't rewrite a test each term. Often the tests used may just be scrambled questions from old tests. The prepared student has an easy *A*.

Many students find the use of homemade flash cards ideal, because they are portable and often fun to use. You might put a possible test question on one side and the answer on the other. Make notes on any data you seem to forget easily. Certain things appear very easy to remember, and others seem easy to forget. But remember, if you forget it once, you will forget it again unless you write it down.

A positive attitude is crucial the few days prior to an exam. The upcoming test is not an execution: It is a chance to show what you have learned. Your instructors want you to get good grades because it reflects on their teaching success. Most instructors feel badly when students do poorly because that mirrors their failure to communicate important concepts. Look at the exam as a challenge and an opportunity to show what you have learned. If you admit to yourself that you probably won't know the answer to every question you won't get discouraged when you can't find the correct response.

LAST HOURS

You have already run the hardest part of the race. If you have kept up during the term, you have already passed the exam; now it is the difference between an *A* and a *B*. Others may have exam fever, but you can relax a bit. Get a full night's sleep and be sure to eat and get some exercise the day of the exam. That encourages better blood circulation and hence a better supply of oxygen to your brain during exam time. You will be able to think more clearly. It is best to exercise in moderation so that you are invigorated rather than exhausted. A brisk walk before the test is a good way to get exercise. Eat good foods, but eat lightly or not at all within an hour of your test. If you do eat, your body's energy and blood supply will be drawn toward your stomach for digestion instead of toward your brain, where it is needed during test time.

Be sure to review all notes and texts. Browse through each chapter, making certain to expose your mind to as much information as possible. If you have kept up, this will be a review and cramming won't be necessary. Your confidence and calm mental attitude will encourage recall at test time. A review on the night before the test should only take two to three hours. On the day of the exam, arrive five to ten minutes early at your class. The best way to relax is to prepare mentally. Get the seat you want in class and practice recalling.

EXAM

Now you can cash in your efforts. First, look over the entire exam. This will help you allot your time wisely. Note the types of questions, which are given the most point value, and which are most difficult. Do not pick up your pen for a few minutes. Stop to think about your attack plan. Be relaxed and calm while you plan your approach. A good test taker doesn't fight tests; the secret is to relax.

Interpret and rephrase questions several ways to be sure you understand them. Then, start with the easiest problems first, and work quickly and neatly. Be sure to keep in mind the test directions as you answer. Don't overread questions by assuming they are more complex than they appear at first. Read them for what you believe is the intent of the question. Notice critical or key words in each question, such as "show," "contrast," "define," and other similar directions. Try to answer every question unless you have absolutely no idea of the answer; points are often subtracted from your grade for wrong answers.

Taking Objective Tests

Objective tests are those that include questions in a true-false, multiple-choice, matching, or fill-in format. The answer is usually provided, but the student must decide among several possibilities.

TRUE-FALSE

True-false questions are the easiest test questions for the obvious reason that you have at least a fifty-fifty chance of getting the right answer. First, be sure you have read the question correctly. Look for such words as *always* or *never*: These words often indicate a false answer. Such words as *often*, *usually*, *rarely* and *sometimes* can indicate a true answer. Decide if the statement is totally true before you mark it true. Answer what the tester intended, not what you read into the question. For example, the statement, "General Motors produces compact cars," is true. If the question had read, "General Motors *alone* produces compact

cars," then it would have been false. On true-false questions, stick with your first impression. Studies have shown over and over that your first impression is usually right, so be slow to change your answer, if at all. Remember, a statement is more likely to be true if it is a fairly long statement; it takes more qualifiers to make a true statement than a false one.

MULTIPLE-CHOICE

An important rule to remember when answering multiple-choice questions: Read the answers first. This way, you'll view each answer separately and equally, without "jumping" on the first and easiest one. Look for an answer that not only seems right on its own, but completes the question smoothly. If the question asks why something occurs, then your answer must be a cause. Try to eliminate any obviously poor answers. Suspect as a possible right answer such phrases as "all of the above," "none of the above," or "two of the above." Check the wording of questions to notice qualifying phrases, such as "all of the following are true *except*" or "which two of the below are *not*." Statistically, the least likely correct answer on a multiple-choice question is the first choice. When in doubt, pick the longer of two answers. But, just as in true-false sections, always put something down. Even an educated guess is better than leaving the question blank and getting it wrong for sure.

SENTENCE COMPLETION

These generally ask for an exact word from memory. They don't allow for much error, so make sure your answer is a logical part of the sentence as a whole. Use the length and number of blanks given as a hint. Make sure the grammar is consistent. When in doubt, guess. Even if it's a generalized guess, you may get partial credit. If you are unsure of two possibilities, include both and hope for half-credit.

ESSAY TESTS

When answering questions on an essay test, begin by making an outline. Assemble and organize the main points. Check the wording of the question to make sure you are interpreting the question correctly. For example, if the question asks you to compare and contrast, do not give a description or a discussion. Begin your essay by using the same words in your answer that are in the question. Keep your answer to the point. Always write something in answer to a question, even if you don't have much to say.

Think and write by using this format:
1. Introduction—Introduce your topic.
2. Background—Give historical or philosophical background data to orient the reader to the topic.
3. Thesis and Arguments—State the main points, including causes, effects, methods used, dates, places and results.

4. Conclusion—Include the significance of each event, and finish up with a summary.

When totally stumped for an answer on an essay, think about book titles, famous names, places, dates, wars, economics, and politics. Usually something will trigger ideas. If you know nothing about the essay question, invent your own question on the subject and answer it. You'll usually get at least partial credit. That's better than nothing.

AFTERMATH

When you complete a test, be sure to reread all your answers. Check the wording of the questions again. Eliminate careless errors, and you can save a lot of disappointment later. Take as much time as you need. When you think you have finished the test, turn it upside down on your desk. Think about it for a few minutes, giving your mind some time to relax and come up with some answers. If you still agree with what you have written, then turn it in. But sometimes those few moments spent just thinking about the questions will help you recall the answer that gets an *A*.

Once your corrected test is returned, look it over. Check your errors, and find out not what they were, but what *kinds* of errors they were. Were they from answering questions too quickly, poor organization, a missed assignment, or incorrect notes? Understand why you made errors, and avoid the problem on the next test.

Review These Points

Preparing for Tests

1. First few weeks of classes:
   Find out about your instructor.
   Read ahead.
   Take notes before class.
2. Midcourse:
   Study every day.
   Ask questions.
   See your teacher.
   Read background material.
3. The last week before the test:
   Find out about exam format.
   Rework notes.
4. Last few days before test:
   Brush up on your weak areas.
   Think positively.
5. Hours before the exam:
   Sleep well.
   Exercise.
   Eat lightly.
   Review your notes.
6. Exam time:
   Read thoroughly.
   Budget your time.
   Interpret questions.

Review These Points

Taking Objective Tests

1. True-false:
   Look for key words.
   Trust your first impression.
2. Multiple choice:
   Read answers first.
   Eliminate poor choices.
   Check wording of question.
3. Sentence completion or fill-in:
   Make sure answer is logical.
   Make sure grammar is consistent.
   When in doubt, guess.

Taking Essay Tests

1. Outline.
2. Assemble and organize.
3. Write your introduction, background, thesis and conclusion.
4. Reread.

Term Papers: Steps to Success

What Is a Term Paper?

A term paper or research paper is an opportunity for you to show several things: (1) that you can examine a topic in detail, (2) that you know research methods, (3) that you know your way around a library, (4) that you can organize a bulk of information in a proper way, and (5) that you can write clearly. So remember that a research paper is an opportunity to show how good a student you are. Do not approach the task of writing one as a terrible burden, a task to be avoided as long as possible.

When you are preparing a research paper, you will be reading books and articles written by others about your topic. You will be tempted to use their knowledge as if it were your own. If you do, you may be guilty of plagiarism.

It is inevitable, however, that you use the ideas that others have thought about your topic. The way to do so honestly, avoiding plagiarism, is to tell your readers who created the ideas you are using. The way to tell your readers is to write footnotes or end notes, giving the name of the work and the author whose ideas you have used. Later in this chapter you will find information about the form such notes should take.

Nine Steps

Like other jobs you have as a student, the task of writing a research paper can be broken down into sequential steps. There are nine steps in research.

1. The first is to read general literature in the subject area you choose to examine. It may seem strange to begin reading before you have chosen a topic, but you will find that by reading general information on the subject, you will be able to choose a specific topic that interests you and for which there is sufficient material to do a paper.

   In order to read general literature, you must have an idea about your topic. For example, if you have received an assignment in history to write a paper on something that happened in the years from 1609–1865, you should think about the specific era you want to examine. Is it the Revolution, the War of 1812, or the writing of the Constitution? Then, once you have chosen the general area, you go to the reference section of your library and read articles in the encyclopedias and specialized reference works dealing with U.S. history, such as the *Dictionary of American Biography*. You can also read sections of a standard textbook on U.S. history.

2. As you read the general literature, you should be looking for a suitable topic. Finding your topic is the second step in writing a paper.

   After you have chosen your topic, limit it. Think about the particular aspect you are going to examine. For example, if you decided to do research on the writing of the U.S. Constitution, you could limit your topic to the role of James Madison in the writing of the Constitution, or the seventeenth century political philosophers who influenced the writers of the Constitution, or perhaps the role of Benjamin Franklin in the writing of the Constitution. By limiting your topic, you are making it specific. You will be able to guide your research and avoid reading works that pertain to your general area of research, but not to your specific topic. This limiting of your topic becomes a great time saver.

3. The next step in the process of writing a research paper is to write a working outline. A working outline is a preliminary organizer for your research. You will make your thesis statement, saying what it is that you will try to prove, and then divide your topic into its natural, general divisions. You do not need to make this outline detailed—merely a statement of the major areas of the topic. For example, to continue, let's see what a preliminary outline might be for the topic, "the role of James Madison in writing the Constitution."

   I. Thesis statement: Madison, the "architect" of our Constitution
   II. Early life
       A. Childhood, adolescence, things Madison studied
       B. What Madison did during the Revolution
   III. How the Constitution was written
       A. Nature of government under "Articles of Confederation"; failure of that government
       B. Convening of the Constitutional Convention
       C. How the Convention operated
           1. Factions
               a. Supporters of "Articles"
               b. "Federalists"
           2. Major ideas that were proposed
   IV. Role of Madison
       A. His faction
       B. Importance to that faction
       C. His accomplishments
           1. When Convention opened
           2. As the Federalists' proposals came forth
       D. Madison's proposals
   V. Final form of Constitution
       A. Brief survey of theoretical model of U.S. government
       B. Madison's contribution
   VI. Conclusion showing that thesis statement is proved

4. The fourth step in doing a research paper is to write bibliography cards of the books and articles you will read. Use 3 x 5 cards, one book or article per card.

   To find the names of the books, use all the resources of the reference room of the library. Encyclopedia articles will recommend books to read for further study; indexes, such as the *Reader's Guide to Periodical Literature*, will provide help. Use the card catalogue of the books in the library. Ask the reference librarians for help; they are a resource, too!

   When you have found a likely book or article, put down all the publisher's information on your card. For a book, put the full name of the author, the full title (including subtitle), the name of the publisher, the place of publication, and the copyright date. For articles, write the name of the author (if given), title of the article (if given), the name of the magazine or encyclopedia, the date of issue of the particular magazine or encyclopedia, the page numbers of the article. If you are reading an encyclopedia article, include all the publishing information that you would include for any book. These bibliography cards will contain all the information you need when writing footnotes or bibliographies.

5. The fifth step is to read the works and take notes. Take your notes on 5 x 8 or 4 x 6 cards, one note to a card. Write only on one side of the card. If your note runs over one card, write on a second card rather than on the back of the first card. That way, when you lay the cards on your desk as you write, you won't have to turn them over to see what is on the back, and you will save time.

   At the top of each card, write an abbreviation of the title of the work cited and the pages in the work from which the note came. Write down direct quotations if you must, but it is better to put the notes in your own words. Keep your cards in a box or packet—don't lose them.

6. After you have taken your notes, write a detailed outline of your paper. This outline is the one from which you will write your paper, so make it as detailed as you can. Make the arrangement of your ideas clear and logical.

7. Then assemble your note cards, putting them in the order of your final outline, and begin to write your first draft.

8. After your rough draft, revise and revise again, until you are satisfied with your paper.

9. Finally, put your paper in the form required by your teacher, using acceptable footnote and bibliography formats.

Date Due	Step Number	Description of Step	Check to Show Step Done
	1	Read general lit.	
	2	Select & limit topic	
	3	Write a working outline	
	4	Collect working bibliography	
	5	Read and take notes	
	6	Write detailed outline	
	7	Write rough draft	
	8	Revise, revise and revise	
	9	Put final draft in required form	

Being Systematic

The first thing you should do when assigned a research paper is to write down a schedule. Allot time for each of the nine steps, allowing about one-third of the total time for steps 1–4, about one-third for reading and taking notes, and the remaining third for composing the paper, steps 6–9.

To allot time for the steps, start your estimates from the date the paper is due and work backward. For example, you have received an assignment from your history professor and have been told that the research paper must be turned in on the last day of the term, nine weeks later.

Write a schedule like the one below, and put the date the paper is due next to step 9. Then, next to step 5, put the date of the day that is three weeks before the end of the term. Then, next to step 4, put the date of the day that is six weeks before the end of the term.

After you have divided the available time into the major parts, subdivide the major areas. In our example you were given nine weeks to complete the assignment. Your division would be something like this: Of the three weeks for steps 1–4, allow yourself about five days for general reading, about two days for selecting your working bibliography; of the three weeks you allow yourself for writing, estimate that your outline will take five days, composing the rough draft about five days, revising about six days, preparing the final copy about five days, and preparing the final copy about five days.

Once your schedule is in place, you are ready to begin. As you search through the general literature, be systematic in your efforts. Being systematic is perhaps the key to success in doing research. Look carefully at all the available general literature, and then when you begin to collect your bibliography, be systematic in the writing of the cards. When you are writing your notes, be systematic again. Make sure every notation is *clear*, especially the page numbers, so that you will not have to retrace your steps and redo some research because you couldn't remember from which source a good idea came.

Footnotes and Bibliography

You must give the source for every idea and quotation you use in your paper. Otherwise you are being academically dishonest.

Give the sources for the ideas you use in proper footnotes or end note form. Footnotes and end notes follow the same form. However, they appear in different places in your paper. As the names suggest, footnotes are put at the foot of the page on which the citation occurs, and end notes at the end of the paper. Use whichever type your professor prefers.

Footnotes and end notes must contain the following information:

For a book:
1. Author's complete name, first name first
2. Title of work underlined
3. Editor, compiler, or translator, if there is one ("edited by," etc.)
4. Series, if any, volume in the series
5. Edition number, if book is not the first edition (2nd ed., e.g.)
6. Number of volumes, if there are more than one.
7. Publication facts, in parentheses:
   city of publication
   publisher
   publication date
8. Volume number, if there is more than one volume
9. Number of page on which the idea or quotation appears

For an article:
1. Author's name, if given
2. Article title, in quotation marks
3. Title of magazine or journal (underlined) in which article appears
4. Volume number and issue number of magazine or journal
5. Page number on which idea or quotation appears.

Here are two footnote examples.

For a book:
   John J. Audubon, <u>Birds of America</u>, (New York, Macmillan, 1946), p.14.

For an article:
   Allan Devoe, "Our Feathered Friends," <u>Nature Magazine</u> 21 (October 1951) pp. 21–23.

It is likely that you will want to cite the same work a number of times in the course of your paper. It would be awkward and time consuming to write the full citation each time. To save yourself time and effort, you may use shortened references. The first time a reference to a book or an article appears, it must be given in full; however, subsequent references may appear in shortened form.

There are two methods of shortening references. One involves giving the last name of the author, a shortened version of the book or article title, and the appropriate page number. For example:
   1. Albert Einstein, <u>The World As I See It</u> (Princeton University Press, 1949), p. 84. becomes
   2. Einstein, <u>The World</u>, p. 104.

The second method involves omitting the book or article title and giving only the author's last name followed by a comma and the appropriate page reference.

You should be aware that some scholars still use certain abbreviations to shorten footnote and bibliography references, but this practice has fallen out of use to a great degree. The following list is given only to make you aware of these abbreviations. The three most frequently used are *ibid.* (Latin, meaning the same place), *op. cit.* (Latin, meaning the work cited or quoted), and *loc. cit.* (Latin, meaning in the place cited). Here are some more examples:

anon.—anonymous
c. or ca.—circa (about: used only with dates)
cf.—compare or confer
ch., chaps.—chapter, chapters
col., cols.—column, columns
e.g.—exempli gratia (for example)
et. seq.—et sequens (and following)
f., ff.—following page, following pages
fac.—facsimile
fig., figs.—figure, figures
l, ll—line, lines
id, idem.—in the same place
i.e.—id est (that is)
ms., mss.—manuscript, manuscripts
n.—note
n.b.—nota bene (note well)
n.d.—no date
no., nos.—number, numbers
n.p.—no publisher
n.s.—new series
p., pp.—page, pages
pseud.—pseudonym
sec., secs.—section, sections
sic—thus
[sic]—error in original

v.—verse
viz.—namely
vol., vols.—volume, volumes

Footnotes, like a sound bibliography, make your paper more scholarly and interesting. It is better to use too many than too few, but they can be overdone. Use them to reflect your honesty in recognizing the important sources from which you have gathered information and to add interest to your theme. Look at one or two of your textbooks or several scholarly books in your school library for effective methods of footnotes and bibliographies.

At the end of your paper you will write a list of the books you used. This list is called the bibliography. There are two kinds of bibliographies: One contains only those works from which you quoted or got ideas (all properly footnoted, of course), and the other contains those works that you consulted. This latter type includes all the works you cited and also other works that pertain to your topic, but which you did not use as sources. Make sure to ask your teacher which kind of bibliography is required for your paper.

Again, as in footnoting, a proper format is necessary. You must include all information necessary for someone else to be able to find the book or magazine in a library. The form of the bibliography entry is slightly different from the footnote entry.

For a book:
   1. Author's complete name, last name first, followed by a period
   2. Title of work, underlined, followed by a period
   3. Editor, compiler, or translator, if there is one, followed by a period
   4. Edition, if not the first, followed by a period
   5. Number of volumes, if more than one, followed by a period
   6. Publication facts:
      city of publication, followed by a colon
      publisher, followed by a comma
      publication date, followed by a period

For an article:
   1. Author's name, last name first, followed by a period
   2. Article title, in quotation marks, followed by a period
   3. Publication facts:
      Name of magazine, journal or book, underlined, followed by a comma
      Volume number of magazine or journal
      Publication date, in parentheses, followed by a comma
   4. Page numbers, inclusive, of the article, followed by a period

Below are two examples of bibliography entries:
Audubon, John J. <u>Birds of America</u>. New York: Macmillan, 1946.
Devoe, Allan. "Our Feathered Friends." <u>Nature Magazine</u>, 21 (October 1951), pp. 21–23.

Bibliographies are usually divided into sections—books first and then articles. Sometimes they are divided into sections for primary sources (eyewitness accounts) and secondary sources (people writing about something that they themselves did not witness). In each section of the bibliography the entries are alphabetical, according to the last name of the author, or if the author's name is not given, according to the first word of the title.

A Word Of Caution

The term paper or research theme, if approached by the student as a difficult and time-consuming burden, usually turns out to be a boring and padded piece of work that boldly betrays the writer's lack of interest. If the theme is looked upon as a challenge and a chance for discovery and creative work, the product is what one would expect—a well-written essay, reflecting wide reading and grasp of material, and intellectually stimulating to the instructor who reads it.

Originality in the term paper is always of great value, but your grade is probably derived more from the scope of the paper—scope referring to the extent of the writer's reading on the subject before he or she starts to write. Originality, like all other inventiveness, is not the gift of all, but there is no student who cannot read widely and fulfill the basic obligation of having a good working knowledge of the subject. Only by first doing extensive study does the writer ever arrive at the place where the imaginative consideration of the ideas of others may bring into existence new ideas. A new idea is usually born from combining ideas from other sources, so the student who is deluded by thinking that he or she can write a successful paper without extensive background reading will doubtless be rudely disillusioned by a poor grade.

Practice for Better Term Papers

1. Make a schedule of the nine steps in research, and assign a date for completion of each step. Put the schedule in your workplace.
2. Allow one-third of your allotted time for writing.
3. Use all the resources of your library, including the librarian.
4. If you find you have chosen a topic for which you can't gain ready access to information, *change your topic*, and revise your work schedule. You should be able to tell whether you need to change when you try to compile your working bibliography. If you can't find many books and articles, take the hint—you will have a difficult time gathering notes and writing your paper.
5. Be systematic in taking your notes. Make sure that every page number is accurate and that you will be able to find the passage cited if you are asked to do so.

The Library: How to Use It

How to Find a Book

Your libraries provide both atmosphere and incentive for serious study. The library habit could become one of your best study habits. It is the purpose of this section to prepare you to find what you want in the library and make you familiar with what is available there.

Knowing the parts of a book—title, author, publisher, date of publication, edition—is the first step toward finding what you want in the library. With this information you are prepared to determine whether the book you want is in the library, and for this you use the card catalogue.

The card catalogue is an alphabetical index to all the books in the library. Cards are filed alphabetically, beginning with the first important word of the title. In addition to the title card there are also author and subject cards. The title card is the quickest if you know what book you want:

```
        TITLE CARD
598.2   Audubon bird guide
P       Pough, Richard G.
        Audubon bird guide; eastern land birds
        Doubleday, 1946
```

Suppose you read the book and decide that you would like to read some more of the author's works. You return the book you have read to the library and check the *author card* for additional books. There is an author card for each separate work of the author. For example, let us imagine you have read John Kieran's *An Introduction to Birds* and are checking the author cards for more books by him. On the author card his name is listed *Kieran, John*. If the library has his *Birds of New York City*, it will be first. The next author card will probably list *Footnotes on Nature*; and the third, arranged alphabetically, will be the book you have just returned, *Introduction to Birds*. The author card usually gives the most complete information regarding the book, but it may contain the same facts as the other cards:

```
        AUTHOR CARD
598.2   Pough, Richard H.
        Audubon bird guide; eastern land birds
        Doubleday, 1946
        Birds
```

Suppose you wish to pursue your study of birds but do not know authors or titles. A third card is available to help you. It is called *the subject card*, and it may be indexed as a general subject (BIRDS) or as a specific subject (SONGBIRDS). Subject cards are either printed with the subject in capitals or in red ink to distinguish them:

SUBJECT CARD
BIRDS
598.2 Pough, Richard H.
P   Audubon bird guide; eastern land birds
      Doubleday, 1946

SUBJECT CARD
(MORE COMPLETE)
AMERICAN FOLKWAYS
917.63 Kane, Harnett Thomas 1910–
K   Deep Delta Country, Duell 1944
      XX, 283 p. maps. Selected bibliography
      pp. 273–80

Subject cards are not used for fiction, except historical novels of critically recognized merit.

You cannot carry the file to show the librarian what you want. You must write (sometimes special forms are provided) the following information: (1) call number, (2) author's name, (3) title,
(4) volume and edition, and (5) your own name.

The numbers on the cards are symbols in a classification system, providing you with a call number by which you request the book. The same number tells the librarian in what section of the library, on what shelf, and in what specific place on the shelf the book is to be found.

Systems of Classification

There are two widely used systems of classification: the Dewey Decimal system and the Library of Congress system. The Dewey Decimal system is the one you will probably use most often. It was developed at Amherst College in 1873 and catalogues all knowledge under *ten divisions*, each division being assigned a group of numbers.

If you go to the section of the library shelving Applied Science, 600–699, you see immediately that each division is further divided. For example,

Dewey Decimal System

Numbers	Main Divisions	Subdivisions
000–099	General Works	Almanacs, encyclopedias, bibliographies, magazines, newspapers; materials that cannot be narrowed to a single subject
100–199	Philosophy	Logic, history of philosophy, systems of philosophy, ethics, and psychology
200–299	Religion	Sacred writings (the Bible), mythology, history of religions, all religions and theologies
300–399	Sociology (Social Sciences)	Group dynamics, law, government, education, economics
400–499	Philology (Study of Lingustics)	Dictionaries dealing with words (not of biographies); grammar and technical studies of all languages
500–599	Science (Subject and Theoretical)	Astronomy, biology, botany, chemistry, mathematics, physics, etc.
600–699	Applied Science (Useful Arts)	Agriculture, all types of engineering, business, home economics, medicine, nursing, etc.
700–799	Fine Arts (Professional and Recreative)	Architecture, painting, music, performing arts, sports, etc.
800–899	Literature	All types of literature— drama, essays, novels, poetry, etc.—in all languages of all countries
900–999	History	All history, biography, geography, and travel, etc.

600–610 has general books or collections dealing with applied science. Medicine is classified under 610. Books on engineering begin with 520 and are further broken down by smaller decimals. A glance at the history shelves reveals that 900–909 includes general works of history; 910 is geography; and so on by decimal subdivision. English is subdivided into literature of nations, then further catalogued. For example, English literature is 820; English poetry 821; English drama 822; and so on to 829.99. English poetry, 821, is further subdivided: 821.1 is early English poetry; and so on to 821.9, each subdivision designating a specific period. A little observation will make it easy for you to find the exact spot in a particular section of the library where your subject can be pinpointed.

The Library of Congress system of classification designates the main divisions of knowledge by letters instead of numbers. Subdivisions in the Library of Congress system are made by the addition of a second letter and whole numbers. No detailed explanation is given of this system beyond the letter classification of knowledge.

Library of Congress System

Letter	Main Divisions
A	General Works
B	Philosophy and Religion
C	History—Auxiliary Sciences
D	History—Topography (except American)
E–F	American History—Topography
G	Geography—Anthropology
H	Social Sciences
J	Political Sciences
K	Law
L	Education
M	Music
N	Fine Arts
P	Language—Literature (nonfiction)
Q	Sciences
R	Medicine
S	Agriculture
T	Technology
U	Military Science
V	Naval Science
Z	Bibliography and Library Science
P–Z	Literature (fiction)

Fiction and Biography

Fiction and biography are usually arranged in a section set aside for each, and the cataloguing is usually simplified. This is always true of fiction. In the fiction section, the books are arranged alphabetically by the author's last name. In case of two or more books by the same author, they are shelved alphabetically by title. Some libraries use the classification symbol *F* or *Fic* plus the first letter of the author's last name.

Biography is usually classified by the letter *B* or the number *92*. However, some libraries classify individual biographies under *921* and collective bi-

ographies under *920*. The *B* and *92* classifications also carry the first letter of the last name of the person written about. Thus, a biography of Abraham Lincoln is designated *B* or *92*. Biographies are arranged on the shelf alphabetically by the last name of the person written about. In case of more than one biography written about the same man, arrangement is alphabetical by the author's name. Collective biographies are arranged alphabetically according to the author or compiler's name.

Here is a card for collective biography. Some of the information is explained below:

  ① \
920   Rome—Biography \
P   Plutarch \
        Plutarch's Lives. The translation \
        called Dryden's. Corrected from Greek \
        and revised by A.H. Clough— \
        ② 5 v. Boston, Little, Brown and Co. 1872 \
        ③ L.C. DE7. P5 1872   8—1460l

① Call number \
② Five volumes \
③ Library of Congress Catalogue number \
④ Copyright number

With this information fresh in your mind, visit your library. Discover the ease with which you can find your way from one section to another and remember it so you will not have to roam. Wandering from section to section and from shelf to shelf each time you visit the library wastes your time and is probably annoying to people who are trying to concentrate on their work.

Reference Books

Reference books provide invaluable help to the student by making important information easily accessible. This is the whole function of the reference section of the library. As you prepare themes, reports, essays, or research papers, you can help yourself get a good start by using these books. They not only give you general information about a topic, but direct you to other works that cover your topic in greater depth.

Reference sections of libraries contain many different kinds of works, and what follows here is merely a guide to some basic kinds of reference books.

Perhaps the first book to catch your eye in the reference section of the library will be an unabridged dictionary, a book of such size that it has its own special rack. An unabridged dictionary contains nearly all the words in the language, giving definitions, showing pronunciation, and presenting information about the origin and history of each word. As well as entries about words, such a dictionary contains biographical and geographic information, abbreviations, tables of weights and measures, and commonly used foreign phrases. Two unabridged dictionaries often found are Merriam-Webster's unabridged dictionary and the Random House unabridged dictionary of the English language. The most comprehensive of all the dictionaries is the *Oxford English Dictionary*. It is many volumes long, and because of the exhaustive length and the high quality of its scholarship, it is the most respected authority on words.

In order to use these massive books, you need to know the abbreviations the editors have used. Abbreviations and their meanings are listed in either the front or back. Be sure to consult this list whenever you are in doubt about the meaning of an entry.

In addition to dictionaries, reference sections of libraries may contain thesauruses of words, usually Roget's or a modernized version of this work. A thesaurus is a compilation of synonyms and so is valuable to anyone doing any kind of writing.

Another source of good information about words is *The New Century Cyclopedia of Names*, which provides an abundance of information about the origins, history, and meaning of names used in English. Two sources of information about English as spoken and written in the United States are H.L. Mencken's *The American Language* and Bergen Evans' *Dictionary of Contemporary American Usage*.

In your English class you may be asked to write essays about works of literature. The reference section of the library contains many examples of literary criticism and much information about authors. *Contemporary Literary Criticism* is a collection of reviews of books by living authors. *Twentieth Century Literary Criticism* contains biographical essays about authors, as well as collections of reviews of works but is filled with biographical information about living authors, including lists of titles of their written works. *Book Review Digest* is perhaps the standard reference of literary criticism, for it contains excerpts from reviews of almost all published nonfiction and fiction. Any work of nonfiction that receives two reviews in periodicals or journals is listed, and so is any work of fiction that receives four reviews.

Whenever you are asked to do a research paper, one place to look for a topic is in general encyclopedias. Encyclopedias, their very name derived from the Greek *enkyklios* (encircle) and *paideia* (education), enclose in one volume or set of volumes masses of information on nearly any conceivable topic.

Every reference section of libraries contains encyclopedias; some libraries have several. Most common are *World Book*, especially written for younger people, *Americana*, *Britannica*, and *Colliers*, but there are others as well. Most encyclopedias update their information by adding a volume, called an annual or a yearbook, each year for a decade or so after publication.

All encyclopedias are arranged alphabetically by subject, and most contain indexes to both topics and contributing authors. The essays in encyclopedias are written by experts, give information in a clear, compact form and often contain a brief bibliography of other works that pertain to the essay's topic.

In addition to these encyclopedias of many volumes, there is an excellent single-volume work, *The Columbia Encyclopedia*. It covers the vast array of human knowledge, but necessarily devotes less space to topics than a multiple-volumed work.

There are also specialized encyclopedias that deal with particular subjects and are limited to particular fields of knowledge, such as art, science, technology, music, or history. Libraries sometimes have encyclopedias that limit their scope to particular religions and ethnic groups, such as the *Catholic Encyclopedia* or the *Jewish Encyclopedia*.

For information on contemporary events you can turn to one or another of the yearbooks that you might find in the reference section. *Facts on File* is an annual collection of digests of news articles on current events, and all subjects are indexed for easy use. Annuals, such as the *World Almanac*, contain up-to-date statistics, some valuable facts about government agencies and personnel, sports, scientific developments, and information on many other topics. Both national and state governments produce yearbooks of various kinds. You will find all of these works to be of great assistance if you have to prepare a paper on contemporary developments.

Most reference sections contain numerous biographical dictionaries. Some volumes are specifically devoted, for example, to musicians, writers, or statesmen. Others give sketches of noteworthy persons from every walk of life. *Who's Who in America*, *Dictionary of American Biography*, *Webster's Biographical Dictionary*, and *Chamber's Biographical Dictionary* are general works. The *Dictionary of National Biography* is devoted to noteworthy citizens of Great Britain. *Current Biography*, published in magazine form several times a year, and put in book form by years, is a place to gather facts on someone who has become prominent in the immediate present.

In addition to contemporary material afforded by yearbooks, there are many interesting and valuable articles in magazines and newspapers. The *Reader's Guide to Periodical Literature* is the standard reference to magazine articles. The *Reader's Guide* is published twice a month and lists alphabetically, by author, subject, and title, the significant articles from more than a hundred magazines. The *New York Times Index* is a guide to the articles found in that newspaper. The *Index* is published monthly and lists alphabetically, by subject, articles and editorials that appeared in the newspaper.

Records and Films

Many libraries have good audiovisual departments containing recordings of famous speeches, color slides of paintings, architectural illustrations, and other pictures relating to geography, history, and all other aspects of knowledge. Ask the librarian for help in unlocking their treasure chest of visual materials.

A great deal of material is available to libraries through microfilms and microcards. Vast quantities of information have been reduced in volume and in cost by these techniques, and so many libraries have been able to expand their holdings. Most microfilm or microcard holdings are of newspapers, periodicals, or rare books. As you do research for history papers or perhaps for an English paper, you may find the articles you want to read are on film. Ask your librarian for help in finding the articles you want and in using the microfilm reading machine.

Tests given to both high-school and college students reveal that those who make the highest marks are those who know how to use the library and do use it. It is the place most conducive to study, the place that provides the greatest storehouse of material from which to learn; so learn to use it, and use it to boost your marks, widen your horizons, and enlarge your life.

Better Library Use

1. Form the library habit. It is a place for quiet study and exciting discovery.
2. Learn the meaning of "call number" and the use of author, title, and subject catalogue cards.
3. Know the Dewey Decimal system and the location of the several divisions in your school or public library.
4. Know the methods of arranging fiction and biography used by your library; arrangements vary from one library to another.
5. Study the reference section to learn generally what is available, its location, and the use to which the various materials may be put.
6. Learn to make a working bibliography as you find material on the topic you are studying. For a model bibliography, check several at the ends of articles in one or two encyclopedias. Use the card method (3 × 5 index cards) of making your bibliography so you can rearrange at will. Know the difference between a working and an exhaustive bibliography (an exhaustive bibliography lists everything ever written on the topic). Choose a limited topic, some significant yet not too well known historical character, and discover the excitement and methodical investigation involved in preparing a complete bibliography. Be sure to limit your topic—not *Financiers of the American Revolution*, rather *Haym Saloman*—not the *Mimic* (Mimidae) *Family* of birds, rather the *Mockingbird*.

USEFUL TABLES

COMPOUND INTEREST
Compounded Annually

Principal $100

Period	4%	5%	6%	7%	8%	9%	10%	12%	14%	18%
1 day	0.011	0.014	0.016	0.019	0.022	0.025	0.027	0.033	0.038	0.044
1 week	0.077	0.096	0.115	0.134	0.153	0.173	0.192	0.230	0.268	0.307
6 mos	2.00	2.50	3.00	3.50	4.00	4.50	5.00	6.00	7.00	8.00
1 year	4.00	5.00	6.00	7.00	8.00	9.00	10.00	12.00	14.00	16.00
2 years	8.16	10.25	12.36	14.49	16.64	18.81	21.00	25.44	29.96	34.56
3 years	12.49	15.76	19.10	22.50	25.97	29.50	33.10	40.49	48.15	56.09
4 years	16.99	21.55	26.25	31.08	36.05	41.16	46.41	57.35	68.90	81.06
5 years	21.67	27.63	33.82	40.26	46.93	53.86	61.05	76.23	92.54	110.03
6 years	26.53	34.01	41.85	50.07	58.69	67.71	77.16	97.38	119.50	143.64
7 years	31.59	40.71	50.36	60.58	71.38	82.80	94.87	121.07	150.23	182.62
8 years	36.86	47.75	59.38	71.82	85.09	99.26	114.36	147.60	185.26	227.84
9 years	42.33	55.13	68.95	83.85	99.90	117.19	135.79	177.31	225.19	280.30
10 years	48.02	62.89	79.08	96.72	115.89	136.74	159.37	210.58	270.72	341.14
12 years	60.10	79.59	101.22	125.22	151.82	181.27	213.84	289.60	381.79	493.60
15 years	80.09	107.89	139.66	175.90	217.22	264.25	317.72	447.36	613.79	826.55
20 years	119.11	165.33	220.71	286.97	366.10	460.44	572.75	864.63	1,274.35	1,846.06

DISCOUNT FACTORS

For calculating present values at different rates of interest

Year	Rate of Interest %																			
	5	5½	6	6½	7	7½	8	8½	9	9½	10	11	12	13	14	15	16	17	18	19
1	0.952	0.948	0.943	0.939	0.935	0.930	0.926	0.922	0.917	0.913	0.909	0.901	0.893	0.885	0.877	0.870	0.862	0.855	0.847	0.840
2	0.907	0.898	0.890	0.882	0.873	0.865	0.857	0.849	0.842	0.834	0.826	0.812	0.797	0.783	0.769	0.756	0.743	0.731	0.718	0.706
3	0.864	0.852	0.840	0.828	0.816	0.805	0.794	0.783	0.772	0.762	0.751	0.731	0.712	0.693	0.675	0.658	0.641	0.624	0.609	0.593
4	0.823	0.807	0.792	0.777	0.763	0.749	0.735	0.722	0.708	0.696	0.683	0.659	0.636	0.613	0.592	0.572	0.552	0.534	0.516	0.499
5	0.784	0.765	0.747	0.730	0.713	0.697	0.681	0.665	0.650	0.635	0.621	0.593	0.567	0.543	0.519	0.497	0.476	0.456	0.437	0.419
6	0.746	0.725	0.705	0.685	0.666	0.648	0.630	0.613	0.596	0.580	0.564	0.535	0.507	0.480	0.456	0.432	0.410	0.390	0.370	0.352
7	0.710	0.687	0.665	0.644	0.623	0.603	0.583	0.565	0.547	0.530	0.513	0.482	0.452	0.425	0.400	0.376	0.354	0.333	0.314	0.296
8	0.676	0.652	0.627	0.604	0.582	0.561	0.540	0.521	0.502	0.484	0.467	0.434	0.404	0.376	0.351	0.327	0.305	0.285	0.266	0.249
9	0.645	0.618	0.592	0.567	0.544	0.522	0.500	0.480	0.460	0.442	0.424	0.391	0.361	0.333	0.308	0.284	0.263	0.243	0.225	0.209
10	0.614	0.585	0.558	0.533	0.508	0.485	0.463	0.442	0.422	0.404	0.386	0.352	0.322	0.295	0.270	0.247	0.227	0.208	0.191	0.176
11	0.585	0.555	0.527	0.500	0.475	0.451	0.429	0.408	0.388	0.369	0.350	0.317	0.287	0.261	0.237	0.215	0.195	0.178	0.162	0.148
12	0.557	0.526	0.497	0.470	0.444	0.420	0.397	0.376	0.356	0.337	0.319	0.286	0.257	0.231	0.208	0.187	0.168	0.152	0.137	0.124
13	0.530	0.499	0.469	0.441	0.415	0.391	0.368	0.346	0.326	0.307	0.290	0.258	0.229	0.204	0.182	0.163	0.145	0.130	0.116	0.104
14	0.505	0.473	0.442	0.414	0.388	0.363	0.340	0.319	0.299	0.281	0.263	0.232	0.205	0.181	0.160	0.141	0.125	0.111	0.099	0.088
15	0.481	0.448	0.417	0.389	0.362	0.338	0.315	0.294	0.275	0.256	0.239	0.209	0.183	0.160	0.140	0.123	0.108	0.095	0.084	0.074
16	0.458	0.425	0.394	0.365	0.339	0.314	0.292	0.271	0.252	0.234	0.218	0.188	0.163	0.141	0.123	0.107	0.093	0.081	0.071	0.062
17	0.436	0.402	0.371	0.343	0.317	0.292	0.270	0.250	0.231	0.214	0.198	0.170	0.146	0.125	0.108	0.093	0.080	0.069	0.060	0.052
18	0.416	0.381	0.350	0.322	0.296	0.272	0.250	0.230	0.212	0.195	0.180	0.153	0.130	0.111	0.095	0.081	0.069	0.059	0.051	0.044
19	0.396	0.362	0.331	0.302	0.277	0.253	0.232	0.212	0.194	0.178	0.164	0.138	0.116	0.098	0.083	0.070	0.060	0.051	0.043	0.037
20	0.377	0.343	0.312	0.284	0.258	0.235	0.215	0.196	0.178	0.163	0.149	0.124	0.104	0.087	0.073	0.061	0.051	0.043	0.037	0.031
21	0.359	0.325	0.294	0.266	0.242	0.219	0.199	0.180	0.164	0.149	0.135	0.112	0.093	0.077	0.064	0.053	0.044	0.037	0.031	0.026
22	0.342	0.308	0.278	0.250	0.226	0.204	0.184	0.166	0.150	0.136	0.123	0.101	0.083	0.068	0.056	0.046	0.038	0.032	0.026	0.022
23	0.326	0.292	0.262	0.235	0.211	0.189	0.170	0.153	0.138	0.124	0.112	0.091	0.074	0.060	0.049	0.040	0.033	0.027	0.022	0.018
24	0.310	0.277	0.247	0.221	0.197	0.176	0.158	0.141	0.126	0.113	0.102	0.082	0.066	0.053	0.043	0.035	0.028	0.023	0.019	0.015
25	0.295	0.262	0.233	0.207	0.184	0.164	0.146	0.130	0.116	0.103	0.092	0.074	0.059	0.047	0.037	0.030	0.024	0.020	0.016	0.013
30	0.231	0.201	0.174	0.151	0.131	0.114	0.099	0.087	0.075	0.066	0.057	0.044	0.033	0.026	0.020	0.015	0.012	0.009	0.007	0.005
40	0.142	0.117	0.097	0.081	0.067	0.055	0.046	0.038	0.032	0.027	0.022	0.015	0.011	0.008	0.005	0.004	0.003	0.002	0.001	0.001
50	0.087	0.069	0.054	0.043	0.034	0.027	0.021	0.017	0.013	0.011	0.009	0.005	0.003	0.002	0.001	0.001	0.001	0.000	0.000	0.000

TEMPERATURE CONVERSION TABLE

Celsius		Fahrenheit	Celsius		Fahrenheit
−273.2	−459.7	....	15.6	60	140
−184	−300	....	21.1	70	158
−169	−273	−459.4	23.9	75	167
−157	−250	−418	26.7	80	176
−129	−200	−328	29.4	85	185
−101	−150	−238	32.2	90	194
−73.3	−100	−148	35.0	95	203
−45.6	−50	−58	36.7	98	208.4
−40.0	−40	−40	37.8	100	212
−34.4	−30	−22	43	110	230
−28.9	−20	−4	49	120	248
−23.3	−10	14	54	130	266
−17.8	0	32	60	140	284
−12.2	10	50	66	150	302
−6.67	20	68	93	200	392
−1.11	30	86	121	250	482
4.44	40	104	149	300	572
10.0	50	122			

AMERICAN, BRITISH & CONTINENTAL CLOTHING SIZE EQUIVALENTS

Note: Size equivalents are approximate. Glove sizes are the same in every country.

Men's Suits and Overcoats

American	36	38	40	42	44	46
British	36	38	40	42	44	46
Continental	46	48	50	52	54	56

Shirts

American	14	14½	15	15½	16	16½	17
British	14	14½	15	15½	16	16½	17
Continental	36	37	38	39	41	42	43

Socks

American	9½	10	10½	11	11½
British	9½	10	10½	11	11½
Continental	38-39	39-40	40-41	41-42	42-43

Men's Shoes

American	8	8½	9½	10½	11½	12
British	7	7½	8½	9½	10½	11
Continental	41	42	43	44	45	46

Children's Clothes

American	4	6	8	10	12	14
British						
Height (in)	43	48	55	58	60	62
Age	4–5	6–7	9–10	11	12	13
Continental						
Height (cm)	125	135	150	155	160	165
Age	7	9	12	13	14	15

Women's Suits and Dresses

American	8	10	12	14	16	18
British	10	12	14	16	18	20
Continental	38	40	42	44	46	48

Women's Stockings

American	8	8½	9	9½	10	10½
British	8	8½	9	9½	10	10½
Continental	0	1	2	3	4	5

Hats

American	6¾	6⅞	7	7⅛	7¼	7⅜	7½
British	6⅝	6¾	6⅞	7	7⅛	7¼	7⅜
Continental	54	55	56	57	58	59	60

Women's Shoes

American	6	6½	7	7½	8	8½
British	4½	5	5½	6	6½	7
Continental	38	38	39	39	40	41

Pantyhose

American	A small	B aver.	C/D long	plus E	plus F
British	small petite	med. med.	large tall	extra 5.0–5.4	large 5.5–5.8
(ft and in)					
Continental	1	2	3	4	5

TABLES OF METRIC WEIGHTS AND MEASURES

Linear Measure

10 millimeters (mm)	= 1 centimeter (cm)
10 centimeters	= 1 decimeter (dm) = 100 millimeters
10 decimeters	= 1 meter (m) = 1,000 millimeters
10 meters	= 1 dekameter (dam)
10 dekameters	= 1 hectometer (hm) = 100 meters
10 hectometers	= 1 kilometer (km) = 1,000 meters

Area Measure

100 square millimeters (mm²)	= 1 square centimeter (cm²)
10,000 square centimeters	= 1 square meter (m²) = 1,000,000 square millimeters
100 square meters	= 1 are (a)
100 area	= 1 hectare (ha) = 10,000 square meters
100 hectares	= 1 square kilometer (km²) = 1,000,000 square meters

Fluid Volume Measure

10 milliliters (mL)	= 1 centiliter (cL)
10 centiliters	= 1 deciliter (dL) = 100 milliliters
10 deciliters	= 1 liter (L) = 1,000 milliliters
10 liters	= 1 dekaliter (daL)
10 dekaliters	= 1 hectoliter (hL) = 100 liters
10 hectoliters	= 1 kiloliter (kL) = 1,000 liters

Cubic Measure

1,000 cubic millimeters (mm³)	= 1 cubic centimeter (cm³)
1,000 cubic centimeters	= 1 cubic decimeter (dm³) = 1,000,000 cubic millimeters
1,000 cubic decimeters	= 1 cubic meter (m³) =1 stere = 1,000,000 cubic centimeters = 1,000,000,000 cubic millimeters

Weight

10 milligrams (mg)	= 1 centigram (cg)
10 centigrams	= 1 decigram (dg) = 100 milligrams
10 decigrams	= 1 gram (g) = 1,000 milligrams
10 grams	= 1 dekagram (dag)
10 dekagrams	= 1 hectogram (hg) = 100 grams
10 hectograms	= 1 kilogram (kg) = 1,000 grams
1,000 kilograms	= 1 metric ton (t)

TABLES OF U.S. CUSTOMARY WEIGHTS AND MEASURES

Linear Measure

12 inches (in)	= 1 foot (ft)
3 feet	= 1 yard (yd)
5½ yards	= 1 rod (rd), pole, or perch (16½ feet)
40 rods	= 1 furlong (fur) = 220 yards = 600 feet
8 furlongs	= 1 statute mile (mi) = 1,760 yards = 5,820 feet
3 miles	= 1 league = 5,280 yards = 15,840 feet
6076,11549 feet	= 1 International Nautical Mile

Liquid Measure

4 gills	= 1 pint (pt) = 28.875 cubic inches
2 pints	= 1 quart (qt) = 57.75 cubic inches
4 quarts	= 1 gallon (gal) = 231 cubic inches = 8 pints = 32 gills

Area Measure

144 square inches	= 1 square foot (ft²)
9 square feet	= 1 square yard (yd²) = 1,296 square inches
30¼ square yards	= 1 square rod (rd²) = 272¼ square feet
160 square rods	= 1 acre = 4,840 square yards = 43,560 square feet
640 acres	= 1 square mile (mi²)
1 mile square	= 1 section (of land)
6 miles square	= 1 township = 36 sections = 36 square miles

Cubic Measure

1 cubic foot (ft³)	= 1,728 cubic inches (in³)
27 cubic feet	= 1 cubic yard (yd³)

Gunter's or Surveyors' Chain Measure

7.92 inches (in)	= 1 link
100 links	= 1 chain (ch) = 4 rods = 66 feet
80 chains	= 1 survey mile (mi) = 320 rods = 5,280 feet

Troy Weight

24 grains	= 1 pennyweight (dwt)
20 pennyweights	= 1 ounce troy (oz t) = 480 grains
12 ounces troy	= 1 pound troy (lb t) = 240 pennyweights = 5,760 grains

Dry Measure

2 pints (pt)	= 1 quart (qt) = 67.2006 cubic inches
8 quarts	= 1 peck (pk) = 537.605 cubic inches = 16 pints
4 pecks	= 1 bushel (bu) = 2,150.42 cubic inches = 32 quarts

Avoirdupois Weight

27¹¹⁄₃₂ grains	= 1 dram (dr)
16 drams	= 1 ounce (oz) = 437½ grains
16 ounces	= 1 pound (lb) = 256 drams = 7,000 grains
100 pounds	= 1 hundredweight (cwt)*
20 hundredweights	= 1 ton = 2,000 pounds*

In "gross" or "long" measure, the following values are recognized.

112 pounds	= 1 gross or long hundredweight*
20 gross or long hundredweights	= 1 gross or long ton = 2,240 pounds*

TABLES OF EQUIVALENTS

Lengths

1 angstrom (A)	0.1 nanometer (exactly) 0.000 1 micrometer (exactly) 0.000 000 1 millimeter (exactly) 0.000 000 004 inch
1 cable's length	120 fathoms (exactly) 720 feet (exactly) 219 meters
1 centimeter (cm)	0.3937 inch
1 chain (ch) (Gunter's or surveyors)	66 feet (exactly) 20.1168 meters

Lengths (continued)

1 chain (engineers)	100 feet 30.48 meters (exactly)
1 decimeter (dm)	3.937 inches
1 degree (geographical)	364,566.929 feet 69.047 miles (avg.) 111.123 kilometers (avg.)
-of latitude	68.708 miles at equator 69.403 miles at poles
-of longtitude	69.171 miles at equator
1 dekameter (dam)	32.808 feet
1 fathom	6 feet (exactly) 1.8288 meters (exactly)

TABLE OF EQUIVALENTS CONTINUED

Lengths (continued)

1 foot (ft) ....0.3048 meters (exactly)
10 chains (surveyors) (exactly)
660 feet (exactly)
1 furlong (fur)...............⅛ statute mile (exactly)
201.168 meters
1 hand (height measure for horses from ground to top of shoulders) ....4 inches
1 inch (in)............................2.54 centimeters (exactly)
0.621 mile
1 kilometer (km)......................................3,281.5 feet
3 survey miles (exactly)
1 league (land)..........................4.828 kilometers
7.92 inches
1 link (Gunter's or surveyors) .... (exactly)
0.201 meter
1 link (engineers)...................................1 foot
0.305 meter
39.37 inches
1 meter (m)...1.094 yards
1 micrometer (mm)
[the Greek   0.001 millimeter (exactly)
letter mu] ....0.000 039 37 inch

Lengths (continued)

0.001 inch (exactly)
1 mil............................0.025 4 millimeter (exactly)
1 mile (mi) (statute or land)................5,280 feet (exactly)
1.609 kilometers
1 international nau-   1.852 kilometers (exactly)
tical mile (nmi) ....1.150779 survey miles
6,076.11549 feet
1 millimeter (mm)................................0.039 37 inch
1 nanometer (nm)......0.001 micrometer (exactly)
0.000 000 039 37 inch
1 pica (typography).................................12 points
1 point (typography)...0.013 837 inch (exactly)
0.351 millimeter
16½ feet (exactly)
1 rod (rd), pole, or perch ....5.029 meters
1 yard (yd)..........................0.9144 meter (exactly)

Areas or Surfaces

43,560 square feet (exactly)
1 acre ....4,840 square yards
0.405 hectare
119.599 square yards
1 are (a).......................0.025 acre

Lengths

1 international foot   = 0.999 998 survey foot (exactly)
1 survey foot   = 1200/3937 meter (exactly)
1 international foot   = 12 × 0.0254 meter (exactly)

Units	Inches	Links	Feet	Yards	Rods	Chains	Miles	cm	Meters
1 inch =	1	0.126 263	0.083 333	0.027 778	0.005 051	0.001 263	0.000 016	2.54	0.025 4
1 link =	7.92	1	0.66	0.22	0.04	0.01	0.000 125	20.117	0.201 168
1 foot=	12	1.515 152	1	0.333 333	0.060 606	0.015 152	0.000 189	30.48	0.304 8
1 yard =	36	4.545 45	3	1	0.181 818	0.045 455	0.000 568	91.44	0.914 4
1 rod=	196	25	16.5	5.5	1	0.25	0.003 125	502.92	5.029 2
1 chain =	792	100	66	22	4	1	0.012 5	2011.68	20.116 8
1 mile =	63 360	8000	5280	1760	320	80	1	160 934.4	1808.344
1 cm=	0.3937	0.049 710	0.032 806	0.010 936	0.001 988	0.000 497	0.000 006	1	0.01
1 meter=	39.37	4.970 960	3.280 840	1.093 613	0.196 838	0.049 710	0.000 621	100	1

Areas or Surfaces

Units	Sq. inches	Sq. links	Sq. feet	Sq. yards	Sq. rods	Sq. chains
1 sq. inch =	1	.015 942 3	0.006 944	0.000 771 605	0.000 025 5	0.000 001 594
1 sq. link =	62.726 4	1	0.435 6	0.0484	0.0016	0.000
1 sq foot =	144	2.296 684	1	0.111 111 1	0.003 673 09	0.000 229 568
1 sq. yard =	1296	20.661 16	9	1	0.033 057 85	0.002 066 12
1 sq. rod =	39 204	625	272.25	30.25	1	0.062 5
1 sq. chain =	627 264	10 000	4 356	484	16	1
1 acre =	6 272 640	100 000	43 560	4 840	160	10
1 sq. mile =	4 014 489 600	64 000 000	27 878 400	3 097 600	102 400	6400
1 sq. cm =	0.155 000 3	0.002 471 06	0.001 076	0.000 119 599	0.000 003 954	0.000 000 247
1 sq. meter =	1550.003	24.710 44	10.763 91	1.195 990	0.039 536 70	0.002 471 044
1 hectare =	15 500 031	247 104	107 639.1	11 959.90	395.367 0	24.710 44

Units	Acres	Sq. mile	Sq. cm	Sq. meters	Hectares
1 sq. inch =	0.000 000 159 423	0.000 000 000 249 10	6.451 6	0.000 645 16	0.000 000 065
1 sq. link =	0.000 01	0.000 000 015 625	404.685 642 24	0.040 468 56	0.000 004 047
1 sq. foot =	0.000 022 956 84	0.000 000 035 870 06	929.034 1	0.092 903 41	0.000 009 290
1 sq. yard =	0.000 206 611 6	0.000 000 322 830 6	3 361.273 6	0.836 127 36	0.000 083 613
1 sq. rod =	0.006 25	0.000 009 765 625	252 929.5	25.292 95	0.002 529 295
1 sq. chain =	0.1	0.000 156 25	4 046 873	404.687 3	0.040 468 73
1 acre =	1	0.001 562 5	40 468 73	4 046.873	0.404 687 3
1 sq. mile =	640	1	25 599 881 103	2 589 968.11	256.996 811 034
1 sq. cm =	0.000 000 024 711	0.000 000 000 038 610	1	0.000 1	0.000 000 01
1 sq. meter =	0.000 247 104 4	0.000 000 386 102 2	10 000	1	0.0001
1 hectare =	2.471 044	0.003 861 006	100 000 000	10 000	1

Weights or Masses

1 assay ton (AT).....................................29.167 grams
1 bale (cotton measure) ....{ 500 pounds in U.S.
{ 750 pounds in Egypt
1 carat (c) ....{ 200 milligrams (exactly)
{ 3.086 grains
1 dram avoirdupois (dr avdp) { 27¹½ (= 27.344) grains
gamma, see microgram ....{ 1.772 grams

1 grain...64.799 milligrams
1 gram ....{ 15.432 grains
{ 0.035 ounce, avoirdupois
1 hundredweight, gross or   { 112 pounds (exactly)
long*** (gross cwt)................{ 50.802 kilograms
1 hundredweight, net or short........{ 100 pounds (exactly)
(cwt. or net cwt.) ....{ 45.359 kilograms

Weights or Masses *(continued)*

1 kilogram (kg)......................... 2.205 pounds
1 microgram (μm [The Greek letter mu in combination with the letter g]) ....0.000001 gram (exactly)
1 milligram (mg)..0.015 gram
1 ounce, avoirdupois (oz avdp) .... { 437.5 grains (exactly) / 0.911 troy ounce / 28.350 grams
1 ounce, troy (oz t).................. { 480 grains (exactly) / 1.097 avoirdupois ounces / 31.103 grams
1 pennyweight (dwt) .... 1.555 grams
1 pound, avoirdupois (lb avdp) .... { 7,000 grains (exactly) / 1,215 troy pounds / 453.592 37 grams (exactly)
1 pound, troy (lb t) .... { 5,760 grains (exactly) / 0.823 avoirdupois pound / 373.242 grams

1 ton, gross or long*** (gross ton) .... { 2,240 pounds (exactly) / 1.12 net tons (exactly) / 1.016 metric tons

***The gross or long ton and hundredweight are used commercially in the United States to only a limited extent, usually in restricted industrial fields. These units are the same as British "ton" and "hundredweight."

1 ton, metric (t) .... { 2,204.623 pounds / 0.984 gross ton / 1.102 net tons
1 ton, net or short (sh ton) .... { 2,000 pounds (exactly) / 0.893 gross ton / 0.907 metric ton

Capacities or Volumes

1 barrel (bbl) liquid ....31 to 42 gallons*
1 barrel (bbl), standard, for fruits, vegetables, and other dry commodities except dry cranberries .... { 7,056 cubic inches / 105 dry quarts / 3.281 bushels, struck measure
1 barrel (bbl), standard, cranberry .... { 5,826 cubic inches / 86⁴⁵⁄₆₄ dry quarts / 2.709 bushels, struck measure
1 board foot (lumber measure)................a foot-square board 1 inch thick
1 bushel (bu) (U.S.) (struck measure)..................... { 2,150.42 cubic inches (exactly) / 35.239 liters
[1 bushel, heaped (U.S.)] { 2,747.715 cubic inches / 1.278 bushels, struck measure*
*Frequently recognized as 1¼ bushels, struck measure.
[1 bushel (bu) (British Imperial) (struck measure)] .... { 1.032 U.S. bushels struck measure / 2,219.36 cubic inches
1 cord (cd) firewood.............................128 cubic feet (exactly)
1 cubic centimeter (cm³)................................0.061 cubic inch
1 cubic decimeter (dm³)........................61.024 cubic inches
1 cubic inch (in³)..................... { 0.554 fluid ounce / 4.433 fluid drams / 16.387 cubic centimeters
1 cubic foot (ft³) .... { 7.481 gallons / 28.317 cubic decimeters
1 cubic meter (m³) ....1.308 cubic yards
1 cubic yard (yd³) ....0.765 cubic meter
1 cup, measuring .... { 8 fluid ounces (exactly) / ½ liquid pint (exactly)
[1 dram, fluid (fl dr) (British)] .... { 0.961 U.S. fluid dram / 0.217 cubic inch / 3.552 milliliters
1 dekaliter (daL)................................... { 2.642 gallons / 1.135 pecks
1 gallon (gal) (U.S.) .... { 231 cubic inches (exactly) / 3.785 liters / 0.833 British gallon / 128 U.S. fluid ounces (exactly)

[1 gallon (gal) British Imperial] .... { 277.42 cubic inches / 1.201 U.S. gallons / 4.546 liters / 160 British fluid ounces (exactly)
1 gill (gi)..................... { 7.219 cubic inches / 4 fluid ounces (exactly) / 0.118 liter
1 hectoliter (hL)................. { 26.418 gallons / 2.838 bushels
1 liter (L) (1 cubic decimeter exactly)... { 1.057 liquid quarts / 0.908 dry quart / 61.025 cubic inches
1 milliliter (mL) (1 cu cm exactly)......... { 0.271 fluid dram / 16.231 minims / 0.061 cubic inch
1 ounce, liquid (U.S.).................... { 1.805 cubic inches / 29.573 milliliters / 1.041 British fluid ounces
[1 ounce, fluid (fl oz) (British)] { 0.961 U.S. fluid ounce / 1.734 cubic inches / 28.412 milliliters
1 peck (pk) ....8.810 liters
1 pint (pt), dry .... { 33.600 cubic inches / 0.551 liter
1 pint (pt), liquid .... { 28.875 cubic inches (exactly) / 0.473 liter
1 quart (qt) dry (U.S.) .... { 67.201 cubic inches / 1.101 liters / 0.969 British quart
1 quart (qt) liquid (U.S.)........... { 57.75 cubic inches (exactly) / 0.946 liter / 0.833 British quart
[1 quart (qt) (British)] .... { 69.354 cubic inches / 1.032 U.S. dry quarts / 1.202 U.S. liquid quarts
1 tablespoon .... { 3 teaspoons (exactly) / 4 fluid drams / ½ fluid ounce (exactly)
1 teaspoon .... { ⅓ tablespoon (exactly) / 1⅓ fluid drams

LARGE NUMBERS

U.S.	Number of zeros	French British, German	U.S.	Number of zeros	French British, German
million	6	million	sextillion	21	1,000 trillion
billion	9	milliard	septillion	24	quadrillion
trillion	12	billion	octillion	27	1,000 quadrillion
quadrillion	15	1,000 billion	nonillion	30	quintillion
quintillion	18	trillion	decillion	33	1,000 quintillion

ROMAN NUMERALS

I	— 1	VI	— 6	XI	— 11	L	— 50	CD	— 400	X̄	— 10,000
II	— 2	VII	— 7	XIX	— 19	LX	— 60	D	— 500	L̄	— 50,000
III	— 3	VIII	— 8	XX	— 20	XC	— 90	CM	— 900	C̄	— 100,000
IV	— 4	IX	— 9	XXX	— 30	C	— 100	M̄	— 1,000	D̄	— 500,000
V	— 5	X	— 10	XL	— 40	CC	— 200	V̄	— 5,000		

GREEK ALPHABET

A	α	alpha	N	ν	nu
B	β	beta	Ξ	ξ	xi
Γ	γ	gamma	O	ο	omicron
Δ	δ	delta	Π	π	pi
E	ε	epsilon	P	ρ	rho
Z	ζ	zeta	Σ	σ	sigma
H	η	eta	T	τ	tau
Θ	θ	theta	Y	υ	upsilon
I	ι	iota	Φ	φ	phi
K	κ	kappa	X	χ	chi
Λ	λ	lambda	Ψ	ψ	psi
M	μ	mu	Ω	ω	omega

WORLD TIME ZONES

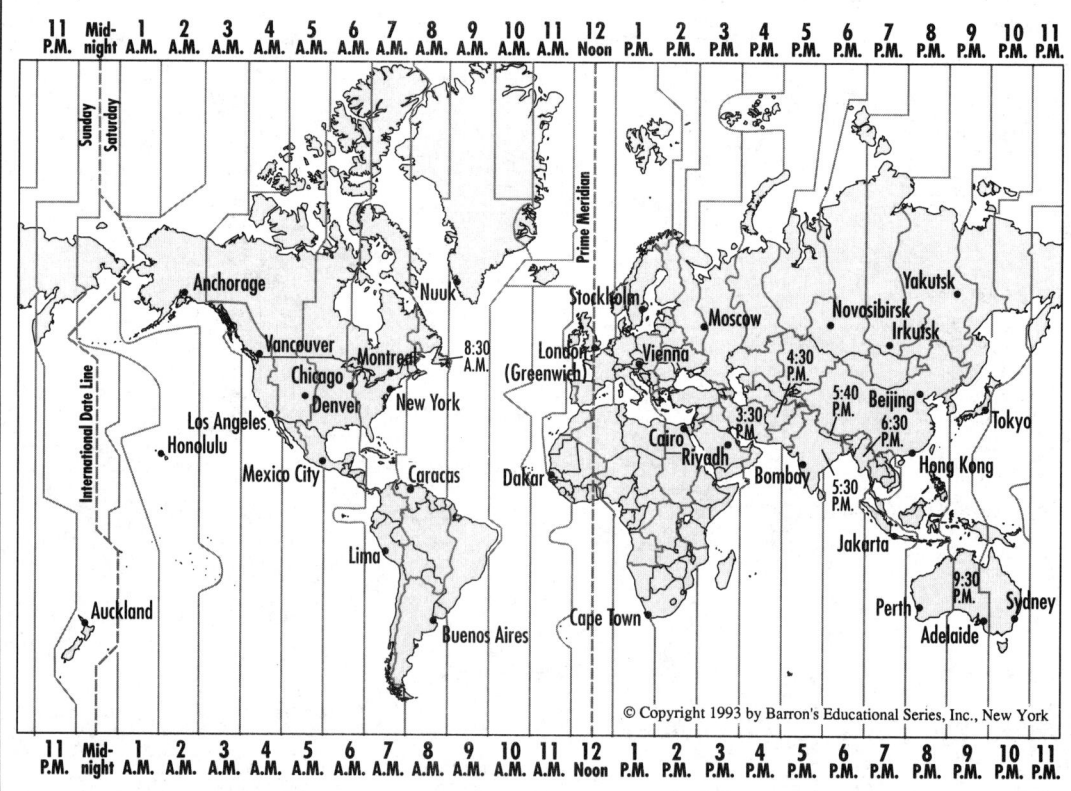

© Copyright 1993 by Barron's Educational Series, Inc., New York

The world is divided into 24 time zones, each one hour apart.

14-40

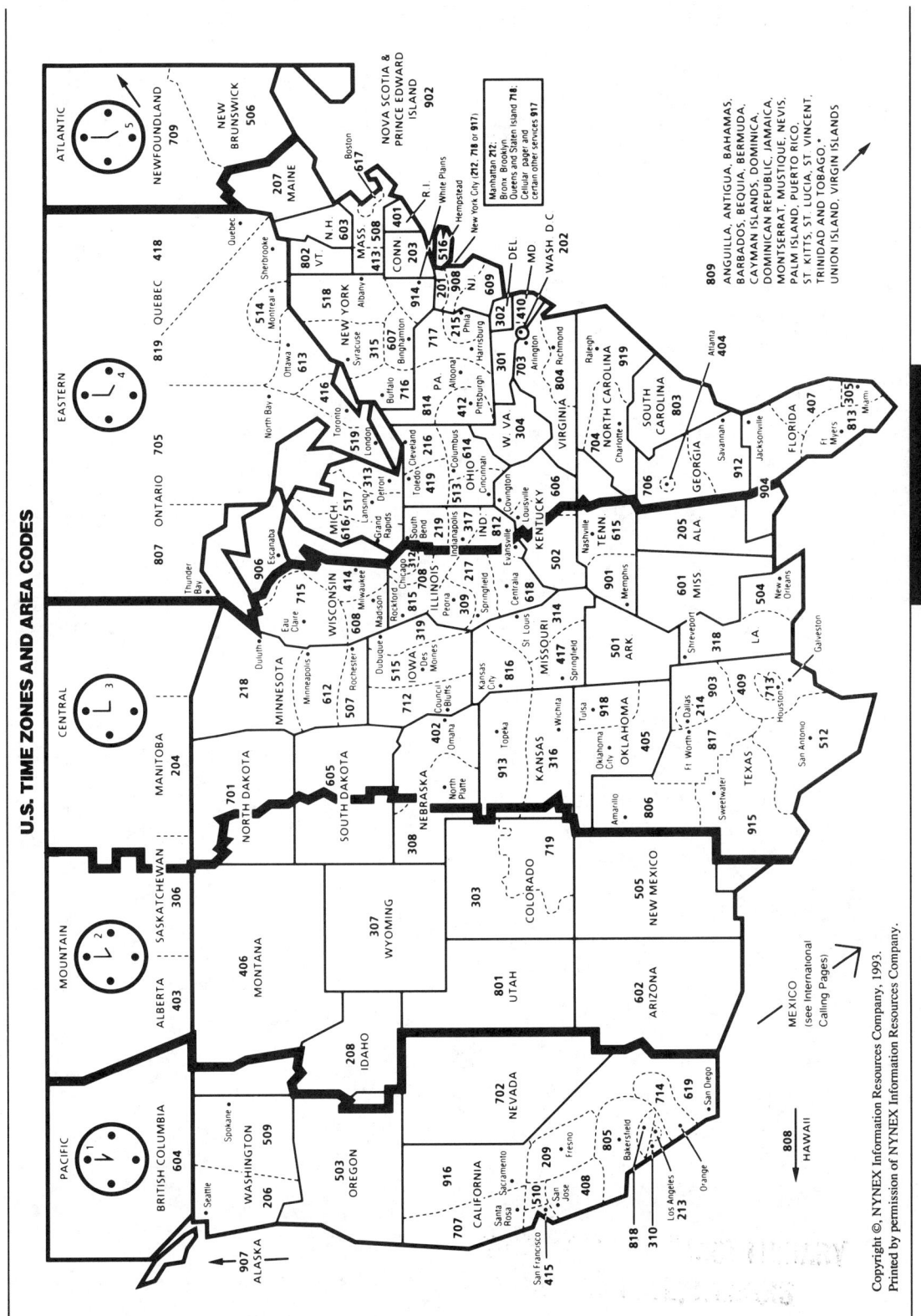

U.S. TIME ZONES AND AREA CODES

LIFE SKILLS

LITERATURE

Abstract poetry Poetry that uses words for their sound qualities rather than for their meaning. Like abstract painting, which uses colors and shapes to convey meaning but represents no specific objects, abstract poetry does not attempt to convey meaning in the traditional sense:

The Pterodactyl made its nest
And laid a steel egg in her breast—
Under the Judas colored sun.

Dame Edith Sitwell

Absurd, the Literature or drama that has as its basic premise the meaninglessness of life in the 20th century, where man is separated from his religious and philosophical roots and therefore lives in isolation in an alien world. Works that depict the absurd use nightmarish fantasy, inconsistencies, and even banal repetitions to suggest the absurdity of modern life. *See* **Beckett, Samuel; Ionesco, Eugene**.

Accent Vocal prominence or emphasis given to a syllable, word, or phrase. In poetry, accented syllables form metrical patterns by contrasting with unstressed syllables. Accented syllables are indicated by the symbol ´.

Cŏme líve wiťh me aňd be m̌y lóve.

Marlowe

Act A major division in a drama; minor divisions within an act are called scenes.

Adage A short, quotable, wise saying that is well known from wide use over a long period of time; usually of anonymous authorship.

Haste makes waste.
Absence makes the heart grow fonder.

Adams, Henry (1838–1918) American historian and man of letters, the grandson and great-grandson of presidents, he wrote studies of the Jefferson and Madison presidencies. He also wrote *The Education of Henry Adams* (1918), an autobiography in which he declared himself to be out of tune with his times. (Also considered noteworthy because he never refers to his wife.)

Adaptation A literary or dramatic work rewritten for another medium.

Addison, Joseph (1672–1719) Essayist, who, together with Richard Steele, was part of the most celebrated British literary partnership. Together they worked on *The Tatler* and *The Spectator,* in which the essay as a literary form was perfected.

Aeneid, Vergil This important Roman epic poem tells of the wanderings of Aeneas, an exile from Troy after the Trojan War. Traveling with his father and his son, Aeneas has a vision of founding a new empire in Italy. When he arrives there, he is opposed by the local prince Turnus, but eventually kills his enemy and founds the Roman Empire.

Aeschylus (524–456 B.C.) The earliest Greek dramatist, he composed about 90 plays, of which seven survive. Among these are *Prometheus Bound,* about the sufferings of the Titan who stole fire from the gods to give to mankind and was punished by a vengeful Zeus, and *The Oresteia,* the only trilogy existing today from Greek tragedy, consisting of *Agamemnon, The Libation-Bearers,* and *Eumenides.*

Aesop Little is known of this Greek writer of fables except that he was reputed to have been a slave and legend associates him with wild adventures. His short and charming moralistic tales have survived through the centuries and Aesop's "lessons" are passed from generation to generation.

Aesthetic distance Refers to the "space" that must necessarily exist between the work of art and the reader or viewer. Such a distance is necessary so that there is no confusion between "art" and "life." A theatergoer might well become enraged at a sadistic character on stage, but he remains knowledgeable enough not to storm down the aisle and threaten the blackguard. Too great an identification with a work of art leads to subjective feelings that will distort the view of the artistic creation, but a lack of participation, a "removal" from what is being presented, will also diminish the experience of the work. *See* **Suspension of disbelief**.

Aiken, Conrad (1889–1973) This poet and novelist, a Georgia native, underwent a traumatic experience at age 11, when his doctor father killed his mother and then himself. Aiken devoted himself entirely to writing, and his poetry was strongly influenced by T.S. Eliot. He had a strong interest in both medicine and modern psychology. His major works were *Punch* (1921) and *Collected Poems* (1953).

Albee, Edward (b. 1928) Adopted into a wealthy family, this clever and satiric American playwright was sent to expensive boarding schools, as a child, but broke at 20 with his parents. Author of *The Zoo Story,* his greatest success came with *Who's Afraid of Virginia Woolf?* in 1962.

Alcott, Louisa May (1832–1889) The daughter of Amos Bronson Alcott, idealist, optimist, transcendentalist, and vegetarian, she grew up in Massachusetts in the experimental colony Fruitlands. She worked as a seamstress before becoming a popular children's writer. *Little Women* (1868) is her best-known work.

Alexandrine A line of poetry with six iambic feet, used widely in the 12th and 13th centuries to eulogize Alexander the Great. Spenser used it as a longer ninth line, following eight iambic pentameter lines, to conclude each Spenserian Stanza.

Alexander Pope parodies the use of the Alexandrine in the couplet:

A needless Alexandrine ends the song,
That, like a wounded snake, drags its slow length along.

Alice in Wonderland (1865), Lewis Carroll A wonder-filled children's classic, peopled by such outrageous characters as the Mad Hatter, Tweedledum and Tweedledee, and the Cheshire Cat, next to whom Alice, whose wanderings hold the tale together, is only a pale, if lovely, player. Although this work can also be read on satiric and symbolic levels, it is still valued primarily as a delightful children's fantasy.

All Quiet on the Western Front (1929), Erich Maria Remarque This German novel captured the spirit of disillusionment that affected all of the West in the wake of World War I. It is related by a young soldier who with the others in his squad, becomes hard and cynical. At the end of the novel, the narrator returns home to find his mother dying of cancer, a symbol of the diseased society awaiting the returning soldiers.

Allegory A narrative poem or prose work in which persons, events, and objects represent or stand for something else, frequently abstract ideas.

Alliteration The repetition of consonants in a series of words in poetry or music.

> The *m*oan of doves in i*mm*e*m*orial
> el*m*s and *m*ur*m*uring of innu*m*erable
> bees.
>
> Tennyson

Note: Alliteration frequently refers only to the initial consonant sound, as in "three tread tightly together." *Compare* **Assonance.**

Allusion An indirect or casual reference to a famous person or event in history, the Bible, a literary work, mythology, or another known source. The allusion may be obvious:

> But sweeter than the Lids of Juno's
> eyes
> Or Cytherea's breath.
>
> Shakespeare

It may also be esoteric:

> April is the cruelest month,
> Breeding violets out of the dead land.
>
> T.S. Eliot

The Ambassadors (1903), Henry James This novel tells the story of a man past middle age who is made to realize through a visit to Paris how much of life he has missed. In this work, as in many James novels, Europe stands for experience and sophistication and America for both virtue and brashness.

An American Tragedy (1925), Theodore Dreiser This novel is a study of social classes and of an individual's effort to rise from one class to another; it also deals with the moral problem of guilt. Clyde Griffiths impregnates a young factory girl and, when the opportunity arises for him to marry a wealthy heiress, he kills his mistress. Ultimately, he is tried and executed for the crime.

Anachronism The representing in literature of a person, scene, object, etc., in a time period that would have been impossible historically (Macbeth wearing a Bulova watch).

Analogy An (implied) comparison between two different things that resemble each other. Sometimes expressed as a *simile:* Joe is *as* crazy as an old hooty owl.

Anapest In poetry, a metrical foot with two unaccented syllables followed by a stressed syllable.

> Oň ă bénch | iň thě párk | iň thě
> sún | iň thě spríng.

Anderson, Sherwood (1876–1941) Born in Ohio, with almost no formal education, Anderson was the manager of a paint factory when he decided to give up business and become a writer. In 1919 his collection of stories, *Winesburg, Ohio,* brought him both critical and popular acclaim.

Anna Karenina, Leo Tolstoy Written between 1875 and 1877, this Russian novel details the moral tragedy of Anna, who leaves her husband and young son to live with and eventually to marry a handsome young count. But, unable to cope with her decision and unsure of her second husband's love, she commits suicide.

Anouilh, Jean (b. 1910) This French playwright's chief contribution to modern drama is his part in the revival of the tragic principle in the theater, especially his concept of the tragic hero—in his work often an individual who will not compromise. Further, he is interested in the relationships between illusion and reality. His best-known works are *Antigone* (1944), *The Lark* (1955), and *Becket* (1960).

Antagonist The major "villainous" character in a work who opposes the hero (protagonist). In Melville's *Moby Dick,* Captain Ahab is the "hero" and the whale in the title is the antagonist.

Anticlimax The arrangement of details so that less important and trivial matters come after the most important item. Also, frequently a lofty tone to one that is followed by one much more mundane.

Used unintentionally, anticlimax can be a serious fault in the plot of a story, but it was often used effectively for humor in satirical poetry of the 18th century, as follows:

> Not louder shrieks to pitying heaven
> are cast,
> When husbands, or when lap dogs
> breathe their last.
>
> Pope

Antigone (442 B.C.), Sophocles This Greek tragedy deals with the struggle between Creon, the king of Thebes, who forbids the burial of Polyneices, one of those who tried to unseat him. Polyneices' sister Antigone contrives to give the body a burial and is ordered shut up alive in a vault. Her fiance, Haemon, the son of Creon, and Creon's wife Euridice then kill themselves. Simply put, the theme is the conflict between public and private duty. Jean Anouilh's *Antigone,* written during the German occupation of France, is a reexamination of this ancient theme.

Antistrophe The second part of the classical Greek choral ode, one of the stanzaic forms accompanying the strophe and the epode.

Antithesis A device in which sharply contrasting ideas are linked in parallel words, phrases, or clauses.

> Worth makes the man, and want of it,
> the fellow;
> The rest is all but leather or prunella.
>
> Pope

Apostrophe In literature, the addressing of an absent person, an abstract quality (like melancholy), or a nonexistent or mythological personage (like the muse) as though present.

> O Goddess! hear these tuneless numbers, wrung
> By sweet enforcement and remembrance dear.
>
> Keats

Apothegm A concisely worded and often witty saying that is instructive and usually more practical than an aphorism.

> Civility costs nothing and buys
> everything.
>
> Lady Mary Wortly Montagu

Argument A paragraph in prose, placed at the beginning of a long poetic work, summarizing the action that is to follow.

Aristophanes (448–380 B.C.) This Greek playwright, considered the master of Old Comedy, wrote approximately 44 plays, of which 11 survive. A conservative, he was not a fan of popular democracy nor of the Peloponnesian War, but his works abound with wholesomeness and good sense. Among his best known plays are *Lysistrata* and *The Frogs*.

Aristotle (384–322 B.C.) A Greek philosopher and a student of Plato, he is important in literary history because of his work *The Art of Poetry*. In that treatise he gives an extended definition of tragedy, influential even in the 20th century.

Arnold, Matthew (1822–1888) English poet and literary critic, the son of a famous teacher and headmaster of Rugby, he attended Oxford and was subsequently offered the professorship of poetry there. He later became the foremost spokesman for the humanities against the rise of science that characterized his century. His most famous poem is "Dover Beach," which is an excellent example of Arnold's beautiful and quiet music.

The Art of Poetry, Aristotle This work by the Greek philosopher originally had three sections, dealing with the epic, tragedy, and comedy. It survives only in a mutilated form so that the section on tragedy is all that remains more or less intact. It allegedly urged on the tragic and dramatic unity of action, time, and place, and states that tragedy must arouse fear and pity to bring about a catharsis of those emotions in the audience.

Asimov, Isaac (1920–1992) This Russian-born American science-fiction writer was as diverse as he was creative. After publishing his first novel, *Pebble in the Sky* in 1950, he went on to explore further the world of science fiction and also to write nonfiction works on science and technology, Bible Studies, humor, and mysteries. In 1979, the publication of *Opus 200* marked his 200th book in print.

Assonance The close repetition of similar vowel sounds, as in H*o*w n*o*w br*o*wn c*o*w or L*i*ke a d*i*amond in the sky.

Auden, Wystan Hugh (W.H.) (1907–1973) English poet (first influenced by Gerard Manley Hopkins and later by T.S. Eliot), who wrote in both an allegorical and allusional style. In 1939, when he abandoned England for America, he deliberately turned to writing for the general public, using delicate irony as his signature.

Austen, Jane (1775–1817) This British novelist, daughter of a clergyman, was unable to attend a university because of her sex and had great difficulty in publishing the six books she wrote. She was the first realist in the English novel and was a foe of the Romantic Movement. Her best-known works are *Sense and Sensibility* (1811), *Pride and Prejudice* (1813), and *Emma* (1816), thought to be her greatest work.

Autobiography A story of a person's life written by that person; also called memoirs. *Compare* **Biography**.

B **Babbitt** (1922), Sinclair Lewis This novel is a study of the American suburban middle class. Babbitt is a real estate salesman in Zenith (Duluth, Minnesota) who is aggressive, optimistic, and enthusiastic. At the age of 46 he begins to realize the superficiality of his life, dabbles in radicalism, and has a brief affair. But social pressures are too much

for him and he sinks back into the life of complacent vulgarity he has tried to escape. In his son, however, he sees hope for a different future.

Baldwin, James (1924–1987) Born in Harlem, New York to a father who was a factory worker and a lay preacher, Baldwin at 14 entered a ministry that was to last for three years. After trying unsuccessfully to support himself in America, this black novelist, essayist, and playwright, went to Paris in 1948: there he wrote some of his best work, including the novel *Go Tell It on the Mountain* (1953). He returned to the United States in 1957.

Ballad A poem that tells a story, often of folk origin, and is written to be sung. A ballad has simple stanzas, and often a refrain. See early American folk ballads "Barbara Allen" and "Tom Dooley," and literary ballads that include Keats's "La Belle Dame Sans Merci" and Coleridge's "The Rime of the Ancient Mariner."

Ballad stanza A four-line stanzaic form used in the popular ballad, or folk ballad, rhyming *abcb*. The first and third lines have four accented syllables, the second and fourth only three.

> Now Robin Hood is to Nottingham
>   gone, *(a)*
> With a link-a-down and a day, *(b)*
> And there he met a silly old
>   woman, *(c)*
> Was weeping on the way. *(b)*

Balzac, Honoré (1799–1850) French novelist who, in his youth, worked as a law clerk, publisher, and printer. In the 1830s he established his reputation with *Eugénie Grandet* (1833) and *Père Goriot* (1835). During this period he had a busy life as a man-about-town, a prodigious spender, and a furious worker, often putting in 14–16 hours a day writing. He gradually developed the idea of grouping his work so that it would form a unity titled *The Human Comedy,* of which his greatest novel, *Cousin Bette* (1846), is a part. He is considered France's finest novelist.

The Barber of Seville (1775), Beaumarchais This French comedy is important less for its plot, involving a young couple's love triumphant over various obstacles, than for the character of Figaro. Although from the lower class, Figaro is far more intelligent and adroit than his so-called betters. Further, he mouths a philosophy of equality rather shocking for the time.

Baroque A style in art, architecture, literature, and music characterized by flamboyancy, elaborate ornamentation, and a symmetrical arrangement. The baroque is a blend of the wild and fantastic with an ordered, formal style as in the poetry of John Donne and the music of Bach.

Barrie, Sir James M. (1860–1937) British playwright and novelist who, although criticized during his lifetime for his use of fantasy, is now held in high esteem for that very "failing." His children's classic, *Peter Pan* (1904), has been told and retold in this country from the Broadway stage to the Disney animated film. Barrie's reputation as a novelist was established in 1891 with the publication of *The Little Minister,* and his most lauded work is the tragicomedy *Dear Brutus,* which is a skillful mix of humor and realism.

Baudelaire, Charles (1821–1867)   This French Symbolist writer became the first modern poet, his influence towering in the early 20th century. An important influence on him was Poe, some of whose work he translated. His masterwork was *The Flowers of Evil*, for many years considered depraved and obscene. His primary theme is the inseparable nature of beauty and corruption.

Beat generation   The 1950–1960 decade of American writers (primarily poets) who expressed their feelings of alienation from society. "Beat"— to be "beaten" by modern life. Jack Kerouac was the undisputed leader of this literary movement, which also included such fascinating figures as Allen Ginsberg and Lawrence Ferlinghetti. Beat literature at first shocked some readers with its frequent use of four-letter words and explicit references to drugs and sex.

Beaumarchais, Pierre Augustin Caron (1732–1799)   From a working-class family, he went from watchmaker to music tutor of the royal family, and finally was in the king's secret service. His most famous works were the two comic dramas *The Barber of Seville* (1775) and *The Marriage of Figaro* (1784).

Beauvoir, Simone de (1908-1986)   French existentialist author, closely associated with Sartre. *The Mandarins* (1956) explores the existential dilemma in fiction and *The Second Sex* (1950) is a brilliant nonfiction study of the status of women.

Beckett, Samuel (1906–1989)   An Anglo-French playwright and novelist, born near Dublin. Beckett was an expatriot who eventually settled in Paris. His themes reflect the absurdity of the human condition through painful observations of man's solitude. In his plays he seeks to combine a vaudevillian with poignant tragedy. *Waiting for Godot* (1952), *Endgame* (1957), *Krapp's Last Tape* (1959), and other works earned him the Nobel Prize in Literature in 1969.

Bellow, Saul (b. 1915)   Born in Quebec Province in Canada, Bellow was raised in the slums of Montreal until his family moved to Chicago in 1924. He attended the University of Chicago and Northwestern and has taught at New York University and Princeton. Considered by critics to be America's best contemporary novelist, his works include *The Adventures of Augie March* (1953), *Seize the Day* (1956), and *Herzog* (1964). He won the Nobel Prize in Literature in 1976.

Benet, Stephen Vincent (1898–1943)   Born in Pennsylvania, educated at Yale and at the Sorbonne, he published poetry as an undergraduate. His long epic, *John Brown's Body*, for which he won a Pulitzer Prize in 1929, made him famous overnight. His short story "The Devil and Daniel Webster" (1937) is frequently anthologized and taught in many high-school English classes.

Bennet, Enoch Arnold (1867–1931)   In his autobiography, this British novelist stated that he wrote only to make money and some critics have indeed called his work journalistic. His best novel is *The Old Wives' Tale* (1908), a story of two sisters, which alternates between England and Paris.

Beowulf   This Old English folk-epic deals with a Scandinavian hero and dates from about 1000, although the combination of Christian and pagan elements leads scholars to believe it was written some centuries earlier. It consists of three parts: Beowulf's fight with the monster Grendel, the fight with Grendel's mother, and 50 years later, Beowulf's mortal combat with the Fire Dragon.

Bierce, Ambrose (1842–1914?)   American journalist, satirist, and short story writer, Bierce was born in Ohio. He served in the Civil War and then became a journalist in San Francisco. A weary melancholy pervaded the latter part of his life, and in 1914 he went to Mexico and was never heard of again. His excellence lies in satire and the chilling and savage horror inherent in his short stories. See such works as *Cobwebs from an Empty Skull* (1874) and *Can Such Things Be?* (1893). Bierce is also greatly anthologized.

Bildungsroman   A novel, usually autobiographical, that covers the principal subject's life from adolescence to maturity; also called an apprenticeship novel.

Billy Budd   (1924, published posthumously), Herman Melville   Based on an actual incident, this short story, or novella, with a seafaring background is essentially a tale of a paradise lost and then regained, where Billy symbolizes the figures of both Adam and Christ.

Biography   Strictly, the life of one person as related by another. The modern biography is comparatively recent in form in that it is both carefully researched and written in a dispassionate manner, as compared to the subjectivity of Romantic biographers who produced biographies that attempted to explore the psychology of their subjects.

Black humor   A type of writing whose popularity began in the early 1960s and in which the grotesque and the horrifying live side by side with elements that are humorous or farcical. Black humor seeks to shock and disorient readers while also making them laugh at the recognition of an absurd and disoriented world. Joseph Heller, Vladimir Nabokov, and Nathaniel West are among the American writers who have achieved fame in this genre.

Blake, William (1757–1827)   Born the son of a hosier, this British poet had visions from childhood on and wrote his first poetry at age 12. In addition to being a poet, he was also an engraver and painter and issued nearly all of his own poems in volumes designed, illustrated, and hand-colored by himself. He rejected 18th-century Neoclassicism completely and urged frenzy and imagination as the only roads to wisdom. His best-known poem is "The Tiger."

Blank verse   A type of poetry in which rhyme is not used. Instead, each line has ten syllables with an *iambic* rhythm (an unstressed syllable followed by a stressed syllable in each poetic foot, as in "abóut thĕ tówn").

   Shakespeare's *Othello* was written in blank verse, as in this excerpt:
> If I quench thee, thou flaming
>   minister
> I can again thy former light restore.

Wordsworth's *The Prelude* includes the lines:
> The leafless trees and every icy crag
> Tinkled like iron, while far-distant
>   hills
> Into the tumult sent an alien sound....

Compare **Free verse**.

LITERATURE

Boccaccio, Giovanni (1313–1375)   Italian poet and storyteller who emulated his great friend Petrarch and immortalized in verse and prose his lifelong love for Fiammetta, who supposedly introduced him at court and urged him to write. His most famous work is "The Decameron."

Böll, Heinrich (1917–1985)   Inducted into the German army in 1939, he was wounded on the Russian front and, as an infantry corporal, became an American prisoner of war in eastern France. After the war he worked as a carpenter and as a statistician until his first work, the novella *The Train Was on Time,* was published in 1949. A Catholic and a pacifist, Böll's highly moral vision of society alienated many groups. Among his other works are the novels *Adam, Where Art Thou? (1951),* and *Billiards at Half-Past Nine (1959),* and *The Clown* (1965). Böll won the Nobel Prize for Literature in 1972.

Bombast   Inflated, extravagant, pompous, and grandiloquent speech, found in most Elizabethan poems and plays and in many political speeches.

> O thou art fairer than the evening air,
> Clad in the beauty of a thousand stars,
> Brighter art thou than flaming Jupiter....
> Marlowe

Borges, Jorge Luis (1899–1986)   Hailed as the greatest contemporary Spanish-American poet and writer, his literary ancestors range from Kierkegaard to Joyce, Kafka to Beckett. Although modest and a deprecator of his own work, the mastery and genius of Borges is revealed in his creation of expressionistic and artistic dreams and mythical fantasies that in his hands often turn to wit and elegance. Most famous among his works are *The Aleph* (1949) and *Labyrinths* (1962).

Boswell, James (1740–1795)   The son of a wealthy Scots judge, he attended Edinburgh University and in 1763 met Samuel Johnson, whose biographer he was to become. *The Life of Samuel Johnson, LL.D.* is considered one of the greatest of all biographies. A new Boswell emerged with the discovery of his diaries and private papers and their publication after World War II.

Bradstreet, Anne (1612–1672)   Born in England, she came to America in 1630 with her husband who was to become governor of the Massachusetts colony. Bradstreet is historically famous in colonial literature for being the first American woman to devote herself to writing poetry, despite raising a large family in a land that was then little more than a wilderness.

Brave New World (1932), Aldous Huxley   A nightmare utopia classic of the 25th century when science and technology have achieved a complete tyranny over humanity. It is noteworthy that many of the futuristic devices depicted in this novel (television, helicopters, and so on) are already in operation, and that psychological conditioning of the masses has been widely used in totalitarian countries.

Brecht, Bertolt (1898–1956)   A German playwright and poet, Brecht won fame for the effect of alienation that he sought to achieve in his plays by his constant reminders that the audience was to think and analyze, not feel. Because of his politics he had to leave Germany from 1938–1947—time he spent in Scandinavia and the United States. His best-known plays are *The Threepenny Opera* (1928) and *Mother Courage and Her Children* (1939).

Brontë, Charlotte (1816–1855)   One of five daughters of an English clergyman, she and her sisters Emily and Anne issued a joint volume in 1846 under the pen names of Currer, Ellis, and Acton Bell; the book had no great success, but all three turned to novel writing, Charlotte's *Jane Eyre* (1847) being the most popular of her works.

Brontë, Emily (1818-1848)   One of the five daughters of a British clergyman, she joined her sisters Charlotte and Anne in publishing a volume of verse under the pen names of Currer, Ellis, and Acton Bell. Although the book had no success, all three began writing novels and Emily's *Wuthering Heights* was published in the year of her death. Succeeding years have proven her to be the most outstandingly talented Brontë with a genius for capturing mood and passion.

Brooks, Gwendolyn (b. 1917)   Poet laureat of Illinois since 1968, Brooks became the first black to win a Pulitzer Prize in 1950 for her poetry, *Annie Allen*. Also a novelist, short-story writer, and author of juvenile books, her works include *Maud Martha* (1953), *A Sesquecentennial Poem* (1968), *The Tiger Who Wore White Gloves* (1974), *Primer for Blacks* (1980), and *Young Poets Primer* (1981).

The Brothers Karamazov (1880), Feodor Dostoyevsky   This Russian novel deals with the landowner Fyodor Karamazov and his four sons Aloysha, a model of loving kindness, Dmitri, a vulgar bully, Ivan, who cannot accept the cruelty of the world, and the bastard Smerdyakov, the embodiment of the sinister. It is perhaps the most profound study in the field of the novel of the conflict between Good and Evil in man's soul.

Browning, Elizabeth Barrett (1806–1861)   English poet who, because of her delicate health, was kept as a semi-invalid by her tyrannical father. After an intense correspondence with Robert Browning, he came to the family residence on Wimpole Street in London and ardently wooed Elizabeth. Defying her father, they married and moved to Italy where her health improved. Her most famous work, *Sonnets from the Portuguese,* contains the often-quoted line, "How do I love thee? Let me count the ways."

Browning, Robert (1812–1889)   This English poet, the son of a bank clerk, spent the first 28 years of his life at home, where he read voraciously. He had his first success with his second volume of poetry, *Paracelsus* (1835), and for a time wrote for the stage, without great results. In 1845 he began his correspondence with Elizabeth Barrett and, after a courtship, greatly opposed by her father, they were eventually married and went to Italy to live. Among Browning's most famous works are *The Ring and the Book* (1868–1869) and *Bells and Pomegranates* (1841) in which he gives us "Pippa Passes," with its much quoted line, "God's in his heaven/ All's right with the world!" Browning is also noted for his dramatic monologues, such as "My Last Duchess" (1841).

Bryant, William Cullen (1794–1878)   American nature poet, born in Massachusetts, the son of a country doctor, he was raised in a conservative

(Federalist) household. In 1829 he became editor of the New York *Evening Post,* a position he held for half a century and in which he usually espoused liberal causes. He is best known, however, as a poet whose romantic themes were nature and humanity. His best known work is "Thanatopsis," written before he was 21.

Buck, Pearl (1892–1973) Born of missionary parents and raised in China, she won world acclaim for her novel on Chinese peasants, *The Good Earth* (1931) and was awarded the Nobel Prize for Literature in 1938. She wrote several novels with American settings, but they were less well received. Her works have greatly contributed to world culture in that they have promoted racial understanding.

Buddenbrooks (1900), Thomas Mann This German novel shows the decline of a German merchant family through four generations. In 1835 the family headed by the old grain merchant Johann Buddenbrook, is prosperous and vigorous. Johann's son Thomas dabbles in aesthetics and philosophy and his brother Christian becomes insane. The line eventually ends in little Hanno, delicate and hypersensitive, who dies of typhus. This was the novel that made Mann's reputation.

Bunin, Ivan (1870–1953) A 19th-century Russian realist who wrote in a detailed and conservative manner, but whose themes are both personal and metaphysical, rather than social. He drew much inspiration from Western literature and was a translator of Longfellow; he also read widely in French literature and thus is quite cosmopolitan in outlook although Russian in temperament. His chief works are *The Village* (1910) and *The Gentleman from San Francisco and Other Stories* (1915), the latter being widely translated and reprinted.

Bunyan, John (1628–1688) An English prose writer of religious allegories, he was almost unhinged by reading gloomy Puritan theology. Bunyan was restored to mental health by a Baptist minister and began to preach in small villages. He was put into prison for 12 years for unlicensed preaching, during which times he wrote nine books. Upon his release he became the pastor of a small church but was arrested again. The second time, he began the composition of his masterwork, *Pilgrim's Progress* (1678 and 1684), an allegory often considered one of the world's great books. His prose combines biblical eloquence with contemporary language.

Burlesque A form of comic drama or fiction in which an elevated subject is treated in a trivial way or a low subject is treated with mock dignity. In both cases exaggeration and distortion are used for the sake of ridicule. Cervantes's *Don Quixote* is an example.

Burns, Robert (1759–1796) A Scottish poet, born in poverty, Burns had only three years of schooling, but was an avid reader and even taught himself French. He became a collector of Scottish folk songs and published his first volume of poetry in 1786. Eventually, he went to Edinburgh, where he was lionized as a peasant-genius. Among his best known poems are "My Luv is Like a Red, Red Rose," "Auld Lang Syne," and "Comin' Thro' the Rye."

Byron, Lord (George Gordon Nuel) (1788–1824) This English romantic poet, the son of a profligate father and a hysterical mother, was born with a club foot. He became notorious for a flamboyant and dissolute life, his cavalier treatment of women, and his liaison with his half sister. In 1812 he published the first two cantos of *Childe Harold's Pilgrimage* and became famous overnight. However, his masterpiece is considered to be *Don Juan,* an epic satire that combines Byron's lyricism with his detest of convention. He spent most of his time on the Continent after 1819 and died during the Greek war of independence.

C Cabell, James Branch (1879–1958) American novelist who achieved notoriety with his novel *Jurgen* (1919), a book of medieval fantasy that some sought to ban on the grounds of obscenity. Much of Cabell's work fought to exist in an age of Naturalism, but he was a writer of great talent, whose works might one day look forward to a revival.

Cacophony A term used either in criticism of poetry to characterize a jarring, discordant, unharmonious combination of sounds, or to illustrate the poetic language used to create a particular effect.

> A tap at the pane, the quick sharp
>   scratch
> And blue spurt of a lighted match.
>
> Browning

Cadence The natural rhythm of language. Used in verse to refer to rhythms of speech falling into patterns. *See* **Free verse**.

Caesura A pause in a line of verse, usually occurring near the middle of the line, indicated by a parallel slash, in books about poetry scansion.

> A little learning/
> Is a dangerous thing.
>
> Pope

The Call of the Wild (1903), Jack London This novel concerns a sled dog who reverts to savagery. Buck, a California sheepdog, is sent to the north in the '96 gold rush. After much mistreatment, he becomes the leader of a pack of savage dogs and then finally falls into the hands of a kind master. But his owner is killed by the Indians, several of whom Buck kills, and he joins a pack of wolves, to return once a year to mourn beside the river that is his master's grave.

Camus, Albert (1913–1960) Although as an existentialist Camus sees the causation of human destiny as unknowable and irrational, there is an optimism in his work lacking in others of the school. Born in Algiers, he was active in the resistance throughout World War ll, and died tragically in an automobile accident when he was 47. His most famous works are *The Stranger* (1942) and *The Myth of Sisyphus* (1955). He was awarded the Nobel Prize for Literature in 1957.

Candide (1759), Voltaire Written partially in response to the great Lisbon earthquake of 1755, in which 60,000 died, this French novel, a world masterpiece of wit and skepticism, is an attack on the point of view that "'everything is for the best in this best of possible worlds.'" It satirically recounts the misadventures of Candide, the archetypal innocent who encounters all manner of chicanery, falsity, and cruelty and finally concludes that a measure of

LITERATURE

peace can only be found if a man is able to lose himself in useful work.

The Canterbury Tales (1388), Geoffrey Chaucer   Chaucer comes across a group of 28 pilgrims at the Tabard Inn in Southwark, just across the Thames from London. They are on their way to the shrine of Thomas à Becket in Canterbury. The host of the inn and the poet (Chaucer) decide to join them, and the host suggests that the pilgrims (who together represent a cross-section of 14th-century English life) tell tales on the way to and from the shrine to entertain the company. Their stories range from the humorous fable to the serious lesson.

Pilgrims made famous by Geoffrey Chaucer's *Canterbury Tales.*

Canto   A major division of a long poem; from the Latin word *cantus,* meaning song.

Capote, Truman (1924–1984)   Born in New Orleans, Capote spent his childhood in Alabama and much of his work is reflective of the greatest in Southern literary tradition. His first short story, "Miriam," was published when he was 20. Though he wrote plays and filmscripts, he is perhaps best known for his "nonfiction novel," *In Cold Blood,* published in 1966. However, his later writing never achieved the greatness of *Other Voices, Other Rooms* and *The Grass Harp* (1951).

Carew, Thomas (1594–1639)   One of Britain's Cavalier poets, i.e., those who backed the king against the Puritans. One of his favorite themes is the tricks time plays on beauty and youth and the admonition that one should seize the pleasure of the moment.

Carlyle, Thomas (1795–1881)   Born into poverty in Scotland, he entered Edinburgh University and later taught for some time until he became interested in German literature, which he introduced almost single-handedly to England. His best known work, *Sartor Resartus* (1833 and 34) is a spiritual autobiography in which he views the material world as the mere cloth for the spiritual one. His lectures, *Heroes and Heroworship* (1841), express his belief that the great of the past have intuitively shaped destiny and served as spiritual leaders of the world.

Carroll, Lewis (Charles Lutwidge Dodgson) (1832–1898)   A lecturer at Oxford on mathematics, Carroll was a loner who loved children and wrote his classic *Alice in Wonderland* (1865, illustrated by Sir John Tenniel) for Alice, a friend's daughter. *Through the Looking Glass* (1871) is a sequel to this work. Carroll also wrote popular humorous verses and is considered to be a master of literary satire.

The Castle (1926), Franz Kafka   This posthumous novel tells the story of a man called K., who has been hired as a land surveyor to a count who lives in a mysterious castle. When he presents himself at the castle, however, no one seems to know who he is or why he is there. K. never does get inside the building, and he never comes to an understanding of what his quest is all about. The novel is usually seen as an allegory of man's efforts to know God.

Catastrophe   The concluding part of a tragedy, usually involving the death of the hero. Hence, the term has come to mean a tragic event in real life. Sophocles' *Oedipus Rex* and *Antigone* and Shakespeare's *Hamlet* all conclude with catastrophic events.

Catcher in the Rye (1951), J.D. Salinger   A sensitive 20th-century masterwork about the pain of growing up with the isolated feeling of being different from everyone else. Told in the first person, "Catcher" is an unparalleled example of the extended monologue. It relates the odyssey of Holden Caulfield, whose adolescence is a sad and poignant journey, but also one filled with wit and insight. Part boy, part man, Holden is not accepted by the adult world, nor does he fit into prep-school life with his contemporaries—an alienation that leads to the gradual breakdown of his personality.

Catharsis (also spelled *katharsis*)   A term first used by Aristotle to describe the purging or cleansing of the emotions that a spectator experiences while attending a tragic drama. There are two interpretations of catharsis: one being that the spectator cleanses his emotions by vicariously sharing the tragic consequences of the evil action depicted onstage and learns to avoid such action, the other holds that the spectator forgets his own conflicts and inner agitation by expending pity and fear on the tragic hero. Although some literary critics would argue that Willy Loman, in Arthur Miller's *Death of a Salesman,* is not a tragic hero (because he is a traveling salesman and not a king or military leader), many theatergoers seem to have experienced a true catharsis in seeing Willy's downfall.

Cather, Willa (1873–1947)   American novelist and short-story writer who captures the spirit of 1880s–1890s pioneering life in the Midwest in such highly praised novels as *O Pioneers!* (1913) and *My Antonia* (1918). Cather, a fine craftsperson who displayed great lucidity and discipline, wrote warmly and richly of the human experience.

Cavalier poetry   Refers to verse (written between 1625–1649, during the reign of Charles I) of exalted diction in a brief, concise form, which was most frequently in praise of wine, women, and song. Herrick and Lovelace are two Cavalier poets.

Cervantes Saavedra, Miguel (1547–1616)   The major figure in Spanish literature was a novelist, playwright, and poet. He became a soldier after leaving school, spent five years as a captive of the Turks, and returned to Spain in 1580. *Don Quixote* (1605–1615), his world-renowned work, had an indelible effect on the development of the European novel. Cervantes also wrote tales of piracy, gypsies, and deep emotion—garnered from his own experience and crafted with expertise.

Characterization   The creation of a fictional character through various techniques, including a description of his or her physical presence and actions, as well as a transcription of the character's thoughts and conversations. E.M. Forster distinguished between flat characters, who are not fully developed and are little more than names, and round characters, who have depth and complexity. In Dickens's novel *Oliver Twist*, Oliver is a well-rounded, fully developed character, while the Artful Dodger is a flat character, almost a caricature.

Chaucer, Geoffrey (1340–1400)   One of the most important figures in English literature, he was the son of a wealthy wine merchant. Chaucer spent many years in the service of a king. His masterwork is *The Canterbury Tales* (1387–1400), but because of the development of modern English, his brilliant storytelling and poetic technique were not fully appreciated until the 18th century.

Cheever, John (1912–1982)   This outstanding American novelist and short-story writer was a grandly perceptive chronicler of suburban lifestyles (see *The Wapshot Scandal* and *The Wapshot Chronicle*). His keen vision is illustrated in *The Collected Short Stories*, an outstanding anthology in contemporary fiction in its breadth of theme and clarity of insight.

Chekhov, Anton (1860–1904)   A physician as well as a writer, this Russian artist is best known today as a dramatist, but he is also considered the world master of the short story and the greatest Russian writer after Tolstoy and Dostoyevsky. His plays include *The Cherry Orchard* (1904) and *The Three Sisters* (1901), both dealing with people ill-equipped to handle the circumstances life forces on them in a static and dull society (a favorite theme of Chekhov's). Also a master of mood, he was a realist whose stories are remarkable both for their irony and their sympathetic viewpoints.

The Cherry Orchard (1904), Anton Chekhov   This Russian drama deals with Madame Ranevsky, the owner of an estate on which there is a large cherry orchard, symbolizing the old order in Russia. A speculator wishes to buy the orchard to erect inexpensive summer bungalows, and as Madame Ranevsky, her family, and friends are unable to adjust to the trend of the times, the orchard is eventually sold. As the curtain falls the ominous strokes of an ax are heard reverberating in the theater.

Chesterton, Gilbert Keith (1874–1936)   The leader of the Catholic movement in English letters in the 20th century was born near London and attended the University there. During the early part of his career, he made his living as a journalist, writing book reviews, essays, and political pieces, but by 1905 Chesterton emerged as an important novelist. His best work is *The Man Who Was Thursday* (1908). A fervent Catholic, his dogmatic views are often concealed by his light and witty style.

Chorus   A group of singers and dancers who appear in classical Greek and Roman dramas to provide background information and exposition of action taking place offstage; also the songs or odes sung by the chorus. Any drama by Aeschylus, Sophocles, or Euripides provides abundant examples of choruses. From Elizabethan times onward, the role of the chorus was taken over by a single actor, when comments on the action were necessary to the dramatist's purpose. A more recent example is the stage manager in Thornton Wilder's *Our Town*.

The Cid (1636), Pierre Corneille   This classic French drama, like many of the plays by Corneille, revolves around the conflict between love and duty. Rodrigo, the protagonist, kills the father of the girl he loves to avenge an insult to his own father. Eventually the girl pleads for his life and the king pardons him.

Civil Disobedience, Henry David Thoreau   In 1846, the year of the Mexican War, Thoreau spent a night in jail for his refusal to pay the poll tax, which then was paid for him. In 1849 he published this essay on the subject, stating that the individual must place his conscience above established formulas and traditions—a point of view that influenced Indian leader Mohandas Gandhi and Martin Luther King, Jr.

Classicism   Originally, simply the literature of Greece and Rome, but later referred to as Greco-Roman imitators, and finally applied to any work "ancient" in concept and form. Today it is used to describe literature characterized by balance, restraint, unity, and proportion. Past masters of classicism include Virgil, Homer, Pope, and Johnson.

Climax   The point of highest interest or conflict in the plot of a short story, novel, or play. A climactic arrangement of words and phrases in a sentence has the ideas occurring in an order of rising importance, with the most important item being the climax. The end of the work, its conclusion, where all matters are resolved follows the climax.

Closed couplet   A pair of rhymed lines of poetry containing a complete statement, structurally independent of lines that come before and after.

> Had we but world enough, and time,
> This coyness, lady, were no crime.
> Marvell

> All human things are subject to
>   decay,
> And when fate summons, monarchs
>   must obey.
> Dryden

Closet drama A dramatic work, usually written in poetry, intended to be read rather than acted on the stage. Also, a play that has survived as literature rather than theatre.

Coleridge, Samuel Taylor (1772–1834) When Coleridge met Wordsworth in 1797 the two became close friends and colleagues in the publication of *Lyrical Ballads* in 1798, the work that inaugurated the Romantic Movement in England. The volume contained his most famous work, *The Rime of the Ancient Mariner*. He was a passionate and erratic artist, beginning many works [like the fragment poem "Kubla Khan" (1797)] that he left unfinished. Because of ill health he became addicted to laudenum (opium) at a young age and that habit became one of the factors that eventually helped to paralyze his poetic gifts in later years. "Christabel" is another of his uncompleted master works.

Collins, Wilkie (1824–1889) An English novelist who for a while worked under Dickens on magazine stories. Collins is best known for his skillful storytelling and intricate plots. Although his characterization has been criticized, his novels are a fine blend of Gothic atmosphere, mystery, and unforesaken love.

Comedy A branch of drama or fiction in which the characters are treated humorously. There is a happy ending, and the audience is amused.

Comedy of manners A type of satirical comedy, especially popular in the Restoration and Neoclassical periods, concerned with the manners of a highly sophisticated and artificial society and characterized by witty dialogue.

Comedy of situation Usually a comedy in which the plot or the situation in which the characters are placed is more important than characterization. Although modern television "sitcoms" (situation comedies) have a continuing set of more or less well-defined characters, they typify this kind of comedy.

Comic relief A comic scene or incident that a playwright inserts in a serious drama to relieve tension and to provide a contrast to the seriousness of the play.

Commedia Dell'Arte (masked comedy) An early form of post-classical drama, the "Commedia" was performed by medieval Italian troupes of about a dozen actors who played stereotypic roles largely through improvision. Masks and traditional costumes were worn and most of the "plays" centered around a pair of young lovers who, with the help and interference of their clever servants, managed to overcome their families and live happily ever after.

Compton-Burnett, Ivy (1892–1969) Born near London, she published the first of her unconventional novels, *Dolores,* in l911, beginning to reveal her use of irony and satire to portray an embittered, hypocritical world. Her novels are known for their lack of plot and description and the use of stylized dialogue to advance the story. Other works include *Brothers and Sisters* (1929) and *Two Worlds and Their Ways* (1949).

Conceit An elaborate or extravagant image that is often part of a grandiose analogy. See the following quote from John Donne as an example of conceit

carried to its outermost borders. In what follows, a flea has just bitten and sucked blood from the poet and his lady, who is about to kill it.

> Oh stay, three lives in one flea spare,
> Where we almost, yea, more than
> 　married are
> This flea is you and I, and this
> Our marriage bed, and marriage tem-
> 　ple is.
> 　　　　　　　　　　　　　　Donne

Concordance An index of the most important and relevant words in a text (e.g., the Bible) listed alphabetically.

Conflict In drama or fiction, the collision between opposing forces (usually the protagonist against the antagonist).

Congreve, William (1670–1729) Educated in Ireland at Trinity College, this Anglo-Irish playwright won acclaim with his first comedy, *The Old Bachelor* (1693), and even more with *Love for Love* (1695). But his finest work, *The Way of the World* (1700), a masterpiece of Restoration comedy, received only lukewarm recognition, and he never wrote anything of consequence again.

Conrad, Joseph (Teodor Josef Konrad Korzeniowski) (1857–1924) Born in Poland, Conrad went to sea as a youth, became involved in gunrunning escapades for the Spaniards, and eventually joined the English merchant marine, where he served for 20 years. Writing in English, his second language, he established himself as a master of fiction, his best novels being *Lord Jim* (1900) and *Victory* (1915). Using the sea as the background for many of his books, his writing is a mixture of Realism and Romanticism, acutely portraying those who suffer from isolation and loneliness.

Consonance The close repetition of consonant sounds before and after different vowels—slip, slop; sometimes the repetition of this sound at the end of words—mid, wed. *Compare* **Assonance**.

Convention A literary practice, style, or technique that has become, through frequent use, an accepted method of literary expression, as the soliloquy in drama in which a character speaks to the audience but is accepted as being unheard by the other characters on stage.

Cooper, James Fenimore (1789–1851) The 12th of 13 children born to a wealthy landowner, this American novelist was brought up in Cooperstown, New York. He attended Yale, but was expelled in his junior year, and then went to sea. He married a wealthy woman and settled in Westchester County. His first great success was *The Spy,* (1921) a Revolutionary War novel. His reputation rests, however, on the *Leather-Stocking Tales* [which includes *The Last of the Mohicans* (1826) and *The Deerslayer* (1841)], five novels about the American frontier, which brought him a worldwide reputation. Considered by some to be the first great American novelist, Cooper has been criticized for his conventional characters and extravagant plots.

Corneille, Pierre (1606–1684) The first of France's classic dramatists of the 17th century, his theme was frequently the conflict between love and duty. His masterpiece, *The Cid,* was first produced in 1636.

Couplet Two successive rhyming lines of poetry, usually having the same meter.

> Lizzie Bordon with an axe,
> Hit her father forty wacks.

Courtly love Exemplified in Renaissance and Medieval literature by a pale and languishing knight made bold because of his veneration and passion for a lady of noble birth who spurs him on to feats of greatness. Once his feelings were returned by the damsel (who was almost always wed to another), adultery rarely became an issue, and the knight was content to pursue only his innocent adoration.

Cousin Bette (1846), Honoré de Balzac Considered by some critics to have replaced *Vanity Fair* as the masterpiece novel in world literature, this work is an indictment of the corrupt Parisienne society in the 1800s, seen through the eyes of the jealous Bette and the decadent Hulot.

Crane, Hart (1899–1932) Always more esteemed by the critics than the general public, this poet was born in Ohio and at age 16 went to New York to make a living as a writer. In spite of holding many menial jobs, he often had to depend on the financial support of friends. He published *White Buildings* (1926) and *The Bridge* (1930), the latter his major work. His career was complicated by alcoholism, and the struggle with his homosexual tendencies. In 1932 he committed suicide by jumping overboard on a ship bound from Mexico. Known as one of the great 20th-century poets, Crane was greatly influenced by Dada, an art movement in France that gave him an excuse to abandon the form and coherence of modern poetry.

Crane, Stephen (1871–1900) American novelist, born in Newark, New Jersey, the son of a Methodist minister, Crane worked as a newspaper reporter in New York and then became an overseas war correspondent; he died of tuberculosis in Germany. His best-known work is *The Red Badge of Courage* (1895), the emotional account of a young soldier in battle, amazing in its perceptions and feelings because Crane had never experienced war.

Crime and Punishment (1866), Feodor Dostoyevsky This Russian novel deals with the murder of an old woman by the impoverished student Raskolnikov and his apprehension by the subtle and unrelenting questioning of a dedicated policeman. The novel is characterized by profound psychological insights dealing with guilt and extreme suffering and the repentance that can lead to a regeneration of the soul.

Criticism Simply, the evaluation of a piece of literature according to its artistic style, its form or structure, and the "value" it is assessed to have. Although the view of every critic must be partially subjective, there are several "schools" of critical thought by which a work might be judged:

(a) *Moral.* This is the Platonic view of art as an agent that shapes man's spiritual and moral attitudes. Art is the teacher, serving an important function in society by acting as the guard of social convention.

(b) *Aesthetic* (Impressionistic). In the late 1800s, a form of criticism that was purely subjective and personal, based only on the particular critic's feelings and impressions regarding a work.

(c) *Biographical.* A literary work judged by the critic's knowledge of the facts and feelings of its creator's life. The critic, here, attempts to draw analogies between an author's work and the way he lives.

(d) *Sociological* (Historical). A work of art viewed as a reflection of its historic, societal background.

(e) *Psychological.* A 20th-century post-Freudian critical approach couched in psychoanalytic terms that attempts to relate an author's work to his unconscious activities during the period of creation.

(f) *Archetypal.* The famous psychologist Carl Jung influenced this mode of criticism that sought to follow universal and collective (inherited and shared racial "memories") unconscious symbols as recurrent themes or motifs in literature.

(g) *Formalist.* Concerned mostly with the organization and structure of a work as a vehicle of language and effect, rather than what the word "speaks" about, or in what ways it seeks to communicate.

Croce, Benedetto (1866–1952) Perhaps the greatest Italian literary figure of the 20th century, Croce was an author, a philosopher, and a critic. As an idealist, he saw the universe, including all human experience, as essentially spiritual, yet he was not a romantic. One of his few biases was an antagonism toward excessive emotionalism in literature.

Cummings, e e (Edward Estlin) (1894–1962) One of the most highly individual and original poets of the 20th century, cummings (all lower-case letters with no end punctuation after initials) was an enemy of complacent middle-class respectability: "...the dull are the damned." The structure, content, and typography of his poems break tradition and proclaim his spontaneous individualism. A lifelong hedonist, his works [which include *Tulips & Chimneys* (1923) and *Poems—1954*] speak of the joy he found in freedom, love, springtime, and sensual pleasure.

Cyrano de Bergerac (1897), Edmond Rostand A verse tragedy whose situations and ideas reflect 19th-century Romanticism. Here are five acts of elegant language, dramatic theatrical devices, and exaggeration that leave the reader or the theatergoer with the desire to jump on stage or between the pages and present Cyrano with the lovely Roxanne over whom he spends almost his entire life in unrequited love.

D

Dactyl A foot in poetry that has one accented syllable followed by two unaccented ones.

> Cárrÿĭnğ, béarăblé.

Dante, Alighieri (1265–1321) Considered the greatest Italian poet, Dante was born to a family of noble background in Florence, but for political reasons he was exiled in 1302. His inspiration for much of his work was Beatrice Portinari, whom he loved from afar as the idealized portrait of womanhood. His masterwork begun during his exile—*The Divine Comedy,* an allegory in verse, consisting of 100 cantos—was written over a period of 20 years.

Daudet, Alphonse (1840–1897) A French naturalist, whom Zola called a "charmer," and who was himself greatly influenced by Dickens (so much so that he was criticized for it). His works, permeated by humor and irony, have virtually all been translated into English.

David Copperfield (1850), Charles Dickens This novel, considered by many critics to be Dickens's masterpiece, is said to reflect many autobiographical elements. The boy David is sent by his stepfather Mr. Murdstone to work in a warehouse and board with the Micawber family, whose head is like Dickens's father, improvident but optimistic. After many adventures and an unsuccessful marriage to Dora, a dependent, childlike woman, David finally weds a woman he has loved all his life.

Dead Souls (1842), Nikolai Gogol This social satire is Russia's great comic novel. It rests on a quirk in the law under serfdom, when souls (as serfs were called) were taxed between censuses even if they were dead. Pavel Tchitchikoff, the protagonist, having discovered that souls will be mortgaged, sets out to buy dead souls. Eventually however, his plan fails and he is ruined.

Death in Venice (1913), Thomas Mann Mann's masterful novella symbolically explores the connection between love and death as von Aschenbach, a writer filled with ennui and seeking excitement, travels to Venice where he meets Tadzio, a beautiful Polish youth with whom he becomes obsessed. When cholera spreads through Venice, Aschenbach, heedless of his own fate, stays and eventually succumbs to the fatal disease. One of the themes of this novella is the conflict between reason (Aschenbach) and vice (personified by the evil Tadzio).

Death of a Salesman (1949), Arthur Miller This Pulitzer Prize-winning American play concerns Willy Loman, a salesman who in his declining years, has become tired and ineffectual. All his life he has filled his sons with the philosophy that being well liked, being handsome, and having a ready smile will lay life at your feet. But his sons, one disillusioned and the other unwilling to admit the emptiness of his father's vision, have not turned out to be what Willy hoped. Seeing himself as a failure, he commits suicide so that his sons will have money to start their own business. This sacrifice turns into an empty gesture.

Decadence A term used by literary historians to denote the decline of any period in art or literature (as contrasted with a former age of excellence).

Decameron ("Ten Days") (1353), Giovanni Boccaccio A collection of 100 prose stories that Boccaccio supposedly wrote as a tribute to the kind friends who were of great comfort to him when he suffered at the cruel hand of his beloved. He wished to offer his readers similar consolation. Because of the plague of 1348, ten storytellers (seven women, three men) are thrown together for an extended period of time, and they serve as the framework of the book. Banding together to live in the country, away from the virulent disease, they spend the hot afternoons storytelling. In the relating of these tales, we have a collection of stories, current at the time, that Boccaccio picked up and retold for no other purpose than to provide sheer amusement. It has been

written that somewhere between *The Divine Comedy* and *The Decameron* lies the truth about human love.

Defoe, Daniel (1660–1731) The son of a butcher, this British novelist and essayist did not begin to write until he was over 30, but produced more than 250 works and probably had a hand in 150 more. Besides being a writer, he was a secret agent, spying for the Whigs and the Tories and sometimes both simultaneously. Unfortunately, his contemporaries considered him to be only a semiliterate scribbler. His most popular works were *The Life and Strange Surprising Adventures of Robinson Crusoe* (1719) and *The Fortunes and Misfortunes of the Famous Moll Flanders* (1722).

Denouement Literally, the "untying of the knot;" the final outcome, solution, or unraveling of the principal dramatic conflict in a literary work.

De Quincey, Thomas (1785–1859) An English essayist who became addicted to opium while at Oxford and achieved literary excellence with the publication of *Confessions of an English Opium-Eater* (1822). De Quincey, a hypersensitive, eccentric man, lived an anguished life from which he sought solace in long lonely walks and drug-induced fantasies. His prolific prose is highly polished, intelligent, and imaginative.

De Staël, Madame (Germaine Necker, Baroness of Staël-Holstein) (1766–1817) She was France's first important woman writer, establishing her reputation with *On Literature* (1800) and consolidating it with *Germany* (1810). The daughter of the Swiss banker and financial expert who tried to help save the monarchy's tottering finances before the revolution, she was a special irritant to Napoleon, who finally drove her into exile. Her style is so conversational that at times it seems more like journalism than literary prose.

Deus ex machina Literally, "god from a machine"; the use of an unexpected and unforeshadowed person or thing to provide a contrived, artificial solution to a dramatic conflict that is often apparently unsolvable. In early Greek drama, when the conflict became hopeless, a god was lowered to the stage from a machine or structure above to rescue the hero or untangle the plot. In more recent literature the use of the deus ex machina indicates inadequacy in the author's devising of the plot. In late Victorian melodramas, when a long-lost relative, newly wealthy, appeared on the scene just in time to save the family farm from being sold by the sheriff, the deus ex machina was exemplified.

Dickens, Charles (1812–1870) Generally considered England's greatest novelist, he worked in a warehouse as a child, was apprenticed to a solicitor and then tried newspaper reporting. In 1833 he started publishing in a magazine a series of impressions of contemporary life, later collected as *Sketches by Boz*. Most of his novels appeared in monthly installments, complete with cliff-hangers and dramatic chapter endings, before being published in book form. Dickens was also a social critic, attacking injustice and hypocrisy. He has been so greatly loved and read that the names of many of his characters have virtually become household words. Some of his more important novels are

Illustration from *A Christmas Carol* by Charles Dickens.

Oliver Twist (1838), *David Copperfield* (1850), and *A Tale of Two Cities* (1859).

Dickinson, Emily (1830–1886) Generally considered one of America's greatest poets, she spent most of her life in seclusion in her Amherst, Massachusetts, home. It was probably during the Civil War period that she began to write, but less than fifteen of her hundreds of poems were published during her lifetime. Her poetic language is one of economy, short lines that speak of passion and the spirit, and many of her poems reflect her unresolved battle with God and faith. All of her poetry and many of her letters have been published in numerous hardcover and paperback editions.

Didactic The term used to describe a piece of literature that attempts to serve a cause that is moral, political, social, and so on. A quiet war has been raging since the time of Plato over whether literature should presume to teach, or exist only as aesthetics. Some of the greatest literary works (Dante's *Divine Comedy*, Milton's *Paradise Lost*) have intended didacticism, but that is only a part of the total experience of those classics.

Diderot, Denis (1713–1784) The coauthor/editor of *The Encyclopedia* with Jean d'Alembert, this French essayist began work with his collaborator in 1750 and directed it alone after 1757. In its time it was the only compendium of human knowledge, and was finally completed in 1772.

Dinesen, Isak (Karen Blixen) (1885–1962) Danish master storyteller who wrote in English and whose life [see *Out of Africa* (1937)] was as illustrious as her tales. She is characterized by an elite and highly polished style and an interest in the mystical and supernatural, as exemplified in *Seven Gothic Tales* (1934).

Dirge A brief song or lyric of lamentation, usually intended to accompany funeral rites, such as Tennyson's "Tears, Idle Tears," and in music, Chopin's "Funeral March."

Dissonance A harsh, unpleasant sound used in poetry, sometimes intentionally for effect, as in the poetry of Browning.

> Fee, faw, fum! bubble and squeak!
> Blessedest Thursday's the fat of the
>   week.
> Rumble and tumble, sleek and rough,
> Stinking and savory, smug and gruff.
>   Browning

Often a synonym for cacophony, dissonance also largely refers to the juxtaposition of closely related sounds.

The Divine Comedy (ca. 1320), Dante Alighieri Considered to be the masterpiece of verse (taking almost 20 years in the writing), this allegory describes the poet's journey through Hell, where his guide is the Roman poet Vergil, through Purgatory and into Paradise, where he is led by Beatrice, his idea of womanhood. The "Comedy" is seen both as Dante's spiritual autobiography and the drama of humanity's search for perfection.

Dr. Faustus (1588), Christopher Marlowe Encouraged to dark ambitions, the title character conjures up Mephistopheles, the servant of Lucifer (the Devil). Dr. Faustus offers Mephistopheles his soul in exchange for 24 years of having his every wish fulfilled. Repentance at the end does him no good, and the Devil carries him off.

Doggerel Sometimes unintentionally humorous verse, written by someone lacking experience or more concerned with humor and/or sentiment than the skillful creation of a poem. Bad limericks are an example.

A Doll's House (1879), Henrik Ibsen This Norwegian drama is considered a landmark in the movement for women's rights. The heroine, Nora, is treated by Torvald (her husband) in a gentle, condescending manner. He spoils her; she is incompetent and forced to live a diminished life in a "doll's house." But gradually Nora's strength emerges as she secretly borrows money for a trip that will save Torvald's life. At the end, because of her husband's lack of faith in her and because they are strangers to each other, she leaves him, independently slamming the door on her marriage.

Donne, John (1573–1631) The greatest British Metaphysical poet, he studied at both Oxford and Cambridge, but could not take degrees because he was a Catholic. Finally he took orders in the English Church and was ordained in 1615. Although Donne wrote lyrics that were often cynical or sensual (also some that were almost playful), the greatest strength and beauty of his work is to be found in his spiritual and religious poems; he was also one of the most eloquent ministers of his day. His volume *Devotions* (1624) reflects his intense concern with death and damnation.

Don Quixote de la Mancha (1605 and 1615), Miguel de Cervantes This picaresque and humorous romantic satire deals with the adventures of the elderly gentleman Alonzo Quixano, whose mind has been filled with images of the age of chivalry. He changes his name to Don Quixote and sets out to be a knight, putting on an old suit of armor and mounting an ancient horse named Rosinante. Accompanied by his servant, Sancho Panza, he undertakes many deeds of valor, all of them colored by his fantasies and illusions. At the end, he retires from adventure and begins to believe that chivalry is absurd.

Dos Passos, John (1896–1970) Born in Chicago, this American novelist and essayist graduated from Harvard and served in World War I. His first important work was *Three Soldiers,* a pacifist novel, but he gained acceptance as a major novelist with the trilogy *U.S.A.* [*The 42nd Parallel* (1930), *1919* (1932), *The Big Money* (1936)], a blend of stream of consciousness, narrative, newspaper quotations, and biographies of the first thirty years of 20th-century America. Dos Passos's politics changed from ardent Marxism to right-wing conservatism.

Dostoyevsky, Feodor (1821–1881) The Russian novelist had his first success with *Poor Folk* (1845). Four years later he was arrested and sentenced to death for attending the secret meetings of a group of radical utopians; however, his sentence was commuted to penal servitude in Siberia, where he suffered great physical and mental pain coupled with attacks of epilepsy. He returned to St. Petersburg in 1859 to create masterpieces in world literature: *Crime and Punishment* (1866), *The Idiot* (1864), and *The Brothers Karamazov* (1879–1880). A writer with existential undertones, Dostoyevsky's work is particularly relevant today because of his understanding of the complexities of the human mind and conscience.

Doyle, Sir Arthur Conan (1859–1930) English author and the creator of Sherlock Holmes, the brilliant theatrical detective who raised the craft of deductive reasoning to the sublime. Holmes is a cult figure, with clubs all over the world devoted to discussions of his expertise—the most famous being the Baker Street Irregulars. In later life, Doyle became a dedicated spiritualist and wrote a history on the subject. He was knighted in 1902.

Drama Generally, a work written to be acted on the stage. Specifically, a play of serious intent that, although it may deal with a problem, or problems, never reaches the heights of tragedy.

Dramatic monologue A type of lyrical poem or narrative piece that has a person speaking to a select listener and revealing his character in a dramatic situation. See, for example. many of the poems of Browning (who brought the dramatic monologue to its highest level), and T.S. Eliot's "Love Song of J. Alfred Prufrock."

Dreiser, Theodore (1871–1945) A major figure in American literature, Dreiser is significant not only for his naturalistic works like *Sister Carrie* (1900) and *An American Tragedy* (1925), but also because of the many battles he waged against censorship and puritanism. The objection to many of his books was not that they were obscene, but that vice is often rewarded while virtue is punished. Born into a background of poverty, he was attracted to Communism, but too conscious of its drawbacks to become a fervent devotee.

Dryden, John (1631–1700) From a Puritan family, this British poet, playwright, and critic took a degree at Cambridge and, after the Restoration, was made poet laureate and historiographer royal by Charles II. He wrote verse and drama, but his criticism was most influential and earned him the reputation as literary dictator of his time. His best work is *An Essay of Dramatic Poesy* (1668).

Dumas, Alexandre (Dumas *père*) (1802–1870) French novelist and dramatist who gave people of all ages *The Three Musketeers* (1844) and *The Count of Monte Cristo* (1845), two historical novels (translated into all languages) that were scorned by the critics of the day who preferred the talents of Dumas *fils* as a playwright.

Dumas, Alexandre (Dumas *fils*) (1824–1895) Following his father, also a French novelist and playwright, he was the key creator of the modern comedy of manners. His most famous and important play, *La Dame aux Camélias* (1852; known in English as *Camille*), was based on his novel of the same title, published in 1848. It was eventually made into an opera, Verdi's *La Traviata*, and a lovely if moody film starring Greta Garbo.

Durrell, Lawrence (b. 1912) Born in India to an English father and an Irish mother, he was sent to England to school at age 11. As an adult, this novelist hopped about the Mediterranean from Corfu to Crete to Rhodes to Cyprus. His best-known work is a tetralogy titled "The Alexandria Quartet" [*Justine* (1957), *Balthazar* (1958), *Montolive* (1960), *Clea* (1960)], which won fame more for its ornate language and the weirdly exotic atmospheres he created than for his exploration and analysis of human emotion.

E   **Eclogue** Originally, a short poem, in the Renaissance it came to mean any verse dialogue whose theme was pastoral. By the 18th century the term only referred to a dialogue form of verse.

Elegy A long and formal poem meditating on the dead; often written to commemorate the death of a particular person, such as Gray's "Elegy in a Country Churchyard."

Eliot, George (Mary Ann Evans) (1819–1880) Considered the first of the modern English novelists, she dared to lead an independent life in Victorian society, living by her own standards and highly developed moral code. However, she shocked that age by her long and happy liaison with G.H. Lewis. Eliot's works are mostly bucolic in setting and her major characters are extremely fascinating because of her psychological investigation of them. *Middlemarch* (1872) is considered by some critics to be her masterwork, but others proclaim the superiority of *The Mill on the Floss* (1860). *Silas Marner* (1861) is most familiar as compulsory reading for many high-school students.

Eliot, T.S. (1888–1965) Claimed by both America and England, and often regarded as the greatest 20th-century poet, Eliot was born in St. Louis, Missouri and educated at Harvard and the Sorbonne. In 1915 he became an expatriot, living in London and earning his living as a teacher, free-lance writer, and editor. He published his first collection of poetry, *Prufrock and Other Observations* (1917) and had his greatest success with *The Waste Land* (1922). Eliot believed that writers must reach beyond their own social climate and reflect the consciousness of

EXHIBIT 15.2
Periods of English Literature

428–1000	Old English Period
1000–1350	Anglo-Norman Period
1350–1550	Middle English Period
1485–1509	Early Tudor Age
1550–1660	The Renaissance Period
1558–1603	Elizabethan Age
1608–1625	Jacobean Age
1625–1650	Caroline Age
1650–1660	The Commonwealth Interregnum
1660–1790	The Neo-Classical Period
1660–1700	The Restoration Age
1700–1750	The Augustan Age
1750–1798	The Age of Johnson
1790–1870	The Romantic Period
1799–1830	The Age of the Romantic Triumph
1830–1870	The Early Victorian Age
1870–1915	The Realistic Period
1870–1915	The Edwardian Age
1915–present	The Contemporary Period

EXHIBIT 15.3
Poets Laureate of England

Edmund Spenser	1591–1599
Samuel Daniel	1599–1619
Ben Jonson	1619–1637
William Davenant	1638–1668
John Dryden	1670–1689
Thomas Shadwell	1689–1692
Nahum Tate	1692–1715
Nicholas Rowe	1715–1718
Laurence Eusden	1718–1730
Colley Cibber	1730–1757
William Whitehead	1757–1785
Thomas Warton	1785–1790
Henry James Pye	1790–1813
Robert Southey	1813–1843
William Wordsworth	1843–1850
Alfred Lord Tennyson	1850–1892
Alfred Austin	1896–1913
Robert Bridges	1913–1930
John Masefield	1930–1967
C. Day Lewis	1967–1972
Sir John Betjeman	1972–1984
Ted Hughes	1984 (until his death)

all ages. To achieve these ends in his own poetry he combines myth, literary allusion, and religious symbolism. In his later works [*Ash Wednesday* (1930), *The Four Quartets* (1935–1942)] he turned from the desolation of the spirit to a hopeful outlook concerning the revitalization of man and his ultimate salvation. As a playwright Eliot successfully attempted the rebirth of verse drama with such plays as *Murder in the Cathedral* (1935) and *The Cocktail Party* (1950). He won the Nobel Prize for Literature in 1948 and is considered one of the most influential poets in the English language.

Ellison, Ralph (b. 1914) Born in Oklahoma City, this black American novelist studied music at Tuskegee Institute in Alabama from 1933–36; he then went to New York to study sculpture. After World War II, a fellowship enabled him to devote himself to his only major work, *The Invisible Man* (1952).

Emerson, Ralph Waldo (1803–1882) This poet and essayist was the central figure of American Transcendentalism. Born in Boston, the son of the pastor of the First Church of Boston, Emerson attended Harvard, where because of poor health he was a mediocre student. Later he taught school, and eventually went to Germany to study for the ministry. Although Emerson found he had little vocation, he still became a preacher, but soon gave up the pulpit, traveled in Europe with Carlyle, Coleridge, and Wordsworth and, on his return, moved to Concord, Massachusetts, where he began to write. His works expressed his ardent belief in Nature's mystical unity and that man could find forgiveness within his own soul.

End rhyme Rhymes occurring at the ends of lines of poetry, which is the usual case.

> I was angry with my friend:
> I told my wrath, my wrath did end.
> I was angry with my foe:
> I told it not, my wrath did grow.
>
> Blake

Epic An extended narrative poem, written in an elevated style, recounting the deeds of a legendary or actual hero. Some illustrious epics are Homer's *The Iliad* and *The Odyssey,* Virgil's *Aeneid,* and Milton's *Paradise Lost. Compare* **Mock epic.**

Epigram A short poem or statement, often satirical, dealing with a single thought or event and often ending with a clever turn of phrase.

> The greatest pleasure I know is to do
> a good action by stealth and to have
> it found out by accident.
>
> Charles Lamb

Epilogue A concluding section that completes the design of a literary work; also a speech in early drama spoken by an actor addressing the audience at the conclusion of a play.

Epiphany Joyce began the use of this term to refer to "a sudden spiritual manifestation;" an intuitive perception of the essential nature or meaning of something; an instant grasp of reality through a sudden happening or event.

Epistolary novel A novel in which the story is carried forward entirely through letters from one or more persons.

Epitaph Originally, a verse inscription on a gravestone, this term also is used to mean a poem to commemorate the dead.

Epithalamium (or Epithalamion) A song or poem written to honor a bride and bridegroom.

Epithet A word or phrase used to characterize a person or thing; sometimes used in conjunction with the object or person, at other times used in place of the name or thing; for instance, Jack the Ripper, or rosy-fingered dawn.

Essay A prose composition, usually brief, dealing with a particular theme or topic. Essays vary widely and may be descriptive, narrative, expository, or argumentative.

Ethan Frome (1911), Edith Wharton This American novella concerns Ethan, a New England farmer, married to Zenobia, who is a whining and domineering hypochondriac. When Mattie Silver, his wife's pretty young cousin comes to work for them, Ethan falls in love with her. But because their love is doomed, Mattie compulsively persuades Ethan to commit suicide with her. However, the sleighing accident that is to accomplish this fails and the two are left crippled, more than ever in Zenobia's power.

Eugénie Grandet (1933), Honoré de Balzac   Eugénie, the daughter of a psychopathic miser, is forced to lead a lonely life of self-deprivation. When her penniless cousin Charles shows her some little kindnesses she gives him her collection of gold pieces that she received, a coin at a time, on each birthday. Swearing marriage and unending love, Charles leaves to seek his fortune. In the intervening years, Eugénie's father dies, leaving her a wealthy heiress, awaiting Charles. When he finally does write, it's to ask that he be released from his promise and Eugénie resigns herself to solitude, her great wealth meaning nothing to her because of the Spartan life she has led.

Euphemism   The substitution of an innocuous or pleasant word or phrase for one considered offensive or impolite: "passed away" for "died;" "in a family way" for "pregnant."

Euphony   A pleasing and harmonious combination of sounds. Euphonious phrases avoid excessive alliteration and the stringing together of harsh consonants and use instead combinations that are pleasing to the ear.

> When in silks my Julia goes,
> Then, then methinks how sweetly
>   flows
> The liquefaction of her clothes.
>
>   Herrick

Euripides (480–406 B.C.)   Considered the last of the great Greek tragic dramatists, he is the most modern because of his interest in human emotions. His total output is unknown, but 18 of his works have survived, among them *Medea* (431 B.C.) and *The Trojan Women* (415 B.C.). According to one legend, he studied with the philosophers Socrates and Protagoras, from whom his religious skepticism was derived.

Everyman (ca. 1525)   A morality play, as in medieval drama, written primarily in rhyming couplets that tells the story of how God, dissatisfied with the worldliness of His creatures, sends Death for Everyman, who has been forsaken by the "characters" of Fellowship, Knowledge, Beauty, and Strength. Only Good Deeds accompanies him when he goes to meet God's judgment. All earthly things are thus proved to be vanity.

Existentialism   Although writers of this school markedly differ in attitudes, in general the Existentialism espoused by Kierkegaard, Heidegger, and Sartre presupposes that one has free will and is therefore completely responsible for one's actions. Most existentialists believe that one forms one's essential being (or essence) by choosing a particular course and pattern in life. Sartre's plays *The Flies* and *No Exit* broach the problem of human freedom and responsibility; Camus's story *The Fall* explores the problem of man's guilt and the extent of his freedom.

Exposition   A tool the playwright uses to give the audience necessary background information about characters, or events that don't take place on stage. Shakespeare uses undisguised exposition by having a character address the audience directly, but contemporary theater is usually more circumspect, and expository scenes must be handled with great technical skill; information is slipped in rather than blatantly presented.

Expressionism   A literary movement of the early 20th century, found mostly in drama, dedicated to revealing the depths of the human mind (after the discoveries of Freud). Expressionist theater uses unreal atmospheres, distortion, and oversimplification to depict external representations of extreme psychological states. (Expressionism was also an important force in the visual arts.)

 **Fable**   A brief tale in prose or poetry that emphasizes a moral and usually has animals as the principal characters. Aesop's *Fables,* for example, or Joel Chandler Harris's *Uncle Remus Stories.*

The Fairie Queene (1590, 1596), Edmund Spenser   Originally intended to consist of 12 books, this English work was left unfinished at the poet's death. It is an allegorical epic, told in verse and based on a series of knightly exploits, with the hero-knight of each adventure representing one of the cardinal virtues described by Aristotle.

The Fall of the House of Usher (1840), Edgar Allan Poe   This American short story concerns a family and a mansion that have both declined and are near disintegration. On a stormy night, Roderick Usher, the last of his line, dies at the moment when the house is demolished by a whirlwind.

Fantasy   Any work of literature that takes place in or involves a nonexistent or unreal world, peopled by unusual, strange, or grotesque characters. Fairy tales and *Peter Pan* are examples of fantasies. Also a type of prose made especially popular in the serial novels of the 1980s.

Farce   A type of low comedy with broad and obvious satire, humor, and much physical action. Shakespeare's *Comedy of Errors* is almost entirely a farce.

A Farewell to Arms (1929), Ernest Hemingway   This American novel is the story of an American lieutenant in the Italian ambulance corps during World War I. He meets an English nurse and they begin a casual affair. However, when he is wounded their relationship becomes more serious, and eventually they escape together to the mountains of Switzerland, where they find happiness for a time. But the nurse dies in childbirth, leaving her lover disillusioned and cynical. The structure of this novel is one of classic tragedy, and in that respect it has been compared to *Romeo and Juliet.*

Farrell, James T. (1904–1979)   Born on Chicago's South Side, at the time a brutal slum, Farrell attended Catholic high schools, the University of Chicago, and De Paul University. The American novelist held a series of odd jobs, including gas station attendant, retail store clerk, advertising salesman. He achieved fame with the publication of the *Studs Lonigan* trilogy (1937). He also did a series based on Danny O'Neill, a South Side boy who escapes the influence of the slums.

Faulkner, William (1897–1962)　Born in Mississippi to a distinguished family, this American novelist and short-story writer had his first critical success with *The Sound and the Fury* in 1929; however, the book did not sell well. Among his other novels are *As I Lay Dying* (1930) and *Sanctuary* (1931). Faulkner, who frequently employs stream-of-consciousness in his works, wrote in a beautiful and brooding style of the decadence and anguish of the South since the Civil War. He explores the disintegration of Southern society on all levels. In 1933 he made the first of several trips to Hollywood to work as a screenwriter and won the Nobel Prize for Literature in 1950.

Faust (1808 and 1831), Johann Wolfgang von Goethe　This German drama is in two parts. It is based on the medieval legend of a man who sold his soul to the devil in return for the opportunity to experience all of life's pleasures.

Fielding, Henry (1707–1754)　The author of the finest novel of the 18th century, *The History of Tom Jones, A Foundling* (1749), this English writer was adept in his use of burlesque and comedy. He had a varied career as playwright, novelist, political journalist, and magistrate.

Figurative language　Language that is not meant to be taken literally; "figures of speech" used by an author to clarify and intensify an image.

> The soul's dark cottage, batter'd and
> decay'd
> Lets in new light through chinks that
> time has made.
> > Edmund Waller

Fitzgerald, Edward (1809–1883)　Born into a wealthy family, this English poet attended Cambridge. After graduation, he learned to read Persian and, starting in about 1857, he began a translation of some of the work of the 12th-century Persian poet Omar Khayyam. Two years later, he published *The Rubaiyat of Omar Khayyam*, which is as much an original poem as a translation, since he added ideas from other Persian poets and some of his own. "The Rubaiyat" urges one to take enjoyment in the pleasures of the moment and to disregard the future.

Fitzgerald, F. Scott (1896–1940)　Considered the literary spokesman for America's "Jazz Age" (the Lost Generation), a period from the close of World War I to the stock-market crash of 1929. In 1920 he married Zelda Sayre, an extravagant, creative woman who had battles with mental health for most of her life. They lived abroad for a time and Fitzgerald ended up in Hollywood, where he wrote screenplays. He died of a heart attack, aggravated by alcoholism. His novels include *This Side of Paradise* (1920), *The Great Gatsby* (1925), and *Tender is the Night* (1934).

Flashback　An interruption of the narrative flow in order to present scenes or incidents that occurred prior to the beginning of the work.

Flaubert, Gustav (1821–1880)　A French novelist who lived in near seclusion because of a serious nervous illness, Flaubert published *Madame Bovary* (1856) and was brought to trial on a charge of "immorality" because of the subject matter in this novel. He was a scrupulous writer, spending much time evoking the exact word (*le mot juste*) needed, and his objectivity is considered unparalleled.

Foot　A unit of rhythm in poetry.

Foreshadowing　A plot device that warns or prepares the reader for what will eventually happen. Dickens frequently employed foreshadowing in his lengthy serialized novels to give an indication of the exciting events that would take place in episodes to follow. In this way, foreshadowing was a "cliffhanger" device; however, Shakespeare often used it as the portent of doom to come (see the opening scene from *Macbeth*, where the witches stir up prophecies).

Forster, E.M. (Edward Morgan) (1879–1970)　A British novelist, his works are concerned with the unenlightened emotional attitudes of the English middle class. *A Passage to India* (1924) is considered by many critics to be his outstanding work. After World War I, Forster virtually abandoned the novel and pursued critical studies and essays on literature instead. Shortly after his death in 1970 a novel about homosexuality, *Maurice*, was published. It was Forster's stipulation that this work be issued posthumously.

France, Anatole (Jacques Anatole Thibault) (1844–1924)　The best-known French man of letters of his time, his work ranges from poems to novels, and his style underwent an equal variety of changes from sentimentality through political satire. His best-known work is *Penguin Island* (1908). France was elected to the French Academy in 1896 and was awarded the Nobel Prize for Literature in 1921.

Franklin, Benjamin (1706–1790) One of America's Founding Fathers.　The fifteenth of his father's seventeen children, he was apprenticed to his older brother, a printer, but fled to Philadelphia and eventually to England, where he lived for two years. On his return, he began a remarkable career as a writer, publisher, scientist, inventor, and politician, and played a major role in the writing of the Constitution. His best-known literary work is *Poor Richard's Almanac* (1732–57), and he also composed a disorganized *Autobiography* (complete version 1868).

Free verse　A verse form without regular meter, which takes its poetic language from the cadence of stressed and unstressed syllables and the rhythms that exist in everyday speech. Walt Whitman's *Leaves of Grass* is an excellent example of free verse.

Freneau, Philip (1752–1832)　Often referred to as the earliest important American lyric poet, Freneau's early works were clearly imitative of British models. However, in 1781 after he had served as a prisoner of war during the American Revolution, he began to write as a propagandist and satirist of Jeffersonian Democracy. He is known today both for his poetry and his political characterizations.

The Frogs (405 B.C.), Aristophanes　This Greek comedy is principally an attack on the dramatist Euripides, whom the author compares unfavorably with Aeschylus. The god Dionysus goes to Hades, from which he is to bring back the best tragic dramatist. After a sort of literary contest, he decides on the older, more conservative playwright, Aeschylus.

Frost, Robert (1875–1963) Although regarded as the archetypal New England poet, Frost was born in San Francisco. He was taken to Massachusetts when still a boy, attended both Dartmouth and Harvard, and then worked as a mill hand, teacher, and farmer. He went to England in 1912 and his first poetry was published there. Among his most famous poems are "Birches," "The Death of the Hired Man," and "Stopping by Woods on a Snowy Evening." By the time of his death he was regarded by some critics as America's most illustrious poet.

Fry, Christopher (b. 1907) Fry the playwright is virtually indistinguishable from Fry the poet. This English dramatist made two important contributions to 20th-century theater. He helped alleviate it from its slump into social preoccupation and he restored to drama something of the scintillating language of the Elizabethan stage. *The Lady's Not for Burning* (1949) is one of his most famous plays.

Gallows humor *See* **Black humor**.

Galsworthy, John (1867–1933) Concerned with the life of well-to-do people and the decline of the upper class, this British author wrote both novels and plays on that subject. His masterpiece is considered to be the *Forsyte Saga,* which began with *The Man of Property* (1906) and concluded with *End of the Chapter* (1934). As a dramatist his best-known works are *Justice* (1910) and *Loyalties* (1922). He won the Nobel Prize for Literature in 1932.

Garcia Lorca, Federico (1899–1936) Lorca was a Spanish poet who turned to the stage to secure a wider audience. His themes are those common to the greatest Spanish literature: blood and pain, passionate and sensual love, fertility and barrenness, pomp and hypocrisy. He spent time in both the United States and Latin America before he was shot by the Franco forces in the Spanish Civil War. His best-known works are the plays *Blood Wedding* (1933) and *The House of Bernarda Alba* (1936).

Gargantua and Pantagruel (1532–1562), François Rabelais This mock-heroic chronicle tells of the giant Gargantua and his son Pantagruel, also a giant, both known for their enormous appetites for food and drink. The adventures of father and son, in war and peace and at the table, are the subject of this world masterpiece, a collection of familiar legends (both serious and humorous) on education, philosophy, and politics.

Garland, Hamlin (1860–1940) Born in a log cabin near Salem, Wisconsin, Hamlin was one of the first American novelists to treat regional material realistically and without romanticizing. His best-known work is *A Son of the Middle Border* (1917); his *A Daughter of the Middle Border* (1922) won a Pulitzer Prize.

Gaskell, Elizabeth Cleghorn (1810–1865) The wife of a cleric in Manchester, this English novelist was well acquainted with the appalling conditions in industrial England. Her *Mary Barton* (1848), about the wretchedness and starvation among mill workers, brought her to the attention of Charles Dickens, who aided her career. Her best-known work is *Cranford* (1851–53).

Genet, Jean (1910–1986) A French dramatist who spent his formative years unsuccessfully avoiding reformatories and prisons. In 1948, through the efforts of Sartre, Gide, and Cocteau, he was pardoned from a sentence of life imprisonment. Genet, an outspoken homosexual, presents characters out of the seamier side of life, and his dramas are enactments of revolt against everything that leaves man subservient and helplessly alone. *Flowers* (1945) is one of his autobiographical works, and two of his best-known plays are *The Balcony* (1957) and *The Blacks* (1959).

Genre A type or classification of literary work. Until recently writers were expected to adhere to the established rules of the genre in which they were working, but modern eclecticism has broken down this tradition.

Gide, André (1869–1951) The son of a Protestant father and a Catholic mother, this novelist and leader of French liberal thought was raised in an upper-middle-class home. His work is difficult to categorize because he moved from symbolism to a complete hedonism to asceticism and for some time he flirted with Communism. His chief works are *The Counterfeiters* (1926) and *Strait Is the Gate* (1909).

"The Gift of the Magi" (1906), O. Henry One of the short stories in *The Four Million,* this is the tale of a poor young American couple, Jim and Della, who have only two treasures: Della's beautiful long hair and Jim's gold watch. For Christmas, Della sells her hair to buy a chain for his watch and he sells his watch to buy her a comb for her hair. But both have "the gift of the Magi," the sacrifice of love.

Giraudoux, Jean (1882–1944) A lifelong pacifist and an enemy of Nationalism, it is ironical that this French novelist and dramatist should have died at the hands of the Germans. He felt that few ideals are worth a war and that crusades usually cause more misery than happiness. His most famous works are the highly imaginative and impressionistic plays *The Madwoman of Chaillot* (1945) and *Tiger at the Gates* (1955).

Glasgow, Ellen (1874–1945) Born in Richmond, Virginia, this American novelist was a sickly child and was unable to attend school. Largely self-educated, her most critically acclaimed novel was *Barren Ground* (1925). In her works, Glasgow attempted to reject the Southern ideals of chivalry and male supremacy and to present the emergence of a strong and dominating middle class. Her other works include *Vein of Iron* (1935) and *In This Our Life* (1941), for which she received the Pulitzer Prize.

The Glass Menagerie (1945), Tennessee Williams The beautifully lyrical story of Amanda Wingfield, a personification of fading Southern gentility, her daughter Laura, who lives in a world of illusion, to which she escapes through her menagerie of glass animals, and, incidentally, her son Tom, the narrator of the play and the catalyst who brings the "gentleman caller" into Laura's life.

Gloss An explanation in the margin or between the lines of difficult works to explain obscure meanings by substituting a familiar word or phrase for an obscure one. The famous marginal gloss in Coleridge's *The Rime of the Ancient Mariner,* which summarizes almost the entire story, begins "An ancient

Mariner meeteth three Gallants bidden to a wedding feast, and detaineth one."

Goethe, Johann Wolfgang von (1749–1832) Considered Germany's greatest literary figure, he began his career in the so-called Sturm und Drang (Storm and Stress) period. He is esteemed for his many lyric poems, his enormously influential novel *The Sorrows of Young Werther* (1774), read throughout Europe, and his masterwork, the drama *Faust* (1808 and 1831).

Gogol, Nikolai (1809–1852) Early in his career, this first important Russian novelist and dramatist was a romantic, but he turned to Realism with such works as the novel *Dead Souls* (1842), considered to be the finest comic work in Russian literature. He also wrote the satirical drama *The Inspector-General* (1836).

Golding, William (b. 1911) The son of a head-master, this English novelist attended Oxford and then became a teacher. In the late 1930s he did some writing, acting, and producing for a London theater and then served in the British navy in World War II. His primary literary exploration deals with the eternal nature of man. This original author's best-known work is *Lord of the Flies* (1954), an allegorical novel. His other works include *The Inheritors* (1955) and *Pincher Martin* (1956). He won the Nobel Prize for Literature in 1983.

Goldsmith, Oliver (1730–1774) One of the most versatile literary men of his time, he was the author of essays, the poem *The Deserted Village* (1770), the novel *The Vicar of Wakefield* (1766), and the highly successful comedy *She Stoops to Conquer* (1771).

The Good Earth (1931), Pearl S. Buck A Pulitzer Prize-winning novel depicting the lives of Wang Lung, a hard-working Chinese peasant, and his wife O-lan, both passionately attached to the soil and struggling to raise themselves from the poverty of their class. At the end of the book Wang Lung, now widowed, exhorts his sons never to relinquish the land, but they are from a different age and have already planned how they will use the money they will receive from the sale of their inheritance.

"A Good Man Is Hard To Find," Flannery O'Connor The most frequently anthologized of her short stories (also appears in a collection with the same title), it tells of the almost casual murder of a family by an escaped criminal called Misfit. The horror here lies in the everyday language and feeling O'Connor creates, contrasted with the bloody deeds being carried on "off-stage," out of the eye of the reader.

Gorky, Maxim (1868–1936) The only major writer of Russia's pre-Revolutionary period who remained popular under the Soviet regime, Gorky was the first Russian writer to find philosophers and poets in the factory and the boardinghouse. In his works he stresses the eternal kinship of all humanity, even the most wretched and rejected. His best-known work is the drama *The Lower Depths* (1902).

Gothic novel A type of novel, first popularized in the late 18th century by Horace Walpole [*Castle of Otranto* (1764)]. The gothic novel is characterized by thrill-provoking and supernatural events, often taking place in a Medieval castle. Mary Shelley's *Frankenstein* (1817), although having a more serious theme, is an excellent example of gothic literature, as are the works of the Brontë sisters in Victorian England. In contemporary life "gothics" have come to mean women's romances in the style of Mary Stewart or Phyllis Whitney, where the dark and brooding lord of the manor becomes, at the end of the tale, the charming and delightful lover who sweeps the unprotesting, love-besotted heroine off her feet.

Grand guignol Refers to dramatic theater where the action of the play and its characters is gruesome and macabre. Originally, the name of an 18th-century puppet who in turn lent his name to a theater in the Montmartre section of Paris.

The Grapes of Wrath (1939), John Steinbeck This American novel concerns the Joad family, itinerant farmers, "Oakies" of the dust bowl during the Depression, lured to California by leaflets promising well-paying jobs. On arrival, they find little work, but much violence and labor strife. Tom, the son, is involved in a murder and becomes a fanatic labor agitator. The most famous scene in this Pulitzer Prize-winning book is the final one, involving the beautifully depicted Rose of Sharon, who is Tom's daughter-in-law. It is this scene (plus some shocking dialogue) that created Steinbeck's fame.

Grass, Günter (b. 1927) Grass was born in Danzig, then a German city, now a part of Poland. He was forced into the Hitler Youth, drafted into the Luftwaffe at age 16, subsequently taken prisoner, and then released in 1946. He began a career as a painter and sculptor and wrote a number of plays before he turned to the novel with *The Tin Drum* (1959), which had a major success. Other important works of this off-beat and often bizarre author include the novella *Cat and Mouse* (1961) and *Dog Years* (1963).

Graveyard school of poetry A school of mid-18th-century poets in whose works melancholy and sullen doom prevail. Gray's churchyard elegy is an excellent example of this type of poetry.

Gray, Thomas (1716–1771) After studying at Cambridge this English author published his first volume, *Six Poems* (1753). He was offered the post of poet laureate in 1757, but being a loner who sought seclusion, he declined it. In 1768 he was named professor of history and modern languages at Cambridge and continued to write poetry, but not in quantity. His most famous poem is "The Elegy Written in a Country Churchyard" (1750). Gray illustrates the move in English poetry from Classicism to Romanticism.

The Great Gatsby (1925). F. Scott Fitzgerald This American novel is a study of a nouveau riche Long Islander who has made his fortune by various shady means and who eventually is killed. It is an examination of success and its poisoning effect on character as well as a picture of the manners of the Long Island (New York) rich during the 1920s.

Greek tragedy This drama form is built in the following way. (a) Prologue: to introduce the play, (b) Parodus: during which the chorus enters and tells the story of the play or provides foreshadowing, (c) Episodes: the action of the drama, (d) Exodos: the ending—it is in this part of the tragedy that the deus ex machina, if one is to be used, appears.

Greene, Graham (1904–1991)   Born the son of a headmaster, this English novelist attended his father's school and then Oxford. He became a convert to Roman Catholicism in 1926 and that religion played a major role in almost all of his serious novels after that time. His best work of fiction is considered to be *The Power and the Glory* (1940) and he also wrote what he termed "entertainments," of which *Brighton Rock* (1938) and *The Third Man* (1950) are the best. Much of Greene's work is a combination of psychological insight and the spy or detective thriller, although the recurrent themes are almost always of sin and salvation.

Gulliver's Travels (1726), Jonathan Swift   This English political and social satire is a savage picture of humankind written in four books. The first concerns the voyage to Lilliput, the land of tiny people; the second, the voyage to Brobdingnag, the land of giants; the third, the voyage to Laputa, the land of philosophers; the fourth, the voyage to the country of the Houyhnhnms.

H **Haiku**   A Japanese form of unrhymed poetry that seeks through bare imagery to create one acutely perceived moment. Although there is no formal structure to haiku, most poems of this type are in three lines, with from five to seven syllables per line.

> Lightning in the sky!
> In the deeper dark is heard
> A night-heron's call.
>
>   Basho

Haley, Alex Palmer (1921–1992)   Born in Tennessee, this autobiographical writer began his career as chief journalist in the U.S. Coast Guard from 1949 to 1959. Best known as the 1977 Pulitzer Prize-winning author of *Roots: The Saga of an American Family*, the genealogical account of his ancestors from Africa to this country, Haley also assisted in writing *The Autobiography of Malcolm X*.

Hamlet (1600–1602), William Shakespeare   This English drama is acclaimed as one of the poet's four great tragedies. Hamlet, prince of Denmark, is obsessed with avenging the death of his father, slain by his uncle Claudius, now married to Gertrude, Hamlet's mother. Eventually Hamlet does kill Claudius, but the end of the play brings the death of Gertrude and Hamlet too. The character of Hamlet has brought analyses from such important theorists as Goethe and Freud.

Hardy, Thomas (1840–1928)   The last of England's great Victorian novelists began and ended his career as a poet, but is best remembered for his fiction. *Far from the Madding Crowd* (1824) brought him fame as a novelist, but he reached his highest stature with such works as *The Return of the Native* (1878), *Tess of the D'Urbervilles* (1891), and *Jude the Obscure* (1895), all of which met with violent disapproval because of their supposed indecency and immorality. Hardy's works are set in the gloomy, sullen landscape of Wessex. He used the combination of characters and place to depict man's constant battle against the forces of nature—his own and those in the external world.

Engraving of scene from *Hamlet* by William Shakespeare.

Harte, Bret (1836–1902)   American Western writer of humorous verse, comic ballads, and short stories who had a keen eye and a journalistic style. Although his stories frequently lacked depth, he cannot be criticized because he sought more to entertain than to soul search. Two of his most famous tales, "The Outcasts of Poker Flat" and "The Luck of Roaring Camp" appear in most American literature anthologies.

Hawthorne, Nathaniel (1804–1864)   Born in Salem, Massachusetts, this moralistic American novelist and short-story writer used as his themes the hidden sinfulness of mankind and the horror of isolation from God and man. His best-known works are *The Scarlet Letter* (1850) and *The House of the Seven Gables* (1851), both of which are steeped in the atmosphere of Puritan New England and are an exploration of the dark psychological effects such a setting can produce.

Hazlitt, William (1778–1830)   Born the son of a Unitarian minister in England, he became a master of the familiar essay, writing on politics, philosophy, the fine arts, and daily life. He was the most important literary critic of his time, especially in the field of the drama.

Hedda Gabler (1890), Henrik Ibsen   This Norwegian drama presents a controlling and manipulative woman married to Tesman, a colorless, ineffective man. Her husband's rival has written an outstanding book, which may cause Tesman to lose his appointment for a history professorship. Hedda, who has always yearned to mold a destiny, burns the manuscript and eventually encourages its author to commit suicide. Threatened with exposure, Hedda shoots and kills herself.

Hellman, Lillian (1905–1984) This New Orleans native, playwright, and autobiographer, wrote *The Children's Hour* (1934), a controversial play that created a great sensation because of its homosexual implications. Even more successful was her drama *The Little Foxes* (1939). Hellman's long time love affair with novelist Dashiell Hammett, her testifying before the House Committee on Un-American Activities (always a leftist, she denied being a Communist Party member, but refused to discuss her associates in left-wing causes), and her eventual life are all discussed in her autobiographical trilogy: *Pentimento* (1973), *An Unfinished Woman* (1974), and *Scoundrel Time* (1976).

Hemingway, Ernest (1899–1961) Born near Chicago, the son of a physician, this American novelist and short-story writer worked briefly as a journalist. During World War I he served as an ambulance driver in Italy, where he was severely wounded. Returning to America, he became a newspaperman again, but in 1921 left for Paris. As an American expatriate, he was considered a representative of the "Lost Generation." His novels include *The Sun Also Rises* (1926), *A Farewell to Arms* (1929), and *For Whom the Bell Tolls* (1940). Hemingway's style is hard and tense, and his themes are much concerned with virility, courage, and man's challenge with both life and death. He won the Nobel Prize for Literature in 1954 and committed suicide in 1961.

Henry, O. (William Sydney Porter) (1862–1918) Often considered to be the father of the American short story, O. Henry was a master of the surprise ending, which he achieved by withholding an important piece of information from the reader. His tales are based almost entirely on plot; mood and character are of incidental importance. It is often as if he took an anecdote and extended it with skill, irony, and humor. Some of his best and most anthologized stories are "The Gift of the Magi" (1906) and "The Ransom of Red Chief" (1910); *Cabbages and Kings* (1904) and *The Four Million* (1906) are two of his important collections.

Hero In myth and early literature, a character filled with courage and idealism. Often a favorite of the gods and sometimes partly divine himself, the hero worked as a symbol of man overcoming threatening obstacles in an angry world; he was also the image of the societal values and morals of his time. Through the years the concept of the hero has changed, and in the 20th century we have the anti-hero, lacking the traditional qualities of his predecessor and frequently depicted as a foolish, sad, often antisocial figure.

Heroic couplet A pair of rhymed lines written in iambic pentameter.

> One science only will one genius fit;
> So vast is art, so narrow human wit.
>
> Pope

Herrick, Robert (1591–1674) One of the most gifted of the English Cavalier poets (those who sided with the king against the Puritans), he was educated at Cambridge. His most famous poem is "To the Virgins, To Make Much of Time" (1648), with its often-quoted line, "Gather ye rosebuds while ye may."

Hesse, Hermann (1877–1962) Born in Germany, he settled in Switzerland in 1912 and became a citizen of that country. Much of his work deals with the subject of the estranged and lonely artist in the contemporary world, who struggles against a materialistic society to reach an aesthetic ideal. His lyric prose novels fall loosely into two categories: the psychoanalytic novel and the novel of intellectual symbolism. His best-known works are *Siddhartha* (1922), *Steppenwolf* (1927), and *Magister Ludi* (1943). In 1946 he won the Nobel Prize for Literature.

Hexameter In Classical Latin and Greek poetry, an elaborately patterned, rhythmic line; now merely a line of poetry with six metrical feet. Alexandrines are hexameter lines.

> Not fit for speedy pace, or manly
> exercise.
>
> Spenser

Historicism A type of literary criticism that examines the historical context in which a work was produced and attempts to determine the influence of social and cultural forces on that work. Another form of historicism attempts to ascertain the applicability of a literary work of the past to present-day readers.

Holmes, Oliver Wendell (1809–1894) Until Holmes was almost 50, he worked as a physician and Harvard professor. His fame as a writer began when he published *The Autocrat of the Breakfast Table* (1857). He was also esteemed for his light poetry, and was the father of Oliver Wendell Holmes, Jr. (U.S. Supreme Court Justice), and the author of many works on jurisprudence.

Holograph An original manuscript of a piece of literature, valued greatly by scholars in their pursuit of the development of a work.

Homer (10th–9th century B.C.) The earliest Greek writer whose works have survived, he was the author of the two major epics, *The Iliad* and *The Odyssey*, both about events connected with the Trojan War. According to one legend, Homer was blind and was thus an inheritor of the tradition of the oral transmission of poetry characteristic of primitive societies.

Hopkins, Gerard Manley (1844–1889) While a student at Oxford, this English poet became a Roman Catholic and joined the Jesuit order. When he became a priest, he burned much of his early passionate lyric poetry and determined not to write again, a promise he couldn't keep. Hopkins turned his poetic voice to the glorification of God in such beautiful lines as "Glory be to God for dappled things/For skies of coupled color like a brinded cow," from "God's Grandeur." He was constantly at war with himself both as a poet and as a man unable to give himself completely to God, and he refused to have his poetry published during his lifetime. Today he is considered one of the most modern and influential poets of the 19th century, largely for the beauty created by his glorified imagery.

Horace (65–8 B.C.) The foremost Roman lyric poet studied in Rome as a youth and, after serving in the military, supported himself as a clerk. He was given a farm by a wealthy patron of the arts, and was primarily the author of Odes, Epodes, and Satires.

LITERATURE

The House of Bernarda Alba (1936), Federico Garcia Lorca   It should be noted that in Spanish the title of this play, *La Casa de Bernarda Alba,* is filled with the letter *-a-,* the feminine ending in that language. It is the study of a house full of women controlled by the forceful female who tyrannizes over her mother and daughters, denying the one of marriageable age the right to see suitors and trying to marry off an older, less attractive girl. Eventually the younger girl kills herself, but Bernarda is unmoved.

Houseman, Alfred Edward (1859–1936)   Educated at Oxford, this English poet was one of the finest classical scholars of his time. His poetry is distinctive for his combination of humor and sadness, his main theme being the passing of youth. *A Shropshire Lad* (1896) is the more famous of his two volumes of verse, including such well-known poems as "When I was One and Twenty."

Howells, William Dean (1837–1920)   Born in Ohio, the son of a printer, this American author worked as a typesetter and printer as a youth before he began writing poetry. He went to Boston and became editor of *The Atlantic Monthly* when his novels began to appear, the best-known being *The Rise of Silas Lapham* (1884) and *Through the Eye of the Needle* (1907).

Hubris (also spelled *Hybris*)   A Greek term that denotes the excessive pride leading to the downfall of the hero in a tragic drama. For example, Macbeth's pride and excessive ambition, which led to calamitous results, and Doctor Faustus, whose pride led him to sell his soul to the devil in exchange for power and magical knowledge.

Hughes, Langston (1902–1967)   This black American author of poetry, short stories, plays, an autobiography, novels, and translations was a native of Missouri who eventually moved to Harlem, New York, which became his home base. His writing is characterized by his use of dialect and his cadence is often expressed in the rhythms of jazz.

Hughes, Ted (b. 1930)   British poet who spent a considerable amount of time in the United States, Hughes was once married to Sylvia Plath. He was recently made poet laureate of Great Britain.

Hugo, Victor (1802–1885)   This illustrious member of the French Academy, son of a general in Napoleon's army, wrote poetry, drama, and novels, but his most enduring works are fiction, particularly *The Hunchback of Notre Dame* (1831) and *Les Misérables* (1862). He was the most important writer of the French Romantic school and also won fame as a political speaker and writer. Hugo spent the years from 1851–1870 in exile because of his political views, but returned triumphantly to France to be greeted as a national hero. He continued his career as a writer whose style was expressed with vigor and beauty until his death in 1885.

Humours   Descriptive of "moods" that appear frequently in the plays of Jonson and Shakespeare, this concept of bodily fluids affecting man's physical and mental attitudes dates back to the Middle Ages and the Renaissance. When the fluids (blood, phlegm, yellow, and black bile) were balanced, a person's temperament would be ideal, but an excess of one and/or the dearth of another could produce unpleasant results.

Excess	Personality	Characteristics
Blood	Sanguine	ecstatic, highly loving
Phlegm	Phlegmatic	intellectual, dull, frightened, unresponsive
Yellow Bile	Choleric	obstinate, filled with rage and vengeance
Black Bile	Melancholic	gloomy, sad, brooding

The Hunchback of Notre Dame (1831), Victor Hugo   This French novel tells of the hideously ugly hunchback Quasimodo and his unrequited love for Esmerelda, a Gypsy dancer. She is eventually hanged as a witch, and united in death with the hunchback. Hugo is saying that spiritual goodness may be found even in the ugliest human being.

Huxley, Aldous (1894–1963)   Born into a distinguished British literary and scientific family, he was educated at Oxford. At 18 he almost became blind and had visual problems for the rest of his life. His first successful novel was *Crome Yellow* (1921). In 1938 he established himself in America and made that his headquarters for the rest of his life. His best-known novel is *Brave New World* (1932). Many of his books are biting critiques of a decadent society, and it is often through humor that he reflects his cynicism and disillusionment. In his late works [for example, *Brave New World Revisited* (1958)] Huxley delved into Mysticism and Eastern philosophy.

Hyperbole   A figure of speech. A deliberate exaggeration, usually to stress a point, as in "that's as funny as a crutch."

I | **Iambic**   A metrical foot that has two syllables, with the accent or stress on the second. The term is used in conjunction with another word to denote the rhythm and number of stressed syllables in a line of poetry: e.g., iambic pentameter (five iambic feet). Examples of iambs are: ăgáin, prŏmóte, ĕnfórce.

Ibsen, Henrik (1828–1906)   The father of modern realistic drama (today highly esteemed as a feminist playwright), this Norwegian playwright had little success with his early works. It was not until he became a voluntary exile in 1864, spending 27 years in Rome, Dresden, and Munich, that he became a successful playwright. His best-known works are the realistic plays *A Doll's House* (1879) and *Hedda Gabler* (1890) and the symbolic *The Master Builder* (1892). Ibsen was far ahead of his time in writing plays about truths that his society did not wish to acknowledge. He found his greatest success in creating the "new" 19th-century woman [*see Hedda Gabler* (1890)], who struggled against the roles she was forced to assume.

Idyll   A short lyrical poem that takes as its setting a scene of pastoral or rural life. Sometimes referred to as pastoral poetry; see Marlow's "The Passionate Shepherd to His Love."

Idylls of the King (1859–1888), Alfred Tennyson   A series of verse tales about the illustrious King Arthur, the adventures of Lancelot, and the Knights of the Round Table, the fabled Camelot with its Queen Guinevere, and the ultimate destruction and corruption that brought about the failure of a dream.

The Iliad, Homer   The earliest work of Greek literature that has survived intact, this epic poem deals with an episode in the tenth year of the Trojan War. The subject is stated in the beginning of the poem: the wrath of Achilles, whose friend Patroclus is killed and who in turn slays the Trojan hero Hector.

Illusion   The necessary intellectual deception played on a reader or an audience by the talents of an author who convinces his audience that the make-believe is real, or at least appears to be so through the length of a book, or the unfolding of a play. *See* **Suspension of disbelief**.

Imagery   Descriptive language used to create pictures in the mind of the reader or to evoke various emotions.

Imagists   A group of American poets (e.g., Sandburg, Williams, Pound) prominent from 1909–1918 and dedicated to producing poems employing the language of common speech, new rhythms, new subject matter, and strong concrete imagery.

Imitation   A concept of art that originated with Aristotle's dictum that art imitates nature. The term also refers to the practice—acceptable in the Greek and Roman schools of rhetoric—of learning composition by imitating literary models.

The Importance of Being Earnest (1865), Oscar Wilde   An extremely clever comedy, filled with wit and paradox; one of the few 19th-century plays to be preserved as a classic, bringing as much delight today as it did over a hundred years ago. "Earnest" is a complex verbal network of relationships and misunderstandings, a true comedy of manners.

In Cold Blood (1966), Truman Capote   A nonfiction novel that brought a new dimension to the modern genre as Capote revealed the mythic significance of facts by simply stating them and allowing the reader to understand that, as Thoreau wrote "Reality is fabulous." The work of a "literary photographer," who is the opposite of the subjective novelist. Here the eye of the camera (Capote) is open and quite passive. The novel relates the story of two men who brutally murder a family in the American Midwest.

Interior monologue   A technique used in the writing of a novel or short story to record the inner thoughts and emotional responses of a character; also called stream of consciousness, it is used frequently in Virginia Woolf's novels and in the Molly Bloom section of James Joyce's *Ulysses*.

The Invisible Man (1952), Ralph Ellison   An American novel that owes some of its inspiration to Dostoevsky and the existentialists in the way in which it deals with a man alienated from his society.

Invocation   Occurs at the beginning of an epic poem, usually as an appeal to one of the muses, when the poet wishes to elicit divine assistance for his work.

Ionesco, Eugene (b.1912)   Considered to be the supreme representative of the Theater of the Absurd, his plays combine a surrealistic technique with a clarity of language and thought to create a picture of man standing on the edge of the abyss. He is best known for *Rhinoceros* (1959) and *The Bald Soprano* (1948).

Briseis of the Fair Cheeks.

Irony   A figure of speech used as a literary device in which the meaning stated is contrary to the one intended. In drama, irony is perceived by an audience when a character makes statements not fully understood by himself. In Shakespeare's *Othello,* Act III, scene iii, the audience knows that Iago is about to deceive the hero in a terrible way, but Othello says of Iago: "I know thou'rt full of love and honesty."

Irving, Washington (1783–1859)   The first American writer to gain a literary reputation in Europe, this novelist, short-story writer, and essayist was also the first American to make his living as a writer. Using the nom de plume Diedrich Knickerbocker, in 1809 he published *A History of New York,* a satire acclaimed as the greatest comic work written by an American. His most famous and popular work was *The Sketch Book* (1820), containing the stories "Rip Van Winkle" and "The Legend of Sleepy Hollow."

Isherwood, Christopher (1904–1986)   This English novelist's *Berlin Stories* (1946) beautifully recounted the political unrest and the decadence of Germany during the rise of Nazism. One of Isherwood's great concerns was for the intellectual in an oppressive society. His characters (note Sally

Bowles in *Berlin Stories*) are always both eccentric and charming.

Italian sonnet Also called Petrarchan, this type of sonnet is divided into an octave, which always rhymes *abbaabba,* and a sestet, which usually rhymes *cdecde.*

On His Blindness

When I consider how my light is spent	(a)
Ere half my days in this dark world and wide,	(b)
And that one talent which is death to hide	(b)
Lodged with me useless, though my soul more bent	(a)
To serve there with my Maker, and present	(a)
My true account, lest He returning chide,	(b)
"Doth God exact day-labor, light denied?"	(b)
I fondly ask. But Patience, to prevent	(a)
That murmur, soon replies, "God doth not need	(c)
Either man's work or his own gifts. Who best	(d)
Bear his mild yoke, they serve him best. His state	(e)
Is kingly: thousands at his bidding speed,	(c)
And post o'er land and ocean without rest;	(d)
They also serve who only stand and wait."	(e)

Milton

J **Jabberwocky** A word taken from a poem by Lewis Carroll and extended to mean any part of writing or speech that is not intelligible. 'Twas brillig, and the slithy toves/Did gyre and gimble in the wabe."

James, Henry (1843–1916) Born the son of a theological writer and the brother of the noted philosopher William James, this American novelist and short-story writer grew up in wealth and began writing in the 1860s when he moved to London. James believed that things European were, in general, finer than things American, although he admired the honesty, directness, and energy that was typically American. His work falls into three periods: the realistic stage, the stage of "psychological realism," and the experimental stage. His best-known works are *The Europeans* (1878), *Washington Square* (1881), *The Portrait of a Lady* (1881), *The Ambassadors* (1903), and *The Turn of the Screw* (1898).

Jane Eyre (1847), Charlotte Brontë A gothic Victorian novel in which Jane Eyre, a young governess, is in love with her employer, the dark and brooding character of Rochester. Mrs. Rochester the mad wife, almost literally holds sway above her husband in the attic rooms of the gloomy mansion, and so the story unfolds, with elements of fear, mystery, and romance.

Jargon A term usually used negatively to describe corporate or trade language, etc., filled with technical, lofty, often obscure terminology; e.g., "computerese" terms such as "interface."

Jeffers, Robinson (1887–1962) Born in Pittsburgh, this American poet went to California and was attracted to the Monterey Peninsula; much of his work centers on that region. He was deeply influenced by Freudian and Jungian psychology and had a strong interest in Greek classic theater. One of his most popular works was an adaptation of Euripides' *Medea* (1947).

Johnson, Samuel (1709–1784) The literary dictator of his time, this eccentric English novelist and essayist (reputed to have atrocious manners and a deplorable appearance) worked as a literary hack until he was finally able to publish his *Dictionary of the English Language* (1755). In 1763, he met James Boswell, who became his disciple and who was to become his brilliant biographer. His last great literary work was *The Lives of the Poets* (1779–1781), ten small volumes of subjective but valuable criticism.

Jonson, Ben (1573–1637) Born into poverty, this British author became a bricklayer, managed to study at Cambridge, fought with the army in France, and eventually became a playwright. He was a favorite of King James I and provided many entertainments for the court. Jonson loved to depict the London of his time with a satirical eye; this talent can be witnessed in two of his best works, *Volpone, or the Fox* (1606) and *The Alchemist* (1610).

Ben Jonson.

Journalese Style once associated with newspaper writing, marked by trite phrases and affectations.

Joyce, James (1882–1941) Born in Dublin, this Irish novelist and playwright was destined for the priesthood, but rebelled against everything connected with his environment and spent his life in self-imposed exile on the Continent. He lived in poverty and suffered from near blindness while he worked on his masterpieces, facing rejection after rejection (because of obscenity charges) before he was able to have his masterpiece *Ulysses* published in Paris in 1922. Its publication was banned in the United States until 1933. Among various literary techniques, this work heavily uses stream of consciousness and the interior monologue, methods extended and elaborated on in *Finnegan's Wake* (1939). Both works require scholarly study if they are to be appreciated in their totalities. The more accessible works of Joyce are *The Dubliners* (1914) and *Portrait of the Artist As a Young Man* (1916).

The Jungle (1906), Upton Sinclair　Said the author of this American novel, "I aimed at the public's heart and hit it on the stomach." It is the story of Jurgis Rukhus, a Lithuanian immigrant who goes to work in a Chicago packing house, where sanitation is all but unknown. Losing his job, he becomes a vagabond and petty criminal, but sees a way out when he attends a socialist meeting. Sinclair's description of methods used in the meat-packing houses was instrumental in the passage of the Pure Food and Drug Act.

Juno and the Paycock (1924), Sean O'Casey　A play that concerns the Irish civil riots against Great Britain; a poetic tragicomedy that follows the decline and eventual disintegration of the Boyle family in the Dublin slums of 1922.

Juxtaposition　In strict definition, the act of placing two or more things (words, images, phrases) side by side. In literary tradition, it is the unusual effects created by linking unlike subjects. Pope was the master of juxtaposition.

Kafka, Franz (1883–1924)　Born in Prague to an unusually strong father who exercised an influence over him all his life, he took a degree in law before his health began to deteriorate; by 1916 he was diagnosed as tubercular. Kafka destroyed much of what he had written during his lifetime although he did publish *The Metamorphosis* (1915), and asked his friend Max Brod to burn the rest after his death. Brod ignored this wish and, among the works that survived, the best known are the novels *The Trial* (1925) and *The Castle* (1926). His prose presents a world that is both real and surreal in which man's feelings of guilt and isolation deny him personal salvation.

Kazantzakis, Nikos (1883–1957)　A Greek author born in Crete, who studied law and philosophy, Kazantzakis was intensely religious. He was a poet, dramatist, and novelist whose dual nature is reflected in his battle between the sensual and the ascetic. *Zorba the Greek* (1953), popularized in the United States by the novel, stage play, and film, is an example of his exuberant affirmation of life.

Keats, John (1795–1821)　Born in London, this great English Romantic poet was an orphan by age 13. His guardians removed him from school and apprenticed him to a surgeon, with whom he studied for five years until he decided to give up surgery to write poetry. His work is filled with lyric beauty and sensuous imagery and, despite personal unhappiness, a sense of joy and an uplifting recreation of beauty. Keats's great love for Fanny Browne was interrupted by his failing health. In 1818 he was diagnosed as tubercular, and in 1821, at the age of twenty-seven, he died. Some of his greatest and

best-known poems are "Endymion" (1818), and, in 1820, "La Belle Dame Sans Merci," "Ode on a Grecian Urn," and "The Eve of St. Agnes."

King Lear (1605–1606), William Shakespeare　This Elizabethan drama is said to be Shakespeare's greatest creation of the tragic spirit. Its largest theme is man's inhumanity to man, as illustrated by filial treason. The story is of Lear and his three daughters, Goneril, Regan, and Cordelia; a tale of love and madness and great pain as the aging king tests the boundaries of his daughters' affections for him. The play ends with the tragic deaths of the four main characters.

Kingsley, Sidney (Sidney Kieschner) (b.1906)　Born in New York City, this American playwright was educated at Cornell. After graduation he worked as a script writer for Columbia Pictures. In 1933 his first major play, *Men in White,* was a great success and two years later he scored an even greater triumph with *Dead End.* Not incidentally, he is also the author of *Detective Story* (1949), a play that is frequently revived to much critical acclaim.

Kipling, Rudyard (1865–1936)　Born in India, this English author drew from his years in that colony much of the material he used as a writer. He achieved fame with his second book, *Plain Tales from the Hills* (1887), a collection of short stories on life in India. He wrote many collections of poetry and short stories, but may be best remembered for such imaginative children's stories as *The Jungle Book* (1894) and *Captains Courageous* (1897). He won the Nobel Prize for Literature in 1907.

Koestler, Arthur (1905–1983)　Born into a Jewish family in Budapest, Hungary, Koestler worked on a collective farm in Palestine and then became a journalist. He joined the Communist Party in 1931, but left it in 1939 at the time of the Russo-German treaty. He served in the British army in World War II and became a British citizen. His best-known work is *Darkness at Noon* (1941). He is renowned for his understanding of and participation in the great movements of his time, and his writing is characterized by a sense of elegant journalism.

Kyd, Thomas (1557–1594)　Author of *The Spanish Tragedy,* one of the most important and influential Elizabethan plays. It established the "tragedy of blood" (or the "blood and thunder tragedy") as the most popular type of Elizabethan tragedy, characterized by violent action and the appearance of ghosts. Shakespeare's tragedies (although they both transform and transcend the type) are written in this tradition.

LaFontaine, Jean (1621–1695)　The reputation of this French creator of fables rests principally on the plots he used, which were drawn from the Greek Aesop and from Oriental fabulist writers.

Lamb, Charles (1775–1834)　English essayist who occasionally collaborated with his sister, Mary, for whom he was guardian and companion. Mary suffered from mental illness, and in a fit of temporary insanity she killed their mother and wounded their father. Although sister and brother were close friends, her madness overshadowed their lives. Lamb, considered one of the masters of the English essay, wrote his observations of life with a mix of humor and sadness. There are few students who have not been exposed to his delightful "Dissertation Upon Roast Pig."

Lament   Usually refers to a poem written as an expression of mourning or grief, as in Shelley's lines to Keats: "Oh weep for Adonais, he is dead."

Lampoon   In prose or poetry, a vicious character sketch or satire on a person. The literary figures of 17th–18th-century England were famous for lampooning, and the style has come into its own again in 20th-century America. One of Harvard's literary publications is entitled *The Lampoon.*

The Last of the Mohicans   (1826), James Fenimore Cooper   One of the five novels constituting the "Leather-Stocking Tales," this American work centers on three elements—the siege of Fort William Henry in 1757 and the massacre of its garrison, a love affair between wealthy characters, and the exploits of Natty Bumppo and his Indian companion Chingachgook.

Lawrence, D.H.   (David Herbert) (1885–1930)   Influential because of his espousal of the psychoanalytical theories of Freud and his school, this highly renowned English novelist, poet, and short-story writer became one of the most controversial authors of the early 20th century. He achieved recognition with his first book, *Sons and Lovers* (1913), but his next, *The Rainbow* (1915) caused such a scandal that Lawrence determined to leave England and spent the rest of his life moving from place to place, staying in Italy, Mexico and the United States. His novel *Lady Chatterley's Lover* (1929) was not published in this country until many years after it was written. Lawrence's works are noted for their intense involvement with sexuality and their sensual/sensuous content.

Lear, Edward   (1812–1888)   The "most pure" of nonsense poets, this English versifier is responsible for the popularity of the limerick. His poetry is addressed almost entirely to the ear. His best-known poem is "The Owl and the Pussycat," and *The Book of Nonsense* (1846) is one of his delightful verse volumes.

Leaves of Grass   (1847–1892), Walt Whitman   A poetic work, greatly revised and augmented by Whitman, which was highly criticized in its time because of the poet's glorification of sex. Today, literary criticism proclaims "Leaves" as a masterpiece in its exaltation of the common man and its veneration of freedom. Famous poems from this work include "Song of the Open Road," "Out of the Cradle Endlessly Rocking," and "Song of Myself."

Legend   A story that is popularly regarded as historical, and indeed has its roots in fact, but one in which imagination also comes largely into play. Often legends involve folk heroes, e.g., Paul Bunyan and Johnny Appleseed.

The Legend of Sleepy Hollow   (1819–1820), Washington Irving   This tale from *The Sketch Book* recounts the story of the rivalry between Ichabod Crane, a Connecticut schoolmaster, and Brom Bones, for the hand of a Dutch heiress. Crane is not only covetous, but superstitious, and one night returning home he encounters the "ghost" of a headless horseman and is so frightened that he leaves the country.

Les Misérables   (1862), Victor Hugo   Written in exile and acclaimed "the greatest epic and dramatic work of fiction ever created," this lengthy and beautiful novel is a moving appeal to the common humanity of man through the character of Jean Valjean. Valjean, imprisoned for stealing a loaf of bread, is released after 19 years, having received a 14-year penalty because of his attempts to escape. The novel is also the story of Inspector Javert, who is unrelenting in his search for Valjean.

Lessing, Gotthold Ephraim   (1729–1781)   This first major figure of modern German literature made his reputation as both a dramatist and a critic. His works include the plays *Miss Sarah Sampson* (1755), the first German tragedy of the middle class, and *Nathan the Wise* (1779), a plea for religious tolerance, as well as a book of criticism *The Hamburg Dramaturgy* (1769), a major influence on German theater history.

Lewis, Sinclair   (1885–1951)   Born in Minnesota, this American novelist and short-story writer graduated from Yale and then held various jobs in journalism and magazine publication. He had his first great success with *Main Street* (1920) and continued to produce works both naturalistic and satirical about American life at the rate of one every two years, including *Babbitt* (1922), *Arrowsmith* (1925), and *Elmer Gantry* (1927). He was the first American to win the Nobel Prize for Literature, in 1930.

Lexicography   The editing or the making of a dictionary, or lexicon; the principles of dictionary making. Samuel Johnson's *Dictionary of the English Language* (1755) is considered the most important early work of lexicography in English.

Libretto   The text, spoken and sung, of a work for the musical theater, such as an opera, operetta, or a musical comedy. Sir William S. Gilbert wrote the libretti for Sir Arthur Sullivan's music in the Gilbert and Sullivan comic operas.

Limerick   A humorous five-line poem rhyming *aabba.* A limerick is sometimes written in four lines, combining the two short lines into one.

> There was a young lady of
>   Tottenham,   (a)
> Who'd no manners, or else she'd
>   forgotten 'em,   (a)
> At tea at the vicar's   (b)
> She tore off her knickers,   (b)
> Because, she explained, she
>   felt 'ot in 'em.   (a)

Lindsay, Vachel   (1879–1931)   A unique figure in 20th-century American poetry, Lindsay wrote some of his works to be chanted and for years traveled around the country as a modern-day troubadour, presenting them and his drawings and trying to return poetry to the general public; he called his performances a "Higher Vaudeville." His published works include *General William Booth Enters into Heaven* (1913) and *The Congo and Other Poems* (1914).

Litotes   A figure of speech that uses understatement to make a point stronger, usually by stating the opposite of the point being affirmed, as in "New York cheesecake is not a bad dessert." In the Book of the

LITERATURE

Acts of the Apostles in the Bible is the example, "A citizen of no mean city."

Livy (59 B.C.–A.D. 17)   A teacher and writer, Livy is considered the only important prose writer of the Age of Augustus, the golden age of Latin literature. A teacher as well as a writer, he wrote *The History of Rome* in 142 books, of which only 35 are extant. He is the chief source of information about Rome's early years.

Lolita (1955), Vladimir Nabokov   This American novel created a sensation when it was first published. It concerns Humbert Humbert, a dissolute European who is sexually attracted to nymphets, girls between 9 and 14. After an affair with Lolita and some further sexual escapades on her part, Humbert eventually crosses her path again to find her married and pregnant. He kills her husband and consequently goes to prison. Some have interpreted the story as a satirical look at the American fascination with youth.

London, Jack (1876–1916)   Born in San Francisco, the illegitimate son of an eccentric astrologer, this American novelist and short-story writer left home at 15, was jailed for vagrancy, worked as an "oyster pirate," sailed as a seaman on a sealing voyage, and in 1896 joined the gold rush in the Klondike. His first work was published in 1899, but his reputation was made with *The Call of The Wild,* which became a best seller in 1903. He wrote 50 novels; his stories are romantic adventures in realistic settings, with an underlying theme of the struggle for existence, the survival of the fittest, and the class struggle.

Long Day's Journey Into Night (1956), Eugene O'Neill   This drama, published in 1956, but written some years before, was intended by the playwright not to be shown in his lifetime. It is a thinly disguised portrait of O'Neill's family and shows how a family built on deceit can rapidly crumble. Yet in the end they are held together by a fierce, irrational affection which is stronger than their hostile feelings for one another.

Longfellow, Henry Wadsworth (1807–1882)   Born in Maine, this American poet and translator was a professor of modern languages at Harvard. His best-known works include *Evangeline* (1847), *Hiawatha* (1855), "The Wreck of the Hesperus," and "Paul Revere's Ride." His reputation has declined steadily since his death. Although his poetry today is considered simplistic, Longfellow is still widely read, and he was the first American to have his bust placed in the poet's corner of Westminster Abbey.

Look Homeward Angel (1929), Thomas Wolfe   Long autobiographical novel of a young man growing up in North Carolina and gradually being introduced to the world of ideas. Wolfe (Eugene in the book) delves deeply into family life in his portrayal of his parents, two sisters, and three brothers. The sequel to this work is *Of Time and The River* (1935).

Lord Jim (1900), Joseph Conrad   The hero, Jim, is endowed by his minister father with a puritanical conscience, and is dogged all his life by a sense of guilt over a youthful transgression. This psychological novel has the sea as its setting.

Lord of the Flies (1954), William Golding   A "classic" in its own time, this work is concerned with moral evil and the darkness in the human heart, made more terrifying because the characters are children, wrecked on a desert island, who gradually make this natural paradise into a hell as they degenerate into primitive and bloodthirsty savagery.

Lost generation   A term created by Gertrude Stein and then brought to popular usage by such writers as Hemingway and Fitzgerald. The Lost Generation refers to the spirit of alienation and the feeling of disillusion prevalent in literature and life after World War I.

Lovelace, Richard (1618–1657)   A Cavalier poet (siding with the English king against the Puritans), he was imprisoned in 1648 and there wrote his famous poem "To Althea," containing the lines "Stone walls do not a prison make/Nor iron bars a cage." He was released in 1649 and published his poems in a volume entitled *Lucasta.*

The Love Song of J. Alfred Prufrock (1915), T.S. Eliot   "Will there be time after tea and ices/to force the moment to its crisis?" Prufrock, a symbol of impotence and banality, wonders, in this evocative and more "accessible" poem of Eliot's. Here a man seeking to rebel in a heroic fashion also fails through ennui and half measures. This poem is an excellent introduction to the beautiful and intricate designs of T.S. Eliot's work.

Lowell, Amy (1874–1925)   Born into one of Massachusetts' leading families, this American poet's first book, *A Dome of Many-Colored Glass* (title taken from a poem by Shelley), was published in 1912, but it was her 1914 collection *Sword Blades and Poppy Seed,* written after her meeting Ezra Pound, that established her as one of the leading imagist poets. Lowell, however, has been criticized for her use of "precious" language and overly abundant sentiment. Her finest work is thought to be her two-volume biography of Keats (1925).

Lowell, James Russell (1819–1891)   This romantic poet, critic, satirist, and wit was born in Cambridge, Massachusetts and attended Harvard University. His best-known work is *The Biglow Papers* (1846–48), an attack on the Mexican War and the southern states. He also served as the first editor of the *Atlantic Monthly.*

Lowell, Robert (1917–1977)   An American poet whose rich use of symbolism in highly individualistic and intense poetry is reflected in the volume *Lord Weary's Castle* (1946), for which he received the Pulitzer Prize.

Lyric   A short, melodic, imaginative poem, usually characterized by intense personal emotion, that creates for the reader a unified impression. Lyric poems include sonnets, songs, ballads, odes, and elegies.

Lysistrata (411 B.C.), Aristophanes   This Greek play takes place toward the end of the long war between Athens and Sparta. The women of Athens, led by Lysistrata, decide that they will withhold their sexual favors from their husbands till the war is ended; they are joined in support by the women of Sparta until the war is finally brought to a close.

EXHIBIT 15.4
Nobel Literature Prizes
(Including Notable Works)

1901 Sully-Prudhomme (René Prudhomme), French poet: *La Justice*, (1878), *Le Bonheur* (1888)

1902 C.M.T. Mommsen, German historian: *History of Rome* (1854–1856)

1903 Björnstijerne Björnson, Norwegian author: novel, *The Fisher Girl* (1868); poem, *Arnljot Gelline (1870)*

1904 Frédéric Mistral, French poet: *Miréio* (1859) José Echegaray, Spanish dramatist: *The Great Galeoto* (1881)

1905 Henryk Sienkiewicz, Polish novelist: *Quo Vadis?* (1895)

1906 Giosué Carducci, Italian poet: *Odi barbari* (1877)

1907 Rudyard Kipling, British author: poetry, *Barrack-Room Ballads* (1892), *If* (1910); novel, *The Light That Failed* (1890)

1908 Rudolf C. Eucken, German philosopher: *The Truth of Religion* (1901)

1909 Selma Lagerlöf, Swedish novelist: *The Story of Gösta Berling* (1891)

1910 Paul J. L. Heyse, German novelist: *The Fury* (1855), *Children of the World* (1873)

1911 Count Maurice Maeterlinck, Belgian author: play, *The Blue Bird* (1909)

1912 Gerhart Hauptmann. German author: play, *Before Dawn* (1889), novel, *The Fool in Christ. Emanuel Quint* (1910)

1913 Rabindranath Tagore, Indian author: philosophy, *Sadhana, The Realization of Life* (1913)

1914 No award

1915 Romain Rolland, French author: novel, *Jean-Christophe* (1904–1912)

1916 Carl G. von Heldenstam, Swedish author: poetry, *New Poems* (1915)

1917 Karl A. Gjellerup, Danish poet and novelist: *The Pilgrim Kamanita* (1906) Henrik Pontoppidan, Danish novelist: *Kingdom of the Dead* (1912–1916)

1918 No award

1919 Carl F. G. Spitteler, Swiss poet: *Olympian Spring* (1900–1906)

1920 Knut Hamsun, Norwegian novelist: *Growth of the Soil* (1920)

1921 Anatole France, French author: novel, *Penguin Island* (1908)

1922 Jacinto Benavente, Spanish dramatist: *Bonds of Interest* (1907), *The Passion Flower* (1913)

1923 William Butler Yeats, Irish poet and dramatist: poetry, *The Wild Swans at Coole* (1919)

1924 Wladyslaw S. Reymont, Polish author: novel, *The Peasants* (1902–1909)

1925 George Bernard Shaw, British (Irish-born) author: plays, *Man and Superman* (1905), *Pygmalion* (1913)

1926 Grazia Deledda, Italian novelist: *After the Divorce* (1902), *Ashes* (1904)

1927 Henri Bergson, French philosopher: *Creative Evolution* (1907)

1928 Sigrid Undset, Norwegian (Danish-born) novelist: *Kristin Lavransdatter* (1920–1922)

1929 Thomas Mann, German novelist: *Buddenbrooks* (1901), *The Magic Mountain* (1924)

1930 Sinclair Lewis, U.S. novelist: *Main Street* (1920), *Babbitt* (1922)

1931 Erik A. Karlfeldt, Swedish poet: *Songs of the Wilderness and Love* (1895)

1932 John Galsworthy, British author: novels, *The Forsyte Saga* (1922), *A Modern Comedy* (1928)

1933 Ivan A. Bunin, French (Russian-born) author: novel, *The Village* (1910); short stories, *The Gentleman from San Francisco* (1916)

1934 Luigi Pirandello, Italian author play, *Six Characters in Search of an Author* (1920)

1935 No award

1936 Eugene O'Neill, U.S. dramatist: *Mourning Becomes Electra* (1931), *Strange Interlude* (1927)

1937 Roger Martin du Gard, French novelist: *The World of the Thibaults* (1922–1940)

1938 Pearl S. Buck, U.S. novelist: *The Good Earth* (1931)

1939 Frans E. Sillanpää, Finnish novelist: *Meek Heritage* (1919), *People in a Summer Night* (1934)

1940–43 No award

1944 Johannes V. Jensen, Danish author: novel, *The Long Journey* (1908–1922)

1945 Gabriela Mistral, Chilean poet: *Desolación* (1922), *Tala* (1938), *Lagar* (1954)

1946 Hermann Hesse, Swiss (German-born) author: novels, *Steppenwolf* (1927) *Death and the Lover,* (1930)

1947 Andre Gide, French author: novels, *The Immoralist* (1902), *Strait is the Gate* (1909)

1948 T.S. Eliot, British (U.S.-born) poet: *The Waste Land* (1922), *Four Quarters* (1935–1942)

1949 William Faulkner, U.S. novelist: *The Sound and the Fury* (1929), *Sanctuary* (1931)

1950 Bertrand Russell, British philosopher: *Marriage and Morals* (1929), *The Conquest of Happiness* (1930)

1951 Pär F. Lagerkvist, Swedish author: novels, *The Dwarf* (1944), *Barabbas* (1950)

1952 Francois Mauriac, French author: novels, *The Desert of Love* (1925), *Vipers' Tangle* (1932)

1953 Sir Winston Churchill, British statesman and historian: *The Second World War* (1948–1953)

1954 Ernest Hemingway, U.S. novelist: *A Farewell to Arms* (1929), *For Whom the Bell Tolls* (1940)

1955 Halldór K. Laxness, Icelandic novelist: *Salka Valka* (1931–1932), *Independent People* (1934–1935)

1956 Juan Ramón Jiménez, Spanish poet: *Unidad* (1925), *Sucesión* (1932), *Presente* (1935)

1957 Albert Camus, French author: novels, *The Stranger* (1946), *The Plague* (1948)

1958   Boris L. Pasternak, Russian poet and novelist (Prize declined): novel, *Doctor Zhivago* (1957)

1959   Salvatore Quasimodo, Italian poet: *Acque E Terra* (1930)

1960   Saint-John Perse, French poet: *Eloges* (1911), *Anabase* (1924), *Exil* (1944)

1961   Ivo Andríc, Yugoslavian novelist: *The Bridge on the Drina* (1945), *Vizier's Elephant* (1960)

1962   John Steinbeck, U.S. novelist: *The Grapes of Wrath* (1939), *East of Eden* (1952)

1963   George Seferis, Greek poet: *Strophe* (1931), *Mithistorima* (1935)

1964   Jean-Paul Sartre, French author (Prize declined): novels, *The Age of Reason* (1945), *The Reprieve* (1945); play, *The Respectful Prostitute* (1947)

1965   Mikhail Sholokhov, Russian novelist: *The Silent Don* (1928–1940)

1966   Shmuel Yosef Agnon, Israeli (Austrian-born) author: novels, *The Bridal Canopy* (1919), *A Guest for the Night* (1938)
Nelly Sachs, Swedish (German-born) poet: *In the Apartments of Death* (1947)

1967   Miguel Angel Asturias, Guatemalan author: novels, *El señor presidente* (1946), *Strong Wind* (1950)

1968   Yasunari Kawabata, Japanese novelist: *The Izu Dancer* (1925) *Snow Country* (1956)

1969   Samuel Beckett, French (Irish-born) author: play, *Waiting for Godot* (1952); novels, *Murphy* (1938), *Molloy* (1951)

1970   Aleksandr I. Solzhenitsyn, Russian author: novel, *One Day in the Life of Ivan Denisovich* (1962); nonfiction, *The Gulag Archipelago* (1974)

1971   Pablo Neruda, Chilean poet: *Crepusculario* (1919), *Canto General* (1950), *Elementary Odes* (1954)

1972   Heinrich Böll, German author: novels, *Adam, Where Art Thou?* (1951), *Billiards at Half Past Nine* (1959)

1973   Patrick White, Australian novelist: *The Happy Valley* (1939) *Vivisector* (1970)

1974   Eyvind Johnson, Swedish novelist: *Romanen om Olov* (1934–1937)
Harry Edmund Martinson, Swedish author: poetry, *Aniara* (1956), *Flowering Nettle* (1936)

1975   Eugenio Montale, Italian poet: *Poesie* (1958), *The Butterfly of Dinard* (1960)

1976   Saul Bellow, U.S. (Canadian-born) novelist: *The Adventures of Augie March* (1953), *Herzog* (1964), *Humboldt's Gift* (1975)

1977   Vicente Alexandre, Spanish poet: *Environment* (1928) *Swords of Lips* (1932)

1978   Isaac Bashevis Singer, U.S. (Polish-born) author: novels, *The Family Moskat* (1950), *Enemies: A Love Story* (1972)

1979   Odysseus Elytis, Greek poet: *The Sovereign Sun* (1974)

1980   Czeslaw Milosz, U.S. (Polish-born author: novel, *The Issa Valley* (1981) poetry, *The Bells of Winter* (1978)

1981   Elias Canetti, Bulgarian author: novel *Auto da fe* (1935)

1982   Gabriel García Marquez, Colombian novelist: *One Hundred Years of Solitude* (1967) *The Autumn of the Patriarch* (1975)

1983   William Golding, British novelist: *Lord of the Flies* (1954)

1984   Jaroslav Seifert, Czech poet: *The Plague Monument* (1980), *The Casting of Bells* (1983)

1985   Claude Simon, French author: *The Cheater* (1956), *The Flanders Road* (1960)

1986   Wole Soyinka, Nigerian dramatist, novelist, and poet: plays, *The Swamp Dwellers* (1957), *The Lion and the Jewel* (1957), *The Trials of Brother Jerol* (1960); novels, *The Interpreters* (1965), *The Man Died* (1972)

1987   Joseph Brodsky, U.S. (Russian-born) essayist and poet: *A Part of Speech* (1980), *Less Than One: Selected Essays* (1986)

1988   Naguib Mahfouz, Egyptian novelist and short-story author: novels, *Midaq Alley* (1966), *Mirrors* (1978), *Wedding Song* (1981); short stories, *God's World* (1973)

1989   Camilo José Cela, Spanish novelist and essayist: *La familia de Pascual Duarte* (*The Family of Pascual Duarte*) 1942, *La colmena* (The Hive) 1953, *Los sueños vanos, los ángeles curiosos* (1979)

1990   Octavio Paz, Mexican essayist and poet: *The Siren and the Seashell, and Other Essays on Poets and Poetry* (1974), *A Draft of Shadows* (1979), *The Labyrinth of Solitude and Other Essays* (1982)

1991   Nadine Gordimer, South African novelist and short-story author: novels, *A Sport of Nature* (1987), *My Son's Story*, 1990; short stories, *Something Out There* (1984), *Jump* (1991)

1992   Derek Walcott, West Indian poet and playright: poems, *The Castaways and Other Poems* (1965), *Collected Poems 1948–1986* (1986), *Omeros* (1990); plays, *Dream on Monkey Mountain and Other Plays* (1971), *Three Plays* (1986)

Macauley, Thomas Babington (1800–1859)   Born into a wealthy family, this English historian and essayist attended Cambridge and was admitted to the bar. His greatest work was *History of England from the Accession of James II* (1848, 1855, 1861), renowned for its brilliant narrative style and its realistic recreation of 17th-century society.

Macbeth (1606), William Shakespeare   One of Shakespeare's most brilliant tragedies, this drama recounts the story of a man capable of goodness, who loses his virtue through his and Lady Macbeth's ambition. Macbeth is hurled from crime to crime as he desperately clings to the throne and searches for the appeasement of his conscience.

Machiavelli, Niccolò (1469–1527)   An Italian Renaissance author who was tortured for his unproved complicity in a plot against the Medici. His master-work is *The Prince* (1532), in which he displays his love for liberty. The adjective "Machiavellian" has come to mean the display of amoral cunning as a justification for power, a phrase that too easily simplifies a very complex man.

MacLeish, Archibald (1892–1982)　An American poet who believed that poetry must serve higher ends than the mere communication of subjective impressions. He was both intellectual and political, and his "You Andrew Marvell" has been called the finest American short poem of the 20th century. MacLeish also wrote a famous verse play, *J.B.* (1958), the story of a contemporary Job, and his "Ars Poetica" is often quoted by students in praise of the line, "A poem should not mean but be."

Madame Bovary (1857), Gustave Flaubert　In this French masterwork of Realism, Charles Bovary, a country doctor and a widower, marries a beautiful farmer's daughter, educated better than most of her class. She conducts an affair with a wealthy libertine and another with a young lawyer. Unable to repay her debts, Emma commits suicide and her husband, learning of her infidelities, dies soon afterward.

Madrigal　A short lyric, usually designed to be sung with musical accompaniment, which generalIy has a pastoral or love motif. In Elizabethan times madrigals were sung a cappella by five or six voices, with a complex interweaving of words and melody.

The Madwoman of Chaillot (1945). Jean Giraudoux　This French fantasy presents good and evil in a clear-cut way: Financiers with their stock manipulations are evil, while the dispossessed, including eccentric old ladies, peddlers, and ragpickers are good. In the play, the Madwoman and her friends frustrate a plot by speculators to destroy Paris in order to tap oil wells beneath the city.

The Magic Mountain (1924), Thomas Mann　This German novel, generally regarded as Mann's masterwork, tells the story of Hans Castorp, a young German engineer who goes to a tuberculosis sanatorium in Switzerland to visit his cousin. Planning to stay for only three weeks, he discovers traces of the disease in himself and stays for seven years. Each of the persons he meets is the personification of some broader force, so at the end of his stay Castorp has come into contact with every aspect of European culture.

Magister Ludi (1943), Hermann Hesse　This allegorical fantasy has as its background pastime—"The Glass Bead Game" (translation of the German title) in which members of a future civilization concern themselves with preserving the cultural and intellectual heritage of the past. This novel is an intellectual work, with the barest of plots, relying heavily on dialogue to uncover its themes.

The Magnificent Ambersons (1918), Booth Tarkington　This American novel is typical of many by this author. lt tells of the founding of a "Gilded Age" (around 1875–1880) and its eventual decline as a new class emerges: the industrial and mechanical generation of the 20th century. The last of the line is George Minafer, who has neither the intellect nor the drive to succeed.

Mailer, Norman (b. 1923)　Born in New Jersey, this American novelist, essayist, and journalist grew up in Brooklyn, New York and graduated from Harvard. He served for two years in the Pacific theater in World War II and in 1946 published his finest novel, *The Naked and the Dead.* Since then he has written a number of books (both fiction and nonfiction)—including *An American Dream* (1965), *Armies of the Night* (1968), and *The Executioner's Song* (1979)—as well as nonfiction books and articles. Mailer frequently shows himself as a bitter critic of American society.

Main Street (1920), Sinclair Lewis　This American novel (a satire on the midwest) tells of Carol Kennicott, a city-bred woman married to a small-town doctor, who tries to serve as a missionary of culture to her husband's town with no success. She runs away to Washington, but grows nostalgic for the town and returns, prepared to adjust to life there. This work is a potent picture of middle-class life in America.

Malamud, Bernard (1914–1986)　This Brooklyn-born American novelist achieved his first success with *The Natural* (1952), an allegorical story of a baseball player. In later novels [i.e., *The Fixer* (1966) for which he won a Pulitzer prize], he works through his most prevalent themes: a preoccupation with the dignity of the common man and the Jewish tradition reflected in America.

Malapropism　A humorous misuse of language that results from substituting an incorrect word for one with a similar sound; named for a character, Mrs. Malaprop, in Richard Sheridan's comedy, *The Rivals.*

Malraux, André (1901–1976)　This French novelist, essayist, and propagandist is essentially a Marxist who sees human conflicts chiefly as struggles between social classes. His main characters often struggle with questions of duty, action or nonaction, and individual or group morality. His most famous works are *Man's Fate* (1933) and *Man's Hope* (1938).

Mann, Thomas (1875–1955)　Born into a middle-class commercial family in north Germany, Mann became aware of the contrasting qualities of his bourgeois father and his exotic mother, who was of Creole extraction. Much of his work deals with this dichotomy (exploring the inner self against changing European culture and psychological values). However, while he developed a contempt for middle-class values, he could never become fully Bohemian. He won fame with his first novel, *Buddenbrooks* (1900), followed by other great successes like the novella *Death in Venice* (1911), and his masterwork *The Magic Mountain* (1924). He was awarded the Nobel Prize for Literature in 1929.

Mansfield, Katherine (1888–1923)　British short-story writer who was born in New Zealand. Although she died young of tuberculosis, Mansfield produced many lyrical and delicate short stories whose simple form can be contrasted with their intense subject matter. Two of her well-known collections are *Bliss* (1920) and *The Garden Party* (1922).

Markham, Edwin (1852–1940)　Born in Oregon, the son of pioneer parents, Markham was taken to California as a child and educated there. He won fame in 1899 with his poem "The Man with the Hoe," inspired by the painting by Millet with the same title.

Marlowe, Christopher (1564–1593) A poet and dramatist, he was the first to use blank verse on the stage, thus influencing Shakespeare. His best-known plays are *Dr. Faustus* (1588) and *The Jew of Malta* (1589). He was killed in a tavern brawl at age 29. Marlowe wrote with great lyrical beauty of the Renaissance spirit. He is considered to be the greatest dramatist before Shakespeare.

Marquand, John P. (1893–1960) This American novelist's first important work (a popular and critical success) was *The Late George Apley* (1937), a satirical look at Boston society that won a Pulitzer. He also wrote the Mr. Moto series of detective stories. His books often aimed at deflating the ego of the white collar worker.

The Marriage of Figaro (1784), Beaumarchais This sequel to *The Barber of Seville* involves many of the same characters, especially Count Almaviva, who has designs on his wife's lady-in-waiting Suzanne, and Figaro, who is to marry Suzanne. After much intrigue involving confused identities, Figaro and his intended are finally married.

Marvell, Andrew (1621–1678) An English metaphysical poet who was one of the prime wits and satirists of his generation, and who strongly espoused individual freedom. Today Marvell is known for his lyric poetry, of which the famous "To His Coy Mistress" is an excellent example.

Masefield, John (1878–1967) The son of a provincial lawyer, this British poet left school at thirteen to become a merchant marine officer. In 1895 he gave up the sea and took a series of menial jobs in New York and London. His publication of *Salt-Water Ballads* (1902) made his reputation, and in 1930 he was appointed poet laureate of Great Britain, a post he held until his death. Masefield's poetry was largely narrative and realistic.

Masque A courtly form of entertainment in early 17th-century England utilizing lavish costumes and spectacular song and dance galas. Involved machinery was used to produce such special effects as moving clouds and blooming flowers. These spectacles were usually performed in praise of the King.

Masters, Edgar Lee (1869–1950) An American poet, born in Kansas, Masters was taken as a child to Lewiston, Illinois, which became the town of Spoon River in his most famous poetic work, *Spoon River Anthology* (1914), a collection of free verse epitaphs that created an enormous sensation as a literary masterwork reflecting small-town life in America.

Mather, Cotton (1663–1728) The grandson of a Puritan clergyman and the son of another, Mather saw himself as the protector of morals for New England. Today history paints him as the prototype of the intolerant Puritan, largely because of his *Memorable Providences Relating to Witchcraft and Possessions* (1693; new ed. 1956), which, although it did not support the witchcraft trials, helped to bring on waves of hysterical fear. Mather published more than 450 books and wrote many more that have never been published.

Maugham, William Somerset (1874–1965) Urbane English novelist who was a masterful storyteller and technician. Maugham's cynical view of life was often tempered by his wit and his ironic portrayals. He had written eight books before his partially autobiographical masterwork *Of Human Bondage* was published in 1915. Some of his famous novels include *The Moon and the Sixpence* (1919), based on the life of French painter Paul Gaugin, and *The Razor's Edge* (1944). Two of his more well-known short stories were made into illustrious films: "Miss Thompson" (1921, later called "Rain") and "The Letter."

Maupassant, Guy de (1850–1893) French short-story writer and novelist who produced a tremendous volume of work until he went mad in 1811 and subsequently died in an asylum. Maupassant's style was classic and simple and his technique with the short story is unsurpassed. His most frequently anthologized story is "La Parure" ("The Necklace"). It is to be noted that Maupassant's realism had a great impact on all European literature.

McCullers, Carson (1917–1967) An American Southern novelist whose unusually imaginative works reflect another aspect of man's isolation, the spiritual malaise that is the underscript to the human condition. *The Ballad of the Sad Cafe* (1943) is one of her more famous novels. Here one of her themes is that the most outlandish people can be the stimulus for love, and that love does not have to be reciprocal to benefit and change the lover. McCullers died at the age of fifty from a series of tragic misfortunes, leaving behind some of the most brilliantly felt literature to come out of the modern South, including the sensitive and lyrical *The Member of the Wedding* (1946).

Medea (431 B.C.), Euripides This Greek play concerns the revenge of the former princess of Colchis, Medea, who aided Jason in his quest for the Golden Fleece, married him, and was rejected for another woman. It is essentially a tale of love turned to hate and has strong elements of horror.

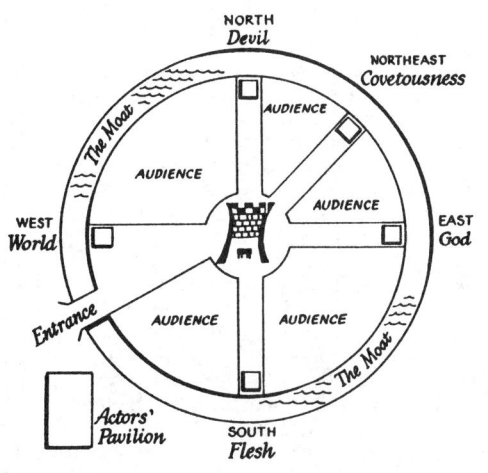

EXHIBIT 15.5
Medieval Theater in the Round

NORTH *Devil*

NORTHEAST *Covetousness*

The Moat

AUDIENCE

AUDIENCE

AUDIENCE

AUDIENCE

WEST *World*

EAST *God*

Entrance

AUDIENCE

AUDIENCE

The Moat

Actors' Pavilion

SOUTH *Flesh*

In medieval times plays were performed in theaters in the round. The audience watched from hills inside the moat.

Melodrama　Although the term literally means "a play with music," melodrama today denotes a play with stereotyped characters and highly charged emotion, usually with a romantic plot and a happy ending. It is also used to describe a thrilling play that evokes horror.

Melville, Herman (1819–1891)　Born into a wealthy merchant family in New York, this American novelist and short-story writer worked as a bank clerk, salesman, farm-hand, teacher, and seaman aboard a whaling ship. His masterwork, the novel *Moby Dick* (1851), Melville's vision of the world symbolically told, is considered by some to be the greatest American novel. Like all of his works, however, it was not recognized until some 30 years after his death. His other novels include *Typee* (1846) and *Billy Budd,* written just before his death and not published until 1924.

The Member of the Wedding (1946), Carson Mc-Cullers　The story of Frankie (F. Jasmine Addams), the tomboy girl who experiences both joy and frustration as she passes through the impossible business of growing up. She is guided and loved by the beautifully drawn character of Bernice, the black housekeeper who represents the voice of experience in Frankie's hesitant search for maturity.

Mencken, H.L. (1880–1956)　Called "The Sage of Baltimore," he was the most influential American critic of the 1920s and early 1930s with a strong admiration for European literature and a pungent distaste for the ideals of American bourgeois culture. In his essays published in *The Smart Set* and *The American Mercury* he applied his energies not only to literary criticism, but also to social, economic, and political affairs.

The Metamorphosis (1915), Franz Kafka　One of the only works that the Czech author published during his lifetime, this novella is about one Gregor Samsa, who awakens one morning to find that he has been transformed into a gigantic bug. As the story progresses, he becomes more and more of a trial to his family and progressively less human. He dies and is disposed of by a charwoman. This compelling and provocative story exists on many levels, one of them being man's inability to communicate.

Metaphor　A figure of speech implying a comparison between two different objects by saying one object *is* another, not *like* another (*See* **Simile**). Bertram is a tiger when he gets angry. His wife is a shrew. *See also,* **Mixed metaphor.**

Metaphysical poetry　Generically, this is any poetry of a philosophical or spiritual nature, although the term is more specifically applied to poets of 17th-century England, with John Donne being the master worker in this genre. Everyday speech combined with puns and paradoxes is the language of Metaphysical poetry. In romantic poems of this school, one often finds elaborate, extended metaphors (conceits) used to depict the union of lovers' souls and explanations of the tensions expressed in physical love.

Metonymy　A figure of speech in which a word that is closely associated with a term is substituted for the term itself. For instance, "We insure you from the cradle to the grave." Here, *cradle* stands for birth, and *grave* stands for death.

Metrics　The branch of poetical study that deals with patterns of rhythm and accent.

The Mill on the Floss (1860), George Eliot　The beautifully told story of Maggie and Tom Tolliver, a brother and sister whose father owns the mill on the river Floss. This novel centers around the responsibilities people take for their lives and the moral choices (Maggie's doomed love for Philip) they are forced to make.

Millay, Edna St. Vincent (1892–1950)　Born in Maine, she was educated at Barnard and Vassar. In 1912 "Renascence," written when she was only nineteen, brought her deserved fame. Upon graduation from Vassar, she went to New York, where she became a central figure in the Bohemian life of Greenwich Village in the 1920s. She was a member of the Provincetown Players, appeared in some of their productions, and wrote three verse dramas for the group. Millay published frequently throughout her life and is read and reread for her exquisite sonnets and lyrics.

Miller, Arthur (b.1915)　A New York native, this American dramatist worked in a warehouse to save money for college and attended the University of Michigan, where he began writing plays. Returning to New York, he turned to radio writing for a living until he had his first broadway success with *All My Sons* (1947). His greatest triumphs, however, came with *Death of a Salesman* (1949) and *The Crucible* (1953), a dynamic drama of the Salem witchcraft trials. In addition to drama, Miller has also written fiction and the filmscript for *The Misfits* (1961).

Miller, Henry (1891–1980)　Born in New York, he was a drifter as a youth, but later worked in his father's tailor shop, was a newspaper reporter, and opened a speakeasy in Greenwich Village. He visited Europe in 1928 and returned to Paris and London for a nine-year stay in 1930. Eventually he settled in Big Sur, California. His best-known books are *Tropic of Cancer* (1931) and *Tropic of Capricorn* (1930), both autobiographical novels that were banned in the United States for many years. Miller's highly controversial works, menages of sexual description, were meant to enforce the enlightenment and liberty of natural men.

Milne, Alan Alexander (A.A.) (1882–1956)　English author who created the classic children's book *Winnie-the-Pooh* (1926) and gave adults as well as the younger world the delightful and captivating characters of Pooh Bear, Piglet, and Eeyore. Milne's detective novel, *The Red House Mystery* (1921), is also a classic in its genre.

Milton, John (1608–1674)　The son of a scrivener and a composer of music, Milton, one of the greatest British poets, composed some of his best works from 1632–1638. These included *L'Allegro, Il Penseroso* and *Lycidas*. A universally acclaimed poet, Milton's theology, although Protestant in background, was considered highly unorthodox and his public life was the subject of much controversy. He became blind in 1652 and wrote his masterwork *Paradise Lost* (1665) despite this handicap. Other major works include *Paradise Regained* and *Samson Agonistes* (both published in 1671).

Minstrel　In the Middle Ages, a wandering musician or poet.

Miracle play   A type of drama, common in Medieval England, that depicts a miracle performed by a saint, or an incident in the saint's life. These plays usually are not based strictly on scriptural accounts.

The Misanthrope (1666), Molière   This French comedy of manners is unusual in that it does not have the happy ending characteristic of most of Molière's comedies. It concerns Alceste, an incorruptible and unreasonable hero, and his love for the bewitching but self-centered coquette Célinère. This play is essentially a comedy of the antisocial man, written with wit and sparkling with dialogue.

Mixed metaphor   A figure of speech that combines two or more inconsistent or incongruous metaphors, as in Shakespeare's "to take arms against a sea of troubles."

Moby Dick (1851), Herman Melville   This American novel, called the attempt to search the unsearchable ways of God, tells the story of Captain Ahab, driven to find and destroy the great white whale Moby Dick, to whom he lost his leg. Told by Ishmael, a young sailor, the only survivor of the wreck of Ahab's ship, the voyage is clearly symbolic, as is the whale.

Mock epic   A long poem, intended to be humorous, that treats a trivial subject in the lofty and exalted style of the epic poem. The mock epic imitates and burlesques the traditions of the true epic. *See* Pope's *The Rape of the Lock.*

Molière (Jean-Baptiste Poquelin) (1623–1673)   In his youth, Molière spent a dozen years touring the French provinces with an acting troupe. He established himself as an actor and director in Paris in 1658, his company eventually becoming the Comédie Française. He was often summoned to the court for which he wrote farces, comedies, and ballets on short notice. Molière is best known for his great comic character portrayals in which he ridicules a vice by caricaturing a person who is the embodiment of the vice. He wrote about 30 comedies of which the best known are *The Misanthrope* (1666) and *The Middle-Class Gentleman* (1670).

Molnár, Ferenc (1878–1952)   A Hungarian playwright and novelist best known for his intriguing *Liliom,* a masterpiece of psychological fantasy. Molnár is most highly praised for his appealing and astute characterizations and his beautiful dialogue.

Monologue   A discourse either oral or written by one speaker only; also called a soliloquy. Many of the poems of Robert Browning, such as "My Last Duchess," are dramatic monologues. Hamlet's speech beginning "To be, or not to be" is a famous soliloquy.

Montaigne, Michel (1533–1592)   Considered France's foremost essayist and in many senses the father of the modern essay. His early works are concerned with death and pain, leading to a period of skepticism, and finally an acceptance of life as the reward man receives when he discovers his own nature. His *Essays* were published in 1580 and 1588.

The Moonstone (1896), Wilkie Collins   Considered the first full-length detective novel in English and among the best of its genre. A work that drew high praise from T.S. Eliot.

Moore, Marianne (1887–1972)   A Missouri native who was educated at Bryn Mawr and taught for some years at the Carlisle Indian School in Pennsylvania. From 1918 on this American poet lived in New York City, first in Greenwich Village and then in Brooklyn. She published many volumes of verse in which she showed herself to be a descendant of the imagists by her cleverly designed poems written in an intellectual and witty style.

Morality play   A type of drama, popular in Medieval England, characterized by a pronounced use of allegory to point up a moral teaching. Abstractions like Conscience, Death, the Seven Sins, and so on, appear as speaking persons, who are usually involved in a struggle for a human soul. *Everyman* is the best-known medieval morality play.

Moravia, Alberto (b.1907)   Italian novelist who reflects the conflict between the creative and the sensual, and whose undervoice expresses the despair and ennui of modern man. Some of his more famous translated novels are *The Woman of Rome* (1949), *Two Women* (1958), and *The Empty Canvas* (1961).

Mother Courage and Her Children (1939), Bertolt Brecht   This German chronicle of the Thirty Years' War tells of a tough old canteen woman who trails after the mercenary armies in Sweden, Poland, and Germany. All three of her children are killed but Mother Courage clings materialistically to her livelihood because it is all that she knows.

Motif   The recurrence of a theme, word pattern, or character in a literary work. This term may also be applied to a major theme that runs through a number of different works. For instance, the isolation of modern man is a frequent motif in contemporary literature.

Mourning Becomes Electra (1931), Eugene O'Neill   Often considered this playwright's most important work, this trilogy is based on the Agamemnon myth as found in *Oresteia* by Aeschylus; however, the setting is a small American town at the end of the Civil War. This drama is an attempt to recast the Greek tragedy into the terms of modern psychology. Lavinia, the central character, comes to destruction basically through the bad blood bequeathed her by her father, but this hereditary taint operates through the medium of psychological obsessions and fixations which make her unfit for normal life.

Muses   The nine muses of Greek poetry were Clio (history), Calliope (epic poetry), Erato (love poetry), Euterpe (lyric poetry), Melpomene (tragedy), Polyhymnia (songs to the gods), Terpsichore (dance), Thalia (comedy), and Urania (astronomy). Ancient poets would appeal to a particular muse for assistance with their creativity.

My Antonia (1918), Willa Cather   This American novel concerns Antonia Shimerda, daughter of Bohemian immigrants in the Nebraska prairieland who assumes the burden of the farm work after her father commits suicide. Later the family moves to town and Antonia becomes a hired girl. She has an illegitimate child and returns to the country where she eventually marries and has more children.

The Mysterious Stranger (1916), Mark Twain   The author's most tenacious attempt to pluck out the heart of the mystery of this fiendish world. Twain withheld the novel from publication because he believed it to be too audacious—it was published the

LITERATURE

year after his death. The novel tells of the visits of an angel to three boys in an Austrian village in 1590. To begin with the boys are steeped in medieval piety and ignorance; at the end they have had revelations about the meanness of mankind and the ugliness of the world that destroy their innocent, happy illusions.

Mystery play A type of medieval play based on Biblical stories, such as the sacrifice of Isaac, the death of Abel, the birth of Christ, and the trial and crucifixion of Jesus. These plays were the most important form of drama in the Middle Ages and continued to be popular into the Renaissance. They were most often performed in cycles associated with great cathedral towns: York, Chester, and Coventry.

Mysticism The theory that some forms of knowledge, such as the knowledge of God, can be received only by means outside the human senses. For example, the works of William Blake, the 19th-century poet and artist, reflect an intense mysticism.

Myth Stories that come anonymously from the remote past; myths stir the subconscious in powerful ways because such folklore and folk beliefs are based on a kind of primitive truth that once explained inexplicable psychological and scientific truths to distant ancestors. The myth of Prometheus attempts to explain how man received fire and the ability to use it; the myth of Pandora's box explains the cause of disorder in the world.

N **Nabokov, Vladimir** (1899–1977) Born in Russia, he studied at Cambridge in England and became a United States citizen in 1945. He then taught at Harvard, Wellesley, and Cornell until the great success of his novel *Lolita* (1955) made it possible for him to stop teaching. Called an anti-novelist by Jean-Paul Sartre, he used parody in all his works and was particularly interested in creating puzzles for his readers. Other novels include *Pale Fire* (1962) and *Ada, or Ardor* (1969).

The Naked and the Dead (1946), Norman Mailer This American work is generally considered the best American novel about World War II. Like the best novels of World War I, it follows a typical squad of men, of diverse character and backgrounds, into a combat situation and analyzes their individual reactions to the experience. The general themes are that war is a meaningless sacrifice, most officers are incompetent, and combat is a senseless waste of effort.

Narrative verse Poetry that tells a story as in *The Canterbury Tales*. In the contemporary world the novel has functioned as usurper of the poetic narrative, and poets seem reluctant to tell tales that can be treated, possibly more expertly, in prose.

Native Son (1940), Richard Wright This American novel concerns Bigger Thomas, a product of the Chicago ghetto who gets a job as a chauffeur for the wealthy Dalton family and accidentally kills the family's young daughter. He is executed for the murder, and here Wright is elegant and incisive about the role society played in the crime.

Naturalism A type of realistic fiction that developed in France, America, and England in the late 19th and early 20th centuries. It presupposes that human beings are like puppets, controlled completely by external and internal forces. Naturalism differs from Realism in that characters in the latter have a measure of free will.

Nemerov, Howard (1920–1991) Chancellor of the Academy of American Poets beginning 1976 and poet laureate of the United States for two terms, 1988–1990, Nemerov also won the Theodore Roethke Award (1968), National Book Award (1978), Pulitzer Prize (1979), Bollingen Prize (1981), and National Medal of the Arts (1987). His works, which spanned six decades, include: novels, *The Melodramatists* (1949), *The Homecoming Game* (1957); poetry, *Mirrors and Windows* (1958), *Sentences* (1980), *Inside the Onion* (1984); and essays, *Figures of Thought* (1978). Nemerov was a visiting lecturer at several American colleges, as well as professor of English at Brandeis University (1966–1969).

Neoclassicism A term used to describe a set of literary characteristics that flourished in the age between the Restoration (beginning in 1660) and the publication of Wordsworth's *Lyrical Ballads* (1798), which signaled the triumph of Romanticism in English literature. Neoclassical literature is characterized by a kind of elegance, wit, common sense, reason, and a careful control of emotions. Dryden and Pope are two renowned neoclassicists.

New Criticism, The A school of literary criticism espoused by the critics John Crowe Ransom, Allen Tate, and Robert Penn Warren, the name comes from Ransom's book *The New Criticism* (1941). This type of literary criticism emphasizes a close analysis of the text of the work, which is considered complete in itself and independent of other works, with no historical and biographical contexts.

New novel This term refers to a concept of the novel that rejects such classic ingredients as plot structure and character delineation. The new novel was born from the fires of writers like Joyce and Faulkner who expressed visions of a disorderly world peopled by characters who had lost their identity.

1984 (1949), George Orwell Much of the power of this novel of a "future" society stems from its use of understatement as well as from its tongue-in-cheek irony. "Big Brother" watches over a nightmare society whose thoughts, recreation, and activities are totally controlled by a small party of the elite.

No Exit (1944), Jean-Paul Sartre This one-act French existential play has very few characters. Garcin, a Latin-American revolutionist, is shown into a closed room and realizes he is dead and has gone to Hell. He is presently joined by two women, Estelle and Ines, who, like him, tortured other people while they were alive. The three are thus condemned to spend eternity together, each loathing the other.

Nonfiction novel *See In Cold Blood*.

Norris, Frank (1870–1902) A dedicated admirer of French novelist Emile Zola, Norris became the foremost exponent of Naturalism in American letters. His best-known novel is *The Octopus* (1901), which concerns the struggle between wheat farmers and the railroad. Another work, *McTeague* (1891), is a novel about the laboring class.

Novella A term frequently used to denote the early tales or short stories of French and Italian writers; a short novel.

Oates, Joyce Carol (b. 1938) One of the most highly acclaimed authors of the latter part of the 20th century, Oates writes novels inhabited by realistic, although often bizarre, characters, so frustrated by modern culture that their suppressed energies frequently erupt in violence. She dissects her characters psychoanalytically and depicts them against desolate and destructive backgrounds. Her novel *Them* won the National Book Award in 1969, but some of her earlier works [*With Shuddering Fall* (1964), A Garden of Earthly Delights (1967), and *Expensive People* (1968)] transcend the later books in their lyrical qualities.

Objective correlative A literary term coined by T.S. Eliot to denote the technique of indirectly and unemotionally eliciting a desired emotional response from the reader through a pattern of objects, symbols, or events. The response is suggested rather than directly prescribed.

O'Casey, Sean (1880–1964) Born in Dublin into a poor family, this Irish playwright, prominent in the Irish rebellions for independence, worked at back-breaking manual labor until he was over 40. His first play to be accepted by the Abbey Theater was *The Shadow of a Gunman* (1923), followed by his greatest play, *Juno and the Paycock* (1924), a grim, satiric comedy. A riot at one of his later plays angered him and he left Ireland never to return, battling the established society from a distance.

Occasional verse Poetry written for a special occasion, usually to honor royalty or to commemorate the death of a national hero.

O'Connor, Flannery (1925–1964) This brilliant Southern American short-story writer and novelist was deeply concerned with the spiritual battle between good and evil. She has been called a "theological" writer, but it is not easy to tell if she used theology for fictional purposes or fiction for theological purposes. O'Connor frequently poses the question (found in one of her collections of short stories, *A Good Man Is Hard To Find*): "Is it the Devil who has many protean forms...? Or is it perhaps even Christ the tiger...?" O'Connor died tragically of lupus at the age of thirty-nine. *Wise Blood* (1952) and *The Violent Bear It Away*, (1960) are her two intense, moving novels.

Octameter A line of poetry containing eight feet.
>A mán in clóthes so óld and thín and
>worn and lápsed in stýle and táste.

Octave A poetic stanza with eight lines; now primarily used to denote the first eight-line division of an Italian sonnet.

Ode A sustained lyric poem with a noble theme and intellectual tone. There are three principal variations: the regular ode, or Pindaric Ode; the irregular ode, or Cowleyan Ode; and the Horatian Ode.

Odets, Clifford (1906–1963) This Philadelphia native began as an actor and in 1930 was one of the organizers of the Group Theater. He won a play contest with *Waiting for Lefty* (1934) and the following year that play and the earlier *Awake and Sing* were both produced on Broadway, establishing him as a gifted social-protest dramatist. He worked for some years in Hollywood and in later life divided his time between the East and West Coasts, writing plays and film scripts.

The Odyssey, Homer This epic deals with the wanderings of the Greek hero Odysseus (Ulysses) after the Trojan War. It was he who had ended the war with his use of the so-called Trojan Horse. In his wanderings he encounters such figures as the Cyclops and the enchantress Circe and arrives home in time to prevent his wife's remarriage.

Oedipus the King, Sophocles This tragedy dates from the middle of the 5th century B.C. and has generally been judged the finest Greek drama. It concerns the king of Thebes, upon whose city a plague has fallen, because the killer of the former king, Laius, is living in the city. Oedipus discovers that it is he who has killed the king and that he has married his own mother. The play has drawn renewed interest in this century because of the Oedipus-complex theory developed by Sigmund Freud.

Of Human Bondage (1915) Somerset Maugham The dominant theme of this moving novel lies in the protagonist's (Philip's) effort to discover his own nature through the many passions that torment him and his resentment of a world that mocks him. In the end he is freed by his choice to live in happy obscurity rather than wage a frantic battle for fame.

O'Hara, John (1905–1970) Born in Pottsville, Pennsylvania, which appears in his novels as Gibbsville, O'Hara worked as a newspaperman and was for a time the football editor of *Time* magazine. In 1934 he turned to screen writing and worked for four different studios in Hollywood. His best-known works are the many short stories he composed and the novels *Appointment in Samarra* (1934), *Butterfield 8* (1935), and *Ten North Frederick* (1955). Although he was a brilliant craftsman in terms of characterization and plot, O'Hara's novels miss if one seeks depth and soul.

O. Henry (William Sidney Porter) (1862–1910) This American short-story writer is best described as the originator of the trick ending, a device he used to the delight of his readers. Born in North Carolina, he went to Texas, where he worked for a bank and then became a newspaper writer. He was charged with embezzlement, fled the country, returned, and spent three years in an Ohio prison. On his release he went to New York (1902), where he died of alcoholism. "The Gift of the Magi" is his most famous short story.

Oliver Twist (1838), Charles Dickens This English novel deals realistically with the criminal class in its depiction of an orphan boy who is led into crime and then saved from that life. Also, the character of the cruel Fagin remains as a literary immortal. This work is seen as the author's first fictional attack on social injustices and a plea for a new order of society.

Omeros (1990), Derek Walcott Reflecting West Indian culture, this poetic literary work uses classics (character names from Homer's *The Iliad* and *The Odyssey*), folklore, history, and native language in a contemporary tone to capture "the whole experience of the people of the Caribbean."

One Day in the Life of Ivan Denisovich (1962), Alexander Solzhenitsyn This Russian novel, in the first person, relates the story of one day in the life of a man held in a Soviet prison camp in the tenth year of his sentence. The concentration is on the details of the present—food, keeping warm, work, sick call—the elements of survival. Critics have suggested that Solzhenitsyn intended to draw an analogy between life in the camps and life outside the camps, both featuring material and spiritual squalor.

O'Neill, Eugene (1888–1953)   The son of a famous actor, O'Neill is considered to be one of the greatest and most important American playwrights. His works are deeply poetic and exemplify the mind and feelings of a tragic artist. Early in his career, he became associated with the Provincetown Players, a group that went to New York and produced ten of his plays. He won the Nobel Prize for Literature in 1936. *The Emperor Jones* (1921), *The Hairy Ape* (1922), *Desire Under the Elms* (1924), *Ah! Wilderness* (1932), and *The Iceman Cometh* (1946) are among his plays.

Onomatopoeia   A word whose sound is descriptive of its sense or meaning. Onomatopoeic words add a vivid quality to poetry: hiss, splash, murmur.

Oresteia, Aeschylus   Written in 458 B.C., this is the only surviving trilogy in Greek drama and deals with the eventual lifting of the curse on the house of Atreus. In the first play, *Agamemnon,* the king of Argos and his slave-concubine Cassandra are killed by his wife Clytemnestra. The second play, *The Libation-Bearers,* tells of the death of Clytemnestra at the hands of her son Orestes, abetted by his sister Electra. In the third play, *Eumenides,* Orestes goes to Athens, where, with the aid of the goddess Athena, he is absolved of the murder of his mother.

Orwell, George (Eric Blair) (1903–1950)   Born in India, this British novelist and short-story writer was sent to school in England and then went out to Burma to serve in the British security police. He then went to Paris and held a series of odd jobs there and in England and fought in the Spanish civil war. All of Orwell's works are concerned with the struggle for human freedom. His best novels are *Animal Farm* (1946) and *1984* (1949).

Osborne, John (b.1929)   Leaving school at 16, this English playwright became an actor, and eventually began to write plays on his own. The great success of his *Look Back in Anger* (1956) generated the concept of "The Angry Young Man" in the modern world. Among his other well-known works are *The Entertainer* (1957) and *Epitaph for George Dillon* (1958), in both of which Osborne reflects man's growing anger and frustration at having to live in a shallow world of false values.

Othello (1604), William Shakespeare   This English tragedy is more closely plotted than most of Shakespeare's great dramas. Desdemona, the daughter of a Venetian senator, is married to the Moorish general Othello. Iago, jealous at having been bypassed for a promotion, resolves to poison Othello's peace by making him suspect his wife's fidelity. He succeeds in this and consequently Othello kills Desdemona. However, learning at last that she had been faithful, the devastated Othello commits suicide.

Other Voices, Other Rooms (1948), Truman Capote   This beautiful lyric novel is the story of a boy's search for his father (for someone to love him), the incredible misfortune of finding him, and his subsequent initiation into an adult world of evil and deformity.

Ottava rima   A poetic stanza with eight iambic pentameter lines rhyming *abababcc*. Supposedly invented by Boccaccio, it was used widely by Milton, Keats, and Byron.

Our Town (1938), Thornton Wilder   This play by a master storyteller is a tribute to American life—a microcosm of life and death and love and marriage in a "typical" New England village. Wilder uses the device of "Stage Manager" as a narrator who speaks directly to the audience in order to break down the invisible wall between stage and audience so that theatergoers feel a sense of participation in the drama. This strategy was also used successfully by Pirandello in *Six Characters in Search of an Author,* and is found in much of Brecht.

Ovid (43–18 B.C.)   Ovid began his career as a highly successful poet, known for his insights into human nature and his wit and humor, but ended it in disgrace and in exile at the command of the emperor. His best known works are *Metamorphoses,* the retellings of virtually all the famous Greek myths, and *The Art of Love.*

Oxymoron   A figure of speech that employs two opposing terms in a paradox, often to strengthen a point or create an emotion, as in

> Why then, O brawling love! O loving
> hate!
> O any thing of nothing first create.
> O heavy lightness! serious vanity!
> > Shakespeare

Oxymorons can also be found in regular conversation: "His absence is a presence."

Paine, Thomas (1737–1809)   Born in England, this American essayist and pamphleteer was trained to be a corsetmaker, served in the British navy in the Seven Years War, and worked as a tax-collector, teacher, and preacher. In 1774 he met Benjamin Franklin, who urged him to emigrate to America, which he did. In 1776 he wrote *Common Sense* and from 1776–1783 *The Crisis,* with its famous opening line, "These are the times that try men's souls." A supporter of the French revolution, Paine was declared an honorary French citizen, but was imprisoned for a time by the revolutionaries. He returned to America in 1802, where he was not warmly received.

Palindrome   A word or sentence that reads the same from left to right or right to left. "Madam, I'm Adam;" "Able was I ere I saw Elba."

Pamela (*Virtue Rewarded*) (1742), Samuel Richardson   This, the first English novel, was more or less an accident. Richardson, a middle-aged printer, had planned a book of model letters addressed to people in humble walks of life. In order to give some unity to the letters, he conceived the idea of connecting them with a story. And so *Pamela* was born. To his astonishment, it took the London public by storm, and so the epistolary form of novel writing remained thereafter one of the most popular. Pamela is a "good" girl, in the service of a "bad" man—one with dishonorable intentions. Happily, she falls in love with him and he with her, her virtue is preserved, and they marry. Richardson was something of a psychologist in dealing with his heroine, depicting her inner struggles with far more insight than many of his successors showed.

Panegyric   A written or oral composition that highly praises a person or place. In Greek literature panegyrics were most often for the dead; in Roman literature, for the living.

Parable   A story told to illustrate a moral truth or lesson. The Bible has the best-known parables: e.g., the sower, the prodigal son, the Good Samaritan.

Paradise Lost (1662), John Milton   The greatest epic poem in English has as its subject matter the first disobedience of Man and his subsequent loss of paradise. Its purpose is to "justify the ways of God to men." The entire physical universe is the background for the events of this epic, as the reader is taken to heaven, to hell, to the depths of chaos, and finally to the Garden of Eden.

Paradox   A statement that appears to be absurd or self-contradictory but is true on a higher level; often used for special emphasis. "He who would save his life must lose it."

Parody   A humorous literary work that ridicules a serious work by imitating and exaggerating its style. In media, a parody is a "take-off" on a particular person, event, etc.

Pasternak, Boris (1890–1960)   The son of a Jewish art professor and portraitist and a concert pianist, this Russian author originally thought of a career in music, but turned instead to poetry and fiction. Under the Stalinist regime, he earned his living principally as a translator and, when he submitted his novel *Doctor Zhivago* to the censors, it was rejected. Sent to the West, it was published to great acclaim in 1957. Two years later, Pasternak won the Nobel Prize for Literature, but was forced to reject it.

Pastoral   A poem about shepherds and rural life, derived from ancient Greek poetry. The pastoral sometimes takes the form of a lament for a dead friend, a dialogue between two shepherds, or a monologue. The word also can describe poetry marked by nostalgia for lost innocence.

Pastoral elegy   A serious poem written in an elevated, formal style and employing conventional pastoral imagery to commemorate the death of a friend, usually a poet. For example, Shelley's *Adonais* (written on the death of Keats).

Pathos   The literary quality that causes the reader (or the theatergoer) to experience feelings of pity and sympathy. For instance, in *Wuthering Heights,* the death of Cathy and Heathcliffe's intense grief. (The character that inspires pathos is usually controlled by his suffering, while the tragic hero eventually resolves and overcomes his pain with nobility.)

Penny dreadful   Particularly in Victorian England, a short mystery or novel, printed inexpensively on cheap paper and having a large distribution.

Pentameter   A line of poetry containing five metrical feet.

Pepys, Samuel (1633–1703)   A graduate of Cambridge and born the son of a tailor, this English diarist became an important naval official and served in the House of Commons. On his death he gave his books to Cambridge and more than a century later a clergyman discovered a diary of his in shorthand, which was subsequently published in 1825. It is an account of the years 1660 to 1669, the period of the Restoration, the great fire, and the great plague.

Periphrasis   A method of stating an idea in an indirect, excessively wordy manner. Literally translated, it means "roundabout speaking." For example, "The answer is in the negative" is a periphrasis for the word "no." The phrase "the year's penultimate month" is a periphrasis for "November."

Persona   In fiction, the term is used to refer to the person through whom the narrative is told. The persona may narrate the story in the first person, but this is not always the case. In all cases the person is a "mask" through which the author speaks.

Personal essay   A type of informal, autobiographical essay that is self-revealing and is usually written in a conversational, often humorous style.

Personification   A figure of speech that gives human forms and characteristics to abstractions, objects, animals, etc. For example, John Keats, in his "Ode on a Grecian Urn," personifies the urn as an "unravished bride."

Petrarch, Francis (1304–1374)   Described as the "Father of the Renaissance" or "the first modern man," Petrarch is remembered today chiefly for the sonnet form that bears his name, and for his love for Laura, the lady of so many of these poems, to whom he became "enslaved through devotion."

Phaedra (1677), Jean Racine   This is a 17th-century French dramatization of the classic Greek legend about Phaedra, the daughter of the king of Crete who married Theseus, killer of the Minotaur, and fell in love with her stepson Hippolytus. After much court intrigue, Hippolytus is banished, then slain by a monster, and Phaedra commits suicide.

Phenomenology   A philosophical system based on the premise that objects have a reality and a meaning only in the consciousness of the person perceiving them. Therefore, to analyze a work of art accurately, the phenomenologist critic must carefully exclude all prejudgments or inferences that come from outside his own intuition. In other words, a work of art exists only as it appears in the mind of the viewer or reader.

Picaresque novel   A type of novel whose structure is a loosely strung together series of incidents concerning a hero who is usually a clever rascal of little means but of endless wiles. For instance, Daniel Defoe's *Moll Flanders* and Mark Twain's *Huckleberry Finn.*

The Picture of Dorian Gray (1891), Oscar Wilde   An English novel of extraordinary wit that hints just enough at mysterious wickedness to have ensured its enthralling the public. Dorian Gray, the decadent bon vivant, lives out his life in the beauty and perfection of his youth, while the famous portrait of him bears the ravages of his decadence.

Pilgrim's Progress, John Bunyan   This simple allegory, published in two parts, the first in 1678, the second in 1684, concerns the hero Christian, who flees the City of Destruction to find the City of God. On his way he meets Faithful, Ignorance, Lord Hate-Good, and Mr. Greatheart. The second part follows Christian's wife Christiana and their four sons as they set out with their neighbor Mercy for the same destination, and how Mr. Greatheart helps bring them there.

Pinter, Harold (b.1930) The son of a Jewish tailor, this British playwright left school at 16 to train for the stage at the Royal Academy of Dramatic Arts, after which he acted with repertory companies. At age 26 he began writing plays, whose everyday settings are infused with an ambience of terror, mystery, and the grotesque. His most successful plays have been *The Caretaker* (1960), *The Birthday Party* (1957), and *The Homecoming* (1965).

Pirandello, Luigi (1867–1936) The Italian dramatist began his career as a Sicilian folklorist and short-story writer, but during the period of World War I he began to write dramas where he portrayed life as consisting merely of a succession of illusions that, put together, constitute what the ordinary person sees as reality. He won the Nobel Prize for Literature in 1934 and his best-known works are *It Is So! (If You Think So)* (1916) and *Six Characters in Search of an Author* (1921).

The Plague (1947) Albert Camus This French political and social allegory is laid in the Algerian seaport of Oran. A physician, Bernard Rieux, recognizes the epidemic that hits the city as bubonic plague. The city, isolated for eight months by the plague, becomes a sort of microcosm of modern society, and the plague is a symbol of the evils that men must band together to fight.

Plath, Sylvia (1932–1963) Plath's suicide at an early age brought great attention to her poetry and her novel *The Bell Jar* (1963). Howard Moss wrote of her as "someone who had faced horror and made something of it as well as someone who had been destroyed by it." *Ariel* is her most famous volume of poetry.

Platonism A term that denotes the idealistic philosophical doctrines of Plato, whose ideas have influenced many English poets.

Poe, Edgar Allan (1809–1849) This American poet, critic, and short-story writer is acknowledged today as one of the great men in American letters. Poe's life and work were both overshadowed by his use of alcohol; even very mild drinking interfered with his writing. His frequently macabre themes, his sense of the violent and quiet horror present in the dark night of the soul pervade his short stories and poetry to give his works an all-encompassing feeling of doom. Among his best-known short stories are "The Murders in the Rue Morgue," "The Fall of the House of Usher," and "The Telltale Heart." "The Raven" and "Annabelle Lee" are two of his most riveting and intense poems.

Poetic justice In a work of fiction (or in real life), an occurrence in which virtue is rewarded and/or vice is punished in an unusual and unexpected way. In almost any Victorian novel (such as those of Dickens) there is a happy ending achieved by poetic justice: e.g., in *Oliver Twist* when the villainous Sikes accidentally hangs himself while trying to escape.

Poetic license Primarily a practice, used by poets, of violating a rule of pronunciation, rhyme, spelling, or normal word order to achieve a desired metrical pattern. This term has also been extended to incorporate any liberty a writer might wish to take in his work.

Poet laureate Originally an English appointment of a poet by the monarch, to serve for life and write verse for state occasions. In 1986, the United States began the appointment of a poet laureate (Robert Penn Warren), to serve on a yearly basis, and help the Library of Congress acquire important works of poetry. (*See* **Exhibit 15.8**, page 15-53.) Ted Hughes is the present poet laureate of Great Britain. *See* **Exhibit 15.3**, page 15-15.

Point of view A phrase used to denote the vantage point from which an author presents the action in a work of fiction. In the *first person* point of view, the author uses the pronoun *I*, and is part of the story. In the *third person* point of view, the author anonymously chronicles the actions and dialogue of his characters. In the *omniscient point of view*, the author enters the minds of his characters, while taking a third person point of view.

Poor Richard's Almanac, Benjamin Franklin Issued annually from 1732–1757, this almanac became the best-known and most-quoted publication in the colonies. Like most periodicals of the sort, it contained weather predictions and horoscopes, but was unusual in presenting a fictional mouthpiece, "Poor Richard" Saunders, who offered such aphorisms as "God helps them that help themselves."

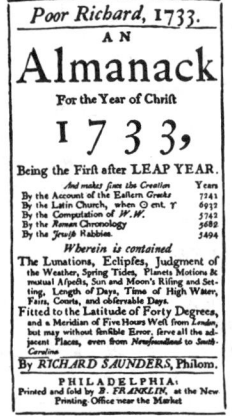 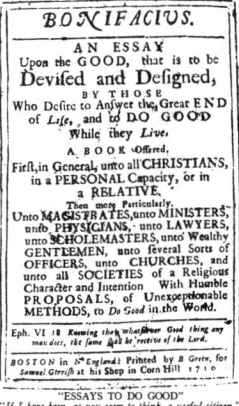

Pages from *Poor Richard's Almanac*, published by Benjamin Franklin.

Pope, Alexander (1688–1744) Because he came from a Roman Catholic family, this English poet could not attend a university and so was privately educated. A serious illness in his childhood left him an invalid for the rest of his life: He never grew taller than four and a half feet and was humpbacked, and only rarely was free from some ailment. He had his first great success with *Essay on Criticism* in 1711. The following year he had even greater success with his mock heroic epic *The Rape of the Lock*. His last major work was the philosophical poem *Essay on Man* (1732–34).

Pornography Greek *porne* (prostitute) and *graphos* (writing). This type of writing, disregarded by some critics, is often referred to as the negation of literature. "Hard-core porn" robs characters of all dimension but the sexual, taking no account of man's complexities. [It is to be remembered that distinctions must be made between erotic passages in literature (i.e., in Joyce's *Ulysses,* banned for many years), often used to enhance and give lyric qualities to a work, and simple pornographic trash, written to titillate the emotions and stimulate sexual fantasies.]

Porter, Katherine Anne (1894–1980)   Born in Texas, she was educated in various convent schools and published her first story in 1922. This American Southern writer is considered one of the most distinguished masters of the short-story form. *Pale Horse, Pale Rider* (a novella, 1939) and *Ship of Fools* (a novel, 1962) are her best-known works. The latter is a long novel that recreates the elements of several societies in a world on the edge of war.

Portmanteau words   A phrase coined by Lewis Carroll to describe words made up of two existing words. The new word carries shades of both previous meanings. *Smog* is a combination of the words smoke and fog. In the poem "Jabberwocky," Carroll uses *slithy* to mean a combination of lithe and slimy. He also uses *mimsy* to denote both flimsy and miserable.

Portrait of a Lady (1881) Henry James   James's finest accomplishment and considered to be a masterpiece of the novel form, this is the story of Isabel Archer, whom the author has created as a bright, eager young American with all the naive expectations in what James saw as our national character.

Potboiler   An inferior literary work written solely in order to provide the author with money.

Pound, Ezra (1885–1972)   One of the most influential poets and controversial figures of the 20th century, Pound published an anthology titled *Des imagistes* which was instrumental in starting the imagist movement in Britain and the United States. He lived in Paris as an expatriate and became a great admirer of the Italian dictator Mussolini, even broadcasting Fascist propaganda tirades from Italy. At the end of the war, he was charged with treason, but adjudged insane. His best-known work is the *Pisan Cantos* (1948), an attempt to recreate civilization's history through myriad threads of myth, Eastern poetry, ballads, jargon, etc.

Précis   A brief summary of a work.

Preface   A brief introductory statement or essay at the beginning of a book that allows the author to introduce the work to the reader, to make acknowledgments, and to acquaint the reader with any special information needed to understand the purpose of the book.

Prelude   A brief introductory poem placed before a lengthy poem, or a lengthy section of a poem.

Pride and Prejudice (1803), Jane Austen   The best-known work of this fascinating and gifted English master. The delightful workings of the Bennet girls, their suitors, and their families have been praised by generations of readers.

Prologue   An introductory speech that precedes plays to give the audience pertinent facts necessary for understanding the characters and action. Prologues are monologues delivered by an actor. The expository speeches of the Stage Manager in Thornton Wilder's play *Our Town* are like prologues except that they occur throughout the play, unlike choruses in Greek dramas.

Prometheus Bound, Aeschylus   Probably written about 478 B.C., this Greek tragedy recounts the sufferings of the hero who stole fire from the gods to give to mankind. Prometheus, chained to a rock throughout the play, paints a picture of Zeus, ruler of the gods, as a harsh and unjust tyrant.

Prose poem   The elements (figures of speech) of poetry, written in prose form.

Prosody   A word applied to the theory and principles of writing poetry and that especially pertains to forms of rhythmic, accented, and stanzaic patterns.

Protagonist   The leading character, usually the hero or heroine, in a work. *See* **Antagonist**.

Proust, Marcel (1871–1922)   One of the great literary figures of the modern age, as a young man this French novelist was very active in society, but after 1905 he lived mainly in a room lined with cork, and devoted himself to work on his 16-volume cyclic novel *The Remembrance of Things Past* (1913–22). This work (considered an extended interior monologue) is highly personal and psychological, and delves deeply into the connection between external and internal realities.

Proverb   A brief statement of an important truth relevant to practical daily living. A proverb is usually an ancient statement, often carried down through oral tradition.

Pun   A play on words that employs the similarity of sounds between words of different meanings in a clever and unexpected way. For example, this quote of Thomas Hood's: "They went and told the sexton and the sexton tolled the bell."

Pure poetry   A term applied to a poem that is written only for the beauty of its sound and imagery. It does not teach a moral truth or have conceptualized thoughts. Edgar Allen Poe's poem "Annabel Lee" is pure poetry; this term was first used, in fact, by Baudelaire in an essay on Poe's poetry.

Pushkin, Alexander (1799–1837)   Considered the greatest Russian poet, he came from a noted family, one of his ancestors having been the black general of Czar Peter I. His best-known works include the drama *Boris Gudonov* (1831), the basis for the opera, and *Eugene Onegin* (1831), a novel written in verse, filled with clever and insightful pictures of 19th-century society in Russia. He also wrote romances, historical poems, and folk tales and the famous short story, "The Queen of Spades" (1834).

Pygmalion (1912), George Bernard Shaw   This English comedy concerns Professor Henry Higgins, a linguist and philologist, who determines to take a young girl from the streets and, by teaching her upper-class speech, pass her off as a lady. He succeeds, but complications arise when she falls in love with him, a feeling he does not initially reciprocate. Obviously, the play is a satire on the English class system.

EXHIBIT 15.6
Pulitzer Prizes

Fiction

1918	*His Family*, Ernest Poole
1919	*The Magnificent Ambersons*, Booth Tarkington
1921	*The Age of Innocence*, Edith Wharton
1922	*Alice Adams*, Booth Tarkington
1923	*One of Ours*, Willa Cather
1924	*The Able McLaughlins*, Margaret Wilson
1925	*So Big*, Edna Ferber
1926	*Arrowsmith*, Sinclair Lewis
1927	*Early Autumn*, Louis Bromfield
1928	*The Bridge of San Luis Rey*, Thornton Wilder
1929	*Scarlet Sister Mary*, Julia Peterkin
1930	*Laughing Boy*, Oliver La Farge
1931	*Years of Grace*, Margaret Ayer Barnes
1932	*The Good Earth*, Pearl S. Buck
1933	*The Store*, T.S. Stribling
1934	*Lamb in His Bosom*, Caroline Miller
1935	*Now in November*, Josephine Winslow Johnson
1936	*Honey in the Horn*, Harold L. Davis
1937	*Gone With the Wind*, Margaret Mitchell
1938	*The Late George Apley*, John Phillips Marquand
1939	*The Yearling*, Marjorie Kinnan Rawlings
1940	*The Grapes of Wrath*, John Steinbeck
1942	*In This Our Life*, Ellen Glasgow
1943	*Dragon's Teeth*, Upton Sinclair
1944	*Journey in the Dark*, Martin Flavin
1945	*A Bell for Adano*, John Hersey
1947	*All the Kings Men*, Robert Penn Warren
1948	*Tales of the South Pacific*, James A. Michener
1949	*Guard of Honor*, James Gould Cozzens
1950	*The Way West*, A.B. Guthrie, Jr.
1951	*The Town*, Conrad Richter
1952	*The Caine Mutiny*, Herman Wouk
1953	*The Old Man and the Sea*, Ernest Hemingway
1955	*A Fable*, William Faulkner
1956	*Andersonville*, MacKinlay Kantor
1958	*A Death in the Family*, James Agee
1959	*The Travels of Jaimie McPheeters*, Robert Lewis Taylor
1960	*Advise and Consent*, Allen Drury
1961	*To Kill a Mockingbird*, Harper Lee
1962	*The Edge of Sadness*, Edwin O'Connor
1963	*The Reivers*, William Faulkner
1965	*The Keepers of the House*, Shirley Ann Grau
1966	*Collected Stories of Katherine Anne Porter*, Katherine Ann Porter
1967	*The Fixer*, Bernard Malamud
1968	*The Confessions of Nat Turner*, William Styron
1969	*House Made of Dawn*, N. Scott Momaday
1970	*Collected Stories*, Jean Stafford
1972	*Angle of Repose*, Wallace Stegner
1973	*The Optimist's Daughter*, Eudora Welty
1975	*The Killer Angels*, Michael Shaara
1976	*Humboldt's Gift*, Saul Bellow
1978	*Elbow Room*, James Alan McPherson
1979	*The Stories of John Cheever*, John Cheever

1980	*The Executioner's Song*, Norman Mailer
1981	*A Confederacy of Dunces*, John Kennedy Toole
1982	*Rabbit Is Rich*, John Updike
1983	*The Color Purple*, Alice Walker
1984	*Ironweed*, William Kennedy
1985	*Foreign Affairs*, Alison Lurie
1986	*Lonesome Dove*, Larry McMurtry
1987	*A Summons to Memphis*, Peter Taylor
1988	*Beloved*, Toni Morrison
1989	*Breathing Lessons*, Anne Tyler
1990	*The Mambo Kings Play Songs of Love*, Oscar Hijeulos
1991	*Rabbit at Rest*, John Updike
1992	*A Thousand Acres*, Jane Smiley

Drama

1918	*Why Marry?*, Jesse Lynch Williams
1920	*Beyond the Horizon*, Eugene O'Neill
1921	*Miss LuLu Bett*, Zona Gale
1922	*Anna Christie*, Eugene O'Neill
1923	*Icebound*, Owen Davis
1924	*Hell-Bent Fer Heaven*, Hatcher Hughes
1925	*They Knew What They Wanted*, Sidney Howard
1926	*Craig's Wife*, George Kelly
1927	*In Abraham's Bosom*, Paul Green
1928	*Strange Interlude*, Eugene O'Neill
1929	*Street Scene*, Elmer L. Rice
1930	*The Green Pastures*, Marc Connelly
1931	*Alison's House*, Susan Glaspell
1932	*Of Thee I Sing*, George S. Kaufman, Morrie Ryskind, and Ira Gershwin
1933	*Both Your Houses*, Maxwell Anderson
1934	*Men in White*, Sidney Kingsley
1935	*The Old Maid*, Zöe Akins
1936	*Idiot's Delight*, Robert E. Sherwood
1937	*You Can't Take It With You*, Moss Hart and George S. Kaufman
1938	*Our Town*, Thornton Wilder
1939	*Abe Lincoln in Illinois*, Robert E. Sherwood
1940	*The Time of Your Life*, William Saroyan
1941	*There Shall Be No Night*, Robert E. Sherwood
1943	*The Skin of Our Teeth*, Thornton Wilder
1945	*Harvey*, Mary Chase
1946	*State of the Union*, Russel Crouse and Howard Lindsay
1948	*A Streetcar Named Desire*, Tennessee Williams
1949	*Death of a Salesman*, Arthur Miller
1950	*South Pacific*, Richard Rodgers, Oscar Hammerstein II, and Joshua Logan
1952	*The Shrike*, Joseph Kramm
1953	*Picnic*, William Inge
1954	*The Teahouse of the August Moon*, John Patrick
1955	*Cat on a Hot Tin Roof*, Tennessee Williams
1956	*The Diary of Anne Frank*, Frances Goodrich and Albert Hackett
1957	*Long Days Journey Into Night*, Eugene O'Neill
1958	*Look Homeward, Angel*, Ketti Frings
1959	*J. B.*, Archibald MacLeish

1960	*Fiorello!*, George Abbott, Jerome Weidman, Jerry Block, and Sheldon Harnick
1961	*All the Way Home*, Tad Mosel
1962	*How to Succeed in Business Without Really Trying*, Frank Loesser and Abe Burrows
1965	*The Subject Was Roses*, Frank D. Gilroy
1967	*A Delicate Balance*, Edward Albee
1969	*The Great White Hope*, Howard Sackler
1970	*No Place to Be Somebody*, Charles Gordone
1971	*The Effect of Gamma Rays on Man-in-the-Moon Marigolds*, Paul Zindel
1973	*That Championship Season*, Jason Miller
1975	*Seascape*, Edward Albee
1976	*A Chorus Line*, Conceived by Michael Bennett
1977	*The Shadow Box*, Michael Cristofer
1978	*The Gin Game*, Donald L. Coburn
1979	*Buried Child*, Sam Shepard
1980	*Talley's Folly*, Lanford Wilson
1981	*Crimes of the Heart*, Beth Henley
1982	*A Soldier's Play*, Charles Fuller
1983	*Night, Mother*, Marsha Norman
1984	*Glengary Glen Ross*, David Mamet
1985	*Sunday in the Park with George*, Stephen Sondheim and James Lapine
1987	*Fences*, August Wilson
1988	*Driving Miss Daisy*, Alfred Uhry
1989	*The Heidi Chronicles*, Wendy Wasserstein
1990	*The Piano Lesson*, August Wilson
1991	*Lost in Yonkers*, Neil Simon
1992	*The Kentucky Cycle*, Robert Schenkkan

Poetry

1918	*Love Songs*, Sara Teasdale
1919	*Old Road to Paradise*, Margaret Widdemer; *Corn Huskers*, Carl Sandburg
1922	*Collected Poems*, Edwin Arlington Robinson
1923	*The Ballad of the Harp-Weaver*; *A Few Figs from Thistles*; eight sonnets in *American Poetry, 1922, A Miscellany*, Edna St. Vincent Millay
1924	*New Hampshire: A Poem With Notes and Grace Notes*, Robert Frost
1925	*The Man Who Died Twice,* Edwin Arlington Robinson
1926	*What's O'Clock*, Amy Lowell
1927	*Fiddler's Farewell*, Leonora Speyer
1928	*Tristram*, Edwin Arlington Robinson
1929	*John Brown's Body*, Stephen Vincent Benét
1930	*Selected Poems*, Conrad Aiken
1931	*Collected Poems*, Robert Frost
1932	*The Flowering Stone*, George Dillon
1933	*Conquistador*, Archibald MacLeish
1934	*Collected Verse*, Robert Hillyer
1935	*Bright Ambush*, Audrey Wurdemann
1936	*Strange Holiness*, Robert P.T. Coffin
1937	*A Further Range*, Robert Frost
1938	*Cold Morning Sky*, Marya Zaturenska
1939	*Selected Poems*, John Gould Fletcher

1940	*Collected Poems*, Mark Van Doren
1941	*Sunderland Capture*, Leonard Bacon
1942	*The Dust Which is God*, William Rose Benét
1943	*A Witness Tree*, Robert Frost
1944	*Western Star*, Stephen Vincent Benét
1945	*V-Letter and Other Poems*, Karl Shapiro
1947	*Lord Weary's Castle*, Robert Lowell
1948	*The Age of Anxiety*, W. H. Auden
1949	*Terror and Decorum*, Peter Viereck
1950	*Annie Allen*, Gwendolyn Brooks
1951	*Complete Poems*, Carl Sandburg
1952	*Collected Poems*, Marianne Moore
1953	*Collected Poems, 1917–1952*, Archibald MacLeish
1954	*The Waking*, Theodore Roethke
1955	*Collected Poems*, Wallace Stevens
1956	*Poems—North & South*, Elizabeth Bishop
1957	*Things of This World*, Richard Wilbur
1958	*Promises; Poems, 1954–1956*, Robert Penn Warren
1959	*Selected Poems; 1928–1958*, Stanley Kunitz
1960	*Heart's Needle*, William Snodgrass
1961	*Times Three: Selected Verse From Three Decades*, Phyllis McGinley
1962	*Poems*, Alan Dugan
1963	*Pictures From Breughel*, William Carlos Williams
1964	*At the End of the Open Road*, Louis Simpson
1965	*77 Dream Songs*, John Berryman
1966	*Selected Poems*, Richard Eberhart
1967	*Live or Die*, Anne Sexton
1968	*The Hard Hours*, Anthony Hecht
1969	*Of Being Numerous*, George Oppen
1970	*Untitled Subjects*, Richard Howard
1971	*The Carrier of Ladders*, William S. Merwin
1972	*Collected Poems*, James Wright
1973	*Up Country*, Maxine Winokur Kumin
1974	*The Dolphin*, Robert Lowell
1975	*Turtle Island*, Gary Snyder
1976	*Self-Portrait in a Convex Mirror*, John Ashbery
1977	*Divine Comedies*, James Merrill
1978	*Collected Poems*, Howard Nemerov: Poems, 1976–1978
1979	*Now and Then*, Robert Penn Warren
1980	*Selected Poems*, Donald Rodney Justice
1981	*The Morning of the Poem*, James Schuyler
1982	*The Collected Poems*, Sylvia Plath
1983	*Selected Poems*, Galway Kinnell
1984	*American Primitive*, Mary Oliver
1985	*Yin*, Carolyn Kizer
1986	*The Flying Change*, Henry Taylor
1987	*Thomas and Beulah*, Rita Dove
1988	*Partial Accounts: New and Selected Poems*, William Meredith
1989	*New and Collected Poems*, Richard Wilbur
1990	*The World Doesn't End*, Charles Simic
1991	*Near Changes*, Mona Van Duyn
1992	*Selected Poems*, James Tate

Q **Quatrain** A stanza or a poem with four lines, with many possible rhyme schemes.
The Quiet Don, Mikhail Sholokhov Written over a period of 14 years, this Russian epic series of novels was published between 1928 and 1940. The best-known of the novels is *And Quiet Flows the Don*, published in the United States in 1934. The story concerns Grigory, a young Cossack who has little sympathy with the revolution led by the Bolsheviks and even fights against them. At the end of the novel tedium and disillusionment claim him.

R **Rabelais, François** (1490–1553) A French monk, physician, archaeologist, and scholar, Rabelais's major work is the burlesque novel *Gargantua and Pantagruel*, which mingled the most serious and profound ideas with broad satire and even scatalogical jokes. The work, in five books, was published between 1533 and 1563, the last volume being posthumous, although its authenticity is contested by some.

Racine, Jean (1639–1699) Considered by the French their greatest writer of tragic drama, Racine was the epitome of classical drama. His simple diction and the realism of his characters accounted for the popularity of his plays. In 1677, after writing ten plays, he retired from the theater and became the king's historiographer. His best-known plays are *Phaedra* (1677) and *Andromache* (1667); he also wrote lyric poetry.

Ransom, John Crowe (1888–1974) Tennessee poet who founded *The Kenyon Review*. A Southerner both by instinct and choice, his poetry combines innovation with the aristocratic traditions of the antebellum South. Ransom, a difficult poet to read, used wit and irony to convey his expression. His works include *Chills and Fever* (1924) and *Selected Poems* (1945, 1963, 1969).

The Rape of the Lock (1712), Alexander Pope Considered to be the most brilliant English poetical satire, in which the heroic couplet has never been managed with greater elegance or wit. This poem in five cantos gives us one of the most brilliant pictures we have of the foibles and artifices of the aristocracy in Pope's day.

Realism A term generally applied to any literature that is true to life. It is specifically applied to a movement in France, England, and America in the latter half of the 19th century, when novelists paid great attention to describing life as it really is. The realists were reacting against what they considered to be the unreal excesses and exaggerations of Romanticism. Examples are the novels of Balzac in France, George Eliot in England, and William Dean Howells in America.

The Red and the Black (1830), Stendhal This psychological French novel deals with Julien Sorel, who is torn between a career in the military (the red) and the clergy (the black). He leaves his mistress and impregnates the daughter of his wealthy employer, who eventually finds out about the mistress and refuses to have Sorel in the family. At the end Sorel shoots his ex-mistress and is subsequently executed.

The Red Badge of Courage (1895), Stephen Crane Concerns the adventures of a young Union soldier, Henry Fleming, in the American Civil War battle of Chancellorsville, although the action is never identified by that name. In his first encounter with the enemy, Henry is afraid and runs away; behind the battle lines he is wounded by another retreating soldier. He returns to his regiment and is acclaimed a hero because of his wound and, as the battle resumes, fights like a true hero. This remarkable emotional account of a young man in battle becomes even more remarkable when one learns that Crane himself had never been involved in war. This is the first modern, realistic treatment of war in American literature.

Refrain A regularly repeated phrase or line of poetry that recurs frequently in a poem or ballad, especially in old folk ballads and songs.

Remarque, Erich Maria (1898–1970) This German novelist fought in World War I and was wounded five times. After the war, he was a teacher for a time, wrote automotive advertising, and became the editor of a general sports magazine. In 1929 his best work, *All Quiet on the Western Front*, appeared and made him famous throughout the world. He became a permanent exile when the Nazis took over in Germany and eventually became a U.S. citizen.

Repetition A device used in writing poetry or prose in which an idea is repeated for emphasis.

> Cannon to the right of them,
> Cannon to the left of them
> Cannon in front of them
> Volleyed and thundered.
>
> Tennyson

Requiem A solemn chant or dirge; a prayer for the soul of the dead, sung at funerals. The word is from the Latin phrase *Requiem aeternam dona eis, Domine* ("Give eternal rest to them, O Lord").

> Slow, slow, fresh fount, keep time
>   with my salt tears...
> Like melting snow upon some craggy
>   hill,
>   Drop, drop, drop, drop,
> Since nature's pride is, now, a withered
>   daffodil.
>
> Ben Jonson

Restoration comedy A term applied to English plays from 1660 (when the monarchy was restored) until the early 1700s, when a sentimental type of comedy arose. Restoration comedies are elegant and witty, and very frequently involved with sexual matters.

The Return of the Native (1878), Thomas Hardy This beautifully executed and tempestuous story of Eustacia Vye and her love for Clym Yeobright illustrates one of Hardy's most deeply felt themes: that the immutable will of man is solely responsible for his catastrophes. However, Hardy is so fine an artist that he never sermonizes, and the reader watches with understanding and compassion the slow unfolding of his characters' downfall.

Rhyme A similarity or correspondence in the vowel sounds of two words that have differing consonantal sounds.

Rhyme scheme The recurring pattern in which rhymes are placed in a stanza or poem. The pattern is normally indicated by using the letter *a* to indicate the first rhyme word, *b*, the second, and so on.

> There has fallen a splendid tear　　(a)
> From the passion-flower at the
> 　gate.　　(b)
> She is coming, my dove, my dear;　(a)
> She is coming, my life, my fate;　(b)
> The red rose cries, "She is near,
> 　she is near";　　(a)
> And the white rose weeps,
> 　"She is late";　　(b)
> The larkspur listens, "I hear,
> 　I hear";　　(a)
> And the lily whispers, "I wait."　(b)
> 　　　　　　　　　　　　　Tennyson

Rice, Elmer (Elmer Reizenstein) (1892–1967) This American playwright was born and grew up in New York. He graduated from law school, but never practiced. After 11 years of failures, he had his first success with *The Adding Machine* (1923), probably the most important American expressionistic play, and added to his reputation with *Street Scene* (1929), a realistic drama.

Richardson, Samuel (1689–1761) *See Pamela.*

Rilke, Rainer Maria (1875–1926) This German poet was a part of the Symbolist movement of the 1890s. In some of his earlier works the poet adopted a technique comparable to that of the American imagists. As time went by, his subjects changed from the despair of the lover and the struggles of the poet to antagonism toward the bourgeois virtues. His greatest poetic works are in *Duino Elegies* (1923) and *Sonnets to Orpheus* (1923).

The Rime of the Ancient Mariner (1898), Samuel Coleridge　Derided in its day by critics as "the strangest story of cock and bull we ever saw on paper," this work is today considered a great poetic achievement. It is the story of an ancient mariner who detains a wedding guest and holds him with "glittering eye" while he tells his tale of horror and the sea.

Rip Van Winkle, Washington Irving　This tale from *The Sketch Book,* published in seven installments between 1819 and 1820, tells of an amiable Dutch loafer who prefers wandering in the Kaatskill Mountains with his dog to providing for his family. On one of his trips, he encounters the crew of Hendrick Hudson, who give him a magic potion. On awakening, he finds that he has slept for 20 years and when he returns to his village, nothing is the same.

The Rise of Silas Lapham (1885), William Dean Howells　This is the story of a wealthy American businessman, who has difficulties dealing with success and personal ethics. The theme is the conflict between the new race of industrial millionaires and traditional New England aristocracy.

Rising action　That part of the plot of a story or drama in which the conflict between the hero or heroine (the protagonist) and the villain (the antagonist) becomes increasingly complicated. In Hemingway's *The Old Man and the Sea* the rising action begins when the old man hooks the tremendous fish and the battle between man and nature begins.

Robinson Crusoe (1719), Daniel Defoe　A Scottish sailor named Alexander Selkirk published a book of his experiences on an island off Chile, where he had lived for five years after being shipwrecked there. The English novelist Defoe picked up the story and wrote a novel based on the same situation.

Robinson, Edwin Arlington (1869–1935) Born in Maine, the son of an amateur spiritualist, this American poet published his first book of poetry at his own expense, but his later work brought him wide acceptance and three Pulitzer Prizes. Although he composed many long poems, his more popular works are such shorter ones as "Richard Cory" and "Miniver Cheevy," in which he explores man's complex nature and the frustration and agony of the human dilemma.

Roethke, Theodore (1908–1963)　This Michigan poet's career was frequently interrupted by manic-depressive episodes, but they did not affect the lyricism, vision, and wit inherent in his poetry. His best-known works are *Praise to the End!* (1951) and *Words for the Wind* (1958).

Roman à clef　A novel based on real persons and events.

Romance　Originally a term denoting a Medieval narrative in prose or poetry dealing with a knightly hero; but now, any fiction concerning heroes, exotic subjects, passionate love, or supernatural experiences.

Romantic movement　A literary movement that began in England in the beginning of the 19th century and whose expression is realized by Wordsworth, who wrote, "All good poetry is the spontaneous overflow of powerful feelings." Further, this literary school upheld man's natural goodness. The glorification of nature and the spirit are two principal themes of romantic poets such as Blake, Coleridge, Byron, and Shelley. The latter typified the essence of this movement when he wrote of the soul "clasping its hands in ecstasy."

Roots (1976), Alex Haley　Regarded as an ancestral chronology of Afro-American heritage, this novel views its major character, Kunta Kinte, on his journey from Africa in the 18th century, through enslavement, and is seen as one black family's struggle for equality in America.

Rossetti, Charles Dante Gabriel (1828–1882) The son of an Italian political refugee in England and the brother of Christina Rossetti, he looked on painting as his profession and poetry as his hobby. Rossetti studied art at the Royal Academy, where he and two other students formed the Pre-Raphaelite Brotherhood, based on the theory that the best painting had been done in Italy before the Renaissance, a group that attracted many disciples. His best-known poem is "The Blessed Damozel" (1850).

Rossetti, Christina (1830–1894)　An English poet who composed more than 900 poems in English and 60 in Italian, her poetry falling into three categories—those of fancy, religious exaltation, and passion. Most of her work is religious.

Rousseau, Jean-Jacques (1712–1778)　The major influence on the development of Romanticism in the 19th century, this French philosopher articulated the notion of the natural man, unspoiled by society. Civilization, he felt, caused equality between men to disappear and laws were invented to preserve that inequality. Although today Rousseau is thought to have suffered grave mental disturbances, his friends merely believed him to be eccentric. His major works are *The Social Contract* (1762), the novel *Emile* (1762), and his autobiographical work, *Confessions* (1765).

Ruskin, John (1819–1900) Born into a wealthy English family, he gave most of his money away to support causes he believed in. Educated at Oxford, Ruskin became a critic of the arts, but he gradually became more interested in social reform. His masterwork is generally considered to be *The Stones of Venice* (1851–53), a defense of Gothic architecture.

Saga A prose narrative of heroic and legendary events in ancient Norway and Iceland; or any modern narrative that resembles Nordic sagas in style and subject matter.

Salinger, J.D. (Jerome David) (b.1919) Born in New York, this important and reclusive 20th-century literary figure published *Catcher in the Rye* (1951), a first-person novel that relates with humor and wit the pain and struggles of its narrator, Holden Caulfield, on his odyssey through adolescence. Salinger was involved with the isolated figure in society; he wrote of the intense loneliness and frustration experienced by his characters as they face a world of conformity and banality. *Nine Stories* (1953) is a brilliant collection that deals particularly with the Glass family. *Seymour: An Introduction* (1963) (about Seymour Glass) is his last published work.

Sand, George (Lucile-Aurore Dupin) (1804–1876) A French novelist who defies classification, Sand was eulogized as "…a woman who observed her own life, and gave it expression …She wrote as she breathed." This quotation notwithstanding, she has frequently been classified as a romantic, writing with great passion of the misunderstood woman, and also creating many pastoral romances [*The Haunted Pool* (1848) and *The Master Bellringers* (1852)]. Her liaison with Chopin was both famous and notorious: Sand wrote about it in her work *A Winter in Majorca* (1842).

Sandburg, Carl (1878–1967) Born in Illinois, this major 20th-century American poet had to earn his own living from age 13. He wrote without conventional meter and his sources were largely historical, although he also was lauded for recreating the contemporary American scene. His *Complete Poems* (1950) won a Pulitzer Prize. After 1928, he concentrated on producing a monumental biography of President Lincoln.

Sappho (7th century B.C.) This poet from the island of Lesbos is the only major female writer whose works have survived from classical Greece and Rome. According to legend, she was married and had a daughter, but much of her poetry concerns her love for women (hence the term "lesbian").

Sarcasm A literary device that uses irony to state in a negative and bitter way the opposite of the intended meaning. "Surely," said the poet to the mendicant, "you are a gentleman of great learning and moral attitude."

Saroyan, William (1908–1981) Born in California, this Armenian-American novelist, playwright, and short-story writer spent some time in an orphanage during his youth. Saroyan dealt with the American dream in a manner both lyrical and sentimental. He published his own first volume of short stories, *The Daring Young Man on the Flying Trapeze* (1934). *The Human Comedy* (a novel, 1934) and *The Time of Your Life* (a play, 1939) are among his most noted works.

Sartre, Jean-Paul (1905–1980) Whether Sartre is a philosopher who wrote belles lettres or a belletrist who had a philosophical system is moot. A French professor of philosophy, he was influential in popularizing an Existentialism that is atheistic, pessimistic, and yet also one with humanistic and progressive elements. His best-known works are the one-act play *No Exit* (1944) and the multivolume novel series titled *The Roads to Freedom,* which he began publishing in 1945.

Satire A type of literary work that uses sarcasm, wit, and irony to ridicule and expose the follies and foibles of mankind, often in an attempt to reform society. *See* Alexander Pope's **The Rape of the Lock** and Jonathan Swift's **Gulliver's Travels**.

Scansion The analysis of poetry or verse to show its metrical pattern. A scansion of the line "Double, Double, toil and trouble," from the incantation of the witches in *Macbeth* would read: *Dóuble dóuble tóil and tróuble.* The marks indicate there are four trochaic feet in the line.

The Scarlet Letter (1850), Nathaniel Hawthorne Set in 17th-century Boston, where adultery was a capital crime, this work, considered to be a major American novel, is the story of Hester Prynne, convicted of adultery and sentenced to wear a scarlet A on the bosom of her garment. She refuses to name her partner, but after seven years the local minister, Arthur Dimmesdale, confesses his guilt and eventually dies. At Hester's death, the letter A is inscribed on her tombstone.

Scenario Outline of the plot of a play, involving the characters and the order of the scene.

Scene A subdivision of an act of a play. In motion pictures a scene is a single situation or unit of dialogue.

Schiller, Friedrich (1759–1805) Germany's most important and esteemed playwright, he is best known for his tragedies *Don Carlos* (1787) and *Wallenstein* (1799). Schiller also wrote plays about Mary Stuart, William Tell, and Joan of Arc, works of history, philosophy, and poems. Of the latter the best known is "Ode to Joy" (1785), used by Beethoven for the choral movement of his Ninth Symphony.

Science fiction A form of fantasy in fiction in which scientific theories, hypotheses, and logic are used to create settings on other planets and galaxies and to depict the future on Earth. Novels and short stories by Ray Bradbury, Arthur C. Clarke, Isaac Asimov, and Ursula LeGuin are typical of the genre.

Scott, Sir Walter (1771–1832) Born in Scotland, this novelist and poet won fame with *The Lady of the Lake* (1810). He turned to writing novels in 1814 and in the next 17 years produced 17 books, which made him the most popular author of his time. Best known among them is *Ivanhoe* (1820).

Self-Reliance, Ralph Waldo Emerson　This, the author's most famous essay, was published in the collection *Essays: First Series* (1841). The piece extols as the highest law being true to the self, whether or not that effort entails nonconformity. This essay contains the famous sentence "A foolish consistency is the hobgoblin of little minds."

Semiotics　The study of symbols and signs in works of literature.

Seneca (4 B.C.–A.D. 65)　Born in Spain, he became the tutor of the future emperor Nero and an important power in the government during the first years of Nero's reign. Later he lost the emperor's favor and eventually committed suicide. His tragedies leaned heavily on Greek drama and were written to be read, not performed. The subject matter of his plays had an important influence on the dramas of Elizabethan England.

Sentimentality　In literature, an overabundance of blatantly stated feeling designed to evoke an emotional response. Wilde criticized Dickens's description of Little Nell's death in *The Old Curiosity Shop:* "That man has no soul who can read of the death of Little Nell without laughing."

Serenade　A song written expressly to be sung beneath the window of a lady's boudoir.

Sestet　A six-line stanza (also called a sextet) commonly found as the concluding six lines of a sonnet. The sestet is also used as a stanzaic form in itself and as a stanza in a poem.

> I wandered lonely as a cloud
> That floats on high o'er vales and
> 　hills,
> When all at once I saw a crowd,
> A host, of golden daffodils;
> Beside the lake, beneath the trees,
> Fluttering and dancing in the
> 　breeze.
> 　　　　　　　　　　　Wordsworth

Setting　The physical background of a narrative. A setting includes the historical epoch in which the action occurs, as well as the social class or condition of the characters.

Seuss, Dr. (Theodor Seuss Geisel) (1904–1991)　An early illustrator for *Life, Redbook,* and *Saturday Evening Post* magazines, Geisel is known by children and parents around the world for his whimsical, often rhyming, easy-to-read fiction, which he authored and illustrated for seven decades. Books under his pen name, Dr. Seuss, include: *The Cat in the Hat* (1957), *Yertle the Turtle* (1958), *Green Eggs and Ham* (1960), *There's a Wocket in My Pocket* (1974), and *Oh, the Places You'll Go!* (1990); and, as Theo Le Sig: *Ten Apples up on Top* (1961), *The Eye Book* (1968), and *The Tooth Book* (1981).

Sexton, Anne (1928–1974)　This American Pulitzer Prize-winning poet [*Live or Die* (1966)] committed suicide in 1974 at the age of 46, after living a passionate and tortured life in and out of psychiatric hospitals. Her lyric strengths and the force of her gut-level poetry can be found in *All My Pretty Ones* (1962) and *Love Poems* (1969).

Shakespeare, William (1564–1616)　Shakespeare is the towering figure in English literature, considered both the greatest dramatist and the greatest poet. Married at 18, the poet left his home, Stratford-on-Avon, soon after and by 1588 he was in a company of actors in London; he wrote plays and poems from 1594 till his death. Shakespeare quickly became the most popular and successful dramatist of his time. After 1608 he began to spend more and more time at Stratford, probably not composing much after 1611. His 37 plays consist of tragedies like *Hamlet,* histories like *Richard II,* and comedies like *Twelfth Night,* and his *Sonnets* are considered to be unequaled in their expression of love and beauty.

EXHIBIT 15.7
The Plays of Shakespeare

The following plays are the accepted canon of Shakespeare. The classification and dates are generally agreed on by scholars.

Comedies

Love's Labour's Lost (1590)
The Comedy of Errors (1591)
Two Gentlemen of Verona (1592)
A Midsummer Night's Dream (1594)
The Merchant of Venice (1595)
The Taming of the Shrew (1596)
The Merry Wives of Windsor (1599)
Much Ado About Nothing (1599)
As You Like It (1600)
Twelfth Night (1600)
All's Well That Ends Well (1602)
Measure for Measure (1604)

Histories

King Henry VI, Parts I, II and III (1592)
King Richard III (1593)
King Richard II (1594)
King John (1594)
King Henry IV, Part I (1597?)
King Henry IV, Part II (1598)
King Henry V (1599)
King Henry VIII (1611)

Tragedies

Romeo and Juliet (1593)
Titus Andronicus (1594)
Julius Caesar (1599)
Troilus and Cressida (1602)
Hamlet (1602)
Othello (1604)
King Lear (1605)
Macbeth (1606)
Antony and Cleopatra (1607?)
Coriolanus (1608)

Romances

Pericles (1608)
Cymbeline (1610?)
The Winter's Tale (1610?)
The Tempest (1611)

LITERATURE

Shaw, George Bernard (1856–1950) Born in Dublin, Shaw established himself in England in 1876 and worked as a drama and music critic, during which time he became interested in Socialism, a major concern throughout his life and works. The first of his plays to be produced was *Widowers' Houses* (1892). Among his principal works were *Man and Superman* (1903), *Pygmalion* (1912) and *Saint Joan* (1924). He won the Nobel Prize for Literature in 1925. He is noted for his brilliant "Shavian" wit, impudence, and social consciousness.

Shelley, Percy Bysshe (1792–1822) An English Romantic poet who was strongly influenced by the writings of the radical William Godwin (he married Godwin's daughter, Mary) and throughout his life retained the faith in a better tomorrow. Shelley wrote with a lyric sense of joy, creating images ("life like a dome of many-colored glass stains the white radiance of eternity...") that remain in the mind. He drowned tragically in a boating accident in Italy. His greatest work is generally considered to be the poetic drama *Prometheus Unbound* (1819). Among his famous individual poems are "Ozymandias," "Ode to the West Wind," and "To a Skylark."

Sheridan, Richard Brinsley (1751–1816) Generally considered the best British dramatist of the 18th century, Sheridan had a playwriting career which lasted only from 1773 to 1780, during which time he wrote the comedies *The Rivals* (1775) and *The School for Scandal* (1777). In 1780 he entered Parliament, but eventually had to give up his seat because of his debts, for which he spent time in prison.

Sherwood, Robert (1896–1955) The New Rochelle, New York, native came from a well-to-do family and he was educated at Harvard. He served in World War I and was seriously wounded. The success of his first play, *The Road to Rome* (1927) made it possible for him to live as a playwright. Both *Idiot's Delight* (1936) and *Abe Lincoln in Illinois* received Pulitzer Prizes. A lifetime liberal, he served under President Roosevelt during World War II, writing many of the president's speeches.

Sholokhov, Mikhail (1905–1984) The winner of the 1965 Nobel Prize for Literature wrote chiefly about life in the Don Cossack region. This Russian author's major work, strongly influenced by Tolstoy's *War and Peace,* is *The Silent Don* (in two volumes, 1934 and 1942), which attempts a panoramic look at life in one region of the Soviet Union during and after the revolution. A Communist Party member, Sholokhov was generally in favor with the Kremlin during his writing years.

Short story A brief narrative, ancient in origin, which includes fables, parables, tales, and anecdotes. The short story as a conscious art form began to appear in the 19th century in the works of Hawthorne, Poe, and Balzac, whose short stories are carefully plotted and written for a calculated effect on the reader.

Sidney, Sir Philip (1554–1586) Scholar, diplomat, poet, courtier, soldier, and gentleman, this English poet was an influential figure under Queen Elizabeth. An artist himself, he was also a patron of the arts and greatly encouraged Edmund Spenser. His major works are *Astrophel and Stella,* a sonnet sequence, and *Arcadia,* a pastoral.

Simile A figure of speech in which an object of one type is said to be like another.

> My love is like a red, red rose.
>
> Burns

Simon, Neil (b. 1927) Born on July 4 and raised in Washington Heights (Manhattan), this prolific playwright began his career as a comedy writer for television. Well known on Broadway for five decades, Simon won the Tony Award for his plays *The Odd Couple* (1966), as well as *Biloxi Blues* (1985)—part of his autobiographical trilogy that includes *Brighton Beach Memoirs* and *Broadway Bound.* Simon won the 1991 Pulitzer Prize for Literature in drama for *Lost in Yonkers.*

Sinclair, Upton (1878–1968) Born in Baltimore and raised and educated in New York, this ardent socialist made the best-seller list with *The Jungle* (1906). The ideas in his work are those of traditional Socialism: the perfidy of big business interests, the strangling influence of monopoly, and business's general disregard of the common citizen. He died leaving behind some 90 published works.

Singer, Isaac Bashevis (1904–1991) This Polish-born Nobel Prize-winning novelist wrote mostly of the passionate, lyrical heritage of the Polish Jews—their spirituality, their color, and the folkways of their daily life. Singer, a master of language and feeling, is best known for *Gimpel the Fool* (1957) and *The Magician of Lublin* (1960).

Six Characters in Search of an Author (1921), Luigi Pirandello In this Italian play the line between theater and life disappears completely, with a play in rehearsal as the curtain rises. A family of six arrive, claiming to be fictional characters, and demand to be put into a play. Their story is told by various members of the family and then the actors attempt to make a play of it; but, as soon as they begin acting, the truth is distorted and illusion takes over.

Soliloquy A monologue delivered by an actor alone on stage. The intention of the speech is to reveal what is going on in the character's mind.

Solzhenitsyn, Alexander (b.1918) After serving in the Soviet army during World War II, this Russian novelist and essayist was arrested for making anti-Stalin comments in a letter. He served eight years in Siberia and subsequently was a teacher of mathematics and physics. Cured of cancer, he has used both his imprisonment and his hospitalization as subjects. His best-known work is the novel *One Day in the Life of Ivan Denisovich* (1962). Solzhenitsyn now resides in the United States.

Sonnet A poem of 14 iambic pentameter lines with a rigidly prescribed rhyme scheme. The two main types of sonnets are the Italian (or Petrarchan) and the English (or Shakespearean).

> When in disgrace with fortune and men's
>   eyes,
> I all alone beweep my outcast state,
> And trouble deaf Heaven with my bootless
>   cries,
> And look upon myself, and curse my fate,

Wishing me like to one more rich in hope,
Featur'd like him, like him with friends possess'd,
Desiring this man's art, and that man's scope,
With what I most enjoy contented least,
Yet in these thoughts myself almost despising,
Haply I think on thee—and then my state
(Like to the lark at break of day arising
From sullen earth) sings hymns at heaven's gate;
For thy sweet love remember'd such wealth brings,
That then I scorn to change my state with kings.

                Shakespeare

Sophocles (496–405 B.C.) This Greek dramatist was the author of some 125 plays, of which seven survive. He is considered most important in the history of theater because he deemphasized the chorus, which had played the major role in the works of his predecessor Aeschylus, and, without abandoning the *function* of the chorus, placed the major stress on his central characters. His two most important plays are *Oedipus the King* and *Antigone.*

The Sound and the Fury (1929), William Faulkner This American stream-of-consciousness novel has an extremely complex structure. It is divided into four sections, each a reflection from the mind of a different character; there are also many flashbacks and switches in chronology. The title of this work is from *Macbeth,* "...a tale told by an idiot, full of sound and fury, signifying nothing," and the story deals with the lyric depravity of the Compson family.

Spender, Steven (b.1909) This English poet and critic speaks with lyrical intensity about social injustices, and writes with passion about the contemporary world. He achieved fame with his autobiography, *World Within World* (1951), and some of his more famous works are the *Collected Poems 1928–1953* (1955) and *The Making of A Poem* (1955).

Spenser, Edmund (1552–1599) This great poet of Britain's Elizabethan age was deeply moral in point of view, and a strict craftsman of meter and language. His masterwork is *The Faerie Queene,* which began publication in 1590, was continued in 1596, but was never finished.

Spenserian stanza A nine-line stanzaic form consisting of eight iambic pentameter lines followed by an Alexandrine, or a line of six iambic feet. The form was invented by Spenser and used in the 3,848 stanzas of *The Faerie Queene.* It rhymes *ababbcbcc.*

Full on this casement shone the wintry moon,   (a)
And threw warm gules on Madeline's fair breast,   (b)
As down she knelt for Heaven's grace and boon;   (a)
Rose-bloom fell on her hands, together prest,   (b)
And on her silver cross soft amethyst,   (b)
And on her hair a glory, like a saint;   (c)

She seem'd a splendid angel, newly drest,   (b)
Save wings, for heaven: Porphyro grew faint: (c)
She knelt, so pure a thing, so free from mortal taint.   (c)

                Keats

Spondee A type of poetic foot composed of two syllables, both of which are stressed: *Néw Yórk, wávelíke, cátlíke.*

Spoon River Anthology (1915), Edgar Lee Masters This American work is a series of short poetic characterizations in the form of epitaphs from an Illinois village graveyard; each of the personalities is allowed to describe him- or herself. Among the better-known entries are "Anne Rutledge," "Lucinda Matlock," and "Petit, The Poet." At the time of its publication it was highly innovative, and both *Our Town* (Thornton Wilder) and *Under Milkwood* (Dylan Thomas) subsequently reflected similar techniques.

Spoonerism An accidental and often humorous interchanging of the initial sounds of two or more words; named for Dr. W.A. Spooner of New College, Oxford, who often made such transpositions in his lectures. A "well-boiled icicle" for a "well-oiled bicycle;" a "blushing crow" for a "crushing blow."

Sprung rhythm As reflected in the poetry of Hopkins, a rhythm measured in feet, with each foot having only one accented syllable (the initial one). Any number of unaccented syllables may be used in addition to create an effect. It is the rhythmic language of everyday speech, prose, and music.

Stanza A group of lines of poetry arranged as a melodic unit that follows a definite pattern. The number of lines in a stanza can vary from 2–12 (a few rare exceptions have even more).

Steele, Richard (1672–1729) Together with Joseph Addison, he was half of the most successful literary partnership in English literature. He attended Oxford and then made his great reputation as editor of the periodicals *The Tatler* (1709) and then *The Spectator* (1711), on which he worked with Addison.

Stein, Gertrude (1874–1946) Born in Pennsylvania, Stein spent her childhood in Vienna, Paris, and San Francisco. After attending Radcliffe, she went on to study medicine at Johns Hopkins, but in 1903 she left the United States for France, where she remained with her constant friend and lover, Alice B. Toklas, for the rest of her life. Stein was the central figure in a circle of outstanding artist and writer expatriates in Paris. Her best-known work is *Three Lives* (1909), which is notable, as are all of Stein's literary productions, for its redundancies, emphasizing rhythms and sounds rather than sense.

Steinbeck, John (1902–1968) Born in California, this outstanding American author gained fame with *Tortilla Flat* (1935) and *Of Mice and Men* (1937), but he had his greatest triumph with *The Grapes of Wrath* in 1939. Compassion for the downtrodden of the world was to be Steinbeck's signature as an author. He remained for most of his life in Monterey and Los Gatos, California, where he wrote novels and stories about the life of the region. He won the Nobel Prize for Literature in 1962.

Stendahl (Marie Henri Beyle) (1783–1842) The son of a lawyer, this French novelist idolized his mother, who died when he was seven. He served in Napoleon's army and afterwards attempted to write drama, but had no success at it. Subsequently he turned to fiction and composed two of the most successful psychological novels of the 19th century: *The Red and the Black* (1830) and *The Charterhouse of Parma* (1839).

Stevens, Wallace (1879–1955) This American poet from Pennsylvania attended Harvard and eventually became a vice president of the Hartford Accident and Indemnity Company. Stevens was a poet concerned with creating order from chaos; his best-known works were *Harmonium* (1923) and *Ideas of Order* (1935).

Stevenson, Robert Louis (1850–1894) Born in Scotland, Stevenson had delicate health even as a boy. To please his family he took up engineering and then was admitted to the bar; however, he gave up law because he had contracted tuberculosis. He died in the South Seas when he was forty-four. His most famous works are *Treasure Island* (1883), *A Child's Garden of Verses* (1885), and *The Strange Case of Dr. Jekyll and Mr. Hyde* (1886).

Stock character A character that has become standard and customary in certain types of literature. A cruel stepmother and a Prince Charming are stock characters in fairy tales, and fainting heroines in sentimental novels.

"Stopping by Woods on a Snowy Evening" (1928), Robert Frost The American poet's best-known short work. The narrator stops his sleigh and sees the deep, almost religious beauty of the frozen woods, but realizes that practical duties call him from the contemplation of nature, as he reflects that he has "miles to go before I sleep."

Stowe, Harriet Beecher (1811–1896) The daughter of one of Connecticut's most prominent clergymen, she had only a haphazard and sketchy education. Stowe lived for 18 years in Cincinnati, a portal of travel between North and South, where she first became aware of slavery. Her fame rested principally on the novel *Uncle Tom's Cabin* (1852), the first best-seller in the United States.

The Stranger (1942), Albert Camus This French novel is about an existential man, a stranger in the universe, named Mersault, indifferent to everything except physical sensations. He kills an Arab, but experiences no remorse or guilt. Sentenced to die, he comes to the realization that this life is all there is, a belief that typifies the existential movement.

Stream of consciousness A type of psychological prose that presents the inner thoughts of a character in an uneven, endless stream (or flow) that stimulates the character's consciousness. *See* Virginia Woolf's *To the Lighthouse*, William Faulkner's *The Sound and the Fury*, and James Joyce's *Ulysses*.

A Streetcar Named Desire (1947), Tennessee Williams This play, considered to be the greatest and most lyrical of American dramas, concerns Blanche Dubois, daughter of a faded and impover-ished Southern family, who visits her sister and her earthy brother-in-law after the family home has been lost through debt. The audience learns of her desire for both drink and men and, when Stella, her sister, goes to the hospital to have a baby, her husband, Stanley, rapes Blanche, who then loses all touch with reality. At the end of the play, as she is being taken to a psychiatric hospital, she looks from one attendant/captor to the other and speaks the memorable lines, "I have always relied on the kindness of strangers."

Stress The accent or emphasis given to a syllable or word in poetry or other rhythmic writing.

Strindberg, August (1849–1912) Beginning as a naturalist, this Swedish playwright and novelist turned to an early type of Expressionism in the middle of his career. After working as a tutor, teacher, telegrapher, journalist, and librarian, he won renown through the publication of *The Red Room*. Married three times, he had an almost pathological attitude toward women, expressed in several of his plays. His best-known works are *The Father* (1887), *Miss Julie* (1888), and *The Dream Play* (1902).

Strophe A special designation for a stanza; in Pindaric odes the strophe is the first stanza and every subsequent third stanza (fourth, seventh, and so on).

Sturm und Drang German, literally "storm and stress." A literary movement in the late 1700s expressing turbulent emotion. Essences of this school are found in Goethe and Schiller.

Style Each author's unique method of expression to convey the meaning he wishes. Eventually, when "breaking down" a great writer's style, one comes finally to the man himself. "Style is the man," is a famous and often confusing quote.

Styron, William (b. 1925) Born in Virginia, Styron attended Duke University. His first novel, *Lie Down in Darkness* (1951) brought him great acclaim; he then stirred much controversy with *The Confessions of Nat Turner,* for which he won a Pulitzer Prize in 1967. Thirteen years passed before the publication of *Sophie's Choice*, where as in "Confessions" he dealt with another subject foreign to his background (this time, the experience of a Nazi death camp, for which he won both critical accolades and disapproval).

Subplot A secondary dramatic conflict that runs through a story as a subordinate complication and that is less important than the main plot. In Shakespeare's play, Hamlet's conflict with Laertes is a subplot.

Suspension of disbelief A literary phrase popularized first by Wordsworth, it asks the reader to enter into a work of literature without barring his own way by creating walls that say, "It couldn't have happened that way," or "How could my heart dance with the daffodils?" Suspending disbelief is to willingly appreciate the work for what it is, reserving subjective judgments.

Swenson, May (b. 1927) An American poet raised in Utah of Mormon parents. Swenson experiments with form (the typography of the poem on the page) and tries many different techniques. Her poetry is filled with evocative images. Some of her better-known works are *Half Sun Half Sleep* (1967) and *New and Selected Things Taking Place* (1979).

Swift, Jonathan (1667–1745) One of the great British literary figures, Swift was born in Dublin into abject poverty after the death of his father. An uncle sent him to Trinity College and he was then ordained in the Church of England. In 1713 he was named dean of St. Patrick's in Dublin, where he remained for the rest of his life, although he reputedly hated Ireland. His masterpiece was *Gulliver's Travels,* written during the 1720s.

Swinburne, Algernon Charles (1837–1909) From a noble family, Swinburne's publication of *Poems and Ballads* (1866) was viciously attacked in Victorian England for its extreme sensuality and anti-Christian sentiments; however, other factions of English critical life had nothing but praise for the beauty of Swinburne's language and the infusion of vitality he brought to poetry. Some of his poetry has been criticized for an overabundance of language, but his weakness did not hinder the success of his overall body of poetry and criticism.

Symbol Something that is a meaningful entity in itself and yet stands for, or means, something else. In literature there are so-called universal symbols and others that suggest special meanings because of the way they are used in a novel or other literary work. A flag is a symbol for a particular country; a voyage, a universal symbol for life. The scarlet letter in Hawthorne's novel assumes a special literary symbolism to those who know the novel thoroughly. Standing for the first letter in the word *Adultery,* the mark of shame gradually becomes a symbol of the bigotry and oppressive puritanism of a society.

Symbolism A literary movement in France in the latter part of the 19th century that was influenced by Edgar Allan Poe. Symbolists believed that unique and highly personal emotional responses, conveyed to the reader by means of a system of subjective symbols, were the main substance of literature. Works of the French writers Mallarmé, Rimbaud, and Baudelaire abound in this kind of symbolism. Baudelaire held that man lives in a "forest of symbols."

Synge, John Millington (1871–1909) Born in Dublin of Protestant parentage, this playwright attended Trinity College and then wandered for several years in Germany, Italy, and France until in 1898 he was persuaded by William Butler Yeats to return to Ireland. It was such plays as *In the Shadow of the Glen* (1903) and *The Playboy of the Western World* (1907) that brought success and fame to Synge and to the Abbey Theater in Dublin. His *Riders to the Sea* (1904) is considered one of the greatest tragedies ever written. Synge died of tuberculosis when he was thirty-eight.

T**arkington, Booth** (1869–1946) Born in Indiana, Tarkington attended both Purdue and Princeton and lived in Indianapolis most of his life. In his novels [e.g., *The Magnificent Ambersons* (1918)] he showed himself a skilled social satirist dealing with the urban middle and upper-middle classes. However, he has been criticized for his sentimentality and his Victorianism in matters of decorum.

Teasdale, Sara (1884–1933) Born in St. Louis, this poet was a sometime habitue of Chicago poetic circles, where she was once courted by Vachel Lindsay. Works of her sensitive and very personal lyrics include the critically acclaimed collection *Flame and Shadow* (1920) and *Strange Victory* (1933)

Tennyson, Alfred (1809–1892) The son of a clergyman, this British poet's first publication was *Poems by Alfred Tennyson* (1832); it was received badly by the critics and he published nothing again until *Poems* (1842). Other works include *In Memoriam* (1850), *Idylls of the King* (1859–1872), and *Enoch Arden* (1864). In 1883 he was elevated to the peerage by Queen Victoria. His writings are considered most representative of the Victorian Age.

Illustration from *Idylls of the King* by Alfred Tennyson.

Tercet A stanza of poetry with three lines. The most common rhyme schemes of the tercet are *aaa, aba, aab,* and *abb.*

Terza rima A special type of tercet that has interlocking rhymes in a continuous rhyme scheme: *aba bcb cdc ded,* and so on.

O wild West Wind. thou breath of Autumn's being,	(a)
Thou, from whose unseen presence the leaves dead	(b)
Are driven, like ghosts from an enchanter fleeing,	(a)
Yellow, and black, and pale, and hectic red,	(b)
Pestilence-stricken multitudes: O thou,	(c)
Who chariotest to their dark wintry bed	(b)
The winged seeds, where they lie cold and low,	(c)

Each like a corpse within its
grave, until (d)
Thine azure sister of the Spring
shall blow (c)
Shelley

Tetrameter   A line of poetry with four poetic feet.
Běhóld hěr, sínglě ín thě fíeld,
Yŏn sólitáry híghland láss.
Wordsworth
(These lines are in iambic tetrameter.)

Textual criticism   An activity in which a literary
scholar seeks to reconstruct an original manuscript
and establish the authoritative text of the literary
work. This process could involve a close study of
an original manuscript or, if that is lost, a conjecture based on the various versions of the printed
text.

Thackeray, William Makepeace (1811–1863)
Born in India, this English novelist was sent to
school in England and studied at Cambridge, where
he found his chief interest was in drawing. He went
to Paris to study art and began to write there, illustrating his own books. He married, but his wife became insane after the birth of their third daughter.
His major works are the novels *Vanity Fair* (1848)
thought to be among the greatest works of all time,
and *Henry Esmond* (1853).

Theater of the absurd   An innovative form of experimental theater that arose after World War II, exhibited by the work of such master playwrights as
Ionesco, Beckett, and Genet. Plays of this genre
combine the grotesque, the ridiculous, and the
meaningless to depict man as isolated in an alien
universe. "Literature of the Absurd" can be found
in some portions of Kafka and Joyce.

Thomas, Dylan (1914–1953)   This major Anglo-
Welsh poet took his beautiful and complex imagery
from Freud and witchcraft, from Welsh legend and
Christian symbol, creating his own unique voice
and mythology. His zest for life, warm humor, and
lyric voice were all eclipsed when he was 39 and
died after an unsuccessful struggle with alcoholism.
Some of his most famous works are *A Child's
Christmas in Wales* and his strikingly dramatic
verse play, *Under Milkwood*. His *Collected Poems*
appeared in 1953.

Thoreau, Henry David (1817–1862)   A native of
Concord, he attended Harvard and became an early
convert to Transcendentalism. This American essayist and naturalist was a teacher, lecturer, and then
a handyman at Emerson's home. He made a trip to
New York to make his fortune as a literary man, returned to Concord to work in the family business,
and spent two years living in a cabin he built near
Walden Pond, about which he wrote in *Walden*
(1854). His best remembered essay is "Civil Disobedience" (1849).

The Three Sisters (1901), Anton Chekhov   This
Russian drama concerns three sisters living in a
Russian provincial town near an army camp. Their
father has died a year before and they feel that there
is little to keep them in the town. As they dream of
going to Moscow, they carry on a sort of social life,
with army officers as their principal guests. However, in a typically arrested gesture, they never make
the move out of their dull, small-town existence.

The Threepenny Opera (1928), Bertolt Brecht
Based on the 1728 English work *The Beggar's
Opera* by John Gay, this German play with music
by Kurt Weill is the story of Mackie Messer (Mack
the Knife), who married Polly Peachum, daughter
of a receiver of stolen goods, but is betrayed by the
other women he has deserted. Mack escapes, is
recaptured, but saved from hanging by the queen's
pardon.

The Tin Drum (1959), Günter Grass   This German
novel is usually interpreted as an allegory of German history from the early 20th century through the
Nazi period. The story is told by the dwarf Oskar
Matzerath, who is in a mental institution. He relates the tale of his life in a lively style, with an ironic
view of middle-class German values and much humor of the sort often called gallows humor.

To the Lighthouse (1927), Virginia Woolf   Considered Woolf's major work, this stream-of-consciousness novel lyrically presents the author's
conviction of the impermanence of all things.

Tolstoy, Leo (1828–1910)   From a wealthy noble
family, this great Russian novelist, short-story
writer, and essayist served in the military and spent
much of his youth in dissipation. He began to express a desire for social reform while still in his 20s,
and after his marriage, he retired to his family estate,
where he composed his two greatest works, *War and
Peace* (1865–69), a novel of the Napoleonic Wars,
and *Anna Karenina* (1875–77), a tragic novel based
on the high society of St. Petersburg.

**Tom Jones (The History of Tom Jones, a
Foundling)** (1749), Henry Fielding   Acclaimed
not only as Fielding's best novel, but as the greatest
work of the century, this breezy and engaging book
is a potpourri of many different characters, plots,
and subplots in addition to the interspersion of a
series of delightful essays on all manner of subjects.
An unending variety of incidents occur between the
separation of Tom from his sweetheart, Sophia, at
the beginning of the novel, and his being reunited
with her at the end.

Tragedy   A serious drama, in prose or poetry, about
a person, often of a high station in life, who experiences sudden personal reversals. Tragedies always
end with a catastrophic event. *See* Sophocles's
Antigone; Shakespeare's *Hamlet* and *King Lear*;
and Arthur Miller's *Death of a Salesman*.

Tragic force   The incident or event in a tragic
drama that triggers an action that results in the
hero's downfall. In Shakespeare's *Macbeth* the escape of Fleance marks the beginning of the catastrophic end of the hero, Macbeth.

Tragic irony   A form of irony that occurs when a
character in a tragedy uses words that mean one
thing to him and something more meaningful to
those who are listening. When Oedipus vows to find
the murderer of his father, he doesn't know that he
himself is the murderer.

Tragicomedy   A type of drama that is initially
serious in tone or theme, until it becomes apparent
that the tragic events will end happily rather than
with a catastrophic event. Shakespeare's *The
Merchant of Venice* ends without Shylock exacting
his "pound of flesh," which would have been tragic
for Antonio.

Transcendentalism A belief that human beings may learn higher truths in ways that transcend the senses, including intuition and mysticism. See the writings of Emerson and Thoreau, in America; Coleridge, in England; and Goethe, in Germany.

The Trial (1925), Franz Kafka Published after the author's death, this Czech novel is the story of a man condemned for a sin or a crime he never understands. The novel can be interpreted as treating the universal sense of human guilt, but some see it as the fate of contemporary man controlled by an anonymous and unfeeling bureaucracy.

Trilogy A literary work with three parts, each a complete unit. For instance, John Dos Passos's *U.S.A.*

Trimeter A line of poetry containing three metrical feet.

Trochee A metrical foot with a stressed syllable followed by an unstressed syllable.

The Trojan War (415 B.C.), Euripides This Greek tragedy has been called by critics less a drama than a tragic pageant; it is judged one of the most compelling antiwar plays. The setting is immediately after the fall of Troy, and the play deals with the wives and children of the conquered, about to become slaves and/or concubines of the Greek conquerors.

Trollope, Anthony (1815–1882) This English writer was the author of about 50 novels, of which the best are in the so-called "Barsetshire Series," which reproduced scenes of the life in a small English cathedral town. The most successful of these were *The Warden* (1855) and *Barchester Towers* (1857).

Troubadour A lyric poet of 12th- and 13th-century France who wrote chivalrously of love for a woman of noble birth.

Turgenev, Ivan (1818–1883) This Russian novelist and short-story writer is best known for his collection of short pieces, *A Sportman's Sketches* (1852), critical of serfdom, and his novel *Fathers and Sons* (1861), in which he wrote of the social revolt in Russia. This novel, his masterwork, was so ill-received that he spent most of his later years outside of Russia.

Twain, Mark (Samuel L. Clemens) (1835–1910) Born in Missouri, this novelist, essayist, and short-story writer was a pilot on the Mississippi River boats in his 20s (his pseudonym was actually a riverboat call for two fathoms) and then became a journalist in Nevada and California. His first popular success was *Innocents Abroad* (1869), written after a trip to the Holy Land. He lived in New York and finally settled permanently in Hartford, Connecticut, where he became one of the most famous lecturers and after-dinner speakers in the country, and wrote his two best-known works, *The Adventures of Tom Sawyer* (1876) and *The Adventures of Huckleberry Finn* (1884). Mark Twain, the great American humorist, baffled critics with the publication of *The Mysterious Stranger* (published posthumously, 1916). This novel was a marked contradiction between the familiar friendly humorist and the avowed misanthrope depicted in the work.

U *Ulysses* (1922), James Joyce This major Irish stream-of-consciousness novel concerns one day, June 16, 1904, in the life of Leopold Bloom, Dublin citizen. All that happens externally, to the uninitiated eye, is that he meets Stephen Dedalus (Joyce) and patches up a quarrel with his wife Molly. The novel, banned in the United States for many years on the charge of obscenity, employs many different literary techniques. Every incident in the book is a parallel of an occurrence in *The Odyssey* of Homer.

Uncle Tom's Cabin (1851–1852), Harriet Beecher Stowe This American novel may have been prompted by the passage of the Fugitive Slave Act of 1850, which hardened abolitionist sentiment in the North. Mrs. Stowe's aim in writing the book, a survey of both the good and evil sides of slavery, was to create more of a treatise than a literary work. The hero is Tom, a slave who undergoes both decent and cruel treatment, and dies feeling that heaven is his only haven.

Poster for *Uncle Tom's Cabin* by Harriet Beecher Stowe, showing Eliza's escape.

Under Milk Wood (1954), Dylan Thomas A masterful verse drama that covers one spring day in the life of a community, from before dawn to nightfall and dark. In this rich and colorful play, characters eulogize themselves, each other, and the town in such poetry as "...moonless night in the small town, starless and bible-black, the cobblestreets silent and the hunched...limping invisible down to the sloeback, slow, black, crow-black, fishing boat-bobbing sea."

Underground writing Usually refers to a facet of journalism popular in the last half of the 20th century in the United States. Such papers as *The Village Voice* (particularly at its inception) and *The East Village Other* concern themselves with liberal political beliefs, experimental forms of drama and literature, and radical ideologies in general.

Understatement　A form of irony, also called litotes, in which something is represented as less than it really is, with the intent of drawing attention to and emphasizing its meaning. For example, Helen of Troy was not a bad-looking woman.

Updike, John (b. 1932)　This Pennsylvania-born short-story writer, novelist, and poet worked for *The New Yorker* before the publication of his first novel, *The Poorhouse Fair* (1959), a book that attacked man's apathy to the aged and the welfare state. In subsequent works the critically-acclaimed Updike has written of the married and the immature, the professor and the clergyman, in his oftentimes brilliant and stylistic fiction. Some of his well-known books are the Rabbit series [*Rabbit, Run* (1960), *Rabbit Redux* (1971), and *Rabbit is Rich* (1981 Pulitzer prize winner)], and the short-story collections *Pigeon Feathers* (1962) and *Museums and Women* (1972).

U.S.A., John Dos Passos　This trilogy, published between 1930 and 1936, is actually a single novel divided into three parts: *The 42nd Parallel* (1930), *Nineteen-Nineteen* (1932), and *The Big Money* (1936). The purpose of the work is to paint a picture of the United States from 1900 into the 1930s. Into the text are woven various types of documentary materials: biographies, "newsreels" and "the camera eye," in addition to semi-autobiographical impressions.

V *Vanity Fair* (1848), William Makepeace Thackeray　Hailed as the greatest novel in English, *Vanity Fair* is subtitled by its author "A Novel Without a Hero." But it has a new kind of heroine, the incomparable, wicked, brilliant, and half-tragic Becky Sharpe, through whose meteoric rise to the heights of social success the reader views the crass stupidity of English aristocracy.

Variorum　An author's work containing, besides the text, interpretive remarks and critical commentaries. Students often use variorums when beginning to study the work of a difficult or esoteric writer.

Vergil (70–19 B.C.)　After studying in Rome and Naples, Vergil was fortunate enough to secure the patronage of two wealthy men so that he was able to devote himself to being a man of letters. His first important works were *Eclogues* and *Georgics,* but his masterwork was the epic *Aeneid.* Perhaps written at the request of the emperor Augustus and considered to be the best in Latin, this poem tells the story of the founding of Rome.

Verse　A general name given to all metrical (or poetic) compositions. Used specifically, the word means a line of poetry or the stanza of a song; used generally, it suggests a lower order of poetry, e.g., the limerick.

Versification　The making of verses; also used as a synonym for prosody to denote all the elements of poetic composition. In the latter sense, versification includes accent, rhythm, meter, rhyme, stanza form and so on.

Victorian age　Refers to 19th-century England under Queen Victoria's reign (1837–1901). An age typified by cluttered parlors, starched doilies, and prim manners, Victorian England is also viewed by some critics as seething with decadence beneath the horsehair sofa and the tightly drawn mouth. Hardy and Dickens were Victorians, as were Arnold and Swinburne.

Vignette　A sketch or a short work of literature that is noted for its precise detail. May also be part of a longer work.

Villanelle　A French form of poetry, originally with a pastoral setting. Now often used for light verse, it adheres to its own strict form.

Villon, François (1431–1480)　Student, clerk, but also highwayman and murderer, Villon is considered France's first outstanding poet. His works, of which the "Little Testament" (1456) and the "Great Testament" (1461) are the best known, are admired for the simplicity and realism Villon employs in his approach to passion and to death.

Voltaire, François Marie Arouet (1694–1778)　The major figure of the French Enlightenment, Voltaire was twice unjustly imprisoned in the Bastille. The second time he was released only because of his promise to go to England, where he lived for several years. A rationalist philosopher, he was also a novelist, historian, and poet of note. His collected works comprise 52 volumes, including his best-known work, *Candide* (1759).

Vonnegut, Kurt, Jr. (b. 1922)　A brilliant and witty 20th-century American novelist who uses the ideas of science fiction to satirize man's need for empathy and caring. Vonnegut is also adept at employing surrealism, black comedy, and nihilism to achieve his points. Some of his best-known works are *Cat's Cradle* (1963), *God Bless You, Mr. Rosewater* (1965), and *Happy Birthday, Wanda June* (1970).

W *Waiting for Godot* (1952), Samuel Beckett　This short Irish play presents two tramps, an ardent materialist and his servant. There is little plot as the characters hope for the arrival of Godot (although the audience never learns who or what that is) and show themselves in the grip of what existentialists term "the absurd." The closing scene is typical: The tramps decide to go, but do not move.

Walcott, Derek (b. 1930)　Born on the Caribbean island of St. Lucia and educated in the British tradition, Walcott was the founding director of the Little Carib Theatre/Trinidad Theatre Workshop (1959–1976). An Obie Award-winning, West Indian playwright and poet, Walcott is known for his "melodious and sensitive" style and "multicultural commitment" to the universal human condition. His epic poem *Omeros* (1990) and other writings earned Walcott the 1992 Nobel Prize in Literature.

Walden (1854), Henry David Thoreau　The theme of this master work is Thoreau's contention that men ought to lead sincere and joyous lives instead of workworn, sham existences. Here Thoreau celebrates the unique in man and challenges him to march to the tune of a different drummer—the one he hears inside himself that is different from all others.

Walpole, Horace (1717–1797)　Walpole is the father of the English "Gothic" novel, the novel of mystery and terror. His major work, *The Castle of Otranto* (1764), with a medieval setting and many trappings of suspense, initiated a vogue that was important in starting the Romantic Movement. Walpole also wrote a Gothic tragedy in blank verse, *The Mysterious Mother* (1768).

Walton, Izaak (1593–1683) Although he was a Royalist, the British author managed to steer clear of the controversies of his lifetime. In 1670 he published a book of biographies, which included lives of John Donne and George Herbert. He is best known, however, for *The Compleat Angler* (1653), a book he wrote ostensibly about his hobby of fishing that is also a philosophical work on the virtues of peace. "The Angler," in hardcover and paperback, is still widely read.

War and Peace (1865–1869), Leo Tolstoy This epic Russian novel, acclaimed the best ever written by many critics, covers the fate of four families, the Rostovs, Bolkonskis, Kuragins, and Bezukhovs, during the period of the Napoleonic Wars. The central romantic interest is Natasha Rostov, who eventually marries the kind but weak Pierre Bezukhov. The composition of the novel took six years, 1864–1870.

Warren, Robert Penn (1905–1989) Born in Kentucky, he attended Vanderbilt University, where he became a member of the "Fugitive Group," a coterie of young Southern writers, and then spent most of his career as a university professor. His poetry has won critical esteem and his 1946 novel *All the King's Men* had considerable popular success. Named America's first poet laureate, Warren won the Pulitzer Prize for his fiction in 1947 and for his poetry in 1958 and 1979.

EXHIBIT 15.8
Poets Laureate
of the United States*

Robert Penn Warren	1986–1987
Richard Wilbur	1987–1988
Howard Nemerov	1988–1990
Mark Strand	1990–1991
Joseph Brodsky	1991–1992
Mona Van Duyn	1992–

*Established in 1986, this post is appointed as a one-year term that is renewable.

The Waste Land (1922), T.S. Eliot Eliot's early master poetic work whose theme is the banality and barrenness of the contemporary world contrasted with the richness of traditional spiritual and mythological forces.

Waugh, Evelyn (1903–1966) From a literary family, this English novelist attended Oxford, the setting of many of his novels. Waugh's faultless command of the English language, his brilliantly bitter wit, and conservative viewpoint are best seen in novels like *Decline and Fall* (1928). His best work is generally considered to be *Brideshead Revisited* (1945).

Wells, H.G. (Herbert George) (1866–1946) A fervent believer in the idea that science could bring about man's ultimate happiness, this British novelist and essayist had his early successes with such science fiction as *The Time Machine* (1895) and *The War of the Worlds* (1898). He then wrote realistic studies of middle-class Englishmen like *Tono Bungay* (1909) and novels on his Utopian dreams for society. His output was enormous.

Welty, Eudora (b. 1909) Born in Mississippi, this Southern American novelist and short-story writer held a number of jobs in advertising and radio before returning to her native state to write. She was also in frequent demand as a lecturer and visiting professor at various universities. The charm of Welty's Southern characters lies both in their eccentricities and their grotesqueries. Her best-known works are *Delta Wedding* (1946) and *The Ponder Heart* (1953).

West, Nathanael (Nathan Weinstein) (1903–1940) Born in New York City, West graduated from Brown University and eventually went into hotel management. His first novel was privately printed in 1931; his second, *Miss Lonelyhearts* (1933) won great critical acclaim but did not sell. In 1939 he went to California where he wrote the screenplay for his book *The Day of the Locust*. The next year he and his wife were killed in an auto accident. Never a financially successful author during his lifetime, his fame and popularity rose greatly after his premature death.

Wharton, Edith (1862–1937) An artist of the interior world whose interest is in the psychological and spiritual motivations of her characters, this American novelist's work can be divided into three groups: novels of humble people in rural settings, novels about World War I, and novels of society life in New York and Europe. She was born in New York, married a Bostonian, but spent most of her later life in France, where she wrote her major works. These include *The House of Mirth* (1905) *Ethan Frome* (1911), and *The Age of Innocence* (1920).

Wheatley, Phyllis (1753–1784) The first American Negro poet to gain celebrity, Wheatley was born in Africa and sold as a slave in Boston, where her master taught her to read and write and drilled her in New England piety. By the time she was thirteen she translated her learning into verses which were both published and admired.

White, E.B. (Elwyn Brooks) (1899–1984) Born in Mount Vernon, New York, and educated at Cornell University, White began his career as a reporter, production assistant, and free-lance writer, with contributions to the *New Yorker* and *Harper's Magazine*. An essayist, poet, and author, White's works include *The Lady is Cold* (1929), *The Elements of Style* with William Strunk, Jr. (1959), and *Letters of E.B. White* (1976). His well-known children's books, *Stuart Little* (1945), *Charlotte's Web* (1952), and *The Trumpet of the Swan* (1970), have delighted readers for decades. White was the recipient of numerous honorary degrees and awards, including the National Medal for Literature (1971) and a Pulitzer Prize special citation (1978).

Whitman, Walt (1819–1892) Born on Long Island (New York), Whitman left school at the age of eleven to become a printer's devil, after which he taught school and became a newspaper editor. In 1855 *Leaves of Grass* was published at his own expense and was universally criticized because of its sexual subject matter and its innovative use of free verse. Whitman's work is filled with his concepts of freedom and the dignity of man. "When Lilacs Last in the Dooryard Bloomed" and "O Captain! My Captain!" (1866) are two of his famous poems. A poet who celebrated life and himself, Whitman, who was homosexual, is today claimed as one of the few truly great American men of letters.

Whittier, John Greenleaf (1807–1892) Born in a small town near Boston, Whittier spent most of his years in the country. His poetic themes were the experiences undergone by the common people of his area, and he was one of the better-known anti-slavery writers. In later life, after the Civil War, which he backed although he was a Quaker, he wrote of New England, its past and its countryside, as in *Legends of New England* (1831) and *Snowbound* (1866).

Wilde, Oscar (1854–1900) Educated at both Trinity College in Dublin and Oxford, this Irish playwright, poet, and novelist made himself the spokesman and the symbol of the "art for art's sake" movement. His best-known novel, *The Picture of Dorian Gray* (1891) was a great popular success and of his plays, *The Importance of Being Earnest* (1895) is judged the best. After serving a prison sentence for homosexual immorality, Wilde spent the rest of his life in France. He was a man and a writer of great art and flair.

Wilder, Thornton (1897–1975) Born in Wisconsin, this American novelist and playwright was educated in China (where his father was a diplomat), at the University of Califomia, Oberlin, Yale, the American Academy in Rome, and Princeton. He later taught at a private school until he was able to support himself on the income from his writing. His best-known novel is *The Bridge of San Luis Rey* (1927), and his plays *Our Town* (1938) and *The Skin of Our Teeth* (1942), utilized nonrealistic theatrical techniques.

Williams, Tennessee (1911–1983) Considered the greatest American playwright, Williams's first successes were with *The Glass Menagerie* (1945) and *A Streetear Named Desire* (1947). In both of those dramas, as in all of the works of this poetic and brilliant writer, the recurring themes are those of intense passion and pain, and the deterioration of Southern gentility into decadence. A master of dialogue and character creation, Williams also wrote the acclaimed *Cat on a Hot Tin Roof* (1955) and *Night of the Iguana* (1961), among other notable theatrical works.

Williams, William Carlos (1883–1963) This American poet was born in Rutherford, New Jersey, where he remained all his life, supporting himself as a physician from 1910–1952, when he retired. His major poetic effort was the long narrative poem *Paterson,* about the New Jersey city. It is a poem by a close observer of American life whose impressions are recorded in a clear and vital style.

Wilson, August (b. 1945) Founder of the Black Horizons Theatre Co. in Pittsburgh (1968), this prolific playwright has won the Pulitzer Prize twice: *Fences* (1987) and *The Piano Lesson* (1990).

Winesburg, Ohio (1919), Sherwood Anderson A set of connected stories or sketches dealing with the inhabitants of a fictional American town. The central figure is young George Willard, reporter for the *Winesburg Eagle,* who is the observer and commentator for most of the stories. It becomes clear that Anderson sees the American small town as a suppressed volcano of frustrations, passions, and bitterness.

Wolfe, Thomas (1900–1938) Born in Ashville, North Carolina, Wolfe was sent to the state university at 15, graduated at 20, and did graduate work at Harvard. He taught English at New York University until the publication of his first novel, *Look Homeward, Angel* (1929), which was both a critical and popular success. Only one other novel was published during his lifetime, [*Of Time And The River* (1935)] in part because of the difficulty of editing his enormous manuscripts. Posthumously published were *The Web and the Rock* (1939) and *You Can't Go Home Again* (1940).

Woolf, Virginia (1882–1941) The daughter of a noted scholar and the wife of a distinguished journalist, this English writer was an original and influential force in the modern novel. Her principal concern in two of her best novels [*Mrs. Dalloway* (1925) and *To the Lighthouse* (1927)] was to recreate the world of the inner consciousness of her characters. She took her own life by drowning.

Wordsworth, William (1770–1850) Born in England's Lake District, this British poet was educated at Cambridge. During the French Revolution he was introduced to the ideas of Rousseau, which affected him deeply. In 1798 he published *Lyrical Ballads* with Coleridge, the book that is considered to have begun the Romantic Movement in Britain. He was named poet laureate in 1843. Some of the exquisite lyricism in Wordsworth's poetry can be found in "Daffodils" and the well-known Lucy poems.

Wouk, Herman (b. 1915) Born in New York, Wouk, a novelist, has lived most of his life in that city. He graduated from Columbia University and then worked for six years as a radio writer. He served four years in the Pacific in World War II, an experience that served him in the writing of his best novel, *The Caine Mutiny* (1951).

Wright, Richard (1908–1960) Born in Mississippi, this black novelist, essayist, and short-story writer attended school only through the ninth grade. He went to Memphis and then to Chicago, where he worked as a dishwasher, porter, postal clerk, and salesman. He joined the Communist Party in 1932 and left it in disillusionment in 1944. Wright had his first success with *Native Son* (1940). He lived in New York and then in Paris.

Wuthering Heights (1848), Emily Brontë The passionate and tempestuous Gothic tale of Cathy and Heathcliffe, whose love for each other bordered on madness and obsession. A lyric novel of intense mood and beauty.

 **Yeats, William Butler** (1865–1939) Born in Dublin, Yeats was educated in London. His family was Protestant and he constantly sought to find a connection between religion and art. His early poetry was symbolist with a certain mystical quality; his later work is more romantic. Besides poetry, he also wrote drama and became a central figure in the Irish literary revival at the end of the 19th century.

Yeats was awarded the Nobel Prize for Literature in 1923. His *Collected Poems* were published in 1953.

Yevtushenko, Yevgeny (b. 1933)   This Russian poet has had success not only in his homeland, but also overseas. His first work was published in 1949 and his first collection, *Scouts of the Future,* in 1952. Two visits to Cuba in 1960 and 1961 produced *Verses About Fidel.* He has continued to write, although he has been criticized in the Soviet press for "over-originality."

Zola, Emile (1840-1902)   The leader of the French naturalistic school, deemphasizing the role of free will in human life, Zola was also an influential pamphleteer. His best-known novel is *Nana* (1880) in which, as in his other works, he is precisely descriptive of different societal milieus. A social reformer, his part in the Dreyfus Affair [*J'accuse* (1898)] was his most eloquent public statement.

LITERATURE

MATHEMATICS

ARITHMETIC

Whole Numbers

The numbers 0,1,2,3, . . . are called whole numbers or integers.

This set of numbers represents the whole numbers. In other words, the set of whole numbers consists of 0 and all the natural numbers.

If the integer k divides m evenly, then we say m is divisible by k or k is a factor of m. For example, 12 is divisible by 4, but 12 is not divisible by 5. 1, 2, 3, 4, 6, 12 are all factors of 12.

If k *is* a factor of m, then there is another integer n such that $m = k \times n$; in this case, m is called a multiple of k.

Since $12 = 4 \times 3$, 12 is a multiple of 4 and also 12 is a multiple of 3; 5, 10, 15, and 20 are all multiples of 5 but 15 and 5 are not multiples of 10.

Any integer is a multiple of each of its factors.

Any whole number is divisible by itself and by 1. If p is a whole number greater than 1, which has only p and 1 as factors, then p is called a prime number. 2, 3, 5, 7, 11, 13, 17, 19, and 23 are all primes. 14 is not a prime since it is divisible by 2 and by 7.

A whole number which is divisible by 2 is called an even number; if a whole number is not even, then it is an odd number. 2, 4, 6, 8, 10 are even numbers, and 1, 3, 5, 7, and 9 are odd numbers.

A collection of numbers is consecutive if each number is the successor of the number which precedes it. For example, 7, 8, 9, and 10 are consecutive, but 7, 8, 10, 13 are not. 4, 6, 8, 10 are consecutive even numbers. 7, 11, 13, 17 are consecutive primes. 7, 13, 19, 23 are not consecutive primes since 11 is a prime between 7 and 13.

Some postulates for the natural numbers are:
The commutative property of addition:

$$a + b = b + a$$

for any two numbers a and b.
The commutative property of multiplication:

$$a \times b = b \times a$$

for any two numbers a and b.
The associative property of addition:

$$(a + b) + c = a + (b + c)$$

for any three numbers a, b, and c.
The associative property of multiplication:

$$(a \times b) \times c = a \times (b \times c)$$

for any three numbers a, b, and c.
Any whole number can be written as a product of factors which are prime numbers.

To write a number as a product of prime factors:
(A) Divide the number by 2 if possible; continue to divide by 2 until the factor you get is not divisible by 2.
(B) Divide the result from (A) by 3 if possible; continue to divide by 3 until the factor you get is not divisible by 3.
(C) Divide the result from (B) by 5 if possible; continue to divide by 5 until the factor you get is not divisible by 5.
(D) Continue the procedure with 7, 11, and so on, until all the factors are primes.

The least common multiple (L.C.M.) of two numbers is the smallest number which is a common multiple of both numbers. To find the least common multiple of two numbers k and j:

Write k as a product of primes and j as a product of primes.

If there are any common factors delete them in one of the products.

Multiply the remaining factors; the result is the least common multiple.

A number m is a common multiple of two other numbers k and j if it is a multiple of each of them. For example, 12 is a common multiple of 4 and 6, since $3 \times 4 = 12$ and $2 \times 6 = 12$. 15 is not a common multiple of 3 and 6, because 15 is not a multiple of 6.

A number k is a common factor of two other numbers m and n if k is a factor of m and k is a factor of n.

Fractions

A fraction is a number which represents a ratio or division of two whole numbers (integers). A fraction is written in the form $\frac{a}{b}$. The number on the top, a, is called the numerator; the number on the bottom, b, is called the denominator. The denominator tells how many of these equal parts there are (for example, parts of a pie); the numerator tells how many of these equal parts are taken. For example, $\frac{5}{8}$ is a fraction whose numerator is 5 and whose denominator is 8; it represents taking 5 of 8 equal parts, or dividing 8 into 5.

A fraction cannot have 0 as a denominator since division by 0 is not defined.

A fraction with 1 as the denominator is the same as the whole number which is its numerator. For example, $\frac{12}{1}$ is 12, $\frac{0}{1}$ is 0.

If the numerator and denominator of a fraction are identical, the fraction represents 1. For example, $\frac{3}{3} = \frac{9}{9} = \frac{13}{13} = 1$. Any whole number, k, is represented by a fraction with a numerator equal to k times the denominator. For example, $\frac{18}{6} = 3$, and $\frac{30}{5} = 6$.

Mixed Numbers

A mixed number consists of a whole number and a fraction. For example, $7\frac{1}{4}$ is a mixed number; it means $7 + \frac{1}{4}$ and $\frac{1}{4}$ is called the fractional part of the mixed number $7\frac{1}{4}$. Any mixed number can be changed into a fraction:

(A) Multiply the whole number by the denominator of the fractional part.

(B) Add the numerator of the fraction to the result of step (A).

(C) Use the result of step (B) as the numerator and use the denominator of the fractional part of the mixed number as a denominator. This fraction is equal to the mixed number.

A fraction whose numerator is larger than its denominator can be changed into a mixed number.

(A) Divide the denominator into the numerator; the result is the whole number of the mixed number.

(B) Put the remainder from step (A) over the denominator; this is the fractional part of the mixed number.

We can regard any whole number as a mixed number with 0 as the fractional part. For example, $\frac{18}{6} = 3$.

Multiplying Fractions

To multiply two fractions, multiply their numerators and divide this result by the product of their denominators. For example, $\frac{2}{3} \times \frac{5}{7} = \frac{10}{21}$.

Dividing Fractions

One fraction is a reciprocal of another if their product is 1. So $\frac{1}{2}$ and 2 are reciprocals. To find the reciprocal of a fraction, simply interchange the numerator and denominator (turn the fraction upside down). This is called inverting the fraction. So when you invert $\frac{15}{17}$ you get $\frac{17}{15}$. When a fraction is inverted the inverted fraction and the original fraction are reciprocals. Thus $\frac{15}{17} \cdot \frac{17}{15} = \frac{255}{255} = \frac{1}{1} = 1$.

To divide one fraction (the dividend) by another fraction (the divisor), invert the divisor and multiply.

Dividing and Multiplying by the Same Number

Since multiplication or division by 1 does not change the value of a number, you can multiply or divide any fraction by 1 and the fraction will remain the same. Remember that $\frac{a}{a} = 1$ for any nonzero number a. Therefore, if you multiply or divide any fraction by $\frac{a}{a}$, the result is the same as if you multiplied the numerator and denominator by a or divided the numerator and denominator by a.

If you multiply the numerator and denominator of a fraction by the same nonzero number the fraction remains the same.

If you divide the numerator and denominator of any fraction by the same number, the fraction remains the same.

When we multiply fractions, if any of the numerators and denominators have a common factor we can divide each of them by the common factor and the fraction remains the same. This process is called canceling and can be a great time-saver.

Equivalent Fractions

Two fractions are equivalent or equal if they represent the same ratio or number. In the last section, you saw that if you multiply or divide the numerator and denominator of a fraction by the same nonzero number the result is equivalent to the original fraction. For example, $\frac{7}{8} = \frac{70}{80}$ since $70 = 10 \times 7$ and $80 = 10 \times 8$.

To find a fraction with a known denominator equal to a given fraction:

(A) Divide the denominator of the given fraction into the known denominator.

(B) Multiply the result of (A) by the numerator of the given fraction; this is the numerator of the required equivalent fraction.

Reducing a Fraction to Lowest Terms

A fraction has been reduced to lowest terms when the numerator and denominator have no common factors. For example, $\frac{3}{4}$ is reduced to lowest terms, but $\frac{3}{6}$ is not because 3 is a common factor of 3 and 6.

To reduce a fraction to lowest terms, cancel all the common factors of the numerator and denominator. (Canceling common factors will not change the value of the fraction.) Sometimes canceling common factors can be helpful in multiplying fractions. For example,

$$\frac{1}{3} \times \frac{3}{4} = \frac{3}{12} = \frac{\overset{1}{\cancel{3}} \times 1}{\cancel{3} \times 4} = \frac{1}{4}$$

Canceling before multiplying gives the product in lowest terms:

$$\frac{1}{\cancel{3}} \times \frac{\overset{1}{\cancel{3}}}{4} = \frac{1}{4}$$

Adding Fractions

If the fractions have the same denominator, then the denominator is called a common denominator. Add the numerators, and use this sum as the new numerator with the common denominator as the denominator of the sum. If the fractions don't have the same denominator, you must first find a common denominator. Multiply all the denominators together; the result is a common denominator. There are many common denominators; the smallest one is called the least common denominator. Once you have found a common denominator, express each fraction as an equivalent fraction with the common denominator, and add as you did for the case when the fractions had the same denominator.

Subtracting Fractions

When the fractions have the same denominator, subtract the numerators and place the result over the denominator. When the fractions have different denominators:

Find a common denominator.
Express the fractions as equivalent fractions with the same denominator.
Subtract.

Rules for Operations on Fractions:

$$\frac{a}{b} \times \frac{c}{d} = \frac{ac}{bd}$$

$$\frac{a}{b} + \frac{c}{b} = \frac{a + c}{b}$$

$$\frac{a}{b} + \frac{c}{d} = \frac{ad}{bd} + \frac{bc}{bd} = \frac{ad + bc}{bd}$$

$$\frac{a}{b} - \frac{c}{d} = \frac{ad}{bd} - \frac{bc}{bd} = \frac{ad - bc}{bd}$$

$$\frac{a}{b} \div \frac{c}{d} = \frac{a}{b} \times \frac{d}{c} = \frac{ad}{bc}$$

Complex Fractions

A fraction whose numerator and denominator are themselves fractions is called a complex fraction.

For example, $\frac{2/3}{4/5}$ is a complex fraction. A complex fraction can always be simplified by dividing the numerator by the denominator.

Decimals

A collection of digits (the digits are 0, 1, 2, . . . 9) after a period (called the decimal point) is called a decimal fraction. For example, .503, .5602, .32, and .4 are all decimal fractions.

Every decimal fraction represents a fraction. To find the fraction that a decimal fraction represents:
(A) Take the fraction whose denominator is 10 and whose numerator is the first digit to the right of the decimal point.
(B) Take the fraction whose denominator is 100 and whose numerator is the second digit to the right of the decimal point.
(C) Take the fraction whose denominator is 1,000 and whose numerator is the third digit to the right of the decimal point.
(D) Continue the procedure until you have used each digit to the right of the decimal point. The denominator in each step is 10 times the denominator in the previous step.
(E) The sum of the fractions you have obtained in (A), (B), (C), and (D) is the fraction that the decimal fraction represents.

You can add any number of zeros to the right of a decimal fraction without changing its value.

We call the first position to the right of the decimal point the tenths place, since the digit in that position tells you how many tenths you should take. (It is the numerator of a fraction whose denominator is 10.) In the same way, we call the second position to the right the hundredths place, the third position to the right the thousandths, and so on. The various digits represent different numbers depending on their position: the first place to the left of the decimal point represents units, the second place to the left represents tens, and so on.

The following diagram may be helpful:

T	H	T	U	T	H	T
H	U	E	N	E	U	H
O	N	N	I	N	N	O
U	D	S	T	T	D	U
S	R		S	H	R	S
A	E			S	E	A
N	D				D	N
D	S				T	D
S					H	T
					S	H
						S

A decimal is a whole number plus a decimal fraction; the decimal point separates the whole number from the decimal fraction. For example, 4,307.206 is a decimal which represents 4,307 added to the decimal fraction .206. A decimal fraction is a decimal with zero as the whole number.

A fraction whose denominator is a power of 10 is equivalent to a decimal. A power of 10 is a product of two or more 10s, for example, 100, or 1,000, or 10,000. The number of zeros in the power of 10 tells you how many places to the left the decimal point in the numerator must be moved. For example, $\frac{12.5}{100} = .125$ and $\frac{213}{1,000} = \frac{213.}{1,000} = .213$.

If the numerator does not have enough digits, add the appropriate number of zeros before the first digit of the numerator.

For example, $\frac{4}{100} = \frac{04}{100} = .04$

Adding Decimals

Decimals are much easier to add than fractions. To add a collection of decimals:
(A) Write the decimals in a column with the decimal points vertically aligned.
(B) Add enough zeros to the right of the decimal point so that every number has an entry in each column to the right of the decimal point.
(C) Add the numbers in the same way as whole numbers.
(D) Place a decimal point in the sum so that it is directly beneath the decimal points in the decimals added.

Subtracting Decimals

To subtract one decimal from another:
(A) Put the decimals in a column so that the decimal points are vertically aligned.
(B) Add zeros so that every decimal has an entry in each column to the right of the decimal point.
(C) Subtract the numbers as you would whole numbers.
(D) Place the decimal point in the result so that it is directly beneath the decimal points of the numbers you subtracted.

Multiplying Decimals

Decimals are multiplied like whole numbers. The decimal point of the product is placed so that the number of decimal places in the product is equal to the total number of decimal places in all of the numbers multiplied. To multiply a decimal by 10, just move the decimal point to the right one place; to multiply by 100, move the decimal point two places to the right and so on.

Dividing Decimals
To divide one decimal (the dividend) by another decimal (the divisor):
(A) Move the decimal point in the divisor to the right until there is no decimal fraction in the divisor (this is the same as multiplying the divisor by a power of 10).
(B) Move the decimal point in the dividend the same number of places to the right as you moved the decimal point in step (A).
(C) Divide the result of (B) by the result of (A) as if they were whole numbers.
(D) The number of decimal places in the result (quotient) should be equal to the number of decimal places in the result of step (B).
(E) You may obtain as many decimal places as you wish in the quotient by adding zeros to the right in the dividend and then repeating step (C). For each zero you add to the dividend, you obtain one more decimal place in the quotient.

To divide a decimal by a whole number, divide them as if they were whole numbers. Then place the decimal point in the quotient so that the quotient has as many decimal places as the dividend.

To divide a decimal by 10, move the decimal point to the left one place; to divide by 100, move the decimal point two places to the left, and so on.

Converting a Fraction into a Decimal
To convert a fraction into a decimal, divide the denominator into the numerator. For example, $\frac{3}{4} = \frac{3.00}{4} = .75$. Some fractions give an infinite decimal when you divide the denominator into the numerator, for example, $\frac{1}{3} = .333\ldots$ where the three dots mean you keep on getting 3 with each step of division. $.333\ldots$ is an infinite decimal.

If a fraction is an infinite decimal, use the fraction in any computation.

You should know the following decimal equivalents of fractions:

$\frac{1}{100} = .01$	$\frac{1}{6} = .1666\ldots$	$\frac{1}{2} = .5$
$\frac{1}{50} = .02$	$\frac{1}{5} = .2$	$\frac{5}{8} = .625$
$\frac{1}{25} = .04$	$\frac{1}{4} = .25$	$\frac{2}{3} = .666\ldots$
$\frac{1}{20} = .05$	$\frac{1}{3} = .333\ldots$	$\frac{3}{4} = .75$
$\frac{1}{10} = .1$	$\frac{3}{8} = .375$	$\frac{7}{8} = .875$
$\frac{1}{8} = .125$	$\frac{2}{3} = .4$	

Percentage

Percentage is another method of expressing fractions or parts of an object. Percentages are

expressed in terms of hundredths, so 100% means 100 hundredths or 1, and 50% would be 50 hundredths or $\frac{1}{2}$.

A decimal is converted to a percentage by multiplying the decimal by 100. Since multiplying a decimal by 100 is accomplished by moving the decimal point two places to the right, you convert a decimal into a percentage by moving the decimal point two places to the right. For example, $.134 = 13.4\%$.

If you wish to convert a percentage into a decimal, you divide the percentage by 100. There is a shortcut for this also. To divide by 100 you move the decimal point two places to the left.

Therefore, to convert a percentage into a decimal, move the decimal point two places to the left. For example, $24\% = .24$.

A fraction is converted into a percentage by changing the fraction to a decimal and then changing the decimal to a percentage. A percentage is changed into a fraction by first converting the percentage into a decimal and then changing the decimal to a fraction. You should know the following fractional equivalents of percentages:

$1\% = \frac{1}{100}$	$25\% = \frac{1}{4}$	$80\% = \frac{4}{5}$
$2\% = \frac{1}{50}$	$33\frac{1}{3}\% = \frac{1}{3}$	$83\frac{1}{3}\% = \frac{5}{6}$
$4\% = \frac{1}{25}$	$37\frac{1}{2}\% = \frac{3}{8}$	$87\frac{1}{2}\% = \frac{7}{8}$
$5\% = \frac{1}{20}$	$40\% = \frac{2}{5}$	$100\% = 1$
$8\frac{1}{3}\% = \frac{1}{100}$	$50\% = \frac{1}{2}$	$120\% = \frac{6}{5}$
$10\% = \frac{1}{10}$	$60\% = \frac{3}{5}$	$125\% = \frac{5}{4}$
$12\frac{1}{2}\% = \frac{1}{8}$	$62\frac{1}{2}\% = \frac{5}{8}$	$133\frac{1}{3}\% = \frac{4}{3}$
$16\frac{2}{3}\% = \frac{1}{6}$	$66\frac{2}{3}\% = \frac{2}{3}$	$150\% = \frac{3}{2}$
$20\% = \frac{1}{5},$	$75\% = \frac{3}{4}$	

When you compute with percentages, it is usually easier to change the percentages to decimals or fractions.

Interest and Discount
Two of the most common uses of percentages are in interest and discount problems. The rate of interest is usually given as a percentage. The basic formula for simple interest problems is

interest = amount × time × rate

You can assume the rate of interest is the annual rate of interest unless the problem states otherwise; so you should express the time in years.

There is another method of computing interest called compound interest. In computing compound interest, the interest is periodically added to the amount (or principal) which is earning interest.

Compounded annually means that the interest earned during one year is added to the amount (or principal) at the end of each year. The interest on $1,000 at 5% for one year is $(1,000)(.05) = $50. So you must compute the interest on $1,050 (not $1,000) for the second year. The interest is $(1,050)(.05) = $52.50. Therefore, during the third year interest will be computed for $1,102.50. During the third year the interest is $(1,102.50)(.05) = $55.125 = $55.13. Therefore, after 3 years the original $1,000 will be worth $1,157.63.

If you calculated simple interest on $1,000 at 5% for three years, the answer would be $(1,000)(.05)(3) = $150. Therefore, using simple interest, $1,000 is worth $1,150 after 3 years. Notice that this is not the same as the money was worth using compound interest.

You can assume that interest means simple interest unless a problem states otherwise.

The basic formula for discount problems is

$$\text{discount} = \text{cost} \times \text{rate of discount}$$

If we know the list price of an item and its discounted price, we can find the rate of discount by using the formula

$$\text{rate of discount} = \frac{\text{list price} - \text{selling price}}{\text{cost}}$$

After an item has been discounted once, it may be discounted again. This procedure is called successive discounting.

Rounding Off Numbers

Many times an approximate answer can be found more quickly and may be more useful than the exact answer. For example, if a company had sales of $998,875.63 during a year, it is easier to remember that the sales were about $1 million.

Rounding off a number to a decimal place means finding the multiple of the representative of that decimal place which is closest to the original number. Thus, rounding off a number to the nearest hundredth means finding the multiple of $\frac{1}{100}$ which is closest to the original number. Rounding off to the nearest tenth means finding the multiple of $\frac{1}{10}$ which is closest to the original number. After a number has been rounded off to a particular decimal place, all digits to the right of that particular decimal place will be zero.

To round off a number to the rth decimal place:
(A) Look at the digit in the place to the right of the rth place;
(B) If the digit is 0, 1, 2, 3, or 4, change all the digits in places to the right of the rth place to 0 to round off the number.
(C) If the digit is 5, 6, 7, 8, or 9, add 1 to the digit in the rth place and change all the digits in places to the right of the rth place to 0 to round off the number.

For example, the multiple of 100 which is closest to 5,342.1 is 5,300. Most problems dealing with money are rounded off if the answer contains a fractional part of a cent. This is common practice.

Signed Numbers

A number preceded by either a plus or a minus sign is called a signed number. For example, +5, –6, –4.2, and $+\frac{3}{4}$ are all signed numbers. If no sign is given with a number, a plus sign is assumed; thus, 5 is interpreted as +5.

Signed numbers arc also called directed numbers. You can think of numbers arranged on a line, called a number line, in the following manner.

Take a line which extends indefinitely in both directions, pick a point on the line and call it 0, pick another point on the line to the right of 0 and call it 1. The point to the right of 1 which is exactly as far from 1 as 1 is from 0 is called 2, the point to the right of 2 just as far from 2 as 1 is from 0 is called 3, and so on. The point halfway between 0 and 1 is called $\frac{1}{2}$; the point halfway between $\frac{1}{2}$ and 1 is called $\frac{1}{4}$. In this way, you can identify any whole number or any fraction with a point on the line.

All the numbers which correspond to points to the right of 0 are called positive numbers. The sign of a positive number is + . If you go to the left of zero the same distance as you did from 0 to 1, the point is called –1; in the same way as before, you can find –2, –3, $-\frac{1}{2}$, $-\frac{3}{2}$, and so on.

All the numbers which correspond to points to the left of zero are called negative numbers. Negative numbers are signed numbers whose sign is –.

0 is neither positive nor negative; any nonzero number is positive or negative but not both. So –0 = 0.

Absolute Value
The absolute value of a signed number is the distance of the number from 0. The absolute value of any nonzero number is positive. For example, the absolute value of 2 is 2; the absolute value of –2 is 2. The absolute value of a number a is denoted by $|a|$, so $|-2| = 2$. The absolute value of any number can be found by dropping its sign, $|-12| = 12$, $|4| = 4$. Thus $|-a| = |a| = a$ for any number a. The only number whose absolute value is zero is zero.

Adding Signed Numbers
Case I. Adding numbers with the *same sign:*
(A) The sign of the sum is the same as the sign of the numbers being added.
(B) Add the absolute values.
(C) Put the sign from step (A) in front of the number you obtained in step (B).

Case II. Adding two numbers with *different signs:*
(A) The sign of the sum is the sign of the number which is largest in absolute value.
(B) Subtract the absolute value of the number with the smaller absolute value from the absolute value of the number with the larger absolute value.
(C) The answer is the number you obtained in step (B) preceded by the sign from part (A).

Case III. Adding more than two numbers with different signs:
(A) Add all the positive numbers; the result is positive (this is Case I).
(B) Add all the negative numbers; the result is negative (this is Case I).
(C) Add the result of step (A) to the result of step (B), by using Case II.

To illustrate,
1. $(-3) + (-5) = -8$ (Case I)
2. $(+1) + (-4) = -3$ (Case II)
3. $(+2) + (-5) + (-1) = (+2) + (-6)$ (Case III)
$\qquad = -4$

Subtracting Signed Numbers

When subtracting signed numbers:
(A) Change the sign of the number you are subtracting (the subtrahend) to its opposite.
(B) *Add* the result of step (A) to the number being subtracted from (the minuend) using the rules of the preceding section.

So we subtract a negative number by adding a positive number with the same absolute value. For example, $(+5) - (-4) = (+5) + (+4) = +(9)$. We subtract a positive number by adding a negative number of the same absolute value. For example, $(+7) - (+2) = (+7) + (-2) = (+5)$.

Multiplying Signed Numbers

Case I. Multiplying two numbers:
(A) Multiply the absolute values of the numbers.
(B) If both numbers have the same sign, the result of step (A) is the answer—i.e., the product is positive. If the numbers have different signs, then the answer is the result of step (A) with a minus sign.

Case II. Multiplying more than two numbers:
(A) Multiply the first two factors using Case I.
(B) Multiply the result of (A) by the third factor.
(C) Multiply the result of (B) by the fourth factor.
(D) Continue until you have used each factor.

The sign of the product is + if there are no negative factors or there is an even number of negative factors. The sign of the product is − if there is an odd number of negative factors. To illustrate:
1. $(+5)\ (+3) = +15$ (Case I)
2. $(+5)\ (-3) = -15$ (Case I)
3. $(+5)\ (-3) + (-2) = (-15)\ (-2)$ (Case II)
$\qquad\qquad = +30$ (Case I)

Dividing Signed Numbers

Divide the absolute values of the numbers; the sign of the quotient is determined by the same rule as you used to determine the sign of a product. Thus,

+	÷	+	=	+
−	÷	−	=	+
+	÷	+	=	−
−	÷	+	=	−

Rational Numbers

Suppose a and b are any two integers (except that b cannot be zero). Then any number that can be written in the form a/b is a rational number.

The signs of a fraction:

$$\frac{-a}{-b} = \frac{a}{b} \quad \left(\text{since } \frac{-1}{-1} = 1, \text{ and } \frac{(-1)\times(-a)}{(-1)\times(-b)} = \frac{a}{b}\right)$$

$$\frac{-a}{b} = -\frac{a}{b}$$

$$\frac{a}{-b} = -\frac{a}{b}$$

$$-\frac{-a}{-b} = -\frac{a}{b}$$

Averages and Medians

Mean

The average or arithmetic mean of a set of N numbers is the result of dividing the sum of all the numbers in the set by N.

The Median

The number which is in the middle if the numbers in a set of numbers are arranged in order is called the median. The median of the set of numbers 4, 5, 8, 13, 15 is 8. The average of these numbers is

$$\frac{4 + 5 + 8 + 13 + 15}{5} = \frac{45}{5} = 9$$

If the number of objects in the set is even, the median is the average of the two numbers in the middle of the array. For example, the median of 64, 66, 72, 75, 76, and 77 is the average of 72 and 75, which is 73.5.

In general, the median and the average of a set of numbers are different.

Powers, Exponents and Roots

Powers

If b is any number and n is a whole number greater than 0, b^n means the product of n factors each of which is equal to b. Thus,

$$b^n = b \times b \times b \times \cdots \times b,$$

where there are n copies of b. If $n = 1$, there is only one copy of b so $b^1 = b$. Here are some examples:

$$2^5 = 2 \times 2 \times 2 \times 2 \times 2 = 32,$$

$$(-4)^3 = (-4) \times (-4) \times (-4) = -64,$$

$$\frac{3^2}{4} = \frac{3 \times 3}{4} = \frac{9}{4},$$

$1^n = 1$ for any n, $0^n = 0$ for any n, except $n = 0$.

b^n is read as "b raised to the nth power." b^2 is read "b squared." b^2 is always greater than 0 (positive) if b is not zero, since the product of two negative numbers is positive. b^3 is read "b cubed." b^3 can be negative or positive.

You should know the following squares and cubes:

1^2	$= 1$	8^2	$= 64$
2^2	$= 4$	9^2	$= 81$
3^2	$= 9$	10^2	$= 100$
4^2	$= 16$	11^2	$= 121$
5^2	$= 25$	12^2	$= 144$
6^2	$= 36$	13^2	$= 169$
7^2	$= 49$	14^2	$= 196$
		15^2	$= 225$

1^3	$= 1$	3^3	$= 27$
2^3	$= 8$	4^3	$= 64$
		5^3	$= 125$

If you raise a fraction, $\frac{p}{q}$, to a power, then

$$\left(\frac{p}{q}\right)^n = \frac{p^n}{q^n}$$

Exponents

In the expression b^n, b is called the base and n is called the exponent. In the expression 2^5, 2 is the base and 5 is the exponent. The exponent tells how many factors there are.

Some **laws of exponents** are:

$x^a x^b = x^{a+b}$ $\qquad$ $(x^a)^b = x^{ab}$

$\dfrac{x^a}{x^b} = x^{a-b}$ $\qquad$ $(xy)^a = x^a y^a$

$b^0 = 1$ for any nonzero number b.

(Note: 0^0 is not defined.)

$x^{-a} = \dfrac{1}{x^a}$

$x^0 = 1$

(Note that x^n is not defined if $n \le 0$ and $x = 0$.)

$b^{-n} = \dfrac{1}{b^n}$.

Multiplying by b^{-n} is the same as dividing by b^n.

Scientific Notation

Scientific notation is useful when it is necessary to express very large numbers or very small numbers close to zero in a compact form. To express a number in scientific notation, write the number as the product of a power of 10 and a number between 1 and 10. Examples: $8.066 \times 10^2 = 806.6$, $9.46 \times 10^{-3} = 0.00946$.

Roots

If you raise a number d to the nth power and the result is b, then d is called the nth root of b, which is usually written $\sqrt[n]{b} = d$. Since $2^5 = 32$, then $\sqrt[5]{32} = 2$. The second root is called the square root and is written $\sqrt{\ }$; the third root is called the cube root. There are two possibilities for the square root of a positive number. Since the square of any nonzero number is positive, the square root of a negative number is not defined as a real number. Thus $\sqrt{-2}$ is not a real number. There are cube roots of negative numbers. $\sqrt[3]{-8} = -2$, because $(-2) \times (-2) \times (-2) = -8$.

You can also write roots as exponents; for example,

$$\sqrt[n]{b} = b^{1/n}; \quad \text{so} \quad \sqrt{b} = b^{1/2}, \quad \sqrt[3]{b} = b^{1/3}$$

The following formula is the basic formula for simplifying square roots, cube roots, and so on:

$$a^{1/n} \times b^{1/n} = (a \cdot b)^{1/n} \text{ or } \sqrt[n]{a \times b} = \sqrt[n]{a} \times \sqrt[n]{b}$$

The name real numbers is used for the set containing all of the rational numbers and all of the irrational numbers. Each real number corresponds to exactly one point on a number line. Real numbers can be represented as decimal fractions that either terminate, endlessly repeat a pattern, or continue endlessly with no pattern. The results of measurements of physical quantities (such as distance, time, mass, or energy) will be real numbers.

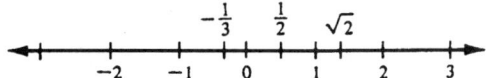

Operations on Radicals

In the radical expression $\sqrt[3]{7}$, 3 is called the index and 7 is called the radicand. In the radical $\sqrt{5}$ (the square root of 5), the index is understood to be 2.

Like radicals have the same index and same radicand.

Like radicals may be added by adding their coefficients:

$$3\sqrt{5} + 4\sqrt{5} = 7\sqrt{5}$$

Radicals with the same index may be multiplied (or divided) by multiplying (or dividing) their coefficients and multiplying (or dividing) their radicands:

$$(3\sqrt{2})(4\sqrt{5}) = 12\sqrt{10}$$

$$14\sqrt{6} \div 7\sqrt{2} = 2\sqrt{3}$$

Factors of the radicand may be removed from under a radical sign by taking the indicated root of the factor and using it as a factor of the coefficient: $5\sqrt{18} = 5\sqrt{9(2)} = 5(3)\sqrt{2} = 15\sqrt{2}$.

Rationalizing Denominators

If a radical sign appears in the denominator of a fraction, you can rewrite the fraction so that there are no radicals in the denominator. For example,

$$\frac{1}{\sqrt{2}} = \frac{1}{\sqrt{2}} \times \frac{\sqrt{2}}{\sqrt{2}} = \frac{\sqrt{2}}{2}$$

Matters are slightly trickier if there is a sum involving a radical in the denominator. For example, consider the fraction

$$\frac{3}{6+\sqrt{5}}$$

To simplify, multiply the top and bottom by $(6 - \sqrt{5})$:

$$\frac{3}{(6+\sqrt{5})}\frac{(6-\sqrt{5})}{(6-\sqrt{5})} = \frac{3(6-\sqrt{5})}{6^2-5} = \frac{18-3\sqrt{5}}{31}$$

In general,

$$\frac{1}{\sqrt{a}+\sqrt{b}} = \frac{\sqrt{a}-\sqrt{b}}{a-b}$$

and

$$\frac{1}{\sqrt{a}-\sqrt{b}} = \frac{\sqrt{a}+\sqrt{b}}{a-b}$$

ALGEBRA

Algebraic Expressions

T and $2J$ are examples of algebraic expressions. An algebraic expression may involve letters in addition to numbers and symbols; however, in an algebraic expression a letter always stands for a number. Therefore, you can multiply, divide, add, subtract, and perform other mathematical operations on a letter. Thus, x^2 would mean x times x. Some examples of algebraic expressions: $2x + y$, $y^3 + 9y$, $z^3 - 5ab$, $c + d + 4$, $5x + 2y(6x - 4y + z)$.

When letters or numbers are written together without any sign or symbol between them, multiplication is assumed. Thus $6xy$ means 6 times x times y.

$6xy$ is called a term; terms are separated by + or – signs. The expression $5z + 2 + 4x^2$ has three terms, $5z$, 2, and $4x^2$. Terms are often called monomials (mono = one). If an expression has more than one term, it is called a polynomial (poly = many).

The letters in an algebraic expression are called variables or unknowns. When a variable is multiplied by a number, the number is called the coefficient of the variable. So in the expression $5x^2 + 2yz$, the coefficient of x^2 is 5, and the coefficient of yz is 2.

A polynomial in x is a multinomial in which each term contains x raised to a whole-number power.

Simplifying Algebraic Expressions

Case I. Simplifying expressions which don't contain parentheses:

(A) Perform any multiplication or division before performing addition or subtraction. Thus, the expression $6x + y \div x$ means add $6x$ to the quotient of y divided by x. Another way of writing the expression would be $6x + \frac{y}{x}$ This is not the same as $\frac{6x+y}{x}$.

(B) The order in which you multiply numbers and letters in a term does not matter. So $6xy$ is the same as $6yx$.

(C) The order in which you add terms does not matter; for instance, $6x + 2y - x = 6x - x + 2y$.

(D) If there are roots or powers in any terms, you may be able to simplify the term by using the laws of exponents. For example, $5xy \cdot 3x^2y = 15x^3y^2$.

(E) Combine like terms. Like terms (or similar terms) are terms which have exactly the same letters raised to the same powers.

(F) Algebraic expressions which involve divisions or factors can be simplified by using the techniques for handling fractions and the laws of exponents. Remember: dividing by b^n is the same as multiplying by b^{-n}.

Case II. Simplifying expressions which have parentheses:

The first rule is to perform the operations inside parentheses first. So $(6x + y) \div x$ means divide the sum of $6x$ and y by x. Notice that $(6x + y) \div x$ is different from $6x + y \div x$.

The main rule for getting rid of parentheses is the distributive law, which is expressed as $a(b + c) = ab + ac$. In other words, if any monomial is followed by an expression contained in parentheses, then each term of the expression is multiplied by the monomial. Once we have gotten rid of the parentheses, we proceed as we did in Case 1.

If an expression has more than one set of parentheses, get rid of the inner parentheses first and then work out through the rest of the parentheses.

Adding and Subtracting Algebraic Expressions

Since algebraic expressions are numbers, they can be added and subtracted.

The only algebraic terms which can be combined are like terms.

Multiplying Algebraic Expressions

When you multiply two expressions, you multiply each term of the first by each term of the second. If you need to multiply more than two expressions, multiply the first two expressions, then multiply the result by the third expression, and so on until you have used each factor. Since algebraic expressions can be multiplied, they can be squared, cubed, or raised to other powers.

In the FOIL method for multiplying binomials:

$$(a + b)(c + d) = ac + ad + bc + bd$$

The result has four terms: first times first, outside times outside, inside times inside, and last times last. The order in which you multiply algebraic expressions does not matter. Thus $(2a + b)(x^2 + 2x) = (x^2 + 2x)(2a + b)$.

Factoring Algebraic Expressions

Because $(x + 2)(x - 3) = x^2 - x - 6$, $x + 2$ and $x - 3$ are said to be factors of $x^2 - x - 6$. If an algebraic expression is the product of other algebraic expressions, then the expressions are called factors of the original expression. We can always check to see if we have the correct factors by multiplying the factors and comparing the product to the original expression. We need to be able to factor algebraic expressions in order to solve quadratic equations. Factoring also can be helpful in dividing algebraic expressions.

To factor a polynomial, first remove any monomial factor which appears in every term of the polynomial.

Example

$3x + 3y = 3(x + y)$: 3 is a monomial factor.

You may also need to factor expressions which contain squares or higher powers into factors which contain only linear terms. (Linear terms are terms in which variables are raised only to the first power.) The first rule to remember is that since $(a + b)(a - b) = a^2 + ba - ba - b^2 = a^2 - b^2$, the difference of two squares can always be factored.

Example

Factor $(9m^2 - 16)$.

$9m^2 = (3m)^2$ and $16 = 4^2$, so the factors are $(3m - 4)(3m + 4)$.

You also may need to factor expressions which contain squared terms and linear terms, such as $x^2 + 4x + 3$. The factors will be of the form $(x + a)$ and $(x + b)$. Since $(x + a)(x + b) = x^2 + (a + b)x + ab$, you must look for a pair of numbers a and b such that $a \cdot b$ is the numerical term in the expression and $a + b$ is the coefficient of the linear term (the term with exponent 1).

Example

Factor $x^2 + 4x + 3$.

You want numbers whose product is 3 and whose sum is 4. Look at the possible factors of 3 and check whether they add up to 4. Since $3 = 3 \times 1$ and $3 + 1$ is 4, the factors are $(x + 3)$ and $(x + 1)$. Remember to check by multiplying.

There are some expressions which cannot be factored, for example, $x^2 + 4x + 6$.

Division of Algebraic Expressions

The main things to remember in division are the following.

1. When you divide a sum, you can get the same result by dividing each term and adding quotients. For example,

$$\frac{9x + 4xy + y^2}{x} = \frac{9x}{x} + \frac{4xy}{x} + \frac{y^2}{x} = 9 + 4y + \frac{y^2}{x}.$$

2. You can cancel common factors, so the results on factoring will be helpful. For example,

$$\frac{x^2 - 2x}{x - 2} = \frac{x(x - 2)}{x - 2} = x.$$

You can also divide one algebraic expression by another using long division.

Postulates of Equality

Any number is equal to itself. In symbols, if a is any number, then

$a = a$

(The technical name for this property is the reflexive property of equality.)

You can reverse the two sides of an equation whenever you feel like it. (Technical name: symmetric property of equality.) In symbols, if a and b are any two numbers,

$a = b$ means the same thing as $b = a$.

If two numbers are both equal to a third number, they must be equal to each other. (Technical name: transitive property.) In symbols, if a, b, and c are any three numbers, and if

$a = c$ and $b = c$, then $a = b$.

If $a = b$, then you can substitute a in the place of b anywhere that b appears in an expression. The technical name for this is the substitution property.

Equations

An equation is a statement that says two algebraic expressions are equal. $x + 2 = 3$, $4 + 2 = 6$, $3x^2 + 2x - 6 = 0$, $x^2 + y^2 = z^2$, $\frac{y}{x} = 2 + z$, and $A = LW$ are all examples of equations. We will refer to the algebraic expressions on each side of the equal sign as the left side and the right side of the equation. Thus, in the equation $2x + 4 - 6y + x$, $2x + 4$ is the left side and $6y + x$ is the right side.

If we assign specific numbers to each variable or unknown in an algebraic expression, then the algebraic expression will be equal to a number. This is called evaluating the expression. For example, if you evaluate $2x + 4y^2 + 3$ for $x = -1$ and $y = 2$, the expression is equal to $2(-1) + 4 \cdot 2^2 + 3 = -2 + 4 \cdot 4 + 3 = 17$.

If we evaluate each side of an equation and the number obtained is the same for each side of the equation, then the specific values assigned to the unknowns are called solutions of the equation. Another way of saying this is that the choices for the unknowns satisfy the equation.

There are some equations that do not have any solutions that are real numbers. Since the square of any real number is positive or zero, the equation $x^2 = -4$ does not have any solutions that are real numbers.

Equivalence

One equation is equivalent to another equation, if they have exactly the same solutions. The basic idea in solving equations is to transform a given equation into an equivalent equation whose solutions are obvious.

The two main tools for solving equations are the following:

If you add or subtract the same algebraic expression to or from each side of an equation, the resulting equation is equivalent to the original equation.

If you multiply or divide both sides of an equation by the same nonzero algebraic expression, the resulting equation is equivalent to the original equation.

An equation of the form $ax + b = 0$, in which x represents an unknown number and a and b represent known numbers, is said to be a linear equation.

The most common type of equation is the linear equation with only one unknown. Using this information, you can solve a linear equation in one unknown in the following way:

1. Group all the terms which involve the unknown on one side of the equation and all the terms which are purely numerical on the other side of the equation. This is called isolating the unknown.
2. Combine the terms on each side.
3. Divide each side by the coefficient of the unknown.

You should always check your answer in the original equation.

If you do the same thing to each side of an equation, the result is still an equation but it may not be equivalent to the original equation. Be especially careful if you square each side of an equation. For example, $x = -4$ is an equation; square both sides and you get $x^2 = 16$ which has both $x = 4$ and $x = -4$ as solutions. Always check your answer in the original equation.

If the equation you want to solve involves square roots, get rid of the square roots by squaring each side of the equation. Remember to check your answer since squaring each side does not always give an equivalent equation.

If an equation involves fractions, multiply through by a common denominator and then solve. Check your answer to make sure you did not multiply or divide by zero.

Some special equations are true for all possible values of the unknowns they contain. Equations of this kind are called identities. Sometimes an equal sign with three bars ($\equiv$) is used in place of the regular equal sign to indicate that an equation is an identity. For example, the equation $2x + 5 + x = 4 + 3x + 1$ is an identity.

A statement of the form "x is less than y," written $x < y$, or "a is greater than b," written $a > b$, is called an inequality. The arrow in the inequality sign always points to the smaller number. Inequalities containing only numbers will either be true (for example, $10 > 7$) or false (for example, $4 < 3$). Inequalities containing variables (such as $x < 3$) will usually be true for some values of the variable but not for others.

The symbol $\leq$ means "less than or equal to," and the symbol $\geq$ means "greater than or equal to."

A true inequality will still be true if you add or subtract the same quantity from both sides of the inequality. The inequality will still be true if both sides are multiplied by the same positive number.

Solving Two Equations in Two Unknowns

You may have to solve two equations in two unknowns. Use one equation to solve for one unknown in terms of the other; now change the second equation into an equation in only one unknown which can be solved by the methods of the preceding section.

Example

Solve for x and y: $\begin{cases} \dfrac{x}{y} = 3 \\ 2x + 4y = 20 \end{cases}$

The first equation gives $x = 3y$. Using $x = 3y$, the second equation is $2(3y) + 4y = 6y + 4y$ or $10y = 20$, so $y = \frac{20}{10} = 2$. Since $x = 3y$, $x = 6$.

Sometimes we can solve two equations by adding them or by subtracting one from the other. If we subtract $x + y = 4$ from $2x + y = 5$, we have $x = 1$.

You can also solve a two-equation two-unknown system by multiplying one of the equations by a number chosen so that you can eliminate one of the variables by adding or subtracting the two equations.

Suppose we have an equation system of the general form

$$a_1 x + b_1 y = c_1$$

$$a_2 x + b_2 y = c_2$$

In general, there will be one pair of values for x and y that will be a solution to both equations simultaneously. These values can be found from the formulas

$$x = \frac{b_2 c_1 - b_1 c_2}{a_2 b_1 - a_1 b_2}, \qquad y = \frac{a_2 c_1 - a_1 c_2}{a_2 b_1 - a_1 b_2}$$

However, it is possible that the equation system will have no solutions. This will occur if the graphs of the two equations are parallel lines.

It is also possible that the system will have an infinite number of solutions. This will occur if the two equations actually define the same line.

Solving Quadratic Equations

If the terms of an equation contain squares of the unknown as well as linear terms, the equation is called quadratic. Some examples of quadratic equations are $x^2 + 4x = 3$, $2z^2 - 1 = 3z^2 - 2z$, and $a + 6 = a^2 + 6$.

To solve a quadratic equation:

1. Group all the terms on one side of the equation so that the other side is zero.
2. Combine the like terms on the nonzero side.

3. Factor the expression into linear expressions.
4. Set the linear factors equal to zero and solve.
The method depends on the fact that if a product of expressions is zero then at least one of the expressions must be zero.

Suppose you are given an equation of the form

$$x^2 + bx + c = 0$$

(x is unknown; b and c are known). To find the solution, think of two numbers m and n that when multiplied together give c and when added together give b. (In symbols: $mn = c$ and $m + n = b$.) Then the polynomial can be factored into the two factors $(x + m)$ and $(x + n)$, and the equation can be written

$$(x + m)(x + n) = 0$$

The two solutions are $x = -m$ and $x = -n$.

You can also solve quadratic equations by using the quadratic formula. The quadratic formula states that the solutions of the quadratic equation

$$ax^2 + bx + c = 0 \text{ are } x = \frac{1}{2a}(-b + \sqrt{b^2 - 4ac})$$
$$\text{and } x = \frac{1}{2a}(-b - \sqrt{b^2 - 4ac})$$

This is usually written $x = \frac{1}{2a}(-b \pm \sqrt{b^2 - 4ac})$.

Note that if $b^2 - 4ac$ *is* negative, then the quadratic equation $ax^2 + bx + c = 0$ has no real solutions because negative numbers do not have real square roots.

The quadratic formula will always give you the solutions to a quadratic equation. If you can factor the equation, factoring will usually give you the solution in less time.

Functions

If a relationship exists between two variables, x and y, such that for every permissible value of x there is one and only one value of y, then y is said to be a function of x. $y = 5x + 2$ is a function; $y^2 = x$ is not a function since each real value of x corresponds to two values of y: $+\sqrt{x}$ and $-\sqrt{x}$.

The set of all possible values of x, the independent variable in a function, is called the domain of the function. The set of all possible values of the dependent variable, y, is called the range of the function.

Word Problems

The general method for solving word problems is to translate them into algebraic equations. The quantities you are seeking are the unknowns, which are usually represented by letters. The information you are given in the problem is then turned into equations. Words such as "is," "was," "are," and "were" mean equals, and words like "of" and "as much as" mean multiplication.

Distance Problems

A common type of word problem is a distance or velocity problem. The basic formula is

distance traveled = rate × time

The formula is abbreviated $d = rt$.

Work Problems

In this type of problem you can always assume all workers in the same category work at the same rate. The main idea is: If it takes k workers 1 hour to do a job, then each worker does $\frac{1}{k}$ of the job in an hour, or he works at the rate of $\frac{1}{k}$ of the job per hour. If it takes m workers h hours to finish a job, then each worker does $\frac{1}{m}$ of the job in h hours so she does $\frac{1}{h}$ of $\frac{1}{m}$ in an hour. Therefore, each worker works at the rate of $\frac{1}{mh}$ of the job per hour.

Number Problems

An example of one type of counting problem is: 50 students signed up for both English and math. 90 students signed up for either English or math. If 25 students are taking English but not taking math, how many students are taking math but not taking English?

In these problems, "either . . . or . . . " means the people taking both English and math are counted among the people taking either math or English.

You must avoid counting the same people twice in these problems. The formula is the following:

the number taking English or math
       = the number taking English
       + the number taking math
       − the number taking both.

You have to subtract the number taking both subjects since these students are counted once with those taking English and counted again with those taking math.

A person taking English is either taking math or not taking math, so there are 50 + 25 = 75 people taking English, 50 taking English and math, and 25 taking English but not taking math. Since 75 are taking English, 90 = 75 + number taking math − 50; so there are 90 − 25 = 65 people taking math. 50 of the people taking math are taking English so 65 − 50 or 15 are taking math but not English.

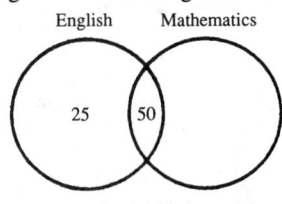

English   Mathematics

25   50

Total = 90

The figure shows what is given. Since 90 students signed up for English or mathematics, 15 must be taking mathematics but not English.

If an event can happen in m different ways, and each of the m ways is followed by a second event which can occur in k different ways, then the first event can be followed by the second event in $m \cdot k$ different ways. This is called the fundamental principle of counting.

Ratio and Proportion

Ratio

A ratio is a comparison of two numbers by division.

The ratio of a to b is written as $a : b = \frac{a}{b} = a \div b$. We can handle ratios as fractions, since a ratio is a fraction. In the ratio $a : b$, a and b are called the terms of the ratio.

Since $a : b$ is a fraction, b can never be zero. The fraction $\frac{a}{b}$ is usually different from the fraction $\frac{b}{a}$ (for example, $\frac{1}{2}$ is not the same as $\frac{2}{3}$) so the order of the terms in a ratio is important.

A ratio is a number, so if you want to find the ratio of two quantities they must be expressed in the same units.

If two numbers measure different quantities, their quotient is usually called a rate. For example, $\frac{50 \text{ miles}}{2 \text{ hours}}$, which equals 25 miles per hour, is a rate of speed.

Proportion

A proportion is a statement that two ratios are equal. For example, $\frac{3}{12} = \frac{1}{4}$ is a proportion; it could also be expressed as $3 : 12 = 1 : 4$. In the proportion $a : b = c : d$, the terms on the outside (a and b) are called the extremes, and the terms on the inside (b and c) are called the means.

In a proportion the product of the extremes is equal to the product of the means.

Finding the products ad and bc is also called cross multiplying a proportion: $\frac{a}{b} \diagdown \frac{c}{d}$. So cross multiplying a proportion gives two equal numbers. The proportion $\frac{a}{b} = \frac{c}{d}$ is read "a is to b as c is to d."

Two variables, a and b, are directly proportional if they satisfy a relationship of the form $a = kb$, where k is a number. The distance a car travels in two hours and its average speed for the two hours are directly proportional, since $d = 2s$ where d is the distance and s is the average speed expressed in miles per hour. Here $k = 2$. Sometimes the word "directly" is omitted, so a and b are proportional means $a = kb$.

Any two units of measurement of the same quantity are directly proportional.

You can always change units by using a proportion. You should know the following measurements:

Length:　1 foot = 12 inches
　　　　　1 yard = 3 feet
Area:　　1 square foot = 144 square inches
　　　　　1 square yard = 9 square feet
Time:　　1 minute = 60 seconds
　　　　　1 hour = 60 minutes
　　　　　1 day = 24 hours
　　　　　1 week = 7 days
　　　　　1 year = 52 weeks
Volume:　1 quart = 2 pints
　　　　　1 gallon = 4 quarts

Weight:　1 ounce = 16 drams
　　　　　1 pound = 16 ounces
　　　　　1 ton = 2,000 pounds

Two variables, a and b, are indirectly proportional if they satisfy a relationship of the form $k = ab$, where k is a number. So the average speed of a car and the time it takes the car to travel 300 miles are indirectly proportional, since $st = 300$ where s is the speed and t is the time.

If two quantities are directly proportional, then when one increases, the other increases. If two quantities are indirectly proportional, when one quantity increases, the other decreases.

It is also possible to compare three or more numbers by a ratio. The numbers A, B, and C are in the ratio $2 : 4 : 3$ means $A : B = 2 : 4$, $A : C = 2 : 3$, and $B : C = 4 : 3$. The order of the terms is important. $A : B : C$ is read A is to B is to C.

Sequence and Progressions

A sequence is an ordered collection of numbers. For example, 2, 4, 6, 8, 10, . . . is a sequence. 2, 4, 6, 8, 10 are called terms of the sequence. We identify the terms by their positions in the sequence; so 2 is the first term, 8 is the 4th term, and so on. The dots mean the sequence continues.

An *arithmetic progression* is a sequence of numbers with the property that the difference of any two consecutive numbers is always the same. The numbers 2, 6, 10, 14, 18, 22, . . . constitute an arithmetic progression, since each term is 4 more than the term before it. 4 is called the common difference of the progression.

If d is the common difference and a is the first term of the progression, then the nth term will be $a + (n - 1)d$. So a progression with the common difference 4 and initial term 5 will have $5 + 6(4) = 29$ as its seventh term.

A sequence of numbers is called a *geometric progression* if the ratio of consecutive terms is always the same. So 3, 6, 12, 24, 48, . . . is a geometric progression since $\frac{6}{3} = 2 = \frac{12}{6} = \frac{24}{12} = \frac{48}{24}, \ldots$. The nth term of a geometric progression is ar^{n-1} where a is the first term and r is the common ratio. If a geometric progression started with 2 and the common ratio was 3, then the fifth term should be $2 \cdot 3^4 = 2 \cdot 81 = 162$.

We can quickly add up the first n terms of a geometric progression which starts with a and has common ratio r. The formula for the sum of the first n terms is $\frac{ar^n - a}{r - 1}$ when $r \neq 1$. (If $r = 1$ all the terms are the same so the sum is na.)

Inequalities

$a > b$ means the number a is greater than the number b; that is $a = b + x$ where x is a positive number. If we look at a number line, $a > b$ means a is to the right of b. $a > b$ can also be read as b is less than a, which is also written $b < a$. For example, $-5 > -7.5$ because $-5 = -7.5 + 2.5$ and 2.5 is positive.

The notation $a \leq b$ means a is less than or equal to b, or b is greater than or equal to a. For example, $5 \geq 4$, also $4 \geq 4$. $a \neq b$ means a is not equal to b.

If you need to know whether one fraction is greater than another fraction, put the fractions over a common denominator and compare the numerators.

Inequalities have certain properties which are similar to equations. We can talk about the left side and the right side of an inequality, and we can use algebraic expressions for the sides of an inequality. For example, $6x < 5x + 4$. A value for an unknown satisfies an inequality if, when you evaluate each side of the inequality, the numbers satisfy the inequality. So if $x = 2$, then $6x = 12$ and $5x + 4 = 14$ and since $12 < 14$, $x = 2$ satisfies $6x < 5x + 4$. Two inequalities are equivalent if the same set of numbers satisfies both inequalities.

The following basic principles are used in work with inequalities:

Adding the same expression to *each* side of an inequality gives an equivalent inequality (written $a < b \leftrightarrow a + c < b + c$ where $\leftrightarrow$ means equivalent).

Subtracting the same expression from *each* side of an inequality gives an equivalent inequality $(a < b \leftrightarrow a - c < b - c)$.

Multiplying or dividing *each* side of an inequality by the same *positive* expression gives an equivalent inequality $(a < b \leftrightarrow ca < cb$ for $c > 0)$.

Multiplying or dividing each side of an inequality by the same *negative* expression *reverses* the inequality $(a < b \leftrightarrow ca > cb$ for $c < 0)$.

If both sides of an inequality have the same sign, inverting both sides of the inequality *reverses* the inequality.

$$0 < a < b \leftrightarrow 0 < \frac{1}{b} < \frac{1}{a}$$

$$a < b < 0 \leftrightarrow \frac{1}{b} < \frac{1}{a} < 0$$

If two inequalities are of the same type (both greater or both less), adding the respective sides gives the same type of inequality.

$(a < b$ and $c < d$, then $a + c < b + d)$

Note that the inequalities are *not* equivalent.
If $a < b$ and $b < c$ then $a < c$.
Some inequalities are not satisfied by *any* real number. For example, since $x^2 \geq 0$ for all x, there is no real number such that $x^2 < -9$.

If there is any property of inequalities you cannot remember, try out some specific numbers. If $x < y$, then what is the relation between $-x$ and $-y$? Since $4 < 5$ but $-5 < -4$, the relation is probably $-x > -y$.

Probably the most common mistake is forgetting to reverse the inequalities if you multiply or divide by a negative number.

GEOMETRY

Geometry is an example of a postulational system, in which postulates (axioms), undefined terms and defined terms are used to prove new relationships that are expressed as statements called theorems. In turn, these theorems, the postulates, and the defined and undefined terms are used to prove other theorems.

The "first" terms of geometry are *point, line*, and *plane*. They are undefined since they can be described but cannot be defined using previously defined words.

A point indicates position but has no physical dimensions.

A line is a continuous set of points that extend indefinitely in two opposite directions.

A plane is a flat surface that extends indefinitely in all directions.

Angles

If two straight lines meet at a point they form an angle. The point is called the vertex of the angle and the lines are called the sides or rays of the angle. The sign for angle is $\angle$ and an angle can be denoted in the following ways:

(A) $\angle ABC$ where B is the vertex, A is a point on one side, and C a point on the other side.

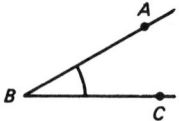

(B) $\angle B$ where B is the vertex.

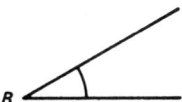

(C) $\angle 1$ or $\angle x$ where x or 1 is written inside the angle.

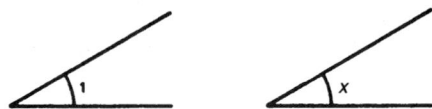

Angles are usually measured in degrees. We say that an angle equals x degrees, when its measure is x degrees. Degrees are denoted by °. An angle of 50 degrees is $50°$, $60' = 1°$, $60'' = 1'$ where ' is read minutes and " is read seconds.

Two angles are adjacent if they have the same vertex and a common side and one angle is not inside the other.

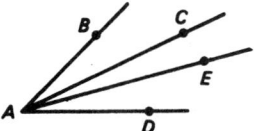

∠*BAC* and ∠*CAD* are adjacent, but ∠*CAD* and ∠*EAD* are not adjacent.

If two lines intersect at a point, they form four angles. The angles opposite each other are called vertical angles. ∠1 and ∠3 are vertical angles. ∠2 and ∠4 are vertical angles.

Vertical angles are equal.

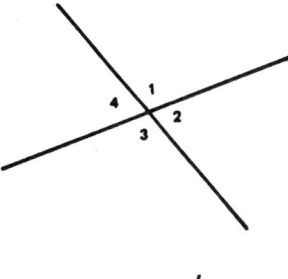

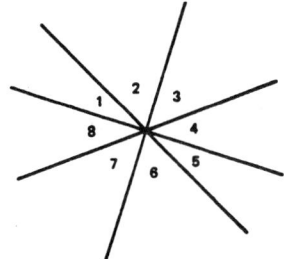

so ∠1 = ∠5, ∠2 = ∠6, ∠3 = ∠7, ∠4 = ∠8.

A straight angle is an angle whose sides lie on a straight line. A straight angle equals 180°.

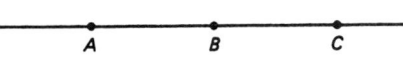

∠*ABC* is a straight angle.

If the sum of two angles is a straight angle, then the angles are supplementary and each angle is the supplement of the other.

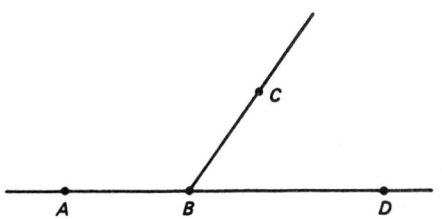

∠*ABC* and ∠*CBD* are supplementary. Note that two angles need not be adjacent to be supplementary.

If an angle of $x°$ and an angle of $y°$ are supplementary, then $x + y = 180$.

If two supplementary angles are equal, they are both right angles. A right angle is half of a straight angle. A right angle = 90°.

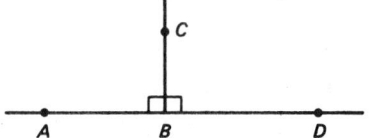

∠*ABC* = ∠*CBD* and they are both right angles. A right angle is denoted by ∟. When two lines intersect and all four of the angles are equal, then each of the angles is a right angle.

If the sum of two adjacent angles is a right angle, then the angles are complementary and each angle is the complement of the other.

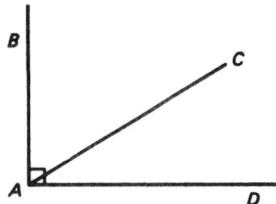

∠*BAC* and ∠*CAD* are complementary.

If an angle of $x°$ and an angle of $y°$ are complementary, then $x + y = 90$.

Example

If the supplement of angle x is three times as much as the complement of angle x, how many degrees is angle x?

Let d be the number of degrees in angle x; then the supplement of x is $(180 - d)°$, and the complement of x is $(90 - d)°$. Since the supplement is 3 times the complement, $180 - d = 3(90 - d) = 270 - 3d$ which gives $2d = 90$, so $d = 45$.

Therefore, angle x is 45°.

If an angle is divided into two equal angles by a straight line, then the angle has been bisected and the line is called the bisector of the angle.

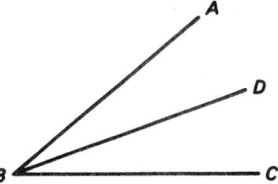

BD bisects ∠*ABC*; so ∠*ABD* = ∠*DBC*.

Two lines in the same plane are parallel if they do not intersect no matter how far they are extended.

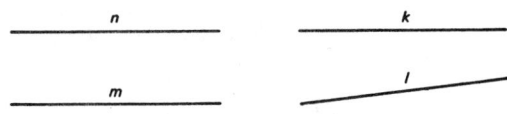

m and n are parallel, but k and l are not parallel since if k and l are extended they will intersect.

Parallel lines are denoted by the symbol ‖; so $m \parallel n$ means m is parallel to n.

If two lines are parallel to a third line, then they are parallel to each other.

If a third line intersects two given lines, it is called a transversal. A transversal and the two given lines form eight angles. The four inside angles are called interior angles. The four outside angles are called exterior angles. If two angles are on opposite sides of the transversal they are called alternate angles.

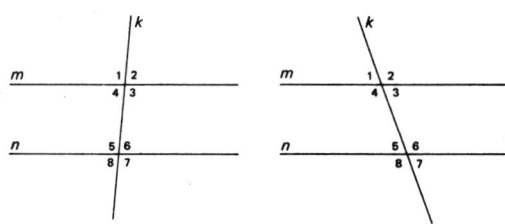

k is a transversal of the lines m and n. Angles 1, 2, 7, and 8 are the exterior angles, and angles 3, 4, 5, and 6 are the interior angles. $\angle 4$ and $\angle 6$ are an example of a pair of alternate angles. $\angle 1$ and $\angle 5$, $\angle 2$ and $\angle 6$, $\angle 3$ and $\angle 7$, and $\angle 4$ and $\angle 8$ are pairs of corresponding angles.

If two parallel lines are intersected by a transversal then:

1. Alternate interior angles are equal.
2. Corresponding angles are equal.
3. Interior angles on the same side of the transversal are supplementary.

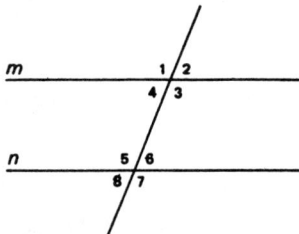

If we use the fact that vertical angles are equal, we can replace "interior" by "exterior" in (1) and (3). m is parallel to n implies:

1. $\angle 4 = \angle 6$ and $\angle 3 = \angle 5$
2. $\angle 1 = \angle 5$, $\angle 2 = \angle 6$, $\angle 3 = \angle 7$, and $\angle 4 = \angle 8$
3. $\angle 3 + \angle 6 = 180°$ and $\angle 4 + \angle 5 = 180°$

The converse is also true. Let m and n be two lines which have k as a transversal.

1. If a pair of alternate interior angles are equal, then m and n are parallel.
2. If a pair of corresponding angles are equal, then m and n are parallel.
3. If a pair of interior angles on the same side of the transversal are supplementary, then m is parallel to n.

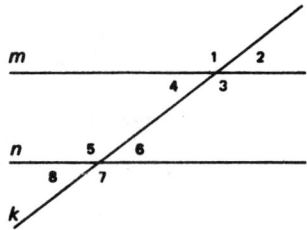

If $\angle 3 = \angle 5$, then $m \parallel n$. If $\angle 4 = \angle 6$ then $m \parallel n$. If $\angle 2 = \angle 6$ then $m \parallel n$. If $\angle 3 + \angle 6 = 180°$, then $m \parallel n$.

When two lines intersect and all four of the angles formed are equal, the lines are said to be perpendicular. If two lines are perpendicular, they are the sides of right angles whose vertex is the point of intersection.

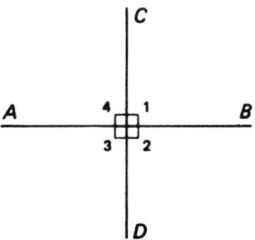

AB is perpendicular to CD, and angles 1, 2, 3, and 4 are all right angles. $\perp$ is the symbol for perpendicular, so $AB \perp CD$.

If two lines in a plane are perpendicular to the same line, then the two lines are parallel.

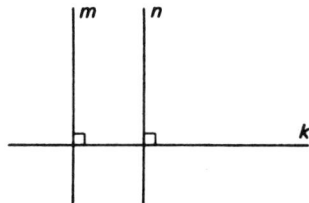

If $m \perp k$ and $n \perp k$, then $m \parallel n$.

If *any one* of the angles formed when two lines intersect is a right angle, then the lines are perpendicular.

Polygons

A polygon is a closed figure in a plane which is composed of line segments which meet only at their endpoints. The line segments are called sides of the polygon, and a point where two sides meet is called a vertex (plural: vertices) of the polygon.

Some examples of polygons are the following:

A polygon is usually denoted by the vertices given in order.

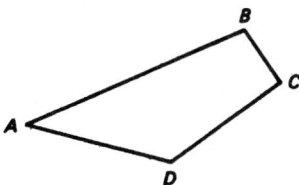

ABCD is a polygon.

A diagonal of a polygon is a line segment whose endpoints are nonadjacent vertices. The altitude from a vertex to a side is the line segment having the vertex as an endpoint and which is perpendicular to the side.

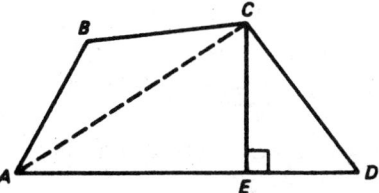

AC is a diagonal, and *CE* is the altitude from *C* to *AD*. A median of a triangle is the segment from a vertex to the midpoint of the side opposite the vertex.

Polygons are classified by the number of angles or sides they have. A polygon with three angles is called a triangle, a four-sided polygon is a quadrilateral, a polygon with five angles is a pentagon, a polygon with six angles is a hexagon, and an eight-sided polygon is an octagon. The number of angles is always equal to the number of sides in a polygon, so a six-sided polygon is a hexagon. The term *n*-gon refers to a polygon with *n* sides.

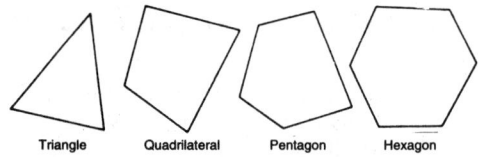

| Triangle | Quadrilateral | Pentagon | Hexagon |

If the sides of a polygon are all equal in length and if all the angles of a polygon are equal, the polygon is called a regular polygon.

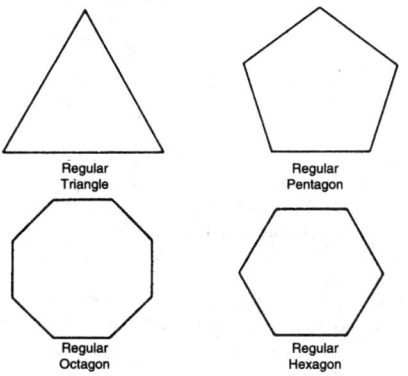

| Regular Triangle | Regular Pentagon |
| Regular Octagon | Regular Hexagon |

If the corresponding sides and the corresponding angles of two polygons are equal, the polygons are congruent. Congruent polygons have the same size and the same shape.

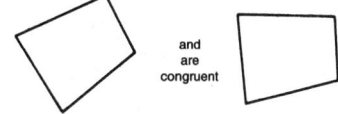

and are congruent

If all the corresponding angles of two polygons are equal and the lengths of the corresponding sides are proportional, the polygons are said to be similar. Similar polygons have the same shape but need not be the same size.

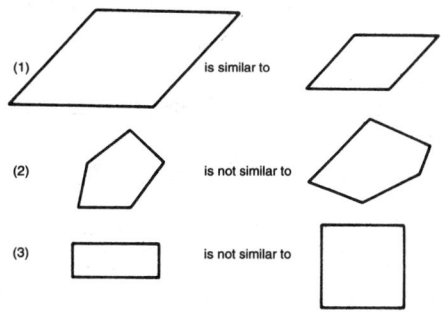

(1)   is similar to

(2)   is not similar to

(3)   is not similar to

The sum of all the angles of an n-gon is $(n - 2) \, 180°$. So the sum of the angles in a hexagon is $(6 - 2) \, 180° = 720°$.

Triangles

A triangle is a three-sided polygon. If two sides of a triangle are equal, it is called isosceles. If all three sides are equal, it is an equilateral triangle. If all of the sides have different lengths, the triangle is scalene. When one of the angles in a triangle is a right angle (90°), the triangle is a right triangle. If one of the angles is obtuse (between 90° and 180°) we have an obtuse triangle. If all the angles are acute (between 0° and 90°), the triangle is an acute triangle.

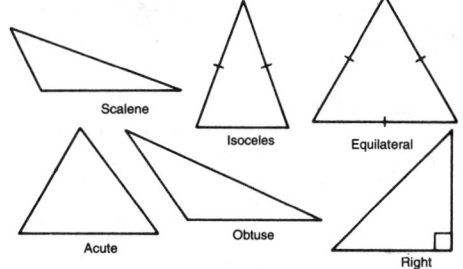

Scalene

Isoceles

Equilateral

Acute

Obtuse

Right

The symbol for a triangle is △; so △*ABC* means a triangle whose vertices are *A, B,* and *C*.

The sum of the angles in a triangle is 180°.

The sum of the lengths of any two sides of a triangle must be greater than the length of the remaining side.

If two angles in a triangle are equal, then the lengths of the sides opposite the equal angles are equal. If two sides of a triangle are equal, then the angles opposite the two equal sides are equal. In an equilateral triangle all the angles are equal and each angle = 60°. If each of the angles in a triangle is 60°, then the triangle is equilateral.

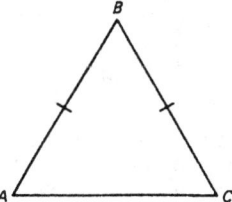

If $AB = BC$, then $\angle BAC = \angle BCA$.

If one angle in a triangle is larger than another angle, the side opposite the larger angle is longer than the side opposite the smaller angle. If one side is longer than another side, then the angle opposite the longer side is larger than the angle opposite the shorter side.

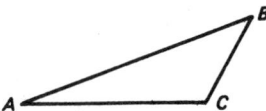

$AB > AC$ implies $\angle BCA > \angle ABC$.

In a right triangle, the side opposite the right angle is called the hypotenuse, and the remaining two sides are called legs.

The Pythagorean theorem states that the square of the length of the hypotenuse is equal to the sum of the squares of the lengths of the legs.

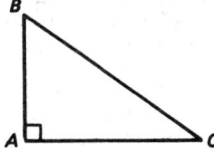

$(BC)^2 = (AB)^2 + (AC)^2$

If the lengths of the three sides of a triangle are a, b, and c and $a^2 = b^2 + c^2$, then the triangle is a right triangle where a is the length of the hypotenuse.

Congruence

Two triangles are congruent if two pairs of corresponding sides and the corresponding included angles are equal. This is called Side-Angle-Side and is denoted by S.A.S.

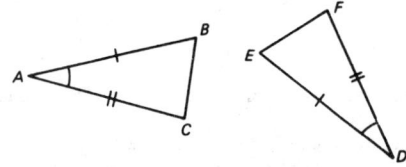

If $AB = DE$, $AC = DF$, and $\angle BAC = \angle EDF$, then $\triangle ABC \cong \triangle DEF$. The symbol $\cong$ means congruent.

Two triangles are congruent if two pairs of corresponding angles and the corresponding included

sides are equal. This is called Angle-Side-Angle or A.S.A.

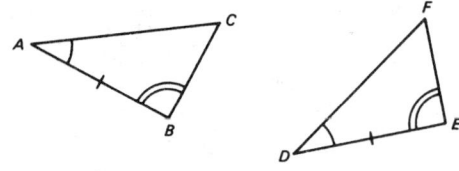

If $AB = DE$, $\angle BAC = \angle EDF$, and $\angle CBA = \angle FED$ then $\triangle ABC \cong \triangle DEF$.

If all three pairs of corresponding sides of two triangles are equal, then the triangles are congruent. This is called Side-Side-Side or S.S.S.

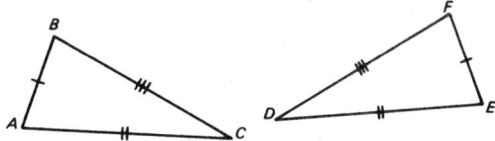

If $AB = EF$, $AC = ED$, and $BC = FD$, then $\triangle ABC \cong \triangle EFD$.

Because of the Pythagorean theorem, if any two corresponding sides of two right triangles are equal, the third sides are equal and the triangles are congruent.

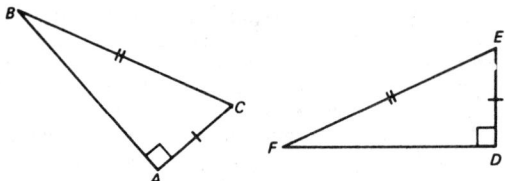

If $AC = DE$ and $BC = EF$, then right $\triangle ABC \cong$ right $\triangle DFE$.

In general, however, if two corresponding sides of two triangles are equal, we cannot infer that the triangles are congruent.

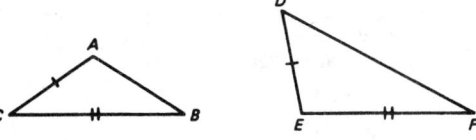

$AC = DE$ and $CB = EF$, but the triangles are not congruent.

Similarity

Two triangles are similar if all three pairs of corresponding angles are equal. Since the sum of the angles in a triangle is 180°, it follows that if two corresponding angles are equal, the third angles must be equal.

If you draw a line which passes through a triangle and is parallel to one of the sides of the triangle, the triangle formed is similar to the original triangle.

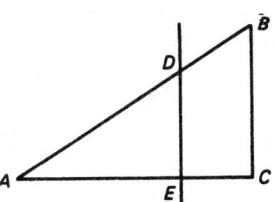

If *DE* ∥ *BC* then △*ADE* ~ △*ABC*. The symbol ~ means similar.

Quadrilaterals

A quadrilateral is a polygon with four sides. The sum of the angles in a quadrilateral is 360°. If the opposite sides of a quadrilateral are parallel, the figure is a parallelogram.

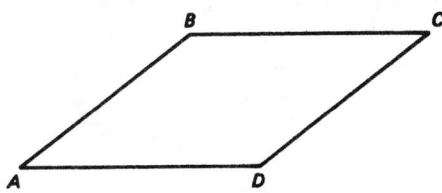

ABCD is a parallelogram.
  In a parallelogram:
1. The opposite sides are equal.
2. The opposite angles are equal.
3. Any diagonal divides the parallelogram into two congruent triangles.
4. The diagonals bisect each other. (A line bisects a line segment if it intersects the segment at the midpoint of the segment.)

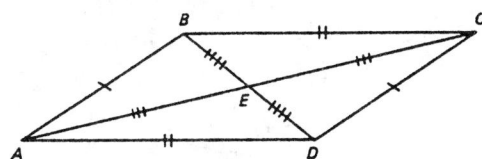

ABCD is a parallelogram.
1. *AB* = *DC*, *BC* = *AD*.
2. ∠*BCD* = ∠*BAD*, ∠*ABC* = ∠*ADC*.
3. △*ABC* ≅ △*ADC*, △*ABD* ≅ △*CDB*.
4. *AE* = *EC* and *BE* = *ED*.
  If *any* of the statements 1, 2, 3, and 4 are true for a quadrilateral, then the quadrilateral is a parallelogram.
  If all of the sides of a parallelogram are equal, the figure is called a rhombus.

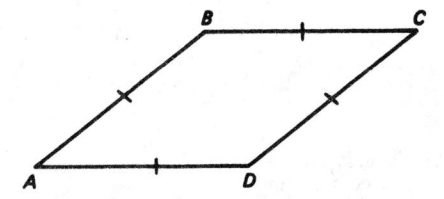

ABCD is a rhombus.

The diagonals of a rhombus are perpendicular.

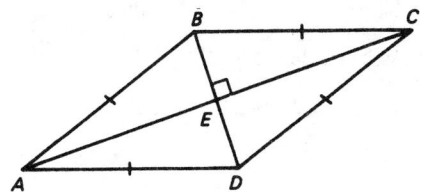

BD ⊥ AC; ∠*BEC* = ∠*CED* = ∠*AED* = ∠*AEB* = 90°.
  If all the angles of a parallelogram are right angles, the figure is a rectangle.

ABCD is a rectangle.
  Since the sum of the angles in a quadrilateral is 360°, if *all* the angles of a quadrilateral are equal then the figure is a rectangle. The diagonals of a rectangle are equal.

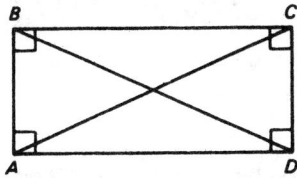

If *ABCD* is a rectangle, *AC* = *BD* and $(AC)^2 = (AD)^2 + (DC)^2$.
  If all the sides of a rectangle are equal, the figure is a square.

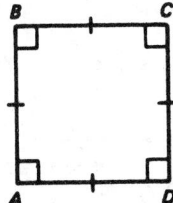

ABCD is a square.
  If all the angles of a rhombus are equal, the figure is a square. The length of the diagonal of a square is $\sqrt{2}s$, where *s* is the length of a side.

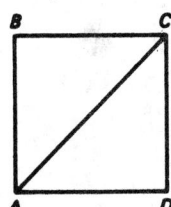

In a square *ABCD*, *AC* = $(\sqrt{2})AD$.

A quadrilateral with two parallel sides and two sides which are not parallel is called a trapezoid. The parallel sides are called bases, and the non-parallel sides are called legs.

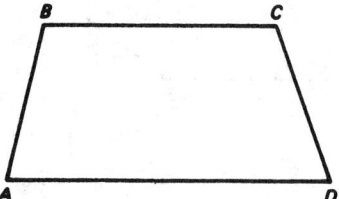

If *BC* ∥ *AD* then *ABCD* is a trapezoid; *BC* and *AD* are the bases.

Circles

A circle is a figure in a plane consisting of all the points which are the same distance from a fixed point called the center of the circle. A line segment from any point on the circle to the center of the circle is called a radius (plural: radii) of the circle. All radii of the same circle have the same length.

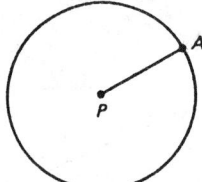

This circle has center *P* and radius *AP*.

A circle is denoted by a single letter, usually its center. Two circles with the same center are *concentric*.

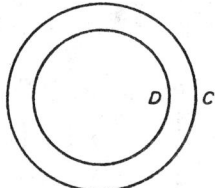

C and *D* are concentric circles.

A line segment whose endpoints are on a circle is called a *chord*. A chord which passes through the center of the circle is a *diameter. The length of a diameter is twice* the length of a radius. A diameter divides a circle into two congruent halves which are called *semicircles*.

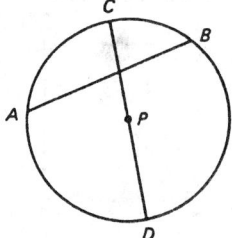

P is the center of the circle.

AB is a chord and *CD* is a diameter.

A diameter which is perpendicular to a chord bisects the chord.

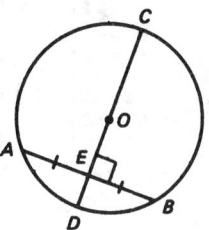

O is the center of this circle and *AB* ⊥ *CD;* then *AE* = *EB*.

If a line intersects a circle at one and only one point, the line is said to be a tangent to the circle. The point common to a circle and a tangent to the circle is called the point of tangency. The radius from the center to the point of tangency is perpendicular to the tangent.

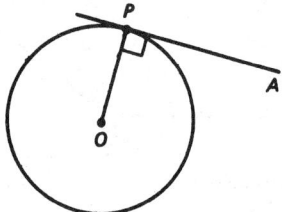

AP is tangent to the circle with center *O*. *P* is the point of tangency and *OP* ⊥ *PA*.

A polygon is inscribed in a circle if all of its vertices are points on the circle.

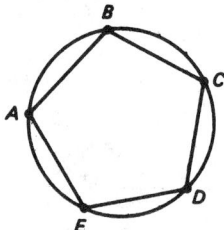

ABCDE is an inscribed pentagon.

An angle whose vertex is a point on a circle and whose sides are chords of the circle is called an inscribed angle. An angle whose vertex is the center of a circle and whose sides are radii of the circle is called a central angle.

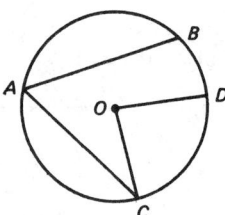

∠*BAC* is an inscribed angle.
∠*DOC is* a central angle.

An arc is a part of a circle.

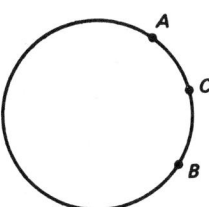

ACB is an arc. Arc ACB is written $\overset{\frown}{ACB}$.

If two letters are used to denote an arc, they represent the smaller of the two possible arcs. So $\overset{\frown}{AB} = \overset{\frown}{ACB}$.

An arc can be measured in degrees. The entire circle is 360°; thus an arc of 120° would be $\frac{1}{3}$ of a circle. The notation $m\overset{\frown}{AB}$ denotes the degree measure of arc AB.

A central angle is equal in measure to the arc it intercepts.

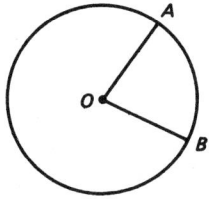

$m\angle AOB = m\overset{\frown}{AB}$

An inscribed angle is equal in measure to $\frac{1}{2}$ the arc it intercepts.

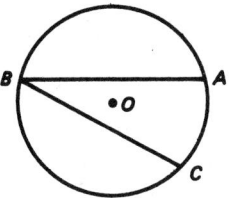

$m\angle ABC = \frac{1}{2}m\overset{\frown}{AC}$

An angle inscribed in a semicircle is a right angle.

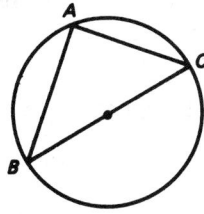

If BC is a diameter, then $\angle BAC$ is inscribed in a semicircle, so $m\angle BAC = 90°$.

Area and Perimeter

The area A of a square equals s^2, where s is the length of a side of the square. Thus, $A = s^2$.

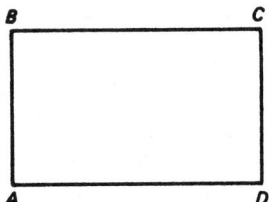

If $AD = 5$ inches, the area of square $ABCD$ is 25 square inches.

The area of a rectangle equals length times width; if L is the length of one side and W is the length of a perpendicular side, then the area $A = LW$.

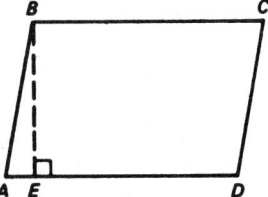

If $AB = 5$ feet and $AD = 8$ feet, then the area of rectangle $ABCD$ is 40 square feet.

The area of a parallelogram is base × height; $A = bh$, where b is the length of a side and h is the length of an altitude to that side.

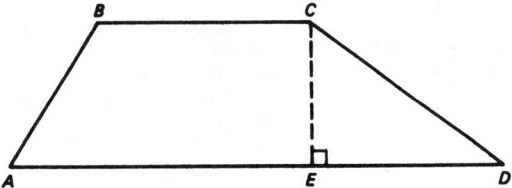

If $AD = 6$ yards and $BE = 4$ yards, then the area of parallelogram $ABCD$ is 6 · 4 or 24 square yards.

The area of a trapezoid is the (average of the bases) × height. $A = [(b_1 + b_2)/2]h$, where b_1 and b_2 are the lengths of the parallel sides and h is the length of an altitude to one of the bases.

If $BC = 3$ miles, $AD = 7$ miles, and $CE = 2$ miles, then the area of trapezoid $ABCD$ is equal to $[(3 + 7)/2] \cdot 2 = 10$ square miles.

The area of a triangle is $\frac{1}{2}$(base × height); $A = \frac{1}{2}bh$, where b is the length of a side and h is the length of the altitude to that side.

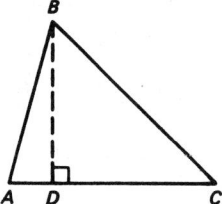

If $AC = 5$ miles and $BD = 4$ miles, then the area of the triangle is $\frac{1}{2} \times 5 \times 4 = 10$ square miles.

Since the legs of a right triangle are perpendicular to each other, the area of a right triangle is one-half the product of the lengths of the legs.

If we want to find the area of a polygon which is not of a type already mentioned, we break the polygon up into smaller figures such as triangles or rectangles, find the area of each piece, and add these to get the area of the given polygon.

The area of a circle is πr^2, where r is the length of a radius.

The symbol π, which is the Greek letter pi (pronounced pie), represents a fundamental irrational number that is approximately equal to $\frac{22}{7}$ or $3.14159\ldots$.

The number π is a special type of number called a transcendental number. A transcendental number cannot be written in the form a^b, where a and b are both rational numbers. Note that all square roots and other roots, such as $\sqrt{2}$ and $\sqrt[4]{15}$, are not transcendental even though they are irrational. Most values for logarithmic functions are transcendental numbers, and most values of trigonometric functions are transcendental numbers. If you study calculus you will discover another fundamental transcendental number called e, which is about $2.71828\ldots$.

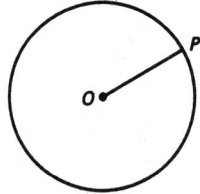

If $OP = 2$ inches, then the area of the circle with center O is $\pi 2^2$ or 4π square inches.

The portion of the plane bounded by a circle and a central angle is called a sector of the circle.

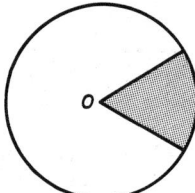

The shaded region is a sector of the circle with center O. The area of a sector with central angle $n°$ in a circle of radius r is $\frac{n}{360} \pi r^2$.

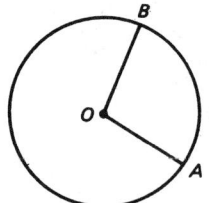

If $OB = 4$ inches and $\angle BOA = 100°$, then the area of the sector is $\frac{100}{360} \pi \cdot 4^2 = \frac{5}{18} \cdot 16\pi = \frac{40}{9} \pi$ square inches.

The perimeter of a polygon is the sum of the lengths of the sides.

The perimeter of a rectangle is $2(L + W)$, where L is the length and W is the width.

The perimeter of a square is $4s$, where s is the length of a side of the square.

The perimeter of a circle is called the circumference of the circle. The circumference of a circle is πd or $2\pi r$, where d is the length of a diameter and r is the length of a radius.

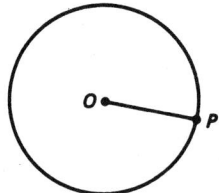

If O is the center of a circle and $OP = 5$ feet, then the circumference of the circle is $2 \times 5\pi$ or 10π feet.

The length of an arc of a circle is $(n/360)\,\pi d$, where the central angle of the arc is $n°$.

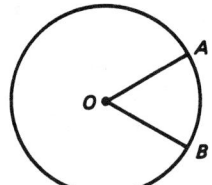

If O is the center of a circle where $OA = 5$ yards and $\angle AOB = 60°$, then the length of arc AB is $\frac{60}{360} \pi \times 10 = \frac{10}{6} \pi = \frac{5}{3} \pi$ yards.

Volume and Surface Area

The volume of a rectangular prism or box is length times width times height.

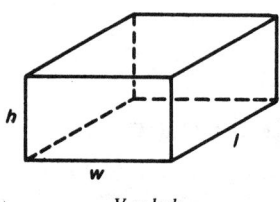

$V = lwh$

If each of the faces of a rectangular prism is a congruent square, then the solid is a cube. The volume of a cube is the length of a side (or edge) cubed.

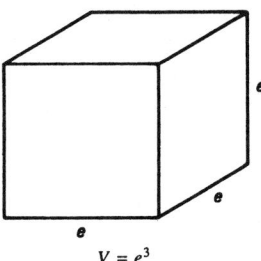

$$V = e^3$$

If the side of a cube is 4 feet long, then the volume of the cube is 4^3 or 64 cubic feet.

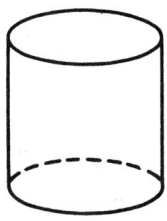

This solid is a circular cylinder. The top and the bottom are congruent circles. Most tin cans are circular cylinders. The volume of a circular cylinder is the product of the area of the circular base and the height.

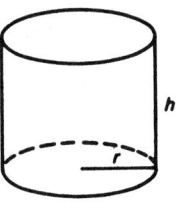

$$V = \pi r^2 h$$

A sphere is the set of points in space equidistant from a fixed point called the center. The length of a segment from any point on the sphere to the center is called the radius of the sphere. The volume of a sphere of radius r is $\frac{4}{3}\pi r^3$.

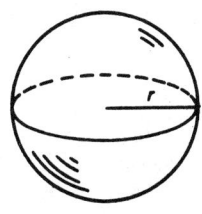

$$V = \frac{4}{3}\pi r^3$$

The volume of a sphere with radius 3 feet is $\frac{4}{3}\pi 3^3 = 36\pi$ cubic feet.

The surface area of a sphere of radius r is $4\pi r^2$.

The surface area of a rectangular prism is $2LW + 2LH + 2WH$, where L is the length, W is the width, and H is the height.

The surface area of a cube is $6e^2$, where e is the length of an edge.

The area of a circular part of a cylinder is called the lateral area. The lateral area of a cylinder is $27\pi rh$, since if we unroll the circular part, we get a rectangle whose dimensions are the circumference of the circle and the height of the cylinder. The total surface area, which is the lateral surface area plus the areas of the circles on top and bottom, is $2\pi rh + 2\pi r^2$.

Coordinate Geometry

In coordinate geometry, every point in the plane is associated with an ordered pair of numbers called coordinates. Two perpendicular lines are drawn; the horizontal line is called the x-axis and the vertical line is called the y-axis. The point where the two axes intersect is called the origin. Both of the axes are number lines with the origin corresponding to zero. Positive numbers on the x-axis are to the right of the origin, negative numbers to the left. Positive numbers on the y-axis are above the origin, negative numbers below the origin. If the coordinates of a point P are (x, y), then P is located by moving x units along the x-axis from the origin and then moving y units up or down. The distance along the x-axis is always given first.

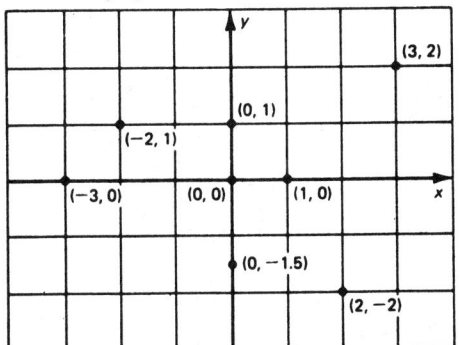

The numbers in parentheses are the coordinates of the point. Thus "$P = (3, 2)$" means that the coordinates of P are $(3, 2)$.

Distance Formula

The distance between the point with coordinates (x, y) and the point with coordinates (a, b) is $\sqrt{(x-a)^2 + (y-b)^2}$.

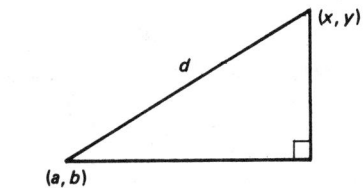

$$d = \sqrt{(x-a)^2 + (y-b)^2}.$$

Slope Formula

The slope, m, of the line joining the points (x_1, y_1) and (x_2, y_2) is given by $m = \dfrac{y_2 - y_1}{x_2 - x_1}$.

Midpoint Formulas

The coordinates, $(\overline{x}, \overline{y})$ of the midpoint of the line joining the points (x_1, y_1) and (x_2, y_2) are given by

$$\overline{x} = \frac{x_1 + x_2}{2}, \; \overline{y} = \frac{y_1 + y_2}{2}.$$

To calculate the slope of a line do the following:
1. Pick any two points on the line—call them (x_1, y_1) and (x_2, y_2).
2. Calculate the distance the line goes up between those two points.
3. Divide by the distance it goes sideways:

$$\text{slope} = \frac{\text{distance up}}{\text{distance sideways}} = \frac{y_2 - y_1}{x_2 - x_1}$$

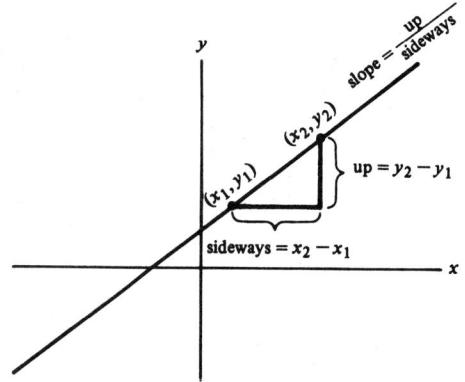

The slope-intercept form of the equation is written in general as:

$y = mx + b$
where $m = slope$, $b = y$-intercept.

The x-axis and the y-axis divide a plane into four regions called quadrants. The quadrant where both x and y are positive is called Quadrant 1. The other three quadrants are labeled as shown.

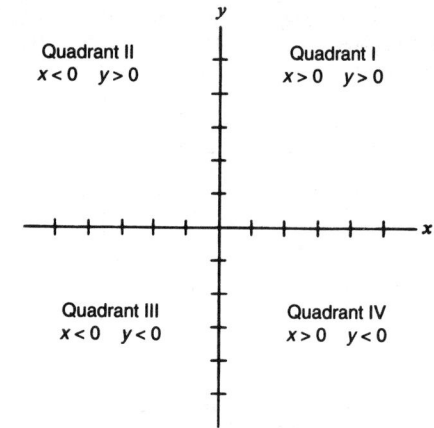

Note that the quadrants are numbered in counter-clockwise order.

Important Mathematical Formulas

Interest = Principal × Time × Rate
Discount = List Price × Rate of Discount
Selling Price = List Price × (100% – Rate of Discount)
Price = Cost × (100% – Rate of Discount)

$$x = \frac{1}{2a}\left(-b \pm \sqrt{b^2 - 4ac}\right) \text{ (quadratic formula)}$$

Distance = Rate × Time
$a^2 + b^2 = c^2$ when a and b are the lengths of the legs and c is the length of the hypotenuse of a right triangle (Pythagorean theorem)
Diameter of a circle = 2 × Radius
Area of a square = s^2
Area of a rectangle = LW
Area of a triangle = $\frac{1}{2}bh$
Area of a circle = πr^2
Area of a parallelogram = bh
Area of a trapezoid = $\frac{1}{2}(b_1 + b_2)h$
Circumference of a circle = πd
Perimeter of a square = $4s$
Perimeter of a rectangle = $2(L + W)$
Volume of a box = lwh
Volume of a cube = e^3
Volume of a cylinder = $\pi r^2 h$
Volume of a sphere = $\frac{4}{3}\pi r^3$
Surface area of a box = $2LW + 2LH + 2WH$
Surface area of a cube = $6e^2$
Surface area of a cylinder = $2\pi rh + 2\pi r^2$
Surface area of a sphere = $4\pi r^2$
Distance between points (x, y) and (a, b) is

$$\sqrt{(x - a)^2 + (y - b)^2}$$

ADVANCED ALGEBRA

POLYNOMIAL EQUATIONS

A polynomial curve of degree n has a maximum of $n - 1$ turning points.

If the degree of the polynomial is even, then the curve will have an odd number of turning points.

If the degree of the polynomial is odd, then the curve will have an even number of turning points.

For example, a first-degree polynomial (line) has zero turning point, a second-degree polynomial (parabola) has one turning point, a third-degree polynomial has zero or two turning points, a fourth-degree polynomial has one or three turning points, and a fifth degree polynomial has zero, two, or four turning points.

If the degree of the polynomial is odd, then the equation must have at least one real solution.

If the degree of the polynomial is even, then the equation may have no real solutions.

Synthetic Division

Synthetic division is a short way of dividing a polynomial by a binomial of the form $x - b$. For example, to find

$$\frac{2x^3 - x^2 - 2x - 8}{x - 2}$$

proceed as follows.

First, write the coefficients on a line, reversing the sign of the divisor's coefficient:

$$
\begin{array}{rrrr|r}
2 & -1 & -2 & -8 & 2 \uparrow\\
\hline
\end{array}
$$

      Answer Line   *divisor's constant term*

Second, rewrite the first coefficient of the polynomial on the "answer line" vertically underneath it:

$$
\begin{array}{rrrr|r}
2 & -1 & -2 & -8 & 2\\
\downarrow & & & &\\
\hline
2 & & & &\\
\end{array}
$$

Third, multiply the 2 in the answer line by the 2 in the divisor, and then add:

$$
\begin{array}{rrrr|r}
2 & -1 & -2 & -8 & 2\\
 & 4 & & &\\
\hline
2 & 3 & & &\\
\end{array}
$$

Fourth, repeat the multiplication and addition process for the next two places:

$$
\begin{array}{rrrr|r}
2 & -1 & -2 & -8 & 2\\
 & 4 & 6 & 8 &\\
\hline
2 & 3 & 4 & 0 &\\
\end{array}
$$

The farthest-right entry in the answer line is the remainder (in this case 0). The remaining elements in the answer line are (from right to left) the coefficients of x^0, x^1, and x^2, so in this case the answer is $2x^2 + 3x + 4$.

Rational Root Theorem

The rational root theorem says that if the polynomial equation

$$a_n x^n + a_{n-1}x^{n-1} + a_{n-2}x^{n-2}$$
$$+ \cdots + a_2 x^2 + a_1 x + a_0 = 0$$

(where a_0, a_1, . . . , a_n are all integers) has any rational roots, then each rational root can be expressed as a fraction in which the numerator is a factor of a_0 and the denominator is a factor of a_n. This theorem sometimes makes it easier to find the roots of complicated polynomial equations, but it provides no help if there are no rational roots to begin with.

Remainder Theorem

If $f(x)$ is a polynomial in x and we perform the division $f(x)/(x - r)$ the remainder is $f(r)$. (This result is called the remainder theorem.)

Series

Summation Notation

$$\sum_{i=1}^{20} i$$

This symbol means: Add up all the integer values of i, starting at $i = 1$ and continuing until $i = 20$. For example,

$$\sum_{i=1}^{5} i = 1 + 2 + 3 + 4 + 5 = 15$$

This is called summation notation.

Arithmetic Series

$$S_n = a + (a + d) + (a + 2d) + (a + 3d) + \cdots$$
$$+ [a + (n - 1)d]$$

A series such as this, in which the difference between any two successive terms is always the same, is called an arithmetic series. $S_n = \frac{n}{2}(a + l)$, where l is the nth term, that is, $l = a + (n - 1)d$.

Geometric Series

A series in which the ratio between two consecutive terms is always the same is called a geometric series.

$$S_n = a + ar + ar^2 + ar^3 + \cdots + ar^{n-1}$$

The general formula for the geometric series:

$$S_n = a + ar + ar^2 + \cdots + ar^{n-1} = \frac{r^n - 1}{r - 1}$$

We can also write that another way if we want to:

$$S_n = a\,\frac{1 - r^n}{1 - r}$$

Infinite Geometric Series

When will a geometric series have an infinite sum?

Clearly the series can have an infinite sum only if it has an infinite number of terms. Also if the ratio between successive terms was greater than 1, then the sum of an infinite series would have to be infinity, since each term would be larger than the last one. An infinite geometric series can have a finite sum only if r is less than 1. The formula for the sum of a geometric series if $|r| < 1$ and $n \to \infty$ is

$$S = \frac{a}{1 - r}.$$

Permutations, Combinations, and the Binomial Theorem

Factorial Function
The factorial of a whole number n (written $n!$) is the product of all of the whole numbers from 1 up to and including that number:

$$n! = n \times (n - 1) \times (n - 2) \times \cdots \times 4 \times 3 \times 2 \times 1$$

Permutations
A permutation is an arrangement of objects in which order matters. The number of permutations of n objects taken j at a time is $\dfrac{n!}{(n - j)!}$

Combinations
A combination is a selection of objects in which the identity, rather than the order, of the objects is significant. The number of combinations of n objects taken j at a time is represented by the symbol $\binom{n}{j}$ or by the symbol $_nC_j$.

$$_nC_j = \binom{n}{j} = \frac{n!}{(n - j)!j!}$$

The expression $\binom{n}{j}$ is sometimes read "n choose j," because it tells you the number of different ways of choosing j objects from a group of n objects.

$$\binom{n}{j} = \binom{n}{n - j}$$

Binomial Theorem
The binomial theorem tells us how to find the powers of a binomial.

$$(a + b)^n = \binom{n}{0} a^n + \binom{n}{1} a^{n-1}b + \binom{n}{2} a^{n-2}b^2$$

$$+ \binom{n}{3} a^{n-3}b^3 + \cdots + \binom{n}{n-1}ab^{n-1}$$

$$+ \binom{n}{n} b^n$$

$$= a^n + na^{n-1}b + \binom{n}{2} a^{n-2}b^2$$

$$+ \cdots + nab^{n-1} + b^n$$

For example,

$$(a + b)^2 = a^2 + 2ab + b^2$$
$$(a + b)^3 = a^3 + 3a^2b + 3ab^2 + b^3$$
$$(a + b)^4 = a^4 + 4a^3b + 6a^2b^2 + 4ab^3 + b^4$$

The Method of Mathematical Induction
This method can be used to prove that a particular formula is true for every whole number. The steps of the method are the following:
1. Show that the method works for 1.
2. Next, assume that the formula is true for an arbitrary number j.
3. Show that *if* the formula is true for the number j, then it must also be true for the number $j + 1$.

Once you have completed these steps, the formula has been proved to be true for all whole numbers.

Exponential Functions and Logarithms

Exponential Functions
An exponential function is a function in which the independent variable x appears as an exponent. For example,

$$y = f(x) = 2^x$$

An exponential function is a function of the form

$$y = f(x) = b^x$$

Here b is a constant number called the base of the function; b can be any positive number (except 1). The domain of the function is the set of all real numbers. The range of this function is the set of all positive numbers. (In other words, the value of the function can never be negative or 0.) Regardless of the value of b, it is always true that $f(0) = 1$. If $b > 1$, then

$$f(x) > 1 \quad \text{if} \quad x > 0$$
$$f(x) < 1 \quad \text{if} \quad x < 0$$

Solution of Exponential Equations
Exponential equations can be solved in one of two ways:
1. If the equation consists of two equivalent powers whose bases can be made the same, then their exponents are equal. For example, if $2^{x+2} = 8^x$, then $2^{x+2} = 2^{3x}$, and x + 2 = 3x.
2. A solution can be accomplished by taking logarithms of both sides of the equation. For example, if $2^{x+3} = 7$, then (x + 3) log 2 = log 7.

Logarithms

Definition of a Logarithm
If $x = b^y$, then y is the logarithm of x to the base b. This can be expressed as $y = \log_b x$. In words, the logarithm of a positive number x to a base b is the exponent to which b must be raised to equal the number.

Common Logarithms

Common logarithms are logarithms in which 10 is used as the base: $y = \log_{10} x$. The subscript 10 is usually omitted so that $y = \log x$ is understood to mean that y is the common logarithm of x.

Common logarithms have the advantage that they can be divided into two parts:

1. The decimal part, called the mantissa, depends only on the sequence of digits in the number regardless of the position of the decimal point in the number. The mantissa of a common logarithm is found by looking up its sequence of digits in a table of common logarithms.
2. The whole number part of a common logarithm is called the characteristic. The characteristic for a number containing one digit before the decimal point, for example, 3.18, is 0. All other characteristics are equal to the power of 10 when the number is expressed in scientific notation. For example, the characteristic for 3180.2 is 3 because $3180.2 = 3.1802 \times 10^3$; the characteristic for 0.0318 is –2 (which is written as 8. – 10 for purposes of calculation) because $0.0318 = 3.18 \times 10^{-2}$.

If a common logarithm must be divided by a number, care must be taken to keep the resulting characteristic as an integer. If a log such as 8.2327 – 10 is to be divided by 3, for example, the log is rewritten as 28.2327 – 10 before division, thus permitting a quotient of 9.4109 – 10.

Properties for logarithm functions:

1. $\log (xy) = \log x + \log y$
2. $\log (x/y) = \log x - \log y$
3. $\log (x^n) = n \log x$

$$\log (\sqrt[n]{x}) = \frac{1}{n} \log x$$

Natural Logarithms

Natural logarithms are logs in which e, a special transcendental number that is approximately 2.71828, is used as the base. $\ln x$ is used as the symbol for the natural log of x ($\ln x = \log_e x$). Natural logs are particularly useful in calculus.

Matrices and Determinants

Matrices

We use boldface roman letters, such as **A** and **B**, to represent matrices. For example, we may have

$$\mathbf{A} = \begin{pmatrix} 5 & 3 & 2 \\ 3 & 6 & 1 \\ 0 & 5 & 0 \end{pmatrix} \qquad \mathbf{B} = \begin{pmatrix} 1 & 12 & 5 \\ 4 & 5 & 6 \end{pmatrix}$$

(In these examples, **A** is a 3-by-3 matrix and **B** is a 2-by-3 matrix. In identifying the size of a matrix, we always write the number of rows first.)

Each number in a matrix is called an element of the matrix. We can easily add two matrices together by adding together their corresponding elements—provided that each matrix has the same number of rows and columns. For example, suppose

$$\mathbf{A} = \begin{pmatrix} 10 & 15 \\ 12 & 17 \end{pmatrix} \quad \text{and} \quad \mathbf{B} = \begin{pmatrix} 5 & 3 \\ 4 & 2 \end{pmatrix}$$

Then

$$\mathbf{A} + \mathbf{B} = \begin{pmatrix} 10 + 5 & 15 + 3 \\ 12 + 4 & 17 + 2 \end{pmatrix} = \begin{pmatrix} 15 & 18 \\ 16 & 19 \end{pmatrix}$$

Given a set of simultaneous equations:

$1x + 1y - 1z = 6$

$2x - 1y + 3z = 11$

$4x + 2y - 3z = 14$

a matrix is formed from the coefficients: Each row represents an equation. The first column contains the coefficients of x, the second column contains the coefficients of y, the third column contains the coefficients of z, and the last column contains the terms from the right-hand side of the equations.

$$\begin{pmatrix} 1 & 1 & -1 & 6 \\ 2 & -1 & 3 & 11 \\ 4 & 2 & -3 & 14 \end{pmatrix}$$

In order to solve 3 linear equations in 3 unknowns:

Write down a matrix with 3 rows and 4 columns to represent the equations. Each row represents one equation. The first column contains the coefficients of x, the second column contains the coefficients of y, the third column contains the coefficients of z, and the last column contains the terms from the right-hand side of the system.

The basic move is to multiply one row by a number and then add that row to another row. Choose suitable multipliers and continue the process until one row contains two zero elements (it represents an equation in one variable which is solvable) and another row contains at least one zero element (it represents an equation in two variables which can now be solved).

Consider two matrices **A** and **B**. Suppose that **A** has m rows and n columns and **B** has n rows and p columns. Then you can find the matrix product **AB**. (Note that the product **AB** exists only if the number of columns of **A** is the same as the number of rows of **B**.)

Here is the procedure to find the matrix product:

1. Start with the first row of **A** and the first column of **B**. (Note that each of these will contain n elements.)
2. Multiply the corresponding elements of this row and this column.
3. Add all the products together. The result will be the element in the first row and first column of the product matrix **AB**.
4. Repeat this process to find each element of **AB**, using the ith row of **A** and the jth column of **B** to get the element in the ith row and jth column of **AB**. (The resulting matrix will have m rows and p columns.)

$$\begin{pmatrix} a_1 & b_1 & c_1 \\ a_2 & b_2 & c_2 \\ a_3 & b_3 & c_3 \end{pmatrix} \begin{pmatrix} x \\ y \\ z \end{pmatrix} = \begin{pmatrix} a_1x + b_1y + c_1z \\ a_2x + b_2y + c_2z \\ a_3x + b_3y + c_3z \end{pmatrix}$$

If the number of columns in **A** is different from the number of rows in **B**, then the product matrix **AB** won't exist. Matrix multiplication doesn't obey the commutative property. The product matrix **AB** won't necessarily be the same as **BA**.

MATHEMATICS

An identity matrix for multiplication is a square matrix such as

$$\begin{bmatrix} 1 & 0 & 0 \\ 0 & 1 & 0 \\ 0 & 0 & 1 \end{bmatrix}$$

that has 1 for each of its main diagonal elements and 0 for each remaining element.

If **I** is an identity matrix, and **A** is any other matrix with the same number of rows as **I**, then $IA = A$. Also, if **B** has the same number of columns as **I**, then $BI = B$.

Determinants

The determinant of a 2-by-2 matrix is defined as:

$$\begin{vmatrix} a_1 & b_1 \\ a_2 & b_2 \end{vmatrix} = a_1 b_2 - a_2 b_1$$

The solution to the system of equations

$$a_1 x + b_1 y = c_1$$
$$a_2 x + b_2 y = c_2$$

is

$$x = \frac{\begin{vmatrix} c_1 & b_1 \\ c_2 & b_2 \end{vmatrix}}{\begin{vmatrix} a_1 & b_1 \\ a_2 & b_2 \end{vmatrix}} = \frac{b_2 c_1 - b_1 c_2}{a_1 b_2 - a_2 b_1}$$

$$y = \frac{\begin{vmatrix} a_1 & c_1 \\ b_2 & c_2 \end{vmatrix}}{\begin{vmatrix} a_1 & b_1 \\ a_2 & b_2 \end{vmatrix}} = \frac{a_2 c_2 - a_2 c_1}{a_1 b_2 - a_2 b_1}$$

The value of the determinant is unchanged if you add a multiple of one row to another row.

Start with the 3-by-3 matrix

$$\begin{pmatrix} a_1 & b_1 & c_1 \\ a_2 & b_2 & c_2 \\ a_3 & b_3 & c_3 \end{pmatrix}$$

The determinant of the matrix is calculated from the formula

$$a_1 b_2 c_3 + a_2 b_3 c_1 + a_3 b_1 c_2$$
$$- a_3 b_2 c_1 - a_2 b_1 c_3 - a_1 b_3 c_2$$

Note that the determinant is a number, not a matrix. A determinant is symbolized by writing all the elements inside straight vertical lines:

$$\det \mathbf{A} = \begin{vmatrix} a_1 & b_1 & c_1 \\ a_2 & b_2 & c_2 \\ a_3 & b_3 & c_3 \end{vmatrix}$$

Here is a method for finding the determinant of a matrix. The minor of a matrix element a_{ij} is the matrix consisting of all of the elements in the original matrix except for the elements in row i and column j. For example, the minor of the element 1 in the 3-by-3 matrix

$$\begin{pmatrix} 1 & 2 & 3 \\ 4 & 5 & 6 \\ 7 & 8 & 9 \end{pmatrix}$$

is the matrix

$$\begin{pmatrix} 5 & 6 \\ 8 & 9 \end{pmatrix}$$

To calculate the determinant of a matrix, start with the first element in the first row. Multiply that element by the determinant of its minor. Then subtract the product of the second element and the determinant of its minor, add the product of the third element and its minor, and keep going in the same way. For example, a 3-by-3 determinant can be found from the following expression:

$$\begin{vmatrix} a_1 & b_1 & c_1 \\ a_2 & b_2 & c_2 \\ a_3 & b_3 & c_3 \end{vmatrix} = a_1 \begin{vmatrix} b_2 & c_2 \\ b_3 & c_3 \end{vmatrix} - b_1 \begin{vmatrix} a_2 & c_2 \\ a_3 & c_3 \end{vmatrix} + c_1 \begin{vmatrix} a_2 & b_2 \\ a_3 & b_3 \end{vmatrix}$$

This method will work for a matrix of any size. However, note that you will need to calculate four 3-by-3 determinants in order to calculate a 4-by-4 determinant. You don't have to use the first row for this process, though; you can use any row or column. It's usually easiest to pick a row with a lot of zeros.

To solve a system of three equations in three unknowns by determinants, the following method may be used.

Calculate the determinant of the matrix of coefficients. That determinant will be the denominator for each solution.

To find the solution for x, replace the coefficients of x in the coefficient matrix with the column of constants from the right-hand side. Then, calculate the determinant of that matrix. That determinant will be the numerator of the solutions for x. Follow the same procedure to find the solutions for y and z:

$$x = \frac{\begin{vmatrix} d_1 & b_1 & c_1 \\ d_2 & b_2 & c_2 \\ d_3 & b_3 & c_3 \end{vmatrix}}{\begin{vmatrix} a_1 & b_1 & c_1 \\ a_2 & b_2 & c_2 \\ a_3 & b_3 & c_3 \end{vmatrix}} \quad y = \frac{\begin{vmatrix} a_1 & d_1 & c_1 \\ a_2 & d_2 & c_2 \\ a_3 & d_3 & c_3 \end{vmatrix}}{\begin{vmatrix} a_1 & b_1 & c_1 \\ a_2 & b_2 & c_2 \\ a_3 & b_3 & c_3 \end{vmatrix}} \quad z = \frac{\begin{vmatrix} a_1 & b_1 & d_1 \\ a_2 & b_2 & d_2 \\ a_3 & b_3 & d_3 \end{vmatrix}}{\begin{vmatrix} a_1 & b_1 & c_1 \\ a_2 & b_2 & c_2 \\ a_3 & b_3 & c_3 \end{vmatrix}}$$

(This solution method is called Cramer's rule.)

TRIGONOMETRY

Trigonometric Functions

Definitions of Functions of Acute Angles

For an acute angle A, such that $0° < A < 90°$, the trigonometric functions, sine A, cosine A, tangent A, cotangent A, cosecant A, and secant A are defined as ratios of the lengths of sides in a right triangle in which A is one of the acute angles.

Draw a right triangle. Pick one of the angles to be the angle of interest (call that angle A).

Let x represent the length of the adjacent side, y represent the length of the opposite side and h represent the length of the hypotenuse. Then,

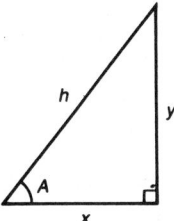

$$\sin A = \frac{\text{opposite side}}{\text{hypotenuse}} = \frac{y}{h}$$

$$\cos A = \frac{\text{adjacent side}}{\text{hypotenuse}} = \frac{x}{h}$$

$$\tan A = \frac{\text{opposite side}}{\text{adjacent side}} = \frac{y}{x}$$

$$\cot A = \frac{\text{adjacent side}}{\text{opposite side}} = \frac{x}{y}$$

$$\sec A = \frac{\text{hypotenuse}}{\text{adjacent side}} = \frac{h}{x}$$

$$\csc A = \frac{\text{hypotenuse}}{\text{opposite side}} = \frac{h}{y}$$

A table of the values of the trigonometric functions, rounded off to the nearest fifth decimal place, appears on page 16-56.

Functions of Special Angles

Certain angles, notably 0°, 30°, 45°, 60°, and 90°, appear very often in applications using trigonometry. Also, the values of their trigonometric functions can be represented precisely by the use of fractions and/or radicals instead of being approximated by the decimal values in the table. Therefore, users of trigonometry generally commit the functions of these special angles to memory:

$$\sin 0° = 0 \quad \cos 0° = 1 \quad \tan 0° = 0$$

$$\sin 90° = 1 \quad \cos 90° = 0 \quad \tan 90° = \text{undefined}$$

$$\sin 45° = \frac{1}{\sqrt{2}} \quad \cos 45° \frac{1}{\sqrt{2}} \quad \tan 45° = 1$$

$$\sin 30° = \frac{1}{2} \quad \cos 30° \frac{\sqrt{3}}{2} \quad \tan 30° = \frac{1}{\sqrt{3}}$$

$$\sin 60° = \frac{\sqrt{3}}{2} \quad \cos 60° \frac{1}{2} \quad \tan 60° = \sqrt{3}$$

Special Right Triangles

Two special right triangles, the 45°-45°-90° and the 30°-60°-90°, provide formulas for side lengths which, if memorized and applied in the definitions of the trigonometric functions, instantly provide the precise values for the functions of 30°, 45°, and 60°.

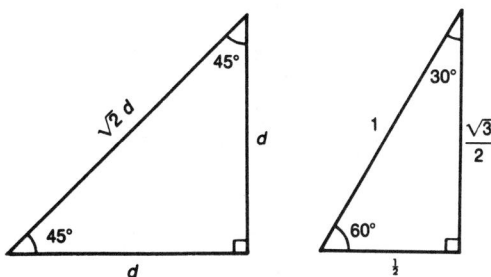

General Definitions of the Trigonometric Functions

The trigonometric functions may be defined for angles of all sizes, including those larger than 90° and even those larger than 360°, by the use of more general definitions than those given above for acute angles. This is done by considering the plane to be divided into four quadrants:

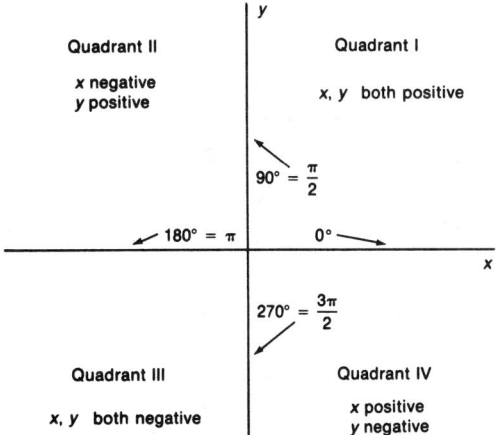

Any angle is then represented in standard position in the quadrants by placing its vertex on the origin and making its initial side coincide with the positive direction of the x-axis. A positive angle is then represented by the counterclockwise rotation from its initial side to the location of its terminal side. A negative angle is represented by the clockwise rotation from its initial side to the location of its terminal side. Angles terminating in each of the four quadrants are pictured below in standard position:

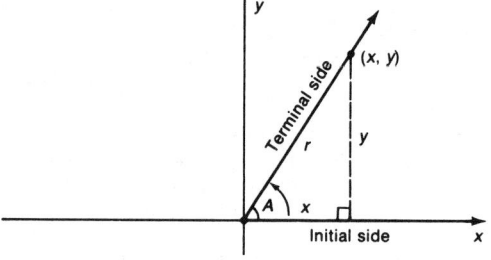

Quadrant I

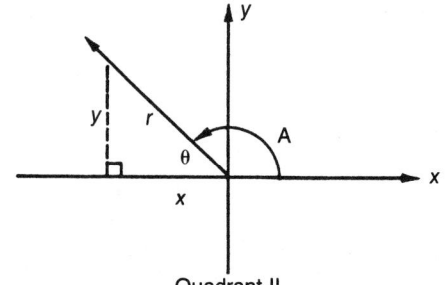

Quadrant II

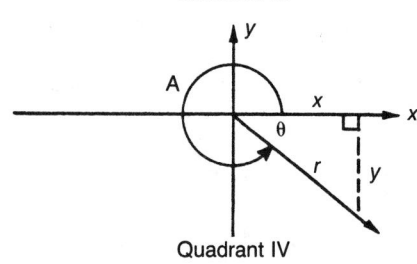

Quadrant III

Quadrant IV

For all four quadrants, the trigonometric functions are defined as follows:

$$\sin A = \frac{y}{r} \qquad \cos A = \frac{x}{r} \qquad \tan A = \frac{y}{x}$$

$$\csc A = \frac{r}{y} \qquad \sec A = \frac{r}{x} \qquad \cot A = \frac{x}{y}$$

Note that r is always considered to be positive, but since x and/or y may be negative in some quadrants, a trigonometric function of an angle larger than 90°

can be negative. The signs of the functions in Quadrants I, II, III, and IV are shown below:

Quadrant	sin	cos	tan	csc	sec	cot
I	+	+	+	+	+	+
II	+	−	−	+	−	−
III	−	−	+	−	−	+
IV	−	+	−	−	+	−

The acute angle between the terminal side of an angle in standard position and the x-axis is called the reference angle. The reference angles are labeled θ in Quadrants II, III, and IV above. In Quadrant I, angle A is its own reference angle. To find a trigonometric function of an angle greater than 90°, find the trigonometric function of its reference angle and then prefix the proper sign for that quadrant. For example, to find cos 210°, note that 210° terminates in Quadrant III where the cosine is negative. The reference angle for 210° is 210° −180° or 30°. Therefore, cos 210° = −cos 30° = −0.8660 (using the table on page 16-58) or

$$\cos 210° = -\cos 30° = -\frac{\sqrt{3}}{2} \text{ (using the 30°-60°-90°}$$
triangle).

The same procedure is used to find trigonometric functions of negative angles. For example, to find sin(−200°), note that −200° is represented by a clockwise rotation so that its terminal side lies in Quadrant II, where the sine is positive. The reference angle is 200° − 180° = 20°. sin(−200°) = +sin 20° = 0.3420.

Angles Larger than 360°

An angle of 360° + A° is represented in standard position by one complete rotation plus A degrees more. The trigonometric functions of such an angle are therefore the same as the functions for A°.

360° is the same as 2π radians (see discussion of radian measure below). Angles larger than 360° are generally denoted in radians in the form $2\pi + A$, $4\pi + A$, and so on; this calls attention to the fact that the angle represents one or more complete rotations plus A radians.

Coterminal Angles

Consider any angle A. This angle is coterminal with the angles $(2\pi + A)$, $(4\pi + A)$, $(6\pi + A)$, and $(8\pi + A)$, and so on. In general, the angle $(2n\pi + A)$, where n can be any integer, will be coterminal with A. The values of the trigonometric functions for an angle will be the same for all angles that are coterminal with the original angle. In particular,

$$\sin A = \sin(2n\pi + A)$$
$$\cos A = \cos(2n\pi + A)$$
$$\tan A = \tan(2n\pi + A)$$

for any value of A.

Radian Measure

In elementary work, angles are usually measured in degrees, where $1° = \frac{1}{360}$th of a complete rotation. In advanced mathematics, especially in calculus, it is advantageous to use a different unit of measure, the radian, to indicate the size of an angle.

Definition of Radian

Draw a circle of radius r. Draw an angle with the vertex at the center of the circle. (This type of angle is called a central angle.) The two sides of the angle will cut across the circle and form an arc. Let s represent the length of the arc, and r the radius of the circle. Then the radian (rad) measure of the angle is

Size of angle in radians $= \dfrac{s}{r}$

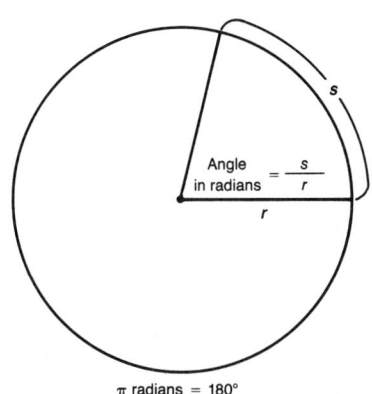

π radians = 180°

When the size of an angle is written as a number without a degree symbol, then it is understood that the angle is being measured in radians. Therefore, you can say that the size of an angle is "π/2" instead of having to say "π/2 radians."

Converting Radians to Degrees and Conversely

π radians= 180°

This relationship can be written in two ways:

$$1 \text{ radian } = \dfrac{180°}{\pi} \qquad 1° = \dfrac{\pi}{180} \text{ radians}$$

If we have an angle of x radians, we can convert it to degrees by using the left equation:

x radians $= \dfrac{180x}{\pi}$ degrees. If we have an angle in degrees, we can convert it to radian measure by using the right equation:

$x° = \dfrac{\pi x}{180}$ radians.

Applications Using Trigonometric Functions

Trigonometry of the Right Triangle

If some parts (angles or sides) of a right triangle are known and another part is to be found, a trigonometric function involving an angle and two sides can be chosen so that it includes the part to be found and two known parts. Solving the resulting equation will yield the value of the part to be found.

Many problems making use of the trigonometry of the right triangle involve either an angle of elevation or an angle of depression.

The angle of elevation of an object is the angle between the horizontal and the line connecting your position to the object (assuming that the object is above you). If you are looking at an object that is below you, you may calculate the angle of depression.

Component Vectors

In science and engineering, forces are represented by vectors (lines indicating direction and magnitude of a force). It is frequently necessary to convert such forces into two components whose combined effect is equivalent to the original force. This may be done by the application of trigonometric functions in the appropriate triangle.

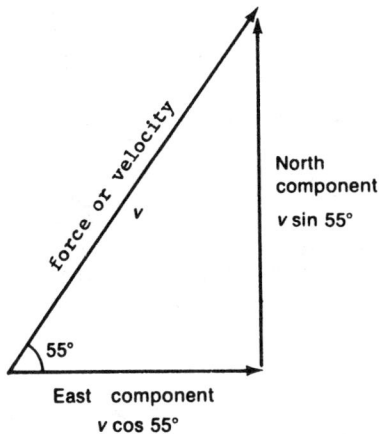

Resultant Vector

When two forces act simultaneously, they can be represented by two vectors and their combined effect will be represented by their "vector sum," known as the resultant vector. If the magnitudes and directions of the two component forces are known, the magnitude and direction of the resultant can be computed using trigonometry. If the components act at right angles to each other, the procedures outlined for the trigonometry of the right triangle can be used. If the components act at an oblique angle, the Law of Sines or the Law of Cosines must be used (*see* next page).

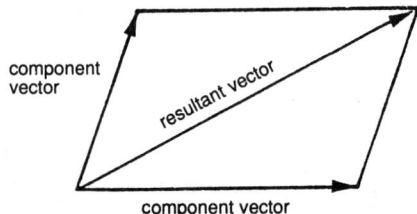

If two component vectors are used as the sides of a parallelogram, the diagonal of the parallelogram which issues from their common origin will represent their resultant.

Velocity Components

Velocities are often broken up into components.

Suppose you have decided on two directions called the x direction and the y direction. (For example, the x direction might represent east and the y direction north, or the y direction might represent up and the x direction horizontal motion in a particular direction. These two directions must be at right angles to each other.) Then, suppose that r represents a velocity vector in a particular direction. Then you may find the x component and the y component of the velocity vector according to the formulas

$r_x = r \cos A$

$r_y = r \sin A$

Solution of Oblique Triangles

Triangles that are not right triangles are called oblique triangles. If the sizes of three of their parts, at least one of which must be a side, are known, the other sides and angles can be found. This is usually accomplished by using the Law of Cosines or the Law of Sines.

Law of Cosines

The law of cosines is useful when you know two sides of a triangle and the angle between those two sides. Let a and b represent the lengths of the two sides, and let C represent the angle between these two sides. Then the third side (c) can be found from the formula

$c^2 = a^2 + b^2 - 2ab \cos C$

Two other forms of the law can be used:

$a^2 = b^2 + c^2 - 2bc \cos A$

$b^2 = a^2 + c^2 - 2ab \cos B$

If the three sides of a triangle are known, use of the Law of Cosines makes it possible to find each of the angles.

Law of Sines

Let a, b, and c be the lengths of the sides of a triangle, and let A, B, and C be the angles opposite those sides. Then,

$$\frac{a}{\sin A} = \frac{b}{\sin B} = \frac{c}{\sin C}$$

By setting any two of the fractions equal, for example, $\dfrac{a}{\sin A} = \dfrac{b}{\sin B}$, three different forms of this law may be obtained. If two sides of a triangle and the angle opposite one of them are known, the angle opposite the other one (and hence the third angle of the triangle also) can be found by using the Law of Sines. If two angles and the side opposite one of them are known, the Law of Sines makes finding the side opposite the other possible.

Identities

General Definition of Identities

Some special equations are true for all possible values of the unknowns they contain. Equations of this kind are called identities.

The trigonometric equation

$$\sin A = \cos \left(\frac{\pi}{2} - A \right)$$

is an identity because it is true for any value of A. The equation

$$\sin A = \frac{1}{2}$$

is not an identity because the only solutions are $A = \pi/6$ and $A = 5\pi/6$ and the other angles coterminal with those angles.

Trigonometric Identities

Many identities exist among the trigonometric functions. They are useful in simplifying trigonometric expressions and also in solving equations in which the variables are trigonometric functions. The trigonometric identities are listed here, grouped by types. These identities are equations which are true for every possible value of the angles A and B, except for angles that make the denominator of a fraction have a value of 0.

Reciprocal functions:

$\sin A = \dfrac{1}{\csc A}$ $\csc A = \dfrac{1}{\sin A}$

$\cos A = \dfrac{1}{\sec A}$ $\sec A = \dfrac{1}{\cos A}$

$\tan A = \dfrac{1}{\cot A}$ $\cot A = \dfrac{1}{\tan A}$

Cofunctions (radian form):

$\sin A = \cos \left(\dfrac{\pi}{2} - A \right)$ $\cos A = \sin \left(\dfrac{\pi}{2} - A \right)$

$\tan A = \cot \left(\dfrac{\pi}{2} - A \right)$ $\cot A = \tan \left(\dfrac{\pi}{2} - A \right)$

$\sec A = \csc \left(\dfrac{\pi}{2} - A \right)$ $\csc A = \sec \left(\dfrac{\pi}{2} - A \right)$

Note the following: $\dfrac{\pi}{2} - A$ and A are complementary angles. The cofunction group of identities may be summarized by saying that cofunctions of complementary angles are always equal.

Negative angle relations:

$\sin(-A) = -\sin A$

$\cos(-A) = \cos A$

$\tan(-A) = -\tan A$

Quotient relations:

$$\tan A = \frac{\sin A}{\cos A}$$

$$\cot A = \frac{\cos A}{\sin A}$$

Pythagorean identities:

$$\sin^2 A + \cos^2 A = 1$$
$$\tan^2 A + 1 = \sec^2 A$$
$$\cot^2 A + 1 = \csc^2 A$$

Functions of the sum of two angles:

$$\sin(A + B) = \sin A \cos B + \sin B \cos A$$
$$\cos(A + B) = \cos A \cos B - \sin A \sin B$$

$$\tan(A + B) = \frac{\tan A + \tan B}{1 - \tan A \tan B}$$

Functions of the difference of two angles:
$$\sin(A - B) = \sin A \cos B - \sin B \cos A$$
$$\cos(A - B) = \cos A \cos B + \sin A \sin B$$

Double-angle formulas:
$$\sin(2A) = 2 \sin A \cos A$$
$$\cos(2A) = \cos^2 A - \sin^2 A$$
$$= 1 - 2 \sin^2 A$$
$$= 2 \cos^2 A - 1$$

$$\tan(2A) = \frac{2 \tan A}{1 - \tan^2 A}$$

Half-angle formulas:

$$\sin\left(\frac{A}{2}\right) = \pm \sqrt{\frac{1 - \cos A}{2}}$$

$$\cos\left(\frac{A}{2}\right) = \pm \sqrt{\frac{1 + \cos A}{2}}$$

$$\tan\left(\frac{A}{2}\right) = \pm \sqrt{\frac{1 - \cos A}{1 + \cos A}}$$

Graphs of the Trigonometric Functions

The graphs of the trigonometric functions are periodic, that is, their shape involves a cycle which is repeated over and over. The trigonometric functions are thus useful in representing many physical phenomena which have this property, for example, alternating current electricity, oscillations, and wave motions.

In the case of the sine and cosine curves, the maximum height of the curve is called the amplitude of the function, and the number of degrees (or radians) in the cycle that is repeated is called the period of the function.

Basic Trigonometric Function Graphs

Graph of $y = \sin x$:

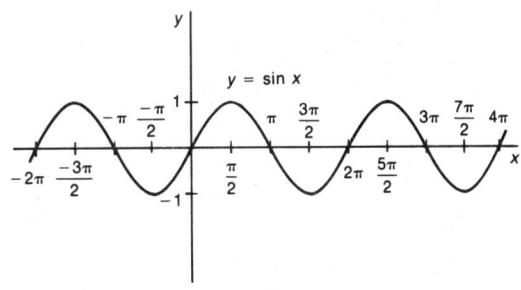

Amplitude = 1; period = 360° or 2π radians.

Graph of $y = \cos x$:

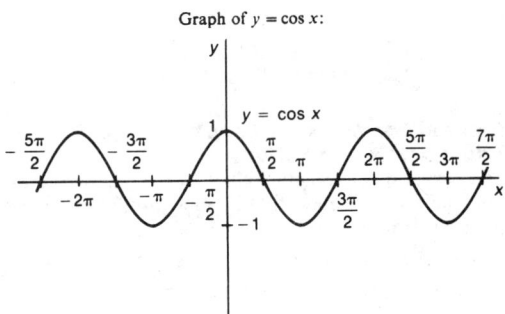

Amplitude = 1; period = 360° or 2π radians.

Graph of $y = \tan x$:

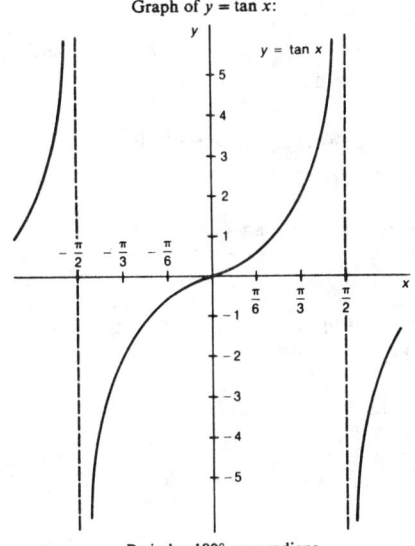

Period = 180° or π radians.

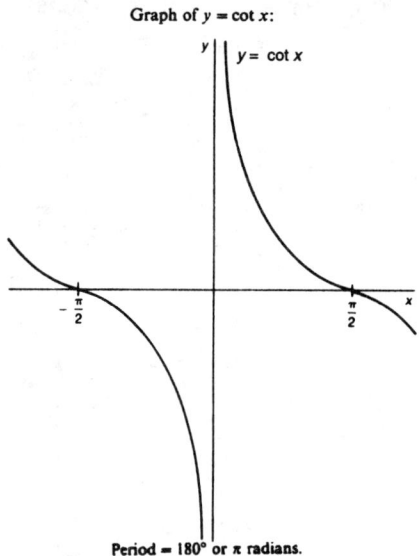

Graph of $y = \cot x$:

Period = 180° or π radians.

General Formulas for Graphs of Trigonometric Functions

The basic equations and shapes of the trigonometric functions may be modified by changing coefficients in the equations.

The general formula for a sine curve is $y = a \sin bx$, where a = the amplitude and $\frac{2\pi}{b}$ = the period in radians $\left(\text{that is } \frac{360°}{b}\right)$. For example, the the graph of $y = 2 \sin 3x$ would have an amplitude of 2 and a period of $\frac{360°}{3} = 120°$ or $\frac{2\pi}{3}$ radians.

The maximum height of the curve would be 2 and it would reach a minimum value of −2. The cycle would repeat every 120° or $\frac{2\pi}{3}$ radians.

The general formula for a cosine curve is $y = a \cos bx$, where a = the amplitude and $\frac{2\pi}{b}$ = the period in radians $\left(\text{ that is } \frac{360°}{b}\right)$.

Inverse Trigonometric Functions

Definition of Inverse Function

The inverse of a function is the relation obtained by interchanging the domain and range of the original function. This is equivalent to interchanging the two numbers in each of the ordered pairs that comprise the original function.

The inverse of a function may be a relation that is not itself a function. To constitute a function, each value of the domain must have one and only one value in the range. Interchanging values of the range and domain may result in more than one value of the new range being paired with the same value of the new domain, in which case the relation is not a function. If the inverse of a function is itself a function, it is called the inverse function of the original function.

Inverses of Trigonometric Functions

The inverse trigonometric functions are represented by the following notation using "arc" prefixed to the name of the function:

If $s = \sin A$, then $A = \arcsin s$.

If $c = \cos A$, then $A = \arccos c$.

If $t = \tan A$, then $A = \arctan t$.

Inverse trigonometric functions can also be represented by another notation:

$\arcsin s = \sin^{-1} s$

$\arccos c = \cos^{-1} c$

$\arctan t = \tan^{-1} t$

The −1 to the upper right of each function stands for inverse function. However, if you use this notation you must be careful that you do not confuse the −1 used to represent inverse function with a −1 used as an exponent.

Principal Values

Since many angles have the same sine, the inverse function, arcsin s, would not be a true function unless we restrict the domain in some way. We do this by the use of principal values for the angles in each of the inverse trigonometric functions.

We specify principal values for each of the inverse trigonometric functions. (In some books the inverse trigonometric functions are written with capital letters if the principal values are meant. In that notation, Arctan t means "the principal value of arctan t.") The principal values of the Arctan function are between $-\pi/2$ and $\pi/2$ inclusive. In other words, the expression Arctan t would mean the value of A between $-\pi/2$ and $\pi/2$ inclusive such that tan A = t. The principal values of the Arcsin function are also between $-\pi/2$ and $\pi/2$ inclusive. The principal values of Arccos x are between 0 and π inclusive.

Graphs of Inverse Trigonometric Functions

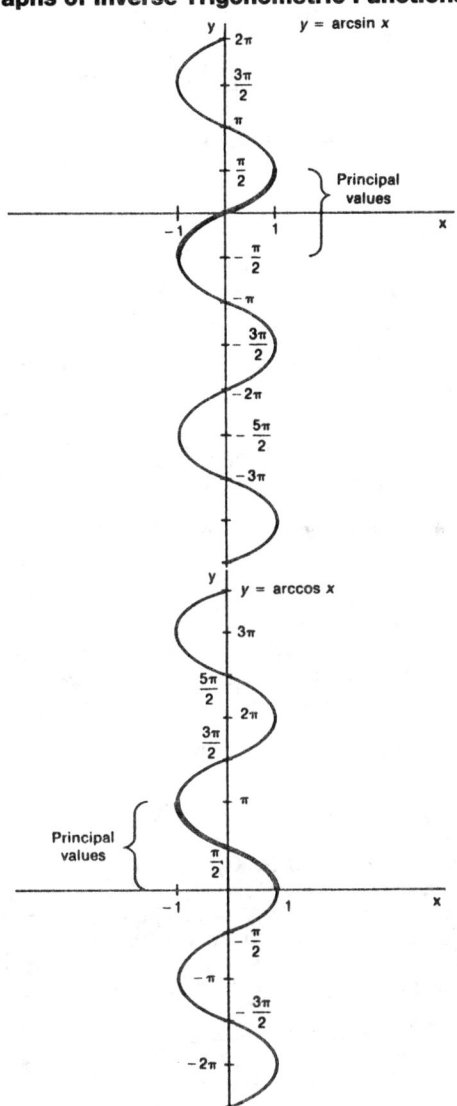

Polar Coordinates

The Polar Coordinate System

In the Cartesian or rectangular coordinate system, any point is represented by (x, y) where x is the abscissa and y is the ordinate. Any point in a plane can also be identified by two numbers under the polar coordinate system. First, pick a point to represent the origin. Then, pick a direction to represent the 0° direction. We will always draw the 0° direction as pointing directly right from the origin. Then, any point in the plane can be identified by two coordinates called r and θ. The symbol θ is a Greek letter called theta.

r = distance from the origin to the point.

θ = the clockwise angle between the 0° line and the line drawn from the origin to the point.

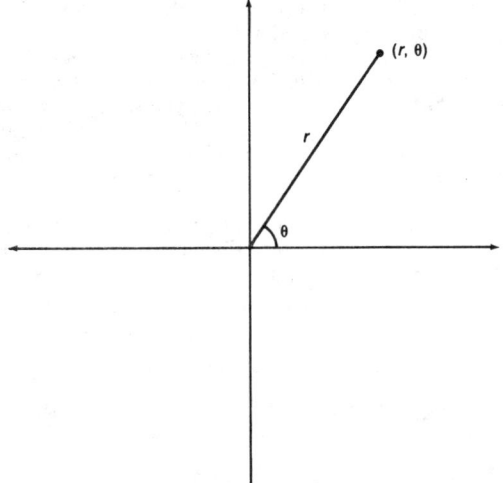

Conversions Between Rectangular and Polar Coordinates

To convert rectangular coordinates (x, y) to polar coordinates (r, θ), let

$$r = \sqrt{x^2 + y^2} \text{ and } \theta = \arctan\frac{y}{x}$$

To convert polar coordinates (r, θ) to rectangular coordinates (x, y), let

$$x = r\cos \text{ and } \theta\, y = r\sin\theta$$

Complex Numbers

The Imaginary Number i

Every real number corresponds to a point on a number line, and a real number can be represented as a decimal fraction that either terminates, repeats the same pattern, or continues endlessly without ever repeating a pattern. However, there is no real number equal to the square root of −1. In other words, the equation $x^2 = -1$ has no real-number solutions. So, we use a new number, called i, such that $i^2 = -1$. Some powers of i:

$i^0 = 1$	$i^5 = i$
$i^1 = i$	$i^6 = -1$
$i^2 = -1$	$i^7 = -i$
$i^3 = -1 \times i = -i$	$i^8 = 1$
$i^4 = -i \times i = 1$	$i^9 = i$

The powers keep repeating the same pattern.

Definition of a Complex Number

A complex number is a number of the form

$a + bi$

where a and b are both real numbers. We call a number of the form bi a pure imaginary number. A complex number is formed by adding a real number and a pure imaginary number.

The number $a - bi$ is called the complex conjugate of the number $a + bi$. In other words, to find the conjugate of a complex number, you simply reverse the sign of the imaginary part. Conjugates have the useful property that the product of any complex number and its conjugate is a non-negative real number.

If you are allowed to use complex numbers, you can factor any nth-degree polynomial as the product of n factors. For example:

$$x^2 + 1 = (x - i)(x + i)$$
$$x^4 - 1 = (x - 1)(x + 1)(x - i)(x + i)$$
$$x^3 - 3x^2 + 2x - 6 = (x - 3)(x + \sqrt{2}i)(x - \sqrt{2}i)$$

However, note that the factors are not necessarily all distinct. For example:

$$x^2 + 2x + 1 = (x + 1)(x + 1) = (x + 1)^2$$

The equation $x^2 + 2x + 1 = 0$ is said to have the double root $x = -1$. If double roots are counted as two roots, triple roots as three roots, and so on, it is easy to see that every nth-degree polynomial equation has n (real or complex) roots.

Representation of Complex Numbers

A complex number can be represented on a two-dimensional diagram. The horizontal axis is the real axis and the vertical axis is the imaginary axis. The number $a + bi$ is represented by a point drawn a units to the right of the origin and b units up.

The absolute value of a complex number is the distance from the origin to the point representing that number, We will use r to represent the absolute value. Then,

$$r = \sqrt{a^2 + b^2}$$

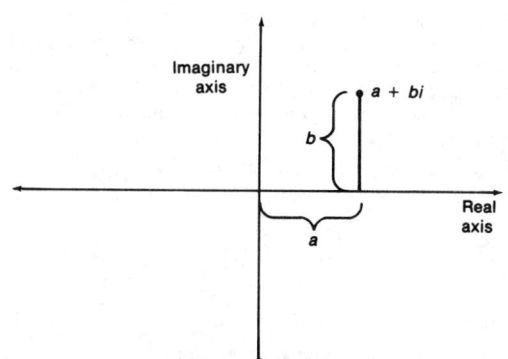

Polar Form of Complex Numbers

A complex number can be expressed in polar coordinate form by listing two numbers: the absolute value r and the angle θ.

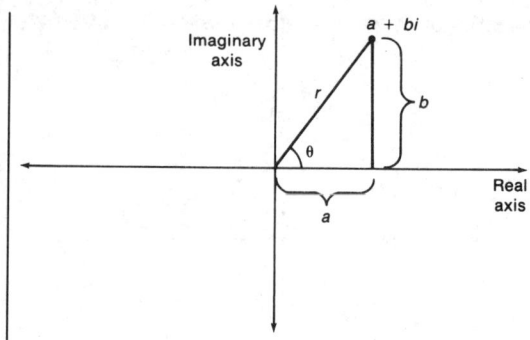

To convert from the polar form to the rectangular form:

$$a = r \cos \theta$$

$$b = r \sin \theta$$

We can also convert the rectangular form to the polar form:

$$r = \sqrt{a^2 + b^2}$$

$$\theta = \arctan \frac{b}{a}$$

Normally we write polar-form complex numbers like

$$r(\cos \theta + i \sin \theta)$$

Properties of and Operations on Complex Numbers

Some of the operations on complex numbers are easier to perform if the numbers are represented in polar form, $r(\cos \theta + i \sin \theta)$, than if they are represented in rectangular form, $a + bi$.

Multiplying Complex Numbers

To multiply two complex numbers written in polar form,

$$[r_1(\cos \theta_1 + i \sin \theta_1)][r_2(\cos \theta_2 + i \sin \theta_2)]$$
$$= r_1 r_2 [\cos (\theta_1 + \theta_2) + i \sin (\theta_1 + \theta_2)]$$

That is, to obtain the absolute value of the product, multiply the two absolute values. To obtain the angle of the result, add the two angles.

For example, the product of $3(\cos 20° + i \sin 20°)$ and $2(\cos 30° + i \sin 30°)$ is obtained by multiplying their absolute values and adding their angles. The product is $6(\cos 50° + i \sin 50°)$.

Powers of Complex Numbers

Powers of complex numbers may be obtained from the formula $[r(\cos \theta + i \sin \theta)]^n = r^n(\cos n\theta + i \sin n\theta)$. This means that raising the complex number $[r(\cos \theta + i \sin \theta)]$ to the nth power requires only the raising of its absolute value r to the nth power while its angle is multiplied by n.

Example
$$[2(\cos 20° + i \sin 20°)]^4 = 2^4[\cos(4 \times 20°)$$
$$+ i \sin(4 \times 20°) = 16(\cos 80° + i \sin 80°)].$$

Roots of Complex Numbers

A complex number has a total number n of nth roots. For example, a complex number has one first root (itself), two square roots, three cube roots, four fourth roots, five fifth roots, and so on. Consider the complex number

$$r(\cos \theta_0 + i \sin \theta_0)$$

The n roots all have absolute value $r^{1/n}$. The n values of the angle θ can be found from the formula

$$\theta = \frac{360m + \theta_0}{n} \text{ degrees } \text{ or}$$

$$\theta = \frac{2\pi m + \theta_0}{n} \text{ radians.}$$

The factor m takes on successively the values of all of the integers from 0 to $n - 1$ to produce each of the nth roots.

ANALYTIC GEOMETRY

Conic Sections

The four curves—circles, ellipses, parabolas, and hyperbolas—are the conic sections.

Relation to Cones

These four curves are called conic sections because they can be formed by the intersection of a plane with a right circular cone. If the plane is perpendicular to the axis of the cone, the intersection will be a circle. If the plane is slightly tilted, the result will be an ellipse. If the plane is parallel to one element of the cone, the result will be a parabola. If the plane intersects both nappes of the cone, the result will be a hyperbola. (Note that a hyperbola has two branches.)

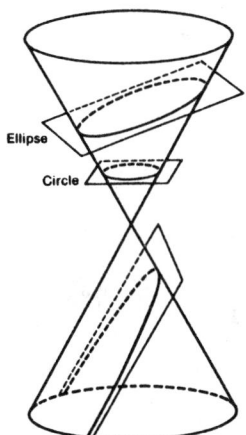

Parabola

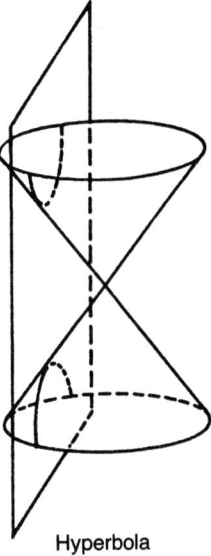

Hyperbola

Circles

A circle is the set of points in a plane that are all the same distance r from a fixed point called the center. The equation of a circle with center at the origin can be written

$$x^2 + y^2 = r^2$$

where r is the radius of the circle.

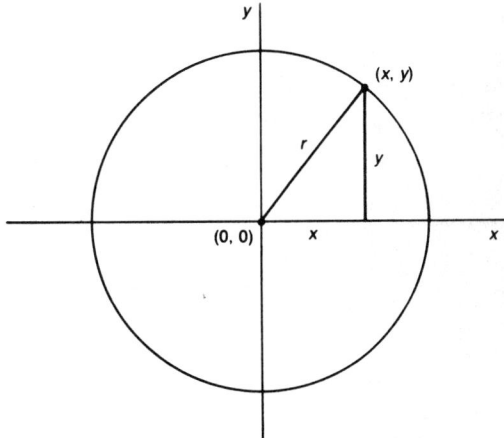

Ellipses

An ellipse is the set of points in a plane such that the

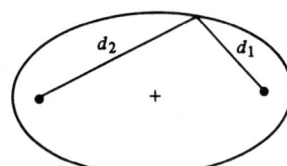

sum of the distances to two fixed points is constant. The two fixed points are the focal points. The point halfway between the two focal points is called the center. The longest distance across the ellipse is the major axis; half this distance is the semimajor axis. The shortest distance across the ellipse is the minor axis; half this distance is the semiminor axis. The equation of an ellipse with its center at the origin, a semimajor axis of length a, and a semiminor axis of length b is

$$\frac{x^2}{a^2} + \frac{y^2}{b^2} = 1$$

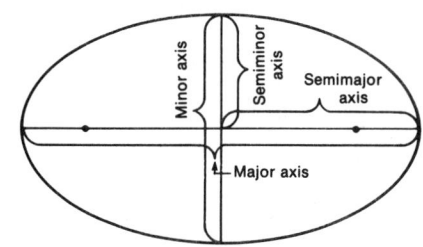

Parabolas

A parabola is the set of all points in a plane that are the same distance from a fixed line (the directrix) and a fixed point (the focus). The point on the parabola closest to the focus is the vertex. If the focus of a parabola is the point $(0, a)$ and the directrix is the line $y = -a$, then the vertex is at the point $(0, 0)$ and the equation of the parabola is

Hyperbolas

$$y = \frac{x^2}{4a}$$

A hyperbola is the set of all points in a plane such that the difference between the distances to two fixed points is a constant. The general equation for a hyperbola with center at the origin is
The meanings of a and b are shown in the diagram.

$$\frac{x^2}{a^2} - \frac{y^2}{b^2} = 1$$

The two diagonal lines are asymptotes. As x gets larger and larger, the positive branch of the curve will come closer and closer to the asymptotes, but it will never actually touch them.

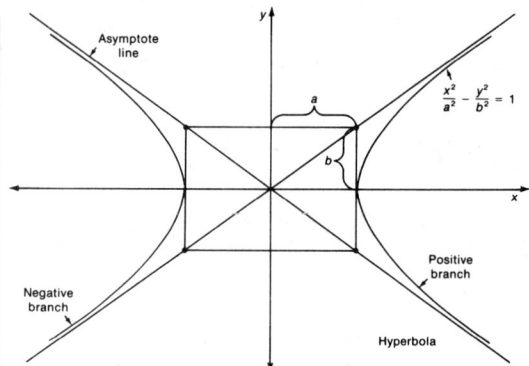

Translation of Axes

In the equations for ellipses, circles, and hyperbolas, we assumed that the center was at the origin. The equation for parabolas assumes that the vertex is at the origin. However, it will often be convenient to find equations for conic sections located anywhere in the plane. Mathematicians think of moving the center of a curve from $(0, 0)$ to a point (h, k) as a translation of the x and y axes. The y-axis is "moved" h units to the left and the x-axis is "moved" k units down if the center of the curve is (h, k).

In general, the equation of a circle with center at the point (h, k) can be written as

$$(x - h)^2 + (y - k)^2 = r^2$$

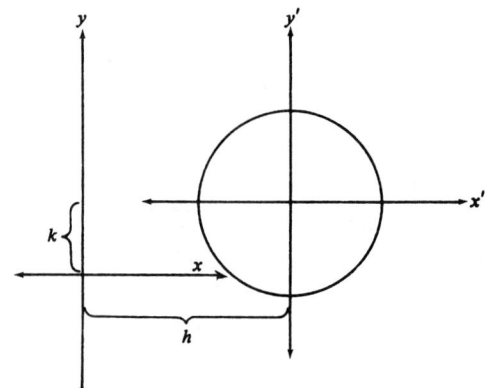

Example

An equation of the circle with center at $(3, -2)$ and radius 5 is

$$(x - 3)^2 + (y + 2)^2 = 25.$$

The equation of an ellipse with center at the point (h, k) can be written as

$$\frac{(x - h)^2}{a^2} + \frac{(y - k)^2}{b^2} = 1$$

Example

$$\frac{(x+1)^2}{16} + \frac{(y-3)^2}{9} = 1$$

is an equation of an ellipse with center at $(-1, 3)$, semimajor axis = 4, and semiminor axis = 3.

The equation of a parabola with vertex at the point (h, k), focus at the point $(h, k + a)$, and directrix at the line $y = k - a$ can be written as

$$y - k = \frac{(x-h)^2}{4a}$$

The equation of a hyperbola with center at the point (h, k) can be written as

$$\frac{(x-h)^2}{a^2} - \frac{(y-k)^2}{b^2} = 1$$

CALCULUS

Derivatives of a Function

Definition of Derivative
If a function is $y=f(x)$, the derivative of the function is the slope of the line that is tangent to the graph of the function. The slope of a

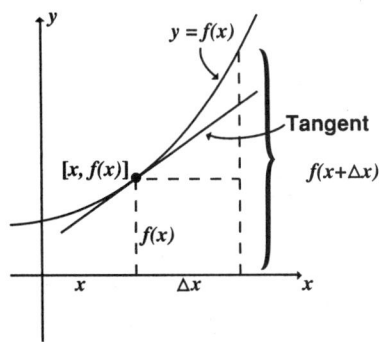

secant joining the point $(x, f(x))$ and the point $(x + \Delta x), f(x + \Delta x)$ is $\dfrac{f(x + \Delta x) - f(x)}{\Delta x}$. As $x \to 0$, the secant approaches the position of a tangent at $(x, f(x))$. Thus, a formal definition of the derivative is

derivative = slope of tangent line

$$= \lim_{\Delta x \to 0} \frac{f(x + \Delta x) - f(x)}{\Delta x}$$

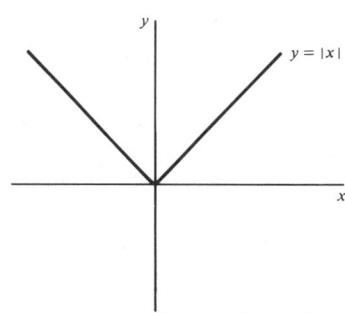

It is important to note that the derivative can be defined for a particular function only if the limit

$$\lim_{\Delta x \to 0} \frac{f(x + \Delta x) - f(x)}{\Delta x}$$

has a definite value. Some functions, such as $y = |x|$ (the absolute value, defined by $y = x$ for $x \geq 0$ and $y = -x$ for $x < 0$), will not have derivatives defined at all points of the function. In this case, the function has no derivative at the point where $x = 0$.

In general, any function with a cusp in it will not have a derivative defined at the point where the cusp is located.

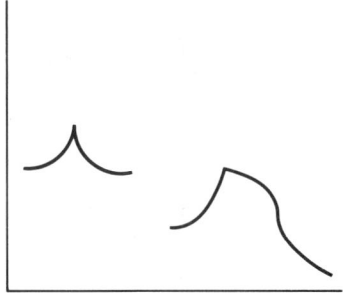

Symbols for the Derivative
For a function $y = f(x)$, the derivative is represented by y' or $f'(x)$ or $\frac{dy}{dx}$. Thus,

derivative $y' = f'(x)$ $\dfrac{dy}{dx}$ $= \lim_{\Delta x \to 0} \dfrac{f(x + \Delta x) - f(x)}{\Delta x}$

Finding Derivatives of Functions
The process of finding a derivative is called differentiation. Listed below are the four rules which permit differentiation of any polynomial function at sight. In this table, note that c represents a constant.

Function	Derivative
$y = c$	$y' = dy/dx = 0$
$y = cx$	$y' = dy/dx = c$
$y = f(x) + g(x)$	$y' = dy/dx = f'(x) + g'(x)$
$y = cx^n$	$y' = dy/dx = cnx^{n-1}$

Example

If $y = 4x^3 - 3x^2 + 7x - 8$, then

$$y' = \frac{dy}{dx} = 12x^2 - 6x + 7.$$

Second Derivative

The derivative, $\frac{dy}{dx}$, of a function $f(x)$ is itself a function of x. It is called the first derivative *of f(x)*. If the derivative of $\frac{dy}{dx}$ is taken, the result is called the second derivative of $f(x)$. The usual notation is

function: $y = f(x)$
derivative: $y' = f'(x) = dy/dx$
second derivative: $y" = f"(x) = d^2y/dx^2$

Example

Let a function be $y = f(x) = 2x^3 - 5x^2 + 3x - 4$. The first derivative is

$$y' = f'(x) = \frac{dy}{dx} = 6x^2 - 10x + 3.$$

The second derivative is

$$y" = f"(x) = \frac{d^2y}{dx^2} = 12x - 10.$$

Drawing Curves by Using Derivatives

The graph of a function $f(x)$ can be sketched by using information obtained from the values of the first derivative $f'(x)$ and of the second derivative $f"(x)$.

Rules for Curve Drawing

1. When the first derivative is positive, the value of the function is increasing.
2. When the first derivative is negative, the value of the function is decreasing.
3. When the first derivative is zero, the curve has a horizontal tangent at that point.

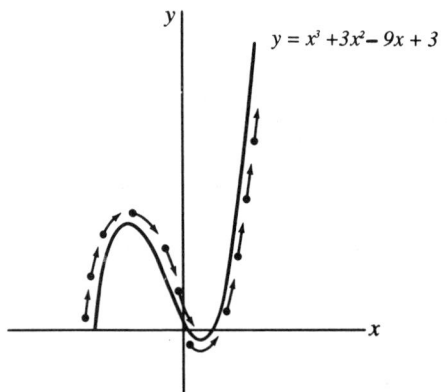

$y = x^3 + 3x^2 - 9x + 3$

4. When the second derivative is positive, the curve is concave upward (and it holds water).
5. When the second derivative is negative, the curve is concave downward (and it spills water).

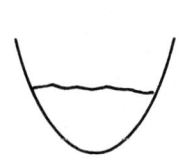

concave–upward curve: holds water   concave–downward curve: does not hold water

6. When the second derivative is zero, the curve has a point of inflection.
7. When the first derivative is zero and
   (a) the second derivative is positive, the point is a local minimum.
   (b) the second derivative is negative, the point is a local maximum.

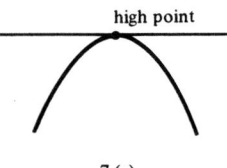
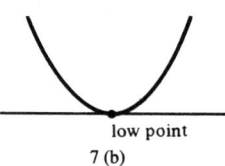

high point

low point

7 (a)   7 (b)

   (c) the second derivative is zero, the point is a point of inflection with horizontal tangent.

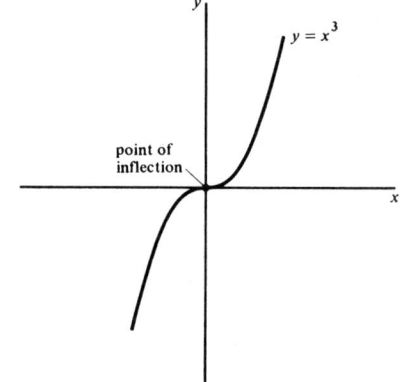

$y = x^3$

point of inflection

In symbols:
$y' = 0$, $y"$ positive, point is a minimum
$y' = 0$, $y"$ negative, point is a maximum

The highest point a curve ever reached is called the absolute maximum.

The second derivative of a position function is known in physics as the acceleration because it represents the rate at which the first derivative (the velocity) is changing.

Derivatives of Complicated Functions

Product Rule

If $f(x) = u(x) \cdot v(x)$ then $\dfrac{df}{dx} = u\dfrac{dv}{dx} + v\dfrac{du}{dx}$,

Example

If $f(x) = (3x^2 + 2x - 1)(2x + 3)$, then

$$\frac{df}{dx} = (3x^2 + 2x - 1)(2) + (2x + 3)(6x + 2).$$

Quotient Rule

If $f(x) = \dfrac{u(x)}{v(x)}$ then $\dfrac{df}{dx} = \dfrac{v\dfrac{du}{dx} - u\dfrac{dv}{dx}}{v^2}$.

Example

If $f(x) = \dfrac{3x^2 + 2x - 1}{2x + 3}$, then

$$\frac{df}{dx} = \frac{(2x + 3)(6x + 2) - (3x^2 + 2x - 1)(2)}{(2x + 3)^2}.$$

Chain Rule
A function embedded in another function, for example, $y = f(g(x))$, is called a composite function. The chain rule enables us to differentiate composite functions.

The chain rule states that if $y = f(g(x))$, let $u = g(x)$ so that the function becomes $y = f(u)$, Then

$$\frac{dy}{dx} = \frac{dy}{du} \cdot \frac{du}{dx}$$

Example

If $y = 3(4x^2 - 1)^3$, let $u = 4x^2 - 1$.

$$\frac{dy}{dx} = 9(4x^2 - 1)^2(8x).$$

Power Rule
If $f(x) = x^n$, where n is any rational number, then $f'(x) = nx^{n-1}$. The power rule is valid for any real number exponent, including irrational numbers, such as π or $\sqrt{2}$.

Example

If $y = 3x^{3/2}$, then $\dfrac{dy}{dx} = 3\left(\dfrac{3}{2}\right)x^{1/2}$.

Implicit Differentiation
The function $f(y) = g(x)$ is called an implicit function because it is not explicitly solved for y in terms of x.

If $f(y) = g(x)$, then $\left(\dfrac{df}{dy}\right)\left(\dfrac{dy}{dx}\right) = \dfrac{dg}{dx}$ will yield an

expression that can be solved for $\dfrac{dy}{dx}$.

Example

$x^5 + 4y^3 - 2y^5 = 3$ is an implicit function of y with respect to x.

Differentiating with respect to x:

$$5x^4 + 12y^2\left(\frac{dy}{dx}\right) - 10y^4\left(\frac{dy}{dx}\right) = 0.$$

This can be solved for $\dfrac{dy}{dx}$: $\dfrac{dy}{dx} = \dfrac{-5x^4}{12y^2 - 10y^4}$.

Exponential Functions
If $y = e^u$, where u is a function of x, then

$$\frac{dy}{dx} = e^u\frac{dy}{dx} \text{ (e is the base of the natural logarithm).}$$

If $y = a^u$, then $\dfrac{dy}{dx} = (\ln a)a^u\dfrac{du}{dx}$.

(ln a is the natural logarithm of a.)

Example

If $y = e^{2x+1}$, then $\dfrac{dy}{dx} = e^{2x+1}(2)$.

Example

If $y = 5^{8x^3}$, then $\dfrac{dy}{dx} = (\ln 5)5^{8x^3}(24x^2)$.

Logarithmic Functions
If $y = \ln u$, where u is a function of x, then

$$\frac{dy}{dx} = \frac{1}{u}\frac{du}{dx}.$$

Example

If $y = \ln(2x - 3)$, then $\dfrac{dy}{dx} = \dfrac{1}{2x - 3}(2)$.

Logarithmic Differentiation
Some functions can be differentiated by taking the natural logarithms of both sides of the equation and then using implicit differentiation. For example, if $y = x^x$, taking natural logs gives $\ln y = x \ln x$. Then implicit differentiation gives

$$\frac{1}{y}\frac{dy}{dx} = x\frac{1}{x} + \ln x. \text{ Hence } \frac{dy}{dx} = x^x + (\ln x)x^x.$$

Derivatives of Trigonometric Functions

If $y = \sin x$: $\dfrac{dy}{dx} = \cos x$

If $y = \cos x$: $\dfrac{dy}{dx} = -\sin x$

If $y = \tan x$: $\dfrac{dy}{dx} = \sec^2 x$

If $y = \text{ctn } x$: $\dfrac{dy}{dx} = -\csc^2 x$

If $y = \sec x$: $\dfrac{dy}{dx} = \tan x \sec x$

If $y = \csc x$: $\dfrac{dy}{dx} = -\text{ctn } x \csc x$

If $u = f(x)$:

$y = \sin u$: $dy/dx = (\cos u)\, du/dx$

$y = \cos u$: $dy/dx = (-\sin u)\, du/dx$

$y = \tan u$: $dy/dx = (\sec^2 u)\, du/dx$

$y = \text{ctn}\ u$: $dy/dx = (-\csc^2 u)\, du/dx$

$y = \sec u$: $dy/dx = (\tan u \sec u)\, du/dx$

$y = \csc u$: $dy/dx = -(\text{ctn}\ u \csc u)\, du/dx$

Example

If $y = \cos(3x^4 + 5)$, then

$$\frac{dy}{dx} = [-\sin(3x^4 + 5)](12x^3).$$

Some Applications of Derivatives

The Mean Value Theorem
The mean value theorem states that, if a function $y = f(x)$ has a derivative defined everywhere between $x = a$ and $x = b$, then there is some value of x (call it x_0) such that $a < x_0 < b$ and $f'(x_0)$ equals the slope of the secant line between the points $(a, f(a))$ and $(b, f(b))$.

L'Hôpital's Rule
This rule enables us to determine the limit approached by a function that takes on the indeterminate value $\frac{0}{0}$ at the point being approached.

L'Hôpital's rule states that, if $h(x) = f(x)/g(x)$, and $\lim_{x \to a} f(x) = 0$ and $\lim_{x \to a} g(x) = 0$, then $\lim_{x \to a} h(x) = \lim_{x \to a} f(x)/\lim_{x \to a} g(x)$.

Example

If $h(x) = \dfrac{x^2 - 4}{x - 2}$, then $h(2) = \dfrac{0}{0}$, but

$$\lim_{x \to 2} h(x) = \frac{\lim_{x \to 2}(2x)}{\lim_{x \to 2}(1)} = \frac{4}{1} = 4.$$

Newton's Method
Newton's method provides an iterative method for estimating the x intercept of complicated functions. The goal of the method is to find x_0 such that $f(x_0) = 0$. First, make a guess (x_1) that is reasonably close to the true value of x_0. Then calculate a better guess according to the formula $x_2 = x_1 - f(x_1)/f'(x_1)$. The method can be repeated to yield a still better guess, $x_3 = x_2 - f(x_2)/f'(x_2)$. Keep going until you are satisfied that the result is close enough to the true answer.

Related Rates
If a relationship involving two variables is differentiated implicitly with respect to time t, the rates of change of the two variables will be related. For example, if a 20-foot ladder slides down a wall, $x^2 + y^2 = 20^2$. Differentiating with respect to t gives

$2x \dfrac{dy}{dt} + 2y \dfrac{dy}{dt} = 0$. Hence, $\dfrac{dy}{dt} = -\dfrac{x\, dx}{y\, dt}$.   The rate of change of y is related to the rate of change of x.

If the rate of change of $x \left(\dfrac{dx}{dx} \right)$ is known, the rate of change of y can be determined from this equation for any specific values of x and y.

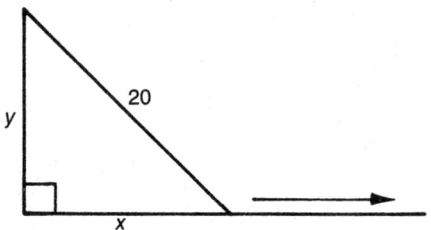

Integral of a Function

Definition of Indefinite Integral
The integral of a function $f(x)$ is another function, $F(x)$, such that the derivative of $F(x)$ is $f(x)$. The function $F(x)$ is the integral or antiderivative of $f(x)$ and satisfies the condition $\dfrac{d\,F(x)}{dx} = f(x)$.

Notation tor Integrals
The symbol $\int f(x)\, dx$ represents the indefinite integral of $f(x)$, and it is equal to $F(x) + C$, where $F(x)$ is the antiderivative and C is any constant number (it is known as the arbitrary constant of integration).

The constant C can be determined if you know an initial condition.

Finding Integrals of Functions
The process of finding the integral of a function is called integration. Listed below are some of the rules for integrating the more common functions:

Sum rule for integrals

$$\int (f(x) + g(x))\, dx = \int f(x)\, dx + \int g(x)\, dx$$

Multiplication rule for integrals

$$n \int f(x)\, dx = \int n f(x)\, dx$$

(where n is any constant number)

However, if n is a variable, then it may *not* be taken outside the integral sign, and $\int n f(t)\, dt \neq n \int f(t)\, dt$.

Perfect integral rule

$$\int dt = t + C$$

Power rule for integrals

$$\int x^n \, dx = \frac{1}{n+1} x^{n+1} + C, \text{ provided that } n \neq -1$$

Example

$$\int 3x^4 \, dx = \frac{3}{5} x^5 + C$$

The integral of $\frac{1}{x}$:

$$\int x^{-1} \, dx = \ln |x| + C$$

Note the following: ln |x| is the natural logarithm of the absolute value of x. $\ln x = \log_e x$, where $e \approx 2.718$.

Trigonometric integrals

$$\int \sin x \, dx = -\cos x + C$$

$$\int \cos x \, dx = \sin x + C$$

$$\int \tan x \, dx = -\ln |\sec x| + C$$

$$\int \sin x \, dx = \ln |\sec x + \tan x| + C$$

Integration by substitution
If you face an integral of the form $\int u^n \, dx$, where u is a function of x, you cannot use the power rule directly until you have converted the dx into a du. First, find the derivative of u, (du/dx), and write that derivative using differential notation. Then make the substitution $dx = (dx/du) \, du$, so the integral becomes equal to

$$\int u^n dx = \int u^n \frac{dx}{du} \, du$$

If dx/du is a constant, it can be moved outside the integral sign:

$$\int u^n dx = \left(\frac{dx}{du}\right) \int u^n du = \frac{dx}{du} \frac{1}{n+1} u^{n+1} + C$$

(If dx/du is not a constant, as in $\int \sqrt{1 - x^2} \, dx$, other methods must be used.)

Example

$$\int (5x^2 + 3)^2 \, x \, dx = \int (5x^2 + 3)^2 \frac{(10x) \, dx}{10}$$

$$= \frac{1}{10} \int (5x^2 + 3)^2 (10x) \, dx$$

$$= \frac{1}{30} (5x^2 + 3)^3 + C.$$

The Definite Integral

Definition of the definite integral
$\int_a^b f(x) \, dx$ is called the definite integral of $f(x)$ over the closed interval from a *to* b. By definition, $\int_a^b f(x) \, dx = F(b) - F(a)$, where $F(x)$, is the indefinite integral of $f(x)$.

Example

$$\int_2^5 (3x + 2) \, dx = \left(\frac{3x^2}{2} + 2x \right)_2^5$$

$$= \left[\frac{3(25)}{2} + 2(5) \right] - \left[\frac{3(4)}{2} - 2(2) \right]$$

$$= \left(\frac{75}{2} + 10 \right) - (6 - 4) = 47\frac{1}{2} - 2$$

$$= 45\frac{1}{2}$$

Geometric Interpretation of the Definite Integral
Assume the area under the curve $y = f(x)$ between $x = a$ and $x = b$ to be divided up into n strips, each with a width of Δx. Then the area under $y = f(x)$ from $x = a$ to $x = b$ is approximately equal to the sum of the areas of n rectangles, each with a width of Δx and with altitudes of $f(a)$, $f(a + \Delta x)$, $f(a + 2 \Delta x)$, . . . , $f(a + n \Delta x)$. The actual area under the curve is

$$\lim_{\substack{\Delta x \to 0 \\ x \to \infty}} \sum_{i=1}^{n} \Delta x \, f(a + i \, \Delta x) = \int_a^b f(x) \, dx$$

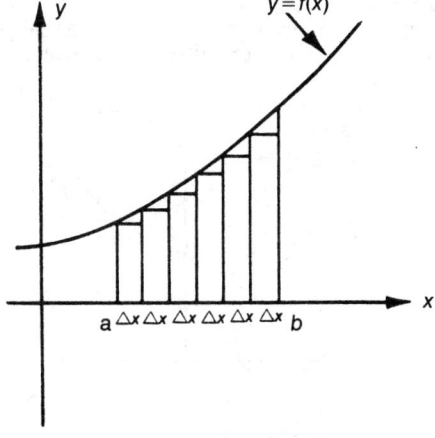

Thus, the definite integral of $f(x)$ between a and b is the area above the x-axis and under the graph of $y = f(x)$ from $x = a$ to $x = b$.

Fundamental Theorem of Integral Calculus
The area below the curve $y = f(x)$, above the line $y = 0$, to the right of the line $x = a$, and to the left of the line $x = b$ equals $A = F(b) - F(a)$, where $F(x)$ is the antiderivative function such that $dF(x)/dx = f(x)$.

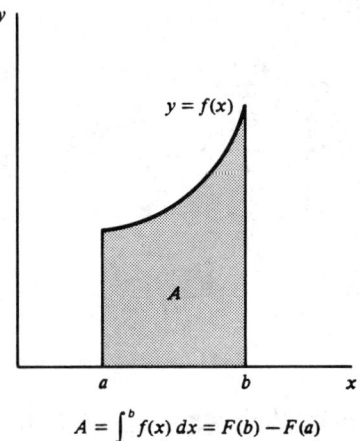

$$A = \int_a^b f(x)\,dx = F(b) - F(a)$$

Notice that the definite integral $\int_a^b f(x)\,dx$ represents the area under the curve $f(x)$ only if $b > a$ and $f(x) > 0$ for all $a < x < b$. If the function is negative everywhere in the interval from $x = a$ to $x = b$, then the value of the definite integral will be the negative of the area between the curve and the x axis. If the function is positive at some places and negative at other places in the interval $x = a$ to $x = b$, then the value of the definite integral will be equal to the total area under the positive part of the curve minus the total area between the negative part of the curve and the x-axis. The final result may be positive, negative, or zero. Sometimes you will be interested in the algebraic value of the definite integral, in which case you really will want the negative areas to cancel out the positive areas.

Area between Two Curves
The area between two curves is the definite integral of a function equal to the difference between the two curves.

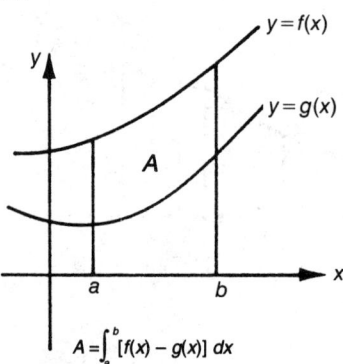

$$A = \int_a^b [f(x) - g(x)]\,dx$$

Special Methods for Integrating Complicated Functions

Integration by Parts
When an integral defies any other means of solution, split it into two parts: call one part u, and the other part dv (which must include the differential—

the d-variable term). Then differentiate u to obtain du, and integrate dv to get v. Then use the formula:

$$\int u\,dv = uv - \int v\,du$$

If $\int v\,du$ looks simpler than the original integral ($\int u\,dv$), you are making progress and can proceed to a solution. If the integral $\int v\,du$ looks more complicated than the original integral, you should either (a) choose new values for u and dv, or (b) try another method.

Example

$\int x \cdot e^x\,dx$. Let $u = x$ and $dv = e^x\,dx$. Then $du = dx$ and $v = e^x$.

$$\int x \cdot e^x\,dx = x \cdot e^x - \int e^x\,dx = x \cdot e^x - e^x + C.$$

Integration by Trigonometric Substitution
For an integral such as

$$A = 4b \int_b^a \sqrt{1 - x^2/a^2}\,dx,$$

let $\dfrac{x}{a} = \sin\theta,$

$$x = a\sin\theta,$$
$$dx = a\cos\theta\,d\theta,$$
$$\theta = \arcsin\left(\frac{x}{a}\right).$$

Then

$$A = 4b \int_{ar\sin(0/a)}^{arcin(a/a)} \sqrt{1 - \sin^2\theta}\,a\cos\theta\,d\theta$$

which can be integrated.
For an integral of the form

$$A = 4ab \int_0^{\pi/2} \cos^2\theta\,d\theta,$$

substitute

$$\cos^2\theta = \tfrac{1}{2}(1 + \cos 2\theta)$$

to get

$$A + 4ab \int_0^{\pi/2} \tfrac{1}{2}(1 + \cos 2\theta)\,d\theta$$

which is integrable.

For an integral of the form

$$z = \frac{1}{a} \int \frac{1}{\sqrt{1 + b^2 x^2/a^2}}\,dx,$$

substitute

$$x = \frac{a\tan\theta}{b}$$

$$dx = \frac{a}{b}\sec^2\theta\,d\theta$$

For an integral of the form

$$z = \int \frac{1}{1 + x^2}\, dx,$$

let $x = \tan\theta$,

$$\theta = \arctan x,$$

$$dx = \sec^2\theta\, d\theta,$$

For an integral of the form

$$z = \int \frac{1}{\sqrt{1 + x^2}}\, dx,$$

let $x = \sin\theta$,

$$\theta = \arcsin x,$$

$$dx = \cos\theta\, d\theta.$$

Integration by Partial Fractions

The method of partial fractions is useful when the integrand contains a proper rational function, that is, a fraction with a polynomial in the numerator of degree less than the degree of the polynomial in the denominator:

$$\int \frac{a_m x^m + a_{m-1}x^{m-1} + a_{m-2}x^{m-2} + \cdots + a_1 x + a_0}{b_n x^n + b_{n-1}x^{n-1} + b_{n-2}x^{n-2} + \cdots + b_1 x + b_0}\, dx$$

$$(m < n)$$

The goal of the method is to break the integrand into a sum of fractions that are much simpler. The first step is to factor the denominator. The result will be a product of some linear factors and some quadratic factors. All the numbers that result will be real, but there is no guarantee that they will be rational. The integrand can then be resolved as a sum of partial fractions as follows:

1. If a linear factor (such as $ax + b$) occurs once in the denominator, then there will be a partial fraction of the form $A/(ax + b)$.
2. If the linear factor ($ax + b$) occurs k times in the denominator, then there are k partial fractions of the form $A_1/(ax + b)$, $A_2/(ax + b)^2$, . . . , $A_k/(ax + b)^k$.
3. If a quadratic factor (such as $ax^2 + bx + c$) occurs once in the denominator, then there is a partial fraction of the form $(Ax + B)/(ax^2 + bx + c)$. [Note that $(b^2 - 4ac)$ is negative in this case. Otherwise, the quadratic factor can be broken into a product of two linear factors.]
4. If the quadratic factor ($ax^2 + bx + c$) occurs j times in the denominator, then there are j partial fractions of the form $(A_1x + B_1)/(ax^2 + bx + c)$,

$$(A_2x + B_2)/(ax^2 + bx + c)^2, \ldots ,$$
$$(A_jx + B_j)/(ax^2 + bx + c)^j$$

The numerators of the partial fractions can be solved for by equating the original integrand with the equivalent sum of partial fractions. Once the integrand has been broken up into partial fractions,

each integral can be solved individually. The integrals with linear denominators can be evaluated with logarithms, and the integrals with quadratic denominators can be evaluated by trigonometric substitution, using the secant-tangent identity.

Example

To evaluate by partial fractions

$$\int \frac{5x - 7}{x^2 - 3x + 2}\, dx,$$

factor the denominator and then split up the integrand into partial fractions as follows:

$$\frac{5x - 7}{(x - 1)(x - 2)} = \frac{A}{x - 1} + \frac{B}{x - 2}$$

$$= \frac{A(x - 2) + B(x - 1)}{(x - 1)(x - 2)}$$

$$= \frac{(A + B)x + (-2A - B)}{(x - 1)(x - 2)}$$

Equating coefficients and constant terms gives

$$A + B = 5$$
$$-2A - B = -7$$

This is a two-equation, two-unknown system, which has the solution $A = 2$, $B = 3$. Therefore,

$$\int \frac{5x - 7}{(x - 1)(x - 2)}\, dx = \int \frac{2}{x - 1}\, dx + \int \frac{3}{x - 2}\, dx$$

$$= 2\ln|x - 1| + 3\ln|x - 2| + C$$

Note if the degree of the numerator is greater than the degree of the denominator, the function is called an improper rational function. An improper rational function can always be written as the sum of a polynomial plus a proper rational function.

Applications of the Definite Integral

Finding the Position of an Object if Velocity Function Is Known

Suppose that an object moves with a velocity v such that $v = f'(t)$, t being a variable representing time.

Find an indefinite integral (or antiderivative) of the velocity function.

$$x = \int v\, dt = \int f'dt = f(t) + c.$$

Find the position of the object at the start. (This is called the initial condition.) When $t = 0$, $x = x_0$.

Solve for the indefinite integral constant by inserting the initial condition into the indefinite integral equation. From $x = f(t) + c$, $x_0 = f(0) + c$ or $c = x_0 - f(0)$.

Volumes of Solids of Revolution

If V = volume of paraboloid:

$$V = \pi \int_{-100}^{0} x^2\, dy$$

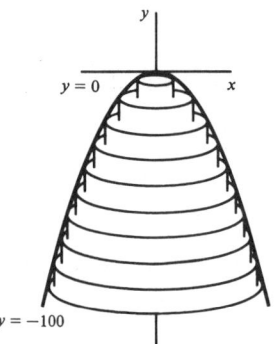

Paraboloid formed by revolving parabola about y - axis, $y = \frac{1}{2} x^2$

Surface Areas

To find the surface area of the paraboloid formed by revolving $x = y^2$ about the x-axis, think of the paraboloid as being cut into slices which are frustums of cones:

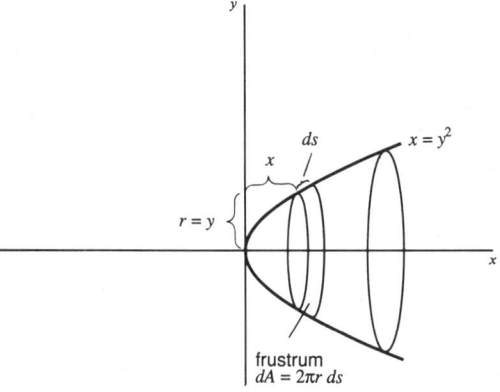

frustrum
$dA = 2\pi r\, ds$

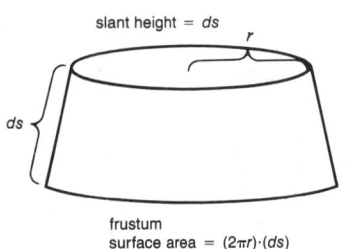

slant height = ds

frustum
surface area = $(2\pi r)\cdot(ds)$
r = average radius

$$dA = 2\pi r\, ds$$

$$ds = \sqrt{1 + (dy/dx)^2}\, dx$$

$$dA = 2\pi r \sqrt{1 + (dy/dx)^2}\, dx$$

$$dA = 2\pi y \sqrt{1 + (dy/dx)^2}\, dx$$

$$A = \int_0^a 2\pi y \sqrt{1 + (dy/dx)^2}\, dx$$

Volumes by Summation of Slices

If $A(z)$ is the cross-sectional area of a region determined by a plane intersecting a solid at z, then the volume of the solid, from a to b, is given by the formula

$$V = \int_a^b A(z)\, dz$$

Consider the problem of finding the volume of a pyramid whose base is an isosceles right triangle. Let s represent the length of each leg of the base, and h the altitude of the pyramid.

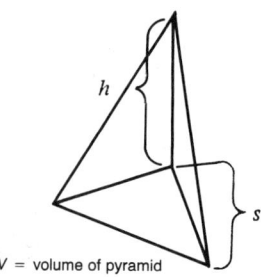

V = volume of pyramid

If we take a slice of the pyramid that is parallel to its base, the cross-sectional region is an isosceles right triangular segment. Let

x = the length of a leg of this triangular segment,

z = the distance from the top of the pyramid to the triangular segment,

dz = the "thickness" of the triangular segment.

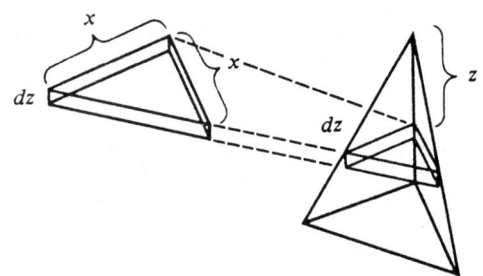

The volume of the differential triangular element is

$$dv = \frac{1}{2} x^2 dz$$

To express variable x in terms of variable z, use similar triangles to establish that $\frac{z}{h} = \frac{x}{s}$, or $x = \frac{sz}{h}$.

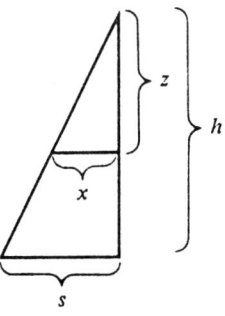

side view of pyramid

Thus,

$$dV = \frac{1}{2}x^2\, dz = \frac{s^2}{2h^2} z^2\, dz$$

Integrate along z, from $z = 0$ to $z = h$:

$$V = \int_0^h \frac{s^2 z^2}{2h^2}\, dz$$

$$= \frac{s^2}{2h^2} \int_0^h z^2 dz$$

$$= \frac{s^2}{2h^2} \frac{1}{3} z^3 \Big|_0^h$$

$$= \frac{s^2 h^2}{6h^2}$$

$$= \frac{s^2 h}{6}$$

Arc Lengths

$$\text{length} = S = \int ds = \int \sqrt{dx^2 + dy^2}$$

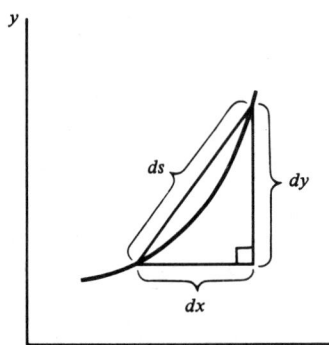

length of curve from $x = a$ to $x = b$

$$= S = \int_a^b \sqrt{1 + (dy/dx)^2}\, dx$$

Centroid and Center of Mass

The centroid $(\bar{x}, \bar{y})$ of a plane figure is given by

$$\bar{x} = \frac{\int x\, dA}{\int dA}$$, where dA is the area of a slice of the figure taken parallel to the y-axis.

$$\bar{y} = \frac{\int y\, dA}{dA}$$, where dA is the area of a slice of the figure taken parallel to the x-axis.

If the plane figure is a plate of uniform density, then $(\bar{x}, \bar{y})$ are the coordinates of its center of mass, often called the center of gravity.

STATISTICS

Statistics is the study of the ways to collect, organize, analyze, and present data. There are two branches of statistics: statistical inference and descriptive statistics. *Statistical inference* refers to the process of using a sample drawn from a larger population to draw conclusions about the entire population. *Descriptive statistics* deals with methods of organizing and summarizing the properties of a given list of numbers without drawing any conclusions about a larger set of numbers. The mean (average), median (middle value in an ordered list of numbers), and mode (most frequently occurring number a list of numbers) are examples of descriptive statistics.

Another descriptive statistic which is the sample standard deviation, measures the degree of "spread-out-ed-ness" (called dispersion) of a set of n numbers $x_1, x_2, \ldots, x_i, \ldots x_n$ using the formula

$$\sqrt{\frac{1}{n} \sum_{i=1}^{n} (\bar{x} - x_i)^2}$$

where $\bar{x} = \text{mean} = \frac{1}{n} \sum_{i=1}^{n} x_i$.

The variance of the set of numbers is equal to the square of the standard deviation.

Random Variables

A random variable, usually denoted by a single capital letter, is a variable that takes on a particular value when a specified random event occurs. A random variable is discrete or continuous.

A discrete random varible may assume only a finite number of possible values. If X represents the face value that will appear on a die after it is rolled, then X is a discrete random variable whose possible values are limited to 1, 2, 3, 4, 5, and 6.

A continuous random variable can take on any value on a continuous interval of numbers. If T represents the length of time until a light bulb burns out, then T is a continuous random variable since it may have such values as 750 hours, 750.1 hours, 750.01 hours, and 750.001 hours.

Density Functions

The probability density function of a discrete random variable X is a function $f(x)$ whose value for a particular number a is the probability (Pr) that the random variable will be equal to a; that is, $f(a) = \text{Pr}(X = a)$. The binomial distribution is an example of a discrete probability distribution. Its density function is

$$f(x) = \text{Pr}(X = x) = \binom{n}{x} p^x (1 - p)^{n-x}$$

where X is a random variable that represents the number of successes that occur in n identical trials of a two-outcome experiment in which the probability of a success in each trial is p.

If X is a continuous random variable, then its density function is the function $f(x)$ such that

$$\text{Pr}\,(a < x < b) = \int_a^b f(x)\,dx$$

and, since the probability of a certainty must be 1,

$$\int_{-\infty}^{\infty} f(x)\,dx = 1$$

Some important examples of probability distributions for continuous random variables are the normal distribution, the chi-square distribution, and the t-distribution.

A cumulative distribution function $F(x)$ gives the probability that a random variable x will be less than or equal to a specific value, say a:

$$F(a) = \text{Pr}(X \le a)$$

It follows that $\text{Pr}(X > a) = 1 - \text{Pr}(X \le a) = 1 - F(a)$.

If $F(x)$ represents the cumulative distribution function of a continuous random variable whose density function is $f(x)$, then the area under the graph $y = f(x)$, to the left of the line $x = b$, to the right of the line $x = a$, and above the x-axis is numerically equal to the probability that x will lie between a and b.

Area under $f(x)$ from a to b = $\text{Pr}(a < X < b)$

$$= \int_a^b f(x)\,dx$$

$$= F(b) - F(a)$$

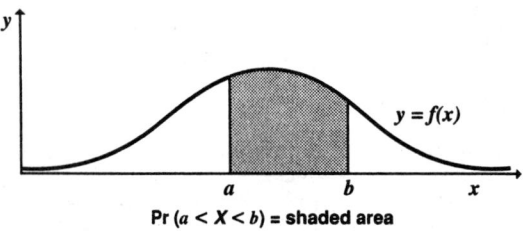

Pr $(a < X < b)$ = shaded area

Normal Distribution

A random variable X has a normal distribution if its density function is

$$f(x) = \frac{1}{\sigma\sqrt{2\pi}}\, e^{-(x-\mu)^2/2\sigma^2}$$

The mean (or expectation) of X is μ, and its variance is σ^2. If $\mu = 0$ and $\sigma = 1$, then X is said to have the standard normal distribution, which has the density function

$$f(x) = \frac{1}{\sqrt{2\pi}}\, e^{-(1/2)x^2}$$

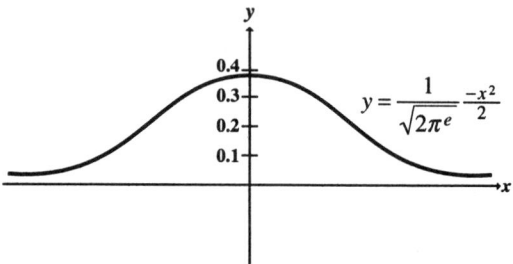

$$y = \frac{1}{\sqrt{2\pi e}}\frac{-x^2}{2}$$

The figure shows a graph of the standard normal density function.

Suppose that Z is a random variable with a standard normal density function. Since a standard normal density function is symmetric about $\mu = 0$, we can see that $\text{Pr}(Z > 0) = 1/2$. If we need to know the probability that Z is between 0 and 1, then we must calculate the area under the curve between 0 and 1.

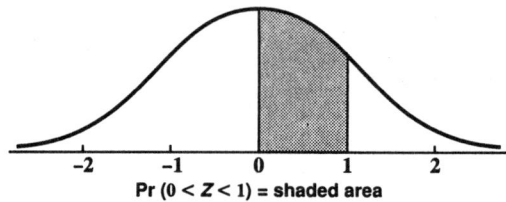

Pr $(0 < Z < 1)$ = shaded area

Unfortunately, there is no simple formula that gives us the area of this region. We have to look up the results in a table such as Exhibit 16.4 at the back of this section. The table gives the cumulative distribution function, which tells you the probability that Z will be less than a particular value. [The Greek letter Φ (phi) is often used to represent this function; $\Phi(z)$ equals $\text{Pr}(Z < z)$.] The table gives only values for positive values of z, but we can use the formula $\Phi(-z) = 1 - \Phi(z)$ to determine the value of the function for a negative number.

The probability that Z will be between any two numbers a and b can be found from the formula

$$\text{Pr}(a < Z < b) = \Phi(b) - \Phi(a)$$

We have already figured out that $\Phi(0) = .5$. We can see from the table at Exhibit 16.4 on page 16-64 that $\Phi(1) = .8413$. Therefore, the probability that Z will be between 0 and 1 is $.8413 - .5000 = .3413$.

Because of the symmetry of the density function, we can see that there is also a .3413 probability that Z will be between -1 and 0. We can add these two probabilities together:

$$Pr(-1 < Z < 0) + Pr(0 < Z < 1) = .3413 + .3413$$
$$Pr(-1 < Z < 1) = .6826$$

Pr ($-1 < Z < 0$) = Pr ($0 < Z < 1$)

Therefore, there is approximately a 68 percent chance that a standard normal random variable will be between -1 and 1. In other words, there is a 68 percent chance that the value of a standard normal random variable will be within one standard deviation of its mean. (In this case the mean is 0 and the standard deviation is 1.)

This particular property also holds for *any* normal random variable, regardless of its mean and standard deviation: There is a 68 percent chance that any normal random variable will be within one standard deviation of its mean. For example, if X is a normal random variable with mean 200 and standard deviation 30, then there is a 68 percent chance that X will be between 170 and 230.

We can also use Exhibit 16.4 to show that there is a 95 percent chance that Z will be between -1.96 and 1.96. In general, we can say that any normal random variable has a 95 percent chance of being less than about two standard deviations away from its mean.

The probability that a standard normal random variable will be between $-a$ and $a,$ where a is a particular number, is given in Exhibit 16.5. For example, Exhibit 16.5 shows that there is a .3830 probability that Z will be between -0.5 and 0.5.

The value of the standard normal random variable could conceivably be anything, since the density function never quite touches the axis. There is no number k such that $Pr(Z > k) = O$. However, the table shows that there is only a .0002 probability that Z will be greater than 3.5, and larger values are even less likely.

We can use the standard normal tables to find the probabilities for any normal random variable by using the following trick. Suppose Y has a normal distribution with mean 6 and variance 9, and we need to know the probability that Y will be between 5 and 8. We can create the random variable Z:

$$Z = \frac{Y - \bar{Y}}{\sigma} = \frac{Y - 6}{3}$$

which will have a normal distribution with mean 0 and variance 1 because of the addition property. It should be clear that if Y is between 5 and 8, Z will be between $-1/3$ and 2/3. Now we can look up the probability in a table (*see* **Exhibit 16.4** on page 16-64):

$$Pr(5 < Y < 8) = Pr(-1/3 < Z < 2/3)$$
$$= \Phi(.6667) - \Phi(-.3333)$$
$$= .7486 - (1 - .6293)$$
$$= .7486 - .3707$$
$$= .3779$$

In general, if X is a normal random variable with mean μ and variance σ^2, then $(X - \mu)/\sigma$ is a standard normal random variable.

Example
The number of hamburgers a cafeteria sells is given by a normal random variable with mean 200 and variance 1,600. We would like to know the probability that the cafeteria sells more than 230 hamburgers.

Let X represent the number of hamburgers sold. Since $\mu = 200$ and $\sigma = 40$, we can create a standard normal random variable Z as follows:

$$Pr(X < 230) = \left[Pr \frac{X - 200}{40} > \frac{230 - 200}{40} \right]$$
$$= Pr(Z > .75)$$
$$= 1 - Pr(Z < .75)$$
$$= 1 - .7734 \text{ (from Exhibit 16.4)}$$
$$= .2266$$

Chi Square

If $X_1, X_2, \ldots , X_n$ are independent and identically distributed standard normal random variables, then the random variable

$$S = X_1^2 + X_2^2 + \cdots + X_n^2$$

will have chi square distribution with n degrees of freedom. The chi-square distribution with n degrees of freedom is symbolized by χ_n^2, since χ is the Greek letter chi. For the χ_n^2-distribution, $E(X) = n$ and $Var(X) = 2n$ (*see* **Exhibit 16.6** on page 16-66).

t-Distribution

If Z is a random variable with a standard normal distribuiton, and x is a χ^2-distribution with n degrees of freedom, then the random variable

$$X = \frac{Z}{(Y/n)^{1/2}}$$

has a *t*-distribution with n degrees of freedom (*see* **Exhibit 16.7**). As n approaches infinity, the density function for the *t*-distribution approaches the density function of a standard normal random variable. When X has the *t*-distribution with n degrees of freedom, then

$$E(X) = 0 \quad \text{if } n > 1,$$

and

$$Var(X) = \frac{n}{n - 2} \quad \text{if } n > 2.$$

Confidence Interval

A confidence interval is an interval based on obser-vations of a sample so constructed that there is a specified probability that the interval contains the unknown true value of a population parameter. It is common to calculate confidence intervals that have a 95 percent probability of containing the true value.

Example
You are trying to estimate the mean weight of loaves of bread produced at a bakery. It would be too expensive to weigh every single loaf, but you can estimate the mean by selecting and weighing a random sample of loaves. Suppose that the weights of the entire population of loaves have a normal dis-tribution with a mean mu (μ), whose value is unknown, and a standard deviation sigma (σ), whose value is known. Suppose also that you have selected a sample of n loaves and have found that the average weight of this sample is $\bar{x}$. Because of the properties of the normal distribution, $\bar{x}$ will have a normal distribution with mean μ and standard deviation $\sigma/\sqrt{n}$.
Now define Z as follows:

$$Z = \frac{\sqrt{n}(\bar{x} - \mu)}{\sigma}$$

Z will have a standard normal distribution. There is a 95 percent chance that a standard normal random variable will be between -1.96 and 1.96:

$$\Pr(-1.96 < Z < 1.96) = .95$$

Therefore:

$$\Pr\left(-1.96 < \frac{\sqrt{n}(\bar{x} - \mu)}{\sigma} < 1.96\right) = .95$$

which can be rewritten as

$$\Pr\left(\bar{x} - \frac{1.96\sigma}{\sqrt{n}} < \mu < \bar{x} + \frac{1.96\sigma}{\sqrt{n}}\right) = .95$$

The last equation tells you how to calculate the confidence interval. There is a 95 percent chance that the interval from $\bar{x} - 1.96\sigma/\sqrt{n}$ to $\bar{x} + 1.96\sigma/\sqrt{n}$ will contain the true value of the mean, μ.
However, in many practical situations you will not know the true value of the population standard devi-ation, σ, and therefore cannot use the preceding method. Instead, after selecting your random sample of size n, you will need to calculate both the sample average, x, and the sample standard deviation, s:

$$s = \sqrt{\frac{(x_1 - \bar{x})^2 + (x_2 - \bar{x})^2 + \cdots + (x_n - \bar{x})^2}{n - 1}}$$

The confidence interval calculation is based on the fact that the quantity $T = \sqrt{n}(x - \mu)/s$ will have a t-distribution with $n - 1$ degrees of freedom. Note that the quantity T is the same as the quantity Z used

above, except that the known value of the sample standard deviation s has been substituted for the population standard deviation, σ, which is now unknown.
Now you need to look in a t-distribution table for a value (a) such that $\Pr(-a < T < a) = .95$, where T has a t-distribution with the appropriate degrees of free-dom. See **Exhibit 16.8** at the back of this section. Then the 95 percent confidence interval for the unknown value of μ is from

$$\bar{x} - \frac{as}{\sqrt{n}} \quad \text{to} \quad \bar{x} + \frac{as}{\sqrt{n}}$$

Example

You are investigating the mean commuting time along a particular route into the city. You have recorded the commuting times for 7 days: 39, 43, 29, 52, 35, 38, 39, and would like to calculate a 95 percent confidence interval for the mean commuting time. Calculate the sample average, $\bar{x} = 39.286$. Then calculate the sample standard deviation $s = 7.088$. Look in Exhibit 16.8 for a t-distribution with $7 - 1 = 6$ degrees of freedom to find the value of $a = 2.447$. Then the 95 percent confidence interval is

$$39.286 \pm 2.447 \times \frac{7.088}{\sqrt{7}}$$

which is from 32.730 to 45.841.

Hypothesis Testing

Often a researcher needs to test a hypothesis about the nature of the world. Frequently it is necessary to use a statistical technique known as hypothesis test-ing for this purpose.
The hypothesis that is being tested is termed the *null hypothesis*. (The other possible hypothesis, which says "The null hypothesis is wrong," is called the *alternative hypothesis*.) Here is an example of a null hypothesis: "There is no significant difference in effectiveness between Brand X cold medicine and Brand Z medicine."
The term "null hypothesis" is used because the hypothesis that is being tested is often of the form "There is no relation between two quantities," as in the example above. However, the term "null hypoth-esis" is used also in other cases, whether or not it is a "no-effect" type of hypothesis.
In many practical situations it is not possible to determine with certainty whether the null hypothesis is true or false. The best that can be done is to col-lect evidence and then decide, correctly or incorrect-ly, whether the null hypothesis should be accepted or rejected. A situation where the null hypothesis has been rejected, but it is actually true, is referred to as a *type 1 error*. The opposite type of error, called a *type 2 error*, occurs when the null hypothe-sis has been accepted, but it is actually false. The probability of committing a type 1 error is called the *level of significance* of the test.
The normal procedure in hypothesis testing is to calculate a quantity called a *test statistic*, whose value depends on the values that are observed in the

sample. The test statistic is designed so that, *if the* null hypothesis is true, then the test-statistic value will be a random variable that comes from a known distribution, such as the standard normal distribution or a t-distribution. After the value of the test statistic has been calculated, that value is compared with the values that would be expected from the known distribution. If the observed test-statistic value might plausibly have come from the indicated distribution, then the null hypothesis is accepted.

Suppose that we are conducting a test based on a test statistic Z, which will have a standard normal distribution if the null hypothesis is true. There is a 95 percent chance that the value of a random variable with a standard normal distribution will be between 1.96 and –1.96. Therefore, we will design the test so that the null hypothesis will be accepted if the calculated value of Z falls between –1.96 and 1.96, since these are plausible values. However, if the value of Z is less than –1.96 or greater than 1.96, we will reject the hypothesis because the value of a random variable with a standard normal distribution is unlikely to fall outside the –1.96 to 1.96 range. The range of values for the test statistic where the null hypothesis is rejected is known as the *critical region*. In this case the critical region consists of two parts. (The two regions at the end of the distribution are called the tails of the distribution.) Notice that there still is a 5 percent chance of committing a type 1 error. If the null hypothesis is true, then Z will have a standard normal distribution, and there is a 5 percent chance that the value of Z will be greater than 1.96 or less than –1.96. Also, there is a 1 percent chance that the value of Z will be greater than 2.58 or less than –2.58.

Example

We wish to test whether a particular coin is fair (that is, equally likely to turn up heads or tails). Our null hypothesis is "The probability of heads is .5." The alternative hypothesis is "The probability of heads is not .5." To conduct our test, we will flip the coin 10,000 times. Let X be the number of heads that occurs; X is a random variable. If the null hypothesis is true, then X has a normal distribution with mean 5,000 and standard deviation 50. We define a new random variable Z as follows: $Z = (X - 5000)/50$. Now Z will have a standard normal distribution. If the calculated value of Z is between –1.96 and 1.96, we will accept the null hypothesis that the coin is fair; otherwise we will reject the hypothesis. For example, if we observe 5063 heads, then $X = 5063$, $Z = 1.26$, and we will accept the null hypothesis. On the other hand, if we observe 5104 heads, then $X = 5104$, $Z = 2.08$, and we will reject the null hypothesis because the observed value of Z falls in the critical region.

Chi-square Testing

The chi-square test is used to test the hypothesis that there is *no* significant difference between two or more groups. In other words, any observed difference in the proportion of each group belonging to a particular category arose solely by chance.

Example

You are given a table with m rows (categories) and n columns (groups):

	Group 1	Group 2	Group 3	...	Group n
Category a	a_1	a_2	a_3	...	a_n
Category b	b_1	b_2	b_3	...	b_n
Category c (and so on)	c_1	c_2	c_3	...	c_n

1. Calculate the total number of observations in each category:

$$a_{\text{total}} = a_1 + a_2 + \cdots + a_n$$
$$b_{\text{total}} = b_1 + b_2 + \cdots + b_n$$

and so on.

2. Calculate the total number of observations in each group:

$$t_1 = a_1 + b_1 + c_1 + \cdots$$
$$t_2 = a_2 + b_2 + c_2 + \cdots$$
$$\cdots\cdots\cdots\cdots\cdots$$
$$t_n = a_n + b_n + c_n + \cdots$$

3. Calculate the grand-total number of observations:

$$T = t_1 + t_2 + t_3 + \cdots t_n$$

4. Calculate the proportion in each category: and so on.

$$p_a = \frac{a_{\text{total}}}{T}$$

$$p_b = \frac{b_{\text{total}}}{T}$$

5. Calculate the predicted frequency of occurrence for each cell:

$$f_{a1} = p_a t_1 \quad f_{a2} = p_a t_2 \quad f_{an} = p_a t_n$$
$$f_{b1} = p_b t_1 \quad f_{b2} = p_b t_2 \quad f_{bn} = p_b t_n$$
$$\cdots$$

6. Calculate the value of the chi-square statistic S:

$$S = \frac{(a_1 - f_{a1})^2}{f_{a1}} + \frac{(a_2 - f_{a2})^2}{f_{a2}} + \cdots + \frac{(a_n - f_{an})^2}{f_{an}}$$
$$+ \frac{(b_1 - f_{b1})^2}{f_{b1}} + \frac{(b_2 - f_{b2})^2}{f_{b2}} + \cdots + \frac{(b_n - f_{bn})^2}{f_{bn}} + \cdots$$

7. If the null hypothesis is true, the statistic S will have a chi-square distribution with $(m - 1) \times (n - 1)$ degrees of freedom. Look up the critical value in Exhibit 16.6. If the observed value is greater than the critical value, reject the hypothesis.

Goodness-of-Fit Tests

The chi-square test can also be used to test whether or not a particular probability distribution fits the observed data very well. This type of test is called a *goodness-of-fit test*. Once again, we want to compare the observed frequencies f of a particular occurrence with the frequencies f^* that are predicted to occur if the alleged distribution really does fit the data well. Once again, we compute the statistic

$$\sum_{i=1}^{n} \frac{(f_i - f_i^*)^2}{f_i^*}$$

If the null hypothesis is true, this statistic will have approximately a chi-square distribution. If the value of the test statistic turns out to be too large, that means there is too much of a discrepancy between the actual results and the predicted results, so we can reject the hypothesis that the predicted distribution fits the data. The number of degrees of freedom for the chi-square statistic is

$n - 1 - $ (number of parameters that you have to estimate using the sample

F-Distribution

The *F*-distribution is a continuous random variable distribution that is frequently used in statistical inference. There are many different *F*-distributions. Each one is identified by specifying two quantities, called the degree of freedom for the numerator (listed first) and the degree of freedom for the denominator. Exhibit 16.9 at the back of this section lists some values. For example, there is a 95 percent chance that an *F*-distribution with 5 and 20 degrees of freedom will be less than 2.71.

If X is a random variable with a chi-square distribution with m degrees of freedom, and Y has a chi-square distribution with n degrees of freedom that is independent of X, then this random variable

$$\frac{X/m}{Y/n}$$

will have an *F*-distribution with m and n degrees of freedom.

Analysis of Variance

Analysis of variance (ANOVA) is a procedure used to test the hypothesis that three or more different samples were all selected from populations with the same mean. The method is based on a *test statistic*:

$$F = \frac{nS^{*2}}{S^2},$$

where n is the number of members in each sample, S^{*2} is the variance of the sample averages for all of the groups, and S^2 is the average variance for the groups. If the null hypothesis is true and the population means actually are all the same, this statistic will have an *F*-distribution with $(m - 1)$ and $m(n - 1)$ degrees of freedom, where m is the number of samples. If the value of the test statistic is too large, the null hypothesis is rejected. Intuitively, it is clear that a large value of S^{*2} means that the observed sample averages are spread further apart, thereby making the test statistic larger and the null hypothesis less likely to be accepted.

The test described above is called one-way analysis of variance. If there are two possible sources of variations for each observation, it is helpful to perform a test called two-way analysis of variance.

EXHIBIT 16.1
Table of Squares and Square Roots

No.	Square	Square Root	No.	Square	Square Root	No.	Square	Square Root
1	1	1.000	51	2,601	7.141	101	10,201	10.050
2	4	1.414	52	2,704	7.211	102	10,404	10.100
3	9	1.732	53	2,809	7.280	103	10,609	10.149
4	16	2.000	54	2,916	7.348	104	10,816	10.198
5	25	2.236	55	3,025	7.416	105	11,025	10.247
6	36	2.449	56	3,136	7.483	106	11,236	10.296
7	49	2.646	57	3,249	7.550	107	11,449	10.344
8	64	2.828	58	3,364	7.616	108	11,664	10.392
9	81	3.000	59	3,481	7.681	109	11,881	10.440
10	100	3.162	60	3,600	7.746	110	12,100	10.488
11	121	3.317	61	3,721	7.810	111	12,321	10.536
12	144	3.464	62	3,844	7.874	112	12,544	10.583
13	169	3.606	63	3,969	7.937	113	12,769	10.630
14	196	3.742	64	4,096	8.000	114	12,996	10.677
15	225	3.873	65	4,225	8.062	115	13,225	10.724
16	256	4.000	66	4,356	8.124	116	13,456	10.770
17	289	4.123	67	4,489	8.185	117	13,689	10.817
18	324	4.243	68	4,624	8.246	118	13,924	10.863
19	361	4.359	69	4,761	8.307	119	14,161	10.909
20	400	4.472	70	4,900	8.367	120	14,400	10.954
21	441	4.583	71	5,041	8.426	121	14,641	11.000
22	484	4.690	72	5,184	8.485	122	14,884	11.045
23	529	4.796	73	5,329	8.544	123	15,129	11.091
24	576	4.899	74	5,476	8.602	124	15,376	11.136
25	625	5.000	75	5,625	8.660	125	15,625	11.180
26	676	5.099	76	5,776	8.718	126	15,876	11.225
27	729	5.196	77	5,929	8.775	127	16,129	11.269
28	784	5.291	78	6,084	8.832	128	16,384	11.314
29	841	5.385	79	6,241	8.888	129	16,641	11.358
30	900	5.477	80	6,400	8.944	130	16,900	11.402
31	961	5.568	81	6,561	9.000	131	17,161	11.446
32	1,024	5.657	82	6,724	9.055	132	17,424	11.489
33	1,089	5.745	83	6,889	9.110	133	17,689	11.533
34	1,156	5.831	84	7,056	9.165	134	17,956	11.576
35	1,225	5.916	85	7,225	9.220	135	18,225	11.619
36	1,296	6.000	86	7,396	9.274	136	18,496	11.662
37	1,369	6.083	87	7,569	9.327	137	18,769	11.705
38	1,444	6.164	88	7,744	9.381	138	19,044	11.747
39	1,521	6.245	89	7,921	9.434	139	19,321	11.790
40	1,600	6.325	90	8,100	9.487	140	19,600	11.832
41	1,681	6.403	91	8,281	9.539	141	19,881	11.874
42	1,764	6.481	92	8,464	9.592	142	20,164	11.916
43	1,849	6.557	93	8,649	9.644	143	20,449	11.958
44	1,936	6.633	94	8,836	9.695	144	20,736	12.000
45	2,025	6.708	95	9,025	9.747	145	21,025	12.042
46	2,116	6.782	96	9,216	9.798	146	21,316	12.083
47	2,209	6.856	97	9,409	9.849	147	21,609	12.124
48	2,304	6.928	98	9,604	9.899	148	21,904	12.166
49	2,401	7.000	99	9,801	9.950	149	22,201	12.207
50	2,500	7.071	100	10,000	10.000	150	22,500	12.247

EXHIBIT 16.2
Common Logarithm Table
The table gives log $(a + b)$.

a	b: .00	.01	.02	.03	.04	.05	.06	.07	.08	.09
1.0	.0000	.0043	.0086	.0128	.0170	.0212	.0253	.0294	.0334	.0374
1.1	.0414	.0453	.0492	.0531	.0569	.0607	.0645	.0682	.0719	.0755
1.2	.0792	.0828	.0864	.0899	.0934	.0969	.1004	.1038	.1072	.1106
1.3	.1139	.1173	.1206	.1239	.1271	.1303	.1335	.1367	.1399	.1430
1.4	.1461	.1492	.1523	.1553	.1584	.1614	.1644	.1673	.1703	.1732
1.5	.1761	.1790	.1818	.1847	.1875	.1903	.1931	.1959	.1987	.2014
1.6	.2041	.2068	.2095	.2122	.2148	.2175	.2201	.2227	.2253	.2279
1.7	.2304	.2330	.2355	.2380	.2405	.2430	.2455	.2480	.2504	.2529
1.8	.2553	.2577	.2601	.2625	.2648	.2672	.2695	.2718	.2742	.2765
1.9	.2788	.2810	.2833	.2856	.2878	.2900	.2923	.2945	.2967	.2989
2.0	.3010	.3032	.3054	.3075	.3096	.3118	.3139	.3160	.3181	.3201
2.1	.3222	.3243	.3263	.3284	.3304	.3324	.3345	.3365	.3385	.3404
2.2	.3424	.3444	.3464	.3483	.3502	.3522	.3541	.3560	.3579	.3598
2.3	.3617	.3636	.3655	.3674	.3692	.3711	.3729	.3747	.3766	.3784
2.4	.3802	.3820	.3838	.3856	.3874	.3892	.3909	.3927	.3945	.3962
2.5	.3979	.3997	.4014	.4031	.4048	.4065	.4082	.4099	.4116	.4133
2.6	.4150	.4166	.4183	.4200	.4216	.4232	.4249	.4265	.4281	.4298
2.7	.4314	.4330	.4346	.4362	.4378	.4393	.4409	.4425	.4440	.4456
2.8	.4472	.4487	.4502	.4518	.4533	.4548	.4564	.4579	.4594	.4609
2.9	.4624	.4639	.4654	.4669	.4683	.4698	.4713	.4728	.4742	.4757
3.0	.4771	.4786	.4800	.4814	.4829	.4843	.4857	.4871	.4886	.4900
3.1	.4914	.4928	.4942	.4955	.4969	.4983	.4997	.5011	.5024	.5038
3.2	.5052	.5065	.5079	.5092	.5105	.5119	.5132	.5145	.5159	.5172
3.3	.5185	.5198	.5211	.5224	.5237	.5250	.5263	.5276	.5289	.5302
3.4	.5315	.5328	.5340	.5353	.5366	.5378	.5391	.5403	.5416	.5428
3.5	.5441	.5453	.5465	.5478	.5490	.5502	.5515	.5527	.5539	.5551
3.6	.5563	.5575	.5587	.5599	.5611	.5623	.5635	.5647	.5658	.5670
3.7	.5682	.5694	.5705	.5717	.5729	.5740	.5752	.5763	.5775	.5786
3.8	.5798	.5809	.5821	.5832	.5843	.5855	.5866	.5877	.5888	.5899
3.9	.5911	.5922	.5933	.5944	.5955	.5966	.5977	.5988	.5999	.6010
4.0	.6021	.6031	.6042	.6053	.6064	.6075	.6085	.6096	.6107	.6117
4.1	.6128	.6138	.6149	.6160	.6170	.6180	.6191	.6201	.6212	.6222
4.2	.6232	.6243	.6253	.6263	.6274	.6284	.6294	.6304	.6314	.6325
4.3	.6335	.6345	.6355	.6365	.6375	.6385	.6395	.6405	.6415	.6425
4.4	.6435	.6444	.6454	.6464	.6474	.6484	.6493	.6503	.6513	.6522
4.5	.6532	.6542	.6551	.6561	.6571	.6580	.6590	.6599	.6609	.6618
4.6	.6628	.6637	.6646	.6656	.6665	.6675	.6684	.6693	.6702	.6712
4.7	.6721	.6730	.6739	.6749	.6758	.6767	.6776	.6785	.6794	.6803
4.8	.6812	.6821	.6830	.6839	.6848	.6857	.6866	.6875	.6884	.6893
4.9	.6902	.6911	.6920	.6928	.6937	.6946	.6955	.6964	.6972	.6981
5.0	.6990	.6998	.7007	.7016	.7024	.7033	.7042	.7050	.7059	.7067
5.1	.7076	.7084	.7093	.7101	.7110	.7118	.7126	.7135	.7143	.7152
5.2	.7160	.7168	.7177	.7185	.7193	.7202	.7210	.7218	.7226	.7235
5.3	.7243	.7251	.7259	.7267	.7275	.7284	.7292	.7300	.7308	.7316
5.4	.7324	.7332	.7340	.7348	.7356	.7364	.7372	.7380	.7388	.7396
5.5	.7404	.7412	.7419	.7427	.7435	.7443	.7451	.7459	.7466	.7474
5.6	.7482	.7490	.7497	.7505	.7513	.7520	.7528	.7536	.7543	.7551
5.7	.7559	.7566	.7574	.7582	.7589	.7597	.7604	.7612	.7619	.7627
5.8	.7634	.7642	.7649	.7657	.7664	.7672	.7679	.7686	.7694	.7701
5.9	.7709	.7716	.7723	.7731	.7738	.7745	.7752	.7760	.7767	.7774

a b:	.00	.01	.02	.03	.04	.05	.06	.07	.08	.09
6.0	.7782	.7789	.7796	.7803	.7810	.7818	.7825	.7832	.7839	.7846
6.1	.7853	.7860	.7868	.7875	.7882	.7889	.7896	.7903	.7910	.7917
6.2	.7924	.7931	.7938	.7945	.7952	.7959	.7966	.7973	.7980	.7987
6.3	.7993	.8000	.8007	.8014	.8021	.8028	.8035	.8041	.8048	.8055
6.4	.8062	.8069	.8075	.8082	.8089	.8096	.8102	.8109	.8116	.8122
6.5	.8129	.8136	.8142	.8149	.8156	.8162	.8169	.8176	.8182	.8189
6.6	.8195	.8202	.8209	.8215	.8222	.8228	.8235	.8241	.8248	.8254
6.7	.8261	.8267	.8274	.8280	.8287	.8293	.8299	.8306	.8312	.8319
6.8	.8325	.8331	.8338	.8344	.8351	.8357	.8363	.8370	.8376	.8382
6.9	.8388	.8395	.8401	.8407	.8414	.8420	.8426	.8432	.8439	.8445
7.0	.8451	.8457	.8463	.8470	.8476	.8482	.8488	.8494	.8500	.8506
7.1	.8513	.8519	.8525	.8531	.8537	.8543	.8549	.8555	.8561	.8567
7.2	.8573	.8579	.8585	.8591	.8597	.8603	.8609	.8615	.8621	.8627
7.3	.8633	.8639	.8645	.8651	.8657	.8663	.8669	.8675	.8681	.8686
7.4	.8692	.8698	.8704	.8710	.8716	.8722	.8727	.8733	.8739	.8745
7.5	.8751	.8756	.8762	.8768	.8774	.8779	.8785	.8791	.8797	.8802
7.6	.8808	.8814	.8820	.8825	.8831	.8837	.8842	.8848	.8854	.8859
7.7	.8865	.8871	.8876	.8882	.8887	.8893	.8899	.8904	.8910	.8915
7.8	.8921	.8927	.8932	.8938	.8943	.8949	.8954	.8960	.8965	.8971
7.9	.8976	.8982	.8987	.8993	.8998	.9004	.9009	.9015	.9020	.9025
8.0	.9031	.9036	.9042	.9047	.9053	.9058	.9063	.9069	.9074	.9079
8.1	.9085	.9090	.9096	.9101	.9106	.9112	.9117	.9122	.9128	.9133
8.2	.9138	.9143	.9149	.9154	.9159	.9165	.9170	.9175	.9180	.9186
8.3	.9191	.9196	.9201	.9206	.9212	.9217	.9222	.9227	.9232	.9238
8.4	.9243	.9248	.9253	.9258	.9263	.9269	.9274	.9279	.9284	.9289
8.5	.9294	.9299	.9304	.9309	.9315	.9320	.9325	.9330	.9335	.9340
8.6	.9345	.9350	.9355	.9360	.9365	.9370	.9375	.9380	.9385	.9390
8.7	.9395	.9400	.9405	.9410	.9415	.9420	.9425	.9430	.9435	.9440
8.8	.9445	.9450	.9455	.9460	.9465	.9469	.9474	.9479	.9484	.9489
8.9	.9494	.9499	.9504	.9509	.9513	.9518	.9523	.9528	.9533	.9538
9.0	.9542	.9547	.9552	.9557	.9562	.9566	.9571	.9576	.9581	.9586
9.1	.9590	.9595	.9600	.9605	.9609	.9614	.9619	.9624	.9628	.9633
9.2	.9638	.9643	.9647	.9652	.9657	.9661	.9666	.9671	.9675	.9680
9.3	.9685	.9689	.9694	.9699	.9703	.9708	.9713	.9717	.9722	.9727
9.4	.9731	.9736	.9741	.9745	.9750	.9754	.9759	.9764	.9768	.9773
9.5	.9777	.9782	.9786	.9791	.9795	.9800	.9805	.9809	.9814	.9818
9.6	.9823	.9827	.9832	.9836	.9841	.9845	.9850	.9854	.9859	.9863
9.7	.9868	.9872	.9877	.9881	.9886	.9890	.9894	.9899	.9903	.9908
9.8	.9912	.9917	.9921	.9926	.9930	.9934	.9939	.9943	.9948	.9952
9.9	.9956	.9961	.9965	.9969	.9974	.9978	.9983	.9987	.9991	.9996

EXHIBIT 16.3
Trigonometric Function Table

Degrees	Sin	Cos	Tan	Radians
0.0	0.00000	1.00000	0.00000	0.00000
0.2	0.00349	0.99999	0.00349	0.00349
0.4	0.00698	0.99998	0.00698	0.00698
0.6	0.01047	0.99995	0.01047	0.01047
0.8	0.01396	0.99990	0.01396	0.01396
1.0	0.01745	0.99985	0.01746	0.01745
1.2	0.02094	0.99978	0.02095	0.02094
1.4	0.02443	0.99970	0.02444	0.02443
1.6	0.02792	0.99961	0.02793	0.02793
1.8	0.03141	0.99951	0.03143	0.03142
2.0	0.03490	0.99939	0.03492	0.03491
2.2	0.03839	0.99926	0.03842	0.03840
2.4	0.04188	0.99912	0.04191	0.04189
2.6	0.04536	0.99897	0.04541	0.04538
2.8	0.04885	0.99881	0.04891	0.04887
3.0	0.05234	0.99863	0.05241	0.05236
3.2	0.05582	0.99844	0.05591	0.05585
3.4	0.05931	0.99824	0.05941	0.05934
3.6	0.06279	0.99803	0.06291	0.06283
3.8	0.06627	0.99780	0.06642	0.06632
4.0	0.06976	0.99756	0.06993	0.06981
4.2	0.07324	0.99731	0.07344	0.07330
4.4	0.07672	0.99705	0.07695	0.07679
4.6	0.08020	0.99678	0.08046	0.08029
4.8	0.08368	0.99649	0.08397	0.08378
5.0	0.08716	0.99619	0.08749	0.08727
5.2	0.09063	0.99588	0.09101	0.09076
5.4	0.09411	0.99556	0.09453	0.09425
5.6	0.09758	0.99523	0.09805	0.09774
5.8	0.10106	0.99488	0.10158	0.10123
6.0	0.10453	0.99452	0.10510	0.10472
6.2	0.10800	0.99415	0.10863	0.10821
6.4	0.11147	0.99377	0.11217	0.11170
6.6	0.11494	0.99337	0.11570	0.11519
6.8	0.11840	0.99297	0.11924	0.11868
7.0	0.12187	0.99255	0.12278	0.12217
7.2	0.12533	0.99211	0.12633	0.12566
7.4	0.12880	0.99167	0.12988	0.12915
7.6	0.13226	0.99122	0.13343	0.13264
7.8	0.13572	0.99075	0.13698	0.13614
8.0	0.13917	0.99027	0.14054	0.13963
8.2	0.14263	0.98978	0.14410	0.14312
8.4	0.14608	0.98927	0.14767	0.14661
8.6	0.14954	0.98876	0.15124	0.15010
8.8	0.15299	0.98823	0.15481	0.15359
9.0	0.15643	0.98769	0.15838	0.15708
9.2	0.15988	0.98714	0.16196	0.16057
9.4	0.16333	0.98657	0.16555	0.16406
9.6	0.16677	0.98600	0.16914	0.16755
9.8	0.17021	0.98541	0.17273	0.17104
10.0	0.17365	0.98481	0.17633	0.17453
10.2	0.17708	0.98420	0.17993	0.17802
10.4	0.18052	0.98357	0.18353	0.18151
10.6	0.18395	0.98294	0.18714	0.18500
10.8	0.18738	0.98229	0.19076	0.18850

Degrees	Sin	Cos	Tan	Radians
11.0	0.19081	0.98163	0.19438	0.19199
11.2	0.19423	0.98096	0.19801	0.19548
11.4	0.19766	0.98027	0.20164	0.19897
11.6	0.20108	0.97958	0.20527	0.20246
11.8	0.20450	0.97887	0.20891	0.20595
12.0	0.20791	0.97815	0.21256	0.20944
12.2	0.21132	0.97742	0.21621	0.21293
12.4	0.21474	0.97667	0.21986	0.21642
12.6	0.21814	0.97592	0.22353	0.21991
12.8	0.22155	0.97515	0.22719	0.22340
13.0	0.22495	0.97437	0.23087	0.22689
13.2	0.22835	0.97358	0.23455	0.23038
13.4	0.23175	0.97278	0.23823	0.23387
13.6	0.23514	0.97196	0.24193	0.23736
13.8	0.23853	0.97113	0.24562	0.24086
14.0	0.24192	0.97030	0.24933	0.24435
14.2	0.24531	0.96945	0.25304	0.24784
14.4	0.24869	0.96858	0.25676	0.25133
14.6	0.25207	0.96771	0.26048	0.25482
14.8	0.25545	0.96682	0.26421	0.25831
15.0	0.25882	0.96593	0.26795	0.26180
15.2	0.26219	0.96502	0.27169	0.26529
15.4	0.26556	0.96410	0.27545	0.26878
15.6	0.26892	0.96316	0.27920	0.27227
15.8	0.27228	0.96222	0.28297	0.27576
16.0	0.27564	0.96126	0.28675	0.27925
16.2	0.27899	0.96029	0.29053	0.28274
16.4	0.28234	0.95931	0.29432	0.28623
16.6	0.28569	0.95832	0.29811	0.28972
16.8	0.28903	0.95732	0.30192	0.29322
17.0	0.29237	0.95631	0.30573	0.29671
17.2	0.29571	0.95528	0.30955	0.30020
17.4	0.29904	0.95424	0.31338	0.30369
17.6	0.30237	0.95319	0.31722	0.30718
17.8	0.30570	0.95213	0.32106	0.31067
18.0	0.30902	0.95106	0.32492	0.31416
18.2	0.31233	0.94997	0.32878	0.31765
18.4	0.31565	0.94888	0.33266	0.32114
18.6	0.31896	0.94777	0.33654	0.32463
18.8	0.32227	0.94665	0.34033	0.32812
19.0	0.32557	0.94552	0.34433	0.33161
19.2	0.32887	0.94438	0.34824	0.33510
19.4	0.33216	0.94322	0.35216	0.33859
19.6	0.33545	0.94206	0.35608	0.34208
19.8	0.33874	0.94088	0.36002	0.34557
20.0	0.34202	0.93969	0.36397	0.34907
20.2	0.34530	0.93849	0.36793	0.35256
20.4	0.34857	0.93728	0.37190	0.35605
20.6	0.35184	0.93606	0.37587	0.35954
20.8	0.35511	0.93483	0.37986	0.36303
21.0	0.35837	0.93358	0.38386	0.36652
21.2	0.36162	0.93232	0.38787	0.37001
21.4	0.36488	0.93106	0.39190	0.37350
21.6	0.36812	0.92978	0.39593	0.37699
21.8	0.37137	0.92849	0.39997	0.38048

Degrees	Sin	Cos	Tan	Radians
22.0	0.37461	0.92718	0.40403	0.38397
22.2	0.37784	0.92587	0.40809	0.38746
22.4	0.38107	0.92455	0.41217	0.39095
22.6	0.38430	0.92321	0.41626	0.39444
22.8	0.38752	0.92186	0.42036	0.39793
23.0	0.39073	0.92051	0.42447	0.40143
23.2	0.39394	0.91914	0.42860	0.40492
23.4	0.39715	0.91775	0.43274	0.40841
23.6	0.40035	0.91636	0.43689	0.41190
23.8	0.40354	0.91496	0.44105	0.41539
24.0	0.40674	0.91355	0.44523	0.41888
24.2	0.40992	0.91212	0.44942	0.42237
24.4	0.41310	0.91068	0.45362	0.42586
24.6	0.41628	0.90924	0.45784	0.42935
24.8	0.41945	0.90778	0.46206	0.43284
25.0	0.42262	0.90631	0.46631	0.43633
25.2	0.42578	0.90483	0.47056	0.43982
25.4	0.42893	0.90334	0.47483	0.44331
25.6	0.43209	0.90183	0.47912	0.44680
25.8	0.43523	0.90032	0.48342	0.45029
26.0	0.43837	0.89879	0.48773	0.45379
26.2	0.44151	0.89726	0.49206	0.45728
26.4	0.44463	0.89571	0.49640	0.46077
26.6	0.44776	0.89415	0.50076	0.46426
26.8	0.45088	0.89259	0.50514	0.46775
27.0	0.45399	0.89101	0.50952	0.47124
27.2	0.45710	0.88942	0.51393	0.47473
27.4	0.46020	0.88782	0.51835	0.47822
27.6	0.46330	0.88620	0.52279	0.48171
27.8	0.46639	0.88458	0.52724	0.48520
28.0	0.46947	0.88295	0.53171	0.48869
28.2	0.47255	0.88130	0.53619	0.49218
28.4	0.47562	0.87965	0.54070	0.49567
28.6	0.47869	0.87798	0.54522	0.49916
28.8	0.48175	0.87631	0.54975	0.50265
29.0	0.48481	0.87462	0.55431	0.50615
29.2	0.48786	0.87292	0.55888	0.50964
29.4	0.49090	0.87121	0.56347	0.51313
29.6	0.49394	0.86950	0.56808	0.51662
29.8	0.49697	0.86777	0.57270	0.52011
30.0	0.50000	0.86603	0.57735	0.52360
30.2	0.50302	0.86428	0.58201	0.52709
30.4	0.50603	0.86251	0.58670	0.53058
30.6	0.50904	0.86074	0.59140	0.53407
30.8	0.51204	0.85896	0.59612	0.53756
31.0	0.51504	0.85717	0.60086	0.54105
31.2	0.51803	0.85536	0.60562	0.54454
31.4	0.52101	0.85355	0.61040	0.54803
31.6	0.52399	0.85173	0.61520	0.55152
31.8	0.52696	0.84989	0.62003	0.55501
32.0	0.52992	0.84805	0.62487	0.55850
32.2	0.53288	0.84619	0.62973	0.56200
32.4	0.53583	0.84433	0.63462	0.56549
32.6	0.53877	0.84245	0.63953	0.56898
32.8	0.54171	0.84057	0.64446	0.57247

Degrees	Sin	Cos	Tan	Radians
33.0	0.54464	0.83867	0.64941	0.57596
33.2	0.54756	0.83676	0.65438	0.57945
33.4	0.55048	0.83485	0.65938	0.58294
33.6	0.55339	0.83292	0.66440	0.58643
33.8	0.55630	0.83098	0.66944	0.58992
34.0	0.55919	0.82904	0.67451	0.59341
34.2	0.56208	0.82708	0.67960	0.59690
34.4	0.56497	0.82511	0.68471	0.60039
34.6	0.56784	0.82314	0.68985	0.60388
34.8	0.57071	0.82115	0.69502	0.60737
35.0	0.57358	0.81915	0.70021	0.61086
35.2	0.57643	0.81715	0.70542	0.61436
35.4	0.57928	0.81513	0.71066	0.61785
35.6	0.58212	0.81310	0.71593	0.62134
35.8	0.58496	0.81106	0.72122	0.62483
36.0	0.58778	0.80902	0.72654	0.62832
36.2	0.59061	0.80696	0.73189	0.63181
36.4	0.59342	0.80489	0.73726	0.63530
36.6	0.59622	0.80282	0.74266	0.63879
36.8	0.59902	0.80073	0.74809	0.64228
37.0	0.60181	0.79864	0.75355	0.64577
37.2	0.60460	0.79653	0.75904	0.64926
37.4	0.60738	0.79442	0.76456	0.65275
37.6	0.61014	0.79229	0.77010	0.65624
37.8	0.61291	0.79016	0.77568	0.65973
38.0	0.61566	0.78801	0.78128	0.66322
38.2	0.61841	0.78586	0.78692	0.66672
38.4	0.62115	0.78369	0.79259	0.67021
38.6	0.62388	0.78152	0.79829	0.67370
38.8	0.62660	0.77934	0.80402	0.67719
39.0	0.62932	0.77715	0.80978	0.68068
39.2	0.63203	0.77495	0.81558	0.68417
39.4	0.63473	0.77273	0.82141	0.68766
39.6	0.63742	0.77051	0.82727	0.69115
39.8	0.64011	0.76828	0.83317	0.69464
40.0	0.64279	0.76604	0.83910	0.69813
40.2	0.64546	0.76380	0.84506	0.70162
40.4	0.64812	0.76154	0.85107	0.70511
40.6	0.65077	0.75927	0.85710	0.70860
40.8	0.65342	0.75700	0.86318	0.71209
41.0	0.65606	0.75471	0.86929	0.71558
41.2	0.65869	0.75242	0.87543	0.71908
41.4	0.66131	0.75011	0.88162	0.72257
41.6	0.66393	0.74780	0.88784	0.72606
41.8	0.66653	0.74548	0.89410	0.72955
42.0	0.66913	0.74315	0.90040	0.73304
42.2	0.67172	0.74081	0.90674	0.73653
42.4	0.67430	0.73846	0.91312	0.74002
42.6	0.67688	0.73610	0.91955	0.74351
42.8	0.67944	0.73373	0.92601	0.74700
43.0	0.68200	0.73135	0.93251	0.75049
43.2	0.68455	0.72897	0.93906	0.75398
43.4	0.68709	0.72658	0.94565	0.75747
43.6	0.68962	0.72417	0.95229	0.76096
43.8	0.69214	0.72176	0.95896	0.76445

MATHEMATICS

Degrees	Sin	Cos	Tan	Radians
44.0	0.69466	0.71934	0.96569	0.76794
44.2	0.69716	0.71691	0.97246	0.77144
44.4	0.69966	0.71447	0.97927	0.77493
44.6	0.70215	0.71203	0.98613	0.77842
44.8	0.70463	0.70957	0.99304	0.78191
45.0	0.70711	0.70711	1.00000	0.78540
45.2	0.70957	0.70463	1.00700	0.78889
45.4	0.71203	0.70215	1.01406	0.79238
45.6	0.71447	0.69966	1.02116	0.79587
45.8	0.71691	0.69717	1.02832	0.79936
46.0	0.71934	0.69466	1.03553	0.80285
46.2	0.72176	0.69214	1.04279	0.80634
46.4	0.72417	0.68962	1.05010	0.80983
46.6	0.72657	0.68709	1.05747	0.81332
46.8	0.72897	0.68455	1.06489	0.81681
47.0	0.73135	0.68200	1.07237	0.82030
47.2	0.73373	0.67944	1.07990	0.82379
47.4	0.73610	0.67688	1.08749	0.82729
47.6	0.73845	0.67430	1.09514	0.83078
47.8	0.74080	0.67172	1.10284	0.83427
48.0	0.74314	0.66913	1.11061	0.83776
48.2	0.74548	0.66653	1.11844	0.84125
48.4	0.74780	0.66393	1.12633	0.84474
48.6	0.75011	0.66131	1.13428	0.84823
48.8	0.75241	0.65869	1.14229	0.85172
49.0	0.75471	0.65606	1.15037	0.85521
49.2	0.75699	0.65342	1.15851	0.85870
49.4	0.75927	0.65077	1.16672	0.86219
49.6	0.76154	0.64812	1.17499	0.86568
49.8	0.76380	0.64546	1.18334	0.86917
50.0	0.76604	0.64279	1.19175	0.87266
50.2	0.76828	0.64011	1.20024	0.87615
50.4	0.77051	0.63742	1.20879	0.87965
50.6	0.77273	0.63473	1.21742	0.88314
50.8	0.77494	0.63203	1.22612	0.88663
51.0	0.77715	0.62932	1.23490	0.89012
51.2	0.77934	0.62660	1.24375	0.89361
51.4	0.78152	0.62388	1.25268	0.89710
51.6	0.78369	0.62115	1.26168	0.90059
51.8	0.78586	0.61841	1.27077	0.90408
52.0	0.78801	0.61566	1.27994	0.90757
52.2	0.79015	0.61291	1.28919	0.91106
52.4	0.79229	0.61015	1.29852	0.91455
52.6	0.79441	0.60738	1.30794	0.91804
52.8	0.79653	0.60460	1.31745	0.92153
53.0	0.79864	0.60182	1.32074	0.92502
53.2	0.80073	0.59902	1.33673	0.92851
53.4	0.80282	0.59623	1.34650	0.93201
53.6	0.80489	0.59342	1.35636	0.93550
53.8	0.80696	0.59061	1.36632	0.93899
54.0	0.80902	0.58779	1.37638	0.94248
54.2	0.81106	0.58496	1.38653	0.94597
54.4	0.81310	0.58212	1.39678	0.94946
54.6	0.81513	0.57928	1.40713	0.95295
54.8	0.81714	0.57643	1.41759	0.95644

Degrees	Sin	Cos	Tan	Radians
55.0	0.81915	0.57358	1.42815	0.95993
55.2	0.82115	0.57071	1.43881	0.96342
55.4	0.82314	0.56784	1.44958	0.96691
55.6	0.82511	0.56497	1.46046	0.97040
55.8	0.82708	0.56208	1.47145	0.97389
56.0	0.82904	0.55919	1.48256	0.97738
56.2	0.83098	0.55630	1.49378	0.98087
56.4	0.83292	0.55339	1.50512	0.98436
56.6	0.83485	0.55048	1.51658	0.98786
56.8	0.83676	0.54756	1.52816	0.99135
57.0	0.83867	0.54464	1.53986	0.99484
57.2	0.84057	0.54171	1.55169	0.99833
57.4	0.84245	0.53877	1.56365	1.00182
57.6	0.84433	0.53583	1.57574	1.00531
57.8	0.84619	0.53288	1.58797	1.00880
58.0	0.84805	0.52992	1.60033	1.01229
58.2	0.84989	0.52696	1.61283	1.01578
58.4	0.85173	0.52399	1.62547	1.01927
58.6	0.85355	0.52101	1.63826	1.02276
58.8	0.85536	0.51803	1.65119	1.02625
59.0	0.85717	0.51504	1.66428	1.02974
59.2	0.85896	0.51204	1.67751	1.03323
59.4	0.86074	0.50904	1.69090	1.03672
59.6	0.86251	0.50603	1.70446	1.04022
59.8	0.86427	0.50302	1.71817	1.04371
60.0	0.86602	0.50000	1.73205	1.04720
60.2	0.86777	0.49697	1.74610	1.05069
60.4	0.86949	0.49394	1.76032	1.05418
60.6	0.87121	0.49090	1.77471	1.05767
60.8	0.87292	0.48786	1.78929	1.06116
61.0	0.87462	0.48481	1.80404	1.06465
61.2	0.87631	0.48175	1.81899	1.06814
61.4	0.87798	0.47869	1.83413	1.07163
61.6	0.87965	0.47563	1.84946	1.07512
61.8	0.88130	0.47255	1.86499	1.07861
62.0	0.88295	0.46947	1.88072	1.08210
62.2	0.88458	0.46639	1.89666	1.08559
62.4	0.88620	0.46330	1.91282	1.08908
62.6	0.88781	0.46020	1.92919	1.09258
62.8	0.88942	0.45710	1.94578	1.09607
63.0	0.89101	0.45399	1.96261	1.09956
63.2	0.89259	0.45088	1.97966	1.10305
63.4	0.89415	0.44776	1.99695	1.10654
63.6	0.89571	0.44464	2.01448	1.11003
63.8	0.89726	0.44151	2.03226	1.11352
64.0	0.89879	0.43837	2.05030	1.11701
64.2	0.90032	0.43523	2.06859	1.12050
64.4	0.90183	0.43209	2.08716	1.12399
64.6	0.90333	0.42894	2.10599	1.12748
64.8	0.90483	0.42578	2.12510	1.13097
65.0	0.90631	0.42262	2.14450	1.13446
65.2	0.90778	0.41945	2.16419	1.13795
65.4	0.90924	0.41628	2.18418	1.14144
65.6	0.91068	0.41311	2.20448	1.14494
65.8	0.91212	0.40992	2.22510	1.14843

Degrees	Sin	Cos	Tan	Radians
66.0	0.91355	0.40674	2.24603	1.15192
66.2	0.91496	0.40355	2.26730	1.15541
66.4	0.91636	0.40035	2.28890	1.15890
66.6	0.91775	0.39715	2.31086	1.16239
66.8	0.91914	0.39394	2.33317	1.16588
67.0	0.92050	0.39073	2.35585	1.16937
67.2	0.92186	0.38752	2.37890	1.17286
67.4	0.92321	0.38430	2.40234	1.17635
67.6	0.92455	0.38107	2.42617	1.17984
67.8	0.92587	0.37784	2.45042	1.18333
68.0	0.92718	0.37461	2.47508	1.18682
68.2	0.92849	0.37137	2.50017	1.19031
68.4	0.92978	0.36813	2.52570	1.19380
68.6	0.93106	0.36488	2.55169	1.19729
68.8	0.93232	0.36163	2.57815	1.20079
69.0	0.93358	0.35837	2.60508	1.20428
69.2	0.93483	0.35511	2.63251	1.20777
69.4	0.93606	0.35184	2.66045	1.21126
69.6	0.93728	0.34857	2.68891	1.21475
69.8	0.93849	0.34530	2.71791	1.21824
70.0	0.93969	0.34202	2.74747	1.22173
70.2	0.94088	0.33874	2.77760	1.22522
70.4	0.94206	0.33545	2.80832	1.22871
70.6	0.94322	0.33216	2.83964	1.23220
70.8	0.94438	0.32887	2.87160	1.23569
71.0	0.94552	0.32557	2.90420	1.23918
71.2	0.94665	0.32227	2.93747	1.24267
71.4	0.94777	0.31896	2.97143	1.24616
71.6	0.94888	0.31565	3.00610	1.24965
71.8	0.94997	0.31234	3.04151	1.25315
72.0	0.95106	0.30902	3.07767	1.25664
72.2	0.95213	0.30570	3.11462	1.26013
72.4	0.95319	0.30237	3.15239	1.26362
72.6	0.95424	0.29904	3.19099	1.26711
72.8	0.95528	0.29571	3.23047	1.27060
73.0	0.95630	0.29237	3.27084	1.27409
73.2	0.95732	0.28903	3.31215	1.27758
73.4	0.95832	0.28569	3.35442	1.28107
73.6	0.95931	0.28234	3.39769	1.28456
73.8	0.96029	0.27899	3.44201	1.28805
74.0	0.96126	0.27564	3.48740	1.29154
74.2	0.96222	0.27228	3.53391	1.29503
74.4	0.96316	0.26892	3.58158	1.29852
74.6	0.96410	0.26556	3.63046	1.30201
74.8	0.96502	0.26219	3.68059	1.30551
75.0	0.96593	0.25882	3.73203	1.30900
75.2	0.96682	0.25545	3.78483	1.31249
75.4	0.96771	0.25207	3.83904	1.31598
75.6	0.96858	0.24869	3.89473	1.31947
75.8	0.96945	0.24531	3.95194	1.32296
76.0	0.97030	0.24192	4.01076	1.32645
76.2	0.97113	0.23853	4.07125	1.32994
76.4	0.97196	0.23514	4.13348	1.33343
76.6	0.97278	0.23175	4.19754	1.33692
76.8	0.97358	0.22835	4.26350	1.34041

Degrees	Sin	Cos	Tan	Radians
77.0	0.97437	0.22495	4.33145	1.34390
77.2	0.97515	0.22155	4.40149	1.34739
77.4	0.97592	0.21814	4.47372	1.35088
77.6	0.97667	0.21474	4.54823	1.35437
77.8	0.97742	0.21133	4.62516	1.35787
78.0	0.97815	0.20791	4.70460	1.36136
78.2	0.97887	0.20450	4.78670	1.36485
78.4	0.97958	0.20108	4.87159	1.36834
78.6	0.98027	0.19766	4.95942	1.37183
78.8	0.98096	0.19424	5.05034	1.37532
79.0	0.98163	0.19081	5.14452	1.37881
79.2	0.98229	0.18738	5.24215	1.38230
79.4	0.98294	0.18395	5.34342	1.38579
79.6	0.98357	0.18052	5.44853	1.38928
79.8	0.98420	0.17709	5.55773	1.39277
80.0	0.98481	0.17365	5.67124	1.39626
80.2	0.98541	0.17021	5.78935	1.39975
80.4	0.98600	0.16677	5.91231	1.40324
80.6	0.98657	0.16333	6.04046	1.40673
80.8	0.98714	0.15988	6.17414	1.41023
81.0	0.98769	0.15644	6.31370	1.41372
81.2	0.98823	0.15299	6.45956	1.41721
81.4	0.98876	0.14954	6.61213	1.42070
81.6	0.98927	0.14608	6.77193	1.42419
81.8	0.98978	0.14263	6.93946	1.42768
82.0	0.99027	0.13917	7.11531	1.43117
82.2	0.99075	0.13572	7.30010	1.43466
82.4	0.99122	0.13226	7.49458	1.43815
82.6	0.99167	0.12880	7.69950	1.44164
82.8	0.99211	0.12533	7.91574	1.44513
83.0	0.99255	0.12187	8.14426	1.44862
83.2	0.99297	0.11841	8.38617	1.45211
83.4	0.99337	0.11494	8.64266	1.45560
83.6	0.99377	0.11147	8.91509	1.45909
83.8	0.99415	0.10800	9.20506	1.46258
84.0	0.99452	0.10453	9.51424	1.46608
84.2	0.99488	0.10106	9.84469	1.46957
84.4	0.99523	0.09758	10.19860	1.47306
84.6	0.99556	0.09411	10.57880	1.47655
84.8	0.99588	0.09063	10.98800	1.48004
85.0	0.99619	0.08716	11.42990	1.48353
85.2	0.99649	0.08368	11.90850	1.48702
85.4	0.99678	0.08020	12.42860	1.49051
85.6	0.99705	0.07672	12.99590	1.49400
85.8	0.99731	0.07324	13.61710	1.49749
86.0	0.99756	0.06976	14.30040	1.50098
86.2	0.99780	0.06628	15.05540	1.50447
86.4	0.99803	0.06279	15.89420	1.50796
86.6	0.99824	0.05931	16.83150	1.51145
86.8	0.99844	0.05582	17.88590	1.51494

Degrees	Sin	Cos	Tan	Radians
87.0	0.99863	0.05234	19.08060	1.51844
87.2	0.99881	0.04885	20.44590	1.52193
87.4	0.99897	0.04536	22.02100	1.52542
87.6	0.99912	0.04188	23.85860	1.52891
87.8	0.99926	0.03839	26.02980	1.53240
88.0	0.99939	0.03490	28.63530	1.53589
88.2	0.99951	0.03141	31.81900	1.53938
88.4	0.99961	0.02792	35.79910	1.54287
88.6	0.99970	0.02443	40.91510	1.54636
88.8	0.99978	0.02094	47.73610	1.54985
89.0	0.99985	0.01745	57.28550	1.55334
89.2	0.99990	0.01396	71.60780	1.55683
89.4	0.99995	0.01047	95.47760	1.56032
89.6	0.99998	0.00698	143.20900	1.56381
89.8	0.99999	0.00349	286.37600	1.56730

EXHIBIT 16.4
The Standard Normal Distribution

If Z has a standard normal distribution, the table gives the value of $\Pr(Z < z)$.

z	$\Pr(Z < z)$	z	$\Pr(Z < z)$	z	$\Pr(Z < z)$	z	$\Pr(Z < z)$
0.01	.5040	0.29	.6141	0.57	.7157	0.85	.8023
0.02	.5080	0.30	.6179	0.58	.7190	0.86	.8051
0.03	.5120	0.31	.6217	0.59	.7224	0.87	.8079
0.04	.5160	0.32	.6255	0.60	.7257	0.88	.8106
0.05	.5199	0.33	.6293	0.61	.7291	0.89	.8133
0.06	.5239	0.34	.6331	0.62	.7324	0.90	.8159
0.07	.5279	0.35	.6368	0.63	.7357	0.91	.8186
0.08	.5319	0.36	.6406	0.64	.7389	0.92	.8212
0.09	.5359	0.37	.6443	0.65	.7422	0.93	.8238
0.10	.5398	0.38	.6480	0.66	.7454	0.94	.8264
0.11	.5438	0.39	.6517	0.67	.7486	0.95	.8289
0.12	.5478	0.40	.6554	0.68	.7517	0.96	.8315
0.13	.5517	0.41	.6591	0.69	.7549	0.97	.8340
0.14	.5557	0.42	.6628	0.70	.7580	0.98	.8365
0.15	.5596	0.43	.6664	0.71	.7611	0.99	.8389
0.16	.5636	0.44	.6700	0.72	.7642	1.00	.8413
0.17	.5675	0.45	.6736	0.73	.7673	1.01	.8438
0.18	.5714	0.46	.6772	0.74	.7704	1.02	.8461
0.19	.5753	0.47	.6808	0.75	.7734	1.03	.8485
0.20	.5793	0.48	.6844	0.76	.7764	1.04	.8508
0.21	.5832	0.49	.6879	0.77	.7794	1.05	.8531
0.22	.5871	0.50	.6915	0.78	.7823	1.06	.8554
0.23	.5910	0.51	.6950	0.79	.7852	1.07	.8577
0.24	.5948	0.52	.6985	0.80	.7881	1.08	.8599
0.25	.5987	0.53	.7019	0.81	.7910	1.09	.8621
0.26	.6026	0.54	.7054	0.82	.7939	1.10	.8643
0.27	.6064	0.55	.7088	0.83	.7967	1.11	.8665
0.28	.6103	0.56	.7123	0.84	.7995	1.12	.8686

z	Pr(Z < z)	z	Pr(Z < z)	z	Pr(Z < z)	z	Pr(Z < z)
1.13	.8708	1.44	.9251	1.75	.9599	2.06	.9803
1.14	.8729	1.45	.9265	1.76	.9608	2.07	.9808
1.15	.8749	1.46	.9279	1.77	.9616	2.08	.9812
1.16	.8770	1.47	.9292	1.78	.9625	2.09	.9817
1.17	.8790	1.48	.9306	1.79	.9633	2.10	.9821
1.18	.8810	1.49	.9319	1.80	.9641	2.11	.9826
1.19	.8830	1.50	.9332	1.81	.9649	2.12	.9830
1.20	.8849	1.51	.9345	1.82	.9656	2.13	.9834
1.21	.8869	1.52	.9357	1.83	.9664	2.14	.9838
1.22	.8888	1.53	.9370	1.84	.9671	2.15	.9842
1.23	.8907	1.54	.9382	1.85	.9678	2.16	.9846
1.24	.8925	1.55	.9394	1.86	.9686	2.17	.9850
1.25	.8944	1.56	.9406	1.87	.9693	2.18	.9854
1.26	.8962	1.57	.9418	1.88	.9699	2.19	.9857
1.27	.8980	1.58	.9429	1.89	.9706	2.20	.9861
1.28	.8997	1.59	.9441	1.90	.9713	2.25	.9878
1.29	.9015	1.60	.9452	1.91	.9719	2.30	.9893
1.30	.9032	1.61	.9463	1.92	.9726	2.35	.9906
1.31	.9049	1.62	.9474	1.93	.9732	2.40	.9918
1.32	.9066	1.63	.9484	1.94	.9738	2.50	.9938
1.33	.9082	1.64	.9495	1.95	.9744	2.60	.9953
1.34	.9099	1.65	.9505	1.96	.9750	2.70	.9965
1.35	.9115	1.66	.9515	1.97	.9756	2.80	.9974
1.36	.9131	1.67	.9525	1.98	.9761	2.90	.9981
1.37	.9147	1.68	.9535	1.99	.9767	3.00	.9987
1.38	.9162	1.69	.9545	2.00	.9773	3.10	.9990
1.39	.9177	1.70	.9554	2.01	.9778	3.20	.9993
1.40	.9192	1.71	.9564	2.02	.9783	3.30	.9995
1.41	.9207	1.72	.9573	2.03	.9788	3.40	.9997
1.42	.9222	1.73	.9582	2.04	.9793	3.50	.9998
1.43	.9236	1.74	.9591	2.05	.9798		

EXHIBIT 16.5

The Standard Normal Distribution

The table gives the value of $\Pr(-z < Z < z)$

z	Pr(−z < Z < z)	z	Pr(−z < Z < z)
0.10	.0796	1.30	.8064
0.20	.1586	1.40	.8384
0.30	.2358	1.50	.8664
0.40	.3108	1.60	.8904
0.50	.3830	1.70	.9108
0.60	.4514	1.80	.9282
0.70	.5160	1.90	.9426
0.80	.5762	1.96	.9500
0.90	.6318	2.00	.9546
1.00	.6826	2.50	.9876
1.10	.7286	3.00	.9974

EXHIBIT 16.6
The Chi-square Cumulative Distribution Function

If X has a chi-square distribution with n degrees of freedom, the table gives the value x such that $\Pr(X < x) = p$. For example, if X has a chi-square distribution with 10 degrees of freedom, there is a probability of .95 that X will be less than 18.3.

n	$p=.005$	$p=.01$	$p=.05$	$p=.25$	$p=.50$	$p=.75$	$p=.90$	$p=.95$	$p=.975$	$p=.99$
2	0.01	.02	.10	.57	1.38	2.77	4.60	5.99	7.87	9.21
3	0.07	.11	.35	1.21	2.36	4.10	6.24	7.80	9.33	11.31
4	0.20	.29	.71	1.92	3.35	5.38	7.77	9.48	11.14	13.27
5	0.41	.55	1.14	2.67	4.35	6.62	9.23	11.07	12.83	15.08
6	0.67	.87	1.63	3.45	5.34	7.84	10.64	12.59	14.44	16.81
7	0.98	1.24	2.17	4.26	6.35	9.04	12.02	14.07	16.01	18.48
8	1.34	1.65	2.73	5.07	7.34	10.22	13.36	15.51	17.54	20.09
9	1.73	2.09	3.33	5.90	8.34	11.39	14.68	16.92	19.02	21.67
10	2.16	2.56	3.94	6.74	9.3	12.5	15.9	18.3	20.5	23.2
11	2.60	3.05	4.57	7.58	10.3	13.7	17.3	19.7	21.9	24.7
12	3.07	3.57	5.23	8.44	11.3	14.8	18.6	21.0	23.3	26.2
13	3.56	4.11	5.89	9.30	12.3	16.0	19.8	22.4	24.7	27.7
14	4.08	4.66	6.57	10.17	13.3	17.1	21.1	23.7	26.1	29.1
15	4.60	5.23	7.26	11.04	14.3	18.2	22.3	25.0	27.5	30.6
16	5.14	5.81	7.96	11.91	15.3	19.4	23.5	26.3	28.8	32.0
17	5.70	6.41	8.67	12.79	16.3	20.5	24.8	27.6	30.2	33.4
18	6.26	7.02	9.39	13.68	17.3	21.6	26.0	28.9	31.5	34.8
19	6.85	7.63	10.12	14.56	18.3	22.7	27.2	30.1	32.9	36.2
20	7.43	8.26	10.85	15.45	19.3	23.8	28.4	31.4	34.2	37.6
21	8.03	8.90	11.59	16.34	20.3	24.9	29.6	32.7	35.5	38.9
22	8.64	9.54	12.34	17.24	21.3	26.0	30.8	33.9	36.8	40.3
23	9.26	10.19	13.09	18.14	22.3	27.1	32.0	35.2	38.1	41.6
24	9.89	10.86	13.85	19.04	23.3	28.2	33.2	36.4	39.4	43.0
25	10.52	11.52	14.61	19.94	24.3	29.3	34.4	37.7	40.7	44.3
30	13.79	14.95	18.49	24.48	29.3	34.8	40.3	43.8	47.0	50.9
40	20.70	22.16	26.51	33.66	39.3	45.6	51.8	55.7	59.3	63.7
50	27.99	29.70	34.76	42.94	49.3	56.3	63.2	67.5	71.4	76.2
60	35.53	37.48	43.19	52.29	59.3	67.0	74.4	79.1	83.3	88.4
70	43.27	45.44	51.74	61.70	69.3	77.6	85.5	90.5	95.0	100.4
80	51.18	53.54	60.38	71.15	79.3	88.1	96.6	101.9	106.6	112.3
90	59.19	61.74	69.12	80.62	89.3	98.7	107.6	113.2	118.1	124.1

EXHIBIT 16.7
The *t*-distribution

If X has a t-distribution with n degrees of freedom, the table gives the value of x such that $\Pr(X < x) = p$. For example, if X has a t-distribution with 15 degrees of freedom there is a 95 percent chance X will be less than 1.753.

n	$p = .750$	$p = .900$	$p = .950$	$p = .975$	$p = .990$	$p = .995$
1	1.000	3.078	6.314	12.706	31.821	63.657
2	0.817	1.886	2.920	4.303	6.965	9.925
3	0.765	1.638	2.353	3.182	4.541	5.841
4	0.741	1.533	2.132	2.776	3.747	4.604
5	0.727	1.476	2.015	2.571	3.365	4.032
6	0.718	1.440	1.943	2.447	3.143	3.707
7	0.711	1.415	1.895	2.365	3.000	3.499
8	0.706	1.397	1.860	2.306	2.896	3.355
9	0.703	1.383	1.833	2.262	2.821	3.250
10	0.700	1.372	1.812	2.228	2.764	3.169
11	0.697	1.363	1.796	2.201	2.718	3.106
12	0.695	1.356	1.782	2.179	2.681	3.055
13	0.694	1.350	1.771	2.160	2.650	3.012
14	0.692	1.345	1.761	2.145	2.600	2.977
15	0.691	1.341	1.753	2.131	2.600	2.947
16	0.690	1.337	1.746	2.120	2.584	2.921
17	0.689	1.333	1.740	2.110	2.567	2.898
18	0.688	1.330	1.734	2.101	2.552	2.878
19	0.688	1.328	1.729	2.093	2.539	2.861
20	0.687	1.325	1.725	2.086	2.528	2.845
21	0.686	1.323	1.721	2.080	2.518	2.831
22	0.686	1.321	1.717	2.074	2.508	2.819
23	0.685	1.319	1.714	2.069	2.500	2.807
24	0.685	1.318	1.711	2.064	2.492	2.797
25	0.684	1.316	1.708	2.060	2.485	2.787
26	0.684	1.315	1.706	2.056	2.479	2.779
27	0.684	1.314	1.703	2.052	2.473	2.771
28	0.683	1.313	1.701	2.048	2.467	2.763
29	0.683	1.311	1.699	2.045	2.462	2.756
30	0.683	1.310	1.697	2.042	2.457	2.750
35	0.682	1.306	1.690	2.030	2.438	2.724
40	0.681	1.303	1.684	2.021	2.423	2.704
50	0.679	1.299	1.676	2.009	2.400	2.678
60	0.679	1.296	1.671	2.000	2.400	2.660
100	0.677	1.290	1.660	1.984	2.364	2.626
120	0.677	1.289	1.658	1.980	2.358	2.617

EXHIBIT 16.8
The *t*-distribution

If X has a t-distribution with n degrees of freedom, the table gives the value of x such that $\Pr(-x < X < x) = p$.

n	$p = .95$	$p = .99$	n	$p = .95$	$p = .99$
1	12.706	63.657	20	2.086	2.845
2	4.303	9.925	21	2.080	2.831•
3	3.182	5.841	22	2.074	2.819
4	2.776	4.604	23	2.069	2.807
5	2.571	4.032	24	2.064	2.797
6	2.447	3.707	25	2.060	2.787
7	2.365	3.499	26	2.056	2.779
8	2.306	3.355	27	2.052	2.771
9	2.262	3.250	28	2.048	2.763
10	2.228	3.169	29	2.045	2.756
11	2.201	3.106	30	2.042	2.750
12	2.179	3.055	35	2.030	2.724
13	2.160	3.012	40	2.021	2.704
14	2.145	2.977	50	2.009	2.678
15	2.131	2.947	60	2.000	2.660
16	2.120	2.921	100	1.984	2.626
17	2.110	2.898	120	1.980	2.617
18	2.101	2.878			
19	2.093	2.861			

EXHIBIT 16.9
The *F*-distribution

If F has an F-distribution with m and n degrees of freedom, then the table gives the value of x such that $\Pr(F < x) = .95$.

n	$m = 2$	$m = 3$	$m = 4$	$m = 5$	$m = 10$	$m = 15$	$m = 20$	$m = 30$	$m = 60$	$m = 120$
2	19.00	19.16	19.25	19.30	19.40	19.43	19.45	19.46	19.48	19.49
3	9.55	9.28	9.12	9.01	8.79	8.70	8.66	8.62	8.57	8.55
4	6.94	6.59	6.39	6.26	5.96	5.86	5.80	5.75	5.69	5.66
5	5.79	5.41	5.19	5.05	4.74	4.62	4.56	4.50	4.43	4.40
6	5.14	4.76	4.53	4.39	4.06	3.94	3.87	3.81	3.74	3.70
7	4.74	4.35	4.12	3.97	3.64	3.51	3.44	3.38	3.30	3.27
8	4.46	4.07	3.84	3.69	3.35	3.22	3.15	3.08	3.01	2.97
9	4.26	3.86	3.63	3.48	3.14	3.01	2.94	2.86	2.79	2.75
10	4.10	3.71	3.48	3.33	2.98	2.85	2.77	2.70	2.62	2.58
15	3.68	3.29	3.06	2.90	2.54	2.40	2.33	2.25	2.16	2.11
20	3.49	3.10	2.87	2.71	2.35	2.20	2.12	2.04	1.95	1.90
30	3.32	2.92	2.69	2.53	2.16	2.01	1.93	1.84	1.74	1.68
60	3.15	2.76	2.53	2.37	1.99	1.84	1.75	1.65	1.53	1.47
120	3.07	2.68	2.45	2.29	1.91	1.75	1.66	1.55	1.43	1.35

MUSIC

Absolute music   Music without direct reference to anything outside itself, i.e., not having words and not being illustrative music depicting story, scene, etc.

Accidental   A sharp, flat, double-sharp, double-flat, or natural sign occurring temporarily in the course of a piece, and not forming part of the key signature. It conventionally refers only to the bar in which it occurs—not to any succeeding bars, unless repeated there.

Acoustic   Term sometimes used to distinguish a "normal" (non-electric) instrument from its electric counterpart—e.g., acoustic guitar.

Acoustics   (1) The science of sound; (2) the sound properties of a building, etc.

Adagio (It.)   Slow, a slow movement; slower than Andante, faster than Largo. *Adagio for Strings*, title of an orchestral work (in elegiac vein) by Barber, first performed 1938, originally the slow movement of a string quartet.

Aerophone   Term used scientifically to classify an instrument in which a vibrating column of air produces the musical sound—including organ, accordion, etc., as well as conventional mouth-blown woodwind and brass instruments.

Air   A simple tune for voice or instrument. The *Air on the G String* is a name given to an arrangement by Wilhelmj (1871) of the 2nd movement of Bach's Suite No.3 in D for orchestra. In this arrangement, for violin and piano, the piece is transposed from D to C and the violinist plays on the lowest (G) string.

Alberti bass   The spreading out of a left-hand keyboard chord in a rhythmical pattern; e.g.,

♫ ♫♫♫♫♫♫ from ♩♩♩

Named after Domenico Alberti (1710–1740), Italian composer who used it extensively.

Aleatory   Dependent on chance or on the throw of the dice (Lat., *alea*). This is rather loosely applied to a tendency (since the 1950s) of some composers to leave elements in their compositions in an indeterminate state. But it might be more strictly confined to compositions in which random chance genuinely plays a part in performance (*see* **Cage, John**), not to those in which a decision of the performer replaces a decision of the composer. See **Indeterminacy.**

Alla breve   A tempo-direction (chiefly 18th century) indicating that, in a bar nominally of four beats, the pace is so fast that it seems to have two beats only (on the original first and third beats).

Allegro (It)   Lively, i.e., rather fast (but not as fast as Presto).

Allemande   Dance-movement often opening the baroque Suite in moderate 4-4 time. It was divided into two sections, and usually began with a short note just before the bar-line. The term is French for "German," but this is not the same as a German dance.

Alto (It., high)   (1) An unusually high type of adult male voice, employing falsetto; (2) the lower type of female voice, so designated in choirs; elsewhere usually contralto; also, sometimes, the corresponding child's voice; (3) in a "family" of instruments,

having range approximately that of an alto voice, e.g., *alto* flute, *alto* saxophone; (4) *alto* clef, written ♯; it is the normal clef for viola but is otherwise little used; (5) Fr. viola.

Andante (It., going)   At a walking pace, at moderate speed (between Allegretto and Adagio).

Appoggiatura (It., a leaning)   (1) Musical ornament (chiefly 18th century, now obsolete) consisting of an unharmonized auxiliary note falling (or less frequently, rising) to an adjacent note that is harmonized or implied to be so. Appoggiatura can be either *written,* using an auxiliary note in smaller type—e.g.,

♪♪   *played*   ♪♪

or *unwritten,* i.e., to be inserted by the performer according to conventions of the period, for example, a recitative in Handel or Mozart ending

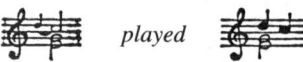 was intended to be sung as ♪♪♪

(2) (derived from above) Term used in modern harmonic analysis for accenting a non-harmonized note like the D in the first example (whether or not notated in the above obsolete way) adjacent to following harmonized notes less accented than itself.

Aria (It.)   Air, song, especially one of some complexity in opera or oratorio; *da capo aria* (as used, e.g., by Handel), one in which the first section is finally repeated after a contrasting section.

Arpeggio (It., from preceding)   A chord (on piano, etc.) that is performed "spread out," i.e., the notes are not sounded simultaneously but in succession (nearly always starting at the bottom), as normally on the harp.

Ars antiqua (Lat., old art)   Term for the style of Western European medieval music (based on Plainsong and organum) practiced, e.g., by Pérotin and preceding the Ars nova.

Ars nova (Lat., new art)   Term for the musical style current in 14th-century France and Italy, free from the restrictions of Ars antiqua, introducing duple (instead of only triple) time and having much independence of part-writing; practiced, e.g., by Landini, Machaut.

Atonal   Not in any key; hence *atonality, atonalism.* (The term *pantonal,* indicating the synthesis of all keys rather than the absence of any, was preferred by Schoenberg but has never won general acceptance.) Twelve-note music developed as a systematization of atonal music.

Augmentation   The treatment of a melody in such a way as to lengthen (usually doubling) the time-values of its notes. The device is used in some fugues.

Babbitt, Milton (b. 1916)   American composer (also influential theorist and teacher), pupil of Sessions. Works include 4 string quartets; piano pieces; *Philomel* for soprano, recorded soprano, and synthesized accompaniment on tape.

Bach   When used alone (e.g. Bach's Cello Suites), it means Johann Sebastian Bach, German composer (1685–1750). Bach was a prolific composer, as required of his post as official church organist and musical director of St. Thomas's Church. Bach was part of a very musical family, including his uncle Johann Christoph Bach (an organist also), and his second wife Anna Magdalena (a music transcriber and instructor). Bach fathered 20 children, not all of whom survived. Of his surviving children, 3 achieved some success as musicians: Karl Philipp Emanuel Bach, an appointed musician of Frederick the Great, soon followed his father's footsteps and became a church organist also; Johann Christian Bach, a composer who eventually settled in England; and Wilhelm Friedemann Bach, eldest son and least known of the Bachs, he was mainly an instructor of music. Some of J.S. Bach's works include the Brandenberg Concertos, the Goldberg Variations, and his cantatas.

Johann Sebastian Bach

Bagatelle (Fr., trifle)   A short, light piece, often for piano. Beethoven wrote 26 bagatelles.

Ballad (derived as ball, i.e., from dancing)   (1) Old song (often a Folk song) telling a story, the music being repeated for each verse; hence (2) a self-contained song of a narrative nature, e.g., Goethe's *The Erl King* as set by Schubert or Loewe; (3) song of narrative, explanatory type characteristically found in French opera and also, e.g., in Wagner's *The Flying Dutchman (Senta's Ballad)*; so Stravinsky called his narrative cantata on Abraham and Isaac a "sacred ballad"; (4) sentimental English song of 19th-century "drawing-room" type (also found in English operas of the period), so *ballad concert,* mainly devoted to such songs.

Ballet (1) Form of dancing of Italian origin, becoming established at French court in the 16th century and evolving into a recognized art form with its own traditional technique and conventions; it normally uses orchestral music (specially composed or otherwise) and appropriately full resources of stage decoration. The term is now used in Britain for almost any piece of stage dancing having an artistic purpose and substantial length; but in the United States it is commonly withheld from works not based on the "classical" technique of dancing, e.g., the so-called modern dance. Hence *opera-ballet* and *ballet-pantomime,* 18th-century French terms differentiating ballet with and without sung words, the term *opera-ballet* is also applied to certain modern ballets with singing, e.g., Prokofiev's *Cinderella.* (But note that the simple classification *ballet* does not exclude the use of voices— as in Ravel's *Daphnis and Chloe*—and that Falla's *Love, the Sorcerer* is styled *ballet-pantomime,* although it has vocal solos.) (2) an alternative spelling of Ballett, and so pronounced.

Bar (1) A metrical division of music, marked on paper as the distance between two vertical lines; so "two beats in the bar," etc; (2) such a vertical line itself. (In general the first of these uses is English, the second American: Eng. *bar* equals U.S. *measure;* U.S. *bar* equals Eng. *bar-line.* But two vertical lines close together, indicating the end of a piece or section, are called even in English *double bar,* not *double bar-line.*) (3) A meaning unconnected with previous two, a medieval German unit of song construction, two similar sections being followed by one in contrast.

Barber, Samuel (1910–1981)   American composer, formerly also singer (e.g., in his own setting, for voice and string quartet, of Matthew Arnold's Dover Beach). Studied in Italy and United States. Works include operas *Vanessa, A Hand of Bridge, Antony and Cleopatra,* 2 symphonies, 2 essays for orchestra, *Adagio for Strings,* overture to Sheridan's *The School for Scandal,* cello concerto, *Capricorn Concerto* (flute, oboe, trumpet, and strings), piano sonata, ballet *Medea* (also known as *Cave of the Heart),* cantata *Prayers of Kierkegaard.*

Barcarolle (Fr., from It.)   A boating-song, especially associated with Venetian gondoliers; a song or instrumental piece suggestive of this, in swaying 6/8 time (e.g., the famous one in Offenbach's *The Tales of Hoffman).*

Baroque   Term borrowed from architecture (where it has connotations of twisting, elaborate, heavy, involved construction) and used to describe characteristics of musical style roughly corresponding to this around 1600–1750. Applied, e.g., to Monteverdi, Purcell, and J.S. Bach, although the liberality of such application makes precise definition awkward. (*Compare* **Rococo**.) The term *baroque organ* is applied to the type of this period, more brilliant in tone and less heavy than 19th-century type, with lighter wind pressure and greater reliance on mutation stops. (This is a 20th-century use of the word *baroque.* In the 18th century the word meant uncouth, odd, rough, and antiquated in taste.) Baroque music generally involves Continuo.

Bartók, Béla (1881–1945)   Hungarian composer settled in the United States, 1940, dying there a poor man. From youth, a virtuoso pianist. Cultivated and developed Hungarian national musical style; partly in association with Kodály, collected and edited Hungarian folk songs, showing them to be different from the gypsy music borrowed by Liszt, Brahms, etc. Active in investigating other folk music, too. His own works—often atonal and cultivating extreme dissonance, especially in his middle life—include opera *Bluebeard's Castle,* mime plays *The Wooden Prince* and *The Miraculous Mandarin;* much piano music including *Mikrokosmos, Out of Doors,* and works for children; orchestral dance suite; *Concerto for Orchestra; Music for Strings, Percussion* and *Celesta,* 3 piano concertos, 2 violin concertos, viola concerto (posthumous, edited by T. Serly), 6 string quartets, trio *Contrasts,* songs and folksong arrangements. *See also* **Cantata.**

Bass   (1) The lowest male voice; (2) the lowest note or part in a chord, a composition, etc.; (3) the lower regions of musical pitch generally, especially in antithesis to treble, (4) Of a "family" of instruments, having low range, e.g., *bass* clarinet, *bass* saxophone; *bass flute,* usually a misnomer for *alto flute;* (5) colloquial abbreviation for double bass, or (in military and brass bands) for the tuba (either size); (6) *bass clef,* clef written 𝄢 and indicating F below middle C as the top line but one of the staff (and so sometimes also called *F clef*); it is normally used for bass voice, for most lower pitched instruments, for the left-hand part of piano music, etc.

Ludwig van Beethoven

Beethoven, Ludwig van (1770–1827) German composer, born in Bonn; son and grandson of musicians. Published a piano piece at the age of 12; worked shortly afterward as pianist, organist, viola player. Went to Vienna, 1792 (to study with Haydn, but did not stay with him), and remained and died there. Many love affairs, but never married. Brought up as Roman Catholic but came to hold unorthodox deistic views. From 1801, developed deafness, becoming total by about 1824—after composition of symphony no. 9 (*Choral*) but before the last five

quartets. Vastly extended the form and scope of the symphony (he wrote 9, not including *Wellington's Victory;* no. 3 is the *Eroica*), and also of the piano concerto (he wrote 5; no. 5 the so-called *Emperor*), the string quartet (16 and *Great Fugue*), the piano sonata (32). Other works include opera *Fidelio;* ballet *The Creatures of Prometheus;* Mass (*Missa solemnis*) in D and a smaller Mass in C; oratorio *Christ on the Mount of Olives;* violin concerto, triple concerto (piano, violin, cello); *Choral Fantasia;* theater music; *Name-Day* overture; *Equali* for trombones; 10 violin sonatas (no. 9, *Kreutzer*); *Archduke* and *Ghost* piano trios; songs; piano pieces, including *Diabelli* and *Prometheus* variations. The so-called *Jena* symphony is not by him. His works are indexed by Kinsky.

Bel canto (It., beautiful singing) Term used, often vaguely, by teachers, authorities on singing, etc., referring to a finely cultivated voice, particularly to imply suitability to the agile and smooth voice-production demanded in the operas of Bellini, Donizetti, etc.

Berceuse (Fr.) A cradle-song, lullaby; instrumental piece suggestive of this.

Berg, Alban (1885–1935) Austrian composer; born, worked, and died in Vienna; pupil of Schoenberg, whose methods he developed. Used a free-atonal idiom combined with very closely worked structures (passacaglia, variation, etc.) in opera *Wozzeck,* completed 1922; shortly afterward turned to strict twelve-note technique, e.g., in *Chamber Concerto* (piano, violin, winds), completed 1925. Other works include twelve-note opera, *Lulu;* a string quartet and (also for string quartet) *Lyric Suite;* songs with orchestra and with piano; violin concerto "in memory of an angel" (i.e., Manon Gropius, 18-year-old daughter of Mahler's widow by her second marriage), written shortly before his own death and not performed until after it (1936).

Berlioz, [Louis] **Hector** (1803–1869) French composer; learned guitar, and had general musical training at Paris Conservatory, but became proficient neither on piano nor on any orchestral instrument—yet a great master and innovator in orchestration (on which he wrote a book); also noted as conductor and music critic. Nearly all his works have some literary or other extramusical allusion (typical Romantic trait; *compare* **Schumann**). His love for the English Shakespearian actress Harriet Smithson is expressed in his *Fantastic Symphony,* 1830; he married her in 1833 and separated from her in 1842. Other works include operas *Benvenuto Cellini, Beatrice and Benedick, The Trojans;* choral works including *The Damnation of Faust* (in which occurs his arrangement of the *Rákóczi March*), *The Childhood of Christ,* and *Requiem;* symphony *Romeo and Juliet; Harold in Italy* for viola and orchestra; *Lélio* (intended sequel to the *Fantastic Symphony*) for reciter, singers, and orchestra; *Roman Carnival, The Corsair, King Lear,* and other overtures; songs with orchestra and with piano.

Binary In two sections; *binary form,* classification used of a simple movement (e.g., in an early 18th-century keyboard suite) in two sections, the first modulating to another key and the second returning to the original key. (*Compare* **Ternary.**) The form developed historically into sonata-form, an alternative name for which is, accordingly, *compound binary form.*

Bitonality   The use of two keys (*see* **Tonality**) simultaneously; for example, Stravinsky's famous early use in *Petrushka,* (1911), Holst, and Milhaud.

Bolero   Spanish dance, usually with a triplet on the second half of the first beat of the bar. The accompaniment includes dancers' voices and castanets. Ravel's purely orchestral *Bolero* (1928) is for ballet, not for dancing an actual bolero. Chopin's *Bolero* (1834) is for piano.

Borodin, Alexander [Porphyrevich] (1833–1887) Russian composer—also professor of chemistry, so could spare little time for music. Illegitimate son of a prince; pupil of Balakirev; one of the "nationalist" group of composers known as the mighty handful. Works include opera *Prince Igor* (unfinished; completed by Rimsky-Korsakov and Glazunov), which includes the *Polovetsian Dances*; 3 symphonies (no. 3 unfinished, but 2 movements of it advanced enough to be completed by Glazunov); symphonic poem *In the Steppes of Central Asia*; 2 string quartets; songs.

Bourrée (Fr.)   Dance-movement (found, for example, in the baroque Suite) in quick duple time beginning with an up-beat.

Brahms, Johannes (1833–1897)   German composer, also pianist; born in Hamburg, where as a youngster he played in sailors' taverns; pupil of Marxsen. In 1853 met Joachim, Liszt, Schumann, and others who became interested in him, visited Vienna 1862, settled there 1863 (also died there). Never married. Entirely devoted to composition from 1864, but did not write the first of his 4 symphonies until 1875. Composed no opera and did not follow widely prevalent Lisztian ideal of Program music, but developed the forms of Beethoven's period and showed notable rhythmic originality. Works include two piano concertos, violin concerto, double concerto (violin and cello); *Academic Festival* and *Tragic* overtures; *Variations on the St. Anthony Chorale* (orchestra or 2 pianos), formerly known as *Variations on a Theme of Haydn*; variations on themes by Handel and by Paganini for piano, and many other piano works; chamber music; songs (including *Four Serious Songs*) and part-songs; choral works, including *A German Requiem* and *Alto Rhapsody.*

Brandenburg Concertos   Six works by J.S. Bach for varying instrumental combinations, of which no two are alike; dedicated to the Margrave of Brandenburg. These are often classified as concerto grosso. They are not really typical, having a wide variety of styles and forms.

Bravura (It. courage, swagger)   A *bravura passage* is one calling for a bold and striking display of an executant's technique.

Bruckner, Anton (1824–1896)   Austrian composer; also organist: played at Royal Albert Hall, London, 1871. At first, church choirboy; went to Vienna and studied with Sechter (with whom Schubert had intended to study) and from 1868 settled in Vienna, becoming professor at the Conservatory there. Heard Wagner's *Tristan and Isolde,* 1865, and became his fervent disciple: wrote, however, no operas but 9 symphonies (no. 3 nicknamed his *Wagner Symphony,* no. 4, *Romantic*), not including 2 unnumbered early works later rejected by him. No. 9 (only 3 of 4 movements finished) is dedicated "to God," Bruckner always retaining devout Roman Catholicism and certain unsophisticated "country" ways. Symphonies nos. 7, 8, 9 use Wagner tubas. There are important differences between the shortened published versions of his symphonies and the "authentic" texts published after his death. Other works include 5 masses, a Te Deum, and a string quintet.

Buffo, buffa (It., comic)   *Basso buffo, tenore buffo,* comic bass, comic tenor (in opera). (Buffo by itself is sometimes found in the list of singers required for an Italian opera, and then indicates a comic bass.) *Opera buffa* means literally "comic opera."

C **Cadence**   A progression of chords (usually two giving an effect of closing a "sentence" in music. Thus *perfect cadence*, progression of dominant chord to tonic chord; *plagal cadence*, subdominant to tonic; *imperfect cadence*, tonic (or other chord) to dominant; *interrupted cadence*, dominant to submediant (or to some other chord suggesting a substitution for the expected tonic chord); *Phrygian cadence*, progression (deriving from the Phrygian Mode) which, in the key of C major, leads to the chord of E major (and correspondingly with other keys). Note that (1) some of these definitions are open to differences between authorities; (2) the *feminine cadence* is not a specific kind of harmonic progression, as the others, but any cadence in which the final chord comes on a weaker beat than its predecessor (instead of, as normally, the other way round).

Cadenza (It., cadence, but pronounced as English and used in a different sense)   A solo vocal or instrumental passage, either of an improvised nature or in some other way suggesting an interpolation in the flow of the music—used particularly, today, in concertos for solo instrument and orchestra. In these, however, genuine improvisation has been very rare for 150 years, as cadenzas have been written out in full instead of by the composer, the actual performer, or a third person.

Cage, John (b. 1912)   American composer (also pianist and writer), pupil of Schoenberg. Has written for ordinary instruments and for his invention, the Prepared piano; is especially noted for "music" that seems to involve the abdication of the composer, e.g., his *Imaginary Landscape* for 12 radio sets, first performed in 1951, requiring 24 performers (2 to each set) and conductor—dynamics, and the ratio of sound to silence, being stipulated but the result obviously depending on chance. See **Aleatory**. Other works include *Renga with Apartment House 1776* for large orchestra (for U.S. bicentennial, 1976).

Canon   Contrapuntal composition, or section of a composition, in which a melody given by one voice (or instrument) is repeated by one or more other voices (or instruments) each entering before the previous voice has finished, so that overlapping results. A *canon at the unison* is when the "imitating" (i.e., following) voice enters at the same pitch as the first voice; a *canon at the fifth* is when the imitating voice enters a fifth higher than the original. A *canon four in one* indicates four voices entering successively on the same melody; a *canon four in two* (or *double canon*) has two different simultaneous canons for two voices each. So also *accompanied canon*, when there are simultaneous other voices or instruments performing but not taking part in the canon; *perpetual canon*, when each voice as it comes to the end begins again; *canon by augmentation, diminution, inversion*, etc., canon in which the theme is treated in the imitating voice in one of those ways; *riddle* (or *enigma* or *puzzle*) *canon*, one in which only the opening voice is written out, leaving the notation of the other entries to be deduced.

Cantata (It., a sung piece) An extended choral work, with or without solo voices, and usually with orchestral accompaniment. This is the later meaning of the term; Italian baroque usage (e.g., Alessandro Scarlatti) indicates solo voice(s) and Continuo, and Bach's cantatas have solo voice(s) with accompanying instruments, with or without chorus. The term is much more rarely used as an actual title than its counterpart, Sonata, but Stravinsky composed a Cantata (2 solo singers, female chorus, 5 instrumentalists) to old English texts (1952) and Bartók a *Cantata Profana* (subtitled "The Enchanted Stags," on a legend symbolizing a plea for political freedom) for 2 soloists, chorus, and orchestra (1930). Britten's *Cantata Academica* (in Latin) was written for the 500th anniversary of Basle University, Switzerland (1960).

Cappella (It., chapel) In 17th-century usage, a near synonym for ripieno, i.e., full performing forces; later use, *a cappella*, *alla cappella*, in the chapel style, i.e., unaccompanied (of choral music).

Cavatina (It.) (1) An operatic song in slow tempo, either complete in itself or (e.g., in Bellini and Verdi) followed by a faster, more resolute section: hence (2) a rather slow, song-like instrumental movement; the title, for example, of a movement in Beethoven's string quartet in B flat, op. 130 (1826) and of a once-famous piece (originally for violin and piano) by Raff, and of the slow movement of Rubbra's string quartet No. 2.

Chaconne A piece (originally for dancing) in slow 3-beat time, in which composers often chose to repeat a given theme several times in the bass (i.e., a ground bass). In such works as the Chaconne that forms the final movement of Bach's Partita No. 2 in D minor for violin alone (c.1720), the theme is harmonically implied even at those points when it is not actually present. The term is applied by modern historians also to vocal numbers ("When I Am Laid in Earth" in Purcell's *Dido and Aeneas*) having a similar pattern of repetition. *See also* **Passacaglia**.

Chamber music Music intended for a room (in fact, called by Grainger "room music," very sensibly), as distinct from a large hall, theater, church, bandstand, ballroom, etc.; hence, particularly, music calling for "intimate" presentation, having only a few performers, and treating all these as soloists on equal terms. Conventionally, works for 1 or 2 performers only are excluded. (The term is not precisely defined. There is every reason for including in

it the appropriate kind of vocal music, e.g., madrigal singing with 1 or 2 voices to each part.) Note that Hindemith gave the actual title *Chamber Music* (Ger. *Kammermusik*) to each of a set of 7 compositions for various instrumental combinations, 1922–1930.

Chanson (Fr.) A song, in particular a type of polyphonic song, sometimes with instruments, current in France from the 14th to 16th centuries. During the latter part of that period Italy and England had the corresponding but different form of the Madrigal. The *chanson de geste*, however, was a type of heroic verse chronicle set to music, popular in the 11th and 12th centuries.

Chopin, Frédéric François [French form of Polish *Fryderyk Franciszek*] (1810–1849) Polish composer and pianist of partly French descent. Born at Zelazowa Wola, near Warsaw; studied in Warsaw; settled in Paris, touring from there (e.g., to England and Scotland). Never revisited Poland (under Russian occupation) but was keen patriot and student of Polish literature. Never married; met George Sand (Aurore Dudevant) 1838, and lived with her until 1847; suffered from consumption, gave his last public concert in 1848, and died in Paris. Works—nearly all for piano, and equally remarkable for harmonic imagination and for use of piano technique—include 3 sonatas (no. 2, in B♭ minor, including a funeral march), 4 scherzos, 25 preludes, 27 studies, 19 nocturnes, 19 waltzes, 10 polonaises, at least 55 mazurkas (these and some other works influenced by Polish music), 4 ballads; also 2 piano concertos, sonata for cello and piano, songs, etc. Contributor to the hexameron.

Chorale (1) German *Choral*, i.e., type of traditional German metrical hymn-tune for congregational use, as in *Ein' feste Burg* (*A Stronghold Sure*), perhaps composed by Martin Luther. This tune, like many others, was used by Bach. Also a *chorale prelude*, an instrumental piece (usually for organ) based on a chorale. For *Passion chorale, see* **Passion**. (2) A choir or choral society—a French word, also used in the title of some U.S. (and, recently, British) choirs.

Chordophone Term scientifically used to classify an instrument in which a vibrating string produces the musical sound; e.g., harp, violin, piano.

Chromatic Pertaining to intervals outside the diatonic (major or minor) scale; *chromatic scale*, ascending or descending by semitones, *chromatic compass*. So also *chromatic progression*, a chord progression that involves departure from the prevailing diatonic scale; *chromaticism*, tendency of a piece or a composer toward the use of intervals outside the prevailing diatonic scale, and thus often toward a plentiful use of modulation (but the term is not used to cover Atonal music, etc.) So also *chromatic harmonica, chromatic harp*.

Classic(al), classicism Terms commonly used very vaguely, but with three main areas of meaning: (1) as distinct from, e.g., "popular" or "folk," serious, learned, belonging to a sophisticated and written tradition; (2) as opposed to Romantic, aesthetically dependent supposedly more on formal attraction than on emotional stimulation; (3) *Viennese classic*, belonging to the period and predominant musical style of Haydn, Mozart, and Beethoven, around 1770–1830. So also the *classical concerto* (Mozart's); so too (as abstraction) *classicism. See also* **Neoclassic**.

Coda (It., tail) In musical analysis, a section of a movement considered to be added at the end as a rounding off rather than as a structural necessity. Thus in Sonata-form, the coda (if there is one) occurs only after both principal subjects have been recapitulated in the tonic key. (As with all such terms of analysis, the meaning here given is of value only as an approximation: Beethoven's codas, for instance, have great importance in his musical design and do not strike the listener as "stuck on" at the end.)

Coloratura (It.) Term applied to an agile, florid style of vocal music or to its performance. A *coloratura soprano* refers to a soprano with a voice suited to this.

Compound time Any musical meter not classifiable as Simple time, in which the beat unit divides into 2. Thus 12/8 is a compound time, because the unit of beat is ♩. (the bar having 4 of these) and this divides not into two but into three subunits (♫). (The term is, however, now more academic than practical: it is of no use in analyzing, say a score by Stravinsky, or in classifying a rumba, in which the beat is of nonuniform length.)

Concertant (Fr.) In a concerted form, with interplay between instruments—term used, for example, by Stravinsky, *Duo Concertant* (1932) for violin and piano, avoiding terms like "sonata" or "suite"; also (feminine form) *concertante*, as in F. Martin's *Petite Symphonie Concertante* for harp, harpsichord, piano and 2 string orchestras (1945).

Concertmaster The first violinist of an orchestra (following the German term *Konzertmeister*); leader.

Concerto (It., a concert, a concerted performance) (1) In general modern usage, a work making contrasted use of solo instrument(s) and orchestra—generally in 3 movements and generally keeping to certain structural principles of which Mozart is regarded as the classic exponent; (2) earlier use, an orchestral work in several movements, with or without solo instruments, (3) term used apart from this by composers for exceptional reasons of their own, e.g., Bach's *Italian Concerto*, which, although for a single player, employs an effect of instrumental contrast between the two manuals of a harpsichord; Bartók's *Concerto for Orchestra* (1944), so-called because of the solo functions filled by individual orchestral instruments.

Concord A chord that seems harmonically at rest; its opposite, *discord,* seems jarring, thus requiring a Resolution to another chord. What constitutes a concord is not something fixed: throughout history composers have tended to admit more and different chords as concords, and in, e.g., much twelve-note music, the ideas of concord and discord need not have structural relevance for the composer.

Concrete music (Fr., *musique concrète*) Type of quasi-musical organization of real, "concrete" sounds (from nature or manmade environment) recorded and arranged on tape—a technique developed chiefly by Pierre Schaeffer at the Paris radio

station in 1948–1949. The process is now absorbed in Electronic music.

Continuo (It., abbr. of *basso continuo*) A type of accompaniment (current particularly around 1600–1750) played from a bass line, most commonly on a keyboard instrument. From the bass notes, the player worked out the correct harmonies, sometimes aided by numerical shorthand indications provided by the composer (*see* **Figured bass**). To *play the continuo*, therefore, is not to play a particular kind of instrument; it is to play on a keyboard instrument (or lute, etc.) a harmonized accompaniment from this type of bass—or to reinforce (e.g., on cello and double bass) this bass line without the chords. Hence *continuo group* of such instruments, e.g., in a Monteverdi opera orchestra. The historic English equivalent for continuo is "thorough-bass," i.e., "through-bass," but *continuo* has now acquired standard usage in English.

Copland, Aaron (b. 1900) American composer, pupil of R. Goldmark and (in Paris) N. Boulanger; also pianist, lecturer, and writer, prominent in general championing of American music. Born in Brooklyn. His work variously shows an indebtedness to jazz (*Music for the Theatre*, 1925), to cowboy songs and similar indigenous American tunes (ballets *Rodeo* and *Appalachian Spring*), and to Latin American music (*El Salón México*, clarinet concerto); but elsewhere it is sometimes completely abstract, fiercely dissonant, and devoid of "popular" influences—e.g., piano variations, piano sonata. Other works include opera *The Tender Land*, 3 symphonies, *Quiet City* (orchestral suite), *A Lincoln Portrait* (with narrator), piano quartet and other chamber music, film scores.

Counterpoint The simultaneous combination of 2 or more melodies to make musical sense, one melody then being spoken of as *the counterpoint of* or *in counterpoint to* another. So *double counterpoint*, when 2 melodies, one above the other, can exchange position; similarly, *triple, quadruple counterpoint* (etc.), where 3, 4 (etc.) melodies can take up any positions relative to each other: all these are kinds of *invertible counterpoint*, as practiced in Fugue. A certain academic discipline abstracted from 16th-century practice is called *strict counterpoint: free counterpoint* denotes counterpoint not bound by this.

Counter-tenor A rare male voice higher than tenor, current in England in Purcell's and Handel's time and revived in the 20th century in concerts and opera; called male alto in, for example, Anglican cathedral usage.

Country and western American form of popular music with origins in the country dance music of the British Isles and France. Country and western music grew out of such American folk forms as bluegrass, cowboy songs, and what was derisively termed "mountain music." It leans toward the use of steel guitars, acoustic guitars, violins (called fiddles), and accordions. Country and western began to grow in popularity in the 1930s and now encompasses many genres such as Cajun music and country rock. Some popular country and western artists include Hank Williams, Patsy Cline, Emmylou Harris, Johnny Cash, and the Oak Ridge Mountain Boys.

Courante (Fr.) Dance in triple time occurring in the baroque Suite.

Cowell, Henry [Dixon] (1897–1965) American composer and pianist, given to musical experiment; developed the idea of clusters of adjacent notes played, e.g., with forearm on the piano, and also extended this to orchestral technique, co-inventor of the "Rhythmicon," electrical instrument reproducing predetermined rhythms. Prolific composer for orchestra, band, and various instrumental groups; works (some with synthesized titles like *Synchrony*, *Tocanta*) include 21 symphonies, *Hymns and Fuguing Tunes* (after Billings), opera, works for piano; also teacher and writer.

Cycle (1) Name given to a set of works, especially songs, intended to be performed as a group and often linked musically or by other means; (2) name given to certain post-1950 pieces in which the performer begins at a point of his or her own choosing, goes through the written score and concludes at the same point—e.g., Stockhausen's *Cycle* (Ger., *Zyklus*) for percussionist, 1959; (3) term used in the expression *cycle of fifths*, the "chain" by which (given equal Temperament) a succession of perfect fifths upward or downward leads back to the original note again (at a higher or lower octave) after passing through all the other 11 notes of the chromatic scale. *See also* **Cyclic form**.

Cyclic form (1) Form of a work in which a theme does duty (often in new guise) in more than one movement, e.g.. Franck, Symphony; Elgar, Symphony no. 1; (2) obsolete (*see* **Cycle**, 1), form of any work with more than one movement.

Debussy, Claude-Achille [born Achille-Claude] (1862–1918) French composer, also noted as critic; born near Paris, worked and died in Paris; visited Russia 1881. Worked out new outlook on harmony and musical structure, of which Impressionism reveals its kinship with contemporary visual art; he also has affinity with such poets as Verlaine and Baudelaire. Was first pro- then anti-Wagner; his opera *Pelleas and Melisande* is unlike any predecessor although seemingly indebted to Mussorgsky for cultivation of natural speech inflections. Achieved first marked success with *The Afternoon of a Faun*, 1894; had already composed cantata *The Blessed Damozel*. Also wrote *Iberia*, *The Sea*, *Nocturnes*, and other works for orchestra; 2 books of piano preludes (with picturesque titles) and other piano works including *Suite bergamasque* and *Children's Corner*; string quartet, violin sonata, cello sonata; music to *King Lear* and *The Martyrdom of St. Sebastian*.

Degree Classification of a note with reference to its position in the scale. Thus the notes of the scale of C major (upward, C-D-E-F-G-A-B-C) are called the 1st, 2nd (etc.) degrees of the scale, returning eventually to the 1st degree, i.e., C. The alternative names for the 1st–7th degrees (major or minor scale) are Tonic, Supertonic, Mediant, Subdominant, Dominant, Submediant, Leading note. Other names are used in the tonic sol-fa system.

Descant (1) Medieval term—*see* **Discant**. (2) An additional part sung (sometimes improvised) above a given melody, as above a hymn-tune; *descant recorder*.

Development The section of a movement (as in Sonata-form) between the initial statement of themes and their final recapitulation, during which the themes are developed, i.e., expanded, modified, combined, broken up, etc.

Diatonic Pertaining to a given major or minor key (opposite of Chromatic); so *diatonic scale*, any one of the major or minor scales; *diatonic harmony*, harmony made up predominantly from the resources of the prevailing key, without much use of notes outside its scale, similarly *diatonic discord*, discord arriving from clashes within the key itself. Hence *diatonicism*, a pronounced use of diatonic harmony.

Discant A developed form of the type of medieval part-writing called organum. The most reliable medieval theorists describe it as essentially a homophonic, measured style.

EXHIBIT 17.1
Musical Terms

Absolute (perfect) pitch The recreation of a musical note (sung or played) as a result of an individual working only from ear and memory.

Allegro A musical pace described as lively and quick.

Andante A piece played in medium tempo, at a moderate pace.

Cadenza A brief passage at the end of a musical piece, meant to sound spontaneous.

Castrato The past practice of castrating a young boy to preserve and enhance his natural soprano range.

Chord A blending of two or more notes.

Concerto A musical piece written for a particular instrument and played in three movements with the accompaniment of an orchestra.

Crescendo Music that becomes louder gradually.

Diminuendo Music that slowly becomes softer.

Étude A solo instrumental piece, often performed, but used primarily to improve the technique of a student.

Fortissimo Music that is very loudly played.

Fugue A musical composition in which one or two themes are repeated by different interweaving voices.

Lento Music played slowly.

Madrigal A musical composition written for two or more voices and performed without accompaniment.

Nocturne Literally, "night piece." A melancholy musical composition written for one or more instruments.

Oratorio A religious composition written for a combination of chorus, orchestra, and soloists.

Presto A musical direction that means to play fast, or quickly.

Rhapsody A romantic musical composition, poetic in quality, that usually has only one movement.

Serenade Light listening music, usually played outdoors. Also, music sung by a lover.

Sonata A musical work in three or four movements usually performed by a violin or a cello with piano accompaniment.

Symphony A grand orchestral work in four movements.

Dominant The 5th note of the scale, in relation to the keynote: thus if the key is C (major or minor), the dominant is G. So *dominant seventh*, chord of the (minor) 7th on the dominant (in this case G, B, D, F) resolving normally to the Tonic chord (in this case C major or minor). So also *secondary dominant*, term sometimes encountered as translation of Ger. *Wechseldominante* (literally exchange dominant), meaning the dominant of the dominant, e.g., the note D in key C (major or minor).

Drone Pipe(s) sounding note(s) of fixed pitch continuing as a permanent bass on various forms of bagpipe; hence, a similar effect (drone bass) in other forms of music.

Dufay, Guillaume (before 1400–1474) Franco-Flemish composer, also singer in Papal choir at Rome, 1428–1437; also canon of the Church. In 1440s, in service to the court of Burgundy. Noted teacher, e.g., of Ockeghem. Works include Masses (one on *L'Homme Armé*), other church music (some with accompanying instruments), and chansons.

Dulcimer (1) Type of instrument (old, but still in use for traditional music, as in Eastern Europe), in which strings stretched over a soundboard are struck with hammers. The Hungarian kind, sometimes seen in the concert hall, is the cimbalom; (2) The name given to an American 3-string folk instrument of the zither type ("Appalachian dulcimer"), with strings plucked by the player's right hand.

Dunstable, John (ca. 1390–1453) English composer of European repute (also mathematician and astrologer); spent some time on the Continent. Works, displaying notable melodic invention within smoothly consonant contrapuntal style, include motets and other church music and three-part secular songs. Name also spelled Dunstaple.

Duple time Time in which the primary division is into 2 or 4—e.g., 2/4, 4/4—as distinct particularly from triple time (primary division into 3). Note especially that 6/4 indicates a bar of two dotted half notes, i.e., ♩. + ♩. and 3/2 indicates a bar of three half notes, i.e., ♩ + ♩ + ♩—giving different accents although both total six quarter notes.

Dvořák, Antonín (1841–1904) Czech composer; 1866–1873, viola player in Czech National Theatre orchestra, conducted by Smetana, who influenced him; 1874, became friend of Brahms. Wrote cantata *The Spectre's Bride* for use in England, which he visited 9 times (Mus.D., Cambridge, 1891). Director of Prague Conservatory, 1891; director of the National Conservatory in New York, 1892–1895, composing the *American* string quartet and the symphony no. 9 in E minor (*From the New World*) at this time. Until after World War II this was known as no. 5 and the previous four symphonies were numbered in a chronologically wrong order; in addition there are four earlier symphonies of his that remained unpublished at the composer's death and were not numbered. Current practice is to number all chronologically: 1 in C minor (*The Bells of Zlonice*), 2 in B♭, 3 in E♭, 4 in D minor, 5 in F, 6 in D, 7 in D minor, 8 in G. Wrote also *Slavonic Dances* and *Slavonic Rhapsodies* in a Czech "national" style that also appears in, but does not dominate, his other works. These include piano concerto, violin concerto, cello concerto in B minor (and an-

other early cello concerto), cycle of 3 concert overtures; 10 operas including *Armida* and *The Rusalka; Mass, Requiem;* 4 piano trios; 14 works for string quartet, a piano quintet, etc.; piano pieces and many songs and part-songs.

Electronic music Term applied not to every musical performance or experience involving electronic apparatus, but to a type of composition (increasingly widespread from mid-1950s) in which musical elements are assembled under the composer's direction on recorded tape, the playback of the tape then functioning as performance, no written score being necessary. (A score or diagram or other readable instruction *may*, however, be made.) The original sound sources may be taken from a conventional instrument, a street noise, or whatever, and treated by tape manipulation (this use of "real" sources being formerly termed Concrete music), or may be themselves electronically produced under laboratory conditions. The process may be facilitated by voltage-controlled synthesizer (*see* **Synthesizer**) and by computer. The eventual playback may be subject to modification under concert conditions (*live electronics*). Modern electronic composers include: Laurie Anderson, Philip Glass, Steve Reich, Pauline Oliveros, Luciano Berio, and Milton Babbitt.

Electrophonic (word compounded from modern *electric* + Gk. *phone* sound, as in *monophony*, etc.) Term used to describe technically those instruments of which the notes are transmitted through electronic circuits ending in transducers (e.g., loudspeakers). They may be divided into (1) *electroacoustic*, in which the tone of a conventional instrument, or one slightly modified, is converted into electrical vibrations and then subjected to controlled amplification and modification, e.g. electric guitar (and bass guitar), electric violin, electric piano; (2) *electromechanical*, those with electrostatic, electromagnetic, or photoelectric tone generators, e.g., Compton and certain other electric organs; (3) *electronic*, those with electronic tube tone generators.

Elgar, Edward (1857–1934) English composer, all but self-taught; Roman Catholic, but was much associated with the Three Choirs Festival (based on Anglican cathedrals). The *Enigma Variations* and *The Dream of Gerontius* established him, 1899–1900. Had already written song cycle *Sea Pictures*. Later wrote oratorios *The Apostles* and *The Kingdom* (intended as the first two parts of an uncompleted trilogy); cantata *The Musicmakers;* 2 symphonies, symphonic study *Falstaff*, overtures *Cockaigne* and *In the South*; recitation with orchestra *Carillon; Introduction and Allegro for Strings*; violin concerto, cello concerto, chamber music, etc. The *Severn Suite* for brass band is one of his few post-1919 works. Knighted 1904; Order of Merit, 1911; Master of the King's Music, 1924; baronet, 1931. Evolved a forthright style that won recognition as "national" (although not indebted to folk song), and unashamedly wrote "popular" works, such as the 5 *Pomp and Circumstance* marches.

Enharmonic Description of the difference between, e.g., F♮ and E♯ or D♯ and E♭ —i.e., on the piano and other fixed-note instruments, a difference only of notation, not of pitch; and on other instruments, and voices, possibly a very small change of pitch also, as may be required to adjust to new harmony. Hence *enharmonic change*, the change of a note in a performer's part e.g., from D♯ to E♭; and similarly, *enharmonic modulation*, involving such a change, as in the two top notes bracketed here:

Ensemble (Fr., together) (1) The quality of teamwork in performance ("their ensemble was poor"); (2) an item in opera for several soloists, with or without chorus; (3) a group of performers, the term implying a group of no fixed number, and not so numerous and regularly constituted as to deserve the name of orchestra or choir.

Episode A section in a piece of music considered to have a subordinate role; in particular, (1) in a Rondo, a contrasting section between recurrences of the main theme; (2) in a Fugue, a section occurring between the entries of a subject.

Equal temperament *See* **Temperament**.

Étude Study. An instrumental piece (usually solo), written to demonstrate the facility of the performer in certain techniques, but sometimes having artistic value as well. For example, Chopin composed 3 sets (27 in all) for piano.

Exposition (1) That part of a Sonata-form or similar movement in which the main themes are initially stated before they undergo development; (2) in a Fugue, the initial statement of the subject by all the "voices" in turn.

Expressionism Term borrowed from painting and applied to literature, drama, and music; involving the expression of the artist's state of mind by means of external symbols not necessarily in normal relation to each other. (The application of the term, e.g., to Schoenberg's music, alludes apparently to an extreme *emotionalism* and to a "hard" sound, supposedly opposite to the Impressionism of Debussy's muted, more liquid style.)

Figured bass A standardized notation for continuo, practiced especially in the 17th and 18th centuries, and also used today, e.g., in academic training and as a kind of harmonic shorthand. Figures with a bass note indicate the distance above that bass note of the other notes to be sounded. If the key is C major, e.g., and the bass note is C, the figure 5 would indicate G, and 5♯ would indicate G♯, but the choice of the particular octave in which this G or G♯ is to be placed is left to the musicianship of the performer. Various abbreviations and other conventions are also used. (The chord symbols used in modern pop music, although similar in being a kind of shorthand, are not the same. They are named after chords—major, minor, augmented, etc.—irrespective of which note of these chords comes in the bass; *figured bass* symbols are invariably relative to a particular bass note.)

Fine (It., end) Term sometimes occurring in the middle of music as notated, in conjunction with some instruction at the end of the music type to go back to an earlier point and proceed from there to the point where *fine* occurs.

Flat Term indicating a lowering in pitch, either (1) indeterminately, as when a singer is said to sing flat, by mistake; or (2) precisely by a semitone, as represented by the sign ♭ ; so B♭ (B flat), the note a semitone lower than B♮ (B natural); so also, e.g., C♭ , a notation sometimes called for through adherence to the "grammar" of music, although on the piano, e.g., the note is identical with B♮ (B natural). So *double-flat*; *flat keys*, those having flats in their key signatures, *in three flats*, in the key of E♭ major or C minor, the key signature of which is three flats (and similarly with other keys), flatted seventh, the lowering of the seventh degree of the scale by a semitone.

Florid Term descriptive of melody that is full of Ornaments—whether such are written in by the composer or, as common in 17th- and 18th-century Italian opera, intended to be added at the preference of the performer.

Folk music, song, tune Terms implying that the work concerned has been transmitted aurally among "the people" from one generation to the next and can be ascribed to no particular composer. As this definition suggests, (1) a folk song must be, or have been, "popular," but not every popular song is a folk song; (2) folk song flourishes among a "primitive" population, where music does not generally take a written form, (3) because of aural transmission, a folk song is likely to exist in several differing versions. Folk song, although "national" in character, has tended to show wide international similarities: in particular it has preserved the Modes longer than "composed" music. It is arguable that certain composed and written songs, e.g., Stephen Foster's, have in a sense become folk songs: i.e., they have been transmitted aurally, they circulate in several versions, and the composer's name is unknown to many who know the songs. Note that (1) this definition of folk songs, etc., does not necessarily coincide with the use of parallel words in other languages; e.g., *Volkslied* (Ger.) takes in a wider variety of traditional popular song; (2) the post-1945 revival of what is called "folk" admits many new songs (in traditional style) by named composers, who are often also performers.

Form The layout of a piece of music considered as a succession of sections. A simple song may thus be said to have a *form* consisting of, say, one line, another line, the first line repeated, then another line; a more involved piece may be said to have a *form* corresponding to one of various basic types: *see*, e.g., **Binary**; **Ternary**; **Fugue**; **Sonata-form**; **Variation**; or such a piece may be said to be "free" in form, i.e., unrelated to such a "set" type. Note that *form* as thus conventionally defined takes in only the "horizontal" aspects of music, not the "vertical" (harmony, counterpoint) and does not fully deal with rhythm; it would be better (and more analogous to terminology in, e.g., painting) if *form* were to be defined as taking in these also, i.e., as concerned with the totality of significant relationships between notes.

Fortepiano An early Italian name meaning the same as pianoforte. Its use in English to denote the late 18th-century piano is arbitrary. (*Fortepiano* is, however, the standard Russian word for the normal instrument.)

Frequency Term in acoustics for the number of complete vibrations undergone by an air column or a resonating body in 1 second. The unit of measurement (one cycle per second) is the Hertz, abbreviated Hz. As frequency increases, the pitch of the note sounded is raised, so pitch can be defined by frequency; by international agreement (1939) the A commonly used for tuning (i.e., that above middle C) is fixed at 440 Hz. *See* **Pitch**.

Fugue A type of contrapuntal composition for a given number of parts or "voices" (so-called, whether the work is vocal or instrumental). Hence *fugue in three voices,* a *four-part fugue*, etc. The essential feature of a fugue is the entries of all the voices successively in Imitation of each other. The opening entry is in the tonic key and is called the *subject*; the imitative entry of the next voice, in the dominant, is called the *answer*; similarly with the entries of subsequent voices (if any) alternately. Commonly there are several complete entries of all voices (with the order changed) in the course of a fugue; the complete entries are separated by *episodes*. Commonly also each voice, having announced the *subject* or *answer*, passes to another fixed thematic element called the *countersubject*, the countersubject being heard in the first voice simultaneously with the answer in the second voice, etc. But the great masters of fugue, such as Bach, do not confine the fugue to a strict pattern, although time-wasting academic theorists have done so.

Galliard A lively dance dating back to the 15th century, usually but not always in 3/2 time. It's often contrasted with, and sometimes built from the same musical material as, a Pavan (which is slower). The dance is obsolete, but has been revived, e.g., by Vaughan Williams in *Job*.

Gavotte An old dance in 4/4 time beginning on the third beat of the bar; sometimes (but not always) a constituent of the baroque Suite and occasionally revived in modern times, e.g. by Prokofiev in his *Classical Symphony*.

Gershwin, George (1898–1937) American pianist and composer of many popular songs; extended his range (especially in applying jazz idioms to concert works) in *Rhapsody in Blue* (1924), piano concerto, *Cuban Overture, An American in Paris*, opera *Porgy and Bess*, piano preludes. (The orchestration of *Rhapsody in Blue* is by F. Grofé; of the other works, by Gershwin himself.) Studied with R. Goldmark but was mainly self-taught. Died after an unsuccessful brain operation.

Glissando (mock-It. from Fr. *glisser*, to slide) Sliding up and down the scale, or making a quick uninterrupted passage up or down the scale, as on the piano, harp, xylophone, trombone. The effect of Portamento on stringed instruments is not the same, since it implies only the smooth linking of two notes, not the deliberate sounding of the notes in between.

Gluck, Christoph Willibald [von] (1714–1787) German composer, born in Bavaria but possibly of Bohemian origin; traveled much—London, 1745; Paris, 1773–1779, where his followers opposed those of Piccinni, settled and died in Vienna. Was consciously an operatic reformer, stressing importance of subordinating music to dramatic needs and also dispensing with dry Recitative; his *Alkestis* (1767) has a famous preface expounding his ideas. This opera, like its predecessor *Orpheus* was originally in Italian; both were later revised, with French texts. Other operas include *Iphigenia in Aulis*, *Iphigenia in Tauris*, and *Armida*, all in French. Wrote in all more than 45 stage works; also instrumental pieces, etc.

Grace-note A note considered additional to the melody, inserted as an Ornament.

Graphic notation Term describing certain newer (post-1950) types of musical notation, especially those that pictorialize the action required of the performer or represent duration by comparative length of a printed line or other visual symbol.

Gregorian chant Type of Plainsong associated with Pope Gregory I (otherwise St. Gregory; approximately 540–604), which became standard in the Roman Catholic Church.

Grieg, Edvard Hagerup (1843–1907) Norwegian composer whose Scottish great-grandfather's name was Greig; also pianist, particularly as accompanist to his wife (and cousin) Nina, who sang his songs. Encouraged by Ole Bull, went to study in Leipzig; later, pupil of Gade in Copenhagen. Became "nationalist" in music. At Ibsen's request, wrote music for *Peer Gynt*. Wrote an early symphony; works also include piano concerto, *Holberg Suite* for strings, music to Bjørnson's Sigurd Jorsalfar; choral works: *Bergliot* (text by Bjørnson) for reciter and orchestra; 3 violin sonatas, many songs and piano works, various Norwegian folk music arrangements. Had Norwegian government pension. Often visited Britain; Hon. D.Mus., Cambridge, 1894.

Ground bass A bass pattern that is persistently repeated while upper parts proceed as, for example, in 17th-century England "Divisions on a ground," i.e., a piece in variation-form constructed by this means. (*Compare* **Chaconne**.)

Guido d'Arezzo (approximately 991–after 1033) Italian monk (long resident in Arezzo, hence the name) and musical theorist. Inventor of two devices greatly facilitating the practice of music: (1) the names *ut, re, mi*, etc. (ancestors of modern do, re, mi) as indication of the relative positions of the notes of the scale: *ut* to be either G, C, or F, bottom notes of the hexachords then used; (2) the "Guidonian hand", an aid to memory whereby the tips and joints of the fingers are given the names of various notes.

Handel, George Frideric [form of name adopted in England by Georg Friederich Händel or Haendel] (1685–1759) Composer born at Halle, Germany; first visited England 1710 and was naturalized there in 1727. Precocious musical activity, at first against his father's wishes. Violinist in Hamburg Opera orchestra, 1703. Visited Italy

1706–1710. Wrote Italian operas for London, including *Rinaldo* (his first there), *Alcina, Berenice, Julius Caesar, Orlando*, and *Xerxes*. "Invented" English biblical oratorio with *Esther*, 1732; other oratorios include *Saul, Israel in Egypt, Messiah, Samson, Judas Maccabaeus, Solomon, Susanna, Theodora*, and (last) *Jephtha.* (*See* **Oratorio**.) Other vocal works include *Acis and Galatea, Semele*, and *Alexander's Feast*: 4 coronation anthems including *Zadok the Priest*. Noted harpsichordist and organist; played his organ concertos as intermissions in oratorio. Wrote for orchestra his *Water Music, Fireworks Music*, and works of concerto grosso type (for strings alone and for wind and strings); also composed *The Harmonious Blacksmith* (later so called), other harpsichord pieces, etc. Worked within the prevailing style of his time, based on Italian vocal line. Made some unacknowledged "borrowings" from other composers, and also reused parts of his own works. Became partially blind, 1751; totally so, 1753. Died in London.

George Frideric Handel

Harmonic (noun) Harmonic tone. One of the tones of the Harmonic series. The lowest such tone, or "fundamental," is called the *first harmonic*, the next lowest the *second harmonic*, etc. But in such phrases as "playing in harmonics" on stringed instruments, the allusion is to harmonics with the exclusion of the first—since the first is the "normal" sound requiring no special directions. To obtain these harmonics other than the first, it is necessary to set the string vibrating not as a whole length but in fractional parts of its length. (*See* **Harmonic series**.) A violinist, etc., does this by placing a finger lightly at a given point of a vibrating string: when the string is an open string (i.e., not otherwise fingered) then the result is called a *natural harmonic*, but when the string is a stopped string (one finger used for stopping and another for "lightly placing") then the result is an *artificial harmonic*. The harmonics obtainable on the

harp (also by lightly placing the finger on a vibrating string) are in this sense natural harmonics.

Harmonic series The set of tones (called *harmonic tones* or simply *harmonics*) produced by a vibrating string or air column, according to whether this is vibrating as a unit through its whole length or in fractional parts (1/2, 1/3, 1/4, etc.). Vibration of the whole length gives the lowest ("fundamental") tone, or first harmonic. The other tones, or "upper partials," i.e., the second, third, fourth, and higher harmonics, are at fixed intervals above the fundamental—an octave above it, then a perfect fifth above that, and so on, decreasingly, ad infinitum. If the fundamental is the C in the bass staff, e.g., the series will begin as follows:

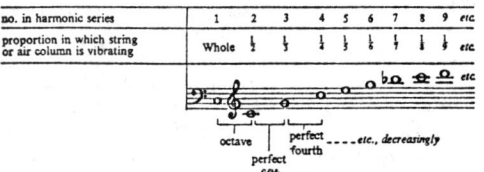

(Not all of these, however, correspond exactly to the notes as tuned in modern European scales.) The importance of the series lies in the following points (among others): (1) the basic technique of brass instruments is to produce the various harmonics by varying the mode of blowing; on, e.g., a bugle this one harmonic series yields all the notes available, but on, e.g., a trumpet and trombone the range is made more complete by use of valves and slide, respectively; (2) the use of the upper partials also forms an important device in string playing (see preceding entry); and these tones are also used on woodwind instruments—in the simplest instance, "blowing harder" on a tin whistle to produce a higher octave means the use of the second harmonic; (3) every note of normal musical instruments consists not of a "pure" tone (like that of a tuning fork) but of a blend of the fundamental and certain upper partials, the precise blend differing between instruments. In fact this difference in blend determines the difference between tone colors of instruments.

Haydn, [Franz] **Joseph** (1732–1809) Austrian composer (not, despite some writers, of Croatian descent). Born at Rohrau; cathedral choirboy in Vienna; became pupil of Porpora; married an unappreciative wife, 1760. Took post with Hungarian noble family of Esterházy, 1761–1790, first at Eisenstadt (Austria) then at Eszterháza (Hungary). Achieved European reputation there, especially for his symphonies and string quartets; he established the now "classical" concept of both these types. Visited Britain 1791–1792 and 1794–1795, presenting in London the last 12 of his 104 catalogued symphonies and also other works; received honorary Oxford degree. Handel's oratorios in London influenced him toward his own *The Creation* and *The Seasons*, written on his return to Vienna, where he died. Nicknames have been given to many of his symphonies (see *Bear, Clock, Drumroll, Farewell, Hen, Horn Signal, Hunt, Imperial, Lamentation, Laudon, London, Maria Theresa*,

Military, Miracle, Morning, Mourning, Oxford, Passion, Philosopher, Queen, Roxolane, Schoolmaster, Surprise) and to his Masses (see *Drum Mass, Creat Organ, Little Organ, Nelson Mass, Wind-Band Mass*), in which he characteristically combines cheerfulness and devotion. Also wrote 2 cello concertos, various other concertos, about 80 string quartets (see *Emperor, Fifths, Frog, Lark, Razor, Tost*), 125 trios with Baryton, more than 20 Italian and German operas (e.g., *Armida, The World of the Moon, Deceit Outwitted*, It. *L'lnfedeltà delusa*); songs, some in English; *Emperor's Hymn*; *The Seven Last Words*; etc. (Very prolific throughout unusually long career.) See *Toy Symphony* for a work mistakenly ascribed to him. Brother of Michael Haydn. Six string quartets called Haydn's op. 3 are now thought to be not by him but by Hoffstetter. His works are indexed by Hob. numbers (Hoboken).

Hindemith, Paul (1895–1963) German composer, formerly violinist and viola player (soloist in first performance of Walton's viola concerto, 1929); teacher in Berlin from 1927. Banned by Nazis as musically "degenerate" (although not Jewish); taught in Turkey from 1933, settled in United States 1939. Noted teacher and theoretician. Composed operas *Mathis the Painter* (on the life of the painter Grünewald) and *The Harmony of the World* (on the life of the astronomer Kepler): he based a symphony on each of these.

Holliday, Billie (Eleanor Gough McKay) (1915–1959) Black American jazz singer of the Harlem Renaissance era. While touring the southern states with Benny Goodman she wrote, *Strange Fruit*, which caused great controversy for being "too political." The title refers to the bodies of lynched blacks she saw from the window while traveling on the bus. Because it was banned in the South, and considered too controversial for airplay in the North, it was removed from future pressings. It only recently has become available. She died of a drug overdose in 1959.

Holst, [originally von Holst] **Gustav** [Theodore] (1874–1934) English composer of partly Swedish descent, pupil of Stanford, at various times pianist, trombonist, teacher (especially at Morley College, London), and conductor of Boston Symphony Orchestra, 1922. Interested in oriental philosophy and made various settings of the Hindu scriptures in his own translations. Bold harmonic experimenter. e.g., in Polytonality; finally cultivated a markedly austere style, e.g., in *Egdon Heath* for orchestra. Other works include operas *At the Boar's Head* (after Shakespeare's *Henry IV*), *The Perfect Fool*, and *Savitri*; *The Planets* for orchestra; *St. Paul's Suite* for strings; choral *Hymn of Jesus* and a *First Choral Symphony* (words by Keats; there is no second); music for military and brass band; songs (4 for voice and violin), etc.

Homophony (from Gk. for same sounding) Term used as opposite of Polyphony, i.e., signifying that (as for instance in an English hymn tune) the parts move together, presenting only a top melody and chords beneath, as distinct from the contrapuntal interplay of different melodies simultaneously. So also *homophonic*; *compare* **Monophony**.

Hornpipe A lively English dance formerly with 3 in the bar, now (as in the well-known *Sailor's Hornpipe* and as in Sullivan's *Ruddigore*) with 2 beats in the bar. The dance was named a "hornpipe" because it was originally accompanied by a pipe made from an animal's horn.

Idée fixe Term used by Berlioz, e.g., in the *Fantastic Symphony*, for what is usually called motto theme.

Idiophone Term used in the scientific classification of instruments to mean "self-sounding," e.g., cymbals, xylophone, whether hit, rattled, stroked, etc. (But drums, in which a membrane is stretched and an airspace is fully or partly enclosed, are Membranophones.)

Imitation A composer's device in part-writing: one voice repeats (if not literally, then at least recognizably) a figure previously stated by another voice. Canon and Fugue employ imitation according to strict and regular patterns.

Impressionism Term borrowed from painting (applied, e.g., to Monet, Degas, Whistler) and used to describe the works, e.g., of Debussy and Ravel insofar as they seem to interpret their titles not in a narrative or dramatic way (like the Romantics) but as though an observer were recording the impression on him or her at a given point. *See also* **Expressionism**.

Improvise (or "extemporize") Perform according to spontaneous fancy, not from memory or from written copy—although often a performer improvises "on" (i.e., around) a given tune. Hence *improvisation*: this term is sometimes also used as title of an actual written piece presumably intended to convey the roving spirit of genuine improvisation.

Indeterminacy The principle, employed by some modernistic composers from the 1950s, of leaving elements of the performance either to pure chance (*see* **Aleatory**) or to the decision of the performer.

Interval The "distance" between two notes, insofar as one of them is higher or lower than the other. Thus the interval from C to the G above it is a fifth, to the A above it a sixth, etc. (These are calculated by counting upward and by including in the count the notes at both extreme ends.) The names fifth, sixth, etc., are themselves further defined: *see* **Perfect**; **Major, minor**. Intervals above an octave (eighth) are called *compound intervals,* being "compounded" of so many octaves plus a smaller interval. Thus the interval from C to the next G above it but one (twelve notes, counting the extremes) is called a twelfth and is a compound interval made of an octave (C–C) and a fifth (C–G).

Intonation Tuning (of pitch); thus a singer's or violinist's intonation is praised if the notes are pitched with a high degree of precision. *See also* **Just intonation**.

Invert Turn upside down; thus (1) a chord not in its "root position" is said to be in one or other *inversion*—*see* **Position** (3); (2) two melodies in counterpoint may be mutually *inverted* by the upper becoming the lower and vice versa (counterpoint capable of making sense under this treatment is called *invertible counterpoint* and forms the stuff of, e.g., Fugue); (3) a single melody may be *inverted* by being performed upside down, i.e., with all its successive intervals applied in the opposite direction. Thus an upward interval of a major third (say D–F♯) when inverted would be replaced by a downward interval of a major third (D–B♭), or by an upward interval of a minor sixth, which would produce the same note (D–B♭) although in a higher octave. A melody so inverted is called the *inversion* of the original, often abbreviated *I* in the theory of twelve-note technique.

Isorhythmic (from Gk., equal-rhythmed) Term applied to certain medieval motets, e.g., by Machaut, of which the rhythms are repeated according to a strict scheme not corresponding to repetition in the melody.

Ives, Charles [Edward] (1874–1954) American composer of music that, all written before 1920, anticipates later devices, e.g., Polytonality, Polyrhythm, quarter-tones. Was organist and choirmaster and had business career, his work being little recognized until his *Concord* piano sonata was played in 1939 and his symphony no. 3 in 1946. Works include 5 symphonies, *Three Places in New England* for orchestra, and songs.

J   **Jazz** American music that grew out of American black idioms such as blues and ragtime. Jazz is characterized by the use of syncopated rhythms; some of them are simple (as in early blues music), others are highly developed and complex (as in bebop music). Instruments typically used by jazz bands include clarinet, drums, trombone, trumpet, electric guitar, and/or piano. The term jazz is now used as an umbrella term, and can mean bebop, swing, ragtime, blues, rhythm and blues, and fusion. Jazz influenced many classical composers such as Satie, Ravel, and Copeland. Famous jazz musicians include Billie Holliday, Dizzy Gillespie, Tommy Dorsey, Fletcher Henderson, Jelly Roll Morton, and Dinah Washington.

Jongleur (Fr., juggler) Medieval wandering minstrel who was singer, instrumentalist (chiefly on a form of fiddle), acrobat, juggler, etc.

Josquin (ca. 1440–1521), in full Josquin des Prez (and other spellings, "Josquin" being properly a diminutive forename). Flemish composer, pupil of Ockeghem, and singer at the Papal Church in Rome. Composed Masses, motets (one on the *Stabal Mater* text), chansons, etc. His work is notable for an expressiveness new at that time: *see* **Musica reservata.**

Just intonation The adoption in performance of the "natural" nontempered scale (*see* **Intonation; Temperament**). This is theoretically possible on voices, bowed-string instruments, etc., in which the pitch of the notes is not mechanically fixed.

K   **K.** Abbreviation (1) of Köchel (in numbering Mozart's works), and (2) of Kirkpatrick (in numbering D. Scarlatti's).

     Key (1) A lever, e.g., on piano, organ, or a woodwind instrument, depressed by finger or foot to produce a note. (2) A classification of the notes of a scale, the most important note called the *keynote* and the others functioning in relation to it. If the keynote is C, then the key may be either C major or C minor, according to whether the major or

minor scale is used basically in the music concerned (*see* **Major, minor**); notes outside the "basic" scale are said to be foreign to the key. The sharps and flats appertaining to the key are displayed in a Key signature, other sharps, flats, and naturals occurring "casually" in the music are written as Accidentals. The major and minor keys were the only two types of note-ordering generally used in Western music between approximately 1600 and 1900; earlier, the Modes prevailed, and later certain composers began to dispense with key altogether (*see* **Atonal**).

Keyboard A continuous arrangement of keys—*see* **Key** (1)—either for the fingers, as on the piano or for the feet, as on the "pedal keyboard" of an organ. So also *keyboard of light*, instrument throwing colors on a screen in Scriabin's *Prometheus*. The term *keyboard* is also used as a general term for a "keyboard instrument," especially in such context, as "Bach's keyboard works," where the works may be suitable for more than one type of keyed instrument.

Key signature The indication in written music of the number of sharps or flats in the prevailing key, such indication normally being placed at the beginning of each line of music (or at any point when the key signature is changed). Thus flat signs on the lines or spaces in the staff denoting B, E, and A indicate that these notes are to be played as B♭, E♭, and A♭ — unless an indication to the contrary is given by an Accidental. Here the key of E♭ major or C minor is indicated, since only these have all these three notes flat (and no others). Thus it is the "natural" form of the minor scale that is used to determine key signature. *See* **Major, minor.**

Kirkpatrick, Ralph (1911–1984) American harpsichordist (also performer on piano and clavichord) whose biography of D. Scarlatti (1953) incorporated a catalogue of Scarlatti's works that has become standard. Thus these works are referred to by their Kirkpatrick or K or Kk numbers. (This has superseded the Longo numbering).

Klavier (Ger.) A piano, harpsichord, or other keyboard instrument. Also spelled *clavier*. For Bach's *Das wohltemperierte Klavier*, *see* **Well-Tempered Clavier The**.

Köchel, Ludwig von (1800–1877) Austrian scholar who compiled a catalogue of Mozart's works (published 1862) that has become standard. Such works are now referred to as K (followed by a number). The German usage is sometimes K.V., for *Köchel-Verzeichnis*, i.e., Köchel Index. (The latest revision of this catalogue was issued in 1964.)

Kodály, Zoltán (1882–1967) Hungarian composer. Collected and edited Hungarian folk songs partly in collaboration with Bartók; developed a strongly national idiom based on these songs, but less harsh and explosive than Bartók's. Achieved a national status as composer, particularly with his *Psalmus Hungaricus* and his opera *Háry János*. Other works include 2 other operas, *Concerto for Orchestra*, symphony, *Dances of Galánta*, variations on Hungarian folk song *The Peacock*, and other orchestral works; *Dances of Marosszek* for piano (afterward orchestrated), *Missa Brevis*, and other choral works; chamber music, songs, etc.

Koto A Japanese plucked stringed instrument of the zither type, usually with 13 strings, placed horizontally and played by three plectrums worn on the thumb and two fingers.

L **Landini, Francesco** [or Landino] (1335–1397) Italian organist, lutenist, and composer (also poet); blind from early childhood. Wrote concerted vocal music of various kinds, and was an exponent of Ars nova. Born, lived, and died in Florence.

Largo (It., broad)   Slow.

Lassus, Roland de (Italianized form, Orlando di Lasso) (ca. 1528–1594)   Flemish composer. Choirboy in Mons, his birthplace; afterwards choirmaster at the Church of St. John Lateran, Rome; worked in Antwerp before serving at the Bavarian court in Munich. He settled there (traveling to Italy, however), and died in Munich. His works, all for two or (usually) more voices, number more than 2,000 and include madrigals and similar works, French, German, and Italian poetry, and religious music: masses, motets, miscellaneous biblical settings in Latin, settings of various texts in Italian, etc. He was preoccupied with such religious settings toward the end of his life.

Leading note   The seventh degree of the major scale, so called because it seems to lead upward to the Tonic a semitone above it. In the minor scale this note (e.g., B ♮ in the key of C minor) is commonly used in ascending but not in descending. *See* **Major**.

Ledger line   Short line written above or below the staff to accommodate notes outside the staff, as in

(This is the correct spelling, but *leger line* is also encountered.)

Leitmotiv (English, leading-motive)   Generally used when speaking of works by Wagner, who assigned specific musical themes (called *leitmotivs*) for characters, places, and situations in his operas. Wagner helpfully arranged these leitmotivs in a book, so that anyone seeing his operas may be able to determine which character is about to enter onstage.

Lent, lento (Fr., It.)   Slow.

Léonin (also Lat., Leoninus)   French composer active about 1163-1190 as church musician in Paris: wrote a cycle of two-part organa for all the principal church feasts of the year.

Libretto (It., booklet)   The text of an opera, or sometimes of an oratorio or other non-stage work. Plural *libretti* (It.) or *librettos* (anglicized).

Lied (Ger., pl. *Lieder*)   Song; specifically, in the non-German-speaking world, the type of song with piano composed by, e.g., Schubert, Schumann, and Wolf. The term is dubiously applied also to songs not in German but of a similar kind, e.g., by Grieg.

Liederkranz, Liederkreis (Ger.)   Song-cycle. *Liederkreis* is used as the actual title of two cycles by Schumann (op. 24, op. 39), to poems by Heine and by Eichendorff (both 1840).

Ligature   (1) A slur mark indicating a group of notes all sung to the same syllable (term sometimes also used in instrumental music when the slur indicates that notes are to be phrased together); (2) on the clarinet, saxophone, etc., the metal band that secures the reed to the mouthpiece.

Liszt, Ferencz [Germanized as Franz] (1811–1886) Hungarian pianist and composer. As child prodigy pianist, visited France and Britain. Lived with the Countess d'Agoult 1833–1844; one of their children (Cosima) later becoming Wagner's wife. From 1848 lived with the Princess Sayn-Wittgenstein, whose eventual effort to secure a divorce from her husband failed; Liszt separated from her in 1861, never married, and in 1865 took minor orders in the Roman Catholic Church and was referred to as "the Abbé Liszt." He revisited London in 1886. He consistently aided new composers from Berlioz to Grieg, and made Weimer a highly important center when he was court musical director there, 1848–1859. His piano works include a sonata (pioneering one-movement form), also *Dante Sonata*, 20 *Hungarian Rhapsodies*, *Mazeppa* (also for orchestra), and other pieces with allusive titles; and many operatic paraphrases, transcriptions of other composers' work, etc. Arranged Schubert's *Wanderer Fantasy* in a version for piano and orchestra. Also composed *The Preludes, Orpheus, Hamlet, Dante Symphony, Faust Symphony, Episodes from Lenau's Faust*, etc., for orchestra; 4 *Mephisto Waltzes*; *Malediction* for piano and orchestra; *Via Crucis* and other church works; more than 70 songs in French, German, Italian, Hungarian, and English (Tennyson's "Go not, happy day"); and much else. Was a bold harmonic innovator, especially in late years. His "Hungarian" music is chiefly of a gypsy, not an authentically peasant, character.

EXHIBIT 17.2
Musical Instruments

Percussion	**Woodwind**	**Stringed**
Snare drum	Oboe	Cello
Bass drum	Flute	Violin
Brass	Piccolo	Bass
French horn	Recorder	
Trombone	Clarinet	

Longo, Alessandro (1864–1945)   Italian pianist and composer who supervised the publication of a complete edition of D. Scarlatti's keyboard works, these being referred to as "Longo No...." or "L...." (followed by a number). This numbering has been superseded by that of Kirkpatrick.

Luening, Otto (b. 1900)   American composer who studied in Munich and in Zurich (pupil of Busoni); was also flutist and conductor. Has made much use of electronic music, e.g., *Fantasy in Space* (flute on tape) and, composed jointly with Ussachevsky, *Poem in Cycles and Bells* for tape and orchestra; earlier, wrote 3 string quartets, serenade for 3 horns and strings, opera *Evangeline*, etc.

Lully, Jean-Baptiste [originally Giovanni Battista Lulli] (1632–1687)   Italian-born composer who was taken in boyhood to France and first worked there as a scullion, then as a violinist. Went into service of Louis XIV, 1652, naturalized French, 1661; achieved the supreme musical position at court, 1662. Himself a dancer, collaborated with Molière in comedy ballets, including *Le Bourgeois Gentil-homme*; from 1673 wrote operas including

Alceste and *Armida*. Wrote also church music, dance music, etc., and established the "French Overture." A brilliant intriguer; obtained a monopoly of opera production in France; made a fortune by speculation; injured his foot with the long staff he used for beating time on the floor, and died of the resulting abscess.

Lyric (1) Strictly, relating to vocal performance with the lyre, i.e., sung; hence *lyric drama*, occasional synonym for opera (especially in French, as *drame lyrique*); hence also *the lyric stage*, i.e., the operatic stage; (2) of a poem, not epic, not dramatic, but fairly short and expressing the writer's own feelings; hence (term taken over from poetry into music) *Lyric Piece* (Grieg), *Lyric Suite* (A. Berg), etc.; (3) as vocal description, e.g., *lyric soprano, lyric tenor*, term indicating intermediate vocal "weight" between light and "dramatic" (heavy); (4) *lyrics*, as noun, the words of a song in a musical, etc.; so *lyricist*, writer of such lyrics.

M MacDowell, Edward [Alexander] (1860–1908) American composer, also pianist. Trained in France and Germany. Wrote many short piano pieces, somewhat after Grieg's manner, which once had wide popularity; also 2 piano concertos, *Hamlet and Ophelia* and other symphonic poems, songs, etc. The MacDowell Colony, a peaceful working place for composers and other artists, in New Hampshire, was organized in his memory.

Machaut, Guillaume de [also Machault] (ca. 1300–1377) French composer, also poet and priest, latterly Canon of Rheims. Considered the chief exponent of Ars nova in France. His Mass for 4 voices is almost the earliest surviving polyphonic mass. Composed also other vocal music to religious and secular texts, some to a very intricate scheme of construction (*see* **Isorhythmic**, a term applying to some of his work).

Madrigal (1) A 16th–17th century type of contrapuntal composition for several voices, originating in Italy but flourishing also in England—mostly self-contained in vocal texture, but some later examples (e.g., by Monteverdi) having independent instrumental accompaniment. The words are usually secular, chiefly amorous, although some *madrigali spirituali* (sacred) exist; (2) term also used for the Italian forerunner of the above type, from the 14th century (after which the term fell out of use until revived as above); (3) term also used in various looser senses, e.g., the so-called madrigals in operettas by Sullivan and German, which pay homage to an older manner without reviving it.

Maestro (It., master) Title given in Italy to recognized conductors and composers (and used in the United States as a loose honorific for conductors). The *maestro al cembalo* was the musician who in the 18th century and thereabouts directed concerts or operas while playing the harpsichord; so also *maestro di cappella*, the musical director of a chapel, a prince's establishment, etc. (but not used today in such a wide sense as its German equivalent, *Kapellmeister*).

Mahler, Gustav (1860–1911) Austrian (Bohemian-born) composer; also noted conductor Vienna Opera, 1897–1907. Jewish, but became Roman Catholic.

Attended Bruckner's university lectures and admired him, but was never a direct pupil; his own music, of an intensely expressive and chromatically inclined type, is incidentally regarded as the forerunner of Schoenberg's and thus of twelve-tone music. Most of his works have a literary or other nonmusical link. Wrote 9 completed symphonies notable for length, large forces used, highly individual orchestration, and some employment of progressive tonality. Nos. 2 (*Resurrection*), 3 and 8 (*Symphony of a Thousand*) employ vocal soloists and chorus, no. 4 a soprano soloist. No. 10, left unfinished, was completed by Deryck Cooke and first performed entirely in this form in 1964. The *Song of the Earth*, although formally a song cycle with orchestra, is also of symphonic dimensions. Wrote also cycles *Songs of a Wayfarer* and *Songs on the Death of Children*, both with orchestra, and other songs; little else.

Major, minor Terms contrasting with one another and having various musical applications. (1) Scales. The *major* scale of C (i.e., treating the note C as its point of repose) is

C D E F G A B C

(and the same notes descending). The *minor* scale is divided for theoretical purposes into three types, of which the *natural minor* scale of C is

C D Eb F G Ab Bb C

(and the same notes descending). The *melodic minor* scale of C differs in its ascending and descending forms:

C D Eb F G A B C

C Bb Ab G F Eb D C

The *harmonic minor* scale of C is

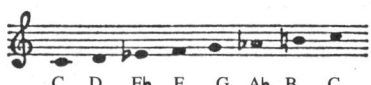

C D Eb F G Ab B C

(and the same notes descending). Similarly with scales beginning on the other notes; i.e.. all major scales are internally alike, the distances (Intervals) between successive notes being the same, although the note of starting differs. All scales belonging to one of the three types of minor scale are, similarly, alike.

(2) Keys. The Key of *C major* is that in which the notes of the scale of C major are treated as "normal," other notes entering only for special purpose. The

key of *C minor* bears a like relation to the scale of C minor: but, although there are three types of minor scale, there is only one type of minor key (the three types of scale corresponding to different aspects of it). The Key signature of a minor key is determined by the *natural minor* scale (above); e.g., for C minor it is three flats (B♭, E♭, A♭):

3) Chords. A *major* or *minor* chord is one that, being built out of the major or minor scale, may serve to identify that scale. More particularly, the *common chord of C major*, or just *chord of C major*, or *C-major triad* means the notes, C, E, G—as contrasted with the *common chord of C minor* (*chord of C minor, C-minor triad*). C, E♭, G. (4) Intervals. The intervals second, third, sixth, and seventh are classified as either *major* or *minor*, the latter a semitone less than the former. Thus, measuring upward from C, the major and minor intervals (in that order) are: second, C–D, C–D♭; third, C–E, C–E♭; sixth, C–A, C–A♭; seventh, C–B, C–B♭. Likewise, of course, measured upward or downward from any other note.

Mannheim school   Name given by modern historians to a group of mid-18th century composers centered at the court of Mannheim (Germany) and notable for (1) the cultivation of a type of symphony forerunning the classical (Haydn-Mozart) type: (2) refinement of orchestral technique—the clarinet and the controlled orchestral crescendo supposedly making here their first entry into this type of music. The founder of the school is generally considered to be J.W. Stamitz, a Bohemian; the other members (including F.X. Richter) were all either Bohemian or Austrian, except for Toeschi, an Italian.

Martenot   Convenient English name for the instrument otherwise called '"Martenot Waves" (Fr., *Ondes Martenot*), after its French inventor, Maurice Martenot (1898–1980). It is an Electronic instrument sounding only one note at a time, played with a keyboard. Brought out in 1928, it has achieved occasional usage as a solo and orchestral instrument, e.g., by Honegger in *Joan of Arc at the Stake*.

Mass   Form of religious service that, although occasionally found in other ecclesiastical contexts, is chiefly important as the principal service of the Roman Catholic Church; High Mass is sung, Low Mass said. The musical setting of the "Proper" of the Mass, varying with the occasion, has normally been left to the traditional plainsong—except for the Requiem Mass, to which new settings have been frequently composed. The unvarying part, called the "Ordinary" or "Common" of the mass and consisting of 5 sections (Kyrie, Gloria, Credo, Sanctus with Benedictus, and Agnus Dei), has been frequently set in the Latin text, which was in universal use until the decrees of the Second Vatican Council took effect in the 1970s. Such settings of the Ordinary are usually called simply (e.g.) *Mass in C* (Beethoven's early setting), or they may have titles or nicknames (e.g., Haydn's *Nelson Mass*) for ease of identification. Bach's so-

called Mass in B minor was not so named by him (nor is it preponderantly in B minor).

Mediant   Name for the third degree of the scale, e.g. E in C major—so called because it stands midway between the tonic (or keynote) and dominant, i.e., between the first and fifth degrees. *Compare* **Submediant**.

Melisma (Gk., song; pl. *melismata*)   A group of notes sung to a single syllable. (Term also sometimes applied more loosely, to any florid vocal passage in the nature of a cadenza). *Melismata* is also the title of a collection of English vocal pieces published by T. Ravenscroft in 1611.

Melody   A succession of notes varying in pitch and having a recognizable musical shape. Thus the three "dimensions" of music are often thought of as (1) melody, (2) rhythm, (3) harmony and counterpoint. The term is also used as a title for certain rather simple pieces, e.g., *Melody in F*, the almost sole survivor of Anton Rubinstein's piano solos, being no. 1 of *Two Melodies*, op. 3 (1853).

Membranophone   Term used in the scientific classification of instruments for those in which a stretched skin (or something similar) is set in vibration, by stick or otherwise, e.g. drums.

Mendelssohn [Bartholdy], [Jakob Ludwig] **Felix** (1809–1847)   German composer, a grandson of the Jewish philosopher Moses Mendelssohn, but was brought up as a Lutheran. Noted pianist and organist; also conductor, head of Leipzig Conservatory (1843), and amateur painter. Born in Hamburg; boy prodigy, composing the overture to *A Midsummer Night's Dream* at 17 (the other music to it later). Visited Scotland, 1829 (see *Scotch Symphony*, *Hebrides*) and afterward revisited Britain nine times, conducting the first performance of Elijah in 1846. Other works include operetta *Son and Stranger*; oratorio *St. Paul*; 5 symphonies (no. 2 *Hymn of Praise*, no. 3 *Scotch*, no. 4 *Italian*, no. 5 *Reformation*); *Ruy Blas* and other overtures; 2 piano concertos; violin concerto in E minor (a youthful concerto in D minor, left in manuscript, was resuscitated by Menuhin) and string octet (scherzo later scored for orchestra) and other chamber music; *Songs Without Words* and other piano solos; organ works, songs. Combined Romantic ardor with a classical decorousness of form, but did not fulfill all his early promise, and in the 20th century underwent a severe decline in popularity.

Menotti, Gian-Carlo (b. 1911)   Italian-born composer living mainly in the United States since 1928, but latterly in Scotland. Has won international success as composer of operas (with his own librettos) in a "realistic" vein sometimes reminiscent of Puccini's (*see* **Verismo**). These include *Amelia Goes to the Ball*, with libretto originally in Italian, and successors, nearly all in English, including *The Old Maid and the Thief*, *The Medium*, *The Telephone*, *The Consul*, *Amahl and the Night Visitors* (for television), *Maria Golovin*, *The Last Savage*, *Help, help, the Globolinks!*, and *Martin's Lie* (for church performance, mainly with child performers); also *The Unicorn, The Gorgon, and the Manticore*, sung offstage, mimed onstage; has also written piano

MUSIC

Gian-Carlo Menotti

concerto, etc. Acts as stage director for his operas, and directed the film of *The Medium*. Founder-director of music festival at Spoleto, Italy, 1958.

Messiaen, Olivier [Eugène Prosper Charles] (1908–1992)   French composer and also organist and writer on music. Member of the former "Young France" group. Influenced by Indian music, and cultivated great rhythmical complexity. Used almost literal orchestral imitation of bird song in various works, including *The Awakening of the Birds* for piano and orchestra. Had also written various works with Roman Catholic associations, including church music, *Visions of the Amen* for 2 pianos, *Twenty Looks at the Child Jesus* for one piano; also songs, organ works, etc.

Meter   Term used in prosody to cover the relationship between accented and unaccented beats, and sometimes similarly used in music; e.g., 3/8 and 6/8 being ascribed as different kinds of *meters*. Usually the term Rhythm is so defined as to cover this relationship along with others, but some writers define *rhythm* and *meter* as mutually exclusive, *meter* concerned with the basic unvarying pulse (as above) and *rhythm* with the actual time patterns of notes effected by the composer with reference to this basic pulse. The usage "common meter," etc., with reference to hymns, alludes to the verse, not to the music.

Metronome   Apparatus for sounding an adjustable number of beats per minute. The one commonly in use is that patented in 1814 by J.N. Maelzel (1772–1838), who stole the invention from D.N. Winkel. There is also a pocket type consisting simply of an adjustable pendulum. A composer wishing for 60 quarter-note beats in 1 minute writes "M.M. [Maelzel's Metronome] ♩= 60." Metronome marks for early works are added by modern editors.

Meyerbeer, Giacomo [originally Jakob Liebmann Meyer Beer] (1791–1864)   German composer of opera in Italian, German, and especially French, including *Robert the Devil, The Huguenots, The Prophet, The African Woman* (*L'Africaine*). These are noted for spectacle and for a striking use of the orchestra. Visited Italy; settled in Paris 1826 and died there, was also active in Berlin from 1842 as musical director to the King of Prussia. Also wrote church music, marches, songs, etc.

Microtone   An interval smaller than a semitone. (An alternative name is "fractional tone.") Quarter tones have been systematically exploited by A. Hába and other Czechs and have also had occasional use in more "orthodox" contexts, e.g., the string parts of Bloch's chamber music; see also Carrillo (whose experiments in this field have extended to much smaller intervals) and Ohana.

Milhaud, Darius (1892–1974)   French composer, born at Aix-en-Provence; became a member of the group of composers called the Six. Associated with various important literary figures, especially Claudel (opera *Christopher Columbus*, play *Proteus*, and other works), and Cocteau (ballets, etc.). Visited Brazil and the United States, and influenced by jazz as early as 1922–1923 (ballet *The Creation of the World*) and also by Latin American music (see *Scaramouche*). Notable exponent of Polytonality. Very prolific composer. His other works include operas *Bolivar* and *David*; an arrangement of *The Beggar's opera* in French; 18 symphonics, one for wordless chorus with oboe and cello; various concertos, one for a marimba-and-vibraphone player; 18 string quartets, of which nos. 14–15 can be played separately or together; Jewish liturgical music; many songs. In the United States during World War II and frequently afterward.

Minnesinger (Ger., sing. and pl.; also as English word)   Type of minstrel flourishing in guilds in 12th- and 13th-century Germany. By social origin these singers were aristocratic; the mastersingers who flourished afterward were of the merchant class.

Minor   Term opposed to "major" and applied to scales, keys, chords, and intervals; for all these usages *see* **Major, minor**.

Mode   A name used for scales that essentially move one octave on the keyboard using only the white keys. The modes in common use during the Middle Ages were:

$$
\begin{array}{rcl}
D-D &=& \text{Dorian} \\
E-E &=& \text{Phrygian} \\
F-F &=& \text{Lydian} \\
G-G &=& \text{Mixolydian} \\
A-A &=& \text{Aeolean} \\
C-C &=& \text{Ionian}
\end{array}
$$

These modes were revised 3 times: In the 4th century by St. Ambrose, in the 6th century by St. Gregory, and by Henry of Glarus in the 16th century. In modern music, modes are employed to evoke a "high church" feel to music.

Moderato (It.)   At a moderate pace. It is also used after another tempo direction, e.g., *allegro moderato*, implying a moderate allegro, i.e., that the word *allegro* is not to be taken in an extreme sense.

Modulate   To change from one key to another in the course of a composition, such a change being accomplished by "continuous" musical means (i.e., not simply by starting afresh in another key) and having a definite validity in the structural organization of the music. Hence *modulation*.

Monody (from Gk. for single song)   Term used to describe the melody and Continuo style of writing (e.g., in early 17th-century Italian opera) in contrast to the earlier polyphonic style when all parts were held as of equal importance (none simply as accompaniment). So also *monodic*.

Monophony (from Gk. for single sound)   Term used of music with a single line of melody (with neither harmonic support nor other melodies in counterpoint). It is sometimes also used even when a simple accompaniment is present, provided that the melody is self-sufficient. So also *monophonic*. *Compare* **Homophony**; **Polyphony**.

Monteverdi, Claudio (1567–1643)   Italian composer, notable in the history of opera, harmony, and orchestration. Choirboy at his birthplace. Cremona: afterward held various state and church musical positions in Mantua and elsewhere—finally in Venice, where he died. Became a priest, 1632. His operas (usually considered history's first major operas) include *Orpheus, The Combat of Tancred and Clorinda, The Return of Ulysses to his Country*, and (when he was 75) *The Coronation of Poppaea*, known in various modern editions. Some other operas are lost. Wrote also more than 250 madrigals (some with independent instrumental parts; *see* **Madrigal**), including a few *madrigali sprituali* (to religious words); masses, 2 settings of the Magnificat, and other vocal works with varying accompaniment—and often with "daringly" expressive harmony. Wrote no purely instrumental works.

Moog, Robert (b. 1934)   Inventor of Synthesizer named after him.

Motet   (1) Normal current use, type of church choral composition, usually in Latin, to words not fixed in the liturgy; corresponding in the Roman Catholic service to the Anthem (in English) in the Anglican service; (2) exceptionally, type of work related to the preceding but not exactly conforming to it, e.g., Parry's *Songs of Farewell* (designated by the composer as *motets*), which are choral and "serious" but not ecclesiastical; (3) Medieval use, a vocal composition defined not so much by its function as by its particular form—it was based on a "given" (not newly composed) set of words and melody to which were added one or more melodies (with other words) in counterpoint. Sometimes, even in works for church use, the given melody was taken from a secular song. The motet in this sense superseded the conductus, being in a freer style.

Motif (Fr.)   Term sometimes used in English for leading motive and sometimes simply for *theme*, etc.; better avoided because of its ambiguities.

Motion   Term used to describe the course upward or downward of a melody or melodies. A single melody is said to move by *conjunct motion* or *disjunct motion* according to whether a note moves to an adjacent note or to some other note (i.e., by a "step" or by a "leap"). Apart from this, two melodies move by *similar motion* (in the same direction, i.e.,

up or down together), or by *contrary motion* (one up, one down), or by *oblique motion* (one remaining on the same note, the other not). *Parallel motion* is similar motion of such a kind that the parts not only move up and down together, but do so "in parallel," preserving the same interval between them.

Motiv, motive (Ger., Eng.)   A short recognizable melodic or rhythmic figure; term used especially to indicate the smallest possible subdivision in musical analysis, one Theme possibly having several *motives*. But the term Leading motive conveys a larger type of unit and a different meaning.

Movement   The primary self-contained division of a large composition, usually each having a separate indication of speed, hence the name. A large composition without any such division is said to be "in one movement." The word is used as a title in Stravinsky's *Movements for Piano and Orchestra* (short work in 5 sections, 1958–1959).

Wolfgang Amadeus Mozart

Mozart, Wolfgang Amadeus [christened Joannes Chrysostomus Wolfgangus Theophilus] (1756–1791)   Austrian composer, born in Salzburg. His father took him and his sister on tour to Paris, London, etc., chiefly as harpsichord prodigies, in 1763–1766. He had already begun to compose (including opera *Bastien and Bastienne*); by 1773, he had thrice visited Italy and had entered the service of the Prince Archbishop of Salzburg. Disliked this and left it after a quarrel, 1781, settling in Vienna. Visited Prague (where *Don Giovanni* and *The Clemency of Titus* were produced), Berlin, and elsewhere; died, poor, in

Vienna, of typhus. Other operas include *Idomeneo, Abduction from The Seraglio, The Impresario, The Marriage of Figaro, Cosi Fan Tutte, The Magic Flute.* Also wrote up to 28 concertos for piano, 1 for clarinet and various others, more than anyone else establishing classical concerto form. (Four further, juvenile piano concertos are arrangements of others' music.) His symphonies (including those nicknamed *Haffner, Linz, Prague, Paris, Jupiter*) have been numbered up to 41, but some of these are spurious and some other works of this kind are not so numbered. Composed various serenades; *A Musical Joke*; 24 string quartets (some nicknamed, e.g., *Prussian Quartets*), 1 clarinet quintet, 6 string quintets, and other chamber works; sonatas for violin and for harpsichord (or piano); *Requiem* (unfinished, completed by Süssmayr), 17 masses, some works for Masonic use, isolated arias with orchestra and songs with piano. Some works are misattributed to him. His compositions are indexed by K. numbers.

Multimedia   Term applied to mixtures of musical, visual, poetic, and other events as practiced by such composers as Berio and Lejaren Hiller, mainly from the early 1960s—often incorporating electronic means and excluding traditional "mixtures," such as opera and ballet.

Music   (1) "An arrangement of, or the art of combining or putting together, sounds that please the ear" (*Chambers Essential English Dictionary*, 1968); (2) as in "Master of the Queen's Music," an old English name for a band of musical performers.

Musica ficta (Lat., feigned music)   In old music (up to 16th century) the practice of treating certain notes in performance as though they were marked with flat or sharp signs. This practice was necessary to avoid certain harmonic anomalies that would otherwise result in polyphonic writing and was carried out by performers according to the recognized conventions of the period. Editors of old texts for modern usage now write in the alterations necessary.

Musica reservata (Lat., reserved music)   Term originating in the early 16th century of which the exact meaning is now unknown: applied to the expressive style associated with Josquin and to the manner of performance appropriate to it and thought to refer to (1) the maintenance of rules governing proper musical interpretation of emotions, and (2) the "reserving" of music to connoisseurs of the new style. The term has been borrowed as the name of a London ensemble devoted mainly to Renaissance and early baroque music, giving its first performances in 1960.

Music-drama   Term used by Wagner to describe his operas after *Lohengrin*, as he considered the term "opera" itself to be inadequate or inappropriate to his intended new type of drama set to continuously expressive music based on leading-motives (as distinguished from the old division into operatic "numbers").

Musicology   Musical scholarship: A 20th century word useful in such contexts as "to study musicology," implying an academic discipline different from that in "to study music." So also *musicologist* (usually implying someone whose activity is more "learned" than that of a mere critic), *musicological*, etc.

Mussorgsky, Modest Petrovich (1839–1881) Russian composer; at first army officer, later a civil servant, but studied briefly as a young man with Balakirev. (Both were members of The Mighty Handful, the group of 5 "nationalist" composers.) Expressed sympathy with "the people" and showed it in various works, including his masterpiece, the opera *Boris Godunov*. Evolved, partly from Russian speech inflection, a highly individual musical idiom misunderstood by many contemporaries—Rimsky-Korsakov "correcting" (misleadingly) much of his work after his death and fathering on him a piece called *Night on the Bare Mountain*. His other works include unfinished operas *The Kovanschina Affair, The Fair of Sorochinsk*, and *The Marriage: Pictures at an Exhibition* for piano (orchestrated by others); many songs including *Songs and Dances of Death*. Died after alcoholic epileptic fits.

Mute   A contrivance to reduce the volume of an instrument and/or modify its tone: on bowed instruments, a pronged damper placed at the bridge: on brass instruments, an object of wood, metal, or fiber (there are various types) placed in the bell. To depress the soft pedal of a piano or to muffle a drum is also in effect to apply a mute. (So also *to mute*, as verb.)

N   **Nationalism, nationalist**   Terms applied to music that (usually through elements dervied from folk music) suggests supposed national characteristics. The terms are particularly applied to the work of such 19th-century composers as Smetana, Liszt, Balakirev, and Grieg, with the implication of national "emancipation" from the domination of German-Austrian musical concepts. Also, The Mighty Handful (five Russian composers: Balakirev, Borodin, Cui, Mussorgsky, and Rimsky-Korsakov) took up a consciously nationalist standpoint in music, drawing much on Russian history, literature, folk music, and folklore generally.

Natural   (1) Of a note or key, not sharp or flat: designated by the sign ♮; (2) of a horn, trumpet, etc., not having valves, keys, or other mechanism, and so producing only the notes of the Harmonic series as determined by the length of the tube; (3) a type of "harmonics" in string-playing—*see* **Harmonic**.

Neoclassic(al), neoclassicism   Terms used of a trend in musical style manifesting itself particularly in the 1920s. Its characteristics include preference for small rather than large instrumental forces; use of concerto grosso technique; emphasis on contrapuntal values; avoidance of "emotionalism." In the hands of Stravinsky, Hindemith, and others this had analogies, with Bach's rather than Mozart's (the so-called Viennese classical) period and might be better labeled *neobaroque*. See **Baroque**; **Classic(al)**.

Neum(e)   Generic name for each of the various signs in medieval musical notation (superseded by modern staff notation) showing the note(s) to which a syllable of vocal music was to be sung. As surviving in plainsong notation, the *neums* give precise indication of pitch; but, originally, from the 7th century, they were only approximate reminders of the shape of the melody.

Nocturne A night piece: (1) generally, in Italian, *notturno*, 18th-century composition of serenade type for several instruments in several movements; (2) short lyrical piece, especially for piano, in one movement—a sense originated by Field, and adopted by Chopin; (3) term applied at the composer's fancy—e.g., to the third movement of Vaughan William's *A London Symphony*, which is headed *Scherzo (Nocturne)*, and in Britten's song cycle with orchestra (1958) entitled *Nocturne*.

Obbligato (It., obligatory) Term used for an instrument having a compulsory, unusual, and special role; e.g., song with flute *obbligato* (where *obbligato* is really an adjective qualifying flute). It should be noted (1) that, by contrast, "flute ad lib." would imply optional, not compulsory, use of the instrument; (2) that occasionally the word *obbligato* is encountered actually meaning *ad lib.*—quite wrongly; (3) that the spelling is not "obligato".

Obrecht, Jacob [latinized as Obertus] (approximately 1451–1505) Netherlandish composer who worked mainly in Flanders but also visited Italy and died of plague there. Wrote masses, motets, and secular songs, showing some emotional characteristics foreshadowing the expressive art of Josquin.

Ockeghem, Jean de [or Okeghem] (ca. 1410–1497) Flemish composer, in service to the French court; also visited Spain. Of great influence; called "the Prince of Music" in his own day; his pupils included Josquin. Wrote masses and motets, sometimes chosing a secular tune as cantus firmus; also wrote French chanson.

Octave The interval that is considered as having eight (Lat., *octo*) steps, counting both the bottom and top notes; according to our notation, notes an octave apart from each other have the same letter names, the note an octave above A being also called A, etc. This naming corresponds to the fact that notes an octave apart seem to the ear like the same note sounded at different pitches, not like entirely different notes. Strictly, the interval from A to the next A above is the *perfect octave*; from A up to A♭ and from A up to A♯ are respectively the *diminished* and *augmented octave*. Thus also *double octave*, two octaves; *at the octave*, (performed) an octave higher than written; *in octaves*, (performed) with each note double one or more octaves above or below; *octave coupler*, device on organ or harpsichord whereby the note struck is doubled an octave higher (sometimes called *superoctave coupler*, to distinguish from *suboctave coupler* doubling at the octave below); *octave key*, finger lever on woodwind instruments giving player access to a higher octave.

Opera (1) obsolete, opus; (2) a company performing opera as defined below; so *Vienna State Opera*, etc.; or an opera house itself, e.g., the Opéra (building) in Paris, opened in 1875; (3) principal meaning, type of drama in which all or most characters sing and in which music constitutes a principal element having its own unity. The first works properly so classified are those arising in Italy about 1600. Various synonyms or near synonyms for the term opera are to be met, their precise significance often depending on historical context. The apparent subdivisions of opera have seeming inconsistencies that are similarly to be resolved only by their differing historical contexts.

Opera buffa (It.) A comic opera, particularly the 18th-century Italian kind as represented by Pergolesi's *The Maid as Mistress*.

Opera seria (It.) Term literally signifying "serious opera," as opposed to *opera buffa*, but used particularly for a specific type of opera flourishing in the 18th century and up to Rossini's *Semiramis* (1823), for example. This type is characterized by (1) an Italian libretto; (2) a heroic or mythological plot; (3) formality in music and action; (4) often, leading roles for Castrato singers.

Opus (Lat. a work: abbr. op.) Term used, with a number, for the enumeration of a composer's works, supposedly in the order of their composition. If an "opus" comprises more than one piece, a subdivision may be used ("Opus 40, No. 2"). Occasionally the letters *a* and *b* are used to indicate different but equally valid versions of the same work. Confusion arises because various composers have (a) failed to number their works, (b) numbered only some and not others, (c) allowed their works to appear with numbers not representing their real order of composition.

Oratorio (1) Type of musical composition (originating about 1600 in performances at the Oratory of St. Philip Neri in Rome, hence the name) consisting of an extended setting of a religious text set out in more or less dramatic form—usually for soloists, chorus, and orchestra; originally requiring scenery, costumes, and action, but later customarily conceived and given in concert form; (2) term also used for a type of work similar to the above but on a nonreligious, although usually "elevated" subject; e.g., Handel's *Semele*, Tippett's *A Child of Our Time*, and certain Soviet Russian works to patriotic texts.

EXHIBIT 17.3
Vocal Ranges

Alto Usually a voice tone associated with young boys, alto is the shortened form of contralto, a female vocal range.

Baritone A male voice with a range between tenor and bass; middle range.

Bass Lowest tone of male singers.

Castrato Term used to describe male singers who had been castrated at an early age in order to preserve their naturally high soprano voice. The last remaining castrato died in the 1930s.

Coloratura soprano Light rapid voice quality, considered virtuoso singing.

Contralto Lowest female singing range.

Falsetto A voice used by a man to imitate a woman's voice, often for humorous effect.

Mezzo A medium-range voice, neither loud nor soft.

Mezzo soprano A woman's voice with a range between soprano and contralto.

Tenor Highest male singing range.

Orchestra A numerous mixed body of instrumentalists. As a more or less stable institution, the orchestra originated in early 17th-century opera, being afterward continually modified (obsolete instruments being replaced by new ones), enlarged, and resystematized. So *symphony orchestra*, standard large orchestra of 19th and 20th centuries, able to play symphonies, etc., as opposed, e.g., to *chamber orchestra* (small size) or *string orchestra* (strings only). The term *theater orchestra* customarily indicates not an opera orchestra (which is ideally of "symphonic" size) but a smaller orchestra used for musicals, etc., commonly including saxophones. A combination of wind instruments only, or any combination for dancing to, is commonly called not an orchestra but a band—the occasional 20th century use of *dance orchestra* being pretentious. Note that *philharmonic orchestra*, unlike symphony orchestra, is not a type of orchestra. Although composers may vary both the kind and numbers of instruments used (variety being especially noticeable in the percussion section), the forces standardized by the requirements of 20th-century (and late 19th-century) symphonic music are found in Exhibit 17.4.

EXHIBIT 17.4
Orchestral Instruments

Woodwind:	3 flutes, 1 doubling piccolo
	3 oboes, 1 doubling English horn
	3 clarinets, 1 doubling bass clarinet
	3 bassoons, 1 doubling contra-bassoon
Brass:	4 (sometimes 6) horns
	3 trumpets
	3 trombones (2 tenor, 1 bass)
	1 tuba
Percussion:	3 kettledrums (1 player)
	snare drum, bass drum, cymbals, gong, triangle, xylophone, vibraphone, etc. (2 or more players)
Unclassified:	2 harps
	1 piano
Strings:	first violins (about 14)
	second violins (about 14)
	violas (about 12)
	cellos (about 10)
	double basses (about 8)

Such works as Tchaikovsky's symphony no. 6 (1893), Elgar's symphony no. 1 (1908), Bartók's *Concerto for Orchestra* (1944), and Shostakovich's symphony no. 15 (1972) could all be encompassed by these forces. The order is that observed in conventional modern printing of a score, except that there is no standard order in percussion.

Orchestration The art of writing suitably for an orchestra, band, etc.; or of scoring for these a work originally designed for another medium. So *orchestrate*, *orchestrator*.

Orff, Carl (1895–1982) German composer, chiefly for the stage; also conductor, editor of old music, and musical educator. A specially devised educational range of percussion instruments bears his name, and his own music is also conspicuous for the use of percussion. His works include the operas *The Clever Girl* (*Die Kluge*), *The Moon*, *Oedipus the Tyrant*, *Antigone*, and others; incidental music to *A Midsummer Night's Dream*; scenic choral works, *Carmina Burana*, *Catulli Carmina* (Lat., *Songs of Catullus*), *Trionfo di Afrodite* (It., *Triumph of Aphrodite*) The last three are grouped as *Trionfi* (*Triumphs*), the second having an orchestra consisting solely of percussion including 4 pianos.

Organ (1) Keyboard instrument in which wind is blown by a bellows through pipes to sound the notes; made in various sizes down to the medieval "portative", i.e., portable, carried by the player. Tone is varied by the selection and combination of different stops on different keyboards; a pedal keyboard, originating in Germany before 1500, has gradually become standard as well as up to 5 (very rarely more) manual keyboards. These 5 are called choir, great, swell, solo, and echo (reading upward), but it is common to find only two (great, swell) or three (choir, great, swell). The 19th and 20th centuries have not only brought mechanical improvements, e.g., electricity to work the bellows, but have also much increased the power and variety of organs—not necessarily with comparable artistic gain. The *extension organ* or *unit organ*, a type of organ built for economy of space and expense. (2) Term for each component tone-producing part of the instrument described above. e.g., the *great organ*, *pedal organ*, meaning the great and pedal keyboards plus the pipes controlled by them and the appropriate machinery. (3) Term for an instrument controlled by keyboard, and imitative of the organ as described above, but pipeless, e.g., reed organ, Hammond organ.

Ostinato (It., obstinate) A persistently repeated musical figure or rhythm; also *basso ostinato*, a bass having this characteristic, or a ground bass. (The term *pizzicato ostinato* in the third movement of Tchaikovsky's *Symphony No. 4*, as an exception, means only "persistent pizzicato" not implying repetition.)

Overture (1) Piece of orchestral music preceding an opera or oratorio; since Gluck, usually musically allusive to what follows; (2) similar piece preceding a play; (3) since Mendelssohn's *Hebrides*, also a type of one-movement orchestral work composed for the concert hall and usually having a title revealing a literary, pictorial, or emotional clue. (This last type is specifically called *concert overture*). So *French overture*, 17th–18th century form of (1) above, in two movements, slow-fast (sometimes with final return to slow tempo): *Italian overture*, quick-slow-quick (the form from which the symphony evolved).

Pachelbel, Johann (1653–1706) German organist and composer of keyboard music (including preludes on Lutheran chorales), church music, etc. Teacher of Bach's elder brother Johann Cristoph, who in turn was the teacher of Bach himself in his boyhood.

Paganini, Niccolò (1782–1840) Italian violinist, called by Schumann "the turning point of virtuosity"; enormously successful, although, with the subsequent advance in the general level of performers' skill, his feats are no longer regarded as freakishly difficult. Was also guitarist (wrote 3 string quartets with guitar part) and viola player: he commissioned, but never played, Berlioz's *Harold in Italy*. Compositions include at least 6 violin concertos (the composer referred to 8) of which apparently only 4 survive in full orchestral score (no. 2 in B minor contains the *Bell Rondo*); variations for violin called *The Carnival of Venice*; and 24 Capricci (i.e., studies) for violin unaccompanied. One of the latter, in A minor, is the source of (1) Brahms's *Studies in Piano Technique: Variations on a Theme of Paganini*, 1866; (2) Rakhmaninov's *Rhapsody on a Theme of Paganini* for piano and orchestra (also in variation form), 1934; (3) Blacher's orchestral *Variations on a Theme of Paganini*, 1947; (4) Lutoslawski's *Variations on a Theme of Paganini* for 2 pianos, 1941. Liszt, Schumann, Busoni, and others also transcribed his works for piano. His music has a certain intense, "demonic" quality, emphasized in his lifetime by the legends of his being inspired by the Devil, etc. Died in Nice.

Palestrina, Giovanni Pierluigi da (approximately 1525–1594) Italian composer who took the name Palestrina from his native town, near Rome. Was choirboy and spent all his musical life in service of the Church, but also proved an able businessman. Became choirmaster of the Julian Chapel at St. Peter's, Rome, and a member of the Papal chapel; later held other high positions. Much honored in his lifetime and described on his coffin as "Prince of Music." After his first wife died he entered the priesthood, but abandoned it and remarried. Apart from a few madrigals his works are all Latin church music for unaccompanied choir, nearly 100 masses (including *Missa Papae Marcelli* and a mass on *L'Homme Armé*), motets, a Stabat Mater, psalms, etc. Posthumous veneration of him led to various fanciful legends.

Parody Misleading term employed by some musical authorities to denote a composer's straightforward imitation or adaptation of his own or someone else's work (without any implication of mockery). But only one example apparently exists (from the 16th century) of a composer's own use of *parody* in this sense on his title page, and it is clearly erroneous.

Partita (It.) Suite or set of variations. A term commonly used in the 18th century, occasionally revived since.

Part writing The laying out of a composition so that each part progresses euphoniously. (The U.S. term is "voice leading," introduced as translation of Ger. *Stimmführung* by immigrant musicians unaware of the established English term.)

Passacaglia (It.) An instrumental piece (originally a dance) in which a theme stretching over several bars is continually repeated, usually, but not necessarily always in the bass. The opposite of *Chaconne*. The two terms, though of different origin, are now often used almost interchangeably, except that *passacaglia* seems never to have been applied to a vocal work.

Passion A musical setting of the biblical story of the suffering (Lat., *passio*) and death of Jesus, prop-

erly meant to be sung in churches during the week before Easter.

Pedal (1) (in harmony) A note sustained below (at the foot of) changing harmonies. This is called a pedal or pedal point or pedal bass. If it is thus sustained but not in the bass it is an inverted pedal; (2) the lowest ("fundamental") note of the harmonic series, especially with reference to the playing of brass instruments; (3) a foot-operated lever.

Pedal point *See* **Pedal** (1).

Pentatonic (from Gk., *pente*, five) Term used for a scale comprising only five notes, particularly that represented by the five black keys of the piano (or other notes in the same position relative to each other). This form of pentatonic scale is widely used in folk music of many countries—Scottish, Chinese, American Negro (e.g., *Swing Low, Sweet Chariot*), etc.

Percussion Collective name for instruments in which (usually) a resonating surface is struck by the player—in most cases directly by hand or stick, but sometimes through leverage as in the type of bass drum used in dance bands, operated by a pedal. The piano and celesta come technically within this definition of percussion instruments but are not conventionally so classified: however, the piano is sometimes said to be "employed as a percussion instrument" (i.e., for percussive rather than melodic effect) in such 20th-century works as Stravinsky's *The Wedding*. Percussion instruments as used today in the symphony orchestra, dance band, etc., may be tuned to a definite pitch (e.g., kettledrum, tubular bell, glockenspiel, xylophone, vibraphone, marimba) or may be of indefinite pitch, e.g., triangle, gong, castanets, whip, rattle, anvil, and the following drums: side drum, tenor drum, bass drum, tabor, tambourine, bongo; the tomtom may be of definite or indefinite pitch, the normal cymbals are of indefinite pitch but the so-called ancient cymbal is not. Instruments that are shaken rather than struck, e.g., maraca, rattle, are also placed within the percussion section of an orchestra, as are certain freak instruments, e.g., motor horn, iron chains, when (exceptionally) employed.

Perfect (1) Term used to describe the intervals of a fourth, fifth, and eighth (octave) in their "standard" dimensions, e.g., C up to F, to G, and to C, respectively. They become diminished if lessened by a semitone and augmented if enlarged by a semitone. (2) Type of cadence (*see* **Cadence**). (3) Term used in the phrase "perfect time," meaning (in medieval music) triple time. (4) Term used in the phrase "perfect pitch" (*see* **Pitch**).

Pergolesi, Giovanni Battista (1710–1736) Italian composer, also violinist and church organist who wrote serious and comic operas, including the enormously successful *The Maid as Mistress* (*La Serva padrona*). Imported into France, it provoked a quarrel between supporters of French and Italian opera—the so-called "War of the Buffoons." After his death, in order to capitalize on his popularity, many works not his were ascribed to him and still commonly are. These included the opera *The Music Master*, concertinos for strings, the songs "Se tu m'ami" (used by Stravinsky in *Pulcinella*) and "Tré giorni son che Nina." Authentic works include a Stabat Mater for male soprano and alto with orchestral accompaniment.

Pérotin [Latinized as Perotinus] French composer active in the early 13th century; composed liturgical music showing a high degree of structural organization, in the style later known as Ars antiqua.

Phrase A small group of notes forming what is recognized as a unit of melody, so *to phrase* and *phrasing*, terms used in regard to a performer's correctly observing the division of a melody into phrases. So also *phrase mark*, a line linking written notes and indicating that they belong to one phrase.

Piano (It.) (1) Soft, abbr. *p*; so *pianissimo* or *pp*, very soft. (2) Common English word for the keyboard instrument called in Italian *pianoforte* (literally soft-loud), the shorter term being more convenient than the longer, and no worse English. The instrument, distinguished, e.g., from harpsichord and clavichord by having its strings struck with hammers, was invented shortly after 1700 (*see also* **Fortepiano**), and by 1800 had almost displaced the harpsichord. The modern piano is iron framed and normally has 88 keys; it is either *upright* (i.e., the strings are vertical) or *grand* (i.e., they are horizontal). It has a "sustaining pedal" (wrongly called "loud pedal") operated by the right foot to prolong the sound by holding off the dampers; and a "soft pedal" (left foot) lessening the volume by causing fewer than the normal number of strings to be struck or by bringing the hammers nearer the strings before they start their movement. On a minority of pianos, there is also a center pedal enabling selected notes to be sustained independently of others.

Pitch The property according to which notes appear to be (in the conventional phrase) "high" or "low" in relation to each other—a property scientifically determined by the frequency of vibrations of the sound-producing agent (*see* **Frequency**). So *concert pitch* is the standard of pitch to which instruments are normally tuned for performance. By international agreement of 1939, the tuning note A (directly above middle C) is fixed at a frequency of 440 Hz; this makes middle C 261.6 Hz, and the C higher 523.2 Hz. (i.e., twice the frequency of the octave below, as is the invariable rule). But in scientific investigation it is found mathematically convenient to suppose this C to have a frequency of 512 Hz (i.e., 2^9). Certain wind instruments are said by dealers to have *low pitch*: this means that they are built to modern concert pitch, not to the *high pitch* (nearly a semitone higher) formerly used by military bands and still used by some brass bands. *Old Philharmonic* and *New Philharmonic pitch* are the names of two higher standards of pitch, now obsolete. *Absolute pitch* or *perfect pitch*, term for the faculty possessed by those who on hearing a note can identify it by name: it would be better to call this not *absolute pitch* but *an absolute sense of pitch*, etc.—although in fact such a faculty of identification is really not absolute but relative (to the nearest whole tone, semitone, etc.)

Plague cadence *See* **Cadence**.

Plainchant, plainsong Type of medieval church music that in its final form called Gregorian chant became standard in Roman Catholic use. It consists of a single line of vocal melody (properly unaccompanied) in "free" rhythm, not divided into regular bar lengths; it has its own system of notation. (The ritual music of the Greek church, called Byzantine music, and of the Jewish synagogue, although of a somewhat similar type, is not called plainsong.)

Polyphony Term literally meaning (from Gk.) any simultaneous sounding of different notes—and correctly used, e.g., in reference to instruments: *polyphonic synthesizer* (*see* **Synthesizer**). But, as commonly used, it implies the presence of counterpoint—opposite of Homophony, in which melodic interest is virtually confined to one "line" of music, the other sounds acting as accompaniment. Hence historical references to the *polyphonic period*, an imprecise term usually indicating a period from about the 13th to the 16th or early 17th centuries, ending with (e.g.) Palestrina, Lassus, and Byrd. (The style of such a later composer as Bach is also polyphonic, but there the polyphony is governed by the harmonic scheme, whereas in the earlier period the polyphony supposedly "comes first" and gives rise to the harmony.)

Polyrhythm The systematic exploitation of several rhythms performed simultaneously, especially in the 20th century, sometimes with the aid of mechanical devices. But there are earlier examples, notably Mozart's three different simultaneous dance rhythms in *Don Giovanni*.

Polytonality The simultaneous use of more than one key (an effect used systematically, e.g., by Holst, Milhaud). When only two keys are involved the more precise term is "bitonality." *See* **Tonality**.

Position (1) In string playing, term used to specify how far along the fingerboard the left hand should rest in order to play a given passage, *first position* being that nearest the pegs; *second,* etc. progressively farther away; (2) in trombone playing, term specifying how far the slide should be pushed out (*first position* the least extended); (3) in *harmony*, the "layout" of a chord, determining which note comes at the bottom, e.g., with the chord consisting of the notes C, E, G, B♭ (i.e., the dominant seventh chord in key F) if the note C (regarded as the "root" of the chord) is at the bottom, then the chord is in *root position*; if E is at the bottom then it is in the *first inversion*; if G is at the bottom, the *second inversion*; if B♭, the *third inversion*. It is solely which note is at the bottom that determines these "positions"; the order of the upper notes is irrelevant.

Postromantic(ism) Terms applied to musical styles seeming to continue on Romantic lines even after the original "wave" of romanticism in music apparently reached its climax in Wagner. The allusion is particularly to the employment of large forces and the linking of music to an emotional message and philosophical or similar ideas (e.g., in Mahler).

Preclassic(al) Terms used of composers (e.g. C.P.E. Bach, J.C. Bach) whose style is considered later than Baroque and leading to the "Viennese Classical" style of Haydn and Mozart.

Prepared piano A piano in which the strings are "doctored" with various objects in order to produce tone qualities other than normal, sometimes with the addition of unusual techniques of playing; e.g., reaching over the keyboard and plucking the strings by hand. Its originator was Cage.

Presto (It., fast)　In, e.g., Mozart, this approximates to the meaning "as fast as possible"; later composers have tended to convey this meaning by *prestissimo*.

Programmatic music, program music　Music interpreting a story, picture, etc. A better term, because self-explanatory and avoiding the confusion with "concert program", etc., is "illustrative music."

Prokofiev, Sergey [Sergeyevich] (1891–1953) Russian composer, also pianist. Pupil of Rimsky-Korsakov and others. Lived abroad from 1918 until settling again in Russia in 1934; his style then became more straightforward and "popular," e.g., in *Peter and the Wolf* and violin concerto no. 2. Nonetheless, some of his later works, e.g., his symphony no. 6, were officially condemned for "formalism" in 1948, along with works by other leading Soviet composers, and his last opera *The Story of a Real Man*, was publicly produced only after his death, 1960. His previous operas include *The Fiery Angel*, *The Duenna*, and *War and Peace*. Also composed 7 symphonies (no. 1, *Classical Symphony*), 5 piano concertos, 2 violin concertos, cello concerto, concertino sinfonia concertante for cello and orchestra; *Cinderella*, *Romeo and Juliet*, and other ballets; songs, patriotic cantatas (e.g., *Alexander Nevsky*); 9 piano sonatas, 2 violin sonatas and other instrumental works; film music.

Psalmody　The study, etc. of the psalms; or an arrangement of psalms for singing.

Cover illustration for Giacomo Puccini's opera *Tosca*.

Puccini, Giacomo [Antonio Domenico Michele Secondo Maria] (1858–1924)　Italian composer, pupil of Bazzini and Ponchielli. In youth a church musician. Works almost entirely operatic, including (in this order) *Manon Lescaut* (1893), *La Bo-*

hème, *Tosca*, *Madam Butterfly*, *The Girl of the Golden West*; a "triptych" (It., *trittico*) (*The Cloak*, *Sister Angelica*, *Gianni Schicchi*) intended to form a single bill; *Turandot* (1924, unfinished). Became one of history's most successful opera composers through a gift for "strong" melody wedded to forceful dramatic plots (*see* **Verismo**): was also original harmonist and orchestrator.

Purcell, Henry (1659–1695)　English composer; boy chorister; pupil of Humfrey and of Blow, whom he succeeded as organist of Westminster Abbey in 1679. Said to have died through a cold caused by being locked out of his own house at night. Wrote short opera *Dido and Aeneas* for a Chelsea girls' school; also semioperas (music not altogether predominant) including *The Fairy Queen*, *King Arthur*, *Dioclesian*, *The Indian Queen*, and music for various plays. Other works include *Odes for St. Cecilia's Day* and other cantatas; songs, keyboard works; trio-sonatas (some described as in 3 parts and some as in 4, but identical in scoring), including the *Golden Sonata*; anthems (including *Bell Anthem*) and other church music. His subtlety of rhythm (especially in the treatment of English words) and harmony has contributed to his high 20th century repute; he notably influenced Holst Britten, and others. Purcell's work is indexed by Z (Zimmerman) numbers.

Q　**Quarter-tone**　Half a semitone, an interval not used in Western music until the 20th century, and then only exceptionally. *See also* **Microtone**.

Quodlibet (Lat., *quod libet*, what is desired)　Piece containing several popular tunes put together in unusual and (usually) ingenious fashion, such as that which ends Bach's *Goldberg Variations*, incorporating two well-known tunes of his day.

R　**Ragtime**　Name given to an early type of jazz, particularly associated with piano playing, with characteristic syncopations; e.g., *Maple Leaf Rag* (Joplin). In vogue around 1890–1920 revived in 1970s. Stravinsky's *Ragtime for 11 instruments* and *Piano-Rag-Music* (indebted to this type of work) date from 1918 and 1919 respectively.

Rakhmaninov, Sergey Vassilievich (1873–1943) Russian composer and pianist. (The spellings *Rachmaninoff*, etc., are inconsistent with the now standard system of transliteration from Russian.) Wrote his piano prelude in C♯ minor at age 20. Left Russia, 1918, disliking Soviet regime, and lived mainly in Switzerland and in the United States, where he died. Nevertheless he conspicuously aided the Russian anti-Nazi effort in World War II. He always maintained a Russian outlook and wrote in an emotional (and sometimes melancholy) Romantic style. Works include 4 piano concertos, *Rhapsody on a Theme of Paganini* for piano and orchestra (*see* **Paganini**), many piano solos (including transcriptions from other composers), and some 2-piano works; also 3 symphonies, symphonic poem *The Isle of the Dead*, 3 operas, choral work *The Bells* (after Poe), songs.

Rameau, Jean Philippe (1683–1764)　French composer, also organist, harpsichordist, and writer of an important *Treatise on Harmony* and other theoretical works. At 50, began his succession of more than 20 operas and opera-ballets, including *The Courtly Indies* (*Les Indes galantes*) and *Castor and Pollux*. His champions and those of Pergolesi clashed in the so-called War of the Buffoons (Fr. *Guerre des bouffons*). Other works include chamber music; dance music and other pieces for harpsichord; cantatas and church music.

Ravel, [Joseph] **Maurice** (1875–1937)   French composer. His family moved from the Pyrenees to Paris before he was 1. Pupil of Fauré and others at the Paris Conservatory. Failed in three attempts for the French Rome Prize, and was unfairly barred (although he had already had works published and performed) from a fourth try. Notable for Impressionist technique (more clear-cut, however, than Debussy's), mastery of orchestration, and innovations in exploiting the sonorities of the piano. Piano works include 2 concertos (one for left hand), sonatina, suites *Gaspard de la Nuit* and *Mirrors* (including *Alborada del gracioso*); also (all later transcribed for orchestra) *Pavan for a Dead Infanta, Valses Nobles et Sentimentales*, and *The Grave of Couperin*. Other works include *Bolero, Spanish Rhapsody*, and *La Valse* for orchestra; *Mother Goose* (for piano duet, later orchestrated); operas *The Spanish Hour* and *The Child and the Spells;* ballet *Daphnis and Chloe*; septet including harp (also called *Introduction and Allegro*) and other chamber music; songs, some with orchestra. Orchestrated Mussorgsky's *Pictures at an Exhibition*. Visited England (Hon.D.Mus., Oxford 1928) and the United States; died in Paris. Refused the Legion of Honour.

Realism   Stylistic term of at least two meanings: (1) the use in opera of characterization and stories based on contemporary life as it is actually observed (not forgetting "life in the raw"), as distinct from "remote" subjects and "refined" treatment: in this sense the term indicates a correspondence with the literary outlook, e.g., of Zola, and is used, e.g., of Italian opera of the Puccini-Mascagni type (*see* **Verismo**); (2) the philosophic attitude of mind considered "correct" for composers under Soviet officialdom: showing optimism, sympathy with "the people," a desire to be comprehensible, an avoidance of such faults as Formalism, etc.; in this sense the term is opposed both to "distortions" in art and to "crude naturalism" (e.g., musical imitations of noises).

Recapitulation   A section of a composition that repeats (in something like their original shape) themes that were originally presented in an earlier section but have undergone "development." The term is used particularly in the scheme of construction called Sonata-form, and variations of it.

Recitative   Type of speechlike singing written in ordinary notation but in which a certain freedom in rhythm (and sometimes also in pitch) is allowed in performance; used particularly in opera, oratorio, etc., as preliminary to a song (so "recitative and air," etc.) and for dialogue. Its two chief kinds are *accompanied recitative* (It., *recitativo accompagnato* or *stromentato*) with normal orchestral accompaniment, and *dry recitative* (*recitativo secco*), which, e.g. in 18th century Italian opera, had merely an accompaniment of "punctuating" chords from a harpsichord (the bass line sometimes also reinforced by

other instruments). (The word is commonly pronounced to rhyme with "thieve," probably on the mistaken supposition that it is French; as it is only English, it might well be made as English-sounding as "narrative.") *Compare* **Speech-song**.

Related   Term used as a measure of one key's harmonic nearness to (or distance from) another. Hence, e.g., G major is more nearly related to D major (a difference of only one sharp in the key signature, meaning that the modulation between them is of the simplest kind) than either is to A♭ major. The use of the term categorically (as when two keys are spoken of as "related," and another two as "not related") is inadvisable, since all keys are related at a greater or lesser remove, and the historical evolution of harmony has been to lessen the difficulty of transition between them. *See also* **Relative**.

Relative   Term used to indicate that a common key signature is shared by one major and one minor key: e.g., E minor is termed the *relative minor* of G major, and G major as the *relative major* of E minor, both having a key signature of one sharp, and modulations between them being accordingly of a simple kind.

Renaissance (Fr., rebirth)   Term used by historians of visual arts to identify the rediscovery and reapplication of "classical" (ancient Greek and Roman as opposed to Christian) images and values in the 14th–16th centuries and the emergence of a more individualistic and wordly art; analogously used by music historians to denote a period of style between "medieval" and Baroque—from early 15th century (e.g., Dunstable, Dufay) to early 17th.

Resolution   The progression from a discord to a concord or to a less acute discord; so *to resolve* a discord.

Respighi, Ottorino (1879–1936)   Italian composer, pupil of Rimsky-Korsakov in Russia; also conductor, teacher, and editor of old Italian music. Works include orchestral suites *The Birds, Three Botticelli Pictures, Fountains of Rome, Pines of Rome*; 9 operas, 2 violin concertos, many songs. Arranged the music to the ballet *The Fantastic Toyshop*.

Resultant tone   Name given to either of two acoustical phenomena: (1) when two loud notes are sounded, another note may sometimes also be heard, lower in pitch, which corresponds to the difference in vibration between the original two and is called "differential tone"; (2) another note, higher than the original two, may also be heard corresponding to the sum of their vibrations ("summational tone").

Retrograde   Term used of a theme when performed backward—a device prominently used, e.g., in the Middle Ages, in Bach's *The Art of Fugue*, and in twelve-tone technique. In this last, both *retrograde* and *retrograde inversion* are standard procedures, the latter meaning that the theme is turned upside down as well as played backward (*see* **Invert**).

Rhythm   That aspect of music concerned not with pitch but with the distribution of notes in time and their accentuation. (*See also* **Meter**.) Hence such phrases as *a strongly marked rhythm* or (by ellipsis) *a strong rhythm*; *two-beat rhythm* (accent on every other beat); a *five-bar rhythm* (each five bars making a regular rhythmic unit); *waltz rhythm* (accent on the first of every three beats, at waltz pace); *free rhythm*, rhythm not determined by the regular incidence of bar lines but arrived at by the performer according to the natural or conventional flow of the notes (as in plainsong). So also *a sense of rhythm*, implying a performer's ability to convey the rhythmic element of a composition intelligibly; *rhythm section* of a (prewar) dance band, collective term for those instruments more concerned with giving the beat than with melody: normally piano, drums and other percussion, guitar, double bass.

Ricercar(e) (It., to search)   Type of contrapuntal instrumental composition current in the 16th–18th centuries, usually in the strictest style of Imitation.

Rimsky-Korsakov, Nikolay Andreyevich (1844–1908)   Russian composer, also conductor; member of the "nationalist" group of composers called The Mighty Handful. In early life was naval officer, and picked up much of his musical technique *after* being appointed professor at the St. Petersburg Conservatory, 1871. His compositions usually have some literary or other extramusical idea behind them and are distinguished by rich orchestration: he wrote a textbook on orchestration with examples entirely from his own work. Wrote operas including *The Maid of Pskov, The Snow-Maiden, Sadko, Mozart and Salieri, The Legend of Tsar Saltan, The Legend of the Invisible City of Kitezh,* and *The Golden Cockerel* (this last banned for its "seditious" satire until after his death). Other works include 3 symphonies (no. 2, *Antar*), *Russian Easter Festival* overture, suite *Sheherazade, Spanish Caprice*, piano concerto, folk song arrangements. Also editor, orchestrator, and reviser (not always scrupulous by modern standards) of other composers' works.

Rock   Type of popular music (originating from "rock 'n' roll"), which from U.S. roots has spread over the Western world since about 1950; based on solo voice and guitars (mainly electric), and mainly diffused by phonograph recording. *Rock'n'roll* is now applied only to a subtype, with particular rhythmic and other features. Fusions with other popular music are indicated by such terms as *folk-rock* and *jazz-rock*. The term "pop" overlaps but is not quite synonymously used; to rock practitioners, pop may denote a more commercialized, more juvenile, and more easily assimilable product than rock.

Rococo   Term originally alluding to fancy rock work (Fr. *rocaille*) and applied in visual art to the predominantly diverting—rather than elevating—style of, e.g., Watteau (1684–1721) and to related styles in architecture. It has been borrowed by writers on music and applied, e.g., to F. Couperin (1668–1733): in all cases the allusion is to a decorative and light art style succeeding the massiveness and constructive ingenuity of Baroque.

Romantic(ism)   Terms alluding to an artistic outlook discernible in European literature toward the end of the 18th century and taken over to describe a supposedly similar outlook in music, principally in the 19th century. One of its literary aspects, that of harking back to the Middle Ages, is rarely found in musical contexts—apart from Bruckner's *Romantic Symphony* (no. 4 in E♭, 1874), a nickname bestowed after the composer's description of the opening in

terms of a scene of medieval chivalry. Another literary aspect, that of cultivation of the supernatural, is evident, e.g., in Weber but not in other composers supposedly no less typed as Romantic, e.g., Chopin. The main musical implication is that the composer is more concerned with the vivid depiction of an emotional state (often linked with a narrative or some other extramusical element) than with the creation of aesthetically pleasing structures. (Such structures must, however, be the result if not the aim of any successful method of composition.) The attempt at more and more "vividness" led to (1) a trend to the evocation of "extreme" emotions, (2) an expansion of orchestral resources for this purpose. Romanticism is thus contrasted with Classicism; it is also, less clearly, differentiated from Impressionism. Composers such as Stravinsky, disclaiming a connection between music and the portraying of emotions, are said to be *anti-Romantic*. For a late variety of Romanticism, *see* **Postromantic**.

Rondo   (properly spelled, in Italian, *rondò*, itself an Italianized form of Fr., *rondeau*) A form of composition, especially an instrumental movement, in which one section recurs intermittently. (The French spelling *rondeau* was used by Bach.) By Mozart's time the rondo had evolved into a standard pattern and was much used, as in the last movement of a sonata or concerto. A simple rondo is built up in the pattern of ABACADA...(etc.), where A represents the recurring section (called *rondo-theme*) and B, C, D... represent contrasting sections, called *episodes*. (The rondo-theme can undergo some variation in its reappearances.) A combination of this with Sonata-form led to what is called the *sonata-rondo* (used, for example, by Mozart and Beethoven). Occasionally in Italian opera (e.g., Mozart, Rossini), *rondò* is used to designate an aria in which a slow section is succeeded by a faster one (i.e., without an implication of recurrence).

Rossini, Gioacchino [Antonio] (1792–1868)   Italian composer, born at Pesaro. His operas appeared in various Italian cities; he visited England in 1823–1824, and after 1829 lived partly in Paris, where he died. Successful in opera from 1810, although *The Barber of Seville* (1816) was at first a failure. Other operas include *The Silken Ladder, Tancred, The Italian Girl in Algiers, Otello, Cinderella, The Thieving Magpie, Armida, Moses, Semiramis, Count Ory, William Tell* (1829, in French, after which success he lived for nearly 40 more years but wrote no more operas). Other works include Stabat Mater and a few other church works; a few songs and duets (among them the collection *Soirées Musicales*) and piano pieces, etc. Exploiter of the orchestral crescendo, and noted in his day for "noisy" effects.

Salieri, Antonio (1750–1825)   Italian composer who lived mainly in Vienna and died there: Beethoven and Schubert were among his pupils. He intrigued against Mozart, but the idea (as expressed in Rimsky-Korsakov's opera *Mozart and Salieri*) that he poisoned Mozart is false. Wrote mainly Italian operas (including a *Falstaff*, after Shakespeare's *The Merry Wives of Windsor*), but also 6 masses, a Passion oratorio in Italian, 2 piano concertos, etc.

Saltarello, salterello Type of Italian dance. In its most common meaning, a lively dance incorporating jumps, the music similar to Tarantella but not so smoothly flowing. The finale of Mendelssohn's Italian Symphony is so styled. The preferred modern Italian spelling is *salterello*, but Mendelssohn wrote *saltarello*, as did older Italian composers.

Saraband, sarabande (Eng., Fr.) Dance that came to the rest of Europe from Spain; forming a regular constituent of the old Suite. It is slow and in 3/2 time.

Satie, Erik (Alfred Leslie) (1866–1925) French composer. For a time he worked as a café pianist, etc., and at 39 became a pupil of Roussel and d'Indy. He influenced younger composers toward a cool, clear style and away from the lushness sometimes associated with Impressionism. His piano solos and duets mostly have eccentric titles. such as *3 Pear-shaped Pieces*. Several of these were orchestrated by Poulenc and others. He also wrote ballets, including *Relâche* (the word displayed by French theatres when they are closed), operettas, Mass (*Messe des pauvres*), and a symphonic drama, *Socrates*.

Scale A progression of single notes upward or downward in "steps". (Compare It. *scala*, stairway.) So *scalic*, e.g.. "a scalic figure," progressing upward or downward in steps. For the *major scale* and *minor scale*, *see* **Major, minor**. *See also* **Chromatic; Diatonic; Pentatonic; Mode**.

Scaramouche Title of suite for 2 pianos by Milhaud: so called because the music is based on music by Milhaud for a play, *The Flying Doctor*, produced in Paris, 1937, at the Théâtre Scaramouche.

Scarlatti, Alessandro (1660–1725) Italian composer who worked chiefly in Naples: reckoned the founder of the type of Italian opera that conquered all Europe in the 18th century. Composed more than 100 operas, many now lost; 600 cantatas for solo voice and continuo; various other cantatas, oratorios, masses, madrigals, etc.; also chamber music. Possibly a pupil of Carissimi in boyhood. Held various court and church posts. Father of Domenico Scarlatti.

Scarlatti, [Giuseppe] **Domenico** (1685–1757) Italian composer; at first wrote Italian opera, etc., on the model of his father (*see* **Scarlatti, Alessandro**), and was known also as a harpsichord virtuoso; but went in 1720 to Portugal and later to Spain (dying in Madrid) and there wrote the greater number of his single-movement harpsichord sonatas. These, numbering over 550, and in their time also called "Exercises" (It., *Esercizi*), exploit with great variety the capabilities of the Binary-form movement, and foreshadow later Sonata-form. (For the numbering of the sonatas, *see* **Kirkpatrick, Ralph**.) Other works include a Stabat Mater and other church music.

Scherzo (It. joke) A type of lively movement that historically, chiefly through Haydn and, especially, Beethoven, developed from the minuet as used in symphonies, string quartets, etc. Usually, therefore, it is in the characteristic minuet form, AABA; and the B section is called the Trio (as in the minuet). Usually also it is in 3/4 time. The original implication of humor is not always maintained, but fast tempo is obligatory and sentimentality is avoided. Examples of the scherzo exist also, not as a movement of a larger work, but as an independent work of its own, notably Chopin's four for piano.

Schoenberg, Arnold (1874–1951) Austrian-born composer who worked in Germany and then (driven out by the Nazis as a Jew and a composer of "decadent" music) from 1933 in the United States, thereafter changing the spelling of his name from the original Schönberg. Died in Los Angeles. At first composed in postromantic style (e.g., in *Transfigured Night, Gurrelieder*); by 1908, however, had developed a technique of atonality (keylessness) shown, e.g., in *Pierrot Lunaire*; afterward systematized this into twelve-tone technique (from about 1923); later of great influence internationally. He himself varied in strictness of adherence to this technique, relaxing it (i.e., admitting the idea of key), e.g., in his late *Ode to Napoleon*. Several works use Speech-song, invented by him (and also influential). Other works include opera *Moses and Aaron*, monodrama *Expectation* (*Erwartung*), cantata *A Survivor from Warsaw*, piano concerto, violin concerto, symphonic poem *Pelleas and Melisande*, 2 chamber symphonies, 4 string quartets, various songs and piano pieces. Also writer of textbooks on music, etc.

Schubert, Franz [Peter] (1797–1828) Austrian composer who was born and died in Vienna, and hardly ever left it. At first a choirboy. Never held an official musical post, and gained little recognition in life. But matured early: wrote song *Gretchen at the Spinning Wheel* (*Gretchen am Spinnrade*) at 17. Often worked very fast, once producing 8 songs in a day. Composed more than 600 songs of great range and subtlety, regarded as founding the type of 19th-century German song (*Lied*). Showed high individuality also in piano pieces, including sonatas, dances, *Wanderer Fantasy, Impromptus, Moments Musicaux*; also wrote works for piano duet. His admiration for Rossini is evident, e.g., in his *Overture in the Italian style*; for Beethoven, in his string quartets (15 including *Death and the Maiden*, and also a *Quartet Movement*) and symphonies—of which he never heard a performance of no. 8 (*Unfinished*) or of no. 9 (and last) the *Great C Major*. (This is sometimes called no. 7, but the symphony properly so called is in E, left in skeleton form, and completed, e.g., by J.F. Barnett and by Weingartner.) The Tragic Symphony is no. 4. Other works include *Alfonso and Estrella* and other operas; music to the play *Rosamunde, Princess of Cyprus*; piano quintet (*Trout*) and other chamber music; 6 Latin masses, and other church music. Unmarried. Died of typhus. His works are indexed by D. numbers (Deutsch).

Schumann, Clara [Josephine] (born Wieck; 1819–1896) German pianist and composer, chiefly for piano; daughter of the composer Friedrich Wieck (1788–1873), and wife of R. Schumann (*see* **Schumann, Robert**). Made many visits to Britain; internationally noted as a performer of her husband's and other works, and also as teacher.

Schumann, Robert [Alexander] (1810–1856) German composer, also pianist, conductor, and noted as critic with wide sympathies. Married Clara Wieck (*see* **Schumann, Clara**), 1840. Developed mental instability, in 1854 throwing himself into the

MUSIC

Rhine; afterward was in a mental asylum, where he died. His work shows Romantic outlook and literary associations: compare the fanciful titles (some given after composition, however) of various piano works, e.g., *Abegg Variations, Carnival, Carnival Jest from Vienna, Kreisleriana, Papillons, Scenes of Childhood.* Other works include many songs (some in cycles, e.g., *Poet's Love, Woman's Love and Life*); 3 string quartets, piano concerto, cello concerto, violin concerto (not heard until 1937, being suppressed by Clara Schumann and Joachim as unworthy); 4 symphonies (no. 1 *Spring Symphony*, no. 3 *Rhenish*; no. 4 originally written directly after no. 1, later rescored); cantata *Paradise and the Peri*, opera *Genoveva, Scenes from Goethe's Faust*, incidental music to Byron's *Manfred.*

Schütz, Heinrich (1585–1672)   German composer who studied under G. Gabrieli in Venice and worked mainly as the court composer in Dresden; influential in introducing Italian musical ideas (as to vocal declamation, concerted instrumental writing, etc.) to Germany. His works include the earliest German opera, *Daphne* (music now lost); Italian madrigals; *Sacred Symphonies*, etc., for voices and instruments; 3 Passions (Matthew, Luke, John), "Resurrection" and Christmas Oratorios.

Scordatura   (It. mis-tuning)   The tuning of a stringed instrument to notes other than the normal, for special effects. Used in the 17th century and revived in modern times, e.g. in Mahler's Symphony no. 4, a solo violinist has to tune all his strings up a tone to represent the unearthly fiddling of a "dance of death."

Score   A music copy combining in ordered form all the different parts allotted to various performers of a piece; so (e.g., in an orchestral library) *score and parts*, meaning both the combined music copy (for the conductor) and the separate copies containing just the music for particular instruments. So also *full score*, a score displaying every different participating voice and instrument; *short score*, a compressed version of the preceding, such as a composer may write out at first, when the outlines of the instrumentation are decided on but not the details; *open score*, a score displaying every part on a separate line—particularly for study or academic exercise, in cases when normal reasons of economy and convenience would suggest compression on to fewer staves; *miniature score* or *pocket score* or *study score*, one that reproduces all the details of a full score but is of a size more suitable for study than for a conductor's desk; *vocal score* (or *piano-vocal score*), one giving all the voice parts of a work but having the orchestral parts reduced to a piano part; *piano score*, one in which not only the orchestral parts but also the vocal parts (if any) are all reduced to a piano part. So also *to score*, to arrange a work for a particular combination of voices and/or instruments (whether this is part of the process of original composition or in itself a process of arrangement of an already existing work).

Segovia, Andrés (1893–1987)   Spanish guitarist, for whom many works (e.g. by Falla, Castelnuovo-Tedesco) have been specially written. His artistry was chiefly responsible for the 20th-century revival of the guitar as a "classical" instrument.

Sequence   (1) The repetition of a phrase at a higher or lower pitch than the original: if the intervals within it are slightly altered in the repetition to avoid moving out of key it is a *tonal sequence*, if they are unaltered it is a *real sequence*; (2) hymnlike composition with nonbibical Latin text, sung during the Roman Catholic High Mass or Requiem Mass; some sequences have been set by various composers. (3) term used by Berio (It., *sequenza*) as title of a series of works for different solo instruments, unaccompanied.

Series   A set of notes treated in composition not mainly as a recognizable theme, but as a kind of plastic material from which the composition is made. The *order* of the notes in the series is considered its main characteristic: although the series can be turned upside down, backward, etc., a relationship to this order must be preserved. The "tone row" in twelve-tone technique is the main example of such a series, but other serial techniques are possible. Hence *serialism*, usually referring to the practice of twelve-tone technique. The term *multiserialism* or *total serialism* is applied to composition in which not only pitch is treated serially, but also other dimensions ("parameters") of music, e.g., time values, volume, force of attack, these being similarly placed in a given mathematical order (e.g., certain works of Boulez, Berio, Nono in the 1950s).

Sharp   Term indicating a raising in pitch, either (1) indeterminately, as when a singer is said to sing sharp, by mistake; or (2) precisely by a semitone, as represented by the sign ♯; so G♯ (G sharp), the note a semitone higher than G♮ (G natural); so also, e.g., B♯, a notation sometimes called for through adherence to the "grammar" of music, although on the piano, e.g., the note is identical with C♮ (C natural). So double sharp; *sharp keys*, those having sharps in their key signatures; *in four sharps*, in the key of E major or C♯ minor, the key signature of which is four sharps (and similarly with other keys); *sharped fourth*, the raising of the fourth degree of the scale by a semitone.

Shostakovich, Dmitry [Dmitrievich] (1906–1975) Russian composer (pupil of Glazunov); also pianist. At 19, wrote very successful symphony no. 1 (14 others followed, including no. 7 Leningrad Symphony; no. 13 *Babi Yar*; no. 14 for soprano and bass soloists with chamber orchestra). Denounced by Soviet officialdom for unmelodiousness, freakishness, etc., in 1936 (after his opera *Lady Macbeth of the Mtsensk District*), again denounced, for formalism and other "faults," in 1948 (after such works as his orchestral *Poem of Fatherland*). In each case admitted his "errors" and endeavored to find a style reconciling his individuality and Soviet offical views on what music should be like. Also composed other operas; *The Golden Age* and other ballets; *Songs of the Forests* and other cantatas to patriotic Soviet texts; songs and piano pieces (including 3 sets of preludes and fugues); concerto for piano, trumpet, and orchestra; 2 violin concertos; 15 string quartets, piano quintet; film music, etc. Reorchestrated Mussorgsky's *Boris Godunov* and made a completion and orchestration of Mussorgsky's *The Kovanschina Affair*. His son Maxim (b.1938) is a pianist and conductor.

Sibelius, Jean [Johan Julian Christian] (1865–1957) Finnish composer who studied in Berlin and Vienna. Because of a Finnish government grant, he was able to give up teaching and concentrate on composing from 1897. Much of his work has Finnish "national" associations, sometimes relating to the *Kalevala* (Finnish national epic poem), e.g., *A Saga*, *Karelia* (overture and suite), *The Swan of Tuonela*, *Lemmin-Käinen's Homecoming*, *Finlandia*, *Pohjola's Daughter*, *Tapiola*. After the last-named work, first performed in 1926, he published almost nothing. Of his 7 symphonies, the last is in one movement only. Other works include violin concerto; small orchestral pieces, including *Valse triste*; an unpublished opera; many songs in Finnish and Swedish; incidental music to A. Paul's *King Christian II*, Maeterlinck's *Pelleas and Melisande*, H. Procope's *Belshazzar's Feast*, Shakespeare's *The Tempest*, and other plays.

Simple time A scheme of time division in which the beat unit is divisible by 2: e.g., 4/4, in which the beat time is the quarter note divided into 2 eighth notes. *Compare* **Compound time.**

Six, The (Fr. *Les Six*) Name given to the French composers, Auric, Durey, Honegger, Milhaud, Poulenc, and Tailleferre. It was invented in 1920 by the French critic Henri Collet (after these composers had together published an album of pieces) on the analogy of the Russian "five" composers. Collet claimed that, inspired by Satie and Jean Cocteau, the "Six" had brought a renaissance of French music. In fact, the "Six" did not remain a group, and only Honegger, Milhaud, and Poulenc achieved wide fame.

Smetana, Bedrich (1824–1884) Czech composer, also conductor and pianist; encouraged by Liszt. Took part in the unsuccessful Czech revolt against Austria (1848) and later worked for some years in Sweden; but from 1861 settled again in Prague. Became totally deaf in 1874 but continued to compose, e.g., cycle of symphonic poems, *My Country*, 2 string quartets (No. 1 *From My Life*), opera *The Kiss* and others. Previous works include operas, *The Bartered Bride* and *Dailbor*, choral works, many piano pieces. He cultivated, and is regarded as having founded, a Czech national style influenced by folk-music.

Solfége, solfeggio French and Italian terms for a method of ear training and sight-reading by which the pupil names each note of a melody (*do* for C, *sol* for G, etc.) as he or she sings it. The Italian is the original term; the French, derived from it, is also used in a broader sense to take in the whole system of rudimentary musical instruction in which it is a prime element. The name *solfeggio* is also given to a vocal exercise written for this method of study.

Solmization The designation of musical notes by a system of syllabic names—as applied to a nomenclature devised by Guido of Arezzo in the 11th century and now to a development of this. Such a development is represented by the current Italian *do, re, mi, fa, sol, la, si* (representing the notes from C up to B), paralleled in English tonic sol-fa by *doh, ray, me, fah, soh, lah, te* (although these are not fixed in pitch but relative, *doh* representing C in C major, D in D major, etc., the other notes ascending from it).

Sonata (It., a piece sounded; as distinct from *cantata*, a piece sung) Originally (in Italy, around 1600) any instrumental piece not in a prevailing form (e.g., Canzona. Ricercar, or dance form). Later, since the Haydn-Mozart era (regarded as the "classic" era for this type of work), usually a work in 3 or 4 movements, or, following the example of Liszt's piano sonata (1852–1853), in one movement deliberately conceived as equal to (and about as long as) several "normal" movements combined. Only a work for 1 or 2 players is now normally called a sonata; a work of this type for 3 is called a trio, for 4 a quartet, etc., and for an orchestra a Symphony. Such terms as *violin sonata*, *cello sonata* normally also assume the participation of a piano. Characteristic of the sonata is the use (normally in the first movement and often in others too) of what is called Sonata-form or a modification of it. Among the notable forerunners of this now standard type are D. Scarlatti's short one-movement keyboard works, now usually also called sonatas; and in the immediate paving of the way for the Haydn-Mozart sonata, a chief part is ascribed to C.P.E. Bach. Earlier, the suite rather than the sonata was the prevailing type of instrumental piece in several movements; and indeed the 17th-century and early 18th-century *chamber sonata* (It., *sonata da camera*) represents virtually a suite (mainly in the form of dance movements) for 2 or more stringed instruments with keyboard accompaniment, the restriction of the term to 1 or 2 players not having yet arisen. The *church sonata* (It., *sonata da chiesa*) was similar but of a "graver" type, avoiding dance movements. The pre-Haydn usage of sonata as applied to a work for orchestra or smaller ensemble has occasionally been revived since 1950.

Sonata-form Term used to describe a certain type of musical construction normally used in the first movement of a Sonata and of a Symphony (which is in effect a sonata for orchestra) and similar works. An alternative name is *first-movement form*, but the form is also found in movements other than first movements, just as it is also found in works not called sonatas. It may also be called *compound binary form* (*see* **Binary**). The essential of sonata-form is the division of a movement (sometimes after an introduction) into 3 parts—exposition, development, recapitulation. The exposition, having its first theme in the "home" key of the movement, moves into another key normally presenting a fresh (second) subject in that key, and ends in that key; the next section "'develops" or expands the material already presented; the last section is basically a varied repetition of the first, but ending in the home key, normally by bringing the second subject into that key. Afterward may follow a further section, called coda ("finishing off" the movement). The key into which the first section moves is normally the dominant (if the piece is in the major key) or the relative major (if the piece is in the minor key). It will be gathered that sonata-form consists basically in the relationship of keys: if the term is applied to keyless (Atonal) music, then it must be with an altered significance.

Song Any short vocal composition, accompanied or not, usually for one performer. The word has no precise meaning but is effectively defined in various contexts by contrast with other terms, e.g., *songs and duets* (implying vocal solos and vocal duets). In opera the word "aria" or "air" is more usual. When, as normally, a song repeats the same tune for successive stanzas of a poem, it is said to be "strophic"; if not, then the term "through-composed" (from Ger. *durchkomponiert*) is sometimes applied to it (*see* **Strophic**). A *song cycle* is a set of songs grouped by the composer in a particular order (usually with reference to the sense of the words) and intended to be so performed. The term *song* is also applied in a generalized sense to certain large-scale works. The *Song of the Three Holy Children* is a book of the Apocrypha (also known in Anglican church use as the Benedicite) supposedly representing a prayer sung in the furnace by Daniel and his brothers.

Soprano (It., upper) (1) The highest type of female voice, with approximate normal range from middle C upward for two octaves; or a child's high voice; (2) *male soprano*, type of male adult voice of similar range, produced by castration as used for some operatic and church singers, e.g., in the 17th and 18th centuries; (3) *soprano clef*; name of a clef (now obsolete) having middle C on the bottom line of the staff; (4) name given, in a "family" of instruments (i.e., a group of different sizes), to the one with a range approximating to the soprano voice, and usually also carrying the implication of being higher than the "normal"-sized instrument, e.g., *soprano cornet, soprano recorder, soprano saxophone*; the small clarinet in E is occasionally (though not commonly) called a *soprano clarinet* for the same reason.

Sotto voce (It. under the voice) Whispered, barely audible; term used of instrumental as well as vocal music.

Sousa, John Philip (1854–1932) American band conductor and composer of marches (*The Washington Post, Stars and Stripes Forever*, etc.); also of *El Capitán* and other operettas. The story that his name was a fabrication to include the letters USA is itself a fabrication.

Speech-song Type of vocal utterance midway between speech and song, originated by Schoenberg and used in the *Gurrelieder, Pierrot Lunaire*, and later works; the voice touches the note (usually notated in a special way, e.g. ♩) but does not sustain it. The German term is *Sprechgesang*, and a voice part employing it is designated *Sprechstimme*.

Stamitz German form of surname adopted by a Czech family of musicians (originally named *Stamic*), whose chief members were (1) Jan Vaclav Stamic [or Johann Wenzel Stamitz] (1717–1757) violinist and composer of violin concertos, symphonies, harpsichord sonatas, etc., who became musical director at the court of Mannheim, 1745, and is regarded as the founder of the Mannheim school; (2) his son Karel Stamic [or Karl Stamitz] (l745–1801), violinist and composer of symphonies, operas, etc.

Stochastic (from Gk.) Governed by the mathematical laws of probability; term applied by Xenakis to procedures whereby, having determined a total massive sound, a composer makes a mathematical calculation (worked out by hand or by computer) to decide the distribution of its component sounds over many moments and/or performers. This is Xenakis's own procedure in *Metastaseis* and other works for large numbers of individual players.

Stockhausen, Karlheinz (b. 1928) German composer, pupil of F. Martin and (in Paris) of Messiaen. Highly influential in trends of form, sound content, use of electronics: he was the first composer to have any electronic "score" (or rather diagram) published, 1956. Later active in exploring spatial possibilities in music and a measure of free choice by performers, e.g., in *Groups* (Ger., *Gruppen*) for 3 orchestras (and 3 conductors); *Cycle* (*Zyklus*) for one percussion player who may begin on any page (*see* **Cycle**). Other works include *Stimmung* ("atmosphere", "tuning") for vocal ensemble, stage piece *Inori* ("adorations" for soloist and orchestra).

Strauss, Johann (the younger; 1825–1899) Austrian violinist, conductor, and composer of enormously successful waltzes in noticeably artistic style, including *The Blue Danube, Roses from the South*, and *Tales from the Vienna Woods*; called the Waltz King. Wrote also polkas (*Tritsch-Tratsch, Thunder and Lightning*, etc.) and other dances; and 16 operettas including *Die Fledermaus* and *The Gypsy Baron*. Other operettas, e.g., *Vienna Blood*, have been made by others from his music. Toured much (London, 1869; United States 1872). Son of Johann Strauss. Collaborated in a few works with his brother Josef Strauss.

Strauss, Richard [Georg] (1864–1949) German composer, also conductor; no relation to the other Strausses. Born in Munich, later settling in Garmisch (also in Bavaria) where he died. Became the most celebrated German composer of his generation. After early leaning toward "traditional" forms, took up and developed the *Symphonic Poem*, composing, e.g., *Macbeth, Don Juan, Death and Transfiguration, Til Eulenspiegel, Thus Spake Zarathustra* (Ger., *Also sprach Zarathustra*), *Don Quixote, Ein Heldenleben*. Also of the character of symphonic poems are his *Symphonia Domestica* and *Alpine Symphony* (1915), his last work of this illustrative type. His early operas (e.g., *Salome, Elektra, Der Rosenkavalier*) have a grandiloquent, Wagner-influenced style and a tendency to "shocking" subjects; but from *Ariadne auf Naxes* (1912), there are signs of the more intimate manner that characterizes especially certain very late works, e.g., horn concerto no. 2. symphony for wind (both in neo-Mozartian style). Wrote also incidental music to *Molière's Le Bourgeois gentilhomme; Metamorphoses* for strings; many songs, several with his own orchestral accompaniments various further operas, including *Arabella, Intermezzo, Capriccio*; ballet *The Legend of Joseph*.

Stravinsky, Igor [Fedorovich] (1882–1971) Russian-born composer; also pianist, conductor, and author of autobiographical and other writings. Pupil of Rimsky-Korsakov; left Russia 1914; lived mainly in Paris, naturalized French 1934; settled in the United States 1939, naturalized there 1945. Prodigiously successful and influential composer, initially winning fame with pre-1914 ballets *The Firebird, Petrushka*, and (using enormous orchestra and "savage" dynamic elements) *The Rite of*

MUSIC

Igor Stravinsky

MUSIC

Spring. Later developed Neoclassical tendency (compact forms, small forces, aversion from "emotion"; *see* **Symphony**), although the austerity of this was modified from the 1930s. Showed interest in jazz (e.g., in *The Soldier's Tale*); based ballet *Pulcinella* on music supposedly by Pergolesi; adopted a deliberate back-to-Mozart style in opera *The Rake's Progress* (1951). Other works include *Symphony of Psalms* (with chorus), *Dumbarton Oaks Concerto*, *Ebony Concerto* (for dance band); opera-oratorios *Oedipus Rex* and *Persephone*; ballets *Apollo Musagetes*, *Orpheus*, *Agon*; mass. Notable rhythmic and harmonic innovator, but long adhered to tonality; however, from the choral and orchestral *Canticum sacrum* (*Holy Canticle*, in Latin, for St. Mark's, Venice), 1955, he adopted a twelve-tone technique indebted to Webern's. Later works included ballet *Agon*; *Movements* for piano and orchestra; *Threni*; *The Flood*; *Sacred Ballad* (in Hebrew, on the biblical story of Abraham and Isaac) for baritone and small orchestra; *Elegy for J.F. Kennedy*. *See also* **Ragtime**. His son, [Svyatoslav] Soulima Stravinsky (b. 1910), is a pianist, composer, and teacher.

Stretto (It. drawn together)   (1) Direction that the pace is to become faster; (2) term used of the overlapping of entries in certain examples of Fugue or similar composition, the subject beginning in one voice before the preceding voice has finished uttering it. A *stretto maestrale* (magisterial) occurs when the full length of the subject, and not just the first part of it, is subjected to overlapping.

Strophic   Term used of a song in which the same music is repeated (exactly or almost exactly) for each successive stanza of a poem. The opposite

type, in which the music progresses continually, has usually been called in English a "through-composed song" (from Ger., *durchkomponiert*).

Subdominant   Name for the fourth degree of the scale. e.g., F in key C (major or minor). It is so called because it dominates the scale to an extent subordinate to the Dominant or fifth degree.

Submediant   The sixth degree of the scale, e.g., A in the key of C major, A♭ in the key of C minor. So called because it is halfway between the keynote and the subdominant (working downward), whereas the Mediant (third degree of the scale) is halfway between the keynote and the dominant (working upwards).

Subotnick, Morton (b. 1933)   American composer, active in electronic music (his *Silver Apples of the Moon*, 1967, is thought to be the first electronic work composed for issue as a phonograph record). Has also written a series of works (for different performing groups) each called *Play!*; a *Ritual Game Room* with tape, lights, dancer, 4 game players and no audience, etc.

Suite (Fr., a following)   The most common name for an instrumental piece in several movements, usually (in older use) a sequence of dances. Its characteristic in the 17th and 18th centuries was the inclusion of the dance forms "allemande," "courante," "sarabande" and "gigue" (these French names were widely used) with optional additions. The Binary form characteristic of these dances was expanded in the mid-18th century into Sonata-form, and the suite was succeeded as the prevailing instrumental form by the sonata (and symphony, i.e., sonata for orchestra, etc.). Since then *suite* has lost a strict specification, and in the 19th and 20th centuries has often been used for a work rather lighter or more loosely connected than a work of sonata type; it may describe a set of movements assembled from an opera or ballet score, etc.

Supertonic   The second degree of the scale, e.g., the note D in the key C (major or minor), lying immediately above the Tonic (first degree).

Symphonic poem   Term introduced by Liszt for an orchestral work that is approximately of the size and seriousness customarily associated with a symphony, but which is meant as an interpretation of something nonmusical, e.g., a work of literature.

Symphony   Term literally meaning "a sounding-together", formerly indicating (1) an overture, e.g., to an opera; (2) the instrumental section introducing, or between the verses of, a vocal work. Occasionally such archaic meanings are revived, e.g., in Stravinsky's work entitled *Symphonies for Wind Instruments* (1920) or Gordon Crosse's entitled *Symphonies for Chamber Orchestra*. But, in general, since the mid-18th century, the word has ordinarily indicated an orchestral work of a serious nature and a substantial size, in the shape of a Sonata for orchestra. Most such works are in 4 movements; some are in 3; some are in 1 ("telescoping" a larger number of movements together) or 5; other numbers are very rare. Symphonies may have a name (e.g., Beethoven's *Pastoral* Symphony), or may include vocal parts (since Beethoven's *Choral* Symphony); but such remain the minority. A *symphony orchestra* (or, in the

United States, just "a symphony") is an orchestra numerous enough to play symphonies and having a repertory of "serious" music (*see* **Orchestra**); a *symphony concert* is one including a symphony or other work of similar type.

Syncopation   A displacement of accent onto a beat that is normally unaccented.

Synthesizer   General word for an electronic apparatus by which any one of a number of musical sounds can be put together from its physical components (harmonic constituents, characteristics of attack and decay, etc.) at such a speed and with such convenience as to make possible the performance of a piece from a musical score; generally (e.g., Moog synthesizer) with a pianolike keyboard. Most such instruments can perform only one note at a time, but *polyphonic synthesizers* began to be marketed about 1976.

T **Tablature**   A system of writing music by symbols that represent not the pitch (as in ordinary modern notation) but the position of the performer's fingers. Such a system was formerly used for the lute, and another one for keyboard. The diagrammatic notation now used in popular music for guitar and ukulele is a tablature.

Pyotr Ilyich Tchaikovsky

Tchaikovsky, Pyotr Ilyich (1840–1893)   Russian composer, aloof from the overt nationalism of The Mighty Handful group, but nevertheless writing in a distinctively Russian style. A homosexual, left his wife a few weeks after marriage (1877); 1876–1890, carried on an extensive correspondence with Nadezhda von Meck, a wealthy widow who gave him a monetary allowance—but they hardly met. Visited the United States, 1892; England, 1893 (D.Mus., Cambridge). Developed cholera after drinking unboiled water (perhaps deliberately?) in St. Petersburg, and died there a few days after the first performance of his last symphony, the *Pathetic*. His second symphony is nicknamed *Ukrainian* (or "Little Russian"), and his third *Polish*, his *Manfred*

Symphony is unnumbered. Other works, notable for vivid, forceful scoring and for an often-expressed melancholy, include 3 piano concertos (no. 1 the popular one, no. 3 unfinished), violin concerto; orchestral works; *Eugene Onegin, The Queen of Spades, Idanta, Mazeppa*, and 7 other operas; ballets *Swan Lake, The Sleeping Beauty, The Nutcracker*; chamber works, songs.

Telemann, Georg Philipp (1681–1767)   German composer of 40 operas, many oratorios, church cantatas, concertos, and other vocal and instrumental works. His chamber music includes instrumental suites called *Musique de table*. Friend of Bach. Held a leading church music post in Hamburg from 1721 until his death.

Temperament   The "tempering" (i.e., slight lessening or enlarging) of musical intervals away from the "natural" scale (that deducible by physical laws), in order to fit them for practicable performance. In particular the piano, the modern organ, and other fixed-pitch modern instruments are tuned to *equal temperament*, meaning that each semitone is made an equal interval. In this way the notes D♯ and E♭ are made identical, and other pairs similarly (although by physical laws they differ slightly); it is therefore equally easy to play in any key or, having started in one key, to modulate to any other. (Bach's 48 preludes and fugues, called *The Well-Tempered Clavier*, were among the first works to require some such system as this, being set in all the major and minor keys.) The previously prevalent system was *mean-tone temperament*, which gave a nearer approximation to natural tuning than does equal temperament for C major and keys nearly related to it; but it was so far out for keys remote from C major that playing in them was virtually impossible, unless such devices as separate notes for D♯ and E♭ were adopted (as they were on some old organs). It is to be noted that instruments in which the notes are not "pre-set" (e.g., the violin family) can have no "system" of temperament, since the player determines the pitch of the note and checks it by ear: and the player may, indeed, get nearer to "natural" intonation than a keyboard's fixed notes allow.

Tenor   (1) The highest normal male voice, apart from the Alto (which uses falsetto), so named because, when polyphonic music emerged in the late Middle Ages, its function was to hold (Lat., *tenere*) the plainsong or other "given" tune while the other voices proceeded in counterpoint to it; (2) name given, in "families" of instruments, to that instrument considered to have a position parallel to that which the tenor voice has among voices: so *tenor saxophone, tenor trombone*, etc.; the word tenor by itself means in a danceband the tenor saxophone, in a brass band the tenor saxhorn, and in obsolete English usage meant the viola; (3) *tenor clef*, type of clef (now little used, but sometimes encountered for cello, bassoon, tenor trombone) written

in which the note middle C is indicated on the top line but one of the staff.

Ternary   In three sections; *ternary form*, classification used of a movement in three sections of which the third is a repetition (exact or near) of the first:

i.e., a movement that may be represented as ABA or ABA´. Note that the term is also used even if the first section is initially stated twice (AABA or AABA´) as in the conventional "minuet and trio," in which the minuet section is given twice on its first statement but only one on its return. *Compare* **Binary**.

Tessitura (It. texture)   The range of notes to which a particular singer's voice naturally inclines ("he has a high *tessitura*"), although exceptional notes may be produced outside it, similarly, the general range (not counting exceptional notes) of a vocal part.

Tetrachord   An obsolete scale pattern (ancient Greek, also medieval) grouping 4 adjacent notes a whole tone or semitone apart. (Originally from *tetrachordon*, Greek four-stringed instrument.)

Theme   A group of notes constituting (by repetition, recurrence, development, etc.) an important element in the construction of a piece. In some types of musical analysis it is broadly equated with subject; but it is sometimes also applied to separately recognizable elements within a subject. In the phrase *theme and variations* it refers to the whole musical statement on which the variations are based (i.e., something much longer than *theme* in most other senses). *Metamorphosis of themes*, the process by which a theme can be altered in character (e.g., by changing its rhythm, say, to suit the dramatic progress of a Symphonic poem) while retaining its essence, e.g. in Liszt's symphonic poems; *representative theme*, a theme that carries some extramusical indication (e.g. a person, object, or emotion) for dramatic or narrative purpose, e.g. the Wagnerian Leading motive. In the term *theme song* (recurring in a musical play, etc., in association with a particular character) the word *theme* is used in a general and not a technical musical sense.

Theremin (or *thereminovox*)   Type of Electronic instrument having an upright sensitive "pole" that produces sound from the motion of the hand in space around it; invented in Russia, 1920, by Lev Sergeyevich Termin (b. 1896), who adopted Theremin as the Western form of his name and patented an improved version of the instrument in the United States, 1928. Composers using it in ensemble have included Varèse (*Equatorial*, 1934) and Martinau (*Phantasy* with string quartet, oboe, piano, 1945). It has a range of 5 octaves and a diversity of tone color.

Thorough-bass   *See* **Continuo**.

Time signature   Sign at the beginning of a composition or movement (and thereafter only when a change has to be indicated) conveying by means of figures the kind of beats in the bar and (above it) the number of such beats; e.g., 3/2 indicates 3 half notes to the bar, 3/8 indicates 3 eighth notes. *See also* **Duple time**.

Toccata (It.)   An instrumental piece, usually for one performer and usually consisting of a single rapid movement exhibiting the player's touch (It. *toccare*, to touch); there are specimens, e.g., by Bach for harpsichord, which are in several movements, and here the term is of imprecise significance.

Tonality   Key, especially in the effect made on the listener by the observance of a single key, as op-

posed (in the 20th century) to Polytonality (simultaneous use of several keys) or Atonality (absence of key).

Tone color   The quality that distinguishes a note as performed on one instrument from the same note as performed on other instruments (or voices). The French word *timbre* is also used in English in this sense. On analysis the differences between tone colors of instruments are found to correspond with differences in the harmonics represented in the sound (*see* **Harmonic series**).

Tone poem   Symphonic poem.

Tonic   The first degree, or keynote, of the scale, e.g., F in the keys of F major and F minor.

Transition   (1) (in analysis) A passage serving mainly to join two passages more important than itself; (2) a change of key, particularly a sudden one, not going through the regularly ordered process called "modulation." *See* **Modulate**.

Transpose   To write or perform music at a pitch other than the original. So certain instruments on which the player produces a note different from the written note are called transposing instruments, and an English horn, e.g., playing a perfect fifth below the written note, is said to *transpose down a fifth*. A song is often *transposed* to a higher or lower key to suit a singer's convenience. So also a piece written in one of the old Modes may be said to be in, e.g., the "Dorian mode transposed", meaning with the same intervals as the Dorian mode but ending elsewhere than D where the Dorian ends. So also *transposing keyboard*, one on which the performer can transpose by mechanical aid: the keys are struck as usual, but the sideways shifting of the keyboard causes strings higher or lower than normal to be struck.

Trautonium   Trade name for a type of electronic instrument invented in Germany in 1930; it produced only one note at a time. It could be fixed to a piano, one hand playing each instrument. Hindemith wrote for it.

Triad   A three-note chord consisting of a particular note plus its third and fifth above, e.g., C–E–G, which is called the "common chord" of C major, no matter whether C remains the bass-note or is replaced by one of the other notes. Similarly C–E♭–G is the "common chord" of C minor. Also *augmented triad*, containing the augmented fifth (e.g. C,E,G♯); *diminished triad*, containing the diminished 5th (e.g., C, E♭, G♭).

Trio-sonata   Type of composition favored in the late 17th and early 18th centuries, usually for 2 violins and a cello (or bass viol), with a keyboard instrument also playing the bass-line and supporting it with harmonies worked out by the player. *See* **Continuo**.

Twelve-tone   Term used to describe a technique of compositon in which all twelve notes within the octave (i.e., the seven white and five black notes of the piano) are treated as "equal," i.e., are subjected to an ordered relationship that (unlike that of the major-minor key system) establishes no "hierarchy" of notes (but see below). One such technique was invented by J.M. Hauer, but the term is now virtually confined to the technique invented by Schoenberg, described by him as a "method of composing with twelve notes that are related only to one another." This method works through the "tone-row" (or Series), in which all the twelve notes are placed in a particular order as the basis of a work. No note is repeated within a row, which accordingly consists of twelve different notes and no others. The tone-row does not necessarily form a theme or part of one, but is used as the "tonal reservoir" from which the piece is drawn. It may be used as it stands, or transformed (*see* **Invert**; **Retrograde**) or transposed. The total structure of the work, not merely the shape of the particular melody, must conform to the observance of the tone-row. Originally the twelve-tone technique was developed as a standardization of Atonal music; but certain composers (e.g., Dallapiccola, F. Martin), while using twelve-tone methods of construction, have allowed the resulting music to present a definitely implied relation to the major-minor key system; and many composers who do not follow twelve-tone technique in Schoenberg's rigorous sense have nevertheless deployed complete series of all the twelve notes without repetition of any one note, e.g., Walton, violin sonata; Britten, *The Turn of the Screw*.

U **Unison** A united sounding of the same note: thus *unison song*, a song for several people all singing the same tune (not harmonizing). Expressions such as s*inging in unison* are generally (but loosely) also applied to the singing of the same tune by men and women an octave apart—where "singing in octaves" would be more strictly accurate.

V **Varése, Edgard** (1883–1965) French-born composer (pupil of d'Indy and Roussel) who settled in the United States, 1915, and cultivated music involving extremes of dissonance, unusual instrumentation, and (often) "scientific" titles, e.g., *Ionization* (percussion instruments only) *Density 21.5* (flute solo, referring to specific gravity of platinum), *Octandre* (Fr. form of Lat. *Octandria*, plant with 8 stamens). Was also an influential pioneer in the use of taped and electronic music: *see* **Theremin**.

Variation A passage of music intended as a varied version of some "given" passage. So *Variations on*...a tune (whether or not the tune has been specially composed by the composer of the variations), the tune being called the "theme" of the variations. Such variations may diverge only slightly from the theme, mainly by melodic ornamentation (as in Mozart), but usage since the mid-19th century has tended to a looser type allowing a much freer form of composition, e.g., Elgar's *Enigma Variations*. The terms *chaconne*, *ground bass*, and *passacaglia* also imply variations, of a specific type, and the term *rhapsody* may do so.

Vaughan Williams, Ralph (1872–1958) English composer, pupil of Stanford, Bruch (in Berlin), and Ravel (in Paris). Close associate of Holst; much influenced by English folk music, some of which he collected and arranged. Based his *Sinfonia Antartica* (symphony no. 7) on his score for the film *Scott of the Antarctic*, and brought out his last symphony (no. 9) at the age of 85. He numbered only the last, identifying the others by key or by name. Other works include operas *Hugh the Drover*, *Riders to the Sea*, *Pilgrim's Progress*, *Sir John in Love*; ballet *Job*; many choral works; *Serenade to Music*, originally for 16 solo voices and orchestra; orchestral works with solo instruments, including *Floscampi*, *The Lark Ascending*, *Romance* (harmonica solo), tuba concerto; *Fantasia on a Theme of Tallis* for strings; Latin mass; hymns, including *For All the Saints*; 2 string quartets; songs, including *Linden Lea* and cycle *On Wenlock Edge*. Also conductor, especially choral, and hymnbook editor. O.M., 1935.

Verdi, Giuseppe [Fortunino Francesco] (1813–1901) Italian composer, born in Busseto of a poor family; became organist and composer in boyhood, but rejected by Milan Conservatory as overage and insufficiently gifted. First opera, *Oberto*, 1839. Later operas—grafting an individual mastery (vocal, orchestral, and dramatic) onto traditional Italian models—include *Nabucco*, *Macbeth*, *Rigoletto*, *Il Trovatore*, *La Traviata*, *Simon Boccanegra*, *A Masked Ball*, *The Force of Destiny*, *Don Carlos*, *Luisa Miller*, *Aida*, *Otello*, and *Falstaff*. The last two are products of his 70s, and rely less on the appeal of successive "set" numbers. Wrote also *Requiem* and a few other works to religious texts, although not himself a churchman; also string quartet—little else. In his earlier operas he became the symbol of resurgent Italian nationalism and frequently clashed with censors suspecting revolutionary implications: in 1860–1865, he himself sat as deputy in that part of Italy already unified. But later lived in seclusion. Founded a home for aged musicians in Milan. After early death of his first wife, lived with and then married the singer Giuseppina Strepponi. Died in Milan.

Verismo (It. realism) Term applied particularly to Italian opera of about 1900 (e.g., Mascagni, Puccini) with reference to its "contemporary" and often violent plots, sometimes amid sordid surroundings; e.g., Puccini's *The Cloak*, aboard a canal barge.

Villa-Lobos, Heitor (1887–1959) Brazilian composer; the first South American composer to become world-famous; was also a pianist and teacher. Prolific output, including operas, ballets, 12 symphonies, 17 string quartets, songs, etc., in varied styles but frequently with pronounced "national" flavor. Composed 14 works called *Choros* for various combinations (some including Brazilian native instruments), explaining the title as synthesizing "the different modalities of Brazilian, South American Indian and popular music, and having for principal elements rhythm and any typical melody of popular character." His *Bachianas Brasileiras* are supposed evocations of Bach in a Brazilian spirit. Wrote also *New York Skyline Melody* (on a melodic "shape" suggested by the skyline) for piano or orchestra; works for piano solo, for guitar, etc.

Viol Type of bowed stringed instrument of various sizes, current up to 1700 and thereafter superseded by instruments of the violin type; revived in the 20th century, however, for old music. The viols differ from the violin family in shape, in having frets, and in the kind of bow and style of bowing used. The three principal sizes (often encountered in ensemble) were the *treble viol*; *tenor viol*; and *bass viol*. All, being rested on or between the legs, are properly called *viola da gamba* (...for the leg) although that term most commonly indicates the bass viol (approximately cello size). *Viola da braccio* (...for the arm) indicates not a viol but a violin or viola. The *division viol* was a small bass viol suitable for solos (such as the playing of Divisions, i.e., variations); the *violone* was a larger (double-bass) viol. Note that the *bass viol* may occasionally (in nonspecialist usage, chiefly U.S.) indicate modern double-bass.

Viola d'amore (It. love-viol) Bowed stringed instrument related primarily not to the modern viola but to the Viol family, but, unlike them, having no frets, and played under the chin. It usually has 7 strings touched by the bow, and 7 "sympathetic" strings beneath them (hence the instrument's name) whose vibration is induced by the sounding of the upper set. The instrument is occasionally encountered in music of the 17th–18th centuries and there are some later exceptional uses (e.g., in Meyerbeer's *The Huguenots*).

Violin Bowed four-stringed instrument, the principal (and highest) member of the family of instruments (called "the violin family") that superseded the Viols from about 1700. The other members are the viola, cello, and double-bass, which has a superficial resemblance to the corresponding member (*violone*) of the viol family. The violin is prominently used in the orchestra (where the players normally divide into first and second violinists, a division usually corresponding to higher- and lower-pitched parts) and in solo and chamber music. Its range is from the G below middle C, upward for three and a half octaves and more.

Virginal(s) (1) Term in English 16th-century sources for all types of keyboard instruments, including *virginal* proper (*see* 2), harpsichord, and even organ; (2) 16th- and 17th-century keyboard instrument of harpsichord type (i.e., the strings being plucked), but smaller and of different shape—oblong, and with its one keyboard along the longer side of the soundboard (not at the end). Revived for old music in the 20th century. Named possibly from Lat. *virga*, rod or jack; possibly from being played by maidens (or because some analogous instrument had been so played); but certainly not from the Virgin Queen, as it was known before her time. The Italian term *spinetto* is used both for this and for the wing-shaped but otherwise similar instrument; but the best practice is to confine the term spinet to the latter type.

Virtuoso (It.) A performer of exceptional skill, especially in the technical aspects of performance.

Vivace (It.) Lively.

Vivaldi, Antonio (1678–1741) Italian violinist and composer; also priest, nicknamed "the red priest" (*il prete rosso*) from the color of his hair. Pupil of Legrenzi, Long in charge of music at an orphanage conservatory in Venice, but died in obscure circumstances in Vienna. Wrote more than 450 concertos (broadly conforming to the concerto grosso type) with various solo instruments, many with illustrative titles, e.g., *The Four Seasons*; also operas, church music, oratorios, including *Juditha Triumphans*. Bach admired him and transcribed many of his works (e.g., Bach's concerto for 4

harpsichords and strings is a transcription of Vivaldi's concerto for 4 violins and strings); and there has been a notable revival of interest in his works in the mid-20th century. His works have been variously catalogued and numbered, most recently by Ryom, whose numbering is preceeded by RV, *Ryom-Verzeichnis* (Ger., index).

Voice (1) The human (and animal) means of sound production using the two vibrating agents called the vocal cords (not "chords"); hence (2) a separate "strand" of music in harmony or counterpoint, whether intended to be sung or played. Thus a Fugue is said to be in, say, four voices (or four parts), whether its four strands are sung by individual voices, sung by several voices each, played by instruments, or all played on one instrument (e.g., piano). (3) (verb) Adjust a wind instrument or organ in the process of construction so that it exactly fits the required standards of pitch, tone color, etc.

Richard Wagner

Wagner, [Wilhelm] **Richard** (1813–1883) German composer, also writer (of his own librettos and of essays on musical and philosophical topics); also noted conductor, in which function he earned a living and visited London in 1855 and 1877. Born in Leipzig, traveled much, met much opposition. From *Rienzi* (1842) went on to write successful operas *The Flying Dutchman*, *Tannhäuser*, and *Lohengrin*; then, exemplifying his new theories of the proper relation of music and drama, composed *Tristan and Isolde*, *The Ring* (cycle of 4 operas), and *Parsifal*. These show a "symphonic" conception of opera, proceeding by leading motives (i.e., themes) not through the contrast of set "numbers". Wagner aimed at the *Gesamtkunstwerk*, the work of art uniting all the arts; the Festival Theater at Bayreuth (opened 1876) was built to his own revolutionary design with this in mind. His only mature comic opera is *The Mastersingers of Nuremberg*. Other compositions include *A Faust Overture*, *Siegfried Idyll*, and 5 song settings (with piano) of poems by Mathilde Wesendonk, at that time his mistress. Afterward he took as mistress Cosima, wife of Bülow and daughter of Liszt, and married her when his first wife died. He died in Venice. Influenced the course of music as much as any composer—as to operatic structure, harmony, and orchestration. Introduced the Wagner tuba.

Weber, Carl Maria [Friedrich Ernst] **von** (1786–1826) German composer, pupil of M. Haydn and Vogler; also conductor and pianist. Exponent of German Romantic opera, particularly in *Der Freischütz*, a lasting international success. Other operas include *Abuhassan*, *Euryanthe*, and *Oberon*—the last written in English for England; Weber died in London after superintending the first production. (He had poor health, and was financially driven to overwork.) Also wrote incidental music to plays, includlng *Preciosa* and *Turandot*; 2 concertos and *Concert Piece* for piano and orchestra; 2 concertos and 1 concertino for clarinet and orchestra; bassoon concerto; *Invitation to the Dance* and other piano solos; church music, songs, etc. Also writer on music; wrote an unfinished novel *A Composer's Life*, criticism, poems.

Webern, Anton von (1883–1945) Austrian composer, pupil of Schoenberg, whose twelve-tone technique he adapted to an individual style much concerned with establishing the relationship between a particular tone quality and a particular note. His works, mainly vocal or in the nature of chamber music, are few and tend to extreme brevity; no. 4 of his *Five Pieces for Orchestra* (1913) scored for 9 instruments including mandolin, takes 6 bars and lasts 19 seconds. Other works include a symphony; variations for orchestra; cantatas; 5 works for string quartet; canons for voice, clarinet, and bass clarinet; songs. He was accidentally shot dead in the Allied occupation of Austria. His posthumous influence on younger composers (and older, e.g., Stravinsky) has been conspicuous.

Weil, Kurt (1900–1950) German-born composer, pupil of Humperdinck and Busoni. Using some jazz-based idoms, he had early success with *The Three-penny Opera* (Ger., *Die Dreigroschenoper*), and with *Rise and Fall of the City of Mahagonny*, both to texts by Brecht with satirical criticism of capitalist society. Persecuted by the Nazis as a Jew and a composer of "decadent" music, he settled in the United States in 1935. His American works include the folk-ish opera *Down in the Valley* and music to various Broadway musical plays including *Lost in the Stars*. Other works include the cantata *Lindbergh's Flight* (1929) and 2 symphonies.

Well-Tempered Clavier, The (Ger., *Das wohltem perierte Clavier*) Title given by Bach to his 24 preludes and fugues, 1722, in all the major and minor keys, and applied also to a further similar 24 (1744); the title is thus now applied to the two sets together, which are also known as "the forty-eight." The use of all the major and minor keys demonstrated the facilities offered by the (then new) system of "equal temperament." The word *clavier*, meaning any keyboard instrument, is correct here—not clavichord, Bach not intending the work exclusively for that instrument.

Whole-tone The interval of 2 semitones, e.g., from C up to the adjacent D, divisible into the 2 semitones C–C♯ and C♯–D. So *whole-tone scale*, a scale progressing entirely in whole-tones, instead of partly in whole-tones and partly in semitones like the major and minor scales and the old Modes. Only two such whole-tone scales are possible—one "beginning" on C, one on C♯, although in fact each scale can begin equally well on any of its notes, since (owing to the equal intervals) there is no note that presents itself as a point of rest equivalent to a note. Debussy and other composers have used the whole-tone scale pronouncedly for chords and short passages, but not consistently for an entire piece.

Wolf, Hugo (1860–1903) Austrian composer chiefly of songs, usually grouped by their literary sources, e.g., Italian songbook and Spanish songbook (German translations of Italian, Spanish poems), Mörike songs (57), and songs to texts by Goethe (51). These are reckoned as a peak within the general German Romantic type of song; as in Schumann's, the piano parts are very important. A few of the songs also have orchestral (as well as piano) versions of the accompaniments. Wolf also wrote opera *The Corregidor*; *Italian Serenade*; and a few other works. Lived largely in poverty; proved himself unfitted to conducting; was an aggressive music critic (extolling Wagner, decrying Brahms); became insane in 1897 and was confined from 1898 until death.

World music Term used in modern musical criticism to catagorize pop music from around the world; e.g. Zulu Jive music from South Africa, Port Au Beuil music from Ireland, and Filmi music from India. The term world music is not used to define classical or courtly musical forms such as Indian Ragas or Japanese Bugaku. One outstanding characteristic of world music is that it is generally danceable and entertaining.

Wuorinen, Charles (b. 1938) American composer of octet and much other chamber music; various concertos including one for tuba, 12 wind instruments, 12 drums; *Making Ends Meet* for piano duet; electronic music. Is also pianist and conductor.

MYTHOLOGY

Achates The faithful friend and companion of Aeneas. In Vergil's *Aeneid* he is often called *fidus Achates,* "faithful Achates."

Achilles The son of Peleus and the Nereid Thetis, and king of the Myrmidons, a Thessalian tribe. He is the hero of Homer's *Iliad* and became the prototype of the Greeks' conception of manly valor and beauty. He took part in the Trojan War on the side of the Greeks as their most illustrious warrior, and slew the Trojan hero Hector. Achilles had been dipped in the Styx by his mother, which rendered him invulnerable except in the heel by which she held him and where he was fatally wounded by an arrow shot by Paris, Hector's younger brother, or, according to another version of the story, by the god Apollo, who had assumed Paris' shape.

Actaeon A celebrated huntsman, son of Aristaeus and Autonoë, the daughter of Cadmon. Having seen Diana bathing, he was changed by her into a stag and torn to pieces by his own dogs.

Adonis A beautiful youth, beloved by Venus. When he was killed by a wild boar, Venus changed his blood into the flower which is still called *Adonis* after him.

Aeneas A Trojan hero, the son of Anchises and Venus. He is the hero of Vergil's *Aeneid,* which describes his exploits after the fall of Troy until his arrival in Italy. He is revered as the ancestral hero of the Romans.

Aeolus King of the Aeolian islands, father of Halcyone; appointed by Jupiter keeper of the winds and later considered to be the wind god. He received Ulysses hospitably and gave him, tied up and made harmless in a leather bag, all the ill winds which were later let out by his companions.

Aesculapius The god of medicine. Son of Apollo and Coronis and father of Machaon. His foster father was the Centaur Chiron. He became a great healer, able to restore life to the dead. Alarmed by this, Pluto, the lord of the realm of the dead, induced Zeus to kill him. At the request of Apollo he was placed among the stars. His oracles on earth were numerous.

Agamemnon King of Mycenae, brother of Menelaus and leader of the Greek expedition against Troy. Because of his refusal to release Chryseis, Achilles withdrew from the fight. Things went bad for the Greeks. Agamemnon, like most of the other leaders, was wounded, but finally he managed to reconcile Achilles. After the return of the victorious Greek army, Agamemnon was killed by his wife's, Clytemnestra's, lover Aegisthus.

Ajax (Gr. **Aias**) Son of Telamon; as a hero in the Trojan War second only to Achilles. He was sent to placate Achilles after the latter's quarrel with Agamemnon. He had an undecided encounter with the Trojan hero Hector and later defended and rescued the bodies of Patroclus and Achilles. He died by his own hand after having seen the coveted armor of Achilles go to Ulysses. From his blood sprang the Hyacinth, which bears the letters "ai" on its leaves, the first letters of his name and also the Greek for "woe."

Alcestis Daughter of Pelias, wife of Admetus, who had won her by driving a chariot drawn by lions and boars. When Admetus fell ill, Alcestis saved his life by agreeing to die in his stead. Hercules saved her by laying in wait for Death, whom he forced to abandon his prey. According to another version, Persephone released her from the underworld.

Amazons A word of unknown origin, interpreted by the Greeks as signifying "without breast." A legendary race of warlike women forming a state from which men were excluded, and dwelling on the coast of the Black Sea. Many Greek heroes got involved with them. One of Hercules' labors was the task to fetch the girdle of the Amazon Queen Hippolyta, whom he had to kill in the process. Theseus carried off the Amazon Queen Antiope and had to give battle to her female warriors in the heart of Athens. Achilles slew the Amazon Queen Penthesilea who had come to the assistance of the Trojans.

Amaterasu Japanese sun goddess. Literally, "the great illuminating queen of heaven." Child of Izanami and Izanagu, the first man and woman of Shinto mythology. She is the mythological ancestress of the Japanese Imperial Family. Frequently shown in masculine dress and invoked before battle, she is also the goddess of weaving. After her brother, the moon god Tsukinoye, murdered her favorite lady in waiting, she hid in a cave. Without sun, the crops withered and died, and the Gods began to age. Finally, she was tricked into coming out by Ama-No-Uzume (literally, queen of laughter), who performed a bawdy dance. When she heard laughter, she followed the sound and saw Ama-No-Uzume dancing. Amaterasu laughed so hard she fell down and rolled out of the cave.

Ambrosia Celestial food used by the gods.

Amphitrite One of the Nereids. As the wife of Neptune, she was the successor to Tethys, the wife of Oceanus, who had been the Titan ruling over the watery element. She was a daughter of Nereus and Doris, and the mother of Triton.

Anansi African spider god. Intermediary god of the Ashanti, he helped to create the world by molding some of his spider webbing. He is a trickster diety who gave mankind fire by tricking the gods. His mythology survives in the "Aunt Nancy" stories of the old South.

Andromache The wife of Hector and mother of Astyanax. After Hector's death and the fall of Troy she was allotted to Neoptolemus of Epirus, but eventually became the wife of Hector's brother Helenus.

Andromeda The daughter of Cepheus and Cassiopeia. To placate Neptune she had to be chained to a rock, but was delivered by Perseus who married her and killed his rival Phineus. After death she was placed among the stars.

Antaeus A gigantic wrestler (son of Earth and Sea, Ge and Poseidon), whose strength was invincible so long as he touched the earth. Hercules succeeded in killing him by lifting him up from the earth and squeezing him to death.

Antigone Daughter of Oedipus, and the Greek ideal of filial and sisterly fidelity.

Antilochus Son of Nestor and friend of Achilles. He was chosen to break to Achilles the news of Patroclus' death. Antilochus himself was killed by

Memnon, the son of Aurora and Tithonus. The three friends, Antilochus, Achilles, and Patroclus were buried in the same mound. Ulysses saw them walking together in the underworld.

Anubis   Egyptian god of embalming, son of Nephtys and Osiris. His aunt Isis taught him the art of embalming. He is one of the most important gods of the underworld because he leads the dead soul to judgment and lies in wait to eat the souls of those whose evil deeds outweigh their good ones.

Aphrodite   *See* **Venus**.

Apollo   One of the great gods of Olympus, son of Jupiter and Latona; like his sister Diana, born on Delos, which is sacred to him. He was the god of archery, prophecy, music, and healing. As the leader of the Muses, he was given the lyre which Mercury had invented, and in turn gave music to woman when she was created. The musician Orpheus was his son. As the god of healing he bore the name of Paeon, sharing it with other gods, and became the father of Aesculapius. He was the successor of Hyperion as sun god and became identified with Helios, in whose stead he was considered the father of Phaëthon. *See also* **Phoebus**.

Apollo's exploits in myth and poetry are numerous. He killed the serpent Python; he loved the nymph Daphne and changed her at her request into a bay tree, he supplied king Midas with a pair of asses' ears for having voted for Pan and against Apollo in a trial of musical skill; inadvertently he killed Hyacinthus; with his sister he took revenge on Niobe for having insulted his mother; for one year he was the servant of king Admetus to atone for his unjust attack on the Cyclops who had made the bolt with which Jupiter killed Apollo's son Aesculapius; he induced Diana to kill Orion; in the Trojan war he intervened on behalf of Chryseis and thus precipitated the quarrel of Agamemnon and Achilles; he healed Hector and assisted him in his struggle with Patroclus; he guided the arrow which killed Achilles; it was he who gave Cassandra, whom he loved, the gift of prophecy; etc.

Apollo was the incarnation of the Greek ideal of youthful manhood. As such he became a favorite subject of Greek and later art.

Apollo, oracles of   Apollo had several oracles: one in Ionia, one on the island of Delos, and one famous one in Delphi, known as the Delphic or Delphian oracle.

Arachne   A maiden skilled in weaving, who was changed to a spider by Minerva for having the presumption to challenge the goddess to a contest in weaving.

Arcadia   A district of the Peloponnesus which, according to Vergil, was the home of pastoral simplicity and happiness.

Ares   Called Mars by the Romans. The Greek god of war, and one of the great Olympian deities.

Argonauts   Jason's crew in search of the Golden Fleece.

Ariadne   The daughter of King Minos of Crete. She fell in love with Theseus and gave him a sword and a clew of thread with which to kill the Minotaur and find his way out of the labyrinth. Theseus fled with her to Naxos and abandoned her there. Her laments aroused the compassion of Bacchus, who married

her and gave her a crown which after her death was transformed into the celestial constellation of the crown of Ariadne.

Artemis   A Greek deity identified by the Romans with Diana. *See* **Diana**.

Atalanta   A beautiful maiden who participated in the Calydonian boar hunt. When Meleager bestowed on her as trophies the head and the hide of the boar which he had killed, she became the innocent cause of a conflict in which Meleager and two of his uncles lost their lives. According to another legend, Atalanta had been warned by an oracle not to marry. In order to make things difficult for her suitors she promised to be the prize in a race. She lost the race to Hippomenes, who then forgot to thank Venus and was changed into a lion as was also his bride.

Athena (Athene)   The goddess of wisdom and of the arts and sciences in Greek mythology, corresponding to the Roman Minerva. She sprang full-armored from the head of Zeus. Athens was called after her as the result of a contest in which the prize went to the deity that had bestowed upon man the most useful boon. Athene's was the olive tree; Neptune's the horse.

Athena

Athens   The capital of Attica, about four miles from the sea, between the small rivers Cephissus and Ilissus.

Atlantis   A mythic island of great extent which was supposed to have existed in the Atlantic Ocean. It is first mentioned by Plato (in the *Timaeus* and *Critias*), and Solon was told of it by an Egyptian priest, who said that it had been overwhelmed by an earthquake and sunk beneath the sea 9000 years before his time.

Atlas   One of the Titans warring against the gods and condemned to uphold the heavens on his shoulders. He was a brother of Prometheus, son of Iapetus and father of the Pleiades. A king by the name of Atlas had the garden of the Hesperides in his realm and was their uncle or father.

Attica   A division of ancient Greece, the chief city of which was Athens.

August Personage of Jade   Chinese god of heaven, husband of Wang Muyiang. Lord of the sky, he rules over humankind and lives at the center of the earth.

Aurora   Identical with Eos, goddess of the dawn.

Bacchus In Roman mythology, the god of wine, the Dionysus of the Greeks, son of Jupiter and Semele, also known as Libus. Semele, at the suggestion of Juno, asked Jupiter to appear before her in all his glory, but the foolish request proved her death. Jupiter saved the child which was prematurely born by sewing it up in his thigh until it came to maturity. His foster-father was Silenus. Bacchus entered Thebes in a chariot drawn by elephants, and, according to some accounts, he married Ariadne after Theseus had deserted her in Naxos.

Baldur   Norse sun god.   Son of Freya and Odin, he was compassionate to a fault. At his birth, which was witnessed by all living beings, Freya made them all individually swear not to harm her son. The one object she forgot to ask was mistletoe. Loki, jealous at Baldur's popularity with the gods, remembered this and dared a blind man to throw a sprig of mistletoe at Baldur. Baldur instantly fell dead. However, he was resurrected after Ragnarok and placed in charge of the new earth that had sprung from the disaster.

Baucis   *See* **Philemon and Baucis**.

Bellerophon   A grandson of Sisyphus. Riding on Pegasus he slew the fire-breathing Chimaera. He was worshipped as a demigod at Corinth.

Bellona   The Roman goddess of war, represented as the sister or wife of Mars.

Boreas   A personification of the north wind. He tried to be gentle with the nymph Orithyia, whom he loved dearly, but he could not breathe soothingly or sigh softly, and, true to his real character, he carried her off and became by her the father of Zetes and Calais. Boreas is at times called a son of Aeolus, the ruler of the winds, who lived in a cave in Mount Haemus in Thrace.

Cadmus King of Phoenicia and Telephassa, by his wife Harmonia father of Actaeon and Ino. He was reputedly the introducer of the Greek alphabet. Seeking his sister Europa, carried off by Jupiter, he had strange adventures—sowing in the ground teeth of a dragon he had killed, which sprang up as armed men who slew each other. The five survivors helped him to found the city of Thebes.

Caduceus   The staff of Mercury, which he received from Apollo in exchange for the lyre. It was originally of olive wood. Its garlands were later replaced by serpents. At the top there were two wings.

Calliope   One of the nine Muses, mother of Orpheus by Apollo; the patroness of epic poetry.

Calypso   The queen of the island Ogygia, on which Ulysses was wrecked. She kept him there for seven years, and promised him perpetual youth and immortality if he would remain with her forever.

Cassandra   The daughter of Priam and Hecuba, gifted with the power of prophecy; but Apollo, whose advances she had refused, brought it to pass that no one believed her predictions, although they were invariably correct, as in the case of the coming of the Greeks.

Castor and Pollux   Twin brothers, offspring of Leda and Jupiter in the guise of a swan. Castor was famous as a horseman. Pollux as a pugilist. They accompanied the Argonauts and became the patron deities of seamen and voyagers. They were the brothers of Clytemnestra and Helen, whom they rescued when she was carried off by Theseus. During their war with Idas and Lynceus, Castor was slain. Pollux being inconsolable, Jupiter placed both brothers among the stars. They are also known as the Dioscuri (sons of Zeus) and Tyndaridae after Tyndareus, their mother's husband.

Centaurs   Originally, an ancient race, inhabiting Mount Pelion in Thessaly; in later accounts, they are represented as half horse and half man.

Cerberus   Watch dog at the entrance to Hades; offspring of Typhaon and Echidna; generally represented with three heads, a mane of serpents' heads and a serpent's tail.

Ceres   The Roman name of *Mother Earth*, the protectress of agriculture and of all the fruits of the earth; later identified with the Greek Demeter.

Ceridwen   Welsh mother goddess, and mother of the famous bard Taliesin. She is usually portrayed stirring a cauldron, which contains simmering herbs that grant wisdom to the drinker. She is featured briefly in *The Mabinogion*, a collection of Welsh myths.

Chaos   Original Confusion in which earth, sea, and air were mixed up together. It was personified by the Greeks as the most ancient of the gods. The egg of Nyx, the daughter of Chaos, was floating on Chaos and from it arose the world.

Charon   The son of Erebos, who conveyed in his boat the shades of the dead across the rivers of the lower regions.

Charybdis   A sea monster which sucked in and discharged the sea three times a day in a terrible whirlpool. Charybdis was a maiden above but ended in a fish begirt with dogs. Together with Scylla she was placed in the Strait of Messina.

Chimaera   A fire-breathing monster of divine origin. It was part lion, part goat, and part dragon. It dwelled in Lycia and was finally killed by Bellerophon bridling Pegasus with a golden bridle given him by Minerva. Aeneas found it in the infernal regions.

Chiron   The wisest of the centaurs, son of Cronos and Philyra. He was instructed by Apollo and Diana and became in turn the teacher of Aesculapius and many distinguished Grecian heroes. He helped Peleus to win the hand of the goddess Thetis. On his death he was placed by Jupiter among the stars where he appears in the shape of the constellation Sagittarius.

Circe   A sorceress, sister of Aeetes, who lived in the island of Aeaea. When Ulysses landed there, Circe turned his companions into swine, but Ulysses resisted the metamorphosis by virtue of a herb called *moly*, given him by Mercury.

Clio   One of the nine Muses, the patroness of history.

Clotho   One of the three Fates, daughter of Themis (Law). Her name signifies "spinner." She spins the thread of human life.

Clytemnestra The wife of Agamemnon, whom she and her paramour Aegisthus murdered after his return from Troy. She was slain by her son Orestes.

Corn Mother Native American. According to this myth, corn was created when a warrior, who had gone into the forest seeking a vision to save his people from starvation, was met by a warrior woman dressed in silky white strands, who challenged him to wrestle with her. Not wanting to harm a woman, at first he was very gentle, until she told him that if he could not defeat her, she would kill him. After he had defeated the warrior woman in battle, she told him to take her body and bury it because it would become food for his people.

Cornucopia Also called the horn of plenty or the horn of Amalthaea. According to one legend it was broken off the goat Amalthaea by the infant Jupiter, who endowed it with the magic power of becoming filled with whatever its owner wished, and gave it to his nurses.

Crete One of the largest islands of the Mediterranean Sea, lying south of the Cyclades.

Cronus One of the Titans, son of Uranus and Ge, father (by Rhea) of Hestia, Demeter, Hera, Hades, Poseidon, and Zeus. He dethroned his father as ruler of the world, and was in turn dethroned by his son, Zeus or Jupiter. By the Romans he was identified with Saturn.

Cupid The god of love in Roman mythology (Lat. *cupido,* desire, passion), identified with the Greek Eros; son of Mercury and Venus. He is represented as a winged boy, carrying a bow and arrows. One legend says that he wets with blood the grindstone on which he sharpens his arrows. *Cupid and Psyche* is an episode in the *Golden Ass* of Apuleius. *See* **Psyche**.

Cybele Anatolian earth goddess. Cybele's priests were called Corybantes, and they ritually castrated themselves to make themselves more like her.

Cyclopes Creatures with one circular eye in the middle of their foreheads, of whom Homer speaks as a gigantic and lawless race of shepherds in Sicily, who devoured human beings; they helped Vulcan to forge the thunderbolts of Zeus under Aetna.

D **Daedalus** Literally, the cunning worker. A personification of skill in the mechanical art; the patron of artists' and craftsmen's guilds. As the hero of legends and tales, Daedalus was an inventive Athenian, son of Metion and grandson of Erechtheus, who originated axes, awls, bevels, and the like. He was the architect who built the labyrinth for King Minos of Crete. Imprisoned in it himself, Daedalus fashioned wings for himself and his son Icarus and escaped to Sicily. Icarus fell into the sea, but his father reached Sicily safely. Daedalus also had a nephew, Perdix, of whose skill he was envious. He tried to kill him by pushing him off a tower but Minerva intervened, saving the boy's life by changing him into a partridge.

Danäe Daughter of King Acrisius of Argos who did not want her to marry and kept her imprisoned because he had been told that his daughter's son would kill him. Jupiter came to her in the disguise of a shower of gold and she became the mother of Perseus. She and her child were set adrift in a chest and saved by a fisherman on the island of Seriphos.

Daphne A nymph, daughter of a river god and loved by Apollo, who killed his rival Leucippus. Daphne escaped and was later changed into a laurel or bay tree which remained henceforth the favorite tree of the sun god.

Delphi A town of Phocis at the foot of Mount Parnassus, famous for a temple of Apollo and an oracle which was silenced only in the 4th century A.D.

Demeter One of the great Olympian deites of Greece, identified with the Roman Ceres. She was the goddess of vegetation and the protectress of marriage. Persephone (Proserpine) was her daughter. *See* **Proserpine**.

Diana A Roman goddess, later identified with the Olympian Artemis, who was daughter of Zeus and Leto, and twin-sister of Apollo. She was the goddess of the moon and of hunting, protectress of women, and—in earlier times at least—the great mother goddess of Nature.

Dido The name given by Vergil to Elissa, founder and queen of Carthage. She fell in love with Aeneas, who was compelled by Mercury to leave the hospitable queen. Elissa, in grief, burns herself to death on a funeral pyre.

Dionysus *See* **Bacchus**.

Dryad A nymph whose life was bound up with that of a tree. Also called *hamadryad* or in English, wood nymph.

E **Echo** The nymph of Diana, who, shunned by Narcissus, faded to nothing but a voice. She was punished by Juno because her prattling had prevented Jupiter's irate wife from surprising him in the company of the nymphs; she was condemned never to speak first and never to be silent when anyone else spoke.

The nymph Echo

Electra   Daughter of Agamemnon and Clytemnestra. Electra, with the help of her brother, Orestes, avenged Clytemnestra's murder of Agamemnon by murdering, in turn, Clytemnestra and her new husband, Aegisthus.

Elysium   A happy land, where there is neither snow, nor cold, nor rain. Hither favored heroes like Menelaus, pass without dying, and live happy under the rule of Rhadamanthus. In the Latin poets, Elysium is part of the lower world, and the residence of the shades of the blessed.

Erebus   A place of darkness through which the souls passed on their way to Hades. Hence loosely, the nether regions of which Proserpine and Pluto were the rulers. Personified, Erebus was among the first beings, son of Chaos, brother of Nyx, and, dwelling in Hades, father of Aether and Day.

Erinys   *See* **Fury**.

Eris   The goddess of discord, sister of Ares or Mars. At the wedding of Peleus and Thetis, Eris, being uninvited, threw into the gathering an apple bearing the inscription "For the Fairest," which was claimed by Juno, Venus, and Minerva. Paris, being called upon for judgment, awarded it to Venus.

Eros   The Greek god of love, the youngest of all the gods; equivalent to the Roman Cupid. *See* **Cupid**.

Eteocles and Polynices   The two sons of Oedipus. After the expulsion of their father, they agreed to reign alternate years in Thebes. Eteocles took the first turn, but at the close of the year refused to resign the scepter to his brother. This was the cause of the "Seven against Thebes." Eteocles and Polynices met in combat and each was slain by the other's hand.

Eumenides   Literally, the gracious ones. A euphemistic term, used by the Greeks to refer to the terrible Erinyes or Furies in order to propitiate them. *See* **Fury**.

Europa   A daughter either of Phoenix or of Agenor, famed for her beauty. Jupiter in the form of a white bull carried her off and swam with her to the island of Crete. She was the mother of Minos, Rhadamanthus and Evandros and according to some forms of the legend, of the Minotaur.

Eurydice   The wife of Orpheus. Fleeing from an admirer, she was killed by a snake and borne to Tartarus, where Orpheus sought her and was permitted to bring her to earth if he would not look back at her following him. He could not resist, however, and Eurydice was forced to return to the shades.

Eurynome   Female Titan, the wife of Ophion.

Eurytion   The Centaur, who, at the marriage feast of Pirithous with Hippodamia, became intoxicated and offered violence to the bride, thus causing the celebrated battle of the Lapithae and Centaurs. Eurytion was also the name of the giant guarding Geryon's cattle and slain by Hercules.

Fates   The three goddesses determining the course of human life. They are described as daughters of Night—to indicate the darkness and obscurity of human destiny—or of Zeus and Themis, that is, "daughters of the just heavens." They were Clotho, who spun the thread of life; Lachesis, who held it and fixed its length; and Atropos, who cut it off.

Faunus   In Roman mythology, a rural deity; son of Picus, grandson of Saturn and father of Acis, the suitor of Galatea, and of Latinus, the father of Lavinia. He, as well as Silvanus, came to be more and more identified with the Greek Pan, with whom he had many traits in common. His priests were the Luperci, his main festival the Lupercalia. When not viewed as an individual, he appeared in the multiformity of the fauns, possibly under the influence of the Greek panes, satyrs, etc., in their relation with Pan.

Freya   Warrior goddess and goddess of marriage in Teutonic mythology. Wife of Odin, she was the mother of Baldur and a formidable warrior, often fighting beside Odin and Thor. She was the goddess to whom the Valkyries brought the fallen heroes before whisking them away to Valhalla. Loki frequently promised her to various giants and monsters in order to get his way. Friday is named after her.

Frigga or Frigg   In Scandinavian mythology, the supreme goddess, wife of Odin. She presided over marriages, and may be called the Juno of Asgard. In Teutonic mythology she is confused with Freya.

Fury   The Furies, in Greek Erinyes or euphemistically Eumenides, were avenging spirits of retributive justice. Their names, when in course of time their number had come to be fixed at three, were Alecto, Megaera, and Tisiphone. Their task was to punish crimes not within the reach of human justice. Through Aeschylus the tradition developed that after the time when they had intervened in the case of Orestes, their functions no longer covered cases of "guiltiness" free from moral guilt. In spite of their inexorable sternness, they wept when they heard Orpheus implore the deities of the underworld to restore Eurydice to life.

Gaea or Ge   The personification of the Earth, called Tellus by the Romans; described as the first being that sprang from Chaos. She gave birth to Uranus and Pontus. Gaea and Uranus, that is Earth and Heaven, were the parents of the Titans. According to another story, Gaea, Erebus, and Love were the first of beings. By Gaea's powers plants potent for enchantment are produced. To her as to Neptune, Themis, and others prophetic influence was attributed.

Ganymede   The most beautiful of all mortals. He was carried off to Olympus that he might fill the cup of Zeus and live among the immortal gods.

Gemini   The constellation *Twins*, that is, the brothers Castor and Pollux, whom Jupiter rewarded for their brotherly attachment by placing them together among the stars when Castor was slain and Pollux was inconsolable.

Golden Fleece   The story is that Ino persuaded her husband, Athamas, that his son Phryxus was the cause of a famine which desolated the land. Phryxus was ordered to be sacrificed but made his escape over sea on the winged ram, Chrysomallus, which had a golden fleece. At Colchis, he sacrificed the ram to Zeus and gave the fleece to King Aeetes. It later formed the quest of Jason's Argonautic expedition, and was stolen by him.

Gorgons   Three monstrous females with huge teeth, brazen claws, and snakes for hair, the sight of whom turned beholders to stone; Medusa, the most famous, was slain by Perseus.

Graces   Three goddesses who enhanced the enjoyments of life by refinement and gentleness; they were Aglaia (brilliance), Euphrosyne (joy), and Thalia (bloom).

EXHIBIT 18.1
Greek Gods and Goddesses

Aphrodite	Goddess of beauty and love
Apollo	God of music, poetry, and healing arts
Ares	God of war
Artemis	Goddess of wild things
Athena	Goddess of wisdom
Demeter	Goddess of crops, fertility of the land
Eros	God of love
Hecate	Goddess of witches
Hera	Protector of women
Hermes	Messenger of the gods
Hestia	Goddess of the hearth fire
Hymen	God of marriage
Pan	God of pastures, forests, flocks, and herds
Persephone	Goddess of sleep
Poseidon	God of the sea
Zeus	King of the gods

Grail or **Graal**   The Holy Grail or Sangreal is the cup from which the Saviour drank at the Last Supper. It was taken by Joseph of Arimathea to Europe, where it was lost. Its recovery became the sacred quest for King Arthur's knights.

Gryphon or **griffin**   A fabulous animal, with the body of a lion and the head and wings of an eagle, dwelling in the Rhipaean mountains, between the Hyperboreans and the one-eyed Arimaspians, and guarding the gold of the North.

Hades Originally, the god of the nether world. Later the name was used to designate the gloomy subterranean land of the dead. After the river Styx; also called Stygian realm.

Halcyone   Daughter of Aeneas and wife of Ceyx. When Ceyx was drowned, she flew to his floating body, and the pitying gods changed them both into birds, kingfishers, who nest at sea during a certain calm week in winter, the "halcyon days."

Harmonia   The daughter of Venus and Mars; given by Jupiter in marriage to Cadmus of Thebes. Vulcan's wedding gift to her was a necklace which proved fatal to all its successive owners.

Harpies   Winged monsters, half women, half birds, armed with sharp claws, and defiling everything they touched. They were driven away by the Argonauts from their victim Phineus and withdrew to an island where Aeneas found them, one of them predicting dire sufferings for the Trojans. In the legends of Charlemagne, Astolpho freed king Senapus of Abyssinia from the Harpies that had blinded him and snatched away his food.

Hebe   The goddess of youth, and cup-bearer of the immortals before Ganymede superseded her. She was the wife of Hercules, and had the power of making the aged young again.

Hecate   One of the Titans, the only one that retained her power under the rule of Zeus. She was the daughter of Perses and Asteria, and became a deity of the lower world after taking part in the search for Persephone. She taught witchcraft and sorcery, was a goddess of the dead, and became identified with Selene, Artemis, and Persephone.

Hector   Eldest son of Priam, the noblest of all the Trojan chieftains in Homer's *Iliad*. After holding out for ten years, he was slain by Achilles, who dragged the dead body thrice around the walls of Troy.

Hecuba   In Homer's *Iliad*, second wife of Priam, and mother of nineteen children, including Hector. When Troy was taken by the Greeks she fell to the lot of Ulysses. She was afterwards metamorphosed into a dog, and threw herself into the sea.

Helen of Troy   The daughter of Zeus and Leda, wife of Menelaus, king of Sparta. She eloped with Paris and brought about the destruction of Troy, which forms the subject of Homer's *Iliad*. After the Trojan War Helen returned to Menelaus. Later legends state that Helen did not accompany Paris all the way to Troy but was detained in Egypt.

Helenus   In Vergil's *Aeneid*, the prophet, the only son of Priam that survived the fall of Troy. He was allowed to marry Andromache, his brother Hector's widow.

Helios   Ancient Greek sun god. He drove his chariot from East to West each day. The center of his worship was Rhodes. His position as sun god was gradually assumed by Apollo.

Hera   The Greek Juno, daughter of Cronus and Rhea, the wife and sister of Zeus. The word means "chosen one."

Hercules

Hercules A mighty Greek hero, son of Jupiter and Alemena, who took part in the expedition of the Argonauts and won immortality by accomplishing twelve feats which are known as the Labors of Hercules. He was killed by Deianira, his wife, who gave him the fatal garment steeped in the blood of Nessus which she thought to be a love-spell. After death, Hercules was placed among the stars. He was worshiped as the god of physical strength. *See also* **Pillars** and **Labors of Hercules**.

Hermes *See* **Mercury**.

Hero and Leander Hero, a priestess of Venus, fell in love with Leander, who swam across the Hellespont every night to visit her. One night he was drowned, and heartbroken Hero drowned herself in the same sea.

Hippolyta The queen of the Amazons who consented to yield her girdle to Hercules and was slain by him when he thought erroneously that she had betrayed him. Hippolyta is also given instead of Antiope as the name of the queen of the Amazons whom Theseus espoused.

Hippolytus The son of Theseus. He repulsed the advances of his stepmother Phaedra, the daughter of Minos, who thereupon managed to arouse falsely the jealousy of her husband. At Theseus' request Neptune frightened Hippolytus' horses, thus causing a fatal accident. When the innocence of the youth became evident, Aesculapius with the help of Diana restored him to life, and Phaedra committed suicide.

Hippomenes The youth who won Atalanta in a foot race, beguiling her with golden apples thrown for her to pick up. Failing to thank Venus, he was changed into a lion, as was also his bride.

Homer The blind poet of Greece, about 850 B.C.

Horus The Elder (Hor) Egyptian sky god. He was usually represented as a falcon and his eyes were the sun and the moon. He was the god of goodness and light, and Egyptian kings were believed to be incarnations of him.

Horus The Younger Egyptian god, born to Isis and Osiris. Best known as the avenger of Osiris, he fought Set (Osiris's brother and murderer) and returned him to the desert. Horus is usually portrayed as a child suckling at Isis's breast.

Hydra A monster of the Lernean marshes, in Argolis. It had nine heads, and it was one of the twelve labors of Hercules to kill it. As soon as he struck off one of its heads, two shot up in its place.

Hygeia Goddess of health and daughter of Aesculapius. Her symbol was a serpent drinking from a cup in her hand.

Hyperboreans Literally, those beyond the north wind. A happy people, living in the north in blissful inaccessibility, in a land of sunshine and abundance, exempt from disease and the ravages of war. Their lives lasted a thousand years which they spent in the worship of Apollo.

Hyperion A Titan, son of Uranus and Ge, father of Helios, Selene, and Eos, precursor of Apollo the sun god. He was the owner of the island of Thrinakia where Lampetia and Phaëthusa tended his cattle.

Icarus The son of Daedalus. He flew with his father from Crete; but the sun melted the wax with which his wings were fastened on, and he fell into the sea, hence called the Icarian.

Iliad Epic poem of the Trojan War by Homer.

Ilium *See* **Troy**.

Io The beautiful daughter of Inachus, king of Argos. Jupiter, who had been flirting with her, changed her into a heifer to conceal her from Juno. Argus, who had a hundred eyes, was charged by Juno to watch the heifer. Mercury, at Jupiter's request, killed Argos, and Juno sent a gadfly to chase the heifer all over the world. On the Nile Io finally recovered her shape and was returned to her family after Jupiter had promised not to pay her any more attentions. Io was by Jupiter the mother of Epaphus, the ancestor of Aegyptus, Damaus, Cepheus, and Phineus. In the allegorical interpretation of mythology Io is the moon.

Iris Goddess of the rainbow; the messenger of the gods when they intended discord. The rainbow is the bridge or road let down from heaven for her accommodation.

Isis Egyptian goddess of magic, wife of Osiris, sister of Nephtys. As the Egyptian goddess of magic, she was invoked by the priests of ancient Egypt. In her most famous myth, her brother Set, jealous of her husband, Osiris, murdered him and tore his body into 14 pieces so that Isis would not be able to find them. With her sister Nephtys, she roamed all of Egypt until she found the pieces. Putting them back together, she embalmed him and gave him a proper burial.

Ithaca The home of Ulysses and Penelope.

Janus A solar deity; doorkeeper of heaven and patron of the beginning and end of things. He had two faces, one for the rising sun and one for sunset. The first month of the year was named for him. The gates of his temples were kept open in time of war. He was the builder of the Janiculum, which Aeneas saw when he set foot on Italian soil.

Jason Son of the Thessalian king Aeson and nephew of the usurper Pelias. He took part in the Calydonian Hunt and was the leader of the Argonautic expedition to secure the Golden Fleece from Aeetes, king of Colchis. This he accomplished with the help of Aeetes' daughter Medea, whom he married and later deserted for the Corinthian princess Creusa. *See* **Medea**.

Jove Another name of Jupiter, the latter being *Jovis pater,* father Jove. *See* **Jupiter**.

Juno The "venerable ox-eyed" wife of Jupiter, and queen of heaven, of Roman mythology. She is identified with the Greek Hera, was the special protectress of marriage and of woman, and was represented as a war goddess.

Jupiter From *Jovis pater,* "father Jove." Also called Jove and, in Greek, Zeus. The supreme deity of classical antiquity, father of gods and men; son of Saturn and Rhea, brought up by the daughters of King Melisseus of Crete on the milk of the goat Amalthea, escaped the fate of his brothers and sisters who were swallowed by their father, defeated the Titans and banished them to Tartarus, and installed himself with his wife, Juno, on Olympus, where Themis (Law) occupies a place near his throne. He is the father of Vulcan by Juno, of the Muses by Mnemosyne, of Apollo by Latona, of Mercury by Maia, of Rhadamanthus and Minos by

Europa, of Perseus by Danaë, of Hercules by Alemena, of Castor, Pollux, Helen, and Clytemnestra by Leda, of Bacchus by Semele, of Amphion by Antiope, etc., and of Minerva, who sprang from his head without a mother. In his flirtations, as with Io and Callisto, he is troubled by Juno's jealousy and appears often in the shape of an animal. He carries away Europa as a bull, appears before Leda as a swan, and escapes the monsters in the shape of a ram. Jupiter wields the thunder and has used it to kill Phaëton, Aesculapius, Capaneus, and many others. He has the power to place mortals among the stars and did so, for instance, in the case of Chiron, Orpheus, and the Pleiades. His activities are varied and numerous. He created woman and sent her as a punishment to Prometheus; he brought about the Deucalian Flood; he fastened the floating island of Delos; instituted the Olympian games, etc. His oracle was at Dodona. He was identified with the Egyptian god Amen as Jupiter Ammon. The Sibylline books were kept in his temple at Rome. His statue by Phidias is known as the Olympian Jupiter.

K **Khnum** Egyptian creator god. He created humankind out of clay and is frequently depicted at a potter's wheel.
Kwan-Yin Chinese goddess of compassion. She is frequently depicted in Chinese statues as sitting on a lotus flower, sometimes carrying a child in her arms. She was one of the first goddesses assimilated into Buddhist culture, and she is called "The Buddha of Compassion" because she sacrificed her treasures in heaven to come to the aid of mankind. In the famous Chinese saga *The Journey to the West*, which talks about the journey of a T'ang priest and his disciple the Monkey King, she frequently comes to their aid.

L **Labors of Hercules** The twelve tasks which won Hercules immortality. They were: (1) to slay the Nemean lion; (2) to kill the Lernean hydra; (3) to catch the Arcadian stag; (4) to destroy the Erymanthian boar; (5) to cleanse the stables of King Augeas; (6) to destroy the cannibal birds of the Lake Stymphalis; (7) to capture the Cretan bull; (8) to catch the horses of the Thracian Diomedes; (9) to get possession of the girdle of Queen Hippolyta of the Amazons; (10) to capture the oxen of the monster Geryon; (11) to get possession of the apples of the Hesperides; (12) to bring up from Hades the monstrous dog Cerberus.

Laius Greek king, father of Oedipus, he was cursed by the gods because he raped the young son of a neighboring king. Because of his crime, Apollo cursed him; telling him that his son would murder him and marry his mother. In order to avoid this, he sent a footman with his son, Oedipus, into the wilderness with orders that the child be left on a mountaintop to die. The footman felt pity on the baby, and gave it to a nearby shepherd, who raised him as his own son. Oedipus, at maturity, met his father on the road and, not knowing who he was, killed him, thereby fulfilling the prophecy.

Latinus In Roman legend, a king of Latium, the son of Faunus and father of Lavinia. He was told in a dream by his father that his daughter's union with

a foreigner would produce a race destined to subdue the world. That foreigner was Aeneas.

Leda Wife of Tyndareus and mother of Helen, Clytemnestra, Castor and Pollux. In later legends the father of her children was the Swan, under which disguise Jupiter concealed himself.

Legba African god of crossroads. Literally, "tricky spirit." He is the son of Yemoja, the sea goddess, and Obatala, the sky god of Nigerian mythology. He is usually portrayed as a "court jester" and brings messages from the gods to man. (*See* **Mercury**.) In African art, he is portrayed wearing traveling clothes in black and red. These are not his colors, but the colors of his best friends, Oggun (god of iron) and Chango (god of thunder).

Lethe One of the rivers of Hades, which the souls of all the dead taste, that they may forget everything said and done when alive. Gr. *letho*, *latheo*, *lanthano*, to cause persons not to know.

Loki Norse god of fire. In Norse mythology, it is Loki who sets the wheel of fate in motion, causing many problems along the way. Loki was originally a friend of the other gods, sometimes helping them (as in the case of Thor's hammer) or harming them (Loki's murder of Baldur). During Ragnarok (The Twilight of the Gods mentioned in Warner's operas), he sided with the giants and wolves who were destroying the castle in which the gods lived.

Lotus-eaters or **Lotophagi** Name of a people who ate the fruit of a plant called lotus. The companions of Ulysses who landed among them and partook of their food lost all memory of home and had to be dragged away before they would continue their voyage.

M **Mars** The Roman god of war; identified in certain aspects with the Greek Ares. He was also the patron of husbandmen.
Medea A sorceress, daughter of Aeetes, king of Colchis and possessor of the Golden Fleece. By her sorcery she helped Jason to secure the Golden Fleece. As Jason's wife, she rejuvenated her father-in-law Aeson and killed Jason's uncle Pelias. When Jason deserted her to marry the Corinthian princess Creusa, Medea sent her a poisoned robe, killed her own and Jason's children, and, after setting fire to the palace, escaped to Athens, where she married Aegeus, the father of Theseus. As Aegeus' wife, she tried to make her husband poison his own son. Detected in her scheming she had to flee to Asia where the country called Media still bears her name.

Medusa One of the Gorgons. Once a beautiful maiden, a goddess punished her by changing her hair into serpents and herself into a frightful monster, the sight of which turned all living things into stone. Perseus cut off her head which was then fixed in Minerva's Aegis. From her blood sinking into the earth, the winged horse Pegasus arose.

Megaera In Greek mythology, one of the Furies. *See* **Fury**.

Menelaus King of Sparta and husband of Helen of Troy, one of the principal figures in the Trojan conflict.

Mentor A friend of Ulysses whose form Minerva assumed when she accompanied Telemachus in his search for his father.

Medusa

Mercury The Roman equivalent of the Greek Hermes, son of Maia and Jupiter, to whom he acted as messenger. He was the god of science and commerce, patron of travellers and rogues, vagabonds and thieves.

Metamorphoses A series of tales in Latin verse by Ovid, chiefly mythological, beginning with the creation of the world, and ending with the deification of Caesar and the reign of Augustus.

Midas A king of Phrygia, son of Gordius and Cybele. He assisted Bacchus' teacher Silenus, whereupon the grateful god granted his wish that everything he touched should turn into gold. When he found that even his food was not exempt from his new influence, he managed to have it transferred to the river Pactolus. In a contest between Apollo and Pan, Midas insisted that the prize should go to Pan. Thereupon Apollo had his ears changed into asses' ears.

Milo A Greek athlete of the last part of the sixth century B.C. He was born in Crotona and led the triumphant army of his native city against the city of Sybaris in 510 B.C. He won six prizes as a wrestler at the Olympic games, six more at the Pythian games, and crowned his glories by carrying a four-year-old heifer through a huge stadium, then killing it and eating it all in a single day. He was eaten by wolves while his hands were caught in a split tree which he had tried to tear apart.

Minerva The Roman goddess of wisdom, patroness of the arts and trades, sprung fully armed from the head of Jupiter. She is identified with the Greek Athene, and was one of the three chief deities, the others being Jupiter and Juno. The most famous statue of this goddess was by Phidias, and was anciently one of the Seven Wonders of the World.

Minos A legendary king and lawgiver of Crete, the son of Jupiter and Europa, who became after his death one of the judges in the underworld. He is often identified with his grandson, the father of Ariadne and Phaedra, who built the labyrinth for the Minotaur and exacted a tribute from the Athenians until Theseus intervened and killed the monster. The word Minos is now generally considered to have been a title rather than a proper name.

Minerva

Minotaur A monster, half bull and half man, offspring of a bull sent by Neptune and Pasiphaë, the wife of King Minos of Crete. Hence the name (Gr. *tauros*, "a bull"). Minos kept it in the labyrinth built by Daedalus and fed it human bodies exacted as a tribute from the Athenians. When Theseus arrived as one of the victims, he managed to kill the monster with the help of Minos' daughter Ariadne, who had fallen in love with him.

Monkey King Chinese trickster god. A popular god with the Chinese, he was also assimilated into the Buddhist pantheon. He frequently gets into trouble because of his insatiable hunger and has a longstanding friendship with Kwan-Yin, goddess of compassion. In one of his most famous myths, he found out about the banquets given by Wang Muyiang, goddess of jade. Arriving before everyone else, he took bites out of all the foods displayed, including the peaches of immortality. When the Imperial Court of Heaven realized what he had done, they tried to destroy him with fire, thunder, and water but could not because he had eaten of the peaches and was now immortal. Because of his ability to see through the disguises of demons, he was sent to the west with the T'ang priest as a disciple and protector.

Morpheus Ovid's name for the son of Sleep and god of dreams; so called from Gr. *morphe,* form, because he gives these airy nothings their form and fashion.

Muses Daughters of Jupiter and Mnemosyne (Memory). They were goddesses of memory and later of the arts and sciences. Their number came eventually to be fixed as nine. They lived on Mt. Helicon and were put in charge of Pegasus by Minerva. Their names and special domains were: Calliope—epic poetry; Clio—history, Erato—love poetry; Euterpe—lyric poetry; Melpomene tragedy; Polyhymnia—sacred poetry; Terpsichore—choral dance; Thalia—comedy; and Urania—astronomy. Apollo was their guardian and leader and was hence called Musagetes.

Mycenae Ancient Greek city, capital of Agamemnon's kingdom.

N **Naiad** A nymph of a lake, river, fountain, etc. The naiads derived their vitality and in turn gave life to the water in which they dwelled.

Narcissus The son of Cephisus; a beautiful youth who saw his reflection in a fountain, and thought it the presiding nymph of the place. He gradually pined away for love of this unattainable spirit, and nothing remained but a flower which the nymphs called by his name. He was beloved by Echo and his fate was a punishment for his cruel indifference to her passion.

Nemesis The goddess of just distribution. Because of her persecution of the excessively rich or proud, she came to be regarded as a goddess of retributive justice. She was represented with wings, the wheel of fortune, in a chariot drawn by griffins, and was often confused with Adrastea, the goddess of the inevitable.

Nephtys Egyptian goddess of the desert, sister of Isis, mother of Anubis. Although she was the wife of Set, he could not give her children, and so with Isis's help, she bore a son (Anubis) by Osiris. After Osiris's murder she left Set in disgust and joined the house of Isis.

Neptune The Roman god of the sea, corresponding with the Greek Poseidon.

Nereids Sea nymphs, beautiful daughters of Nereus and Doris. They were fifty (or one hundred) in number; they played, danced, and were wooed by the Tritons. The most famous were Amphitrite, Thetis, and Galatea.

Nestor A king of Pylos, son of Neleus, renowned for his wisdom, justice, and knowledge of war, the oldest councilor of the Greeks before Troy.

Niobe Daughter of Tantalus, proud Queen of Thebes, whose seven sons and seven daughters were killed by Apollo and Diana, at which Amphion, her husband, killed himself, and Niobe wept until she was turned to stone.

Nu Kua Chinese goddess of marriage and gardening. Originally half-woman, half-dragon, she created the race of human beings with legs and liked the legs so much that she fashioned a pair for herself. She taught humankind to garden so that she would not have to feed them herself.

Nymphs Beautiful maidens, lesser divinities of nature: dryads and hamadryads, tree-nymphs; naiads, spring-, brook-, and river-nymphs; Nereids, sea-nymphs; oreads, mountain- or hillnymphs.

O **Odin** Chief god of the Norse, though not necessarily the most popular (*see* **Thor**), he is best known for the ways in which he gained wisdom. In one myth, he gave his eye to the blind keeper of the Well of Wisdom in order to take a drink. In another, he hung upside down from the "world tree"— Yggdrasil—so that he might be able to read the rune stones that lay at its base.

Odysseus *See* **Ulysses**.

Odyssey Homer's epic poem, relating the wandering of Ulysses from the end of the Trojan War until his return to Ithaca.

Oedipus Greek hero and king. Son of Laius and Jocasta. Because of a curse placed upon his father, Laius, Oedipus was sent into the wilderness, not knowing that he was the son of royalty. On the road to Thebes, he met Laius, who demanded that Oedipus get out of the way. In the ensuing argument, Oedipus killed his father. Once he arrived at Thebes, he answered the riddle of the Sphinx and was unknowingly allowed to marry Jocasta, Queen of Thebes and his mother. They had four children— Ismene, Antigone, Eteocles, and Polynices. When a plague struck Thebes, the Delphic oracle (the oracle of Apollo) declared that until the murderer of Laius was found, the plague would continue. It was then that Tiresias, the blind seer of Thebes, revealed to Oedipus who he really was. His wife and mother, Jocasta, hung herself in remorse at her unknowing crime, and Oedipus blinded himself with the pins from her gown. Oedipus fled to Colonus with his two daughters and was welcomed there. However, Creon, Laius's brother and the new king, kidnapped Ismene and Antigone. It was at Colonus that Oedipus was taken into heaven by the gods. His daughters remained with Creon, while his grown sons, Eteocles and Polynices, fought over the kingdom and eventually killed one another in battle.

Olympus The dwelling-place of the dynasty of gods of which Zeus or Jupiter was the head, corresponding to the Norse Valhalla.

Ophion The king of the Titans who ruled Olympus until dethroned by the gods Saturn and Rhea.

Oracles Answers from the gods to questions from mortals seeking knowledge or advice on the future. They were usually given in equivocal form so as to fit any event. Also, the places where such answers were given forth by a priest or priestess.

Orestes The son of Agamemnon and Clytemnestra. Because of his crime in killing his mother he was pursued by the Furies until purified by Minerva.

Orion A giant and hunter, son of Neptune. In the attempt to gain possession of Merope, he was blinded by her father Oenopion but restored to sight by Apollo. He became a favorite with Diana, whose brother Apollo made her kill him inadvertently. Diana placed him among the stars where he appears as the constellation Orion with dog Sirius following him.

Orpheus A Thracian poet, son of Apollo and Calliope, whose music moved even inanimate objects. He took part in the Argonautic expedition and appeased a storm. When his wife, Eurydice, died, he charmed Pluto, who released her on condition that he would not look back. He did turn round and lost her again. He perished, torn to pieces by infuriated Thracian maenads.

Osiris Egyptian god of the dead, brother of Set and Nephtys, husband of Isis, father of Horus the Younger. Osiris was the god of vegetation, until his death at the hands of his brother. Out of compassion for his sister Nephtys, who was childless, he lay with her in order that she might have a child.

Ovid A Latin poet in the time of Augustus who wrote the poetical fables called *Metamorphoses*.

Pallas Athene   *See* **Minerva**.

Pan   Called Faunus by the Romans, the Greek god of nature and the universe.

Pandora   Literally, the all-gifted. The first woman, dowered with gifts by every god, yet entrusted with a box she was cautioned not to open. Curious, she opened it, and out flew all the ills of humanity, leaving behind only hope, which remained. She is to be compared with Eve.

Paris   The son of Priam, king of Troy, and Hecuba; through his abduction of Helen he is the cause of the Trojan War. It was he who awarded the Apple of Discord and the title of "Fairest" to Venus, who in return assisted him to carry off Helen, for whom he deserted his wife, Oenone. At Troy, Paris earned the contempt of all by his cowardice; he killed Achilles with a poisoned arrow and suffered the same fate at the hands of Philoctetes when the city was taken.

Parnassus   A mountain near Delphi, Greece, with two summits, one of which was consecrated to Apollo and the Muses, the other to Bacchus.

Parthenon   The great temple on the Acropolis at Athens to Athene *Parthenos* (i.e.,the Virgin).

Patroclus   The loyal friend of Achilles. When Achilles refused to fight to annoy Agamemnon, he sent Patroclus in his own armor to the battle. Patroclus was slain by Hector.

Pegasus   The winged horse of the Muses, born of the sea foam and the blood of the slaughtered Medusa. He was caught by Bellerophon, who mounted him and destroyed the Chimaera, when Bellerophon attempted to ascend to heaven, he was thrown from the horse, and Pegasus mounted alone to the skies to become the constellation of the same name. When the Muses contended with the daughters of Pieros, Mount Helicon rose heavenward, Pegasus gave it a kick and brought out of the mountain the soul-inspiring waters of the fountain Hippocrene.

Pele   Hawaiian fire goddess. One of the most important of the Hawaiian pantheon and one of its few survivors. She created the Hawaiian archipelago as a result of her ongoing feud with her sister Na-Maka-Ka-Ahi, the ocean.

Pelias   Jason's uncle, who usurped the Argonaut's kingdom, promising to return it to him if Jason would bring him the Golden Fleece.

Penelope   The wife of Ulysses, who, waiting twenty years for his return from the Trojan War, put off the suitors for her hand by promising to choose one when her weaving was done, but unravelled at night what she had woven by day.

Persephone   *See* **Proserpine**.

Perseus   Son of Jupiter and Danaë, slayer of the Gorgon Medusa, and deliverer of Andromeda from the sea-monster

Phaedra   The daughter of Pasiphaë and King Minos of Crete; sister of Ariadne. She became the wife of Theseus and fell in love with her stepson Hippolytus. When her advances were repulsed, she aroused the jealousy of her infatuated husband and Hippolytus was killed. When his innocence became evident, Phaedra committed suicide and Aesculapius with the help of Diana restored Hippolytus to life.

Pegasus

Phaëthon   The son of Phoebus, who undertook to drive his father's chariot, but was upset and would have set the world on fire had not Zeus transfixed him with a thunderbolt.

Philemon and Baucis   Poor cottagers of Phrygia, husband and wife, who entertained Jupiter so hospitably that he promised to grant them whatever request they made. They asked that both might die together. Philemon became an oak, Baucis a linden tree, and their branches intertwined at the top.

Philoctetes   A famous archer, to whom Hercules, at death, gave his arrows. He joined the Greeks against Troy but was left behind on Lemnos because of the offensive smell of a festering wound. An oracle having declared that only the arrows of Hercules could fell Troy, Philoctetes was sent for. He went to Troy, slew Paris, and the prophecy came true.

Phoebus   (from Greek *phoibos*, "bright"). An epithet of Apollo, particularly in his quality as the sun god. *See* **Apollo**. The name often stands for the sun personified.

Phoenix   A messenger to Achilles; also, a miraculous bird, dying in fire by its own act and springing up alive from its own ashes.

Pillars of Hercules   Two mountains facing each other; one, Calpe (now the Rock of Gibraltar), on the southwest corner of Spain in Europe, the other, Abyla, on the northern coast of Africa.

Pleiades   Seven of Diana's nymphs who were changed into stars.

Pluto   Identical with Hades and Dis. The ruler of the infernal regions, son of Saturn, brother of Jupiter and Neptune, and husband of Proserpine.

Plutus   In Greek mythology, the son of Iasion and Demeter. He was associated with Irene, the goddess of peace. Jupiter blinded him to make sure that he would bestow his gifts indiscriminately on good men and bad.

Polynices *See* **Eteocles and Polynices**.

Polyphemus   One of the Cyclopes, a giant with only one eye in the middle of his forehead, who lived in Sicily. He was in love with Galatea and crushed his successful rival Acis with a rock. He was blinded by Ulysses, whom he had taken prisoner with twelve members of his crew.

Poseidon   The Greek god of the sea; son of Cronus and Rhea, brother of Zeus and Pluto, husband of Amphitrite. In Roman mythology, he became assimilated to Neptune. *See* **Neptune**.

Priam   In Greek legend, king of Troy when that city was sacked by the Greeks, husband of Hecuba, and father of fifty sons and many daughters, among whom were Hector, Helenus, Paris, Deiphobus, Agenor, Polyxena, Troilus, Cassandra, and Polydorus. When Hector was slain, the old King went to the tent of Achilles and made a successful plea for the body of his dead son. After the gates of Troy were thrown open by the Greeks concealed in the wooden horse, Pyrrhus, the son of Achilles, slew the aged Priam.

Procrustes   A robber of Attica who seized travelers and bound them on his iron bed, stretching the short ones and cutting short the tall. Thus he was served himself by Theseus.

Prometheus   Literally, "forethought." One of the Titans, son of Iapetus and Clymene. Jupiter entrusted him with the task of making men out of mud and water. Out of pity for their state, he gave them fire, stealing it from heaven, and was punished by being chained to Mount Caucasus, where an eagle preyed on his liver. He was finally released by Hercules.

Proserpine   (Greek **Persephone**) One of the greater goddesses; daughter of Ceres and wife of Pluto, who carried her off to his realm against the will of her mother and, by intervention of Jupiter, had to agree to a compromise by which she was to pass half the time (winter) with her husband and the other half (summer) with her mother. At times she was identified with Hecate. While queen of the infernal regions, Theseus tried to carry her off. When Venus sent Psyche to her to fetch some of her beauty in a little box, it developed to be a bit of Stygian sleep.

Proteus   Neptune's herdsman, an old man and a prophet, famous for his power of assuming different shapes at will.

Psyche   A beautiful maiden, personification of the human soul, sought by Cupid (Love), to whom she responded. She lost him through curiosity, wanting to see him though he only came to her by night, but was finally, through her prayers, made immortal, and restored to him. Psyche is a symbol of immortality.

Pygmalion   A sculptor, in love with a statue he had made, which was brought to life by Venus; also, a brother of the Queen Dido.

Pyramus   Lover of Thisbe, his nextdoor neighbor. Their parents opposing, they talked through cracks in the housewall, and agreed to meet in the near-by woods. There Pyramus, finding a bloody veil and thinking Thisbe slain, killed himself, and she, seeing his body, killed herself. (Burlesqued in Shakespeare's *Midsummer Night's Dream*).

Python   A monstrous serpent which arose from the mud left by the deluge of Deucalion. It lurked in the caves of Mount Parnassus and was slain by Apollo.

 **Ra**   Egyptian sky god. By himself, he created the set of nine deities known as the Ennead. These include Shu, god of air; Tefnut, goddess of rain; Geb, god of the earth; Nut, goddess of the sky; Horus the Elder; Nephtys, goddess of the desert; Isis, goddess of magic; Osiris, god of the dead; and Set, god of the desert. When Ra began to age, the Ennead feared that he would die. Isis agreed to cure him if he taught her his secret name, known only to himself. Only when he was near death would Ra give Isis his name. With this, Isis created a spell and saved the dying king.

Remus   Twin brother of Romulus. *See* **Romulus**.

Rhea   A female Titan, wife of Cronus, her brother, and "Mother of the Gods," for example, of Jupiter, Neptune, Juno, Ceres, etc. She became identified with the Asiatic Cybele.

Romanus   In legend, the son of Histion, grandson of Japhet, great grandson of Noah, and ancestor of the Romans.

Romulus   With his twin brother, Remus, the legendary founder of Rome. They were sons of Mars and Rhea Silvia. They were suckled by a she-wolf, and eventually set about founding a city but quarrelled over the plans, and Remus was slain by his brother. Romulus was taken to the heavens by his father in a fiery chariot, and was worshipped by the Romans under the name of Quirinus.

Sagittarius   A southern constellation, partly in the Milky Way, representing an archer (Lat. *sagittarius*, "archer") who is identified as the Centaur Chiron, placed after his death among the stars by Jupiter. Also known by the English name Archer.

Sappho   Greek poetess who leaped into the sea from the promontory of Leucadia in disappointed love for Phaon.

Saturn   A Roman deity, identified with the Greek Cronus (time). He devoured all his children except Jupiter (air), Neptune (water), and Pluto (the grave). The reign of Saturn was celebrated by the poets as a "Golden Age."

Satyrs   A race of immortal goatmen who dwelt in the woodlands. The most famous satyr was Silenus.

Scylla   A sea-nymph beloved by Gilaucus, but changed by the jealous Circe to a monster and finally to a dangerous rock on the Sicilian coast, facing the whirlpool Charybdis. Many mariners were wrecked between the two. Also, the daughter of King Nisus of Megara, who loved Minos, besieging her father's city; he, however, disliked her disloyalty and drowned her. Also, a fair virgin of Sicily, friend to the sea-nymph Galatea.

Set   Egyptian god of the desert, brother of Isis and Osiris, husband of Nephtys. Set was jealous and envious of his brother Osiris, and angered that he had been given the barren desert to reign while his brother was given the fertile Nile area. He therefore murdered Osiris and made sure to scatter the pieces so that Isis, with her magic, would not be able to find and bury him. Because of his crime he was banished to the desert forever.

Seven against Thebes, Expedition of the   An expedition against the city of Thebes by the heroes Adrastus (the only survivor), Polynices, Tydeus, Amphiaraus, Hippomedon, Capancus, and Parthenopaeus.

Sibyl   Any of a number of prophetesses whose special function it was to intercede with the gods on behalf of human supplicants. The most famous is the Cumaean Sibyl whom Aeneas consulted before descending to Avernus.

Silvanus or **Sylvanus**   In Roman mythology, the divine protector of woods, fields, cattle, etc. His characteristics were very much the same as those of the Greek Pan.

Sirens   Sea-nymphs, whose singing charmed mariners to leap into the sea; passing their island, Ulysses stopped the ears of his sailors with wax, and had himself lashed to the mast so that he could hear, but not yield to, their music.

Sirius   Orion's dog, which was changed into the Dog-star.

Sisyphus   A legendary king of Corinth, condemned in Tartarus to perpetually roll up hill a big rock which, when the top was reached, rolled down again.

Somnus   In classic myth, the god of Sleep, the son of Night (*Nox*) and the brother of Death (*Mors*).

Sphinx   A monster, waylaying the road to Thebes, and propounding riddles to all passers on pain of death for wrong guessing. She killed herself in rage when Oedipus guessed correctly.

Styx   The river of Hate (Greek *stugein*, to hate)—that flowed nine times round the infernal regions. The five rivers of hell are the Styx, Acheron, Cocytus, Phlegethon and Lethe.

Tantalus   Son of Jupiter and Pluto (daughter of Himantes); father of Pelops and Niobe. As a king of Mount Sipylus in Lydia, he revealed the secrets of the gods and was punished in Tartarus by having to stand under a loaded fruit tree up to his chin in water, the fruit and water retreating whenever he tried to satisfy his hunger or thirst.

Tartarus   The infernal regions of classical mythology; used as equivalent to Hades by later writers, but by Homer placed as far beneath Hades as Hades is beneath the earth. It was here that Zeus confined the Titans.

Telemachus   The only son of Ulysses and Penelope. He went to Pylos and Sparta in search for his father and helped him on his return to Ithaca to slay Penelope's suitors.

Terra   Goddess of the earth.

Thalia   The Muse of comedy and bucolic poetry. Thalia is also the name of one of the three Graces. It signifies "blooming."

Thebes   The chief city of Boeotia, Greece, founded by Cadmus, the Tyrian.

EXHIBIT 18.2
Roman Gods and Goddesses

Apollo	God of music, poetry, and healing arts
Bacchus	God of wine, fertility
Ceres	Goddess of fertility of the earth
Cupid	God of love
Diana	Goddess of the moon and the hunt
Juno	Protector of women
Jupiter or **Jove**	The supreme deity
Mercury	Messenger of the gods
Minerva	Goddess of wisdom
Neptune	God of the sea
Pluto	Ruler of the underworld
Proserpine	Goddess of sleep
Venus	Goddess of love and beauty
Vesta	Goddess of the hearth fire
Vulcan	God of crafstmen, fire

Theseus   Chief hero of Attica; son of Aegeus and Aethra; a great hero of many adventures.

Thetis   The chief of the Nereids. By Peleus she was the mother of Achilles.

Thor   Warrior god of thunder. The most popular of the Norse gods because of his patronage of sailors and laborers, who prayed to him for protection before going to work. With his hammer, he broke up the icy rivers each spring. In one of his myths, he dressed as a woman in order to fool the giants who had stolen his hammer. The giant demanded Freya in marriage in return for the magic hammer. So Thor, dressed as a young bride, went to the wedding as Freya. When the giant placed the hammer in the "bride's" lap, Thor leapt up from the seat and destroyed the giant.

Tiresias   A Theban seer. He had seen Minerva bathing and was blinded by her. Relenting, but unable to withdraw the punishment, she compensated him by giving the gift of second sight. After his death, Ulysses, at the request of Circe, consulted him in Hades.

Titans   A race of primordial deities, children of Heaven and Earth, finally overcome by the thunderbolts of rebellious Jupiter, who banished them to Tartarus, where they lie prostrate at the bottom of the pit. According to the oldest accounts there were twelve Titans, six male and six female: Oceanus, Coeus, Crius, Hyperion, Iapetus, Cronus, Theia, Rhea, Themis, Tethys, Mnemosyne, Phoebe.

Triton   The son of Neptune and Amphitrite, represented as a fish with a human head. It is this sea god that makes the roaring of the ocean by blowing through his shell.

Trojan horse   *See* **Wooden Horse**.

Trojans   Inhabitants of Troy, whose adventures under the leadership of Aeneas, after the fall of their city, form the subject matter of Vergil's *Aeneid*.

Trojan War   The legendary war sung by Homer in the *Iliad* as having been waged for ten years by the

The Trojan horse

Ulysses

confederated Greeks against the men of Troy and their allies, in consequence of Paris, son of Priam, the Trojan king, having carried off Helen, wife of Menelaus, king of Lacedemon (or of Sparta). The last year of the siege is the subject of the *Iliad*; the burning of Troy, and the flight of Aeneas is told by Vergil in his *Aeneid*.

Troy   City in Asia Minor, held to be identical with the Greek Ilium. In Greek legend, the capital of King Priam and object of the Trojan War.

Typhon   A fire-breathing monster, the father of the Sphinx, the Chimaera, and other monsters. He is often identified with Typhoeus, a son of Tartarus and Gaea, who begot the unfavorable winds or, according to other stories, is himself one of them. As a hundred-headed giant he warred against the gods and was banished by Jupiter to Tartarus under Mount Aetna. Typhon is also the name used by the Greeks for the Egyptian Set, the god of evil, who killed his brother (or father) Osiris.

U **Ulysses**   The Roman name of the Greek Odysseus, of hero of Homer's *Odyssey,* and a prominent character in the *Iliad*.

Unicorn   (Latin *unum cornu*, one horn). A mythical animal, represented as having the legs of a buck, the tail of a lion, the head and body of a horse, and a single horn in the middle of its forehead. The oldest author that describes it is Ctesias (400 B.C.).

Uranus   A personification of Heaven. The son of Gaea or Earth and by her the father of the Titans.

V **Valhalla**   "Hall of Warriors," a heavenly resting place for Norse warriors who had died bravely in battle. Warriors were chosen and carried to Valhalla by Valkyries, who were warrior demi-goddesses. There, they sat at tables and were given heavenly mead to drink.

Valkyries   Norse demi-goddesses, daughters of Odin and Erda. They were nine in number, the most famous being Brunhilde, who was Odin's favorite. The Valkyries were trained as warriors by Odin and Thor themselves. They rode the heavens on winged horses searching the battlefields for warriors who had died bravely to bring into Valhalla, the final resting place of valiant men.

Venus   In Roman mythology, the goddess of beauty and love. Originally of minor importance, she became through identification with the Greek Aphrodite one of the major characters in classical myths. She was the daughter of Jupiter and Dione. According to another view (influenced by association with the Greek term *aphros*, "foam") she had sprung from the foam of the sea at Cyprus. Jupiter gave her in wedlock to Vulcan. She was the mother, by Vulcan, of Eros and Anteros; by Mars, of Harmonia; by Anchises, of Aeneas; etc. She wore a magic girdle which enabled its wearer to arouse love in others. She plays an important part in many legends and stories: she gave beauty as a gift to Pandora, the first woman; she fell in love with Adonis and after his death changed his blood into the anemone; she first objected and finally consented to her son Cupid's (Eros) love for Psyche; she had Atalanta and Hippomenes changed into lions; she consoled Ariadne and gave her Bacchus as her husband; she competed against Juno and Minerva for the apple of discord and was given the prize by Paris; she destined Helen, the wife of Menelaus, for Paris and caused thus the Trojan war; she sided with the Trojans against the Greeks and enlisted the help of her admirer Mars; etc.

Vergil   Publius Vergilius Maro (70–19 B.C.) Famous Roman epic and idyllic poet. Author of the *Aeneid*, which relates the adventures of Aeneas after he left Troy.

Vesta   In Roman mythology, one of the chief divinities, corresponding to the Greek Hestia. She was the virgin goddess of the hearth and presided over the central altar of family, city, tribe, and race. The vestals were her priestesses.

Vestals   Six stainless virgins, who watched as priestesses over the sacred fire in the temple of Vesta. The fire had originally been brought to Rome by Aeneas. When it went out, it was rekindled from the rays of the sun.

Vesuvius, Mount   A famous volcano near Naples, Italy.

Virgil   *See* **Vergil.**

Virgo   Constellation of the Virgin, representing Astraea, goddess of innocence and purity.

Vulcan   A son of Jupiter and Juno, husband of Venus, god of fire and the working of metals, identified with the Greek Hephaestus, and called also Mulciber, for example, the softener. His workshop was on Mount Etna where the Cyclops assisted him in forging thunderbolts for Jove.

Wang Muyiang   Chinese goddess of heaven and weaving. It is Wang Muyiang who gives the banquets attended by all in heaven. At the banquets, the peaches of immortality are served as dessert, as well as elixirs and potions of immortality. With her daughters, she weaves all of the garments of the Imperial Court of Heaven.

Wooden Horse   It was filled with armed men and left outside Troy as a pretended offering to Minerva when the Greeks feigned to sail away. It was accepted by the Trojans and brought into their city, but at night the hidden Greek soldiers destroyed the town.

Zephyrus   A personification of the west wind; the gentlest of all the sylvan deities. Also known as Favonious. He fans the inhabitants of Elysium and is the lover of Flora. When Apollo played at quoits with Hyacinthus Zephyris was jealous and drove the missile Apollo had pitched so that it killed Hyacinthus. He bore Psyche from her lonely mountain refuge to the flowery dale where Cupid was waiting for her and also brought her sisters to see her.

Zeus   The Grecian Jupiter. The word means the "living one" (Sanskrit, *Djaus*, heaven). *See* **Jupiter.**

PHILOSOPHY

A posteriori   Knowledge that comes "after," or only through, experience. Our knowledge of the details of the external world is taken to be *a posteriori*.

A priori   Knowledge that comes "prior to," or independently of experience. Mathematical and logical knowledge are often taken to be *a priori*.

Absolutism   The doctrine that truth or values are objective or absolute rather than merely relative or subjective.

Academy   Plato's school of philosophy, so named after the grove where he lectured. The teachings of Plato's successors are conventionally divided into the Old Academy, which clove closely to Plato's positions, and the New Academy, begun by Arcesilaus in the 3rd century B.C., which was characterized by Scepticism. *See* **Plato; Scepticism.**

Aesthetics   That branch of philosophy dedicated to the study of art and artistic values. "An aesthetics" is also used to designate a particular theory of art or a particular approach to artistic values.

Agape   A Greek word originally meaning "love." Among the early Christians, it came to be applied to the "love feast," a ritual where the faithful commemorated the Last Supper of Jesus and his disciples. From this, it took on connotations of brotherly love (for fellow Christians), filial love (for God), and charity.

Agent   In ethics, a term used to designate a person who is acting in a certain situation or who is contemplating action in a certain situation.

Al-Fārābī (ca. 873–950)   Islamic philosopher of Turkish origin. He studied with Christian Aristotelians in Baghdad. Following their teachings, his system asserted a unity between Platonic and Aristotelian writings. He introduced Aristotelian logic to the Islamic world, distinguished philosophy from theology, attempted proofs of the existence of God using Aristotle's *Metaphysics*, based his political philosophy on Plato's *Republic* and *Laws*, explained creation as a process of emanation along Neoplatonic lines, and subordinated revelation to reason. Such was his fame that he was called "the second Aristotle."

Alienation (estrangement)   Hegel, Feuerbach, and Marx were the first thinkers to discuss alienation explicitly and shaped current discussions. According to them, the things man produces become alien to him, they are other than him, thus every act of production is an instance of alienation. Since for these thinkers man is what he does, by being alienated from what he produces, man is also alienated from his producing and thus from himself. In coming to know himself as what he does, however, man overcomes his alienation from himself and comes to recognize himself in his products. Today "alienation" is often used in psychology to refer to a state of mind in which one feels like an alien in the world. Some say that alienation is more than just a feeling—that it is an objective fact. *See also* Psychology section, page 21–3.

Althusser, Louis (1918–1986)   French structuralist or analytical Marxist of the 1960s. Rejected Marx's early writings as humanistic, ideological, and Hegelian. Also rejected Hegelian readings of Marx. He focused instead on Marx's later work, especially *Capital*, which he saw as very different from the early work and from which he believed he could develop a truly scientific Marxism, one untainted by the "ideological" conceptions that he believed characterized the early Marx. In rejecting Marx's humanism, he saw the human individual as no more than a location and function within the structure of the relations of production.

Altruism   Action for the sake of others; the opposite of egoism. In some contexts (for example, sociobiology) altruism has come to be used for other-regarding action of all types, whether ultimately arising from a genuine concern for others or from more selfish motives.

Analytic philosophy   The dominant tradition of philosophy in England, America, and parts of Europe. Bertrand Russell, Ludwig Wittgenstein, W. V. O. Quine, and Saul Kripke are prominent representatives. Although historically the tradition has emphasized linguistic or conceptual analysis, it is best characterized in terms of a general concern with clarity and precision rather than by any specific methods or theses that all analytic philosophers are bound to accept.

Analytic proposition   A proposition or statement necessarily true by virtue of the meaning of its terms. "All bachelors are unmarried" is the common example.

Anarchism   A political philosophy that holds that freedom is the highest political value and that hierarchy is anathema. More narrowly, anarchism is identified with the position that all government is tyrannical and that people can arrange their lives cooperatively. Some anarchists have been individualists (*e.g.*, Max Stirner), some socialists (*e.g.*, Michael Bakunin), some communists (*e.g.*, Emma Goldman).

Anselm (ca. 1033–1109)   Scholastic philosopher, born at Aosta in Italy. A Benedictine monk, he was abbot at Le Bec in Normandy, and became Archbishop of Canterbury in 1093. Anselm is most famous for his formulation of the ontological argument for the existence of God. In his wider theological interests, he followed Augustine in asserting the harmony of revelation and reason. His works include the *Proslogion* and the *Monologion*. *See* **Ontological argument, The**.

Antecedent   The "if" clause in a conditional or "if-then" statement. Symbolically expressed, P is the antecedent of the conditional "if P then Q."

Antirealism   The view that science or other bodies of belief do not represent or correspond to an independent reality—"the world"—or that there is no such reality to which science or other bodies of belief can correspond.

Antithesis   In German Idealism, the second moment of the dialectic. The antithesis appears in opposition to the thesis. Out of this opposition emerges the synthesis, which is to be the supersession of the thesis and antithesis and of their opposition, but which, at the same time, is to contain this opposition within itself.

Apodictic knowledge   Knowledge of matters of necessity, as opposed to matters of contingency; knowledge of what must be the case, as opposed to what simply happens to be the case.

Apollonian   One of the two spirits distinguished by Nietzsche in *The Birth of Tragedy*, the other

PHILOSOPHY

being the Dionysian. The Apollonian is the spirit of rationality, intelligence, harmoniousness, restraint and moderation. It harnesses and tries to keep control of the irrational Dionysian spirit. *See* **Nietzsche.**

Apology A spoken or written defense. Plato's *Apology* is written as a presentation of Socrates' defense of himself against charges of corrupting the youth of Athens and believing in gods other than those recognized by the state.

Appeal to authority A fallacy in which one attempts to support a claim not by rational argument in its behalf but merely by citing some expert or renowned text as holding it.

Aquinas, Thomas *See* **Thomas Aquinas.**

Arendt, Hannah (1906–1975) German political and social theorist. Studied with Heidegger and Jaspers. Fled from the Nazis first to Paris and then to the United States, where she settled in New York. She lectured at a number of universities, finally taking a permanent position as a professor of political philosophy at the New School for Social Research in 1948. Author of *The Origins of Totalitarianism*, *Eichmann in Jerusalem*, *On Violence*, and *The Human Condition*, she theorized about public versus private space, totalitarianism, and the "banality of evil."

Aristotle

Aristotle (384–322 B.C.) Greek philosopher, born at Stagira in Macedon. The son of a physician, he came to Athens to study with Plato. In 342 B.C., he joined the court of Phillip II of Macedon, where he taught Phillip's heir, later known as Alexander the Great. He returned to Athens in 335 B.C. and founded his own school in a peripatos (covered walk) at the Lyceum in Athens; thus, his followers were called Peripatetics. His work encompasses not

only areas we would associate with philosophy, such as logic, metaphysics, and ethics, but also physics, astronomy, biology, and psychology. Aristotle divides knowledge into the theoretical (knowledge for its own sake), the practical (knowledge for the sake of action), and the productive (knowledge for the sake of producing something). The theoretical includes such knowledge as metaphysics (the study of being) and physics (the study of motion). The practical includes ethics and politics, which describe happiness and how to attain it. Analytics, or logic, is a preliminary to all knowledge; Aristotle's major contribution to logic is the syllogism. Aristotle's influence on these and other matters was immense among the ancients and especially among medieval Islamic and Christian philosophers. *See also* **Categories; Cause; Essence and Existence; Faculty; Form; Metaphysics; Prime Mover; Substance and Attribute; Summum bonum; Syllogism; Teleology; Universals.**

Asceticism The practice of self-denial for spiritual good. Such practices are common to many of the world's religions; in Buddhism and Christianity, they are connected to a monastic tradition. Among philosophers, the Cynics argued that asceticism was the means to a virtuous life, and Schopenhauer held that asceticism was a means of quieting the will and thus ending pain.

Atomism The view that nature is composed of simple units, or atoms. The Pre-Socratic philosophers Leucippus and Democritus (5th century B.C.) held that atoms differ only in size and shape, are indivisible, and are so small as to be imperceptible. Empedocles, Anaxagoras, and Epicurus hold similar positions.

Attribute A property. The attributes of a thing are the properties it has. For example, sweetness is an attribute of sugar.

Augustine of Hippo (354–430) Christian theologian, born at Tagaste in what is now Tunisia. Augustine's life was characterized by the Roman world's final transition from paganism to Christianity. Although raised a Christian, he became first a Manichaean and later a Sceptic. He returned to Christianity in 386 and became bishop of Hippo in 396. Augustine's philosophy was a Platonism in the service of Christianity. His Platonism manifests itself in various ways: His belief that understanding can lead us to faith, and that faith can lead us to understand, recalls Plato's dialectic; his argument that we can discover the nature of the Trinity through examination of our own nature recalls the theory of forms. His works include his autobiographical *Confessions*, *The City of God*, and *On the Trinity*.

Aurelius, Marcus *See* **Marcus Aurelius.**

Autonomy Self-determination in choice and action, independent of external coercion or constraint. In ethics, the principle of autonomy is that people's own choices regarding their own lives should take priority. As such, a principle of autonomy is opposed to paternalism.

Averroës (Arabic *Ibn Rushd*) (ca. 1126–ca. 1198) Islamic commentator on Aristotle, born at Córdoba. He came from a family of judges and lawyers; tradition holds that he studied law, theology, medicine, and philosophy. He became associated with the caliphate in Marrakesh, which commissioned his commentaries. His own philosophy was largely Aristotelian. Averroës' commentaries had tremedous influence on later medieval Christian Aristotelianism.

Avicenna (Arabic *Ibn Sīnā*) (980–1037) Islamic physician and philosopher of Persian origin, born in Bukhara. Avicenna's reputation as a philosopher in the Islamic world was so great that he was called "the third Aristotle" (al-Fārābī being the second). He wrote a comprehensive system that was primarily Aristotelian. He distinguished between necessary and contingent being, and in so doing first elaborated the distinction between essence and existence. He had a great influence upon the Scholastics.

B **Bacon, Francis** (1561–1626) English statesman and philosopher of science, known for his repudiation of traditional speculative philosophy and his insistence on the acquisition of knowledge by means of induction. Bacon's outline of induction stressed empirical observation, inference, and verification through repeated observation and experiment. The obstacles to such a route to knowledge and to rationality generally, Bacon termed "idols": "the Idols of the Tribe," common to people in general and including the mistaken notion that sense-perception affords direct access to reality; "the Idols of the Den," including the tendency of each individual to interpret data according to his own "peculiar and singular disposition"; "the Idols of the Marketplace," including dangers to rationality from ambiguous and ill-defined language; and "the Idols of the Theater," including errors based on the dogmas of traditional philosophical systems.

Beauvoir, Simone de (1908–1986) French existentialist and feminist philosopher. Founded the review *Les Temps Modernes* with Jean-Paul Sartre, her life-long companion, and Maurice Merleau-Ponty. Best known for her seminal work in feminist philosophy, *The Second Sex* (1949), which discusses the facts and myths of women's lives, examining both the problems they face and the possibilities open to them. She argued that women's subjectivity has been conceived as the "other" of male subjectivity, which has been taken to be subjectivity in general. De Beauvoir's work has been influential on several generations of feminists and continues to shape feminist thought today.

Begging the question A fallacious pattern of reasoning in which one argues for a position only by in some way presupposing or assuming that very position as given. *See also* **Circular argument.**

Behaviorism In psychology, behaviorism is the view that psychology as a science need deal only with behavior, as opposed, for example, to the data of introspection. In philosophy, analytical behaviorism is the view that "mental" terms (think, believe, imagine, remember) refer ultimately only to behavior.

Being and Becoming For the Greeks, something that is, or has *Being*, is permanent and unchanging; something that *becomes* is impermanent and changes. Sometimes Being is contrasted with Not-Being, and change is seen as an effect of Not-Being. Reconciling Being and Becoming or Not-Being was a problem for Greek philosophy. For Par-

menides, Being is real and Not-Being an illusion; for Heraclitus, Becoming is regulated by a permanent principle; for Plato, Becoming is a pale reflection of Being; for Aristotle, Becoming is real and manifests itself in the change from potentiality to actuality.

Bentham, Jeremy (1748–1832) English thinker best known as a utilitarian. His followers, known as Benthamites, became a powerful political force in England and included James Mill and his son, John Stuart Mill. Bentham saw British law as chaotic and illogical and hoped to introduce legal reforms based on utilitarian principles. He considered the existing penal code and civil laws to be based on "moral laws" that did not take the consequences of actions into account. His most famous contribution to utilitarian theory was the "hedonic calculus" which gave a way to judge between courses of action based on their consequences for the pleasure and pain of all the people affected. Every pain and pleasure is assigned a certain number of units, allowing one to judge which is the better action—which produces the lowest pain and/or the highest pleasure.

Bergson, Henri (1851–1941) French philosopher of science, especially of biological evolution. His most famous work is *Creative Evolution*, in which he puts forth a theory that there was an "original impetus of life" that pervades the whole evolutionary process. This *élan vital*, or vital impetus, is a "current of consciousness" that has penetrated matter, thus giving rise to living bodies, and that is carried from one generation to the next through reproduction. For Bergson, man (or beings "of the same essence" as man) is the goal of evolution. He considers creative evolution to be a cosmic process, occurring on many planets besides Earth. Bergson also considered intuition to provide knowledge of the real while the intellect only provides knowledge of appearance.

Berkeley, George (1685–1763) Irish philosopher and Anglican bishop. Considered to be the founder of "idealism," though he preferred to call his position "immaterialism." He denied the possibility of material substance. In order for something to exist, it must either be perceived or be a perceiver. Thus there is no material world independent of the mind. All apparently material things are, in fact, passive ideas that God causes to exist in our minds and that he sustains when no one is perceiving them. Thus for Berkeley there are only two kinds of thing in the universe: passive ideas and active minds or spirits.

Boethius (ca. 475–524) Roman statesman and philosopher, born at Rome. In 510, Boethius rose to the post of consul under Theodoric. He was imprisoned for treason in 523, a charge he denied. He was executed in 524. His most famous work is the *Consolation of Philosophy*, in which the imprisoned Boethius is visited by Philosophy personified, who argues that temporal pleasure is fleeting and true happiness is found in God. The text contains Neoplatonic, Stoic, and Aristotelian elements. Boethius, who was a Christian, is sometimes called the first Scholastic; he was also a translator of Greek texts into Latin, a commentator, and a logician.

Buddhism   A philosophy originating in the teachings of the Gautama Buddha (India, ca. 563–ca. 483 B.C.). "Buddha" means "enlightened one"; Buddhism is thus the seeking of enlightenment. According to Buddhism, life is characterized by suffering, which has its origin in desire; desire can be quenched, suffering ended, and enlightenment achieved through the Buddha's teaching. This release from suffering, and ultimately from the cycle of rebirth, is called nirvana. Various Buddhist schools advocate different paths to enlightenment. The Theravada school, located in Sri Lanka and southeast Asia, teaches that enlightenment is achieved through solitary meditation. The Mahayana school, found in China, Korea, and Japan, emphasizes good works and compassion for others. Vajrayana Buddhism, centered in Tibet, has a highly developed metaphysic and accompanying rituals that are necessary for the good progress of the soul. *See also* Religion section, page 22–4.

C **Carnap, Rudolf** (1891–1970)   Born and educated in Germany, Carnap became an active member of the Vienna Circle but emigrated to the United States with the rise of Naziism. A prominent logical positivist and later logical empiricist, Carnap is known particularly for work in logic and his attempts to outline the logical framework of a scientific understanding of the world. His major works include *Logische Aufbau der Welt* and *Logische Syntax der Sprache*.

Categorical Imperative   *The* moral law that admits of no exceptions, proposed by Kant. It is formulated in Kant's work in a number of different ways that are supposed to be equivalent, but the simplest is, "Act only in such a way that the maxim of your act should become a universal law." In other words, do not do anything that you cannot, without contradiction, will everyone to do. For example, it would be a violation of the categorical imperative to tell a lie because if everyone lied, truth would have no meaning and no one would believe anyone. The whole point of a lie is that everyone think that you are telling the truth, thus lying is contradictory.

Categories   For Aristotle, the various ways a thing can be named or described. He posits 10 categories. For Kant, the various ways a thing can be thought or conceived *a priori*. Kant postulates 12 such pure concepts of the understanding.

Cause   In contemporary contexts, a cause is that event which produces another as its effect. Much philosophical work has made it clear that whether an event *c* causes an event *e* is not to be identified either with mere correlation or with the simple question of whether *e* would not have occurred had *c* not occurred. For Aristotle, a cause is a principle of explanation. He distinguishes between four causes: the *efficient cause*, that which makes, or begins, or moves a thing; the *material cause*, its physical substrate; the *formal cause*, that which gives a thing its structure or essence; and the *final cause*, the end to which it strives or the purpose for which it is made. Thus, the efficient cause of a statue is the sculptor; the material cause, the bronze from which it is made; the formal cause, the shape it has; and the final cause, the happiness a thing of beauty brings. The contemporary sense of cause would thus belong among Aristotle's efficient causes.

Cicero (Latin *Marcus Tullius Cicero*) (106–43 B.C.)   Roman orator, statesman, and philosopher, born at Arpinum. He was educated in philosophy and law at Rome, Athens, and Rhodes; he then entered upon a public life. He opposed both Julius Caesar and Marc Antony; he was executed at Antony's request when Octavian, later Augustus, took Rome. He is the most renowned of the Roman orators. In philosophy, Cicero was openly eclectic; believing that the Greeks had explored all philosophical possibilities, he presented them to a Roman audience. He inclined variously to Scepticism, Stoicism, and Peripatetic teachings, but rejected Epicureanism.

Circular argument   A fallacious pattern of reasoning in which one argues in a circle by arguing for a position only by assuming or presupposing that very position. Begging the question is form of circular argument.

Cognitive Science   The study of human intelligence from perception to language and reasoning. The field has grown enormously in recent years due to Chomsky's theoretical innovations in linguistics and to computer science. Cognitive science brings together people from disciplines as diverse as neurophysiology, psychology, linguistics, philosophy, and anthropology.

Coherence theory of truth   The theory that the truth of a claim or belief consists merely in its coherence with an entire body of claims or beliefs.

Communism   A social system in which property is held by the community rather than the individual. Modern Communists advocate the abolition of the state, which they consider, as Lenin put it, "the means by which one class oppresses another." (*State and Revolution*) Lenin considered communism to be the final goal of revolution and characterized it with the slogan, "From each according to his ability, to each according to his needs." (*Ibid.*) Marx, considered by many to be the father of communism, said that communism is "not a state of affairs which is to be established, an ideal to which reality will have to adjust itself," but rather is "the real movement that abolishes the present state of things." (*German Ideology*)

Comte, Auguste (1798–1857)   French positivist philosopher and mathematician. Comte did a historical study of the progress of the human mind, by which he meant the progress of the sciences. For Comte, the history of the sciences could be seen to pass through three stages: the theological, the metaphysical, and the positive, which is characterized by the study of laws "of relations of succession and resemblance." This final stage is one that we are always approaching but that we can never reach. Comte also attempted to show that each science is dependent on a previous one—physics on astronomy, biology on chemistry. Comte believed that the mind can only be understood in terms of what it has done—a position fundamentally different from that of Descartes and his followers.

Conditional   Any "if-then" statement. For example, "If this is copper, then it conducts electricity."

Confucianism   An ethical and political philosophy originating in the teachings of the Chinese thinker K'ung Fu-tzu, or Confucius (551–479 B.C.). Confucianism proper, as set forth in the aphoristic *Analects*, describes the path to a harmonious society through good government and ultimately through the virtuous character of the individual. Neo-Confucianism (960–1912) broadened the movement's traditional realm to include metaphysics and cosmogony. *See also* Religion section, page 22–6.

Consciousness   Used in a number of different ways, it can mean self-knowledge, self-awareness, or introspection. Consciousness is, then, an awareness of thinking, believing, doubting, perceiving, etc. The term *consciousness* can also be used to refer to any mental state regardless of whether or not one is aware of it.

Consequent   The "then" clause in a conditional or "if-then" statement. Symbolically expressed, *Q* is the consequent of the conditional "if *P* then *Q*."

Continental philosophy   Philosophy based on traditions coming from continental Europe, particularly France and Germany, in the 19th and 20th centuries, including phenomenology, existentialism, structuralism, post-structuralism, hermeneutics, critical theory, deconstruction, and post-modernism. The term "continental philosophy" is usually opposed to "Anglo-American" or "analytic" philosophy. It is usually considered to have begun with Kant and Hegel.

Contingent   Possible but not necessary. A contingent event is one that could occur but could also fail to occur. A contingent proposition is one that is possibly true but not necessarily true. In the work of Leibniz, and in contemporary semantics for modal logic, a contingent proposition is one true in some possible world and not true in some other.

Contradiction   An explicit contradiction is a proposition of the form "*P* and not-*P*," which involves both the assertion and denial of the same proposition *P*. The Law of Non-Contradiction is the principle that no contradiction can be true.

Contrary   Two statements are contraries if both cannot be true but both can be false. "All people are likeable" and "No people are likeable" are contraries.

Correspondence theory of truth   The theory that the truth of a claim or belief consists in its correspondence to reality or to the facts.

Cosmological argument   An argument attempting to prove the existence of God from the existence of the world. In the *Summa Theologiae*, Aquinas presents several forms of the cosmological argument. In one, he argues that all phenomena have an efficient cause; nothing causes itself, and an infinite regress of causes is impossible; therefore, there must be a first efficient cause, which is God. Others to put forward cosmological arguments include Plato, Aristotle, Descartes, and Locke.

Cosmology   The branch of philosophy devoted to the study of the universe and its origins. Cosmology traditionally includes questions of whether the universe is infinite in space and time, for example, as well as questions of whether all things can be contingent or whether there must in some sense be an initial necessary cause or "first mover." Why is there something rather than nothing? is perhaps the ultimate cosmological question.

Counterfactuals   Conditional statements with false antecedents: "Had this dime been made of copper, it would have conducted electricity," "Had Nixon not resigned, he would have been impeached." Important contemporary work has been stimulated by the fact that it is easy to find both true and false counterfactuals, although all material conditionals with false antecedents are counted as true in classical logic.

Critical theory   The views of the Frankfurt School, which began with the Institute for Social Research founded in Frankfurt in 1923. Since most of the Institute's members left Nazi Germany before the war, it was reestablished in New York in 1936. Max Horkheimer took over the school in 1930 and gave it its theoretical definition. Under him members of the school reexamined Marxism from a Hegelian perspective and in light of their disillusionment with both the West and the Soviet Union. They also attempted to integrate Marxism and psychoanalysis, doing a great deal of work on the authoritarian personality (the title of a book by Adorno). They did not emphasize revolution but instead emphasized tolerance. They also focused attention on the role and function of the family in bourgeois society. Critical Theory is also very influential in the philosophy of art and aesthetics. It particularly addresses the phenomenon of mass culture in the United States and compares it to fascism, particularly in its erasure of the distinction between public and private and the fact that it was not created by the people but was forced upon them and dominates them. A contemporary critical theorist is Jurgen Habermas.

Cynicism   A movement in Greek philosophy from the 4th century B.C. to the 6th century A.D. The Cynics held that happiness was to be found in the virtuous life, which was the natural life. They viewed Greek social conventions as unnatural and preached asceticism and self-sufficiency. The Cynics proceeded less by argument than by practice, diatribe, and satire; thus, the Cynic Diogenes of Sinope is said to have searched by daylight with a lamp for a human being. Other Cynics included Antisthenes, Crates, and Hipparchia. Cynicism had a great influence on Stoicism.

Dasein   German word literally meaning "there-being." It is used by Hegel to refer to a determinate being rather than being in general. It is also used, particularly by Heidegger, to refer to man or human being in the sense that man is already a being active in his world before we bring philosophical reflection to bear upon him.

Deconstruction   An anti-institutional philosophical practice, first undertaken by Jacques Derrida, which calls into question the basic ideas and beliefs that give legitimacy to current forms of knowledge, particularly in philosophy. It emphasizes what has been marginalized, bringing what is on the margins of philosophy to the center.

Deduction   A pattern of inference from premises to conclusion in which, if the premises be true, it is impossible for the conclusion to be false.

Definition   In contemporary use, a definition is taken as giving the meaning of a term or necessary and sufficient conditions for its application. In Aristotle and other traditional works, definition is taken as giving the essence of a thing.

Deism   Broadly, the belief in a God who is impersonal, transcendent, and not involved in the world—that is, in a God who is an "absentee landlord." More narrowly, a strain in 17th and 18th century philosophy in England and France that held that reason proves the existence of God, and there need be no recourse to revelation. Deism is conventionally contrasted with theism.

Deontology   Literally, "the science of duty." Deontological ethics holds that some acts are morally obligatory regardless of their consequences. Kant's categorical imperative is a deontological principle—the morally good action is the one done out of respect for the moral law, and the consequences of such action are immaterial to its moral goodness. For such a deonotologist, it is the reason for an action and not its consequences that we must judge either good or bad.

Derivation   In formal logic, an ordered list of formulae or set of steps, each of which is either an axiom of the system at issue or follows from previous steps by a rule of inference of the system. Derivations are often called "proofs."

Derrida, Jacques (b. 1930)   French philosopher, Directeur d'Études at the École des Hautes Études en Sciences Sociales, Paris. Founder of deconstruction. Influenced by and has written on Hegel, Nietzsche, Saussure, Freud, and Husserl. Received his doctorate only in 1980, based on his many publications including *Speech and Phenomena*, *Writing and Difference*, and *Of Grammatology*. Derrida is highly critical of the western philosophical tradition, its institutional nature and its exclusivity. He is considered by many to be a literary theorist rather than a philosopher. His work remains far more influential in the United States than in France.

René Descartes

Descartes, René (1596–1650)   French philosopher, considered to be the founder of modern philosophy. He was concerned with the question of what we can know with certainty. In order to answer this question he developed a "method of doubt" whereby he attempted to doubt the truth of everything he did not know clearly and distinctly. In his most famous work, the *Meditations on First Philosophy*, this method of doubt left him with the knowledge of only one thing—his own existence. He could not doubt that because even in doing so someone had to be doubting, hence his famous dictum from *Discourse on Method*: "I think, therefore I am." (*Cogito ergo sum.*) From this one thing that he finds he knows clearly and distinctly, he attempts, using the laws of reason, to deduce the truth of everything he doubted. Descartes equates "I" with the "thing that thinks" or the mind and says that it is a distinct substance from the body. This mind/body dualism pervades modern philosophy. For Descartes the most troubling question to which this gives rise is that of how these two separate substances interact. He concludes that it must be through the pineal gland, but he is unsure exactly how. This dualism also leads to the conclusion that mind and body exist independently of each other. Without the mind or soul the body is, for Descartes, a mechanical system. Since animals have no souls or minds they are, for Descartes, mere machines.

Determinism   The doctrine that all events, including all human choices, are necessitated; that none happens by chance, and none could possibly have failed to occur as it did. Most familiarly, causal determinism is the doctrine that all events are necessitated by earlier causes; given those causes, they could not have failed to occur.

Dewey, John (1859–1952)   American philosopher, especially of education. Dewey focused on experience as fundamental to life. Knowledge is only one type of experience. Human experience is one of the kinds of transactions that constitute nature, the others being the physicochemical and psychophysical. People are involved in constant transactions with the whole of nature, and they can come to understand nature through systematic inquiry. For Dewey, knowledge requires experimentation rather than contemplation. He developed an "instrumental" or "experimental" logic, the function of which was to study the ways in which we are most successful in gaining knowledge. There are no first principles. Rather, knowledge is rational because it proceeds by a self-corrective process—we must constantly test our claims and check them with others. He was critical of the approach to education in late 19th century America, which treated the child as a passive recipient of information, but he was equally critical of theories of education that said that children should be allowed to choose what they want to learn—such an approach ignores the immaturity of children's experience. Dewey saw children as naturally curious and explorative and thus thought that a child should "learn by doing."

Dialectic   For Socrates, argument by means of question and answer, with the goal of displaying the weaknesses of the argument of the person questioned. For Plato, rational discourse, which attempts to apprehend the essence of things, and ultimately, the idea of the Good. For Aristotle, a form of reasoning whose premises are based on generally accepted opinion. The modern notion of dialectic as the triad of thesis, antithesis, synthesis was first introduced by the German philosopher Fichte in 1794. The Hegelian dialectic, however, is not mechanical in this way but is organic and involves concepts passing over into their opposites and the achievement of a higher unity in this opposition. For Hegel, dialectic is not simply a process of thought but a world process—one through which history and the universe as a whole proceeds. While Marx used this Hegelian notion of dialectic, Engels and many later Marxists reverted to the mechanical movement of thesis-antithesis-synthesis.

Dionysian   One of the two spirits distinguished by Nietzsche in *The Birth of Tragedy*, the other being the Apollonian. The Dionysian is the spirit of irrationality, absurdity, ecstasy, and excess. Dionysian festivals are associated with drunkenness and debauchery and sometimes with frenzied insanity. The Dionysian spirit in man is that of his irrational and animal instincts, and must be harnessed and channeled by the rational, Apollonian spirit.

Dogma   Originally, a Greek term meaning "opinion" and "public decree." For the Greeks, it came to mean the teachings of the philosophical schools. For the Christians, it meant the teaching of the church. For Kant, dogmatism is the position that reason is able to proceed from concepts alone, without reference to the sensibility or to experience. Following Kant, dogma has taken on the pejorative meaning of a rigidly held belief based on authority, not on reason or experience.

Dualism   Any doctrine that asserts a pair of irreducible categories. Plato's distinction between the sensible and intelligible worlds is a form of dualism, as is Manicheanism's opposition of the principles of light and darkness. Similarly, Descartes's distinction between mind and body is a dualism of substance. Kant posits an epistemological dualism between the activity of the understanding and the passivity of the sensibility. Dualism is often contrasted with monism.

E **Egalitarianism**   The doctrine that all people are equal, and so should be given equal rights, opportunities, liberties, etc.

Egoism   Psychological egoism is the theory that people in fact seek only their own good or pleasure. Ethical egoism is the theory that people ought to seek only their own good or pleasure.

Emotivism   The theory that all ethical language is merely emotive; that it serves only to express likes and dislikes, rather than to describe any ethical state of affairs. A simple form of emotivism appears in A. J. Ayer's *Language, Truth, and Logic*. A more sophisticated form appears in Charles Stevenson's *Ethics and Language*.

Empiricism   A philosophical position that holds that sense experience rather than reason is the source of all knowledge. It is opposed to rationalism and is exemplified in modern philosophy by Locke, Berkeley, and Hume. Kant is also considered by many to be an empiricist in that he believes that experience is necessary to knowledge.

Enlightenment   In general, the term may be used for any cultural period that celebrates reason as a central human virtue and attempts to expand human horizons by rational human efforts alone. The Enlightenment is often used to designate a particular period of this sort in 17th and 18th-century European history, fostered particularly by English, Dutch, French, and German philosophers.

Epicureanism   A school of Hellenistic philosophy founded in 306 B.C. in Athens by Epicurus (341–270 B.C.). It survived at least until the second century A.D. Epicureanism held that knowledge originates through the senses; that all things, including the soul, are composed of atoms; and that happiness consists in pleasure, especially peace of mind. Although Epicureanism is often associated with debauchery, the school in fact emphasized peace of mind to an extent that resembled asceticism. Besides Epicurus, the most famous member of the school is Lucretius.

Epistemology   The branch of philosophy that concentrates on knowledge and knowing, including questions of what knowledge is (or what various types of knowledge are), and how we come to know, and the relation between knowledge and certainty.

Essence and existence   For Aristotle, essence is the nature of a thing, or what it is. Following Aristotle, Aquinas holds that essence is the nature of a thing, and existence is the being of a thing. God bestows existence on essence to create corporeal things. God's essence, on the other hand, *is* existence: otherwise put, it is his nature to be.

Essential property   In contemporary use, an object has an essential property if that object could not have existed and failed to have that property. The color this table is painted is not an essential property of it: This table could have existed and been painted another color. Arguably, this table's being made of wood *is* an essential property: nothing could have been *this table* and not have been made of wood.

Essentialism   The doctrine that some properties of things are essential to them. In contemporary usage, essentialism is taken as coextensive with the view that there are *de re* necessities, or real necessities in the things themselves, rather than merely linguistic necessities based on how they are described.

Ethical relativism   The doctrine that ethical values are relative to cultures or individuals, rather than objective or absolute. Descriptive relativism is the anthropological theory that ethical beliefs vary with time and culture. Ethical relativism proper is the theory that the truth of ethical claims varies with time and culture; in an extreme form, that there are no ethical claims truly applicable independent of culture and time.

Ethics   The branch of philosophy that concentrates on moral questions: questions of right and wrong, good and bad action, virtues and vices, and rights and obligations. Descriptive ethics in a psychological, sociological, or anthropological attempt to characterize what it is that people happen to believe about right and wrong, virtues and vices, and the like. Normative ethics, in contrast, is a more properly philosophical discipline in which the attempt is to find out the *truth* about right and wrong, virtues and vices, and rights and obligations.

Excluded Middle　The Law of Excluded Middle is the principle that every proposition must be either true or false; that there is no middle value. The Law of Excluded Middle is the defining principle of bivalent logic. *See* **Logic**.

Existentialism　A philosophical movement usually considered to have been founded by Kierkegaard. Heidegger and Sartre are the best-known 20th-century existentialists. The movement is perhaps best characterized by the slogan "existence precedes essence," which means that there is no self before action, that we are what we do and no more. Existentialists also hold that reality cannot be fully comprehended, that the universe does not make sense, and that there is no underlying rationality. In existentialism there is no answer to the question "Why are things as they are and not otherwise?"

F　**Faculty**　A power, ability, or part of the mind or soul. The theory of such abilities is called faculty psychology. For Aristotle, each living thing has a soul, and the soul's faculties include self-nutrition, sensation, locomotion, and the power of thought. For Kant, the powers of the mind include sensibility, imagination, understanding, and reason.

Fallacy　Any generally flawed or unreliable step of reasoning, especially one that is commonly used to draw illegitimate conclusions or that has a deceptive appearance of validity.

Feminism　In philosophy, a position and method of critique that holds that women have been left out of philosophy, and that when male philosophers spoke of the Human Subject and Mankind they were actually speaking about men. Many of these traditional philosophers have even asserted that women are not rational (or are at least less rational than men), are weak-minded, overly emotional, and childlike. Feminist philosophy is concerned to point out the male-centeredness of the western philosophical tradition and to discuss women's experience, subjectivity, and their role in the world. It is also concerned with the nature and meaning of gender, particularly with whether it is an essential category or is socially constructed, and with the differences between women (*e.g.* class, race, and sexual orientation). Mary Wollstonecraft wrote her *Vindication of the Rights of Women* in the 18th century, but it was not until Simone de Beauvoir's *Second Sex* (1949) that feminism became a philosophical rather than solely a political and social endeavor. It is only since the 1980s that the philosophical establishment has begun to accept, or at least tolerate, feminist philosophy as genuine philosophy.

Final Cause　*See* **Cause**.

Form　For Plato, an idea perceived by the intellect, as distinguished from an object perceived by the senses. We merely have opinions about sensible objects, because they change; we *know* forms because they are eternal and unchanging. Just as sensible objects belong to the sensible world, forms belong to an intelligible world. The intelligible world, because it is eternal, unchanging, and knowable, is the ultimate reality; the sensible world is merely an ephemeral image, sensible things merely inadequate copies of forms. The relation between a sensible object and a form is called participation. For example,

a beautiful thing participates in the idea of beauty. For Aristotle, form is the pattern or structure of a thing, to be distinguished from matter, or its physical substrate.

Foucault, Michel (1926–1984)　French structuralist philosopher and psychopathologist. Died of AIDS. Foucault saw human history as a series of *epistemes* or world views that determined everything, including what is true, within it. Within any given *episteme* there are things that cannot be known because they are not caught by the conceptual web or framework that makes sense of the world. In this way an *episteme* could be compared to Thomas Kuhn's notion of "paradigm." (*See* page 19–16.) Foucault puts forth this view in *The Order of Things*. His other works include *The Archaeology of Knowledge*, *The History of Sexuality*, *Discipline and Punish*, *The Birth of the Clinic*, and *Madness and Civilization*.

Free will　Doctrine opposed to determinism that holds that our actions are freely chosen and not determined by anything other than our own act of choosing.

Frege, Gottlob (1848–1925)　Regarded as a major founder of contemporary logic and a continuing influence in philosophy of language. Frege's logical work introduced the predicate calculus using rules of inference in much their modern form, as well as the standard quantifiers and propositional functions crucial to Russell and Whitehead's *Principia Mathematica* and later work. In philosophy of language Frege distinguished between *Sinn* and *Bedeutung* —at least roughly, the sense and reference of a term. Frege maintained that two names may have the same reference though a different sense, as, for example, in "The Morning Star is the Evening Star." Frege's major works are the *Begriffsschrift*, *Grundlagen der Arithmetik*, and *Grundgesetze der Arithmetik*.

Freud, Sigmund (1856-1939)　Austrian psychiatrist and founder of psychoanalysis, a theory which has had an immense impact on contemporary continental philosophy, particularly in France. Freud theorized the distinction between the *id* or irrational desires, the *ego*, and the *superego* or moral/social norms that create guilt. He also theorized the unconscious, which is a much larger psychic space than consciousness and is responsible for dreams, hysterical symptoms, phobias, and neuroses. Freud also discussed the sexuality of infants, which was revolutionary because previously children were not thought to have sexual urges until puberty. Among his other important discussions are those about the roles of repression, the Oedipus complex (the desire for one's mother and the hatred and fear of one's father), the death instinct, inhibition, aggression, and the reality principle in psychic life.

G　**Gnosis**　A Greek word meaning "knowledge." In Plato's *Republic*, it denotes knowledge of the intelligible realm, in opposition to opinion (*doxa*) of the sensible. For the Gnostic movement, which began in the first and second centuries, it came to mean direct knowledge of the divine. The Gnostics were radical dualists: They held that matter is intrinsically evil and that through individual revelation we can attain gnosis of the true God, who is alien to this world. This gnosis can be either a return to an original unity with God, as in Valentinianism, or release from an original dualism, as in Manichaeanism.

Gödel's Theorem Kurt Gödel (1906-1978) Gödel's first theorem (in semantic form) is that any formal system adequate for number theory, if sound, will be incomplete: if all theorems of that system are true on interpretation, there will be some formula that expresses a truth on interpretation and yet does not appear as a theorem. Gödel's second theorem is that no consistent formal system adequate for number theory can contain as a theorem a statement expressing the consistency of that system in a certain straightforward sense.

Good, the For Plato, the highest and best of the ideas, desired for its own sake, through which all other ideas are beneficial, useful, knowable, and possible. In the *Republic*, Plato argues that the Good is to the intelligible world as the sun is to the sensible world: The Good makes the forms knowable, just as the sun makes objects visible. Later Platonists identify the Good with the Beautiful and the One.

Greatest Happiness Principle The central principle of classical utilitarianism: That act is right that produces the greatest amount of pleasure for the greatest number of people. In other forms of utilitarianism, it may be rules or institutions that are evaluated rather than acts, and happiness or pleasure may be replaced by more complicated notions of the good.

Habermas, Jürgen (b. 1929) German philosopher and well-known critical theorist, best known for his work on "communicative ethics." For him society can only be rational if its policies are subject to public control, which occurs within a framework of open discourse, free from manipulation and domination. Major works: *Theory of Communicative Action, Legitimation Crisis.*

Hedonism From the Greek word *hedone*, which means pleasure. There are two forms of hedonism, ethical and psychological. Ethical hedonism holds that pleasure is the highest good, and pain is intrinsically undesirable. Epicurean and Utilitarian ethics can be considered hedonist; the former focuses on the pleasure of the individual, the latter on collective or universal pleasure. Psychological hedonism holds that pleasure is the end of all action, whether good or evil. Ethical and psychological hedonism thus differ in that the former is prescriptive and the latter descriptive.

Hegel, Georg Wilhelm Friedrich (1770–1831) German philosopher, often wrongly considered to be an apologist for the Prussian state and a totalitarian. Hegel was, in fact, an absolute idealist who considered Mind/Spirit (*Geist*) to be the world. According to Hegel, human knowing is Mind coming to know itself while nature is Mind becoming other, a necessary moment in coming to know itself. Hegel's *Phenomenology of Spirit* shows the progression of human consciousness from the standpoint of immediacy to that of being in a position to know itself as the actualization of Spirit in a community of people in a relation of mutual recognition, a community of individuals characterized by being a "we that is 'I' and an 'I' that is we." Hegel's other works include *Philosophy of Right, Encyclopedia of the Philosophical Sciences*, and *Science of Logic.*

Heidegger, Martin (1889–1976) German philosopher, phenomenologist, and existentialist. Also a Nazi collaborator. Heidegger was concerned with the nature of being (What is it to be?). In his most famous work, *Being and Time*, Heidegger undertakes an analysis of man or Dasein because only man asks about the nature of being. Man is always already active in the world when he starts to ask about his being. He is also projecting himself into the future so, in an important sense, his being consists in what he is not yet. In his everyday life, man is bound up with the public and occupied with petty concerns. He is therefore alienated from his authentic self most of the time. This is what Heidegger calls inauthentic existence, as opposed to authentic existence, which is characterized by dread (*Angst*), brought about by realizing that he will die. Death and the relation to it is authentic because it is the only event in a man's life that is his own and no one else's.

Hempel, Carl (b. 1905) Best known for work in philosophy of science, particularly in theory of explanation and theory of confirmation. Hempel is known for the Nomological-Deductive model of scientific explanation, according to which a set of statements (the *explanans*) offer a scientific explanation of another statement (the *explanandum*) just in case the statements of the explanans have empirical content and are true, entail the explanandum, and contain at least one general law actually used in the entailment. Hempel's major papers are collected in *Aspects of Scientific Explanation.*

```
┌─ All copper conducts electricity (law) ┐  explanans
│  This penny is copper                  ┘

entail ──────────────────────────────
  └→ This penny conducts electricity  ── explanandum
```

N-D model of a scientific explanation
for the fact that this penny conducts electricity.

Heraclitus (6th–5th centuries B.C.) Pre-Socratic philosopher, from Ephesus in what is now Turkey. Heraclitus held that the world is in constant flux, that this flux takes place through a unity and interchange of opposites, and that it is regulated by a principle alternately identified as reason or fire.

Hermeneutics Traditionally a term associated with Biblical interpretation, within philosophy the term is applied to the art and/or science of interpretation generally. In recent continental philosophy, the German philosopher Hans-Georg Gadamer has been the best-known theorist. It is most influential in philosophy of art and philosophy of literature.

Hermeticism The teachings of the legendary Hermes Trismegistos (Greek, Thrice-great Hermes), often identified as an Egyptian priest. These teachings supposedly form the *Hermetica*, a collection of pagan, magical, Platonic, and Gnostic texts written in Greek and compiled between the 1st and 3rd centuries A.D. The term "hermeticism" came to be associated with any magically inclined Platonism, especially that of the Renaissance.

Hinduism   English term for the majority religion of India. Hinduism is amazingly diverse, and easily accommodates conflicting theological and philosophical viewpoints. The minimum standard of Hindu orthodoxy is acceptance of the Vedas, the most ancient Hindu texts. Popular Hinduism can be further characterized by polytheism, a belief in reincarnation, and the caste system. Traditionally, there are six orthodox schools of Hindu philosophy. Yoga is theistic and concerns the discipline of the self. Sāṃkhya, although atheistic, treats the metaphysical underpinnings of Yoga. Mīmāṃsā is concerned with the systematic exegesis of Veda Vedānta, which is actually a collection of schools, supplies a theological framework for Veda The Nyāya school deals with logic. Vaiśeṣika doctrine is atomistic.

Hobbes, Thomas (1558–1679)   English empiricist philosopher. Hobbes had an extreme fear of anarchy and civil war, which motivated his political theory. He insisted on a strong state to guarantee the security of its citizens, even at the expense of their liberty. He distinguished between two kinds of person— natural and artificial. The natural person is the one whose words and actions are his own. The artificial person is one whose words and actions are another person's. The state is an artificial person— the sovereign or Leviathan (after which Hobbes' book *The Leviathan* is named). Natural persons give up their right to govern themselves and allow an artificial person, the sovereign, to govern them. This involves a contract both between the natural persons, whereby they agree to accept governance by the sovereign, and between them and the sovereign, whereby the sovereign guarantees their security. This arrangement is called a commonwealth. Hobbes considered his political theory to be continuous with his materialism; he wanted to produce a unified science in which political institutions would be deduced from facts about human nature.

Humanism   Any view that emphasizes human flourishing and human happiness on earth as a primary good to be pursued, as opposed, for example, to goals of serving God or seeking rewards in an afterlife. In contemporary usage, the term is also used to designate an explicitly atheistic view that considers the good of all earth's humanity as the supreme ethical goal and emphasizes methods of science, reason, and democratic decision making.

Hume, David (1711–1776)   Scottish empiricist philosopher. Hume was troubled by the existence of concepts that do not seem to be derivable from experience, like God and causation. His work was an attempt to resolve this problem. His empiricism is often summed up by the slogan "No ideas without impressions," which means that there can be no mental contents without sense experience. For Hume, ideas are, in fact, faded impressions. So, for example, the idea of a sound is the faded impression of a sound. Since the imagination consists in the manipulation of ideas, which are faded impressions, it is more limited than we usually think. Even a concept like "God" is really just an exaggeration of empirical ideas of certain human powers. Our idea of causation comes from repeated experience of *B* following *A* so that it becomes a habit to expect *B* to follow *A*. The idea of causation, then, is the impression of expectation that *B* will follow *A*. Hume's most famous works are *Enquiry Concerning Human Understanding* and *Treatise on Human Nature*.

Husserl, Edmund (1859–1938)   German philosopher, considered the founder of phenomenology. Searched for the foundation of human knowledge, which he called the Archimedean point. His work was a constant search for a beginning—both of knowledge and of his work itself—so he abandoned his earlier views on several occasions to begin again in order to be sure that he was beginning correctly. Husserl considered the self to be the source of all knowing acts. He considered philosophy to be a nonempirical science, which he called phenomenology. According to Husserl, once we adopt a reflective attitude to the world, which he called the phenomenological reduction, we discover the "transcendental ego" or "pure consciousness." Everything in the world is only an object for this pure consciousness. The transcendental ego is the Archimedean point from which all study can begin.

Hypatia (ca. 370–415)   Neoplatonic philosopher, mathematician, and astronomer, born at Alexandria. She became head of the Neoplatonic school at Alexandria at an early age. A pagan, she was murdered by a band of Christian monks. She is said to have lectured on both Plato and Aristotle in addition to mathematics, geometry, and astronomy.

I   **Idealism**   The philosophical position that ideas rather than matter are what is fundamental or real in the universe. Leibniz and Berkeley are considered idealists in this sense. Kant's idealism, which he called "formal," "critical," or "transcendental," is somewhat different. For Kant, we cannot know the world through rational thought alone, but neither can we know it only through sense experience. Perception requires organization by the intuitions of space and time and by the categories of the understanding. German philosophers Fichte, Schelling, and Hegel developed Absolute Idealism out of Kant's idealism. Fichte believed that the starting point of philosophy must be a free intelligent ego rather than space, time, and the categories of the understanding with which Kant had started. Schelling considered the mind, unlike everything else, to be undetermined and absolute. The most influential absolute idealist was Hegel. According to Hegel, "The finite is not genuinely real." Mind or the Absolute Idea, which is infinite, is what is genuinely real. The tradition of absolute idealism was continued by the "neo-Hegelians" or "British Idealists," particularly W. T. Harris, T. H. Green, F. H. Bradley, Bernard Bosanquet, Josiah Royce, and John McTaggart in the late 19th century and the first half of the 20th century in the United States and Great Britain.

Ideology   A word first used by Destutt de Tracy in 1796 to refer to his program of reductive semantic analysis, which would lead to institutional reforms in France. Napolean opposed the *idéologistes*, dismissed them, and persecuted them, ridiculing them with the name *idéologues*. Marx adopted this contemptuous view of ideology but did not consider it to be ineffective. He considered ideology to be a mystification of nature and society with institutional causes used as a means to keep certain groups in power. For Marx, ideology is an all-encompassing power from which it is very difficult to escape.

Iff   A common abbreviation for "if and only if." *See* **Logic.**

Indexical   A term the referent of which depends on the person, time, place, etc., of its use. If two different people both say "I am sick," the term "I" has a different referent in each case. "Here" and "now" are other common examples of indexicals.

Induction   The process of coming to a generalization regarding all things of some larger class on the basis of a smaller sample. The standard scientific practice of confirming universal generalizations such as "All white male cats are deaf" on the basis of a finite and limited sample of white male cats is considered induction.

Innate Ideas   Ideas that are in some way genetic, "hard-wired" into the mind, and that do not need to be learned. At various times it has been proposed that God, immortality, space, time, and basic forms of linguistic structure are innate ideas.

Intuitionism   Associated most strongly with the work of W. D. Ross, ethical intuitionism is the view that ethical rightness or wrongness is based on inherent ethical qualities, rights, obligations, etc., which can be directly intuited. More broadly, intuitionism is any view that grounds knowledge in certain basic intuitions.

J **James, William** (1842–1910)   American philosopher and psychologist, founder of pragmatism, and older brother of novelist Henry James. Perhaps most often quoted for his assertion that without language to order our experiences, the world would be a "bloomin', buzzin' confusion." His major work is usually considered to be *Principles of Psychology*, although *Pragmatism: A New Name for Some Old Ways of Thinking* and *The Varieties of Religious Experience* are also quite famous.

K **Kabbalah**   The mystical tradition of Judaism, especially the school of esotericism and theosophy that originated in the Middle Ages. The latter is founded largely on the *Sefer ha-Zohar*, or Book of Splendor, a 12th-century compilation of texts, the largest part of which are mystical exegeses of the Torah. Kabbalism's method is the elaboration of the attributes of the deity; its goal is contemplation of (and rarely, union with) God. The sources of medieval Kabbalah include not only Judaism, but Zoroastrianism, Neoplatonism, Christianity, and Gnosticism.

Kant, Immanuel (1724-1804)   German philosopher. Kant lived his entire life in Königsberg, where he taught at the university for many years. He credited Hume with having awakened him from his dogmatic slumbers. Kant is considered to have been responsible for the Copernican Revolution in philosophy. In his *Critique of Pure Reason*, he set out to find the proper limits of reason. He wanted to know just what reason could and could not do. This meant that he needed to find the conditions for the possibility of knowledge. He combined the positions of the empiricists and the rationalists by insisting that sense experience and the categories of the understanding are both necessary for

Immanuel Kant

knowledge. For Kant, we can never know what things are apart from our understanding of them. His moral philosophy, as put forth in the *Critique of Practical Reason* and *Groundwork of the Metaphysics of Morals*, is founded upon an absolute moral law, the binding force of which we cannot understand but which we can nonetheless feel. We must believe our wills to be free, the soul to be immortal, and God to exist in order to act, but we cannot know these things as they are part of the realm of things-in-themselves. Kant's third critique, *Critique of Judgment*, contains his aesthetic theory and a discussion of teleology. These three critiques constitute the Kantian system, called critical or transcendental idealism.

Kierkegaard, Søren (1813–1855)   Danish philosopher and religious thinker, regarded as a founder of Existentialism. Several of Kierkegaard's works are written as if by other authors, representing opposing characters in his overall view of man's relation to rationality and religion. One prominent Kierkegaardian theme is the "leap of faith" required to transcend the aesthetic and ethical stages into truly religious existence. Another is the claim that truth is subjectivity. Major works include *Either/Or*, *Fear and Trembling*, and *Sickness Unto Death*.

Kripke, Saul (b. 1941)   McCosh Professor of Philosophy at Princeton University, Kripke developed the semantics for modal logic based on Leibniz's notion of "possible worlds" while still in high school. His best-known book work is *Naming and Necessity*, in which he argues that reference rather than description gives proper names their meaning. He has also argued against the materialist idea that mental states are identical with brain states.

Kuhn, Thomas S. (b. 1922)   Philosopher and historian of science at MIT. His landmark *The Structure of Scientific Revolutions*, in which he describes how science moves from one world view or paradigm to another, has changed the philosophy of science and social science enormously since its publication in 1962. Kuhn argues that science is not a steady accumulation of knowledge but is rather a process of relatively stable periods of knowledge advancement and revolutionary periods during which the entire world view changes, as for example with the Copernican revolution, when the Earth came to be seen as revolving around the sun, or when quantum physics replaced Newtonian physics.

Lacan, Jacques (1901–1981) French psychoanalyst in the Freudian tradition who focused on language. For Lacan, castration is not just sexual, as it is for Freud, but linguistic— we can only signify ourselves in a symbolic system that we do not command but that commands us. For Freud, only women are castrated; for Lacan, everyone is. Lacan's emphasis on the phallocentrism of language has made him influential among some feminists.

Leibniz, Gottfried Wilhelm (1646–1716) German philosopher, scientist, mathematician, historian, and diplomat. A rationalist, Leibniz is best known for his *Monadology*, in which he proposes that the fundamental stuff of the universe is monads. Monads are unitary forces that are not in space and time and thus not material. Leibniz was also the first philosopher to talk about possible worlds. He considered the actual world to be "the best of all possible worlds," because God, being all good, could not have made anything less than the best world actual.

Locke, John (1632–1704) English empiricist philosopher. In his *Essay Concerning Human Understanding*, Locke inquired into "the origin, certainty, and extent of human knowledge, together with the grounds and degrees of belief, opinion and assent." In doing this he put forth a number of ideas, including the distinction between primary and secondary qualities. Primary qualities are inseparable from the thing that has them—for example, extension, solidity, figure, and mobility. These qualities really exist in the thing itself. Secondary qualities are the powers a thing has to produce certain sensations in us—for example, color, odor, sound, warmth, and smell. These qualities do not exist in the thing but are rather produced in us by the thing. Locke is perhaps best known, however, as a political thinker. His *Two Treatises On Government* were written, at least in part, to justify England's Glorious Revolution of 1688, resulting in the ascension to the throne of Mary and William of Orange. In the second treatise, Locke theorized that all men are originally in a state of nature and come together to form a social contract to create a body politic. It is important that this contract is between free and equal men. The purpose of the contract is to preserve the life, freedom, and property of everyone. This idea heavily influenced the American Declaration of Independence and the foundation of the United States of America.

Logic The study of patterns of reasoning and argument, particularly with an eye to deductively valid patterns of reasoning and argument. Traditional logic, starting with Aristotle and continuing through the Middle Ages, is based on categorizations of arguments in terms of valid and invalid syllogisms.

Contemporary formal or symbolic logic includes as its simplest form the propositional or sentential calculus, which attempts to formalize axiomatically the logical relations represented by English connectives "and," "or," "not," "if-then," and "if and only if." Predicate calculus attempts to expand this formal treatment to the quantifiers "all" and "none." Various systems of modal logic attempt to handle "necessary" and "possible" (alethic modal logic) and "permissible" and "obligatory" (deontic modal logic). Classical logics of all of these forms share (a) an assumption of bivalence—that sentences or propositions have only one of two values, true or false—and (b) a certain treatment of the conditional, taken as representing "if-then" sentences.

Logical positivism A set of views associated with the Ernst Mach Society or Vienna Circle of the 1920s, which included prominently Otto Neurath, Moritz Schlick, Rudolf Carnap, and A. J. Ayer as an informal English spokesman. The general tone of logical positivism is antimetaphysical and proscientific, in one form rejecting as literally meaningless all propositions that are neither (a) *a priori* propositions of logic and pure mathematics, nor (b) propositions capable of empirical verification. Under the influence of logical positivism, metaphysics became a derogatory term for idle and meaningless mental confusion, with philosophy taken as a therapeutic attempt to dispel such confusion. Because the model of knowledge was scientific knowledge, important attempts were made to characterize scientific knowledge precisely.

Lucretius (Latin *Titus Lucretius Carus*) (99–55 B.C.) Epicurean philosopher of Roman origin. His poem, *On the Nature of Things*, is an exposition of Epicurean philosophy. According to Jerome, a love potion drove Lucretius mad and he composed the poem during periods of sanity.

Lukàcs, Georg (1885–1971) Hungarian Marxist philosopher. Considered a Hegelian Marxist, Lukàcs was very critical of the emphasis on natural necessity and the "dialectics of nature" propounded by Engels and his followers, such as Lenin. Major work: *History and Class Consciousness*.

Lyotard, Jean-Francois (b. 1924) French philosopher, Professor Emeritus of Philosophy at the University of Paris VIII, and Professor of Comparative Literature at the University of California at Irvine. Considered a postmodernist, he is concerned with "pagan" ethics, with how we treat those who are different and how we can have a society that includes them without doing violence to their difference. His best-known work is *Postmodern Condition*.

Machiavelli, Niccolò (1469–1527) Italian statesman and author, born at Florence. Born to a prominent family, he held office under the Florentine republic. He was dismissed when the Medici returned to power and lived out his life on a country estate. In *The Prince*, he gives practical advice on how a monarch might best keep power. He argues that a prince should rule with little regard for virtue or vice because at times virtue can work against, and vice for, his interests. In the *Discourses*, he describes how a republican form of government may improve itself.

Niccolò Machiavelli

MacIntyre, Alasdair (b. 1929)   A contemporary philosopher known for critical and historical studies in ethics and social philosophy. One strand of MacIntyre's work involves the claim that current ethical debate results in irresolvable conflicts because we have inherited conflicting fragments of ethical intuition from earlier traditions, torn from the social contexts in which they once made sense. Major works include *Against the Self-Images of the Age*, *After Virtue*, and *Whose Justice? Which Rationality?*

Maimonides (Hebrew *Moses ben Maimon*) (1135–1204)   Medieval Jewish philosopher, commentator, and physician, born at Córdoba. His family fled Spain after the conquest of the Islamic Alhmohads, and eventually settled in Cairo, where he became court physician to the vizier of Saladin and head of the Egyptian Jewish community. His main philosophical work is the *Guide of the Perplexed*; in it, he attempts to reconcile Judaism and Aristotelianism. He held that no positive attribute can be predicated of God; and that where reason and scripture seem to be in contradiction, either ambiguous scripture must be understood as allegory or inconclusive philosophical arguments must give way to scripture. Maimonides also produced a commentary on the Mishnah; the *Mishneh Torah*, a codification of Jewish oral law; some medical treatises; and a work on logic.

Manichaeanism   A form of Gnosticism, founded by the Persian prophet and martyr Mani (ca. 216–ca. 276). It posits two coeternal principles: one of darkness, matter, and evil; the other of light, soul, and good. These two principles are at war, and this war results in the mixture of principles that is our universe. Our bodies are of the darkness, and our souls of the light; the path from darkness to light is gnosis, or knowledge of the divine, which was revealed first by Zoroaster, then Buddha, then Jesus, and finally Mani. Today the term Manichaeanism is used to attack positions perceived as dualistic.

Marcus Aurelius (Latin *Marcus Aurelius Antoninus*) (121–180)   Roman emperor and late Stoic philosopher. His aphoristic *Meditations* were written in Greek while the emperor was at war. His views are less concerned with logic and physics, and more disposed to a kindly providence, than earlier forms of Stoicism.

Marcuse, Herbert (1898–1981)   German philosopher who emigrated to the United States in the 1930s. Marcuse was the most famous exponent of critical theory (*see* page 19-6) and the most revolutionary. He undertook a detailed study of Hegel, which resulted in his first major work, *Reason and Revolution*. He was a Hegelian Marxist who tried to reconcile Freud and Marx in his *Eros and Civilization*, in which he discussed psychological categories that had become political categories. Marcuse's most influential work was *One-Dimensional Man*, in which he claimed that advanced industrial society is totalitarian because it manipulates needs. In the 1960s Marcuse became known as the ideologue of campus revolutions in the United States and Europe.

Karl Marx, German economist and author of *Das Kapital*.

Marx, Karl (1818–1873)   German philosopher, social and economic theorist. The father of communism, Marx spent his life in exile, first in Paris, then in Brussels, and finally in London. He was heavily influenced by Hegel, whose dialectical method he used throughout his work. Most famous for his criticism of capitalism and bourgeois society, Marx worked with Friedrich Engels to produce the *Communist Manifesto* in 1848, which was to become one of the most influential works for world politics. It is an analysis of capitalism and a call to revolution—a call that Lenin, Mao, and Che Guevara, among others, heard. Among Marx's most influential works was his enormous analysis of capitalism, *Das Kapital* or *Capital*.

PHILOSOPHY

Marxism A philosophical/political/social theory based on the work of Karl Marx. Marxism comes in two distinct varieties, but what both have in common is a critique of capitalism. The first of the two main kinds of Marxism is Hegelian Marxism, which focuses a great deal of attention on Marx's early work and his links with Hegel. Georg Lukàcs, Herbert Marcuse, Jean-Paul Sartre, and Maurice Merleau-Ponty are all considered Hegelian Marxists. The other main form is orthodox Marxism, which actually begins with Engels rather than with Marx. Orthodox Marxism focuses on causal and deterministic laws that drive history and is critical of Hegelianism, dismissing the early Marx as dangerously influenced by Hegel. Lenin and Stalin are well-known orthodox Marxists. It is important to remember that Marx himself claimed that he was not a Marxist.

Materialism The metaphysical view that all that ultimately exists is physical or material; that anything apparently mental, spiritual, or abstract is ultimately reducible to the purely physical or material. Nineteenth- and twentieth-century science are often accused, rightly or wrongly, of presupposing a materialist metaphysics.

Mead, George Herbert (1863–1931) American pragmatist philosopher and social behaviorist. Professor of philosophy at University of Chicago from 1892, Mead published very little during his lifetime. His lectures and notes were edited by friends and students and published posthumously. In his best-known work, *Mind, Self and Society*, Mead was concerned with the emergence of mind and self out of social activity. Mead's social behaviorism was an attempt to account for introspection within an essentially behavioristic framework.

Meinong, Alexius (1853–1920) Known for the view that there literally are things that don't exist, such as unicorns, round squares, and the (imaginary) golden mountain. Meinong held that objects may either "exist" or "subsist," with the latter category reserved for nonexistent items such as unicorns and round squares. Meinong also held that certain entailment relations must hold, however, so that the round square must be both round and square.

Merleau-Ponty, Maurice (1908–1961) French philosopher, existentialist, and phenomenologist. He believed that the body is that through which we live, as opposed to Sartre, who saw the body as something other than the self. For Merleau-Ponty, we cannot have disembodied experience of the world. All of our experiences are through our senses and are thus sensuous. The French word *sens* means both sense and meaning. Meaning then is always sensuous, which is why Merleau-Ponty says, "We are condemned to meaning."

Metaphysics The study of being as such, that is, of what it means for something *to be*. For Aristotle, metaphysics is primarily the study of substance, because substance is that which *is*; everything else that is said to be is an attribute or determination of substance. Aristotle called this discipline first philosophy and theology; it received its popular name because it comes after (Greek *meta*) the *Physics* in the Aristotelian corpus. After Aristotle, the term came to be used for any theory of the nature and structure of reality, at times including ontology, cosmology, and theology.

Mill, John Stuart (1806–1873) English philosopher, administrator for the East India Company, and Member of Parliament. Mill was rigorously educated by his father, who started teaching him Greek at the age of three and Latin at eight. By the time he was 14, he had read most of the Greek and Latin classics, studied history extensively, and worked intensively in logic and mathematics. At 15 he read Jeremy Bentham's *Traite de legislation*, which made him decide to become a world reformer. At 20 he suffered a nervous breakdown and spent the next few years tempering his analytic training with the poetry of Wordsworth and Coleridge—what he considered an education of the feelings to balance his education of the intellect. Mill was an empiricist who held that all inference is ultimately induction. He formulated five methods of induction in his *System of Logic* (the method of agreement, of difference, of agreement and difference, of concomitant variation, and of residues). His *Utilitarianism* has been one of the most influential works in ethics. Mill is also well known for his *On Liberty*, which focused especially on freedom of thought and discussion. Mill was also an advocate of women's rights and was heavily influenced by his friend and wife, Harriet Taylor.

Mind-Body Problem The recurring problem in philosophy of how the mind and the body are related. Answers have varied from Descartes's mysterious connection through the pineal gland to the denial of any mind apart from brain processes, and from Berkeley's denial of the existence of material substance to Leibniz's idea of a preestablished harmony such that mind and body appear to be linked even though they are in fact independent. The mind-body problem continues to interest and trouble philosophers today.

Monism Any doctrine that asserts unity. Monism can be the simple assertion that only unity is conceivable, as with Parmenides. It can maintain that plurality is derivable from unity, as with Plotinus. It can claim that mind and matter are the manifestations of a single substance, as with Spinoza, or a single process, as with Hegel. Monism is often contrasted with dualism.

More, Thomas (1478–1535) English statesman and author, born in London. Culminating a distinguished career as a statesman, More was lord chancellor to Henry VIII from 1529–1532. He was imprisoned in 1534 and later beheaded for refusing to acknowledge Henry as head of the Church of England. He is most remembered as a thinker for *Utopia* (1516), a work written in Latin that purports to chronicle a visit to an ideal republic. As is typical with Renaissance philosophers, More draws heavily on the ancients, including Plato, Cicero, and Epicurus.

Mysticism A diverse group of doctrines calling for direct knowledge or experience of, or union with, the ultimate reality. Stereotypically, mysticism is theistic, other-worldly, and antirational; this is not necessarily the case, however. Mysticism can be theistic (Pseudo-Dionysios) or atheistic (Theravāda Buddhism); it can be otherworldly (Teresa of Ávila)

PHILOSOPHY

or involved with the world (Mahāyāna Buddhism); and in various forms of mysticism, intellect either can know the ultimate reality (Gnosticism) or it cannot (Plotinus).

Natural Law   The doctrine that some or all standards for human conduct can be derived from human nature. Thus, Stoicism draws its ethics from natural human rationality. Thomas Aquinas argues that there is a natural law imprinted by the Creator on all people, Christian and Gentile; this natural law is supplemented by human and especially divine law. Natural law is often contrasted to convention and to positive law.

Necessary   A necessary event is one that cannot but occur; a necessary proposition is one that cannot but be true. It is impossible for a necessary event *not* to occur, and impossible for a necessary proposition *not* to be true. In the work of Leibniz and in contemporary semantics for modal logic, a necessary proposition is one true in all possible worlds. In theology, a necessary being is one the existence of which is necessary.

Negation   The negation of a sentence that asserts that *p* is the case is a sentence that asserts that *p* is not the case. In logic, negation is represented by ~ or ¬.

Neoplatonism   A philosophical movement in late antiquity, lasting from approximately the 3rd to the 6th centuries A.D. Neoplatonism is a modern term; the Neoplatonists considered themselves to be propounding the true doctrine of Plato. It is characterized by monism and the doctrine of emanation. Plotinus, often called its founder, held that all reality is an emanation of the One, which he identified with the Platonic form of the Good. Our task is to turn from the sensible world and achieve union with the One, which is not possible through the intellect. Iamblichus (3rd–4th centuries) is most known for his view that theurgy, or magical practice, is a path to the One. Representative of Athenian Neoplatonism is Proclus (ca. 410–485), who elaborated the theory of emanation into an extremely complex and subtle system. Alexandrian Neoplatonism, which included Hypatia, was focused on scholarship. The movement largely ended in 529, when Justinian closed the pagan schools of learning. Neoplatonism underwent a revival in the Renaissance.

Nietzsche, Friedrich (1844–1900)   German philosopher. In his first work, *The Birth of Tragedy* (1872), he distinguished between the Apollonian and Dionysian spirits. Nietzsche is also well known for his discussion of the *Superman* (Übermensch), a human being who has ordered his passions and affirms life, that is, who has his act together and gets things done. The Superman sees perfection as a task and sets about to achieve it. Another important conception in Nietzsche's philosophy is *the will to power*, which is man's basic motive and can be found in all living things. All people want power as embodied in self-possession, fearlessness, and an ability to change the lives of those around them. Nietzsche is falsely considered by some to have been a proto-Nazi as a result of his sister's creative editing of some of his writings during his illness and after his death. Plagued by bad health,

poor eyesight, and frequent migraines, Nietzsche went mad in 1889. Nietzsche's works include *Thus Spake Zarathustra*, *Beyond Good and Evil*, and *Genealogy of Morals*.

Nihilism   A general term for negative or pessimistic views regarding existence, meaning, and value. In an extreme form, nihilism is the view that nothing exists. In a more common ethical form, nihilism is the view that nothing has any genuine value or meaning.

Nirvana   A Sanskrit word meaning "extinguishing," as of the flame of a lamp. In Buddhism, it is the state of enlightenment. We are endlessly reborn to lives of suffering because of desire; each life is likened to a lamp, desire to its fuel, and we pass from life to life as a flame passes from lamp to lamp. Nirvana is attained by the elimination of desire so that suffering and rebirth may end, just as the absence of fuel extinguishes the flame. Desire is eliminated by following the Buddha's teachings, especially that of contemplation.

Noesis and Noema   In Husserl, *noesis* is an intending act while *noema* is the intended meaning or sense. For example, the act of wishing that the house were on the hill is the *noesis*, while the wished-for house (as wished for) is the *noema*.

Non-Contradiction, Law of   The principle that no contradiction can be true; that any sentence of the form "*P* and not *P*" must be false.

Noumenon   In Kant, anything that cannot be known by experience—any object as it is in itself independent of our experience of it, as opposed to *phenomenon*.

Ockham's Razor   The principle that plurality is not to be posited without necessity, associated with the English scholastic William of Ockham (ca. 1285–1359). In other words, an explanation with fewer assumptions is preferable to one with more, where possible. It is also known as the principle of economy and of parsimony.

Ontological argument, The   An argument attempting to prove the existence of God from his essential nature. It was first put forward by Anselm in his *Proslogion*. Anselm argues that God is that than which nothing greater can be thought; that than which nothing greater can be thought must include existence, for if it did not, something greater could be thought; therefore, God necessarily exists. Duns Scotus, Descartes, and Leibniz also put forth forms of the ontological argument. *See also* **Anselm**.

Ontology   The theory of being. Ontology is often used as a synonym for metaphysics.

Pantheism   The doctrine that God is the cosmos and the cosmos, God. Hinduism has a pantheistic moment in the Vedic concept of Brahman, the unity behind all illusory plurality. Spinoza can be considered a pantheist in identifying substance with God and reducing thought and extension to attributes of substance. On some readings, the Hegelian Absolute Idea is a pantheist conception. Pantheism is often contrasted with the narrow sense of theism.

Paradigm   A word used by Thomas Kuhn to refer to a scientific world view. It can be used to refer to any set of laws and principles that form a coherent view. A paradigm can also be a model, as a blueprint is a paradigm for a building, or can be an exemplary case, as one could say that a particularly bright, hard-working student is a paradigm of what all students should be.

Paradox   In general, a paradox consists of two contrary propositions with apparently compelling arguments for each, or an unacceptable proposition for which there appears to be a compelling argument. Perhaps the oldest paradox is the paradox of the Liar, consisting of the following sentence:

This statement is false.

Is the exhibited sentence true, or false? If true, it must be false, since it *says* it's false. If false, on the other hand, it must be true, since that's was it *says* it is. It appears that the sentence must be either true or false, but either assumption leads to contradiction. Other classical paradoxes include the Sorites, or paradox of the heap, and Zeno's paradoxes of motion. Among paradoxes important for the development of twentieth-century set theory are Russell's paradox of the set of all sets which are not members of itself (is *it* a member of itself, or not?), Cantor's paradox of the set of all sets, and Burali-Forti's paradox of the greatest cardinal number.

Parmenides (6th–5th centuries B.C.)   Pre-Socratic philosopher, lived at Elea in Italy. For Parmenides, being is one, and change and multiplicity are illusions. In his poem, *The Way of Truth*, he argues the following: that which is thought must have being, for that which is not cannot be thought; being is changeless, for change requires not-being; and being is one, for multiplicity requires not-being. Parmenides founded the Eleatic school; the most famous of his students was Zeno of Elea.

Particulars   Individual things, often understood as instances of general concepts, or universals.

Pascal, Blaise (1623–1662)   French philosopher, mathematician, physicist, and inventor. Pascal invented an early calculating machine, made contributions to number theory, probability, and geometry, and conducted experiments on air pressure and the vacuum. His later religious and philosophical writings have overshadowed these achievements, however, and he is most widely remembered today for his reflections on human existence and God in his *Pensées*.

Peirce, Charles Sanders (1839–1914)   American philosopher and mathematician, one of the founders of pragmatism. Peirce is remembered best for seminal work in logic and philosophy of science, though these were always for him part of larger philosophical systems.

Perception   A general term for seeing, hearing, tasting, feeling, or otherwise sensing.

Personal identity   The character of being the same person, which an individual retains through various mental and bodily changes. The problem of personal identity is that of specifying what conditions are required in order for an individual at one point and an individual at another to be the same person.

Phenomena   In Kant, things as they are for human experience as opposed to how they are in themselves.

Phenomenalism   A view according to which statements about the world are ultimately only statements about actual and potential perceptions, phenomena, or appearances, or the view that all that exists is ultimately composed of such phenomena or appearances. In a weaker sense, phenomenalism is the view that at any rate the only knowledge possible is knowledge about actual and potential perceptions, phenomena, or appearances, rather than about things in themselves.

Phenomenology   The study or science of phenomena. The term was first used by German philosopher Johan Heinrich Lambert in 1764. Hegel was the first to make the term well known in his *Phenomenology of Spirit* (1807). Here he shows that by coming to know Mind or Spirit as it appears, we come to know it as it *is*. Husserl made phenomenology into a method of philosophy, which is usually what people consider phenomenology to be today. Phenomenology in this sense is a method of description whereby one describes phenomena by means of direct awareness. The phenomenologists' slogan is "Return to the things themselves," by which they mean that philosophers should get back to philosophy and describe things as phenomena rather playing around with language and logic. Martin Heidegger, Jean-Paul Sartre, and Maurice Merleau-Ponty all considered themselves to be phenomenologists, though they used the term somewhat differently from Husserl and from each other.

Philosopher-king   Plato writes in the *Republic* that a just state is impossible unless kings are philosophers and philosophers are kings. He then elaborates a system of education that will create these philosopher-kings, and thus a just state. This education culminates in dialectic, which prepares the rulers to know the idea of the Good.

Philosophy   From a Greek term meaning "love of wisdom." Broadly, philosophy involves theoretical or conceptual examination, often of questions that arise in other contexts or disciplines. This definition may seem overly broad, since philosophy so defined would apparently include aspects of science and art as well. Traditionally, however, much of what was considered philosophy also qualifies as art (Plato's dialogues, for example) or natural science (parts of the Aristotelian corpus). At present, philosophy appears as a university discipline that deals with past and present systematic theorizing. As such, it includes as subfields logic, metaphysics, epistemology, ethics, politics, aesthetics, and philosophy of language.

Philosophy of language   A branch of philosophy concentrating on questions regarding language: What is meaning? What is reference? Is a perfect language possible? Is necessity purely linguistic? An even more focused subbranch is philosophy of linguistics.

Philosophy of law   A branch of philosophy that concentrates on questions about the nature and function of law and legal systems: What is required for a legal system? Does the law have ethical force? Under what conditions is civil disobedience justified? Is the death penalty justifiable? In many instances philosophy of law merges with theoretical jurisprudence.

EXHIBIT 19.1
Philosophers' Quotes

Hope is a waking dream. —Aristotle

A likely impossibility is always preferable to a convincing possibility. —Aristotle

I wish that every human life might be pure transparent freedom. —de Beauvoir

One is not born a woman, one becomes one. —de Beauvoir

The greatest happiness of the greatest number is the foundation of morals and legislation. —Bentham

The absurd is the essential concept and the first truth. —Camus

It is not rebellion itself which is noble but the demands it makes upon us. —Camus

Do not wait for the last judgment. It takes place every day. —Camus

The four conditions of happiness: (1) life in the open air, (2) the love of another being, (3) freedom from all ambition, and (4) creation. —Camus

The highest possible stage in moral culture is when we recognize that we ought to control our thoughts. —Darwin

The greatest minds are capable of the greatest vices as well as of the greatest virtues. —Descartes

From fanaticism to barbarism is only one step. —Diderot

Man is sometimes extraordinarily, passionately, in love with suffering. —Dostoevski

So long as man remains free he strives for nothing so incessantly and so painfully as to find someone to worship. —Dostoevski

In philosophy, it is not the attainment of the goal that matters, it is the things that are met with by the way. —Ellis

The good or ill of man lies within his own will. —Epictetus

First say to yourself what you would be; and then do what you have to do. —Epictetus

The longest journey
Is the journey inwards
Of him who has chosen his destiny. —Hammarskjöld

Beauty in things exists in the mind which contemplates them. —Hume

I have often thought that the best way to define a man's character would be to seek out the official mental or moral attitude in which, when it came upon him, he felt himself most deeply and intensely active and alive. At such moments there is a voice inside which speaks and says: "This is the real me!" —James

Nothing on earth consumes a man more quickly than the passion of resentment. —Nietzsche

The heart has its reasons which reason knows nothing of. —Pascal

The life which is unexamined is not worth living. —Plato

Mankind answers injustice fearing that they may be the victims of it, and not because they shrink from committing to it. —Plato

Fear is the main source of superstition, and one of the main sources of cruelty. To conquer fear is the beginning of wisdom. —Russell

Happiness is the only sanction of life; where happiness fails, existence remains a mad and lamentable experiment. —Santayana

Fantacism consists in redoubling your efforts when you have forgotten your aim. —Santayana

Man can do nothing unless he has first understood that he must count on no one but himself; that he is alone, abandoned on earth in the midst of his infinite responsibilities, without help, with no other aim than the one he sets himself, with no other destiny than the one he forges for himself on this earth. —Sartre

I know of no more encouraging fact than the unquestionable ability of man to elevate his life by a conscious endeavor. —Thoreau

It is only by risking our persons from one hour to another that we live at all. And often enough our faith beforehand in an uncertified result is the only thing that makes the result come true. —James

There is only a single categorical imperative and it is this: Act only on that maxim through which you can at the same time will that it should become a universal law. —Kant

Morality is not properly the doctrine of how we may make ourselves happy, but how we may make ourselves worthy of happiness. —Kant

The absurd...is not identical with the improbable, the unexpected, the unforeseen. —Kierkegaard

There is no such thing as absolute certainty, but there is assurance sufficient for the purposes of human life. —Mill

Liberty consists in doing what one desires. —Mill

Man is a rope stretched between the animal and the Superman – a rope over an abyss. —Nietzsche

Philosophy of religion   A branch of philosophy that concentrates on questions about theology and religion: Is there a God? Is belief in a God rational? Is the existence of a God consistent with the existence of evil?

Philosophy of science   A branch of philosophy that concentrates on questions about the character of scientific knowledge: What is a theory? Under what conditions is a hypothesis confirmed? What constitutes a scientific explanation? What is the difference between science and pseudoscience?

Plato (ca. 427–ca. 347 B.C.)   Greek philosopher, born at Athens. The son of an aristocratic family, he was a follower of Socrates. In 388 B.C. he traveled to the court of the tyrant of Syracuse, hoping to put his theories into practice; he made two more visits later in life. He founded his school, the Academy, after his first such visit. Among his students was Aristotle. It is difficult to make generalizations about Plato's work, given its literary character; however, provisional remarks about its form and content are possible. Plato's chosen literary form was the dialogue, usually a dramatic account of a philosophical conversation. The main character is often Socrates. A striking feature of many dialogues is that the characters regard the conversation as inconclusive. Among the dialogues are the *Apology*, *Republic*, *Symposium*, and *Timaeus*. The literary form of the dialogue is a reflection of Plato's method: rational discourse that attempts to apprehend the essence of things. Plato's doctrine is referred to as the theory of forms. He argues that ideas alone are real, and that sensible objects are mere images of ideas; true knowledge is of the intelligible world, and the good man and the good state act in accord with the idea of the Good. His work predates later distinctions among disciplines within philosophy; thus, the theory of forms is simultaneously ethics, politics, ontology, logic, and epistemology. *See also* **Academy; Dialectic; Form; the Good.**

Plotinus (ca. 205–270)   Neoplatonic philosopher, born in Egypt, studied at Alexandria. After an aborted attempt to travel east to study Persian and Indian philosophy, Plotinus settled at Rome. He is generally considered the founder of Neoplatonism. His position is characterized by monism and the theory of emanation and is set forth in the *Enneads*, which were edited by his student Porphyry. Disagreeing with Gnostic dualism, Plotinus held that all reality is an emanation of the One, which he identified with the form of the Good. Emanation undergoes several stages, termed *hypostases*. The first of these is the One; the second, Intellect; the third, Soul. The sensible world, although a result of the process of emanation: is not considered a separate hypostasis. Our task is to seek union with the One. This is achieved by turning away from the sensible world and the body, and turning first to Soul, then Intellect, and finally the One. Although Plotinus' system is rational, final union with the One is beyond Intellect or reason.

Political Philosophy   The branch of philosophy that deals with political life, especially with the essence, origin, and value of the state.

Popper, Karl (b. 1902)   In philosophy of science, known for the falsifiability criterion, according to which a theory qualifies as scientific not if it is verifiable but if it is falsifiable—that is, if it is incompatible with certain possible results of observation. Popper's main work is *Logic of Scientific Discovery*.

Pragmatic theory of truth   Associated with the work of Charles S. Peirce and (more clearly) William James. In a simple form, it is the theory that the truth of a claim or belief consists in whether it works in practice.

Pragmatism   A philosophical movement founded by C. S. Peirce and William James. "The pragmatic method tries to interpret each notion by tracing its practical consequences." (James, *Pragmatism*.). The consequences of any idea are its meaning.

Premise   In an argument, one of the propositions of the set from which a conclusion is drawn.

Pre-Socratics   A group of Greek thinkers who lived in the 6th and 5th centuries B.C. and are united by an interest in the constituent principles of nature. Although their name implies that they lived and taught before Socrates, some were his contemporaries. *See also* **Atomism; Heraclitus; Parmenides; Pythagoras; Thales; Zeno of Elea.**

Prime Mover   The unmoved source of all movement, or God. In the *Physics*, Aristotle argues that all movement has a cause; since an infinite regress of causes is unthinkable, there must be an original, unmoved source of movement, or Prime Mover; since movement is continuous and eternal, this Prime Mover must be one and eternal. Nor does it have magnitude: eternal movement requires infinite force, infinite force cannot reside in a finite magnitude, and infinite magnitude cannot exist. In the *Metaphysics*, Aristotle argues that the Prime Mover is the source of change in that it is the primary object of desire and of thought; it is the final cause of the universe, alive, actual, and good; it is immaterial; it is thought thinking itself; it is, in fact, God.

Property   Any characteristic of an object; some attribute that it has. The color, size, and shape of an object are all properties it has.

Proposition   A statement, or that which is expressed by a declarative sentence. Sometimes it is said that it is propositions expressed by sentences, rather than sentences themselves, that are true or false. Propositions are also taken to be what is believed or known.

Psychoanalysis   Psychological/philosophical theory/practice developed by Sigmund Freud. Psychoanalysis emphasizes achieving self-knowledge through conversation with an analyst. It is a method of investigation that consists in bringing out the unconscious meaning of a person's words, actions, and the products of imagination using free association. It is also a method of psychotherapy that brings things repressed in the unconscious to consciousness, allowing the patient to work through them and thus curing the patient of the physical and/or psychological symptoms they cause.

Pythagoras (6th century B.C.)   Pre-Socratic philosopher, lived at Croton in Italy. He was founder of the school of Pythagoreanism. The teachings of the school had both philosophical and religious aspects. These included the doctrines that the universe is based on number and arranged according to mathematical ratio and musical harmony; that number itself is based on a fundamental mathematical and moral dualism between the limited and the unlimited; that the soul is immortal and undergoes reincarnation; and that one should observe certain taboos (*e.g.,* abstention from beans). The Pythagoreans had a great influence on mathematics, hence the geometrical theorem that bears their name.

Quine, W.V.O. (b. 1908)   American philosopher and logician, professor of philosophy at Harvard. Quine is sceptical of the distinction between analytic truths, which are true by definition (like "all bachelors are unmarried men"), and synthetic truths, which are true as matters of fact (like "Albany is the capital of New York"). Quine was also concerned with problems of translation, encapsulated in the "indeterminacy of translation": it is possible to compile incompatible manuals for translating one language into another, all of which seem to work, and therefore none of which can be called the one right manual. Quine's most famous work is his *Word and Object.*

Rationalism   An approach to philosophy that takes reason alone, unaided by experience, to be primary in the search for truth. Descartes, Leibniz, and Spinoza are paradigmatic rationalists, all of whom attempted to reconstruct philosophical thought on a mathematical model.

Rawls, John (b. 1921)   A contemporary political philosopher known for a theory of justice with affinities to social contract theory, sometimes interpreted as a defense of liberalism. On Rawls's theory, roughly, a policy is just if it is in accord with principles that would be agreed to by a group of free and rational individuals in an "original position," in which under "a veil of ignorance" they do not yet know what position they will take in a society. His major works are "Justice As Fairness," and *A Theory of Justice.*

Realism   In the most common contemporary sense, realism is the view that science and similar bodies of belief do represent or correspond to an independent reality—the world—against which they are judged and which they can more or less adequately mirror. Realism has also been used to label the view that atoms, quarks, the weak force, and other things apparently designated by nonobservational or theoretical terms are nonetheless real. In one traditional sense, realism is the view that universals are real—that general categories exist in their own right, rather than merely the individual things that belong to those categories.

Reason   The power of thought. It is sometimes conceived of as thinking abstractly, thinking logically, or thinking dialectically. Reason is variously opposed to appetite (the power of desire) and sensation (the power of sensing objects). The conclusions of reason are sometimes contrasted to the conclusions of intuition, of revelation, and of faith.

Relativism   The doctrine that truth or value is relative to cultures or individuals, rather than objective or absolute. In an extreme form, relativism is the view that there is no truth, there are only views held by one or another group.

Renaissance   A term from French meaning "rebirth." It is applied to a period in Western European history from approximately the 14th to the 17th centuries and is often considered a rebirth of intellectual and aesthetic culture after the Middle Ages. Renaissance thought is characterized both by a return to the ancients and by humanism. Part of the age's rebirth was the rediscovery of ancient Latin and Greek texts: Aristotle's writings, which the medievals knew through commentators, were available in a more complete form; Plato's writings, which the medievals knew through the attacks of the commentators, were available for the first time. Thus, a Renaissance Aristotelianism arose (*e.g.,* Pomponazzi), and more importantly, a Renaissance Platonism (*e.g.,* Ficino and Pico). Renaissance humanism was a turning from a focus on God and the next world to human beings and this world. It was therefore openly antagonistic to Scholasticism.

Rousseau

Rousseau, Jean-Jacques (1712–1778)   Swiss-born philosopher best known for his book on education, *Emile,* and his book on political theory, *Social Contract.* Rousseau considered man to be a free and rational being by nature and thought that his participation in society must be consistent with that fundamental nature. A political society must be the result of a social contract—a free association of intelligent people. Because they have chosen to form this society, its members owe it their allegiance. This society must, however, be one that leaves its members free, obeying not another person, but the general will, which is always directed toward the general good. Only in obeying the general will are individuals truly free because only then are they obeying a law that they have given to themselves. This democratic notion of society was very influential in the formation of the United States.

Russell, Bertrand (1872–1970)   Known primarily for work in logic and the foundations of mathematics, culminating in *Principles of Mathematics* and *Principia Mathematica* (with Alfred North Whitehead). Russell later did work in epistemology, including *Our Knowledge of the External World* and *An Inquiry into Meaning and Truth*, as well as authoring a range of popular works in ethics, politics, and education.

Sartre, Jean-Paul (1905–1980) French existentialist philosopher and writer. Founded the journal *Les Temps Modernes* with Simone de Beauvoir, his lifelong companion, and Maurice Merleau-Ponty. Sartre was heavily influenced by Hegel, Marx, Husserl, and Heidegger. He was interested in human beings and sought to describe their mode of being. His fundamental definition of the self could be summed up "You are what you do." His most famous philosophical works are *Being and Nothingness* and *Critique of Dialectical Reason*. He is also well known for his play *No Exit*, for his novel *Nausea*, and for his collection of stories, *The Wall*.

Scepticism   The position that knowledge is limited or impossible. The many historical forms of scepticism include Academic, Pyrrhonian, Cartesian, and Humean scepticism. Academic scepticism (3rd to 1st centuries B.C.), associated with the New Academy, argued that certainty is impossible because the senses are fallible and the most we can hope for is probability. Pyrrhonian scepticism (1st to 3rd centuries A.D.) argued that we should suspend judgment about all that is not immediate in appearance, such as logical or causal connection, because there is no way of ascertaining its certainty. René Descartes' method of universal doubt can be called sceptical, although it is ultimately in the service of certainty and rationalism. David Hume advocated a mitigated form of scepticism. He argued that the excesses of Pyrrhonian scepticism had to be corrected by common sense and reflection, and our enquiries limited to the capabilities of the human understanding.

Scholasticism   A movement in medieval Christian thought. It lasted from the 11th to 15th centuries, although anticipations exist as early as the 6th century and survivals as late as the 18th. Scholasticism can be characterized in four ways. First and foremost, scholasticism was Christian. Its overriding concerns were theological, and it sought to systematize the truths of faith and relate them to the truths of philosophy. Second, it was rational. In the service of faith, it made use of non-Christian philosophy. These sources included not only Greek philosophy generally and Aristotle in particular but also Islamic philosophers such as Avicenna and Averroës. Third, it was systematic. This manifested itself in forbidding technical language, in voluminous commentary, in precise logical disputation, and especially in great systematic works called *summae*. Fourth, scholasticism was associated with universities, or "schools"; hence the name of the movement. *See also* **Anselm; Cosmological argument; Essence and existence; Natural Law; Ontological argument, The; Thomas Aquinas; Universals.**

Semantics   In a general sense, the study of the meaning of linguistic signs or symbols. In logic, the semantics for a formal system provides a model or set of models that afford a valuation, usually in terms of "true" and "false," for the formulae of the system. As a subdiscipline of logic, formal semantics is that branch of logic involving the study of interpretations or valuations for formal languages, and is roughly coextensive with model theory.

Semiotics   Also known as semiology. The science of signs. *Semiotics* appears in the work of C. S. Peirce at the end of the nineteenth century and *semiology* in Ferdinand de Saussure, a Swiss linguist, in his *Course on General Linguistics* (1910–1913). For Saussure, linguistics is only a part of semiology—all human behavior and production is significant and can be studied as such by semiotics. Roland Barthes further developed semiotics in his *Elements of Semiology* (1964). For him, however, all significant behavior is already language, thus all questions about significance are already questions about language. For Saussure, the sign is the relation of signifier and signified. A sign is not just a word but the word and the concept that goes with it. Umberto Eco is perhaps the best-known semiotician today.

Social contract   An original agreement whereby people existing in a "state of nature" agree to build a society together or to establish mutual social relations. The idea of a social contract is central to the social philosophy of Hobbes and Locke, but appears also in Rousseau, Kant, and in a contemporary form in the work of John Rawls. Typically, the role of such an idea, which need not be held to reflect an actual historical event, it to gauge the justice of certain social structures or governmental policies by seeing if they would accord with the rational decisions made in a social contract.

Socialism   A social and political position, originating with Robert Owen in 1827, to the effect that existing society is unjust and corrupt because of an unequal distribution of wealth and property and that a better society can be created, which will improve mankind instead of corrupting it. This society would be characterized by equality. After Marx and Engels' *Communist Manifesto*, socialism changed. They dismissed previous socialists as utopians and advocated a "scientific" socialism. Lenin said that socialism would be just a step on the way to communism, a step that could be characterized by the slogan "From each according to his ability, to each according to his contribution," and by the gradual withering away of the state.

Socrates (ca. 470–399 B.C.)   Greek philosopher, born at Athens. Socrates himself wrote nothing; what we know of him comes through Plato, his student, and Xenophon, his apologist. Excepting time spent at war, he lived his entire life at Athens. He spent his days in philosophical disputation, and in so doing attracted a number of followers and made a number of enemies. In 399, he was charged with corrupting the youth and disbelieving in the gods of the state. His defense, or apology, is reported by both Plato and Xenophon. He was convicted and sentenced to death, which he carried out by drinking hemlock. Plato wrote a number of dialogues in which Socrates is the chief character; it is therefore difficult to separate Socrates's position from the one Plato attributes to him. Plato and Xenophon agree, however, on what has been called the Socratic method, or dialectic: disputation by means of question and answer, especially to show weaknesses in the answerer's position. Socrates has been taken as the seminal figure in Greek philosophy; thus, all philosophy prior to his is characterized as "Pre-Socratic."

Solipsism The doctrine that the only things that exist are aspects of "my" consciousness; that reality does not extend beyond what I perceive, and that there are no other selves or beings apart from me and my consciousness.

Sophist Originally, a Greek term meaning "wise man," in the 5th and 4th centuries it came to mean "teacher," especially one hired to teach young Athenian male citizens. The course of study included rhetoric at the very least. The goal of the Sophist was to prepare the young man for a political life. According to Plato, the sophist's means to this was to teach him to argue for or against any position whatsoever, often to destructive effect. Following the criticisms of Plato and others, the reputation of the Sophists suffered, and the term became a synonym for quibbler and intellectual cheat.

Sound An argument is sound where it both is valid and has true premises.

Baruch Spinoza

Spinoza, Baruch or Benedict (1632–1677) Known for a philosophical system presented in an axiomatic deductive style and concluding that the universe is a single deterministic entity, with infinite attributes, that can be thought of as either Nature or God. As a Jew living in Holland, Spinoza had little contact with his Dutch neighbors. Because he had been expelled from the synagogue for unorthodox opinions, moreover, he had little contact with the rest of the

Jewish community. Spinoza earned his living as a lens grinder, refusing the chair in philosophy at Heidelberg in 1673 because he thought it would cost him his independence and tranquility of mind. Major work: *Ethics.*

State of nature The state of humanity as it would be if there had never been any social or political institutions. The idea of a state of nature is used by a number of political philosophers, most notably Locke, Rousseau, and Hobbes. In Locke and Rousseau, the state of nature is used as an argument for basic rights, including rights to liberty. In Hobbes, a quite different conception of the state of nature is used to argue for the necessity of a government with virtually unlimited powers over the individual.

Stoicism A school of Hellenistic philosophy, founded by Zeno of Citium (ca. 336–ca. 265 B.C.), which flourished from the third century B.C. to the second century A.D. It derives its name from the painted porch, or *stoa poikile,* in Athens, where Zeno taught. The Stoics conceived of nature as a rational whole. In line with this, they developed a propositional logic. In ethics, they held that the path of virtue is the path of nature, that is, of reason. By eschewing conventional goods for the rational, natural life, one can avoid both pain and pleasure and attain peace of mind. In addition to Zeno, Stoic philosophers include Epictetus and Marcus Aurelius.

Structuralism A philosophical standpoint of the continental tradition. It had its origins in the linguistic studies of Ferdinand de Saussure and Roman Jakobsen, who investigated the structure underlying language. Its basic premise is that in order to understand society, one has to understand the implicit structure that all human activity presupposes. Anthropologist Claude Levi-Strauss used this concept of structure in his analysis of primitive societies, as did Jacques Lacan and Michel Foucault in psychology and epistemology.

Subject, the The self, the "I." All self-conscious human beings who act, speak, and know themselves are *subjects.*

Subjective idealism A philosophical position that rests on the assumption that the object of perception is part of the mind. Fichte was considered a subjective idealist in that he considered the ego to be the source of all things. *See* **Idealism.**

Subjectivism In ethics, the view that ethical values are merely a matter of the subjective impressions and preferences of individuals and have no objective or independent status apart from the subjective states of individuals. Linguistically expressed, the view is that ethical statements are merely statements about subjective impressions and preferences.

Substance and attribute The distinction between substance and attribute comes from Aristotle. In the simplest case, a substance is an individual thing—for instance, Socrates. Wisdom, on the other hand, is an attribute we predicate of Socrates in saying "Socrates is wise." Aristotle and later thinkers also offer more complicated accounts of substance and attribute, however.

Summum bonum A Latin phrase meaning "the greatest good." In ethics, it is the good that is valued as an end in itself, not as a means to another end. As such, it forms the foundation of various systems of ethics. Thus, for Aristotle, happiness is the greatest good; for the Epicurean, pleasure; for the Stoic, peace of mind. Kant calls the good will the highest good; Mill, the greatest happiness for the greatest number.

Syllogism　A form of valid deductive argument that consists of two premises and a conclusion. The argument "All Greeks are wise; Socrates is a Greek; therefore, Socrates is wise" is a syllogism. First formulated by Aristotle, the syllogism dominated Western logic until the 19th century.

Syntax　In logic, the syntax of a system is defined by a grammar that specifies certain strings of symbols as well-formed formulae, or *wffs*. Syntax is also taken as the study of properties of formal systems dependent only on the form of its formulae, independent of interpretation. In this broader sense, the study of syntax is roughly correlate to proof theory.

Synthetic proposition　A proposition that, if true, is true as a matter of fact or because of the way the world is, rather than solely in virtue of the meaning of its terms.

T **Tarski, Alfred** (b. 1902) Polish-American logician known for his work in formal semantics, the notion of meta-languages, and truth. Tarski is well known for his *T-schema*. Although actually developed in a formal context, the T-schema is widely interpreted informally as specifying, given a sentence *P* and name "*P*" for that sentence, that "*P*" is true if and only if *P*. Tarski's theorem is that the notion of arithmetical truth is not arithmetically definable; *i.e.*, that within any consistent formal system adequate for arithmetic there can be no formula *f* such that it is a theorem for all and only those formulae taken as true on the standard interpretation that formula *f* applies to them.

Tautology　Informally, a definitional or analytic truth. In logic, a compound sentence true regardless of what truth values are assigned to its components: "If *P* then *P*," for example. More generally, the term is used to designate any similarly trivial truth, such as "Either Bill will win class president or he won't."

Teleology　A doctrine that seeks to explain phenomena through ends, goals, or purposes. Through the concept of final causality, Aristotle argued that not only is human activity purposive, but that all things in nature have a purpose or end (*e.g.*, the purpose of teeth is to chew, the goal of a seed is the mature plant). In fact, he argues, all things have a common goal in their desire for the Prime Mover, or God. Hegel argues that the goal of history is the realization of freedom and reason. Teleology is often contrasted with mechanism, which seeks to explain all phenomena through efficient causality.

Thales (6th century B.C.)　Pre-Socratic philosopher from Miletos in what is now Turkey. Tradition holds not only that he was the founder of the Ionian school of philosophy, but also that he was the first Western philosopher. He was also a mathematician and astronomer. None of his work survives. Many of the Ionians attempted to explain the workings of nature through recourse to a single principle, and Aristotle reports that Thales held that water is the persisting substrate of all things.

Theism　Broadly, the position that there is a God. This view can be based on reason, on revelation, or both. Variants include monotheism (that there is one God), polytheism (that there are many Gods), and pantheism (that the whole is God). More narrowly, theism is the belief in a God who is personal, transcendent, and active in the world. In this latter sense it is contrasted with pantheism and deism.

Theology　The systematic study of the truths of religion, sometimes limited to the study of God's nature, attributes, and relation to the world. Theology as a discipline originated in late antiquity, when Jewish and Christian intellectuals attempted to explain and understand their religions through philosophy. Medieval theologians—Islamic, Jewish, and Christian—were concerned with the relation of theology (and its realm, revealed truth) to philosophy (and its realm, truth found by reason).

Theorem　In logic, a provable formula, or one that appears as the last line of some derivation.

Thomas Aquinas (1225–1274)　Scholastic philosopher, born at Roccasecca near Naples. The youngest son of a noble family, Aquinas was educated by Benedictines and eventually became a Dominican. He studied theology at Paris and taught at the university there; he also he spent time at the papal court. Aquinas was the creator of a synthesis of Aristotelianism and Catholicism. He held that, although separate, theology and philosophy are at harmony, with faith supplementing and correcting reason; that reason can know nature, for the senses perceive particulars, from which the intellect abstracts universals; that the intellect cannot know God positively in this life, but only negatively and by analogy; and that things are a combination of essence and existence. His works include the *Summa Contra Gentiles* and the *Summa Theologiae* (often incorrectly called the *Summa Theologica*). Thomism, as his position is called, is the dominant philosophy in the Roman Catholic Church.

Thoreau, Henry David (1817–1862)　American essayist and philosopher, one of the Concord transcendentalists. Thoreau is best remembered for his eloquent and outspoken individualism. Major works: *On Civil Disobedience, Walden*.

Transcendentalism　An American intellectual movement centered around Concord, Massachusetts, and flourishing from about 1836 to 1860. The roots of transcendentalism are many and various, though it draws most strongly from the romanticism of Goethe, Wordsworth, Coleridge, and Carlyle. For the most part it constitutes a moralistic theme rather than a philosophical position—a theme of idealistic striving beyond the bonds of provincial conservatism. Foremost among the transcendentalists were Ralph Waldo Emerson, Henry David Thoreau, William Ellery Channing, and George Ripley.

Truth　*See* **Coherence theory of truth; Correspondence theory of truth; Pragmatic theory of truth.**

U **Universals**　General concepts or ideas. Universals are often contrasted with *particulars*. The origin and nature of universals is a long-standing debate in philosophy. Among the ancients, Plato held that ideas had objective reality apart from sensuous things, while Aristotle argued that universals exist only as common properties of particulars. The problem of universals, however, is most commonly known as a Scholastic debate. There were three basic positions in this debate: Nominalism, Conceptualism, and Realism. Nominalism held that universals were arbitrary names given to particulars. William of Ockham is often read as a Nominalist. Conceptualism held that although universals exist only as concepts of the mind, they are not arbitrary, but follow on similarities in the world. Peter Abelard was of this school. The moderate Realism of Thomas Aquinas held that universals exist only in particular things, from which they are abstractions.

Utilitarianism   Classical utilitarianism (as in the work of Jeremy Bentham) is the view that an act is right if it produces the greatest amount of pleasure for the greatest number of people. In other forms of utilitarianism (including John Stuart Mill, G. E. Moore, and contemporary authors), it may be rules or institutions that are evaluated rather than acts, and happiness or pleasure may be replaced by more complicated notions of the good.

Utopia   A neologism from Greek that means either "good place" (*eutopia*) or "no place" (*outopia*). It was coined by Thomas More for his book *Utopia* (1516), which purported to chronicle a visit to an ideal republic. The term has come to mean any ideal social structure. Utopian literature became a powerful tool for social criticism in the Renaissance and modern periods; the term is sometimes applied to certain ancient arguments as well (e.g., Plato's *Republic*).

Valid   A deductively valid argument is one in which it is impossible for all of its premises to be true and its conclusion to be false; if its premises are true, its conclusion *must* be true. More generally, an argument is said to be valid if its conclusion legitimately follows from its premises.

Virtue   Greek theories of virtue are based on the term *arete*, which means "goodness," "excellence," and "virtue." The goodness or virtue of a thing is that by which it performs its function well. Thus, the function of a knife is to cut; a good, or "virtuous," knife cuts well. Plato argues in the *Republic* that when reason rules the soul, as is its function, the soul is virtuous; as such, it possesses wisdom, bravery, temperance, and justice. For Aristotle, the ethically virtuous soul habitually chooses its path of action according to a rational mean between two vices. Thus, when faced with a fearful situation, it chooses the mean, which is courage, rather than wallow in an excess of fear, which is a vice called cowardice, or proceed heedlessly and fearlessly, which is rashness.

Weber, Max (1864–1920)   German sociologist. Against Karl Marx, Weber denied that any form of social activity could be purely economic, though he did think that all activities have an economic aspect. His most famous work was *The Protestant Ethic and the Spirit of Capitalism*, in which he argued that capitalism is largely the result of the ascetic secular morality associated with Calvinism.

Whitehead, Alfred North (1861–1947)   British mathematician and philosopher known for work in the foundations of mathematics with Bertrand Russell (*Principia Mathematica*) and for later work in metaphysics, most notably in *Process and Reality*.

Wittgenstein, Ludwig (1889–1951)   Austro-English philosopher. The two major periods of Wittgenstein's philosophical life are marked by the *Tractatus Logico-Philosophicus* and *Philosophical Investigations*. The *Tractatus* is an attempt to lay out the structure of any language that mirrors the world, with implications drawn regarding what can be said and what can only be shown. The *Philosophical Investigations* is a posthumously published and much looser collection of ideas centering on the social nature and function of language, with attention to implications for both the content and proper practice of philosophy.

Wollstonecraft, Mary (1759–1797)   Educator and first major philosophical feminist. Born and raised in a poor farming family in rural England, she was self-educated and worked as a governess and then as a freelance writer and translator. She was condemned by many for her Bohemian lifestyle, which included being independent, living with a man, and giving birth to a child out of wedlock. She married William Godwin only a few months before her death from complications following childbirth. The child she had with William Godwin was her second daughter, Mary Wollstonecraft Godwin, who eventually married the poet Percy Bysshe Shelley and wrote the Gothic novel *Frankenstein*. Mary Wollstonecraft was concerned with women's education and with the fact that middle class and aristocratic women are expected and trained to be useless, feeble, and weak-minded. Wollstonecraft's arguments for women's emancipation, put forth most famously in her *Vindication of the Rights of Women* (1792), earned her the admiration of some and the hostility of many, who called her such things as "a hyena in petticoats" and "a philosophizing serpent." Wollstonecraft was also a supporter of the French Revolution and was highly critical of social systems based on the assumption that some people are born better than others. Mary Wollstonecraft's life and work continue to inspire feminists today.

Yoga   A Sanskrit word meaning "yoking," given both to a set of Indian practices and to a school of Hindu philosophy. Broadly, Yoga is an ascetic and contemplative discipline whose goal is enlightenment. In this sense, it is current in Hinduism, Jainism, and Buddhism. More narrowly, Yoga is one of the six schools of Hindu philosophy. It was first elaborated in Patañjali's *Yoga-sūtras*, perhaps in the 2nd century B.C. It argues that liberation from suffering comes about through yogic discipline, which includes regularized breathing and physical postures; liberation itself, unlike that of Buddhism, consists in the pure isolation of the eternal self. The physical forms of Yoga are considered preliminaries to the mental discipline of meditation, the goal of which is to reach a state in which not only awareness of one's surroundings but the awareness of being in that state is removed. Reaching this state consists in a progression of stages of emptying the mind.

Zen A term meaning "contemplation," given to a Japanese form of Mahayana Buddhism. It was introduced to Japan from China in the twelfth and thirteenth centuries. Zen emphasizes meditation and discipline, often as a means to sudden enlightenment. The object of meditation is the *koan*, a question meant to transcend intellectual distinctions.

Zeno of Elea (ca. 490–ca. 430 B.C.) Pre-Socratic philosopher. A student of Parmenides, he is most famous for a series of paradoxes of motion. In one, Zeno argues that a runner cannot traverse the length of a stadium: In order to reach the finish line, a runner must pass over an infinite number of points; it is impossible to pass over an infinite number of points in a finite time; thus, the runner cannot reach the finish line. He is not to be confused with Zeno of Citium, founder of Stoicism.

PHYSICS

Absolute temperature *See* **Kelvin scale**.

Absolute zero The lowest possible temperature, –273.16°C, which is also called 0 K (zero on the Kelvin scale). Absolute zero has been approached to within a thousandth of a degree, but it is theoretically impossible to ever actually reach this temperature.

AC *See* **Alternating current**.

Acceleration The rate of change in velocity. Since acceleration is a velocity divided by a time, its units must be (m/s)/s, or m/s². A change in velocity can be either a change in speed or a change in direction. For discussion of changes in speed, *see* **Linear acceleration**; for changes in direction, *see* **Centripetal acceleration**.

Acceleration due to gravity In a given gravitational field, all objects in free fall have the same acceleration. Near the surface of the earth, the acceleration due to gravity is g_0, = 9.8 m/s². It is slightly greater at the poles than at the equator.

The acceleration due to gravity near any celestial body varies inversely as the square of the distance from the center of the body. What is the acceleration due to gravity g at an altitude of 3000 km above the earth? The distance from the center of the earth is 3000 km + the radius of the earth (6400 km) = 9400 km. Setting up the inverse square ratio gives

$$\frac{g}{9.8 \text{ m/s}^2} = \left(\frac{6400 \text{ km}}{9400 \text{ km}}\right)^2$$

from which g = 4.5 m/s².

Note that the acceleration of an object in free fall is always directed straight down, regardless of the direction of its velocity. If the object is falling straight down, its velocity increases at the free fall rate. If it is rising, its velocity decreases at that rate. If its motion has a horizontal component, in a uniform gravitational field, the downward acceleration gives it a parabolic path.

See also **Orbit**; **Trajectory**.

Accelerators Devices to accelerate charged particles by the application of electric fields. A linear accelerator consists of a series of evacuated pipes, placed end to end, in which the electric field is applied as the particle passes through the gap between two pipes. In a cyclotron, the path of the particle is made circular by the application of magnetic fields. In large, high-energy accelerators, such as the synchroton, particles travel through small tubes. The path is made circular by strong electromagnets spaced at intervals, and the particles are accelerated by electric fields across gaps between sections of the tube. Synchrotons carry the particles through tubes formed into a circle several miles in diameter. *See also* **Supercollider**.

Alpha decay One of the modes of radioactive breakdown of atomic nuclei. In this reaction, a large, unstable nucleus emits a helium nucleus, called an alpha particle, consisting of two protons and two neutrons. *See* **Radioactivity**.

Alpha particle A helium nucleus produced in the radioactive breakdown of a large nucleus. *See* **Radioactivity**.

A stream of alpha particles was used by Rutherford to investigate the structure of matter, an experiment that resulted in the discovery of the atomic nucleus. *See* **Rutherford's experiment**.

Alternating current An electric current consisting of a longitudinal wave in a wire, carried by electrons. The electrons vibrate back and forth, so that the current flows first in one direction and then the other, alternating at some definite frequency. For electric power transmission, the frequency is usually 60 Hz, but in electronic equipment, it can be many megahertz.

Alternating current, or AC, is now universally used for power transmission because its potential can be changed with high efficiency by transformers. This makes it possible to transmit large amounts of electric energy with high efficiency. The reason is that the power lost in the transmission line is equal to I^2-R, where I is current and R is the resistance of the line. Thus, reducing the current drastically reduces the loss in the line. The power delivered to the load is IV, so large amounts of power can be delivered at a small current by using very high potentials, such as 250,000 V.

For discussion of the meaning of the measured values of AC, *see* **Effective value**.

Ammeter An instrument for measuring electric current. The most common type of ammeter consists of a Weston galvanometer, which measures current in the microampere range, with a low-resistance shunt. The shunt is in parallel with the meter, so it carries most of the current around the galvanometer, but the part of the current that goes through the galvanometer movement is a constant fraction of the total. Thus, the ammeter scale can be calibrated in terms of the total current.

Ampere (A) The SI unit of electric current. It is the current at a point when charge flows past that point at the rate of 1 coulomb per second.

The ampere is an SI basic unit, defined operationally. Specifically, it is the current in a parallel pair of wires if the magnetic force between them in each meter of wire is 10^{-7} newton when the wires are 1 m apart. *See* **Magnetic force**.

Amplitude The maximum displacement of a vibration or a wave. For example. the amplitude of the oscillation of a pendulum is the distance from the equilibrium position, at the center of the swing, to the end of the swing.

The amplitude of a vibration is a measure of its energy. The energy is proportional to the square of the amplitude. The amplitude of a sound wave is the maximum displacement of an air molecule due to the passage of the wave. It determines the loudness of the sound. In a sound wave in open air, amplitude decreases linearly with distance from the source.

The amplitude of an electromagnetic wave at any given point is the maximum strength of its electrical field at that point. At a given wavelength, the amplitude of a light wave determines the brightness of the light. *See also* **Wave**.

Angle of incidence In the ray model of light, the angle that a light ray makes on arriving at an interface. The angle is always measured with respect to the normal, that is, with a line drawn perpendicular to the surface. In the figure, the angle marked i is the angle of incidence. *See* **Reflection**; **Refraction**.

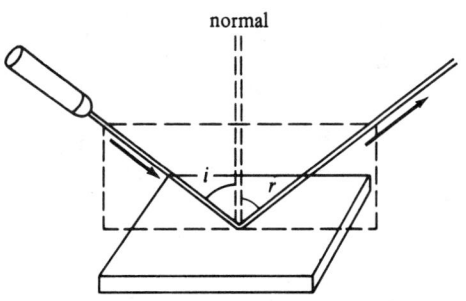

normal

Angle of reflection   *See* **Reflection**.

Angle of refraction   *See* **Refraction**.

Angular momentum   A vector quantity that expresses the tendency of an object to resist changes in its rotation. It is changed by the application of a torque. (*See* **Vector**; **Torque**.)

The simplest case is represented by a point mass moving in a circular path. The angular momentum, measured from the center of the circle, is then equal to *mvr*, the product of the object's mass, its speed, and the radius of the circle in which it is traveling. The direction of the angular momentum vector is defined as perpendicular to the plane of the object's path. For a real rotating object, the angular momentum is found by summing all the *mvr*'s for all points in the object.

In the absence of an externally applied torque, angular momentum is conserved. The classical example of the conservation of angular momentum is shown in the figure. The skater is spinning with arms outstretched. Bringing the arms close to the body results in a great increase in the rate of rotation. Since no torque was applied, there is no change in the angular momentum. Although the *r*'s have decreased; the angular momentum, the sum of the *mvr*'s, is maintained by an increase in the *v*'s.

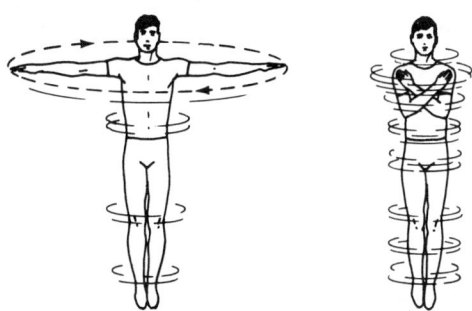

At the atomic level, angular momentum is quantized. The spins of electrons, protons, and so on can change only by jumps equal to $h/2\pi$, where h is Planck's constant. The Bohr model of the hydrogen atom was developed on the sole assumption that the angular momentum of electrons in an atom is quantized. *See* **Bohr model**.

Antinodal line   A line along which a standing wave in two dimensions forms antinodes. *See* **Two-point interference**.

Antinode   A point of maximum destructive interference. *See* **Interference**; **Standing wave**.

Armature   The rotating part of a motor or generator.

Atmospheric pressure   The pressure exerted by the atmosphere against all surfaces. (*See* **Hydrostatic pressure**.) Atmospheric pressure is measured with a barometer. The usual form of barometer is made by filling a tube about 1 meter long with mercury and immersing it in a dish of mercury, as shown in the figure. The mercury level in the tube drops, leaving an evacuated space above the surface.

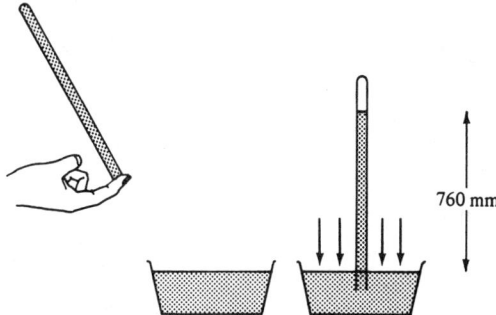

760 mm

The pressure at the open surface of the dish is provided by the atmosphere and must be equal to the pressure at the same level in the mercury. Therefore, the pressure in the atmosphere is equal to *hDg* where *h* is the distance from the top of the mercury column to the open surface of the mercury dish. The density of mercury is $13.6 \text{ g/cm}^3 = 13.6 \times 10^3 \text{ kg/m}^3$. At sea level, the average level of the mercury stands at 760 mm, so the pressure of 1 atmosphere is

$(0.760 \text{ m})(13.6 \times 10^3 \text{ kg/m}^3)(9.8 \text{ N/kg})$
$= 1.013 \times 10^5 \text{ Pa or } 101.3 \text{ kPa}$

In the units used in meteorology, this is 1013 millibars. It is also expressed as 760 mm Hg or 29.9 inches of mercury or 760 torr.

Although pressure in a gas is ordinarily considered constant throughout, this rule does not hold when the gas extends vertically for a considerable distance. The usual rule for hydrostatic pressure still holds, and the pressure is equal to *hDg*. This expression cannot be applied directly, because the density increases with pressure and is greater at lower levels. Roughly, the pressure in the earth's atmosphere decreases about 11% for each kilometer of rise. The actual value depends on temperature and many other conditions.

Atom   The smallest part of an element. Atoms are about 10^{-10}m in diameter and consist of a central nucleus about 10^{-14}m across surrounded by a cloud of electrons.

The nucleus of the atom contains most of its mass and has a positive electric charge. The charge on the nucleus specifies the element to which the atom belongs. Charges of natural nuclei range from 1 unit (hydrogen) to 92 units (uranium). Electrons surrounding the nucleus have negative charges, each exactly one single unit. The number of electrons is the same as the number of units of positive charge on the nucleus, so that the atom as a whole has no electric charge.

Atoms combine in various ways to form compounds. The modes of combination are determined by the arrangements of the electrons, which are different for each element. It is the number and arrangement of its electrons that determine the chemical properties of the element.

For further details, *see* **Electron**; **Nucleus**.

Atomic bomb   *See* **Nuclear bomb**.

Atomic energy   *See* **Nuclear energy**.

Atomic mass number   The total number of nucleons in an atomic nucleus. *See* **Nucleus**.

Atomic number   The number of protons in an atomic nucleus. *See* **Nucleus**.

Avogadro's number   *See* **Mole**.

B

Balmer series   The set of bright lines in the visible part of the spectrum of atomic hydrogen. The frequencies of the lines can be represented by a simple equation. For details about how this observation led to the quantum model of the atom, *see* **Bohr model**.

Barometer   *See* **Atmospheric pressure**.

Battery   Originally, a group of electric cells, connected together. The word is now also used for a single cell.

Beats   A phenomenon heard when two sound sources at slightly different frequencies are sounded together. At the ear, the sound waves arrive alternately in and out of phase. Thus, interference is alternately constructive and destructive, as shown in the figure. The sound gets louder and softer at a definite beat frequency, equal to the difference between the frequencies of the two waves. Thus, if tuning forks of 256 and 259 Hz are sounded together, for example, the listener will hear three beats per second.

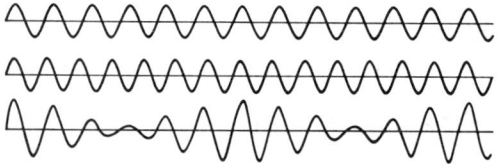

Beta decay   Radioactive breakdown of a nucleus in which electrons ("beta rays") are produced. The electrons come from the disintegration of a neutron in the nucleus into an electron and a proton. *See* **Radioactivity**.

Beta rays   Electrons produced by radioactive elements. *See* **Radioactivity**.

Big bang   The event with which, most scientists believe, the universe began. *See* Earth and Space Science section, page 5-4.

Binding energy   The energy needed to separate the parts of a system. For example, work must be done to peel an orange. The amount of work needed to separate the skin from the edible part is the binding energy holding the skin to the fruit.

In a crystal, every molecule is bound in place by intermolecular forces. It takes work to break a crystal. The crystal can be broken down by adding heat to the system, making it melt. The heat needed to melt the crystal, the latent heat of fusion, is the binding energy of the molecules (or ions) in the crystal. Similarly, the latent heat of vaporization is the binding energy holding the molecules within the surface of the liquid phase. *See* **Latent heat**.

Every chemical bond has a certain amount of binding energy. In water, for example, the hydrogen can be separated from the oxygen by supplying the binding energy in the form of an electric current. Conversely, hydrogen and oxygen can combine to form water, releasing the binding energy in the form of an explosion.

In an atomic nucleus, the protons and neutrons are held together by the strong nuclear force. Since this is extremely powerful, the binding energies of nuclei are very great. Therefore, it is extremely difficult to split a nucleus.

The theory of relativity tells us that energy and mass are interchangeable according to the formula $E = mc^2$. This means that mass, corresponding to the binding energy, must be added to separate the parts of an atomic nucleus. The difference between the binding energies of nuclei is the source of nuclear energy. *See* **Mass deficit**; **Nuclear energy**.

Black hole   *See* Earth and Space Science section, page 5-5.

Bohr model   A model of the hydrogen atom that explains the spectrum of atomic hydrogen by assuming that the angular momentum of electrons is quantized. This model introduced the concept that electrons in atoms can occupy only certain energy states and that they jump from one state to the next.

The crucial bit of experimental evidence that led to the Bohr model of the hydrogen atom was the Balmer series. This is a formula that represents the frequencies of the light in the line spectrum of atomic hydrogen. The formula can be written as

$$f \propto \frac{1}{n_1^2} - \frac{1}{n_2^2}$$

where n's are integers. When $n_1 = 2$, the frequencies correspond to the Balmer series. Other values of n_1 yield values for spectral lines in the ultraviolet and infrared.

According to the Bohr model, the n's stand for the energy levels of the electron in the hydrogen atom. When the electron jumps from one level to another, a photon must be emitted or absorbed. The energy of the photon is hf, where h is Planck's constant (*see* **Photon**; **Planck's constant**). The equation tells us the energy (and therefore the frequency) of photons emitted when the electron drops from one energy level to a lower one. Then the energy of all levels is given by the formula

$$E = \frac{13.6 \text{ eV}}{n^2}$$

Energy Levels for Hydrogen

		eV
$n = \infty$	Ionization	0.0
$n = 5$		-0.54
$n = 4$		-0.85
$n = 3$		-1.5
$n = 2$		-3.4
$n = 1$	Ground State	-13.6

The chart shows the hydrogen energy levels derived from this formula. The chart (or the equation) can be used to calculate the wavelengths of the lines of the spectrum of atomic hydrogen. For example, what are the wavelength and the color of the light emitted when a hydrogen electron drops from level 5 to level 2? From the chart, the energy difference between the two levels, and thus the energy of the emitted photon, is 3.4 eV – 0.54 eV = 2.86 eV and

$$f = \frac{E}{h} = \frac{2.86 \text{ eV}}{4.14 \times 10^{-15} \text{ eV·s}} = 6.90 \times 10^{14} \text{ Hz}$$

which is a line in the Balmer series at the borderline of the ultraviolet.

Boiling point The temperature at which a liquid and its vapor can remain in equilibrium. Boiling point is a function of pressure, increasing as the pressure rises. Boiling point at a pressure of 1 atmosphere is called normal boiling point.

If water is kept in a closed container, it will evaporate until the air above the water is saturated. This means that the liquid is in equilibrium with the vapor. However, the temperature may be far below the *normal* boiling point. This is so because the water vapor is only a small part of the air. Since the partial pressure of the water vapor is much less than 1 atmosphere, equilibrium with the liquid is reached at a low temperature.

If a liquid is in an open container, the pressure inside it is 1 atm. Bubbles of water vapor can remain in equilibrium with the liquid only at the normal boiling point. Adding heat causes additional liquid to vaporize, forming bubbles, but the temperature will not rise.

Normal boiling point is measured by means of a thermometer suspended in the space above the boiling liquid. The liquid is boiled until all the air is driven out of the vessel, so that the space is filled with the vapor. As the vapor condenses onto the thermometer, heat transfers to the thermometer. When equilibrium is reached, no further condensation takes place and the thermometer stops rising.

The normal boiling point of water is taken as the definition of 100°C.

Boltzmann's constant *See* **Gas law.**

Brownian motion The random vibratory motion of microscopic-sized particles suspended in a liquid or gas. It results from the random, unequal impacts of the molecules of the liquid or gas.

Bubble chamber A device for recording the path of a charged subnuclear particle. It consists of a tank containing a fluid kept just below its boiling point. If the pressure in the fluid is suddenly decreased, bubbles of vapor will form in it. If a charged particle passes through the fluid at that moment, bubbles will form along the path of the particle. The properties of the particle, such as its energy, momentum, and lifetime (down to extremely small fractions of a second), can be determined by studying the bubble tracks.

The most sophisticated bubble chambers, used with giant particle accelerators, are cubical chambers about 15 feet on a side, filled with liquid hydrogen. When the pressure is reduced, flash photographs are taken from several positions. The device can record up to 10 events per second. Some-

times, hundreds of such photographs must be scanned in the search for information about the breakdown of a particular kind of particle.

**Calorie** A unit of energy, now defined as 4.18605 joules. It is primarily used in measurements of heat, as it is very nearly equal to its original definition: the amount of heat needed to raise the temperature of 1 gram of water from 14.5°C to 15.5°C.

In calculations, little error is made by assuming that the ratio between heat added and temperature change is constant as long as the water is liquid.

Example

How much energy must be added to 250 g of water to raise its temperature from 20°C to the boiling point (100°C)?

The pertinent equation (for water only) is

$$H = m \, \Delta T$$

where H is the energy added (called heat in this context), m is the mass of water, and ΔT is the change in temperature. Thus,

$$H = (250 \text{ g}) (80°C) = 20,000 \text{ cal}$$

This can be converted to the SI unit of energy:

$$(20,000 \text{ cal}) (4.19 \text{ J/cal}) = 83,800 \text{ J or } 84 \text{ kJ}$$

The "calorie" used in dietetics is really a kilocalorie, or 1,000 calories. *See also* **Heat; Latent heat; Specific heat.**

Candela The unit of luminous intensity, one of the six base units of the SI. It is defined as the intensity of the light emitted from 1/600,000 of a square meter of a black body at a temperature of 2,046 K.

Capacitor A device for storing electric charge. It consists of two flat conducting plates separated by an insulator. Capacitors take many forms; for example, some have movable plates with only air for insulation, and others are made of layers of foil separated by waxed paper.

When the two plates of a capacitor are connected to points of different potential, electrons flow into one plate and out of the other. The capacitor is then said to be charged. One use for this device is an electronic flash gun. It takes a few seconds to charge a capacitor, and the charge is then used to produce a bright flash of light lasting a few milliseconds. Capacitors are also used in filters in electronic circuits, since they block low frequencies of alternating current and pass the higher frequencies.

Cathode ray A stream of electrons from a negative terminal in an evacuated tube. The stream can be narrowed to a fine beam and its direction controlled by the application of electric and magnetic fields. In a cathode ray oscilloscope, the beam strikes a fluorescent screen and causes it to glow. The oscilloscope is used to form a visual representation of cyclically varying potentials. This is how the picture is formed in a television picture tube.

Cell An enclosed chamber in which a reaction takes place. An electric cell uses a chemical reaction to produce electricity. It consists of two different metals (or one metal and carbon) immersed in an ionic solution called an electrolyte. The chemical reaction removes electrons from one terminal and deposits them on the other. The reaction comes to a stop when an equilibrium is reached, with one terminal at a higher potential than the other. The potential difference between the terminals varies from about 1.2 to 2.5 V, depending on the chemicals used.

When a complete conducting circuit from one terminal to the other is established, electrons flow out of the negative terminal and into the positive terminal. Since electrons are negatively charged, this flow constitutes a current going the other way. As charge is drawn off the terminals, the equilibrium is disturbed, and the reaction starts up again.

The common dry cell has a carbon rod as the positive terminal and a zinc can, enclosing the electrolyte, as the negative terminal. The electrolyte is ammonium chloride, in a paste of other materials. In the storage battery used in automobiles, the terminals are lead and lead oxide, and the electrolyte is sulfuric acid. This is called a storage cell because it can be recharged by running the current through it in the reverse direction. Many other kinds of cells are also in use.

Celsius scale   The temperature scale (formerly called centigrade) in which the melting point of ice is defined as 0° and the normal boiling point of water is taken to be 100°. This is the scale used in most of the world and in scientific work. For the relationship of the Celsius scale to the SI units, *see* **Kelvin scale**.

Center of gravity   A point in any object from which the torque produced by the weight of the object can be calculated. If an object has uniform density and a simple geometric shape, the center of gravity is at its geometric center.

If an object is pivoted at some point other than under the center of gravity, the weight of the object produces a torque that tends to make the object rotate. The torque is found by multiplying the entire weight of the object by the horizontal distance between the center of gravity and a vertical line through the pivot.

Example

How much torque is produced by the weight of a uniform 160 kg steel beam 4.0 m long if the beam is pivoted at a point 1.2 m from one end?

The center of gravity is at the geometric center of the beam, 2.0 m from each end. The radius vector of the center of gravity, the horizontal distance from the pivot point to the center of gravity, is 0.8 m. Then the torque τ (the Greek letter tau) produced by the weight of the beam is

$$\tau = (160 \text{ kg})(9.8 \text{ N/kg})(0.8 \text{ m}) = 1250 \text{ N·m}$$

Centigrade scale   *See* **Celsius scale**.

Centrifugal force   A fictitious force in rotating frames of reference. On a merry-go-round, for example, people are accelerated centripetally, toward the center of the motion. They will experience a gravitylike force pushing them outward from the center. The force exists only in the frame of reference in which the people consider themselves at rest. The person who experiences the force must say, "I am at rest; the world is rotating

around me, causing me to be pulled outward." An observer outside the merry-go-round, however, explains all events without reference to a thing called centrifugal force.

Centripetal acceleration   A change of velocity in which only the direction of the velocity is changing, not its magnitude. If acceleration is constantly perpendicular to velocity, speed does not change, but the object travels in a circular path. Acceleration is then called centripetal because it is directed toward the center of the circle. The magnitude of centripetal acceleration can be calculated from the speed v and the radius of the circle r according to the equation

$$a_c = \frac{v^2}{r}$$

Example

What is the centripetal acceleration of a motorcycle travelling at 25 m/s in a circular path of radius 150 m?

$$a_c = \frac{v^2}{r} = \frac{(25 \text{ m/s})^2}{150 \text{ m}} = 4.2 \text{ m/s}^2$$

Centripetal force   Any force acting perpendicularly to the velocity of an object, thus giving the object a centripetal acceleration and causing it to move in a circular path at constant speed. (*See* **Centripetal acceleration**.) If you tie a rock to the end of a string and swing it around, the centripetal force on the rock is the tension in the string. In a so-called "centrifugal" clothes dryer, the clothes are kept going around in a circular path by the centripetal force exerted on them by the wall of the tub. The centripetal force that keeps planets orbiting the sun instead of going off in a straight line is the sun's gravitational attraction. *See* **Orbit**.

Centripetal force, like any force, is the product of mass and acceleration (*See* **Inertia**). For example, if the rock you tied to a string and swung around has a mass of 0.30 kg, is at the end of a string 0.50 m long, and is traveling at 3.4 m/s, the tension in the string is

$$F = ma = \frac{mv^2}{r} = \frac{(0.30 \text{ kg})(3.4 \text{ m/s})^2}{0.50 \text{m}}$$
$$= 6.9 \text{ kg·m/s}^2 = 6.9 \text{ N}$$

Chain reaction   A nuclear reaction that is self-regenerating. A chain reaction is possible because of a special property of two nuclear fuels, uranium-235 and plutonium. When a nucleus of either of these two elements is struck by a slow neutron, the nucleus splits, releasing large amounts of energy. The special property is that, in splitting, the nucleus also releases two or three additional neutrons. These may strike other nuclei, so that more fissions occur, and still more neutrons are released. In a nuclear bomb, this chain reaction can build up so quickly that the nuclei of an entire mass of fuel will split in a few seconds. In a nuclear power plant, the reaction is controlled by inserting rods of a neutron-absorbing material into the reaction chamber. *See* **Nuclear bomb**; **Nuclear energy**; **Nuclear fission**; **Nuclear reactor**.

Charge   *See* **Electric charge.**

Coherent light   Light of a single frequency in which all the waves are in phase at every point in space. This is the light of a laser. Its special properties give it a wide variety of uses. Coherent light can be formed into a narrow beam that spreads very little and can be focused to a microscopic point. It can be used to form a hologram which is a photographic record of the actual structure of the light waves. The light beam may be so intense that it can be used for cutting hard materials and for surgery. It can be modulated to transmit many telephone conversations through a single optical fiber, or to record music on a compact disk.

Cohesion   *See* Earth and Space Science section, page 5-7.

Color   The sense perception based on the combinations of light frequencies entering the eye. The retina has three kinds of color receptors, most sensitive to red, green, and blue, respectively. These are called the primary colors. All color perception is produced by stimulating various combinations of these three kinds of cells.

Commutator   A device attached to the rotating armature of a motor or a generator. In a motor, the commutator feeds current into each armature coil at the right moment to produce maximum torque; in a generator, the commutator converts the AC of the armature into a direct current output.

In the figure, a simple split-ring commutator feeds current into the single-coil armature of a simple motor. When the armature has turned halfway around, the current will be fed into the other side of the commutator. In this way, the current always goes into whichever side of the coil will receive the force of the field in the right direction to keep the motor turning. In a real motor, the commutator has many segments, each pair feeding a different coil.

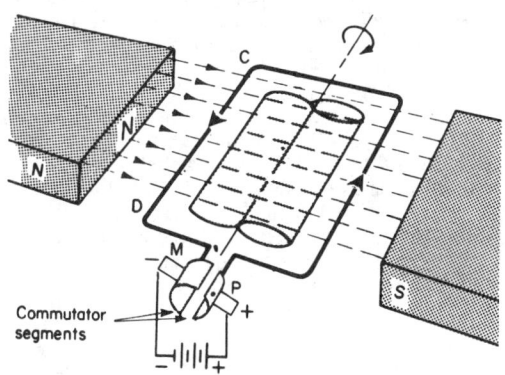

Commutator segments

Component   A part of a vector quantity acting in some direction other than along the vector itself. For example, you may travel in a northeast direction and would want to know how your trip has affected the time of sunrise. The distance north is of no significance; your answer depends only on the eastward component of your motion.

Suppose you travel 350 mi in a direction 30° west of north, as shown in the figure. How far north have you come?

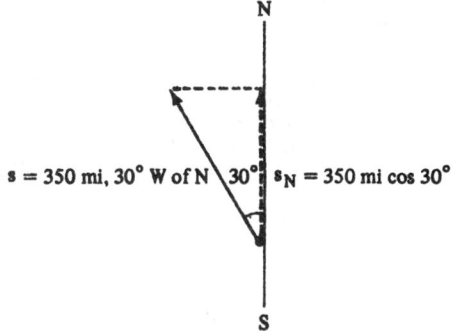

s = 350 mi, 30° W of N s_N = 350 mi cos 30°

The answer is (350 mi) cos 30° = 303 mi. In general, if a vector **V** makes an angle θ_x with any X axis, the component of the vector on that axis is

$$V_x = \mathbf{V} \cos \theta_x$$

It is often important to find another component of the vector on a Y axis perpendicular to the X axis. It will be

$$V_Y = \mathbf{V} \sin \theta_x$$

Thus, the distance west traveled in the trip above is (350 mi) sin 30 = 175 mi.

Two components at right angles to each other are called rectangular components. The Pythagorean theorem tells us that

$$V^2 = V_X^2 + V_Y^2$$

Concave lens   A lens that is thinner in the middle than at the edges. When divergent light from an object enters such a lens, it emerges with a greater angle of divergence.

The concave lens can form only one kind of image: virtual, erect, and smaller than the object. The figure shows how this image can be located. One ray from a point on the object enters the lens parallel to the principal axis. It diverges in such a way that it seems to be coming from the principal focus. A second ray from the same point passes undeflected through the center of the lens. Since the emerging rays are divergent, they do not come to a focus, and no real image can be formed. However, if an observer looks through the lens, the rays entering the eye will appear to be coming from a point between the lens and the object. Each point on the object is represented by a point in this virtual image. *See* **Focal length; Lens formula.**

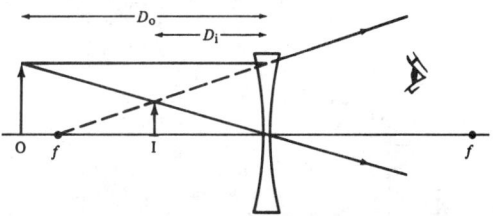

Concave mirror   A mirror that converges the light that reflects off its surface. Thus, it forms the same kinds of images as a convex lens. If the object distance is greater than the focal length, the image is real, inverted, and in front of the mirror. It can be cast onto a screen or a photographic plate. This is the image used in astronomical telescopes and mirror "lenses" for cameras. If the object distance is less than the focal length, the image is virtual, behind the mirror, and enlarged. This is the reason that a concave mirror can be used for shaving or putting on makeup. *See* **Focal length**.

Conduction   (1) The passage of an electric current through a metal. The special property of metals is that they have many free electrons in their structure, electrons that can move easily from place to place. If the two ends of a wire are at points of different potential, all the free electrons shift their positions, so there is a net displacement of negative charge toward the high-potential end. Conduction occurs as electrons flow into the wire at the low-potential end and out at the high-potential end. (2) The passage of heat through a material. If one part of a substance is at a higher temperature than another, the atoms at the higher temperature are vibrating more violently. They will transmit this violent motion to adjacent atoms, until the effect is felt in the colder region. The net result is that heat is passed toward the colder region. Metals are the best conductors of heat because their free electrons participate in passing the energy along.

Conductor   A substance that permits the free passage of electricity or heat. The best solid conductors are metals, especially (in order) silver, copper, aluminum, and gold. Ionic solutions and molten ionic substances are also good conductors of electricity, but not necessarily of heat. Diamond is one of the best conductors of heat, but does not conduct electricity at all. *See also* **Conduction**.

Conservation law   A basic law of physics specifying that in closed systems certain quantities do not change. In macroscopic systems, the conserved quantities are mass-energy, momentum, angular momentum, and electric charge. There are additional conserved quantities in subatomic systems.

Constructive interference   *See* **Interference**.

Convection   The movement of liquids and gases resulting from temperature differences. *See* **Heat**.

Convex lens   A lens that is thicker in the center than at the edges. The effect of such a lens on light is to converge the rays that enter. Four kinds of effects produced by convex lenses may be distinguished.

Parallel rays of light entering the lens, such as those coming from a distant star, are brought to a focus at a distance equal to the focal length of the lens. In a camera focused at infinity, the distance from the film to the lens is the focal length of the lens. In this condition, the rays from each point on the object are essentially parallel as they enter the lens. Each point on the object is represented by a point on the image, forming a real image of the object.

Diverging rays enter from the principal focus of the lens. This is the converse of the first case. The rays emerging from the lens are parallel, and no image is formed. The best narrow beam from a searchlight is produced by a small source of light, such as an arc lamp, placed at a distance from the lens equal to the focal length.

Diverging rays from a point farther away than the focal length do not diverge as strongly as those coming from the principal focus, and they can be brought to a focus. Each point on the object is represented by a point on a real image. The figure shows how

the location of the image can be found. D_o is the object distance; D_i is the image distance; and f is the focal length of the lens. One ray from a point on the object enters the lens parallel to the principal axis and passes through the principal focus on emerging. A second ray passes undeflected through the center of the lens. The point of intersection of these two rays specifies the location of the image point.

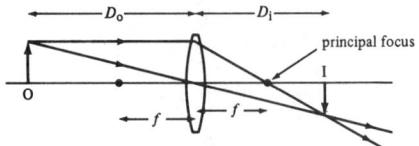

Rays coming from a point closer to the lens than the focal length diverge so strongly on entering the lens that they are still divergent— although less so—on leaving, as shown in the next figure. They do not come to a focus. However, they form a virtual image. An observer looking through the lens sees rays that appear to be coming from a point behind the object. The image is enlarged and erect. This is a magnifying glass.

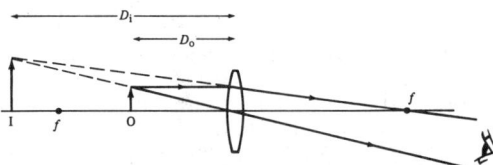

For methods of calculating the size and position of the images, *see* **Lens formula; Focal length**.

Convex mirror   A convex mirror, such as that used as a right-side mirror on automobiles, diverges the light that strikes it. Since it diverges light, it forms the same kind of images as a concave lens. The image in the mirror is virtual, erect, and behind the mirror at a distance less than the object distance. A car seen in such a mirror looks farther away than it is because the image is so small.

Coulomb (C)   The SI unit of electric charge. It is defined as the amount of charge delivered by a current of 1 ampere flowing for 1 second.

Coulomb's law   The law established by Charles Augustin de Coulomb, about 1820, stating that the electric force between charged objects is directly proportional to the product of the charges and inversely proportional to the square of the distance between them. It can be written as

$$F = \frac{kq_1q_2}{r^2}$$

where the q's are charges, r is the distance between them, and k is the universal electric constant of free space, equal to 9.00×10^9 N·m²/C².

Example

What is the force between two pith balls bearing charges of 3.0 and 4.5 nC, respectively, when the balls are 20 cm apart?

$$F = \frac{(9.00 \times 10^9 \text{ N·m}^2/\text{C}^2)(3.0 \times 10^{-9} \text{ C})(4.5 \times 10^{-9} \text{ C})}{(0.20 \text{ m})^2}$$

$$= 3.0 \times 10^{-6} \text{ N}$$

Current *See* **Electric current**.
Cyclotron *See* **Accelerators**.

Dalton (Dl) A unit convenient for expressing the mass of an object of atomic size. It is defined as ½ of the mass of a nucleus of carbon 12. The conversion to SI is 6.024×10^{26} Dl = 1 kg. The atomic "weights" given in tables are actually the average atomic masses and are expressed in daltons.

Density A property of materials, the ratio of mass to volume. It is usually expressed in grams per cubic centimeter.

Example

What is the density of a cubical block of wood 6.0 cm on a side, if its mass is 185 g?

$$D = \frac{m}{V} = \frac{185\,g}{(6.0\ cm)^3} = 0.86\,g/cm^3$$

Destructive interferences *See* **Interference**.
Deuterium *See* **Nuclear fission**; *see also* Earth and Space Science, page 5-10.
Diffraction The process by which waves, encountering an obstacle, bend around corners. The figure shows the diffraction, around a barrier, of a wave generated by a point source and traveling along a circular front.

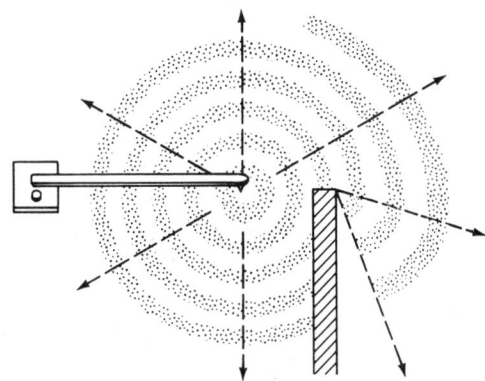

Diffraction is greater at longer wavelengths. If a barrier is not much bigger than a wavelength, the wave will bend completely around it as though it were not there. If a wave goes through an opening not much bigger than a wavelength, as in the next figure, the opening acts like a point source, and the wave on the other side spreads out along a circular front.

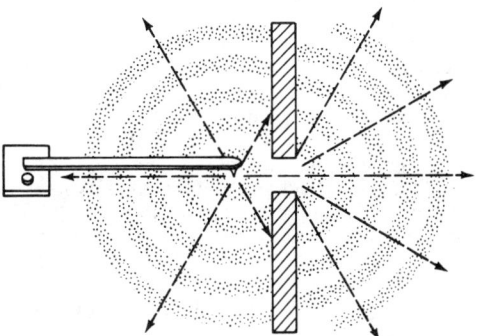

Diffraction grating A sheet of transparent material, or a mirrored surface, ruled with a great many very fine parallel grooves, typically over 500 to the millimeter. When light strikes the grating, it is diffracted, each groove acting like a point source. The result is a pattern of nodal and antinodal lines much like that shown under **Two-point interference**.

If light strikes the grating along the normal, some of it ($n = 0$) goes straight through, and some is diffracted off to both sides, at specific angles. The angles θ_n are specified by the equation

$$\sin \theta_n = \frac{n\lambda}{d}$$

where λ is the wavelength, d is the distance between grooves, and n is a whole number.

Example

A grating is ruled 580 lines per millimeter, and violet light of wavelength 4.60×10^{-7} m shines on it. What are the diffraction angles?

The groove spacing is $d = 1/580$ mm, or 1.724×10^{-6} m. Therefore,

$$\sin \theta_n = \frac{n(4.60 \times 10^{-7}\,m)}{1.724 \times 10^{-6}\,m}$$

Substituting integral values of n gives

$$\theta_0 = 0$$
$$\pm\theta_1 = \pm 15.5^0$$
$$\pm\theta_2 = \pm 32.3^0$$
$$\pm\theta_3 = \pm 53.2^0$$

There are no other values, since the equation gives $\sin \theta_4 > 1$. Thus, there are a total of seven antinodal lines. When the light falls on a screen, it forms seven bright violet bars.

Since the diffraction angles depend on wavelength, every color of light is diffracted to a different angle. A mixture of wavelengths, such as white light, is separated out into separate bright bars. The diffraction grating spreads white light into a broad spectrum. The diffraction grating provides an extremely accurate method of measuring the wavelengths of light.

Dimensionality The property of a measurement that defines the kind of quantity being measured. The dimensionality of any physical quantity (except those involving light intensity) can be expressed in terms of six basic SI units: kilogram (kg), meter (m), second (s), ampere (A), kelvin (K), and mole (mol).

Consider, for example, measurements of mass. The measurement might be made in kilograms, milligrams, slugs, or pound-mass. All these measurements have the same dimensionality. This means that it is possible to convert the units from any one to any other. It is meaningful, for example, to ask which is larger, 22 kg or 6 slugs. Also, the two quantities can be added by converting slugs to kilograms, or vice versa. However, it makes no sense to ask which is larger, 30 cm or 16 g, because the two quantities have different dimensionality. The units cannot be interconverted. Quantities with different dimensionality cannot be compared, added, or subtracted.

Any quantities can be multiplied or divided, and the outcome is always a new dimensionality. For example, volume is always the product of three linear measures, so its dimensionality is cubic meters (m^3). This is not the same dimensionality as meters (m), and lengths cannot be added to volumes. Volumes can also be expressed in liters, cubic centimeters, acre-feet, or cubic miles, however, and any of these measurements can be converted to cubic meters. All have the dimensionality m^3.

Most physical quantities have complex dimensionality, with several different basic quantities combined. For example, a force is a mass times an acceleration, so its dimensionality is $kg \cdot m/s^2$. Specific heat is energy per unit mass per unit temperature change, and its dimensionality works out this way:

$$\frac{kg \cdot m^2}{s^2} \div kg \cdot K = \frac{m^2}{s^2 \cdot K}$$

Dimensional analysis provides an extremely useful means of checking the results of a theoretical calculation.

For example, an engineer does some theoretical work and concludes that the pressure (force per unit area) in a pipe can be found as the product of the density of the fluid in the pipe and its velocity. He can check his result this way:

$$\frac{force}{area} = density \times velocity.$$

$$\frac{kg \cdot m}{s^2} \div m^2 = \frac{kg}{m^3} \times \frac{m}{s}$$

Since the dimensionalities on the two sides of the equation are different, the equation cannot be true.

Direct current (DC)   Electric current flowing steadily in one direction. All batteries produce direct current, flowing steadily from the high potential to the low potential terminal. In a generator, the current in the armature is always alternating. If a generator is to produce direct current, the output of the armature must be fed through a commutator, which will reverse its connections every half-cycle.

Dispersion   The sorting out of waves according to the speed at which they travel. In most media, higher frequency waves travel slower. In glass, red light travels faster than violet. As shown in the figure, white light entering the prism is bent toward the normal (*see* **Refraction**). The violet is bent more than the red. On emerging from the prism, the light speeds up and bends away from the normal. However, because the sides of the prism are not parallel, the rays bend twice in the same direction. This amplifies the dispersion effect, and the light is sorted out into a full spectrum.

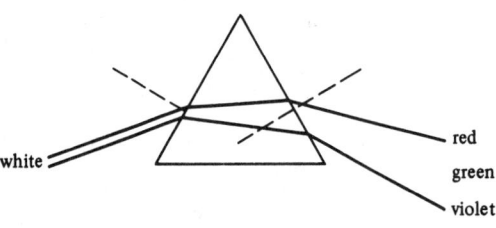

white   red

green

violet

Doppler effect   The change in frequency of a wave due to the motion of the source or of the observer. The figure shows that if a moving object emits a sound wave, the crests will be crowded together on the side toward which the object is moving. This means that the wavelength is shorter on that side, so the frequency is higher. Conversely, the frequency heard by the observer on the other side will be lower than the frequency emitted by the source. If a car moves past the observer while sounding its horn, the observer will hear a sudden drop in pitch as the car passes.

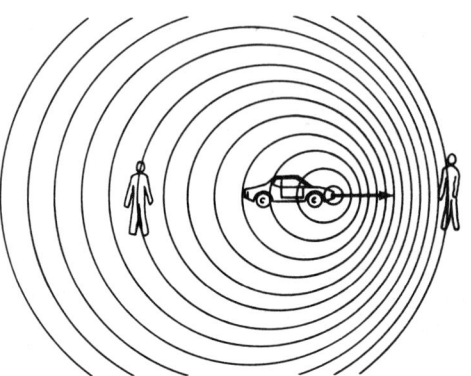

A similar effect is noted if the source is at rest and the observer is moving. If the observer is moving toward the source, his or her ear will intercept crests of the wave at a higher frequency than the one at which they are being emitted.

The Doppler shift of the frequency of light plays an important role in cosmology. Astronomers note that the light from distant galaxies is "red-shifted." This means that the frequencies received are lower than those emitted by the galaxies. Since all galaxies are thus seen to be moving away from us, the whole universe must be expanding.

Double-slit interference   The pattern of alternate bright and dark bars produced by constructive and destructive interference of the light passing through two slits close together. Many slits close together form a diffraction grating, which produces the same pattern.

Dry cell   The cell of an electric battery made in such a way that its electrolyte is a paste instead of a liquid, so that it will not spill. See **Cell**.

E

Effective value   A measure of current or potential difference, applied to an alternating current, indicating that it produces the same heating effect as a direct current with that value. For example, if a sine-wave current constantly changes from +5 A to –5 A and back, it produces the same heat as a 3.5 A direct current. Its effective value is therefore 3.5 A.

If an alternating current registers on a meter as 7.0 A, that is its effective value. Its maximum is found by multiplying the effective value by $\sqrt{2}$. Thus a 6.0 A alternating current is constantly changing from +8.5 to –8.5 A and back. AC potentials follow the same rule.

Efficiency   For a system, the ratio of the useful energy output to the energy input. Every device that converts energy always wastes some in the form of low-temperature heat discharged into the environment (*see* **Second law of thermodynamics**).

Example 1

In using a chain hoist to lift an 85 kg engine 0.6 m, a mechanic pulls 18 m of chain through the hoist, using a force of 45 N. What is the efficiency of the hoist?
The work output of the machine is

(85 kg)(9.8 N/kg)(0.6 m) = 500 J

The work input is

(45 N)(18 m) = 810 J

The efficiency is therefore

$\dfrac{500 \text{ J}}{810 \text{ J}} = 0.62$ or 62%

Example 2

An electric motor operating on 120 V uses 2.2 A to operate a pulley that lifts a 370 kg bale a distance of 12 m in 4.5 minutes. What is the efficiency of the system?
The energy input is

(120 V)(2.2 A)(270 s) = 71,300 J

The energy output is

(370 kg)(9.8 N/kg)(12 m) = 43,500 J

Then the efficiency of the system is

$\dfrac{43.500 \text{ J}}{71.300 \text{ J}} = 0.61$ or 61%

These two examples illustrate mechanical efficiency. *See also* **Thermal efficiency**.

Elastic energy   The potential energy stored by the distortion of the shape of a solid. An archer does work by pulling on the bow. This stores elastic energy, which is transferred to the arrow when it is fired.
   The simplest case is a spring. As the spring is stretched, work is done on it. In its stretched condition, therefore, the spring is storing elastic energy. The energy stored is equal to the work done in stretching the spring. As the spring is stretched through a distance Δl, the force increases from 0 to $k \, \Delta l$ (*see* **Elastic recoil**). The average force is thus $k \, \Delta l/2$, and the work done is this quantity times the distance.

Example

How much energy is stored in a spring if its constant is 80 N/m and it is stretched from 8.0 to 14.0 cm?
Since the length increase is 0.060 m, the force exerted when the spring is stretched is

$F_{elas} = k \, \Delta l = (80 \text{ N/m})(0.060 \text{ m}) = 4.8 \text{ N}$

The average force is half this, or 2.4 N, exerted over a distance of 0.060 m. Therefore, the energy stored is

$W = F \, \Delta s = (2.4 \text{ N})(0.060 \text{ m}) = 0.14 \text{ J}$

Elastic recoil   The force exerted by a solid as a result of the distortion of its shape. *See* **Force**.
The simplest case is the behavior of a spring. Within a definite limit, the elastic recoil of a spring is di-

rectly proportional to the increase in its length. The ratio of force to increase in length is called the constant, k, of the spring. It is expressed in N/m:

$F_{elas} = k \, \Delta l$

Example

A spring, unstretched is 12 cm long. It is needed to operate a lever in such a way that it exerts a force of 70 N when it is stretched to 14.5 cm. What must be the constant of the spring?
   The increase in length is 2.5 cm, so

$k = \dfrac{F}{\Delta t} = \dfrac{70 \text{ N}}{0.025 \text{ m}} = 2800 \text{ N/m}$

The constant of a spring depends on the kind of metal of which it is made and on its dimensions. The equation holds until the spring is stretched beyond its elastic limit. At that point, a permanent rearrangement of its crystal structure takes place, and the spring does not return to its original shape.

Electric cell   *See* **Cell**.

Electric charge   The property of particles that enables them to exert and respond to electric forces. There are two kinds of charge, designated positive and negative. Objects are neutral, or uncharged, when they contain equal amounts of positive and negative charge. Electric charge is conserved; that is, the total amount of charge in an isolated system does not change. For example, stroking a rubber rod with wool gives the rubber rod a negative charge, but the wool acquires an equal positive charge. The total charge is still zero.
   Electric charge is measured in coulombs (C). In static situations, such a charge would be very large; the more common units are the microcoulomb ($1\mu C = 10^{-6}$ C) and the nanocoulomb ($1 \text{ nC} = 10^{-9}$ C). Charge is quantized, so that every particle has an integral number of unit charges. This unit, known as the charge on the electron, is 1.60×10^{-19} C.

Electric constant of free space   *See* **Coulomb's law**.

Electric current   The flow of electric charge through a conductor. Current is expressed in amperes and can be measured by an ammeter. *See* **Alternating current; Direct current**.
   The direction of an electric current is defined as the direction of flow of positive charge. The movement of negative charge in one direction has exactly the same effect as the movement of positive charge the other way. Therefore, when electrons move through a wire from right to left, the direction of the current is from left to right. When there is a current in an ionic solution, there may be two currents. Positive ions flow from high potential to low, and negative ions flow from low potential to high. Both currents are from high potential to low.

Electric energy   The energy stored in separated electric charges. Since it takes work to separate a positive charge from a negative charge, the potential energy of the system is highest when charges are separated. Conversely, the energy stored in similar charges is greatest when they are closest together.
   A battery uses chemical energy to separate electric charge, placing a negative charge on one terminal and a positive charge on the other. If a conducting path is established from one terminal to the other,

charge will flow through it from the positive terminal to the negative terminal. (This flow of charge, if in a wire, will consist of electrons going from the negative terminal to the positive terminal.) When the charges reunite, the electric energy has been converted into other forms, such as heat, or (in a motor) kinetic energy.

A generator is also a charge-separating mechanism. It converts kinetic energy to electric, using its magnetic field as a means to exert the forces that separate the charges.

The amount of electric energy is often calculated as the product of power and time. The usual unit is the kilowatt-hour (kWh), defined as the energy converted in an hour at the rate of 1000 watts. Thus, if you use a 350 W television set for 4 hours a day, the energy used during a month is

$$E = Pt = (350 \text{ W})(4 \text{ hours/day})(31 \text{ days})$$
$$= 43{,}400 \text{ watt-hours or } 43.4 \text{ kWh}$$

See also **Electric potential**; **Electric power**.

Electric field   A region of space in which an electric charge will experience a force. The field strength $\mathscr{E}$ at any given point is defined as the force that the field would exert on a unit positive charge at that point:

$$\mathscr{E} = \frac{F}{q}$$

The electric field strength may be expressed in newtons per coulomb (N/C), but is more commonly given in volts per meter (V/m). The two units are identical. Consider two points in a uniform electric field separated by a distance s. According to the definition of potential difference, the energy stored is qV. This must be equal to the work that would have to be done to move the charge from one of the points to the other, which is $Fs = \mathscr{E}qs$. Then

$$qV = \mathscr{E}qs \quad \text{so} \quad \mathscr{E} = \frac{V}{s}$$

In other words, the electric field is equal to the gradient of the potential. The greater the potential difference between two points and the closer together they are, the stronger is the field between them.

Example

If a charge of 20 nC is in an electric field between two flat, parallel plates separated by 1.5 cm and charged to a potential difference of 360 V, what is the force on the charge?

The electric field between flat, parallel plates is uniform, so the field between them is

$$\mathscr{E} = \frac{360 \text{ V}}{0.015 \text{ m}} = 24{,}000 \text{ V/m} = 24{,}000 \text{ N/C}$$

and the force on the charge is

$$F = \mathscr{E}q = (24{,}000 \text{ N/C})(20 \times 10^{-9}\text{C})$$
$$= 4.8 \times 10^{-4}\text{N}$$

The direction of an electric field at any point is the direction of the force on a positive charge. The force on a negative charge is in a direction opposite to the field. Thus, the field pushes a positive charge

toward lower potentials and a negative charge toward higher potentials.

Electric field lines   Lines drawn as a way of representing the properties of an electric field, as shown in the figure. The lines are drawn in such a way that the field at any point is tangential to the line, and the lines are closest together where the field is strongest. All lines originate on positive charges and end on negative charges.

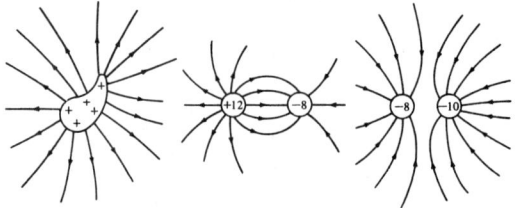

Electric force   *See* **Coulomb's law**.

Electric potential   Electric energy per unit charge. It is expressed in joules per coulomb, called volts (V).

In most problems dealing with electricity, a crucial datum is the difference between the potential at one point and the potential somewhere else. When we say, for example, that a battery produces 12 V, we mean that the potential at the positive terminal is 12 V higher than the potential at the negative terminal. Every coulomb of charge that flows from the high potential terminal to the low potential terminal, through an external circuit, delivers 12 joules of energy to the circuit. The equation for the calculation of energy delivered is thus

$$E_{\text{elec}} = qV$$

where E_{elec} is the energy converted from electric to other forms (or vice versa), q is the amount of charge that flows, and V is the potential difference.

Example

How much energy is stored when a chemical reaction in a 12 V battery removes 20,000 C of charge from one terminal and places it on the other terminal?

$$E_{\text{elec}} = (20{,}000 \text{ C})(12 \text{ J/C}) = 240{,}000 \text{ J}$$

Electric power   The rate at which electric energy is converted into other forms. Whenever electric charge moves to a point of lower potential, it loses an amount of energy equal to qV, where q is the charge and V is the difference in potential (*see* **Electric potential**). A current, which is a continuous flow of charge, must steadily lose electric energy, converting it into heat (as in a light bulb) or motion (as in a motor; *see* **Electric current**). The rate at which this energy is converted is electric power. Accordingly, the power is the amount of energy converted divided by the time, or

$$P = \frac{qV}{t}$$

and, since current (I) is q/t,

$P = IV$

If current is in amperes and potential difference is in volts, power is in joules per second, called watts (W).

Electrolyte   *See* **Cell.**

Electromagnet   A magnet consisting of a coil of wire wrapped around a core of iron or other strongly magnetic material. The current in the wire creates a magnetic field identical with that of a bar magnet, as shown in the figure. The iron core greatly strengthens the field.

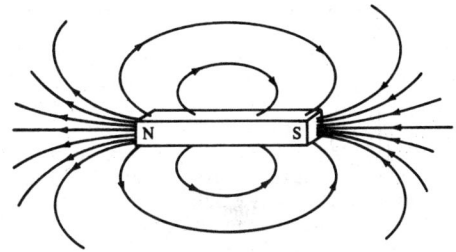

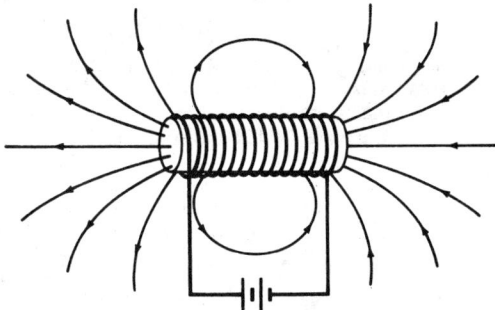

To determine the polarity of the electromagnet, wrap the fingers of the right hand around the core, with the fingers following the direction in which the current circulates. As shown below, the thumb points in the direction of the field lines inside the coil. The end of the electromagnet at which the field lines emerge is the north-pointing (N) pole.

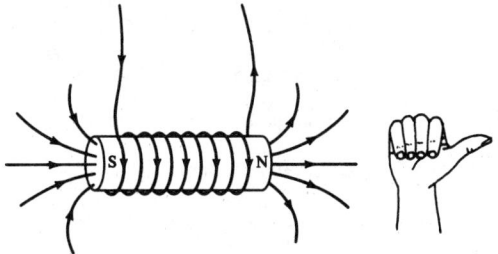

See also **Ferromagnetism.**

Electromagnetic induction   The process by which a changing magnetic field produces an electric field. In many applications, the field can be detected as a potential difference.

A simple demonstration of electromagnetic induction is shown in the figure, where X represents a magnetic field directed into the page. A bar, perpendicular to the field, is moved to the right. This is equivalent to the magentic field's changing by moving past the bar to the left. The bar contains free electrons. Since the electrons in the bar are moving to the right, the magnetic field exerts forces on them, pushing them to the bottom of the bar, and leaving the upper end of the bar positive. There is then a potential difference between the ends of the rod.

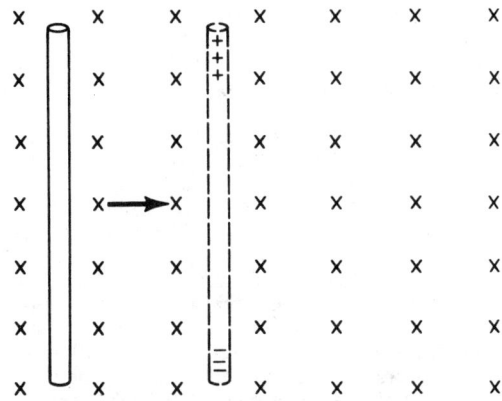

Michael Faraday generalized the rules of induction to produce the following law: The potential difference between the ends of a loop is proportional to the rate at which the magnetic field within the loop is changing. This is demonstrated in the next figure. If the bar magnet is moving into the solenoid, it is changing the magnetic field inside the loops of wire. This induces potential differences across loops, which add up. If the circuit is completed by connecting the ends of the solenoid through a galvanometer, a current will register on the galvanometer. The current exists only as long as the magnet is moving.

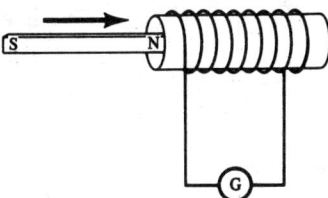

In the third figure, the bar magnet has been replaced by an electromagnet. The electromagnet is now called a primary coil. As long as the primary coil is moving, there will be current in the other solenoid, the secondary coil. Another way to change the magnetic field is to change the current in the primary. As long as the primary current is changing, there will be a current in the secondary, proportional to the rate of change of the primary current.

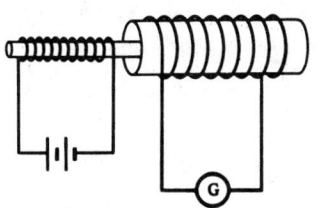

For applications of the induction principle, *see* **Generator; Induction coil; Transformer.**

Electromagnetic radiation *See* **Electromagnetic waves.**

Electromagnetic spectrum The full list of electromagnetic waves, arranged according to frequency. Waves of different frequencies are produced by different natural processes. Exhibit 20.1 shows how the complete spectrum is divided roughly into sections according to frequency. Wavelengths are also given; note that frequency × wavelength always gives 3×10^8 m/s, the speed of the waves.

Electromagnetic waves Waves, or radiation, emitted by accelerated electric charges. The waves consist of oscillating electric and magnetic fields, oriented at right angles to each other. Both kinds of fields are perpendicular to the direction of travel, so the waves are transverse. They propagate through empty space, following the rule that changing magnetic fields produce electric fields and changing electric fields produce magnetic fields. In empty space, they travel at the speed of 2.998×10^8 m/s.

The source, properties, and effects of the waves vary according to their frequency. The waves vary greatly in frequency, from about 10^2 to 10^{23} Hz. For details, *see* **Electromagnetic spectrum.**

Electron A fundamental particle bearing a single negative charge. The charge on the electron (1.60×10^{-19} C) was determined by measuring the force exerted on tiny oil drops by an electric field, *see* **Millikan's oil drop experiment.** The mass (9.1×10^{-31} kg) was found by measuring the radius of the circle in which electrons travel in a magnetic field; *see* **Mass spectrometer.**

Electrons comprise the part of all atoms that surrounds the nucleus. An element is defined by the number of electrons in each of its atoms. All chemical reactions result from interactions of the outer electrons of the atoms. The movement of electrons is responsible for electric current and the accumulation of charges. Electrons are also produced in radioactive decay.

See also **Atom; Beta decay; Cathode ray; Conductor; Electric charge; Electric current; Fundamental particles; Ion.**

Electron volt (eV) A unit of energy, equal to the work done in moving an electron through a potential difference of 1 volt.

The usual expression for calculation of electrical energy is $E_{elec} = qV$. If V is in volts and q is in elementary charges, E_{elec} will be in electron volts. Thus, if an electron is accelerated through a potential difference of 25,000 V in the electron gun of a picture tube, it emerges with 25,000 eV of energy. To do the calculation in joules, it would be necessary to express q for an electron in coulombs (1.60×10^{-19} C). Thus, it turns out that 1 eV = 1.60×10^{-19} J.

The electron volt is a convenient unit to use in the physics of elementary particles, since most of them have just one unit of elementary charge. Other units in use are the mega-electron-volt (1 MeV = 10^6 eV) and the giga-electron-volt (1 GeV = 10^9 eV).

Electrophorus A device for storing electric charge by means of electrostatic induction. It consists of a "sole plate," usually of some sort of wax or plastic, and a metal plate that rests on the sole plate. The metal plate has an insulating handle.

To charge the metal plate, first charge the sole plate by stroking it with fur or wool. This gives it a

EXHIBIT 20.1
The Electromagnetic Spectrum

Band	Frequency	Wavelength	Method of Production	Use
AC	10^2 to 10^4 Hz	10^4 to 10^6 m	generators	power, heating
Long wave	10^5 to 10^6 Hz	300 to 3000 m	electronic circuits	AM radio, navigation
Shortwave	10^6 to 10^7 Hz	10 to 300 m	electronic circuits	CB, taxis, police, etc.
Very high frequency	10^7 to 10^8 Hz	1 to 10 m	electronic circuits	TV, FM radio
Ultrahigh frequency	10^8 to 10^9 Hz	10 cm to 1 m	electronic circuits	TV, airports
Microwave	10^{10} to 10^{11} Hz	1 mm to 10 cm	electronic circuits	radar, telephone
Infrared	10^{12} to 10^{14} Hz	7×10^{-7} m to 1 mm	hot objects	space heating
Visible light	10^{15} Hz	4.5×10^{-7} to 7×10^{-7} m	outer electron transformation	seeing, photography
Ultraviolet	10^{16} to 10^{18} Hz	10^{-10} to 10^{-8} m	outer electron transformations	sterilization, tanning
X rays	10^{19} to 10^{21} Hz	10^{-11} to 10^{-13} m	inner electron transformations	medical imaging, treatment
Gamma rays	10^{21} to 10^{23} Hz	10^{-13} to 10^{-15} m	nuclear transformations	medical

negative charge that will not be removed easily. Then place the metal plate on the sole plate and touch the metal plate momentarily with the finger. The field of the sole plate induces a separation of charge between the metal plate and the body. Electrons are repelled from the metal plate into the finger, leaving the metal plate with a positive charge.

Electroscope A device for detecting electric charge by mutual repulsion of parts. In the gold-leaf electroscope shown in the figure, any excess charge will be conducted down to the delicate gold leaves. They repel each other and move apart. In other kinds of electroscopes, a carefully balanced vane rests upright against a metal post. When the electroscope is charged, the vane is repelled from the post and rotates to form an angle with the post. The angle is a rough measure of the potential.

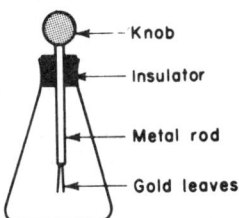

- Knob
- Insulator
- Metal rod
- Gold leaves

An electroscope can be charged by contact with a charged object. For example, if a rubber rod is charged negatively by stroking it with wool, the rod can be used to charge the electroscope. Stroking the charged rod against the knob of the electroscope makes the leaves move apart. Negative charge has been transferred to the electroscope. Touching the knob removes the charge.

It is also possible to charge the electroscope by electrostatic induction. Touch the electroscope knob with the finger, and bring the charged rubber rod near the knob. The field of the rod produces a charge separation, so that electrons flow out of the electroscope and into the body. If the finger is removed while the rod is still in place, the electroscope is left with a positive charge.

Electrostatic induction Separation of charge produced by an electric field. For example, a charged rubber rod is brought near a scrap of paper. The field produced by the rod repels electrons in the paper, so that the part near the rod becomes positive and the other end becomes negative. The rod can pick up the paper because the positive part is nearer the rod, so the force of attraction is stronger than the force of repulsion. If the scrap of paper is cut in half while in contact with the rod, one half has a net positive charge and the other half is negative. *See* **Electrophorus; Electroscope.**

Elementary charge The quantum of electric charge, equal to 1.60×10^{-19} C. This is the charge of a proton, an electron, and any other charged particle. All electric charges are integral multiples of the elementary charge.

Energy A conserved physical quantity, having the dimensions of work. Its SI unit is the joule, equal to 1N·s, or $1 \text{ kg·m}^2/\text{s}^2$.

When work is done on a system, the energy of the system increases by an amount equal to the work

done. For example, pushing an object through a distance does work. If the object is on a horizontal, frictionless surface, the only effect of this work is an increase in speed. Thus. speed is a measure of the energy of the system. *See* **Kinetic energy.**

Work done in lifting results in a change in the position of an object in a gravitational field. Therefore, the separation of an object from the earth is a measure of the energy of the system. *See* **Gravitational energy.**

It takes work to separate positive and negative electric charges, so opposite charges have more energy when separated than when they are together. *See* **Electric energy.**

Where there is friction, work done on a system will result in a rise in temperature. It follows that temperature is a measure of the energy of a system. *See* **Heat.**

The molecules and atoms of materials exert forces on each other and are in constant motion. It follows that they possess kinetic energy and various kinds of potential energy as well. Changes in these forms of molecular energy are observable as changes in temperature, phase, size, and certain other properties. *See* **Internal energy.**

Energy takes all these forms, each expressible by a mathematical formula. In an isolated system, energy may be converted from one form to another, but the total amount of energy remains constant. This rule is known as the first law of thermodynamics. *See* **Energy conversions.**

Relativity theory produced the important conclusion that mass represents an extremely concentrated form of energy, which can be converted into other forms of energy by nuclear transformations. *See* **Mass-energy.**

Not all forms of energy are equally useful. Although energy is always conserved, it becomes degraded into a less useful form every time it is used. *See* **Second law of thermodynamics.**

Energy conversions Changes in the form of energy. According to the first law of thermodynamics, the total amount of energy in any isolated system never changes. However, energy may be converted from one form into another.

An example is the conversion of gravitational into kinetic energy as an object falls freely. Suppose an object is at rest at a height h above some level, where its energy is taken to be zero. Then its gravitational energy is mgh. If the object is allowed to drop, it reaches the zero level with no gravitational energy, but with kinetic energy $mv^2/2$. For uniformly accelerated motion, $v = \sqrt{2as}$. In this case, $s = h$ and $a = g$. Then $v^2 = 2gh$, and $mv^2/2 = mgh$. The gravitational energy lost is equal to the kinetic energy gained, and the total energy is unchanged.

Example 1

A pendulum is swinging, and its speed is 2.5 m/s at the bottom of its path. How high does it rise?

As the pendulum rises, its kinetic energy is converted into gravitational energy; it stops when it has no more kinetic energy. Set the initial kinetic energy equal to the final gravitational energy:

$$\left(\frac{mv^2}{2}\right)_{initial} = (mgh)_{final}$$

Note that the mass does not matter. Then,

$$\frac{(2.5 \text{ m/s})^2}{2} = (9.8 \text{ m/s}^2)h$$

$$h = 0.32 \text{ m}$$

Example 2

An immersion heater uses 1.4 A on a 120 V circuit to heat 240 g of water. How long will the water take to go from 20°C to the boiling point?

The amount of energy needed (*see* **Specific heat**) is

$$cm \, \Delta T = (4.19 \text{ J/g·K}) \, (240 \text{ g}) \, (80 \text{ K}) = 80,400 \text{ J}$$

Energy is being supplied at the rate of

$$P = IV = (1.4 \text{ A}) \, (120 \text{ V}) = 168 \text{ W} = 168 \text{ J/s}$$

Then the time needed is

$$\frac{80,400 \text{ J}}{168 \text{ J/s}} = 480 \text{ s}$$

Example 3

If a waterfall is 65 m high, how much does the temperature of the water increase as it strikes the bottom?

Set the lost gravitational energy equal to the increase in thermal energy:

$$(mg\Delta h)_{lost} = (mc \, \Delta T)_{gained}$$

Since the mass drops out of the equation,

$$(9.8 \text{ m/s}^2) \, (65 \text{ m}) = (4.19 \text{ J/g·K}) \, \Delta T$$

so $\Delta T = -0.15 \text{ K}$

Equilibrium   The state of a system in which oppositely acting influences cancel each other out so that the system is not undergoing any change.

When all the forces acting on an object add up to zero, the object will remain at rest or in uniform motion; its acceleration is zero. *See* **Translational equilibrium**.

When all the torques acting on an object add up to zero, the object will continue its state of nonrotation or uniform rotation. *See* **Rotational equilibrium**.

When all parts of a system are at the same temperature, there will be no transfer of heat from one part to another. *See* **Heat**; **Specific Heat.**

Equipotential surface   The surface of an object in a state in which all points are at the same electric potential. When a metal has an excess charge, the charge distributes itself in such a way that the entire object, inside and out, is at the same potential. This condition is reached when all the charge is on the surface and the charge is most concentrated where the curvature is greatest. Since curvature is great at a projecting point, charge accumulates on any projection. This is the principle of the lightning rod.

Equivalence principle   The rule that, at a point in space, no experiment can distinguish between the effects of a gravitational field and those of the

acceleration of the frame of reference. This is the basis of the general theory of relativity.

Einstein's analysis of this situation uses an elevator in outer space, drawn upward by a cable. Suppose the elevator is being accelerated at 3 m/s². If an observer in the elevator suspends a kilogram from a spring scale, the scale must be exerting a force to accelerate the kilogram, thus keeping it at rest within the elevator. The force the scale exerts is $ma = (1 \text{ kg})(3 \text{ m/s}^2) = 3 \text{ N}$. This is precisely what the scale would read in a gravitational field of 3 N/kg.

This thought experiment implies a resolution of a question that had been troubling physicists since Newton. The force of gravity acts on the *gravitational* mass of the object, according to the equation $w = m_{gravitational}g$. On earth, this equation tells us that a kilogram weighs 9.8 N. If the kilogram is attached to a spring scale in outer space and accelerated at 9.8 m/s², the scale reads 9.8 N. The accelerating force is acting on the *inertial* mass of the kilogram, according to the equation $F = m_{inertial}a$. The equivalence principle tells us that there is no way to determine whether the scale reading is weight or accelerating force. Then inertial and gravitational mass must always be identical. This was always suspected, but the equivalence principle showed that it *must* be true. *See also* **Mass**.

Escape velocity   The speed that an object must have if it is rising against the pull of gravity so rapidly that it will not return. Since infinite separation is defined as zero gravitational energy, escape represents an increase in gravitational energy from a negative value to zero. *See* **Gravitational energy**.

How fast must a bullet be fired upward if it is to escape from the earth's gravity?   As the bullet rises, it loses kinetic energy and gains gravitational energy, *see* **Kinetic energy**; **Gravitational energy**. If its total energy is greater than zero, it will still have kinetic energy when its gravitational energy is zero. Therefore, the condition for escape is zero total energy:

$$\frac{mv^2}{2} - \frac{GmM}{r} = 0$$

where M is the mass of the earth (or other planet), v is the escape velocity, r is the starting distance from the center of the earth, and G is the universal gravitation constant. Note that all objects have the same escape velocity; the mass of the object, m, cancels out. Solving for v to get the escape velocity from the surface of the earth, we have

$$v = \sqrt{\frac{2GM}{r}}$$

$$= \sqrt{\frac{2(6.67 \times 10^{-11} \text{ N·m}^2/\text{kg}^2)(6.0 \times 10^{24} \text{ kg})}{6.4 \times 10^6 \text{ m}}}$$

$$= 11,200 \text{ m/s}$$

Evaporation   The change of phase from liquid to vapor. *See* **Boiling point**.

 **Fahrenheit scale**   The temperature scale in common use in the United States. Its fixed points are the melting point of ice, defined as 32°F, and the normal boiling point of water, 212°F.

The following formula will convert Fahrenheit temperatures to Celsius:

$$\frac{5}{9}(°F - 32) = °C$$

Faraday's law of induction   See **Electromagnetic induction**.

Ferromagnetic domains   See **Ferromagnetism**.

Ferromagnetism   The property of certain materials of greatly increasing the strength of any magnetic field in which they are placed. This is the property that makes it possible to use these materials to make strong magnets.

There are several ferromagnetic elements, including iron, cobalt, and nickel. None of them can form permanent magnets. As soon as they are removed from the magnetic field, they lose their magnetism. Permanent ferromagnets, which remain magnetic when removed from the field, are made of certain alloys, such as steel, alnico, and Magnequench. Some ceramics, which are complex oxides of iron and other metals, can also be made into permanent magnets.

All elements have some sort of magnetic property, produced by the rotation and revolution of their electrons. The molecules of ferromagnetic substances are strongly magnetic because they have several unpaired electrons, revolving in the same direction. The molecules interact strongly with each other, so that adjacent molecules tend to line up in the same direction. They form groups of parallel molecules called ferromagnetic domains. An ordinary piece of iron is not magnetic because its domains are randomly oriented. If it is placed in a magnetic field, the molecules at the borders between domains rotate to line up with the field. This enlarges those domains that are aligned parallel to the field, at the expense of neighboring domains. When all domains are completely aligned with the external field, the iron is magnetically saturated and cannot be made any stronger.

Fictitious force   A prerelativity designation for a force resulting from acceleration of the frame of reference. For example, when you step on the brake of a car, the car undergoes an acceleration to the rear. Objects in the car experience a force pushing them forward.

The fictitious force exists only in the accelerated frame of reference. An observer in the earth frame describes the events differently. The outside observer sees the passengers in motion. When the car slows, the passengers simply continue to move the way they were going. This is just the inertia principle, which does not invoke any force. See also **Centrifugal force**.

In the general relativity theory, there are no fictitious forces. Acceleration of the car alters the gravitational field in the car's frame of reference. The fictitious forces are indistinguishable from gravitational forces. See **Equivalence principle**.

Field   A region of space in which some physical quantity has a definite value at every point. Fields can be mapped in various ways. For example, a contour map is a plot of an altitude field; the map specifies the altitude at every point in the field.

Vector fields have both magnitude and direction at each point. For the properties of some important vector fields, see **Electric field**; **Light rays**; **Gravitational field**; **Magnetic field**.

Field lines   Lines drawn in a vector field to indicate the magnitude and direction of the field at each point. The line is drawn so that it is tangential to the field at every point. The magnitude of the field is represented by spacing; the closer together the lines, the stronger the field. For details, see **Electric field lines**, **Light rays**; **Magnetic field lines**.

First law of thermodynamics   The law that the total energy in a closed system does not change. See **Energy**; **Energy conversions**.

Focal length   The distance from the center of a lens or curved mirror to the principal focus. All light rays entering a convex lens parallel to the principal axis are refracted in such a way that when they emerge, they pass through the principal focus of the lens. The focal length can be found by focusing an image of a distant object onto a screen. When the image is sharp, the distance from the lens to the image is the focal length of the lens.

A concave lens does not bring light to a focus. Parallel rays entering the lens diverge. The principal focus of the lens is the point from which the rays appear to be diverging. It can be found by tracing these rays coming out of the lens and extending them to a point of convergence behind the lens. The focal length of a concave lens is always given as a negative number.

Mirrors reflect the light, not refract it. They produce the same sorts of effects as lenses. A concave mirror converges light, so it behaves like a convex lens. Conversely, a convex mirror is like a diverging lens. In either ease, focal lengths are defined as in lenses. The focal length of a spherical mirror is twice the radius of curvature of the mirror.

Force   Roughly, a push or a pull exerted on an object. When a single force is exerted on any object, it changes the object's velocity. Force is a vector quantity, and its effect depends on the direction in which it is exerted. If the force is directed in the same direction as the velocity, the object speeds up. If the force is in the opposite direction, the object slows down. If the force is perpendicular to the velocity, the object changes direction without a change in speed (see **Centripetal force**).

The measure of a force is the acceleration it produces on an object of a given mass. This is expressed in Newton's second law of motion:

$$F = ma$$

where F is the force, expressed in newtons, m is the mass, in kilograms, and a is the acceleration in m/s². This equation defines the newton as equal to a kg·m/s².

Example

A 15 kg frictionless cart on a horizontal surface is pushed from rest to a speed of 6.8 m/s in 4.0 s. How much force was applied?

The acceleration of the cart was

$$a = \frac{\Delta v}{\Delta t} = \frac{6.8 \text{ m/s}}{4.0 \text{ s}} = 1.7 \text{ m/s}^2$$

so the applied force was

$$F = ma = (15 \text{ kg})(1.7 \text{ m/s}^2)$$
$$= 26 \text{ kg·m/s}^2 = 26 \text{ N}$$

Every force is one-half of an interaction pair. Newton's third law of motion states that for every action there is an equal and opposite reaction. What this means is that if object A exerts a force northward on object B, then B must exert an equal southward force on A. For example, you cannot bat a ball without having the ball exert a force on the bat. If you swing and miss, there is no force on either the ball or the bat.

Forces may be classified according to how they are produced.

Gravity is a force exerted by two masses on each other. The force on each is directed toward the other. The magnitude of the force depends on the masses of the objects and the distance between them. The gravitational force of the earth on objects near it is called *weight*. For further details, *see* **Gravity**.

Elastic recoil is the force exerted by a solid when an applied force deforms it. An obvious example is a spring. If you stretch the spring, it tends to return to its original shape. It will exert a recoil force against whatever force was applied to stretch it. A less obvious example: you are standing on a floor; your weight distorts the shape of the floor and the floor reacts by pushing up against you with a force equal to your weight. All elastic recoil forces can be reduced to two kinds: tension, in which the object is stretched; and compression, in which forces are exerted toward each other. For further information, *see* **Elastic recoil**.

Electromagnetic forces are exerted by electrically charged objects and by electric currents. *See* **Coulomb's law**; **Magnetic force**.

Hydrostatic force is the force exerted by a liquid or a gas against the walls of its container. For details *see* **Hydrostatic pressure**.

Buoyancy is an upward force on any object immersed in a liquid or a gas. It is the net hydrostatic force, resulting from the fact that the upward hydrostatic force is always larger than the downward force. This is the force that makes ships float and helium-filled balloons rise.

Friction is a retarding force acting on any object in motion. It results from the rubbing of the object against other things, and it always acts in a direction opposite to the relative velocity. This is the force that makes moving objects slow down and eventually come to rest.

Viscous drag is a frictionlike force, retarding the motion of any solid moving through a liquid or a gas.

All these forces, except gravity, result from the electromagnetic interactions between molecules. On a macroscopic scale, there are thus only two basic forces: electromagnetism and gravity. On the nuclear scale, there are two others; *see* **Strong nuclear force**; **Weak interaction**.

When there is more than one force acting on an object, the F in $F = ma$ is the vector sum of all the forces. If the vector sum is zero, the acceleration of the object is zero. This is expressed as Newton's first law of motion: a body at rest will remain at rest, and a body in motion will remain in motion at constant speed in a straight line unless acted on by an outside force. For details of these states, *see* **Translational equilibrium**.

Frame of reference A specified position, arbitrarily designated as being at rest, from which measurements are made. We commonly take the local surface of the earth as a frame of reference, as when we give someone instructions for driving from one place to another. We know, however, that the earth is in motion, and that for describing the motions of the planets, the sun is a more convenient frame of reference. The sun is also in motion, however. For many purposes in astronomy, it is convenient to take the fixed stars as a frame of reference. They are also in motion, but their relative positions change very slowly.

In doing theoretical or practical physics, any frame of reference may be selected. For details, *see* **Galilean relativity**; **Special relativity**.

Free fall The condition in which an object is moving under no other influence except gravity. *See* **Acceleration due to gravity**.

Frequency For any repeating or cyclic event, the number of repetitions per unit of time. The usual unit is the hertz (Hz), equal to one cycle per second. The highest audible frequency, for example, is about 18,000 Hz, meaning that the air vibrates 18,000 times every second. *See* **Wave**; **Sound wave**.

Friction *See* **Force**.

Fundamental particles To a chemist, there are just three fundamental particles that make up all matter: proton, neutron, and electron. Of these, the neutron is unstable, breaking down with a half-life of 11 minutes. Physicists, however, have found an enormous zoo of subnuclear particles in cosmic rays and in the output of particle accelerators. All of these particles are unstable, breaking down with half-lives as short as 10^{-22} second.

It is now possible to simplify and organize the knowledge of these particles. The systematic scheme, called the Standard Model, says that there are just three families of fundamental particles. Each family consists of just two types of quarks and two leptons. All the other particles, hundreds of them, are combinations of quarks.

The first family consists of the "up" and "down" quarks; the leptons are the electron and the neutrino. A particular combination of three kinds of quarks forms a proton; a different combination of three quarks makes a neutron. These are massive particles, with angular momenta of 1/2, 3/2, and so on. Particles made of three quarks are classified as baryons. In any sort of recombination of parts, the total number of baryons never changes.

Various combinations of two quarks each make up the unstable particles called mesons, which can have spins of 0, 1, 2, and so on. Interactions of particles can change the number of mesons. A lepton is a lightweight particle; an electron has small mass and a single negative charge. A neutrino has no charge, and no rest mass has ever been detected for it.

Every particle also has an antiparticle, identical except that it has the opposite electric charge. Many baryons are made up of antiquarks combined with quarks.

The second family of particles is just like the first, except that its quarks and leptons have about 10 times the mass of those in the first family. The third family, in turn, has 10 times the mass of the second. The heavy families also form baryons and mesons by making combinations of quarks. For further information, *see* **Quark**.

Galilean relativity The principle, established by Galileo, that the laws of mechanics are the same in any frame of reference moving with constant velocity. Consider, for example, an experimenter in a train moving at constant velocity. If she drops a ball, she will see it fall straight down, in her frame of reference. It will strike the floor of the train at her feet. She sees exactly the same result as if the train were at rest. No experiment that she can perform completely inside the train will tell her whether the train is moving.

This does not mean that the motion of the ball is the same in any frame of reference. An observer outside the train will see that the ball was in motion when it was dropped. In the earth frame of reference, the ball moves forward as it falls, taking a parabolic path. It lands at the feet of the experimenter inside the train because the experimenter was also moving forward. The observers disagree on the motion of the ball; they agree on the laws of nature that control it.

For the application of this principle when things are moving at speeds close to the speed of light, *see* **Special relativity**.

Galvanometer A device for measuring small electric currents. The common type is the Weston galvanometer, illustrated in the figure. It consists of a permanent magnet with a cylindrical soft-iron core between its poles. A coil of wire placed around the core is free to rotate. When there is current in the coil, the magnetic field exerts a torque on the coil. The coil turns against the restraint of a spring (not shown). The greater the current, the farther the coil turns before coming to rest. A pointer attached to the coil indicates the current against a scale.

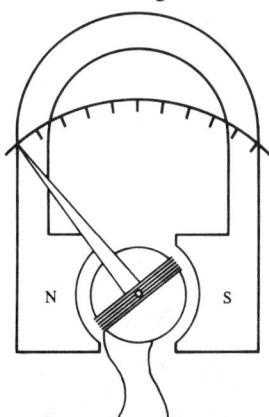

The Weston galvanometer is extremely sensitive and can measure currents in the microampere range. By combining it with other circuitry, it can be used to measure large currents, potentials, resistance, power, and any other quantity that can be converted

into a small-current analog. *See* **Ammeter**; **Voltmeter**.

Gamma rays Extremely high frequency electromagnetic waves emitted in the radioactive transformation of a nucleus. *See* **Electromagnetic waves**; **Electromagnetic spectrum**; **Radioactivity**.

Gas A phase of matter in which the substance will spread out indefinitely unless confined inside a container. This behavior contrasts with that of a solid, which has a definite shape, and with that of a liquid, which is confined by an upper surface. A gas exerts a hydrostatic pressure against its container, or any other object in contact with it. The pressure depends on the temperature and can be changed by altering the volume occupied by the gas. *See* **Gas law**.

Gases have extremely low density. Water vapor, for example, occupies about 1000 times as much volume as an equal mass of liquid water. This implies that the molecules of a gas are very far apart. The distance between the molecules is so great that there is very little attraction between them. This is why gases spread out indefinitely. The pressure they exert is attributed to repeated impact of the gas molecules against the surface. It is evidence that the molecules of a gas are constantly in random motion. For more details, *see* **Kinetic theory of gases**.

In a liquid, there is an upper surface because the molecules are close enough together to attract each other. A gas has more internal energy than the liquid because energy is required to separate the molecules when a liquid is converted to a gas. For calculations dealing with this additional binding energy, *see* **Latent heat**.

Gas law An empirical or theoretical rule relating pressure, volume, temperature, and other properties of gases. The simplest form is the "ideal" gas law. This is an approximation of the behavior of gases that produces good accuracy as long as the temperature is high and the pressure is low.

The ideal gas law can be represented as a single equation,

$$pV = nkT$$

where p is the pressure, V is the volume, n is the number of molecules in the sample, k is a universal constant (the Boltzmann constant), and T is the kelvin temperature. The value of k is 1.38×10^{-23} joule per molecule per kelvin.

Applications of the gas law often involve changes in only two of the variables, so that problems can be treated simply as proportionalities.

Example 1

A sealed bottle contains 2 liters of hydrogen at 1 atm pressure and 20°C. What will the pressure be if the hydrogen is heated to 160°C?

Since the bottle has a fixed volume, V will not change; n and k are also constant. Therefore, p/T is constant, and

$$\frac{p_i}{T_i} = \frac{p_f}{T_f}$$

where the subscripts indicate initial and final values respectively. In substituting values, it is essential that the Celsius temperatures be converted in kelvins by adding 273. Then the equation becom

$$\frac{1 \text{ atm}}{293 \text{ K}} = \frac{p_f}{433 \text{ K}}$$

from which $p_f = 1.5$ atm

Sometimes three variables will change.

Example 2

A cylinder contains 2.4 liters of chlorine at 20°C and a pressure of 35 pounds per square inch (psi). What must the pressure be to raise the temperature to 240°C while allowing the gas to expand to occupy 5.6 liters?

Since neither n nor k changes, pV/T is constant:

$$\frac{p_i V_i}{Ti} = \frac{p_f V_f}{T_f}$$

and, using kelvin temperatures,

$$\frac{(35 \text{ psi})(2.4 \text{ liters})}{293 \text{ K}} = \frac{p_f (5.6 \text{ liters})}{513 \text{ K}}$$

which gives $p_f = 26$ psi.

Example 3

A steel cylinder contains 12 g of hydrogen sulfide gas at a pressure of 1400 kPa and a temperature of 35°C. A valve is opened to allow 7.5 g to flow out, and the temperature drops to 10°C. How much is the pressure?

Since V and k are constant, p/nT is constant. The mass drops from 12 to 4.5 g, so n_f is $\frac{4.5}{12}$ of n_i, or $0.375 n_i$.

$$\frac{1400 \text{ kPa}}{n_i(308 \text{ K})} = \frac{p_f}{(0.375 n_i)(283 \text{ K})}$$

so $p_f = 482$ kPa.

Geiger counter   A device for detecting charged particles. It consists of a gas-filled chamber, with a metal shell and a wire down the center. The wire and shell are kept at a potential difference just too small to ionize the gas. When a charged paticle passes through the gas, it will ionize at least one atom. The ions produced accelerate in the electric field; when they strike other atoms, they produce additional ionizations. This cascade of charged particles produces a pulse of current from the shell to the wire. The current is detected in the external circuit, which is connected to a counting mechanism.

General relativity   The theory of relativity extended to deal with accelerated frames of reference. Its basic premise is the equivalence principle, the identity of the effects of gravitational fields and acceleration of the frame of reference. (*See* **Equivalence principle.**) General relativity is a new theory of gravitation. It makes no use of the concept of force. In this theory, the effects of gravity are expressed in terms of gravitational fields only. The mathematical language describes the fields in terms of four variables, three of space and one of time. The motion of an object in a gravitational field is determined by the geometry of this space-time continuum.

Large masses, such as the sun, distort the geometry of this four-dimensional space-time continuum. Any object in free fall in this space follows a path marking the shortest space-time distance from one point to another.

The earliest trial of Einstein's formulation of the general relativity theory tested its prediction of the bending of light by a gravitational field. As the light from a star passes near the sun, it should bend in the sun's field. This phenomenon, visible as an apparent displacement of the star in the sky, can be seen only during a total eclipse of the sun, when starlight passing near the sun is visible. The test has been made a number of times. Other predictions of the theory have been made, and so far it has withstood all challenges.

Generator   A device for converting mechanical energy into electric energy, using the principle of electromagnetic induction. A simple generator is shown in the figure. A loop of wire (the armature) is placed between the poles of a magnet. In the position shown, none of the magnetic field lines passes through the loop. To generate electricity, the loop is turned. When it has turned through 90, a maximum number of field lines go through the loop. In another 90, there is once again no field in the loop. According to Faraday's law of induction, the potential difference between the ends of the loop is proportional to the rate at which the field passing through the loop is changing.

The potential difference between the ends of the armature loop increases, decreases, and reverses, making a complete cycle of a sine wave for every revolution of the armature. In the circuit shown, the circuit is completed through a lamp. An alternating current thus flows through the lamp. If direct current is needed, the output passes into a commutator that rotates with the armature. This reverses the connection to the lamp every half-cycle, so that the current in the external circuit is always in the same direction.

In the large generators of a commercial power station, an electromagnet produces the magnetic field. A small part of the armature current is used for the field magnets. The armature remains stationary, and the field magnet rotates around it. Typically, the armature output is about 20,000 V alternating current. With the armature stationary, this large potential can be drawn off by means of firm, nonmoving connections to the armature terminals instead of slip rings. *See* **Electrogmagnetic induction.**

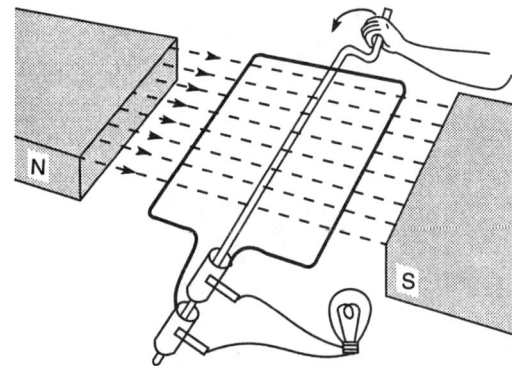

Grating spectroscope   *See* **Diffraction grating.**

Gravitational energy   The potential energy of a system due to the position of masses with respect to each other. In the most common case the energy of an object is due to its position with respect to the earth. This can be expressed in terms of its position in the gravitational field of the earth.

If an object is lifted vertically, work must be done on it equal to the force needed to lift it multiplied by the vertical distance it moves. The force is equal to the weight, of the object, mg, where m is its mass and g is the earth's gravitational field. Then the formula for any change in gravitational energy is

$$\Delta E_{grav} = mg\, \Delta h$$

where Δh is the vertical distance through which the object moves. No work is done when the object moves horizontally, since the force is always vertical and work is done only in motion in the direction of force (see **Work**).

Example 1

How much does the gravitational energy of a 120 kg wheelbarrow load increase if the wheelbarrow is pushed for 30 m up an incline of 22°?
   The vertical distance the load moves is

$$(30 \text{ m}) \sin 22° = 11.2\text{m}$$

and the increase in the gravitational energy is

$$mg\, \Delta h = (120 \text{ kg})(9.8 \text{ N/kg})(11.2 \text{ m}) = 13{,}200 \text{ J}$$

If some zero level of gravitational energy is arbitrarily chosen, a value can be assigned to the gravitational energy. Then,

$$E_{grav} = mgh$$

where h is the vertical distance above the zero level.
   If the object is below the zero level, the energy is negative.

Example 2

If a 60 kg man has zero gravitational energy while on the street, how much energy does he have when he walks down into a basement 12 m below street level?

$$E_{grav} = mgh = (60 \text{ kg}) (9.8 \text{ N/kg}) (-12\text{m})$$
$$= -7100 \text{ J}$$

When the vertical distance moved is very large, the formula given above for gravitational energy cannot be used. The reason is that the value of g decreases as separation gets greater. In astronomical systems, where distances are large, gravitational energy is given by

$$E_{grav} = -\frac{Gm_1m_2}{r}$$

where G is the universal gravitation constant (= 6.67×10^{-11} N·m²/kg²; see **Gravitational force**) the m are any two masses, and r is the distance between them. The zero value for gravitational energy is taken at complete separation of the objects (r = infinity). Since the gravitational energy decreases as the objects come closer together, all other values are negative.

Example 3

How much work is required to lift a 45,000 kg rocket into orbit at an altitude of 3800 km? The work

needed is the difference between the final gravitational energy and the initial gravitational energy:

$$\Delta E = -\frac{Gm_1m_2}{r_f} - \left(-\frac{Gm_1m_2}{r_i}\right)$$

$$= Gm_1m_2\left(\frac{1}{r_i} - \frac{1}{r_f}\right)$$

where the m are the masses of the rocket and the earth. The distance r_i is the radius of the earth; for r_f, add to this the altitude of the rocket:

$$Gm_1m_2 = \left(6.67 \times 10^{-11} \text{ N·m}^2/\text{kg}^2\right)$$
$$\times \left(6.0 \times 10^{24} \text{ kg}\right)(45{,}000 \text{ kg})$$
$$= 1.80 \times 10^{19} \text{ N·m}^2$$

$$\Delta E = \left(1.80 \times 10^{19} \text{ N·m}^2\right)$$
$$\times \left(\frac{1}{6.4 \times 10^6 \text{ m}} - \frac{1}{10.2 \times 10^6 \text{ m}}\right)$$
$$= 1.0 \times 10^{12} \text{ J}$$

Gravitational field   A region of space in which any object is subjected to a gravitational force. Every object is surrounded by a gravitational field that depends on its mass. The fields are generally too small to detect except for those of very large objects, such as the earth.

The magnitude of the field (γ, the Greek letter gamma) at any position is a vector. It is defined as the force acting on each unit of mass at that position. The direction of the field is the same as the direction of the force. The force exerted by the field is called the *weight* of the object. Thus, to find the weight of anything, multiply its mass by the field at its position in space:

$$w = m\gamma$$

Example 1

What is the weight of a 55 kg woman near the surface of the earth?
   The field near the surface of the earth is 9.8 N/kg, so her weight is

$$w = (55 \text{ kg})(9.8 \text{ N/kg}) = 540 \text{ N}$$

If an object is in free fall, the only force acting on it is its weight. Then, according to the law of inertia, it must accelerate, obeying the equation

$$F = ma$$

In free fall, weight is the only force, so $F = w$. Also, the acceleration is due to gravity, so $a = g$. Therefore

$$w = m\gamma$$

It follows that $g = \gamma$. Acceleration due to gravity is identical with gravitational field. This result provides empirical evidence for the identity of inertial mass (= F/a) with gravitational mass (= w/g) (see **Mass; Equivalence principle**).

The gravitational field around any astronomical object varies inversely as the square of the distance from the center of the object. This can be seen from Newton's equation for gravitational force. See

Gravitational force. Since the field is F/m, where m is the mass of an object in the field, dividing the gravitation equation by m gives the field:

$$g = \frac{Gm}{r^2}$$

where G is the universal gravitation constant, m is the mass of (for example) the earth, and r is the distance from its center.

A convenient way of calculating the gravitational field at any altitude above the earth is to make use of the inverse square proportionality. Since Gm is constant, gr^2 has the same value in all the space around the earth, including the surface. Use the surface of the earth as a reference point, then g_0 (gravitational field at the surface)=9.8 m/s² and r_0 (radius of the earth) is 6.4×10^6 m.

Example 2

How much is the gravitational field at an altitude of 2800 km above the earth?

The value of r is the altitude plus the radius of the earth. Then,

$$gr^2 = g_0 r_0^2$$

$$g\left(9.2 \times 10^6 \, \text{m}\right)^2 = \left(9.8 \, \text{m/s}^2\right)\left(6.4 \times 10^6 \, \text{m}\right)^2$$

$$g = \left(9.8 \, \text{m/s}^2\right)\left(\frac{6.4}{9.2}\right)^2$$

$$g = 4.7 \, \text{m/s}^2$$

Thus, at that altitude, any object in free fall will have an acceleration of 4.7 m/s² and each kilogram will weigh 4.7 newtons.

Gravitational force   The mass-dependent force of attraction between any two objects. This is the force that holds the earth together and holds everything down to the earth. It is also the force that holds the planets in their orbits around the sun. *See* **Orbit**.

Any two objects attract each other with a force that varies directly as the product of their masses and inversely as the square of the distance between them. The classical formula for gravitational force is

$$F_{\text{grav}} = \frac{Gm_1 m_2}{r^2}$$

where the m are the masses, r is the distance between them, and G is the universal gravitation constant, equal to 6.67×10^{-11} N·m²/kg².

Application of this equation to objects of ordinary size shows that the forces between them are too small to take into account.

Example

How much is the gravitational attraction between a 60 kg man and a 1200 kg automobile when they are 5 m apart?

$$F_{\text{grav}} = \frac{\left(6.67 \times 10^{-11} \, \text{N·m}^2 / \text{kg}^2\right)(60 \, \text{kg})(1200 \, \text{kg})}{(5\text{m})^2}$$

$$= 1.9 \times 10^{-7} \, \text{N}$$

Gravitational force becomes significant when objects are large. The weight of any object on earth is the gravitational force between the object and the earth. Gravitation is the chief force that must be considered in dealing with astronomical systems. The formulation above, developed by Isaac Newton, is an action-at-a-distance theory. It implies that one object can act on any other in the universe, regardless of distance, instantaneously. The first step in dealing with this problem was a reformulation of the theory. *See* **Gravity**.

Gravity   An effect causing unconstrained objects to move through space when no other apparent cause exists.

The earliest treatment of gravity, by Isaac Newton, explained the motion of objects through space as the result of a force of attraction. All objects, in this theory, attract each other with a force that is proportional to the two masses and inversely proportional to the distance between them. This theory was extremely successful in explaining weight, the motions of the heavenly bodies, the tides, the trajectories of objects in free fall, and many other phenomena. *See* **Gravitational force**.

Newton's formulation required physicists to conceive of a force acting instantaneously through unlimited space. This was troubling, and a new formulation was produced. Each mass was thought of as the origin of a gravitational field. Any object in the field is acted on by the field. Thus, the earth, being a large object, produces a strong gravitational field. The weight of anything on earth is the force of the earth's field acting on the mass of the object. *See* **Gravitational field**.

In the most modern theory of gravity, produced by Albert Einstein, the concept of force is not used. Large masses, such as the earth, curve the space around them. A falling object follows the curvature of space. *See* **General relativity**.

Half-life   The length of time it takes for half of any given sample of a radioactive material to decay. For example, half-life of radium-226 is 1600 years; of uranium-238, 4.5 billion years, and of beryllium-8, 2×10^{-16} second.

The radioactive breakdown of a given nucleus is unpredictable and can be stated only in terms of probability. If there are a great many nuclei in a sample, the number that will decay during any time interval can be accurately predicted, but it is not possible to state which ones.

Example

The half-life of polonium-84 is 3 minutes. If a sample contains 16 mg of polonium-84, how much will be left after 12 minutes?

The 12 minute interval is four half-lives, so the amount of polonium is reduced to one-half four times. The amount remaining is

$$(16 \, \text{mg})\left(\tfrac{1}{2}\right)^4 = 1 \, \text{mg}$$

Heat   Energy transferred from one place to another because of a difference in temperature. Heat always flows from the higher temperature to the lower unless energy is expended to reverse the direction. When all parts of the system are at the same temperature, heat transfer stops and the system is in a state of thermal equilibrium.

When heat enters a system, it increases the internal energy of the system. This can be detected as an increase in temperature (*see* **Specific heat**), as a change in phase (*see* **Latent heat**), or by a number of other changes. For discussion of the measurement of heat, *see* **Calorie**.

There are three means of transfer of heat. *Conduction* is transfer through a material. This can be seen when a spoon is placed in hot coffee. The other end of the spoon will become warm. Metals are good conductors of heat, but most other materials are not. Heating one end of a metal spoon greatly increases the random vibrations of its free electrons, and these vibrations are transmitted to neighboring electrons. (*See* **Conduction**.)

Another method of heat transfer is *convection*. This is confined to fluids, that is, liquids and gases. When a fluid is heated at the bottom, it expands there and its density becomes less. The result is that the warmer fluid rises and the colder material above sinks. If heat is applied continuously at the bottom, a continuous convection current carries heat upward. This can be seen in a pot of water, heated on a stove. Eventually, the whole mass of water will reach the boiling point. If the heat is applied from above, as in a broiler, only the water at the top will become warm. There is no convection current, and the water will boil at the top while it is still cold at the bottom. Changes in weather result from convection currents in the atmosphere produced by uneven heating of the earth's surface.

Radiation is transfer of heat in the form of an electromagnetic wave. All warm objects produce radiant heat, mostly as infrared waves. When these waves are absorbed by a colder object, they cause a rise in internal energy. Transfer of heat by radiation is most effective in empty space, and this is the mechanism that carries heat to us from the sun. For details, *see* **Radiation**.

Heat of fusion   *See* **Latent heat**.

Heat of vaporization   *See* **Latent heat**.

Heisenberg uncertainty principle   *See* **Quantum theory**.

Hertz (Hz)   The SI unit of frequency, equal to 1 cycle per second.

Horsepower (hp)   A unit of power, equal to 550 foot-pounds per second, or about 746 watts.

Hydrostatic pressure   The pressure exerted by liquids and gases against solids in contact with them. In liquids, the pressure increases linearly with depth and depends on the density of the liquid. The pressure is exerted against any surface, regardless of the direction it faces or the shape of the containing vessel. It is found by the expression

$$P = hDg$$

where h is the depth of the liquid, D is its density, and g is the gravitational field.

Pressure can be very great at large depths.

Example

How much pressure is exerted against the bottom of a dam if the water there is 66 m deep?

The density of water is 1 g/cm^3 = 10^3 kg/m^3, so

$$p = (66 \text{ m})(10^3 \text{ kg/m}^3)(9.8 \text{ N/kg})$$
$$= 6.5 \times 10^5 \text{ N/m}^2$$

This is 650 kPs (kilopascals), or about 6.5 atm.

The density of gases is so low that in any container of reasonable size, the pressure is uniform throughout. *See* **Gas law**; **Kinetic theory of gases**. However, in the earth's atmosphere the pressure decreases with altitude. *See* **Atmospheric pressure**.

I **Image**   An analog of an object formed by rays of light. Images are formed by optical instruments. When you look into a mirror, your image looks back at you. When you take a picture, an image forms on the film and is rendered permanent by chemical development.

There are two kinds of images: real and virtual. The figure shows how a real image is formed. Light from point A, the tip of the candle, spreads out in all directions. Some of that light enters the lens as a bundle of divergent rays. The lens refracts the light in such a way as to bring these rays together at a point A´. Point B is not self-luminous, but it reflects the light that strikes it. Reflection is diffuse, meaning that light from that point scatters in all directions. Some of these light rays enter the lens and are brought to a point at B´. Every point on the object is represented by a point on the image. If a film is placed at the image point, a sharp picture of the candle will be recorded. *See* **Convex lens**; **Concave mirror**.

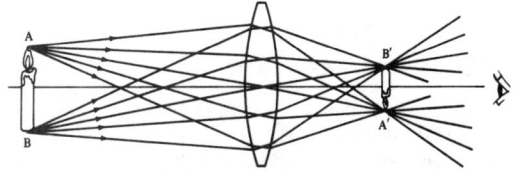

There is no light coming from a virtual image. When you look into a mirror, your image is behind the mirror. Surely no light is coming from there through the glass to your eye. The light only *seems* to be coming from the image. The image formed by a magnifying glass or a telescope is also virtual. *See* **Concave lens**; **Convex lens**; **Plane mirror**.

Impulse   The product of force and time. *See* **Momentum**.

Inclined plane   A sloping surface or ramp used as a means of lifting a weight. In the figure, the plane is inclined at an angle θ to lift the load to a height h while pushing it through a distance l.

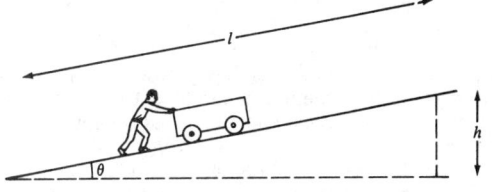

The next figure shows how to find the mechanical advantage of an inclined plane. The weight of the load mg is a force vector that can be resolved into two components, one parallel to the plane and the other perpendicular to it. The angle θ in this figure is the same as the angle θ in the first figure.

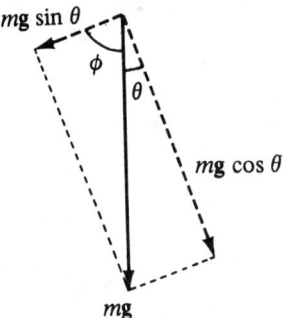

In the vector diagram, the component parallel to the plane is $mg \sin \theta$. This is the force that must be exerted to push the load up the ramp.

The mechanical advantage of the ramp is thus

$$MA = \frac{\text{load}}{\text{effort}} = \frac{mg}{mg \sin \theta} = \frac{1}{\sin \theta}$$

In the second figure, $l/\sin \theta$ is l/h. This agrees with the expectation that the mechanical advantage should be the ratio of effort distance l to load distance h.

Example

A ramp 2.8 m long is used to push a 240 kg cart up to a platform 0.8 m high. How hard must the cart be pushed?

The load is

$(240 \text{ kg})(9.8 \text{ N/kg}) = 2350 \text{ N}.$

The mechanical advantage is $(2.8 \text{ m})/(0.8 \text{ m}) = 3.5$. The effort, then, is $(2350 \text{ N})/3.5 = 670 \text{ N}$. It would actually be somewhat more because of the friction in the system. Clearly, this is a job for two strong men.

Induction   *See* **Electromagnetic induction; Electrostatic induction**.

Induction coil   Two coils wrapped around an iron core to produce a high-potential spark. The primary is made of thick wire so that it can carry a large current. The secondary is made of far more turns of very fine wire. When the current in the primary is interrupted, the magnetic field in the core suddenly collapses. This rapidly changing field induces a potential difference into the secondary. Because of the very large number of turns, the potential may be quite large. Typically, the induction coil of the ignition system of an automobile uses the 12 V of the battery to produce a 20,000 V spark. *See* **Electromagnetic induction**.

Inertia   Roughly, the tendency of objects to resist changes in their motion. It can be defined precisely as the ratio of force applied to the acceleration produced: $I = F/a$.

Careful experimentation has shown that inertia is always proportional to the gravitational property, the mass of an object. To produce a given acceleration takes a much larger force acting on a bowling ball than on a tennis ball. Because this proportionality is truly universal, it is possible to express inertia in the same units as mass; a 5 kg object always has five times as much inertia as a 1 kg object. Therefore, inertia can be expressed in kilograms, and the law of inertia can be written as $F = ma$. *See* **Force**.

Infrared   *See* **Electromagnetic spectrum; Heat**.

Insulation   Material used to prevent the passage of electricity or heat. Electric wires are embedded in a coating of rubber or plastic insulation so that the current will not leave the wire.

Effective insulation against heat loss must prevent all three modes of heat transfer. Conduction is easily prevented by using a nonconductor, such as the wooden handle of a frying pan. Convection can be prevented by eliminating fluids or by preventing the movement of the fluid. This is the principle of the woolen blanket. The wool is a poor conductor, and the air it traps is even poorer. The fibers prevent the air from flowing. Household insulation, which usually consists of a thick layer of fibers, uses the same principle but also includes a layer of aluminum foil. This is an excellent reflector, so it prevents the passage of infrared rays.

The most effective insulating device is the vacuum bottle, or Dewar flask. It consists of two bottles, one inside the other, with an evacuated space between them. The vacuum effectively prevents both conduction and convection. Radiation is prevented by the silver coating on both bottles. Coffee will stay hot, or liquid nitrogen cold for many hours.

Integrated circuit   An entire miniaturized electronic circuit made as a single unit. By various etching and deposition processes, conductors and insulators are deposited onto a thin wafer of crystalline silicon. The circuit may consist of many thousands of resistors, capacitors, and transistors, each microscopic in size and all connected together. The whole circuit that operates a desk-top computer can be on a chip the size of a dime.

Interference   The phenomena observed when two identical waves arrive at a point simultaneously. If they arrive out of phase, as in the figure, the crests of one wave cancel out the troughs of the other, and there is no vibration at that point. This is called *destructive interference*. On the contrary, if the waves arrive in phase, crests reinforce crests and troughs add to troughs. Interference is *constructive*, and there is maximum vibration at that point.

When two point sources near each other produce identical waves, the medium will display a pattern of regions of constructive and destructive interference. *See* **Two-point interference**.

If the frequencies of the two waves are slightly different, the waves are alternately in and out of phase. *See* **Beats**.

When two equal waves pass through each other in opposite directions, destructive and constructive interferences alternate along the path. *See* **Standing wave**.

When light diffracts through a narrow opening or around an edge, the shadow region contains alternate zones of constructive and destructive interference. *See* **Interference fringes**.

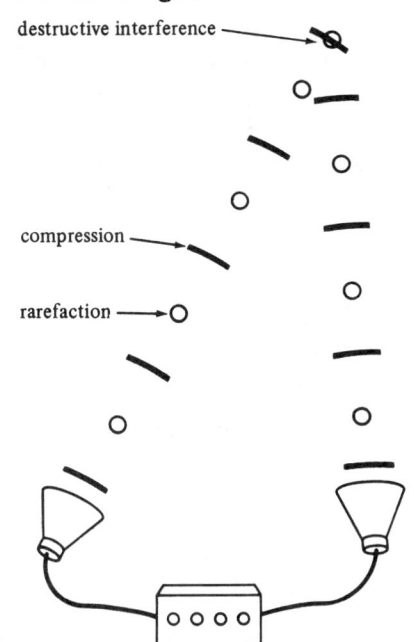

destructive interference

compression

rarefaction

When light passes through a grating made of very fine lines close together, an interference pattern is formed that makes it possible to measure wavelength. *See* **Diffraction grating**.

Interference fringes　A series of alternate dark and light bands in the region where light is diffracted around an edge. The figure is a photograph of the interference fringes produced by light of a single frequency that has passed through a tiny hole.

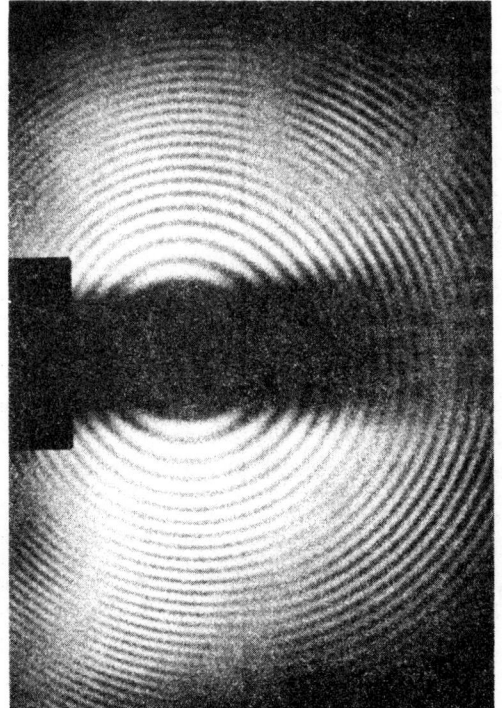

The fringes are produced by alternate constructive and destructive interference of the diffracted light.

If the light is not monochromatic, each wave length forms fringes at different points. As a result, the fringes are colored, like a rainbow. A diffraction grating makes use of this interference phenomenon to measure the wavelength of light.

Internal energy　The kinetic and potential energy of the molecules of an object. Changes in internal energy can be detected in a number of ways. A change in temperature represents a change in the kinetic energy of molecules (*see* **Kinetic theory of gases**; **Specific heat**). Changes in the potential energy are seen as changes in phase (*see* **Latent heat**), crystal structure, physical state, or chemical composition.

Invariant　A physical quantity that has the same value in any frame of reference. Temperature is an example. If someone in a relativistically moving train takes the temperature of an object at rest in the train, he will get a definite value. An observer at rest in the earth frame who measures the temperature of the same object will get the same answer. It was a shock to physicists to learn that the speed of light is invariant, but mass, length, and time are not. *See* **Special relativity**.

Ion　An atom or group of atoms that has acquired an electric charge. Negative ions have one or more excess electrons; positive ions have lost one or more electrons.

Metals, in forming chemical combination, lose one or more electrons from each atom. Some typical metallic ions are copper (Cu^{1+} or Cu^{2+}) silver (Ag^{1+}), iron (Fe^{2+} or Fe^{3+}), and mercury (Hg^{1+} or Hg^{2+}). Other positive ions are formed by hydrogen (H^{1+}) and ammonium ($NH_4)^{1+}$. Some typical negalive ions are chlorine (Cl^{1-}) phosphorus (P^{3-}). carbonate ($CO_3)^{2-}$, and oxygen (O^{2-}).

Ionic substance　A material composed entirely of ions, not molecules. An example is ordinary table salt. Crystals of salt consist of ions of sodium (Na^{1+}) and chloride (Cl^{1-}) alternating in a checkerboard pattern. Many ionic substances dissolve readily in water. Their ionic character can be shown by the fact that the solutions conduct electricity readily.

Isotope　An atom of an element that differs from other atoms of the same element in atomic mass number, but not in atomic number. Any given element has a definite atomic number, equal to the number of protons in its nucleus. Different isotopes of the element, however, have different numbers of neutrons and, therefore, different atomic mass numbers.

The name of the element and its isotopic composition are represented by its chemical symbol, a subscript, and a superscript. For example. the fissionable isotope of uranium is $^{235}_{92}U$. This indicates that its atomic number is 92 and its atomic mass number is 235. The nucleus has 92 protons and $235 - 92 = 143$ neutrons.

The number of electrons in an atom is always equal to the atomic number. Since chemical reactions involve only the electrons, all isotopes of any given element will have the same chemical properties. Isotopes can be separated by various means, all of which depend on the difference in mass of the nuclei. *See* **Mass spectrometer**; **Nucleus**.

PHYSICS

Joule　The SI unit of energy. *See* **Energy**.

Kelvin scale　The SI temperature scale. It differs from other temperature scales in that its zero is a real zero, the lowest possible temperature.

The unit in which temperature is measured in the SI is the kelvin (K). For simplicity, the kelvin has been defined so that any temperature interval in kelvins is numerically equal to the measure of the same interval in degrees Celsius.

To achieve this equivalence, the fixed point of the Kelvin scale, the temperature at the triple point of water, is defined as 273.16 K.

A constant-volume hydrogen thermometer can be used to calibrate the Kelvin scale. It consists of a glass bulb, containing hydrogen gas, connected to a manometer to measure pressure. When the bulb is in water at its triple point, the pressure reading is taken as a definition of 273.16 K. Other temperatures are determined by setting pressure proportional to temperature.

Example

Suppose the pressure at 273.16 K is 18.5 mm Hg. When the thermometer is immersed in a boiling liquid, the pressure in the thermometer rises to 33.8 mm. What is the boiling point of the liquid? To find the temperature,

$$\frac{T}{33.8 \text{ mm}} = \frac{273.16 \text{ K}}{18.5 \text{ mm}} \quad \text{and } T = 499 \text{ K}$$

Since the temperature at the triple point of water is 0.01°C, to convert from degrees Celsius to kelvins, it is only necessary to add 273.15.

Because it has a natural zero, the Kelvin scale can be used meaningfully to state ratios of temperatures. For example, twice 200 K is 400 K. However, this process makes no sense at all in the Celsius scale. What temperature is three times as great as −10°C? Surely, the answer cannot be −30°C which is smaller, not larger. The only meaningful answer has to be based on a scale with a natural zero:

$$-10°\text{ C} + 273 = 263 \text{ K}$$
$$263 \text{ K} \times 3 = 789 \text{ K}$$

If the answer is wanted in degrees Celsius,

$$789 \text{ K} - 273 = 516°\text{C}$$

Kepler's laws　*See* Earth and Space Science section, page 5-22.

Kilogram (kg)　The SI unit of mass. It is one of the SI base units and is the only base unit not defined in terms of an atomic measurement that can be repeated in many different laboratories. The reason is that it has not yet been possible to measure the mass of any subnuclear particle with sufficient accuracy. The kilogram is defined as the mass of the International Prototype Kilogram, a platinum-iridium block kept at the International Bureau of Standards in Paris.

Kilopascal (kPa)　*See* **Pressure**.

Kilowatt (kW)　*See* **Power**.

Kinetic energy　The energy possessed by a mass because of its motion. It is calculated as $\frac{1}{2}mv^2$, where m is mass and v is speed. Since energy is scalar, the direction of the speed is not significant.

The equation for kinetic energy may be demonstrated this way. Assume a mass m to be accelerated from rest on a horizontal, frictionless surface. The law of inertia tells us that

$$F = ma$$

Since the only change produced by the work done is the increase in speed, the work done must be equal to the kinetic energy produced. Work is force times distance (s), so

$$E_{\text{kin}} = W = Fs = mas$$

We know that for uniformly accelerated motion starting from rest,

$$v^2 = 2as$$

and substitution into the preceding equation gives

$$E_{\text{kin}} = \frac{mv^2}{2}$$

Kinetic energy can be converted into any of the other forms of energy. A moving object can be brought to rest only if its kinetic energy is converted. On a level surface, friction will convert the kinetic energy to heat. If a moving object is rising up a hill, its kinetic energy is converted into gravitational energy. *See* **Energy conversions**.

Example

On a frictionless surface, a 60 kg cart is pushed a distance of 12 m with a force of 220 N. It is released and then rises up a hill. How fast will it be going when it has risen 2.5 m?

Set the work done equal to the sum of kinetic and gravitational energy produced:

$$Fs = mgh + \frac{1}{2}mv^2$$
$$(220 \text{ N})(12 \text{ m}) = (60 \text{ kg})(9.8 \text{ N/kg})(2.5 \text{ m})$$
$$+ \frac{(60 \text{ kg})v^2}{2}$$

from which $v = 6.2$ m/s.

Rotational motion also has kinetic energy. It is calculated as the work done in producing a given angular velocity.

At speeds approaching the speed of light, the kinetic energy formula needs a correction. This is represented by a converging series of terms. The first term is the standard formula, and the second is $\frac{3}{8}(mv^4/c^2)$. Subsequent terms have still higher powers of c in the denominator and are rarely needed in calculations This is one of the consequences of the special theory of relativity.

See also Earth and Space Science section, page 5-22.

Kinetic theory of gases　The theory that explains the properties of gases and the gas laws on the assumption that a gas consists of molecules in random motion.

The kinetic theory starts with basic assumptions about the nature of a gas: (1) it consists of separate molecules in random motion; (2) the molecules are so far apart that they do not exert any attraction on each other; (3) the molecules occupy only a very small part of the space in which the gas is confined; (4) all collisions between molecules and with the walls of the container are completely elastic; that is, there is no loss of kinetic energy.

The molecules are bouncing around very rapidly and repeatedly strike the walls of the container. It is this impact that produces the hydrostatic pressure. An analysis of the mechanics of the molecules yields a mathematical expression for the pressure.

The more molecules there are, the more impacts there will be. Therefore, the pressure is proportional to n, the number of molecules in the sample.

The force of the impact depends on the momentum of the molecules, so the pressure is proportional to mv.

The faster the molecules are moving, the more often they will hit any given wall. The pressure is proportional to their average velocity v.

The larger the container, the farther the molecules have to travel between impacts, so the pressure is inversely proportional to the volume V.

Careful analysis combines these proportionalities into a single equation:

$$p = \frac{nmv^2}{3V}$$

(The 3 comes in because of the three dimensions of space.)

The ideal gas law, arrived at empirically, is

$$pV = nkT$$

(*See* **Gas law**.) Solving both equations for pV/n gives

$$\frac{pV}{n} = kt = \frac{mv^2}{3}$$

and since $E_{\text{kin}} = \frac{mv^2}{2}$

$$E_{\text{kin}} = \tfrac{3}{2} kT$$

Since k is a universal constant, the equation tells us that the temperature of a gas depends *only* on the average random kinetic energy of its molecules.

Example

What is the average speed of oxygen molecules at a temperature of 20°C?

Find the average kinetic energy of the molecules:

$$E_{\text{kin}} = \tfrac{3}{2} kT = \tfrac{3}{2}\left(1.38 \times 10^{-23}\,\frac{\text{J}}{\text{K}}\right)(293\ \text{K})$$

$$= 6.07 \times 10^{-21}\ \text{J}$$

The mass of an oxygen molecule is 32 daltons, or

$$\frac{32\ \text{Dl}}{6.02 \times 10^{26}\ \text{Dl}/\text{kg}} = 5.32 \times 10^{-26}\ \text{kg}$$

Then

$$E_{\text{kin}} = \frac{mv^2}{2}$$

$$6.07 \times 10^{-21}\ \text{J} = \frac{(5.23 \times 10^{-26}\ \text{kg})v^2}{2}$$

From which $v = 480$ m/s.

Latent heat The difference in internal energy between one phase of a substance and another. The latent heat of fusion—330 J/g for water—is the heat that must be added to ice at 0°C to melt it. The latent heat of vaporization—2300 J/g for water—is the heat that must be added to water at 100°C to vaporize it.

The reason ice is such an effective cooling agent is that it has a high latent heat of fusion. While melting, it absorbs heat from its surroundings without changing its temperature. It will absorb heat until thermal equilibrium is reached. When enough ice is put into a drink, the drink cools to the melting point.

Example 1

How much ice melts if ice cubes are put into 350 g of water at 20°C?

Transfer of heat stops when the water has cooled down to 0°C. Then,

Heat lost by water = heat gained by ice

$$(cm\Delta T)_{\text{water}} = (mL)_{\text{ice}}$$

where L is the latent heat of fusion of ice, c is the specific heat of water, and ΔT is the temperature change. Then

$$(4.19\ \text{J/g·K})(350\ \text{g})(20\ \text{K}) = m_{\text{ice}}\,(330\ \text{J/g})$$

$$m_{\text{ice}} = 89\ \text{g}$$

In changing phase from vapor to liquid or from liquid to solid, latent heat is released, with no change in temperature.

Example 2

What final temperature is reached if 40 g of steam at 100°C is introduced into 550 g of water at 15°C?

The water heats to some final temperature T_f; the steam condenses into water, and the newly formed water must then cool down to the final temperature. Again, the heat lost is equal to the heat gained:

Heat gained by water = heat lost by condensation of steam + heat lost in cooling down of condensed steam

$$(cm\Delta T)_{\text{water}} = (mL)_{\text{steam}} + (cm\Delta T)_{\text{condensed steam}}$$

$$(4.19\ \text{J/g·K})\,(550\ \text{g})\big(T_f - 15\,°\text{C}\big) =$$

$$(40\ \text{g})(2200\ \text{J/g}) + (4.19\ \text{J/g·K})\,(40\ \text{g})\big(100\,°\text{C} - T_f\big)$$

The units J and g drop out. Then

$$2300\,\frac{T_f}{\text{K}} - 34{,}600\,\frac{°\text{C}}{\text{K}} = 92{,}000 + 16{,}800\,\frac{°\text{C}}{\text{K}} - 168\,\frac{T_f}{\text{K}}$$

$$2468\,T_f = 51{,}400\,°\text{C} + 92{,}000\,\text{K}$$

$$T_f = 20.8\,°\text{C} + 37.2\,\text{K} = 58\,°\text{C}$$

Law of inertia The second law of motion, which states that the acceleration of an object is proportional to the force applied. See **Force**; **Inertia**.

Lens formula A pair of equations relating the sizes and positions of object and image formed in a lens or a curved mirror. If D_i and D_o are object and image distances (measured from the lens), f is the focal length, and S_i and S_o are the sizes, the equations are

$$\frac{1}{f} = \frac{1}{D_i} + \frac{1}{D_o} \quad \text{and} \quad \frac{S_i}{S_o} = \frac{D_i}{D_o}$$

Example 1

A camera with a 7.5 cm lens is being used to photograph a vase 25 cm high onto a film 9.0 cm high. Where should the vase be placed so that the image will fill the film?

First, find the ratio of the two distances:

$$\frac{9.0\,\text{cm}}{25\,\text{cm}} = \frac{D_i}{D_o}$$

$$D_i = 0.36 D_o$$

Then substitute this value into the distance formula:

$$\frac{1}{7.5\,\text{cm}} = \frac{1}{0.36 D_o} + \frac{1}{D_o}$$

$$\frac{1}{7.5\,\text{cm}} = \frac{1+0.36}{0.36 D_o}$$

$$D_o = 28\,\text{cm}$$

Example 2

What are the size and the location of the image of a baby 45 cm long, formed by a concave lens of focal length −20 cm, if the baby is 150 cm from the lens?

First, find the location:

$$\frac{1}{-20\,\text{cm}} = \frac{1}{150\,\text{cm}} + \frac{1}{D_i}$$

$$D_i = -17.6\,\text{cm}$$

The negative sign for location indicates that the image is in front of the lens. Now solve for size:

$$\frac{45\,\text{cm}}{S_i} = \frac{150\,\text{cm}}{-17.6\,\text{cm}}$$

$$S_i = -5.3\,\text{cm}$$

The negative sign indicates that the image is virtual.

Lenz's law The rule that the direction of a potential difference induced electromagnetically into a coil must be such as to oppose the change that produced the potential difference. For example, suppose the N pole of a bar magnet is inserted into a solenoid. If the ends of the solenoid are connected together by a wire, a current will be induced while the magnet is moving in. The current must be in such a direction as to oppose the motion of the magnet; that is, it must produce an N pole at the end where the magnet is inserted. Conversely, while the magnet is being removed, the induced current must attract the magnet, so that end of the solenoid must be an S pole.

An important application of Lenz's law occurs in electric circuits containing coils. When a switch is closed to send current from a battery into an electromagnet, the field inside the electromagnet is building up. This induces a potential difference into the coil, in the opposite direction from the current supplied by the battery. The result is that the increase in the current is slowed. Conversely, when the switch is opened, the collapse of the magnetic field induces a current in such a direction as to oppose the decrease in the current. The current continues to flow, and there will be a spark across the switch terminals.

Lever A rigid bar used as a machine to change the amount of effort needed to do a given amount of work. In the example shown in the figure, using the pole as a lever makes it possible to lift the boulder.

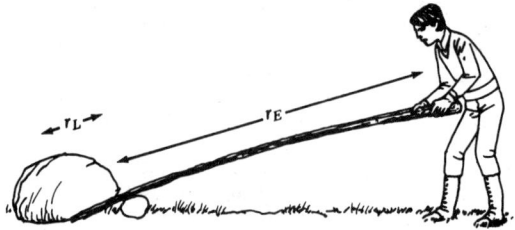

As in any machine, the ideal mechanical advantage can be found as the ratio of the distance the effort moves to the distance the load moves. A little geometry shows that in the case of the lever, this ratio is also

$$MA = \frac{r_E}{r_L}$$

where MA is the mechanical advantage, r_E is the effort arm (distance from effort to fulcrum), and r_L is the load arm (distance from load to fulcrum).

Example

If the mass of the boulder is 240 kg and it must be lifted 10 cm, how much force is required to lift it, and how far will that force have to be moved?

The pole is 2.6 m long, and the fulcrum is 0.4 m from the boulder. The effort arm is thus 2.2 m, and the load arm is 0.4 m. Then,

$$MA = \frac{2.2\,\text{m}}{0.4\,\text{m}} = 5.5$$

The distance the effort must move is thus (10 cm)(5.5) = 55 cm. The effort needed is (240 kg)(9.8 N/kg)/5.5 = 430 N. It will actually be somewhat larger because of the friction in the system.

Many levers are in common everyday use. They are classified according to the relative positions of the effort, load, and fulcrum. The figure shows three common lever-operated instruments, each with the fulcrum in a different position.

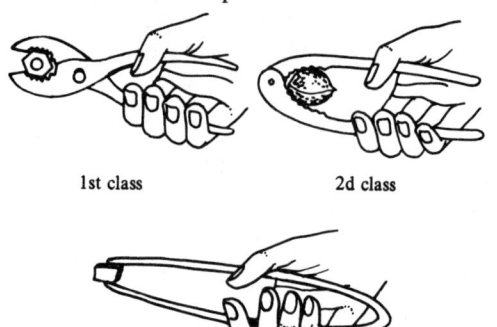

1st class   2d class

3d class

Light rays A convenient means of dealing with light in optical systems. A light ray is drawn in such a way that its direction at any point indicates the direction of travel of the light waves. The density of the light rays indicates the brightness of the light. The light ray can be thought of as the field line of the Poynting vector. *See* **Poynting vector**.

A basic property of light rays is that they are straight, unless bent by either reflection or refraction. Light rays are a useful invention as long as diffraction effects do not enter the picture. In other words, the ray model of light cannot be used unless objects or slits are substantially larger than the wavelength of the light.

Light waves Electromagnetic waves of those frequencies that are visible to the human eye. The color seen depends basically on the wavelength of the waves. The wavelengths range from 4.5×10^{-7} m (violet) to 7.0×10^{-7} m (red). *See* **Electromagnetic spectrum**.

Linear acceleration The rate of increase or decrease in the speed of an object. In the simplest case, an object starts at rest and accelerates with acceleration a for time t while traveling a distance s and reaching a speed v. A set of three equations can be used to describe this motion:

$$a = \frac{v}{t}$$

$$s = \tfrac{1}{2}at^2$$

$$v = \sqrt{2as}$$

Example 1

How fast is a motorcycle going if it accelerates uniformly from rest at 4.5 m/s^2 while traveling 40 m?

$$v = \sqrt{2as} = \sqrt{2(4.5 \text{ m/s}^2)(40 \text{ m})} = 19.0 \text{ m/s}$$

The same equations can be used if the object is coming to rest with uniform acceleration.

Example 2

What is the acceleration of a car that applies its brakes and comes to rest with uniform acceleration while traveling 75 m in 6.0 s?

$$s = \tfrac{1}{2}at^2$$

$$75 \text{ m} = \tfrac{1}{2}a(6.0 \text{ s})^2$$

$$a = 4.2 \text{ m/s}^2$$

In this case, it would be appropriate to use a negative sign for the acceleration to show that it is in the opposite direction from the velocity.

Line of force *See* **Magnetic field**.

Longitudinal wave A wave in which the vibrations of the medium are parallel to the direction of travel of the wave. A longitudinal wave consists of a series of compressions and rarefactions traveling outward from the source. The figure shows a longitudinal wave in a spring. As the hand moves back and forth, it alternately compresses and rarefies the spring. The oscillations of the separate gyres of the spring are phased to transmit these compressions and rarefactions.

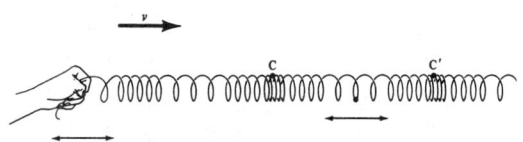

The most familiar longitudinal wave is a sound wave in air. A vibrating object compresses the air near it at its own frequency of vibration and starts the wave moving outward. Another example is an alternating current in a wire. Here the medium is the free electrons in the wire. A generator applies an alternating potential to the electrons, causing them to vibrate and transmit a wave away from the generator. *See* **Sound wave**.

Machine A device for changing the amount of force required to do a given amount of work. For examples, *see* **Inclined plane; Lever; Pulley; Wheel-and-axle**.

The work input to a machine is the product of the effort applied to the machine and the distance through which the effort moves. The work output is the product of the force the machine exerts on its load and the distance through which the load moves. Ideally, the work output is equal to the work input. Usually, the function of the machine is to make it possible to do the required work using a smaller force than would be needed without the machine. This always involves exerting the force over a larger distance, so that the amount of work done on the machine is still equal to the work done by it. Some machines, such as a bicycle, do the converse, using a larger force to increase the distance moved at the output end. *See* **Mechanical advantage**.

In a real machine, friction and other losses always produce some loss in work. Extra effort is needed to compensate for losses, so the work input is always larger than the work output. *See* **Efficiency**.

Magnet *See* **Electromagnet; Ferromagnetism**.

Magnetic field A region of space in which an electric current, properly oriented, will experience a force. A magnetic field will act on a permanent magnet. The direction of the field can be defined as the direction that the field exerts on an N pole. The force on an S pole is in the opposite direction. The result is that a compass needle placed in a magnetic field will oscillate back and forth and come to rest with its N pole pointing in the direction of the field.

Fundamentally, a magnetic field exerts a force only on a moving electric charge. A permanent magnet contains moving electric charges in orbit around the nucleus of every atom. These electrons are the moving charges on which the magnetic field acts.

The magnitude of a magnetic field is defined as the maximum force it exerts per unit current per unit length of wire. The unit field is therefore the newton per ampere-meter, which is given the special name of tesla (T): 1 N/A·m = 1 T. A field of 1 T is very strong, and the more common unit of measure is the millitesla (mT).

The figure shows a magnetic field B in which a current I flows. The field is represented by field lines. The force on the current is a maximum when the current is perpendicular to the field. There is no force if the current is parallel or antiparallel to the field. The force is perpendicular to both the current and the field. The direction of the force can be found by pointing the fingers of the right hand in the direction of the field, with the thumb indicating the direction of the current. The palm then shows the direction of the force.

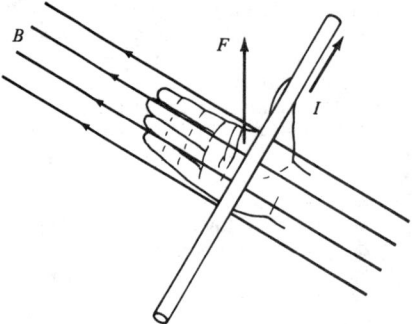

When the current is perpendicular to the field, the magnitude of the force is $F = BIl$, where l is the length of the current in the field and I is the current.

Example

How much force is exerted by a field of 25 mT on a wire 30 cm long carrying 12 A of current perpendicular to the field?

$$F = BIl = (25 \times 10^{-3} \text{ T})(0.30 \text{ m})(12 \text{ A})$$

$$= 0.090 \text{ N}$$

Every electric current is surrounded by a magnetic field. The compasses shown in the next figure, placed near the current, show that the direction of the field is tangential: that is, the field at any point is perpendicular to a line drawn from the current to the point. To find the direction of the field, point the right thumb in the direction of the current, and wrap the fingers around the wire. The fingers will point in the direction of the field. To see how currents can be used to make stronger fields, *see* **Solenoid**.

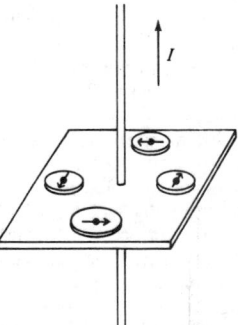

Magnetic field lines Lines drawn to help in visualizing the properties of a magnetic field. They are drawn in such a way that the field is tangent to the line at every point, and the lines are closest together wherever the field is strongest.

The figure shows the field around the current I, plotted as field lines. The lines form circles centered on the current. They show an important property of magnetic field lines: they never terminate, but always form closed loops because there are no isolated magnetic poles.

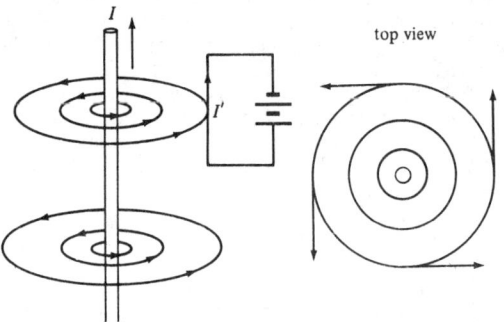

top view

The field around a bar magnet, and the identical field around a solenoid are shown in the figure on page 20–13. The lines are concentrated at the poles, where the field is strongest. They come out of the N pole and enter the S pole, and they are continuous through the center of the solenoid or the bar magnet.

Magnetic force The force between electric currents. Parallel currents attract; antiparallel currents repel each other. There is no force when the currents are perpendicular to each other. The force per unit length of parallel or antiparallel currents (F/l) is given by

$$\frac{F}{l} = \frac{2k'I_1 I_2}{r}$$

where the I are the two currents, r is the distance between them, and k' is the magnetic constant of free space, equal to exactly 10^{-7} N/A^2. (*See* **Ampere**.)

This formula represents an action-at-a-distance formulation. It is often more meaningful and more convenient to express the force differently using the language of magnetic fields. In this formulation, a current produces a magnetic field which then exerts a force on another current. *See* **Magnetic field**.

Magnetism of earth The earth is surrounded by a magnetic field similar to that of a bar magnet, as shown in the figure. The field is strongest and vertical at a point in northern Canada called the magnetic

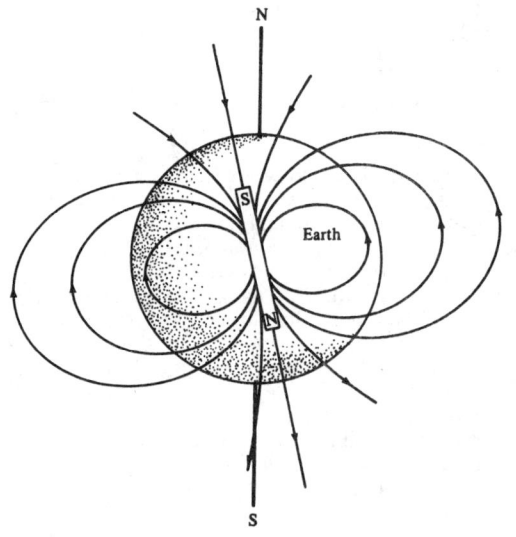

north pole. Since the field lines enter the earth here, the north magnetic pole is an S pole. At the equator, the earth's field is approximately horizontal. The source of the field is convection currents in charged material inside the earth, but the details are poorly understood.

Mass Roughly, the quantity of matter in anything. In classical physics, mass has two distinct definitions:

Gravitational mass is the property of an object that determines its weight in a gravitational field. Weight is the product of gravitational mass and gravitational field. This is the property that is used to provide an operational definition of mass. Two masses are identical, by definition, if when they are put on opposit pans of an equal-arm balance, the balance is level.

Inertial mass (or just *inertia*) is the property by which an object resists changes in its velocity. It is symbolized by m in the law of motion, $F = ma$. In the absence of a gravitational field, as in an orbiting space craft, only this property can be used to measure mass.

The identity of these two definitions of mass is shown by the empirical observation that all objects in free fall have the same acceleration. In this condition, the only force acting is gravity, and that is the weight of the object; therefore $w = F$. As always, the weight in a gravitational field is $w = m_{gravitational}g$. Since the acceleration of an object in free fall depends only on the gravitational field, it follows that the inertial mass is universally proportional to the gravitational mass. For that reason, both kinds of mass can be expressed in the same units.

Classical physics provided no explanation for this identity of the two forms of mass. The general theory of relativity does. *See* **Equivalence principle**.

Mass is a conserved quantity; the total mass never changes in any chemical or physical interaction. However, in one interpretation, mass increases as an object approaches the speed of light and all forms of energy have mass. *See* **Special relativity**; **Mass-energy**.

Mass deficit The difference between the mass of a nucleus and the sum of the masses of its separate nucleons. Mass deficit corresponds to the binding energy according to the formula $E = mc^2$. When nucleons combine to form a nucleus, binding energy must be released.

Example

What is the binding energy of the helium nucleus?

2 protons: $2 \times 1.6724 \times 10^{-27}$ kg	=	3.3448×10^{-27} kg
+ 2 neutrons: $2 \times 1.6748 \times 10^{-27}$ kg	=	3.3496×10^{-27} kg
=		6.6944×10^{-27} kg
− mass of helium nucleus		6.6438×10^{-27} kg
= mass deficit		0.0506×10^{-27} kg

$\times (3.0 \times 10^8$ m/s$)^2$ = binding energy = 4.6×20^{-12} J

or

$+1.60 \times 10^{-19}$J/ev gives 2.9×10^7 ev

This is the amount of energy released every time two protons and two neutrons combine to form a helium nucleus. This reaction is the source of the energy of the sun. The energy of chemical reactions is

typically a few electron volts per molecule, but this nuclear reaction produces millions of electron volts. *See* **Nuclear energy**.

Mass-energy Classical chemistry developed the law of conservation of mass, which states that in an isolated system, the total amount of mass does not change. Classical physics produced the law of conservation of energy. Relativity theory has revealed that these two laws are actually two aspects of the same law, the conservation of mass-energy.

As work is done on an object, its energy, by definition, increases. A force producing acceleration increases kinetic energy. However, according to special relativity, the speed of light is an absolute limit on speed. As an object approaches the speed of light, it takes larger and larger forces to produce any increase in speed. As the speed of light is approached, the applied force can no longer produce a proportional increase in speed. Instead, it increases the mass. Therefore, mass must be a form of energy.

The theory supplies an equation for calculating the energy equivalent of any quantity of mass:

$$E = mc^2$$

when m is mass, c is the speed of light, and E is the energy equivalent of the mass. A small amount of mass corresponds to an enormous amount of energy. Consider a grain of sugar, which might have a mass of a milligram:

$$E = (10^{-6}\text{kg})(3.0 \times 10^8 \text{ m/s})^2 = 9 \times 10^{10} \text{ J}$$

Conversely, what is the mass increase of a 3000 kg jet plane going 600 miles an hour? The speed is 270 m/s, so

$$E = \frac{mv^2}{2} = \frac{(3000 \text{ kg})(270 \text{ m/s})^2}{2} = 1.1 \times 10^8 \text{ J}$$

To get the corresponding mass,

$$m = \frac{E}{c^2} = \frac{1.1 \times 10^8 \text{ J}}{(3.0 \times 10^8 \text{ m/s})^2} = 1.2 \times 10^{-9} \text{ kg}$$

Surely there is no way to detect that extra microgram.

When elements combine to form compounds, energy is released. Since all energy has mass, the mass of the compound should be less than the mass of the elements that make it up. Chemists have never found this difference because it is too small to detect. In nuclear reactions, the picture is different. The binding energy of the nucleus is extremely large, so the loss of mass is detectable. *See* **Mass deficit**.

Mass spectrometer A device for using a magnetic field to measure the mass of charged particles. The principle, first used to determine the mass of the electron, is illustrated in the figure. An electron beam is accelerated in an electron gun by using a positive potential V to attract the electrons. They acquire a kinetic energy equal to eV, where e is the electronic charge. They pass through a hole into a magnetic field B. Since the particles are in motion, the field exerts a force on them equal to Bev where v is their velocity. The force is perpendicular to the velocity, making the electrons travel in a circular path. Since the force is centripetal, it must be equal to mv^2/r, where m is the electron's mass and r is the radius of the circle.

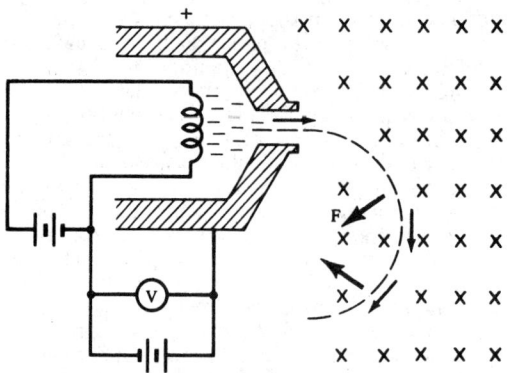

Since Bev is a centripetal force,

$$Bev = \frac{mv^2}{r} \quad \text{so} \quad v = \frac{Ber}{m}$$

Also, the kinetic energy of the electrons, unaffected by the magnetic field, is eV, so

$$eV = \frac{mv^2}{2}$$

Substituting the expression for v found above gives

$$eV = \frac{mB^2e^2r^2}{2m^2} \quad \text{so} \quad m = \frac{B^2er^2}{2V}$$

Since B, e, and V are known, the mass of the electrons can be found by measuring the radius of the circle in which they travel.

The principle is now used in the commercial mass spectrometer, which measures the number of particles of given mass in any mixture. The material is gasified and ionized by a hot filament. The ions have a single positive charge because each gives up an electron. They are accelerated by a negative potential and pass into a magnetic field. There they travel in a half-circle. The mass of each particle determines the diameter of the circle in which it travels, so they form separate beams according to mass. Each beam is a current because the particles are charged. The currents are measured and plotted on a graph according to the diameter of the half-circle in which they have traveled.

Matter wave   A stream of particles possessing wave properties. According to the duality principle (*see* **Quantum theory**), wave and particle are two complementary ways of describing the same set of phenomena.

A moving particle has a wavelength. To find out what it is, consider the case of a photon, which is just another kind of particle. The photon, has no rest mass since it is never at rest. However, it is affected by a gravitational field, so it has gravitational mass. Also, it has momentum and can exert a force, so it has inertial mass. It has only relativistic mass, related to its energy by the equation $E = mc^2$. The photon theory tells us that its energy is hf. Therefore, $hf = mc^2$. The momentum is mass times velocity, so

$$mc = \frac{hf}{c}$$

Since c/f is the wavelength, the equation becomes

$$mc = \frac{h}{\lambda}$$

For a particle with rest mass, such as an electron, the momentum is mv. Therefore the equation for the wavelength of an electron beam becomes

$$\lambda = \frac{h}{mv}$$

The theory that matter has wave properties was justified with the discovery of an interference phenomenon produced by an electron beam. When the beam was reflected from a crystal, which acted as a diffraction grating, it formed a complete set of interference fringes. Since interference is strictly a wave property, the electron beam must be behaving like a wave. Measurement of the diffraction angles gave the wavelength, which agreed with the equation above.

The matter wave theory provided a new explanation for the energy levels in the hydrogen atom (*see* **Bohr model**). The wave model conceives of the electrons orbiting the nucleus to form standing waves. The correct interference relationships are possible only if the circumference of the orbit is a whole number of wavelengths. This assumption gives the correct values for the size of the hydrogen atom and the energy levels. More complex atoms demand a more advanced theory.

The wave property of an electron beam has turned out to be of great practical value. The resolving power of a microscope is limited by the wavelength of the light. Using visible light, this is around 5 x 10^{-7} m. Consider the wavelength of an electron beam accelerated through a potential difference of 60 V. Each electron reaches a kinetic energy

$$\frac{mv^2}{2} = qV$$

Multiplying both sides of the equation by $2m$ gives

$$m^2r^2 = 2qVm$$

Taking the square root of both sides of the equation gives the following expression for momentum:

$$mv = \sqrt{2qVm}$$

$$= \sqrt{2(1.60 \times 10^{-19}\,C)(60\,J/C)(9.1 \times 10^{-31}\,kg)}$$

$$= 4.2 \times 10^{-24}\ kg{\cdot}m/s$$

Now find the wavelength:

$$\lambda = \frac{h}{mv} = \frac{6.6 \times 10^{-34}\ J{\cdot}s}{4.2 \times 10^{-24}\ kg{\cdot}m/s} = 1.6 \times 10^{-10}\ m$$

which is 3000 times smaller than the wavelength of light. A microscope using an electron beam can thus provide a much more detailed look at tiny objects. Since the beam is charged, it can be focused and controlled by magnetic fields. The electron microscope has revolutionized the study of the biology of living cells.

Mechanical advantage   The ratio of force output to force input in a machine. In common usage, the term usually refers to the ideal case, in which there is no loss of work in the operation of the machine itself.

Consider the problem of lifting a 1200 N engine a distance of 3.0 m. The work needed to do the job is (3.0 m)(1200 N) = 3600 J. The load is very heavy, and the job can be made feasible by attaching the load to a pulley with a mechanical advantage of 4. Then the effort, or input force, is 1200 N/4 = 300 N. However, it will be necessary to pull the rope of the pulley through a distance of 12.0 m, not just 3.0 m. The work input is then (12.0 m)(300 N) = 3600 J, the same as the work output.

The worker using the pulley will actually have to pull somewhat harder than 300 N to allow for the friction in the pulley and the weight of the pulley itself. This has no effect on the ideal mechanical advantage, which is still 4. In all cases, the ideal mechanical advantage can be found as the ratio of the input distance to the output distance. In the case cited, it is (12.0 m)/(3 .0 m) = 4. *See* **Efficiency**.

Meter (1) A measuring instrument, usually reading out on a dial or a digital display. *See*, for example, **Galvanometer**. (2) The SI unit of length, abbreviated as **m**. It is a base unit, now defined as the distance light travels in a specified time interval.

Microwave *See* **Electromagnetic spectrum**.

Millikan's oil drop experiment In 1909, Robert Millikan measured the extremely tiny charge on an electron. The apparatus consisted of a pair of horizontal metal plates with an adjustable potential difference between them. Droplets of oil were sprayed into the space between the plates through a small hole in the upper plate. Millikan watched a single droplet through a microscope. By measuring its rate of fall in air, he could determine its weight. Then he turned on the potential difference and adjusted it until thc droplet stood still. In that condition, its weight was equal to the upward electric force on it. This force is qV/d, where q is the charge, V is the potential difference between the plates, and d is the plate separation. *See* **Electric field**.

Using this technique, Millikan measured the charge on thousands of droplets. He found it always to be equal, within experimental error, to some integral multiple of 1.60×10^{-19}C. He concluded that this is the charge on a single electron.

Mole (Mol) The SI basic unit of amount of substance, defined as the number of particles in 0.012 kg of carbon 12. The number is called Avogadro's number and is approximately 6.024×10^{23}. This number defines the number of atomic mass units, or daltons, in a gram.

Molecule The smallest part of a substance (however, *see* **Ionic substance**). The composition of a molecule is given as a formula expressing the number and kind of atoms in each molecule. For example, oxygen gas has the formula O_2 indicating that each molecule contains two atoms of oxygen. The chemical formula for ethane is C_2H_6, indicating that each molecule is composed of two atoms of carbon and six atoms of hydrogen.

Many of the properties of materials are explained in terms of the interactions of molecules with each other or with their surroundings. For discussion of the properties of gases, *see* **Kinetic theory of gases**.

The electromagnetic attraction between molecules constitutes the force that holds solids in a crystalline structure, giving them a definite shape. In liquids, attraction prevents the free escape of molecules, establishing an upper surface. *See* **Latent heat**.

Momentum The product of mass and velocity. It is a conserved vector quantity. Consider the law of inertia in a slightly different form:

$$\mathbf{F} = m\mathbf{a} = \frac{m\Delta\mathbf{v}}{\Delta t} \qquad \text{or} \qquad \mathbf{F}\Delta t = \Delta m\mathbf{v}$$

$\mathbf{F}\Delta t$, the product of a force and the time during which it acts, is called impulse, and $m\mathbf{v}$ is momentum. The equation says that the amount that the momentum of an object changes is equal to the impulse applied to it.

This principle makes it possible to solve complex problems by considering only the initial and final states, without dealing with all the changes between them.

Example 1

A rocket in outer space consists of a 220 kg payload and 80 kg of fuel. It is going 160 m/s. Some fuel is burned for 12s, providing a thrust of 340N, and the remaining fuel burns for 16s and gives a thrust of 200 N. How fast is the payload then traveling?

This is an extremely complex problem that can be solved simply by making use of the impulse and momentum relationship:

Initial momentum = (300 kg)(160 m/s) = 48,000 kg·m/s

$\quad$ + impulse = (340 N)(12 s)

$\qquad\qquad$ + (200 N)(16 s) $\qquad$ = 7280 N·s

$\quad$ = Final momentum $\qquad\qquad$ = 55,280 kg·m/s

(Note that kg·m/s = N·s.)

55,280 kg·m/s = (220 kg)v_{final}

and

v_{final} = 251 m/s

Since impulse is equal to the change in momentum, it follows that if no impulse is applied to any system, the total momentum of the system will not change. This rule is called the law of conservation of momentum. The law is extremely useful in dealing with systems in which only the initial and final states need be considered.

Example 2

A 45 kg girl on roller skates is going 3.0 m/s and collides with a 62 kg boy coming toward her at 4.8 m/s. After the collision, they are traveling together. How fast are they traveling?

The total momentum before the impact must equal the total momentum afterward:

(45 kg)(3.0 m/s) + (62 kg)(–4.8 m/s)

$\quad$ = (107 kg)v_{final}

(If the girl's direction is positive, the boy's must be negative.)

v_{final} = –1 .5 m/s

The negative sign indicates that they are traveling together in the boy's original direction. Momentum is a vector quantity, and in cases in which the action is not along a single line, vector mathematics must be used.

Motor A device for converting electric energy into mechanical energy using the force a magnetic field exerts on a current. The principle of the electric motor is illustrated in the figure. The current in the loop flows in on one side of the loop and back on the other. The result is that the magnetic field exerts forces on the current in opposite directions on the two sides of the loop. This produces a torque, which makes the loop turn. When it has gone halfway around, the commutator switches the current to the opposite side of the loop. In this way, the current in the loop is kept constantly in the proper direction to keep the loop turning.

In a real motor, there are a number of loops, all wound around an iron core. The assembly is called an armature. A commutator split into many segments supplies current to whichever loop is in the

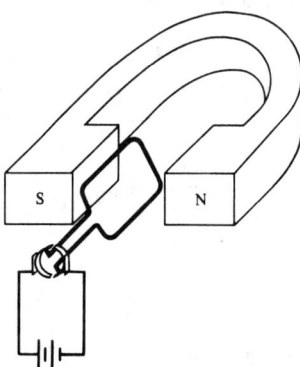

best position at any moment. The magnet, in most cases, is an electromagnet.

Neutrino A tiny particle with no charge, emitted from radioactive nuclei during beta decay, and in other processes. Whether neutrinos have any rest mass is still under debate. They are produced in enormous quantities in the nuclear reactions in stars and may constitute a substantial part of the mass of the universe. Neutrinos are extremely difficult to detect because they do not interact strongly with matter. Most of the neutrinos that strike the earth pass right through it unaltered. Nevertheless, several experiments have managed to trap and identify neutrinos, and there is no doubt of their existence. It now appears that there are three kinds of neutrinos.

Neutron A fundamental particle having a little more mass than a proton and no electric charge. Neutrons are components of all atomic nuclei except the hydrogen nucleus. The neutron is stable inside the nucleus, but when free, it decays with a half-life of 11 minutes to form a proton and an electron.

The mass of an isotope varies only according to the number of neutrons in the nucleus. *See* **Isotope**; **Nucleus**; **Strong nuclear force**. In a nuclear reactor, the flow of neutrons keeps the reaction going; *see* **Nuclear energy**.

Newton *See* **Force**.

Newton's laws The laws of motion developed by Isaac Newton in the seventeenth century. These laws are the foundation of the science of physics. They incorporate all the known rules of planetary motion, as well as the motion of objects on earth. All these motions, as well as the tides, the trajectories of cannonballs, the swinging of a pendulum, and many

other phenomena, are explained on the basis of just two general principles: *inertia* and *gravitation*.

Inertia is really a single idea but is usually expressed in three parts known as the laws of motion: (1) A body in motion will continue in motion at constant speed in a straight line unless acted on by an outside force. (2) If a force does act, the acceleration of the object is directly proportional to the force and inversely proportional to its mass. (3) For every force exerted on an object, it exerts a force equal in magnitude and opposite in direction on another object. *See also* **Inertia**.

Owing to *gravitation*, all objects in the universe attract each other. *See* **Gravitational force**.

Nodal line A line along which interference is destructive. *See* **Two-point interference**.

Node A point of destructive interference. *See* **Standing wave**.

Normal A line drawn perpendicular to a surface; *see* **Reflection**; **Refraction**.

Nuclear bomb An explosive device deriving its energy from a chain reaction of fission of large nuclei. The fuel may be uranium-235, but is now most often plutonium-239. *See* **Nuclear fission**; **Plutonium**.

Any stray neutron can start a chain reaction in plutonium-239 or uranium-235. However, if the mass of fuel is small, the chain reaction will stop because too many neutrons escape from the surface before striking another plutonium nucleus. In a bomb, the plutonium is kept in a loose, spongy mass, which allows many neutrons to escape. The bomb is detonated by an implosion: a charge of an explosive on all sides of the plutonium squeezes the fuel into a compact mass. The chain reaction follows immediately. To make the bomb effective, the mass of plutonium must be contained in a strong, solid shell for a long enough time to allow the chain reaction to develop.

The energy produced by a nuclear bomb is expressed in terms of the equivalent explosive power of trinitrotoluene (TNT). A small bomb produces the equivalent of 100,000 tons of TNT, and larger ones are measured in megatons. The largest, the hydrogen bombs, use the fission bomb to provide the high temperature needed for a fusion reaction. *See* **Nuclear fusion**.

Nuclear energy Energy obtained by nuclear transformations that increase the nuclear binding energy. *See* **Mass deficit**; **Nuclear fission**; **Nuclear fusion**; **Nuclear reactor**; **Nucleus**.

Nuclear fission The process by which large nuclei are split into smaller ones, with a release of energy. The principle is that the nuclei most tightly bound are those of medium size. In large nuclei, the large number of protons, all repelling each other, makes the binding energy per particle small. Splitting the nucleus into smaller, more tightly bound nuclei thus releases considerable binding energy.

Many kinds of large nuclei can be made unstable by adding a neutron. For example, a slow neutron added to uranium-235 may produce this reaction:

$$^{235}_{92}\text{U} + ^{1}_{0}\text{n} \rightarrow ^{141}_{56}\text{Ba} + ^{92}_{36}\text{Kr} + 3^{1}_{0}\text{n}$$

Uranium-235 may undergo fission in other ways as well. These reactions are the basis for nuclear reactors. Uranium-235 is known as a fissionable material because, when it splits, it produces two or three neutrons per fission. Each of these, when slowed down, can enter another nucleus and cause it to split. In a short fraction of a second, there is an enormous flux of neutrons and many fissions are going on at once. This is called a chain reaction. It is the basis on which all atomic bombs and nuclear energy installations depend. *See* **Nuclear bomb**; **Nuclear reactor**.

Nuclear fusion The process of combining small nuclei to form larger ones. The larger nuclei have more binding energy per particle, so a great deal of energy can be converted into other forms.

For example, lithium deuteride is a salt of lithium and deuterium (hydrogen-2). If this salt is exposed to an atomic bomb explosion, neutrons from the explosion react with the lithium to produce helium and tritium (hydrogen-3):

$$_3^6\text{Li} + _0^1\text{n} \rightarrow _2^4\text{He} + _1^3\text{H}$$

The high temperature, millions of kelvins, sets the atoms in such violent vibration that the deuterium and tritium nuclei are often brought into the range of the strong nuclear force. They will fuse and produce a helium nucleus and a neutron:

$$_1^3\text{H} + _1^2\text{H} \rightarrow _2^4\text{He} + _0^1\text{n}$$

The helium nucleus has a large mass deficit, so enormous amounts of energy are released, in the form of heat and blast.

So far, large-scale nuclear fusion has been achieved only in bombs. In many laboratories, strong efforts are under way to produce nuclear fusion reactions under controlled conditions. The greatest problem is achieving the enormous temperatures while keeping the fuel confined. If this problem can be solved, a limitless supply of safe, nonpolluting energy will be available.

Nuclear reactor An installation that produces energy from a chain reaction of controlled fission of uranium-235. (*See* **Nuclear fission**; **Chain reaction**.) There are a number of different designs of nuclear reactors. The reactor in nuclear power plants in the United States uses metallic uranium as a fuel and graphite as a moderator.

The fuel is long rods of uranium, enriched to 3% $_{92}^{235}\text{U}$. Natural uranium is $_{92}^{238}\text{U}$, with only 0.7% $_{92}^{235}\text{U}$ mixed in. Natural uranium can be used, but $_{92}^{238}\text{U}$ absorbs neutrons. If natural uranium is used as a fuel, the reactor must be very large and carefully designed to reduce the loss of neutrons from the surface and to other parts. By using enriched uranium, a greater loss of neutrons to other causes can be tolerated.

To enrich natural uranium, $_{92}^{235}\text{U}$ must be separated from $_{92}^{238}\text{U}$. This cannot be done chemically since all isotopes of uranium have the same chemical properties. The separation is done by processing the uranium in the form of uranium hexafluoride, a gas. The gas is allowed to diffuse through a porous barrier. The smaller molecules go through a little faster, so the uranium on the other side of the barrier is slightly enriched. The process is repeated until the desired degree of enrichment is achieved.

In the reactor the fuel rods are inserted into a large block of graphite, the reactor core. The graphite is the moderator. When neutrons are released from the

fission of a nucleus, they are going too fast to enter another nucleus. The moderator slows them down.

Cadmium rods, inserted into the reactor core, control the rate of the reaction. Cadmium absorbs neutrons. The reactor can be shut off instantly by dropping the cadmium rods all the way into the core.

Energy is removed from the reactor core in the form of heat. Pipes carry water into the core. It emerges as superheated steam, which is fed into an ordinary steam turbine to spin the generators.

Nuclear fuel is far less expensive than coal or oil. The fuel rods last about a year before they must be replaced. When the first nuclear chain reactions were made, it was thought that the price of electric energy would drop to practically nothing. Experience has shown that this is not so. The cost of safety devices and disposal of nuclear waste has driven the price up to that of electricity produced by conventional means.

Nucleon One of the particles, neutrons and protons, that make up the nucleus of an atom.

Nucleus The central part of an atom, containing nearly all its mass. The nucleus consists of two kinds of particles strongly bound to each other: protons and neutrons. The nucleus always has a positive charge, equal to the number of protons in it. The number of protons in the nucleus is the atomic number of the nucleus, which defines the element of which the atom is a sample. The total number of nucleons (protons and neutrons) defines the atomic mass number of the nucleus. This will be different for different isotopes of the same element.

The composition of a nucleus is represented symbolically by one or two letters that identify the element, a subscript giving the atomic number of that element, and a superscript giving the atomic mass number. Thus, $_{17}^{35}\text{Cl}$ stands for the isotope of chlorine having seventeen protons (like all chlorine nuclei) and eighteen neutrons.

Since the protons are positively charged, they repel each other. The nucleus is held together by a special, extremely strong force of attraction. (*See* **Strong nuclear force**.) The nucleus holds together because the attraction between all nucleons is strong enough to counteract the repulsion between protons.

Large nuclei can hold together only because they contain many more neutrons than protons. All elements of atomic number greater than 82, as well as some isotopes of smaller elements, are unstable. They spontaneously break down, emitting high-energy fragments. *See* **Radioactivity**.

Because the strong nuclear force is so large, the binding energy of a nucleus is extremely great. The result is that the mass of a nucleus is measurably smaller than the masses of its separate particles (*see* **Mass deficit**). Nuclear reactions, including radioactive decay, can take place if the products are more strongly bound than the reactants. The excess binding energy is released as kinetic and electromagnetic energy. *See* **Nuclear fission**; **Nuclear fusion**, **Radioactivity**.

 **Ohm** The SI unit of electrical resistance, represented by the Greek letter capital omega (Ω). It is defined as the resistance of a conductor in which a potential difference of 1 V produces a current of 1 A. This definition implies that the po-

tential difference across any conductor (in volts) is equal to the product of its resistance (in ohms) and the current in the conductor (in amperes).

Ohm's law   The rule that, in a metallic conductor at constant temperature, the current is proportional to the potential difference between the ends. *See* **Resistance**.

Orbit   The path taken by a particle moving through a field. Most commonly, it is the path of a planet around the sun, or a satellite around the earth, held in place by gravitational attraction. A planet or satellite in orbit is in free fall. It is accelerated toward its primary by the force of gravity. Its centripetal acceleration is the acceleration due to gravity at its altitude. The shape of the orbit, in general, is an ellipse. If the speed is precisely right, the ellipse becomes a circle. If the speed is greater than needed for a circular orbit by a factor of the square root of 2, the curve opens up into a hyperbola and the satellite escapes.

At any given altitude, only one velocity will produce a circular orbit.

Example

How fast must an artificial satellite be made to travel in order to go into circular orbit at an altitude of 5500 km?

First, find the acceleration due to gravity at that altitude (*see* **Gravitational field**). Since the acceleration due to gravity is inversely proportional to the distance from the center of the earth,

$$gr^2 = g_0 r_0^2$$

$$g(5500 \text{ km} + 6400 \text{ km})^2 = (9.8 \text{ m/s}^2)(6400 \text{ km})^2$$

$$g = (9.8 \text{ m/s}^2)\left(\frac{64}{119}\right)^2$$

$$= 2.8 \text{ m/s}^2$$

Since the acceleration is centripetal,

$$g = \frac{v^2}{r} \quad \text{and} \quad v = \sqrt{gr}$$

Therefore,

$$v = \sqrt{(2.8 \text{ m/s}^2)(11.9 \times 10^6 \text{ m})} = 5800 \text{ m/s}$$

There is one orbit for artificial satellites that is much in demand and is becoming crowded. This is the stationary orbit, in which a satellite remains above the equator in the same position relative to the earth. The period of the orbit is 24 hours, so that it just keeps pace with the earth's rotation. This is the orbit for relay satellites. A TV receiving antenna can remain pointing at such a satellite without moving. To find the altitude of the stationary orbit, note that its acceleration must be

$$g = \frac{g_0 r_0^2}{r^2}$$

and its acceleration, where T is its period, is

$$a = \frac{4\pi^2 r}{T^2}$$

Equating these two values of acceleration and solving for r gives

$$r = \left(\frac{g_0 r_0^2 T^2}{4\pi^2}\right)^{1/3}$$

Substituting $g_0 = 9.8 \text{ m/s}^2$, $r_0 = 6.4 \times 10^6$ m, and $T = 86,400$ s gives $r = 4.2 \times 10^7$ m which is an altitude of 36,000 km above the surface.

For information about the laws of the orbits of the planets, *see* **Kepler's laws**, Earth and Space Science section, page 5-22.

Oscilloscope   *See* **Cathode ray**.

Parallel circuit   An electric circuit in which the current branches into two or more different lines. The figure shows a circuit of this sort. With the switches open, there is no current because there is no complete circuit. Since all points on the upper wire are connected to the positive terminal of the battery and all points on the lower wire to the negative terminal, there will be a potential difference of 60V across each switch.

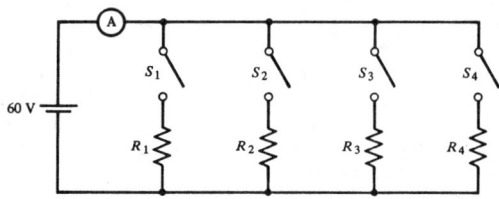

Closing switch S_1 makes a complete circuit. The 60 V potential difference is now applied to the resistor R_1, and the current will flow through the resistor. The amount of current, from Ohm's law, is 60 V/R_1. (*See* **Resistance**.)

If switch S_2 is now closed, there is a second complete circuit. The current in R_2 is 60 V/R_2. The total current coming out of the battery is the sum of the currents in the two resistors.

Closing any switch applies the same 60 V potential difference to the resistor. The rule for potential differences in a parallel circuit, then, is that all elements have the same potential difference as the source:

$$V_{\text{total}} = V_1 = V_2 = V_3 = \cdots$$

Each branch has its own current, depending on its resistance. The total current is the sum of all the separate currents:

$$I_{\text{total}} = I_1 + I_2 + I_3 + \cdots$$

Since in each case $I = V/R$,

$$\frac{V_{\text{total}}}{R_{\text{total}}} = \frac{V_1}{R_1} + \frac{V_2}{R_2} + \frac{V_3}{R_3} + \cdots$$

and since all the V are the same,

$$\frac{1}{R_{\text{total}}} = \frac{1}{R_1} + \frac{1}{R_2} + \frac{1}{R_3} + \cdots$$

Note that every time a switch is closed, the current increases. This means that the total resistance is always less than the smallest of the individual resistances.

Example

Three resistors, of 12, 20, and 24 Ω, are connected in parallel to a 24 V battery. Find (1) the total current and (2) the total resistance.

The total current is the sum of the separate currents, each of which is V/R:

$$I_1 = \frac{24\ V}{12\ \Omega} = 2.0\ A$$

$$I_2 = \frac{24\ V}{20\ \Omega} = 1.2\ A$$

$$I_3 = \frac{24\ V}{24\ \Omega} = 1.0\ A$$

So the total current is 4.2 A. Then the total resistance is

$$R = \frac{V}{I} = \frac{24\ V}{4.2\ A} = 5.7\ \Omega$$

Another way to find the total resistance is the following:

$$\frac{1}{R_{total}} = \frac{1}{12\ \Omega} + \frac{1}{20\ \Omega} + \frac{1}{24\ \Omega}$$

$$= \frac{10 + 6 + 5}{120\ \Omega}$$

$$R_{total} = \frac{120\ \Omega}{21} = 5.7\ \Omega$$

Partial pressure   *See* Earth and Space Science section, page 5-27.

Particle detector   A device for recording the presence or passage of a charged subatomic particle. *See* **Geiger counter**; **Spark chamber**; **Bubble chamber**.

Pendulum   A concentrated mass suspended at the end of a low-mass string and set to swinging back and forth. If the dimensions of the bob are small, the string is long, and the angle through which the pendulum swings is small, the period of oscillation of the pendulum, T, is given by

$$T = 2\pi \sqrt{\frac{l}{g}}$$

where l is the length of the string and g is the acceleration due to gravity. Note that the mass of the bob does not matter. The pendulum is used to make very sensitive measurements of the gravitational field.

Period   The duration of a single cycle of any repetitive process. Period is the reciprocal of frequency.

Phase   A time relationship between two oscillatory motions. If two pendulums are swinging in such a way that their motions are always parallel, they are said to be in phase. If one swings *to* while the other is going *fro*, they are out of phase.

The phase relationship is usually expressed as a fraction of a cycle, given in degrees. For example, if one pendulum lags behind the other by just 1/4 of a cycle, it is said to be 90° out of phase.

Here is an example of the use of the concept of phase: Two pendulums are both swinging with a period of 1.6 s. One of them reaches its peak just 0.2 s behind the other. What is the phase difference? The phase difference is a fraction of a cycle, expressed as a fraction of 360°:

$$\text{phase angle} = \left(\frac{0.2\ s}{1.6\ s}\right) 360° = 45°$$

In a wave, all parts of the medium are oscillating. The wave travels because the successive points in the medium are out of phase with each other. For details, *see* **Wave**; **Standing wave**.

Phases of matter   *See* Earth and Space Science section, page 5-28.

Photoelectric effect   The emission of electrons from a metal as a consequence of illumination by visible or ultraviolet light. Albert Einstein was awarded the Nobel Prize for his discovery of the laws governing photoelectric emission.

The basic rule is that each electron is released from the surface by the energy of a single photon. The energy of the photon must be more than the binding energy of the electron. The excess energy becomes the kinetic energy of the electron.

Since the energy of a photon depends only on its frequency, it is only the frequency of the light that determines whether or not an electron will be emitted. The higher the frequency of the incident light, the greater the energy of the emitted electrons. Making the light brighter will increase the number of electrons emitted, but it will not change their energy.

The figure is a diagram of a circuit in which the photoelectric effect can be studied. Light falls on the metallic surface, which emits electrons. The electrons are collected by a filament at the center of curvature of the metal surface. They flow back to the emitting surface through an ammeter, which measures their rate of flow. To get through the ammeter, however, the electrons must flow through an adjustable battery. They enter the negative terminal of the battery. This means that they must lose energy as they pass through the battery. As the battery is made more negative, the less energetic electrons are unable to get through, and the current diminishes. The current stops altogether when the reverse potential is enough to stop the most energetic electrons. This potential is called the cutoff potential V_{cutoff}.

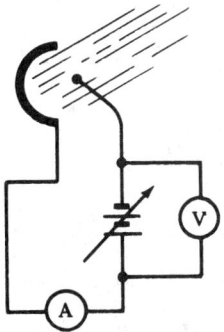

The cutoff potential is a measure of the energy of the most energetic electron emitted from the surface. The energy lost as this electron passes into the battery is eV_{cutoff}, where e is the charge on the electron. This energy must be the amount of energy the electron has as it leaves the surface. It is less than the energy of the photon because the electron is bound. Part of the photon energy is used to release the electron. The binding energy is called the work function of the metal surface. No electron will be emitted unless the photon energy is greater than the metal's work function.

Example

What is the photoelectric work function of a metal if the cutoff potential is 2.6 V when the metal is illuminated by ultraviolet light of wavelength 1.5×10^{-7} m?

First, find the energy of the photons (*see* **Photon**):

$$E_{photon} = hf = \frac{hc}{\lambda}$$

$$= \frac{\left(4.14 \times 10^{-15} \text{ eV·s}\right)\left(3.0 \times 10^{8} \text{ m/s}\right)}{1.5 \times 10^{-7} \text{ m}}$$

$$= 8.3 \text{ eV}$$

Since the most energetic electron was stopped by a reverse potential of 2.6 V, the energy it had when it was free from the surface was

$$eV = (1 \text{ electron charge})(2.6 \text{ V}) = 2.6 \text{ eV}$$

Therefore the energy it lost in leaving the surface, the work function of the metal, is

$$(8.3 \text{eV} - 2.6 \text{eV}) = 5.7 \text{ eV}$$

Photon   A package of energy, a part of the energy of an electromagnetic wave. Every electromagnetic wave is composed of these tiny packages of energy. The amount of energy in each photon depends only on the frequency of the wave, according to this formula

$$E_{photon} = hf$$

where f is the frequency of the wave and h is a universal constant known as Planck's constant.

Example

What is the photon energy of the yellow line in the sodium spectrum?

The wavelength of the line is 5.9×10^{-7}m. First, determine its frequency:

$$f = \frac{c}{\lambda} = \frac{3.0 \times 10^{8} \text{ m/s}}{5.9 \times 10^{-7} \text{ m}} = 5.1 \times 10^{14} \text{ Hz}$$

Then apply the photon equation :

$$E_{photon} = \left(6.62 \times 10^{-34} \text{ J·s}\right)\left(5.1 \times 10^{14} \text{ Hz}\right)$$

$$= 3.4 \times 10^{-19} \text{ J} \quad \text{or} \quad 2.1 \text{ eV}$$

Visible light is produced by energy transitions in the outer electrons of atoms. The energy states are quantized; that is, the electrons must jump from one energy state to another without passing through any intermediate stages. When an electron drops from a higher state to a lower one, it emits a photon that carries away the lost energy. Conversely, an electron can be driven to a higher energy state by absorbing a photon with just the right amount of energy. This is why a colored object absorbs certain frequencies of light and reflects others. If the photon energy is large enough, it can produce ionization, leading to a chemical change (*see* **Bohr model; Planck's constant**).

The photon energies of visible light are of the order of a few electron volts. This is in the range of energies of chemical changes. Single-cell batteries produce potential differences of 1 or 2 V. The photon energy of visible light is enough to produce

chemical change in a green leaf or a photographic film. Each photon ionizes a single molecule. Infrared rays have much lower frequencies, so their photon energies are much smaller (*see* **Electromagnetic waves**). They cannot produce ionization, and the effects of single photons are never seen.

At the other extreme, gamma rays have extremely high frequencies, and their photon energies are in the millions of electron volts. The energy packages are so large that they can be counted separately, by various instruments. Gamma rays are produced by the extremely high energy transitions that take place within atomic nuclei.

Pitch   The subjective sensation of the note of a sound. Pitch is expressed in terms of notes of the scale, designated as letters. Each pitch corresponds to a definite frequency of the sound. Middle C on the piano, for example, is the pitch produced by a sound wave with a frequency of 261.6 Hz.

The note one octave higher than C is designated C'. Its pitch is just twice that of C. Doubling the frequency of any note raises the pitch by one octave.

The piano is tuned in such a way that it can be played in any key. This is accomplished by tuning it in the scale known as the equal-tempered chromatic scale. The frequencies of the twelve notes of this scale, including the black notes, form a geometric series. Each half-tone is higher by a factor of $2^{1/12}$. Repeating this factor twelve times completes the octave.

Planck's constant   The fundamental constant that appears in all calculations in quantum physics. It is equal to 6.63×10^{-34} joule-second, or 4.14×10^{-15} electron volt-second.

Plane mirror   A flat metallic surface that reflects light specularly. (*See* **Reflection**.) The mirror forms a virtual image, as shown in the figure. Some of the rays reflected diffusely from the book are reflected from the mirror and reach the eye. They appear to be diverging from a point behind the mirror, forming a virtual image.

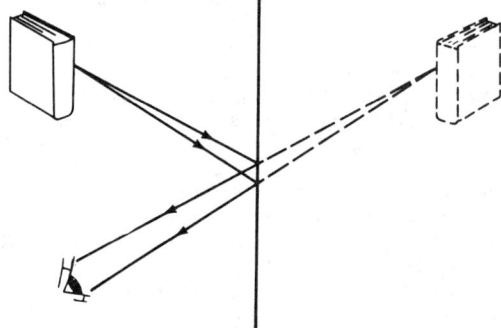

The image is erect, the same size as the object, and the same distance behind the mirror as the object is in front of it. Contrary to popular belief, it is not reversed right to left. The reversal is front to back, since each point on the object is represented by a point on the image at the same distance from the mirror.

Planet   A nonluminous astronomical body in orbit around a star, such as the sun. For the rules governing the motions of the planets in their orbits, *see* **Kepler's laws**, Earth and Space Science section, page 5-22; **Orbit**.

Plutonium   The element of atomic number 94. It is not found in nature but is produced by the bombardment of uranium-238 with fast neutrons. This is the reaction:

$$^{238}_{92}U + ^{1}_{0}n \rightarrow ^{239}_{92}U$$

Uranium-239 undergoes beta decay with a half-life of 23 minutes to produce neptunium-239:

$$^{239}_{92}U \rightarrow ^{239}_{93}Np + ^{0}_{-1}e$$

Another beta decay, half-life 2.3 days, produces plutonium-239:

$$^{239}_{93}Np \rightarrow ^{239}_{94}Pu + ^{0}_{-1}e$$

Plutonium is relatively stable. With a half-life of 24,000 years, it undergoes alpha decay to turn into $^{235}_{92}U$ (*See* **Radioactivity**.)

In a nuclear reactor, the neutron flux bombards the uranium-238. As the reactor functions, it generates plutonium. The plutonium can be separated from the spent fuel rods by chemical means. Plutonium, like uranium-235, is fissionable. When it is bombarded by a slow neutron, it splits and releases two or three neutrons. A reactor can thus produce more fissionable nuclear fuel than it uses.

Plutonium is one of the most dangerous substances in the world. First, it is extremely poisonous. Second, it is the fuel for nuclear bombs. The nuclear industry must keep careful track of every ounce of plutonium produced.

Polarization   The process by which a transverse wave is constrained to oscillate in a single plane. Consider, for example, the electromagnetic wave produced by a vertical radio antenna. The electric component of the wave is strictly vertical; the wave is polarized. On the other hand, the light emitted by a flashlight pointed straight up will have waves with electric components in all possible horizontal directions. Some will be oriented east-west, others north-south, and still others everywhere in between. The wave is not polarized.

An unpolarized light wave can be polarized, as shown in the figure. The wave is passed through a special kind of crystal that has its molecules oriented in such a way as to absorb the horizontal components of the light. The light that passes through the crystal is vertically polarized. Polaroid is a proprietary material made of such crystals aligned and embedded in plastic.

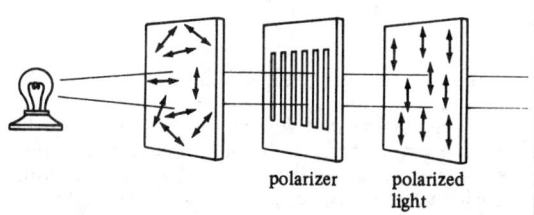

polarizer   polarized light

The human eye cannot detect polarization of light. The next figure shows how polarization can be demonstrated. If polarized light is passed through a Polaroid filter, oriented at right angles to the polar-

ization, none of the light will get through. Rotating the filter through 90° to bring it into the same orientation as the polarizer will allow the light to pass.

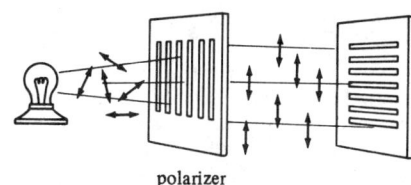

polarizer

Two natural processes polarize the light around us. One is reflection. Light reflected at certain angles from horizontal surfaces will be polarized horizontally when it comes off. Good examples are the glare from the surface of water and the glare from a wet roadway. A filter polarized vertically will eliminate this glare, a fact that finds its use in sunglasses. Photographers use polarizing filters to eliminate surface glare.

The second natural process that polarizes light is scattering from tiny particles. For example, water made cloudy by the addition of a few drops of milk will scatter light. If a light is shone into the liquid from above, the scattered light coming out the sides of the container is polarized horizontally. The blue light of the sky is produced by scattering from dust particles, and it will be found to be polarized if viewed at an angle of 90° from the sun.

Polaroid   A proprietary sheet material that polarizes light; used in filters, sunglasses, and so on. *See* **Polarization**.

Positron   An electron with a positive charge.

Potential   *See* **Electric potential**.

Potential energy   The energy due to position in a force field. Any time a force is required to move something from one place to another, its potential energy increases. The amount of the increase is the work done, the force times the distance moved. If anything is released and falls to a new position, its potential energy is decreasing.

It takes a force to lift something, moving it away from the earth. *See* **Gravitational energy**.

An electric charge in an electric field has a force on it, and work must be done to move it. *See* **Electric energy**.

Work must be done to distort the shape of a solid, as in stretching a spring. *See* **Elastic energy**.

Molecules are held in position in solids and within a surface in liquids, and work must be done to remove them. *See* **Latent heat**.

Power   The rate of doing work or transforming energy. It is expressed in joules per second, called watts (W). Power is the amount of energy converted (ΔE) divided by the time taken (Δt):

$$P = \frac{\Delta E}{\Delta t}$$

Example

An engine is able to do work at the rate of 600 W. Using appropriate machinery, how long will it take the engine to pump 2500 kg of water to a height of 6.0 m?

The work to be done is

$$mgh = (2500 \text{ kg})(9.8 \text{ N/kg})(6.0 \text{ m}) = 147{,}000 \text{ J}$$

Then,

$$\Delta t = \frac{\Delta E}{P} = \frac{147{,}000 \text{ J}}{600 \text{ W}} = 245 \text{ s}$$

This gives the ideal time. In practice, the machinery would have to be designed to pump at a lower rate, since part of the power will be consumed in the machinery itself. *See* **Efficiency**.

The power concept is used in electricity, as the rate of converting electric energy into other forms. For example, a 100 W light bulb uses 100 J of electric energy every second, converting it into heat and light. *See* **Electric energy**.

Poynting vector   A vector representing the speed and direction of a light wave or other electromagnetic wave at a given point in space. Light rays are lines drawn at all points tangent to the Poynting vector.

Pressure   Force exerted per unit area. The SI unit is the pascal (Pa) = N/m², but many other units are also in use. A convenient unit is the atmosphere (atm), which is the average pressure exerted by the atmosphere at sea level. All of the following units are equal to 1 atm:

101.3 kilopascal (kPa)
1013 millibars
14.7 pounds per square inch (psi)
760 millimeters of mercury
760 torr

We use a number of devices whose purpose is to reduce pressure by spreading a force out over a larger area. A man on skis will not sink into the snow because his weight is distributed.

Example

What is the pressure exerted by a 60 kg man if he is standing on (1) a three-legged stool, or (2) skis?

The area of contact of the leg of a stool might be about 5 cm², so the pressure he exerts is

$$P = \frac{F}{A} = \frac{(60 \text{ kg})(9.8 \text{ N/kg})}{15 \text{ cm}^2} \times \left(\frac{100 \text{ cm}}{\text{m}}\right)^2$$

$$= 3.9 \times 10^5 \text{ N/m}^2 = 390 \text{ kPa}$$

A ski is about 10 cm wide and 2 m long, so the area of two skis is about 0.4 m². Then the pressure on the snow is

$$P = \frac{F}{A} = \frac{(60 \text{ kg})(9.8 \text{ N/kg})}{0.4 \text{ m}^2} = 150 \text{ Pa}$$

The concept of pressure is most often used in dealing with liquids (*see* **Hydrostatic pressure**) and gases (*see* **Gas law**).

Primary coil   *See* **Electromagnetic induction**.

Principal focus   *See* **Focal length**.

Proton   A fundamental particle with a positive charge and a large mass, about 1800 times the mass of an electron. Protons are components of all atomic nuclei; *see* **Nucleus**.

The proton has been considered to be one of the very few stable particles. Recent theories, however, propose that the proton breaks down into smaller particles with half-lives far greater than the age of the universe.

Pulley   A machine that uses wheels and ropes to divide the weight of the load to provide a mechanical advantage. The basic principle is illustrated in the figure. The man supports half the weight; the other half is held up by a fixed support. The mechanical advantage is thus 2. For each meter that the load is lifted, the man will have to pull 2 meters of rope.

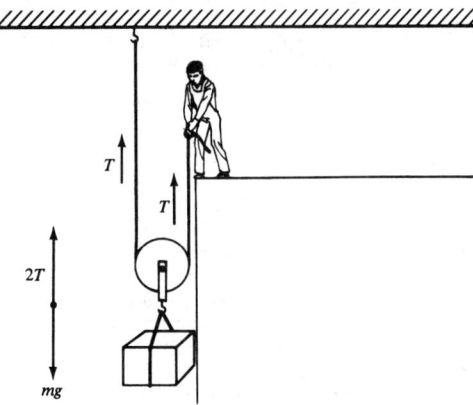

In an ordinary pulley system, the mechanical advantage can be determined by counting the number of strands supporting the load. In the next figure, for example, there are five strands. The strand the man is pulling on does not count because it is not connected to the load.

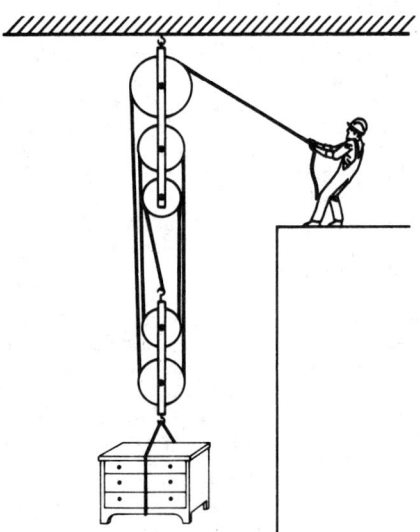

Suppose the bureau he is lifting has a mass of 85 kg and he has to lift it a distance of 20 m. How hard does he have to pull, and how much rope must he pull through? To raise the load 1 m, he must pull enough rope to shorten all five strands supporting the load by 1 m. Therefore, to raise the load 20 m, he must pull through (5 × 20 m) = 100 m of rope. The ideal effort force is (85 kg)(9.8 N/kg)/5 = 167 N. He will have to pull a lot harder than that, since he must lift the pulley wheels and rope and must overcome the friction in the system.

Quantum theory The modern theory of submicroscopic particles. It incorporates several interconnected basic principles:

Quantization of energy. Changes in energy levels do not occur smoothly, but in jumps. In any given subatomic system, only certain energy levels are possible. In jumping from one level to another, the system emits or absorbs electromagnetic energy. The quantization of energy states was first observed in the study of emission of electromagnetic waves from hot objects (*see* **Radiation**). The energy of the electromagnetic wave is also quantized, so that light has certain properties characteristic of particles. For more details, *see* **Bohr model**; **Photon**.

Duality principle. Wave and particle are two alternative ways to describe physical phenomena. An electromagnetic wave consists of particles called photons. Depending on the particular experiment, either the wave or the particle model may be used. Conversely, a beam of particles has wave properties, and in some experiments these must be considered. *See* **Matter wave**.

Heisenberg uncertainty principle. It is not possible to specify both the position and the momentum of a particle simultaneously with arbitrary accuracy. This leads to the strange result that the laws of nature must be expressed in terms of probability rather than absolute prediction. In an electron beam, for example, you cannot state where any given electron will land. The wave equations express the probability that an electron will take some particular path. When there are a large number of electrons, the pattern becomes predictable using wave equations.

The strangest aspect of quantum theory, made evident by many experiments, is that there are always two mutually incompatible ways of describing events. The wave-particle duality is an example. Depending on what experiment is being done, a beam of light or of electrons must be considered either a wave or a particle. The nature of the system is not defined until the experimenter looks at it. Quantum systems have no properties of their own apart from the means used to observe them. *See* **Radiation**; **Bohr model**; **Photoelectric effect**.

Quark One of a class of particles that make up protons, neutrons, and other hadrons. There are six kinds of quarks and six antiquarks, each of which can exist in three different "colors." This has nothing to do with the ordinary meaning of "color." In this context the term is simply a convenient way to name the different kinds of quarks. A quark has 1/3 or 2/3 unit of elementary charge. Neutrons, protons, and other kinds of particles are made of three quarks each, and mesons are made of two quarks. Free quarks have never been observed; apparently, quarks exist only in combinations of two and three. *See* **Fundamental particles**.

Radiation (1) Any electromagnetic wave; (2) specifically, heat transferred by infrared waves. Radiant energy is emitted by any object warmer than its surroundings and absorbed by anything colder than its surroundings. The efficiency of absorption and radiation depends on the nature of the surface. A white or shiny surface efficiently reflects the radiation, whether it is coming from the inside or from the outside. A black surface is one that allows all radiation to pass, either in or out. This means that a black object will warm or cool faster than a white one. The cooling fins of an engine, for example, are painted black to encourage radiant cooling. Also, a solar heating panel is painted black to provide the most effective absorption of sunlight. Conversely, household insulation incorporates a sheet of shiny aluminum foil. This prevents heat from entering in the summer or leaving in the winter.

Theoretical and practical studies of radiation have been done with the physicist's nearest approach to an ideal black body: a can with a hole in it, painted black in the interior. The hole is an ideal absorber, since any light that enters is most unlikely to find its way out again. If the can is heated to redness, the hole is the ideal radiator and will look brighter than any other part of the system. The rate of energy loss from an ideal black body is proportional to the fourth power of the kelvin temperature.

It was the study of black body radiation that initiated the era of quantum physics. The problem was to account for the measured distribution of wavelengths of the emitted radiation. Max Planck, in 1900, was able to produce a formula that fit his observed data to high accuracy. Previous theories were unable to account for the absence of the ultraviolet and shorter wavelengths. Planck's equations were derived on the assumption that the vibrating molecules that produced the waves could occupy only certain definite energy states and that they had to jump from one state to the next. This was the first experimental evidence for the existence of quantized energy states. Planck's constant, $h = 6.6 \times 10^{-34}$ J·s, defined these states. This constant now appears in every equation of quantum physics. *See also* Earth and Space Science section, page 5-30.

Radioactivity The spontaneous breakdown of atomic nuclei, with the release of subnuclear particles. Nuclei are held together by a delicate balance between the mutual repulsion of the protons, due to their charge, and the strong nuclear attraction between all nucleons. Not all combinations are stable. Large nuclei especially, with their many protons, are subject to disintegration.

Alpha decay is the emission of a helium nucleus, called an alpha particle, from a large nucleus. The helium nucleus is composed of 2 protons and 2 neutrons, so the emission of an alpha particle reduces the atomic number of the parent nucleus by 2, and its atomic mass number by 4. An example is the decay of uranium-238 to form thorium-234:

$$^{238}_{92}U \rightarrow \, ^{234}_{90}Th + \, ^{4}_{2}He$$

When decay is over, the thorium nucleus may be left in an excited state. It will return to its lowest energy state by emitting a very high-frequency photon known as a gamma ray. The combined energies of the alpha and gamma particles always have one of several definite values. This indicates that there are quantized energy states in the nucleus.

A second kind of radioactive decay is beta emission. The nucleus comes to a more stable condition by emitting an electron. The electron is formed by the breakdown of one of the neutrons into an electron and a proton. This does not change the atomic mass number, but with one more proton in the nucleus, the atomic number increases by 1. An example is the beta decay of bismuth-83 to form polonium-84:

$$^{210}_{83}\text{Bi} \rightarrow ^{210}_{84}\text{Po} + ^{0}_{-1}e + \bar{\nu}$$

The emitted electron may have various amounts of energy, but it always less than would be expected by comparison of the masses of the particles. The extra energy is released in the form of a tiny particle with no charge and little or no rest mass (*see* **Neutrino**).

The product of a radioactive decay may itself be radioactive. When a uranium-238 nucleus decays, it enters on a whole series of alpha and beta decays until it has turned into a completely stable nucleus of lead-206. In Exhibit 20.2, the arrows pointing diagonally down to the left represent alpha decays, and the arrows moving horizontally one space to the right are beta decays.

New kinds of nuclei are created by bombardment with neutrons or other particles, and many of these are radioactive. They may decay by other modes, such as the emission of a positive electron or by capture of an orbital electron by the nucleus.

Although it is not possible to predict when any given nucleus will decay, the probability of decay during any time interval is known. *See* **Half-life**.

Radio waves *See* **Electromagnetic spectrum**.

Reaction *See* **Force**.

Reactor *See* **Nuclear reactor**.

Reflection The process by which light, or other waves, bounce off a surface. In analyzing the behavior of light, it is convenient to use the concept of a ray (*see* **Light rays**).

Specular reflection, as shown in the figure, occurs when a beam of light strikes a smooth, flat surface—a mirror. The lines marked *N* are normals, lines drawn perpendicular to the surface. The angle that the incoming ray makes with the normal is called the angle of incidence; the angle the outgoing ray makes with the normal is the angle of reflection. These two

angles are equal. If a beam of parallel rays, for example from a laser, strikes a mirror, the reflected beam will still consist of parallel rays.

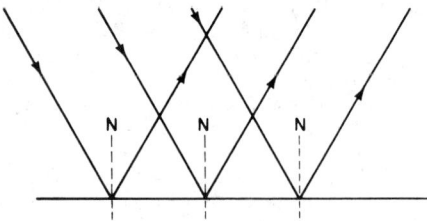

Specular Reflection

Because the angle of incidence and the angle of reflection are equal, light that comes from an object and strikes a mirror forms a virtual image of the object. *See* **Plane mirror**.

When a surface is irregular, as in the next figure, the rays reflect in all directions. The light is diffused, scattered in all directions from every point on the object. All ordinary objects scatter reflected light in this way. We see things because a small part of the light scattered from objects enters our eyes. The lens of the eye uses the scattered light to form an image on the retina. To see how this works, *see* **Convex lens**.

See also **Total internal reflection**.

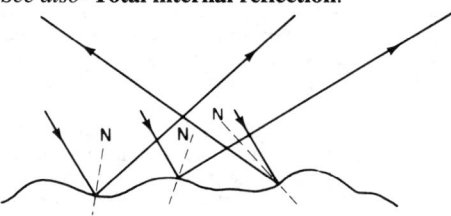

Diffuse Reflection

Refraction The bending of a light beam as it passes from one medium into another. The beam bends because the speed of the light is different in the two media. The figure shows the refraction of a beam as it enters, and again as it leaves, a glass plate.

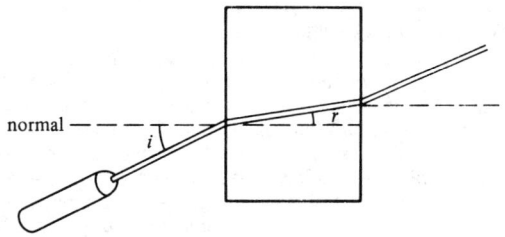

normal

The angle marked *i* is the angle of incidence, *r* is the angle of refraction. As the beam slows on entering the glass from air, it bends toward the normal, so that $r < i$. When it emerges from the glass, it speeds up and bends away from the normal.

Consider a ray of light at an interface between two media. It obeys a simple rule regardless of which way it is traveling. It travels with speed v_A in medium *A* and makes an angle with the normal θ_A the other medium its speed is v_B and the angle is θ_B. Then,

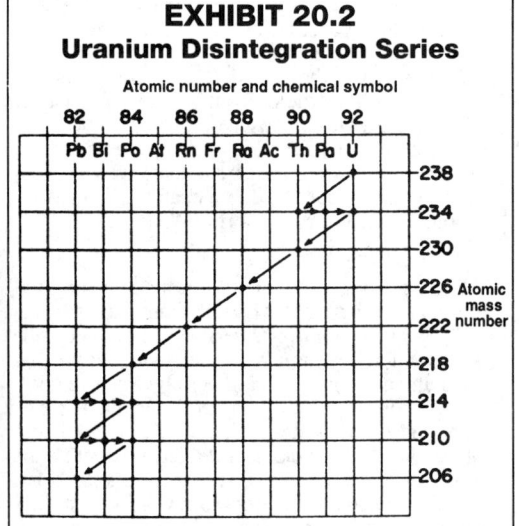

EXHIBIT 20.2
Uranium Disintegration Series

Atomic number and chemical symbol

82	84	86	88	90	92

| Pb | Bi | Po | At | Rn | Fr | Ra | Ac | Th | Pa | U |

238
234
230
226 Atomic
mass
222 number
218
214
210
206

$$\frac{v_A}{v_B} = \frac{\sin\theta_A}{\sin\theta_B}$$

For every medium, an index of refraction n can be specified. This is defined as the ratio of the speed of light in a vacuum to the speed in the medium. Then the following ratio of sines of angles applies:

$$n = \frac{c}{v} = \frac{\sin\theta_c}{\sin\theta_m}$$

where θ_c is the angle a ray makes on entering or leaving the medium and θ_m is the angle in the medium.

Suppose a beam of light enters a piece of crown glass, index of refraction 1.62, from air, making an angle of incidence of 55°. How much is the angle of refraction?

$$1.62 = \frac{\sin 55°}{\sin\theta_m}$$

which gives $\theta_m = 30°$

What happens if a beam passes from one medium into another? If the two indices of refraction are known, the answer can be found. Suppose a beam leaves a diamond ($n_D = 2.50$) at an angle of 22° and passes into water ($n_w = 1.33$). What is the angle of refraction?

$$\frac{\sin\theta_W}{\sin 22°} = \frac{v_W}{v_D}$$

But $v_w = c / n_w$ and $v_D = c / n_D$. Substituting these values gives

$$\frac{\sin\theta_W}{\sin 22°} = \frac{n_D}{n_w} = \frac{2.50}{1.33}$$

from which $\theta_w = 45°$

On entering a medium of lower index of refraction, the ray bends away from the normal. If the angle of incidence is large enough, the ray may bend so far that it does not leave the medium at all. *See* **Total internal reflection**.

In most media, the longer wavelengths of light travel faster. This makes it possible to separate the colors of light by refraction. *See* **Dispersion**.

Relativity   The principle that the laws of nature are the same in any frame of reference. Measurements are meaningful, in other words, only if they are made relative to some specified frame of reference. In the sixteenth century, Galileo put it this way: If you are in the cabin of a ship sailing on a smooth sea, there is no way you can tell whether the ship is moving unless you look out. *See* **Galilean relativity**.

Albert Einstein extended this principle to include electromagnetic phenomena in nonaccelerated frames of reference. He made one additional assumption: that the speed of light in a vacuum is an invariant law of nature. *See* **Special relativity**.

In extending the relativity principle to include accelerated frames of reference, Einstein came up with a new way of looking at space and time and an improved theory of gravity. *See* **General relativity**.

Resistance   In an electric conductor, the ratio of potential difference to current:

$$R = \frac{V}{I}$$

where V is potential difference in volts (V), I is cur-

rent in amperes (A), and R is the resistance in ohms (Ω the Greek letter omega). Suppose a resistor of 30 Ω is connected in a circuit in such a way that a current of 65 mA flows through it. What is the potential difference between its ends?

$$V = IR = (65 \times 10^{-3} A)(30\ \Omega) = 1.95\ V$$

This equation is often called Ohm's law, but this is somewhat misleading. The law that current is proportional to potential difference applies only to metallic conductors kept at a constant temperature. In many other devices, resistance depends on current. Even in metals, it increases with temperature. The resistance of a 100 W light bulb at room temperature is about 1 Ω at room temperature. How much is it when the bulb is operating at its rated 120 V? Since the power is IV, the current is

$$I = \frac{P}{V} = \frac{100\ W}{120\ V} = 0.83\ A$$

and the resistance is

$$R = \frac{V}{I} = \frac{120\ V}{0.83\ A} = 145\ \Omega$$

Resistivity   The property of a material that determines its resistance at any given set of dimensions. The resistance of a wire is proportional to its length and inversely proportional to its crosssectional area:

$$R = \frac{\rho l}{A}$$

where ρ, the Greek letter rho, is the resistivity of the material. The resistivity of aluminum at room temperature, for example, is 2.8×10^{-8} $\Omega\cdot m$. What is the resistance of a wire 26 m long and 0.40 mm² in cross section?

$$R = \frac{\rho l}{A} = \frac{(2.8\times10^{-8}\ \Omega\cdot m)(26\ m)}{0.40\ mm^2}\left(\frac{1000\ mm}{m}\right)^2$$

$$= 1.8\ \Omega$$

Resistivity increases with temperature. In boiling water, the wire would have a resistance of 2.5 Ω.

Resistor   An electric conductor specifically made to provide a definite amount of resistance in a circuit. Resistors are rated according to their resistance and the largest amount of power they can dissipate in the form of heat.

RMS value   The root mean square value of an AC current or potential. For a sine wave, this is the effective value. *See* **Effective value**.

Rotational equilibrium   A situation in which the rate of rotation does not change because the sum of all torques on an object is zero. In the absence of friction, a spinning object will rotate forever; the earth has been doing so for a long time. To change the rate of rotation, a torque must be applied (*see* **Torque**).

Only the simplest cases will be treated here.

Example 1

Consider a seesaw 6.0 m long, pivoted at the center. A 32 kg girl is sitting at one end, and her 25 kg brother is 60 cm from her. Where on the other side must their 55 kg father sit, to produce balance?

PHYSICS

Assume the children produce clockwise torques. All radius vectors (r) must be measured from the center of rotation. Then the total clockwise torque is

$$(32 \text{ kg})(9.8 \text{ N/kg})(3.0 \text{ m}) = 941 \text{ N·m}$$
$$(25 \text{ kg})(9.8 \text{ N/kg})(2.4 \text{ m}) = \underline{588 \text{ N·m}}$$
$$= 1529 \text{ N·m}$$

The father must produce an equal torque in the opposite direction:

$$(55 \text{ kg})(9.8 \text{ N/kg})r = 1529 \text{ N·m}$$
$$r = 2.8 \text{ m}$$

from the pivot.

Note that it was not necessary to include g in the problem since all the torques are produced by weight only.

Example 2

A telephone pole 7.5 m long has a mass of 920 kg and its center of gravity is 2.8 m from the broad end. How much force is required to lift the narrow end off the ground?

The clockwise torque is the total weight times the distance from the center of gravity to the pivot at the broad end:

$$(920 \text{ kg})(9.8 \text{ N/kg})(2.8 \text{ m}) = (7.5 \text{ m})F$$
$$F = 3400 \text{ N}$$

Ruling engine A device for ruling lines on a film for the purpose of making a diffraction grating.

Rutherford's experiment The discovery of the atomic nucleus. A radioactive substance was placed at one end of an evacuated glass tube and a fluorescent screen at the other. Between them was a very thin sheet of gold foil. The radioactive material emitted alpha particles, which went through the foil and struck the screen. Every time a particle hit the screen, it produced a flash of light.

About 99.9% of the alpha particles went straight through the foil, indicating that the foil was mostly empty space. For the one particle in a thousand that was deflected, the angle of deflection was measured. The distribution of these angles showed that the deflection was produced by an inverse-square repulsion. Since alpha particles are positively charged, this indicated that they were being deflected by a positive charge. Rutherford concluded that the foil contained positively charged nuclei about one ten-thousandth as big across as the atom as a whole. The atom is about 10^{-10} m in diameter, while the size of the nucleus is 10^{-14} m.

Scalar A quantity that has magnitude but no direction, as opposed to vectors. Some scalar quantities are time, volume, energy, potential, and charge.

Second (s) The basic SI unit of time. It is now defined in terms of the oscillation of a molecule in an atomic clock.

Secondary coil *See* **Electromagnetic induction.**

Second law of thermodynamics The principle that every time energy is transformed, it becomes less useful. For example, when electric energy is used to operate a motor, no more than 80% of the electric energy can be converted into kinetic energy. The rest becomes heat, which is discharged into the environment. Low-temperature heat is always one outcome of an energy transformation. This is why we need supplies of high-quality energy all the time. The total amount of energy never changes, but the amount of useful energy always diminishes. *See* **Efficiency.**

Heat can be used as a source of usable energy as in a steam engine or an automobile engine. However, it is never possible to convert heat into other forms of energy 100%. A steam engine takes in very hot steam, but the water it discharges is never at absolute zero. The amount of useful energy that can be obtained from heat depends on the difference between the input and output temperatures (*see* **Thermal efficiency**). Every heat engine takes in a working substance at a high temperature and discharges some of the input energy in the form of useless heat at the ambient temperature. Furthermore, temperature differences always tend to disappear because heat moves spontaneously from higher temperatures to lower. Therefore, energy is always becoming less useful.

Series circuit An electric circuit in which the same current flows successively through more than one conductor, with no branching. Consider, for example, the circuit shown in the figure. When the switch is closed, the circuit is completed through all four resistors. Since there is no branching, the current leaving one resistor has no place to go except into the next one. The first rule for a series circuit, then, is

$$I_{total} = I_1 = I_2 = I_3 = \cdots$$

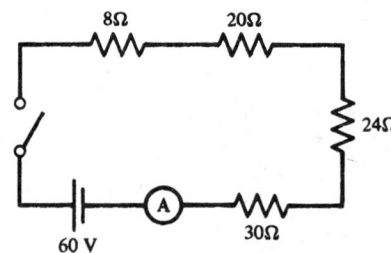

As the current passes through each resistor in turn, it gives up some of its energy to each. It must return to the battery at a potential 60 V lower than when it started out. The potential drops across each resistor, and the total drop has to be 60 V. The rule for potentials, then, is

$$V_{total} = V_1 + V_2 + V_3 + \cdots$$

Since each resistor obeys Ohm's law, each V in the equation above can be replaced by IR. All the I are the same, so

$$R_{total} = R_1 + R_2 + R_3 + \cdots$$

In the circuit shown, then, the total resistance is

$$R_{total} = 8 \text{ Ω} + 20 \text{ Ω} + 24 \text{ Ω} + 30 \text{ Ω} = 82 \text{ Ω}$$

Now it is possible to find the current:

$$I_{total} = \frac{V_{total}}{R_{total}} = \frac{60 \text{ V}}{82 \text{ Ω}} = 0.73 \text{ A}$$

With this information, the potential differences across all of the resistors can be found:

$V_1 = IR_1 = (0.732\ \text{A})(\ 8\ \Omega) = 5.86\ \text{V}$
$V_2 = IR_2 = (0.732\ \text{A})(20\ \Omega) = 14.64\ \text{V}$
$V_3 = IR_3 = (0.732\ \text{A})(24\ \Omega) = 17.57\ \text{V}$
$V_4 = IR_4 = (0.732\ \text{A})(30\ \Omega) = \underline{21.96\ \text{V}}$
$60\ \text{V}$

SI *See* **Système internationale**.

Solenoid A long coil of wire in which a current flows, creating a magnetic field. The field is strongest inside the solenoid. It is uniform inside, except near the ends. The magnitude of the field depends only on the current and the number of turns of wire per unit length of solenoid. *See* **Electromagnet**; **Magnetic field lines**.

Sonic boom A loud noise produced by an airplane flying at or faster than the speed of sound. As shown under Doppler effect, the compression zones of a sound wave produced by a moving object are crowded closer together in the region in front of the object. If the plane is moving at the speed of sound, or faster, all those compression zones unite to form a single, enormous, V-shaped compression, like the wake of a boat. When this compression zone reaches the ground, a loud, explosionlike sound is heard. *See* **Doppler effect**.

Sound wave A longitudinal wave in air propagated by the vibration of air molecules, producing an alternate series of compressions and rarefactions. In the figure, the vibrations of the tuning fork compress the air and the wave moves out along a spherical front.

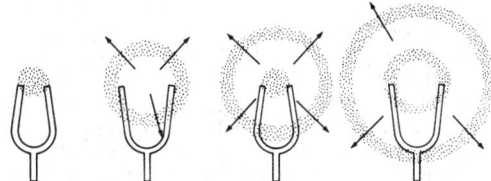

The speed of a sound wave in air depends chiefly on the temperature. It is 331 m/s at 0°C, plus 0.6 m/s for each degree. The frequency of the wave is fixed by the frequency of vibration of the source.

Example

What is the wavelength of the sound produced by an oboe sounding A (= 440 Hz) to tune up an orchestra if the temperature is 22°C?

The speed of the sound waves is

$331\ \text{m/s} + (0.6)(22\ \text{m/s}) = 344\ \text{m/s}$

The wavelength is the speed of the wave divided by its frequency:

$$\lambda = \frac{v}{f} = \frac{344\ \text{m/s}}{440\ \text{Hz}} = 0.78\ \text{m}$$

The young human ear can detect sounds in the range from about 18 to 18,000 Hz. The ability to hear the higher frequencies diminishes with age. Musical pitch is determined by the frequency (*see* **Pitch**).

Spark chamber A device for detecting and recording the passage of a subnuclear particle. It consists of a set of metal plates, set parallel to each other and separated by small gaps. Each plate is at a higher potential than the one below it, so that there is a gradient of potential through the whole chamber. When a charged particle goes through the chamber, it ionizes the air, and a spark jumps from each plate to the one above it, following the path of the particle. The spark is photographed, and the path can be analyzed.

Special relativity The relativity principle applied to non-accelerated motion at speeds close to the speed of light. The relativity principle states that the laws of nature are the same in any frame of reference. *See* **Galilean relativity** for application of the relativity principle at normal speeds; for its application in accelerated motion, *see* **General relativity**; **Equivalence principle**. According to this rule, the usual velocity addition theorem does not apply at speeds approaching the speed of light. Suppose, for example, you are in a car going 30 m/s and fire an arrow forward, which is given a speed of 50 m/s by the bow. In the earth frame of reference the speed of the arrow is

$30\ \text{m/s} + 50\ \text{m/s} = 80\ \text{m/s}$

The starting point of special relativity is the assumption that the speed of light is a law of nature, and thus must be the same in any frame of reference.
Imagine, however, you are in a car going 2.5×10^8 m/s and fire an arrow that goes 2.8×10^8 m/s. The velocity addition theorem of special relativity says the speed of the arrow is not 5.3×10^8 m/s but is 2.95×10^8 m/s. The speed can never be greater than 3.0×10^8 m/s, the speed of light. Even worse, if you, in your car, turn on your headlights, the speed of the light in your frame of reference is 3.0×10^8 m/s. It is the same in the earth frame—or any other!

The logical consequences of this assumption were so strange that it took a long time and a great deal of experimental evidence before physicists could accept them. They involved a complete revision of all notions of space, time, mass, and energy. The theory gave equations for transformations of measurement data from one frame of reference to another. The transformations all involved a quantity

$$\beta = \sqrt{1 - \frac{v^2}{c^2}}$$

where v is the relative speed of the frame of reference and c is the speed of light. For example, let us assume there is a rocket ship traveling overhead at 2×10^8 m/s, which gives $\beta = 0.75$.

The first consequence is space contraction. If someone in the rocket ship measures its length and gets a value of 60 m, this is the length in a frame of reference at rest with respect to the rocket ship. An observer on the ground will find the length to be 60 m $\times \beta = 45$ m. If the pilot of the ship measures an identical ship on the ground, the one on the ground is in motion in a frame of reference connected to the rocket ship. The ship on the ground, measured by the pilot, will be only 45 m long. Space contraction had been noted experimentally but was never explained until the theory of special relativity appeared.

The second consequence is time dilation. If an event in the rocket ship takes 10 s, the observer timing it from the ground will measure its duration to be $10 \text{ s}/\beta = 13$ s. Time dilation has been tested experimentally by measuring the half-lives of particles moving near the speed of light. The evidence shows that it works.

The third consequence is relativistic mass increase. A pilot in the rocket ship might determine her own mass to be 50 kg. As measured from the ground, it would be $50 \text{ kg}/\beta = 67$ kg. Conversely, if she measures a 50 kg person on the ground, she will find the mass of the person to be 67 kg. Mass increase is an important design consideration in particle accelerators, which push protons and electrons up to nearly the speed of light.

The relativistic mass increase led to another startling conclusion: the equivalence of mass and energy. This was the theory that led to nuclear energy. *See* **Mass-energy**.

Specific gravity   *See* Earth and Space Science section, page 5-35.

Specific heat   A property of a material indicating the amount of increase of temperature it achieves per gram for a given quantity of heat added. The pertinent equation is

$$\Delta H = cm \, \Delta T$$

where ΔH is the amount of heat added, c is the specific heat, m is mass, and ΔT is the increase in temperature. The specific heat is usually given in calories per gram-degree Celsius. Since this is always a change in temperature, $^\circ\text{C} = \text{K}$.

Example 1

The specific heat of aluminum, for example, is 0.92 J/g·K. How much heat is required to raise the temperature of a 450 g aluminum pot from 20 to 210°C?

The temperature increase is 190 K, so

$$\Delta H = cm \, \Delta T$$
$$= (0.92 \text{ J/g·K}) (450\text{g})(190 \text{ K}) = 79{,}000 \text{ J}$$

Specific heat may be used to solve problems in which a mixture of materials at different temperatures comes to equilibrium.

Example 2

When 350 g of hot iron ($c = 0.48$ J/g·K) is dropped into 200 g of water at 20°C, the mixture comes to a final temperature of 64°C. What was the initial temperature of the iron?

Set up an equation in which the amount of heat lost by the iron is equal to the heat gained by the water. The specific heat of water is 4.19 J/g·K.

$$(0.48 \text{ J/g·K})(350\text{g}) \, \Delta T_{\text{iron}} = (4.19 \text{ J/g·K})(200\text{g})(44 \text{ K})$$

which gives $\Delta T_{\text{iron}} = 219$ K. Since the iron cooled to 64°C, it must have started at 283°C.

Spectrum   An array of waves arranged according to wavelength. *See* **Electromagnetic spectrum**.

The spectrum of visible light covers a very small part of the total electromagnetic spectrum, from about 450 to 700 nm (1 nanometer = 10^{-9} m) The human eye can distinguish 50 or more separate hues in the spectrum. The long-wavelength end looks red, and it shades gradually into orange, yellow, green,

and blue. The spectrum becomes violet at the short-wavelength end.

White light contains all these visible wavelengths. The separate colors can be made visible by a prism (*see* **Dispersion**) or a diffraction grating. For accuracy in the measurement of wavelength, a diffraction grating spectrometer is far superior. *See* **Diffraction grating**.

Substances excited by heat or electric current produce light, and the wavelength content of the spectrum is unique for each kind of material. The spectrum can reveal much information about the structure's of the atoms and molecules. For the simplest example, *see* **Bohr model**.

Speed   The magnitude of velocity, the distance traveled per unit time without reference to direction. Average speed is total distance traveled divided by the total time:

$$v_{\text{av}} = \frac{\Delta s}{\Delta t}$$

Example

You ride a bike 60 m in 11 s, rest for 10 s, and then ride another 150 m in 18 s. What was your average speed?

$$v_{\text{av}} = \frac{60 \text{ m} + 150 \text{ m}}{11 \text{ s} + 10 \text{ s} + 18 \text{ s}} = 5.4 \text{ m/s}$$

Instantaneous speed v may vary greatly during any one trip. It cannot change very much during a short time interval. The average speed during a very short time interval is the best approximation for the instantaneous speed during that interval. For methods of dealing with changing speed, *see* **Acceleration**. For effects due to the direction of travel, *see* **Velocity**.

Spring constant *See* **Elastic recoil**.

Standing wave   When two identical waves pass through each other in opposite directions, the medium is set into a special kind of oscillation. As shown in the figure, points of maximum vibration (antinodes) alternate with points of no vibration (nodes). The figure represents a rope or a taut string that can be set into this kind of vibration.

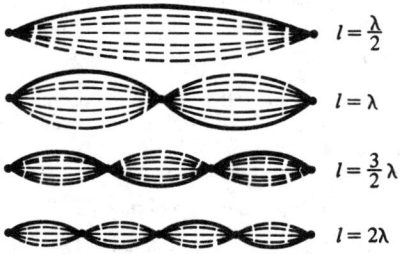

In any such standing wave, the distance from one node to the next is a half-wavelength. Since the string is clamped at the ends, the ends must be nodes. This places a limitation on the possible wavelengths. The length of the string must be an integral number of half wavelengths.

When a guitar string is plucked, waves of all frequencies start out toward both ends of the string. They reflect from the ends, bouncing back and forth from one end to the other. All frequencies die out immediately except those that can form standing waves with nodes at the ends of the string. All the possible modes of vibration shown in the figure, and many others, occur in the string simultaneously. The sound produced is a mixture of all the frequencies.

Example

A guitar string is 80 cm long, and the wave in it travels at 260 m/s. What are the frequencies in the sound?

First, the string vibrates with nodes at each end and an antinode in the middle. The string is a half wavelength long, so the wavelength is twice the length of the string, or 1.60 m. The frequency of this mode of vibration (the fundamental mode) is

$$f = \frac{v}{\lambda} = \frac{260 \text{ m/s}}{1.60 \text{ m}} = 162.5 \text{ Hz}$$

At the second mode of vibration, the wavelength is half that of the fundamental. The speed of the wave is no different, so the frequency is twice as much, 325 Hz. The next mode has three half-wavelengths in the string, so its frequency is three times the fundamental. All the frequencies form a series in which each member is an integral multiple of the fundamental.

Strong nuclear force An extremely strong force between certain kinds of subatomic particles. Since the discovery of the electron, hundreds of kinds of particles have been found. Three of them—neutrons, protons, and electrons—make up normal matter. The others have been found in cosmic rays or produced in high-energy particle accelerators. The strong nuclear force acts only on an important group of particles call hadrons. Neutrons and protons belong to this category. Electrons and other leptons are not affected by the nuclear force.

The strong nuclear force acts only over distances as small as a nucleus. The neutrons and protons are composed of three smaller particles called quarks. Other hadrons, such as the pi meson, are made of a quark and an antiquark. The strong nuclear force that binds the quarks together to form hadrons is so strong that it may not be possible ever to separate the quarks. Within a nucleus, the interactions between quarks make it possible for the strong nuclear force to bind all the nucleons to each other. See **Fundamental particles.**

Supercollider An enormous particle accelerator being constructed near Dallas, Texas. It will consist of a ring-shaped tunnel 80 kilometers long, and will cost at least 8 billion dollars. Subnuclear particles will be accelerated through the tunnel, with extraordinary accuracy. The particles will be speeded up by electric fields, and their path will be bent and controlled by huge superconducting electromagnets. Collisions of enormous energy will be produced by causing two streams of particles to go around in opposite directions, so that they collide. Experiments with this device are expected to produce new kinds of subnuclear particles that will provide a deep insight into the events that occurred at the origin of the universe.

Superconductivity The complete disappearance of all electric resistance in certain substances kept at very low temperatures. A current can be started in a

superconducting ring, and it will continue to flow forever with no further external source of energy.

Superconductivity was discovered in materials immersed in liquid helium, at a temperature of 4 K. For many years, superconductivity was observed only at such extremely low temperatures, near absolute zero. In 1986, however, a great breakthrough was made with the discovery that certain ceramics become superconductive at much higher temperatures. The current record is 120 K. Cheap liquid nitrogen can be used for cooling, rather than the enormously rare and expensive liquid helium.

Système Internationale (SI) The metric system of measurements, standardized for uniform usage. The system is founded on seven basic units, defined operationally. All other units are derived from them by definition. Only multiples and submultiples of units that are powers of 10 are allowed.

The basic units of the SI are as follows:
meter (m), measuring distance
kilogram (kg), measuring mass
second (s), measuring time
kelvin (K), measuring temperature
ampere (A), measuring current
candela (cd), measuring luminous intensity
mole (mol), measuring amount of substance

Some examples of derived SI units are as follows:

liter (L) = 10^{-3} m³, measuring volume
newton (N) = kg·m/s², measuring force
coulomb (C) = A·s, measuring electric charge
watt (W) = kg·m²/s³, measuring power
pascal (Pa) = kg/m·s², measuring pressure
volt (V) = kg·m²/A·s³, measuring potential

These are some of the prefixes that are allowed:
nano (n) = 10^{-9}
micro (μ) = 10^{-6}
milli (m) = 10^{-3}
centi (c)= 10^{-2}
kilo (k) = 10^{3}
mega (M) = 10^{6}
giga (G) = 10^{9}

 **Temperature** The property that determines the direction of flow of heat. The basic definition is that two systems are at the same temperature if no heat flows from one to the other. In the SI, temperature is defined operationally only, and its unit of measure, the kelvin (K), is one of the basic units of the system.

Three temperature scales are in common use: see **Fahrenheit scale** for the one commonly used in the United States; see **Celsius scale** for the one used in scientific work and in most of the rest of the world; see **Kelvin scale** for the only scale that has a natural zero. Temperature intervals can be measured in any scale, but multiplication and division by temperatures can be done only in the Kelvin scale.

It is now known that temperature can be interpreted in terms of molecular motion. Temperature is the average random translational energy of the molecules. As such, it is a statistical property and applies only to large aggregates of particles. See **Kinetic theory of gases.**

Thermal efficiency The theoretical upper limit to the conversion of heat into work. In a heat engine, such as a steam turbine, heat is put in, and some of it comes out in the form of useful work. The efficiency of the engine is

$$\text{Efficiency} = \frac{\text{work}_{out}}{\text{heat}_{in}}$$

However, there is always some heat coming out. The water coming out of the turbine is never at absolute zero. Ideally, the difference between the heat that goes in and the heat that comes out is the work done:

$$W = H_{in} - H_{out}$$

It can be shown that the greatest possible efficiency of a heat engine depends on the difference between the temperature of the steam going in and that of the water coming out:

$$\text{Thermal efficiency} = \frac{T_{in} - T_{out}}{T_{in}}$$

This indicates that if we want to get the most possible work out of a steam engine, we want the steam to be as hot as possible when it goes in and as cold as possible when it comes out. The same rule applies to gasoline engines or to any other engine that converts heat to work.

For example, suppose steam enters a turbine at 650°C (= 923 K) and is discharged as warm water at 40°C (= 313 K). The thermal efficiency is

$$\frac{923\text{ K} - 313\text{ K}}{923\text{ K}} = 0.66$$

This 66% is the ideal efficiency. In practice it will be less for the usual reasons, including friction and imperfect insulation.

What this tells us is that the usefulness of heat as a source of other kinds of energy depends on temperature differences. The oceans contain enormous amounts of internal energy, but their temperature varies so little that the energy cannot be used efficiently. Since heat always tends to flow from high temperature to low, there is a constant tendency for differences in temperature to disappear. Therefore, energy is constantly becoming less useful.

Thermal equilibrium The condition in which no heat flows from one part of a system to another because all parts are at the same temperature. *See* **Heat; Specific heat.**

Thermocouple Two wires made of different metals, with their ends twisted together. When the coupled ends are heated, a potential difference is generated. Connecting the other ends of the wires to a sensitive voltmeter indicates the potential produced, which can serve as a measure of the temperature at the thermocouple.

Thermometer A device for measuring temperature. The common mercury-glass thermometer consists of a small bulb containing mercury connected to a tube with an extremely fine bore. When the mercury in the bulb expands, the additional volume rises into the tube. Small expansion produces a substantial rise because the bore of the tube is so narrow. A Celsius thermometer is calibrated by marking the melting point of ice as 0°C and the boiling point of water as 100°C. The space between them is divided into 100 equal spaces.

There are many other kinds of thermometers. The most accurate thermometer for calibration in SI is a constant-volume hydrogen thermometer (*see* **Kelvin scale**). Other thermometers measure temperature by the resistance of a platinum wire, the current generated by the thermocouple, the color of a flame, and so on. *See also* **Stellar temperature**, Earth and Space Science section, page 5-36.

Time *see* Earth and Space Science section, page 5-39.

Torque The property of a force by which it produces changes in rotation. The amount of torque depends on the magnitude of the force applied, but also on the direction of the force and the point of application. In the figure, both pictures show the same forces applied to the rings. It is obvious, however, that the ring at *a* will not turn, but the one at *b* will. The forces on the *b* ring produce a torque.

Torque must be measured around some pivot point. A wheel mounted on an axle is constrained and must spin around its axle or not at all. A force applied on a line through the axle produces no torque. To get the most torque, the force must be applied tangentially, that is, perpendicular to a radius of the wheel. The farther away from the axle the force is applied, the more torque it produces.

For a force applied tangentially, the torque is the product of the force and the radial distance of the pivot point. It is measured in newton-meters.

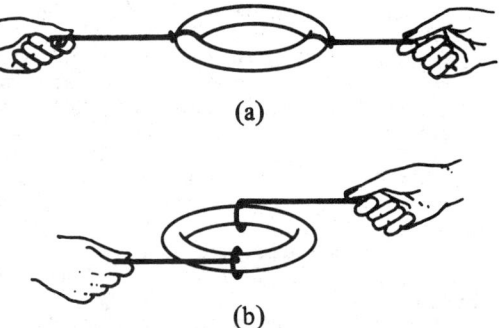

(a)

(b)

Example

What is the torque if the radius of the Wheel of Fortune is 1.5 m and a contestant pushes it tangentially with a force of 12 N?

$$\tau = (12\text{ N})(1.5\text{ m}) = 18\text{ N·m}$$

For applications *see* **Rotational equilibrium.**

Total internal reflection Reflection of a light ray when it approaches a medium of lower index of refraction at a high angle. When light emerges from a medium of high index of refraction into one of lower index, it bends away from the normal (*see* **Refraction**). Rays *B*, *C*, and *D* in the figure show this. Ray *D* bends so far that it emerges along the surface, with an angle of refraction of 90°. At any larger angle of incidence such as that at ray *E*, the ray cannot emerge at all. It is reflected back into the medium in which it travels more slowly.

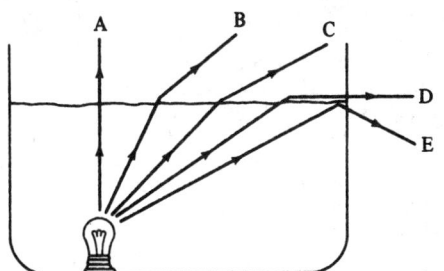

Total internal reflection is useful in optical equipment because it is the most efficient reflection available. There is less loss than at a mirrored surface. In a light pipe, light can be confined as long as the conducting medium is not bent too sharply at any point. Very fine filaments of highly transparent glass, embedded in plastic of lower index, can carry light for miles. They are replacing electric wires for carrying telephone messages.

The angle of incidence of ray D is called the critical angle of incidence i_c. At any angle higher than this, the light is totally reflected. This is the angle at which the angle of reflection is 90°. Therefore,

$$n = \frac{c}{v} = \frac{\sin 90°}{\sin i_c} \quad \text{and} \quad \sin i_c = \frac{1}{n}$$

Trajectory   The path of a particle in free fall. If the velocity has a horizontal component, this component does not change, but the vertical component increases at the rate of acceleration due to gravity. The path of the motion, assuming a uniform gravitational field, is thus a parabola. High velocities at high altitudes result in elliptical trajectories. *See* **Orbit**.

Transformer   A device that uses magnetic fields to convert alternating current potentials to higher or lower values. It consists of two coils of wire, usually wrapped around an iron core. An alternating current is introduced into one coil, the primary. This generates an alternating magnetic field in the core. The secondary coil is also wrapped around the core. The alternating magnetic field in the core induces an alternating potential difference in the secondary. If the secondary circuit is completed, there will be current in the secondary and in its load.

The potentials across the coils are in direct proportion to the number of turns of wire in the coils.

Example

A primary is made with 600 turns of wire and is to be used to step 120 V alternating current up to 15,000 V alternating current for use in a gas discharge tube. How many turns of wire must there be in the secondary?

$$\frac{V_p}{V_s} = \frac{N_p}{N_s} \quad \text{so} \quad \frac{120 \text{ V}}{15,000 \text{ V}} = \frac{600 \text{ turns}}{N_s}$$

which gives an answer of 75,000 turns for the secondary.

Since the transformer cannot create power, in the ideal case the power output is equal to the power input: $V_p I_p = V_s I_s$. This means that if the potential is stepped up, there must be more current in the primary than in the secondary. The currents are inversely proportional to the number of turns. If the gas discharge tube uses 20 mA at 15,000 V, how much current must be supplied to the primary coil?

$$\frac{I_p}{I_s} = \frac{N_s}{N_p} \quad \text{so} \quad \frac{I_p}{20 \text{ mA}} = \frac{75,000 \text{ turns}}{600 \text{ turns}}$$

so the primary current is 2500 mA, or 2.5 A. Actually, it will be a little more because some energy is lost in the production of heat owing to the resistance of the wires and the repeated reversing of the magnetization of the core. This might be very small; large transformers manage efficiencies up to 95%.

Transformers may step potentials down as well as up. The effect depends on which coil has more turns.

Transistor   A solid-state device used in the amplification and control of electronic signals. Except for certain specialized functions, transistors have completely replaced vacuum tubes.

A transistor consists of a sandwich, with a material of one kind placed between layers of another. In one form, the middle layer, called the base, is doped with an impurity that gives it an excess of electrons. The other two layers, the emitter and the collector, are doped with a material that has a deficiency of electrons; they are said to have electron "holes."

To use a transistor as an amplifier, a potential difference is placed between the emitter and the base, and another between the collector and the base. To amplify an AC signal, the signal is inserted into the emitter current, which flows through the base. Since the collector current also goes through the base, this circuit also carries the fluctuations in the emitter current. The collector has a much higher resistance than the emitter. The result is that the same current, in both circuits, has a much higher potential difference coming out of the collector circuit than going into the emitter circuit.

Translational equilibrium   A condition in which the velocity of an object does not change because the vector sum of all forces on it is zero.

Example 1

Consider the 2.2 kg brick in the figure being pulled along a tabletop at constant speed. The string has 12 N of tension in it and makes an angle of 18° with the table. What are the friction and the elastic recoil of the tabletop?

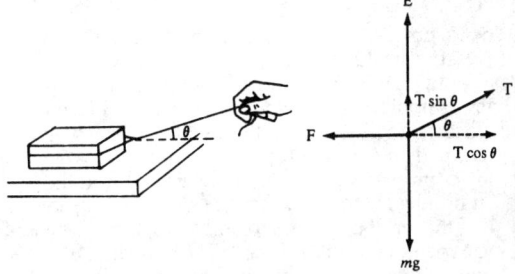

A vector diagram shows the magnitudes and directions of the forces acting on the brick. Friction acts to the left, retarding the motion. The elastic recoil of the tabletop pushes straight up, supporting the weight of the brick. Gravity, the weight of the brick, acts straight down. The tension in the string acts along the string, at 18° to the horizontal.

Since the velocity of the brick is not changing, it is in equilibrium. In this state, the sum of all the forces acting along any axis must be zero. To determine the amount of friction, consider the forces on a horizontal axis. Friction **F** pulls to the left; the horizontal component of the tension **T** pulls to the right. There are no other horizontal forces. Therefore,

$$\mathbf{F} = \mathbf{T} \sin \theta = (12 \text{ N})(\sin 18°) = 3.7 \text{ N}$$

(*See* **Component**.) To determine the elastic recoil, consider the vertical forces. Upward: elastic recoil + vertical component of tension; downward: weight. Then,

$$\mathbf{E} + (12 \text{ N})(\cos 18°) = (2.2 \text{ kg})(9.8 \text{ N/kg})$$

so **E** = 10.1 N

Example 2

What is the tension in the rope holding up the 22 kg sign in the figure if the rope makes an angle of 55° with the bar?

Neglect the weight of the bar. All we need is the forces on the vertical axis. Down: the weight of the sign; up: the vertical component of the tension.

$$\mathbf{T} \cos 55° = (22 \text{ kg})(9.8 \text{ N/kg})$$

and **T** = 380 N.

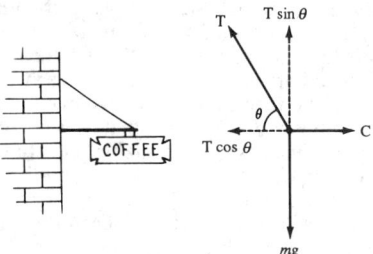

Transverse wave   A wave in which the vibrations are perpendicular to the direction of travel of the wave. Mechanical transverse waves can be sustained only in solids, since liquids and gases have no tensile strength. Electromagnetic waves are transverse and require no medium at all. The standing wave in a string is transverse; the wave velocity is along the length of the string.

Triple point   The combination of temperature and pressure at which all three phases of a substance can exist in equilibrium. To get water to its triple point, for example, a small amount of water is placed in a closed container, and the air above the water is pumped out. Since the boiling point is lower at lower pressures, removal of the air will start the water boiling at room temperature. As pumping continues, the water continues to boil, extracting its heat of vaporization from the liquid. The temperature of the liquid drops. Eventually, the liquid reaches its freezing point, and boiling continues while some of the liquid freezes. The heat of fusion is supplying the heat of vaporization, and the water is at its triple

point. The temperature is 0.01°C, and the pressure is 0.610 kPa, or about 0.006 atm.

Two-point interference   When two point sources are oscillating in phase, they produce a definite pattern of constructive and destructive interference. This can be demonstrated in a ripple tank, as shown in the figure. The waves spread out from the sources on circular fronts. Along the lines marked R_0, R_1, and R_2, the waves arrive in phase. These are antinodal lines, where interference is constructive and oscillation is a maximum. *A* is a nodal line, where the waves arrive out of phase, and destructive interference produces regions of no oscillation.

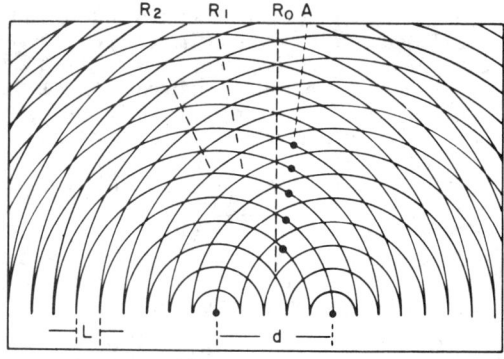

Waves from Two Point Sources in Phase

To produce constructive interference, the wave from one source must travel some whole number of wavelengths farther than the wave from the other. This is the condition that defines the location of the antinodal lines. Nodes occur wherever the path difference is an odd number of half-wavelengths.

Interference in optical systems produces alternating nodal and antinodal lines. (*See* **Diffraction grating**; **Interference fringes**.)

Units   *See* **Système Internationale**.

Vector   A physical quantity having both magnitude and direction. Some examples are displacement, velocity, acceleration, force, momentum, area, angular momentum, electric field, gravitational field, and magnetic field. All vectors obey a special rule of addition, shown in the figure. **A** and **B** are vectors; their lengths represent their magnitudes, and each has a direction. **C** is a vector representing the vector sum **A** + **B**.

The vector sum of **A** and **B** can be visualized by thinking of the vectors as displacements. Imagine you start at the tail of **A** and walk a distance and direction represented by **A**. From there, walk a distance and direction represented by **B**. Where are you with respect to your starting point? Here is the rule for adding **A** + **B**: Move **B**, without changing its direction or magnitude, to a position such that its tail is at the head of **A**. Draw **C** from the tail of **A** to the head of **B**. Now **C** represents your distance and direction from your starting point. The third diagram shows that **B** + **A** also gives **C**.

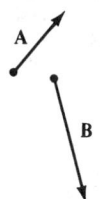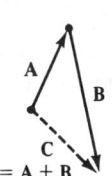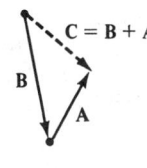

Example

The boat in the figure is traveling at 4.0 m/s across a river that is flowing at 5.5 m/s. What is the net velocity of the boat?

Since velocity is a vector quantity, the two velocities must be added by the rules of vector mathematics, as shown in the vector diagram. When the two velocities are at right angles to each other, the easiest way to add them is by the theorem of Pythagoras:

$$v = \sqrt{(4.0 \text{ m/s})^2 + (5.5 \text{ m/s})^2} = 6.8 \text{ m/s}$$

and the direction, measured with respect to the cross-stream axis, is

$$\arctan \frac{5.5}{4.0} = 54°$$

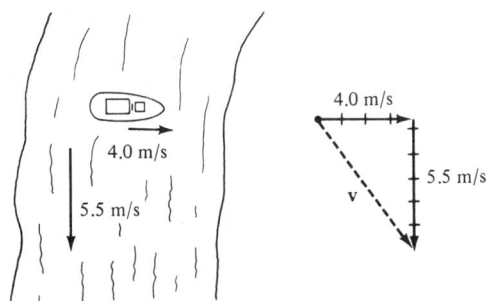

For more information about vectors, *see* **Component**; for more applications, *see* **Translational equilibrium**.

Velocity   A vector quantity representing speed (distance traveled per unit time) in a particular direction. Velocities obey the usual rules of vector addition. For example, if you are walking south at 3 m/s on a train going north at 9 m/s, your net velocity with respect to the earth is "6 m/s north." Since velocity is a vector, it is not completely stated unless the direction is given.

Now suppose you are walking west in that train. The two velocities to be added are now at right angles to each other. Following the rules for vector addition, the magnitude of your net velocity is

$$\sqrt{(3 \text{ m/s})^2 + (9 \text{ m/s})^2} = 9.5 \text{ m/s}$$

and the direction is

$$\arctan \frac{3}{9} = 18° \text{ west of north}$$

For details, *see* **Vector**.

Volt   *See* **Electric potential**.

Voltmeter   An instrument for measuring electric potential difference. The most common kind consists of a Weston galvanometer with a very high resistance placed in series. The galvanometer measures current. When the voltmeter is connected between two points in a circuit, the current through it is very small because of the high resistance. This is necessary so that the meter does not distort the parameters of the circuit. The current is proportional to the potential difference between the two connection points, so the scale of the instrument can be calibrated in volts.

**Wave**   A disturbance propagated through a medium. The wave in the rope of the figure is a paradigm. As the hand moves up and down, it pulls the rope up and down. Each segment of the rope pulls on the next one down the line. The result is that every piece of the rope is moving up and down, with

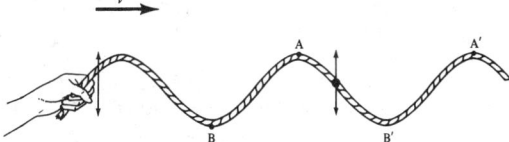

a time delay from each point to the next. The wave is moving to the right, but each point on the rope moves only up and down. A wave is described by certain parameters:

Frequency f is the rate of vibration. It is measured in cycles per second, called hertz (Hz). Every point on the wave has the same frequency, which is determined by the frequency of the source (the hand).

Velocity v is the rate at which any given crest moves through the medium (the rope), measured in meters per second (m/s). Velocity is determined primarily by the nature of the medium, although in many media, waves of higher frequency move faster (*see* **Dispersion**).

Wavelength λ (the Greek letter lambda) is the distance in meters between two points in the same phase. It can be found most easily by measuring the distance between crests, as between points *A* and *A'*. Wavelength is determined by the velocity and frequency according to the equation $v = f\lambda$

Example

In the figure above, the speed of the wave in the rope is 6.4 m/s and the hand is shaking the rope at the rate of 4.0 vibrations per second. What is the wavelength of the wave?

$$v = f\lambda \quad \text{so} \quad 6.4 \text{ m/s} = (4.0 \text{ Hz})\lambda$$

and λ = 1.6 m.

Amplitude is the maximum displacement of any point, the distance from the equilibrium position to the top of a crest. It is determined by the amplitude of the vibration that produced the wave. The energy carried by the wave is proportional to the square of the amplitude. If the wave loses energy as it travels (as all real waves must) the amplitude decreases with distance from the source. The process of losing energy is called *damping*.

Waves can be classified according to whether the motion of the particles is parallel or perpendicular to the wave velocity. *See* **Longitudinal wave; Transverse wave.** *See also* **Sound wave; Electromagnetic waves.**

Wavelength *See* **Wave.**

Weak interaction One of the four basic forces of nature. This is an extremely short range force, confined to the interior of subnuclear particles. The weak interaction is responsible for the radioactive decay of large nuclei and of all particles except the proton, electron, neutrino, and photon. It acts by altering one of the quarks in the particle, making it unstable. Recent theory has found that the electromagnetic and weak interactions are aspects of a single basic force. *See also* **Strong nuclear force.**

Weight *See* **Gravity.**

Wheel-and-axle A simple machine consisting of a wheel of large diameter mounted on an axle of small diameter. The mechanical advantage is the ratio of the two diameters.

Work The product of the distance an object moves and the force pushing it in the direction it is going. If the force is in newtons and the distance in meters, the work is in joules.

For example, if a force of 160 N is required to slide a crate along a floor, and if that force is applied to shove the crate 12 m, the work done on the crate is

$$W = F\Delta s = (160 \text{ N})(12 \text{ m}) = 1920 \text{ J}$$

Work is scalar. If the crate is shoved back to its original position, it takes another 1920 J to do so, even though there has been no net change in position.

It is important to note that only the force in the direction of motion counts. If you hold up a box weighing 50 N without moving it, you are pushing it upward but doing no work. If you carry it horizontally, your force is still upward and the distance is horizontal. No work is done because the force is perpendicular to the displacement. There is no force in the direction of movement.

Work can be thought of as a mechanism for transferring energy from one system to another. The crate gains energy (heat produced by friction), and the person pushing it loses an equal amount. *See* **Energy.**

PSYCHOLOGY

Aberration The act of wandering or straying from the normal course. Idiosyncratic or peculiar behavior.

Abnormal Literally, any departure from the norm or the normal. The term is largely used to denote deviant behavior patterns in individuals. Although this latter reference has been the dominant one in psychology for a long time, there has been some reluctance recently on the part of clinicians to use it. For example, within classical psychoanalysis, homosexuality is classified as abnormal; within a social learning theory analysis it is not. Also, Einstein would of necessity be called abnormal. The years have layered onto this term too many value judgments; any of a number of synonyms are preferable—*maladaptive, maladjusted, deviant, dysfunctional*, etc.

Abusing parent A label for a parent or guardian who has physically or psychologically mistreated or neglected a child. Research has not identified any common characteristics of these individuals other than they were likely to have been abused themselves as children. *See* **Child abuse**.

Acarophobia A fear of small insects or animals. Occasionally, the delusion that one's skin is infested with mites or fleas.

Accident prone A term loosely used to describe persons who display a somewhat higher than average rate of accidents. Such individuals may indeed contribute to their high accident rates by any number of conscious or unconscious reasons or they may be simply unlucky.

Achievement test Any test designed to evaluate a person's current state of knowledge or skill. Contrast with aptitude test, which is designed to evaluate potentialities for achievement independent of current knowledge.

Acting out Either a rather irrational, impulsive display of temperament in children or adults, or a display of feeling and emotion that has previously been inhibited. Here the term is used with a positive connotation, in that self-expression is regarded as healthy and therapeutic, particularly to a doctor, observing the manifestations of emotional illness.

Acute brain disorder A cover term for any disability due to a reversible (hence, temporary) impairment of brain tissue.

Addiction Any psychological or physiological overdependence of an organism on a drug. Originally the term was used only for physiological dependencies in which the drug had altered the biochemistry of the individual such that continued doses (often of increasing size; *see* **Tolerance, drug**) were required, as is the case with drug opiates and alcohol. However, the line between the purely physiological addiction and the psychological dependence is far from clear. The confusion led the World Health Organization to recommend recently that the term "dependence" be used, with proper qualifiers when drugs are involved. *See* **Methadone; Withdrawal; Dependence, physiological; Dependence, psychological**.

Adler, Alfred (1870–1937) Austrian psychologist, founder of the school of individual psychology. Adler joined Freud and then split with him in 1911 over a difference in psychoanalytic judgment regarding inferiority feelings and striving for power. Adler addressed himself to the educated layman, and much of his approach was directed toward the welfare of children; he was the founder of many child-guidance clinics. *Individual psychology* is concerned with three phases of mental disease: understanding, prevention, and treatment. This school lays stress on the early development of the child and the feeling of helplessness that later produces inferiority complexes. Inferiority then leads to overcompensation and eventually produces the superior and hostile attitudes that characterize the delinquent or criminal personality. Adler's emphasis is on family: an older sibling being pushed aside to make way for the new baby, the importance of the mother figure as the first social contact. Diagnosis in individual psychology relies heavily on the patient's earliest memory as illustrative of his first attempts at problem solving. Dreams are seen as reflective of attempts to cope with problems.

Affective disorder A broad psychiatric diagnostic category used to denote disturbances of mood or emotional tone to the point where excessive and inappropriate depression or elation occurs. Current terminology is mood disorder. *See* **Bipolar disorder; Cyclothymic disorder**.

Affective psychosis Loosely, any psychosis with severe disturbances in mood or feeling. The classic example is the manic-depressive reaction. Current terminology is bipolar disorder. *See* **Bipolar disorder; Cyclothymic disorder**.

Aggression An extremely general term used for a wide variety of acts that involve attack, hostility, etc. Typically, it is used for such acts that can be assumed to be motivated by any of the following: (a) fear or frustration; (b) a desire to produce fear or flight in others; or (c) a tendency to push forward one's own ideas or interests.

Agoraphobia Generally, a fear of open spaces. Agoraphobia is the most commonly cited phobic disorder of those persons who seek psychiatric or psychological treatment. It has a variety of manifestations, the most common a deep fear of being caught alone in some public place (indeed, this is regarded by some authorities as the defining feature of the disorder). Help for this phobia is now easily available through clinics and groups treating the syndrome.

Alcohol abuse A general label for any pathological syndrome associated with excessive alcohol use. A variety of characteristics is found in serious cases, including a daily need for alcohol, continuing consumption in the face of physical disorders or impairments in social and occupational functioning, "blackouts" or periods of amnesia, extended alcoholic "binges" lasting several days, repeated but unsuccessful attempts to quit drinking and overall mental and emotional deterioration.

Alcohol amnestic disorder Memory impairment associated with prolonged, excessive consumption of alcohol.

Alcoholic jealousy An irrational, paranoid-like jealousy often observed in cases of chronic alcohol abuse.

Alcoholic psychosis A general term used to cover the serious, disabling outcome of excessive, chronic alcohol abuse.

Alcohol idiosyncratic intoxication A disorder the defining feature of which is a marked change in mood and behavior following ingestion of an amount of alcohol too small to produce intoxication in most people. The intoxicated state is typically manifested by a dramatic shift toward aggressiveness and hostility that is not typical of the person and there is usually subsequent amnesia for the episode.

Alcohol withdrawal An organic mental disorder characterized by tremor of the hands, eyelids, and tongue, nausea, weakness, sweating, depressed mood, anxiety, and irritability. It follows, usually within a few hours, cessation of alcohol intake in an individual who has been drinking for several days or longer.

Alcohol withdrawal delirium Delirium resulting from sudden cessation of alcohol intake following an extended period of alcohol abuse. Typically, symptoms are hallucinations (usually visual), rapid and irregular heartbeat, agitation, tremors, sweating, and high blood pressure.

Alienation Most contemporary usage reflects the standard dictionary meanings: a feeling of strangeness or separation from others; a sense of a lack of warm relations with others. Existentialists, however, have made the term a central construct in their psychology and appended a subtle but important meaning to the term. Rather than concentrate solely upon alienation of one human from others, they also stress the alienation of a person from him- or herself. This separation of the individual from the presumed "real" or "deeper" self is assumed to result from preoccupation with conformity, the wishes of others, and the pressures from social institutions. *See* **Existential psychology and therapy.**

Alzheimer's disease A progressive disease that is superficially similar to senility except that it strikes relatively early in life (usually in the 40s and 50s). The first sign is impaired memory, usually followed by disturbed speech and thought and ultimately complete helplessness.

Amnesia Generally, any partial or complete loss of memory. A number of specific forms of amnesia are recognized, each denoting a particular kind of deficit in memory. Note, however, that amnesia can be physiological, caused by some form of damage to brain tissue, or psychogenic and caused by any of a variety of factors, including neurotic reactions.

Amphetamines A class of drugs including benzedrine, dexedrine, and methedrine that act as central nervous system stimulants. Amphetamines suppress appetite, increase heart rate and blood pressure, and, in larger doses produce a feeling of euphoria and power. Therapeutically, they are used to alleviate depression. They are also used to treat Attention Deficit Hyperactive Disorders (ADHD) in children. Amphetamine abuse is common, and chronic use leads to paranoid psychosis. *See* **Tranquilizers, minor.**

Analysis The particular set of techniques and procedures used in the practice of psychoanalysis. The process is designed to reveal root causes of mental illness.

Androgyny From Greek *andros* (= man) and *gyne* (= female), the condition in which some male and some female characteristics are present in the same individual.

Anger Very generally, a fairly strong emotional reaction that accompanies a variety of situations, such as being physically restrained, being interfered with, having one's possessions removed, being attacked or threatened, etc. Anger is often defined by a collection of physical reactions including particular facial grimaces and body positions.

Angst German for *anxiety*, *anguish*, or *psychic pain*. In the existential school, this mental turmoil is regarded as *the* fundamental reality of beings who must confront life as a battleground within which personal choice is essential and the responsibility for decisions made must be borne.

Anima Originally, the soul. In the early writings of Carl Jung, one's inner being, that aspect of one's psyche in intimate association with one's unconscious. In Jung's later writings, the feminine archetype, which was differentiated from *animus*, the masculine archetype. In arguing for this essential bisexuality of all persons, Jung hypothesized that both components were present in both sexes.

Anorexia nervosa An eating disorder characterized by intense fear of becoming obese, dramatic weight loss, obsessive concern with one's weight, disturbances of body image such that the patient "feels fat" when of normal weight or even when emaciated. The classic anorexic is young (rarely over 30), female (roughly 95 percent of all cases) and from a middle- or upper-class family. They frequently are described as "model children." The disorder is rather resistant to treatment and can have an unremitting course leading to death, although in the large majority of cases there is spontaneous full recovery. *See* **Bulimia; Eating disorders.**

Antianxiety drugs A general term for several classes of drugs that function primarily to reduce anxiety. The term is preferred by many, rather than minor tranquilizers, on the grounds that they are not so "minor" and can have serious side effects, particularly when taken in large doses or in combination with alcohol.

Antidepressant drugs A general psychopharmacological classification of drugs used in fairly severe depressive disorders. The most common are tricyclic compounds and monoamine oxidase inhibitors. Some classification systems include the amphetamines as antidepressants, although they are more commonly grouped with the stimulants; others include lithium because of its use in the treatment of manic-depressives. *See* **Lithium; Tranquilizers, major; Tranquilizers, minor.**

Antipsychotic drugs A general term covering all those drugs used in the treatment of psychoses. The major tranquilizers, such as Thorazine and Mellaril, are included in this group. *See* **Lithium; Tranquilizers, major; Neuroleptic medication.**

Antisocial personality disorder A personality disorder characterized by a history of chronic antisocial behavior (often observed in childhood), the essential feature of which is the violation of the rights of others. Strictly speaking the term is only used when the onset is before age 15 and continues into later life. Typical patterns of behavior are truancy from school, an inability to hold a job, lying, stealing, aggressive sexual behavior, drug and alcohol abuse, vagrancy and a high rate of criminality. *See* **Psychopath**; **Criminal psychopath**; **Psychopathic personality**.

Anxiety   Most generally, a vague, unpleasant emotional state with qualities of apprehension, dread, distress, and uneasiness. Frequently known as panic, anxiety is often distinguished from fear in that an anxiety state is often objectless, whereas fear assumes a specific feared object, person or event. In existential theory, anxiety is characterized as the emotional accompaniment of the immediate awareness of the meaninglessness, incompleteness, and chaotic nature of the world in which we live. *See* **Generalized anxiety disorder**; **Hyperventilation**.

Anxiety, free-floating   The kind of vague, nebulous anxiety associated with the generalized anxiety disorders. Also called neurotic anxiety. *See* **Generalized anxiety disorder**.

Anxiety neurosis   A subclass of anxiety disorders characterized by recurrent periods of intense anxiety. Usually included in this category are panic disorders, generalized anxiety disorders and obsessive-compulsive disorders.

Anxiety-relief response   A term coined by behavior therapists for a learned operant response that relieves feelings of anxiety. The technique is to associate the response (usually saying out loud or thinking a word like "calm" or "relax") with the cessation of a painful stimulus (like an electric shock). With the response now connected to a feeling of relief it can (at least in principle) be used in other anxious moments or circumstances.

Anxiety, tolerance of   A loose term used for the extent to which an individual can put up with anxiety-provoking situations without having them adversely affect ability to function.

Aphasia   A general term covering any partial or complete loss of language abilities. The origins are always organic, namely, a lesion in the brain. There are literally dozens of varieties of aphasia.

Apoplexy   An acute, abrupt loss of consciousness and subsequent motor paralysis caused by brain hemorrhage, embolism, or thrombosis.

Applied psychology   Basically, an umbrella term used for all those subdisciplines within psychology that seek to apply principles, discoveries, and theories of psychology in practical ways in related areas, such as education, industry, marketing, opinion polling, sport, therapy.

Archetype   In Jung's characterization of the psyche, the inherited, unconscious racial ideas and images that are the primitive components that rise as symbols from the collective unconscious.

Asexual   Literally, without sex or lacking sexuality.

Asocial   Without regard to society or social issues. This meaning is used to describe situations, events, behaviors, or people that operate independently of (although not in opposition to: antisocial) social values and customs. An asocial person is one who is withdrawn from society.

Assertiveness training   A set of techniques used as both a treatment for certain disorders and as a general training program to teach individuals how to assert themselves.

Association, free   Any seemingly unrelated association made between ideas, words, thoughts, etc. In a free-association test the subject is given a word and asked to reply with the first word that comes to mind. It has been used primarily in psychoanalysis, where it serves mostly as a device to explore the client's unconscious.

Asthma   A general term for any of several varieties of bronchial disorders characterized by a spasm of the upper respiratory system with difficult, labored breathing. Asthmatic attacks often accompany allergic reactions and occasionally are secondary complications of respiratory infections. However, asthma is usually classified as a psychosomatic disorder because of the tendency for asthmatic reactions to accompany anxiety and psychoneurotic conflicts.

Attention Deficit Hyperactive Disorder (ADHD)   A general psychiatric syndrome characterized by a child's displaying developmentally inappropriate lack of attention, excessive motor activity, and a lack of impulse control. The term Attention Deficit Disorder (ADD) is used with children who show problems only with impulse control and/or attention deficits and are not overactive. This is a common disorder and frequently results in behavior and/or performance problems in the school setting. Typically the hyperactivity diminishes as the child reaches middle school, but the attentional difficulties and impulsiveness often persist until the late teenage or early adult years. This disorder has had previous names, such as hyperkinesis, hyperactive syndrome, hyperkinetic syndrome of childhood, and minimal brain dysfunction. *See* **Hyperactivity**; **Hyperkinesis**.

Aura   A subjective experience that frequently precedes an epileptic seizure or an impending migraine headache. The aura may occur anywhere from a few hours to several seconds prior to onset and usually consists of a variety of sensory-based hallucinations (e.g., a flash of light).

Autism   The general meaning is reflected by the roots of the word: aut- = self, and -ism = orientation or state. Hence, the tendency to be absorbed in oneself; a condition in which one's thoughts, feelings, and desires are governed by one's internal apprehensions of the world. The term implies that the internal state is in conflict with reality and that the individual sees things in terms of fantasies and dreams, wishes, and hopes, rather than in terms of a reality shared by and with others. The term was originally coined by E. Bleuler for schizophrenia.

Automatic speech   Speech produced without conscious reflection on what is being said. Easily seen with extremely well-learned material, as with counting, saying the alphabet. Also, speech that emerges devoid of conscious control. It is observed in some psychoses, in advanced senility, and occasionally in highly emotional states.

Autosuggestion   Literally, self-suggestion. The term comes from a system of self-improvement developed by a Frenchman, Emile Coué (1857–1926), that was very popular in the 1920s and 1930s. The heart of Coué's rather simplistic system was contained in the phrase, "Every day in every way I am getting better and better," which he counseled people to repeat twenty to thirty times a day.

Aversion therapy A general term for any of a number of behavior-modification techniques that use unpleasant or painful stimuli in a controlled fashion for the purpose of altering behavior patterns in a therapeutic way. The use of such procedures has been primarily restricted to such disorders as alcoholism, drug abuse, and cigarette smoking (and in a few questionable cases, homosexuality) and, generally speaking, they have not been very successful.

Avoidant-personality disorder A personality disorder characterized by a hypersensitivity to rejection that is so extreme that the individual avoids contacts with others and shies away from forming relationships unless given strong guarantees of uncritical acceptance. There is typically low self-esteem, a tendency to devalue accomplishments and inappropriate distress over personal shortcomings—all accompanied by a desire for affection and acceptance.

B

Babinski reflex An upward extension of the toes upon stroking the sole of the foot. A normal reflex in infants but a symptom of certain classes of organic disorders in adults.

Barbiturates A very large group of drugs classified as *hypnosedatives*. Of the over 2,500 barbiturates that have been catalogued, roughly 15 are currently used, in a variety of conditions, including (most commonly) as an aid for sleeping, as an anesthetic, and in the symptomatic treatment of epilepsy. Generally, barbiturates depress the activity of all excitable cells. Barbiturates can be divided into three classes, depending on speed and duration of action. The long-acting include *phenobarbital* and *mephobarbital*. These produce their effects slowly (approximately one hour after ingestion) and last roughly 8-12 hours. The intermediate-acting (15-30 minute onset time; 3-5 hour action) include *pentobarbital*, *secobarbital* and *amobarbital*. The ultra-short-acting (1–2 seconds; 15–30 minutes) include *thiopental* and *methohexital*. Those in this last group are used primarily as anesthetics and administration is usually intravenous. With long-term use all the barbiturates produce tolerance as well as both psychological and physiological drug dependence.

Barbiturate withdrawal A syndrome classified as an organic mental disorder that appears following cessation of intake of barbiturates after a history of prolonged and heavy use. The symptoms are virtually identical with those of *alcohol withdrawal* and include nausea, weakness, tachycardia, sweating, anxiety, and confusion. *See* **Alcohol withdrawal**; **Alcohol withdrawal delirium**; **Withdrawal**.

Behaviorism The approach to psychology that argues that the only appropriate subject matter for scientific psychological investigation is observable, measurable behavior. It was with John B. Watson in the 1910s that behaviorism was born. It is represented in contemporary thinking by the perspective of the late B.F. Skinner.

Behavior modification Changing behavior by applying techniques based on learning theory.

Behavior therapy That type of psychotherapy that seeks to change abnormal or maladaptive behavior patterns by the use of positive and negative reinforcers. The focus is on the behavior itself rather than on underlying conflicts. All behavioral disorders are assumed to result from "unfortunate" contingencies in the life of the individual leading to the acquisition of maladaptive behaviors. There is no need to explore underlying conflicts; effective therapy should aim at modification of the behavior(s) that the patient currently manifests. A large array of specific therapeutic procedures and modification techniques exists.

Bestiality Most broadly, any beastly behavior of a person. More specifically, sexual behavior between humans and animals. The latter is the usual meaning.

Binet, Alfred (1857–1911) French psychologist who developed the first standardized intelligence test. At the turn of the century, Binet began research on individual differences, which eventually led him to develop his renowned intelligence scale in 1905. For intelligence investigation, he studied the differing mental levels and processes of his daughters, using pictures, word tests, and ink blots. The *Stanford-Binet Scale* is a revision of the original Binet and Simon test, widely adapted for use in most countries.

Biofeedback Feedback providing information about bodily functioning through sensory channels or outside sources (e.g., EEG).

Biorhythms A general label covering all periods of biological systems. The most intensely studied are the *circadian rhythms*, although many biological functions show a period other than a daily one, for example, menstrual cycles, bird migrations, protective-coloring changes, etc. Note that in recent years this term has become "contaminated" by the emergence of a pseudoscience of the same name. Using the so-called biorhythm methods its practitioners claim to be able to predict a person's performance on a task on any given day, on the basis of a chart of their biorhythms from their day of birth. An utter lack of supportive evidence for these claims has, predictably, had little impact on public acceptance but it has led scientific researchers to cast about for a new label for their field.

Bipolar disorder A major affective disorder in which both manic and depressive episodes occur. Also known as *manic-depression* and *manic-depressive* psychosis. *See* **Affective disorder**; **Affective psychosis**; **Cyclothymic disorder**; **Hypomanic disorder**; **Lithium**; **Mania**; **Manic episode**.

Bisexual *Hermaphrodite*. Also, an individual whose sexual preferences include members of his or her own sex as well as members of the opposite sex.

Body language The complex system whereby information about feelings and emotions is communicated through nonverbal channels involving gestures, body position, facial expressions, etc. Despite the often misleading and trivial discussions about it that have unfortunately impressed themselves upon the lay public, it is possible to approach this topic in a reasonable and scientifically responsible fashion.

Borderline personality disorder A personality disorder in which the individual chronically lives "on the borderline" between normal, adaptive functioning and real psychic disability. Usually such a person is identified by any of a number of instabilities with no clear features; e.g., interpersonal relations tend to be unstable, self-image may be disturbed, displays of anger and temper are common, impulsive acts that are self-damaging, like gambling or shoplifting, are frequent.

Brain lesion Any damage to brain tissue produced by injury, disease, surgery, etc.

Bulimia An eating disorder in which an individual goes through recurrent episodes of rapidly consuming a large quantity of food and then purging (e.g. vomiting, using laxatives). Episodes are usually associated with depression and are followed by guilt, self-deprecation and overconcern with body shape and weight. *See* **Anorexia nervosa**; **Eating disorders**. *See also* Health & Medicine, page 8-19.

C**affeinism** Caffeine intoxication. Symptoms are nervousness, anxiety, insomnia and psychomotor agitation. In sensitive persons as little as 250 mg (roughly 2–3 cups of coffee or 3–5 cups of tea) is sufficient to produce these effects.

Castration complex In classical (Freudian) psychoanalytic theory, the fear associated with loss of one's genitals. In the male the complex is supposedly manifested as anxiety surrounding the possibility of loss, in females as the guilt over having already experienced the loss. The original position with regard to males has, of course, been critiqued rather severely but is still, generally speaking, a part of the standard psychoanalytic theory; the position with regard to females has been so vigorously attacked, especially by female analysts, that it is rarely taken seriously any longer. *See* **Penis envy**.

Catatonia The term refers literally to muscular rigidity or extreme tension. It is observed as a syndrome in catatonic schizophrenia where the patient in a so-called catatonic state may remain in a fixed position for long periods. *See* **Schizophrenia, catatonic (type)**.

Catharsis From the Greek meaning *purification*, *purging*. In psychoanalytic theory this meaning was borrowed to refer to the release of tension and anxiety resulting from the process of bringing repressed ideas, feelings, wishes, and memories of the past into consciousness. Lay usage has broadened the meaning a bit and one often sees the term used to refer to any satisfying emotional experience.

Cerebellum Literally, the Latin diminutive "little brain." It is involved in muscle coordination and the maintenance of body equilibrium.

Cerebrum The largest and most prominent structure of the brain. The inner core is composed of white matter: the outer covering is made up entirely of gray matter. The human cerebrum consists of perhaps 15 billion cells and is the latest brain structure to have evolved. It is involved in processing and interpretation of sensory inputs, control over voluntary motor activity, consciousness, planning, and execution of action, thinking, ideating, language, reasoning, judging, and the like; in short, all of those functions most closely associated with the so-called higher mental functions.

Child abuse Generally, any form of physical or psychological mistreatment or neglect of a child by parents or guardians. The most common form involves severe and repeated physical injury (contusions, broken bones). Other forms of mistreatment such as starvation, locking the child away in attics or closets, burning with cigarettes or other hot objects, sexual assault, and emotional and psychological degradation are also included. *See* **Abusing parent**.

Chronic brain disorder (or **syndrome)** One of the standard classifications of behavior disorders. It refers to disorders resulting from large, long-lasting brain damage such as those caused by syphilis, brain tumors, strokes, or drugs. The most common by far are those due to changes occurring in old age (senile psychosis) and alcohol (alcoholic psychosis).

Claustrophobia Fear of closed spaces.

Client-centered therapy Also known as nondirective therapy. Developed by Carl Rogers. The therapist does not advise or direct the clients. Working on the assumption that clients are best able to deal with their personal problems, the therapist is nonjudgmental and accepting and reflects the clients' feelings and concerns in order to clarify points and encourage them. *See* **Rogers**.

Clinical psychology The area of psychology concerned with aberrant, maladaptive or abnormal human behavior. Within the vast umbrella of clinical practices are diagnosis, classification, treatment, prevention, and research. Although recent years have reflected a trend toward the empirical approach, in which the clinician draws on the findings and methodology of the researcher, clinical psychology largely reflects its historical lineage, which is predominantly medical in orientation. However, to appreciate the enormous range available to the practicing clinician (and even more bewilderingly, to the person seeking psychotherapy), other recognized and widely practiced therapies should be consulted: behavior, client-centered, encounter, Gestalt, group, psychoanalysis (various forms), existential, cognitive, etc.

Codependency A situation in which one person develops a dependency on another person who is also dependent. This usually occurs in dysfunctional relationships and the term is frequently used in the area of substance abuse. For example, a spouse has a neurotic need to maintain a bad marriage relationship and is unwilling to challenge the substance-dependent partner's dysfunctional behavior.

Cold turkey Slang for the process of terminating a physiological *drug dependence* by abruptly ceasing to take the drug with no support from other drugs. Depending on the severity of the dependence and the form of drug involved, such a process can be a most trying experience. This is particularly true in the case of opiates, amphetamines. and alcohol. *See* **Withdrawal**.

Collective unconscious Jung's term for that aspect of the unconscious shared by all. This racial unconscious (as it is also called) was assumed by Jung to be inherited and, in his conceptualization, to consist of the residue of the evolution of man. Its components were termed *archetypes*.

Comparative psychology A subdiscipline of psychology concerned with the investigation of the behavior of various species of animals by drawing comparisons (similarities and distinctions) between them. The approach draws on other areas in psychology, such as learning theory, and on other disciplines, including ethology, physiology, genetics and zoology. *See* **Lorenz.**

Compulsion Behavior motivated by factors that compel a person to act against his or her own wishes. Differentiate from *obsession*, in which the focus is more on thoughts and feelings than on behavior, and from *impulse*, in which the compelling quality is more sudden and satisfiable. Compulsion usually carries the connotation of repetitiveness and irrationality. *See* **Obsession**; **Obsessive-compulsive disorder**.

Conditioning A generic term for a set of empirical concepts, particularly those that specify the conditions under which associative learning takes place. Often divided into two separate types: *classical conditioning* (or *Pavlovian*) and *operant* (or *Skinnerian*). The basic difference between the two is that in classical conditioning the outcome of a trial always occurs regardless of how the organism responds—Pavlov's dogs received food whether or not they salivated. In operant conditioning the outcome of a trial is contingent upon the organism making a specified response—Skinner's pigeons were not given food unless they pecked the key the requisite number of times under the proper stimulus conditions. In classical conditioning, the conditioned response (e.g., eye blink, salivation, knee jerk) is generally reflexive, primitive, autonomic, and lacking in volition, and it is elicited by the conditioned stimulus. In operant conditioning, the response (e.g., bar pressing, maze running) is more voluntary, nonreflexive, and emitted by the organism in the presence of the appropriate stimulus. *See* **Skinner**; **Pavlov.**

Congenital Present at birth. Note that the term is not necessarily synonymous with *innate* or *hereditary*. A congenital condition may be due to factors other than heredity, e.g., retardation produced by the mother's contracting German measles early in pregnancy.

Consciousness Generally, a state of awareness. This is the most general usage of the term and is that intended in phrases like "he lost consciousness." It is also a domain of mind that contains the sensations, perceptions, and memories of which one is momentarily aware, that is, those aspects of present mental life to which one is attending. The term has a distinctly checkered history. It has sometimes represented the central focus of pychology (*structuralism*) and at others been banned from the psychologist's lexicon as representing nothing more then the flotsam of bodily activity; (*see* **Behaviorism**). The ongoing fascination with it, however, stems from the compelling sense that consciousness is one of the fundamental defining features of our species: that to be human is to possess not only self-awareness but the even more remarkable capacity to scan and review mentally that of which we are aware.

Control group A group in an experiment that is as closely matched as possible to the experimental group except that it is not exposed to the independent variable(s) under investigation.

Conversion disorder A disorder in which an individual's psychic conflict is exhibited in somatic form whereby the physical symptoms will appear to have superficial causes with no true organic source.

Countertransference In psychoanalysis, the analyst's displacement of affect (i.e., *transference*) onto the client. More generally, the analyst's emotional involvement in the therapeutic interaction. In the former sense countertransference is a distorting element in a psychoanalysis and can be disruptive; in the latter sense it is considered benign and, by some, inevitable. Freud supported the former sense, and Jung the latter. Most current analysts see it as inevitable and even as therapeutically useful.

Cranial nerves The 12 nerves that enter and leave the brain directly rather than through the spinal cord. They are numbered and individually named:

  I *Olfactory*: smell
  II *Optic*: vision
  III *Ocumotor*: eye muscles
  IV *Trocular*: oblique muscles of eye
  V *Trigeminal*: face, nose, and tongue
  VI *Abducens*: rectus muscles of eye
  VII *Facial*: facial muscles, taste buds, anterior part of the tongue
  VIII *Auditory-vestibular*: hearing and balance, also called *vestibulocochlear*
  IX *Glossopharyngeal*: the throat, taste buds, posterior part of the tongue
  X *Vagus*: heart, lungs, thorax, larynx, pharynx, external ear, and abdominal viscera
  XI *Spinal accessory*: neck muscles
  XII *Hypoglossal*: tongue muscles

Cranium That portion of the skull enclosing the brain.

Criminal psychopath An individual whose illegal acts stem from uncontrollable psychological problems, e.g., the disorders of kleptomania, pyromania; exhibitionism and rape are included. Also called *criminal sociopath*.

Cyclothymic disorder An affective disorder characterized by cyclic mood swings or by a fairly consistent elation or depression. Distinguish from manic-depression, in which the range of the emotions is much more extreme. Cyclothymia is used as a psychiatric label only when there has been extended observation (usually two years or more) by the physician of the patient's mood swings. Cyclothymic patients rarely experience together more than two months of behavior not categorized as either elated or depressed. Not meant to apply to acute emotional reactions. Also called *cyclic disorder* or *cyclothymia*. One of the bipolar disorders. *See* **Bipolar disorder.**

D **Defense mechanism** A term applied to any enduring pattern of protective behavior designed to provide a defense against the awareness of that which is anxiety producing.

Delirium A disoriented condition with clouded consciousness, often accompanied by hallucinations, illusions, misinterpretations of events, and a generally confused quality with reduced capacity to sustain attention to things in the environment. Delirium is frequently of fairly rapid onset (often after head injury or a seizure) but may also develop slowly over time.

Delirium tremens   An acute *delirium*, with all of its characteristic symptoms, that is associated with excessive alcohol abuse. Some writers have used the term (and its slang abbreviation, the *d.t.'s*) as though the syndrome were caused by alcohol consumption, which is true but only in a misleading manner. The proper usage is for a delirium whose onset follows, usually by a day or two, the cessation of alcohol intake after many years of alcohol abuse.

Delusion   A belief that is maintained in spite of argument, data, and refutation that should (reasonably) be sufficient to destroy it. Care should be taken in the use of the term—one person's delusion may be another's salvation.

Delusions of grandeur   Delusions of exaggerated greatness, power, influence; *megalomania*.

Delusions of persecution   Delusions of the paranoid type; the person feels that others are out to "get" them, thwart their efforts to achieve, and somehow inflict pain or injury on them. Typically a rich, systematic conspiracy is imagined. *See* **Paranoia**.

Dementia   Generally, a loss of intellectual capacity to the extent that normal social and occupational functions can no longer be carried out. The term is reserved for multifunctional disorders in which reasoning, judgment, and other "higher mental processes" are lost. Typically, alterations in personality and modes of social interaction accompany these cognitive deficits.

Dementia, senile   A general term for any dementia associated with the aged. Senile dementias are of the primary degenerative type and are associated with a variety of causes, including Alzheimer's disease, Pick's disease, certain vitamin deficiencies, and cerebrovascular pathologies.

Dependence, physiological   Drug dependence produced by alterations in physiological states resulting from repeated administrations of the drug. The characteristic that marks such dependence and differentiates it from *psychological dependence* is that severe physiological dysfunctions emerge if the drug is suddenly discontinued. Opiates and the barbiturates both produce such dependence with prolonged use. Also referred to as *physical dependence*. The term is preferred over the previously used *addiction* and *drug addiction. See* **Addiction**.

Dependence, psychological   Drug dependence characterized by a rather pervasive drive to obtain and take the substance. The term is usually used for dependences on drugs whose action does *not* produce fundamental biochemical changes such that continued doses of the drug are required for normal functioning. Drugs like marijuana are commonly cited as ones likely to produce psychological dependence with habitual use. *See* **Addiction**.

Dependency, morbid   Karen Horney's term for extreme, neurotic surrender of self to another, such that one person becomes pathologically reliant on another for things social and emotional.

Dependent personality disorder   A personality disorder characterized by the sufferer's passively allowing others to take over responsibility for his or her life. Such individuals are typically lacking in self-confidence, unsure of their abilities and willing to allow decision making in all matters to be taken over by others.

Depersonalization   The dominant meaning is that of the existentialists, who used the term to characterize the feeling of loss of self or of personal identity, the sense that one is but a number in a computer memory bank, or mere cog in a blundering, dehumanized, social machine. In psychiatric terms, it represents an emotional disorder in which there is a loss of contact with one's own personal reality, accompanied by feelings of strangeness and an unreality of experience. In severe cases, parts of one's body feel alien or altered in size and one may have the experience of perceiving oneself from a distance.

Depression   Generally, a mood state characterized by a sense of inadequacy, a feeling of despondency, a decrease in activity or reactivity, pessimism, sadness, and related symptoms. In this sense depressions are quite normal, relatively short-lived, and (damnably) frequent. In psychiatry, any of a number of affective disorders in which the above characteristics of mood are extreme and intense. Depression in this sense may be symptom of some other psychological disorder. Note that *Anhedonia* (general lack of interest in the pleasures of life) is an essential characteristic of depression.

Depression, agitated   A depression in which the individual displays psychomotor agitation as a dominant symptom. The overt symptoms are irritability, excitability, and restlessness.

Depression, neurotic   "Ordinary" severe depression. A mildly out-of-date term used as a cover for any depression that is not a *psychotic depression*; i.e., one in which there is no loss of contact with reality.

Depression, psychotic   Severe depression in which the individual loses contact with reality and suffers from an array of impairments of normal functioning.

Depression, reactive   Depression resulting from events occurring in one's life. The use of the term *depression* in this label is clinical and connotes that the affective reaction is inappropriate given the events themselves, thus differentiating the meaning of the term from that of *grief*.

Depression, retarded   Depression characterized by psychomotor retardation as the dominant symptom. The individual tends to be lethargic, laconic, and slow to initiate action.

Depression, unipolar   A *major depressive episode*. The qualifier *unipolar* is used when the depressive episodes recur without the appearance of the manic phase that is observed in the classic form of *bipolar disorder*.

Depressive anxiety   A psychoanalytic term for anxiety provoked by a sense of fear concerning one's own hostile feelings toward others. The usage here derives from the oft-stated interpretation that "depression is hostility turned inwards."

Depressive episode, major   In psychiatry, *depression* with all of the classic symptoms: sleep disturbances, lethargy, feelings of worthlessness, despondency, morbid thoughts, appetite disturbance, impaired concentration, and, on occasion, suicide attempts. The term is reserved for cases in which there is no known organic dysfunction.

Developmental psychology   Strictly speaking, the field of psychology concerned with the lifelong process of change. "Change" here means any qualitative and/or quantitative modification in structure and function: crawling to walking, babbling to speaking, illogical reasoning to logical, infancy to adolescence to maturity to old age, birth to death. When first articulated as a substantive subdiscipline in psychology by G.S. Hall around the turn of the century, it was quite explicitly this kind of "cradle-to-grave" field of investigation. However, it should be noted that most of the scientists who call themselves *developmental psychologists* are interested in childhood, indeed so much so that for many the term *developmental psychology* has become equivalent to *child psychology.*

Dewey, John (1859–1952)   The founder of the functionalist movement, which was one of the leading schools of psychology in the first half of the twentieth century. *Functionalism* is a very practical psychological movement that emphasizes the usefulness of mental processes in the adaptation of the organism (the entire human) to its environment.

Diagnostic and Statistical Manual (DSM I, II, III and III-R)   The full name is Diagnostic and Statistical Manual of Mental Disorders (DSM). It is the official system for classification of psychological and psychiatric disorders prepared by and published by the American Psychiatric Association. The latest revision, DSM III-R, was completed in 1987 and is the major guide for the classification, treatment, and prognosis of psychological/psychiatric disorders.

Dipsomania   Uncontrollable craving for alcoholic beverages. Distinguish from *alcoholism*, dipsomania occurs in widely spaced "attacks" of relatively short duration.

Directive therapy   A general label for any therapeutic approach when the therapist gives advice to the client and directs the client to change.

Disorientation   Inability to orient oneself with regard to spatial, temporal, and contextual aspects of the environment. Acute disorientation brought on by alcohol, drugs, or dramatic alterations in one's circumstances is not uncommon and not abnormal; long-term progressive disorientation is a symptom of a variety of psychological and/or neurological disorders.

Dissociation   Used generally to characterize the process (or its result) whereby a coordinated set of activities, thoughts, attitudes, or emotions becomes separated from the rest of the person's personality and functions independently. More extreme forms are observed in the *dissociative disorders* (e.g., Multiple personality disorder, fugue, amnesia). H.S. Sullivan used the term to characterize the process whereby thoughts or memories that produce anxiety are cut off from consciousness. *See* **Multiple personality.**

Down's syndrome   A congenital condition characterized by a flat skull, stubby fingers, an unusual pattern of skin folds on the palms of the hands and the soles of the feet, folds on the eyelids, a fissured tongue, and often severe mental deficiency.

Dream   A lot of people have wrestled with this one; let us define it simply as "imagery during sleep." Dreaming appears to occur in many organisms and is intimately related to rapid-eye movement (or REM) sleep.

Dream analysis   A technique originally used in psychoanalysis whereby the contents of dreams are analyzed for underlying or disguised motivations, symbolic meanings, or evidence of symbolic representations. In typical dream analysis the individual relates a dream and then free associates about it with the aim of deriving insight into underlying dynamics. Freud, quoting the old proverb, "pigs dream of acorns and geese dream of maize," assumed that dreams were expressions of wish-fulfillment. However, according to the standard theory, since most wishes had been repressed, the deep meaning of dreams (*dream content*) had to be interpreted through a veil of censorship, disguise and symbolism. *See* **Dream symbolism.**

Dream content   According to psychoanalytic theory the contents of a dream are of two types: (a) *manifest*—that known to the dreamer, the "surface" of the dream; and (b) *latent*—the deep, hidden aspects that presumably need to be interpreted before their meanings can be made clear.

Dream symbolism   Within the various psychoanalytic approaches, the disguised expressions in dreams wherein one thing is a "stand-in" or a symbol for something else. The usual interpretation is that the symbols are necessary for deeply repressed wishes to escape censorship. There are "standard" interpretations for some commonly occurring dream symbols—towers, pencils, pistons, and other entities that share functional, physical, or linguistic similarities are almost universally taken as phallic symbols, likewise boxes, doorways, and tunnels as vaginas. However, it is misleading to generalize blindly the symbolic elements of dreams. If dream analysis is to be of value it needs to be carried out with a sensitivity to the dreamer's own life and to the manner in which the free-associations to the dream unfold. "Pop psychology" books on dream symbolism and meaning should be avoided.

Drug interaction   The effects of two (or more) drugs taken together, when their combined effects are different from what would be produced by only one of them taken alone. The classic example is that of alcohol and a sedative: their interaction produces central nervous depression far greater than either drug alone would yield.

Dysfunctional   A term recently coined and often used in substance abuse situations. It implies abnormal, difficult, faulty, inappropriate, etc. functioning (e.g., dysfunctional family, dysfunctional behavior).

Dyslexia   A learning disability that is characterized by a disturbance in the process of reading or interpreting letters or words. This term is reserved for individuals who have significant problems reading when there is no evidence of any generally debilitating disorder, like mental retardation, major brain injury, severe emotional problems, or cultural factors. The dyslexic individual shows a cluster of specific characteristics with the major symptom of an inability to read. Some of the other symptoms are: reading or writing words, letters or numbers backwards, mispronouncing words, fine-motor coordination problems, memory problems, inability to repeat words or sounds that are heard. *See* **Learning disability.**

PSYCHOLOGY

Eating disorders A general term used to cover a variety of conditions characterized by serious disturbances in eating habits and appetitive behaviors, e.g., *anorexia nervosa*. See **Anorexia nervosa**; **Bulimia**.

Eclectic Generally, not following any one system but selecting and using whatever is considered best in all systems. In clinical psychology and psychiatry an eclectic therapist is one who will use whatever therapeutic procedures seem most applicable to the case. This may mean taking a psychoanalytic bent with one client but a more direct, behavioral approach with another. In general, eclecticism is regarded as healthy, especially in fields like psychology, which are at too immature a level to expect that any one of its theories or procedures could be universally applicable.

Educable mentally retarded (EMR) A label for a child who scores below the "normal" range on a standard IQ test and although formally still classified as mentally retarded can still profit from education and instruction. Contrast with *trainable mentally retarded* (TMR), which is used for those considered to be sufficiently below normal so as not to be able to profit from a standard education but who can be trained in a minimally demanding skill. Generally the IQ range for the EMR is 50–69; the TMR label is reserved for those scoring between 35 and 49. Current terminology for EMR includes Mild Mentally Handicapped or Disabled and for TMR, Moderate Mentally Handicapped or Disabled. *See* **Intelligence quotient**; **Mental retardation**.

Ego From the Latin for *I*, the "I" or "self" conceptualized as the central core around which all psychic activities revolve. Also, one of the components in the Freudian tripartite model of the psychic apparatus (along with the *id* and *superego*). In this conceptualization the ego serves as an executive who functions adaptively to maintain psychic balance. Today, the ego is conceived of as a kind of psychological touchstone that serves as a basis for one's interests, values, attitudes, desires, etc. This is the meaning captured in terms like *egocentric*, *egoistic*, and *egotistical*.

Ego development The gradual emerging awareness by the child that he or she is a distinct, independent person. The manner in which this takes place is not so easily stated, however. Classical psychoanalysis assumes that the process is one in which the ego progressively acquires functions that enable the individual to master impulses and to learn how to function independently of parents.

Ego ideal A notion of positive ideals one would like to be or accomplish.

Electra complex *See* **Oedipus complex**.

Electroconvulsive therapy (ECT) The use of electroconvulsive shock as a therapeutic procedure for psychiatric disorders. The technique consists of applying weak electric current (20–30 milliamps) to the temperofrontal region of the skull until a *grand mal* seizure results. The patient is sedated using an ultra-short-acting barbiturate, and a muscle relaxant is administered to minimize the intensity of the muscular reactions. ECT produces a period of drowsiness, temporary confusion, and disorien-

tation, and a variety of memory deficits, some of which the patient recovers over time, although gaps may remain indefinitely. In the past there have been rigorous protests over the uncontrolled and unwarranted use of ECT, particularly in many large, understaffed mental institutions where its primary function is to produce docility in patients when they are threatened with it. While it has in the past been seen as a treatment of last resort for depressed people who do not respond to drug therapy, it is recently regaining some respectability.

Electroencephalogram (EEG) A record of the changes in electrical potential of the brain. Electrodes are generally attached to (or occasionally just under) the scalp, and the wavelike potentials are amplified and transferred to paper. Detailed EEG analyses have revealed that the brain undergoes systematic changes in the kinds of potential exhibited during various activities.

Encounter group A small group that focuses on intensive interpersonal interactions (or "encounters"). The group usually has as its goals the removal of psychological barriers and defenses, achieving openness, honesty, and the willingness to deal with the difficulties of emotional expression. Group members are encouraged to deal with "here-and-now" and to eschew intellectualization and personal history. Encounter groups and their use in psychotherapy began with the *human potential movement*.

Erikson, Erik H. (b. 1902) American psychoanalyst born in Germany who studied with the Freudians and eventually became a professor of human development and lecturer on psychiatry at Harvard. Erikson is especially important for his involvement with child development, his writings on the identity crisis, and his revision of Freud's psychosexual theory. The *Ego Psychology* of Erikson recasts Freudian theories into what is known as a psychosocial form, tracing the child's development into adulthood through trust/distrust, autonomy/shame and doubt, initiative/guilt, industry/inferiority, personal identity/role confusion, intimacy/isolation, creativity/stagnation, and ego integrity/despair. Each stage is representative of a critical point in development, and a positive adaptation (i.e., to trust rather than distrust, which the child learns from the first encounter with the parents) at each stage is instrumental in attaining mental health in adulthood.

Eros The Greek god of love. In Freudian theory, Eros refers to the whole complex of life-preservative instincts. Included among them, of course, are the sexual instincts. *See* **Thanatos**.

EST An acronym for Erhard Seminar Training. A form of psychotherapy based on the "theories" of Werner Erhard (*né* Jack Rosenberg, a one-time sales manager). The procedure consists of large group sessions of rather extraordinary intensity. For up to 60 hours several hundred people are gathered in a large hall and subjected to physical privation, guided (some would say forced) meditation, and fervent diatribes on the EST way to "get in touch" with one's inner sense of personal responsibility. It would be remiss not to add here a cautionary note—the EST program is more of a mass psychological religion than a true therapeutic procedure (it has been called "the McDonald's of Zen"), and the pressure and intensity of an EST session holds genuine dangers for persons with severe emotional problems.

Existential psychology and therapy　To treat this broad and varied spectrum of contemporary psychology and psychologists, it is necessary to have a brief but working knowledge of existentialism, a philosophical movement of the twentieth century. Simply put, existentialism contends that a human lives in an unknowable universe, that he or she must make choices and assume responsibility for decisions, and that he or she must exercise free will without living under absolute certainties of right or wrong. *Existential psychology* is based on the premise that existence takes precedence over essence, that nothing is determined, and that freedom of choice is paramount. This school does not deal with abstractions and opposes the intellectualism of classic psychoanalysis. *Existential therapy* has no rigid set of tenets in its approach to mental health. Most therapists are in general eclectic and in particular adhere to existential doctrine. Since "being" is prime in the movement, the interaction of the patient to the inner and outer world is deeply explored, with the knowledge that he or she is able to determine his or her own future. Because freedom of choice is stressed, a natural anxiety arises on the part of the patient as to risk taking, etc., and fears that are generated are dealt with in sessions. A goal is eventually to shed the past by emphasizing the present and the future. Self-fulfillment is considered of primary importance.

Extraversion-introversion　A hypothesized dimension of personality with two theoretical poles, *extraversion* and *introversion*. Originally the dimension was entertained as reflecting two unitary personality types that were presumed opposites of each other. Today most theorists doubt that either exists as a singular type, and instead regard both as collections of a number of different patterns of behavior. Moreover, it also seems unlikely that the two poles can be validly regarded as opposites since many increase in their display of behaviors reflective of one pole, without necessarily diminishing the display of behaviors reflective of the other. *See* **Introversion**.

F

Family therapy　A generic term for a variety of therapeutic approaches to treating the family as a unit.

Fantasy　A term generally used to refer to the mental process of imagining objects, symbols, or events not immediately present. However, it is also used to refer to the symbol or image itself. In general, fantasy is assumed to be normal, even indicative of psychological stability and health. It is usually pleasant, often whimsical, and frequently creative. The pathological aspects that are often cited are restricted to when the fantasy becomes delusionary or when it dominates a person's mental life and serves as a retreat from reality rather than an adjunct to it.

Father figure　One who takes the place and hence the role of the real father. It may be used with either of two connotations: (a) The sense that the person has taken over the full complement of functions of the real father who was replaced; e.g., a stepfather or a foster father. (b) The sense that the individual fulfills psychologically important functions, usually that of becoming the male adult with whom one identifies. As the word "figure" in the term connotes, meaning (b) is the dominant one and indeed may be what is intended even when the father figure is in the role described in (a).

Father fixation　An excessive focusing of emotional attachment to the father. The term implies a rigid focusing, so that there is difficulty in shifting affective attention away from the father to other more socially accepted persons. The equivalent process centered on the female parent is called, not surprisingly, *mother fixation.*

Fetal alcoholic syndrome (FAS)　A cluster of abnormal developmental features of a fetus resulting from severe alcoholism in the mother. The high level of alcohol in the blood combined with a generally reduced level of normal nutrients can produce any (or all) of a number of anatomic and psychological deficits including growth deficiencies, learning disabilities, mental retardation, hyperactivity, heart murmurs, and skeletal malformations.

Fetishism　Generally a fetish is an object of blind devotion or reverence. Fetishism thus connotes a kind of religious activity that emphasizes the worship of inanimate objects believed to have magical or transcendent powers. A *paraphilia* (a mode of sexual expressions) characterized by obtaining sexual arousal and satisfaction with some object or some part of the body not directly erogenous. Fetishes are usually articles used by others, often but not always of the opposite sex (shoes, gloves, handkerchiefs), or parts of the body (hair, feet). *See* **Paraphilia**.

Fixation, affective　As derived from classical psychoanalytic theory (Freudian theory), the process whereby one becomes excessively attached to (or "fixated" on) some object or person that was appropriate for an earlier stage of development. This condition is assumed to produce a variety of neurotic behaviors, such as excessive or irrational attachments to people or objects and an inability to form normal, mature relationships. Within the psychoanalytic frame of reference the full term is often (usually) shortened to *fixation*. Within such contexts modifiers are often used, e.g., *father fixation*, *oral fixation*.

Flooding　*See* **Implosion therapy**.

Freud, Sigmund (1856–1939)　The Viennese neurologist and founder of psychoanalysis whose early works (i.e., *General Introduction to Psychoanalysis*) explored his initial theories regarding the unconscious, dreams, hysteria, sex, and the libido, for all of which he was roundly ostracized. The ban of Freud's methods and thinking lasted until 1908, when the first International Congress of Psychoanalysis convened, and thereafter analysis and the therapeutic exploration of the mind eventually became an accepted and occasionally even a revered form of medical practice. As conceived by Freud, psychoanalysis is a psychological method that seeks the basis for human behavior and motivation in the unconscious mind. Analysis begins with the *libido*, defined as sexual energy, as it passes in development through all forms of love and into the individual's overall adjustment to life. The earliest libidinous stage is termed the oral stage, in which pleasure is sought at the primal levels of sucking, chewing, etc., followed by the anal and genital stages, in which the satisfactions obtained from bowel excretion are followed by the pleasures of early masturbation. Eventually, Oedipal and Electra complexes develop in the child's relationship to the parent, and when these are of necessity thwarted, the child becomes more of a social animal, which marks the beginning of the end of the infantile period and the start of puberty. Freud traces the workings of the mind on three levels: conscious, unconscious, and subconscious. The libido and all repressed memories reside in the unconscious, considered the most important level. The personality rises from the unconscious, developing from the *id*, or the animalistic aspect of the child. The *ego* develops from the id and is seen as the facet of the personality that seeks to gratify the id while dealing with reality. The *superego* (which could be termed the Freudian conscience) is the part of the personality that places prohibition and restrictions on the individual and endeavors to curtail the activity of the lustier id by its mediator, the ego. Freud believed that neuroses occur when the ego breaks down through a struggle with the id and through harboring repression. The ego weakens and no longer has sufficient energy to deal with reality. Freudian psychology seeks to release the energies of the ego by uncovering and overcoming repressions so that the individual can live a more healthy and complete life. Free association and dream interpretation are two psychoanalytic means to achieve this desired end.

Sigmund Freud

Freudian slip   Any minor slipup or error; most typically observed in speech, writing, small accidents, memory lapses, etc. According to Freud, these were no mere innocent gestures but the result of the operations of unconscious wishes or conflicts that could often be used to reveal the functioning of the unconscious in the normal healthy individual. Also known as *parapraxis*.

Future shock   A term coined by Toffler as a way of expressing the view that we in Western society are becoming overloaded, in terms of what we can process. The "shock" produced by the rapid changes in social structures, social values, and consumer products is so great that, Toffler argued, many persons simply cannot cope or adapt.

Gender-identity disorder   A psychiatric label for those disorders characterized by a sense of inappropriateness and attendant discomfort concerning one's sex anatomy and one's sex role. Usually included in this category are *transvestism* and *transsexualism*. See **Transvestism**; **Transsexualism**.

Generalized anxiety disorder   A subclass of *anxiety disorders* characterized by persistent "free floating" anxiety and a host of unspecific reactions such as trembling, tension, sweating, lightheadedness, feelings of apprehension and irritability. Also called, simply, *anxiety reaction*. See **Anxiety**, **free-floating**.

Genius   Loosely used, the term refers to the highest level of intellectual or creative functioning or to a person possessing such capabilities. Although there have been several efforts at giving an explicit definition (e.g., at one time an IQ of 140 or over was used), such attempts provide only illusory objectivity. Unfortunately (or fortunately) there does not appear to be a clear set of attributes that defines genius; all behaviors, including the intellectual and creative, are subject to a variety of "noncognitive" factors, such as motivation, temperament, emotion, and the demand characteristics of the environment, and people who display "genius" in one setting do not necessarily display it in others. Furthermore, the common language has played such havoc with the term that its usefulness is now suspect even in the most technical context.

Gestalt psychology and therapy   *Gestalt psychology* (the term "Gestalt" was originated by Charles von Ehrenfels in 1890) is a school of thinking that contends that the psychological makeup of an individual is based on the unity and wholeness of behavior combined with experience. Limited analytic judgments are permitted, but not to the detriment of the entire "organism," i.e., as long as they do not fragment or break down the unity of the personality. *Gestalt therapy* is associated with the work of Frederick (Fritz) Perls, based loosely on concepts of unity and wholeness. Treatment (usually in groups) focuses on attempts to broaden the awareness of self by using past experiences, memories, emotional states, bodily sensations, etc.—everything that could contribute to the totality of meaningful awareness.

Group therapy   A very general term used to cover any psychotherapeutic process in which groups of individuals meet together with or without a therapist/leader. The interactions among the members of the group are assumed to be therapeutic and in many cases to be more effective than the traditional client-therapist diad.

Halfway house   Originally, a facility for persons released from institutions (mental, penal, drug- and alcohol-related) designed to ease the transition back into the community. Many such facilities function more broadly, however. Rather than being only "halfway out" houses they may also serve as semiprotective environments for those "halfway in" persons who can still function productively in the community but need a supportive caring shelter.

Hallucination   A perceptual experience with all the compelling subjective properties of a real sensory impression but without the normal physical stimulus for that sensory modality. Hallucinations are taken as classic indicators of a psychotic disturbance and are a hallmark of various disorders like schizophrenia. Hence, the term is not usually applied to a variety of other "false perceptions" that occur normally, like the images that often accompany the transition from waking to sleeping (hypnagogic) or those that occur when first awakening (hypnopompic) or those that occasionally accompany vivid religious experiences. In actual usage the term is generally modified so that the particular modality involved is specified, e.g., *auditory hallucination, tactile hallucination. Distinguish from* **Delusion**.

Hallucinogen   Loosely, any of a large group of psychoactive chemical compounds capable of producing hallucinations, e.g., LSD, mescaline, psilocybin. *See also* Health & Medicine, page 8-35.

Hedonism   In psychology proper, the theory that behavior is motivated by approach toward pleasure and avoidance of pain. In ethics, the doctrine that the goal of human conduct ought to be the striving for pleasure and the avoidance of pain.

Heredity-environment controversy   A debate of long standing over the relative contributions of experience (nurture, environment, learning) and inheritance (nature, heredity, genetic predisposition) to the makeup of an organism, especially a human organism.

Histrionic personality disorder   A personality disorder usually characterized by immaturity, self-centeredness, attention getting, manipulativeness, and, quite often, a vague seductiveness. Such persons are overly dramatic, reactive and intense in their interpersonal relationships, and frequently play out classic roles like "princess" or "victim." Also called, especially in older texts, *hysterical personality*.

Homophobia   When from the Latin root of *homo*, fear of man. When from the Greek root, an irrational fear of homosexuality. The term is used in this sense rather broadly and may refer to (a) fear of one's homosexual tendencies or feelings, (b) fear of homosexual persons, or (c) a general undifferentiated fear of homosexuality. Strictly speaking it applies to females or males, although there is a tendency to use it only for men. *Androphobia* is fear of man or the male sex.

Homosexuality   The term is used rather generally to refer to sexual contact between persons of the same gender. This "contact" may be fleeting, nonorgasmic, and occasional or it may represent an individual's dominant (if not exclusive) mode of sexual expression. In a very real sense, then, the term may be found in the psychological literature covering persons ranging from those who have had one or two half-hearted experiences to those for whom heterosexual contacts have been nonexistent. Comprehensive surveys suggest that perhaps 40 percent of the population have had at least one homosexual experience leading to orgasm whereas perhaps 5 to 10 percent of the sexually active population is exclusively homosexual. There has historically been a strong antisocial bias against the homosexual, as evidenced by the inclusion, until the 1980 edition of the *Diagnostic and Statistical Manual of the American Psychiatric Association*, of homosexuality in the compendium of mental illnesses. The more recent, enlightened perspective tends to regard it simply as a particular manifestation of sexual preference, without entailing any clinical judgment. Note that there is a tendency in popular literature and even in some technical writings to reserve the word *homosexual* for a male and to use *lesbian* for a female. The term *gay* has become common as a general and inclusive label.

Horney, Karen   (1885–1952)   A German psychiatrist who came to the United States in 1932 and was associate director of the Chicago Institute of Psychoanalysis before going on to be a lecturer at the New School for Social Research in New York and dean of the American Institute for Psychoanalysis. As a neo-Freudian, Horney laid stress on culture and environment rather than biology as the initiators of neuroses. She defined anxiety as any person or thing that blocked an individual's means of gaining security. In a neurotic state a person will hold firmly to the safety devices he or she has created, and although this adherence will serve as a protection in some ways, it will also render one both helpless and vulnerable in other areas. Horney's psychoanalytic theories are well defined and described in her works, some of which are *The Neurotic Personality of Our Time* (1936), *Self-Analysis* (1942), and *Neurosis and Human Growth* (1950).

Hostility   A long-lasting emotional state characterized by enmity toward others and manifested by a desire to harm or inflict pain upon those at whom it is directed. Often distinguished from *anger* on the grounds that anger is a more intense and momentary reaction.

Human-potential movement   A general label covering the vast array of presumably therapeutic techniques, such as encounter groups, sensitivity training, and assertiveness training. Actually, the number of different theories, techniques, and orientations that are part of this essentially eclectic movement is growing daily and in unpredictable ways. Advocates of the movement see it as the cutting edge of a new humanism; critics view it as largely an irresponsible commercial enterprise that preys upon people's vulnerabilities and fears.

There have been enough positive results from the use of some of the techniques for a number of them (particularly sensitivity training) to have actually been introduced into schools and businesses. However, many authorities are highly critical of the movement as a whole because of its tendency to follow the intuitions of practitioners who tend to accept uncritically the claimed virtues of such disparate approaches as Zen Buddhism, psychodrama, art, dance, poetry, mysticism, yoga, meditation, fasting, acupuncture, rolfing, astrology, or just plain "letting it all hang out" independent of any coherent theoretical analysis, controlled experimentation, or systematic follow-up on the efficacy of these techniques. The movement, nevertheless, remains strong.

Hydrophobia   Fear of water; rabies.

Hyperactivity   Vigorous, inappropriate motor activity. *See* **Attention Deficit Hyperactive Disorder (ADHD)**.

Hyperkinesis   Excessive and inappropriate motor activity, extreme restlessness; usually accompanied by poor attention span and impulsivity. *See* **Attention Deficit Hyperactive Disorder (ADHD)**.

Hypermnesia   Literally, excessive memory. Hence: a characteristic of some *idiots savants* in which there is an extraordinary ability to recall names, dates, places, etc. An extremely detailed recollection of a particular past experience. It is observed occasionally in the manic phase of bipolar disorders, during hypnosis, and during certain neurosurgical procedures. There are questions as to whether these experiences ought to be classified as true memory phenomena in that the conditions under which they occur make it nearly impossible to determine whether they are real hypermnesic effects or merely elaborations of events. *See* **Idiot savant**; **Manic episode**.

Hyperorexia   Excessive appetite. *Contrast* **Anorexia nervosa**.

Hyperventilation   Excessive respiration rate; the feeling of "breathlessness" that frequently accompanies panic (anxiety) attacks. *See* **Anxiety**; **Generalized anxiety disorder**.

Hypnosis   Few terms in the psychological lexicon are so thoroughly wrapped in mysticism and confusion. The problems arise from the tendency that dates back to the discoverer, Franz Anton Mesmer (1733–1815), to regard the process of hypnotism as one that transports the subject into a separate "state of mind." Further complications emerged because the phenomenon attracted a coterie of charlatans, faith healers and, more recently, entertainers, who make unsubstantiated claims and show a singular reluctance to use proper controls in their work. The present view is that a hypnotic "state" does exist. It is somewhat less dramatic than often portrayed but does, in general, display the following characteristics: (a) although it superficially resembles a sleep-like state (which is how it got its name), the EEG pattern does not resemble any of the stages of sleep; (b) normal planning functions are reduced—a hypnotized person tends to wait passively for instructions from the hypnotist; (c) attention becomes highly selective—the individual may hear only one person to the exclusion of others; (d) role playing is readily accomplished, the hypnotized person frequently becoming quite thoroughly immersed in a

suggested role; and (e) post hypnotic suggestion is often observed, frequently a specific amnesia in which the subject cannot recall things he or she has been told to forget.

It should be noted that all of these effects are of a kind in that they are also characteristic of a "normal" person who has voluntarily given up conscious control, a person who evidences extreme suggestibility. Not surprisingly, then, there is a school of thought that argues that there is nothing at all special about this "state" but that it merely represents an extreme pole on the scale of normal suggestibility.

Hypnotherapy   A general term for any psychotherapy that makes use of hypnosis. Hypnotherapy is generally classified as a directive therapy since hypnosis tends to produce a passivity during which the patient accepts direction from others.

Hypochondriasis   A condition characterized by imagined sufferings of physical illness or, more generally, an exaggerated concern with one's physical health. The hypochondriac typically displays a preoccupation with bodily functions, such as heart rate, sweating, bowel and bladder functions, and the occasional minor problems like pimples, headaches, a simple cough, etc. All such trivialities are interpreted as signs of symptoms of more serious diseases. "Doctor shopping" is common; assurances of health are futile.

Hypomanic disorder   A mild form of the bipolar disease, characterized by excitement, energetic behavior, creativity, and an elevated rate of productivity. *See* **Bipolar disorder**.

Hypothalamus   A relatively small (peanut-sized) but extremely complex structure at the base of the brain that is intimately involved in control of the autonomic nervous system and a variety of functions that are crucially related to survival, including temperature regulation, heart rate, blood pressure, feeding behavior, water intake, emotional behavior, and sexual behavior.

Hysteria   Of all psychiatric disorders hysteria has the longest and most checkered history. Deriving originally from the ancient Greeks it was, until relatively recently, assumed to be solely a dysfunction of women and caused by a "wandering" uterus (*hysteron* = uterus). Psychoanalytic theory helped in providing a more reasonable etiology, but the link between gender and the disorder was not completely severed, males were rarely so diagnosed. The symptoms that have been cited most often are hallucinations, somnambulism, paralysis, and dissociation. This has become relatively rare in industrialized societies.

Id   In the Freudian model of the mind, the primitive, animalistic, instinctual element, the pit of roiling, libidinous energy demanding immediate satisfaction. It is regarded as the deepest component of the psyche, the true unconscious. Entirely self-contained and isolated from the world about it, it is bent on achieving its own aims. The sole governing device here is the pleasure principle, the id being represented as the ultimate hedonist. The task of restraining this single-minded entity is a major part of the ego's function.

Idée fixe French for *fixed idea*. A firmly held idea that is maintained without rational reflection and despite the existence of sufficient contrary evidence to persuade a reasonable person of its untenability.

Identity crisis An acute loss of the sense of one's identity, a lack of the normal feeling that one has historical continuity, that the person here today is phenomenologically the same as the one here yesterday.

Idiot savant From the French meaning *knowledgeable idiot*. The incongruity of the term characterizes the incongruity of the syndrome. An *idiot savant* is one whose overall mental capabilities are quite limited (occasionally to the point of requiring institutionalization) but who possesses some extraordinary talent, such as a computerlike ability to perform arithmetic calculations or a seemingly limitless memory for names or dates. *See* **Hypermnesia**.

Illusion Distorted perception of a real physical stimulus.

Implosion therapy A procedure in which an individual in inundated with experiences in order to develop an aversion to an unwanted habit (e.g., continuously smoking cigarettes until the thought or sight of a cigarette makes one feel sick) or to extinguish the disabling anxiety associated with a phobia (e.g., a person who fears snakes is continuously presented with the feared stimulus until it no longer elicits anxiety). This procedure is also called flooding.

Impulse-control disorder A class of disorders all marked by failure to resist an impulse or temptation to engage in some act that ultimately proves harmful to oneself. Generally included here are *pathological gambling*, *kleptomania*, and *pyromania*. Typically, the individual feels a highly increased sense of tension prior to the act and a pleasurable, gratifying feeling afterward. Guilt may or may not be experienced following the act.

Incest Sexual relations between close relatives such as parents and children or siblings.

Incest survivor An individual who has been sexually abused by a close relative. This term is used as an alternative to the term *victim* in order to eliminate connotations of helplessness and promote active healing.

Inferiority complex As originally coined by Adler, the term described a collection of repressed fears stemming from organ or bodily inferiority that gave rise to feelings, attitudes, and ideas of a more general inferiority. Popular usage has badly mangled the original sense by using the term to refer to any sense of inadequacy or feelings of inferiority.

Inferiority feelings Loosely, any attitudes toward oneself that are critical and generally negative. Strictly speaking, this is the term that should be used in popular discourse when, for example, someone claims to have an "inferiority complex."

Inhibition From the Latin for *restraint*. Hence, very generally, the restraining, preventing, repressing, or prohibiting of any process. In psychoanalysis, the control of instinctual id (primitive impulses) impulses by the action of the superego.

Inkblot test A generic term used for any of the several projective tests that use inkblots. The most widely used is, of course, the Rorschach test. *See* **Rorschach test**.

Innovative therapies Over the years almost every conceivable form of doing, believing, acting, reacting, hoping, touching, fighting, loving, moving, emoting, provoking, etc., ad nauseam, has been turned into some form of psychotherapy—this term acts as an umbrella for them all. A few of these have shown their worth in controlled settings and with proper evaluation and follow-up of cases (e.g., sex therapy); others serve mainly as sources of income for therapists and as something new to try for people who drift psychically about looking for someone somewhere to inject some meaning into their lives. Some of the more exotic forms extant (as of this writing anyway, most are shortlived) are body therapy, poetry therapy, encouragement therapy, rebirthing therapy, and imagination therapy. One hardly knows what to make of these. There are essentially no attempts made to validate the techniques used, no basis for determining success or lack of it, and, most damning, no reasonable theoretical basis for assuming that any of them ought to work—short of plain old common sense. After all, poetry is certainly a good thing, and reading, writing and understanding poetry would probably have therapeutic value for anyone. Psychology as a pure and applied science is certainly not served well by what has been called this "southern Californiaizing" of society.

Instinct A term with a tortured history indeed. The root is Latin, *instinctus* meaning to *instigate* or *impel*, with the implication that such impulses are natural or innate. There are four general, distinguishable meanings of the terms: (a) an unlearned response characteristic of the members of a given species, (b) a tendency or disposition to respond in a particular manner that is characteristic of a particular species, (c) a complex, set of acts found within a given species that emerges under specific stimulus conditions, and (d) any of a number of unlearned, inherited tendencies that are motivational forces behind complex human behaviors. This sense, of course, is that expressed by classical psychoanalysis.

Intellectualization A defense mechanism whereby problems are analyzed in remote, intellectual terms while emotion, affect, and feelings are ignored.

Intelligence quotient An age-related measure of intelligence level. It is sometimes defined as 100 times the mental age (MA, determined by a standardized test) divided by the chronological age (CA). Note that this procedure establishes the average as 100. Nearly always abbreviated as IQ. Some problems were encountered with the above method of determining IQ, and most modern tests use a Deviation IQ. This procedure obtains an IQ by statistical comparison. The individual's test performance is compared with scores of other individuals the same age and an IQ is derived. The approximate ranges of intelligence are: Very Superior (IQ of 130 and above), Superior (IQ between 120 and 129), High Average (IQ between 110 and 119), Average (IQ between 90 and 109), Low Average (IQ between 80 and 89), Borderline (IQ between 70 and 79), Mild Mental Retardation (IQ between 50 and 69), Moderate Mental Retardation (IQ between 35 and 49), Severe Mental Retardation (IQ between 20 and 34) and Profound Mental Retardation (IQ below 20). *See* **Wechsler**

Intelligence Scales; Educable mentally retarded; Mental retardation; Genius.

Intentional forgetting *Forgetting* due to *repression*. Here the notion of *intentional* is compromised somewhat in that it usually carries the connotation of awareness, whereas repression denotes an unconscious process. Also, directed forgetting, forgetting of material following instructions to do so. This is a touchy issue; it evokes images of the old joke about instructing someone *not* to think about pigmy elephants.

Introversion A turning inward. Used in personality theory to refer to the tendency to shrink from social contacts and become preoccupied with one's own thoughts. Although presumably a "normal" characteristic, there are many who believe that extreme forms of introversion border on the pathological, e.g., autism. *See* **Extraversion-introversion**.

Intuition A mode of understanding or knowing characterized as direct and immediate and occurring without conscious thought or judgment. There are two distinct connotations that often accompany this term: (a) that the process is unmediated and somehow mystical; (b) that it is a response to subtle cues and relationships apprehended implicitly, unconsciously. The former borders on the unscientific and is not recommended, although it is certainly common enough in the nontechnical literature; the latter hints at a number of difficult but fascinating problems in the study of human behavior in the presence of complex situations.

Isolation Generally, separateness, apartness. In psychoanalysis, a defense mechanism that operates unconsciously and functions by severing the conscious psychological ties between some unacceptable act or impulse and its original memory source. In this sense, the original experience is not forgotten but it is separated from the affect originally associated with it. The classical theory views this mechanism as a common one in obsessional neuroses. In Jung's terms, a feeling of psychological estrangement from others. Also called *psychic isolation*, Jung argued that it derived from deep secrets, originally from the collective unconscious, which one feels must be kept from others. In existential psychology, isolation is akin to alienation, a feeling of being separate in an absurd universe.

James, William (1842–1910) A philosopher and psychologist, James established the first psychology laboratory in America. In the field of psychology, he is best known for his work, *Principals of Psychology* (1890), and his "stream-of-consciousness" belief that mentality must be seen as an ongoing process, and not fragmented into bits of consciousness. James held that an emotion is evidenced by the internal conflict that arises from a person's reaction to a particular emotional situation. Out of this theory grew his legendary argument that a man meeting a bear in the woods does not run because he is afraid, but rather is afraid because he runs. It is the running itself that initiates the visceral reaction of fear, which produces the emotion.

Jocasta complex Jocasta was the mother and wife of Oedipus, and in keeping with psychoanalytic tradition the term stands for the mother's role in the playing out of the *Oedipus complex*.

Jung, Carl (1875–1961) The Swiss psychologist whose renown has challenged Freud, with whom he broke ties in 1913 after severe disagreements about the nature of the libido and the unconscious. The movement known as *analytical psychology*, founded by Jung, defines the libido as the primal "life urge," not necessarily wholly aligned with the sexual drive, as espoused by Freud. Jung saw the psychological energy process translated by symbols that arise from the unconscious, some of which (the archetypes) are evidence of the "collective unconscious" of man. That is, "the inherited" inner visions of myth and symbol that extend back to the beginning of time. These archetypes are universal (i.e., the Mother, the Shadow, the Hero, and the Cross) and Jung could trace their patterns through the world of art and literature, where human repressions are exhibited by the unconscious working through the creatively conscious mind. Like Freud, Jung used free association and dream interpretation in his analysis: however, unlike Freud, he did not stress the role of the past as an explanation for disturbances of the psyche, but rather he used dreams as a tool to understand the present and as evidence of a precognitive future. Jung sought the individuation of the psyche, which means the integration and balance of the individual parts of the mind to create a healthy adjustment to the world and to the self. He believed that for a person to be whole and fulfilled, a harmony between the conscious and the unconscious (a delicate balance) must be achieved.

Kleptomania A *disorder* characterized by recurrent inability to resist impulses to steal. A defining feature of the disorder is that there is no immediate need or use for what is stolen. Typically there is little or no planning involved, merely a sudden, acute impulse that is acted on.

Latent Existing in hidden form, dormant but capable of being evoked or developed.

Learning disability A syndrome in which individuals of average or above average intelligence do not learn the way most people learn and experience difficulty learning specific skills or academic areas. It usually results from lags in the development of skills or abilities necessary for learning. Learning disabilities are more common in males than females and cover a wide range of learning problems. Sometimes they affect reading (dyslexia), writing (dysgraphia) or math (dyscalculia). This syndrome is often abbreviated as LD. *See* **Dyslexia**.

Libido In psychoanalysis, the hypothesized mental energy that, being derived from the id, is most fundamentally sexual. Freud, who introduced the term, considerably modified his usage of it in his later works so that the purely sexual component became less prominent and it took on a meaning closer to *life* energy. Within the larger scope of psychoanalysis these later modifications never dominated thinking to the extent that the early theory did, the libido itself has tended to retain its strongly sexual connotations. It is frequently taken simply to represent any sexual or erotic desire or pleasure, or any psychic energy independent of sexuality.

Lithium (salts) Usually classified as *antipsychotics* containing the element lithium compounds are used primarily in the treatment of *bipolar disorders*, particularly the manic aspect. Lithium's manner of action in the body is unknown. It does, however, compete with the sodium salts and changes the composition of body fluids. It can also be toxic and dosage must be carefully controlled by taking lithium blood levels. Note that some authorities classify the lithium salts with the *antidepressants*. See **Bipolar disorder**; **Tranquilizers, major**.

Lobotomy, prefrontal A surgical procedure severing a portion of the brain. The original operation was developed by A.E. Moniz in the 1930s and was so heralded as a psychosurgical procedure for severe psychological disorders that he received the Nobel Prize for his work. With the accumulation of data from tens of thousands of lobotomies the general conclusion is that the procedure does not work. Whatever beneficial results may occasionally be obtained must be balanced against the negative side effects of apathy, insensitivity, impaired judgment, and seizures, all of which are irreversible. Recent years have fortunately witnessed its gradual demise.

Lorenz, Konrad (b. 1903) An Austrian zoologist who gained fame through his study of animal and human behavior by the method of comparative zoology. Lorenz traced behavioral patterns on an evolutionary continuum, and his later work on aggression was highly esteemed because of the understanding it lent to the eruption of violence in cities and, on a more universal scale, because of its application to the prevention of war.

M**Magical thinking** The belief that thinking is equated with doing. Seen in children as a normal stage of development during which they believe that their thoughts and hopes are the cause of events happening about them. Also observed in adults in a variety of psychiatric disorders.

Mania Loosely and nontechnically, madness, violent, erratic behavior. Also, mood disorder characterized by a variety of symptoms including inappropriate elation, extreme motor activity, impulsiveness, and excessively rapid thought and speech. It is a component of *bipolar disorder*.

Manic-depressive See **Bipolar disorder**.

Manic episode A distinct period during which the predominant mood is *mania*. Characterized by grandiose explosions of feelings and actions. See **Bipolar disorder**; **Hypermnesia**.

Maslow, Abraham H. (1908–1970) An American psychologist who veered away from psychoanalysis and behaviorism to stress the element of *humanism* in psychology, a force that addresses itself to self-realization and the exalted motives that seek knowledge and aesthetics. Maslow downgraded feelings of isolation and alienation and sought to replace them with a joyous and nonconformist attitude toward life, coupled with mysticism and a spirit of creativity. When a person is able to experience such peak attitudes, he or she is in the midst of an awakening that is first awesome and then becomes conducive of the living of a healthy and happy life. Such

an awakening may take place in the near frenzy of creation or it may be a part of a meditative or contemplative life.

Masochism The term derives from the name of the Austrian novelist, Leopold von Sacher-Masoch (1835–1895), and refers most broadly to any tendency to direct that which is destructive, painful, or humiliating against oneself. Special uses abound: *Sexual masochism* is used when erotic pleasure is associated with the treatment; *moral masochism* is used when the person seeks to alleviate guilt by subjecting himself or herself to continuous punishment; *psychic masochism* is used for any kind of hostility or destructive impulse tuned upon oneself, a usage that is very general; *mass masochism* refers to whole populations subjecting themselves to pain and hardship.

Mass behavior Collective behavior of a *mass* without any obvious direct or personal communication or mutual influencing of the individuals making up the mass. Fads and fashions, dress styles, political movements, etc., are examples. The assumption is that mass communication systems are the channels through which the societal influences occur. Also called *mass contagion*.

Maternal-deprivation syndrome A group of symptoms, including stunted physical growth and retarded emotional development, associated with infants who have been deprived of handling and nurturing. Interestingly, the syndrome also emerges with species other than humans and has been documented in several mammals, including monkeys and mice.

Megalomania An exaggerated self-evaluation or sense of self-worth. A common component in narcissistic personality disorder.

Melancholia From the classic Greek for *black bile*. Today the term refers to a pronounced depression with feelings of foreboding and a general insensitivity to stimulation.

Memory, racial A hypothesized storehouse of memories, feelings, ideas, etc., that, according to Carl Jung, we have inherited from our ancestral past. Racial memory in Jung's theory is a part of the *collective unconscious*.

Menninger, Karl Augustus (b. 1893) American psychiatrist who, with his brother William Claire (1899–1966), founded the Menninger Foundation (1941) in Topeka, Kansas, for the purpose of research and training and to educate the public in the field of psychology. The foundation soon became the key psychiatric center of the United States and functioned not only as a mental hospital, but also as the largest psychiatric training school in this country.

Mental retardation The contemporary term of choice as the umbrella label for all forms of below-average intellectual functioning as assessed by a standard IQ test. The classification system currently in use in the United States specifies four levels: *mild* (approximate IQ range of 50–69), *moderate* (35–49), *severe* (20–34), and *profound* (below 20). See **Educable mentally retarded**; **Intelligence quotient**.

Methadone A synthetic narcotic that blocks the effects of other narcotics. It is used for the treatment of heroin addiction in what are called *methadone maintenance* programs. However, methadone itself produces a drug dependence of the morphine type and withdrawal from it is just as traumatic as withdrawal from any other opiates. See **Addiction**.

Microphobia　Fear of small objects.

Monophobia　Irrational fear of being left alone.

Mood disorder　See **Bipolar disorder**.

Multiple personality　A relatively rare disorder in which one's personality becomes so fragmented that two (or more) relatively independent subpersonalities emerge. The condition of multiple personality is an abnormality that is not to be confused with the pronounced changes in style, behavior, and reactivity shown by most normal persons as they move between different social situations and different social roles. The pathological condition is marked by circumstances in which these varied manifestations of self become so divided that the sense of underlying integrity is lost. Lay people often confuse multiple personality with schizophrenia, probably because of the persistent and erroneous use of the colloquialism "split personality" for schizophrenia (the "split" in schizophrenia is between affect and thought, not between "personalities"). See **Dissociation**.

Murphy's laws　A number of semihumorous "laws" that, alas, are true entirely too often. Although long lists of variations on the legendary Murphy and his laws exist, the three original ones are: Anything that can possibly go wrong will go wrong. Anything that goes wrong will do so at the worst possible time. Anything you plan will cost more and take longer. Anyone with the slightest familiarity with probability theory or even a touch of fatalism about the outcome of the most carefully planned research will appreciate the *a priori* truth of these laws.

N　**Narcissism**　The term comes from the Greek myth of a young man's unfortunate emotional investment in his own reflections. In its most general sense it stands for an exaggerated self-love. However, the term may have any of a variety of meanings depending on the particular orientation of the author. Psychiatrically, a narcissistic neurosis is characterized by such extensive self-love that normal love for others is impossible.

Narcissistic personality disorder　A personality disorder characterized by patterns of grandiosity, a need for attention and admiration, preoccupation with success and power, lack of empathy, interpersonal exploitivity, sense of entitlement, and hypersensitivity to the criticism of others.

Narcoanalysis　A form of psychoanalysis carried out under the influence of drugs that produce a sleeplike stupor, most commonly one of the barbiturates. The principle behind the procedure, at least in theory, is that the client's defenses are less effective in this state and hence he or she may be more willing or able to probe into areas normally avoided and be more open to suggestions from the analyst.

Narcolepsy　An abnormal condition characterized by recurrent, uncontrollable, brief episodes of sleep. Although some narcoleptics appear normal except for these transient episodes, many others display related symptoms, including excessive daytime sleepiness and disturbed nighttime sleep.

Necrophobia　A pathological generalized fear of death. Specifically, an irrational fear of dead things, particularly human corpses.

Neo-Freudian　A term descriptive of any psychoanalytic approach, theory, or individual analyst that significantly departs from or modifies the orthodox *Freudian* position. Those analysts who emphasized social, cultural, and interpersonal factors while maintaining a basically dynamic point of view such as Horney, are so labeled. Those who made a clean break from Freud and established their own schools of thought, like Jung and Adler, are not so classified.

Nervous　Loosely and largely nontechnically, descriptive of persons of elevated emotionality, hyperexcitability, tenseness. By extension, referring to a broad class of disorders whose origins may be either neural or emotional. The looseness of usage has led to a gradual abandonment of this term in the technical literature, although it survives in popular parlance, e.g., *nervous breakdown* for a serious acute emotional disorder and *nervous energy* for an elevated level of drive and activity.

Nervous breakdown　A nontechnical term for a severe emotional disorder. See **Nervous**.

Neuroleptic medication　A general term encompassing all drugs used in the treatment of psychosis. See **Antipsychotic drugs**; **Antidepressant drugs**; **Tranquilizers, major**.

Neuropsychology　A branch of physiological psychology that studies the interrelationships between behavior and neurological processes.

Neurosis　A disease of the nerves, now referred to as personality or mental disturbance *not* due to any known neurological or organic dysfunction, i.e., a *psychoneurosis*. This meaning, dominant since Freud, has been used to denote an identifiable symptom that, although distressing and painful, is relatively benign in that reality testing is intact. Recent years have seen the use of the phrase *neurotic disorder* as a generic cover term for any enduring mental disorder that is distressing, recognized by the individual as unacceptable and alien, but contact with reality is maintained and there is no demonstrated organic disorder.

Normal　Conforming to that which is characteristic and representative of a group; not deviating markedly from the average or the typical. Free from disease, mental disorder, mental retardation or other psychological dysfunction. The latter meaning includes behavior that reflects the typical patterns that are observed in society. Unfortunately, many who use the term allow their theories of behavior or their own beliefs about the "quality of life" to determine the boundary that separates normal and abnormal. One interesting attempt to deal with this problem has suggested the specification of the *norm group*. For example, one may deem cannibalism "normal" among certain peoples in New Guinea but not in, say, Canada. If there is a resolution to this that may work, it lies in the desire of many psychologists to characterize that which is normal in a manner that blends the group norm idea with the consideration of the individual. i.e., to ask the question: "Is the behavior functional and adaptive for that person in that social system?'' If so, then it will be considered *normal* and if not, it will be regarded as *abnormal*.

Nymphomania   An exaggerated sexual desire in females. The term is used almost unconscionably loosely, often attached to sexually active women whose erotic desires and behaviors happen to exceed one's own particular preferences about what is right and proper. As a true clinical syndrome, it is rare and is generally regarded as a manifestation of some deep psychological disorder accompanied by other symptoms.

Obsession   Any idea that haunts, hovers, and constantly invades one's consciousness. Obsessions are seemingly beyond one's "will" and awareness of their inappropriateness is of little or no avail. *Compare with* **Compulsion**; **Obsessive-compulsive disorder**.

Obsessive-compulsive disorder   A *disorder* with two essential characteristics; recurrent and persistent thoughts, ideas, and feelings, and repetitive, ritualized behaviors. Attempts to resist a compulsion produce mounting tension and anxiety, which are relieved immediately by giving in to it. The term is not properly used for behaviors like excessive drinking, gambling, eating, etc. on the grounds that the ''compulsive gambler,'' for example, actually derives considerable pleasure from gambling; one burdened with a true obsessive-compulsive disorder derives no pleasure from it other than the release of tension.

Occupational therapy   Simply, therapy based on giving the individual something purposeful to do. It may be either physical therapy, in which the tasks are designed to exercise and develop certain muscles and sensory motor coordination, or psychologically oriented therapy, in which the work is designed to improve one's general sense of self. In psychiatric hospitals, this therapy seeks to have patients interrelate in organized groups while preforming a skill (ceramic making) or taking part in an activity (volleyball). It is meant to alleviate stress and boredom and absorb the patient in meaningful activity.

Oedipus complex   A group or collection (i.e., a *complex*) of unconscious wishes, feelings, and ideas focusing on the desire to "possess" the opposite-sexed parent and "eliminate" the same-sexed parent. In the traditional Freudian view, the complex is seen as emerging during the Oedipal stage, which corresponds roughly to ages 3–5 and is characterized as a universal component of development irrespective of culture. The complex is assumed to become partly resolved, within this classical view, through the child making an appropriate identification with the same-sexed parent, with full resolution theoretically achieved when the opposite-sexed parent is "rediscovered" in a mature, adult sexual relationship. In Freud's view, a variety of neurotic fixations, sexual aberrations, and debilitating guilt feelings were theoretically traceable to an "unresolved" Oedipus complex. Interestingly, the theoretical genesis of the complex—which derives its name from the mythical figure Oedipus, the hero of two of Sophocles' tragedies who unknowingly killed his father and married his mother—was Freud's own self-analysis, carried out after his father's death. At first,

Oedipus referred only to the male complex, *Electra* being used for the female. Today, however, both are subsumed under *Oedipus* largely for convenience, although it should be noted that Electra's sins were different from Oedipus'. Rather than directly murdering her mother, she urged her brother to do it. Contemporary psychoanalytic theory places somewhat less importance on the complex than did Freud and his immediate followers.

Omnipotence of thought   In psychoanalytic theory, the belief that one's wishes, hopes, or thoughts can affect reality. Some theorists assume that it is a normal stage of childhood (*magical thinking*); others regard it as a sign of alienation from and even denial of reality. Freud thought that it was a fundamental aspect of the development of magic and religion.

Opiates   A class of drugs including (a) the naturally occurring opiates, all of which are derived from the opium poppy; morphine is the drug of reference here, codeine the other commonly found alkaloid of opium; (b) the semisynthetic opiates, including heroin and various other preparations; (c) the synthetic opiates, including methadone, a wholly synthetic compound with a morphine-like pharmacological profile. As a class the opiates all have both analgesic and narcotic effects; they also produce (often rapidly) both *drug tolerance* and *drug dependence*.

Organic mental disorder   An umbrella term in contemporary psychiatry for a large number of disorders all of which are associated with brain dysfunction, either transitory or permanent. Note that in contemporary clinical psychology and psychiatry most researchers and practitioners operate on the presumption, taken as an article of faith rather than on any definitive evidence, that ultimately all serious disorders (or psychoses) will be shown to be organic in origin.

Overanxious disorder   An anxiety disorder of childhood characterized by excessive and inappropriate anxiety and fearfulness that is not focused on or associated with a specific situation or object. Children with the disorder display an inordinate concern with future events, are overly concerned about their own performance (scholastic, social, athletic) and often have a variety of psychosomatic complaints.

Pain principle   The striving for death or for nirvana. In Freud's early psychoanalytic formulations this notion is only hinted at; later it was made explicit in the form of Thanatos, the death instinct, which was conceived of as operating along with Eros, the life instinct. There are some terminological confusions to be found in the writings of psychoanalysts, with regard to the pain principle. On one hand it is used as here, but compare *pleasure-pain principle*, for which there are rather different connotations.

Panic disorders   A class of *anxiety disorders* characterized by recurrent panic attacks, which usually occur unpredictably. They may be quite severe and accompanied by a severe sense of dread, heart palpitations, sweating, trembling, and a feeling of unreality. Typically, they are short in duration, but fear of another attack may persist and may also precipitate the attack.

Paranoia In standard psychiatric terms, a functional disorder in which the symptoms of delusions of jealousy and delusions of either grandeur and/or persecution cannot be explained by other disorders, such as schizophrenia, organic mental disorder, or organic brain syndrome. In the classic form, the delusions develop insidiously and become knit together into a rational and coherent set of beliefs that is internally consistent and, once the initial set of assumptions is accepted, compelling and vigorously defensible. In paranoia, intellectual functioning is otherwise unimpaired and the paranoid is quite capable of coherent behavior within the delusional system.

Paranoid anxiety A psychoanalytic term for anxiety produced by fear of attack from hostile others. Also called *persecutory anxiety*.

Paranoid ideation The typical pattern of thinking displayed in cases of paranoia, it is characterized by suspiciousness and beliefs that one is being followed, plotted against, persecuted, etc.

Paraphilia An umbrella term for any mode of sexual expression in which arousal is dependent upon what are generally considered socially unacceptable stimulating conditions. Typically a paraphiliac is not one who simply enjoys an exotic passing fancy with something "offbeat" but is rather obsessively concerned with and responsive to the particular erotic stimuli of his or her sexual mode. Human sexual expression is extraordinarily varied and a large number of paraphilias has been identified and studied (e.g., pedophilia, voyeurism, sadism). *See* **Fetishism**; **Sadism**; **Sado-masochistic**; **Voyeurism**.

Parapsychology A more or less (with the emphasis on the *less*) accepted branch of psychology concerned with paranormal phenomena; that is, those that are presumed to be unexplainable using known laws and principles. Generally included are extrasensory perception (ESP), telepathy, precognition, telekinesis, clairvoyance, and the like. Although there is a great deal of interest in parapsychology and many actively pursue the scientific basis of the various claims that have been made, the majority of psychologists are deeply skeptical and for good reason. First, the results of the individual experiments that have reported positive findings have proven notoriously difficult to replicate. Second, no mechanism has ever been proposed that could explain these purported paranormal phenomena in any way that is coherent in view of the rest of scientific knowledge. Precognition, for example, invites the hypothesization of time travel by the mind. Third, and this reason is perhaps unfortunate, many charlatans and fakes argue strongly for paranormal phenomena and many of the purported effects have been shown to be the result of outright fraud.

Passive-aggressive A general label descriptive of a person who is lacking in independence and tends to react to events rather than initiate them—the reactions often being aggressive in nature. Descriptive of patterns of behavior in which aggressiveness is displayed but in an indirect rather than in an active manner. It is commonly seen in persons in a relatively low power position in which overt aggressiveness would surely lead to reprisals.

Pavlov, Ivan P. (1849–1936) A Russian physiologist and experimental psychologist who by his work on the nervous stimulation of the gastric system discovered the *conditioned reflex*, and extended this theory into studies in such areas as conflict and sleep theories, greatly influencing American behaviorists. A conditioned reflex occurs as a response that is learned through a particular stimulation, i.e., a dog salivating at the sound of a tuning fork, by associating the tuning fork with the food that the animal is given just after the sound occurs. Pavlov believed that the processes of the psyche could be investigated by means of conditioning, since he held that psychic and physiological processes are identical. *See* **Conditioning**.

Ivan Petrovich Pavlov

Penis envy The hypothesized envy of the penis. The primary usage is with regard to women who, according to the classical Freudian view, are universally afflicted with a repressed wish to possess a penis. This position, stemming as it does from Freud's characterization of women as incomplete men, has been vigorously criticized and is rarely taken completely seriously any more. The secondary usage is with respect to young boys, who often display envy of the adult male. *See* **Castration complex**.

Persona From the Latin, meaning *person*. In classical Roman theater, it was a mask which the actor wore expressing the role played. By extension of this notion, Jung used the term in his early formulations to refer to the role a person takes on by virtue of the pressures of society. It is meant to refer to the role that society expects one to play in life, not necessarily the one played at a psychological level. The persona is public, the face presented to others.

Personal unconscious   Jung's term for an individual person's unconscious as distinguished from the collective unconscious. Jung conceived of the personal unconscious as consisting of repressed, suppressed, forgotten, or even ignored experiences and believed that material in it could and often did enter consciousness.

Pervasive developmental disorder (psychotic) A class of childhood disorders characterized by a serious distortion of basic psychological functioning. The notion of distortion here is a general one and may involve social, cognitive, perceptual, attentional, motor, or linguistic functioning.

Peter principle   The notion that a person is promoted up through the ranks of an organization until he or she reaches his or her level of incompetence.

Phobia   A term from the Greek for *fear* or *dread*; in keeping with this etymology specific phobias are properly given Greek root qualifiers, e.g., *pyrophobia* = fear of fire, *nyctophobia* = fear of the night, etc. In standard psychiatric work, a reaction requires several factors before it is properly classified as a phobia. Specifically, the fear must be a compelling need to flee or avoid the phobic object or situation, and the fear must be irrational, not based on sound judgment. *See also* Health & Medicine, Page 8-49.

Phobic character   A psychoanalytic term for an individual who tends to deal with difficult or anxiety-provoking situations by the simple expedient of avoiding them, usually by restricting his or her activities in life and seeking a protective environment.

Physiological psychology   A branch of psychology that is oriented toward description and explanation of psychological phenomena based on physiological and neurological processes. It shares much of its subject-matter and many of its techniques with biology and physiology and typically reflects either a *correlational* orientation, in which the search is for the physiological correlates of behavior, or *reductionistic* orientation, in which the final explanation for action and thought is sought in physiological principles.

Piaget, Jean (b. 1896)   A Swiss psychologist well noted for his work in the field of child psychology. Utilizing a clinical method to question children, Piaget was able to make detailed diagnoses of their intelligence. His theory of *cognitive development* traces the ability of the child to think on more and more complex levels. The first stage of development is the sensorimotor stage (birth–2), when the child learns to move objects and have the beginnings of perception about time and space. Stage 2 (2–7) reflects simple thinking, with little flexibility of thought, and the third level (7–11) is the concrete stage when the child first begins to master concepts. The fourth and final stage of development (11 and after) involves the start of adult reasoning and abstract thinking.

Placebo   A preparation with no medicinal value and no pharmacological effects. In studies on the effects of a drug or other substance, a placebo con-

trol condition is invariably used to separate the true pharmacological effects from the psychological effects of the subject believing that a real drug is being administered. In contemporary usage, placebo has also come to mean a medication prescribed for its psychological rather than its physiological effect. Used for its "pacifying" effect and in the treatment of hypochondria. Although this term was first introduced in the context of drug research, it has been widely used and may be found in situations having nothing to do with the study of drugs.

Pleasure-pain principle One often sees this term in its shortened form *pleasure principle*. The reference here is to a hypothetical early and primitive id function that seeks to satisfy any need either by direct means or through hallucination and fantasy— with the implication that at this point in an infant's development there is a failure to differentiate the fantasy from the reality. According to the standard Freudian model, the primitive, pleasure-seeking, pain-avoiding operations gradually become modified by the *reality principle* as ego functions are developed and the child comes to replace the fantasized wish fulfillment with more appropriate and reality-oriented adaptive behavior. Note also that the *pain* of the principle is different in meaning from the *pain* in the *pain principle*, where a striving *for* pain is hypothesized, not an avoidance of it. *See* **Reality principle**.

Postpartum depression   Loosely, any acute depression occurring within three months following childbirth. If psychotic symptoms are present, such as delusions, hallucinations, marked illogical thought, loosening of associations, the term *postpartum depression* may be used. Note, the three-month criterion is not universally adhered to and a variety of time periods may be cited as diagnostically relevant.

Post Traumatic Stress Disorder (PTSD)   An anxiety disorder resulting from having experienced an event that is beyond the realm of usual human experience (e.g., war, physical trauma). It is characterized by reexperiencing the traumatic event, avoidance of stimuli associated with the trauma, sleep disturbances, and persistent increased arousal.

Primal anxiety   In psychoanalytic theory, the anxiety experienced immediately after birth when the infant is expelled from the protective womb and thrust into the frenetic stimulation of the outside world. Note that some psychoanalytic theorists have continued to maintain that this primal experience (the so-called *birth trauma*) is the source of all anxiety; Freud himself revised his thinking on this issue considerably in his later writings.

Primal scream   Janov's term for the presumably therapeutic howl that occurs when a patient in *primal therapy* makes contact with the *primal trauma* hypothesized to lie at the core of all neuroses.

Primal therapy   A form of psychotherapy based upon the theory of Arthur Janov. The procedure consists basically of an intense therapeutic interaction between client and therapist focused on a single goal, for the client to recognize and then express his other deepest emotions toward the parent, to make contact with the *primal trauma*. Typically this contact is manifested as a gut-tearing, infantile, agonized *primal scream.* The therapy tends to be rather single-minded in practice, with many aspects—problems of daily life, dreams, fantasy, transference, etc.—being neglected which has subjected the approach to considerable criticism from other quarters.

Primal trauma   A term used very generally in psychoanalytic approaches to refer to some painful childhood experience. The experience of birth, an especially severe punishment, the death of a parent, witnessing parental coitus, the knowledge that your parents do not love you, etc., have been so labeled by various theorists.

Primary process   According to psychoanalytic theory, this term describes the mental functioning of the id, which is described as unconscious, irrational, and regulated by the pleasure principle.

Psyche   The oldest and most general use of this term is by the early Greeks, who envisioned the psyche as the soul or the very essence of life. More conventionally, the connotation is limited to *mind*, in the psychological sense.

Psychedelic   An invented term constructed by combining the Greek words *psyche* meaning *mind* and *delos* meaning *manifest* or *visible*; hence, *mind-manifesting*. It is used for drugs that are self-administered for the primary purpose of producing changes, mood, perception, and judgment, e.g., *LSD, mescaline, marijuana.*

Psychiatric social work   A specialization within social work in which the social worker is trained to diagnose and treat emotional/behavioral disorders. Also called clinical social work. The social workers treat clients independently or in collaboration with psychiatrists and clinical psychologists.

Psychiatrist   A person trained in medicine who specializes in the prevention, diagnosis, and treatment of mental disorders. The actual practice of the psychiatrist and the clinical psychologist overlap considerably, the primary difference being that the psychiatrist, by virtue of the medical license, is legally authorized to prescribe drugs but the clinical psychologist is not.

Psychiatry   A specialization within medicine encompassing prevention, diagnosis, treatment, and research of mental disorders. Psychiatry, although parallel in many respects to *clinical psychology* has been historically and is at present a branch of medicine. Psychiatrists hold the MD degree, whereas clinical psychologists hold a PhD or other professional degree. The historical issue here is more important than many realize, for psychiatry has traditionally taken the point of view that emotional and behavioral disorders are medical problems and that a person with a serious behavioral or emotional disability is mentally ill. As such, the psychiatrist is trained specifically in abnormalities and their prevention and cure, and little training is received in theories of normal behavior, experimental design, collection and analysis of data, etc. The practice of psychiatry is extremely broad and includes aspects that are indeed strictly medical such as drug treatment, electroconvulsive shock therapy, legal issues of institutionalization and hospitalization, and organic disabilities with psychological manifestations. However, it also includes many aspects that have little to do with the domain of medicine in a strict

sense including behavior modification therapy and psychoanalysis. Indeed, in these endeavors the practicing psychiatrist is little different from the practicing clinical psychologist.

Psychic trauma   A general term used for any painful psychological experience. Typically used with the implication that the impact of the experience is long lasting and that it interferes with normal functioning.

Psychoanalysis   A set of techniques for exploring the underlying motivations of human behavior, or a method of treatment of various mental disorders. It is used for the comprehensive theory of Sigmund Freud although it may be found referring to any of a variety of related dynamic theories that are derivative of Freudianism.

Psychoanalyst   A term reserved for persons who have psychoanalytic training at a recognized institute. They may have had any of a number of different forms of training prior to the psychoanalytical, e.g., an MD degree with a psychiatric residency, a doctorate or other advanced degree in psychology, or even a master's degree in social work or counseling. The term *lay analyst* is often used for practitioners who have not taken a medical degree.

Psychodrama   A psychotherapeutic technique developed by J.L. Moreno in which the individual acts out certain roles or incidents in the presence of a therapist and, often, other persons who are part of a therapy group. The procedures are based on the assumption that the role taking allows the person to express troublesome emotions and face deep conflicts in the relatively protected environment of the therapeutic stage. Common variations are *group psychodrama,* in which all the actors are in the therapy group, and *family groups* in which difficult domestic scenes are enacted.

Psychologist   Determining just to whom this term applies is no simple matter. The difficulties stem from the fact that some who claim it do so because they *practice* psychology, others because they *apply* it, others because they *teach* it, and still others because they *research* it. The standard characterization of a psychologist that is usually offered is that he or she is one who (a) holds at least a master's degree or preferably a doctorate and (b) studies psychological processes.

Psychology   Psychology simply cannot be defined; indeed, it cannot even be easily characterized. Even if one were to do so today, tomorrow would render the effort inadequate. Psychology is what scientists and philosophers of various persuasions have created to try to fulfill the need to understand the minds and behaviors of various organisms from the most primitive to the most complex. As a distinct discipline it finds its roots a mere century or so back in the faculties of medicine and philosophy. From medicine it took the orientation that explication of that which is done, thought, and felt ultimately must be couched in biology and physiology; from philosophy it took a class of deep problems concerning mind, will, and knowledge.

Psychopath   A term with two uses, both of which are falling out of favor; (a) A general label for a person with any severe mental disorder. This usage is now absent from technical writings but still occurs in popular literature; (b) An individual diagnosed as having a *psychopathic personality*. Note, however, that that term has been largely superseded by *antisocial personality disorder*. See **Antisocial personality disorder**; **Criminal psychopath**; **Psychopathic personality**.

Psychopathic personality   A personality disorder characterized by amorality, a lack of affect, and a diminished sense of anxiety and/or guilt associated with the commission of transgressions. *See* **Antisocial personality disorder**; **Criminal psychopath**; **Psychopath**.

Psychopharmacology   Generally, any form of psychotherapy that treats behavioral and mental disorders with drugs and chemicals, such as tranquilizers or anti-depressants. Some therapists view most, if not all, abnormal reactions as being, in the final analysis, due to biochemical imbalances and will argue that they should be treated likewise. Others take a less definitive position and will use these drugs as a way of producing a temporary quiescent state during which more traditional therapy techniques may be employed; broadly to cover any technique based on chemicals, for example in the treatment of cancer. *See* **Tranquilizers, major**; **Tranquilizers, minor**.

Psychotherapy   In the most inclusive sense, the use of absolutely any technique or procedure that has palliative or curative effects upon any mental, emotional, or behavioral disorder.

Psychotic disorders   A general cover term for a number of severe mental disorders of organic or emotional origin. In contemporary psychiatric terminology, the defining feature of these disorders is gross impairment in *reality testing*. That is, the person makes incorrect inferences concerning external reality, makes improper evaluations of the accuracy of his or her thoughts and perceptions, and continues to make these errors in the face of contrary evidence. Classic symptoms include delusions, hallucinations, severe regressive behaviors, dramatically inappropriate mood, and markedly incoherent speech. The standard clinical literature lists as psychoses: *manic-depression* (or *bipolar disorder*), *paranoia, schizophrenia,* various *organic mental disorders, pervasive developmental disorder,* and some of the *affective disorders*.

Psychotic episode   A general term for a relatively short-duration emotional or mental disorder when there is a transient break in some aspect of reality testing.

Pyromania   An *impulse-control disorder* characterized by a recurrent failure to resist impulses to set fires and deep fascination with watching them burn. A defining feature of the disorder is that the fire setting is undertaken without obvious motivations, such as money, revenge, or political ideology.

R   **Rage**   A term usually taken to refer to the extreme end of the domain of emotion denoted by *anger,* i.e., anger that has gotten out of control. It is usually identified by the same patterns of visceral and muscular responses as anger, but the pattern is more extreme and more intense and an attack response is considered more likely.

Rational-emotive therapy   A form of psychotherapy developed by Albert Ellis that focuses on the rational, problem-solving aspects of emotional and behavioral disorders. Ellis's approach is highly directive, consisting in large measure of telling the client what he or she must do in order to be happy and then "encouraging" him or her, often through confrontation and encounter, to act and think accordingly .

Reality principle   According to psychoanalytic theory, this term describes the child's recognition of the real demands of the environment and the need to accommodate them.   This is seen as normal development, as the reality principle serves to modify or decrease the more primitive, unreal pleasure principle. *See* **Pleasure-pain principle**.

Reality-testing   Very generally, any process by which an organism systematically assesses the limits upon its behavior that the external environment imposes. In psychoanalytic theory, a set of ego functions that enable the child to distinguish between subjective impression and external reality and to adjust the primitive subjective components to the constraints of the objective environment.

Regression   The core meaning of the term which underlies the various specialized uses is that of reverting, a going backward, a retreating; the opposite of *progression*. Thus, a reverting to an earlier, more primitive or more childlike pattern of behavior in psychoanalytic theories, it has a negative implication, i.e., the notion that stress or anxiety is causing the individual to flee from reality into a more infantile state, but in cognitive/developmental theories, it refers to a temporary falling back upon an earlier form of thinking in order to begin to learn how to deal with new complexity, and is viewed as a way-station in an ultimately progressive development of cognitive processing.

Reich, William (1897–1957)   Austrian psychiatrist who eventually broke with Freud and settled in New York City. Reich's theories involved the permeation of the universe by what he termed *orgone energy,* a primal phenomenon that required dispersal through sexual release. If such a release was not possible, or if it was withheld, neurosis and irrational social behavior would develop. Reich, a lecturer at the New School for Social Research in New York City and the founder of the Orgone Institute in 1942, invented an "orgone box," which he claimed would restore depleted energy. He was deemed a fraud, and in 1956 was tried for contempt of court and sentenced to two years in a federal penitentiary, where he died at the age of sixty.

Relaxation therapy   Generally, any psychotherapy that emphasizes techniques for teaching the client how to relax, to control tensions. The procedure used is based upon E. Jacobson's *progressive relaxation techniques* in which the individual learns how to relax muscle groups one at a time, the assumption being that muscular relaxation is effective in bringing about emotional relaxation. Jacobson's techniques are often used in various forms of behavior therapy.

Repression   In all depth psychologies from the classical Freudian model onward, a hypothesized mental process or operation that functions to protect the individual from ideas, impulses, and memories that would produce anxiety, apprehension, or guilt were they to become conscious. Repression is considered operative at an unconscious level, that is, not only does the mechanism keep certain mental contents from reaching awareness, but its very operations lie outside conscious awareness. An important corollary is that that which is repressed is not deactivated but continues to have a lively existence at the unconscious level, making itself felt through projections in disguised symbolic form, in dreams, for example.

Resistance   In psychoanalysis, opposition to making what is unconscious conscious. Note that some psychoanalysts also use the term somewhat more pragmatically to refer to the opposition to accepting the interpretations made by the analyst. In either case, the resistance is generally regarded as caused by unconscious factors. It is also regarded as universal in psychoanalysis.

Rogers, Carl (b. 1902)   American psychologist who developed the self theory of personality, a nondirective approach to therapy. The patient sits across from the therapist in a nonclinical atmosphere meant to be conducive to easy and free speech. The purpose is to unfold to the individual a greater understanding of him or herself. The role of the doctor in modifying and interpreting is minimal; the patient, by listening to himself, is viewed as being his own therapist. Rogers believed that individual experiences that were either repressed or remembered in a distorted way resulted in feelings of panic (anxiety) and proved to be decisive to the self. Conflict must be alleviated before growth can continue, and potentialities are allowed to come to fruition through counseling that is nondirective, so that the individual eventually comes to regard himself in a positive way and therefore value the person he has discovered.

Romeo and Juliet effect   The increase in the attractiveness between two people resulting from an attempt on the part of their parents or others to keep them apart.

Rorschach test   The grandfather of all tests designed with an unstructured set of stimuli to which the patient is requested to respond in an unrestricted way. Designed and developed by the Swiss psychiatrist Hermann Rorschach (1884–1922), the administration of the test consists of a structured interview using a series of ten standardized ink blots (black or white and colored). Each blot is presented to the subject, who is requested to state freely what he or she sees either in the blot as a whole or in any part of it. Extremely complex scoring and interpretation systems have been developed and lengthy training is required to become proficient in its use. According to the classical interpretation, responses to color are supposedly reflective of emotional responsiveness of the subject to the environment; form and location responses are taken as indices of overall orientation to life; movement responses are assumed to reflect tendencies toward introversion; originality theoretically reflects intelligence, but bizarre originality is seen as indicative of neurotic tendencies, etc.

There is a certain fascination with this test that affects all, professional and lay alike. In some ways,

particularly among lay people, it is seen as a symbol of psychology itself. It reflects that strange belief that many have that psychologists and psychiatrists can somehow tell you something about yourself that you would never be able to ascertain on your own, as if they possessed some mysterious ability to read through the veils of defenses and posturing that are opaque to all but these shamans and their testing procedures. Yet there is essentially no evidence whatsoever that the test has even a shred of validity. It seems not unreasonable to assume that the test can be of value in a clinical setting, but perhaps not necessarily because of any intrinsic property of the Rorschach itself nor of the manner of its administration. Rather, it is likely the case that the test provides an opportunity for an extended, unbounded interaction between client and therapist, with the ink blots acting as the vehicle for the interaction. Given such an intensive, open setting, particularly when the client believes the test has a valid psychological role to play in the ongoing dialogue, the perceptive clinician can gain insight into the personality characteristics of the client. Thus, the usefulness of the Rorschach will depend upon the sensitivity, empathy, and insightfulness of the Rorschach itself. An intense searching dialogue about the wallpaper or the rug would do as well. *See* **Inkblot test**.

Sadism   The association of sexual pleasure from the inflicting of pain upon another. Note that *pain* here may take many forms other than the purely physical. As the term is used, psychic pain, humiliation, debasement, exploitation, etc. may all be regarded as sadistic acts. The term derives from the rather singular sexual orientation of the notorious essayist, novelist, and revolutionary, Donatien Alphonse François, the Marquis de Sade (1740–1814). Somewhat more generally, the derivation of pleasure from the inflicting of pain and suffering on others. *See* **Paraphilia**.

Sado-masochistic   A hybrid term reflecting the oft-noted tendency for sadistic and masochistic manifestations to occur together in the same person. Also characterizing a relationship between persons in which one enacts the role of sadist and the other the role of masochist. *See* **Paraphilia**.

Schizoid personality disorder   A personality disorder characterized by a restrictive range of emotional experience and expression, withdrawal, and indifference to social relationships and intimate attachment.

Schizophrenia   A general label for a number of psychotic disorders with various cognitive, emotional, and behavioral manifestations. The term originated with Eugen Bleuler, who offered it in 1911 as a replacement for *dementia praecox*. It literally means *splitting in the mind* and was chosen by Bleuler because the disorder seemed to reflect a cleavage or dissociation between the functions of feeling or emotion on one hand and those of thinking or cognition on the other. Although there are various distinguishable schizophrenias certain features are taken as hallmarks of all: (a) deterioration from previous levels of social, cognitive, and vocational functioning; (b) onset before the age of 45; (c) a duration of at least six months; and most tellingly,

(d) a pattern of psychotic features including thought disturbances, bizarre delusions, hallucinations (usually auditory), disturbed sense of self, and a loss of reality testing. The borderline that distinguishes schizophrenia from other disorders is fuzzy, and differential diagnosis is problematical. Note also that many authorities are convinced that a relatively straightforward (although largely uniform) neurochemical cause exists for the disorder.

Schizophrenia, catatonic (type) A type of schizophrenia characterized by a tendency to remain in a stupor-like state during which the patient may hold a particular posture, sitting or lying in the same position for extended periods of time, sometimes for weeks or even months. Frequently the catatonic state gives way to short periods of frenetic activity during which the patient is capable of considerable damage to others as well as to him or herself. See **Catatonia**.

Schizophrenia episode, acute A general diagnostic category used for relatively brief (a few weeks or months) episodes of schizophrenic symptoms, typically, clouding of consciousness, emotional turmoil, and disorganized thought.

Schizophrenia, paranoid (type) A type of schizophrenia characterized primarily by delusions of persecution or grandiosity or hallucinations with persecutory or grandiose content. Delusional jealousy is often part of the disorder, and any of a number of associated symptoms many be found, including unfocused anxiety, anger, argumentativeness, doubts about gender identity, stilted formal quality, aloofness. Unlike many other forms of schizophrenia, the patient is usually of relatively normal appearance and clean in habits and if the delusions are not acted on impairment in functioning may be minimal.

Schizophrenia, simple A form of schizophrenia characterized by an extreme lack of what are considered normal emotional reactions to the real world. Emotions of joy, sadness, anger, resentment, and the like are missing; ambition and initiative likewise; apathy, indifference, and resignation dominate. With social and economic impoverishment, vagrancy often results.

Secondary process According to psychoanalytic theory, this term describes the rational, logical, conscious mental functioning associated with the ego and the reality principle.

Sedatives A class of drugs all of which produce drowsiness and are prescribed most frequently in cases of insomnia. All these drugs function similarly to depress, nonselectively, central nervous system functioning. Depending on the size of the dose, they produce mild sedation, "hypnotic" sleep, anesthesia, coma, and death from respiratory failure. All are subject to buildup of tolerance, so that increasing doses are needed to maintain the same effect, and all produce drug dependence. They also diminish sensory-motor skills and interact strongly with many other drugs, significantly alcohol. Other drugs are occasionally included in the category of sedatives, in particular *antihistamines,* which have drowsiness as a side-effect, and some *tranquiliz*ers, which may aid sleep by reducing anxiety and agitation. See **Tranquilizers**.

Self-acceptance Quite literally, an acceptance of oneself. The term is used with the specific connotation that this acceptance is based on a relatively objective appraisal of one's unique talents, capabilities, and general worth, a realistic recognition of their limits, and a rich feeling of satisfaction with both these talents and their boundaries.

Self-awareness Generally, the condition of being aware of or conscious of oneself—in the sense of a relatively objective but open and accepting appraisal of one's true personal nature.

Self-consciousness Generally, *self-awareness* but with a "twist," the additional realization that it is possible that others are similarly aware of oneself. Specifically, a sense of embarrassment or unease that derives from when the individual suspects that the awareness that others have contains critical evaluative aspects that are incompatible with one's own personal self-assessment or reveals one to be inadequate.

Self-deception The deceiving of oneself in the sense of the inability to have accurate insights into one's limitations; a self-deceiver cannot display *self-acceptance.*

Self-denial The practice of deliberately forgoing pleasures and satisfactions. Typically practiced by those who value asceticism, who argue that they forsake the superficial and trivial pleasures for greater psychological gain.

Self-expression The acting out of one's inner feelings, beliefs, attitudes, etc. In many contemporary psychotherapeutic orientations, such a display is assumed to have therapeutic value. Also any behavior carried out for the sheer pleasure and satisfaction that it provides for the individual.

Self-identification The process whereby one develops affection and admiration for another person who possesses qualities and traits that resemble those of oneself. That is, one sees (identifies) oneself in another; there is no suggestion of confusion in personal identity, however.

Self-image The imagined self; the self one supposes oneself to be. Many models of neurosis, particularly that of Karen Horney, are built on the commonly observed circumstances in which a person's real self is rather dramatically incongruent with their self-image.

Senile psychosis In the past this term was used to cover a range of disorders of the aged characterized by memory impairment, stubbornness, irritability, and a generally erratic pattern of affect. The preferred psychiatric category is *dementia, Senile.* See **Dementia, senile**.

Separation anxiety In psychoanalysis, the hypothesized anxiety on the part of the infant or child concerning possible loss of the mother object. By extension, anxiety over the possible loss of any other person or object upon whom one has become dependent.

Sex therapy A general term used to cover any therapeutic enterprise aimed at the relief of sexual dysfunctions or disturbances. Included are therapies aimed at altering one's attitudes toward sex and sexual behavior, for example, to relieve irrational fears or guilt feelings that inhibit performance and enjoyment, therapies specifically concerned with

PSYCHOLOGY

identifiable dysfunctions, such as impotency, premature ejaculation, or orgasmic dysfunctions, therapies which focus on communication and interactive difficulties that a married couple may be experiencing, and so forth.

Sexual identity One's identity with respect to sexual preferences. The term is usually restricted to labeling oneself as hetero-, homo-, or bisexual.

Skinner, Burrhus F. (1904–1990) American psychologist responsible for a system of operant conditioning, an experimental laboratory arrangement consisting of the "Skinner box," in which an animal is placed and the need (i.e., for food) gratified when it learns to operate a simple mechanism that when depressed will provide it with a pellet to eat (the reward). The idea is that responses will increase through positive reinforcement. *See* **Behaviorism; Conditioning.**

Social psychology That branch of psychology that concentrates on any and all aspects of human behavior that involve persons and their relationships to other persons, groups, and social institutions and to society as a whole. Gordon Allport captured this general sense in his now classic definition of social psychology as the discipline that "attempts to understand and explain how the thought, feeling or behavior of individuals are influenced by the actual, imagined or implied presence of others."

Stress interview Quite literally, an interview in which the person being interviewed is deliberately put under considerable emotional stress to evaluate their ability to handle such tension in real-life situations.

Sublimation In classical psychoanalysis, the process whereby primitive, libidinous impulses and aggressive drives are redirected and refined into new, learned, "noninstinctive" behaviors. Typically, the term is used with the understanding that the learned behaviors are socially acceptable whereas the deep, primitive impulses would not be. Freudian theory regards creative and artistic tendencies as manifestations of sublimation. Also generally, and more loosely, any redirection of energy from the socially unacceptable to the acceptable.

Success, fear of A term coined by Matina Horner for a fear of accomplishing one's goals or of succeeding in society's eyes. She originally argued that women displayed this fear more than men since striving for success places a woman in a conflict between a general need for achievement and social values that tell her that she should not achieve "too much." More recent research seems to indicate that men are just as likely to show this hypothesized fear. It should be pointed out, however, that it is far from clear how thoroughly one can divorce this fear from *a fear of failure*, particularly when each new "success" in life carries with it greater potential for greater failure.

Suicide A person who intentionally kills himself or herself. Emile Durkheim, the first to study suicide systematically, distinguished three different types, depending on what motivates the act of self-destruction: *altruistic, anomic* and *egoistic;* definitions of each are found below.

Suicide, altruistic Durkheim's term for suicide based on sacrificing oneself for the good of others.

The soldier who hurls himself upon a grenade to save others and the ritual suicide, such as hara-kiri, which is designed to save one's family from shame, are classic examples.

Suicide, anomic Suicide that results, in Durkheim's analysis, from the sense that life no longer has meaning, from a sense of anomie, loneliness, isolation, and loss of contact with the norms and values of society. Also called *normless suicide.*

Suicide, egoistic In Durkheim's classification system, suicide resulting from a sense of deep personal failure, a feeling that one is personally responsible for not living up to societal and personal expectations.

Superego In the Freudian model of the psyche the hypothetical entity associated with ethical and moral conduct and conceptualized as responsible for self-imposed standards of behavior. The superego is frequently characterized as an internalized code or, more popularly, as a kind of *conscience* punishing transgressions with feelings of guilt. In the classical psychoanalytic literature, the superego is assumed to develop in response to the punishments and rewards of significant persons (usually the parents), which results in the child becoming inculcated with the moral code of the community. Whereas the *id* is conceptualized as concerned with the pleasurable and the *ego* with the actual, the superego is viewed as being concerned with the ideal.

Superiority complex The conviction that one is better than or superior to others. Although there are (indeed, must be) persons who are in fact superior in various ways and who recognize their talents, the term is typically not used for them. Rather, it is reserved for those who have an exaggerated and unrealistic sense of themselves and is generally interpreted as a defense against deeper feelings of inferiority.

Suppression In psychoanalysis, conscious exclusion of impulses, thoughts, and desires that are to be unacceptable to the individual. The classic theory distinguished suppression from *repression* in that the former is a conscious process and the latter, unconscious.

Systematic desensitization A behavioral technique that serves to decrease anxiety toward a feared stimulus by exposing the individual to a series of approximations to the anxiety-producing stimulus under relaxed conditions until the anxiety reaction is extinguished.

Talking cure A half-joking term used to refer to the psychoanalytic therapy in that the person's neuroses seem to be "cured" by their simply talking to the analyst. The usage has extended beyond pure psychoanalysis and is occasionally applied to other therapies based on having the individual talk through problems.

Talking out The full and spontaneous discussion of one's emotional and behavioral problems. Usually the term is restricted to the therapeutic setting but it is flexible enough to be applied in other situations, e.g., with a counselor, a friend, a teacher.

Tardive dyskinesia A disorder characterized by involuntary and rhythmic movements of the face and upper body.

PSYCHOLOGY

Thanatomania A homicidal or suicidal mania. Also, wasting away and ultimate death following awareness that one has transgressed seriously some societal taboo or believing that one has been bewitched. In this sense, it is also called *voodoo death*.

Thanatos The Greek god of death. In Freud's usage, Thanatos refers to the theoretical generalized instinct for death as expressed in such behaviors as denial, rejection, and the turning away from pleasure. *Compare with* **Eros**.

Therapy An inclusive label for all manners and forms of treatment of disease or disorder. Because the term is so broad, both connotatively and denotatively, it is typically used with qualifiers to designate the form of therapy referenced.

Therapy, active A general term for any therapeutic approach in which the therapist takes an active, directing role, e.g., *rational-emotive therapy*. Also called *directive therapy*.

Therapy, didactic A kind of *directive therapy* in which the therapist instructs the client, explains things in detail, and attempts to teach the client various specific ways to overcome his or her problems.

Therapy, passive Generally, any therapy in which the therapist maintains a low profile and makes little or no attempt either to control the direction of therapy or to direct changes in the client.

Therapy, physical Generally, the use of any physical agent in a therapeutic fashion, e.g., massage, exercise, heat.

Therapy, preventive Any therapy that is designed to prevent a serious condition from developing.

Tic disorder A term used to describe a set of neurological disorders that are characterized by one or more of several forms of tics. Tics are defined as involuntary, sudden, rapid, recurrent, nonrythmic motor movements (e.g., eye blinking, arm movements, head jerking, finger or hand movements, facial twitches) or vocalizations (e.g., grunting, throat clearing). Compulsive behavior and obsessive thinking may also be part of this disorder. Transient tics are temporary, come and go, and may last only a few weeks or months. Chronic tics are unchanging and may persist for several years. *See* **Tourette syndrome**.

Tolerance, drug A condition of diminished responsiveness to a particular drug resulting from repeated exposure to it. Once tolerance has developed, increased doses are required to produce the effects achieved earlier with small doses.

Tourette syndrome A neurological disorder characterized, in mild form, by involuntary tics and movements and, in advanced cases, by large involuntary bodily movements, noises like barks and whistles, and in instances, an uncontrollable urge to utter obscenities. *See* **Tic disorder**.

Tranquilizers A generic label used for any of several classes of drugs, all of which have one or more of the following properties: antianxiety, sedative, muscle relaxant, anticonvulsant, antiagitation. Tranquilizers are generally grouped into the *minor tranquilizers*, which are used primarily for the treatment of anxiety, and the *major tranquilizers*, which are used for the more serious psychiatric disorders, such as schizophrenia and bipolar disorder.

Tranquilizers, major A general label for those drugs that are used primarily to improve the mood and behavior of patients with severe psychiatric disorders. In a sense the term *tranquilizer* is misleading, since the drugs that are included in this category have rather different actions and effects than that of simply tranquilizing. As a result, the contemporary, preferred term is *antipsychotic drug*, because their most significant function is the alleviation of many of the symptoms of various psychoses. The drugs in this category function to alleviate symptoms, they do not "cure" the disorders for which they are prescribed. They ameliorate the confusional states, disturbed thinking, and erratic affect of various pyschoses and produce a general quietude, a slowing of responsiveness to external stimuli, and a lessening of attentiveness without major changes in wakefulness or arousability. They also have a variety of side effects that can be troublesome, such as muscular disorders, tremors, dry mouth, hypotension, and various toxic allergic reactions. *See* **Antipsychotic drugs**; **Antidepressant drugs**; **Lithium**; **Neuroleptic medication**.

Tranquilizers, minor A general term for any of several classes of drugs that are used primarily in the treatment of anxiety and psychiatric disorders that have an anxiety-related component. They are most frequently prescribed for relief of tension and anxiety and are commonly referred to collectively as *antianxiety drugs*. The pharmacology of these drugs is similar to that of the *barbiturates*, but they are generally safer, with greater latitude for tolerance and lesser likelihood of development of dependency. Their primary action is to produce muscle relaxation through the central nervous system; they do not act upon the muscles themselves. *See* **Antianxiety drugs**; **Antidepressant drugs**.

Transactional analysis (TA) A form of psychotherapy originally developed by Eric Berne. It is practiced in a straightforward group setting in which the primary goal is to have the client achieve an adaptive, mature, and realistic attitude toward life, to have, in Berne's words, "the adult ego maintain hegemony [authority] over the impulsive child."

Transference Most generally, the passing on, displacing, or "transferring" of an emotion or affective attitude from one person onto another person or object. Within psychoanalysis, the displacement of feelings and attitudes applicable toward other persons (usually one's parents but also siblings, a spouse, etc.) onto the analyst. Transference here is often termed either *positive* or *negative*, depending upon whether the person develops pleasant or hostile attitudes toward the analyst. Its conspicuousness in psychoanalysis, they argue, is attributable simply to the calculated neutrality of the analyst, which allows it to be more unambiguously observed. Freud believed the transference mechanism to be of the highest importance in a successful analysis; however, he died before he had reached any conclusions on how to terminate a positive transference between doctor and patient.

Transsexualism A condition characterized primarily by a belief that one is of the wrong sex. Several criteria have been proposed for identifying the true transsexual: (a) discomfort with one's sexual anatomy; (b) a persistent, deep desire to be a member of the opposite sex; (c) a wish to change one's genitalia; and (d) absence of other psychological disorders or genetic anatomical abnormalities such as hermaphroditism. *See* **Gender-identity disorder**.

Transvestism   A condition marked by a persistent desire to dress in the clothes generally regarded by society as appropriate to the other sex. Considered a *gender-identity disorder,* the label is reserved for those who (a) derive sexual pleasure from such cross-dressing and (b) have no desire to change their anatomic sex. Note that male professional entertainers who work as *female impersonators* may or may not be transvestites; the terms are not synonymous. Note that homosexuality (now considered by the American Psychiatric Association as an alternate life style, not a condition for therapy) and transvestism are in no way synonymous. *See* **Gender-identity disorder**.

U **Unconscious**   A state characterized by a lack of awareness. In psychoanalysis, a domain of the psyche encompassing the repressed id functions, the primitive impulses and desires, the memories, images, and wishes that are too anxiety provoking to be accepted into consciousness. Characterizing these primordial, repressed desires, memories and images. Note that the unconscious is assumed to be populated by two varieties of psychic entities, those that were once conscious but had been exiled from awareness and those that were never in consciousness.

V **Voyeurism**   A *paraphilia* characterized by a pattern of sexual behavior in which one's preferred means of sexual arousal is the clandestine observing of others when they are disrobing, nude or actually engaged in sexual activity. Interestingly, a voyeur does not usually derive pleasure from striptease shows, public nudity, or pornography; arousal is dependent upon the observed person(s) not being aware of their being observed. *See* **Paraphilia**.

W **Watson, John Broadus** (1878–1958) Watson, an American psychologist in favor of militant behaviorism, saw psychology as the "science of behavior." He believed human responses could be predicted by (a) observation, (b) conditioned reflexes, (c) verbal methods, and (d) testing. His studies of children and animals were innovative because structuralists and behaviorists had virtually neglected these two groups. He worked on the conditioning of childhood fears, and his advances with animals opened the way to the development of comparative psychology. *See* **Behaviorism**.

Wechsler Intelligence Scales   A general label for various Wechsler tests of intelligence. All of the Wechsler scales are individually administered tests. The Wechsler Adult Intelligence Scale—Revised (WAIS-R) is for adults. The Wechsler Intelligence Scale for Children—Third Edition (WISC-III) is used with children 6 to 16 yeas of age, and the Wechsler Preschool and Primary Scale of Intelligence—Revised (WPPSI-R) is designed to be used with children below the age of 6. *See* **Intelligence quotient**.

Will to power   Adler's term for the desire to dominate others or the striving for superiority over them.

Wish fulfillment   In psychoanalysis, a complex process whereby id impulses are satisfied and, as a result, psychic tension is reduced. In the classical Freudian conception, dreams are vehicles for the action of the wish fulfillment. In dreaming, for example, the primal id fails to distinguish between fantasies, images, or hallucinations and reality and so the dreamer may represent as fulfilled in symbolic form wishes that would otherwise have disrupted sleep because of their unacceptability.

Withdrawal   A pattern of behavior characterized by the person removing him or herself from normal day-to-day functioning, with all of its attendant frustrations, tensions, and disappointments. Here the sense is of neurotic removal of self from normal social discourse, accompanied by uncooperativeness, irresponsibility, and often a reliance on drugs and alcohol to facilitate this social remoteness. Pertaining to drug or alcohol usage, a general term covering any of the effects or symptoms observed when the administering of a substance upon which one has become dependent is discontinued. *See* **Addiction**; **Alcohol withdrawal**; **Alcohol withdrawal delirium**; **Barbiturate withdrawal**; **Cold turkey**; **Delirium tremens**.

Wundt, Wilhelm (1832–1920)   Considered by some to be the founder of modern psychology, Wundt was the leader of the school of structuralism, which contended that psychology is human experience studied from the point of view of the person doing the experiencing. Introspection and self-exploration are stressed. Structuralists in general believed in the separation of mind and body, without interaction, but conceived of in such a way that a parallel structure is formed: For each conscious experience of the mind, a corresponding reaction occurs in the body. It must be remembered that the mind does not cause physical reactions any more than the body alters states of consciousness. Between 1890 and 1920 in the United States, structuralism was the dominant school of psychological thought, eventually replaced because of its narrow perspective by functionalism and behaviorism in America and Gestalt psychology in Germany.

X **Xenophobia**   A pathological fear of strangers or strange places.

RELIGION

Abbey   A monastery that houses at least twelve monks. It includes a church, guesthouse, infirmary refectory, etc. Ruled by an abbot elected for life through a secret ballot.

Absolution   In the Roman Catholic church, the priestly power to remove the sin of a believer and grant reconciliation with the church. Absolution follows the act of penance.

Acolyte   A member of the laity who prepares the wine and water for mass or services and assists in the service itself. These tasks are now usually performed by an altar boy.

Adam   From the Hebrew "Adamah," earth. The father of the earth; the first man. In Jewish tradition, the symbol of man's unity and equality, whose fall represented human imperfection. Note: In Judaism, Adam's fall was not caused by imperfection (sin), but is seen as a parable of inherent human foibles.

Advent   In Christianity, the observance of four Sundays before Christmas. A period of time for contemplation before the birth of Jesus.

Adventists   A Christian sect based on the teachings of William Miller (1782–1849). He believed in the immanent return of Christ and the renewal of the earth as a home for the redeemed who will be physically resurrected from the dead. Miller took the prophetic and apocalyptic passages in the Bible literally. By calculations based on the *Book of Daniel*, he concluded that the second advent of Christ would occur between 1843 and 1844. A great number of people throughout New England believed his ideas.

Agape   A Greek word meaning "selfless love." In Greek, there are several words for love, each having a unique meaning. *Eros* is usually associated with desire and erotic love. *Philia* has the connotation of love between good friends. *Agape* stands as the most noble of all loves: It is love that loves regardless of another's qualities, despite the lack of physical or intellectual beauty.

Agnosticism   Literally meaning "to not know," it is the state of suspended belief. Primarily, it means suspended belief with respect to the existence of God.

Agnus dei   Latin for "Lamb of God." The symbol of the sacrificial Christ as a lamb. As an invocation: the Lamb of God that takes away the sins of the world.

Allah   The name for God in Aramaic and Islam. Used by Arabians in ancient times as a supreme god and latter by Mohammed as the only God. It is also used as the name for God by Arabic-speaking persons of other faiths.

All Saints' Day   Occurring on November 1, a day on which Christian groups celebrate saints not otherwise mentioned on liturgical calendars.

All Souls' Day   A solemn holy day of the Catholic church to commemorate departed souls in limbo; usually November 2.

Altar   Originally a place to commune with a god through a sacrificial offering. Earliest forms were created from rock, a ground covered with sweet grasses and herbs, or stones made into a mound. Always found outdoors, as the first gods were conceived of as embodied in the powers of nature.

Anabaptists   A third branch of Protestantism in the Reformation, initiated in Zurich, and holding that Luther, Calvin, and Zwingli had not gone far enough in their reforms. Two leaders of the movement, Grebel and Blaurock, friend of Zwingli, argued for two fundamental points: (1) that baptism should not be given to infants but only to those who had made a decision to follow Christ (believers' baptism), and (2) that the church should be free from civil magistrate control.

Ancestor worship   In primitive religions, the belief that the spirits of the dead hovered near their earthly homes. They had the power to bless and protect those within who cared for them with offerings of food and drink.

Angelus   Prayer, or the bell rung for three daily prayers to celebrate the Annunciation. A practice in convents and monasteries.

Annunciation   The angel Gabriel's announcement to Mary that she was to give birth to Jesus. The Catholic church celebrates this festival on March 25.

Anthropomorphism   Literally, the form of a man. The term is used in religion to mean giving God the characteristics and traits of man. For instance, ascribing hunger or sorrow to God.

Antichrist   Primarily, one who denies or is in opposition to Christ. This term actually refers to one, evil in purpose, who will meet defeat by the acts of Christ in the second coming. References to the Antichrist can be found in *The Book of Revelation*.

Antisemitism   Prejudicial actions or verbalizations against the Jews. Antisemitism has existed throughout history; in the contemporary world it found life in Fascism.

Apostle   Literally, "one sent out." Usually referring to the twelve chosen by Jesus. According to the book of Acts, to be an apostle one had to have been an immediate disciple of Jesus and a personal witness of the Resurrection.

Ark   The sacred chest of God in the Hebrew Bible containing the Ten Commandments, which were written on stone tablets. Today the Ark is placed in the synagogue in the eastern wall as the container of the scrolls of the Law. Also the term for the boat that Noah built by command of God so that he and his family could escape the Flood.

Ascension   In the Catholic church, celebrated 40 days after Easter Sunday when the risen Christ ascended into heaven from Mount Olivet.

Ash Wednesday   The first day of Lent in the Christian church. The beginning of 40 days of deprivation in preparation for the Crucifixion and Easter Sunday. Traditionally in the Catholic church, the day individuals begin the sacrifice of one or more pleasures throughout Lent.

Atheism   Disbelief in the existence of God. From the Greek *a* (not) and *theos* (God). In ancient times atheists were those who did not accept the existence of the popular gods. The early Christians were called atheists because they denied the many gods of the Roman culture. In modern times, an atheist is usually one who denies the existence of the one supreme being as held in Judaism, Christianity, and Islam.

Atman   A Sanskrit term that signifies "the self." The Upanishads and Vedantic philosophy understands Atman and Brahman, the ruler of all things, to be one and the same.

Atonement   A theological doctrine meaning the reconciliation between God and persons marked with sin. In the New Testament, the death of Jesus atoned for the sins of the world; he was a substitute for humanity and allowed for God and humanity to have fellowship and harmony. Generally, the understanding of atonement differed between Eastern and Western Christianity. Immediately after the schism in 1054, Anselm, the Archbishop of Canterbury, developed a juridical theory of the atonement that was further developed by John Calvin. This juridical emphasis in Western theology has been characteristic of most Western Christians, both Roman Catholic and Protestant. For Western Christians, and especially those in the Augustinian/Calvinist tradition, sin is primarily something God punishes humanity for. On the contrary, Orthodox Christianity understands sin as primarily something God rescues humanity from.

Atonement, Day of   An annual ceremony in the Hebrew Bible that renews the people's relationship with God by cleansing the temple, priesthood, and people of their sins. The day is accompanied by fasting and sacrifice. In modern Judaism, the ceremony is on Yom Kippur, the holiest day of the year.

Avatar   A divine incarnation. From the Sanskrit word *avatara*, meaning "descent." In Hinduism, the term refers to the manifestation of Vishnu, of which nine have occurred, the tenth being expected.

B

Baptism   A rite of dedication and induction of an individual into a circle of social and religious privilege. The rite is usually of a ceremonious nature with pledges given, prayers said, and accompanied by some visible sign (such as water, symbol of purification, or wine, honey, oil or blood) sealing the bond of fellowship. In its earliest form the rite probably symbolized not only an initiation but the magical removal of some tabu or demon possession. In Christian circles the rite has assumed the status of a sacrament, the supernatural rebirth into the Divine Kingdom. Various forms include sprinkling with water, immersion, or the laying on of hands. In some Christian circles it is considered less a mystical rite and more a sign of a covenant of salvation and consecration to the higher life.

Baptists   A Protestant sect that originated in the early 17th century, stressing the total separation of church and state; also baptism by immersion for the cleansing of sin, rebirth, and the acceptance of Christ as personal Saviour.

Bar mitzvah   A Jewish male thirteen years of age. A bar mitzvah is considered an adult with moral and religious responsibilities. The term also applies to the ceremony that initiates a boy as a bar mitzvah.

Bat mitzvah   The ceremony for a girl that is similar to a bar mitzvah. *See* **Bar mitzvah**.

Beatitudes   The collective name for the proclamations of Jesus in the Sermon on the Mount. All of the nine "sayings" begin in the same way: "Blessed are the..." and proceed to exemplify ideal Christian concepts. For example, "Blessed are the meek, for they shall inherit the earth."

Beelzebub   A name for the Devil in the New Testament, synonomous with Satan.

Benedictines   The name of the oldest religious order of monks, founded in the 6th century by St. Benedict. Benedictine monks remain in the same monastery for life; they are known for scholarship and the cultivation of art and religion.

Bhagavad Gita   From the Sanskrit, "Song of the Blessed." An epic poem dated from the 6th century B.C. that contains a dialogue between Arjuna and his charioteer, the God Krishna in disguise. The theme of the poem is love of God, which can be expressed through paths of knowledge, devotion, and duty. These paths lead to salvation, which is called nirvana. In the poem the divine reality appears in two forms: Krishna, the divine in human form, and Brahman, the impersonal absolute. According to the Bhagavad Gita, the attainment of nirvana is the awareness of the divine as an impersonal absolute and results in the loss of individual identity as the "self" realizes it is Brahman. *See* **Nirvana**.

Bible, the   Derived from the Greek word *biblia* (the books). Refers to the Hebrew and Christian scriptures. The Hebrew scriptures contain 39 books, which are grouped in three sections: the Law, Prophets, and Writings. The Christian scriptures contains 66 books; 39 books in the Old Testament (which is the Hebrew Bible) and 27 in the New Testament. However, the Roman Catholic church recognizes several additional Hebrew writings as part of their Old Testament.

EXHIBIT 22.1
Books of the Bible

OLD TESTAMENT
STANDARD VERSIONS

Genesis	Ecclesiastes
Exodus	Song of Solomon
Leviticus	Isaiah
Numbers	Jeremiah
Deuteronomy	Lamentations
Joshua	Ezekiel
Judges	Daniel
Ruth	Hosea
I Samuel	Joel
II Samuel	Amos
I Kings	Obadiah
II Kings	Jonah
I Chronicles	Micah
II Chronicles	Nahum
Ezra	Habakkuk
Nehemiah	Zephaniah
Esther	Haggai
Job	Zechariah
Psalms	Malachi
Proverbs	

NEW TESTAMENT
STANDARD VERSIONS

Matthew	I Timothy
Mark	II Timothy
Luke	Titus
John	Philemon
Acts	Hebrews
Romans	James
I Corinthians	I Peter
II Corinthians	II Peter
Galatians	I John
Ephesians	II John
Philippians	III John
Colossians	Jude
I Thessalonians	Revelation
II Thessalonians	

Bible belt   A colloquial expression for the fundamentalist Protestant sects of the South and Midwest.

Bodhisattva   In Sanskrit *bohi* (wisdom) and *satva* (existence in). A Buddhist doctrine describing one's refusal to enter Buddhahood in order to help others.

Book of Common Prayer   The Anglican (Episcopal) book of worship that describes the sacraments and other rites of the church.

Brahma, the creator of the world and humankind.

Brahma   One of the personal gods of the Hindu faith. *See* **Hinduism**.

Brahman   Associated in the Veda writings with wind, breath, and sun, Brahman is the fundamental essence of reality. In the Upanishads and Vedantic philosophy, all appearances or worldly things are identical with Brahman. Hence, the belief that humanity's experience of the world is illusion. An Indian philosopher by the name of Shankara (788–820) firmly established the philosophy of Advaita Vedanta, which emphasized that reality (Brahman) is undifferentiated and has no qualities. Reality is, therefore, completely beyond the mind's categories and conceptualization.

Buddha, Gautama Siddhartha (560–477 B.C.) The founder of Buddhism. Born in southern India near the Himalayas. After his first child was born, he renounced his life of pleasure and adopted ascetic practices. He realized that enlightenment could not be attained through deprivation of the body, and later became a beggar. After seven years, one day while sitting under the Bode-tree, he was enlightened and became the Buddha, or the Awakened One. Those who had practiced an ascetic life with Gautama soon became his disciples. Later, females were permitted to be disciples as well. Upon his death, he spoke these words to his disciples: "I take my leave of you; all the constituents of being are transitory; work out your salvation with diligence." Several interpretations of his teachings arose, forming the Hinayana and Mahayana sects. Suffering permeates life and keeps an individual from salvation or enlightenment. To experience enlightenment, one must eliminate suffering. The cause of suffering is ignorance, and it can be eliminated by the cessation of consciousness, perception, bodily senses, sensation, and finally the cessation of all desire. At this point, one ceases to have any sense of attachment to the world, and to cease all bodily senses and intellect is to cease existence. Without existence, one has no birth, no death, no misery or despair. The way out of ignorance is to follow the "Noble Eight-fold Path": (1) right faith, (2) right resolve, (3) right speech, (4) right action, (5) right living, (6) right effort, (7) right thought, and (8) right concentration. To be enlightened means to realize that one is free from rebirth and in the state of nirvana. According to the Buddha, all affirmative and negative descriptions of nirvana are wrong. Nevertheless, it is the case that in nirvana one is not an individual being with personal identity.

Buddahood. *See* **Buddha, Gautama Siddhartha**.

Bodhisattva.

Buddhism   A religion founded by Gautama Buddha in the 6th century B.C. in eastern India. Later, Buddhism was carried from India and became dominate in China and other eastern regions, although it was in a way absorbed into Hindu thinking since many claimed the Buddha to be an avatar (*see* **Avatar**) spreading enlightenment to all creatures. In early Buddhism, there were two main branches, Hinayana and Mahayana. In the Hinayana school, discipline is more strict; karma and rebirth are possible without an individual self, and nirvana is an extinction of one's personal existence. Mahayana stresses more the idea of universal compassion in the teaching of the bodhisattva, the savior who delays nirvana in order to work for the salvation of others. Nirvana, in addition to it being the end of rebirth, is understood more in terms of complete compassion and wisdom and the peace of tranquility. *See also* **Karma**; **Nirvana**.

Caliph   A title given to the successor of Mohammed. The secular and religious ruler of a Moslem state.

Calvary   The name of the place where Christ was crucified.

Calvin, John (1509–1564)   A French theologian of the Reformation, who experienced what he termed a "sudden conversion" that caused his departure from Catholicism. In 1541 he moved to Geneva and established a theocratic type of government. Along with Luther, Calvin was one of the forerunners of Protestantism. His principal writing, called *The Institutes of the Christian Religion*, maintains that humanity is lost in the state of sin and totally depraved. In this state, humanity cannot only not save itself, but it cannot even will to be saved. Therefore, salvation is the result of God's decision to bestow grace upon an individual through the death of Christ. Involved in this grace is also the gift of faith, since no one can will to believe because all are completely evil. For Calvin, then, God predestines some to receive grace and be saved, whereas others God predestines to damnation. Philosophically, under the doctrine of providence, God is the primary cause of every event in the world. Although Calvin admits to secondary causes, every event can be connected to its primary and sufficient cause, which Calvin says is God.

Canonization   A decree of the Pope that a particular believer is be venerated as a saint. The necessary requirements for canonization are the achievement of beatification and two miracles brought about by intercession after death of the person to be canonized.

Cantor   In the synagogue, the leader of liturgy or a soloist; the servant of the synagogue. Cantor is a term used by many faiths or groups of people.

Cardinal virtue   The four are justice, temperance, fortitude, and prudence—known in Greek philosophy and theology as the prime virtues from which all other moral virtues issue. Generally joined with them are the three theological virtues of faith, hope, and charity.

Catechism   Literally, from the Greek, meaning "to teach by word of mouth." In Jewish, Eastern Orthodox, Roman Catholic, and Protestant practice, it is a collection of religious instruction usually arranged in the form of questions and answers.

Catholic   A term meaning all-inclusive or universal. In religion, catholic means the one, universal Christian church. It can be used in a contemporary context, but it usually describes the early church before divisions arose such as the split between the East and the West in 1054 and the many divisions after the Reformation in the 16th century. The term was first used for the Christian church in the 3rd century by Cyprian. *See also* **Roman Catholic church**.

Chasidism   The mystic movement among Polish Jews in the late 1700s that spread into eastern Europe by the mid 1800s. It stressed spiritual exaltation and the joy of complete surrender to God.

Chesterton, Gilbert Keith (1874–1936)   An English writer who wove philosopher and theology into his essays, short stories, and novels. Chesterton is famous for his Father Brown mystery stories, where a priest is involved in solving mysteries through the use of wit, theology, and a good sense of human nature. An academic journal dedicated solely to Chesterton, called *The Chesterton Review*, is published by the G. K. Chesterton Society.

Christening   The act of baptism in the Christian church, usually of an infant and including the giving of a name.

Christianity   One of the world's major religions centered around the worship of and belief in Jesus Christ, founder of the religion, as the son of God. It is believed that Catholicism (the first leading branch of Christianity), was begun when Jesus turned to his apostle Peter and declared, "Upon this rock [the name "Peter" meaning rock] I will build my church." Jesus Christ preached morality based on compassion in disregard for the rituals and laws of Judaism. Christ considered himself to be a reformer of Judaism, and "King of the Jews." However, Jesus Christ was careful to point out that his kingdom was a heavenly one and "not of this world." Because of this emphasis on a heavenly kingdom, he was rejected as the Messiah, and he was crucified by the Romans. Christianity can be divided into two major sects: Catholicism and Protestantism. The split between Catholicism and Protestantism began in 1517 with Martin Luther and the publishing of the 95 theses. (This period was called the Reformation.) Some major areas of disagreement between the two Christian groups include the intepretation of the Bible and who should interpret it, and the institution of priesthood.

Christian Science   A religious philosophy initiated by Mary Baker Eddy. *Science and Health*, the authoritative work for the movement, was published in 1875. As a philosophy, it is maintained that God's goodness means that God cannot have created nor be responsible for darkness. In fact, the dark things of life do not really exist. The concept that nothing is real and eternal but God and that evil has no reality is developed in detail in *Science and Health*. Humanity is "God's spiritual idea" and when in right alignment with God there is neither sickness, sin, sorrow, nor death, all of which are errors of the mind. The primary teaching of Christian Science is the resolution of what philosophers and theologians have called the problem of evil.

Christmas   The celebration of the anniversary of the birth of Jesus, observed on December 25. The precise date of Jesus' birth cannot be determined. Some scholars argue that December 25 was the holy day celebrated in Mithraism, the official religion of the Roman Empire in 307 A.D. In 312 Constantine became emperor and soon thereafter made Christianity the state religion.

Communion   *See* **Lord's Supper**.

Confession   In the Roman Catholic and Anglican churches, the acknowledgment of one's sins to a priest. Confession is only one part of the act of penance, which is performed by the believer in order to expiate sins committed after baptism.

Confirmation   The completion of baptism by the laying on of hands or unction (or both), thus bestowing full initiation into Christian discipleship with its gift of the Holy Spirit—so understood in the early and Medieval church on the basis of Acts 8:14–17, 19:1–7.

Confucius (551–479 B.C.)　A Chinese philosopher born in the state of Lu and town of Tsou. He was the first Chinese teacher to offer education to any who wanted to learn. Teachings included poetry and ritual, conduct, and honesty. Graduates received positions in a number of Chinese cities. His teachings can be found in the Lun-Yü (Analects), recorded by his students and followers.

Confucianism　A movement that has dominated Chinese culture for 2000 years. It has also permeated Korea and Japan. Based on the teachings of Confucius, the philosophy has as its goal harmonious social relations and the good society. The Confucian principle "What you do not want done to yourself, do not do to others" has permeated many cultures. Individual moral reform is seen as the key to an ordered family and society. *Li* is the way of right action or proper behavior and is instrumental in the keeping of ceremonies and the fulfillment of one's duties in life. The five cardinal relations are sovereign and subject, father and son, elder and younger brother, husband and wife, and friend and friend. For Confucius, poetry and music were important for the building of character. In short, the building of character can be seen as a process beginning with poetry, being established by *Li*, and finalized with music. The philosophy of Confucianism is not concerned with supernatural beings or eternal personalities; instead, it is humanistic and promotes the true order of human life so there can be harmony with the universe.

Congregationalism　A Protestant movement that can be loosely dated from 1550. The sect migrated from England to New England and founded the Plymouth Bay Colony. Jonathan Edwards is associated with this movement that took leadership in the founding missions and the developing of education.

Consubstantiation　Martin Luther's doctrine that the body and blood of Jesus are "in real substantial presence" with the bread and wine of the Eucharist, in contrast to the Roman Catholic doctrine of transubstantiation. *See* **Transubstantiation**.

Cross　Used as a synonym in the New Testament of the death of Jesus. Along with the apostolic writings, in the Gospels, the writers depicted Jesus as referring to the word "cross" theologically, in that one must symbolically carry the cross if one is to be a follower of Jesus.

Crucifix　Any representation of Jesus on the cross.

D **Decalogue**　The Ten Commandments that Moses received from God on Mount Sinai. Written on tablets of stone, they are held to be the foundation for Jewish and Christian morality.

Deism　A term meaning the belief in a god who created the world but does not interact with it physically, morally, or by the promising of life after death. In contemporary usage, Deism refers to the 17th and 18th century movement that advocated the reign of reason rather than revelation, most particularly the Hebrew and Christian Bible. However, originally, the term was developed by the Scocinians in the 16th century in order to distinguish their position from atheism.

Devil　In the Christian church, the source of all evil, bent on enslaving mankind.

Dharma　Sanskrit word with several meanings. In general, it can mean "law," but it is also culture, custom, justice, and religion. Dharma is used to signify the right path and the proper relation of individual things. Employed in the Vedic *Sutras* and in Buddhism.

Dies Irae　A Latin hymn used in funeral masses.

Doxology　A hymn or formal statement of praise to God. Used traditionally, by Jews and Christians at the end of public prayer. "Praise God from whom all blessings flow" is the most familiar form of the doxology.

E **Easter**　The day Christians observe the resurrection of Jesus, celebrated on the Sunday following the first full moon on or after March 21.

Eastern Orthodox churches　The group of churches that separated from the Roman Catholic church in 1054. Their orthodoxy is derived from the first seven Ecumenical Councils. In each region a bishop presides over the Orthodox Church. The regions included the churches of Albania, Alexandria, America, Antioch, Bulgaria, Cyprus, Constantinople, Czechoslovakia, Georgia, Greece, Jerusalem, Poland, Romania, Russia, and Serbia.

Epiphany　This feast day officially commemorates Jesus as the Son of God. It is represented by the adoration of the Magi who arrived in Bethlehem on the Twelfth Night, or January 6, the date of the feast.

Episcopal church　(Church of England, Anglican) A Protestant denomination that has retained the ancient Catholic sacraments, creeds, and orders. The basic beliefs are affirmed in the Apostles Creed, the Nicene Creed, and the *Book of Common Prayer* (a book of services and rites of the faith).

Eschatology　From Greek meaning "knowledge of last things." In both Judaism and Christianity, the term applies to the doctrine surrounding death, resurrection, the end of the age, and judgment.

Ethical Culture Societies　A movement initiated by Felix Adler in 1876 in New York City, stressing ethics as the primary concern of religion. The Society has been acknowledged as a religion, thereby making its property and financial activities tax exempt. The New York society was involved in social activism. In particular, it struggled for reforms in such areas as the elimination of child labor, adult education, and the improvement of the African-American condition.

Eucharist　From the Greek *eucharistus*, meaning "thanksgiving." Over time, this term became an expression for the Lord's Supper, relating the breaking of the bread by Jesus.

Excommunication　Partial or total exclusion from a religious body for transgressions or acts of willful disobedience.

Exorcism　This term denotes the expulsion of malevolent spirits or demons from possessed persons by certain rites in which the aid of more powerful spirits or deities is sought.

 **Faith**　Derived from the Latin *fidere*, which means "to trust." Religiously, faith is associated with the act of personally trusting in the nature and activity of God. It is often applied to the act of

accepting something on the basis of little or no justification or evidence. However, traditionally the concept of faith was more sophisticated. Three Latin
phrases were used to explain the uniqueness of faith
more clearly: (1) *credo Deo* (I believe God), (2)
credo Deum (I believe of God that), and (3) *credo in
Deum* (I believe in God). These three phrases correspond respectively to the Latin terms *notitia* (to notice), *assensus* (to assent), and *fiducia* (to have faith).
Before one has faith in God, one first notices that
God exists, then one believes that God is a certain
type of being (knowledge of the nature of God). Faith
is simply trust in the person of God. Hence, faith can
be seen as putting one's trust in a person or object
that one has first noticed and secondly understood.
By analogy, it could be said that one believes that a
bank exists, believes that it has certain functions, and
lastly has faith that the bank will keep one's money
safe. Contrary to popular thought, faith does not necessarily mean belief without rational justification,
for many classical and contemporary theists have
used reason to explain the nature of God and justify
the belief in the existence of that type of being.

Fatalism The belief in the inevitability of events,
with or without causes.

Father Divine An African-American religious
leader who formed a cult in Harlem in the first half
of the 20th century. He achieved notoriety because
of the emotional excesses of his religious meetings,
and also because of the alleged healings and miracles that were supposed to have taken place during
them. Father Divine's true name was George Baker,
the Georgian son of slave parents. He was frequently arrested on various charges, was once sentenced to a chain gang, and later tried for insanity
because of his messianic claims. In court, he refused
either to deny or confirm that he was God.

Fetishism The use of a material object (conceived
of as being the temporary or permanent housing of
a soul) as a means of worship, or acquiring values.
The term is most synonymous with idol or amulet. A
fetish is selected because of its origin, e.g., an animal's tooth or claw, because of its unusual character, or because of a particular experience on the part
of its owner. A priest or shaman may persuade a
spirit to enter the object, and the fetish may be specialized to provide only one specific wish or value to
the person who owns it. Most generally, fetishes are
of general usefulness in giving protection, preventing, or healing disease, assuring success, etc. When
a fetish fails, it is usually discarded.

Final Judgment The time when all people, both
the living and dead, will be judged before God according to their faith and deeds.

Fish, as symbol The Greek word *ichtys* contains
(as an acronym) the first letter of the Greek words
that translate "Jesus Christ, God's Son, Savior," one
of the reasons the emblem of the fish was employed
by the early Christians. Another reason why it was
used as a symbol is the relation between fish, water, and the Christian life through baptism.

G **Gandhi, Mohandas Karamchand**
(1869–1948) Though a devoted Hindu,
Gandhi found support for his doctrine of
nonviolence in the Sermon on the Mount,
and he frequently used the New Testa-

ment, along with the Bhaghavad Gita, for spiritual
guidance. In India, Gandhi was popularly titled Mahatma (Great Soul).

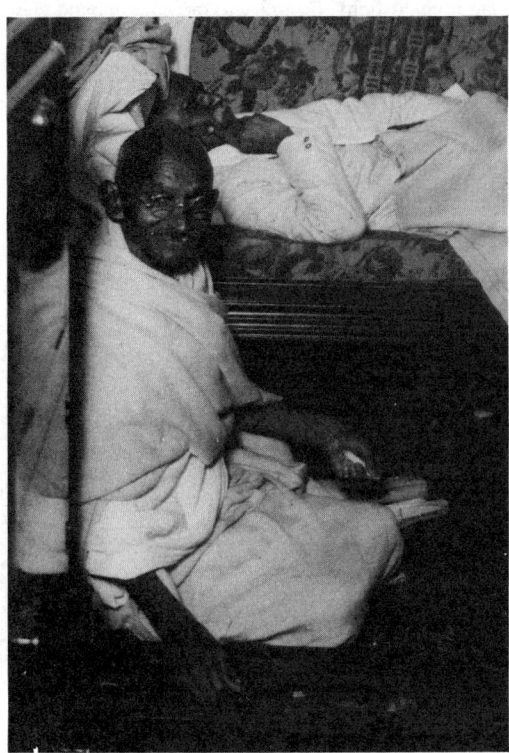

Mahatma Gandhi, on his arrival in England, September, 1931.

Gautama Buddha *See* **Buddha, Guatama
Siddhartha**.

Gideons, the An international layman's association organized in 1899 in Wisconsin. Its program includes a ministry of evangelism and the purchase
and distribution of Bibles that are placed in hotels,
hospitals, and prisons.

Gnosticism A philosophical-religious movement
similar to the mystery religions and aimed at personal salvation. Gnostics claimed to have secret
knowledge and wisdom. At the end of the 2nd century B.C., it seriously competed with Christianity.
There were many types of Gnosticism. Some Gnostic beliefs are: Good and evil are two opposing
forces. There are seven powers or angels that come
from God and from which come darkness. By certain knowledge and defiance of the physical world,
the initiate is lifted toward God. In some Gnostic circles where the Goddess of Heaven, the Great
Mother, played a key role, religious prostitution was
involved.

God A name for the ultimate basis of reality. The
concept of God can be understood in two general
ways: God as a transcendent absolute, or as the most
perfect being, the latter being more compatible with
the scriptural revelation in Judaism, Christianity,
and Islam. As a transcendent absolute, God is beyond the concept of human reason and admits of no
duality. Any characteristics such as personality and

love are false descriptions of that which cannot be described. The notion of God as absolute is often found in the history of Jewish, Christian, and Islamic philosophy. Contrary to the nondualistic view of God, a philosophical tradition becoming ever more influential in contemporary philosophy is the view that God is a being who has all compossible perfections. The word compossible indicates the adherence to principles of coherence and reason. A perfection is a great making quality, which is generally understood to be something considered better to have than to lack. Therefore, God would have the qualities of perfect power, knowledge, and love, to name a few. Personality is also considered as perfect quality, which means that God has the ability to truly interact in human history and to communicate to humanity.

Good Friday   The Friday before Easter. Traditionally, the day when Jesus was crucified.

Gospel   Originally a reward paid the one who brought good news. Later, it came to mean the good news itself. In the New Testament, it is the message of salvation through Christ. Gospels is the term used for the four books that give accounts of Jesus' life: Matthew, Mark, Luke, and John.

Grace   In theology, the favor of God to humanity, or the compassion of God despite God's anger over iniquity. The Hebrew Bible contains many instances when God gives grace to people, and the sacrificial institution is a symbol of God's grace and forgiveness. In the New Testament, grace is often contrasted with works. It is important to emphasize, however, that in the New Testament, the apostle Paul did not consider (as is still thought to be the case by many today) Judaism to be a religion without God's grace, in contrast to the new era of grace through Christ. In addition to meaning the simple gift of acceptance by God apart from any merit, grace can also mean the continuous divine assistance and love given to sustain the world and, specifically, believers.

Guru   A teacher or spiritual guide in Hinduism. Sometimes a guru is thought to be an incarnation of God. The term generally means any spiritual leader or philosophical guide.

Hades   The realm of the dead in the underworld. From the Greek name for its mythical leader in the New Testament, Hades refers to a vast dark region in the depths of the earth that is not a place of punishment, but one of comfortless doom.

Hadith   The collection of sayings of the prophet Mohammed. Modern Islam recognizes anywhere from 4000 to 600,000 hadiths, depending on the sect.

Hammurabi, Code of   A legal document based on ancient material and originated between 2100–1800 B.C. Of the 282 laws, many have serious retributive punishment.

Hanukkah   An eight-day Jewish holiday celebrating the rededication of the Jerusalem Temple in 165 B.C., after the Syrian Greeks were defeated by the Maccabees.

Heresy   In religion, heresy is a denial of a fundamental belief of a particular church. Historically in the Roman Catholic church, one was called a heretic if one denied a "revealed truth."

Hegira   The flight of Mohammed from Mecca in 622 A.D. After his death, the Moslem calendar was dated from this event, and history is written as A.H. (year of Hegira).

Hillel   (Hillel the Elder) (30 B.C.–10 A.D.) The most prominent Jewish teacher of the 1st century and one of the keenest masters of the Bible, Hillel was the founder of an influential school that bears his name (Beth Hillel). He is revered for his inspiring saintliness, humbleness, and love for his fellow man.

Hinduism   The traditional religion of India. Hinduism does not have a founder. Historically, there were various stages of Hindu development: (1) Vedic, (2) Brahmanic, (3) Philosophic, (4) Devotional or Sectarian, and (5) Reformed Hinduism, which includes Herctica Hinduism and the Buddhist and Jain movement. Hinduism consists of a diversity of beliefs, ranging from polytheism to monotheism to complete monism. Its principal scriptures are the Vedas, which contains three parts, the *Samhitas*, *Brahamanas*, and the *Upanishads*.

Holiness   Essentially, the universal meaning of this term distinguishes the sacred from the profane. In the course of moral and religious development holiness has come to mean ethical purity and moral perfection of character. It remains, however, an essentially religious concept, denoting the perfect and loving righteousness that characterizes God's nature and power. Insofar as the term is applicable to men, it refers to that moral likeness to God that is the fruit of his grace, bringing man into perfect moral sonship and obedience to God.

Holy Grail, the   The medieval legend pertaining to the cup that Jesus drank out of during the Last Supper. The legend can be broken into two different stories. The first centers on the Grail and is associated with Joseph of Arimathea. The second is that of two knights of King Arthur's Round Table, Perceval and Galahad, and their quest for the Grail.

Holy Spirit   The roots of this concept can be found in primitive religion where at times men worked themselves into a frenzy likened to madness. This was explained by the presence in the world of a mysterious power that might enter a man and make him its instrument. In the Hebrew Bible this power was attributed to the strength of Samson. Later this power was associated with the frenzy in which a prophet uttered divine proclamations. It eventually came to mean the "mood" of the prophet: divine impulse, knowledge, and action. Only after the death of Jesus did the concept of the Holy Spirit come to mean (through the writings of Paul) the spirit of love (God) abiding in the believer.

Holy water   In the Catholic church, ordinary water that has been sanctified by a blessing. Salt is added to ordinary water to signify that the water is preserved from corruption. Holy water is used extensively in ceremonies of blessing.

Homily   A term in use from the early Christian church to designate an informal talk on church doctrine or a passage from scripture, etc. To be contrasted with a sermon, which is more formal.

Hospice   In the 5th century, a building set aside for use of travelers, the sick, and the unfortunate. The term came from "hospitality," which was practiced by monasteries. In the last half of the 20th century, hospices are once again in use throughout the United States as shelters for the ill and the incurable.

Host   The unleavened bread used in the celebration of communion, either to symbolize or to become through consecration the body of Christ.

I Ching   *The Book of Changes.* A classic book in Chinese antiquity that deals with the practice of divination. Written between the 6th and 3rd centuries B.C., the book contains 64 hexagrams that are based on eight trigrams.

Icon   Particularly in the Eastern Orthodox churches, mosaics of Jesus Christ, paintings, bas-reliefs, and any image of the Virgin Mary or Saints is considered an icon. In the 11th century split between the Eastern and Western churches, the issue of icons was serious. The West tended to shy away from the use of images, but the East made it a doctrinal point to distinguish between the false practice of worshipping icons and the proper way of veneration.

IHS   From the Greek, an abbreviation of Jesus' name, which has served as a symbol for him.

Imam   Those individuals who are in the true succession of Mohammed. The final Imam will be the one who brings the worldwide reign of Islam. A Shi'ite tradition claims that in 873 B.C. an Imam disappeared and is now called the "hidden Imam." He will appear again as the final Imam, called the Mahdi. *See* **Shi'ite.**

Immaculate Conception   A Roman Catholic doctrine set forth officially by Pope Pius IX in 1854 holding that the Virgin Mary was from the moment of conception not tainted by original sin.

Imitation of Christ   Attributed to Thomas à Kempis (1380–1471). Christian devotional literature that, apart from the Bible, is the most widely read Christian book. Rich in spiritual counsel, it stresses that the road to salvation can only be taken by those prepared to suffer with Christ, and that the "lusts" of the world must be forsaken.

Incense   Incense is the granulated resin of certain tropical and eastern trees that is used in religious services. When it is burned in a covered vessel its scent is released. The aromatic fragrance signifies virtue, and zeal is symbolized by the act of burning. The rising smoke reflects prayer ascending to heaven.

Islam   A religion founded by Mohammed, an Arabic man who believed himself to be the final prophet. The truth of Islam was revealed by the one true God to Mohammed, and once the revelations were written down, the writing was called the Koran. Islam recognizes the truth of Judaism and Christianity, but only as interpreted through the Koran and Mohammed. Central to Islam is the concept of God and law. God is a complete unity, completely holy, and demanding of dedication and obedience. God is the uncreated one, and all else has been created and is dependent on God. On a day in the future that only God knows, there will be a resurrection leading to judgment, some being thrown into eternal fire and others entering the Garden. Some schools of Islamic thought hold that the prayers of the Prophet for his followers will allow those not guilty of idolatry or apostasy to enter paradise. Legal obligations in Islamic practice cannot be underemphasized.

Sharia, or religious law, touches the areas of family, inheritance, and ritual. The primary Islamic obligations are called the five pillars: (1) to pronounce the testimony "There is no other God but Allah, and Mohammed is his prophet;" (2) ritual prayer facing Mecca, which is performed five times a day (at dawn, noon, afternoon, sundown, and evening); (3) almsgiving, of a fixed percentage but varying according to the different law schools and functioning as a governmental tax for the benefit of the community; (4) fasting during the month of Ramadan; and (5) pilgrimage to Mecca at least once in one's lifetime so long as one is capable. The fifth pillar is indicative of the spiritual importance of geographic location. Like the city of Jerusalem in Judaism, Islam gives spiritual importance to the city of Mecca. *See also* **Koran**; **Mohammed**; **Shi'ite**; **Sufi**; **Sunni**.

Jehovah's Witnesses   Protestant sect begun in 1874 by Charles Russell Taze, founded upon the idea that only a select few will be spared the thousand-year judgment that will take place when Christ returns to earth. In the early days of the religion, Russell declared that Christ had already returned but was invisible. Jehovah's Witnesses are excluded from having to salute the flag at public events, believing that allegiance is owed only to God and not to anything of this world. Jehovah's Witnesses put a strong emphasis on the study of the bible by laymen, and have developed a number of free or low-cost manuals for the student. These are frequently distributed door-to-door or on street corners in urban areas. This proselytizing is an important part of the religion. The Jehovah's Witnesses' house of worship is called "The Kingdom Hall."

Jesuits   A Roman Catholic religious order (founded by St. Ignatius Loyola in the 1500s), whose motto is "To the greater glory of God." Today Jesuits are considered to be the scholars of the church, their work in the field of education is highly renowned.

Jesus Christ   Jesus was a Jewish teacher from Nazareth in the first century A.D. who taught for only one to three years. Jesus chose twelve disciples who called him "the Christ" (a title meaning "anointed of God") and later claimed that he, after being put to death on the cross by the Romans and buried, rose from the dead, spoke, and ate with them several times. The sayings of Jesus are recorded in the Gospels. In the first three Gospels, Matthew, Mark, and Luke, Jesus taught about the kingdom of God, that love of God was necessary for salvation, and that he, as the "son of man" was instrumental in the desire of God to save the world from darkness. In the Gospel of John, Jesus is outspoken about his unity, or identity with God. Here he states that if one has seen him, then one has seen the Father. In all Gospel accounts, Jesus is the chosen one of God who has come to save the Jews and the world from sin.

Joan of Arc   (1412–1431)   Born in Domrémy, of farmer stock, Joan grew up in a desperate time for France in its war with England. Apparently a normal, though grave, child at 13, she received voices and visions (St. Michael, St. Catherine, and

St. Margaret) that by 1428 commanded her to deliver and free her country. Assuming male attire, she overcame the reluctance of army leaders and courtiers, and after being examined by theologians was commissioned by the king. Between April and July of 1429 she routed the English from Orléans, captured Troyes, and saw Charles VII crowned at Rheims. Her power seemed to wane with her failure to relieve Paris, the continuous opposition at court, and finally with her capture (at Compiégne) by a Burgundian who sold her to the English. Pierre Cauchon, bishop of Beauvais, instituted proceedings for heresy against her at Rouen, a subtler and for a time more effective way of discrediting Charles than killing Joan outright. Her trial is infamous for treachery, bigotry, and cruelty, in which the University of Paris played a regrettable part. Joan's good sense and candor (on all but her steadfast affirmation of visions) in her responses have added to her fame. The 70 propositions against her, condensed to 12, included condemnation of her male attire and of her voices and visions as "false and diabolical," and she was particularly attacked for her alleged responsibility to God alone and not the church. Because of this last indictment, Joan was tricked into relapsing into "heresy." She was burned at the stake May 30, 1431. In 1456 there was a complete reversal of the judgment of 1431. She was beatified in 1909 and canonized in 1920.

Judaism   The Jewish religion. The origin of Judaism can be tied to the account in the Hebrew Bible of Abraham and his descendants. According to the book of Genesis, God called Abraham out of the city of Ur in order to establish a special people of God. From Abraham came Jacob, who settled the Israelites in Egypt. They flourished under the protection and kindness of the Egyptians. As time passed however, later pharaohs changed in attitude toward the descendants of Jacob, and the Egyptians put the Israelites into slavery. From here God called Moses to lead the Israelites out of slavery into a new land. Their journey unfolded into what is called the Tribal League period, where twelve distinct tribes existed in political and spiritual partnership. After much turmoil, the Israelites settled in the land which is modern Israel and established a kingdom. Central to Judaism is the practice of the Law, which is contained in the Pentateuch, the first five books of the Hebrew Bible. The Law calls for a priestly class to carry out necessary sacrifices for the sins of the Jewish people. In addition to the written Law, there was an oral tradition of interpretation of the law that gradually unfolded, eventually being written down as the Talmud. After the destruction of the Temple in 70 A.D. by the Romans, Jewish practice changed, with less emphasis on sacrifice and more on the interpretation of the law. This was the period of Rabbinic Judaism, when the synagogue and the interpretation of tradition become the primary focus. From here, one of Judaism's great philosophers emerged, Maimonides. Despite the destruction of the Temple and the Jewish dispersion, it should be noted that the land of Israel, and especially Jerusalem, is regarded as spiritually a holy land. The Hebrew Bible describes this entire history as an intimate relationship between Israel and God. The most

important elements of the Jewish faith are monotheism and the Mosaic law. The Jewish faith described in the Hebrew Bible can be said to hold that God personally has been revealed in history, that humanity is responsible for unrighteousness, and that justice will be completely dealt with in the world to come. Judaism has gone through shifts in its religious orders and practices.

Judaism, Conservative   Founded in 1913, this branch of Judaism recognizes the authority of the Law in the Bible through the Talmudic and later Rabbinic periods and even into modern times. It is sometimes said to combine the ideals of Orthodoxy and Reform in agreeing to the principle of progress yet holding to tradition. The Law is open to change and development, although the essential character of Judaism is said to be maintained. Basically characteristic of Conservative Judaism is the change in attitudes toward the language of prayer, dietary laws, and the Messianic hope. Some conservative circles practice the segregation of men and women.

Judaism, Orthodox   The Jewish branch that adheres to faithful observation of the Mishnaic and Talmudic traditions. It is usually associated with the attempt to exclude new influences on Judaism and to preserve the practice of medieval Judaism. Along with a strong scholarly and rationalist tradition are strict Sabbath observance and a liturgy of daily prayers in Hebrew, usually conducted in the synagogue. As ingrained in strong tradition, it always upholds the segregation of men and women in worship, and women cannot be counted among the ten required for public worship.

Judaism, Reform   A shift in Jewish thinking that adapted to the change brought about by the European Enlightenment. Abraham Geiger (1810–1874) was the principal instigator. Revelation and tradition were not considered fixed or even binding in all matters. Some in Reform Judaism do not believe in the unique role Judaism is thought to have in the revelation of God to the world. In addition to aligning itself with a faith in reason, Reform Judaism adhered strongly to the rational tradition in Judaism. Along with the conducting of services in the vernacular, the synagogue liturgy was revised. The main task of Reform Judaism is now an adjustment to modern times, which includes the critical and scientific interpretation of the written and oral law and the reaffirmation of Judaism in a secular world.

 **Kabbalah** (Cabala)   A term signifying the body of mystical doctrines developed and books written within Judaism between the intertestamental period and the 14th century. As anti-Orthodox, Kabbalistic doctrine generally arises from the concept of emanation, which is the philosophical position that different levels and qualities of being have come from God's essence and are commonly identified with God's essence. Specifically, grades of wisdom mediate between God and creation, with levels of angels and demiurges that assist communion between humanity and God. Sin is the separation from God. Although a clear dualism is maintained, the nature of God, however vaguely defined, resembles the monism found in most strains of mysticism. The Kabbalah literature is contained

in the *Gilgulim*, *Hekhaloth*, *Sefer Yesira*, *Sefer hab-Bahir*, the *Book of Raziel*, *Shi'ur Koma*, and *Zohar*, the primary text of the Kabbalah and also known as *The Book of Splendor*.

Kaddish   Originally an ancient Jewish prayer to sanctify God's name and the coming of his kingdom. Its opening words parallel the Lord's Prayer, pointing to a traditional prayer form from which both stem. From medieval times Kaddish has been said as the mourner's declaration of faith.

Karma   In Buddhist teachings, the dynamic manifestation of mental and physical energy that produces good, evil, or neutral effects, according to the inherent state of the manifestation; *i.e.*, an action that is positive will eventually create a positive effect. This effect then becomes the course for further effect, making the self a process of unceasing transformation from one life to another in the wheel of transmigration—a continual process of becoming. Thus, Karma is action (energy, manifestation) and the evolving entity of the individual.

Kiss of peace   A salutation as an act of Christian brotherhood, also known as the "Kiss of Charity"and the "Holy Kiss."

Koran (Quran)   The scriptures of Islam, written in Arabic, which were revelations recited by Mohammed in 622 A.D. It appears that parts of the Koran were written by Mohammed during the Medinan period, while the rest was written between 622 and 632 A.D. According to the Orthodox view, God is the speaker, Mohammed the recipient, and the angel Gabriel the intermediary for the revelation. Contrary to this and popular belief, the Koran never identifies Gabriel as an angel and does not claim that angels were agents of revelation (although XVI, 2 comes the closest). Critical examination of the texts shows the matter to be quite complex. No speaker or source of the revelation is given for the oldest parts of the Koran. Some passages do not give indication that the message is from God (XCI, I-10, CI, CII, etc.). However, from LIII, I0, LXXXI, 23, Mohammed had visions of God and it seems that in the Meccan years he heard the voice of God instead of an intermediary. The Koran praises the greatness of God, describes the joys of heaven and the horrors of hell, contains civil, criminal, and ceremonial law, and denounces the deification of any human being. It contains many literary forms, although its arrangement makes it difficult to classify precisely in parts. The way of salvation is through the prophets, from Moses, Christ, and then to the final prophet, Mohammed. The Koran makes use of didactic stories that are variations of Arabian, Jewish, and Christian stories.

Kosher   Literally, "fit," or "fit to be eaten according to Jewish ritual." Jewish law prohibits the use of certain animals for food; it also requires that meat and milk foods be separated and that all meat be cleansed of surface blood before being eaten. Kosher food is prepared in accordance with the rules of the Talmud.

Krishna   One of the last two incarnations of Vishnu. In the Bhagavad Gita, Krishna eventually becomes Brahman. He is represented in Hindu literature and drawings as a slayer of dragons, a warrior, a cowherd, and a lover.

 **Latter Day Saints**   A religious sect founded by Joseph Smith in Fayette, New York in 1830, when he received revelations instructing him to establish a new church. He received a set of gold plates that contained what is now the Book of Mormon. The book connects the settlement of America with a group of Israelites 600 years before Christ. Smith and his cohorts encountered much difficulty, especially because of the integration of polygamy into their doctrine. In 1844 Smith was killed, and Brigham Young led the believers to Utah and founded Salt Lake City in 1848. After much controversy with federal laws regarding polygamy, in 1890 the Latter Day Saints publicly denounced the doctrine. Theologically, there is an acceptance of the Christian Bible although mostly interpreted through the primary scriptures, the Book of Mormon. Hence, terminology can be extremely similar to that of Christianity while the meaning behind the doctrinal terms are at times different. For example, the understanding of God is different in that Latter Day Saints consider God to be a created being who has increased in wisdom, power, and knowledge over time. It could be said the Latter Day Saints' theology is lacking a philosophical tradition that attempts to reconcile the concept of God with analytic reasoning. Finally, since God is not an uncreated being, it is clear that Jesus is not uncreated and neither is he identified with the nature of God, except in that he resembles one who is close to attaining the status that the present God holds.

Laying on of hands   In the Christian church, a method used by a qualified person to transmit a blessing to another. Also, as a rite of exorcism before baptism and to impart the Holy Spirit to the newly baptized.

Lent   Forty days from Ash Wednesday to the eve of Easter. In the early Christian period, Lent was a period of preparation for baptism at Easter and of public deeds of goodness by those who were being disciplined by the church. Today, some Christians voluntarily give up certain pleasures (types of food or a special interest) as a symbol of sacrifice.

Limbo   The resting place for souls excluded from heaven through no fault of their own. Primarily, in the Catholic church, those who die without baptism and therefore in a state of original sin.

Liturgy   A group of readings and a formalized pattern for a religious service.

Lord's Prayer   A popular name for the prayer of Jesus in Matthew 6:9–13 and in Luke 11:2–4.

Lord's Supper   The central rite of Christian worship (also called the Eucharist, Holy Communion, and the Mass). This service developed historically out of the Last Supper of Jesus and His disciples before the Crucifixion and has traditionally been related to the words: "This is my body...This is my blood...Do this in remembrance of Me." In Protestant sects bread and wine or grape juice are given to the congregation as symbols of the body and blood of Christ. In Catholicism, the priest, through an act known as transubstantiation, offers his congregation the consecrated host.

Lutheranism   The first Protestant sect, it was founded in 1530 by Martin Luther, a scholar of the

Bible who laid out his disagreements with the Catholic church on the subject of indulgences in his 95 theses. In Luther's time, these indulgences (basically pardons for sins committed) were sold at the local church. In writing his 95 theses, Luther hoped to point out to the clergy the biblical reasons for discontinuing this practice. Instead, he found himself having to debate the church on this subject, causing him to leave the church. His main disagreement with the church lay in the church's use of priests to grant dispensations, believing that only God could forgive sin, and that confession to a priest was not needed. In 1530, with the support of noblemen, he gave his permission for his followers to use the name "Lutheranism" to describe the beliefs written out in his catechism. *See* **Luther, Martin**.

Martin Luther, author of the 95 theses that began the Protestant Reformation.

Luther, Martin (1483–1546) A German churchman who sought to reform the Roman Catholic church. Although his father wanted him to become a lawyer, Luther entered an Augustinian order after his A.B. and M.A. degree in literature and philosophy. In 1507 he was ordained as a priest. In 1512, after some time teaching at the University of Wittenberg on the subjects of philosophy and scrip-

ture, Luther attained the degree of Doctor of Theology. Throughout his life Luther struggled with his understanding of sin and the way one's broken relationship with God was restored. Specifically, Luther struggled with the concept of contrition, the act of feeling sorry for one's sinful thoughts and deeds and the desire not to sin again. He could never resolve how much contrition was enough to please God, or what one could do in the case of one's not having appropriate contrition. After lecturing on the books of Romans, Galatians, and Hebrews, Luther discovered what he considered the most amazing revelation in his entire life, namely, that one is justified by faith, and faith alone, instead of works. Paul's use of the phrase "justification by faith" became the cornerstone of Luther's theology. Because of his discovery, Luther began to see official church practices that were contrary to his understanding of the gospel, which prompted him to plead with the Pope and other church authorities to reform their teachings and practices. Indulgences, one of these practices, were letters written for the absolution of the sin of individuals who did not have adequate merit. They came with a price, and were often sold for large amounts of money. It was claimed by those giving indulgences that the overabundance of good deeds and righteousness of particular saints could be applied to others in the present. The sale of indulgences was the motivating factor in Luther's famous 95 theses, posted on the Wittenberg door in 1517. Later in his life, Luther developed a theological position of "the priesthood of all believers," which stood in contrast to the Catholic view that one can approach God only through a priest. In 1520, he published three important works: (1) *An address to the Nobility of the German Nation*, (2) *On the Babylonian Captivity of the Church of God*, and (3) *On the Liberty of a Christian Man*. As made clear by the titles, Luther had now seriously doubted that the Church would reform and made a political plea to those of his German homeland. For an explanation of the creation of the Lutheran church, *see* **Reformation**.

M**Mammon** In the New Testament, this term was taken by medieval writers to mean the devil, or covetousness. From the 16th century to the present, it has been used to indicate the evil influence of wealth.

Mantra A word applied to hymns and prayers to the gods. It also came to mean a spell or charm with magical significance. Mantras vary from those expressing noble religious aspirations to those of clearly magical power. They are heavily relied on in Hindu religious rites.

Martyr One who suffers persecution for his faith; a person willing to undergo torture or death for his religious convictions. The first martyrs were the victims of Roman persecutions during the first three centuries of Christianity.

Mass From the Latin *missa* (dismissal). It refers most often to the Roman Catholic service including the Eucharist, but also to the Anglican Communion service. Mass consists of liturgical texts, sometimes spoken and at other times sung.

EXHIBIT 22.2
Major World Religions

Buddhism   One of the great Oriental philosophies and religions, founded in India by Prince Siddhartha Gautama (560–580 B.C.), who is known as Buddha, "The Enlightened One." One of the main tenets of Buddhism is the recognition of necessary suffering as an integral part of life. Man can only be partially freed from suffering through releasing himself into an upward spiral of spiritual, mental, and emotional purity. The central Buddhist writings are collected in a set of sacred scriptures known as the *Pali Canon*. In the Eastern world today there are over 250 million members of different branches of this faith, including such sects as Zen and Mahayana Buddhism.

Christianity   A religion based on the teachings of the divine prophet Jesus Christ (ca. 6 B.C.–30 A.D.), whose sacred scriptures exist in the Old and New Testaments of the Bible. The two main branches of Christianity are Roman Catholicism and Protestantism (encompassing many smaller sects). This religion stresses obedience to the will of God and salvation through faith and good works. The population of the Christian world numbers over eleven hundred million.

Confucianism   Based on the spiritual and ethical sayings of Confucius (ca. 551–479 B.C.), the teachings of this religion are founded in the *Analects*, an ancient document of the moral and religious sayings of Confucius which stress the virtue of man and the state above all other precepts. Most of the over 170 million followers of this religion are Chinese.

Hinduism   Founded in India, and one of the most ancient of the living religions of the world, Hinduism has no single founder. It evolved over a period of seven thousand years and its tenets are set forth in a collection of works known as the *Veda* ("Knowledge"). These scriptures and the caste system are adhered to by all members of the faith. Throughout the world today there are more than 450 million Hindus.

Islam   A monotheistic religion founded by Mohammed (570–632 A.D.), believed to be the final prophet. Its adherents are called Moslems. The revelations given to Mohammed by God, called Allah in the Arabic-speaking world, are written in the Koran. The precepts of religious law found there permeate all aspects of personal and social life. Islam accepts the truth of Judaism and Christianity, but only as interpreted through Koran. Today there are some 800 million Moslems, mainly in North Africa and Near and Middle East.

Judaism   A religion based on a belief in one God, who was revealed to Moses and Abraham over 375 thousand years ago. The rites, beliefs, and traditions of Judaism are found recorded in the Torah (a book explaining the will of God as stated in the first five books of the Old Testament) and the Talmud (the authorized writings of Jewish traditions). Worldwide, there are more than 15 million people of the Jewish faith.

Taoism   Lao Zi (ca. 600 B.C.), a Chinese religious philosopher, was the founder of this contemplative faith that puts great emphasis on the Way (Tao, pronounced dow), which is the orderly and natural unfolding of the workings of the Universe. Today there are over 19 million Taoists throughout the world.

Zoroastrianism   A religion (6th century B.C.) founded in Persia by Zoroaster, a prophet whose teachings centered on the battle between good and evil, in which the good works of man act in a way that is universally redeeming. The scriptures of this faith are known as the *Zend Avesta* and are written in Iranian. In the East today there are more than 250 Zoroastrians.

Meditation   The sustained contemplation of God or a spiritual theme or ideal. Meditation requires a composed mind and abstraction from sense experience. The goal of meditation is to be aligned with the true nature of reality, whatever one's beliefs may be. Hence, meditation is not necessarily associated with mysticism, as is often thought to be the case.

Menorah   A seven-branched candelabrum, the light from which, in popular tradition, symbolized the presence of God within the temple. In Jewish thought and literature, the flaming menorah is a fitting symbol of the unquenchable and illuminating spirit of Judaism.

Messiah   In the Hebrew Bible, a term meaning "anointed one" and applied to kings and high priests. The word is even used for King Cyrus, whom the Biblical writers saw as a being used to accomplish God's purposes. In the New Testament, Messiah is replaced with the Greek word "Christ," and is the title given to Jesus.

Methodists   A Protestant denomination that was originally a reform movement within the Church of England. Initiated by Charles and John Wesley, George Whitefield, and others in the late 1720s at Oxford. In 1738 there were public meetings held outside by Whitefield because the English church refused to allow him to speak in its churches. After John Wesley joined these meetings, a new movement was formed, which was at first spread by traveling preachers. After spreading to Ireland and Scotland, Methodism was brought to North America by lay assistants and then later by appointed ministers, two being the famous Thomas Coke and Francis Asbury. Theologically, Methodism is anti-Calvinist, in that it supports free will, although much of the focus in Methodism is away from theology and concentrated on direct experience of God. The church is now worldwide and is one of the largest Protestant churches in the United States.

Miracles   The intervention of the Divine into the realm of the natural that appears contrary to natural laws. A miracle, therefore, could be an occurrence caused by God either in line with the laws of the universe or contrary to natural laws.

Mohammed   An Arabian man born in Mecca who believed that there is only one God and that God had chosen him to be his last prophet. The decisive point in Mohammed's life came when he overthrew the idols in Mecca and was forced to leave, but convinced many people to follow his revelations of the one God. He then formed a mosque and an army in Medina. The combination of a religious force and an army allowed his teachings to conquer the city of Mecca and spread out through the Middle East, uniting much of Arabia. In addition to establishing a new religion, Mohammed can be credited with abolishing the common practice of female infanticide. Today, the religion of Mohammed is called Islam and numbers as one of the three great theistic religions. *See* **Islam**.

Monotheism The belief that there is only one God. The rise of monotheism occurred first in Judaism. Scholars differ on whether the concept of one God developed early in Jewish history or late. The Egyptian pharaoh, Ikhnaton (1375–1358 B.C.) was thought by some to be monotheistic in demanding that all worship Aton, the sun god. It is more likely that Ikhnaton's belief was *henotheistic*, believing in a supreme god while not denying the existence of other gods.

Moses The Jewish man in the book of Genesis who lived with an Egyptian family from infancy and was taught Egyptian culture, but who was called by God to lead the Jewish people out of Egypt. Through Moses, God brought the terrible plagues against Egypt, gave Moses the Ten Commandments, and led the Jewish people to a new land, modernday Israel.

Moslem A believer in the one God as revealed to Mohammed and recorded in the Koran. One who submits to the faith of Islam.

Mosque An Islamic place of worship. Also refers to the group gathered to worship in an Islamic temple.

Mufti An Islamic judge who interprets Islamic religious law.

Mullah An Islamic spiritual teacher. Part of the class of learned religious scholars. Used as a title.

Mystery religion A term used to describe esoteric religions during the Hellenistic and Roman eras. Usually focusing on the dying and rising of a savior, mystery religions advocated a type of hidden knowledge and a particular ritual that permitted one to be united with God and to gain immortality. Mithraism, the cult of Eluesis, Isis-Osiris, and the cult of Dionysus are but a few of the many mystery religions.

Mystic A term meaning "one who is initiated into the mysteries." The term *mysticism* was first used in the *Dionysius Areopagitica*, a group of writings from the 5th and 6th centuries A.D. that advocated the theology of the "negative way." This theology held that God's transcendence is such that no one can understand what God is by use of reason. Instead, God can be known in terms of negation—God is not limited in knowledge, power, or in any way. God's nature is beyond the duality of reason. From here, mysticism became associated with the nonrational approach to religious experience and devotion. Two general types of mysticism can be distinguished: esoteric and exoteric. The esoteric mystic is one who attempts to have union with the transcendent God or principal of the universe. Exoteric mysticism is based on a materialistic pantheism, the universe being the whole of reality, and where one seeks union with everything. In general, mysticism involves the union between the self and the ultimate principle of reality. This union typically involves the blending of one's personality with the nature of God or ultimate reality to the point where there is no distinction and self-identity is lost. However, there is a small mystical tradition in the West that, although seeking a union with the personal and knowable God, maintains a distinction between God and believer.

Natural theology The idea that the study of God begins with the existence of the world, humanity, and reason. In contrast to theology, which studies the concept of God derived from scripture, natural theology focuses primarily on reason. William Paley, author of *Natural Theology*, is a good example of a natural theologian having much influence, especially remembered for his argument from design for the existence of God.

Neophyte One who is a recent convert or religious novice. The term can also mean one recently ordained as a Roman Catholic priest.

New Testament The authoritative collection of Christian scriptures. Most scholars believe that the evidence suggests these writings were collected over several centuries after the first apostles died. The letters were written by individual apostles and believers. Most were not universal letters but sent to particular churches, such as the Corinthian, Phillipian, and Galatian letters. These churches kept the letters, circulated them among the local believers, and then the letters most likely found their way into the hands of other churches because of their value in teaching and because of the writer's spiritual leadership. Most scholars agree that it was the Christians who invented the book, or codex. As the number of letters began to accumulate, along with the proliferation of apocryphal letters claiming authority, and during the serious struggle with Marcionism, Christians were forced to begin deciding which letters were authoritative and then to put them together in one book. One of the criteria the early church had for deciding a writing was authoritative was if it was the work of an apostle. But this was not absolute because it was believed by many the book of Hebrews was not written by Paul, as is thought today, yet it was added to the canon. The greatest concern was whether the writing agreed with the teachings of the first church, the accepted Gospels, and letters of Paul. Some letters, such as Revelations, were not canonized until the 3rd or 4th century. As mentioned above, the New Testament is a book containing letters written to people for a particular purpose and on a particular occasion. Hence, a letter can only be understood by understanding the context in which it was written—not only the spiritual and political world of the first century but also the audience and the peculiar circumstances under which the letter was written.

New Year, Jewish The first day of the civil year and the first day of the seventh month of the ecclesiastical year (generally occurring in September), described as "a memorial proclaimed with the blast of the horn, a holy convocation," upon which no servile work is permitted. Invested with the character of a Day of Divine Judgment, it acquired great solemnity. The sounding of the ram's horn (shofar) during the morning service stirs the people to thoughts of repentence. The elaborate liturgy of the day dwells upon God's sovereignty, providence, revelation, and redemption. Orthodox Jews observe two days of Rosh Hashanah.

Nirvana   From the Sanskrit, meaning "blown out." Mentioned in the Bhagavad Gita and in the Vedas, nirvana is usually associated with Buddhism. Hinayana and Mahayana Buddhism both have varying interpretations of nirvana. Sometimes it is thought to be literal extinction while others see it as a state of perfect bliss. What is sure, however, is that the state of nirvana is devoid of individual personal awareness and distinctiveness.

Novena   In the Catholic church, a nine-day devotion made by an individual for some specific purpose, or in honor of a saint.

Old Testament   The Christian term for the Hebrew Bible. Established as official canon by the end of the 2nd century A.D. It is comprised of 39 books written mostly in Hebrew, but some in Aramaic. The Roman Catholic Old Testament differs from Old Testament of the early church and of Protestant churches in that several intertestamental and apocryphal books are added, such as I and II Maccabees. The Hebrew Bible and Old Testament consist of what are traditionally called the five books of Moses, the prophets, and the psalms and proverbs. Its authorship is complex in that it was written over long period of time, although most scholars consider the bulk of the writings to have been written during the kingdom period and during the Babylonian exile.

EXHIBIT 22.3
Old Testament Apocrypha

The First Book of Esdras
The Second Book of Esdras
Tobit
Judith
The Rest of the Book of Esther
The Wisdom of Solomon
Ecclesiasticus
Baruch
The Song of the Three Holy Children
The History of Susanna
The History of Bel and the Dragon
The Prayer of Manasses
The First Book of the Maccabees
The Second Book of the Maccabees

Om   Originally *aum*, a Sanskrit term meaning "assent." A mystical symbol of high importance in Hinduism. It stands for the whole of reality, including Atman and Brahman. Om is often pronounced, sometimes with prolonged syllables, during various types of Indian meditation.

Omnipotence   One of the classical attributes of God in Judaism, Christianity, and Islam. From the Latin, meaning "all powerful." Many medieval philosophers considered omnipotence to be the power to do all that is possible, inferring that some things are not possible, like the creation of a round square. Hence, some hold that omnipotence does not mean the power to create contradictions precisely because this is not a possible power in reality.

Omnipresence   One of the classical attributes of God, meaning that God is present to all things in all places or the attribute of being everywhere. Usually in classical philosophy of religion, omnipresence is qualified in that God is said to be present to the world yet distinct from it. In other words, God is in all places but is not identical with the world.

Omniscience   A classical attribute of God, meaning "to know all things." In classical philosophy, it is held that God knows ever specific detail of past, present, and future. In contemporary philosophy of religion, some philosophers who hold a temporal view of God, such as Charles Hartshorne, have a different view of omniscience. They maintain that time is an aspect of God's existence and that God does not know the actual future, except those specific actions that God has decided to perform in the future, and also that God knows all possibilities that the future may bring. Hartshorne's teacher, the philosopher Alfred North Whitehead, developed a view of time, different from that of his contemporary, Einstein, that allowed for experience to be extended instead of broken in points. This allowed him to posit the view that God's presence is infinitely extended and continuously "coming to be," not temporally, but as one present experience. Hence, God knows the future only in terms of a multiplicity of possibilities that may come to be.

Ontology   The study of being, or the fundamental stuff of existence. The problem of reality.

Oracle   Particularly in ancient times, the answers given by certain divinities to inquiries by pilgrims coming to their shrines. Usually, in dealing with the future, these replies were obscure and capable of being interpreted in accordance with the event. The Delphic Oracle was the most famous Greek oracle, one who had great influence on all the city-states.

Original sin   In Christian theology, the infection of sin into all future humanity, caused by Adam and Eve's choosing to disobey God. After sinning against God, the two were put out of the Garden of Eden and forced to labor upon the land and deal with a corrupted nature. The apostle Paul originated the idea of universal infection by writing, "in Adam all have sinned, so in Christ all can be saved." In Western theology, original sin is seen almost as a genetic inheritance. In Orthodox and Eastern theology, it is seen more as environmental.

Ormazd (or Ahura Mazda)   The creator of the world in Zoroastrianism; the highest deity and source of all light and goodness. Ormazd is in eternal combat with Ahirman, also known as Angra Mainyu, who is the evil spirit and source of darkness. *See* **Zoroastrianism**.

Orthodoxy   (Gr. orthos, right, straight; doxa, opinion) Correctness of religious belief, according to an authoritative standard. The Roman Catholic regards himself as orthodox in contrast with the Protestant, while the Trinitarian Protestant looks on himself as orthodox with respect to the Unitarian. Orthodoxy varies, too, with time, what is unorthodox at one period may be orthodox in a later one. Christ was unorthodox with respect to the Judaism of his day and yet was to become the founder of a new orthodoxy.

Pagan (Derived from Latin "country man") The term was first applied to those who clung to Greek and Roman faiths. Since Christianity first spread in the cities, this was true for more of the rural than the urban population. The term "pagan" is now applied to one who does not belong to an organized religion. In contrast to "heathen" it implies a disinterested rather than a hostile point of view.

Palm Sunday The Sunday before Easter. In the Gospels, as Christ rode into Jerusalem on the back of a donkey (to fulfill the prophecy in Isaiah), his way into the city was strewn with branches of palm.

Pantheism From the Greek *pan* (everything) and *theos* (God), meaning that everything in the world is identical with God. Two general types of pantheism can be distinguished: materialistic and idealistic pantheism. However, pantheism is mostly associated with idealism, where the world of appearance is illusion and all things are really identical. Since religious idealism is most prevalent in the Eastern world, pantheism in the East is almost always idealistic as seen in Hinduism and Buddhism. The West, being inundated with a strong materialistic world view, tends to produce a pantheistic view that admits to the existence of the material reality, claims the world is God, and sees everything as identical. Examples of materialistic pantheism are 17th and 18th century materialism and the contemporary ecological movement called "Deep Ecology." In the pantheistic view, no qualitative distinction can be coherently made between anything in existence. The qualitative identity of all things means that the concept of the whole is very important in determining the fundamental nature of reality. Of course, if everything is identical, there is a problem with individual identity. What is more, most pantheistic systems hold that the whole is an impersonal unity, meaning that human qualities of love, communication, and personality are either transcended or denied. More specifically, there have been many pantheists and various types of pantheism in the history or philosophy and religion, from the early Greek philosopher Parmenides to Hegel. In addition to the many pantheists in the East, a short list of Western pantheists, varying in type, is as follows: Parmenides, Heraclitus, Cleanthes, the Neoplatonists, Erigena, Averroës, the Kabalah, Meister Eckhart, Nicholas of Cusa, Giorgano Bruno, Paracelesus, Spinoza, Goethe, Hegel, Schleiermacher, Josiah Royce, and Teilhard de Chardin.

Parable Usually an expanded simile in story form used as an allegory for the purposes of teaching a spiritual or moral lesson.

Parish The area or district within which a regularly installed pastor or priest exercises his pastoral office.

Paschal Lamb In Judaism, a lamb slaughtered, cooked, and eaten at Passover. In the book of Exodus, when the Israelites were in captivity under the Egyptians, it is recorded that God instructed all those who would hear to sprinkle the blood of a lamb on their household entrance so that God's vengeance against the Egyptians, which would be the killing of every firstborn, would pass over that house.

Passion The sufferings of Christ from the Last Supper to his death on the cross. Also applicable to the sufferings of the martyrs. The term is often used for the narrative or dramatic performance of Christ's sufferings.

Passover celebrates Jewish freedom.

Passover In Judaism, the observance of the story in Exodus 12, where God's wrath "passed over" the houses with the blood of a lamb sprinkled on their entrance. It is traditionally celebrated for eight days with special meals including unleavened bread and a ritual of prayers and hymns.

Penance A sacrament of the Roman Catholic church dealing with the expiation of sins after baptism that involves contrition, confession, and satisfaction. Contrition is sorrow for one's sins and the desire to sin no more. Confession is the acknowledging of sin to a priest, who grants absolution. Satisfaction is the performing of certain good works, such as prayer, fasting, and almsgiving, as assigned by a priest.

Penitence The feeling of remorse and sorrow over one's sinful deeds, including the desire not to sin again.

Pentecost, Christian The feast that takes place the seventh Sunday after Easter to celebrate the descent of the Holy Spirit onto the apostles. Also considered to be the birthday of the Catholic church.

Polemics Arguments among Christians in an effort to determine the true Christian view with regard to specific questions.

Pope The word "pope" is derived from the old ecclesiastical Latin "papa," from the Greek *papas*, meaning father; hence the expression as applied to the Pope "Father of Christendom." Catholic theologians maintain that all the prerogatives—Primacy, Infallibility, Universal Power, etc., accorded by Christ to St. Peter—are also the pope's in virtue of his being the successor of Peter as Bishop of Rome.

Prayer   Communication with God in the form of worship, thankfulness, and petition.

Predestination   Mostly in Christian and Islamic theology, the view that the salvation or damnation of persons has been determined beforehand by God. Some forms of predestination include the concept of providence, the belief that God is in control of worldly events, and posit a divine determinism of all events. The doctrine can be found in Augustine and Calvin; it then makes its way into some forms of Presbyterianism. Augustine promulgated the individualistic and deterministic view of predestination in his theology and commentary on the book of Romans. Contrary to his interpretation, the apostle Paul used predestination closely with the term election in the sense that God had the freedom to bring salvation to the Gentiles and that he had predestined this act of grace from all eternity.

Presbyterianism   A form of Protestantism coming from the teachings of John Calvin. Some have described their early attitude toward church and the Presbyterians' state as a passionate theocentrism. In the church there are four primary positions of authority: (1) the pastor, who is the only one allowed to preach or administer the sacraments, (2) teachers, (3) presbyters (or elders), those with disciplinary authority, and (4) deacons. By 1645 all English speaking churches used the *Westminster Confession* as their standard of doctrine. There is a strong emphasis on infant baptism and communion as being central in God's working of grace. Predestination could be the most important doctrine in that it sums up the inability of humanity to even will to love God and describes the total dependency of all events on the will of God. Not all Presbyterians agree with Calvin on every point. The late theologian Karl Barth could not agree with Calvin on the issue of election. There is no fixed liturgy, and today the church has several different subdenominations.

Priest   In the Roman Catholic, Orthodox, and Anglican churches, a priest is one who by the grace of God is ordained a bishop, who is considered to be an apostolic successor. In many Protestant churches, a priest, or pastor, is usually chosen by an individual congregation.

Prophets   In the Hebrew Bible, those who spoke for God, usually independent of the priestly class and the King, but sometimes associated with the priests or part of the king's court. The prophets spoke against the iniquity of Israel by speaking publicly and sometimes by addressing the king of Israel personally. In the Hebrew Bible, the prophets are divided into the minor and major prophets, terms denoting only the length of a book and not its importance.

Protestantism   One of the three major branches of Christianity, consisting of hundreds of divergent denominations and sects, each having its own interpretation of the Bible and its own theological beliefs and ritualistic practices. Most, however, agree to the

---

EXHIBIT 22.4
Protestant Sects

Baptists   A denomination that began in England out of dissatisfaction with both the Church of England and the Roman Catholic church. Baptists believe the Bible to be the ultimate authority and lay great stress on baptism as a public symbol of faith in Christ as personal Savior.

Congregationalists   (The United Church of Christ). A Protestant sect whose members recognize Christ as the head of the church and the Bible as the spiritual inspiration of God's work in the world. Sin is viewed as the indifference of man to the will of God.

Episcopalians   (Anglicans) Most of the early leaders of the United States (Washington, Madison Monroe, etc.) were Episcopal—a Protestant sect that embraces many Catholic sacraments and creeds. The Book of Common Prayer is used in worship and contains all the services of the church.

Jehovah's Witnesses   A sect that believes in only one God (Jehovah, as proclaimed by Isaiah). Witnesses contend that Jesus died as a sacrifice to God and later (in 1914) Christ rid heaven of Satan, which caused tremendous trouble and unrest on Earth. When God reigns again, Satan will be destroyed forever.

Lutherans   A denomination born after the split in the Roman Catholic church caused by the Reformation that was led by Martin Luther. This religious community puts great emphasis on the doctrine of salvation through faith; they conceive of God as a loving, benevolent Father.

Methodists   John Wesley was the first leader of this church in the 1700s. He preached the doctrine of God's mercy and man's desire to strive for perfection in order to find contentment.

Mormons   This church was founded under the leadership of Joseph Smith, in 1820. Mormons believe in the second coming of Christ and use The Book of Mormon as a complement to the Bible. Baptism in the faith takes place when an individual is old enough to understand the meaning of the ceremony.

Presbyterians   A religion that began in the 1600s and recognizes communion and baptism as the only two celebrated religious sacraments. Presbyterians believe that salvation is an act of God, and therefore unable to be achieved through human effort.

Seventh-Day Adventists   The members of this sect believe that the world is coming to an end imminently, and that people must align their wills to the will of God as revealed in the Bible. Adventists adhere to a literal interpretation of the Scriptures, and believe the dead are in a limbo to be judged at the Second Coming of Christ.

Unitarian Universalists   A religious body whose individual beliefs are a matter of personal choice. Most members believe in the teachings of Jesus rather than in his divinity and conceive of God as a unity not a trinity. They view heaven and hell as the mental conditions of man, expressed by such differences in thought as tyranny and love.

basic claims of Orthodoxy, namely that there is one God and that Jesus was God's only son who rose from the dead to free humanity from darkness. The term comes from the Reformation, where those against the abuses of the Roman Catholic church were said to "protest." The most central Protestant belief is the emphasis on the Bible as the revealed teaching of God, and that an individual believer can stand alone and discover the truth of the Bible. With this view, it is often said, or at least implied by practice, that the commentary on the scriptures by other believers and the decrees of the early church, including the later Roman Catholic church, are of little or no importance. This can be seen especially in Baptist theology, where even the creeds of the early church such as the Apostles Creed and the Nicean Creed are not recited or used. Even though each type of Protestantism varies in its view of the significance of church history, it can generally be said that Protestants, because of their emphasis on personal interpretation of scripture, either gloss over or have disdain for any writings or church pronouncements during the Roman Catholic era, specifically from Augustine to the Reformation, but also including the Apostolic Fathers of the 2nd century.

Purgatory   In Roman Catholicism, a punishment after death for an unspecified period of time for venial sins (minor sins committed without deliberation).

Puritanism   The Puritans were a sect formed because they wished to purify English Protestantism by removing all traces of Catholic forms and ceremonies. Puritanism emphasized the Bible instead of tradition or reason as the chief source of authority, and their moral code was very strict.

R **Rabbi**   In Hebrew, meaning "master." It became a title of ordination for teachers of authority in Judaism.
Recluse   A popular term for one withdrawing from the world, especially for the purpose of religious dedication. In a technical sense, this term refers to monks and nuns who are allowed to undertake permanent seclusion in their cells.

Redemption   A term describing the act of God's saving humanity from sin and the darkness of the world. It is most commonly associated with the theistic religions of Judaism, Christianity, and Islam. The Hebrew Bible contains a sacrificial system that God accepted as sufficient for the sins of the people. In the New Testament, Paul thought Jesus, the anointed one of God, was the final sacrifice that saved the world from sin. He understood redemption to mean the glorious result of Jesus' sacrificial death. Redemption in Christianity is tied to the concept of Atonement and must be understood as a unit. In addition to the Western religions, one could say Hinduism and Buddhism contain the concept of redemption. Humanity is tied to the law and effects of Karma and is condemned to subsequent rebirths. With the realization of true reality, or enlightenment, one can be liberated, or redeemed, from the wheel of birth, death, and rebirth.

Reformation   A European movement initiated by Martin Luther in 1517, which resulted in the establishment of a Lutheran church and other churches based on various leaders such as Luther. Although Luther's actions finally created a separate church, it was Luther's sincere intention to reform the Roman Catholic church. Only later, after his pleas for reform were ignored and then dealt with by personal attack and persecution, did Luther turn to the people of his German homeland for assistance in rebellion against the pope and Rome. With the prodding of the landowners against Rome, Luther secured the help of the feudal lords and princes. In short, without a political uprising, the Reformation might have had a much different conclusion. But, the Reformation was also happening in other parts of Europe. Zwingli was at work in Switzerland, Calvin in France and later in the city of Geneva, and John Knox in Scotland. The many different churches that sprang from the Reformation are the Protestant denominations.

Relic   An object regarded as reverent because of its association with a martyr or saint. Relics can be part of the body of a saint (i.e., a fragment of bone), any part of the clothing belonging to a saint, or something intimately connected to one.

Repentance   Being sorry. In Christianity, it is turning from a life of disobedience to God to the service of God. Repentance can also be understood as the abhorrence of sin, a direct change in one's direction, once headed toward sin and now toward faith and love of God.

Requiem   A mass for the dead at funerals and on All Souls' Day, November 2.

Resurrection   To bring the dead back to life in bodily form. A doctrine in Judaism, Christianity, and Islam, according to which upon the decree of God the dead come back to life. Contrary to other Near Eastern religions, there is no particular geographic location where the dead will rise or where they will live. In Judaism, the concept of resurrection unfolded most prominently in the intertestamental apocalyptic writings. In Christianity, Jesus rose from the dead and had a unique heavenly body, one capable of walking through material objects like doors but also a body that could partake of eating and physical contact with the world. The apostle Paul held that at the resurrection the followers of Jesus would be given heavenly bodies.   In all three theistic religions, all of the dead, both the good and the evil, will rise again to meet God, some being accepted and others rejected.

Revelation   The revealing of that which was previously hidden. In Jewish, Christian, and Islamic theology, revelation is the act of God in history by either word or deed. Hence, these accept the necessity of a personal God who can interact with humanity and be involved in history. Today there are two ways of understanding revelation: one being the very acts of God and the other being the recorded acts of God. As scribes began to write down and make copies of what many believed God had done, the view became ingrained in orthodox belief that revelation was not only the specific historical events and persons that God was involved with, but also that revelation was the sacred writings themselves. In addition to this specific revelation, theologians also speak of a general revelation. General revelation is the presence of God in the world in terms of humanity's understanding of goodness, beauty, truth, and reason, along with the very existence of humanity, which is made in the image of God.

Roman Catholic church   One of the three major branches of Christianity. It teaches that God redeemed the world by sending Jesus Christ and that Jesus founded the church. The ministering of the church is effected through: (1) the sacraments (baptism, confirmation, Eucharist, penance, holy orders, marriage, and anointing of the sick), which are outward signs instituted by Jesus Christ and through which the believer demonstrates his faith and receives an inner grace; (2) the Church's works of assisting people to live in grace.

Rosary   In the Roman Catholic church, a prayer on beads usually on a necklace that contains symbols of the recitation of five or fifteen Hail Marys. An Our Father precedes each decade and is followed by a Gloria. Throughout this prayer the power and mystery of Christ is part of the contemplation.

Rosh Hashanah   *See* **New Year, Jewish**.

S

Sabbath   The sacred day of rest in Judaism on the last day of the week, sunset Friday to sunset Saturday. It consists of services Friday at sundown and Saturday morning, when there is reading from the Torah scroll and scripture lessons are presented to the congregation. The beginning of the Sabbath is marked by the lighting of candles or oil lamps, and its conclusion is sealed by wine, fragrant spices, and candle flames. In the Hebrew Bible, specific ordinances are written on how to observe the Sabbath, notably the prohibition against any type of work. Some Christians celebrate the Sabbath on Sunday and usually do not follow the ordinances in the Hebrew Bible, their Old Testament.

Sacrament   Certain rites in Christianity that have special meaning for the believer. It is usually understood to be an outward sign of God's grace. Christian churches differ on the efficacy of the sacraments and the number; however, all agree that baptism and the Eucharist, or communion, are sacraments.

Sacrilege   The desecration of a sacred thing. The Hebrew Bible contains many examples of sacrilege and punishments that resulted from it. In ancient times the term also referred to the theft of sacred property. In English law sacrilege is breaking into a place of worship with intent to steal.

Salvation   Derived from the Latin word *salvare*, which means "to save." In religion, salvation can refer to any belief that considers there to be a need for humanity to be saved from something, whether it be sin as in Judaism, Christianity, or Islam, or the wheel of samsara in Hinduism and Buddhism.

Samsara   A Sanskrit word meaning "cycle of existence." The cycle involves birth, death, momentary rest, and then birth again in the form of a new body. Samsara is associated with the word "reincarnation" (the rebirth in a new body after one's death) which is, contrary to many popular beliefs in the Western world, not desirable.

Savior   In the ancient world, associated with the names of Egyptian rulers and with the character of the gods in the mystery religions. It is now used as another name for Jesus Christ.

Scripture   The authoritative writings of a religion.

Seder   The order of the home service on the first and second nights of Passover.

Seven deadly sins   The list, traditionally, is composed of pride, envy, anger, sloth, avarice, gluttony, and lust.

Seventh-Day Adventists   The contemporary Protestant sect that follows the basic theological teachings of the Adventists movement. *See* **Adventists**.

Shaman   The priest or medicine man found among such people as the American Indians.

Shi'ite   Islamic sect that believes only the literal descendants of Ali (the spiritual successor to Mohammed) have the right to lead and make decisions that are binding on the religious life of Muslims. Shi'ites follow the proclamations of the Ayatollah, who is the earthly representative of the Imam, who is in heaven. Shi'ites, who have appointed Ayatollahs since the disappearance of the twelfth Imam, believe that he will return. As such he is called the Muntazar, or "Awaited One." Modern Shi'ites number 60 million and are the second largest Islamic sect next to the Sunni. Modern Shi'ites find their largest numbers in Iraq, Afghanistan, and Iran, where it is the official state religion.

Shinto   A formal set of religious practices associated with shrines in Japan. The rituals involve a type of ancestor worship and sometimes Japanese deities. Shintoism was introduced into Japan in the 6th century A.D. Today it is deeply ingrained in the culture of Japan, both politically and spiritually in terms of personal practice.

Shiva   A Hindu god and the god of worship in Saiva Hinduism. Shiva is the destroyer, one god of the Hindu trinity, along with Brahma the creator and Vishnu the preserver.

Sikh, Sikhism   A reform movement within Hinduism around 1500 A.D. Nanak (1469–1538) was the founder and a follower of the poet Kabir. Both Kabir and Nanak taught that the way of salvation was through *bhakti*, the way of faith or devotion. Nine teachers succeeded Nanak, at which point the tenth, Govind Singh, claimed that from then on only the scriptures, the *Granth*, would teach. Sikhism is monotheistic and rejects idols and incarnations. It also rejects the caste system, tobacco, wine, and pilgrimages.

Sin   Any transgression against God. To violate the nature and law of God.

Society of Friends (Quakers)   A religious movement founded in the later stages of the Protestant Reformation in England by George Fox (1635–1691). Theologically, Quaker theology has its roots in English liberal Protestantism. It focuses on what Fox called the "doctrine of the inner light," which puts one into direct relationship with God over and above any church or state authority.

Stigmata   Physical wounds resembling those Jesus received on the cross that reputedly appear on persons (frequently saints) to signify a particular intimacy or suffering with God.

Sufi   One of the many unorthodox offshoots of Islam. Sufism places its emphasis on a personal union with Allah in earthly life and strives to experience a mystical knowledge of Allah. The corpus of Sufi tradition consists of the Koran and the Hadith, or sayings of the prophet. Sufis are generally not interested in the details of Mohammed's life as they pertain to his government, etc. (the Sunnah), and are interested only in the details of Mohammed's direct experiences with Allah. Sufis have created a large body of written work, emphasizing Allah as love and light, which is couched in lush, ecstatic imagery. Sufis are known for their ecstatic dancing (Dervish), which is supposed to provoke the follower into union with the divine.

Sunnah   The part of Islamic tradition that deals with the governance of Mohammed and the historical events in his life. Modern Islamics look to the Sunnah not only for clues as to how to interpret secular law, but also for guidance on how to conduct themselves in worldly matters.

Sunni   The largest sect of Islam, which places emphasis on the literal interpretation of the Koran. The Sunni also regard the historical events of Mohammed's life (the Sunnah) and his sayings (the Hadith) as an integral part of their tradition. Unlike Shi'ites, Sunnis do not have a messianic tradition.

Synagogue   A Greek term meaning "an assembly" or "to bring together." It was first used to mean a community of Jews. Today a synagogue is more specifically a place for Jewish worship or a gathering of Jews inside a place of worship, and it takes the place of the Temple in Israel. Instead of Temple sacrifices or a priestly class, there is prayer, and the reading and study of the Hebrew Bible. The synagogue became the focus of Jewish religious, social, and intellectual life. Sometimes it served as an elementary school, law court, or communal center. Since the first Christians were Jews, the synagogue became the model for the type and manner of worship of Christianity.

Tabernacle   A portable tent sanctuary used by the Israelites during their desert wanderings. In Catholicism it is the repository for the Blessed Host.

Talmud   A collection of Jewish tradition supplementing the Hebrew Bible after the text of the Mosaic Law was fixed in the 5th century A.D. Summarizing some seven centuries of Jewish culture, its emphasis is on interpretation of the Torah, Jewish civil and religious law, and also on the subjects of ethics, social institutions, history, and science. In the *Talmud* is found the *Mishnah* and the *Gamara*. The *Mishnah* summarizes the Jewish oral law from the 5th century B.C. to the 2nd century A.D. The *Gamara* amplifies and explains the details of the *Mishnah*. There are two versions of the *Talmud*, the Palestinian *Talmud* (5th century A.D.) and the Babylonian *Talmud* (7th century A.D.).

Taoism   An ancient Chinese religion and philosophy dating to the 2nd century B.C. and founded by Lao Tzu, who is said to have written the principal Taoist text, the *Tao Te Ching*. The text is replete with Chinese mysticism. The emphasis is away from reason and toward being in harmony with nature. Central to Taoist thought is the *Tao* and the *Yin* and *Yang*. The *Tao* is the fundamental nature of existence, that from which all things have come, and it is something which cannot be named or described—it is an undifferentiated unity from a Western logical analysis. From the *Tao* has come

Yin and *Yang*, the dualistic principles that permeate the universe. Ritually, Taoist practice involved magic charms for health cures and alchemy, which resulted in the development of metallurgy, gunpowder, and pharmaceuticals.

Theism   From the Greek *theos*, meaning "God." In contrast to pantheism, where God is identical to everything, theistic conceptions maintain that God is present to the world yet distinct from it. *See* **God**; **Omniscience**; **Omnipresence**; and **Omnipotence**.

Theses, Ninety-Five   A writing that was posted on the Wittenberg church door by Martin Luther in 1517 in response to the sale of indulgences by the Dominican John Tetzel. The theses make four main points: (1) indulgences cannot take away the guilt or punishment of sin; (2) indulgences cannot take away the sin of those in purgatory; (3) the power of the Holy Spirit is the only thing that can give the believer merit and, therefore, the pope can only remit ecclesiastical penalties; (4) the true repentance that Christ demands is sufficient for God's pardon and makes indulgences unnecessary and a blasphemy to the grace of Christ. *See* **Luther, Martin**.

Torah   The Mosaic law that contains the first five books of the Hebrew Bible. Traditionally, it is considered to have been written by Moses. Many scholars today think it is was written much later, using a combination of oral material from Moses' time and later scribal additions.

Transmigration   The rebirth of a spirit or personality into another being after death. One can be reborn into the same or different species. Prevalent in the many forms of Hinduism, in Buddhism, and in the West in the Pythagoreans, Plato, and the Kabalah. Also called Metempsychosis.

Transubstantiation   A Roman Catholic doctrine according to which the bread and wine in the Eucharist become the body and blood of Christ.

Trinity   In Christianity the belief that God is one but exists in three persons: the Father, Son, and Holy Spirit. Although official doctrine in Orthodox, Roman Catholic, and most Protestant thinking, the Trinity was not a singular doctrine throughout the early history of the church. In Hinduism, it is the gods Brahma, Vishnu, and Shiva. In Buddhism, it is the Mahayana doctrine of Buddha as the Body of Transformation, Bliss, and Dharma.

Unitarianism   The doctrine that God is one and that Jesus was only human, in contrast to the orthodox understanding of the Trinity and the full divinity and humanity of Jesus. A doctrine that arose after the reformation, appeared in England in 1682, and flourished in the 1700s at Harvard College in America. It is thought that in the early 1800s most of the ministers in Boston were Unitarian. Classical Unitarianism should be distinguished from contemporary Unitarianism. Before the 20th century, Unitarians generally agreed that a personal God existed. Therefore, classical Unitarianism was quite transcendent. Today, Unitarians usually do not think a belief in a God of unity is important. Rather, emphasis is placed on personal freedom and tolerance with respect to belief. In fact, contemporary Unitarianism leans toward nontranscendence, or toward agnosticism or atheism. As the church stepped further away from theological issues, attention was placed on personal satisfaction through a good character, political reform, and education.

Upanishads   The philosophical text of Hinduism. Also called the *Vedanta*.

V **Vedanta**   From the Sanskrit meaning "the end of knowledge." A philosophical system in Hinduism that concerns itself with the 555 sutras of the *Vedanta Sutra*, also called the *Bhrama Sutra* since the doctrine of Brahman and the self is dealt with. The most widespread view is that of Shankara, a monist interpretation that sees Brahman as the only reality. Contrary to Shankara, Ramanuja held that individual persons and the world exist as extensions of the body of God.

Vedas   Sanskrit word meaning "knowledge." A collection of ancient Indian writings and hymns that address religious ritual, regulation, and philosophical subjects. There are five general divisions: (1) the Samhitas, hymns to gods and goddesses; (2) the Brahmanas, rules for sacrifices; (3) the Aranyakas, explanations of the meaning of the Vedic sacrifices; (4) the Upanishads, philosophical writings; and (5) the Sutras, later writings expressing important religious and social duties. The Vedas are a lengthy and complex group of writings that may date to the 7th or 8th century B.C.

Virgin Mary   A title given to Mary, the mother of Jesus, because of the belief that she did not conceive Jesus by natural means but was miraculously made pregnant by the power of God.

The incarnation of the god Vishnu in the form of Rama.

Vishnu   The supreme god of the Vishnuite sect of Hinduism, although a minor sun god in the Vedas. He is the Preserver in the Hindu Trinity, along with Brahma and Shiva. Tradition has it that Vishnu has appeared in many different incarnations, sometimes in animal or half animal form, as the fish, tortoise, and boar. His incarnations are also said to have been as Krishna, Rama, and Buddha. An important philosopher of the Vishnu sect is Ramanuja. Vishnusim is one of the two major theistic sects in Hinduism, with some forms being monotheistic.

Vishnuism, Vaisnavism   *See* **Vishnu.**

W **Worship**   The adoration of a deity, in personal solitude or in a group of individuals. Worship is usually initiated by prayers and ceremonies that assist one in expressing love to God.

Y **Yahweh**   In Hebrew, "YHWH" is the name of God as written in the Hebrew Bible. The vowels "a" and "e" are thought by some to be the correct pronunciation of YHWH. The name Jehovah is an alternate interpretation of the sound of the Hebrew YHWH.

Yin and Yang   A Chinese symbol from ancient times that stands for the principle of duality that permeates the entire universe. *Yin* is the feminine, passive, weak, and destructive side of reality, while *Yang* is the masculine, strong, and constructive aspect of reality. Yin and Yang can be found in the Taoist writing, the *Tao-Te Ching*, where the principles have come from the indescribable *Tao*, and also in the *Yin Yang* philosophy. *See* **Taoism.**

Yoga   A Sanskrit term meaning "union" or "to yoke." A practical way of bringing the individual self in union with ultimate reality. With Patanjali as founder, it is one of the six orthodox schools in Indian thought. There are many different types of Yoga, but a general perspective can be gained by the following. The individualistic human mind, the ego, is made up of *citta*. The ego exists because of *Avidya* (the confusion of the noneternal with the eternal), *Dvesa* (having worries about fear and death), and *Raga* (attachment to pleasures and pleasurable things). The goal of Yoga is to be free from *citta*, destroy the ego, and become the true self. The various types of Yoga, each having its own specific doctrine, are *Astanga*, *Asparsha*, *Shiva*, *Bhagavad Gita*, *Kundalini*, *Laya*, and *Mantra Yoga*.

Z **Zen**   The name in Japan for a type of Buddhism originating in India and called Ch'an in China. In the 5th century A.D. Bodhidharma brought Zen to China, where it became a growing force. In the early 7th century, two schools developed, the northern school led by Shen-hsiu and the southern school led by Hui-neng. The school of Shen-hsiu emphasized the importance of effort and practice that led to gradual enlightenment. Hui-neng stressed sudden enlightenment without the burden of meditation and the reciting of sutras. The southern school eventually overcame the northern school, making Hui-neng's understanding the way of Zen. Later, in 1191 Zen was carried to Japan by Ei-sai. Today, Zen is prevalent throughout Japanese culture. Zen has many interesting sutras, pithy sayings, and stories for teaching the true nature of reality. The basic philosophy of Zen is the negation of all concepts and things so that everything is "no-thing." This idea can be understood as a negative synthesis. In language there is affirmation and denial, or thesis-antithesis. Some philosophies advocate the combining of thesis-antithesis in order to create a new reality. In Zen, reality is neither thesis nor antithesis. Zen philosophy believes reality must be understood as neither/nor. The nature of reality that corresponds to this principle is called emptiness. Everything is nothing because everything has emptiness. Enlightenment is the realization that one's individual self is the dreamlike manifestation of emptiness, and once this is realized, one can follow the middle path, reject asceticism, and partake in the splendor of everything just as it is.

Zoroastrianism   A religion founded by Zarathushtra (also called Zoroaster), ca. 1000 B.C. It remained strong until 636 A.D., when an Islamic invasion began persecutions. According to the Zoroastrian scriptures, the Avesta, king of Vishtaspa of east Iran supported Zoroaster. With this support Zoroaster gained a powerful following and soon his beliefs became the national religion of eastern Iran. The philosophy can be summarized as follows: In the beginning of time, two powerful spirits battled, one good and the other evil. The good spirit that brings life, law, order, and truth, is Ahura Mazda, and the evil spirit, bringing evil and darkness, is Angra Mainyu. Both spirits have a host of helpers, sometimes associated with other personal beings while at others resembling Platonic concepts. This struggle between the good side and the dark side is continued in the world. At this time both powers are in a balance, but eventually Ahura Mazda and the forces of goodness will have victory, finally condemning the evil spirit and his followers to destruction. Zoroaster challenged all to choose the good or the evil side in the battle. Allegiance to the good side was made by good thoughts, good words, and good deeds. In addition to the final judgment of Angra Mainyu, there is the judgment upon individual death when one's deeds are weighed. If there is more good than evil, then one enters into life, but in the case of more evil, there is death.

UNITED STATES AT A GLANCE

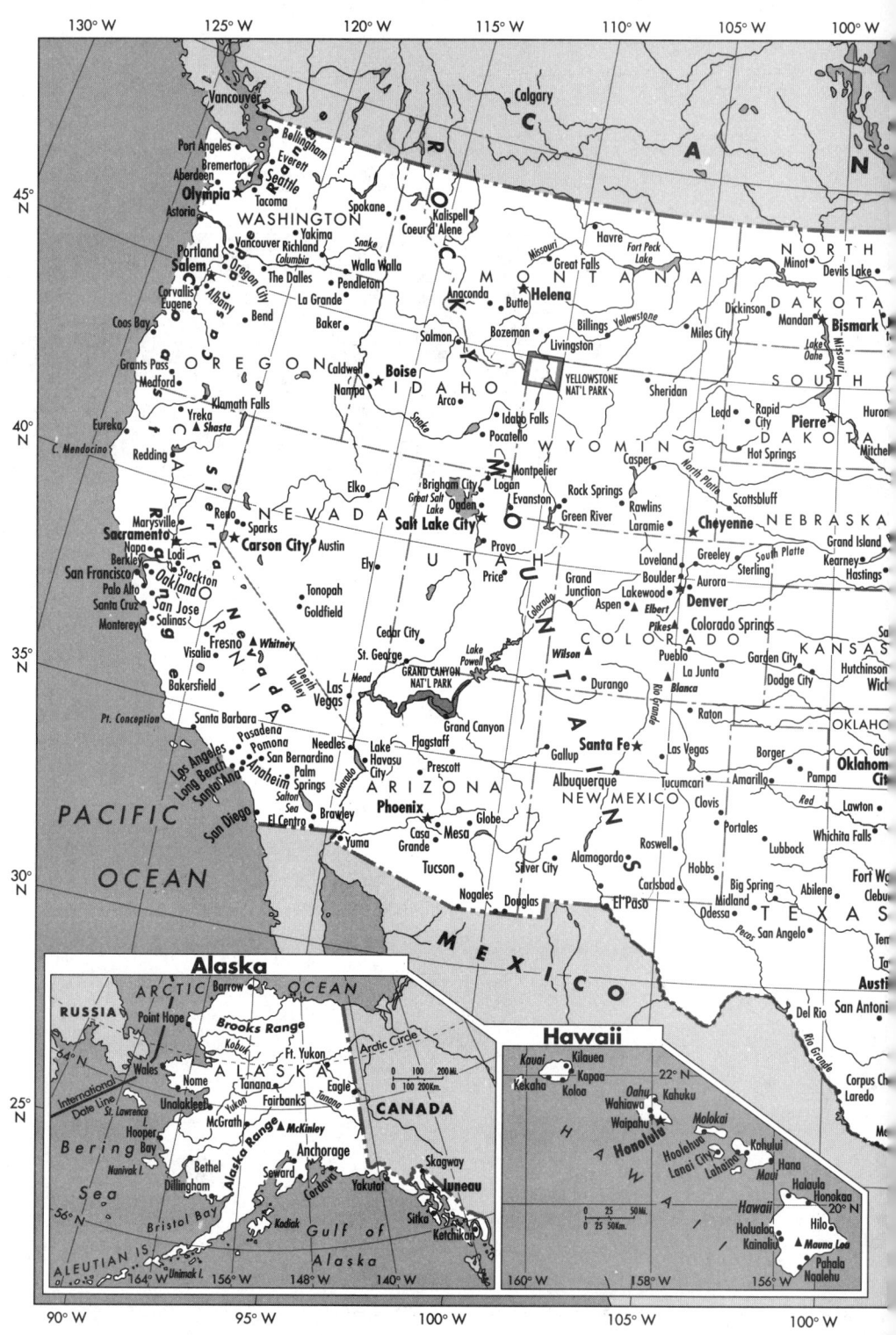

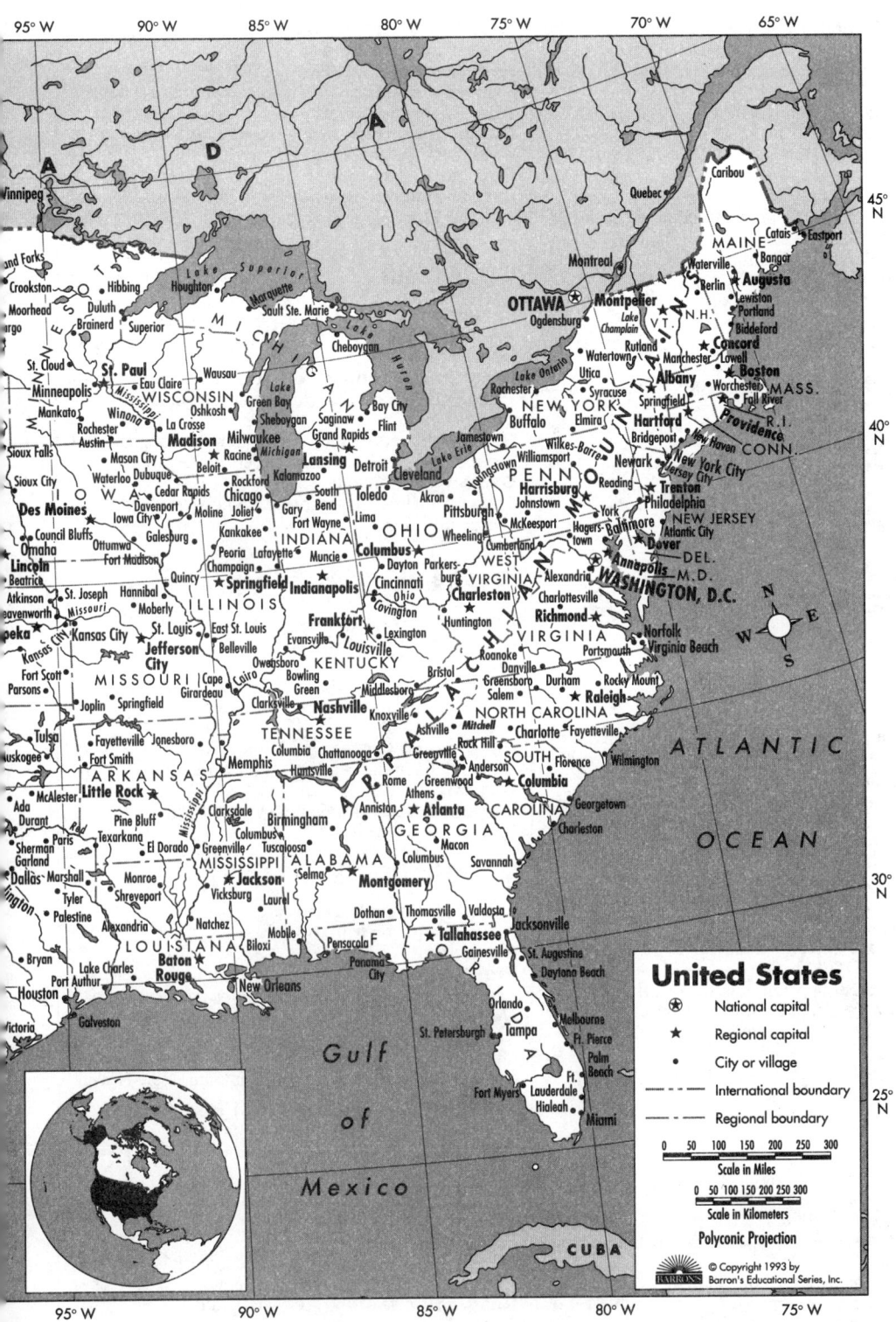

United States

⊛ National capital
★ Regional capital
• City or village
—·—·— International boundary
—··— Regional boundary

| 0 | 50 | 100 | 150 | 200 | 250 | 300 |
Scale in Miles

0 50 100 150 200 250 300
Scale in Kilometers

Polyconic Projection

© Copyright 1993 by
Barron's Educational Series, Inc.

United States: An Overview

Location   Central North America, bordered on the North by Canada, on the South by Mexico
Area   3,615,123 square miles
Population   256,000,000
Government   Federal Republic
Largest cities   New York, Los Angeles, Chicago, Philadelphia, Houston, Detroit, Washington, D.C. (capital)
Languages   English, Spanish
Ethnic groups   European descent, African descent, Amerindian
Religions   Protestant, Roman Catholic, Jewish
Chief industries   Heavy industry, light manufacturing, electronics, mining, agriculture, forestry, livestock-raising, food processing
Chief crops   Grains, sugar, potatoes, soybeans, fruit
Minerals   Coal, oil, copper, gold, silver, natural gas, lead, zinc, uranium
Leading exports   Machinery, vehicles, armaments, grains, aircraft, chemicals
Leading imports   Oil, automobiles, electronic equipment
Monetary unit   Dollar

Alabama

Location   Southeast
Area in square miles   51,609
Population   4,089,000
Principal products   Iron, steel, textiles, hydroelectric power, cotton, cattle, poultry, pulp, wood products
Geographic features   Coastal plain in the South, hills in the North
Capital   Montgomery
Largest cities   Birmingham, Mobile, Montgomery

Alaska

Location   Northwestern North America, not contiguous to the mainland 48 states
Area in square miles   586,412
Population   570,000
Principal products   Oil, natural gas, fish, lumber
Geographic features   Central plateau, Pacific and Arctic Mountains, frozen tundra in the North
Capital   Juneau
Largest cities   Anchorage, Fairbanks, Juneau

Arizona

Location   Southwest
Area in square miles   113,909
Population   3,750,000
Principal products   Copper, molybdenum, cotton, livestock, lumber
Geographic features   Plateau in the North, desert in the Southwest
Capital   Phoenix
Largest cities   Phoenix, Tucson, Mesa, Tempe

Arkansas

Location   South central
Area in square miles   53,104
Population   2,372,000
Principal products   Chemicals, furniture, cotton, rice, soybeans, lumber
Geographic features   Prairie in the East, Ozark Mountains in the West
Capital   Little Rock
Largest cities   Little Rock, Fort Smith, Fayetteville, Hot Springs

California

Location   West coast
Area in square miles   158,693
Population   30,380,000
Principal products   Aircraft, electronic equipment, oil, natural gas, citrus fruits, vegetables, wine, computers
Geographic features   Mountains on the coast and in the East, central valley, desert in the South
Capital   Sacramento
Largest cities   Los Angeles, San Diego, San Francisco, San Jose

Colorado

Location   West central
Area in square miles   104,247
Population   3,377,000
Principal products   Livestock, grains, sugar beets, sand and gravel, computer and electronic equipment
Geographic features   High plateau in the East, mountains in the central region and West
Capital   Denver
Largest cities   Denver, Colorado Springs, Aurora

Connecticut

Location   New England
Area in square miles   5,009
Population   3,291,000
Principal products   Aircraft, submarines, electrical and electronic equipment, tobacco, lumber
Geographic features   Coastal plain, Berkshire Mountains in the Northwest
Capital   Hartford
Largest cities   Bridgeport, Hartford, New Haven, Waterbury

Delaware

Location   Middle Atlantic region
Area in square miles   2,057
Population   680,000
Principal products   Synthetic materials, luggage, autos, soybeans, vegetables, chemicals
Geographic feature   Coastal plain
Capital   Dover
Largest cities   Dover, Wilmington, Newark

Florida

Location Southeast
Area in square miles 58,560
Population 13,277,000
Principal products Citrus fruits, vegetables, electrical and electronic equipment, textiles, livestock
Geographic features Coastal plain, tropical climate in the South
Capital Tallahassee
Largest cities Jacksonville, Miami, Tampa, Saint Petersburg

Georgia

Location Southeast
Area in square miles 58,876
Population 6,623,000
Principal products Lumber and other forest products, fruits, textiles, poultry, cotton, corn, peanuts
Geographic features Coastal plain, Blue Ridge Mountains in the Northeast
Capital Atlanta
Largest cities Atlanta, Columbus, Savannah, Macon

Hawaii

Location Mid-Pacific Ocean, not contiguous to the mainland 48 states
Area in square miles 6,450
Population 1,135,000
Principal products Sugar, pineapple, tropical fruits, clothing
Geographic feature Volcanic mountains
Capital Honolulu
Largest cities Honolulu, Hilo

Idaho

Location Northwest
Area in square miles 83,557
Population 1,039,000
Principal products Potatoes, silver, antimony, lead, cobalt, grains, sugar beets, livestock
Geographic features Plains in the South, mountains in the central and northern regions
Capital Boise
Largest cities Boise, Pocatello, Idaho Falls

Illinois

Location North central
Area in square miles 83,557
Population 11,543,000
Principal products Machinery, electric and electronic equipment, grains, vegetables, livestock, farm implements
Geographic features Prairie and fertile plains, hills in the South
Capital Springfield
Largest cities Chicago, Rockford, Peoria, Springfield

Indiana

Location North central
Area in square miles 36,291
Population 5,610,000
Principal products Iron, steel, petroleum products, automobile parts, limestone, grains, livestock, vegetables
Geographic features Plains, with hills in the South
Capital Indianapolis
Largest cities Indianapolis, Fort Wayne, Gary, Evansville

Iowa

Location Midwest
Area in square miles 56,290
Population 2,795,000
Principal products Grains, livestock, tires, agricultural equipment, food products, lumber
Geographic feature Prairie
Capital Des Moines
Largest cities Des Moines, Cedar Rapids, Davenport, Sioux City

Kansas

Location Midwest
Area in square miles 82,264
Population 2,495,000
Principal products Grains, livestock, oil, salt, zinc, lead, aircraft, processed foods
Geographic feature Prairie
Capital Topeka
Largest cities Wichita, Kansas City, Topeka

Kentucky

Location East central
Area in square miles 40,395
Population 3,713,000
Principal products Tobacco, horses, alcoholic beverages, textiles, clothing, electric equipment
Geographic features Mountains in the East, hills in the North, flatlands in the central region
Capital Frankfort
Largest cities Louisville, Lexington, Owensboro

Louisiana

Location South
Area in square miles 48,523
Population 4,252,000
Principal products Oil, natural gas, sulfur, rice, sugarcane, pecans, salt, chemicals, lumber
Geographic features Mississippi delta in the South, coastal plain, hills in the Northeast
Capital Baton Rouge
Largest cities New Orleans, Baton Rouge, Shreveport, Lafayette

Maine

Location New England
Area in square miles 33,215

Population 1,235,000
Principal products Potatoes, berries, apples, wood products, fish
Geographic features Sandy seacoast, mountains elsewhere
Capital Augusta
Largest cities Portland, Lewiston, Bangor

Maryland

Location Middle Atlantic
Area in square miles 10,577
Population 4,860,000
Principal products Seafood, chickens, vegetables, sand, gravel, electronic equipment
Geographic features Coastal plain, mountains in the West
Capital Annapolis
Largest cities Baltimore, Rockville, Hagerstown

Massachusetts

Location New England
Area in square miles 8,257
Population 5,996,000
Principal products Machinery, electric and electronic equipment, vegetables, poultry, cranberries
Geographic features Coastal plain, with hills in the West
Capital Boston
Largest cities Boston, Worcester, Springfield, New Bedford, Cambridge

Michigan

Location North central
Area in square miles 58,216
Population 9,368,000
Principal products Motor vehicles, cereals, machine tools, iron, copper, fruits, sugar beets, salt, lumber, furniture
Geographic features Lower Peninsula: flatlands in the South, hills in the North; Upper Peninsula: flatlands in the East, hills in the West
Capital Lansing
Largest cities Detroit, Grand Rapids, Warren, Flint, Lansing

Minnesota

Location North central
Area in square miles 84,068
Population 4,433,000
Principal products Iron, grains, machinery, plastics, processed foods
Geographic features Plains in the South and Northwest, hills in the Northeast
Capital St. Paul
Largest cities Minneapolis, St. Paul, Duluth, Bloomington

Mississippi

Location South
Area in square miles 47,716
Population 2,592,000

Principal products Lumber, furniture, cotton, clothing, soybeans, rice
Geographic features Coastal delta, prairie in the central region, hills in the Northeast, prairie in the Northwest
Capital Jackson
Largest cities Jackson, Biloxi, Hattiesburg

Missouri

Location Midwest
Area in square miles 69,686
Population 5,158,000
Principal products Aerospace equipment, shoes, beer, livestock, timber, soybeans, grains
Geographic features Prairie in the North, hills in the South
Capital Jefferson City
Largest cities St. Louis, Kansas City, Springfield, Independence

Montana

Location Northwest
Area in square miles 147,138
Population 808,000
Principal products Lumber, plywood, copper, lead, zinc, livestock
Geographic features Hilly plains in the East, Rocky Mountains in the West
Capital Helena
Largest cities Billings, Great Falls, Butte, Missoula

Nebraska

Location Midwest
Area in square miles 77,227
Population 1,593,000
Principal products Grains, livestock, electric and electronic equipment, farm machinery
Geographic features Prairie, with hills in the North
Capital Lincoln
Largest cities Omaha, Lincoln, Grand Island

Nevada

Location West
Area in square miles 110,540
Population 1,284,000
Principal products Copper, oil, livestock
Geographic features Mountains in the West, desert in the East and South
Capital Carson City
Largest cities Las Vegas, Reno, Sparks, Carson City

New Hampshire

Location New England
Area in square miles 9,304
Population 1,105,000
Principal products Dairy products, poultry, vegetables, leather goods, machinery, plastics

Geographic features   Coastal plain, with White Mountains in the North
Capital   Concord
Largest cities   Manchester, Nashua, Concord, Portsmouth

New Jersey

Location   Middle Atlantic
Area in square miles   7,836
Population   7,760,000
Principal products   Chemicals, pharmaceuticals, petroleum products, machinery, vegetables
Geographic features   Coastal plain with Palisades in the East, mountains in the Northwest
Capital   Trenton
Largest cities   Newark, Jersey City, Paterson, Elizabeth, Trenton

New Mexico

Location   Southwest
Area in square miles   121,666
Population   1,548,000
Principal products   Machinery, lumber, potassium, copper, gold, silver, livestock, cotton
Geographic features   Plains in the East, Rocky Mountains in the central region, plateau in the West
Capital   Santa Fe
Largest cities   Albuquerque, Santa Fe, Las Cruces, Roswell

New York

Location   Middle Atlantic
Area in square miles   49,576
Population   18,058,000
Principal products   Textiles, printed matter, clothing, automobile and aircraft components, fruit, machinery, chemicals, vegetables, livestock, wine
Geographic features   Coastal plain, with Catskill and Adirondack Mountains in the North and center, plateau in the West
Capital   Albany
Largest cities   New York, Buffalo, Rochester, Yonkers, Syracuse

North Carolina

Location   South
Area in square miles   52,586
Population   6,737,000
Principal products   Machinery, electronic equipment, furniture, lumber, tobacco, textiles, corn, cotton
Geographic features   Coastal plain, with Blue Ridge and Great Smoky Mountains in the West
Capital   Raleigh
Largest cities   Charlotte, Raleigh, Greensboro, Winston-Salem

North Dakota

Location   North central
Area in square miles   70,665
Population   635,000

Principal products   Grains, coal, natural gas, metal fabrication, farm equipment
Geographic features   Prairie in the East, plateau in the West
Capital   Bismarck
Largest cities   Fargo, Bismarck, Grand Forks

Ohio

Location   Midwest
Area in square miles   41,222
Population   10,939,000
Principal products   Rubber, automobile and aircraft parts, steel, glass, soybeans, grains, livestock, coal
Geographic feature   Plains
Capital   Columbus
Largest cities   Cleveland, Columbus, Cincinnati, Toledo, Akron

Oklahoma

Location   Southwest
Area in square miles   69,919
Population   3,175,000
Principal products   Oil, meat, construction and oil equipment, wheat, cotton, peanuts
Geographic features   Plains, low mountains in the East
Capital   Oklahoma City
Largest cities   Oklahoma City, Tulsa, Lawton, Norman, Enid

Oregon

Location   West coast
Area in square miles   96,981
Population   2,922,000
Principal products   Lumber, fish, fruits, machinery, aluminum, fabricated metals, wood products
Geographic features   Mountains in the East and West, plains in the central region
Capital   Salem
Largest cities   Portland, Eugene, Salem, Medford

Pennsylvania

Location   Middle Atlantic
Area in square miles   45,333
Population   11,961,000
Principal products   Steel, machinery, coal, oil, natural gas, livestock, poultry, vegetables
Geographic features   Coastal plain in the East, Allegheny Mountains in the West
Capital   Harrisburg
Largest cities   Philadelphia, Pittsburgh, Erie, Allentown, Scranton, Reading

Rhode Island

Location   New England
Area in square miles   1,214
Population   1,004,000
Principal products   Jewelry, silverware, textiles, fish, electronic equipment, apples, potatoes
Geographic feature   Coastal plain

Capital   Providence
Largest cities   Providence, Warwick, Cranston, Pawtucket

South Carolina

Location   South
Area in square miles   31,055
Population   3,560,000
Principal products   Machinery, textiles, forest products, apparel, tobacco, fruits, cotton, peanuts
Geographic features   Coastal plain in the East, Blue Ridge Mountains in the West
Capital   Columbia
Largest cities   Columbia, Charleston, Greenville, Spartanburg

South Dakota

Location   North central
Area in square miles   77,047
Population   703,000
Principal products   Electric equipment, grains, livestock, lumber
Geographic features   Plains in the East, Black Hills in the West
Capital   Pierre
Largest cities   Sioux Falls, Rapid City, Aberdeen

Tennessee

Location   Southeast
Area in square miles   42,244
Population   4,953,000
Principal products   Machinery, chemicals, textiles, apparel, soybeans, grain, cotton, tobacco
Geographic features   Great Smoky Mountains in the East, plateau, then plains in the West, also Gulf coastal plain
Capital   Nashville
Largest cities   Memphis, Nashville, Knoxville, Chattanooga

Texas

Location   Southwest
Area in square miles   267,339
Population   17,348,000
Principal products   Machinery, transportation equipment, oil, natural gas, livestock, hides, sulfur, salt, cotton, chemicals, fruits, vegetables
Geographic features   Coastal plains, prairies in the East and central regions, Rocky Mountains in the West
Capital   Austin
Largest cities   Houston, Dallas, San Antonio, El Paso, Fort Worth

Utah

Location   West
Area in square miles   84,916
Population   1,770,000
Principal products   Oil, copper, silver, gold, metal products, foodstuffs, electrical and aerospace equipment

Geographic features   Rocky Mountains in the Northeast, salt flats in the West, plateau and Wasatch Mountains in the central region
Capital   Salt Lake City
Largest cities   Salt Lake City, Provo, Ogden, Orem

Vermont

Location   New England
Area in square miles   9,609
Population   567,000
Principal products   Computer equipment, granite, marble, livestock, dairy products, maple syrup, lumber
Geographic feature   Green Mountains throughout
Capital   Montpelier
Largest cities   Burlington, Rutland, Barre, Montpelier

Virginia

Location   Middle Atlantic
Area in square miles   40,817
Population   6,286,000
Principal products   Chemicals, textiles, tobacco, cotton, coal, lumber
Geographic features   Coastal plain, with Blue Ridge Mountains in the West
Capital   Richmond
Largest cities   Norfolk, Richmond, Virginia Beach, Newport News

Washington

Location   West coast
Area in square miles   68,192
Population   5,018,000
Principal products   Aircraft, lumber, fruits, livestock, ships, chemicals
Geographic features   Olympic Mountains in the West, Cascade Mountains in the East, lowland in the central region
Capital   Olympia
Largest cities   Seattle, Spokane, Tacoma, Bellevue, Everett

West Virginia

Location   East central
Area in square miles   24,181
Population   1,801,000
Principal products   Coal, steel, aluminum, lumber, chemicals, plastic and wood products
Geographic feature   Allegheny Mountains throughout
Capital   Charleston
Largest cities   Charleston, Huntington, Wheeling, Parkersburg

Wisconsin

Location North central
Area in square miles 56,154
Population 4,955,000
Principal products Milk, butter, cheese, automobiles, beets and other vegetables, beer, furniture, machinery
Geographic features Plains, with hills in the Southwest
Capital Madison
Largest cities Milwaukee, Madison, Green Bay, Racine, Kenosha

Wyoming

Location West
Area in square miles 97,914
Population 460,000
Principal products Oil, natural gas, petroleum products, wool, livestock, grains, meat, leather goods
Geographic features High plateau with Rocky Mountains in the West
Capital Cheyenne
Largest cities Casper, Cheyenne, Laramie, Rock Springs

UNITED STATES
AT A GLANCE

WORLD
AT A GLANCE

Abyssinia

(*See* **Ethiopia**)

Afghanistan

Location   Central Asia, bordered by Turkmenistan, Uzbekistan, and Tajikistan on the North, China on the East, Pakistan on the East and South, Iran on the West

Area   250,000 square miles

Population   16,400,000

Government   Republic, in transition

Largest cities   Kabul (capital), Kandahar, Herat

Languages   Pashto (Iranian), Dari Persian, Uzbek (Turkic)

Ethnic groups   Pashtoon 50%, Tajik 25%, Uzbek 9%, Hazara 9%

Religion   Muslim

Chief industries   Carpets, textiles, cement

Chief crops   Barley, corn, sugar, wheat, cotton, fruit, nuts

Minerals   Natural gas, copper, lead, coal, zinc, iron

Leading exports   Cotton, carpets, natural gas, fruits and nuts

Leading imports   Petroleum products, machinery, food products

Monetary unit   Afghani

Albania

Location   Balkan peninsula, bordered by Yugoslavia on the North and East, Macedonia on the East, Greece on the South; on the East coast of the Adriatic

Area   11,100 square miles

Population   3,300,000

Government   Republic

Largest cities   Tirane (capital), Durres, Vlorë

Language   Albanian

Ethnic groups   Albanian 95%, Greek 2.5%

Religions   Muslim, Greek Orthodox, Roman Catholic

Chief industries   Textiles, timber, chemicals, construction materials

Chief crops   Corn, cotton, tobacco, wheat, sugar beets, potatoes, fruits

Minerals   Chrome, copper, coal, oil

Leading exports   Minerals, fuels, tobacco, foodstuffs

Leading imports   Machinery, foodstuffs, minerals

Monetary unit   Lek

Algeria

Location   North Africa, bordered on the West by Morocco, on the East by Tunisia and Libya, on the South by Mauritania, Mali, and Niger

Area 919,595 square miles
Population 26,000,000
Government Republic; military rule
Largest cities Algiers (capital), Oran, Constantine, Annaba, Setif
Languages Arabic, Berber, French
Ethnic groups Arab 75%, Berber 25%
Religion Muslim (state religion)
Chief industries Petrochemicals, steel, textiles, fertilizers, plastics
Chief crops Wheat, barley, grapes, fruits, olives
Minerals Oil, natural gas, iron, mercury, zinc
Leading exports Oil, gas
Leading imports Food, consumer goods
Monetary unit Dinar

Andorra

Location Southwestern Europe on southern slope of the eastern Pyrenees, between France and Spain
Area 179 square miles
Population 55,000
Government Principality; co-princes are the President of France and the Bishop of the See of Urgel in Spain
Largest city Andorra la Vella (capital)
Languages Catalan, French, Spanish
Ethnic groups Catalan 61%, Spanish 30%, Andorran 6%, French 3%
Religion Roman Catholic
Chief industries Tobacco products, tourism
Chiet crops Tobacco, fruits
Mineral Mineral water
Leading export Hydroelectric power
Leading import Foodstuffs
Monetary units French franc and Spanish peseta

Angola

Location Southwest Africa on the Atlantic Coast, bordered on the North and East by Zaire, on the East by Zambia, Namibia on the South
Area 481,350 square miles
Population 8,900,000
Government Republic
Largest city Luanda (capital)
Languages Portuguese, Bantu
Ethnic groups Ovimbundu 38%, Kimbundu 23%, Bakongo 13%, European 1%, Mestizo 2%
Religions Roman Catholic, Protestant, Animist
Chief industries Oil, diamond mining, fish processing, cement
Chief crops Coffee, sisal, bananas, cotton, corn
Minerals Diamonds, copper, phosphates, oil, sulphur, manganese
Leading exports Diamonds, oil, coffee, fish products
Leading imports Machinery, electrical equipment, clothing, food
Monetary unit Kwanza

Antigua and Barbuda

Location Eastern Caribbean Sea, about 30 miles North of Guadaloupe

Area 170 square miles
Population 100,000
Government Constitutional monarchy, with the Queen of England as the sovereign, a cabinet, and a parliament
Largest city St. John's (capital)
Language English
Ethnic group Antiguan
Religion Christian, predominantly Church of England
Chief industries Tourism, manufacturing
Chief crops Cotton, fruit, vegetables
Leading exports Petroleum products, manufactures
Leading imports Food, fuel, machinery
Monetary unit East Caribbean dollar

Argentina

Location Southern South America, bordered by Chile on the West, Bolivia and Paraguay on the North, Brazil and Uruguay on the East
Area 1,070,000 square miles
Population 32,600,000
Government Republic
Largest cities Buenos Aires (capital), Cordobar, Rosario, Mendoza
Language Spanish
Ethnic groups European descent 85%, Indian, Mestizo
Religion Roman Catholic
Chief industries Meat processing, cement, motor vehicles, textiles, chemicals
Chief crops Wheat, corn, cotton, beef cattle, grapes, sugar, tobacco, rice
Minerals Oil, lead, zinc, iron, copper, tin
Leading exports Meats, grains, hides and skins, industrial products
Leading imports Machinery, steel, fuel
Monetary unit Austral

Armenia

Location Formerly in the U.S.S.R., bordered by Georgia on the North, Azerbaijan on the East, Iran on the South, Turkey on the West
Area 11,500 square miles
Population 3,376,000
Government Republic
Largest cities Yerevan (capital), Kumayri, Kirovakan
Language Armenian
Ethnic groups Armenian 88%, Azerbaijani 6%
Religion Mostly Christian
Chief industries Mining, chemicals
Chief crops Cotton, figs, grain
Minerals Copper, zinc, molybdenum
Leading exports Data not available
Leading imports Data not available
Monetary unit Ruble, pending Armenian currency

Australia

Location South Pacific Ocean
Area 2,966,200 square miles

Population   17,800,000
Government   Democratic, federal state system. Parliamentary government with the Queen of England as the sovereign, an elected Prime Minister, and a parliament
Largest cities   Canberra (capital), Sydney, Melbourne, Brisbane, Adelaide, Perth
Languages   English, aboriginal languages
Ethnic groups   European 95%, Asian 4%, Aborigine 1.5%
Religions   Anglican, Roman Catholic, other Protestant
Chief industries   Machinery, steel, textiles, chemicals, motor vehicles
Chief crops   Wheat, barley, oats, corn, cattle, wool, meat, sugar, fruits, vegetables
Minerals   Gold, iron, bauxite, zinc, oil, uranium, coal, lead, nickel, tin, tungsten
Leading exports   Wool and other agricultural products, ores, coal
Leading imports   Machinery, consumer goods
Monetary unit   Australian dollar

Austria

Location   Central Europe, bordered by Switzerland and Liechtenstein on the West, the Czech Republic on the North, Hungary on the East, Slovenia and Italy on the South
Area   32,374 square miles
Population   7,900,000
Government   Federal Republic, Parliamentary Democracy
Largest cities   Vienna (capital), Graz, Linz, Salzburg
Language   German
Ethnic groups   German 98%, Slovene, Croatian
Religion   Roman Catholic
Chief industries   Steel, chemicals, machinery, paper and pulp
Chief crops   Grains, livestock, sugar beets
Minerals   Iron, oil, magnesite, aluminum, coal, lignite, copper
Leading exports   Iron, steel, machinery, textiles, lumber
Leading imports   Automobiles, foodstuffs, petroleum products
Monetary unit   Schilling

Azerbaijan

Location   Formerly in the U.S.S.R., bordered by Russia and Georgia on the North, Iran on the South, Armenia on the West, the Caspian Sea on the East
Area   33,400 square miles
Population   7,000,000
Government   Republic
Largest cities   Baku (capital), Gyandzha, Sumgait
Language   Azeri, Turkish, Russian
Ethnic groups   Azerbaijanis 83%, Russians and Armenians
Religion   Mostly Muslim
Chief industries   Oil refining, heavy machinery, building materials
Chief crops   Grain, cotton, rice, silk, tobacco

Minerals   Iron, copper, lead, zinc
Leading exports   Data not available
Leading imports   Data not available
Monetary unit   Ruble, pending Azerbaijan currency

Bahamas

Location   Atlantic Ocean, 50 miles East of the United States
Area   5,380 square miles
Population   255,000
Government   Commonwealth, with parliamentary system, with the Queen of England as the sovereign, an elected parliament, and a prime minister
Largest city   Nassau (capital)
Language   English
Ethnic groups   Black 85%, White including British, Canadian, American
Religions   Anglican, Baptist, Roman Catholic
Chief industries   Tourism, rum, pharmaceuticals, banking
Chief crops   Fruits, vegetables
Mineral   Salt
Leading exports   Fish, pharmaceuticals, rum
Leading imports   Food, fuels, manufactured goods
Monetary unit   Bahamian dollar

Bahrain

Location   Persian Gulf, off the coast of Saudi Arabia
Area   262 square miles
Population   500,000
Government   Emirate
Largest city   Manama (capital)
Languages   Arabic, Persian, English, Urdu
Ethnic groups   Arab 73%, Iranian 6%, Indian, Pakistani 13%
Religion   Muslim
Chief industries   Oil refining, aluminum processing
Chief crops   Fruits, vegetables
Minerals   Oil, natural gas
Leading exports   Oil, aluminum, fish
Leading imports   Machinery, food, motor vehicles
Monetary unit   Dinar

Bangladesh

Location   Southern Asia, bordered by India on the West, North, and East and Burma on the Southeast
Area   55,598 square miles
Population   111,400
Government   Parliamentary Republic
Largest cities   Dacca (capital), Chittagong, Khulna
Languages   Bengali, English
Ethnic groups   Bangali 98%, Bihari tribes
Religions   Muslim, Hindu
Chief industries   Jute, textiles, leather goods manufacture, cement, fertilizers
Chief crops   Rice, jute, tea, sugar, grains
Minerals   Natural gas, uranium, timber
Leading exports   Jute goods, tea, leather goods
Leading imports   Foodstuffs, fuels, cotton
Monetary unit   Taka

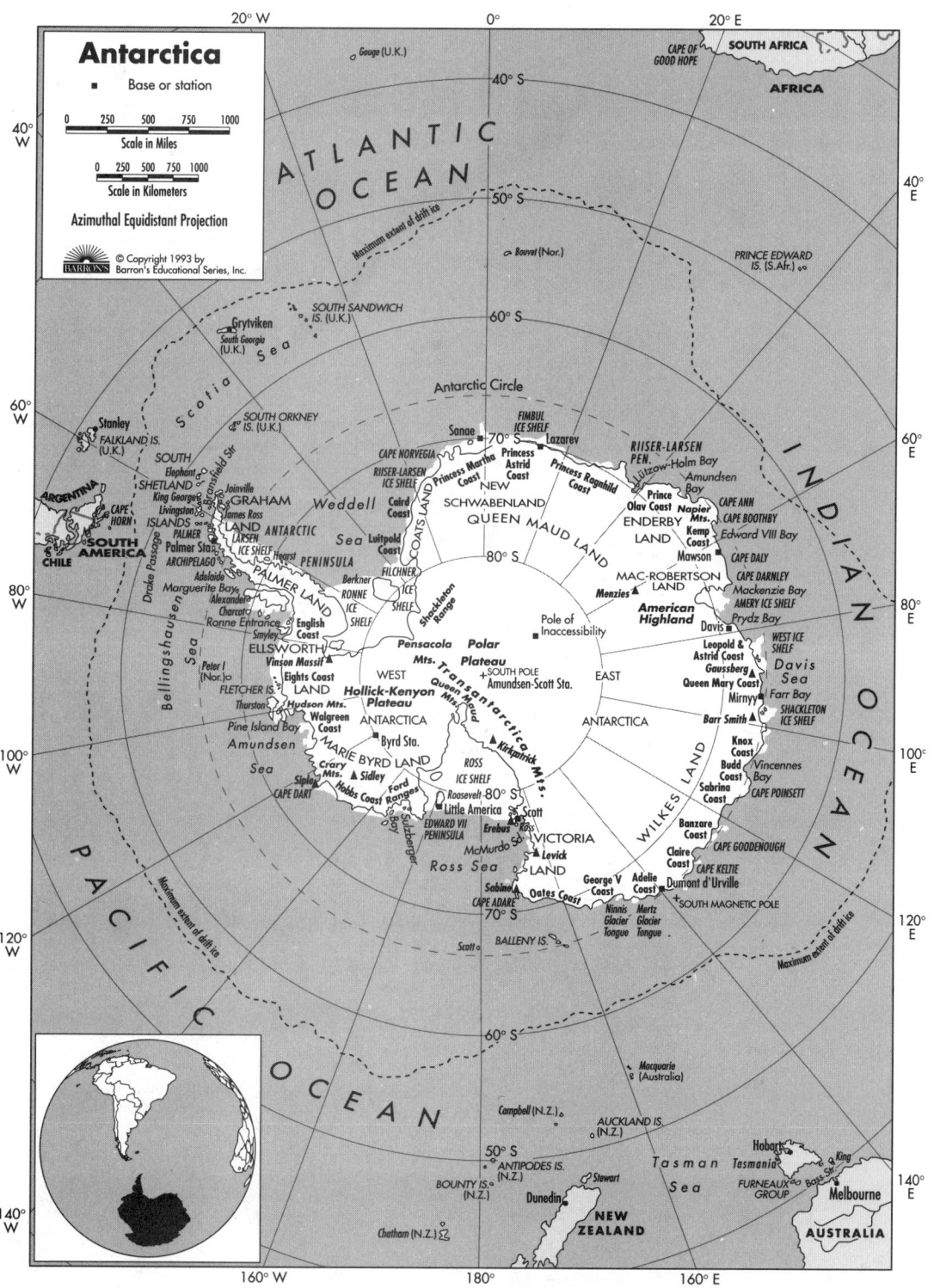

Antarctica

■ Base or station

Scale in Miles
Scale in Kilometers

Azimuthal Equidistant Projection

© Copyright 1993 by
Barron's Educational Series, Inc.

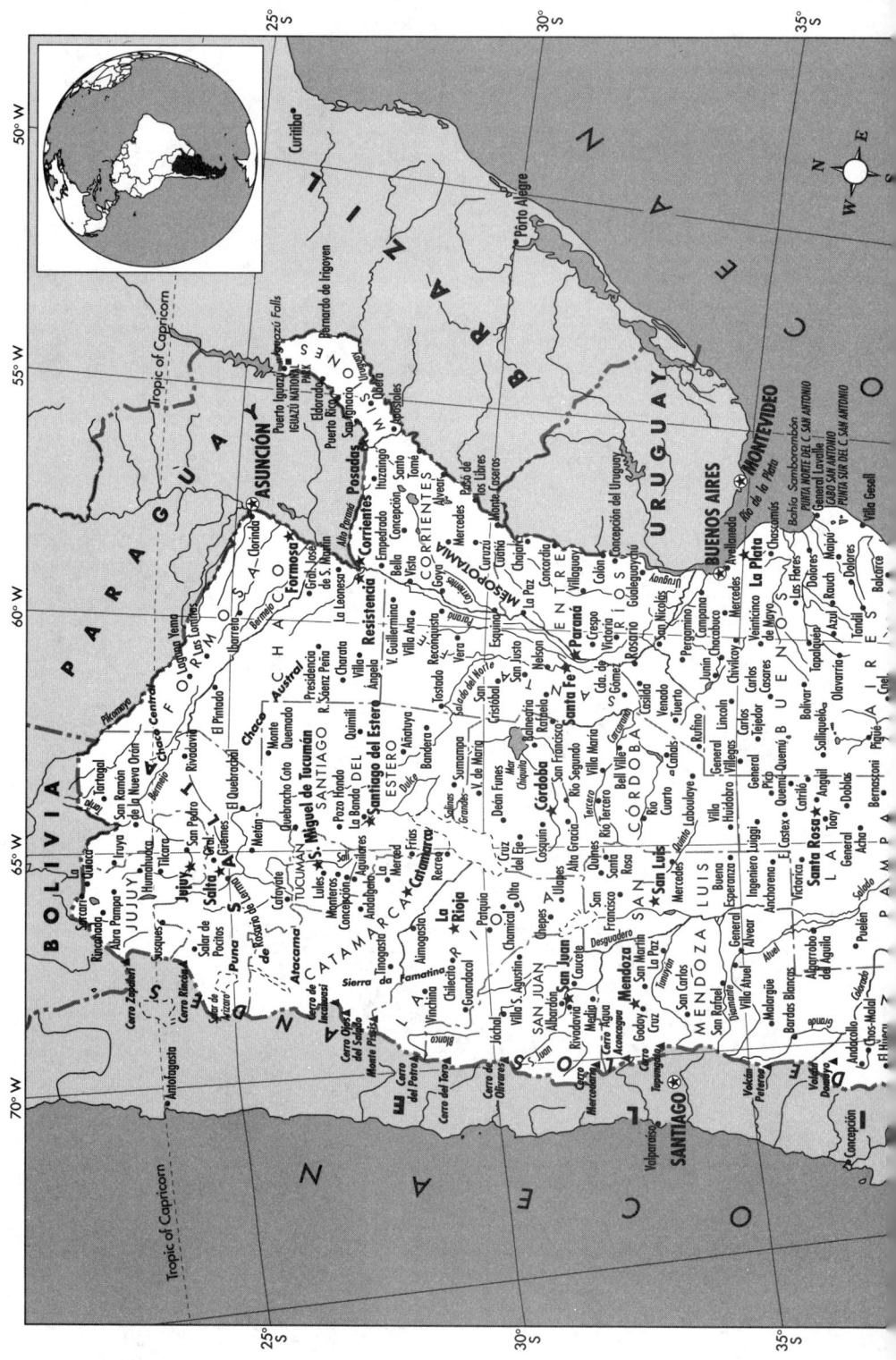

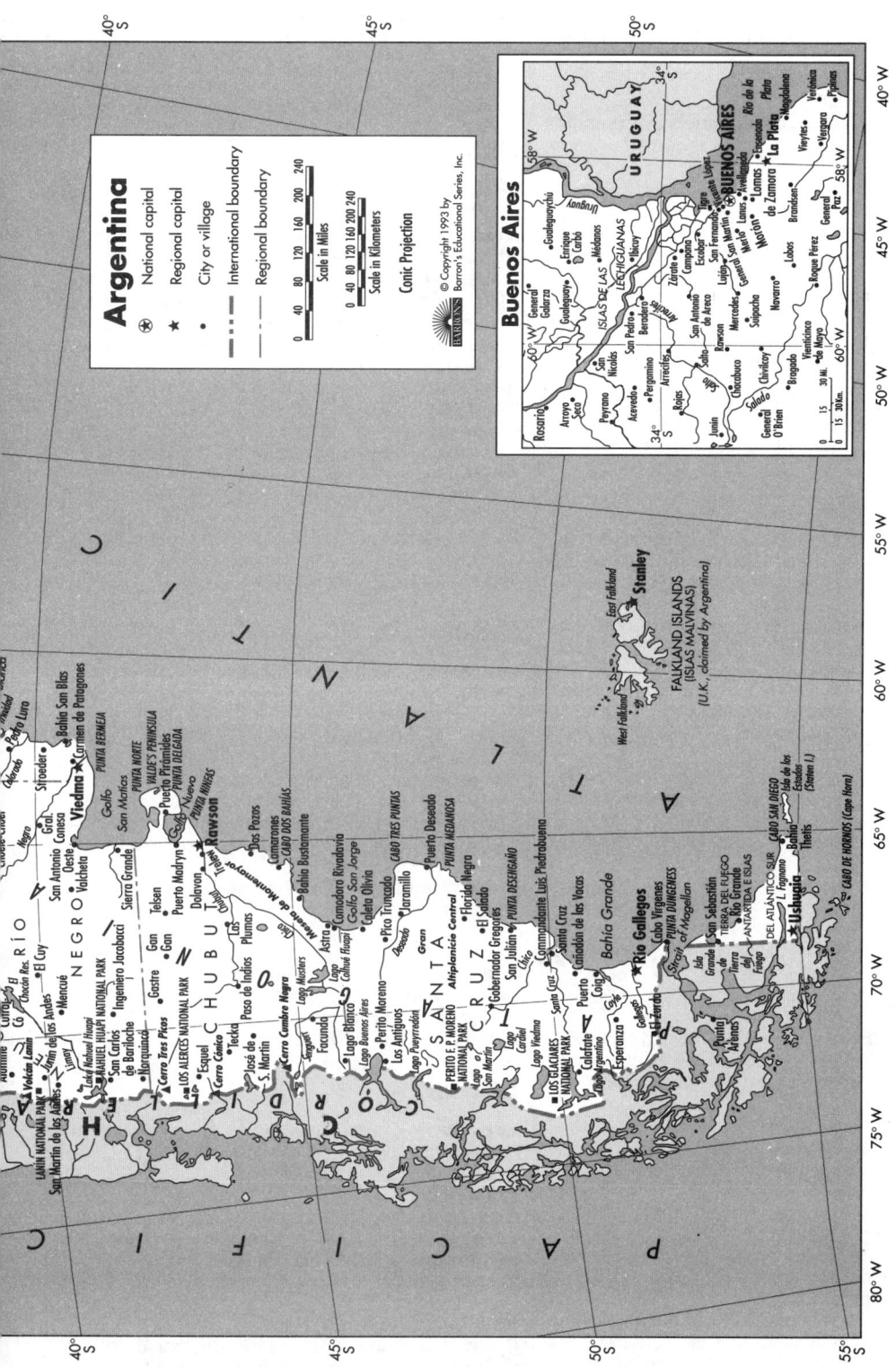

Barbados

Location   Atlantic Ocean, 300 miles North of Venezuela
Area   166 square miles
Population   300,000
Government   Independent nation in Commonwealth with a parliamentary system, with the Queen of England as the sovereign, an elected legislature, and a prime minister
Largest city   Bridgetown (capital)
Language   English
Ethnic groups   African 80%, mixed 16%, Caucasian 4%
Religions   Anglican, Methodist, Roman Catholic
Chief industries   Light manufacturing, sugar milling, tourism
Chief crops   sugarcane, foods, cotton
Mineral   Lime
Leading exports   Sugar, molasses, rum, textiles
Leading imports   Foods, machinery, oil
Monetary unit   Barbados dollar

Belarus

Location   Formerly in the U.S.S.R. as Byelorussia, bordered by Latvia and Lithuania on the North, Poland on the West, Ukraine on the South, Russia on the East
Area   80,200 square miles
Population   10,300,000
Government   Republic
Largest cities   Minsk (capital), Gomel, Vitebsk
Languages   Belarusian, Russian
Ethnic groups   Belarusian 78%, Russian 13%, Polish 4%
Religion   Eastern Orthodox
Chief industries   Agricultural machinery, textiles, chemical products
Chief crops   Potatoes, vegetables, flax, grains, sugar beets
Mineral   Limestone
Leading exports   Data not available
Leading imports   Data not available
Monetary unit   Ruble, pending Belarus currency

Belgium

Location   Northwest Europe, bordered by France on the West and South, Luxembourg on the Southeast, Germany on the East, the Netherlands on the North
Area   11,781 square miles
Population   10,000,000
Government   Constitutional monarchy with a parliamentary system
Largest cities   Brussels (capital), Ghent, Charleroi, Liège, Antwerp, Bruges
Languages   Flemish, French
Ethnic groups   Fleming 58%, Walloon 41%
Religion   Roman Catholic
Chief industries   Steel, glassware, textiles, chemicals, diamond cutting
Chief crops   Grains, flax, fruit, vegetables, potatoes, sugar beets

Mineral   Coal
Leading exports   Iron and steel, cut diamonds, textiles, glassware, chemicals
Leading imports   Motor vehicles, machinery, fuels
Monetary unit   Belgian franc

Belize

Location   Central America, bordered by Mexico on the North, Guatemala on the West and South
Area   8,867 square miles
Population   200,000
Government   Commonwealth with a parliamentary system, with the Queen of England as the sovereign, an elected parliament, and a prime minister
Largest cities   Belize City, Belmopan (capital)
Languages   English, Spanish, Creole
Ethnic groups   African, Mestizo, Maya, Creole
Religions   Roman Catholic, Methodist, Anglican
Chief industries   Processed foods, timber products including furniture, rum
Chief crops   Sugarcane, fruits, corn, rice
Leading exports   Sugar, molasses, lumber, fruits, fish, clothing
Leading imports   Fuels, foodstuffs, machinery, textiles
Monetary unit   Belize dollar

Benin

Location   West Africa, bordered by Togo on the West, Burkina Faso and Niger on the North, Nigeria on the East
Area   43,484 square miles
Population   5,000,000
Government   Republic
Largest cities   Cotonou, Porto-Novo (capital)
Languages   French, African languages
Ethnic groups   Fons, Adjas, Baribas, Yoruba
Religions   Animist, Christian, Muslim
Chief industries   Palm oil processing, textiles
Chief crops   Oil palms, peanuts, coffee, cotton, tobacco, corn, rice
Minerals   Lime, oil
Leading export   Palm products
Leading imports   Fuels, foodstuffs, consumer goods, machinery
Monetary unit   CFA franc

Bhutan

Location   Central Asia, bordered by India on the West and South, China on the North
Area   17,992 square miles
Population   1,600,000
Government   Monarchy
Largest city   Thimphu (capital)
Languages   Dzongkha, Nepali
Ethnic groups   Bhotia 60%, Nepalese 25%, Lepcha, Indian
Religions   Buddhist, Hindu
Chief industries   Mining, cement manufacture
Chief crops   Rice, grains, potatoes, fruit
Minerals   Dolomite, coal

Leading exports Fruits, timber, gypsum, cement, handicrafts
Leading imports Fuels, machinery, vehicles
Monetary unit Ngultrum

Bolivia

Location West central South America, bordered on the West by Peru and Chile, on the East by Brazil, on the South by Paraguay and Argentina
Area 424,165 square miles
Population 7,800,000
Government Republic
Largest cities Suere and La Paz (capitals), Santa Cruz, Cochabamba
Languages Spanish, Quechua, Aymara
Ethnic groups Quechua 30%, Aymara 25%, Mestizo 30%, European 14%
Religion Roman Catholic
Chief industries Petroleum refining, food processing, tin, textiles
Chief crops Potatoes, sugar, coffee, bananas, rice, corn, coca
Minerals Tin, antimony, bismuth, oil, copper, silver, tungsten, lead
Leading exports Tin, lead, zinc, silver, antimony
Leading imports Foodstuffs, machinery, consumer goods
Monetary unit Boliviano

Bosnia and Herzegovina

Location Formerly part of Yugoslavia, bordered by Croatia on the North, Croatia and the Adriatic Sea on the West, Yugoslavia on the South and East
Area 19,741 square miles
Population 4,300,000
Government Republic
Largest cities Sarajevo (capital), Banja Luka, Mostar (capital of Herzegovina)
Language Serbo-Croatian
Ethnic groups Muslim Slavs 43%, Serbian 31%, Croatian 17%
Religions Eastern Orthodox, Roman Catholic, Muslim
Chief industries Mining, timber products, leather goods
Chief crops Grains, sugar beets, fruit, cotton, tobacco
Minerals Coal, iron, bauxite, lead, zinc, mercury, manganese
Leading exports Data not available
Leading imports Data not available
Monetary unit Dinar

Botswana

Location South central Africa, bordered by Namibia on the North and West, South Africa on the South, Zimbabwe on the Northeast
Area 231,800 square miles
Population 1,400,000
Government Republic, Parliamentary Democracy
Largest city Gaborone (capital)
Languages English, Tswana
Ethnic groups Tswana, Kalanga

Religions Animist, Christian
Chief industries Processing of diamonds, copper, nickel, salt
Chief crops Livestock, sorghum, corn, peas, beans
Minerals Diamonds, copper, nickel, salt, coal
Leading exports Diamonds, cattle, copper, nickel
Leading imports Foodstuffs, textiles, machinery, petroleum products
Monetary unit Pula

Brazil

Location Eastern half of South America, bordered by every nation on the continent except Chile and Ecuador
Area 3,286,470 square miles
Population 151,000,000
Government Federal Republic
Largest cities Cirainflex, Brasilia (capital) São Paulo, Rio de Janeiro, Belo Horizonte, Recife, Porto Alegre, Salvador
Languages Portuguese, English, German, Italian
Ethnic groups European descent, African descent, Mulatto, Indians, Arabs, Japanese
Religion Roman Catholic
Chief industries Steel, automobiles, chemicals, appliances, petrochemicals
Chief crops Coffee, cotton, soybeans, sugar, cocoa, oranges, livestock
Minerals Iron, manganese, gold, uranium, diamonds, coal, chromium, bauxite
Leading exports Coffee, cocoa, soybeans, sugar, beef, industrial products, transport equipment
Leading imports Oil, grains, machinery, chemical products, coal
Monetary unit Novo Cruzado

Brunei Darussalam

Location North coast of the island of Borneo, bordered on landward sides by Sarawak
Area 2,226 square miles
Population 300,000
Government Sultanate
Largest city Bandar Seri Begawan (capital)
Languages Malay, Chinese, English
Ethnic groups Malay, Chinese
Religions Muslim, Buddhist, Christian
Chief industry Oil
Chief crops Rice, bananas, cassava
Minerals Oil, natural gas
Leading exports Oil, liquified natural gas
Leading imports Machinery, foodstuffs, manufactured goods
Monetary unit Brunei dollar

Bulgaria

Location Eastern Balkan peninsula, bordered by Yugoslavia on the West, Romania on the North, Turkey on the South
Area 42,823 square miles
Population 8,900,000
Government Republic

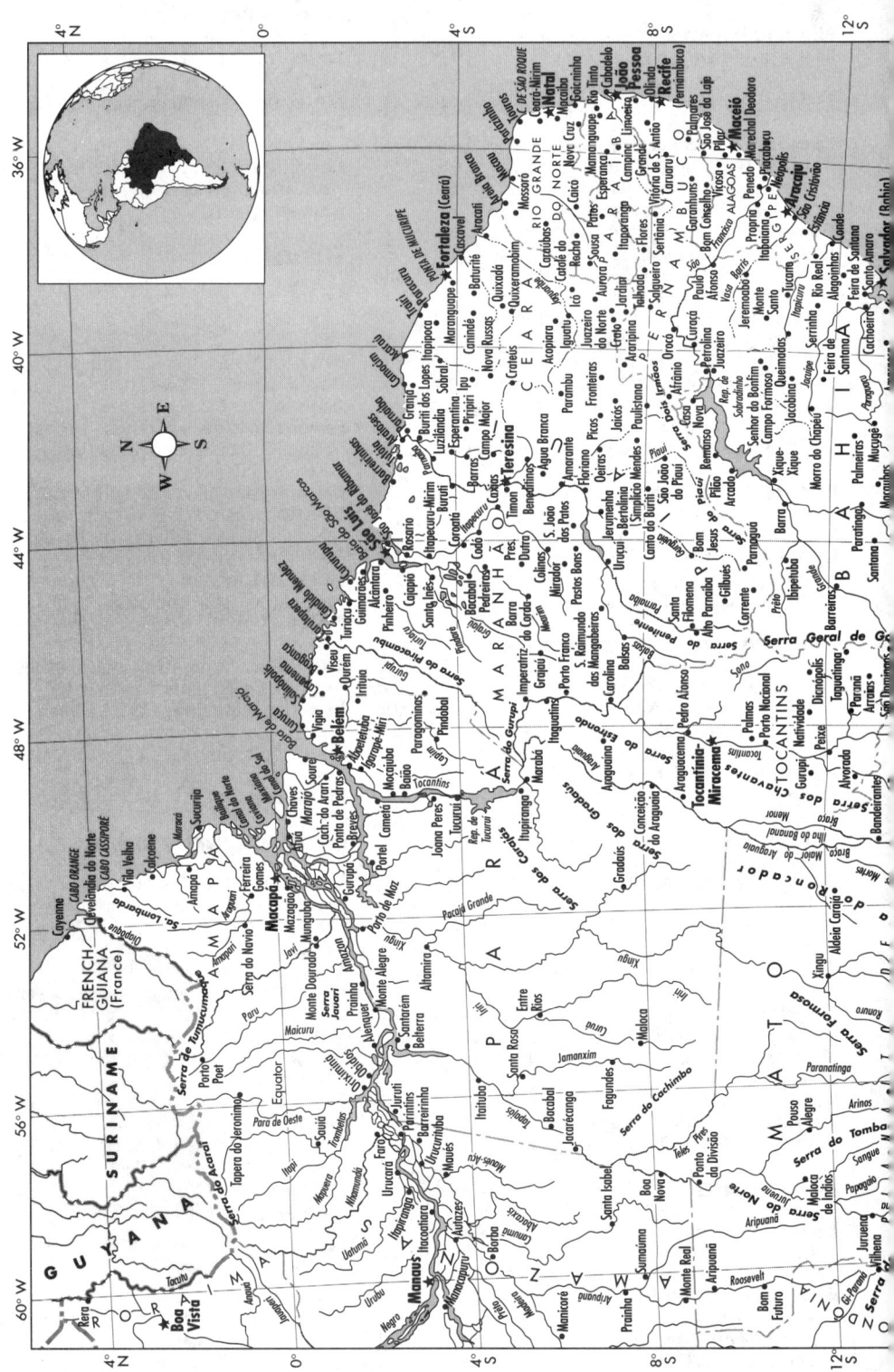

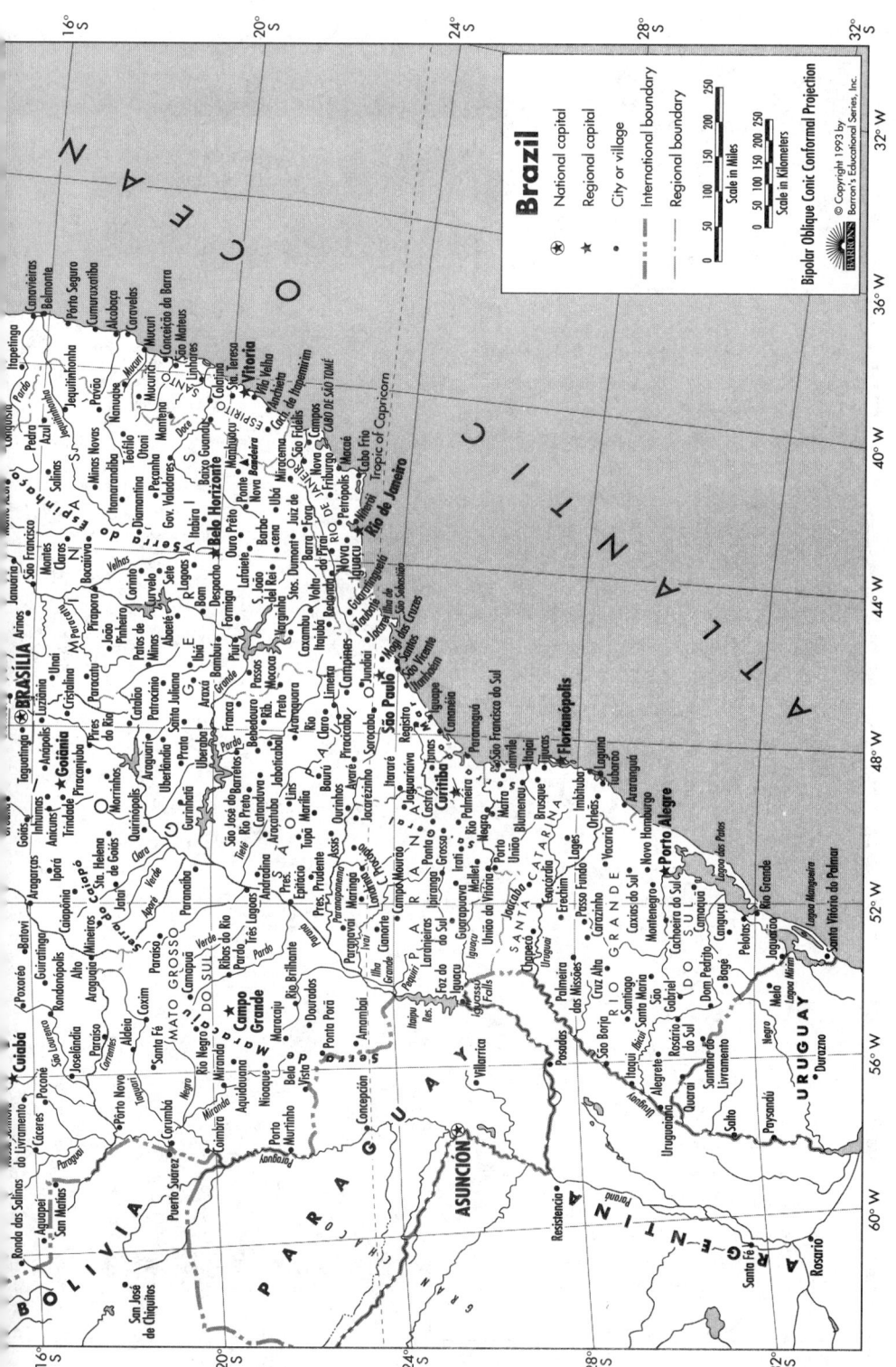

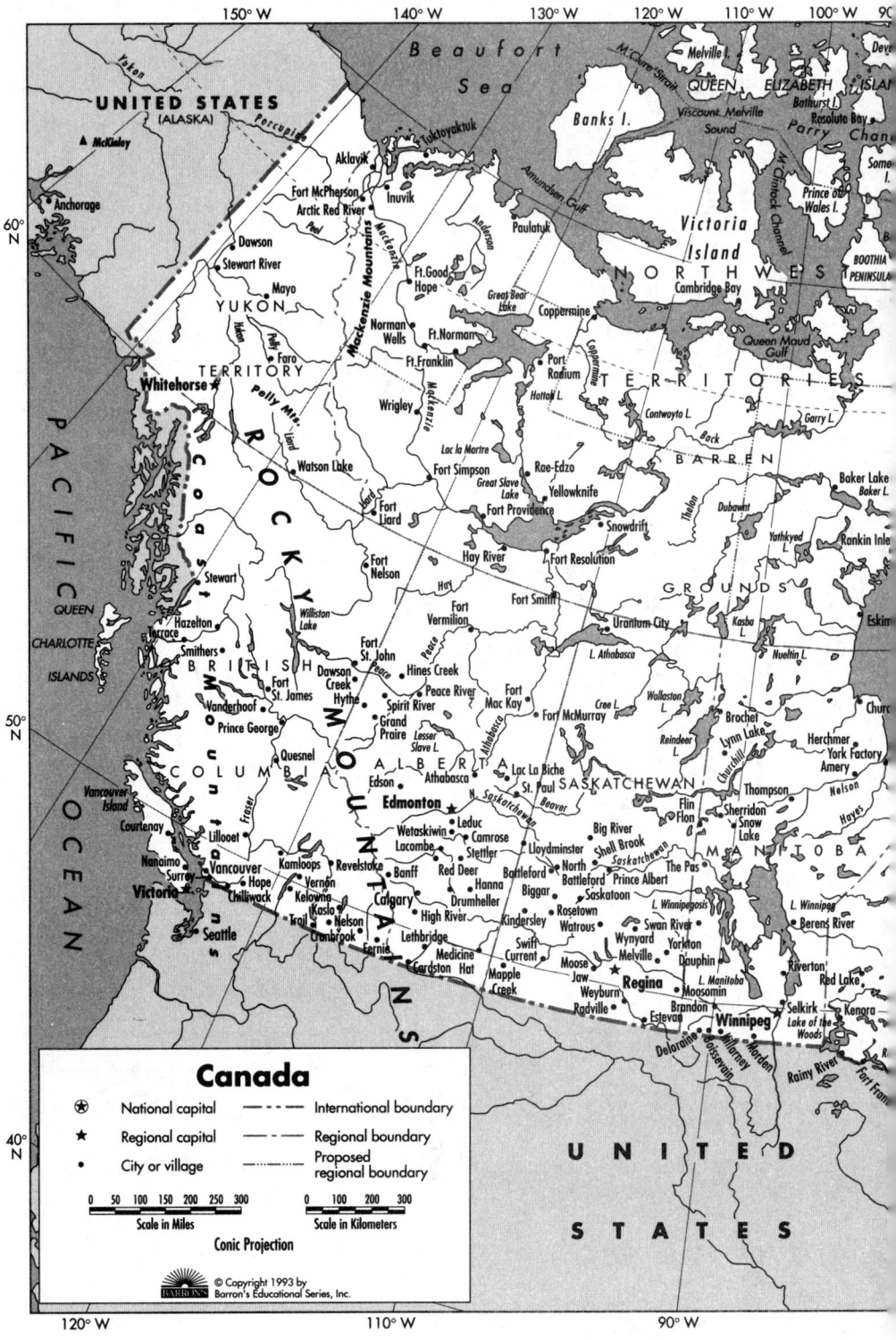

Canada

✪	National capital	—·—·—	International boundary
★	Regional capital	—··—··—	Regional boundary
•	City or village	·········	Proposed regional boundary

0 50 100 150 200 250 300
Scale in Miles

0 100 200 300
Scale in Kilometers

Conic Projection

© Copyright 1993 by
Barron's Educational Series, Inc.

Queen Elizabeth Islands

WORLD AT A GLANCE

Largest cities   Sofia (capital), Plovdiv, Varna, Ruse
Languages   Bulgarian, Turkish
Ethnic groups   Bulgarian 85%, Turk 8.5%
Religions   Eastern Orthodox, Muslim
Chief industries   Chemicals, machinery, metals, textiles
Chief crops   Grains, fruit, corn, potatoes, tobacco
Minerals   Lead, coal, oil, manganese, lignite
Leading exports   Machinery, minerals, transport equipment, agricultural products
Leading imports   Machinery, fuels, raw materials, metals
Monetary unit   Lev

Burkina Faso

Location   Western Africa, South of the Sahara, bordered by Mali and Niger on the North, Benin, Togo, Ghana, and the Ivory Coast on the South
Area   105,869 square miles
Population   9,500,000
Government   Military, in transition to republic
Largest cities   Ouagadougou (capital), Bobo-Dioulasso
Languages   French, Sudanic tribal languages
Ethnic groups   Voltaic groups (Mossi, Bobo, Lobi, Gurunsi), Mande groups (Samo, Marka, Boussance, Dioula)
Religions   Animist, Muslim, Roman Catholic
Chief industries   Agriculture, light manufacturing
Chief crops   Millet, sorghum, rice, peanuts, sugarcane, cotton
Minerals   Manganese, gold, limestone, bauxite, copper
Leading exports   Livestock, peanuts, cotton, oilseeds
Leading imports   Textiles, food, machinery, fuels
Monetary unit   CFA franc

Burma

(*See* **Myanmar**)

Burundi

Location   East central Africa, bordered by Rwanda on the North, Zaire on the West, Tanzania on the East
Area   10,747 square miles
Population   5,800,000
Government   Republic
Largest city   Bujumbura (capital)
Languages   French, Kirundi, Swahili
Ethnic groups   Hutu 85%, Tutsi 14%, Twa (Pygmy) 1%
Religions   Roman Catholic, Animist
Chief industries   Agriculture, fishing
Chief crops   Coffee, cotton, tea
Mineral   Nickel
Leading exports   Coffee, cotton, tea
Leading imports   Foodstuffs, petroleum products, consumer goods
Monetary unit   Burundi franc

Cambodia (Kampuchea)

Location   Southeast Asia, bordered by Thailand and Laos on the North and Vietnam on the East and South
Area   69,898 square miles
Population   8,000,000
Government   Coalition government, in transition
Largest city   Phnom Penh (capital)
Language   Khmer, French
Ethnic groups   Khmer 90%, Vietnamese, Chinese
Religions   Buddhist, Animist
Chief industries   Agriculture, forestry, textiles, cement
Chief crops   Rice, rubber, corn, sugar
Minerals   Iron, manganese, copper
Leading exports   Rubber, rice, wood
Leading imports   Foodstuffs, fuel, machinery
Monetary unit   Riel

Cameroon

Location   West Africa, bordered by Nigeria on the North, Chad and the Central African Republic on the East, Congo, Gabon, and Equatorial Guinea on the South
Area   183,569 square miles
Population   12,000,000
Government   Republic, one-party presidential regime
Largest cities   Douala, Yaounde (capital)
Languages   French, English, Bantu, Sudanic
Ethnic group   Bantu
Religions   Christian, Animist, Muslim
Chief industries   Aluminum processing, agriculture, small manufacturing
Chief crops   Coffee, cocoa, peanuts, tea, cotton, bananas, tobacco
Minerals   Bauxite, oil
Leading exports   Cocoa, coffee, lumber, aluminum, oil
Leading imports   Consumer goods, transport equipment, fuel, machinery
Monetary unit   CFA franc

Canada

Location   North America, bordered by the United States on the South and West
Area   3,851,809 square miles
Population   27,000,000
Government   Commonwealth with a parliamentary system, with the Queen of England as sovereign, an elected parliament, and a prime minister
Largest cities   Toronto, Montreal, Vancouver, Ottawa (capital), Winnipeg, Edmonton, Calgary, Quebec
Languages   English, French
Ethnic groups   European descent, Amerindian
Religions   Roman Catholic, Protestant
Chief industries   Manufacturing, mining, agriculture, forestry
Chief crops   Beef cattle, wheat, milk, barley, corn, vegetables, fruits
Minerals   Nickel, zinc, copper, gold, petroleum, natural gas, iron, uranium

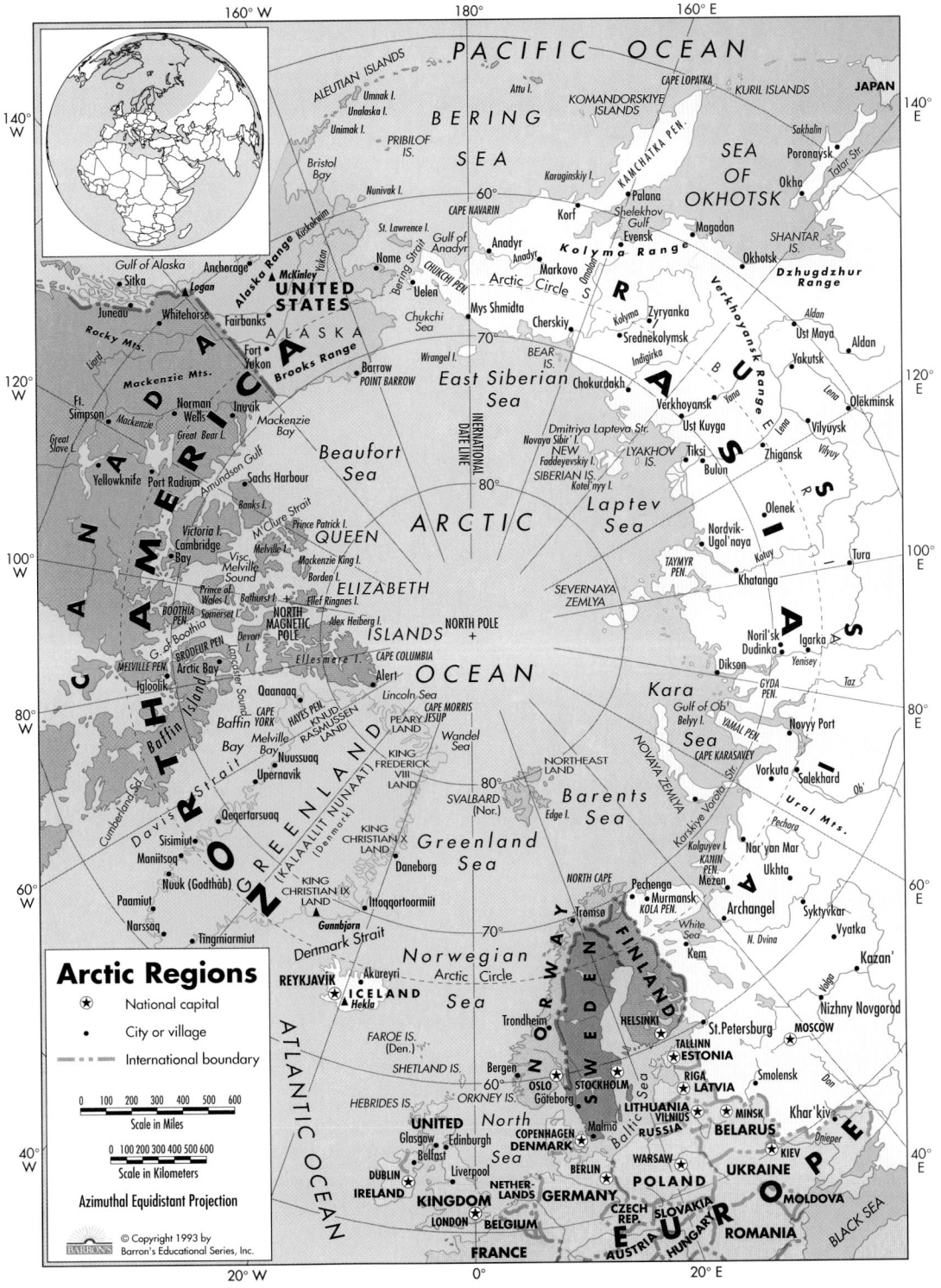

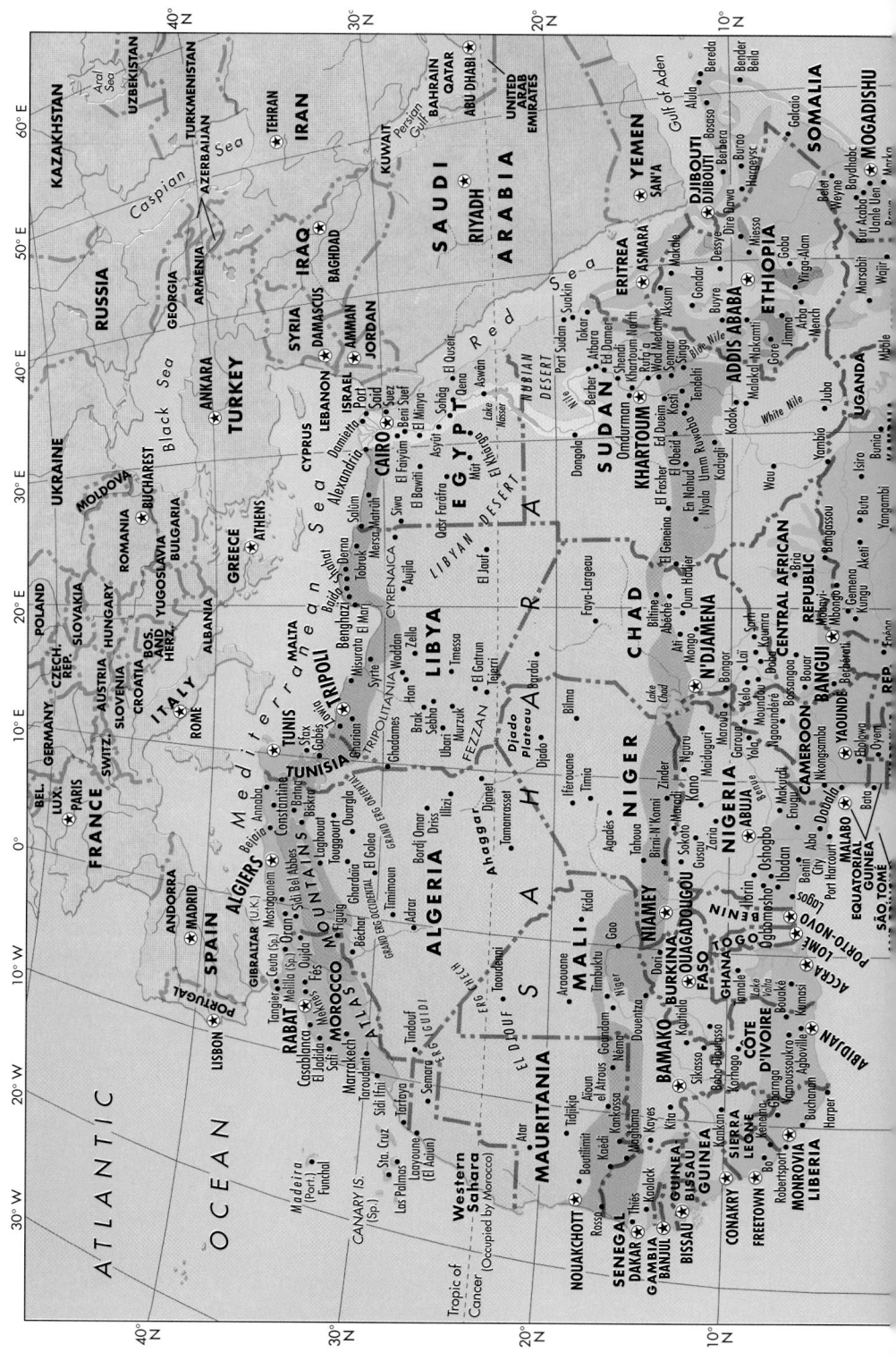

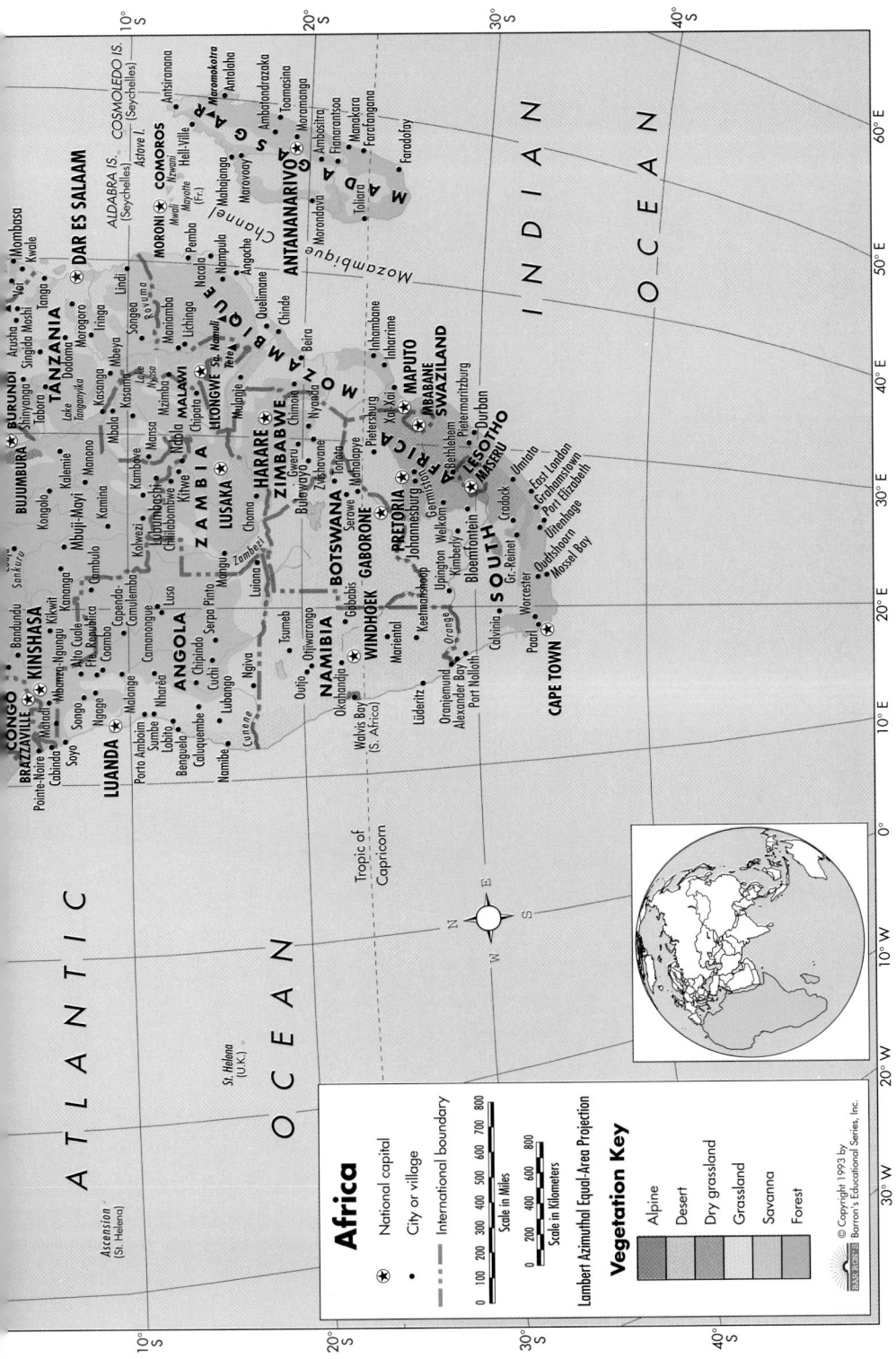

Africa

⊛ National capital
• City or village
–·–·– International boundary

Scale in Miles
0 100 200 300 400 500 600 700 800

Scale in Kilometers
0   200   400   600   800

Lambert Azimuthal Equal-Area Projection

Vegetation Key

Alpine
Desert
Dry grassland
Grassland
Savanna
Forest

© Copyright 1993 by
Barron's Educational Series, Inc.

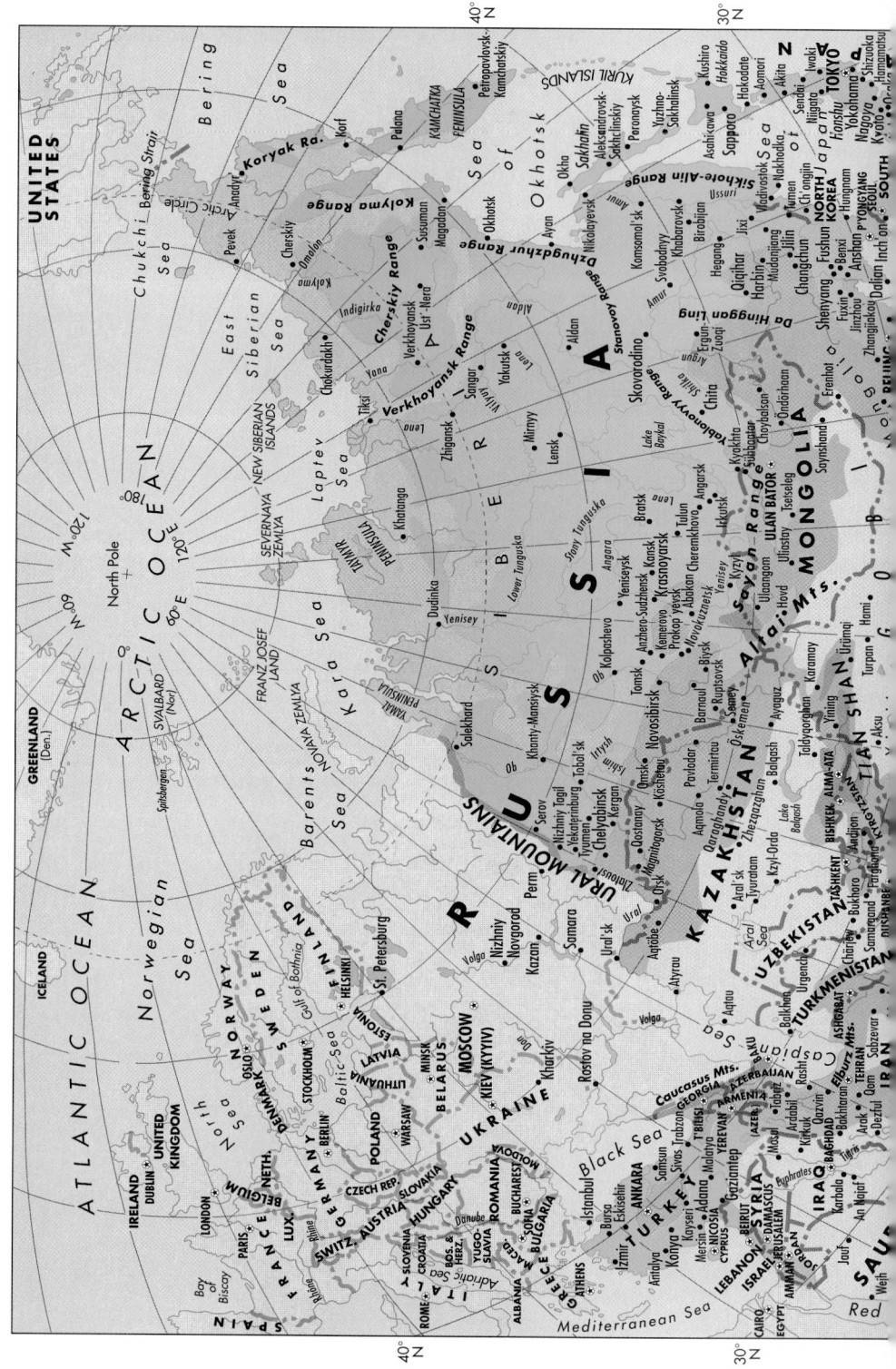

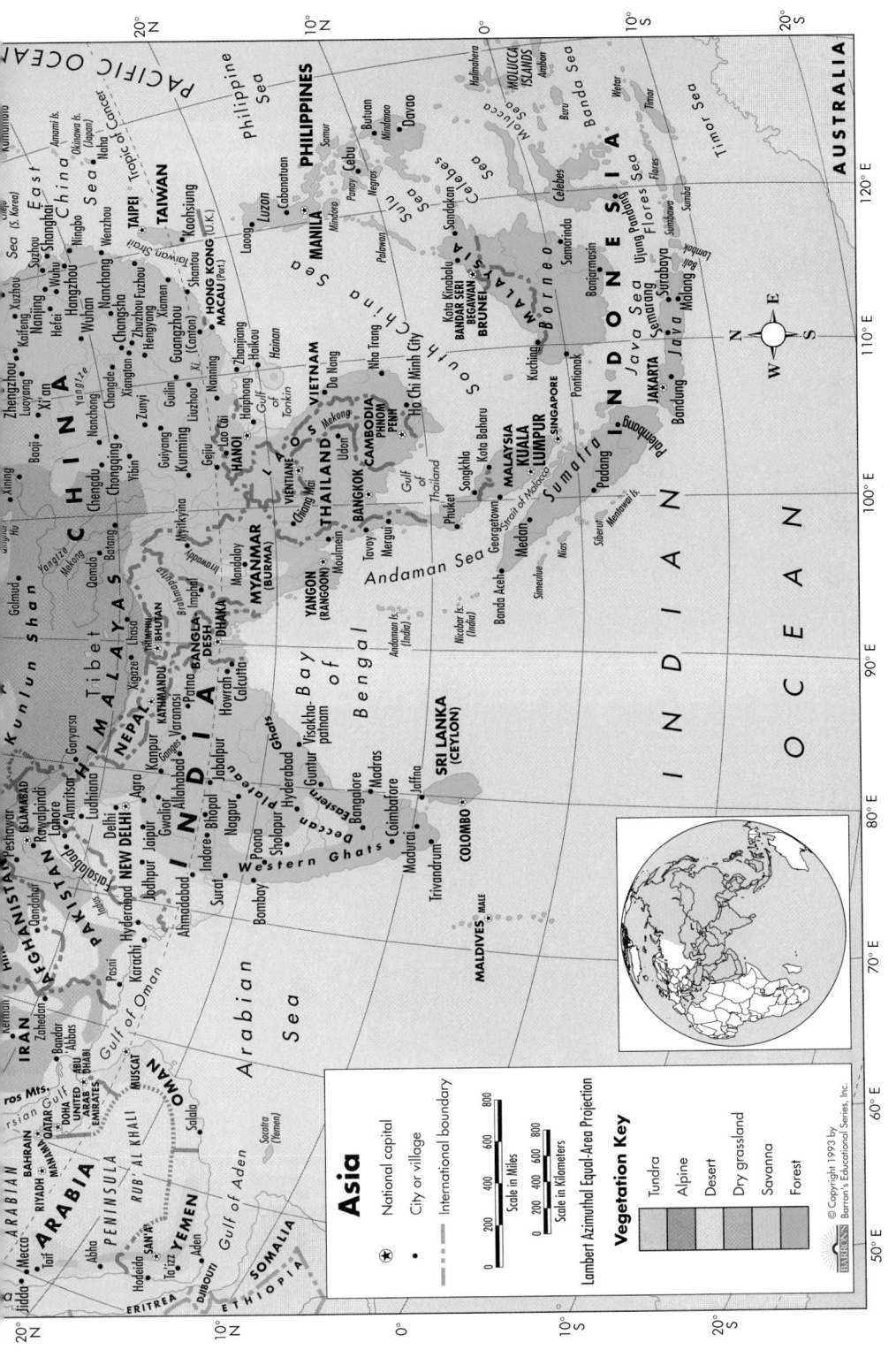

Asia

✦ National capital
• City or village
- — International boundary

Scale in Miles
0   200   400   600   800

Scale in Kilometers
0   200 400 600 800

Lambert Azimuthal Equal-Area Projection

Vegetation Key

Tundra
Alpine
Desert
Dry grassland
Savanna
Forest

© Copyright 1993 by
Barron's Educational Series, Inc.

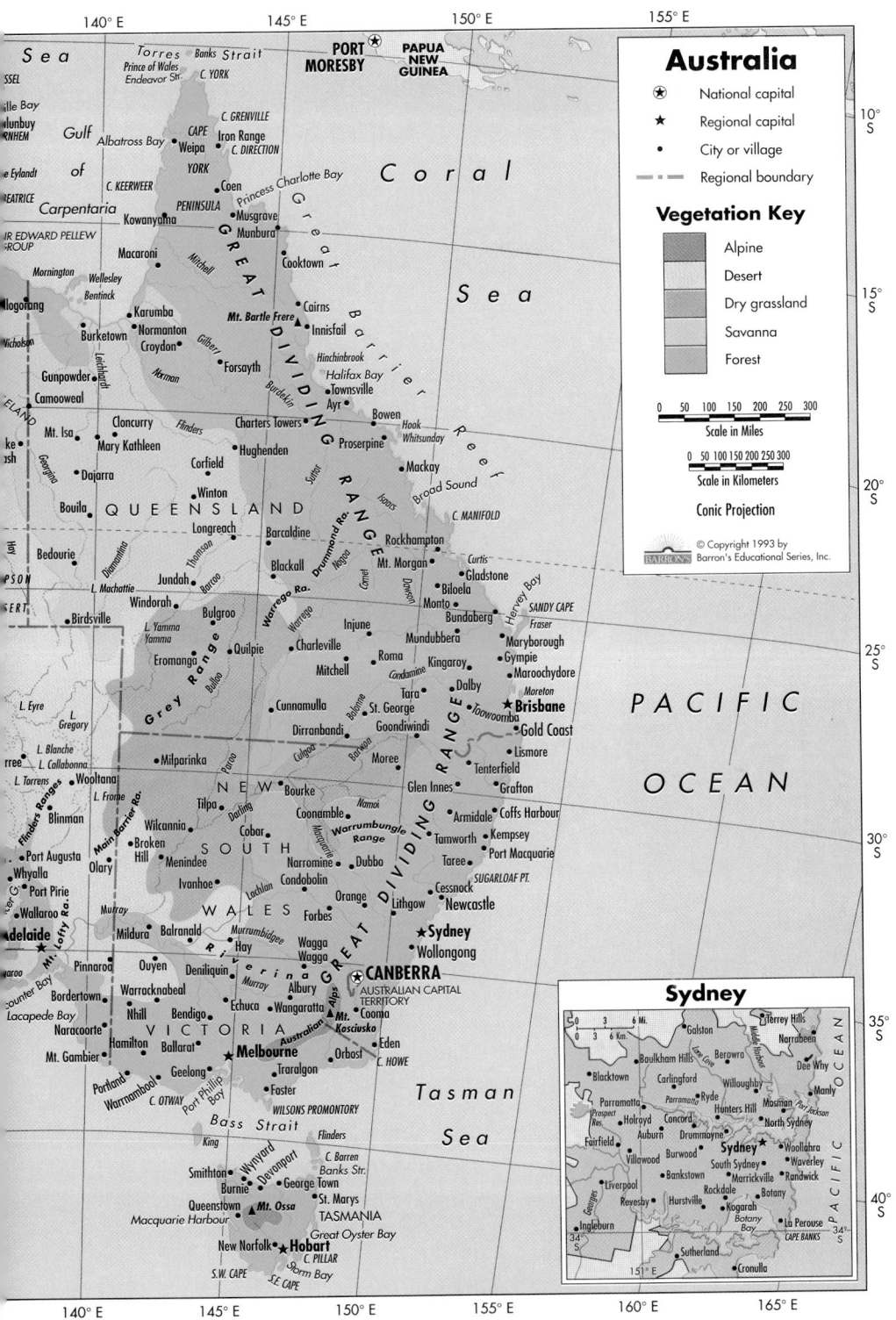

Australia

⊛ National capital
★ Regional capital
• City or village
–·–·– Regional boundary

Vegetation Key

Alpine
Desert
Dry grassland
Savanna
Forest

0 50 100 150 200 250 300
Scale in Miles

0 50 100 150 200 250 300
Scale in Kilometers

Conic Projection

© Copyright 1993 by
Barron's Educational Series, Inc.

Sydney

Europe

Vegetation Key

⊛ National capital

• City or village

- - - International boundary

	Ice and snow
	Tundra
	Alpine
	Desert
	Dry grassland
	Grassland
	Forest

0   100   200   300   400
Scale in Miles

0   100 200 300 400
Scale in Kilometers

Polyconic Projection

© Copyright 1993 by
Barron's Educational Series, Inc.

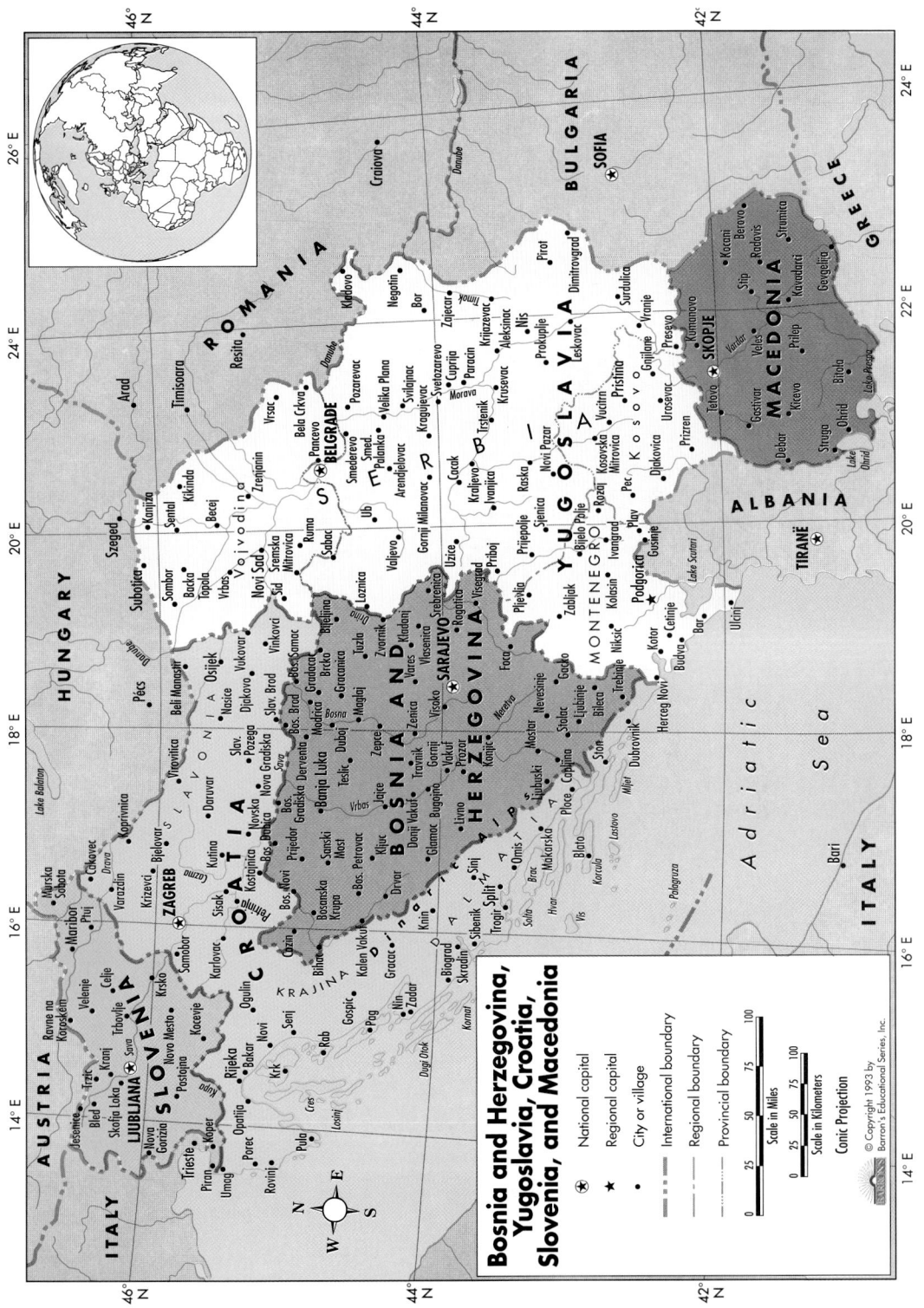

Bosnia and Herzegovina, Yugoslavia, Croatia, Slovenia, and Macedonia

⊛ National capital
★ Regional capital
• City or village

━ ━ ━ International boundary
─ ─ ─ Regional boundary
⋯⋯⋯ Provincial boundary

Scale in Miles
0 25 50 75 100

Scale in Kilometers
0 25 50 75 100

Conic Projection

© Copyright 1993 by
Barron's Educational Series, Inc.

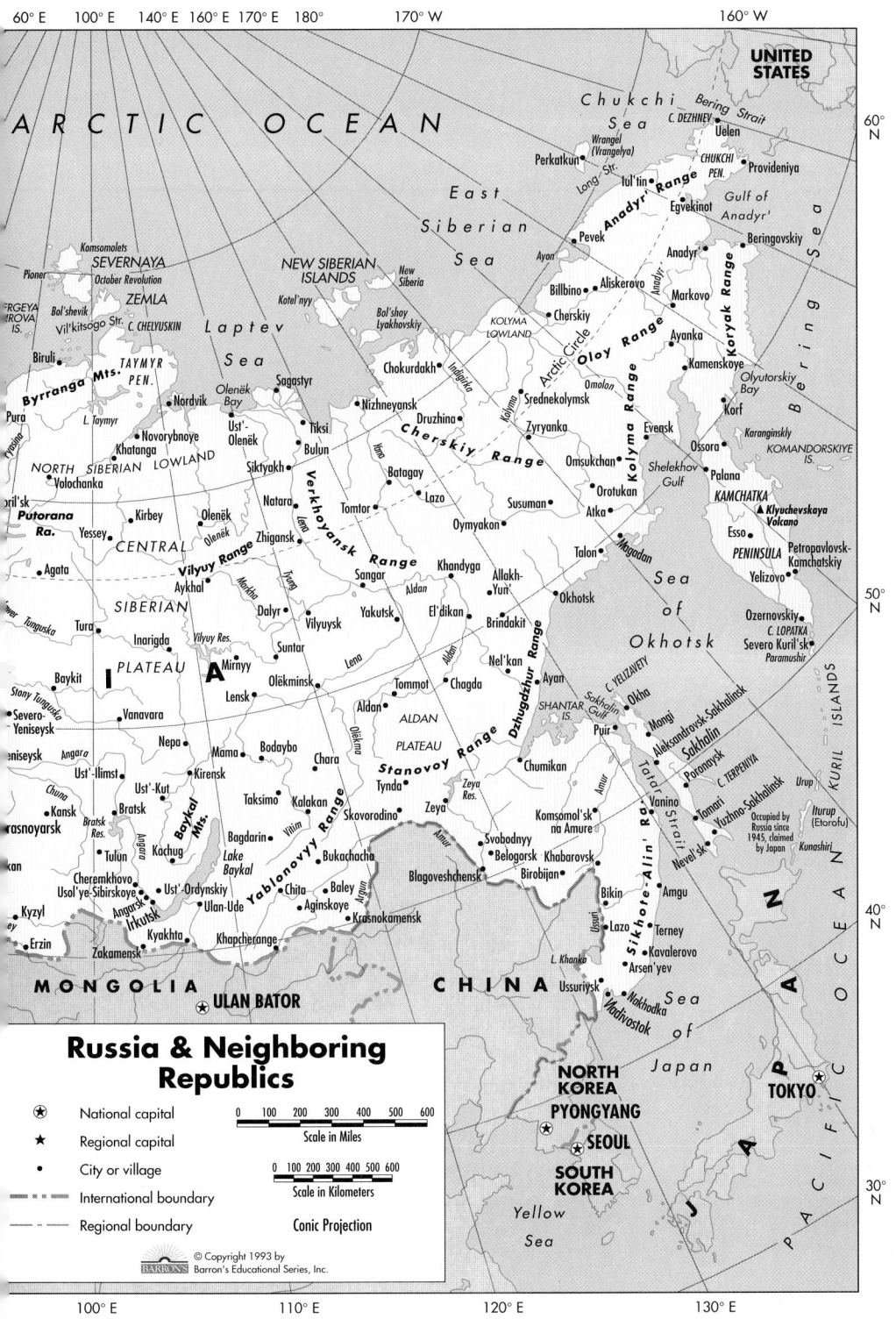

Russia & Neighboring Republics

⊛	National capital
★	Regional capital
•	City or village
—··—··—	International boundary
—·—·—	Regional boundary

0 100 200 300 400 500 600
Scale in Miles

0 100 200 300 400 500 600
Scale in Kilometers

Conic Projection

© Copyright 1993 by
Barron's Educational Series, Inc.

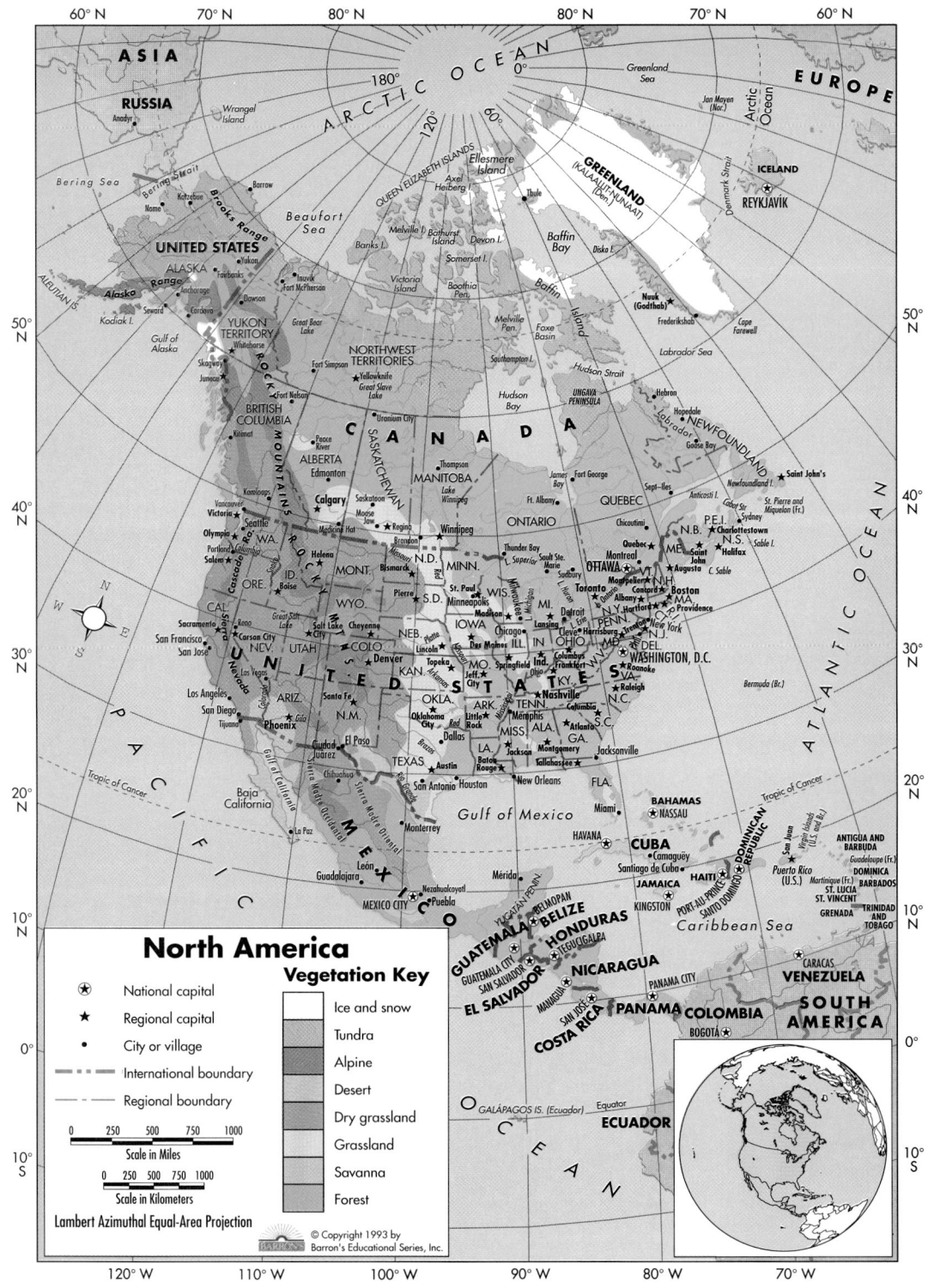

North America
Vegetation Key

⊛	National capital
★	Regional capital
•	City or village
▬·▬·▬	International boundary
▬·▬	Regional boundary

Scale in Miles
0 250 500 750 1000

Scale in Kilometers
0 250 500 750 1000

Lambert Azimuthal Equal-Area Projection

	Ice and snow
	Tundra
	Alpine
	Desert
	Dry grassland
	Grassland
	Savanna
	Forest

© Copyright 1993 by
Barron's Educational Series, Inc.

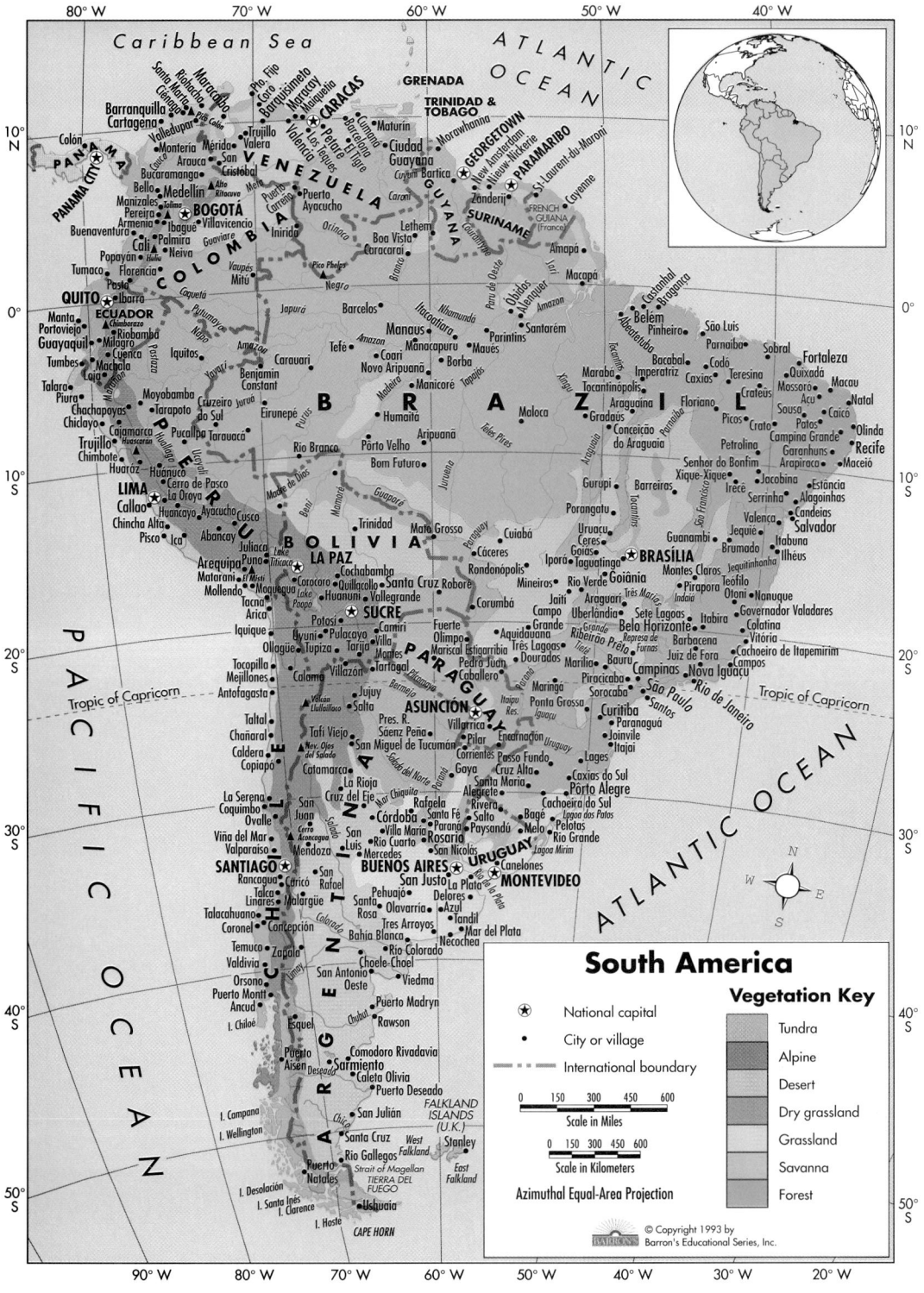

South America — Vegetation Key

- ⊛ National capital
- • City or village
- –·–·– International boundary

Scale in Miles
0 150 300 450 600

Scale in Kilometers
0 150 300 450 600

Azimuthal Equal-Area Projection

Vegetation Key
- Tundra
- Alpine
- Desert
- Dry grassland
- Grassland
- Savanna
- Forest

© Copyright 1993 by
Barron's Educational Series, Inc.

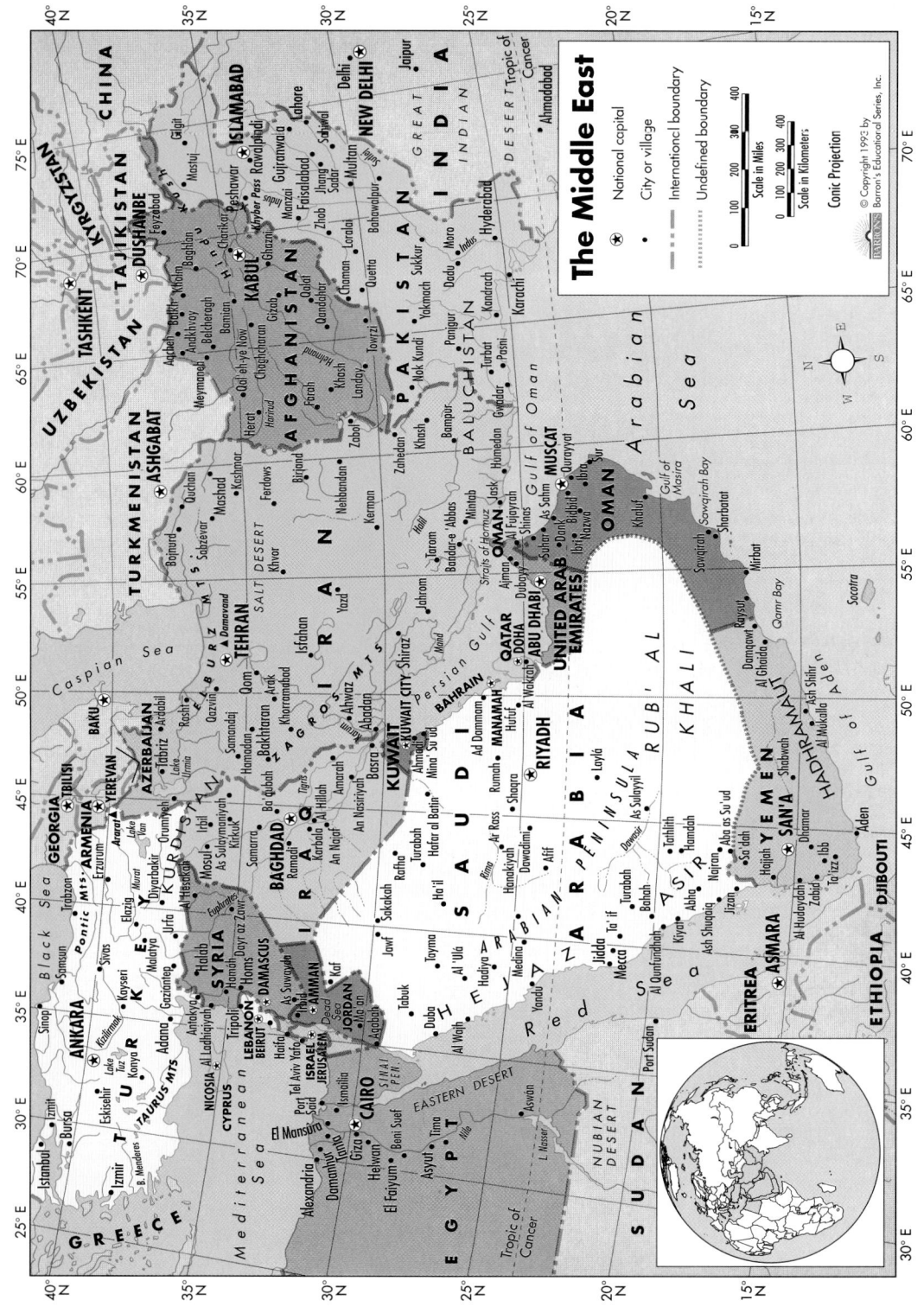

The Middle East

⊛ National capital
• City or village
International boundary
Undefined boundary

Scale in Miles
0   100   200   300   400

Scale in Kilometers
0   100   200   300   400

Conic Projection

© Copyright 1992 by
Barron's Educational Series, Inc.

Leading exports Manufactured goods, newsprint, wood, wheat, natural gas, ores, motor vehicles
Leading imports Electronic equipment, processed foods, chemical products, machinery
Monetary unit Canadian dollar

Cape Verde

Location Atlantic Ocean, off western tip of Africa
Area 1,557 square miles
Population 386,000
Government Republic
Largest cities Mindelo, Praia (capital)
Languages Portuguese, Crioulo
Ethnic groups Creole 71%, African 28%, European 1%
Religion Roman Catholic
Chief industries Agriculture, fishing, salt mining
Chief crops Bananas, coffee, sugarcane, corn, beans
Mineral Salt
Leading exports Fish, bananas, coffee, salt
Leading imports Fuel, foodstuffs, consumer goods
Monetary unit Escudo

Central African Republic

Location Central Africa, bordered by Cameroon on the West, Chad on the North, Sudan on the East, Congo and Zaire on the South
Area 240,530 square miles
Population 3,100,000
Government Republic, in transition from military rule
Largest city Bangui (capital)
Languages French, Sangho, Hansa, Swahili
Ethnic groups Banda 27%, Baya 34%, Mandia 21%, Sara 10%
Religions Protestant, Roman Catholic, Animist
Chief industries Agriculture, mining, light manufacturing, forestry, textiles
Chief crops Cotton, coffee, peanuts, corn, sorghum
Minerals Diamonds, uranium
Leading exports Diamonds, cotton, coffee, wood
Leading imports Machinery, textiles, petroleum products
Monetary unit CFA franc

Chad

Location North central Africa, bordered by Niger, Nigeria, Cameroon on the West, Libya on the North, Sudan on the East, Central African Republic on the South
Area 495,755 square miles
Population 5,200,000
Government Military
Largest city N'Djamena (capital)
Languages French, Arabic
Ethnic groups Sudanese Arab 30%, Sudanic tribes 25%, Nilotic, Saharan tribes
Religions Muslim, Animist, Christian
Chief industry Agriculture
Chief crops Cotton, sugar, peanuts, livestock
Minerals Oil, uranium, salt

Leading exports Cotton, cattle
Leading imports Machinery, petroleum products, food, motor vehicles
Monetary unit CFA franc

Chile

Location Western coast of southern South America, bordered on the North by Peru, on the East by Bolivia and Argentina
Area 292,250 square miles
Population 13,500,000
Government Republic
Largest cities Santiago (capital), Valparaiso, Concepción, Antofagasta
Language Spanish
Ethnic groups Mestizo 66%, Spanish 25%, Indian 5%
Religions Roman Catholic, Protestant
Chief industries Steel, textiles, wood products, mining
Chief crops Grains, sugar beets, potatoes beans, fruits
Minerals Copper, iron, nitrate, coal, iodine, cobalt, zinc
Leading exports Copper, iron ore, nitrates, wood products, fruits
Leading imports Machinery, chemical products, wheat, vehicles, fuels
Monetary unit Peso

China

Location East Asia, bordered on the North by Mongolia, Russia, Kazakhstan, Uzbekistan, and Kyrgyzstan, Afghanistan, Tajikistan, and Pakistan on the West, North Korea on the Northwest, India, Nepal, Bhutan, Burma, Laos, and Vietnam on the South
Area 3,700,000 square miles
Population 1,160,000,000
Government Marxist people's republic
Largest cities Shanghai, Beijing (capital), Tianjin, Canton, Wuhan, Shenyang
Language Mandarin and local dialects
Ethnic groups Chinese 94%, Mongol, Manchu, Korean
Religions Confucian, Buddhist, Taoism, officially atheist
Chief industries Iron and steel, plastics, agricultural implements, textiles, armaments
Chief crops Rice, grains, cotton, tea
Minerals Coal, iron, tungsten, antimony, oil, natural gas
Leading exports Oil, iron, steel, textiles, minerals
Leading imports Machinery, grains, fertilizers, industrial raw materials
Monetary unit Yuan

Colombia

Location Northwestern South America bordered by Panama on the North, Brazil and Venezuela on the East, Ecuador and Peru on the South
Area 439,730 square miles
Population 34,000,000

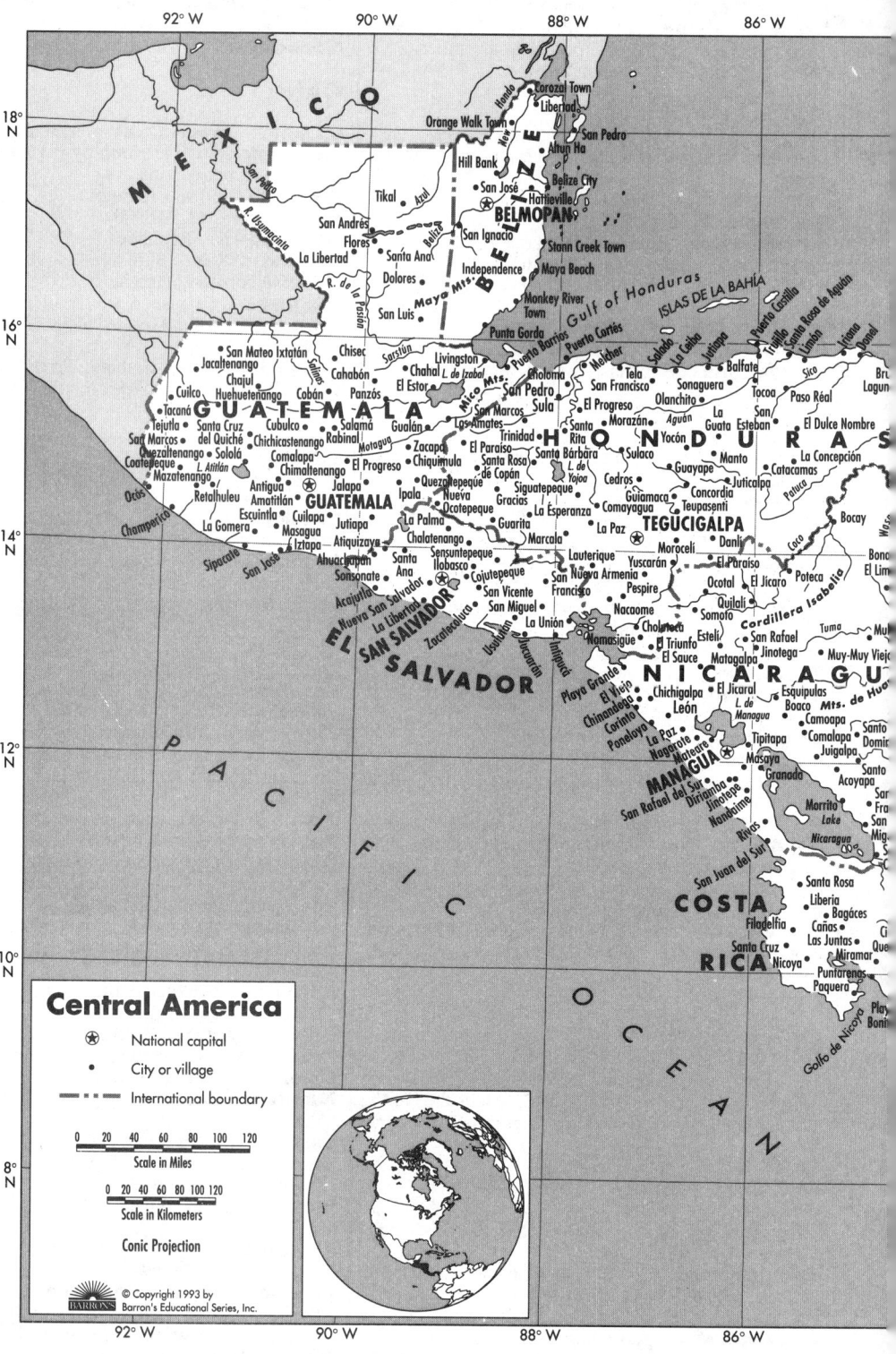

Central America

⊛   National capital

•   City or village

–··–··–   International boundary

0 20 40 60 80 100 120
Scale in Miles

0 20 40 60 80 100 120
Scale in Kilometers

Conic Projection

© Copyright 1993 by
Barron's Educational Series, Inc.

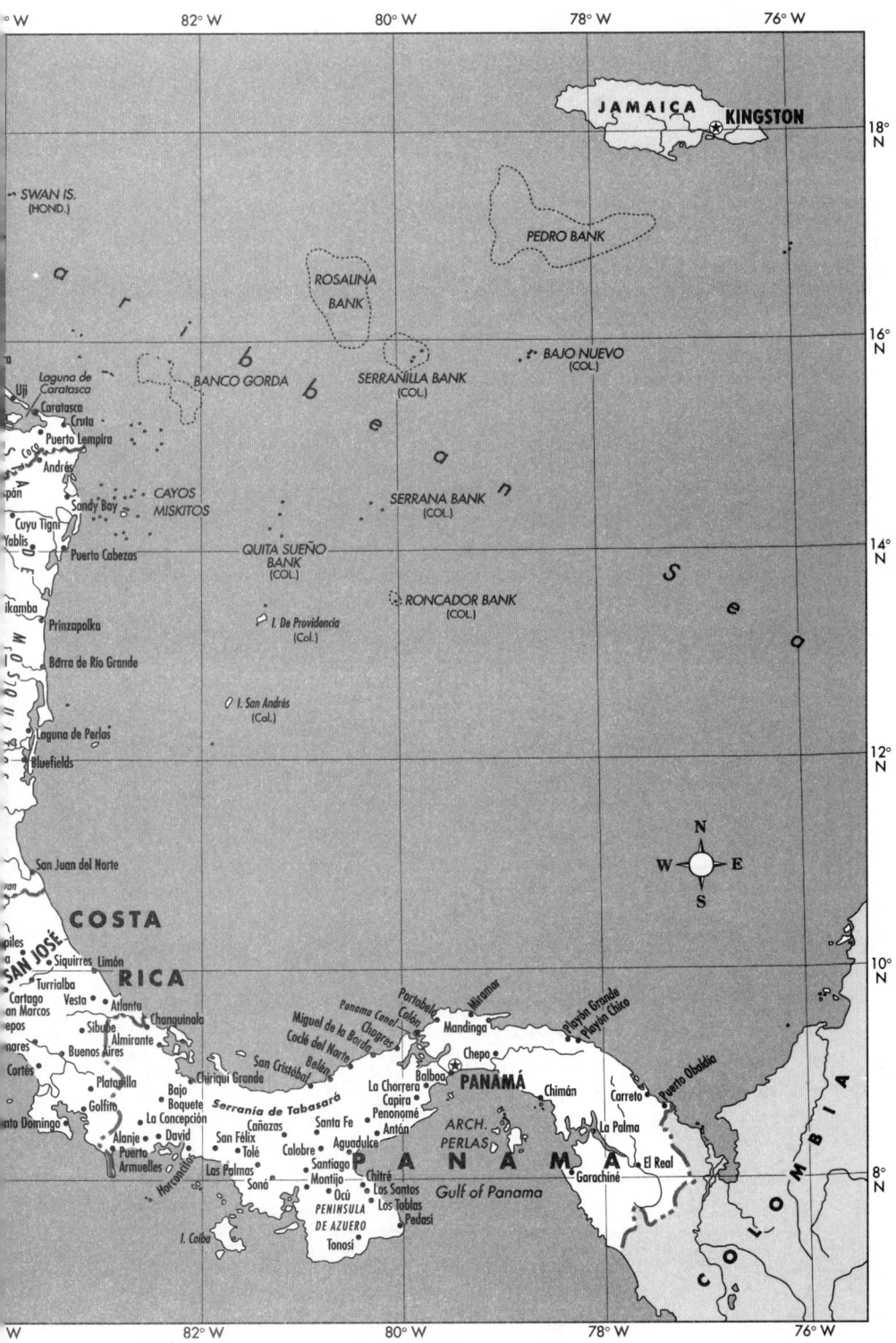

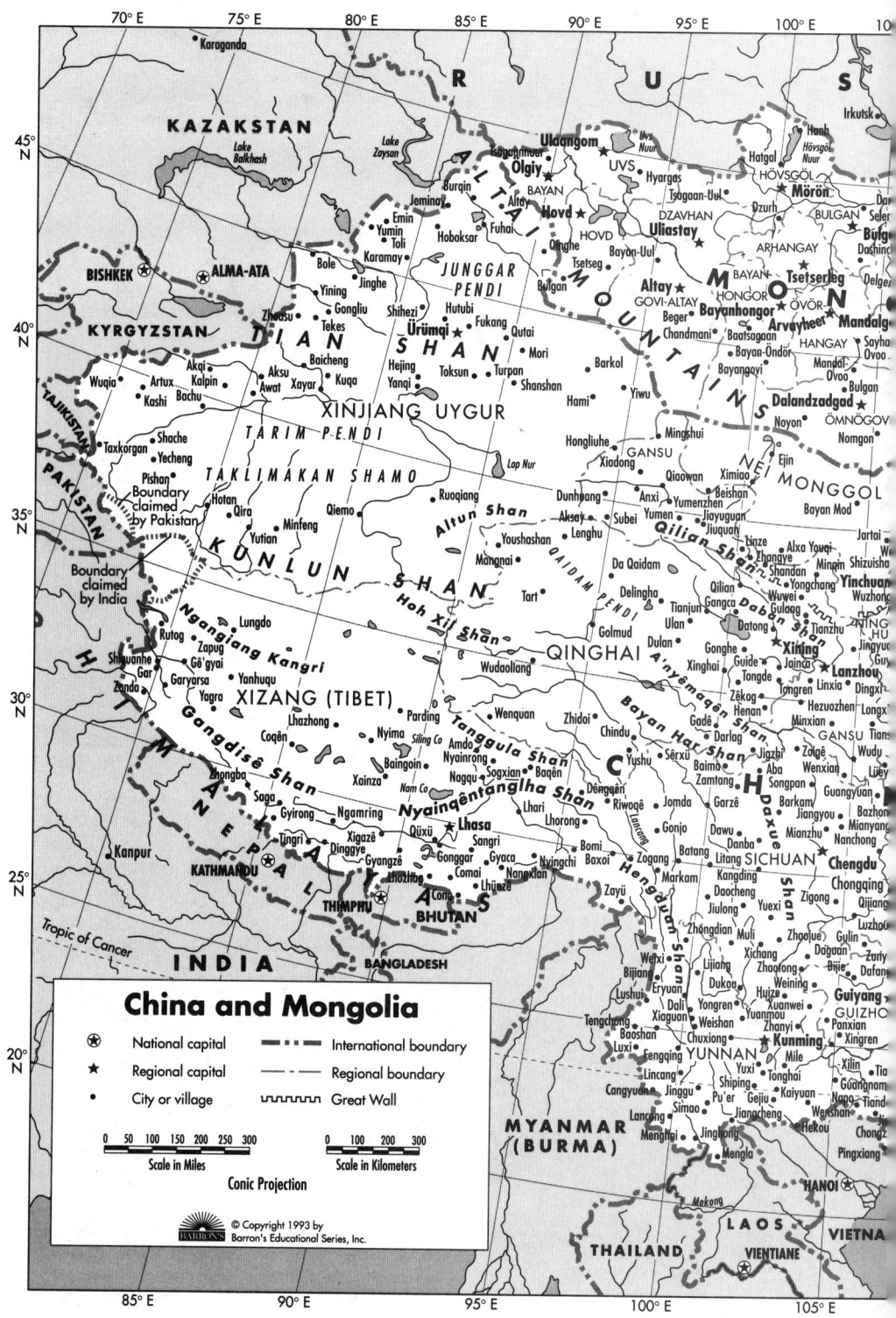

China and Mongolia

⊛ National capital
★ Regional capital
• City or village

▪▪▪▪ International boundary
▪—▪— Regional boundary
wwww Great Wall

Scale in Miles
0 50 100 150 200 250 300

Scale in Kilometers
0 100 200 300

Conic Projection

© Copyright 1993 by
Barron's Educational Series, Inc.

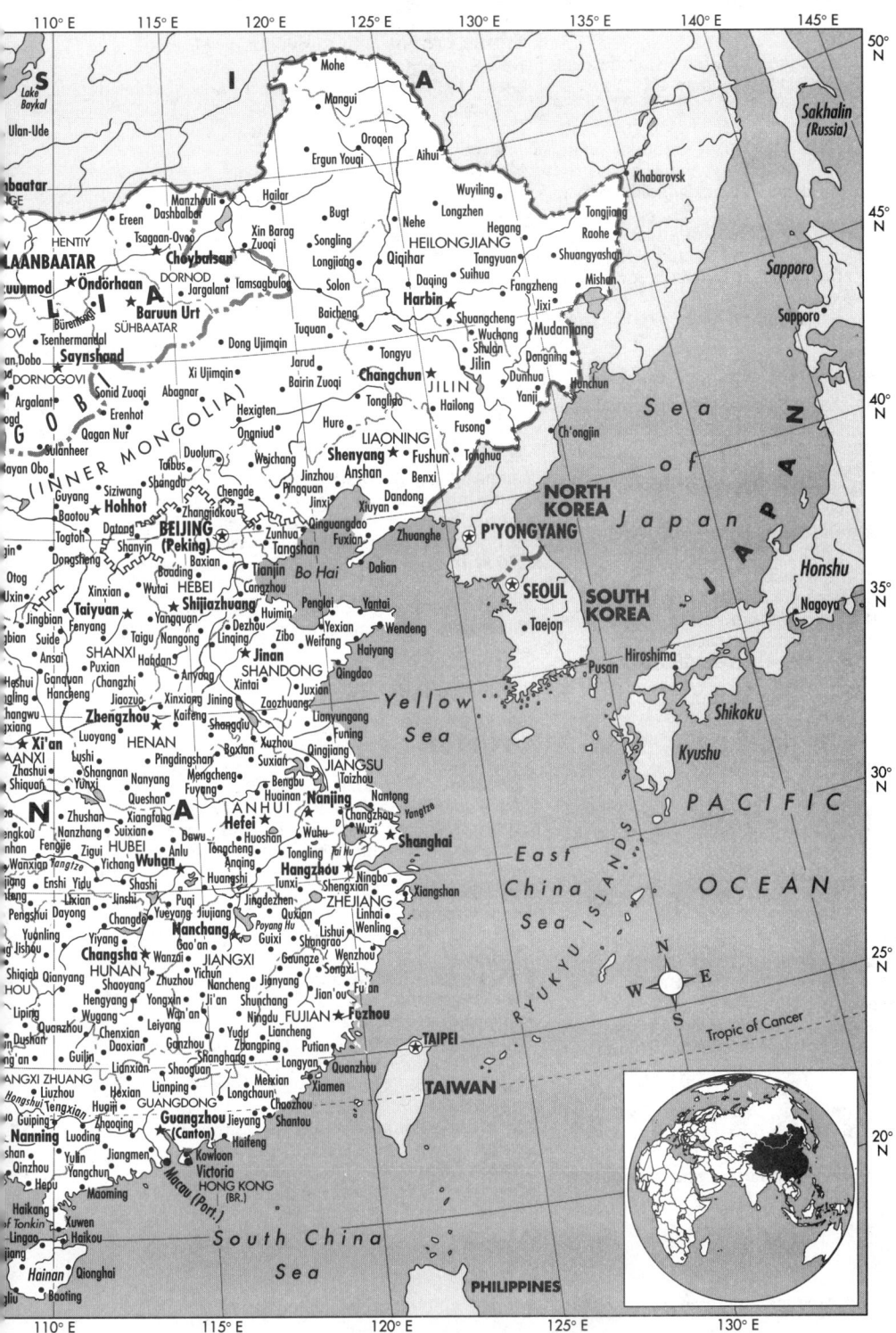

Government　Republic
Largest cities　Bogotá (capital), Medellin, Cali Barranquillá, Cartagena
Language　Spanish
Ethnic groups　Mestizo 58%, European descent 20%, Mulatto 14%, Black 4%, Indian 1%
Religion　Roman Catholic
Chief Industries　Textiles, steel, hides, chemicals
Chief crops　Coffee, rice, tobacco, cotton, sugar, bananas
Minerals　Oil, natural gas, emeralds, gold, copper, lead, coal, iron
Leading exports　Coffee, coal, oil, sugar
Leading imports　Machinery, chemical products, metal products, paper products, transport equipment
Monetary unit　Peso

Comoros

Location　Three islands in the Mozambique channel of the Indian Ocean between Mozambique and Madagascar
Area　838 square miles
Population　500,000
Government　Republic
Largest city　Moroni (capital)
Languages　Arabic, French, Comoran
Ethnic groups　Arab, African, East Indian
Religions　Muslim, Roman Catholic
Chief industry　Perfume distillation
Chief crops　Vanilla, copra, perfume plants, fruits
Leading exports　Perfume essence, vanilla, copra
Leading imports　Fuels, foodstuffs, consumer goods, petroleum products
Monetary unit　CFA franc

Congo

Location　West central Africa, bordered by Gabon and Cameroon on the West, Central African Republic on the North, Zaire on the East, Angola on the South
Area　132,046 square miles
Population　2,400,000
Government　Republic
Largest cities　Brazzaville (capital), Pointe-Noire
Languages　French, Bantu dialects
Ethnic groups　Bakongo 45%, Bateke 20%, M'Bochi, Sangha
Religions　Roman Catholic, Animist, Muslim
Chief industries　Agriculture, forestry, mining
Chief crops　Palm kernels, coffee, corn, bananas, rice, cassava, peanuts, tobacco
Minerals　Oil, natural gas, potash
Leading exports　Oil, lumber, tobacco, coffee, cocoa
Leading imports　Machinery, consumer goods, foodstuffs
Monetary unit　CFA franc

Costa Rica

Location　Central America, bordered on the North by Nicaragua, on the South by Panama
Area　19,575 square miles
Population　3,200,000

Government　Republic
Largest city　San José (capital)
Language　Spanish
Ethnic groups　Spanish descent, Mestizo
Religion　Roman Catholic
Chief industries　Processed foods, textiles, fertilizers
Chief crops　Coffee, bananas, sugarcane, rice, cacao
Minerals　Salt, gold, sulfur, iron
Leading exports　Coffee, bananas, sugar, beef
Leading imports　Machinery, pharmaceuticals, chemicals, fuels
Monetary unit　Colón

Côte d'Ivoire (Ivory Coast)

Location　Western Africa, bordered by Liberia and Guinea on the West, Mali and Burkina Faso on the North, Ghana on the East
Area　124,503 square miles
Population　13,000,000
Government　Republic
Largest city　Abidjan (capital)
Languages　French, African tribal languages
Ethnic groups　Baules, Bete, Senufo, Milinke
Religions　Tribal, Muslim, Christian
Chief industries　Food processing, timber logging, oil refining
Chief crops　Coffee, cocoa, corn, beans
Minerals　Diamonds, iron ore, oil, manganese
Leading exports　Coffee, cocoa, wood, oil
Leading imports　Consumer goods, fuels
Monetary unit　CFA franc

Croatia

Location　Formerly part of Yugoslavia, bordered by Slovenia and Hungary on the North, the Adriatic Sea on the West, Yugoslavia on the East, Bosnia and Herzegovina on the South and East
Area　21,829 square miles
Population　4,700,000
Government　Republic
Largest cities　Zagreb (capital), Split, Rijeka, Osijek
Language　Serbo-Croatian
Ethnic groups　Croats, Serbs
Religion　Roman Catholic
Chief industries　Aluminum products, oil refining, food processing, shipbuilding
Chief crops　Olives, grapes, grains, sugar beets, potatoes
Minerals　Bauxite, copper, coal, iron ore
Leading exports　Data not available
Leading imports　Data not available
Monetary unit　Croatian dinar

Cuba

Location　West Indies, North of Caribbean Sea; 90 miles South of the United States
Area　44,218 square miles
Population　10,800,000
Government　Marxist people's republic

Largest cities   Havana (capital), Santiago de Cuba, Camagüey
Language   Spanish
Ethnic groups   Spanish, African descent
Religion   Roman Catholic
Chief industries   Oil refining, textiles, chemicals, food processing, sugar refining
Chief crops   Sugar, tobacco, coffee, pineapples, citrus fruits, rice
Minerals   Nickel, iron, copper, manganese, cobalt
Leading exports   Sugar, coffee, shellfish, nickel, tobacco
Leading imports   Oil, foodstuffs, machinery
Monetary unit   Peso

Cyprus

Location   Eastern Mediterranean Sea, about 50 miles South of Turkey
Area   3,572 square miles
Population   710,000
Government   Republic
Largest city   Nicosia (capital)
Languages   Greek, Turkish, English
Ethnic groups   Greek 80%, Turk 18.7%, Armenian
Religions   Greek Orthodox, Muslim
Chief industries   Wine, clothing, asbestos mining
Chief crops   Grains, grapes, citrus fruits, potatoes
Minerals   Copper, asbestos, gypsum
Leading exports   Clothing, citrus fruit, wine
Leading imports   Machinery, petroleum products, cotton, consumer goods
Monetary unit   Pound

Czech Republic

Location   Formerly part of Czechoslovakia, bordered by Germany on the West, Poland on the North, Austria on the South, Slovakia on the East
Area   30,441 square miles
Population   10,314,000
Government   Republic
Largest cities   Prague (capital), Pizen, Brno, Ostrava
Language   Czech
Ethnic groups   Czech, Moravian
Religions   Roman Catholic, Protestant
Chief industries   Manufacturing, iron, steel, oil products, motor vehicles, chemicals, food processing, mining, agriculture
Chief crops   Grains, potatoes, sugar beets, hops
Minerals   Coal, lignite
Leading exports   Data not available
Leading imports   Data not available
Monetary unit   Koruna

Czechoslovakia
(*See* **Czech Republic; Slovakia**)

Denmark
(includes Greenland)

Location   Northern Europe, bordered by Germany on the South, Norway and Sweden on the North (Greenland, a province of Denmark is 1,300 miles away off the Northeast coast of North America)

Area   16,630 square miles (Greenland 840,000 square miles)
Population   5,200,000 (Greenland 56,000)
Government   Constitutional monarchy
Largest cities   Copenhagen (capital), Arhus, Odense
Language   Danish
Ethnic group   Scandinavian
Religion   Lutheran
Chief industries   Machinery, textiles, electronics, furniture (Greenland fishing, sealing)
Chief crops   Barley, beef and dairy cattle, oats, potatoes, wheat
Minerals   Oil, zinc, lead, coal, cryolite
Leading exports   Meat and dairy products, manufactured goods (Greenland fish and fish products)
Leading imports   Machinery, steel, oil, foodstuffs (Greenland oil, machinery, foodstuffs)
Monetary unit   Krone

Djibouti

Location   Eastern Africa, bordered by Ethiopia on the West and North, Somalia on the South
Area   8,494 square miles
Population   400,000
Government   Republic
Largest city   Djibouti (capital)
Languages   French, Afar, Somali, Arabic
Ethnic groups   Somali 60%, Afar 35%, European, Arab
Religion   Muslim
Chief industries   Agriculture, dock work, goat and sheep herding
Mineral   Salt
Leading exports   Hides, cattle
Leading imports   Machinery, foodstuffs, fuels
Monetary unit   Franc

Dominica

Location   Eastern Caribbean Sea
Area   290 square miles
Population   90,000
Government   Republic
Largest city   Roseau (capital)
Languages   English, French patois
Ethnic group   African descent
Religion   Roman Catholic
Chief industries   Agriculture, tourism
Chief crops   Bananas, citrus fruits, coconuts
Leading exports   Bananas, grapefruit, coconut oil
Leading imports   Machinery, foodstuffs, fuels
Monetary unit   East Caribbean dollar

Dominican Republic

Location   West Indies, occupying the Eastern half of the island of Hispaniola, bordered on the West by Haiti
Area   18,704 square miles
Population   7,400,000
Government   Republic
Largest cities   Santo Domingo (capital), Santiago de los Caballeros
Language   Spanish

Ethnic groups European 16%, Mulatto 73%, Black 11%
Religion Roman Catholic
Chief industries Sugar refining, cement, textiles, tourism
Chief crops Sugarcane, coffee, cocoa, tobacco, rice
Minerals Nickel, gold, silver, bauxite
Leading exports Sugar, nickel, coffee, cocoa
Leading imports Foodstuffs, oil, machinery, cotton, chemicals
Monetary unit Peso

Ecuador

Location Northwestern South America, bordered by Colombia on the North, Peru on the East and South
Area 104,510 square miles
Population 10,500,000
Government Republic
Largest cities Guayaquil, Quito (capital)
Languages Spanish, Quechuan, Jivaroan
Ethnic groups Mestizo 55%, Indian 25%, European and African descent
Religion Roman Catholic
Chief industries Processed foods, textiles, fishing
Chief crops Bananas, coffee, rice, sugar, corn
Minerals Oil, copper, iron, lead, silver
Leading exports Oil, bananas, coffee, cocoa, fish products
Leading imports Machinery, textiles, vehicles, oil
Monetary unit Sucre

Egypt

Location Northeast Africa, bordered by Libya on the West, Sudan on the South, Israel on the East
Area 386,660 square miles
Population 56,000,000
Government Republic
Largest cities Cairo (capital), Alexandria, Giza, Shubra el Khema, Port Said
Languages Arabic, English
Ethnic groups Egyptian, Bedouin, Nubian
Religion Muslim
Chief industries Textiles, chemicals, cement, food processing
Chief crops Cotton, rice, grains, vegetables, sugar, fruits, beans
Minerals Iron, phosphates, oil, gypsum, manganese, limestone
Leading exports Oil, cotton, textiles
Leading imports Machinery, foodstuffs, fertilizers, iron and steel
Monetary unit Pound

El Salvador

Location Central America, bordered by Guatemala on the West, Honduras on the North
Area 8,260 square miles
Population 5,500,000
Government Republic
Largest cities San Salvador (capital), Santa

Miguel, Santa Ana
Language Spanish
Ethnic groups Mestizo 89%, Amerindian 10%, Caucasian 1%
Religion Roman Catholic
Chief industries Food processing, textiles, oil refining
Chief crops Coffee, cotton, sugar, corn, rice, sorghum
Leading exports Coffee, cotton, sugar
Leading imports Machinery, oil, foodstuffs, fertilizer
Monetary unit Colón

Equatorial Guinea

Location Western Africa, bordered by Cameroon on the East and North, Gabon on the South; also comprises several islands in the Gulf of Guinea
Area 10,830 square miles
Population 380,000
Government Military rule
Largest city Malabo (capital)
Languages Spanish, Fang, English, Bubi
Ethnic groups Fang 80%, Bubi, also several other groups
Religion Roman Catholic Traditional
Chief industries Agriculture, timber
Chief crops Cocoa, wood, coffee, rice, yams
Leading exports Cocoa, wood, coffee
Leading imports Machinery, foodstuffs, textiles, oil
Monetary unit Bipkwele

Estonia

Location Formerly in the U.S.S.R., bordered by the Baltic Sea on the North and West, by Russia on the East, Latvia on the South
Area 17,413 square miles
Population 1,600,000
Government Republic
Largest cities Tallinn (capital), Tartu, Narva
Languages Estonian, Russian
Ethnic groups Estonian, Russian, Ukrainian
Religion Lutheran
Chief industries Oil shale processing, fertilizers, wood processing
Chief crops Grain, vegetables
Minerals Oil shale, limestone, phosphorite
Leading exports Data not available
Leading imports Data not available
Monetary unit Ruble (pending Estonian currency)

Ethiopia (Abyssinia)

Location Eastern Africa, bordered by Sudan on the West, Kenya on the South, Somalia and Djibouti on the East
Area 471,800 square miles
Population 53,000,000
Government In transition from Marxist military rule
Largest cities Addis Ababa (capital), Asmara
Languages Amharic, Tigre, Galla, Arabic
Ethnic groups Oromo 40%, Amhara 25%, Tigre

12%, Somali, Afar, Sidama
Religions Ethiopian Orthodox Christian, Muslim, Animist
Chief industries Cement, textiles, sugar refining, food processing
Chief crops Coffee, grains, sugarcane, cotton, livestock
Minerals Potash, salt, gold, platinum, copper
Leading exports Coffee, hides, skins
Leading imports Oil machinery, foodstuffs
Monetary unit Birr

Fiji

Location Southwestern Pacific Ocean
Area 7,056 square miles
Population 750,000
Government Commonwealth with a parliamentary system, with the Queen of England as the sovereign, an elected parliament, and a prime minister
Largest city Suva (capital)
Languages English, Fijian, Hindustani
Ethnic groups Indian 50%, Melanesian-Polynesian 45%, European 2%
Religions Christian, Hindu, Muslim
Chief industries Sugar refining, tourism
Chief crops Sugar, bananas, ginger
Minerals Gold, copper
Leading exports Sugar, coconut products, gold, lumber
Leading imports Machinery, foodstuffs, fuels
Monetary unit Dollar

Finland

Location Northern Europe, bordered by Sweden on the West, Norway on the North, Russia on the East
Area 130,119 square miles
Population 5,000,000
Government Republic
Largest cities Helsinki (capital), Tampere, Turku
Languages Finnish, Swedish
Ethnic groups Finn, Swede, Lapp
Religion Lutheran
Chief industries Machinery, metals, shipbuilding, clothing
Chief crops Grains, potatoes, dairy products, sugar beets
Minerals Copper, iron, zinc
Leading exports Paper, wood products, machinery, ships, clothing
Leading imports Oil, electronics, foodstuffs, textiles, chemicals
Monetary unit Markka

France

Location Western Europe bordered by Spain and Andorra on the South, Luxembourg and Belgium on the North, Germany, Switzerland and Italy on the East
Area 211,208 square miles
Population 56,900,000
Government Republic

Largest cities Paris (capital), Marseilles, Lyons, Toulouse, Nice, Strasbourg
Language French
Ethnic group French
Religion Roman Catholic
Chief industries Chemicals, automobiles, iron and steel, aircraft, textiles, wine, perfume, electronic equipment
Chief crops Grains, grapes and other fruit, vegetables
Minerals Coal, iron, bauxite
Leading exports Automobiles, wine, clothing, iron and steel
Leading imports Oil, machinery, chemicals, agricultural products
Monetary unit Franc

Gabon

Location Western Africa, bordered by Equatorial Guinea and Cameroon on the North, Congo on the East and South
Area 103,346 square miles
Population 1,100,000
Government Republic
Largest city Libreville (capital)
Languages French, Bantu dialects
Ethnic groups Fang 25%, Bapounon 10%, others
Religions Tribal beliefs, Christian
Chief industries Agriculture, mining
Chief crops Sugarcane, wood, palm, rice, cocoa, coffee, peanuts
Minerals Oil, uranium, iron, manganese
Leading exports Oil, wood, manganese, uranium
Leading imports Foodstuffs, vehicles, machinery
Monetary unit CFA franc

The Gambia

Location Western Africa, bordered on three sides by Senegal
Area 4,361 square miles
Population 875,000
Government Republic
Largest city Banjul (capital)
Languages English, Mandingo, Wolof
Ethnic groups Mandingo 42%, Fula 16%, Wolof 14%, others
Religions Muslim, tribal, Christian
Chief industries Agriculture, fishing, tourism
Chief crops Peanuts, rice, palm kernels, bananas, cassava, corn
Leading exports Peanuts, palm kernels, fish
Leading imports Machinery, textiles, foodstuffs, fuel
Monetary unit Dalasi

Georgia

Location Formerly in the U.S.S.R., bordered by Russia on the North, the Black Sea on the West, Turkey and Armenia on the South, Azerbaijan on the East
Area 26,900 square miles
Population 5,500,000
Government Republic
Largest cities Tbilisi (capital), Kutaisa, Batumi

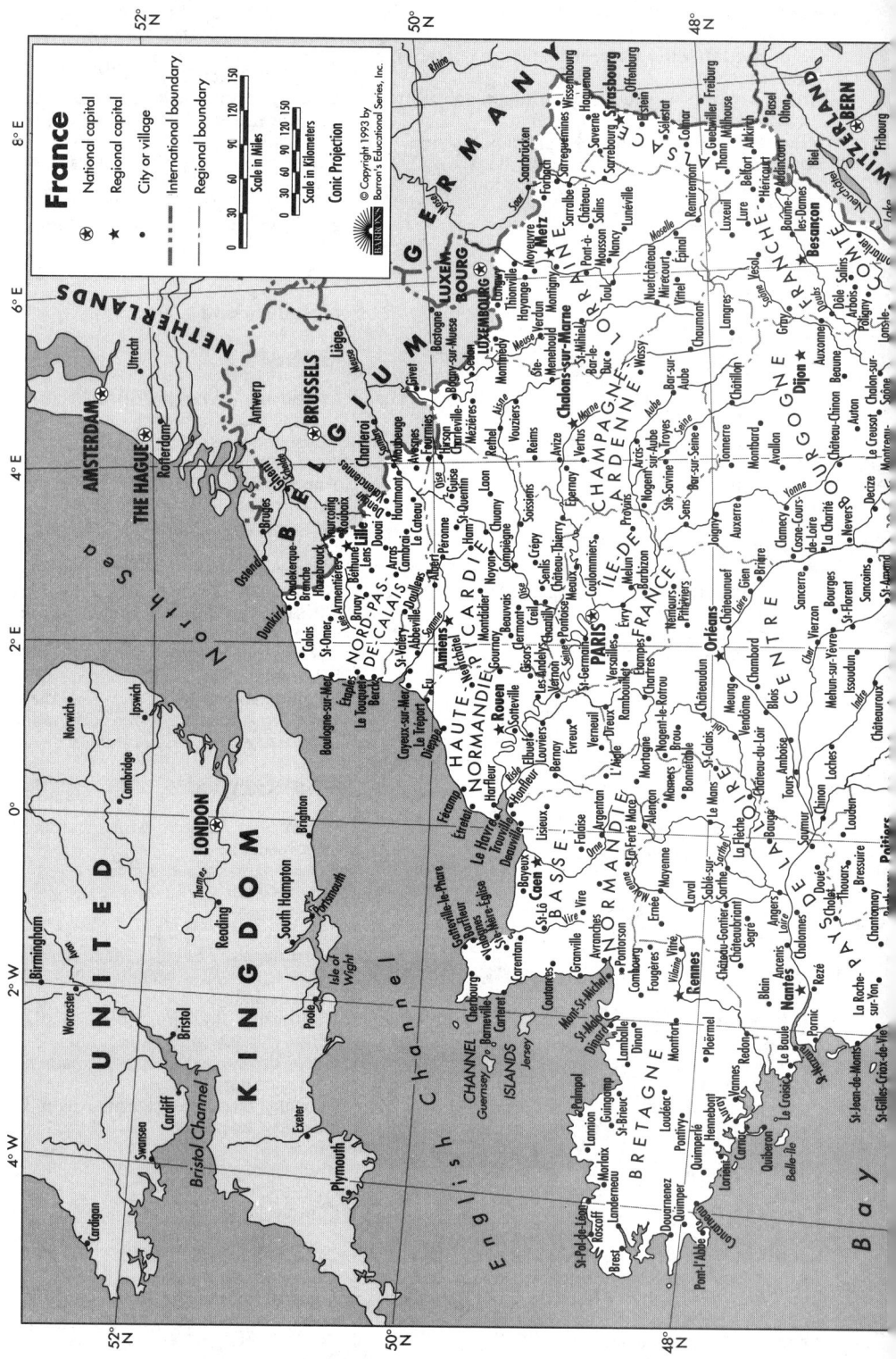

France

- ⊛ National capital
- ★ Regional capital
- • City or village
- ·—·—· International boundary
- —·—· Regional boundary

© Copyright 1993 by
Barron's Educational Series, Inc.

Scale in Miles
0   30   60   90   120   150

Scale in Kilometers
0   30   60   90   120   150

Conic Projection

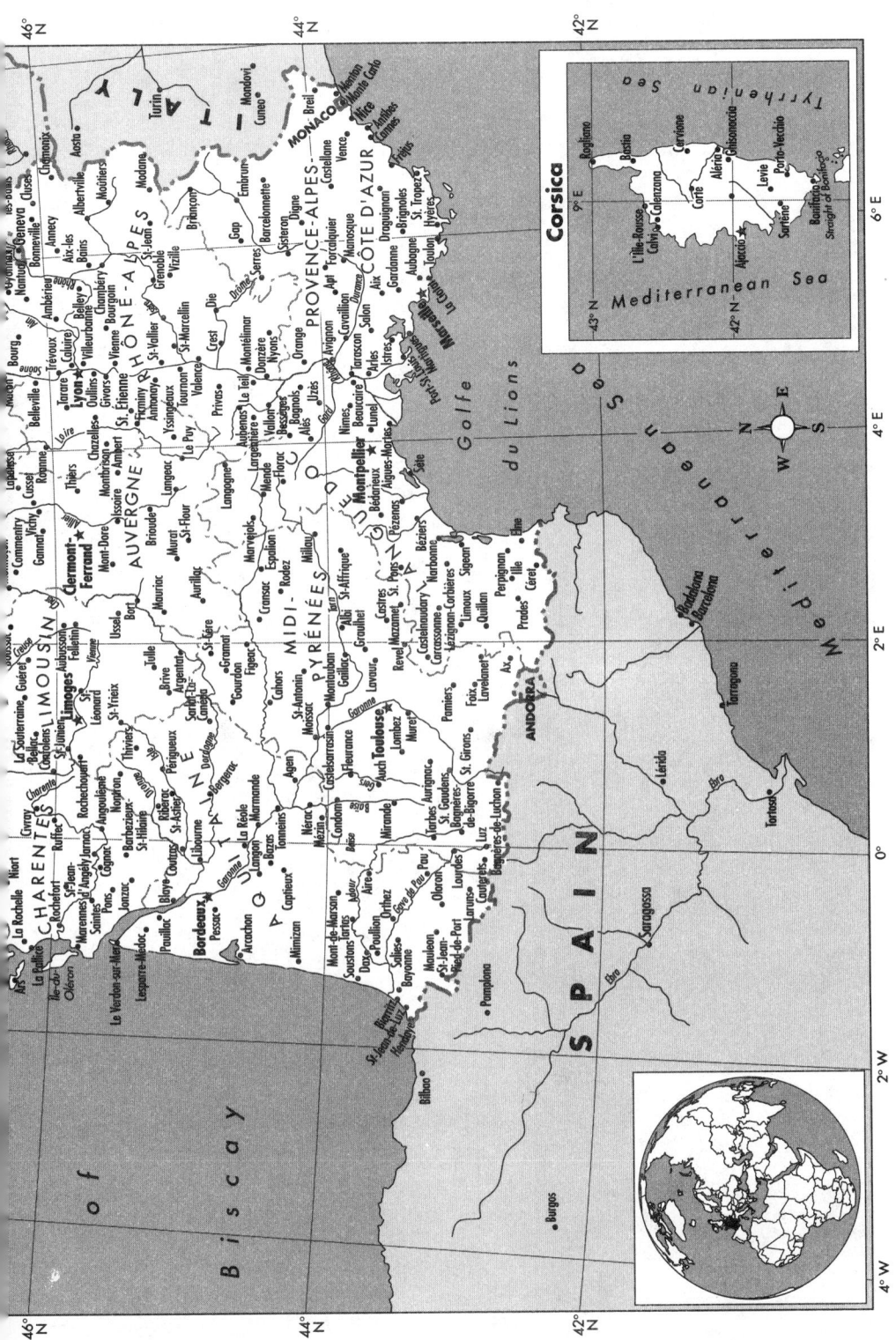

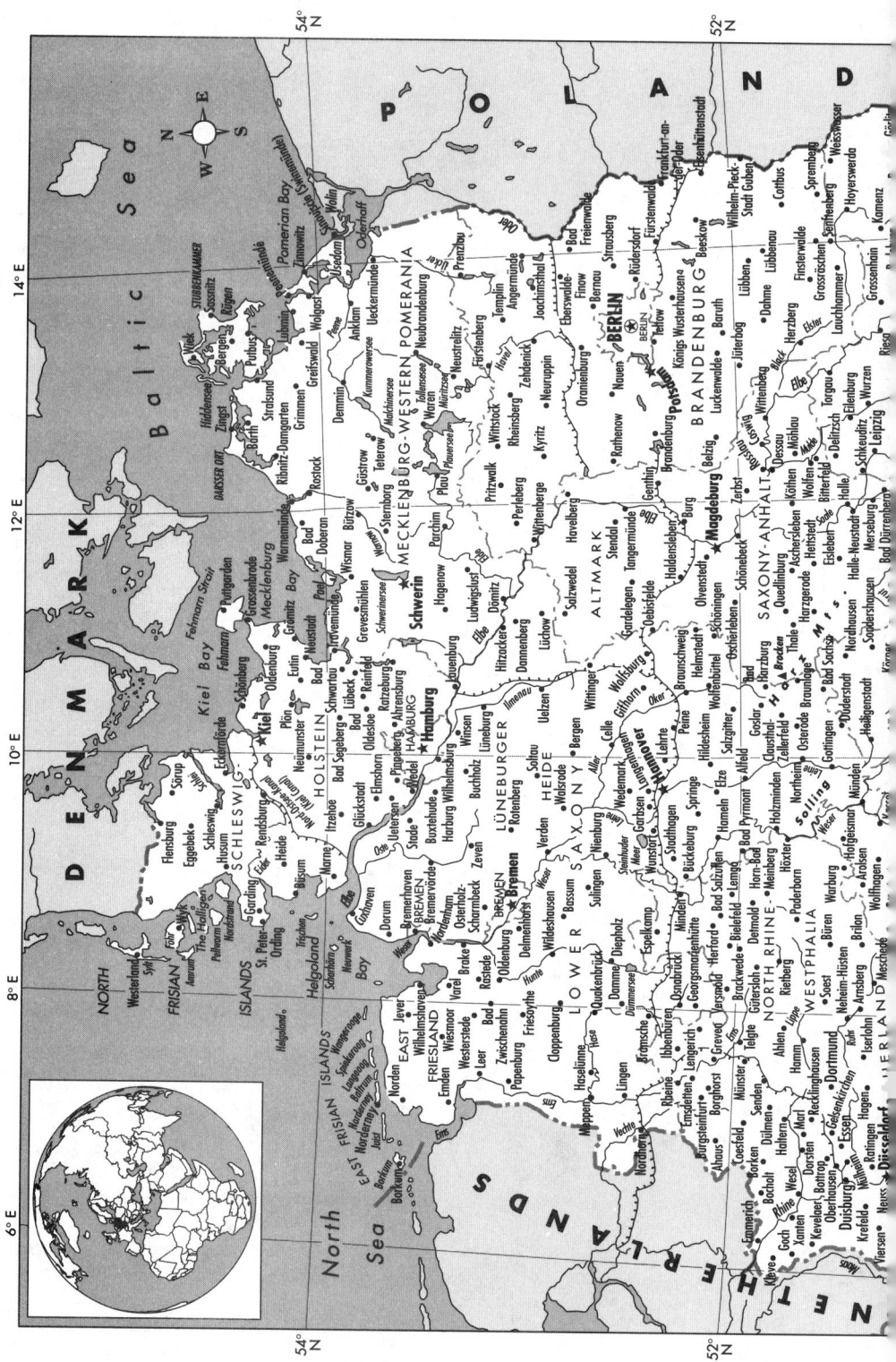

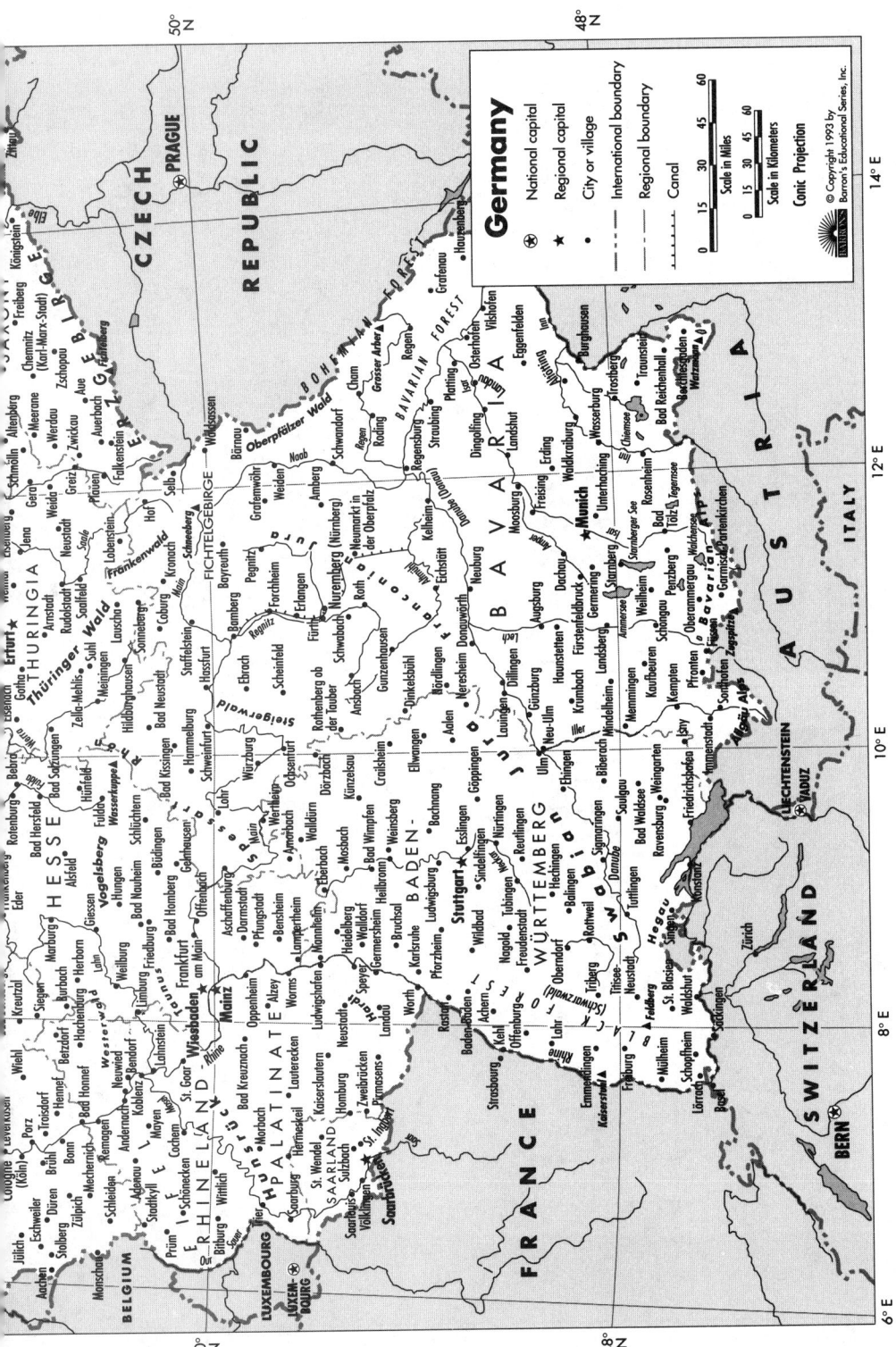

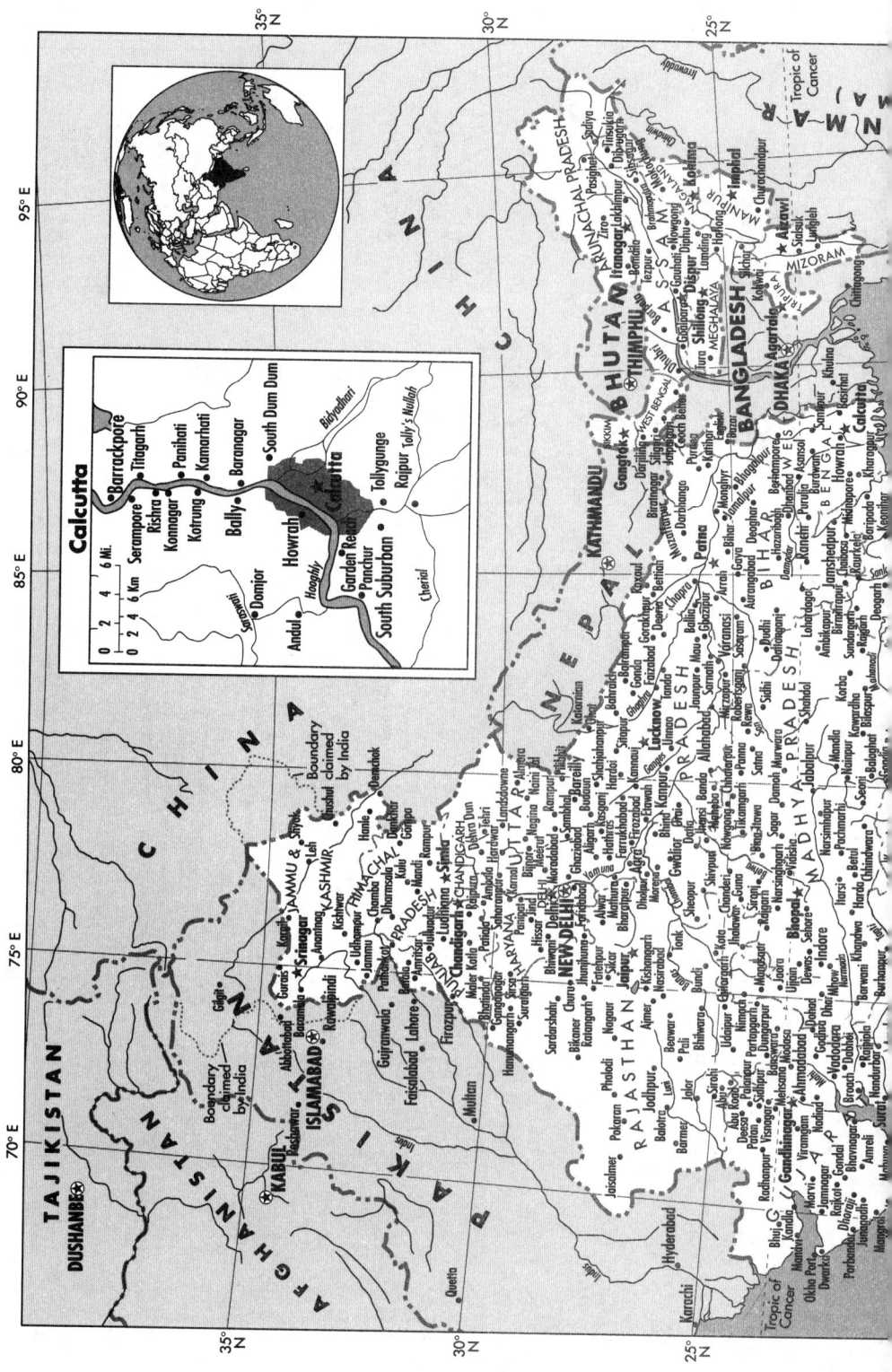

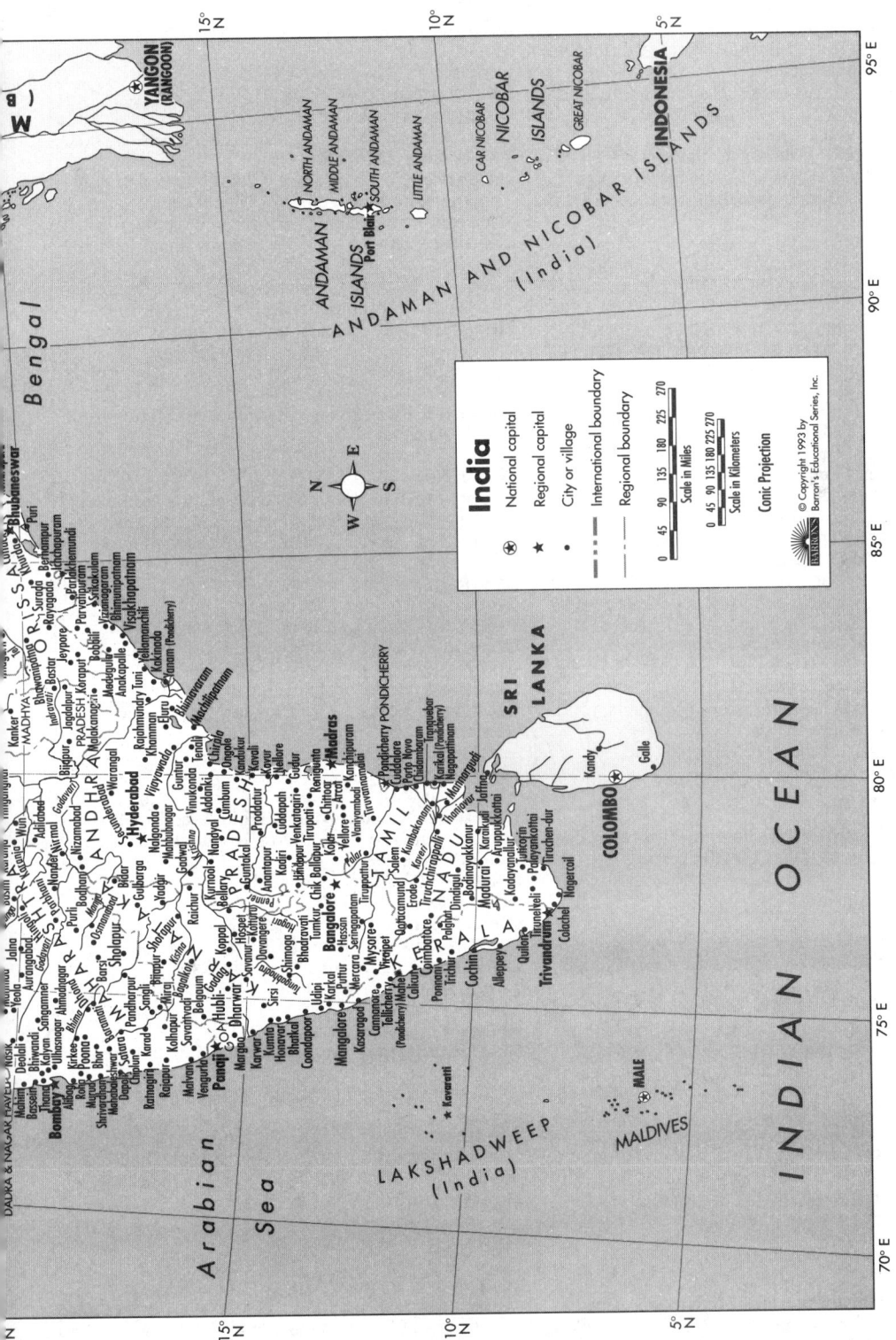

Languages   Georgian, Russian
Ethnic groups   Georgian, Armenian, Russian
Religion   Eastern Orthodox
Chief industries   Mining, metal fabrication, chemicals, building materials
Chief crops   Citrus fruits, grapes, tea, tobacco, grains
Minerals   Manganese, coal
Leading exports   Data not available
Leading imports   Data not available
Monetary unit   Ruble, pending Georgian currency

Germany

Location   Central Europe, bordered by Denmark and the Baltic Sea on the North, the Netherlands, Belgium, Luxembourg, and France on the West, Austria and Switzerland on the South, Poland and the Czech Republic on the East
Area   137,838 square miles
Population   80,000,000
Government   Federal Republic
Largest cities   Berlin (capital), Hamburg, Munich, Colone, Essen, Frankfurt
Language   German
Ethnic group   German
Religion   Protestant 49%, Roman Catholic 45%
Chief industries   Chemicals, machinery, vehicles, mining, steel production
Chief crops   Grains, potatoes, vegetables, sugar beets
Minerals   Iron, coal, potash, lignite
Leading exports   Machines, precision tools, vehicles, iron and steel products
Leading imports   Manufactured products, foodstuffs, raw materials, fuels
Monetary unit   Mark

Ghana

Location   Western Africa, bordered by Ivory Coast on the West, Burkina Faso on the North, Togo on the East
Area   91,843 square miles
Population   15,800,000
Government   Military rule
Largest cities   Accra (capital), Kumasi, Tamale
Languages   English, tribal languages
Ethnic groups   Akan 44%, Moshi-Dagomba 16%, Ewe 3%, Ga 8%
Religions   Christian, tribal beliefs, Muslim
Chief industries   Agriculture, mining, aluminum
Chief crops   Cocoa, coffee, coconuts, cassava, rice, palm kernels
Minerals   Gold, diamonds, manganese, bauxite
Leading exports   Cocoa, gold, timber, aluminum
Leading imports   Machinery, foodstuffs, medicines, consumer goods, oil
Monetary unit   Cedi

Greece

Location   Balkan peninsula, bordered by Albania, Macedonia and Bulgaria on the North, Turkey on the East
Area   51,000 square miles

Population   10,200,000
Government   Republic
Largest cities   Athens (capital), Salonika, Piraeus, Patras
Language   Greek
Ethnic group   Greek 98.5%
Religion   Greek Orthodox
Chief industries   Textiles, chemicals, metals, wine, processed foods
Chief crops   Grains, rice, corn, cotton, olives, citrus fruits, tobacco, grapes
Minerals   Bauxite, oil, manganese, lignite
Leading exports   Fruits, textiles, manufactured goods
Leading imports   Machinery, oil, chemicals, foodstuffs, consumer goods
Monetary unit   Drachma

Grenada

Location   Caribbean Sea, about 100 miles from South America
Area   133 square miles
Population   100,000
Government   Commonwealth with a parliamentary system, with the Queen of England as sovereign, an elected parliament, and a prime minister
Largest city   St. George's (capital)
Languages   English, patois
Ethnic group   African descent
Religions   Roman Catholic, Protestant
Chief industries   Agriculture, tourism, fishing
Chief crops   Spices, cocoa, bananas
Leading exports   Nutmeg, cocoa beans, mace
Leading imports   Oil, foodstuffs, machinery
Monetary unit   Caribbean dollar

Guatemala

Location   Central America, bordered by Mexico on the North and West, Belize, Honduras and El Salvador on the East
Area   42,042 square miles
Population   9,400,000
Government   Republic
Largest city   Guatemala City (capital)
Languages   Spanish, Mayan dialects
Ethnic groups   Mayan 54%, Mestizo 42%, White 4%
Religion   Roman Catholic
Chief industries   Agriculture, textiles, chemicals, rubber, plastics
Chief crops   Coffee, cotton, sugar, bananas, corn, beans
Minerals   Nickel, oil
Leading exports   Coffee, cotton, sugar, bananas
Leading imports   Machinery, oil, pharmaceuticals
Monetary unit   Quetzal

Guinea

Location   Western Africa, bordered by Guinea-Bissau, Senegal, and Mali on the North, Ivory Coast on the East, Liberia on the South
Area   94,925 square miles
Population   7,500,000

Government   Republic, under military rule
Largest city   Conakry (capital)
Languages   French, tribal languages
Ethnic groups   Fulani 35%, Malinke 30%, Sousous 20%
Religions   Muslim, tribal, Christian
Chief industries   Agriculture, mining
Chief crops   Rice, coffee, bananas, pineapples, corn, palm nuts
Minerals   Bauxite, iron, diamonds, gold
Leading exports   Bauxite, aluminum, pineapples, bananas, coffee
Leading imports   Machinery, foodstuffs, oil, textiles
Monetary unit   Guinean franc

Guinea-Bissau

Location   Western Africa, bordered by Senegal on the North, Guinea on the East and South
Area   13,948 square miles
Population   1,000,000
Government   Republic
Largest city   Bissau (capital)
Languages   Portuguese, Criolo, tribal languages
Ethnic groups   Balante 30%, Fula 20%, Mandyako 14%, Mandingo 13%
Religions   Tribal, Muslim
Chief industry   Agriculture, food processing
Chief crops   Peanuts, cotton, rice
Minerals   Bauxite, phosphates
Leading exports   Peanuts, palm kernels, fish, wood
Leading imports   Oil, foodstuffs, manufactured goods
Monetary unit   Peso

Guyana

Location   Northern South America, bordered by Venezuela on the West, Suriname on the East, Brazil on the South
Area   83,000 square miles
Population   800,000
Government   Republic
Largest city   Georgetown (capital)·
Languages   English, Amerindian dialects
Ethnic groups   East Indian 51%, African descent and mixed 43%
Religions   Christian, Hindu, Muslim
Chief industries   Agriculture, mining, textiles
Chief crops   Sugar, rice, citrus fruits
Minerals   Bauxite, gold, diamonds
Leading exports   Sugar, bauxite, rice, gold, timber
Leading imports   Oil, machinery, foodstuffs
Monetary unit   Dollar

Haiti

Location   West Indies, occupying the western end of the island of Hispaniola, with the Dominican Republic on the East
Area   10,714 square miles
Population   6,300,000
Government   Republic, in transition from military rule

Largest city   Port-au-Prince (capital)
Languages   French, Creole
Ethnic group   African descent 95%
Religions   Roman Catholic, Protestant, voodoo
Chief industries   Agriculture, textiles, sugar refining, light industry
Chief crops   Coffee, sugarcane, bananas, cocoa, tobacco, rice
Minerals   Bauxite, copper
Leading exports   Coffee, sugar, light industrial products
Leading imports   Foodstuffs, oil, machinery
Monetary unit   Gourde

Herzegovina
(*See* **Bosnia and Herzegovina**)

Honduras

Location   Central America, bordered by Guatemala on the West, El Salvador and Nicaragua on the South
Area   43,277 square miles
Population   5,200,000
Government   Republic
Largest cities   Tegucigalpa (capital), San Pedro Sula
Languages   Spanish, Amerindian dialects
Ethnic groups   Mestizo 90%, European descent, Black, Indian
Religion   Roman Catholic
Chief industries   Agriculture, clothing, textiles, forest products
Chief crops   Bananas, coffee, corn, beans, sugarcane
Minerals   Gold, silver, lead, zinc, antimony
Leading exports   Bananas, coffee, sugar, lumber, minerals
Leading imports   Oil, machinery, chemicals
Monetary unit   Lempira

Hungary

Location   Central Europe, bordered by Austria and Slovenia on the West, Slovakia on the North, Romania and Ukraine on the East, Croatia and Yugoslavia on the South
Area   35,919 square miles
Population   10,500,000
Government   Republic
Largest cities   Budapest (capital), Miskolc, Debrecen
Language   Magyar
Ethnic groups   Magyar 92%, German 2.5%, Gypsy 3%
Religions   Roman Catholic, Protestant
Chief industries   Steel, chemicals, machinery, pharmaceuticals, textiles
Chief crops   Grains, potatoes, beets, vegetables, grapes, sunflowers
Minerals   Bauxite, coal, natural gas
Leading exports   Machinery, tools, bauxite
Leading imports   Machinery, oil, consumer goods
Monetary unit   Forint

Iceland

Location   North Atlantic Ocean
Area   39,760 square miles
Population   280,000
Government   Republic
Largest city   Reykjavik (capital)
Language   Icelandic
Ethnic group   European descent
Religion   Lutheran
Chief industries   Fishing, agriculture, mining
Chief crops   Hay, potatoes, turnips
Mineral   Diatomite
Leading exports   Fish and fish products, diatomite
Leading imports   Food, machinery, oil, textiles
Monetary unit   Krona

India

Location   Southern Asia, bordered by Pakistan on the West, China, Nepal and Bhutan on the North, Burma and Bangladesh on the East
Area   1,269,219
Population   870,000,000
Government   Republic
Largest cities   Calcutta, Bombay, New Delhi (capital), Madras, Bangalore
Languages   Hindi, with 14 other languages recognized, including English
Ethnic groups   Indo-European 72%, Dravidian 25%, Mongoloid 3%
Religions   Hindu, Muslim, Christian, Sikh
Chief industries   Textiles, steel, cement, machinery, chemicals, fertilizer
Chief crops   Rice, grains, cotton, jute, tea, sugarcane, spices, oil seeds
Minerals   Iron, coal, manganese, bauxite, chromium, mica
Leading exports   Fish products, tea, iron, textiles
Leading imports   Machinery, chemicals, oil
Monetary unit   Rupee

Indonesia

Location   Southwestern Pacific Ocean
Area   741,101 square miles
Population   190,000,000
Government   Republic
Largest cities   Djakarta (capital), Surabaja, Bandung, Medan
Languages   Malay, Javanese
Ethnic groups   Malay, Javanese, Chinese, Papuan
Religion   Muslim
Chief industries   Agriculture, food processing, textiles, mining
Chief crops   Rice, cassava, sugarcane, coffee, peanuts, spices, rubber
Minerals   Oil, tin, nickel, bauxite, natural gas, copper
Leading exports   Oil, rubber, coffee, timber, textiles
Leading imports   Machinery, chemicals, manufactured goods
Monetary unit   Rupiah

Iran

Location   Southwest Asia, bordered by Turkey and Iraq on the West, Turmenistan, Armenia, and Azerbaijan on the North, Afghanistan and Pakistan on the East
Area   636,293 square miles
Population   59,400,000
Government   Islamic republic
Largest cities   Teheran (capital), Esfahan, Mashhad, Tabriz
Languages   Farsi, Turk, Kurdish, Arabic, English, French
Ethnic groups   Persian 63%, Turkoman and Baluchis 19%, Kurd 3%, Arab 4%
Religion   Muslim
Chief industries   Agriculture, mining, manufacturing, oil refining, petrochemicals
Chief crops   Grains, rice, sugar beets, cotton, dates, livestock
Minerals   Oil, natural gas, iron, chromium, lead, manganese
Leading exports   Oil, textiles, carpets
Leading imports   Machinery, pharmaceuticals, wheat
Monetary unit   Rial

Iraq

Location   Middle East, bordered by Jordan and Syria on the West, Turkey on the North, Iran on the East, Kuwait and Saudi Arabia on the South
Area   167,920 square miles
Population   19,000,000
Government   One-party republic
Largest cities   Baghdad (capital), Basra, Mosul, Kirkuk
Languages   Arabic, Kurdish
Ethnic groups   Arab 75%, Kurd 15%, Turk
Religion   Muslim
Chief industries   Oil refining, petrochemicals, textlles, construction materials
Chief crops   Grains, livestock, rice, cotton, dates
Minerals   Oil, natural gas, sulfur, phosphates
Leading exports   Oil, wool, cement
Leading imports   Manufactured goods, food
Monetary unit   Dinar

Ireland

Location   Western Europe in the Atlantic Ocean
Area   17,130 square miles
Population   3,500,000
Government   Republic, with a parliamentary system
Largest cities   Dublin (capital), Cork, Limerick
Languages   English, Irish
Ethnic group   Irish
Religion   Roman Catholic
Chief industries   Agriculture, food processing, metals, electronics, beverages, machinery, tourism
Chief crops   Grains, sugar beets, potatoes
Minerals   Zinc, lead, natural gas, copper, gypsum, limestone
Leading exports   Machinery, textiles, chemicals, dairy products
Leading imports   Machinery, oil, iron, steel
Monetary unit   Pound

Israel

Location Asia Minor, bordered by Egypt on the West, Lebanon on the North, Syria and Jordan on the East
Area 8,000 square miles
Population 4,500,000
Government Republic
Largest cities Jerusalem (capital), Tel Aviv, Haifa
Languages Hebrew, Arabic
Ethnic groups Jewish, Arab
Religions Jewish, Muslim, Christian
Chief industries Diamond cutting, textiles, processed foods, chemicals, plastics, electronics, agriculture
Chief crops Citrus fruits, grains, olives
Minerals Potash, lime, copper, phosphates
Leading exports Polished diamonds, citrus fruits, textiles, processed foods, fertilizer
Leading imports Diamonds, oil, ships, foodstuffs, iron and steel
Monetary unit Shekel

Italy

Location Southern Europe, bordered by France on the West, Switzerland and Austria on the North, Slovenia on the East
Area 116,300 square miles
Population 58,000,000
Government Republic
Largest cities Rome (capital), Milan, Naples, Turin, Genoa, Palermo, Bologna
Language Italian
Ethnic group Italian
Religion Roman Catholic
Chief industries Manufacturing, food processing, textiles, automobiles, tourism, agriculture
Chief crops Grapes, grains, citrus fruits, olives
Minerals Mercury, potash, gas, marble, sulfur
Leading exports Automobiles, clothing, shoes, machinery, citrus fruits
Leading imports Oil, machinery, foodstuffs, chemicals
Monetary unit Lira

Ivory Coast
(*See* **Côte d'Ivoire**)

Jamaica

Location West Indies
Area 4,250 square miles
Population 2,500,000
Government Commonwealth with a parliamentary system, with the Queen of England as the sovereign, an elected house of representatives, and an appointed prime minister
Largest city Kingston (capital)
Languages English, Jamaican Creole
Ethnic groups African 76%, mixed 15%, Chinese, Caucasian, East Indian
Religions Protestant, Roman Catholic
Chief industries Tourism, sugar refining, beverages, light manufacturing

Chief crops Sugarcane, coffee, bananas, citrus fruits
Minerals Bauxite, gypsum, limestone
Leading exports Bauxite, sugar, bananas
Leading imports Oil, consumer goods, machinery
Monetary unit Dollar

Japan

Location Sea of Japan, off the East coast of Asia
Area 145,800 square miles
Population 124,000,000
Government Constitutional monarchy with a parliamentary system
Largest cities Tokyo (capital), Yokohama, Osaka, Nagoya, Sapporo, Kyoto
Language Japanese
Ethnic group Japanese
Religions Shinto, Buddhist
Chief industries Electrical and electronic equipment, automobiles, machinery, chemicals
Chief crops Rice, grains, vegetables, fruits
Leading exports Ships, electrical and electronic equipment, automobiles, steel, synthetic fabrics
Leading imports Oil, coal, wood, iron, cotton, foodstuffs
Monetary unit Yen

Jordan

Location Western Asia, bordered by Israel on the West, Syria on the North, Iraq on the East, Saudi Arabia on the South
Area 37,735 square miles
Population 3,500,000
Government Constitutional monarchy
Largest cities Amman (capital), Zarka, Irbid
Language Arabic
Ethnic group Arab
Religions Muslim, Christian
Chief industries Textiles, cement, food processing
Chief crops Grains, fruits, vegetables, olives
Minerals Phosphate, potash
Leading exports Phosphates, vegetables, fruit, fertilizer
Leading imports Oil, foodstuffs, consumer goods, textiles, machinery
Monetary unit Dinar

Kampuchea
(*See* **Cambodia**)

Kazakhstan

Location Formerly in the U.S.S.R., bordered by Russia on the North, Kyrgyzstan, Uzbekistan, and Turkmenistan on the South, China on the East, the Caspian Sea on the West
Area 1,049,000 square miles
Population 16,700,000
Government Republic
Largest cities Alma-Ata (capital), Karaguada, Chimkent, Semipalatinsk
Languages Kazakh, Russian

Ethnic groups   Kazakh, Russian, German, Ukrainian
Religion   Muslim
Chief industries   Mining, manufacturing, agriculture
Chief crops   Grain, cotton, rice, grapes, sugar beets, livestock
Minerals   Coal, tungsten, copper, zinc, lead, nickel
Leading exports   Data not available
Leading imports   Data not available
Monetary unit   Tanga

Kenya

Location   Eastern Africa, bordered by Uganda on the West, Sudan and Ethiopia on the North, Somalia on the East, Tanzania on the South
Area   224,960 square miles
Population   25,000,000
Government   Republic
Largest cities   Nairobi (capital), Mombasa
Languages   Swahili, English, other African languages
Ethnic groups   Kikuyu 21%, Luo 13%, Luhya 14%, Kelenjin 11%, Kamba 11%
Religions   Protestant, Roman Catholic, Muslim, tribal
Chief industries   Agriculture, textiles, oil refining, food processing, tourism
Chief crops   Coffee, sisal, tea, cotton, corn
Minerals   Gold, lime, salt, diatomite
Leading exports   Coffee, tea, refined petroleum
Leading imports   Oil, machinery, iron and steel
Monetary unit   Shilling

Kiribati

Location   Southwest Pacific Ocean
Area   270 square miles
Population   72,000,000
Government   Republic, with a parliamentary system with the Queen of England as the sovereign, an elected parliament and a president
Largest city   Tarawa (capital)
Languages   English, Gilbertese
Ethnic groups   Micronesian, Polynesian
Religions   Roman Catholic, Protestant
Chief industries   Agriculture, fishing
Chief crops   Copra, vegetables, coconuts, breadfruit, bananas
Mineral   Phosphates
Leading exports   Phosphates, fish, copra
Leading imports   Fuel, foodstuffs
Monetary unit   Australian dollar

Korea, North

Location   Eastern Asia, bordered by China and Russia on the North, South Korea on the South
Area   46,540 square miles
Population   22,000,000
Government   Marxist people's republic
Largest city   Pyongyang (capital)
Language   Korean
Religions   Buddhist, Confucian, Chondokyo

Chief industries   Manufacturing, agriculture, mining, petrochemicals
Chief crops   Rice, corn, vegetables, fruits, potatoes
Minerals   Coal, iron, lead, zinc, graphite, tungsten
Leading exports   Minerals, chemicals, foodstuffs
Leading imports   Oil, machinery, wheat, coal
Monetary unit   Won

Korea, South

Location   Eastern Asia, bordered by North Korea on the North
Area   38,025 square miles
Population   43,600,000
Government   Republic
Largest cities   Seoul (capital), Pusan, Taegu, Inchon
Language   Korean
Religions   Buddhist, Confucian, Christian
Chief industries   Agriculture, fishing, manufacturing, mining, electronics, textiles
Chief crops   Grains, vegetables, rice
Minerals   Iron, copper, tungsten, graphite, coal, gold, silver
Leading exports   Textiles, automobiles, steel, electronics
Leading imports   Machinery, oil, grains, chemicals, cotton
Monetary unit   Won

Kuwait

Location   Southwestern Asia, bordered by Iraq on the North, Saudi Arabia on the South
Area   6,880 square miles
Population   1,800,000
Government   Sheikhdom
Largest cities   Hawalli, Kuwait (capital), as-Salimiyah
Languages   Arabic, English
Ethnic groups   Arab 84%, Iranian, Indian, Pakistani
Religion   Muslim
Chief industry   Oil refining
Chief crops   Wheat, dates, vegetables
Minerals   Oil, natural gas
Leading export   Oil
Leading imports   Foodstuffs, oil refinery equipment, automobiles
Monetary unit   Dinar

Kyrgyzstan

Location   Formerly in U.S.S.R., bordered by Kazakhstan on the North, China on the East, Uzbekistan on the West, Tajikistan on the South
Area   76,642 square miles
Population   4,400,000
Government   Republic
Largest city   Bishkek (capital)
Languages   Kyrgyz, Russian
Ethnic groups   Kyrgyz, Russian, Uzbek
Religion   Muslim
Chief industries   Tanning, mining, textiles, agriculture, herding
Chief crops   Grains, sugar beets, tobacco, cotton

Minerals Coal, mercury, antimony, lead, zinc, tungsten, uranium
Leading exports Data not available
Leading imports Data not available
Monetary unit Ruble

Kuwait

		0 20 40 60 80
✪	National capital	Scale in Miles
•	City or village	0 20 40 60 80
	International boundary	Scale in Kilometers
	Intermittent river flow	Mercator Projection

© Copyright 1993 by
Barron's Educational Series, Inc.

Laos

Location Southeast Asia, bordered by Thailand on the West, Burma and China on the North, North Vietnam on the East, Kampuchea (Cambodia) on the South
Area 91,429 square miles
Population 4,200,000
Government Marxist people's republic
Largest city Vientiane (capital)
Languages Lao, French
Ethnic groups Lao 48%, Mon-Khmer tribes 25%, Thai 14%, Meo and Yao 13%
Religions Buddhist, tribal
Chief industries Agriculture, forestry, mining
Chief crops Rice, corn, tobacco, cotton
Mineral Tin
Leading exports Tin, coffee, teak
Leading imports Rice, oil, machinery, fuels
Monetary unit Kip

Latvia

Location Formerly in the U.S.S.R., bordered by Estonia and the Baltic Sea on the North, the Baltic Sea on the West, Lithuania and Belarus on the South, Russia on the East

Area 24,900 square miles
Population 2,700,000
Government Republic
Largest city Riga (capital)
Languages Latvian, Russian
Ethnic groups Latvian, Russian
Religions Lutheran, Roman Catholic
Chief industries Machinery, metal working, light industry, dairy products
Chief crops Grains, potatoes
Minerals Limestone, dolomite, clay
Leading exports Data not available
Leading imports Data not available
Monetary unit Ruble, pending Latvian currency

Lebanon

Location Asia Minor, bordered by Syria on the East, Israel on the South
Area 4,015 square miles
Population 3,384,000
Government Republic
Largest cities Beirut (capital), Tripoli
Languages Arabic, French
Ethnic groups Lebanese 82%, Armenian 5%, Palestinian 9%
Religions Muslim, Christian
Chief industries Trade, agriculture, food processing, textiles
Chief crops Fruits, grains, tobacco, olives, grapes
Mineral Tin
Leading exports Fruits, vegetables, textiles
Leading imports Machinery, foodstuffs
Monetary unit Pound

Lesotho

Location Southern Africa, bordered on all sides by South Africa
Area 11,720 square miles
Population 1,850,000
Government Constitutional monarchy under military rule
Largest city Maseru (capital)
Languages Sotho, English
Ethnic group Sotho 99%
Religions Protestant, Roman Catholic
Chief industries Diamond polishing, food processing
Chief crops Grains, sorghum, beans
Mineral Diamonds
Leading exports Wool, cattle, mohair, diamonds, hides
Leading imports Machinery, foodstuffs, clothing
Monetary unit Maloti

Liberia

Location Western Africa, bordered by Sierra Leone on the West, Guinea on the North, Ivory Coast on the East
Area 43,000 square miles
Population 2,750,000
Government Republic, in transition from military rule

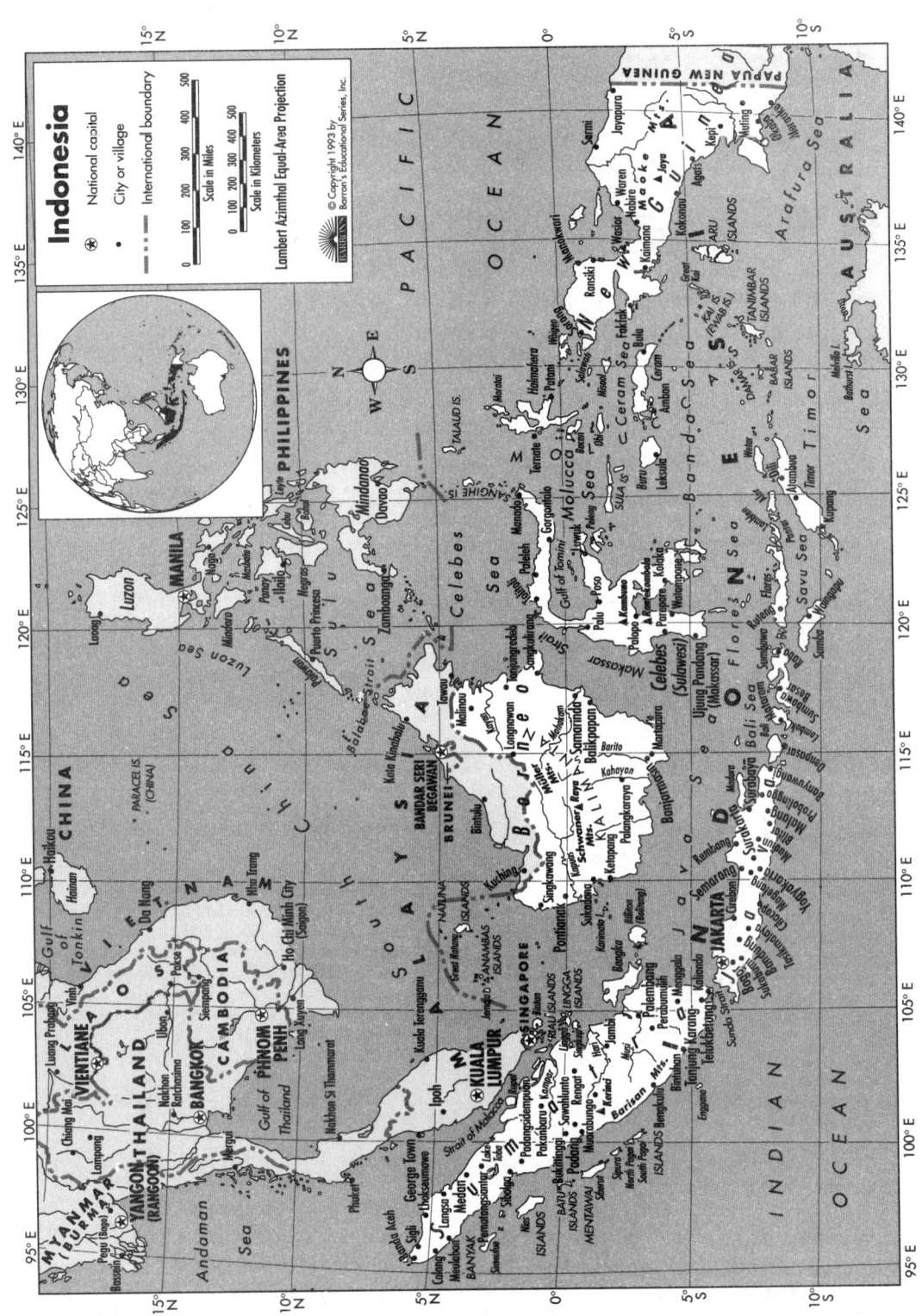

Golan Heights and East Jerusalem have been occupied and annexed by Israel. The West Bank and Gaza Strip are occupied by Israel.

Israel

⊛ National capital
★ Regional capital
• City or village
⬥ Ruin
–·–·– International boundary
–·–·– Regional boundary
Salt flat

Scale in Miles
0 10 20 30 40

Scale in Kilometers
0 10 20 30 40

Conic Projection

© Copyright 1993 by
Barron's Educational Series, Inc.

Jerusalem

24-53

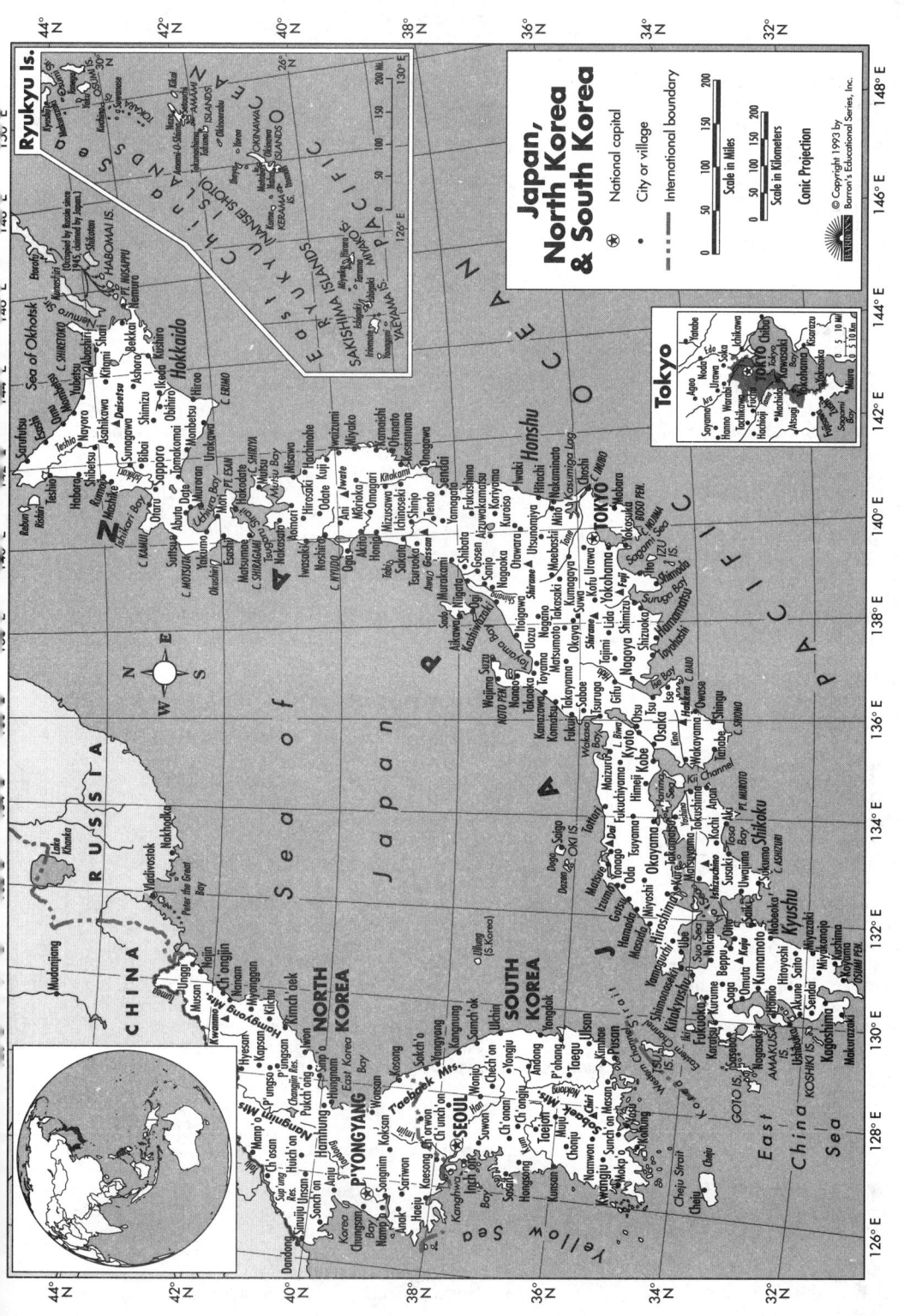

Japan,
North Korea
& South Korea

⊛ National capital
• City or village
International boundary

Scale in Miles
Scale in Kilometers
Conic Projection

© Copyright 1993 by
Barron's Educational Series, Inc.

Ryukyu Is.

Tokyo

Largest city   Monrovia (capital)
Languages   English, tribal
Ethnic groups   African tribes 95%, Afro-American descent 5%
Religions   Tribal beliefs, Muslim, Christian
Chief industries   Rubber processing, food processing, agriculture, mining
Chief crops   Rice, cassava, coffee, cocoa, sugar
Minerals   Iron, diamonds, gold
Leading exports   Iron ore, rubber, timber, coffee
Leading imports   Machinery, manufactured goods, fuels
Monetary unit   Dollar

Libya

Location   Northern Africa, bordered by Tunisia and Algeria on the West, Egypt on the East, Niger and Chad on the South
Area   679,359 square miles
Population   4,400,000
Government   Socialist military dictatorship
Largest cities   Tripoli (capital), Benghazi
Language   Arabic
Ethnic group   Arab-Berber
Religion   Muslim
Chief industries   Oil refining, textiles, agriculture
Chief crops   Grains, dates, olives, citrus fruits, grapes
Minerals   Oil, natural gas, gypsum
Leading exports   Oil, hides
Leading imports   Machinery, foodstuffs, manufactured goods
Monetary unit   Dinar

Liechtenstein

Location   Central Europe, bordered by Switzerland on the West, Austria on the East
Area   62 square miles
Population   28,000
Government   Constitutional monarchy
Largest city   Vaduz (capital)
Language   German
Ethnic groups   German 95%, Italian 5%
Religion   Roman Catholic
Chief industries   Manufacturing of precision instruments and chemicals, ceramics, forestry, banking
Chief crops   Grains, vegetables, livestock
Mineral   Salt
Leading exports   Stamps, dental equipment, pottery, machinery
Leading imports   Machinery, textiles, processed foods
Monetary unit   Swiss franc

Lithuania

Location   Formerly in the U.S.S.R., bordered by Latvia on the North, Belarus on the East and South, the Baltic Sea on the East, Russia and Poland on the South
Area   25,174 square miles
Population   3,750,000
Government   Republic
Largest cities   Vilnius (capital), Kaunas

Languages   Lithuanian, Russian
Ethnic groups   Lithuanian, Russian, Polish
Religion   Roman Catholic
Chief industries   Shipbuilding, farm machinery, food processing, dairy products
Chief crops   Grain, potatoes, vegetables, sugar beets
Minerals   Clay, limestone, dolomite, gypsum
Leading exports   Data not available
Leading imports   Data not available
Monetary unit   Ruble, pending Lithuanian currency

Luxembourg

Location   Western Europe, bordered by Belgium on the West, Germany on the East, France on the South
Area   998 square miles
Population   390,000
Government   Constitutional monarchy
Largest city   Luxembourg (capital)
Languages   Luxembourgian, French, German
Ethnic groups   French, German
Religion   Roman Catholic
Chief industries   Agriculture, steel, chemicals, metal products, glass
Chief crops   Corn, grapes, livestock
Mineral   Iron
Leading exports   Steel, chemicals, rubber products
Leading imports   Oil, coal, foodstuffs, consumer goods
Monetary unit   Franc

Macedonia

Location   Formerly in Yugoslavia, bordered by Yugoslavia on the North, Albania on the West, Greece on the South, Bulgaria on the East
Area   9,928 square miles
Population   1,900,000
Government   Republic
Largest cities   Skopje (capital), Bitola, Gostivar
Language   Macedonian
Ethnic groups   Macedonian, Albanian, Turkish
Religion   Eastern Orthodox
Chief industries   Agriculture, mining, textiles
Chief crops   Tobacco, cotton, fruits, vegetables, grains
Minerals   Chromium, lead, silver, antimony, lignite
Leading exports   Data not available
Leading imports   Data not available
Monetary unit   Dinar

Madagascar

Location   Indian Ocean, off southeastern coast of Africa
Area   226,657 square miles
Population   12,000,000
Government   Republic
Largest city   Antananarivo (capital)
Languages   Malagasy, French
Ethnic groups   Malayan-Indonesian tribes, Arab, African
Religions   Animist, Christian, Muslim

Chief industries   Agriculture, textiles, processed foods, fishing
Chief crops   Coffee, cloves, vanilla, rice, sugar, sisal, tobacco
Minerals   Graphite, chromium, coal, bauxite
Leading exports   Coffee, cloves, vanilla, chromite
Leading imports   Machinery, chemicals, foodstuffs, oil
Monetary unit   Franc

Malawi

Location   Southeastern Africa, bordered by Zambia on the West, Tanzania on the North Mozambique on the South
Area   45,747 square miles
Population   9,100,000
Government   Republic
Largest cities   Blantyre, Lilongwe (capital)
Languages   English, Chichewa
Ethnic groups   Chewa 90%, Nyan ja, Lomwe and other Bantu tribes
Religions   Christian, Muslim, tribal
Chief industries   Agriculture, fishing, sugar refining
Chief crops   Tea, tobacco, cotton, corn, sugar
Minerals   Limestone, uranium, coal, bauxite
Leading exports   Tobacco, sugar, tea
Leading imports   Machinery, oil, foodstuffs, consumer goods
Monetary unit   Kwacha

Malaysia

Location   Southeastern Asia, bordered by Thailand on the North, Indonesia on the South
Area   127,320 square miles
Population   18,000,000
Government   Constitutional monarchy with a parliamentary democracy
Largest cities   Kuala Lumpur (capital), George Town, Ipoh
Languages   Malay, Chinese, English, Indian languages
Ethnic groups   Malay 59%, Chinese 32%, Indian 12%
Religions   Muslim, Buddhist, Hindu, Christian
Chief industries   Rubber processing, mining, forestry, light manufactures
Chief crops   Rubber, palm oil, rice, lumber, copra, pepper
Minerals   Oil, tin, copper
Leading exports   Rubber, oil, lumber, palm oil, electronics
Leading imports   Machinery, rice, chemicals, capital equipment
Monetary unit   Ringgit

Maldives

Location   Indian Ocean
Area   115 square miles
Population   200,000
Government   Republic
Largest city   Male (capital)
Language   Divehi

Ethnic groups   Sinhalese, Dravidian, Arab
Religion   Muslim
Chief industries   Fish and coconut processing, tourism
Chief crops   Coconuts, fruits, sweet potatoes
Leading exports   Fish, clothing
Leading imports   Grains and other foodstuffs, consumer goods, petroleum products
Monetary unit   Maldivian rupee

Mali

Location   Western Africa, bordered by Senegal and Mauritania on the West, Algeria on the North, Niger on the East, Guinea, Ivory Coast and Burkina Faso on the South
Area   478,765 square miles
Population   8,400,000
Government   Republic, in transition from military rule
Largest city   Bamako (capital)
Languages   French, African languages
Ethnic groups   Mande 50%, Peul 17%, Voltaic 12%, Songhai 6%
Religions   Muslim, tribal
Chief industries   Agriculture, mining
Chief crops   Millet, rice, peanuts, cotton
Minerals   Bauxite, iron, manganese, gold
Leading exports   Cotton, peanuts, livestock
Leading imports   Textiles, foodstuffs, machinery, petroleum products
Monetary unit   CFA franc

Malta

Location   Mediterranean Sea, South of Italy
Area   122 square miles
Population   380,000
Government   Republic
Largest cities   Valletta (capital), Sliema
Languages   Maltese, English
Ethnic groups   Italian, Arab, French
Religion   Roman Catholic
Chief industries   Agriculture, textiles, plastics, electronic equipment manufacture
Chief crops   Fruits and vegetables, grains
Minerals   Limestone, salt
Leading exports   Textiles, clothing, wine
Leading imports   Foodstuffs, oil
Monetary unit   Maltese lira

Marshall Islands

Location   Southwestern Pacific Ocean
Area   70 square miles
Population   49,000
Government   Republic
Largest city   Majura (capital)
Languages   Marshallese, English
Ethnic group   Micronesian
Religion   Christian
Chief industries   Fishing, agriculture
Chief crops   Coconut palms, fruits, vegetables
Leading export   Copra
Leading imports   Foodstuffs, consumer goods
Monetary unit   U.S. dollar

Mauritania

Location   Northwestern Africa, bordered by Morocco on the North, Algeria and Mali on the East, Senegal on the South
Area   397,954 square miles
Population   2,000,000
Government   Republic, in transition from military rule
Largest city   Nouakchott (capital)
Languages   Arabic, French
Ethnic groups   Arab-Berber 80%, Black African 20%
Religion   Muslim
Chief industries   Agriculture, fish processing
Chief crops   Millet, corn, rice, dates, livestock
Minerals   Iron, copper, gypsum
Leading exports   Iron ore, copper, fish, gum arabic
Leading imports   Machinery, oil, foodstuffs
Monetary unit   Ouguiya

Mauritius

Location   Indian Ocean
Area   790 square miles
Population   1,100,000
Government   Commonwealth, with a parliamentary system with the Queen of England as the sovereign, largely elected legislature, and appointed prime minister
Largest city   Port Louis (capital)
Languages   English, French, Creole, Hindi
Ethnic groups   Indo-Mauritian 68%, Creole 27%
Religions   Hindu, Roman Catholic, Muslim
Chief industries   Agriculture, sugar processing, rum, tourism
Chief crops   Sugarcane, tea
Leading exports   Sugar, tea, molasses, fish
Leading imports   Foodstuffs, consumer goods
Monetary unit   Mauritian rupee

Mexico

Location   Central America, bordered by the United States on the North, Guatemala and Belize on the South
Area   761,600 square miles
Population   89,000,000
Government   Republic
Largest cities   Mexico City (capital), Guadalajara, Monterrey, Ciudad Juarez
Language   Spanish
Ethnic groups   Mestizo 55%, Amerindian 29%, European 10%
Religion   Roman Catholic
Chief industries   Agriculture, mining, food processing, chemicals, textiles, oil refining
Chief crops   Corn, cotton, coffee, sugarcane, fruits, rice
Minerals   Oil, silver, gold, lead, zinc, copper
Leading exports   Oil, cotton, sugar, coffee
Leading imports   Machinery, foodstuffs, electrical equipment
Monetary unit   Peso

Micronesia

Location   Southwestern Pacific Ocean
Area   271 square miles
Population   105,000
Government   Republic
Largest city   Kolonia (capital)
Languages   Micronesian dialects, English
Ethnic group   Micronesian
Religion   Christian
Chief industries   Fishing, agriculture, mining
Chief crops   Coconut palms, fruits, vegetables
Mineral   Phosphates
Leading exports   Phosphates, copra
Leading import   Foodstuffs
Monetary unit   U.S. dollar

Moldova

Location   Formerly in U.S.S.R., bordered by Ukraine on the North, East and South, Romania on the West
Area   13,000 square miles
Population   4,400,000
Government   Republic
Largest cities   Chisinau (capital), Tiraspol, Beltsy
Languages   Romanian, Ukrainian
Ethnic groups   Moldovians, Ukrainians, Russians
Religion   Eastern Orthodox
Chief industries   Agriculture, wine-making, food processing, textiles
Chief crops   Grapes, grains, sugar beets, fruits
Minerals   Lignite, gypsum
Leading exports   Data not available
Leading imports   Data not available
Monetary unit   Ruble, pending Moldovan currency

Monaco

Location   Western Europe, bordered by France on the West, North and East
Area   0.6 square mile
Population   29,700
Government   Principality with a constitutional monarchy
Largest city   Monaco-Ville (capital)
Language   French
Ethnic groups   French 47%, Italian 16%, Monegasque 16%
Religion   Roman Catholic
Chief industries   Tourism, gambling, precision instruments
Leading import   Foodstuffs
Monetary unit   French franc

Mongolia (formerly Outer Mongolia)

Location   East central Asia, bordered by Russia on the North, China on the South
Area   604,250 square miles
Population   2,300,000
Government   In transition from a Marxist people's republic
Largest cities   Ulan Bator (capital), Darhan
Languages   Mongolian, Russian, Chinese

Ethnic groups   Mongol 83%, Kazakhs 5%
Religion   Buddhist
Chief industries   Agriculture, textiles, cement, food processing, herding
Chief crop   Grains
Minerals   Coal, copper, molybdenum, tungsten, iron, lead, gold
Leading exports   Livestock, animal products, metals
Leading imports   Machinery, oil
Monetary unit   Tugrik

Morocco

Location   Northwestern Africa, bordered by Algeria on the East, the western Sahara on the South
Area   175,000 square miles
Population   26,000,000
Government   Constitutional monarchy
Largest cities   Casablanca, Rabat (capital), Fez, Marrakech
Languages   Arabic, Berber, French, Spanish
Ethnic group   Arab-Berber 99%
Religion   Muslim
Chief industries   Agriculture, mining, fishing, textiles, chemicals, food processing
Chief crops   Grains, citrus fruits, vegetables, dates, grapes
Minerals   Antimony, lead, cobalt, oil, coal, phosphates, manganese
Leading exports   Phosphates, fruits, fish and fish products, canned fruits and vegetables
Leading imports   Machinery, oil, foodstuffs, consumer goods
Monetary unit   Dirham

Mozambique

Location   Southeastern Africa, bordered by Malawi, Zambia, and Zimbabwe on the West, Tanzania on the North, South Africa and Swaziland on the South
Area   309,494 square miles
Population   16,300,000
Government   Marxist people's republic
Largest city   Maputo (capital)
Languages   Portuguese, Bantu languages
Ethnic group   Bantu
Religions   Traditional beliefs, Christian, Muslim
Chief industries   Agriculture, cement, textiles, food processing
Chief crops   Cotton, cashew nuts, peanuts, sugar, copra, tea
Minerals   Coal, bauxite, titanium
Leading exports   Nuts, cotton, sugar, tea
Leading imports   Machinery, textiles, oil, food
Monetary unit   Metical

Myanmar (formerly Burma)

Location   Southeast Asia, bordered by India and Bangladesh on the West, China, Laos and Thailand on the East
Area   261,789 square miles
Population   42,500,000

Government   Military
Largest cities   Yangon (capital), Mandalay, Moulmein
Language   Burmese
Ethnic groups   Burman 72%, Karen 7%, Shan 6%, Indian 6%
Religions   Bhuddist, Animist, Christian
Chief industries   Processed foods, petroleum products, textiles
Chief crops   Cotton, cashew nuts, sugar, tea
Minerals   Oil, natural gas, tin, antimony, zinc, copper, gemstones
Leading exports   Rice, teak, oilseeds, rubber
Leading imports   Machinery, manufactured goods, food
Monetary unit   Kyat

Namibia

Location   Formerly Southwest Africa, bordered by Angola and Zambia on the North, the Atlantic Ocean on the West, South Africa on the South, Botswana on the East
Area   318,261 square miles
Population   1,500,000
Government   Republic
Largest city   Windhoek (capital)
Languages   Afrikaans, English, German, tribal languages
Ethnic groups   Ovambu, Kavango, Herero, Damara
Religion   Christian
Chief industries   Mining, food processing, herding
Chief crops   Corn, millet, sorghum
Minerals   Diamonds, copper, lead, zinc
Leading exports   Diamonds, copper, lead, zinc, hides, beef
Leading imports   Foodstuffs, fertilizer, construction material
Monetary unit   South African rand

Nauru

Location   Western Pacific Ocean
Area   8 square miles
Population   9,400
Government   Republic
Largest city   Yaren (capital)
Languages   Nauruan, English
Ethnic groups   Nauruan 57%, Pacific Islander 26%, Chinese 8%, European 8%
Religion   Christian
Chief industry   Phosphates
Mineral   Phosphates
Leading export   Phosphates
Leading imports   Foodstuffs, fuel
Monetary unit   Australian dollar

Nepal

Location   Central Asia, bordered by China on the North, India on the South
Area   54,362 square miles
Population   19,800,000
Government   Constitutional monarchy

Largest cities　Katmandu (capital), Pokhara
Language　Nepali
Ethnic groups　Indian, Tibetan, central Asian descent
Religions　Hindu, Buddhist
Chief industries　Agriculture, hydroelectric power, jute milling
Chief crops　Rice, grains, jute, sugarcane
Mineral　Quartz
Leading exports　Clothing, leather goods, grain
Leading imports　Petroleum products, fertilizer, machinery
Monetary unit　Rupee

The Netherlands

Location　Northwestern Europe, bordered by Germany on the East and Belgium on the South
Area　15,770 square miles
Population　15,200,000
Government　Constitutional monarchy with a parliamentary system
Largest cities　Rotterdam, Amsterdam (capital), The Hague, Utrecht
Language　Dutch
Ethnic group　Dutch
Religions　Roman Catholic, Protestant
Chief industries　Agriculture, manufacturing of metal products, chemicals, electronic equipment, diamond cutting
Chief crops　Grains, sugar beets, potatoes, vegetables, fruits, flowers
Leading exports　Machinery, foodstuffs, textiles, natural gas
Leading imports　Oil, chemicals, minerals, raw materials, consumer goods
Monetary unit　Guilder

New Zealand

Location　Southwestern Pacific Ocean, off the coast of Australia
Area　103,736 square miles
Population　3,300,000
Government　Parliamentary system, with the Queen of England as the sovereign, an elected parliament, and a prime minister
Largest cities　Manukau, Christchurch, Auckland, Wellington (capital)
Languages　English, Maori
Ethnic groups　European descent 87%, Maori 9%
Religions　Protestant, Roman Catholic
Chief industries　Livestock, food processing, textiles, forestry
Chief crop　Grains
Minerals　Gold, coal, oil, natural gas
Leading exports　Wool, meat and meat products, dairy products
Leading imports　Machinery, consumer goods, petroleum products
Monetary unit　New Zealand dollar

Nicaragua

Location　Central America, bordered by Honduras on the North and Costa Rica on the South

Area　50,193 square miles
Population　3,900,000
Government　Republic
Largest city　Managua (capital)
Language　Spanish
Ethnic groups　Mestizo 69%, European 17%, Black 9%, Indian 5%
Religion　Roman Catholic
Chief industries　Agriculture, mining, forestry, food processing
Chief crops　Bananas and other fruits, cotton, coffee, sugar, rice, beans
Minerals　Gold, silver, copper, tunsten
Leading exports　Cotton, sugar, coffee, meats
Leading imports　Machinery, pharmaceuticals, oil, chemicals
Monetary unit　Cordoba

Niger

Location　Western Africa, bordered by Mali and Burkina Faso on the West, Libya and Algeria on the North, Chad on the East, Benin and Nigeria on the South
Area　489,200 square miles
Population　8,200,000
Government　Military rule
Largest city　Miamey (capital)
Languages　French, Hausa, Fulani
Ethnic groups　Hausa 56%, Djerma 22%, Fulani 8%, Tuareg 8%
Religions　Muslim, Christian
Chief industries　Agriculture, mining, herding
Chief crops　Peanuts, cotton, livestock, cassava, rice
Minerals　Uranium, tin, coal, iron
Leading exports　Uranium, livestock, hides
Leading imports　Machinery, oil, foodstuffs, consumer goods
Monetary unit　CFA franc

Nigeria

Location　Western Africa, bordered by Benin on the West, Niger on the North, Chad and Cameroon on the East
Area　356,669 square miles
Population　88,500,000
Government　Military rule, in transition
Largest cities　Abuja (capital), Lagos, Ibadan
Languages　English, Hausa, Yoruba, Ibo
Ethnic groups　Hausa 21%, Yoruba 20%, Ibo 17%, Fulani 9%
Religions　Muslim, Christian
Chief industries　Oil, food processing, agriculture, vehicle assembly
Chief crops　Cocoa, peanuts, cotton, grains, cassava, livestock
Minerals　Oil, natural gas, coal, iron, limestone
Leading exports　Oil, cocoa, rubber, timber
Leading imports　Foodstuffs, chemicals, consumer goods, steel, textiles
Monetary unit　Naira

Norway

Location Northern Europe, bordered by Finland and Russia on the North, Sweden on the East
Area 128,181 square miles
Population 4,250,000
Government Constitutional monarchy with a parliamentary system
Largest cities Oslo (capital), Bergen, Trondheim, Stavanger
Languages Norwegian, Lapp
Ethnic groups Norwegian, Lapp
Religion Lutheran
Chief industries Fishing, forestry, mining, agriculture, food processing, oil, shipbuilding
Chief crops Grains, potatoes, livestock
Minerals Oil, natural gas, copper, nickel, iron
Leading exports Oil, gas, fish, paper, pulp, ships
Leading imports Machinery, foodstuffs, chemicals, consumer goods
Monetary unit Krone

Oman

Location Arabian peninsula, bordered by United Arab Emirates, Saudi Arabia, and Yemen on the West
Area 82,030 square miles
Population 1,700,000
Government Absolute monarchy (Sultanate)
Largest cities Matrah, Muscat (capital)
Languages Arabic, English, Urdu
Ethnic groups Arab 87%, Baluchi 4%, Persian 3%, Indian 2%, African 2%
Religion Muslim
Chief industries Oil, agriculture, fishing
Chief crops Dates, bananas, grains, vegetables
Minerals Oil, copper, marble
Leading exports Oil, fish, citrus fruits
Leading imports Machinery, foodstuffs, consumer goods
Monetary unit Omani rial

Pakistan

Location Southern central Asia, bordered by Afghanistan and Iran on the West, China on the North, India on the East
Area 310,403 square miles
Population 119,000,000
Government Republic
Largest cities Karachi, Lahore, Faisalabad, Rawalpindi, Hyderabad, Islamabad (capital)
Languages Urdu, Punjabi, English
Ethnic groups Punjabi 66%, Sindhi 13%, Pathan 8.5%, Urdu 7.6%, Baluch 2.5%
Religion Muslim
Chief industries Agriculture, manufacturing, mining, textiles
Chief crops Cotton, rice, wheat
Minerals Natural gas, iron
Leading exports Cotton, rice, textiles
Leading imports Machinery, oil, chemicals
Monetary unit Rupee

Panama

Location Central America, bordered by Costa Rica on the West, Colombia on the East
Area 29,760 square miles
Population 2,400,000
Government Republic
Largest cities Panama City (capital), Colón
Languages Spanish, English
Ethnic groups Mestizo 70%, West Indian 14%, European 10%, Indian 6%
Religion Roman Catholic
Chief industries Agriculture, sugar refining, fishing, oil refining
Chief crops Bananas, pineapples, cocoa, corn, sugar, coffee
Mineral Copper
Leading exports Refined oil, bananas, shrimp, coffee, sugar
Leading imports Machinery, foodstuffs, oil
Monetary unit Balboa

Papua New Guinea

Location Southwestern Pacific, eastern half of the island of New Guinea, bordered by Indonesia on the West
Area 178,260 square miles
Population 3,900,000
Government Commonwealth with a parliamentary system, with the Queen of England as the sovereign, an elected parliament, and a prime minister
Largest city Port Moresby (capital)
Languages English, native dialects
Ethnic groups Papuans, Melanesians, Pygmies
Religions Protestant, Roman Catholic
Chief industries Agriculture, fishing, mining, forestry
Chief crops Coffee, coconuts, tea, copra
Minerals Copper, gold, silver
Leading exports Coffee, copper, gold, lumber, fish
Leading imports Machinery, foodstuffs, fuels
Monetary unit Kina

Paraguay

Location Central South America, bordered by Bolivia on the North, Brazil on the East, Argentina on the South
Area 157,047 square miles
Population 4,650,000
Government Republic under military rule
Largest city Asunción (capital)
Languages Spanish, Guarani
Ethnic group Mestizo 95%
Religion Roman Catholic
Chief industries Agriculture, forestry, mining, food processing
Chief crops Grains, cotton, beans, peanuts, tobacco, soybeans
Minerals Iron, manganese, limestone
Leading exports Cotton, timber, soybeans, coffee
Leading imports Machinery, foodstuffs, fuels, motor vehicles
Monetary unit Guarani

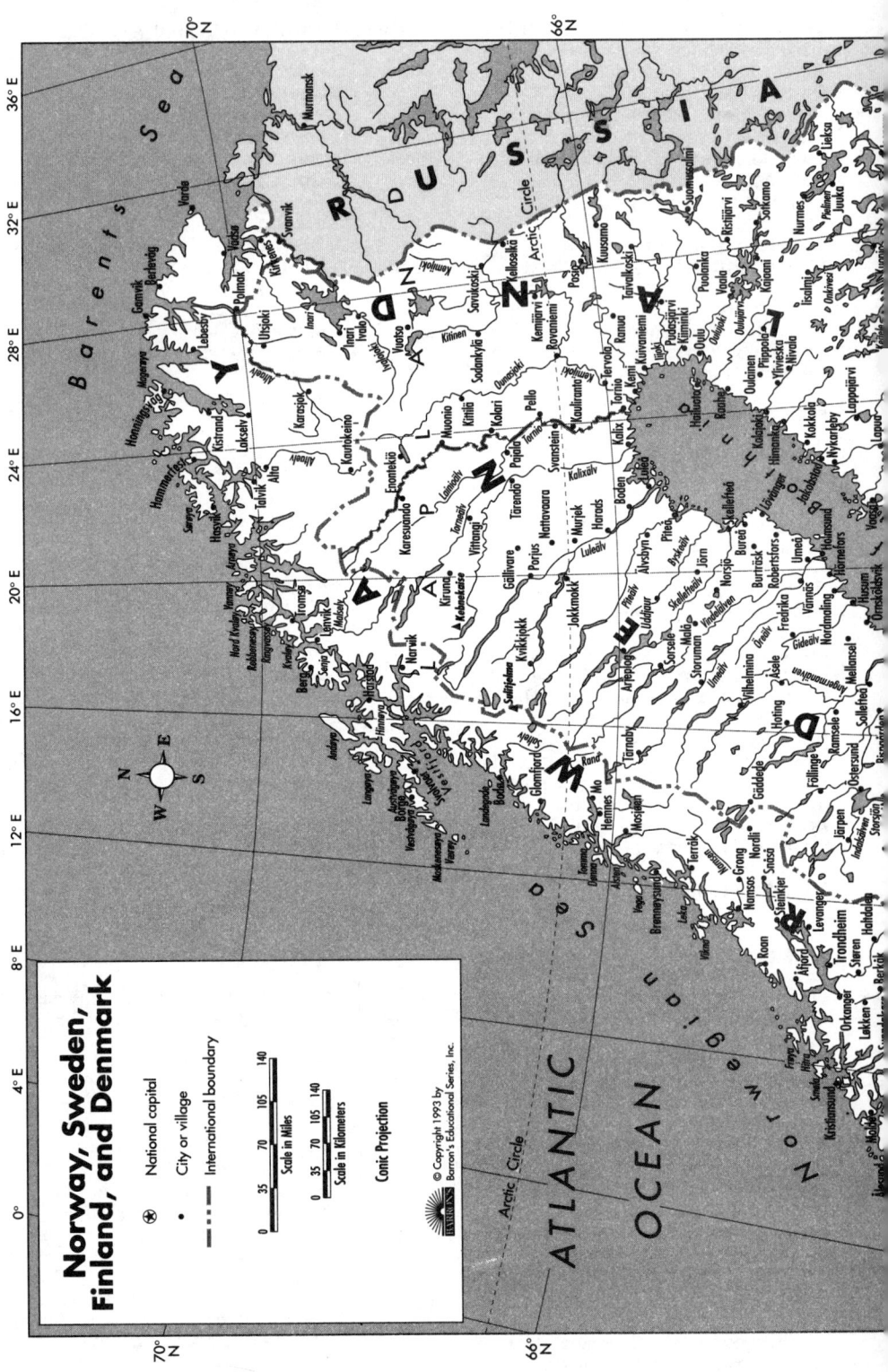

Norway, Sweden, Finland, and Denmark

⊛ National capital

• City or village

▪–▪ International boundary

Scale in Miles
0 35 70 105 140

Scale in Kilometers
0 35 70 105 140

Conic Projection

© Copyright 1993 by
Barron's Educational Series, Inc.

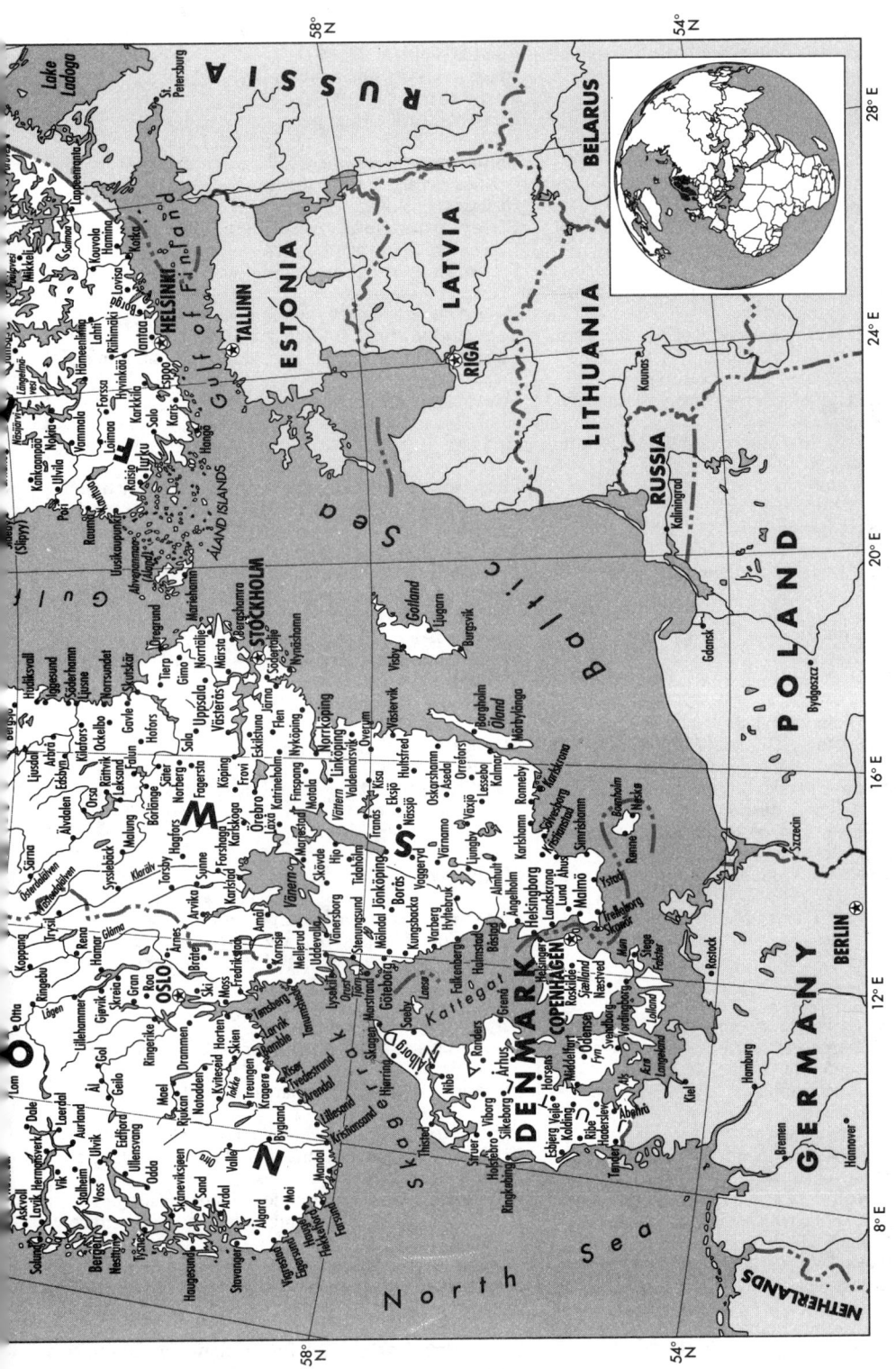

Peru

Location   Western South America, bordered by Ecuador and Colombia on the North, Bolivia on the East, Chile on the South
Area   496,222 square miles
Population   22,400,000
Government   Republic under presidential dictatorship
Largest cities   Lima (capital), Arequipa, Callao
Languages   Spanish, Quechua
Ethnic groups   Amerindian 45%, Mestizo 37%, European 15%, Black, Asian
Religion   Roman Catholic
Chief industries   Agriculture, mining, fishing, light manufacturing
Chief crops   Cotton, sugarcane, coffee, rice, corn, grains
Minerals   Copper, lead, silver, zinc, oil
Leading exports   Oil, copper, sugar, cotton, zinc, lead
Leading imports   Machinery, foodstuffs, chemicals, pharmaceuticals
Monetary unit   Sol

The Philippines

Location   Pacific Ocean off the southeastern coast of Asia
Area   115,830 square miles
Population   65,000,000
Government   Republic
Largest cities   Manila (capital), Quezon City, Davao
Languages   Filipino, English
Ethnic groups   Malay, Chinese, European descent
Religions   Roman Catholic, Protestant
Chief industries   Agriculture, food processing, textiles, clothing, light industry
Chief crops   Sugar, rice, corn, pineapples, bananas
Minerals   Oil, gold, silver, copper
Leading exports   Coconut products, wood, textiles
Leading imports   Foodstuffs, oil
Monetary unit   Peso

Poland

Location   Eastern Europe, bordered by Germany on the West, Belarus and Ukraine on the East, the Czech Republic and Slovakia on the South
Area   120,727 square miles
Population   38,100,000
Government   Republic
Largest cities   Warsaw (capital), Lodz, Krakow, Wroclaw, Poznan, Gdansk
Language   Polish
Ethnic groups   Polish 98%, German, Ukrainian
Religion   Roman Catholic
Chief industries   Agriculture, mining, manufacturing, food processing
Chief crops   Grain, sugar beets, potatoes
Minerals   Coal, sulfur, natural gas
Leading exports   Coal, coke, machinery
Leading imports   Oil, wheat, foodstuffs
Monetary unit   Zloty

Portugal

Location   Southwestern Europe, bordered by Spain on the North and East
Area   35,553 square miles
Population   10,400,000
Government   Republic
Largest cities   Lisbon (capital), Pôrto
Language   Portuguese
Ethnic group   Portuguese
Religion   Roman Catholic
Chief industries   Agriculture, forestry, textiles, metal products, fishing
Chief crops   Grains, potatoes, olives, grapes, rice
Minerals   Tungsten, uranium, iron
Leading exports   Wine, cork, fish
Leading imports   Oil, machinery, cotton, iron and steel
Monetary unit   Escudo

Qatar

Location   Arabian peninsula, bordered by Saudi Arabia on the West, United Arab Emirates on the South
Area   4,400 square miles
Population   500,000
Government   Independent emirate
Largest city   Doha (capital)
Languages   Arabic, English
Ethnic groups   Arab 40%, Pakistani 18%, Indian 18%, Iranian 10%
Religion   Muslim
Chief industry   Oil
Minerals   Oil, natural gas
Leading export   Oil
Leading imports   Machinery, foodstuffs, consumer goods
Monetary unit   Riyal

Romania

Location   Southeastern Europe, bordered by Hungary and Yugoslavia on the West, Ukraine and Moldova on the North and East, Bulgaria on the South
Area   91,699 square miles
Population   23,000,000
Government   Republic, in transition from Marxist regime
Largest cities   Bucharest (capital), Brasov, Timisoara
Languages   Romanian, Hungarian, German
Ethnic groups   Romanian 88.1%, Hungarian 7.9%, German 1.6%
Religions   Eastern Orthodox, Roman Catholic
Chief industries   Manufacturing, agriculture, mining, forestry
Chief crops   Grains, potatoes
Minerals   Oil, coal, natural gas, iron, salt, copper
Leading exports   Machinery, chemicals, furniture, shoes, lumber
Leading imports   Oil, iron, machinery, consumer goods
Monetary unit   Leu

Russia

Location   Formerly in the U.S.S.R., bordered by the Arctic Ocean on the North, Norway, Finland, Estonia, Latvia, Belarus and Ukraine on the West, Georgia, Azerbaijan, Kazakhstan, China, Mongolia and North Korea on the South, the Pacific Ocean on the East

Area   6,592,800 square miles

Population   148,500,000

Government   Republic

Largest cities   Moscow (capital), St. Petersburg, Novosibirsk, Samara, Rostov, Volgograd

Language   Russian

Ethnic groups   Russian, Tatars, Ukrainians

Religion   Eastern Orthodox

Chief industries   Manufacturing, mining, light and heavy industry, automobiles, oil refining, agriculture, forestry

Chief crops   Grains, sugar beets, fruits, vegetables, cotton, potatoes

Minerals   Oil, natural gas, coal, iron, lead, zinc, nickel, bauxite, gold, platinum

Leading exports   Data not available

Leading imports   Data not available

Monetary unit   Ruble

Rwanda

Location   Central Africa, bordered by Zaire on the West, Uganda on the North, Tanzania on the East, Burundi on the South

Area   10,169 square miles

Population   7,800,000

Government   In transition from a one-party republic

Largest city   Kigali (capital)

Languages   Kinyarwanda, French

Ethnic groups   Hutu 90%, Tutsi 9%, Twa 1%

Religions   Christian, traditional beliefs, Muslim

Chief industries   Agriculture, mining, food processing

Chief crops   Coffee, tea

Minerals   Tin, wolfram, gold

Leading exports   Coffee, tea, tin, tungsten

Leading imports   Oil machinery, textiles, foodstuffs

Monetary unit   Franc

Saint Kitts-Nevis

Location   Caribbean Sea

Area   101 square miles

Population   40,000

Government   Commonwealth, with a parliamentary system with the Queen of England as the sovereign, an elected prime minister, and a parliament

Largest cities   Basseterre (capital), Charlestown

Language   English

Ethnic group   African descent 95%

Religion   Protestant

Chief industries   Agriculture, tourism

Chief crop   Sugar

Leading export   Sugar

Leading imports   Oil, foodstuffs, machinery

Monetary unit   East Caribbean dollar

Saint Lucia

Location   Caribbean Sea

Area   238 square miles

Population   170,000

Government   Commonwealth, with a parliamentary system with the Queen of England as sovereign, an elected parliament, and a prime minister

Largest city   Castries (capital)

Languages   English, patois

Ethnic group   African descent

Religion   Roman Catholic

Chief industries   Agriculture, fishing, light industry, food processing, tourism

Chief crops   Bananas, coconuts, cocoa, citrus fruits, spices

Leading exports   Bananas and other fruits, coconuts, spices, cocoa

Leading imports   Foodstuffs, oil, machinery, metals

Monetary unit   East Caribbean dollar

Saint Vincent and the Grenadines

Location   Caribbean Sea

Area   150 square miles

Population   107,000

Government   Commonwealth, with a parliamentary system with the Queen of England as sovereign, an elected parliament, and a prime minister

Largest city   Kingston (capital)

Language   English

Ethnic group   African descent

Religions   Protestant, Roman Catholic

Chief industries   Agriculture, tourism, fishing, food processing

Chief crops   Bananas, arrowroot, coconuts

Leading exports   Bananas, arrowroot, copra

Leading imports   Foodstuffs, textiles, oil, machinery

Monetary unit   East Caribbean dollar

San Marino

Location   Southern Europe, bordered on all sides by Italy

Area   24 square miles

Population   23,000

Government   Republic

Largest city   San Marino (capital)

Language   Italian

Ethnic groups   San Marinese 88%, Italian 11%

Religion   Roman Catholic

Chief industries   Postage stamps, tourism, light manufacturing, woolen goods

Leading exports   Wine, textiles, ceramics, postage stamps

Leading imports   Manufactured consumer goods

Monetary unit   Italian lira

São Tomé and Principe

Location   Atlantic Ocean off the West coast of Africa

Area   372 square miles
Population   114,000
Government   Republic
Largest city   São Tomé (capital)
Language   Portuguese
Ethnic group   Portuguese-African descent
Religion   Christian
Chief industries   Agriculture, fishing, fish processing
Chief crops   Cocoa, coconuts, copra, coffee
Leading exports   Cocoa, coconut products, coffee
Leading imports   Foodstuffs, fuels, machinery, consumer goods
Monetary unit   Dobra

Saudi Arabia

Location   Arabian peninsula, bordered by Jordan, Kuwait, and Iraq on the North, United Arab Emirates and Qatar on the East, Yemen and Oman on the South
Area   840,000 square miles
Population   17,000,000
Government   Monarchy
Largest cities   Riyadh (capital), Jeddah, Mecca
Language   Arabic
Ethnic group   Arab
Religion   Muslim
Chief industries   Agriculture, oil refining, manufacturing, mining, herding
Chief crops   Dates, grains, fruits
Minerals   Oil, copper, gold, iron
Leading exports   Oil, petroleum products
Leading imports   Machinery, manufactured food goods
Monetary unit   Riyal

Senegal

Location   Western Africa, bordered by Mauritania on the North, Mali on the East, Guinea and Guinea-Bissau on the South
Area   75,750 square miles
Population   7,900,000
Government   Republic
Largest city   Dakar (capital)
Languages   French, tribal languages
Ethnic groups   Wolof 36%, Serer 17%, Peulh 17%, Diola 9%, Mandingo 9%
Religion   Muslim
Chief industries   Agriculture, fishing, mining, food processing
Chief crops   Peanuts, grains, sorghum
Minerals   Phosphates, iron ore
Leading exports   Peanuts, phosphates, canned fish
Leading imports   Foodstuffs, machinery, oil
Monetary unit   CFA franc

Seychelles

Location   Indian Ocean, northeast of Madagascar
Area   171 square miles
Population   80,000
Government   One-party republic
Largest city   Victoria (capital)

Languages   French, English, Creole
Ethnic group   Creole
Religion   Roman Catholic
Chief industries   Food processing, fishing, tourism
Chief crops   Coconuts, spices, patchouli
Leading exports   Cinnamon, vanilla, copra, fish
Leading imports   Foodstuffs, machinery, oil
Monetary unit   Rupee

Sierra Leone

Location   Western Africa, bordered by Guinea on the North and East, Liberia on the South
Area   27,699 square miles
Population   4,300,000
Government   Military rule
Largest cities   Freetown (capital), Bo, Kenema, Makeni
Languages   English, tribal languages
Ethnic groups   Temne 30%, Mende 29%
Religions   Animist, Muslim
Chief industries   Agriculture, mining, tourism
Chief crops   Cocoa, coffee, rice, ginger, palm kernels
Minerals   Diamonds, bauxite, iron ore
Leading exports   Diamonds, bauxite, coffee, cocoa
Leading imports   Oil, machinery, rice
Monetary unit   Leone

Singapore

Location   Southeastern Asia
Area   224 square miles
Population   2,750,000
Government   Republic
Largest city   Singapore (capital)
Languages   Chinese, Malay, English, Tamil
Ethnic groups   Chinese 77%, Malay 15%, Indian 6%
Religions   Buddhist, Tao, Muslim, Hindu, Christian
Chief industries   Shipbuilding, banking, tourism, food and rubber processing, oil refining, light industry
Chief crops   Vegetables, fruits, rubber
Leading exports   Petroleum products, rubber products, electronics, computers
Leading imports   Crude oil, machinery, manufactured goods
Monetary unit   Dollar

Slovakia

Location   Formerly part of Czechoslovakia, bordered by Poland on the North, the Czech Republic and Austria on the West, Hungary on the South, Ukraine on the East
Area   18,919 square miles
Population   5,297,000
Government   Republic
Largest cities   Bratislava (capital), Kosice
Languages   Slovak, Hungarian
Ethnic groups   Slovak, Hungarian
Religions   Roman Catholic, Protestant, Eastern Orthodox

Chief industries Heavy industry, armaments, iron, steel, chemicals, mining, leather goods, agriculture, herding, forestry
Chief crops Grains, potatoes, sugar beets
Minerals Coal, lignite
Leading exports Data not available
Leading imports Data not available
Monetary unit Koruna

Slovenia

Location Formerly in Yugoslavia, bordered by Austria on the North, Hungary on the Northeast, Croatia on the South, Italy and the Adriatic Sea on the West
Area 7,819 square miles
Population 1,970,000
Government Republic
Largest cities Ljubljana (capital), Maribor
Languages Slovenian, Serbo-Croatian
Ethnic groups Slovenes, Croats, Serbs
Religion Roman Catholic
Chief industries Manufacturing, mining, textiles, agriculture
Chief crops Grains, potatoes, fruit
Minerals Coal, iron, mercury
Leading exports Data not available
Leading imports Data not available
Monetary unit Tolar

Solomon Islands

Location Southwestern Pacific, East of New Guinea
Area 11,640 square miles
Population 375,000
Government Commonwealth, with a parliamentary system, with the Queen of England as the sovereign, an elected parliament, and a prime minister
Largest city Honiara (capital)
Languages English Melanesian languages
Ethnic groups Melanesian 93%, Polynesian 4%
Religions Protestant, Roman Catholic
Chief industries Agriculture, fishing, fish canning
Chief crops Coconuts, rice, bananas, cocoa, yams
Minerals Gold, bauxite, copper
Leading exports Fish, timber, copra, palm oil
Leading imports Oil, machinery, foodstuffs
Monetary unit Dollar

Somalia

Location Eastern Africa, bordered by Djibouti, Ethiopia, and Kenya on the West
Area 246,199 square miles
Population 7,900,000
Government Republic, in transition following clan-based civil war
Largest city Mogadishu (capital)
Languages Somali, Arabic
Ethnic group Hamitic
Religion Muslim
Chief industries Agriculture, herding
Chief crops Bananas, sorghum, grains, sugarcane
Minerals Tin, uranium
Leading exports Bananas, livestock, hides
Leading imports Foodstuffs, oil, machinery
Monetary unit Shilling

South Africa

Location Southern Africa, bordered by Namibia, Botswana, and Zimbabwe on the North, Mozambique, and Swaziland on the East
Area 471,445 square miles
Population 41,000,000
Government Republic
Capitals Cape Town, Pretoria, and Bloemfontein
Largest cities Johannesburg, Cape Town, Durban, Pretoria
Languages English, Afrikaans, African languages
Ethnic groups Bantu, European descent, Indian descent
Religions Christian, Hindu, Muslim
Chief industries Mining, manufacturing, agriculture
Chief crops Grains, tobacco, sugarcane, peanuts, fruit
Minerals Gold, diamonds, chromium, antimony, coal, iron, nickel
Leading exports Gold, diamonds, foodstuffs
Leading imports Oil, machinery, chemicals, textiles
Monetary unit Rand

Spain

Location Southwestern Europe, bordered by Portugal on the West, France and Andorra on the North
Area 194,897 square miles
Population 39,380,000
Government Constitutional monarchy with a parliamentary system
Largest cities Madrid (capital), Barcelona, Valencia, Seville
Languages Spanish, Catalan, Galician, Basque
Ethnic groups Spanish 72.8%, Catalan 16.4%, Galician 8.2%, Basque 2.3%
Religion Roman Catholic
Chief industries Manufacturing, agriculture, fishing, herding
Chief crops Grains, citrus, fruits, olives, vegetables, grapes
Minerals Coal, uranium, mercury, iron, gypsum, zinc, copper
Leading exports Fruits, textiles, shoes, machinery, timber, chemicals
Leading imports Oil, machinery, chemicals, steel
Monetary unit Peseta

Sri Lanka

Location Indian Ocean, south of India
Area 25,332 square miles
Population 17,500,000
Government Republic
Largest cities Colombo (capital), Kandy, Jafna
Languages Sinhala, Tamil, English
Ethnic groups Sinhalese 75%, Tamil 18% Moor 7%
Religions Buddhist, Hindu, Christian, Muslim
Chief industries Agriculture, forestry, light manufacturing, mining
Chief crops Tea, coconuts, rubber, rice, spices
Minerals Graphite, gems, limestone

WORLD AT A GLANCE

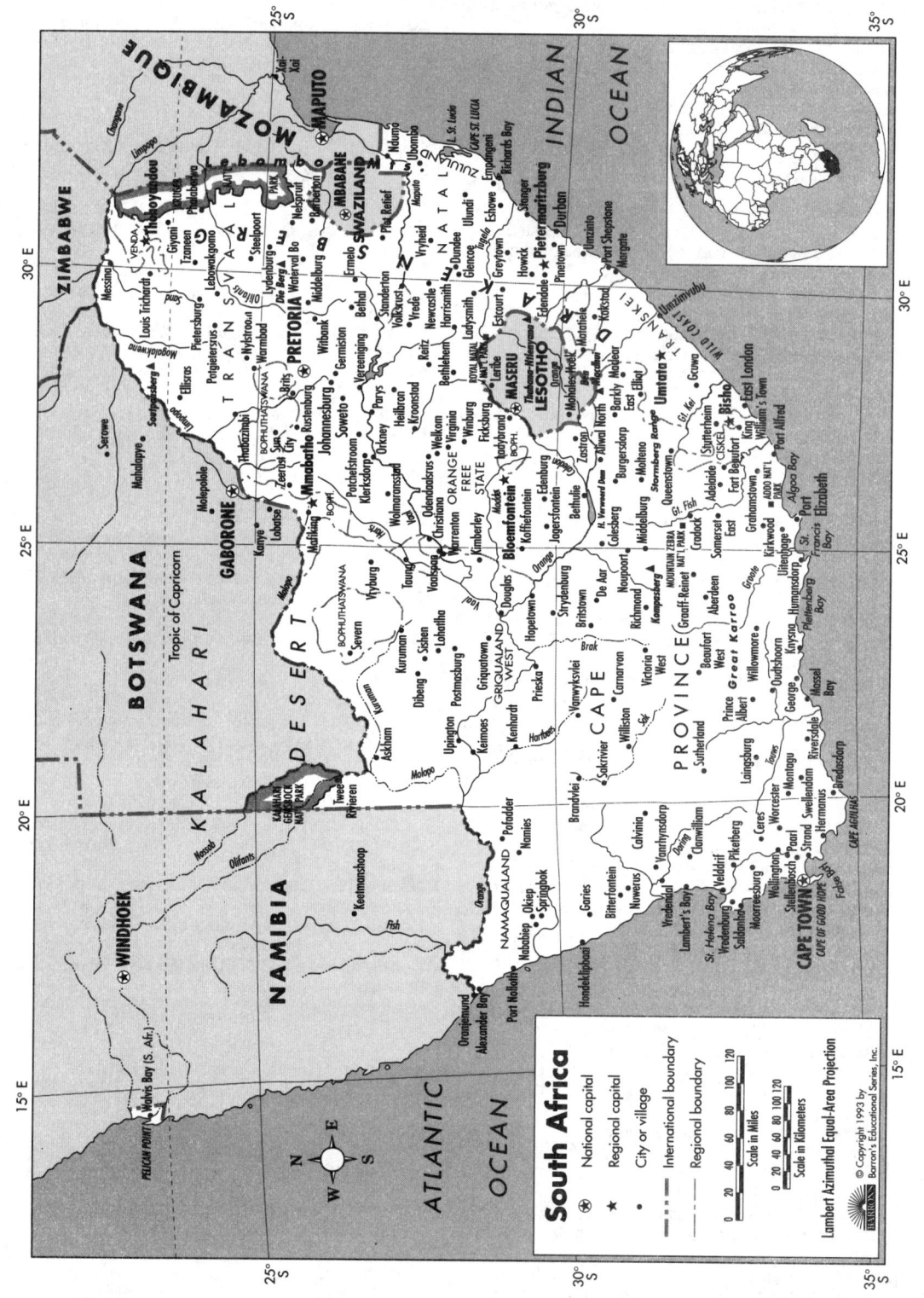

South Africa

⊛ National capital
★ Regional capital
• City or village
–⋯–⋯ International boundary
–·–·– Regional boundary

Scale in Miles
0 20 40 60 80 100 120

Scale in Kilometers
0 20 40 60 80 100 120

Lambert Azimuthal Equal-Area Projection

© Copyright 1993 by
Barron's Educational Series, Inc.

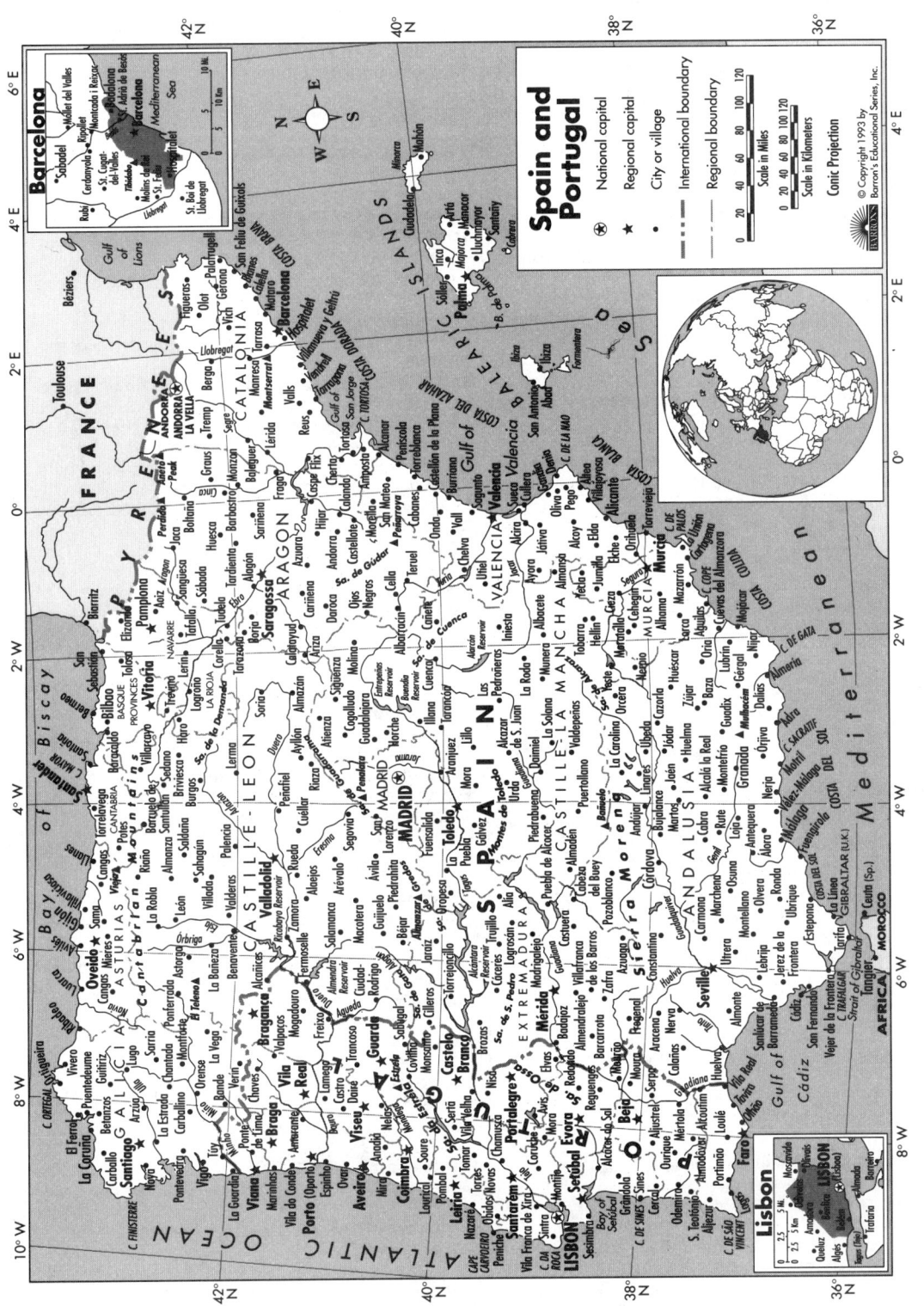

Barcelona

Spain and Portugal

⊛ National capital
★ Regional capital
• City or village
—·—·— International boundary
———— Regional boundary

Scale in Miles
0   20   40   60   80   100   120

Scale in Kilometers
0   20   40   60   80   100   120

Conic Projection

© Copyright 1993 by
Barron's Educational Series, Inc.

Lisbon

Leading exports Tea, rubber, coconuts, textiles
Leading imports Machinery, oil, sugar
Monetary unit Rupee

Sudan

Location Northern Africa, bordered by Libya, Chad, and Central African Republic on the West, Egypt on the North, Ethiopia on the East, Zaire, Uganda, and Kenya on the South
Area 967,500 square miles
Population 27,000,000
Government Military rule
Largest cities Khartoum (capital), Omdurman, Port Sudan
Languages Arabic, English, tribal languages
Ethnic groups Arab, Nubian, Nilotic, Sudanic
Religions Muslim, Animist, Christian
Chief industries Agriculture, light manufacturing, mining
Chief crops Gum arabic, cotton, peanuts, sesame seeds, grains
Minerals Iron, copper, chrome, oil
Leading exports Cotton, peanuts, gum arabic
Leading imports Chemicals, oil, machinery
Monetary unit Pound

Suriname

Location Northeastern South America, bordered by Guyana on the West, French Guiana on the East, Brazil on the South
Area 63,037 square miles
Population 400,000
Government Republic
Largest city Paramaribo (capital)
Languages Dutch, Surinamese, English
Ethnic groups Hindustani 37%, Creole 31%, Javanese 15%
Religions Muslim, Hindu, Christian
Chief industries Agriculture, forestry, mining, fishing
Chief crops Rice, coffee, sugar, fruits
Minerals Bauxite, iron
Leading exports Bauxite, aluminum, rice, lumber
Leading imports Oil, cotton, foodstuffs, consumer goods
Monetary unit Guilder

Swaziland

Location Southern Africa, bordered by South Africa on the West, North, and South, Mozambique on the East
Area 6,704 square miles
Population 830,000
Government Monarchy
Largest city Mbabne (capital)
Languages Swazi, English
Ethnic groups Swazi 90%, Zulu 2.3%, European 2.1%
Religions Christian, Animist
Chief industries Forestry, agriculture, sugar refining
Chief crops Sugar, rice, cotton, corn, citrus fruits, livestock

Minerals Asbestos, coal, iron, diamonds
Leading exports Iron, asbestos, sugar, wood products
Leading imports Foodstuffs, oil, machinery
Monetary unit Lilangeni

Sweden

Location Northern Europe, bordered by Norway on the West, Finland on the East
Area 173,730 square miles
Population 8,600,000
Government Constitutional monarchy with a parliamentary system
Largest cities Stockholm (capital), Göteborg, Malmö
Languages Swedish, Finnish
Ethnic groups Swedish 91%, Finnish 3%, Lapp
Religion Lutheran
Chief industries Manufacturing, forestry, mining, automobiles, steel, shipbuilding
Chief crops Grains, potatoes, sugar beets
Minerals Iron, coal, copper, zinc, lead
Leading exports Machinery, paper, wood pulp, iron and steel products, automobiles
Leading imports Machinery, fuels, foodstuffs, oil
Monetary unit Krona

Switzerland

Location Central Europe, bordered by France on the West, Germany on the North, Liechtenstein and Austria on the East, Italy on the South
Area 15,941 square miles
Population 6,800,000
Government Federal republic
Largest cities Zurich, Basel, Geneva, Bern (capital), Lausanne
Languages German, French, Italian, Romansh
Ethnic group European
Religions Roman Catholic, Protestant
Chief industries Manufacturing, agriculture, banking, tourism, herding
Chief crops Grains, sugar beets, potatoes
Mineral Salt
Leading exports Precision instruments, watches, machinery, chemicals, pharmaceuticals, textiles
Leading imports Oil, iron, steel, foodstuffs, chemicals
Monetary unit Franc

Syria

Location Middle East, bordered by Lebanon and Israel on the West, Turkey on the North, Iraq on the East, Jordan on the South
Area 71,498 square miles
Population 13,300,000
Government Socialist Republic under one-party rule
Largest cities Damascus (capital), Aleppo, Homs, Hama
Languages Arabic, Kurdish, Armenian, French, English
Ethnic groups Arabs 90%, Kurd, Armenian, Turkish, Circassian, Assyrian

Religions   Muslim, Christian
Chief industries   Agriculture, herding, manufacturing
Chief crops   Cotton, grains, fruits, sugar beets
Minerals   Oil, phosphate, chrome, manganese
Leading exports   Oil, textiles, phosphate
Leading imports   Machinery, fuel, foodstuffs
Monetary unit   Pound

Taiwan

Location   China Sea, off the East coast of Asia
Area   13,900 square miles
Population   20,800,000
Government   Republic
Largest cities   Taipei (capital), Kaohsiung
Languages   Chinese, Taiwanese, Hakka dialects
Ethnic group   Chinese
Religions   Confucian, Tao, Buddhist
Chief industries   Manufacturing, agriculture, food processing, forestry, tourism
Chief crops   Rice, sugarcane, tea, fruits
Minerals   Coal, limestone, marble
Leading exports   Textiles, electronic equipment, plywood
Leading imports   Machinery, oil, cotton, metals
Monetary unit   Taiwan dollar

Tajikistan

Location   formerly in the U.S.S.R., bordered by Uzbekistan and Kyrgyzstan on the North and West, Afghanistan on the South and East, China on the East
Area   55,300 square miles
Population   5,300,000
Government   Republic
Largest cities   Dushanbe (capital), Khodzhent
Languages   Tajik, Russian
Ethnic groups   Tajik, Uzbek, Russian
Religion   Muslim
Chief industries   Manufacturing, textiles, agriculture, herding
Chief crops   Grains, cotton, vegetables
Minerals   Coal, lead, natural gas, gold
Leading exports   Data not available
Leading imports   Data not available
Monetary unit   Ruble

Tanzania

Location   Eastern Africa, bordered by Rwanda, Burundi, and Zaire on the West, Kenya and Uganda on the North, Zambia, Malawi, and Mozambique on the South
Area   364,900 square miles
Population   27,100,000
Government   Republic
Largest city   Dar es Salaam (capital)
Languages   Swahili, English
Ethnic group   African
Religions   Muslim, Christian, traditional beliefs
Chief industries   Agriculture, mining, light manufacturing, herding, food processing
Chief crops   Coconuts, grains, cotton, coffee, cashew nuts, tea, sisal

Minerals   Diamonds, gold, nickel, iron, coal
Leading exports   Cotton, coffee, diamonds, cloves, sisal
Leading imports   Machinery, steel, oil
Monetary unit   Shilling

Thailand

Location   Southeastern Asia, bordered by Burma on the West, Laos on the North, Cambodia on the East, Malaysia on the South
Area   198,456 square miles
Population   56,500,000
Government   Constitutional monarchy, with a parliamentary system
Largest city   Bangkok (capital)
Languages   Thai, Chinese, English
Ethnic groups   Thai 75%, Chinese 14%, others 11%
Religion   Buddhist
Chief industries   Agriculture, mining, forestry, textiles, food processing, fishing
Chief crops   Rice, rubber, corn, tapioca
Minerals   Natural gas, tin, tungsten, gems
Leading exports   Rice, rubber, tin, tapioca, fish products
Leading imports   Machinery, oil, iron, steel, chemicals
Monetary unit   Baht

Togo

Location   Western Africa, bordered by Ghana on the West, Burkina Faso on the North, Benin on the East
Area   21,925 square miles
Population   3,800,000
Government   One-party republic
Largest city   Lomé (capital)
Languages   French, tribal dialects
Ethnic groups   Ewe 35%, Kabye 22%, Mina 6%
Religions   Traditional, Christian, Muslim
Chief industries   Agriculture, mining, light manufacturing
Chief crops   Cocoa, coffee, manioc, millet, peanuts, cotton, rice, yams
Minerals   Phosphate, marble, manganese
Leading exports   Phosphates, cocoa, coffee, cotton
Leading imports   Machinery, foodstuffs, consumer goods, fuels
Monetary unit   CFA franc

Tonga

Location   Southwestern Pacific Ocean
Area   270 square miles
Population   99,000
Government   Constitutional monarchy
Largest city   Nukualofa (capital)
Languages   Tongan, English
Ethnic groups   Tongan 98%, Polynesian, European
Religions   Protestant, Roman Catholic
Chief industries   Agriculture, fishing
Chief crops   Tropical fruits, spices, coffee, coconuts

Leading exports   Copra, bananas, tropical fruits
Leading imports   Textiles, foodstuffs, lumber, fuels, machinery
Monetary unit   Pa'anga

Trinidad and Tobago

Location   Caribbean Sea
Area   1,980 square miles
Population   1,300,000
Government   Republic
Largest city   Port-of-Spain (capital)
Languages   English, Hindi, French, Spanish
Ethnic groups   African descent 40%, East Indian 40%
Religions   Roman Catholic, Protestant, Hindu, Muslim
Chief industries   Mining, agriculture, tourism
Chief crops   Sugarcane, fruits, coffee, cocoa
Minerals   Oil, natural gas, asphalt
Leading exports   Oil, fertilizers
Leading imports   Foodstuffs, machinery, consumer goods
Monetary unit   Dollar

Tunisia

Location   Northern Africa, bordered by Algeria on the West and Libya on the South
Area   63,170 square miles
Population   8,300,000
Government   Republic
Largest cities   Tunis (capital), Bizerte, Sfax
Languages   Arabic, French
Ethnic group   Arab 98%
Religion   Muslim
Chief industries   Agriculture, mining, food processing, textiles
Chief crops   Grains, olives, citrus fruits, dates, grapes
Minerals   Oil, phosphates, iron, lead
Leading exports   Oil, phosphates, iron, citrus fruits
Leading imports   Machinery, foodstuffs, consumer goods
Monetary unit   Dinar

Turkey

Location   Asia Minor, bordered by Bulgaria and Greece on the West, Georgia and Armenia on the North, Iran on the East, Iraq and Syria on the South
Area   301,381 square miles
Population   58,900,000
Government   Republic
Largest cities   Istanbul, Ankara (capital), Izmir, Adana, Bursa
Languages   Turkish, Kurdish, Arabic
Ethnic groups   Turk 85%, Kurd 12%
Religions   Muslim, Christian
Chief industries   Agriculture, mining, light manufacturing, herding, tourism
Chief crops   Tobacco, cotton, grains, fruits, nuts, potatoes, sugar beets
Minerals   Oil, coal, chromite, copper

Leading exports   Tobacco, cotton, fruits, textiles, leather
Leading imports   Oil, machinery, foodstuffs, fuels, fertilizer
Monetary unit   Lira

Turkmenistan

Location   Formerly in the U.S.S.R., bordered by Kazakhstan on the North, Uzbekistan on the North and East, Iran and Afghanistan on the South, the Caspian Sea on the West
Area   188,500 square miles
Population   3,700,000
Government   Republic
Largest city   Ashkhbad (capital)
Languages   Turkish, Russian
Ethnic groups   Turkmen, Russian, Uzbek
Religion   Muslim
Chief industries   Oil refining, textiles, agriculture, herding
Chief crops   Grains, cotton, grapes
Minerals   Oil, natural gas, sulfur, potassium
Leading exports   Data not available
Leading imports   Data not available
Monetary unit   Ruble

Tuvalu

Location   Southwestern Pacific Ocean
Area   10 square miles
Population   9,300
Government   Commonwealth, with a parliamentary system, with the Queen of England as the sovereign, an elected parliament, and a prime minister
Largest city   Funafuti (capital)
Languages   Tuvaluan, English
Ethnic group   Polynesian
Religion   Protestant
Chief industries   Agriculture, fishing
Chief crop   Coconuts, copra
Leading export   Copra
Leading imports   Foodstuffs, fuels, machinery
Monetary unit   Australian dollar

Uganda

Location   Eastern Africa, bordered by Zaire on the West, Sudan on the North, Kenya on the East, Tanzania and Rwanda on the South
Area   91,134 square miles
Population   17,100,000
Government   Military rule (republic)
Largest city   Kampala (capital)
Languages   English, Swahili, Luganda
Ethnic groups   Bantu, Nilotic, Nilo-Hamitic, Sudanic tribes
Religions   Christian, Muslim, Traditional
Chief industries   Agriculture, mining, food processing
Chief crops   Coffee, cotton, tobacco, tea, bananas, sugarcane
Minerals   Copper, cobalt, limestone
Leading exports   Coffee, copper, cotton, tea
Leading imports   Oil, machinery, textiles, food
Monetary unit   Shilling

U.S.S.R. (Former)

(*See* specific republics formed from, e.g., **Azerbaijan, Belarus, Kazakhstan, Russia, Tajikistan**)

Ukraine

Location   Formerly in the U.S.S.R., bordered by Belarus on the North, Russia on the North and East, Romania and Moldova on the Southwest, the Black Sea on the South and Hungary, Slovakia and Poland on the West

Area   233,100 square miles

Population   52,100,000

Government   Republic

Largest cities   Kiev (capital), Kharkiv, Donetske, Odessa

Languages   Ukrainian, Russian

Ethnic groups   Ukrainian, Russian

Religions   Eastern Orthodox, Ukrainian Catholic, Muslim

Chief industries   Iron and steel, heavy machinery, light industry, mining, agriculture

Chief crops   Grains, sugar beets, potatoes

Minerals   Iron, manganese, chromium, coal, copper, zinc, titanium

Leading exports   Data not available

Leading imports   Data not available

Monetary unit   Hryvnia

United Arab Emirates

Location   Arabian peninsula, bordered by Saudi Arabia on the West and South, Qatar on the North, Oman on the East

Area   32,000 square miles

Population   2,400,000

Government   Federation of Emirates

Largest city   Abu Dhabi (capital)

Languages   Arabic, Farsi, English, Hindu, Urdu

Ethnic groups   Arab, Iranian, Pakistani, Indian

Religion   Muslim

Chief industries   Agriculture, fishing, oil refining

Chief crops   Dates, vegetables, fruits

Mineral   Oil

Leading exports   Oil, dates, fish

Leading imports   Foodstuffs, machinery, consumer goods

Monetary unit   Dirham

United Kingdom

Location   Atlantic Ocean, off northwestern coast of Europe

Area   94,300 square miles

Population   56,500,000

Government   Constitutional monarchy with a parliamentary system

Largest cities   London (capital), Birmingham, Glasgow, Leeds, Sheffield, Liverpool

Languages   English, Welsh, Gaelic

Ethnic groups   English 81.5%, Scottish 9.6%, Welsh 1.9%, Ulster 1.8%, Irish 1.4%

Religions   Protestant, Roman Catholic

Chief industries   Manufacturing, mining, fishing, steel, metals, vehicles, chemicals

Chief crops   Grains, vegetables, sugar beets

Minerals   Coal, oil, natural gas

Leading exports   Machinery, oil, chemicals, transport equipment

Leading imports   Foodstuffs, machinery, consumer goods

Monetary unit   Pound

United States

Location   Central North America, bordered on the North by Canada, on the South by Mexico

Area   3,615,123 square miles

Population   256,000,000

Government   Federal Republic

Largest cities   New York, Los Angeles, Chicago, Philadelphia, Houston, Detroit, Washington, D.C. (capital)

Languages   English, Spanish

Ethnic groups   European descent, African descent, Amerindian

Religions   Protestant, Roman Catholic, Jewish

Chief industries   Heavy industry, light manufacturing, electronics, mining, agriculture, forestry, livestock raising, food processing

Chief crops   Grains, sugar, potatoes, soybeans, fruit

Minerals   Coal, oil, copper, gold, silver, natural gas, lead, zinc, uranium

Leading exports   Machinery, vehicles, armaments, grains, aircraft, chemicals

Leading imports   Oil, automobiles, electronic equipment

Monetary unit   Dollar

Uruguay

Location   Southern South America, bordered by Argentina on the West, Brazil on the North

Area   68,037 square miles

Population   3,100,000

Government   Republic

Largest city   Montevideo (capital)

Language   Spanish

Ethnic groups   Europeans 89%, Mestizo 10%, Mulatto and Black

Religion   Roman Catholic

Chief industries   Agriculture, meat packing, light manufacturing, herding, textiles

Chief crops   Grains, citrus fruits, rice, vegetables

Leading exports   Meat, rice, leather, shoes, wool

Leading imports   Oil, chemicals, machinery

Monetary unit   New Peso

Uzbekistan

Location   Formerly in the U.S.S.R., bordered by Kazakhstan on the North and West, Kyrgyzstan and Tajikistan on the East, Turkmenistan and Afghanistan on the South

Area   172,700 square miles

Population   20,500,000

Government   Republic

Largest cities   Tashkent (capital), Samarkand

Languages   Turkic, Russian

Ethnic groups   Uzbek, Russian

United Kingdom and Ireland

⊛ National capital
★ Regional capital
• City or village
▬▪▬▪▬ International boundary
▬▪▬▪▬ Regional boundary

Scale in Miles
0 20 40 60 80 100 120

Scale in Kilometers
0 20 40 60 80 100 120

Bonne Projection

© Copyright 1993 by
BARRON'S Barron's Educational Series, Inc.

London

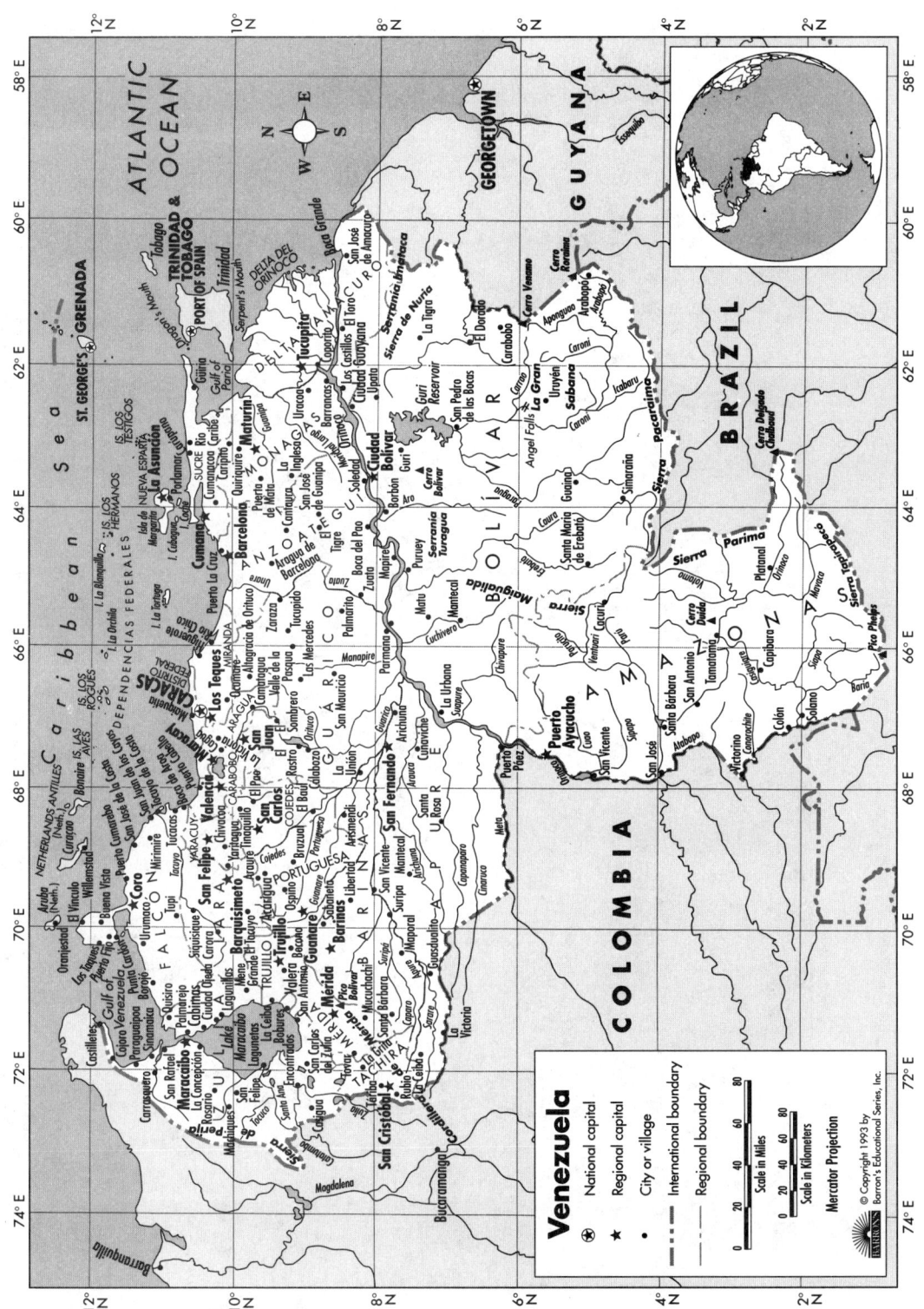

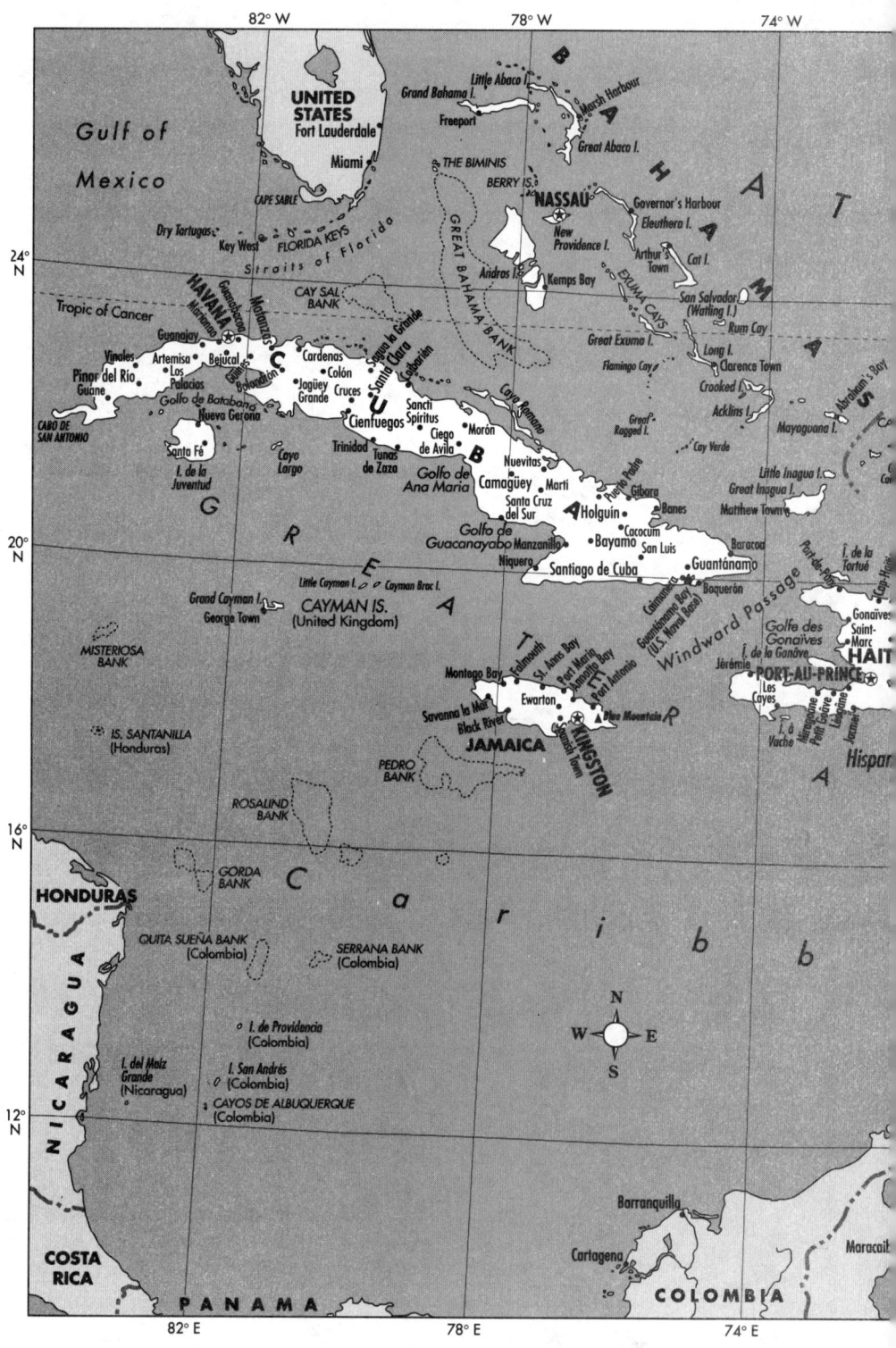

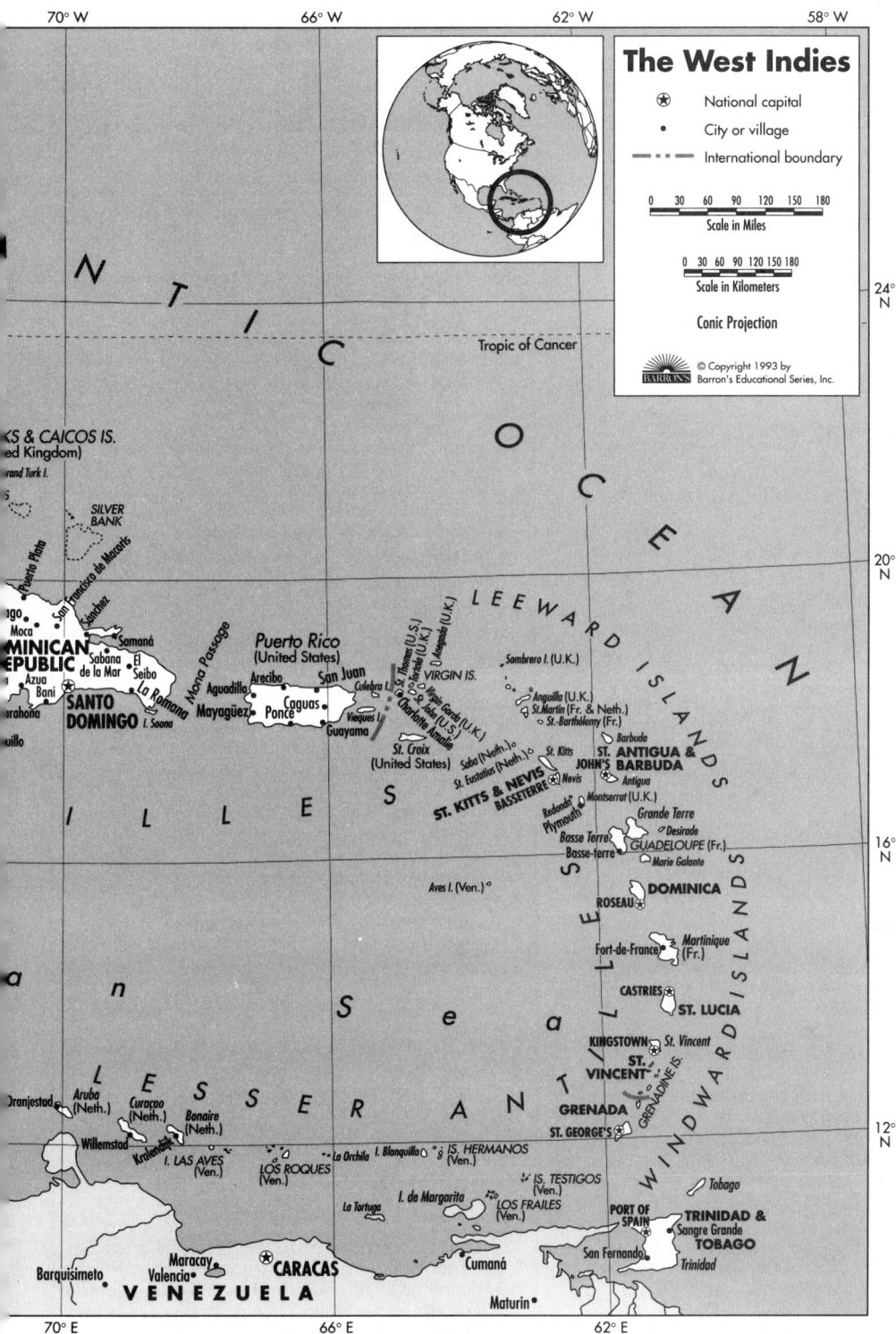

The West Indies

⊛ National capital

• City or village

— International boundary

0 30 60 90 120 150 180
Scale in Miles

0 30 60 90 120 150 180
Scale in Kilometers

Conic Projection

© Copyright 1993 by
Barron's Educational Series, Inc.

Religion Muslim
Chief industries Manufacturing, textiles, agriculture
Chief crops Cotton, rice, grains, grapes
Minerals Coal, copper, natural gas
Leading exports Data not available
Leading imports Data not available
Monetary unit Ruble

Vanuatu

Location Southwestern Pacific Ocean
Area 5,700 square miles
Population 170,000
Government Republic
Largest city Vila (capital)
Languages Bislama, French, English
Ethnic group Melanesian
Religions Protestant, Roman Catholic, Animist
Chief industries Agriculture, fishing, fish processing
Chief crops Copra, cocoa, coffee
Mineral Manganese
Leading exports Copra, coffee, processed fish
Leading imports Foodstuffs, machinery
Monetary unit Vanuatu franc

Vatican City

Location Central Italy, in Rome
Area 0.17 square mile
Population 778
Government Independent papal state
Languages Italian, Latin
Ethnic groups Italian, Swiss
Religion Roman Catholic
Monetary unit Lira

Venezuela

Location Northern South America
Area 352,143 square miles
Population 19,700,000
Government Republic
Largest cities Caracas (capital), Maracaibo, Valencia
Languages Spanish, Indian languages
Ethnic groups Mestizo 69%, European 20%, Black 9%, Indian 2%
Religion Roman Catholic
Chief industries Agriculture, manufacturing, oil refining
Chief crops Rice, coffee, sugarcane, bananas
Minerals Oil, iron, natural gas
Leading exports Oil, iron, bauxite
Leading imports Machinery, foodstuffs, chemicals
Monetary unit Bolivar

Vietnam

Location Southeast Asia, bordered by Laos and Cambodia on the West, China on the North
Area 128,000 square miles
Population 68,500,000
Government Marxist people's republic
Largest cities Ho Chi Minh City, Hanoi (capital)

Languages Vietnamese, French, English
Ethnic groups Vietnamese 84%, Chinese 2%, Muong, Thai, Khmer, Man, Cham
Religions Buddhist, Confucian, Tao, Roman Catholic
Chief industries Agriculture, light manufacturing, mining, forestry, food processing
Chief crops Rice, rubber, fruits, vegetables, sugarcane
Minerals Phosphates, bauxite, coal, iron
Leading exports Coal, rubber, agricultural products
Leading imports Machinery, chemicals, grain, fertilizer, oil
Monetary unit Dong

Western Samoa

Location Southwestern Pacific Ocean
Area 1,133 square miles
Population 190,000
Government Republic with a parliamentary system
Largest city Apia (capital)
Languages Samoan, English
Ethnic groups Samoan 88%, Euronesian 10%, European
Religions Protestant, Roman Catholic
Chief industries Agriculture, forestry, fishing, food processing
Chief crops Cocoa, coconuts, bananas, taro
Leading exports Copra, cocoa, bananas, lumber
Leading imports Foodstuffs, machinery
Monetary unit Tala

Yemen

Location Formed by the unification of Yemen Arab Republic and the People's Democratic Republic of Yemen, bordered by Saudi Arabia on the North, Oman on the East, the Arabian Sea on the South, the Red Sea on the West
Area 203,850 square miles
Population 10,200,000
Government Republic
Largest cities San'a' (capital), Aden
Language Arabic
Ethnic groups Arab, Indian, Somali
Religion Muslim
Chief industries Oil refining, agriculture, fishing, herding
Chief crops Grains, fruits, cotton, coffee, dates
Mineral Salt
Leading exports Cotton, coffee, hides, dried fish
Leading imports Consumer goods, foodstuffs
Monetary unit Dinar and rial

Yugoslavia

Location Made up of Serbia and Montenegro, the two remaining members of the former federation of six republics, bordered by Hungary on the North, Romania and Bulgaria on the East, Albania and Macedonia on the South, Croatia, Bosnia and Herzegovina on the West
Area 39,000 square miles
Population 10,000,000

Government Republic
Largest cities Belgrade (capital), Titograd
Language Serbo-Croatian
Ethnic groups Serb, Montenegrin
Religion Mostly Eastern Orthodox
Chief industries Manufacturing, mining, agriculture, herding
Chief crops Grains, tobacco, sugar beets
Minerals Coal, copper, iron, lead
Leading exports Data not available
Leading imports Data not available
Monetary unit Dinar

Zaire

Location Central Africa, bordered by Congo on the West, Central African Republic and Sudan on the North, Uganda, Rwanda, Burundi, and Tanzania on the East, Zambia and Angola on the South
Area 905,500 square miles
Population 37,850,000
Government Republic in transition from one-party rule
Largest cities Kinshasa (capital), Kananaga, Lubumbashi
Languages French, Bantu dialects
Ethnic groups Bantu 80%, other tribes
Religions Christian, Muslim, tribal
Chief industries Agriculture, mining, forestry, light manufacturing
Chief crops Rubber, coffee, bananas, cocoa, cotton, sugarcane
Minerals Cobalt, copper, zinc, tin, diamonds, gold, oil, coal, iron
Leading exports Copper, cobalt, diamonds, coffee
Leading imports Foodstuffs, textiles, motor vehicles, machinery
Monetary unit Zaire

Zambia

Location Southern Africa, bordered by Angola on the West, Zaire on the North, Tanzania, Malawi, and

Mozambique on the East, Zimbabwe and Namibia on the South
Area 290,586 square miles
Population 8,400,000
Government Republic
Largest cities Lusaka (capital), Kitwe, Ndola Chingola
Languages English, Bantu dialects
Ethnic group Bantu
Religions Animist, Roman Catholic
Chief industries Agriculture, mining
Chief crops Rubber, corn, tobacco, peanuts, cotton, fruit, rice
Minerals Cobalt, copper, zinc, gold, lead, coal
Leading exports Copper, cobalt, lead, zinc, tobacco
Leading imports Machinery, consumer goods, foodstuffs
Monetary unit Kwacha

Zimbabwe

Location Southeastern Africa, bordered by Botswana on the West, Zambia on the North, Mozambique on the East, South Africa on the South
Area 150,800 square miles
Population 10,500,000
Government Republic with a parliamentary system
Largest cities Harare (capital), Bulawayo
Languages English, Shona, Sindebele
Ethnic groups Shona 80%, Ndebele 19%
Religions Tribal, Christian
Chief industries Agriculture, mining, light manufacturing, herding
Chief crops Tobacco, cotton, corn, sugar, wheat, tea
Minerals Gold, copper, chrome, nickel, tin, asbestos, iron, coal
Leading exports Copper, tobacco, asbestos, clothing, gold, meat
Leading imports Textiles, oil, machinery, vehicles
Monetary unit Dollar

EXHIBIT 24.1
Total Population and Population Density of the World's Ten Largest Nations

Nation	Population (1991 est.)	People per Sq. Mi.
China	1,160,000,000	314.2
India	870,000,000	703.3
United States	256,000,000	69.6
Brazil	151,000,000	45.9
Russia	148,500,000	22.6
Argentina	32,600,000	30.5
Canada	27,000,000	7.0
Sudan	27,000,000	27.9
Australia	17,000,000	6.0
Kazakhstan	16,700,000	15.9
World	5,423,000,000	93.7

EXHIBIT 24.2
Actual and Projected Population of World Regions

Region	1980	1990	2000 (est.)
Asia	2,583,447,000	3,112,695,000	3,712,542,000
Africa	477,231,000	642,111,000	866,585,000
Europe*	749,973,000	786,966,000	818,378,000
Latin America**	362,685,000	448,076,000	538,439,000
North America	251,909,000	275,866,000	294,712,000
Oceania	22,800,000	26,481,000	30,144,000
World	4,448,048,000	5,292,195,000	6,260,800,000

*Includes the former U.S.S.R.
**Includes Mexico, Central America, and the Caribbean

EXHIBIT 24.3
1980–1990 Average Annual Growth Rate for World Regions

Africa	3.0%	Latin America	2.1%	Oceania	1.5%
Asia	1.9%	Europe	0.3%		
North America	0.8%	U.S.S.R.	0.8%	World	1.7%

EXHIBIT 24.4
Racial Groups by Geographic Location

	Some characteristics	Place where group developed
African	Medium to dark brown skin color; dark hair, which may be curly or tightly coiled	Africa south of the Sahara
American Indian	Light to dark brown skin color; dark, straight hair	North America and South America
Asian	Light brown skin color; dark, straight hair; eyes that appear almond shaped	Asia, except South Asia and the Middle East; part of northern North America
Australian	Medium to dark brown skin color; light to dark hair; generally small	Australia
European	Light to medium skin color, blond to dark hair, which may be straight or curly	Europe, the Middle East, and North Africa
Indian	Light to dark brown skin color; dark hair	South Asia, particularly India
Melanesian	Dark brown skin color, dark hair	New Britain, New Guinea, and the Solomon Islands
Micronesian	Dark brown skin color; curly hair; generally small	The Caroline, the Gilbert, the Mariana, and the Marshall Islands
Polynesian	Light brown to medium skin color; dark hair; somewhat tall	Hawaii and widely scattered islands in the Pacific Ocean

EXHIBIT 24.5
The Continents

Continent	Sq. Mi.
Asia	17,297,000
Africa	11,708,000
North America	9,406,000
South America	6,883,000
Antarctica	5,405,000
Europe	3,835,000
Australia	2,968,000

EXHIBIT 24.6
Largest Countries in Area

Country	Sq. Mi.
Russia	6,592,800
Canada	3,831,033
China	3,691,500
United States	3,678,896
Brazil	3,286,487
Australia	2,967,909
India	1,237,061
Argentina	1,068,301
Kazakhstan	1,049,000
Sudan	967,500

EXHIBIT 24.7
Smallest Countries in Area

Country	Sq. Mi.
Vatican City	0.2
Monaco	0.6
Nauru	8.2
Tuvalu	10
San Marino	24
Liechtenstein	62
Marshall Islands	70
St. Kitts-Nevis	101
Maldives	115
Malta	122

EXHIBIT 24.8
The Oceans

Ocean	Sq. Mi.	Greatest Depth-Ft.
Pacific	63,800,000	36,161
Atlantic	31,800,000	30,249
Indian	28,900,000	24,441
Arctic	5,400,000	17,881

EXHIBIT 24.9
Principal Mountains of the World

Mountain	Country	Ht.-Ft.
Europe		
Elbrus, Mount	Russia	18,510
Dyhtau	Russia	17,070
Blanc, Mont	France-Italy	15,781
Rosa, Monte	Italy-Switzerland	15,200
Matterhorn	Italy-Switzerland	14,692
Asia		
Everest, Mount	China-Nepal	29,029
K2 (Godwin Austen)	China-Pakistan	28,251
Kanchenjunga	India-Nepal	28,207
Dhaulagiri	Nepal	26,811
Annapurna	Nepal	26,503
Africa		
Kilimanjaro	Tanzania	19,341
Kirinyaga (Mount Kenya)	Kenya	17,057
Margherita Peak	Uganda-Zaire	16,795
(Ruwenzori Range)		
Ras Dashen	Ethiopia	15,157
Toubkal	Morocco	13,671
North America		
McKinley, Mount	United States	20,320
Logan, Mount	Canada	19,849
Orizaba, Pico de	Mexico	18,701
(Volcán Citlaltépetl)		
Popocatépetl Volcan	Mexico	17,887
Whitney, Mount	United States	14,494
South America		
Aconcaqua, Cerro	Argentina	22,853
Ojos de Salado,	Argentina-Chile	22,516
Nevado		
Huascarán, Nevado	Peru	22,205
Chimborazo, Volcán	Ecuador	20,561
Christóbal Colón,	Colombia	19,029
Pico		
Oceania		
Wilhelm, Mount	Papua, New Guinea	14,793
Cook, Mount	New Zealand	12,349
Kosciusko, Mount	Australia	7,310
Antarctica		
Vinson Massif	Antarctica	16,864
Jackson, Mount	Antarctica	13,750

EXHIBIT 24.10
Principal Islands of the World

Island	Sq. Mi.	Island	Sq. Mi.
Greenland	840,004	Java	51,038
New Guinea	303,090	North Island	44,297
Borneo	288,243	Cuba	44,218
Madagascar	226,658	Newfoundland	43,359
Baffin	183,810	Luzon	40,420
Sumatra	182,860	Iceland (Island)	39,769
Great Britain	87,870	Mindanao	36,537
Honshu	87,805	Ireland	32,588
Ellesmere	82,119	Hokkaidó	30,144
Victoria	81,930	Sakhalin	29,498
Celebes	73,057	Hispaniola	29,418
South Island	58,093		

EXHIBIT 24.11
Principal Rivers of the World

River	Location	Length-Mi.
Nile-Kagera	Africa	4,145
Yangtze	China	3,915
Amazon-Ucayali	Brazil-Peru	3,902
Mississippi-Missouri-Red Rock	United States	3,741
Yellow (Huang He)	China	3,395
Ob-Irtysk	China-Russia	3,362
Rio de la Plata-Paraná	S. America	2,920
Mekong	Asia	2,796
Paraná	S. America	2,796
Amur	China-Russia	2,744
Lena	Russia	2,734
Mackenzie	Canada	2,635
Congo (Zaire)	Africa	2,610
Niger	Africa	2,585
Yenisey	Russia	2,543
Mississippi	United States	2,348
Missouri	United States	2,315
Ob	Russia	2,287
Volga	Russia	2,194
Murray-Darling	Australia	2,169

EXHIBIT 24.12
Major Lakes of the World

Lake	Country	Sq. Mi.	Depth-Ft.
Caspian Sea	Iran-Kazakhstan-Russia	143,200	3,363
Superior	Canada-United States	31,820	1,333
Victoria	Africa	26,293	262
Aral Sea	Kazakhstan	25,676	223
Huron	Canada-United States	23,010	750
Michigan	United States	22,400	923
Tanganyika	Africa	12,700	4,711
Baikal	Russia	12,162	5,315
Great Bear	Canada	12,096	1,356
Nyasa	Africa	11,892	2,224
Great Slave	Canada	11,031	1,834
Erie	United States-Canada	9,940	210
Winnipeg	Canada	9,417	60
Ontario	Canada-United States	7,540	802
Ladoga	Russia	7,104	738

EXHIBIT 24.13
Waterfalls of the World

Waterfall	Country	River	Ht.-Ft.
Angel	Venezuela	Churun	3,189
Tugela	South Africa	Tugela	3,110
Yosemite	United States	Yosemite Creek	2,425
Sutherland	New Zealand	Arthur	1,900
Gavarnie	France	Gave de Pau	1,381
Lofoi	Zaire	Lofoi	1,260
Krimml	Austria	Krimml	1,250
Takakkaw	Canada	Yoho	1,248
Staubbach	Switzerland	Staubbach	1,001
Mardalsfoss	Norway	—	974
Gersoppa	India	Sharavati	830
Kaieteur	Guyana	Potaro	810

EXHIBIT 24.14
World Climate Regions

Climate Region	Location (Examples)	Climate	Description	Human Use
Low latitudes Tropical rain forest	Near the Equator: Amazon River Basin; Congo River Basin; west coast of Colombia and Ecuador; Indonesia, the Philippines; west coasts of India, Burma and Malaysia	Rainy, hot all year: "Night is the winter of the Tropics"	Jungle—tall trees, dense foliage, rivers	Rivers—most important highways; hardwood forests—rubber, bananas; shifting cultivation—"slash and burn"
Wet and dry tropical (tropical savanna)	North and south of tropical rain forests: Sahel—West Africa; llanos in South America, India, Southeast Asia	Winters, dry; summers, rainy; Hot all year	Tall grasslands, some trees; East African plateau, low grass savanna	Cattle raising, sugarcane, paddy rice; thinly populated except in India
Tropical desert	North and south of savannas: Sahara—North Africa, west coasts of continents—southwest Africa, southwest South America, southwest United States, southwest Asia—Arabian Desert	Hot, with little or no rain	Vast sandy areas (Erg Desert), vast rocky dry areas (Hamada Desert); desert shrubs, some low grasses	Nomad cattle herders move from watering place (oasis) to watering place; irrigation needed for agriculture
Middle latitudes Maritime	West coast of continents: Great Britain, northwest Europe, U.S. Pacific Northwest; Southern half of Chile	Rainy, moderate temperatures	Mixed forest, good farmland, low grasses	Farming, manufacturing: northwest Europe, one of most densely populated areas in the world; wheat, fruits, sugar beets, grazing
Humid continental	Two-thirds of United States—Northern United States, east coast United States; Western Russia, Belarus	Hot summers, cold winters, dependable, moderate rainfall	Plains—mixed forest, low grasses	"bread baskets" of United States and Russia—wheat, corn grazing; also industrial center of United States and Russia
Continental steppe	Far inland, often on plateaus: Great Plains—central North America; Ukraine, Kazakhstan	Very hot summers, very cold winters, light and undependable rainfall	Low grasses, shrubs; trees along streams	Grazing, herding; grains grown with irrigation
Continental desert	North and south of continental steppe (Asian Gobi Desert)	Dry—extreme temperatures	Very little vegetation	Grazing, herding, mining
Mediterranean (subtropical)	West side of continents near the sea: southern Europe, central Chile; southern California	Mild wet winters, very hot summers	Grasses, evergreen trees	Olives, wheat, grapes need for irrigation
Humid subtropical	East coasts of North America, Asia, (China, Japan); pampas of South America	Long humid summers, short mild winters	Mixed forest, low grassland	Rice, cotton, citrus fruits, vegetables, tobacco, grazing
High latitudes Taiga (forest)	North of humid continental areas in North America, Europe, Asia, Russia, Canada, Alaska	Low rainfall, snow and ice, long cold winters, short cool summers	Evergreen forests, snow and ice covers land most of year	Thinly settled; mining, lumbering, fishing hunting, herding
Tundra	North of taigas	Little rainfall, long cold winters, short cool summers	"Arctic prairie"; few trees, permafrost—land frozen	Thinly settled; hunting, fishing, herding; permafrost prevents farming
Polar ice cap	Coasts of Arctic region, Greenland, North Canada, Siberia in Russia	Very cold, very short frost-free summer	Permafrost: moss, lichens, shrubs	Fishing, trapping, hunting, oil

INDEX

References are to pages, e.g., 21-2, and to exhibits, e.g., Exh. 18.6.

References are to pages, e.g., 21-2, and to exhibits, e.g., Exh. 18.6.

INDEX

References are to pages, e.g., 21-2, and to exhibits, e.g., Exh. 18.6.

INDEX

References are to pages, e.g., 21-2, and to exhibits, e.g., Exh. 18.6.

References are to pages, e.g., 21-2, and to exhibits, e.g., Exh. 18.6.

References are to pages, e.g., 21-2, *and to exhibits, e.g.,* Exh. 18.6.

References are to pages, e.g., 21-2, *and to exhibits, e.g.,* Exh. 18.6.

INDEX

References are to pages, e.g., 21-2, and to exhibits, e.g., Exh. 18.6.

INDEX

References are to pages, e.g., 21-2, and to exhibits, e.g., Exh. 18.6.

References are to pages, e.g., 21-2, and to exhibits, e.g., Exh. 18.6.

G

References are to pages, e.g., 21-2, and to exhibits, e.g., Exh. 18.6.

References are to pages, e.g., 21-2, *and to exhibits, e.g.,* Exh. 18.6.

References are to pages, e.g., 21-2, and to exhibits, e.g., Exh. 18.6.

References are to pages, e.g., 21-2, and to exhibits, e.g., Exh. 18.6.

INDEX

References are to pages, e.g., 21-2, *and to exhibits, e.g., Exh. 18.6.*

References are to pages, e.g., 21-2, and to exhibits, e.g., Exh. 18.6.

References are to pages, e.g., 21-2, *and to exhibits, e.g.,* Exh. 18.6.

References are to pages, e.g., 21-2, and to exhibits, e.g., Exh. 18.6.

References are to pages, e.g., 21-2, and to exhibits, e.g., Exh. 18.6.

INDEX

INDEX

INDEX

References are to pages, e.g., 21-2, and to exhibits, e.g., Exh. 18.6.

References are to pages, e.g., 21-2, and to exhibits, e.g., Exh. 18.6.

INDEX

The World

⊛ National capital

• City or village

–·–·– International boundary

Scale in Miles
0 625 1250 1875 2500

Scale in Kilometers
0 625 1250 1875 2500

Robinson Projection

© Copyright 1993 by
Barron's Educational Series, Inc.